W9-BKT-796

JUN 2004

JUN 09

JUL X X 2015

WITHDRAWN

demo
$3.00
11/15/93

WORLD AUTHORS 1975–1980

Biographical Reference Books from
The H. W. Wilson Company

American Reformers

Greek and Latin Authors 800 B.C.–A.D. 1000
European Authors 1000–1900
British Authors Before 1800
British Authors of the Nineteenth Century
American Authors 1600–1900
Twentieth Century Authors
Twentieth Century Authors: First Supplement
World Authors 1950–1970
World Authors 1970–1975
World Authors 1975–1980

The Junior Book of Authors
More Junior Authors
Third Book of Junior Authors
Fourth Book of Junior Authors and Illustrators
Fifth Book of Junior Authors and Illustrators

Great Composers: 1300–1900
Composers Since 1900
Composers Since 1900: First Supplement
Musicians Since 1900
American Songwriters

Nobel Prize Winners

World Artists 1950–1980

World Film Directors: Volumes I, II

CUMBERLAND COUNTY COLLEGE LIBRARY
P.O. BOX 517
VINELAND, N.J. 08360

WORLD AUTHORS
1975–1980

A Volume in the Wilson Authors Series

Editor
VINETA COLBY

REFERENCE
NOT TO BE TAKEN FROM
THIS ROOM

THE H. W. WILSON COMPANY

NEW YORK

1985

Ref
PN
451
W66
V.3

93-417

Copyright © 1985 by The H. W. Wilson Company.

All rights reserved. No part of this work may be reproduced or copied in any form or by any means, including but not restricted to graphic, electronic, and mechanical—for example, photocopying, recording, taping, or information and retrieval systems—without the express written permission of the publisher, except that a reviewer may quote and a magazine or newspaper may print brief passages as part of a review written specifically for inclusion in that magazine or newspaper.

Second Printing 1988

Library of Congress Cataloging in Publication Data

Main entry under title:

World authors, 1975–1980.

   (The Wilson authors series)
   "Companion to the four volumes in the Wilson
authors series."—Pref.
   Includes bibliographies.
   1. Literature, Modern—20th century—Bio-bibliography.
2. Literature, Modern—20th century—History and
criticism. I. Colby, Vineta. II. Series.
PN451.W672 1985   809´.04   85–10045
ISBN 0–8242–0715–7

PRINTED IN THE UNITED STATES OF AMERICA

Acknowledgments

The lines from "West and East: A Dream" on page 11 are by Adonis and can be found in *An Anthology of Modern Arabic Poetry* (Berkeley: University of California Press, 1974) translated and edited by Mounah H. Khouri and Hamid Algav

The lines beginning "O miserable alphabet, O twenty . . . " and the lines from "Resurrection and Ashes" on page 11 are by Adonis and can be found in *Modern Arabic Poets 1950–1975* (Washington, DC: Three Continents Press, 1976) translated and edited by I.J. Boullata

The lines beginning "Tourists stream in . . . ," the lines from "This is" and the lines from "Table Prayer" on pages 34–35 are all from *Selected Poems* (Princeton, NJ: Princeton University Press, 1975) by Benny Anderson, translated by Alexander Taylor

The lines from "The Doves," from "The Light of Home," and from "What Is Poetry" on page 62 are from *God's Shadow: Prison Poems* (Bloomington: Indiana University Press, 1976) by Reza Baraheni

The lines on page 76 from *Descartes and the Animals* (London: Platform, 1954) are by Bernard Bergonzi

The lines from "Her First Calf" and from "Manifesto: The Mad Farmer Liberation Front" on page 82 are from *The Country of Marriage* (New York: Harcourt Brace Jovanovich, 1973) by Wendell Berry

The lines from "Uncle Red Milton and the Pup" on page 82 are from *Sayings and Doings* (Frankfort, KY: Gnomon Press, 1975) by Wendell Berry

The lines from "God Sent My Fathers Here, to a Bewilderment of Blood, to Links of Hatred" on page 125 are from *The World's Flesh* (Melbourne: Cheshire, 1954) by Vincent Buckley

The lines from "To Praise a Wife" on page 125 are from *Masters in Israel* (Sydney: Angus and Robertson, 1961) by Vincent Buckley

The lines from "Parents" on page 125 are from *Arcady and Other Places* (Melbourne: Melbourne University Press and London, New York: Cambridge University Press, 1966) by Vincent Buckley

The lines from "Stand Up and Be Counted" on page 126 are from *Golden Builders and Other Poems* (London: Angus & Robertson, 1976) by Vincent Buckley

The lines beginning "Leaves . . . " on page 151 are from *Plight* (New Rochelle, NY: Elizabeth Press, 1969) by Cid Corman

The lines from "The Islands" on page 160 are from *Songs of Cifar and the Sweet Sea* (New York: Columbia University Press, 1979) by Pablo Antonio Cuadra

The lines from "Mouth of Light" on page 178 by René Despestre can be found in *Negritude: Black Poetry from Africa and the Caribbean* (New York: October House, 1970) by Norman Shapiro

The lines beginning "The grid of narrative . . . " on page 193 are from *Burn This* (London: Hutchinson, 1982) by Thomas M. Disch

The lines from "Knife in the Sun," from "Sunflower" and from "Wings" on page 94 are all from *Orchard Lamps* (New York: Sheep Meadow Press, 1978) by Ivan Drach, translated by Daniel Halpern and others

The lines from "Girls in White" on page 202 are from *The Bright Plain* (Chapel Hill: University of North Carolina Press, 1942) by Charles Edward Eaton

The lines from "Topaz" on page 202 are from *The Shadow of the Swimmer* (New York: Fine Editions Press, 1951) by Charles Edward Eaton

The lines from "Late Afternoon with a Cat" on page 211 are from *Homage to Fats Navarro* (New York: New Rivers Press, 1978) by Richard M. Elman

The lines from "Washington Square Park" on page 227 are from *Indiana* (Los Angeles: Black Sparrow Press, 1969) by Clayton Eshleman

The lines beginning "Beastlike motor cars . . . " and the lines from "Snake" by Feng Zhi on pages 236–237 can be found in *Modern Chinese Poetry: An Introduction* (Seattle: University of Washington Press, 1972) by Julia C. Lin

The lines from "Intermission" on page 273 are from *Harsh World and Other Poems* (Princeton, NJ: Princeton University Press, 1977) by Angel González, translated by Donald D. Walsh

The lines from "Feeling and Form" on page 30 are from *Taking Notice* (New York: Knopf, 1980) by Marilyn Hacker

The lines from "Apologia pro opere suo" on page 308 are from *Presentation Piece* (New York: Viking, 1974) by Marilyn Hacker

The lines from "On the Divide" and from "Poem" on page 310 are from *Winter News* (Middletown, CT: Wesleyan University Press, 1966) by John Haines

The lines from "Lies" and from "A Poem Like a Grenade" on page 311 are from *The Stone Harp* (Middletown, CT: Wesleyan University Press, 1971) by John Haines

The lines from "Dusk of the Revolutionaries" on page 311 are from *Cicada* (Middletown, CT: Wesleyan University Press, 1977) by John Haines

The lines from "Where Is My Woman Now: For Billie Holiday" and from "Dead-Day: Malcolm, Feb. 21" on page 317 are from *Dear John, Dear Coltrane* (Pittsburgh: Pittsburgh University Press, 1970) by Michael S. Harper

The lines from "The Faculty Club, Portland, Oregon" and from "Don't Explain: Culture as Science as Language as Cannibal" on page 318 are from *History Is Your Own Heartbeat* (Champaign, IL: University of Illinois Press, 1971) by Michael S. Harper

The lines from "Love Letters: The Caribou Hills, the Moose Range" on page 318 are from *Song: I Want a Witness* (Pittsburgh: University of Pittsburgh Press, 1970) by Michael S. Harper

The lines beginning "Who's seen a house . . . " and "Old symbols are torn . . . " on page 324 are from *Crossing the River Twice* (Cleveland, OH: Cleveland State University Poetry Center, 1976) by Stratis Haviaras

The lines from "Docking at Palermo" on page 345 are from *Good Luck in Cracked Italian* (New York: World, 1969) by Richard Hugo

v

The lines beginning " . . . black men . . . " on page 374 are from *Highlife for Caliban* (Ann Arbor, MI: Ardis, 1973) by Lemuel Johnson

The lines from poem "number XXIV" on page 375 are from *Hand on the Navel* (Ann Arbor, MI: Ardis, 1978) by Lemuel Johnson

The lines from "Bath" on page 393 are from *Of Rhymes of a Pfc* (New York: New Directions, 1964) by Lincoln Kirstein

The lines beginning "syrinx charmer of grass snakes . . . ," the lines beginning "In the orchards . . . ," and the lines from "Mission Accomplished" on pages 431–432 are all by Paul-Marie Lapointe and can be found in *The Terror of the Snows* (Pittsburgh: University of Pittsburgh Press, 1976) translated by D.G. Jones

The lines from "The Star with Two Names the Name of Two Stars" by Enrique Lihn (translated by John Felstner) on page 457 can be found in *The Dark Room and Other Poems* (New York: New Directions, 1978) collected by Patricio Lerzundi

The lines from "When the Saints Come Marching In" on page 460 are from *Cables* (London: P. Breman, 1970) by Audre Lorde

The lines from "Coal" on page 460 are from *Coal* (New York: Norton, 1976) by Audre Lorde

The lines from "Black Mother Woman" on page 461 are from *From a Land Where Other People Live* (Detroit: Broadside Press, 1973) by Audre Lorde

The lines from "Poem 19" and "Poem 32" on page 470 and from "Poem 55" on page 471 are from *Poems to Eimhir* (London: Gollancz, 1971) by Sorley Maclean, translated by Ian Crichton Smith

The lines from "Van Gogh in the Borinage," from "The Death of Marilyn Monroe," from "A Disused Shed in Co. Wexford," lines beginning "We could all be saved by keeping an eye on the hill . . .," lines beginning "But the hills are still the same . . . ," lines beginning "Demanding that I inhabit . . . ," lines beginning "Elocution, Logic Political Science . . . ," the lines from "Carrowdore Churchyard" and from "North Wind: Portrush" on pages 483–484 are all by Derek Mahon and can be found in *Poems 1962-1978* (Oxford, New York: Oxford University Press, 1979) by Derek Mahon

The lines from "Letter from North Queensland: 1892" on page 488 are from *The Year of the Foxes and Other Poems* (New York: Braziller, 1979) by David Malouf

The lines from "Breathing Exercises" on page 548 are from *Returning Your Call* (Princeton, NJ: Princeton University Press, 1975) by Leonard Nathan

The lines from "To My Craft" by Agnes Nemes Nagy on page 553 are from *Selected Poems* (University of Iowa: International Writing Program, 1980) translated by Bruce Berlind

The lines from "Twelve Years" on page 557 are from *Day of Sirens* (Manchester, England: Carcanet, 1973) by Margaret Newlin

The lines from "Words" and from "The Airy Bedroom" on page 557 are from *The Book of Mourning* (Ann Arbor, MI: Ardis, 1982) by Margaret Newlin

The lines from "Occupation: Housewife" and from "Wishing for Vermeer, Breughel" on page 557 are

from *The Fragile Immigrants* (Oxford: Carcanet, 1971) by Margaret Newlin

The lines from "Over the Garden Wall" on page 572 are from *The Dainty Monsters* (Toronto: Coach House Press, 1967) by Michael Ondaatje

The lines beginning "See the rat in the jelly . . . " on page 573 are from *Rat Jelly* (Toronto: Coach House Press, 1973) by Michael Ondaatje

The lines beginning "Imagine if you dug him up . . . " on page 573 are from *The Collected Works of Billy the Kid* (New York: Norton, 1974) by Michael Ondaatje

The lines from "In Memoriam Professor G.H.K." by István Örkény (translated by Carl Erickson) on page 576 can be found in Albert Tezla's *Ocean at the Window* (Minneapolis: University of Minnesota Press, 1981)

The lines from "The Balcony" on page 590 by Sandro Penna can be found in *This Strange Joy* (Columbus: Ohio State University Press, 1982) by W.S. Di Piero

The lines from "Fish in the Net" and from "Passion of Ravensbrück" by Janos Pilinszky (translated by Peter Sherwood) on pages 593–594 can be found in Albert Tezla's *Ocean at the Window* (Minneapolis: University of Minnesota Press, 1981)

The lines from "A Martian Sends a Postcard Home" and from "In the Mortuary" on page 617 are from *A Martian Sends a Postcard Home* (Oxford, New York: Oxford University Press, 1978) by Craig Raine

The lines from "The Onion, Memory" on page 617 are from *The Onion, Memory* (Oxford, New York: Oxford University Press, 1978) by Craig Raine

The lines from "She Speaks" on page 630 are from *Nu-Plastik Fanfare Red and Other Poems* (St. Lucia, Brisbane: University of Queensland Press, 1973) by Judith Rodriguez

The lines from "Occasion for Elegy" on page 630 are from *Water Life* (St. Lucia, Brisbane: University of Queensland Press, 1976) by Judith Rodriguez

The lines from "Father and Son" on page 662 are from *The Wounded Stag* (Manila: Capital Publishing House, 1956) by Bienvenido Santos

The lines from "Light from Canada" on page 667 are from *The Crystal Lithium* (New York: Random House, 1972) by James Schuyler

The lines on page 667 from *The Morning of the Poem* (New York: Farrar, Straus & Giroux, 1980) are by James Schuyler

The lines beginning "Ever since I realized . . . " on page 677 are from *For Colored Girls Who Have Considered Suicide When the Rainbow Is Enuf* (San Lorenzo, CA: Shameless Hussy Press, 1975) by Ntozake Shange

The lines from "In Memory of Your Body" on page 679 are from *Poems from Deal* (New York: E. P. Dutton, 1969) by David Shapiro

The lines from "Flowers of the Mediterranean" on page 680 are from *A Man Holding an Acoustic Panel* (New York: E.P. Dutton, 1971) by David Shapiro

The lines from "The Devil's Trill Sonata" on page 680 are from *Lateness* (Woodstock, NY: Overlook Press, 1978) by David Shapiro

The lines on page 691 from *Dying: An Introduction* (Boston: Little, Brown, 1968) are by L. E. Sissman

The lines from "Field" on page 706 are from *The Elements of San Joaquin* (Pittsburgh: University of Pittsburgh Press, 1977) by Gary Soto

The lines from "Mexicans Begin Jogging" on page 707 are from *Where Sparrows Work Hard* (Pittsburgh: University of Pittsburgh Press, 1981) by Gary Soto

The lines beginning "Let me go down to them and learn . . ." and the lines from "The Almond Tree" on page 709 are from *A Familiar Tree* (Oxford, New York: Oxford University Press, 1978) by Jon Stallworthy

The lines from "The Almond Tree Revisited" on page 709 are from *Hand in Hand* (London: Chatto and Windus, 1974) by Jon Stallworthy

The lines from "Three Priests in April" on page 711 are from *Three Priests in April* (Baltimore: Contemporary Poetry, 1956) by Stephen Stepanchev

The lines beginning "It is subtle and slow . . ." on page 711 from *Mining the Darkness* (Los Angeles: Black Sparrow Press, 1975) are by Stephen Stepanchev

The lines from "Living in America" on page 713 are from *Living in America* (Ann Arbor: Generation, 1965) by Anne Stevenson

The lines from "England" on page 713 are from *Reversals* (Middletown, CT: Wesleyan University Press, 1969) by Anne Stevenson

The lines from "The Mudtower" on page 713 are from *Enough of Green* (Oxford, New York: Oxford University Press, 1977) by Anne Stevenson

The lines from "Green Mountain, Black Mountain" on page 714 are from *Minute by Glass Minute* (Oxford, New York: Oxford University Press, 1982) by Anne Stevenson

The lines from "Cecie" on page 735 are from *Love and Other Deaths* (London: Elek, 1975) by D. M. Thomas

The lines from "Force (2): Song" on page 759 are from *Ordinary Things* (New York: Farrar, Straus & Giroux, 1974) by Jean Valentine

The lines from "Night" on page 759 are from *Pilgrims* (New York: Farrar, Straus & Giroux, 1969) by Jean Valentine

The lines from "To My Soul" on page 759 are from *Dream Barker and Other Poems* (New Haven: Yale University Press, 1965) by Jean Valentine

The lines from "Letter from a Stranger" on page 760 are from *The Messenger* (New York: Farrar, Straus & Giroux, 1979) by Jean Valentine

The lines from "Aphrodite," from "Magdalen" and from "My Sun" on page 761 are by Kóstas Várnalis and can be found in *Modern Greek Poetry* (New York: Simon and Schuster, 1973) by Kimon Friar

The lines from "The Secret" on page 765 are from *The French Girls of Killíni* (Boston: Little, Brown, 1967) by Arturo Vivante

The lines from "Never Offer Your Heart . . ." on page 775 are from *Good Night, Willie Lee, I'll See You in the Morning* (New York: Harcourt Brace Jovanovich, 1979) by Alice Walker

The lines from "Three Dollars Cash" on page 775 are from *Revolutionary Petunias* (New York: Harcourt Brace Jovanovich, 1973) by Alice Walker

The lines beginning "And then more lovely than a well-played flute . . ." on page 776 are from *Perennia* (Cambridge: Golden Head Press, 1962) by Francis Warner

The lines from "Of What Is Past" on page 793 are from *Lies* (New York: Houghton Mifflin, 1969) by C. K. Williams

The lines from "The Spirit the Triumph" on page 793 are from *I Am the Bitter Name* (New York: Houghton Mifflin, 1972) by C. K. Williams

The lines from "Waking Jed," the lines beginning "The Baskets on their Court are Still intact at least . . ." and the lines from the title poem "Tar" on pages 793–794 are all from *Tar* (New York: Vintage Books, 1983) by C. K. Williams

The lines beginning "By our crawling . . ." on page 799 are from *Beat Drum Beat Heart* (London: Cresset Press, 1946) by Sheila Wingfield

The lines from "One's Due" on page 800 are from *Admissions* (London: John Calder, 1977) by Sheila Wingfield

The lines from "April" on page 807 are from *China Trace* (Middletown, CN: Wesleyan University Press, 1977) by Charles Wright

The lines from "The New Poem" on page 807 are from *Hard Freight* (Middletown, CN: Wesleyan University Press, 1973) by Charles Wright

The lines from "Amanita Phalloidus" on page 827 are from *The Dark Side of the Earth* (New York: Harper & Row, 1974) by Paul Zweig

The lines from "Afraid that I Am Not a Poet" and from "The Natural History of Death" on page 827 are from *Against Emptiness* (New York: Harper & Row, 1971) by Paul Zweig

KEY TO PRONUNCIATION

ā   āle
â   câre
a   add
ä   ärm

ē   ēve
e   end

g   go

ī   ice
i   ill

ᴋ   German *ch* as in
      ich (iᴋ)

ɴ   Not pronounced, but
      indicates the nasal
      tone of the preced-
      ing vowel, as in the
      French *bon* (bôɴ)

ō   ōld
ô   ôrb
o   odd
oi   oil
o͞o   o͞oze
o͝o   fo͝ot
ou   out

th   then
th   thin

ū   cūbe
û   ûrn; French eu, as in
      jeu (zhû), German
      ö, *oe*, as in *schön*
      (shûn), *Goethe*
      (gû´te)
u   tub

ü   Pronounced approxi-
      mately as ē, with
      rounded lips: French
      u, as in *menu*
      (mə·nü); German ü,
      as in *grün*

ə   the schwa, an un-
      stressed vowel rep-
      resenting the sound
      that is spelled
      a as in sofa
      e as in fitted
      i as in edible
      o as in melon
      u as in circus

zh   azure

´   = main accent

˝   = secondary accent

CONTENTS

NECROLOGY

Arbuzov, A. N. Apr. 20, 1986
Ding Ling Mar. 4, 1986
Francis, R. July 13, 1987
Nagel, E. Sept. 20, 1985
Seifert, J. Jan. 10, 1986

Authors

PREFACE

World Authors 1975–1980 is a companion to the four volumes in the Wilson Authors Series that provide information on writers of this century: *Twentieth Century Authors* (1942) and its supplement (1955); *World Authors 1950–1970* (1975); and *World Authors 1970–1975* (1980). The editorial policy established by Stanley J. Kunitz and Howard Haycraft in *Twentieth Century Authors* "to provide . . . authentic biographical information on the writers of this century, of all nations, whose books are familiar to readers of English," has not changed, although the range of subjects has grown steadily wider and more cosmopolitan. The editor of this volume has also continued the practice of her predecessors by inviting every living writer who could be reached to contribute an autobiographical sketch. About a third of the 379 writers in the volume responded, and many who did not choose to write assisted us by providing biographical and bibliographical information. Autobiographies that have been translated from foreign languages have been rendered literally. The remaining sketches were written by a large number of contributors who are acknowledged below, many of them scholars specializing in the literature on which they wrote. We have not followed a consistent policy of length in individual entries. When authors have contributed, it seemed desirable to let them speak in their own voices, even if at greater length than in our third-person sketches.

This volume also follows the general policy of the series in selecting writers whose work is of great popular interest or literary merit, and who came to prominence in the years 1975–1980. We have also included several, however, whose achievements pre-date the time span of the title, and whose reputations, for a variety of reasons, have lagged behind their work. Inevitably, lack of space or failure of judgment have caused us to overlook some writers, but these omissions will be rectified in later volumes.

In recent years the republic of letters, and the world of *World Authors,* has been greatly expanded by the efforts of translators and scholars, and the widening literary interests of the English-speaking public. It is especially gratifying to be able to include in this volume many writers from what, until a decade ago, had been undiscovered literary territory—the People's Republic of China—as well as to extend our coverage of writers from Southeast Asia, the Soviet Union, Africa, and Latin America. Our sole criterion for selection has been the existence of a portion of their work in English translation. In discussing foreign-language writers we have cited principal works in the original language, giving in parentheses the titles of English translations or, when there are none, literal English language equivalents. In listing works about the author we have not given an exhaustive bibliography but a selection intended to guide the reader to useful and accessible biographical and critical sources.

It is a particular pleasure to acknowledge the contributions of those who cooperated in the planning, writing, editing and production of this book: Howard Batchelor, Bruce R. Carrick, John Jamieson, Andrew C. Kimmens, Ellen Lehman, John Wakeman and Roslyn Wegweiser.

V.C.
May 1985

xv

CONTRIBUTORS

Stephen Akey
Fernando Alegría
Roger Allen
Benedict Anderson
Anna Louise Andrade
Steven Anzovin
Miriam Bachner
Ruth Beizer-Bohrer
Thomas E. Bird
William Bischoff
Robert Bledsoe
Antonina Bouis
Eugene Braigen
Jerome Brooks
Malcolm Compitello
Miriam Cooke
Elizabeth D. Crawford
Angela DellePiane
Victor Dmitriev
Tamara S. Evans
Yi-tsi Mei Feuerwerker
Andres Franco
Sada Fretz
Lita Friedman
Robin Fulton
Janet Garton
Van C. Gessel
Eamon Grennan
Mitzi Hamovitch
Frank Hugus
William P. Kelly
Walter Kendrick
Rolf Kieser
Andrew C. Kimmens

Bernard R. Kogan
Theresa S. Kubis
Frank Laraque
Robert E. Long
A. J. Liehm
Torberg Lundell
Sigurdur A. Magnùsson
Shirley Mangini-Gonzalez
Myron Matlaw
Verne Moberg
George O'Brien
Tatiana Patera
Janet Podell
Ritva Poom
Blossom R. Primer
Marguerite Raben
Janet E. Rasmussen
Charles E. Reagan
Yvonne L. Sandstroem
William Scherzer
Grace Schulman
Richard Sheldon
C. K. Stead
Irwin Stern
Edward Tallman
Albert Tezla
Nancy J. Tomes
Paul I. Trensky
Timothy Tung
Richard Wall
Claire Nicolas White
Eleanor Withington
Zhu Hong

ABRAMS, M(EYER) H(OWARD) (July 23, 1912–), American scholar, critic, and educator, was born in Long Branch, New Jersey, to Joseph and Sara (Shanes) Abrams. Early attracted to the humanities, he went to Harvard, where he took his B.A. in 1934 with a senior honors thesis that was published the same year by Harvard University Press as *The Milk of Paradise: The Effects of Opium Visions on the Works of De Quincey, Crabbe, Francis Thompson, and Coleridge.* This first book defined the field to which Abrams has devoted his career in scholarship—English literary romanticism, on which he has expounded widely and significantly in many studies, the most important of which are *The Mirror and the Lamp* and *Natural Supernaturalism.*

Abrams spent the academic year 1934–35 in England at Cambridge University as a Henry Fellow and returned to Harvard for his M.A. in 1936. He began his teaching career as instructor in English at Harvard in 1938 while completing his doctoral thesis on romantic theories of poetry and criticism. He received his Ph.D. in 1940 and continued to work on this subject, enlarging it to what finally emerged as *The Mirror and the Lamp: Romantic Theory and the Critical Tradition* in 1953. During World War II Abrams was a research associate at Harvard's Psycho-Acoustic Laboratory, and in 1945 he returned to full-time teaching as assistant professor of English at Cornell University. Cornell has remained his academic home ever since—with leaves for visiting lectureships and research fellowships. These include a year (1953) as Fulbright lecturer at the Royal University at Malta, and lecture series at Indiana University in 1963, the University of Toronto in 1964, and UCLA in 1975. A recipient of a Rockefeller Postwar Fellowship in 1946, a Ford Foundation Fellowship in 1957, two Guggenheim fellowships (1957, 1960), a fellowship at the Center for Advanced Study in the Behavioral Sciences at Stanford in 1967, and a visiting fellowship at All Souls College, Oxford in 1977, he has also been honored for his books, receiving the Phi Beta Kappa

M.H. ABRAMS

Christian Gauss prize for *The Mirror and the Lamp* in 1954 and the Modern Language Association's James Russell Lowell Prize in 1972 for *Natural Supernaturalism.* In 1978 the University of Rochester awarded him an honorary Doctorate of Humane Letters.

These academic honors testify to Abrams' achievements as scholar and critic, but to them must be added his distinction as a teacher of English literature to several generations of undergraduate and graduate students at Cornell, where he became full professor in 1953, then the first Frederic J. Whiton Professor of English Literature in 1960, and in 1963 the Class of 1916 Professor. When he was the subject in 1978 of a two-day symposium at Cornell under the sponsorship of the Society for the Humanities, one of Abrams' former students noted his personal qualities, his "robust enjoyment in the life of the mind and of the spirit," which he communicates to students, colleagues, and readers in general. As a teacher, Abrams has written, he spends much of his time "in teaching method—that is, the forms of sound reasoning in a humanistic discipline, the kinds of questions that are relevant, and the nature and weight of the evidence for and against answers to these questions." Thus as both teacher and scholar-critic, he has adopted an essentially pluralistic approach that is solidly in the humanistic tradition. In a paper delivered at a conference of the University Center for Rational Alternatives in 1973, at a time when traditional humanism was under widespread challenge, he voiced his suspicions of relativistic attacks on "certainty" and "values." While conceding that certainty was impossible, he argued for "an essential pluralism in the humanistic pursuits," a recognition of differences: "In comparison with the hot world of prophecy, the world of the humanist is a cool world." He urged open-minded recognition of "multiple interpretations" that broaden and enrich our understanding of literature and a "secure balance and a firm will to conduct, rationally, a discipline in which many of the premises, procedures, and conclusions are essentially contestable, without surrendering either to an all-dissolving skepticism or to the inviting dogmatism of the visionary and the fanatic."

The four main fields in which Abrams has worked are Wordsworth and Coleridge studies, the history of ideas, critical theory, and the teaching of English literature. To this last, in addition to classroom teaching, he has contributed especially with his essay on "Theories of Poetry" written for the *Princeton Encyclopedia of Poetry and Poetics* (1965) and his collaboration on the widely used *Norton Anthology of English Literature,* of which he is general editor and for which he prepared the sections on romanticism, providing comprehensive and lucid introductions and carefully edited selected texts that balance the needs of the undergraduate student with the demands of rigorous scholarly methodology. A fellow scholar-critic-teacher, Wayne Booth, has written: "To me Abrams is the best historian of ideas, as ideas relate to literature and literary criticism, that the world has known." Moving out from literature, sometimes from a single poem (as he does with a passage from Wordsworth's "The Recluse" in *Natural Supernaturalism*), he seeks the essence of romanticism, as another scholar writes, "by describing parallels in form and idea in the works of the poets and philosophers of the period," that is, in the social and intellectual contexts of a work or of an entire literary movement. *The Mirror and the Lamp* began, Abrams wrote in the preface, with a study of the critical writings of Dr. Johnson and Coleridge and grew, over more than ten years, into a history of aesthetic thought from ancient times to the romantic era. Its title combines "two common and antithetical metaphors of mind"—the mirror, a metaphor for mimetic and pragmatic theories of art (those that regard literature as a record of external reality as the artist perceives it), and the lamp, a metaphor for expressive or emotional theories (illuminating what the artist perceives). Abrams' thesis is that romanticism marks a distinct shift from one to the other: whereas in the eighteenth century a work of art was "comparable to a mirror presenting a selected and ordered image of life," romanticism reversed the image and offered in its place a subjective aesthetic in which the artist's creative imagination brought clear and penetrating light to the nature of things. Abrams supports his thesis with extensive analysis of the critical writings of the major romantics (European as well as English), with special emphasis on Wordsworth and Coleridge, and he concludes with an examination of certain timeless critical questions of poetic "truth" and the uses of poetry. The impact of *The Mirror and the Lamp* in 1953 on a generation nurtured on the New Criticism, with its emphasis on the literary object alone apart from any special context and generally indifferent to the writings of the romantics, was described by the critic Jonathan Culler: "We needed precisely such a guide as *The Mirror and the Lamp,* which would judiciously explain romantic theory, enabling us to see its relation to other theories of poetry and to see romantic literature as a comprehensible historical phenomenon." Since its initial appearance, *The Mirror and the Lamp* has been regarded as an exemplary theoretical study of literature.

Taking his stand firmly for traditional humanism and critical pluralism, Abrams invited challenges from structuralist and deconstructionist critics with his *Natural Supernaturalism: Tradition and Revolution in Romantic Literature.* The title, from a chapter in Carlyle's *Sartor Resartus,* suggests the primary concern of the book—"the secularization of inherited theological ideas and ways of thinking." In this phenomenon, specifically in the Christian symbolism of man's fall, redemption, and rebirth, the romantics reformulated their faith in their creativity and their relationship to nature in spite of the disillusion and alienation that followed the French Revolution and marked the spirit of their age. Abrams writes: "Despite their displacement from a supernatural to a natural frame of reference, however, the ancient problems, terminology, and ways of thinking about human nature and history survived, as the implicit distinctions and categories through which even radically secular writers saw themselves and their world, and as the presuppositions and forms of their thinking about the condition, the milieu, the essential values and aspirations, and the history and destiny of the individual and of mankind." Concentrating upon Wordsworth's autobiographical poem *The Prelude,* but framing it in the intellectual history of its time, Abrams (with wide reading in French and German poets and philosophers as well as in English literature) sought both to define romanticism and to establish the continuity of the Judaeo-Christian tradition. As Wayne Booth wrote: "Showing us where we came from, demonstrating that it was a place of greatness in our past, transmitting forgotten connections that join us to that past, *Natural Supernaturalism* becomes a portrayal of who and where we are. . . . It makes life itself, in a post-romantic age, tangibly, demonstrably livable."

Even the critics who challenged the thesis of *Natural Supernaturalism* acknowledged the book's importance. Calling it "the best book on romanticism I have ever read," Morse Peckham proceeded to reject its thesis for over-emphasizing secular redemptionism, relying too heavily on analogy, and failing to explore the complexities of romanticism. Thomas McFarland concluded that *Natural Supernaturalism* is "correct in most of its major contentions" and sheds "genuine light on major aspects of romantic attitude and practice." But the principal value of the book, in his judgment—namely, Abrams' extensive use of German sources—is also its weakness: "The same willingness to record analogies rather than explore relationships leads to some rather surprising omissions . . . a Germanic tendency to press recalcitrant materials into *à priori* schemes."

Abrams' most formidable critic was J. Hillis Miller, whose review was a deconstructionist attack on all traditional forms of criticism. He too praised the book as "in the grand tradition of humanistic scholarship . . . learned, elegantly and lucidly composed, equable and sane throughout, generously humane in its appreciation of the great works of the past and in its desire to perpetuate their values through our dark time. . . ." Nevertheless, he argued, Abrams "oversimplified the problem" with romantic "presuppositions" and a narrow view of language as mimetic and of a literary text as communicating direct and unequivocal meaning: "In place of the theory of interpretation presupposed in *Natural Supernaturalism,* Derrida, Nietzsche, and the others [deconstructionist critics] would put the notion that a text never has a single meaning, but is the crossroads of multiple ambiguous meanings." To this Abrams replied that for deconstructionism, " . . . any history which relies on written texts becomes an impossibility. If a production is to be accounted a history, it must be a history of something determinate and determinable; and the elementary assumption that a cultural historian must make is that he is able to understand, in the sense that he is at least able to approximate, the core of meanings that certain writers at certain times expressed in their writings."

The aim of any good aesthetic theory, Abrams has written, is "to establish principles enabling us to justify, order, and clarify our interpretation and appraisal of the aesthetic facts themselves." As a pluralist acknowledging that literary criticism can never be scientifically "true," he nevertheless defends literary criticism: "The criterion is not the scientific verifiability of its single propositions, but the scope, precision, and coherence of the insights that it yields into the properties of single works of art and the adequacy with which it accounts for diverse kinds of art." Abrams admits that he relies "on taste, tact, and intuition rather than a controlling method." He has described his *Natural Supernaturalism* as "an effort of imagination to understand a great romantic enterprise by looking at it from within." This is not subjectivism, however, but a rejection of what he calls "analytical metacriticism," which questions interpretation and evaluative judgments and would reduce all criticism to a linguistic analysis or what he calls "a language-game." His main caveat against such a method, as he wrote in an essay of 1968 called "What's the Use of Theorizing about the Arts?", is that "while criticism involves the use of logic and scientific method, it must go far beyond their capacities if it is to do its proper job." It must "deal with all the important human concerns with art . . . our common humanity, our sense of what life and the world are really like, and how people really act, our deep moral convictions and even religious beliefs (or lack of them)." If indeed criticism is a "language game," he concludes the essay, "the name of this game is the humanities."

Abrams married Ruth Gaynes in 1937. They have two daughters. Professor emeritus since July 1, 1983, Abrams lives in Ithaca, New York, working on the Cornell Wordsworth edition and other scholarly projects.

PRINCIPAL WORKS: The Milk of Paradise, 1934; The Mirror and the Lamp, 1953; A Glossary of Literary Terms, 1957; Natural Supernaturalism, 1971. *As editor*—The Poetry of Pope: A Selection, 1954; Literature and Belief: English Institute Essays, 1958; English Romantic Poets: Modern Essays in Criticism, 1960; (with others) The Norton Anthology of English Literature, 1962–   ; Wordsworth: A Collection of Critical Essays, 1972; (with J. Wordsworth and S. Gill) William Wordsworth: The Prelude, 1979.

ABOUT: Booth, W. C. Critical Understanding: The Powers and Limits of Pluralism, 1979; Borklund, E. Contemporary Literary Criticism, 1982; Contemporary Authors 57–60, 1976; Jordan, F. (ed.) The English Romantic Poets: A Review of Research and Criticism, 1972; Lipking, L. (ed.) High Romantic Argument: Essays for M. H. Abrams, 1981; Who's Who in America, 1983–84. *Periodicals*—Critical Inquiry 2, 1976; 3, 1977; Diacritics 2, 1972; Studies in Romanticism 13, 1974; Yale Review 61, 1972.

ACHDIAT KARTA MIHARDJA

*ACHDIAT KARTA MIHARDJA (March 6, 1911–   ), Indonesian novelist and short story writer, writes: "I was born into a class-ridden colonial society, when the national political awareness of my people started to emerge and developed rapidly. The classes were based on political and economic power which coincided with racial differences and were sustained by an accordingly discriminating legal system. At the top were the Dutch rulers and other European nationals who, peculiarly enough, also included the Japanese. Down at the bottom were the 'inlanders' (natives). In between this lowest and the top class of Europeans there were three other classes; one the so-called 'half bloods' or 'Indo-Europeans,' another one the Chinese, and the third the so-called 'foreign Orientals' comprising Indians, Arabs and other Asians. They were all above the 'inlanders.'

"Strikingly enough, the class of the 'inlanders' were also divided into several strata. The *priyayis* or the native administrators and bureaucrats with the *bupati* (regent) and his relatives were at the top of the social ladder, while far below them were the poverty-stricken classes of peasants, small traders, fishermen, artisans, labourers, coolies, etc. who constituted the great majority of the Indonesian people. As a class the native administrators were the descendants of the feudal aristocracy who ruled the country with authority delegated by a sovereign lord. But since the Dutch seized power they had been transformed into mere tools in the hands of the colonizers. I hailed from this feudal *priyayi* class.

"I happened to be born in the month Safar of the Arabic calendar, believed to be an ill-fated month, the month for dogs to mate. A baby born within that month was bound to become very naughty as a child and wicked as a grown-up person. But that could be prevented by conducting certain ceremonies which in my case took place in one morning when as a boy of four my naughtiness seemed to be intolerable anymore for my parents. After the ceremony everybody was happy; and somehow, my father didn't flog me as often as he had done before. As a matter of fact the whole matter was pure superstition

which was strange to me, because my parents and the whole family were very devoted Moslems. When in 1911 the first Islamic political party was founded both my father and the other male members of the family, including my two grandfathers, joined immediately as party members. Like most nationally conscious Moslems of the time, they felt that we musn't be governed by a foreign race of *kafirs* (unbelievers) any longer.

"When I reached the age for attending school, I was sent to a Dutch-Native School. I was not entitled to attend the more prestigious European school. Already in the lower classes of the school, a sort of inferiority complex towards the Europeans as a race was implanted systematically and effectively into my system. To learn the Dutch language for instance the class was given a textbook full of pictures with captions in simple sentences. The pictures were juxtaposed on the same page—one picture depicted a European, and the other an 'inlander.' The European was always pictured as a handsome looking and neatly attired person, while in contrast the native was constantly ugly and hungry looking, miserable, dirty and poorly dressed. Accordingly the captions were also contrasting statements—favourable for the European, and negative, even humiliating and insulting for the 'inlander.'

"Fortunately, during my formative years nationalism was flaring up. Already when I was a schoolboy, I used to attend political public gatherings where leaders like Sukarno and others gave fiery and inspiring speeches.

"Inspired by such speeches I joined Sutan Syahrir's nationalistic youth organization. (He

°äk´ dē ät, kä´ tä mē hä´ jä

was later the first prime minister of the Republic of Indonesia; 1945–47). Then, counteracting the divide and rule policy, the youths took a pledge in 1928, acknowledging that they belonged to one Indonesian nation, that Indonesia was their one and only fatherland, and that they adopted the Indonesian language as the unifying national language. The severe depression of the 1930s put my father on pension, and I had to look for a job. There was a good chance for me to start a career as a *priyayi*. But I abhorred the idea of becoming a tool of the colonial government. Instead I joined the Taman Siswa in Jakarta—a non-Dutch school system with strong nationalistic sentiments and ideals. Through subjects such as national history, geography, arts and culture, the students were taught to love their country and culture. However, there was to my feeling, too much Javanese traditionalism in the whole system, and not enough modernism of the West, which I thought should be adopted as one of the prominent characteristics of Indonesian culture as distinct from traditional cultures, such as Javanese, Balinese, Minangkabau, and the countless established traditional cultures of the various ethnic groups, which were scattered all over the archipelago. So, I left Taman Siswa. Incidentally, it was by this time that the controversial problem of East-West cultures was being discussed zealously among Indonesian intellectuals which later I compiled in a book titled *Polemik Kebudayaan* (Polemics on Culture), published in 1948.

"Having no job nor money to live on in Jakarta, I came home to live a parasitical life with my parents in the small country town of Garut, waiting for something to turn up that would give me an income. I killed my boredom with a lot of reading. Fortunately my father was a great lover of good books. He had a good collection of some of the works (in Dutch translations) of Shakespeare, Tolstoy, Dostoyevsky, Turgenev, Dumas, Zola, Multatuli, Vondel and some others, beside works of Sundanese and Indonesian writers of the time. I had ample time to read many of them. I also had more opportunity to observe and think about my family's religious life.

"My family belonged to the austere mystical Sufi order of Kadiriyah-Nakshabandiyah. Unlike Quran reading, I found listening to the discussions about sufism very interesting. The discussions used to be held in my parents house when the guru who lived in the village came over to our town and stayed with us for one or two days. I was told that unless I joined the order I wouldn't be together with the other members, including my parents, as one family in the hereafter. Hence everybody was very happy when I was initiated into the order. To me, however, it

simply meant that the order would bind us together in the same spiritual climate here in the present life, and had nothing to do with the hereafter, in which I had less interest.

"When in the late 1950s President Sukarno appealed for every Indonesian to manifest himself as a *manusia komplit* (a complete man) stressing the importance and necessity of having a strong political awareness, I responded in a paper that I read to a conference on culture in Salatiga in 1959, expounding that the 'complete man' was to me identical with the *insan kamil* who took care and constantly perfected all aspects of his identity—the intellectual, the moral, the aesthetical and the physical.

"'Life is not meant to be easy.' The phrase was doubly true during the depression for a jobless 'colonized' person. At one stage I succeeded in getting a press-card as a correspondent for the Dutch press agency Aneta. I was still living with my parents in Garut. One day I sent in a news item about an Indonesian boy who had been crushed to pieces by a running train. The chief editor shouted through the telephone that the accident was non-news. I was angry. Only a couple of days before, Aneta reported extensively the news of two missing Dutch boys in the mountains. Dutch newspapers printed big headlines on the front page about it. And the government had even sent a whole company of the army to search for them, which I commended for humanitarian reasons. But still I returned my press-card immediately.

"Then I became a member of the editorial board of the Indonesian daily paper *Bintang Timur* (East Star) in Jakarta. I found the job as an editor as satisfying as that of teacher in regard to educating my people and implanting a national consciousness in them. For understandable political reasons the paper failed to attract advertisements from the European business community. It went bankrupt. To make ends meet, I picked up odd jobs—salesman, auctioneer, teaching Europeans who wanted to learn Sundanese, and so on. In the meantime I had married a girl who was very efficient in making a small income. While from time to time I earned some money with writing, she delivered home-made cakes to restaurants and did some catering for wedding parties and the like. The Pacific War was already imminent by the time. Everybody in the nationalist circles started to speculate on what effect the war would have on our people and country. I agreed with the opinion of some political leaders that the war would constitute a sort of 'God's blessing in disguise.' Indonesia would then be free from the shackles of the Dutch. But then what next? Freedom? Or another country, the winner of the war, would take over the role of the Dutch as a new colonizer and oppressor? Mohammad Hatta (later the vice-president of the Republic) gave a warning from his exile on the island of Banda in the Moluccas about the danger of Japanese expansionism and fascism. That changed my optimism for freedom into apprehension. With that threat in mind I accepted an offer for a job in Bandung as a translator for a Dutch propaganda journal against the Japanese. But not for long. I got another job as an editor at the government publishing house Balai Pustaka. I moved back to Jakarta.

"Soon afterwards the Japanese occupying forces ruled over the country. Life became more difficult. Oppression became harsher; exploitation more cruel. People died from hunger and disease, or were tortured to death by the dreadful military police. Humanity had lost its dignity. I often pondered on the meaning of life, the meaning of the phrase that man was 'God's beloved creature,' why God allowed man to behave and act in a way worse than even the way of the wildest animals, whether God existed at all. Concerned about all these problems I later wrote the novel *Atheis* (An Atheist). Thanks to an Indonesian member of the board of censorship who quite often turned a blind eye to what was actually written in the text, and also due to the fact that the Japanese members of the board didn't have a good enough command of Indonesian to catch the subtle shade of meanings of the words or innuendoes, I managed to have my writings pass their scrutiny. My satirical doggerels and lampoons were even allowed to be broadcast through the military radio station. Similarly with a radio play I adapted from Multatuli's famous short story 'Saidjah and Adinda.' A play depicting the feelings and sufferings of a young couple, just married, who were forced to break up their honeymoon because the husband had to go to war, was also allowed to be produced on the stage. Except for the national spirit those writings were of little literary value, if any. But that very spirit turned out to be decisive for the success of the revolution for independence which exploded in August 1945.

"Perhaps due to the hardships, both spiritual and physical, I contracted tuberculosis, just a couple of months before the fall of Japan. I was hospitalized. When the revolution broke out, I was convalescing with my family in Garut, up in the beautiful mountainous area of West Java. Soon after independence was proclaimed by Sukarno and Hatta on the 17th of August 1945, a vacuum in authority occurred in various places of the country. A period of insecurity arose, pervaded by suspicion, false allegations, vengeance and violence. Although I was still convalescing, I deemed myself strong enough to join exercises in guerrilla fighting. Like many young Indonesian men and women at the time, I learned how to handle fire-arms and a bit of the theory and tactics of guerrilla fighting. Considering my physical condition, still handicapped by the effect of t.b., I felt that I wouldn't be able to become a good guerrilla fighter with fire-arms in my hand. I decided to fight with my pen instead. I wrote pamphlets, worked as an editor of a daily paper and a semi-weekly journal. The former was in the Indonesian language, and the latter in the local Sundanese language. Both papers were at the beginning financially self-supporting, but eventually sponsored by the ministry of defense in Jakarta. Beside writing I gave talks on political ideologies and social systems to keep the national spirit and revolutionary morale alive among the fighters and the ordinary people.

"After independence I resumed my work as an editor of the Balai Pustaka. I was active in literary and cultural circles, attended lectures on philosophy at the university, studied hard about literary theories, culture, and other social sciences I needed for my growth as an autodidact and writer, sat consecutively in the editorial boards of several literary-cultural magazines, became chairman of the Indonesian Centre of the International PEN-Club, deputy chairman of the Indonesian Writers Association, a member of the Institute of National Culture, head of the literary section of the advisory board of the Indonesian Broadcasting Commission, and a member of the Executive Committee of the National Commission for UNESCO. In politics I became a member of the Socialist-Democratic Party, characteristically labelled by the Communists as a party of 'stooges' of the British capitalist-imperialists, and eventually banned by Sukarno. In 1957 my collection of stories *Keretakan dan Ketegangan* (Fissures and Tensions) won the B.M.K.N. (Institute of National Culture) Literary Prize. And in 1970 the government granted me the Indonesian Literary Award. From 1959 to 1961 I lectured in modern Indonesian literature at the University of Indonesia in Jakarta. By the end of 1961 I was offered a lectureship at the Australian National University, Canberra, to teach the same subject. Occasionally I also gave lectures at various other universities and institutes as a 'visiting lecturer,' including at the I.S. S.I. (Indonesian Studies Summer Institute) held under auspices of the Ohio University at Athens, Ohio, during Summer 1981.

"Although I have a keen interest in literature, culture, politics, and the like, my main concern has always been the human condition, which is deteriorating constantly. I always wonder whether it's high time for man to think more in terms of cooperation and peace than in terms of competition and war."

———

The theme of alienation that dominates Achdiat Mihardja's short novel *Atheis* (An Atheist), a work described as "a major landmark in modern Indonesian literature," is echoed in his own life history. Like his hero Hasan, an idealistic Sundanese who settles in the modern, semi-Westernized city of Bandung, and like many other educated modern Indonesians, Achdiat found himself in conflict. Breaking away from the strict Moslem faith of his family, exposed to challenging new political ideas of socialism and communism, confronted with an authoritarian regime in his own land, yet reluctant to abandon the mysticism and idealism of his past, Achdiat became an expatriate and now lives in Australia. Hasan suffers a more tragic fate. He breaks his ties with his devoutly religious family, becomes an atheist, and marries an emancipated young woman. His wife is unfaithful and leaves him for an anarchist lover. Meanwhile, tormented with guilt for what he feels was his betrayal of his father and his ideals, and suffering from tuberculosis, he loses his will to live and, rushing out into the street during an air-raid, he is killed by a Japanese soldier. The question with which the novel begins: "Isn't it futile to torture oneself with remorse when it is no longer possible to rectify mistakes or expiate a sense of guilt?" is answered by Hasan's friend Rusli: "Relieve yourself by working harder, by working for humanity," a statement that echoes the philosophy by which its author lives.

Atheis, published in 1949, was received by Indonesian readers as "the first post-war novel of real interest, a definite attempt at genuine, sound literature." A. Teeuw writes in his survey of modern Indonesian literature that "the old theme of the conflict between old and new, between traditional society and modern culture, is presented here in an entirely new way, and is based on a broader and deeper knowledge and a more general training than had been the case before the war." The novel is narrated in part by Hasan, in part by people who knew him, and in part by a first-person voice who is the author himself, balancing the subjective account of his protagonist with an objective overview of a country torn by war, struggling to shake off the colonialism of its past and come to terms with the clashing ideologies of communism and democracy. Western readers have criticized the long discussions Achdiat introduces—debates among the characters on Marx, Freud, religion,

and atheism—as intrusive and didactic, but Teeuw observes that to Indonesians in 1949 "these things were probably so novel that the author could only incorporate them in his story by making them explicit in conversations."

Achdiat's more recent work, mainly short stories that treat of both current Indonesian society and the problems of Indonesian expatriates, has been characterized by George Quinn as wry, satirical, "colored by fatalism and pessimism, but relieved by humor and a tentative faith in the power of love." Teeuw calls his *Keretakan dan Kategangan* "one of the best post-war collections to have appeared in modern Indonesia," but he feels that with *Kesan dan Kenangan* (Impressions and Reminiscences, 1961), written after his exile from his native land and his travels in the United States, Achdiat "has so long lacked daily contact with the reality of Indonesia that these later stories strike one as being far-fetched and not very relevant." Nevertheless Teeuw finds that the 1973 collection *Debu cinta bertebaran* (Dust of Love Scattered) "paints an appealing picture" of the life of Indonesian expatriates in Australia.

Achdiat has translated into Indonesian short stories by Jack London, Chekhov, Faulkner, and Hemingway, and Thornton Wilder's novel *The Bridge of San Luis Rey.*

WORKS IN ENGLISH TRANSLATION: *Atheis* (1949) was translated into English by R.J. Maguire in 1972 in the Asian and Pacific Writing series published by the University of Queensland Press. Some short stories by Achdiat have been published in *Treasury of Modern Asian Stories,* edited by Daniel Milton and William Clifford, 1961, and *Fifty Great Oriental Stories,* edited by by G.Z. Hanrahan, 1965.

ABOUT: Dictionary of Oriental Literature, III, 1974; Encyclopedia of World Literature in the 20th Century I, 1981; Teeuw, A. Modern Indonesian Literature, 1967; Wilding, M. Introduction to *Atheis,* 1972. *Periodicals*—Twentieth Century Autumn 1970.

*ACZEL, TAMAS (December 16, 1921–   ), Hungarian poet, novelist, and journalist, was born in Budapest. His father, a minor executive at a large bank, was a lifelong social-democrat who held strong opinions about social justice. Aczel's high-school years were unhappy ones, frequently marked by conflicts with his teachers, mainly over political and economic issues. A poor student, he concentrated on the study of German, French, and English, and was able to speak all three by the time he graduated. Unable to attend the university, he became an assistant reception clerk at a hotel, where he again had

°äk´ zel, tō´ mäsh

difficulties with his superiors, chiefly over their poor treatment of employees. He left his position to become an electrician's apprentice; on completing his training, he joined the ironworker's trade union. Aczel wrote his first poems during this time and succeeded in publishing some of them in *Népszava* (People's Voice) by the age of eighteen. A soldier for a time during World War II, he was caught trying to get in touch with the Communist underground and sent to the Mauthausen labor camp, where he wrote many poems, all of them lost there.

After returning to Budapest in August 1945, Aczel became a reporter for *Szabadság* (Liberty) and participated in the workers' movement. He next obtained a position in the publishing section of the Cooperative Center and, making many visits to the provinces, became very familiar with the hard life of the peasantry. In 1948 he joined the educational section of the Employees Cooperative, but after a few months he accepted the literary editorship of *Szikra* (Spark), which gave him time for his own writing. He also obtained a degree in comparative literature from Péter Pázmány University in 1948 and a master's degree in the history of ideas from Loránt Eötvös University in 1950, and lectured at the latter from 1950 to 1952 and at the Hungarian Academy of Dramatic Art from 1953 to 1955. His active support of the Communist government began to grow in 1948. He was editor-in-chief of *Csillag* (Star), the Party's literary monthly (1950–53) and secretary of the Hungarian Writers Federation (1953–54). He made his living as a free-lance writer and journalist from 1954 to 1956. During the 1956 uprising Aczel was press secretary to Prime Minister Imre Nagy, and when the government collapsed in November, he defected, escaping to Czechoslovakia in a car he had purchased with money he received as a winner of the Stalin Prize in 1952. He settled in London editing the *Hungarian Literary Gazette* (1957–64) and making his living as a writer, translator, and lecturer (1964–66). In 1966 Aczel joined the English Department of the University of Massachusetts.

His post-war writings showed his deep commitment to the objectives of the Communist Party and his espousal of socialist realism. In a newspaper article (1949), he declared that the eminence of an author was no longer dependent on the literary past or cliques but solely on the quality of his writings, and he acknowledged that young authors owed "a special responsibility to our country," requiring "the faithful reflection of the reality of our people's democracy and the presentation of a clear picture of the emerging [socialist] man." Aczel's second book of poems, *Eberség, hüség* (Vigilance and Faith, 1949),

for which he received the Kossuth Prize, and the two that followed in 1951 and 1956 deal directly with the social and economic environment, acclaiming the achievements of Marxist-Leninist ideology. Viewed by some critics as playing a vital role in establishing socialist literature in the early years of Hungarian democracy, Aczel describes everyday events and the labors of the working man in his poems from 1945 to 1949. They celebrate the collectivization of agriculture, various Party congresses, visits with workers and miners, and the virtues of Stalin. Two of his novels from this period also confirm his commitment to socialist realism: *A szabadság árnyékában* (In the Shadow of Liberty, 1949), for which he was awarded the Stalin Prize, and *Vihar és napsütés* (Storm and Sunshine, 1950). They are parts of a cycle originally planned to present the development of socialism and the new socialist man in Hungary after the war. Concerned with the period 1944 to 1946, they attempt an epical presentation of the involvement of every level of Hungarian society in events at a time of physical and social ruin. Though widely accepted, both novels were often condemned by official critics of the József Révai school for attempting too much, for lavishing excessive attention on the ruling classes at the expense of the working class, and for failing to produce a socialist hero sufficiently worthy of imitation by readers, one of the major requirements of socialist realism.

Aczel's most important development as a literary artist occurred after he took up permanent residence in the West, when he was thirty-six. Two novels give clear proof of his giant strides in subject matter and narrative technique. *The Ice Age*, set in the Stalinist "ice age" of 1953–56 in Hungary and written in London between January 1959 and July 1962, portrays the power of unlimited authority to subvert the human spirit to the point where only survival matters. Aczel allows no illusions to sustain anyone rendered suspect by their relationships with Dr. Antal Karolinszky and his sister, Rezi, who are themselves falsely under suspicion regarding the natural death of a party official. For the sake of self-preservation all of their associates are ready to denounce them. Using the episodic method of narration, Aczel probes in an almost surrealistic manner the characters' connections with the doctor and his sister. He condemns power relentlessly: " . . . the fundamental of power is envy: the fewer the people who have the right and the means to give full vent to their instincts, the more enjoyable it becomes to those who possess that right and that means. That is why power is never sustained by illusions, but power always supports illusions: namely, the hope that one day it will be your turn to do as you like." One of Aczel's major points about the political system in which he once participated is that its "aimlessness" produces a paralyzing effect: "What was astonishing about the system was not how aimless power had become but how flexibly the rigid dogma of power adapted itself to its aimlessness. Fear, centrally organized and directed, was used to make the individual mind accept this aimlessness as a natural state of being." W. M. Kunstler, writing in the *New York Times Book Review,* found a warning for Americans in the novel: "Aczel's terrified people could be all of us who run for cover when the shells fall close. . . . Fear is hardly parochial. . . . When courage begins to fail, Budapest may be considerably closer to New York, Chicago and San Francisco than the map would indicate."

The second novel, *Illuminations,* the first Aczel wrote in English, chronicles the life of Dr. Feldheimer, a dentist who also appeared in *The Ice Age,* and other exiles from Central Europe after World War II. Now a resident of London and blinded in an auto accident, Feldheimer recounts his activities, ranging from the mundane to the bizarre, and often informs the reader about his past in Hungary, including his life with his father and mother and his role as an important functionary in the Communist Party. Aczel's command of the English language is so remarkable by now that he spins sentences into paragraphs, often with parenthetical material. He displays his learned vocabulary almost to a fault; for example, he entitles the chapters in the last section Myopia, Hypernetropia, Nyctalopia, Hemeralopia, Ambylopia, and Presbyopia, with each intended to reflect the meaning of the chapter. Frequently, episodes are interrupted by other events, often flashbacks, and then are resumed without warning. Reviewers generally found the work perplexingly symbolic, to the point where it is difficult to determine what Feldheimer's life is actually intended to illuminate. The reviewer in the *New York Review of Books* found its fundamental value to lie in those longer episodes in which the author writes social comedy about the lives of the exiles and "the panegyrics about bits of London, doubledecker buses, Covent Garden roses, Swiss Cottage traffic jams." The reviewer for the *Times Literary Supplement* faulted the novel for making the protagonist's past "infinitely richer and more exciting than is his present or . . . his future will ever be," and, like the previous reviewer, considered the novel "most readable . . . where a novelette is inserted into the uneven flow of the narrative," forcing him to speculate that Aczel's talents may be "more suited to short, conventional stories."

Aczel has also written on the problems of the intellectual in Eastern Europe and the Soviet Union. With Tibor Meray, he wrote *The Revolt of the Mind,* in which the resistance of intellectuals behind the Iron Curtain is explored. He has also edited and contributed to *Ten Years After: The Hungarian Revolution in the Perspective of History.* In 1984 he is nearing the end of a new novel and intends "to go back to an old idea of writing a kind of 'political autobiography.'"

Since coming to the United States, Aczel has been teaching creative writing and modern European literature, especially drama and fiction, at the University of Massachusetts in Amherst. He often lectures in various parts of the country. He is married to Olga Gyarmati, winner of an Olympic Gold Medal in the long jump, and has two children, Julia, who was born in Budapest in 1953, and Thomas, who was born in London in 1960.

WORKS IN ENGLISH TRANSALTION: Aczel's first novel, *The Ice Age,* was translated into English by John Simon (and others), 1965. His second novel, *Illuminations,* published in 1982, was written in English, as were his nonfiction work *The Revolt of Mind* (with T. Meray), 1959, and his editions of *Ten Years After,* 1966, and *Poetry from the Russian Underground,* 1973.

ABOUT: Contemporary Authors 49–52, 1975; Tezla, A. Hungarian Authors: A Bibliographical Handbook, 1970. *Periodicals*—New York Review of Books December 3, 1981; New York Times Book Review June 13, 1965; December 3, 1981; Saturday Review July 31, 1965; November 1981; Times Literary Supplement, March 12, 1982; World Literature Today Summer 1982.

ADONIS or ADUNIS (pseudonym of Ali Ahmad Esber or Saïd) (1930–), Lebanese poet, critic, and journalist, writes (in Arabic): "Seen from a forty-year distance, my life as a poet seems born out of a coincidence, a kind of fairy tale: 1930—I was born in a village reminiscent of man's beginnings: huts made of stone which we called houses, surroundings where trees mingled with people, where man's body was but nature's alter ego. Each season the mud on our house would crack and each season fresh mud was added to help the house in its fight against rains and winds. The roof was wooden sticks covered with thorny branches, covered first with dirt, then mud to make sure the rain would not pierce it. Nevertheless, the rain seeped through invisible cracks and fell, drop by drop on our heads: my father's, my mother's and sisters whether we were eating, sleeping or just resting. I could well say I grew up like a tree or a plant,

ADONIS

the house being nothing but a frail barrier between myself and nature's anger, rain and thunder, or nature's favors when the elements subsided.

"Our house was too small for the family so we built a wooden bed where we could all sleep. Its wooden legs were high enough for the cow to live under it. I remember vividly staring at the cow when it returned from pasture at sunset and went to sleep before I did. I remember thinking that the cow was happier, specially in the light of my daily visits to the village teacher who taught me how to read and write. He used to keep me next to him by placing the tip of his cane between my feet . . . a noose that nailed me to the ground, just in case I thought of running away to the fields, which I usually did whenever I had a chance.

"Until I turned fourteen I had never attended school, seen a car, listened to a radio or seen one, and of course had no idea what a city was all about. I discovered my body rather early. I must have been twelve or thirteen when I learned my first lesson in the encounter of two bodies. Afterwards and even before, I used to rub my body against the grass as if it were a woman's garb. Then the fairy tale I mentioned earlier (I won't write the story here) brought me to the city. I found myself enrolled in the French Lycée at Tartus, one of the few modern schools in the area. In those days, only the rich bourgeois kids attended the Lycée because it was heavily endowed by their families. It took me two months to acquire a proper city outfit. Meanwhile, I went around in my long village robe. The students looked at me in a strange way which, I must admit, was not devoid of admiration.

"1950—Graduation year. I received a baccalauréat degree, which is to say, I completed my pre-college curriculum in just six years, since I was enrolled in the Lycée in the midst of 1944 at age fourteen. Upon graduation, I entered Law School at the University of Damascus, utterly convinced that the Arabic department had nothing useful to offer me. I had, since early childhood, studied Arabic poetry, memorized the most beautiful poems of great Arab poets, become conversant with the intricacies of the Arabic language, its rules and syntax. This almost perfect command of Arabic I owe to my father, who had supervised my education with relentless heed. But before the year was over, my inability to bridge the gap between law and poetry became quite obvious; I therefore decided to study philosophy.

"1952—My father's death. Unexpected and utterly distressing. He was, later, to become an essential part of my life and thinking. In fact, I really got to know him after he had passed away. Only then did I discover that he was more of a friend than a father: inspiring rather than dictating, never guiding but merely hinting. My father was truly a unique poem.

"1954—I graduated from the University of Damascus with a license in Philosophy and joined the army the same year. I spent one year of my service in jail, the other in that second jail we call military establishment. At the end of my two-year service, I was filled with doubts about the very concept of systems, governments and specially the military. I came out of the whole experience lost and almost crushed.

"1956—I married Khālida Sāleh and together we left Damascus for Beirut where I recovered my Lebanese citizenship (my family is of Lebanese origin). We decided to settle in Beirut where we still live today. Our two daughters were born there, Arwād in 1958 and Neanāre in 1971. Khālida, who is a literary critic, teaches Arabic literature at the Lebanese university. Also in 1956 I met the Lebanese poet Yussif al-Khal and together we launched *Shi'r*, a poetry journal. The first issue came out in 1957. *Shi'r* will remain the one publication that played a decisive role in establishing a divider between two periods of Arabic literature: the 'classical' and the 'modern.'

"1968—With a vanguard of Arab writers, I started publishing *Mawakif*, a journal meant to widen the experience initiated by *Shi'r*, give it multiple dimensions and a more radical stand than the one adopted by *Shi'r*. *Mawakif* is still being published today.

"1971—I was appointed to the Lebanese university where I taught pre-Islamic and contemporary Arabic literature which I still do. The necessities of academic life (legal and administrative) required that I get a Ph.D. which I did in 1973 from St. Joseph University, in Beirut. The subject of my thesis was 'Permanence and Change in Arabic Thought and Literature.'"

—trans. M. Ghossein

———

Roger M. Allen writes of Adonis that "perhaps no other writer living in the Arab world today combines so effectively the roles of poet and critic." Born in Qassabin, near the city of Latakia, in Syria, he settled in Lebanon in 1956, where he soon distinguished himself both as a poet and an editor, publishing poetry journals and a three-volume anthology of classical Arabic poetry. His pen-name Adonis, adopted early in his career, reflects his interest in mythology and especially in themes of rebirth. Considered one of the most influential of contemporary Arabic poets, he writes poetry remarkable for its careful workmanship and purity of diction. He is a visionary, a metaphysical poet, describing poetry as a "leap outside of established concepts, a change in the order of things and in the way we look at them." Although in his early poetry especially Adonis has drawn on ancient tradition (Greek and biblical as well as Arabic), he is an experimenter in language and poetic forms, often writing a kind of lyrical prose-poetry.

In his influential critical writings Adonis has emphasized the importance of innovation in language; he seeks to free poetry from the rigid conventions of Arabic tradition. Along with other contemporary Arabic poets, Adonis began to write a revolutionary "free verse," abandoning conventional meter for a basic musical unit created by the arrangement of words and images in patterns developing out of the idea of the individual poem. This kind of poetry reflects a quest for an expression that transcends the traditional formalism of Arabic literature:

O miserable alphabet, O twenty—
nine reeds, with what can I further burden you and what forest can I plant you to be?
I give up to nature's beast and drag myself behind you.

—trans. I. J. Boullata

This break with the past is reflected also in Adonis' sense of social commitment. I. J. Boullata writes that the modern Arab poet is "mindful that he is a member of a resurgent old nation, of a society that is changing, and ultimately of a world that is fragmented." The result in Adonis' verse is a subjective expression that is often complex and even obscure to many readers, but that nevertheless communicates his spiritual self-searching. In a long poem called "Resurrection and Ashes" he addresses the symbolic phoenix:

O Phoenix, when fire is born in your beloved wing
What pen do you hold?
How do you replace your lost down?
Do you erase the dry error in its book?
When ashes embrace you, what world do you feel?

—trans. I. J. Boullata

The personal and the political merge in the intensity of a poem called "West and East: A Dream":

There was something stretched along history's buried path,
Something adorned but charged,
Bearing its poisoned infant of oil,
With a poisonous merchant singing his luring song

There was an East that like a child
Begged and cried for help,
With the West as its unerring master.
The map has changed;
The whole world is aflame,
And in its ashes
East and West are gathered
In a single tomb.

—trans. M. A. Khouri and H. Algar

In such poetry, M. M. Badawi writes of Adonis and the *Shi'r* group, "the private world of the poet and the society in which he lives are so inextricably bound up together . . . that the personal salvation he seeks in his poetry is at one and the same time the salvation of his community." Mirene Ghossein considers "liberty"—"a liberty with themes, a liberty with words themselves through the uniqueness of poetic vision"—to be Adonis' main contribution to contemporary Arabic poetry. As a result of this new freedom, she writes, "it is possible to talk of an Adonisian vision of the world where mysticism and existentialism, socialism and individualism, and poetry and reality actually coexist. . . . " More than perhaps any other poet writing in Arabic, Adonis has assimilated Western influences yet produced an Arabic poetry that preserves its personal as well as its national identity.

Adonis' first volume of verse, *Dalīla* (Dalilah), was published in 1950. This was followed by a number of other collections, one of the most interesting of which, to Western readers, is *Qabr min ajl New York* (A Tomb for New York, 1971). Here, writing a prose-poetry that reveals, as M. M. Badawi points out, "obvious biblical influences in rhythm and structure of sentence," he speaks out passionately against "the horrors of New York and American civilization" and condemns American intervention in Vietnam and the Middle East. His complete works were published in two volumes as *al Āthār al-Kāmila* in 1971. A collection of his critical essays *Zaman al Shi'r* (The Time for Poetry) was published in 1972.

WORKS IN ENGLISH TRANSLATION: Adonis received the second Syria-Lebanon award (the first went to Fazil Dağlarca, the Turkish writer, in 1968) of the International Poetry Forum, which sponsored the publication of an English translation or "transposition" of his selected poems by Samuel Hazo as *The Blood of Adonis* in 1971. English translations of some of his poems are in *An Anthology of Modern Arabic Poetry,* 1974, edited by Mounah H. Khouri and Hamid Algar, and in I. J. Boullata's *Modern Arabic Poets 1950–1975,* 1976.

ABOUT: Badawi, M. M. A Critical Introduction to Modern Arabic Poetry, 1975, *and* An Anthology of Modern Arabic Verse, 1970; Boullata, I. J. Modern Arab Poets 1950–1975, 1976; Dictionary of Oriental Literature III, 1974; Encyclopedia of World Literature in the 20th Century (rev. ed.) I, 1981; Ghossein, M. *Introduction to* The Blood of Adonis, 1971; Khouri, M.A. and H. Algar An Anthology of Modern Arabic Poetry, 1974.

*AHLIN, LARS (April 4, 1915–   ), Swedish novelist, short story writer, dramatist, and essayist, was born in Sundsvall, an industrial town near the coast of northern Sweden. His mother left home when Ahlin was five. His father was a traveling salesman. Ahlin had to drop out of school at age thirteen to help support himself, and he became involved with the Communist youth movement after brief association with a Christian youth group. Belonging to the school Erich Auerbach labels "Christian realism," exemplified by Dostoevsky, whose work made a great impact on him, Ahlin combines in his work a radical criticism of traditional social structure based on hierarchy with a deep religious consciousness. Such realism features grotesque elements that arise from the conflict between spiritual qualities and the instincts of the flesh and demonstrate the co-existence of irreconcilable extremes within one person. Among other influences on Ahlin's formative years are Thomas Mann, André Gide, Henri Poincaré, Martin Luther, and the Swedish classics. He also studied Karl Barth and Kierkegaard.

Ahlin briefly attended a "folkhögskola," a uniquely Scandinavian form of boarding school for the economically disadvantaged adult student, but was largely self-educated. His summers were spent peddling poems to get money for school. During this period Ahlin saw himself "as worthless, outside society," a feeling reflected by many of his fictional characters. Ahlin's work also conveys his belief that diverse and ex-

LARS AHLIN

treme human qualities should be given equal existential value. As a writer he tries to function as an "intercessor" between the socially inferior and superior. His views on social equality assisted in forming the philosophical framework of the Swedish welfare state.

In 1936 Ahlin moved to Stockholm and spent the following seven years doing odd jobs and continuing to study while he tried, unsuccessfully, to establish himself as a writer. His first published novel, *Tåbb med Manifestet* (Tåbb and the Manifesto, 1943), introduced the type of existential inquiry Ahlin has pursued throughout his career. In his first six novels he explores the dynamics of death and failure. His protagonists in these novels suffer from low self esteem because their self image is dependent on their conforming to an ideal which they cannot live up to for reasons beyond their control. Tåbb, for example, is unemployed and thus does not belong to the working class as defined by the Communist Manifesto. Ideals, then, tend to degrade rather than inspire because there are too many uncontrollable factors preventing man from realizing his ideals, especially social and human imperfections. Ahlin therefore wants to demonstrate that the ideals we choose for our self image are only arbitrary definitions of what is inferior and what is superior. His characters' distorted view of self is symbolized in a series of grotesque events and their encounters with feeble and decadent people. Their view of self begins to change when they experience a form of death, figurative or real. Their notion of "thing-ness" in a Barthian sense is then replaced with a more positive appreciation of self. Tåbb moves back to the

°äh lēn

country where he finds satisfaction in "patient, insistent, everyday work," an attitude that is more Lutheran than Marxist. Death, then, signifies a change, a liberation from man's dependence on institutions or ideals for his sense of meaningful identity.

Aron in *Fromma mord* (Pious Murders, 1952) is not as successful as Tåbb. He returns to his home town to restore proper relations between himself and various components of his life. Among other things, he wants to put a stone on his father's grave. But his notion of an ideal restruction of his life makes him pious, i.e. he perceives the world too narrowly, expecting from it a simplistic consistency which it does not have. In the end he sinks into a swamp tied to his father's gravestone, unable to liberate himself from traditional value systems and therefore doomed to perish as an individual human being. In two other novels from this period, Ahlin presents his philosophy in terms of parent/child relationships. One of them, *Om* (If, About, or Around, 1946) is Ahlin's most experimental novel. Bengt wants to save his father, Peter, from a life of illusions and false ideals. But Peter needs to fit into a socially defined system here symbolized in his search for a woman who will consent to function as Bengt's "real" mother after Bengt's real mother has rejected them both. In the end, Peter abandons Bengt in favor of a woman, taking Bengt's maternal inheritance with him and accusing Bengt of destroying his life with moralism. Peter's moral collapse signifies the collapse of father values, i.e. traditional social values, thus leaving the son free either to repeat the life of the father or to follow a new course.

Om represents Ahlin's most ambitious attempt to create an alternative to the Flaubertian novel of illustration. Putting into practice his theories on the novel, Ahlin here presents a shifting narrative point of view through a three-part subject consisting of a name and two pronouns whose reference never remains constant or consistent. Thus Ahlin tries to keep the reader aware of the text as construct. By this method he also involves the reader in giving the text its final significance. This he also seeks to accomplish through three-part verb clusters where the effect or nature of a given activity is not absolutely defined, but meant to change with each reader's choice of dominant word from the cluster. Following this structurally avant-garde novel, Ahlin published two of his most traditionally composed works, *Jungfrun i det gröna* (Nigella Damascena, 1947) and *Egen spis* (A Stove of One's Own, 1948), also his most entertaining comedy of human interaction. Sören in the earlier novel, as the critic Arne Melberg points out, resembles

Tåbb in his final achievement of a "form of inner readiness to accept the imperfection both in terms of personal qualities and social conditions."

Stora glömskan (The Great Amnesia, 1954) forms a transition between the two major thematic perspectives in Ahlin's work. Previously he focused on death and failure with love as a possibly redeeming factor. After *Stora glömskan,* love becomes the focal point of discussion. In this novel we meet the thirteen-year-old Zackarias, who accepts life with its inconsistencies and ambiguities, pain and joy. He learns about the nature of love from a decrepit washerwoman whose love for her deceased husband, paradoxically, was mixed with contempt for his weakness. She represents one of Ahlin's many old and often feeble women who articulate a Lutheran-inspired notion of love. Later Zackarias learns from another old person that love creates cosmic harmony in its power to unite two fundamentally different principles, male and female. The father in *Stora glömskan* represents playfulness, irregularity, wisdom, and freedom from conventions. He, like Bengt's father, illustrates the corruptibility of society, but unlike Peter he also stands for spiritual freedom gained by rejecting social standards.

Stora glömsksan was followed by four novels about love. In these novels Ahlin further explores the notion of love acquired from his readings of Anders Nygren's *Eros and Agape,* Luther, and St. Paul. We find, especially, love as *agape* reflected in his work. This term defines God's love of man which is given regardless of merit or rank, creating worth, as Luther wrote, by regarding "as very precious the thing that is loved." It is paradoxical in that though love is a desirable state of being, it does not necessarily bring bliss, but pain and suffering instead. Through work love is given a place in everyday life and is thereby removed from the realm of ideals. Love, like death, is a force which creates equality between people because they touch a person only as an individual being with total disregard for his social status.

After *Kvinna kvinna* (Woman Woman, 1955) Ahlin published his most ambitious work on love, *Natt i marknadstältet* (Night in the Market Tent, 1957). The novel centers on Paulina, another of Ahlin's many lower-class women embodying love, and the young Zackarias, who largely functions as an observer of the events. His struggle with detachment from personal involvement culminates during the night in the market tent, a setting also used by the classic writer Almqvist, as the critic Hans-Göran Ekman points out, to reflect the poet's necessary emotional detachment from his work. Zackarias learns about the paradox of love from Paulina, whose love for her husband Leopold leads her to kill him because his value system is perverted by what Karl Barth called his "social lusts"—man's longing to express himself individually in order to appreciate his self. This leads him to regard a crime to obtain money as less shameful than to receive Paulina's love while he is poor and without social significance.

In the following novel, *Gilla gång* (Normal Course, 1957), Ahlin uses neologisms and unconventional word formations to symbolize how love creates its own form of existence. In *Bark och löv* (Bark and Leaves, 1961), his most philosophical novel, he explores the relationship between art and love. Erik, a writer, realizes that his life is not complete without love, while Aino, a painter, refuses to give love or receive it because she believes that "to love is to die," i.e. if she loves Erik she will die as an artist. Conversely, her emotional involvement with her art prevents her from emotional involvement with Erik. In *Bark och löv,* also a structurally innovative work, the events are tied together by linguistic devices rather than rational continuity of plot.

Ahlin published three collections of short stories in the 1940s: *Inga ögon väntar mig* (No Eyes Are Waiting For Me, 1944), *Fångnas glädje* (The Joy of the Imprisoned, 1947), and *Huset har ingen filial* (The House Has No Annex, 1949). They gained immediate critical acclaim and admiration for their concision and clarity in dealing with the same problems he explores in his novels. Ahlin's stories are written in the style of Hemingway—"a new artful version of naturalism," as Ahlin says, though he questions the tenability of this new literary style. Two of his plays have been performed: *Lekpaus* (Break in the Game, 1948) and a radio play, *Eld av eld* (Fire from Fire, 1949).

In the 1940s Ahlin also published a number of essays outlining his theories of the novel. Here he labels himself as "identifier" to describe a writer who wants to avoid emotional identification between reader and character. He seeks to accomplish this by, for example, letting his characters speak a language inconsistent with their level of education or social background. Their speech is also in many ways interchangeable, thus making them appear to be different forms of the same consciousness, ultimately the writer's own. His next period of essay production took place during the 1960s, beginning with a speech at a writers' conference in 1961. He perpetuated and developed his earlier theories in articles and a series of unpublished radio lectures in 1966. In an article published in 1970, *In på benet* (To the Bone), Ahlin for the first time made public his mystical vision of 1933 which made a profound and lasting impact on his concept of self and man in society. This philosophical production coincides with a total artistic silence which lasted over twenty years until the early 1980s. During this time, however, his work was subject to growing critical appreciation and discussion.

Ahlin's creative silence was broken in 1983 when he published *Hannibal-segraren* (Hannibal, the Victor) in collaboration with his wife, Gunnel. This novel constitutes a new achievement for him. His language, at times criticized for verbosity, here achieves a new dimension of beauty and stringency, maintaining its poetical qualities while seeming less an outburst of untamed perceptions. The novel explores the dynamics of desire for power. It also constitutes a discussion of the formation of the image of power as the narrator/scribe presents the actions and consequences of Hannibal's steps in his quest for power. It constitutes a new direction of Ahlin's philosophical inquiry into the human condition.

In recognition of Ahlin's important contribution to Swedish letters Ahlin and his family received the prestigious Övralid prize in 1984. He also received the "De nios" prize in 1960, and the "Boklotteriets" prize in 1962. He received a State artist's award of annual income for life in 1964. In 1969 Ahlin was made Honorary Doctor of Philosophy at the University of Umea.

WORKS IN ENGLISH TRANSLATION: None of Ahlin's major works have been translated, but essays and excerpts from his fiction are available in English. These include Naomi Walford's translation of "Tåbb Knocks at the Door," and "How to Win a Layabout for Science," in *Sweden Writes,* edited by Lars Bäckström and Göran Palm, 1965; "After Years of Silence," from *Fångnas glädje,* translated by Frederic Fleisher, and "Progress without Apostasy," translated by Karin Petherick in *Arts, Drama, Architecture, Music International Review,* 31, 1966; "Polluted Room," from *Inga ögon väntar mig,* translated by Walter Johnson in the *Literary Review* 9, 1965–66.

ABOUT: Bäckström, L. and G. Palm (eds.) Sweden Writes, 1965; Columbia Dictionary of Modern European Literature, 1980; Encyclopedia of World Literature in the 20th Century (rev. ed.) I, 1981; Gustafson, A. A History of Swedish Literature, 1961; Lundell, T. Lars Ahlin, 1977; Nielsen, E. A. Lars Ahlin, 1968. *Periodicals*—Cambridge Quarterly 9, 1979; Scandinavian Studies 47, 1975; Scandinavica 14, May 1975.

*AICHINGER, ILSE (November 1, 1921–   ),
Austrian novelist, poet, short story writer, and
radio playwright, was born in Vienna and spent
her childhood in Linz. After the "Anschluss," she
and her family were persecuted, and she was
forced to do compulsory service during World
War II. When the war ended, she studied medicine but dropped out in the fifth semester to
complete her first novel, *Die grössere Hoffnung*
(*Herod's Children*) in 1948. From 1949 to 1950
she worked as a reader in the editorial department of the publishing house S. Fischer, first in
Vienna, then in Frankfurt. Later she became
one of the founders of the Hochschule für Ges-
taltung in Ulm. In 1953 she married the German
poet Günter Eich (1907–1972), whom she had
met as a fellow member of the post-World War
II writers' association "Gruppe 47." They had
two children.

Among the major characteristics of Ilse Aichinger's literary works are their unobtrusiveness,
clarity, and complete absence of artistic pretension, but her works are not simple or easy to understand. Early critics frequently associated her
narrative prose with the works of Kafka, whom
she resembles in her meta-psychological treatment of complex situations. However, Kafka's
references to his own life are lacking from all
Aichinger's works except *Herod's Children*,
which bears some autobiographical elements in
the story of a young girl, Ellen, who has Jewish
grandparents and lives in a country overrun by
the Nazis. A the end of the book Ellen is killed
by a shell. Her martyrdom and the suffering of
other rejected children is seen under the utopian
sign of "the greater hope" which cannot materialize in the lifetime of those who hope.

In Aichinger's later stories all references to her
personal life are absent. Her first novel establishes a possible relationship with the thinking of the
French existentialists, especially with Sartre's
concept of human bondage which is reflected in
her 1953 story *Der Gefesselte* (*The Bound Man*),
in which the protagonist, chained and imprisoned, renounces free movement and learns to
live with his fetters. The topic of the acceptance
of human bondage recurs in several other stories.
Aichinger, "the sceptical narrator," as she has
been called by Hans Wolfschütz, has not
changed her style throughout the years of writing. John C. Alldridge writes: "In all her works
the reader's sympathy is sought in a language
which uses no histrionics, no extreme devices of
syntax to heighten its effect and to stress the
meaning. Limitation of vocabulary to the experience of everyday life and of persons of humble
position enables Aichinger to render her meaning and appeal direct." In *Spiegelgeschichte*
(Mirror Story, 1954) the events of a dead girl's

ILSE AICHINGER

life are traced back from deathbed to birth (in
anticipation of Christa Wolf's *The Quest for
Christa T.*) in patterns of perception. This important story won her the "Gruppe 47" prize in
1953. In several of her short stories—*Zu keiner
Stunde* (Never at any Time, 1957); *Besuch im
Pfarrhus* (Visit to the Parsonage, 1961); *Wo ich
wohne* (Where I Live, 1963); *Eliza, Eliza,* 1965;
Auckland, 1969; *Nachricht vom Tag* (News of
the Day, 1970), the narrator assumes various
identities in exploring perception and states of
mind. In retrospect, this aspect of Aichinger's
narrative technique looks like an anticipation of
the *nouveau roman*.

In 1953 Aichinger presented her first radio
play, *Knöpfe* (Buttons), the story of a group of
workers in a button factory imprisoned in the
monotony of their work, which prevents them
from realizing that they themselves gradually
turn into buttons. Two short radio plays, *Weisse
Chrysanthemen* (White Chrysanthemums,
1960) and *Französische Botschaft* (French Embassy, 1960), were followed by a radio dramatization of her short story *Besuch im Pfarrhaus* in
1961, which explores, in a dialogue between two
children, the range of consciousness of human
beings, adult and infantile, confronting visible
and imagined threats. *Die Schwestern Jouet*
(The Jouet Sisters, 1969), a play for three female
voices, is an attempt ot create a new world as a
world of wishful thinking. Similar speculations
with wishful images, with space, time, and possibilities, occur in *Nachmittag in Ostende* (An Afternoon in Ostende, 1968). *Auckland* (1969) is a
study of a series of unsuccessful efforts to establish a dialogue between dependents.

°ī´kin gə´, ēl´ sə

Even in early works like *Wo ich wohne* and *Eliza, Eliza,* Aichinger garnished her stories and dialogues with poetry. Her poems, like her other writings, do not burst upon the scene. Rather they live in a quiet verbal magic which borders surrealism but lacks its frequent pretentiousness. Undeterred by lack of acclaim (which leaves a number of her works still unpublished), Aichinger continues to write her cryptic poems, for example:

Escarpment
For what would I do
if it were not for the hunters, my dreams,
who, in the morning,
descend on the other side of the mountains,
in the shadows.
—trans. J. C. Alldridge

As Alldridge puts it: "The effect on the reader or audience is one of surprise that such gems of sensitive understanding of the human spirit, expressed in such precise language, should not have attracted attention before."

Ilse Aichinger's most recent volumes of poetry are *Schlechte Wörter* (Bad Words, 1976) and *Verschenkter Rat* (Free Advice, 1978). She has received many literary prizes, among them the Osterreichicher Staatspreis für Literatur (1952), the Literaturpreis des Kulturkreises im Bundesverband der Deutschen Industrie (1953), the Literaturpreis der Freien und Hansestadt Bremen (1953), the Immermann-Preis der Stadt Düsseldorf (1955), the Literaturpreis der Bayerischen Akademie der Schönen Künste (1961). She is a member of the Academy of Arts in Berlin and of the West German PEN Club, and lives in Bayerisch Gmain, Upper Bavaria.

WORKS IN ENGLISH TRANSLATION: *Herod's Children* was translated into English by Cornelia Schaeffer in 1963 and *The Bound Man and Other Stories* by Eric Mosbacher in 1956. James C. Alldridge translated her *Selected Short Stories and Dialogues* in 1968 and A. H. Chappel translated *Selected Poetry and Prose* in 1983. Herman Vinke's *The Short Life of Sophie Scholl* (1984), translated by Hedwig Pachter, contains an interview with Aichinger.

ABOUT: Alldridge, J. C. Ilse Aichinger, 1969; Best, A. and H. Wolfschütz (eds.) Modern Austrian Writing, 1980; Cassell's Encyclopedia of World Literature, 1973; Columbia Dictionary of Modern European Literature, 1980; Contemporary Authors 85–88, 1980; Encyclopedia of World Literature in the 20th Century (rev. ed.) I, 1981; Fourth Book of Junior Authors and Illustrators, 1979; Langer, L. L. *Introduction to Aichinger's Selected Poetry and Prose*, 1983; Opel, A. (ed.) Anthology of Modern Austrian Literature, 1981; Ungar, F. (ed.) Handbook of Austrian Literature, 1973.

*AITMATOV, CHINGIZ (December 12, 1928–), Soviet writer of fiction, essays, and drama, was born in the small Kirghiz settlement of Sheker. Aitmatov's father, Torekul, had studied in Moscow, spoke Russian fluently, and occupied high posts in the Communist Party of Kirghizia. He died in 1937, a victim of Stalin's terror, then at its height. Aitmatov's mother, Nagima, and the four children subsequently lived with his father's sister. Both women greatly influenced the future writer by acquainting him with traditional Kirghiz customs and works of folk literature. From his father the boy inherited a love for Russian literature. He attended Russian school, but was forced by the war to leave in 1942. He worked as a tax agent, clerk for a tractor brigade, and secretary of a village Soviet.

Immediately after the war Aitmatov returned to his studies and in 1946 attended a veterinary technical school, after which he entered the Agricultural Institute of Kirghizia. In 1952 he began work as a veterinary technician. He published his first story in the same year. Although not yet thinking of a literary career, he worked on his Russian a great deal, took an interest in questions of linguistics, and translated extensively from Kirghiz to Russian and from Russian to Kirghiz. After three years' work on a livestock farm and with several stories in the local press to his credit, Aitmatov began attending advanced courses at the Gorky Literary Institute in Moscow. In 1958 he returned home to write for the newspaper *Soviet Kirghizia* and as correspondent for *Pravda*.

Aitmatov's work may be divided into three periods. During the first (1952–1957), he wrote stories which he himself would later characterize as "weak and imitative." They include: "Gazetchik Dziuio" (Dziuio the Newsboy, 1952), "Asnim" (1953), "Bely dozhd" (White Rain, 1954), "Sypaichi" (1954), "Nochnoi poliv" (Night Watering, 1955), "Trudnaya pereprava" (A Difficult Crossing, 1954), and others. Except for the first, which concerns a Japanese newsboy, they all deal with the generation gap that results from the intrusion of modern socialist culture into the patriarchal feudal life of the Kirghiz. In perfect agreement with the then current official theory of "lack of conflict," by which conflict within Soviet society is possible only between the good and the better, clashes in these stories generally end either in the complete reconciliation of the generations, or in the victory of honest, conscientious workers over others who are slightly less so. Already in these stories, however, Aitmatov tried to avoid the schematic by fully dramatizing all conflicts, so that their happy resolution would not seem externally imposed.

°īt´mä tôf, chin´giz

CHINGIZ AITMATOV

Beginning in 1957 with the story "Litsom k litsu" (Face to Face), Aitmatov's prose changes key. The question of a character's individual freedom, of the very possibility of choice, becomes important for him. Seide, the heroine of the story, hides her husband, an army deserter, from her fellow villagers, and sees no crime in it: such action is sanctioned by ancient custom. On learning, however, that he was robbing people exhausted and weak from hunger, she turns him over to the authorities. Seide breaks with custom here not because her husband's desertion violated Soviet law, but because he was acting against the well-being of the Kirghiz people. The old, not the new, ideology governs the heroine's action. Whereas in the early stories moral evaluation of the hero's actions depended on their relation to the new ideology, Aitmatov now locates the hero's larger freedom within the Kirghiz ethical tradition. This tendency determined the future course of his work.

The second period is illustrated in the stories written between 1958 and 1963 collected in *Povesti gor i stepei* (*Tales of the Mountains and Steppes*) which was awarded the Lenin Prize for 1963. The book opens with the long story "Jamilya." Significantly, its original name was "Song." Daniyar, a convalescent officer, has won the heart of Jamilya with his songs. Jamilya then commits an act which from the point of view of Kirghiz custom would be unthinkable: she leaves the village with her lover shortly before the return of her wounded husband from the front. The fundamental point of the story is that in violating ancient custom, the heroine does not act immorally. Her heart is a prisoner to the Kirghiz

spiritual tradition with its age-old emphasis on an essentially aesthetic perception of reality and its embodiment in art. The singer and sung poetry have always been valued very highly in Kirghizia. Thus in resolving the problem of freedom, Aitmatov proceeds not by breaking with Kirghiz tradition or subordinating it to the new socialist reality, but by immersing himself deeply in the old order with all its conflicts.

Since Aitmatov had challenged both ordinary Kirghiz custom and the new socialist morality (the husband whom Jamilya betrayed was a front-line soldier), the editors of the journal *Ala-too* refused to publish the story, claiming that "Kirghiz women do not behave that way." Mukhtar Auezov, a noted Kazakh writer and Aitmatov's friend and literary sponsor, had to intervene before it could be published in Kirghiz. A Russian translation appeared in the journal *Novy Mir,* then under the distinguished editorship of Alexander Tvardovsky. It evoked a very favorable response in the Soviet press and, in the fall of 1961, appeared in *L'Humanité,* the newspaper of the French Communist Party. Louis Aragon, who did the French translation, wrote that it is "the most beautiful love story in the world."

Aitmatov is always on the side of characters who cherish the idea of kinship, not only in the sense of family connections but in an emotionally heightened sense with historical, epic and mythic implications as well. In one of his stories, ("Verbliuzhy glaz"/The Camel's Eye) Kemel decides to work as a field hand rather than go on to an institute after finishing school. His education and high-mindedness greatly irritate the brutal and obtuse tractor-driver Abakir. Their mutual antagonism forms the central conflict of the narrative. Kemel often thinks of his old history teacher, whose invisible presence in the field helps sustain him in his struggle. This theme is also developed in the long story "Pervy uchitel" (The First Teacher). A leading scholar, Altynai Sulaimanova, gratefully recounts the story of her first teacher, a man who could barely read and write but possessed wisdom, not merely rational knowledge, and the strength of character of the heroes of the old folk epics, in whom an intuitive knowledge of the truth and even the gift of prophecy are combined with a will of iron. Aitmatov has written, " . . . I consciously idealized the character of the Communist, selflessly devoted to the cause of the revolution." But in his idealization of the character he proceeds from the standpoint of Kirghiz epic tradition, not Communist ideology. The long story "Materinskoe pole" (Mother's Field) logically concludes the second period of Aitmatov's work. Job-like, old Tolgonai heroically suffers the loss of three sons and then of her husband, the agonizing death of her widowed daughter-in-law, hunger and back-breaking drudgery on a collective farm. What is new about this story is the way the mytho-epic side of the heroine's consciousness ceases to be a mystery to her, whereas before only the author understood it.

The third period of Aitmatov's work begins with the long story "Proshchai, Gulsary!" (*Farewell, Gulsary!*, 1966). It also includes the following works: "Bely parakhod" (*The White Ship*, 1970), *Voskhozhdenie na Fudziyamu* (*Ascent of Mt. Fuji*, 1973), "Rannie zhuravli" (The Cranes Fly Early, 1975), "Pegi pyos, begushchi kraem morya" (A Spotted Dog, Running at the Edge of the Sea, 1977), *I dolshe veka dlitsa den* (The Day Lasts More Than a Hundred Years, 1980).

Like "Jamilya," *Farewekk, Gulsary!* was first published in Alexander Tvardovsky's *Novy Mir*. The narrative structure consists of the conversation of an old collective-farm worker, Tanabai Bakasov, with his dying horse Gulsary, which conveys the parallel tragedies of man and horse. Tanabai naively thought that when the nomadic way of life was brought to an end, its ideals of kinship and brotherhood would live on in the collective farm. But he has come to feel that, instead of uniting people, collectivization had divided them and turned them into slaves of the state. Tanabai is expelled from the Party as punishment for an act of "rebellion" when, exhausted by a futile attempt to save a flock of sheep, he tries to beat with a pitchfork the local public prosecutor, an arrogant, well-fed bureaucrat who has insulted him. After this incident he withdraws into himself for good. Gulsary also "rebels" by refusing to serve the perpetually drunken collective-farm chairman as saddle horse and running off to regain the freedom of the herd. At the chairman's order the stallion is castrated. This scene and the scene of Tanabai's rebellion are the climactic moments of the story. Old and exhausted, Gulsary dies on the road; his master is now alone. The story concludes as Tanabai recalls an old Kirghiz song about a she-camel who had lost her calf and goes calling for it over the steppe, milk streaming from her over-full udder onto the ground. It expresses his loss and sense of waste in a way that links them to the age-old traditions of his race, to the eternal realm of mytho-epic reality.

For Aitmatov this reality finds its ideal embodiment in the consciousness of animals and children. The main character of *The White Ship* is a seven-year-old boy. High in the mountains in a forest preserve stand the three cabins of three families, joined by ties of blood both close and distant. In charge is the forester Orozkul, whom everyone thoroughly detests and fears for his stolid cruelty. Orozkul's father-in-law Momun works as his subordinate and is raising a grandson, whose parents have abandoned him. The boy lives in two worlds: that of the myths which his grandfather tells him and the real world, which seems cruel and senseless. Family scenes of fighting and cursing weigh on the boy's spirits, but cannot destroy his inner world, at the foundation of which lies a feeling of harmony with nature and direct kinship with river, rocks and trees. The boy believes that the ancestress of their clan is Horned Deer Mother, who left the mountains when people killed off all her children, their own brothers. Moreover, he identifies Horned Deer Mother with his own missing mother, as he identifies his father with the white ship that passes every day on the lake below. When a doe appears in the forest preserve, the boy and his grandfather decide that Horned Deer Mother has forgiven the people. But Orozkul orders the grandfather to shoot the doe, and after an ineffectual attempt at opposition, Momun complies. Expecting to turn into a fish and join his father, the white ship, the boy throws himself into the river and drowns. Thus Momun pays with his grandson's life for his own irresolution. Aitmatov is opposed to compromise with evil, but in this somber tale it clearly cannot always be avoided.

Having demonstrated the harmony of mytho-epic thought, Aitmatov once again proceeds to show its tragedy in modern historical circumstances. The main character of the novel *I dol'sše veka dlitsja den'* (*The Day Lasts More Than a Hundred Years*), the railroad worker Edigei Buranny makes a long journey across the steppe to an old Kazakh cemetery where he wants to bury his best friend. On the way he recalls his long, hard life. Another story takes place on a parallel level of science fiction about a pair of astronauts—one Soviet, the other American—who leave their common space ship without permission from Center and land on a distant planet at the invitation of its inhabitants. When they want to return to earth as emissaries of the alien civilization, Center refuses to accept them on orders of the Sovet and American governments, which fear the superior alien civilization's threat to their hierarchical dominance of earth. A defensive rocket cordon is thrown around the earth, and the astronauts cannot return.

In addition to the real and science-fiction levels, the novel has a third, mytho-epic level. Aitmatov introduces an ancient legend about a mother who tries to rescue her captive son when he is turned by his enemies into a *mankurt*, a man without memory. At his captors' instigation the *mankurt* shoots his own mother with arrows and kills her. Are the *mankurt's* arrows similar to the rockets speeding into space? Have the men who launched them denied their mother earth? To Aitmatov this barbaric act is conditioned by a "loss of memory," a lack of respect for the past. In a conversation with an agent of the secret police, Edigei Buranny maintains that historical memory is essential. The agent has just arrested the teacher Abutalip for sitting up late at night writing about folk traditions, an incomprehensible and therefore suspicious act in the repressive atmosphere of the time. Thus in the terms of the novel, Stalinist secret police agents are associated with *mankurts.* Edigei is not permitted to bury his friend in the old cemetery. Surrounded by barbed wire, it is scheduled to be destroyed because of its proximity to a rocket base. A second legend occupies an important place in the novel: the legend of the love of the great Kazakh poet Raimaly for the young poetess Begimai. Through it Aitmatov returns to the problem raised in "Jamilya" of the tragic conflict between custom and individual spiritual freedom. Although as a whole the novel is more complex and polyphonic than *Farewell, Gulsary!,* the narrative device of Edigei's recollections during his journey is similar. Moreover, his relations with his camel Karanar are not less "fraternal" than those of Tanabai with his horse Gulsary. The novel has considerable political interest for Westerners. On its first publication in *Novy Mir* it was hailed in the USSR as a plea for the Soviet peace movement, but in its attack on Orwellian thought-control (in the preface Aitmatov condemns the Maoist Cultural Revolution, which attempted to make *mankurts* out of China's populace), Aitmatov—as Mary Seton-Watson wrote in a review in the *Times Literary Supplement*—"affirms the individual Soviet citizen's right to think for himself, to make his protest against official bureaucracy, to join individuals of other nations in the common struggle for greater sanity in world affairs."

Western readers know Aitmatov mainly through the publication and production (in London and in Washington, D.C.) of his play, written in collaboration with Kaltsi Mukhamedzhanov, *The Ascent of Mount Fuji* (1973). The scene is a reunion of some old friends held on top of a Kirghiz mountain—a history professor, a teacher, an artist, an actress, and a journalist. What they have in common is that some years earlier they had renounced their brilliant friend, a poet, and one of the group had betrayed him to the authorities. The informer's identity is not known, and as the group explores their attitudes and reactions, they begin a painful "ascent" to truth and self-knowledge. What most impressed

Westerners was the fact that an officially approved Soviet drama could be so free of ideological argument and so universally interesting and appealing. The suspense, drama critic Irving Wardle wrote in the (London) *Times,* "arises directly from its undisguised moral purpose: namely, that citizens should not hand their conscience over to the state."

Aitmatov's writings trace an evolution from an initially favorable attitude toward collectivization, Russification, and the introduction of a settled, nonnomadic way of life, to one of increasing hostility toward these tendencies; from a mythologizing perception of various elements of Soviet life (komsomol, collective farm, Party, city committee, tractor station), to the reestablishment of Kirghiz mythology, through the prism of which he shows the gradual moral degradation of his people. Soviet criticism remains silent of these developments, which begin to appear in works of Aitmatov's third period, after he had been accorded enormous fame and popularity. He is necessary to official Soviet ideology as the representative of a national minority and its culture, but in the eyes of the ordinary Soviet reader, he seems in fact a Russian writer, raising problems important to the Russian people, and indeed writing largely in Russian. In Aitmatov's work the literary tradition of nineteenth-century Russian realism mediates the conflict between religiously determined consciousness and the new order, with its opposition to tradition and its pretensions to taking over the entire world. In his numerous articles and interviews Aitmatov acts as an apologist for socialist realism and emphasizes his loyalty to the ideas of the Party. All in all, there is no hypocrisy in this; he is a loyal follower of Lenin who considers the norms and spirit of Lenin's party to have been distorted. He often defends the Kirghiz language, indirectly attacking the intensifying process of Russification.

Aitmatov's works have been published in many languages and countries, and a number have been successfully adapted to stage and screen, often by Aitmatov himself. According to UNESCO data, he is one of the most widely read authors in the world. He lives in Frinze, Kirchiz, with his wife Keres, a physician. They have two sons.

WORKS IN ENGLISH TRANSLATION: English-language versions of *Jamila* and *Tales of the Mountains and Steppes* were published in Moscow in 1959 and 1969 respectively. In England, where Aitmatov is better known than in the United States, *Farewell, Gulsary!* was translated by John French in 1970, and T. and G. Feifer translated *The White Steamship* in 1972. The latter was published in the United States in Mirra Ginsberg's translation in the same year as *The White Ship*. In 1983 John French's translation of *The Day Lasts More Than a Hundred Years* was published. The drama *The Ascent of Mount Fuji* was translated by Nicholas Bethell in 1975. A number of Aitmatov's short stories and non-fiction pieces have been published in the journal *Soviet Literature* since 1962.

ABOUT: Brown, D. Soviet Russian Literature Since Stalin, 1978; Clark, K, *Foreword to* The Day Lasts More Than a Hundred Years, 1983; Contemporary Authors 103, 1982; Encyclopedia of World Literature in the 20th Century (rev. ed.) I, 1981; Great Soviet Encyclopedia I, 1973; International Who's Who, 1983–84; Shneidman, N. Soviet Literature in the 1970s, 1980; Slonim, M. Soviet Russian Literature, 1977; Zhukov-Breschinsky, Z. A. Modern Encyclopedia of Russian and Soviet Literature I, 1977. *Periodicals*—Books Abroad 49, 1975; Culture and Life 7, 1959; New York Times July 30, 1970; Russian Literature Triquarterly 16, 1979; Times Literary Supplement November 4, 1983; World Literature Today 56, 1982.

DAMASO ALONSO

*ALONSO, DAMASO (October 22, 1898–), Spanish scholar, critic, and poet, was born in Madrid, the son of well-to-do middle-class parents. Though he began his university studies in the sciences, he soon changed to the humanities, obtaining his *licenciatura* (1921) and his doctorate (1928) from the University of Madrid. From 1921 to 1923 he was a lecturer in Spanish at the University of Berlin, and from 1923 to 1925 and again from 1928 to 1929 he held a similar post at Cambridge. A disciple of the eminent scholar Ramón Menéndez Pidal, he collaborated with him at the Centro de Estudios Históricos. In 1933 he obtained the chair of Spanish Language and Literature at the University of Valencia, and in 1939 he became Professor of Romance Linguistics at the University of Madrid, taking over the chair of Menéndez Pidal. Elected to the Royal Spanish Academy of the Language in 1945, he succeeded his former mentor as its president in 1968. He has been a member of the Royal Spanish Academy of History since 1954. He has taught as a visiting professor at numerous universities outside of Spain, including Oxford, Leipzig, Stanford, Columbia, Yale, Johns Hopkins, and Harvard. Various foreign institutions have bestowed honorary degrees on him, among them the universities of Lima, Bordeaux, Oxford, Hamburg, and Rome. He has served as editor of the *Revista de Filología Española* and the Biblioteca Románica Hispánica series of the Gredos publishing house.

As a scholar and critic, Alonso distinguished himself in the fields of linguistics and literature. His work in linguistics has resulted in numerous monographs on aspects of historical grammar,

dialectology, and lexicology, as well as on various topics of Romance philology. Dámaso Alonso is without a doubt contemporary Spain's foremost literary critic, with a reputation that extends far beyond that country's borders. Influenced by the methods of I. A. Richards and William Empson, he established his own credentials as a critic with his early writings on the poetry of Luis de Góngora, which were largely responsible for rescuing the Baroque poet from oblivion. His book *La lengua poética de Góngora* (Góngora's Poetic Language), which sprang from the same matrix as his doctoral dissertation on Góngora's syntax, was awarded the National Prize for Literature in 1927, the year which marked the three hundredth anniversary of the great poet's death. His edition of Góngora's *Soledades* (Solitudes) appeared that same year. During the following decade, in addition to writing numerous articles on Góngora and other subjects, he edited a series of works which include the *Enchiridion* and the *Paraclesis* of Erasmus, as well as an anthology of traditional and medieval Spanish poetry.

Alonso's most important critical works appeared, however, after the Spanish Civil War (1936–39). Building on his knowledge of literature and literary theory, as well as of linguistics and historical methodologies, he began to elaborate a stylistic approach to literary analysis which was already discernible in his previous work. These developing techniques are applied in his *La poesía de San Juan de la Cruz* (The Poetry of Saint John of the Cross), which came out in 1942. Between 1944 and 1951, he published a series of books and articles which contain the

° ä lôn´sō, dä mä´sō

essence of his method of stylistic analysis. *Poesía española. Ensayo de métodos y límites estilísticos* (Spanish Poetry. Essay on Stylistic Methods and Limits), which appeared in 1950, is considered his most fundamental critical work. With the publication of this book, he clearly established himself as the founder of the Spanish stylistic school. The type of criticism developed by Dámaso Alonso is not limited to a restricted number of objective linguistic patterns. It is an ample yet precise approach which utilizes multiple techniques. As he himself has stated, it involves "the study of everything which individualizes a work of literature." In another key work, *Seis calas en la expresión literaria española* (Six Penetrations into Spanish Literary Expression), written in collaboration with Carlos Bousoño and published in 1951, he concentrates on a more specific and technical form of stylistic analysis. Throughout the same period in which he was developing the critical approach explified by *Poesía española* and *Seis calas,* he continued his work in linguistics and in the historical setting of literature. His life-long interest in Góngora culminated in *Góngora y el "Polifemo"* (Góngora and the "Polyphemus"), which comprises an edition of Góngora's *Fable of Polyphemus and Galatea,* a biography of the poet, a general study of his style, a review of the criticism of Góngora, and detailed notes and analysis of the poem. Originally published in 1960, it has been expanded in subsequent editions and now fills three volumes. It is the standard reference work on Góngora. While he has covered the whole range of Spanish literature as regards periods and genres, Alonso's primary critical interest has been poetry. His work as a teacher, which has been closely connected with his scholarship and criticism, has left a deep imprint on several generations of students, both Spanish and foreign.

Even if he were not a major scholar and critic, Dámaso Alonso would still occupy a prominent place in twentieth-century Spanish letters as a poet. He belongs to a brilliant group of Spanish poets who emerged in the 1920s—Pedro Salinas, Jorge Guillén, Gerardo Diego, Federico García Lorca, Rafael Alberti, Vicente Aleixandre, and Luis Cernuda. His first book of poetry, *Poemas puros, poemillas de la ciudad* (Pure Poems, Little Poems of the City), appeared in 1921, when the influence of Juan Ramón Jiménez was at its height. Despite the title and date of publication, the book bears little relation to the "pure poetry" then in vogue and shows only a slight indebtedness to the work of the older poet. Though twenty-three years elapsed before the publication of Alonso's next two books of verse, *Poemas puros* anticipated both the themes and techniques of

his later production. The contrast between an idealized conception of existence and a harsh, prosaic reality is repeated throughout the book and is a prefiguration of a conflict which is at the very core of his mature poetry, the conflict between a religious view of life and an existential one. The simple, neat, formalistic exactness of these early compositions reveals a basic characteristic of all Alonso's poetry: the use of images in which symbolic and metaphorical functions overlap and become fused. The use of prosaic vocabulary for poetic effect is also evident.

Alonso matured late as a poet and he did not publish another book of poems until 1944. The appearance that year of *Hijos de la ira* (Children of Wrath) had a profound impact on the renewal of post-Civil War poetry in Spain. Its dominant tone is one of existential anguish. The language is ordinary and often prosaic, the style seemingly direct, and the images, with their surrealist echoes, suggest a nightmarish reality, which is reinforced by the syncopated rhythms of the free verse. In one of the most quoted poems in the book, "Insomnio" ("Insomnia"), Madrid is described as a city of "more than one million cadavers." Though the overall view of existence expressed in this volume is pessimistic, God is not totally absent, nor is man deprived of all hope. *Hijos de la ira* constitutes a modern version of the mystical journey, in which the poet-protagonist undergoes total humiliation in order to achieve salvation. The book moves between two poles: on the one hand, a yearning for religious and personal transcendence; on the other, a tendency toward egotism, pettiness, and destruction. Humor is utilized in some of the poems to avoid sentimentality and to emphasize the poet-protagonist's self-awareness, but Alonso made even greater use of this device in his later work. *Hijos de la ira* was one of the most widely read books of verse in post-Civil War Spain and ushered in an important current of existential poetry which would remain vigorous well into the 1950s.

Oscura noticia (Dark Message) also appeared in 1944, but contains several poems written much earlier. As in *Poemas puros* and other poems he wrote during the same era, we perceive a clash between an idealistic vision of life and a prosaic one. Now, however, the poet is more explicit in relating this conflict to such basic problems of human existence as time, death, and love. Like *Hijos de la ira, Oscura noticia* is also marked by religious preoccupations. *Hombre y Dios* (Man and God, 1955) constitutes a passionate dialogue with God on the eternal themes of suffering, freedom, injustice, and death. As in *Hijos de la ira,* the poet sometimes abandons his anguished tone for a humorous one. His most recent book of poetry, *Gozos de la vista* (The Joys of Sight), has not yet been published in its entirety. It focuses on, as its title suggests, the subject of human sight, its marvels and limitations. On a deeper level, it treats a theme of even wider scope, the dual nature of man's existence, its virtues and shortcomings. Several works of fiction round out the body of his creative work.

Dámaso Alonso has long had a special interest in English literature. In 1926 he published, under a pseudonym, a translation of James Joyce's *Portrait of the Artist as a Young Man.* He has also translated works by several English-speaking poets: Gerard Manley Hopkins, T. S. Eliot, D. H. Lawrence, and William Butler Yeats. Certain similarities between his own work and that of some of these writers has been pointed out.

As the author of *Hijos de la ira,* Dámaso Alonso played a crucial role in the development of Spanish poetry after the Civil War. With the majority of the leading poets of the previous period either dead or in exile, he, along with Vicente Aleixandre, remained in Spain and paved the way for younger writers who were not satisfied with the cold formalism which prevailed in Spanish poetry in the years immediately following the Civil War. They recognized in his poems their own painful experience of a world ravaged by war and destruction. *Hijos de la ira* remains one of the key works of contemporary Spanish poetry.

WORKS IN ENGLISH TRANSLATION: *Children of Wrath* was published in a bilingual edition with an English translation by Elias L. Rivers in 1970. Little of Alonso's critical writing is available in English. Two essays have been published: "Tradition or Polygenesis," in *Modern Humanities Research Association Annual Bulletin,* 1960, and "Towards a Knowledge of Literary Works," in *The Critical Moment: Literary Criticism in the 1960s,* 1965.

ABOUT: Brown, G. G. Literary History of Spain: Twentieth Century, 1972; Columbia Dictionary of Modern European Literature, 1980; Contemporary Authors 110, 1984; Contemporary Literary Criticism 14, 1980; Debicki, A.P. Dámaso Alonso, 1970; Dust, P. H. Dámaso Alonso's Quest for Meaning, 1970; Encyclopedia of World Literature in the 20th Century (rev. ed.) I, 1981; International Who's Who 1983–84; Morris, C. B. A Generation of Spanish Poets, 1920–1936, 1967. *Periodicals*—Books Abroad Spring 1974; Times Literary Supplement May 31, 1974.

*ALTHER, LISA (July 23, 1944–   ), American novelist, was born in Kingsport, Tennessee, the daughter of John Shelton (a surgeon) and Alice (Greene) Reed. She attended public schools in Kingsport, an industrialized community of 40,

°al´ ter

LISA ALTHER

000 inhabitants in rural northeastern Tennessee. An eager joiner of clubs, she also aspired to be a writer, and felt an early attraction to the novels of Flannery O'Connor. She left the South to attend Wellesley College, Massachusetts, from which she received her B.A. in 1966. Two months later she married Richard Philip Alther, a New Jersey-born painter and former advertising copywriter. During the following year they lived in New York City where Lisa Alther worked as a publishing assistant at Atheneum. They then moved to a four-acre farm in Vermont, where their daughter, Sara Halsey, was born two years later. It was after the birth of her daughter that Alther settled down to establish herself as a writer. She did free-lance writing for magazines, but her fiction went unsold for a number of years. By the time her novel *Kinflicks* was accepted she had written two other novels, as well as dozens of short stories, and collected 250 rejection slips.

Kinflicks was written both at the Vermont farm and in a rented room in Montreal, where Alther holed up with pen and paper one week out of every six to write for hours at a time. In an interview Alther spoke of writing "for fourteen or sixteen hours a day, getting into these highs and just staying there." The appearance of *Kinflicks* was a publishing event; the novel became a best-seller in hardcover before selling a million and a half copies in paperback. The jacket of the novel also carried an endorsement from Doris Lessing that would be the envy of any author of a first novel. "I very much liked this book," Lessing wrote, "and am sure Alther will be recognized as a strong, salty, original talent.

Is the word I am looking for balanced? She does fuse qualities, being robustly despairing, tenaciously critical, yet vigorously creative, firm but comical—she had me laughing at four in the morning. No man could have written it, but it is very far from being 'a woman's book,' and it made me wonder what *Tom Jones* would be like, written now. It is the size and scope of the territory Alther claims which is impressive."

The twenty-seven-year-old heroine of *Kinflicks* is Virginia ("Ginny") Babcock, who, at the opening of the novel, returns to her home town of Hullsport, Tennessee, to be with her dying mother. A series of flashbacks reveals Ginny's development from her early years as a cheerleader and flag-waver at local football games through her college experiences in the North, and her participation in the social, political, and sexual turmoil of the early 1960s. Ginny's sexual rites of passage in the small southern town seemed to many critics writing of an extraordinary kind. "It is safe to call this section," Doris Grumbach declared, "the best 100-or-so pages on adolescent mores and attitudes, sex and sensibilities, since Salinger took us on Holden Caulfield's journey."

Because of its dramatic rendering of the tumultuous age of the 1960s, *Kinflicks* made a strong impression and was praised in many reviews. John Leonard, in the *New York Times*, called it "a very *funny* book, not at all savage, about serious matters, full of people one would like to meet, and oddly invigorating. The tone of voice throughout is a tone that has been missing in American fiction for years—it is the speech of breezy survivors, of Holden Caulfield, Augie March and, ultimately, Huckleberry Finn." Other critics, however, found *Kinflicks* flawed in one respect or another, its comedy too often slapstick. *Kinflicks* also aroused spirited controversy among feminists. Erica Jong hailed the novel as a modern feminist classic, but Germaine Greer was decidedly displeased by Alther's "picaresque novel of a *femme moyenne sensuelle* whose adventures are chiefly remarkable in that they do not raise her consciousness one notch."

Alther's more recent novels, *Original Sins* and *Other Women*, treat many of the same themes of *Kinflicks*, but handle them more somberly. Instead of having one protagonist, *Original Sins* has five. They are, in fact, called "The Five" when they are children together in the southern town of Newland, perched in the branches of a weeping beech tree and dreaming happily of the future. As they grow older, they drift apart, suffering disappointment and alienation in their lives.

Paul Gray, in *Time*, wrote that he found *Original Sins* an impressive novel, superior to *Kinflicks*. "As she cuts back and forth between the adventures and peregrinations of her characters," he remarked, "Alther constructs a broad social portrait of nearly two decades of American life. She covers civil rights, Vietnam, women's lib, the sexual revolution, radical politics . . . with page-turning verve and intelligence." But Mary Cantwell, in the *New York Times*, and J. A. Avant, in the *Nation*, expressed disappointment. Avant commented that Alther attempts "doggedly to work out what she thinks has to go into the novel: Tennessee valleys, cotton mill machinery, Upper West Side apartments, feminist consciousness-raising sessions, voter registration drives," but the effect was "static," and the characters stereotypes. Critics expressed similar reservations about *Other Women*, in which her middle-aged heroine experiments with marriage, motherhood, lesbianism, fantasizing, and psychotherapy. Nancy Evans, who found the plot conventional and the characters unconvincing, especially regretted the absence of the comic detachment that had distinguished her earlier work.

Despite her celebrity, Lisa Alther lives quietly near Hinesburg, Vermont (population 2,000) with her husband and daughter, and is very protective of their privacy. Andrew Feinberg, in a recent interview, describes Alther as "a big-boned, five-foot-eight-and-one-half-inch woman who still seems tomboyish. . . . Although several of her Vermont friends are writers, she finds no great pleasure in shop talk. She would rather hike, ski . . . or play poker." A "calm, funny, casual person," she teaches southern fiction, when she is not at her typewriter, at Saint Michael's College in Winooski, Vermont. There is perhaps some irony that she should live in Vermont while teaching the literature of the South, but it is an irony that goes far back in her life—her father having been a Virginian while her mother came from upstate New York. Inner conflict and the tension of opposites, however, seem an integral part of Alther's writing. Her sense of the unused potentialities in women coexists with her hard-headed knowledge of human limitations.

PRINCIPAL WORKS: Kinflicks, 1976; Original Sins, 1981; Other Women, 1984.

ABOUT: Contemporary Authors 65–68, 1977; Contemporary Literary Criticism 7, 1977; Janet Todd (ed.) Gender and Literary Voice, 1980. *Periodicals*—Atlantic May, 1976; Harper's May 1976; Horizon May, 1981; Nation April 25, 1981; New Republic June 13, 1981; New Statesman August 27, 1976;

New York Review of Books April 1, 1976; May 3, 1981; New York Times March 16, 1976; July 30, 1976; New York Times Book Review March 14, 1976; November 11, 1984; New Yorker March 29, 1976; Newsweek March 15, 1976; Rolling Stone April 22, 1976; Spectator September 12, 1981; Time March 22, 1976; April 27, 1981; Times Literary Supplement August 27, 1976; June 26, 1981; Village Voice March 8, 1976.

RICHARD ALTICK

ALTICK, RICHARD D(ANIEL) (September 19, 1915–), American scholar and educator, was born in Lancaster, Pennsylvania, the son of Edward Charles and Laura (Reinhold) Altick. He received his B.A. from Franklin and Marshall College in 1936 and his Ph.D. in English literature from the University of Pennsylvania in 1941. Altick was an instructor in the English Department at Franklin and Marshall from 1941 until 1945, when he joined the English Department at Ohio State University, where he was Professor of English from 1950 to 1968 and Regents' Professor of English until he retired in 1982.

"Believing that every work of art must be seen from without as well as from within," Richard Altick writes of the scholar in his *Art of Literary Research,* "he seeks to illuminate it from every conceivable angle, to make it as intelligible as possible by the uncovering and application of the data residing outside itself." As a teacher, Altick has communicated his enthusiasm for scholarship to several generations of students and colleagues. As a writer specializing in Victorian culture, he has made his knowledge accessible to a wide nonacademic audience. The gap commonly assumed to exist between scholarship and teaching, between the scholar's dedication to specialized studies and the teacher's responsibility to educate students of widely varied backgrounds and interests, does not exist for Altick. "Learning without teaching is sterile," he concludes in that book, "and teaching without learning is merely a way of passing time. The true scholar finds that the two are, in fact, inseparable; and his life necessarily has room for both." As a specialist in Victorian literature and culture, Altick has worked appropriately in a tradition established by Thomas Carlyle, Matthew Arnold, and Robert Browning—bringing the past back to life, restoring the social and historical context of English literature, and moving toward the achievement of what he calls "the supreme goal of Victorian scholarship, the weaving of a seamless web of historical knowledge that embraces all aspects of the age's life and expression."

Altick came to the study of Victorian literature as a young English instructor trained in eighteenth-century and romantic literature, assigned to teach a course in Victorian poetry because nobody else had requested it. His qualifications, he recalled in an essay written forty years later, "Victorians on the Move; Or, 'Tis Forty Years Since," "hovered between the minimal and the non-existent." Learning as he taught, he found himself in what was then a relatively little explored area of scholarship. If, as he notes, "not actually present at the creation," he both witnessed and played a significant part in the establishment of Victorian studies during the next several decades. Among his most important contributions is an ambitious book that required ten years of research and writing, *The English Common Reader: A Social History of the Mass Reading Public, 1800–1900.* Here he investigated the gradual spread of literacy in nineteenth-century England and the responses to this development within English society—fears, for example, of a literate working class demanding social change, and of the dangers of moral corruption and the degradation of taste, all associated with popular reading. Working through the vast archives of the period—newspapers, periodicals, broadsides, the documents of the public education and library movements, the records of publishers and circulating libraries—Altick assembled his material into a book that the *Times Literary Supplement* found an "entertaining examination of Victorian reading habits [that] is also an attempt to collect the kind of information essential to understanding the popular taste of any age," and that Frank Luther Mott, historian of American popular reading, praised for its careful research as well as its surprising readability and grace.

Altick has both worked intensively with single literary works—as in *Browning's Roman Murder Story: A Reading of "The Ring and the Book"* (written in collaboration with James F. Loucks), a comprehensive critical examination of the massive poem that demonstrates its coherence and artistic structure—and dealt with more general ideas in such books as *Victorian Studies in Scarlet,* described by the *Times Literary Supplement* as "an admirable exposition of the astonishing extent to which murder figured in the popular imagination during the 19th century," and *Lives and Letters,* a history of English and American literary biography. Leon Edel, writing in the *New York Times Book Review,* found this study especially valuable for "Altick's demonstration of the extent to which biography in England and America has been invariably the product of the cultural climate," noting that while he is not himself a biographer, "he is an unabashed and fervent admirer, a constant reader." Social history was again Altick's focus in *Victorian People and Ideas,* a book frequently consulted by students of the period, and most notably in *The Shows of London,* a large, profusely illustrated book that records the hitherto neglected history of popular exhibitions in England from 1600 to 1862—dioramas, panoramas, "pleasure domes," freak shows, and menageries. As Altick points out in his introduction, the book complements *The English Common Reader:* "There I dealt with what the English people paid to read; here, I am concerned with what Londoners paid to gaze at. Both volumes, therefore, are studies in the history of English popular culture." By the 1860s, Altick points out, with the success of the Crystal Palace Exhibition of 1851, this whole phase of English life began to disappear, as occasional shows were replaced by public museums. He records this history in a wealth of fascinating detail, with a storyteller's finesse and critical tact. Well received by both American and English reviewers, the book won the George Freedley Memorial Award in 1980.

Discovering the life of scholarship, as he has done of literature, was Altick's purpose in *The Scholar Adventurers,* a widely read book that treats notable scholarly discoveries of the past and the scholars who made them: the spectacular find of James Boswell's manuscripts at Malahide Castle, the record of Mrs. Hawthorne's "censorship" of her husband's *Notebooks,* the tracking down of famous forgeries, the mysterious circumstances surrounding the murder of Christopher Marlowe, and the "untold" stories of Byron's adventures. Though Altick does not include his own scholarly adventures in the book, his capsule definition of the literary scholar—"a lively imagination focused in the art of literature, and a scientific devotion to truth in its minutest detail"—certainly describes him.

Altick married Helen W. Keller in 1942; they have two daughters. Among his academic honors are fellowships from the Newberry Library, the American Council of Learned Societies, and the Guggenheim Foundation, and visiting professorships at New York University (1950) and Stanford (1956). In 1964 he received a Litt. D. from Franklin and Marshall College. In 1984 Ohio State University Press published a volume of essays in his honor by noted scholars of Victorian literature — *Victorian Literature and Society.*

PRINCIPAL WORKS: A Preface to Critical Reading, 1946; The Cowden Clarkes, 1948; The Scholar Adventurers, 1950; The English Common Reader, 1957; (with Andrew Wright) Selective Bibliography for the Study of English and American Literature, 1960; (with W. R. Matthews) Guide to Doctoral Dissertations in Victorian Literature, 1880–1958, 1960; The Art of Literary Research, 1963; Lives and Letters: A History of Literary Biography in England and America, 1965; (with J. F. Loucks) Browning's Roman Murder Story: A Reading of 'The Ring and the Book,' 1968; To Be in England, 1969; Victorian Studies in Scarlet, 1970; Victorian People and Ideas, 1973; The Shows of London, 1978. *As editor*—Carlyle, T. Past and Present, 1965; Browning, R. The Ring and the Book, 1971, 1981.

ABOUT: Contemporary Authors, new revision series 4, 1981. *Periodicals*—American Literature March, 1964; Atlantic, September 1966; Dickens Studies Annual 10, 1982; New Statesman January 29, 1949; New York Review of Books December 17, 1970; October 12, 1978; New York Times March 13, 1949; August 6, 1964; New York Times Book Review December 10, 1950; February 2, 1964; November 14, 1965; October 25, 1970; Spectator November 26, 1948; May 25, 1974; Times Literary Supplement October 24, 1968; April 13, 1973; July 5, 1974; October 27, 1978; Victorian Studies Summer 1979; Yale Review Winter 1979.

*AMALRIK, ANDREI (ALEKSEYEVICH) (May 12, 1938–November 11, 1980), Russian writer, was born in Moscow into a family of nonconformists. His father, a distinguished historian, was dismissed from his university post because of his criticism of the Stalin regime—this in spite of his service in the Battle of Stalingrad. Growing up amid the dangers and privations of the German invasion of the USSR in World War II, Amalrik came into conflict with authorities early on. He managed, however, to enroll at Moscow University in 1959 where he was an outstanding student. But in 1963 his dissertation on Russian history offended authorities because it concluded that Scandinavian and Byzantine-Greek civilizations had contributed significantly to Russian culture. This thesis was in direct con-

°ä mäl′ rik, än dryä′ ē

ANDREI AMALRIK

flict with the accepted, party-endorsed, view of Russian culture as exclusively Slavic. Informed that his research was brilliant but the conclusion unacceptable, Amalrik refused to remove the offending passages and was expelled from the university. He attempted to send his dissertation abroad through the Danish embassy, but his plan was discovered and he was put into a precarious position with the KGB.

This was the beginning of Amalrik's lifelong struggle with the system. In the course of his dissident activities during the 1960s and early 1970s, Amalrik published his writings only in the West. In the Soviet Union they circulated through the underground *samizdat* (self-published). The best known of these are a collection of plays (1962–63); *NezheLannoe puteshestuie v Sibiz* (*Involuntary Journey to Siberia*, 1966), describing his exile to Siberia; an essay *Prosushchestvuet Li Sovetskii Soiuz do 1984 goda?* (*Will the Soviet Union Survive Until 1984?*, 1970) and his major work *Zapiski dissidenta* (*Notes of a Revolutionary*, 1976), another autobiographical account of his last years in the Soviet Union. These works are the record of an almost incredible stuggle against ceaseless harassment, frail health, and the rigors of prison life. They are all the more remarkable for the indomitable spirit they express, for the will to survive against impossible odds.

Amalrik's plays are his earliest and only works of imaginative literature. The collection *Nos! Nos! N-o-s!*, published in English translation as *Nose! Nose? No-se!*, includes seven plays, six conceived and written by him, the seventh adapted for the stage from Nikolai Gogol's nine-

teenth-century classic short story "The Nose." Amalrik's plays are written in an absurdist style, befitting the absurd reality of Soviet life as the playwright sees it. He misses none of the possibilities offered by Soviet environment, especially in his attacks on the ever-compromising and equivocating Soviet intelligentsia whom he despises for cowardliness and lack of resolution in the face of oppression. In his view these people are guilty of complicity because, unlike the working classes, they have the intellectual sophistication to identify the problem but lack the courage to act upon this knowledge. In one of the plays, "My Aunt Is Living in Volokolansky," Amalrik writes a tragedy familiar to many Russians. The central character, a professor, is a prototype of a man destroyed through years of pressure and compromise. From the seemingly trivial and innocuous dialogue among the four characters, the reader draws the inescapable conclusion that advancement within the confines of the Soviet system can come only at the expense of individual dignity and independence.

The autobiographical *Involuntary Journey to Siberia* is an account of Amalrik's arrest on charges of pornography and "parasitism,"—failure to hold a regular job—his mockery of a trial, and his predetermined sentence to a *kolkhoz* (collective farm) in Siberia for forced labor. There are vivid sketches of the officials, the judges, on the one hand, and of the dissidents, artists, prostitutes, and vagrants who shared his sentence, and of Siberia itself, a backward rural Russia, stagnating in the wholesale application of an inapplicable ideology. Once released, Amalrik returned to his proudly defiant life, supporting himself and now his wife, a painter, Gyuzel Makudinova, with odds jobs, ranging from delivering mail to free-lance journalism. A collector of avant-garde Russian painting, he established ties with Western European artists which made him highly suspect in the USSR. Even more daringly, he came to the defense of Andrei Sinyavsky and Yuri Daniel when they went on trial for their writings, and shortly after, he published the essay *Will the Soviet Survive until 1984?*, challenging the idealistic liberal democratic movement in the USSR which believed that the system would weaken as a result of its inflexibility and complex bureaucracy and of threats from outside the country, especially from China. Not surprisingly Amalrik was re-arrested in 1970 and this time condemned to a severe prison sentence. Living under almost intolerable conditions of filth and starvation, he became very ill and nearly died. He managed to survive, however, and even to continue to resist the authorities, and at the end of his three-year term he was arrested again, charged with criti-

cizing the Soviet Union, and sentenced to another three-year term. All this is recounted in
graphic detail in *Notes of a Revolutionary,*
which also describes his release from confinement in 1975. He returned to Moscow, without
a residence permit, and with his wife managed
a precarious existence until 1976, when the KGB
reluctantly gave him permission to leave the
USSR. He and his wife flew to Amsterdam
where they received a tumultuous welcome and
moved on from there to Utrecht and then to the
United States where he lectured a Harvard and
other universities. He settled with his wife in
southern France, where he worked on a biography of Rasputin. In 1980, driving to Madrid to
participate in a conference on the Helsinki Accords, he was killed in an automobile accident.
In a brief Preface to the English translation of
Notes of a Revolutionary, Amalrik summed up
the essence of his short but memorable life:

> After my longtime negative attitude toward the word
> "revolution," I became a participant in what is perhaps one
> of the most significant radical changes of our times. No one
> yet knows whether this agonizing attempt to create a new
> ideology will succeed, or whether it will end in a blind al-
> ley. The crisis of Christianity gave birth to the Enlighten-
> ment, and the crisis of the Enlightenment engendered
> Marxism. But can we yet affirm with confidence that
> Marxism's crisis will be solved by transformation of the
> "person" from an element in the "system" into a true per-
> son? The philosophy of totalitarianism is still spreading
> through the world. But in the land where it first triumphed,
> the process of overcoming it has begun, not "from the
> right" but "from the left," in a movement that gropes its
> way along but in a forward direction.

WORKS IN ENGLISH TRANSLATION: *Will the Soviet Union Survive Until 1984?* was published in Hilary Sternberg's
translation in 1970; Manya Harari and Max Heyward
translated *Involuntary Journey to Siberia* also in 1970.
Guy Daniels translated *Notes of a Revolutionary* in
1982. Amalrik's *Nose! Nose? No-se! and Other Plays*
was translated by Daniel Weissbort in 1973. Amalrik's
unfinished book on Rasputin was translated into
French by Basile Karlinsky in 1982.

ABOUT: Columbia Dictionary of Modern European Lit-
erature, 1980; Current Biography, 1974; Jacoby, S.
Introduction to Notes of a Revolutionary, 1982.
Periodicals—New York Times November 13, 1980;
New York Times Book Review July 11, 1982; New
Yorker March 26, 1984.

*ANDAY, MELIH CEVDET (July 1915–   ),
Turkish poet, playwright, novelist, essayist, and
translator writes: "I was born in Istanbul, where
I had my primary and secondary schooling. Istanbul, with its unique historical heritage, gave
me the opportunity of experiencing the real taste
of Byzantine and Ottoman cultures. I loved the
sea, the ships, the sunshine and the clouds. In

MELIH CEVDET ANDAY

1931 my family moved to Ankara, the capital of
new Turkey. Ankara was a barren city with
sharp light, short showers and marvellous sun-
sets. It was not as tenderhearted as Istanbul perhaps, but it gave me the sensation of our ancient
Anatolian history and taught me the strong character of our people and its interesting fate. I attended the local lycée there and finished it. I
went to Belgium (Brussels) to read sociology;
however I returned to my country after a short
stay, because the Second World War broke out.
In Ankara I was employed as a civil servant, and
at the same time I resumed my studies at the
Law School of Ankara University. I could not get
my degree, because of the intervention of my
national service which lasted for approximately
four years. Nevertheless this provided me with
the opportunity of getting to know Anatolian villages. After the termination of my national service I again returned to Ankara and during the
1940s and 1950s the major position I held was
acting as the publication consultant for the Ministry of Education. Later I moved to Istanbul
and established myself there as a journalist. I edited art pages and particularly wrote articles and
essays on artistic, literary and social problems,
together with serialized articles on the social life
of Istanbul. Then I taught Turkish phonetics and
diction at the drama department of Istanbul
Conservatory for twenty-five years. I have been
selected as a board member of Turkish Radio-
TV. My last post was at the Turkish Embassy in
Paris and I acted as the cultural counsellor there.
Now I contribute regularly to *Cumhuriyet,* an
influential Istanbul daily, and devote the rest of
my time to writing poems, novels and plays.

°än´ dä, mä lē´ chäv´ dä

"I began writing poems very early, but my first poem was published in 1936, in a famous literary review, *Varlik* (Existence), in Ankara. This first poem used meter for the sake of meter and I continued in the same way for a year; however, I later wanted to revolutionize Turkish poetry and I collaborated with two colleagues of mine—two distinguished poets [Orhan Veli Kanik and Oktay Rifat]—to find a new way in this direction. We aimed at altering the whole structure of our poetry from its very foundations, so we eliminated traditional meters and verse forms, as well as the conventional stock of epithets and metaphors. We reduced rhyme to a base minimum and we adopted the man in the street as our hero. In an effort to communicate to the common man we utilized rhythms and idioms of colloquial speech.

"The Ottoman language was a mixed one, Turkish, Arabic and Persian, and our classic poets wrote their poems with this mixed language. During Atatürk's period we purged these Arabic and Persian words from Turkish on a large scale. But our great poets like Ahmet Hasim and Yahya Kemal, who are leaders of modern Turkish poetry, have got a lot of foreign words in their poems. The first problem for us was to create a people's language used in literature. That is why all we young poets and writers nearly became linguists. When asked at a Balkan literary conference held in Sofia what I considered to be the classic works of Turkish literature, I replied, 'We have no classics,' and went on to explain: 'It is not easy to call a literature classical when it does not give us early examples of the language we speak, of the art form we use, or of a universal significance illumined by the light of the intellect.' This was an irritating statement in the eyes of most of our intellectuals, because in reality our poetry begins in the thirteenth century, but we have to bear in mind that our popular poetry also begins in the same century. Unfortunately our intellectuals did not pay any attention to it after the Tanzimat period (Ottoman reformation and westernization in 1839).

"The subject was not a formalistic problem, but also was the realism in verse and social justice in politics. Mr. Talat S. Halman (a Turkish poet who translated some of my poems into English) says in the introduction to *On the Nomad Sea*: 'Throughout the 1940s and much of the succeeding decade, his poetry dwelt on the socioeconomic plight of the vast majority of the Turkish population. In poem after poem Anday vented his imagination over inequality and injustice.' We burst on the scene with a joint book of poems entitled *Garip* (Strange, 1941). After a short while, it became the name of a new current in Turkish literature; in fact the Garip move-

ment was considered the most drastic change Turkish poetry has ever experienced. These poems have been written in a humoristic style in general.

"My own first poetry book, *Rahati Kaçan Ağac* (The Tree Ill at Ease), was published in 1946, exactly five years after the appearance of *Garip*. Then other books followed it: *Telgrafhane* (Cable Office, 1952), *Yanyana* (Side by Side, 1956). Halman says: 'The metamorphosis in Anday's aesthetics came in a six year period—from 1956 to 1962. After much soul searching, he gradually evolved from a poet of social criticism to one of intellectual explorations and abstract formulation. Although he never abandoned his humanism, his affirmation of life, and his lucid diction, everything else about his poetry—substance, style, syntax—changed radically. The final break with his past came in 1962 with the publication of *Kollari Bağli Odiseus* (Odysseus Bound).' I handled in this poem the famous theme of Odysseus' return to Ithaca, and in an another poem which came after, 'Horses at the Trojan Gates,' a similar theme of Homer about the Trojan War. I take ancient Anatolian history as our own historical heritage, and to me these Homeric themes are contemporary happenings. With this view, I believe, I have reached a new understanding of our past. And I recently treated the story of Gilgamesh, with this view in mind, in my latest poetry book. One can think that I am trying to synthesize Western and Eastern cultures. This may be true. Yet, although I like English and American poetry so much ever since my younger days—I translated a lot of poems from English into Turkish—I prefer to use the term 'planetarisation' in place of 'westernization,' since my target is world poetry."

When Melih Cevdet Anday made his radical break with the poetic realism that had characterized his early poetry, he moved away not from Turkish literature but toward what he calls "world poetry"—an attempt to absorb his native culture into a universal vision that is conceptual and intellectual rather than primarily socioeconomic. For that reason, his retelling of the Odysseus myth in terms of modern man's struggle to end his alienation from the universe is a work of profound significance in modern Turkish literature. Drawing upon and assimilating his wide reading in Western literature—ranging from Homer and the Old Testament to Baudelaire, Pound, Eliot, and Wallace Stevens (a poet to whom he has been specifically compared)—into traditional Turkish poetry, Anday wrote a richly complex and abstract poem, actually a collection of poems that explores the conscious functioning of the human mind. Alienated from nature, society, and himself, modern man has failed to create a new or alternative universe and has become a mere bystander: "Fallen apart from nature, man keeps quiet." He cannot enjoy experience or selfhood, but can know only the sensation of observing, looking on. Pessimistic and unresolved as his Odysseus-Everyman seems to be, Anday is not without hope, because of his faith in the power of the human intellect: "To create your immortality," he writes in this poem, "Defend yourself with words/ On the side of reality."

As a novelist, Anday has been concerned primarily with the breaking down of the traditional social hierarchies of Turkish life. His *Aylaklar* (The Idlers, 1965) traces four generations in the life of a traditional upper-class Turkish family stubbornly resisting the realities of social change and ultimately losing their home and status. Anday has also published a book about his travels in the Soviet Union, Bulgaria, and Hungary (1965), as well as two plays—*Icerdikiler* (Those Who Are Within, 1965) and *Mikado'nun Cöpleri* (The Mikado Game, 1967)—in which characters discuss abstract philosophical questions but, thanks to Anday's dramatic craftsmanship, manage to maintain the reader's interest. Though few have been translated into English, Anday's works have been widely read in Russian, Rumanian, Hungarian, German, and French translations, and in 1971 he was named by UNESCO as "one of the prominent figures of world literature"—along with Dante, Shakespeare, Cervantes, and—among the moderns—Nobel prize winners Kawabata and Seferis.

WORKS IN ENGLISH TRANSLATION: *On the Nomad Sea: Selected Poems* was translated by Talat Sait Halman in 1974. Other poems by Anday are published in English in *Literature East and West* (March, 1973) and in *The Penguin Book of Turkish Verse*, 1978. *Rain One Step Away*, a collection of poems, was translated by Talat Halman and Brian Swann in 1980.

ABOUT: Columbia Dictionary of Modern European Literature, 1980; Dictionary of Oriental Literature 3, 1974; Encyclopedia of World Literature in the 20th Century IV, 1975; Reader's Encyclopedia of World Drama, 1969. *Periodicals*—Books Abroad 39, 1965.

*ANDERSCH, ALFRED (February 4, 1914– February 21, 1980), German novelist, editor, essayist, poet, short-story, and radio, film, and TV writer, was born and raised in Munich, where he went to elementary school and attended the

°än´dersh

ALFRED ANDERSCH

Gymnasium until 1928; he left school because of low grades and became apprenticed to a bookseller. His father, a merchant, an insurance agent, a political conservative who had been an officer in World War I and subsequently a supporter of the German commander-in-chief, Erich von Ludendorff, died early. Andersch's joblessness from 1931 to 1933 coincided with the beginning of his own political activities. At the age of eighteen, shortly after his father's death and in protest against his "petit-bourgeois family," he became the leader of the Communist youth organization of Southern Bavaria. Following the burning of the Reichstag (Feb. 27, 1933), he was sent to the Dachau concentration camp for a three-month term and was released "with nothing worse than a black eye." After a brief second arrest in September 1933 and under Gestapo surveillance, Andersch broke with the Communist party, felt driven to introversion, and "for years . . . lived on the island of [his] soul." He pursued a number of clerical jobs, first in Munich and then in Hamburg; in 1940 he was drafted into the German army, released in 1941, and drafted again in 1943. Staging his entirely "private twentieth of July," Andersch deserted from the Wehrmacht near Nettuno on June 6, 1944 and voluntarily became a prisoner of war. In his first book, *Die Kirschen der Freiheit* (The Cherries of Freedom, 1952), Andersch gives a Sartrian interpretation of his life up to 1944 when he threw away his gun in the Italian hills "to perform an act of freedom, an act situated in the no man's land between the captivity [he] came from and the captivity into which [he] was going." "Freedom," Andersch concluded, "lies in the wilderness," and the fruits of the cherry tree he came across as he made his way towards the American lines, he baptized "the wild cherries of [his] freedom."

During his internment in the United States from 1944 to the end of 1945, Andersch wrote numerous contributions for *Der Ruf* (The Call), the journal of German prisoners of war in the United States. In the fall of 1945 the American authorities sent Andersch to Fort Getty, Rhode Island, to participate in a course in basic spoken English, German and American history, and the outlines of American military government administration in occupied Germany. At Fort Getty, "less a POW-camp than an unacknowledged member of the Ivy League," writes J. D. Wilkinson, Andersch was profoundly impressed by the Americans' "unspoken belief in the possibility of change through teaching, which presupposes a faith in the positive forces in man." Upon his return to Germany, Andersch became Erich Kästner's editorial assistant for *Neue Zeitung* (New Times) in Munich and then, together with Hans Werner Richter, coeditor of the postwar periodical *Der Ruf* (1946–47). Next he helped to found the literary movement of Gruppe 47 from which he disassociated himself eventually because it had developed into "an instrument of power." For ten years (1948–58) Andersch did his own experimental programming for German radio networks and thereby "contributed decisively to shaping ideas and forms of Germany's reviving intellectual life," as Peter Demetz observes. He moved to Berzona, a small village in a remote valley in the Italian-speaking part of Switzerland, in 1958 to concentrate on his writing and received Swiss citizenship in 1972. Five years later he fell gravely ill, underwent a kidney transplant and died of kidney failure in Berzona in 1980. Alfred Andersch was survived by four children and his wife Gisela Dichgans, a painter and photographer, with whom he had written a number of travel books.

In his books and essays that deal with recent history, Andersch time and again criticized society from an antifascist point-of-view; but he followed no program, served no party, institution or ideology. As he put it in "The Cherries of Freedom": "I hope I shall always refrain from any attempt to convince people. One can only try to show them the possibilities they have to choose from." Freedom, escape, and rescue are the central themes of Andersch's work. In contrast to Andersch's own interpretation, Marcel Reich-Ranicki was the first to express the now generally accepted view that it is not Andersch's desertion in 1944 which accounts for the motif of escape in his novels, short stories, and radio plays, but his escape in 1933 from politics into

art, from the reality of life into introversion. As a rule, then, his heroes are loners and outsiders, disappointed and bitter and desperate beings, as well as extreme individualists. Often they fail to find a place for themselves in society, and they consider themselves to be failures.

Andersch's first novel, *Sansibar oder Der letzte Grund* (*Flight to Afar*, 1957), highly praised by German critics and translated into eleven languages, established his literary reputation. On an October day in prewar Nazi Germany, in a small town on the Baltic, five people face decisions that are to change their lives; and in the span of twenty-four hours they become intimately involved with each other because they need each other's help to carry out their choices. They are Judith Levin, a young Jewish girl from Hamburg who, after the suicide of her mother, has come to Rerik to find transportation for her escape to Sweden; Gregor, a young communist functionary on his last trip in the service of the illegal party; an old communist fisherman, Knudsen, whose beliefs have been dwindling; Pastor Helander, who is determined to save a wooden statue of a young monk reading, made by a sculptor (probably Barlach) persecuted by the regime; and, finally, a young boy who reads Mark Twain and yearns to leave for the great unknown which he calls Zanzibar "beyond the open seas." The fisherman brings the Jewish girl and the precious statue to the coast of Sweden; he himself, however, decides to return to whatever awaits him in Rerik; the young boy enjoys an hour of supreme freedom in the Swedish woods but realizes that his escape would spell trouble for the fisherman and therefore rejoins Knudsen, who will be his new father. Gregor breaks with his organized past by engineering Judith's escape and the rescue of the statue as a "private undertaking," and he consequently decides to resist on his own. The pastor takes his army revolver to shoot those men in black uniforms who come to arrest him at dawn. "From the net of interrelationships," according to Peter Demetz, "the statue . . . emerges as a symbolic image of normative attitudes: disciplined yet free, attentive to knowledge and yet ready at any moment to get up and act in accordance with his inner self." Demetz makes the convincing point that the central meaning of *Sansibar* is ironically hidden in the party message Gregor is to bring to his comrades in Rerik: "As Nazi political pressure was increasing, the party had decided to rebuild the network of illegal combatants in small cells of five who would be unknown to other cells and thus have a better chance of surviving. Contrary to the expectations of the party, Gregor indeed helps to build a compact group, consisting of five people who have chosen freedom by making spontaneous choices. They are the exemplary 'cell' of five on whom the future of mankind rests." In contradistinction to Reich-Ranicki, who praised the novel as a "parable about man's free will and his individual responsibility, about his capacity to choose and to decide," Demetz ultimately maintains a more critical stance, arguing that Andersch failed to capture with equal success "the differentiated autonomy of [the] consciousness of the five characters involved" and that "the existentialist pattern to be demonstrated triumphs all too easily over the loose ends of life."

Andersch's second novel, *Die Rote* (*The Redhead,* 1960), is a tale of personal flight. Franziska Lukas, a beautiful German woman and a highly qualified interpreter, impulsively escapes from an unhappy marriage with Herbert, a German corporation man of aesthetic pretensions, as well as from a long affair with his boss Joachim. Abandoning her husband in a café in Milan, she takes the train to Venice to start her own life. There, in the bleak wintertime atmosphere of this fabulous city, she is unwittingly drawn into the conflict between Patrick O'Malley, a former member of the British Counterintelligence Service, and Kramer, a onetime Gestapo officer whose past ties him irrevocably to Patrick. Staggering from the fatal scene of their final encounter, Franziska almost instinctively seeks refuge in the embrace of Fabio Crepaz, a violin player who once commanded the partisans of the region but is now cut off from the commitments of the past and in search of a new direction for his life. At the house of Fabio's proletarian parents in Mestre, Franziska gives birth to her child, whose father, Herbert, she divorces and goes on living as a working girl in a local soap factory. Suspense, murder, and the unexpected fulfillment of Franziska's hidden dream of the simple life mark the climax of this novel which Peter Demetz praised for its "austerity and considerable sophistication" and which Reich-Ranicki condemned for its simplistic Rousseauean juxtapositions and its superficial, tendentious social criticism.

Efraim (*Efraim's Book,* 1967), his next novel, received the Nelly Sachs prize in Germany and was translated into twelve languages. Georg, alias George Efraim, born of a Jewish family in Berlin in the early twenties, is sent as a child to England to be saved from Nazi persecution. While he goes to school in London and becomes a journalist later on, his mother perishes in Theresienstadt and his father in Auschwitz. Separated from Meg, his British wife, Efraim lives in Rome as correspondent for a London weekly, but he becomes thoroughly weary of his profession. As in Andersch's earlier novels, recent history and social criticism play a certain role; but Efraim, the narrator of the novel, is preoccupied with his private life: his loss of interest in his career, the failure of his marriage, the whole purpose of his life. Finding it impossible to believe in destiny, since he attributes little importance to free will and prefers to watch how chance rules the world, he finds no answers to his questions. During the Cuban missile crisis Efraim is sent to Berlin to report on the mood of the city and to track down a young Jewish girl who disappeared from her mother's house long before the persecutions began. He never completes his dual assignment; instead he begins to discover himself and to rediscover his German identity. Composing the novel of his life (writing in German again after many years) he is forced to uncover his intellectual and sexual frustrations without compromise and thus, as one reviewer describes it, "regains a precarious balance of mind through the act of telling his story." *Efraim* received largely favorable reviews in Germany as well as in the United States, where Robert J. Clements praised the novel for its "leisured narrative of time past cleverly woven together with flashbacks, repetitions, echoes, and cinematic techniques." However, the critic Reich-Ranicki objected to *Efraim's* transparent similarities with Andersch's earlier novels, to its compilations of clichés, and to an embarrassing lack of taste, especially in Andersch's treatment of the Jewish theme; Reich-Ranicki contends that in the case of *Efraim* "*kitsch* has become a moral category."

Andersch's last novel, *Winterspelt* (1974), is about the last days of World War II. The year is 1944; the place, Winterspelt, a small village on the Belgian border which is also the German front line. (Andersch's wife had been evacuated to Winterspelt in 1944.) To everyone involved, Germans and Americans alike, it is obvious that Germany has lost the war. Thus communication between the two sides, although not yet realized, begins to seem a distant possibility. The central character, Major Dincklage, grows obsessed with the idea of surrendering his battalion to the Americans. Through three civilians—a schoolteacher with whom he falls in love, a Communist organizer, and a man whose daily routine includes nonchalant journeys into enemy territory—he approaches the American commander with his strange vision. But he has not reckoned with the patriotic paranoia of a German corporal, or the consequences of the Battle of the Bulge, and the peaceful surrender never takes place. The German commander's symbolic act, one that speaks for life amid the machinery of death, is the crucial issue of this story. Far from confirming historical determinism, the novel—

in Andersch's own words—points to an escape from "the dictatorship of the indicative." For only by imagining how something might possibly have been, can we conceive of better possibilities at all. As Rhys Williams puts it, "the major's plan failed not because it had to, but because history tells us that it did." Positive reviews by leading critics outweighed more reserved assessments. Jean Améry went as far as to call *Winterspelt* "the most essential novel to have come out of World War II."

Andersch's literary reputation is based not only on his novels but also on his short stories, many of which reveal his interest in formal experimentation. In *Geister und Leute* (Spirits and People, 1958) and *Ein Liebhaber des Halbschattens* (Lovers of Half-Shadows, 1963), two of his collections which were combined and published in the United States as *The Night of the Giraffe and Other Stories,* the settings range from a concentration camp to a post-war German bourgeois home and the châteaux of the Loire. Their concern lies chiefly with social and existential problems of individuals: a lonely and desperate professor who takes a fateful trip through a forbidden part of East Germany; a Frenchman who, in a night of unrest and violence in Paris, tries to expose the truth behind the uprising in Algeria and is himself exposed to a sudden and terrifying moment of truth; a strange and wonderful old woman, living out her life on the remote, tide-washed shore of the North Sea, who has an unannounced visitor in the night. Many of the tales in *Mein Verschwinden in Providence: Neun neue Erzählungen* (*My Disappearance in Providence and Other Stories,* 1973) concern the effect of World War II on the generation that came of age in Germany in the late thirties. Several of these stories are autobiographical and deal with Andersch's central themes of change, flight, liberation, and "disappearance." All of the works collected here reveal his mastery of the short story form. Their pointillist technique anticipates *Winterspelt,* and, according to Robert Neumann, Andersch reached "his full stature" as a narrator with these "nine new stories."

When Andersch received the Literaturpreis der Bayerischen Akademie der schönen Künste in 1975, he was hailed as "an author of the first hour after 1945," who had "substantially contributed to provoke the German world of letters with critical and political impulses and had thus furthered the formation of a democratic public." In retrospect, these words not only summarized Andersch's past achievement; they also foreshadowed the role he was to play in the remaining years of his life. For with the poem "Artikel 3(3)" in the collection *Empört euch der Himmel ist blau* (Rise Up in Revolt the Sky in Blue, 1977), Andersch took a determined stance against the so-called "Radikalenerlass," a law introduced in 1976 to discriminate against political radicals, which signaled to him the possible beginning of a new era of anti-liberalism, and he thereby triggered considerable political controversy. In this poem, "a people of ex-Nazis" is once again engaged in its "favorite sport": "the persecution of / communists / socialists / humanists / dissidents / leftists," and "the new concentration camp" has already been built. Andersch hoped that "Artikel 3(3)" would be one of those texts that will prevent the acceptance of a new totalitarian system because it provokes public debate.

Andersch's life and work are characterized by the tension between aesthetics and politics. On the one hand he advocates artistic autonomy; on the other hand he attempts to make—at least indirectly—a political statement. On the level of form this tension expresses itself in Andersch's enthusiasm for simple narrative techniques and the communicative potential of popular literature, e.g. detective fiction, as well as for highly abstract and experimental forms. Both these aspects come together in his writing, somewhat to the detriment of his reputation: his work is exposed to attacks by political as well as aesthetic purists. Rhys Williams, however, has argued that Andersch's duality is precisely his strength: "In his successful role as editor he aimed at introducing Sartre and Beckett to the broader public while simultaneously rehabilitating popular literature (*Trivialliteratur*) among educated readers. With the eclectic taste of the autodidact, Andersch displays in his essays an openness to foreign literature, to film and painting, to science and philosophy. Political differences are subordinated to aesthetic affinities so that Ernst Jünger can find the same recognition as Hans Magnus Enzensberger and Peter Weiss, even though ideological considerations of a broader nature are never absent from his work."

The fact that moral austerity and sensuous pleasure in the sheer diversity of life stand side by side in Andersch's works has contributed to a degree of uncertainty in their critical appraisal. One group of critics accepts his philosophical position but takes the sensuous component for *kitsch*; another group objects to his politics while praising the plasticity of his descriptions; and a third group raises the question whether Andersch was successful at integrating these two elements on the artistic level. Whereas the early Andersch attempted to mediate between these two opposites, toward the end of his life he accepted this tension as a necessary part of his literary creativity. In his defense for the imprisoned writer Peter Paul Zahn, "Meine Himbeeren und

Peter Paul Zahn" (My Raspberries and Peter Paul Zahn, 1979), the personal and the public, the sensuous and the political stand, as the title indicates, simply side by side. In earlier years, Andersch worked towards a synthesis of the two; now however, according to Rhys Williams, "they remain as antinomy, as provocation, as unsolved and unsolvable contradiction."

WORKS IN ENGLISH TRANSLATION: Andersch's novels *Flight to Afar* and *The Redhead* were translated into English by Michael Bullock in 1958 and 1961 respectively. *The Night of the Giraffe and Other Stories* was translated by Christa Armstrong, 1964; *Efraim's Book* by Ralph Manheim, 1970; *Winterspelt* by Richard and Clara Winston, 1978; *My Disappearance in Providence and Other Stories* (including the first English translation of "The Cherries of Freedom") was translated by Ralph Manheim, 1978.

ABOUT: Arnold, L. H. (ed.) Alfred Andersch, 1979; Columbia Dictionary of Modern European Literature, 1980; Contemporary Authors, first revision series 33–36, 1978; Encyclopedia of World Literature in the 20th Century (rev. ed.) I, 1981; Demetz, P. Postwar German Literature: A Critical Introduction, 1970; Wilkinson, J. D. The Intellectual Resistance in Europe, 1981. *Periodicals*—Australian Universities Modern Language Association, 1983; Modern Languages 58, 1977; New German Studies 9, 1981; New York Times Book Review November 15, 1964; July 30, 1978; Orbis Litterarum 29, 1974; Saturday Review August 19, 1970.

ANDERSEN, BENNY (ALLAN) (November 7, 1929–   ), Danish poet, novelist, and short story writer, writes: "I was born on the outskirts of the twenties, bordering onto the dismal shadows of recession and unemployment of the thirties, in a Copenhagen suburb, bordering on countryside with fields, forests, and a large mysterious marsh, Uttersley Marsh. My father was a bricklayer's assistant, formerly reserve postman, and even earlier a cabin boy on Danish ships en route to and from America. As a child of artisans' and workers' stock it was assumed that I would leave school at an early age and be an artisan's apprentice. However, I grew up to be a passionate bookworm, reading all that was within reach, children's books, western series, old magazines and novels, and apparently showed no ability for practical work.

"When I was twelve years old my mother rented a piano in order to brush up her technique and recapture happy hours spent playing on my grandmother's old piano. I was immediately drawn to the instrument and seriously tried to play on it. Seeing this my parents offered me lessons at an aunt's and I accepted the offer.

BENNY ANDERSEN

They had no idea what they were letting themselves in for. While most young pupils feel piano exercises to be more punishment than pleasure, I practiced voluntarily in ecstacy for three to four hours every afternoon, when I came home from school. This must have been a great strain on the family, as we were four children and two grown-ups living in a small two-room apartment. When my father returned home exhausted after a hard day's work and looked forward to relaxing with the newspaper, as had been his custom, he now had to sit in the tiny kitchen, because I was practicing. However, I have no recollection of ever being told to 'stop the noise.' Music and literature thus became my main interests during my early youth and later determined my career. Even though my background cannot be said to be particularly literary or musical, there was nevertheless a personal relationship to words and music. As mentioned before, my mother was a music lover, and my father also played the banjo. He played and sang many old and new songs for us during the periods when the banjo wasn't at the pawnshop. Books were regularly borrowed from the public library rather than bought and kept on the shelves in the home. But several members of the family, including my father, were very clever at producing their own songs for weddings, birthdays and other festive occasions within the family.

"After finishing my seventh year in school, around fourteen years old, I worked as a messenger boy at a grocer's shop and an engineering firm. At the same time I took a course in typewriting at evening school; this perhaps due to some vague premonition of my future life. Finally I became an office clerk in an advertising agency where I discovered that I wanted to further my studies.

"During the following four years I attended night school and there achieved an advanced level certificate in 1948. It was very exhausting having both a full-time job and a full school syllabus, so when I received my certificate I gave up studying and skipped my intentions of becoming an M.A. in comparative philology. Instead, nineteen years old, I started working as a bar pianist in a provincial town far away from Copenhagen, and so began thirteen years of roaming existence as a musician, both as a solo piano player or as a member of a trio touring Scandinavia. During the period at night school, lectures in Danish literature were centered on the classical authors, so for my own pleasure I read the works of contemporary writers—only God knows how I found time for this! I was fascinated by the modern lyrics and began to write poems of my own, a few of which were printed in the literary magazine *Heretica* in 1952. While traveling around Scandinavia I continued to write poems and short stories using motifs from my surroundings and musician's life. In 1960 I had my first collection of poems published. This had been encouraged and supported by the publisher Jarl Borgen, who had read some of my poems in literary supplements. Two years later, in 1962, I took the plunge and became a full-time author. In as small a speech area as Danish, this can only be done successfully if one is very diligent and possesses equal shares of versatility, talent and good luck, particularly if one has a family to support! In addition to poems and short stories I have written children's books, a novel, feature articles and translations, plays for stage, radio, television, children's theater and film manuscripts. Within recent years I have also spent some time writing and composing songs for three LP records with the singer Povl Dissing. One can probably say that I have resumed, to some extent, my former career as a touring pianist, as Dissing and I have given concerts in Denmark, Norway, Iceland and the Faroes. We have also performed for the Danish colony in Brussels and for interested groups and students of Scandinavian languages at universities in England and Scotland. People often wonder how I am able to cope with the contrast between the author's quiet introverted life and the hectic extroverted life of a musician on the road. But for me the rhythm between these two sides of my work is as natural as exhaling and inhaling and the seasonal changes in the Nordic countries."

Acknowledged as "Denmark's most popular poet," Benny Andersen has bridged the gulf between pop culture and high art. His experiences as a jazz pianist and as a traveling poet-musician have brought him into touch with the major trends in popular culture in Europe and America, but Andersen remains essentially a native Dane, writing out of his personal experiences and observations of daily life in Copenhagen. He comments wryly but sympathetically on the lot of the common man—alienated, bemused, reaching out for companionship and love: "This is the large city where we live," his poem "This Is" begins, and it proceeds to list the directions in which life leads—

and this is me
in the middle of a sentence
in the middle of a TO that stretches in all directions. . . .

all pointing to another—"and this is you." The poem ends with a quiet plea for human love: "Reach me a little finger."

In his fiction as in his poetry, Andersen usually portrays nameless characters drifting alone and reaching out for relationships only to be frustrated by the "machinery" of society. His short story "The Passage," for example, is a first-person account of a life so lonely that the narrator survives only by eavesdropping on the conversations of others and picking their pockets for the scraps of life these contain: "These I can take hold of and feel, taste, use, these things I dare accept as genuine, with these (and other) fragments I shall restore my life, build up a new existence instead of the one my facile memory and my meticulous memories allot me, and which becomes more and more indifferent to me." Such writing is representative of much Danish "modernism," described as "an unmasking process" which attempts to strip away the superficial ease and well-being of contemporary life to show the grotesque absurdity of reality. "I . . . became a citizen in the land of the smile," Andersen writes in a poem satirizing Danish advertising campaigns to promote tourism:

tourists stream in
to see smiling traffic victims
the chuckling homeless
the cackling bereaved.

Grim as Andersen's vision seems to be, it is more accurately described by one critic as "mournfully humorous." His work is lively, full of colloquialisms and linguistic playfulness, with coined words like "dregsmorning" to describe a morning-after hangover and metaphors like "the telephone's snake head ready to strike." It is also profoundly simple and moving, as in his "Table Prayer":

Give me today
my bread to butter.
Soft and hard shall meet
in my hands
and the butter's sunshine overwhelm
the bread's darkness.
Let me touch what we live on,
brown bread, yellow butter,
love.

—all translations by A. Taylor

A member of the Danish Academy, Andersen
has received various honors for his work, including the Workers Fellowship and Critics prizes
and, in 1964, the Louisiana Prize. He married
the painter Signe Boesen in 1950, and they have
two children.

WORKS IN ENGLISH TRANSLATION: Alexander Taylor translated Benny Andersen's *Selected Poems* in 1975. There
are selections from his poems in L. Jennen's anthology
Contemporary Danish Poetry, 1977. Andersen's short
story "The Passage" is translated in S. Holm's *The Devil's Instrument and Other Danish Stories*, 1971, and a
volume of *Selected Stories* appeared in 1983.

ABOUT: Contemporary Authors 101, 1981; Columbia
Dictionary of Modern European Literature, 1980; Encyclopedia of World Literature in the 20th Century
(rev. ed.) I, 1981; Taylor, A. *Preface to* Selected Poems,
1975. *Periodicals*—Times Literary Supplement October 15, 1976; World Literature Today 52 (1978).

ANGELL, ROGER (September 19, 1920–   ),
American editor, fiction writer, and baseball columnist, was born in New York City, the son of
Ernest and Katharine Shepley (Sergeant) Angell.
His father was a well-known New York attorney;
his mother, a member of an old Boston family
and a graduate of Bryn Mawr, was the *New
Yorker's* first fiction editor. Mrs. Angell later
married E. B. White, the essayist, and was an influence not only on her husband's work but also
on that of James Thurber and a large number of
contributors to the *New Yorker.*

Angell attended the Pomfret School, from
which he graduated in 1938. He received his
B.A. degree from Harvard University in 1942. In
October 1942 he married Evelyn Ames Baker,
by whom he has two daughters, Caroline and Alice. Following their divorce in 1963, Angell married Carol Rogge, by whom he has a son, John
Henry. From 1942–46 he served with the United
States Army Air Force in the Pacific theater. Angell was an editor at the Curtis Publishing Company's *Magazine X* in 1946, and from 1947–56
a senior editor at *Holiday* magazine. Since 1956
he has been fiction editor and general contributor at the *New Yorker.*

His first book, *The Stone Arbor, and Other
Stories* comprises a dozen short stories originally

ROGER ANGELL

© Thomas Victor

published in the *New Yorker* between 1946 and
1960. The critic for the *Times Literary
Supplement* was highly impressed by the volume. "Everywhere," he wrote, "there are traces
of deliberateness, of pondered carefulness. Always the reader is aware of being in the presence
of an artist patiently searching for—and often
finding—the exact, and clinching, detail." A. W.
Phinney, in the *Christian Science Monitor*, remarked that "the stories are marked by craftsmanship, by a certain urbanity, and most of all
by their precise focus on a milieu which has become almost solely *New Yorker* property in recent years—the domestic lives of fairly sensitive,
educated, slightly troubled people moving along
in the middle of this century." Robie Macauley,
however, thought that Angell's careful control in
the stories was as much a fault as a virtue, and
would have preferred Angell to have taken
greater risks. Daniel Talbot, in an acidulous review, complained of the "sketchy quality" of the
tales, and of Angell's failure to probe deeply into
the characters' inner states.

The Stone Arbor was followed a decade later
by a short, whimsical volume entitled *A Day in
the Life of Roger Angell.* It consists of twenty-
one parodies that originally appeared in the
New Yorker. The title sketch, a jewel-like piece,
describes the trivia of the author's waking,
breakfasting, and collapse back into bed in an inflated, momentous style that pokes fun at the
newspaper columnist Jim Bishop. Other parodies include spoofs of the *Reader's Digest* and
the *New York Review of Books.* John Avant was
particularly charmed by Angell's send-up of
Lawrence Durrell's *Alexandria Quartet,* and de-

clared that "much of [the book] is equal in literary value to Dwight Macdonald's wonderful anthology *Parodies*." Some reviewers found the pieces uneven in quality, but Victor Navasky credited Angell in all of them with "perfect pitch, an eye for detail, flawless style."

In 1962 Angell proposed to the editors of the *New Yorker* that he write an article on baseball, an assignment that led to his regular coverage of the sport for the magazine. *The Summer Game* collects twenty-one of these pieces written at various times during the previous decade. Many of the great stars of the period are evoked sharply and memorably by Angell—Carl Yastrzemski, Tom Seaver, Sandy Koufax, Vida Blue, Brooks Robinson, Johnny Bench, Lou Brock. But *The Summer Game* is reporting with a difference, since it elevates baseball writing into a fine art. Angell's metaphors leap out startlingly at the reader—as when he describes the Mets fans at the beginning of the season looking at their opening-day opponents in "much the way Sicilian farmers look over their shoulders at Mount Etna before beginning the spring plowing."

The Summer Game received remarkably favorable notices. The reviewer for the *Saturday Review* called Angell "baseball's finest reporter"; and Keith Cushman commented that "Angell is simply the most elegant, stylish, and intelligent baseball writer in the country today." Ray Robinson remarked that Angell's "subtle, striking word portraits of the fans, star players, the brooding, manipulative managers, and other accessories of The Game, have to be among the best ever composed about the sport." In his review on the front page of the *New York Times Book Review*, Ted Solotaroff wrote that "page for page, *The Summer Game* contains not only the classiest but also the most resourceful baseball writing that I have ever read."

In *Five Seasons*, Angell extended his chronicle with sixteen pieces covering the seasons between 1972 and 1976. The volume contains firsthand accounts of the heroes and headline stories of baseball during the time, and includes sketches of such players as Catfish Hunter, Pete Rose, Tom Seaver, Hank Aaron, Nolan Ryan, and Luis Tiant. Angell follows the seasons from spring training camps to the World Series games, travels with a baseball scout, reveals the deadening influence of the television industry on the game, and the destructive struggle of the club owners to preserve their absolute control over the players. As in the previous book, Angell writes as a lively stylist who, at one point, notes that "the moment [Reggie] Jackson hit his shot, he dropped his bat at his feet and stood stock-still at the plate, watching the ball go, more or less

in the style of Sir Kenneth Clark regarding a Rembrandt." His ear for speech is sharp and exact, and he brings players and managers to life in quick, deft portraits. His wit shines through many of the anecdotes he relates.

Praise for *Five Seasons* was lavish, many reviewers calling it even better than *The Summer Game*. Peter Andrews remarked that "Angell brings to his work the two indispensable qualities for top flight baseball writing: a keenly analytical mind that can dissect the sport in all its facets, as well as a passionate concern for the game itself and how it should be played." Joel Oppenheimer wrote that Angell "combines a love of the game with a love of language and a wildly perceptive ability to make pictures that hold. . . . We want to be able to rebuild a particular game in our minds or to rebuild the game itself, with its excellences and tensions and its absence of time as we know it—so that we can reenter that world the game creates. It's this that Angell gives us . . . a sense of being in the ball park."

Late Innings collects sixteen of Angell's *New Yorker* essays covering baseball seasons from 1977 to 1982. A number of the pieces focus on the problems and dislocations of the game—soaring player salaries and bitter labor conflicts, which culminated in the players' strike that closed down the sport for fifty days in the summer of 1981. The World Series games are covered, including the final game of the 1977 Series in which Reggie Jackson hit three home runs. Angell observes the emergence of young stars like George Brett and Goose Gossage, and bids farewell to such old stars as Willie Mays and Thurman Munson. *Late Innings* was favorably reviewed, but this time round some reservations were expressed. Although calling Angell "the most astute and graceful chronicler the sport has known," Jonathan Yardley thought that his spring-training and post-season pieces were becoming somewhat routine and formulaic. Mark Harris commented that "journalism, even for the *New Yorker*, is subject to limitation, and inevitably these selections, sound and solid and satisfying as they are, lack the unity of a premeditated book."

Today, as fiction editor, Angell works in the office at the *New Yorker* once occupied by his mother, to whom he refers within the office precincts as "Mrs. White." In his account of Angell (and Katharine and E. B. White) in *Here at The New Yorker* (1975), Brendan Gill describes Angell as "intensely competitive. . . . Any challenge, mental or physical, exhilarates him." At various times, including a period during the late 1970s, Angell has written film criticism for the *New Yorker* in addition to his other assignments.

He has also been active in PEN and the Authors League, and is currently vice president of the national council of the Authors Guild. He was the recipient in 1981 of the George Polk award for commentary.

PRINCIPAL WORKS: The Stone Arbor, and Other Stories, 1960; A Day in the Life of Roger Angell, 1970; The Summer Game, 1972; Five Seasons, 1977; Late Innings, 1982.

ABOUT: Contemporary Authors 57–60, 1976; Who's Who in America, 1983–84. *Periodicals*—Atlantic August 1977; (Washington Post) Book World August 1, 1972; June 5, 1977; May 23, 1982; National Review October 14, 1977; New York Review of Books May 23, 1982; New York Times Book Review March 26, 1961; June 12, 1972; May 15, 1977; May 23, 1982; Newsweek May 22, 1972; Times Literary Supplement July 28, 1961.

MAYA ANGELOU

*ANGELOU, MAYA (April 4, 1928–   ), American memoirist and poet, was born Marguerite Ann Johnson in St. Louis, the daughter of Bailey Johnson, a doorman and later a naval hospital worker, and Vivian Baxter Johnson, a woman of extraordinary energy and resourcefulness. At the age of three, she and her four-year-old brother, Bailey, were sent by their parents, who had divorced, from Long Beach, California, to Stamps, Arkansas, to live with their paternal grandmother. Maya—her brother gave her the name—was brought up in this entirely segregated community (as well as for a short while in St. Louis), graduated from the Lafayette County Training School at the age of twelve, then moved with her brother back to San Francisco to live with their mother, who had remarried. She graduated from Mission High School at sixteen. Two months later, in the summer of 1944, she gave birth to a son, Guy—"the best thing that ever happened to me," she has said. "One would say of my life," she told an interviewer in 1972, "born loser, had to be; from a broken family, raped at eight, unwed mother at sixteen. . . . It's a fact but it's not the truth. In the black community, however bad it looks, there's a lot of love and so much humor."

She wrote eloquently of this childhood in her first volume of memoirs, *I Know Why the Caged Bird Sings,* a classic of American autobiography and an immediate critical and popular success. James Baldwin sensed after reading it "the beginning of a new era in the minds and hearts and lives of all Black men and women." The book, to him, "liberates the reader into life simply because Maya Angelou confronts her own life with such moving wonder, such a luminous dignity.

I have no words for this achievement, but I know that not since the days of my childhood, when people in books were more real than the people one saw every day, have I found myself so moved. . . . Her portrait is a Biblical study of life in the midst of death." R. A. Gross wrote that the "book is more than a tour de force of language or the story of childhood suffering. It quietly and gracefully portrays and pays tribute to the courage, dignity and endurance of the small, rural Southern black community in which she spent most of her early years in the 1930s."

In *Gather Together in My Name,* Angelou takes her life's story four years further on. She describes the bitter disillusionment of the black community as the wartime move toward economic equality with white Americans vanished with the coming of peace. Through this wasteland of disappointment moves the very young woman with her infant son. She tries a variety of jobs—Creole cook, cocktail waitress, and even the amateur and absentee madam for two lesbian prostitutes. Annie Gottlieb, calling the book "engrossing and vital, rich and funny and wise," particularly praised "the palpability, the precision and the rhythm of this writing. The reader is rocked into pleasure, stung into awareness. And the migrant, irresolute quality of the story—a faithful reflection of her late adolescence in the forties—resolves into a revelation. The restless, frustrated trying-on of roles turns out to have been an instinctive self-education, and the book ends with Maya Angelou finally gaining her adulthood by regaining her innocence."

Singin' and Swingin' and Gettin' Merry Like Christmas carries her life into the 1950s. She

°an´ jə l͞oo, mī´yə

writes of her short-lived marriage (the origin of her Greek surname), her endless efforts to support her family, and the genesis of her theatrical career. She studied dance with Martha Graham, Pearl Primus, and Ann Halprin, and drama with Frank Silvera and Gene Frankel. She sang and danced in nightclubs in San Francisco, Chicago, and New York, and was a member of a State Department-sponsored production of Gershwin's *Porgy and Bess* during a twenty-two country tour of Europe and Africa in 1954–55. In a review of *Singin' and Swingin'*, Linda Kuehl remarked that Angelou "is a self-conceived picaresque heroine. She lives her life as though it were a story, which is one reason why it transcribes so naturally to the printed page." The entire autobiography, which is still far from finished, is a tribute to the author's strong faith, personal courage, talent, and thoroughgoing sense of self-worth.

Angelou has published several collections of poetry, beginning with *Just Give Me a Cool Drink of Water 'Fore I Diiie*, in which the contents are divided into two sections, poems of love and poems of racial confrontation. Chad Walsh called Angelou "a poet whose work is a moving blend of lyricism and harsh social observation. The first [part] is the more personal and tender. . . . The second part, 'Just Before the Worlds Ends,' has more bite—the anguished and often sardonic expression of a black in a white-dominated world." The *Choice* reviewer, however, expressed a more general critical view in terming the thirty-nine poems "craftsmanlike and powerful though not great poetry."

Oh Pray My Wings Are Gonna Fit Me Well is also composed of sections, in the publisher's words, "poems of love and memory; poems of racial confrontation; poems of misplaced patriotism; songs of the street and songs of the heart." Some critics remarked on the poems' sense of excitement when read aloud, and praised their vivid images; another called the author an unfortunate example "of the dangers of success": "The public voice," wrote J. F. Cotter, "drowns out the private emotion." And S. M. Gilbert, in a lengthy review, remarked, "I can't help feeling that Maya Angelou's career has suffered from the interest her publishers have in mythologizing her. [This] is such a painfully untalented collection of poems that I can't think of any reason, other than the Maya Myth, for it to be in print."

The similarity of the collection *And Still I Rise* to the earlier ones confirmed most critics in the view that Angelou is a far more convincing writer of prose than of verse. "The poems that work," wrote J. B. Blundell, "have language close to speech or more nearly to song, while the others get mired in hackneyed metaphor and forced rhyme. Despite its unevenness, the book succeeds as a statement of one black woman's experience, and of her determination not only to survive but to grow." "Many young people," in Ellen Lippmann's opinion, "will identify with Angelou's description of black city life and will be cheered by her enthusiasm. However, Angelou is more adept at prose than verse, and the strength here is even more evident in her autobiographical *I Know Why the Caged Bird Sings*."

Among other facets of her varied career, Angelou served in 1960–61 as northern coordinator for the Rev. Dr. Martin Luther King, Jr.'s Southern Christian Leadership Conference, a position that involved much traveling and fundraising. She covers this experience—the early years of the black liberation movement—in the fourth volume of her autobiography, *The Heart of a Woman*, in which she also describes her experiences in Africa. These began in 1961, when she worked for a year on *The Arab Observer*, an English-language weekly in Cairo. In 1962 she entered a brief common-law marriage to Vuzumi Make, an African freedom fighter, and lived in Ghana, where she wrote for the *Ghanian Times* and the Ghanian Broadcasting Company and served as an administrator at the University of Ghana until her return to the United States in 1966.

Angelou has also produced and acted in a number of plays—the most distinguished being the prize-winning off-Broadway production of Jean Genet's *The Blacks* in 1961. She acted for one of the largest television audiences on record in 1977 when she played Kunta Kinte's grandmother in the series based on Alex Haley's *Roots*. As a writer she has created the screenplays *Georgia, Georgia* (1972), the story of a black singer on tour in Sweden; *All Day Long* (1974); an as yet unfilmed version of *I Know Why the Caged Bird Sings*; and the television scripts for the educational series *Blacks, Blues, Black* (1968), *Assignment America* (1975), *The Legacy* and *The Inheritors* (both 1976). She is a popular lecturer on American college campuses where her work is well-known to students because many of her writings are on college reading lists. Holder of honorary degrees from several universities, she served on President Ford's American Revolution Bicentennial Council and on President Carter's National Commission on the Observance of International Women's Year. In 1983 she was named Woman of the Year in Communications in the field of books. Angelou married Paul Du Feu in 1973 and lived for several years in Berkeley, California. She now lives in Winston-Salem, North Carolina, where she is Reynolds Professor of American Studies at Wake Forest University.

PRINCIPAL WORKS: *Memoirs*—I Know Why the Caged Bird Sings, 1970; Gather Together in My Name, 1974; Singin' and Swingin' and Gettin' Merry Like Christmas, 1976; The Heart of a Woman, 1981. *Poetry*—Just Give Me a Cool Drink of Water 'Fore I Diiie, 1971; Oh Pray My Wings Are Gonna Fit Me Well, 1975; And Still I Rise, 1978; Shaker, Why Don't You Sing, 1983.

ABOUT: Contemporary Authors 65–68, 1977; Current Biography, 1974; Evans, M. (ed.) Black Women Writers: 1950-1980, 1984; Living Black American Authors, 1973; Who's Who Among Black Americans, 1977–78; Who's Who in America, 1983–84. *Periodicals*—America February 7, 1976; Atlantic June 1974; Black American Literature Forum Fall 1983; Book World April 9, 1972; Choice April 1972; September 1974; January 1976; Essence May 1983; Intellectual Digest June 1973; Library Journal March 15, 1970; October 15, 1971; May 15, 1974; September 1, 1976; September 1, 1978; New York Times March 24, 1972; New York Times Book Review June 16, 1974; New Yorker June 15, 1974; Newsweek March 2, 1970; Poetry August 1976; Saturday Review October 30, 1976; Viva March 1974.

AHARON APPELFELD

APPELFELD, AHARON (1932–), Israeli novelist, was born in Czernowitz (now Chernovtsy), the chief city of the former province of Bukovina in the foothills of the Carpathian Mountains of northern Rumania, now a part of the Ukrainian S.S.R. His parents were well-to-do, educated, and liberal Polish Jews, his father a successful mill owner. In the summer of 1940, when the family was staying in their country house outside Czernowitz, the German Army overran the area. His mother was shot, and he and his father were sent to a labor camp in Transnistria (now the Moldavian S.S.R.), where they were separated from each other. He escaped from the camp after a few months. "For two years," Appelfeld said in an interview in 1980, "from the ages of eight to ten, I wandered about from place to place as a shepherd boy, afraid to speak to anyone. As soon as people began to know me in any one place or I struck up some kind of friendship, I instinctively understood I had to move on. I knew that if the peasants discovered I was Jewish, they would kill me." After serving in the field kitchens of the Red Army from 1944, he spent a couple of years in refugee camps in Yugoslavia and Italy before emigrating to Palestine in 1947 where his father, who had miraculously survived, later joined him. Appelfeld began to study Hebrew at a youth farm near Jerusalem (he was fourteen on his arrival, and had never been to school), fought in the 1948 Arab-Israeli war, then entered Hebrew University, where he studied Yiddish and Hebrew.

Appelfeld has published, in Hebrew, ten novels and several collections of short stories. The four novels that have appeared in English concern the complacent, assimilated world of Central European Jews before the Holocaust. *Badenheim 1939* describes the dreadful foreboding that comes over a Jewish resort near Vienna during the summer before the war. Using a quiet, orderly narrative style, the author relates detail after banal detail as he builds a picture of the bemused inhabitants trying to enjoy their holiday, while a faceless, sinister Department of Sanitation very gradually rounds up all the Jews—using the most transparent ruses—and deports them to Poland. At the end, as the remaining guests are being crammed into "four filthy freight cars," several among them continue to insist that nothing whatever is amiss. Irving Howe called the short novel "a small masterpiece," and the author "a spiritual descendant of European modernism." He discerned Appelfeld's affinities with Thomas Mann "with regard to setting and character" and with Franz Kafka, "who provides the terms of vision for this remarkably gifted writer."

The air of tragedy is even more pervasive in *The Age of Wonders,* whose intelligent, prescient narrator describes the slow, relentless destruction of his family, his childhood, his entire world. His narrative is eerily calm and filled with ominous detail; the reader realizes that it is the boyhood recollection of a grown man who has somehow survived the Holocaust (a word that is never used). His story begins just before the war, as he travels home with his mother in a first-class railway car: they have been expelled from their habitual summer resort for being

Jews. His mother is a frightened but indomitable woman, his father a celebrated Austrian writer, liberal intellectual, and Jewish anti-Semite who blames the *petit-bourgeois* merchant class and Eastern European Jewish immigrants for his own gradual ostracism by literary society. The town the family lives in is minutely described, and the book's first part ends as its Jewish inhabitants, locked up in their temple awaiting deportation, turn on the rabbi, assaulting and torturing him. In the second part, entitled "Many Years Later, When Everything Was Over," the boy has become a man, and because of a renewal of interest in Austria in his father's books, returns from Israel to visit his old home town. He is cold, factual, and scathingly judgmental as he describes what he sees around him, how little the town has changed although all its Jewish inhabitants are gone. "Strange, he reflected, objects survive longer; they are passive. Otherwise how could they withstand such changes?" He leaves the town for good after a few weeks, with nothing resolved about the appalling past.

"Appelfeld's subject," according to A. Alvarez in a review of the novel, "is Jewish anti-Semitism—not a topic that has been much encouraged since the Holocaust and one, perhaps, that still can be handled with impunity only by an Israeli novelist writing in Hebrew." Joel Agee agreed: "What, in fact, is a Jew? . . . The question rings as a silent subtext through every page of the book. It is a mark of Mr. Appelfeld's artistic integrity that he never proffers a didactic or dogmatic answer, but allows the question a wide range of emotional and philosophical inflections; and that is a major source, as well, of the novel's power." "With this book," wrote Gabriel Josipovici, " . . . post-war writing has come of age, for it has grasped and made palpable for us the relation of the great modernist tradition of Kierkegaard, Nietzsche, Proust, and Kafka to the crucial events of modern times, and has done so not by being clever but by being wise, not by numbing us with images and ideas but by looking quietly and steadily at what is central to our lives."

Anti-Semitism is also present in *Tzili*, "as remorseless and inevitable," in Joyce Carol Oates' words, "as any event in nature, in which human wishes count for very little." This is the story, told in Appelfeld's characteristically elegiac, unemotional style, of a young Jewish girl, "devoid of charm and almost mute," the last child in a large, impoverished family of assimilated, areligious Jews who consider academic distinction to be life's greatest prize. Because Tzili does poorly at school, she is ridiculed by others in the family, and alone of all the children is given religious instruction. The family abandons her after the be-

ginning of the war, and she wanders from place to place, abominably treated by everyone she meets, her absolute passivity finally suggesting a kind of transcendent wisdom, an inner reservoir of endurance that simply allows her to survive. At the end of her story, she joins a boatload of other survivors bound for Palestine, where "everything will be different." Her baby has been born dead, an event that nearly drives her mad, but the fact that she has a future at all allows the novel to end on a note almost of hope: "The wound in her stomach was apparently healing. The pain was bad but not unendurable." Oates writes: "It is a measure of Aharon Appelfeld's uncanny skill that a narrative so deliberately shorn of familiar human relations and emotions should bear so much power. This is fiction in the service of a stern and highly moral vision, in which details yield to a larger design and individuals participate in a historical tapestry they cannot comprehend. . . . "

The Retreat offers a similar but even more devastating portrait of the pre-war Jewish community. Here a group of Austrian Jews assemble in a "sanatorium" whose manager, a Polish Jew formerly a horse trader, promises that "within a short space of time he would painlessly eradicate embarrassing Jewish gestures and ugly accents." His aim is "to turn the sickly members of his race into a healthy breed," but ultimately he himself becomes as "sickly" as his guests. Most of them, including the manager, die as victims of spiritual inanition more than of real disease. Yet there are survivors, one of whom—a former actress—finds contentment in her capacity simply to endure. *The Retreat* seems to sum up Appelfeld's vision. As the novelist Jakov Lind put it in his review: "The tragic self-delusion of the emancipated and assimilated Jew culminated in passive resignation to the inevitable." For Lind the book is "a small masterpiece, the vision of a remarkable poet on a passage of our contemporary history, given in an unassuming little volume of elegant prose."

Appelfeld teaches Hebrew literature at Ben-Gurion University, Beersheba, and lives with his wife and three children in Mevaseret Zion, a suburb of Jerusalem.

WORKS IN ENGLISH TRANSLATION: Appelfeld's novels have been translated into English by Dalya Bilu: *Badenheim 1939* in 1980; *The Age of Wonders* in 1981; *Tzili* in 1983; and *The Retreat* in 1984.

ABOUT: *Periodicals*—Christian Century July 1–8, 1981; Christian Science Monitor April 7, 1982; Library Journal December 1, 1980; December 15, 1981; Nation January 31, 1981; New Republic February 14, 1981; New York Review of Books February 5, 1981; February 4, 1982; New York Times December 9, 1980; New York Times Book Review November 23, 1980; December 27, 1981; February 27, 1983; May 20, 1984; Newsweek December 29, 1980; December 14, 1981; Saturday Review November 1981; Times Literary Supplement November 20, 1981; November 19, 1982; Time December 28, 1981.

*ARBUZOV, ALEKSEI NIKOLAEVICH (May 26, 1908–), Russian dramatist, writes (in Russian) in 1983: "I was born in Moscow. My father, Nikolai Kirovich Arbuzov, was a strange man. He was of the nobility, though he did not possess a fortune, and was constantly undertaking commercial enterprises that he soon abandoned. For some reason, he knew Turkish well, and in mid-century, he served in Constantinople in the Russian embassy. Consequently, he published sketches of Constantinople life in one of the periodicals. Later on, he wrote a few short stories in the spirit of Turgenev. I was told that all his life he dreamed of becoming a writer. At the time of my birth, my parents were no longer young. I was the only child in the family. My father was much older than my mother, and she was over thirty when I was born. My mother, Nadezhda Vladimirovna Mandraki, an engineer's daughter, was only the wife of my father and knew no other responsibilities.

"I do not remember the reasons for my parents' leaving Moscow in the fall of 1914, when I was seven. We moved to Petrograd, where I spent my childhood, adolescence, and youth. In the fall of 1916, I was sent to a private gymnasium. I did not like school. I did not find any friends in the classroom; the teachers irritated me. I would run away from lessons and roam around the streets. I did not notice that the relationship between my parents was becoming more difficult. At the end, my father left us. I never saw him again. He died in 1920 in Moscow of an apoplectic stroke. At home everything went to pieces. My mother became sick and our financial means were soon exhausted. We moved to a smaller apartment and sold our possessions. I witnessed the October revolution in the street and, squeezed in a crowd, I watched the taking-over of the Winter Palace. Then came the hard days of Petrograd—blockade and hunger. I had typhus, typhoid, relapsing fever, scurvy, Spanish flu. My mother started working in a hospital, but shortly afterward, she grew ill and was herself admitted to the hospital, where she stayed up to her death in 1938. So, at eleven years of age, I was alone. I traded at the market with whatever I could get; I lived wherever I could. I chopped wood and delivered bundles of it to various places, and finally I joined a settlement of delinquent children.

ALEKSEI N. ARBUZOV

"My salvation came to be the theater. During one of the hungriest years, I got into the Bolshoi Dramatic Theater to see Schiller's *Robbers,* staged for Red Army soldiers who were leaving for the front. An introduction was delivered by the poet Alexandr Blok. The performance was a thunderous success, the soldiers refusing to leave the theater. That day decided my destiny. I understood the power the theater had. That night I started to dream about my future in theater. I saw the entire repertoire of the Bolshoi Dramatic Theater, sneaking in without a ticket, and became a confirmed theater fan. In school I did not study. My days were free, and I secretly would get into the theater gallery and watch the rehearsals, trying to remember all that I heard and saw. My mother's sister had taken me into her family and more or less adopted me. In providing for my destiny, her role was priceless.

"In the beginning of the twenties, Moscow theater groups became constant visitors in Petrograd and this theatrical feast drove me out of my mind and excited my imagination. I devoured theatrical literature. At fourteen, I stepped onto the stage for the first time, as an extra at the Mariinskii Theater. I remember when, in the ballet *Egyptian Nights,* I walked with a giant fan following Cleopatra's sedan-chair, which was carried by two students who subsequently became famous, Evgenii Mravinskii and Nikolai Cherkasov. At sixteen, I got into one of the dramatic workshops which were then numerous in Leningrad. This workshop was splendidly named 'United Art,' and in it I diligently practiced *commedia del'arte.* Later, I moved on to Palestra [a traveling theater studio], directed by

°är byoo′ zôf, e lyik′sä

P. P. Gaideburov and N. F. Skarskaia. They were real promoters of Russian theatrical culture who in 1903 had organized the first theater for workers with a model classical repertory. To these people I owe all that I achieved in my theatrical career.

"In the fall of 1927, I completed my work at Palestra and joined the Gaideburovski Theater Troupe. I became more and more attracted to the agit-prop theater. My young acting contemporaries and I organized a live theatrical newspaper, and we appeared at factories and mills. In the spring of 1928, I left the Gaideburovski Theater, and together with a group of theatrical youths organized a theater which was proudly named 'the guild of experimental drama.' There I directed two works, A. Faiko's *Uchitel' Bubus* (Teacher Bubus) and an adaptation of Jack London's *Belye Volki* (White Wolves). Subsequently, our group fell apart, and part of it decided definitively to go over to the camp of agit-prop theater. Together with my friends, I took part in organizing a theater on wheels, an 'agit-wagon' named 'Maksim Gork'i.' Traveling by rail, we presented performances in villages and small towns.

"I became a dramatist by chance. Playing our small scenes, we strove for the highest degree of realism. We did not have a dramatist with us, and I myself had to take up a pen. Captivated by writing, there on the agit-train I started composing my first multiple-act play, *Klass* (Class), which was completed within a few weeks. Now, fifty-three years later, I am afraid to look at the yellowed pages of the play, which was a presumptuous, clumsy concoction of a pulp writer. But at that time it delighted the actors and directors and was staged successfully in about ten different cities. However, at its première in Leningrad, in 1931, at the Krasnyi Theater, where it appeared under the title *Bol'shaia Zhizn* (Big Life), it was a total failure. At that time, I left Leningrad and went to Moscow where I became resident playwright of the Proletkult Theater. In the spring of 1932, I married Tania Evteeva, a young actress. A daughter, Galina, was born to us.

"I am inclined to consider the early part of my Moscow life as a happy one. I made many friends there. Even though I had a desperate need of money, I worked hard and diligently. I wrote long plays, *Syny Otechestva* (Sons of the Fatherland), *Serdce* (Heart), *Idilliia* (Idyll), and several one-act plays. But none of these was produced because I had frightened the theater too much by the downfall of my first opus.

"Success came suddenly. In total penury, my wife and I went to a collective farm theater. The time we spent there provided me with an abundance of material for my work. Upon our return to Moscow, in the summer of 1934, I wrote my first comedy, *Shestero Liubimyh* (Six Loves). This was a simple vaudeville piece with a small number of characters from which I did not expect much. However, the play was unexpectedly staged in Moscow and Leningrad and then played in many cities in the Soviet Union. Encouraged, I began writing a new comedy, *Dal'niaia Doroga* (Distant Road) in 1935. I did not have to go far to collect my material. This was a play about young builders of the first Moscow metro. It was staged in 1936 simultaneously by three Moscow theaters. The reception by the press was mixed. It was reported that the work had a lyrical note, unusual for a so-called 'industrial play.' The public reacted favorably, and the play was staged often and successfully.

"At that time, I began work on *Tania*, a play which I secretly considered as decisive for me because for the first time I was writing a play about myself, and that stirred my imagination. Another inspiration was my decision to write a role for an actress who had been the idol of my youth, Mariia Ivanovna Babanova. The play was written over a two-year period. After the work was finished, I timidly telephoned Babanova, whom I did not know, and announced that I had written a play for her. What was I expecting? She was famous, the first actress of Moscow, and I was an unknown playwright. But that very evening, she came to me, listened to the reading of the play, and then and there, without hesitating, said that she would act in it. The work was produced by the Theater of the Revolution in April 1939. Babanova brought us a huge success and the play had over a thousand performances and remained on the stage for more than fifteen years.

"However, the success of *Tania* at the end of the thirties did not bring us tranquility. Troubled by the general status of our theaters, in the summer of 1938 we decided to form a new theater-workshop. After rounding up young amateur actors, students from theatrical schools, we undertook a daring experiment. Because we were dissatisfied with the contemporary condition of dramaturgy, we created a play collectively and invited our theatrical friends to one of the rehearsals. Very soon, *Pravda* published an article about us. There were also a number of encouraging newspaper reviews and on February 5, 1941, the play *Garod na Zare* (City at Dawn) opened. This was the happiest day of my life, triumphantly rewarding our three-year effort. A new theater, destined to become the favorite of the students and theatrical youth, was created in Moscow and we, the directors of the studio, V. N. Pluchek and I, happily embraced each other.

"Our happiness was short-lived. The war began and almost all of the male members of the troupe ended up in the army. With those remaining, we organized a theater, 'Moskovskaia Studiia' (Moscow Workshop) for the soldiers at the front, and I wrote two plays: *Bessmertnyi* (Immortal), in collaboration with A. Gladkov, and *Domikna Okraine* (Cottage on the Outskirts). The second one played for a long time after the war in the Maiakovsky Theater. The workshop was active until almost the end of the war. It was only because of illness that I had to interrupt my work there. Then came a difficult post-war period. My family situation changed; before the war I had married for a second time. She was a student, A. Bogacheva. In 1940, a daughter, Varvara, was born to us, and ten years later, a son, Kiril. During the first post-war years, it was difficult to write and no easier to live. In eight years, there were only two premières: a staging of Turgenev's novel *Nakanyne* (*On the Eve*) at the Vahtangov Theater in 1948, and a comedy, *Vstrechas Unost'iu* (A Meeting with Youth) at the Central Theater of the Soviet Army and the Theater of Satire in 1947. The main work of those years was the creation of the play *Gody Stranstvii* (*The Years of Wandering*), written over a period of five years and finished in 1950, but not staged until 1954. This was a major success and meant a great deal in my future life. I became one of the most frequently staged authors of the time.

"In 1957, *Gorod na Zare* (City at Dawn) got a new life on the stage of the Vahtangov Theater. This marked the beginning of a long and fruitful connection with the members of the Vahtangov where seven of my plays were staged. Especially significant was the *Irkutskaya Istoria* (*The Irkutsk Story*), in 1959, which proved to be very popular. Following this play, the Vahtangov staged *Dvenadzatyii Chas* (*The Twelfth Hour*) in 1960, and *Poteriannyii Syn* (Lost Son) in 1961. In that same year *Irkutskaya Istoria* (*The Irkutsk Story*) opened in Bratislava under the direction of I. Budskii. This was an incomparable, imaginative production which completely transcended the play itself. The first time that I saw one of my plays on a foreign stage was on the occasion of the première of *The Twelfth Hour* in England. All worked out successfully, thanks to the direction of Frank Hauser, and the memorable performance of Judi Dench in the role of Anna.

"In 1964, after working for three years, I completed what I think is my best play, *Moi Bednyii Marat* (My Poor Marat). It was staged by the director Anatolii Efros in the Moscow theater named after Lenin's Komsomol and caused a controversy. The London première of *Marat*

(under the title of *Obeshchanie* [*The Promise*]) turned out to be the best production that I have ever seen. Again it was under the direction of Frank Hauser and again it featured Judi Dench, this time with the brilliant Ian McKellen and Ian McShane. The tragic essence of the play was captured with startling precision. *The Promise* had more than three hundred performances in London and the English critics called it the play of the year. It toured New York and other English and American cities, as well as Scandinavia, France, Italy, the Federal Republic of Germany, Japan, India, and Latin America, and was filmed in England in 1969.

"In 1965, my third marriage, to the actress M. U. Lifanova, changed my life. My play *V Etom Milom Starom Dome* (In This Dear Old House, 1972) was dedicated to her; in it she played the role of Iulia. At this time I became increasingly involved in community work. My most fulfilling occupation was the Organizacia Studii Molodyh Dramaturgov (Young Dramatists' Study Organization); this group was in existence for more than ten years. Even now we continue to meet, argue, and read our plays. Dramatists are a heterogeneous clan. They need personal intercourse. The success of any one of us is everybody's success, and in that lies our happiness."

—trans. B. Kogan, E. Braigen

By his own account, Arbuzov has had no occasion to rebel against Soviet censorship or outright repression. Unlike celebrated self-exiles like Vladimir N. Voinovich, Alexandr I. Solzhenitsyn, and Anatoly V. Kuznetsov, he seems to have felt himself at ease in the USSR. Having made his accommodation with Soviet-Marxist ideology and practice early in life, he has written a number of plays whose positive theme, as one biographical account put it, "is the formation of the spiritual makeup of Soviet youth as well as the formation of Communist morality." These plays deal with contemporary Soviet realities and thus, in the main, represent accepted Soviet "realism."

Two of Arbuzov's best-known and most frequently performed works illustrate his subject matter and techniques and his relationship with the ever-present Russian literary censors. *The Irkutsk Story,* the hit of Moscow's 1961 season and also the hit of the season in London in 1968 (as *It Happened in Irkutsk*), is typical in reflecting Soviet workers' lives. It has to do with a love triangle involving two employees in a hydroelectric station and a young girl who serves as a cashier in a small food shop near the station. Arbuzov's tone in this play is sentimental. And at the end, as one reviewer observed with some flippancy, when the girl snaps back from imminent tragic collapse and enters the collective bosom of her comrades, the audience is overcome: "Men, women, even children, with tears streaming down their faces—all of them applauding as they blow their noses."

My Poor Marat or, as Western audiences know it, *The Promise*, by far Arbuzov's best-known play, has had a different history. Written and produced in Moscow in 1964, it soon became a great success in the USSR and abroad. Arbuzov seems most questioning and least congratulatory here. Yevgeni Surkov, writing in the New York *Times*, February 14, 1965, characterizes Arbuzov's style as "lyrical, soft, inclined to romantic sensitiveness and, at the same time, highly theatrical, passionate." The name character in this play is not the Marat of the French revolution, but a contemporary Russian who asks questions not ordinarily asked on the Soviet stage or in Soviet novels: why his life has not been more fulfilled, why the hopes and dreams of his youth have not been adequately realized. Surkov continues: "Why do people sometimes go astray? Why do they swindle, losing themselves, their truthful human nature? Aleksei Arbuzov seeks an answer to these questions together with his audience."

But that he did so publicly did not sit well with the arbiters of Soviet culture, the overseers of drama and the other arts. Arbuzov was taken to task for writing considered "negative," "nihilistic," and "emphasizing the insecurities and maladjustments of life." In 1965, both *Pravda* and *Izvestia*, the official Communist party newspaper and the official USSR government newspaper, published a series of reviews and articles berating fiction and drama which "give a distorted view of life in the Soviet Union." The literary journals *Yunost* (Youth) and *Novy Mir* (New World) were singled out for publishing such dissident works; and among individual writers castigated were the poet Andrei Voznesensky and Arbuzov. Voznesensky was criticized chiefly for "excessive experimentation and obscurity of content" and Arbuzov for suggesting that ideals are changing in Soviet society. Arbuzov was charged specifically with implying in *The Promise* that "the devotion of modern Soviet youth to the revolutionary ideals of the past is becoming dissipated." Despite these statements of censure, however, Arbuzov's freedom to express himself seems never to have been in any real danger. *The Promise* continued on into the seventies, at least, as a popular Soviet theatrical attraction.

On a visit to New York in 1964, Arbuzov told a *New York Times* interviewer: "The American theater is an actor's theater. The British theater is a director's theater. The Soviet theater is an audience's theater; the audience is better than the theater and deserves better than it gets." He also commented favorably on productions he saw of *Hello, Dolly!* ("a very professional work, very dynamic") and Arthur Miller's *Incident at Vichy*. His own plays have had greater success in England and in France than in the United States. In 1976, marking the fiftieth anniversary of his career, the Royal Shakespeare Company produced his comedy about the romance between an aging circus performer and her physician, *Old World* (*Sraromodnaya Comediya*) in London with Peggy Ashcroft and Anthony Quayle in the leading roles, but the New York production, retitled *Do You Turn Sommersaults?*, with Mary Martin and again Anthony Quayle in 1978, was a failure. It fared better in the Paris production that same year starring Edwige Feuillière.

Arbuzov's life-work is an illustration of how a creative writer in the USSR can maintain his artistic and moral integrity and flourish despite minor brushes with the establishment. Essentially an honest man and no toady, he has apparently had no need to quarrel unduly with the political and cultural hierarchies. Like Voznesensky and the composer Dmitri Shostakovich, he has accepted official criticism of his work, but has found it entirely compatible with his artistic and political beliefs to remain in the Soviet Union and pursue his prolific career.

WORKS IN ENGLISH TRANSLATION: Over many years Ariadne Nicolaeff, a lifelong friend of Arbuzov's, has translated a number of his plays into English. Among them—some published separately, some collected in his *Selected Plays*, 1982—are *The Promise, Once Upon a Time, Confession at Night, The Irkutsk Story, Cruel Games, Old World* or *Do You Turn Sommersaults?*. R. Prokofieva's translation of *It Happened in Irkutsk* is in *Three Soviet Plays*, published in Moscow in 1961; and R. Daglish's translation of *Evening Light* is in *Nine Modern Soviet Plays*, edited by V. Kommissarzhevsky, 1977. A translation of *Years of Wandering* appears in the periodical *Soviet Literature*, IX, 1954.

ABOUT: Columbia Dictionary of Modern European Literature, 1980; Contemporary Authors, first revision series 29–32, 1978; McGraw-Hill Encyclopedia of World Drama, I, 1984; Matlaw, M. (ed.) Modern World Drama, 1972; Oxford Companion to the Theatre (4th ed.) 1983. *Periodicals*—New York Times December 4, 1964; Times Literary Supplement June 17, 1983; Washington Post August 21, 1977.

ARLEN, MICHAEL J. (December 9, 1930–), American essayist, was born in London, the son of Michael Arlen, author of the popular romantic novel *The Green Hat* (1924) and other works, and the former Atalanta Mercati. He graduated from St. Paul's School in Concord, New Hampshire, in 1948 and from Harvard in 1952. Beginning his journalistic career as a staff reporter for *Life* magazine (1952–56), Arlen then moved in 1957 to the staff of the *New Yorker,* where he has remained ever since as contributor of a regular television column, and where most of his books originally appeared in serial form.

The first collection of Arlen's writing on television was *Living-Room War,* in which he expounded his theory that "Television has a transforming effect on events. It has a transforming effect on the people who watch the transformed events." Michael Janeway wrote that as a TV critic Arlen is "artful and free of supercilious condescension" and "disdains the easy way to kick the box. . . . As one watches the medium through Arlen's eyes, one begins to share his perception that what is most wrong with television is that its voices are all unnatural, and that to it, we are all children. The best of these pieces, 'Television's War,' defines this perception in a vivid metaphor." In fact, the book's unifying theme is the way in which the medium distorted and denatured the Vietnam War. Edward Mapp remarked that while Arlen's essays "may not prove his thesis," they are always "fascinating reading, . . . witty, engaging, . . . suited to the informed layman."

Arlen's other books of television criticism are *The View from Highway 1: Essays on Television,* which covers, among other matters, the announcing styles of Howard Cosell and Tom Snyder, the sexual content of detergent commercials, and "All in the Family"; and *The Camera Age: Essays on Television.* In his introduction to the latter book he asks the thematic questions, "Is television then a window on the world? Or is it a space we have found to hide in from the twentieth century?" Richard Gilman, reviewing *The Camera Age,* called Arlen "an admirable man doing unenviable work," but remarked that "the note of despair" discernible in his early essays on the medium, "muted though it still is, has grown increasingly audible." The book's title represents to Gilman "an idea, unexceptionable if not especially fertile, of the camera as dominating our era, influencing our perceptions when it isn't actually creating them, more and more substituting a 'look' of things for their truth."

Two of Arlen's books are concerned with his family, particularly his father, a celebrated writ-

MICHAEL J. ARLEN

er in his day who was born Dikran Kouyoumjian but put his Armenian heritage behind him for the rest of his life. *Exiles* was compared by Elizabeth Janeway to "looking through a heap of photographs, except that these photographs come alive, for Arlen has more than enough of his father's gift to recreate brilliantly this history of exile. It is not just a nostalgic work of filial piety, but a report on the strange shifting world which makes and unmakes its heroes restlessly. It is also an affirmation of a sort of private heroism and humanism that the world can't spoil." The *Harper's* reviewer wrote that the author resisted the temptation to present his father "as a romantic figure, resisted the desire to invest him with a greatness that was not there. . . . The book ends in peace—with a glimpse of his father as he must have been when all was going well. It is a small, perfect stroke, the last of many in this poignant, funny, open, intriguing book that rescues a man from legend, restoring him to our consciousness in a way he could never manage himself. What finer task for a son to complete?" Geoffrey Wolff remarked that "the great thing about *Exiles* is not what it reveals about either of the Michael Arlens but what it confirms about this author's strange and eloquent style. He neither writes like his father nor writes against him. He has not let English public schools or American private schools skim or dilute his prose. . . . Rather, he seems to be an unusually gifted writer in whom both sinew and vulnerability reside."

A father, though not specifically his own father, figures significantly in Arlen's first novel, *Say Goodbye to Sam.* The hero-narrator, a journalist moving into middle age, brings his new wife to the Southwest to visit his father, a tough and irascible Hollywood film director with whom he has always had a distant and uneasy relationship. Although the father-son conflict is not resolved smoothly, the younger man survives his own stormy rites of passage into maturity. The extent to which Arlen has drawn upon his own experiences here is conjectural, but, as Ivan Gold remarked in his review of the novel, he "has done much for our understanding of fatherhood and of the difficult business of growing up with a famous artist as a parent." Christopher Lehmann-Haupt rated the book "a solid first novel," with promise that Arlen will move forward in this form as well as in journalism.

Passage to Ararat charts Arlen's discovery of the Armenians and their tragedy; through this understanding he comes to a new appreciation of his father. The book, which won the National Book Award for current affairs in 1976, is partly an anthology of Armenian history, including the massacres of the 1890s and the wholesale genocide which began in 1915. P. S. Prescott identified Arlen's unifying preoccupation as "an attempt by the author to see himself and the rest of us precisely, and to examine both our seemingly inexhaustible need to rearrange reality and the evasions and technologies that we constantly develop to ease our self-deceptions. I cannot think of a more important undertaking for a writer just now." By confronting the genocide, what it means to be "hated unto death," Arlen better understands what he sees as the modern Armenian's "characteristic attributes of excitability and gloomy introspection"; in Peter Gardner's words, "self-pity and self-hatred; he sees them as symptoms of trapped rage—trapped as a result of the Turks' refusal to acknowledge their crimes and the world's indifference to them." In recovering the history of his people, he has, according to Stefan Kanfer, "performed a series of brilliancies: his research is irreproachable, his ear infallible. His writing retains a clarity and fury that animates each line. The tribes of the Bible leap from the page: the victims of mass murder speak out after decades of silence."

Arlen's other books include *An American Verdict*, a passionate account of the 1969 murder by the Chicago Police Department of two prominent leaders of the Black Panthers and of the subsequent trial of the Illinois state's attorney for obstruction of justice, and *Thirty Seconds*, an account of the making of a television commercial, which the *Choice* reviewer called "enlightening, entertaining, even astonishing. So much effort and expense—by a great many actors, technicians, song-writers, singers, advertising men, and miscellaneous helpers—were

combined to help A. T. & T. spend nearly a million dollars in the hope of earning more billions by asking America to 'reach out and touch someone' via long-distance telephone." Much of the book's humor derives from Arlen's letting the shallow admen speak for themselves. P. S. Prescott called it "an exquisite comedy of commercial manners, a comedy in which the actors make verbs of 'Polaroid' and 'vignette' and say things like 'Temperamentally, I'm very well adjusted to the creative side' and 'I did some of the early Coke.'"

Arlen has been married twice; he has four daughters from his first marriage, in 1957, to Ann Warner, from whom he was divorced in 1971, and four stepchildren from his second marriage, in 1972, to Alice Albright Hoge. For several years he has lived on the North Side of Chicago. From 1969 to 1972 he served on the jury for the Columbia University-Dupont awards for broadcast journalism, and in 1980 he was on the faculty of the Bread Loaf Writers Conference. He has won, in addition to the National Book Award, the Screen Directors Guild award for TV criticism in 1968, and the Prix Brémond in 1976.

PRINCIPAL WORKS: Living-Room War, 1969; Exiles, 1970; An American Verdict, 1973; Passage to Ararat, 1975; The View from Highway 1, 1976; Thirty Seconds, 1980; The Camera Age, 1981; Say Goodbye to Sam, 1984.

ABOUT: Contemporary Authors 61–64, 1976; Who's Who in America, 1983–84. *Periodicals*—America June 13, 1981; Atlantic February 1969; Choice September 1980; Harper's June 1970; Library Journal January 15, 1969; Nation May 2, 1981; New Republic October 6, 1973; March 12, 1977; New York Review of Books July 16, 1981; New York Times October 5, l984; New York Times Book Review May 4, 1969; May 10, 1970; September 30, 1973; June 17, 1975; October 10, 1976; April 12, 1981; October 21, 1984; Newsweek May 11, 1970; October 8, 1973; August 18, 1975; December 27, 1976; May 5, 1980; Saturday Review September 6, 1975; Time August 18, 1975; October 8, 1984.

*ARMAH (GEORGE) AYI (AREY) KWEI (October 28, 1939–), Ghanaian novelist and poet, was born in the twin harbor city of Sekondi Takoradi, in western Ghana, of Fante parents. A brilliant student, he attended the prestigious Achimota College, whose alumni include Kwame Nkrumah, Ghana's first president, and the distinguished writer Kofi Awoonor. In the year following Ghana's independence, he went on scholarship to the Groton School, Groton, Massachusetts, which he attended during the academic year 1958–59, and from which he graduated

°är´ mäh, ï´ kwä

AYI KWEI ARMAH

magna cum laude. He then entered Harvard University, which awarded him a bachelor's degree in social studies in 1963, again with honors. After graduation he went to Algeria, where he worked as a translator for the magazine *Révolution Africaine.* Armah returned to Ghana in 1964 and briefly tried a career in journalism but was unsuccessful. He taught for a while at the University of Cape Coast. This was his last extended residence in Ghana. He returned to the United States and obtained his M.F.A. in creative writing at Columbia University in 1970. That same year he embarked on almost a decade of teaching and writing in East Africa, at the College of National Education, Chamg'ombe, Tanzania, and then at the National University of Lesotho. His last three novels were written during his time in East Africa. Armah returned to the United States in the early 1980s, this time to the University of Wisconsin. He now lives in Dakar, Senegal. As a matter of principle, he does not grant interviews, and has revealed little of his personal life.

Poet, short story writer, essayist, Armah is best known for his five novels, and is generally regarded as one of the most talented and controversial novelists of the second generation of African writers, after Chinua Achebe and Wole Soyinka. He is widely praised for his sense of style, his powerful symbols, for his characterization and structure, his sense of humor, and above all for the extremely high moral integrity of his political vision. At the same time, he is said to "epitomize an era of intense despair," to represent "an eternal exile," and is assailed for his penchant for nauseous (in Sartre's sense) images.

Some critics feel that he betrays a personal disillusionment and an ire that occasionally go beyond acceptable literary boundaries.

His first and best known novel is *The Beautyful Ones Are Not Yet Born,* published in 1968. The protagonist is nameless and is simply called "the man." He is characterized by an almost preternatural rectitude and is the only moral being in a sea of corruption and material greed. His principal opponents are his family and loved ones, who urge him on to accept the norms of a rapacious society, and he is thus left isolated from human sympathy save for the critical figure called "the Teacher." The society is mirrored both by the family and by a certain former schoolmate named Joseph Koomson, a semiliterate, bombastic adventurer who manages to master the bureaucratic labyrinth powerfully represented by the sewer. The sewer becomes a pervasive scatalogical symbol throughout the novel. The use of this symbol for the anonymous but representative African country and the general hopelessness that envelopes the action aroused vitriolic reaction among African critics; even Achebe gently chided him. The beautiful depiction of the protagonist, however, and the book's many stylistic felicities established him as an important writer. Armah's second novel, *Fragments,* published two years later, is obviously autobiographical. The protagonist, Baako, is a writer who, after five years in the United States, returns home. He is a "been-to," a local son who has gone abroad for study and enrichment and who is supposed to come home laden with material goods. Baako's grandmother, Naana, like the Teacher in *The Beautiful Ones,* is a blind-seer, who both deeply loves and understands Baako and who stands in living contact with the ancestors. The Puerto Rican psychiatrist Juana also understands him and has a deep sensual attraction for him. Baako meets another "been-to," with the Hemingway-sounding name of Henry Robert Hudson Brempong, who has been to Europe several times, and who plays the role of "osagfeyo" or "redeemer," as Baako spiritualizes it. Baako wishes to devote himself to the people as a journalist, but his mother Efua and the people want something more tangible. Torn between his own integrity and the crass materialism of the society, Baako finally descends into madness. Robert Fraser calls this work "his most unified, structurally, and thematically."

The African *déraciné* makes his appearance again in Armah's third novel, *Why Are We So Blest?* A young Ghanaian intellectual, Modin Dofu, has recently dropped out of Harvard, disillusioned that its elite system has spiritually separated him from his people. In a fictitious North African city with the tearful name of Laccryville he is thrown together with two other *déracinés,* a Portuguese black African named Solo, and a white American girl, Aimée Reitsch, herself a dropout from Radcliffe. Solo has already suffered a mental breakdown, obsessed with the notion of who wins and loses wars; Aimée is torn between a rather tepid devotion to the revolution and ardent pursuit of her sexual needs. Modin, aloof from Solo, is caught between the racial condescension of Mr. Oppenhardt, the foundation chairman who is surprised that Modin is both African and intelligent, and the prurient interest of Mrs. Jefferson, a professor's wife, who is intrigued by his sexuality. In this novel Solo is the lonely and rejected writer. The central relation is that between Modin and Aimée. Fraser points out that one of the chief weaknesses of the novel is the reduction of Aimée as a single-minded tool of destruction. She obsessively urges Modin out into the desert where he is picked up by O.A.S. revolutionaries, who castrate and kill him.

The controversy surrounding Armah's work has intensified with his two later novels, *Two Thousand Seasons,* and *The Healers.* The most ambitious effort so far is certainly *Two Thousand Seasons.* Not a novel in the usual sense, it is an epic covering a period of one thousand years of African history and is engaged in what Soyinka calls "racial retrieval." Fraser is persuaded that Armah is the most French of African writers in English and that the literary progenitors of *Two Thousand Seasons* are André Schwartz-Bart's *Le Dernier des justes,* and Yambo Ouologuem's *Le Devoir de violence.* The latter work, by the Malian writer, was very badly received in the United States, and it is widely believed that Armah wrote *Two Thousand Seasons* as a direct refutation of its thesis. Both authors trace the history of Africa over hundreds of years and several countries and cultures, and are particularly concerned with the collusion between Arab and European oppressors of Africans. However, for Ouologuem all three groups are equally "bound to violence" and destruction. For Armah, the great Ashante kingdom, filled with energy and life, is the harbinger of Africa's future. Fraser's judgment of *Two Thousand Seasons* is ultimately negative; he argues that the historical distance, the lack of a clearly defined protagonist, the "plural voice," have diminished the fine powers and style that we have come to appreciate in Armah, and everyone finds great patches of the novel dull and verbose. Soyinka is at once more sympathetic and more critical. He sees a certain venom in Armah's depiction of Arab oppressors of Africans and at times a nearly gratuitous violence, but he thinks that a corrective reading of history is necessary. "Its vision,"

Soyinka says of *Two Thousand Seasons,* "is secular and humane. Most remarkable of all . . . is Armah's insistence on a revolutionary integrity, a refusal to be trapped into promoting the increasingly fashionable rhetoric of violence for its own sake." *The Healers* continues the epic mode of *Two Thousand Seasons* and is frankly directed to an African audience for what critics calls a therapeutic purpose. Mixing fact and fiction, it reenacts the war between the Ashante and Fante peoples that culminated with the fall of the celebrated Ashante empire. The healers in question are groups of men devoted to both the land and to the people, who see fragmentation as the lethal disease of Africa. It is a cautionary tale, which Bernth Lindfors considers to have finally refuted Armah's early reputation for being a prophet of doom.

Armah is clearly a writer of enormous talent and a major figure in the development of the contemporary African novel. This is a genre, according to Awoonor, in search of "political excellence," an excellence that remains as elusive in society as it is in literature. Armah's Virgil in this quest has been the tragic genius Frantz Fanon, healer, visionary, writer, on whom Armah has written a major essay. He has been tutored, too, by the civil rights movement in the United States, and by the early euphoria of Africa's independence, which coincided with his own adolescence. His is a vision of a socialist state of almost monastic purity and spirituality whose growing remoteness has left him saddened in his scriptorium.

PRINCIPAL WORKS: The Beautyful Ones Are Not Yet Born, 1968; Fragments, 1970; Why Are We So Blest?, 1972; Two Thousand Seasons, 1973; The Healers, 1979.

ABOUT: Contemporary Authors 61–64, 1976; Contemporary Literary Criticism 5, 1976; Encyclopedia of World Literature in the 20th Century (rev. ed.) I, 1981; Fraser, R. The Novels of Ayi Kwei Armah, 1980; Herdeck, D. E. (ed.) African Authors, 1973; Soyinka, W. Myth, Literature and the African World, 1976.

*ARREOLA, JUAN JOSE (September 21, 1918–   ), Mexican novelist, short story writer, and dramatist, was born in Ciudad Guzmán, state of Jalisco, "among chickens, pigs, goats, guajolotes, cows, asses and horses." Self-educated, he did not formally finish elementary school due to the chaos created in his province by the Cristera Revolution. In accord with the views of his devoutly Catholic family, he could not attend the state-run lay schools. From the age of twelve he was compelled to work, first as an apprentice to a bookbinder and subsequently

°är´´ rä ō´lä, hwän hō sä´

at a print shop. The boy loved the theater and had a prodigious memory equalled only by his avidity for reading. In 1941 Arreola began teaching in his native town and trying his hand at writing short stories. His models were Baudelaire, Walt Whitman, Giovani Papini; other influences were Marcel Schwob, Theophile Gautier, Knut Hamsun, Selma Langerlöf, Sartre, Proust, Kafka, Joyce, and Gide. Between 1943 and 1945 Arreola worked on a newspaper in Guadalajara, where he met Juan Rulfo. They became close friends and collaborators on the magazine *Pan.* Arreola also worked as a professional actor and in 1945, through the help of the French actor and director Louis Jouvet, the young Arreola realized the dream of every cultured Latin American: a scholarship that took him to Paris to study acting. A year later, back in Mexico, he began to proofread for the very powerful Mexican publisher Fondo de Cultura Económica, a job which brought him to the attention of the faculty of the prestigious El Colegio de México. This institution provided Arreola with a fellowship that allowed time for him to finish and publish his first book-length collection of short stories— *Varia invención* (Various Inventions, 1949). Under the influence of better organized reading, which his work at the Fondo imposed upon him, Arreola systematized and reorganized his knowledge. What he calls his "cultured" stage had begun. In 1952 Arreola published the first edition of his most celebrated book of short stories— *Confabulario.* In 1962 both books, together with a third— *Bestiario,* were pubblished under the title *Confabulario total* (Total Confabulario), which also included a one-act play, *La hora de todos* (Everybody's Hour, 1954). In the same year Arreola published a new collection, *Los presentes* (The Current Ones), which launched works of unknown young Mexican writers such as Carlos Fuentes. In 1963 he published his novel, *La feria* (*The Fair*). His last published book, in 1971,— *Palindroma* (Palindrome)—continued in the same vein as that of his previous books, namely the fantastic, a genre that, like Borges, to whom he has been compared, he favors because of his belief that through the efforts of the imagination one can best explain and reveal a reality that cannot otherwise be perceived. In this respect, aestheticism in Arreola's work does not imply either evasion or preciosity. It is based upon an intrinsic belief in the value of language. As he explains: "I love language above all." This is not only an aesthetic pronouncement but an ethical one, since Arreola considers literature to be a medium that transcends both the real as well as the imaginary. This can be well seen in *Confabulario.*

Confabulario is a metaphorical title that unites the original meaning of "telling fables" with the other meaning of "confabulate," to conspire. In the short stories of *Confabulario* the alienation of contemporary man is not shown directly but obliquely and suggestively through the presentation of imaginary absurd situations which unveil the fragility of human beings *vis-á-vis* the dangers of an arbitrary and chaotic world. Mixing the grotesque and the ordinary, Arreola denounces everything that inhibits man's freedom. Fantastic distortion highlights the author's response to the problems of today's world. Arreola's short stories reveal an appeal to universal values achieved not through the terrestrial picturesque, but through a series of narrative situations which are pure imaginative games. Arreola is capable of conferring verisimilitude on the unbelievable. His subjects generally derive not from reality but from his reading; they distill the intellectual stimuli provided by his reading. He thereby deals with the dangers of alienation that challenge the existence of both the individual and society. Arreola trivializes that which we are accustomed to perceive as logical and just. He separates himself through irony, confronting his reader with his own personal alienation and the alienation of the outside world. The "El guardagujas" (The Switchman) in *Confabulario,* one of the most widely read Spanish-American tales and the most famous of this volume, presents through a process of literary inversion the abnormal as normal. The strange and the equivocal confer poetic dimension upon reality, and serve to liberate reality. For some critics this short story is a modern allegory of Christianity; for others it is "a satire of the political reality of any country whose circumstances are similar to those shown in the story." For some others it is "an interpretation of the world in the middle of the twentieth century." Finally, another critic considers that Arreola with this short story was formulating his essential ideas which are, no doubt, existentialist, in accord with a philosophical focus that is the trademark of most of today's Spanish-American narratives and essays.

La feria (*The Fair*) is Arreola's only novel. Written in the form of apparently independent vignettes, it confounded some critics. In fact, *The Fair* has a complex narrative structure: short texts (from one line to as much as fifty-four) separated by asterisks (in the Spanish editions, and by black lines in the English translation). An inattentive reader confronted with a constantly interrupted narrative sequence could easily see the book as a series of vignettes, but a more attentive sophisticated reader of contemporary fiction will discover relationships among the fragments. Thus, the structure of *The Fair* can be considered ingenious, similar to that of Julio Cortázar's *Hopscotch* published just five months earlier. Like *Hopscotch, The Fair* can be read in several ways—for its humor, satire, vivid descriptions, and rich style. But the reader can also discover and follow one or several of the different plots, reading sequentially only these parts. *The Fair* is a labyrinthine novel. Nevertheless, to voyage through it the reader needs no clues, since the text provides a very obvious central theme—that of the failure of the social structure. This theme is expressed through the lives of people in a typical provincial town—Zapotlán el Grande (today Ciudad Guzmán), in the state of Jalisco, the author's native town. This material is treated in a satirical manner, the satire being only one of the elements which confer unity to the book. The juxtaposition of the different sequences can be compared to a mosaic, which viewed from a distance shows both texture and meaning. No one before Arreola had attempted anything like this in Mexican literature. It brings to mind the *USA* trilogy of John Dos Passos, for Arreola interweaves not only different plots but also different historical times—the Colonial, the nineteenth century, the present. In time, the failure of the social fabric is shown to have become pervasive, to the point of evolving into a way of life within a rigid although unconscious structure. This failure affects all the social classes; not only do the Indians fail but also those who have enslaved them. All their lives are tragic moral failures. In this truly *comédie humaine* the middle class fail, the poor fail, even the priest, the physician, the elderly rich religious lady, the young lover, the poet, the historian—all fail. Institutions—including the church—also fail. There is no ideal society in Zapotlán, and ultimately the religious event intended to celebrate the patron saint, Señor San José, fails when "a small band of malicious persons burst into the plaza . . . [and] in a matter of seconds they . . . splash kerosene at the base of the four pillars supporting the platform on which stood the *castillo,* and set fire to them." All that remains from the solemn fair are red hot coals, smoke, ashes. The fair is the central motif about which —like a medieval dance of death—all the characters dance, complaining, praising Señor San José, plotting against each other, fighting for their rights, challenging a hostile nature but always ending up in failure. Yet, astonishingly, the tone of the novel is not tragic but satirical and humorous.

Juan José Arreola directs a creative writing workshop at the National Autonomous University (UNAM) in Mexico City. He also has a TV program—"El mundo a los ojos de Arreola" (The World As Seen By Arreola) in which he discusses an assortment of topics—art, religion, philoso-phy, urban problems, politics, women, the young, and even TV itself. Arreola's TV presence has been described as forceful; his face "illuminates the small screen every night for a few minutes. His energetic clear voice dramatizes every commentary with histrionics."

WORKS IN ENGLISH TRANSLATION: In 1964 George G. Schade translated *Confabulario and Other Inventions,* which includes "Bestiary" and "Various Inventions," as well as other stories by Arreola. John Upton translated *The Fair* in 1977.

ABOUT: Brushwood, J. S. Mexico in its Novel, 1966; Foster, D. W. and V. (eds.) Dictionary of Contemporary Latin-American Literature, 1975; Sommers, J. After the Storm: Landmarks of the Modern Mexican Novel, 1968. *Periodicals*—Americas 16, 1964; Arizona Quarterly 12, 1956; 16, 1960; 18, 1962; Books Abroad 37, 1963; 38, 1964; 47, 1973; Hispania 38, 1955; 42, 1959; 48, 1965; 55, 1972; Journal of Spanish Studies: 20th Century 7, 1979; New York Times Book Review June 5, 1966; Saturday Review August 1, 1964; Studies in Short Fiction 8, 1971.

*BA JIN (also rendered as PA CHIN, pseudonym of LI FEI-KAN) (November 25. 1904–   ), Chinese novelist, short story writer, essayist, and translator, writes: "I was born into a big family of bureaucratic landlords in Chengdu, Sichuan Province. I spent my childhood among twenty or thirty so-called 'superior people' and twenty or thirty so-called 'inferior people.' In the wealthy environment I got in touch with the miserable lives of the man servants and porters and heard the groans of young people under the suppression of my hypocritical and selfish elders. I left my old-style family as if I got rid of a terrible dark shadow. In the spring of 1927, I left Shanghai for Paris where I was a stranger, in the hope of finding a way to save myself as well as others. I lived on the fifth floor of a small apartment house in the Latin Quarter. In the room, which barely received any sunshine, I suffered from extraordinary loneliness, mental agony and thoughts of my motherland and dear ones. I could not pour out my feelings and I could not express my love and hatred, as though I had fallen into an infinite sea of bitterness where I found no place to set my heart. I often stood before the bronze statue of Rousseau, telling my despair and agony to this 'Genevan citizen' who 'dreamed of eliminating suppression and inequality.' Listening to the deep-toned bell of Notre Dame de Paris that tolled the hour, I began to write something of novel scenes, transforming suffering, loneliness and passion into lines of words inscribed on paper. My past love and hatred, sorrow and joy, suffering and compassion, hope and struggle, all came to my pen.

°bä jin

BA JIN

"In the August of the following year, my virgin novel *Miewang* (Destruction) was completed. The novel was serialized in *Xiaoshuo Yuebao* (Story Monthly), the then authoritative magazine. At the end of 1928, I returned to Shanghai, settled down there and plunged myself into writing and translation. I wrote and wrote without stop, with countless pathetic pictures in my mind's eye. The sufferings of the majority and myself were like a whip thrashing my heart. Day and night passion was burning within my body, and I had a feeling that many people wanted to vent their grievances through my pen. I finished the novel *Jia* (Family), which amounted to the opening of the graves of my family. I described truthfully my grandfather and my eldest brother, a what-I-say-goes autocratic patriarch and an always submissive and filial youngster. I voiced grievances for those relentlessly crushed young lives and 'my denunciation' of a moribund social system. At the end of 1934, I travelled to Japan and spent several months in Tokyo and Yokohama and came back in the autumn of 1935. Together with some of my friends, I launched Cultural Life Publishing House. After the anti-Japanese War broke out in 1937, I went in a round-about way to Chongqing and other places in southwest China and was back in Shanghai in 1945.

"Since the founding of the New China, I have been living in Shanghai all the time. In July of 1949 I attended the Congress of the Chinese Literary and Art Workers in Beijing. In 1952 I gathered material in the Korean battlefield. I was forced to stop writing during the period of ten chaotic years beginning 1966. I was able to publish my writings again in 1977.

"I was Chairman of the Shanghai Federation of Art and Literary Circles, Editor-in-chief of *Shouhuo* (Harvest), a literary magazine, Vice-Chairman of the Chinese Writers' Association, Vice-Chairman of the Federation of Literary and Art Circles, member of the Standing Committee of the National People's Congress. Now I am Vice-Chairman of the Chinese People's Political Consultative Conference, Vice-Chariman of All-China Federation of Literary and Art Circles and Chairman of the Chinese Writers' Association."

From 1919, when the teen-aged Ba Jin was caught up in the tide of the revolutionary May Fourth movement, to his eighties (as he writes in the sketch above), he has pursued what he calls in his memoirs "his own true vocation . . . the concept of social justice." Inspired by Kropotkin's "Address to the Young" and other revolutionary writings, he coined his pen-name from the syllables of the names of *Ba*kunin and Kropot*kin*. His first novel, *Miewang* (Destruction, 1927), is the story of a young anarchist that was largely a self-projection. The protagonist, Du Daxin (or Big Heart), "a Byronic hero in proletarian dress," as C. Y. Hsia describes him, deliberately chooses death in a vain assassination attempt as a way out of an emotional impasse. Ba Jin's year in Paris was also marked by his strong involvement in the wave of protest over the internationally publicized Sacco and Vanzetti case. He corresponded with the latter in Boston, and when the two men were executed, Ba Jin was prostrated with shock.

After his return to China during the ebb of the anarchist movement in the thirties, Ba Jin's intense romantic and revolutionary fervor was channeled into creative writing. As he says in his memoirs, his "feelings must find an outlet, and his love and hate must be poured out." The years from 1927 to 1946 were the most productive in Ba Jin's writing career. He published in all twenty full-length novels and novelettes, twelve collections of short stories, and seventeen collections of essays, as well as translations. Of these works the most important are the two trilogies *Aiqing Sanbugu* (Love) and *Jiliu* (Torrent, or Turbulent Stream). The Love trilogy, comprising *Wu* (Fog), *Yu* (Rain), and *Dian* (Lightning), with a short interval called *Lei* (Thunder), treats of what Hsia calls the "intellectual debates, romantic entanglements and revolutionary conspiracies" of a group of radical youths. Much of his material was drawn from his own observations and from the lives of his friends. As Nathan K. Mao points out, "He uses his characters to voice his points of view." Among the issues he treats are the conflicts between love and duty among the younger generation and the emergence of educated, liberated Chinese women. Although, as Mao writes, "Pa Chin seldom makes direct reference to sexual relationships," he introduced ideas of free love and women's sexuality which "must have been shocking to . . . Chinese readers in the 1930s."

In his most famous trilogy, *Jiliu* or "Torrent," Ba Jin turns to his own family history for inspiration. The three parts of this trilogy—*Jia* (Family, 1931), *Chun* (Spring, 1938), and *Qiu* (Autumn 1940)—relate the story of the Kao clan, concentrating mainly on the fates of the young generation, those who suffer and die under the feudal tyranny and those who rebel and break away from the family, while the last volume closes on a note of melancholy and resignation. The "Torrent" trilogy, especially "Family," has been widely adapted for the stage and screen in China. The death of a maid servant who drowns rather than marry an old roué, and the death of the eldest daughter-in-law in childbirth by being subjected to a cruel superstitious custom, are among some of the most affecting scenes in the trilogy. Ba Jin says that "in writing 'Family,' I have suffered together with my characters and took part in their struggle against the yoke. I have laughed with these lovable young people and cried with them." In his Foreword to the 1937 edition, he wrote: "Here I am, flinging my own 'j'accuse' to a dying system." In the "Torrent" trilogy, Ba Jin created a galaxy of characters who faithfully reflect the generation of young people during the May Fourth Movement of 1919, their rebelliousness against the old order, and their struggle for individual freedom and social democracy. It is impossible to overrate the impact of his fiction on the young; it inspired many of them to take the path of revolution. Olga Lane writes that "more than any other modern Chinese writer, [his] works present a composite portrait of the young men of China in a transitional period, a counterpart of the portrait of western young men in nineteenth-century European literature." In 1936, Lu Xün, the most honored Chinese critic of his day, praised Ba Jin as "a fervent, progressive writer, who takes his place among our handful of good writers."

After the 1940s, Ba Jin's writings calmed down from the impassioned outbursts of the thirties to a more detached and calm mood. *Qiyuan* (Leisure Garden), *Disi Bingshi* (Ward Number 4), *Han-ye* (Cold Nights), and the *Huo* (Fire) trilogy are products of this period. The "Fire" trilogy (1940–43) treats of the war of national resistance against the Japanese aggression. In a postscript to Part I of "Fire," Ba Jin writes that in this novel he "wanted to communicate his own fervor and indignation, stimulate other people's courage and strengthen their faith." He acknowledged that, "frankly, I wanted to write a work of propaganda," and highly impassioned propaganda it was.

"Cold Nights" is undoubtedly the best of this group. It focuses on the lives of three characters: the husband, a petty clerk, weak and consumptive but good-natured and well-educated, his sensitive and sensuous wife, and his domineering mother—a stock situation which Ba Jin brings to life in all its painful details, not only relating the breakup of the family but exposing the disintegration of the corrupt society of the late 1940s. At the end, the departure of the wife with her rich lover and the death of the husband bring out the fate of the "small fry" in an icy cold reality. C. T. Hsia comments that "with this novel Pa Chin has become a psychological realist of great distinction . . . he also succeeds to a remarkable degree in giving his novel symbolic dimensions: the fate of the three principal characters is not only a parable of China in her darkest hour of defeat and despair, but a morality play about the insuperable difficulties facing Everyman walking the path of charity."

Ba Jin is an impassioned writer who believes in art but not in craftsmanship. His writing flows naturally, sometimes rushing forward impetuously, often clear and tranquil, but always natural, never overwrought. He says of his own work: "I lack the temperament of an artist; I cannot compose a novel as if it were a work of art. When I write, I forget myself and become practically an instrument; I have really neither the leisure nor the detachment to choose my subject and form. As I said in my preface to *Quangming* (Light) [a collection of his short stories], at the time of writing I myself no longer exist. Before my eyes looms a dark shadow, and it expands until it becomes a series of pathetic pictures. My heart becomes, as it were, whipped by a lash; it palpitates, and my hand moves rapidly along the paper, beyond my control. Many, many people are taking hold of my pen to express their sorrows. . . . Do you think I can still pay attention to form, plot, perspective, and other such trivial matters? I am almost beside myself. A power drives me on, forcing me to find satisfaction in 'mass production'; I have no way of resisting it, and it has become a habit with me."

Ba Jin is one of those modern Chinese writers most influenced by Western culture. He has read widely in Russian and European classics (Tolstoy and Dostoevsky are among his favorites) and has translated into Chinese the writings of Turgenev, Gorky, Wilde, and the German poet and short story writer Theodor Storm, among others. During the Cultural Revolution, when he was under attack and unable to write or publish, he translated surreptitiously the *Reminiscences* of the nineteenth-century Russian revolutionary Alexander Herzen as an oblique protest against the despotism of the "Gang of Four." When he was exiled to the countryside, he recited passages from Dante's *Divine Comedy* to comfort and strengthen himself.

During the years after the Liberation, from 1949 to the outbreak of the Cultural Revolution, when he was prevented from writing, Ba Jin tried hard to remold himself and serve the Chinese people by his writings. That the works of this period lack the compelling quality of the earlier masterpieces is probably due to the fact that he was handling material with which he was unfamiliar. His total literary output runs to some four million words and has been published in fourteen volumes (*Ba Jin Wenji*) in Peking in 1958–62 and in Hong Kong in 1970.

With the overthrow of the "Gang of Four" in 1976, Ba Jin won new recognition as a veteran writer who had survived the ordeal. He was elected president of the Writers' Union and chairman of the China branch of PEN, and his works have been translated into English, French, German, Spanish, Russian, Italian, Swedish, Serbian, Rumanian, as well as Esperanto. In 1975 he was among the nominees for the Nobel Prize in Literature. In 1982 Ba Jin received the Dante International Prize, and in 1983 during French President Mitterand's visit to China, Ba Jin was awarded the medal of the Legion of Honor. As he approached the age of eighty he remained active on the literary scene, serving as chairman of the Chinese Writers Association, and working on another translation of Herzen and a new novel.

WORKS IN ENGLISH TRANSLATION: Two of Ba Jin's novels have been translated into English—*The Family* by Sidney Shapiro in 1958, reprinted in 1972, and *Cold Nights* by Nathan K. Mao and Liu Ts'un Yan in 1978. English translations of some of his short stories were collected by Wen I and published in Shanghai in 1941 as *Short Stories by Pa Chin*; one short story, "The General," is in *Modern Chinese Stories and Novellas, 1919–1949*, edited by J. S. M. Lau and C. T. Hsia in 1981. Additional short stories have been translated in *Living China*, edited by Edgar Snow in 1936, and in the periodical *Chinese Literature* 5, May 1962; 6, June 1963; 8, August 1979; and 12, 1982. A collection of his journalism, mainly reports on the Korean War, was published in China in 1954 as *Living Amongst Heroes*. A bibliography of Ba Jin's writings in Chinese appears in Nathan K. Mao's book on him in the Twayne World Authors Series, listed below.

ABOUT: Biographical Dictionary of Republican China, 1967–1971, 1972; Dictionary of Oriental Literature I, 1974; Hsia, C. T. A History of Modern Chinese Fiction, 1971; Lang, O. Pa Chin and His Writings, 1967; Mao, N.K. Pa Chin, 1978; Prusek, J. (ed.) Studies in Modern Chinese Literature, 1964; Yang, W. and N.K. Mao Modern Chinese Fiction, 1981. *Periodicals*—Chinese Literature 6, June 1973; Journal of the Chinese Language Teachers Association May 1976.

BAKER, ELLIOTT (Dec. 15, 1922–   ), American novelist, short story writer, and dramatist, writes: "Being born in Buffalo in the middle of December is a good introduction to the bleaker side of life. My love of horse racing came from my father and my feelings about literature from my mother. She'd grown up in Elmira when Mark Twain lived there. Having had childhood glimpses of the great man and the citizenry's deference to him, she was convinced that an author was the most wonderful thing a person could be. It still saddens me that she died shortly before my first book was published.

"My pitching arm took me from Buffalo to Indiana University. This and some other growing-up experiences are chronicled in the slightly fictionalized reminiscences of my *Unrequited Loves*. Having no high school qualifications for such noble things as Liberal Arts, I wallowed in the School of Business. So I can boast of having had little formal education, and I still lump most professors with most doctors, movie producers, and critics as fools or knaves—or both. In my junior year, I first met Robert Frost. I'd written enough bad verse to be admitted to a seminar he conducted. I last saw him in 1958. We spent a long evening together and he was much kinder then about my attempts at poetry. It would be romantic to claim him as an influence.

"After a brief stint in professional ball (Cincinnati Reds), I went into the army. My war was spent as an infantry rifleman, walking most of the way from Omaha Beach to Czechoslovakia. A few incidents from this period appear in my books, but I never wanted to write *that* war novel. Nor did I wish to do an 'early' novel. I'd won a playwriting competition for servicemen and became interested in the theatre. It was to be more than a dozen years before one of my plays appeared on Broadway. But my early efforts for the stage proved good preparation for the advent of the 'golden age' of television. I wrote a number of plays for the new medium during the 1950s.

"My first novel was completed in 1959 and was promptly turned down by every publisher in the land. It was published five years later by one of the rejectors (on the recommendation of

ELLIOTT BAKER

a British publisher I've never met) and became what is called an 'international success.' I mention this when I guest-lecture at universities as an encouragement to those students who are already collecting rejection slips. I enjoy these lectures, but refuse to play any other parts of the literary game—no savaging another author's efforts with a clever review, no serving on awards committees, no attending launching parties in order to hobnob with influential critics.

"I write slowly, discard a great deal and constantly experiment with structure. So a book takes me two to three years of total concentration. Between books, I've been fortunate to obtain screenplay assignments. These have allowed me to live alternately in southern California and England, and I'm well-known to the race track attendants in both places. I find I write more easily in a broken-down cottage in West Sussex than in a luxurious house in Beverly Hills—another testimonial to the perversity of my nature.

"I am not analytical about writing, about my own or anyone else's—living or dead. There are too many complexities involved and I don't want to tamper with them as long as the words are coming right. Auden said somewhere that the most difficult feat in writing is to be simultaneously comical and sad. I hope this is true, because I believe I've achieved it at times.

"My attitudes hardened young, and I've found no reasons to alter most of them. They should appear consistent throughout my work. A novel to me remains a magic box filled with people and events. Adding a few of these to the world, thus making some permanence of one's observations and sensibilities, seems to me a worthy accomplishment of a single lifetime."

Elliott Baker's best-known novel, *A Fine Madness,* is the story of a nonconformist poet, Samson Shillitoe, who commits himself to a mental sanitarium where he hopes to find the leisure in which to complete an epic poem. A victim of a group of experimenting psychiatrists, he is lobotomized but ironically survives to write his poem and to father a child. "Life and creation vanquish death and destruction," William J. Schafer writes of the novel. This theme informs Baker's work, for his heroes—more accurately anti-heroes—are usually exposed to a less than "fine" madness and often survive in even more damaged shape than Shillitoe. Baker's humor is satiric, often black. His novels usually center on a protagonist who becomes a pawn in some sinister yet primarily realistic power struggle. In a group of related short stories, *Unrequited Loves,* his "most genial and optimistic book," the adolescent protagonist (named "Elliott Baker") is initiated into the rites of modern American society of the period 1932–1945—baseball, love, sex, war. The reader responds with horror yet laughter, the belly laugh turning (as *Newsweek* commented) "into a deeply satisfying gut reaction."

The human-bizarre figures strikingly in much of his writing and suggests comparisons with Joyce Cary (several critics were reminded by Shillitoe of the eccentric painter Gulley Jimson in *The Horse's Mouth*), J.P. Donleavy, and Joseph Heller. His unhappy American salesman Wendell Pocock, for example, of *Pocock and Pitt,* survives a heart attack in London to become Winston Pitt and start a new and even more absurdly terrifying life as a pawn in a sinister international blood bank that is preparing for "the ultimate bomb." *Pocock and Pitt,* as Robert E. Long observed in *Saturday Review,* "is essentially a cultural fairy tale, raising the question, 'Can man survive as a human entity in an anti-human world he himself has created?'" Long found the novel brilliant in evoking "the grotesque underside of reality" but flawed overall by a contrived plot which reduces the serious theme to farce. The problem of sustaining a balance between farce and moral parable rises again in *Klymt's Law,* where a psychology professor experiments with extrasensory perception to devise a plan to beat the system at Las Vegas. "Baker's way with follies," William Feaver wrote in the *Times Literary Supplement,* "is to circle them like a coyote scenting prey, observing at a distance before closing in for the punchlines and showdowns."

A more tempered and realistic novel, *The Penny Wars* is the story of a sixteen-year-old boy growing up in a small town on the eve of World War II. Vividly recreating the drabness and provinciality of America in the late 1930s, the book offers a sensitive portrait of an adolescent who dreams of fighting for democracy against the forces of Fascism but lives in a reality only peripherally affected by the world outside. The boy encounters his own battles—sexual awakening, conflicts with a bigoted teacher, and a tragic German-Jewish dentist neighbor, a refugee from Nazism—which expose him to the other side, the penny side as it were, of war. The result was a deceptively quiet novel that, Stanley Kauffmann wrote in the *New Republic,* "explodes and reverberates," and where seemingly bland episodes become "the demonic jest, all the more demonic because those who are stabbed by it can now see the joke."

Baker has written for radio and television both in the United States and in England, for motion pictures, and for the stage. *A Fine Madness* was made into a film in 1966, with Baker's screenplay; Sean Connery and Joanne Woodward played the leading roles. It was a critical though not a commercial success, much admired for its fast pace and sharp satire. His dramatization of his novel *The Penny Wars* had a brief run on Broadway in 1969.

PRINCIPAL WORKS: *Novels*—A Fine Madness, 1964; The Penny Wars, 1968; Pocock and Pitt, 1971; Klymt's Law, 1976; And We Were Young, 1979. *Short Stories*—Unrequited Loves, 1974. *Plays*—The Delinquent, the Hipster, the Square, and the Sandpile Series, 1962.

ABOUT: Contemporary Authors 45–48, 1974; Meyers, J. The Enemy, 1980; Vinson, J. (ed.) Contemporary Novelists, 1982. *Periodicals*—New Republic August 24, 1968; San Francisco Chronicle August 25, 1968; Times Literary Supplement November 18, 1976.

TONI BAMBARA

BAMBARA, TONI CADE (March 25, 1939–), American novelist and short-story writer, writes: "Toni Cade Bambara is the daughter of a community-developer mother, currently training senior citizen performing arts troupes in Atlanta, and a natural comedian father, now deceased; sister of painter Walter Cade III; and mother of an ancient wise woman who travels under the guise of a dancing kid called Karma.

"I spent my formative years in the Harlem, Bedford-Stuyvesant, and South Jamaica sections of New York and in a Jersey City slum whose physical and psychological landscape even yet bewilders me whenever I spy a Jersey license plate saying 'The Garden State.' Growing up in the streets of Harlem under the gaze of adults who were our guidance counselors ('So, what do you plan to do with your energetic self that's gonna make a difference for us, Sweetheart? Hmmm?'), social workers, therapists, teachers, travel guides long before we ever heard those titles and heard that salaries were supposed to be attached to same, I learned to appreciate the crucial difference between the Ghetto (acoustic broadcasters mounting the soapbox on Speaker's Corner, the university of the neighborhood, translated each race/class/sex/socio-politico-economic power play in terms of its impact on remote-controlled Harlem) and the Community (in beauty parlors, kitchens, laundry basements and other female terrain, women said in various idioms that bespoke their roots and training, 'Ideologies may come and go, Sugar, cause oppression's just a temporary thing. But the laws of hospitality, kinship obligations and caring neighborliness remain eternal, cause first and foremost there's us, community;' and the men, on the slightest uncalled-for shift in breeze blowing through the streets, would stride out of the barber shops, pool halls, corner candy stores and other male terrain to hitch up their pants, tug at the brim of their hats, and give a look guaranteed to straighten out even the most hard-head, triflin, mischievous or downright evil blowhard troublemaker). This double-eyed approach to locale and character prompted reviewers and critics and now student readers of my stories in *Gorilla, My Love* and *The Seabirds Are Still Alive* to remark: 'An uncompromising realism coupled with a commitment to the ideal,' 'harrowing and at the same time warmly comic and celebratory.'

"At sixteen, having done hard time in day and evening school busting rock the summer of 1955,

I entered Queens College and picked cotton on that particular academic plantation for four years. In a great hurry since kindergarten to get my 'formal education' behind me so I could devote full attention to my anything-but-casual-education that would clarify what my work in this world would be, I raced up and down the snatch rows bagging biology, chemistry, languages, theatre, anthropology and music, then took my pittance—a degree in Old Ethnic studies (as opposed to the 'new' Ethnic Studies of today); that is, I got a B.A. in Anglo-Saxon Studies, or as they call it the academic trade, English Lit. I went on to become a social worker, titled and salaried unlike my childhood mentors who persisted in contributing their problem-solving and healing genius to the community without 'proper' training and 'official' accreditation. I continued the education begun in my mother's kitchen, my godparents' living room, the Apollo's balcony, Michaux's Liberation Bookstore, on Speaker's Corner at 125th and 7th, and in various lodge halls and auditoriums where my mother took us to hear Paul Robeson, Claudia Jones, Langston Hughes, Gwen Brooks and others. Along the way I earned a second set of working papers certifying that I had mastered the gist of certain European-American cultural constructs and sociopolitical myths and paradigms; in short, an M.A. in American Lit.

"Upon return from a European sojourn, I worked in psychiatric and drug therapy programs, directed a settlement house, and was doing youth-leadership organizing work with street forces in Brooklyn, Harlem, and the Lower East Side when the first wave of Black Power Movement swept us all up. I followed street forces into City College's SEEK program and joined the campus forces that would achieve within the academic community what cultural workers would achieve within the arts community—a redefinition of American History, American Literature, American Language, which all U.S. citizens and overseas people too have heretofore been encouraged to experience in monocultural terms only. A pluralistic dialect began to inform the new arts criticism and the new scholarship as well. Formerly a student who wrote, an occupational therapist who wrote, a street worker who wrote, I became a teacher who wrote. I fashioned language materials to augment standard texts being used in the classroom, wrote plays for The Theatre of Black Experience of Harlem, scripts for children's programs on WNYC, monthly book reviews and occasional movie reviews for Dan Watts' *Liberator;* and short stories, some of which were published in *Negro Digest, Massachusetts Review, Prairie Schooner,* and now defunct small

journals whose names and issues are known only to an intrepid young Ph.D. candidate who has taken over my file cabinet since the publication of *The Salt Eaters* in 1981 and ignores disclaimers on my part such as, 'I'm not a good subject. Yet. I've only just hit my stride. Surely you want a more seasoned veteran for your dissertation. Come back in ten years. Give me a break. Give me some air. Get off my bones.'

"After the publication of two anthologies, *The Black Woman* in 1970 and *Tales and Short Stories for Black Folks* in 1971, and the first story collection, *Gorilla, My Love,* in 1972, I began appearing with some regularity in 'mainstream,' as they say, periodicals, *New York Times, Washington Post, Redbook,* either as the writer of stories, articles, reviews, or as the subject. I felt a shift off center. Though the pitch, pace, stress, and shape of my works were clearly in the Afro-centric modes derived from community story telling and tradition, the interpretive genius of our songsters, particularly be-bop musicians, and though I was being kept on course by my more-than-teaching work with the Black community of Livingston College at Rutgers University, nonetheless, I was listing to the side with one ear cocked toward the applause from 'establishment' circles. A dangerous or at least comic posture for someone serious about balance. In the mail, together with letters from expatriates gone to Africa and the Caribbean, letters from prisoners, from students, and other sectors of my readership, came letters from former professors and classmates of my undergraduate days congratulating me for 'realizing the promise I'd shown as winner of the John Golden Award for fiction in 1959,' invoking the names of Joyce, Robert Penn Warren, Ring Lardner and others who at best were tangential, certainly 'otherly' to the tradition I was attempting to plumb, do justice to, and find my equilibrium in. I stepped up my involvement in Black Studies, the Black Aesthetic and Small Press movements. And in the summer of 1973, declined an invitation to return to Paris, London, and Rome, and went instead to Cuba and soon thereafter Vietnam, Brazil, and Africa.

"'The community that names you daughter, sister, mama is the community that accredits you, enables you, and keeps you whole,' my elders had taught me. This struggle to stay whole, stay centered with a capacity to enable others, especially in the teeth of conspicuous defections and massive burnout, informs *The Seabirds* collection, especially 'Broken-Field Running,' a story of trying to keep vision vibrant in the mute-and-me seventies, about two Pan-African schoolteachers and their children. It became too the motive force behind the novel *The Salt Eaters* that asks straightaway, what constitutes

wholeness for a systematically damaged people?
The answer lies within the best of one's cultural
traditions. The regenerative source, the healing
spa, the spirit that gives rise to the rites of renewal can be found at that core. So argues the book,
if not the entire body of work to date, as pointed
out by the illuminating finger of our most singular critic Eleanor Traylor [see *Studies in Contemporary Black Women's Writings,* listed
below].

"I do not know at what point I recognized that
I was a writer, recognized that it was a potent
way to participate in community development,
a way to join with forces all over the world in the
disarming/dismantlement of the exploitive arrangement of unequal access to the means and
the benefits of development, a weapon with
which to arrest the psychopaths determined to
annex the whole globe to madness and/or blow
it up. I have no dates. Nor can I pinpint that moment in childhood when I realized that people
wrote books, real people with families and passions and contradications and constituencies. But
somewhere between *Gorilla* in '72 and *Seabirds*
in '77, I became a writer who taught, a writer
who organized, a writer who developed the in-
tellectual/creative/psychic resources of young
folks. The move from New York to Atlanta in
1974 had much to do with the shift in self definition. Having done what I went to Livingston
College of Rutgers University to do, namely, to
help set up an institution within an institution
within an institution so a number of evolved people could have time and space to develop a cadre
of competent, conscious, committed, principled
change agents (500 strong, have yet to skip a
beat)—I headed South, threw a 4-by-8 sheet of
pine across three sawhorses, sat down and wrote.
By the time the bulk of critical feedback on *Salt*
turned my once cheery mailman into a hump-
backed grump, I understood that writing had
become the central activity in my life.

"While I can't pinpoint the gee-mom-I'm-a-
writer moment, I can say with some precision
when the idea of being a film maker began to
take hold. It was three weeks after the big snow
of 1947 and two weeks before my eighth birthday. I was fidgeting in the movie dark of the
Sunset on 125th Street while Michael Curtiz'
1940 action-packed, revisionist version of events
leading up to the Civil War 'The Sante Fe Trail'
played. Fidgeting and muttering because the
story of the Harpers Ferry campaign, of Harriet
Tubman who mapped it, of Mary Ellen Pleasants who bankrolled it, of Frederick Douglass
who critiqued it, and of John Brown who moved
too soon and all but blew it was as familiar to me,
given the brand of mentors who've been on my
path from day one to this morning, as 'Goldi-

locks' is to any random sampling of the non-
adult U.S. population, as they say in the sosh
trade. *Sante Fe Trail* was all wrong. Not only
were Tubman, Pleasants, Douglass, Black abolitionists and Underground Railroad operatives
absent, but Raymond Massey was playing John
Brown as a crazed, fanatic, bugged out looney.
I'd heard the word that Brown, though he often
broke discipline, was, even so, one of white
America's few true transformation models—
important, since the preference is usually for,
not conscious human beings with moral conscience, but rather laboratory inventions ala the
Frankenstein Monster and 6 Million Dollar Man.
The movie got weirder. Ronald Reagan played
General Custer, Errol Flynn played Jeb Stuart,
the writer and director played havoc with dates,
places, and events and figures. It was a mess.
'I'm gonna make a movie about Harpers Ferry,'
said I. I knew nothing yet about making a film.
But I knew it wouldn't be a western. We had geography in the fourth grade.

"The Harpers Ferry script is scheduled for
production in 1985, according to my work
schedule. In the meantime, I'm scripting Toni
Morrison's novel *Tar Baby,* produced by Jonathan Sanger (*Frances, The Elephant Man*) and
starring Howard E. Rollins (*Ragtime, The Med-
gar Story*); putting into copy production a yet
untitled work documenting the community's
story of the Atlanta Missing and Murdered Children Case; and assembling a collection of stories,
international in setting, to be titled 'The Faith of
the Bather.'"

———

Toni Cade took the name Bambara—an African tribe living in the Niger River region—from
a signature that she found among papers in a
trunk belonging to her great-grandmother. It is
an affirmation of her ethnic identity as bold and
resonant as her writing. She is not easy to read.
Her prose is explosive with energy and sometimes rage, sometimes humor. Her ear catches
the idioms and rhythms of the street speech of
northern blacks and small-town southern blacks,
and, as a reviewer of *The Salt Eaters* observed
in the *Times Literary Supplement,* she makes
few concessions to "the uninitiated." Robie Macaulay wrote in the *New York Times Book
Review*: "Shrewd, tough, cat-smart and, at the
same time, both sentimental and humane, she's
an original."

In "A Sort of Preface" to *Gorilla, My Love,*
Bambara described her fiction as
"straight-up . . . cause I value my family and
friends, and mostly cause I lie a lot anyway."
Her first collection of short stories, this volume

pointed the direction in which her future work would move. The stories recreate her world of family, urban ghetto-life a street childhood in Harlem, New York city public schools, blues singing, movies (the title story refers to a movie she saw in her childhood that was *not* about a gorilla, much to her and her friends' dismay). "Bambara writes with pride, wit, and a generous portion of human warmth," the *Saturday Review* observed. And Bell Gale Chevigny in the *Village Voice*, while noting a kind of over-writing "by classical standards" in these stories, nevertheless praised the collection: "She fools with an excess of understatement that makes her tone unique—zealously cool, ardently tough. But once you're won by its rhythm, it runs on with a breathless ease and self-acceptance that needs no more authority." The short stories in *The Sea Birds Are Still Alive* range more widely to reflect her own widening horizons, especially her travels to Africa and Vietnam. They retain, however, their steady focus on the black experience (although the title story here is a portrait of the wartime sufferings of the Vietnamese). Some reviewers found her use of the Black idiom and her rambling, informal narrative manner unnecessarily obscure and self-indulgent, but overall it was judged an impressive collection. Her novel *The Salt Eaters* gave Bambara the opportunity to direct her energies into the single theme of racism. It is the story of a woman's recovery from a suicide attempt but also of the generations of black women who have been part of the struggle for freedom, concentrated here in the Civil Rights demonstrations of the 1960s. The novel—as is characteristic of Bambara—nevertheless swings wildly in time and scene, from impressionistic sketches of violent racial confrontations to dreams, the conscious and the unconscious, the real and the mystic. It is perhaps overly ambitious in its aim, but as Susan Lardner wrote in the *New Yorker:* "The force of the book, however, is a result of this determination. Piecing together fragments of events, dialogue, memories, dreams, premonitions, nostalgia, folklore, religious and political and literary allusions and old songs, Bambara sails along, for the most part smoothly, toward the apocalyptic thunderstorm and 'burst cocoon' of her finale."

Toni Cade Bambara has a B.A. from Queens College (1959) and an M.A. from City College (1963) of the City University of New York. In addition to her teaching at City College and at Rutgers University, she has been visiting professor in Afro-American Studies at Duke and at Atlanta universities. She has worked in dance, theater, and film as well as in numerous community and social activist organizations; and she has lectured all over the United States on Black culture. She lives with her daughter Karma in Atlanta, Georgia.

PRINCIPAL WORKS: *Short stories*—Gorilla, My Love, 1972; The Sea Birds Are Still Alive, 1977. *Novel*—The Salt Eaters, 1980. *As editor*—The Black Woman, 1970; Tales and Short Stories for Black Folks, 1972.

ABOUT: Contemporary Authors, first revision series 29–32, 1978; Contemporary Literary Critics 19, 1981; Evans, M. (ed.) Studies in Contemporary Black Women's Writings, 1980, and Black Women Writers: 1950-1980, 1984; Living Black American Authors,1973; Sternberg, J. (ed.) The Writer and Her Work, 1980; Tait, C. (ed.) Black Women Writers at Work, 1983; Who's Who Among Black Americans, 1977–78. *Periodicals*— First World Magazine Summer 1981; New York Times Book Review March 27, 1977, June 1, 1980; New Yorker May 5, 1980.

BANDYOPADHAY, BIBHUTIBHUSAN
See BANERJI, BIBHUTIBHUSAN

*BANERJI (or BANERJEE), BIBHUTI-BHUSAN

BANERJI (or BANERJEE), BIBHUTI-BHUSAN (September 12, 1894–November 1, 1950), Bengali novelist and short story writer whose family name is formally spelled Bandyopadhay, was born in Muratipur, a village north of Calcutta. Although his father Mahananda Banerji, a member of the Brahmin caste, was a man of some education and musical talent, the family was very poor. The struggle for existence which Banerji depicted so movingly in his later writings was his own family's, and the memories of his childhood in an impoverished but loving family form the novel *Pather Panchali,* a work known best to Westerners in a film version by the distinguished Indian director Satyajit Ray.

In spite of his family's poverty, Banerji managed to get a good education, moving from a tiny village school to Ripon College in Calcutta, where he received a B.A. degree in 1918 and entered law school. Having to support his mother, a younger brother, and his young wife, he abandoned law studies to become a clerk in a real estate office, an inspector for the Society for the Protection of Animals, and finally a school teacher—a profession he followed for most of his life, even while writing some twenty volumes of short stories, seventeen novels, essays, travel books, a Bengali grammar, and a translation of Sir Walter Scott's *Ivanhoe*. Widowed early in life, Banerji remarried in 1940 and had one son.

The factual records of Banerji's life are skimpy, but *Pather Panchali* and some of his later books offer a record that is rich with sensitive

°ban´ə jē, bē bōō´ tē bōō´´ san

and realistic detail. His first sketches of childhood in a remote Indian village were rejected by many publishers because they lacked a clearly developed story. In 1928 the magazine *Vichitra* accepted them conditionally with the understanding that the work would be discontinued if there was too little reader interest. But, as Satyajit Ray recalls, the story "was a hit from the first installment." Published as a book in 1929, *Pather Panchali* was an enormous success and has remained an Indian favorite among adults and—in two shortened versions—with children as well. Although Banerji wrote many more novels, including a sequel to *Pather Panchali—Aparajita* (The Unvanquished), this single work established him, in the judgment of his English translator T.W. Clark, "as one of the greatest of the 20th-century prose writers in Bengali, a company which includes Rabindranath Tagore and Saratchandra Chatterji." Tagore himself had high praise for the book: "I felt in it the true flavour of story-telling. It does not set out to teach anything; it helps one to see things—trees and shrubs, highways and byways, men and women, their joys and woes—in a wholly new and fresh light cleansed of their humdrun triviality."

Episodic as its title, which can be translated loosely as "Song of the Road" (*pather* meaning "of the road," *panchali* a genre of Indian narrative poems handed down from generation to generation) suggests, *Pather Panchali* is a series of sketches of the family life of Opu, a boy growing up in a rural village. His adventures, along with those of his charming, slightly older sister Durga, are simple but so poetically and evocatively described that the book bears comparison with Wordsworth's *Prelude* and Dickens' *David Copperfield* as a register of the growth of a child's mind and sensibilities and his awakening to the natural world around him. "I chose *Pather Panchali* for the qualities that made it a great book," Satyajit Ray wrote of his film version, citing "its humanism, its lyricism, and its ring of truth." In reshaping it for film, Ray retained "the rambling quality of the novel because that in itself contained a clue to the feel of authenticity; life in a poor Bengali village does ramble." If the novel rambles, it nevertheless has a focus in the child Opu's consciousness: "Mere awareness of distance was enough to fill his little mind with a feeling of wonder and make him happy," Banerji writes. "He could not explain what he felt, but whenever he thought of things or places which were a long way off he seemed to be lifted out of himself and transported to another world. But . . . whenever this fascination of distance took possession of him, his thoughts suddenly turned to his mother who always seemed to be left behind when he went on his long journeys." Terrified by his discovery of his isolation, he rushes home "across the verandah into the kitchen, and threw his arms round his mother who was in the middle of her housework." The metaphor of the road, the journey through life, is sustained for Opu and his sister playing in the lush natural surroundings of the countryside: "They were journeying towards an unknown horizon along a road that twisted on its long unending way like the serpent of the world; and at every bend there was something waiting to welcome them, fruit or flowers, laughter or sympathy, with a welcome that was always new."

Pather Panchali is not entirely idyllic. The family is often hungry; the mother is thoughtlessly cruel to a dependent elderly relative; and Opu's sister dies of fever. The novel ends with the family leaving the villege to make the long train journey to a new life in the city of Benares. Banerji resumed his chronicle in *Aparajita* in 1932, which carries Opu's story into his young manhood, his marriage, his wife's death in childbirth, and his growing desire to become a writer. When Ray filmed the novel in 1952 he conceived it as a trilogy. *Pather Panchali* was released in 1955 to international acclaim (including a Cannes Film Festival award in 1956). *Aparajita* in 1956, and *Apur Sansar* (*The World of Apu*) in 1959, were equally distinguished films. A later novel of Banerji's, *Ashani Sanket*, a poetic but grimly realistic story of the Bengali famine of 1943, was filmed by Ray in 1973 under the English title *Distant Thunder*.

After *Pather Panchali* the most popular of Banerji's novels in Bengali is *Aranyak* (Wilderness, 1934), a story of a wild wood which shelters and controls the lives of its inhabitants. Though selected by the Sahitya Akademi of New Delhi for translation into all major Indian languages, it has not appeared in English. One short story, "Megh-Mallar," translated in *Green and Gold: Stories and Poems from Bengal,* edited by Humayun Kabir (1958), illustrates another aspect of his work—his taste for the occult and for astrology. The title refers to a raga song which the hero plays on a flute, entrapping a goddess whom he releases only with the sacrifice of his own life. As Pabitra Sarkar points out, however, Banerji's treatment of reincarnation and the supernatural "is sharply distinct from that of the Hindu faith." Rather, it reflects the vision of the child in pristine innocence, preternatural yet, like Opu in *Pather Panchali*, never totally removed from the real world of nature in which he lives.

WORKS IN ENGLISH TRANSLATION: Most of Banerji's writings remain unavailable to English language readers. *Pather Panchali* was translated into English in 1968 under the auspices of UNESCO. Another and much freer version of the work (incorporating parts of *Aparajita*) was "transcreated" into English by the Indian poet Monika Varma in 1973 and published by the Calcutta Writers Workshop in three small volumes.

ABOUT: Bose, B. An Acre of Green Grass, 1948; Clark, T. W. Introduction to Pather Panchali; Contemporary Indian Literature: A Symposium, 1959; Encyclopedia of World Literature in the 20th Century IV, 1975; Kripalani, K. Modern Indian Literature, 1968; Narasimhaiah, C. D. (ed.) Awakened Conscience: Studies in Commonwealth Literature, 1978. *Periodicals*—Sight and Sound, Spring 1957.

REZA BARAHENI

*BARAHENI, REZA (December 11, 1935–), Iranian poet, novelist, and critic, writes: "I was born in a Turkish-speaking family in Tabriz, Iran's second largest city, in the province of Azarbayjan on the border of the Soviet Union and Turkey. The ancient character of the city, along with its revolutionary history of the last hundred years, have become part and parcel of my writing. Except for one year, 1945–46, the local dialect of Azari Turkish, spoken by the entire population of Azarbayjan, was banned by the Pahlavi regime. So, like most writers of my native province I learned to read and write in Persian. Except for some pieces of poetry in Azari Turkish, and two books (*The Crowned Cannibals* and *God's Shadow: Prison Poems*) and about two dozen articles in English, all my writing has been done in Persian, the official language of all Iranians.

"I was sent to school by a philanthropic merchant, who paid for my entire elementary and high school education. The family was so poor that I had to work from the age of five to help support it. All summer and in between school hours and on holidays I worked in several tea-packing factories where my father worked. The family was extremely religious and not radical or revolutionary of any sort. Of the eleven children my mother gave birth to, seven died, all of them casualties of peace-time poverty. The Soviets were in northern Iran for almost the entire period of World War Two. In 1945–46, Azarbayjan was an autonomous region. I wrote my first poems in my native tongue when I was ten. When the region's autonomy was overthrown by the Iranian regime with assistance from the U.S., I suddenly found I had no language. At seventeen I began to write in Persian, the 'national' language, and this has been my main literary language for the past thirty years. Then I began learning English from Iranian teachers, as well as Americans and Englishmen. At age twenty-four I took a Ph.D. in English from the Interna-

tional University of Istanbul. Since then I have been assistant, associate and full professor in several Iranian and American universities. I left a tenured professorship in creative writing at the University of Maryland to participate in the Iranian revolution of 1979. The experience I gained from the revolution, no university could provide. I had been in the Shah's prisons before the revolution. Two years after the revolution I was in prison again, this time for signing a statement on democracy. Six months after my release I was dismissed from my professorship at Tehran University for the same reason. I stay at home in Tehran now, write novels and poetry, and live on what my publishers give me.

"Two cities present themselves as the main focus of my writing, Tehran and Tabriz. I have two main characters in these writings: one who fights for freedom, and the other who fights against the first one. Hope belongs to the first one, although he dies; and history belongs to the second one, although he kills. My vision of history is not parricidal; it is infanticidal, i.e. old people kill young people so that the authority of the past will be the law of the present. Behind the Iranian cult of martyrdom lies the inherent deep structure of gerontocracy. I consider myself a revolutionary writer because I stand by the youth, watch their struggle and celebrate the upsurge of their blood against their oppressors. Therefore I am a writer of the ancient battle between Eros and Thanatos. Literature is the battlefield between these two. Turn history upside down and inside out, and you will find my novels and my poetry.

"At twelve I had my first vision of what the

°bä ´ rä hä ´´ nē, rä zä

major character of a novel would be like. Going to school on an extremely cold winter morning, I was taken out to watch a young revolutionary who was being hanged by the Shah's goons. The man's image entered my soul like the ghost of an ancient hero entered the Underworld. He stood there with his eyes bursting out, and his mouth closed tightly, biting on a tongue that was long, blue and red. Thus my unconscious was formed by history, revolution, experienced personally, as personal hatred and love are experienced. However, I am a satirist, and a comedian. I am also a very good mimic, and I make people laugh when I talk. I combine in fact the ancient roles of the bard and the clown to please the company of my spectators. But that archetypal image is there. It is like leaving a theatre with a tragedy playing, and going to another theatre with a comedy on, and then leaving the one with the comedy to go back and watch the one with the tragedy. I call this the tragi-comedy of creative imagination.

"I am a suitable carcass for future editors, researchers, writers of doctoral theses. Half of what I have written has gone unprinted (all governments think I am an anarchist, while I myself think I am simply a writer), half of what I have printed has been left unpublished (again because of what governments think that a writer should do and should not do). I sometimes think that only if Jean Genet and Samual Beckett were, correspondingly, president and prime minister, would I be fully published and circulated. Otherwise, I stay as the tip of my own iceberg, hoping that posterity will show that underneath I am indeed an island turned upside down, with a golden volcano hidden in my fist, with unique minerals for the use of future centuries.

"I have in my blood the legacy of Rumi and Hafiz, Pound, Joyce, Proust and Virginia Woolf, and a bit of Faulkner. But the visionary nature of my poetry and prose belongs entirely to my past tradition. To be a modern writer one has to go to the roots, the essentials of the act of writing itself. Therefore Rumi, Dante, Shakespeare, Whitman, Proust, Joyce, Pound and Neruda are all the contemporaries of a writer who knows the poetics of the essentials of writing, i.e. how to have a vision.

"Another portion of my autobiography of some interest belongs to my rather long stay in the U.S. (1974–79). I worked very closely with such prominent men and women of letters and advocates of human rights as Arthur Miller, Jerzy Kosinski, Kurt Vonnegut, the late Muriel Rukeyser, Denise Levertov, Allen Ginsburg, Lawrence Ferlinghetti, Kay Boyle and Daniel Ellsberg. The release of writers in prison was a primary goal for all of us. I worked with Amnesty International and the American Branch of PEN, an international organization of poets and writers. These men and women and their organizations have released many a writer from jails all over the world. I admire such men and women who fight on the frontiers of freedom for all. But I think that the writer of the Third World is a totally new species. His or her main concern is life and death. He doesn't receive awards because his genius is suppressed. He doesn't receive world recognition because he doesn't have human rights. This strange species carries his last testament in his pocket when he walks out. He carries his epitaph with him. Somehow, I think he is the martyr who wants to be heard posthumously. His life and death symbolize the entirety of the human predicament. I am an expert in knowledge of such artists and writers. They shine from their dark hemispheres with fragile suns as their epitaphs. They are simply lovely, and their mission for the future is future history."

––––––––

The novelist E. L. Doctorow, in his introduction to *The Crowned Cannibals: Writings on Repression in Iran,* cites Reza Baraheni as an example of "the writer-witness," one of an alarmingly large number of authors who are generating a new art in the twentieth century that sings of political oppression, imprisonment, and torture: "the *Lieder* of victims of the state." Baraheni, Doctorow writes, "is chronicler of his nation's torture industry and poet of his nation's secret police force." In 1977 when *The Crowned Cannibals* was published, the Shah of Iran was in firm control of his country, and Baraheni was an exile living in the United States after being released in 1974 from 102 days of imprisonment. During his stay in the United States, Baraheni was a powerful voice of protest, lecturing and giving poetry readings and teaching in the creative writing programs of the University of Iowa (1974), the University of Indiana (1975–77), Bard College (1977), and the University of Maryland (1977–79).

The Crowned Cannibals is a collection of a few poems and several substantial essays, including "Masculine History," on the cultural disintegration of his country, and "The Strangulation of Iranian Writers," critical essays that established him as, in Doctorow's words, "the virtual founder of modern literary criticism" in Iran. Among his other critical writings published in Tehran but not translated into English are studies on the writing and the poetics of fiction, analytical criticism, and creativity in poetry. Of these essays Ehsan Yar-Shater writes: "Baraheni's daring and trenchant critiques must be considered an important literary event in themselves." British and American readers know him primarily as a poet. His *God's Shadow: Prison Poems* was written for the most part when he was working with Paul Engle at Iowa. Introduced by an essay in which Baraheni describes his imprisonment and torture in harrowingly graphic detail, the poems are a cry of pain and protest. "I call them poems of factuality," he writes, "for they are concerned with genuine experience—not things that I have imagined, not abstract or ideological matters." Two of the poems, he recalls, "I wrote on prison walls with my fingernails, memorizing each stanza, erasing it so that I wouldn't get caught." One of these is "The Doves"—

outside doves perch everywhere
it is clear from
their cooings of love and delight
it is clear from
the whirr of their wings
wings which seem to fan me in my prisoner's   sleep
it is clear outside
doves perch everywhere

the night is like a day on the other side of the   bars
on this side the day is like the night

The other poem, "The Light of Home," has for its refrain "take me back home! / take me back home," with a number of images of animal and human suffering:

where is home?
home suggests the concrete in the lower depths
home is the correlative of chains blood
prison home is torture from coast to coast
home is dawn executions death and martyrdom

All of the poems in *God's Shadow* are stark and brutally (for some critics shockingly) frank in imagery and language, but the tone is consistent with Baraheni's vision of his art. His poem "What Is Poetry" begins:

poetry
is a shark's fin cutting a prisoner's throat
delicately and precisely.

A play by Baraheni, "Play No Play," was given an English-language performance in Salt Lake City in 1973 but not published—nor has any full-length novel of his appeared in English. A chapter, however, of a novel "The Infernal Times of Aga-ye Ayyaz" (1972), was published as "The Dismemberment," translated by Carter Bryant, in *New Writing from the Middle East* (1978). It is a grisly allegory of a ritual human sacrifice, obscure and symbolic but unmistakably political, ending with an anguished cry—"my nation, my passive nation."

Baraheni has translated many works of for-

eign literature into Persian, among them Shakespeare's *Richard III*, Ivo Andrić's *The Bridge Over Drina*, and writings by Saint-Exupéry and Lévi-Strauss. His parents, who were Moslems, were Mohammed-Taghi and Zarasoltan (Shokoohetaze) Baraheni. His first marriage, in 1959, to Angela Marangozidi, ended in divorce in 1966; he married Sanaz Sihhati, a teacher, in 1971, and they have two children.

WORKS IN ENGLISH TRANSLATION: God's Shadow: Prison Poems, 1976; The Crowned Cannibals: Writings on Repression in Iran, 1977.

ABOUT: Contemporary Authors 69–72, 1978; Doctorow, E. L. *Introduction to* The Crowned Cannibals, 1977; Hamalian, L. and J. D. Yohannan (eds.) New Writings from the Middle East, 1978; Yar-Shater, E. Iran Faces the Seventies, 1970. *Periodicals*—Harper's May 1977; New York Times December 16, 1973; June 17, 1977; June 20, 1977.

*BAROLINI, ANTONIO (May 29, 1910– January 21, 1971), Italian poet, novelist, short-story writer and journalist, was born in the city of Vicenza in northeastern Italy, the son of Giuseppe Barolini, a naval officer of Venetian ancestry, and Maria Lucia Albarello Barolini, whose family was from Padua and Vicenza. He had to work as an adolescent and had little formal schooling. He worked for a time in a bank as a young man, but also came to be on intimate terms with the anti-Fascist literary world of his native city. His first book of poetry, *La gaia gioventù e altri versi agli amici* (The Happy Youth and Other Verses to Friends, 1938), had five poems deleted from it by the Fascist censors. (A corrected edition appeared in 1953.) His next, *Il meraviglioso giardino* (The Marvelous Garden, 1941, revised 1964), made his reputation as a poet by attracting the favorable attention of Benedetto Croce and the critic Pietro Pancrazi. He lived in German-occupied Venice during the war, much of which he spent in hiding, but managed then and later to produce several more books: the stories in *Giornate di Stefano* (Stefano's Days, 1943), *Poesie di dolore* (Poems of Sadness, 1943), *Viaggio col veliero San Spiridione* (Voyage on the Sailboat San Spiridione, 1946), and *Il veliero sommerso* (The Sunken Sailboat, 1949). Several of these were brought out by the underground publisher Il Pellicano. For collaborating with this house and for other anti-Fascist crimes, Barolini was sentenced in absentia to fifteen years' imprisonment late in the war by a special tribunal of the Italian Social Republic based in Salò.

Beginning in 1951, Barolini lived for fourteen

* bă rō lē´ nē

years in the United States, working as a correspondent for the Turin daily *La Stampa.* He published two more books of poetry during this period, *Elegie di Croton* (Croton Elegies, 1959), named for his home in Croton-on-Hudson, New York, and *Poesie alla madre* (Poems to Mother, 1960), which won the Bagutta prize. Most of his poems may be found in the combined edition of *L'angelo attento* (The Attentive Angel) and *Il meraviglioso giardino* published by Feltrinelli in 1968. This book includes many unpublished poems along with the greater part of earlier published collections.

Barolini was seen from the beginning as outside the poetic mainstream, although his amiable, conversational style owes much to the school of hermeticism that flourished in his youth. The critic Pancrazi welcomed him as "an agile and modern poet, but not one who is in fashion, which is indeed an index of his distinction." A decade later Pier Paolo Pasolini, reviewing the corrected edition of *La gaia gioventù,* saw in Barolini "a prefiguration of a new language of (potential) realism; of an imaginary realism; in short, of a taste for the prosaic as an extreme extenuation of the taste for the poetic." The critic Geno Pampaloni, in an introduction to the 1964 revision of *Il meraviglioso giardino,* praised Barolini's "faculty for transcending his own images' facility and accessibility. . . . His poetic metaphor is a unitary image of man, in which one can find . . . a nonviolent cohabitation of contraries, the irrational and the responsible, the poetic and the prosaic, the ordinary beside the mark of God." For Pampaloni, Barolini's chief qualities are "his continuity, his internal coherence, the constant strength of his voice, [and] the instinctive faithfulness of his return to essential themes." Eugenio Montale, in a 1962 review entitled "Poeta sperso fra gli nomini" (A Poet Lost Among Men), emphasized Barolini's basic spirituality: "In a world where sin no longer exists because it is seen as only one of many forms of illness, that is, irresponsibility, he continues to feel himself a sinner and guilty of misdeeds of which no one, not even he, is aware. . . . In a world which pretends to extend to every man the faculty of making a god of himself, he merely trims and reduces the margins of the real to leave intact a habitat in which man, being the master and author of nothing, may look without shame into the face of his natural unhappiness."

In 1950, the year before he left Vicenza for America, Barolini married Helen Frances, an American writer of Italian ancestry. She bòre him three daughters during their time in New York, and became his close collaborator and sole English translator. "I want to declare," he once said, "that any success of mine in the English language is due entirely to my wife, Helen." From 1956 to 1959 he published in the *New Yorker* seven interconnected short stories of provincial life in the Veneto of his childhood. These he joined with two other stories that had appeared in the *Reporter* to form his first book in English, *Our Last Family Countess and Related Stories.* When the Italian version of the book appeared in 1968, Barolini's gentle "unmalicious humor" was widely appreciated. One story in particular, "La grande schidionata del cugino Canal" (The Great Bird Barbecue of Cousin Canal) was rated a masterpiece by Montale.

Barolini's novels were best-sellers in Italy. *Una lunga pazzia (A Long Madness,* 1962) told a searing story of love, betrayal, madness, and religious intolerance and superstition. Also set in the Veneto, its characters are two generations of a large and passionate family. The novel's theme was stated by Barolini in a foreword: "The ritualization of what is properly the soul's secret life leads, indifferently, to aberration, madness." Montale greatly admired this novel as well, finding in it "that explicative intent that was never lacking in the old naturalists; the wish to say everything, to leave nothing for the reader to guess." Contrasting Barolini with the avant-garde novelists of alienation, Montale concluded that *Una lunga pazzia* was "a book which does not resemble any other books of today and which, scandalously, makes a mark in a literary landscape dominated by a heavy conformism."

His other novels are *Le notti della paura* (The Nights of Fear, 1967), a fictional account of his clandestine life in Venice during the Nazi occupation, and *La memoria di Stefano* (The Memory of Stefano, 1970), which won the Prato prize. This last work, combining the earlier stories of Stefano with a later, philosophic addition, was seen by the critic Giacinto Spagnoletti as best showing the spiritualism that was characteristic of the author late in his life. "Barolini's Catholicism is not ascetic and combative, like that of Simone Weil, nor is it in the dramatic or cosmic line of a Claudel or a Papini. Rather it is like that subtle, tormented Jansenist vein that comes to the surface in the novels of Graham Greene, a writer whom [Barolini] loved greatly." His writings about the recovery of his Catholic faith were delivered to the publisher Vallecchi just before his death, and appeared the following year as *Il paradiso che verrà: momenti di un'esperienza religiosa* (The Paradise to Come: Moments of a Religious Experience, 1972).

Barolini was the prime mover behind a literary controversy that occurred in 1968. Nominated for the Strega prize, one of Italy's most prestigious literary awards, he attacked the system of judging for its bias and cronyism. Accompanied by three of the four other nominees, he attempted as a mark of protest to withdraw his book *L'ultima contessa di famiglia* (*Our Last Family Countess*) from consideration. The writers' action led to a reform of subsequent prize competitions.

After his return to Italy in 1965, Barolini worked with Diego Fabbri on the review *Fiera letteraria,* wrote frequent columns for the Milan daily *Corriere della Sera,* and published several articles in the magazine *Il Mondo* on America and on various religions. He also devoted considerable time to television. He was responsible, with Silvano Giannelli, for the televised literary discussion program "L'approdo" in 1966–67, and was afterward, until his death, a valuable member of the program's directing committee.

Barolini suffered a severe heart attack in 1964 which kept him an invalid for several months. Although he seemed to recover most of his former energy, another heart attack proved fatal in 1971.

WORKS IN ENGLISH TRANSLATION: Helen Frances has translated two volumes of Barolini's work—*Our Last Family Countess and Related Stories* in 1960, and his novel *A Long Madness* in 1964.

ABOUT: Columbia Dictionary of Modern European Literature, 1980; Contemporary Authors, new revision series 1, 1981; Pampaloni, G. *in* I contemporanei V, 1974; Pozza, N. Antonio Barolini 1910–1971, 1973 (reprints all important Italian criticism, including obituary selections).

BARRETT, WILLIAM (C.) (December 30, 1913–), American philosopher and critic, was born on Long Island and raised in Queens, the son of John Patrick Barrett, an engineer, and Delia Connolly, both of whom were of Irish-Catholic descent. As a teen-ager, he became interested in philosophy and read Aristotle, where he discovered "the *power* of a philosophical concept" to shape the destinies not only of individuals but of entire civilizations. Barrett majored in philosophy at City College of New York, receiving a B.A. in 1933, and at Columbia University, where he took his Ph.D. in 1938 with a dissertation on Aristotle. For the next two years he was a philosophy instructor at the Chicago campus of the University of Illinois, and taught at Brown University from 1940 to 1942, when he was inducted into the United States Army. During World War II, Barrett was stationed in Italy as a member of the Office of Strategic Services.

Having been educated in New York City during the Great Depression, Barrett absorbed the

WILLIAM BARRETT

leftist political culture that flourished at City College and in the bohemian quarters of Greenwich Village, and embraced Marxism, as did many intellectuals of his generation. Barrett's ideological development, though, was to carry him to the right—to anti-Stalinist Trotskyism in the later 1930s, to anticommunist leftism in the period of the Cold War, and finally, in the late 1960s, to neoconservatism. "It was our Marxist decade," Barrett wrote of the 1930s in his memoir, *The Truants*; "yet the irony was that its experience of Marxism was of something remote and distant—either intellectually in the intricacies of theory that didn't mesh with our actual life, or romantically remote in the deeds of socialist heroes in far-off lands."

Apart from socialism and Western philosophy, the formative influence on Barrett in his youth was the poet Delmore Schwartz. They met in 1933 and soon became "spiritual brothers," to use Barrett's phrase. Drawn to Schwartz's brilliance—within five years he would be known as the most promising young writer in America—and because he was "the most magical human being I've known," Barrett shared his friend's ardor for modern literature, especially the poetry of T. S. Eliot. They also saw themselves as vanguard intellectuals who had shed middle-class mores, a lofty self-regard for which they found theoretical justification in the Marxian concept of alienation. The mid- to late 1930s, when Barrett and Schwartz attended graduate school, were the halcyon days of their friendship. Although Schwartz and Barrett were to serve together as associate editors of *Partisan Review* from 1945 to 1952, their lives diverged in the post-war years. Whereas Barrett became caught up in the teaching of philosophy at New York University and in writing about existentialism, Schwartz was increasingly susceptible to alcoholism and fits of paranoid schizophrenia, diseases that dried up his creativity and eventually killed him. By the late 1950s Schwartz had renounced his old friends, including Barrett, and in 1966 he died in virtual obscurity.

When Barrett joined the editorial staff of *Partisan Review*, it was the nation's most influential literary magazine, committed, Barrett wrote, to "the two M's . . . , Marxism in politics and Modernism in art." Founded in 1934 as an organ of the Communist Party, *Partisan Review* became a dissident journal of the left in 1937, after its principal editors, William Phillips and Philip Rahv, broke with the Moscow-dictated party line in both politics and art. According to Barrett, the writers who formed the nucleus of *Partisan Review* "were attacking Stalin and the Soviet Union from the point of view of a purer Marxism, and it was above all the purity of their radicalism that lured me on." In the years immediately after World War II, Phillips and Rahv also advanced the cause of "internationalizing" American literature, and they hired Barrett for his familiarity with contemporary European thought and his ability to elucidate abstruse philosophical concepts. Thus, when Rahv and Phillips introduced existentialism and the post-war writings of its leading French spokesmen—Jean-Paul Sartre, Simone de Beauvoir, Maurice Merleau-Ponty, and Albert Camus—to the North American intellectual community, Barrett became the magazine's chief exponent of that school of thought.

Initially, Barrett conceived of existentialism, with its dramatic emphasis on the freedom of the individual in his concrete situation, as a philosophy compatible with liberal or democratic Marxism. In the late 1940s and fifties, however, he underwent a spiritual crisis which led to the gradual withering away of his Marxism. He developed a preference for liberal writers like Camus, an advocate of what he called "ordinary values . . . , those elemental feelings of decency without which the human race could not survive," over radical thinkers like Sartre, whom Barrett now saw as a "rampant ideologue" who "had gone too far in encircling himself in his system of ideas to see beyond them." And as Barrett came to regard existentialism as "a symptom of the central question that haunts . . . our civilization . . . , the religious question, either God or Nihilism," he realized that to pass "into a new world-epoch that will succeed the last twenty-five hundred years of Western philosophy that have brought us to our present period of science

and technology," we must "recast our fundamental . . . attitudes towards Being. . . . " For that revaluation of values Barrett turned primarily to the German philosopher Martin Heidegger, who offered *Gelassenheit,* a passive, surrendering resignation, the will to let being be, as an ontological counter-principle to Western philosophy's stress on scientific progress and technological achievement.

In his major philosophical studies—*Irrational Man, What Is Existentialism?, Time of Need,* and *The Illusion of Technique*—Barrett examines modern man's alienation from nature through the literature of existentialism, depicting that philosophy as a protest against the pervasive rationality of postindustrial society, with its soulless, depersonalizing reliance on instrumental forms of reason and the domination of nature by technology [technical means]. Because existentialism "place[s] the reality of human existence in the individual," Barrett saw it as a way to regain the unity of thought and being that has been lost in philosophy since Descartes severed subject from object and "gave us pure mathematical logic as both the essence of truth and the technique for discovering truth," to quote a *Newsweek* reviewer of *The Illusion of Technique.* Furthermore, in his analysis of the roots of existentialism, Barrett argues that the Enlightenment ridded the world of ancient superstitions but also ushered in the scientific revolution, which, in the cultural realm, culminated in Ludwig Wittgenstein's systems of linguistic analysis and mathematical logic, and in the social sphere has produced the technocratic state, in which technique and the cold spirit of abstraction rule the soul of man in place of nature. And in *The Illusion of Technique* Barrett warns that, unless the idea of freedom is rehabilitated, the antinatural trajectory of technological civilization could bring about the hellish utopias described by Alexander Solzhenitsyn in *The Gulag Archipelago,* which documents the perfection of techniques for controlling life in totalitarian states, and by B. F. Skinner in *Beyond Freedom and Dignity,* a blueprint for ordering society by means of behavioral engineering.

In *Irrational Man: A Study in Existential Philosophy* Barrett traces the historical sources of the existential school in ancient thought, in nineteenth-century romantic poetry, and in the modern art and literature of Baudelaire, Picasso, Joyce, Beckett, and Hemingway. Because of the lucidity with which he inventoried existentialism's basic doctrines and explained the views of its principal theoreticians—Kierkegaard, Nietzsche, Sartre, and Heidegger—*Irrational Man* has become the most popular introduction to the philosophy in the English language. In *What Is*

Existentialism? Barrett analyzes the contemporary phenomenon of nihilism in the light of the later writing of Heidegger, whose ideas he discussed more fully in *The Illusion of Technique.*

Barrett again confronted the question of nihilism in *Time of Need: Forms of Imagination in Twentieth Century Literature,* linking its rise to the dissolution of man's partnership with God in the nineteenth century and to the heedless pursuit of technological advantage that has caused modern man to desert his true nature. According to Barrett, modern literature testifies that man hungers to be reunited with vital impulses that are "primal, primordial, primitive." In *Commentary* magazine John Wain wrote that Barrett sees this leitmotif "in Hemingway's preoccupation with the concrete, in the revolt of Camus from the abstractions of urban intellectual life and his kinship with 'the world of the sea and the stars,' in the blood-and-kinship rituals of Faulkner, in the mythopoeic imagination of Joyce. . . . We, as a species, are making a determined effort to enclose ourselves in an envelope of technology from which we exclude the remnants of primitive consciousness within us."

The Illusion of Technique: A Search for Meaning in a Technological Civilization is Barrett's culminating critique of the cultural drift toward total reliance on technique, which he defines as an abstract set of rules or automatic procedures that threatens to extinguish human freedom. The book's interpretive structure, as James Atlas observed in *Time* magazine, is provided by the author's account of the ideas of Wittgenstein, Heidegger, and William James, all of whom "shared Kant's conviction that freedom was the principal issue philosophy had to address." After turning away from the logical positivism of his youth, Wittgenstein had attempted to illuminate the nature of being through the exploration of ordinary language. However, John Murray Cuddihy wrote in the *New York Times Book Review* that "Wittgenstein . . . remains, on Barrett's reading, trapped in his own 'behavioristic' metaphor: words are tools." Barrett next turned to Heidegger for a new conception of being that would enable Western man to confront the [indissolubly linked] questions of God and nihilism. Although Barrett felt that the principle of *Gelassenheit* could help us "recast our ideas of . . . Being," he now concluded that "the will to let Being be" was fatally bereft of any ethical imperative, and wrote: " [Heidegger's] conception of freedom is detached from the will to action." For a modern definition of the moral will, Barrett drew upon William James, whose "will to believe" Barrett converted into a "will to prayer," one that might help the believer to find the "faith to will."

"When Barrett's search for meaning ends," wrote Cuddihy, "he is able to say with James that freedom is the one fact in human life 'where belief in the thing and the reality of the thing coincide.' Human freedom, then, is a fragile thing because—like meaning—its being is uniquely dependent upon man's continuing belief in it."

The Truants: Adventures Among the Intellectuals is Barrett's insider's chronicle of the *Partisan Review* coterie when it gained cultural influence in years following World War II. Widely praised for its portraits of Philip Rahv and Delmore Schwartz, Barrett's memoir was also called by Hilton Kramer in the *New York Times Book Review* "very much a text for *our* time . . . because our culture is still beset by so many illusions that were spawned and codified in the milieu that . . . Barrett has set out to describe. . . . " According to Kramer, one of the illusions that Barrett, when he was a leftist editor of *Partisan Review* and after he endorsed neoconservatism, polemicized against is the tendency of "the intellectual left to ascribe all blame for the cold war to the evil designs of American foreign policy, and to acquit the Soviet Union of all malevolent intent." Indeed Barrett appended an essay he had published in the Summer 1946 issue of *Partisan Review,* entitled "The 'Liberal' Fifth Column," to *The Truants* because "the post-War period . . . is a unified era; and nowhere is this unity exhibited more markedly than in the continuity of the Liberals' attitude toward the Soviet Union." Barrett attributes the rise of both modernism and nihilism to the death of God, and in *The Truants* he speculates that the disappearance of God might account for "that very troubling and paradoxical phenomenon of our time: the Liberals' susceptibility to totalitarianism . . . Liberals . . . may be suddenly driven to carry utopian hankerings into the field of politics. They may even aspire to bring about heaven on earth for the dream of heaven they have lost."

Barrett taught in the philosophy department of New York University until his retirement in the late 1970s. He has since then served as a senior fellow at the National Humanities Center and as visiting professor at Pace University, New York City. He lives in Tarrytown, New York .

PRINCIPAL WORKS: Irrational Man: A Study in Existential Philosophy, 1958; What Is Existentialism?, 1964; (with D. Yankelovich) Ego and Instinct: The Psychoanalytic View of Human Nature, 1970; Time of Need: Forms off Imagination in Twentieth Century Literature, 1972; The Illusion of Technique: A Search for Meaning in a Technological Civilization, 1978; The Truants: Adventures Among the Intellectuals, 1982. *As editor*—Zen Buddhism, 1956; Philosophy in the 20th Century, 1971.

ABOUT: Atlas, J. Delmore Schwartz, 1977; Barrett, W. The Truants, 1982; Contemporary Authors 13–14, 1964; Current Biography, 1982; Phillips, W. A. Partisan View: Five Decades of the Literary Life, 1983. *Periodicals*—Atlantic June 1983; Christian Science Monitor March 19, 1964; Commonweal June 8, 1979; Nation February 27, 1982; New Republic October 14, 1978; Newsweek October 2, 1978; New York Review of Books April 2, 1964; March 22, 1979; New York Times May 24, 1982; December 26, 1983; New York Times Book Review December 24, 1978; February 7, 1982.

BAYLEY, JOHN (OLIVER) (March 27, 1925–   ), British literary critic, was born in Lahore, in present-day Pakistan, the son of Frederick Bayley, an officer in the Indian Army, and the former Olivia Heenan. He attended Eton, then joined the British Army in 1943, serving in the Grenadier Guards and Special Intelligence until 1947 when he went up to New College, Oxford. In 1950 he took a first-class honors degree in English. A member of St. Antony's and Magdalen colleges, Bayley was elected to a fellowship at New College in 1955 and remained there as tutor in English until 1974. In that year he became Warton professor of English literature and took up that chair's accompanying fellowship at St. Catherine's College, Oxford.

In his lectures, essays, and books, Bayley is seen by many critics as typifying the Oxford style of literary criticism, which is steadily illuminating rather than flashy, eclectic yet learned, and rather unsystematic in its discursiveness. *The Romantic Survival,* Bayley's first book, described as "a study in poetic evolution," is a wide-ranging investigation into literary and cultural history. It examines literary romanticism both in the light of its origins in the developing self-consciousness of Wordsworth and Coleridge and of its later expression in Victorian and in modern poetry. In spite of the counter-reaction of classicists like T. E. Hulme and T. S. Eliot, Bayley finds a revival of romanticism emerging in Yeats, Auden, and Dylan Thomas—a "mind-created structure" of the creative imagination.

Bayley scored one of his greatest successes with his second critical work, *The Characters of Love: A Study in the Literature of Personality,* an analysis of the treatment of love and lovers in Chaucer's *Troilus and Criseyde,* Shakespeare's *Othello,* and James' *The Golden Bowl,* in which Bayley argues for an emotional involvement of the author with his characters—"an intense interest in the personalities" combined with "a sort of detached solicitude, a respect for their freedom." It is this quality of "an author's love

for his characters" that Bayley finds lacking in contemporary writers. The novelist and critic William Golding found the study "subtle and perceptive," especially admiring the concluding chapter on "Character and Nature," which he called "not only casually learned and astonishingly penetrating, but likely to be of great help and incitement to the practising writer." The reviewer for the *Times Literary Supplement,* however, was not in sympathy with the book, terming it "attractive, ingenious and maddening" and objecting to its lack of sustained, systematic argument. Nevertheless, this review contained a prophetic conclusion: "Mr. Bayley's feelings about many things could well point the way to the opening up of a new phase in English literary criticism, with a predominant emphasis rather different from that of the past forty years—it would certainly not come in without welcome. But even a writer who wants us to give up much of what is now seen as a proper part of literary criticism must use the language of criticism to make his case; and Mr. Bayley has taken only the first steps towards doing that."

In *The Characters of Love* Bayley cites Tolstoy as a novelist who loves his characters, and in *Tolstoy and the Novel* he examines the great Russian novelist's achievement within the framework of the Russian literary tradition, comparing him to Dostoevsky and both of them to Pushkin. The works of numerous Western novelists are then studied according to Tolstoy's "relation" to them; they include Goethe, Flaubert, Proust, and Sartre; Jane Austen, Emily Brontë, Dickens, James, Lawrence, Forster, Evelyn Waugh, and Anthony Powell. Bayley's final chapter treats Pasternak's *Doctor Zhivago* as exemplifying Tolstoy's fictional legacy. Kathryn Feuer remarked that Bayley "is superbly the 'good reader' for whom Tolstoy longed, sympathetic and stimulating even in the occasional interpretations which seem strained or, simply, wrong. . . . Reading Mr. Bayley, we come to understand what we feel when reading Tolstoy." She felt, however, that the author was considerably less successful at placing Tolstoy "within nineteenth-century Russian literature." The *Times Literary Supplement* reviewer congratulated Bayley for avoiding "the big set-piece battles of Form and Structure and Symbolism in favour of the skirmishes of paradox and local attacks of sharp penetration. . . . The informality of his essentially unsystematic approach is well suited to discussing the qualities which he recognizes and admires in Tolstoy: self-sufficiency, happy ease, self-confidence, lack of strain."

Bayley pursued his interest in Russian literature in *Pushkin: A Comparative Commentary,* described by the publishers as the first detailed study in English of Pushkin's writing. The book discusses the Russian's accomplishment and compares it with the standards and traditions of the European literature of his day, while examining closely the various styles and genres attempted by the versatile Pushkin—lyric and narrative poetry, the verse and prose novel, tragedy, the short story, and history. One critic commended Bayley's "broad cosmopolitan approach," remarking that "his prose translations of selected passages are impeccable, even if they fail to convey the full flavor of the originals." Helen Muchnic called the book "brilliant" and "provocative," adding that the author's enthusiasm and admiration for Pushkin are "ardent enough to satisfy even a Russian."

In *The Uses of Division: Unity and Disharmony in Literature*, Bayley discusses the "involuntary divisions, amounting to total disunity," the sense of a writer at odds with himself, which he sees as a characteristic of much great literature. The writers considered include the novelists Dickens, Kipling, and Lawrence; the poets Keats, Lowell, Larkin, and Berryman; and, for the last fifty pages, Shakespeare. *An Essay on Hardy* described a new approach to Hardy as poet and novelist, based on the difference Bayley perceives between Hardy the private "noticer" of his surroundings and Hardy the professional author and interpreter of reality. Bayley's most acclaimed recent work, however, is *Shakespeare and Tragedy*, which contends that Shakespeare employed the idea of tragedy in several different ways, distinguished as tragedies of consciousness (*Macbeth* and *Othello*), tragedies of construction (*Julius Caesar* and *Coriolanus*), and several tragedies of mixed type. In addition to the plays above, he discusses *Hamlet, King Lear, Troilus and Cressida,* and *Timon of Athens*. Robert M. Adams, in an enthusiastic review, called this book "the subtlest and most steadily enlightening piece of literary discussion that I've encountered in a long time. It is a work of the highest imaginative quality, unpretentious in its methods, and rich in literary sensitivity. . . . It deals undeviatingly with the plays, their language, the quality of the minds represented in them, and the responses to those imagined persons that Shakespeare is able to evoke from us." Adams goes on to characterize the author's critical style as including "a large element of the speculative and hypothetical. Incidental comments are apt to be no less suggestive than major theses, and the alert reader will frequently profit from Bayley's statement of a case, even when it doesn't fully answer to his own experience of the text. Quiet observations repeatedly strengthen the argument." J.I.M. Stewart

wrote that "Professor Bayley seems to me to be with Coleridge, and not least in creating the impression of a swiftly moving mind operating in the interest of a subtle and extended dialectic performance. . . . Here is Shakespeare criticism of the order of Bradley's and Wilson Knight's." One reviewer, however, writing in *Choice*, expressed considerable exasperation with Bayley's unsupported "oracular assertions": "With each book, [he] gets more indirect, more elusive, or, to put it differently, more meditative and more private and less concerned with clearly arguing a case for the general reader."

The publication of Bayley's *Selected Essays* in 1983 gave George Steiner occasion for a critical assessment of his work. Writing in the *Times Literary Supplement,* he confessed to a certain ambivalence, calling Bayley's stance "distinctive but not readily definable." Though creditably free, in Steiner's judgment, from the obscurantism of currently fashionable deconstructionists, Bayley's own idiom is "highly self-conscious and, at times, recherché," reflecting an "acrobatic strain [that] is both exhilarating and inhibiting." He is at his best as a comparatist, especially strong on Russian and American poetry, where he "finds the native ground under persistent influence, pressure, contrastive illumination from other tongues and traditions."

Bayley has written one novel, *In Another Country*. It is the story of Oliver Childers, a gentle, intelligent man; his career as an intelligence officer during the British occupation of the Ruhr; his forbidden romance with Liese, a young German woman; and his friendship with a charming, egotistical rogue, Duncan Holt, who betrays Oliver both in Germany and again after their return to Britain. The book was admired by critics in both Britain and the United States, who liked its quietly ironic style and allusive wit. Several of them wrote that they expected great things from the young novelist, but in nearly thirty years he has published no other work of fiction.

In 1956, Bayley married Iris Murdoch, the novelist and philosopher. They live in the village of Steeple Aston, near Oxford.

PRINCIPAL WORKS: *Criticism*—The Romantic Survival: A Study in Poetic Evolution, 1956; The Characters of Love, 1961; Tolstoy and the Novel, 1966; Pushkin, 1971; The Uses of Division, 1976; An Essay on Hardy, 1978; Shakespeare and Tragedy, 1981; Selected Essays, 1984. *Fiction*—In Another Country, 1955. *Poetry*—El Dorado; The Newdigate Prize Poem 1950, 1951.

ABOUT: Borklund, E. Contemporary Literary Critics, 1982; Contemporary Authors 85–88, 1980; Who's Who, 1983–84. *Periodicals*—Choice May 1967; November 1971; September 1978; November 1981; Commonweal December 2, 1955; July 28, 1967; Economist March 11, 1978; Encounter July 1978; July 1981; Library Journal October 1, 1955; May 15, 1961; May 15, 1967; November 15, 1971; September 1, 1976; December 15, 1978; New Republic May 27, 1978; New Statesman March 12, 1955; February 3, 1961; October 28, 1966; August 6, 1971; May 11, 1976; March 24, 1978; May 15, 1981; New Yorker December 17, 1955; New York Review of Books September 14, 1967; October 7, 1971; October 22, 1981; New York Times Book Review April 23, 1967; Saturday Review January 7, 1956; July 22, 1978; Spectator March 18, 1955; February 10, 1961; Times Literary Supplement April 29, 1955; February 24, 1961; December 8, 1966; July 30, 1971; July 23, 1976; July 28, 1978; July 3, 1981; April 20, 1984; Virginia Quarterly Review Summer 1967; Yale Review October 1967.

© Thomas Victor

ANN BEATTIE

BEATTIE, ANN (September 8, 1947–), American novelist and short story writer, was born in Washington, D.C., the daughter of James A. and Charlotte (Crosby) Beattie. Beattie, who was an only child, has said of her adolescence in the suburbs of Washington that she was interested in writing and painting, "but it wasn't until I got to college that I began to take writing seriously—not my own, but literature." She received her B.A. degree from the American University in Washington in 1969, and an M.A. (1970) from the University of Connecticut, where she spent two additional years in the doctoral program. Instead of writing her dissertation, however, she spent her time "secretly writing stories." In 1972 she married David Gates, a psychiatrist, and at approximately the same time had her first story published in the *New Yorker,* after the magazine had "rejected twenty stories in a row." While a visiting writer and lecturer at the University of Virginia from 1975 to 1977, she published her first two books—*Distortions,* a collection of short stories, and *Chilly Scenes of Winter,* a novel.

Distortions collects nineteen of her stories, thirteen of which appeared originally in the *New Yorker.* Witty, sometimes almost surrealistic, the tales combine the pedestrian with the bizarre: two dwarfs marry, a woman is afraid she might disappear while her husband is away, a divorced man fills his brother's apartment with animals, spacemen come to earth to take nude pornographic pictures. One reviewer describes the characters of these stories as passionless people who "very nearly sleepwalk through their lives as they let things happen to them, feel little, think less." Several reviewers hailed the appearance of the stories as a literary event, marking the emergence of an original new talent, but others mixed praise with reservations. Susan Horo-

witz noted Beattie's "instinct for the grotesque that verges on the edge of real wit and pain," but found the stories fragmented, many of them lacking "an emotional core." Kristan Hunter commented that the stories are too often "a series of static scenes . . . still-lifes of people who do not have any meaningful connection to humanity, and do not move, feel, or grow," with the result that the reader feels little empathy with them.

Chilly Scenes of Winter, Beattie's first novel, takes place in an unnamed city that might be Washington, D.C., and centers on a young man named Charles, a survivor of the turbulent sixties who now finds himself, at twenty-seven, pursuing an existence of listless dislocation. He works at a white-collar government job, takes care of his mother who is mentally unstable and regularly attempts suicide, consorts with his friend Sam who work in a men's clothing store and seems to have little independent life at all, and mourns his separation from his girlfriend Laura. What is particularly notable about the work is that it relies for its effect hardly at all upon plot (which would imply a purposive world), and instead is related in short, present-tense sentences that eventually numb the mind and adumbrate the state of its lost characters.

In his review of the novel, John Updike praised *Chilly Scenes of Winter* elaborately, remarking that Beattie's "details—which include the lyrics of songs the characters overhear on the radio and the recipes of the rather junky food they eat—calmly accrue; her dialogue trails down the pages with an uncanny fidelity to the low-level heartbreaks behind the banal; her resolutely unmetaphorical style builds around us a maze of familiar truths that nevertheless has something airy, eerie, and in the end lovely about it. . . . [Its characters] are exquisitely modulated studies in vacancy." It was commonly said that in *Chilly Scenes of Winter* Beattie had created a mirror for her generation, but reviews of the novel were not uniformly favorable. The critic for the *Atlantic* commented that "the structure of the novel is slack, . . . limply giving in to the downward pull of its mood. When, at the end, a bit of sunshine seems about to break through the wintry clouds of Charles's life, the change is false and flatly incredible." Margo Jefferson, in *Newsweek,* found Beattie's social details more "decorative than substantial." "Her taut, present-tense sentences," she wrote, "can be wearing: there is little resonance between them."

In 1977–78 Beattie was Briggs-Copeland lecturer in English at Harvard University, and in 1979 published her second collection of stories, *Secrets and Surprises.* The stories in the collection (eight of the fifteen appeared originally in the *New Yorker*) extend Beattie's range as a chronicler of the disaffected maturity of the sixties generation. Her characters, usually couples in their thirties who live in New York City or the suburbs, privileged in some ways, moderately well-off, can make no sense of their lives or find any meaning in the social order outside themselves. In reviewing the book, E. S. Duvall spoke of the "unrelieved passivity of the characters," in whom Beattie is yet able to compel one's interest; and the reviewer for the *Virginia Quarterly Review* noted that Beattie's great achievement in the stories was her persuading the reader that "eventlessness is the rhythm of life itself." Other reviewers were impatient with Beattie's method. Gail Godwin remarked that Beattie's characters, in their eventless lives, are committed to things rather than to people, and that these things are "too often a mere catalogue of trends. . . . Miss Beattie has a coolly accurate eye for the *moeurs* of her generation. . . . But a sharp eye for *moeurs* doesn't add up to a full fiction any more than the attitude of irony can be said to represent a full human experience."

Falling in Place, a novel about the disintegration of the Knapp family in suburban New York, was written, Beattie has said in an interview, in a series of eighteen-hour sessions over the course of a single month. Once again, reviewers disagreed strongly. Richard Locke, in the *New York Times Book Review,* declared that *Falling in Place* "is stronger, more accomplished, larger in every way than anything [Beattie has] done. . . . There is a new urgency to the characters' feelings and a much greater range and number of characters and points of view. . . .

Inevitably these studies in domestic sorrow recall the stories of J. D. Salinger or John Cheever or John Updike: Ann Beattie's world, like theirs, is a miserable suburban purgatory inhabited by grieving wraiths." Among the dissenting reviewers, Robert Towers complained of "diminishing returns" in the work. "So much passivity, aimlessness, and narcissism," he wrote, "is easier to take in small doses—Ann Beattie's short stories for instance—than in a novel of this length." Jack Beatty found the incident in which the Knapp son half accidentally shoots his sister merely melodramatic violence, following which the novel aimlessly "drifts on . . . for another 100 pages."

The Burning House, Beattie's most recent volume of short stories, covers the same terrain as her earlier collections, but reveals a somewhat more sympathetic attitude toward her characters. Some critics maintained that it confirmed Beattie's place as a foremost stylist in contemporary "minimalist" fiction, whereas others objected to the lack of moral values in her work. Margaret Atwood, who praised the book, noted that "no one is better at the plangent detail, at evoking the floating, unreal ambiance of grief [than Beattie]." Jonathan Yardley, on the other hand, believed that Beattie was repeating herself tediously. "The members of her generation," he wrote, "are unlikely to find a more observant or perceptive chronicler than Ann Beattie, but there is precious little in what she writes to persuade us that they are worth such attention."

In 1979 Beattie's novel *Chilly Scenes of Winter* was adapted as a film by Joan Miklin Silver and released by United Artists under the title *Head Over Heels.* It was poorly received and was recalled after five weeks, except in Boston, where it became a kind of cult film. A newly edited version, entitled *Chilly Scenes of Winter,* with the "happy ending" deleted, was released in 1982, and enjoyed a highly successful run—adding to Beattie's growing reputation.

Beattie had a Guggenheim fellowship in 1977 and in 1980 received an award from the American Academy and Institute of Letters. In recent years she has lived in Connecticut and in New York City.

PRINCIPAL WORKS: Chilly Scenes of Winter, 1976; Distortions 1976; Secrets and Surprises, 1979; Falling in Place, 1980; The Burning House, 1982.

ABOUT: Contemporary Authors 81-84, 1979; Dictionary of Literary Biography Yearbook, 1982; Who's Who in America, 1983-84. *Periodicals*—Atlantic June 1980; (Washington Post) Book World September 19, 1982; Commentary February 1979; July 1980; Harpers May 1980; Horizon December 4, 1982; New Leader January 15, 1979; New Republic June 7, 1980; Newsweek August 23, 1976; New Yorker November 29, 1976; June 9, 1980; New York Review of Books May 15, 1980; New York Times Book Review August 15, 1976; May 11, 1980; September 26, 1982; Saturday Review August 7, 1976.

BECK, BEATRIX (July 30, 1914–   ), Belgian novelist and journalist, writes (in French): "I was prematurely and accidentally born in Villars-sur-Ollon, Vaud, Switzerland. My parents returned to France with me three weeks later. Apparently they were able to find transportation even at that time of general mobilization. Christian Beck my father, who died of galloping consumption in 1916 at the age of thirty-seven, was a writer and a friend of André Gide.

"Among my memories of World War I are the neighbors running to see an aeroplane that crashed in the small pine wood behind our house in the Ile de France, and a long procession of refugees from the north, some walking, some riding in carts. Above all I remember an old woman pushing a wheelbarrow and a little girl carrying a bird in a cage. The refugees were offered food from every side; sometimes bread and butter or fruit, sometimes a glass of wine. The Germans were shelling Paris with 'Big Bertha,' and the grown-ups were saying 'This is the end.' There was talk of people who had been suffocated between two mattresses because they had Spanish influenza, otherwise called the plague. I sported two little woolen mascots, Nénette and Rintintin, in my buttonhole.

"I attended rural schools at Fourqueux and at Saint-Nom-la-Bretèche, and received my secondary schooling at the lycée of Saint-Germain-en-Laye. I imagined that one day I would discover a new art comprising all existing arts, and that I would recount the life of a human being from the moment of conception to death without omitting an instant. I also dreamed of writing a book that would consist entirely of onomatopoeic words. At the same time I was fascinated by the wager of Pascal, that terrifying genius [who proposed that one has nothing to lose by believing in God, and everything to gain]. I also hoped that, like Pascal, I would discover God through mathematics.

"Soon after I became an adult my mother killed herself by taking Gardénal and Dial-Ciba, drugs that were freely available at that time. She left a brief note to say that my father's calls from beyond the grave had become more and more pressing. While studying at the University of Grenoble I married Naum Szapiro, a stateless Jew from Gradno (once in Poland, now in the

BEATRIX BECK

USSR) who was a student at the Polytechnic Institute. Our daughter Bernadette was born on the morning of Christmas day 1936. Naum, drafted into the French army, was killed on April 3, 1940 at Blombay in the Ardennes. He was just twenty-eight, I was twenty-five, and Bernadette was three years of age. To earn a living, and to be able to pay for Bernadette's board and lodging with a peasant family in order to conceal her from the Gestapo raids that took place in our Nazi-occupied town, I took various menial jobs as factory worker, carton assembler, artist's model, and clerk. The wives of Gestapo officers, who wore sky-blue raincoats, specialized in kidnapping Jewish children.

"I raised enough money by selling André Gide's correspondence with my father to support myself while writing my first book *Barny* in 1948. I then wrote several autobiographical narratives, stories for children, and, having rid myself of the autobiographical impulse, novels. When *Léon Morin, prêtre* (Léon Morin, Priest, 1952) won the 1953 Goncourt prize I was able to buy a home of my own. My daughter and I had been 'camping out' in a friend's apartment above a shop. Later, *Léon Morin* was made into a film by Jean-Pierre Melville.

"I was André Gide's last secretary, and then worked as a journalist, a reader for television, and a literary advisor. I have taught at the University of California at Berkeley, at Hollins College in Virginia, at the Universities of Laval and Sherbrook in Quebec, and at Laurentian University in Ontario. Now I live in the Normandy countryside in a small house made larger by a garden enclosed by a hedge. The animals seem to belong to another, more robust age. The crows have immense wingspans; the butterflies are like birds of prey. Seen close up, the dragonflies remind me of military helicopters. The field mice display a subtle intelligence in escaping the cat's claws, dashing into cracks in the brickwork or under doors. I never thought that I would see pear trees outgrow houses. My daughter, who now has a student daughter of her own, has continued the tradition of our family by publishing a book, *La première ligne* (The Front Line). It concerns her father who, just before his death, demanded that he be stationed in the front line."

—trans. H. Batchelor

English-language readers know Béatrix Beck only from one novel, her Prix Goncourt-winning *The Passionate Heart,* a translation of *Léon Morin, prêtre.* The book is, however, characteristic of all her work—short, impressionistic, episodic novels which explore with rare sensitivity and realism the inner and outer worlds of a single character, Barny, who is a recognizable persona for Beck. Although Barny's life is one of personal tragedy and terrible hardship—a childhood impoverished by World War I, a young womanhood impoverished by life in occupied France in World War II, the deaths of her parents and her young husband—she responds to life affirmatively for the most part, sometimes even joyously. Beck's novels register those responses in all their depth and variety. Barny, an uncommonly intelligent and thoughtful woman, may not fulfill her creator's youthful ambition to "recount the life of a human being from the moment of conception to death without omitting an instant," but she is a richly developed character as well as a fictional record of Beck's life experiences. The eyes of the child in her first novel, *Barny,* register the suffering of her widowed mother who struggles to raise and educate her sickly, dreamy child and to preserve her own very tenuous sanity. At the end of the novel Barny is a young woman, now pregnant herself, and her mother has committed suicide. Transcending the harsh reality of her life is Barny's quest for religious faith. Told in the simple language of a young child, the novel seems half dream, half reality: Barny brings her father back to life in her imagination, lives fantasies that shield her from the cruel circumstances of her life, questions whether God has abandoned her, but never abandons her quest for Him. As an adolescent, Barny studies mathematics and philosophy, with Pascal and Jesus as her ideals. What kept her steadfast in her faith, she writes, was the fear "not of losing the world, which I held contemptible, but of deceiving myself, of not being in the truth." Resolving even then to become a writer, she makes lofty plans to write spontaneously but impeccably, "to reunite all the arts in mine."

Barny won the admiration of distinguished critics, among them the essayist and philosopher Georges Bataille and the novelist André Gide. It was followed in 1951 by *Une mort irrégulière* (An Irregular Death), centering on Barny's husband, a refugee Jew killed in World War II. With *Léon Morin, prêtre* in 1952, Beck carried Barny's life record into her widowhood in wartime France as she struggles to raise a young daughter and to resolve her religious doubts: "My spirit was as tormented as my body. . . . The faithful and their priests seemed to defy me. They live on paper currency. I had to have gold." Restless and tormented, she wanders into a church confessional, determined to defy religion. "Religion is the opium of the people" are her first words to the priest. But because the priest, Léon Morin, is so sympathetic, so eager to engage her in examining her ideas, he guides her back to her faith. In the course of that journey they fall in love, but he honors his vows, leaving her in the end lonely but strengthened.

In its English translation by Constantine Fitz-Gibbon the book found enthusiastic readers. Brendan Gill, in the *New Yorker,* compared Beck with François Mauriac and Graham Greene, judging her work, however, less grim and despairing. Henri Peyre, in *Saturday Review,* found it a "harsh" book, "stripped of ornaments and rhetoric, purposely devoid of grace, written with concise sobriety, but one which faithfully renders the moods and atmosphere of France under the occupation and the spiritual aspirations of people crushed by material worries." Beck has continued to trace Barny's life, sometimes as center but often now as witness to the spiritual journeys of others, in Belgium and in England where she has relatives—*Des accommodements avec le ciel* (Working Things Out with Heaven, 1954), and *Le Muet* (The Mute, 1963). In her recent work, *Noli,* 1978, and *La Décharge* (The Discharge, 1979), she has concentrated more particularly on the world of childhood and the consciousness of the sensitive, developing young child.

WORKS IN ENGLISH TRANSLATION: The only work of Béatrix Beck's available in English is Constantine FitzGibbon's translation of *Léon Morin, prêtre,* published in 1953 in the United States under the title *The Passionate Heart* and in England as *The Priest.*

ABOUT: Cassell's Encyclopedia of World Literature 2,

1973; Columbia Dictionary of Modern European Literature, 1980.

*BENET GOITIA, JUAN (October 7, 1927–   ), Spanish novelist and essayist, was born in Madrid, the son of Tomás Benet and Teresa Goitia. His life, like that of so many Spaniards of his generation, was directly influenced by the Spanish Civil War (1936–39) that uprooted his family—his father died in the conflict's early days—and imposed at its conclusion the repressive Francoist regime that ruled Spain from 1939 to 1975, and to which many of Benet's works respond directly or indirectly. He began his early studies in San Sebastián, where his family had moved during the war, and continued them in Madrid upon his return there at the war's conclusion. In 1948 Benet enrolled in the University of Madrid's School of Civil Engineering from which he graduated in 1954. Most of the period between graduation and 1966, when he returned to Madrid permanently, was spent directing large public works projects, mostly in the northwest of Spain. This experience years later provided the real geography into which Benet would place the coordinates of his fictitious "Región" where the majority of his important literary pieces are set. His directing of public works projects was interrupted by his trips abroad to gain more practical engineering experience. Benet's more recent travels have expanded to include speaking engagements on literary topics in both Europe and the Americas.

Benet's literary avocation was encouraged by his reading of works recommended by his older brother Francisco who had an important influence on his early intellectual formation, through his contacts with various young intellectuals during his university days in Madrid, and through his attendance during the same period at various literary meetings or "tertulias." During these formative years he began to acquire his extensive knowledge of Western literature through his reading of Sir James Frazer, Thomas Mann, Faulkner, Kafka, Proust, and the classics. His contacts with Spanish writers and intellectuals of his generation, among them Luis Martín-Santos, Ignacio Aldecoa, and Carmen Martín-Gaite, kept him abreast of intellectual trends in and out of Spain. It was this contact that led to the publication of his first literary work *Max*, a short play, published in a prestigious literary magazine in 1953.

It was almost a decade later that Benet's first volume of narrative prose appeared. *Nunca llegarás a nada* (You Will Never Get Anywhere, 1961), a collection of short stories the majority

JUAN BENET GOITIA

of which are set in "Región," serves mainly to introduce this place to his readers. A period of almost eight years separates the publication of this work from the appearance of his first novel, *Volverás a Región* (You Will Return to Región, 1967), on which he had been working for a number of years. This book is now almost universally recognized as his greatest literary achievement, and one of the most important novels produced in Spain in the last half-century. An hermetic and enigmatic work, it sets the main lines that his major fiction followed. As with almost all his important writing it takes place in "Región." It is a complex chronicle of the effects of the Spanish Civil War, and the decadence and decay its outcome portended, on the lives of a group of characters, many of whom appear in other novels of what has been called the "Región cycle."

But it was only the awarding of the prestigious Seix Barral prize in 1969 to his second novel, the equally hermetic *Una Meditación* (A Meditation, 1970) that began to focus critical attention on the work of this writer by avocation, whose novels, because of their baroque structural complexities, seemed so distinct from much of what his contemporaries were writing. In 1971, Benet published the novelette *Una Tumba* (A Tomb), a work with strong ties to the tradition of ghost stories and horror fiction, and also a collection of theatrical works. *Un viaje de invierno* (A Winter Journey), the third novel of the "Región" cycle, appeared the following year. It, like the first two major works of fiction, requires that the reader be capable of understanding all the references and allusions to other works of literature upon which a complete comprehension of the text depends. This novel gained Benet his second literary award, the Nueva Crítica prize. In 1972 Benet published another volume of short works, *5 narraciones y 2 fábulas* (5 Narratives and 2 Fables), and also the fourth novel of the "Región" cycle, *La otra casa de Mazón* (The Mazón's Other House) and another volume of short stories, *Sub rosa*. The former continues to pose difficulties of comprehension through its structural complexities. The latter demonstrates Benet's debt to such writers as Conan Doyle, Stevenson, and Melville. *En el estado* (In the State), the author's fifth novel, appeared in 1977. It too requires a reader capable of deciphering a complex literary organization, and one who is aware of the parodic use Benet makes of a myriad of other cultural texts from Kleist to Flaubert.

The second half of the volume *Del pozo y del Numa* (Of the Well and of Numa, 1978) is a narrative centered on El Numa, the mysterious character derived from *The Golden Bough*, who plays a fundamental role in *Volverás a Región*. In 1980 Benet again published two novels. The first was the enigmatic *Saul ante Samuel* (Saul Before Samuel). Another of the "Región" cycle novels, it recounts in an extremely complex manner a history of fratricide, with links to the biblical characters to whom the work's title refers. *El aire de un crimen* (Air of a Crime), runner-up for the Planeta prize, Spain's most lucrative, was, by design, an almost complete departure from the type of narrative Benet had previously written. Due to its accessible style, structure, and subject matter it gained Benet a wider readership than any of his previous works, and thus served to introduce the writer to an audience to whom his works were unknown. *Trece fábulas y media* (Three and a Half Fables), another collection of short pieces, appeared in 1982, and was followed in 1983 by the novelette *En la penumbra* (In the Shadow).

Benet's latest literary endeavor is a multivolume work entitled *Herrumbrosas lanzas* (Rusty Lances). This novel is also set in "Región" during the Spanish Civil War, but is different from the other novels that use "Región" as their setting in that its style and structure are much more reminiscent of *El aire de un crimen*. Closer examination reveals that behind its easily comprehensible nature are typical Benetian complexities, and that the parodic use he makes of other writers' texts is here extended to include his own previous writing on "Región," especially *Volverás a Región*. The first part of this work appeared in 1983 and won Benet the Critic's Prize for narrative.

Benet has also gained a considerable reputation as an essayist. His most important collection

is undoubtedly *La inspiración y el estilo* (Inspiration and Style), first published in 1966. In this volume Benet develops a series of literary precepts that direct his approach to literature and the arts. The essays in this collection show that Benet opts for a literature of imagination that ostensibly breaks with realist norms, and that he sets the primacy of style and imagination over content that directly projects social problems. Benet seemingly eschews any direct links between literature and socio-political projects. Subsequent volumes continue to develop these ideas while also ranging far afield and expressing his views on a myriad of cultural topics, including Shakespeare, Chomskian linguistics, classical painting, and Cervantes. These collections include *Puerta de tierra* (Door of Dust, 1970); *El ángel del Señor abandona a Tobías* (The Angel of the Lord Abandons Tobit) and *En ciernes* (In Blossom), both 1976, and *La moviola de Eurípides* (Euripides' Replay Machine, 1982). Benet's essays also reflect his concern with his own environment, and with recent Spanish history.

This is best seen in the monograph *¿Qué fue la guerra civil?* (What Was the Civil War?, 1976). His views on the lamentable state of Spanish letters, the result of Spanish writers' desire to affect political events, is also voiced in a number of his essays. Benet also writes extensively for the Spanish press on topics of general interest. The majority of his contributions are now found in Spain's highly regarded daily *El País*. A number of his articles have recently been collected in the two volumes *Artículos 1962–1977*, 1983, and *Sobre la incertidumbre* (Above Uncertainty, 1983).

Both the quantity of material he has published, and its intrinsic merit have led critics to rank Benet among the most important writers of his generation. In fact, the distinguished Hispanist Ricardo Gullón has stated that when one speaks of the Spanish novel the 1970s belong to Benet. Only the next few years will tell if that assessment can be carried over into the next decade. A first reading of Benet's essays and fiction would lead one to the general conclusion offered by the majority of critics of his work who see him as an elitist and extremely hermetic author whose baroque prose poses substantial and sometimes insoluble enigmas for the reader. Yet it must be kept in mind that beyond Benet's denial of any connection between his narrative and social conditions lies the possibility that the narrative and essayistic project which rejects a relationship between text and context is not based on the presumption that such a link is impossible, but on the fact that others who have attempted it have failed because they have subordinated literature to extra-literary values. Benet's own work might be seen as the exception that disproves his rule. His novelistic world elaborates certain structural constants which, deciphered and calibrated with Benet's acerbic comments on his own environment—most especially the repressive Francoist regime that governed Spain until 1975—demonstrates how that criticism is given life in a narrative that on the surface seems remote from conditions in contemporary Spain.

Juan Benet is one of Spain's most polemical, difficult, and respected authors, one who has consistently broken with norms of literature and who continues to chart new ground. Benet's wife died in 1974. He has three sons and a daughter.

WORKS IN ENGLISH TRANSLATION: Only one of Benet's works is available in English—*A Meditation,* translated by Gregory Rabassa, 1982.

ABOUT: Cabrera, V. Juan Benet, 1983; Compitello, M. A. Ordering the Evidence, 1983; Herzberger, D. K. The Novelistic World of Juan Benet, 1977; Manteiga, R., Herzberger, D. K. and Compitello, M. A. (eds.) Critical Approaches to the Writings of Juan Benet, 1984. *Periodicals*—American Hispanist 3, 1979; Denver Quarterly 17, 1982; Hispanic Review, 47, 1979; New York Times Book Review May 23, 1982.

BERGONZI, BERNARD (April 13, 1929–   ), English critic, poet, and novelist, writes: "I wanted to be a writer long before I ever thought of being an academic. I was born and grew up in a featureless inner suburb of South London, a hilly district of long streets of terraced houses (somewhere far beneath them were the traces of a Saxon settlement), though well provided with parks and open spaces. Fashionable London, only a few miles away across the Thames, seemed very remote. My social origins were at the uncertain point where the respectable, aspiring working class touched the lowest rung of the lower middle class. My father, who was the son of Italian immigrants and had been a dance-band musician in the twenties, held a white-collar job in a local factory; my mother was the youngest member of a large working-class family. She had grown up in considerable poverty and had little formal education; but she had a keen, restless intelligence and was widely read. Both my parents were Catholics; I was brought up a Catholic and have remained one in my own way; see my contributions to *Why I Am Still a Catholic* (edited by Robert Nowell, London, 1982). We were not, however, a typical Catholic family, as I was an only child.

"My schooling was disrupted by prolonged

BERNARD BERGONZI

periods of severe illness as a child and again in my teens, and on more than one occasion I nearly died; what effect this had on my temperament and sensibility I do not know, but I have enjoyed good health all my adult life. The Second World War also interfered with my education, and I left school shortly before I was sixteen. No one in my mother's large extended family had ever been to university, nor had anyone I knew personally apart from a cousin on my father's side, and it did not seem a possible option. But after several years of working in low-level clerical jobs in London offices, and publishing poems and reviews in little magazines, I was persuaded by some far-sighted literary friends that it would be possible and desirable for me to continue my education. I managed to spend a year at an adult college in Scotland, where the poet Edwin Muir was Warden and teacher of literature. Then at the age of twenty-six I won a mature student's scholarship to Oxford [Wadham College, B.Litt. 1961, M.A. 1962]. I was absorbed or seduced by academic life; after my earlier experiences I found it remarkable to be paid for doing what I enjoyed doing. I still do from time to time. In 1959 I was appointed an assistant lecturer at Manchester University, where Frank Kermode was then head of the English Department. In 1960 I married Gabriel Wall, daughter of the Catholic writers Barnard and Barbara Wall. We have a son and two daughters.

"Coming to intellectual maturity in the fifties I was influenced by the young writers of what was then known as the 'Movement': men such as John Wain, Kingsley Amis and Donald Davie, whom I met and whose example I wanted to follow, in combining the teaching of English in a university with the writing of literary criticism and poetry or fiction. (Before long, though, Wain and Amis gave up teaching.) I moved to the new University of Warwick in 1966, and became known as a critic and literary historian, though I continued to write poems, if at infrequent intervals, and I published my first novel, *The Roman Persuasion,* in 1981, after years of writing about other people's fiction. Liking a diversified life, I have taken a hand in academic administration, which I find less taxing than teaching or writing, and was a pro-vice-chancellor at Warwick between 1979 and 1982. I have also taught in America, at Brandeis, Tulsa and Stanford.

"As a critic I suppose I am in a familiar British tradition: empirical, unemphatic, judicious, lucid, conversational. I regard criticism as a useful but essentially secondary activity, and I marvel at, without admiring, the self-important airs assumed by top French or American critics. Roger Sale, reviewing a book of my essays in the *Hudson Review* in 1973, came up with what looks to me like a fair assessment of my qualities and limitations as a critic: 'Out of respect and love for his subjects, Bergonzi tends to accept them all, and so he is often cautious where a more lavish or decisive evocation is needed, polite where he could often afford to be rude, graceful and intelligent in ways that seem to have seldom led him to ask why he does as he does.' I would like to think I have sharpened my manner a little since then; certainly I have become more concerned with theoretical and speculative questions. The critical book of mine that I find most interesting is the latest, *Reading the Thirties,* a short work which tries to bring recent Continental influences to bear on the native style of criticism and literary history that I learnt in the fifties. Criticism has changed a lot and has become very conscious of fashion. I am interested in intellectual fashions, though I do not feel obliged to follow them."

———

Bernard Bergonzi is a critic whose tastes are shaped more by a deep love for literature than by any doctrinaire critical system. In *The Situation of the Novel,* a comparative study of contemporary British and American fiction, he draws upon a wide range of reading to support his thesis that the English novel remains traditional, "both backward- and inward-looking, with rather little to say that can be instantly translated into universal statements about the human condition." Writing about modern English fiction thus becomes, for Bergonzi, "an attempt to define what it means to be English at the present time." Without using the novel as a documentary source, he nevertheless explores what he calls "the relation between the small world of the novel and the large world from which it draws its life"; that relationship, he reminds the reader, "is rarely simple and can be remarkably complicated."

Bergonzi's poetry shares some of the qualities of lucidity and thoughtfulness that characterize his criticism. Lyrical, usually rhymed and formal in structure, the poems draw on local scenes (the British Museum, London Bridge, Charing Cross Road, Blackheath), his travels in Italy, artists he admires (Vuillard, Klee), sometimes with humor, more often with genuine wit. In "Descartes and the Animals," he imagines the philosopher sitting quietly in a garden thinking ("He thought and was. . . . He thought in thought"). Interrupted by a noisy hunting party, he pities the panting hart but recalls that animals do not think and therefore his pity is in vain. The poem closes:

Man, born to think, and out of thinking born,
was that one beast that felt its natural part.
And from the woods a shrill triumphant horn
sounded for the swift and broken hart.

Bergonzi's first novel, *The Roman Persuasion,* is a study of a cultivated English Catholic family (the father edits a literary journal) in the mid-1930s, clinging to their traditions and values under the challenges of the Spanish Civil War and the political crises of that age. "These contemporary details," Ian Scott-Kilvert wrote in a review of the book, "are accurately portrayed and judiciously selected; the result is a convincing portrait of a strikingly closed world."

PRINCIPAL WORKS: *Non-fiction*—The Early H.G. Wells, 1961; Heroes' Twilight: A Study of the Literature of the Great War, 1965; The Situation of the Novel, 1970; Anthony Powell, 1971; T.S. Eliot, 1972; The Turn of a Century, 1973; Gerard Manley Hopkins, 1977; Reading the Thirties, 1978; *Novel*—The Roman Persuasion, 1981. *Poetry*—Descartes and the Animals, 1954; Years: Sixteen Poems, 1979.

ABOUT: Contemporary Authors, first revision series 17–20, 1976; Hudson Review, Winter 1973–74; Times Literary Supplement June 3, 1977; December 1, 1978; March 20, 1981.

BERMANT, CHAIM ICYK (February 26, 1929–), English novelist and journalist, writes: "I was born in Lithuania into a family in which the only form of writ was holy so that my thoughts about being a writer verged on the blas-

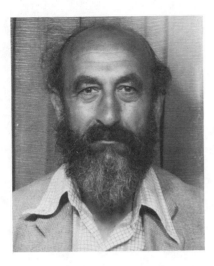

CHAIM BERMANT

phemous. We settled in Scotland in 1938 and I took to writing in English even before I could speak it. Although I enjoyed the benefits of a good Scottish education (and nowhere is good English taken more seriously than in Scotland), I have never mastered the intricacies of English syntax, or even spelling, and I only achieved my breakthrough as a writer when I joined Scottish television in 1958 and was provided with a literate secretary. I was never particularly happy in television, because I am a word man and in television, or at least in good television, the pictures should speak for themselves.

"After accumulating what I thought was sufficient capital, I left to devote myself to novels, and my first book *Jericho Sleep Alone* was published in 1964. I spent a number of years in journalism before becoming a full-time, self-employed writer in 1966. I value the disciplines of journalism. The prospect of a dead-line concentrates the mind wonderfully, as does the need to say as much as possible in as few words as possible. A generous contract for a book, on the other hand, can make one self-indulgent and often does. I still maintain my contacts in journalism and am a regular contributor to two London papers, and eight of the twenty-four books I have written (e.g. *Troubled Eden, The Cousinhood, Ebla*) were either inspired by newspaper articles I have written or are enlarged forms of them. My first novels were concerned with lower-middle class Jewish life, my later ones with middle-middle class which I believe reflects not so much my own personal progress, as the upward move of Jewry in general. I do not care to be type-cast as a Jewish writer (though I am pre-

cisely that) and have attempted to escape from time to time from Jewish subjects and I think I may have succeeded with my fourth novel, *Diary of an Old Man,* possibly because when men reach a certain age they transcend their particular qualities and acquire a peevish self-centeredness which is quite universal. I used to produce about two books a year, which was regarded as unforgivable by most U.K. critics, especially where they failed to produce any themselves. It is, however, true that I used to attack my typewriter without sufficient consideration and perhaps even without sufficient cause, and have rushed books into print (e.g. *Here Endeth the Lesson* and *Now Dowager*) which might have been best put aside, or even torn asunder, yet my most successful book (*Diary of an Old Man*) took but a month to write. My U.S. publisher (Tom McCormack, of St. Martin's Press), felt that my books were too short and bore every mark of hurried work, and with a generosity which—in my experience at least—is rare in the publishing trade (and a recklessness which is even rarer) he advanced me a large sum so that I might slow down. And slow down I did, partly because of age, partly because of fatigue, but largely because I took the trouble to research the background to my stories, instead of letting everything pour forth from my own sweet head. It has meant that my books are now much larger, and sell better; I only wish I could be sure that they are better, and I have yet to be convinced that fecundity is a fault. A more serious fault is that I strain too eagerly for a laugh. Laughs are rare in contemporary fiction and I think a certain amount of strain is forgivable, provided (a): it is not the reader who is being strained, and (b): the pay-off pays off, and it is possible that I sometimes fail in both respects, though I think I succeed often enough to be forgiven for trying. The number of people who can read may be growing, but the number of those who do is declining, and I feel anyone who derives his livelihood from books owes a duty to them. I lack the moral depth to make them better men, the sagacity to make them wiser, or even the authority to make them more informed, but I like to think I have the flair to keep them amused and that I can keep at least some people happy some of the time."

———

Readers for whom the epithet a "charmingly old-fashioned novel" (applied by one reviewer to *The Second Mrs. Whitberg*) is not a patronizing dismissal but a real compliment have long welcomed Chaim Bermant's portraits of contemporary Anglo-Jewish life. His characters are not the *angst*-driven intellectuals of much current American-Jewish fiction but simple, forthright people going about the business of living as comfortably and happily as they can in the modern world—as Bermant describes them: "hapless but not helpless, beset by many small calamities which somehow never amount to an irreversible disaster and which certainly do not diminish their hope that even if the worst is not over, the best is yet to come." His more recent non-fiction has focused more seriously, but not without humor too, on journalism and sociology—the modern state of Israel and studies of Jewish life in England. In his autobiography, *Coming Home,* he describes a year in which he and his family lived in Israel. Although the account is straightforward and almost journalistic, it is a work of candid self-analysis, for Bermant discovered during this period that home for him, in spite of his Jewish roots, was not Israel but the England where he had, until then, felt himself an alien. "Is it a moral crime to leave Israel?" he asks himself. "In a sense it is for any Jew who has any pretensions to being a Zionist, or who draws reassurance and pride—as I do—from the existence of Israel." But for Bermant, a writer, England "will always have its pecular hold . . . I am at home in English in a way that I shall never be in Hebrew, no matter how lovely its cadences and how ancient its echoes."

Bermant was educated at Glasgow Rabbinical College, Glasgow University (M.A. 1955, M. Litt. 1960), and the London School of Economics (M. Sci. 1957). He married Judith Weil in 1962, and they have four children.

PRINCIPAL WORKS: *Autobiography*—Coming Home, 1976. *Fiction*—Jericho Sleep Alone, 1964; Berl Make Tea, 1965; Ben Preserve Us, 1965; Diary of an Old Man, 1966; Swinging in the Rain, 1967; Here Endeth the Lesson, 1969; Now Dowager, 1971; Roses Are Blooming in Picardy, 1972; The Last Supper, 1973; The Second Mrs. Whitberg, 1976; The Squire of Bor Shacor, 1977; Now Newman Was Old, 1978; The Patriarch, 1981; The House of Women, 1983. *Non-fiction*—Israel, 1967; Troubled Eden: An Anatomy of British Jewry, 1969; The Cousinhood: The Anglo-Jewish Gentry, 1971; The Walled Garden, 1974; Point of Arrival: A Study of London's East End, 1975; The Jews, 1978; (with M. Weitzman) Ebla, 1979.

ABOUT: Contemporary Authors 57–60, 1976; Vinson, J. (ed.) Contemporary Novelists, 1982; Who's Who, 1983–84.

*BERNHARD, THOMAS (February 9, 1931–), Austrian novelist, short story writer, playwright, and poet, was born in Heerlan (Holland), the son of Austrian parents. His maternal

°bern´ härt, tō´ mäs

THOMAS BERNHARD

grandfather was the writer Johannes Freumbichler (1881–1949). His father, a carpenter of peasant descent from Henndorf near Salzburg, died in Frankfurt (Oder) in 1943. Thomas Bernhard grew up with his maternal grandparents in Vienna and Seekirchen (Wallersee). His mother remarried. From 1943 to 1944 Bernhard lived in a boarding school. Between 1944 and the end of World War II, he worked as a gardener and entered the Johanneum Gymnasium in Salzburg. In 1947 he dropped out of the Gymnasium and started apprenticeship with a grocer, but two years later he became ill and had to enter the tuberculosis sanatorium Grafenhof. In the same year his grandfather died, and a year later his mother. While at the sanatorium Bernhard began to write poetry, short narratives, and plays. After being released from the sanatorium, he began his studies in music and acting at the Mozarteum Academy in Salzburg, where he completed a thesis on Artaud and Brecht. While studying he also worked as a courtroom reporter for the leftist newspaper *Demokratisches Volksblatt* (Salzburg). From 1957 on Bernhard turned to literature and traveled extensively in Europe, especially in Poland and England. In 1965 he settled on a farm in Ohlsdorf (Upper Austria).

Together with his fellow countryman Peter Handke, Thomas Bernhard is the most prolific author in contemporary German literature. He had an obscure and modest start. His first literary publications, *Die heiligen drei Könige von St. Vitus* (The Three Wise Men of St. Vitus, 1955); *Der Schweinehüter* (The Swineherd, 1956), almost went unnoticed. These early works contained most of the topics and motifs that were to become Bernhard's trademarks in later stories and novels: despair over the coldness of the world, the dreariness of a chaotic globe devoid of God, and the attempt of isolated individuals to break through their isolation at least temporarily by the use of language. Bernhard's characteristic reduction of language is evident even in this early writing. After the publication of three volumes of poetry reflecting melancholy and suffering—*Auf der Erde und in der Hölle* (On Earth and in Hell, 1957); *In hora mortis* (In the Hour of Death, 1958); *Unter dem Eisen des Mondes* (Under the Iron of the Moon, 1958); and the stage text *Die rosen der einöde* (The Roses of the Wilderness, 1959)—Bernhard turned to prose fiction and won his first critical recognition. In *Frost* (1963), the report of a medical student about a doomed painter, and in *Amras* (1964), another story about illness, Bernhard uses Novalis' motto "the essence of sickness is as dark as the essence of life." In *Verstörung* (Perturbation, translated as *Gargoyles,* 1967), a collection of stories on illness, brutality, and crime, there is a monologue of a mental patient who ventures into "infinite space." The narrator is the son of a doctor with whom his father visits small villages in Steiermark (a possible influence of Hemingway's stories comes to mind). The patients respond in various ways according to their social backgrounds, their illnesses, their levels of sensitivity, and their degrees of literacy. But for the son, a student of mathematics, they all serve as introductions into the essence of illness. The sick visitations turn into a demonstration of a general perturbation culminating with the visit of the sick prince who, in a monologue, recognizes the senselessness of the world and of his own efforts to improve it, but also intuits the approach of his own mental and physical decline.

After a number of works that appeared at short intervals—*Die Jause* (The Afternoon Snack, 1965); *Prosa,* 1967; *Ungemach* (Trouble, 1968); *An der Baumgrenze* (At the Timber Line, 1969); *Watten* (Mud Flats, 1969); *Ereignisse* (Events, 1970)—Bernhard wrote in his first major novel, *Das Kalkwerk* (The Lime Works, 1970), about yet another catastrophe. It is the story of the murderer Konrad who has killed his crippled wife and, retired into his lime works, tries in vain to express the motives for his deed. For the first time in Bernhard's work, an element of grotesque humor arises from the contrast between the active and the contemplative life, represented by the existence of Konrad on the one hand, and of his wife on the other. The novel is, metaphorically speaking, the depiction of an artist's existence in an epoch of thorough utilitarianism. The lime works contain the abso-

lute antitheses of the artist's existence: they are his asylum as well as his prison, his idyll and his hell, the condition for his being able to write down his experiences and at the same time the guarantee of his failure.

In 1970 Thomas Bernhard shocked the theater world with his first play, *Ein Fest für Boris* (A Party for Boris), which, in an obvious reference to Artaud's theater of cruelty, is written for fifteen cripples in wheelchairs, their legs amputated, planning a celebration for one of their own. Again, grotesque humor prevails in a world of utter despair and imprisonment. The sickness which afflicts the characters of Bernhard's second and third plays is art, or rather, the pursuit of artistic virtuosity for its own sake. In *Der Ignorant und der Wahnsinnige* (The Ignoramus and the Madman, 1972) a brilliant opera singer has perfected herself into a self-obsessed *Koloraturmaschine* (singing machine). Yet her pathological concern with technical perfection eventually makes her fail in her career, which leads to the author's conclusion: "We can only exist by taking our minds off the fact that we exist." In *Die Macht der Gewohnheit* (The Force of Habit, 1974), the theme of obsessive perfectionism is treated in a somewhat lighter manner. It takes place in a circus where a relentless ring master satisfies his pretensions to "high art" by drilling an assortment of circus artists into an ensemble of virtuosi. The reference to Herbert von Karajan and the culture industry of the Salzburg Festivals (where *Der Ignorant* was first produced and booed) reflect Bernhard's ambiguous relationship to Austria in general and to his hometown Salzburg in particular. His dramas have been called "satyr-plays to his novels" (Bernhard Sorg) because they deal with the same topics, such as dissolution (*Ein Fest für Boris*), darkness (*Der Ignorant und der Wahnsinnige*), dullness (*Die Macht der Gewohnheit*), and death (*Der Präsident* (The President, 1975). In *Die Jagdgesellschaft* (The Hunting Party, 1974) an aging general is confronted with the fact that after his having wasted his life he is already spiritually dead: "Life is a torment, . . . on the other hand only in our states of fear do we really face up to ourselves." The "Worldimprover" (*Der Weltverbesserer,* 1979) is a latter-day Voltaire waiting in self-enchantment and hypochondria for the visit of academic dignitaries who are to bestow upon him an honorary degree. This is a repetition of the topic of hypocrisy and public award-giving as treated in Bernhard's hilarious comedy *Immanuel Kant* (1978) in which the immortal philosopher travels by ocean liner to New York to receive an honorary doctorate from Columbia University. Kant is accompanied by his wife and a parrot who preserves the philosophical theses of his master for posterity while the latter is engaged in endless pseudo-intellectual small talk with his fellow passengers. *Vor dem Ruhestand* (Before Retirement, 1979) also focuses on a single festive moment: Himmler's birthday, commemorated every year by Judge Rudolf Höller (the name contains a reference to hell in contrast to "Himmler" which, grotesquely, implies the meaning of "heaven") and his two incarcerated sisters.

Honors and public recognition have been awarded to Bernhard himself, who has accepted them cynically. After receiving many honors— the Oesterreichische Staatspreis für Literatur (1967), the Anton-Wildgans-Preis der Österreichischen Industrie (1967), the Georg-Büchner-Preis (1970), and the Franz-Theodor-Csokor-Preis (1972)—Bernhard set out to dispel any notion that he approves of the mores of official Austria. In *Der Stimmenimitator* (The Voice-mime, 1980) he depicts an Austrian mentality which is far removed from the proverbial Viennese charm and elegance. In a miniature, anecdote-like sketches of persons and places, of macabre, farcial, and grotesque incidents, he paints the picture of a merciless, inhumane, and humorless society of hypocrites and philistines. In 1975 Bernhard started a series of autobiographical stories which cover the first nineteen years of his life in great detail. In five volumes—*Die Ursache* (The Cause, 1975); *Der Keller* (The Basement, 1976); *Der Atem* (The Breath, 1978); *Die Kälte* (The Cold, 1981); *Ein Kind* (A Child, 1983)—he goes back in time until he reaches his earliest childhood memories (*Ein Kind*). His intention clearly is a reckoning with his country, his time, and his contemporaries. The autobiographical stories serve as a kind of footnote to Bernhard's literary work: we find out about the illegitimacy of his birth, which caused his mother to hide in Holland to escape the scandal of being an unwed mother in her own village. We hear about wartime and Allied bombings in Salzburg, about Nazi Austria, brutal schooling, tuberculosis, the Catholicism of Salzburg, which is seen by Bernhard as the passive form of Fascism, and the cracked myth of Salzburg as a beautiful center of culture. "My home city," he concludes in *Der Keller*, "is in reality a deadly disease." In *Der Atem* he describes the horrible bungling by the doctors who treated his pleurisy and explains his recovery as an act of will. A further description of the excruciating ineptitude of doctors follows in *Die Kälte*. The provocation of the autobiographical works lies in the fact that they are as close to the truth as Bernhard feels he can get. The ring of personal authenticity more than compensates for the impossibility of historical truth. As Bernhard put it in *Der Keller*:

What I am describing here is the truth and yet it is not the truth, because it cannot be the truth. In all our reading we have never read a sentence of truth, no matter how many books we have read about actual events. Lies are repeatedly presented as truth, the truth as lies et cetera. It's a question of *whether we want to lie or tell and write the truth*, even if it can never be the truth, never is the truth.

Most recently Bernhard has returned to what one critic called "the perfidiously perfect syntactical construction" of his prose fiction. In *Beton* (*Concrete*, 1983) Bernhard again lashes out against hypocrisy and vulgarity in Austria, which he calls the stinking public lavatory of Europe, yet he also describes the problem of a writer (the protagonist Rudolf who actually plans to write about Felix Mendelssohn but ends up writing *Beton*) who is a successful member of a much despised society, biting the hand that is feeding him, a misanthrope whose despair ironically also turns against his own hypochondriac obsession: "The question is really only how we are to survive the winter as painlessly as possible. And the much crueller spring. And summer we have always hated. Then autumn takes everything away from us again."

Among the literary influences on Bernhard (he mentions Robert Walser; George Steiner refers to parallels in the sadomasochistic Austria of Robert Musil's *Young Törless*), repeated references to Wittgenstein were obvious long before his most recent essay on *Wittgenstein's Neffe: Eine Freundschaft* (Wittgenstein's Nephew: A Friendship, 1983), consisting of a seamless block of one paragraph, 164 pages long. Like Büchner and Kleist before him, Bernhard proves himself a master of the accelerating monotone whose anaphoric power, as it was the case with Kafka, devastates the reader. In *Wittgenstein's Neffe*, the genius of the nephew is pitted against the fame of his uncle. Bernhard's own conclusion bears, as usual, autobiographical features:

The one, Ludwig, was *perhaps* more philosophical; the other, Paul, was *perhaps* crazier. But it may be that we only believe the one Wittgenstein to have been a philosopher because he made public his philosophy and not his derangement, whereas we believe the other, Paul, to have been mad only because he suppressed and did not publish his philosophy but made visible his derangement.

Ingeborg Bachmann, the great Austrian poet who, like Bernhard, was influenced by Wittgenstein, was one of the first critics to recognize the importance and literary rank of her fellow countryman. In 1969 she wrote about Bernhard's novels: "How closely these books are depicting their time (a result that is not intentioned by the author), only a later time will be able to appreciate, in the same way as only a later time was able to appreciate Kafka. In these books everything is precise, of a most ominous precision. Only, we do not know yet the situation which is described here so precisely; that is, we do not know ourselves. . . . The novels are full of pathos, provided one still knows what this word really means: they are full of suffering, and the bearable and the unbearable are closely related to it. Above all, since there is more than one expected and there is so little to expect in these times, there is a great embarrassment in the end. Is there anything laudable here? Is there a coming fame, the fame of German literature which, like everyone else, had to wait for its sidereal times?"

WORKS IN ENGLISH TRANSLATION: English translations of Thomas Bernhard's writings include Richard and Clara Winston's *Gargoyles* in 1970; Sophie Wilkins' *The Lime Works,* 1973; Neville and Stephen Plaice's *The Force of Habit: A Comedy,* 1976; Sophie Wilkins' *Corrections,* 1979; and David McLintock's *Concrete,* 1984.

ABOUT: Cassell's Encyclopedia of World Literature, 1973; Columbia Dictionary of Modern European Literature, 1980; Contemporary Authors 85–88, 1980; Encyclopedia of World Literature in the 20th Century (rev. ed.) I, 1981. *Periodicals*—German Life and Letters 25, 1971–72; Modern Austrian Literature 11 (1978); Modern Drama January 1981; New York Times Book Review July 1, 1984.

BERRY, WENDELL (ERDMAN) (August 5, 1934–   ), American poet, novelist, and agriculturalist, was born in Henry County, in the north-central part of Kentucky, northeast of Louisville. He attended the University of Kentucky at Lexington, earning both his bachelor's (1956) and master's (1957) degrees there. From 1964 to 1977 he was a faculty member at that institution.

After several years of living in New York City, Berry decided to return permanently to Port Royal, Kentucky, the hill country where he was born. He settled on a small farm which had once been part of the land his family owned, and worked it. With his several books of published poetry and his essays on agriculture, Berry has become a highly respected figure in the ecological movement (Noel Perrin calls him one of the "gurus" of the environmental movement) concerned to demonstrate, as he wrote in the preface to one of his best-known books, *The Unsettling of America,* "that agriculture is an integral part of the structure, both biological and cultural, that sustains human life, and that you cannot disturb one part of that structure without disturbing all of it."

Berry's novels, *Nathan Coulter, A Place on Earth,* and *The Memory of Old Jack,* are straightforward character studies of honest

WENDELL BERRY

country people. In the last-named of these, Jack Beechum, a ninety-two-year-old farmer, moves slowly and reflectively through the last day of his life, reexperiencing the pain of his loveless childhood, his unhappy yet lasting marriage, and a sad love affair; the reader is always conscious of his deep identification with the land he has worked on all his life. Beechum's original, according to Berry, was his own father. R. E. Clayton praised the novel's "masterfully controlled style at once simple and taut" and its "characters who rise from the printed page of vibrant life in elegant richness of detail." Greil Marcus thought the book's genius lies "in Berry's voice, a tone that harmonizes Beechum's adventures into the past with his last hours in the present."

Critics have tended to divide rather sharply over the merits of Berry's poetry. Hayden Carruth discerned two strains in his work: "long-line poems that approximate very loosely to blank verse, and short-line poems in acutely toned and measured phrasings, influenced by the work of Denise Levertov." To R. W. French, "Berry's poems are pastorals of withdrawal, advising us to retreat to the earth, where salvation may be found. . . . What can a man do in times of crisis? He can enrich the earth. . . . What Berry is talking about, finally, is a sense of culture." Others have expressed irritation at the prosy flatness of the poems' language, at the unmodulated way in which Berry pursues his single theme. Reviewing *Farming: A Hand Book,* William H. Pritchard complained, "Eventually one feels smothered in goodness and sincere human response to The Land. . . . In general, everything is so designedly moving and humble and always wise, so wise that I could only feel depressed." Edwin Fussell, writing of *The Country of Marriage,* was antagonized by the poems' easy certainty: "Berry appears to have no politics, except implicitly. I am bored, annoyed, angry (by turns), with his male chauvinism, obsessions with male primogeniture, and all the blather about marriage with virtually no reference to women. I like even less statements that the Berrys have labored this land six generations, meaning, I suppose, that a Californian can't understand either the land or the Berrys."

Yet *The Country of Marriage* in many ways shows the author at his best. His sense of the interconnectedness of all living things reverberates even through an account of the birth of a domestic animal:

He stands, and his legs
wobble. After the months
of his pursuit of her, now
they meet face to face.
From the beginnings of the world
his arrival and her welcome
have been prepared. They have always
known each other.
                                        ("Her First Calf")

And there is the frequent appearance in this book of one of Berry's most engaging personas, the Mad Farmer, an ironic character much given to final-sounding pronouncements. In "Manifesto: The Mad Farmer Liberation Front," the poem's beginning is angry and derisive, an echo, perhaps, of the life Berry left behind when he came back to the farm, the way of the outside world:

Love the quick profit, the annual raise,
vacation with pay. Want more
of everything ready made. Be afraid.
to know your neighbors and to die.
And you will have a window in your head.
Not even your future will be a mystery
any more. Your mind will be punched in a
    card
and shut away in a little drawer.
When they want you to buy something
they will call you. When they want you
to die for profit they will let you know.

Similar high spirits may be found in the collection *Sayings & Doings,* which contains "Uncle Red Milton and the Pup," a lengthy poem with a hilarious ending, and such short sketches as this untitled exchange between a country farmer and his child:

"Pap, health officer said
you got to get them damn
hogs out of the house.
It ain't healthy."
"You tell that sonavabitch
I've raised a many
a hog in this house,
and ain't lost one yet."

Such earthy humor is generally not to be found in Berry's books of essays, where he is at his most earnest. *The Hidden Wound* is a reflection on racism in America, centered on his own remembered relations with the black people who worked on his grandfather's farm. J. W. Hattmann called the book "a sensitive and convincing study of the terrible harm the white man does to himself by the evil of his racism. It is compassionate and understanding in its approach, but it insists that white America must cease to exist as a racist society or it will destroy itself." In *A Continuous Harmony: Essays Cultural and Agricultural,* Berry treats, among other subjects, contemporary American nature poets, among whom he names Gary Snyder, Denise Levertov, and A. R. Ammons. They "characteristically approach their subject with an openness of spirit and imagination, allowing the meaning and the movement of the poem to suggest themselves out of the facts. Their art has an implicit and essential humility, a reluctance to impose on things as they are, a willingness to relate to the world as student and servant, a wish to be included in the natural order rather than to 'conquer nature,' a wish to discover the natural form rather than to create new forms that would be exclusively human." The primary theme of *The Unsettling of America: Culture & Agriculture* is the imminent and probably inevitable "deliverance of American agriculture into the hands of corporations. The cost of this corporate totalitarianism in energy, land, and social disruption will be enormous." Berry then shows a clear understanding of what America has come to mean to many ecologists: the betrayal of all values for the sake of the dollar: "If it does happen, we are familiar enough with the nature of American salesmanship to know that it will be done in the name of the starving millions, in the name of liberty, justice, democracy, and brotherhood, and to free the world from communism. We must, I think, be prepared to see, and to stand by the truth: that the land should not be destroyed for *any* reason, not even for any apparently good reason." In *The Gift of Good Land: Further Essays Cultural and Agricultural,* Berry reports having seen on his travels away from Port Royal proof that good farms and farmers still exist, and that an ecologically responsible agriculture is indeed possible, despite the continued ascendancy of agribusiness in the world. In a review of this book, Roger B. Swain wrote, "Although Berry's thinking runs clear and deep, he is the first to admit that 'solutions have perhaps the most furtive habits of any creatures,' and adds his own prejudice that 'they reveal themselves very hesitantly in artificial light, and never enter air-conditioned rooms.'"

In 1982–83 Northpoint Press published three books by Berry—poems, essays, and a revised, shortened version of his earlier novel *A Place on Earth*. Noel Perrin, reviewing all three in the *New York Times Book Review*, found the novel the best of them—"magical," tender, comic, tragic, with "an overwhelming sense of place . . . a masterpiece." Perrin was pleased with but not as enthusiastic about *Standing by Words*, a collection of Berry's essays, mainly on poetry—an unpretentious, "eloquent and clear" group, "very much out of harmony with the prevailing thought of our time," which will not persuade "the fashionable majority." Berry's collection of poems, *The Wheel*, Perrin found "no worse and perhaps a little better" than his earlier poems. Some of them "seem indistinguishable from prose," but one long poem, "Elegy," in Perrin's judgment, "is a true addition to our literature."

Berry married Tanya Amyx in 1957; they have a daughter and a son. He has received a Rockefeller fellowship (1965), the Bess Hokin prize given by *Poetry* magazine (1967), and a grant in 1969 from the National Endowment for the Arts.

PRINCIPAL WORKS: *Poetry*—November Twenty-six, Nineteen Hundred Sixty-three, 1964; The Broken Ground, 1964; Openings, 1969; Findings, 1969; Farming: A Hand Book, 1970; The Country of Marriage, 1973; The Eastward Look, 1974; To What Listens, 1975; Sayings & Doings, 1975; The Kentucky River, 1976; There Is Singing Around Me, 1976; Clearing, 1977; Three Memorial Poems, 1977; A Part, 1980; The Wheel, 1982. *Novels*—Nathan Coulter, 1960; A Place on Earth, 1967 (revised ed. 1983); The Memory of Old Jack, 1974. *Non-fiction*—The Long-legged House, 1969; The Hidden Wound, 1970; The Unforeseen Wilderness: An Essay on Kentucky's Red River Gorge, 1971; A Continuous Harmony, 1972; The Unsettling of America, 1977; The Gift of Good Land, 1981; Standing By Words, 1983.

ABOUT: Contemporary Authors 73–76, 1978; Dictionary of Literary Biography: American Poets Since World War II, Part 1, 1980; Vinson, J. (ed.) Contemporary Poets, 1980. *Periodicals*—Atlantic October 1977; Best Sellers December 1, 1970; March 15, 1974; Choice April 1974; June 1974; October 1977; Christian Science Monitor September 30, 1981; Library Journal August 1969; August 1970; September 1, 1970; December 15, 1972; January 15, 1974; February 15, 1977; July 1977; September 15, 1980; Nation November 9, 1970; September 28, 1974; National Review November 14, 1977; New Republic April 6, 1974; New York Times Book Review March 31, 1974; November 25, 1977; December 20, 1981; December 18, 1983; Parnassus Spring/Summer 1974; Poetry November 1970; May 1974; Times Literary Supplement April 10, 1981; Virginia Quarterly Review Winter 1971; Autumn 1974.

*BERTON, PIERRE (July 12, 1920–   ), Canadian journalist, historian, and television personality, is the son of Francis George Berton and Linda (Thompson) Berton. His father, a civil engineer and amateur naturalist, was one of the thousands who converged on Dawson in the late 1890s to seek their fortune in the great Klondike gold rush. Like most, he found no gold, but he stayed in the Northwest, becoming the government's registrar of mining claims and, for a time, one of the area's few dentists. Berton was born in Whitehorse on the Yukon River and spent his youth in Dawson, by then in rapid economic decline from its brief heyday as the Mecca of the Canadian Klondike.

In a 1970 *Maclean's* magazine article, Berton recalled that, as a writer, he was "hooked early. I was telling stories aloud to my parents at the age of four and writing them down on paper as soon as I learned to spell." He regularly published his own small newspapers, even during his hitch with the Canadian Army during World War II, so, when he escaped from the dreary life of Dawson to the relatively bustling city of Vancouver as a young man, he naturally entered journalism. After graduating from the University of British Columbia, he joined the *Vancouver News Herald* (1941–42), then the *Vancouver Sun* (1946–47), where he was chief reporter. A glib stylist and talented organizer who found the act of writing "fun," Berton often wrote six stories a day. Scott Young of *Maclean's* lured him away to Toronto in 1947; by 1958 he was the magazine's managing editor. From 1958 to 1962 he was associate editor and daily columnist for the *Toronto Daily Star*.

The Royal Family, Berton's first book, had modest Canadian sales. The next two, *The Golden Trail: The Story of the Klondike Rush* and *The Mysterious North*, provided background which he used to write *The Klondike Fever*, a commercial and critical success. Reviewers immediately accepted *The Klondike Fever* as the definitive popular history of the period, capturing, according to Maurice Dolbier, the gold rush's "abysmal foolishness and incredible bravery, [which had] some of the qualities of an epic and many of the cliches of the dime novel." Berton grounded his book in personal knowledge of the Klondike as well as determined digging into old newspapers and public documents, unpublished journals, diaries and period autobiographies, and the occasional lucky interview—as when he discovered one of the last surviving "Klondike Queens," now a wizened old woman, living in a suburb of Seattle. This painstaking preparation, wrote Dolbier, enabled Berton to separate "the lively and astonishing facts from the dross of Klondike fictions. . . . This last

°bâr tôN

PIERRE BERTON

segments and interviewed some 2,000 guests;
their remarks were not edited in postproduction,
giving the show a freshness and bite lacking in
similar American programs. Berton, who had
quickly absorbed each guest's background and
issues on the morning of the show, would invariably ask pertinent questions and ferret out the
areas of greatest controversy. When his own interest was aroused, usually in matters of Canadian history, Berton himself became the
entertainer, expounding volubly and with animation on odd bits of historical lore.

As an author, Berton struck gold with his best-
selling two-volume chronicle of the heroic construction of the Canadian Pacific Railroad, *The
National Dream, 1871–1881* and *The Last Spike,
1881–1885,* finished in 1971. Ecstatically received in Canada—one reviewer revealingly
called it "a terrifically *enviable* achievement"—Berton's history garnered equally good
notices in the United States, where books on
purely Canadian subjects are rarely reviewed,
much less read. "Berton is Canada's most widely
read nonfiction author," noted *Library Journal,*
"and this history demonstrates why. He is always
readable, and at times his prose has real grandeur; he is lucid, making easy sense of political
and financial complexities; and he has a splendid
sense of humor, good timing, and an ear for interesting anecdotes. To all of this, he adds here
a firm grasp of the history of the period." William French of the *Toronto Globe and Mail* perceived an overall pattern to Berton's choice of
subjects. "It's clear that when Pierre Berton
wrote [*The Klondike Fever*] . . . he embarked
on the major literary work of his career. The
grand design of that work is now emerging—an
epic, multi-volume history of the opening and
settlement of the Canadian West after Confed-
eration. . . . Berton, consciously or not, is accomplishing in these books what few other
historians writing about Canada have been able
to achieve—instill in his readers a compelling
sense of our heritage." The two volumes, plus a
lavishly illustrated abridgement, constituted
something of a publishing phenomenon in Canada, selling in excess of 250,000 copies.

great gold rush was one of the oddest chapters
in the history of modern man, and in Pierre Berton it has received its best historian." A National
Film Board documentary on the gold rush, *City
of Gold* (1958), which Berton wrote and narrated, won forty awards, including the Grand Prix
at Cannes. In 1972 the author made use of the
material yet again—his frank recycling and revision of earlier work has enabled him to produce a book a year since 1960 while carrying on
several other careers—in *Klondike: The Last
Great Gold Rush, 1896–1899.*

In the early and mid-1960s Berton published
several collections of his newspaper and magazine articles and a number of genial attacks on
the stodgier aspects of Canadian society, notably
The Comfortable Pew, a wry look at religious
conservatism, and *The Smug Minority,* a kind of
socialist-populist critique of Canada's capitalist
upper classes (to which Berton, by this time, belonged). Given their controversial subjects, both
were surprising commercial successes. Even a
cookbook written in 1966 with his wife, a restaurant owner, did well and was reissued in 1972.

Not only as a best-selling author, but also as a
regular contributor to *Maclean's,* a member of
the board of McClelland and Stewart, one of
Canada's largest publishing houses, editor-in-
chief of the Canadian Centennial Library, a daily radio commentator, the host of two television
talk shows, and a panelist on a third, the energetic Berton completely dominated Toronto publishing and journalism circles in the 1960s and
1970s. During its twelve-year run, "The Pierre
Berton Show" was the most popular non-
network show in Canada. The host taped 1,600

In 1973 Berton left his television shows—he
claimed, out of boredom—to concentrate on his
writing and to finish work on the eight-part CBC
adaptation of *The National Dream,* which he
narrated. Widely praised by Canadian reviewers—critic Blaik Kirkby typically called it "a series which will be talked about for years and will
stimulate many Canadians to feel a chest-
swelling pride in their nation"—for its historical
scope and accuracy and its high-quality production, the series was, with Berton's full support,
intended to prove that Canadian television could

equal American programming in technical polish and exceed it in depth.

Berton himself made a trip with his family into his own past in 1972, taking power rubber rafts down the Yukon River to Whitehorse and Dawson. He wrote of the expedition in *Drifting Home,* in which, according to Scott Young, "we meet him really where he lives, as we all do, in a complicated web of family legend, fact and experience, and understand better the things in life that have made him, at one extreme, an iconoclast, and at the other, a very gentle man." *The Dionne Years: A Thirties Melodrama,* an account of the unusual public furore over quintuplets born in Ontario during the Depression, marked something of a departure for him. The Dionne children were plagued from birth by manipulative doctors, pushy journalists, eager promoters, and legions of the idly curious. Ironically, despite the Dionnes' personal humiliations, the hordes of tourists who traveled to Ontario to catch a glimpse of them infused the region with desperately needed cash, saving it from bankruptcy. Novelist Margaret Atwood thought the book "a compulsive read," but also felt that while reading it "you have the greasy feeling that by doing so you become part of that snoopy exploitation which has dogged the Dionnes all their lives, and which you, of course, do not approve. But if such a book should be, *The Dionne Years* is all such a book should be." Berton's central concern, she continued, was "what causes the public, at any given time, to adopt this or that figure, this or that hero or heroine, as its symbol and totem."

Berton tackled the Canadian-American conflict during the War of 1812 in *The Invasion of Canada 1812–1813* and *Flames Across the Border: The Canadian-American Tragedy 1813–1814.* The author was, in the words of Doug Fetherling, "at the height of his powers" when chronicling the ultimately unsuccessful campaign of "a bunch of American yahoos—warlike, intemperate, ignorant for the most part" against the "bridesmaid" of Britain, Canada. (Several critics have noted that Berton has made American depredations on Canada a central theme of his works.) Though ostensibly "social history," the books were faulted for their characteristic emphasis on anecdote and swift character sketches over solid socio-historical analysis; nonetheless, the majority of reviewers agreed with R. L. Burr's opinion that "American and Canadian readers alike will be delighted by this admirable account of . . . 'the strangest of all the wars fought by the English-speaking people.'"

Berton married Janet Walker in 1946; they have five daughters and two sons and currently live in Kleinburg, near Toronto. Explaining his fascination with Canadian history, Berton told Blaik Kirkby in 1971: "One of the reasons I write about Canadian subjects is that I am trying to show Canadians who we are. A lot of people are going to psychiatrists because they're rootless and they don't know who they are, and this is true of nations, too.

"That's why Canadians have been lacking in confidence. The only way to find it is to go back to our childhood, 1867 and beyond, and find out who we are."

PRINCIPAL WORKS: The Royal Family, 1954; The Golden Trail: The Story of the Klondike Gold Rush (U.S., Stampede for Gold), 1955; The Mysterious North, 1956; The Klondike Fever, 1958; Just Add Water and Stir, 1959; Adventures of a Columnist, 1960; (with Henri Rossier) The New City: A Prejudicial View of Toronto, 1961; The Secret World of Og (juvenile), 1961; Fast Fast Fast Relief, 1962; The Big Sell, 1963; The Comfortable Pew, 1965; My War with the Twentieth Century, 1965; The Centennial Food Guide, 1966 (also as Pierre and Janet Berton's Food Guide, 1974); Remember Yesterday, 1966; The Cool, Crazy Committed World of the Sixties, 1966; The Smug Minority, 1968; A Pierre Berton Omnibus (collection), 1969; The National Drama 1871–1881, 1970; The Last Spike 1881–1885, 1971; The Impossible Railway: The Building of the Canadian Pacific, 1972; Klondike: The Last Great Gold Rush 1896–1899, 1972; Drifting Home, 1973; Hollywood's Canada: The Americanization of the National Image, 1975; The Dionne Years: A Thirties Melodrama, 1977; The Wild Frontier, 1978; The Invasion of Canada 1812–1813, 1980; Flames Across the Border: The Canadian-American Tragedy 1813–1814, 1981; Why We Act Like Canadians, 1982. *As editor*—Historic Headlines: A Century of Canadian News Dramas, 1967.

ABOUT: Canadian Who's Who, 1983; Contemporary Authors, new revision series 2, 1980; Oxford Companion to Canadian Literature, 1983. *Periodicals*—Library Journal September 15, 1980; Maclean's March 1968; September 1970; October 12, 1981; September 1984; New York Herald Tribune October 25, 1958; New York Review of Books October 26, 1978; New York Times January 19, 1979; New York Times Book Review November 12, 1972; December 10, 1978; Saturday Night November 1970; November 1971; October 1977; Toronto Globe and Mail June 14, 1958; September 14, 1970; November 20, 1971; September 23, 1972; May 28, 1973; September 22, 1973; September 28, 1973; March 1, 1974; May 8, 1978.

*BICHSEL, PETER (March 24, 1935–), Swiss short story writer, novelist, and journalist, was born in Lucerne, the son of Willi Bichsel, a painter, and the former Lina Bieri. He attended the teachers' college in Solothurn, a city to the

°bik´sel

north of Bern, and from 1955 to 1968 taught in primary schools, first in the town of Zuchwil, then in Solothurn. Since 1968 he has devoted all his time to writing.

Bichsel had been writing seriously for several years when, in 1964, he read some of his prose miniatures at a meeting in Sigtuna, Sweden, of Gruppe 47, the well-known German-language writers' conference founded after World War II by Hans Werner Richter and Alfred Andersch and which counted among its most loyal members such writers as Günter Grass, Heinrich Böll, and Uwe Johnson. Bichsel's reductionist language and extreme, almost surreal, stylistic compression, both firmly in the service of a social criticism, made a great impression on the conference's participants.

The stories he read were among the twenty-one published the same year as *Eigentlich möchte Frau Blum den Milchmann kennenlernen* (*And Really Frau Blum Would Very Much Like to Meet the Milkman*), which in 1965 was awarded the Gruppe 47 prize during the conference's annual meeting in Berlin. The length of the title is at comic variance with the book's diminutive size: even with large print and very wide margins, the English-language edition comprised barely eighty-eight pages. The stories are each typically fewer than five hundred words in length and describe situations that may seem ominous or frivolous—sometimes both—but which never expatiate upon the visions or ideas they raise. The point of view in them is never made explicit. "The Milkman," the story from which the book's title is derived, describes the quintessentially banal relationship between a milkman and one of his customers. "The milkman knows the dented pan, it's the one belonging to Frau Blum, she usually takes two liters and a hundred grams of butter. The milkman knows Frau Blum. If anyone were to ask him about her he'd say: 'Frau Blum takes two liters and 100 grams, she has a dented milk-pan and a legible handwriting.' The milkman doesn't worry, Frau Blum doesn't run up any debts. And when it happens—and it can happen—that she leaves one penny less than the right amount, he writes on a scrap of paper: 'One penny short.' Next day he finds the penny without fail and a note saying: 'Sorry.' 'Don't mention it' or 'Never mind,' the milkman thinks then, and would write it on a scrap of paper, and that would amount to a correspondence. He does not write it. . . . " In its original German, the passage is in many ways typical of Bichsel's style, with its frequent use of the subjunctive to indicate possibility or potentiality (usually, and unavoidably, rendered in English by the conditional "would" or "could") and its playing

with various permutations of the verb *kennen* ("to know"). While Frau Blum would like to "know" the milkman better—she doesn't even "know" his name—the milkman "knows" Frau Blum quite as well as he needs to. The bleakness of this carefully modulated social observation is reinforced by the laconic dryness of the author's description. Other stories in the collection treat subjects that are no more or less banal in the same compressed, suggestive manner: in "Herr Gigon" the narrator, with assiduous neutrality, describes a man's religious hypocrisy; "The Knife" tells a new convict's one-sided encounter with a prison guard; in "San Salvador" a man, trying out a new fountain pen, writes a farewell note to his wife, but he is waiting for her as usual when she returns home. In one anomalous story, however, "The Animal Lover," the narrator is strongly present, as is a febrile note of authorial irony, as he describes "another opportunity to write down the story about the animal lover, the story about the man with the two dogs, the story about the man who takes the dogs for a walk. . . . When no other story occurs to me I look for the one about the animal lover. I have the impression that it's turning into my story, that it's inevitable. . . . What is disagreeable is having to write a story, and having to write this particular story, being under a compulsion. That's why I let the opportunity pass again..."

The same situation—a writer at a loss for a subject—is a theme of Bichsel's most important novel, *Die Jahreszeiten* (The Seasons, 1968). A man tries, and continually fails, to write a novel. He minutely describes his house and the way the seasons change its appearance, quotes extensively from insurance policies and manuals of house painting, lists his many household rules and regulations, and mulls over what characters he might or might not include in his narrative, which is never in fact completed, or even really begun. "It is an anti-novel," wrote the reviewer for the *Times Literary Supplement*, "in the sense of querying the traditional values of fiction. But he has a sense of the inevitable: one never feels that the author does anything for the sake of being different; one knows that this is the only way he can write and one respects him for it, hard as he makes it for us to follow him." The same reviewer commented extensively on Bichsel's style, which in its "peculiar blend of melancholy and caprice" seems very like Gertrude Stein's. "His vocabulary, like hers, is sparse to the point of miserliness. His sentences receive their tensile strength from omissions. We read on, fascinated, wondering what it is that he wants to hide from us, only to discover that he hides nothing: he simply sees the world that way, as a pattern of diminutively few verifiable points strung together by elastic bonds of assumption. Caught in this spiderweb are the creatures of whom he writes." Siegfried Mandel, however, in *Die Jahreszeiten,* thought less highly of Bichsel's work: "[Here] the limited range of his technique and his materials becomes obvious and the narrations fail to muster the earlier charm and unpretentious tenderness. A recipe, even a tasty soufflé, cannot be indefinitely repeated without losing its original novelty, which is the case, I am afraid, with Bichsel's miniatures. Perhaps Bichsel's manner is too self-conscious, and instead of letting the reader discover essences, he reveals his own discovery of them and blurs the edges of fiction with his prose commentary."

An even shorter book than his first story collection is his second, *Kindergeschichten,* 1969 (*Stories for Children*; translated in U.S as *There Is No Such Place as America*). These seven stories, considerably more developed than the sketches in his earlier work, feature characters whose dilemmas seem markedly more universal in their description of experience, more emblematic of the human condition. The best pieces treat the difficulty of communication and the personalness and intractability of language. "A Table Is a Table" is about an old man "who has given up talking, who has a tired face, too tired for smiling and too tired for frowning." Enraged at the sameness of his life, he finds a new happiness in giving everyday things new names, but the names he chooses are of other everyday things. "Then he learned the new names for all kinds of things and forgot more and more of the right ones. He now had a new language that belonged to him alone. Now and again he began to dream in the new language, and then he translated the songs of his school days into his own language and sang them softly to himself. But soon even translating became difficult for him, he had almost forgotten his old language. . . . And he was frightened of talking to people. He had to search his mind for a long time for the names that people call things. . . . And that's why he gave up talking. He kept quiet, spoke only to himself, no longer so much as nodded to people when he passed them." "The Man with the Memory" tells of a human phenomenon who memorizes thousands of railroad timetables, then deliberately forgets all he has learned in order to travel everywhere "so as to count the steps of stairs all over the world, to know something that nobody knows and no official can look up in books." "Jodok Sends His Love" is a charming fantasy in which the narrator tells of his late grandfather who spoke constantly about his own brother Jodok and came eventually to call everyone and everything by that name. "He no longer said: 'I've quite an appetite today,' but 'I've

quite a Jodok today.' Later he gave up saying 'I,' but instead: 'Jodok has quite a Jodok today.' . . . And even if at the end he couldn't say anything but Jodok, the two of us always got on very well. I was very young and grandfather was very old, he sat me on his knees and jodoked Jodok the Jodok of Jodok Jodok—that is, 'He told me the story of Uncle Jodok,' and I enjoyed the story very much. . . . But I'm very sorry to say that this story isn't true, my grandfather wasn't a liar, nor did he live to a great age." The reviewer for the *Times Literary Supplement* described the components of this collection as "brilliantly executed variations on basic human conditions, which pinpoint the moral complexities of life, . . . characterized by supremely deceptive simplicity. These plain, unadorned sentences embrace universal life and truth, describing attitudes and states of mind rather than events; a lot happens, and nothing happens. Bichsel is not interested in reality, but in the relationship individuals have to it."

Bichsel is the author of a regular column in *Zürcher Woche,* a popular weekly, in which he is much more overt than in his stories in criticizing what he sees as the boring stolidity of his countrymen and their institutions. "Literature is political," he has written, "in the sense that it holds a dialogue with men . . . and occupation with language in itself is always a form of one's occupation with humans."

Bichsel married Therese Spörri in 1956; they have a daughter and a son.

WORKS IN ENGLISH TRANSLATION: Michael Hamburger has translated two collections of Bichsel's stories: *And Really Frau Blum Would Very Much Like to Meet the Milkman,* 1968, and *There Is No Such Place as America* (U.K. *Stories for Children*), 1969.

ABOUT: Columbia Dictionary of Modern European Literature, 1980; Contemporary Authors 81–84, 1980; Mandel, S. Group 47: The Reflected Intellect, 1973. *Periodicals*—Christian Science Monitor August 14, 1969; Times Literary Supplement November 7, 1968; July 11, 1971.

*BIOY CASARES, ADOLFO (September 15, 1914–), Argentinian novelist and short story writer, was born in Buenos Aires to a rich landowners' family and passed his infancy in the city and at the family ranch (*estancia*) in the province of Buenos Aires. A very imaginative boy, he not only invented friends, but also found the evening skies, pictures of dead people, and mirrors to be connections with a marvelous world. He considered the supernatural to be terrifying and sad, but at the same time compelling and at-

bē oy´ käs˝ är res´, ä dol´ fō

tractive. Analogous feelings were awakened in the young Bioy by his readings, which compelled him, at seven years of age upon reading *Petit Bob* by Gyp, to write his plagiarized version, similar even in its typography. During his years in high school he was attracted particularly to mathematics, but his love of writing remained paramount.

Bioy's first literary piece was finished in 1928. It was a "fantastic thriller" entitled *Vanidad o una aventura terrorífica* (Vanity or a Terrifying Adventure), and the following year he published his first short book, entitled *Prólogo* (Prologue). He was then beginning to discover the literature of the Spanish novelists of the nineteenth century, the Bible, Dante's *Commedia,* Joyce's *Ulysses,* and Argentinian classics as well as comic strips and pulp novelettes. Like every Argentinian of the upper classes, he began studies at the School of Law of the University of Buenos Aires, but not being successful then switched to the Faculty of Philosophy and Letters. Nevertheless, he never finished any university career, being most happy managing his father's *estancia.*

In 1932 Bioy met Jorge Luis Borges, starting a close friendship which has lasted till the present, a fruitful relationship from which they jointly created a literary *persona*—H. Bustos Domecq. Borges convinced Bioy that literary creation excluded any other activity. Together they established a publishing firm Destiempo (Against Time), which was totally unsuccessful. During those years Bioy read avidly under Borges' tutelage, giving credit to the literary influences of Johnson, Gibbon, De Quincey, Butler, Stevenson, Kipling, Wells, Conrad, Proust, Hawthorne, James, and, above all, Borges and Kafka. In 1933 he published a book of short stories *Diecisiete disparos contra lo porvenir* (Seventeen Shots at the Future) concealing his identity with a pseudonym. This was followed, in 1935, by *La nueva tormenta* (The New Storm), illustrated by the artist and writer Silvina Ocampo, whom he married in 1940, and subsequently by a book almost every year—*La estatua casera* (The House Statue) in 1936, *Luis Greve, muerto* (Luis Greve, Deceased) in 1937.

Bioy has always denied his first books, so that for him his literary career began in 1940 with the publication of one of the most widely read Argentinian literary classics—*La invención de Morel* (*The Invention of Morel*) which was awarded the Municipal Prize, and was immediately translated into French and Italian. In that same year, Bioy wrote and published, together with Borges and Silvina Ocampo, an important volume—*Antología de la literatura fantástica* (Anthology of Fantastic Literature). In 1942 the first volume of short stories by H. Bustos Domecq appeared—*Seis problemas para Don Isidro Parodi* (Six Problems for Don Isidro Parodi), but it was not well received by the critics, who did not know the identity behind the pseudonym. In 1945, Bioy published one of his best novelettes—*Plan de evasión* (*A Plan for Escape*), and accepted the direction, together with Borges, of a series published by one of the most eminent firms of Argentina, Editorial Emecé. The series, appropriately called *El séptimo círculo* (The Seventh Circle), brought to the Argentinian public the best English thrillers. The next year, Bioy and Silvina Ocampo produced a detective novel—*Los que aman, odian* (Those Who Love, Hate) and, with Borges under the pseudonyms B. Suárez Lynch and H. Bustos Domecq, he wrote *Un modelo para la muerte* (A Model for Death) and *Dos fantasías memorables* (Two Memorable Fantasies). In 1948 appeared a volume of short stories under the title of one of them, *La trama celeste* (The Celestial Plot). The book was a great success and, in Bioy's own perception, it marks the moment in which he had really found his voice. About this time he conceived another novel which was not to be ready for publication until 1954, *El sueño de los héroes* (The Dream of the Heroes). In 1956 appeared *Historia prodigiosa* (Prodigious Story), a collection of six short stories. Three years later another group of short stories appeared under the title *Guirnalda con amores* (Garland with Love), a miscellanea of pieces centered on love, through which Bioy thought to free himself from fantastic literature only to relapse to it again with a book published in 1962, a winner of the second National Literary Award—*El lado de la sombra* (The Side of the Shade). In 1967 appeared another volume of short stories, *El gran Serafín* (The Great Serafim), which won first place in the National Literary Award contest. In 1968 Bioy published a group of critical essays, *La otra aventura* (The Other Adventure) and in 1969 he returned to the novel with a best-seller, *Diario de la guerra del cerdo* (*Diary of the War of the Pig*), followed in 1973 by *Dormir al son* (Asleep in the Sun)—for which he received the much coveted Great Prize by SADE (Argentinian Society of Writers). Many of Bioy's short stories and novels have been made into full length films and/or TV films in his native country and in Italy. Since 1980, Bioy Casares has published *El héroe de las mujeres* (The Women's Hero) and has been working on a new novel—"Irse" (Leaving); "in spite of" himself he continues to write short stories. There is a compilation of some of his writings from 1969 published in Venezuela under the title *Adversos milagros* (Adverse Miracles).

Bioy's first novel, *The Invention of Morel,* is largely responsible for his fame. It is in the form of notes written by a man who, in order to escape police persecution, finds refuge on a presumed desert island in the middle of an ocean. Soon he discovers that on the land there are very strange buildings populated by people who seem totally unaware of his presence. Those people, under very unusual circumstances, seem to take part in a ritual of intrigues and social conventional routines. The escapee falls in love with one of the static figures (Faustine) but finally discovers— after an hallucinatory pilgrimage which confronts him with the fantastic phenomena of parallel suns—that the people are not really human beings. They are only images projected by Morel's complex machine, which is regulated by the sea tides. He also discovers that Morel was able to build a sort of circular paradise in which the actions and the gestures of the figures repeat themselves with the inexorable periodicity of the lunar tides. But before arriving at this conclusion, the character's imagination is populated by a series of suspicions and conjectures which he consigns to a diary, that which we are reading presumably after his death. All of this lends suspense to the narrative and a peculiar, surrealistic atmosphere. It is easy to conjecture that Bioy Casares was paralleling very closely H. G. Wells' *The Island of Dr. Moreau* as well as Jules Verne's *The Castle on the Carpathian Mountains,* in which a scientist creates *homunculi* and uses scientific techniques to reproduce human figures which give the narrative its fantastic overtones. Within the framework of Argentinian literature of the time, *The Invention of Morel* initiated Argentinian science fiction, a genre in which that country has over the last fifty years made the most striking contribution in the Spanish-speaking world. On another level, since secondary to the science-fictional aspect of the book there is a revelation of an enigma and strange, fearful circumstances, *The Invention of Morel* is structurally close to the Gothic novel and the *who-dun-it.* As Jorge Luis Borges states in his foreword to the first edition of Bioy's book: "The odyssey of marvel [that Bioy Casares] unfolds seems to have no possible explanation other than hallucination or symbolism, and he uses a single fantastic but not supernatural postulate to decipher it." Borges ends by flatly asserting that "[t]o classify [*The Invention*] as perfect is neither an imprecision nor a hyperbole."

El perjurio de la nieve ("The Perjury of the Snow"), first published in 1944, is a *novella* which, under the disguise of a mystery, tackles both the problem of the impossibility of understanding reality beyond appearances, as well as the inevitability of interpreting reality in elusive ways due to its multiplicity. Following a sort of circular path, of frames that somehow attract the reader's attention away from the central plot which takes place in a Patagonian *estancia,* one narrator, Bioy Casares, who signs the narration with his own initials, and another narrator called Juan Luis Villafañe, confirm at every step of the tale the ambivalent and unknowable character of reality. The whole tale is a well-designed paradox with allusions to De Quincey, Coleridge, an "occult king of the universe" whose decisive actions are inscrutable, and to the archetypal subject of the eternal return.

Plan de evasión (*A Plan for Escape,* 1945) returns to an atmosphere similar to that of *The Invention of Morel.* Set on Devil's Island at the turn of the century, it is the chronicle of a nightmare with a dual structure: on one hand, it offers the diary of the thoughts evoked in Enrique de Nevers by the strange conduct of Governor Castel, and de Nevers' suspicions of a possible prisoner's rebellion. On the other hand, the novel gives the explanation of the events offered by Governor Castel himself. The narration is thus achieved through different kinds of narrative discourses: the entries of de Nevers' diary, flashbacks of past situations, letters of de Nevers, documentary texts adduced by Governor Castel, and the letter of Xavier Brissac with posthumous clues as to the destiny of the heroic de Nevers. The Governor in this narrative, like Morel in the earlier book, has conceived and constructed a fantasy that envelops the tale, achieved by the author through imagination and a rigorous style.

La trama celeste (The Celestial Plot, 1948) is a volume of short stories; the title story is considered a classic of Spanish science fiction. The plot develops the idea of a plurality of worlds imagined as "bundles of spaces and parallel times" combined with magical elements. It is structured through contrasts of esoteric worlds with a detailed Buenos Aires geography in which streets, squares, parks of the populous city are easily recognizable. An Argentinian test pilot flys his plane from the military airfield of El Palomar, through a "pass" that has somehow made his plane jump to "another world," and, incredibly, he returns from it. The key to this strange event is given indirectly: the work of the French economist and politician Louis Auguste Blanqui, *L'éternité par les astres* (Eternity through the Stars), explains the thesis of parallel universes.

Diario de la guerra del cerdo (*Diary of the War of the Pig,* 1969) is totally different from the earlier narratives. This focusing of Bioy Casares on subjects more connected with Argentinian reality and with the destiny of man had begun in 1954 with the novel *El sueño de los héroes* (The Dream of the Heroes). *Diary* is a somber book because it portrays a world in which man has no right to be old, in which society destroys old age. The novel, nevertheless, as always for this author, has room for love and, perhaps (as the open end might suggest), for hope. Taking place during a week of street fighting in Buenos Aires, the narrative is enhanced by strong characterizations and by the anxieties, humiliating defeats, and terror it depicts.

In *Dormir al sol* (Asleep in the Sun, 1973), Bioy Casares seems to have gone back to the fantastic genre mixed with the mysterious, the gothic, and the pseudoscientific (phrenology). The novel tells the story of Lucio Bordenave, an ex-bank employee and present clock salesman who leads a happy if humdrum life in the petitbourgeois neighborhood of Flores in Buenos Aires. Suddenly—and almost without justifiable reasons—his wife is taken to the Phrenology Institute, a strange place with odd practices. From that moment on, Bordenave's life changes from routine to unbelievable episodes in which he becomes aware that around him strange transfers and mutations of bodies and souls are taking place. Compared with the black irony of *Diary*, this novel is full of light humor and, as the critics have pointed out, Bioy Casares displays sparkling imaginative capacity to create hallucinatory fantasies.

Bioy Casares has confessed that for him life and literature are the same, that he is indebted to books for many intense moments in his life. He writes seriously but with gusto: "I do not know the anguish of the blank page. I always have more subjects than the ones I write about." He usually rewrites his texts several times until achieving the tone he searches for. He believes that in the future the short story will surpass the novel as a literary genre, this because the short story can have all of the excellences of the novel without its defects, mainly its length. Bioy Casares, who lives in Buenos Aires with his wife and daughter, was awarded the coveted Italian Award Mondello, together with the Italian writer Italo Calvino, in 1984.

WORKS IN ENGLISH TRANSLATION: Relatively little of Bioy Casares' work has been translated. Ruth C. L. Simms translated *The Invention of Morel and Other Stories* in 1964. Gregory Woodruff and Donald A. Yates translated *Diary of the War of the Pig*, 1972; and Suzanne Jill Levine translated both *A Plan for Escape*, 1975, and *Asleep in the Sun*, 1978.

ABOUT: Contemporary Authors, revised series 29–32 r, 1978; Contemporary Literary Criticism 4, 1975; Encyclopedia of World Literature in the 20th Century (rev. ed.) I, 1981; Foster, D. W. and V. (eds.) Dictionary of Contemporary Latin American Authors, 1975; Mac-

Adam, A. Modern Latin American Narratives: The Dreams of Reason, 1977. *Periodicals*—Bulletin of Hispanic Studies 70, 1975; Hispanic Journal 4, 1982; Modern Fiction Studies 19, 1973.

*BJØRNEBOE, JENS (October 9, 1920–May 10, 1976), Norwegian novelist, dramatist and poet, was born in Kristiansand in south Norway, the son of shipowner and consul Ingvald Bjørnebo [sic] and the former Maja Svenson. The conservative provincialism of his home town was inimical to his independent nature, and he became a rebel early in life. After being expelled from several schools, he ran away to sea at the age of sixteen. He returned to his father's deathbed in 1939 and began studying—first in Oslo and then, during the German occupation, in Sweden. His first ambition was to become a painter; but on his return to Norway after the war he began to write.

Bjørneboe's rebellious nature is evident in nearly everything he wrote. But he was a rebel with a purpose; he was fired throughout his life by a burning sense of fury at injustice and at the oppression of individual freedom, which he saw wherever he looked. He conducted his literary career like a series of campaigns, leaving behind him a trail of scandals, court cases and outraged authorities. His main object of attack was always authoritarianism—the power-seekers whose sole ambition was personal aggrandizement, and the system, which set out to impose uniformity and destroy those who did not fit in. And his heroes were the misfits, the deviant personalities who refused to be moulded into model citizens but insisted on being different. They, maintained Bjørneboe, are the pioneers and creators, the guardians of freedom and the bearers of culture.

While still an adolescent Bjørneboe became aware of the German atrocities committed in the concentration camps; and after the war he felt compelled to investigate the topic in his first novel, *Før hanen galer* (Before the Cock Crows, 1952). Here he attacks the "ethical schizophrenia" of the German camp doctors who could cold-bloodedly experiment on Jews during the day while being loving husbands and fathers at night. It is a paradox that haunts him in many of his later works too. His first meeting with man's inhumanity in the shape of Nazi brutality became an obsessive nightmare; as late as 1966 he was still proclaiming: "Germania is the cross on which I am nailed." Yet his obsession with Germany did not make him into a Norwegian patriot; on the contrary, he denounced his fellow countrymen regularly for their narrow-mindedness and callousness—and never more

°byurn´ bō, yens

fiercely than in his other war novel, *Under en hårdere himmel* (Beneath a Harsher Sky, 1957). The violence of his denunciation of Norwegian persecution of Nazi sympathizers after the war earned him many bitter enemies.

During the 1950s Bjørneboe earned his living as a teacher at the Steiner school in Oslo. At this time he was much interested in Rudolf Steiner's anthroposophical philosophy, and particularly in his educational theories which were put into practice at the school. The state educational system was in his eyes one of the repressive institutions which set out to destroy individuality and creativity; the Steiner school encouraged free expression and tolerance. Bjørneboe's experiences during this period crystallized in the novel *Jonas* (1955, *The Least of These,* 1955), a blistering attack on the "salamanders" of the school system and a sensitive evocation of the sufferings of the young misfit Jonas. Bjørneboe also published three volumes of poems during this decade, but they are generally regarded as being among his less important productions; they are classical in form and subject matter, and often derivative.

After a few years traveling in southern Europe, Bjørneboe returned to Norway to live by his pen from 1960 to the end of his life. The plays and novels of this period represent his central literary achievement, though he was also an indefatigable essayist and journalist. His attacks on the authoritarian system were unabated; among his targets were the penal system with its emphasis on vindictive punishment rather than rehabilitation (*Den onde hyrde*—The Bad Shepherd, 1960), the judicial system that is concerned with victimization rather than justice (*Tilfellet Torgersen*—The Torgersen Case, 1973), and the puritanical code of sexual morals that brands free expression of sexuality as perversion (*Uten en tråd*—*Without a Stitch,* 1966). The last-mentioned work was the subject of a pornography trial in Norway in 1967 that provided its author with a splendid platform from which to proclaim his views. He lost the case, and the novel was banned.

From the beginning of his literary career, Bjørneboe wished to write for the stage; but he met with such discouragement from Norwegian theaters that he abandoned the idea until the early sixties, when he began writing plays in earnest. With the plays that he wrote then, particularly *Til lykke med dagen* (Congratualtions, 1965) and *Fugleelskerne* (The Bird Lovers, 1966), he emerged as Norway's most innovative dramatist since the war. He had a wide-ranging knowledge of European theater and was strongly influenced by Brecht, whose Berliner Ensemble he particularly admired. His style of dramatic writing, like Brecht's, was an energetic, fast-moving and physical form of theater, in which the action is interspersed with cabaret-style satirical songs and ballads. In *Til lykke med dagen,* a dramatization of *Den onde hyrde,* the plight of the young offender Tonnie becomes a stark portrayal of an outcast whose dialogues with representative figures of authority strip away his illusions and leave him ever more isolated, and the sterotyped reactions of the authorities turn into a grotesque pantomime of self-importance and moral hypocristy *Fugleelskerne* presents the conflict between morality and economic advantage in a group of former Italian resistance fighters faced with the return of their German torturers, now offering to turn their village into a German tourist resort. The clash between humanity and barbarity is savagely underlined in the hard-hitting songs:

Our rational, thrifty nation can really work apace;
They're amazingly efficient at getting the job done!
You can say what you like about Goethe's race—
At building crematoriums they're second to none!

Bjørneboe's first two plays were received with interest, though the unusual form and the controversial treatment of sensitive subjects made the critics cautious. They were more unreservedly enthusiastic about his next play, *Semmelweis* (1968—first performed 1969), an account of the Austrian doctor who discovered the cure for child-bed fever—another misfit and pioneer who was hounded to death by institutionalized authority, and whom history has vindicated. By now Bjørneboe was recognized as a major innovative dramatist—although paradoxically this play is more naturalistic in form than his first two. *Amputasjon* (Amputation, 1970), a demonstration in visual and concrete terms of the maiming and crippling effects of an authoritarian system on the mind of the individual, is again more pantomimic and acrobatic—and was castigated by critics: "it all drowns in blood and bestiality."

Bjørneboe's relationship with the Norwegian theater remained an uneasy one throughout his life; "the dictatorship of mediocrity" was the kindest term he could find for it. He drew much of his inspiration from his reading of foreign playwrights, and from his collaboration with foreign directors—the Israeli Issy Abrahami (*Til lykke med dagen*), the German Carl Maria Weber (*Fugleelskerne*), the Swedes Allan Edwall (*Semmelweis*) and Martha Vestin (*Amputasjon*).

Although many of his novels aroused furious debate because of the controversial nature of their subject matter, Bjørneboe did not achieve his real breakthrough as a novelist until 1966 with the publication of the first part of his major trilaogy, *Frihetens øyeblikk* (*Moment of Freedom*). The next two parts, *Kruttårnet* (The Powder Magazine) and *Stillheten* (The Silence) followed in 1969 and 1973. In this trilogy Bjørneboe attempted to confront on a more universal scale the problem which had obsessed him since he was a boy: man's seemingly endless capacity for cruelty towards his fellow men. "The History of Bestiality" he called it; and through the three novels, with their three different narrators, the quest widens and deepens in space and time. *Frihetens øyeblikk* is set in a courtroom in a small European principality and takes as its central theme the Second World War and the evil embodied in nazism. *Kruttårnet,* which takes place in a lunatic asylum in Alsace, concentrates on the history of the religious persecutions carried out in the name of Christianity. *Stillheten* moves to Africa to investigate the white man's guilt—the history of colonization of the Third World and wholesale destruction of civilizations involved. It is a gruesome and shocking catalogue, strongly marked by the debilitating depression to which its author was a constant prey; yet it bears witness too to an indomitable spirit which can look steadily at the darker side of man's nature and still hope. For however unfathomable the evil in the world, it is counterbalanced by an equally unfathomable good.

With this trilogy Bjørneboe moved away from the traditional realism of his earlier novels. Indeed he did not call these works novels at all; the first part is subtitled "The Heiligenberg manuscript," the second part a "scientific postscript and final protocol," and the third—somewhat desperately—an "anti-novel and absolutely final protocol." And as the work progresses, the structure almost disintegrates; the narrative is used to link more and more tenuously a selection of documentary material, including lectures, historical essays, and statistics. The reassuring story-line of the novel, which it is so easy to dismiss as "mere fiction," breaks down under the urgency of Bjørneboe's message. *Frihetens øyeblikk* is one of the forerunners of the documentary novel in Scandinavia.

The writing of the "History of Bestiality" took a heavy toll on Bjørneboe; his health suffered from years of overwork and depression, which he tried to deaden with alcohol. Yet he found the energy to write one more novel, which many critics declared to be his best: *Haiene* (The Sharks, 1974), a stirring tale of adventure on board a sailing ship bound from Manila to Marseilles in 1899, involving shark-hunting, mutiny and shipwreck. In the tradition of Conrad and Melville, it engrosses the reader in the age-old conflict between man and the sea. It is a tale of greed, hatred and brutality; yet also of compassion and humanity. The narrator, Peder Jensen, who has prided himself on owing no affection to any human being, adopts a half-starved ship's boy and discovers how to receive as well as give. The novel ends with a utopian vision as the sailors, cast away on a desert island after the shipwreck, build up a new and just society where no one is master and no one servant: the classless egalitarian community which was Bjørneboe's ideal alternative to the power structures of authoritarian capitalism.

It was, however, but a transitory hope for Bjørneboe, which could not be sustained against the ever-encroaching despair. He took his own life in May 1976 at the age of fifty-five. Since his death he has, like so many other controversial individualists, become much more acceptable; he has been claimed by many groups as a representative of their ideas. But in his life he always refused to be a member of any group, living out his own anarchistic ideals of individual freedom and commitment to "that truth, which is my own truth, that which *only I* know, because only *I* am I, and only *I* can see the world in *my* way."

WORKS IN ENGLISH TRANSLATION: *The Least of These* was translated into English by Bernt Jebsen and Douglas K. Stafford, 1959; *Without a Stitch* by Walter Barthold, 1969; *Moment of Freedom* by Esther Greenleaf Mürer, 1975. Bjørneboe's short story "Life and the Youth" is published in J. W. McFarlane's *Slaves of Love and Other Norwegian Short Stories,* 1982.

ABOUT: Columbia Dictionary of Modern European Literature, 1980; Contemporary Authors 69–72, 1978; Garton, J. Jens Bjørneboe, 1985; Lyngstad, S. (ed.) Review of National Literatures 12: Norway, 1983. *Periodicals*—Scandinavica 2 1984; Scandinavian Studies 1 1976.

BLACKWOOD, CAROLINE (July 16, 1931–), British novelist and essayist, was born Lady Caroline Hamilton-Temple-Blackwood, daughter of the Marquess and Marchioness of Dufferin and Ava. She grew up at Clandeboye, the family's rather rundown estate in County Down, Northern Ireland, and was educated at private schools in England and Ulster. In her early twenties she married the painter Lucian Freud; after a divorce she married the American composer Israel Citkovitz, by whom she had three daughters. After another divorce she fell in love in 1970 with the American poet Robert Lowell, at that time married to the writer Elizabeth Hardwick. She and Lowell had a son the following year and in 1972 were married. Lowell, who described their relationship in *The*

CAROLINE BLACKWOOD

Dolphin (1973), died in 1977. Since then Blackwood, who for many years spent a great deal of time in New York, has lived mainly in London.

Her first book, *For All That I Found There*, is an odd mixture of five short stories and eight journalistic essays. The pieces, arranged into sections entitled Fiction, Fact, and Ulster, are all infused with a terse, sardonic wit that is not compassionate but gets at the truth by willfully refusing to accept conventional wisdom. She describes a visit to a chaotic free school in Harlem, a contentious radical-moderate split at a feminist meeting, the horrors of a Surrey hospital for burned patients. The chapters on Ulster are mostly childhood memories: she has not lived there since the age of seventeen. Many of the characters in her stories, whatever their class background, appear to be remarkably cold, cruel, and vulgar. According to Carole Horn, "Those who appear most intense, most lovely, are as likely as any to be rotted within, to suffer the psychological equivalent of that macabre form of leprosy in which a person, though riddled with the disease, appears perfectly normal until he suddenly, horribly disintegrates."

The Stepdaughter, Blackwood's first novel, seemed a departure from her previous writing in its Manhattan setting and epistolary form. An unnamed woman, abandoned by her husband for a younger woman, describes the disarray of her life in angry letters to no one. She focuses much of her hatred on his lumpish, unhappy teen-age daughter, whom he has also abandoned in the luxurious high-rise apartment. She determines at first to get her out of the apartment, then discovers that the girl is in fact not her hus-

band's child, and finally relents and decides to tolerate her "in my life," but by that time the child is gone, swallowed up by the city. The woman's shocked acceptance of her terrible guilt closes the novel; a harsh atonement is possibly hinted at in the last line of her last letter: "Will only write again if I have good news."

Male reviewers generally admired the novel's sharpness of observation. Michael Wood called it "an intelligent work by a writer with a very distinctive voice"; James Price even contended that, "with its unblinking view of man's selfishness and woman's dependence, *The Stepdaughter* is a notable contribution to the women's movement." Women reviewers, however, discerned in it a flinty, unyielding quality wholly devoid of feeling. Jane Larkin Crain thought the author's tone one of "icy hauteur" and saw in the book "a facile, monochromatic nastiness that robs it of resonance. . . . One is invited to look down from a great height and remark how unappetizing is the life the author surveys, and with what thoroughgoing wit she dismisses it. The book manifests a disdain for the way we live now that seems too easily won, and that defuses its rather brilliant bitchiness."

Blackwood's second novel is *Great Granny Webster*, in which the narrator attempts to reconstruct the history of her aristocratic family by concentrating on what she knows of her maternal forebears. Great Granny Webster, a cold and joyless Victorian matriarch, had a daughter who set fires and went mad, a beautiful granddaughter who tried to be a free spirit but ended up a suicide, and a great-granddaughter who spent only a single summer at Dunmartin, the gloomy, dilapidated family seat. Anne Duchêne thought Blackwood's writing "so easy and unassertive that the wit and the images and the sharply honed points of the sentences seem to come naturally from a steady look at things. . . . The failure of the family implies the failure of strength in a whole society; which is a very high aim in a very small book." Janet Wiehe considered all the characters, even the brief sketches of the servants, "sharply observed" and the somewhat "grim" story "delightfully funny."

The Fate of Mary Rose is a thoroughly macabre novel, short and sharp in its observations and, again, often grimly humorous. The narrator is a successful historian, a cold, fault-finding man, who lives in London, near his mistress, while his wife, an obsessive perfectionist, lives in a beautiful Kentish village with their six-year-old daughter, the timid and impressionable Mary Rose. The rape and murder of a little neighbor girl precipitates the complete disintegration of these three unbalanced lives, collectively and individually. The hollow meaninglessness of the family's existence together is constantly exposed, as are the conflicts permeating the narrator's false and selfish life. The book's purpose, according to Patricia Craig, is "to set out clearly the most extreme consequences of an act of violence. . . . It is never less than interesting; and now that she has added narrative control to her other attributes, Caroline Blackwood joins that small group of distinguished women novelists . . . whose task is to comment obliquely on the dangers and infirmities of contemporary life."

In quite another mood but no less acerbic, Blackwood and Anna Haycroft have written a cookbook for the busy and fashionable set, *Darling, You Shouldn't Have Gone to So Much Trouble.* The authors' friends, apparently, are forever "dropping in" on one another in large numbers, and the hostesses generally advise plying them with strong drink in odd mixtures (brandy and champagne, for example), separating them from their children, and giving the latter such fare as spam casserole in the kitchen, while saving the good stuff—instant mashed potatoes, ersatz caviar, salads "expanded" by leftovers—for their now-comatose elders. The book is written in an unappetizing style, brusquely and as if in a great hurry, and seems positively to delight in the stodgy monotony of mass-produced British food. It sold, of course, very well. "Someone," said Blackwood in a 1981 interview, "said we should do one on sex with the same title." One British reviewer remarked that, having read Blackwood's novels, she wouldn't be caught within miles of her chic Earl's Court kitchen.

In early 1984 Blackwood visited a group of women camping out, under the most rigorous conditions, on Greenham Common to protest the installation of American cruise missiles on British soil. Her report on this visit, *On the Perimeter,* described by one reviewer as "partisan, but far from one-sided," was based on interviews with the protestors as well as with some of the civilians, police, and soldiers defending the base. The book raised challenging questions on the intense emotionalism of both sides—the dogged persistence of the women, the rage of their opponents—all of this presented in what the *Times Literary Supplement* reviewer called an "absorbing, witty and compassionate narrative."

Blackwood has been working for several years on a biography of the Duchess of Windsor. Her wide acquaintance among the aristocracy, reportedly the repository of most of the secrets about Wallis Simpson and her husband the Duke of Windsor, seems to promise that the veils of discretion will at last be lifted on the "love" story of the century.

WORKS: *Fiction*—The Stepdaughter, 1976; Great Granny Webster, 1977; The Fate of Mary Rose, 1981; Good Night Sweet Ladies, 1983; Corrigan, 1984. *Non-fiction*—For All That I Found There, 1973; Darling, You Shouldn't Have Gone to So Much Trouble, 1980; On the Perimeter, 1984.

ABOUT: Contemporary Authors 85–88, 1980; Contemporary Literary Criticism 6, 1976, and 9, 1978; Dictionary of Literary Biography 14, 1983. *Periodicals*—Christian Science Monitor November 2, 1977; Encounter September 1976; January 1978; Listener May 20, 1976; London Magazine October-November 1974; London Review of Books March 5–19, 1981; New Statesman November 30, 1973; June 4, 1976; August 28, 1977; March 6, 1981; New York Review of Books September 15, 1977; November 9, 1978; New York Times Book Review September 18, 1977; July 26, 1981; New Yorker October 17, 1977; Observer February 22, 1981; Times (London) March 26, 1981; Times Literary Supplement April 5, 1974; May 21, 1976; September 2, 1977; February 27, 1981; September 21, 1984; October 19, 1984.

BLYTHE, RONALD (November 6, 1922–), English essayist and novelist, writes: "I was born and brought up in Suffolk, and come from ancient rural roots on my father's side which have been associated with this eastern part of England for many centuries. My mother came from London and I like to think—I have no proof that it was so—that it was the mixture of her love of reading and my father's farming background which created the necessary clash of opposites which initially formed me as a writer. I was born during the great farming depression which lasted, except for the government-assisted war years of 1914–1918, from the 1870s to the 1940s, and so all my boyhood recollections are of extreme poverty and, at the same time, a very beautiful and still unspoiled countryside. Also of country people who had more in common with the characters in Hardy's novels than with those of villagers today. Like most writers, I cannot pinpoint some moment of decision in my life when I 'began,' as it were. Looking back, even to earliest childhood, I see myself, more or less, as I still am, imaginative, tougher than I look, or am thought to be, disciplined, and solitary. A great watcher and listener. I have always had a strong and not very comfortable feeling of separateness, or perhaps I should call it an unwanted feeling of separateness, of being a bit isolated where I most belong. This too is a common condition of the writer.

RONALD BLYTHE

"I have remained within the same few miles all my life, not for a passion for my own background but due to such humdrum motives as economics and the familiarity of a local routine and society which allows me to exist without needing to explain myself. When I was twenty I began work in a large provincial public library where I eventually became the reference librarian, and where I began to write, poetry and short stories mostly. I consider these years as those of my true education. I read enormously, everything from contemporary literature to the Greek and Latin authors in the Loeb translations, and French writing particularly, discovering Proust, Flaubert and the French poets. During this time I was drawn into a distinguished group of artists and writers who lived in East Anglia. They included W. R. Rodgers the Irish poet, James Turner, John Nash and Benjamin Britten. Influenced by their way of life, I gave up my job at the library and went to work as a freelance writer on the Suffolk coast, a jerseys, jeans and bicycle existence, during which I wrote my first novel and kept myself by working for Britten (editing the programme for the Aldeburgh Festivals, etc.) and being a publisher's reader, a job found for me by W. R. Rodgers.

"Eventually, I drifted to a tiny village in central Suffolk and there, due to the founding of the Penguin English Library in the mid-sixties and the success of a history of the inter-war years which I had written for them, and called *The Age of Illusion,* I began to edit the classics. My life at this point seemed to fulfil two different aspects of my nature, the bookish and scholarly, and the purely creative and imaginative. In *Akenfield* I appear to have pulled or welded these two strands of myself together without, at the time, realizing that I was doing so. This book, which to my astonishment became so well known, is essentially autobiographical and a statement about the family and the society which I came from. It is a book of witness of what I had seen and heard, and of what my parents and grandparents had seen and heard. It is local history as interpreted by a local man who is also part-novelist and part-poet.

"One of the best things about *Akenfield* was that it eased me back into the ordinary life of the district, and out of the study. Although rather reclusive and shy, I found that I was able to take classes sometimes in the local schools and colleges on English Literature, and to assist at the church, etc. While writing *Akenfield* I became fascinated by the achievement/predicament of old age, and of time versus the flesh, and eventually used the same method to write *The View in Winter,* which repudiates the modern concept of aging as a mostly medico-economic dilemma. My good fortune as a writer has been to see my regional or even parochial books given such a wide acceptance. My misfortune (personally speaking!) is in not being able to quite categorize myself. I have learnt how to observe human nature from the old fixed centre of a rural community—and beyond. The 'beyond' part of the observation derives from another culture altogether, of course, that of music, painting, poetry, novels, (chiefly) Christian philosophy and the huge dilemmas of the modern world, such as hunger and nuclear war."

Ronald Blythe describes his first two books, the novel *A Treasonable Growth* and the story collection *Immediate Possession,* as "formal yet odd and unlike traditional village-centered fiction, being both sophisticated and simple at the same time." British critics, he recalls, "at once recognized [them] as something new in that very large field known in Britain as 'country writing,' . . . and . . . described [them] as full of secret threads that bind people to their environments."

The Age of Illusion: England in the Twenties and Thirties, 1919–1940 is a collection of essays on notable characters and events of the interwar period, among them Sir William Joynson-Hicks, a militant prude; Amy Johnson, an early woman aviator; the often-told story of Edward VIII and Mrs. Simpson; and the burial of the Unknown Soldier. The reviewer for the *Economist* wrote, "Plainly, while Mr. Blythe was writing there was hovering about him the shade of Lytton

Strachey," the author of the short biographies that comprise *Eminent Victorians,* but Strachey "did his homework on the facts better than Mr. Blythe has sometimes done. . . . Much of this is fun and some of it shrewd, but too little of it gets under the skin of what went on." Malcolm Muggeridge, in a characteristically bad-tempered reaction, wrote, "The large and variegated cast are assembled, put on their costumes and their makeup, speak their lines. But what of the play? What is the point of this so foolish, expensive, bloody and destructive spectacle? If point there be, it has eluded Mr. Blythe."

Akenfield: Portrait of an English Village, Blythe's second book of nonfiction, was much better received: it was the subject of many reviews in both Britain and the United States, almost all of them highly favorable. A great variety of villagers is included, most of them in portraits made of their own words. The whole, according to a reviewer in the *Times Literary Supplement,* amounts to "a composition as complicated in its way as a major Breughel." The reviewer complains of "some gaps in the pattern, inevitably, and perhaps they could be filled only by an author less politically compassionate and less involved with some of his subjects than this author has become. Without that involvement, however, he could hardly have won the confidence which gives reality to the stories of the younger village lads of the new generation as well as the survivors of other and harder times." James (now Jan) Morris exulted that the book "provides an invaluable and horridly enjoyable corrective to the standard rose-pub-and-quaintness notion of bucolic England. I can imagine few societies in the Western world less enticing than the society of Akenfield." The book's strong impact, to Morris, was accomplished by "lovingly drawing apart the curtains of legend and landscape" to reveal "the inner, almost clandestine, spirit of the village behind," which is "somewhat akin to life in a bed of rather wilted poison ivy." Blythe considers *Akenfield* to be "the fashioning out of the talk of the writer's own people of a spiritual statement about themselves."

Blythe calls *The View in Winter: Reflections on Old Age* a collection of "talk from a very different country, that of the very old, placing this talk against what literature itself has recorded on human aging from the earliest times." The book is oral history, as is *Akenfield,* but contains rather more of the author's own commentary as well as a kind of anthology of thoughts on the subject by other writers, including Dickens, Shaw, and Simone de Beauvoir. V. S. Pritchett thought the book "neither a clinical nor a statistical social study [but] essentially an unflinching, inquiring, and reflective essay, graced by wide reading of the poets, novelists, and philosophers and brought sharply to life by interviews in which the old cottager, farmer, miner, the matron, the nurse, and others of all classes talk about their experience and their dreads. These are the survivors of that almost extinct 'brotherhood,' the men who fought in the 1914 war, an engineer, a senior neurologist, an actor, many widows and priests—all add their story—and between these voices which are rich in the accent of real lives looking back on their memories, the essay advances an enquiry which is tender and subtle, and happily without dogmatism." Barbara Grizzuti Harrison went further, predicting "that *The View in Winter,* a wide and beautiful book, splendid in its conception, lyrical in its prose, will become a classic in the literature of old age." She considered the book "unexcelled social history" and praised Blythe's "unerring instinct for structure."

From the Headlands (U.S., *Characters and Their Landscapes*) is a collection of essays on various topics, some on Blythe's favorite writers (Hardy, Hazlitt, Clare, Crabbe, Tolstoy, and others), some on little-remembered utopian socialists (Henry George and Thomas Davidson), others on the country life and attitudes to it. P. J. Kavanagh objected to a strain of self-effacement in the essentially personal essays: "Certainly there is a strong autobiography vein but almost as soon as he calls our attention to himself he modestly withdraws behind his subject so that we are left wishing for more autobiography or for none at all. . . . The impression stays . . . that this book, these pieces, are really about Blythe, and no harm in that."

Blythe is president of the John Clare Society and a member of the Fabian Society; he is also a fellow of the Royal Society of Literature, whose Heinemann Medal he won for *Akenfield.*

PRINCIPAL WORKS: *Fiction*—A Treasonable Growth, 1960; Immediate Possession, 1961. *Non-fiction*—The Age of Illusion, 1963; Akenfield, 1969; The View in Winter, 1979; From the Headlands, 1982 (U.S. Characters and Their Landscapes).

ABOUT: Contemporary Authors, first revision series 5–8, 1969; *Periodicals*—Atlantic September 1969; September 1983; Economist November 30, 1963; New Republic October 4, 1969; December 15, 1979; New Statesmen November 15, 1963; May 30, 1969; New York Review of Books January 1, 1970; November 8, 1979; New York Times Book Review May 10, 1964; September 21, 1969; October 14, 1979; January 29, 1984; New Yorker February 27, 1984; Times Literary Supplement December 5, 1963; June 5, 1969; November 23, 1979; November 26, 1982.

*BODELSEN, ANDERS (February 11, 1937–), Danish novelist and short-story writer, was born in the Frederiksberg section of Copenhagen. His father was Dr. C. A. Bodelsen, a noted professor of English, his mother, Merete Bodelsen, a well-known art historian. Bodelsen was thus exposed to the arts as a child and wrote a collection of short stories at the age of seven. From 1956 through 1960 Bodelsen attended the University of Copenhagen where he studied law, economics, and comparative literature without, however, taking a degree. Since 1959 he has contributed to various Copenhagen newspapers, most recently to *Politiken*. Bodelsen has also worked regularly for radio and television, having written plays for both media and having supplied several scripts for the popular television series about the police force in a small, fictitious Danish town, *En by i provinsen* (A Town in the Provinces, 1977–1979). He married Eva Sindahl-Pedersen in 1975.

Bodelsen made his literary debut while still a university student with the imaginative, perceptively written first-person novel *De lyse naetters tid* (The Time of the Light Nights, 1959), a reflective work dealing with the painful maturation process of its youthful protagonist. In this novel, Bodelsen accurately chronicles the coming of age of his own somewhat pampered generation which was born shortly before World War II. Although it ends on an optimistic note, *De lyse naetters tid* leaves unanswered the question of whether this generation has indeed matured, a question to which the author returns in several works written some twenty years later.

Bodelsen's second novel, *Villa Sunset* (1964), represents a radical departure, both thematically and stylistically, from *De lyse naetters tid* and seems not to have been understood by its readers. Nonetheless, *Villa Sunset* along with the collection of short stories *Drivhuset* (The Greenhouse, 1965) provides the key to much of Bodelsen's subsequent work; for these two contain the themes and motifs that became dominant in Bodelsen's output during the 1960s and 1970s: social disintegration, institutional corruption, human isolation, the moral imperative, futurism, and the vulnerability of the individual. *Villa Sunset* depicts the sham and hypocrisy of the establishment and the exploitation of the "little man" by wealthy manufacturers. Two stories in *Drivhuset* evoke quite strikingly the mood of the collection: "Alt er tilladt" (Everything Is Allowed) and "Agurke-tid" (Summer Doldrums). In the former the insidious sophistries of the amoral Jacob seduce the narrator into believing that there is no such thing as right or wrong. In the latter the ambitious young crime reporter of the newspaper *Ekspressen* becomes so ob-

ANDERS BODELSEN

sessed with solving a series of grisly sex-murders that he destroys his own promising career; the murderer himself is never identified. Both *Villa Sunset* and *Drivhuset* are, moreover, written with subtle humor and irony and are imbued with that sense of absurdity that characterizes most of Bodelsen's pre-1980 works. In these two volumes we meet for the first time some of the characters and institutions that recur in many of Bodelsen's writings from the 1960s and 1970s: Little Lotte, Uncle Svend, Mr. Sunshine, and the newspaper *Ekspressen*.

Bodelsen solidified his reputation as a serious writer in 1967 with the collection of short stories *Rama Sama*. Composed lucidly and with attention to detail, the stories of *Rama Sama* show their middle-class protagonists at critical junctures in their lives when they must either reassess their situations or rationalize the (frequently unethical) actions which they are about to take. "Succes" (Success) reveals the inner workings in the mind of the striver, Thykjaer, at a board meeting as he maneuvers his way up the corporate ladder. In "Snyd" (Cheating) the schoolboy protagonist rejects society's moral principles and cheats on his math examination because, as he tries to convince himself, if he does not cheat his entire future will be ruined.

In a gripping series of novels and short stories from the 1960s and 1970s Bodelsen examines the question of personal versus societal loyalties from a variety of standpoints. Henrik Mork, who accidentally runs down and kills a man with an automobile in the novel *Haendeligt uheld* (1968, *One Down* or *Hit and Run Run Run*), elects to protect himself, his family, and above all his career instead of confessing his crime, even though his actions lead to the death of another human being. Simon Borck, the seemingly unassuming bank-teller who engineers the robbery which deprives both his own bank and the actual stick-up man of several hundred thousand *kroner* in the novel *Taenk på et tal* (*Think of a Number*, 1968) is an amoral rebel against the constraints of an all-too-regimented society and a demeaning professional situation.

The stories of *Lov og orden*, subtitled *Kriminalnoveller* (Law and Order: Criminal Stories, 1973), present an assortment of otherwise average Danes who resort to unlawful means to achieve their goals: Martin Simonsen, yet another frustrated bank employee, progresses from petty vandalism to political assassination in the stories "Den tavse mand" (The Silent Man) and "Lov og orden"; for him as for other similar characters (even those who commit no crimes), the law is a meaningless and unwelcome intrusion in the individual's striving to live as he sees fit. It is disturbingly clear in many of these stories that the social fabric is unraveling.

Bodelsen also wrote novels during the 1960s and 1970s about the innocent individual against whom the full weight of the criminal-justice system is thrown. Martin Bendix of *Bevisets stilling* (*Consider the Verdict*, 1973) is wrongly accused of sexually abusing and murdering a young woman. Even though he is eventually cleared of the crime for lack of evidence, he is ultimately destroyed by the stigma of the accusation and by his devastating experience in solitary confinement. Symbolically, Martin Bendix dies alone on the last page of the book.

In the novel *Borte borte* (Gone, Gone, 1980) Bodelsen combines the theme of the individual's responsibility to society with that of the victim of the system. The protagonist, the store-owner Niels Møller, lets himself be persuaded to have his warehouse of unsellable electric organs torched so that he can collect the insurance. Tragically, however, the arson takes three innocent lives. Møller's pangs of conscience eventually prove too great for him and he cycles off to make his confession at the conclusion of the novel.

Occupying a unique place in Bodelsen's work is the novel *Straus* (1971). Written rapidly in a fit of pique at his fellow Danish author, Klaus Rifbjerg, who had made Bodelsen the butt of an unflattering portrayal in one of his own short stories, *Straus* explores the questions of identity, jealousy, and insanity more intensely than in any of Bodelsen's other writings. Perhaps not surprisingly there are parallels between Bodelsen's *Straus* and Rifbjerg's *Anna (jeg) Anna* (*Anna (I)*

Anna, 1969) which treats these same questions. There are close stylistic similarities as well: the narration shifts erratically between first and third persons, for instance, and the telling is disjointed and hectic. Significantly, both *Straus* and *Anna (jeg) Anna* are constructed around the voyage undertaken by the central character to discover him/herself—not coincidentally Bodelsen's protagonist assumes the guise of a woman just prior to killing his literary rival, Straus (who, one is tempted to speculate, really symbolizes the narrator's better self).

Representing yet another facet of Bodelsen's authorship are his futuristic works, in which he addresses himself primarily to the fate of the welfare society. This aspect of his art was already apparent in *Villa Sunset*, which takes place during an abnormally cold winter that Bodelsen equates with the great "fimbul winter" of Old Norse mythology, one of the harbingers of the end of the world. Villa Sunset itself, an old house which is about to be razed to make room for the new order (in the form of a garbage incinerator), is inhabited by an odd assortment of eccentrics and self-styled social misfits who are as out of touch with the world around them as is the house itself (with its symbolic address on Nirvanavej—"Nirvana Road"). The novel ends grotesquely with Villa Sunset's resident nihilists cruising the early spring streets in a reconditioned Dusenburg loaded with plastic explosives. The world seems about to dissolve into a kind of anarchistic absurdity. *Frysepunktet* (*Freezing Down* or *Freezing Point*, 1969) deals primarily with the relationship between Bruno, the fiction editor of a weekly magazine, and his balletdancing paramour Jenny, both of whom are scientifically "frozen down" (placed in a state of suspended animation) until their physical ailments can be cured medically. At each thawing, however, Bruno finds the world more and more alien and increasingly devoid of a meaning for the "eternal life" which the elite of its citizenry seem to have procured for themselves. In fact, beyond the walls of the clinic in which he is essentially interned, a revolution is taking place, one which Bruno instinctively supports although he is totally powerless to participate in it.

That Bodelsen's critique of society also occasionally manifests itself in his crime stories is understandable; assaults on social institutions, such as banks and insurance companies, are ultimately, in Bodelsen's view, attacks on the stability of society as a whole. The final story in the collection *Lov og orden*, for example, shows a society coming apart at the seams, with acts of sabotage, assassinations, and hijackings all commonplace events. In 1977 and 1978 Bodelsen published a two-volume work of almost epic proportions which describes in realistic detail the decade of the 1960s. *De gode tider* (The Good Times, 1977) chronicles the successful business venture launched by the two friends, Bo and Arne. In *År for år* (Year by Year, 1978), however, the enterprise had gone bankrupt, and Bo has made a shambles of his personal life while Arne, his marriage of convenience intact, seems intent on avoiding life's unpleasantnesses. These two novels contain none of the chilling predictions of society's imminent collapse that characterize Bodelsen's futuristic works, nor do they address themselves to questions of the moral imperative or the individual's reponsibility to society. They are soberly and objectively written and faithfully reproduce the spirit of the recent Danish past. Bodelsen firmly anchors *De gode tider* and *År for år* in the 1960s by referring to many of the salient events of the decade: the Kennedy assassination and the Vietnam conflict.

Over regnbuen (Over the Rainbow, 1982) continues the theme of *År for år*: the prosperity of the 1960s was a brief, illusory respite which will never return to Denmark. In this novel the same hard economic times that were so fateful for Bo and Arne in *År for år* have overtaken the Nedergaard family, all of whose members (with the exception of six-year old Marianne) feel as if they have reached a dead end. Urged by an old friend, they decide to emigrate to Australia and begin anew. The real protagonist of the novel is seventeen-year-old Klaus, on whom the decision has a positive, although unexpected effect: he emerges from his inner exile of self-doubt as the "strongest" member of the family. At the end of *Over regnbuen* Klaus, who has decided not to emigrate but to stay in Copenhagen and finish high school, seems ready to accept the challenge that faces his generation and work to "save" Denmark. The older generation (the same one portrayed in *De lyse naetters tid*) may have given up, but, the author seems to be saying, there is hope in the country's youth.

Bodelsen's unpretentious, realistic style makes him accessible to a large segment of the reading public. That most of his works are set in the middle-class milieu of contemporary Denmark also explains his popularity in his native land. Yet, even while writing about specifically Danish themes, Bodelsen is able to speak to a more broadly based, international audience, for many of the crises which afflict Denmark and its citizens are also felt in much of the rest of the Western world. Bodelsen has received several prestigious literary awards, among them the Grand Prix de la Littérature Policière in 1971 and the Søren Gyldendal Prize in 1981.

WORKS IN ENGLISH TRANSLATION: The following novels by

Bodelsen have been translated into English: *Think of a Number* by David Hohen, 1969; *Hit and Run Run Run* or *One Down* by Carolyn Bly, 1970; *Freezing Down* or *Freezing Point* by Joan Tate, 1971; *Straus* by Nadia Christensen and Alexander Taylor, 1974; *Consider the Verdict* by Nadia Christensen, 1976; and *Operation Cobra* by Joan Tate, 1976. His collection of short stories, *Rama Sama*, was published in English translation in 1973, and the story "Success," in Paula Hostrup-Jessen's translation, is included in Sven Holm's collection *The Devil's Instrument and Other Danish Short Stories*, 1971.

ABOUT: Columbia Dictionary of Modern European Literature, 1980; Encyclopedia of World Literature in the 20th Century (rev. ed.) I, 1981.

BOGARDE, DIRK (stage name and pseudonym of Derek Jules Gaspard Ulric Niven Van den Bogaerde) (March 28, 1921–   ), British novelist, memoirist, and actor, was born in the borough of Hampstead, London, son of Ulric Jules Van den Bogaerde, for many years art editor of the London *Times,* and Margaret Niven, who had been an actress. He had a varied education, first at University College School, London, then at Allen Glen's, a technical school in Glasgow, which he hated. From the age of twelve he developed his talent for drawing and painting at the Chelsea School of Art, London, and at sixteen won a scholarship to the Royal College of Art.

From early childhood, however, his real love was acting. His father agreed to support him during a two-year apprenticeship in the theater, but his fledgling career was interrupted by war just after it began late in 1939. Bogarde spent the war as a member of the Queen's Royal Regiment in Europe and the Far East, was assigned for a time to Air Photographic Intelligence, and was discharged with the rank of major in 1946. He soon resumed his acting career, and after nearly four decades and more than sixty films, has established himself as one of the most distinguished screen actors of his time. He has played the lead in such highly acclaimed films as *Victim* (1961), *The Servant (1963), Darling* (1965), *Accident* (1967), *Death in Venice* (1971), *The Night Porter* (1973), *Providence* (1976), and, in what many consider his finest work, as the hero of Rainer Werner Fassbinder's haunting version of Nabokov's *Despair* (1979).

Bogarde began writing his autobiography in the late 1960s. The first volume to be published, *A Postillion Struck by Lightning,* covered his early youth and adolescence and ended with his entry into the army, with a postscript chapter showing the actor, nearly forty, trying to make

DIRK BOGARDE

sense of his impersonation of Franz Liszt in the unmemorable Hollywood bio-epic, *Song Without End* (1960). Suzanne Lowry called the book "romantic, modest, and funny. Bogarde must be the least name-dropping autobiographer the cinema has yet produced." Caroline Seebohm thought that American readers would greatly appreciate the book's "extreme Englishness: not only of the descriptions of an upbringing in which parents are distant, elegant figures who leave most of the child-rearing to a nanny, and where 'homesick' means literally a longing for the house not the parents, but also of Bogarde's psychological development. 'Life before 1934, the Summer Life if you like . . . had seduced me into a totally unreal existence of constant happiness, simplicity, trust and love. What I clearly needed, and what I got, was a crack on the backside which shot me into reality. . . . To be sure, it was a violent crack, but it did not, I trust, find me weak; amazingly the Summer Life had made me strong.' This is gung-ho, stiff-upper-lip stuff," concludes Seebohm, "and whether or not it will withstand the test of time, I can't help thinking it is admirable."

The second instalment of the autobiography was *Snakes and Ladders,* covering Bogarde's army service and his accession to stardom. "I have never been an extrovert actor," he writes, "always an introvert; instinctive rather than histrionic. . . . I discovered, to my amazing and lasting delight, that the camera actually photographed the mind process however hesitant it was, however awkward. . . . The people I played had minds, of some sort or another, and I became completely absorbed in trying to find

those minds and offer them up to the camera." In addition to such exacting descriptions of his craft, he is expert at dialogue, at recreating the personalities of his directors and fellow actors, and much of the book is taken up by sharp portraits of Luchino Visconti, Kay Kendall, Julie Christie, Noel Coward, and Judy Garland. Moira Hodgson called Bogarde "an intelligent writer, thoughtful and modest without exaggerated self-deprecation" yet also thought him "cautious and guarded about his famous friends" and about himself: "there's much," she wrote, "that he passes over in silence." This sense of reticence has been remarked by other reviewers of his books, and Hodgson cites a passage from *Snakes and Ladders* which suggests that the dehumanizing effects of fame and stardom may be one cause of it: "I now lived in an alien world . . . in which all the standards and beliefs we had been brought up to respect as right and honourable were almost completely redundant . . . it came as a major shock to discover on my rise towards the giddy elevation to the canopy of the Odeon Leicester Square that these rules did not apply to public property like politicians, jockeys, footballers, boxers, murderers, the entire Royal Family and its appendages and above all to film stars . . . by placing ourselves from choice apparently, in the glare of the spotlight, we had automatically forfeited our privacy, and for the most part, our lives."

An Orderly Man, the final volume of the autobiography, is much concerned, as are the first two, with Bogarde's parents and his homes. He describes a long correspondence with a woman—Mrs X, he calls her—who was the first person to encourage him to write. His daily letters to her, filled with the detail of his childhood and later life, were all returned to him after Mrs X's death in 1972 and formed the core of his autobiography. Craig Brown thought it "refreshing" that the book was "so sparing in its devotion to glamour, so idiosyncratic and so thoughtful," yet strongly restated the old complaint about the author's personal reticence. "His presence is there beside his mother's hospital bed, or filming with Fassbinder, or sifting through scripts, and an abundance of dialogue and detail is faithfully jotted down, but under the sensitively rendered commotion, his character remains in hiding."

Bogarde's first published novel was *A Gentle Occupation,* which takes place on an imaginary island in the Dutch East Indies just after World War II, when units of the British and Indian armies, according to the author's note, "found themselves involved in trying to 'hold the ring' in the crumbling Dutch Empire in South-East Asia, and suffered heavy casualties in killed, wounded and missing." He creates a varied, international cast of characters who live under the constant threat of violence, and in what Robert Kiely called "an atmosphere of fear, suspicion, tentative hope, but, above all, of confusion." Kiely wrote that the novel contains "fine vignettes: beautifully composed comic scenes and moments of compelling action. But by failing to provide not merely a conventional hero but a single consciousness of depth or sensitivity through which events are perceived or interpreted, Bogarde allows his material to slip away into repetitious, conventionally ironic fragments."

Voices in the Garden, set in the south of France, is a novel, in Rachel Billington's words, "structured around a theme of deception" and dealing "with characters and a society of apparent silliness and superficiality. This is a tale of facades, of the false posing as the true and eventually becoming real." An elderly woman, lonely and incurably ill, the wife of a distinguished historian, is saved from suicide by a handsome young man, who is then taken, along with his girlfriend, into her home. One of the book's most entertaining characters is a greasy and villainous Italian film director, Umberto Grottorosso, who appears on the scene with a fawning retinue and a lavishly appointed yacht. Billington felt that the principal characterizations lacked sufficient depth: "Appearances, meaning in this instance the literals of dress and flank, are given undue importance but stop short of meaning anything deeper. The minds, plumbed only rarely, turn out to be empty." Yet she called the descriptions "always excellent. The color, the touch, the smell of the south of France is vivid around us. Even the unconvincing has a kind of physical reality, like, one can't help feeling, a film whose intentions have been realized with admirable form but little content. The cadences of speech move with their own entirely successful swing and balance. It is clear that Mr. Bogarde must be judged as a writer rather than as an actor writing."

In a 1981 interview, Bogarde spoke of the satisfaction he has found in writing: "There's been the satisfaction of finding at my age a new career. Writing is sure as hell hard work, but so was acting. I haven't done badly." He tries to keep his prose "as simple, witty, and civilized as possible." For the past several years he has lived on a small farm near Grasse, in the hills above Cannes on the French Riviera.

PRINCIPAL WORKS: *Fiction*—A Gentle Occupation, 1980; Voices in the Garden, 1981. *Memoirs*—A Postillion Struck by Lightning, 1977; Snakes and Ladders, 1979; An Orderly Man, 1983.

ABOUT: Contemporary Authors, 77–80, 1979; Current Biography, 1967; Dictionary of Literary Biography 14, Part I, 1983; Who's Who, 1982. *Periodicals*—Guardian March 23, 1977; New York Times April 29, 1980; September 12, 1981; New York Times Book Review October 9, 1977; July 8, 1979; June 29, 1980; October 18, 1981; October 9, 1983; People October 26, 1981; Saturday Review August 8, 1970; Times Literary Supplement September 18, 1981; April 29, 1983.

BOOTH, WAYNE C(LAYSON) (February 22, 1921–   ), American critic and educator, writes: "It's hard for me to say what kind of an author I am, but it's fairly easy to list the myths I use in order to keep on writing. The first says that I've done it all on my own, against the grain of my upbringing, and that I deserve immense credit for every word that comes out of an empty mind. Almost as much a bully of humility as Mr. Bounderby, 'born and bred in a (cultural) ditch, sir,' I produce every work with an almost miraculous exertion of pure character. No background. No Latin. Even less Greek. Ignorant of all history. Unable to finish *The Faery Queen.* Surrounded by reference books and guides to pure style, dodging the thrusts of the howler-spotters, constantly fearing the exposure that threatens every autodidact, 'Here I am, Mrs. Gradgrind, anyhow, and nobody to thank for my being here but myself.' Obviously I must work like a demon to make up for not having lived in—shall we say—Bloomsbury?

"This myth lives in some discomfort with a second one: whenever I publish *anything,* no matter how poor it is, I am fulfilling the fondest dreams of my family and my Mormon culture. All of my family on both sides were devout Mormons, descendants of pioneers who had been converted in Great Britain in the 1850s. Matthew Arnold claimed, in *Culture and Anarchy,* that the very existence of people like my great-grandparents, the ignorant, superstitious emigrants who fled by the tens of thousands through England's ports each year, confirmed his theses about England's cultural plight. If he had visited American Fork, Utah, at any time during my childhood about fifty years later, he would surely have thought his judgment confirmed.

"But what he would have overlooked—what perhaps no one could have discerned at the time—was the intense though almost secret drive for a literary culture that families like mine were enacting—enacting by their very faith in a new church founded on a miraculously delivered *book.* A family legend has it that my paternal great-grandfather, required to work throughout childhood in England's dark Satanic mills, learned how to work one lever with his foot, freeing one hand to hold—a book. He grew

WAYNE C. BOOTH

up with a bad limp, and all of us believe that it was caused by the years of sitting twisted over that machine, reading his books—French was mentioned, and medicine, and history.

"His children, the great aunts and uncles I listened to as they sat around on Sunday afternoons telling stories about their childhood in pioneer days, were all scribblers. We still have some of their wonderful long letters, a few of them in surprisingly competent verse. Great Uncle Wilford made a good long start on a Miltonic epic about a book of Mormon heroes. And when my Aunt Relva died not long ago, in her eighties, we found fragments of stories in her trunk; only then did we remember that she had sometimes mentioned a 'childhood' desire to 'be a writer.'

"In college, choosing a career, I simply ignored all of this. Living in a cultural desert, surrounded by philistines and barbarians, I decided to go against my traditions, march to a different drummer, and become not only a teacher (like my father and mother, six aunts and uncles, and one grandfather) but an *author.*

"The third myth is that I am not really a critic or rhetorician or even a teacher but a failed novelist. I keep hoping to discover the secret of how to complete, with honor, any one of the fragments that languish in my files. I am convinced that all those "world authors" out there somehow took in that secret with their nurse's milk. Maybe if I try out enough different projects, I'll stumble into something really good, like Cervantes hitting his stride with *Don Quixote* in his late fifties. . . .

"The plain truth is that at sixty-one my days are as full of writing projects as were those of the

'projectors' Swift mocked in his time. Poems, short stories, novels (no plays), political satires, a book touting the perfect undergraduate curriculum, hoaxes, three different kinds of autobiography (all rich in Mormon lore), two novels, three more books of criticism, two textbooks, a book about teaching, a defense of the humanities, a guide to good writing, a book of rhetorical theory to end all rhetorical theory, an anthology of political speeches, with analyses that attempt once more that great American task of educating public citizens, a rhetoric of the TV commercial, a revision of *Modern Dogma* to make my critique of modernism more cogent, a history of political satire.

"None of that, even if completed, is likely to change the profession I list on my passport: it's been 'teacher' (with an implied 'novelist manqée') all the way."

––––––––

The son of Wayne Chipman and Lillian (Clayson) Booth, Wayne Booth was born in American Fork, Utah. He received his B.A. from Brigham Young University in 1944 and, following military service in World War II, taught and did graduate work in the English Department of the University of Chicago (M.A. 1947, Ph.D. 1950). After three years as assistant professor of English at Haverford College, he moved on to Earlham College, where he was professor of English and head of the department from 1953 to 1962. He returned to the University of Chicago in the latter year as George M. Pullman Professor of English. From 1964 to 1969 he was dean of a college of the University and in 1970 was appointed Distinguished Service Professor. He has held a number of guest professorships (Indiana, Princeton, the University of California at Berkeley and at Irvine) and received many academic honors including Ford, Rockefeller, NEH, and Guggenheim fellowships and, in 1962 for *The Rhetoric of Fiction,* the Christian Gauss Award of Phi Beta Kappa. From 1980 to 1982 he was president of the Modern Language Association of America. Booth has been married since 1946 to Phyllis Barnes, a clinical psychologist, whose interest in his work he has acknowledged in the prefaces to several of his books ("she has so often helped me clear up my ideas and my style that she is a Chicago critic by osmosis"). They have two daughters.

As a graduate student at the University of Chicago in the late 1940s, Booth came under the intellectually challenging influence of what has come to be known as the "Chicago School" of criticism. Not a school in any formal sense, this was a group of academics headed by Professors

Ronald S. Crane and Richard McKeon, whose "rigorous, exasperating, terrrifying year-long seminar" (as Booth describes it) trained graduate English students in literary criticism on Neo-Aristotelean principles. Booth wrote his doctoral dissertation under Crane on Sterne's *Tristram Shandy,* and although in his subsequent work he has moved on to develop his own critical theories, he never fails to acknowledge his debt to his mentors who taught him "not conclusions, but rather some ways of thinking, and ways of thinking about ways of thinking."

The Rhetoric of Fiction, first published in 1961 and many times reprinted, with a second edition in 1983, has become what the *Times Literary Supplement* called "a major influence" in modern literary criticism. Rarely has a contemporary critical examination of an art form so widely extended and refined the possibilities of understanding within that form. Booth employs a firmly controlled discipline, concentrating upon what the novelist has done to guide and direct the reader's responses to the work itself. Booth's method demands close critical reading, but in contrast to much currently fashionable literary criticism, it is pluralistic and humanistic, restoring to the novelist his identity as "a kind of public self" whose principal concern is the communication of his vision of life to his readers. For Booth, "rhetoric"—i.e. the technical means by which the novelist "makes [readers] see what they have never seen before, moves them into a new order of perception and experience altogether"—is not a calculated device to manipulate the reader's responses. It neither dismisses nor denies the aesthetic integrity of literature, its purity as a work of the creative imagination. Rhetoric, instead, is an artistic means by which the author achieves the principal purpose of his creative vision—which is communication between author and reader.

The result of Booth's wide-ranging reading in *The Rhetoric of Fiction* from Chaucer, Boccaccio, and Cervantes through the major European, English, and American novelists of the eighteenth, nineteenth, and twentieth centuries, is enlightening and stimulating, offering students and teachers of literature alike a useful critical methodology. His concepts, for example, of the "implied author" (the image the novelist "creates of himself" as narrator) and the "reliable and unreliable narrator" (*reliable* when he speaks or acts in accordance with the norms of the work—which is to say, the implied author's norms—*unreliable* when he does not) are applied in close readings of specific novels. That such an approach has its critical limitations Booth was quick to acknowledge, writing in his Preface that he has "rigorously" excluded many

major questions of the social context of novels and the psychology of readers and authors alike: "My excuse is that only in doing so could I hope to deal adequately with the narrower question of whether rhetoric is compatible with art." Critics of his work have challenged his premises, arguing that novels are not "self-expression" or "sophisticated specimens of 'communication'" between author and reader (John Killham in the *British Journal of Aesthetics,* 1966), that Booth offers a didactics rather than an aesthetics of fiction (Donald Pizer in *College English,* 1967), that interpretation is not "a major ingredient of all fiction" (Bernard Paris, *Novel,* 1968), that he wishes to be "a moral re-educator" (Morse Peckham, *The Triumph of Romanticism,* 1970). In response to much of this criticism Booth offers not a defense but an appeal for critical pluralism and what he calls "cumulative discourse" among literary critics of any and all schools.

Rhetoric remains Booth's primary focus in his subsequent critical examinations not only of literature but of contemporary society as well. A practicing teacher and administrator, he has confronted the crises in American higher education at first hand. As dean of a liberal arts college in the late 1960s, he found himself grappling "not simply with political assumptions" but with "modernist dogmas about belief and consent." To the students (and many of his academic colleagues) who demanded revolution not reform in the universities, who rejected traditional reasoning and humanistic education, Booth replied with an appeal to rhetoric: "the art of discovering warrantable beliefs and improving those beliefs in shared discourse." He urged a rhetoric of "systematic assent" rather than negation, based on communion among thinking human beings, "the community of those who want to discover good reasons together" (*Modern Dogma and the Rhetoric of Assent*). Addressing student groups during this period he argued "in defense of a rational persuasion" in "a world in which men show little esteem for logic, little respect for facts, no faith in anyone's ability to use thought or discourse to arrive at improving judgments, commitments, and first principles."

PRINCIPAL WORKS: The Rhetoric of Fiction, 1961, 1983; Now Don't Try to Reason with Me: Essays and Ironies for a Credulous Age, 1970; A Rhetoric of Irony, 1974; Modern Dogma and the Rhetoric of Assent, 1974; Critical Understanding: The Powers and Limits of Pluralism, 1979.

ABOUT: Borklund, E. Contemporary Literary Critics, 1982; Contemporary Authors, new revision series 3, 1981; Who's Who in America, 1983–84. *Periodicals*—Profession, 1982.

*BORGEN, JOHAN (April 28, 1902–October 16, 1979), Norwegian novelist and journalist, was born in Kristiania (later Oslo), the son of the lawyer and property owner Paul Holst Borgen and the former Andrea Bommen. In later life he depicted his early childhood in the affluent West End of the capital with some nostalgia in the autobiographical *Barndommens rike* (The Kingdom of Childhood, 1965). His first years were relatively stable and happy, though troubled by his awareness of the discord between his parents and a growing antipathy towards their privileged and affluent existence. This stability came to an abrupt end with the beginning of the First World War, which for Borgen, as for many of his contemporaries, meant the disintegration of what had seemed a timelessly secure society.

After the war he began to study law, though without enthusiasm; his real interests lay in writing. He worked as a journalist for several newspapers, traveled abroad, and wrote his first short stories—which bore clear traces of Knut Hamsun. It took Borgen some time to find his own literary style; in the period between the wars he experimented with plays, short stories and novels, as well as continuing with a frenetic journalistic career. During the 1930s he was one of the best known journalists on *Dagbladet,* Oslo's largest newspaper. It was not until after World War II that he gave up his job in order to devote himself to creative writing—although he remained a regular contributor to the paper throughout his life.

Borgen was no ivory tower writer—he was deeply interested in social and political issues and never afraid to speak out. This is most clearly demonstrated in his "causeries" in *Dagbladet,* which he wrote under the name of Mumle Gåsegg; sly, humorous anecdotes which concealed beneath their urbane and polished surface a biting criticism of social mores or political dishonesty. When the Germans occupied Norway in 1940 his criticisms continued unabated, to the extent that he was imprisoned and tortured at the German prison camp at Grini, before being released and fleeing with his family to Sweden.

Throughout his life Borgen's main base was in Oslo or in country houses not far from the capital; yet he traveled extensively and had an extraordinarily wide circle of friends. He was one of the most cosmopolitan Norwegians of his age. His affection for Denmark was particularly strong, and the Danish authors Kjeld Abell and H. C. Branner were among his closest friends. He was constantly on the move in Norway too, seeking solitude in order to immerse himself in the creative process of a new book or involved in productions of his own and others' plays. Dur-

JOHAN BORGEN

ing the 1930s Borgen was actively involved with the theater and wrote the majority of his plays. Most of them were ephemeral and only moderately well received; but the remarkable *Mens vi venter* (While We're Waiting, 1938) was a critical success. It is an existential drama set in a station waiting-room, which becomes a metaphor for a suspended state of existence in which the central character is waiting to make an informed choice of action—until he discovers that he has waited so long that *that* has become his choice.

By the middle of the 1950s Johan Borgen had become a household name in Norway, largely due to his journalism and his radio broadcasts. But it was not until then that he emerged as a major author, with the publication of the first part of his trilogy *Lillelord* (1955). The other two parts followed swiftly: *De mørke kilder* (The Dark Springs) came out in 1956 and *Vi har ham nå* (We Have Him Now) in 1957. In these novels Borgen focuses his attention on the complicated mental life of a man at war with himself. Like the hero of *Mens vi venter,* Lillelord—alias Wilfred Sagen—is a man who postpones choosing until the very postponement becomes a way of life. It is a study of a dual personality, a split fostered by his environment and early influences between Lillelord, the sensitive, gifted upper-class mother's darling, and Wilfred, the cynical and amoral exploiter who revels in the company of drop-outs and criminals. The trilogy follows the course of his life against a broad panorama of twentieth-century Norway. In the first part, set in Oslo in the stable era before 1914, he is an adolescent, discovering his own mental and physical possibilities and the thrill, which be-

°bôr´ gen, yō hän

comes a craving, of playing a dangerous double game; yet at the same time he is still vulnerable and uncertain, and becomes almost fatally trapped in the "nets" laid for him by his concerned family.

Nets are a favorite image of Borgen's; his characters are continually on the run, in both concrete and metaphorical terms. Wilfred's fear of being caught develops into a pathological terror of commitment of any kind, which undermines all his attempts to find a direction for his life. He is exceptionally gifted; in *De mørke kilder* it becomes clear that he could with almost equal ease have attained fame as an actor, writer, musician or painter. Yet he cannot take any of it seriously. In his element in the rootless existence of post-1914 Europe, he wanders from place to place and from opportunity to opportunity, always moving on when it seems that he is about to succeed. He is a consummate lover, able to respond not only physically but also emotionally to the moods and needs of his partner. (This instinctive ability to guess thoughts and wishes is another recurring theme in Borgen's works; to him, "guessing" [å gjette] is an essential part of any human intimacy.) Yet in this area too Wilfred is ultimately a failure; his inability to commit himself totally poisons even his deepest love—for Miriam, a Jewish musician who has achieved that oneness with her art which he can never attain.

Vi har ham nå is set during the German occupation of Norway, and depicts the logical conclusion of Wilfred's schizophrenic behavior as he becomes simultaneously a resistance fighter and a Nazi collaborator. The war provides him with the ideal opportunity to be on both sides at once, to save lives and to end them with impartial efficiency. At the end of the war, as the resistance group comes to collect him, he holds a gun to his head without knowing if it is loaded. He dies, but even now without having chosen; his death, like his life, is a game of chance.

The problem of identity, of deciding who one is—or rather of choosing whom to be—is central to Borgen's writing. He saw personality not as a fixed and immutable element but as something fluid and impermanent, the result of a deliberate self-restriction: "Personally I believe that man's fascination for art lies in our unsatisfied desire for identity. I believe that our unarticulated longing for freedom, our painful and impractical and completely unreasonable longing for freedom derives simply from the fact that we are shut up inside that system of apparent necessities which is called our personality, or which we call our personality, because we need to fasten a fine-sounding name to the cage in which we have shut ourselves up. . . . We live a crippled life, shut up inside the narrow cage of considerations, caught in the net of expectations." (*Ord gjennom år*, Words Through the Years, 1966) Borgen was fascinated by states of mind in which the gratuitousness of the adoption of a fixed personality becomes apparent and returned again and again to the depiction of a mind in crisis, at a crossroads of choice. To choose is necessary; the refusal to do so leads to the sterile and pathless no-man's land in which Wilfred languishes. The right choice is the one which heals the split, which leads back to spiritual harmony and away from the distracting tension of being continually "beside oneself."

The search for self-coincidence is at the center of Borgen's next and most powerful novel, *Jeg* (I, 1959). Here the split in personality is mirrored in the form of the novel itself; the identity of the central character Matias Roos splits into two parts, an "I" and a "he," so that he is simultaneously the narrator and the central actor in the drama. The passive narrator remains in the forest, watching and commenting as his active self sets off on a pilgrimage. Matias Roos is one of the "guilty ones," guilty in a Kafkaesque sense not because of an evil he has committed but by the very act of existing as he has done. He seeks to atone for this guilt; and chronology and reality break down as he searches through fragments of past and present in order to find out where his life went wrong. He expiates his guilt by taking upon himself the punishment for a crime he has not committed, or only vicariously committed. Finally he returns to the forest and becomes reunited with his other self, perhaps at the moment of death.

Jeg is a novel which leaves many questions unanswered; it is the most experimental and disturbing of Borgen's works, taking the reader into a nightmare landscape of the mind where chaos threatens to overwhelm the control of reason. In the novel *Blåtind* (Blue Peak, 1964) he explores the theme of the fragility of identity in a much more concrete fashion. Two of the novel's central characters have literally lost their identities: the Jewish girl Nat, who has been made a concentration camp prostitute, has no memory of her earlier self, and Ole, a resistance worker who has been tortured and brainwashed, has had his personality systematically destroyed. But ironically it is a third character, Peter, who is least sure of who he really is; his apparent strength is but a facade which conceals his hollowness. A sense of self depends upon an inner strength which in many of Borgen's works is shown to be possessed by women more readily than by men.

After *Blåtind* Borgen wrote several more novels which were well received. By this time he had become the Nestor of Norwegian letters. *Den røde tåken* (*The Red Mist*, 1967) centers on a man who seems to be on the run from the police, and who returns to the scene of his crime—not the crime of which he has been convicted, but the undiscovered crime for which he has endured a lifetime's guilt. The journey becomes a voyage back into his own consciousness, which is not complete until he has thrown himself off a huge monument and arrives at the truth about himself in the last moments of his life. *Min arm min tarm* (My Arm, My Intestine, 1972) and *Den store havfrue* (The Large Mermaid, 1973) are more lighthearted novels which take a sometimes comical, sometimes satirical look at the problems of surviving in modern society.

Despite the seriousness of his themes, Borgen's novels are not gloomy and despondent. He is an engaging storyteller and a supreme stylist. The quick-wittedness and love of repartee which made him such a successful journalist are in evidence in his novels too, where his lightness of touch makes them compelling and—with the exception of *Jeg*—easy reading. He is also a master of the short story form; indeed, in the opinion of some critics it is his short stories that represent the pinnacle of his achievement. He wrote short stories throughout his life, from his first published work (*Mot mørket*—Towards Darkness, 1925) to his last (*I dette rom*—In this Room, 1975). Some of the best are collected in *Noveller i utvalg 1936–61* (Selected Short Stories 1936–61, 1961). The themes of the short stories are similar to those of the novels; among his best are warmly sympathetic cameos of lovers and their intuitive understanding, such as "Elsk meg bort fra min bristende barndom" (Release Me Through Love From My Crumbling Childhood) and "I gresset" (In the Grass), where the ability to "guess" the moods of the other creates a sympathy deeper than words. Stories of people "on the run" and searching for themselves are frequent too, for example "Korridorene" (The Corridors) in which a girl who has been running away all her life finally finds the courage to take a stand and make her choice; and "Passet" (The Passport) in which a ridiculous confusion about passports leads to the narrator being faced with the question "Who are you—really?" and finding himself unable to answer it.

Johan Borgen died in 1979 after a long illness, having become almost a myth in his own lifetime. After his death his wife Annemarta wrote an account of their life together, *Deg* (You, 1981), which is at the same time a fascinating study of Norwegian cultural life over fifty years from 1930 to 1980.

WORKS IN ENGLISH TRANSLATION: Borgen's *The Red Mist* was translated by Oliver Stallybrass in 1973; *Lillelord* by Elizabeth Brown Moen and Ronald E. Peterson in 1982. A short story, "In the Grass," is in J. W. McFarlane's *Slaves of Love and Other Norwegian Short Stories*, 1982.

ABOUT: Birn, R., Johan Borgen, 1974; Columbia Dictionary of Modern European Literature, 1980; Encyclopedia of World Literature in the 20th Century (rev. ed.) I, 1981, Synnes, M., and J. E. Vold, Johan Borgen 1902–1962, 1962. *Periodicals*—Scandinavian Studies 1, 1974; Scandinavica 2, 1975.

BRADLEY, DAVID (September 7, 1950–), American novelist, was born in Bedford, Pennsylvania, son of David Henry and Harriette (Jackson) Bradley. As a black family, the Bradleys were in a small minority in their community; no more than a hundred blacks lived in the entire, largely rural, county. Bradley's father, who influenced him in becoming a writer, was a minister and historian who attended the University of Pittsburgh and New York University and was the author of several privately published books on the history of the Methodist church. David Bradley attended local schools and in 1968 entered the University of Pennsylvania, from which he received his B.A., summa cum laude, in 1972. During the following year he was a guest lecturer at the University of Warwick and the University of Nottingham in England, and at the University of Edinburgh in Scotland; and he studied at the Institute for United States Studies, King's College, University of London. He received an M.A. degree from the University of London in 1974.

Bradley was an asssistant editor in Philadelphia and New York with J. P. Lippincott, the publisher, from 1974–76; and in 1975 a visiting lecturer at the University of Pennsylvania. In 1975, at the age of twenty-five, he published his first novel, *South Street*, which introduced him to the American reading public. The novel is set in Philadelphia's black ghetto and deals with a young, educated, middle-class black man, Adlai Stevenson Brown, who decides to investigate the down-and-out life of the city. At Lightnin' Ed's bar, Brown skirmishes with such characters as Leroy Briggs, a local numbers king; Big Betsy, a prostitute; Jake the wino; and Rayburn the cuckold. Complications quickly proliferate. The pace of the novel is manic, its style bawdy and Rabelaisian.

Almost all of *South Street*'s reviewers were impressed by its surging energy, humor, and backstreet realism. The critic for *Choice* remarked that "nothing like the author's fresh and witty

© 1980 Thomas Victor

DAVID BRADLEY

use of similes has occurred in American fiction since the publication of Guy Owen's *Ballad of the Flim-Flam Man.* With all his senses keenly alert, he has captured and presented the *allegro con brio* of that part of Philadelphia best known to the black community. The book is a strong social document as well as a beguiling work of fiction." The reviewer for *Booklist* noted that "the strongest [features] of this novel are atmosphere and dialogue. The street is alive, indeed it is the central character, and the talk is funny and [the action] fast moving. . . . The slim plot may be overlooked in the sheer joy of the richness of the characters. Brown . . . is perhaps the least well done, but the focus is mostly on the people around him in an impressive first novel pulsing with vitality."

Reviews of *South Street* in the *New York Times* were admiring, although with reservations. Mel Watkins called *South Street* a "fine first novel [that] displays a versatile fictional talent within which control and technique are matched with an incisive eye for detail and an oblique viewpoint both refreshing and entertaining. . . . Mr. Bradley uses satire, burlesque and a perfectly pitched ear for ghetto dialect to establish a narrative tone that is both delightfully humorous and poignantly revealing." But he faulted the novel for the thinness of its plot, and found the central character drawn with "less conviction" than the peripheral ones. Jerome Charyn, also in the *Times,* called *South Street* an "ambitious, scraggly novel," whose hero "is a thin creation, predictable in his language and his suffering. . . . Still, he doesn't destroy the legitimacy of Lightnin' Ed's; the preachers, whores

and hoodlums claw at us with their vitality and the harsh power of their voices."

In 1976–77, Bradley was visiting instructor at Temple University in Philadelphia, and in 1980–81 visiting lecturer at San Diego State University. In 1981 he published his second novel, *The Chaneysville Incident,* a work which he says involved eleven years of research and writing. The book is based on an event brought to light by Bradley's mother, a local historian in Bedford, Pennsylvania. She learned of thirteen runaway slaves who had been intercepted near Chaneysville in their flight for freedom along the Underground Railroad in the mid-1800s. The slaves, who had told their captors that they would rather die than be sent back into slavery, were taken at their word and executed. After Mrs. Bradley informed her son that she had discovered the slaves' burial site, he decided to write their story. Bradley attempted several approaches, including a straightforward historical novel, before casting the work in the form of a black family saga beginning in the present and constantly inquiring back into the past in a suspenseful search for answers to a number of mysteries. *The Chaneysville Incident* is thus not so much history as history conjured with, imagined and pondered creatively. Its hero is a young black historian named John Washington, who searches for the meaning of his father's suicide and the even stranger death of his grandfather, a runaway slave.

A large and at times powerful novel, *The Chaneysville Incident* attracted a considerable amount of attention; and at least one critic wrote that it "rivals Toni Morrison's *Song of Solomon* as the best novel about the black experience in America since Ellison's *Invisible Man* nearly thirty years ago." Vance Bourjaily remarked that whatever else may be said about Bradley, it is clear that "the man's a writer. What he can do, at a pretty high level of energy, is synchronize five different kinds of rhetoric, control a complicated plot, manage a good-sized cast of characters, convey a lot of information, handle an intricate time scheme, pull off a couple of final tricks that dramatize provocative ideas, and generally keep things going for 200,000 words. That's about two and a half books for most of us." Bourjaily was particularly impressed by the "beautifully rendered and wildly adventurous chase" in the later part of the book; but he found some of the plotting "a bit Victorian," and objected to the rather heavy-handed "white-baiting . . . which only those white readers far gone in guilt and masochism will find gratifying or even interesting."

Mary Helen Washington found the novel ambitious in its scope and partly in its achievement; but she was stung by the small and slighting role assigned to women in the work. "If [the narrator's] past is filled with shadowy women," she wrote, "his present is worse. The main women in the frame story, his mother Yvette and his white lover Judith, are . . . exercises in depreciating women. . . . Can we tolerate a history of black people in which the major event of each generation is the begetting of a first-born son, . . . in which all the proud, defiant, heroic gestures are accomplished by men?" Phoebe-Lou Adams also found fault with Bradley's characterization of Judith, a woman who "listens" worshipfully as the hero recreates history and is denied any life of her own. She "was no doubt necessary to the action," Adams observed, "but Lord, she is a bore." Thomas M. Gannon went further, and questioned whether the historical passages were "fully assimilated" into the structure of the novel. "For long periods," he commented, "the novel stands still for the recitation of history within the novel. [But] the novel's problems are not limited to structure. Washington and his lover are racial stereotypes. He is the standard variety superblack, a Renaissance man from the other side of the tracks, a brilliant scholar, an accomplished woodsman, a mighty hunter. . . . Finally, the novel's ending creaks with contrivance." But however varied the reviews, it was generally felt that Bradley had written an arresting book, and placed himself in the forefront of the younger generation of black American novelists.

Bradley is professor of English at Temple University and a frequent contributor to national magazines, including the *New York Times Magazine.* He has said in an interview that he is partial to novels that "give you a lot of information," among which he includes Alex Haley's *Roots.* His earliest literary passion was science fiction, particularly the works of Robert Heinlein, who taught him "that to write a story you must create a world, one that has internally consistent rules." He particularly admires Faulkner, Jean Toomer, and Robert Penn Warren, especially *All the King's Men,* a discernible influence on *The Chaneysville Incident.* Bradley's recent work in progress is a novel about the upheavals of the late 1960s.

PRINCIPAL WORKS: South Street, 1975; The Chaneysville Incident, 1981.

ABOUT: Contemporary Authors 104, 1982. *Periodicals*—America May 30, 1981; Atlantic May 1981; Book World April 12, 1981; Choice December 1975; Christian Science Monitor May 20, 1981; Library Journal October 15, 1975; New York Times October 4, 1975; New York Times Book Review September 28, 1975; April 19, 1981; May 13, 1984; Saturday Review July 1981.

*BREYTENBACH, BREYTEN (September 16, 1939–), South African poet, prose writer, and painter, was born in Bonnievale, in western Cape Province. His family has been a prominent part of the Cape Dutch ascendancy since the seventeenth century; his brother, today a general in the South African army, commands a well-known Black unit of anti-guerrilla commandoes that has made frequent raids into Angola and Zimbabwe. Young Breytenbach received a conventional Afrikaner schooling, but did not go on to attend Stellenbosch University, as would have been expected for someone of his background; he instead enrolled as a student of poetry and fine arts in the English-language University of Cape Town.

Breytenbach dropped out of university, however, at the age of twenty and left by freighter for Europe, where he worked, in England and on the Continent, in a variety of jobs—railway porter, factory hand, even cook on a yacht—before settling in Paris in 1961. There he began seriously to paint and write, and met and married Yolande Ngo Thi Hoang Lien, whose father was for a time finance minister of South Viet Nam in the government of Ngo Dinh Diem. From 1962 until well into the 1970s Breytenbach's highly regarded paintings were often seen in solo and group exhibitions in Paris, Brussels, Amsterdam, and Edinburgh.

Breytenbach published his first two books in 1964: a collection of poems, *Die Ysterkoei Moet Sweet* (The Iron Cow Must Sweat) and a group of short prose pieces, *Katastrofes* (Catastrophes). The books had an immediate impact in his homeland, and established him as one of the chief writers of the *Sestigers,* the brilliant literary generation of the 1960s. Both poems and stories combine fairly transparent political allegory with an astonishing linguistic grace and flexibility. He has been from the beginning resolutely unrealistic in his treatment of every theme, a characteristic he shares with many of his countrymen in their various considerations of their brutalized culture. Among the most famous of the *Katastrofes* are two absurdist, hallucinatory companion pieces, "The Fascist Pumpkin" and "The Totalitarian Pumpkin" (the work *pampoen* in Afrikaans means also, colloquially, "fool"). The pumpkins and the men who want them for their birthdays are different in each story, but the men's situations, it is clear, are ultimately identical. In the "totalitarian" story, the man is in jail, and when his wife brings him the longed-

°brī´ ten bäk, brī´ ten

BREYTEN BREYTENBACH

for gift, it is quickly destroyed: "The warder has cut the pumpkin open and scooped out pumpkin. The warder has taken out a saw without teeth and three drained dreams wrapped in a manuscript and a pistol full of little hallelujahs and a moustache and a Playboy and a pellet of marijuana and on top of that a future and an escape and three ounces of sympathy from an unknown sympathiser." The best of his poems speak directly to his fellow Afrikaners, destroying their complacency, making them think about things they would always prefer to ignore. Among the most powerful is "Breyten Prays for Himself" which includes the lines:

There is no need for Pain Lord
We could live well enough without It
A flower has no teeth

It is true we are only fulfilled in death
But let our flesh stay new as fresh cabbage
Make us firm as a fish's pink body
Let us spellbind each other with eyes deep butterflies

Pardon our mouths our guts our brains
Let us regularly taste the sweet evening air
Swim in tepid seas, be allowed to sleep with the sun
Ride peacefully on bicycles through bright Sundays

And gradually we will rot like old ships or trees
But keep Pain far from Me o Lord
That others may bear it
Be taken into custody, Shattered
              Stoned
              Hanged
              Lashed
              Used
              Tortured
              Crucified
              Interrogated
              Placed under house arrest
              Made to slave their guts out

Banished to obscure islands till the end of their days
Wasting in damp pits down to slimy green imploring bones
Worms in their stomachs heads full of nails
But not *Me*
Never give us Pain or complain

The "others" who must "bear it," who are "banished to obscure islands" are, of course, the leaders of South Africa's black majority. Their cause had become, even as early as 1964, Breytenbach's own.

He published several books of poems over the next decade, whose very titles suggest the force of his condemnation: *Die Huis van die Dowe* (The House of the Deaf, 1967); *Kouevuur* (Gangrene—literally, Cold Fire, 1969); *Oorblyfsels* (Remnants, 1970); *Skryt* (which means both Write and Cry, 1972); and *Met Ander Woorde* (In Other Words, 1973). His poetry has appeared in English in several collections: in translations by various hands in *Sinking Ship Blues* and *And Death White as Words*; and in *In Africa Even the Flies Are Happy,* a British edition combining poetry and prose with some of the original Afrikaans retained.

Breytenbach remained in exile in Paris—his wife's official classification by the regime as "non-white" was an important reason for his reluctance to return home. In 1973, however, the couple was granted a three-month visa, and Breytenbach was able to see his own country for the first time in fourteen years. At the first general meeting of the *Sestigers,* held at the University of Cape Town, he delivered a famous address, "The View from Outside," in which he warned his fellow Afrikaners that their racist society was doomed, and urged them to understand this fact and write about it. Having been an active supporter of the anti-apartheid movement in Europe, Breytenbach also made or renewed contacts with foes of the regime throughout the country.

The most extraordinary part of Breytenbach's story occurred in 1975, when he returned to South Africa in disguise, carrying a forged French passport and using the name Christian Galaska. He had been for several years under surveillance by the South African security police, who arrested him as he was about to leave the country. Charged under the infamous Terrorism Act with being a founder of Okehela (a Zulu word meaning "spark"), allegedly a white wing of the banned African National Congress, he was forced to plead guilty to reduced charges (the prosecutor told him he would otherwise be hanged) and was sentenced to nine years in prison. In 1977, after a year and a half in solitary confinement next to the death cell, he was again put on trial, charged under the Terrorism, Riotous Assemblies, and Prisons acts with an incredible list of crimes: trying to escape; recruiting a warder to aid him in such a purpose; promoting an underground movement to fight apartheid while in prison; plotting to blow up the Afrikaans Language Monument in Paarl; planning a Soviet submarine attack on Robben Island, where the country's black leaders have been imprisoned for decades; and smuggling out poems and letters. To everybody's surprise, he was acquitted of all but the last charge, for which he received a nominal fine.

The poems Breytenbach wrote in prison constitute his finest work. His poetry had been growing increasingly brief and allusive, verging on the gnomic. The prison poems, however, are full of expansive energy and rage, yet take unerring aim at their targets and retain a painful sense of irony. The greatest among them is perhaps "Taalstryd" (The Struggle for the Taal), a long, passionate poem which describes the history and predicament of Afrikanerdom and how the Taal, the Afrikaners' beloved language, has become an almost mystic vehicle of intolerance and repression:

We ourselves are aged.
Our language is a grey reservist a hundred years old and more
his fingers stiff around the triggers—
and who will be able to sing as we sang
when we are no longer there? . . .

From the structure of our conscience
from the stores of our charity
we had black contraptions built for you, you bastards—
schools, clinics, post-offices, police-stations—
and now the plumes blow black smoke
throbbing and flowing like a heart.

But you have not fully understood.
You have yet to master the Taal.
We will make you say the ABC all over again,
we will teach you the ropes
of Christian National Education . . .

And you will please learn to use the Taal,
with humility use it, abuse it . . .
because we are down already, the death-rattle's
throb and flow
on our lips . . .

As for us, we are aged . . .

In 1976, while still in prison, Breytenbach published 'n Seisoen in die Paradys (A Season in Paradise), both a rediscovery, in the style of Rimbaud, of his remembered youth and a record of his ninety-day return to South Africa in

1973. The first of his books so far published in the United States, it seemed too dense in theme and style to serve as an introduction to Breytenbach and his work. Paul Theroux, reviewing the book, called it "a teeming narrative, because no idea and hardly a sentence is uttered before it is overtaken by a new thought or impression. . . . The whole effect is a careening into South Africa's fortress wall of a simple soul in a state of nerves reduced to fragments of blood and brain." In a moving introduction to the translation, the South African poet and novelist André Brink writes that Breytenbach is "a man . . . closer to me than any brother." The most constant source of inspiration for the poet, Brink remarks, has been Zen Buddhism. His work "is a dazzling marriage of the real, the ordered, the rigorously disciplined world of the senses on the one hand, and the mystical and imaginary on the other. Essentially, Breytenbach's is an imagination prodded and prompted by the visual—one is never allowed to forget that this is a painter at work—while, in its turn, the visual is infused and informed by fantasy, much in the same way as it occurs in the paintings of that astounding medieval modernist, Hieronymus Bosch, another pervading influence in the work of Breytenbach."

Breytenbach was allowed to write while in prison, although he was forced to turn over all his manuscripts to the authorities. Upon his release his writings were returned to him, and they became the basis for his book Mouroir: Mirrornotes of a Novel. The title is a composite word of the French mourir (to die) and miroir (mirror), signifying, he explains, a dying place "where people go simply to finish their sentence." A collection of fragments of prose described by its author as "the inner exteriorization of disintegration," Mouroir is full of obscurities. Breytenbach provides few clues: "The texts have no symbolic intent; they only mirror and establish situations and images, situations made up of images." Neal Ascherson found it "an elusive kind of fiction. . . . Scenes emerge, detailed in the strong moonlight of Breytenbach's imagination, which then dissolve into other, disconnected scenes in a way that is literally dreamlike." As evidence, however, of the continuing growth of his creative powers, unchecked by seven years of confinement, Mouroir is a significant work. Ascherson describes it as "a writer's book of prose exercises, or a sculptor's yard full of seasoned blocks of old nightmare ready to be carved."

Throughout his imprisonment, the French government had been putting pressure on Pretoria, first to improve the conditions of the poet's incarceration, then to secure his release. This pressure intensified after the accession to power in mid-1981 of President François Mitterand and his Socialist government. Finally, in December 1982, Breytenbach, in the words of Donald Woods, "became one of the twenty-seven political prisoners, and the first white, to be released before full expiration of sentence in the first such commutation in thirty years."

In an interview soon after in Paris with Woods, a well-known South African English-language journalist and enemy of apartheid, Breytenbach spoke of his plans to write from then on mostly in French and English. When asked whether he was thus abandoning Afrikaans, he gave a grim reply: "I'd never reject Afrikaans as a language, but I reject it as part of the Afrikaner political identity. I no longer consider myself an Afrikaner. Actually, I prefer to consider myself a citizen of the world. I feel at home here in Paris. I'm a Parisian! But Afrikaans—I've long felt there was hope for it only if it were used in resistance to apartheid, but I think it is now too late. For blacks, it is a denial of reality and a humiliation. Afrikaans as the youngest prince of the Germanic languages? The prince has been poisoned. What remains is a language for use on tombstones." As to his imprisonment, he spoke of it as a necessary expiation for any white South African opposed to apartheid: "We need this for ourselves, independently of any general wish to serve the black cause and see justice done. It is for our own inner selves as well. We need it for our own redemption."

WORKS IN ENGLISH TRANSLATION: A selection of Breytenbach's prose and poems 1964–1977 was published in 1978, in Denis Hirson's English translation, as *In Africa Even the Flies are Happy.* Another collection, *A Season in Paradise,* translated by Rike Vaughan, was published in 1980. Also available in English are *Sinking Ship Blues,* 1977, with translations by André Brink, Ria Leigh-Loohuizen, and Denis Hirson, and a bilingual selection of his works, *And Death White as Words,* edited by A.J. Coetzee in 1978 and his prose work *Mouroir: Mirrornotes of a Novel,* 1984.

ABOUT: Brink, A. *Introduction to* A Season in Paradise, 1980; Coetzee, A.J. *Introduction to* And Death White as Words, 1978. *Periodicals*—Guardian Weekly December 19, 1982; New Statesman October 3, 1980; New York Review of Books October 25, 1984; New York Times March 31, 1980; December 6, 1982; New York Times Book Review March 30, 1980; May 1, 1983.

BRICKNER, RICHARD P(ILPEL) (May 14, 1933–), American novelist, was born in New York City the son of Richard M. and Ruth (Pilpel) Brickner. Brickner, whose parents were both psychiatrists, grew up in comfortable cir-

RICHARD P. BRICKNER

cumstances in New York City, where he attended the Fieldston School of the Ethical Culture Society. He entered Middlebury College in 1951. In 1953, while a sophomore, he became partially paralyzed as a result of an automobile accident. Although told that he should expect to live the life of an invalid, he made a limited recovery and fought stubbornly to reenter the active world. Paralyzed from the waist down and confined to a wheelchair, he enrolled at Columbia University, where he overcame many obstacles to become an editor of the college humor magazine, and graduate as an English major in 1957. From 1957 to 1961 he worked as an editor at Doubleday in New York City, but left to begin a career as a writer.

His first novel, *The Broken Year,* is a fictionalized autobiography whose hero, Eric Green, has an upper-middle-class New York upbringing, is infatuated with the theater, and works in a summer stock production as he pursues his interest in acting. On the brink of his first success, he falls down a flight of stairs, breaking his neck, and his future seems doomed. He is saved, however, by his vitality, which enables him to struggle back to active life.

From 1967 to 1970 Brickner was a lecturer at the City University of New York and, from 1970, a member of the faculty at the New School for Social Research. In 1972, he published his second novel, *Bringing Down the House,* which is concerned with the world of the theater and mocks the vulgar cultural pretensions of New York society. Bogus pre-Raphaelite prints are offered in supermarkets; Pound's *Cantos* are printed on dresses. The central characters include an art critic-politician, Alastair Hughes, who has moderated a YMHA symposium on "Kitsch and the Cold War"; a multimillionaire arts patron, Goddard Moss, who dictates his memoirs while speeding to his office in a chauffeur-driven limousine; and a playwright, Gregory Lubin, who writes jeremiads on the American scene. Elliott Baker, writing in the *New York Times Book Review,* called the work "wise and delightful," and described Brickner as a "gifted satirist."

The Broken Year and *Bringing Down the House* received few reviews, but Brickner's third book, *My Second Twenty Years: An Unexpected Life,* an autobiography, was reviewed widely and brought him national attention. *My Second Twenty Years* tells of Brickner's auto accident in 1953, his painful effort to reenter life, and his growth as a human being, which amounted to a remaking of himself. Leonard Kriegel called the book "a memorable achievement, a brilliant autobiography that is certainly among the most incisive books ever written about the process of becoming a cripple." The reviewer for *Booklist* wrote that *My Second Twenty Years* was "a searing, lyrical . . . gripping portrait of Everyman's climb from adolescence to maturity. . . . A beautiful, haunting document."

One of the most extraordinary and upredictable features of *My Second Twenty Years* is Brickner's candid account of his sexual life after his accident. Eric Moon commented that "the central sphere of the battle is his frustrating, difficult search for a rewarding sex life, and this he recounts with a stark honesty and sensitivity which can rarely have been matched in literature. It is a brilliant, moving, incredibly revealing and superbly written story." *My Second Twenty Years* was also praised by Jane Richmond, Lis Harris, and Joseph Epstein, the last of whom, in the *New York Times Book Review,* commented that "suffering understood has always been one of literature's great subjects, and Richard Brickner does not demean it."

In Brickner's *Tickets,* a light-hearted romance that by the end becomes dark, an attractive couple meet in New York—Alan Hoffman, a journalist, and Betsy Ring, who has just written her first novel. Alan, who is an aficionado of the opera, finds life imitating opera librettos. Daphne Merkin remarked that *"Tickets* is an elegantly written, deeply observed book about the difference between irony in art and in life. Brickner's prose reads like the best sort of talk, alternating between high sobriety and high jinks, and implicitly trusting the reader to understand what he is up to. He is up to a lot here, for there is little cultivated pleasure and its attendant pain that he misses." The reviewer for the *New Yorker,* much less pleased, felt that Brickner failed to transcend the operatic situations in which he portrays his characters.

Richard Brickner lives on the East Side of Manhattan, and teaches at the New School for Social Research. In addition to his books, he has contributed humorous pieces to the *Saturday Review* and published reviews of books in the *New York Times Book Review* and other publications. His pronounced interest in music and the theater is reflected in his novels. In 1983–84 he was a Guggenheim fellow.

PRINCIPAL WORKS: The Broken Year, 1962; Bringing Down the House, 1972; My Second Twenty Years, 1976; Tickets, 1981.

ABOUT: Contemporary Authors, first revision series 5–8, 1963; new revision series 2, 1981. *Periodicals*—Harper's April 1981; Library Journal September 15, 1962; New Leader May 1, 1972; April 20, 1981; New Republic February 19, 1977; New Yorker December 6, 1976; March 23, 1981; New York Herald Tribune October 7, 1962; New York Times Book Review January 30, 1972; September 12, 1976; March 8, 1981; Partisan Review Winter 1977.

BRINK, ANDRÉ (May 29, 1935–), South African novelist, writes: "I was born in a small village in the arid central region of South Africa. My father, a magistrate, was transferred every five or six years, so that I grew up in quite a succession of villages—all resembling each other in their conservative Protestantism, and in the generosity and narrow-mindedness that characterize the inhabitants of such places all over the world. After seven years at a small Calvinist university the watershed in my life came when, from 1959–1961, I did postgraduate research in Comparative Literature at the Sorbonne in Paris. The experience of suddenly finding myself remote from everything that had been familiar to me, and especially the trauma of witnessing the Sharpeville massacres in South Africa (March 1960) at such a distance, forced me to reexamine all the convictions and beliefs I had previously taken for granted.

"Returning to South Africa, I became involved in an exciting movement of literary renewal, known as the revolt of the "Sestigers" (writers of the sixties), which challenged all the existing moral and religious taboos then prevailing in Afrikaans literature and society. Towards the end of the sixties I returned to Paris for another year, this time with the intention of exploring the possibilities of settling permanently in Europe. Suddenly I found myself right in the midst of the student revolt of May, 1968. This

ANDRÉ BRINK

experience, which involved above all the asessment of the relationship between the individual and his society as a whole, prompted a new and agonizing soul-searching in myself. I realized that, if writing was really important to me—and by then it had already become a way of life to me, a way of coming to grips with the meaning of experience—I could not do it outside my own society, for to do so would be a form of luxury, an indulgence. I had to return to South Africa to assume my full responsibility, for every word I write, within my society.

"The very first novel to merge from this decision, *Kennis Van Die Aand* (1973), later translated as *Looking on Darkness*, was banned by the censors—the first book in the Afrikaans language ever to be dealt with in this way. At the same time a systematic process of intimidation and harassment was instituted against me, resulting in constant surveillance, interception of mail, the tapping of my telephone, a house search, interrogations by the Security Police, the confiscation of notes and correspondence and even of my typewriters. All of this made me more and more resolute to fight the ideology of apartheid with every weapon at my disposal. Cut off from my habitual readers through censorship, I was forced to start writing in English alongside of Afrikaans, in order not to be engulfed by silence. Throughout the seventies I wrote every book in both languages, taking them through three or four drafts in Afrikaans first, then translating (no, much more: reworking, rethinking, refeeling) them into English and, after two or three more versions, retranslating them into Afrikaans. In *A Chain of Voices*, I used En-

glish for some of the thirty different 'voices' speaking in the story, and Afrikaans for others, eventually disentangling the book into two separate versions.

"Since *Looking on Darkness* was first published in London in 1974 and in New York the following year, my work has been translated into more than twenty languages. My most gratifying experince as an author so far has been to see *A Dry White Season* awarded both the British Martin Luther King Memorial Prize and the French *Prix Médicis Étranger* in 1980. But what really gives one the sustenance to go on is the continuing overwhelming reaction from readers, especially those who bear the burden of oppression in my country. The discovery of touching the minds and sensibilities of individuals, which surely is the prerequisite for any significant social change, has been a profoundly moving and inspiring one.

"In the most recent past, possibly as a result of, among other reasons, the success of my work abroad, the conditions of my personal life in South Africa have eased somewhat. Which is not, of course, a reason to relax and enjoy it!—on the contrary, it makes it all the more imperative to continue the ceaseless and unremitting struggle against the lie, against injustice, and against unfreedom, which I have made my own."

———

Writing in two languages, English and his native Afrikaans, André Brink lives in two worlds. His home is in Grahamstown, South Africa, where he is professor of Afrikaans and Dutch literature at Rhodes University. His readership is international, his works published in more than twenty foreign countries, and his public voice, both as a novelist and a spokesman for human rights, is powerful. With his contemporaries the novelists Etienne le Roux, J. M. Coetzee, and the poet Breyten Breytenbach, who also write in Afrikaans, he belongs to a smaller and until recently less widely known group of writers than the celebrated English-language South African writers Alan Paton, Nadine Gordimer, Doris Lessing, and Dan Jacobson. But his intense, passionate, and action-packed novels have attracted a large public who might otherwise have ignored the social issues with which he is so deeply concerned.

Like William Faulkner and William Styron (in *The Confessions of Nat Turner*), he writes on an epic scale of the violence and brooding guilt of the oppressed blacks and the oppressing whites. His fiction, many critics complain, is often marred by melodrama and sensationalism (Jane Kramer describes it as "apartheid gothic"), but few have denied its impact upon readers.

Looking on Darkness, the first of Brink's novels to be published internationally, is the story of a South African "colored" who has won fame abroad as an actor but is destroyed when he returns to his native country to work for his own people. Told in flashbacks in the first-person from a prison cell where he awaits execution for the murder of his white mistress, it offers a brutal and chilling picture of South African life. "There are failings in the novel," C. J. Driver wrote in the *Times Literary Supplement:* "imaginative credibility slips, the control of the narrating 'I' wavers and pity becomes self-pity . . . But within its context this is a brave and important novel and in any terms a fine one." The same quality of genuine moral outrage against apartheid redeems the otherwise lurid, violence-filled and sexually explicit *Rumours of Rain.* Here a ruthless and bigoted white Afrikaaner who represents contemporary ruling society is seen against a natural landscape of alternating drought and torrential rain that serves as a metaphor for the ominous fate of his country. In *A Dry White Season* an idealistic white Afrikaaner teacher becomes a martyr when he attempts to investigate the mysterious death in prison of a black friend, an activist in the struggle for racial freedom. Although the plot strikingly recalls the death in prison of the black leader Stephen Biko in 1976, Brink had begun the novel a year earlier and the news of Biko's death, he told an interviewer, "came as such a shock to me that for a long time I couldn't go back to writing."

Conceived on a more epic scale, Brink's historical novels, *An Instant in the Wind,* a story of the love between a white woman and a runaway black slave set in the Cape colony in the eighteenth century, and *A Chain of Voices,* trace the roots of the tragedy of modern South Africa. In *A Chain of Voices* Brink drew on the records of a slave uprising in 1825, with multiple narrators—Belgian, British, Dutch, black—recounting the story of an "archetypal" slave who leads a small band in an inevitably unsuccessful revolt against his masters' tyranny. The theme of the novel is articulated by an elderly slave woman, surrogate mother of the doomed hero: "'We go on talking and talking, an endless chain of voices, all together yet all apart, all different yet all the same, and the separate links might lie but the chain is the truth.'" Described (in the *New York Times Book Review*) by Julian Moynahan as a "powerful and disturbing book," *A Chain of Voices* struck other readers as excessively polemical, marred, Roger Owen wrote (in the *Times Literary Supplement*) by "glaring" faults: "derivativeness; a proneness to cliché; a striving for 'fine' writing; a certain woodenness of style."

These are aesthetic risks which Brink has taken consciously and deliberately in all his writing as he has taken personal risks in his choice to live and write in South Africa. A member of South African PEN. and president since 1978 of the Afrikaans' Writers Guild, Brink said, in his speech accepting the Martin Luther King Memorial Prize: "I have tried to be totally honest in accepting the responsibility a man owes to his society and his time. . . . Writing is an affirmation, not only of the individual, but, through him, of the nameless and voiceless multitude who must rely on him to define the validity of their right to be." A number of Brink's essays on South African life, particularly on his experiences as an Afrikaaner confronting the traditional racism of his culture, were collected in *Mapmakers: Writing in a State of Siege.*

Married since 1970 to Alta Miller, Brink has four children, two from two earlier marriages which ended in divorce. In addition to his writing and teaching, Brink has taken an active interest in theater (several of his plays in Afrikaans have been staged) and writing for films and television. He has also translated into Afrikaans writings by Shakespeare, Cervantes, Henry James, Graham Greene, and others. His translation of Lewis Carroll's *Alice Through the Looking Glass* won an award from the South African Academy in 1970.

PRINCIPAL WORKS IN ENGLISH OR ENGLISH TRANSLATION: *Novels*—File on a Diplomat, 1965; A Portrait of a Woman as a Young Girl, 1973; Looking on Darkness, 1974; An Instant in the Wind, 1976; Rumours of Rain, 1978; A Dry White Season, 1979; A Chain of Voices, 1982; The Wall of the Plague, 1984. *Non-fiction*—Mapmakers, 1983.

ABOUT: Cassell's Encyclopedia of World Literature 2, 1973; Contemporary Authors 104, 1982. *Periodicals*—International Herald Tribune June 3, 1982; New York Review of Books December 2, 1982; New York Times Book Review June 13, 1982; Times Literary Supplement September 16, 1983; October 5, 1984; Washington Post May 28, 1982.

BROOKNER, ANITA (July 16, 1938–), British art historian and novelist, is the only child of Newson and Maude Brookner. She was educated at James Allen's Girls' School, at King's College of London University, and at the Courtauld Institute of Art. She was a lecturer in art history at Reading University in 1959–64, and since 1964 has been employed at the Courtauld Institute, where since 1977 she has held the post of reader with the rank of professor. She was Slade Professor at Cambridge University in

© 1985 Thomas Victor

ANITA BROOKNER

1967–68 and is a fellow of New Hall, Cambridge.

Brookner has concentrated professionally on French painting of the late eighteenth and early nineteenth centuries, a field in which she has become internationally respected, in particular for her masterly biographical-critical studies of Jean-Baptiste Greuze and Jacques-Louis David. Her first book, *Watteau*, a brief introductory study, was followed by an interesting exercise in comparative criticism, *The Genius of the Future: Studies in French Art Criticism—Diderot, Stendhal, Baudelaire, Zola, the Brothers Goncourt, Huysmans*, which grew out of her Slade lectures at Cambridge. The six concomitant essays study, one by one, the personalities and accomplishments of the subjects, none of whom was known primarily as an art critic. The greatest space is devoted to Baudelaire, perhaps the most energetic and passionate of them all: "in his own lifetime," remarked Philip Covisbee, "he was one critic among many others in the Paris of the 1840s and 1850s, whereas now he is somehow *the* critic." "In the case of Stendhal at least," wrote the reviewer for the *Times Literary Supplement*, "it is to his major literary works that one must turn for a key to his artistic temperament and an indication of what he expected of art. . . . This is significant for, with all the writers whom Dr. Brookner discusses, one gets the feeling that their criticism of painting and sculpture was an overflow from their feelings about their own medium."

Greuze: The Rise and Fall of an Eighteenth-Century Phenomenon accomplished nothing less than a revival of modern understanding, after more than five decades of critical neglect, of one of the most widely admired painters of pre-Revolutionary France. The artist, according to Brookner's introduction, "appealed to a vein of feeling that has now become extinct" and "his progress charts the evolution of painting from the moment when bourgeois taste was in full command to the triumph of the Puritan revolution." Though she calls him a "not very lovable painter," she is able to interest the reader in his life, which she considers "a genuine tragedy, beginning in provincial isolation, progressing to European fame, and ending in unpopularity and financial ruin." Brookner is especially persuasive on the intellectual and social background to Greuze's art, on the way it exemplifies the cult of *sensibilité* and its bizarre religious forerunner, quietism. She concludes that the artist "tried, clumsily, but with a marked if brief success, to reintroduce into the heartless dexterity of mid-eighteenth-century French painting concepts of a nostalgic regard for his own simple background and a desire to harness this nostalgia to more abstract intellectual ideas." The book, revealed the *Times Literary Supplement* reviewer, "was begun . . . as a doctoral thesis primarily concerned with the literary sources of Greuze's subject paintings in the *drame bourgeois* of the Abbé Prévost and Nivelle de la Chaussée's *comédie larmoyante*. But the reader should not be led by this to expect a display of bookish pedantry. Miss Brookner's style is sharp, elegant and often witty."

A universally enthusiastic critical reception greeted *Jacques-Louis David*, the first full-length study of this great artist to appear in English. Brookner had already elaborated on the close connection that existed between David and Greuze, who was ultimately unsuccessful in elevating his own style of sentimental genre painting to the heights to which the Academy assigned history painting. She conceives *David* as "an apologia" for an artist "who subsumed into his remarkable life many of the fundamental preoccupations of the eighteenth century in terms of thought, belief, and behavior. The book is intended for the general reader whose eye has been arrested by David's images and whose mind has been haunted or irritated by their supernal energy and conviction." She concludes with remarks on David's "power of sensibility, of excitability, of emotional generosity, which has its roots in the Enlightenment itself." The artist is one of the Happy Few, a concept dear to Stendhal and one Brookner had put to good use in her 1974 British Academy lecture, *Jacques-Louis David: A Personal Interpretation*. "The Happy Few," the book concludes, "are those who remain emotionally alive, who never compromise, who never succumb to cynicism or the routine of the second-hand. The Happy Few are not necessarily happy, but they are never corrupted and rarely bored."

Even Brookner's most fleeting obiter dicta on painters have an unmistakable ring of familiarity and authority and are invariably expressed with a witty and trenchant sympathy. She writes of Watteau that "we should still like to know why he painted scenes of love and flirtation when he seems to have felt so utterly miserable all the time." Chardin she calls the "most painterly of painters, whose *matière* has the dry creaminess of certain cheeses." Boucher is "the only painter of the eighteenth century whose reputation is still unrevised; in a sense he is his own greatest connoisseur, loving the immaculate paint, the fine materials, and beautiful surfaces that go to make his pictures so glossily attractive." More than almost any art critic of her time, she has the ability to bring to vibrant life the long-dead masters whose works fill our museums. She is also among the most consistently informative, readable, and incisive of the many regular book reviewers for the *Times Literary Supplement.*

The three slim, sharply intelligent novels Brookner has published since 1981 have been an agreeable surprise to many. Her heroines are industrious, somewhat wistful single women who have reached turning points in their lives. Dr. Ruth Weiss, of *A Start in Life* (U.S., *The Debut*), is the daughter of immigrants from Berlin who have settled in London. Sensitive and introspective, she spends her time teaching and writing about Balzac and looking after her incompetent father. She yearns constantly for "her adventure, the one that was to turn her life into literature." Kitty Maule, in *Providence,* is the granddaughter of immigrants and a professional student of the Romantic tradition and of Benjamin Constant's *Adolphe.* She is headed for a permanent career in the university, "an easy life doing difficult things," yet she has no understanding of the place love and beauty should play in her life, and because she is rejected by a cool, unselfconscious egomaniac—Brookner is wonderful at portraying these academic monsters—she retreats from the possibility of a fully interactive life and faces "a future of careful, creative dessication," in Galen Strawson's words. Frances Hinton, in *Look at Me,* is a reference librarian in a medical research institute with a burning need to be noticed. She becomes for a time the center of attention of a colleague's wife, a bored, insatiable devourer of people. Frances also retreats from life after being dissected and rejected, and determines to write a novel about her erstwhile friends. *Look at Me,* according to Mary

Cantwell, "is a horror story about monsters and their victims told in exceptionally elegant prose. It is a great pleasure to read, especially when one considers that Frances, in becoming a writer, may end up the biggest monster of them all." These novels have been praised for their full-length portraits, their deft and ironic characterizations; Brookner's greatest weakness as a novelist is generally held to be the lack of broad narrative scope.

In 1984 Anita Brookner received the prestigious Booker Prize for her novel *Hôtel du Lac.*

PRINCIPAL WORKS: *Criticism*—Watteau, 1968; The Genius of the Future, 1971; Greuze, 1972; Jacques-Louis David, 1980. *Fiction*—A Start in Life, 1981 (U.S., The Debut); Providence, 1982; Look at Me, 1983; Hôtel du Lac, 1984.

ABOUT: Who's Who, 1984. *Periodicals*—Choice June 1972; June 1973; June 1981; Economist December 25, 1971; Encounter April 1981; Harpers July 1983; February 1984; Library Journal April 1, 1972; New York Times Book Review May 22, 1983; March 18, 1984; New Republic May 30, 1981; March 26, 1984; New Statesman January 21, 1972; Times Literary Supplement November 26, 1971; October 13, 1972; January 9, 1981; May 28, 1982; Village Voice January 22, 1985.

BROOKS, JOHN (NIXON) (December 5, 1920–), American novelist and journalist writes: "I was born in New York City and grew up in Trenton, New Jersey. Many of my forebears were clergymen or lawyers; none that I have heard of were writers, other than of sermons and briefs. My first ambition, beginning in my teens, was to be a newspaperman. This had to do chiefly with a vision of myself smoking a lot of cigarettes, drinking a lot of whiskey, and wearing a hat in my office. Of course, I do none of those things, nor have I ever really been a newspaperman. At Princeton University, I studied English literature and managed to become editor of the campus daily. The experience inoculated me against ever wanting to be in charge of anything again, other than my own thoughts. (I have made one exception: from 1975 to 1979 I served as president of the Authors Guild of America, a fine and useful organization.) In the military service in Europe during the Second World War, I deluged American magazines with manuscripts, and amassed the usual collection of rejection slips.

"Back home in 1945, I got my first and only writing job through the familiar combination of influence and luck. I had an introduction to the managing editor of *Time* magazine; that was the influence. I happened to walk into *Time*'s offices

JOHN BROOKS

(still wearing my military uniform) at a moment when a senior editor had just fired five or six writers he disliked on the strength of his belief that the end of the war would bring a sudden glut of writers his way; that was the luck. I worked for *Time* as a writer for two years. It was a rather unhappy experience, but a richly rewarding one. First, seeing my own words (often considerably rearranged) in print in a famous magazine gave me confidence that I *could* become a writer, and my very unhappiness on the job provided the theme of my first real product of my own, my novel *The Big Wheel*. With that book's publication, my career pattern was set: I became a staff contributor (not an employee) of the *New Yorker*, more or less regularly taking leave of absence from that post to write books. That is pretty much the way it has been ever since.

"After three novels had been published, I abandoned fiction—at least as far as publication is concerned—and since then have devoted myself entirely to non-fiction, with excursions into book reviewing. I can't explain this change except by saying that it seemed to be the natural evolution of my career. I have certain regrets about it, and may have a nostalgic fling at fiction one of these days.

"Meanwhile, in writing about American society, often from the perspective of the world of business and finance, I strive above all for elegance, simplicity, fairness, and humor. (Irony I need not strive for, because it comes to me naturally.) I have found the writing life to be a thorny but rewarding one. Financially, it has enabled me to live not richly but more than tolera-

bly well and to pay my children's tuition. (Having no talent or taste for teaching or lecturing, I have never earned any substantial sum from anything but writing.) Spiritually, it has provided pain and pleasure in what I suppose are the usual proportions. The worst agony for me is not the familiar one of facing a blank page with a blank mind; it is, rather, the round-the-clock nagging depression that comes when the writing is not going well and I can't figure out why. The reward is the elation that comes when a problem suddenly solves itself, or a strong passage pops up apparently out of nowhere—or, best of all, when a long work that passes one's own muster is completed.

"My favorite among my books is *Showing Off in America,* but then maybe that is because it is the most recent of them. When I have occasionally been tempted by offers to augment or replace the writing profession with some other—for example, editing—I have found it easy to refuse. To abandon writing seems not only undesirable but impossible."

———

The crisp documentary style of John Brooks' novels conceals a thoughtful and thought-provoking novelist who records contemporary life (popular journalism on a weekly news magazine in *The Big Wheel,* family relationships in upper-class American society in *A Pride of Lions,* business and high finance in *The Man Who Broke Things*) out of a conviction "that nothing should be lost, that the essences of one's time as well as its facts and figures should be set down, that the timeless struggles of the human heart should be seen exactly as they existed under a certain set of conditions." These are Brooks' words, quoted from his essay "Some Notes on Writing One Kind of Novel." That kind of novel is the novel of manners—not merely a journalistic record of surface life but a work that takes an attitude toward social behavior to reflect a deeper concern with morality itself. "For what are most manners," Brooks asks, "than a conscientious effort to do the right thing, and what is that but morality, however misdirected?" James W. Tuttleton suggests that as a novelist Brooks works in the same tradition as Fitzgerald, Lewis, Marquand, O'Hara, and Cheever.

Brooks developed his skills as a non-fiction writer in a number of articles for the *New Yorker* that leaven factual expository prose with shrewd wit and an engaging quasi-novelistic interest. Because he often blurs the borders between journalism and social history, he has risked the disapproval of specialist critics. Economist J. K. Galbraith, for example, wrote of his *Seven Fat Years: Chronicles of Wall Street,* "Mr. Brooks regards financial transactions as a kind of amiable game played out for his delectation." Writing what historian E. F. Goldman describes as "free-wheeling commentary," he has tackled challenging subjects like corporate history (*The Fate of the Edsel, Telephone*), international banking and finance (*The Games Players*), and—most formidable of all—the "multiple revolutions" in American society since World War II (*The Great Leap*). Probably his most ambitious book, *Showing Off in America,* examines contemporary American society's "conspicuous consumption," following the precedent of Thorstein Veblen's classic *Theory of the Leisure Class* (1899). Brooks discovers that in the studied casualness and iconoclasm of pop art, high tech, and blue jeans, American society of the 1960s and seventies had a consumption more conspicuous and class conscious than Veblen could ever have imagined.

Brooks received the Loeb Magazine Award in 1964 and again in 1968 for his articles in the *New Yorker.* The son of John Nixon and Bessie (Lyon) Brooks, he took his B.A. at Princeton in 1942 and spent the following three years in the U.S. Army serving in Europe. He has been twice married—to Anne Curtis Brown (divorced 1952) and to Rae Alexander Everitt (divorced 1975) and has a son and a daughter from his second marriage. He lives in Greenwich Village in New York.

PRINCIPAL WORKS: *Novels*—The Big Wheel, 1949; A Pride of Lions, 1954; The Man Who Broke Things, 1958. *Non-fiction*—The Seven Fat Years: Chronicles of Wall Street, 1958; The Fate of the Edsel,1963; The Great Leap: The Past Twenty-Five Years in America, 1966; Business Adventures, 1969; Once in Golconda: A True Drama of Wall Street, 1920–1938, 1969; The Go-Go Years, 1973; Telephone, 1976; The Games Players: Tales of Men and Money, 1980; Showing Off in America: From Conspicuous Consumption to Parody Display, 1981.

ABOUT: Contemporary Authors, first revision series 13–16, 1975; Tuttleton, James W. The Novel of Manners in America, 1972; Who's Who, 1982–83.

BROWN, DEE (ALEXANDER) (February 28, 1908–), American novelist and historian writes: "Bienville Parish, Louisiana, was my birthplace, but at an early age I was removed to southern Arkansas where I grew up amidst the boisterous oil boom towns of the 1920s. Thanks to a grandmother who had been a schoolteacher I was taught to read at the age of four, and

DEE BROWN

thanks to an editor-printer whose newspaper establishment was nearby I learned to set type before I was in my teens. This combination engendered a life-long attachment to printed words. I was also fortunate enough to attend public schools during the period when all students were taught to read, and the writing of at least one page of prose was a daily requirement. Consequently I graduated with the impression that everyone was expected to write as much as possible in order to keep printers in full employment.

"I became a printer myself soon after leaving high school, working for a small daily newspaper in the Ozark Mountains. There I started my education all over again. This was tornado country, and one night I joined a party of rescuers sent to dig people out of the storm wreckage of a neighboring town. Although I was very late getting back to work the next day, I'd had the presence of mind to collect a few vital facts about the disaster which I intended to pass on to the editor of the paper. To my surprise he asked me to write the story. With press time bearing down upon us, I composed it hastily upon a linotype, and the story with all its unproofed typographical errors went into the front page under a black banner headline. This was a memorable event in my young life. And because the lone local reporter disliked to visit scenes of accidents, shootings, or other violent occurrences, I was soon being asked to cover these incidents for the newspaper.

"After a year or so of this, I went off to college to study journalism. American history soon seduced me away from that objective, however, particularly the history of the American West. Each summer I traveled the West with a young history professor whose head contained the whole panorama of exploration and settlement beyond the Mississippi. I became convinced that the sweep of Europeans across America from east to west was mankind's greatest folk epic, a continuous adventure tale of raw endurance, of triumphs and tragedies that included every element of good and evil. My discovery of the West and its past was like an exciting dream that I hoped would never end.

"Graduating into the Great Depression of the 1930s, I worked at dozens of temporary jobs until eventually I found employment as a librarian, an absorbing profession that I followed for about forty years, interrupted by three years of military service during World War II. Throughout my career I wrote articles, short stories, books of fiction and non-fiction. Except for three histories about the American Civil War, almost everything published was Western Americana, and the Civil War histories dealt with the Western theater operations. Much of the fiction was based upon actual events in the West. Never did I consider writing to be a way to earn a living; it was something that I enjoyed doing, a most satisfying avocation.

"From childhood I had been fascinated by American Indians, and those I had the good fortune to know added to my admiration for these remarkable survivors of America's inglorious treatment of them. Although the books I wrote in the early years dealt mainly with explorers, settlers, cowboys, cavalrymen, and frontier women, Indians usually played significant roles in them. Consciously and subconsciously for a quarter of a century I gathered information about the various tribes, trying to view events in American history as these events must have appeared to the Indians. Finally I believed I had enough information to write a history of the West from the viewpoint of the American Indians, and that was *Bury My Heart at Wounded Knee.* Soon after its publication I lost my amateur status; my avocation became my vocation."

The Americana of Dee Brown's novels and non-fiction is a highly colored and dramatic record, but it is drawn from extensive research in historical archives. Beginning with a mere interest in westward exploration and settlement, he wrote his first book, *Wave High the Banner,* a novel, about Davy Crockett, and then plunged into the study of frontier history—publishing from 1948 to 1955 (in collaboration with M. F. Schmitt) a trilogy of documents and

photographs—*Fighting Indians of the West, Trail Driving Days,* and *The Settlers' West.* With *Grierson's Raid,* drawn from the unpublished private papers of Benjamin Henry Grierson, an obscure music teacher who led a group of Union soldiers in a daring raid into Confederate territory in 1863, Brown established himself as a historian. Since then he has shuttled comfortably between history and fiction with lively Westerns and several books for children. His most successful book, *Bury My Heart at Wounded Knee,* is a history of the American West seen from the point of view of the Indian. A powerful indictment of the United States government's treatment of the Indian from 1860 to 1890, the book was a best-seller, awakening its many readers to the systematic exploitation and destruction of the native American population.

In 1980 Brown returned to fiction with a long and ambitious novel, *Creek Mary's Blood,* that spans a century in the life of an Indian woman and her two sons, tragic witnesses to the destruction of their culture. Though fiction, the book draws heavily on fact: Creek Mary, the matriarch, organized a group of warriors in a rebellion in Georgia, and the details of their flight west, pursued by government troops, were drawn from historical records. "What a role serendipity plays in research!" Brown told an interviewer for *Publishers Weekly.* "I was looking something up, and there was Creek Mary . . . an American epic that needs to be told."

Brown received a B.S. degree in Library Science from George Washington University in 1937 and an M.S. from the University of Illinois in 1952. Since his retirement from the library staff of the University of Illinois in 1972, he has lived in Little Rock, Ark. He married Sally B. Stroud in 1934; they have two children.

PRINCIPAL WORKS: *Fiction*—Wave High the Banner, 1942; Yellowhorse, 1956; Cavalry Scout, 1958; They Went Thataway, 1960 (re-issued as Pardon My Pandemonium, 1984); The Girl from Fort Wicked, 1964; Creek Mary's Blood, 1980; Killdeer Mountain, 1983. *Non-fiction*—Grierson's Raid, 1954; The Gentle Tamers: Women of the Old Wild West, 1958; The Bold Cavaliers: Morgan's Second Kentucky Cavalry Raiders, 1959; Fort Phil Kearny: An American Saga, 1962; The Galvanized Yankees, 1963; Showdown at Little Big Horn, 1964; The Year of the Century: 1876, 1966; Action at Beecher Island, 1967; Bury My Heart at Wounded Knee, 1970; The Westerners, 1974; Hear the Lonesome Whistle Blow, 1977. *Children's books*—Andrew Jackson and the Battle of New Orleans, 1972; Tales of the Warrior Ants, 1973; Teepee Tales of the American Indian, 1979.

ABOUT: Contemporary Authors, first revision series 13–16, 1975; Current Biography, 1979; Dictionary of Literary Biography Yearbook, 1980; Who's Who in America, 1983–84. *Periodicals*—New York Times Book Review April 13, 1980; Publishers Weekly March 21, 1980; Wilson Library Bulletin March 1978.

BROWN, ROSELLEN (May 12, 1939–), American poet and novelist, was born in Philadelphia, the third child and only daughter of David H. and Blossom (Lieberman) Brown. She was ten weeks old when the family moved to Allentown, the first of a number of such disruptions that left the author with the concern for place and roots that runs through her published work. By the time Rosellen was a teen-ager, the Brown family had settled in New York City, and she went to Barnard College, earning her B.A. in 1960. She had expected to become a journalist, but when a freshman English assignment required her to write a sonnet, she discovered her talent for poetry. Awarded a Woodrow Wilson fellowship upon leaving Barnard, she went on to Brandeis University, intending to earn a Ph.D. However, she disliked graduate school and, deciding that she might better spend her energies on her own writing rather than a thesis, she completed her studies with an M.A. (1962).

Rosellen Brown married Marvin Hoffman, a teacher, on March 16, 1963. In 1965, she and her husband moved to Mississippi to teach literature at Tougaloo College. In the center of the civil rights movement and passionately committed to its aims, she found in poetry a way to express the concern she felt. "I've never been able to commit myself wholly to an ideology or a movement," she has said, "nor am I very good at activist *business,* so writing about people with whom I deeply empathize is a way for me to try to give them a voice when they are inarticulate or kept from speaking for themselves. If you can't do anything particularly useful . . . you can at least make an imaginary record." Her Mississippi experience (1965–1967) made a lasting impression and became a source of material for later works.

The Hoffman family (by now their first daughter, Adina, had been born) returned north and settled in Brooklyn. Some of Brown's poems were printed in the *Nation* and in the *Atlantic Monthly,* and in 1970 the University of Massachusetts Press published a collection of poetry from the Mississippi-Brooklyn years entitled *Some Deaths in the Delta and Other Poems.* The book was an award winner in the National Council on the Arts Selection Program of the Association of American University Presses. The collection, like Brown's subsequent work, elicited mixed—though respectful—critical reac-

ROSELLEN BROWN

tions. One reader found the poems notable, a good example for other poets who wished to treat social issues. Another found the book "insufficient as a liberation of the poet's feeling," and concluded that the work "is ultimately unsuccessful but promising."

The publication of *Street Games* in 1974 brought Brown widespread attention. Set in a changing Brooklyn neighborhood much like the one she lived in, the loosely connected stories focus on different individuals who live on a street that, once fine, has slipped into poverty and is now beginning to attract the middle class. Sharp observations of the tensions and cross-currents among people of widely different backgrounds show the author's sociological interests. The importance of place, so central in all her work, is already evident: the neighborhood is the link for all the stories, the framework within which people live or from which they seek escape, and it assumes the force of a character in itself. Also evident is a penchant for the catastrophic event that has often bothered Brown's critics. Her concern for language, her ear for it and her sensitivity to the feelings that produced it, won praise from the critics. Jane Larkin Crain, writing in *Saturday Review/World,* summed up the reactions: "To be sure, Brown concentrates almost unwaveringly on the stormier, more wrenching aspects of the experience of life represented, but her stories seek to enlarge rather than to diminish the people portrayed in them, and it is from this impulse of her writing that the primary seriousness and effectiveness derive."

Some of the *Street Games* stories had been published in periodicals before the book appeared. Three, "A Letter to Ismael in the Grave," "Mainlanders," and "Why I Quit the Gowanus Liberation Front," were included in the O. Henry Prize Stories collections for 1972, 1973, and 1976 respectively. "How to Win" was chosen for *Best American Short Stories, 1975.* "Mainlanders" had been written as a series of sketches that were not fiction, though they held together as a story. When Brown decided to develop her material into a set of stories, she mined "Mainlanders" for four of them, "as I often do," she told Tom LeClair in an interview. "My words are my words." Observant readers may encounter certain striking images in the poetry that later turn up in a story or a novel. Sometimes whole passages may reappear. Thus the story called "The Bird Is Closing Its Eye," which was published in *North American Review* in 1972, appears with some changes as an episode in her *Tender Mercies,* published in 1978.

By the time *Street Games* came out, Brown and her family had moved to Peterborough, New Hampshire. A second daughter, Elana, had been born, and Brown was at work on her first novel, *The Autobiography of My Mother.* The narrative alternates between two voices: that of Gerda Stein, who by tenacity and hard work has risen from a poor, immigrant background to become a nationally known lawyer for social causes but who is incapable of warmth or love for individuals; and that of her daughter, Renata Stein, a promiscuous hippie whose whole life has been a rebellion against Gerda and who punishes her mother for her rejection by being completely passive. The novel begins when Renata returns home after an exile of eight years, bringing with her an illegitimate daughter. It explores the conflict between the two women and culminates in the accidental death of the grandchild, just as Gerda is about to attempt to gain custody of her because Renata is an unsuitable mother. Both women are too full of past injuries to see that they are perpetuating these in the lives of their daughters. Hence the title, which the author characterizes as a Möbius strip.

The reviews of *The Autiobiography of My Mother* were admiring, and praise of its intelligence, subtlety, meticulousness, psychological insight, and talent occurred even in the otherwise unfavorable ones. One reader spoke of Brown's "candor and ease, never retreating for one moment from her conviction that family is an accident from which the victims can never recover." Anatole Broyard found the mother larger than life, the daughter smaller, and felt that when the book ended, he had been left not knowing how he was supposed to feel about them. Joseph Epstein, while he praised the novel's intelligence and the author's gifts, found that

it lacked a real story and "might more accurately have been entitled 'Two Characters in Search of a Novel'. . . . It is only at the end . . . that through a twist with the fatal air of contrivance to it, something like a plot emerges. . . . Still," he concluded, "her novel does make one indisputable point, and this is that Rosellen Brown is a novelist worth reading." The novel won its author the Great Lakes Colleges New Writer's Award in 1976. The American Library Association chose it as one of its Best Books for Young Adults the same year.

Another book of poetry, *Cora Fry,* was published in 1977. Again Brown ventured in a different direction, for this cycle of poems described the life of a New Hampshire woman, her frustration with its constricting smallness, her attempts to escape, and her return. Brown has referred to the cycle as "a fiction writer's poem, strung on a narrative frame, devoted to the construction of a character by an accretion of fragments, tiny increments of daily observation enlarged by imagery." Reaction was respectful, if not wholeheartedly enthusiastic, for Cora's plain-speaking struck critics as prosaic, or even dull. Nevertheless, Cora's dissatisfactions are ones felt by many women, and both *Redbook* and *Ms* excerpted large sections of *Cora Fry* for their readers. Brown does not deny an interest in feminism, but she emphatically denies any polemical purpose when she writes. Her concern is for the characters she is writing about, and she writes for the joy of writing itself. The writer must listen to his or her own voice. Afterward, "anyone who wants to claim the work when it is finished is free to do so; it's the solicitation of my attention before it's finished that I want to resist."

With the publication of *Tender Mercies* in 1978, Brown showed considerable technical development and met with the best critical success she had received yet. The story deals with a marriage—"at flashpoint," the author says—paralyzed when an accident, caused by the husband in a moment of braggadocio, renders the wife quadriplegic. Somehow the family must pull itself together again. Laura and Dan Courser must adjust to her helplessness and work through the rage, blame, regret, guilt, and fear to come to terms with what has happened and see how they can go on. Brown told interviewer Tom LeClair, "I think what I am doing is telling the ultimate scary story . . . and then proving to myself (and anyone else who's still listening) that the really lovable parts of ourselves can always, though at great cost, be redeemed. . . . I wanted *Tender Mercies* to affirm, against all odds, that our love for each other can exist independent of 'function,' or household service or

physical accomplishment. It *persists . . .* "
Joyce Carol Oates, though she had reservations
about the novel, called it "haunting," containing
"prose as masterful, and as moving, as any being
written today." Another reviewer noted that it
"is an experience of language at a depth of feeling you rarely encounter in modern fiction."
Katha Pollitt summed up the general tenor of reviews when she wrote that the Coursers' story
"has none of the self-consciousness or histrionics
that have marred Brown's fiction in the past.
The language is spare and clean, with flashes of
quiet poetry, perfectly suited to the plain but by
no means simple New Englanders it portrays.
Brown . . . seems to have found herself."

In 1982 the novelist and her family moved on
again, this time to Houston, Texas, where she
teaches creative writing at the University of
Houston. For her next novel she turned to the
years she had spent in Mississippi in the sixties.
Describing it to Tom LeClair before its completion, she said, "It has at its center again an emotionally extravagant occurrence. I was having
difficulty writing about a couple of superannu-
ated civil rights workers trying to deal with the
'ordinariness' of their lives after the excitement
of their activist youth. . . . The couple finds
themselves guardians of two children whose parents were killed in an accident. I bring these kids
from a very different life . . . into this family,
to prod them to reflect on their post-movement
life and political engagement. . . . I use an extraordinary circumstance to push the characters
to remember what their ordinary lives were like
before everything was changed by a stroke." Entitled *Civil Wars*, the novel was published in
1984.

Looking back over her career, Rosellen Brown
described her goals as a writer to Tom LeClair:
"I still write for the same reason I wrote when
I was nine years old: to speak more perfectly
than I really can, to a listener more perfect than
any I know. . . . I want to *move* you. I may do
some sociological business, a little humor on the
side, but I'm happiest when someone says to me,
'I was moved by that book.' . . . [A] book is a
good place to try for the whole story, the compassionate history of the interior, the invisible
pain of the one who inflicts pain. . . . You have
a better chance of understanding people in your
writing than you ever do in your life."

Rosellen Brown received a grant from the
George and Eliza Howard Foundation for the
years 1971–1972, a creative writing grant from
the National Endowment for the Humanities for
1973–1974, and a fellowship from the John Simon Guggenheim Memorial Foundation for
1976–1977. She was a fellow at the Radcliffe Institute from 1973 to 1975.

PRINCIPAL WORKS: *Poetry*—Some Deaths in the Delta and
Other Poems, 1970; Cora Fry, 1977. *Novels*—The Autobiography of My Mother, 1976; Tender Mercies,
1978; Civil Wars, 1984. *Stories*—Street Games, 1974.

ABOUT: Contemporary Authors 77–80, 1979; LeClair,
T. and McCaffery, L. (eds.) Anything Can Happen,
1983. *Periodicals*—Chicago Review Winter 1972;
Hudson Review Winter 1976–77; New York Times
June 18, 1974; May 26, 1976; New York Times Book
Review June 20, 1976; December 10, 1978; Saturday
Review October 28, 1978; Saturday Review/World
June 29, 1974; Southwest Review Summer 1979; Writ-
er September 1977.

BRUNNER, JOHN (September 24, 1934–   ),
British science-fiction writer, was born in Pres-
ton Crowmarsh, Oxfordshire, the son of Anthony and Felicity (Whittaker) Brunner. Like many
another writer of this genre, he got his first taste
of science from reading *The War of the Worlds*
by H. G. Wells, and by the age of thirteen he had
begun sending his own stories to magazines. He
studied modern languages at Cheltenham College, Gloucestershire, but left at the age of seventeen, telling his headmaster that his schooling
interfered with his education. By that time, he
had published a paperback novel under a pseudonym, buying a typewriter with the proceeds.
His first published short story, "Thou Good and
Faithful," appeared in the prominent American
magazine *Astounding Science Fiction* (now
Analog Science Fiction) in 1953. After two years'
service as a pilot in the Royal Air Force (1953–
55), he went to work in London as a technical ab-
stractor at the Industrial Diamond Information
Bureau (1956) and then as an editor for Spring
Books (1956–58), meanwhile continuing to write
and publish stories. In 1958 he became a free-
lance writer of conventional space thrillers for
the American paperback house Ace, producing
some two dozen novels over the next few years.

Brunner's transition from pulp writer to serious novelist came about largely as a result of his
work for the Campaign for Nuclear Disarmament, the activist group cofounded by Bertrand
Russell. In 1959, he and his wife Majorie Rosamond Sauer, whom he had married the previous
year, toured Western Europe with an exhibition
entitled "No Place to Hide." "Living night and
day with images of horror and destruction,"
Brunner writes, "stamped permanently on my
mind the truth that we inhabit a planet too small
to be further shrunk by nationalism, intolerance
and prejudice. . . . Writing mainly about the
future, I have a vested interest in there being a
future for me to write about." The galactic empires and warring planets of his earlier work

JOHN BRUNNER

important work to appear from the SF ghetto since it was formed in 1926," according to the American Modern Library Association, Brunner confirmed his growing reputation as one of the field's top writers. This sprawling and ambitious work, the first book by a non-American to win the Hugo Award (1969), follows the intertwined lives of three major characters, all Americans: a black executive charged with supervising the economic development of a suspiciously tranquil African nation; a dropout social philosopher who discovers the key to human survival in a chemical secreted in the Africans' sweat; and a timid white scholar who is trained as a spy and sent to kill an Asian scientist who has found a way to breed superhuman embryos. The world they inhabit is not far removed from that of the United States in the late 1960s, troubled by overpopulation, widespread drug use, the breakdown of the family, race riots, and an undeclared war with China in the mid-Pacific.

Brunner constructed this complex world by means of a montage of styles and voices, including expository prose, poetry, graffiti, news clippings, television scripts, and snippets of conversation. "My task," wrote Brunner in an essay in the magazine *Extrapolation,* "[was] to throw at my reader information about my future world from as many sides as the real world can hit him from." His use of these "contrasted modes of presentation," as he calls them, was influenced by the work of John Dos Passos and by the stylistic experiments of the writers of the British "New Wave," including Michael Moorcock, J. G. Ballard, and Brian Aldiss.

Reflections on social problems and the use of unconventional writing styles were features of his next three major books as well. *The Jagged Orbit,* set a few decades farther into the future than *Stand on Zanzibar,* portrays a paranoid America where racial violence is encouraged by weapons manufacturers and the mass media. "Here the very fabric of language registers instability—a frequent Brunner tactic," as Pfeiffer explained. In *The Sheep Look Up,* the United States, drowning in its own polluted wastes, sinks rapidly into ecological ruin and finally self-destructs. The America of the twenty-first century, in *The Shockwave Rider,* is dominated by a computerized "data net" that contains records on every person in the country; the net is controlled by the government and big business, both of which, in turn, are controlled by organized crime.

The Shockwave Rider ends on a more upbeat note than either *Stand on Zanzibar* or *The Sheep Look Up*: a small group of people, including the hero, a computer "virtuoso," wrest control of the

were gradually replaced by explorations of such themes as the possibility of global disaster, the collusion between corrupt governments and their selfish populations in perpetuating disastrous policies, and the abuse of technology for political ends.

The first of these "cautionary fictions," as he calls them, was *The Squares of the City* (published in 1965 but written in 1960), which depicts an authoritarian state whose citizens are manipulated by subliminal images flashed on their television screens. The hero, an urban planner, discovers that the leaders of the two ruling factions are using people as literal pawns in a power struggle disguised as a chess game. Brunner modeled the game on an actual one that was played in 1892. The *New York Times* called the book "a first-class fantasy thriller that will hold the reader through to its disturbing climax." It was especially well received in France, where Brunner has since had a large following.

The protagonist of *The Whole Man* (U.K., *Telepathist,* 1965) is a deformed orphan who uses his immense telepathic powers to cure mental illness in other people. John R. Pfeiffer, in a contribution to the essay collection *The Happening Worlds of John Brunner,* called *The Whole Man* "one of the best examples in all science fiction [of] wish-fulfillment romps of this sort." The reviewer for the *Times Literary Supplement* noted that "Mr. Brunner writes with considerable distinction, an acute psychological insight, and in those passages where delusioning images, either probed or projected, are being described, with a rich poetic imagination."

With *Stand on Zanzibar,* "perhaps the most

data net from the criminals and make information accessible to all. The book suffered, in the opinion of some critics, from overlong passages of didactic exposition, considered a common fault in Brunner's writing, and from a lack of conviction in the second half. Wrote reviewer Gerald Jonas in the *New York Times,* "If a 'slice-of-future-life' has any esthetic or intellectual value, it should be allowed to stand by itself. At the first hint that the author is merely being arbitrary in his choice of details—in his meticulous descriptions of what people will wear and eat and talk about 100 years from now—the whole fictional edifice collapses like a house of cards." But *Library Journal* claimed that in *The Shockwave Rider* "Brunner has once again asserted his claim to a place at the top of serious speculative writing."

In addition to these major works, Brunner has published a score of shorter science-fiction novels, ten collections of short stories, four volumes of verse, nine suspense novels, a film script (*The Terrornauts,* 1967), translations from the French, a number of essays on writing science fiction, and numerous songs, including the antinuclear anthem "The H-Bombs' Thunder." His honors include the British Fantasy Award (1965), the British Science Fiction Association Award (1970 and 1971), the Prix Apollo from France (1973), the Cometa d'Argento from Italy (1976 and 1978), and the Europa Award (1980). Formerly the chairman of the British Science Fiction Association and the advisory vice president of the Science-Fiction Foundation at North-East London Polytechnic, he is a member of the Science Fiction Writers of America and in 1980 was elected copresident of the European Science Fiction Convention. He has also been a contributing editor of *Sanity,* the journal of the Campaign for Nuclear Disarmament.

About the importance of science fiction as literature, Brunner has written, in a statement in *Twentieth-Century Science-Fiction Writers,* "It has been well said that the great contribution of SF to the corpus of literature is 'the future as metaphor.' I entirely agree, and though in the past I have had my doubts I do not currently feel that I shall ever exhaust the possibilities opened up to us by that discovery. . . . Even metaphors drawn from an obsolete future can be invaluable in preparing us for eventual reality."

PRINCIPAL WORKS: *Novels*—Threshold of Eternity, 1959; The World Swapper, 1959; Echo in the Skull, 1959 (rev. ed. Give Warning to the World, 1974); The Hundredth Millenium, 1959 (rev. ed. Catch a Falling Star, 1968); The Brink, 1959; The Atlantic Abomination, 1960; Sanctuary in the Sky, 1960; The Skynappers, 1960; Slavers of Space, 1960 (rev. ed. Into the Slave

Nebula, 1968); Meeting at Infinity, 1961; Secret Agent of Terra, 1962 (rev. ed. The Avengers of Carrig, 1969); The Super Barbarians, 1962; Times Without Number, 1962; The Space-Time Juggler, 1963; The Astronauts Must Not Land, 1963 (rev. ed. More Things in Heaven, 1973); Castaways' World, 1963 (rev. ed. Polymath, 1973); The Rites of Ohe, 1963; The Dreaming Earth, 1963; Listen! The Stars!, 1963 (rev. ed. The Stardroppers, 1972); Endless Shadow, 1964; To Conquer Chaos, 1964; The Crutch of Memory, 1964; The Whole Man, 1964 (U.K. Telepathist, 1965); The Altar on Asconel, 1965; The Day of the Star Cities, 1965 (rev. ed. Age of Miracles, 1973); Enigma from Tantalus, 1965; The Repairmen of Cyclops, 1965; Wear the Butcher's Medal, 1965; The Long Result, 1965; The Squares of the City, 1965; A Planet of Your Own, 1966; Born Under Mars, 1967; Out of My Mind (stories), 1967; The Productions of Time, 1967; Quicksand, 1967; Bedlam Planet, 1968; Stand on Zanzibar, 1968; Father of Lies, 1968; Double, Double, 1969; The Jagged Orbit, 1969; Timescoop, 1969; The Evil That Men Do, 1969; Black is the Color, 1969; Blacklash, 1969 (U.K., A Plague on Both Your Causes); The Devil's Work, 1970; The Gaudy Shadows, 1970; Good Men do Nothing, 1970; Honky in the Woodpile, 1971; The Dramaturges of Yan, 1971; The Wrong End of Time, 1971; The Traveler in Black, 1971; The Sheep Look Up, 1972; The Stone That Never Came Down, 1973; Total Eclipse, 1974; Web of Everywhere, 1974; The Shockwave Rider, 1975; Interstellar Empire, 1976; The Infinitive of Go, 1980; Give Warning to the World, 1980; Players at the Game of People, 1980; *Stories*—No Future in It and Other Science Fiction Stories, 1962; Now Then!, 1965; No Other Gods but Me, 1966; Out of My Mind, 1967; Not Before Time: Science Fiction and Fantasy, 1968; From This Day Forward, 1972; Entry to Elsewhen, 1972; Time Jump, 1973; The Book of John Brunner, 1976; Foreign Constellations, 1980; Players at the Game of People, 1980; The Long Result, 1981; Manshope, 1982; The Webs of Everywhere, 1983; The Crucible of Time, 1983. *As "Keith Woodcott"*—I Speak for Earth, 1961; The Ladder in the Sky, 1962; The Psionic Menace, 1963; The Martian Sphinx, 1965. *Non-fiction*—Horses at Home, 1958. *Other*—Trip: A Cycle of Poems (verse), 1966; The Terrornauts (screenplay), 1967; Life in an Explosive Forming Press (verse), 1971; (translator) Gerald Klein, The Overlords of War, 1973; A Hastily Thrown-Together Bit of Zork (verse), 1974; (editor) The Best of Philip K. Dick, 1977; Tomorrow May Be Even Worse (verse), 1978.

ABOUT—Aldiss, B., Billion Year Spree, 1973; Bleiser, E.F. (ed.) Science Fiction Writers, 1982; DeBolt, J. (ed.), The Happening Worlds of John Brunner, 1975; Contemporary Literary Criticism 8, 1978, and 10, 1979; Contemporary Authors, new revision series 2, 1981; Smith, C. (ed.), Twentieth-Century Science-Fiction Writers, 1981. *Periodicals*—New York Times, October 27, 1968; Times Literary Supplement, August 8, 1971, August 23, 1974; Mother Jones, August 1976; New Republic, October 30, 1976; Science Fiction Review 8, 1979; Science Fiction Studies 3, 1976; 5, 1978; Yale Review, March 1978.

BUCKLEY, VINCENT (THOMAS) (July 8, 1925–   ), Australian poet and critic, was born in Romsey, Victoria, Australia, the son of Patrick and Frances Buckley. He took his B.A. from the University of Melbourne in 1950, his M.A. in 1954. From 1955 to 1957 he studied literature at Cambridge University, but took no degree there. The following year he returned to his Australian university, where he has been Lockie fellow (1958–60), reader in English (1960–67), and, since 1967, professor of English.

Buckley's first book, *The World's Flesh,* was a disparate collection in which he seemed to be trying out various poetic voices. In general, the persona is deeply, rather traditionally Christian and Catholic, highly intelligent and ratiocinative, yet quite lacking in true fire. One critic remarked on the poems' "rhetorical slackness." The centerpiece of the collection is undoubtedly the nine-poem sequence "Land of No Fathers," which linked his immigrant ancestors' quest for a home with De Quiros' search for the southern continent. The land's alien, threatening feeling is strongly conveyed throughout, especially in the third segment, "God Sent My Fathers Here, to a Bewilderment of Blood, to Links of Hatred":

And though my father settled here, he
      could not choose
(Exile before him, and behind the sea)
The little cares that put men's hearts at peace,
But sorrows founded on absurdity,

A style of living grown so corporate
There's no more room for any thwarted thing
To wrench or cry its heart out, or berate
The rain through unseen mountains burrowing
Into the warmth of evil. God sent him down
In a field without flowers, that his soul might taste
The drawn-out venom of a country town. . . .

By the time his next book of poems, *Masters in Israel,* was published, Buckley had been to Europe and returned. These poems seem more relaxed in tone, less insistent on making a point, and they possess a warmer intelligence. The longest, "In Time of the Hungarian Martyrdom," is one of his first forays into overt political commentary, a vein he would continue to explore, but his personal reflections are more effective, especially the biting but never bitter humor of "To Praise a Wife," with its opening "motto":

To praise a wife, what things must enter in:
Pity and work, the vanity she'll reprove;
The gaunt affection, the sturdy sin,
The rage at others, and the central love.

Yet these odd powers, which run to complete
   a man,
Spill over the poem, as water brims a glove.
So, in despair, I end where I began:
That point of anger that's the quick of love.

Arcady and Other Places is a memorable col-lection in which, according to Chris Wallace-Crabbe, "the different kinds of poetic impulse began to cohere into a compelling style, a manner that truly delivered the goods." Several of the poems Buckley contributed to *Eight by Eight,* a cooperative anthology of the work of eight Melbourne poets "united only by friendship and geography," were later included in *Arcady.* Especially fine is the section "Eleven Political Poems" (originally entitled "Eleven Anti-Political Poems"), which castigate the outrageous politics and politicians of the 1960s without straining too hard at capturing specific personalities.

Buckley's poetic voice is perhaps most endearing in *Arcady* when he is writing, in a fully engaged yet determinedly unsentimental way, of his parents. The univeral experience of a grown-up child's visit home is re-created with deft and moving particularity in "Parents":

My father asks me how I stand it all,
The work, the debts, the spite. My mother
      talks
As though I were a famous man and yet
Unguarded somehow, too fragile to touch.
It's their needs, not mine, that flutter here
In the questions and the anecdotes. I stare
At the rust encroaching on the walnut
      branches
Or the pile of litter where the biggest pinetree
Used to stand, before my absence killed it.
Their door has a vine over it; they murmur
Endearments to the animals, and cry
At small wrongs. Which is the oldest of us
      three?

Yet another remarkable section of *Arcady* is "Versions from Catullus," eight poems in which Buckley manages to preserve the direct and impassioned sincerity of the Roman lyric poet's originals.

The title poem of *Golden Builders and Other Poems* takes up about half the book. Divided into twenty-seven sections, it is a dramatic meditation on the city of Melbourne, a place infused by the poet with great symbolic force. Wallace-Crabbe, himself a Milburnian and one of the poets who joined Buckley in *Eight by Eight,* considers "Golden Builders" a subtle triumph of autobiography: "autobiography, that is, constructed mosaically, spatially, without chronology or causal sequence. What it creates is something like Freud's city of memory, 'a mental entity . . . in which nothing once created has perished, and all the earlier stages of development had survived alongside the latest.' Friends, loved ones, acquaintances, trees, swathes of townscape, all are set down in vivid juxtaposition by the poet, 'the Montale watcher-figure,' himself shaped by it all." The result is a visionary portrait of a city, somewhat in the manner of Blake, but the reader who is not Australian will perhaps appreciate better the shorter poems in the collection, the best of which are simple statements of thought or experience, pared of rhetorical flourish. "Stand up and be counted" captures the rueful predicament of every politically engaged human:

"Stand up and be counted," they keep
    saying,
and every time I stand up
and every time I'm counted, and every time
I count only as one.
Wouldn't it be better for the Cause
if I squatted back with the others,
lifting my hand only in unison,
happier, and looking like a million?

Buckley's criticism includes *Essays in Poetry, Mostly Australian*, a lively attempt to establish a canon of twentieth-century Australian poets; *Poetry and Morality: Studies in the Criticism of Matthew Arnold, T.S. Eliot, and F.R. Leavis,* which came down firmly on the side of the moral evaluators among literary critics; and *Poetry and the Sacred,* in which he explores the concept of the sacred in literature and studies those writers who best manifest it in their works—Wyatt, Donne, Blake, Melville, Yeats, and others. The reviewer for the *Economist* wrote, "The book as a whole bears the imprint of a mind that comes to its own conclusions, not in ignorance or disregard of other critical estimates, but with integrity of judgment." He also published in 1961 a critical study of the Australian woman novelist Henry Handel Richardson (1870–1946), author of *The Getting of Wisdom* and *The Fortunes of Richard Mahony.*

Buckley has been married twice, the second time in 1976 to Penelope Curtis. He is the father of four children. He won the gold medal of the Australian Literature Society in 1959 for *Masters in Israel* and the Myer award in 1967 for *Arcady.*

PRINCIPAL WORKS: *Poetry*—The World's Flesh, 1954; Masters in Israel, 1961; Arcady and Other Places, 1966; Golden Builders, 1976; Late Winter Child, 1980; Pattern, 1980; Selected Poems, 1981. *Criticism*—Essays in Poetry, Mainly Australian, 1957; Poetry and Morality, 1959; Henry Handel Richardson, 1961; Poetry and the Sacred, 1968.

ABOUT: Contemporary Authors 101, 1981; Vinson, J. (ed.) Contemporary Poets, 1980. *Periodicals*—Choice February 1970; Economist January 18, 1969; Times Literary Supplement December 19, 1968; June 9, 1978.

BYATT, A(NTONIA) S(USAN DRABBLE)

(August 24, 1936–   ), English novelist and critic, was born in Sheffield, in the north of England, the daughter of John Frederick Drabble, a circuit judge and also a writer, and Kathleen Marie Bloor Drabble, an English teacher. She is the elder sister of the novelist and critic Margaret Drabble. Both girls were educated at the Mount School, a Quaker institution in York, and both took bachelor's degrees with first-class honors at Newnham College, Cambridge. Antonia pursued graduate study at Bryn Mawr College in Pennsylvania in 1957–1958 and at Somerville College, Oxford, in 1958–59. In July 1959 she married Ian Charles Rayner Byatt, an economist. Following a divorce in 1969, she married Peter John Duffy. She has one daughter from her first marriage and two daughters from her second marriage.

Shadow of a Sun, her first novel, is still regarded by some as her best. It tells of seventeen-year-old Anna Severell, brilliant but unsure of herself, her unhappy relationship with her father Henry, a famous novelist, and her nearly disastrous passage to maturity. "To create a memorable character," wrote R. D. Spector, "is an achievement that eludes most writers in their literary lifetime, but A. S. Byatt has managed it in her first attempt. Her portrait of the novelist Henry Severell . . . has a Dickensian exaggeration that startles and arouses the imagination. . . . Henry dominates the reader's mind just as surely as he does the fictional characters who live in his shadow." The reviewer for the *Times Literary Supplement,* employing a characterization now rarely heard, called her "a very feminine writer, careful to give us not only the visual detail (which she does very well) but also the emotional convolutions behind each utterance of her characters. . . . [She] feels deeply for her characters and has a thoughtful, unhurried way of conveying precisely why they are worth caring about."

Malcolm Bradbury thought *The Game,* published four years later, "a deep and able book, . . . the sensibility romance in its more traditional guise." It is the story of two sisters whose long-running childhood rivalry flares again, fatally, at the reappearance of a man they had both once loved. Bradbury admired Byatt's perception and her craftsmanship: "For her creativity is a species of living, and the way in which individuals compose themselves to meet the situations that demand or test this creativity is of the essence. The characters are thus under perpetual pressure and in perpetual growth, and if at times the literariness of the novel makes it lumpish, she is also capable of real and intense achievement in these scenes." He concluded that the novel is "a *tour de force,* and the impressive

A. S. BYATT

exactness of its detailing of sensibility shows a remarkable resource in a young novelist."

Byatt's longest and most challenging novel to date is *The Virgin in the Garden,* the 428-page story of the coming of age in Yorkshire of two sisters and a brother during the coronation year of 1953. Iris Murdoch, to whose own novels Byatt's have often been compared, thought it "a very good book, . . . a large, complex, ambitious work, humming with energy and ideas, . . . a highly intellectual operation, . . . a strong, confident, very long traditional novel, a remarkable achievement." Michael Irwin thought it a "careful, complex novel" whose "narration everywhere displays knowledge and intelligence," but complained that the latter virtue "proves a weakness as well as a strength. The author's commitment is to her ideas rather than to the imaginative life her story is apparently intended to have. . . . The recurrent emotional and psychological insipidity is closely connected to the fact that this is a very bookish novel. Most of the main characters are chronically literary." Daphne Merkin, in a somewhat hard-bitten American reaction, echoed Irwin's reservations: Byatt, she wrote, is "too self-consciously literary. Her book is crammed with bits and pieces of higher learning and sounds alarmingly donnish on occasion. Her characters cannot get into bed without invoking T. S. Eliot or D. H. Lawrence; they are relentlessly cultured, given to talking rather than doing. If for American tastes they are ludicrously cerebral, nevertheless behind all the erudite chatter lurks the sad knowledge 'that poetry had no answer to pain.'"

Byatt, who teaches literature at University College, London, has published a study of Iris Murdoch: *Degrees of Freedom: The Novels of Iris Murdoch.* She began the book, she explains in the introduction, "with a nagging curiosity to know exactly what Miss Murdoch was talking about, what sort of moral statement she was making, what were the ideas behind her novels." Granville Hicks thought Byatt "particularly enlightening on Miss Murdoch's various attempts to combine symbolism and realism." The *Times Literary Supplement* reviewer called the book "an attempt by an ordinary reader—that is to say, someone who reads for pleasure—to get to grips with the philosophical ideas of a professional philosopher. . . . Even if the potentiality is not realized, to have tackled the whole question of what fiction can do, especially in the context of philosophical ideas now current, makes Mrs. Byatt's book worthwhile—not least because it offers a provoking network of suppositions in the light of which to criticize other experiments in art."

Another critical study by Byatt is *Wordsworth and Coleridge in Their Time,* a collection of six essays on early nineteenth century English life, the background of the two chief formulators of English romanticism. "The virtue of the book," wrote the *Choice* reviewer, "for beginning students and experienced scholars, is the lavish and fascinating supply of information and lore about the poets and their world: if the information is not new, there is no other book on either poet that brings so much of it together."

PRINCIPAL WORKS: *Fiction*—The Shadow of a Sun, 1964; The Game, 1968; The Virgin in the Garden, 1979. *Criticism*—Degrees of Freedom: The Novels of Iris Murdoch, 1965; Wordsworth and Coleridge in Their Time,1973.

ABOUT: Contemporary Authors, first revision series 13–16, 1975; Dictionary of Literary Biography 14, Part I, 1983; Who's Who, 1984. *Periodicals*—Best Sellers April 1, 1968; Book Week August 30, 1964; Choice September 1973; September 1979; Encounter July 1968; May 1979; New York Times Book Review August 2, 1964; March 17, 1968; April 1, 1979; New Statesman November 3, 1978; New Yorker September 26, 1964; Times Literary Supplement January 9, 1964; July 29, 1965; January 19, 1967; November 3, 1978; Saturday Review October 30, 1965.

CALDER, NIGEL (DAVID RITCHIE) (December 2, 1931–), British science writer, is the son of Peter Ritchie-Calder, Baron of Balmashannar, himself a noted science writer, and Mabel Jane Forbes McKail. He was born in London, attended Merchant Taylor's School, and served

NIGEL CALDER

a year (1950–51) as a lieutenant with the British Army. Inspired by his father's love of science, Calder studied physics at Sidney Sussex College, Cambridge University, receiving a B.A. in 1954 and an M.A. in 1957.

After two years as a research physicist with the Mullard Research Laboratories in Surrey, Calder joined the staff of the journal *New Scientist,* first as a writer (1956–60), then as science editor (1960–62)and editor-in-chief (1962–66). Calder helped establish the journal as a youthful, iconoclastic alternative to the renowned but conservative *Nature,* the leading British journal of science. From 1959 to 1961, and again from 1966 to 1971, Calder was the science correspondent for the *New Statesman.* Already the author of seven popular books on scientific topics, he began in the late 1960s a successful venture in films and publishing, writing the scripts for a number of well-received BBC science programs and spinning off related books. He has presented two series, "The Whole Earth Show" and "Spaceships of the Mind," from which he also derived books. David Attenborough and Carl Sagan, among others, have since used this strategy with similar success.

Calder is widely considered Britain's best science popularizer, and his reputation there may be compared with that of Isaac Asimov in the United States. Like Asimov, he is prolific and versatile, writing on topics as diverse as radio astronomy, particle physics, behavior modification, weather control, plate tectonics, and the causes and effects of nuclear war. Most reviewers agree that his books fulfill the basic requirements of popular writing on science. He conveys

the drama and excitement of the latest scientific discoveries, avoiding the misrepresentation of speculative theory as fact and describing complex developments and procedures in terms comprehensible to lay readers. His own fields of greatest competence are physics and astronomy. "Calder's particular and enviable talent," wrote John Keegan in the *New Republic* (September 27, 1980), "is for turning abstruse technicalities into everyday language without damage to the subtlety of the specialist's language."

His first three books, *Electricity Grows Up, Robots,* and *Radio Astronomy,* were basic introductions for readers of high-school age. Drawing on the writings of such diverse thinkers as Thomas Malthus, R. Buckminster Fuller, Rachel Carson, and Robert Ardrey, in *Eden Was No Garden: An Inquiry into the Environment of Man,* Calder broadly surveyed the ecological and social impact of new technologies and scientific fields. By the end of the twentieth century, he claimed in this study, traditional means of securing food and material wealth, coupled with an ever-increasing human population, will be in danger of exhausting the resources of the entire planet. He advocated the automation of agriculture in vast "food factories" and the dismemberment of the earth's sprawling cities and suburbs in favor of high-density arcologies, giant structures housing hundreds of thousands of people. The land thus cleared would be returned to a global wilderness, benignly managed by humanity. Reviewer Harold Bloomquist called it "an urbane and intelligent book" (London *Times,* June 1, 1967), in which Calder "leads his reader down a tortuous path of science, engineering, and political science with an admirable lucidity . . . Calder is not satisfied with merely criticizing: he offers a full-blown Utopian vision of what the world might be; and truthfully, it looks pretty good."

Technopolis: Social Control of the Uses of Science was Calder's appraisal of the ways in which the practice of science and technology can or should be controlled, and by whom. Science, he optimistically asserts, will ultimately assume enlightened control over itself: "It is scarcely credible that the well-informed, research-trained, interconnected committees of the foreseeable future should tolerate men in power who have simple-minded theories of society, or who seek to profit from the differences between men." A year earlier, however, he had painted just the opposite future in *Unless Peace Comes: A Scientific Forecast of New Weapons,* an admonitory collection of essays by scientists and international weapons specialists on the rapid development of novel means of mass destruction. Calder has since demonstrated an abiding concern with arms control and other ways of avoiding nuclear annihilation. He has covered the activities of the Pugwash group of anti-nuclear scientists for the *Bulletin of the Atomic Scientists,* and in 1979 published *Nuclear Nightmares,* a chilling pessimistic overview of current nuclear-weapons strategies and how these strategies make a total nuclear war all too likely.

The author's BBC collaborations began with *The Violent Universe: An Eyewitness Account of the New Astronomy.* Both the book and the program (eventually shown in the United States on public television, as were most of his subsequent productions) were critically well-received. Carl Sagan, writing in *Book World,* called the book "by far the best, the most readable, the most up-to-date account of the new astronomy," while noting Calder's "remarkable talent for the apt analogy and the appropriate phrase: Space is the abyss that starts at the top of our hair; a globular cluster is likened to a swarm of gnats; research on controlled nuclear fusion is an attempt to put the fire of the sun in a bottle." In the *Washington Post* radio astronomer Frank Drake wrote: "I know of no other book where one can get a feeling for the present astronomical world; where one can feel the enthusiasm and thinking of the real scientists; where one can appreciate the breadth of activities in astronomy's golden age." Calder repeated this formula—a strongly visual, easy-to-understand television program sketching the most glamorous developments in a particular scientific field, supplemented by a lavishly illustrated, more detailed text—with a dozen more projects, including *The Restless Earth, The Weather Machine, The Human Conspiracy,* and *Einstein's Universe,* produced in honor of the Einstein centenary.

Due perhaps to the very nature of popularization, Calder has occasionally failed to satisfy scientific reviewers as to the accuracy or tone of his material. Television viewers were reported to have enjoyed the broadcast version of *The Weather Machine,* for example, but in reviewing the book for the *Times Literary Supplement,* T. J. Chandler claimed that "in interpreting the often highly complicated theories of past climates and meteorological processes, Nigel Calder has sometimes simplified to the point of misrepresentation." Jeremy Bernstein, a scientist and fellow science writer, had harsh words for both the book and the program of *Einstein's Universe.* The television version featured Peter Ustinov improbably sporting a silver lamé jumpsuit while explaining the intricacies of special and general relativity. "Many people seem to like Calder's productions," wrote Bernstein in the *New York Times Book Review,* but "I find them too busy. Things are constantly lighting up and going off. It is like trying to practice science in a discotheque." However, David Quammen of the *Christian Science Monitor* considered the book "casual in style but not condescending, abundantly thought-provoking, and concise. [The author] has held himself to a high standard of lucidity while juggling a prodigiously complex assemblage of fact and theory and paradox and conjecture, from Galileo's study of falling objects to Stephen Hawking's latest inspiration concerning black holes."

Among Calder's recent books are *The Comet Is Coming!* an irreverent view of cometology, and, in particular, superstitions about Halley's Comet; and *1984 and After: Changing Images of the Future,* which was prepared for an exhibition of the same name that toured U.S. museums in early 1984.

A member and former chairman of the Association of British Science Writers, Calder was awarded the Kalinga Prize by UNESCO in 1978 for the popularization of science. In 1954 he married Elisabeth Palmer; they have five children and live in West Sussex.

PRINCIPAL WORKS: Electricity Grows Up, 1958; Robots, 1958; Radio Astronomy, 1958; (ed.) The World in 1984, 1965; Eden Was No Garden, 1967 (U.K. The Environment Game); (ed.) Unless Peace Comes: A Scientific Forecast of New Weapons, 1968; Technopolis: Social Control of the Uses of Science, 1969; The Violent Universe: An Eyewitness Account of the New Astronomy, 1969; Living Tomorrow, 1970; The Mind of Man, 1970; The Restless Earth: A Report on the New Geology, 1972; (ed.) Nature in the Round: A Guide to Environmental Science, 1973; The Life Game, 1973; The Weather Machine, 1974; The Human Conspiracy, 1975–76; The Key to the Universe: A Report on the New Physics, 1977; Spaceships of the Mind, 1978; Einstein's Universe, 1979; Nuclear Nightmares, 1979; The Comet Is Coming!, 1980; Timescale: An Atlas of the Fourth Dimension, 1982; 1984 and After: Changing Images of the Future, 1984.

ABOUT: Contemporary Authors 21–24, 1976; Who's Who, 1983–84. *Periodicals*—Book World March 1, 1970; Christian Science Monitor April 9, 1979; Nation October 28, 1968; New Republic July 13, 1970; New York Review of Books November 23, 1978; New York Times Book Review June 16, 1967; July 28, 1968; March 11, 1979; Newsweek July 13, 1970; Saturday Review June 14, 1975; Scientific American May 1971; Times Literary Supplement December 20, 1974; Wall Street Journal July 30, 1976.

CARO, ROBERT A. (October 30, 1936–), American biographer, was born and raised in Manhattan, the son of Benjamin Caro, a Polish immigrant and New York real estate broker, and an American-born mother who died when he was eleven. He attended the Horace Mann School and Princeton University, where he majored in English and graduated in 1957. After working for a time on a daily newspaper in New Brunswick, New Jersey, in 1960 Caro joined the staff of the Long Island daily *Newsday,* where he became an investigative reporter and won acclaim for a series of articles exposing the selling of worthless land in Arizona that led to the indictments of thirty-seven people and corrective state and federal legislation.

Caro was beset during his newspaper career by the space limitations on his writing, which conflicted with his natural prolixity. "I couldn't tell people the complete truth" in a newspaper format, he recalled in 1982. While at Harvard on a Nieman fellowship in 1965, he realized the future course of his career. Listening to a discussion of highway construction in a planning seminar, he remarked, "Wait a minute! That's not how highways get built. They get built because Robert Moses *wants* them built!" After obtaining a one-year Carnegie Foundation grant and a modest publisher's advance, he left *Newsday* and spent the next seven years working on the biography of Moses, the New York master builder and politician of legendary power, who was by some accounts the most powerful nonelected public official in American history.

The 1,246 pages (600,000 words, which an editor cut down from more than a million) of *The Power Broker: Robert Moses and the Fall of New York* are the result of this painstaking effort. Caro was extremely fortunate in getting Moses to agree to be interviewed (several would-be biographers had seen their plans scuttled by Moses' adamant refusal to talk for the record), and during eleven months in 1967 and 1968 Moses talked freely to Caro and permitted his associates to do likewise. "The visits were extraordinary," he recalled in 1974. "Moses would sit and talk for hours on end, . . . telling anecdotes from his days in power—stories of Al Smith, of the legislatures, of the mayors he worked with." Yet as a result of other research Caro concluded that "much of what he was telling me was at variance with the records." A confrontation resulted in the termination of all contact between author and subject, but Caro had by that time more than enough information to complete his book. He presents Moses as a classic American type: an early idealist who lost hold of his principles in trying to realize his dreams, his fall derived from the corruption inherent in misused power.

ROBERT A. CARO

The book caused considerable controversy. Moses issued a 3,500-word denunciation in advance of publication, thundering that the book was "full of mistakes, unsupported charges, nasty baseless personalities, and random haymakers thrown at just about everybody in public life." Reviewers were unanimous in their praise of the book's great readability—one New York critic likened it to reading about "a gunfight at Gracie Mansion"—but divided over its merit as history. Christopher Lehmann-Haupt felt "its virtues are carried to excess. Mr. Caro's thoroughness in documenting the case against his subject leads him to make accusations that seem irrelevant in their contexts, . . . and suggests nothing so much as vindictiveness on the author's part. His eagerness to render his story melodious leads him to pump away at his drama as if he were a piper putting air into his bag; to repeat and repeat certain notes long after the reader has grasped their point; and to arrange his passages and juggle his time sequences to a point where one begins to wonder what else in his evidence he may have arranged and juggled." Robert C. Wade, though critical of the book's "inordinate length," commended it as "the first successful entry to the highly guarded confines of the Robert Moses public works empire. Caro unravels the complicated legislation that created it, explains the expansion of its power, describes the unique life-style it bred and assesses its pervasive impact on the nation's largest metropolis. In the future, the scholar who writes the history of American cities in the twentieth century will doubtless begin with this extraordinary effort." *The Power Broker* won the Pulitzer prize for biography and the Francis Parkman prize of the Society of American Historians.

Caro labored for another seven years on the first volume of his next project, a three-volume biography of President Lyndon B. Johnson. He and his wife, Ina Joan Caro, moved to Austin, Texas, site of the massive Johnson archives, and spent years interviewing nearly everyone who had ever known LBJ. During breaks from examining the thirty-two million documents in the presidential archives, they would venture into the hill country of Blanco County, west of Austin, where Johnson was born. The Caros found no hostility among the people there, he recalled in 1982, "but they were reluctant. They were telling me the rehearsed stories, stories about Johnson being a popular campus leader and how everyone knew he'd grow up to be president. It wasn't what I wanted." His persistence led to greater candor on the part of his sources, and gradually a portrait of the young Johnson began to emerge that was quite unlike any suggested by the several dozen biographies already written. *The Path to Power,* volume one of *The Years of Lyndon Johnson,* requires 882 densely printed pages to cover the first thirty-three years of the subject's life, from his birth in 1908 (which does not occur until chapter four) to his election to the Senate in 1941. Johnson, Caro concludes, was possessed of a hunger for power "so fierce and consuming that no consideration of morality or ethics, no cost to himself—or to anyone else—could stand before it." The book's most sensational revelations were excerpted before publication in the *Atlantic Monthly,* including an accusation that Johnson, while in office, had regularly accepted "envelopes stuffed with cash." Several reviewers reacted with ill-concealed fury, much of it directed at Caro. "When we were very young," wrote Douglass Cater, former special assistant to President Johnson, "we played a childish game where every word or deed of one's playmate was ascribed to the basest motivation. I sense such game-playing in Caro's account. What was intended to be a love affair has gone so sour that no pejorative is too strong, no insinuation too farfetched. It is as if Robert Caro has become a chameleon for the monster he imagines: exaggerating beyond the point of hyperbole; manipulating facts when the facts don't fit his conclusions. Ten thousand footnotes cannot close this credibility gap." To David Herbert Donald, Caro "makes only the most casual attempts to probe Johnson's character or to understand his motivations." Donald felt that the biography's "imbalance derives from Mr. Caro's view of the biographer as a judge—and in this case a hanging judge. . . . For those who seek to understand this remarkably complex, singu-

larly gifted and tragically limited man, Mr. Caro's book will seem more like a caricature than a portrait." Robert R. Harris, however, took the more representative view that the book is "controversial, highly opinionated, exhaustively documented and magisterial." And Murray Kempton called Caro "the most Dreiserian of our chroniclers. He proceeds in the same plodding, laborious, heroic way, which makes *The Path to Power*'s arrival at fashion something of an astonishment. . . . Caro's Johnson, like Dreiser's Frank Cowperwood, is a creature liberated from moral prejudices, and, unless we set aside our own, we will miss each one's lesson. . . . Caro has thrown a dead cat into the garden of Franklin D. Roosevelt's centennial. *The Path to Power*'s truly resonant message is that the richest rewards of social reform are reserved for the enterpriser with the wit and detachment to find his main chance in the spirit of his age."

Caro lives in New York, where he is working on the second volume of the Johnson trilogy and on a novel about an investigative reporter.

PRINCIPAL WORKS: The Power Broker; Robert Moses and the Fall of New York, 1974; The Path to Power (The Years of Lyndon Johnson, vol. 1), 1982.

ABOUT: Contemporary Authors 101, 1981; Current Biography, 1984. *Periodicals*—America September 21, 1974; Christian Science Monitor September 18, 1974; December 3, 1982; National Review December 6, 1974; April 15, 1983; Nation September 28, 1974; New Republic September 7, 1974; February 7, 1983; New York Review of Books October 17, 1974; February 17, 1983; New York Times August 21, 1974; September 9, 1974; May 6, 1975; September 22, 1981; New York Times Book Review September 15, 1974; November 21, 1982; Newsday October 25, 1974; November 21, 1982; Newsweek September 16, 1974; November 29, 1982; People January 17, 1983; Publishers Weekly November 25, 1983; Saturday Review October 18, 1974; March-April 1983; Time September 16, 1974; November 29, 1982; Times Literary Supplement January 17, 1975; March 25, 1983; Washington Post November 21, 1982; November 25, 1982; December 9, 1982; March 8, 1983.

CARVER, RAYMOND (May 25, 1938–), American short story writer and poet, was born in Clatskanie, Oregon, the son of Clevie and Ella (Casey) Carver. He was educated at local schools in Yokima, Washington, where his father worked in a lumber mill and his mother was a waitress. In an account of his early years in the fall 1982 issue of *Syracuse Scholar,* he speaks of working at a variety of usually manual jobs after finishing high school—as a deliveryman, service station attendant, janitor, and laborer at a saw-

RAYMOND CARVER

mill. In 1957 he married Maryann Burk, and with his wife, and later their two children, Christine and Vance, he continued to support himself by miscellaneous jobs while he began writing fiction at night. In 1959, he moved from Oregon to Paradise, California, where he enrolled in a fiction writing course taught by John Gardner at nearby Chico State College. According to Carver, Gardner gave impetus to his early work as a short story writer for little magazines.

Carver, who writes so intimately of the grinding existence of working-class people, had his own long and painful struggle for his education and for the leisure he needed to do his writing. He recalled in an interview in the *New York Times Magazine:* "I learned a long time ago when my kids were little, and we had no money, and we were working our hearts out and weren't getting anywhere, even though we were giving it our best, my wife and I, that there were more important things than writing a poem or a story. That was a very hard realization for me to come to. But it came to me, and I had to accept it or die. Getting milk and food on the table, getting the rent paid, if a choice had to be made, then I had to forgo writing." Somehow he managed never to forgo writing completely. He also managed to get a B.A. from Humboldt State College in 1963. By then, having published some short stories in little magazines, he was encouraged to enter the writing program at the University of Iowa, from which he received an M.F.A. in 1966. In 1971–72 he was a lecturer in creative writing at the University of California, Santa Cruz; and during the next year was visiting lecturer in fiction writing at the University of Cali-

fornia at Berkeley. In 1973–74 he was a lecturer at the Writers Workshop at the University of Iowa. At this early point in his career, he published two volumes of stories—*Near Klamath* and *Winter Insomnia*—and a volume of stories—*Put Yourself in My Shoes*—in small-press editions. He was the recipient in 1971 of a grant for poetry, from the National Endowment for the Arts, and in 1973–74 held the Wallace Stegner fellowship in creative writing.

Ironically, at the very point when his fortunes seemed to be turning most favorable—the mid-1970s with the publication, to excellent reviews, of *Will You Please Be Quiet, Please?*—Carver suffered a series of severe bouts with alcoholism and depression. Several times hospitalized, separated from his wife and children, living on borrowed money, he was, as he recalls, "finished as a writer." In June 1977, after an especially harrowing period, he stopped drinking. He told a *Paris Review* interviewer in 1983: "I'm prouder of that, that I've quit drinking, than I am of anything in my life." In the 1970s Carver divided his time between teaching and writing. From 1977 to 1980 he taught in the English department at Goddard College, and in the following year was visiting writer at the University of Texas (El Paso). From 1980 to 1983 he was professor of English at Syracuse University. During the late 1970s and early 1980s he has come into increasing prominence; his work has appeared in a number of the volumes of *The Best American Short Stories* and *The O. Henry Prize Stories,* and he has received a series of awards, including a National Endowment for the Arts award in fiction (1980) and a Guggenheim fellowship (1979–80). The expansion of Carver's reputation on a national level, however, was indicated most dramatically by his selection, in January 1983, as a recipient of one of the prestigious "Mildred and Harold Strauss Livings," which provide a tax-free stipend of $35,000 a year for a minimum of five years. The "Strauss Livings" are conferred by a special panel of the American Academy and Institute of Arts and Letters. They stipulate that recipients must resign their positions and may not work, the annual stipend freeing them to devote their full time to writing.

Carver has come to attention principally through his short story collections—*Will You Please Be Quiet, Please?, What We Talk About When We Talk About Love,* and *Cathedral. Will You Please Be Quiet, Please?,* which was nominated for a National Book Award, and *Cathedral,* a National Book Critics Circle nominee, introduce the reader to a starkly existentialist world of everyday life, in which characters—mainly white- and blue-collar workers, salesmen, waitresses—are unable to communicate with others and take their natures from the dehumanizing and hostile society in which they live—a world, Thomas R. Edwards wrote, "whose people worry about whether their old cars will start, where unemployment or personal bankruptcy are present dangers . . . where making a living is hard and the texture of life drab." Geoffrey Wolff emphasized not only the marginal nature of Carver's characters' lives, but also the inner terror with which they seem condemned to live. Though very brief, the stories explore complex human tensions and emotions repressed in the course of humdrum daily modern life. Yet they have a quality that Wolff describes as "menacing," reminding him of the brooding ominous mood of Kafka or Harold Pinter. Dean Flower compared Carver's laconic prose in *Will You Please Be Quiet, Please?* with "Hemingway's purified style," but while Hemingway implies "volumes of unspoken knowledge," Carver's work hints at a disturbing absence of the "knowable." A husband suspects his wife of infidelity and spies on her but neither confirms nor dismisses his suspicions. Another man simply plans to go duck hunting and spends an evening thinking about his empty, aimless life: "All he does is smoke cigarettes, try to read a few poems, listen to the rain, stare at the wall. Carver's gift is to make these routine emptinesses terrible."

With the publication of *What We Talk About When We Talk About Love* Carver achieved celebrity. Reviews were generally extremely favorable. Hailing him as "one of the true contemporary masters of an exacting genre," Robert Towers described the seventeen stories that make up the collection as "low-rent tragedies" involving "people who read *Popular Mechanics* and *Field and Stream,* people who play bingo, hunt deer, fish, and drink. They work at shopping centers, sell books, have milk routes, or try, drunkenly, to manage a motel. . . . Their ordinariness is unredeemed, their failures and fatalities of a sort that goes unnoticed except, perhaps, for an occasional paragraph in some small-town newspaper." David Kubal remarked that Carver's stories record "the great disenchantment of the middle class"—their "sense of betrayal; that life has not fulfilled its early promise of peace, order, and love." But Kubal also expressed some reservations, complaining that the cumulative effect of so many stories of a similar "tone, theme, and structure" tends to produce an effect of monotony. James Atlas remarked that "at its best, [Carver's] willfully simple style concentrates our attention, requires us to supply our own conclusions. And he manages to articulate the longings of inarticulate people." But, like Kubal, he referred to the reductiveness of Carver's style and fictional world. "One is left," he said, "with a hunger for richness, texture, excess."

With *Cathedral,* his fifth short story collection, Carver showed signs of a more emotionally enriched and expansive spirit. There is no reversal, no abrupt shift to hopefulness and cheer, but there is less despair. As Irving Howe described these stories in the *New York Times Book Review,* they "suggest he is moving toward a greater ease of manner and generosity of spirit." The hard force of his will is still present, also the laconic manner, what Howe calls "the dry intensity," but at least a few of the stories in *Cathedral* "venture on a less secure but finer rendering of experience." Carver has yet to publish a novel (he has worked on one from time to time) and in 1984, living on the outskirts of the quiet fishing and logging town of Port Angeles on Washington's Olympic peninsula, he was reported to be writing poetry once again.

PRINCIPAL WORKS: *Poetry*—Near Klamath, 1968; Winter Insomnia, 1970; At Night the Salmon Move, 1976. *Fiction*—Put Yourself in My Shoes, 1974; Will You Please Be Quiet, Please?, 1976; Furious Seasons and Other Stories, 1977; What We Talk About When We Talk About Love, 1981; Cathedral: A Raymond Carver Reader, 1983; *Prose & Poetry*—Fires: Essays, Poems, Stories 1966–1982, 1983.

ABOUT: Contemporary Authors, first revision series 33–36, 1978; Contemporary Literary Criticism 22, 1982; Current Biography, 1984; Who's Who in America, 1983–84. *Periodicals*—America January 30, 1982; American Book Review January 1982; Atlantic June 1981; Hudson Review Summer 1976; Autumn 1981; Iowa Review Summer 1979; Nation July 4, 1981; National Review December 11, 1981; New Republic April 25, 1981; Newsweek April 26, 1976; April 27, 1981; New York Review of Books April 1, 1976; May 14, 1981; New York Times Book Review March 7, 1976; April 26, 1981; September 11, 1983; New York Times Magazine June 24, 1984; Paris Review Summer 1983; Partisan Review Fall 1982; Village Voice September 18, 1978.

CASTRO, JOSÉ MARIA FERREIRA DE
See FERREIRA DE CASTRO, JOSÉ MARIA

CHAO SHU-LI *See* ZHAO SHULI

CHARYN, JEROME (May 13, 1937–), American novelist and short story writer, writes: "Until the age of seven I could neither read nor write. English was not my native tongue. I had

JEROME CHARYN

no native tongue. My mother and father howled in some private tongue that might have been Polish but was more a language of wounds they'd picked up in America. It was this grumbling song that I learned from them and tried to manipulate into school talk. I failed. My teachers thought I was a wolf child out of the city cellars. They sent me to a speech clinic in the Bronx. The clinicians were just as baffled by my song. They administered an ink blot test. I growled at the pictures those blots produced, and that's how I became a dealer of words.

"My own writing has that primitive grunt of a child looking at ink blots in his head. I do not believe in building up vocabularies. I prefer to dismantle them. And so my novels are like disrupted kindergarten texts, grown-up games for children. The meaning of the text can only come from the music it supplies. I feel like a hurdy-gurdy grinder, playing out his primitive melodies on some faulty machine. That machine is all I have."

Jerome Charyn is the son of Sam Charyn, a furrier, and the former Fannie Paley. He was raised in the Bronx, and was, he told *Columbia College Today,* "an illiterate wild child, a Classics Comics graduate, a reader of gangster novels, and a Marlon Brando fan." Still, he did well enough to get accepted into Columbia, where he read Sophocles and Rabelais, started writing fiction, and graduated with honors in 1959. After teaching high school in New York for a few years and working as a recreation leader for the Parks Department, he had his first novel published in 1964 at the age of twenty-seven.

That novel, *Once upon a Droshky,* is a realistic, Dickensian tale of New York tenants fighting off an eviction notice in the 1930s. It was praised for its verbal authority and poignant comedy, and it set the mold for Charyn's next two books. These showed the same talent for characterization and story-telling that Charyn had revealed in *Once upon a Droshky,* though he did try to move beyond his native milieu by setting *On the Darkening Green* in a reform school in upstate New York. *The Man Who Grew Younger and Other Stories* returned to the Bronx and Manhattan, perhaps a more fruitful milieu for Charyn.

Charyn's fourth book, *Going to Jeruslaem,* begins in the (for him) familiar territory of south Brooklyn, but soon takes off to follow its chief protagonists, a six-year old chess prodigy and his traveling companion (a former Nazi) on a bizarre chess-playing tour of the country. Although many critics considered *Going to Jerusalem* rather a hodgepodge, it remains an important work, for it marked Charyn's break, however confused, with the realist tradition. Henceforward his name would be linked more often with the Hawkes/Nabokov school than with the Bellow/Malamud one that had nurtured him.

If *Going to Jerusalem* was a tentative toeing of the avant-garde waters, *American Scrapbook* was a full and—most reviewers agreed—unsuccessful plunge. The novel's subject is the United States' internment of Japanese-Americans during World War II, and the treatment is a multiple voice narration similar to Faulkner's in *As I Lay Dying.* It seems that Charyn had not mastered this exacting technique, and the result came closer to confusion than a hard-won success. *Eisenhower, My Eisenhower* was drawn along the lines of *American Scrapbook* and met with a similar reception, although some critics praised it for its sheer energy.

Charyn's next work, *The Tar Baby,* was no less daring than its two predecessors, but much more controlled. The novel purports to be a memorial issue of a third-rate academic journal, complete with its own title page, letters to the editor, and classified ads, and dedicated to the memory of a campus security guard and sometime Wittgenstein scholar. In a 1974 essay on Charyn and some of his contemporaries in *TriQuarterly,* Albert J. Guerard took exception to those critics who dismissed *The Tar Baby* as a pale imitation of Nabokov. Although conceding that it was "derivative in spots and perhaps in overall inspiration," he could still claim it as "a small masterpiece." "There is not one rendered scene of present action," he wrote, "on which we can absolutely depend; the reader must turn from mirror to mirror, attendant to shifting profiles, measuring distortion. Yet the whole is rich, comic, sardonic, meaningful. We are entertained; we believe; we care. The Tar Baby does contain that fragment of truth for which we have forgotten to ask."

Summarizing Charyn's first decade as a writer and finding it paradigmatic of a turn in recent American fiction away from realism, Guerard might well have wondered how Charyn would consolidate his gains in the decade to come. Blue Eyes was an indication. Ostensibly a thriller about a New York City policeman investigating a white slavery ring, Blue Eyes respects its conventions while transcending them. As Thomas LeClair wrote in the New York Times Book Review, "Blue Eyes would have been only a modest study of police deals and dealings—a novel of public information—had not Charyn maintained an intensity of language that characterizes our best novels of private creation." The same could more or less be said for the remaining books (Marilyn the Wild, The Education of Patrick Silver, and Secret Isaac) in what came to be a tetralogy centering on the Manhattan police inspector Isaac Sidel and his friends and enemies. Reviewers differed widely in their assessments of the individual books, but a pattern did emerge. Charyn seemed to be making greater concessions to plot, to "readability," yet these concessions were artfully contrived to suggest much larger concerns. Josephine Hendin detected this pattern in her discussion of Marilyn the Wild in the Harvard Guide to Contemporary American Writing when she wrote, "Youth against age and authority and the weird cast of New York types (the novel boasts an albino negro pyromaniac) put Charyn's novel, for all its gross, police-blotter realism, solidly on the side of the surreal."

Charyn's prolific output has not diminished in recent years, and his subject matter has become ever more varied. He has taken on historical figures in The Franklin Scare (Eleanor and Franklin D. Roosevelt) and Darlin' Bill (Wild Bill Hickok); mythologized his own past in The Catfish Man; fantasized a Polish brothel on the West Side of Manhattan in the first third of this century in Panna Maria; and mythologized himself again (as Jerome Copernicus Charyn) in Pinocchio's Nose which, as Saul Maloff pointed out, demands of its readers "forbearance, avuncular indulgence of a willful writer's shenanigans, the strength to endure, and a willingness to give him all the rope he asks for." As is often the case with Charyn, reviewers disagreed over

these novels. This lack of agreement perhaps supports the widely-held contention that Charyn writes too much, that he sometimes spreads his talent thin, and that he has yet to produce the major work he is capable of.

Nevertheless, the books Charyn has written since The Tar Baby show no falling off in vigor or experimentation. The Seventh Babe is perhaps the most satisfying of these later novels. It begins as a seemingly conventional baseball story about the ups and downs of a rookie third baseman for the 1923 Boston Red Sox. But Charyn once again sets up conventional expectations and neatly side-steps them, for The Seventh Babe turns into a fabulous account of the outlaw leagues, where the great Cincinnati Colored Giants travel with their own witch doctor and create baseball diamonds out of cemeteries. William Plummer in the New York Times Book Review noted the influence of Gabriel García Marques here, and said that Charyn had successfully appropriated the Colombian novelist's "peculiar flair for the comic sublime."

Since 1972 Jerome Charyn has been the executive editor of Fiction, and he has also edited two anthologies of contemporary fiction, The Single Voice and The Troubled Vision. In 1968 he joined the English Department of Lehman College of the City University of New York, becoming a full professor in 1978, and he has taught creative writing at Princeton and the University of Texas. He lives in Greenwich Village and is married to Marlene Phillips, a writer.

PRINCIPAL WORKS: Novels—Once upon a Droshky, 1964; On the Darkening Green, 1965; Going to Jerusalem, 1967; American Scrapbook, 1969; Eisenhower, My Eisenhower, 1971; The Tar Baby, 1973; Blue Eyes, 1975; Marilyn the Wild, 1976; The Education of Patrick Silver, 1976; The Franklin Scare, 1977; Secret Isaac, 1978; The Seventh Babe, 1979; The Catfish Man, 1980; Darlin' Bill, 1980; Panna Maria, 1982; Pinocchio's Nose, 1983. Short stories—The Man Who Grew Younger and Other Stories, 1967. As editor—The Single Voice, 1969; The Troubled Vision, 1970.

ABOUT: Contemporary Authors, first revision series 5–8, 1969; Contemporary Literary Criticism 5, 1976; 8, 1978; 18, 1981; Dictionary of Literary Biography Yearbook, 1983; Hoffman, D. (ed.) Harvard Guide to Contemporary American Writing, 1979; Vinson, J. (ed.) Contemporary Novelists, 2d ed., 1976; Who's Who in America, 1983–84. Periodicals—Columbia College Today Winter–Spring 1971; New York Times Book Review February 9, 1975; May 6, 1979; July 17, 1983; Tri-Quarterly Spring 1974.

CHATWIN, (CHARLES) BRUCE (May 13, 1940–), English novelist and travel writer, was born in Sheffield, the son of Charles Leslie and Margharita (Turnell) Chatwin. In a detailed and revealing self-portrait in the *New York Times,* Chatwin explained that the Chatwins were "Birmingham worthies," professional people, chiefly architects and lawyers, who did not go into trade. His father was a lawyer and during World War II served on a minesweeper in Cardiff Harbor, while the mother and son moved about, staying with relatives and friends, in various parts of England. By 1944, and for some time thereafter, Chatwin lived with two great-aunts in Stratford-on-Avon. His most memorable early experiences were attending productions of Shakespeare's plays at the Stratford-on-Avon theater—which included performances by Gielgud, the Oliviers, Peggy Ashcroft, and Paul Robeson. Chatwin was educated in British private schools, where he says that he was "considered a dimwit and dreamer," due partly to his failure to master Greek and Latin. His parents urged him to follow a family tradition and train as an architect, but in 1958, at the age of eighteen, he went to work as a porter at Sotheby & Co., the London auction house.

Chatwin's progress at Sotheby & Co. was extraordinary. He rose rapidly in the firm to art auctioneer, head of the Impressionist department, and by 1965 to one of the company's directorships. A year later, he gave up his job to study archeology at the University of Edinburgh but left soon after to travel and write a book that he claims was "unintelligible" and was never published. In 1973, he was hired by the *Times* of London to write articles for its Sunday magazine, a free-lance career that sent him to exotic parts of the world, and eventually led to his first book, *In Patagonia,* which received the Hawthornden Prize of the British Society of Authors and won him an international reputation.

In Patagonia records Chatwin's wanderings in the southernmost sections of Argentina and Chile, an exotic and partly desolate region. There he encountered hundreds of strange peopled—transplanted Welsh villagers, Boers, gringos, and a German farmer who lives so much in the past that he earnestly toasts Mad King Ludwig. His travels also occasion a wealth of variegated lore about the area—ranging from Darwin's sojourn in Patagonia, in the course of developing his theory of the origin of species, to the legends surrounding Butch Cassidy and the Sundance Kid, who fled to Patagonia to evade capture. The book's odd tales, bizarre characters, and haunting vignettes are presented in ninety-seven brief chapters, many of them only a page in length, but which together impart a sense of rich observation and reflection.

BRUCE CHATWIN

In Patagonia was greeted with unanimous critical acclaim, and described by many viewers as an instant classic; "a little masterpiece," as one critic said, "of travel, history, and adventure." Walter Clemons remarked that Chatwin's interweaving of "remote past and gritty present . . . is mesmerizing"; Sybille Bedford called it "one of the most exhilarating travel books I have read"; and Joseph Tetlow commented that Chatwin's mingling of "the utterly usual with the weird" creates the most fascinating narrative "since Lawrence wrote about Arabia." Alastair Reid praised Chatwin's remarkable gift for condensation, his "clear-cut cameos" that have the effect of seeming "almost surreal." Like other "traveler's tales of the past," he wrote, Chatwin's miniaturist episodes evoke "the strangeness on the earth's surface." Hilton Kramer noted that Chatwin "writes about the past and present, the mythical and the historical, the land and the people—in a style that is ultimately grave and comical but always precise and pictorial."

In 1979 Chatwin received the E. M. Forster Award from the American Academy and Institute of Arts and Letters, which enabled him to visit the United States. But he found that the frenetic pace of New York City life did not allow him the quiet he needed to write, and he departed for Africa, where his second book, *The Viceroy of Ouidah,* is set. The subject of the book is the Marxist state of Benin, formerly Dahomey, the center in the early nineteenth century of the African slave trade. The central figure of Chatwin's account is a Brazilian slave trader, Francisco de Souza, who arrived in Dahomey's port city of Ouidah in 1812 and allied himself with an insurgent prince. Upon coming to power, the prince named him viceroy of Ouidah and overlord of the country's slave trade. De Souza enjoyed vast wealth for a time before dying a street beggar, and leaving behind him "sixty-three mulatto sons and an unknown quantity of daughters whose ever-darkening progeny, now numberless as grasshoppers, were spread from Luanda to the Latin Quarter." In Benin, Chatwin attempted to do research on de Souza's bizarre career, but was arrested as a "suspicious" foreigner and ejected from the country, following which he cast de Souza's story in the form of a novel, the main figure of which is a Francisco Manoel da Silva.

The Viceroy of Ouidah was described by Phoebe-Lou Adams as "a cool, tense, terrifying novel about the mutually corrupting effects of the partnership between a slave-merchant and the Dahomean king who supplied his human goods. This is Conrad's *Heart of Darkness* seen through a microscope." W. L. Webb, in the *Guardian,* called the book "in every sense a very superior piece of work"; and the critic for the *New Yorker* found it "a truly wonderful novel. . . . Mr. Chatwin has a powerfully visual and aural style; sights and sounds crowd his sentences to the point that the book almost breathes. The narrative of da Silva's rise and fall may be full of ironies and surprise turns and of outré incidents, but the real excitement is in the prose." Ronald Nevans, however, objected to the skeletal and murky narrative, to Chatwin's straining "for a serio-comic, mythic quality. . . . The hard, lean prose of *In Patagonia* here becomes arch and pretentious." Walter Clemons, too, found Chatwin's "reportorial gifts" stronger than his imaginative ones: "His best pages are his robust first-hand observations of the family reunion at the start. His later narrative is bejewelled with glinting ironies and bizarre details, but the effect is thin and fancy."

In Chatwin's novel *On the Black Hill,* set in the Border Country between Wales and England, eccentricity appears to fascinate him, and he looks upon it with a cool English eye. The main characters are twin brothers, Lewis and Benjamin Jones, who are born in 1900, remain unmarried, and bound closely to the soil, until they are eighty—even sharing the same parental bed for forty-two years. V. A. Pritchett was quick to note that *On the Black Hill* plays off a peculiarly Welsh imagination, which is "mythical and Biblical," against a modern one of civilization and "progress." Suspicion of modernity guides the lives of the twin brothers, who remain tenaciously insular while the twentieth-century world changes around them. "Strangeness plainly stated," Pritchett remarked, "is the key to Mr. Chatwin's . . .

chronicle, the mixing of outward and inner life. . . . The whole book is at once grave, sparkling, and ingeniously contrived."

Reaction of other critics to the book was varied. Frances Taliafero called it "a frieze of country life and people. . . . Conventional plot structure and character development have little part here; we know Lewis, Benjamin, and their neighbors as we know some permanent figures of our own lives, not by dramatic revelation but by long association and accumulated sympathy." John Updike, in the *New Yorker,* praised Chatwin's "wonderfully sharp and knowing small scenes," and commented that his chiseled, "studied style . . . touches on the epic." The critic for the *Virginia Quarterly Review,* however, felt that the novel lacked momentum, and that the story, although "vividly and poetically imagined," was not deeply moving. Robert Towers, in the *New York Times Book Review,* who admired many aspects of the work, also felt that the reader was not "profoundly moved" by the story, since the characters "are seen mostly from the outside—and with a dispassionate curiosity that keeps the reader's sympathies at a certain distance."

In 1965, Chatwin married Elizabeth Chanler, and they live on a farm in Gloucestershire, England—when he is not traveling. Most recently, fascinated by their nomad culture, he has lived among the Australian aborigines; and he now thinks of himself as a nomad too. "There was a time," he told an interviewer, "when I collected antiquities. I raced like mad through the bazaars of Cairo, Baghdad and Teheran till I found what I wanted. Now I own almost nothing."

PRINCIPAL WORKS: In Patagonia, 1977; The Viceroy of Ouidah, 1980; On the Black Hill, 1983.

ABOUT: Contemporary Authors 85–88, 1980. *Periodicals*—Guardian October 23, 1980; Newsweek December 15, 1980; New Yorker October 9, 1978; March 21, 1983; New York Review of Books November 9, 1978; January 20, 1983; New York Times Book Review July 30, 1978; December 14, 1980; January 2, 1983; February 27, 1983; Saturday Review November 1980; Virginia Quarterly Review Summer 1983.

CHAVIARAS, STRATES *See* HAVIARAS, STRATIS

*CHEN JO-HSI ("RUOXI") (LUCY H.C. TUANN) (November 15, 1938–   ), Chinese short story writer, naturalized Canadian, writes: "I was born in a village in Taiwan at a time when

---

°chen jō shē

CHEN JO-HSI

the island was occupied by Japan. Being the daughter of a poor carpenter, I grew up with workers and farmers, and was well acquainted with the frustrations of poverty and ignorance. Tha Japanese occupation had also provided me with strong feelings of political and social awareness. From a very young age, I had the full taste of the bitterness of being a Chinese and one of the poor. After World War II, Taiwan was restored to China, but it has been separate from the Chinese mainland since 1949 when the latter became Communist. I worked as a tutor through college, Taiwan University, majoring in English literature. I began writing stories as a freshman and published *Modern Literature,* a literary bimonthly, with fellow classmates to promote contemporary western literature. In my last year of college, I became fascinated by Hemingway's writing and decided to go the United States for further studies of twentieth-century American fiction.

"In 1962 I arrived in the U.S. with a scholarship from Mount Holyoke College but transferred the next year to Johns Hopkins University, which offered creative writing courses. I was married soon after and received a Master's degree from the university in 1965. The liberal atmosphere of the American campus in the sixties, together with the Vietnam war and the civil rights movement, greatly influenced me; in fact, they caused me to switch from literature to politics. Socialism was a fad then and books of Mao Zedong were a must in my reading list. Convinced that the most meaningful life of an intellectual was to work with and for the broad masses, I decided to go to China, following Mao's teaching 'to serve the people.'

"In the fall of 1966 my husband and I went to Beijing when China launched the Cultural Revolution. For two and one half years we were left alone in a hotel to watch the revolution, which eventually turned into a civil war. In 1969 we were sent to teach in college. As schools were shut down then, teachers were ordered either to participate in endless political campaigns or put to work in farms. It was not until 1972 that I began teaching English to students newly enrolled in college. The radical Mao style of education brought nothing but confusion and frustration to college; politics took over knowledge. I felt that I was not a teacher but only a tool for political propaganda. Besides, intellectuals were downgraded to the very bottom of all walks of life; those who had studied abroad were suspected as foreign agents and people like us who had been to the United States especially were under tremendous pressure. Moreover, children of the intellectuals were deprived of high school and college education and were doomed to spend their lives in the countryside. Being the mother of two sons, this hurt me more than anything else. The Mao style of revolution and socialism had turned out to be nothing but disillusion. In the winter of 1973, after more than seven years in China, our family left the country for Hong Kong.

"I taught high school for a living in Hong Kong. This is the most crowded city in the world, full of Chinese, yet I felt very lonely there. I missed the people I left behind. When the summer holiday came, I wrote my first story on the Cultural Revolution, 'Mayor Yin,' in a mood similar to that of Marcel Proust when he wrote *Remembrance of Things Past.* At that time China was still shrouded in the glory of the revolution. The revelation of its horror through the story shocked the overseas Chinese community. Many urged me to write more while some branded me a 'traitor' because I exposed the dark side of China. As I continued to write, some Chinese officials even termed me 'people's enemy.'

"In 1976 Mao Zedong died and soon his four close associates, including his wife, were arrested and tried as the Gang of Four. Under new leadership, stories about the Cultural Revolution made a debut in 1978 and the theme soon dominated the Chinese literary scene. My writings were thus classified as the earliest ones of this category. To convince me that China had gone through great changes and improved, I was invited to pay the country a visit in 1982. During my forty-two-day trip in China, I found that, though my books have been banned, they were, however, known among literary circles and the intellectuals who had access to outside information.

"Ever since the Chinese writers have devoted themselves to writing and analyzing the Revolution, I ceased writing about it. The overseas Chinese, particularly the intellectuals in North America, have provided me with the most fascinating topic for fiction writing. I am interested in their life and struggles in an affluent yet foreign society, and for the time being am satisfied with them as characters of my fiction."

While a graduate student at Johns Hopkins University, Chen Jo-hsi met a fellow Chinese student, Shih-yu Tuann, who was working on a doctorate in fluid mechanics. They married and, inspired by the ideological struggles of Maoist communism, returned to China. Their disillusionment with the Cultural Revolution was the inspiration for her stories collected in *The Execution of Mayor Yin*. (The title story has been translated into French, German, Japanese, Swedish, Danish, Norwegian, and Dutch, as well as English.) With quiet, almost chilling restraint, Chen records the betrayal of the ideals of the revolution. Her characters are simple, decent people too unsophisticated to cope with the ruthless power struggles of a totalitarian bureaucracy. Betrayed by their innocent but brainwashed children, by well-meaning friends, or by their own ideals, they do not fit into the new society and live in fear or die in despair. Yet for all their grimness, Chen's stories celebrate the survival of the human spirit and her love for her native country. "Being Chinese," she told an interviewer in 1978, "I do not want to accuse China. There is much there that is good, and the government has reason to be proud of many things. But I must criticize what I see that is wrong." Though now settled with her family in California after living for some years in Vancouver, Chen maintains a close and passionate interest in both mainland Chinese and Taiwanese politics. In January 1980, she led a group of Chinese writers and scholars now living in the United States in a plea for leniency for sixty-five Taiwanese accused of anti-government rioting.

WORKS IN ENGLISH TRANSLATION: *The Execution of Mayor Yin and Other Stories from the Great Proletarian Cultural Revolution* was translated by Nancy Ing and Howard Goldblatt in 1978 in the Chinese Literature in Translation series published by Indiana University Press. A collected *Stories of Chen Jo-hsi* was published in Taiwan in 1982, and the Chinese University Press of Hong Kong published stories and excerpts from her work in *Two Writers and the Cultural Revolution: Lao She and Chen Ruoxi* in 1980.

ABOUT: *Periodicals*—New York Review of Books July 20, 1978; New York Times Book Review July 30, 1978; The Province (Vancouver, B.C.) May 16, 1978; Time June 26, 1978; Times Literary Supplement June 9, 1978.

---

*CHESSEX, JACQUES** (March 1, 1934–), Swiss novelist and poet, writes (in French): "Jacques Chessex was born in Payerne, in the Canton of Vaud, Switzerland. His ancestors on both his mother's and his father's side were country people. Pierre Chessex, Jacques' father, was at the time of his son's birth a professor of Latin and history, and a writer of articles on history and the study of place-names. This learned and intellectually curious man had a great influence on his son. A country childhood. In 1943 the family moved to Lausanne, where Jacques Chessex obtained his certificate at the Collège Classique Cantonal in 1950, followed by a baccalaureate at the Collège Saint-Michel in Fribourg in 1952, then a degree in literature at the University of Lausanne in 1961. His subjects were philosophy, the history of art, and French, with a thesis on Francis Ponge. Jacques Chessex taught for several years at the Béthusy secondary school in Lausanne, and since 1969 he has been professor of French language and literature at the Gymnase Cantonal de la Cité.

"Jacques Chessex devoted himself to literature very early. In 1954 he published his first collection of poems, *Le Jour proche* (The Approaching Day), soon followed by two important volumes of poetry that the critics received very favorably—*Une Voix la Nuit* (A Voice at Night) and *Batailles dans l'air* (Battles in the Air, 1957, and 1959). Thereafter Chessex's faithful, attentive public has steadily increased, especially since the time he began to write novels.

"From the 1960s onward his production has been copious. His works in order of publication include: *La Tête ouverte* (The Open Head, 1962), a tale; the poems *La Jeûne de huit nuits* (The Fast of Eight Nights, 1966) and *L'Ouvert obscur* (The Dark Opening, 1967); an essay of poetic criticism, *Charles-Albert Cingria* (1967); and a novel that became famous, *La Confession du Pasteur Burg* (Pastor Burg's Confession, 1967). In 1969 came *Portrait des Vaudois* (Portrait of the People of Vaudois, new edition 1982), a book of memory and savage humor where figures of the land, the metaphysics of an entire people, and the most routine daily events are combined in a kind of epic, a modern legend in which Chessex's fellow citizens deciphered and rediscovered themselves. In 1970 there was the scandal of *Carabas*, which is still remarkable today for its frankness, its linguistic extremes, its

---

°chess´ex, zhäk

JACQUES CHESSEX

autobiographical confessions, its clever and obsessive eroticism.

"In 1973 his most celebrated novel, *L'Ogre*, received the prestigious Prix Goncourt. This was followed by the widely read collections of short stories and novels: *L'Ardent Royaume* (The Ardent Kingdom, 1975), *Les Yeux jaunes* (Yellow Eyes, 1979); *Judas le transparent* (Transparent Judas, 1982), as well as two collections of short novels: *Le Séjour des morts* (Dwelling of the Dead, 1977), *Où vont mourir les oiseaux* (Where the Birds Go to Die, 1980), and several tales for children. Poetry questioning the meaning of life and death, sharp perceptions of the limits of man and his mystery, a taste for the wondrous and the sordid that links him to the baroque, firmness of writing and a singular subtlety in the pursuit of form—these are some of the traits that critics have pointed out, always more pronounced in each of Chessex's publications.

"At present Chessex is writing poems, short stories, and a more personal work doubtless prefigured in *Bréviaire* (Breviary, 1976), where the figure of his father, who committed suicide in 1956, has an elegiac dimension that is very moving and memorable.

"Jacques Chessex founded the review *Ecriture* with Bertil Galland in Lausanne in 1964. He has contributed to a number of periodicals, reviews, and literary journals: *La Nouvelle Revue Française, Les Cahiers du Sud, Les Nouvelles littéraires, Le Monde, Match, La Gazette de Lausanne, Le Journal de Genève, Webster Review, Sud,* etc. His work has been translated into English, German, Italian, Spanish, Portuguese, Rumanian, Czech, Yugoslavian, Hungarian, Turkish, and Japanese. Besides the Prix Goncourt [of which he was the Swiss winner] he has received the Prix Schiller (1963), and the Prix Alpes-Jura (1971)."

—trans. H. Batchelor

Jacques Chessex's father, himself a writer of books on the land and culture of the Vaud, haunts the writings of his son. In *Bréviaire,* a collection of poetic prose essays and poems, he is the shadow ("Portrait d'une Ombre") who floods his imagination and memory with feelings of guilt for not having loved him enough when he was alive or for not having been able to tell him of his love. It is a vastly different image from the lustful, physically powerful doctor-father of his novel *L'Ogre*, yet it reflects the love-hate paradox of all father-son relationships: "For Jean Calmet loved his father. He loved him, he loved that massive, watchful strength . . . he loved that domineering voice at the same time he feared it. A rather cowardly fear prevented him from running to the doctor, from snuggling into his arms. This cowardice shamed him like a betrayal." Even when dead, the memory of Jean Calmet's father—the Ogre—continues to dominate him, and at thirty-eight a Latin teacher in Lausanne, unloved and incapable of loving, he at last confronts his impotence in a tortured affair with a young student. Unable to exorcize the now castrating ghost of his father, he commits suicide. While some American reviewers found the novel "harrowing" and more a case history than a character study, almost all its readers were impressed by its power and intensity.

The conflict implicit in *A Father's Love* reflects the striking contrast in Chessex between his rural Calvinistic background, the austere and serene Vaud region, and what has been described as "the repressed baroque Catholic side" of his nature. Contradictions, wild oscillations between moods, and a language almost classically pure and severe characterize his writings. Perhaps his most revealing work is *Carabas,* a collection of bravura pieces on politics, drunkenness, travels, mustaches, God, and women. His *Confession du pasteur Burg,* a portrait of a thirty-seven-year-old clergyman torn between his religious vocation and his physical desires, created a scandal in Swiss Protestant circles. A scholar and critic as well as a creative writer, Chessex has written on several fellow Swiss-French (*romand*) writers—Ramuz, Velan, Cingria—establishing once and for all the existence of a genuine *romande* literature.

PRINCIPAL WORKS IN ENGLISH TRANSLATION: Chessex's novel

L'Ogre was translated into English by Martin Sokolinsky in 1975 with the title *A Father's Love.*

ABOUT:Columbia Dictionary of Modern European Literature, 1980; Contemporary Authors 65–68, 1977; Garcin, J. Entretiens avec Jacques Chessex, 1979. *Periodicals*—French Review May 1975.

*CHIAROMONTE, NICOLA (July 12, 1905–January 18, 1972), Italian political and literary critic, was born in the southern town of Rapolla, in Potenza province, the son of a doctor. He was educated at first by the Jesuits, then continued to study Greek, Latin, and classical philosophy at the University of Rome, obtaining a diploma in law. As a student he belonged to a group of young playgoers calling themselves I Schiacalli (The Jackals), who went together to the theaters about Rome to boo nearly everything presented, except for the iconoclastic works of their hero Pirandello whose plays always remained supreme in Chiaromonte's scale of dramatic values. A committed and vocal anti-Fascist of the anarchist persuasion from the beginning of Mussolini's rule in 1922, he first began to publish articles in the reviews *Il Mondo* and *Conscientia* in 1925, but the Fascists soon blacklisted him. He returned to print in the early 1930s in the pages of *Fiera letteraria,* where from 1931 to 1934 he wrote articles on English literature and served as film critic. In 1933–34 he also wrote for *Solaria* and *Scenario.* His clandestine collaboration with the anti-Fascist group Giustizia e libertà (Justice and Liberty), whose review *Quaderni* was published in Paris, led to his flight into exile in 1934. He and his wife established themselves in Paris, where he became a close friend of the Russo-Italian philosopher Andrea Caffi, and continued with Carlo Rossi to edit *Quaderni.* He fought on the Republican side in the Spanish Civil War as a pilot in the air squadron organized and commanded by André Malraux. In Malraux's novel *Man's Hope* (1937), the character Scali, the art historian who reads Plato at the front, is based on Chiaromonte.

The Nazi invasion of France in 1940 forced Chiaromonte to flee to the south, then unoccupied by the Germans, where his wife died. He then continued to North Africa, where in Algeria he became a friend of Albert Camus. Finally, in 1941, he managed to reach the United States. He soon became a regular contributor to the most important journals of the anti-Communist left: *Partisan Review, New Republic* and Dwight Macdonald's one-man effort, *Politics.* His closest friends were also drawn from the democratic left of the New York literary world,

and included Macdonald, James T. Farrell, Meyer Schapiro, and Mary McCarthy. From 1943 to 1945 he also coedited from New York, with Gaetano Salvemini and Enzo Tagliacozzo, the weekly *Italia libera.*

Chiaromonte left the United States in 1948 to go back to Paris, where until 1952 he worked as an international civil servant for UNESCO. He returned to live in Rome only in 1953 and became drama critic on the liberal weekly *Il Mondo* from the time of its reappearance in that year until 1968. From then until his death he wrote regular drama criticism for *L'Espresso* and an occasional column for the Turin daily *La Stampa.* From 1956 to 1968 he coedited, with Ignazio Silone, the monthly *Tempo presente.*

Although Chiaromonte was a widely read and highly respected journalist, he published only two books in his lifetime. The first of these was *La situazione drammatica* (The Dramatic Situation, 1960), a collection of his theater reviews from 1953 to 1958. His approach to theater, indeed to all literature, was that of a traditional intellectual: austere, elitist, and decidedly unproletarian. The critic Leon Wieseltier wrote that "Chiaromonte expects of literature a logical cogency and architectural pattern in its rendering of experience." He rejected most theatrical experimentalism as well as the tendency to exalt stars and directors at the expense of the play's integrity. The essential quality of all good theater is its success at *azione ragionante* (reasoning action), by which the surface reality of life is stripped away. He was no admirer of illusionism—costume, props, or elaborate stage machinery—what Mary McCarthy calls "the naive or else false importance given to externals, not only of dress and furnishings but of events and happenings." Admiring most of all the works of Jean Genet, Samuel Beckett, and of course Pirandello's theater "of judgment and reflection," he reserved his greatest scorn for political ideology masquerading as theater, which he felt negated the works of Bertolt Brecht and his politically committed followers.

Chiaromonte was invited to give the Christian Gauss lectures at Princeton University in 1966. His difficult subject was the idea of history and man's changing perception of his relation to it, as expressed in novels by Stendahl, Hugo, Tolstoy, Roger Martin du Gard, Malraux, and Boris Pasternak. He concluded that the general loss of a sense of history is a principal cause of the emptiness, sham, and alienation found in the modern human condition. These lectures were the basis for his second book, *The Paradox of History,* which appeared the same year in Italy as *Credere e non credere.*

°kē''ä rō mon´ tä, nē´ kō lä

Chiaromonte's death occurred after a sudden heart attack in the studios of the Italian state radio, where he had just participated in a panel discussion. His widow, Miriam, an American he had met while in exile in New York, received a grant from the Giovanni Agnelli Foundation to prepare for publication three volumes of his uncollected criticism. These appeared as *Scritti politici e civili* (Political and Civil Writings, 1976), *Scritti sul teatro* (Writings on the Theater, 1976), and *Silenzio e parole* (Silence and Words, 1978). Preceded by a lengthy introduction by Mary McCarthy, selections from his literary and political essays appeared in English as *The Worm of Consciousness and Other Essays* (1976).

Chiaromonte's politics are hard to catalog. A lifelong enemy of the right, he was also sharply critical of the left. He retained the anarchist's severe skepticism of most organizations and ideologies. Indeed, ideology seems to him the most besetting and destructive of the twentieth century's ills. Leon Wieseltier sees him as a spokesman for "liberalism, and of an old-fashioned kind," pointing to his total confidence in reason and his "respect for measure in argument and action." Chiaromonte understood the causes of the youth revolt in Italy during the 1960s: he had always despised the shabby corruption of the Christian Democrats' self-perpetuating governments. Yet he refused to sanction mob action, and advocated instead "the only truly revolutionary solution," a general withdrawal from centralized politics and systems into decentralized groups, which would make possible an ethical revival in collective life. He also recommended the same kind of decentralization as the theater's best chance for salvation from superficiality and the baneful effects of mass culture.

WORKS IN ENGLISH TRANSLATION: The Paradox of History, 1971; The Worm of Consciousness and Other Essays, 1977; Trevelyan, R. (ed.) Italian Writing Today, 1967.

ABOUT: Columbia Dictionary of Modern European Literature, 1980; Luti, G. Chronache letterarie fra le due guerre, 1966. *Periodicals*—Dissent Winter 1974; New York Review of Books February 20, 1975; May 13, 1976; February 14, 1985.

CH'IEN CHUNG-SHU *See* QIAN ZHONG-SHU

*CHILDRESS, ALICE (October 12, 1920–), American playwright and novelist, was born in Charleston, South Carolina. As a

° chil´dres

ALICE CHILDRESS

child she moved with her family to Harlem, in New York City, where she attended public school and appeared in school theatricals and amateur presentations. In 1940 Childress joined the American Negro Theatre in Harlem as an actress and member of its technical staff. From 1941 to 1952, she was director of the theatre, and acted in a number of its productions, having featured roles in *On Strivers' Row* (1940), *Natural Man* (1941), *Three's a Family* (1943), *Anna Lucasta* (1946), *Rain* (1947), and *Almost Faithful* (1948). During this period, she supported herself through a variety of jobs—as an apprentice machinist, governess, saleslady, and insurance agent.

Her first (one-act) play, *Florence*, was presented at the American Negro Theatre in 1949, and was favorably reviewed for its realistic dialogue and strong characterization. It was followed a year later by *Just a Little Simple*, based on Langston Hughes's novel *Simple Speaks His Mind*, a collection of dialogue narratives focused on Jesse B. Semple ("Simple"), a black man with keen insight into the follies of prejudice and hypocrisy. Childress' first play produced outside Harlem was *Trouble in Mind*. Presented at the Greenwich Mews Theatre in 1955 and directed by Childress, it dealt with a group of black actors who rehearse a "white liberal" play about blacks containing stereotypes of black people. The drama centers on the problem of black performers who have few opportunities to use their talents in the contemporary theater and are often forced into appearing in works in which they cannot believe. *Trouble in Mind* won the 1956 Obie award for the best original Off-Broadway play. Sally R. Sommer has remarked of *Trouble in Mind* that "the best parts of the play . . . prefigure the tough black style of the '60s plays—naturalistic dramas that hit hard, inset with sermonlike arias for solo performers."

Childress' *Wedding Band* was first produced at the University of Michigan in 1966, and presented in 1972 at the Public Theatre in New York, where it was co-directed by Childress and Joseph Papp. *Wedding Band* is concerned with an interracial relationship in Charleston in 1918, involving a black woman and a white man who cannot marry because of segregationist laws in the South. Clive Barnes, who was impressed by its humor and compassion, described it as a "love story about hard, dusty times in a hard, dusty place." Edith Oliver found the richness of the drama in its "small scenes of byplay among the neighbors" rather than in the principal characterizations. "For the most part," she commented, "Miss Childress . . . [succeeds] in creating a whole style of life at that time and in that place. The first act is splendid, but after that we hit a few jarring notes, when the characters seem to be speaking as much for the benefit of us eavesdropping as for the benefit of one another." In an astringent review, Walter Kerr noted that "Childress is at her best with the peripheral figures. . . . The play moves only at its edges; the center feels, and is, impotent, a joint surrender rather than a joined battle."

Childress' later stage works include *The World on a Hill; String,* a one-act play which adapts de Maupassant's story "The Piece of String" to a contemporary situation and black idiom; *Mojo;* and *When the Rattlesnake Sounds,* a play about Harriet Tubman for a juvenile audience. The title comes from Tubman's own words: "Child, you lookin at a woman who's been plenty afraid. When the rattlesnake sounds a warnin . . . it's time to be scared"—lines that reflect Childress' almost magical rendering of black speech. Mary M. Burns called *When the Rattlesnake Sounds* "a beautifully crafted work"; and Zena Sutherland remarked that the play was "moving despite its lack of action" because of the deftness with which Childress summoned up character and situation. *Wine in the Wilderness,* which was shown on Boston television in 1969, and produced on the New York stage in 1976, was considered particularly effective in its depiction of the heroine, a young Harlem woman battered by life, but with great powers of survival. James V. Hatch noted that Childress had created "a *new* black heroine who emerges from the depths of the black community, offering a sharp contrast to the typically strong "Mama" figure that dominates such plays as *Raisin in the Sun.*"

Although best known as a playwright, Childress has also published a number of novels. Her first, *Like One of the Family: Conversations from a Domestic's Life,* comes out of her work in the theater, since it is narrated in a series of satiric monologues by a black maid who vents her views, often hilariously and spiritedly, on racist attitudes in America. *A Hero Ain't Nothin' but a Sandwich,* written in part for young adults, concerns a thirteen-year-old boy in Harlem, Benjie Johnson, who is already a drug addict. The work is narrated in sections, in which Benjie and the important people around him alternately relate their "side of the matter." At the same time the work depicts the boy's first rejection of his stepfather Butler, and then his discovery that Butler represents something of the "hero" figure he has needed. The basic concern of *A Hero* is a struggle for self-respect in a ghetto environment, and its implications go beyond the boy himself, who, as Miguel Ortiz wrote, "is hurting, in trouble, and worthy of our sympathy." *A Hero* was nominated for a National Book Award and received the Jane Addams award for a young adult novel in 1974.

A Short Walk, Childress' most ambitious novel, follows its heroine from her teenage years in Charleston in the early years of the twentieth century, through her marriage to a dull man of property, her flight from him to the then-forming northern ghetto, involvement in Marcus Garvey's black nationalist movement, her life in a traveling minstrel show, to her death of a heart attack on the streets of New York after World War II. *A Short Walk* is a chronicle of black life in America during the first half of the twentieth century as it is experienced by a woman who has had to make her own way. The character of the heroine, Cora James, was considered by reviewers to be the finest part of the work. James Park Stone referred to the "inner radiance [that] never quite leaves her," and Geraldine Wilson noted Cora's "solitariness, that pronounced aloneness which often goes unrecognized in the lives of so many black women." Mary Biggs and Alice Walker, however, considered that the subordinate characters tended to lack dimension; and Walker, in particular, remarked that the sequence of experiences through which Cora passes gives the sense of *déjà vu. Rainbow Jordan* is Childress' account of a fourteen-year-old black girl who is abandoned by her irresponsible mother, and eventually accepts the support and guidance of a middle-aged woman with whom she has been left. Ann Tyler called Rainbow "a heartbreakingly sturdy character," and went on to describe the work as "a beautiful book."

Childress has received a number of honors and awards for her writing, including a playwright's grant from the John Golden Fund (1957), and an appointment for independent study (1966-68) at Harvard's Radcliffe Institute. In 1977 she received the Virgin Islands film festival award for best screenplay for *A Hero Ain't Nothin' but a Sandwich,* and the Paul Robeson Award for outstanding contributions to the performing arts. In the same year she was elected to the Black Filmmakers Hall of Fame, and "Alice Childress Week" was officially observed in Charleston, South Carolina. She has been married for many years to Nathan Woodard, a musician and film editor; and three of her plays—*Martin Luther King at Montgomery, Alabama* (1969), *The African Garden* (1971), and *The Freedom Drum* (1971)—have music written for them by her husband. They have a daughter, Jean (Mrs. Richard Lee). Childress traveled to Russia in 1971 and to mainland China in 1973, but her life is still strongly centered in Harlem, where she is active in many civic groups. In an interview, she has said that in whatever form she works, she is always influenced by the drama.

PRINCIPAL WORKS: *Plays*—Florence, 1949; Just a Little Simple, 1950; Gold Through the Trees, 1952; Trouble in Mind, 1955; Wedding Band, 1966; The World on a Hill, 1968; String, 1969; Wine in the Wilderness, 1969; Mojo, 1970; When the Rattlesnake Sounds, 1975; Let's Hear It for the Queen, 1976; Sea Island Song, 1979. *Novels*—Like One of the Family, 1956; A Hero Ain't Nothin' but a Sandwich, 1973; A Short Walk, 1979; Rainbow Jordan, 1981.

ABOUT: Black American Playwrights, 1800 to the Present, 1976; Black American Writers Past and Present, 1975; Contemporary Authors 45–48, 1974; new revision series 3, 1981; Contemporary Dramatists (3rd ed.), 1982; Directory of Blacks in the Performing Arts, 1978; Evans, M. (ed.) Black Women Writers (1950–1980), 1984; Fifth Book of Junior Authors, 1983; Living Black American Authors, 1973; More Black American Playwrights, 1978; Notable Names in the American Theatre, 1976; Selected Black American Authors, 1977; Something About the Author, 7, 1975; Who's Who in America, 1983–84; Who's Who of American Women, 1974–75, 1973. *Periodicals*:—Book World May 18, 1971; Ms. December, 1979; Nation November 13, 1972; New Republic November 25, 1972; New Yorker November 4, 1972; New York Times November 5, 1955; February 2, 1969; October 26, 1976; February 3, 1978; January 11, 1979; November 11, 1979; April 26, 1981.

CHOU LI-PO See ZHOU LIBO

CLARK, CURT See WESTLAKE, DONALD E.

CLAVELL, JAMES (DU MARESQ) (October 10, 1924–   ), English novelist and filmmaker, was born in Sydney, Australia, the son of Sir Richard Charles and Eileen (Lady Ross) Clavell. Clavell claims descent from Walterus de Claville, a Norman adventurer who landed at Hastings, England with William the Conqueror in 1066. Clavell's father was a Captain in the Royal Navy whose duty carried his family to a succession of Commonwealth port cities. Clavell was educated at secondary schools in England and joined the Royal Artillery regiment in 1941. He was captured by the Japanese in Java in 1942, and spent the next three years in prisoner-of-war camps, chiefly at Changi, outside Singapore, where conditions were so harsh that only 10,000 of the 150,000 prisoners survived. He had decided on a military career when he returned to England in 1945 as a captain, but a motorcycle accident, which left him lame in one leg, resulted in a disability discharge.

In 1946–47 Clavell attended the University of Birmingham to prepare for a career in law or engineering, but after meeting his future wife, April Stride, an actress, he decided to become a film director. During the next few years he worked as a film distributor and made television pilots. In 1952 Clavell married April Stride (by whom he has two daughters, Michaela and Holly), and the couple immigrated to the United States in 1953, becoming naturalized citizens in 1963. After some film production experience in New York City, Clavell went to Hollywood, where he wrote his first produced screenplay, *The Fly* (20th Century-Fox, 1958), a science fiction thriller. Following the commercial success of the film, other writing assignments came in rapid succession. He wrote *Watusi* (MGM, 1959), a remake of *King Solomon's Mines,* and received a Screen Writers award for his collaboration on the screenplay for *The Great Escape* (United Artists, 1963), an account of the escape of Allied prisoners from a German POW camp during World War II. He was also coauthor of screenplays for *633 Squadron* (United Artists, 1968), a World War II thriller, and *The Satan Bug* (United Artists, 1965), a science fiction film.

Clavell's ambition to become a director was realized when he became writer, director, and producer of *Five Gates of Hell* (20th Century-Fox, 1959), about medical personnel during the war in Indochina. As writer-director-producer, Clavell next made *Walk Like a Dragon* (Paramount, 1960), an offbeat Western; *Where's Jack?* (Paramount, 1966), about the career of an eighteenth-century British highwayman; *To Sir With Love* (Columbia, 1967), about a teacher from British Guiana (played by Sidney Poitier) who wins over his problem students in a tough

JAMES CLAVELL

secondary school in London's East End; and *The Happy Valley* (ABC Films, 1971), dealing with the Thirty Years War in Europe.

Clavell drew for the first time on his own experience in writing his first novel *King Rat,* an account of Allied prisoners during the period just before the end of World War II. The novel tests traditional ideals against the need to survive under harsh conditions and makes absolute moral standards seem questionable. *King Rat* shows the influence of Clavell's work in films, since it is strongly visualized and cinematic (it was adapted as a film in 1962 by Byron Forbes), and pays greater attention to dramatic conflict than to depth of characterization. Reviewers were particularly critical of Clavell's use of character stereotypes. The critic for the *New Yorker* remarked that "the suffering of the men [is told] in such detail that individual characters and personalities remain in the shadow, and the few who survive are hardly better known to us at the end . . . than they were at the beginning."

In 1963 Clavell lived with his family in Hong Kong while he began his second novel *Tai-Pan,* which takes place in Hong Kong immediately after the ceding of the island to the British in 1841—a period of opium dealing, trade rivalries, and the forging of a commercial empire. A highly plotted novel involving typhoons and piracy, action and sex, *Tai-Pan* proved an enormously popular work, selling more than two million copies. It fared less well, however, with critics. The reviewer for *Time* remarked that "its very energy and scope command the eye," but was scornful of the content, calling the hero "a kind of Scottish superman."

Tai-Pan was outstripped in popularity nine years later by the publication of Clavell's *Shōgun,* a record-breaking best-seller that in 1980 was adapted for NBC in a five-part, twelve-hour mini-series that captured one of the largest audiences in American television history. *Shōgun* is an exploration of Japanese feudal culture at a time when it was first penetrated by Westerners. The hero is an Englishman, a Captain John Blackthorne, who is shipwrecked and captured by the warlord Toronaga, and then becomes his trusted adviser. The novel depicts the struggle between Toronaga and Ishido to become Shōgun, or supreme military dictator, with Blackstone being instrumental in Toronaga's accession to power.

Without necessarily regarding *Shōgun* as a novel of great literary merit, reviewers were impressed by the graphic writing, and the vast scope of the narrative. The *New Yorker* called *Shōgun* "slick," "ambitious," and a flashy "fact-crammed novel," but conceded that "Mr. Clavell does have a decided gift for story telling." In the *New York Times Book Review,* Webster Schott remarked: "I can't remember when a novel has seized my mind like this one. . . . The imagination is possessed by Blackthorne, Toronaga and medieval Japan. . . . It strives for epic dimension, and occasionally it approaches that elevated state. It's irresistible, maybe unforgettable and, finally, exhausting."

Clavell's *The Children's Story,* a short story published originally in the *Ladies' Home Journal,* depicts the takeover of children's minds by a totalitarian power. Through skillful propaganda, the children are weaned away by a "New Teacher" from a belief in God, country, and parents. *The Children's Story* was reviewed slightingly as "simplistically written"—"a dated throwback," as Joyce Smothers remarked, "to the Cold War mentality of 25 years ago." In the same year Clavell published *Noble House,* a huge novel of 1,200 pages set in Hong Kong during ten days in 1963. Clavell's intricate plot depicts the struggle between rival companies against a background of espionage. Critics regarded *Noble House* as a kind of superior "entertainment," and the reviewer for *Time* noted humorously that *Noble House,* "weighing in at almost four pounds, is . . . an alternative challenge for those who keep vowing to read *War and Peace."* But he went on to say that "few contemporary writers can match Clavell's sense of place."

In addition to his fiction and screenplays, Clavell has written a play, *Countdown at Armegeddon* (1966). He plans to write another Oriental saga, tentatively entitled "Nippon," which will tell of Japan from the 1870s to the 1970s, bringing the *Shōgun* story up to date.

PRINCIPAL WORKS: King Rat, 1962; Tai-Pan, 1966; Shōgun, 1975; The Children's Story, 1981; Noble House, 1981.

ABOUT: Contemporary Authors, first revision series 25–28, 1977; Current Biography, 1981; Who's Who in America, 1983–84; *Periodicals*—Booklist September 15, 1981; Christian Science Monitor August 9, 1962; National Review November 12, 1982; New Yorker September 8, 1962; New York Review of Books, September 18, 1975; New York Times Book Review May 22, 1966; June 22, 1975; May 3, 1981; New York Times Magazine September 13, 1981; Publishers Weekly February 14, 1972; Saturday Review August 11, 1962; Time July 7, 1975.

J.M. COETZEE

COE, TUCKER *See* WESTLAKE, DONALD E.

---

*COETZEE, J(OHN) M. (February 9, 1940–), South African novelist, writes: "Born Cape Town, South Africa. Father a lawyer, mother a schoolteacher; grandparents on both sides farmers. Until 1945 lived in a succession of small towns in the Cape Province, thereafter mainly in the more somnolent suburbs of Cape Town. Educated in English-medium schools, the last of them a Catholic boys' college; emerged from twelve years on hard benches with little to show but an acquaintance with elementary Latin and algebra. Guidance test proved that his vocation was to become a quantity surveyor. Nevertheless proceeded to the University of Cape Town where he irresolutely studied both literature and mathematics. By 1961 had degrees in both but no better idea of what to do in life. Read Eliot and Pound and tried doggedly to understand what people saw in Shakespeare; specialized in statistics but never wholly understood how probability theory could be made to connect with reality. Wrote poetry, encouraged by Guy Howarth; admired the lectures of professors Skewes on number theory and Casson on Middle English phonology.

"Took the mailship to England in 1962. Spent the daylight hours working for I.B.M. as a computer programmer, the evenings in the British Museum reading Ford Madox Ford, and the rest of the time tramping the cold streets of London seeking the meaning of life. In the Everyman Theatre, Hampstead, discovered instead the films of Ingmar Bergman and Satyajit Ray, and (later) Jean-Luc Godard. Gave up poetry June 1963. Spent 1964–65 in the laboratories of a computer company in the countryside outside London. Read Beckett. During a week-long visit to the Mathematical Laboratory at Cambridge University made the dispiriting discovery that everyone there was twice as clever as he was. Gave up mathematics and Britain and enrolled in the graduate program in English at the University of Texas.

"Spent three dull but productive years in Austin getting a professional education. Learned rudiments of criticism from James Sledd. Started to suspect, however, that grammar was more interesting than literature. Read Chomsky, wrote over-hasty dissertation on Beckett's prose style. Played tennis in the cool of the evening, slaved over French and German. Went to Buffalo (SUNY) as assistant professor of English. Learned, from colleagues too numerous to mention, something about the life of the mind, while the bombs went on falling in Vietnam. Began writing *Dusklands*, reading history. Left (with regret) in 1971.

"Back in South Africa, settled down to undergraduate teaching with a definite sense of closing horizons. Completed *Dusklands*. Worked on translations (from Dutch), on academic criticism, on *In the Heart of the Country*. Spent 1979 in the U.S. and wrote most of *Waiting for the Barbarians* there. Lives with two teenage children within walking distance of the University of Cape Town, where he is currently Associate Professor of English."

°cō ĕt´ zē

J. M. Coetzee took his M.A. from the University of Cape Town in 1963, his Ph.D. from Texas in 1969. He taught at Buffalo from 1968 to 1971, and since 1972 has taught English at Cape Town, South Africa's oldest university, an institution for whites only where the language of instruction is English.

Coetzee is of Afrikaner descent, and his novels are widely read as political allegories of the violently racist, schizoid society of his country. *Dusklands* consists of two novellas which treat parallel situations. In the first, "The Vietnam Project," Eugene Dawn, employed by an American research foundation, attempts to extract from the fields in which he is expert practical information which the U.S. government can then use to win the Vietnam War. "People who doubt themselves have no core," he says. "I am doing my best to fashion a core for myself." He tries to impose his will onto everything he encounters, but he has been going mad all along, and, after an act of enormous violence, ends in an insane asylum. The second story, generally considered the better, is "The Narrative of Jacobus Coetzee," a fictional account, set in the 1760s, of the seizure and mastery of the land by a Boer frontiersman. "I move through the wilderness with my gun at the shoulder of my eye and slay elephants, hippopotami, rhinoceros, buffalo, lions, leopards, dogs, giraffes, antelope and buck of all descriptions, hares, and snakes; I leave behind me a mountain of skin, bones, inedible gristle and excrement." The climax of this madman's story is his massacre of an entire tribe of Hottentots because they failed to honor him, because they were indifferent to him. This narrative is the author's attempt to get to the very seed of the violence and hatred which have long been consuming his country and its poeple.

Coetzee's first work published in the United States was *From the Heart of the Country* (its original title is *In the Heart of the Country*), another tale of madness, isolation, and repression. The central character, who tells her story to her diary in a seemingly random, babbling fashion, is Magda, daughter of a white sheepfarmer, forced to remain on the farm in the remote veldt to care for her widowed father, a cold and distant old man. He violates every taboo of his society in a "lunge towards happiness" by seducing his black foreman's wife and bringing her into his house. Magda murders him for this, then gives the foreman and his wife free rein in the house, for which she is raped and utterly humiliated. At the end she is left alone, "a crazy old queen in the middle of nowhere." Tom Paulin saw the novel as "a prophetic account of the historical destiny of South Africa" and "an intellectual lyric which sings the absence of history, the

electric lull before history breaks, rather than a chronicle of a frustrated woman's life—on the level of individual psychology the story is unconvincing but as a piece of cultural psychoanalysis and diagnosis, it's glitteringly precise. It tells of a society turned to stone and of terrible retributions to come." Blake Morrison held that Magda's obsessions, "as she herself acknowledges, inevitably bring certain constrictions and confusions to the narrative: unchecked by irony or humour, hers is at worst 'a history so tedious in the telling that it might as well be a history of silence.' Certainly the interminable questing and questioning are considerably less finely handled than her responses to the physical world. Nevertheless Mr. Coetzee manages through her to present a powerful image of outdated conventions and of the struggle to erode them."

Waiting for the Barbarians was generally seen as an even more oblique parable of his country's predicament. The narrator is a magistrate in a desolate territory who is unaware of any barbarian threat until the arrival of Colonel Joll, a coldly terrifying inquisitor sent by the Third Bureau to prepare for the barbarians' invasion and, if he can, to prevent it by torture. Joll succinctly describes his methods: "First I get lies . . . then pressure, then more lies, then more pressure, then the break, then more pressure, then the truth. That's how you get the truth." The magistrate takes pity on two of Joll's victims, and is himself tortured for his pains. Finally, when Joll and his men abandon the town as indefensible, the magistrate remains behind to care for his fellow citizens, who will be the first victims of the vengeance of the barbarians, when they come. The quietly bitter ending makes clear the meaning of the title, which is taken from one of the most famous poems of the Greek poet Constantine Cavafy:

What does this sudden uneasiness mean,
  and this confusion? . . .

Because it is night and the barbarians have not
  come
and some men have arrived from the frontiers
and they say that there are no barbarians any
  longer
and now, what will become of us without
  barbarians?
These people were a kind of solution.

Some critics of *Waiting for the Barbarians* expressed irritation and even bitterness at Coetzee's calm, careful, and craftsmanlike style, and especially at the simple sympathy he shows for his characters and their dilemma, complaining, as Leon Whiteson for one did, that "white writers who live in South Africa and attack apartheid preach to the converted who live far way. Much applauded abroad, they are of little account at home." But the international attention and honors won by a novel like this—including the James Tait Black memorial prize and the Geoffrey Faber award for 1980—suggest a greater effectiveness in Coetzee's work. Jane Kramer wrote that *Waiting for the Barbarians* is "a reflection on power in the form of a parable of imperial power. Its landscape, which is the moral landscape of Empire, is as particular as Faulkner's Yoknapatawpha County . . . South African fiction is mortgaged to apartheid. By now, it constitutes a sort of genre in itself . . . Coetzee's parable of a nameless magistrate crossing from frontiers of a nameless empire to return a tortured barbarian girl to her people—a pilgrim on a doomed expiatory quest—takes that genre frankly to its limit."

With his *Life and Times of Michael K*, however, Coetzee stretched that limit, writing an allegory that by its title alone suggests comparison with Franz Kafka, and defining his "landscapes of suffering," Cynthia Ozick wrote of the book, "by the little-by-little art of moral disclosure—his stories might be about anyone and anyplace." Michael K is not identified racially, but he is clearly a social pariah—slow-witted, born with a harelip, poor, uneducated, fatherless, with a mother who works as a servant until a war leaves her unemployed and mortally ill, his dependent and burden. Michael K knows nothing except his job as a gardener in a Cape Town park, and the short novel describes his futile but determined struggle to find safety, in a now chaotic and tyrannical society, for his mother and himself. They seek only a bit of dry soil where they may live in peace, but his mother dies on the quest. For a while Michael K, alone and at peace, finds a spot of ground which he cultivates lovingly. There he develops a kind of independence and selfhood, but it is short-lived. The brutal world intrudes upon his freedom, and the novel ends with him in a concentration camp doing forced labor.

The major problem of the novel, in the critical consensus, is Michael K's passivity. Kafka's central characters, to be sure, are also helpless. But, as D. J. Enright observed: " . . . if not exactly masters of their fate, [they] are comparatively brisk, alert and active." But Michael K's life is almost vegetable—so innocent that he is only barely aware of what is happening to him. A gardener, he lives, Coetzee writes, "like an earthworm. . . . Or a mole, also a gardener, that does not tell stories because it lives in silence." Yet the power of the novel—and its terrible relevance to the condition of life in present-day South Africa—is unmistakable. As Ozick observes: "Mr. Coetzee's subdued yet urgent lament is for the sadness of South Africa that has made dependents and parasites and prisoners of its own children, black and white." It is also a lament for a country he chose to return to, with sadness but also with love. "What I missed," he wrote in an article in the *New York Times Book Review* in 1984 describing his American years, "seemed to be a certain emptiness, empty earth and empty sky, to which South Africa had accustomed me."

PRINCIPAL WORKS: Dusklands, 1974; In the Heart of the Country, 1977; Waiting for the Barbarians, 1980; Life and Times of Michael K, 1983.

ABOUT: Contemporary Authors 77–80, 1979. *Periodicals*—America September 25, 1982; Books in Canada August-September 1982; Canadian Forum October 1982; Commonweal May 21, 1982; July 13, 1984; Encounter October 1977; January 1984; Library Journal July 1977; April 15, 1982; New York Review of Books December 2, 1982; February 2, 1984; New Statesman November 7, 1980; New York Times Book Review December 11, 1983; April 15, 1984; New Yorker July 12, 1982; Newsweek May 31, 1982; Observer January 9, 1983; Times Literary Supplement July 22, 1977; November 7, 1980; January 14, 1983; September 30, 1983; World Literature Today Autumn 1981.

COLWIN, LAURIE (1944–), American novelist and short story writer, was born in New York City. Her father, Peter Barnett Colwin, was a fundraiser and executive, and a director of the United Jewish Appeal. Colwin grew up in Long Island, Chicago, and Philadelphia. She attended Bard College briefly, but dropped out in 1963 and went to work in New York, holding a series of jobs in publishing. For a time, she took courses at the Columbia School of General Studies. When she was twenty-five, and "between jobs," she produced short stories she felt were good, and decided to seek a literary agent. She was taken on by the well-known agent Claudia Donadio, who sold one of her stories to the *New Yorker,* and Colwin's career as a writer was launched.

Her first collection of short stories, *Passion and Affect,* published in England as *Dangerous French Mistress and Other Stories,* dealt with characters who discover an irrationality in themselves and others when they form "relationships," usually sexual or marital ones. Reviewers were immediately struck by Colwin's sharply observant, attractive style. Peter Wolfe spoke of her "bright, figured prose . . . her short, terse paragraphs [that] transmit sharp-cut images and bright little rips of meaning." Somewhat similarly, Robert Kirsch noted that Colwin "writes [in a line descended] from Dorothy Parker to John Cheever. The economy, the bright-

LAURIE COLWIN

ness, the wit are all there." Anne Barnes remarked that the stories "seem at first to be like sketches for long, open-ended novels. [Colwin] is precise in her portraits of people but leaves their relationships with each other undefined, so that the reader feels they may change direction at any moment. Almost all the stories are about love, passionate, familiar, or adolescent, yet Miss Colwin is on the whole more interested in separateness than togetherness."

Colwin's first novel, *Shine On, Bright and Dangerous Object,* published only a year after *Passion and Affect,* tells the story of Elizabeth "Olly" Bax, who has been left a widow at twenty-seven with the drowning death in Maine of her risk-taking Boston lawyer husband. She goes to New York, and finds that she must take risks of her own, not only in her musical career but also in her personal life. Disturbingly, she begins an affair with her brother-in-law, Patrick Bax, and later goes to a musician's colony in New Hampshire, and is forced again, in her relationship with a married doctor, to discover the truth of her own emotions. The novel was on the whole received enthusiastically by reviewers. "Though it is loaded with all those motifs about growing and finding oneself," Dorothy Rabinowitz observed, "this bright and elegant novel has been accomplished without a jot of cant. . . . On the surface the plot is slender enough . . . but the drama . . . is complex, the point of view unfaltering."

Colwin's gift for capturing social surfaces deftly was also evident in her second novel, *Happy All the Time,* set in New York. A lighthearted romp, it deals with Guido Morris and

Vincent Cardworthy, and the young women they pursue, Holly Sturgis and Misty Berkowitz. Guido and Vincent, both young, handsome, and rich, are cousins and companions since birth. They have every advantage (degrees, jobs, etc.), but appear unequal to the strong-minded women they pursue. At the end, after much confusion is resolved, they are permitted to live "happily ever after," even to toast their happiness attained and to be. A number of critics were clearly charmed by the liveliness and comic spirit of the work. Frances Taliaferro, for example, called it a "delicious book [having] the sweetness of *Cosi fan tutti* without its shadows"; and Eliot Fremont-Smith described it as "an elegant, fresh, funny tale. . . . Colwin is a wonderful, knowing writer." Lucinda Franks pointed out that one of Colwin's strategies in the novel was her reversal of usual male-female roles. "The women," she wrote, "are cool, aloof, independent, and unemotional, while the men dangle on their every word, torturing themselves with self-doubt." She added, however, that "happiness happens to be serious business, and it comes unbelievably easy here to people who are not quite believable." Walter Sullivan, one of the book's adverse critics, also questioned the characterization: "Colwin . . . knows that her characters ought to be different from one another . . . so she gives each of them a fragment of a personality. . . . Maybe the point of the book is that people as fatuous as these are too self-centered and imperceptive not to be happy . . . but the idea is hardly one on which to build a novel."

Happy All the Time was followed by Colwin's second collection of short stories, *The Lone Pilgrim.* The volume contains thirteen stories that are variations on a single theme: trendy women in their twenties and thirties who discover love are temporarily dislocated by it, and find themselves in its aftermath. They are civilized and decent, do not need to worry about money, and have jobs on the edge of the arts. The men with whom they become involved have solid professional backgrounds and are good providers. The critical reception of *The Lone Pilgrim* was generally favorable. "How pleasant it is," Mitchell Ross wrote, "to acknowledge the talent of someone like Laurie Colwin, who . . . has wit and civility in her bones, and who writes better than the whole mopey lot of feminist fictionists." Letty Pogrebin called attention to Colwin's styling of her female characters, who are "impossibly gifted . . . and blissfully untouched by the sooty shortfalls of life's bank accounts. . . . This is fiction a feminist can love if you are willing to love stories about one woman after another who is brilliant in a different field, quirky in an enchanting new way, and more often than not lives happily ever after with a man who seems clearly to deserve her." But to Joyce Carol Oates, Colwin's women were superficial, an "ebullient catalogue of hairstyles, clothes . . . hobbies, apartment furnishings." Allen Wier found them so self-absorbed that "it is difficult to feel compassion for them."

Family Happiness, Colwin's most ambitious novel to date, revolves about the Solo-Miller clan, an attractive, well-to-do New York Jewish family that makes a self-sufficient world unto itself. Its mainstay is the daughter Polly Solo-Miller Demarest, married to a successful lawyer, and with two small children, Pete and Dee-Dee. She has lived so much within this clan that only when she is thrown into an affair with a painter, Lincoln Bennett, does she begin to recognize how emotionally barren she feels. In the course of the novel, she begins to form a new perception of herself as a person of worth outside the family circle. Kimberly Blake remarked that "Colwin's attention to the details of family domesticity, her dry humor . . . make this novel . . . a delight"; and Gene Lyons wrote that "only a novelist with Laurie Colwin's conciseness, ear for dialogue, and talent for creating a vivid world of minor characters could make so familiar a story as consistently amusing and ultimately as surprising as this one." Victoria Rothschild had more mixed reactions. "The strength of *Family Happiness,*" she remarked, "lies in its asides, in the comic caricatures of minor figures in Polly's life. . . . Where the novel falls short is in its central confrontations. Neither Linky nor Henry the husband has enough substance to become more than agreeably perfect. Compared to the sharp pictures of Polly's family background . . . her main conflicts seem an ordered and pleasing blur." Carolyn See, too, found the principal male characters wooden, but was also critical of the heroine. "Polly is so much a compendium of secondary virtues," she commented, "that she does not quite appear as a human being."

Reflecting on her career in a 1983 interview, Colwin has said that she feels "life is extremely good" to her. After her early experiences as a college dropout, and as a editor in a series of short-lived jobs with publishing houses, she has established an admirably successful, independent life. She lives in Manhattan with her husband Peter Jurjevics, formerly editor-in-chief of Dial Press, whom she married in 1983. In addition to her books, she has published short stories in a variety of magazines, including *Redbook, Mademoiselle, Cosmopolitan,* and the *New Yorker.* She likes to cook, and has many interests outside her writing. In a family tradition, she devotes part of her time to volunteer social work, and is particularly active in the Olivieri Center for Homeless Women in New York.

PRINCIPAL WORKS: *Novels*—Shine On, Bright and Dangerous Object, 1975; Happy All the Time, 1978; Family Happiness, 1981. *Short stories*—Passion and Affect, 1974 (U.K. Dangerous French Mistress and Other Stories); The Lone Pilgrim 1981.

ABOUT: Contemporary Authors 89–92, 1980; Contemporary Literary Criticism 5, 1976; 13, 1980; 23, 1983. *Periodicals*—Book World February 22, 1981; Ms. July 1981; Nation November 20, 1982; New York Daily News May 22, 1981; New York Times Book Review September 19, 1982; Saturday Review June 14, 1975; October 14, 1978; Savvy February 1983; Sewanee Review April 1979; Times Literary Supplement September 5, 1975; June 11, 1976.

CORMAN, CID (June 29, 1924–), American poet and editor of *Origin* magazine, was born Sidney Corman in Boston. He was educated at Boston Latin School and at Tufts University in Medford, Massachusetts, from which he graduated in 1945. After studying literature at the University of Michigan in 1946–47 and the University of North Carolina at Chapel Hill in 1947, he returned to Boston, where he hosted a weekly radio program, "This Is Poetry," on WMEX from 1949 to 1951.

In 1951 Corman founded *Origin,* with the intention of developing a broader audience for poets working in the imagist tradition of William Carlos Williams and Wallace Stevens—"a poetry," he wrote, "that spoke to the ear, the heart, and the intelligence with unswerving devotion and immediacy." The magazine, whose contributors included Robert Creeley, Robert Duncan, Louis Zukofsky, Charles Olson, and Denise Levertov, quickly became an important medium for contemporary American poets (its only rival was *Black Mountain Review,* published in the 1950s). According to Michael Heller, Corman's editorship of *Origin,* which continues to the present day, helped to make him "a central reference point in the poetic battleground of the postwar years," allowing him to serve as "generator, clearing house, arbitrator, and gadfly, presiding at one of the most fertile and creative periods of American poetry."

Corman spent 1954–55 in Paris on a Fulbright fellowship studying at the Sorbonne and 1956-57 in Matera, Italy, as a teacher of English. In 1958 he visited Kyoto, Japan, where he settled two years later. He and his wife Shizumi ran an ice cream and coffee shop there, and their home became a hostel for American poets interested in the Japanese poetic sensibility. From Kyoto he continued to issue *Origin*. The magazine never had a circulation of more than 1,000; it was often much lower. Corman raised money to continue operations by selling collections of valuable manuscripts from the magazine's early years to university libraries.

Corman's own poetry developed slowly and steadily over the three decades following the publication of his first book of poetry. Early on, he patterned his verse after that of William Carlos Williams, building mood through the selection and accumulation of detail. After his move to Kyoto he adoped the succinct, compressed style of Japanese poetry, seeking "only perception mounted upon perception in the joy of language." In the poems of *Sun Rock Man,* inspired by his year in Matera, he "vigorously favors the recording eye over the conceptualizing mind," wrote Michael Heller, making himself an instrument of observation and distillation through which the life of the village is rendered into images. Ann Charters describes him in these poems as "using the situation for 'satori,' sudden glimpses of the nature of reality, where he learns about himself and the world and shapes his insights into poems."

Michael Heller identifies exile—specifically, the homelessness of the poet facing the silence of the unarticulated and inarticulate world—as the theme of Corman's work after *Sun Rock Man.* In his confrontation with the finality of this silence, Corman creates what he calls "felt thought" that "appeals . . . to the each in all and the all in each." "The intelligence of [a Corman] poem," Heller continues, "resolves itself not only ideationally but virtually at the level of the syllable (something Corman has learned well from Zukofsky and Olson), where each moment of development is anticipated musically. In Corman, the minims of speech are deployed much like the quavers of traditional song, as both accents and resistances to plain meaning." This meaning, Heller asserts, "often resides less in a particular line or statement than in the cumulative effect of passage through the poem."

A few critics have noted that Corman's poetry has a limited emotional range and that in his preoccupation with his own position as participant/observer he occasionally crosses the line into self-indulgence. The more successful poems follow his own dictum: "Brevity, immediacy, clarity," as in the example from *Plight*:

Leaves
confetti
one looks

to see
whom heaven
blesses.

Robert J. Griffin says of poems like these that they have "an Oriental flavor so strong . . . that they seem not original works but carefully literal translations." Part of this quality is undoubtedly the result of Corman's work as a translator of the haiku poet Matsuo Bashō and of other poets writing in Japanese, French, German, and Italian.

More than one commentator has noted in Corman's work a tension between two ways of thinking, represented by the cities of Kyoto and Boston—the first fostering contemplation of the natural world coupled with economy and fluidity of poetic expression, the second generating what Hayden Carruth calls "a Yankee toughness and existential lucidity" that allows the poet to "speak what whole libraries have debated about contemporary experience."

Most of Corman's numerous verse collections have been issued by the Elizabeth Press in New Rochelle, New York, and by his own Origin Press in Kyoto, which he describes as "a nonprofit semi-cooperative house producing works of poetry" (other authors published by the press include Ted Enslin, Gary Snyder, and Louis Zukofsky). A volume of his selected poems, *Aegis,* was published in 1982. His critical essays have appeared in *Origin* and in *Massachusetts Review, Kulchur, Caterpillar,* and *Grosseteste Review;* some of them were collected in his *Word for Word: Essays on the Art of Language.* His introduction to *The Gist of "Origin": An Anthology* (1973) was described in *Choice* as "thoughful, specific, candid, and invaluable as social history." *Origin,* now in its fourth series, remains under Corman's editorship in Dorchester, Massachusetts, where he has lived since 1979.

Corman has been the recipient of a Chapelbrook Foundation grant in 1967, a National Endowment for the Arts grant in 1974, and the Lenore Marshall Memorial Prize in 1975. Perhaps because he seeks to write "poetry that makes the role of the critic pointless," little critical attention has been directed to his work. Still, he has had a strong influence on contemporary poetry. According to Heller, his "simplicity of structure and depth of realization marked a maturity of stance that younger poets, in the ongoing literary ferment, have turned to as a kind of spiritual and intellectual benchmark."

PRINCIPAL WORKS: *Poetry*—subluna, 1945; A Thanksgiving Eclogue from Theocritus, 1954; The Precisions, 1955; The Responses, 1956; The Marches, 1957; Stances and Distances, 1957; A Table in Provence, 1959; The Descent from Daimonji, 1959; Clocked Stone, 1959; For Sure, 1959; For Instance, 1962; Sun Rock Man, 1962; In No Time, 1963; In Good Time, 1964; All in All, 1964; For Good, 1964; Nonce, 1965;

Stead, 1966; For You, 1966; For Granted, 1967; Words
for Each Other, 1967; & Without End, 1968; Hearth,
1968; No Less, 1968; The World as University, 1968;
No More, 1969; Plight, 1969; For Keeps, 1970; Nigh,
1970; Livingdying, 1970; Of the Breath Of, 1970; For
Now, 1971; Cicadas, 1971; Out & Out, 1972; Be Quest,
1972; A Language Without Words, 1972; Poems:
Thanks to Zuckerkandl, 1973; So Far, 1973; Three Po-
ems, 1973; RSVP, 1974; Yet, 1974; O/I, 1974; For Dear
Life, 1975; Once and For All: Poems for William
Bronk, 1975; Not Now, 1975; Un Less, 1975; For the
Asking, 1976; Leda & the Swan, 1976; 's, 1976; The Act
of Poetry, 1976; Anyhow, 1976; Word for Word, 1977;
At Their Word, 1978; Auspices, 1979; Aegis, 1982.
Translations—Matsuo Basho, Cool Melon, 1959; (ad-
aptations) Cool Gong, 1959; (with Kamaike Susumu)
Shimpei Kusano, Selected Frogs, 1963; (with C. Eshle-
man) Translations from the Spanish, 1967; Basho, Back
Roads to Far Towns, 1967; (with K. Susumu) Kusano,
Frogs and Others: Poems, 1968; Francis Ponge,
Things, 1971; René Char, Leaves of Hypnos, 1973;
Philippe Jaccottet, Breathings, 1974. *Editor*—Franco
Beltrametti, Face to Face, 1973; The Gist of "Origin":
An Anthology, 1975. *Non-fiction*—William Bronk: An
Essay, 1976; Word for Word: Essays on the Art of Lan-
guage, 1977. *Other*—At: Bottom, 1966.

ABOUT: Allen, D.M. (ed.) The New American Poetry,
1960; Contemporary Authors 85–88, 1979; Dictionary
of Literary Biography 5, 1980; Magill, F.N. (ed.) Critical Survey of Poetry: English Languages Series, 1982;
Taggart, J. A Bibliography of the Works of Cid Corman, 1975; Vinson, J. (ed.) Contemporary Poets, 1975.
Periodicals—Choice November 1975; Madrona, III
December 1975; New York Times Book Review May
16, 1976; Parnassus: Poetry in Review Spring-Summer
1976. Partisan Review Spring 1972.

*COSIC, DOBRICA (December 29, 1921–   ),
Yugoslavian (Serbian) novelist and essayist
writes in Serbian: "I was born (and for this event
I claim no credit and accept no blame) in the
beautiful Serbian village of Velika Drenova,
which lost more than half its mobilized men in
World War I and about a hundred women and
children to epidemics of typhus and the Spanish
flu during the Austro-Hungarian and Bulgarian
occupations. I grew up in the home of peasants
and warriors, exhausted, industrious, and ever
worried people, who were able to express, perfectly, whatever they felt, thought, and saw. My
father and my grandfather taught me to love
plants and freedom; and I realized that life was
more suffering than joy, and man always an uncertainty. My mother taught me to be good to
the weak and to fear the unknown; she assured
me that man can defend himself from human
brutality, egotism, and envy, by his intelligence
and pride. Old men and warriors taught me philosophy, history, and psychology. As I was learning the alphabet in primary school, the presence

DOBRICA COSIC

of the village poor prompted me to ask the painful question: Why is there so little justice in the
world, and why do we, even as children, join
games as unequals? And the village priest, showing me thick volumes from his library, made me
believe that the world was a mystery. This is how
I graduated from my first university, in my village, and I still remember some of the knowledge and the mysteries conveyed to me.

"My father considered the peasant the freest
man on earth, and vine-growing the most wonderful profession. Therefore, instead of sending
me to high school so I could become a clerk, he
had me study viniculture so I could learn about
vines, wine, and become a vine-grower. Shortly
before World War II everybody in my country
was dissatisfied by the way the country was governed and wanted to change and improve the regime. Many young men and women wanted to
destroy the state and establish a new order, following the example of Russia. They had great
hopes for the revolution; as they dreamed of the
new world, their heads were reaching the clouds.
I was one of them.

"In 1941, when my homeland, Yugoslavia,
was invaded by Germans, Italians, Hungarians,
and Bulgarians, I—before I had kissed a girl—
became a Yugoslav partisan and started fighting
for freedom and a new, more just, social order.
In Serbia, where I fought, the Germans avenged
the death of one soldier by killing a hundred
Serbs; fifty Serbs paid with their lives for a
wounded German soldier, and twenty-five for
slashed tires on a German vehicle. The partisan
war from 1941 to 1945 was an additional and
unique university for me: I learned about the un-

known in man and in my people; fear forced me to see in human beings that which I would have never otherwise seen. And I realized: there is no limit to evil in man, and yet the world exists thanks to the spirit and courage of sensible and good men. It was during the war that I started to write: I wrote partisan tracts and one love letter—to my future wife. After the war, I was among the victors in my country, haughty and self-confident, convinced that the realization of our socialistic ideals was in our power. Victory brought me love, and a wife—a devoted friend who knew all my weaknesses and was able to help me live a courageous and honorable life. However, I soon realized that winning a war does not mean winning peace; that power is a vice that cannot be resisted even by the best of us. I worked as a journalist and a politician and came to believe that I had something to say to people.

"In 1951 I published *Daleko je sunce* (The Sun Is Far Away), a novel about the partisan war, in which I attempted to answer—from a psychological and ethical point of view—the following question: Is there any sense in fighting for freedom at any cost? My compatriots showed confidence in me, and since 1951 I have worked as a professional writer—novelist, believing that the novel is 'the mastering of destiny.' In 1954 I published *Koreni* (Roots), a novel depicting the dramatic fate of a Serbian peasant family at the end of the nineteenth century: the tragical aspect of the love between father and son, the pain of existence, the desire to continue living through one's offspring. My daughter—my only child—was born the same year. In 1961 I published *Deobe* (Divisions), a novel in three volumes: the psychological, moral, and social schism in Serbia during World War II; revolution and counter-revolution; the tragedy of civil war. I examined the human condition, attempted to determine the limits of man's capacity for evil, tried to probe the meaning and the absurdity of Abraham's sacrifice. In 1972–1978 I published *Vremi smrti* (*The Time of Death*), a novel in four volumes. Serbia in World War I. The destiny of a people and a nation which, rejecting the laws of history, defended its freedom against a three times stronger adversary, and, refusing to capitulate, made an exodus into Albania, a unique exodus of one nation in modern world history. Man's tragedy of exceeding his powers. In addition to ten volumes of novels, I published five books of articles and essays in which I critically examined contemporary Yugoslavia. My novels have been translated into English, Russian, German, Czech, Slovak, Finnish, Bulgarian, Arabic, and several other languages.

"I live and work in Belgrade, with limited civil rights, searching for the truth about the tragedy of a nation and people who, in their confrontation with history, accomplished more than they were able to, and, thereby exceeding the limits of their powers, remained defeated even in their victories."

—trans. Zoran Minderovic

———

Although Dobrica Ćosić remains a politically controversial figure in Yugoslavia, there is little controversy over his reputation as a major novelist, second perhaps only to Ivo Andrić, whose Bosnian trilogy, *The Bridge on the Drina*, like his own Serbian tetralogy *The Time of Death*, depicted in epic terms the tragic human history of his people. History and fiction merge in his work in a panoramic vision of a Serbia ravaged by foreign conquest, internal division and dissension, disease, and poverty. "What seems to emerge from these works," Vasa D. Mihailovich writes, "is the grand design of a series of novels examining the emergence of the present as the most vital social force in the last century of Serbian history, especially during the two world wars."

Beginning in *Daleko je sunce* with a history of the partisan war of the recent past, he moved backward in time in his second novel, *Koreni*, introducing a nineteenth-century Serbian family whose destiny he traced in later novels. The early novels are realistic and naturalistic, showing first-hand knowledge of peasant life. Without sacrifice of such objective detail, however, he began to develop a more subjective narrative technique, with the use of inner monologues and shifting points of view more in the manner of Joyce and Faulkner than of his earlier masters, Dostoevsky, Leonov, and Sholokhov. In *Deobe*, not only individual characters but the people themselves, identified as one mass, speak monologues in rich colloquial speech—"a kind of modern epic," Svetlana Velmor-Janković writes, remarkable for "its stylistic and linguistic structure."

Ćosić's most ambitious work, *Vreme smrti*, traces in faithful historical detail the unhappy fate of the Serbian army and civilian population in the early years of World War I. The scale is epic and the volumes have been compared, not unreasonably, with Tolstoy's *War and Peace*, centering as they do on a single family caught up in the sweep of history. They and the people their lives touch—both fictitious and historical characters—fill a huge scene and give Ćosić the opportunity to portray almost every facet of Serbian life. The father of the family, Vukašin Katić, is an educated man who had once wanted to write a dissertation on John Locke's conception of democracy but instead decided "to dedicate his life to bringing about changes in Serbia, a land sunk deep in fear, split by rival dynasties, rent by the quarrels of political parties." Idealistic, with faith in education and democratic institutions, "he believed in Progress, in what was New, in Europe." But he learns to his bitter disillusionment that his country is condemned to be a victim of the European war and that "the capacity to endure evil was the most universal of all human capacities." In spite of early victories against the powerful Austro-Hungarian armies—in battles that Ćosić describes in graphic detail in *A Time of Death,* Serbia is weakened by an epidemic of typhus (in *Road to Eternity*) and defeated and ravaged by the German and Bulgarian troops (*South to Destiny*).

English-language readers can appreciate the power of Ćosić's writing and what Celia Hawkesworth (in the *Times Literary Supplement*) calls his "deep sense of moral responsibility and humanity." But it is difficult for them to follow the complex and unfamiliar historical detail. American and English reviewers found fault with the mechanical shifting of scenes, the lengthy "philosophical meditations," and the lack of distinct characterization. Hawkesworth writes that "his characters tend to embody a situation or point of view rather than come to life as individuals. The novels are broad and detailed canvases, full of vigour and colour, but flat, with a uniform tone."

Ćosić's essays and newspaper articles, some of them banned in Yugoslavia, express (in Hawkesworth's judgment) "a thinker and critic of great courage." Active in the Yugoslav Writers Union, he advocated as early as 1964 a greater diversity in Yugoslavian writing and greater cultural contact with other countries. Writers, he argued, should have the right "to organize on different bases according to other similarities and affinities, as long as these are in keeping with the social-ideological tenets of the Yugoslav Writers Union." Sveta Lukić, a prominent Yugoslavian critic and editor, wrote that "the personality and activity of Dobrica Ćosić exemplify the real nature of our modernism and the process of 'spiritual liberation' which took place in the literature of the fifties. Dobrica Ćosić appeared, alone and original, in the silent period following the Cominform expulsion. He was the first to speak about man's fate with greater insight because of experiencing the Yugoslav revolution." In 1977 he was elected to the Serbian Academy of Sciences and Arts.

WORKS IN ENGLISH TRANSLATION: An English translation of *Vreme smrti* by Muriel Heppell was published in three volumes, with Part I condensed by Ćosić in a prologue to the first volume: *The Time of Death,* 1978; *Reach to Eternity,* 1980; *South to Destiny,* 1981. A portion of his novel *Bajka* (1966), a futuristic allegory of a mythical state that has been compared to *Brave New World* and *1984,* was translated as "Freedom" in *New Writing in Yugoslavia,* B. Johnson (ed.) in 1970.

ABOUT: Columbia Dictionary of Modern European Literature, 1980; Encyclopedia of World Literature in the 20th Century (rev. ed.) IV, 1981; Lukić, S. Contemporary Yugoslavian Literature, 1972; Modern Slavic Literatures (Library of Literary Criticism) II, 1976. *Periodicals*—Times Literary Supplement May 27, 1983.

COX, HARVEY (GALLAGHER, JR.) (May 19, 1929–), American theologian, was born in Phoenixville, Pennsylvania, the son of Harvey G. Cox, Sr., a painter, decorator, and transport manager, and the former Dorothea Dunwoody. He graduated with honors from the University of Pennsylvania (1951), took a bachelor of divinity degree cum laude from the Yale Divinity School (1955), and a Ph.D. from Harvard (1963). Ordained a minister in the American Baptist Church in 1956, he worked for the church's Home Mission Society from 1958 to 1963, spent the next two years as assistant professor of theology and culture at Andover Newton Theological School near Boston, then joined the faculty of the Harvard Divinity School, where since 1970 he has been Victor Thomas professor of divinity.

In 1977, writing in *Turning East: The Promise and Peril of the New Orientalism,* Cox recalls the milestones of his spiritual development: "I had been intellectually converted from my own fundamentalism in my junior year in college by reading Reinhold Niebuhr's *Moral Man and Immoral Society* with its withering exposure of pietistic individualism. In my years of graduate study, I developed an admiration for Paul Tillich, who always considered himself a 'religious socialist,' and for Walter Rauschenbusch, the prophet of the American social gospel. Later I came to admire the Reverend Martin Luther King, Jr., and still later I became acquainted with the various schools of 'liberation theology,' including those emanating from the Catholic left of Latin America." These experiences directed Cox's thinking toward the relationship between theology and the secular nature of human society. The result was his first book *The Secular City: Secularization and Urbanization in Theological Perspective.* Here he defines secularization as "the liberation of man from religious and metaphysical tutelage, the turning of his attention away from other worlds and toward

HARVEY COX

this one," but maintains that the technological culture dominating modern life need not entail the destruction of Christianity: secular man may instead serve as an agent of the faith's renewal. The second part of the book considers the dilemma of the church in the secular city, and discusses the ways God may be spoken of in a secular fashion—as a sociological, political, and theological question.

The Feast of Fools: A Theological Essay on Festivity and Fantasy was, in its original form, the William Belden Noble lectures at Harvard for 1968. Cox intended the book as a response to criticisms of the one-sidedness of *The Secular City,* what critics called its "eager activism, its zealous concern for social change, its hyperthyroid extraversion." He perceives "an unnecessary gap in today's world between the world-changers and the life-celebrators": the former "need not be joyless and ascetic" and there is no reason why the latter "cannot also be committed to fundamental social change." He proceeds to study the nature of fantasy and its connection to religion and the utopian vision, and includes a chapter on "Christ the Harlequin," a figure he calls "the personification of festivity and fantasy in an age that had almost lost both." W. J. Sullivan remarked that Cox "wants to do more than comment on festivity and fantasy. It is his intent to fashion a theology of celebration and relate these elements of play to the religious sphere. This he does not in strict, systematic fashion, but through suggestion, example and intuition."

Cox's aim in *The Seduction of the Spirit: The Use and Misuse of People's Religion* was to examine three forms of religion: testimony, peo-

ple's religion, and the value patterns promulgated by the mass media. He believes that "religions serve the human spirit best when they nurture a lively mixture of stories and signals, but . . . our society is suffering from a lethal overload of signals. . . . When signals begin to *pose* as stories, when control cues *pretend* to be something other than what they are," man is confronted by "the seduction of the spirit." James Hitchcock expressed satisfaction with Cox's ostensibly comprehensive sympathy for "those cultural phenomena that are currently fashionable among the American intelligentsia. . . . He has not, however, renounced his right to arbitrate what in popular culture is 'authentic' and what is not." J. M. Cameron wrote that the author had apparently adopted "the view that it is part of his vocation as a theologian today not simply to understand a variety of religious traditions but in a sense to inhabit them. . . . I think there may be something a trifle exalted about his fancy that the authentic theologian is a spiritual guide. And the story that there are strange realms of being with which the shamans and the gurus are acquainted is only supported by remarks about archetypes in the unconscious and about forms of consciousness 'older, richer and more complex than ours.' We seem to be back in the swamp of harmonial religion."

Feeling a need to understand the Eastern religions and cults that have recently exerted so strong an attraction on America's young people, Cox wrote *Turning East: The Promise and Peril of the New Orientalism.* "In the course of my investigation, however, I became aware that many of the hopes and hungers that motivate people to turn toward the East were not just observable in others: they were also present in me." What changed the course of his investigation was his discovery of "the meditational practice [*shamatha*] taught by the Tibetan Buddhists in Colorado." His final accomplishment in the book is to examine the Oriental movements around us from the point of view of his secularist theology. He concludes that we must construct "a postmodern spiritual discipline" out of some very unpromising resources: "the shards and clinkers of a disintegrating culture, the remnants of previously taken paths, the often preoccupied and theologically unsophisticated people around" us; these raw materials, he remarks ruefully, are "all anyone has today." The book provoked contrasting critical responses, one critic holding it to be "for the most part sensible, modest, interesting, and useful," while another found his account "to say the least, very unconvincing, . . . trite and trivial."

Like many other writers in the liberal spirit of

the 1960s and '70s, Cox has revised and indeed reversed some of his thinking in the 1980s. *Religion in the Secular City* moves, as its subtitle promises, "Toward a Postmodern Theology." Not only has religion survived in "the secular city," but it has been strengthened: "No one is quite sure just what the postmodern era will be like, but one thing seems clear. Rather than an age of rampant secularization and religious decline it appears to be more of an era of religious revival and the return of the sacral. No one talks much today about the long night of religion or the zero level of its influence on politics." In Iran, Poland, Latin America, and in the conservative backlash of American politics in the early 1980s, religion has become increasingly social and political; and because new groups—the working-class, the poor, the Third World—are increasingly vocal, religion is addressing itself to the needs and interests of those groups.

In May 1957, Cox married Nancy Nieburger; they have a son and two daughters and live in Cambridge. He has often involved his family in various experiments to develop "a more human way of living": they lived for several years in the Boston ghetto of Roxbury, have attempted a communal arrangement with another married couple, and have periodically forsworn using their telephone, television, and automobile. Cox preaches occasionally at the Baptist Church in Harvard Square, and in recent years has taken leaves from Harvard to teach at the Baptist seminary in Mexico City and at the Catholic University in Lima, Peru. "Theology," he told an interviewer in 1984, "is for me a form of research that combines what has been done in the past by anthropologists or ethnographers—actually looking at real movements and the real people in them—with the traditional theological function of making sense of it all."

PRINCIPAL WORKS: The Secular City, 1965; God's Revolution and Man's Responsibility, 1965; The Feast of Fools, 1969; The Seduction of the Spirit, 1973; Turning East, 1977; Just as I Am, 1983; Religion in the Secular City, 1984.

ABOUT: Contemporary Authors 77–80, 1979; Current Biography, 1968; Who's Who in America, 1982–83; Callahan, D. J., The Secular City Debate, 1966. *Periodicals*—America December 16, 1967; February 24, 1968; December 13, 1969; November 4, 1977; American Scholar Winter 1973–74; Christian Century January 3, 1968; June 12, 1968; January 30, 1974; Commonweal May 18, 1984; December 6, 1968; October 5, 1973; Library Journal October 1, 1967; March 15, 1968; November 15, 1969; July 1973; New Republic September 29, 1973; October 1, 1977; New York Review of Books May 31, 1973; March 7, 1974; October 11, 1984; New York Times Book Review Novem-ber 19, 1967; March 15, 1970; September 25, 1977; March 4, 1984; August 26, 1984; Newsweek October 10, 1977; Times Literary Supplement August 8, 1968; June 26, 1970.

*CROCE, ARLENE (May 5, 1934–   ), American dance critic, is the eldest of three children born to Michael Daniel Croce, a textile worker, and Louise Natalie (Pensa) Croce. A native of Providence, Rhode Island, she was "an art-struck child with my head inside the Philco, listening to *Carmen* live from the Met." She was educated at the University of North Carolina at Greensboro and Barnard College, from which she received a B.A. in English in 1955. For the next ten years she worked in editorial jobs in publishing houses, spending all her evenings in film and ballet theaters. Her fascination with ballet intensified in 1957, when she saw the New York City Ballet present three works choreographed by George Balanchine to music by Igor Stravinsky. "The evening had a physical effect on me: I literally couldn't sleep—maybe for a week—afterward. And I knew that in some way my life's work was going to have to be bound up with some aspect of what had happened that night."

In 1965 Croce founded a quarterly magazine, *Ballet Review*, with the intention of providing a forum for other writers on dance. Eventually she began writing for it herself. "There used to be a parochial smell about dance criticism—the worst tradition, not the best. A protective, jealous, private atmosphere," she told an interviewer for *Vogue*. "But because the dancing I saw was so healthy and impressive, I saw no reason why you couldn't apply to it the same rigorous standards you would apply to the other arts." B.H. Haggin has observed that, with the exception of Edwin Denby, there was no one writing perceptive, illuminating dance criticism until Croce came along. She has remained at the top of the field. "Croce's pre-eminence doesn't have or want the volume of a 'major voice,'" Robert Garis has remarked, "and she doesn't happen to want to speak for any new movement or school of dance. You sense that she would rather enliven the dance scene than dominate it. Yet she has great authority in the exciting way her life-sized voice creates the illusion of embodying and speaking for the best audience there is. You want to belong to that audience. She couldn't create such an illusion if she weren't a first-rate writer and this is perhaps her greatest distinction: As she moves easily from ballet to modern dance to movies to the World's Professional Ballroom Dancing Championships, it's not unlike accom-

°krō´chä

panying Shaw through the musical world of the late nineteenth century, and when I call Croce a superb journalist I have the Shavian standard in mind."

Croce continued to edit *Ballet Review* until 1978. From 1969 to 1971 she also contributed a monthly article to the *Dancing Times* of London, "at a time," she says, "when it was impossible to publish on a regular basis in this country." Articles and reviews by Croce appeared in *Harper's, Playbill, Sight and Sound, Commentary,* and other periodicals. Since 1973 she has written a weekly column for the *New Yorker.*

Croce's first book, published in 1972, was *The Fred Astaire and Ginger Rogers Book,* a discussion of the ten films made by Astaire and Rogers between 1933 and 1949, including analyses of the dance numbers. The book was enlivened by flip sequences of dances in the page corners. Croce "seems to know everything" about the films, Joseph Kanon wrote, and describes them with "a gusto, versatility, and grace that remind one of the way Astaire and Rogers dealt with their own rigid plot formulas." The reviewer for *Choice,* however, thought it only "a minor contribution to the lore of movie-making."

Two collections of Croce's reviews have been published: *Afterimages,* which Lincoln Kirstein called "the most reliable chronicle of theatrical dancing from 1966 to 1977, which is the most prolific epoch of the art in America," and *Going to the Dance,* which extends the chronicle through 1981. Reviewers of both books remarked on Croce's ability to capture in words the image of dancers in motion. "She remembers movement as accurately as others remember lines of poetry," said Anna Shapiro, "and rises nearly to poetry herself in her will to bring what she has seen to the reader." Edwin Denby said, "When I read her, I see what is happening on the stage, moment by moment, as it happens. . . . Her style is conversational in tone but has a Jamesian complexity of structure." To describe Patricia McBride dancing in the intermezzo in George Balanchine's *Brahms-Schoenberg Quartet,* Croce wrote in *Afterimages*: "The intermezzo unfurls in a continuous line indistinguishable from the line of McBride's body; the dance just seems to grow out of the curve of her deeply indented lower back and to shape itself voluntarily in a series of unarrested scroll-like plunges. Over and over she plummets and returns upon herself—up through her partner's hands, behind his shoulder, or caught on his chest—and each time the recovery seems to fix both of them momentarily in a new condition, a new intimacy. In this way, the pas de deux

never loses dramatic tension, never becomes remorselessly physical, but the illusion of drama is created entirely by McBride's steadiness through the variable sweep of the patterns Balanchine has set for her."

Croce is candid about her prejudices: "It's a question of what you're equipped to appreciate." She ridicules practitioners of false dance—cerebral, pretentious, compulsively striving to create excitement through "overenergized kinetics." Her targets include Gerald Arpino, Kenneth MacMillan, Jerome Robbins ("The reason one can't formulate a meaning for what he has put on the stage is that there isn't any"), and Maurice Béjart ("Most nights the audience put on a better show than he did"). Those whose art she considers genuinely intuitive and daring include George Balanchine, Natalia Makarova, Suzanne Farrell, Patricia McBride, Mikhail Baryshnikov, Twyla Tharp, and Paul Taylor; about them, as Martha Duffy noted, "she can write truly rhapsodic prose." McBride "has the body of a pubescent girl, the bones of a sparrow, the stamina of a horse." Nadezhda Pavlova has "paradigmatic legs" that sweep the air in "high-voltage arcs. The energy of the gesture seems to pulsate from hip to point as steadily as a beam from a lighthouse." Of Makarova in the role of Odette in *Swan Lake*: "There is always in Makarova's dancing that mysterious extra stretch from the center— always that central support for the force of a gesture—which remains invisible. Leg extensions at hip height caused not the slightest disturbance in the torso or anyplace else. So she appears as if controlled by some exterior force—the sorcerer, perhaps."

In the opinion of some critics, Croce's admiration for these outstanding figures sometimes leads her to exaggerate both their merits and their faults. Both B. H. Haggin and Robert Garis took issue with Croce's treatment of Suzanne Farrell, whom Croce accused of having adopted a distorted style that mutilated the Balanchine ballets in which she appeared in the 1960s. Garis, while acknowledging "Croce's demandingly accurate eye and her virtually moral sense of fidelity of style and form," objected that "her fine, quick sense of the differences" between ballets had blinded her "to what was in fact a large change in Balanchine's sense of style and technique which he was expressing chiefly through Farrell."

Croce sees dance criticism as a way of reawakening sensibilities that have been dulled by overemphasis on the intellect. "We are educated away from our instincts, not only in seeing dance, but in looking at pictures, listening to music, and all the other direct sensory experiences that one is supposed to have with art." (Robert Craft has noted that Croce's understanding of the arts is encyclopedic—she could, he says, be a drama, film, or graphic arts critic—and that she has an "intuitive sense of the relationship between music and choreography.") Ballet, according to Croce, has the "utmost realism always"—a "realism of the imagination" that "enriches you and stabilizes you and encourages you in life." Edwin Denby has said that for attentive readers "she awakens a kind of natural connoisseurship."

Croce served from 1977 to 1980 as dance panelist of the National Endowment of the Arts. The honors she has received include a Guggenheim fellowship (1971), Princeton University's Hodder fellowship (1971), New York City's Mayor's Award for Art and Culture (1979), and the literary award of the American Academy and Institute of Arts and Letters (1979)—the first time the award was made to a dance critic.

PRINCIPAL WORKS: The Fred Astaire and Ginger Rogers Book, 1972; Afterimages, 1977; Going to the Dance, 1982.

ABOUT: Contemporary Authors 104, 1982. *Periodicals*—Choice May 1973; Commentary August 1978; Hudson Review Summer 1978; Newsweek December 4, 1972; November 14, 1977; New Yorker December 8, 1974; October 23, 1978; December 4, 1978; New York Review of Books November 29, 1973; November 24, 1977; August 12, 1982; New York Times Book Review December 17, 1972; November 27, 1977; August 1, 1982; Saturday Review December 16, 1972; June 1982; Time January 22, 1973; January 9, 1978; July 26, 1982; Vogue June 1979.

CROSS, AMANDA See HEILBRUN, CAROLYN

*CUADRA, PABLO ANTONIO (1912–   ), Nicaraguan poet, journalist, editor, and man of letters, writes (in Spanish): "In my childhood, I was another person, and my greatest adventure was to substitute the other for myself. The poet is a child who can invent his childhood. My fiction-childhood was the time when I could create my world and live in it. My poetry, then, was nothing other than the work of a child: 'The child is father to the man.'

"I was born in 1912, but I was able to change my grandparents at will: I could come from the sea as a cabin boy on a ship, or I could replace my Indian blood with that of the earliest founders, and with them clear the jungle and make a

*kwäd´ rä

PABLO ANTONIO CUADRA

land. I removed 2,000 childhood years from my first works, using tools of obsidian to prepare the place. The child knows the magic of places—and places were what I made. For this is my poetry of place, neither patriotic nor nationalistic. I wanted to give man a place, and that became my work.

"It helped a great deal to have a father with biblical knowledge. Brimming with history, patriarchal, he was a cattleman with an immense library. My father contributed more than a century to my childhood.

"Although I was born in Managua, the capital of Nicaragua, my family is from Granada, the port city of the Great Lake, and from my fourth to my forty-sixth year I lived there. There I studied for my baccalaureate with the Jesuits, then on to a law career. I did not finish, because I was horrified by the practices of the profession. I joined my brother Carlos in making a ranch for cattle-raising and farming, and a sawmill, on the banks of the Lake. In line with this work, we navigated large areas of the Lake, and made friends with the sailors. The language of my poetry was nourished by this life and by my knowledge of Nicaraguan men; also, I dedicated years to studying and investigating, in books, the new indigenous culture—its language and its myths—and the new folklore.

"In Granada in 1929, I founded, with a group of poets, a literary movement called the *Vanguardia*. Our proposals included two apparently contradictory methods: (1) to absorb the literary currents of the world's vanguard, and (2) to seek and affirm a new Nicaraguan identity. The first objective was part of Rubén Darío's heritage: We were continuing his tradition of extension and universality. The second was born of the perennial necessity for young people to form a new generation: for years, Nicaragua had been victim of foreign intervention. The Nicaraguan vanguard movement represented, therefore, a double search: for newness and for roots.

"In 1935, I married Adilia Bendana. I have five children and, to this day, twenty books. I edited the reviews *Vanguardia* (from 1930 to 1932); *Cuadernos del Taller San Lucas* (1943 to 1951); and, from 1961, *El Pez y La Serpiente*. I have traveled a great deal in Europe and in the three Americas. My life seemed to be a pendulum that swung between the plane and the plow, but in 1954 I became editor of the newspaper *La Prensa,* in Managua, together with Pedro Joaquín Chamorro. It was costly to reconcile the writer with the journalist. As I edited the periodical, freedom clashed with a dynasty of dictators. Costly also were fears and anxieties, threats and arrests. In 1978, my companion editor, Chamorro, was assassinated. The entire country rebelled, and *La Prensa* became stronger in its campaign demanding the renunciation of tyranny; in time, Somoza ordered the plant to be bombed and burned. Before he could do so, however, he was thrown out of power by the insurrection of the masses.

"After the triumphant Revolution of 1979, *La Prensa* rose from the ashes, revived under my editorship. In my seventy years, I have not had to compromise with my conscience in my dedication to the light of man: to his dignity, his justice and his freedom."

—trans. G. Shulman

———

Grace Shulman, translator of Cuadra's poetry, contributes the following notes: "The poetry of Pablo Antonio Cuadra incarnates his dream of an autonomous Nicaragua. Wisely, he is never didactic; instead, he sings his country's music and folklore, celebrating its villages and farms. His first book, *Poemas nicaragüenses* (Nicaraguan Poems) appeared in 1934 when he was twenty-one years old. It was the initial book of poetry from the *Vanguardia,* that Nicaraguan literary movement he describes as simultaneously merging with the work of a universal vanguard of writers and renewing his country's poetry. The *Vanguardia,* which also included José Coronel Urtecho and Joaquín Pasos, generated a Nicaraguan literary renaissance and also became a force in creating a literature free from European influence, which was an artistic fulfillment of the political wish to liberate Nicaragua from years of foreign intervention.

"Cuadra's *Poemas nicaragüenses* heralded the rebirth of his country's poetry. It embodied common speech, Nicaraguan customs, and ordinary objects. His art was not a part of the Modernist movement inaugurated by Rubén Darío, whose metaphors referred commonplace things to a realm of ethereal splendor, but in the powerful indigenous tradition of the vanguard group. 'His poetry is a land that speaks,' wrote his countryman, the poet Ernesto Cardenal, and it is the fusion of earth and song, as well as the celebration of ordinary, temporal things, that strengthen Cuadra's early work.

"Cuadra suffered through his country's political struggles from an early age. Before he was twenty, he felt keenly the humiliating presence of the United States Marines, who were stationed in Nicaragua for seventeen years. The young writer was inspired by Augusto César Sandino, the guerrilla fighter who continued his warfare in the northern mountains until the Marines were withdrawn in 1933. Driven by nationalist feeling and a deep desire for Nicaraguan independence, Cuadra backed General Anastasio Somoza, in the hope of initiating a new Nicaragua freed of its false sense of equality and safe from foreign intervention. In 1946, however, disillusioned by the dictatorship of the elder Somoza, Cuadra left Nicaragua for Mexico and Spain, where he described himself as a 'voluntary exile.' He taught poetry and read his work at various universities in the United States and in South America, then returned home in 1950.

"The books of his exile—*La Tierra prometida* (The Promised Land, written in 1952), and *Libro de horas* (The Book of Hours, 1956)—never lost their national identification. And *El Jaguar y la luna* (*The Jaguar and the Moon,* 1959), a book that is built on his country's powerful Indian legends, won the Rubén Darío prize for Central American verse in 1959. Although he has published numerous volumes of poetry and essays, as well as a play, in his country, and his work has appeared in Brazil and in Spain, and has been translated into Portuguese and Italian, *The Jaguar and the Moon* and *Songs of Cifar and the Sweet Sea* are the only book-length English versions of his poetry.

"Like Ernesto Cardenal, the priest who founded a community to serve the poor on the Island of Solentiname, Pablo Antonio Cuadra feels an impassioned unity with the peasants and laborers of Nicaragua. In his poetry he identifies with the *campesinos* he lived and worked among. Cardenal wrote: "Pablo Antonio in his poetry has given universal transcendence to the packsaddle, the flat pan, the grindstone. . . . " And like Cardenal, Cuadra writes out of a pro-

found spiritual conviction. After the active political period of his youth, and his disillusionment
with the elder Somoza, Cuadra went through a
severe spiritual crisis that was reflected in *Canto
Temporal* (Temporal Song, 1943). Of that inner
conflict, Cuadra wrote: 'I used to have faith in
the Faith—but this decisive encounter with
Christ revealed to me faith in love.' The Nicaraguan poet found Christ in the people, believing
that their labors would bring about a new dawn
of peace. And so ends "The Islands," from
Cantos de Cifar (*Songs of Cifar*):

The cocks
are heard in the distance.
                    The wind
blows on the hot coal of the morning star.
Already it seems to be dawn.

"*Songs of Cifar and the Sweet Sea* is a selection
from *Cantos de Cifar* (*Songs of Cifar*), which appeared in two editions, in 1969 and in 1971, and
then in a complete edition in 1971. The cycle of
poems recounts the odyssey of a sailor, Cifar,
who, with a "thirst for horizons," navigates the
waters of Lake Nicaragua. That body of water,
variously called "The Lake" and "The Great
Lake," is fresh water ("sweet sea") that is, won-
drously, filled with dangerous sharks. One of two
freshwater lakes in Nicaragua, it is ninety-two
miles long and thirty-four miles wide. Although
Cuadra portrays real people of the present, dis-
closing actual names of families and places, he
uses a vocabulary that is plain and also elevated
to an epic tone.

"In *Songs of Cifar*, as in many of his works,
Cuadra writes of his land and its people. He envisions herons, white sails, sardines hurled on the
beach, the cormorants, the cliffs, and, always,
the hungry, the poor, the shipwrecked in body
and in spirit.

"In his poetry, Cuadra writes of human freedom, but is never directly political. In fact, his
column on cultural matters for *La Prensa*, 'Escri-
to a Máquina' ('Typewritten,' as opposed to his
poetry, which is handwritten), indicates the division within himself between journalism's immediate impact and art's permanence. *Siete árboles
contra el atardecer* (Seven Trees Against the
Dusk) is his work composed during 1977–79, the
terrible years of Somoza's dictatorship that culminated in the assassination of Pedro Joaquín
Chamorro and in the people's insurrection. The
seven trees found in Nicaragua (*ceiba, jocote,
panamá, cacao, mango, jenísero, jícaro*) are presented in precise detail and also as symbols of the
freedom of the people, and of the dignity of the
land. If he whispers of oppression, he sings out
of the beauty of natural things and of the valiant
life of the common people.

"In his poetry, Cuadra makes original use of
a greater American tradition that has informed
the work of Octavio Paz and César Vallejo, as
well as Walt Whitman and Ezra Pound. Cuadra
envisions the vast empty areas of space that are
central to many poets born in the Americas. He
writes of commonplace objects and things, depicting natural phenomena with startling accuracy. In composing a poetry of Nicaragua,
Cuadra has created a poetry of the Americas
and, beyond that, of the world."

WORKS IN ENGLISH TRANSLATION: Thomas Merton's translation of Cuadra's *The Jaguar and the Moon* was first
published in Merton's *Emblems of a Season of Fury* in
1963, then reprinted as a separate volume in 1971.
*Songs of Cifar and the Sweet Sea: Selections from
Songs of Cifar, 1967–1977*, translated and edited by
Grace Schulman and Ann McCarthy de Zavala, was
published in 1979. Selections from Cuadra's verse are
included in *Poets of Nicaragua: A Bilingual Anthology, 1918–1979*, edited and translated by Steven F.
White, with an introduction by Grace Schulman, 1982.

ABOUT: Foster, D. W. and V., (eds.) Dictionary of Latin-
American Authors, 1975; Merton, T. *Introduction to*
Cuadra's The Jaguar and the Moon, 1971; Schulman,
G. *Introduction to* Cuadra's Songs of Cifar, 1979.
Periodicals—New York Times Book Review March 13,
1983; Poetry Society of America Bulletin Winter 1982.

*DAGLARCA, FAZIL HUSNU (1914–   ),

Turkish poet, was born in Istanbul shortly after
the outbreak of World War I, the fifth child of
an army officer of moderate means. He attended Kuleli Military Lycée and the national military college, and was commissioned a second
lieutenant in 1935. After serving in the infantry
in various parts of Turkey he retired from the
army with the rank of captain in 1950. From
1952 to 1959 Dağlarca worked as an inspector
for the Ministry of Labor. In the latter year he
opened a bookshop in Istanbul, called *Kitap*
(Book), which became a literary magnet over the
following two decades. He was also the founder
and first editor (1960–65) of a literary magazine,
Türkçe (Turkish).

Poetry is a greatly admired and popular art
form in Turkey, and accomplished poets have
often become figures of national prominence
and influence. On the strength of more than six
thousand poems, collected in over sixty volumes,
Dağlarca is reckoned one of the best-known literary figures in the country. His first book of poems, *Havaya Çizilen Dünya* (A World Sketched
in Air, 1935), appeared the very day of his com-
missioning, and he published six further volumes
while still in military service, including what is
generally regarded as his best collection, *Toprak*

°dä glär´kə

FAZIL HUSNU DAGLARCA

Ana (Mother Earth, 1950). Although he has produced acclaimed poems in the epic, lyric, and satiric genres, he is perhaps best loved as an engaged poet of social criticism, and several of the poems in *Toprak Ana,* according to Talât Sait Halman, "exerted a shattering impact on political and intellectual circles by dramatically exposing conditions in [Anatolian] villages." The reality of the harsh deprivation suffered by the peasants—Turkey's forgotten people—had rarely been confronted in published (as opposed to oral) poetry. At the start of "Banks of the Red River" he abruptly negates the widespread, popular, even national myth of happy, carefree peasants:

Brother, what you say isn't so.
This is not the land where people dance and cheer.
Come out to Anatolia,
Come by trucks or ox-carts, but come.
You aren't far from here. . . .

The grim depiction of hunger in "Village without Rain" shocked the country's conscience:

I'm hungry, black earth, hungry, hear me.
With the black ox I'm hungry tonight.
He thinks, and thinking feeds him,
I think, and thinking makes my hunger grow.
    I'm hungry, black earth, hungry, hear me.
    One can't hide it when he's hungry. . . .

Hunger is black on our faces, hunger is hoary.
Meadows and hills hunger.
Rain falls no more and the crops are scorched.
How did we anger the skies far and wide?
    Hunger is black on our faces, hunger is hoary.
    One can't live on it when he's hungry.

Other collections manifesting Dağlarca's

acute social conscience include *Bati Acisi* (The Agony of the West, 1958), which grew out of his trip to France and Italy in the early 1950s and speaks passionately of the sociopolitical consequences of East-West coldness and incomprehension; *Özgürlük Alani* (Freedom Square, 1960), expressing his joy over the 1960 military coup which ended the tyrannical excesses of the Adnan Menderes government; *Cezayir Türküsü* (Song of Algeria, 1961), songs of praise for the struggles of the Algerian people against French colonialism; and *Vietnam Savaşimiz* (Our Vietnam War, 1966), a stridently anti-imperialist collection that gave voice to the rising anti-Americanism among the Turkish people. Particularly notable in the last volume is "Poverty," with its deep understanding of a peasant's stolidity when confronted by extreme violence:

This is combat, from land to sky.
Burn me.
Burn me if you like,
But don't burn the forest that shelters me.

This is combat, do whatever you want.
Burn my sky.
Burn my nights if you like
But don't burn my prize cows.

This is combat, I know.
Burn my heart.
Burn my loves if you like,
But don't burn my rice paddies.

Vietnam Körü (The Blind of Vietnam, 1970) and *Hiroshima* (1970) are also indictments of American imperialism.

In the epic mode, a very popular one in his country, Dağlarca has won national renown with *Çakirin Destani* (The Epic of Çakir, 1945), which he describes as "the story of observing the individual in his society and of abandoning the individual for the sake of the community." The hero here is not the conventional epic hero, but an ordinary man with a modern life full of difficulty and consternation. His other epics are more conventional in their subject matter, such as *Üç Şehitler Destani* (The Epic of the Three Martyrs, 1949), depicting a glorious episode in the 1919–22 Turkish war of independence. This great national struggle is the subject of most of his subsequent epics: *Istiklâl Savaşi* (The War of Independence, 1951), *Yedi Memetler* (Seven Heroes, 1964), and *Çanakkale Destani* (The Epic of the Dardanelles, 1965). *Istanbul Fetih Destani* (The Epic of the Conquest of Istanbul, 1953) commemorates the five hundredth anniversary of the fall of Constantinople to the Turks, and *Kubilay Destani* (The Epic of Kubilay, 1968) pays honor to a rural teacher assassinated by conservative religious fanatics in 1930. The latter poem confirms Dağlarca's political sympathy among his country's progressive secularists, the spiritual heirs of Mustafa Kemal Atatürk.

Dağlarca is regarded by Turkish literary critics above all as a poet *sui generis*: no foreign influences shaped his style or informed his themes, and even as a young man he was seen to have a mature taste and a well-developed sense of individuality. "It would be futile," wrote Yaşar Nabi Nayir, "to attempt to find the effects of any poet or movement on him. Just as he owes nothing to his predecessors, he shares none of the essential features of his major contemporaries." The diversity and great quantity of his poetry, in Nayir's opinion, will necessitate "years of arduous effort by critics in order to elucidate all the subtleties and obscurities." Yet there is still, even in Turkish, no comprehensive assessment of his accomplishment.

In 1974 Dağlarca received Yugoslavia's Golden Wreath award, which had previously been given to W. H. Auden, Pablo Neruda, Eugenio Montale, and others. At the Rotterdam Poetry International gathering of 1977, he was voted poet of the year.

WORKS IN ENGLISH TRANSLATION: A large and representative selection of Dağlarca's poems in English translation, from his first collection to a portion of the 1,243 quatrains of *Haydi* (Come On, 1968), is available in *Selected Poems*, 1969, translated by Talât Sait Halman. Translations of his work have also appeared in French, Dutch, Hungarian, Macedonian, and Estonian.

ABOUT: Columbia Dictionary of Modern European Literature, 1980; Dictionary of Oriental Literatures 3, 1974; Encyclopedia of World Literature in the 20th Century, (rev. ed.) I, 1981; Halman, T. S. (ed.) Contemporary Turkish Literature: Fiction and Poetry, 1982; Menemencioğlu, N. (ed.) The Penguin Book of Turkish Verse, 1978.

DAVENPORT, GUY (November 23, 1927–), American scholar, critic, poet, and short story writer, was born in Anderson, S.C., the son of Guy Mattison Davenport, an express agent, and the former Marie Fant. Except for two years (1950–52) in the U.S. Army Airborne Corps, Davenport has pursued an academic career. A B.A. (1948) from Duke University, he spent the next two years as a Rhodes Scholar at Merton College, Oxford, acquiring a B.Litt. After military service he taught English for three years at Washington University in St. Louis and earned his Ph.D. at Harvard in 1961, becoming a contributing editor of *National Review*. From 1961 to 1963 he was assistant professor of English at Haverford College. Since then he has been professor of English at the University of Kentucky in Lexington.

GUY DAVENPORT

Though he won an undergraduate prize for creative writing, contributed to *Hudson Review* and *Virginia Quarterly Review* under the penname of Max Montgomery, and published translations, criticism, and prize-winning poetry while teaching, Davenport did not attempt to write stories until 1970 during his first sabbatical leave. Even today he considers his published work "extensions of the classroom," seeing the poems as "lessons in aesthetics," the stories as "lessons in history," and himself as an "inveterate explainer"—a teacher who writes rather than a professional writer.

As a teacher-critic he believes that "Art is the attention we pay to the wholeness of the world," and that "within the arts we have the memory of mankind in a way no other continuum of culture has kept the useful past." Sometimes he thinks that "the museum, a twentieth-century parody of a temple, is all . . . we have, physically, of the past." But in his criticism he salutes Ruskin and Pound, "two fierce voices . . . which cried out that the arts are the teachers of morality"; how tragic that because these are "the easiest voices to discount as those of charming cranks," professors are ignoring "the power of the poem to teach not only sensibilities and the subtle movements of the spirit but . . . real lasting *felt* knowledge." As a southerner he "takes a certain amount of unhinged reality for granted" and remains "grateful for a day at St. Elizabeth's" when the paranoiac Pound gave him Leo Frobenius' *Kulturgeschichte Africas* with the covers reversed so that he could read it with impunity on the train home. For Davenport as for Pound, "the past is now; its invisibility is our blindness, not its absence." Where Eliot and Joyce attempted an Inferno and Purgatorio, Pound tried for a Paradiso, a "city in the mind," a Periclean Athens or New Jerusalem, old as Frobenius' walled, "temple-centered city . . . put into place with music and incantation," and lasting from "Jericho to Paterson, N.J. . . . , from Troy to Dublin."

Other writers whom Davenport admires either practice with Pound "a daedalian" art dedicated to a "Renaissance of the archaic" (e.g., Charles Montagu Doughty, Charles Olson, Jonathan Williams) or know as Pound, Joyce, and Eliot did "that tradition is maintained by invention and innovation" (e.g., Louis Zukovsky, Ronald Johnson, David Jones). When Davenport looks for the distinctly American in literature he finds ancient antitheses and analogues. Poe's raven atop the bust of Pallas is "the irrational dominating the intellect," the opposite of the ancient "goddess of field and citadel wearing the sanctuary of her people for a crown." Whitman, "America's archetypal poet," who "combined the contemplation of nature and of civilization . . . into a single intoxicating vision of life, because he always had sight of the transitoriness of all phenomena," is also linked with "erotic camaraderie" old as Plutarch's Theban Sacred Band of Pythagorean democrats who thought of a friend as "another self." And Eudora Welty, whom Davenport calls America's "greatest living writer," gives him in her novels an Ovidian Persephone figure who metamorphoses into Eurydice and then Orpheus in an action "old as agriculture and sin." In a recent interview Davenport confesses that his "greatest inspiration is not America but Kafka's *Amerika,* a created, mythical country "that has nothing in common with the one we know but is, all the same, real."

Interested in photography, cinematography, surrealist painting, collage, and frottage, Davenport seeks "*felt* knowledge" of reality in architectonic structure and organic form, believing with Wittgenstein that "the meaning of the world, is outside" in an imagined world. Anthropology and religion show man dressing "biological imperative in custom and ritual; the artist dresses it in analogy, and finds design in accident and rhythm in casualness." In art "event is pattern and essence melodie." In poetry and storytelling Davenport gives his heart to "styles controlled by artifice"—to the epic "severity and archaic beauty" of Doughty's *Dawn in Britain.* Modern poets who search for a "pure mother English" or profit from the meditations of Stein and Wittgenstein on "the splashed meaning of chattered language" also please him, but as a translator of poetry he mis-

trusts "rhetorical cosmetics, and arbitrary tune for melodramatic coloring." He likes the "passion for objectivity" that Pound praised in Homer, Ovid, Dante, Chaucer—master poets "whose manner is limpid, sharp, . . . simple" and whose art seems to have obliterated the artist. The personal enters such poetry only through "coloration and attitude and characteristic attention."

In expository prose he admires the "practical economy" of Louis Agassiz—"elegantly exact, scrupulous in its details," giving an "eloquence of information" that "has a brilliance all its own which flashes from deep sensibility and sharp awareness of beauty." Writers like these make Davenport ask for teachers ready to talk about "the scientific precision of the poet" and "the poetic precision of the botanist . . . in one context."

Ever since his father taught him reverence for Indian arrowheads on Sunday trips, Davenport has sensed the joys described in his essay "Finding"—the "foraging" joys a scholar-teacher may share with the artist and scientist when fragments recovered from the past or memory's found objects are given a new context. In the same year that he selected, annotated, and introduced *Specimens of Scientific Writing* by Agassiz to prove "that authenticities count, that Agassiz need not be held on trust as a mind which illuminated scientific matters in the nineteenth century and now must live in history as a reputation wholly fabulous," *Poetry* published fourteen of his translations of Archilochus. Some critics thought the translation so free as to be invention and many readers supposed even Archilochus the poet also invented, but Davenport insisted in his "Translator's Note" to the more comprehensive *Carmina Archilochi* published a year later that he had been as "literal as an amateur's Greek could manage" when dealing with shredded stanzas and lines (in two cases a single letter) scattered in quotations of later grammarians, rhetoricians, and critics and on scraps of Alexandrian papyrus once used to wrap and stuff "third-class mummies." Hugh Kenner's "Foreword" saw "a personal affinity" with Archilochus in Davenport's ability to "renew our pleasure in the laconic and the expletive," and Davenport admitted that the urge to translate this satirist, lyricist, and mercenary soldier "with the vocabulary of a paratrooper sergeant" had come "as much from the barracks of the XVIII Airborne Corps and of the 756th Heavey Artillery" as from the classroom.

Whereas Garry Wills freund Davenport's Archilochus "recognizable," F. M. Combellack complained of a "pervasive falseness" because "additions, modifications, and combinations" made Archilochus seem "less fragmentary than he really is." Similar objections were made to Davenport's translation of Sappho (1966), which Charles Fuqua called "as historically misleading as it is aesthetically suggestive," and to the enlarged *Archilochus, Sappho, and Alkman* (1980).

Davenport's own stories, first collected in *Tatlin!, Da Vinci's Bicycle,* and *Eclogues* between 1974 and 1981, gained him a prominent place among neo-modernist writers and raised other questions not only for critics but for their author. In response to a critical essay on *Tatlin!* by Richard Pevear in *Hudson Review,* Davenport considered for the first time "the distinction between storytelling and fiction." A resulting essay, "Ernst Machs Max Ernst" first appeared in *New Literary History* in 1978 as a contribution to "the confrontation of self in imaginative writing," the assigned theme of that issue, and later as the final essay in *The Geography of the Imagination.* This reply to Pevear reviews the collage of fact and fictional images in such stories as "The Aeroplanes at Brescia" and "Da Vinci's Bicycle" and asserts the author's trust in such visual detail to produce a symbolic meaning that he feels, though not always knows, is there.

Whereas Pevear had maintained that Davenport's "wealth of narrative invention" stayed within the bounds of fiction's spell-binding art of "continuity, coherence, persuasion," Davenport feels he is always storytelling, not "projecting an illusory fictional world" that (for Pevear) is "narcotic and propagandistic." The major themes of these stories include the general one of "the Dogon sense that man is a forager trying to find God's complete plan of the universe." *Tatlin!'s* title story grew "out of a political stance" Davenport once took and out of his foraging for "the origins of modernism in painting and sculpture." His Tatlin thinks of himself as the Khlebnikov of constructivism, fusing folklore with "the most revolutionary modernity" and dreaming of opening up the dead closed order of Renaissance architecture and "the static allegory" of the Statue of Liberty with a monumental spiral for the Third International or "a new . . . Pegasus" to replace "the carriage of the aristocracy." As an artist-inventor he tries to "keep translating his models back into the primal reality," a method close to Davenport's own. Though Davenport as storyteller gives himself the role of "a playful Calvinist God" who knows the future and treats Tatlin's aspirations for machinery and society with an irony that could be aimed at his own art, he endows a few historical figures in other stories with a more impressive power to give words to the wordless *logos,* whose language is "harmonic de-sign, trees, light, time, consciousness, attractions like gravity and reproduction." Herakleitos, in the story named for him, and the Dutch philosopher Adriaan van Hovendaal in "The Dawn in Erewhon" have a more truly godlike awareness of some "inner consistency of all dialects of the *logos*"; Kafka and Wittgenstein in "The Aeroplanes at Brescia," and Abbé Breuil in "Robot" (a story about the cave paintings at Lascaux), and the Protean Poe, who calls himself Edgar A. Perry in "1830," all have a more haunted intuition of "what nature, desire, design, and God are saying."

As Davenport surveys his narrative art he sees three questions providing themes subsidiary to that of the foragers: is matter alive or dead? how does it differ in nature and the machine? and how should man reconcile his physical animality with the counter-forces of a mechanical age to "reclaim" a spirit currently lost to his civilization? In the collections after *Tatlin!* these themes persist. Critics appreciate the humor and intellectual excitement given them by Davenport's surrealist imagery and structure, especially in shorter stories like "Robot," "Ithaka," and "The Trees at Lystra." Longer, more ambitious developments like "the Dawn at Erewhon" and "Au Tombeau de Charles Fourier" provoke impatience. Jack Sullivan found the collages of *Da Vinci's Bicycle* "dizzying" and "sometimes wearying in their self-conscious erudition," and George Stade's first impression was that they were derivative and dated in their "high modernism." On a second reading Stade recanted, finding them "very good, by any standard, except that of immediate accessibility"; even Sullivan concluded that "At his best Davenport belongs in the same company as his 'foragers.'" But Hilton Kramer, a critic still favorably disposed to modernism in art, objects to a "hostility to modern society" that Davenport shares with Pound; and George Steiner, who places Davenport beside William Gass, Borges, Raymond Queneau, and Calvino, still thinks his "sprightly elegance defuses" the important question of "what . . . makes high literacy so vulnerable to the siren calls of barbarism." Why, for instance, is the Bolshevik Revolution called "a necessary delirium" and Pound's involvement with "totalitarian Fascist inhumanity" dismissed? Steiner also sees in the stories' "world of *ficciones* and reflections" a "homoeroticism" whose "pressures . . . on the very nerve centers of modern art, thought, and social consciousness" Davenport has yet to articulate and analyze.

PRINCIPAL WORKS: *Criticism*—The Intelligence of Louis Agassiz, 1963; The Geography of the Imagination, 1981. *Translations*—Carmina Archilochi, 1964; Sappho: Songs and Fragments, 1965; Archilochus, Sappho, and Alkman, 1980; The Mimes of Herondas, 1981. *Poetry*—Flowers and Leaves, 1966. *Short Stories*—Tatlin!, 1974; Da Vinci's Bicycle, 1979; Eclogues, 1981; Trois Caprices, 1981; Fifty-seven Views of Fujiyama *in* Granta 4, 1981 and Hudson Review Spring 1983.

ABOUT: Contemporary Authors, first revision series 33–36, 1978; *Periodicals*—Beaux Arts 1983; Classical World September 1964; Hudson Review Spring 1975; Autumn 1980; Spring 1983; National Review June 16, 1964; March 1966; New Yorker November 30, 1981; New York Review of Books March 3, 1966; December 12, 1974; New York Times Book Review October 20, 1974; June 17, 1979; September 6, 1981; Saturday Review July 7, 1979; Shearsman, 7 (1982); Times Literary Supplement April 24, 1981.

LUCY DAWIDOWICZ

DAWIDOWICZ, LUCY (SCHILDKRET)

(June 16, 1915–   ), American writer and historian, writes: "In August 1938, I left New York City, where I had lived all my twenty-three years, to go for a year to Vilna, then in Poland. There I was to study Jewish history and Yiddish. It was a quixotic undertaking. For well over fifty years, the Jewish traffic had been going the other way. Not only geographically, as the East European Jews fled westward to America, but also psychologically, as they fled from their East European origins, their language, and their history.

"What had put me on such a perverse reverse course? Nowadays, we'd call it a search for identitiy. For myself, I look back upon this episode in my life as a search for wholeness. Like most daughters of working-class East European Jewish immigrants, I had gone to Hunter College. There poetry was the love of my life. In 1937, I began working toward a master's degree in English literature at Columbia University. But soon I found that in a world of brutal history whose victims were too often Jews, Wordsworth had become wearisome and even alien.

"The Third Reich was then casting its shadow over Europe. Everywhere in Central and Eastern Europe the Jews were being assaulted by violence and/or administrative edict. Republican Spain was being destroyed by the Fascists. Stalin was murdering his own generals and political leaders, condemning millions of Russians to certain death in concentration camps. What was Wordsworth to me at such time that I should care for him?

"Thrashing around to make sense of my life, I turned for advice to a beloved teacher. Not one of my college teachers, but a man who had taught modern Jewish history at a Jewish high school I used to attend on weekends. It was a sec-

ular Yiddishist school, whose faculty included men of learning and accomplishment. My history teacher was Jacob Shatzky, who in 1922 had earned a doctorate from the University of Warsaw for a dissertation on Polish-Jewish history. (He worked as librarian of the New York State Psychiatric Institite.) I laid my unhappiness before him: What should I do with my life, when Wordsworth no longer spoke to me?

"He advised me go to Vilna, where the headquarters of the Yiddish Scientific Institite—YIVO (an acronym of its Yiddish name)—was then located, to become a fellow at its Research and Training Center. There I could study Jewish history and improve my Yiddish. As a member of the YIVO's board, he would see to it that I got a fellowship and travel expenses.

"My journey to Poland was not only quixotic, but reckless. (My parents disapproved.) In the summer of 1938 Europe was smoldering with war. Hitler had already annexed Austria and was now threatening Czechoslovakia. In the very month that he was hotting up the Czech crisis, I sailed on the Polish liner *Batory* to Gdynia, the port in Poland's narrow corridor to the sea.

"A month later, when I had already settled into my new life in Vilna and begun my studies at the YIVO, the Czech crisis had reached the very precipice of war. The Czech government had ordered full mobilization. The French began to call up all their reserves. At the end of September, a moment—so it seemed—before war erupted, the Munich Conference was convened. It appeased Hitler for the time being by dismembering Czechoslovakia. Neville Chamberlain, Britain's Prime Minister and chief architect of the Munich Agreement, then declared: 'I believe it is peace for our time.'

"My year at the YIVO in Vilna was a year under the sign of history. I lived in a city where even the cobblestones were venerable with history. In the year I lived there, every day dawned with anxiety for the future and darkened with the terror of history. Early in October, in accordance with the Munich Agreement, the Poles seized their share of Czechoslovakia. My friends were ashamed for Poland.

"History was then the frame which defined the space of our lives. It had not yet become a vise. In that Vilna year, history unfolded before me in a dual perspective: the history of the distant past merging into the foreground of contemporary history. For me it was a rich year in the acquisition of new knowledge, new friends, and a new sense of myself. But in that same year the frame of history began to tighten like a vise around our lives and around the landscape of Poland. Hitler's demands on Poland were escalating and his clamor filled the air.

"Planning to return home in October 1939, I took a vacation in August in the countryside near Vilna. It was a pastoral, isolated place, without newspapers or telephones. I don't remember exactly the day, but probably, as I reconstruct it, it was August 22 when my friends in Vilna telegraphed that a registered letter had arrived for me from the American consul in Warsaw. He advised all American citizens to leave Poland because of the imminent danger of war. It apeared that Germany and the Soviet Union had just signed a trade treaty, news enough to startle the world even in those times. Still more ominous was the news that these ideological foes were about to conclude a nonaggression pact.

"Returning to Vilna was no easy matter. Poland had already begun to mobilize. Anything on wheels had already been requisitioned. I think I got back on a farmer's wagon. In Vilna, my friends urged me to leave Poland. I said that I would stay, share their fate, help them. But their response was unsentimental. They said that war would come, there'd be food shortages, life would be hard; I'd be a burden. I remonstrated, then compromised: I'd go to Warsaw to find out from the American consul what was happening. I said I'd return; I left most of my things there. But I never returned to Vilna.

"In Warsaw the American Consul and my friends counselled me to leave. Europe was on the verge of war. I was convinced by the sense of panic in Warsaw, which I had not seen in provincial Vilna. Though I fully appreciated how fortunate I was to be an American, my good fortune in this respect burdened me with guilt for

leaving those I loved behind. Still, I decided to leave Poland. My return steamship ticket was no longer of any use. The port city Gdynia was already closed; passenger ships had been requisitioned for war duty. By then there were fewer exits. I chose to go by train, via Berlin, to Copenhagen. That train was said to have been the last to cross the Polish border into Germany. In Berlin I had to traverse the center city to get from one railroad station to another. The streets were all aswarm with troops, the Berliners possessed with war fever. It was a relief to arrive in Copenhagen. There, with thousands of other stranded Americans, I waited for homeward passage. By the end of September, when Poland had already fallen, I finally came back home.

"A year later Max Weinreich, the only one of the YIVO's three directors to escape the war, reached New York. (Of the other two, Zalman Reisen was arrested in September 1939 when the Russians occupied Vilna; he disappeared forever. The third, Zelig Kalmanovich, remained in Vilna under the Russians, then under the Lithuanians, and finally under the Germans. He and his wife Riva, both of whom I loved as cherished parents, died in a labor camp in Esthonia in 1943.) Max Weinreich and the YIVO board in New York—which included Jacob Shatzky— decided that for the duration of the war YIVO's headquarters should be transferred to New York. Max Weinreich insisted that I come on staff to work for him. Now he saw in me something more than just myself.

"When I left New York in 1938, I had embarked on a search for wholeness. The year in Vilna had achieved that goal. But also something more. By virtue of my quixotic journey and the intervention of history in my life, I had not only found myself, as they say, but I had become a symbol of myself. For now I embodied a specific Jewish continuity, bridging the YIVO's European past and its present American possibilities. I stood between two worlds and was part of both.

"During the six most terrible years in all of Jewish history I worked at the YIVO. The fate of the East European Jews was always at the center of our lives. We published scholarly works about the life and death of the Jews in the Warsaw ghetto. Meanwhile, I went back to Columbia University, and finished my graduate studies, not in English literature, but in Jewish history. By now I was adept in bridging my two worlds.

"A year after the war ended, I quit the YIVO to work in occupied Germany among the Jewish survivors. One of my unexpected tasks was to help identify books from YIVO's Vilna library which the Germans had seized and brought to Frankfurt in 1942. My work speeded up the process of restoring to the YIVO in New York what had remained of the YIVO in Vilna. I felt like a bit player in the great drama of history. With the rightness of poetic justice, my part in the restitution of YIVO's library formed a circle of the Vilna chapter of my life.

"At the end of 1947 I came home. A few days later I married [Szymon M. Dawidowicz] a man from Poland whom I had met when we worked together at YIVO. It was a marriage that integrated my two worlds. Shortly thereafter I worked as a researcher for John Hersey. He was writing a novel about the Warsaw ghetto and needed access to the documentary sources in Yiddish and Polish.

"The rest of my life just seemed to follow inevitably."

What followed inevitably for Lucy Dawidowicz was a career dedicated to Jewish and in more recent years Holocaust studies—research for the American Jewish Committee, teaching at Yeshiva University in New York and visiting professorships at Stanford and the State University of New York in Albany, the writing of articles for *Commentary*, the *New York Times Magazine*, and other journals, and a series of books on Jewish life in America and Europe. Principally it is her work as a historian of modern European Jewry that has brought Dawidowicz international recognition. Her restrained, carefully documented writing makes no attempt to conceal her firm and sometimes controversial moral convictions. Her *War Against the Jews, 1933–1945*, Robert Alter wrote in *Commentary*, "does not neglect the many self-serving actions of the various political and socio-economic groups within the ghettos." Irving Howe has noted in some of her work "a certain hostility toward the Jewish Enlightenment (Haskala) and Jewish Socialism (Bundism) as forces that, in her estimate, hastened the breakup of traditional Jewish life." But Dawidowicz's main thrust is against those who fail to see the Holocaust in its most sweeping and tragic universal dimensions. If her history of the Holocaust is "tendentious" and her reading of modern history "selective," as some critics have suggested, the book nevertheless "embodies high standards of scholarship," Telford Taylor wrote, and "as a whole is a valuable contribution to the literature of the Second World War and the Holocaust" (*New York Times Book Review*, January 24, 1982).

Lucy Dawidowicz is the daughter of Max and Dora Schildkret. She received her B.A. from Hunter College in 1936 and holds honorary degrees from Kenyon, Hebrew Union, and Monmouth Colleges. Her *War Against the Jews, 1933–1945*, received the Anisfield-Wolf Prize in 1976, the year in which she also won a Guggenheim fellowship.

PRINCIPAL WORKS: (with L.J. Goldstein) Politics in a Pluralist Democracy, 1963; (ed.) The Golden Tradition: Jewish Life and Thought in Eastern Europe, 1967; The War Against the Jews, 1933–1945, 1975; (ed.) A Holocaust Reader, 1976; The Jewish Presence: Essays on Identity and History, 1977; The Holocaust and the Historian, 1981; On Equal Terms: Jews in America, 1881–1981, 1982.

ABOUT: Contemporary Authors, first revision series 25–28, 1977; Who's Who in America, 1983–84. *Periodicals*—Book of the Month Club News September 1978; Book Week February 12, 1976; Commentary June 1975; Jerusalem Post (international ed.) July 20–26, 1980; New York Times March 5, 1982; Toronto Star April 30, 1981.

DE GRAMONT, SANCHE *See* MORGAN, TED

*DELBLANC, SVEN AXEL HERMAN (May 26, 1931–), Swedish novelist, playwright, essayist, and critic, was born in Swan River, Manitoba, Canada, the son of immigrant farmer Siegfried Delblanc and Anna Nordefeldt Delblanc. The family soon returned to Sweden, where Delblanc was raised in rural Vagnhärad, Södermanland. He studied literary history at the University of Uppsala, receiving degrees in 1956, 1959, and 1965, after which he published his doctoral dissertation entitled Åre och minne (Honor and Memory, Key Concepts in Eighteenth-Century Swedish Literature) and became a *docent* (assistant professor).

Delblanc has proved to be one of the most prolific and important prose writers of his generation, which came to dominate Swedish writing and attract interest abroad with their social and philosophical concerns. In an interview he described his literary stance: "I regard myself as being in the existentialistic tradition of the forties and fifties, a generally European phenomenon. And the questions discussed at that time seem still urgent to me: problems of human freedom, progress, humiliation, involvement, and other such problems which have been relevant for European existentialists from Dostoevsky and Nietzsche down to our day." These are the issues that Delblanc has discussed in various forms in his large body of writing, now approaching thirty volumes, with translations available in a dozen languages.

°del bläN´, sven

SVEN DELBLANC

His earliest works were mainly novels of ideas, with emphasis on the varieties of freedom and the outsider role of the artist or creator. *Eremitkräftan* (The Hermit Crab, 1962) examines freedom's terms in allegory, with protagonist Axel first confronting the total control of a military dictatorship in his own society, The Prison, then the total lack of restraint in The White City (a community in which absolute freedom reigns), leading to a pessimistic conclusion. Delblanc's first popular success followed: *Prästkappan* (The Clergyman's Gown, 1963), a tragic picaresque novel set in the Europe of Frederick the Great and the Seven Years' War. Quixote-like anti-hero Hermann Anderz evolves from oppressed to oppressor, ultimately finding the confines of the latter role, in his clergyman's gown, as difficult as his original situation. A third novel, *Homunculus* (1965), is "a magic tale" of a chemistry teacher in modern-day Stockholm who manages to perform the medieval feat of artificially creating a human being or homunculus. His independence is threatened when both Great Powers get wind of his plans and set their intelligence police (CIA and KGB) after him in a mad chase through Stockholm. Less of a political satire and more a symbolic work is *Nattresa* (Night Journey, 1967), featuring protagonist Axel Weber, whose trip across the United States in the Vietnam years demonstrates the degree to which the corruption of multinational capitalism has pervaded society, even its antisocial demonstrators. A subsequent novel also imbued with radical America's politics is *Åsnebrygga* (Donkey's Bridge, 1969), utilizing Delblanc's impressions from his stay in Berkeley as a visiting professor at the University of California. Other works from the sixties and early seventies inspired by his California trip and another to pre-Khomeini Iran include his radio plays *Ariadne och påfågeln* (Ariadne and the Peacock, 1964) and *Göm dig i livets träd* (Hide in the Tree of Life, 1965); travel reportage in *Zahak* (1971); and the essay collection *Trampa vatten* (Treading Water, 1972).

Most popular among Swedish readers are the four novels of the Hedeby series from the 1970s, later made into a mini-series for television. These are semiautobiographical, as the early destiny of Axel Weber, the protagonist in *Nattresa* and now a boy in Hedeby, Södermanland, is traced from the late thirties to the mid-forties in *Åminne* (Remembrance, 1970); *Stenfågel* (Stone Bird, 1973); *Vinteride* (Winter Lair, 1974); and *Stadsporten* (The City Gate, 1976). Delblanc not only follows the development of his *alter ego* but also depicts the society's evolution from a small-farm culture to a post-war community transformed by industry. As editor Björn Nilsson puts it: "These novels have the basic broad, rolling structure of rural chronicles, with continual digressions into burlesque tall story, baroque allegory, and philosophical discourse. They have also come to be Sven Delblanc's most beloved books."

The role of the artist is a theme Delblanc investigated imaginatively in subsequent titles including *Primavera* (1973); *Kastrater* (*Castrati*, 1975); *Grottmannen* (The Caveman, 1977); and *Gunnar Emanuel* (1978). Other works from these years are *Gröna vintern* (The Green Winter, 1978); *Kära farmor* (Dear Grandmother, 1979), a portrait of a woman wielding power; the play *Den arme Richard* (Poor Richard, 1978); and *Stormhatten* (The Top Hat, 1979), three Strindberg studies. Another notable political allegory was *Speranza* (1980), described in *Publishers Weekly* as "a forceful novel, spare but memorable." The title is the name of a slave ship at the time of the French Revolution, and the story is about an idealistic young aristocrat on board whose lofty morals disintegrate as gradually he turns into a slaver himself. Several American critics praised the novel's "stylistic finesse" and rich irony.

A major series by Delblanc began with the publication of *Samuels bok* (Samuel's Book, 1981), followed by *Samuels döttrar* (Samuel's Daughters, 1982), and *Kanaans land* (The Land of Canaan, 1984). These semidocumentary novels were written as a tribute to Delblanc's family history, incorporating bits of journals and correspondence into a work that has been called "one of the very few saints' biographies in our Protestant national literature." The main focus is on the title character, Delblanc's grandfather, an inspired Lutheran minister whose credentials were challenged by the church, after which he was demoted to village schoolteacher and eventually became an inmate of an insane asylum. The women of the family carry on his struggle in the spirit of Sweden's pietist movement, a moral orientation that leads the most "intellectual" of the daughters, the battered wife Maria, to follow her brutal husband to the Canadian wilderness. As wheat farmers there, in *Kanaans land,* they fight against the terrible odds of natural and economic devastation through Depression hard times, but finally decide to return to Sweden. The projected fourth volume in the series will chronicle their homecoming. The novels on Samuel's family present an ironic contrast to the classic Swedish emigration tetralogy by Vilhelm Moberg (1949), about earlier, more optimistic pioneers.

Delblanc produced another serious exploration of religion in *Jerusalems natt* (Jerusalem's Night, 1983), written in the tradition of Pär Lagerkvist's *Barrabas* (1950). Delblanc's later novel is set in the year 70 AD during the siege of Jerusalem by the Roman army. The second generation of early Christians emerges as the author dramatizes the birth of a religious movement; with the historical Jesus dead, the mythification of his person proceeds, accelerated by true believers and opportunists too. Such works as *Jerusalems natt,* the *Samuels bok* series, and several earlier works place Delblanc among the most significant writers of this period. He won the Aftonbladet prize for literature in 1965; the Major Novel prize, and the Svenska Dagbladet literary prizes in 1970; the Zorn prize in 1971; and the Sixten Heyman prize in 1974.

He was married in 1955 to Christina Ekegård, a teacher, and lives in Uppsala.

WORKS IN ENGLISH TRANSLATION: Three of Delblanc's novels have been translated into English: *Homunculus* by Verne Moberg in 1969; *The Castrati: A Romantic Tale* by C.W. Williams, 1979; and *Speranza* by Paul Britten Austin, 1983.

ABOUT: Columbia Dictionary of Modern European Literature, 1980; Encyclopedia of World Literature in the 20th Century (rev. ed.) I, 1981. *Periodicals*—Books Abroad 48, 1974; Germanic Review 49, 1974; Sweden Now 2, 1983.

R. F. DELDERFIELD

DELDERFIELD, R(ONALD) F(RED-ERICK) (February 12, 1912–June 24, 1972), English novelist, essayist, and dramatist, was born in London, one of four sons of William

James and Alice (Jones) Delderfield. The Delderfields were a working-class family. His father, a cattle buyer in the Smithfield meat markets of London, was a self-proclaimed political radical, active in the London Council of Bermondsey and in the local Baptist chapel; his Welsh mother was staunchly Tory, and—as Delderfield recalled in his autobiography, *Bird's Eye View*—"I grew up to accept unending yet jovial conflict as a natural state of affairs accompanying marriage and home life." His earliest recollections were of watching the Zeppelin raids on London during World War I. In 1918 his father bought a printing business and small provincial newspaper in Exmouth in Devonshire, and from that time forward Delderfield's roots and heart were in the English countryside. In later years he would draw on that West Country for his most popular novels, huge family chronicles that celebrate its history, legends, and landscapes.

Delderfield's education came far more from his reading than from his schooling. After a few dreary years in schools of little or no academic distinction, he was sent to boarding school at West Buckland, where his lingering Cockney accent and inaptitude for sports convinced him that "I was not equipped for life." Thanks to his mother's enthusiasm for Dickens, Thackeray, and other Victorian novelists and his own early interest in history, he resolved at age thirteen to become a writer. By seventeen, after a brief course at a commercial college, he went to work on his father's newspaper, the *Exmouth Chronicle.* As a reporter he covered funerals, weddings, and trials in the local courthouse, but because Exeter is a center of holiday travel, he also had the opportunity from time to time to interview visiting celebrities—actors, politicians, and, most significant, George Bernard Shaw, who surprisingly gave the fledgling journalist a long and friendly interview. Mainly, however, Delderfield's duties were routine, and he filled his leisure hours with dedicated movie-going ("For me the film that was not worth watching simply did not exist") and scribbling. With more persistence than genius he wrote about fifteen plays during the next ten years, none of them seeing production until 1939 and most of those only brief runs in provincial theaters. When World War II broke out he enlisted in the RAF where he served as a public relations officer and saw action in the last year of the war in Belgium and France.

By 1944, while still in military service, Delderfield was well launched on a playwriting career. A religious drama, *Spark in Judea,* and a play about life on a smalltown newspaper, *Printer's Devil,* had received encouraging critical notices (including praise from James Agate) during their provincial runs. A meeting in 1942 with a professional lyrics and comedy writer, Basil Thomas, led to a successful collaboration, *This Is My Life* (first produced at Wolverhampton under the title *Matron* in 1942). Delderfield's *Worm's Eye View,* a comedy about army life, was his first play to reach the London stage, in 1945; it ran in the West End for a record five and a half years and was made into a motion picture in 1950. When the war ended, Delderfield sold his interest in the family newspaper and became a fulltime writer of plays and radio scripts for the BBC. But he was not happy in the theater, seeing himself, he recalled, "as a stay-at-home entertainer, someone who turned out three- and one-act plays much as a cabinet maker makes something practical from a stock of seasoned timber . . . a kind of extended journalism." His real desire was to write fiction and history—"to project the English way of life in the tradition of Hardy and Galsworthy."

Delderfield's motto as a writer was characteristically forthright: "Believe in yourself, and be yourself on paper." With an industry and energy that rivaled the spirit of the Victorian and Edwardian novelists he admired, he settled down in 1947, at considerable loss of income at first, in an old house in Devon and wrote daily, 365 days a year, from nine to five, producing at an astounding rate of 4,000 words a day some nineteen novels and nine books of non-fiction in twenty years. The results may not have been entirely in the tradition of Hardy and the Victorians (Orville Prescott observed: "At his best he may remind one of Trollope, at his worst of

Hugh Walpole"), but he wrote a number of books of creditable craftsmanship and vigorous narrative. His love for the English scene and character found its voice in what his critics considered "old-fashioned, conventional" novels, but his public found him unfailingly "a good read." And it was a devoted and rapidly growing public, first in England and then in the United States where, perhaps surprisingly, his sagas of English family life, crowded with incident and sweeping panoramically over generations from Victorian to contemporary times, had a large and enthusiastic readership and sold some ten million copies in the 1960s and 1970s.

Delderfield may well have revealed the secret of his success in his own description of one of his novels, *There Was a Fair Maid,* as a challenge to "the sink, braces and bacteria school of postwar realism in drama and fiction." Frankly nostalgic and celebrating the "good old" virtues of romantic love, loyalty, hard work, persistence and patriotism, laced with vigorous and sometimes violent action and rapturous but never explicit sex, they offer the reader escape, entertainment, and a substantial amount of historical detail. Commenting on his popularity, Webster Schott observed in the *New York Times Book Review* that "what Delderfield has given us is English fairy tales for grownups—hopeful, optimistic, wondrous—when we wanted and needed them." Typical of the Delderfield novel is *A Horseman Riding By,* a novel of 1,150 pages which carries its stalwart hero through some sixty years of his life from the Boer War to the 1960s and manages to include a panorama of Devonshire country life, the suffragette movement, and World Wars I and II, with numerous economic and social crises interwoven into the story of a single family. Another family saga, *God Is an Englishman,* along with its sequel, *Theirs Was the Kingdom,* spanning the Victorian age from 1857 to the Diamond Jubilee, also enjoyed record-breaking sales and a friendly but patronizing critical reception. "It is built out of clichés as huge and familiar as the blocks of Stonehenge," Christopher Lehmann-Haupt wrote, but so artfully contrived that "we settle back half knowing what will happen, but wanting to hear every detail just the same." Delderfield's American public grew even larger with the dramatization of his novel about English public school life, *To Serve Them All My Days,* in the Public Broadcasting television series "Masterpiece Theatre" in late 1982.

As a historian Delderfield was less successful. Although his studies of Napoleon's military campaigns and his family life were judged sound in essentials, they were faulted for errors of detail and inadequate documentation. His personal reminiscences, collected in a series of essays—*Nobody Shouted Author, Bird's Eye View, For My Own Amusement,* and *Overture for Beginners*—are chatty and informal, as is his *Under an English Sky,* an affectionate account of a motor trip through England which he unabashedly called "a patriotic testament." Except for visits to America to promote his books, Delderfield rarely traveled abroad: "I can never be absent from Britain for more than twelve hours before I begin to suffer the pangs of homesickness and the older I grow the more mulishly insular I become." Delderfield died at his home in Sidmouth, Devonshire, at the age of sixty. He was survived by his wife, May Evans, whom he had married in 1936, and a son and daughter.

PRINCIPAL WORKS: *Novels*—All Over Town, 1947; Seven Men of Gascony, 1949; Farewell the Tranquil Mind, 1950; The Adventures of Ben Gunn (juvenile), 1956; The Avenue Goes to War, 1958; There Was a Fair Maid Dwelling, 1960 (U.S., Diana); Stop at a Winner, 1961; The Unjust Skies, 1962; The Spring Madness of Mr. Sermon, 1963 (U.S., Mr. Sermon); Too Few for Drums, 1964; The Horseman Riding, 1966 (U.S., A Horseman Riding By); Post of Honor, 1966; The Green Gauntlet, 1968; Come Home Charlie and Face Them, 1969 (U.S., Charlie Come Home); God Is an Englishman, 1970; Theirs Was the Kingdom, 1971; To Serve Them All My Days, 1972; Give Us this Day, 1973. *Non-fiction*—Nobody Shouted Author, 1951; Bird's Eye View, 1954; Napoleon in Love, 1959; The March of the Twenty-Six, 1962 (U.S., Napoleon's Marshals); The Golden Millstones: Napoleon's Brothers and Sisters, 1964; Under an English Sky, 1964; The Retreat from Moscow, 1967; Imperial Sunset: The Fall of Napoleon, 1968; For My Own Amusement, 1968; Overture for Beginners, 1970.

ABOUT: Contemporary Authors 73–76, 1978; For My Own Amusement, 1968; Overture for Beginners, 1970; Something About the Author 20 (1980). *Periodicals*—New York Times June 27, 1972; New York Times Book Review June 9, 1974; Publishers Weekly January 12, 1970.

DE LILLO, DON (November 20, 1936–), American novelist, was born in the Bronx, New York, in 1936, and attended Fordham University, where he received his B.A. in 1958. Since he guards his privacy and until recently has given no interviews, very little information about De Lillo's background is available. De Lillo acquired some recognition with the publication of his first novel, *Americana,* in 1971. The novel's central character and narrator is David Bell, a successful, twenty-eight-year-old television executive who leaves his job and New York to seek his roots in the heartland of America. Bell attempts to reconcile and impose a pattern on the

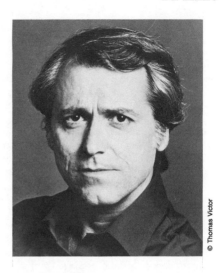

© Thomas Victor

DON DE LILLO

disparate experiences of his earliest and present life—his travels and his memories of youth, marriage, and divorce—by constantly using a movie camera. The unusual quality of *Americana* is its evocation of the characters' dimensionless lives, captured imagistically as if on film. The novel was highly praised by Christopher Lehmann-Haupt and by Joyce Carol Oates, who called it "a robust and intellectually exciting work . . . one of the most compelling and sophisticated first novels that I have ever read."

De Lillo's *End Zone,* published only a year later, begins as a novel about football but becomes an inquiry into metaphysics. De Lillo's football field seems a dream world in which players are encapsulated in visions of a nuclear holocaust. "The combining element," D. K. Oberbeck wrote, "is power; enormous, explosive power, whether pooled on a football field or in missile silos. Behind the automaton-like facades, De Lillo's players are devoured in a chillingly funny way by utterly cosmic preoccupations." The hero of *End Zone,* Gary Harkness, drifts from a college in the East to play ball for Logos College in West Texas, joining other misfits on a team coached by Emmett Creed, who constantly shouts: "play bawl," "get fetal." The players take courses in astrotechnology, and use absurd jargon drawn from nuclear warfare and space exploration to call their plays.

Having explored the vacuousness of such typically American icons as the media executive and the football player, De Lillo turned in *Great Jones Street* to the rock idol. Bucky Wunderlick, rock singer and would-be messiah, leaves his group and retreats to New York's slums, where he becomes involved with a commune of revolutionary drug addicts. R. Z. Sheppard remarked that "by nudging his hero toward the truly mythic, De Lillo overextends a book that is otherwise distinguished by a cool, clinical touch. As he demonstrated in his two previous novels, the author has a knack for chill atmosphere, satiric caricature and witty dialogue." Walter Clemons found *Great Jones Street* a less satisfying work than *End Zone,* but conceded that there is ample evidence in the novel "of a writer stretching himself, accomplishing things he hasn't before."

Yet the experiments of *Great Jones Street* did not prepare for De Lillo's next novel, the large and rambling *Ratner's Star,* whose central character, Billy Twillig, a fourteen-year-old mathematical genius and Nobel laureate, is called to a computer-radio-telescope complex called Space Brain to decode a radio message from a distant planet. At the research facility, Billy encounters Henrik Endor, his predecessor on the code, who now lives in a hole; Orang Mohole, the kingpin of alternate physics; Shazar Lazarus Ratner, a renowned astronomer turned mystic; and Elux Troxl, "a semi-treacherous entrepreneur" who deals in leased computer time, chain letters and bat guano. Amanda Heller called the characters who inhabit *Ratner's Star* "the oddest collection of benign yet sinister zanies this side of the *Looking Glass,*" and found the novel an elegant satire of the scientific mind. Critical reaction to this puzzling novel differed widely. George Stade wrote that "De Lillo's new book is the something else his others were straining to become," a flawed but major work. Peter Prescott thought differently. "Our very best mandarins," he commented, "are stalked by talented disciples: Donald Barthelme by Robert Coover, Thomas Pynchon by Don De Lillo. I have no doubt at all that if we hadn't had *V* and *Gravity's Rainbow* we would not now have *Ratner's Star.* . . . De Lillo knows how to write brilliantly, even movingly, but he doesn't know when he's working dully."

In *Players,* De Lillo returned to the subject of New York City lives. The novel begins with the Wynants, Pammy and Lyle, a successful couple who have begun to worry that they no longer have the ability to experience life directly. Soon Lyle is drawn into association with a group of terrorists who bomb the Stock Exchange, and Pammy goes off to Maine with two homosexual friends. Diane Johnson, writing in the *New York Times Book Review,* called *Players* an "elegant, highly finished novel." But De Lillo's subordination of character to a concern with pattern and ideas was faulted by a number of critics, including James Atlas, who complained that Lyle and Pammy are so devoid of moral or dramatic significance as to leave the reader "indifferent to their fate."

Running Dog, like *Players,* is set in New York, but takes the form of a spy thriller and differs radically from De Lillo's previous novels. "The subject of *Running Dog,*" Thomas Leclair wrote, "is entertainment: the characters want to possess what they believe is a pornographic film of Hitler and his inner circle made just before the fall of Berlin. An old porn merchant named Lightborne wants the film to verify his scholarly research; Senator Percival would add it to his collection of erotica; upstart smut king Richie Armbrister fights the Mafia for it. Caught among the deals and betrayals of these would-be buyers, sellers, and viewers is former CIA agent Frank Selvy . . . who withdraws into what he calls 'the machine of self' and travels to a distant solitude." The reviewer for the *New Yorker* found *Running Dog* a meditation on capitalist consumerism: "Mr. De Lillo is in full command of [a] limited form, and his book, though obscure as to purpose, is a pleasure to read."

The Names is a conundrum of still larger proportions set in Athens, the Near and Middle East, and India. Its hero is a James Axton, a risk analyst whose company insures multinational corporations against the hazards of political upheaval. Axton himself has only a problematic identity. "My life is going by and I can't get a grip on it," he says. "It eludes me, it defeats me . . . Nothing adds up." Of Axton, Michael Wood wrote: "He wants to find a passion that is not an insanity. And yet an insanity is what he pursues." What he finds are an archeologist and a movie maker. With them he discovers an Eastern sect dedicated to murdering victims on the basis of their initials which represent, to them, some kind of symbolic script—a striking parallel to the multinational executives Axton has worked for. J. D. O'Hara described *The Names* as "the best writing De Lillo has ever done," and Robert Towers commented that "nearly every page testifies to De Lillo's exceptional gifts as a writer." Yet even critics who were deeply impressed had reservations. Michael Wood, although calling *The Names* "a powerful, haunting book, formidably intelligent and agile," went on to say that it "often feels like a major work but it also feels a little blurred, its insights scattered rather than collected."

With the publication of *White Noise* in early 1985, De Lillo emerged as one of the most interesting of contemporary American novelists. His readers also became more numerous; the coterie that had admired his earlier books grew into a larger, though not actually large, public. Still personally reticent, reluctant to give interviews and discuss his future literary plans, he nevertheless produced a more "public" novel in *White Noise*—a commentary on present-day American life that is as trenchant and compelling as it is witty and inventive. *White Noise* is set on an American college campus of the 1980s, and its center is a professor who specializes in Hitler studies and fumbles with the problems of raising a family of precocious children and coping with a mass culture. The "white noise" of the title is death. Death seems remote in a sheltered academic environment, yet it actually permeates the atmosphere—literally in a railroad tank car accident that spreads toxic fumes over the area, symbolically both in the professor's work and in the very nature of American life today. For all its seriousness of theme, the novel is, as one reviewer observed, "grimly funny." De Lillo himself, in one of his rare interviews, commented that death as a subject "seemed innately comic, and everything sprang from it. I never felt that I was writing a comic novel before *White Noise*. Maybe the fact that death permeates the book made me retreat into comedy." Certainly it produced a brilliantly ironic novel, funny but also "touching and as serious as death and puff adders," Christopher Lehmann-Haupt wrote in the *New York Times*. Quoting De Lillo, "The nature of modern death is that it has a life independent of us," Jayne Anne Phillips wrote in the *New York Times Book Review:* "What belief can correspond to a fact so irrevocable? *White Noise* offers no answers, but it poses inescapable questions with consummate skill."

De Lillo is married and lives with his wife in a modest residential street in a New York suburb. In 1979 he received a Guggenheim fellowship, and spent several years in Greece, the Middle East, and India while writing *The Names*. He thinks of New York as an "enormous influence" on his work—"the paintings in the Museum of Modern Art, the music of the Jazz Gallery and the Village Vanguard, the movies of Fellini and Godard."

PRINCIPAL WORKS: Americana, 1971; End Zone, 1972; Great Jones Street, 1973; Ratner's Star, 1976; Players, 1977; Running Dog, 1978; The Names, 1982; White Noise, 1985.

ABOUT: Contemporary Authors 81–84, 1979; Contemporary Literary Criticism 8, 1978; Contemporary Novelists, 1982. *Periodicals*—Atlantic August 7, 1976; Christian Science Monitor October 11, 1978; Critique August, 1978; Harper's September, 1977; December, 1982; Horizon October, 1978; Nation September 17, 1977; New Republic October 7, 1978; November 22, 1982; New Yorker May 6, 1972; July 12, 1976; New York Review of Books June 29, 1972; New York Times Book Review May 30, 1971; April 9, 1972; April 22, 1973; June 20, 1976; September 4, 1977; September 1, 1972; October 10, 1982; January 13, l985; Partisan Review 3, 1979.

DELORIA, VINE (VICTOR), Jr. (March 26, 1933–   ), American Indian historian and philosopher, writes: "I was born in Martin, South Dakota, a border town on the Pine Ridge Indian reservation in southwestern South Dakota. My father was an Episcopal missionary on that reservation; my grandfather had been a missionary on the Standing Rock Reservation in the northern part of the state and my great-grandfather had been a Yankton Sioux medicine man with great powers. Almost the turn of the nineteenth century a French lad, survivor of a trapping camp massacre by the Crees in Canada, staggered into a Yankton Sioux camp. The Sioux took him in and he lived the rest of his life with them. In 1858 when my great-grandfather went to Washington to sign a treaty he took the leather pouch of the French ancestor to have the papers inside it read. That is where 'Deloria' came from. In the French it is 'des Lauriers.'

"After a hitch in the Marines I attended Iowa State University and then the Augustana Theological Seminary. Finally I went to the School of Law at the University of Colorado. If I had been younger I would have gone to medical school and become the only doctor, lawyer, Indian chief in the country. But I was too old.

"I began writing accidentally. I was in law school and Stan Steiner's book, *The New Indians,* was released. It dealt with things that a group of us had done and some publishers wanted a militant book by an Indian. So Stan shuttled me over to Macmillan and I began writing. My basic orientation has been to attempt to create a new atmosphere in which philosophical, religious and political concepts of Indians can be understood by people in the larger society. Therefore I do not usually deal with Indian poetry, romantic images of Indians, or secrets of tribes. In dealing with cultural and religious ideas of Indians I make it a rule only to write about things that are already on paper somewhere and not to discuss anything which traditional Indians have not already revealed.

"I believe that Indians had a very sophisticated idea of the human personality and that all their social, economic and political institutions were designed to maximize personal growth. This knowledge can be very useful to us today except that it must be translated and transposed into concepts that we can recognize and understand. That is the overall goal of my writing. I try to reduce the complex ideas which tribes had

VINE DELORIA

would much prefer to be in a Creative Writing program where I could concentrate on helping younger people learn to write. American politics and politicians are so predictable and so dull. I have, however, a good position at Arizona and we have a program we are proud of so I am not unhappy with my present situation.

"My major complaint is that too many people seek me out for a variety of things, mostly public appearances, which takes time away from doing research and thinking about things. In America it seems as if everyone has to be rushing around and no one is allowed the luxury of just reading and thinking. So I try to do what I can when I can find the time to do it. I eventually hope to finish my writing career with a book called 'The Structure of Religious Personality' in which I can examine and compare the great religious figures and their lives and demonstrate the sophistication of Indian religious ways. That book is, unfortunately, a decade or more away."

to more abstract principles of practical relationships. While this task is difficult I find that Indians on the whole appreciate or respect this kind of thinking and writing. Non-Indians are generally looking for exotic thrills or spiritual advice so they often mistake the format of what I present as not really dealing with Indian matters.

"I have a goal of being recognized as a thinker over and above being an Indian. That is exceedingly difficult because most book reviewers tend to take offense when an ethnic writer attempts to move out of his or her category and act as if they were really a person. My book *Custer Died for Your Sins* was very popular because I was playing the pre-assigned role for an Indian writer. My book *The Metaphysics of Modern Existence* is infinitely deeper and took considerably more thought but it was an effort to join the larger intellectual community as a person. Needless to say hardly anyone reviewed it. It nevertheless has been popular among younger Indians who see the need to establish an independent intellectual position for contemporary Indians.

"I have increasingly shunned the spotlight and prefer to work at home reading and thinking about how to make the major connections between Indian values and the larger intellectual world. I take the Indian traditions literally in most instances and have devised a long term system of interpretation of Indian legends which links tribal memories to planetary disturbances and catastrophes. This system would indicate that Indians have a much longer history than orthodox thinkers would allow them to have.

"At present I am a professor of Political Science at the University of Arizona. However I

Vine Deloria, Jr., was educated first in reservation schools, then at the Kent School in Connecticut. From 1954 to 1956 he served in the U.S. Marine Corps; he then enrolled at Iowa State University where he received a B.S. in General Science. In the following years he worked as a welder in Moline, Illinois, and studied for the ministry at the Lutheran School of Theology in Chicago, taking a master's degree in 1963. He worked in Washington, D.C., with the National Congress of American Indians from 1964 to 1967, coming into direct contact (and conflict) with the Department of the Interior's Bureau of Indian Affairs. Recognizing the urgent needs of his people and the frustration of those needs in the bureaucracies of government, he took a law degree (J.D.) in 1970 at the University of Colorado.

With the publication in 1969 of *Custer Died for Your Sins,* Deloria became an articulate and effective spokesman for the American Indians. This bitterly ironic but soundly reasoned and thoroughly documented history of the systematic oppression of the native American was a powerful indictment of white America, written as much in sorrow as in anger: "Until America begins to build a moral record in her dealings with the Indian people, she should not try to fool the rest of the world about her intentions on other continents." This and Deloria's subsequent books did much to dispel the sentimentalizing and romanticizing of the Indian cause.

Deloria's books have increasingly framed profound moral questions on the relationship of Western Christianity to the exploitation not only of Indians but of the land itself. Christianity, he wrote in *God Is Red,* "has avoided any rigorous consideration of ecological factors in favor of continuous efforts to realize the Kingdom of God on earth." It is the failure of the white Christian American to recognize the roots of his identity in the land itself—as the Indian does—that imperils his civilization. "America needs a new religion," he wrote in his Introduction to *We Talk, You Listen,* a religion "in which religious sensitivity is expressed in rigorous adherence to the values of racial and ethnic groups—secularization of religious feelings in political action."

Deloria has published numerous papers, articles, and reports on Indian history and is active in many associations—cultural, religious, and political—that work for education and human rights. He has received honorary degrees from Augustana College (1972), Scholastica College (1976), and Hamline University (1979), the Anisfield-Wolf Award (in 1970 for *Custer Died for Your Sins*), and a special citation from the National Conference of Christians and Jews (in 1971 for *We Talk, You Listen*). He has been married since 1958 to Barbara Jeanne Nystrom; they have two sons and a daughter.

PRINCIPAL WORKS: Custer Died for Your Sins, 1969; We Talk, You Listen: New Tribes, New Turf, 1970; Of Utmost Good Faith, 1971; God Is Red, 1973; Behind the Trail of Broken Treaties, 1974; The Indian Affair, 1974; Indians of the Pacific Northwest, 1977; The Metaphysics of Modern Existence, 1979.

ABOUT: Contemporary Authors 53–56, 1975; Current Biography 1974; Gridley, M.E. Contemporary American Indian Leaders, 1972; Who's Who in America, 1983–84.

DE MILLE, AGNES (1905–), American choreographer, dancer, and writer, was born in New York City, the elder of two daughters of William C. de Mille and Anna (George) de Mille. Her mother was the daughter of Henry George, the political economist and leader of the Single Tax movement. Her father, the younger brother of the film director Cecil B. de Mille, began his career as a playwright and moved to Hollywood with his family in 1914 to become a director himself.

Discouraged from becoming an actress by her father and uncle, de Mille turned to ballet under the inspiration of a performance by the Russian ballerina Anna Pavlova—a "bright unworldly experience [that] burned in a single afternoon a path over which I could never retrace my steps." After graduating from the University of Califor-

AGNES DE MILLE

nia with a degree in English literature, de Mille moved to New York City with her divorced mother, who supported her during the 1930s while she studied with Marie Rambert in London and toured Europe and America giving solo recitals that combined comedic pantomime with dance. Her first major success as a choreographer was *Three Virgins and a Devil* (1941) for Ballet Theatre (now American Ballet Theatre). It was followed in 1942 by *Rodeo, or, The Courting at Burnt Ranch,* for the Ballet Russe de Monte Carlo. Set to music by Aaron Copland, *Rodeo* was the first ballet to combine elements of classical ballet, modern dance, tap, and American folk dance—a ballet, as John Gruen has said, "unmitigatedly reflective of [de Mille's] American roots." It was an immediate hit, as was de Mille in the role of the Cowgirl who can't catch the eye of the Head Wrangler until she puts on a dress.

This new idiom was adapted by de Mille for the Broadway stage in Richard Rodgers' and Oscar Hammerstein's *Oklahoma!* (1943), the first musical to use dance sequences to develop plot and character. "I didn't try just to tell a story," de Mille recalled, "but to increase the dynamics, so to speak, heighten the color, go into a language that just diction and dialogue couldn't achieve."

The events of de Mille's life up to her marriage in 1943 to Walter F. Prude were recounted by de Mille in *Dance to the Piper,* a well-received autobiography. The *New Yorker*'s reviewer observed that it was "written, for the most part, with the wit, bounce and ginger that characterize the dances she has composed." The reviewer for the *Times Literary Supplement* said: "Most fascinating is the revelation of the character of the author—witty, stubborn, perceptive and full of ambition—that is achieved with an apparent literary ease unusual when an artist in one medium is rash enough to tackle another." A sequel, *And Promenade Home*, focused on the years from 1942 to 1945, when de Mille was choreographing some of the best-known musicals of the Broadway stage, including *Carousel, One Touch of Venus,* and *Bloomer Girl;* the book ends with de Mille pregnant with her son Jonathan. "Piercing the narration," wrote Margaret Lloyd, "are incisive comments on the theater of ballet and of life, flashes of verbal brilliance bursting like sudden rockets on a page. Miss de Mille is a distinguished writer as well as a distinguished choreographer."

De Mille went on to choreograph the Broadway hits *Brigadoon* (1947), *Gentlemen Prefer Blondes* (1949), *Paint Your Wagon* (1951), and *110 in the Shade* (1963)—nearly twenty musicals, all of which had dancing as an integral part of the play's development. Her trademark, in addition to the use of movements derived from the Anglo-American folk dance tradition, was comedy (the *New Yorker* called her "a born comedienne, both as a dancer and as an author"). In 1947, with *Allegro,* she became the first woman (and the first dance-director) to stage an entire Broadway musical. The *Encyclopaedia Britannica* notes that de Mille is "concerned with real people" and expresses "their moods and foibles through a ballet-based vocabulary blended with stylized, everyday movement patterns made unexpectedly poignant or humorous by contrasting dynamics, breath pauses, suspensions, sudden thrusts, or slow, sustained strength."

De Mille's ballets, commissioned by a variety of companies, display a wider range of emotion than her musicals. The most famous of them, *Fall River Legend* (1948), commissioned by Ballet Theatre, was a somber enactment and psychological interpretation of the Lizzie Borden murder case. De Mille described her investigation of the crime and her struggle to recreate it as a ballet in *Lizzie Borden: A Dance of Death.* She gave an account of the ballet's reception in the Soviet Union in her *Russian Journals.*

From the 1950s, de Mille was involved in a variety of dance-related activities: touring with the Agnes de Mille Dance Theatre, choreographing for stage, film, and television, teaching, writing, and lecturing; she also served as cofounder and president of the Society of Stage Dancers and Choreographers. At the same time she was raising her son. "If only I could choose," she wrote,

"could live one way or another, cut my pattern clean—be like other women, simply a wife and mother, or, like great artists, sure and undivided. But all parts of me are set against each other." Her *Speak to Me, Dance with Me,* a memoir in letters and commentary of the years 1932 to 1935, when she was studying in London, was published in 1973; R. L. Coombs said of it: "A spirited assortment of glittery theater trivia, gossip-column name dropping . . . and a good deal of rapid, emotional, introspective rambling combine to produce an exceptionally clever, cosmopolitan tête-à-tête and one of the more intelligent and memorable celebrity memoirs of the decade."

In 1973 de Mille founded the Agnes de Mille Heritage Dance Theater, with the intention of building it into a national folk company that would preserve American ethnic and native dance traditions. In May 1975, as she was preparing to deliver a lecture at a dance exhibition to raise funds for the project, she suffered a stroke that paralyzed her right side. The complications of the stroke included a heart attack and a pulmonary embolism. She gave a harrowing account of her illness and partial recovery in *Reprieve.* During her convalescence she worked with great difficulty on *Where the Wings Grow,* a memoir of the summers her family spent in Merriewold, New York, when she was a young child, and the only one of her books not connected with dance.

According to Deborah Jowitt, "de Mille's previous books were witty and sentimental . . . like novels centering around the perils and triumphs of 'Agnes,' the choreographer and woman. They're good theater, good fun, and often deeply moving. *Where the Wings Grow* is a memoir, a gathering of vivid impressions, but, more importantly, it's about the passionate quality of memory itself, about the amazing pungency of sights, sounds and smells recollected. . . . In a curious way, this most private and intuitive of Agnes de Mille's books is also the least self-centered."

In addition to her autobiographical volumes, de Mille is the author of a handbook for aspiring professionals, *To a Young Dancer,* and of two historical surveys, *The Book of the Dance* and *America Dances.* Rosamond Gilder wrote that *The Book of the Dance* "manages to be many things at once: a history from primitive forms through classic ballet to the modern dance, an encyclopedia of great dance names from Louis XIV to Jerome Robbins, a pictorial record of extraordinary wealth, diversity and gaiety, a fascinating presentation of the methods, approaches and techniques of the leading modern choreographers and a highly readable and witty piece of work." *America Dances* grew out of a dance exhibition narrated by de Mille and demonstrated by the members of the Joffrey Ballet for PBS television. A lavishly illustrated book, it surveyed the history of American dance from the early seventeenth century to contemporary times, ranging from folk and popular forms like tap and musical comedy to the work of major American ballet companies, sprinkled with de Mille's personal and often provocative impressions of figures like Martha Graham, Lincoln Kirstein, and Lucia Chase. According to Holly Brubach, "Miss de Mille is a reliable guide through history until she sets foot in her own neighborhood. Then she can't resist polishing her own trophies and settling old scores, and her voice, which is otherwise calm and authoritative, turns shrill, her tone strident." Iris Fanger, on the other hand, thought that de Mille "is best when writing about the people and times she knew."

De Mille, who lives in New York City, has received numerous honorary degrees and other awards, including the Tony Award for best choreography in 1947 and 1962 and the Capezio Award in 1966. In 1981 she was given a lifetime achievement award in the Kennedy Center Honors.

PRINCIPAL WORKS: *Autobiography*—Dance to the Piper, 1951; And Promenade Home, 1956; Russian Journals, 1970; Speak to Me, Dance with Me, 1973; Where the Wings Grow, 1978; Reprieve, 1981. *Other*—To a Young Dancer, 1962; The Book of the Dance, 1964; Lizzie Borden: A Dance of Death, 1968; (with L. Chase) American Ballet Theatre, 35th Anniversary Gala, 1975; America Dances, 1980.

ABOUT: Contemporary Authors 65–68, 1977; Current Biography 1943, 1985; Gwen, J. The World's Greatest Ballets, 1981; Mainiero, L. (ed.) American Women Writers, 1979; Maynard, O. The American Ballet, 1959; Stoddard, H. Famous American Women, 1970; White, J.T. et al. (eds.) Notable Names in the American Theatre, 1984. *Periodicals*—Book Week April 26, 1964; Christian Science Monitor October 9, 1958; October 31. 1963; November 29, 1963; February 18, 1981; Dancemagazine October 1971; September 1973; November 1974; June 1974; February 1981; Library Journal February 15, 1973; October 15, 1981; New Yorker January 12, 1952; December 14, 1963; October 25, 1968; February 6, 1978; New York Times Book Review January 13, 1952; September 16, 1962; December 10, 1968; May 6, 1973; February 5, 1978; February 1, 1981; Times Literary Supplement February 1, 1952.

*DEPESTRE, RENE (August 26, 1926–), Haitian poet, novelist, and essayist, was born in Jacmel. From 1915 to 1934 Haiti was occupied by U.S. troops and, like many other Haitian intellectuals before him, Depestre later took a very strong stand against the violation of his country's sovereignty. Soon after his elementary schooling, Depestre moved to Port-au-Prince, the capital, where he completed his secondary education. In 1945, he published his first collection of poems, *Etincelles* (Sparks), which brought him recognition and fame. From then on , some of the recurring themes of his poetry would be socialist revolution, love, and the cultural, racial, and political aims of the movement known as "Negritude," "the sluggish agony of my roots." In *Sparks,* Depestre continued the new Haitian poetic trend that blended themes of political freedom and of love in such a way as to suggest that the second is almost impossible without the first. He was also editor-in-chief of the newspaper *La Ruche* (The Hive). The vehemence of his poems, and the attacks of the newspaper against the dictatorship of President Lescot were bound to bring him trouble and, along with some friends, he was detained in the police headquarters. A student strike followed and became a general strike that forced the government to resign. Depestre was praised as one of the heroes of the so-called "bloodless revolution." His second collection, *Gerbe de Sang* (Wreath of Blood, 1946) showed disillusionment, but also hope for a "new growth once the dead flesh of corruption is cut away."

The new president granted him a scholarship to the Sorbonne in Paris. This marked the beginning of his first period of exile, 1947–1957. During that decade, he visited many countries, and wrote *Végétations de Clarté* (Luminous Plants) in which politics became a more integral part of his poetry; *Traduit du Grand Large* (Translated from the High Sea), described how his love for his country and his wife Edith, a Rumanian, helped soothe his exile; in *Mineral Noir* (Black Ore) "the proletarian solidarity of the wretched of the earth integrated in its revolutionary process the racial fraternity of all oppressed colored people," according to his friend, the poet Paul Laraque (winner of the 1979 La Casa de las Americas poetry award).

Depestre and his wife were allowed to come back to Haiti in 1957. Threatened by the bloody dictatorship of François Duvalier, however, he once again left Haiti, this time for Cuba, in 1959 for another period of exile, which has so far been uninterrupted. During this second exile, Depestre continued to be a prolific writer. The works of this period include many collections of poems, essays, and novels, as well as translations.

°də pestr, rə nä´

In addition to his writing, Depestre has been a broadcaster at Radio Havana, and a teacher at the University of Havana and at the University of the West Indies in Mona, Jamaica. His new series of poetry collections included *Journal d'un animal marin* (Diary of a Sea-Animal, 1964), a title which is borrowed from Carl Sandburg's definition, "poetry is the diary of a sea-animal that lives on Earth but would like to fly"; *Un arc-en-ciel pour l'Occident Chrétien* (A Rainbow for the Christian West, 1966) deals mainly with the religious and political powers of voodoo gods in the history of Haiti; *Cantate d'Octobre* (October Cantata, 1968), which contains a narrator and a chorus, is a vibrant and rhythmic tribute to his friend Che Guevara's life and death; and *Poète à Cuba* (Poet in Cuba, 1976), which blends eroticism and politics in a challenge to the doctrine of socialism. A humorous critic called it "communist eroticism." This last publication proved very controversial: Claude Roy, who wrote a preface to it, praised the talent of the poet, but criticized his ideology, and the author felt he had to reply in "Letter from Cuba to Claude Roy."

Depestre is also an excellent prose writer. His only novel, *Le Mât de Cocagne* (The Greasy Pole), is allegorical and satirical. In many Haitian cities, the climbing of such a pole is a long tradition that makes fun of the poor. The most wretched are the ones who try to reach the prize tied at the top. As the pole is very greasy, the prize can be gained only by extraordinary effort. In the novel, the winner is a former senator who finds a rifle at the top and shoots some of the well-known thugs of the repressive regime. He is killed, but only after he has shown the way to liberate Haiti. *Alleluia pour une femme-jardin* (Alleluia for a Woman-garden), which won the "Concourt Bourse," is made up of ten short stories (five of them published in 1973), shocking to some reviewers but praised by others for their "happy eroticism." *Pour la Révolution Pour la Poésie* (For Revolution, for Poetry), published in 1974, is an essay dealing mainly with the Cuban revolution and its impact on the author: "those years have been the light arrow that showed me the road to my identity. My arrival in Cuba in March 1959 coincided with the end of my first flush of youth. I had behind me twelve years of an effervescent exile . . . my head was cracking up with negative contradictions." In another essay of 1980, *Adieu à la Négritude* (Farewell to Negritude), he rejects Negritude, denounces racial concepts as mythical traps, and pleads for a pan-human identity.

Despestre's works attest to the influence of Haitian poets such as Jacques Roumain and René Bélance, the Martinican Aimé Césaire, French poets Rimbaud, Breton, and particularly Paul Eluard, and American poets Langston Hughes and Carl Sandburg. Nevertheless, Depestre's art is very personal and not imitative. His great creativity, in terms of the successive and uninterrupted waves of striking images, and his ever-changing style, rank him among the best poets of the French language. The following poem, with its flow of unexpected metaphors, shows the strong influence of surrealism, although Depestre is not a surrealist:

Mouth of light

My mouth mad with systems
mad with adventures
spreads warning-lights
along the most dangerous turns

My mouth black with suffering
black with spit
black as night is black
drinks from its cup of light

My mouth pregnant with songs
pregnant with serpents
from my first childish cry
has uttered things
that split the moon in two

And it is my mouth
filled with its babblings
that tells men
the pain of a world
that is opening its veins

—trans. N. Shapiro

After twenty years in Cuba, Depestre has lived in France since 1979, and works at UNESCO. In a recent essay he indicates a deep skepticism about the possibility of a society combining equitable distribution of wealth and respect for individual rights. He seems to be moving toward more traditional utopian humanism.

WORKS IN ENGLISH TRANSLATION: One volume of Depestre's poetry has been translated into English—*A Rainbow for the Christian West,* by Joan Dayan, in 1977. Selections from his work appear in *Black Poets in French,* edited by M. Collins, 1972, and Norman Shapiro's *Negritude: Black Poetry from Africa and the Caribbean,* 1970.

ABOUT: Dayan, J. *Introduction to* A Rainbow for the Christian West, 1977; Dictionary of Contemporary Latin American Authors, 1975; Garret, N.M. The Renaissance of Haitian Poetry, 1963; Parker, C. A. (ed.) When the Drumbeat Changes, 1981. *Periodicals*—Black Images Spring 1974; French Review October 1979; Modern Language Studies Winter 1979.

*DERRIDA, JACQUES (1930–   ), French philosopher and literary theorist, was born in El Biar, Algeria, of Sephardic Jewish parents. He came to France to complete his military service and stayed on in Paris to study at the École Normale with Jean Hyppolite, the translator of Hegel's *Phenomenology*. Derrida attended Harvard University in 1956–57, and from 1960 to 1964 taught philosophy at the Sorbonne. There he was associated with the group of young intellectuals who published the influential avant-garde journal *Tel Quel*—a relationship that endured until the early 1970s, when Derrida split with the group over *Tel Quel's* increasingly Maoist orientation. Since 1965 Derrida has taught the history of philosophy at the École Normale Supérieure. He is, as well, a founding member of GREPH (*Groupe de recherches sur l'enseignement philosophique*), a student and faculty movement devoted to the defense and improvement of the institutional teaching of philosophy. Derrida has lectured widely in the United States and in England and has been a visiting professor on a regular basis at Johns Hopkins and at Yale.

In a lengthy introduction to his first book, a translation of one section of Husserl's *Die Krisis der europäischen Wissenschaften und die transcendentale Phänomenologie, L'Origine de la géometrie* (*The Origin of Geometry*) in 1962, Derrida launched a far-reaching critique of Western metaphysics, an attack characterized by a profound suspicion of any epistemological foundation of meaning or certainty and a militant rejection of the primacy of the spoken word. In his early *Tel Quel* essays and in three subsequent books—*La Voix et la phenomène* (*Speech and Phenomena*, 1967), a critique of Husserl's theory of signs; *L'Ecriture et la différence* (*Writing and Difference*, 1967), a collection of essays on Lévi-Strauss, Foucault, Freud, and others; and *De la grammatologie* (*Of Grammatology*, 1967), a study of speech and writing in Saussure, Lévi-Strauss, and Rousseau—Derrida extended his subversive reading of the history of Western philosophy. Writing, he argues, has been "debased, lateralized, repressed, displaced" by a philosophic tradition painfully aware of the inadequacies of its own written discourse. Western metaphysicians from Plato, Rousseau, and Hegel to Saussure and Lévi-Strauss, Derrida maintains, have consistently confused their desire for closure with its achievement; their texts record not the *Gelassenheit* they seek but mark a futile longing for absolute presence, a certainty beyond doubt, and indeed, an end to writing itself.

Far from providing a privileged access to unmediated truth—to an exact correspondence between signifier and signified—speech is, for Derrida, as enmeshed in the complex web of language as is writing. Already an echo remote from a recoverable origin, speech is no less fragmentary than writing and no more capable of deferring language's pluralistic and self-referential nature. Both speech and writing are, in his analysis, textual performances in which the gap between what is said and what is meant is endlessly re-presented. The coherence metaphysicians purport to create is, then, achievable only by arbitrarily repressing the polysemous nature of language.

Where Western philosophy finds presence, Derrida discovers a void. Arguing that "there is nothing outside the text," he undermines the foundation of metaphysics by announcing as his primary assertion the absence of any referent or transcendent signified. Meaning, identity, history, and reality itself are simply fabrics of references, webs of signs which point to each other and not to a "reality" beyond themselves. But Derrida's quarrel with the philosophic tradition he surveys is not limited to a dispute over its methods or its intentions. More important to Derrida is the effect of Western philosophy's quest for epistemological certainty. That tradition has fostered, he maintains, a kind of intellectual imperialism by repressing the limitless possibilities of language in the interests of a specific world view. By disrupting the logic of the principal system of Western thought, Derrida attempts to undermine the political structures, social institutions, and ideological assumptions it supports. His emphasis on the inherent excess of language is directed toward persuading his readers to embrace the openness of the world—its ultimate "undecidability"—and to reject any claim for truth or certainty as a restrictive illusion predicated on a naïvely representational theory of language.

The multiplication of meaning is the objective of Derridean analysis. Through the "deconstruction" or "desedimentation" of the texts he analyzes, Derrida seeks to uncover intertextual layerings and thereby counter the narrow bias of Western epistemology. The central texts of that tradition become for him a locus of play and dissemination rather than objects of comprehension. In the absence of a transcendent signified Derrida defends the unorganizable energies of language, and through a dizzying series of allusions, puns, and neologisms, seeks to unsettle conventional frames of reference and overturn the West's accustomed schemata.

Derrida's more recent writing—especially his essays on Plato, Mallarmé, and Sollers (*La Dissémination,* 1972; *Dissemination*) his study of psychoanalysis (*La Carte postale: De Socrate à Freud et au-dela,* 1980; *The Post Card*); his investigation of style in Nietzsche (*Eperons,* 1976; *Spurs*); and his cross-referential reading of Hegel and Genet (*Glas,* 1974; *Glas*)—wages guerrilla warfare against the philosophic edifice he has inherited. His subversive analyses of Western thought reveal a mind at once playful and deadly serious. Resisting authority of any sort, Derrida undermines not only the monolithic discourse he addresses but his own writing as well. By ceaselessly questioning his assumptions and resisting his inclinations toward system and order, Derrida avoids replacing one closed interpretation with another.

Derrida's influence on contemporary philosophy has been significant, but his impact on the practice of literary criticism has been even more extensive. His insistence on the elusiveness of meaning and his dismissal of a text's referential power runs counter to the conventional perception of the critic's role as explicator. And indeed, Derridean analysis has been resisted and harshly attacked in many quarters of the critical establishment. But a number of influential literary theorists, most notably Derrida's colleagues at Yale—Hillis Miller, Paul de Man, Geoffrey Hartman, and Harold Bloom—have employed a deconstruction methodology to redefine critical activity. Two corollaries of Derridean practice have exerted a particularly strong influence in this area. First, by denying the referential function of literature, Derrida has redefined the status of the critic. Casting the reader as the maker of meaning, the orchestrator of the play of the text, Derrida designates the critic as the rival rather than the servant of the author. The deconstructive analyst is no longer devoted to defending the humanistic tradition by preserving the stability of a literary canon and channeling the response of readers. He is rather a provocateur and liberator who speaks for the erotic pleasures of textual encounters. Second, Derridean theory reshapes the function of criticism. Rather than "explaining" texts by tying loose ends, clarifying authorial intention, and eliminating ambiguity, deconstruction defends the text's plurality. It promotes rather than resists literature's own habit of breaking rules, blurring boundaries, and encouraging uncertainty. Where more conventional criticism struggles to double the literary text by crafting a simulacrum which coincides with its content, Derridean practice rejects such neatness as repressive and attempts to open language to its own richness and possibilities. Attentive to the marginal, the contradictory, and the excluded, such readings encourage instability and attempt to generate an excess of meaning. The decon-

structive critic, Derrida writes, "is no longer turned toward the origin, affirms play and tries to pass beyond man and humanism; the name of man being the name of that being who, throughout the history of metaphysics or of onto-theology—in other words, throughout his entire history—has dreamed of full presence, the reassuring foundation, the origin and the end of play."

Derrida's radical revision of philosophic and critical practice has provoked considerable controversy. His position has been assailed as nihilistic and irresponsible, a sterile game in which all meaning and value dissolve. His writing has been attacked as needlessly difficult and perversely unintelligible; his linguistic theory has been rejected as absurdly reductive. Most significant, Derrida has been accused of diagnosing an illness without providing a cure, of involving his readers in a web of complications which reduces the world to a linguistic abyss and impoverishes human experience beyond redemption. To some degree, this reaction has proceeded from a misreading of Derrida's intentions. Indeed, his resistance to system and authority has made his work particularly vulnerable to misinterpretation by his many disciples and popularizers. It is nevertheless true that deconstruction seeks to dismantle the fundamental assumptions of the humanistic tradition and presents a challenge to that belief system which demands response. Perhaps the most enduring result of the Derridean enterprise is that in framing that response, the humanistic community has been forced to respond with greater sensitivity to the possibilities of language and to the complexity of the web of signification that is the world.

WORKS IN ENGLISH TRANSLATION: A considerable number of Derrida's writings have been translated since the early 1970s. These include *Speech and Phenomena,* by David B. Allison, 1973; G. C. Spivak's *Of Grammatology,* 1976; J. P. Leavey, Jr.'s *Edmund Husserl's Origin of Geometry: An Introduction,* 1978, and *The Archeology of the Frivolous: Reading Condillac,* 1981; Alan Bass' *Writing and Difference,* 1978, *Positions,* 1981, and *Margins of Philosophy,* 1983; Barbara Harlow's *Spurs: Nietzsche's Styles,* 1979; Barbara Johnson's *Dissemination,* 1981; Richard Rand's *Signésponge/Sighsponge,* 1984. Translations of *Glas* and *The Post Card* are scheduled to appear in 1985.

ABOUT: Arac, J., et al. The Yale Critics: Deconstruction in America, 1983; Bloom, H., et al. Deconstruction and Criticism, 1979; Columbia Dictionary of Modern European Literature, 1980; Culler, J. On Deconstruction, 1982; de Man, P. Blindness and Insight, 1971; Hartman, G. Saving the Text, 1981; Krupnick, M. (ed.) Displacement, Derrida, and After, 1983; Leitch, V. Deconstructive Criticism, 1983; Lentricchia, F. After the New Criticism, 1980; Smith, S. H. and W. Kerrigan (eds.) Taking Chances: Derrida, Psychoanalysis and Literature, 1984. *Periodicals*—L'Arc 54 (1973); Boundary 2, 4 (1976); Contemporary Literature Spring 1979; Critical Inquiry Summer 1978; London Review of Books February 18–March 3, 1982; Modern Language Notes 91 (1976); New Literary History Autumn 1978; New York Review of Books June 12, 1980; Partisan Review 43, 2 (1976); 46, 4 (1979); 48, 2 (1981); Sub-stance 7 (1973).

*DESAI, ANITA (MAZUMDAR) (June 24, 1937–), Indian novelist and short story writer, was born in Mussoorie, a hill station north of Delhi in the present-day state of Uttar Pradesh, the daughter of D. N. Mazumdar, a businessman, and the former Toni Nime. She took her B.A. at Delhi University in 1957, and the following year married Ashvin Desai, a businessman. They have four children.

Her first two novels, *The Peacock* and *Voices in the City*, were published in Britain by Peter Owen, a publisher specializing in literature of the British Commonwealth and continental Europe. The latter book, set in Calcutta, treats the relationship between a wastrel brother and his two neurasthenic sisters. The reviewer for the *Times Literary Supplement* commended Desai's skill at creating atmosphere and "suggesting rapid fluctuations of consciousness," but complained that "it is often difficult for an English reader to distinguish the indisputable moments of insight through the haze of decorative emotion."

Two succeeding novels, *Bye-Bye, Blackbird* and *Where Shall We Go This Summer?*, were published only in India. Her first work to appear in the United States was *Fire on the Mountain,* a short, highly colored novel that is essentially a character study of Nanda Kaul, a lonely, proud old woman who has retired to a broken-down summer house in the hill country. She is not pleased to be joined there by her great-granddaughter, Raka, a wary, withdrawn, and mysterious child, and for a time they coexist in the same household, unable to touch each other or share their feelings. Everything changes when Ila Das, an old school friend of Nanda's, comes to tea. She is extremely poor, nearly starving on a tiny pension, and her cheerful talkativeness becomes unbearable to her old friend and to Raka, who runs from the room as soon as she can. On her way home, Ila is raped and murdered, and Nanda is informed almost immediately by a telephone call from the police. She has not replaced the receiver before Raka returns with the news that she has set a forest fire with stolen matches. The novel's message may be, according to Gabriele Annan, "that we need to connect,

ANITA DESAI

which both Nanda and Raka have failed to do. What is original is that in their failure they are not presented as a pitiable mess, but each in her way as a dignified, strange and beautiful creature." Katha Pollitt was not satisfied with the book's sensational ending: "The decaying resort and the two disappointed, game old ladies have a real story in them, but not this one, with its pyromania and brutality. Even in masterly hands this plot could produce only the easy thrill of a startling climax; in Anita Desai's talented but less expert hands, it is anything but startling. So the reader has the sense of looking helplessly on as characters of Jane Austen possibilities are marched along to the garish drum of Edgar Allan Poe."

Clear Light of Day is a universally praised novel about family relationships and the power of memory. It describes the visit of Tara and her husband to her decaying family mansion outside Delhi to visit Bim, Tara's elder sister, who looks after their youngest brother, Baba, an autistic, childlike adult. The sisters' memories of the family's past dominate the book, but in the present they often seem estranged from one another, and their mutual love fades and revives throughout their story. Karen Ray called it "a novel of perfect details, of looking at the world through a magnifying glass, of collecting enough small bits to make sense somehow of the whole. . . . Its spirit reaches to the very heart of India and of humanity." Novelist Anne Tyler thought the book "without apparent movement. It hangs suspended, like the family itself, while memories replay themselves and ancient joys and sorrows lazily float past. . . . Anita Desai has created an entire little civilization here from a fistful of memories, from a patch-work of sickroom dreams and childhood games and fairy tales. *Clear Light of Day* does what only the best novels can do: It totally submerges us. It takes us so deeply into another world that we almost fear we won't be able to climb out again."

Desai has also published a collection of short stories, *Games at Twilight,* eleven tales about families and the tensions within them. The title story concerns a children's game of hide-and-seek. One participant, Raki, decides to hide where nobody will find him, and no one does. By the time he emerges, the afternoon has changed to evening, and his siblings are playing at quite another game. Victoria Glendinning called this story "a jewel . . . simply and beautifully done; Mrs. Desai is a writer's writer in that anyone who has ever set pen to paper must ask himself just what it is about the writing that makes the story so memorable, and there is, naturally, no simple answer to the question." To Glendinning, Desai's greatest achievement as a writer is her "gift of being able to transfer an image that catches her own imagination to the imagination of her reader, and making it seem important."

PRINCIPAL WORKS: The Peacock, 1963; Voices in the City, 1965; Bye-Bye, Blackbird, 1968; Where Shall We Go This Summer?, 1975; Fire on the Mountain, 1977; Games at Twilight and Other Stories, 1978; Clear Light of Day, 1980; In Custody, 1984. *Juvenile*—The Peacock Garden, 1974; Cat on a Houseboat, 1976.

ABOUT: Bellioppa, M. The Fiction of Anita Desai, 1971; Contemporary Authors 81-84, 1979; Mukherjee, M. The Twice-Born Fiction, 1972; Sharma, R. S. Anita Desai, 1981; Srinivasa Iyengar, K. Indian Writing in English, 1962; Verghese, P. Indian Writing in English, 1970. *Periodicals*—Christian Science Monitor January 28, 1981; Library Journal November 15, 1977; October 1, 1980; London Times August 3, 1978; New Republic February 21, 1981; New Statesman September 5, 1980; New York Times November 24, 1980; New York Times Book Review November 20, 1977; November 23, 1980; New Yorker November 14, 1977; Times Literary Supplement July 8, 1965; June 17, 1977; September 1, 1978; September 5, 1980; October 19, 1984.

DILLARD, ANNIE (DOAK) (April 30, 1945–), American poet, critic, and nature writer, was born in Pittsburgh, the eldest of three daughters of Frank Doak, a businessman, and the former Pam Lambert. She was brought up in comfortable circumstances—a world, she said in 1977, of "country clubs, girls' schools, that kind of thing." She also developed early on a habit of omnivorous reading. An excellent student at Hollins College in Virginia, she majored

ANNIE DILLARD

in English and was elected to Phi Beta Kappa in her junior year, taking her bachelor's degree in 1967 and her master's the following year, with a thesis on Thoreau's *Walden.* While at Hollins she also studied theology, which attracted her, she told an interviewer, because of its beauty: "Theology is like poetry. It leaps around making joyful connections with the rhythm and the beat of poetry."

At the end of her sophomore year, Annie Doak married her writing instructor, Richard Dillard, who, she has often insisted, "taught me everything I know." Writing poetry and keeping a daily journal "to give me physical access to my thoughts," she lived in a cabin on Tinker Creek in the Roanoke Valley of the Virginian Blue Ridge Mountains and finally decided to rework her journal entries as a book covering her observations of an entire year beside the creek. The first two chapters were placed by an agent with *Harper's* magazine, a third with the *Atlantic.* In 1974 Harper's Magazine Press published *Pilgrim at Tinker Creek,* which won the Pulitzer Prize for nonfiction that year, the same year in which appeared her poetry collection, *Tickets for a Prayer Wheel.* Most of the twenty-one poems in the latter book had been published earlier in magazines and reviews. They are filled with elemental concerns: the mystery, exaltation, and terror of nature, the difficulty and imperative necessity of knowing God. Several times, as in the long title poem at the end of the collection, Dillard describes mystical experiences as highly colored as those of any early Christian anchorite: "The presence of God: / he picked me up / and swung me like a bell. / I saw the trees / on fire,

I sang / a hundred prayers of praise." One critic complained that God "appears a little too often for comfort in her poems" and this presence makes them "looser, breathier, even rambling."

Pilgrim at Tinker Creek, a popular success, prompted very contradictory responses from critics. Many were impressed by Dillard's meticulous style, "so careful of the minute," wrote one, "that her theme [what it is to believe in God] in comparison, borders on the irrational." Eva Hoffman placed the book "squarely in the American tradition of essayistic narratives in which one person . . . tries . . . to make sense of the universe starting from degree zero. Like a true transcendentalist, Miss Dillard understands her task to be that of full alertness, of making herself a conscious receptacle of all impressions. She is a connoisseur of spirit, who knows that seeing, if intense enough, becomes vision." Explicit comparisons were made to Thoreau and Melville. Some critics, however, such as Charles Deemer, thought the book naive and even silly. "Her observations are typically described in overstatement reaching toward hysteria, and the lessons she would impart are at best sophomoric, at worst pompous twaddle. . . . If Annie Dillard wants to change lives, she had better talk sense or breathe spiritual fire. . . . Call this book a meteorological journal of an egomaniac." Eudora Welty made the same observation, although more quietly. After paying tribute to Dillard's "sense of wonder so fearless and unbridled" and the intensity of imagination, she balked at the incomprehensibility of some passages of metaphysical speculation, then came to the heart of her critique, the book's unrelenting self-centeredness: "Annie Dillard is the only person in her book, substantially the only one in her world; I recall no outside human speech coming to break the long soliloquy of the author. Speaking of the universe very often, she is yet self-surrounded, and, beyond that, book-surrounded. Her own book might have taken in more of human life without losing a bit of the wonder she was after. Might it not have gained more?" Finally, Hayden Carruth considered the book, with its professed "affection of nostalgia," to be "dangerous" and "subversive": "To my mind the view of man and nature held by any honest farmer . . . is historically more relevant and humanly far more responsible than the atavistic and essentially passive, not to say evasive, view held by Annie Dillard."

Dillard's marriage ended shortly after the publication of *Pilgrim at Tinker Creek,* and she moved from the Roanoke Valley to Washington State to begin teaching poetry and creative writing at Western Washington University, Bellingham, in the state's extreme northwest. She spent a good deal of time in a primitive log cabin on an island in Puget Sound, and there began fifteen months' work on her second book of prose, *Holy the Firm.* "I know only enough of God to want to worship him, by any means ready to hand" is the author's principal thematic statement; the book covers three days, which are made to relate to the primal myths of Creation, Fall, and Redemption. The first day's central image is a burned moth that itself becomes a candle flame; the second day's, a young friend and neighbor who is horribly burned in a plane crash; on the third day the author tries to reconcile human suffering with God's existence. Frederick Buechner, a novelist and clergyman, found *Holy the Firm* nearly faultless, "a book of great richness, beauty and power. . . . The violence is sometimes unbearable, the language rarely less than superb. Dillard's description of the moth's death makes Virginia Woolf's go dim and Edwardian. One thinks of Gerard Manley Hopkins, among others—nature seen so clear and hard that the eyes tear." Val Morehouse, while paying tribute to the author's energy, wrote of her book as inevitably failing to answer the immense questions it discusses: "We follow a ritualistic, highly contrived and skillfully orchestrated procession of images and ideas, paradoxical, egotistical, sometimes hyperbolic and are left stranded amid the debris of her unanswered questions." He also characterized Dillard as appearing to be "always distant from human warmth, though not from passion."

In 1982, Dillard again published two books in one year, the criticism of *Living by Fiction* and the essays in *Teaching a Stone to Talk: Expeditions and Encounters.* In the former work, she considers first the accomplishment of those writers she calls "contemporary modernists," principally Borges, Calvino, García Márques, and Nabokov, and studies their aims and techniques. Next she proceeds to examine "The State of the Art," concentrating on the analysis of prose style, the importance of critics, and the distinction between literature and entertainment, among other matters. The final section, "Does the World Have Meaning?", manages to pose again all the big questions about literature as a means of salvation and an honest interpreter of the world. Vance Bourjaily thought it "a stimulating book, one of those in which quality of thought and felicity of prose seem consequences of one another." After the first part, he found the book "all fireworks. . . . [It] proceeds like wonderful conversation, moving here and there as the reader's pen continues to fill the margins with response." Andrea Barnet called it "a bold, provocative book that celebrates the necessity of art," adding that "though Dillard allows herself fewer poetic excursions here than in her previous works, she has forfeited none of her eloquence."

Teaching a Stone to Talk comprises fourteen essays on mainly natural events. For the first time, however, other people appear as strong, independent forces in Dillard's writing, although her central images still depict the nonhuman world: the terror and screaming occasioned by a total solar eclipse, the meaning to be extracted from the sight of dozens of water striders in a sunny backwater, the exchange of a long, intense stare with a weasel. The title essay concerns "a man in his thirties who lives alone with a stone he is trying to teach to talk" and moves on to a consideration of God's presence within nature's silence, both of which we are on earth to witness. "That is why I take walks: to keep an eye on things." For Helen Bevington, reviewing the book, Dillard "is a fine wayfarer, one who travels light, reflective and alert to the shrines and holy places after first carefully selecting them for herself. She sets out again and again, seeking other landscapes, other encounters. Or she stays at home, thriving and surviving, no more scared than anybody. 'I have not been lonely yet,' she says, 'but it could come at any time.'"

In 1980, Dillard married for a second time; her husband, Gary Clevidence, is a teacher of anthropology. She taught writing at Wesleyan University in Middletown, Connecticut, from 1979 to 1981, returning there in 1983. She has published about a dozen short stories in various magazines since 1972, and disclosed as long ago as 1977 that she was at work on a novel, but by 1983 had published no fiction. Winner of the Washington Governor's Award for Literature in 1977, she was a member of a State Department cultural delegation to China in May–June 1982, and held a grant from the National Endowment for the Arts in 1982–83.

PRINCIPAL WORKS: *Poetry*—Tickets for a Prayer Wheel, 1974. *Non-fiction*—Pilgrim at Tinker Creek, 1974; Holy the Firm, 1977; Living by Fiction, 1982; Teaching a Stone to Talk: Expeditions and Encounters, 1982; Encounters With Chinese Writers, 1984.

ABOUT: Contemporary Authors, new revision series 3, 1981; Current Biography 1983; Who's Who in America, 1982–83. *Periodicals*—America October 8, 1977; May 6, 1978; Christianity Today May 5, 1978; Commentary October 1974; Library Journal May 1, 1974; November 1, 1977; New Leader June 24, 1974; New York Times November 9, 1977; November 25, 1982; New York Times Magazine May 10, 1982; New York Times Book Review March 24, 1974; September 25, 1977; May 9, 1982; November 28, 1982; Time March 18, 1974; October 10, 1977; Saturday Review March 1982; Virginia Quarterly Review Autumn 1974.

DING LING (also rendered as **TING LING**) (1904–   ), Chinese novelist and short story writer, was born in Linli county, northern Hunan, the home province of many of China's revolutionary leaders. She was named Jiang Bingzhi, Ding Ling being the pen-name she created for herself later. One of modern China's most prominent and controversial writers, her literary career in many respects encapsulates the history of modern Chinese literature as it has developed through six decades of political revolution.

Ding Ling's paternal grandfather and great-grandfather had been officials under the Manchu dynasty, but by the time of her birth, the once-wealthy family had entered a period of precipitous decline. Her father suffered from ill health and died when Ding Ling was three years old. It was the mother who was the great influence on her life, a woman, Ding Ling has often said, much greater than herself. When her husband died, leaving her with a host of debts and two small children—one of them an infant son who died soon after—the young widow took the bold step of attending a normal school to prepare herself for a teaching career. She later became a pioneer educator and founder of elementary schools.

Following her mother about, Ding Ling pursued her education at various schools. For a time she stayed at the home of her maternal uncle. There she discovered an attic filled with old books and translations of foreign novels that she read steadily to pass her days of loneliness. When the "tide of May Fourth splashed against their small town" in 1919, Ding Ling was caught up in its spirit of iconoclasm and the exciting possibilities of a new literature in colloquial language. The May Fourth Movement had begun as student demonstrations in Peking protesting the government's compliance with the decision of the Allies at the Versailles Peace Conference to cede Shangdong province to Japan. As the protest spread to other cities, it grew into a broad cultural movement which profoundly questioned China's traditional past and looked to models from the West in its search for a new order. In the next two decades this cultural movement was to culminate in the resplendent flowering of a new Chinese literature. Under the impetus of May Fourth, Ding Ling became a precocious activist; she took part in demonstrations, meetings, cut her hair short, taught in a school for the poor, and tried her hand at writing in the new style. Two of her poems in the vernacular were published in the local newspaper. With the support of her mother, she defied the elders of her family to break off an arranged marriage, and before graduating from high school she left home for the semi-Westernized

DING LING

metropolis of Shanghai to try out the existence of a liberated woman in the China of the 1920s.

In Shanghai Ding Ling took courses in Western literature at the People's Girls' School and Shanghai University, both founded by leftwing intellectuals, studied painting, and hobnobbed with anarchists. In 1924 she went to Peking to enroll in the university, but she met the fledgling poet Hu Yepin and soon they were living together a life of young love, literary aspirations, and precarious poverty. It was then that Ding Ling began to write the short stories that quickly established her fame.

Ding Ling's early stories won recognition—or notoriety—for the unprecedented audacity and sensitivity with which she depicted the psychology of young women. Her second and perhaps most famous story, "The Diary of Miss Sophie," published in 1928, is an account of a tubercular, high-strung woman's infatuation for a young man with the handsome "exterior of a medieval knight," but a despicable soul. The work exploded, in the words of contemporary critics, like a bomb shell, shattering the quiet of the literary scene. No one had described the sexual fantasies of a young woman in such frank and impassioned terms in Chinese literature before. Some fourteen short stories followed in three years, many focusing on the introspective modern young woman struggling for personal liberation and suffering the crises of love, sex, and identity. But the pressures of external events soon led to a radical change in Ding Ling's fiction.

During the late 1920s the Kuomintang government's persecution of writers and the radicalization of literature were both proceeding apace.

Ding Ling and Hu Yepin had moved to Shanghai, where the protection provided by its foreign settlements allowed a political opposition to exist with a limited degree of impunity. In 1930 both Ding Ling and Hu Yepin joined the newly formed League of Left-Wing Writers. Hu became increasingly active in the Chinese Communist Party while Ding Ling wrote a group of stories on the conflict between love and revolution which also explored the consequent changing concept of literature. Their first child, a son, was born in November 1930. Two months later, on January 17, 1931, Hu Yepin was arrested while attending a meeting, and along with twenty-three or twenty-four alleged Communists he was executed on February 7 in Longhua prison. There were four other young writers besides Hu Yepin among the victims, and the Five Martyrs soon became one of the most powerful emblems of literary persecution in modern Chinese history. Her husband's martyrdom reinforced Ding Ling's commitment to the cause for which he was killed. Active in the League of Left-Wing Writers, she assumed the editorship of its literary periodical, *Beidou* (Big Dipper). Her own writing turned outward from the subjective lives of her characters to the political world in which they lived; she extended her subject matter from alienated young intellectual women to striking factory workers, oppressed peasants, the unjust legal network, the coming socialist revolution. A long story, "Flood," depicting the suffering that drove peasants to rebellion during the disastrous floods in China in 1931, was hailed by Communist critics as a landmark example of the new proletarian fiction. In 1932 Ding Ling joined the Communist Party.

Beidou was suppressed by the Kuomintang authorities after seven issues. On May 15, 1933, Ding Ling was kidnapped by government agents at her home, imprisoned, and widely presumed to have been executed. She was moved to various places of confinement and later placed under house arrest; the main purpose was not to execute her but to persuade her to renounce the Communist Party and place her talents at the service of the Kuomintang government. She refused to cooperate and three years later, in September 1936, she managed a daring escape to the border regions in northwest China where the Communist Party had its headquarters. A few months later the party moved its capital to Yanan, an ancient and isolated town that became the unlikely base from which the Communist revolution dramatically expanded to establish its power over China twelve years later. The proper role of art and literature within this all-encompassing political effort became an urgent issue over the next few years. When the War of

Resistance against Japan broke out in 1937, Ding Ling organized and directed the Northwest Front Service Corps, spending several months with her troupe traveling through the backward mountain villages of the area and performing plays and songs to propagate the message of uniting to fight Japan. Her experience and similar experiments by others discovered a new audience and suggested new uses for literature and art. One member of the troupe was the writer Chen Ming, whom Ding Ling married in 1942.

There was a sharp decline in Ding Ling's fictional output during her Yanan period, although she produced several stories on war and revolution. In 1941 she also served as editor of the literary page of the party's newspaper the *Liberation Daily,* and in that capacity she called for critical essays on society, literature, and art, publishing several that exposed the darker side of Yanan life. Her own critical essay, the famous "Thoughts on March Eight," discussed the plight of women in Yanan, even though they were "better off than in other parts of China." Mao Zedong's answer to these critics and other "bourgeois" writers who had been drawn to Yanan to take part in the revolution was given in his historic "Talks at the Yanan Forum on Literature and Art" in May, 1942; there he stated explicitly once and for all that literature and art must be subordinate to politics and party control. The "Talks" were part of a campaign to correct undisciplined attitudes and impose a firm ideological line, the first of many campaigns the party was to conduct in subsequent decades. Ding Ling underwent self-criticism, and when she resumed writing in 1944, her new pieces were sketches of model labor or production heroes based on uplifting real-life incidents. She was congratulated by Mao for her success in embarking on this new literary path.

When the People's Republic of China was established in 1949, Ding Ling was for a time one of the most prominent members in its cultural hierarchy—vice chairperson of the Writer's Union, editor of important literary journals, and head of the training school for writers. She traveled abroad for the first time in her life, leading delegations to the Soviet Union, Hungary, and Czechoslovakia. In 1951 she was awarded the Stalin prize in literature for her novel on land reform *Taiyang zhao zai Sangganhe shang* (*The Sun Shines on the Sanggan River*). The novel was in large part based on her personal observations, and its depiction of the changes in the peasants' consciousness as they took part in the activated mass struggle to destroy the traditional structure of rural economic and political power can be read as an account in microcosm of the quintessential Chinese revolutionary experience. With its sweeping vision of China in revolution, the novel is evidence of the vast distance, both in ideology and technique, that the author herself had traveled since she began with her stories about the subjective experiences of lonely young women, a distance that reflects the momentous transformations in modern Chinese literature since the 1920s.

The adjusted political orientation of Ding Ling's fiction was not enough to ensure her continuing status in a volatile revolutionary society. Her prestigious position lasted but a few years. In 1957 she was the prime target of the antirightist drive and denounced in a nation-wide campaign. Among the charges against her—immorality, ideological failings, and traitorous conspiracy against the party—one was specifically directed against her attitude towards literature, her alleged exaltation of literature as an individual creation which could be set up in opposition to party leadership. The struggle against her was necessary, it was said, to "protect the socialist line in art and literature." She was expelled from the party in 1958, and immediately faded away to become a nonperson. Her writings were completely banned, her name never mentioned in public; it was as if one of modern China's most prolific and prominent women writers had never written or existed. Not until twenty-one years later—during the period of relative liberalization following the death of Mao Zedong in 1976, when the party acknowledged its mistaken extreme "leftist" tendencies of the past—was Ding Ling, along with many other "rightists," finally rehabilitated. Information about what had happened to her during the two previous decades of silence and invisibility began to emerge. She had been sent to a state farm in the Great Northern Wilderness, the northeast corner of China, just south of the Heilongjiang River bordering Siberia, for labor reform, working first on the poultry brigade, and then later as a teacher in adult literacy classes. During the early phases of the Cultural Revolution (1966–1967) she suffered much physical abuse in "criticism and struggle" sessions; all her manuscripts, notes, and diaries were confiscated and destroyed. In 1970 she was returned to Peking and placed in solitary confinement for five years.

With official rehabilitation in 1979 the ban on Ding Ling's books was lifted and she was permitted, after a hiatus of twenty-three years, to resume her writing career. In 1981 she visited the United States for the first time, spending two months at the International Writing Program at the University of Iowa.

Between 1928 and 1948 Ding Ling published

ten collections comprising some sixty short stories and sketches, two novellas, and two novels
(one remains unfinished). Two volumes of essays
appeared in 1953 and 1954. Most of her fiction
and essays have been republished since her rehabilitation and she has added several volumes of
sketches, reminiscences, addresses, and critical
writings on literature.

WORKS IN ENGLISH TRANSLATION: *The Sun Shines Over the
Sanggan River* was translated by Yang Hsien-yi and
Gladys Yang in 1954; "The Diary of Miss Sophia,"
translated by A.L. Chin, is in Harold R. Isaacs (ed.)
Straw Sandals: Chinese Short Stories, 1918–1933, 1974;
"In the Hospital" and "When I Was in Hsia Village,"
translated by Gary Bjorge, are in Joseph S.M. Lau, C.T.
Hsia, and Leo Ou-fan Lee (eds.) *Modern Chinese Sto-
ries and Novellas, 1919–1949.* Other stories are in
When I Was in Sha Chuan and Other Stories, translat-
ed by Kung Pusheng, n.d.; and in Edgar Snow (ed.)
Living China, Modern Chinese Stories, 1936.

ABOUT: Boorman, Howard L. and Howard, Richard C.
(eds.) Biographical Dictionary of Republican China,
1967–1971; Chang, Jun-mei, Ting Ling: Her Life and
Her Work, 1978; Feuerwerker, Yi-tsi Mei, Ding Ling's
Fiction: Ideology and Narrative in Modern Chinese
Literature, 1982; Goldman, Merle Literary Dissent in
Communist China, 1967; Hsia, C.T. A History of Mod-
ern Chinese Fiction, 2nd ed., 1971; Klein, Donald
Walker and Clark, Anne B. (eds.) Biographic Dictio-
nary of Chinese Communism, 1921–1965, 1971;
Spence, Jonathan D. The Gate of Heavenly Peace: The
Chinese and Their Revolution, 1895–1980, 1981;
Yang, W.L.Y. and N. Mao (eds.) Modern Chinese Fic-
tion, 1981.

*DIOP, BIRAGO** (December 12, 1906–),
Senegalese short story writer and poet, was born
in Ouakam, a suburb of Dakar, at that time the
capital of French West Africa. He was the son
of Ismaël Diop, a master mason and member of
the Wolof tribe, and Sokhna Diawara, whose
family was from Sine-Saloum. He was only two
months old when his father died, and he was
raised, as he said in 1976, in "a matriarchal ambiance composed of affection and authority, and
tempered by a feminine entourage of grand-
mothers, mothers-in-law, aunts, half sisters, and
cousins much older than I." He was a French citizen from birth, and was brought up, as are the
majority of Senegalese, in the Islamic faith. Yet
he found no attraction in Koranic studies, and
soon came to consider himself an animist. Diop
is a common surname in Senegal, and he is not
a close relative of the well-known writers among
his countrymen who also bear the name: Alioune
Diop, Cheikh Anta Diop, and David Diop.

Birago attended primary school in the Rue

BIRAGO DIOP

Thiong, Dakar, then in 1921 won a scholarship
to one of the country's best schools, the coeduca-
tional and multiracial Lycée Faidherbe in Saint-
Louis, a city to the north on the Mauritanian border. He was a student there for seven years until
1928, when he began a year of military service.
He won a scholarship in 1929 to study veterinary
medicine at the University of Toulouse, France,
where he took his doctorate in veterinary surgery in 1933. In 1933–34 he did postdoctoral research at the Institut d'Etudes Vétérinaires
Exotiques in Paris, where he met for the first
time his countryman Léopold Sédar Senghor, a
prime mover behind the then-emerging black
literary and philosophical movement known as
Négritude. Diop was a contributor to the unique
issue of *L'Etudiant noir,* Senghor's highly influential journal. In France he concentrated on
writing poetry: several of his poems were collected by Senghor in the important *Anthologie de las
nouvelle poésie nègre et malgache de langue
française* (Anthology of the New Black and Mal-
agasy Poetry in French, 1948). Among his most
famous works is "Viatique" (Viaticum), recounting in haunting, breathless terms a tribal initiation rite; it was included in Diop's only book of
poetry, *Leurres et lueurs* (Lures and Glimmers,
1960):

With three fingers red in the blood,
Blood of dog,
Blood of bull,
Blood of goat,
My mother touched me three times,
She touched my forehead with her thumb,
With her index my left breast,
And with her second finger touched my navel.
When I had plunged my fingers into the sand,
Into the sand which had gone cold,

°dē ´ op, bir ä gō ´

Then my mother said: "Go through the
world, go!
All your life they will follow your steps."

Returning home in 1934, Diop served until 1942 as head of the government cattle inspection service for the whole of western Mali, a vast area he had to cover by whatever means of transportation was at hand: horseback, automobile, canoe. He recounts how during these travels, "beneath other skies, when the weather was dull and the sun was sick, I often closed my eyes and there would arise from my lips the *Kassaks* which used to be sung in the 'Men's Huts'; and I would hear my mother or my grandmother recounting once again the rebuffs of Bouki the Hyena, that conceited coward, or the misfortunes of Khary Gaye, the orphan girl, the tricks of that wicked child Djabou n'Daw, the triumphs of the diabolical Samba Seytane, and the misadventures of Amary the Devout. This momentary return to my childhood tempered my exile. . . . On my return to my own country, having forgot little of what I had learned as a child, I had the great good fortune to meet, on my long road, the old Amadou Koumba, my family's *griot*. [A griot is a storyteller, genealogist, singer, and repository of a uniquely oral tradition.] Amadou Koumba told me the same stories that had cradled my childhood. He taught me others too, filled with wise sayings and maxims, enclosing all the wisdom of our ancestors." This excerpt from the introduction to Diop's first book, *Les Contes d'Amadou Koumba* (*The Tales of Amadou Koumba,* 1947), has led many critics and even specialists in African literature to suppose that the griot was a real person, encountered, according to Diop's account, near the place where the river Falémé joins the Senegal. The author, however, acknowledged in 1976 that "Amadou Koumba was only a borrowed name, a useful roof to cover goods which had come to me from several sources, of which the first and last were familial. For as to subject matter I owe more to my brother Youssoupha than to my maternal grandmother's griot."

The tales, mainly beast fables, are richly interspersed with much of Diop's best poetry. They resonate with his strong belief in animism; as Joyce Hutchinson wrote, "If his observation of the human comedy is necessarily influenced by his broader knowledge and understanding of humanity, this influence is not intrusive; he is never patronizing. There is nothing artificial about the insistence on respect for tradition which pervades all his stories. The other insistent and pervading theme, which is obviously as important for Diop as it was fundamental for the griot, is the belief that everything, elements, spirits, animals, plants, stones as well as human beings, is endowed with life."

To this first book of tales Diop added three more, *Les nouveaux contes d'Amadou Koumba* (1958), *Contes et lavanes* (1963), and *Contes d'Awa* (1977); Senghor contributed a lengthy and magisterial preface to the first of these. Janheinz Jahn noted that if Senghor was "the first to introduce into French poetry African customs and manners, myths and celebrations personally experienced, also hero figures, chiefs, kings, priests, shrines, spirits, springs, and animals, . . . [then] Birago Diop set a model for prose with his recreation of African stories and myths in the oral style of a professional narrator." John Reed and Clive Wake, however, pointed to the key difficulty confronting the African writer who: "if he writes in English or French, although people from all parts of his country and indeed from many parts of Africa and the rest of the world will be able to read his work, he will not be intelligible to those people even from his own village who have not learnt a European language." Nevertheless, the tales have become extremely popular throughout Africa, and have been translated into six European languages besides French, making Diop one of the world's most widely read African writers.

Diop married in France in 1934 Marie-Louise Pradère, an accountant from the Haute-Garonne; they had two daughters. In 1960, he retired from his governmental post, but the following year accepted President Senghor's invitation to become ambassador to Tunisia, where he served until 1965. He has since managed his own veterinary clinic, while serving as president of the reading board of New African Editions, Dakar, of the Senegalese Writers Association, and of the administrative council of the Senegal office of Authors' Rights. Two volumes of his memoirs have appeared, *La Plume raboutée* (The Piecemeal Pen, 1978) and *A Rebrousse-temps* (Against the Grain of Time, 1981), and a third volume is expected.

WORKS IN ENGLISH TRANSLATION: Nineteen of Diop's short stories were translated into English by Dorothy S. Blair as *Tales of Amadou Koumba* in 1966. R. Guy translated *Mother Crocodile* in 1981. Selections from his poetry are included in *A Book of African Verse,* edited by J. Reed and C. Wake, 1964.

ABOUT: Columbia Dictionary of Modern European Literature, 1980; Contemporary Authors new revision series 10, 1984; Encyclopedia of World Literature in the 20th Century, (rev. ed.) 1, 1981; Herdeck, D. African Authors, 1973; Jahn, J. (ed.) Who's Who in African Literature, 1972; Kane, M. Les Contes d'Amadou Koumba: Du conte traditionnel au conte moderne d'expression française, 1968; Kane, M. Birago Diop:

l'Homme et l'oeuvre, 1971; Zell, H. M. and Silver, H. (eds.) A Reader's Guide to African Literature, 1972.

DISCH, THOMAS M(ICHAEL) (February 2, 1940–), American novelist, science-fiction writer, and poet, writes: "I was born in Des Moines, Iowa, the eldest son of Helen and Felix Disch. I was named for my paternal grandfather, who ran a corner grocery store in Minneapolis. He died before my memory became operational, and my only recollection of him—or rather, of his store—is of my entire satisfaction with a strawberry ice cream cone. My grandmother, his wife, was a crippled, mean-spirited, small-minded German Catholic. Of her my earliest memory is the dread I felt of having to kiss her wrinkled, powdery cheek at the end of a visit. Another vivid memory (though much later) is of Grandma Disch choking on a baked bean she'd swallowed, while all the children at the dinner table—me and my three younger brothers Greg, Jeff, and Gary, but not Nancy, since she would still have been a baby then—laughed uproariously, being of the conviction that Grandma had swallowed her own false teeth. After my grandfather's death Grandma Disch (no one ever called her by her first name, and I don't remember what it was) was supported by her captive daughters, Aurelia and Cecelia, who worked as secretaries. A third daughter, Lorraine, escaped her sisters' fate, first by enlisting in the war effort, then by marrying. She was promptly exiled from Grandma Disch's presence forever: Lorraine's husband was a divorcé, and *we* were Catholics.

"My mother's people were subsistence farmers in the Mille Lacs Lake area of central Minnesota. Their lives and land were poor enough that they could fairly be called peasants. They cut their own firewood and the blocks of ice for the icehouse, got their water from a hand pump, and shat in a privy. Grandpa Gilbertson lived in an immemorial leather-and-oak rocker, a vastly fat, grouchy man who'd been crippled in the Spanish-American War. From that ever-fixed position it was his ever-merry joke to hook me by the neck with his cane whenever I ventured near his rocker. He had heroically stubborn prejudices. My mother's favorite tale of him was that when taken to see a traveling circus he refused to believe that the lion, tiger, and elephant were anything but men got up in costumes. To do him credit (*I* was never at that circus), maybe he was right. Grandma Gilbertson—Emma—was the salt of the earth, a good-tempered robust bustling countrywoman right out of a Breughel painting (though her people, the Bricks, were

THOMAS M. DISCH

Norwegian, like the Gilbertsons). She was utterly capable, deeply loved, an archetypal cook, an unstoppable gossip, and a compulsive game-player in her last years. The farm she presided over has always been my model of pre-lapsarian Eden.

"My father was a door-to-door salesman. He met my mother, the farmer's daughter, in Minneapolis when he was heading a crew selling *Collier's Magazine* and she was working at a drug store soda fountain. After they were married, she traveled with his crew, which is how I came to be born in Des Moines. The earliest home I have any memory of was a downstairs duplex in a St. Paul slum where, being forbidden to cross the street, a colored boy and I played with each other from our opposing curbstones. There too, grazing on the neighborhood lawns in emulation of Bambi, an early role-model, I came down with a bad case of oral poison ivy.

"Before I entered kindergarten we'd moved across the Mississippi to Bryant Avenue in Minneapolis. There on Saturday mornings I would sit staring into the single green eye of our radio, listening to (or call it worshipping) *Let's Pretend*. There I marshalled two sets of bowling pins (children and grown-ups) in my own fairy tales (the big pink pin was a witch; the little blue pin was me). There, at night, I would cross my eyes, stare up at the ceiling, and watch self-projected home movies in wide-screen color (alas, I no longer can regulate my phosphene activity so purposefully).

"In March 1945 my brothers Gregory and Jeffrey were born. That fall I started kindergarten at Incarnation School. The nun in charge told my parents she believed I was possessed by a devil (better a bad review than none at all), but even so I got the starring role in the class play at graduation. I played a priest ('Come with me to Our Lady's garden . . .') and protested mightily at having to wear what I considered a dress. Only the threat of having to appear, instead, as a daisy persuaded me to get into the cassock and recite my lines.

"In the summer of 1945 there was a polio epidemic and I was kept indoors. To keep me occupied my mother taught me to read, and this led, in the next school year, to my being skipped ahead to second grade, to which rupture in the natural order I ascribe all my later overweenings.

"I attended Incarnation only one more year. Then my Gilbertson grandparents decided the farm was too much for them, and so for five months I was to live in that hand-me-down Eden. The raspberry bushes, flower beds, and senile orchards; the sagging barn and haunted chicken coop; the icehouse with the woodpile stacked against it; the bats in the attic, the wrens in the birdhouse, the snakes in the grass; the wood range in the kitchen, the grates in the floor of the upstairs bedrooms, which were their only source of heat: nothing in my childhood remains so clear and dear in memory as that house, the fields and swamps about it, the great reedy lake just down the road. We Disches enjoyed that borrowed splendor for the summer and fall of 1948. We brought in and canned one harvest of vegetables—and then my father's new job, selling insulation and quonset houses, brought us to Fairmont in the more prosperous Corn Belt in the southwest corner of the state.

"I attended St. Paul's Convent School in Fairmont from fourth through eighth grade. The nuns ran a tight ship. Regularly I had to write, as punishment, on the blackboard, 'I must learn to obey.' And so I did. I learned to diagram sentences, served Mass, sang in the choir (St. Paul's did a brisk trade in 8 a.m. requiems), and learned to obey. In those same years I began to earn my living, delivering the *Minneapolis Star* and the *Tribune,* and selling greeting cards and household novelties from door to door. My father instructed me in the arts of salesmanship and in the summers would take me on the road with him to nearby towns, me with my carton of magnetic potholders, him with Britannica Junior (the quonset-house business having hit the skids).

"What I needed my earnings for then (and now too) was movies, books, and restaurants. My very first mortal sin was going to see Cecil B. de Mille's *The Greatest Show on Earth,* which the dread Legion of Decency had rated as a B movie because James Stewart portrayed a mercy killer. My reading, by contrast, was relatively unpatrolled. I read through my mother's stacks of Perry Mason paperbacks, my father's issues of *SatEvePost,* all the animal adventures and sea stories in the children's section of the library, as many Hardy Boy adventures as I could buy or borrow. Comic books, too, of course, though I prudently resisted buying D.C. Comics myself and read those at my best friend's house.

"It was through the same friend, Bruce Burton (who has already since *retired* from being the dean of a St. Paul law school!), that I made the acquaintance of science fiction. SF became my ruling passion during seventh and eighth grades—SF and the theater. For I'd exhausted the children's section of the library and discovered, upstairs, an alcove stuffed with twenty years of Broadway hits. A play can be read almost as quickly as a comic book, and the dialogue is often better. A critic in the *New York Times* has written, in disparagement of my too-developed treatment of character in an SF novel, that it was as though I'd inserted 'one of O'Neill's family dramas . . . into a play by Brecht.' At age twelve I had yet to discover Brecht, but already my concept of total literary sublimity was a bipolar model with *Strange Interlude* to the north and *Brave New World* down under. Though I've added other role-models over the years, I still think that represents a fairly worthwhile ambition and a good plan for the reform of science fiction.

"Just before I entered high school, my family—there were seven of us now, and the Fairmont area had been milked pretty dry of encyclopedia prospects—moved back to the Twin Cities. From being one of eight boys and twenty-three girls in my grade school class, all known quantities, I became one of unknown hundreds in a brand-new suburban school. Try as I might (which was not very hard), I never managed to be popular, though I never stopped believing I ought to be. (My career in a nutshell.) The next year I switched to Cretin, a Catholic military high school named for a former bishop of the diocese. Cretin's Christian Brothers accelerated my departure from the faith of my childhood and from Cretin, but the big Declaration of Independence—the Rubicon of my adolescence—was still to come. It came, or I came to it, in the summer of 1955, when after having been dragooned from my job as a library page in order to provide an audience for a lecture that no one had come to, I fell in love with the lecturer and her subject. That fall I started taking ballet classes from Mrs. Andahazy, formerly of the Ballets Russes de Monte Carlo. It was the next best thing to running away with the circus.

"In retrospect those ballet classes and rehearsals (for I was to top off my dance career preforming in the corps for the Andahazy production of Aurora's Wedding) strike me as having been the major defining experience of my teenage years: in part because they required obstinate self-definition as (at best) a nonconformist; in larger part because by their means the spirit of art became fused with the body's fiber. Most men are obliged to rely on sports for that confirmational, or transubstantive, benefit. I think I had the better bargain. Surely it is to Mrs. Andahazy, more than to any other teacher I've had, that I feel most deeply beholden.

"In the same two last years of high school I was discovering poetry. Shakespeare first, and then, by a happy accident, Pope. In junior year I undertook to memorize 1,000 lines of poetry, wrote a blank verse play that scanned, and did my junior essay on Pope's prosody. In senior year I developed a sense of critical shame and slowed down virtually to a stop, but not before I'd taken my choicest quatrains to Allen Tate at the University of Minnesota and demanded to know if I should set out to become a poet. Bless him, he said I should.

"My twig was bent, and branches pruned, in various others ways in my high school years, but the sum is simple enough: I worked hard at assimilating the elements of a culture not mine of birthright, thought myself miserable (though I was abundantly happy), and as soon as I had my diploma and a bit of cash took off for New York City like an iron filing to a magnet, where I've remained since, except for a few lengthy periods of expatriation. (Six and a half years all told, in five different stretches, chiefly in England and Italy.)

"My ambivalent feelings about New York are on record in my fiction and poetry, and I won't try to express my sense of that debt here, except to say, well, yes, I love New York. I went to NYU's Washington Square College in the Village, a college almost as impersonal, for those who liked it that way, as a computer terminal— first to the evening school (while I worked days at an insurance company); then, when I got a scholarship that paid my tuition, full-time in day school, where I switched my major from English to History. I paid for rent and groceries by checking coats and selling orange juice at the Majestic Theater during the long runs of *The Music Man* and *Camelot*. Of all the jobs I've had to do, that was probably the least onerous. After all, I was on Broadway.

"Just before finals in May 1962 I had what we called in those days a nervous breakdown. That's to say, I'd decided to leave NYU but didn't know how to do so other than by claiming dementia. Over the first weekend of my breakdown I stayed home and wrote what I figured I now *must* write—a story I could sell to a magazine. Two long months later Cele Goldsmith, the editor of *Fantastic*, bought "The Double-Timer" for one-and-a-half cents a word, or $112.50. I didn't study for my make-ups, and I didn't return to NYU. I was now, officially, a writer.

"During the next year I shared an apartment on Riverside Drive with John Clute, whom I'd met in an English course titled 'The Quest for Utopia,' taught by J. Max Patrick. In that course I had met all the friends I was to retain from my college years: John Clute, Jerry Mundis, and Charles Dizenzo. What the four of us had in common was that we all intended to become writers, and we all did.

"I don't know how to tell the story of my apprenticeship, once it had begun in earnest with that first sale, without resorting to self-mythologizing ('There's No Business Like Show Business!') or to some kind of critical self-appraisal, work-by-work, which is liable to be only a discreeter form of self-congratulation. Yet it is one of the great privileges of being an artist that one's life and one's work can form an inextricable tangle, a privilege I'm thankful for every time I'm asked to list separate phone numbers for home and for work. In my case the tangle is complicated by the fact that very often my closest friends have also been collaborators— or, at the very least, literary confidants on a day-to-day, page-by-page basis. Some for-instances. In 1965 and 1966 I wrote *Black Alice* and a paperback gothic in collaboration with John Sladek, all the while we traveled through Morocco, Spain, and England (where John fell in love, got married, and grew roots). Earlier, in summer of 1965, I wrote the opening story of *334* (then called 'Problems of Creativeness') while subletting Jerry Mundis's apartment at 334 East 11th St., and I wrote the very last sub-chapter for that book, literally at the prompting of a nightingale, while I was sharing a cottage with Charles Naylor on a dairy farm in Surrey. For me all these associations of person and place seem relevant—but relevant more, perhaps, to revery than to a *précis* of my career.

"My relation with Charles Naylor has been closer and more sustained than any other in my adult life, and together we have written what I consider 'my' most ambitious and achieved novel, *Neighboring Lives*. That collaboration by no means exhausts the literary debt I owe Charles Naylor, for it has only been through his discerning scrutiny, his exhortations and grimaces, that

I've been able, over the fourteen years we've lived together, to write poetry that has some focus and substance. The larger expression of the debt I owe him can be found diffused among my poems and fictions.

"At the moment of writing this short memoir (March 1983), I have two completed novels—'The Businessman: a Tale of Terror' and 'A Troll of Surewould Forest: a Post-Modern Pantomime for the Reading Impaired'—ready under their canvases, waiting to be unveiled, and soon I must settle down and finish a third novel, 'The Pressure of Time.' To settle, hopefully (and I think it's pedantic to say that 'hopefully' is a solecism; no other single word serves the purpose) in Italy. Maybe Venice this time. Whether or not I get there in the near future, I think it suits my case to end on the prospective note of what is wished-for, awaited, and imagined, for I spend the better part of my mental life daydreaming and carrying on imaginary conversations with people I'm on the way to visit."

———

Tom Disch is regarded as one of the few writers who are breaking down the barriers, erected over decades by critics, between science fiction and the rest of literature. He explained this himself in his introduction to "an anthology of political foreboding," *Bad Moon Rising*: "There are two ways of writing about politics— retrospectively, with a view to what is known to have happened, or prospectively, with a view to the best or worst that yet may be. In other words, the writer of fiction has a simple choice: the historical novel—or science fiction." All of Disch's work is "about politics" in that his major characters suffer as a rule a devastating loss of freedom within a violent or menacing sociopolitical setting. As to his "simple choice," he has opted for both sides, having written masterful historical fiction as well as novels and stories set in the near and distant future. He is best known for the latter sort, which John Calvin Batchelor placed "in the British tradition of dystopian fiction, that is, serious letters about an impaired, make-believe place that is more profoundly modern-times than anything in the media."

Camp Concentration is a dense, multi-layered novel set in 1975 (the near future at the time of publication in 1968) in a subterranean prison camp in Colorado. Disch's friend John Sladek described it thematically as linking "imprisonment and death with artistic freedom and immortality. . . . [It] wades into the largest ethical issues without flinching." Highly literary in its evocations—Dante, the various manifestations of the Faust legend, Aquinas, Joyce, Rilke,

and Rimbaud are among the many complex allusions—the book nevertheless, according to Peter Nicholls, "is genuine, hard-core science fiction. . . . [It] was one of the rare New-Wave works of sufficiently high quality to bridge the gap between the late-1960 young turks of science fiction and the old guard." Originally published in serial form by Michael Moorcock in the influential British magazine *New Worlds*, the novel helped establish Disch as a popular writer in Britain.

Also set in the near future, *334* is an interconnected series of stories about the dazed, defeated inhabitants of a high-rise housing project at 334 East 11th Street (one of the author's former New York addresses). In this book, which one reviewer called "*Last Exit to Brooklyn* plus 50 years," Disch "explores sexual politics," according to Batchelor, "with homosexual men and women loving and agonizing equally with broken families, deserted mothers, and suicidal Third Worlders. Food shortages and degrading governmental supplements are a matter of course, there is little meaningful work, and a black market for corpses thrives. (This is a state of the art novel, and devastating.)" The highly regarded *On Wings of Song*, which critics have compared with Orwell's *1984* and Robert Heinlein's *Stranger in a Strange Land*, is also set in Manhattan, but in the twenty-first century, when technology has enabled people's spirits to fly away (by means of singing) from their bodies, which must then be expensively maintained until their return.

Two novels by Disch are set in Victorian England. He wrote the more famous of these, *Clara Reeve*, under the pseudonym Leonie Hargrave; the imposture was so convincing that hardly any reviewers noticed it, and one of those who did "wondered, momentarily, whether Leonie Hargrave might possibly be G. M. Young or Walter Houghton in drag." Clara, the orphan heroine, suffers unspeakable and very contemporary torments within a finely detailed Victorian and Neapolitan setting. In a lively review, Tom Sharpe declared that to have read the book, "is to know the full meaning of literary prostitution. For 442 pages I was firmly held by the narrative and the delineation of character, . . . fascinated by the brilliance of the imagination that created the Victorian world of Clara Reeve and by the erudition that made that world vivid and alive. . . . [It] is something of a masterpiece; it is also an extremely unsavoury book."

Disch's other "Victorian" novel is *Neighboring Lives*, written with his friend Charles Naylor. It recounts, by means of what one critic called "a montage of small, telling events," the atmosphere of London's Chelsea district between 1830 and 1870. The Carlyles are prominent characters, and Leigh Hunt, John Stuart Mill, the Brownings, and the Pre-Raphaelite poets and painters are also featured. Anthony Burgess described the authors as "in love with the Victorian age, and they are right to be, but their love is of a kind that blots out the grosser blemishes of the beloved. . . . [The authors], concerned with giving us a kind of painless history lesson, emphasize unity of place at the expense of plot. Some of us prefer to get our history straight. . . . [Yet] this is a substantial book, . . . a fine tribute to that most creative region of London, and . . . an admirable rendering of its most creative time. It is not, however, a novel, except in a Pickwickian sense."

A few critics, while admiring the wit and vigor of Disch's longer fiction, have preferred the formal tightness and tense ambiguity of the short stories. Some of these tales, such as "Getting into Death," "The Asian Shore," and "Bodies," are unquestioned classics of the genre.

Disch is also accounted a very accessible poet, often producing what Donald Davie called "cleanly written, intelligently civil and good-humored *verse*. . . . It blows in upon us like a keen and bracing wind." Of the fifty-eight poems in *ABCDEFG HIJKLM NPOQRST UVWXYZ* (the alphabetical inversion is correct), Gavin Ewart wrote, "We are in the presence of a poet of the John Updike, John Fuller or X. J. Kennedy kind—somebody, that is, who is not afraid to write what used to be called Light Verse, somebody with a games-playing mind and an interest in the shapes of poems, somebody, too, who is very accomplished at writing them." One poem in this "abecedary" describes Time as "the school where we pay / attention to the inexorable and are made to write / one hundred million times *I must learn to obey*"—a reference to his own early instruction, which he described in his sketch above. *Burn This*, originally subtitled *& Other Essays in Criticism*, consists of a number of polished verse essays—a long-neglected mode—which, in David Lehman's words, "appeal to that line of writers from Pope to Auden and John Hollander who value urbanity, strike a balance between plain address and epigrammatic prose, and consider criticism far too important to be left entirely to critics." The poems are tough-minded statements of literary belief, leavened considerably by flashes of Disch's vivid imagination:

The grid of narrative
Is not the page on which the text
So interpretably rests, nor yet
The row of inky vocables that printers
String between two margins: it is a frame
Of mind, an imposition of the square

I-Think upon the blank I-Am.
As the linear narrative unreels,
As the words pale to transparence,
A world is formed complete with a table
Set for a dinner of roast goose, fake
Hobbemas on the wall, and passionate
Ping-pong matches with death to the losers!

PRINCIPAL WORKS: *Novels*—(with J. Sladek, as Cassandra Knye) The House that Fear Built, 1966; (with J. Sladek, as Thom Demijohn) Black Alice, 1968; Camp Concentration, 1968; The Prisoners, 1969; 334, 1972; (as Leonie Hargrave) Clara Reeve, 1975; On Wings of Song, 1979; (with C. Naylor) Neighbouring Lives, 1981; The Businessman: A Tale of Terror, 1984. *Short stories*—Under Compulsion, 1968 (U.S. Fun with Your New Head); White Fang Goes Dingo and other Funny S.F. Stories, 1971; Getting into Death, 1976; The Early Science Fiction Stories of Thomas M. Disch, 1977; Triplicity (includes The Genocides, Puppies of Terra, Echo Round his Bones), 1980; Fundamental Disch, 1980. *Poetry*—The Right Way to Figure Plumbing: 50 Poems 1962–67; ABCDEFG HIJKLM NPOQRST UVWXYZ, 1981; Burn This, 1982; Here I am, There you are; Where were we, 1983. *As editor*—The Ruins of Earth: Stories of the Immediate Future, 1971; Bad Moon Rising, 1973; The Improved Sun: An Anthology of Utopian S-F, 1975; (with C. Naylor) New Constellations: An Anthology of Tomorrow's Mythologies, 1976; (with C. Naylor) Strangeness: A Collection of Curious Tales, 1977.

ABOUT: Bleiler, E.F. (ed.) Science Fiction Writers, 1982; Contemporary Authors, first revision series 21–24, 1977; Smith, C. C. (ed.) Twentieth-Century Science Fiction Writers, 1981. *Periodicals*—New Statesman January 24, 1969; September 26, 1975; June 22, 1979; May 22, 1981; New York Times July 23, 1975; New York Times Book Review December 29, 1968; July 27, 1975; October 28, 1979; May 22, 1981; Punch September 7, 1968; Saturday Review February 1981; Time July 28, 1975; Times Literary Supplement May 15, 1981; June 12, 1981; June 19, 1981; August 27, 1982; May 25, 1984; Village Voice August 27–September 2, 1980.

DOMECQ, H. BUSTOS *See* BIOY CASARES, ADOLFO

*DRACH, IVAN (October 17, 1936–   ), Ukrainian poet, was born on a collective farm in the village of Telizhentsi, about a hundred miles from Kiev. His father was a worker in a beet-sugar refinery, his mother a laborer on the farm. Because his father had been able to amass a considerable library, Ivan learned to read and write at an early age and was a precocious student in the local collective school. The Nazi invasion and occupation of the Ukraine scarred his childhood; among his earliest memories, he has written, are "green, sun, soil, screams, and the madness of war." He joined the Komsomol, the Young Communist League, served in the Soviet Army (1955–58), then studied literature and philosophy at the University of Kiev and film-scenario

°dräk

writing in Moscow. He has been a member of the Communist Party since 1959.

Drach made a sensational poetic debut with the publication by the prestigious *Literary Gazette* (June 18, 1961) of his long lyrical narrative "Nizh u sontsi" (Knife in the Sun), a passionate paean to the strength of his people and an interesting thematic combination of folkloric nostalgia and the hard political facts of his country's history. The poet, unsure of himself and his place in the world, in search of his own soul and his land's national identity, lets his imagination carry him beyond "the bluebird and the Dnieper—/Newton's gravity can't hold me,/I break through the galaxy into the unknown." He meets a polite and well-dressed Stranger, clearly the modern devil, who tells him:

I come from the underworld. Like it or not
I'll take you on a journey
that will make you curse your native land,
your motives and your dreams.
You will dig the bones of your ancestors
out of their graves,
you will tear the red flag into shreds
and use it to wrap your feet.
You will throw yourself off a cliff
into the black mouth
of your humble servant.
Then you will writhe
for a hundred centuries. . . .
                    —trans. Daniel Halpern

The devil shows him the pitiable sights of his country: poverty, the suffering of the Russians in war and under the Stalinist oppression. The poet is nevertheless able to transmute the misery he witnesses into a life-affirming force; the strength and resourcefulness he finds in his people enable him in the end to turn the tables on the devil:

So then, what do you have to say, devil?
What do you have to say about my country?

The poem's daring frankness and stylistic originality drew harsh official criticism, despite its appearance in a respected quasi-official journal during the brief cultural thaw of the Khrushchev era. Drach revised and reprinted the poem several times, blunting, in the opinion of some, its passionate and shocking force.

Another of Drach's earliest lyrics, "Sonyashnyk" (Sunflower), from the 1962 collection of the same name, has remained extremely popular and has become almost his signature poem. It is a deft anthropomorphizing of the flower that is one of the Ukraine's most potent folk motifs:

The sunflower had arms and legs,
had a rough, green body.
He raced the wind,
he climbed a pear tree
and stuffed ripe pears into his shirt
and swam near the mill
and lay in the sand

and shot sparrows with his sling-shot.
He hopped on one foot
to shake the water out of his ear—
and suddenly saw the sun
with its golden spindrift of curls,
the beautiful tanned sun
in a red shirt that reached to its knees.
It rode on a bicycle
weaving through banks of clouds . . .

Poetry, my orange sun!
Every minute some boy
finds you for himself
and changes to a sunflower forever.
                    —trans. Daniel Halpern

A gentle yet pervasive irony is among the most attractive aspects of Drach's style. In "Wings," one of his most popular poems, a Ukrainian peasant receives as a New Year's gift a pair of wings. A commonsensical, unimaginative man, he considers them worthless until he finds a radical solution:

he put his ax to the whetstone,
stretched his wings on a log, and hacked them off.

Screech owls gagged, the stars blinked,
and at night, slashing through cotton,
his new [i.e., regrown] wings began to beat.
The old peasant lived by his ax.
He got rich off the wings.
He shingled his roof with wings.
He fenced himself in with wings.
And poets stole the wings
to keep their muse in wings.
Aesthetes worshipped the wings,
and the lopped wings dreamed of heaven. . . .
                    —trans. Paul Nemser and Mark Rudman

Such imaginative freedom, wittily expressed, is typical of Drach at his most compelling. The best of his poems, in Stanley Kunitz's words, "begin with brilliant perceptions, or concrete instances, and climb, with an explosion of images, towards the realm of the transcendent." Drach himself has said of his bent for fantasy: "My strongest horse is fantasy of soul. My horse of reality is weaker, but it keeps me from flying out of sight."

The poets who have most influenced Drach include the nineteenth-century Ukrainian national poet Taras Schevchenko; two other Ukrainian poets closer to his own generation, Mykola Bazhan and Pavlo Tychyna; and Pushkin; also the Americans Walt Whitman and Allen Ginsberg, the Chilean Pablo Neruda, the Italian Salvatore Quasimodo, and the Spaniard Federico García Lorca. He has written an interesting contemporary variation on Whitman's "What think you I take my pen in hand to record?" which describes in almost surreal terms the meeting of two men "on a deserted field, on white snow:/one just stepped out of a spaceship, /the other just stepped off a train . . . /One, just back from a camp, embraced the other just back from the sky." He has also published translations of poems by García Lorca, Quasimodo, and Ginsberg. His entire work (he writes in both Ukrainian and Russian) is comprised in several collections. Following *Sonyashnyk* are *Protuberantsi sertsya* (Protuberances of the Heart, 1965), *Poezii* (Poems, 1967), *Balady budniv* (Workaday Ballads, 1967), *Do dzherel* (Toward the Springs, a retrospective collection, 1972), *Korin i krona* (Root and Treetop, 1974), and *Kyivske nebo* (Kiev Sky, 1976). Kunitz recalls meeting Drach in Kiev in 1967 and attending a reading given by the poet, at which he was "moved by the sonority of his poems and the blazing intensity of his spirit. It was a different music from any that I had heard in Russia..."

WORKS IN ENGLISH TRANSLATION: The most remarkable of Ivan Drach's poems are available in English in only one published volume, *Orchard Lamps,* 1978, with translations by Daniel Halpern and others and illustrations by Jacques Hnizdovsky.

ABOUT: Columbia Dictionary of Modern European Literature, 1980; Encyclopedia of World Literature in the 20th Century (rev. ed.) I, 1981; Kunitz, S. *Introduction to* Orchard Lamps, 1978; Modern Slavic Literatures 2, 1976. *Periodicals*—Library Journal June 15, 1978; New York Times Book Review March 11, 1979.

*DUBOS, RENE J(ULES)** (February 20, 1901–February 20, 1982), American scientist, educator, and writer, was born in Saint-Brice-sous-Forêt, France, to Georges Alexandre and Adeline Madeleine (de Bloedt) Dubos, and spent his early childhood in rural villages of the Ile-de-France. A sickly child, he developed a taste for reading and philosophical speculation early in life and was especially influenced by the writings of the nineteenth-century French critic Hippolyte Taine on folklore and fables. These, Taine believed, reflected the landscape and natural environment out of which they developed. This, and the inspiration of one of his childhood heroes, Louis Pasteur, directed young Dubos' interest toward agriculture and biology. The family moved to Paris in 1914, but the death of his father as a result of injuries received in World War I left them very poor. With the help of scholarships, Dubos was able to attend the Institut National Agronomique where he received a B.S. degree in 1921. After a brief period of service in the French army, he went to Rome in 1922 as assistant editor of a scientific journal published by the International Institute of Agriculture.

In the course of his work in Rome, Dubos dis-

RENE DUBOS

covered his primary interest in bacteriology and in 1924 resolved to continue his studies in the United States. A chance meeting in Rome with the scientist Dr. Selden Waksman led to his appointment as a research assistant and instructor in bacteriology at Rutgers University in New Brunswick, New Jersey. He took his Ph.D. at Rutgers in 1927 with a dissertation on environment and soil organisms, thus launching the studies in ecology for which he became famous. Although he later taught at many universities, including Harvard (professor of Comparative Pathology and Tropical Medicine, 1942–1944) and the University of Michigan School of Public Health (1961), Dubos spent most of his professional career at the Rockefeller Institute (now Rockefeller University) in New York City, which he joined in 1927 and from which he retired in 1971 as professor emeritus. His early research there was on the soil bacteria that cause such human diseases as dysentery, pneumonia, and tuberculosis in an effort to discover the therapeutic agents in swamp soil that would produce immunity from these diseases. Following the work of Alexander Fleming, Dr. Waksman, and other researchers in the field of antibiotics, in 1939 he isolated the active substance tyrothricin which was used in the treatment of various respiratory infections—"a pioneering achievement in immunology," as Paul L. Montgomery described it in the *New York Times.* Dubos' research in tuberculosis bacilli contributed to the development of the vaccine commonly used today and also to chemotherapy, the science of treating diseases with chemical reagents that are toxic to certain micro-organisms. In 1948 he was honored by the

°dü bô, rə nā´

American Public Health Association for his work at the Rockefeller Institute.

Dubos' unique achievement was his success in using his scientific research from the laboratory as the basis of a "humanistic biology," the study of the relationship of environment to health and the survival and well-being of the human race. A gifted writer, he made his highly specialized and technical knowledge accessible to a public increasingly interested in and alarmed about pollution. In more than a dozen books and over 200 articles and lectures, he helped awaken the public to the urgency of what he called his "theology of life on earth." In the enormous progress of modern technology Dubos saw the prospects for the extinction of human values and human life: "Man does not have any idea where he is taking himself, or the dangers involved." His vision of the future was ominous because, as he argued, contemporary science has slighted the study of the long-range effects of the new technology on human behavior and the quality of life. Pollution of our natural resources, noise, waste, ugliness are the most urgent problems of modern civilization: "In my opinion, there is no chance of solving the problem of pollution—or the other threats to human life—if we accept the idea that technology is to rule our future."

A humanist writing for scientists and laymen alike, Dubos called himself "A Despairing Optimist"—the title of a column he published for several years in the quarterly *American Scholar*. Although forever warning of the dangers of technology, he retained an optimistic faith, writing in *The Wooing of Earth* in 1980: "Yet I have faith in the future because I believe that our societies are learning to anticipate the dangers they will face and to deal with them preventively before irreversible damage is done."

Dubos received the Pulitzer Prize in 1969 for *So Human an Animal,* a book that influenced the environmental movement almost as much as Rachel Carson's *Silent Spring* (1962). Here once again he argued that we can change "our suicidal course" only by learning to deal with our environment and "by supplementing the knowledge of things and of the body with a science of human life." This, rather than "pure" research, Dubos wrote in *Reason Awake: Science for Man,* must become the business of science, and he urged scientists and laymen alike to work together towards a holistic science of man to create "new environments that are ecologically sound, aesthetically satisfying, economically rewarding, and favorable to the continued growth of civilization." In *A God Within* he stated that "the biblical injunction that man was put in the

Garden of Eden 'to dress it and to keep it' (Genesis 2:15) is an early warning that we are responsible for our environment. To strive for environmental quality might be considered as an eleventh commandment, concerned of course with the external world, but also encompassing the quality of life."

Some reviewers, professional scientists in particular, have objected that Dubos' writings are repetitious and simplistic, but even within the scientific community he was respected for the cogency and thoughtfulness of his views. "His mode of discourse is characterized less by anger than by a grave and luminous rationality," Spencer Klaw wrote in the journal *Natural History* of *Reason Awake.* Internationally honored for his work, Dubos received more than twenty honorary degrees and numerous awards for individual books, including, in addition to the Pulitzer Prize, the Phi Beta Kappa Award in 1963 for *The Unseen World. His Only One Earth: The Care and Maintenance of a Small Planet,* written in collaboration with Barbara Ward, was the basis for the United Nations Conference on the Human Environment held in Stockholm in 1972.

Described by an interviewer in 1971 as tall, energetic, and animated, Dubos enjoyed gardening and landscaping at his home in Garrison, New York. His first wife, Marie Louise Bonnet, whom he married in 1934, died of tuberculosis in 1942. In 1946 he married Letha Jean Porter, a laboratory technician with whom he collaborated in his book on tuberculosis, *White Plague.* Dubos died in New York City on his eighty-first birthday. A few weeks later, on March 6, 1982, the *New York Times* printed his last article, written from his hospital bed, in which he reiterated his profound faith "that life can be celebrated and enjoyed under the most trying and humble of circumstances." It was his wish, he wrote, that his life's work should be continued by the René Dubos Center for Human Environment which had been established in 1980 in Riverdale, New York: "The assumption behind our forums on energy conservation and land development is that by using the five *E*'s—ecology, economics, energetics, esthetics, and ethics—*homo sapiens* can create 'humanized' environments that are stable, profitable, pleasurable, and favorable to the health of the earth and the growth of civilization."

PRINCIPAL WORKS: The Bacterial Cell, 1945; Bacterial and Mycotic Infections of Man, 1948; Louis Pasteur: Free Lance of Science, 1950; The White Plague: Tuberculosis, Man, Society, 1952; Pasteur and Modern Medicine, 1960; The Dreams of Reason: Science and Utopias, 1961; The Unseen World, 1962; The Torch of Life, 1962; (with M. Pines) Health and Disease, 1965; Man

Adapting, 1965; So Human an Animal, 1968; Man, Medicine and Environment, 1968; Reason Awake: Science for Man, 1970; (with B. Ward) Only One Earth, 1972; A God Within, 1972; Beast or Angel? Choices that Make Us Human, 1974; Of Human Diversity, 1974; The Professor, the Institute and DNA, 1976; The Wooing of Earth, 1980; (with J. P. Escande) Quest: Reflections on Medicine, Science and Humanity, 1980.

ABOUT: American Men and Women of Science, 12th ed., 1972; Contemporary Authors, first revision series 5–8, 1969; Current Biography, 1973; McGraw-Hill Modern Men of Science, 1966; Who's Who in America, 1980–81. *Periodicals*—New York Times October 5, 1966; February 21, 1982; New York Times Magazine October 17, 1971.

DUGGAN, MAURICE (November 25, 1922– December 11, 1974), New Zealand short story writer. C.K. Stead, editor of Duggan's *Collected Stories,* writes: "Maurice Duggan was born in Auckland, New Zealand, of Irish Catholic parents. If one adds the fact that his mother retired in melancholy behind a closed door while he was still an infant, and died before he reached the age of ten, one has sketched a large part of what was to become his subject matter. He rejected the church but it remained a formative part of his experience. Nearly all of his male characters have Irish names and a verbal flair to match. His women are equivocal figures, objects of desire, but also likely to dissolve into identity with that image of the mother who seemed to reject him, or that of the hated stepmother who replaced her. And the scene, urban or rural, is always and unmistakably New Zealand.

"Duggan claimed to have left school at thirteen, though not, apparently, before acquiring some Latin in addition to more basic subjects. (He was later to attend university where he was a successful student, though he left without completing his degree.) His teen-age years were somewhat turbulent, and at least once he left home and lived on a farm where his love affair with the Maori farmer's daughter provided the subject of one of his finest late stories, 'Along Rideout Road that Summer.' A football injury led to osteomylitis and, at the age of seventeen, amputation of one leg. After two years on crutches Duggan was equipped with his first artificial leg which he records 'cost sixty pounds, weighed fifteen pounds' and was 'crippling above all to my vanity.'

"In 1939 New Zealand joined Britain in its war with Germany. Young men were flocking to join the forces. Deprived of the life of action Duggan took more than ever to books. He worked in a bookshop, and at the age of nineteen

MAURICE DUGGAN

made his first attempt to write fiction. In this he was encouraged by Frank Sargeson, then living in Auckland and already established as a fiction writer published in London by John Lehmann's Penguin New Writing and in New York by James Laughlin's New Directions. Duggan's first published stories, which remained uncollected during his lifetime, appeared in periodicals between 1945 and 1949. Two of these appeared in Cork in a periodical called *Irish Writing.*

"At this early stage in his career Duggan's problem was one of style. He was given to verbal elaboration, an Irish 'gift of the gab' combined with a (perhaps Catholic) sense of language as a kind of ritualistic magic, all fostered and encouraged by the dominating influence and example of James Joyce. Fiction as narrative did not much interest him (he was fond of quoting E. M. Forster's weary 'Yes—oh dear yes—the novel tells a story'). But he had to learn, as he put it, to 'murder his darlings.' His language had to be simplified, and the story called 'Six Place Names and a Girl' was the one which taught him an important lesson. Its subject, he later wrote, drawn from his own life, 'moved me strongly enough to force me away from what had become a habit of rhetoric. If it was to be strong it had to be simple; the language must be a focussing glass and not, as had been up to now the case, a sort of bejewelled and empty casket.'

"For the time being, then, Duggan had his subject: it was himself. He left New Zealand in 1949 and during two years in London, with visits to France and Spain, he wrote most of the stories collected in his first book, *Immanuel's Land,* meticulously worked, economically written evocations of an Irish Catholic boyhood in New Zealand.

"A hemorrhage in Spain followed by the diagnosis that he was suffering from pulmonary tuberculosis cut short Duggan's stay in Europe. He returned with his wife (Barbara Platts, whom he had married in 1945) to New Zealand, spent some time in hospital, and was not declared completely free of the disease until 1957. It was during this period that his only child, a son, was born.

"Meanwhile he had been trying to write a novel, still drawing on that childhood material which had served him so well in the stories of *Immanuel's Land*. Like Katherine Mansfield's Burnell family, Duggan's Lenihans are drawn direct from life. Like Mansfield, Duggan hoped to put together a novel using these childhood stories as its prefabricated sections. And like her he abandoned the project which nonetheless left him with some lengthier short fictions than he had previously published. From that point in his career, he says, 'I ceased to be subject.' This is true in the simple sense that he no longer wrote directly autobiographical fiction. But in the stories which followed the abandonment of his Lenihan family there is still a characteristic persona—verbose, New Zealand-Irish, ex-Catholic, wounded, uncomplaining, fatalistic, and tending to alcoholism—who is very close indeed to the character of the author.

"In 1960 Duggan was awarded the Burns fellowship at Otago University in Dunedin. He wrote of it afterwards as the best year of his writing career, and so it was. But that was only after months of sterile labor at a novel, 'Miss Bratby,' which he was to return to with admirable and misplaced persistence for many years before finally abandoning it. His letters of that year record the torment of working conscientiously at 'the cold corpse of Miss Bratby,' and then at last the exhilaration, puzzlement, and alarm at finding himself doing something quite different and unplanned—'bursting away' (as he described it) 'down another cul de sac in search of the ineffable.' This was the brilliant and Beckettesque novella, 'Riley's Handbook,' Duggan's most demanding, most difficult, and most rewarding work, one which ought to put him among the few truly significant writers of fiction in English in recent decades, but which is scarcely known outside New Zealand. In this short novel Duggan adopts the persona of the derelict painter, Riley, escapee from suburbia, marriage, romantic love, and his own reputation, dying of tuberculosis while practicing a strange barbaric kind of love on the body of Myra, who works with him as a cleaner in a pub, and heaping a

hatred which gradually reveals itself as thwarted love upon the memory of his mother who rejected him and died while he was still a child. Here Duggan returned from simplicity to elaboration of language, but with extraordinary vigor and unequaled inventiveness. First published in the periodical *Landfall* in 1961, where it occupied most of one issue, 'Riley's Handbook' was received in New Zealand literary circles with a silence that might have signified respect, puzzlement, or dismay; and though it must have been nearer than anything else he wrote to what might be called the center of his being, and drew on the very best of his literary intelligence, it was not an experiment he was encouraged to repeat.

"Another story written during his tenure of the Burns fellowship, 'Blues for Miss Laverty,' defines the other pole of his fiction. Though written with all of Duggan's linguistic skill and world-weary intelligence, it is a somewhat conventional picture of a lonely woman music teacher on the brink of alcoholism and despair, looking for 'a little human warmth,' a story that would not be out of place, for example, in the *New Yorker*. Reviewers who were silent, perhaps baffled, by 'Riley's Handbook,' lavished praise on 'Blues for Miss Laverty.' Did Duggan know he was being encouraged to do work of a kind which demanded less of himself? He must have suspected as much. He had said firmly in a letter during 1960 that he did not want to write 'conventional fiction.' It was this recognition that had turned him from 'Miss Bratby' to 'Riley's Handbook.' During the 1960s the temptation to do the easier thing and earn immediate recognition and applause must have been strong.

"Duggan's second collection of stories, *Summer in the Gravel Pit*, was published in London in 1965. It contained three stories reprinted from *Immanuel's Land*, two from the abandoned Lenihan novel, and four others including 'Blues for Miss Laverty' and what must be one of the most brilliant of his shorter fictions, 'Along Rideout Road that Summer.' The latter story adopts something like the Riley manner, but in a way which is less esoteric, less demanding on the reader. It combines the story of first love with the question of post-colonial identity—how, that is, does the mind educated to see the world in terms of European literary models, cope with a reality which is non-European? The story is both witty and moving, and marks a new sophistication in the New Zealand consciousness as it manifests itself in fiction.

"During the 1960s Duggan was employed in advertising, work he disliked and at which he was very successful. His tendency to alcoholism increased, and by the end of the decade his writing career seemed finished, though not before he had published another book, *O'Leary's Orchard,* containing 'Riley's Handbook' and two other novellas, one of which, the title story, displays a marvelous wry tolerance of human affairs (and especially the affairs of the sexes) that springs direct from experience.

"In the early 1970s Duggan made one final effort to return to his writing. He 'dried out' successfully and completed one new and original fiction, 'The Magsman Miscellany,' representing a quite new direction in his work, before being stopped once again, this time by a cancer which proved terminal. He died in December 1974 at the age of fifty-two.

"Duggan is remembered among literary circles in Auckland not only as a writer of extraordinary talent but also as a marvelous companion, a great talker—'a brilliant, tender, prickly soul, dazzling in his wit' as Molly Macalister described him; 'a shining man with too few skins.'"

PRINCIPAL WORKS: Immanuel's Land, 1956; Short Story One (stories by Diana Athill, Maurice Duggan, Maurice Gee, and C.K. Stead), 1961; Summer in the Gravel Pit, 1965; O'Leary's Orchard, 1970; Collected Stories (edited by C.K. Stead), 1981. *Fiction for children*—Falter Tom and the Water Boy, 1958; The Fabulous McFanes and other Children's Stories, 1974.

ABOUT: Contemporary Authors 73–76, 1978; Hankin, C. (ed.) Critical Essays on the New Zealand Short Story, 1982; Stead, C.K. *Introduction to* Duggan's Collected Stories, 1981; Vinson, J. (ed.) Contemporary Novelists, 1976. *Periodicals*—Landfall 97, March 1971; 142, June 1982.

DUNNE, JOHN GREGORY (May 25, 1932–), American novelist, journalist, and screen-writer, was born in Hartford, Connecticut, the son of Richard Edwin and Dorothy (Burns) Dunne. Dunne's father, a graduate of the Catholic University and Harvard University Medical School, was a surgeon who raised his family of six children in upper-middle class circumstances in West Hartford. The fifth of the children, Dunne was educated at the Benedictine Portsmouth Priory in Rhode Island, and at Princeton University, where he received his B.A. in 1954. After completing his service in the U.S. Army in 1956, Dunne came to New York, where he worked as a staff writer for *Time* magazine, and in the following year met Joan Didion (see *World Authors 1970–1975),* who had just come to New York to work for *Vogue.* They were married in 1964, and moved to California to work as free-lance writers. In 1966, they adopted a daughter, named Quintana Roo after the state in the Yucatan.

JOHN GREGORY DUNNE

During the 1960s, Dunne contributed to many national magazines, including *Life, Saturday Evening Post, Esquire, Atlantic,* and *Harper's.* In 1966, while traveling through east-central California, he stopped by chance in the town of Delano, where a grape pickers' strike, led by Cesar Chavez, was in progress, and was inspired to chronicle the strike in his book of the following year, *Delano: the Story of the California Grape Strike.* Although *Delano* did not attract a large audience, it was well received, and was the first of the books on Cesar Chavez and his union. Robert Coles called *Delano* "a quiet, well-written book that avoids rhetoric and the easy gratification of polemics in order to tell a story, and tell it fairly, coherently and with an appropriate touch of irony. . . [It] should certainly be read by anyone interested in what happens to people psychologically during a long and sticky fight."

In 1967, Dunne wrote a piece for the *Saturday Evening Post* on 20th Century-Fox and its studio head, Richard Zanuck, that expanded into a book-length project. For one year, with the cooperation of Zanuck, he was given free access to the studio, where he met and listened to the conversation of actors, directors, producers, agents, writers, and top executives. The work that resulted, *The Studio,* a behind-the-scenes account of the inner workings of the American film industry, was praised as a "prose documentary," using a deadpan *cinéma-vérité* style reminiscent of Lillian Ross' *Picture.* Henry Halpern, among others, noted Dunne's gift for recording speech, his "infallible ear for recreating . . . remembered conversation," but the effect of the book was perhaps captured best by Arlene Croce, in the *National Review,* who observed that Dunne's "picture people . . . walk through the pages like the grateful dead." Reading between the lines, one has the impression of an efficiently robotized world of "new" executives and their dependents.

Yet 20th Century-Fox later provided the financing for Dunne's film *Panic in Needle Park* (1971), which he adapted with Joan Didion from the novel by James Mills. The film, an account of the disastrous effect of a "panic" or drug shortage on a community of addicts on Manhattan's West Side, was shot entirely on location in the neighborhood of the West 70s described in the novel. The Dunnes' collaboration was followed by their film version of Didion's novel *Play It As It Lays,* for Universal, in 1972. During this time, however, Dunne found himself running dry as a writer, and in a depressed state gravitated to Las Vegas, which provided the milieu of *Vegas; A Memoir of a Dark Period. Vegas* purports to be a factual account of Dunne's nervous breakdown, but reads almost exactly like a novel. It was praised by a number of reviewers for its evocation of Las Vegas as "the ante-room of Purgatory," a setting in which are concentrated, as Peter Prescott observed, "the tattered, corrupt remnants of the American Dream." Prescott went on to remark that "Dunne's principal skill (he shares it with his wife, Joan Didion) is to create in a paragraph or two an extraordinary narrative of fear and anxiety, a vignette of useless life."

Vegas proved the turning point of Dunne's career, the work in which he found his special subject of alienation in a context of Irish Catholicism. His next book, *True Confessions,* rooted in the culture of Irish Catholicism, made him famous. He had previously been less well known than Joan Didion, but with *True Confessions,* their marriage became a partnership of celebrities. The novel, as one critic summarized it, "is about brotherhood, the loss of innocence, and the frailty of the human condition." Corruption-ridden Los Angeles in the late 1940s provides the background for this tale of two brothers, a policeman and a priest, who find themselves reflected in one another. The plot is complicated, and makes use of shifting panels of time, but the manner of the novel derives from the hard-boiled mysteries of Raymond Chandler—although with a difference, since it is Dunne's very modern dark humor that predominates. Dunne's sharp ear for dialogue and for shocking street speech were noted by many critics, who found *True Confessions* altogether the most striking and vivid novel of its kind to have appeared in years.

Quintana & Friends, published the following year, is a collection of Dunne's non-fiction pieces for various magazines, and was regarded as being modest and coming to life only fitfully. Dunne's second novel *Dutch Shea, Jr.* made a much stronger impression. This novel is often comic, but it is also harrowing in its revelation of the hero's inner life as he is driven ever closer to suicide. Many of the novel's critics found *Dutch Shea, Jr.* a gripping *tour de force,* and praised its dark humor. Other reviewers, however, objected to Dunne's cluttered canvas and gratuitous weirdness, his unconvincingly created hero.

Dunne and Didion read and edit each other's writing, and collaborate on film scripts in between work on their novels. They collaborated on the screenplay for *A Star Is Born,* starring Barbra Streisand, and the film version of Dunne's *True Confessions,* (1981). Called "the best known writing couple in America," and "the First Family of Angst," the Dunnes are a fixture of the Hollywood party circuit, with close friends that include Gore Vidal, Mel Brooks, Carl Reiner, and the film director Tony Richardson.

PRINCIPAL WORKS: Delano: the Story of the California Grape Strike, 1967; The Studio, 1969; Vegas: A Memoir of a Dark Season, 1974. *Novels*—True Confessions, 1977; Quintana & Friends, 1978; Dutch Shea, Jr., 1982.

ABOUT: Contemporary Authors, first revision series 25–28, 1977; Dictionary of Literary Biography Yearbook 1980, 1981. *Periodicals*—Book World November 12, 1967; Commentary May 12, 1978; Esquire July 1982; Horizon January 1981; Hudson Review Spring 1978; National Observer March 8, 1971; National Review December 9, 1977; New Republic December 2, 1967; May 10, 1969; March 9, 1974; Newsweek April 19, 1982; New York Review of Books January 26, 1978; New York Times May 3, 1982; February 3, 1974; Saturday Review October 29, 1977; February 17, 1979; April 1982; Time March 29, 1982; Vogue October 1, 1972; Washington Post April 30, 1982.

EATON, CHARLES EDWARD (June 25, 1916–   ), American poet and short story writer, writes: "I was born in Winston-Salem, North Carolina, where my father was mayor for many years, and I was educated in the public schools. Though my father was a businessman and politician, he could recite more poetry than any college professor I have ever known. My mother and sister were painters and my eldest brother, Clement, a historian. The intellectual suggestiveness of the household, in which I was the last of eight children, provided an atmosphere that

CHARLES EDWARD EATON

no doubt encouraged me to write poems at the age of seven or eight. I was always taught that some achievement other than material was the true purpose of life, and my father and mother gave me the blessing, unusual in America, of saying that they wanted and expected me to be a poet. Even at that early age, I thought of poetry as an organic part of life, as if a particular soma and psyche produced this special kind of fruit.

"At the University of North Carolina, I had the good fortune to study with 'Proff' Koch, founder of the Carolina Playmakers. He produced my first play, *Sea Psalm,* with the added thrill for a seventeen-year-old writer of Tallulah Bankhead's first cousin in the leading role.

"Education was one of the shibboleths of my family, as if life must not travel too lightly or too free of its own history, so Princeton followed and then Harvard. The philosophy of Plato, particularly the *Symposium,* had so persuaded me that this study could be beautiful as well as intellectually profound that I decided as a graduate student at Princeton to become a philosopher. Kant taught me, alas, that philosophy could also sometimes 'clip an Angel's wings,' but I endured and hastened on to Hegel, Nietzsche, and Bergson. Nothing but good, however, came of these rigorous as well as pleasurable studies, and whatever intellectual weight my poems and stories contain owes a good deal to the time spent at Princeton.

"Harvard was another matter—even more intellectually brisk, not to say forbidding, and somehow more pressed round with an exacting world. Harvard, however, could not make a Germanic scholar of me though I was awarded an M.A. in English, and the main thing it gave me was Robert Frost. The bell Gertrude Stein said rang only for authentic genius sounded the first time in his class, though most of its changes and best music came in sessions I spent alone with him in his apartment when he could let himself down from being a great man. Frost brought me to Bread Loaf, launched me, in fact, on my 'professional' career, invited me to record my poems at the Library of Congress when he was poet in residence, visited my classes in creative writing yearly in Chapel Hill, and, in general, kept a cool, mysterious—sometimes remote and starlit—eye on me until his death.

"Between Princeton and Harvard there had been a year teaching high school English in Puerto Rico, mainly conceived as an adventure supported by a job, establishing a life-long pattern of balancing intellectual pursuit with experience. This appetite for 'the world's body' versus the book found its fullest expression when, after teaching creative writing two years at the University of Missouri, I spent over four years as vice-counsul at the embassy in Rio de Janeiro. Stationed in *a cidade maravilhosa,* I traveled all over the country for the embassy as cultural relations officer, and Brazil made as lasting an impression on me as India on E. M. Forster. Thus a character in my first book of stories, *Write Me from Rio,* says: 'For through the years that was what Rio had become to me—the visionary South of all my snow-bound Northern yearning, the fructive center of the earth's body, the pith of appetite, the climate of blessed mornings and benign evenings, the luxuriant frontier of Adventure that blooms at the edge of Order.'

"In 1946, the University of North Carolina lured me home where I met and later married a graduate student of mine in creative writing who became my companion, secretary, and most astute critic, completing, along with my mother and father, the triumvirate of those who have influenced me most. I like to teach, but have found too long a stay in Academe claustrophobic. Five years at the university proved to be enough for a while, and my wife and I moved for a year, and stayed twenty-eight, to Woodbury, Connecticut, the village fictionalized as Meadowmount in my third collection of stories, *The Case of the Missing Photographs.* In a basic pattern of come and go between one nourishing environment and another, we spent winter and spring in Chapel Hill, finally settling there permanently in 1980.

"Summers spent on Cape Cod were always a glorious blending of life and work. In Provincetown, we met Karl Knaths, the American painter, the second man who rang a bell with me loud and clear. Like Frost in his outward simplicity, Knaths had a mind as elegantly sophisticated as Wallace Stevens'. When he died in 1971, my wife and I were inspired to write the catalogue and organize the memorial retrospective circulated nationally by International Exhibitions Foundation. After poetry and prose, painting has remained focal in my life.

"In this brief odyssey of education and art, I have touched on only a few salient points of departure and, perhaps, on some arrivals. Cézanne reminded himself every morning to be 'Sur le motif!' I also believe that my chief underlying drive has always been my work directed by an innate sense of action and assimilation, commitment and withdrawal, as, for example, Brazil, having yielded material for several books, led me back to the American South and my third collection of poetry, The Greenhouse in the Garden. All of my books explore different areas of my experience, though not specifically and certainly not in the contemporary mode of confession, and are my record of a world seen through a certain temperament. I do not have any rigid theories about art, have never followed any school, and though I have been called a modern formalist, I must insist upon the qualifying adjective. I do not admire minimal or reductive art, and believe in working powerfully and freely on one's own terms in a given medium to achieve a full-bodied affect. I agree with Coleridge that a work of art is 'an act of the imagination rather than the will,' and treat this faculty as equal in value with my interest in the world as it is. If I have an idol, an eidolon, an archetypal figure, it is that of the fully articulate man."

———

Charles Edward Eaton is the son of Oscar Benjamin Eaton and the former Mary Hough. He attended Duke University in 1932–33 before transferring to the University of North Carolina at Chapel Hill, where he took an A.B. in 1936. The Bright Plain, his first book of poems, appeared in 1942 as he was completing two years as creative-writing instructor at the University of Missouri and before he became vice-consul in Brazil. "I chart green regions on a barren place," the concluding line of the sonnet "Green Regions," early in the collection, seems to stand as the poet's first statement of intention. His strict control of meter and rhyme and a thorough respect for traditional forms are all surprisingly well-developed in The Bright Plain. There are careful echoes of other poets, as of Emily Dickinson in the vaguely menacing "Girls in White":

O look: the girls in white
With coils of yellow hair!
Where did they sleep last night—
In what house: in whose care? . . .

Someone should stop them now
Before the night comes on;
A stranger with somber brow
Waits beyond the lawn.

Appearing nearly a decade later, Eaton's second collection, The Shadow of the Swimmer, won the Ridgely Torrence Memorial Award of the Poetry Society of America. Many of these poems, such as "Topaz," show an increased faculty for analytical observation, an ability to heighten the moment:

This is a shaft of sunlight caught
Unmoted where it charged the stone:
A tension, stretched sheer-gold, so taut
That three dimensions seem but one.

And because he is so at home with metrical restrictions, he often attains extraordinary results by stretching them:

From bee-sting, spider-bite, thorn-prick,
    hammer-bruise, flesh learns;
Through lip-brush, hand-grasp, the body
    knows.
Nothing there is that touches but goes
Taut, limp, soft, hard, dry, moist, chills or
    burns.

"Who is this Charles Edward Eaton?" asked William Carlos Williams in a review in the Arizona Quarterly of The Greenhouse in the Garden. "He must be some older man whose name I have forgotten, who has lived to learn many tricks of the craft of the poem without succumbing to them." (Eaton was then just forty and hardly the senior figure in American poetry that Williams took him for.) "This Eaton," continued the master, "has LEARNED something without bitterness and incorporated it into his art. He has NOT yielded the essentials which to him are necessary, basic—how to eschew inversions of the normal phrase; he has learned that there does exist an American Idiom which in American mouths must replace the academic." Williams was even more enthusiastic about the poems themselves, "whose subtlety of invention, whose proud modesty, whose deft inventive use of formal qualities is gently infinite." May Swenson, writing in Poetry magazine, admired the book's structure: "An explosive force seems to have sustained the first three parts of the book, finding a relieving conclusion in the final part. . . . The effect is cumulative, the whole being almost like a diary or document."

The critic John Engels wrote of Eaton's "fine passionate intelligence" in a review in Poetry of Countermoves: "It's true that he sometimes writes poems in which one gets the impression they are full of 'work,' as if his intuitions were cliffs in a tropical forest, and he has had to build long and rather dangerous and frightening suspension bridges of words between them. But on the whole he is a skillful, perceptive, and sensational poet who works from an intense formal concern, and with a fine confidence and spontaneity." Then Engels offers an analytical explanation and evaluation of Eaton's technique: "[He] accomplishes [his] tricks usually in terms of a most conservative and orthodox structure, which, however, never seems merely conventional. Most of the poems begin descriptively, with a composition of place, an attempt to see something in the most physical aspect of its being, and to focus the mind on it. And there follows analysis and colloquy, the whole characterized and animated by an imagination always in evidence."

The deceptive conventionality of Eaton's structure and themes is a recurrent motif in the criticism of his poetry. "If Eaton's poetry," wrote Robert D. Spector in *Saturday Review* about *On the Edge of the Knife*, "with its use of rhymed stanzas, appears superficially to belong to a formal tradition, his long, free lines and sometimes brutal imagery and diction, pushing his feelings to their limit, suggest otherwise." Another reviewer, writing of *The Man in the Green Chair*, remarked that "Eaton continues to trap the unwary reader too quickly reassured by conventional rhyme and stanzas; for the tonal and thematic ranges of the poems, their very formal elegance, press home shocking revelations, unsettling human exposures. . . . Eaton's lyrics devastatingly unveil the strangeness within us all."

As a rule, Eaton has published his poems separately before drawing them together in volumes. They have appeared in more than a hundred periodicals, ranging from established magazines such as *Harper's*, *Atlantic Monthly*, and *Saturday Review* to such influential reviews and little magazines as *Sewanee Review, Southern Review, Salmagundi, Poetry*, and *Yale Review*. He and his wife, the former Isabel Patterson, whom he married in 1950 and to whom he has dedicated most of his books, now live in Chapel Hill. He lists his avocational interests as painting (his devotion to painting has resulted in two books of art criticism, one on Karl Knaths and the other on Robert Broderson), swimming, and gardening, all of which are major motifs in his work. "I do not belong to any school," he has said, "and I am neither a traditionalist nor extreme experimentalist. I believe in balance among the elements of poetry, and I am trying to speak in a contemporary voice about matters of lasting interest."

PRINCIPAL WORKS: *Poetry*—The Bright Plain, 1942; The Shadow of the Swimmer, 1951; The Greenhouse in the Garden, 1955; Countermoves, 1962; On the Edge of the Knife, 1969; The Man in the Green Chair, 1977; Colophon of the Rover, 1980; The Thing King, 1983. *Short Stories*—Write Me from Rio, 1959; The Girl from Ipanema, 1972; The Case of the Missing Photographs, 1978. *Other*—Karl Knaths: Five Decades of Painting, 1973; Robert Broderson: Paintings and Graphics, 1975.

ABOUT: Contemporary Authors, new revision series 2, 1981; Contemporary Poets, 1980; Critical Survey of Short Fiction, 1981; International Who's Who in Poetry, 1977–1978; Who's Who in America, 1982–83; Who's Who in the World, 1980–81. *Periodicals*—Arizona Quarterly Spring 1957; Choice December 1977; October 1980; Commonweal August 18, 1978; International Fiction Review 7, no. 1, 1981; Midwest Quarterly Spring 1981; New York Times Book Review July 22, 1951; May 12, 1963; Poetry March 1957; September 1963; Saturday Review March 31, 1956; December 26, 1970; Sewanee Review Winter 1973; Southern Humanities Review Fall 1979; Fall 1981.

* * *

*ECO, UMBERTO (January 5, 1932–   ), Italian semiotician and novelist, was born in Alessandria, a small city east of Turin in northern Italy, the son of Giulio and Giovanna (Bisio) Eco. He studied philosophy and literature at the University of Turin, earning his doctorate of philosophy in 1954. From then until 1959 he worked for Italian television while lecturing (1956–64) in his old department at Turin. Eco moved to Milan as lecturer for one year (1964–65) before being elected professor of visual communications at Florence (1965–69). After two years as professor of semiotics at the Milan Polytechnic, in 1971 he took up his present position as the first professor of semiotics at the venerable University of Bologna.

Eco published early in his career several works on specific historical, literary, and philosophical subjects, among which should be cited his first book, on the aesthetic problem in Thomas Aquinas (1956), a greatly respected work on the poetics of James Joyce (1966), a lighter but nonetheless serious study of the cultural significance of James Bond (1965), and an unusual translation-adaptation of comic books on revolutionary subjects from the People's Republic of China (1971). He is well known in his own country as a trenchant yet unideological critic of Italian society, and has for several years been a regular columnist and reviewer for the popular Milan weekly *Espresso*. Semiotics, the theory of signs, has gradually become the primary focus of Eco's academic work. Although he is now count-

°ā´ kō

UMBERTO ECO

ed among the best-known European experts in that science (or "scientific attitude," as he terms it), he is best appreciated as a generalist and a synthesist, at present a particularly important and influential role in view of the proliferation of highly abstract and analytical semiotic models in diverse fields. His most important book on the subject, *A Theory of Semiotics*, originated, he explains in the introduction, in 1967 as an article on the semiotics of visual and architectural signs, which soon became his first important book, *La struttura assente* (The Absent Structure, 1968), "offering an overall view of semiotics and containing a long epistemological discussion on structuralism." Although seven translations of the book appeared throughout the world, he found each attempt at an English version "unsatisfactory," and so decided "to rewrite the book directly in English." This "truly semiotic project" resulted in "a brand-new work" no longer having "anything to do with *La struttura assente*, and which, to prove this point, has been retranslated into Italian as *Trattato di semiotica generale* (Tractate on General Semiotics, 1975)." *A Theory of Semiotics* is a different book, filled with equations, diagrams, tables, and extensive notes, and organized with extreme philosophical rigor. It aims "to explore the theoretical possibility and the social function of a unified approach to every phenomenon of signification and/or communication." The book examines in considerable detail the semiotic content of such areas as language (formalized, natural, written, coded), paralinguistics, zoosemiotics (animal communication), medicine, kinesics and proxemics, musical codes, cultural codes, text theory, plot

structure, mass communication, aesthetic theory, rhetoric, and several others. Each of these fields or areas of study, of course, has developed its own semioticians, whose work Eco has apparently entirely digested and which he summarizes and uses. Though formidable in its organization, the book is written in lucid, almost simple English.

Eco's most influential work on textual semiotics is *The Role of the Reader: Explorations in the Semiotics of Texts,* a collection of nine essays, previously published between 1959 and 1977, covering various aspects of one of his primary areas of research, the dialectic between "open" and "closed" texts, and the cooperative role of the reader in textual interpretation. The title essay, written especially for the collection, tries to elucidate "the constancy of the theme of interpretative cooperation," though he insists he has much more to say on the subject: "Many of the present text theories are still heuristic networks full of components represented by mere 'black boxes.'" A collection of essays with more general semiotic aims is *Semiotics and the Philosophy of Language,* in which Eco examines the contributions of various philosophers to his chosen topics, which include "Sign," "Symbol," "Code," "Metaphor," and "Isotopy," as well as essays on "Mirrors" and "Dictionary vs Encyclopedia." He also includes a notable definition that insists yet again on the universality of his discipline: "A general semiotics is nothing else but a philosophy of language and . . . the 'good' philosophies of language, from *Cratylus* to *Philosophical Investigations,* are concerned with all the semiotic questions." In Rebecca Posner's words, he "advocates reconsideration of the whole history of philosophy from the viewpoint of semiotics."

In Milan in 1974, Eco organized the first congress of the International Association for Semiotic Studies, an organization with which he has been connected for many years. The proceedings of that congress, *A Semiotic Landscape* (1979), edited by Eco (with Seymour Chatman and Jean-Marie Klinkenberg), comprise an impressive array of 221 essays covering the range of interest in semiotics in all fields. Eco, appropriately, gave the summarizing address at the end of the six days of papers. "I do not know," he confessed, "if semiotics is a science. I prefer to consider it *a scientific attitude,* a critical way of looking at the objects of other sciences. I am not troubled by the suspicion that my science does not have a recognizable and duly registered academic physiognomy. We are not fishing for departmentalization."

After more than a decade of work to bring semiotics to the attention of the academic world,

Eco became internationally famous in the early 1980s as the author of a single novel, his only published work of fiction, *Il nome della rosa* (*The Name of the Rose,* 1980), a medieval murder mystery so engrossing and well made that it became the best-selling novel not only in Italy and several European countries, but in the United States as well. For any first novel to be so successful is virtually unheard of; the characteristics of this one make the feat all the more surprising: it is set in 1327 in a Benedictine monastery whose exact location is never made clear; it contains no significant female characters; it is filled with Latin, only occasionally translated; its many story lines turn upon fine points concerning heresy, fourteenth-century church-state relations, and Aristotelian aesthetics. Love of books, in its many aspects, permeates this first major novel by any semiotician. The story is therefore dense with significant detail, learned argument, and recourse to such older systems of knowledge as numerology, astrology, and gemology; these are lists of herbs and herbals, illuminators and illuminations, heretics and heresies, popes and emperors. "There is nothing more wonderful," writes the novel's narrator, an aged Benedictine monk, Adso, recalling events long past, "than a list, instrument of wondrous hypotyposis." The theme of the novel is expressed near the beginning to the narrator by the hero, an English Franciscan who bears a close physical and mental resemblance to Sherlock Holmes (his name is William of Baskerville): "I have been teaching you to recognize the evidence through which the world speaks to us like a great book. Alanus de Insulis said that 'omnis mundi creatura/quasi liber et pictura/nobis est in speculum'; and he was thinking of the endless array of symbols with which God, through His creatures, speaks to us of the eternal life. But the universe is even more talkative than Alanus thought, and it speaks not only of the ultimate things (which it always does in an obscure fashion) but also of closer things, and then it speaks quite clearly." Late in the story, the hero adds, "I have never doubted the truth of signs, . . . they are the only things man has with which to orient himself in the world." Affirming this, Adso closes his memoir with the rose in its pure beauty as the ultimate signification: "stat rosa pristina nomine, nomina nuda tenemus." A continuous suspense and delightful humor leaven this copious learning; Eco accomplishes the story, in Richard Ellmann's words, "with brio and irony. He has gone to school to the best models, Borges among them." *The Name of the Rose* won both the Strega and Viareggio prizes in Italy and the Médics prize in France.

The Name of the Rose also won Eco an international celebrity far beyond the reputation he had enjoyed as a scholar-philosopher. In 1984 Eco lectured to large audiences in the United States, speaking in only slightly accented English, with wit and sometimes mischievous humor mainly on how he came to write this remarkable novel. Recounting all this in a short book, *Postcript to The Name of the Rose,* he observes characteristically: "I began writing *The Name of the Rose* in March of 1978, prodded by a seminal idea: I felt like poisoning a monk. I believe a novel is always born of an idea like this; the rest is flesh that is added along the way." The added "flesh" included the reconstruction of his own encyclopedic notes collected since 1952 on every conceivable aspect of medievalism, the reading and rereading of medieval romances and chronicles ("to acquire their rhythm and their innocence"), and, probably most challenging, the choice of a narrative voice: "Adso was very important to me. From the outset I wanted to tell the whole story . . . through the voice of someone who experiences the events, records them all with the photographic fidelity of an adolescent, but does not understand them . . . to make everything understood through the words of one who understands nothing." Eco makes no excuses or apology for the obscurities of his novel, but he respects his readers. A humanist in the oldest and truest sense of the word, he is perhaps best represented not in this novel but in a collection of essays written between 1977 and 1983 and published in 1984 as *Sette anni di desiderio* (Seven Years of Desire). These record a deeply troubled time in Italy and in the world— political terrorism, student unrest, crises of belief leading to a "religiosity of the unconscious, of the vortex, of the absence of a center, of radical difference, of absolute otherness, of fracture." His ideas, Gilbert Reid wrote in the *Times Literary Supplement,* "are, as usual, very suggestive; he almost always succeeds in giving intellectual form to the ephemeral and chaotic events of seven crucial years. His command of creative taxonomy is the sign of a civilized and discerning mind."

Eco married Renate Ramge in September 1962; they have a son and a daughter and live in Milan.

WORKS IN ENGLISH TRANSLATION: Eco has done his own English language versions of *Theory of Semiotics,* 1976; *The Role of the Reader,* 1979; and *Semiotics and the Philosophy of Language,* 1984. Other English translations of his writings include his collaboration with G.B. Zorzoli, *The Picture History of Inventions from Plough to Polaris,* by Anthony Lawrence, 1962; *The Bond Affair,* by R. Downie, 1966; and the compilation, with J. Chesneaux and G. Nebiolo, *The People's Comic Book: Red Women's Detachment, Hot on the Trail, and Other Chinese Comics,* by Endymon Wilkinson (who translated the Chinese) and Frances Frenaye (who translated the Italian), 1973. William Weaver published his highly praised translation of *The Name of the Rose* in 1983; and of *Postcript to The Name of the Rose* in 1984.

ABOUT: Bondanella, P. and J. C. (eds.) Dictionary of Italian Literature, 1979; Contemporary Authors 77–80, 1979. *Periodicals*—America August 13, 1983; Choice July-August 1976; Christian Science Monitor November 29, 1963; Harper's August 1983; Library Journal November 1, 1963; May 1, 1976; April 1, 1983; Modern Language Journal September-October 1976; New York Review of Books July 21, 1983; New York Times June 4, 1983; June 15, 1983; New York Times Book Review December 1, 1963; June 5, 1983; July 17, 1983; August 7, 1983; Newsweek July 4, 1983; Science November 8, 1963; Scientific American December 1963; Time July 13, 1983; Times Literary Supplement December 21, 1962; June 15, 1984; October 5, 1984.

JACQUES ELLUL

*ELLUL, JACQUES (January 6, 1912–), French social critic, historian, and theologian writes, in French: "My career as a university teacher, which began in Montpellier in 1937, has been commonplace. I have been a professor of the history and sociology of institutions. But two facts about me are quite unusual.

"In the first place, nothing in my upbringing prepared me for such a career. My family was rather poor, but quite remarkable. My father's wealthy Serbian and Italian forebears had been ruined, and he became a minor office worker. My mother, who was also from an impoverished family that had known better times, was an artist, a professor of painting. I grew up in an aristocratic, but poverty-stricken milieu. My father, although frequently out of work, managed by enormous sacrifice to provide me with a secondary education. At seventeen years of age I was supporting myself. I became a university professor only by great effort. The second unusual fact about my career is that in 1940 I was dismissed from my post by the Vichy government. My wife and I had literally nothing to live on, and we led the lives of peasants in the country for four years. During this period I worked with the Resistance.

"During the years 1929–1940 I had a political and religious orientation. I was not brought up in the Protestant church, and although my mother was very pious she did not influence me. There was only a Bible in our house, which I read by myself. But suddenly, in 1930, I discovered Karl Marx, having begun to read *Capital* by chance. Because my father was then unemployed and we were all very miserable, I found in Marx an explanation for all injustices, and all

miseries. . . . My conversion to Marxism filled me with enthusiasm. Unfortunately, when I approached the Communist Party I discovered I had been much deceived. It was not at all the same thing! No communist that I met had read Marx. They were not interested in theory, and I was not interested in the kind of militant work that they proposed. I therefore did not join the Communist Party. I continued instead to work alone on Marx, and on the Bible! I was engaged in politics, in 1935 on behalf of the Spanish Republicans, and in 1936 for the Popular Front, but I quickly became disenchanted with politics. Some student friends invited me to join a small group of Protestant students and eventually I became converted to a belief in Jesus Christ, and became a member of the Reformed Church. But in terms of interpreting social and economic phenomena I continue to think that Marx was very useful. Since then my entire intellectual life has consisted of a sort of dialogue or dialectical argument between the words of Marx and the testimony of the Bible (I have leaned increasingly on theology to understand the biblical message). I did not closely attach myself to any traditional left-wing political position, and within the realm of Christian philosophy I have for the most part followed Kierkegaard and Barth. These are my roots. The books that I wrote between *Présence au Monde Moderne* in 1947 and *La Foi au Prix du doute* (1980) or *Changer de Révolution* (1982) have all been concerned with this dual interest of mine—in Marx and the Bible. I have written and published about forty books: six works of history, fifteen about the sociology of contemporary society (for example, *La*

Société technologique), and nearly twenty about theology and ethical studies (for example, *Ethique de la Liberté*).

"But there is another side to my life. I am not merely a professor (of history!) and a writer. It is clear that I have worked equally hard on behalf of two causes: the theories of Marx (you must change the world), and the demands of the Gospel (you will be happy if, knowing these things, you put them into practice). Although I have never wanted to take part in political action, I have striven for reform in several fields: in the first place I have attempted to change the French Reformed Church, on whose National Council, its governing body, I have served for twenty years; and secondly I have helped to found what we call in France "Specialized Prevention." This is a voluntary organization committed to helping those young people who are labeled 'maladjusted' or 'drop-outs' by giving them assistance to overcome their crises and problems, and to regain control of themselves. It is well known that our principal problems are drugs and violence. I have worked for these movements for twenty years. To give a point of comparison for the benefit of American readers, the social work that I do is not unlike that of Saul Alinsky. Finally, I am engaged quite deeply in the movements to preserve the environment and to ban nuclear arms, and for several years I have been the director of a movement for the preservation of the French Atlantic coastline. But in all that there is at the same time my basic objective of changing the fundamental elements of society while remaining a witness to Christian faith. I have tried to show how a Christian can become involved in worldly matters in order to express faith in Jesus Christ—that has been, and remains, the center of my life.

"These activities have swallowed up so much of my time that, now I am old, I regret that I did not devote enough time to my family. It is true that my wife and children have been sacrificed in this experience and my wife has paid the heaviest price for accepting this life. At the moment though, I have given up nearly all of my activities, but I am preparing several books: a study of the ethics of holiness and, in the field of sociology, an account of the effects of the information industry on many and society."

—trans. H. Batchelor

———

Introducing a series of extended interviews with Jacques Ellul published as *In Season, Out of Season,* Madeleine Garrigou-Lagrange asked: "Is he right-wing? Left-wing? Everyone ends up confused when they try to assign him a fixed position. He doesn't mind exasperating those who demand a label." Ellul confirms her impression in the first interview: "Basically—and perhaps most significantly—every time I have acquired a belief, in any domain, the first thing I have done is to conduct a criticism of this belief . . . When I meet someone with whom I am in instant agreement, I start by searching for points of disagreement." Ellul's statement is not perverse, however. Rather, it suggests, first, the complexity of a mind which rejects simplistic or dogmatic answers, and, second, a lifetime of rigorous intellectual self-discipline, thrusting him into direct confrontation with the major social and theological issues of our age. Ellul's sociology and Ellul's theology work together in what he calls "a relation of mutual criticism." His principal writings counterpoint each other: "That is why I can say that the reply to each of my sociological analyses is found implicitly in a corresponding theological book, and, inversely, my theology is fed on socio-political experience. But I refuse to construct a *system* of thought, or to offer up some Christian or prefabricated sociopolitical solutions. I want only to provide Christians with the means of thinking out *for themselves* the meaning of their involvement in the modern world" (his italics).

Although a handful of American readers had been acquainted with Ellul's writings since the middle of the 1950s, it was not until the publication of *The Technological Society (La Technique, ou l'enjeu du siècle,* 1954) in 1964 that his work became widely known in the United States. Appearing early in a decade of radical social change, the book was studied in college classes and debated in the press along with "futurologies" like Theodore Roszak's *The Making of a Counter Culture* and Alvin Toffler's *Future Shock* and the writings of Marshall McLuhan and Herbert Marcuse. But Ellul's work differed profoundly from all these. His close and subtle analyses of social phenomena, his erudition, and his sober, even fatalistic, vision of the future were not calculated to win popular enthusiasm. His critics found his work pessimistic—some conjecturing that his fundamentally Calvinistic Protestantism darkened his thinking—and disturbing. His admirers respond that he is misunderstood. The theologian Martin E. Marty writes: "Like the prophet Jeremiah, who considered his challenge a burden and who often reflected on the loneliness his apparent misanthropy caused him, Ellul sends out darts and jabs in his writings that reveal a loving and hoping heart in a time of abandonment."

The Technological Society is a study of the conflict between what Ellul calls "technique" and human freedom. Technique, he explains, is not synonymous with technology; it is "the totality of methods rationally arrived at and having absolute efficiency in every field of human activity . . . the organized ensemble of all individual techniques which have been used to secure any end whatsoever." His survey therefore covers not only the technique of economics but also of politics and human manipulation (i. e. education, propaganda, advertising), showing how this modern "technological society" gradually absorbs into itself all moral values and becomes autonomous and all-powerful. But Ellul offers no future "horror show" of the *1984* type. Although technique has become, like Frankenstein's creature, the monster that threatens its creator, the threat is more mythic than literal because, he believes, man still has the power to act and to transcend his pre-conditioned social environment. In the book which followed one year later, *Propaganda: The Formation of Men's Attitudes* (*Propagandes,* 1962), Ellul argues that modern man's need "to be able to face his condition" can be met by propaganda. While acknowledging the dangers of brain-washing, he looks to a more rational grasp of propaganda to give explanations and values that will help us to understand the vastly complex society that technique has created: "When man can be fully adapted to this technological society, when he will end by obeying enthusiasm, convinced of the excellence of what he is forced to do, the constraint of the organization will no longer be felt by him; the truth is, it will no longer be a constraint, and the police will have nothing to do. The civic and technological good and the enthusiasm of the right social myths—both created by propaganda—will finally have solved the problem of man." In his third major book, *The Political Illusion* (*L'illusion politique,* 1965), Ellul examined the relationship between technique and politics. Although he had earlier argued that technique inevitably creates a form of totalitarianism by absorbing and dominating all aspects of life, he does not envisage "a universal concentration camp" in the future. Rather, he foresees a "political illusion," a politicalization of life in which the state assumes power over all aspects of life and the populace accepts such rule because they believe that as voters they remain in control of the political process.

As a lay theologian (Marty calls him "the quintessential Protestant of his day"), Ellul works within the Judeo-Christian framework, rejecting materialism and pessimism alike. In an interview with David C. Menninger in 1973, he expressed his conviction that man still has the power to act: "And he can change the course of social evolution. Consequently, it's a kind of challenge that I pose to men. It's not a question

of metaphysical fatalism." His theology, like his sociology, demands a constant questioning and challenging of received ideas, but it remains staunchly Christian. He has concentrated upon the Old Testament, writing biblical commentary and continuing his research into natural morality. In *The Meaning of the City* (*Sans feu ni lieu,* 1975), his "composition in counterpoint" to *The Technological Society,* he sees the city as "the supreme achievement of man's technology," but traces its origins, as he does with almost every social and political phenomenon, to the Bible, here specifically to Cain (Genesis 4:9–17: "And he built a city . . . "). From the beginnings of history, Ellul writes, social man has confronted divine revelation: "the city is not just a collection of houses with ramparts, but also a spiritual influence. It is capable of directing and changing a man's spiritual life." Individual freedom has a central place in his Christian ethics, as he points out in *The Ethics of Freedom* (*Ethique de la liberté,* 1973, 1975), and "hope bears witness to us that there is a future." In short, Ellul finds in theology the power to transcend the seemingly deterministic and materialistic nature of modern technique: "When I encounter individuals in total despair," he told Madeleine Garrigou-Lagrange, "crushed by misfortune, by the lack of a future, by injustice or loneliness, I must transmit to them the reason I myself have found to hope and live." Therefore, as David C. Menninger writes of him in an article in *Review of Politics,* his primary purpose is "a concern for the preservation of certain values deeper, more traditional and more basic than rationalism, founded in liberty and hope."

Ellul's parents were Joseph and Marthe (Mendes) Ellul, and he describes himself as "a specimen of what people call a *métèque,* a product of the melting pot." He has spent most of his life in Bordeaux, taking his university degree there in law in 1931 and his doctorate in 1936. From 1944 to 1977 he served as deputy mayor of Bordeaux. He began his teaching career at the University of Montpellier, 1937–1938, and then at Strasbourg in Clermont-Ferrand, from which he was dismissed in 1940 for criticism of the Pétain government. After World War II he returned to the University of Bordeaux as professor of law in 1944 and professor at the Institute of Political Studies in 1947. He has received honorary degrees from the Universities of Amsterdam and Aberdeen and is an officer of the Legion of Honor and the Order of Merit. In 1937 he married Yvette Lensvelt. He credits his meeting with her as "the third great moment of my life"—the first having been his discovery of poverty in 1929, the second his religious conversion: "It was she who helped me take the step that allowed me to stop fleeing as I had done for years in the face of God's revelation."

WORKS IN ENGLISH TRANSLATION: Jacques Ellul writes in French but almost all his work is available in English translation, and many of his articles have been published in English-language journals. For a comprehensive bibliography up to 1980, including some nine doctoral dissertations on him, see Christians and Van-Hook's *Jacques Ellul: Interpretive Essays* listed below. Individual titles include: The Presence of the Kingdom (tr. O. Wyon), 1951; The Theological Foundation of Law (tr. M. Wieser), 1960; The Technological Society (tr. J. Wilkinson), 1964, rev. ed. 1967; Propaganda (tr. K. Kellen and J. Lerner), 1965; The Political Illusion (tr. K. Kellen), 1967; A Critique of the New Commonplaces (tr. H. Weaver), 1968; To Will and to Do: An Ethical Research for Christians (tr. G. E. Hopkin), 1969; Violence: Reflections from a Christian Perspective (tr. C. G. Kings), 1969; Autopsy of Revolution (tr. P. Wolf), 1971; The Judgment of Jonah (tr. G.W. Bromiley), 1971; The Politics of God and the Politics of Man (tr. G.W. Bromiley), 1972; False Presence of the Kingdom (tr. G. E. Hopkin), 1972; Hope in Time of Abandonment (tr. G. E. Hopkin), 1973; The Meaning of the City (tr. D. Pardee), 1975; The New Demons (tr. G. E. Hopkin), 1975; The Ethics of Freedom (tr. G.W. Bromiley), 1976; Apocalypse: The Book of Revelation (tr. G.W. Schreiner), 1977; The Betrayal of the West (tr. M. J. O'Connell), 1978.

ABOUT: Contemporary Authors 81–84, 1979; Christians, C. G. and J. M. VanHook (eds.) Jacques Ellul: Interpretive Essays, 1981; Ellul, J. Perspectives on our Age: Jacques Ellul Speaks on his Life and Work (ed. W.H. Vanderburg, tr. J. Neugroschel), 1981, In Season, Out of Season (ed. M. Garrigou-Lagrange, tr. L. K. Niles), 1982; Holloway, J. Y. (ed.) Introducing Jacques Ellul, 1970; Who's Who in France, 1981–82. *Periodicals*—Commentary August 1970; Review of Politics, April 1975.

ELMAN, RICHARD M(ARTIN) (April 23, 1934–), American novelist, short story writer, poet and journalist, writes: "I was born in Brooklyn, New York. I had an elder brother. My parents were named Edward and Pearl; they'd both been born in Russia and came here at age four. My father was a striver: a high school athlete and excellent in mathematics, he went through college by working at the Crucible Steel Corporation cleaning out the ovens in an asbestos suit. He became a chemical engineer and then a lawyer with offices in the Chrysler Building. For a while he represented a major labor union. Then something happened and he lost his clients and right about then I was born in the midst of a depression: the national economic mess and my father's personal career disaster.

"He did not recuperate from that until I was five or six, and World War II was commencing.

RICHARD ELMAN

We were lower middle-class then and ended up at war's end middle-to upper middle-class. Our first house in Brooklyn was opposite Ebbet's Field, and I used to watch lots of games from the windows of neighbors, and we often had Brooklyn Dodgers for neighbors.

"I did not like my parents. They said I was 'abnormal,' troubled, a pain in the ass. I did poorly in grade school and Midwood High School and went to college finally only through family influence: Syracuse was my father's school. I was initially admitted on probation as a business administration student. Much later I made some interesting friends at Syracuse, and even got to know the writer John A. Williams a little bit, and the painter Keith Sanzenbach, who committed suicide in California before his work was fully appreciated. I did very well there and came under the influence of some very good teachers and writers: Daniel Curley, Donald Dike, Leonard Brown, and decided I wanted to be a writer too. I met my first wife (the painter Emily Schorr) at Syracuse, and we fell in love and caused each other a lot of grief for a number of years.

"After Syracuse I studied with Yvor Winters at Stanford and published my first poems in *Talisman* and the *Paris Review*. I joined the army, served in the field artillery, and published my first writings in the *Nation* magazine about the army, under the pseudonym Erik Pearl. I also wrote and published a short novel then: *A Coat for the Tsar*. I worked in broadcast journalism until 1965 in and around New York City and wrote and published all the while. Since then I've been a writer and sometime teacher and published fourteen books of fiction, journalism, and poetry, and lots in magazines.

"I have two children: Margaret Ruth Elman, age eighteen, student; and Lila Neufeld Elman, two, toddler. My present wife, Alice Goode Elman, is associate professor at Suffolk County Community College in Selden, Long Island.

"The books of mine I like best are *Fredi & Shirl & The Kids, The Man Who Ate New York, An Education in Blood, The Breadfruit Lotteries, The Poorhouse State, Little Lives* (written as John Rowland Spyker), and *Cocktails at Somoza's.* I am a contributor to National Public Radio's 'All Things Considered' and *La Prensa Literaria* of Managua. Since 1963 I have been predominantly a free-lance person and my writing has been my chief source of income. It has subsidized efforts at fine prose and poetry, and sometimes I have had to write strictly commercial work under pseudonyms or anonymously."

Richard M. Elman, who frequently writes pseudonymously and anonymously, is one of a large number of writers whom John Leonard described in the *New York Times* in 1976 as "proletariat," because they are "serious writers who must hustle to survive" by teaching (Elman has taught at Hunter, Bennington, Columbia), journalism, novelizing screenplays, even from time to time clerking, but always writing seriously and professionally. Leonard suggests that Elman "is one of the 200 best writers in this country." He is certainly one of the most prolific. Among his pseudonyms, in addition to the Erik Pearl of his first novel, are John Howland Spyker (*Little Lives,* 1980), Delmas Hanks (*Smokey and the Bandit,* 1981), Michael Lasker (*The Gangster Chronicles,* 1981). With Paul Schrader he "novelized" Martin Scorsese's film *Taxi Driver* in 1967. He has also written under the names Michael Parnell, Varmut Eklund, and Kindell Oken (the last two being for privately printed poetry chapbooks titled respectively *Poems of My Middle Age* and *Bueyes que ye Amo* or *Oxen I Have Loved*). With subsidies from the National Endowment for the Arts and the New York State Council on the Arts, Elman published under his own name a chapbook of his selected poems, *The Man Who Ate New York.*

During his two years as a research associate at the School for Social Work at Columbia University in 1965–66, Elman produced *The Poorhouse State: The American Way of Life on Public Assistance,* a collection of interviews with welfare recipients living on the lower East Side of New York City. An angry and eloquent book, *The Poorhouse State* is an indictment of the welfare system which, Elman contends, humiliates and harasses the poor while perpetuating their poverty. The solutions Elman proposes to this problem—"to provide assistance without humiliation" through some system of direct grants or negative income tax—struck most of his reviewers as vague and unrealistic, but they acknowledged the value of *The Poorhouse State* as polemic: "If this admirable book does no more than educate a hostile electorate to the need for positive reform of the public assistance laws," J. J. Graham wrote in *Commonweal,* "it will be a unique contribution to literature in this field." In 1967 Elman continued his sociological work with *Ill-at-Ease in Compton,* a study of a Los Angeles community bordering on Watts. In Compton, a neighborhood rapidly turning into a black ghetto, he found evidence of the urban decay that is spreading in many other American cities. As in the earlier book, Elman drew his material from interviews with the residents of Compton, producing a lively, sometimes humorous but more often grim and pathetic study that sociologists dismissed as fragmentary and inconclusive, but general readers found moving and enlightening. "Raising many more questions than it answers," B. R. Boylan wrote in the *Saturday Review,* "*Ill-at-Ease in Compton* is a crisply written, thoughtful montage."

Elman established his reputation as a serious novelist with a trilogy of the Yagodah family, Hungarian Jews desperately struggling to survive the Nazi domination of their country during the early 1940s. The first of these novels, *The 28th Day of Elul* (the Hebrew calendar's date for September 12, 1939), is narrated by Alex Yagodah, who has escaped to Israel. Like other contemporary Jewish-American writers who were not personally involved in the Holocaust, Elman found himself re-assessing his identity as a Jew by reconstructing the horrors of the Jewish experience in his imagination. He did this with anger and bitterness, offending some of his Jewish and non-Jewish readers alike with a portrait that emphasizes the vulnerability of his Jewish characters. Descriptions of their sexuality, cowardice, and greed serve to underscore the horror of their plight. Elie Wiesel, in the *New York Times Book Review,* noted the "erotic digressions" but was generally much impressed with Elman's treatment of "the most important human and philosophical questions of our time." He praised the style of the novel, "which is vivid, argumentative, poignant and moving. Sparing no one, he [Elman] provides disturbing insight into the traumatic psychology of certain survivors—who, caught in the web of universal betrayal, are forced into total isolation. They are characters in search of their day." Joel Lieber wrote in the

Saturday Review: "Primed by an ironic, stinging intelligence, sections in *Elul* are nothing short of masterly."

Its first sequel, *Lilo's Diary,* is a short, fragmentary record of Alex Yagodah's cousin and fiancée who is betrayed by her own people for what they wrongly believe will be their saftey: "an extraordinary, angry and tender work of imagination," Clancy Segal judged it in the *New York Times Book Review.*With *The Reckoning,* the concluding novel of the trilogy, Elman turned to another member of the Yagodah family, the middle-aged businessman Newman. His diary chronicles the last days of the Jewish Hungarian community, his desperate efforts to survive, to keep his business going, to conceal from his wife his affair with a gentile mistress, and to make some moral sense out of the chaos of his life. The diary, which begins as a calculated ledger of his materialistic values, is gradually transformed into a record of moral bankruptcy. "The book is terse and faulted for its initial coldness, its lack of humor, its smallness in certain realistic aspects," Victor Burg observed in the *Christian Science Monitor.* Nevertheless, he concluded: "It is striking as a whole; and within its historical context, far exceeds the potential banality of its immediate circumstances."

In a complete reversal of style and subject, Elman wrote a candid and hilarious novel *Fredi & Shirl & The Kids: The Autobiography in Fables of Richard M. Elman* in 1972. "In writing these fables," he says in the foreword, "I have had to imagine myself, and those who knew me, when I was three, six, and twelve, etc. Not to say that I have tried to be untrue, I have wanted to be incontrovertible, and this time around I preferred laughing to crying." Making no attempt to conceal identities (he described the book to *World Authors* as "an accurate account of my life up to age 35"), he writes a near comic-strip caricature of bourgeois New York Jewish family life with himself as archetypal victim—of nagging parents, sadistic older brother, sarcastic teachers, sexual perverts, oversexed women. The language—or "slanguage" as one reviewer described it—of the book is often obscene, but it captures with remarkable fidelity what Albert Goldman described in *Life* magazine as "the rhythm, the energy, the mindless, manic excesses of those playground and street-corner tongues." The same manic mindlessness dominates his journalistic *Uptight with the Rolling Stones,* an account of a 1972 American tour of the Rolling Stones interspersed with their songs and impressionistic sketches of their hysterical fans. A more substantial result of Elman's work as a journalist was *Cocktails at Somoza's,* a "sketchbook" of his impressions of two visits to

Nicaragua. The title refers to the lavish parties that dictator Somoza gave for the foreign press during Elman's first visit in 1978. He returned a year later to report on the Sandinista overthrow of that government in what reviewers agreed was a lively eye-witness account.

Elman's poetry is collected in *Homage to Fats Navarro,* which includes poems from *The Man Who Ate New York.* These deal with a variety of subjects, ranging from a series of impressionistic poems on cities he has visited, "Streets of the Moon," to "Taking out the Garbage" ("My high depends on whether my sack / is half-empty, or full or bursting"). The language also ranges from street argot to standard English but is always strikingly fresh and original. Painting and painting imagery figure prominently in his work ("Its snowing pigments in Vuillard's garden"), and his simple domestic subjects are treated with subtlety and grace:

The cat in the sun can't hear
his purring for the leaves
nearby in the wind moving
over him with slow
soft cat-like sibilance,
as if these branches were caressing
his own stolid cattishness
with their own attentive
shadow pawings. Finally
its the scumbly spot
the cat makes when he moves away
from this place to hear himself
purr that is feline; this
haunch of dark green shadow
dims the crouching eyes
of branches about to spring
down from overhead.

("Late Afternoon with a Cat")

PRINCIPAL WORKS: *Novels*—A Coat for the Tsar, 1959; The 28th Day of Elul, 1967; Lilo's Diary, 1969; The Reckoning, 1969; An Education in Blood, 1970; Fredi & Shirl & The Kids, 1972; The Breadfruit Lotteries, 1980; The Menu Cypher, 1982. *Short stories*—Crossing Over, 1973. *Non-fiction*—The Poorhouse State, 1966; Ill-at-East in Compton, 1967; Uptight with the Rolling Stones, 1973; Cocktails at Somoza's, 1981. *Poetry*—Homage to Fats Navarro, 1978.

ABOUT: Contemporary Authors, new revision series 17–20, 1976; Contemporary Literary Criticism 19, 1981. *Periodicals*—New York Times February 10, 1970.

*EMECHETA, (FLORENCE ONYE) BUCHI (July 12, 1944–), Nigerian novelist, was born in Lagos, the daughter of Jeremy Nwabudike Emecheta, a railway worker, and the former Alice Ogbanje Okwuekwu. Her parents were Ibos from the village of Yaba, seven miles from the capital. Her father died when she was quite young, and for several years she was kept

°em ē´ chē tə

BUCHI EMECHETA

in a condition of virtual servitude, malnourished and cruelly treated, by foster parents. She was betrothed at eleven and married at sixteen; her first son was born the following year. By the age of twenty-two she had had two sons and three daughters.

Always a good student, despite the deprivations of her childhood, she was able to earn enough money to send her new husband to Britain to study accounting. With his parents' permission, she followed him there in 1962, and spent several miserable years in London caring for her children in a succession of one-room apartments that lacked both heat and hot water. Her husband was a failure as an accounting student, then grew violent towards her, and finally, in 1966, they separated. By then civil war was raging in her Ibo homeland, making return to Nigeria out of the question. With the aid of a British government grant, she took a B.Sc. degree in sociology from London University in 1972, while managing all along to house, feed, clothe, and educate her five children. She also began to write.

In the Ditch is a fledgling novel in the form of a diary, in which Emecheta describes, with sharpness and compassion, her experience of British society and its racism. Her first genuine novel, *The Second-Class Citizen,* was also the first of her works to be published in the United States. Like most of her best books, it is highly autobiographical: its story of Adah, a passionate, honest, and sensitive Ibo woman, is in almost every respect a reflection of Emecheta's own life. Her descriptions of the black immigrant experience in Britain are revelatory, as in the wrench-

ing account of the humiliating subterfuges Adah and her husband employ just to rent a single room in the seediest slum of working-class North London. But it is in the African sections, Adah's memories of her home village and the early chapters describing her growing up, that Emecheta's writing becomes richest, most resonant and affecting, with its constant undercurrent of compassionate irony:

The title "United Kingdom" when pronounced by Adah's father sounded so heavy, like the type of noise one associated with bombs. It was so deep, so mysterious, that Adah's father always voiced it in hushed tones, wearing such a respectful expression as if he were speaking of God's Holiest of Holies. Going to the United Kingdom must surely be like paying God a visit. The United Kingdom, then, must be like heaven.

Alice Walker thought *The Second-Class Citizen* an important and informative novel that "raises fundamental questions about how creative and prosaic life is to be lived and to what purpose, which is more than some books, written while one's children are banished from one's life, do."

Although she has remained a resident of North London (she now has an entire house for herself and her children), Emecheta has concentrated in most of her other fiction on Nigeria, on the changes impinging on traditional village life, and, most pertinently and memorably, on the condition of women in that new nation. Her heroines are extraordinary fictional creations: they invariably transcend the West African particularities of their stories, and they stand for unmistakably universal ideals. In *The Bride Price,* Aku-nna is thirteen when her father dies, and the family must leave their apartment in Lagos and return to Ibuza, their native village. There she becomes the virtual property of her father's brother, who permits her to continue her education only because she might thereby fetch a higher bride price—the money any suitor must pay her family. She falls in love with her schoolmaster, but as the descendant of slaves, he is considered an unsuitable match by her family. The lovers elope, and soon Aku-nna dies in childbirth, fulfilling the superstition that a woman whose bride price is not paid will die. Part of the novel's sharp poignancy lies in the constant contrasting of the heroine's image of herself as a modern young woman with the hidebound, impenetrable nature of the societal forces that govern her life. The book's quality, according to Susannah Clapp, "depends less on plot or characterization than on the information conveyed about a set of customs and the ideas which underlay them."

The Slave Girl, set in the 1940s, is the story of Ojebeta, an orphaned Ibo girl, who at the age of seven is sold into slavery by her older brother.

She lives for eight years in reasonable tranquility with her owners until one of them dies, then manages to persuade the bereaved family to let her return to Ibuza, her own village, where she becomes a Christian and meets her future husband, a worker in Lagos for a European company. Her autonomy, however, is still very much in question, as the novel's final sentence makes clear: "So as Britain was emerging from war once more victorious, and claiming to have stopped the slavery which she had helped to spread in all her black colonies, Ojebeta, now a woman of thirty-five, was changing masters." *The Second-Class Citizen, The Bride Price,* and *The Slave Girl* won the Jock Cambell-New Statesman award in 1978.

A particularly grim tale of repression is *The Joys of Motherhood,* which also explores the contrasts between Ibuza, Emecheta's archetypal Ibo village, and Lagos. This is the story of Nnu Ego, daughter of a proud chief, who has no identity in her society because she has produced no son in her marriage. She is sent away from her village to the capital to marry a man employed as a launderer by an English couple. Although she then produces several children, her new husband proves to be ineffectual and a poor provider; her life in the sprawling, confusing city is a saga of endless struggle. Her children, once grown, have no respect for the traditions she has spent her life defending, and her story's ending is unremittingly bleak:

She used to go to the sandy square called Otinkpu, near where she lived, and tell people there that her son was in "Emelika," and that she had another one also in the land of the white men—she could never manage the name Canada. After such wandering on one night, Nnu Ego lay down by the roadside, thinking that she had arrived home. She died quietly there, with no child to hold her hand and no friend to talk to her. She had never really made many friends, so busy had she been building up her joys as a mother.

The reviewer for *West Africa* remarked that Emecheta "looks at things without flinching and without feeling the need to distort or exaggerate. It is a remarkable talent. She is also humorous, against the odds in a story so basically grim." To John Updike, the novel "bears a plain feminist message. . . . As Chinua Achebe, in *Things Fall Apart* and its successors, wrote of the baffled and broken African fathers, so Buchi Emecheta writes of the mothers. . . . In this compassionate but slightly distanced and stylized story of a life that comes to seem wasted, she sings a dirge for more than African pieties. The lives within *The Joys of Motherhood* might be, transposed into a different cultural key, those of our own rural ancestors."

Emecheta's two most recent novels represent radical departures for her talent. *Destination Biafra,* which the publishers term historical fiction, has an ambitious scale: twelve tumultuous years of Nigerian political history, from independence in 1960 through the bitter civil war and its aftermath, are seen through the eyes of a young man and woman who are prime movers in the entire drama. Most critics felt that this rather short novel fell considerably below the quality of the author's previous work. The reviewer for the *Times Literary Supplement* wrote: "A writer whose reputation has been made with fictionalized autobiography must recognize that a leap to historical fiction, and especially to the large canvas of tumultuous public history, may not be easy and may call for a different apprenticeship." *The Rape of Shavi* is an even stranger novel than its predecessor, a futuristic political fantasy set in a mythical sub-Saharan country. A band of white male desperadoes, on the run from a nuclear disaster in Europe, arrive in Shavi, discover the country's wealth, corrupt the people physically and morally, then escape in their freshly repaired plane back to Europe. The Shavian king's son escapes with them as a stowaway, but is arrested on his arrival in Britain (where no catastrophe has occurred) and is imprisoned as an illegal alien. In prison he learns racial hatred and other forms of European corruption, then returns to his country to complete the ruin of his people. The bleakness of the tale is quite unleavened by Emecheta's characteristic irony; her writing here seems oddly awkward and hasty.

PRINCIPAL WORKS: *Fiction*—In the Ditch, 1972; The Second-Class Citizen, 1975; The Bride Price, 1976; The Slave Girl, 1977; The Joys of Motherhood, 1979; Destination Biafra, 1982; The Rape of Shavi, 1984.

ABOUT: Contemporary Authors 81–84, 1979; Contemporary Literary Criticism 14, 1980. *Periodicals*—Book World May 13, 1979; Christian Science Monitor July 5, 1979; Listener July 19, 1979; Ms. January 1976; New Statesman June 25, 1976; October 14, 1977; June 2, 1978; April 27, 1979; New York Times Book Review September 14, 1975; November 11, 1979; New Yorker May 17, 1976; January 9, 1978; July 2, 1979; Times Literary Supplement January 31, 1975; June 11, 1976; February 26, 1982; February 3, 1984.

ENDO, SHUSAKU (March 27, 1923–), a Japanese Catholic novelist, playwright, and critic, was born in Tokyo, but spent the formative years of his youth in Dalian, Manchuria. His most vivid recollection of those days is of seeing his mother practice the violin until blood streamed from her calloused fingertips. The

SHUSAKU ENDO

sternness of her resolve was only part of the spell she cast over her son; after she divorced her husband and took her two sons back to Japan with her, Endō's mother was converted to Catholicism and persuaded her children to follow her example. After a year of indoctrination, Endō was taken to be baptized. Though he claimed to know nothing of the meaning of the teachings he had been hearing, he obediently agreed to the ordinance. Endō wrote: "When the French priest asked me, 'Do you believe in God?' I guilelessly answered, 'Yes, I believe,' just as the other children had. It was like a dialogue in a foreign language textbook: 'Will you eat this candy?' 'Yes, I will eat it.' I had no idea what a momentous decision I was making. I could not begin to imagine the burdens that would be heaped upon me later as a consequence of uttering that simple reply."

Sometime after his graduation from middle school in 1940, Endō began to feel doubts about the Christianity he had so blithely accepted as a child. Japan was asserting its territorial claims in China and Southeast Asia, and attitudes toward foreigners and their religious practices were deteriorating. Sensing keenly at this time that the Christianity which his mother had thrust upon him was very much like "a suit of Western clothes inadequately tailored to my Japanese body," Endō's attendance at Mass dropped off sharply. It was several years before Endō would conclude that stripping off that Western-style clothing would leave him spiritually naked, and that his task as an individual, as a devoted son to his mother, and as a writer would be to re-tailor his adopted wardrobe to fit the contours of his Japanese body.

In 1943, after failing nine successive entrance examinations, Endō was finally admitted to Keiō University, where he fell under the sway of a Catholic philosopher and began reading Maritain and Rilke. He was first impressed at this time by the contrasts between the European and Japanese cultural and religious climates. Although he was called up for a conscription physical in 1945, Endō was ruled unfit for active duty because of a history of pleurisy. That same year he was accepted into the Department of French Literature at Keiō, and began composing essays which examined the philosophical distinctions between East and West; the first of these, "Kamigami to kami to" (The gods and God, 1947), was his lifelong literary theme in a nutshell—the monotheistic heritage of Catholicism struggling to set down roots in the pantheistic soil of Japan.

On June 5, 1950, Endō and three other young Japanese set sail for France as the first Japanese to study abroad after World War II. Endō spent two and a half years at the University of Lyons, studying French Catholic literature and reaffirming his belief that thick walls separated Christian and non-Christian societies. Though intellectually he felt very close to writers such as Mauriac and Bernanos, emotionally he still had a sense of distance from them and the literary worlds they created, as well as from the spiritual traditions of his native land.

Chronic pulmonary problems forced Endō to terminate his studies and return to Japan in 1953. He quickly established himself as an important young critic and published his first fiction, "Aden made" (As far as Aden), in 1954. This was followed by a short novel, *Shiroi hito* (White Men, 1954), which dealt graphically with betrayal and faith in the French Resistance during the German occupation. This work received the prestigious Akutagawa Prize and encouraged Endō to compose a companion work set in Japan, *Kiiroi hito* (Yellow Men, 1955), which contrasts the European Christian conscience with what Endō classifies as a Japanese "numbness to sin and guilt." These questions of conscience are further explored in his first important novel, *Umi to dokuyaku* (The Sea and Poison, 1957), and the 1959 work *Kazan* (*Volcano*).

In 1960 Endō again traveled to Europe to do research, but the recurrence of health problems forced him back to Japan, where he remained in a hospital for nearly three years and underwent three major operations, culminating in the removal of one entire lung. His subsequent writings, however, were distinguished by the introduction of new images, new themes, and a shift in focus from the barriers separating East and West to the potential for the creation of a new Christian ethic in Japan. The first glimmerings of this approach may be found in the short story collection *Aika* (Elegies, 1965), but the full literary exposition of Endō's belief in the universality and adaptability of Catholicism did not appear until 1966, with the publication of Endō's internationally acclaimed novel, *Chimmoku* (*Silence*). This work established Endō's reputation in Japan as a serious thinker and writer, and its translation into a score of foreign languages has earned it a permanent place in world literature.

Since the publication of *Silence*, Endō has maintained a hectic schedule of writing and has combined his literary efforts with a variety of other pursuits. In 1968 he established the largest amateur theatrical troupe in Japan; he served as editor of the important literary journal, *Mita Bungaku*; he was appointed a member of the selection committee for the Akutagawa Prize, and also serves as a permanent director of the Bungeika Kyōkai (the Literary Artists' Association) and the Japan PEN Club. He has received a wealth of literary prizes in both Japan and abroad—his *Iesu no shōgai* (*A Life of Jesus*, 1973) received the Dag Hammarskjold Prize for literature; a companion work, *Kirisuto no tanjō* (The Genesis of the Christ, 1977) was honored with the Yomiuri Literary Prize; and his most recent serious novel, the masterful *Samuri* (*The Samurai*, 1980), was given the prestigious Noma Prize in Japan and earned Endō membership in the Geijutsuin, Japan's Art Academy. Most recently Endō's studies have combined a continuing interest in Japan's seventeenth century "Christian era" with a new absorption in Jungian psychological analysis of human behavior. Translations of his writings have appeared in England, the United States, seven European countries, Scandinavia, Russia, Brazil, Mexico, and Israel, and critical interest in his work has risen in response. Graham Greene, to whom Endō is often superficially compared, has called him "the Japanese writer most approachable for Western readers," while Francis King has described him as "one of the half-dozen leading novelists of the post-war period." Readers have expressed admiration for the surface simplicity of novels that deal with profound moral problems, and Irving Howe has suggested that Endō is "surely one of the most accomplished writers now living in Japan or anywhere else."

An examination of Endō's major writings supports these views and indicates a definite maturation in ideas and literary techniques. The early works, such as *Yellow Man* and *Volcano*, are interesting as problem novels which examine the moral gaps between the European and Japanese

traditions. Endō is ruthless in his condemnation of the Japanese spiritual conscience, which he describes as responsive to direct social pressures but insensitive to any metaphysical considerations. *The Sea and Poison* is particularly scathing, drawing its materials from a series of inhumane operations performed on captured American pilots by doctors at a Kyushu University during World War II. In this novel, Endō is not interested in condemning the individuals involved in the vivisections; rather as a novelist he is drawn to the excesses of human cruelty that stem from a social ethic devoid of a concrete image of God or a sense of individual guilt. *The Sea and Poison* is a stirring work, effectively told from a variety of narrative viewpoints, but the characters tend to be drawn monochromatically and to lack an existence independent of the moral framework to which Endō has assigned them. In fact, according to the critic Saeki Shōichi, most of these early works "lack the dull resiliency of human flesh," and the characters "howl and suffer submissively as they writhe beneath the burden of the themes that have been foisted upon them."

These literary flaws are first corrected in the *Elegy* collection of stories published after Endō's extended hospitalization. Short works such as "Watashi no mono" (My Belongings) and "Yonjussai no otoko" (A Forty-Year-Old Man) from that collection reveal new and significant aspects of Endō's thought—an emphasis on isolated acts of compassion, and the moral consequences of each individual action. The stern, paternal shadings of Western Christianity begin to take on muted tones in his writings, as Endō pursues the image of a maternal, forgiving Christ who will accept human beings in their weakened, sinful state so long as their shortcomings are compensated by a willingness to love others and share in their private burdens.

The most important literary manifestation of this new motif is the apostate Kichijirō, who weaves his way throughout the narrative of *Silence*. Though in Western terms Kichijirō is painted as a Judas figure, to Endō this character's human devotion to the suffering martyrs renders him worthy of a painful but efficacious salvation. When the stern, demanding priest Rodrigues is finally brought down to Kichijirō's level by the tortures of the Japanese authorities, he recognizes that human compassion is more important than fidelity to institutionalized religion, and his "apostasy" is depicted rather as a personal victory. The compelling persuasiveness of Endō's smoothly fashioned plot in *Silence* allows the reader to share in Rodrigues' torment and to relish his final, internalized salvation.

The supremacy of private over institutionalized faith is reiterated in *The Samurai,* which contrasts the active, manipulative Father Velasco with the passive, manipulated Japanese vassal Hasekura. The novel is an intricate, finely honed study in contrasts between East and West, belief and betrayal, pride and humility. Based, like *Silence,* on actual historical occurrences in the seventeenth century, *The Samurai* follows the steps of a trade embassy dispatched to Mexico and Rome by a powerful Japanese warlord. Velasco, who leads the mission, is determined to use this voyage to showcase Western material and spiritual supremacy, while the unsuspecting Hasekura, like Endō, is persuaded to accept Christianity as an expedient. With great delicacy, Endō examines the faint, subtle stirrings of true faith within the heart of this Japanese ambassador, a faith quite unlike that of the overbearing Velasco, yet in the end no less sincere.

Endō has found a variety of literary means to present his views of faith and responsibility. He has written many historical studies, such as *Tetsu no kubikase* (The Iron Pillory, 1976), an interpretive biography of the Christian warrior Konishi Yukinaga; and *Jū to jūjika* (The Musket and the Cross, 1979), an account of the first Japanese seminary and the fate of its graduates. He has also produced a wide array of humorous "entertainments," each of which manages to comment upon some aspect of the Japanese moral ethic. The best of these works include *Obakasan* (*Wonderful Fool,* 1959), *Watashi ga suteta onna* (The Girl I Left Behind, 1963), and *Kuchibue o fuku toki* (*When I Whistle,* 1974). Whatever forms his writings have taken, Endō has remained dedicated to the theme he expounded in his first published essay, "The gods and God." With his roots firmly planted in Japanese soil, which grows thick with a myriad of clamoring gods, Endō continues to hack away at the undergrowth and seeks to catch a clear glimpse of the God he has been unable to cast away. His literary chronicles of that struggle are unique in the history of modern Japanese literature, and provide Endō's many Western readers with a new perspective on their own spiritual roots.

WORKS IN ENGLISH TRANSLATION: *Silence* was translated by William Johnston, 1969; *The Golden Country* and *The Wonderful Fool* by Francis Mathy in 1970 and 1974 respectively. Michael Gallagher translated *Volcano* and *A Life of Jesus* in 1978. In recent years Endō's principal translator has been Van L. Gessel—*When I Whistle,* 1979; *The Samurai,* 1982; and a collection of eleven short stories, *Stained Glass Elegies,* 1984.

ABOUT: Contemporary Authors, first revision series 29–32, 1978; Encyclopedia of Japan, 1984. Updike, J., Hugging the Shore, 1983. *Periodicals*—Monumenta Nipponica Winter 1982; New York Review of Books February 19, 1981; November 4, 1982; New York Times Book Review December 26, 1982; Times Literary Supplement October 26, 1984.

ENGEL, MARIAN (RUTH PASSMORE)

(May 24, 1933–), Canadian novelist and short story writer, writes: "I was born in Toronto. My father was a high school teacher—auto mechanics, drafting, sheet metal. Because of the way things were in the depression, we moved a lot: from Toronto to Thunder Bay to Brantford, Galt, Sarnia, all in Ontario. Sometimes we lived in our trailer because of housing shortages. I had a sister six years older—still do, thank goodness.

"I have always loved books; and when I was about eleven I started to send things to the Sunday School papers, and then to the *Seventeen* magazine contests; sometimes got a prize. In those days it didn't do to mention you were Canadian. But I was—came from a family of nationalists. Father was a pilot in the first world war. Mother was the lieutenant-governor's secretary before she married. She had a typewriter. I was good at school and not much else. I worked summers as a newspaper reporter while I was at McMaster University; went to McGill in Montreal to do an M.A. under Hugh MacLennan, the famous Canadian novelist. Then I taught at Montana State at Missoula for a year. Discovered I hated mountains. I became Miss Passmore the Geography at the Study School in Montreal.

"In 1960 I got a Rotary Foundation fellowship to study in France. I thought I might start a Ph.D. but instead I worked on a television play and a novel, became bilingual, read Proust when I was in bed with jaundice in a room M.F.K. Fisher had inhabited the year before me. I took up with an old McMaster friend, Howard Engel, and we went to England where we could get jobs and a marriage license. Then we went to Cyprus. I mostly worked as a translator in the credit business, but I taught a bit too and I was always writing, writing, writing. We returned to Canada in 1963 and settled in Toronto, where I wrote a publishable book at last, *No Clouds of Glory.* I also had twins, William and Charlotte. And more books.

"Somewhere in there I got divorced. I've also written hundreds of articles, short stories and book reviews, won the City of Toronto book prize, been a library trustee for Toronto, been Chairman of the Writers' Union of Canada and been made an Officer of the Order of Canada.

"I'm tired.

MARIAN ENGEL

"I've sold my archives to McMaster University at Hamilton Ontario. My alma mater. Canadians like my work, and it's nice to be liked. I don't sell as well in the US and UK, where Canadian is a kind of dirty word anyway; and I find that a book that does well in the UK will fail in the US. You can't win them all.

"I've been writer-in-residence at a couple of universities and taught creative writing at the University of Alberta at Edmonton. I'm a stickler about grammar, which my students don't like, but I belong to that dying generation who routinely took three languages as well as English and it bothers me when students can't take their prose apart and reassemble it.

"I write less than I used to because when sales are so poor there's no point in pushing yourself into martyrdom, but I still enjoy making sentences and trying to stack them up in a book. Some day I want to write about theories of paradise. Some day I want to write a poem. Some day I will finish the novel I am working on. Some day I will mail this. . . . "

Marian Engel is the daughter of Frederick Searle Passmore and Mary Fletcher Passmore. She took her B.A. from McMaster in 1955 and her M.A. from McGill two years later. In addition to the teaching jobs she mentions above, she was also, in 1963, a teacher at St. John's School, run by the Royal Air Force, in Nicosia, Cyprus. Most of her novels are slender, with a lapidary, concentrated quality of language that heightens the effects of her rapid narratives and revealing dialogue. "Her terse sentences," according to the entry on her in the *Supplement to the Oxford Companion to Canadian History and Literature,* "have the force of explosives that shatter Canadian middle-class values and the fantasied escape route—a romantic life in Europe." An important theme in her work is the imperative need for an authentic identity—personal, social, political, and national.

Each of Engel's novels focuses on a single woman, whom the reader comes to know thoroughly. Her heroines are tough-minded and intensely self-aware, often with a rueful sense that their lives are flawed or even failed. Each woman is a distinct type; George Woodcock saw them collectively as "a gallery of feminine roles in late 20th-century western society. *No Clouds of Glory* presents the woman as academic, challenging man in the career world; *The Honeyman Festival* the woman as quintessential earth mother; *Monodromos* the woman as divorced wife moving back through surrogate sisterhood to renewed individuality; *Joanne* the woman as wife and mother finding her way through the ruins of a failed marriage; *Bear* the woman as humanity recognizing and seeking unity with its animal nature; *The Glassy Sea* the woman as nun—humanity uniting reluctantly with its angelic nature."

Doris Grumbach, in her review of the widely acclaimed *Bear,* remarked generally on the futility "in précis or paraphrase to attempt to capture the persuasive power of Marian Engel's fiction." Woodcock described *Bear* and *The Glassy Sea* as "written with a brilliance of craftsmanship so sustained and so spare that they emerge as marvellously luminous and self-sufficient artifacts." In *Bear* we meet Lou, a lonely, unhappy young bibliographer assigned one summer to evaluate a library and estate on Cary Island in northern Ontario, an area she had known as a child. Chained behind the house is an enormous bear, which she must look after and whose power and significance she begins to sense immediately. "From this point on," wrote Grumbach, "the narrative is pure magic, an alchemical transformation from fact into folk tale and the rich areas of the human psyche, a metamorphosis so subtle that its sexual shock is completely acceptable to us." Lou comes to describe her love for the animal in explicitly religious terms: "She felt him to be wise and accepting. She felt sometimes that he was God." In the end, after being inadvertently wounded by the bear, who is taken away into the wilderness by his Indian friends, Lou feels reborn; she is able on leaving the island to affirm her humanity.

The Glassy Sea is the story of Marguerite He-ber, an Anglican nun who renounces her vows for an unhappy marriage and a tragic motherhood but eventually returns to the convent. "One is fiercely concentrated on Marguerite," wrote one reviewer, "a symbol of all who triumph over chauvinism and cruelty. She is unforgettable." Woodcock, who praised the novel for "the compassion, the lyricism, the resonance of prose," described its theme as "the search for spiritual perfection. . . . Sister Mary Pelagia has sought faith through the aesthetic route, the way of taste, and found herself forced to return and relive the secular life; when she reenters the religious order, it is not even with manifest faith, but with a plain sense of duty."

Engel made an energetic attempt at comic relief with *The Year of the Child*, about the redevelopment of a rundown Toronto residential area and the zany characters who live there. At the book's center is Harriet Ross, mother of many, who listens to her neighbors' complaints with unflagging patience. Doris Cowen, though holding that Engel "misses the rollicking good cheer, the effect of outrageous farce that she seems to be aiming at," nevertheless felt that the novelist "is not, and never can be, frivolous. Her humor keeps bringing us back to the difficulties of reality. . . . The heart of the book—the story of Harriet and her children—is thoroughly coherent, unaffected by the constellation of subplots around it." Leo Simpson wrote that the novel "manages the fusion of laughter and reality superbly, sparkles wittily throughout, and contains an earnest volume's worth of truth about the way lives are lived by women and children."

Engel has been writer in residence at the University of Alberta (1978–79) and the University of Toronto (1980–81), and has received the Rotary Foundation Fellowship (1961) and the Governor-General's Award for literature (1976).

PRINCIPAL WORKS: *Novels*—No Clouds of Glory, 1968 (reprinted as Sarah Bastard's Notebook, 1974); The Honeyman Festival, 1970; Monodromos, 1973 (U.K. One Way Street, 1975); Joanne, 1975; Bear 1976; The Glassy Sea, 1978; The Year of the Child, 1981 (Canada, Lunatic Villas). *Short stories*—Inside the Easter Egg, 1975. *Juvenile*—Adventure at Moon Bay Towers, 1974; My Name Is Not Odessa Yarker, 1977.

ABOUT: Contemporary Authors, first revision series 25–28, 1977; Contemporary Novelists, 1982; Literary History of Canada 3, 1973; Oxford Companion to Canadian History and Literature, 1983. *Periodicals*—Books in Canada April 1981; Harper's October 1976; Library Journal July 1976; New Statesman April 1, 1977; New York Times Book Review August 15, 1976; Quill & Quire April 1981; Saturday Review September 18, 1976; Times Literary Supplement April 1, 1977.

*ENQUIST, PER OLOV (September 23, 1934–   ), Swedish novelist, dramatist, critic, and essayist, was born in the village of Hjoggböle in the province of Västerbotten in northern Sweden. His father, Elof Enquist, a longshoreman and lumberjack, died six months later, and the author was raised by his mother, Maja Lindgren Enquist, a schoolteacher interested in religion. Attending school in nearby Skellefteå, he passed his *studentexamen* in 1954 and between 1955 and 1964 studied at the University of Uppsala, where he completed an M.A. and a thesis on the crime novels of Thorsten Jonsson. Throughout his youth he was interested in sports and in college competition won a championship in the high jump.

Enquist worked as a literary critic for a number of Swedish newspapers including *Uppsala Nya Tidning* (1960–63); *Svenska Dagbladet* (1966–67); *Expressen* (1967–); and various other papers and journals, including *Aftonbladet*. In 1966 he also edited an essay anthology entitled *Sextitalskritik* (Criticism of the Sixties). Through the 1970s and into the eighties, his voice was among the most articulate heard in debates on literature and politics, and he assumed an increasingly important role in Swedish cultural politics. From 1969 to 1973 he served as a member of the National Arts Council and of the Radio Board, and he has also been on the board of directors of the Swedish Authors' Society.

It was primarily as a novelist that Enquist established his literary reputation, attracting attention with a number of early novels including *Kristallögat* (The Crystal Eye, 1961), a psychological study of a young woman; *Färdvägen* (Thoroughfare, 1963), a kind of picaresque novel influenced by the new French novel; *Magnetisörens femte vinter* (The Magnetizer's Fifth Winter, 1964), a novel based on the life of Frans Anton Mesmer, the founder of mesmerism, but with its exploration of seduction and mass appeal offering contemporary political parallels; the experimental novel *Hess* (1966), a surrealistic depiction of the consciousness of a modern European, writing a dissertation on the Nazi leader Rudolf Hess. The latter works placed Enquist among the most interesting new writers, winning him the BLM Prize in 1964 and compliments from such leading critics as Bengt Holmqvist, Lars Gustafsson, Lars-Olof Franzén, and Karl Vennberg.

In 1968 his work *Legionärerna* (*The Legionnaires*) acquired international acclaim, breaking new ground for the documentary novel. It received the Nordic Council Prize in 1969 as well as other awards and was translated into some ten languages. The novel is the author's exhaustive investigation of a classic moral dilemma

°en′ kwist, pâr

PER OLOV ENQUIST

in recent political history: Sweden's extradition of 167 Baltic refugees in 1946. Mainly from Latvia and Estonia, the men had been drafted into the German army during the war; now, as Russian troops approached, they fled to Sweden for asylum, afraid of the consequences if they returned home. They were interned for eight months and finally put on board a Soviet ship. Enquist's treatment of the story features both "objective" documentation and more subjective elements, as the author explores his own motivation for investigating the case. In reviewing the work for the *Observer*, Anthony Thwaite called it "a masterpiece of concentration, range, and involvement."

From 1970 to 1971 Enquist lived in West Berlin, and Central Europe is the setting of his next novel, the first of two dealing with sports. *Sekonden* (The Second, 1971) tells the story of a world-class Swedish hammer thrower who, in order to improve his results, hollowed out the hammer by a few ounces and in time was exposed. The novel is generally considered to draw a political parallel to the development of Swedish Social Democracy from earlier in the century. Its author, wrote Olof Lagercrantz, had now, at age thirty-seven, achieved "mastery." The second work on sports and politics was a documentary book from the Olympic Games in Munich, entitled *Katedralen i München* (The Cathedral in Munich, 1972). This work was followed by a collection of stories entitled *Berättelser från de inställda upprorens tid* (Tales from the Age of Suspended Rebellions), political stories of the middle class, a few set in Berlin but most in Los Angeles, where the author was a visiting professor at UCLA in 1973.

In Los Angeles, Enquist became a playwright. While rereading Strindberg's works in connection with his teaching, he prepared to discuss the play *The Stronger* and grew fascinated. "I thought it was a play that contained either hypocrisy or else an interesting lie," he commented in an interview. This idea, of the hidden premises Strindberg implanted in his works to argue his own case, became a central theme for the drama *Tribadernas natt* (*The Night of the Tribades,* 1975). Set in Copenhagen in 1889, at a rehearsal of *The Stronger,* Enquist's play examines the relationship between Strindberg, his wife Siri (starring in *The Stronger*), and the Danish actress Marie Caroline David, allegedly a lesbian interested in Siri. David serves as Enquist's spokesperson (" . . . you yourself were the truest men I had ever met. Yet you lied constantly"). But the most interesting thing about this play, according to Clive Barnes reviewing the New York production (1977) in the *New York Times,* was "that it has been written virtually in the style of Strindberg. . . . It will be impossible in the future to see *The Stronger,* or indeed most of Strindberg's work, without recalling the dramatic image Mr. Enquist offers." Within its first years *Tribades* was translated into twenty languages and had more than a hundred productions, including a short run on Broadway. According to Norstedts, the author's publisher, the only other Swedish dramatist to receive so much international attention was Strindberg himself.

Two contemporary political plays followed in collaboration with Anders Ehnmark: *Chez nous* (1976), an attack on the "free" press, and, in the wake of the 1968 student revolt, *Mannen på trottoaren* (The Man on the Sidewalk, 1979), about the elitism of the intellectual left. In 1980, on his own, Enquist brought out a second play in the three-part series begun with *Tribades. Till Fedra* (To Phaedra) is a classical tragedy in a Greek setting based on the Phaedra motif, written in blank verse and dealing with the subject of love in the present time. The third play in this series, *Från regnormarnas liv* (From the Life of the Rain Snakes, 1981) featured Johanne Luise Heiberg (friend of Hans Christian Andersen and wife of author/critic Johan Ledwig Heiberg) as the leading character. Productions in Copenhagen and Stockholm were followed by others in Seattle, Paris, Zürich, Munich, Warsaw, and Vienna; an off-Broadway production was scheduled for 1984.

After some success in the theater, Enquist returned to the novel with *Musikanternas Uttåg* (The Department of the Musicians, 1978), about the early growth of the labor movement in Västerbotten. Conceived as the first in a three-part series, this major novel was highly praised and translated into several languages.

An even more ambitious work is the six-part, eight-hour TV dramatization *Strindberg: Ett liv* (Strindberg: A Life), begun in March 1979 and commissioned by Swedish television. The drama was filmed in Sweden, Denmark, France, and Czechoslovakia and was expected to be released internationally in 1985. Here the thesis of Strindberg's hidden premises, launched in *The Night of the Tribades*, is explained at greater length as Enquist shows the earlier playwright confronting a great number of existential situations.

Enquist's views on Sweden's political status are summed up in his essay "On the Art of Flying Backwards with Dignity," in which he discusses the idea of Sweden as a *förbudsstat* (land of restrictions), a subject of popular debate in the mid-eighties. He also treats this theme in *Dr Mabuses nya testamente* (Dr. Mabuse's New Will, 1982), a satirical novel set in 1888 and written in collaboration with Anders Ehnmark.

In the late 1970s Enquist moved to Copenhagen, where he lives with his second wife, Lone Bastholm, chief of dramatic productions at the Royal Theater.

WORKS IN ENGLISH TRANSLATION: Enquist's novel *The Legionnaires* was published in an English translation by Alan Blair in 1968; Ross Shideler translated his play *The Night of the Tribades* in 1977. His essay "On the Art of Flying Backwards" was translated by Verne Moberg and published in the Winter 1984 issues of *Daedalus*.

ABOUT: Columbia Dictionary of Modern European Literature, 1980; Contemporary Authors 109, 1983; Encyclopedia of World Literature in the 20th Century (rev. ed.) II, 1982. *Periodicals*—Sweden Now 18, 1984.

EPSTEIN, LESLIE (May 4, 1938–   ), American novelist and short story writer, was born in Los Angeles, California, son of Philip G. and Lillian (Targen) Epstein. At the time of Epstein's birth his father and his twin brother Julius were already established in Hollywood as screenwriters. In their long and highly successful collaboration, they wrote the screenplays for such films as *Mr. Skeffington, Arsenic and Old Lace, The Man Who Came to Dinner*, and *Casablanca*, the last of which won them an Academy Award. In a sketch of his life published in the *New York Times Book Review*, Leslie Epstein recalled the southern-colonial house in suburban Los Angeles that his father had bought from Mary Astor, the large upstairs library where his father and uncle wrote their screenplays—his precocious introduction to the life of writing. His childhood

LESLIE EPSTEIN

memories had much to do with films: one of his playmates of that time was Elizabeth Taylor. After attending boarding school Epstein entered Yale University, graduating with a B.A. degree in 1960. He attended Oxford University (1960–62) as a Rhodes Scholar, and in 1963 received his M.A. from the University of California at Los Angeles. He received his D.F.A. from Yale Drama School in 1967, and from 1965 taught in the English Department at Queens College, New York, where he became professor of English in 1976. He is currently director of the Graduate Creative Writing Program at Boston University.

During the early 1970s Epstein called attention to himself as a New York theater reviewer, and as the author of short stories. In 1972 he received a grant for fiction from the National Endowment for the Arts, and in the following year was a Fulbright fellow. His first novel, *P. D. Kimerakov*, tells a bizarre story. Pavel Donatovich Kimerakov is a Russian gerontologist who comes to America as the Soviet representative to the Fourth International Congress on Aging. In New York, after delivering the opening address, he is kidnapped by one Leon T. Kapp, an American impresario having ties with the CIA. The plot moves from imbroglio to imbroglio as Kimerakov becomes enamored of an American dancer named Lauretta, and then returns to the Soviet Union, where Lauretta appears with her American company. The innocent academician ventures increasingly from a sheltered life into an absurdist world. Reviews of the novel were, on the whole, favorable. David Bromwich found the book's hilarity sometimes "forced," and considered the work better in parts than it was as a whole; but he was decidedly impressed by the charm Epstein brought to his conception of the "touchingly awkward" Kimerakov. Maureen Howard called *P. D. Kimerakov* "a bravado display of talent: a balance of the Marx Brothers and Nabokov, of cinematic capers . . . , and of dazzling language."

P. D. Kimerakov was quickly followed by *The Steinway Quintet Plus Four,* a novella and four short stories. The title story, published earlier in periodical form and called by one critic a "short story masterpiece," is set at the Steinway Restaurant, a dairy restaurant on the lower east side of Manhattan, where Sarah Bernhardt had dined and Albert Einstein once sat in on violin, now fallen on hard times. The story is narrated with tragicomic effect by an aging Jewish musician with memories of old Vienna that collide with the hard realities of present-day New York. Two gunmen enter the restaurant as the quintet begins to perform, and culture comes into conflict with violence; music is held hostage to disorder. In a representative review, Katha Pollitt found some of the stories in the collection developed according to "an overly intellectual schema," but considered the title story a jewel, "deft, original and very funny."

In 1976 Epstein began to plan for his next novel, on the Holocaust, by reading as widely as possible on the subject at the Institute for Jewish Research in New York. His research was interrupted for a year, but a Guggenheim fellowship for 1977–78 enabled him to return to the project which, when completed, involved four years of reading and writing. The result, *King of the Jews,* is Epstein's best-known and most ambitious novel to date. *King of the Jews* was suggested by a historical figure, M. C. Rumkowski, head of the Judenrat, or Jewish Council, in Lodz, Poland, during the period of the Nazi persecution of the Jews. Rumkowski, in a sense, collaborated with the Nazis by choosing for them weekly quotas of Jews for deportation to the extermination camps; had he not done so, they would have taken away even larger numbers of victims. Rumkowski's gamble was that he would be able to stave off total annihilation of the ghetto before the end of the war—a gamble he lost, as does Epstein's protagonist I. C. Trumpelman, chairman of the Judenrat in an unnamed Polish city. Trumpelman is a character of larger-than-life size, a man of both strength and weakness who ultimately becomes a tragic figure, ruthlessly exploited by the Nazis, and eventually reviled by his own people. One of the problems raised by the novel is the difficulty of judging such a man who, had his gamble succeeded, and at least part of the ghetto been saved, would have been hailed as a hero.

One of the most striking qualities of *King of the Jews* is its quality as a "Yiddish fairytale." In commenting on this aspect of the work, Edith Milton remarked that "the style is conversational, the tone of someone telling stories to children, but it sounds vaguely as though it is in translation, an English version of Sholem Aleichem. Following the Yiddish story-telling tradition, Epstein frequently steps forward to address us directly. "'Ladies and gentlemen, think of it! No life anywhere' he says, speaking of the expanding universe." At times, *King of the Jews* is as preposterously comic as a Yiddish tale, though the matter it deals with is horrific; it combines the legendary quality of folklore with unspeakable modern reality.

Considered one of the notable novels of the year, a widely discussed and controversial work, *King of the Jews* was both praised and damned. Peter Heinegg, impressed by the novel, called attention to the spell-binding way in which "world-historical horror constantly alternates with farce . . . [Epstein] catches perfectly the hallucinatory feeling of life in a homey human world invaded by irrational nightmare. *King of the Jews* is vivid, generous fiction and a moving exploration of Jewish consciousness. It ranks as a major literary attempt to come to terms with the Holocaust, and it marks the emergence of an important young writer on the American scene." Peter Prescott considered *King of the Jews* an immense feat. The book's "uncommon interest," he wrote, "results from Epstein's storytelling prowess; he has the extraordinary ability to roll from one grand scene to another." Daphne Merkin called the novel "a remarkably emphatic effort of the imagination."

Other reviewers were angered by Epstein's "playful" envisioning of the Holocaust. "As one reads the book," Jane Larkin Crane commented, "it is as if 6,000,000 Jews hadn't really suffered and died at a particular time and place at all, but had merely been conjured up by Leslie Epstein as background for his fanciful exploration of the Eternal Enigma of the Jew. . . . It is in the service of this sort of perversity that the author has felt free to trivialize the Nazi Holocaust." Edith Milton remarked that Epstein's highly styled narration "grates horribly against the enormity of the subject matter. Epstein seems constantly, quaintly, to be tugging at one's sleeve, demanding attention for himself, reminding us to admire his verve, his wit, the clever twists of his story line. . . . At its best this shows itself as a freshness of imagery so intense that it is poetic. At its worst, it appears as a total insensitivity to the texture of European life and Jewish ritual." In a distinctly hostile review, Ruth R. Wisse objected to Epstein's "flat caricatures [and] cabaret style of narration. . . . Had the novel engaged any of the issues it raises, it might have risked literary significance, for Epstein is a professional and engaging writer. But instead, the author has approached his subject with deliberate naivete . . . , and with a boyish nihilism that reduces the Jewish tragedy to a hollow metaphysical joke."

Epstein's next novel, *Regina*, concerns an actress, Regina Singer, née Glassman, once a famous actress, now a film and drama critic, who has been asked to perform in a revival of *The Seagull*, the vehicle of her first triumph twenty years earlier. During the course of a summer heatwave in New York, she is forced to relive the most wounding experiences of her past and to confront a world around her that seems about to topple into chaos. In reviewing *Regina*, Karen Gray Miller wrote that "its ambiguous parable of hope that ends the novel remains unconvincing," and the critic for *Publishers Weekly* noted that "Regina has all the right-minded sentiments— on racism, sexism, nuclear missiles, endangered whales—but she lives continuously on the cutting edge of hysteria, and she is fatally given to the inexplicable melodramatics, the soup in which the novel—despite its many fine moments—too often dissolves, swamping our will to believe." George Stade, on the other hand, regarded *Regina* as a stunning performance, "subtle and convincing. . . . This kind of novel is risky, but Mr. Epstein's control is equal to his daring. . . . In the last few chapters, set during and immediately after opening night, all of Mr. Epstein's motifs come together in a sequence of tremendous literary chords."

Epstein lives in Brookline, Massachusetts, with his family—his wife, the former Ilene Gradman, whom he married in 1969, and their three children, Anya, and twin boys, Paul and Theo. When he is not directing the creative writing program at Boston University, he writes film criticism for *Boston Magazine* and fiction for the *Atlantic, Esquire,* and other magazines. His greatest successes thus far have been in the field of delicate, extravagant whimsy. An early comment on Epstein by David Bromwich, in the *New York Times,* characterizes his work well: "One senses in [Epstein] what is rare enough at any time: the presence of a sly, appealing, grave and humorous talent that will eventually write its own rules."

PRINCIPAL WORKS: P. D. Kimerakov, 1975; The Steinway Quintet Plus Four, 1976; King of the Jews, 1980; Regina, 1982.

ABOUT: Contemporary Authors 73–76, 1978; *Periodicals—* America March 17, 1979; Commentary May 1979; Newsweek January 29, 1979; New Yorker March 26, 1979; New York Review of Books April 5, 1979; New York Times Book Review October 10, 1982; November 21, 1982; Publishers Weekly December 24, 1979; Saturday Review March 31, 1979; Yale Review Spring 1976; Autumn 1979.

*ERDMAN, NIKOLAI ROBERTOVICH (1902–August 10, 1970), Russian playwright and filmscript writer, was born in Moscow. Although he became one of the leading dramatists of the period of the New Economic Policy (NEP), he produced only two plays, one of which was not published or performed in the Soviet Union until 1982. He fell out of party favor early in his career, and little is known about his life.

Erdman first wrote for the theater in collaboration with his brother Boris (1899–1960), a poet who was better known as a set designer. They adapted *Lev Gurych Sinichkin,* a nineteenth–century vaudeville script by D. T. Lensky, to which Nikolai Erdman added skits that parodied contemporary Soviet propaganda drama (agit-prop). It was produced at the Vakhtangov Theater in 1924.

Meyerhold decided in the following year to produce Erdman's first full-length play, *Mandat* (The Mandate). A raucous comedy that satirizes both the old and the new Russian regimes, it elicits laughter with broad farce as well as verbal wit. The family of its simple-minded protagonist, Pavel Guliachkin, used to own a laundry and now wants to "wash away" their petty bourgeois past. He obtains a forged party membership card, the "mandate." Because of it, a Czarist-sympathizing family seeking a Communist connection plan to have their son marry Guliachkin's sister. But then, mistakenly believing the cook Anastasia to be the Czarist heiress, and courting her, they spurn the Guliachkins.

The Czarists and the Guliachkins are made equally ridiculous by the use of both irony and farce. At the end, both families' insignificance is confirmed when all are left empty-handed. "They don't even want to arrest us," Guliachkin wails at the final curtain. "How are we to go on living?"

Both the play and the production were widely acclaimed. Meyerhold considered Erdman's comedy "in the tradition of Gogol and Sukhovo-Kobylin." Gorky invited Erdman for a two-hour talk about his play, leaving him "overjoyed and quite carried away." Stanislavsky praised the play and the production extravagantly, noting that "Meyerhold has accomplished what I myself am dreaming of." Lunacharsky, the Soviet Union's Commissioner

°ärt´ män, nē´ kō lī

NIKOLAI ERDMAN

of Education, gave the play equally high praise, thus officially sanctioning Erdman's triumph.

Although both Stanislavsky and Tairov also were eager to produce Erdman's next play, *Samoubiitsa* (The Suicide, 1931), Meyerhold prevailed. But after eighteen months of work, permission for the play's production was cancelled during dress rehearsals in 1932. Stanislavsky, whose Moscow Art Theater was thought to follow "socialist realism" more faithfully, was licensed to produce it, but his work on the play soon stopped, too. Gorky urged Stalin to permit the production. Stalin wrote: "I do not have a very high opinion of the play *The Suicide*. My closest comrades consider it empty and even harmful." No wonder, for even in the period of the more relaxed standards that prevailed during the NEP, Erdman's sharp satire of the regime was intolerable.

In fact, Meyerhold's aborted production of *The Suicide* was one of the cited offenses that brought about the closing of his theater on January 8, 1938, his subsequent imprisonment, and, ultimately, his murder. Erdman, too, became a victim of the 1930s purges. According to Nadezhda Mandelstam, the proximate cause of his arrest was his authorship of some fables. She quotes his brief, defiant departing fable:

Once the GPU came by
and grabbed old Aesop by the ass.
The moral of this tale is clear—
No more fables needed here.

He was exiled to Kalinin, where he lived in a "poky hole of a room." Eventually he returned to Moscow—at first secretly, once to honor Bul-

gakov's death in 1940 and other times, as Mandelstam relates, to visit "his old women . . . who just loved him."

Like Erdman's first play, *The Suicide* is a wildly farcical comedy that satirizes scheming Russian malcontents. In dramatizing their grievances and those of the "little man" who is the play's protagonist, Erdman also presents a broad picture of the many bureaucratic ills and absurdities of contemporary society. To escape them, Podsekalnikov decides to shoot himself. His cowardice, which repeatedly frustrates his attempts, provides much of the comedy.

At a farewell banquet the drunken Podsekalnikov telephones the Kremlin, demanding to speak to the leader. "Not in? In that case, tell him for me that I read Karl Marx and I didn't like him. . . . Are you listening? My God. He's hung up." Unable to kill himself, Podsekalnikov sneaks into the coffin. Amidst much other grotesque comedy at his funeral, Podsekalnikov unexpectedly arises to embrace one of the mourners and then proclaims that he has lost his desire to die. It is better, he says, to live and reiterate, if only in whispers, "that it's hard to live." The bitter end of the play is the announcement that one of his earlier petitioners *has* committed suicide, his farewell note declaring Podsekalnikov to be right: "Life is not really worth living!"

Though greatly admired by the few who had seen the rehearsals and the mimeographed text, *The Suicide* was not published or produced in Russia until 1982. But their praise—even after the original production was proscribed, Stanislavsky thought it a "splendid play" and Nadezhda Mandelstam called it "the best play in the Soviet repertory"—brought it to the attention of the West. It was first produced in Goteborg, Sweden, in March 1969. Subsequently it received major, favorably reviewed productions in London, New York, and throughout Europe.

Erdman was restored to public favor during the 1950s, but his plays were not. Though he occasionally had ideas for new plots, he refused to risk writing any more plays. Indeed, according to his friend Mandelstam, at their visits Erdman "just sat and drank, without saying a word." But he did resume his earlier interest in writing filmscripts, the most successful of which was *Volga* (1938), written with Misha Volpin and Grigory Alexandrov, and said to have been Stalin's favorite film.

Although Erdman never saw a public performance of *The Suicide*, he lived to see the play achieve a measure of international renown. He died of natural causes in Moscow.

WORKS IN ENGLISH TRANSLATION: Erdman's two plays *The Mandate* and *The Suicide* were translated into English by M. Hoover, G. Genereux, Jr., and J. Volkov in 1975.

ABOUT: Gorchakov, N. A. The Theater in Soviet Russia, 1957; Mandelstam, N. Hope Against Hope, 1970; Segel, H. B. Twentieth-Century Russian Drama, 1979; Yershov, P. Comedy in the Soviet Theater, 1956. *Periodicals*—Russian Literature Triquarterly Winter 1972; International Herald Tribune July 27, 1982.

CLAYTON ESHLEMAN

ESHLEMAN, CLAYTON (June 1, 1935–   ), American poet and translator, writes: "I was born in Indianapolis, Indiana, the only child of Gladys Maine (1896–1970) and Ira Clayton (1895–1970) Eshleman. My mother was a mild yet forceful woman who other than occasional part-time jobs, and singing in the local Fairview Presbyterian Church choir, was a typical midwestern/urban housewife of her times. My father, educated at Purdue University to become a mechanical engineer, spent most of his adult life working on time and motion study in an Indianapolis slaughterhouse. He was also for many years a deacon in the church. My parents had a meager social life, and few interests outside keeping up the home, and church activities. They did not smoke, drink, curse, dance, gamble or associate socially with nonwhite Protestants.

"I don't recall much of my childhood. I think it was probably both introspective and blank; I did not know how to get along with other children, and ever since I was seven or eight, have felt a real burden at being with people in general (except for a few very close friends). My mother got me involved in neighborhood piano lessons when I was six, and these more or less continued until I went to Indiana University in 1953, where I initially, for one year, majored in music. However, from the time I was thirteen or fourteen, typical social anxieties to compete as an athlete distracted me from any serious artful attention to the piano, and from the time I was sixteen my real interest in music turned toward bebop and its world of those who were essentially outcasts in my background and education to that time. Thus a complex and quite slow initiation began to take place in which the 'otherness' of Indiana began to be available in fits and starts, an 'otherness' that via Bud Powell and Lenny Tristano, two avant-garde pianists, would finally lead me to poetry in 1957.

"I suppose that I was a fairly typical i.e. pathetic, teenager of my times, hounded by a need to 'make it' in areas that really held no interest for me (football, track, hanging out with the guys, etc.) There was a sinister centrifugal social force in my WASP world of the late forties/early fifties, designed to keep one away from one's 'self,' or creative possibilities, and finally, with little learned and everything worthwhile compromised, to lock one into the routines of the adult professional or business careers. I now realize that I was extremely unhappy clambering about in this wind-tunnel, but I tried hard to do it because no alternative that I knew how to take hold of was presented. It all came to a head in my case as a freshman at Indiana University when I was a pledge at the Phi Delta Theta fraternity in the days when pledges were regularly beaten with wood paddles, and incessantly abused and bewildered by the clumsy alter-ego of the system the pledges were to enter: as sophomores or (after Hell Week) as actives, and as actives to finally graduate as full-fledged adults.

"For my first three years at Indiana University I more or less leapt around in the Phi Delt cage and ruined everything that I touched. I dropped out of music school after my first year, and spent the next two years drinking and cheating in business school. I counted successes by figuring out how to stay out of the ROTC and the kind of impulsive, inconsiderate sexual adventures that veer between the quick 'screw' and a desperate search for a friend, a mothering-girlfriend.

"I think it was in 1956 that I was thrown out of school for a semester (a combination of terrible grades and too many campus parking tickets on my 1952 yellow Chevrolet convertible), and, thank the gods below, I did not return, tail between legs, to home and parents, but found a room off campus, got a job selling men's clothing, and began to take the first steps on my own.

I ended up rooming with two bitter, bright Korean 'Vets' who ridiculed my Phi Delt ties, and slowly pounded it through my noggin that history, philosophy, and literature existed. When I returned to school I again changed my major, this time to philosophy, still continuing to avoid real study. However, in 1957 a series of coincidences cornered me, and when I tried to get out of the corner, the only way seemed to be through poetry. In a six-month period, I took a twentieth-century American poetry course with Sam Yellin, a creative writing class with Josephine Percy, and met Mary Ellen Solt and Jack Hirschman. Solt was then working on a book on William Carlos Williams, and via her connection to Williams put me in contact with Louis Zukofsky, Cid Corman, Robert Creeley, and less directly, Robert Duncan and Charles Olson. Hirschman, a graduate student from CCNY, was then engaged by an international sense of poetry that included, in one rush, Rilke, Lorca, Mayakofsky, Joyce, Barnes, Nin, Perse, Durrell, as well as young poets Hirschman had known in New York City, David Antin, Robert Kelly, and Jerome Rothenberg. At the first semester vacation after these introductions, I took off for New York City, and met besides the mentioned younger poets, Diane Wakoski, Armand Schwerner, George Economou, and quite importantly, Paul Blackburn, who was clearly not of our generation (for it was as if I was suddenly part of one, almost overnight), but closer at that time to such poets as Kelly and Rothenberg than to the Black Mountain figures of his own generation.

"The following summer, with a couple hundred dollars, and a 25¢ Spanish-English dictionary I hitchhiked to Mexico, trying all at once to learn Spanish, read Pablo Neruda in various translations, and to translate Neruda's *Residencia en la Tierra* myself. By the time I returned to Mexico the following summer, I had discovered the poetry of César Vallejo, decided to be a poet, and back at Indiana University become an editor on the English Department literary magazine *Folio.* The following year I became the main editor of *Folio,* and brought out three issues which demonstrated my new interests in contemporary American and foreign poetries—before the Department itself decided (on the basis of Ginsberg and Zukofsky material) the *Folio* was too wild and obscure and without notifying me eliminated the budget for the following year. So almost at the very point poetry in all its complex magnificence and turmoil was 'there' for me, the 'Spirit of the English Department' asserted itself, and the perennial conflict between the academic and the new presented itself. Yellin informed me that I would never pass my Masters orals, and so to leave with something

at least, I took a Masters of Arts in Teaching and cleared out. I was riding the crest of the first real full-blown enthusiasm in my life.

"Clearing out turned out to mean getting married to Barbara Novak, and figuring out a way to live abroad. Because of my interest in Neruda, Vallejo, and Mexico, I applied to the University of Maryland's overseas Western Division, where if I were accepted I would have taught composition and literature to American military personnel, and had a chance to live in Europe. The only job opening, however, was in Maryland's Far Eastern Division, so I accepted it, and spent the next three years in the Far East: one year teaching in Taiwan, Korea, and the Tokyo area for Maryland, and two years in Kyoto, living in nineteenth-century wooden houses, and making a living teaching English as a foreign language mainly at Matsushita Electric, between Kyoto and Osaka.

"These three years were exotic, difficult, charged, and permeated with study, in a sense, all the study I had not done at Indiana University. Suddenly I was twenty-six years old, a poet, I had been exposed to a tremendous range of twentieth-century poetry as well as to many of the people who will be my poetic companions for the rest of my life—but I had little depth in any single area. In Kyoto, from 1962 to fall 1964, I read Rilke, the I Ching, Joseph Campbell, every inch of *origin* magazine (Corman too was in Kyoto then, doing the second series of *origin,* and I would spend about one evening a week with him at his local hangout, the Muse coffee shop downtown), but I focused my attention on all of William Blake and all that I could find on Blake, and on slowly translating again and again the posthumously published poetry of César Vallejo. These were years in which my whole background was in my throat, and years in which I began to deconstruct my macho Indiana-ego. These were also years in which I struggled to understand the most basic things about my own sexual and creative nature. I learned that I was a strong room of hostility and heldback grief, all of which was bound up with an aggressive and repressed sexuality which my background argued had to be withheld in order for the creative orders to come through. I wrote for hours on end, often sitting and staring at the typewriter for a half day, trying to write a line that did not sound like someone else and was, at the same time, myself—which was of course a complete mystery. I collected caterpillars and studied them for months, and spent a season on a bench regarding an orb-weaving spider in the Okumura's stone garden. I passed out while reading Blake's 'Book of Urizen,' and in short seemed to suffer all the psychic and concomitant physical 'bends' that I had avoided until then. My gamble was that if I was willing to go through the background material, and not try to transcend or deny it, that I could raze the House of Eshleman, and slowly build a new one, a new house of Eshleman, in its place. While I published a number of poems in magazines in the early and midsixties, the big work, which came together only after both my parents died in 1970, was not published until 1973. *Coils* was my response to a kind of 'portrait of the artist as a young man' situation, but shifting the time frame to the years between twenty-five and thirty-five.

"Barbara and I returned to the states in 1964, and spent the next year back in Bloomington, Indiana, where I wrote and translated full-time (except for teaching a few extension courses), and she worked in the university bookstore. By the spring of 1965 I knew that to be responsible to what Vallejo had come to mean to me (I was now on the fourth draft of the translation) I had to spend some time in Peru. With Barbara pregnant and about $300, we left for Lima and stayed there until March 1966. My only child, Matthew, was born in February, 1966, in Lima. While there, I made a living by creating and editing a bilingual magazine for Peruvian and North American poetries, sponsored by the Peruvian North American Cultural Institute—which turned out to be attached to the United States Information Service and refused to allow the first issue of my magazine, *Quena*, to be published unless I withdrew several pages of the poetry of Javier Heraud. While the poems at stake were hardly political at all, in any sense, Heraud had shocked the artistic world of Peru several years before by becoming a Communist while on a grant in Cuba, and on return to Peru, with a tiny band of guerrillas had invaded a northern plantation where he was murdered. Such an editorial controversy went a good deal deeper than the problems with the Indiana University English Department over *Folio*. For to be fighting with the Institute over Heraud's poetry while walking around in the hideous slums of Lima made me aware of not only what poverty could be, but the subtle ways in which North American economic and military imperialism infested the lives of Latin Americans. I refused to withdraw the Heraud poetry; *Quena* was cancelled; Matthew was born; and with the Vallejo translation publication rights rendered impossibly complicated by the poet's half-mad, half-brilliant, intransigent widow, we returned to the States.

"The next four years were spent in New York City; Barbara and I soon separated, and I spent two years in Reichian therapy while teaching English as a foreign language at New York University. Reich was a great discovery for several reasons: his therapy, in the hands of Dr. Sidney Handelman, enabled me to convert my rigidities and unhappinesses into a functioning creative way of being, that I realized could be both sexual and imaginative (in effect, the more you spent the more you had, rather than the other way around). Reich's own writings helped me make connections between the misery I had seen in Peru and sexual/economic manipulation, and the therapy and the writing together led me to realize that I could be aggressive *and* compassionate, could stand up for what I believed *and* be yielding—as long as I was willing to take the consequences. In New York I also participated, at times fulltime, in artist protest activity against the American involvement in Vietnam, and in 1967 started *Caterpillar* magazine, which I mainly edited and typed at night. *Caterpillar* went on for twenty issues (averaging around 200 pages per issue) and was finally my chance, on my own, my money, my editing, to carry through with a magazine project that would enable me to work out a basic sense of poetics in relation to my own and several earlier generations. The first twelve issues were done in New York and the last eight in the Los Angeles area, where I moved in 1970, with my present wife Caryl, after accepting a teaching position at the then new California Institute of the Arts.

"Since then Caryl and I have lived in Los Angeles, with the exception of several extended visits to Europe, mainly France. Once *Coils* was completed in 1972, I began to break up the deconstructive self-portraiture of my writing in the sixties with a series of 'portraits' of other artists and people, for the most part written in the first person, using materials from their lives to think about and construct a sense of the particular weight of their lives, that form the core of *The Gull Wall*, a book that in other respects meditates upon the life and death of my old friend Paul Blackburn who died of cancer at forty-six in 1971. By 1975, I had discovered the Upper Paleolithic cave art of southwestern France and perhaps even more importantly for the years to come, the paucity of imaginative writing about this art, developed between 40,000 and 8,000 BC, when the autonomous imagination and the archetypal patterning that offers us our primary cultural potentials were being worked out. I soon realized that in response to having worked through the suffocating personalism of my Indiana background, I had gone to the most transpersonal realm known. My research on Paleolithic imagination and the construction of the underworld has given a focus to what I consider my most significant books: *What She Means, Hades In Manganese,* and *Fracture.*

"Since 1979 I have been teaching creative

writing to science students at the California Institute of Technology in Pasadena, and since spring 1981 I have edited a new literary triquarterly that is published by the Institute. Besides my teaching, writing, and reviewing for the *Los Angeles Times Book Review*, I have also been working on new translation projects, the most important of which have been a complete poetry of Aimé Césaire, with colleague Annette Smith, and a selected poetry of Michel Deguy."

———

Clayton Eshleman maintains that *Coils* was his first "big work," although he had already published by then no fewer than seventeen books of verse. The characteristics of this early work are similar: the style features uncontrolled free association and deliberate obscurantism; the subject matter is unvaried and personal, with repeated, dispirited references to his unhappy sex life; the dominant tone is extremely anxious and wholly self-regarding. Even the briefest account of a cityscape can manifest all of these characteristics, as in "Washington Square Park," from *Indiana* here quoted in full:

after rain
    pigeons raw
August, graze

Primeval scene—
gouged, rutted-with
earth, covered
    covered

O Barbara
    dried up

Paul Zweig's comments on Eshleman's *Hades in Manganese* are representative of critical reaction to almost all his poetry. Describing his verse as all-inclusive, with "bewildering shifts in tone, leaps and gaps, puns, willful incoherences," he observes that Eshleman "lets go of nothing. He will not cooperate with taste, judgment, esthetic standards, for they are, presumably, the enemy, the suppressors." Yet as Zweig writes of those same excesses in Eshleman's book on Paul Blackburn, *The Gull Wall*: his "dance may be grim and narcissistic, but it contains all of a man's being; it holds nothing back, and the reader looks on uncomfortable, a little irritated, but still looking."

Eshleman's fifteen-year ordeal of translating *The Complete Posthumous Poetry of César Vallejo* resulted in what most critics consider his most mature work. The translations of this major Peruvian poet correct long-standing errors in the received versions of many of the best-known poems, and the whole work, according to A. J. MacAdam, "enables us to see how a poet maturing in the '20s and '30s was drawn irresistibly into politics." The translation won the National Book Award in 1979.

PRINCIPAL WORKS: *Poetry*—Coils, 1973; What She Means, 1978; Hades in Manganese, 1981; Fracture, 1983; Sea Urchin Harakiri, 1984. *Memoirs* (poetry and prose)—The Gull Wall, 1975. *Translations*—Neruda, P. Residence on Earth, 1962; Césaire, A. State of the Union (with D. Kelly), 1966; Vallejo, C. Human Poems, 1969; Vallejo, C. Spain, Take This Cup from Me (with J. R. Barcia), 1974; Cesar Vallejo: The Complete Posthumous Poems (with J. R. Barcia), 1978; Artaud, A. Four Texts (with N. Glass), 1982; Deguy, M. Quadratures, 1984; Deguy, M. Given Giving, 1984; Césaire, A. The Collected Poetry (with A. Smith, 1984).

ABOUT: Contemporary Authors, first revision series 33–36, 1978; Contemporary Literary Criticism 7, 1977; Vinson, J. (ed.) Contemporary Poets, 1980; Dictionary of Literary Biography 5, 1980; Who's Who in America, 1982–83. *Periodicals*—American Book Review May-June 1982; Choice April 1976; October 1979; New York Times Book Review March 23, 1969; February 13, 1972; February 1, 1976; October 11, 1981; Times Literary Supplement January 18, 1980; Virginia Quarterly Review Winter 1980; Winter 1983.

FABRICIUS, SARA *See* SANDEL, CORA

*FALLACI, ORIANA (June 29, 1930–   ), Italian journalist and novelist, writes: "I was born in Florence, Tuscany, the first daughter of two courageous Florentines obsessed with the love for freedom, when Italy had been taken over by Mussolini's Fascism, and this is the first thing to say about me. For better or worse, I am what I am and write as I write because of the place and the time and the parents that generated me. Being born and growing up in Florence is a privilege both from a cultural and a political point of view because it does not only mean belonging to one of the most beautiful cities in the world, it also means belonging to what has been the cradle of our civilization. When Italy was ruled by the feudal system and Europe by crude or even barbaric monarchs, Florence administrated itself with the democratic system of the Comunes and gave birth to artists like Giotto, Dante Alighieri, Petrarca. Almost all the great Italians whose names are known in the world came from Florence and Tuscany. My parents never stopped reminding me that when Caterina de Medici went to marry Henry II in Lyons, she left Florence with dozens of scholars, scribes, painters, musicians, jewelers, tailors, cooks that would teach the court of France how to live and behave: 'If it were not for her, those French

°fä lä ´ chē

ORIANA FALLACI

wouldn't even know how to cut a dress or how to make a wheel of cheese, a bottle of wine.' Maybe they exaggerated a little, but, in spite of the decadence which has mummified the splendor of centuries, when I move among the palaces and the monuments and the bridges and the museums of Florence I feel the deep truth of those words. Because of this I cannot live without Florence, without my apartment beyond the Arno River, without the old rustic mansion I keep in the hills of Greve in Chianti, the town where two other great Italians were born and died: Amerigo Vespucci who gave his name to America and whose house still stands there intact, and Giovanni da Verazzano who discovered New York and whose statue stands in the middle of the square. In that mansion, built in 1700 and surrounded by vineyards, olive trees, chestnut woods, I have written almost all my books. Apart from the fact that I write in Italian and that any language needs its environment, I am incapable of working at some engaging book outside Florence and Tuscany.

"Being born when Fascism had taken over in Italy and growing up under its oppression was a tragic misfortune of course, yet I owe to that misfortune as well as to my parents the cult for freedom which permeates all my writings and which makes up the main leit-motif of all my books. Freedom is a food which is not appreciated when you have it as a daily course; when you are hungry for it, instead, you see it as a dream to materialize, as a kingdom to conquer. Political freedom, individual freedom, freedom of thought and expression, independence of judgment, were the various aspects of the food that

I missed from the time I went to school and the Fascists persecuted my father who had started fighting Mussolini when he was still a teen-ager. I lived my childhood in the expectancy of seeing him arrested or beaten or killed by Mussolini's squads, and because of this I became politically engaged at an age when girls play with dolls. As a matter of fact, I never possessed a doll until I was twenty years old and I bought it as an act of revenge. When I was a child, my dolls were the political fights I saw around me thanks to that incredible father and that incredible mother who never gave in to dictatorship. My mother, Tosca, was the youngest daughter of Augusto Cantini, an anarchist sculptor who was so faithful to his beliefs that in the First World War he chose to be an army deserter and to be sentenced to death by default. My father, Edoardo, was the youngest son of a lieutenant revenue officer who belonged to the Republican party of Mazzini when being a Mazzinian was as revolutionary as being a Maoist today. At the age of twenty, my parents had fallen in love also because of their communion of ideas. From them my sisters and I learned how to hate the fanaticism, the dogmas, the tyranny and to resist fear. Even physical fear. I shall never forget the day when, under a bombing of Florence in 1944, my father stopped my tears of fright with a slap and this phrase: 'A girl does not cry.' Many years later, when I was a war correspondent in Vietnam, in the Middle East, in the Indo-Pakistani War, in the Latin American insurrections, and fear touched me, I always thought of that phrase and felt better.

"*Nothing and So Be It*, my book on Vietnam, was provoked by my experiences in the war as a little girl. I went to Vietnam from 1967 to 1975, in twelve long trips, because I wanted to see again the war as an adult, to tell as an adult the horrors and the stupidities and the noble braveries I had seen as a little girl in Florence. Not by chance, war and death are another leit-motif of my writing and to them I always go back as to the theme of tyranny and freedom.

"Writing was my dream since I was eight years old and I read *The Call of the Wild* by Jack London, so I fell in love with Jack London and I started telling everybody that I would become Jacqueline London; I would have an adventurous life in far countries and I would tell all that in my books. At that time I wrote bizarre fairy tales placed in exotic places like China and Alaska where the hero always won and the tyrant ended in horrible death. I also participated in writing competitions, and once I won the first prize with a composition on a kernel of grain. The prize was five thousand lire, I guess the equivalent of today's fifty dollars, and I never enjoyed it because my mother put it for me in a savings account. When years later we went to withdraw it, inflation had reduced its value to a few cents. As soon as the war was over, and Fascism defeated, and democracy reestablished, I could return to my school, the Liceo Classico Galileo Galilei of Florence, and my talent for writing became then more evident. Every teacher kept saying that, rather than a dream, writing was my destiny.

"In the end, my case is simple because it is the case of a person who has remained essentially rooted to the early part of her existence. The more I think of it, the more I conclude to have never cut the umbilical cord which ties me up to the time of my formation. I haven't even after choosing America (or should I say New York) as my new home—second home. I don't believe in flags, in frontiers, in passports, and I think that the various languages are a curse of mankind. So, I feel perfectly at home both in Florence and in Manhattan, in Europe and in the United States. (By the way, when I go to Italy, I always say 'I go to Europe.' To me they are the same thing.) And I can adapt myself very easily to every country I go, as long as it has some freedom.

"By cultural dualism I do not mean only the two languages in which I think and work: English and Italian. I also mean the two ways of life, the two kinds of education, So, if you ask me which authors influenced me the most in my work I give an answer that mixes together the European literature and the American literature and I make an extravagant potpourri which contains Manzoni and Melville, Flaubert and Jack London, Emily Brontë and Hemingway, Proust and [Margaret] Mitchell. This is not the result of a confused education; it is the result of an absorbed fusion which slowly took place in my mind through my living outside the frontiers of a precise fatherland, then through living an equal time and in an equal way inside two cultures that make me feel better.

"The same can be said of another apparent dualism of mine: my being an author and a journalist at the same time. Am I both really? I don't know. But I know that when I'm asked if I consider myself an author or a journalist I reply, 'I'm a writer.' In fact I never saw myself as a good reporter and I was stunned when Walter Lippmann paid me that compliment calling me 'the best reporter in the world.' I could never have worked for a press agency or even for a daily paper: even in the first years of my career, when I wrote some news I gave it the shape of a story and not of a piece of information. Moreover, I never felt satisfied with the shortness and the synthesis and the immediacy of a newspaper article and I constantly felt handcuffed by the rules of journalism. In fact I never loved it very much, though I owe to it much of my life and of my success.

"In the last years this has become so apparent that I have practically reduced my journalistic activity to the political interviews, though they too leave me kind of unsatisfied. When I talk with a head of State or a political leader, I always try to stay with him or her more than is necessary for a newspaper-interview and, instead of an interview, I would like to write on him or her a long book. In fact, nobody can deny that both in their form and substance, my interviews are nearer to history and theater than to pure journalism. Nobody can deny that in questioning those leaders, I care much more to know about the soul and the story of that man or woman than about the more or less sensational answers they may give me about that particular political moment. Which is why my interviews never get old and after several years are as valid as the first day, and why I feel so hurt when the Americans define me 'the greatest political interviewer of our time.' I am not an interviewer, I am a writer who makes interviews.

"My private life is a land that I prefer to keep for myself: which is the reason why I have always refused, till today, to write my biography. However the main facts are known. I was never legally married, since the death of Alekos Panagoulis I live alone, and I do not have any children. I lost them all, so my only children are my books. I also lost my mother, in 1978, and my family now includes my old father, my three sisters, some nephews, an adorable dog that stays in my country house in Tuscany, and a thousand books. Many of which I have read, many of which I keep promising myself to read in my old age unless I get shot in one of those wars from which I can't keep myself away, or unless I die of cancer as a result of the sixty cigarettes a day that I smoke."

Oriana Fallaci began her career working part-time for a local newspaper to support her education as a medical student at the University of Florence, but she soon discovered her love for journalism and abandoned her medical studies. From routine news reporting she moved rapidly into a highly dramatic and personalized kind of interviewing. At first her subjects were glamorous celebrities of the entertainment, literary, and political world who soon bored her with their shallow egotism. Published as *Gli antipatici* (*The Egoists*) in 1963, these interviews brought her wide attention but gave her little satisfaction.

Fallaci's energies and flair for the dramatic demanded larger international, and sometimes even cosmic, challenges. In the early 1960s, for example, she visited Cape Canaveral to report on NASA and the astronauts in a book that explored not only the achievements but also the paradoxes of space exploration—*Se il sole muore* (*If the Sun Dies,* 1965). Fallaci made no attempt to disguise herself as an objective reporter but wrote in the form of a dialogue between herself and her aging father what she called a "ruthlessly autobiographical" and subjective book on her reactions to the space age. Some reviewers challenged her factual detail and her frankly polemical tone, but all agreed that the book was lively, literate, and in its portrait of the astronauts themselves, as the *New Yorker* critic wrote, "delightfully candid, fresh, shrewd, and full of humor." She regards her "first real book" as the earlier *Il sesso inutile* of 1961 (*The Useless Sex*) on the worldwide status of women, described by a reviewer in *Library Journal* as "a wide-eyed, responsive, but unresearched study of what women do and how they feel about it"; and she takes greatest pride in her account, written in the form of a diary with interviews and frontline reporting, on conditions in Vietnam, which she visited twelve times during the years 1967 to 1975—*Niente e così sia* (*Nothing and So Be It,* 1969). Here the tragedy of Vietnam became a symbol of the futility of human violence even when perpetrated "in the name of democracy, freedom, and Christianity." Reviewers found the book controversial but deeply moving and, in the main, an honest and courageous statement.

Fallaci's fame rests principally on her candid interviews with most of the major figures of world politics of the past two decades. Voluble, provocative, and never awed by the power of her subjects, she confronted Henry Kissinger, the Shah of Iran, Yasir Arafat, Golda Meir, Indira Gandhi, among others, with questions that displayed their vulnerability and offered revealing insights often denied to more objective reporters. Published in Italy in 1974, *Intervista con la storia* (*Interview With History*), the book offended some of its subjects and some reviewers alike. "She wants to be more than a brilliant interviewer; she wants to be an avenging angel," Ted Morgan wrote in the *Washington Post.* In more recent interviews—with the Ayatollah Khomeini for the *New York Times Magazine* in 1978, with Lech Walesa for the London *Sunday Times* in 1981—Fallaci shows no signs of subduing her aggressive style, often turning the interview into a confrontation and debate. Her interviews, she has said, are "my joy, my pride, and commitment."

Always the center of her work, as journalist or novelist, Fallaci revealed her own inner life in two novels—*Lettera a un bambino mai nato* (*Letter to a Child Never Born,* 1975), addressed to the embryo of a child she was carrying and expressing her conflict between her love for the unborn life and her resentment at the sacrifice of her career that motherhood would demand, and *Un uomo* (*A Man,* 1979), a forthright account of her love affair with Alexandros Panagoulis, the poet and Greek Resistance leader who was killed in 1976. A lyrical tribute to a fallen hero, *A Man* was a best-seller in Italy and won the Premio Viareggio literary award; it impressed American reviewers as a story of "bitter, wrenching power," "a work of transcendent Greek tragedy," and—as Elizabeth Peer wrote in *Newsweek*—"a stunning memorial to her dead lover and his cause." This book, Fallaci has told *World Authors,* was the most emotionally demanding of all her works. She rewrote it several times, reliving "the trauma of a grief which had destroyed my life. I lost my peace forever in that book. Not by chance, I used to say that I hate it more than I love it. Such hate, however, does not change the fact that *A Man* undoubtedly is my most important work."

PRINCIPAL WORKS IN ENGLISH TRANSLATION: Almost all of Oriana Fallaci's books have been translated into English. Pamela Swinglehurst translated her novel *Penelope at War* in 1961, *The Useless Sex* in 1964, *The Egoists* in 1968 (published as *Limelighters* in the U.K. in 1967), and *If the Sun Dies* in 1966. Isabel Quigley translated her book on Vietnam, *Nothing and So Be It,* in 1972; John Shepley translated *Interview with History* and *Letter to A Child Never Born* in 1976. William Weaver translated *A Man* in 1980.

ABOUT: Contemporary Authors 77–80, 1979; Current Biography 1977. *Periodicals*—New York Times Book Review November 3, 1980; Publishers Weekly November 7, 1980; Times (London) April 6, 1981.

FARRELL, J(AMES) G(ORDON) (January 23, 1935–August 12, 1979), Irish novelist, was born in Liverpool, England, the son of William and Josephine (Russell) Farrell. He attended the Rossall School, a private school in Lancashire, and although his parents returned to their native Ireland after World War II, he remained at the school until his graduation. He then taught for a year at a Dublin prep school, and for another year worked as a fireman for a construction company on the DEW line in the Canadian Arctic. In 1956 he entered Brasenose College, Oxford, where he played in a center position for his college's rugby team, but by the end of the year

J. G. FARRELL

was stricken with polio, which left him with severely weakened muscles from the waist up; he
was for a time confined to an iron lung. Farrell
received his B.A. degree from Oxford in 1960,
and for the following two years taught English
in France.

Farrell's first novel, *A Man from Elsewhere*,
which takes place in France, is concerned with
a young Communist journalist assigned to visit
a dying novelist who has repudiated his earlier
Communist affiliations. Determined to blacken
the reputation of a man he regards as disloyal to
the Party, and to prevent his adulation by the
non-Communist world, he finds himself increasingly influenced by the dying man and his family. In the end, his own Communist faith
destroyed, he is left disillusioned, confused, and
embittered. John Spurling has described the
novel as a "period piece of the late '50s," but he
also noted that the theme of irreconcilable convictions in the novel was reiterated and became
important in Farrell's later work.

Farrell's second novel, *The Lung*, is a black
comedy based on his own experience as a polio
victim. The novel, John Spurling wrote, "is seen
entirely through the eyes of its hero, Martin
Sands, who is motivated when we first meet him
by an irresistible craving for alcohol and a slightly milder one for women. . . . Sands is essentially a comic figure and Farrell's triumph is to keep
him so through all the vicissitudes of his gradual
cure in a private hospital." A writer in the *Times
Literary Supplement* called attention to the other inmates of Sands' ward, "lost souls who inhabit an up-to-date limbo. Here, attended by a
starched staff with pockets bulging with ther-

mometers and sleeping-pills, they cultivate their
obsessions, contemplate the different kinds of
ruin they have made of their lives, and look rehabilitation shiftily in the face. . . . Mr. Farrell's is an effective, potent brew, compounded
of desperation with a certain wild hilarity."

In 1966 Farrell received a Harkness Fellowship for residence in the United States and spent
a two-year period in New York City. His third
novel, *A Girl in the Head*, was highly praised by
Martin Levin in the *New York Times Book
Review* as a "beautifully-executed symposium
on anti-heroics." Treating in a surrealistic and
grotesque fashion the romantic and sexual adventures of one Count Boris Slattery, the novel
displayed Farrell's "flair for giving the ridiculous an inspired reality," Levin wrote.

In 1968 Farrell returned to London, where he
lived for the next ten years. In 1970 he published
Troubles, which marked a turning point in his
career. In this novel, which was awarded the
prestigious Geoffrey Faber Memorial prize, Major Brendan Archer, an English army officer,
finds himself among the inhabitants of The Majestic, a huge, crumbling resort hotel in Wicklow
on the coast of Ireland in the summer of 1919.
The Majestic, with its atmosphere of paralysis
and decay, is clearly intended to suggest the
British Empire at a point of near impotence.

Farrell elaborated upon his theme of the British Empire in decline in his next novel, *The
Siege of Krisnapur*, set in India during the Sepoy
rebellion. The result of considerable research
(and an extended visit by Farrell to India), *The
Siege of Krisnapur* is notable for the authority of
its historical reconstruction. Yet at the same time
Farrell manages to make his characters seem almost our contemporaries—with the difference
that they do not know all that we do. His use of
a double or ironic focus, Victorian and modern,
caused the novel to be compared to John Fowles'
The French Lieutenant's Woman. Walter Clemons remarked in *Newsweek* that "J. G. Farrell's novel of the Sepoy Mutiny in 1857 begins
as a comedy of Victorian conventions and imperial pride. It accelerates into a terrific narrative
of action as the prolonged siege tests the inmates
of Krisnapur with cholera, stench, despair and
religious mania. Before it ends, steep clefts have
opened in the assumptions of progress and civilized order."

The Singapore Grip, which takes place in the
British colony of Singapore between 1939 and
the surrender to the Japanese in 1942, brings
Farrell's trilogy of the British Empire to a conclusion. Christopher Porterfield thought the
novel was weighed down by its documentation,
its characters, against such detailed back-

grounds, being "mere outlines." Peter Prescott, however, praised the work in *Newsweek* for its "sure sense of place and history."

Farrell, who never married, lived quietly in London and avoided publicity, almost never giving interviews. According to Malcolm Dean's memoir, he liked bicycling, walking, and entertaining friends (he was a connoisseur of fine wine and a cook) at his modest, two-room flat in Knightsbridge. The financial success he achieved with his last novels enabled him to buy an old farmhouse on Sheep's Head peninsula on the isolated West Coast of Ireland. There, four months later, on August 12, 1979, he fell from rocks while fishing, and was swept out to sea by a wave.

In 1981 his last work, *The Hill Station,* dealing with a Victorian clergyman in India, was published posthumously. The manuscript of 50,000 words was said by P. H. Furbank, in the *Times Literary Supplement,* to be in "his best style," but since the novel is merely a fragment, any assessment of it would be difficult to make. *The Hill Station* also contains Farrell's diary of a tour of India in 1971, and essays about him by his friends Malcolm Dean, John Spurling, and Margaret Drabble.

PRINCIPAL WORKS: A Man from Elsewhere, 1963; The Lung, 1965; A Girl in the Head, 1967 (U.S., 1969); Troubles, 1970 (U.S., 1971); The Siege of Krisnapur, 1973 (U.S., 1974); The Singapore Grip, 1978 (U.S., 1979); The Hill Station, 1981.

ABOUT: Contemporary Authors 73–76, 1978; Contemporary Literary Criticism 6, 1976; Contemporary Novelists, 1982; Dictionary of Literary Biography 14, 1983; Who Was Who, 1971–1980 7, 1981. *Periodicals*—Encounter August 1981; Nation November 8, 1971; New Statesman October 9, 1970; September 15, 1978; August 31, 1979; New Yorker November 25, 1974; New York Review of Books December 12, 1974; New York Times Book Review March 23, 1969; September 12, 1971; October 6, 1974; May 27, 1979; Observer October 1965; Newsweek October 21, 1974; May 7, 1979; Times Literary Supplement September 20, 1963; November 11, 1965; January 22, 1971; September 21, 1973; October 6, 1978; May 22, 1981; Spectator April 25, 1981.

FAUST, IRVIN (June 11, 1924–   ), American novelist and short story writer, writes: "I came to writing rather late, in my early 30s, but it worked splendidly for me. I was ready, with plenty in the tank. My first story was 'Into the Green Night,' done in several hours. My wife, Jean, my best and most intuitive critic, liked it, so I sent it out to about twenty-two small magazines, got the familiar thank you, liked it, try us

IRVIN FAUST

again. Around the twenty-third try, Reed Whittemore at the *Carleton Miscellany* said thanks, we'll take it. He took two others. I began to produce fast, banging out stories that the *Transatlantic Review* and *Paris Review* printed.

"I began to get letters from publishers (it seems we're all discovered through the mail). An editor or friend had read my work and liked it, did I have a novel? Nope, no novel, but about ten stories, how about it? See us when you write that novel.

"Finally, a brave gentleman at Random House, Robert Loomis, asked to look at the stories. He liked them and told Bennett Cerf he'd like to do them as my first book. Cerf, despite the TV image, gave his editors, who were very good, autonomy. The result was *Roar Lion Roar and Other Stories* and Random House (and I) even made a few dollars on this 'gamble.'

"The stories ranged all over the place but were unified by the 'adjustment' of their characters to the American scene, a dynamic that most of us would call a maladjustment. In the title story, for example, a newly arrived Puerto Rican boy finds his true self by identifying with the Columbia football team, finally, happily, giving his life for his beloved Lions. For *him* the proper and quite appropriate gesture.

"An idea for a novel finally did strike in 1962 (I was beginning to think, as Salinger put it, I was a sprinter, not a miler). The Cuban missile crisis hit me as a liberating factor and Harold, my protagonist, in one week transforms all his dreams and yearnings into reality. This was *The Steagle.* It told me I could be a miler. Incidentally, it was made into a film in 1971, a pretty good film in its original form. But the money people who had final cut just about killed it, telling me something about Hollywood which, of course, I should have known. Critically, the book was well received.

"I jumped then into the student riots of the late 60s, but from a cop's point of view. *The File on Stanley Patton Buchta.* Poor title, but a rather good book, although the critics didn't think so. I think they wanted the wild, fantastic Faust of *RLR* and *The Steagle.* I gave them a rather passive Wasp who liked to play games, not as sport, but with life. Rather, I think, like America until it is jolted by Pearl Harbor, student riots, etc. Buchta played at being a triple agent, similar to the old Czarist provocateurs. It catches up with him of course, as it always has with this country when we drift, but the book was too different, or perhaps ahead of its time and was a critical and commercial failture. Maybe I'll dig it up one of these days . . .

"I then got hooked on history, that is, the interplay of history and the existential moment. I taught myself how to research (painfully) and dug into the Spanish-American War, a seminal event for this country, but generally thought of as a nice little war. *Willy Remembers* was the result and I raced through it in nine months (if I go much beyond a year with a novel, I'm in trouble). Through the quasi-senile eyes, ears, and mind of a Germanic bigot and veteran of that war, I was able to weave a fabric of history into the present and also to comment on both. *Willy* was a huge success critically and although not a best-seller, did well with the public.

"Still intrigued with history as today, I dived into the Chinese Boxer Rebellion of 1900; the Nixon trip really got me going: two invasions with many parallels. I wrote it as a Chinese puzzle, a book within a book within a book, using a Richard Harding Davis type as my parodistic focus. It worked, for me, and surprisingly, for a number of critics and even the public. I say surprisingly because it is a complex and unsettling book.

"Enough of history, or pre-Faustian history. I thought then that I'd like to look at modern America, but in a special way that would heighten my effects. I chose that native phenomenon, the stand-up comic and came up with *A Star in the Family.* I broke down time and sequence completely, but unified the book by having my man stand aside and do his 'shtik' on what the hell was happening to us.

"The book worked; the critics didn't. They said, 'Christ, another piece on Lenny Bruce, forget it.' Many, I'm sure, didn't read the book. It has *nothing* to do with Lenny (I'm not even a Lenny fan), but that was the kiss of an early and painful death. The book sank without much of a ripple.

"After a decent period of mourning I returned to the watershed event of my generation, World War II. Not the war itself—I'm tired of that—but what it did to my generation and why, largely because of it, we can't communicate with our kids. *Newsreel.* It covers the twenty-two-year readjustment of Speed Finestone who went to war as a scared kid and came back a hero. It came out in 1980 and I was satisfied; it did what I wanted and needed (although it wasn't autobiographical). It also did a pretty fair job with women, which has never been a strong point, along with the rest of my generation.

"I paused then and returned to stories, the first love. The second one I did came out in '81 in the *Atlantic,* and has been picked as an O'Henry Prize Story. That's nice. The old boy hasn't lost his touch. More important, I liked it too."

————

With a doctorate in social psychology and long experience as a guidance counselor to high school students, and—more important perhaps—extraordinary imaginative sympathy, Irvin Faust has created a gallery of characters who mirror, Richard Kostelanitz writes, "how an hysterical consciousness distorts the lines between fantasy and reality so that the reader is never fully sure whether such actions take place in dream or in life." In Kostelanitz' judgment—an opinion shared by other critics—*The Steagle* (the title alludes to the merger of two football teams, the Steelers and the Eagles), with its vivid portrait of a New York City college English professor collapsing into nervous breakdown, "establishes Faust among the most accomplished psychological novelists today."

Faust's fictional world is the contemporary American urban experience—of Jew, Puerto Rican, East Indian, of the alienated young and the lonely disaffected elderly, the educated and the illiterate—translated by his protagonists into the mythology of mass culture. His heroes fantasize themselves into American mythic images—the sports hero, the movie star, the gangster, the stand-up comedian—with comic but usually tragic results. Using interior monologue, Faust inevitably risks "narrative dislocation." As Frank Campenni writes, "The reader must sometimes guess whether events described have taken place at all outside the mind of the central character or whether actual events have occurred just as described." The method proved most successful, however, in *Willy Remembers,* where a ninety-three-year-old veteran of the Spanish-American

War, ranging wildly through American history, becomes a vessel of national memory, remarkable, in R.V. Cassill's judgment, for "Joycean complexity of ambivalences, portmanteau images and concentric legends."

Born in New York City and educated at City College in New York (B.S. 1949) and Columbia University (D. Ed. 1960), Faust taught in New York City and suburban schools. In 1960 he became director of guidance and counseling at Garden City High School on Long Island. Out of this work has come his non-fiction collection of "student-centered" case studies, *Entering Angel's World.* Faust married Jean Satterthwaite in 1959.

PRINCIPAL WORKS: Roar Lion Roar and other Stories, 1965; The Steagle, 1966; The File on Stanley Patton Buchta, 1970; Willy Remembers, 1971; Foreign Devils, 1973; A Star in the Family, 1975; Newsreel, 1980. *Non-fiction*—Entering Angel's World, 1963.

ABOUT: Bruccoli, M. (ed.) Conversations with Writers 2, 1978; Contemporary Authors, first revision series 33–36, 1978; Dictionary of Literary Biography 2, 1978; Vinson, J. (ed.) Contemporary Novelists, 1982; Who's Who in America, 1983–84. *Periodicals*—New York Times Book Review August 29, 1971; TriQuarterly Winter 1967.

© 1985 Layle Silbert

ELAINE FEINSTEIN

FEINSTEIN, ELAINE (October 24, 1930–), British poet, novelist, short-story writer, and translator, was born in Bootle, Lancashire, the daughter of Isidore Cooklin, a shopkeeper, and the former Fay Compton. After taking her B.A. in English at Newnham College, Cambridge, in 1952, she studied law and passed the bar examination, but never entered the profession. Her marriage in July 1957 to Arnold Feinstein, an immunologist, has produced three sons. She worked on the editorial staff of the Cambridge University Press (1960–62), as an English lecturer at a teachers' training college in Hertfordshire (1963–66), then as assistant lecturer in English at the University of Essex, where she was a colleague of the poet and critic Donald Davie, and became associated with a coterie of young poets, including Ed Dorn, Lee Harwood, and Tom Pickard, who aimed at making their work less rhetorical, closer to the spoken word, and more spontaneous in tone. American poetry, particularly the work of William Carlos Williams and Robert Creeley, had a deep influence on Feinstein's development as a writer, one she has fully acknowledged. Her career as a published writer began in 1966, and she has since become highly respected as an accomplished lyric poet and original prose stylist.

Feinstein pays considerable attention in her poetry to details of appearance—punctuation, spacing, line breaks—as well as to the less evident subtleties of tone, rhythm, and syntax. This is particularly evident in her first two collections, *In a Green Eye* and *The Magic Apple Tree.* She keeps meter under strict control, and her persona is usually rational, experienced (though not sophisticated), and resolutely unromantic. She can create a delicate relationship between tone and meaning, as in the involuted, one-sentence poem "Bathroom":

My legs shimmer like fish
my hair floats on the water:
tonight I observe that my
skin is no longer smooth
that blue veins show
in my arms that my
breasts are smaller

and lie seeing still water
meeting a white sky
(my elbows swim for me)
waiting for those
queer trails of thought
that move toward sleep

to where
the unforgiven words are
stored in circuits
of cells that hold
whatever shape there is
of the lost days

Her view of personal experience—often concerning such mundane matters as children, gardening, and marriage (in such poems as "A Dream of Spinsterhood")—is mature and solidly realistic. Poems from the first two collections, as well as from *The Celebrants,* were published in a selection entitled *Some Unease and Angels,* the only volume of her poetry to appear in the United States.

Feinstein worked for many years at the monumental task of translating into English the powerful yet delicate lyrics of Marina Tsvetayeva, a poet many readers of Russian regard as among the greatest of the century. Her edition of the *Selected Poems* was revised and expanded by fourteen poems in another volume, *Selected Poems.* Feinstein knows no Russian, and had to work from elaborate notes on the semantic, phonetic, and metrical characteristics of each poem, notes prepared by her collaborator, Angela Livingstone, and others, whose literal translations accompany Feinstein's poetic "transformations"—her own term for her efforts, borrowed from Octavio Paz. Her work received a very diverse critical reception. According to David McDuff, if her versions "claim to have the status of poetry, then one must insist that with a poet of the uniqueness and greatness of Tsvetayeva they must make at least some gesture in the direction of the formal and prosodic qualities of the original. This, with the possible exception of an eccentrically indented preservation of Tsvetayeva's stanzaic patterns (minus the rhymes), Feinstein's versions singularly fail to do." Henry Gifford, on the other hand, thought the translations "must be among the best of this century into English from any literature."

Feinstein sees her prose as "a channel for the exploration of my humanist concerns"; her early novels are short, economical in their use of language, and thematically diverse. In their unsensational depiction of sexuality and acute consciousness of what she terms, in *The Circle,* her first novel, the "terrible continuous burden of relationship," they recall the work of Iris Murdoch.

She moved to a larger, more international canvas with *Children of the Rose,* a troubling tale of a troubled couple, Alex and Lalka Mendez, Polish Jews, survivors of the Holocaust, rich, attractive, and thoroughly haunted by the past. Alex buys and renovates a French château, once occupied by the Gestapo, then spends his days there reading dense Hasidic tomes, trying to fathom the death of his family. Lalka stays in their Chelsea house, returns to Cracow to confront her past but loses her mind there, and ends up at the château, imbecilic and bedridden. Susannah Clapp remarked on the novel's convolution of plot and extreme stylistic terseness; she felt the author's "limitations are closely bound up with her merits. Much of the distinction of her writing depends on presenting characters who are not just incidentally irritated or pleased

by their dreams and memories, but changed and controlled by them—and some of the most persuasive writing in this novel describes people in the grip of flashback or nightmare. A price has to be paid for this effect. People whose inner life is so active are not always recognizable from the outside: their blunderings and bewilderment when confronted with each other are only too understandable."

"The black drama of the magician," a line from Feinstein's long poem "The Celebrants," might be taken as the theme of *The Shadow Master,* in which some British tourists in Turkey become caught up in the political intrigue and religious fanaticism surrounding a Turkish Jewish mystic who believes he is the reincarnation of Sabbatai Zevi, a seventeenth-century zealot and mystic. The novel includes a plot as complex as any detective story, constant travel back and forth across Europe, a rather conventional love interest, and much speculation on the symbolic mysteries of the Kabbala. British reviewers found the book "exhilarating and dextrous," its dialogue "exact, witty, original." The reviewer for the *New York Times Book Review,* however, wrote that "Everythng in this congested traffic-jam of a book is forced. Even the dialogue seems designed to cause migraine. And the simplest descriptions are clumsy. . . . It moves slowly from the confused to the pretentious."

The Survivors is certainly Feinstein's most ambitious novel to date, a realistic account of three generations of two Liverpool Jewish families from the time of their ancestors' emigration from Odessa at the turn of the century. One family, named Gordon, is highly assimilated, non-religious, middle class, and moneyed; the other, named Katz, is Orthodox and working class. The book is divided into four chronological sections (February 1914, October 1920, March 1934, 1956) which grow shorter and more selective of detail as they approach the present day (the 1970s); more than a third of the novel takes place during World War I. Members of one family rarely meet members of the other, and a range of characters represents several quite distinct ways of life; the final sections depict the academic and worldly success of the intelligent children of each family. Peter Lewis commended Feinstein for stretching her talent by attempting such a family saga, but thought *The Survivors* "more satisfactory in its parts than as a whole. . . . At. times, Feinstein seems to be trying to put a gallon into a pint glass. Ever since Lawrence revolutionized the family novel in *The Rainbow,* the genre has proved very difficult to handle for serious purposes and nowadays is associated mainly with popular, especially romantic, fiction. Feinstein has made a gallant attempt to redeem it, but in so doing she has sacrificed the more imaginative and even fantastic qualities of her recent fiction for pedestrian realism."

Feinstein's collection of short stories, *The Silent Areas,* shows her in top form: her natural tendency toward economy of language seems here utterly natural, congenial to the requirements of the short story. This collection contains the remarkable "Hansel and Gretel," a cunning inversion of the traditional children's story, set in the present, in which a small boy and girl are sent away from a "ranch-style executive house" in Cambridgeshire where their parents have completely run out of food and money. They happen upon a small house in the woods inhabited by an old woman who takes them in and feeds them. They then proceed to lie to her, plot against her, and finally incinerate her in her own fireplace and ransack her house. The story is terrifying and quirky, and has the impact of a great fairy tale.

works: *Novels*—The Circle, 1970; The Amberstone Exit, 1972; The Glass Alembic (U.S., The Crystal Garden), 1973; The Children of the Rose, 1974; The Ecstasy of Dr. Miriam Garner, 1976; The Shadow Master, 1978; The Survivors, 1982; The Border, 1984. *Poetry*—In a Green Eye, 1966; The Magic Apple Tree, 1971; At the Edge, 1972; The Celebrants, 1973; Some Unease and Angels, 1977. *Short Stories*—Matters of Chance, 1972; The Silent Areas, 1980. *Translations and editions*—Selected Poems of John Clare, 1968; The Selected Poems of Marina Tsvetayeva, 1971, revised edition, 1982; Three Russian Poets: Margarita Aliger, Yunna Moritz, Bella Akhmadulina, 1978.

about: Contemporary Authors 69–72, 1978; Dictionary of Literary Biography 14, 1983; Vinson, J. (ed.) Contemporary Poets, 1975. *Periodicals*—Choice June 1974; July–August 1978; Harper's June 1974; Library Journal May 1, 1974; October 1, 1979; Listener June 21, 1973; New Statesman September 22, 1978; November 18, 1981; New York Review of Books April 15, 1982; New York Times Book Review May 19, 1974; November 4, 1979; New Yorker June 3, 1974; Times (London) September 14, 1978; Times Literary Supplement April 25, 1975; February 3, 1978; October 6, 1978; January 8, 1982; February 26, 1982; June 8, 1984.

*FENG ZHI (also rendered as **FENG CHIH**) (September 17, 1905–   ), Chinese lyric poet, German scholar, professor, and man of letters, was born Feng Cheng Zhi, son of a minor clerk in Zhuo county, Hebei province. He recalls the earliest influences that set him on his literary career were his first language teacher, who initiated him into the world of classical literature,

another teacher who revealed to him a totally new world of Western literary modes, and his college professor, who helped him get into print for the first time.

In the summer of 1921 Feng Zhi enrolled in Beijing (Peking) University two years after the May Fourth Movement, a social, ideological, and political rebellion that marks a new era in modern Chinese history. It was, among other things, a movement to bring the vernacular into literary language and usher in a new, modern literature. Among the spate of literary societies then being formed, Feng himself, with a few literary friends, banded together in 1925 to found a literary journal *Chen zhong* or "The Sunken Bell," (the title was taken from Gerhart Hauptmann's play). In this journal Feng published his early poems. Lu Xun, China's most eminent literary critic, always responsive to new writers, took an interest in the work of this group and singled out Feng Zhi as "the most distinguished lyric poet of modern China." He praised the struggles of the short-lived journal (eight years of sporadic publication with thirty-four numbers published) as "the most elastic, sincere, and enduring in China."

In 1927 Feng published his poetry from the years 1921 to 1926 as *Zuori Zhige* (Songs of Yesterday), and in 1929 he published subsequent poems in *Beiyou Ji Qita* (Northern Wanderings and Other Poems). The title poem is a chronicle of the poet's stay in northern China, a sensitive intellectual's response to the sordidness of life in Harbin, a corrupt, semi-colonial city, and evokes echoes of T. S. Eliot's *The Waste Land.* Of Harbin he writes:

Beastlike motor cars
Marauding in the streets,
Bony horses pulling broken carts,
Shrieking with their necks outstretched.
Jewish banks, Greek restaurants,
Japanese drifters, White Russian brothels,
All gather in this strange place
With complete complacency.
Rich Chinese merchants
With their fat smug smiles,
Concubines in outlandish foreign clothes,
Pasty-faced youths in their melon-shaped caps.
. . . . . .
And prostitutes harboring poisonous germs
Gaudily strolling on the streets.
Am I wandering in hell?
Sinking deeper and deeper at every step
The sky is permeated with darkness and cold.
                              —trans. J. C. Lin

Those poems of the first period of his writing were practically unnoticed except by connoisseurs. In 1935, Zhu Ziqing, a scholar-critic, included some of Feng's poems in a collection of modern Chinese literature and in 1959, the famous scholar, poet, and critic He Qifang, de-

°feng jē

scribed Feng as a poet of great sensibility. He quoted the lyrics "Snake" and "Southern Night" as typical of Feng's early poetry, "not elaborate, but stongly moving." Compared with other poets of the times, wrote He Qifang, "some are more impetuous, some more picturesque, some more sophisticated, but such strong shades and shadows conveying such a highly-charged atmosphere which subtly lingers on and on—that is Feng Zhi's own touch." He goes on to say that "Snake" especially brings out the loneliness and depression of the young of the period and is typical of the spirit of the times.

My loneliness is a long snake,
Quiet and speechless.
If you happen to see it in your dream,
Oh by no means be startled.

It is my loyal companion,
Its heart suffers from burning homesickness:
It yearns for that lush plain,
Those crow-black strands of silk on your head!

And like the moonbeams, lightly
It will pass by your side
To steal your dream for me,
A dream that is a flaming crimson flower,
                                        —trans. J. C. Lin

Another aspect of Feng Zhi's early poetry is the lyric ballad. Of these, "The Drapery" (1924) and "The Silkworm Stallion" (1925) were much anthologized. The first portrays the irony of fate as seen in the plight of a young woman who, having voluntarily exiled herself to a nunnery, is inhibited from loving the man she feels she could love. The second, a narrative poem told in a strong romantic vein, is based on a mythological tale of a young maid who turns into a silkworm.

From 1930–35, Feng Zhi studied in Germany, first in Berlin and then in Heidelberg, where he received his doctorate. "It was a restless period in Germany," he recalls, "but I did not heed reality. I sat in Jaspars' lectures on existentialist philosophy, read Kierkegaard and Nietzsche, enjoyed the paintings of Van Gogh and Gauguin, and above all, read the poetry of Rilke with absorbing interest, but was not able to produce anything satisfactory myself."

Back in war-torn China in 1935, Feng first taught in Shanghai, then moved south-west, eventually reaching Kunming where he taught German at the prestigious SouthWest Associated University. It was here in 1941 that he first adapted the sonnet form, for which he was indebted to Rilke (whom he translated), and eventually wrote some of the most beautiful sonnets in modern Chinese literature. These follow the traditional fourteen-line structure but are unrhymed. Their only resemblance to the Western form, as Dominic Cheung points out, is their di-

vision, like the Petrarchan sonnet, into octaves and sestets. Thus Feng entered the second stage of his writing career—the early forties—a period which is noted chiefly for his sonnets.

In the afterword to the republication of the "Sonnets" (first published in 1942) in 1948, Feng revealed how he began these poems: One winter evening, as he walked in the country near Kunming, the appearance of several silver-colored planes in the bright blue sky carried his thoughts back to the legend about someone dreaming of the gigantic bird called the "roc," and that set off his train of thought. The lines that took shape in his mind during that solitary stroll became a variation of the sonnet form. As he put it: "The beginning was accidental, and yet I felt within me a sense of growing responsibility: There are experiences of our minds that return to our consciousness again and again, never stopping"—historical figures, natural scenes, private emotions or musings on the common lot—and to everything that offered something to his experience, he wished to record his gratitude in verse. This resulted in his twenty-seven sonnets written in 1941. Julia C. Liu writes: "If the early Feng Zhi is essentially a romantic lyricist, the later Feng, as revealed in his sonnets, is a poet of rare sensitivity and meditative strength. He has the incomparable gift of endowing the commonplace with freshness and projecting universals out of the tedious routines of life. The sonnets have intellectual and spiritual validity as well as great artistry. Feng belongs to the company of celebrated meditative poets that includes Rilke and, in his own tradition, Wang Wei."

On first publication in 1942 the sonnets were favorably commented on by such prestigious scholars as Zhu Ziqing and Li Quangtian, poets themselves. Li, in an article on "Meditative Poetry," pointed out that the sonnet form "with its layer upon layer of ascent and descent, its gradual concentration and diffusion, its intricacy and order, the winding in and out of its rhythm," is perfectly suited to convey the writer's meaning, giving it form and discipline. Critics have noted in them metaphysical overtones and parallels to Rilke. Of his sonnets, Feng himself feels, after forty years, that "compared to the two previous collections of twenty years earlier, they are more mature, both ideologically and artistically."

During the war, Feng became increasingly conscious of social evil, as is evident in his familiar essays and historical narratives of this period. As Feng recalls, he was then primarily concerned with the view of nature, "but the reality of Chinese society during the war period was such that I could not go on writing about nature. My essays too were gradually taken over by the ugliness of reality, and from writing about nature, I shifted to writing about society."

With the founding of the People's Republic, Feng Zhi, as a leading figure in cultural affairs, threw himself ardently into the task of rebuilding the country. Fully conscious that his life, with that of his country, had entered a new stage, he once again took up the writing of poetry. These poems of his third period of writing, mainly composed in the fifties, were collected first as *Xijiao Ji* (Our Western Suburbs), later rearranged with additions as *Shi Nian Shichao* (Poems of a Decade), 1959. He Qifang holds that of these later poems, "'Han Po the Woodcutter' and 'Drum of Human Skin' preserve the note of his early lyric narratives, but are more refined. Apart from that, it is difficult to trace in these poems any characteristics of Feng's early works." Feng Zhi himself agrees, but thinks that the poems of those ten years "are still fired with genuine feeling." The difficulty lies, perhaps, in the fact that he was striving after new forms to accommodate the new contents, and discarded the forms in which he excelled.

Another aspect of Feng's literary output, relatively unnoticed abroad, is his historical narratives, the most important being "Wu Tsi-Hsu." It is based on a historical legend about the wanderings of a persecuted young noble of the Chu kingdom of the Spring and Autumn period, circa 515 B.C. As Feng recalls, the story had always haunted him, and when he eventually started to write it, he let loose his imagination. Under the influence of Lu Xun's writings, he broke out of the bounds of history and added new material to the story—mainly slightly veiled allusions to current social abuses in the Guomintang area during the war period or scenes borrowed from private life.

One of the major achievements of Feng's postliberation years is his *Dufu Zhuan* (Life of Tu-Fu, 1952). Feng had always been a fine classical scholar, especially well-versed in classical poetry, and the celebrated eighth-century poet Tu-Fu, who sang of the sufferings of the masses, was his special favorite. His "Life of Tu-Fu," written with great sensitivity, is generally considered one of the best literary biographies published in New China. The book, along with a short story on Tu-Fu's late years "Black Strands Reappear in a Head of White Hair" was republished in one volume in the late seventies.

According to a recent interview published in *Wen Yi Bao*, China's leading literary journal, Feng reveals that he writes naturally, the words coming out in an easy flow, but that he is productive only at certain periods. Thus, Feng Zhi's output, taken on the whole, is relatively small. He struggles with the inner vision, combining romantic sensibility with classical restraint. He has produced a rare phenomenon—a combination of modern Western (mostly German) literary influence with Chinese classical scholarship. It is certainly that rare something in him that induced Lu Xun to hail him as "the most distinguished lyric poet of modern China."

Apart from his writing, Feng has had a full career as scholar, professor, and leading man of letters, especially in the field of foreign literature. After 1949, he served as chairman of the foreign language and literature department of Beijing (Peking) University, then from 1964, as director of the Institute of Foreign Literature, Chinese Academy of Social Sciences. He was also elected vice-president of the Writer's Union, and traveled extensively abroad on various delegations, especially in northern Europe, on missions of friendship and cultural exchanges.

Feng Zhi was nominated foreign member of the Academy of Literature, History and Antiquarian Studies in Stockholm in 1980, the first Chinese to be so honored, and then corresponding member of the Academy of Science and Literature of Mainz in 1981. He received the Goethe Medal of the Goethe Institute in 1983.

WORKS IN ENGLISH TRANSLATION: Kai-yu Hsu translated a selection of Feng Zhi's poetry, including a number of his sonnets, in his *Twentieth Century Chinese Poetry*, 1963; and Julia C. Lin includes a few translations (including some of the sonnets) in her discussion of him in *Modern Chinese Poetry: An Introduction*, 1972. The fullest critical discussion of his poetry as well as translations of all twenty-seven of his sonnets is by Dominic Cheung in his book on Feng in the Twayne World Authors Series, listed below.

ABOUT: Biographical Dictionary of Republican China, 1967–1971; Cassell's Encyclopedia of World Literature, 1973; Cheung, D. Feng Chih, 1979; Hsu, K. The Chinese Literary Scene, 1975 and Twentieth Century Chinese Poetry, 1963; Lin, J. C. Modern Chinese Poetry: An Introduction, 1972. *Periodicals*—Chinese Literature 3, 1963.

*FERREIRA DE CASTRO, JOSE MARIA

(May 24, 1898–June 29, 1974), Portuguese novelist and essayist, was born in the village of Oliveira de Azeméis near the town of Salgueiros in northern Portugal. His mother was Maria Rosa Soares de Castro and his father, who died when Castro was eight, was José Eustáquio Ferreira de Castro. At the age of twelve, having completed little more than a primary school ed-

*fer rā´ ē rə de käs´trō

ucation, Castro (along with many of his poverty-stricken compatriots) emigrated from the recently declared First Portuguese Republic (1910) to Brazil, in search of "promised wealth." He spent some four years on a rubber plantation in the middle of the Amazon jungle. Afterwards in Belém, capital of the Brazilian state of Pará, he barely survived, doing odd jobs and selling his own writings door-to-door. Castro returned to Portugal in 1919 poorer than he had left, but certainly more conscious of social issues. After further difficulties, he obtained work as a journalist and initiated the publication of his novels, which over the following five decades established him as a major Portuguese writer and brought worldwide attention to him and to Portuguese literature during the 1930s.

In his *Memórias* (Memoirs, 1933), Castro described his precocious interest in writing: "When I was nine years old, I dreamt of publishing in the town newspaper . . . I only achieved this dream when I was thirteen, on the Madeira River, and I sent a story to a small monthly in Rio Grande do Sul, Brazil, and they published it." His spare moments on the Paraíso rubber plantation were evidently dedicated to avid reading and to sketching what became his first stories and novels. In conservative post-World War I Portugal, his initial publications, reflecting the techniques of the fading naturalist literary school of Zola, were considered somewhat scandalous, verging on pornography. For example, *Carne Faminta* (Starved Flesh, 1922) is a blatant tale of sexual starvation in the Amazon jungle and involved a case of incest. This novel and others of the same ilk, published in 1923, were later rejected by the author for inclusion among his mature works.

Thematically and philosophically, Castro's Amazonian experience always remained at the core of his fiction. Man's mistreatment of his fellow man, which he witnessed both in the emigration process and in the jungle, led him to acknowledge that only the solidarity of mankind—true humanitarianism—could save man from tragedies. *Emigrantes* (*Emigrants*, 1928), Castro's first widely successful novel, presented the plight of men who see themselves obliged to emigrate in order to improve their social lot (as he himself had been). Although his poverty is not absolute, Manuel da Bouça, the novel's protagonist, decides to "temporarily" abandon his wife and daughter in vain pursuit of wealth in Brazil. His perdition is owed not only to his emigrant status in Brazil, but also to his refusal to accept his personal limitations. His years in São Paulo are full of hardship, but the illusion of sudden wealth is all too powerful. Castro stressed the elements of Manuel's story which typify the emi-

grant of any nationality, all of whom, he believed, are both culturally and economically unprepared for the emigrant experience: "The emigration problem . . . is a consequence of a greater and deeper problem. . . . The emigrants seek their adventure because they lack bread or because they convince themselves that in their world only the possessor of gold has a right to life's pleasures. . . . If there is guilt to be established for this situation, it belongs first to Europe."

A Selva (*The Jungle*, 1930) complements the issues of his first novel, but focuses on the origins of specific social and political phenomena. Alberto, the protagonist, flees a possible political jailing in Portugal and seeks refuge in the Amazon. There he confronts victims of centuries-old social, political, and racial persecution. He gradually realizes that a more just society can only be a "classless society." *The Jungle* was an astonishing worldwide success. Commentators and translators, including Blaise Cendrars, noted Castro's impressive descriptive talent. Fred Marsh, who reviewed the 1934 English language version, wrote: "Long passages of the book are given over to rhythmic descriptions of the jungle in winter and summer, when flooded and when parched; to descriptions of the fauna and flora of the Amazonian wilderness; to incidents which illustrate the strange, greedy, generative spirit of this growing mass of vegetation. . . . "

Castro's inclusion of contemporary sociopolitical concerns in his fiction makes him a precursor of the neorealist movement in literature, which began to flourish in the mid-1930s. Neither *Emigrants* nor *The Jungle*, which have overshadowed all of Castro's later works, assumes a solely doctrinal stance. Rather, the action is well balanced to reveal the confluence of socio-political conditions and the personal traits of the characters. Psychological developments are carefully enhanced by Castro to reveal the characters' growing awareness of societal disjunctions and their attempts to rectify such situations. Thus, his characters are presented as possible role models for the reader prepared to take political action .

Eternidade (Eternity, 1933) is set on the island of Madeira in post-World War I. The class and political confrontations which shook Europe are suddenly echoed in edenic Madeira. Juvenal, the main character, is politically astute, but more contemplative than active. He remains on the sidelines until class injustice rouses him to action. His participation in a peasant uprising demanding work and food results in his deportation to the Cape Verde Islands. He is comforted by his belief in the future: "I have a need to believe in the redemption of man by man; without this belief, all life's roads seem to me to be negative and closed; for this reason, I believe in the future, which is the only epoch in which all the anxieties and hopes of all those disinherited from everything can fit."

The locale of *Terra Fria* (Frozen Earth, 1934) is a village in mountainous northern Portugal. Although the inhabitants are simple and poor, they are honorable and religious. The novel's plot once again examines the results of emigration. Here, a wealthy returned emigrant, the "americano," has made the village his personal fiefdom, having taken control of everything. His mania for possessions and total domination results in village tragedies and finally in his death. In *A Lã e a Neve* (The Wool and the Snow, 1947), Castro dealt with the emergence of industrial Portugal, and the consequent conflicts between worker and management. Horácio, a shepherd, feels impelled to abandon his rural flocks to become a weaver in a nearby city. This decision requires him to break with a centuries-old rural family life and to confront abuse and intolerance in his new life. Through these experiences, he gains a greater social consciousness; he realizes the limits of his "worker status" and those imposed upon him from within Portuguese society.

Castro's belief in the possibility of liberty and equality—the aims of proletarian revolution—were dealt another hard blow as a result of the Spanish Civil War (1936–1939). *A Curva da Estrada* (The Curve in the Road, 1950) takes place in Republican Spain of the early 1930s and all the characters are Spanish, although the story might very well be a metaphor for the contemporary Portuguese situation. An elder statesman of the Spanish Socialist Party, Soriano, becomes disillusioned with the turn of events in his party, over which he can no longer exert control. Vanity and the desire for power push him to consider bolting to the opposition party. Only his son's zealous pleading and rationalization of the situation saves him from betraying himself and all those who believed in him. The "Socratic" dialogue between Soriano and Enrique delves into the meaning of political and social commitment and the need for constant evaluation of one's aims and motives. Castro's strong feelings about the disastrous situation of his Iberian comrades are further developed in another impassioned novel, *O Intervalo* (The Intermission), written in 1936 but published only after the 1974 Portuguese revolution, which brought a half-century of dictatorship to a veritably comic end. *The Intermission* was to be the third in a series of novels that were to highlight the paths of the workers' movement since the turn of the century: "In that morbid, anti-intellectual, anti-analytic, uncomprehending atmosphere [of Portugal in the 1930s] . . . which the Spanish Civil War had even further deepened among Lusitanian spirits, my poor book about the proletarian battles in Spain would . . . inevitably have been suppressed. . . . I left it in my files. . . . I tried to write other novels which unconsciously were drawn to similar themes, the prohibited ones—the principal ones of our day . . . and I gave up. It is very difficult, except for the most cynical soul, to be untrue to himself."

Events of the Second World War (perhaps the Nazi bombing of the Spanish town of Güernica) inspired *A Missão* (1954, *The Mission*). The validity of religion and the Church as forces within society is touched upon. Some members of a Christian brotherhood decide to paint the word "Mission" on the roof of their building to save the structure from aerial bombing. Others protest and suggest that it would be more "Christian" to paint the word on the nearby factory and thus save the lives and livelihood of the townspeople. The moral dilemma debated by the brothers revolves around their obligation to "save lives or save souls." The final decision, however, is snatched from them by the sway of events.

In *O Instincto Supremo* (The Supreme Instinct, 1968), his final novel, Castro eulogized his ideal of the humanitarian: the Brazilian Coronel Rondon. The novel describes Rondon's expeditions to the interior of the Amazon to make contact with and pacify the Parintintins Indians. His motto was "To die, perhaps, but never to kill." Castro commented: "Although rooted in true facts, this examination of a moral problem and of popular heroism . . . is an epic of recent days and has been ignored by the world and by the majority of Brazilians. . . . " The epic possibilities of the events become, however, quite secondary to Castro's glorification of the personal and psychological background of the hero. This results in a novel of little vitality. It is, however, notable that Castro's final novel returned once again to a Brazilian theme. Castro was greatly admired in Brazil for *Emigrants* and *The Jungle*, both of which influenced the Brazilian neorealist writers of the 1930s and 1940s.

In addition to these and other novels, which have been translated into seventeen languages, Castro published several collections of essays narrating his travel experiences in Europe, the Middle East, and the Orient. He also wrote popular guides to the world's artistic treasures. One Brazilian critic describes his literary contribution in this manner: "This writer, who always refused to belong to the Academies, is most notable for his ability to hear the feelings, aspirations, problems, and dramas of the people. His work is a continuous communion with the simple and humble rural folk or factory worker, whom he knew well how to motivate as a character and whom he understood quite well."

WORKS IN ENGLISH TRANSLATION: Ferreira de Castro's novel *A Selva* was the first of his works translated into English—as *The Jungle: A Tale of the Amazon Rubber Tapper* by L. Dickson in 1934. *Emigrants* was published in Dorothy Ball's translation in 1962, and *The Mission,* translated by Ann Stevens, was published in 1963.

ABOUT: Columbia Dictionary of Modern European Literature, 1980; Contemporary Authors 102, 1981; Encyclopedia of World Literature in the 20th Century (rev. ed.) I, 1981; Library of Literary Criticism: Modern Romance Literature, 1967. *Periodicals*—New York Times November 18, 1962, July 2, 1974; New York Times Book Review February 3, 1935.

M.F.K. FISHER

FISHER, M(ARY) F(RANCES) K(EN-NEDY) (July 3, 1908–), American memoirist and food- and travel-writer, was born in Albion, Michigan, the daughter of Rex Brenton Kennedy, a journalist and editor, and the former Edith Oliver Holbrook. In 1912 her father sold his share of the family newspaper and moved West with his wife and children. After eighteen months of seeing the sights, they settled down in the Quaker town of Whittier, California, where for the next four decades Rex Kennedy was owner and editor of the *Whittier News.* Mary Frances grew up in an ebullient and literate family, but became eager to escape Whittier's straitlaced confines. In 1929 she married Alfred Fisher, Princeton graduate and son of a Presbyterian minister, and that same year they left for three years in France, spent mostly in Dijon, the chief city of Burgundy, living in a boardinghouse, "very simply with very simple people," as she said in 1981. "I didn't want to pass time, just to marry some nice Pasadena broker. Nope, nope, nope. When I went to France, I really worked. I learned how to study, how to think." She attended the University of Dijon for three years, and her husband earned his doctorate there. They returned to southern California in 1932 so he could take up a teaching post in French at Occidental College, but her writing career had still not begun.

To supplement her husband's $650 annual salary, Fisher took a job in a store that sold pornography. "I didn't care," she recalled. "It didn't interest me at all. . . . I was the front because I looked so sweet." At the same time, on free mornings, she began to do research on food and gastronomy at the Los Angeles Public Library, producing several essays—"little things I'd give to my husband . . . to amuse him." With the help of a family friend, the painter Dillwyn Parrish, these were published in 1937 as *Serve It Forth.* The slim book, filled with recondite gastronomical references and beautifully written, was favorably reviewed by Lucius Beebe, the doyen of American food-writers, who later became irate on learning she was not a man. "Women, he had assumed," she said in 1969, "were supposed to confine themselves to home economics doings and stuff." Soon after becoming a published author, she divorced Fisher and married Dillwyn Parrish, returning to Europe to live in his house outside the Swiss town of Vevey on Lake Geneva. Parrish, however, contracted a fatal illness and died just after the start of World War II. His widow returned to California.

Her books appeared regularly thereafter. *Consider the Oyster* was followed by *How to Cook a Wolf,* on coping with wartime scarcity, and *The Gastronomical Me,* which many consider her best book. Her first four works plus *An Alphabet for Gourmets* were collected in one volume as *The Art of Eating* in 1954 (repr. 1976). During the 1940s she also produced an anthology of good eating, *Here Let Us Feast: A Book of Banquets;* a widely acclaimed annotated translation of Jean Anthelme Brillat-Savarin's classic *The Physiology of Taste;* and her novel *Not Now but NOW,* neglected when it was first published in 1947 but a surprising success in a 1982 reissue. An earlier effort at fiction, *Touch and Go,* had been written with Parrish and published in 1939 under the pseudonym Victoria Berne. She set down her philosophy on food and writing in the preface to *The Gastronomical Me.* In response to the frequent questions "Why do you write about food and eating and drinking? Why don't you write about the struggle for power and security, and about love, the way others do?" she answered, "It seems to me that our three basic needs, for food and security and love, are so mixed and mingled and entwined that we cannot straightly think of one without the other. So it happens that when I write about hunger, I am really writing about love and the hunger for it, and warmth and the love of it and the hunger for it . . . and then the warmth and richness and fine reality of hunger satisfied . . . and it is all one."

Fisher's style has always been praised for clarity, sophistication, and richness of sensuous detail; she herself has called it "pleasant honesty." W. H. Auden said, "I do not know of anyone in the United States today who writes better prose." Although her books often contain unusual recipes, she has never written a cookbook per se. "Recipes in my book," she announced early in her career, "will be there like birds in a tree, if there is a comfortable branch." Her collections of essays on gastronomy in *The Art of Eating* are complemented by *With Bold Knife and Fork*; the early and more autobiographical *The Gastronomical Me* is fleshed out by the memoirs of her Episcopalian girlhood in Quaker Whittier; *Among Friends,* and by *As They Were,* a collection of previously published articles. Most of her books contain some reflections on her travels; two in particular recount her experiences of living in the south of France: *Map of Another Town: A Memoir of Provence* treats the city of Aix-en-Provence, and *A Considerable Town* is a fond memoir of the ancient city of Marseilles. *A Cordiall Water: A Garland of Odd & Old Receipts to Assuage the Ills of Man or Beast,* a serious consideration of naturopathy, herbal medicine, and "the fine line that separates scientific from religious healing," is Fisher's own favorite among her books. "I haven't written anything I'm proud of, ever," she remarked in 1981. "I used to say I'm going to write a good book by the time I'm fifty, then I raised the ante a bit." At the age of fifty-five she went to Mississippi to teach for a year in a segregated black school. "I wanted to see if the South was as rotten as I'd heard it was, and it was. Oh, it was worse!" She has never written about her experiences there.

In the early 1970s, Fisher moved from a large, old house in St. Helena, Napa Valley, to a comfortable two-room house designed for her by the architect David Bouverie on a part of his ranch in Glen Ellen, Sonoma county, in the wine country north of San Francisco. She has always loved wine ("I could and would forgo any other liquid forever, as long as I might drink one humble wine with my daily bread") and wrote *The Story of Wine in California* long before the quality of American wines was widely appreciated.

Her frequent trips to Europe, often shared with her two daughters from her third marriage (to the publisher Donald Friede, whom she also divorced), were discontinued after the mid-1970s, as cataracts, arthritis, and heart trouble began to take their toll. She still, however, writes and cooks copiously and entertains modestly. "I will not bow," she said to Maya Angelou in an interview that appeared in early 1983. "Absolutely not bow. I say, 'Brother Pain, come in and sit down, you and I are going to take this thing in hand. And I will not give in.'" *Sister Age,* her sixteenth book, is a culmination of her long interest in the problems of aging. "I think it is something you must welcome," she said to Angelou, "and I welcome it as a sister. And I am grateful. Other people have done much more and much better, but I'm glad I've lived this life and expect to be around for many others."

PRINCIPAL WORKS: *Non-fiction*—Serve It Forth, 1937; Consider the Oyster, 1941; How to Cook a Wolf, 1942; The Gastronomical Me, 1943; Here Let Us Feast, 1946; An Alphabet for Gourmets, 1949; The Art of Eating, 1954; A Cordiall Water, 1961; The Story of Wine in California, 1962; Map of Another Town, 1964; (*introduction to*) Napa Wine, by Robert Louis Stevenson, 1965; The Cooking of Provincial France, 1968; With Bold Knife and Fork, 1969; Among Friends, 1971; A Considerable Town, 1978; As They Were, 1982; Sister Age, 1983. *Fiction*—(as Victoria Berne) Touch and Go, 1939; Not Now but NOW, 1947. *Translation*—Brillat-Savarin, J. A. The Physiology of Taste, 1949.

ABOUT: Contemporary Authors 77–80, 1981; Current Biography, 1948, 1983. *Periodicals*—Gourmet November 1983; Newsday May 13, 1981; Newsweek February 11, 1980; June 6, 1983; New York Times December 16, 1969; August 31, 1977; May 22, 1978; New York Times Book Review June 6, 1982; May 29, 1983; People January 24, 1983; Quest/81 June 1981; Washington Post Book World December 5, 1971.

FORSYTH, FREDERICK (1938–   ), British novelist and journalist, was born in Ashford, Kent. He attended Tonbridge School, where he excelled in foreign languages, and was a student for five months at the University of Grenada, Spain.

Forsyth joined the Royal Air Force at the age of seventeen, and after flight training was for a

FREDERICK FORSYTH

time the youngest qualified pilot in the corps. Embarking on his career in journalism, he learned the reporting trade on the *Eastern Daily Press* in Norwich, Norfolk (1956–61), then joined Reuters, working as a correspondent in Paris and Central Europe (1961–65). He was hired by the British Broadcasting Corporation in 1965, but had few foreign assignments until July 1967, when he was flown into Biafra just after that province had declared its independence from Nigeria. His reporting on the bloody horrors of the Nigerian civil war was considered by his superiors to be too favorable to the rebels; Sir David Hunt, British high commissioner in Lagos, called it "hopelessly biased" and complained to the Foreign Office and to the BBC, which withdrew him from the war zone. He angrily resigned his job and returned to Biafra as a freelance reporter at the personal invitation of Col. Chukwuemaka Ojukwu, the secessionist leader, whom he greatly admired. In an interview in 1974, Forsyth insisted his reporting was correct: "I described exactly what I saw—which is something that the man on the spot is uniquely in a position to do. I have no time for editors who've never been reporters, any more than pilots have for squadron leaders who've never flown, and that was the position I found myself in at the BBC. There are a lot of time-servers there. The BBC was, and remains, a news-gathering organization that is in a position to 'manage' the news and quite often does so without scruple." *The Biafra Story,* his first book, is a careful yet passionate account of a brave people's doomed struggle for freedom.

Forsyth was in Paris in August 1962 when President Charles de Gaulle was nearly assassinated at Petit-Clamart outside the capital. Rightist extremists asserted they had made the attempt because of de Gaulle's support for Algerian independence, which had occurred the month before. The incident obsessed him for years, and during thirty-five days in 1970 he wrote *The Day of the Jackal,* his first novel, which many critics still consider his best work. It was rejected by four major London publishers before it was bought by Hutchinson, and it became in short order an international best-seller. Several critics complained of its tastelessness and incessant use of clichés, but as Pamela Marsh wrote, it "has all the ingredients for instant readership—unrelenting action, drama, and the inevitable ration of lust and torture." The reviewer for the *Times Literary Supplement* felt that the reader "is almost persuaded he is following the reconstruction of an actual event. Part of the secret is that real people move in and out of the plot. . . . The technique is not new, but Mr. Forsyth handles it with a mature confidence remarkable in a first novel, and reinforces the general aura of plausibility with a fanatical attention to what one might call the logistic details." Precise use of detail has always been a hallmark of Forsyth's fiction.

The Odessa File describes the attempt of Peter Miller, a young German reporter, to penetrate Odessa, a sinister organization protecting the false identities of former Nazi SS officers. He wants in particular to discover the whereabouts of Eduard Roschmann, the ruthless commandant of a death camp in Riga, Latvia, who has become indispensable to a pan-Arab missile program. The novel was another enormous international success, and an exciting espionage movie was made of it starring Jon Voight as the reporter and Maximilian Schell as the evil Roschmann. The novel's critics were, as usual in Forsyth's case, less than kind. Richard P. Bruckner accused him of borrowing "painful, live history in order to spring a few quick thrills," but was obliged to allow that the author "shows two areas of strength. . . . One is the substance of his historical narration. The second is in his knowledge and use of mechanics. Whatever equipment he describes, you know he is describing it authoritatively—thus his burglaries, bombs, murders and forgeries are arresting." Michael Crichton claimed that the "subject matter" of *Odessa* "has never worked well. The constellation of concentration-camp victims, SS officers, and lingering German anti-Semitism has too many reverberations, too many profound moral questions, to fit comfortably in a suspense-novel format. The questions are weightier than the superstructure can support, and the story collapses under the burden."

Forsyth turned to his experiences in West Africa as the inspiration for his next novel, *The Dogs of War*. The "dogs" are a group of white mercenaries hired by a mining tycoon to assassinate a corrupt dictator and replace him with a more tractable puppet. The tycoon's goal is ownership of a mountain of platinum ore in the unnamed country's interior. In an extraordinary real-life development, Forsyth was accused in an article in the *Times* of London of financing, from his home in southeastern Spain, a planned coup d'état in Equatorial Guinea against the regime of Francisco Macías Nguema. The coup never took place, and although he denied his involvement at first, he later admitted he had needed detailed information about organizing such a plot but never intended it to go ahead. The critics were divided in their reaction to this novel. Donald Goddard, in a savage review, called it "meretricious, . . . informed with a kind of post-imperial condescension toward the black man . . . [and] some openly patronizing references to the Africans' fear of fighting in the dark and their 'annoying habit' of shutting their eyes while firing automatic weapons." Edward Bartley, on the other hand, thought *Dogs* a "spellbinder, . . . top drawer. . . . Forsyth's characterizations are finely drawn." John R. Coyne, Jr., called it "ingeniously plotted, an impressive blend of fact and fiction, written in tight, lucid, masculine prose, . . . a first-rate thriller."

The Devil's Alternative, published in 1980, is a novel set in 1982, describing events that bring the world close to nuclear annihilation, including the assassination of the head of the Soviet KGB, the hijacking of a supertanker, and the betrayal of Russian secrets at the highest level. The title is a term used by British intelligence to describe a distasteful solution to a knotty problem. Barbara Conaty thought it "a stupendous entertainment. . . . While the intricately woven themes spin to a smooth and coherent conclusion, the reader is swept into the counsels of the great, the intrigues of the loyal, and the plots of the lowly. Paradoxically, all this is achieved through a modicum of violence and nary a sexy titillation." I. P. Heldman wrote, "As Mr. Forsyth spins his web, he projects us into the hot seats of all the world leaders. We listen with them while their china cups clink, feel the chill in their bones at the prospect of what it will take to avert world disaster. . . . [He] wraps it all up with a double-whammy ending that will take even the most wary reader by surprise. . . . A many-layered thriller."

Forsyth was reported in 1974 to have earned more than two million pounds from his literary endeavors. He and his wife, Carrie, have a son and live on a large estate in County Wicklow, Ireland. To avoid paying heavy British income taxes, he is obliged to spend most of the year outside the United Kingdom. He professes to be very satisfied with his financial success: "I'm a writer with the intent of selling lots of copies and making money. I don't think my work will ever be regarded as great literature or classics. I'm just a commercial writer and I have no illusions about it."

PRINCIPAL WORKS: *Fiction*—The Day of the Jackal, 1971; The Odessa File, 1972; The Dogs of War, 1974; The Devil's Alternative, 1980; The Fourth Protocol, 1984. *Non-fiction*—The Biafra Story, 1969, rev. ed. The Making of an African Legend: The Biafra Story, 1977; *Juvenile*—The Shepherds, 1975.

ABOUT: Contemporary Authors 85–88, 1980; Contemporary Literary Criticism 2, 1974 and 5, 1976. *Periodicals*—Atlantic September 1971; August 1974; Best Sellers August 1, 1974; Christian Science Monitor August 12, 1971; July 31, 1974; Library Journal September 1, 1971; October 1 , 1972; January 15, 1980; National Review November 24, 1972; August 2, 1974; June 13, 1980; New Republic August 31, 1974; New Statesman September 20, 1974; New York Review of Books November 6, 1980; New York Times Book Review August 15, 1971; November 5, 1972; July 14, 1974; February 24, 1980; Newsweek August 16, 1971; July 22, 1974; February 11, 1980; September 2, 1984; Observer June 13, 1971; September 24, 1972; September 8, 1974; Saturday Review September 4, 1971; December 9, 1972; Times Literary Supplement July 2, 1971; October 25, 1974.

FRANCIS, ROBERT (CHURCHILL) (August 12, 1901–), American poet and prose writer, sent the following autobiographical note to *World Authors* in 1982:

"At the age of eighty-one I am involved in more writing projects than ever before in my life. And there is an ever-increasing amount of 'busyness' pertaining to my work. In this I am assisted by a literary aide and also by two advisors who will become my literary co-executors. Aside from this literary activity, I take or make time to care for my grounds and garden, and to do all my housework including the preparation of all my meals. And not only busy; time for friends, interviewers, photographers, as well as for sunbathing and music, my own and other people's."

———

Francis was born in Upland, Pennsylvania, the son of Reverend Ebenezer Fisher Francis, a Baptist minister, and the former Ida May Allen. After living in New Jersey and in Greenport, Long Island, Francis' family, which included his

ROBERT FRANCIS

older sister from his father's first marriage, moved to the Boston area of Massachusetts in 1910, settling in West Medford a year later. Here Francis, a sensitive child, grew up, beginning violin lessons in seventh grade and later developing a "feeling for English," as he states in his autobiography, *The Trouble With Francis*, while taking a Latin course in high school. At Medford High School, he served as editor-in-chief of the school magazine and graduated in 1919 as valedictorian with a straight-A record.

Francis then entered Harvard, where he had the poet Robert Hillyer as his freshman English teacher, was a first violinist in the orchestra, and majored in history, writing some poetry during his senior year. After graduating with an A.B. degree in 1923, he went to Lebanon as a teacher in the prep school of the American University of Beirut. Returning home in poor health in 1924, he began a regimen that included sunbathing, which was to become one of his major pastimes, and at this time he also undertook several musical and literary projects and then attended the Harvard Graduate School of Education, earning a Master's degree in 1926.

Following his graduation, Francis took a position as an English teacher in Amherst High School, but, discontented with teaching, decided after a year to devote himself to writing. He succeeded in having several essays and stories published in magazines, and he also performed on and taught the violin. From 1932 to 1937 he lived in the town of Amherst, rooming in the homes of various elderly landladies. One of these experiences later provided the material for his novel *We Fly Away*.

After making the acquaintance of Robert Frost in 1933, Francis developed an enduring friendship with the older, established poet, who often read Francis' poems and discussed them with him. Francis recorded their conversations in a journal which he published many years later as *Frost: A Time to Talk*. On the recommendation of another Amherst literary friend, the poet and teacher David Morton, Francis' first book of poems, *Stand With Me Here*, was published in 1936. "Overnight," Francis observes in his autobiography, he became "an Amherst poet, a Macmillan poet, an American poet." The volume, which included such poems as "A Broken View," "Cloud in Woodcut," "Bronze," "Prophet," "Artist," "While I Slept," and "Diver," received mixed reviews but was praised by several critics, including William Rose Benét, for its craftsmanship and its feeling for nature. It also won its author a fellowship to the Breadloaf Writers' Conference in August 1937.

Having lived in an old rented house outside the town center of Amherst since 1937, Francis in 1940 had a "small one-man (but not one-room) house" (as he characterizes it in *The Trouble With Francis*) built for him on Market Hill Road in Amherst Township. This house he named Fort Juniper after the juniper tree, which grows so low to the ground that it cannot fall and thus serves "as a symbol of what might he called infallibility." At Fort Juniper, which he considers "an expression of my way of life, and so something of a symbol of myself," Francis, a vegetarian, does all his own housekeeping, meal preparation, and gardening. Adhering to his belief in thrift, he has made it his practice "not to earn much but to spend little." His life-style reflects his intense admiration for Thoreau, who, together with Emerson and Whitman, is one of the "American writers who meant the most" to him.

From 1938 to 1954, Francis contributed monthly essays on country subjects to the Home Forum Page of the *Christian Science Monitor*. Also in 1938 his second book, *Valhalla and Other Poems*, was published, the title piece being a long narrative work about a New England farm family. This volume elicited a letter of high praise from Robert Frost, who regarded a number of the poems as his "idea of perfection." After voluntarily doing noncombatant military service from 1942 to 1943, Francis took several brief teaching assignments, including one at Mount Holyoke College. *The Sound I Listened For*, Francis' next collection, included such poems as "Juniper," "Serpent as Vine," "Spicebush and Witch-Hazel," and "Seagulls," praised by reviewers for their imagery, lyricism, and depth of thought. Although Louis Untermeyer, in the

Yale Review, found strong similarities to Frost, and Milton Hindus, in *Poetry,* found echoes of Emily Dickinson, Frost, and Edwin Arlington Robinson, both of these critics noticed an original voice as well.

From 1946 until the magazine ceased publication four years later, Francis contributed poems and essays to the Philadelphia-based *Forum.* *The Face Against the Glass,* a pamphlet of poems that he had printed privately in 1950, contained "Glass," which expressed his theory of the fusion of poetic form and meaning: "Words of a poems should be glass/ But glass so simple-subtle its shape/ Is nothing but the shape of what it holds." After a period of difficulty in placing his work, he had poems accepted by the *New Yorker* and *Saturday Review* in 1953, the same year in which six of his poems were included in *New Poems by American Poets,* edited by Rolfe Humphries. Three poems by Francis also appeared in *The Faber Book of Modern American Verse,* edited by W. H. Auden. Beginning in 1954, he taught poetry classes for five summers at the Chautauqua Writers' Workshop in New York.

Some of Francis' best-known and most frequently anthologized poems appeared in *The Orb Weaver*—"Swimmer," "High Diver," "Waxwings," "Pitcher," "The Base Stealer," "Two Wrestlers," and "Apple Peeler." The volume was very favorably reviewed, especially in the *Massachusetts Reivew,* where John Holmes made its publication the occasion for a lengthy analysis of the characteristics of Francis' poetry. The first four lines of "Pitcher" illustrate what Holmes regarded as Francis' interest in probing the intention behind an action: "His art is eccentricity, his aim/ How not to hit the mark he seems to aim at,/ His passion how to avoid the obvious,/ His technique how to vary the avoidance." Calling Francis "that rare figure in present-day poetry, both a poet's poet and a reader's poet," Holmes observed that his poems are readable, "have been slowly and thoughtfully made, and kept until ready to go out on their own," are often playful and amusing, and "satisfy every expectation they create."

Come Out Into the Sun: Poems New and Selected contained among the new poems several of a political nature, as well as eight word-count poems. As Francis explains in his autobiography, his device of word-count "is a way of controlling the length of a line of poetry, not by the number of syllables it contains, and not by the number of clusters of syllables called feet, but by the number of whole words." "Museum Vase" and "Icicles," for example, have three words to a line.

A number of political poems appeared in *Like Ghosts of Eagles* in 1974, notably such anti-war pieces as "The Righteous," "Light Casualties," and "Blood Stains." This volume also included examples of his technique, described in *The Trouble With Francis,* of using "a fragmented surface—short phrases or single words—instead of connected discourse" in order to achieve "greater emotional impact." Various reviewers, while seeing him as basically a traditional poet, commented on his epigrammatic style, language play, and experimentation with form. Francis' *Collected Poems, 1936–1976* reproduced the contents of his seven previous books and added a section of new poems. His preface alerted the reader to the poet's development from a "serious young man" to a "bolder and livelier" writer in his later work. Although some critics felt his poetry to be limited by its generally unimpassioned manner, the *Collected Poems* brought new recognition to Francis, who, as several reviewers noted, had long suffered undeserved neglect. Comparing his direct, memorable "lyric-didactic" poetry to that of William Stafford, Robert P. Tristram Coffin, and Guy Owen, Lewis Leary's review in the *New England Quarterly* stated that "Robert Francis remains close to nature and close to truth."

Francis' first book of non-fictional prose was *The Satirical Rogue on Poetry,* a collection of very brief essays. "My hidden motive in writing *The Satirical Rogue,*" he explains in his autobiography, "was to get even with the world of poetry which had caused me so much suffering over the years. To get even with it by pin-pricking and deflating it." The last paragraph of "On Looking Like a Poet" exemplifies his pointed way of doing this: "Self-expression is important to all poets, and looking like a poet is one form of it. If a poet happens not to be writing fine poems or even any poems at all, looking like a poet may be almost the only form of self-expression he has." *The Trouble With Francis* begins and ends with the writer's philosophy. Francis calls himself "a happy pessimist": "I have been growing healthier and happier over the years; yet when I look around me I am more impressed with the ills of life, the injustices, frustrations, and agonies, than with anything else." He also confesses to a dislike for poetry, especially contemporary poetry. One reviewer compared the book to the autobiographies of Yeats and Edwin Muir, and another likened it to *Walden* and Nadezha Mandelstam's *Hope Against Hope.* In the *Nation,* Michael Hamburger wrote that "by providing statistics of his income and expenditure, of the plants he grows and eats, of the things he buys and does not buy, Robert Francis shows how frugality can work in practice on the East Coast of the U.S.A., in 1970; and how its practice can lead to happiness, 'fulfillment and control.'"

Fulfillment has come for Francis in the respect and honors he has achieved over his long career. The American Academy of Arts and Letters awarded him a fellowship to the American Academy in Rome in 1957 and he returned to Italy in 1967 on an Amy Lowell Travelling Scholarship. Elected an honorary member of Phi Beta Kappa at Harvard University, he has been Phi Beta Kappa poet at both Tufts University (1955) and Harvard (1960). In 1970 the University of Massachusetts awarded him an L.H.D., and in 1974 he received the Creative Arts Award in Poetry from Brandeis University. The works and papers of Francis are housed in three places: the Syracuse University Library, which organized The Robert Francis Papers in 1968; the Jones Library, the public library of the Town of Amherst, where Francis has given poetry readings, talks, and violin concerts; and the University of Massachusetts Library in Amherst, home of the principal Robert Francis collection, which is located in Special Collections and in Archives. In 1974 the University of Massachusetts Press established the Juniper Prize in honor of Francis.

PRINCIPAL WORKS: *Poetry*—Stand With Me Here, 1936; Valhalla and Other Poems, 1938; The Sound I Listened For, 1944; The Face Against the Glass, 1950; The Orb Weaver: Poems, 1960; Come Out Into the Sun: Poems New and Selected, 1965; Like Ghosts of Eagles: Poems, 1966–1974, 1974; Collected Poems, 1936–1976, 1976. *Novel*—We Fly Away, 1948. *Non-fiction*—The Satirical Rogue on Poetry, 1968: The Trouble With Francis: An Autobiography, 1971; Frost: A Time to Talk: Conversations & Indiscretions Recorded by Robert Francis, 1972; A Certain Distance, 1976; Francis on the Spot, 1976; Pot Shots at Poetry, 1980.

ABOUT: Contemporary Authors, new revision series 1, 1981; Hamburger, M. Art as Second Nature: Occasional Pieces, 1950–74, 1975; Rosa, A. (ed.) The Old Century and the New: Essays in Honor of Charles Angoff, 1978; Vinson, J. (ed.) Contemporary Poets, 1980. *Periodicals*—Hudson Review Summer 1977; Massachusetts Review August 1960; New England Quarterly June 1977; New York Times Book Review March 10, 1985; Sewanee Review Summer 1977; Western Humanities Review Autumn 1974.

FRANK, JOSEPH (NATHANIEL) (October 6, 1918–), American biographer and literary critic, was born in New York City. Although he attended New York University (1937–38), the University of Wisconsin, Madison (1941–42), and the University of Paris (Fulbright Scholar, 1950–51), without taking a degree, he was none-

JOSEPH FRANK

theless able to earn a doctorate in 1960 from the University of Chicago where he had both Rockefeller and University of Chicago fellowships. He worked as an editor at the Bureau of National Affairs in Washington (1942–50) and was special researcher at the United States embassy in Paris (1951–52). Frank lectured in English at Princeton University from 1954 to 1956 (Christian Gauss lecturer 1954–55), then taught at Minnesota (1958–61) and Rutgers (1961–66) universities before returning (1966) to Princeton to teach in the comparative literature department and direct the Gauss Seminars in Criticism. He is now professor emeritus.

Frank made his mark as a critic with several influential scholarly articles on modern literature, notably "Spatial Form in Modern Literature," first published in Sewanee Review in 1945. His thesis here and in two later essays in Critical Inquiry (1977 and 1978) found its origin in the eighteenth-century German critic Gotthold Lessing's distinction between the temporal and the spatial arts: literature, which the reader apprehends sequentially through time and memory, and painting, which we perceive in space. Modern literature, however—predominantly works of "disharmony and disequilibrium"—moves, Frank writes, "in the direction of spatial form," a tendency he notes specifically in Eliot, Pound, Proust, Joyce, and Djuna Barnes. "All these writers ideally intend the reader to apprehend their work spatially in a moment of time, rather than as a sequence." Their readers therefore must re-orient themselves to a "space logic." "Instead of the instinctive and immediate reference of words and word-groups to the objects or events they symbolize and the construction of meaning from the sequence of these references, modern poetry asks its readers to suspend the process of individual reference temporarily until the entire pattern of internal references can be apprehended as a unity."

This essay, considerably expanded, became the centerpiece of Frank's most important book of criticism, *The Widening Gyre: Crisis and Mastery in Modern Literature,* which was accompanied by an enthusiastic introductory essay by Allen Tate. The remaining contents of the volume attest to a wide-ranging literary interest: two essays on André Malraux; a piece on Thomas Mann's *Dr. Faustus*; critical appraisals of Robert Penn Warren and John Peale Bishop; and evaluations of the critics of R. P. Blackmur and Lionel Trilling. John Simon described some of the essays, especially those on Mann and Blackmur, as "models of sensitive judiciousness and unspectacular but thorough illumination of their subjects. . . . In a critique like the one of Lionel Trilling, Mr. Frank proves himself an adroit polemicist, and in his analysis of [Barnes'] *Nightwood* a master mystagogue."

Frank gives an engaging account of his gradual commitment to studying the life and works of Fyodor Dostoevsky in the introduction to the first volume of his critical biography, *Dostoevsky: The Seeds of Revolt 1821–1849.* Invited to give the Gauss lectures, he chose as his topic "Existential Themes in Modern Literature"; he began his survey with an analysis of Dostoevsky's *Notes from Underground* "as a precursor of the mood and the themes that are found in French Existentialism." Yet he found much in the work "to which an Existentialist reading offered no clue whatever. When I began to write up my lectures, I decided to study *Notes from the Underground* more thoroughly, and to investigate the social-cultural background that so obviously served as Dostoevsky's point of departure. This led me to read whatever I could find about the period in the languages at my disposal, and finally, when the limitations of such sources became apparent, to learn Russian. As time went by, I realized that my interest in Existentialism had greatly diminished, while my fascination with Dostoevsky and Russian culture of the nineteenth century continued to grow by leaps and bounds. I abandoned the idea of writing up my lectures and decided instead to write a book on Dostoevsky. This was the far-away and almost accidental origin of the present book and its successors—though I had no intention of writing a work on any such scale when I started out." The "scale" of the project is vast: its four volumes, "dealing, in chronological sequence, each with another period of Dostoevsky's life," will make it by far the most ambitious non-Russian biography of the great novelist. Frank also states that "a complete version of the entire work already exists in draft, and I hope to be able to publish the remainder . . . within a reasonable number of years." As of 1984 two volumes have appeared.

Frank's conclusions about Dostoevsky differed considerably from the prevailing Western viewpoint. "I see Dostoevsky's work as a brilliant artistic synthesis of the major issues of his time, a personal utterance, to be sure, but one, more than most, oriented by concerns outside himself. It is not simply—as we too often tend to think in the West—the passionately febrile expression of an unbalanced but extraordinarily gifted temperament. Indeed, one way of defining Dostoevsky's genius is to locate it in his ability to fuse his private dilemmas with those raging in the society of which he was a part." His interest in the details of the novelist's personal life is therefore strictly limited: "I deal at length only with those aspects of his quotidian experience which seem to me to have some critical relevance. . . . I do not go from the life to the work, but rather the other way round. My purpose is to interpret Dostoevsky's art, and this purpose commands my choice of detail and my perspective." In twenty-four chapters Frank traces Dostoevsky's youth and education in Moscow, his association as a young man with various literary circles in St. Petersburg, and in the last section, entitled "The Road to Self-Discovery," the mixed critical reception given his earliest works and the relatively high praise heaped on the novel *Netotchka Nezvanova,* which finished serial publication in May 1849, a month after Dostoevsky's arrest for political offenses and shortly before the beginning of his Siberian exile.

The first volume elicited unanimous critical praise. Morris Dickstein called it "a masterful work of cultural biography, . . . it may be the most ambitious book on Dostoevsky undertaken in any language. Essentially, Frank has written three different but overlapping books within a single volume. The first is a lively personal biography, the second a close study of Dostoevsky's intellectual and political development, and the last a thoughtful work of literary criticism on his neglected early novels and stories." V. S. Pritchett thought the biography's first installment "a work of detection and collation at its scrupulous best. Every detail is considered; evidence is weighed and fortunately the author has a pleasant and lucid style, unleadened by the fashionable vice of fact-fetishism."

Volume two of the biography, *Dostoevsky:*

The Years of Ordeal 1850–1859, was not a disappointment to most admirers of its predecessor. At the beginning of the book, Frank goes into considerable detail about the arrest and trial of the young novelist and his fellow radical idealists and analyzes Dostoevsky's amazingly forthright replies during his interrogation by the police. After the trial and the inevitable guilty verdict there occurred the famous mock-execution, then the long, frightful journey to Siberia, four years at hard labor, and a further period of forced military service. The culmination of Dostoevsky's story during these years was his turning away from Western ideas and his conversion to religious belief and Slavophilism: "the rediscovery of the Russian Christ." At the end of the volume, Dostoevsky returns at last to Petersburg, confident that he will again attract the literary fame he enjoyed during the 1840s.

Pritchett reviewed the second volume as enthusiastically as he had the first. "Professor Frank," he wrote, "is scholarly in his inquiry: he is clear, persuasive, and free of academic jargon. Dostoevsky has so often seemed an unreliable and mystifying projector of versions of his life and his beliefs that he can easily strike us as incoherent. Frank's is a patient and ever-curious and sympathetic investigation of a man and a writer who was very much a 'double,' who can easily confuse us with his poses, his powers of self-dramatization, and his contradictions."

Ronald Hingley, however, expressed "certain reservations" in his review—on Frank's "special pleading" that portrays Dostoevsky as a liberal-minded social idealist and his "cool, lucid, analytical approach, his quiet, unimpassioned marshalling of his material," which, while "most admirable," Hingley finds inconsistent with the character of Dostoevsky himself—"the increasingly militant foe of reason."

In May 1953, Frank married Marguérite Straus, a French-born mathematician. They have two daughters and live in Princeton.

PRINCIPAL WORKS: The Widening Gyre, 1963; Dostoevsky: The Seeds of Revolt 1821–1849, 1976; Dostoevsky: The Years of Ordeal 1850–1859, 1983. *As editor*—R.P. Blackmur, A Primer of Ignorance, 1967; Paul Valéry, Masters and Friends, 1968.

ABOUT: Borklund, E. Contemporary Literary Critics, 1982; Contemporary Authors 77–80, 1979. *Periodicals*—America February 5, 1977; Best Sellers March 1977; Book Week July 5, 1964; Choice February 1977; Christian Science Monitor December 27, 1976; Commentary March 1977; Commonweal May 13, 1977; Economist October 22, 1977; Library Journal September 1, 1976; National Review June 10, 1977; New Republic November 20, 1976; New York Review of Books November 11, 1976; February 2, 1984; New York Times Book Review November 21, 1976; New Yorker April 11, 1964; September 12, 1977; Poetry September 1964; Times Literary Supplement September 30, 1977; August 17, 1984; Virginia Quarterly Review Spring 1964; Autumn 1977.

FRANKLIN, JOHN HOPE (January 2, 1915–   ), American historian and educator, contributes the following account of his life: "Franklin was born in the all-Negro town of Rentiesville, Oklahoma. He was named for the great educator, John Hope, who had taught his parents, and who later became President of Morehouse College and Atlanta University. Franklin's father was an attorney, and his mother, a teacher, exposed him early in life to education by having him attend her class before he was of school age. When he was ten the family moved to Tulsa, where his father had already set up practice. When his law office was destroyed in the race riot of 1921, he conducted business from a tent. This example, reinforced by visits to court with his father, pointed Franklin toward the study of law and when he entered Fisk University in 1931, he had already decided on that career. It was then that he came under the influence of his history teacher, Theodore S. Currier, and when Franklin decided on a history career, Professor Currier helped him to gain admission to Harvard University. There, Franklin received his M.A. in 1936 and his Ph.D. in 1941. His dissertation, "The Free Negro in North Carolina, 1790–1860," published in 1943, became the first of his nine major works. His *From Slavery to Freedom: A History of Negro Americans* was published in 1947 and is now in its fifth edition. It is widely regarded as the standard text in courses on Negro history.

"Since his early years on the faculties of Fisk, St. Augustine's College and North Carolina College (now North Carolina Central University), he has been active in organizations such as the American Civil Liberties Union, the NAACP Legal Defense Fund, and the United Negro College Fund. In 1954 he helped prepare the brief in Brown v. the Board of Education that resulted in the Supreme Court's outlawing racially segregated schools.

"His professional activities increased when he joined Howard University in 1947, and Brooklyn College in 1956, where he was Chairman of the History Department. He was a popular guest speaker at university convocations and lecture series, and frequently appeared on the programs of historical associations. He was President of the American Studies Association in 1967, Southern Historical Association (1970–71), Organization

JOHN HOPE FRANKLIN

of American Historians (1974–75), and the American Historical Association (1978–79). He was President of the United Chapters of Phi Beta Kappa from 1973 to 1976, and a founding member of the Fisk University chapter in 1953.

"During his years at Brooklyn Franklin continued to do research and writing, and in 1956 *The Militant South* was published. *Reconstruction After the Civil War* appeared in 1961, followed in 1963 by *The Emancipation Proclamation.* Meanwhile, he was a frequent contributor to scholarly journals. In 1965 he was a co-author of *Land of the Free,* and with the editors of Time-Life Books brought out in 1970 an *Illustrated History of Black Americans.* Appearing in 1976 were *A Southern Odyssey: Travelers in the Antebellum North,* and *Racial Equality in America,* the subject of his Jefferson Lecture in the Humanities.

"Franklin has been on the boards of the American Council of Learned Societies, American Studies Association, Salzburg Seminar in American Studies, and the Board of Foreign Scholarships (Fulbright board), which he represented abroad as program officer for the Near East. He lectured abroad as Fulbright Professor in Australia, and at New Zealand and Indian universities. He was Pitt Professor of American History and Institutions at Cambridge University in 1962–63, and during that year lectured in France, Germany and Italy. As the Lincoln Lecturer for the Board of Foreign Scholarships in 1973 he traveled in Latin America and the Far East.

"He was served several presidential administrations. In 1961 he was appointed to the Board of Foreign Scholarships, and in 1967 was a con-

sultant for the National Advisory Commission on Civil Disorders. From 1972 to 1979 he was on the National Council for the Humanities and in 1977 was appointed to the Presidential Advisory Board on Ambassadorial Appointments. From 1977 to 1981 he was a member of the Advisory Commission on Public Diplomacy, and in 1980 was a delegate to the 21st Conference of UNESCO in Belgrade.

"In 1964 Franklin left Brooklyn College for the University of Chicago, where he was chairman of the department of history from 1967 to 1970 and from 1969 the John Matthews Manly Distinguished Service Professor of History. From 1980 to 1982 he was a Senior Fellow at the National Humanities Center, and in 1982 joined Duke University as the James B. Duke Professor of History. He plans to publish his biography of George Washington Williams, 1849–1891, historian, clergyman, lawyer, legislator, and diplomat. Franklin also plans a study of runaway slaves, and the preparation of his father's autobiography for publication."

———

From the outset of his career as a scholar, John Hope Franklin has been sensitive to the racist bias of earlier white historians. Yet he does not regard himself as a "black" historian: "I don't teach black history . . . I teach the history of the South—black and white," he told an interviewer in 1980. Franklin is not an advocate of black studies programs in American higher education, viewing them as "to a considerable extent, a political response of expediency on the part of universities." In response to criticism by some blacks that he has not been an activist, he points out that he sees himself as a scholar and "role model," and he notes with pride that at Supreme Court Justice Thurgood Marshall's invitation he directed some of the basic research on school segregation that led to the landmark Brown v. Board of Education case in 1954. "I haven't insulated myself in an ivory tower. I write to be read. I have tried to provide as much fuel for the whole civil rights movement as anyone, with my writing."

As early as 1947 in his preface to the first edition of his now classic *From Slavery to Freedom: A History of Negro Americans,* Franklin charted his future course as a historian: "I have made a conscious effort to write the history of the Negro in America with due regard for the forces at work which have affected his development. This has involved a continuous recognition of the main stream of American history and the relationship of the Negro to it." In four revised and enlarged editions of that book that appeared between 1947 and 1980, in its paperback edition and its translations into Indian and Japanese, *From Slavery to Freedom* introduced several generations of students to a long-neglected area of American history. Although his work follows in the tradition of earlier scholars like George B. Woodson, W. E. B. DuBois, and Carter G. Woodson, he has made his distinctive mark. Earl E. Thorpe wrote of Franklin in a review of the work of these black historians, that "the objectivity of the author, his temperateness in tone, thorough grasp of his materials, and scholarly presentation make the work a significant contribution."

Subsequent books and articles have won Franklin the title "doyen of black historians" and an impressive number of academic honors—among them Guggenheim and Mellon fellowships. In 1976, the National Endowment for the Arts named him Jefferson Lecturer in the Humanities. These lectures, published as *Racial Equality in America* in the bicentennial year, were an attempt to epitomize racial relations in the United States, exploring the paradox of the American past with its ideal of human equality and its reality of inequality. The late Roy Wilkins wrote of the lectures; "John Hope Franklin is an uncommon historian who has consistently corrected in eloquent language the misrecording of this country's rich heritage."

Though not a popularizer, Franklin is widely known to readers who are not historians or academic students of history. He participated with a group of internationally eminent psychologists, sociologists, and anthropologists in studies of specific problems of racism, published under his editorship as *Color and Race*. In his introduction, Franklin points out that "consciousness of color" is "an inescapable fact" in human history and within given societies. One of his best known books is a volume in the Chicago History of American Civilization series, *Reconstruction after the Civil War*. In lucid and readable prose he surveys a vast amount of controversial material documenting the activities of black and white members of state legislatures and postwar constitutional conventions, showing that as a consequence of the war the North, now an industrial colossus, was more changed than the South, which was "more than ever attached to the values and outlook that had shaped its history." Franklin concludes: "The Union had been preserved and human slavery had been abolished; but these were achievements of the war. In the postwar years the Union had not made the achievements of the war a foundation for the healthy advancement of the political, social, and economic life of the United States."

Franklin married Aurelia E. Whittington, a librarian, in 1940. They have one son, John Whittington Franklin, who directs the English language program at the American Cultural Center at Dakar, Senegal.

PRINCIPAL WORKS: The Free Negro in North Carolina, 1790–1860, 1943; From Slavery to Freedom, 1947; The Militant South, 1800–1860, 1956; Reconstruction after the Civil War, 1963; The Emancipation Proclamation, 1963; The Emancipation Proclamation, 1963; (with J. W. Caughey and E. R. May) Land of the Free, 1965; Illustrated History of Black Americans, 1970; A Southern Odyssey: Travelers in the Antebellum North, 1976; Racial Equality in America, 1976. *As editor*—The Civil War Diary of James T. Ayers, 1947; Tourgee, A. A. Fool's Errand, 1961; Higginson, T. W. Army Life in a Black Regiment, 1962; Three Negro Classics, 1965; (with I. Starr) The Negro in the Twentieth Century, 1967; Color and Race, 1968; DuBois, W. E. B. The Suppression of the African Slave Trade, 1969; Reminiscences of an Active Life: The Autobiography of John R. Lynch, 1970.

ABOUT: Contemporary Authors, new revision series 1, 1981; Current Biography 1963; Ploski, H. A. and R. C. Brown, Jr. (eds.) The Negro Almanac, 1966; Thorpe, E. Black Historians: A Critique, 1971; Toppin, E. A. Biographical History of Blacks in America since 1528, 1971; Who's Who in America, 1983–84. *Periodicals*—Chronicle of Higher Education January 9, 1978; Integrated Education January-August 1980; People October 29, 1979.

FRANKLIN, (STELLA MARY) MILES

(October 14, 1879–September 19, 1954), Australian novelist, was born at Talbingo, in the High Monaro country thirty miles west of Canberra. She was the eldest of seven children of John Maurice and Susannah (Lampe) Franklin, descendants of Irish and German settlers and members of the "squattocracy," land-owners in the rough cattle-raising bush. A precocious, tomboyish little girl, she had a happy childhood with freedom to ride horses, wander about in the open country, and absorb the sights and sounds that were to figure so prominently in her writing. Her first and to this day most important novel, *My Brilliant Career*, records the spirit if not the letter of those early years. Like her fictitious heroine, she was fiercely independent and rebelled against the restrictions imposed on girls. Also, like her heroine, she was in perpetual conflict with her stern, practical-minded, hardworking mother. Her education was spotty, but she read widely in both the Victorian novelists and such contemporary writers as Hall Caine and Marie Corelli.

From about the age of twelve, Miles Franklin

aspired to a literary career—"to draw attention to myself" and to escape from the intellectually and spiritually confining life of her family. At first she scribbled adolescent romances, but heeding the advice of a visiting Englishman, she turned to her native scene: "The idea sprouted. Huh, I'd show just how ridiculous the life around me would be as story material, and began in sardonically humorous mood a full-fledged novel with the gibing title, *My Brilliant (?) Career* (Preface, *My Career Goes Bung*). The novel, written when she was sixteen and by her own testimony "tossed off on impulse in a matter of weeks," reflected both the inexperience and the refreshing charm of her youth. Told by its high-spirited heroine Sybylla Penelope Melvyn, it describes a life of poverty on a remote dairy farm from which the narrator is rescued by a visit to her more genteel relatives. In their beautiful home Sybylla discovers the joys of ease and refinement without sacrifice of her love for a free life in nature. Her happiness is short-lived, however, because she must return to the bush to help support the family her improvident father cannot provide for. After a grueling experience as "governess" in a family of prosperous but ignorant and uncouth farmers, she goes home to assist her overworked mother. Miserable as her life is, she refuses a highly eligible suitor though she is strongly attracted to him, and stoically accepts her fate as a woman: "My ineffective life will be trod out in the same round of toil—I am only one of yourselves. I am only an unnecessary, little, bush commoner, I am only a—woman!"

It is little wonder that in 1895 such a novel, written by an unknown with much spirit but no literary art or sophistication, could not find a publisher. Undaunted, Miles Franklin sent her manuscript to the Australian poet and short story writer Henry Lawson who found it so "true to Australia" that he took it with him to England where it was published (with the question mark removed from the title) by Blackwood's in 1901. The novel was an immediate success with Australian reviewers but it brought her very little money and very much pain. The autobiographical form—intended by its author as fiction and drawn only loosely from her own life—was taken as fact by many readers, including her own relatives. Instead of bringing her the praise and recognition she sought, *My Brilliant Career* brought the young novelist so much embarrassment that she left home and moved to Sydney and later Melbourne, supporting herself with free-lance journalism and work as a house maid. In an attempt to supply a "corrective" she wrote another novel, *My Career Goes Bung*, with the same heroine now in Sydney reaping the dubious rewards of literary success. As the title suggests, Sybylla becomes disillusioned with society. She returns to her country home to help her family fight a drought, chastened and matured but still determined to fight for her ideals: "Beauty is abroad," she writes at the end of the book. "Under her spell the voices of the great world call me. To them I give ear and go."

Unable to find a publisher for this second "audacious" novel, Franklin put the manuscript aside and forgot it. Forty years later she found a copy her mother had kept in a trunk and in 1946 the novel appeared, an indication, she wrote in the preface, of "how smug behaviour must have been when it was written." Disheartened by these early literary ventures, she left Australia in 1905 for a thirty-year period of self-exile, settling first in the United States, where she worked in Chicago in the trade union movement from 1908 to 1915 (experiences she drew on in her posthumously published novel *On Dearborn Street*). By now an ardent suffragist and social reformer, she wrote only one novel during this period, *Some Everyday Folk and Dawn*, a conventional love story interesting only for its advocacy of women's rights. Shortly after the outbreak of World War I, she moved to England to do social work. In 1916 she volunteered for service with the Scottish Women's Hospital Unit and served in the Balkans, nursing the wounded and victims of a typhus epidemic.

Franklin drew her inspiration from her Australian roots; away from her native land she did little significant writing. One exception was a series of novels, beginning with *Up the Country* in 1928, written while she was living in London and working for the National Housing Council. These were published under the name "Brent of Bin Bin," a pseudonym she never openly acknowledged. The evidence, however, has convinced all her biographers and critics that she was indeed Brent—possibly writing with a collaborator. But the setting, language, and tone of these hearty realistic novels—the country of her girlhood, incidents and details that reappear in her acknowledged books, eccentric "bush" language (*combobulated, ramiparous, ramfeezled*), the ardent feminism—mark them as her work. She concealed her identity, her biographer Marjorie Barnard suggests, because she still suffered embarrassment from the reception of her earlier books. Altogether there were six interconnected Brent novels (one of them published posthumously), forming a saga of squattocracy life in the Monaro region from 1830 to 1928. Loose and discursive, they are nevertheless colorful and lively and had a small but devoted audience.

Miles Franklin did not find a place in her native literature until she returned to Australia in

1933. *All that Swagger*, a long novel chronicling the history of an immigrant family from 1815 to contemporary times, was well received and won the Prior Memorial Award. Several minor works followed (some of these written with collaborators)—novels, plays, a biography of the Australian writer Joseph Furphy, and a series of lectures on the history of Australian literature that she delivered in 1950 to students at the University of Western Australia. This last, published as *Laughter, Not for a Cage*, contains a loving but candid assessment of her country's culture and an impassioned plea for its development: "Without an indigenous literature people can remain aliens in their own soil. An unsung country does not fully exist or enjoy adequate international exchange in the inner life."

Franklin's contribution to that culture might have been all but forgotten except for a combination of circumstances long after her death in 1954. One was the emergence of the feminist movement in the 1960s. *My Brilliant Career*, long out of print and forgotten, was published for the first time in Australia in 1965 and was in a third edition by 1974. Even more significant was its success as a film. Produced in Australia by a group of enterprising women, directed by Gillian Armstrong, with a spirited performance in the leading role by Judy Davis, it was released internationally in 1980. Critics and public alike received the film warmly, not so much as a polemic in the cause of women's rights as a genuinely warm and sensitive portrait of a young woman's struggle for self-fulfillment.

Miles Franklin never married. She spent her last years in her family's house in suburban Sydney, writing and entertaining her friends who described her as an independent, lively, and witty woman with thick curly hair, blue eyes that sparkled behind her glasses, and an undiminished enthusiasm for life. Although a productive writer for most of her life, she is remembered mainly for her first precocious and artless novel. Her later fiction, critics agree, was romantic and adolescent. Perhaps the harshest assessment is Adrian Mitchell's in the *Oxford History of Australian Literature* who wrote that "Franklin's crative imagination did not respond to later times." In her, H. M. Green observed, "one perceives possibilities that have not been realized."

PRINCIPAL WORKS: *Novels*—My Brilliant Career, 1901; Some Everyday Folk and Dawn, 1909; Old Blastus of Bandicoot, 1932; All that Swagger, 1936; My Career Goes Bung, 1946. *By "Brent of Bin Bin"*—Up the Country, 1928; Ten Creeks Run, 1930; Back to Bool Bool, 1931; Prelude to Waking, 1950; Cockatoos, 1954; Gentlemen at Gyang Gyang, 1956. *Non-fiction*—Joseph Furphy, 1944; Laughter, Not for a Cage, 1956; Childhood at Brindabella, 1963.

ABOUT: Barnard, M. Miles Franklin, 1967; Green, H. M. History of Australian Literature I, 1962; Mathew, R. Miles Franklin, 1963; Miles Franklin: A Tribute by Some of her Friends, 1955; Oxford History of Australian Lliterature, 1981.

FRENCH, MARILYN (November 21, 1929–   ), American novelist and critic, writes: "I wanted to write as soon as I could read or perhaps even before, awed that feeling could be aroused by the sound and sense of words. I sat in the grass examining the shapes and colors of flowers, or lay back watching the tops of trees, the clouds, and tried to put words on what I saw and felt. Still, I was surprised when my second-grade 'compositions' turned up in the school newspaper broken into verses—poems, bearing my name! I conceived of literature (a word I may not have known) as lyrical, oblique, disconnected from everyday life, but having the power to lighten or stop the heart. The books I loved most and re-read every year were like this— expurgated versions of Greek and Norse myths, Bible stories, and fairytales. The books offered at school disappointed me: a semester's worth could be gulped in an afternoon, yet leave me unsatisfied. The books in the library were not much better: they purported to be about children's real life but their sweetness had no relation whatever to what I knew and felt. When I wanted truth, I would go to my mother and ask her about her childhood, her parents. Her stories were grim enough to feel true.

"At the same time, I avoided everyday life assiduously. Small, gentle-mannered, and frightened, I trudged fearfully to school, to classes with larger, older children raised more roughly than I had been. Outside school, I withdrew: I read, sketched, practiced the piano, listened to our records over and over: Bizet's *Carmen*, Gounod's *Faust,* and Tchaikowsky's *First Piano Concerto.* I don't know to this day how we managed to acquire them. In summer, I would build a Persian tent in the backyard out of old torn quilts and blankets; I would then be a Persian princess, sipping lemonade and composing poetry. Finding it appropriate to my tent, I tried to brew perfume by soaking flowers in water, refusing to believe my mother's warning about the result. I never was able to learn anything from anyone else.

"As I grew older, my inwardness became more painful, but I persisted in it. It seemed necessary to shut out the silence of my home and the cries and shouts of the street. If the restrained emotion within the house was so terrible, what could unrestrained emotion be like? I wrote ' sonatas,' novels, stories, poems; at ten I tried to pro-

MARILYN FRENCH

duce a weekly newspaper for our block, which I cranked out on a 'printing press' I had begged for Christmas. (As I recall, it was like a mimeograph machine except that one set the type.) This was particularly ironic, because newsworthy items on that block were all unprintable; if there was any light news, I did not know it. What I knew was the real stuff. My mother was the confidante of several neighborhood women. She refused to gossip but needed to talk—so she talked to me. The poverty of the neighborhood I could see for myself, but now I knew which fathers beat their children, which husbands beat their wives; which boy had been arrested, for what. I knew about the man who played the ponies, whose wife hid her earnings from him; and about the widower, the butcher who chained his daughter to the bed when he went out drinking at night. I knew the man two doors down was a drug addict—and I also knew what my mother did not, that he had tried to rape my sister. I knew about the man dying of tuberculosis in the house all the children avoided; and about the tuberculosis of my first crush, Nicky, who died when he was eight.

"Around fourteen, I decided I had to enter the real world. I did this with great trepidation, much pain, utter lack of finesse, and a little success. I would spend Saturday nights dancing the lindy with my girlfriends in one of our livingrooms, while the radio played Glenn Miller, Tommy Dorsey, and Frank Sinatra; and Sunday lying on my stomach on the porch floor reading Thomas Paine, Nietzsche, and Schopenhauer. I did not understand all of what they wrote, but what I comprehended felt true. I still read fic-

tion, but most of the books I found were insubstantial. I devoured them, overeating like an undernourished person, and felt sick afterwards, in a satiation on sweets that was both physical and mental.

"These three elements continued to make up the unromantic triangle of my life: the truths of ideas; the lyrical, artistic world of emotion; and real life, which was made up of people and events. I could not get them together. Even at night, as I lay in bed 'thinking,' I would daydream sugary sequences for myself and my family, and pursue logical, critical arguments about the existence of god, heaven, and hell; the proper organization of the world; and the nature of good and evil. Much of my thinking was a mulling over of what I had been taught. I rejected most of it.

"The same categories continued as I worked in the real world to pay my way through college, vacillated between English and Philosophy as a major (English won, but only because the Philosophy department in my college was at that time dismal, and one of my English professors, a poet, was inspiring), and ended by spending much of my time playing bridge in the real world of the student lounge. I have always found school boring; I would read far beyond the requirements, and often find my teachers' lectures inadequate or wrong. Sometimes I felt impelled to demonstrate this to them. I had a distinct sense that I was regarded as a holy terror.

"This attitude towards me followed me ever after. It made me unhappy, and I determined in my marriage to become a different person. This was probably the greatest mistake of my life, as sweet compliance seemed to dismay my husband. In time, I gave it up. After devoting myself to getting him through law school, by a series of paralyzing office jobs, and to the children, who were born a year apart, I began in 1957 to write seriously, and to make an effort to publish. I had little success. Strongly feminist before there was much comprehension of feminist values, my work puzzled publishers; most of my rejection notices began, 'You write well, but...' Lonely, I went back to college to get my Master's degree and find some intellectual companionship; then I taught for a time. The stormy marriage ended at last, and I went to Harvard for a Ph.D. Because of encouragement from my Harvard advisor, I turned my dissertation on James Joyce's *Ulysses* into a book which was published in 1976. By that time I was in despair about my writing, having published only a few stories and articles in nearly twenty years. I decided to give up obliqueness; to lay on the page in direct, artful prose, with ideas couched in ordinary language, the truth of real life as I saw it.

"The publication of *The Women's Room* changed my life. It allowed me to write without frustration and doubt about publication, and gave me enough security to write whatever I chose without anxiety about money. Most important, the acceptance of this novel was a symbolic acceptance of my various parts. They converged into a circle: real life with its people, events, ideas, and emotion is my truth, which will never again be disconnected."

———

In 1958 Marilyn French read Simone de Beauvoir's *The Second Sex* and was especially moved by her discussion of talented women who are frustrated in their ambition to write and, under family and social pressures, keep postponing literary work. Then a young housewife and mother of two small children, she had behind her a college degree and a conventional middle class background. Born in New York City to E. C. and Isabel (Hazz) Edwards, she married Robert M. French, Jr., a lawyer, in 1950, took a B.A. at Hofstra University in Long Island in 1951, and, like the heroine of her *Women's Room,* settled down to an interlude of domesticity. Divorced in 1967, she went to Harvard for graduate study in English literature, taught English at Hofstra (1964–1968) and at the College of the Holy Cross in Worcester, Mass. (1972–1976), and received her Ph.D. in 1972. Her first book was her thesis on James Joyce, *The Book as World,* a study of the style and narrative point of view in *Ulysses* that critic Hugh Kenner praised as "radically and persuasively original." A carefully documented critical analysis of the novel, *The Book as World* in no way anticipated the sensational popular novel that was to follow it—*The Women's Room,* which sold over 4,000,000 copies, was translated into twenty foreign languages, and made into a television movie in 1980. "I wanted to tell the story of what it is like to be a woman in our country in the middle of the twentieth century," French told an interviewer for the *New York Times.* Whether her version of that reality is accurate or not, it was timely and compelling. *The Women's Room* is Mira Ward's story, but the point of view often blurs with the authorial "I" who tells her story and the stories of the many women she encounters on her voyage of self-discovery: "I sometimes think I've swallowed every woman I ever knew," the narrator says. "My head is full of voices . . . I feel as if I were a medium and a whole host of departed spirits has descended on me clamoring to be let out."

Those voices rush out of French's novel— strident and determined to be heard, to articulate their loneliness, their confusion, and their rage against men. When reviewers of *The Women's Room* objected that her male characters are one-dimensional and stereotypical, she sprang to her defense: "The men are there as women see them and feel them—impediments in women's lives." Unabashedly polemical, the novel chronicles the lives of several generations of women who submitted to male domination until time and the special circumstances of the 1960s (the Civil Rights and anti-Vietnam War movements) liberated them, or at least opened the prospects for their liberation. Tracing her heroine Mira's life from childhood to middle age, she draws a portrait of an intelligent human being trained to submit and repress herself who suddenly finds herself abandoned when her husband asks for a divorce. Wounded but not defeated, Mira builds a new life to which men are incidental. There is no possibility of co-existence between the sexes. In motherhood women find temporary fulfillment, but only because children are an absorbing interest: "Children are the center of a woman's life," she told the *New York Times'* interviewer. "Work is always central. When you have children, they become your work, your opus." But, as Mira discovers, children grow up, and other kinds of work, other channels for a woman's energies, must be found.

The power struggle between the sexes is the subject of French's second novel, *The Bleeding Heart.* The bitterness and tendentiousness that critics noted in *The Women's Room* had been offset by its power and passion. But the second novel was focused not on a large and representative group of women, but on one middle-aged woman, divorced, mother of two grown children, successful in her career as scholar and college professor. This heroine, on sabbatical leave in England to do research in Renaissance literature at Oxford for a book to be called "Lot's Wife: A Study of the Identification of Women with Suffering," regards herself, in spite of her seeming independence, as "the original bleeding heart" and plunges into a love affair with a married man, also American. Both characters are sensitive and vulnerable, survivors carrying scars of their emotional wounding, and French here seems to be striving for a more lyrical vision of man-woman love. But because such relationships carry a burden of tradition—submissive woman/dominant man—the affair is doomed to failure. The novel's fate was little more cheering. Critics who had accepted the "cardboard villains" of *The Women's Room* because of its "jagged realism" and valid, if somewhat stereotypical view of male chauvinism, found *The Bleeding Heart* "heavy handed," didactic, and cluttered with "incessant rhetoric." The novel ends with the hero's offering to divorce his wife to marry the heroine and her rejection of him because she sees no possibility of truce in the war between the sexes: "How could you work it out, the togetherness, the distance? The old way had been to turn the woman into the man's creature: one will, one mind, one flesh: his. But there was no new way, was there?"

At the root of the struggle between the sexes, French suggests in her non-fiction scholarly book *Shakespeare's Division of Experience,* is the polarity between "the masculine and feminine principles," a basic distinction since the beginning of recorded history. The masculine principle is power, resistance to the natural forces of birth and biological change which define the feminine principle. In a long essay introducing this controversial book, French argues that Shakespeare, ambivalent in his treatment of women characters, searched for enduring ideals in a world he viewed as disintegrating, seeking always "to re-integrate human experience. But because he—and his tradition—saw experience in terms of polar opposites, his work has been important in perpetuating the very division he sought to reconcile." Thus, while he admired and even idealized feminine qualities, Shakespeare "never abandoned belief in male legitimacy or horror of female sexuality." Although they praised her ingenuity and thoroughness in covering Shakespeare's works, most reviewers of the book found her thesis dubious and/or limiting. Anne Barton objected, in *New York Review of Books,* that it blinded the author to the subtlety with which Shakespeare treated characters like Rosalind, Juliet, Desdemona, and Isabella, "making them incapable of the growth and change associated with men," and Geoffrey Hartman, in the *New York Times Book Review,* called the book "a lay sermon" easier to appreciate for its "intellectual passion than its bias."

In 1980 Marilyn French told an interviewer for *Publishers Weekly* that she directs her work to helping women and men understand "the difference between philosophical feminism and political feminism." A philosophical rather than political feminist herself, she prefers the novel, the essay, and occasionally the lecture platform as outlets for her views. Her projected studies for the future she said were essays on women, men, and morals.

PRINCIPAL WORKS: *Novels*—The Women's Room, 1977; The BleedingHeart, 1980. *Non-fiction*—The Book as World: James Joyce's *Ulysses,* 1976; Shakespeare's Division of Experience, 1981.

ABOUT: Contemporary Authors, new revision series 3, 1981; Contemporary Literary Criticism 10, 1979; Who's Who in America, 1983–84. *Periodicals*—New York Times October 27, 1977; March 9, 10, 1980; People February 10, 1978; Publishers Weekly March 7, 1980.

* * *

FRIEDAN, BETTY (GOLDSTEIN) (February 4, 1921–   ), American feminist writer, was born to a middle-class family in Peoria, Illinois, the oldest of three children of a jewelry-store owner, Harry Goldstein, and Miriam (Horwitz) Goldstein. Her early years followed a conventional pattern except that as a Jewish family in a small midwestern town the Goldsteins were always (in her words) socially "marginal," and she early developed a "passion against injustice." In high school Betty Goldstein excelled in English, founded and edited the school literary magazine, and graduated as valedictorian. At Smith College, she studied gestalt psychology with Kurt Koffka, edited the college newspaper, and founded another literary magazine. She took her B.A. summa cum laude in 1942 and accepted a research fellowship in psychology to study with Erik Erikson at the University of California at Berkeley, where she once again distinguished herself academically. But after a year of graduate work she decided not to continue for a doctorate. Instead, already subject to the "feminine mystique," that she later described, she followed the pattern set by so many of her sister Smith graduates. She moved to New York, held a succession of jobs in journalism and advertising, lived in a shabby apartment in Greenwich Village, and in 1947 married Carl Friedan, a theatrical producer who later became an advertising executive.

Like the women who furnished case histories for her first book, Betty Friedman settled down to domesticity, had three children, lived in the suburbs, and was one of the many model housewife-mothers of the period, "concentrating on breast-feeding and wheeling Danny, my first baby, to the park, and reading Dr. Spock." Like many such women, she found herself restless and dissatisfied, dimly aware of what she called "the problem that has no name"—the condition, she wrote later, "which defines woman solely in terms of her three-dimensional sexual relationship to man: wife, mother, homemaker—passively dependent, her own role restricted to timeless, changeless love of husband and children."

The problem found its name and definition in *The Feminine Mystique,* a book that evolved from a survey she prepared for a Smith College magazine in 1956–57 of alumnae some years after their graduation. Friedan sent a question-

BETTY FRIEDAN

naire to these women, then to alumnae of other women's colleges, and discovered that her problem was anything but unique. Indeed, the results of that questionnaire and the response from readers to that study and to an expanded article on the subject that she published in *Good Housekeeping* in 1960, stunningly confirmed her impressions. Realizing that this was a far larger problem than her own range of experience had suggested, Friedan plunged into serious research in history, sociology, psychology, and American popular culture. She commuted daily from her suburban home to the New York Public Library where she worked intensively for the next several years on the book that was to become a classic of feminist literature and to win its author international fame. Published in 1963, *The Feminine Mystique* enjoyed a success that was partly a happy accident of time. Earlier writings by Pearl Buck, Mirra Komarovsky, and particularly Simone de Beauvoir's *The Second Sex* had articulated many of the issues raised by Friedan, but in the 1960s, an era of radical social change, Friedan found an extraordinarily large and responsive audience. Within a year of its publication more than 65,000 hardcover and half a million paperback copies had been sold, and by the end of the decade the book had fifteen printings, sales figures in excess of a million, and had been translated into thirteen languages. Its author had become a public figure, a lecturer in demand all over the country, a radio and television celebrity, and the founder of NOW, the largest political-action organization for women.

The Feminine Mystique is a passionate polemic. Establishing—on the basis of her personal domestic life, her questionnaires, her wide reading, and her analysis of the American cultural scene, particularly the contents of women's magazines—an image of the women of post-World War II American society as bored, unfulfilled even in motherhood, and powerless to control their lives, Friedan raised challenging and disturbing questions. "I helped create the image," she wrote in a chapter titled "The Happy Housewife Heroine." "I have watched American women for fifteen years try to conform to it. But I can no longer deny my own knowledge of its terrible implications. It is not a harmless image. There may be no psychological terms for the harm it is doing. But what happens when women try to live according to an image that makes them deny their minds? What happens when women grow up in an image that makes them deny the reality of the changing world?"

The Feminine Mystique offered what its author called "a new life plan for women"—not the familiar nostrums of volunteerism and part-time jobs but "work that is of real value to society—work for which, usually, our society pays." The books ends with a series of ringing rhetorical questions: "Who knows what women will be when they are finally free to become themselves? . . . Who knows of the possibilities of love when men and women share not only children, home and garden, not only the fulfillment of their biological roles, but the responsibilities and passions of the work that creates the human future and the full human knowledge of who they are?" To all this, readers, and many reviewers, responded enthusiastically; but there were also reservations—less about Friedan's general thesis than about the accuracy of specific charges. For example, her charge that during the 1950s male editors of women's magazines conspired to keep women in domesticity by publishing only articles and stories that glorified wife-mother roles, instead of showing women happy in careers, was found unconvincing by more than one reviewer. Her condemnation of Freudian psychology with its emphasis on female anatomy as determining women's destiny was generally approved of, but her attack on Margaret Mead for idealizing the role of motherhood in primitive societies was regarded as unfair in light of Mead's vigorous criticism of the inequality of women's roles in American society. Gerda Lerner wrote that *The Feminine Mystique* was "a-historical," being "no other than the myth of woman's 'proper sphere' created in the 1840s and updated by consumerism and the misunderstood dicta of Freudian psychology." Furthermore, as June Sochen and others pointed out, her focus was narrow: "Betty Friedan's message did not deal with working-class women or black women. Like most feminist writing it appealed to the class of the writer: the middle class." Yet no critic except outright anti-feminists disputed the power and basic validity of Friedan's book and the importance of the questions it raised. As the late Lillian Smith observed in the *Saturday Review*: "Written with a passionate drive, it is worthy of respectful reading . . . a scholarly work appropriate for serious study."

Betty Friedan's feminist career began with a book, but because the issues were, by 1963, so urgent, and because she was herself a forceful presence and an impassioned platform orator, she soon found herself involved in political action. Although in the twenty years since the first publication of *The Feminine Mystique* she wrote many speeches and magazine articles, she produced only two more books, and one of these, *It Changed My Life,* is mainly a collection of those pieces. She reports in the introduction to that book that her commitment to political activism followed her discovery, as she traveled over the country lecturing and meeting thousands of women, that she was truly "needed": "I felt the burden of that expectancy, and the guilt over that second book I should have been writing. Why was I wasting so much time running around the country talking to women? I was supposed to be writing a book on patterns that would enable women to move beyond the feminine mystique. But to be honest, I really hadn't found such new patterns." What Friedan found, however, was that the problems could not be solved "unless society changed," and that women were ready and eager for social change: "I had inadvertently stumbled on the force, the source of energy, that could and would coalesce to change the whole gestalt: the women with those problems, those yearning, helpless, defensive, apologetic, guilt-ridden women, who were unconsciously getting ready to move—just as I was."

In 1966 the National Organization for Women (NOW) was founded, with Betty Friedan as its first president. A reformist not a revolutionary body, NOW worked primarily to achieve equality of opportunity for women, advocating the "de-sexing" of newspaper help-wanted advertisements, the elimination of age restrictions for airline stewardesses, and demanding high-level government appointments for women. It supported the Equal Rights Amendment, the legalization of abortion, child-care centers for working mothers, paid maternity leaves, and tax reform to allow deductions for child care. Although its fundamental concerns were feminist, NOW was open to men on the premise that its causes could benefit both sexes by extending civ-

il rights, reforming alimony laws, and moving toward what its Statement of Purpose calls "a fully equal partnership of the sexes as part of the world-wide revolution of human rights now taking place within and beyond our national borders."

The period of Friedan's tenure as president of NOW was a turbulent one, partly reflecting the general ferment in American life during the late 1960s and partly her own controversial personality. In *It Changed My Life* she describes the internal power struggles of the movement and her reservations about the increasingly radical and militant drift of the feminist movement. Anything but an advocate of passive resistance herself, Friedan was nevertheless alarmed by extremists within the group who, she felt, were giving it an unfavorable public image: "But there was something about this new, abstract ideology of man hatred, sex warfare, that made me uneasy from the beginning . . . [it] seemed to be leading us away from the reality of our movement—and its real possibilities for changing the situation of women." Her critics, however, mainly a younger generation of women, demanded radical social change and considered the philosophy of *The Feminine Mystique* outdated and "hopelessly bourgeois." Other strong women leaders were emerging, and while Friedan remained a central and dominating figure, she was under pressure to step down from the presidency. In early 1970 she did that, explaining that she wanted more time for writing and that her recent divorce (in 1969) had put her under financial pressure. Nevertheless, she spent the next six months organizing the Women's Strike for Equality, a nationwide demonstration on August 26, 1970 commemorating the fiftieth anniversary of women's suffrage.

Since then, though she holds no major office in any feminist group, Betty Friedan has pursued the cause energetically. *It Changed My Life* was a personal account of her activities in the women's movement, interspersed with speeches and articles she had written from 1964 to the year of its publication, 1976. It also included accounts of her visits with Prime Minister Indira Gandhi in 1966, Pope Paul VI in 1974, and Simone de Beauvoir in 1975. The main emphasis of the book, however, was on her ideological differences with other prominent feminists. Insisting that "man is not the enemy," that "sexual politics is highly dangerous and diversionary," and that "female chauvinism denies us full humanity as women," Friedan made a strong case, but weakened it, in the judgment of many reviewers, by her failure to document her charges against the opposition and by her personal animus: "She is bitter about women who question her leadership," Cynthia Harrison wrote in *Library Journal,* "and her egocentrism is overbearing." But Harrison conceded the book's value as an historical record of the founding of NOW. Stephanie Harrington, writing in the *New York Times Book Review,* objected that she "failed to spell out or document" some politically "sensational" charges against her opponents alleging their FBI and CIA affiliations. Yet Harrington too admired her courage "to be a middle-class extremist, determined not to frighten off women with rhetoric equating feminism with lesbianism or with the overthrow of men."

In recent years Betty Friedan has somewhat softened her image. She remains, as before, a rapid-fire, forceful, raspy-voiced speaker, but her tone is less strident as she seeks to educate women and men alike rather than to awaken consciousness. She has taught courses in sociology (not women's studies) at Temple University, Yale University, and Queens College of the City University of New York. From 1979 to 1981 she was a senior research associate at Columbia University's Center for the Social Sciences, in 1982 a fellow of the Kennedy School of Government at Harvard, and in 1982–83 a fellow of Harvard's Center for Population Studies. Her historical papers are in the Schlesinger Library at Radcliffe College. She has been awarded many honors, including a doctorate from Smith College in 1975, but the one in which she may take most satisfaction honors her not as a woman leader but as American Humanist of the Year (1975).

Writing in the early 1980s as a kind of gray eminence of the feminist movement, Betty Friedan offered in *The Second Stage* a candid and searching reevaluation of her views. With a deadlock on ERA, an economy that made full-time remunerative work for women no longer a choice but a necessity, a strong anti-abortion movement, and a general conservative trend in the United States, she felt new urgency for "a second stage" in the women's movement. Observing her own children, now young adults with careers and families, their friends, the whole younger generation that had apparently been "liberated," she found new problems, a need for a new definition of the individual and of the family. Unlike many contemporary observers, she sees no prospect that marriage and family life as we know them will become obsolete. On the contrary, she senses "the new urge of both women and men for meaning in their work and life, for intimacy, yes, for love, and roots in home and family." Her second stage would be a movement of both sexes to create a more flexible society in which working-schedules, child-care centers, community facilities, and extended families (but not communes), subsidized by public and private funds, would help men and women alike to fulfill their desires for useful work and also for children and family life: "The second stage involves coming to new terms with the family—new terms with love and with work. The second stage may not even be a woman's movement. . . . The second stage has to transcend the battle for equal power in institutions. The second stage will restructure institutions and transform the nature of power itself."

Friedan's vision of the future struck some of her readers as unrealistic, too lofty in its idealism. "Mrs. Friedan too often occupies the high ground of rhetoric," M.O. Steinfels wrote in *Commonweal.* But for Erica Jong, in the *Saturday Review, The Second Stage* was "a courageous book," and she admired the author's "insistence on psychological truth rather than political polemicizing, her insistence on seeing the feminist movement in historical perspective. . . . For those of us seeking a new direction for feminism, it is here."

Still much in demand as a lecturer, Betty Friedan keeps a crowded schedule. In April 1983 she traveled to England at the invitation of the Cambridge Union Society to engage in a formal (but often rowdy) debate on how men have benefited from the women's movement. Confronting a good-humoredly hostile audience, Friedan not only held her own but won the debate by a large margin. She lectured on the right to abortion, and consulted with the Minister for Women's Rights in France. In the United States she continues to campaign for ERA. She divides her time between an apartment near Lincoln Center in Manhattan and a house on the eastern shore of Long Island. She is the mother of three children—a daughter in medical school, one son a Ph.D. in theoretical physics, the other an engineer—and a grandmother.

PRINCIPAL WORKS: The Feminine Mystique, 1963; It Changed My Life: Writings on the Women's Movement, 1976; The Second Stage, 1981.

ABOUT: American Women Writers 2, 1980; Contemporary Authors 65–68, 1977; Current Biography 1970; Friedan, B. The Feminine Mystique, 1963, It Changed My Life, 1976; Janeway, E. (ed.) Women: Their Changing Roles, 1973; Sochen, J. Movers and Shakers: American Women Thinkers and Activists 1900–1970, 1973; Walker, G. Women Today, 1975; Who's Who in America, 1983–84. *Periodicals*—Chicago Tribune October 25, 1981; New York Times October 19, 1981; New York Times Magazine November 29, 1970; February 27, 1983.

*FUSSELL, PAUL (March 22, 1924–), American literary critic, essayist, and cultural historian, writes: "I was born into a highly respectable family in Pasadena, California, in the 1920s and 30s very much a middle-class oasis to which fathers working in nearby Los Angeles repaired nightly. The second of three children, I grew up in an atmosphere of comfort and privilege, and during the Great Depression, when everyone else was growing poorer, we seemed to be getting richer. We had a second house at the nearby resort of Newport Beach, and we swam and boated there every summer. Although my father, a corporation lawyer, finally retired a millionaire, I attended public schools, my parents insisting both that these were as good as their private counterparts (probably true in Pasadena in those days) and that they didn't want to risk making snobs of their children.

"As a boy I was enthusiastic and artistic, and I pursued frantically one serious hobby after another—magic, printing, photography, cars, music. But through all this I seemed dimly aware that language was going to be my métier. Incompetent at sports, I gravitated naturally to work on school newspapers and magazines. My interest in words and the arrangements you could make of them received a distinct boost when I spent a year learning printing in the vocational program of my high school. In those days, students still learned to hand-set type in composing sticks from the wooden type-case, and 'making words' this way—reversed and upside-down—I found exciting. At this stage I also fell in love with certain type faces like Caslon Old Style and Garamond, and they have brought me pleasure always regardless of what words are made from them.

"In the fall of 1941 I entered Pomona College, some thirty miles from my home. At roughly the same time the Second World War came to America. At college I majored in government and history, changing my major to English only after the war. Together with my older brother, already installed at Pomona, I edited the college humor magazine. We thought it funnier than its readers. I was enrolled in Infantry ROTC and I was called to active duty in May, 1943. As I've indicated in my essay 'My War,' I trained as an Infantry rifleman, and then went to Fort Benning to train as an Infantry officer. I joined the 103rd Infantry Division in Texas and fought in France as a rifle platoon leader from November, 1944, until March, 1945, when I was wounded in the back and thigh by shell fragments. My life since than had been largely a response to the shock of combat on a twenty-year-old youth and the trauma of wounds. I am forty percent disabled.

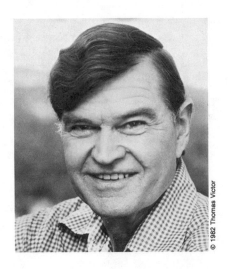

© 1982 Thomas Victor

PAUL FUSSELL

"The sort of reading I was drawn to after the war was mostly in the fault-finding tradition: Mencken, Swift, Bierce, Flaubert, Mark Twain. Anything critical and anti-romantic attracted me immediately, irony and satire especially. I looked for an age and a tradition in which these motifs were dominant. In the English eighteenth century I found it.

"Released from the army in 1946, I finished my final year at college and then entered the Harvard graduate school on the G.I. Bill. I didn't know what I wanted to do, but I thought I might end up teaching at a prep school with an M.A. degree. But as I went deeply into literary scholarship, I knew I had to go as far as I could, and so continued on to the Ph.D. and a career in college teaching. In 1949 I married Betty Harper, a friend from college. We had two children and are now separated. In 1951 I began teaching English at Connecticut College ('for Women,' in those days) and in 1955 moved to Rutgers. I taught there until 1983, when I became Donald T. Regan Professor of English Literature at the University of Pennsylvania.

"Until the 1970s my writing was largely a refraction of my teaching in eighteenth-century English literature, as well as my teaching of poetry. But in the mid-seventies, persuaded that I'd said all I had to say about those matters, I looked around for another topic, and found it in war. The Vietnam War was then in progress, and I thought I might obliquely say something about the waste and criminality of war in general by looking at the myth of the First World War. Thus, *The Great War and Modern Memory*. My writing there and since has depended largely on my own experience. My travels are reflected in *Abroad,* and my continuing obsession with innocence, irony, and elegy in *The Boy Scout Handbook and Other Observations.*

"One of my ambitions is to bring to 'the essay' the sort of seriousness and art normally associated with 'the novel' and 'poetry.' I would like to write something that could be read with illumination and delight a century from now—like Matthew Arnold's *Culture and Anarchy,* for example."

———

With *The Great War and Modern Memory* Paul Fussell moved from literary scholarship, where he had already published several books distinguished for their readability as well as their solid research, to cultural history. Winner of both the National Book Critics Circle and the National Book awards in 1976, *The Great War* examines not only the British literature but also the entire British experience of World War I, engaging the reader, Peter Stansky observed, "at both the intellectual and emotional level . . . Historically he is on solid ground: his detailed knowledge, his range, his humanity—all these make for a book of exciting connections which help one better to understand the past and the present." Fussell has also abridged and edited Siegfried Sassoon's semi-autobiographical novels of World War I, *The Complete Memoirs of George Sherston,* under the title *Sassoon's Long Journey.* In a lighter vein, though again exhaustive in its range of reading, *Abroad: British Literary Traveling Between the Wars* surveys travel books of the 1920s and 30s, the closing days, in Fussell's opinion, of independent, individualistic travel and travel writing, since then reduced to mere tourism and guide book writing. Witty and iconoclastic, Fussell makes no attempt to conceal his scorn for the modern tourist, provoking a fellow travel writer, Jonathan Raban, to remark in his review of *Abroad* that the criticism is "bad-tempered nonsense," though conceding that "Mr. Fussell argues it with such force and clarity that he makes it a pleasure to quarrel with him." In later books Fussell has become increasingly a social critic in the spirit of George Orwell and Edmund Wilson. His collection *The Boy Scout Handbook and Other Observations* ranges widely with irony and humor over such varied topics as the hazards of a writing career, the eccentricities of the British, his personal experience in World War II, and the absurdities of contemporary life. The essay "Notes on Class," for example, comments wryly: "Those delighted to employ the vacuous commercial 'Have a nice day' and those who

wouldn't think of saying it belong manifestly to different classes, no matter how we define them and it is unthinkable that those classes will ever melt. Calvin Coolidge said that the business of America is business. Now apparently the business of America is having a nice day."

PRINCIPAL WORKS: Theory of Prosody in Eighteenth-Century England, 1954; Poetic Meter and Poetic Form, 1965; The Rhetorical World of Augustan Humanism, 1965; Samuel Johnson and the Life of Writing, 1971; The Great War and Modern Memory, 1975; Abroad: British Literary Traveling Between the Wars, 1980; The Boy Scout Handbook and Other Observations, 1982; Class, 1984. As editor—Sassoon's Long Journey, 1983.

ABOUT: Contemporary Authors, first revision series 17–20, 1976; Who's Who in America, 1983–84. *Periodicals*—Publishers Weekly October 3, 1980; Times Literary Supplement February 11, 1983.

GARIOCH, ROBERT (Robert Garioch Sutherland) (May 9, 1909–April 26, 1981), Scottish poet. Robin Fulton, editor of Garioch's *Complete Poetical Works,* contributes the following sketch: "Sutherland was born and grew up in Edinburgh. Of his immediate family background he wrote, in an essay contributed to *As I Remember:* 'My father was a painter, like his father before him. My mother was a music teacher, before she was married. Her father was a company porter in Leith Docks, discharging bulk cargoes of grain. The metters and weighers tipped it into a sack which was placed on the back of the porter, who carried it from the ship across a plank to the shed. My mother used to tell me the full sack weighed two and a half cwt. My father's people had 'always' belonged to Edinburgh; my mother's were Mathewsons, hinds and grieves who circulated from one farm to another, never far from Kelso. My father was a violinist also, a fiddler, to use his own word, a semi-professional of the theatres and picture-houses; he would often come home from work to find himself required as a deputy, then he would clean himself and set off at a trot with his fiddle-case under his oxter, very pleased. My mother had taught the piano, also the mandoline and similar instruments. Miss Kate Mathewson's Mandoline Band was very popular.'

"We can see in this background something of the blend of a strongly practical turn of mind and an intense interest in the arts, and something too of the lifelong sense of belonging to a distinct and familiar locality, which not only characterized Garioch the man as known to his friends but also gave his poetry its individual flavor.

ROBERT GARIOCH

"He took his M.A. in English Language and Literature at Edinburgh University—but these were the Depression years and career options were limited. A large part of his working-life came to be spent as a school-teacher in the London area, both before and after his war experience. Combining school-teaching and writing was not easy for him, but at least he was able to express his frustration in his witty Scots translation of George Buchanan's 'The Humanists' Trauchles in Paris,' to which he added 'Garioch's Repone,' this reply concluding with the MORAL:

Lat onie young poetic chiel
that reads thae lines tak tent richt weill:
THINK TWICE, OR IT'S OWRE LATE!

"In the war Garioch found himself in the North Africa campaign; he was captured and spent the rest of the war as a P.O.W., first in Italy and then in Germany. On leave at the end of the war he wrote an account of the life he had just suffered and survived, *Two Men and a Blanket:* this lay unpublished for thirty years and appeared eventually in 1975. The book is one of the most eloquent accounts of the war from the point of view of the 'common' soldier whose lot is boredom, deprivation and discomfort, with only an occasional glimpse of events in any way dramatic or significant. The eloquence lies in the sober and moderate observation, the very practical attitude to the mechanics of survival, and in the irony that somehow never spills over into bitterness.

"Garioch returned to Scotland in the late 1950s but retired from school-teaching early, in the mid-1960s, after which his livelihood was, if not uncertain, at any rate meager. He worked part-time on a regular basis for the School of Scottish Studies in Edinburgh University, transcribing tapes and assisting in the collection of material for the two dictionaries then in progress, *The Dictionary of the Older Scottish Tongue* and *The Scottish National Dictionary.* From 1971 to 1973 he held the Writer's Fellowship at Edinburgh University, and in the last decade or so of his life he was much in demand for poetry readings. He reviewed and broadcast occasionally, was one of the editors of *Scottish International Review,* and edited an anthology of Scottish poetry, *Made in Scotland,* for Carcanet Press in 1974; for the same press he also prepared a selection of the work of Sir David Lindsay (not yet published).

"Wider recognition for Garioch came slowly and this is reflected in the irregular pattern of his publishing: his writing chronology (as discernible in his notebooks) is not matched by his publishing chronology. One of the first instances of public recognition came in an article by Ian Fletcher in the magazine *Chanticleer* (1954), which concluded: 'Other names in the Scots literary scene may glitter more than his, but no one now is doing more to enlarge and diversify the existing richness of the Lallans tradition than Robert Garioch.' By this time Garioch's separate publications consisted only of two hand-printed, privately-distributed pamphlets: *17 Poems for 6d* (with Sorley Maclean) and *Chuckies on the Cairn.* The Masque of Edinburgh followed in 1954. His Scots translations from the Latin of George Buchanan's *Jephtha* and *The Baptist* appeared in 1950: he was rightly proud of these productions and they deserve more attention than they have received. His first 'proper' collection was his *Selected Poems,* published in 1966 with a warm introduction by Sydney Goodsir Smith. Two single collections, *The Big Music* and *Doktor Faust in Rose Street* followed: some of the work in these two collections was more recent than 1966, some had been written earlier. Then in 1977 came his *Collected Poems,* and it is interesting to note Garioch's own arrangement of his work: he felt free to ignore the order in which the poems had been written and to treat them as, in a sense, contemporaneous, grouping them according to thematic or formal considerations. One reason for this was that he tended to return time after time to certain types or forms of poems (such as the 'Edinburgh Sonnets') and these clearly benefit from being read together. *The Complete Poetical Works* of 1983 retains much of this arrangement but adds material uncollected in 1977 and draws upon the notebooks. *A Garioch Miscellany* gathers a selection of letters, reviews, and short prose pieces.

"In *As I Remember* Garioch recalls: 'I studied Honours English (we didn't "read" in those days) and we used to stick our poems on the board of the English Library. Vexed by the Englishness of other people's poems, I reacted by presenting "Fi'baw in the Street," glottal stops and all. I thought I was being rude, but it was well received. Mr. Murison's *Guid Scots Tongue* tells us how Allan Ramsay's work was one of reaction. I regard mine as a small part of that reaction, which has never quite ceased since Ramsay began it, sometime about 1720.' But Garioch's use of Scots was both more important and less strenuous than a protest: it was rather a natural development of the linguistic surroundings in which he grew up. Elsewhere in the same essay he notes: 'The language spoken in our house was good Scots, by which I mean that it used many words not found in English, and that it was sounded according to Scottish rules.' Whether this made Garioch part of the so-called Scottish Renaissance is arguable. Whether the Scottish Renaissance was cohesive and productive enough to take its place in Scottish literary history as a significant and influential phenomenon is also arguable, and is still much argued over in certain Scottish literary circles. But it is certainly true that from the publication of Hugh MacDiarmid's early Scots lyrics there was a renewed interest in the possibilities of Scots for literary purposes. MacDiarmid's use of Scots was consciously literary: he culled words and expressions from different historical periods and different geographical areas: words like 'synthetic' and 'extended' have been applied to the kind of Scots developed by MacDiarmid. Garioch's use of Scots was no less deliberate but it was less self-consciously literary: except in cases where he would consciously re-employ older stylistic manners (such as the aureate diction of his Greek translations) his Scots is recognizably based on the everyday speech of the non-genteel parts of Edinburgh society. Much as he loved and used dictionaries, it is the talk of the street that we hear in his poems.

"Garioch's use of Scots is only one aspect of a more comprehensive and strongly felt sense of tradition: a sense gained not only from reading but also from living, for Edinburgh is an old city; many writers have lived there, and it is still possible to see buildings and cityscapes as they must have been familiar to those who lived among them generations ago. This feeling of nearness to one's predecessors is celebrated in many of Garioch's poems, perhaps most of all in 'To Robert Fergusson'

My ain toun's makar, monie an airt
formed us in common, faur apairt
in time, but fell alike in hert . . .

"The way in which Garioch celebrates Fergusson by the skillful use of a stanza-form in which Fergusson himself was skilled is but one example of Garioch's own skill in verse-making. At first sight his attitude may seem old-fashioned: in *As I Remember* he declares: 'I do not like to hear metrical poetry read with more attention to full-stops than to line-endings, and hate to hear rhymes hurried over as if they were something not quite nice.' Old-fashioned or not, Garioch was undoubtedly one of the most accomplished verse-craftsmen of his time. The variety of forms he mastered can be appreciated by looking at 'Embro to the Ploy,' 'To Robert Fergusson,' 'Sisyphus,' 'The Humanists' Trauchles in Paris,' 'The Muir,' 'The Big Music,' 'The Traivler,' 'The Lesson,' 'Chalk Farm 1945,' as well as various sonnets, both his own and in translation, where he still engineered a surprise out of a form we may think was dead.

"Indeed, 'old-fashioned' is a term Garioch could well have accepted as a compliment: he found much to admire and imitate in writers of the past. His translations, an important part of his output, are a witness to this. More than that, it can be argued that to Garioch translation offered more than a technical challenge: he had something of the not-so-modern understanding of translation as a way of honoring and communing with writers of the past, and, like many of those writers in their own practices of imitation and translation, he underplayed his own very considerable contribution. The range of his translations is worth noting—Pindar, Hesiod, Anglo-Saxon, George Buchanan, Goethe, Apollinaire, Arthur Johnstone—but his most substantial and remarkable achievement here is his Scots translations from Giuseppe Belli (1791–1863), the Italian poet who produced over two thousand sonnets in Romanesco. Belli had an eye and a nose for street-life and gossip, and an ear for the vigors of local speech; he could combine satire and compassion almost in the same breath: the consanguinity between Garioch and Belli is remarkable. Garioch's 1977 *Collected Poems* contains fifty-two of the sonnets, but in the last years of his life he worked steadily at more, aiming at a separate collection, and by the time of his death he had accumulated no fewer than 120. Garioch's Scots (or rather Edinburgh) versions of Belli's Roman sonnets, it need hardly be said, both scan and rhyme."

PRINCIPAL WORKS: 17 Poems for 6d (with Sorley Maclean), 1940; Chuckies on the Cairn, 1949; The Masque of Edinburgh, 1954; George Buchanan's Jephtha and The Baptist, 1959; Selected Poems, 1966; The Big Music, 1971; Doktor Faust in Rose Street, 1974; Two Men and a Blanket, 1975; Collected Poems,

1977; Fulton, R. (ed.), A Garioch Miscellany, 1983; Complete Poetical Works, 1983.

ABOUT: Garioch, R. Two Men and a Blanket, 1975; Lindsey, M. (ed.) As I Remember, 1979; Smith, S.G. *Introduction to* Garioch's Selected Poems, 1966; Vinson, J. (ed.) Contemporary Poets, 1980. *Periodicals*—Lives Review 62 (1977); Times Literary Supplement September 9, 1977; November 18, 1983.

GAY, PETER (JACK) (June 20, 1923–), American historian, was born in Berlin to Morris Peter Gay and the former Helga Kohnke, a Jewish couple of moderate means. His father's business was expropriated in 1938 by his gentile partner, and the family fled the country "late in April 1939, on the last ship to Cuba," arriving in the United States in 1941. They became naturalized U.S. citizens in 1946. During and after the war, Gay wrote in 1976, "I refused to read anything in the German language. . . . I guarded my memories of Nazi Germany, like secret, privileged wounds, to preserve, with them, my hatred." The family settled on Long Island and Gay recommenced his interrupted education. After receiving a B.A. from the University of Denver in 1946, he studied government at Columbia University, obtaining his M.A. the following year and his Ph.D. in 1951. His dissertation, written under the direction of Professor Franz L. Neumann, became his first book, *The Dilemma of Democratic Socialism: Eduard Bernstein's Challenge to Marx,* about the insoluble differences in German politics between Marxist and non-Marxist socialism, focusing on the political and intellectual career of Bernstein, the foremost theoretician of German democratic socialism.

Weimar Germany has continued to be an important focus of Gay's career as a European intellectual historian, but he has also made seminal contributions to historiography, the principles and methodology of the writing of history, and especially to the modern understanding of the Enlightenment. His interest in the French *philosophes* began with, and has always centered on, the protean figure of Voltaire. *Voltaire's Politics: The Poet as Realist* aimed at placing "Voltaire's political ideas in the framework of his time"; it was widely praised for broad scholarship and incisive argument. Gay's two-volume annotated translation of Voltaire's *Philosophical Dictionary* has become the standard English version of the work; he also translated Voltaire's novel *Candide.*

The Party of Humanity: Essays in the French Enlightenment consisted of three essays on Voltaire, three on the general characteristics of the

PETER GAY

French Enlightenment, and three critiques of contrary views on the Enlightenment, notably a long piece on Rousseau and his modern interpreters. This retrospective collection served as herald for Gay's largest and most highly acclaimed work, *The Enlightenment: An Interpretation.* The first volume, *The Rise of Modern Paganism,* treats the intellectual origins of the movement. It was praised by John Ratte as "that rare work of intellectual history, a book which attempts to shape contemporary thought as much as to analyze and evaluate the thought of the past." It won both the National Book Award and the Frederic G. Melcher Book Award for 1967. Volume two, *The Science of Freedom,* was described by J. W. Burrow as "a comprehensive and magisterial study of the historical matrix from which emerged the belief in critical reason as the lever of human betterment." Always a notable devotee of comprehensive bibliography, Gay appended a separate "Bibliographical Essay" to each volume; together the essays consist of eighteen chapters and 263 pages. *The Bridge of Criticism: Dialogues Among Lucian, Erasmus and Voltaire on the Enlightenment,* intended as a kind of coda or "political epilogue" to the preceding work, was criticized for its unorthodox form and for being "a thinly veiled defense of modern liberalism."

Weimar Culture: The Outsider as Insider was Gay's painstaking re-creation, survey, and critique of the world of his early childhood. The Weimar Republic, which was "born in defeat, lived in turmoil, and died in disaster," produced a remarkable culture he describes as "the creation of outsiders, propelled by history into the inside, for a short, dizzying, fragile moment." It was "a precarious glory, a dance on the edge of a volcano." Walter Laqueur called the book "absorbing" and "clearly a labor of love, . . . despite the difficulties of doing justice to so many disparate trends in various fields, he has succeeded exceedingly well. One could dispute details endlessly. . . . But what matters is the broad outline, and on this count it is difficult to fault Mr. Gay's judgment." *Freud, Jews, and Other Germans: Masters and Victims in Modernist Culture,* a series of chiefly biographical essays on German-Jewish cultural interaction in pre-Nazi Germany, represented a continuation of Gay's interest in the Weimar period, but was not the full-length history he promised to write in *Weimar Culture.*

In two difficult works of the mid-1970s, Gay showed himself a subtle theoretician of his field. *Style in History* was an inductive comparison of the work and style of four historians, Edward Gibbon, Leopold von Ranke, Thomas Babington Macaulay, and Jakob Burckhardt. J. W. Burrow considered "each of the essays . . . an amalgam of intellectual history, psychology and literary analysis which succeeds admirably in avoiding each of the different kinds of available pedantry." The twin conclusions, that stylistic analysis is a valid form of history and that "skepticism about the possibility of genuine historical knowledge" is unwarranted, serve together to further one of the most crucial of Gay's ideas, that history as a discipline is both an art and a science. In *Art and Act: On Causes in History—Manet, Gropius, Mondrian,* the Critique Lectures delivered at the Cooper Union in 1974, Gay attempts "to deal with art as a piece of history." The book was judged a success by Hilton Kramer, who called it "a fresh reading" of the voluminous literature on the three artists, free of art-historical stereotypes. "He has significantly revised the way the modern 'aesthetic object' and its makers will henceforth be perceived. In writing about art as history, he has succeeded in restoring it to life."

On a scale even more ambitious than his earlier work on the Enlightenment is Gay's projected multi-volume study of *The Bourgeois Experience,* the first volume of which was subtitled *Victoria to Freud: Education of the Senses.* Conceived as "history informed by psychoanalysis," Gay's work generated considerable excitement and controversy in 1984, all the more because this volume had sexuality for its subject and challenged a number of widely held views on Victorian life—especially on the alleged frigidity and sexual innocence of Victorian women. Drawing upon contemporary letters, di-

aries, novels, and art, as well as the studies of sexologists, historians, psychologists, and sociologists, Gay offers a wide-ranging portrait of Victorian sexuality. In future volumes he plans to study, or, as he puts it, to "redefine," the bourgeois experience in love, conflict, and aggression.

Gay joined the Columbia faculty in 1947 as a part-time lecturer in government. He switched to the history department in 1956, became professor of history in 1962, and held the William R. Shepherd chair from 1967 to 1969. In the latter year he went to Yale, first as professor of comparative European intellectual history, and from 1970 as Durfee professor of history. He was twice awarded a Guggenheim fellowship (1967–68, 1977–78), was a visiting fellow of Churchill College, Cambridge (1970–71), and a Rockefeller Foundation fellow (1979–80). In 1959 he married Ruth Slotkin, a writer, and they have three daughters. He is a member of several U.S. and French historical societies, and has frequently contributed articles to popular journals, especially the *New Republic.*

PRINCIPAL WORKS: The Dilemma of Democratic Socialism, 1952; Voltaire's Politics, 1959; The Party of Humanity, 1964; A Loss of Mastery, 1966; The Enlightenment, 1966, 1969; Age of Enlightenment, 1966; Weimar Culture, 1968; The Bridge of Criticism, 1970; (with R. K. Webb) Modern Europe, 1973; Style in History, 1974; Art and Act, 1976; Freud, Jews, and Other Germans, 1978; The Bourgeois Experience: Victoria to Freud, 1984. *Translations*—Cassirer, E. The Question of Jean Jacques Rousseau, 1954; Voltaire's Philosophical Dictionary, 1962, and Candide, 1963. *Anthologies*—John Locke on Education, 1964; Deism, 1968; (with G. J. Cavanaugh) Historians at Work, 1972; Eighteenth Century Studies, 1972; (with J. A. Garraty) A History of the World, 1972; The Enlightenment, 1973.

ABOUT: Contemporary Authors, first revision series 13-16, 1975; Who's Who in America, 1983-84. *Periodicals*—Harper's December 1983; History Today August 1984; National Observer March 13, 1967; October 30, 1976; New York Review of Books February 2, 1984; New York Times August 3, 1976; December 21, 1977; New York Times Book Review January 1, 1967; November 24, 1968; August 22, 1976; January 29, 1978; January 8, 1984; Publishers Weekly January 6, 1984; Times Literary Supplement June 20, 1975; December 24, 1976.

GELLNER, ERNEST (ANDRÉ) (December 9, 1925–), British anthropologist and philosopher, was born in Paris, the son of Rudolf Gellner and the former Anna Fantl. He was educated at Balliol College, Oxford, and took his Ph.D. from the University of London in 1961.

His academic career began at Edinburgh University, where he was assistant lecturer from 1947 to 1949. He then moved to the sociology department of the London School of Economics where the study of functional social anthropology was reaching a peak among the first generation of Bronislaw Malinowski's disciples. Gellner has taught at the LSE ever since, and has held the rank of professor since 1962.

Gellner's first book created immense consternation in philosophical circles and established his reputation as a brilliant iconoclast. *Words and Things: A Critical Account of Linguistic Philosophy and a Study in Ideology* strongly attacks the presuppositions and arguments of the analysts of "ordinary language"—the school of linguistic philosophy founded by Ludwig Wittgenstein which has held sway at Oxford since the 1940s. In a lively introduction to the book, Bertrand Russell likened Oxford philosophers to the nihilistic Abecedarian heretics, who "maintained that all human knowledge is evil, and, since it is based upon the alphabet, it is a mistake to learn even the ABC. . . . The Oxford Abecedarians do not reject *all* human learning, but only such as is not required for a First in Greats—i.e., such as has been discovered since the time of Erasmus." *Words and Things* was refused a review in *Mind*, the quasi-official journal of British philosophy, a move that was called "the nearest modern philosophy has come to ceremonial tribal expulsion" by I. C. Jarvie and Joseph Agassi, the editors of three volumes of Gellner's collected essays. The book was, however, discussed at great length throughout the British press; even Oxford philosophy dons were occasionally constrained to admire its argumentative energy and sociological verity, all the while disputing the philosophical content of its criticism.

With *Thought and Change*, Gellner attempts to formulate and criticize a modern philosophy based on the industrialization of society. "We live at a time," he concludes in the book, "when we can see the interdependence of the political, the economic and the cognitive transformations; a time also when transformation has gathered enormous speed and has come to embrace the whole of humanity. Its understanding is certainly the first task of thought. We only possess fragments of such an understanding—enough for a reassurance that understanding is possible, if not for much more. But systems of thought that are constitutionally unable even to perceive the change, let alone to understand it, are worthless." Earlier social thinkers were able to take refuge in stable myths, but modern man, in Gellner's view, "must make a virtue of contingency": the modern "science of society" must become attuned to "transition." Julius Gould remarked that "much of Gellner's own philosophical argument centres on the vexed issue of the relation between facts and values. . . . The central point is this: moral conclusions cannot rest upon solely factual premises—there is always a moral element in the premises themselves." The author's other main work of systematic philosophical speculation is *Legitimation of Belief*, in which his aim is to defend "*critical* monism, the attempt to restore intellectual order by the sustained application of simple, delimited, lucid principles, principles designed to isolate and use the marks of genuine knowledge, an attempt which is mandatory in conditions of intellectual chaos such as in fact often obtain—such monism is absolutely essential for our life. It has nothing to do with a bath in a tepid, cosmic fluid. The systematic obfuscation of this distinction, the attempt to foist the motives, spirit, and criteria of oceanic monism on to critical monism, is one of the gravest and most conspicuous defects of recent thought." He attempts to determine in the book which beliefs are cognitively legitimate, and by what criteria they are warranted.

By general consent, Gellner's greatest work of anthropology is *Saints of the Atlas*, a study of the village life of the Berbers who live in the High Atlas Mountains of Morocco. The author considers these people to be saints of Islam, the embodiments of the Koranic tradition. The chief problem of the study, stated at the beginning of the second chapter, is "how did the Rule of Saints, or Anarchy Mitigated by Holiness, maintain itself and function?" The book, he explains in the introduction, "is concerned mainly with power and belief, and less specifically with wealth. It is concerned with the politics and religion of a tribal people, who are mixed pastoralists and agriculturalists. Their ecology does affect the understanding of local religion and local power, but it enters into this account only to the extent necessary for the understanding of politics and faith." The reviewer for the *Times Literary Supplement* admired Gellner's "refreshingly open-ended way" of exploring "aspects of segmentary Berber politics. . . . Far more than the people he studies, the anthropologist often risks becoming the slave of custom in the sense that, having established what actually happens, he tends to invest this with a finality which defies further questions, or the contemplation of possible alternatives. Professor Gellner never does this. He constantly asks why things are as they are, and what would follow if they were different. This, coupled with a proper respect for the historical perspective, gives his analysis a satisfying richness and depth."

Gellner's interest in Islamic society has widened over the years. In 1973 he edited, with Charles Micaud, *Arabs and Berbers: From Tribe to Nation in North Africa,* an influential collection of fifteen essays by British, French, and American scholars, all concerned to demonstrate the high degree of cultural unity in Northwest Africa. His much-discussed *Muslim Society* examines the dynamics of Islamic society in the contemporary world. He constructs his theoretical model for a sociology of Islam mainly on the *Muqaddima* of Ibn Khaldun, the fourteenth-century cadi of Cairo and prime authority of the interrelationships of Islam. Despite the ostensibly fragmentary nature of the book—except for its powerful organizing introductory essay, it is in the main a collection of previously published articles and reviews—reviewers generally recognized its value. Clifford Geertz called it "the boldest and most ingenious, as well as the most hard-driven, attempt in recent years to present a general account of the fundamental features of social life in the Islamic world. . . . [Gellner] constructs a remarkably unified model of 'the basic rules of the game' as it is played in that world; a model which, whatever else one may say about it, is anyway clear."

Gellner's collected essays, edited by Jarvie and Agassi, appeared in three volumes: the anthropological and sociological essays published as *Cause and Meaning in the Social Sciences*; the political essays as *Contemporary Thought and Politics*; and the philosophical essays as *The Devil in Modern Philosophy* (1974). They show the extremely wide range of his interests as an engaged and original modern thinker. Bernard Crick remarked that each volume "exhibited his polemical as well as his technical ability; he is the master of the comic *reductio ad absurdum* and of homely caricature." Another volume, consisting mainly of polemical pieces and extended book reviews, is *Spectacles & Predicaments: Essays in Social Theory.*

In September 1954, Gellner married Susan Ryan; they have two sons and two daughters. Until ill health forced him to curtail arduous travel, he was a regular visitor to the Berber villages in the mountains of Morocco. He is a member of the Royal Anthropological Institute, of several sociological associations, and is a fellow of the British Academy.

PRINCIPAL WORKS: Words and Things, 1959 (rev. ed.) 1979; Thought and Change, 1964; Saints of the Atlas, 1969; Legitimation of Belief, 1974; Patrons and Clients, 1977; Muslim Society, 1981; Nations and Nationalism, 1983. *Collected essays*—Cause and Meaning in the Social Sciences, 1973; Contemporary Thought and Politics, 1974; The Devil in Modern Philosophy, 1974; Spectacles & Predicaments, 1980. *As editor*—Arabs and Berbers, 1973.

ABOUT: Contemporary Authors, new revision series 4, 1981. *Periodicals*—Choice October 1970; November 1973; February 1974; November 1974; July–August 1975; December 1980; March 1982; Contemporary Sociology May 1982; Encounter May 1965; October 1974; March 1982; Guardian October 16, 1959; Nation September 24, 1960; New Statesman October 31, 1959; January 15, 1965; December 5, 1969; January 24, 1975; New York Review of Books May 27, 1982; Science May 22, 1981; Spectator November 20, 1959; Times Literary Supplement November 20, 1959; March 5, 1970; June 15, 1973; September 21, 1973; August 9, 1974; March 14, 1980; December 11, 1981; October 21, 1983.

GIJSEN, MARNIX *See* GORIS, BARON JAN-ALBERT

GILBERT, MARTIN (October 25, 1936–   ), British historian and biographer, was born in London, the son of Peter Gilbert, a manufacturer of jewelry, and the former Miriam Green. He attended Highgate School and Magdalen College, Oxford, taking his B.A. with first-class honors in 1960. He was senior research scholar from 1960 to 1962 at St. Antony's College, a postgraduate institution in Oxford, and since 1962 has been a fellow and member of the governing body of Merton College.

Also in 1962, Gilbert had the good fortune to be appointed research assistant to Randolph S. Churchill, who had been preparing to write the official biography of his father, Winston S. Churchill. The first volume, *Youth, 1874–1900,* appeared in 1966, the year after the former prime minister's death; volume two, *The Young Statesman, 1901–1914,* was published the following year. Randolph did not long survive his father, however, and in 1968 Gilbert, who had by that time become senior research assistant, was named official biographer. The post carried with it not only immense prestige in historical circles; it also conferred the advantage of exclusive and unrestricted access to the enormous Churchill archive. All other biographers of Churchill of whom there have been a good number, have to rely on published sources.

Volume three of *Winston S. Churchill,* entitled *The Challenge of War, 1914–1916,* was the first of Gilbert's authorship to appear. Covering the latter part of Churchill's tenure as first lord of the Admiralty at the end of Asquith's prime ministry, including the ill-fated Dardanelles expedition, the book was almost universally praised for painstaking scholarship and careful judgment. J. G. Harrison wrote, "The book ably catches and transmits the breathtaking extent of Churchill's genius. Even to dip into it will show what those who scorn history miss to their own impoverishment." The reviewer for the *Times Literary Supplement* called Gilbert "a worthy successor" to Randolph Churchill, "and interestingly enough more partisan than the hero's son," concluding that "every page bears evidence of the immense work of research which backs the book."

The fourth volume, *The Stricken World, 1916–1922*, examines Churchill's return to power in 1916 in David Lloyd-George's government, first as minister of munitions, then as war and air secretary, and finally as colonial secretary. J. E. Harrison considered it "a book of careful and almost endless scholarship, . . . written with great readability." To John Grigg, "The very great merit of Mr. Gilbert as a biographer is that he presents the evidence fairly, lucidly, and in sufficient detail for readers to form their own judgments." *The Prophet of Truth, 1922–1939*, volume five, at more than 1,150 pages the longest installment yet, covered by far the most ground, treating Churchill's performance as chancellor of the exchequer (1924–29) under Stanley Baldwin, and the decade (1929–39), often called his "wilderness years," during which he was out of office. The *Economist* reviewer, once again comparing Gilbert with Randolph Churchill as biographer, found that the former "has brought the story to life. To those who claim . . . that this biography is too long and too big to permit any assessment of the men and matters in it, this life-and-breath is a powerful retort." Stephen Koss commended the book as "Churchillian in technique as well as scope," and Paul Johnson wrote, "Mr. Gilbert also provides scores of biographical notes, which are always useful and often essential. He himself remains in the background, an objective and vigilant impresario, allowing the material to tell its own tale." With volume six, *Finest Hour 1939–1941*, Gilbert described the dramatic events from the outbreak of World War II in Europe to the American declaration of war following Pearl Harbor. Carrying on the biography "magnificently," Gaddis Smith wrote in the *New York Times Book Review*, Gilbert "focuses in a very disciplined way on Churchill himself, citing his published works but letting him speak mostly through unpublished material. Thus the reader follows Churchill through every waking moment." Emerging strikingly in this volume, Smith observes, is "a case study in leadership," with a wealth of detail that draws a portrait of Churchill "on a scale appropriate to its heroic subject."

Gilbert has periodically published fat companion volumes of annotated documentary evidence, reproducing in full the sources of each of his thousands of quotations and adding much collateral evidence as well—the documents accompanying volume three, for example, run to nearly 1,700 pages. The biographical volumes to the end of volume five have taken over 4,000 pages, and there may be that many still to come, for volume six takes Churchill's life only through 1942. Gilbert was appointed official biographer of Sir Anthony Eden, Earl of Avon, in 1977, but will doubtless complete the first massive project before embarking in earnest on the second.

So much careful scholarship comes only after countless thousands of hours of labor, but in addition to his work on Churchill, Gilbert has produced enough other books to equal the entire writing careers of at least a couple of ordinary historians. He is renowned for his contributions to British and European diplomatic history of the interwar period, and especially to the history of the catastrophe suffered by the Jews under the Nazis. He concentrated at first on the British policy of appeasement; *The Appeasers*, written with Richard Gott, was criticized by A.J.P. Taylor as a replaying of "old tunes" and "a rigid diplomatic narrative, ignoring the climate of opinion at the time." *The Roots of Appeasement* seeks to demonstrate the continuity of appeasement as a British political and diplomatic tool in dealing with Germany from 1918. It was a valid enough policy during the 1920s, when Germany was weak, but, as the *Times Literary Supplement* reviewer noted, "it had become an ineffective and psychologically corrosive one well before Munich."

Gilbert began his consideration of the destruction of European Jewry with *Exile and Return: The Struggle for a Jewish Homeland*, a study of both the millennial Jewish yearning for Zion and of the usually repressive British policy toward Zionist aspirations from 1914 to 1948. The extensive examination of public and private British archives "is of such power and importance," wrote Eric Briendel, "that it serves to make *Exile and Return* a major contribution to contemporary history." *The Holocaust: A Record of the Destruction of Jewish Life in Europe During the Dark Years of Nazi Rule* is a slender book of maps and photographs, accompanied by Gilbert's captions, showing the location of the death camps, ghettos, deportation routes—the infrastructure of the Holocaust. *The Final Journey: The Fate of the Jews in Nazi Europe* supplements the pictorial record with lengthy firsthand accounts of the "Final Solution" by victims and survivors. *Auschwitz and the Allies* studies the Allied governments' reluctant discovery of Nazi atrocities against Jews and their belated, woefully inadequate reaction. J. P. Stern called it a "distinguished and eminently sober book. . . . Composed of a vast array of detailed records, many of them previously unpublished, as well as the author's conversations with survivors, Mr. Gilbert's chronicle is written in a sombre and quiet style throughout, . . . yet it has none of that supposedly 'scientific' detachment which so readily deteriorates into callousness."

In addition to all the above books, Gilbert, who lists his only recreation as "drawing maps," has composed a considerable number of highly regarded historical atlases to many disparate regions and periods, including American history (1969), the First World War (1971), Russian history (1972), the Arab-Israeli conflict (1975), the Jews in Arab lands (1975), the Jews of Russia (1976), and Jerusalem history (1977). He has also written major biographies of Lord Allen of Hurtwood (1965) and Sir Horace Rumbold (1973), several biographies for younger readers, and was editor of the *festschrift* for A.J.P. Taylor, *A Century of Conflict* (1966). He has been a frequent contributor of articles and reviews to historical journals. Long concerned with anti-Semitism in the Soviet Union, Gilbert has also been active in recent years in the movement to assist those who have been denied permission to emigrate. These are non-dissident Jews, suffering because they have expressed their wish to leave the U.S.S.R. In the spring of 1984, Gilbert visited New York in support of the efforts of the Conference on Soviet Jewry, and in the same year he published *The Jews of Hope,* which describes his meeting in 1983 with a number of these Soviet Jews.

Gilbert has a daughter from his first marriage, to Helen Constance Robinson, and a son from his second marriage, to Susan Sacher. He has been a visiting lecturer or professor at Budapest University (1961), the University of South Carolina (1965), Tel-Aviv University (1979), and the Hebrew University of Jerusalem (1980), where he has been on the board of governors since 1978. He has served as historical consultant to newspapers and television companies, including Thames Television and the British Broadcasting Corporation, and was known to be responsible for the authenticity of the Southern Pictures television series, *Winston Churchill: The Wilderness Years,* shown in 1980–81. In 1981 he was awarded an honorary doctorate of letters by Westminster College in Fulton, Missouri, where Churchill made his "Iron Curtain" speech in 1946.

PRINCIPAL WORKS: (with Richard Gott) The Appeasers, 1963; Britain and Germany Between the Wars, 1964; The European Powers, 1900–1945, 1965; Plough My Own Furrow: The Life of Lord Allen of Hurtwood, 1965; Servant of India: A Study of Imperial Rule 1905–1910, 1966; The Roots of Appeasement, 1966; Winston S. Churchill, vol. iii, 1914–1916, 1971, companion volume (in two parts) 1973; Sir Horace Rumbold: Portrait of a Diplomat, 1973; Churchill: A Photographic Portrait, 1974; The Arab-Israeli Conflict: Its History in Maps, 1974, 3rd ed. 1979; Winston S. Churchill, vol. iv, 1917–1922, 1975, companion volume (in three parts) 1977; Winston S. Churchill, vol. v, 1922–1939, 1976, companion volume, part one, The Exchequer Years, 1922–1929, 1980, part two, The Wilderness Years, 1929–1935, 1981, part three, The Coming of War 1936–1939, 1982; Winston S. Churchill, vol. vi, Finest Hour 1939–1944, 1983; Exile and Return: The Emergence of Jewish Statehood, 1978; Final Journey, the Fate of the Jews of Nazi Europe, 1979; Auschwitz and the Allies, 1981; Churchill's Political Philosophy, 1981; The Jews of Hope, 1984. *As editor*—A Century of Conflict: Essays Presented to A.J.P. Taylor, 1966; Churchill, 1967; Lloyd George, 1968; Winston Churchill 1970; The Coming of War in 1939, 1973.

ABOUT: Contemporary Authors, first revision series 9–12, 1974. *Periodicals*—America September 21, 1963; Christian Science Monitor October 2, 1963; December 2, 1971; August 8, 1975; Commentary February 1979; November 1981; Economist March 9, 1963; July 3, 1965; November 19, 1966; November 6, 1971; January 20, 1973; May 4, 1974; October 30, 1976; October 17, 1981; Encounter February 1979; New Republic January 17, 1976; May 21, 1977; January 13, 1979; June 16, 1979; New Statesman February 15, 1963; May 26, 1967; October 29, 1971; July 26, 1974; June 6, 1975; October 29, 1976; July 7, 1978; May 11, 1979; October 9, 1981; New York Review of Books October 22, 1981; New York Times April 28, 1984; New York Times Book Review August 18, 1963; November 24, 1974; December 25, 1983; Saturday Review September 7, 1963; Times Literary Supplement July 15, 1965; December 1, 1966; May 29, 1969; March 19, 1971; October 29, 1971; March 9, 1973; October 29, 1976; December 4, 1981; July 1, 1983; Virginia Quarterly Review Autumn 1963; Autumn 1975; Spring 1979.

GLOAG, JULIAN (July 2, 1930–), British novelist, was born in London, the son of John Edwards Gloag, a much-published historian of British architecture and decorative arts, and Mary Gertrude Ward Gloag. During his national service he was a rifleman in the British Army (1949–50) before attending Magdalene College, Cambridge, from which he took his bachelor's degree in 1953. He worked during the next two years in London as a researcher for *Chambers's Encyclopaedia,* then moved to New York, where he was editor at Ronald Press (1956–59) and Hawthorn Books (1961–63). He has been a full-time writer since 1963.

Gloag's first novel, *Our Mother's House,* is a tale of ghoulish deception in which, after the

JULIAN GLOAG

sudden death of a London mother, her seven children bury her in the back garden, then carry on by themselves under the leadership of the eldest, a thirteen-year-old girl. They deceive creditors, insurance companies, and even some highly suspicious neighbors; for solace they develop a sort of cult of the absent mother, and end up turning quite savage. G. M. Casey thought it "a macabre story of inexorable credibility," particularly admiring Gloag's "memorable" portraits "of seven highly individual children . . . [who] are persons, not symbols, and their very vitality is a tribute to their creator's skill as a novelist." Most reviewers, however, considered the novel to be implausible, one remarking that "in such a tale, one must be persuaded or it cannot interest." The novel's similarity to William Golding's *Lord of the Flies* was also noted; Dorrie Pagones believed it lacked "the sustained vision and dramatic power of the Golding masterpiece, for it shifts focus midway and thereafter almost imperceptibly slows its pace."

In *A Sentence of Life,* Gloag tells the story of Jordan Maddox, an apparently respectable London publisher accused of murdering his secretary, who desperately attempts to understand his responsibility in the crime. Martin Tucker maintained that the hero is like the children in *Our Mother's House*: "Fear of the indecency of other people drives a basically decent person into more and more deviant acts of deception. . . . [The] ordinary characters . . . little by little reveal themselves as capable of enormous passion and deceptiveness." Joseph Haas, while praising the "framework of [the] suspenseful murder case and taut trial scenes," felt that Gloag's finest

achievement was the character of Maddox, "a totally realized, memorable man." The entire book "is directed toward the slow revelation of Maddox's soiled innocence. The conclusion . . . holds up a mirror that Mr. Gloag will not permit us to ignore."

Maundy is a frightening novel whose eponymous hero, a well-behaved Home Counties banker, experiences a dangerous mental crisis. In one part of his life he enacts scenes of gross cruelty, sexual abuse, and complete selfishness; these we see alternated with scenes of his other rather genteel and ordinary life with the former sort coming utterly to dominate his existence. Many of the scenes of introspective hallucination are "rendered with terrifying conviction," wrote J. R. Frakes. Although he found the prose often "strained into a self-consciously hysterical attempt at mad lyricism and automatic writing," Frakes concluded that the book is "a very special kind of fiction, reminiscent at times of Harold Pinter and John Hawkes but usually emitting its own private effluvium. The corruption of gentility stinks worse than festering lilies. As the air thickens and suffocates, gross figures emerge from the fog, grotesques that miraculously manage to be simultaneously persuasive, comic and menacing."

Critical reaction was sharply divided over *Sleeping Dogs Lie,* an intricately plotted novel in which Hugh Welchman, a psychiatrist, determines to help a young Cambridge student understand his phobia, a fear of descending stone steps. Evan Hunter thought the book a "triumph": "Welchman is a brilliant creation, . . . [who] must eventually come to grips with his own ghosts as well as those that are haunting his young patient. . . . The shocking and surprising plot twists that propel this compulsively readable novel . . . are as labyrinthine (and ultimately as logical) as the workings of the unconscious itself." David Wilson, however, found the novel distasteful: "These are lives unleavened by humor, and their uncovering is cold and clinical. . . . The bleakness of the emotional landscape is echoed in the description of the physical terrain. . . . It is all rather like a Freudian gloss on an Agatha Christie plot, a whodunit laced with whys and wherefores." Gillian Wilce agreed, remarking on the book's "perfect internal consistency. . . . And yet to what end? . . . Here all are guilty, all are rather unpleasant, wholly self-absorbed and, in spite of their hectic, bloody lives, not very interesting."

Gloag married Danielle J. H. Haase-Dubose, a university professor, in September 1968; they have a son and a daughter and have lived in Paris for several years. He is a fellow of the Royal

Society of Literature and the Royal Society of Arts.

PRINCIPAL WORKS: Our Mother's House, 1963; A Sentence of Life, 1966; Maundy, 1969; A Woman of Character, 1973; Sleeping Dogs Lie, 1980; Lost and Found, 1981.

ABOUT: Contemporary Authors 65–68, 1977. *Periodicals*—Best Sellers May 15, 1963; June 1, 1966; February 15, 1969; Choice November 1969; Library Journal May 15, 1963; February 1, 1969; May 15, 1980; New York Herald Tribune Book Review June 9, 1963; New York Times Book Review May 12, 1963; May 1, 1966; March 9, 1969; July 20, 1980; New Statesman October 25, 1963; June 27, 1969; January 2, 1981; Newsweek May 13, 1963; Saturday Review June 22, 1963; May 7, 1966; February 22, 1969; Time May 10, 1963; Times Literary Supplement November 1, 1963; June 26, 1969; December 12, 1980; October 23, 1981.

GAIL GODWIN

GODWIN, GAIL (June 18, 1937–   ), American novelist and short story writer, was born in Birmingham, Alabama, the daughter of Mose Winston and Kathleen (Krahenbuhl) Godwin. She spent her early years in Asheville, North Carolina, where her mother, deserted by her husband, taught English at local junior colleges and wrote several novels that were not published. After World War II, Kathleen Godwin remarried, and the family lived in Norfolk, Virginia and other Southern localities.

Godwin attended Peace Junior College, Raleigh, North Carolina from 1955 to 1957, and with a scholarship went on to the University of North Carolina at Chapel Hill, from which she graduated with a B.A. in journalism in 1959. She worked for a year (1959–60) as a reporter for the Miami *Herald,* and was subsequently employed (1962–65) by the United States Travel Service at the American Embassy in London. In 1965 she met and married Ian Marshall, a London psychotherapist. "For one year," she wrote in an account of her life in *The Writer on Her Work,* "we did our best to drive each other crazy—and both almost succeeded. Our union was dissolved a year later in a nightmarish vacation in Majorca." The marriage and vacation provided the inspiration later for Godwin's novel *The Perfectionists.*

Following her divorce from Marshall in 1966, Godwin returned to the United States to work as a researcher at the *Saturday Evening Post.* In 1967, she was instructor in English at the University of Iowa where she received her M.S. in 1968 and her Ph.D. in 1971. In 1970, while she was still a graduate student, her first novel, *The Perfectionists,* was published to critical acclaim. Praised by Joyce Carol Oates as "a most engross-

ing novel" that "introduces a young writer of exciting talent," *The Perfectionists* tells the story of an American wife and her English psychotherapist husband, Dr. Empson, who go to Majorca on a belated honeymoon—accompanied by the doctor's three-year-old illegitimate son and one of his female patients. The dissolution of the husband and wife's marriage is accentuated by the heroine's relationship to the strange little boy who will not or cannot speak. Robert Scholes remarked that the *The Perfectionists* "is developed with a satiric and symbolic vigor that suggests a combination of Jane Austen and D. H. Lawrence. The eerie tension that marks the complex relationship is the great achievement of the novel." He added, however, that the reader sees the relationship entirely from the heroine's point of view, making *The Perfectionists* "a woman's novel" in a "constricting" sense.

Upon receiving her Ph.D., Godwin became an Instructor and Fellow (1971–72) at the Center for Advanced Studies at the University of Illinois; and a lecturer (1972–73) at the Writer's Workshop at the University of Iowa. In 1972 she published her second novel *Glass People,* the story of Francesca Bolt, "a pampered young woman who is almost literally dying of emptiness and passivity as the treasured possession of her husband, powerful, remote, all-competent Cameron, who needs her to fulfill the only function he can't perform for himself: to be his flawlessly beautiful wife." The novel traces Francesca's attempt to escape from her role as Cameron's "wife and beautiful object," and to find a life of her own, a pursuit that by the end of the novel seems doomed. *Glass People* was called "both tense and witty," a work related in "a smooth, mocking tone with horror always underneath." Godwin, Genevieve Stuttaford commented, "is drolly neutral, and she makes no judgments." The underlying theme, extending that of *The Perfectionists,* is a woman's search for identity.

That search had its most extended and sympathetic treatment in Godwin's *The Odd Woman.* A study of a sensitive and intelligent young woman, Jane Clifford, with a job teaching English in college, and a married lover, it explores the anomalous position of a modern woman who is professionally independent but emotionally dependent. With its title a distinct echo of George Gissing's novel of 1893, *The Odd Women* (which has a not dissimilar theme), the novel had special relevance for the contemporary feminist movement and has been widely read and discussed in academic circles. It impressed Lore Dickstein, in the *New York Times Book Review,* as a major achievement, comparable "in sensitivity and brilliance, to the best of Doris Lessing and Margaret Drabble. It is a cerebral, reflective novel—most of the action takes place in Jane's mind—and a pleasure to read. Godwin's prose is elegant, full of nuance and feeling, and sparkling with ironic humor." But John A. Avant was less enthusiastic. "Jane's fear that she has closed herself off from life," he wrote, "is recognizable, but Godwin is unable to dramatize it. Jane gets increasingly tiresome as the novel goes on. . . . She learns very little." William Pritchard faulted the book for being too "solemn," and commented that he found it difficult to care deeply about the heroine.

In 1976, while Godwin was in Brazil as an American Specialist for the United States Information Service, her collection of short stories, *Dream Children,* was published. These stories are almost entirely about women: "unhappy women, women lost to disappointment, mildly victimized by their men, betrayed by their expectations." *Dream Children* was regarded generally as a modest book. "The new stories," Katha Pollitt wrote, "are not all well-shaped . . . but the best have the sharp humor and sharp eye that marked her earlier work."

Violet Clay, Godwin's fourth novel, also concerns a young woman in the process of reexamining her life. Although highly readable, *Violet Clay* was found by reviewers to lack the complexity and subtlety of Godwin's best work, its characters tending to be representatives of ideas rather than fully realized people.

Godwin's *A Mother and Two Daughters,* which depicts the closely interrelated lives of Nell Strickland and her daughters Cate and Lydia against the background of a North Carolina town, is a reflective work that touches on many themes of especial interest to women, and it ends affirmatively with the sense of all three women growing, in unpredictable ways, toward greater self-realization. The critic for the *New Yorker* found the characters mere "social specimens," but Walter Clemons, in *Newsweek,* asserted that the clarity of the novel's best scenes "disarms one's annoyance at its failings."

Gail Godwin has been a lecturer at Vassar College (1977) and, since 1978, at the Columbia University Writer's Workshop. She has received a number of awards for fiction, including a grant from the National Endowment for the Arts (1974), a Guggenheim Fellowship (1975), and an award from the American Academy of Arts & Sciences (1981). Her stories and essays have appeared in *Harper's, Esquire, Atlantic, Paris Review,* and many other national magazines.

PRINCIPAL WORKS: *Novels*—The Perfectionists, 1970; Glass People, 1974; The Odd Woman, 1974; Violet Clay, 1978; A Mother and Two Daughters, 1982. *Short stories*—Dream Children, 1976; Mr. Bedford and the Muses, 1983.

ABOUT: American Women Writers 2, 1980; Contemporary Authors, first revision series 29–32, 1972; Contemporary Literary Criticism 5, 1976; 8, 1978; Contemporary Novelists, 1982; Dictionary of Literary Biography 6, 1980; Who's Who in America, 1982; Sternburg, Janet (ed.) The Writer on Her Work, 1980. *Periodicals*—Atlantic May, 1976; (Washington Post) Book World October 1, 1972; National Review September 15, 1978; New Republic January 25, 1975; July 8, 1978; February 17, 1982; New Statesman August 15, 1975; Newsweek January 11, 1982; New Yorker October 7, 1972; New York Review of Books April 1, 1976; July 20, 1978; New York Times Book Review June 7, 1970; October 5, 1972; February 20, 1975; February 22, 1976; May 21, 1978; Saturday Review August 8, 1970; February 21, 1976; October 28, 1977; Time January 25, 1982; Times Literary Supplement July 23, 1971; July 4, 1975; March 5, 1982; Writer December 1983.

*GONZALEZ, ANGEL MUÑIZ (September 6, 1925–), Spanish poet, journalist, and professor, was born in Oviedo (Asturias), Spain, the son of Spanish Republicans. His father, who was a professor of pedagogy in a normal school, died when the poet was a small child. González studied law at the University of Oviedo, and later studied journalism in Madrid. After working in Seville and Barcelona, in 1956 he settled into a job as a civil servant at the Ministry of Public Works in Madrid, a post that he held until 1972. He then began to teach and give lectures in various universities in the United States. In 1974, he

°gôn thä´ läth, äng hel

ANGEL GONZALEZ

was invited to teach at the University of New Mexico in Albuquerque, where he continues to hold the position of professor of Spanish.

While recovering from tuberculosis in the mountains of Asturias as a teen-ager, González began to write poetry. Years later, in 1956, when he arrived in Madrid with his first book—which won the coveted Adonais Prize—he was quickly befriended by other poets. Among them was a childhood friend, Carlos Bousoño, and the Nobel Laureate Vicente Aleixandre. He soon established himself as a member of a group of poets and critics of his age, often labeled "The Generation of 1950" and also "The Children of the Civil War." Influenced by their childhood experiences and the psychological scars produced by the war, the Generation formed a movement that was characterized as "social realist." Highly critical of the Franco government, these writers were constantly observed by the censors because of their political activism against the regime.

González's work expresses the frustration of the life of a dissident intellectual under a repressive regime, though he also writes of the bittersweet memories of lost love, nostalgia for childhood, and optimism about the possibility of a better world. His early readings, nevertheless, were not those of the grim reality of post-civil war Spain. They included such vanguard poets of the early twentieth century as Antonio Machado, Juan Ramón Jiménez, Gerardo Diego, Rafael Alberti, and García Lorca. For González, life and literature were separated by the large gulf that he perceived between life experience and the purely esthetic expression of these avant-garde poets.

Yet González's first book, *Aspero Mundo* (*Harsh World*), published in 1956, reflects the discovery that experience can be communicated through poetic form. He had been reading the "social poets" of the 1940s and '50s by this time—Gabriel Celaya, José Hierro, Blas de Otero, and the Latin American writers Cesar Vallejo and Pablo Neruda. *Aspero Mundo* is a book of love poetry—of experiences more imagined than real, according to the poet himself. Yet it also includes a great deal of autobiographical "poetry of experience," which was to characterize much of the work of his first period. González's early poetry, as he himself has described it, expresses his own personal defeat, as well as the "collective defeat" of his countrymen.

His second book, *Sin esperanza con convencimiento* (Without Hope but With Conviction, 1961) conveys even more clearly a commitment to narrating the history he lived as a child. His style became ironic and allegorical, partly as a way to avoid censorship. Yet it is here that the poet begins to establish a unique voice in Spanish letters. The obsessive theme of time is visible throughout this book. It is a time in the future, one which will bring a better life for Spaniards. The deep socio-political commitment expressed in González's poetry is evident in poems such as "Intermission," where the poet employs the resting period between the scenes of a play to refer to the Franco regime, as explained in this fragment:

The story does not end here.
This is only
a little pause so that we may rest.
The tension is so great,
the emotion released by the plot is so
intense
that all of us,
dancers and actors, acrobats
and distinguished audience,
give thanks to
the conventional truce of the intermission,
and we happily
agree that it was all a lie,
while the musicians tune their violins,
So far we have seen
several quick scenes that foretold death,
we know the faces of certain characters
and we know
something that many of them even do not know:
the motive
for the betrayal and the name
of the betrayer.
                                            —trans. Donald D. Walsh

Grado elemental (Elementary Grade, 1962), *Palabra sobre palabra* (Word upon Word, 1965), and *Tratado de urbanismo* (Treatise on Urban Development, 1967) are also books of social criticism, in which the poet fuses the realm of his experiences with that of the larger social panorama, which he contemplates with a caustic and critical eye. As he once said: " . . . the writer, the poet, of our times must be a rebel, a nonconformist. For me the function of contradicting the common systems of life, the most alienating ones, is one of the central tasks of literature in general and of poetry in particular." His vehement criticism of society is expressed in such poems as "Fables for Animals," where he tells us:

man has already left behind his adolescence
and his western old age could very well
serve as an example to the dog
so that the dog can be
more of a dog,
and the fox more of a traitor,
and the lion more ferocious and bloodthirsty
and the ass as they say the ass is,
and the ox more inhibited and less of a bull.
To every beast that pretends
to improve itself as such
    —be it
with bellicose or peaceful objectives,
with financial or theological plans,
or simply because of its love of art—
I will never cease to give it this advice:
observe the *homo sapiens* and learn.
                    —trans. Shirley Mangini González

González's *Palabra sobre palabra* is also the title of his collected works, published for the first time in 1972, in its fourth printing in 1984. This is also the title of an anthology of his work published in 1968.

Tratado de urbanismo reflects the poet's desire to identify himself with the urban scene and marks the end of the first period in González's poetry. He had lost hope for poetry as a political tool and he became conscious of "the uselessness of all words." Like many of his contemporaries, González abandoned most of his dissident political activity and began traveling and lecturing in Mexico and the United States. He has since returned to Spain only to lecture and to vacation.

The change in González's life view was revealed in the three volumes he wrote between 1969 and 1978. Marked by the use of rhetoric and parody, which are often reminiscent of Confucian riddles and puns, these works repeatedly reveal that poetry's function, though it continues to express a life view, is more ontological than concrete. As the poet has said: " . . . the poem is often an unexpected discovery for its author. It is very possible that the writers who affirm that they have no intentions when they begin writing are sincere, which is equal to saying they don't wish to say anything. But the work, if it is worthwhile, says or means something. I think that what the work means or says is what the author wanted to say unconsciously."

Perhaps the poem which most clearly expresses this new ontological and metapoetic vein in González's latest poetry is "Poetics to which I sometimes apply myself" from a book whose playful title (in English) is *Sample corrected and augmented, of some narrative methods and of the sentimental attitudes that they habitually suffer* (1976) and in Spanish is *Ilusos los Ulises* (The Deluded Ulysses):

To write a poem: to mark the water's skin

Softly, the symbols
are deformed, enlarged
the breeze, the sun, the clouds,
express what they want to
they distend themselves, they become tense, until
the man who looks at them
—a sleeping wind
the light high—
either sees his own face
or—pure transparence, deep
failure—he sees nothing.
                    —trans. Shirley Mangini González

Throughout his poetry, González oscillates between hope and despair. He is caustic, yet benevolent. He accuses the word of being useless, yet he clings to it. His insistent use of irony, as the critic Emilio Alarcos Llorach has said: "is the method by which what the poet is attempting to accomplish reaches the reader with greater force: the distance between the reality which he censures and the ideal which he doesn't even dare to propose." González denounces the hypocrisy of society even in his puns and short poems. As the critic José Olivio Jiménez has pointed out, González discovers through his poetry the contrasting dualities of life, and one of the most important is that of "deceiving appearances and the more profound and true reality," which he constantly expresses in this poetry. In the last poem of *Sample,* the poet tells us sadly:

Always, after a trip,
a terse look fixes itself upon what it is looking for,
and it is a somber nothingness, a frightening light,
that touches the eyes of the one who returns.

Faithfulness, useless toil
Who had the arrogance to attempt it?
No one has been capable
—not even those who have died—
of unraveling the plot
of the days.

Faithfulness, useless toil
Who had the arrogance to attempt it?
                    —trans. Shirley Mangini González

González continues to write poetry. In 1983 he published *Prosemas o menos* (Prose-Poems More or Less) and another book is nearing publication. In addition to his poetry, he has published criticism on the poets Juan Ramón Jiménez, Antonio Machado, Gabriel Celaya, and poets from the Generation of 1927. González has also published numerous journalistic articles on contemporary poetry. His work has appeared in many anthologies of Spanish poets, including *Siete poetas españoles de hoy,* published in Mexico in 1983.

WORKS IN ENGLISH TRANSLATION: A bilingual edition, *"Harsh World" and Other Poems,* with English translations by Donald D. Walsh and an introduction by González, was published in 1977. English translations of individual poems have appeared in *Mundus Articum* (Winter 1974), *New Directions* 28 (1974), and the *Texas Quarterly* (1977).

ABOUT: Alarcos Llorach, E. Angel González, Poeta, 1969; Contemporary Authors 85–88, 1979; Debicki, A. P. Poetry of Discovery, 1982; Jiménez, J. O. Diez años de poesiá española, 1960–1970, 1972. *Periodicals*—New York Review of Books December 21, 1978.

MARY GORDON

GORDON, MARY (December 8, 1949–), American novelist, was born in Far Rockaway, New York, the daughter of David and Anna (Gagliano) Gordon. Her mother, a devout Catholic, was of mixed Irish and Italian descent; although crippled at an early age by polio, she worked as a legal secretary, and was the financial mainstay of the Gordon house. David Gordon was born into a Jewish family in Lorain, Ohio, attended Harvard University, and participated in the American expatriate experience in Paris during the 1920s. He returned to America with a loathing of everything "modern," and became a convert to Catholicism. In interviews, Mary Gordon has recalled her father as a powerful influence on her life. "My father was a gentleman and a scholar," she has remarked, "and he bred me to be a lady and a scholar. He spoke seven languages, he read Greek with his meals, he was besotted with me, his only child." He died of a heart attack, while doing research for a biography of Paul Claudel, when Mary Gordon was eight years old.

Gordon attended the Holy Name of Mary grammar school in Valley Stream, Long Island, and the Mary Louis Academy, a girls' Catholic high school in Jamaica, Queens. At an early age, she aspired to be a nun who would "write poetry in my habit and lead a very disciplined life." By her teenage years, she rebelled against the restrictiveness of the church, and in 1967 won a scholarship to Barnard College, Columbia University. At Barnard, she wrote poetry, studied creative writing with Elizabeth Hardwick, and participated in the student revolt at Columbia in the late 1960s. She received her B.A. degree from Barnard in 1971, and an M.A. in the writing program at Syracuse University in 1973. She worked on a Ph.D. for several years (completing "five sevenths" of a dissertation on Virginia Woolf)—until her academic work conflicted with her desire to write fiction. Woolf indeed proved to be a link between scholarship and creative writing. Reading her as a graduate student, taking notes faithfully on index cards, Gordon says, made her aware of "the rhythms of those incredible sentences—the repetitions, the caesuras, the potent colons, semicolons. I knew it was what I wanted to do." Two other English women writers whom she cites as influences on her work are Elizabeth Bowen and Margaret Drabble.

In 1974, Gordon married James Brain, a professor of anthropology at the State University of New York at New Paltz. From 1974 to 1978 she taught in the English department at the Dutchess Community College, Poughkeepsie, while writing short stories that appeared in *Redbook, Mademoiselle, Ms.,* and other magazines. In 1975 she began writing her first novel, *Final Payments,* which was turned down by several publishers before being accepted, in revised form, by Random House. Elizabeth Hardwick was shown the manuscript and advised that it be changed from a third to a more dramatic first-person narration. In this form, it was published in 1978 to considerable critical acclaim. It was also a resounding popular success; the paperback edition alone had sold more than a million copies by the end of 1979.

Final Payments, which is grounded in the milieu of American Irish Catholicism and deals with feminist themes, tells the story of Isabel Moore, who is thirty when the novel opens. For the last eleven years, she has cared for her bedridden father, a stroke victim who had taught medieval theology at a small Catholic college in Queens. The professor had dominated his daughter's life, isolating her in an atmosphere in which everything secular was scorned, and sexuality was repressed. With his death, Isabel enters the world of New York City, where she has affairs with two men, a disturbing experience that sends her back to a penitential life of caring for her father's old housekeeper Margaret Casey. At the end, Isabel comes to recognize that her attempt to love the unlovable housekeeper is not "religious" but guilty self-punishment; and she prepares to reenter the world.

Many reviewers found *Final Payments* an exceptional first novel. David Lodge called it " a well-made realistic [work] of refined sensibility and moral scruple . . . a rich, thoughtful, stylishly written novel." Martha Duffy remarked that "from the opening rites of burial, laced with fine Irish malice, the reader relaxes, secure in the hands of a confident writer. That assurance lasts right through the book." Wilfred Sheed called *Final Payments* a "comic" novel with a rich gallery of minor characters that come to life quickly and exactly, and compared Gordon's wry depiction of these individuals to the method of Jane Austen, "the patron writer of the cloistered." He added that Gordon is much more than a Catholic novelist in the usual narrow sense, seeing the Roman Catholic church "not as a good or bad place, with batteries of lawyers to prove both at once, but as a multi-layered poem or vision which dominates your life equally whether you believe it or not; which doesn't even need your belief once it has made its point."

Other critics hedged their praise of *Final Payments* with reservations. William Pritchard remarked that Gordon is "fine when dealing with the old people on welfare whom Isabel goes around to interview; they can be presented as grotesquely or humorously or sadly affecting, can be characterized with the sharpness of one-dimensional life. . . . But with her two girlfriends [and the men she becomes involved with] she . . . seems to be flailing the novel along." Something of the same sort was expressed by Maureen Howard, who was impressed by Gordon's capturing of the churchiness of the Moore house in Queens, but found Isabel's "sojourn in the big world . . . less interesting than her bondage." Pearl Bell found a number of the turns of plot, especially Isabel's return to care for the spiteful Margaret Casey, unconvincing. But the objection most often raised was that Gordon was unable to create fully sexual male characters, to endow them with inner dimension or complexity.

With the publication of *Final Payments*, Gordon suddenly found herself a celebrity, constantly sought after for interviews. In the following year, she taught Catholic fiction and creative writing at Amherst College, where she wrote her second novel, *The Company of Women*, published in 1981. *The Company of Women* is similar in some essentials to *Final Payments*, since it describes a bright, sheltered Catholic girl who enters the world, is jolted by what she finds there, and withdraws again into a more sheltered Catholic environment. Its heroine is Felicitas Taylor who, as a fourteen-year-old, fatherless girl, seeks the paternal affection of a priest, Father Cyprian, who has rebelled against the liberalization of the church and devotes himself to the spiritual well-being of a small group of women. In the novel's second section, set in 1969, Felicitas has come of age, enrolls at Columbia and finds herself in the midst of the counterculture. She is seduced by a Maoist political science instructor, Robert Cavendish, is drawn into his free-love "commune," and becomes pregnant. She gives birth to a baby girl and goes back to live among the group of women whose counselor is Father Cyprian. In the final section, set in western New York state, Felicitas attempts to find "ordinary human happiness" by marrying a commonplace man, while her daughter shows promise of becoming the group's hope for the future.

Reviews of *The Company of Women* differed widely in their assessment of the novel. Peter Prescott found flaws in the work, but admired the risks Gordon had taken, and concluded that "on her second time out, [Gordon] looks more impressive than she did in *Final Payments*. G. B. Harrison also acknowledged that the novel could be faulted, but added: "given its scope, depth, and the perfection of its lyrical passages . . . it is fair to call this a brilliant novel." Sally Fitzgerald agreed, calling *The Company of Women* "an even more impressive work, larger in scope, more deeply perceptive, richer in mystery, than the first book." Yet other critics objected to the novel's plot contrivances and to its narrowly conceived characters. R. Z. Shepard noted that "though Cyprian's followers illustrate the spiritual dependency of women in a male-dominated church, they remain only illustration—sketches of romanticized stoicism." Robert Towers observed that "the whole Columbia section rings false—not because the events described could not have happened, but because Mary Gordon abandons the delicacy of perception and the psychological subtlety that deepens the other sections and indulges in . . . melodramatic excess." In a by now familiar criticism, James Walcott pointed out that Gordon fails to bring her male characters to life. "Men are still mysterious beings to her," he wrote, "figures hewn from trees."

In 1979, following her divorce from her first

husband, Gordon married Arthur Cash, a professor of English at the State University of New York at New Paltz. They have a daughter and a son. Gordon divides her time between caring for the children and writing. In interviews, she has said that Jane Austen, Charlotte Brontë, Virginia Woolf, and Ford Madox Ford are her favorite writers; and that Georges Bernanos' *Diary of a Country Priest* is a favorite book.

PRINCIPAL WORKS: Final Payments, 1978; The Company of Women, 1981; Men and Angels, 1985.

ABOUT: Contemporary Authors 102, 1981; Contemporary Literary Criticism 13, 1980; Current Biography, 1981; American Novelists Since World War II, 2nd series, 1980; Who's Who in America, 1982. *Periodicals:*—Commonweal May 9, 1980; Esquire March 1981; Newsweek February 16, 1981; New York Review of Books June 1, 1978; New York Times February 6, 1981; New York Times Book Review February 15, 1981; May 13, 1984; March 31, 1985; Spectator January 13, 1979; Time February 16, 1981.

BARON JAN-ALBERT GORIS

GORIS, BARON JAN-ALBERT (pseudonym **Marnix Gijsen**) (October 20, 1899–), Belgian essayist, novelist, and poet, writes: "My civil name is as above stated; my pen-name is Marnix Gijsen. I was born in Antwerp, alas, in a bourgeois family. At school I revolted against the Jesuits who conducted all their classes in French while the pupils were Flemish and spoke Netherlandish (Dutch). I therefore was expelled from school. Later on, when boys of my age were menaced by being called up for work in Germany, they reaccepted me. My first publications had political connotations, being attacks against my masters. I was active as a literary critic for ten years on *De Standaard.* I was reputed to be the terror of the young poets, but I replied that I defended poetry against their clumsiness. In 1967 I wrote my first novel, *The Book of Joachim of Babylon* (a semiautobiographical story of my first and lamented marriage). From then on I published every year either a novel or a bundle of short stories. *Lament for Agnes* was made into a successful film. *De Nachttrein naar Savannah, Georgia* (The Night Train for Savannah, Georgia) was less well conceived . *De Kroeg van Groot verdriet* (The Café of Great Sorrow) was made into a good film.

"I became a doctor of historic sciences in Louvain in 1925 by presenting a thesis on the development of modern capitalism in Antwerp in the sixteenth century. I came for the first time to the USA as a student in Seattle. I came back in 1939 in an official capacity and remained in the States until 1964 when I left for Canada where I was

president of the sixty-three participating nations [in Expo 67 in Montreal]. I retired from civil service on April 1, 1968.

"As far as my literary career is concerned, I received every prize available including the Great Literary prize [the Priis de Nederlandse Letteren, 1974] for the two Dutch-speaking nations—Holland and Belgium. Books of mine have been translated into fifty languages (many of which I do not understand). Ten years ago I was made a baron by the king. A couple of times I was involved in local politics without the slightest success. I have lived a double life: as a writer and as a civil servant. In both fields I have been very successful. I am a lapsed Catholic and a fervent agnostic. As far as I am concerned, you may apply to me the Jewish story of the two Jews at the wailing wall. Said the one to the other, 'How are things with you?' The other replied: 'I have nothing to wail about.'"

———

Jan-Albert Goris has assumed many identities in his long career, and it is difficult to recognize the same man in the iconoclastic Belgian poet and critic of the 1920s and thirties, the journalist and publicist reporting to American readers on Belgian history and culture and life in occupied Belgium during World War II, the international diplomat, the romantic novelist grieving over a lost youthful love, the cynic challenging traditional beliefs, the moralist deploring the materialism of modern times. Equally articulate in Dutch, English, and French, he is essentially European and cosmopolitan, urban and urbane.

Goris has used the pen-name of Marnix Gijsen, his maternal family name, for his fiction. His childhood was unhappy. Shy and self-conscious, he grew up during the German occupation of his country in World War I, had an unhappy romance (the inspiration for his later novel *Lament for Agnes*), did his military service from 1921 to 1922, and launched a career as a journalist. He began his literary career as a poet with *Het huis* (This House) in 1925, a volume of expressionistic verse that immediately marked him as a controversial and important literary figure. (A much later collection of poems in Dutch, though with the English title *The House by the Leaning Tree,* 1967, is a more traditional series of his reflections during the summer of 1962, when he lived in a country house in West Redding, Conn.)

In the course of post-doctoral research, Goris traveled to France, Switzerland, England, and finally the United States. He returned to Belgium in 1927 and served in various government posts until he came back to the United States in charge of the Belgian exhibits at the 1939 New York World's Fair. With the outbreak of World War II and the second German occupation of his country, he was unable to return home. A stateless emigré, in 1941 he became a journalist and spokesman for his country by assuming the editorship of *News from Belgium,* a small English-language weekly publication of the Belgian Government Information Center. His editorials, written in English, were collected in two volumes—*Belgium in Bondage* and *Strangers Should Not Whisper.* A later series of his editorials in the *Belgian Trade Review,* 1954–64, was collected as *Candid Opinions on Sundry Subjects.* James Hilton, in a preface to the first volume, called his journalism "among the best current writing." In response to this praise, Goris wrote: "I think that the qualities you are kind enough to discover in my writing are mainly due to the fact that my vocabulary is limited and that, therefore, I am forced to express myself as clearly as possible, as I have no way of camouflaging by an abundant use of words." The articles and editorials he published in these journals are a personal voice—the voice of what he called "the new man, the Euro-American homunculus." This creature embodies both cultures; "the blue blood of an old aristocratic culture mixing with the carmine red of a young, vigorous race. He is not lost to Europe; he is not won to America."

This ambivalence is reflected both in his sympathetic reports on numerous aspects of American life ("Columbus Is My Middle Name" is the title of one chapter in *Belgium in Bondage*), and in some of his later novels like *Goed en kwaad*

(Good and Evil, 1950) and *De Vleespotten van Egypte* (The Fleshpots of Egypt, 1952) in which American materialism is treated with considerable cynicism.

As a novelist, Goris/Gijsen assumes a different personality—more personal to the extent that most of his novels have autobiographical elements. His plots are simple, his heroes sensitive, intellectual, reflective. All his novels, R. P. Meijer writes, "are concerned with the search for eternal moral values and at the same time show the hand of a master narrator." The best known of them is a short and witty retelling of the biblical story of Susannah and the Elders, *Het boek van Joachim van Babylon* (*The Book of Joachim of Babylon*).The narrator is Susannah's sorely tried husband Joachim—"who found life as the husband of a paragon of chastity something of a trial." Indeed, Joachim's marriage to a woman who embodies all the beauty and virtue of the ideal wife but who is totally incapable of real womanly love becomes a hell on earth: "Beauty stared me in the face every day in Susannah, and now it looked to me as cold and sterile as she was." The tone of the novel is urbane but not profane, funny but also provocative and serious. Richard Plant wrote of it in the *New York Times:* "Mr. Gijsen succeeded where most historical writers would have failed. He also succeeded in avoiding the pitfalls of rewriters of biblical episodes: he doesn't dress his narrative in pseudoarchaic language, he doesn't sentimentalize, and he is not flippantly psychological."

The only other novel by Goris/Gijsen in English translation is *Klaaglied om Agnes* (*Lament for Agnes*), a book in which he dropped his mask of cynicism to reveal a far more personal self. Set in Antwerp and the Flemish countryside of his boyhood, this short novel is again narrated in the first person by a voice that is far more recognizably that of its creator than is the narrator of *The Book of Joachim.* "Sensitive people are vulnerable all their lives and always in new ways," he writes. Agnes is the fictionalized portrait of the young woman he had been engaged to, who had died of tuberculosis in 1928. The narrator—whose childhood and early career in journalism parallel Goris' own life—falls in love with a young girl. Their relationship is close but never physically intimate, and Agnes remains a shadowy figure, a Eurydice to the narrator's Orpheus—whose death leaves him emotionally barren. The book is "homage to her sweet memory . . . Agnes, my chaste bride, my dead sister, like Eurydice twice lost."

Goris has written some ten other novels and two plays. Though little read today in England and America, his reputation as a major writer in

Netherlandic literature remains solid. "Gijsen's greatest merit," Judica Mendels writes, "besides his mastery of the language, is the warmth and tenderness that lie behind so much irony and bitterness."

WORKS IN ENGLISH TRANSLATION: *The Book of Joachim of Babylon* was translated into English in 1952 by F.G. Renier and A. Cliff. Mrs. W. James-Gerth's translation of *Lament for Agnes* was published in 1975 as volume 6 of the Library of Netherlandic Literature. His principal writings in English are *Belgium in Bondage,* 1943; *Strangers Should Not Whisper,* 1945; and *Candid Opinions on Sundry Subjects,* 1964. In addition, Goris has written a number of pamphlets on Belgian art and literature that were published by the Belgian Government Information Center.

ABOUT: Cassell's Encyclopedia of World Literature 2, 1973; Columbia Dictionary of Modern European Literature, 1980; Encyclopedia of World Literature in the 20th Century (rev. ed.) II, 1982; Krispyn, E. Foreword to Lament for Agnes, 1975; Meijer, R.P. Literature of the Low Countries, 1978.

GOULD, LOIS (1938?–),

GOULD, LOIS (1938?–), American novelist, was born Lois Regensburg in New York City; her father was a cigar manufacturer, her mother the fashion designer Jo Copeland. She began writing in childhood, intending to become a poet or playwright. Educated at Wellesley College, from which she graduated in 1957, she went to work as a police reporter for the *Long Island Star-Journal,* of which she became an editor. In 1959 she married Philip Benjamin, a reporter for the *New York Times,* by whom she had two sons, Tony and Roger. She wrote two non-fiction books—*The Childbirth Challenge* (with W. L. Fielding) and *So You Want to Be a Working Mother!*—and by the mid-1960s was the executive editor of *Ladies Home Journal.*

Gould's career as a novelist began after the death of her first husband and her remarriage in 1967 to Robert E. Gould, a psychiatrist. Her protagonist in *Such Good Friends* was Julie Messinger, the wife of a magazine director. While her husband lies in a coma brought on by an anesthesiologist's error during minor surgery, Julie discovers a diary in which he has recorded, in code, his affairs with her women friends. Attempting to come to terms with her marriage, she takes revenge by systematically seducing her friends' husbands. Gould has said that the novel is concerned "with what people do to each other in the name of friendship, at a time of overwhelming crisis. Love and death occur in the book, but what matters is how those to whom they happen learn to use both of these terrifying forces as masks, to wield them as weapons, and to survive them without the scars of understanding."

The book was a best-seller, in part because of its graphic sex scenes; this kind of candor was still unusual in 1970. Paul D. Zimmerman ascribed Gould's treatment of these scenes to "either innate vulgarity or a cynical bid for sales," and W. G. Rogers suggested that the book was pornography. Several reviewers made comparisons with Philip Roth's *Portnoy's Complaint,* then the standard for boldness of sexual description in literature. Richard Freedman noted that Gould's "extraordinarily sensitive eye for the telling detail . . . goes far to compensate for makeshift plotting and relatively shallow characterization." Joel Lieber, who thought that Gould "writes as idiomatically and naturally and truthfully as an old pro," called *Such Good Friends* a "frantic, cruel recital of modern middle-class woman's lot" and "an imaginative chapter in the feminist struggle. It is also another of the many recent signposts of social and psychological and political change going on." A film version of the novel, directed by Otto Preminger, was released in 1971.

Gould's next two novels were in the same vein of personal crisis, but they were generally considered to be at the level of soap opera. *Necessary Objects* was about four affluent sisters who spend their time destroying one another's marriages. "Gould's prose is several cuts above Jacqueline Susann's," wrote Dorothy Nyren, " . . . but the general mood and content aren't much superior to *Valley of the Dolls.*" Sara Blackburn, describing the characters as "horrible people" whom the author depicts "pitilessly and with an almost ferocious relish," wondered why Gould had "thought their lives worth a novel." Gould has indicated that for her the book was something of an exercise in structure: "I knew the people . . . and in fact it wasn't very important what I did with them. I just wanted to group them and take them apart and put them together again."

Final Analysis, according to the *New Yorker,* is "a slick romance about a lonely, disaffected psychiatrist and his guilt-ridden, weepy ex-patient which is occasionally quite funny but pushes feminism and enlightenment-through-psychiatry in the same way that old-fashioned romances used to push love and moral rectitude." Iris Owens called it "an infatuated account of an obsessed woman's unrelieved self-loathing, an explicit study of masochism, with a rare candor that both excites and repels." L. J. Davis felt that Gould's journalistic talents worked against her in this novel—that her depictions of famous novelists and publishing celebrities (the heroine is a freelance writer) turned the book into "some hideous bout of charades" that detracts from the "far more important book that simply is not getting written."

Final Analysis was the last of what *Publishers Weekly* called Gould's "wry, sardonic, New York-style comedies with a wittily feminist viewpoint." *A Sea-Change* was an elaborately symbolic fable about a submissive wife and mother who is transformed, through the magical intervention of Hurricane Minerva, into the black gunman who raped her (or, as other critics have interpreted it, into an androgynous goddess figure who commands authority over her female lover and her two daughters). This experiment in myth-making was disliked even by those critics who had been sympathetic to Gould's work in the past. "A book which could have been about the dawning of female power, *whatever that is,* is instead about the capture and magical appropriation of male power, which is defined as the only kind of power there is," wrote Annie Gottlieb. "It's a frightening, yet oddly cozy, crawl back and deeper into the sadist/masochist trap Gould delineated so well in *Such Good Friends* . . . And yet, far from being a questioning, an exploration of that trap, it winds up feeling like a strange embrace and acceptance of it." Ella Leffland wrote, "We have no sense of a writer seized by an idea and wrestling with it to the best of her ability; rather, the writer seems to have looked for a surefire project and pulled out occult feminism."

Still more ambitious was *La Presidenta,* a historical novel about Eva Peron, the peasant and prostitute who came to power in Argentina through her alliance with its military leader, and about her successor, Isabel Peron. "This is not simply a fictional rehashing of Argentine history," wrote Charles Michaud; "it is a sustained and often fascinating portrait of a particular woman, her world and place in it, and how she changes both that place and that world." According to Gloria Steinem, "Gould has threaded into her story the themes of power and sexuality, the influence of the church and the mass media, the 'show business' politics, and the interplay between myth and reality in the icon's perception of herself." Gould said of the book, "I've abandoned the things that came easiest to me—humor, playfulness. People tell me they miss those qualities. They're very comforting, but you try not to do comforting things."

After the publication of *A Sea-Change,* Gould wrote a series of essays for the newly inaugurated "Hers" column in the *New York Times.* These formed part of *Not Responsible for Personal Articles,* a collection of Gould's newspaper and magazine pieces on a range of subjects from the electoral defeat of Indira Gandhi to her family's ordeal during an armed robbery; they were written, according to Jane S. Bakerman, with "penetrating insight, thoughtfulness, and wit."

In the same year she published *X: A Fabulous Child's Story,* which originally appeared in *Ms.*

Gould and her husband live on the East Side of Manhattan and on Long Island. In an interview for *Writer's Digest,* she said: "I wrote my earliest books surrounded by people, children, the tritest household work—and I don't know that I could have marshaled that kind of concentration had I not learned in a newspaper office to work with teletype machines going and everyone else talking and telephones ringing." She has contemplated switching from novels to plays, in part because the gestation period of a novel is so long. "The small satisfactions have to mean a great deal to make one survive the other stuff," she told *Writer's Digest.* "If you tried to prorate it, it would come out to about 15 minutes of ecstasy every three years, and I don't know that that's enough to sustain most of us."

PRINCIPAL WORKS: *Fiction*—Such Good Friends, 1970; Necessary Objects, 1972; Final Analysis, 1974; A Sea-Change, 1976; X: A Fabulous Child's Story, 1978; La Presidenta, 1981. *Non-fiction*—(with W. L. Fielding) The Childbirth Challenge, 1962; So You Want to Be a Working Mother!, 1966; Not Responsible for Personal Articles, 1978.

ABOUT: American Women Writers, 1980; Contemporary Authors 77-80, 1978. *Periodicals*—Book World, June 21, 1970; April 14, 1974; Christian Science Monitor September 24, 1970; Harper's October 1976; Library Journal February 1, 1970; August 1972; March 1, 1978; May 15, 1981; Ms. February 1978; July 1981; New York Times Book Review June 2, 1970; October 15, 1972; April 14, 1974; September 19, 1976; February 26, 1978; May 31, 1981; New Yorker April 22, 1974; People April 10, 1978; Publishers Weekly April 17, 1981; Saturday Review June 13, 1970; May 18, 1974; Time June 1, 1970; Village Voice May 18, 1974; August 30, 1976; Writer's Digest September 1980.

GOULD, STEPHEN JAY (September 10, 1941–), American paleontologist, was born in New York City, the son of Leonard and Eleanor (Rosenberg) Gould. He grew up in a lower-middle-class neighborhood of the city where no one in his family or among his acquaintances, he said, ever "knew a college professor." Even at a very early age, however, he was entranced by science. When he was five his father, a court stenographer, took him to the American Museum of Natural History to see a dinosaur exhibition—an experience that left him "awestruck" and inspired his interest in paleontology. His scientific interests were encouraged by his parents and public school teachers before he entered Antioch College, where he graduated with a B.A. in 1963. He pursued graduate studies in the depart-

STEPHEN JAY GOULD

ment of paleontology at Columbia University with a National Science Foundation fellowship, and received his Ph.D. in 1967.

Gould was appointed assistant professor of Geology at Harvard University in 1967 and became a full professor in 1973, at the age of thirty-two. Concurrently he also held the post of Curator of Invertebrate Paleontology at Harvard's Museum of Comparative Zoology. Gould received national attention when, in 1972, with Niles Eldredge of the American Museum of Natural History, he published a paper offering a new explanation for the "missing links" between species. Eldredge and Gould argued that absence of fossil evidence for transitional forms between species suggested that most species had developed relatively quickly (on the scale of geologic time) and have persisted virtually unchanged for millions of years. Their theory of "punctuated equilibrium"—an early, random splitting off of new species from existing ones—challenged traditional views of natural selection.

From the early 1970s, Stephen Jay Gould has been a prolific contributor to scientific journals; and since 1974 has written a column, "This View of Life," for *Natural History* magazine. It was from these columns that he prepared his first book, *Ever Since Darwin,* published in 1977. His principal concern in the book is that Darwin has been "misunderstood, misquoted, and misapplied," because his conception of evolution did not envision a "preordained process" leading to man's dominion and control over other creatures and the earth. The Darwinian spirit, according to Gould, insists that evolution has no moral purpose, "that individuals struggle to in-

crease the representation of their genes in future generations, and that is all." Subjects Gould discusses in separate chapters are extraordinarily wide-ranging—patterns of continental drift, Velikovsky's cosmic theories, man's relationship to African hominids, and the biological concepts of r- and k- selection.

Ontogeny and Phylogeny, published the same year, was written primarily for biologists. In the main section, Gould puts into historical perspective the now discredited theory advanced by Ernst Haeckel in 1920 that "ontogeny recapitulates phylogeny," or, to put it in layman's language, that the various stages of fetal growth repeat the evolutionary development of the species. To the general reader, the most revealing part of the book is Gould's illumination of how Haeckel's recapitulation theory, promulgated in *The Riddle of the Universe,* influenced a great number of thinkers. With its insistence on unity and progressive development in nature, it lent itself to imperialist doctrines and was used by the Nazis to advance their claim to racial supremacy. It also affected Jung's archetypal theory of childhood as "a state of the past"; Freud's conviction that "each individual somehow recapitulates in an abbreviated form the entire development in the human race"; and the educational theory of Piaget. Gould was praised by reviewers for his ability to take a technical issue seemingly of concern to only a limited number of scientists, and demonstrate its relevance to broader cultural topics.

The Panda's Thumb is a second collection of essays taken from Gould's columns in *Natural History.* Like *Ever Since Darwin,* the topics it takes up are of the most varied nature—from the "thumb" (actually an enlarged wristbone) of the panda, to the processes of sexual selection among mites and the anatomical devices with which the Philippine angelfish lured its prey. Typically, Gould begins with a particular natural phenomenon and proceeds to make observations on more general matters. In doing so, he frequently introduces "literary" figures into his discussion (George Eliot, Kant, Lytton Strachey among others), revealing a broader humanistic perspective than is usually found in scientific writing. In 1981 *The Panda's Thumb* received the American Book Award for writing in science.

In the following year Gould published *The Mismeasure of Man,* which received the National Book Critics Award for general non-fiction, and has had the largest impact of any of Gould's books. "The book," James Miller wrote, "is about the abstraction of intelligence as a single entity, its location within the brain, its quantification as one number for each individual, and the use of these numbers to rank people in a single series of worthiness, invariably to find that oppressed or disadvantaged groups—race, classes, or sexes—are innately inferior and deserve their status." In the articulate and often pungently witty early part of *The Mismeasure of Man,* Gould describes the misguided attempts of nineteenth-century scientists to determine intelligence by measuring craniums. The racial bias of the great American naturalist Louis Agassiz is also revealed, and in later sections Gould's history of IQ testing shows that the inherent bias of the tests affected laws restricting immigration of eastern Europeans to the United States. *The Mismeasure of Man* received enthusiastic reviews, but a number of scientists criticized Gould's failure to indicate what he thinks intelligence actually is, and also contended that his allegedly left-wing egalitarianism had predisposed him to misjudge the accuracy and usefulness of aptitude testing.

Gould is a politically committed liberal who writes for *Science for the People* as "Steve Gould," and has more than once been at the center of controversy. During the 1970s he was a leading critic of sociobiology, a discipline founded by his Harvard University colleague Edward O. Wilson. Gould considers the premise of sociobiology, that human behavior can be analyzed as separate traits, each with its own genetic basis and evolutionary justification, as at once too deterministic and too speculative—an invitation to intellectual woolgathering. Gould's own position has been that human potential is limited less by genetic inheritance than by environment. During the early 1980s,Gould found himself involved in an even more vocal controversy concerning the efforts of many church-affiliated groups to augment the teaching of evolution in schools with the teaching of "creationism." He has argued that the so-called "creationism," though it uses a scientific vocabulary, is merely another version of the story of divine creation told in Genesis. It is, Gould insists, not science, but pseudo-science, and he regards it as an attempt to distort intellectual inquiry in education. He has been a leading figure in many scientific committees opposing legislation that would make the teaching of "creationism" mandatory in public schools. In 1982, in recognition of this work, *Discoverer* magazine named Gould "Scientist of the Year."

Gould has received numerous honors and awards, including the Schuchert Award in 1975, for excellence in paleontology. He was one of the first twenty-one "exceptionally talented" people from a variety of fields to receive a MacArthur Foundation Prize fellowship (providing him

with a grant of $38,400 a year for five years, from 1981 to 1986, to use as he wishes). Although Gould is a prolific author he is also a conscientious teacher whose lectures on geology at Harvard receive ovations from his students. He also conducts research in land snails in the Bahamas, where he has reclassified the species Cerion.

Gould married Deborah Ann Lee (an artist) in 1965, and they have two sons, Jesse and Ethan. Gould's commitment to his family is as intense as his many-sided intellectual curiosity. A profile in *Newsweek* refers to his older son's learning disability, and to Gould's nightly efforts to overcome the problem through "sheer will and effort."

PRINCIPAL WORKS: Ever Since Darwin, 1977; Ontogeny and Phylogeny, 1977; The Panda's Thumb, 1980; The Mismeasure of Man, 1981; Hen's Teeth and Horse's Toes, 1983.

ABOUT: American Men and Women of Science 15th ed., 1982; Contemporary Authors 77–80, 1979; Who's Who in America, 1983–84. *Periodicals*—Book World October 12, 1980; Contemporary Psychology July 1978; Discoverer January 1982; New Republic November 11, 1981; Newsweek November 14, 1977; October 13, 1980; November 9, 1981; March 29, 1982; The New Yorker April 12, 1982; New York Review of Books February 19, 1981; October 22, 1981; New York Times Book Review November 20, 1977; September 14, 1980; November 1, 1981; Saturday Review October, 1981; Science March 17, 1978; February 5, 1982; Smithsonian January 1981; Wall Street Journal December 9, 1981.

*GRADE, CHAIM (April 5, 1910–June 26, 1982), Yiddish poet and novelist, was born in Vilna, Lithuania, the son of Schlomo-Motte Grade, a Hebrew teacher of progressive bent, and his second wife, the former Vella Blumenthal. Both parents figure prominently in their son's work, especially Vella, who became a fruit peddler in the Vilna marketplace so that seventeen-year old Chaim could continue his Talmudic studies. Indeed, the importance of Grade's youth in "the Jerusalem of Lithuania" can hardly be overestimated, for almost all of his fiction is set there, and the vanished culture of Eastern European Jewry became his great theme.

Grade's upbringing was orthodox, and he studied at various yeshivas until he was twenty-two. Nevertheless, as his fictional alter-ego Chaim, or Chaikl, Vilner makes clear, he was torn by inner doubts, and his early inclination for aesthetics finally prevailed over his training in religious ethics. In the early 1930s he became involved with a group of writers known as "Young Vilna," who sought to infuse Yiddish lit-

°grä´ də, kĭm

CHAIM GRADE

erature with new currents from European modernism. His poems began appearing in Yiddish magazines in 1932, and in 1936 his first book, *Yo* (Yes), was published. This book was praised for its lyric elegance, but Grade's next work, *Musernikes* (1939), abandoned the lyric mode for the narrative. The central character in this epic poem is the author's younger self, Chaim Vilner, a yeshiva student and follower of Musar, an ascetic and rigorously self-critical movement of Judaism that began in nineteenth century Lithuania. This is a work, writes Israel Ch. Biletzky, "in which prayerful atmospheres and terror, clamorous silence and spiritual wrestling are interwoven." After much turmoil, Chaim Vilner breaks from the Musar fold, as did Chaim Grade, yet Vilner does not lose his faith:

I know the stars are distant, everlasting,
But I who ail and to my blue pane cleave,
Shall my heart, which neither brave is nor believing,
If need be forcibly command: believe!
                                    —trans. I.C. Biletzky

Grade's literary career was abruptly interrupted by the Nazi invasion of 1941, when he fled Vilna for Russia. He returned at the war's end to find that his wife and mother and indeed his whole civilization had perished at the hands of the Nazis. Unable to bear the painful memories there, he moved on to Paris, where he became active in the Yiddish literary community and wrote lacerating poems on the Holocaust. In a perceptive essay in *Commentary*, Ruth R. Wisse speculated that the despair Grade was pouring into these poems, and especially into the book he dedicated to his dead wife, *Mit Dayn Guf oyn Mayn Hent* (With Your Body in My Hands), caused him to turn to prose fiction as a means of gaining greater artistic control over his raw emotions.

Grade's first effort in prose was the short story "My Quarrel with Hersh Rasseyner," which established his reputation in America when it was published in *Commentary* in the early fifties. Again Chaim Vilner is the protagonist. He appears as a secular Jew shaken by the Holocaust who has a chance encounter in the Paris Metro with an old friend from his Musar days, the Orthodox Hersh Rasseyner. The two tear into each other almost immediately over their conflicting ethical and theological beliefs. No resolution is reached; "My Quarrel with Hersh Rasseyner" simply balances one argument against another. Yet, as Irving Howe wrote in the *New Republic,* the story "shows Grade at his best: the dramatic rendering of intellectual struggle, the clash between two modes of thought which brought eastern European Jewry to a high pitch of excitement even when threatening to tear it apart."

After resettling in New York City in 1948, Grade, though not neglecting poetry, turned more and more to fiction. Still, he was reluctant to have his work translated from the Yiddish ("I dwell among my people," he explained in 1979 in *Judaica Book News*) and it was not until 1974 that his first full-length novel, *The Agunah* appeared in English. (It was originally published in 1961 as *Die Agune.*) In the meantime, he settled into his booklined apartment in the West Bronx with his second wife, Inna Hecker Grade, and supplemented his income from writing with lecture tours on literature throughout North and South America, Israel, Europe, and South Africa.

When the English translation of *The Agunah* was published, Elie Wiesel took the occasion in the *New York Times Book Review* to call Grade "one of the great—if not the greatest—of living Yiddish novelists." Wiesel's tacit comparison with Isaac Bashevis Singer may have seemed excessive to some, but almost all of the book's reviewers recognized a major talent in Yiddish literature. *The Agunah* tells the story of a young Vilna woman whose husband is reported missing in action in World War I. Wishing to remarry, she is blocked by a rabbinical law that forbids a woman's remarriage unless an eyewitness can testify to her first husband's death. Drawn to her case are two rabbis, one who interprets the law strictly, the other leniently. As in "My Quarrel with Hersh Rasseyner," ethical viewpoints are embodied in obsessed, passionately committed characters, and the rabbis' inability to compromise brings misfortune on them and tragedy on the woman caught in the middle.

Grade's most ambitious work of fiction is the two-volume *Tsemakh Atlas* (1967–68), translated as *The Yeshiva* (1976–77). The inspiration for the novel, curiously enough, was Melville's *Moby Dick,* for in Captain Ahab Grade saw a character whose fierce, God-obsessed struggles could be transposed to his own protagonist, Tsemakh Atlas. Atlas is an iron-willed Musarnik and Yeshiva principal wrestling with secret doubts, lust, and pride. Opposed to him is his worldly-leaning but equally stubborn pupil, Chaikl Vilner. But in *The Yeshiva,* the two antagonists are reconciled by a third person: the revered Talmudic scholar Reb Avraham-Shaye. In the end, after countless subplots and a Balzacian view of the Polish and Lithuanian ghettos in the 1920s, Atlas and Vilner forsake the punishing Musar creed and return to secular life with a faith strengthened by their contact with the Jewish sage.

Irving Howe and Ruth R. Wisse, Grade's most thoughtful critics, praised *The Yeshiva* for its high moral seriousness and its complex psychological portraits of Atlas and Vilner. Yet Howe objected that the "genre pictures of East European Jewish life seem a little heavy and slap-dash, as if Grade were counting too much on the keyed-in responses of his Yiddish audience." Along these lines, Wisse noted that Grade had become more protective of his past and that the elegiac tone he adopted in parts of the novel helped lay that past to rest instead of keeping it vividly and contentiously alive.

Less panoramic in scale than *The Yeshiva,* more compressed but still intense, are the three novels that comprise the posthumously published *Rabbis and Wives.* Here the stern precepts of the Lithuanian scholars and rabbis come into conflict with the human needs and desires of the congregation. In this last work Walter Goodman (in the *New York Times*) noted "a saving strain of down-to-earth humor," reminiscent but in no way imitative of the style of Isaac Bashevis Singer. Ruth Wisse suggests a more remote but not unlikely comparison with Anthony Trollope's novels of nineteenth-century English church— where individual consciences and church politics often come into conflict—with results that are more wryly humorous than tragic.

The poems that Grade continued to write in the United States still revolved around the tragedy of his people, but he was also moved to write odes on the beauty of the American landscape. Nevertheless, his most famous poem of this period is his most mournful. "Poem about the Soviet Yiddish Writers" was composed in 1962, when Grade learned that five of his literary friends from Moscow had been murdered by the Stalin

regime. The last lines of this long elegy bespeak the special poignance of a poet writing in a doomed language about doomed people:

But your language, that the hangman throttled, silenced,
Stays dumb in the land where poets still sing forever.
So I am left with your language; like the dress of one
that is drowned in the river
— trans. J. Leftwich

Chaim Grade died of a heart attack in New York at the age of seventy-two. Over the years he accumulated many literary prizes, including the William and Janice Epstein Fiction Award from the Jewish Book Council of the National Jewish Welfare Board in 1968 and the Remembrance Award from World Federation of Bergen-Belsen Association in 1969. In addition to his many volumes of poetry and fiction, Grade wrote a highly regarded memoir of his childhood and his experience of the Holocaust, *Der Mames Shabosim* (My Mother's Sabbaths, 1955).

PRINCIPAL WORKS IN ENGLISH TRANSLATION: English translations of Grade's poems are available in R. Whitman's Anthology of *Modern Yiddish Poetry,* 1966, and J. Leftwich's *Anthology of Modern Yiddish Literature,* 1977. His short fiction is represented in *A Treasury of Yiddish Stories,* edited by I. Howe and E. Greenberg, 1954. Curt Leviant translated *The Agunah* in 1974, and *The Yeshiva,* in two volumes, in 1976 and 1977. The English translation of the posthumously published *Rabbis and Wives* was done by Harold Rabinowitz and Grade's wife, Inna Hecker Grade.

ABOUT: Biletzky, I. C. Essays on Yiddish Poetry and Prose Writers of the Twentieth Century, 1969; Contemporary Authors 93–96, 1980; Encyclopaedia Judaica 7, 1972; Encyclopedia of World Literature in the 20th Century (rev. ed.) II, 1982; Liptzin, S. A History of Yiddish Literature, 1972. *Periodicals*—Commentary April 1977; Judaica Book News Spring/Summer 1979; New Republic February 26, 1977; New York Times October 28, 1974; July 1, 1982; New York Times Book Review September 1, 1974; January 8, 1978; November 14, 1982.

*GRAMSCI, ANTONIO (January 23, 1891– April 27, 1937), Italian political theorist, essayist, and journalist, was all but unknown even in Italy until a decade after his death, when his collected writings were published and hailed as a revelation and inspiration to Italian Marxists, themselves re-emerging from the repression of Fascism and the devastation of World War II. It was another thirty years before his work became available in English translation and he received international recognition as "the greatest Western Marxist theorist of our century" (Eugene D. Genovese) and "an extraordinary philosopher, perhaps a genius, probably the most original

°gram′ shē

ANTONIO GRAMSCI

communist thinker of the twentieth century in western Europe" (E. J. Hobsbawm).

Antonio Gramsci was born in the village of Ales, in Sardinia, into a family of the petty bourgeois Italians of Greek-Albanian and Spanish ancestry. His father, Francesco Gramsci, had been a law student who gave up his studies to take a job in the state bureaucracy. When Antonio was only seven, Francesco Gramsci was arrested, probably for political reasons, and sentenced to five years' imprisonment, leaving his wife and seven children in desperate poverty. For a while young Gramsci's mother, working as a seamstress, managed to send the boy to a local school and encourage his love for reading, but when he was eleven he went to work at heavy labor, hauling books in the local law registry. Already suffering from a spinal ailment that left him a hunchback never to grow over five feet tall, he early developed an awareness of social injustice: "From my youth on," he wrote in 1924, "I had an instinct for rebellion against the rich because I, who had made 10s in every subject in elementary school, had been unable to continue studying, while the sons of the butcher, the pharmacist and tailor had gone on." After his father's release from prison, the boy was able to return to a secondary school, and in 1910 he won a scholarship to the University of Turin where he enrolled in the faculty of letters, studying linguistics and philology.

Plagued by ill health and poverty, spending what little money he had only for books and cigarettes, he was a brilliant but irregular scholar. A witness to the struggles of the factory workers of Turin to organize into a labor movement, and

by now a student of Hegel, Marx, Engels, and Lenin, Gramsci became active in the socialist movement. By early 1916, his biographer Giuseppi Fiori writes, "Gramsci the 'professional revolutionary' was born." He abandoned the university for journalism and began writing anonymously or simply under his initials for *Avanti!*, the socialist paper to which young Benito Mussolini, then an ardent socialist, was also a contributor. But Gramsci's humanistic background, his love for languages and literature, and the influence of the Italian critic and scholar Benedetto Croce, prevented him from adhering to rigid political dogma. His contributions to *Avanti!*, especially his brilliant theater criticism (he prided himself on his discovery of Ibsen and Pirandello), distinctly raised the literary tone of that journal. Believing that his working class readers must know their history and their culture before they could effectively organize for political action, Gramsci wrote in "La Città futura" (The City of the Future, 1917) that the aim of socialists must be "the possibility of the integral fulfillment of the whole human personality, as a right of all citizens . . . [to] bring the maximum of liberty with the minimum of constraint."

In 1919, by now a leader of the Turin socialist movement, he became editor of a new journal, *L'Ordine nuovo* (The New Order) and promoter of a factory council movement in which elected workers could organize for revolutionary change. The collapse of the Italian government after World War I and the emergence of the political force of Fascism convinced Gramsci of the need for more effective political action, and he joined the newly formed Italian Communist Party in 1921. In 1922 he was invited to Moscow where he was welcomed as a leader of Italian communism and, because his always frail health had completely broken down, he received desperately needed medical attention. Two years later he returned to Italy to reorganize his divided party in the struggle against the now dominant Fascist Party.

Gramsci settled in Rome editing a new paper, *Unità*, and was elected to Parliament as a Communist in 1924. He was joined in Rome a year later by his wife Giulia Schucht whom he had met while convalescing in a sanatorium in the Soviet Union, and their young son Delio. By 1926, with Mussolini's Fascists in control of the government, it was obvious that his political activities would no longer be tolerated. His wife, now pregnant with a second son, returned to the Soviet Union for safety, but Gramsci remained behind to face inevitable arrest. He lingered in prison for two years before his trial in 1928 when he was condemned to twenty years imprisonment. "For twenty years we must stop that brain from working," the public prosecutor announced before sentence was passed.

Rarely has prophecy proved so wrong. Gramsci spent the remaining years of his life in prison suffering terrible hardship that finally destroyed his already delicate health. He never saw his wife and family again, but thanks to the devotion of his sister-in-law Tatiana Schucht, who lived in Rome, and his loyal friends who kept him supplied with books, he maintained a lively correspondence and managed, under formidable obstacles, to write the letters and notebooks that became his legacy to the world. He wrote hastily with no opportunity for revision and no hope of publication; to outwit the prison censorship he invented circumlocutions—referring to Marx as the "founder of the philosophy of praxis," Lenin as "Ilich" and Trotsky as "Leon Davidovitch" or "Bronstein." He suffered long periods of disabling illness—so severe that in 1936, owing largely to pressure from a few foreigners like the French writer Romain Rolland, he was transferred to a hospital and his sentence reduced by ten years. But he died a week before he was to be freed and was buried in the English Protestant Cemetery in Rome. "Italian Communism will have its great martyr," Rolland had written in "For Those Dying in Mussolini's Jails" in 1934—a prophecy more accurate than the public prosecutor's.

Gramsci left behind him thirty-two notebooks of over 2,800 pages, smuggled out to the Soviet Union after his death by his sister-in-law. They were not published in Italy until 1948, but between then and 1950 six volumes appeared. These included a study of Croce's philosophy, a book on the intellectual and culture, notes on Macchiavelli's politics in the modern state, a history of Italy, another on the Risorgimento, and a collection of essays on literature and national life. Though fragmentary, his writings constitute a single *oeuvre*, fulfilling his resolve at the time of his imprisonment to write a literary work "on an ample scale, disinterestedly, *für ewig!* As much a cultural humanist as a political theorist, he never totally repudiated the influence of Croce (who in turn admired and respected him). But the patrician Croce's idealism and aestheticism seemed to him the source of much of Italy's problem—alienating the intellectual from the working class which must build its own ruling power, its "hegemony." Unlike doctrinaire Marxists, however, Gramsci rejected scientific materialism and economic determinism because these ignore the "philosophy of mind" and the traditions of the past. As he defines his own "philosophy of praxis" (thought developing into practice), it is not isolated but "contains in itself all the fundamental elements needed to construct a total and integral conception of the world . . . and everything that is needed to give life to an integral political organization of society." His "Modern Prince" will not be an autocratic ruler but "the protagonist and organizer of intellectual and moral reform—that is, he proposes the terrain for a further development of the collective national-popular will towards the construction of a superior, all-embracing form of modern civilization."

Gramsci's *Lettere dal carcere* won the Viareggio Prize in 1947. Portions of these letters, published in English translation in 1973 as *Letters from Prison,* reveal him as not only a dedicated political theorist but a sensitive and at times brilliant literary artist. His letters discuss, among other things, his reading ("I read six newspapers each day and eight books a week, as well as illustrated magazines and scholarly journals") ranging over everything from popular fiction, adventure and detective stories, to Dante, Goethe, Dostoevsky, Tolstoy, Chekhov, and Gide. He studied languages and taught courses to his fellow convicts in French, German, history and geography. Without self-conscious literary art, sentimentality or self-pity, he wrote vividly, particularly of his childhood memories of the Italian south, reminding more than one critic of Italy's great novelists Elio Vittorini and Carlo Levi. The prison experience itself enriched his sympathies and his powers of observation. From his cell, he writes in 1927, he has made friends with simple nature, with pet sparrows, two of whom he compares: "The first sparrow was more likeable than the present one. He was very proud and extremely lively. The one I have now is very unassuming, servile, and unenterprising. The first one immediately lorded it over the whole cell. I think his spirit must have been Goethean; he would scale every peak in the cell, settling there awhile to savor a sublime peace of mind . . . My present sparrow, on the other hand, is quite nauseating in his domesticity. He likes to be fed, although he can eat perfectly well by himself; he hops into my shoes and nestles in the cuffs of my trousers, if his wings were unclipped, he would fly onto my knee."

Because Gramsci's principal interest, as he wrote, was "the creative spirit of the people" and the cultivation of that spirit in an enlightened and humane society, it is possible that his poignant *Letters from Prison* will survive as literature when his political theory is forgotten and that it is Gramsci the humanist rather than Gramsci the revolutionary who will be remembered. "Morally my position is excellent," he wrote from prison in 1927. "Some call me satanic, some saintly, but I have no intention of appearing a martyr or a hero. I think of myself as an ordinary man who refuses to barter his deep convictions for anything in the world." But Gramsci was no "ordinary man." For Italian Marxists discovering his work in the 1940s and 50s, like the poet and film-maker Pier Paolo Pasolini who wrote an elegiac poem on him, *Le ceneri di Gramsci* (The Ashes of Gramsci, 1957), he was a lost ideal, a "master," and a kindred spirit. For readers of any or indeed no political ideology whatever, he has become a symbol of the indomitable human spirit.

PRINCIPAL WORKS IN ENGLISH TRANSLATION: Louis Marks translated *The Modern Prince and Other Writings* in 1957. *Selections from the Prison Notebooks of Antonio Gramsci,* edited and translated by Quintin Hoare and Geoffrey Nowell Smith, was published in 1971, and *Letters From Prison,* translated by Lynne Lawner, appeared in 1973. Hoare and John Matthews published *Selections from the Political Writings, 1910–1920* in 1977, and *Selections from the Political Writings, 1921–1928,* translated by Hoare, appeared in 1978.

ABOUT: Adamson, W. L. Hegemony and Revolution: Gramsci's Political and Cultural Theory, 1980; Bondanella, P. and J. C. (eds.) Dictionary of Italian Literature, 1979; Buci-Glucksmann, C. Gramsci and the State, 1980; Clark, M. Antonio Gramsci and the Revolution that Failed, 1977; Columbia Dictionary of Modern European Literature, 1980; Davidson, A. Antonio Gramsci: Towards an Intellectual Biography, 1977; Femia, J.V. Gramsci's Political Thought, 1982; Fiori, G. Antonio Gramsci: Life of a Revolutionary, 1971; Joll, James, Gramsci, 1977; Said, E. W. The World, the Text, and the Critic, 1983; Sassoon, A. S. Gramsci's Politics, 1980. *Periodicals*—Times Literary Supplement August 28, 1948; December 5, 1952.

GRANT, MICHAEL (November 21, 1914–), English classical scholar, writes: "My father, Maurice Harold Grant, was a regular officer of the British army who also wrote comprehensive works on English landscape paintings and a variety of other subjects. My mother died in 1980 at the age of 103. I was born in London and educated at Harrow School which twice sent me to Rome during vacations. Then I studied classics at Trinity College, Cambridge, specializing in ancient history in the latter part of the course. After taking my degree I embarked on graduate study, my subject being the bronze coinage of the Augustan period throughout the empire, with special regard to its historical significance. Since many of the coins were unpublished or little known, my University and College (most generously) enabled me to travel widely in Europe to look at collections. I was elected to a four-year research fellowship in

MICHAEL GRANT

1938, but after only one year of this halcyon existence the second World War broke out. I enlisted in the army and was posted as junior officer to the War Office, where I remained (apart from a short visit to France) until the following year. Then I was transferred to the British Council and, after a brief spell in Egypt, became its first representative in Turkey, with the task of expanding that country's cultural and educational relations with Britain in the middle of the war. I stayed in Turkey for five years (apart from a number of near-eastern travels) and in 1944 married Anne-Sophie Beskau, who was then working in the Swedish Legation at Ankara. In 1945 we returned to London, where I served for two years as deputy controller of the British Council's work in liberated Europe. Our first son was born and my first book (based on my fellowship thesis) was published during this period, and its conclusion saw us in Cambridge, where I started to resume my pre-war research. In 1948, however, we moved to Edinburgh on my appointment as professor of Humanity. Our second son was born. In 1956, on secondment from Edinburgh University, I became the first vice-chancellor of the new University of Khartoum (formerly Gordon College) in newly independent Sudan, where, apart from summer visits to Britain we spent nearly three years. Soon afterwards, we were in Belfast in Northern Ireland, where I took up office as president and vice-chancellor of the Queen's University.

"In 1966, however, I retired, leaving the university career at the age of fifty-one, and we moved to our present home on the lower slopes of the Monte Pisano, not far from Lucca. During the years that have passed (very quickly) since then, I have been engaged, most of the time, in writing, in partnership with my wife. Founded upon my earlier periods of what (I hope!) was original research, the books I have been engaged upon in recent years have been prompted by a different, though related aim. For I have tried to appeal to that considerable body of people—students, teachers, 'educated public,' intelligent but not necessarily in possession of specialized knowledge—who are strongly drawn to the ancient world (in which they see their cultural and spiritual roots) and want to discover more about it, preferably in jargon-free language.

"I think these books of mine can be divided into four more or less distinct but overlapping categories. First, there are general books, some intended for reading and some for reference, on large sweeps of ancient civilization (heavens, how difficult it is to generalize accurately: quite as much of an art, in its way, as detailed research). Secondly, there are what my publishers, with varying degrees of approval, call 'monographs,' which deal with more particular topics relating to Greek and Roman history and culture. Thirdly, I have written a number of translations from Latin authors—Cicero and Tacitus. Finally, I have given expression to a longstanding interest in the Jewish and Christian aspects of the ancient world by writing about Judaism, Jesus and Saint Paul, and trying to decide and set down, with as much objectivity as possible, what actually happened. Letters I receive about these publications range from constructive to irrelevant—and from appreciative to irate.

"All this work (lack of subjects never seems to present a problem) keeps me busy here [Lucca, Italy] for about nine months of every year, as the beautiful seasons change among the vineyards and cypresses and flowers of Galtaiola. We spend the remaining weeks in England (where our sons are living), or sometimes in other countries of Europe, or,—especially often—in the United States, where, in addition to undertaking lecture-tours, I have taught at Stanford University (several times), the University of California (Santa Barbara), the Virginia Military Institute (Lexington), and Hampden-Sydney College in the same state. These are activities, I believe, which reduce the danger of withdrawing into an ivory tower where the only voice one can hear is one's own, or those of our local nightingales."

———

Although a specialist in several recondite fields of classical scholarship—numismatics, iconography, relief portraiture, architecture, philosophy and theology—Michael Grant has eminently succeeded in his aim of reaching "that considerable body of people" who want to learn more about the ancient past in "jargon-free language." Scholar-critics have praised his work for impeccable scholarship combined with a lucid and engaging prose style. Always at the center of his attention is cultural history—the totality and vitality of ancient civilizations. "We feel that we know how the ordinary people really lived and felt," a reviewer in the *New York Times* wrote of his *World of Rome*. "Though he is concise, he tells us all sorts of things we need or want to know," the *New Yorker* observed of his survey of the Greek and Roman historians in *The Ancient Historians*. Equally if not even more important, he stimulates his readers to further reading and study in the classics. Michael Grant was named Officer of the Order of the British Empire in 1946 and Commander in 1958.

PRINCIPAL WORKS: From Imperium to Auctoritas, 1946; Roman Imperial Money, 1954; Roman Literature, 1954; Roman History from Coins, 1958; The World of Rome, 1960; Myths of the Greeks and Romans, 1962; The Civilizations of Europe, 1965; Gladiators, 1967; The Climax of Rome, 1968; The Ancient Mediterranean, 1969; Julius Caesar, 1969; The Ancient Historians, 1970; The Roman Forum, 1970; Nero, 1970; Cities of Vesuvius, 1971; Herod the Great, 1971; Roman Myths, 1971; Cleopatra, 1972; The Jews in the Roman World, 1973; The Army of the Caesars, 1974; The Twelve Caesars, 1975; The Fall of the Roman Empire, 1976; Saint Paul, 1976; Jesus, 1977; History of Rome, 1978; The Etruscans, 1980; Greek and Latin Authors, 1980; From Alexander to Cleopatra, 1983; The History of Ancient Israel, 1984.

ABOUT: Contemporary Authors, new revision series 4, 1981; Who's Who, 1983–84. *Periodicals*—American Historical Review February 1984; Commonweal May 20, 1983; New York Times Book Review May 8, 1983; Times Literary Supplement April 1, 1983.

GRAY, FRANCINE DU PLESSIX

(1930–), American novelist and journalist, writes: "I spent the first ten years of my life in Paris, did not know a word of English until the age of eleven, and still do much of my thinking and all of my counting in my first two languages, French and Russian. My mother [Tatíana Liberman du Plessix] was born in St. Petersburg and came to France in 1926. During the Russian Revolution and the famine that succeeded it, she helped to support her family by reciting poetry to Red Army soldiers in exchange for rations of potatoes and bread. Her passion for poetry, her ability, undiminished to this day, to recite by heart hundreds of lines of Pushkin, Pasternak or

FRANCINE DU PLESSIX GRAY

Mayakovsky may have bred in me that belief in the redemptive and talismanic force of the Word which is at the heart of any writer's vocation.

"My father [Bertrand Jochaud du Plessix] was born into an impoverished, aristocratic family of the French Vendée whose convictions tended to Royalism ('never forget,' he would say, 'that we were knighted in the very *First* Crusade'). He won scholarships to a succession of the most competitive graduate schools in Paris. He was to bear for the rest of his brief life the bitterness of early poverty and failed aspirations. I was born in Warsaw, Poland, during his brief stint in the diplomatic service. I was an only child and we returned to Paris before I was one-year-old. Success continued to elude my father as he tried business, journalism, finance. My mother helped to support us by a small hat-designing enterprise which she ran in a corner of her bedroom in our small flat near the Trocadero. My father died with the Free French Forces in the first weeks after de Gaulle's call and was one of the 900 or so Frenchmen to receive the General's highest military honor—the Croix de la Libération. He had been the idol of my early years, and his untimely death may have stamped my work with its two most pervasive themes—the search for God, the search for the Father.

"My Parisian childhood was characterized by conditions ideal to the making of a writer—solitude, oppression, a constant refuge in books. Until the age of ten I was tutored at home by my father and a tyrannical governess who seldom let me talk to other children for fear that I might catch their germs. My father's death was fol-lowed by our flight to America, my years as the only scholarship student in a prestigious and admirably authoritarian girls' school in which I continued to feel an outsider. Despite these states of alienation so fortuitous for most writers, I seemed destined to spend a few decades searching for my vocation. Between the ages of twelve and twenty-two I aspired to be, in turn, a nun, a dancer, an architect, a war correspondent, a painter, a professor of philosophy, a theologian. My first literary efforts in college were marked by extremely confusing mixed signals of success and failure. I excelled as a critic but did wretchedly in my one class in 'creative writing'—a C minus for stories about situations of which I knew precious little, about middle-aged alcoholic actors who sought redemption in Bowery churches. A wiser teacher steered me towards autobiography and I won the Putnam Creative Writing Award upon graduating from Barnard for some tragi-comic stories about my French childhood. Yet a year later, upon attending a summer session at Black Mountain College, Charles Olson told me they were pure junk. 'If you want to be a writer keep it to a journal,' the giant walrus stormed at me, 'and don't try to publish anything for another ten years!'

"Through some instinctive trust in the advice of a man whose eye was erratic but sometimes admirable, I kept to Big Charles' advice. The decade of journal-keeping I indulged in between 1953 and 1963—years during which I mostly earned my keep as a hack journalist—seemed to have served as a matrix in which I allayed my life's central torment—my simultaneous need to commit emotions to paper and the terror that accompanies that need. But fidelity to the schedule set me by Charles Olson now seems providential. In 1963, a year past his decade deadline, I rewrote one of the stories that had earned me my college prize. It was about my governess and was published in the *New Yorker.* Twelve years and two books of non-fiction later, the same story was to become the first chapter of *Lovers and Tyrants.*

"After twenty years of being labeled 'author' I still feel honored, yet undeserving, of the appellation 'novelist.' And I'm particularly rebellious against the notion that I practice something which could be called 'creative' writing. Edmund, the protagonist of my novel *World Without End,* speaks for me when he attacks the romantic notion of the artist as chosen: 'Divinity of the creator, artist as sacred vessel . . . Debased Faustianism, elitist ooze, kraut metaphysics doled out in seedy art schools!' I look upon myself rather as a craftsperson, a cabinetmaker of texts, and occasionally, I hope, a witness to our times.

"Always that plaguing question: Why do I go on writing, seeing the continuing anguish of the act, the dissatisfaction I feel with most results? Flannery O'Connor answered it best: 'I write because I don't know what I think until I read what I say.' I also write because I'm antediluvian enough to believe that literature can still address such traditional themes as love, honor, compassion, faith, trust, grace—the basic staples of the human condition. I still feel close to the Catholic Church, a multi-layered vision which, once it has made its point, can dominate one's life whether one believes in it or not. I trust in Flaubert's dictum that writing thrives most vigorously within the confines of a rigorously ordered bourgeois life. I have been married for over a quarter of a century to the painter Cleve Gray, and have spent those years in the same New England country house. My favorite escapes from the painful practice of my craft are to grow vegetables and many herbs; play tennis; reread Dostoyevsky, Henry James, St. Paul, Wallace Stevens, Thomas Merton and numerous other sources of inspiration; enjoy the company, and frequently seek counsel, of my two adult sons; enjoy the solace of a few friendships which grow in depth and richness as the years flow on. I go to my work space daily, like a bureaucrat, if only to meditate on the difficulties of the pages at hand. My attitude towards the composing of any text is summed up by an ancient Chinese proverb: 'One must write a poem the way one rules a kingdom, the way one cooks a small fish.'"

The early years of her life that Francine Gray describes are registered in fiction in Stephanie, the heroine of her first novel, Lovers and Tyrants. Much of her development into a mature artist is reflected in her Edmund of World Without End. Both characters are European-born into families of aristocratic background, sheltered then suddenly thrust into the new world of American life, poor but still firmly rooted in the tradition and culture of their European roots, ultimately successful but uncomfortable in both societies. Beyond that, her novels are less autobiography than imaginative expressions of the responses of a sensitive, talented, socially committed human being to the challenging and complex condition of the modern world, European and American.

Francine Gray herself was born in Warsaw, Poland and came to the United States with her mother in 1941. Beginning her career—after education at the Spence School in New York City, Bryn Mawr, Black Mountain and Barnard colleges (with a B.A. in philosophy from the last in

1952)—Gray worked for United Press (1952–54), the French edition of Réalités magazine (1954–55), and as art critic and book editor for Art in America (1962–68). She came to the attention of a larger reading public with the publication of articles in the New Yorker reporting on the American Catholic radical movement of the 1960s, with profiles of the Berrigan brothers and Ivan Illich and essays on the activities of various left-wing Catholic groups. Collected in a book in 1970 as Divine Disobedience: Profiles in Catholic Radicalism, these pieces, which received the National Catholic Book Award, impressed many critics both with their accuracy as reportage and their balanced and tolerant views of Catholicism. "Gray writes with a sharp eye and a romantic pen," Michael Novak commented in Book World. Though sympathetic to the rebels, she is also sympathetic to the Church, leading Novak to compare her to British Catholic writers like Ronald Knox, Hilaire Belloc, G. K. Chesterton, and Evelyn Waugh. In the Saturday Review David Schoenbrun hailed her work as a challenging call to the Catholic Church to awaken and revitalize its worshippers. Written with a sharp reportorial ear and eye, her book, he observed, "is not only a book for Catholics, but for all who seek to reconcile faith and reason, God and Caesar, for believers and nonbelievers."

Also for the New Yorker in 1972 (and published as a book the same year), Gray wrote a short but solidly observed and candid profile of Hawaii: The Sugar-Coated Fortress, which she portrays as "profoundly hedonistic and provincial . . . an autistic Eden, a plastic paradise, in which the militarism and racism of the American empire are cloaked in a deceptive veil of sunshine and flowers." She has also published essays on travel, American politics, manners and morals, book reviews and drama criticism in the Saturday Review, Ramparts, Vogue, Cosmopolitan, and New York Review of Books; and has lectured and conducted writing workshops at Harvard, Yale, California (Berkeley), Indiana and Syracuse universities. From 1975 to 1979 she was on the English faculty of City College of the City University of New York.

Best known, however, as a novelist, Gray attributes her writing of fiction to a solitary childhood in which, under pressures from a domineering governess and a critical and demanding father, she struggled for self-expression, torn between her "need to commit fantasies to paper and the terrors that accompany that need, the leaden slowness of the words' arrival, my struggle with the clamped metal jaws of mouth and mind." Like her Stephanie and Edmund, she conquered those inhibitions in America with a new language and a totally new and different life. *Lovers and Tyrants* takes its protagonist from a sheltered French childhood to her middle age in a radically liberated America of the early 1970s. In the course of that journey Stephanie confronts the main issues of contemporary feminism—the conflict of career and sexual liberation with marriage and family responsibilities. ("I shall never cease to marvel at the way we beg for love and tyranny," Stephanie remarks early in the book.) A "thesis" novel that, Joan Peters wrote in the *Nation*, "beautifully" exploits "the limited strength of the autobiographical novel," it was praised for its wit, intelligence, and "elegant prose." But some critics, notably John Leonard in *Harper's*, objected to the "elegant prose," finding it mannered and self-conscious—"a prose that tries too hard."

In *World Without End*, Gray widens her focus to portray three main characters—Edmund, a painter and art critic, and two women he met in his youth during an idyllic summer on Nantucket—rich, charming and high-spirited Claire, and the brilliant Sophie who becomes an internationally famous television newscaster. The theme of the novel is the idealized friendship of these three, now adults, who take a trip together to Russia as much to discover themselves as to explore a foreign country. The book was aptly described by Doris Grumbach in *Commonweal* as one of a currently rare genre—"the novel of intelligence." That is both its virtue and its failing. Her characters, Grumbach notes, "are so detached and so cerebral, their talk is so elevated and informed . . . that somehow passion is smothered in them." Similarly, Judith Gies in *Saturday Review*, while impressed with the author's intelligence and seriousness of purpose, found it "less a novel than a morality play."

PRINCIPAL WORKS: *Novels*—Lovers and Tyrants, 1976; World Without End, 1981. *Non-Fiction*—Divine Disobedience, 1970; Hawaii: The Sugar-Coated Fortress, 1972.

ABOUT: Contemporary Authors 61–64, 1976; New York Times August 20, 1981; New York Times Book Review September 12, 1982.

GRAY, SIMON (JAMES HOLLIDAY)

(October 21, 1936–), British dramatist, was born on Hayling Island, Hampshire, the son of Dr. James Davidson Gray, a Canadian pathologist, and the former Barbara Cecelia Mary Holliday. He was sent to Canada with his elder brother at the beginning of World War II and remained with his grandparents in Montreal until 1945, when he returned to England to contin-

SIMON GRAY

ue his education. He attended Portsmouth Grammar School, then Westminster, a public school in London. He returned with his family to Canada in the early 1950s, received a B.A. in English from Dalhousie University, Nova Scotia, in 1957, then, after spending a year teaching English at the University of Clermont-Ferrand in France, he entered Trinity College, Cambridge, to read English, taking a second bachelor's degree in 1961. After holding research scholarships at St. John's and Trinity Colleges (1961–63), he taught for a year at the University of British Columbia and was supervisor (tutor) in English at Trinity for another year before being hired as lecturer in English at the University of London's Queen Mary College, in the East End. He has held that post, in which he has mainly concentrated on the Victorian novel, since 1965.

Gray began his writing career with four novels: *Colmain*, a satire about a remote, mythical Canadian province; *Simple People*, a story of life in Cambridge narrated by a Canadian postgraduate; *Little Portia*, about the shocks attendant upon maturity; and *A Comeback for Stark*, an espionage thriller published under the pseudonym Hamish Reade. The speeches in these novels, as well as in the few short stories he has published, are lifelike, their wit and invective smoothly defining of character, but narrative scope and balance, the particular qualities of fiction, are quite foreign to them.

After attending a production of Harold Pinter's *The Homecoming*, Gray decided to concentrate on the drama. Shortly thereafter, in 1966, he reworked one of his stories into a teleplay for the BBC, *The Caramel Crisis*, which turned out to be the first of more than a dozen such projects. Among the most successful was *Death of a Teddy Bear* in 1967, which won the Writers' Guild award and a decade later formed the basis of a stageplay, *Molly,* a retelling of the story of Alma Rattenbury, center of a famous British sex-and-murder scandal of the mid-1930s.

Wise Child, Gray's first theatrical success, began life as a rejected teleplay. A veteran criminal, on the run from the police, decides to dress up as "Mrs. Artminster," a prim and proper middle-class housewife, and pose as the mother of his young confederate, Jerry, a whining psychopath. The themes of dominance and submission and of homosexuality, fully exploited in Gray's later work, make their first appearance here. The London production featured Alec Guinness as the aging transvestite in a famous performance full of comic virtuosity. Five years later the British actor Donald Pleasence attempted the role in New York, but the critics hooted the play from the stage and it closed after only a few performances.

A two-year-long string of failures, described by Gray as "three flops in a row," followed *Wise Child. Dutch Uncle,* in which the principal character longs to leave his job and kill his wife, failed after a short run by the Royal Shakespeare Company; a modernized adaptation of Dostoevsky's *The Idiot,* produced by the National Theatre in 1970, was described by Irving Wardle as "the saddest piece of butchery" he had ever seen at the Old Vic and closed soon thereafter; *Spoiled,* also a rewriting of a teleplay, is the domestic drama of a teacher of French, his pregnant wife, and the meek, exploited schoolboy who comes to him for help to pass an examination. This play closed after a three-week run in London's West End.

Butley was Gray's first unalloyed triumph on both sides of the Atlantic, and Ben Butley is one of his best-developed and most interesting characters, a smugly witty lecturer in English who uses his intellect as a weapon to devastate those around him. He is forced during the course of a single day to realize his serious shortcomings as teacher, husband, and friend. In further observation of the classical unities, the entire action takes place in Butley's office. Although the audience tends to side with the sardonic, clever hero early in the play, his cold and vicious intellectuality becomes repellent before long, and his victims' very human ordinariness engages our sympathy. Clive Barnes, calling the play "a literate and literary comedy with a heart," considered the best part of the work its adroit rendering of the character of Butley: "Where Mr. Gray has been particularly clever is to give

his declining slob all the funny lines. He fights against all comers like a cornered Bugs Bunny full of wisecracks and with a splenetic humor. You can see the tarnished brilliance of the man, the fallen hopes, the eroding self-distrust that spews out a fine comic bitterness upon the world. Unfulfilled and unforgiving, Butley makes his last stand with style and venom."

Simon Hench, hero of Gray's next hit, *Otherwise Engaged,* is a character solidly in the Butley mode. Adept at holding life at bay with a withering, sharp wit, this London publisher finds his planned evening of solitude interrupted by all manner of people, including a loud-mouthed lodger in his house, a desperate wife who confesses adultery, and his brother, a feckless schoolmaster. He demolishes them all in turn, then impassively sits down to his music, with the audience having realized, as Hench himself perhaps does not, that his own life has been emptied of meaning. The London production of this play, directed by Harold Pinter and starring Alan Bates, two frequent collaborators with Gray before and since, ran for more than thirty months. In New York the work won the Drama Critics Circle award for best play of the 1976–77 season.

Although Gray has written an increasingly large number of plays in the years since *Otherwise Engaged,* none has enjoyed the popularity of that work either in Britain or America. *Plaintiffs and Defendants, Two Sundays, Dog Days*—apparently an early draft of *Otherwise Engaged*—*Molly,* and *Close of Play* passed rapidly by in performances chock-full of stars, yet were generally unappreciated by critics and the public. *The Rear Column* concerned, in the author's words, with "five seemingly decent Victorian gentlemen going to pieces in hideous circumstances in the Congo," had a more mixed reception. Much disliked by the London critics, where it had a short, unhappy run, the even shorter-lived off-Broadway New York production was praised for its craftsmanship and sympathetic characterizations. *Stage Struck* is a comic mystery, which many found reminiscent of Ira Levin's *Deathtrap,* about a vengeful ex-stage manager, an expert at creating special effects, plotting to murder his wife, a successful London actress who wants to leave him. *Quartermaine's Terms,* which made many think of plays on similar themes by Terence Rattigan, concerns the dismissal from a low-ranking teaching post of St. John Quartermaine, a sad, unattractive loner forced by circumstances into an unwelcome isolation. The hero is treated by Gray with uncharacteristic gentleness and sympathy. The *Times* reviewer called him "grinning, forgetful, and deeply kind, . . . an inarticulate character of awesome loneliness who rivals the tragic force of Willy Loman." In its New York production it was highly acclaimed and ran for almost a year. In 1984 Gray's *The Common Pursuit,* directed by Harold Pinter, was produced in London. Like many of his earlier works, it centers on the interplay of literature (here a group of writers on a literary magazine) and life. Jeremy Treglown found it an advance on Gray's "previous best, *Butley* and *Otherwise Engaged,* with the same caustic wit," but with "more warmth and generosity . . . than anything Gray has written before."

"Either nobody likes my plays or I always just happen to stand by somebody who doesn't," said Gray in an interview in 1981. He is widely known by his colleagues in the theater as a dogged perfectionist and has put several of his plays through as many as forty drafts before allowing a production. He has also frequently expressed a rueful appreciation of the realities of the theater and especially an abiding hatred of critics. Theater reviewers, he wrote in 1983, "seem not to understand how apart they are from the activity that provides them with their livelihoods. After all, most performances (and frequently the best of them) take place without their assistance. They usually only come once, and only affect what they're to judge by the extent to which their presence undermines it. . . . Not only, therefore, *not* a part of the experience but professionally bound to resist it—as they resist that other witness, the paying audience, whose testimony they either ignore or even despise. But this, I fully understand, is a partial view. There are probably moods in which I might be inclined to see them in a more pathetic light, wondering who could want to lead such a pariah life, even for a column on the *Sunday Times.*"

Gray has been married since 1965 to Beryl Mary Kevern. They have two children and live in Highgate, North London.

PRINCIPAL WORKS: *Drama*—Wise Child, 1968; Sleeping Dog, 1968; Dutch Uncle, 1969; The Idiot, 1971; Spoiled, 1971; Butley, 1971; Otherwise Engaged, 1975; Plaintiffs and Defendants, 1975; Two Sundays, 1975; Dog Days, 1976; Molly, 1977; The Rear Column, 1978; Close of Play, 1979; Stage Struck, 1979; Quartermaine's Terms, 1981. *Fiction*—Colmain, 1963; Simple People, 1965; Little Portia, 1967; A Comeback for Stark, 1968.

ABOUT: Contemporary Authors 21–24R, 1977; Contemporary Dramatists, 1977; Current Biography, 1983; Who's Who, 1983–84. *Periodicals*—Choice May 1973; January 1977; Library Journal February 15, 1973; September 15, 1976; April 1, 1981; New Republic June 20, 1981; New York Times November 1, 1972; August 17,

1975; March 5, 1978; November 19, 1978; February 22, 1981; February 28, 1983; New Yorker February 6, 1978; December 4, 1978; Observer August 3, 1975; October 29, 1978; May 27, 1979; Spectator June 9, 1979; Times (London) July 31, 1975; November 8, 1976; November 24, 1977; November 23, 1979; August 3, 1981; Times Literary Supplement September 2, 1983; July 13, 1984; Village Voice February 14, 1977; February 28, 1977; December 4, 1978.

GREELEY, ANDREW M(ORAN) (February 5, 1928–), American sociologist and novelist, was born in Oak Park, Illinois, the only son of Andrew Thomas Greeley, a corporation executive, and the former Grace Anne McNichols. From early childhood he wanted to be a Catholic priest, and attended Quigley Preparatory Seminary in Chicago and St. Mary of the Lake Seminary in Mundelein, Illinois, where he took the degrees of bachelor of arts (1950), bachelor of sacred theology (1952), and lector of sacred theology (1954). He was ordained a priest in May 1954. From then until 1963 he was assistant pastor of Christ the King Church in Chicago, and during this time completed graduate work in sociology at the University of Chicago (M.A., 1961; Ph.D., 1962). Since 1962 he has been associated with the university's National Opinion Research Center (NORC), and many of his books have drawn on data assembled there. Since 1978 he has divided his time between Chicago and Tucson, where he is professor of sociology at the University of Arizona.

Greeley is a hugely prolific writer on the sociology of religion in the United States. Over twenty-four years he has published more than eighty books and monographs, as well as hundreds of articles for popular magazines and professional journals, regular newspaper columns, and innumerable reviews. He has on occasion been "gently accused," according to Bruce Buursma, "of never having had an unpublished thought." He has written on subjects as diverse as religious education, religious vocation, ecumenicism, death and dying, marital sexuality, church doctrine, American ethnicity, church history, Irish-American history, American Catholic history, papal politics, and Mariology. He has published a catechism, as well as several best-selling novels that feature churchmen as prominent characters.

At the beginning of his writing career, Greeley seemed to focus on the youth of the church as a special area of interest. *Strangers in the House: Catholic Youth in America* analyzes in thirteen essays the U.S. teen-ager's search for security and maturity in an apparently insecure and purposeless society. Much of the book dis-

ANDREW M. GREELEY

cusses ways of preventing juvenile delinquency, then a relatively new middle-American preoccupation. Helen Burgess called the book "an examination of the factors in our culture that have created an apathy at its core." *And Young Men Shall See Visions* comprises sixteen letters to John, a college student, dealing with such questions as personal morality, choice of career, love and marriage, and religious observance. *Letters to Nancy* is a companion volume for the young Catholic woman.

Religion and Career: A Study of College Graduates, the first of Greeley's publications for NORC, presents the results of a statistical survey of the influence of religion on the career and graduate-school plans of U.S. college graduates in June 1961. The most important conclusions drawn by Greeley from his data concern the relatively recent, quite dramatic rise in the economic and social status of U.S. Roman Catholics. The common sociological assumption had been, according to N. J. Demerath, "that Catholics have remained traditionalist laggards in a capitalistic age," but Greeley's study "adds to the mounting evidence for Catholic parity." The author continued his work on American education with *The Education of Catholic Americans,* written with Peter H. Rossi and sponsored by the Carnegie Corporation and the U.S. Department of Health, Education and Welfare, which drew on data collected in personal interviews with 2,753 U.S. Catholics from the ages of twenty-three to fifty-seven and on questionnaires from another 1,000 teen-agers, all the adolescents in the homes of the families sampled. The authors attempt a survey of the consequences of U.S.

Catholic education between about 1910 and 1960—the preconciliar U.S. Catholic church. J. H. Fichter called the book "by far the most useful study that has been attempted in the area of American Catholic education." Other books by Greeley touching on education are *The Changing Catholic College,* another NORC monograph; *From Backwater to Mainstream: A Profile of Catholic Higher Education,* funded by the Carnegie Commission on Higher Education; *Can Catholic Schools Survive?* (with W. E. Brown); *Catholic Schools in a Declining Church* (with C. McCready and K. McCourt), a NORC study; and *Catholic High Schools and Minority Students.*

Delineating the peculiarities of American Catholicism is Greeley's other principal and enduring concern; he has usually approached the subject as a progressive, though he is no radical. The provocative essays in *The Hesitant Pilgrim: American Catholicism after the Council* explained how the Second Vatican Council had changed the U.S. church, and how the council's impetus would continue to change it in the future. *The Catholic Experience: An Interpretation of the History of American Catholicism* explores the thesis that the Americanizers within the American church have always won the important arguments with the conservative traditionalists, but lost the power that ran the church. Two books published in 1969 consider the future of the Catholic church and of religion in general in America. *A Future to Hope For: Socio-Religious Speculations* discusses the main problems facing the contemporary church, including sexuality and the crisis of leadership, that are in urgent need of solution. *Religion in the Year 2000* balances the hostility to traditional religion of the contemporary world against Greeley's sociological projection of present religious trends into the next century. Among the most important of Greeley's NORC studies is *The American Catholic: A Social Portrait,* which was judged remarkable by J. A. Coleman for summarizing so many of Greeley's ideas: " . . . it is all there between two covers—the essential Greeley reader, distilling in one volume his last fifteen years of research." In *The Communal Catholic: A Personal Manifesto,* Greeley takes a rather surprising position against Catholic liberal intellectuals, who have, he believes, betrayed the church. The hope of the church lies in the communal, or grass-roots Catholic, a loyal adherent who is uninterested in church structure or politics. *An Ugly Little Secret: Anti-Catholicism in North America* traces strong anti-Catholic sentiment in America from its roots in nineteenth-century nativism. *Crisis in the Church: A Study of Religion in America* is another sociological summary of the author's views on the difficulties faced by the contemporary church. Finally, in *The Denominational Society: A Sociological Approach to Religion in America,* Greeley develops the thesis that American religion is basically denominational, despite the common set of values held by many Americans. Martin Marty called it "a kind of textbook on the subject."

Because of their sensational content, Greeley's novels have received far more attention than would have been the case if their author had not been a priest and well-known Catholic apologist. *The Cardinal Sins,* the first of them, was widely assumed to be based on Greeley's archdiocesan superior, John Cardinal Cody of Chicago, whom he had described in print as "a madcap tyrant." The appearance of the novel preceded by several months the public announcement of a state investigation into Cody's irregular finances, and its explicit treatment of sex, including a priest who fathers an illegitimate child, as well as its portrait of the venality of the clergy, inevitably offended many Catholics. To their expressions of outrage, Greeley replied (in an interview in the *New York Times*) "I'm saying here's my church, made up of human beings with all the weaknesses and frailties and yet with the capacity to transcend those limitations and to produce great people, great art, great mysticism, and great missionaries. If it shocks people to hear a priest say we're not perfect, then it's high time they be disabused of wrong notions about us." The commercial success of this book and of *Thy Brother's Wife,* also a story of forbidden love among the hierarchy, led to a multivolume fiction contract for Greeley, already surely the best-selling priest-novelist in United States history. On the basis of a survey he conducted among his readers he concluded "that the sex in the books is not overdone and that the mixture of religion and story in the books responds to both market and human needs."

With an independent and very large income from his writing he has adopted a lifestyle that includes a desert home near Tucson, an apartment in Chicago, and a summer house on Lake Michigan. "I don't worry about my lifestyle," he told his *New York Times* interviewer in 1982, "I worry about my life. In my Ash Wednesday sermon I used a line from Faulkner that 'life is nothing more than a preparation for being dead a long time.'" In January of 1984 he established a grant of $850,000 to the University of Chicago to endow a chair in Roman Catholic Studies, all the more generous because the university had denied him tenure some years earlier.

Other Greeley books of note include *The Jesus Myth,* reflections on the person and teachings of Jesus and their meaning for today; *The Sinai Myth,* an attempt to understand the reality behind the events described in Exodus 19–20; *The Devil, You Say! Man and His Personal Devils and Angels,* an analysis of contemporary vices and their corresponding virtues; *Death & Beyond,* a manual of pastoral care replete with much sociological data; *Everything You Wanted to Know about the Catholic Church but Were Too Pious to Ask,* an encyclopedic collection of small essays on a wide variety of contentious Catholic topics; and his foray into Vatican politics, *The Making of the Popes, 1978: The Politics of Intrigue in the Vatican,* a personal account, in the manner of the New Journalism, of his effort to probe the secrets of the two papal conclaves of 1978. He has also collaborated with his sister Mary Greeley Durkin on a book analyzing the problem of declining church attendance, *How to Save the Catholic Church.*

PRINCIPAL WORKS: The Church and the Suburbs, 1959; Strangers in the House: Catholic Youth in America, 1961 (rev. ed.) 1967; (editor with Michael E. Schlitz) Catholics in the Archdiocese of Chicago, 1962; Religion and Career, 1963; Letters to a Young Man, 1964; Letters to Nancy, 1964; (with Peter H. Rossi) The Education of Catholic Americans, 1966; The Hesitant Pilgrim: American Catholicism after the Council, 1966; The Catholic Experience: An Interpretation of the History of American Catholicism, 1967; Changing Catholic College, 1967; And Young Men Shall See Visions, 1968; Crucible of Change: The Social Dynamics of Pastoral Practice, 1968; Uncertain Trumpet: The Priest in Modern America, 1968; Youth Asks, "Does God Talk?," 1968, published as Youth Asks, "Does God Still Speak?," 1970; (with Martin E. Marty) What Do We Believe?, 1968; From Backwater to Mainstream: A Profile of Catholic Higher Education, 1969; A Future to Hope In: Socio-Religious Speculations, 1969; Life for a Wanderer: A New Look at Christian Spirituality, 1969; Religion in the Year 2000, 1969; Why Can't They Be Like Us?: Facts and Fallacies about Ethnic Differences and Group Conflicts in America, 1969; A Fresh Look at Vocations, 1969; The Friendship Game, 1970; New Horizons for the Priesthood, 1970; The Life of the Spirit (also the Mind, the Heart, the Libido), 1970; (with William E. Brown) Can Catholic Schools Survive?, 1970; (with Joe L. Spaeth) Recent Alumni and Higher Education, 1970; Why Can't They Be Like Us?: Americans' White Ethnic Groups (includes portions of Why Can't They Be Like Us?: Facts and Fallacies about Ethnic Differences and Group Conflicts in America), 1971; Come Blow Your Mind with Me, 1971; The Jesus Myth, 1971; The Touch of the Spirit, 1971; What a Modern Catholic Believes about God, 1971; The Denominational Society: A Sociological Approach to Religion in America, 1972; Priests in the United States: Reflections on a Survey, 1972; The Sinai Myth, 1972; That Most Distressful Nation: The Taming of the American Irish, 1972; The Unsecular Man: The Persistence of Religion, 1972; What a Modern Catholic Believes about the Church,

1972; The Catholic Priest in the United States: Sociological Investigations, 1972; The New Agenda, 1973; Sexual Intimacy, 1973; (editor with Gregory Baum) The Persistence of Religion, 1973; Building Coalitions: American Politics in the 1970s, 1974; The Devil, You Say!: Man and His Personal Devils and Angels, 1974; Ecstasy; A Way of Knowing 1974; Ethnicity in the United States: A Preliminary Reconnaissance, 1974; (with Baum) The Church as Institution, 1974; MEDIA: Ethnic Media in the United States, 1974; Love and Play, 1975; May the Wind Be at Your Back: The Prayer of St. Patrick, 1975; The Sociology of the Paranormal: A Reconnaissance, 1975; (with William C. McCready and Kathleen McCourt) Catholic Schools in a Declining Church, 1976; The Communal Catholic: A Personal Manifesto, 1976; Death and Beyond, 1976; Ethnicity Denomination, and Inequality, 1976; The Great Mysteries: An Essential Catechism, 1976; Nora Maeve and Sebi, 1976; (with McCready) The Ultimate Values of the American Population, 1976; The American Catholic: A Social Portrait, 1977; The Mary Myth: On the Femininity of God, 1977; Neighborhood, 1977; No Bigger Than Necessary: An Alternative to Socialism, Capitalism, and Anarchism, 1977; An Ugly Little Secret: Anti-Catholicism in North America, 1977; Everything You Wanted to Know About the Catholic Church but Were Too Pious to Ask, 1978; (editor with Baum) Communication in the Church Concilium, 1978; (with J. N. Kotre) The Best of Times, the Worst of Times, 1978; Crisis in the Church: A Study of Religion in America, 1979; The Making of the Popes, 1978: The Politics of Intrigue in the Vatican, 1979; Women I've Met, 1979; The Magic Cup: An Irish Legend, 1979; (editor) The Family in Crisis or in Transition: A Sociological and Theological Perspective, 1979; Death in April, 1980; The Irish Americans: The Rise to Money and Power, 1980; (with McCready) Ethnic Drinking Subcultures, 1980; The Cardinal Sins, 1981; Thy Brother's Wife, 1982; Catholic High Schools and Minority Students, 1982; How to Save the Catholic Church, 1984; Lord of the Dance, 1984; Virgin and Martyr, 1985.

ABOUT: Contemporary Authors, first revision series 5–8, 1969; new revision series 7, 1982; Current Biography, 1972; Kotre, J. The Best of Times, the Worst of Times: Andrew Greeley and American Catholicism 1950–1975, 1978; Who's Who in America, 1982–83. Periodicals—America January 18, 1964; March 7, 1964; November 26, 1966; February 10, 1968; March 2, 1968; October 11, 1969; September 11, 1971; February 5, 1972; August 5, 1972; November 25, 1972; February 17, 1973; December 8, 1973; November 30, 1974; May 15, 1976; April 9, 1977; September 15, 1979; American Sociological Review August 1964; February 1967; Catholic World December 1961; Chicago Tribune April 4, 1982; Christian Century February 12, 1964; January 11, 1967; January 10, 1968; April 24, 1968; November 17, 1971; October 18, 1972; April 18, 1973; Commentary January 1967; July 1971; August 1973; Commonweal January 10, 1964; November 28, 1969; March 6, 1970; March 10, 1972; June 16, 1972; December 14, 1973; June 18, 1976; May 13, 1977; August 19, 1977; November 5, 1982; Critic February 1964; April 1964; December 1966–January 1967; April 1968; July 1970; November–December 1972; Spring 1977; Spring 1978; September 1979; Harvard Educational Review Summer 1967; National Review September 10, 1971; April 15, 1977; New Republic September 9, 1972; December 29, 1973; New York Review of Books March 4, 1976; New York Times March 22, 1982; New York Times Book Review July 25, 1971; November 14, 1971; April 2, 1972; November 19, 1972; November 11, 1973; February 24, 1974; March 6, 1977; June 24, 1979; July 26, 1981; June 17, 1984; New York Times Magazine May 6, 1984; New Yorker November 20, 1971; March 3, 1973; March 6, 1977; June 24, 1979; July 26, 1981; Saturday Review December 2, 1962; March 16, 1968; May 16, 1970.

GREEN, HANNAH. See GREENBERG, JOANNE

GREEN, MARTIN (BURGESS) (September 21, 1927–   ), English scholar and critic, writes: "I was born in Ealing, a suburb of London, where my father kept a small sweet-shop. When I was seven he had to give that up, because of a nervous breakdown, and we moved to a village in Shropshire where my mother's aunt had a house, having been a schoolteacher there many years. Oddly enough, I was never conscious of my father's illness, but I was deeply affected by my mother's taking on the primary responsibilities, and by the strains this caused. (But this seemed to me in some sense a cultural conflict, for her family and friends, being from Manchester, were more aggressively practical than his, who were from London and had some airs of cockney hedonism, some suggestion of faded boutonnières about them.)

"I got scholarships to grammar school and then Cambridge, by great good fortune becoming eligible for the latter just when money was allotted to County Scholarships, in 1945. But I was an unhappy child and learned by rote rather than by intelligence. However, I did well enough until I got to the university, where my emotional problems caught up with me. Those problems helped me to identify myself with F. R. Leavis (all of whose lectures I attended faithfully) in the under-dog drama he made out of his intellectual career. And so, even as an undergraduate, I found an activity of the mind—not a career—which I could engage in wholeheartedly; to be Leavisite. This activity was more than literary criticism, for Leavis made one see the largest issues of national destiny, and religious values, involved in choosing between him and his enemies. This suited my needs at the time—and since I have observed the same pattern of behaviour in other Leavisites, I have to

MARTIN GREEN

suppose that my own inner conflicts were also typical and cultural. But, just because I saw that in them, as time went by I had to recognize a corrupt source to my sense of mission, and had to extricate myself from that Puritan comradeship.

"After leaving Cambridge, I spent two years doing National Service in the Royal Air Force, and then one year of teacher training. But I was not good in the classroom, and so went for a year to France, and from there to America in 1952. These were moves away from home rather than towards anything. But teaching freshman English at the University of Michigan, I found a kind of teaching I liked, and taking graduate courses (having thought 'study' was all over for me) I found a more authentic pleasure in literature stirring in my mind. Above all, I found friends, and was able, in modest measure, to re-invent myself. A bit carried away with all that success, I wrote a dissertation which the university rejected, threw up the Ph.D., and went back to Europe for a year. But from that time on, I had my second wind, almost a second, American, birth; and I returned to Michigan and wrote my dissertation 1956–7. More important, I began to write—a series of essays comparing England with America, later collected as *Mirror for Anglo-Saxons.*

"That American identity was in some ways fraudulent, being all light, bright, optimism. I managed to live through the years of the McCarthy investigations without paying real attention—for me, America had to be innocent, to justify my escape from England. However, though I now think I was badly deceived about myself and the world, my dealings with literature and ideas still seem to me to have benefited from that influx of playful energy I took from being American. While at Wellesley, where I spent four years after leaving Ann Arbor, I read about the Two Cultures controversy, decided that Leavis was wrong, and went back to Cambridge to do undergraduate science in 1961. This I wrote about in *Science and the Shabby Curate of Poetry*; while at the same time I wrote *Reappraisals,* another "audacious" divergence from Leavis. While at Wellesley I had met a circle of talented people, at a more sophisticated level of literary intelligence than I had known before, and I returned to them in 1963, when I got a job at Tufts. But I still thought of myself as aspiring to a university job in England, and when I got an offer in 1965, from Birmingham, I went home again. (Meanwhile I had written *The Problem of Boston* and some of the essays in *Yeats's Blessings on von Hügel.*)

"Teaching in England, however, proved a disappointment. I didn't like the tutorial system, and found my students sullen, because of their tangle of class resentments. In other words, I still needed the more oxygenated air I breathed in America. Moreover, I married an American in 1967. For all these reasons I returned to Tufts in 1968. I was immediately plunged into problems of political conscience, and found I was unable to take action on what I thought were my convictions. I was no better able to answer the challenge of those years than other people, and realized that my American optimism had betrayed me. Luckily I found a subject to write about in *The von Richthofen Sisters,* which allowed me to treat the themes of that conflict. That book pleased the neo-conservatives, and the next one, *Children of the Sun,* had a similar success. But I realized that in finding an audience I was accepting their version of my intentions. I could not accept myself as a neo-conservative, but I could not go back to the comfortable role of ordinary Leftism. So I began to identify myself with Tolstoy and Gandhi and radical religion. This took the form of the trilogy *The Lust for Power,* of which the final volume, *Tolstoy and Gandhi: Men of Peace,* comes out in May 1983."

———

Martin Green is the son of Joseph William Elias Green and the former Hilda Brewster. His Cambridge college was St. John's, from which he graduated in 1948. He took a teaching diploma from King's College, London, in 1951 and a certificate in French studies from the Sorbonne the following year. His Michigan Ph.D. was conferred in 1957. Green's first book, *A Mirror for Anglo-Saxons: A Discovery of America, a Rediscovery of England,* received wide critical attention on both sides of the Atlantic. American reviewers tended to express satisfaction at what *Harper's* called Green's "avowed preference for the United States" over his mother country. "A book of unquestionable sincerity and insight," commented Barry Spacks in the *New Republic,* "which . . . turns the customary verdict of America's cultural inferiority *vis à vis* the European model neatly upside down. . . . It brings to a head . . . the violent foment [sic] of a new critical generation in England, and offers a vision of America which wonderfully clears the air of self-doubt and self-deprecation." British reviewers, on the other hand, mainly considered his critique either outdated—because of his absence from England during most of the previous decade—or flatly wrongheaded. "His sole consistency," wrote Alan Brien in the *Spectator,* "is a habit of hanging himself from the wrong trees: at every stage he has the right instincts but the wrong reactions, the right solutions to the wrong problems, the right conclusions based on the wrong examples. . . . What is important about his book is the portrait of a split individual which it reveals."

Reaction to *Science and the Shabby Curate of Poetry: Essays about the Two Cultures* was equally mixed. Written after Green had spent a year taking formal courses in science, the book was called by the *Times Literary Supplement* reviewer "a stimulating, austere, intellectual exercise. . . . [Green's] whole manner throughout is exposition at its most eloquent." Other critics, however, complained of the polemical tone of the book: "With the need for a synthesis," remarked Richard Mayne, "it's hard to disagree: but the tired platform tone . . . sounds too much like the phoney, fruity, pass-the-port 'humanism' that Green has denounced on an earlier page."

Green's Roman Catholicism was elementary to his decision to write *Yeats's Blessings on von Hügel: Essays on Literature and Religion,* which, according to the *Times Literary Supplement* reviewer, quoting the preface, is "intended to encourage a new type of Catholic sensibility 'which would complement the executive efficiency of the Church militant with the suppler and more complex sympathies of the literary imagination.'" The other writers treated in the book, besides those in the title, are Nabokov, Sholokhov, Pasternak, and J. F. Powers. Turning to the more obviously secular in *Cities of Light and Sons of the Morning: A Cultural Psychology for an Age of Revolution,* Green offers a historical examination of the development of London,

Weimar, and Edinburgh into great European cultural centers and analyzes some of the principal writers and thinkers they produced. Although some critics found the weight of detail and the mentioning of "scores of names from the past and present" overwhelming and somewhat self-defeating, others paid tribute to the book's originality and learning. In the second, autobiographical part of the work, Green, according to Jeffrey Meyers, "constructs a painfully honest portrait of himself as a characteristic liberal in an age of revolution: twitching with nervous solicitation of students' approval, willing but unable to forge the Faustian pact, nostalgic for the cities of light as well as for the fat cloistered days of the early 1960s, yet fearful and dubious of the radical commitment he believes is now compulsory."

Green is perhaps best known for two biographical studies published in the mid-1970s: *The von Richthofen Sisters; The Triumphant and the Tragic Modes of Love: Else and Frieda von Richthofen, Otto Gross, Max Weber, and D.H. Lawrence, in the Years 1870–1970* and *Children of the Sun: A Narrative of "Decadence" in England after 1918.* The two "modes of love" of the title of the former book exemplify for Green two kinds of rebellion against patriarchal society, but the book reflects far more than the colorful lives and loves of the two women who are its subject. George Levine wrote that "the subject, really, is Green's imagination of the major cultural issues of the past century and the method he has developed to formulate and explore them. . . . He gives us wonderful narrative and anecdotal material about the aesthetic and intellectual stars of prewar Germany and the Weimar republic." The subjects of *Children of the Sun* are the aesthetes Brian Howard and Harold Acton; its theme, according to Green, is "the imaginative life of English high culture between 1918 and 1957, seen in terms of cultural psychology; that is, in terms of the temperamental styles cultivated among intellectuals and artists and their work." Other literary members of the generation who came to maturity just after World War I, including Waugh, Huxley, the Sitwells, Auden, Isherwood, Spender, Betjeman, and Cyril Connolly, are also discussed. "The evocation of a generation's manners and mannerisms," wrote Robert Alter, "with all their contexts and antecedents, is consistently fine," yet he felt that the book lacked "any real critical perspective."

All three volumes of Green's biographical study of Gandhi and Tolstoy, *The Lust for Power,* have been generally well received. In the first volume, *The Challenge of the Mahatmas,* Green writes that the two subjects "are . . . our

Mahatmas by virtue of . . . three themes they develop ["thought," "empire," and "spirit"] which trouble us all, though some of us more than others. Above all, they are my Mahatmas, by virtue of three of my characters: as a man of letters, and so incomplete contemplative, would-be man of peace; as a citizen of England, the supreme imperialist power, now suffering the corruptions of imperial decay; and as, in some vestigial sense, a Christian." The first volume treats the cultural milieu and nexus between the subjects; the second, *Dreams of Adventure, Deeds of Empire,* studies what one critic called "the impact that travel, exploration, imperial endeavor, and related developments have had on literature." These ideas are exemplified for Green in the adventure stories of the past three centuries, especially those by Defoe, Scott, Cooper, Conrad, Tolstoy, Twain, and Kipling. "He brings to bear on his examples," wrote Jonathan Raban, "all the socio-bio-anthropo-econo-critical apparatus he can muster, and there is no one alive who can muster as much of it, or muster it as skillfully, as Martin Green. The trouble is that this huge labor simply doesn't pay off in terms of results. . . . There is very little that is genuinely original. . . . Martin Green's radicalism turns out to reside largely in his tone of voice." The third volume, *Tolstoy and Gandhi, Men of Peace: A Biography* constructs "parallel lives" of the subjects and examines the inner core of religious sensibility shared by them. One critic found the argument "thoughtful and sometimes illuminating," but another, in a familiar objection, thought the book's comparative framework "rather strained": "Green takes subjects of cultural interest and reduces rather than enlarges their significance."

Green married the former Carol Elizabeth Hurd in 1967; they have a son and a daughter. Among the honors he has received are three of the University of Michigan's Hopwood Creative Writing Awards in 1954, two Guggenheim fellowships (1974–75; 1977–78), and a fellowship in 1980–81 at the Woodrow Wilson International Center for Scholars.

PRINCIPAL WORKS: *Non-fiction*—A Mirror for Anglo-Saxons, 1960; Reappraisals: Some Commonsense Readings in American Literature, 1963; Science and the Shabby Curate of Poetry: Essays about the Two Cultures, 1965; The Problem of Boston; Some Readings in Cultural History, 1966; Yeats's Blessings on von Hügel: Essays on Religion and Literature, 1967; Cities of Light and Sons of the Morning, 1972; The von Richthofen Sisters, 1974; Children of the Sun, 1976; The Labyrinth of Shakespeare's Sonnets: An Examination of Sexual Elements in Shakespeare's Language, 1974; Transatlantic Patterns: Cultural Comparisons England with America, 1977; The Challenge of the Mahatmas, 1978; Dreams of Adventure, Deeds of Empire, 1979; Tolstoy and Gandhi, Men of Peace, 1983. *Novel*—The Earth Again Redeemed, 1978.

ABOUT: Contemporary Authors first revision series 17–20, 1976. *Periodicals*—Atlantic October 1960; September 1978; Christian Science Monitor September 22, 1960; June 24, 1965; July 9, 1979; Commentary November 1972; June 1976; Commonweal October 7, 1960; July 2, 1965; February 28, 1968; November 3, 1972; New Republic September 19, 1960; July 20, 1974; February 21, 1976; June 25, 1977; September 29, 1979; New Statesman April 14, 1961; September 6, 1963; October 23, 1964; September 6, 1974; July 6, 1980; New York Review of Books February 13, 1969; April 15, 1976; August 4, 1977; New York Times Book Review October 9, 1960; April 17, 1966; March 10, 1974; January 25, 1976; August 7, 1977; November 12, 1978; May 25, 1979; Newsweek January 26, 1976; Saturday Review September 24, 1960; December 16, 1972; February 7, 1976; August 1978; Spectator April 14, 1961; Times Literary Supplement April 21, 1961; July 26, 1963; November 19, 1964; October 12, 1967; September 13, 1974; July 18, 1980.

GREENBERG, JOANNE (Goldenberg) ("Hannah Green") (September 24, 1932–   ), American novelist and short story writer, writes: "I was born in Brooklyn, New York, [to Julius and Rosalie Goldenberg] and grew up in a house that my grandfather had bought to 'break the block.' We were the only Jews in a neighborhood of people who were horrified by our being there, even though we had been there for over a generation. I don't suppose that the anti-Semitism that I suffered was any worse than what anybody else had; it was just more constant, but it did mean that when I read about Dick and Jane in school, I felt that I was reading about strange and wonderful lives, and probably this sense of serenity in their lives helped my reading. I read other books, mostly boys' adventure books, but it wasn't until I was twelve or so that I really caught the idea of trying to make some of that adventure for myself by writing. This coincided with a move to Manhattan, a city from which I felt profoundly alienated even though there were Jews enough for anybody's taste.

"I went to the High School of Music and Art, and from there to a mental hospital where I stayed for three years, and where I had a much better time, although I didn't learn any more music. I was nineteen when I got out of the hospital, and hit the ground running. I went to American University after that (after taking a year out for a General Education Degree). American University in those days was a small, informal place that had little government research or research assistantships, which meant

JOANNE GREENBERG

that teachers taught our courses and graded our papers, and that meant that I think I got my college education for the most part from people who cared about teaching.

"I feel to a great extent as though I was born in college. Summers I went other places—sometimes working my way out and back. In 1955, I met Albert Greenberg at school, and married him seven months later. After an eight-month honeymoon re-fighting the Second World War through Italy, we came back and settled in Colorado, where we have been ever since. Somehow, we got two kids and a house and a cat. Somehow, I started writing novels.

"Although I had always written poetry, it wasn't very good, and when I decided I did want to write a novel, I had to count the chapters in a novel I was reading at the time to see how many chapters I should have. I didn't end up with the same number that Steinbeck had, though. The book went through six years of study and changes and turned out to be *The King's Persons* which, after seven publishers, was finally accepted by Holt, Rinehart, and Winston. I then decided to see if I could make personal experiences into some kind of artistic form, and wrote *I Never Promised You a Rose Garden*. Charles Schultz's book, *Peanuts*, paid for the publication of *The King's Persons*, and *Rose Garden* paid for the publication of the rest of my books, even though I think that the later ones are better.

"My ambition in life is to keep on writing, getting better all the time, until I hit eighty-five, and then coast. I would also like to finish the ironing. Since I am not a genius, it's still all possible to do. And I hope to spend the rest of the time pounding against the walls of my limitations and, with luck, bending them a little. Wouldn't that be nice?"

———

Joanne Greenberg began her writing career with a novel set among the Jews of York in medieval England (*The King's Persons*) and with the pseudonym "Hannah Green." She abandoned the historical genre in 1964 with her next novel *I Never Promised You a Rose Garden*, and her pseudonym in 1968 when she discovered that there was another writer named Hannah Green. Since then she has written a number of highly praised short stories and several novels, but *I Never Promised You a Rose Garden* remains her most popular book. This sensitive and painfully candid study of a sixteen-year-old schizophrenic and her long and harrowing hospitalization and ultimate recovery is to this day widely read, especially by young adults, and is on the reading lists of many college courses in psychology. Drawn from her own hospital experiences from 1948 to 1951 when she was under treatment for schizophrenia, the novel dramatizes the conflict within her young protagonist between the real world of middle-class loving Jewish family life in which she has grown up and an imaginary world, Yr, which she has peopled with the creatures of her tormented psyche. Under the care of a sympathetic psychiatrist, Dr. Clara Fried, a refugee from Nazi Germany, the girl painfully and gradually is restored to mental health. The doctor in the novel, a character inspired by the psychoanalyst Frieda Fromm Reichwann who treated Joanne Greenberg during her own hospitalization, provides its title. Gently guiding her patient back to sanity, she admits that the reality she offers is a cruel, unjust world: "'I never promised you a rose garden . . . and I never promised you peace or happiness . . . The only reality I offer is challenge, and being well is being free to accept it or not at whatever level you are capable.'"

As a dramatization of "the internal warfare in a young psychotic," novelist R. V. Cassill wrote in the *New York Times, I Never Promised You a Rose Garden* is "marvelous." But, he observes, "convincing and emotionally gripping as this novel is, it falls a little short of being fictionally convincing . . . It is as if some wholly admirable, and yet specialized, nonfictional discipline has been dressed in the garments and mask of fiction." The novel was made into a motion picture in 1977, and its screenplay, by Gavin Lambert and Lewis John Carlino, was nominated for an Academy Award that year.

It is with the vulnerable—the emotionally ill, the physically disabled, the Jew striving to preserve religious tradition in modern America, the Colorado farmer struggling to preserve his farm from the ravages of dust storms, the idealistic social worker and civil rights activist—that Joanne Greenberg's subsequent fiction is mainly concerned. Yet somber as her material often is, she is neither morbid nor doctrinaire. Reviewers have described her work as "charming," "optimistic," and "courageous." Sharing her husband's interest in vocational rehabilitation (he is a professional counselor), her vision of life is perhaps best described by the central charcter of her *A Season of Delight*, a middle-aged Jewish suburban housewife whose children have abandoned their family heritage (the son in a Hare Krishna cult, the daughter a militant feminist). Instead of grieving, the woman devotes herself to life-saving work as a volunteer ambulance driver and to quiet steady loyalty to her husband and his ailing mother: "'We live like modern nobility, in the ancestral castle. There are certain rooms shut off for warmth, and because of the upkeep. We remember those rooms, every inch of them, and everything with which they were furnished, but we don't often unlock them, and we try to live all the more warmly in the rest of the house. Try.'"

PRINCIPAL WORKS: The Monday Voices, 1965; In This Sign, 1971; Founder's Praise, 1976; A Season of Delight, 1981; The Far Side of Victory, 1983. *As Hannah Green*—The King's Persons, 1963; I Never Promised You a Rose Garden, 1964. *Short stories*—Summering, 1966; Tales Told Out of Time, 1966; Rites of Passage, 1972; High Crimes and Misdemeanors, 1979.

ABOUT: American Women Writers 2, 1980; Contemporary Authors, first revision series 5–8, 1969; Contemporary Literary Criticism, 1977; Who's Who in America, 1983–84.

GRUBB, DAVIS (ALEXANDER) (July 23, 1919–July 24, 1980), American novelist and short story writer. The following sketch was written for *World Authors* by Louis Grubb:

"My brother was born in Moundsville, West Virginia to Eleanor and Louis Grubb. Our rather sleepy Ohio River town was a stopping point for our grandfather's steamboat in the 1880s. Dave once said, 'When I was ten my mother took me on trip from Wheeling, West Virginia to Cincinnati, Ohio on the great Queen City, a magnificent Stern Wheeler.' For more than two hundred years our family has lived in that part of the Ohio Valley, and in setting and spirit, it has been the source of his novels. Dave's child-

DAVIS GRUBB

hood was rather typical for a small town in the 1920s, except for occasional summer trips to Lake Chatauqua, a cultural center in New York State, where he met F. Scott Fitzgerald, Thomas Edison, Paul Whiteman, and received a dime from John D. Rockefeller. His father, an architect, came from a prominent Wheeling family.

"Of his work Davis said, 'I have never wavered from a resolution made at the age of seven that I would become a writer. My earliest influences were the tales of old men in my river town.' After a rather uninspired high school record, in Clarksburg, West Virginia, he studied art for one year at Carnegie Tech, in Pittsburgh, Pennsylvania, where, for extra money, he stuffed Brazilian humming birds, and finally left after being told he was color blind.

"He began to write fiction seriously after he tried radio announcing, copywriting, and a year at NBC as a $15-a-week page. He broke into print with a half-hour radio play. Here began a long career of short story writing. He has published over fifty short stories, most of these in *Colliers, American Magazine, Cosmopolitan, Good Housekeeping, Saturday Evening Post, Ellery Queen,* and many anthologies. Three of these stories were seen on 'Alfred Hitchcock Presents.' His 'Horse Hair Trunk' was used on radio and then later on television. The title story from his last collection, 'The Siege of 318,' was produced after his death, on ABC's 'Dark Room.'

"His influences include his love for William Blake, and then Rebecca West, Robert Graves, William Faulkner, John O'Hara, D. H. Lawrence, and Thomas Wolfe. He was an avid reader and book collector.

"Our mother's beliefs and experiences had a great influence on him; she became a child welfare worker in 1936, after the death of our father, and many of Dave's characters came directly from her job experiences. He traveled many miles with her in the hills of West Virginia and packaged surplus food for the poor in the late thirties. All of this, plus a belief in God (not the formal church which he railed against in his last novel, *Ancient Lights*) surfaced in his work. Dave was also a very funny man and knew many comedians. Lenny Bruce was a good friend.

"His eleven published books started with: *Night of the Hunter.* 'Hunter' was loosely based on a man who advertised for widows. The purpose being for marriage and then to swindle them of their money. Finally, murder and burial in his garage. The book's story is of a little boy's father who is hanged for murder, but before he dies he tells a tale. The boy holds a secret, and a soft-voiced preacher with a bloody history stalks the child through a moonlit night, down at Cresaps Landing.

"Nelson Algren described *Night of the Hunter*, 'as compelling a story as I've come across.' Walter Van Tilburg Clark said it was 'a moving and darkly disturbing book. There is power, poetry, imagination here.' 'Hunter' was sold to Charles Laughton and Paul Gregory for a film. It was released in 1955, featuring Shelley Winters, Robert Mitchum, and Lillian Gish. The film is considered a classic. It is in the permanent collection of the Museum of Modern Art. R.C.A. released an L.P. of Laughton reading an abbreviated version which Dave had written. He also wrote two songs for the movie score. A series of pencil sketches done by Dave were the basis for many of the scenes. They were followed by Stanley Cortez, the famous cinematographer. The book was written in Philadelphia in six weeks, while Dave was working as a copywriter at Al Paul Lefton Advertising Agency.

"*A Dream of Kings* was a civil war novel peopled again with family characters and stories (Grandfather Cresap ran away from home at twelve to join the Confederacy but was sent home because of his age). He came back to this period again twenty years later for an, as yet, unpublished novel, 'The Scallop Shell.' *A Dream of Kings* tells of a young man's growth to manhood in a West Virginia river town and of a love story with a first love that he rediscovers after soldiering with Stonewall Jackson. *The Watchman* evolves around a prison (which was, indeed, in our home town, Moundsville—which he renamed 'Glory' for his later books). *Time* said, 'The latest of the author's marrow-chilling tales of good and evil—a mixture of poetic rage against cruelty in man, a song in praise of physi-

cal love, a cry of despair at the blows dealt to the innocent young.'

"*The Voices of Glory* recorded the voices of nearly thirty people—the men, women, and children living in the twenties in the West Virginia river town called 'Glory.' One character, a public health nurse, is the thread that ties all the stories together. She, too, was based on a real nurse. Orville Prescott wrote in the *New York Times*: 'Davis Grubb's *The Voices of Glory* is an overwhelming novel. It overwhelms with torrential eloquence, with tempestuous emotion, with drama and melodrama and pathos. There hasn't been anything like *Voices of Glory* ever—although some may be reminded of the poems in Edgar Lee Masters' *Spoon River Anthology* and others may be reminded of a play, Thornton Wilder's *Our Town*. But those works were efforts to distill in a brief space the essence of human experience. His almost Dickensian quality does not make the people of Glory any the less striking as individuals or their stories any the less dramatic. He is a born storyteller.' *Twelve Tales of Suspense and the Supernatural* were the 'cream,' up until 1964 at least. Dave always wrote with the camera in mind so it is not surprising three of these stories were seen on television. *A Tree Full of Stars* (1965) is a Christmas story, based on a family, again from Moundsville, that kept their Christmas tree lit all year. Strangely, this enraged some people in town. The family was finally forced to leave.

Shadow of My Brother is the story of a young boy brutally murdered in a southern town while five people watch. The author goes back three generations of the Wilson family to build a narrative of terror and evil. Lillian Smith considered it an 'extraordinarily interesting book. One of the best novels ever written on the mind-in-depth of a white racist. Davis Grubb knows the evil and sweetness in the human heart as few writers understand it.' *The Golden Sickle* (1968) is set in post-revolutionary Virginia. The old inn where much of the action takes place was actually run by members of our family and Dave played there as a child. Dave loved the books about pirates by Howard Pyle, and in this story he tells of Ohio River pirates. *Fools' Parade* has for its main character, a convicted murderer, who has served forty-seven years in Glory Prison and earned $25,452.32, saving his meager earnings in the prisoners' 'Work and Hope Savings Plan' at the local bank. The plot revolves around the problems of cashing the check. The story takes place in 1935. James Stewart and George Kennedy made a wonderful film from this book, filming it in Moundsville, West Virginia. Dave went back for the filming and took his dear friend—a Lhasa Apso dog named 'Rowdy Charly.' *The Barefoot Man* is about miners, their women, strike breakers and a character based on Mother Jones. It was said that 'Grubb's new novel is perhaps the most searing and convincing work to come out of the American agony in the thirties since Steinbeck's *The Grapes of Wrath.*

"*Ancient Lights* was Dave's last novel and, in his opinion, his finest. Actual work began in Moundsville where he was working on a grant from the West Virginia Arts and Humanities Foundation. I was asked by friends, before the book was released, 'What is it about?' I found it impossible to describe it in a few words. First, it is his biggest book—540 wonderful pages filled with so many people and places. Let me quote: Stephen King said, ' I found *Ancient Lights* exhilarating, hilarious, amazing—and sometimes shocking, with it image of Christ as a happy-go-lucky bumpkin from Weirton, West Virginia. It's an authentic by-golly-damn tour de force. Grubb, like Heller in *Catch 22,* is inventive, clear, and full of a febrile imagination. His language throws off sparks; it coruscates. I absolutely loved it and envy the people who will read it.' The *Chicago Tribune* called it 'a river of a book, powerful, brilliant in its moments of religious light and insight,' and a reviewer in the *New York Times* wrote '*Ancient Lights* is the kind of book you put down again and again, think about for a while and then resume reading in pursuit of the author's manic vision.'

"Dave died on the eve of his sixty-first birthday, six weeks after delivering the manuscript to Viking. He is buried on a hill with the people he wrote about so well. The hill overlooks the Ohio River and Moundsville, or 'Glory' as he would say."

PRINCIPAL WORKS: *Novels*—The Night of the Hunter, 1953; A Dream of Kings, 1955; The Watchman, 1961; The Voices of Glory, 1962; A Tree Full of Stars, 1965; Shadow of My Brother, 1966; The Golden Sickle, 1968; Fools' Parade, 1969; The Barefoot Man, 1971; Ancient Lights, 1982. *Short stories*—Twelve Tales of Suspense and the Supernatural, 1964; The Siege of 318, 1979.

ABOUT: Contemporary Authors, new revision series 4, 1981. *Periodicals*—New York Times July 25, 1980.

*GUSTAFSSON, LARS (May 17, 1936–   ), Swedish poet, novelist, playwright, and critic, was born in Västerås, the son of Einar and Margareta Gustafsson. In 1958, after graduating from the Västerås *gymnasium* and doing his military service, Gustafsson began studying philosophy at Uppsala University. After he received his *filosophie licentiat* degree in 1961, Gustafsson became an editor for the literary periodical

LARS GUSTAFSSON

Bonniers Litterära Magasin in Stockholm. In 1966, Gustafsson became chief editor, a post which he resigned in 1972. He received a doctorate in philosophy from Uppsala University in 1978 and published his dissertation on language in the nineteenth century, *Språk och lögn* (Language and Lies), the same year. *Filosofier* (Philosophies, 1979) is a more popularly written investigation of similar problems.

Gustafsson is a world traveler, something which is reflected not only in such non-fiction books as *Kinesisk höst* (Chinese Autumn, 1978) and *Afrikanskt försök* (African Attempt, 1980) but also in his novels and poetry. Three of the five novels in what he calls a "novel system," *Sprickorna i muren* (Cracks in the Wall), have American and German settings, and Gustafsson's recent fiction, the short story collection *Berättelser om lyckliga människor* (Stories of Happy People, 1981) and the novel *Sorgemusik för frimurare* (Dirge for Freemasons, 1983) have settings that reflect both his travels and his frequent periods of residence in Germany and the United States. (In 1979 he was visiting professor at the University of Texas.)

Gustafsson's international orientation has not caused him to lose touch with his native country. He contributes regularly to the Stockholm daily *Svenska Dagbladet* on topics of literary and cultural interest, and has published several studies of modern society, including one on which he collaborated with John Myrdal, *Den onödiga samtiden* (The Unnecessary Present, 1974). His 1984 volume of poetry, *Fåglarna* (The Birds), includes as many poems on local Swedish flora and fauna as did his first collection, *Ballongfararna*

°gōos täv son, lärs

(The Balloonists, 1962). Although Gustafsson started publishing as a novelist, it was his early poetry which first brought him critical recognition. In his book-length poem *Kärleksfärklaring till en sefardisk dam* (1970; translated in his *Selected Poems* as "Declaration of Love to a Sephardic Lady"), Gustafsson emerges as a fully mature, important poet who controls all aspects of his craft. The poem contains sections of great lyrical beauty, a trait of Gustafsson's poetry which can be illustrated by a quotation from the poem "Song of the Depth of the World, the Depth of the Eye, and the Brevity of Life":

. . . Like ancient signs,
wonted constellations appear in the sky,
the November wind moves among the brittle
  stalks of reeds that move
with a drying sound. Across the western sky
a falling angel's tracks show like a text.
                    —trans. Yvonne L. Sandstroem

The poem appears in *Artesiska brunnar cartesiska drömmar* (Artesian Wells Cartesian Dreams, 1980), Gustafsson's most impressive and unified volume of poetry. In spite of his background in philosophy—frequently remarked on by literary critics—Gustafsson states (in the foreword to his collected poems, 1982) that not until the 1980 collection did he actually write "philosophy in poetic form." The ending of "Elegy for a Dead Labrador" illustrates this element in Gustafsson's poetry.

One might say, from this more objective
standpoint, we were two organisms.
Two of those places where the universe makes a knot
in itself, short-lived, complex structures
of proteins that have to complicate themselves
more and more in order to survive, until everything
breaks and turns simple once more, the knot
dissolved, the riddle gone. You were a question
asked of another question, nothing more,
and neither had the answer to the other.
                    —trans. Yvonne L. Sandstroem

Gustafsson also published two plays (in 1970), one of which, *Den nattliga hyllningen* (Homage at Night), has been performed not only in Sweden but in Switzerland and in Germany, where it was particularly well received. The play is based on an incident which took place in the author's hometown, Västerås, in 1824. As Gustafsson explains, it is "a play about power. It could not have been written without the events of the '60s and one must consider it against the complete change in the aspects of power which have influenced the mentality of an entire generation. . . ." An unpublished play (performed on Swedish and West German radio in 1973), *Huset i Oneida* (The House in Oneida) employs an American setting once again to examine the problem of power.

Gustafsson's best-known work, the five-

volume "novel system," *Sprickorna i muren* (Cracks in the Wall, 1971–78), is also concerned with power, mainly, as in *Den nattliga hyllningen*, with political power. The first autobiographical novel, *Herr Gustafsson själv* (Mr. Gustafsson Himself, 1971), plays against the background of what Gustafsson considers the corrupt and repressive politics of late 1960s Europe; *Yllet* (Wool, 1973) deals mainly with deteriorating social conditions in the Swedish countryside while *Familjefesten* (The Family Party, 1975) is set among the powerful, the policy makers; the more universal theme of *Sigismund* (1976) is, in Gustafsson's words, "the collective unconscious of our times, its dreams and nightmares." The last volume in the "system," *En Biodlares död* (1978; English translation, *Death of a Beekeeper*, 1981), considered Gustafsson's best novel, focuses on a single individual, a middle-aged retired school teacher who is dying of cancer and who experiences unconventional visions of Paradise during his last days. All of the novels deal with the plight of the European intellectual in a period when what Gustafsson calls "official lies" have created a wall which blocks both sight and communication. As the novel system progresses, the winds of change start to blow and the "cracks in the wall" begin to appear.

Gustafsson's productivity and versatility are both impressive, but it is finally the quality of his work that counts. During the last decade, he has established himself as one of the most important and accomplished European writers, both of fiction and poetry, in his generation.

WORKS IN ENGLISH TRANSLATION: Gustafsson's *Selected Poems*, in Robin Fulton's translation, was published in 1972; Yvonne L. Sandstroem translated his *Varma rum och kalla* as *Warm Rooms and Cold* in 1975; and Robert T. Rovinsky collected his poems in *Forays into Swedish Poetry: Lars Gustafsson*, 1977. Translations of individual poems have appeared in the *New Yorker*, August 24, 1982, and *New Directions* 46, 1983. Seven of his poems are published in *Modern Swedish Poetry in Translation*, edited by G. Harding and A. Hollo, 1979. Translations of Gustafsson's prose include his novels *Death of a Beekeeper* by J.K. Swaffar and G. Weber, 1981; a novella, *The Tennis Players* (*Tennisspelarna*, 1977) translated by Yvonne L. Sandstroem; and *Sigismund*, translated by John Weistock and scheduled for publication in 1985. Shorter works appear in *Fiction* 2, 1973, and *Modern Swedish Prose in Translation*, ed. K. E. Lagerlöf, 1979.

ABOUT: Columbia Dictionary of Modern European Literature, 1980; Contemporary Authors 85–88, 1980; Encyclopedia of World Literature in the 20th Century (rev. ed.) II, 1982; Rossel, S. H. History of Scandinavian Literature 1870–1980, 1982; Rovinsky, R. T. Introduction to Forays into Swedish Poetry, 1977. Periodicals—Scandinavian Studies 44, 1972.

*GYLLENSTEN, LARS (November 12, 1921–), Swedish novelist and essayist, writes: "I was born in Stockholm and have lived in Stockholm all my life. My father was a merchant (director of a large machine company); my mother is a sister of a famous Swedish composer (Ture Rangström, died in 1947). I believe that I have a sympathy for matters of fact and logical thinking from my father and an inclination for arts and fantasy from my mother. I have three younger sisters. I was married in 1946 to Inga-Lisa Hultén, whom I met during my studies of medicine (she is a doctor, neurologist), and we have one daughter, Katarina, who has also become a doctor.

"In my late teens I 'discovered,' like many youngsters in their puberty age, that human life is doomed to death, that most of us have to suffer before we die, that our fates only to a very small and futile degree are in our own control, that we are a prey to illusions, prejudices, cruelty, and ephemeral ambitions, that we ourselves contribute to such evil and wicked self-destructions, sometimes or perhaps most often when we imagine that we are working to realize the highest ideals and to further the welfare of ourselves and our fellow creatures . . . and so on. The Nazi era offered illustrative confirmations—and what followed after, and after. My reactions and attitudes have remained the same ever since—perhaps I have not been cured from puberty, and I fear (and hope) that I never will be. I became an existentialist long before I ever got to know that word.

"My favorite subjects in school were natural sciences—and Swedish. My early readings, when I started to read other things than for pure fun, were philosophy—and my first philosopher, who really fascinated me, was Arthur Schopenhauer. I continued with other Kantian and post-Kantian philosophers, including Nietzsche—and my thinking in matters of epistemology and poetics has been formed in Kantian terms. More modern thinkers, who have influenced me, include Poincaré, Russell, Bohr, Wittgenstein, Popper, and other, more or less Kantian-stained, philosophers committed to the problems of the bases of natural science—theory of science. An important 'discovery,' which I made in the early fifties, was Charles Sanders Peirce. I have been very much stimulated by his theory of knowledge, his 'infinite inquiry' and pragmatism.

"Besides such philosophers as those mentioned above I 'discovered' Sören Kierkegaard at about the same time in my spiritual development. His artistic qualities, his pathetical commitment to 'pubertal' or existential conflicts and themes, the dialectical tensions and paradoxes inherent in his thinking and writings, and, not the least, his lit-

LARS GYLLENSTEN

erary method stimulated me and has continued to stimulate me intensely. I found in his pseudonymic approach, his 'indirect communication,' his experimental use of different inherent writers to explore different 'life attitudes' or 'stages of life' something which in my view corresponded to the method of natural sciences, the model thinking, and which could be used also for a non-Christian writer (like myself) in his strivings to wrestle with the ambiguities of life and the inescapable dilemma of illusion and reality. We live in our own pictures of reality, but behind our own pictures hides a most real reality, more a-human than human, and there is no other way for us to get in touch with that hidden reality than our own illusions, figments, and (verbal) icons.

"All my books could have been written under pseudonym—the 'heroes' of my books are the inherent writers, which explore their life attitudes by means of the verbal projections, the verbal icons, the books they write. I myself am a kind of meta-writer, a super-writer, behind the individual books—but I am involved in the books through the fact that each book, each 'implied writer' *could* be I, could really be I myself. My own life is a vehicle for these 'implied writers'; these could-be-myselves and their life attitudes could be mine.

"After school I wanted to become a writer—but I realized that I ought to have a 'real' profession, in order to have a social relationship and not remain in some sort of ivory tower, in order to secure a living without dependence on the commercial possibilities of my writing, in order not to be obliged to write when I had nothing to say. And I was also attracted by natural science, but I had difficulties in choosing the subject, so I started to study medicine, which I regarded as the best broad-field topic of natural science. I was very fortunate that I could choose like this—most young people never can. My medical studies started in 1940, at the Karolinska Institute, the medical high school of Stockholm. I became involved in basic research—histology, embryology. My scientific researches have concentrated on developmental problems—the production of lymphocytes (immune competent cells) and the control of the growth of the lymphatic system, the postnatal development of the visual system and its dependence on functional stimulation, the cause of 'retrolental fibroplasia' (an eye disease in premature children, most often with complete blindness as final result—a colleague of mine and I could demonstrate that this disease is caused by oxygen poisoning, in our experimental studies on mice), etc. I published my doctor's thesis in 1953, became an assistant professor at the Karolinska Institute in 1953, associate professor in 1955, and left my position as a professor of histology in 1973. Since then I have been only a writer and, from 1977 on, permanent secretary of the Swedish Academy (member of the Academy in 1966).

"My first published book, in 1946, was a fake—a collection of poetry, written in four to five hours together with a friend of mine, without any serious ambition, a pastiche of incomprehensible modernistic poetry. The collection was published under pseudonym, as if it was a serious work of a modernistic young poet. After a couple of months we announced that there were no serious ambitions behind the poems, that they had been written haphazardly in order to ridicule jargon in poetry. Our declaration caused great alarm, and perhaps not altogether to our satisfaction.

"My first serious book was published in 1949, and after that I published twenty-two books, most of them novels, some collections of articles and essays, some of prose poetry.

"My first book (*Moderna myter*—Modern Myths) was a collection of aphorisms, poems, prose poetry, short stories—intended to demonstrate the life view of 'bankruptcy of the naïveté'—lack of faith in anything. The second book, *Det blå skeppet* (The Blue Ship, 1950), had the purpose of exploring the literary fantasies of someone who tried to picture and praise a contrasting attitude: confidence, playfulness, trust in providence or fate, etc. The book is a mosaic of fantastic stories and anecdotes, experienced by a little boy who lives with his beloved and rather adventurous mother on a steamship in the archipelago outside Stockholm. The third book *Barnabok* (Child Book, 1952) is a novel about a desperate man involved in a love story with two women—one representing ordinary, trivial, bourgeois life, the other passion, suffering, and surrendering. The story is told in an expressive style, with naive, infantile, grotesque, fragmented passages, intended to mirror the conflicts and destructiveness of the 'hero.' Later books include a novel about a similarly desperate politician in a fictive totalitarian state, perhaps in the eastern part of Europe, *Senatorn* (The Senator, 1958); a retelling of the death of Socrates, from the point of view of his family, especially his wife and daughter, *Sokrates död* (1960), an anti-heroic philosophy as contrasted with the heroism of Socrates; *Senilia* (1956), with Ahasueros as never-mentioned sub-hero, a man trying to 'disarm the suffering' (horror of death, bad conscience, jealousy etc.) by means of a philosophy according to which nothing is new on earth, everything is the repetition of the same thing which has occurred before, and he tries to feel and perceive like an old man. In later books I have tried to explore the possibilities of a Swedenborgian and/ or Leibnizian philosophy, according to which man as microcosm corresponds with the world as macroanthropos—*Diarium spirituale* (1968), *Palatset i parken* (The Palace in the Park, 1970), *Baklängesminnen* (Backwards Memories, 1978—a man is telling his life story, beginning with watching his own funeral, ending with his own birth). In *I skuggan av Don Juan* (In the Shade of Don Juan, 1975) I have told a story of Don Juan from the point of view of his servant Leporello, an anti-heroic story. In *Grottan i öknen* (The Cave in the Desert, 1973) St. Anthony is the 'hero'—the ancient one and a modern reincarnation of him—and the philosophy has something to do with a life cycle of death and rebirth (asceticism, self-destruction, acedia, exile—and recreation, new faith and trust, vita nuova).

"My books are 'verbal icons.' I try to find consolation and experiences, to praise life, and to find reasons to praise life in spite of everything that seems to say that our life is a cruel, fugitive, illusory, tragicomical, serious-ridiculous exile. They are a combination of play, provocation, philosophy, prayer . . . an 'infinite inquiry.' I could say more about them but everything I say about them must be insufficient and unjust, because if I could tell what they are and explain their meaning I could have abstained from writing them."

———

Since only one of his major works is available

in English, Lars Gyllensten is all but unread in the United States and Great Britain. Yet he is a truly international figure, and both as author and as permanent Secretary of the Swedish Academy (which selects Nobel prizewinners in literature), he is influential on the world scene. Certainly he is one of the best and most widely educated of living writers—a humanist in the true Renaissance sense combining the talents of scientist, philosopher, and creative artist. Although some of his critics have speculated on the oddity of his switching in midlife from a brilliant career in science and medicine to literature, he had in fact no gap to bridge, having since his youth been engaged in what Leif Sjöberg calls "a continuous dialectical inquiry" between the reality of the universe as science knows it and the illusion of reality that literature creates. A passage in his *Testament of Cain*—his only book in English translation and one of his most original and imaginative—confirms his dedication to science even as it acknowledges the illusory nature of life: "In this world of shadows all mysteries are market juggling, for the truth is but hearsay. She must be sought in the pieces that remain when men's superficial pictures of her have been crushed. But the labour that is devoted to mitigating pain and bereaving perdition of its terrors is no illusion, for suffering is no superficial picture and perdition is the goal of all things."

The Testament of Cain is a short but complex and subtle philosophical novel which Gyllensten describes as a kind of "collage," consisting of heterogeneous fragments of alleged historical records and memoirs put together by a narrator who himself undergoes several incarnations in the course of the book. What emerges is, in Hans Isaksson's words, "a witty illustration of the relativity of truth in the form of an account of the Cainites, a sect whose belief in truth is only to be glimpsed through the destruction of petrified creeds." Cain's murder of Abel, which occurs at the end of the book, is the act of ultimate iconoclasm, for Abel is represented as a savage idol-worshipper. It is a challenging, disturbing, profoundly serious book, yet written with a tongue-in-cheek pedantry and detachment that actually heighten its dramatic power. On the whole Gyllensten's novels are somber, his characters haunted by despair and mocked by the ironies of fate, torn between their instinct for struggle and survival and the temptations of surrender. Yet this dialectic, as Isaksson writes, works towards a synthesis: "In the end the tension between surrender and distance goes together with the rhythm from spiritual death and destruction to new life and creation."

WORKS IN ENGLISH TRANSLATION: Keith Bradfield translated *The Testament of Cain* (Kains memoarer, 1963) in 1967. A short selection from other writing by Gyllensten is in K. Lagerlöf's *Modern Swedish Prose in Translation,* 1979. The best English-language introduction to Gyllensten's work is Hans Isaksson's book (listed below) in the Twayne World Authors Series.

ABOUT: Cassell's Encyclopedia of World Literature 2, 1973; Columbia Dictionary of Modern European Literature, 1980; Isaksson, H. Lars Gyllensten (tr. K. Lissbrant), 1978; Rossel, S. H. A History of Scandinavian Literature, 1870–1980 (tr. A. C. Ulmer), 1982. *Periodicals*—American-Scandinavian Review February 1967; World Literature Today Winter 1979; Spring 1981.

HACKER, MARILYN (November 27, 1942–   ), American poet, was born in New York City to Albert Abraham and Hilda (Rosengarten) Hacker, children of Jewish immigrants. Her parents met at City College where both were evening students, taking graduate courses in the sciences. Her mother taught elementary school, and her father worked irregularly in a variety of industrial jobs: "Their vicissitudes were the emotional backdrop of my childhood, while my mother's steady civil servitude paid the bills," Marilyn Hacker recalls. "We lived in three rooms in the middle Bronx; I slept on a folding cot in my parents' bedroom till I was eight, then in the living-room. I'd learned to read when I was three, in spite of terrible vision, corrected with thick glasses two years later." Just before her fifth birthday, she started kindergarten and continued in the New York City public schools. Her high school was the Bronx High School of Science, which she left at age fifteen in order to attend New York University.

Hacker remembers writing poetry at age five: rhymed quatrains dictated to her mother, and she continued writing all through school. Her parents owned books—Modern Library editions—and she read Jack London, Plato, Cellini, Dostoevsky, Dickens, Nietzsche, and Twain. She began to read poetry at age twelve, "thanks to the public library and a dedicated librarian who fed me Hardy, Thomas, cummings, Millay, Eliot. Poetry was only minimally taught in that otherwise academically-intensive high school. But I shared my tastes with equally impassioned friends. We passed just-published *Howl* under the desks; we mythologized Chatterton, Rimbaud, and Keats, we communicated our discoveries in voluminous letters, all-night phone-calls, our own poems."

At eighteen, having completed three years of study at NYU, she married her closest friend,

© 1982 Layle Silbert

MARILYN HACKER

Samuel R. Delany, on August 22, 1961. "He was a brilliant novelist, black, and gay. I graduated two-and-a-half years later, with a major in Romance Languages, and a year as a paperback editor and one at art school [the Art Students League] to my credit. The marriage lasted, on the books, eighteen years [they divorced in 1980] though we never lived together more than two years at a time." Her daughter, Iva Alyxander, was born in London in 1974, and her first book, *Presentation Piece,* was published in the same year.

Presentation Piece was the winner of the 1975 National Book Award and was chosen as the 1973 Lamont Poetry Selection. Using traditional forms (villanelle, sestina, sonnet), Hacker frequently deals with social injustice, sometimes drawing upon historical events to illustrate modern parallels. Peter Meinke, in the *New Republic,* complimented her work: "I suppose it is still fashionable to think that intellect and wit are somehow incompatible with deeply felt poetry—one can't be romantic and ironic at the same time—but *Presentation Piece* encourages me to think that the fashion may be changing." Less impressed with the book was Norma Procopiow, in *Book World,* who found the poet "recondite" and complained that "the poems seem created, not with urgency or commitment, but to display craftsmanship. Yet, it is the craftsmanship which distorts. Hacker's world of sexual liberation sounds somewhat ludicrous propped by seventeenth-century verse forms." Characteristic of the poems in *Presentation Piece* is the feminist sonnet "Apologia pro opere suo," that begins:

It appears that almost all the poets who slighted
the theme of Unrequited Love to say
how more of the land than That Boy or That Lady lay
were poets whom somebody had, in fact, requited.

Of her next work, *Separations,* one reviewer, Hayden Carruth in the *New York Times Book Review,* suggested that perhaps she had been advised to leave out of her first book poems she felt confident enough to publish in the second volume: "Dull poems, too long, and some damnably obscure. It is obscurity of both kinds: the kind that comes from reticence about private affairs (in which case why publish at all?) and the kind that comes from insufficient thought (in which case why not wait till the materials become clearer?). One can't help thinking another year or two between books would have been a good idea." In the same review, however, Carruth says that these poems are in the minority, that her technical skill combined with her "thematic adultness and intelligence, her compelling poems of lust, anger and grief, her sense of experience truly lived, and you have a formidable poet to contend with. *Separations* is the work of a woman whose body and mind are functioning at high intensity, perfectly coordinated."

Taking Notice, like *Separations,* received mixed responses. Stanley Plumly noted that this work "constitutes the last volume in a trilogy. Her concerns are basically the same—esthetic and sexual confrontation. . . . The first book is an introduction to and exploration of relationships, friendly and familial; the second centers on the difficulty and eventual disintegration of a long-distance marriage. This third book, a taking and nailing-up of notice, begins with 'one man, not some indifferent Muse to me' and ends with 'the woman I love, as old, as new to me/ as any moment of delight.'"

Hacker's poems deal with pain, absences, and injustice; she often seems to use her poetry as a way of licking her wounds, simultaneously healing and reopening them. *Taking Notice* extends her own wounds to the world of women as she explores relationships with other women: mother, lover, daughter, friends. This application of the personal to the universal often deprives her poetry of emotional appeal. When she does become personal, as in the opening poem of *Taking Notice,* entitled "Feeling and Form," the effect is touching:

Write
about anything—I wish I could. It's like
the still-lives you love: you don't have to like
apples to like Cezanne. I do like words,
which is why I make things out of words
and listen to their hints, resounding like
skipping-stones radiating circles, drawing context from text, the way I've watched you draw
a pepper shaker on a table, draw

it again, once more, until it isn't like
anything but your idea of a drawing, like an idea of movement, drawing its shape from sequence. . . .

Included in this volume are poems about her
daughter, Iva, which relieve the somber mood
and according to Suzanne Juhasz, in *Library
Journal,* bring out "Hacker's gaiety, as well as
her anger, frustration and deep love."

Hacker is not an easy or accessible poet. Her
vocabulary and references are often arcane and
her lines do not have an easy flow or musicality.
A self-proclaimed radical feminist and lesbian,
she has a vigorous commitment to her work and
the human causes she embraces. In addition to
the writing of her poetry, Hacker has worked as
an antiquarian bookseller, a translator, post-
office clerk, textbook writer, employment counselor, and teacher of English to Cantonese-
speaking children. She and her ex-husband
founded and co-edited *Quark, a Quarterly of
Speculative Fiction* from 1969–71, and she has
been guest editor for *Woman Poet: The East*
published by Women-in-Literature, Inc. in
Reno, Nevada. Her most recent editorship is of
13th Moon, a feminist literary magazine. Among
other honors she has had a National Endowment
for the Arts grant (1973–74), a Guggenheim fellowship (1980–81), and an Ingram-Merrill
Foundation fellowship (1984–85). Hacker participates in poetry readings and teaches writing
at Columbia University's School of General
Studies. She makes her home in New York City
with her daughter.

PRINCIPAL WORKS: Presentation Piece, 1974; Separations,
1976; Taking Notice, 1980.

ABOUT: Contemporary Authors 77–80, 1979; Magill,
F. N. (ed.) Critical Survey of Poetry 3, 1982; Miniero,
L. (ed.) American Women Writers 2, 1980; Vinson, J.
(ed.) Contemporary Poets, 1980. *Periodicals*—American Poetry Review July–August 1981;
Book World May 26, 1974; November 2, 1980; Frontiers 5, Fall 1980; Library Journal August 1980; New
York Times Book Review August 8, 1976; October 12,
1980; Poetry July 1981.

HAINES, JOHN (MEADE) (June 29,
1924–), American poet and essayist, writes: "I
was born in Norfolk, Virginia where my father
was stationed as an officer at the Naval Training
Station. I have one or two pretty clear memories
of this time: of being on the beach with my
mother at about age sixteen months while waiting for my father to come off duty and join us.
I can recall sitting on a blanket spread on the
sand near some rocks, and having a large tin

JOHN HAINES

cracker can to play with. A photograph taken on
that or a similar occasion supports the recollection.

"Somewhat later—but when?—I remember
being carried on my father's shoulders down the
small round hatch of a submarine, and being allowed to look through the periscope. At age two,
what could I have seen? The space inside the
submarine was small, tight, gleaming, oily and
rather mysterious. I think I was not comfortable
in it.

"The family left Norfolk rather soon thereafter, and the next several years were a succession
of moves: to Vallejo, California where my brother was born in 1926; then back east to New London, Connecticut. This migratory life continued
into the 1930s with three and six-month tours at
Long Beach, California; Bremerton, Washington; Honolulu; San Diego; and with two longer
stays in the east, at Washington, D.C. Three autobiographical sketches in my book of essays,
Living Off the Country, deal with these years in
some detail.

"The perpetual restlessness of this childhood
left a lasting mark on my character. The effect
was not wholly negative; nonetheless it carried
with it a good deal of insecurity, the meaning of
which was largely concealed to me until many
years later when I realized that my relations
with people and places were apt to have about
them an all too temporary aspect, as if it were
taken for granted that none of them would last.

"Much could be written about my teens, the
years on the brink of another war (between two
wars), my own three years in the Navy during
World War II, and my subsequent efforts to take

up a career as an artist. In 1946, at age twenty-two, I was still unformed, and undecided. My long-suppressed desire to be at home somewhere finally surfaced a year after the war when an opportunity arose to go to Alaska. This was one of those events in life that, spur-of-the-moment as in my own case it seemed, have about them a kind of absolute certainty; everything else was determined from then on, and all events up to that time found their needed meaning.

"I do not have sufficient space to tell that story adequately here. Any interested reader can follow it for himself in my essays and poems published at intervals during the past twenty years.

"Following my first stay in Alaska, I returned to art school for a while in the early 1950s, but life seemed to me by then pretty well determined by the place I had mapped out for myself at Richardson, seventy miles southeast of Fairbanks. I began writing poetry seriously during my first winter here, and the writing has been fairly continuous since then.

"I came to poetry fairly late, to maturity as a writer later still when compared to many of my contemporaries. My teachers and mentors were the poets best known writing in the modernist mode: Eliot, Pound, Williams, Yeats to mention only the most prominent. Many other poets in languages besides English also contributed to what growth I have been capable of. But I had as teachers also unlettered men: trappers, hunters, rivermen, prospectors and local tellers of tales. These were the old people of a frontier now gone. I have in a sense survived them, with their histories intact. The Alaska I knew and loved has changed considerably in recent years and in ways that I do not always feel comfortable with. But the land still speaks to me, and it is to that as well as to its true citizens that I have mostly listened.

"Through the 1970s I was much of the time absent from Alaska, living and teaching in California, Montana, Seattle and in England. I returned to Alaska in 1980 to write and to observe the fate of this country to which I have given the attention of thirty-five years.

"I have never sought to live a 'remarkable life.' Although it may appear that my life has in some ways been unusual, to me it has seemed for the most part simply a life—difficult, often solitary and lived 'on the edge,' but uncommonly rich also. It has occurred to me at times that I may have tried to live the poetry as well as write it. I am none too certain about these things, but it does seem to me that life at its completest might be 'lived poetry,' and not be merely a source material for the books we write."

———

John Haines is the son of John Meade Haines and the former Helen M. Donaldson. His formal education as a painter was begun after he left the Navy in 1946. He attended the National Art School (1946–47), American University (1948–49), and the Hans Hoffmann School of Fine Art (1950–52).

Karen Sollid, in a preface to *North by West* (1975), a joint retrospective collection of some of Haines' poems with those by William Stafford, wrote that "he originally went to Alaska while he still thought of himself as a visual artist; after living on his homestead for a while, he turned to poetry as a way of expressing the images which became part of his daily life." Haines wrote in 1981 that he had for three decades "thought of my writing as having its primary roots in the soil of Alaska," adding, "The effort in the writing could be broadly described as one person's attempt to identify a particular place, and to define himself in relation to that place—to understand, finally, what *residence* really means."

"Narrative in nature, yet lyrical in feeling" is one critic's characterization of the poems in *Winter News,* an "accurate description of the real and metaphysical life in an immense, quiet land." G. D. McDonald wrote of them as giving "a feeling of new discovery, such as we had when poets first wrote of flying in high altitudes above the clouds." Many of Haines' most familiar motifs—animal life, coldness, and death—first occur in these poems.

I am haunted by
the deaths of animals.

Their frozen, moonlit eyes
stare into the hollow
of my skull; they listen
as though I had
something to tell them
    (from "On the Divide")

The loneliness of life in the vast wilderness is everywhere expressed, always in a restrained, almost elegiac tone:

The immense sadness
of approaching winter
hangs in the air
this cloudy September. . . .

Our berries picked,
the mushrooms gathered,
each of us hides
in his heart a small piece
of this summer,
as mice store their roots
in a place
known only to them.
    (from "Poem")

In *The Stone Harp*, containing poems written during the social turmoil caused by the Vietnam

War, politics appears overtly in Haines' poems for the first time. President Johnson is the thinly veiled subject of "Lies":

The Man from Texas
is a coarse and wrinkled spider;
he spins tales
to children of all ages. . . .

Each time he pulls at a thread
one of his listeners dies.

And in "A Poem Like a Grenade" there is the voice of the authentic revolutionary wielding a new weapon:

It is made to be rolled down
a flight of stairs,
placed under a guilty hat,
or casually dropped into a basket
among the desks
of the wrongheaded statesman. . . .

Its wastepaper soil catches fire,
the hat is blown from its hook.
Five or six faces are suddenly,
permanently changed . . .

Lawrence Raab, reviewing this book, was among the earliest critics to notice one of Haines' most salient virtues, his "effortless and almost transparent style. The best poems are like small streams into which the words fall, like stones, gathering color and revealing their markings as water passes over them." His quiet lyricism has changed little over the years. William Stafford described it in a review of *News from the Glacier: Selected Poems 1960–80*: "Typically the poems drift down the page in free-falling, three-beat lines that play accompaniment to one another with recurrent gritty words."

Concern for the American ecology dominates the collection *Cicada*, which Hayden Carruth called "the mature work of one of our best nature poets, or for that matter one of our best nature writers of any kind, best because he is so much more than a naturalist. Haines knows the ecological crisis as well as anyone, and he knows it is . . . a crisis of consciousness, the human mind in ultimate confrontation with itself." *Cicada* also contains some of his finest political poems, including a moving lament for the lost hopes of the 1960s:

Our hunted names spoken with care
by the few strange youths
who remember,

history for us becomes
the dark side of a mountain,
as the great cloud-utopias
burn out in the west.
     (from "Dusk of the Revolutionaries")

Haines was twice married, to Jo Ella Hussey (in 1960) and to Jane McWhorter (in 1970), and has four children. His major collections have been published by Wesleyan University Press, and individual poems have appeared in numerous reviews and little magazines, notably *Hudson Review, Kayak, San Francisco Review, Chicago Choice, Critic, Ironwood, Stinktree,* and *Cutbank.* Among the honors accorded him were a Guggenheim fellowship (1965–66), a grant from the National Endowment for the Humanities (1967–68), the Amy Lowell scholarship (1976–77), and in 1982 an award by the governor of Alaska for excellence in the literary arts.

PRINCIPAL WORKS: *Poetry*—Winter News, 1966; Twenty Poems, 1971; The Stone Harp, 1971; Leaves and Ashes, 1974; North by West, 1975; In Five Years' Time, 1976; Cicada, 1977; In a Dusty Light, 1977; News from the Glacier, 1982. *Nonfiction*—Living off the Country, 1981; Of Traps and Snares, 1981; Other Days, 1982.

ABOUT: Contemporary Authors 17–20, 1976; Contemporary Poets, 1975; Haines, J. Living Off the Country, 1981. *Periodicals*—American Scholar Summer 1971; Bookweek November 13, 1966; Harper's August 1966; June 1978; Library Journal March 15, 1966; February 15, 1971; August 1977; Nation March 27, 1967; Parnassus Winter 1972–73; Poetry November 1966; May 1972; Seneca Review April 1971; Stinktree November 1972; Virginia Quarterly Review Summer 1966; Summer 1972.

HALEY, ALEX (PALMER) (August 11, 1921–), American biographer, scriptwriter, and popularizer of American black history, was born in Ithaca, New York, to Bertha (Palmer) Haley and Simon Alexander Haley, an agriculture teacher. When Haley was an infant his mother took him to live at her parents' home in the small town of Henning, Tennessee; his father joined them soon after taking his degree from Cornell and later assumed control of his father-in-law's lumber business. Haley, who led a happy rural childhood in Henning, developed a close relationship with his maternal grandmother, Cynthia (Murray) Palmer. Every summer, as he has often related, the Murray sisters and cousins would gather in Henning and discuss the family genealogy, which began, according to Cynthia, with Haley's great-great-great-great-grandfather, an African who was brought by slave-ship to "Naplis" (Annapolis) and sold to a plantation master in Spotsylvania County, Virginia. The African, named "Kin-tay," told his daughter Kizzy something of his life before his capture and taught her a number of his native words, most of which began with a "k" sound. She in turn passed this information on to later generations. The young Haley, "scrunched down, listening, behind Grandma's squeaky chair," was deeply affected by these stories.

ALEX HALEY

In 1929 Haley's father sold the lumberyard and took up college teaching, moving through the South from one black agricultural college to the next. At the age of seventeen, after two years of teachers' college, Haley enlisted in the Coast Guard. He worked his way up from mess boy to cook during World War II. At night and on weekends Haley read constantly, mostly sea tales, to stave off the boredom of shipboard life. He began to write adventure stories himself, basing them on real incidents in naval records. (In so doing he acquired research skills that stood him in good stead later while laying the groundwork for *Roots.*) After eight years of submissions, his first story was accepted for publication. In 1949 the Coast Guard created a new rating for him—Chief Journalist.

After two decades of service, Haley left the Coast Guard in 1959 to become a full-time freelance magazine writer. In his struggling early years he lived hand-to-mouth in a Greenwich Village basement. Around 1960 *Reader's Digest* began giving him regular biographical assignments; then, in 1962, a conversation with the jazz trumpeter Miles Davis was turned by Haley into the first of the now-famous *Playboy* interviews. Haley's first book, *The Autobiography of Malcolm X*, grew out of another *Playboy* interview. Malcolm X, then irrevocably separated from the Nation of Islam (the Black Muslims), attempting to establish his own religious and political organization among American blacks, and in constant fear for his life from white and black racists, slowly came to trust Haley and consented to a year of intensive interviews, from which Haley ghostwrote the text.

Not only a powerful account of Malcolm's life, which followed the archetypal pattern of the downtrodden sinner self-redeemed, enlightened, and then sacrificed (he was killed, probably by rival Black Muslims, a few months before the book's publication), *The Autobiography of Malcolm X* also had an immense effect on the black power movement in the United States. Critics unanimously praised it as an exemplary piece of transcription; Malcolm's own voice could be heard throughout. "Clearly [Malcolm X] had charisma," wrote Nat Hentoff in *Commonweal*, "but powering that charisma was his capacity to understand and articulate his own American experience and so link it with that of other blacks that he was indeed a spokesman . . . the nature of his own experience and its series of 'conversions' . . . is distilled with candor and cutting clarity (with writer Alex Haley serving as an admirably unobtrusive and astute organizer of the material)." In the *New York Review of Books*, political critic I. F. Stone wrote that though Haley's own conventional politics "muted" Malcolm's call for "common action with the rest of the world's colored peoples," the writer "did his job with sensitivity and devotion." *The Autobiography of Malcolm X* has so far sold more than seven million copies in eight languages.

After the success of his first book, Haley approached several publishers with plans for other projects, including a history of American blacks in the South before desegregation. In 1965, while in Washington, D.C. on another assignment, he found his steps directed to the National Archives by the thought of his grandmother's family stories. Going through post-Civil War census records, he stumbled upon the names of his maternal great-grandparents. Aflame with the idea of tracing his own heritage back through slavery to "the African," Haley embarked on the twelve-year odyssey of research and self-discovery, funded in part by lecture tours and advances from *Reader's Digest* and Doubleday, that culminated in *Roots*. Haley followed the linguistic clues passed on to him from his grandmother to a Mandinka-speaking area of Gambia, in western Africa. He traveled by safari to the village of Juffure to meet with a native *griot*, or oral historian, who in reciting the history of the Kinte clan mentioned Haley's own ancestor, "the African," who was named Kunta Kinte. Suddenly embraced as a long-lost son of the village—he was universally addressed as "Meester Kinte," while Haley himself cried "I've found you, Kunta Kinte, I've found you!"—the dazed and excited author returned to the United States convinced he had experienced a revelation of great historical importance. "Back home," Haley wrote, "I knew that what I must write, really, was our black saga, where any individual's past is the essence of the millions'."

After seven more years of grueling research, which included spending several nights naked on a wooden board in the hold of a transatlantic steamer to approximate the experience of a slave's "middle passage" to America, Haley finally published *Roots: The Saga of an American Family* in 1976. Neither a scholarly investigation of the black experience in America, nor a fictional narrative based on his research, the book partook of both: Haley called it "faction," a blend of fact and fiction. He fleshed out the outlines of his family history with the trappings of a historical novel, creating complete characterizations for the major figures and inventing dialogue and events to propel those characters in their inevitable journey to the author himself, whose own life and search is recounted in the last twenty pages of the book.

Roots as a work of literature was successful to the extent that Haley maintained a plausible middle-ground between historicity and fictional vigor. But, initially, readers and reviewers with few exceptions received it not as a conventional work but as a phenomenon, a sociological event defining a stage in the evolution of American social consciousness. One critic called the book "an epic work of classical dimensions" that "will have a serious, sustained impact on Civil Rights in this century and the next." In his *New York Times* review, James Baldwin wrote that "*Roots* is a study of continuities, of consequences, of how a people perpetuate themselves, how each generation helps to doom, or helps to liberate, the coming one—the action of love, or the effect of the absence of love, in time. It suggests, with great power, how each of us, however unconsciously, can't be but the vehicle of the history which has produced us." Arnold Rampersad claimed in the *New Republic* that although *Roots* was "so innocent of fictive ingenuity that it seldom surpasses the standards of the most popular of historical romances," and despite Haley's "twin desires for illumination of truth and cultural propaganda," he was forced to pronounce the work an "unquestionable final success," whose narrative limitations, numerous historical errors, and evident reverse racism paled before the author's "display of intelligence, industry and humanity."

The social impact of Haley's book, already powerful, was increased manyfold with the airing in January 1977 of the David L. Wolper television production of *Roots.* Despite (or perhaps because of) its predominantly black cast, unsympathetic portrayal of whites, and graphic depiction of the degradations of slavery, the miniseries attracted the largest television audience ever, some 130 million viewers. Sales of the book *Roots* skyrocketed—it was rapidly adopted as a text in dozens of college courses—and a second television series, *Roots: The Next Generations,* based closely on the latter chapters of the book (and with Haley acting as script consultant) was shown in 1979. James Earl Jones played Haley in the final segment.

In a minority opinion, Michael Arlen viewed the book and television series in a negative light. "Haley's work seems only incidentally a drama of the progress and the tribulations of black people in America," he wrote in the *New Yorker.* "This is the overlay of the story: the plot; the journalistic message that people tell themselves they are responding to. The deeper energy of the story, and its real strength in terms of audience appeal, proceeds from Haley's own fantasies about Going Home, and above all from his apparent willingness to leave the fantasies intact and unchallenged in much the same way that his audience does. . . . Of course, if Haley had bitten the bullet and broken through the dream he was so movingly trapped in, he would have had to write a different, braver, and almost certainly less popular book; but then he might have given his people, and also other peoples, a truer Kunta Kinte, clothed, however dangerously, in his real humanity, and who knows but that in the long run this might have turned out to be the greater gift?"

The truth and originality of Haley's book faced other challenges. In 1977 reporter Mark Ottaway published a letter in the Sunday *Times* of London which cast doubt on the essential core of Haley's transcendental experience in Africa. The *griot* of Juffure, claimed Ottaway, was a well-known trickster who knew Haley's story beforehand, told him just what he wanted to hear, and arranged for the various "spontaneous" celebrations mounted in the village in Haley's honor. Ottaway noted that inexperienced field anthropologists are often duped in the same way. Haley was also accused of plagiarizing parts of *Roots* from the work of other authors; these suits were settled out of court.

Haley has since embarked on a number of other projects. In the early 1970s he and his two brothers established the Kinte Foundation, which is devoted to the collection and preservation of records pertaining to black American genealogy. Haley also donated $6,000 to the village of Juffure for a new mosque. Among his ongoing literary works are a history of the town of Henning and a biography of Frank Wills, the security guard who discovered the Watergate break-in. A third television series, *Palmerstown, USA* (1980), a collaboration with producer Norman Lear, was based on Haley's boyhood experiences in Henning. The author has twice been married and has three children.

PRINCIPAL WORKS: The Autobiography of Malcolm X, 1965; Roots: The Saga of an American Family, 1976.

ABOUT: Contemporary Authors 77–80, 1979; Contemporary Literary Criticism 8, 1978; Current Biography, 1977; Who's Who in America, 1983–84. *Periodicals*—Commentary December 1976; Ebony August 1976; April 1977; New Republic December 4, 1976; New York Review of Books November 11, 1976; New York Times June 27, 1976; New York Times Book Review September 26, 1976; January 2, 1977; February 27, 1977; New York Times Magazine July 16, 1972; New Yorker March 26, 1979; Newsweek February 14, 1977; March 24, 1980; People June 7, 1982.

BERNHARD HARING

*HARING, BERNHARD (November 10, 1912–), German moral theologian, teacher and writer, writes: "I was born in Bottingen, southwestern Germany, the eleventh child of happy parents. My father, a farmer, felt that there was nothing so satisfying as being a farmer. He was a man to whom many people came seeking advice, asking him to write their letters, or with petitions which he never refused. My mother remains in my memory as a model of gentleness. She had a genius for creative non-violence and for education. She gave us children the greatest freedom to resolve our problems but never tolerated mutual accusations. A fine home-manager, she was also a mother to the poor of our little town. Our parents did everything possible to guarantee us a good education for life, knowing that this is the only stable capital.

"My early memories coincide with the first World War. My oldest brother was conscripted for army service and my second brother volunteered, not out of enthusiasm but to keep our father out of military service: a decision strongly but unsuccessfully opposed by my father. The week after the war's end, and at a time when our mother was very gravely ill, two telegrams came on the same day, each listing a brother as 'missing.' The eldest had been killed, the second captured and later returned as a sick man. This traumatic experience was doubly painful to my father, first because the younger son had volunteered in his place despite his protests, and second, because he had dissuaded his elder son, on a recent furlough home, from his intention to go into hiding rather than return to a lost war. It is no wonder that, like the rest of my family, I became a firm opponent of any kind of militarism.

"As farmers, we did not suffer in the hard years after the war but for a long time we lived very frugally, since our parents could not see poor people's children starve without giving generous help. Not only were they very religious people but they took faith as their rule of life and, by their example, taught us to do the same. In my early years as student I came upon a copy of *Das Kapital* by Karl Marx and read it thoroughly. I was shocked by Marx's worldview but even more by what he told about Christians who not only adhered to the ruthless system of early capitalism but even tried to justify it by religious arguments. My faith did not suffer, for I had experienced 'faith bringing fruit in love and justice' at home. But I conceived a lasting wrath against any use of religion for arguments to favor the overprivileged. I also began to write on themes of social commitment, war and peace. When I had to deliver the graduation address in 1933, four months after Hitler came to power, I chose as topic 'Only the desert experience will bring us to freedom'—referring to the Israelite experience. Some of my professors were furious. Others, however, smiled cautiously among friends.

"I had now decided to enter the Congregation of Redemptorists, founded by Alphonsus de Liguori. Alphonsus, son of a wealthy ambitious nobleman, had lived a radical exodus from the overprivileged class and turned firmly to the poor and oppressed. I realized vividly that in the hard time to come people would need, above all, men dedicated to bring the good news of Christ to the suffering, the oppressed and poor.

"At the Redemptorists' theological seminary I

°här´ ing, bern´ härt

had outstanding teachers except the professor of moral theology whose legalistic casuistry annoyed me. It was a shock, then, when the Major Superior asked me to take my doctorate in moral theology. I told him frankly that this would be my last choice, since I disagreed with the way the moral doctrine was being presented. However, his response disarmed me: 'This is precisely why we make our request. We want someone to initiate a refreshing change.'

"At the theological school of Tübingen I began work on a theme that has remained a focus of all my work: the relationship between the sacred and the good—religion and morality. But my studies were soon interrupted. I was called to the Medical Corps of the German army.

"From 1941 to 1945, I served on the eastern front, mostly in Russia, where I came to love dearly the humble Russian people. Against Hitler's strictest rules, I acted as priest as well as medic throughout the war, both for our soldiers and the civil populations we encountered. Being priest for the priestless Orthodox Christians was a marvellous school of ecumenism.

"Near the war's end we were in Poland. As usual, I held secret religious services for the soldiers and the local Polish people. When Germany surrendered those people made me their pastor and obtained a Polish identity card which later enabled me to return to Germany. Years later I wrote the story in my book *Embattled Witness,* in gratitude to these people.

"Back in Tübingen, after further study I took my doctorate in theology. The book *Das Heilige und das Gute* (The Sacred and the Good), presented the thought of both Protestant and Catholic philosophers and theologians. Its good reception encouraged me to begin a comprehensive work on Christian ethics. Published in 1954, the 1,400-page, three-volume *Das Gesetz Christi* (The Law of Christ), went to eight German editions and thirteen translations.

"My attention turned next to the sociology of religion and of family. *Soziologie der Familie,* the first of my books in this field, had an English translation. In 1958, the German Society for Sociology invited my membership. Since 1957 I have taught at the Academia Alfonsiana in Rome, a graduate and postgraduate school of moral theology with a large student body from all over the world, especially the Third World.

"During the 2nd Vatican Council I had a rather hectic assignment as *peritus* and as coordinating secretary for the commission which worked out the Council's major text, 'The Church in the Modern World.' After the Council I spent a few sabbatical semesters teaching in ecumenical Protestant faculties (Brown University, Yale University, Union Theological Seminary). During a term as Visiting Professor at the Kennedy Institute for Study of Human Reproduction and Bioethics, I wrote *Ethics of Manipulation.* The major part of my almost-five-months 'vacation' was spent working in Africa and Asia, and the minor part in teaching in various North American universities.

"In the seventies, some of my publishers asked for a revised edition of *The Law of Christ.* However, since we had entered a wholly new era with new perspectives and priorities, I proposed instead a new synthesis which could profit from the wider conciliar vision and my own worldwide experiences. Meanwhile, in heart, I had become a 'citizen of the world' while remaining also a citizen of Germany, an honorary citizen of Baltimore, and living among the Italians as 'one of them.'

"A long battle against larynx cancer and finally a complete laryngectomy freed me from other activities to concentrate on the new synthesis, published in three volumes, *Free and Faithful in Christ.* I wrote the text originally in English and then in German (*Frei in Christus*). Several translations are now completed or on the way.

"While seemingly almost 'voiceless,' I am happy and grateful to God that I can still bring to many people the liberating message of a Christian life. It is a special joy for me when I can help other laryngectomized persons to face the difficulties and to rediscover the many joys of life. The magic key which I recommend is gratitude: to see first the many reasons to give thanks before asking the troublesome questions which also have to be brought into light. More than ever I enjoy gardening, music and long daily walks. I intend to spend whatever time and energy God may still grant me for one cause: peace, peace-research and peace-education."

———

Fr. Bernhard Häring is the son of Johannes and Franziska (Flad) Häring. He took his Tübingen doctorate in theology in 1947 and was professor of moral theology and sociology at the Redemptorists' major seminary in Gars-am-Inn, Bavaria, from 1947 to 1957, when he left to assume the professorship of systematic moral theology at the Academia Alfonsiana. Since 1957 he has also been professor of family sociology at the Lateran University in Rome.

The best-known of Häring's early books was undoubtedly *Das Konzil im Zeichen der Einheit* (1963, translated by Edwin G. Kaiser as *The Johannine Council: Witness to Unity*). Upon reading this optimistic analysis of the first session of Vatican Council II, Pope John XXIII is said to have remarked of Häring, "He has the best mind of all the conciliar theologians." The book takes as its prime text the pope's opening address to the council (it is included as an appendix), in which he spoke of the mystery of unity and the necessity of achieving it for all Christians. James Finn remarked on Häring's "warm, open, charitable tone. There is no hint of polemics, no sharp edges, nothing aggressive or hostile. In keeping with the Johannine theme his concern is pastoral and his style reflects this concern. This does not prevent him from expressing firm opinions on some of the thorniest issues with which the council is concerned." Fr. Gustave Weigel also termed the tone "truly fraternal" and "free from polemics" in accordance with the pope's ecumenical spirit.

Häring condensed his magisterial three-volume work *Das Gesetz Christi* (1954, translated by Kaiser as *The Law of Christ*, 1961–67) into a popular edition, *Christ in einer neuen Welt* (1958, translated by M. Lucidia Häring as *Christian Renewal in a Changing World*, 1964). He wrote the book, he says, "for today's Christian who courageously examines and applies moral theology to the concrete situations of real people trying to realize and apply the teachings of the Church in this period of emphasized renewal." R. A. McCormick thought the condensation in a sense "also a purification. . . . His book is simple, serene, beautiful. Surely it is very close to the gospel message. One will not find here precise answers to knotty contemporary problems. He will find what is Father Häring's stock in trade—a spirit, an overarching attitude toward the moral life."

English translations of Häring's popular works of practical theology began to abound in the mid-1960s. *Gabe und Auftrage der Sakramente* (1962, translated by R. A. Wilson as *A Sacramental Spirituality*, 1965) discusses each of the seven sacraments in the light of the Incarnation: *Der Christ und die Obrigkeit* (1956, translated by Patrick O'Shaughnessy as *The Liberty of the Children of God*, 1966) treats the moral bases and presuppositions of mature Christian obedience; *Die gegenwartige Heilsstunde* (1964, translated by Arlene Swidler as *This Time of Salvation*, 1966) is a series of essays on such subjects as tradition and adaptation in Christian life, the spirit of the liturgy and modern technology, the nature of conversion, and sin and holiness as social phenomena; and Häring's popular *Ehe in Dieser Zeit* (1960, translated by Geoffrey Stevens as *Marriage in the Modern World*, 1965) became one of the most widely used Catholic marriage manuals on its publication in English.

Häring began writing some of his books in En-

glish in the late 1960s. *A Theology of Protest*, though criticized for an "anecdotal, rambling, and repetitious" style, was saluted as a much-needed and brave attempt "to find the via media between violent revolution and nonviolent protest." *Morality Is for Persons*, a reworking of lectures Häring gave at Catholic University and Villanova University, attempts to cover the basic principles of Catholic moral theology, situational ethics, the magisterium of the church, and the theory of natural law, among other topics. R. A. McCormick called the latter book "vintage Häring: a shrewd sense of the direction of things, a generous purchase on compassion, understanding, and prudence, but a little less hard analysis than is desirable." Those books he wrote originally in English have often been criticized for opacity of expression; his editors, for failing in their elementary duty of clarification. The English of his translated books is usually far easier to understand.

Häring's most important recent work is the three-volume *Free and Faithful in Christ: Moral Theology for Clergy and Laity*, a systematic attempt to update his earlier *The Law of Christ*, to define and explain the basic laws of Christian ethics in the postconciliar era. Volume one, *General Moral Theology*, was called by J. P. Crossley "a book of wisdom, and like the wisdom literature of the Bible, it is not especially well outlined; the gems are where one happens to find them." Compared with its model, Crossley found in the new work "a more concerted effort to base moral theology on freedom." To David Hollenbach, "the central motif of the book is the biblical, theological and essentially religious heart of the Christian moral life," but this traditional approach "has little to say about the 'hard cases' that have been at the center of so much recent discussion: euthanasia, abortion, human rights and sexuality." The second volume of the series, *The Truth Will Set You Free*, is a discussion of the virtues of faith, hope, and love, and an attempt to formulate an ethics of such diverse subjects as communication, aesthetics, asceticism, evangelization, and sexuality and marriage. The concluding volume of *Free and Faithful in Christ, Light to the World*, treats ethical issues of two kinds: the medical ethical problems of abortion, sterilization, euthanasia, and suicide; and the social ethical issues of public life in the modern world. The *Choice* reviewer remarked that "Häring remains faithful to his irenic, moderate, ecumenical, essentially optimistic outlook in the spirit of Vatican II. . . . The concept of subsidiarity is important in his economic and political outlook. The book is long, but individual sections that could be read separately are brief (sometimes, perhaps, too brief). There are some unfortunate lapses in English style."

Most of Häring's books are regularly translated into many languages. Besides German he speaks English, French, and Latin and reads Spanish, Portuguese, Dutch, and Greek.

PRINCIPAL WORKS IN ENGLISH: The Law of Christ (3 vols.), 1961–1966; The Johannine Council, 1963; Christian Renewal in a Changing World, 1964; Marriage in the Modern World, 1965; A Sacramental Spirituality, 1965; The Liberty of the Children of God, 1966; Toward a Christian Moral Theology, 1966; This Time of Salvation, 1966; Christian Maturity, 1967; What Does Christ Want? 1967; Shalom: Peace, 1967; The Christian Existentialist, 1968; Acting on the Word, 1968; A Theology of Protest, 1969; Love Is the Answer, 1970; The Church on the Move, 1970; Celebrating Joy, 1970; Morality Is For Persons, 1971; Hope is the Remedy, 1972; Faith and Morality in the Secular Age, 1973; Medical Ethics, 1973; Sin in the Secular Age, 1974; Evangelization Today, 1974; Prayer, Integration of Faith and Life, 1975; Ethics of Manipulation, 1976; Embattled Witness, Memoirs of a Time of War, 1976; The Sacraments in a Secular World, 1976; Blessed Are the Pure in Heart, 1977; Mary and Your Everyday Life, 1978; Eucharist and Your Everyday Life, 1978; Discovering God's Mercy, 1980; Free and Faithful in Christ, 1978–81; In Pursuit of Holiness, 1982.

ABOUT: Contemporary Authors, first revision series 5–8, 1969. *Periodicals*—America November 9, 1963; March 27, 1965; January 18, 1966; February 5, 1966; May 7, 1966; April 8, 1967; September 21, 1968; June 27, 1970; September 11, 1971; September 2, 1972; April 24, 1976; December 2, 1978; October 31, 1981; Christian Century March 1, 1967; May 29, 1974; March 7, 1979; April 16, 1980; Commonweal November 8, 1963; February 26, 1965; September 23, 1966; November 25, 1966; October 23, 1970; December 17, 1971; February 15, 1974; Choice March 1976; October 1973; June 1976; April 1979; April 1980; November 1981; Critic December 1963–January 1964; April 1965; February 1966; June 1966; August 1966; April 1967; May 1970; May 1971; May 1979; Library Journal November 1, 1963; August 1968; July 1970; April 15, 1970; May 1, 1971; June 15, 1974; April 1, 1976; February 1, 1979; February 1, 1980; August 1981.

HARPER, MICHAEL S(TEVEN) (March 18, 1938–   ), American poet, was born in Brooklyn, New York, the son of Walter Warren Harper and the former Katherine Johnson. His university education took place in Los Angeles: he earned an A.A. degree (1959) after two years at Los Angeles City College, then B.A. (1961) and M.A. (1963) degrees at the Los Angeles State College of Applied Arts and Sciences, now known as California State University at Los Angeles. Also in 1963 he took an M.A. in creative writing from the Writers Workshop at the University of Iowa. He taught English literature and writing at several West Coast colleges, including

MICHAEL S. HARPER

Contra Costa College, San Pablo, California (1964–68); Lewis and Clark College and Reed College, Portland, Oregon (1968–69); and California State College (now California State University), Hayward (1970). Since 1971 he has been a member of the English department at Brown University, Providence, Rhode Island, a professor since 1973, and since 1983 the first holder of the Israel J. Kapstein professorship of English. He has also been visiting professor at Carleton College and at Cincinnati, Harvard, and Yale universities.

"My poems," wrote Harper of the seventy-one short lyrics comprising his first collection, *Dear John, Dear Coltrane*, "are rhythmic rather than metric; the pulse is jazz; the tradition generally oral; my major influences musical; my debts, mostly to the musicians who taught me to see about experience, pain, and love, and who made it artful and archetypal." The musicians he refers to are the great saxophonist of the book's title, plus, among others, Miles Davis, Billie Holiday, and Bud Powell. The best of the lyrics, when read aloud, sound remarkably like jazz improvisations, as in this excerpt from "Where Is My Woman Now: For Billie Holiday":

poplars lean backward
greener and sparser
on windward side
where is my woman now
caught in northern spit
losing the weak leaves
and winter bark
the rains till the hillside
while the poppies mope
where is my woman now
on the slopes are sparrows
bathing like sheep

in this spring muck
where is my woman now

But frequently in this first collection he lays aside musical analogies and theories of rhythmical-metrical opposition to echo the pain of the racial confrontations of the 1960s. In "Dead-Day: Malcolm, Feb. 21" he conveys a cold bitterness at all the betrayal and loss:

We've placed some Malcomesque
soul brothers near the soul kits;
who walks the schizophrenic line?
What is terror but a black orchid,
a white lightnin' bouquet:
St. Malcolm at the Oracle:
A-um-ni-pad-me-hum:
Another brother gone.

The *Virginia Quarterly Review* called Harper's "a poetry of classically unadorned statement, a direct, unflinching record of a man alive—in his time. When he is at his best, in both his public and his private voice, he creates a language humming with emotion and ennobled by a deeply felt human dignity."

The angry social satirist in Harper's persona seemed to take over the collection *History Is Your Own Heartbeat.* The absurd, anomalous gentility mocked in "The Faculty Club, Portland, Oregon" is a rare instance of the poet's including himself among his targets:

. . . our language is clear, polished,
of cast wax, the breathing measured,
each in his box seat, honed and ready;
academic freedom, black studies;
pup tents on our lawn's meridian,
camped and potted in our orchidean
garden, freshened with insect-manure,
humanities, clean funds from directors
and the government.
The conservatives, the lower division,
always against war, negotiate
our flints, feathered gowns, tenure,
genteel wines, and this song.

More typical is the energized, breathless style—elevated street language—of such cautionary political lyrics as "Don't Explain: Culture as Science as Language as Cannibal":

Herbicides ain't drano;
defoliants ain't aspirin;
pathogenic bacteria ain't crest;
virus ain't contac;
toxins ain't pepto;
napalm ain't vix:

What dem?
What dey do?

The collection *Debridement,* a medical term Harper explains as "the cutting away of dead or contaminated tissue from a wound to prevent infection," consists of three sequences, each exploring a key figure in the black American experience: the abolitionist John Brown, the writer Richard Wright, and Sergeant John Henry Louis. The title section contains the poems about the fictitious Louis, a hero of the Vietnam War and winner of the Medal of Honor, who was shot down on the streets of Detroit by a white shopkeeper who falsely claimed he tried to rob his store. The personal, oblique tone of much of Harper's work is evident in these poems, whose unorthodox punctuation makes their exact meaning even harder to fathom. David Lehman, reviewing the collection, complained that Harper's "work is simply not daring, not sharp, not surprising enough." Laurence Lieberman, on the other hand, called the poet's style "deceptive: when it most wears the guise of expressionless immobility, just under the chilled surface a cunning of insurgency lurks to spring."

Nightmare Begins Responsibility takes its title from the epigraph to "Love Letters: The Caribou Hills, the Moose Range," a long, macho poem about a moose hunt in the far north with "an Indian friend who lives in Happy Valley," a poem reprinted in *Song: I Want a Witness*:

One does not sell the earth upon which
the people walk.

A people's dream died there. There is no
center any longer, and the sacred tree is dead.

Nightmare begins responsibility.

In its new context, as the title poem in another collection, it describes the pitiable tragedy of the poet's family life, how he stood by helplessly at the death of his second son, the second of his sons to die. The poem is painfully moving; many critics think it is Harper's finest work. The collection as a whole, however, was not well received, one critic accusing the author of "opacity"and "sameness," another claiming that "the poet strays too often . . . lapsing into the stiff diction and philosophical abstractions of somebody casting around for subjects to write about."

Images of Kin: New and Selected Poems is a long, retrospective collection that contains only fourteen new poems—gathered under the title "Healing Songs"—among nearly 140 others from his previous books. In these new poems, according to David Ignatow, "he begins looking for his own personal resolution and ease, as if he had found himself at last in tune with his society. . . . The fact that [he] has created this new perspective for himself speaks volumes about a whole new advance in Mr. Harper's career." This book, as was *History Is Your Own Heartbeat,* was nominated for the National Book Award in Poetry.

Harper has been married since December 1965 to the former Shirley Ann Buffington.

Their surviving child is a daughter. In addition to publishing his poems, he has edited, with Robert B. Stepto, *Chant of Saints: A Gathering of Afro-American Literature, Art, and Scholarship,* an anthology of the work of thirty contemporary black writers and visual artists, and the poetry of a black poet of an earlier generation, Sterling A. Brown, who has been called "the Afro-American Poet Laureate." In *Nightmare Begins Responsibility,* Harper included a sequence called "Sterling Letters: For Sterling A. Brown" that showed his appreciation of the older poet, whose "contemporaries and protégés," in the words of Carrington Bonner, "make up the bulk of the black literary establishment."

WORKS: *Poetry*—Dear John, Dear Coltrane, 1970; History Is Your Own Heartbeat, 1971; Photographs: Negatives: History as Apple Tree, 1972; Song: I Want a Witness, 1972; Debridement, 1973; Nightmare Begins Responsibility, 1975; Images of Kin, 1977. *As editor*—Heartblow: Black Veils, 1974, 1978; (with R. B. Stepto) Chant of Saints, 1979; The Collected Poems of Sterling A. Brown, 1980.

ABOUT: Contemporary Authors 33–36R, 1978; Vinson, J. (ed.) Contemporary Poets, 1975; Who's Who Among Black Americans, 1977–78. *Periodicals*—Best Sellers January 1978; Choice June 1975; Freedomways no. 4, 1980; Library Journal April 1, 1970; May 15, 1973; March 15, 1975; October 1, 1979; September 1, 1980; Nation June 21, 1980; New York Times Book Review March 5, 1978; January 11, 1981; Poetry December 1973; Saturday Review August 8, 1970; Times Literary Supplement May 30, 1980; Virginia Quarterly Review Autumn 1970; Yale Review October 1973.

HARRINGTON, (EDWARD) MICHAEL

(February 24, 1928–), American social and political theorist, was born in St. Louis, the son of Edward M. Harrington, Sr., a patent attorney, and the former Catherine Fitzgibbon, who had been a schoolteacher. In an interview in 1964, Harrington spoke of his "Irish New Dealer" parents and the "atmosphere of enlightened Roman Catholicism" in which he grew up. He attended parochial schools in St. Louis, then Holy Cross College, a Jesuit institution in Worcester, Massachusetts, from which he received a B.A. in 1947. He was enrolled for a year at Yale Law School, then transferred to the University of Chicago to study English literature (M.A., 1949). He had been what he called a "Taft conservative" upon entering Yale, but by the end of the decade had become a committed Catholic radical.

After a year of social work in St. Louis, Harrington moved to New York to join the Catholic Worker movement, a dynamic group of socially and politically active Catholics that had been

MICHAEL HARRINGTON

founded by Dorothy Day in the early 1930s. In 1951–52 he worked at St. Joseph's House of Hospitality, a Bowery settlement house, and as an associate editor on the *Catholic Worker*. He was secretary to the Workers Defense League (1953), then in 1954 joined the staff of the Fund for the Republic, where he worked on several research and writing projects, particularly a report on blacklisting in the entertainment industry. He was a conscientious objector during the Korean War.

A well-received article in *Commentary* magazine in 1959, "Our Fifty Million Poor," was expanded by Harrington into his first book, *The Other America: Poverty in the United States,* in which he poignantly describes the plight of "tens of millions of Americans [who] are, at this very moment, maimed in body and spirit, existing at levels beneath those necessary for human decency." The book became a bestseller, thanks in part to a lengthy commentary on it by Dwight Macdonald in the *New Yorker.* The book was read by President John F. Kennedy, who began using in his speeches one of Harrington's phrases, "the invisible poor"; Kennedy set in motion a federal antipoverty initiative that culminated in passage of the landmark Economic Opportunity Act of 1964, the keystone of President Lyndon B. Johnson's War on Poverty. An author's first book has seldom had such a powerful effect.

In *The Accidental Century,* Harrington continued the exploration, begun in *The Other America,* of the gap between the highly developed technological capacity of Western society and the meanness of its social, economic, and religious conscience. Emile Capouya considered the book "as original a work" as its predecessor, "much broader in scope, far more ambitious intellectually. Indeed, the book sets out to draw a moral, psychological, and social portrait of this age of crisis, offering political predictions and even the outlines of political solutions." G. W. Linden felt that the "true quest" of the book is "the spiritual meaning of cybernation." Though quarreling somewhat with Harrington's nomenclature and methodology, Linden described as "beautifully argued" his "main thesis, that the human care of human beings is a desirable and achievable goal. . . . His style is lucid, brilliant, and epigrammatic."

Toward a Democratic Left: A Radical Program for a New Majority appeared in 1968, a year of exceptional turbulence in a turbulent decade. It offered a direction to a new political alliance, to be composed of black-power groups, white youth, white-collar union members, the New Left, and socially committed Christians and Jews. This party of the democratic left would further "a program and a movement which socialists and radicals can—and must—support but which appeals to the more traditional American aspirations for reform as well." William V. Shannon wrote, "Having achieved the intellectual triumph of making radicalism once again seem fresh and pertinent to national issues, Harrington is equally effective in his undoctrinaire approach to international problems of political violence and economic underdevelopment. . . . Once again the author may have written a more topical book than he would have thought possible when he began it."

Harrington was undaunted by the utter failure of the Democratic left to cohere in the U.S. national elections of 1968, and continued to adumbrate his vision of a utopian future. In *Socialism* he offers a "demystification" and what he considers to be an authentic view of Marx and Engels, whose "words are now used to justify theories and practices they would abominate." Garry Wills called this "the most brilliant and important" of Harrington's books. His scathing and penetrating analysis of modern capitalism—its severe limitations as a political philosophy—was continued in *The Twilight of Capitalism* and *Decade of Decision: The Crisis of the American System.* The former book is primarily a painstaking interpretation of the Marxist conceptual framework, and by extension an attack on the vulgar Marxism practiced in many places. Tibor Scitovsky considered it "a tribute to Harrington's judgment and writing skill that the reader emerges alive and the wiser." "The most eloquent pages" of the latter volume, according to Robert Lekachman, "are Harrington's bill of particulars in his indictment of the corporate sector—among other items: neglect of the older cities, favoritism to suburbs and Sunbelt, callous misuse of the environment, worker health and safety, and consumer interest in product reliability. But the central charges link inequality and unemployment."

Poverty on an international scale is the subject of *The Vast Majority: A Journey to the World's Poor,* which examines the histories and future prospects of the nations of the Third World. The rapaciousness of international capitalism will prevent these countries, for the foreseeable future, from attaining economic parity with the developed West. J. S. Allen thought that although Harrington's careful argument "will not compel capitalists to lay their profits in the laps of the poor, it cannot be dismissed as simplistic or doctrinaire; and even confirmed capitalists will recognize in Harrington not a bleeding heart but an informed, subtle thinker—and a good man."

The Next America: The Decline and Rise of the United States is Harrington's response to the resurgence of conservatism in the United States, which he believes will be unable to preserve and protect those traditional values it pretends to champion. The next America, "well to the left of the New Deal," is foreshadowed for Harrington in his analysis of the radical potential of American labor, in the marked improvement of U.S. race relations, and in the proven success of the welfare state with regard to the elderly. "In this 'zero hour of a renascent conservatism,'" wrote Jack Beatty, quoting a line from the book, "it is positively bracing to watch Harrington's dialectical imagination at work, discovering the seeds of the possible in the actual." Harrington offers a less sanguine outlook in his response to the first term of the Reagan administration in *The New American Poverty.* "The new Gradgrinds," (as he calls the advocates of neo-conservatism and supply-side economics) "have created an underclass of technologically untrained and unemployed, of the uprooted and the homeless." Harrington's presentation of the problem was generally praised, but his proposed solution—greater government spending and an extension of social welfare programs—struck most reviewers as more idealistic than practical. *The New American Poverty,* Michael Suridoff observed in the *New York Times Book Review,* will not be read by the incumbent President as *The Other America* was by his predecessor in the '60's. More's the pity."

A self-described atheist and "cultural Catholic," Harrington outlined a political agenda for what he sees as "the spiritual crisis of

Western civilization" in *The Politics at God's Funeral.* In the moral vacuum of the modern era, which he traces from eighteenth-century deism through the emergence in the nineteenth century of nationalism and Marxism to the ultimate secularization of Stalinism, Harrington sees capitalism as the prime agent. He urges a "democratic socialism" that will create the social and economic conditions out of which a "new spirituality" can emerge. Several reviewers of the book challenged both the originality and the political viability of his thesis, but Peter L. Berger, in the *New York Times Book Review,* summed up critical reaction to Harrington when he wrote that in this "as in previous works . . . he comes through as an honest and decent man trying to apply his considerable intellectual powers to making sense of the moral dilemmas of the age."

Harrington married Stephanie Gervis in May 1963; they have a daughter and a son. For several years he has been editor of the *Newsletter of the Democratic Left* and a member of the editorial board of *Dissent.* He has also been, since 1972, a professor of political science at Queens College of the City University of New York.

PRINCIPAL WORKS: The Other America, 1962; The Retail Clerks, 1963; The Accidental Century, 1965; Toward a Democratic Left, 1968; Socialism, 1972; Fragments of the Century, 1974; Twilight of Capitalism, 1976; The Vast Majority, 1977; Decade of Decision, 1980; The Next America, 1981; The Politics at God's Funeral, 1983; The New American Poverty, 1984. *As editor*—(with Paul Jacobs) Labor in a Free Society, 1959; (with Irving Howe) The Seventies, 1972; (with T. F. Lindsay) The Conservative Party, 1918–1970, 1974.

ABOUT: Who's Who in America, 1982–83; Current Biography, 1969; Contemporary Authors, first revision series 17–20, 1976. *Periodicals*—Atlantic October 1984; Commentary January 1966; August 1972; May 1974; March 1978; March 1984; Commonweal June 29, 1962; September 17, 1965; July 26, 1968; May 26, 1972; September 20, 1974; May 9, 1980; Nation March 24, 1962; June 3, 1968; February 4, 1978; March 15, 1980; New Republic July 24, 1965; June 1, 1968; June 3, 1972; January 19, 1974; August 7–14, 1976; January 7, 1978; May 10, 1980; September 9, 1981; New York Herald Tribune Magazine December 27, 1964; New York Review of Books July 11, 1968; July 20, 1972; March 7, 1974; October 26, 1978; New York Times October 7, 1983; New York Times Book Review April 8, 1962; September 12, 1965; May 19, 1968; April 30, 1972; January 27, 1974; May 23, 1976; November 27, 1977; October 9, 1983; August 26, 1984; New Yorker January 19, 1963; Newsweek August 30, 1965; April 15, 1968; May 1, 1972; Saturday Review September 11, 1965; May 13, 1972; July 10, 1976; October 29, 1977; Virginia Quarterly Review Autumn 1965; Village Voice August 26, 1965; Washington Post April 25, 1968.

HARTMAN, GEOFFREY H. (August 11, 1929–   ), American literary critic, was born in Germany, the son of Albert Hartman and the former Agnes Heumann. He emigrated to the United States in 1946, just after the war, and became a naturalized citizen the same year. Hartman received his bachelor's degree in 1949 from Queens College, in the City University of New York, and a doctorate from Yale University in 1953. From 1955 to 1962 he taught English and comparative literature at Yale, then moved to the University of Iowa (1962–65) and Cornell (1965–67) before returning to Yale as professor of English and comparative literature. Karl Young professor since 1974, in early 1984 he succeeded the late Paul de Man as chairman of the department of comparative literature. Hartman married Renée Gross in October 1956; they have a son and a daughter.

Hartman's dissertation, directed by the theoretical critic René Wellek, was published the year after he received his doctorate as *The Unmediated Vision: An Interpretation of Wordsworth, Hopkins, Rilke, and Valéry.* It contains the first general expression of Hartman's aims as a critic. He begins by deploring the fragmenting effect on literature inflicted by criticism and its "formidable legion of variant, if not discordant, *interpretations.* . . . I wondered if . . . there might be found once more a method universal in its appeal, a method of interpretation which could reaffirm the radical unity of human knowledge." Hartman intends that the essays comprising the book should "attempt to present a way to analysis sensitive to each author as individual and to each work of art as such, and a principle of synthesis applicable to all authors and to every literary work of art." Whether he arrives at this laudable goal is debatable—most reviewers thought he did not—but he discusses the ways in which the poets who are the subjects of his study realized that "personal experience becomes the sole authority and source of conviction, and the poet a new intermediary." Each of these poets "has tried to conceive a pure representation distinguished from that of Jewish or medieval Christian thought in that its motive and terminal object is identified not with the God of the Testaments, but with Nature, the body, or human consciousness." The modern poet, for Hartman, "is the Experimenter and, not rarely, the Self-Tormentor. His real mediation is to accept and live the lack of mediation. . . . The experiment has only started which, clearing the mind for the shock of life, would in time overcome every arbitrary god of the intellect, thus to achieve a perfect induction and a faultless faith." In his concluding chapter, a meditation on the Perseus myth, he suggests that

GEOFFREY HARTMAN

only the poet can experience "the shock of life" in an unmediated way: his personal experience becomes for the reader a kind of shield of Perseus, making reality endurable.

Hartman has always been scathing in his denunciation of formalist criticism, which he has called "the new chastity of Eliot and Richards." "Formalism," for Hartman, is any critical method that aims to get at the truth of literature "by a study of its formal properties." He does not name these properties, but we are left in no doubt about who his enemies are and where they practice their craft. "Many," he writes in *Beyond Formalism: Literary Essays 1958–1970,* "in this country, as well as in Europe, have voiced a suspicion of Anglo-Saxon formalism. The dominion of Exegesis is great: she is our Whore of Babylon, sitting robed in Academic black on the great dragon of Criticism, and dispensing a repetitive and soporific balm from the pedantic cup. If our neo-scriptural activity of explication were as daring as it used to be when Bible texts had to be harmonized with strange or contrary experience, i.e., with history, no one could level this charge of puerility. Yet our present explication-centered criticism is indeed puerile, or at most pedagogic: we forget its merely preparatory function, that it stands to a mature criticism as pastoral to epic." Hartman's objections to the New Criticism are not based in any way on that school's supposedly elitist approach to literature; indeed, a common complaint about Hartman as critic lies in what one reviewer called "the unrelenting 'ivory tower' quality of Hartman's mind and approach to literature—a quality reflected in his prose too." Denis Donaghue, a noted an-

tagonist, has termed Hartman's style "too self-regarding to be wholesome." Another reviewer commended *Beyond Formalism* for presenting "a synoptic view that intends to be neither criticism nor literary history but a balance or fusion of both."

A second major theme running through Hartman's criticism is his constant desire to justify—using ever more elaborate means—the critic's reason for being. In a section entitled "Confession" introducing *The Fate of Reading and Other Essays,* he strikes a rather familiar critical pose: "I have a superiority complex vis-à-vis other critics, and an inferiority complex vis-à-vis art. The interpreter, molded on me, is an overgoer with pen-envy strong enough to compel him into the foolishness of print. His self-disgust is merely that of the artist, intensified. 'Joe, throw my book away.' . . . Having discounted other critics, and reduced art to its greatest exemplars, he feels naked enough to say: 'Myself and Art.' Like Emerson, who said that ultimately there was 'I and the Abyss.'" Some of the essays in this collection "comment on the dangerous liaison between literary studies and psychoanalysis"; the connection "between rhetorical studies and literature" he considers "equally dangerous." A major aim in this book is an exploration of the role of literary criticism in society today. The author believes that any critic, "belated or transcendant, . . . owes the great poem or novel an 'answerable style'"; he must protect "the very concept of art from the twin dangers of ideological appropriation and formalistic devaluation. The demand for contemporaneity on the one hand, and endlessly competing formal options on the other, pressure the reader as much as the artist." What he calls "a hygienic response" will not be satisfactory: "It makes us the zealots of a plainstyle criticism shrinking our ability to read intelligently and generously. Even system-making is preferable. System-makers are still makers: the unacknowledged poets of our time. . . . At least they do not feed the inferiority complex so endemic to a profession which writes books about books." The main problem with *Beyond Formalism* and *The Fate of Reading* is that both are essentially collections of essays on disparate topics. Both insist repeatedly on being regarded as complete works of criticism, but their parts only occasionally cohere into an overall critical statement. The general points made by the books are often obscure and logically nonsequential; as with much of Hartman's criticism, their real value lies in the individual perceptions.

Hartman's many years at Yale, "practicing deconstruction without a license," as he says, have produced something of an about-face in his previously apologetic approach to criticism. In *Criticism in the Wilderness* he adopts the stance of a close reader (a technique he now believes may be merely "overperfected") in an attempt "to bring together my reading of criticism with my reading of literature: to view criticism, in fact, as within literature, not outside of it looking in." He presents his general view of critical history: "We have moved from the Arnoldian Concordat, which assigns to criticism a specific, delimited sphere distinct from the creative (which remains superior and the object of millennial hopes), to a New-Critical Reduction, with Eliot as its influential source. Criticism was valued *in* art and only tolerated *outside* art." He claims to see a third phase of modern criticism, which he calls "the Revisionist Reversal," which acknowledges "the intellectual element in art but reinvests criticism with creative potential. It opposes those who abstract creative power from the critical essay. It is not afraid to see criticism as a contaminated creative thinking." He is here, as usual, concerned with bringing Continental philosophical critics to the attention of their Anglo-American counterparts. "Has the tradition of philosophic criticism dominant on the Continent nothing to offer Anglo-American practical criticism? Must every idea 'go up in smoke,' or be subject to the obverse snobbery of an unconventional edginess, an eloquently inarticulate scrutiny?" He concludes by describing his vision of American criticism in the 1980s—a period he sees as one of spurious modernist freedom and potentiality. This criticism "could flourish on a broad and flexible, a 'transnational' base. It has no need to accept the last traces of the genteel tradition. . . . For all criticism entails a rethinking, which is itself creative, of what others hold to be creative: a scrutiny of the presence of the fictive, and of the fiction of presence, in every aspect of learning and life."

In *Saving the Text: Literature/Derrida/Philosophy*, by far his most controversial work, Hartman may be seen as having given himself completely to his continental models. The work is intended to be a committed response to Jacques Derrida's *Glas* (1974), itself an almost impenetrable study of the relation of a work of literature to its critical commentary. Hartman describes *Glas*—which most experts on Derrida regard as being far removed from his most important, earlier work—as having a "beautiful strangeness," as being "an aphoristic sparagmos of form" and "in part an ambitious 'mise en scène' if not 'mise à mort' of Hegel." The book is "a science of remnants," a "Hegelian Rag," a "fashionable meditation in the graveyard of Western culture," "full of strange noises," a "labyrinth"; it "ruins words," it conveys "a sense of débris, which is the obverse of an awareness of the treacherous flow ('glissement') of language." Skeptical readers will perhaps concur from these and many similar passages, with Elmer Borklund's general observation about Hartman's work that while "his sincerity and passion [about literature] are obvious . . . it is sometimes impossible to tell what he is talking about or how he moves from point to point."

PRINCIPAL WORKS: *Criticism*—The Unmediated Vision, 1954; André Malraux, 1960; Wordsworth's Poetry, 1787–1814, 1964; Beyond Formalism, 1970; The Fate of Reading, 1975; Akiba's Children, 1978; Criticism in the Wilderness, 1980; Saving the Text, 1981. *As editor*—Hopkins: Critical Essays, 1966; Wordsworth: Selected Poetry and Prose, 1970; New Perspectives on Coleridge and Wordsworth, 1972; (with D. Thorburn) Romanticism: Vistas, Instances, Continuities, 1973; Psychoanalysis and the Question of the Text, 1978.

ABOUT: Borklund, E. (ed.) Contemporary Literary Critics, 1977; Who's Who in America, 1983–84. *Periodicals*—Choice April 1974; January 1981; July-August 1981; Encounter July 1981; June–July 1982; Library Journal November 15, 1970; October 15, 1973; February 15, 1975; October 1, 1980; June 15, 1981; Nation November 3, 1980; New Republic November 1, 1980; New York Times Book Review April 20, 1975; November 9, 1980; New Yorker October 14, 1974; May 3, 1982; Times Literary Supplement August 22, 1975; World Literature Today Summer 1981; Winter 1982; Yale Review June 1971; March 1974; Autumn 1975; Autumn 1981.

*HAVIARAS, STRATIS (June 28, 1935–   ), Greek-American poet and novelist, was born in Nea Kios, a village in Argos, Greece, to Greek parents who had emigrated from Turkey in the 1920s. He was only nine when the Nazis occupied Greece in World War II, killed his father, a fighter in the Greek Resistance, and sent his mother away to a concentration camp. Living with his grandmother, a superstitious but fundamentally wise woman schooled in the arts of survival, he was witness to the terrors that the enemy imposed upon his country. Often in danger, always hungry, he had little education and learned cruel lessons in the harsh realities of life. He found refuge in playing with paper puppets and flying huge kites, creating illusions of joy and freedom that life itself denied. Death was omnipresent: "We were surrounded by death, and the only way out was dying. The fact of death, following the confusion about the idea of death. So much so that to survive was often an accident." His grandmother explained a village legend that "when a tree sings, it's because somebody dies, or because somebody comes back

°hä vē ä ras´ strä tēs

STRATIS HAVIARAS

from dead." Years later Haviaras recorded these memories in a novel, *When the Tree Sings,* the pain and bitterness of which are relieved only by the freshness and resiliency of the child's point of view through which he captured his past. Terrible as his experiences had been, they fed his imagination: "Stories are good, I thought; all stories are good. Even if a story is about death, it's a good story. But death itself is not, there's no death that's a noble death. . . . Sorry there's nothing in the house to treat you to but words."

When the war ended, Haviaras' mother, now almost a stranger to him, was released and returned to Nea Kios, but conditions were little improved as Greece was torn by civil war. The family moved to Athens where they lived in a slum and the boy, now twelve, worked as a laborer by day and studied at night. Self-taught, he began writing poetry and published his first book, *He kyria me ten pyxida* (Lady with a Compass), in 1963. This was followed by two more books of verse in 1965 and 1967. In 1966, now a draftsman working for an American construction company in Athens, he met and married an American architect, and in the following year he emigrated to the United States, becoming a citizen in 1971.

Life was no easier for Haviaras during his first years in this country. He found a job as a stack attendant in the Widener Library at Harvard University, learned English, and managed to complete a B.A. at Goddard College in Vermont in 1973. In the following year he became curator of the poetry collection of the Harvard College Library, a post which he still holds. Haviaras has developed the collection into one of the finest in

the country, not only for printed books but for recordings of poetry readings as well. From the archives—which contain readings by Pound, Eliot, Stevens, Moore, Frost, and almost every major modern American poet—he assembled cassettes and wrote introductions to some 140 poems that were issued in 1978 as *The Poet's Voice,* now considered a major "document" in the history of American poetry.

Haviaras published one more volume of poems in Greek, *Nekrophaneia* (Apparent Death) in 1972, but since that time he has written in English. Greece, however, still haunts him—his love for the country clashing disturbingly with his bitterness toward the dictatorship of the military junta of the 1970s—"the smell of Greece wounding my nostrils," he wrote. For five years, from 1971–76, he published a poetry quarterly, *Arion's Dolphin,* in Cambridge, and in 1976 his first collection of poems in English, *Crossing the River Twice,* was published.

The book is in two parts: "Prose Poems and Proverbs" and "Soma: An Index," a group of short poems. The volume is appropriately divided to express what Linda Lord, in the *Harvard Magazine,* calls "the identity crisis" that Haviaras experienced in his first years in America, his "soma" or body in a new land, but his poetic genius stifled by his inability to use the language:

Who's seen a house   My homeless tongue—
Hiding its door?   Half moon
Who broke the door   Half knowledge
And found no house?   The language

Haunted by memories of the suffering he had known in Greece, the poet learns "To filter / His horror / Through / Rhythm." But the adjustment is not easy:

Old symbols are torn
Down from the walls
Before the walls
And names out of old torn indexes
Return but resist my voice
Where did I spend the rest of the night?
How did those two scores of years go by?
The words on this backyard wall
May all have been restored
But the answer is missing

Haviaras' first novel, also written in English, *When the Tree Sings,* brought him immediate acclaim. Nominated by the American Book Awards as the best first novel of 1979 and honored by the American Library Association as a Notable Book of the Year, this slim collection of fragments of memory proved to be a powerful and dramatic book, with haunting and lyrical sketches that, as John Leonard wrote in the *New York Times,* "add up to a bitter and beautiful coming of age." Individual scenes, fragmentary as they are, are graphic: the starving boy breaking the neck of a starving sparrow to provide a meager meal, the pathetic deaths of children and helpless old people, a lyrical romantic interlude between the boy and a girl who will soon die, the pagan orgy of victory when the Allies land, the bungling bureaucracy of the occupying Allied forces, the treachery of some Greeks against their own people. Brutal and savage as it is, *When the Tree Sings* is also full of hope, with what the *New Yorker* called "the miraculous resilience of the children of a proud and wily people" and the gallantry of the resistance of the people of an occupied country, leading the reader through "an inexorable emotional ordeal to an eventual celebration of life," as Elaine Kendall wrote of it in the *Los Angeles Times*.

The Heroic Age, Haviaras' second novel and a postlude rather than sequel to his first, centers on a young Greek boy struggling to survive in the post-war but equally turbulent period of Greek civil war. Once again Haviaras posits a brutalized and brutalizing adult world where the innocence of childhood is exploited and corrupted. His hero-narrator, orphaned by the Nazi invaders of his country, and his victimized young friends seek refuge in fantasy-escape. They are fighter-heroes themselves but also pathetic pawns in adult war games. The boy's fantasies (induced by an hallucinogenic drug in some bread he has eaten) carry him into a kind of flight of death and rebirth, a lyrical and poetic metamorphosis that offers temporary escape. In the end, now fifteen and restored to the grim reality of his life, the boy acknowledges that "the heroic age for me was over." Yet the book is neither bitter nor despairing. Reviewers noted the "magic" quality of Haviaras' prose—"harsh but deeply moving." The uniqueness of *The Heroic Age*, Marcelle Thiébaux wrote in the *New York Times Book Review*, "is that the fantasy grows out of mythic memory, with an ease and whimsy that appear as natural as breathing."

Haviaras' first marriage ended in divorce. Since 1977 he has lived in Cambridge with Heather Cole, a librarian at Harvard. They have a daughter Elektra, born in 1981. He is described as a burly, hearty man who "looks a little like Hemingway in his thirties—strong, confident and genial."

PRINCIPAL WORKS: *Poetry*—(ed.) Thirty-Five Post-War Greek Poets, 1972; Crossing the River Twice, 1976; (ed.) The Poet's Voice, 1978. *Fiction*—When the Tree Sings, 1979; The Heroic Age, 1984.

ABOUT: Contemporary Authors 105, 1983. *Periodicals*—Harvard Magazine 82, September–October 1979; Los Angeles Times Book Review June 3, 1979; New York Times June 21, 1979; New York Times Book Review June 24, 1979; June 10, 1984.

HEILBRUN, CAROLYN G(OLD) (pseudonym **Amanda Cross**) (January 13, 1926–), American feminist critic, literary scholar, educator, and mystery novelist, was born in East Orange, New Jersey, the only child of Archibald Gold, an accountant, and Estelle (Roemer) Gold. Describing the early formation of her character, Heilbrun has written that her parents, both the children of poor Eastern European Jewish immigrants, had largely rejected "the whole culture from which [they] had come, with its ignorance, its illiteracy . . . [and] its rigid, distorted beliefs," and that she was so little cognizant of her own Jewish identity that she could not even recognize institutional anti-Semitism when it was practiced against her in college and after. Decisively developed, however, and at the earliest age, was her feminist awareness. With the example of her mother, who urged her to be independent, honest, and wary of "male admiration and approval," Heilbrun "felt that, unlike so many of the women I had read of and know personally, I had been born a feminist and never wavered from that practice. I do not mean, of course, that I expressed feminist views in the dreary masculinist years after World War II. But I never denied that pain to myself, nor lied about my anger."

She attended private schools, then Wellesley College and Columbia University, where she trained in "the strains of moral realism" with Lionel Trilling and earned her Ph.D. in 1959. Except for one year as an English instructor at Brooklyn College, her entire academic career has been at Columbia: starting there as an instructor in 1960, she became a professor of English in 1972. She married James Heilbrun, a professor of economics, in 1945; they have three children, Emily, Robert, and Margaret.

As a writer, Heilbrun has pursued two paralleled careers: as Amanda Cross, mystery novelist, and, under her own name, literary and feminist scholar. Her first two books, *The Garnett Family*, a study of three generations of British editors, writers, and "servants of literature," and a biography of Christopher Isherwood, were well-received but unexceptional. Inspired by the explosive growth of feminist criticism in the 1970s, Heilbrun began to use her knowledge of nineteenth- and early twentieth-century literature to prove that, in her words, "feminism, in the intellectual as well as the political sphere, is at the very heart of a profound revolution." The elucidation of obscure or subliminal sexual biases as important formative agents in fiction is Heilbrun's main contribution to literary criticism. In two influential works of feminist scholarship, *Toward a Recognition of Androgyny* and *Reinventing Womanhood*, she developed a cri-

CAROLYN HEILBRUN

tique, based primarily on literary and psychoanalytic examples, of how cultural bias determines sex roles, and of the continuing failure of women writers and feminism in general to address the deepest problems of woman's sexual self-image.

The three sections of *Toward a Recognition of Androgyny*—"The River of Androgyny," "The Woman as Hero," and "The Bloomsbury Group"—trace the historical development of the bisexual concept of the mind from Homer to D. H. Lawrence to Joan Didion. While offering the universal aspiration toward the ideal of androgyny as the only viable impetus "away from sexual polarization and the prison of gender toward a world in which individual roles and modes of personal behavior can be freely chosen," Heilbrun does not attempt a political assessment of androgyny in the modern world—there is hardly enough material to analyze—but pays particular attention to the androgynous novel, in which "the reader identifies with the male and female characters equally." Of all literary works, she argued, those of the Bloomsbury Group most closely approach the androgynous ideal, since its members attempted to live androgynously in real life. In the last chapter of the book Heilbrun discusses the backlash of recent anti-androgynous American fiction, some written by women, and links it to resentment against the rise of feminism since the 1960s.

"Unlike books screaming 'feminism,'" wrote the reviewer for *Choice*, "this one unobtrusively points to humanism as an option to replace sexual polarization. One gains profound respect for the men and women [described in this book] who are great, because they are dimensional—not ul-

tra-'feminine' or 'masculine.'" Perhaps the biggest single difficulty with *Toward a Recognition of Androgyny* was Heilbrun's loose definition of androgyny itself, which the *Yale Review* called "so idiosyncratic as to be nearly useless . . . sometimes androgyny is 'the equality of the masculine and the feminine impulses'; more often it is 'the recognition of the feminine principle as central.'"

"Womanhood must be reinvented," wrote Heilbrun in *Reinventing Womanhood*. "Woman has too long been content to accept as fundamental the dependent condition of her sex. We avoid aggressive behavior, fear autonomy, feel incomplete without the social status only a man can bestow. I wish [in this book] to name those strictures not wholly societal or cultural which inhibit women from the full formation of a self." The inhibiting strictures that Heilbrun describes are manifest, she claims, in a failure by successful women to maintain solidarity with other women in the face of patriarchal society; with few exceptions, Heilbrun notes, achieving women renounce or deny feminism to gain acceptance as honorary males. In particular, she accuses women writers of failing "to imagine autonomous women characters . . . with even the autonomy that [the writers] themselves have achieved." As examples she cites the diminished women created by Jane Austen, George Eliot, the Brontës, and even Simone de Beauvoir (while, several critics have pointed out, ignoring the heroines created by other writers, such as Doris Lessing, who do not seem to fit her description). Heilbrun concludes: "Woman has not, like Demeter, used what she had to force her rights upon men. Rather, she has willingly relinquished her rights and those of younger women, accepting in their place the role of 'other.'"

Generally considered by feminists a well-argued critique of the movement, *Reinventing Womanhood* nonetheless drew fire for its deliberate, sometimes confusing interweaving of the author's personal history into her arguments, which appeared self-serving to some, and for what Margo Jefferson called the "unsettling practice of draping an oftstated notion or simple observation in the garments of radical originality." Jefferson thought that Heilbrun "falsifies and reduces" the achievements of women writers and the movement in general. Ann Hulbert, writing in the *New Republic*, acknowledged that the book is "frustratingly uneven" but allowed that "Heilbrun sets an inspiring goal: autonomy for the self and imaginative sympathy for a community of women."

Heilbrun's popular murder mysteries are all very consciously styled after those of Dorothy

Sayers (who, like Heilbrun, was a feminist); as much novels of genteel character and clever, erudite conversation as of detection, they belong to that subgenre of mystery usually considered the province of women writers, in which the solution of an intricate puzzle within an artificial world of manners and discourse is the point and the chief pleasure for the reader. Her amateur detective, Professor Kate Fansler, teaches literature at a Manhattan university clearly modeled on Columbia. The ideal feminist—bright, independent, determined, supercompetent in an intellectual field, and a believer in the androgynous ideal—Fansler applies her knowledge of literature and history, as well as her psychological insight, to the solution of the murder in each book. The first, *In the Last Analysis,* has Fansler solving the murder of a former student whose body is found on the couch of a psychoanalyst who was once Fansler's lover. In reviewing the book, Anthony Boucher, himself a mystery novelist, editor, and anthologist, was most impressed with Heilbrun's urbane dialogue. "There is a murder . . . but all anybody ever does is talk about it: and somewhat amazingly, the talk is so very good that the book must be considered a serious candidate for the [Mystery Writers of America's] next first-novel Edgar. Cross acutely perceives university life, psychoanalysis, and the subtle interplay of people; and her Professor Kate Fansler is an amateur detective in the finest tradition." Other critics have found Heilbrun's dialogue to be painfully overwritten, her plotting weak and implausible, and her transplantation of the conventions of the classic British mystery to American soil unnatural, but those same qualities seem to be what her admirers enjoy the most. *In the Last Analysis* was indeed nominated for an Edgar and won a scroll for one of the three best first mystery novels of 1964.

The James Joyce Murder, Poetic Justice, and *The Question of Max* hinge on the unlikely conjuction of scholarship, literature, and murder. In the first, Fansler is asked to handle the literary estate of the first American publisher of Joyce. An original draft of *Ulysses* is stolen, a woman is killed, and Fansler, with the help of her urbane perennial suitor (and eventual husband), New York D.A. Reed Amhearst, and clues from Joyce's own works, finds the criminal. *Poetic Justice,* set, like most of these novels, solidly in academe, mixes student dissent, university power struggles, the poetry of W. H. Auden, and the murder of a fellow professor, while in *The Question of Max* yet another of Fansler's students is killed, and in pursuing the murderer through Oxford she is almost murdered herself. Of *Death in a Tenured Position,* in which Fansler investigates the poisoning of Harvard's first woman

English professor, Jeffrey Burke wrote: "Cross pokes a great deal of pointed fun at a crusty institution, and a little at feminist extremism. When she is not tied down by exposition, her prose is abundantly witty, but several times I found myself wishing that someone would just walk in, order a sandwich, eat it, pay for it, and leave. Still, she writes well, and though I found the solution disappointing, I thought the solving, which depends on psychological insight and sly literary clues, top-notch."

Reviewer Mary Cantwell, explaining the continuing popularity of the Kate Fansler mysteries, called them "the bookish woman's Harlequin Romances. . . . The happy reader will be reminded of her college classes (three to one the reader is a she, five to one she was an English major) and the days when it seemed there wasn't anything that couldn't be solved with a line from *The Duchess of Malfi.* Heilbrun's characters, Cantwell added, "will not dazzle as Sayers' people dazzle—but then Sayers was a kind of genius—but they will charm. Feminism and the life of the mind will be served forth most attractively."

Heilbrun has been a visiting professor at Swarthmore College, the Union Theological Seminary, Yale University, and the University of California, Santa Cruz. She served on the editorial boards of *Virginia Woolf Quarterly, Virginia Woolf Newsletter,* and the feminist journal *Signs,* and has been a fellow of the Guggenheim and Rockefeller Foundations and the Radcliffe Institute. In 1984 she was president of the Modern Language Association of America.

PRINCIPAL WORKS: *Fiction*—(as Amanda Cross) In the Last Analysis, 1964; The James Joyce Murder, 1967; Poetic Justice, 1970; The Theban Mysteries, 1972; The Question of Max, 1976; Death in a Tenured Position, 1980. *Non-fiction*—The Garrett Family, 1960; Christopher Isherwood, 1970; Toward a Recognition of Androgyny (U.K., Toward Androgyny), 1973; Reinventing Womanhood, 1979.

ABOUT: American Woman Writers, 2, 1980; Bargainnier, Earl F. Ten Women of Mystery, 1981; Contemporary Authors, new revision series 1, 1980. *Periodicals*—Book World April 22, 1979; Choice October 1973; Christian Science Monitor September 15, 1976; May 14, 1979; Critic Spring 1977; Harpers April 1967; July 1981; Nation September 3–10, 1983; New Republic June 9, 1979; New Statesman July 7, 1961; February 18, 1977; New York Times Book Review May 24, 1964; March 19, 1967; June 21, 1970; April 1 5, 1973; October 3, 1976; January 8, 1978; May 13, 1979; March 22, 1981; Minnesota Review November 1966; Saturday Review Autumn 1977; Times Literary Suplement September 24, 1964; June 29, 1967; Yale Review June 1973; July 3, 1981.

HELPRIN, MARK (June 28, 1947–   ), American short story writer and novelist, writes: "I am reluctant to talk about myself (though I have at times done so with the drive and speed of a tobacco auctioneer) because, as I age, all things and most glories appear to me to be more and more transient, and the line between self-explanation and self-glorification to grow thinner and thinner. Nonetheless, I can say the following. When I was a boy, I lived on the Hudson, at Eagle Bay, where the river is many miles wide and opens up into farmland and mountains that in the winter are white and in the summer are green. The winter wind descended from Canada (or so we thought), pushing before it displaced mountain lions and bears, freezing the streams, and making the cattails in hidden moonshadowed ravines jingle with ice. On winter nights, everything was covered with silver light, everything was pure. In the summer, I poled rafts across the bay, and saw it, too, turn silver-blue as the mist gave way to the morning sun. I knew painfully little; I had not gone to Harvard or Oxford, or written books, or been awarded honors; I was alone most of the time or (believe it or not) in the company of animals; and my greatest ambition was to see a woman, in daylight, at close hand, fully unclothed. Things have changed a great deal, but not the essential beauty of the Hudson, and the truest statement that I can make about myself is to say that everything I have done since that time, and everything I will do, is with the hope that someday I will return to the Hudson (we will have to move farther north this time, because of the development) and be granted the privilege of watching my children encounter the seasons there, in their beauty, in the same way that I once did, and can never do again. That, as far as I can tell, is the plain and awkward truth, and the heart of my autobiography."

———

Mark Helprin is the son of Morris Helprin, a retired film executive, and the former Eleanor Lynn. He grew up in affluent surroundings in Ossining, New York, graduated from Harvard University in 1969, served in the Israeli Infantry and Air Force in 1972 and 1973, put in time in the British Merchant Navy, and had his first book published at the age of twenty-eight. Helprin's wide travels and experiences have certainly influenced his fiction, though rarely in an autobiographical way. His books show a range of subject matter and setting most unusual in American writers of his generation.

Helprin sold his first short story to the *New Yorker* when he was twenty-one and still at Har-

MARK HELPRIN

vard. His first book, *A Dove of the East and Other Stories,* consists of twenty pieces, most of which originally appeared in the *New Yorker.* The stories range all over the world and treat of characters as diverse as a cattle rancher in Jamaica, a dying priest in Rome, and a Spanish widow in New Mexico. The title story and "A Jew of Persia," which received the highest praise from reviewers, embody Helprin's ethical views of Judaism with particular sharpness. Reviewers tended to think less of the remaining eighteen short stories. Some, like Dorothy Rabinowitz, complained about minor flaws, but others, such as Julia O'Faolain, found Helprin's tales monotonously similar. A few critics were wholly negative. Amanda Heller wrote that "the author affects a dreamy, antique style for the telling of his wispy romances, then turns most of them into shaggy-dog stories by refining atmosphere at the expense (nearly total) of plot and characterization." Perhaps the most representative view was that taken by Duncan Fallowell. He thought the title story was weakened by sanctimoniousness and sentimentality and that a few of the others were "unbeatably vague." But, he wrote, Helprin demands attention because he is "a seeker after truth. Bits of it are squittering out all over the place, sufficiently to fuse into a magnetic center and make one recognize that the book is not written by a fool."

Two years later Helprin's second book and first novel was published; *Refiner's Fire: The Life and Adventures of Marshall Pearl, a Foundling* retains the refined prose of *A Dove of the East,* but puts it to the service of a sprawling, old-fashioned *bildungsroman.* Its immense plot tells the story of Marshall Pearl, an orphan born of a Jewish mother in a refugee ship off the coast of Palestine in 1947. Marshall is sent to America and adopted by a wealthy, childless couple in the Hudson Valley. As soon as Marshall is old enough he sets off on a series of adventures, the first of which involves him in a Rastafarian rebellion while still an adolescent. His subsequent wanderings take him to Harvard, a slaughterhouse in Kansas, and at least two mountain ranges. The novel ends with Marshall struggling for life in an Israeli hospital bed after having been gravely wounded in battle during the October War. *Refiner's Fire,* Helprin insists, is not autobiographical though many readers apparently thought it was. "There is a real Marshall Pearl," he writes. "I pay him a percentage of my royalties. However, the life in the book is not his either."

Some critics thought this plot was too much to digest and the novel received rather mixed reviews. However, Joyce Carol Oates, Peter Ackroyd, and others admired Helprin's recklessness, his freedom from current literary dogma. Oates considered *Refiner's Fire* "a brilliantly sinuous tale" and said, "if the exuberant, extravagent plotting of the novel ever becomes tangled in its own fabulous inventions, and its prodigy of a hero ever comes to seem more allegorical than humanly 'real,' that storytelling command, that lovely voice is never lost." Ackroyd wrote, "Mark Helprin is so sure of his own narrative skills that the novel glows with his permanent presence" and praised the work for its resistance to the Gods of realism and modernism."

Helprin's detractors, on the other hand, were as blunt as they had been with *A Dove of the East.* Pearl K. Bell found "no sustaining idea behind the theatricality" and for her the story became "a numbing bore." John Ryle said, "Female characterization is almost non-existent" and Roger Sale said that the pieces of the novel are held together "by a dreamy romanticism of a silly and bigoted kind."

There were fewer dissenting voices for Helprin's third book, *Ellis Island and Other Stories.* It was an immediate critical and popular success, won the National Jewish Book Award and the *Prix de Rome,* and led to a spate of interviews in popular magazines in which Helprin was able to clarify his intentions. In one of them he told the *New York Times* that he considered himself an outsider, an American Jewish author who had abjured the way of Bellow and Malamud. "I'm not at all like them," he said. "I don't have that introspection. I have no agony and no resentments. Boredom and alienation don't mean a thing to me." Helprin might have said that his concerns are more religious and ethical than social and psychological. "I am trying," he told *New Brooklyn* magazine, "to open a road to God and nature. I could write forever, without stopping, about nature. Nature always seems much more important to me than anything human."

"The Schreuderspitze," the opening story of *Ellis Island,* and one singled out for praise by most reviewers, amply testifies to Helprin's spiritual intentions. It concerns a Bavarian photographer who flees to an Alpine village after the death of his wife and son in an auto accident. There he trains for a climb up the murderous rock face of the Schreuderspitz only to find the actual ascent unnecessary: in a vision of transcendent illumination the photographer stands on the mountaintop and sees his loved ones revealed to him.

Not all or even most of the short stories in *Ellis Island* aspire to this level of spiritual intensity, and at least one critic, Pearl K. Bell, has denied that Helprin is "the essentially religious writer he claims to be." But most were delighted by the virtuosity of setting and incident, religious or not. Other highly regarded pieces were "Letters from the Samantha," an epistolary tale about a captain who takes a mysterious, possibly evil ape on board ship; "Palais de Justice," about an elderly lawyer risking a heart attack in a fierce rowing race on the Charles River; and the title piece, a four-part novella about a plucky Jewish immigrant making his way through turn-of-the-century New York.

It was not until 1983, however, with *Winter's Tale,* that Helprin established himself as one of the important contemporary American fiction writers. His longest (nearly 700 pages) and most ambitious novel to date, *Winter's Tale,* is a boldly imaginative book, full of elements of the picaresque and the fantastic. Its hero journeys through time, sometimes on the back of a flying horse. He lives in pre-World War I America, dies and is reborn near the end of the twentieth century in a New York City that undergoes an ice age and a holocaust, and is itself reborn into a third milennium. *Winter's Tale* is also a lyrical and transcendent love story, not only of the hero's romance with a fairy-tale-like heroine who dies young, but also of his infatuation for New York—a menacing, gangster-ridden jungle that emerges a beautiful "live creature, pale and pink." Alan Bold described the almost indescribable vision of the book, in his *Times Literary Supplement* review, as bringing together the elements of "biblical symbolism, literary fable, realistic narrative . . . in a synthesis that offers imaginative myth as alternative to naturalistic violence." Helprin's writing, he concludes, "has the confidence of the consummate artist and the linguistic presence of the gifted story teller." Other reviewers were similarly impressed by Helprin's virtuosity and "verbal pyrotechnics," and what Andrea Barnet, in the *Saturday Review,* called "the utter exuberance of Helprin's imagination." Barnet, however, had reservations about the total effect: "Helprin's freewheeling use of fantasy at times eclipses his essential seriousness, diminishing the novel as a whole. Yet there is unquestionable genius in the book's marvelous individual pieces." Robert Towers, in the *Atlantic,* though judging that "Helprin's fantasy-spinning apparatus works prodigiously," raised the question of whether the book succeeds as a novel. "My answer must be a slightly qualified negative. Again and again I had the sense that my responses were being coerced, that the author was trying to better me into an acceptance of the book's visionary and poetic powers."

In addition to his fiction Helprin has written on Middle Eastern policy. (He has a master's degree from Harvard's Center for Middle Eastern Studies.) He studies foreign policy several hours a day and envisions a career as a writer/diplomat. Helprin was married in 1980 to Lisa Kennedy, an attorney and vice president of the Chase Manhattan Bank. He writes three hours each day in meticulous, blot-free script, and describes himself as "psychopathically neat." A *Publishers Weekly* writer in a 1981 interview noted that Helprin's resemblance to "a college undergraduate or slightly aging Eagle Scout" belies a different personality: "a man of decided opinions and a will of steel."

PRINCIPAL WORKS: *Short stories*—A Dove of the East and Other Stories, 1975; Ellis Island and Other Stories, 1981. *Novels*—Refiner's Fire: The Life and Adventures of Marshall Pearl, a Foundling, 1977; Winter's Tale, 1983.

ABOUT: Contemporary Authors 81–84, 1979; Contemporary Literary Criticism 7, 1977; 10, 1979; 22, 1982. *Periodicals*—Atlantic Monthly October 1975; September 1983; Commentary June 1981; Life May 1981; New Brooklyn Summer 1982; New Review June 1976; New York Times March 5, 1981; New York Times Book Review January 1, 1978; March 1, 1981; March 25, 1984; May 13, 1984; New York Review of Books February 23, 1978; May 14, 1981; Newsweek February 23, 1981; Publishers Weekly February 13, 1981; Saturday Review September 20, 1975; Spectator April 24, 1976; February 25, 1978; Times Literary Supplement February 17, 1978; November 25, 1983; Vogue March 1982.

HERRIOT, JAMES (pseudonym of James Alfred Wight) (October 3, 1916–), British writer, was born in Sunderland, England, the son of Scottish parents, James Henry and Hannah Wight. When he was three weeks old the family moved to Glasgow, Scotland, where he was educated at local schools. He has remarked in an interview that both of his parents were musicians, and that at an early age he was given piano lessons but showed no particular aptitude. He "decided on being a vet," he said, when he was thirteen. He attended the Glasgow Veterinary College, and after graduation became an assistant to a Yorkshire veterinarian, before long becoming his partner. There he met and in 1941 married Joan Catherine Danbury; their daughter today is a doctor, their son a veterinarian who shares his father's practice.

Herriot rarely leaves Yorkshire, and his books communicate a profound affection for the locality and its people. It was not, however, until he was more than fifty years of age that he began to write of his experiences as a vet. Until then he had written nothing at all, although he had occasionally thought of setting down some of the incidents of his life. His first book, written during spare moments, was sent to an English publisher who, after retaining it for a year and a half, turned it down; a second accepted it enthusiastically. Published in England as *If Only They Could Talk,* it was well received, but did not create any great stir, and was followed by a second book, *It Should Happen to a Vet.* The turning point in Herriot's career came when an American editor, Thomas McCormack, president of St. Martin's Press, read the books and surmised that Herriot's writing might find a responsive audience in the United States. He combined the two books and added three chapters, publishing the single, larger volume under the new title, taken from a well-known hymn, *All Creatures Great and Small.* The book was a phenomenally successful best-seller.

All Creatures Great and Small, which tells the story of Herriot's arrival in Yorkshire to undertake his first professional assignment, his being made a full partner in the veterinary practice, his marriage, and recognition that he had found his rightful place in life, received highly favorable reviews. Nelson Bryant remarked that Herriot's portrayal of Siegfried and Tristan Farnon, the eccentric bachelor brothers with whom he became professionally associated, was "delightful." "Indeed," he went on, "every character in the book emerges with force and clarity. There is humor everywhere." Many critics referred to Herriot's infectious pleasure in working with farm animals, his sense of the rich reward of "hard work and simple living." Ana-

JAMES HERRIOT

tole Broyard praised the book in the *New York Times*, calling Herriot "a natural storyteller" who is "tremendously interested in everything and manages to invest his stories with that interest."

Herriot's *Let Sleeping Vets Lie*, published in England, provided the basis for *All Things Bright and Beautiful*, which was also acclaimed in the United States and became an immediate best-seller. Evelyn Callaway commented that "a sequel rarely attains the same degree of excellence as the first book," but astonishingly, *All Things Bright and Beautiful* did exactly that; she noted that Herriot was an anecdotist of "uncanny skill" whose humor mingles easily with a warmly humane understanding. Edward Weeks found Herriot "such a likable cove, so good-natured in his predicaments, that one rides along with him in effortless enjoyment." Ruth Farwell was impressed by Herriot's ability to make "ordinary things become vastly entertaining, sometimes deeply moving, often hilarious." She went on to remark that "character is what fascinates him. . . . Yorkshire has always bred hard-working, hard-living folk, stout-hearted in adversity and stuffed with idiosyncrasies . . . the people Herriot meets on his daily rounds are a marvelous crew."

From the material of *Vets in Harness* and *Vets Might Fly*, both published in England in 1976, came *All Things Wise and Wonderful*, which received generally favorable reviews but was thought to lack the strong dramatic frame of the earlier books. Herriot's service in the Royal Air Force at the beginning of World War II, which ended in his illness and return to Yorkshire with

a medical discharge, is interlaced in the book with his veterinary experiences; but nothing decisive occurs. The critic for *Business Week* found *All Things Wise and Wonderful* on a par with the earlier books, and called Herriot "a superb writer, evoking whole scenes from a memory that appears capable of total recall." But Richard Lingeman thought Herriot's material "shows signs of wearing thin at the elbows." "What allays one's pleasure," he continued, "is a sense of formulas creeping into the stories, of mechanical plot-shifts, as though Herriot were straining to heighten and point up a diminishing store of materials. . . . On the whole, *All Things Wise and Wonderful* is as ingratiating as [his] previous [books]; niceness still triumphs, but this time round, it's a near thing."

Herriot's fame increased in the late 1970s when the BBC adapted *All Creatures Great and Small* for television, in a thirteen-part series that was widely viewed in both Britain and the United States. In 1979 *James Herriot's Yorkshire* was published—a volume containing more than 200 striking photographs of sites that had stimulated Herriot's writing and locations where the televised version of *All Creatures Great and Small* was filmed. The photographs were accompanied by Herriot's attractively written commentary on Yorkshire. *The Lord God Made Them All* concludes his Yorkshire reminiscences. Although reviewed respectfully, an undercurrent of dissatisfaction runs through the book's notices. "To this abject aficionado," Henrietta Buckmaster wrote, "the latest book is a disappointment." She noted that the hilarious Farnon brothers have now disappeared, and that "James's two young children are not quite substantial enough to take their place. . . . The book is made up of odd bits and pieces, remembered scrappily in most cases." Phillip Johnson noted that "the current volume consists of incidents drawn from Herriot's experience immediately after World War II, plus the diaries of two uneventful trips he took during the sixties, arbitrarily interspersed with the older material. Herriot's readers will be disappointed to discover that the unaffected charm that made his stories popular in the first place has now become a carefully reproduced commodity."

In an interview-story in *Time* magazine in 1981, Stefan Kanfer has observed that Herriot is "the most celebrated resident of Yorkshire since Lassie." His portrayal of the region's laconic inhabitants and his deeply fulfilling work there as a vet, have brought Herriot an international audience. His books have been translated into twelve languages (including Japanese); and in the United States two of his books alone—*All Creatures Great and Small* and *All Things Bright and Beautiful*—have each sold six million copies in paperback. He has also been awarded (1978) an O.B.E. by the British government. Despite his fame and considerable earnings from his writings Herriot continues to live inconspicuously and to devote his days, and sometimes his evenings, to his veterinary practice in the small village of Thirk. Totally unassuming, he has remarked: "I still regard myself as a veterinarian who scribbles in his spare time."

PRINCIPAL WORKS: If Only They Could Talk, 1979; It Shouldn't Happen to a Vet, 1972; All Creatures Great and Small, 1972; Let Sleeping Vets Lie, 1973; All Things Bright and Beautiful, 1974; Vets in Harness, 1976; Vets Might Fly, 1976; All Things Wise and Wonderful, 1977; James Herriot's Yorkshire, 1979; The Lord God Made Them All, 1981; Moses the Kitten, 1984.

ABOUT: Contemporary Authors 77–80, 1979; Contemporary Literary Criticism 12, 1980. *Periodicals*—Christian Science Monitor June 8, 1981; New York Times December 14, 1972; New York Times Book Review February 18, 1973; November 3, 1974; September 18, 1977; Time June 29, 1981; Wall Street Journal December 3, 1979.

HIBBERT, CHRISTOPHER (March 5, 1924–), English historian and biographer, writes: "My childhood was spent very happily in a small village in Leicestershire where my father was a parson. He was very poor, but my mother inherited enough money from my grandfather to send her children to expensive boarding schools. My school career was quite undistinguished, and I was not sorry to leave at seventeen to take up a place at Oxford. My studies being interrupted by the war, I joined the army in the ranks of the Sherwood Foresters, and was afterwards commissioned. My years as an infantry officer in Italy I count as being the most formative in my life. I was wounded twice and awarded the Military Cross. I had thoughts of remaining in the army when the war was over, but chose to return to Oxford which I loved. I obtained my degree in 1948 and married a few months later.

"The need to earn a living for a family which was soon to include three children took me into the profession of surveyor and land agent. I worked in an office in the daytime, and took a correspondence course at home in the evenings. After qualifying I borrowed money to set up in business on my own account, prospered modestly, and took in a partner to whom I subsequently sold my share in order to buy a partnership in a large, old-established firm in London. In the evenings and at week-ends and in the train on

CHRISTOPHER HIBBERT

my journeys to and from London I returned to the writing I had briefly and desultorily practiced at Oxford and in the army. I had some short stories broadcast, some scripts accepted by the BBC, and for a year or so was the television critic of a weekly political journal then edited by an Oxford friend and now defunct. My first book was published in 1957. After the publication of my third, which won a prize from the Royal Society of Literature (and resulted in my being elected a Fellow), I decided to devote my whole time to writing. I have since written some twenty books, mostly historical or biographical, all of which have been published in America as well as in England. I have also contributed articles and literary criticism to newspapers and periodicals in both countries; and my work has been translated into most European languages."

Christopher Hibbert is one of a small group of popular writers who specialize in the genre of "narrative history." Though not an academic historian by profession, he has the training and the skills of a scholar. His many books, which range widely over Chinese, Italian, French, and English history, are fully and carefully documented from primary sources. Many of them are lavishly illustrated, supplementing his notes and bibliographies with "visual documentation." Hibbert's specializations include military history (for which his wartime service provided special preparation), biography (literary as well as historical, with books on Samuel Johnson and Charles Dickens), and general history. Inevitably, such variety and productivity leave purely academic historians suspicious of the soundness of the work, but Hibbert has fared well among his academic critics. Although Lawrence Stone described his biography of Charles I as "pop history . . . a new art form, a combination of surface rhetoric and glossy but irrelevant visual illustration," and the *Times Literary Supplement* called his history of Windsor Castle (*The Court at Windsor*) "royal gossip . . . a first-class book of the admittedly second-class genre," most of Hibbert's books have been acclaimed for their historical soundness as well as for their readability. Hibbert himself makes only modest claims for his work. His second book, a biography of the colorful eighteenth-century criminal Jack Shepherd, *The Road to Tyburn,* was "intended as a work of entertainment rather than of scholarship." *London: The Biography of a City,* he writes, was "mainly intended as an introduction" and "guide-book." And even of his biography of King Edward VII, *The Royal Victorians,* based on unpublished materials in the Royal Archives and in numerous private collections, he writes that he hopes his readers "will be rewarded by discovering some clumps of hitherto disregarded clover amidst the familiar grass."

Other studies, however, were more ambitiously conceived. His two-volume biography of George IV was acclaimed for its illuminating and judicious portrait of a subject rarely treated with such depth and sympathy. His biography of Lord Raglan, for which he received the Royal Society of Literature award in 1962 (the same year in which he won the Heinemann Award for Literature), and his history of the Indian uprisings of 1857, *The Great Mutiny,* in preparation for which he traveled to India and collected much previously unpublished material, are regarded as first-rate historical studies. Even more challenging was his biography of Mussolini, a controversial portrait based on original research in Italian archives and on interviews with people who had known him. The book was partly at least the result of a personal quest: "I wondered how much Mussolini resembled the monstrous buffoon of war-time propaganda and how much the demi-god of fascist doctrine," and concluded with the author's admission that he could not pass judgment on his subject, "even if such a judgment were yet possible." Faulted for lack of balance, a disproportionate emphasis on the dramatic highlights rather than on the whole historical context in which Mussolini figured, it was nevertheless praised for its narrative fluency. Hibbert writes, G. M. Fraser observed of *The Great Mutiny,* "as the best historians do, dispassionately, and lets the facts speak for themselves." But he is also a literary stylist, as Paul Theroux noted of *The Dragon Wakes,* a study of Western visitors to China from 1793 to 1911: "Like our greatest historians, Hibbert has a novelist's sensibilities, a care for the past intensified by a concern for the future."

Married since 1948 to Susan Piggford, Hibbert has two sons and one daughter. He lives in Henley-on-Thames, in Oxfordshire, and when not engaged in research and writing, pursues his avocations—cooking, gardening, painting, and collecting eighteenth- and nineteenth-century caricatures.

PRINCIPAL WORKS: The Road to Tyburn, 1957; King Mob, 1958; Wolfe at Quebec, 1959; Corunna, 1961; The Destruction of Lord Raglan, 1961; Il Duce (U.K., Benito Mussolini), 1962; The Battle of Arnhem, 1962; The Roots of Evil, 1963; Agincourt, 1964; The Court at Windsor, 1964; Garibaldi and His Enemies, 1965; Waterloo: Napoleon's Last Campaign, 1966; The Making of Charles Dickens, 1967; Charles I, 1968; The Grand Tour, 1969; London: The Biography of a City, 1970; (with C. Thomas) The Search for King Arthur, 1970; Anzio: The Bid for Rome, 1970; The Dragon Wakes: China and the West, 1793-1911, 1970; The Personal History of Samuel Johnson, 1971; George IV, Prince of Wales, 1762–1811, 1972; George IV, Regent and King, 1812–1830, 1973; The Rise and Fall of the House of Medici, 1974; Edward VII: A Portrait, 1976; The Great Mutiny: India, 1857, 1978; Disraeli and His World, 1978; The Court of St. James's 1979; The French Revolution, 1981; Africa Explored: Europeans in the Dark Continent, 1769–1889, 1982.

ABOUT: Contemporary Authors, new revised edition 2, 1981; Something About the Author 4, 1973; Who's Who, 1983. *Periodicals*—History Today May 1983; Modern Age Summer/Fall 1983; New Leader October 17, 1983.

HIGGINS, GEORGE V(INCENT) (November 13, 1939–), American novelist and short story writer, was born in Brockton, Massachusetts, to Irish-American parents John Thompson Higgins and Doris Montgomery Higgins, both schoolteachers. George Higgins grew up in Rockland, Massachusetts, and attended the local high school, where his father had recently become the principal. At the urging of his parents, Higgins entered Boston College's premedical school program, but switched to the study of English and graduated in 1961. At Stanford University, where he received a master's degree in writing, he studied under Wallace Stegner.

After briefly working as a soft-drink delivery truck driver, when he learned, he said, "to swear between syllables," he began work as a reporter, first for the Providence, Rhode Island *Journal*

GEORGE V. HIGGINS

and Evening Bulletin (1962–63), then for the Associated Press (A.P.) in a tiny bureau in Springfield, Massachusetts (1963–64). As a reporter, Higgins first encountered the New England underworld that figures so prominently in his novels. While covering local trials for the A.P., Higgins decided he could match or better the performance of the prosecutors he observed, so, after working for the A.P. in Boston, he returned to Boston Colege as a law student. "I had been thinking about it for some time," he told the *National Observer*, "but I decided to go into law school on November 22, 1963. I decided I ought to participate directly, instead of just standing by." He earned his J.D. in 1967, was admitted to the Massachusetts Bar the same year, and immediately began trying cases in Boston for the Massachusetts Attorney General's office. "If you want to be a trial lawyer, like I did," Higgins said in a 1972 interview, "the place for you is in the government. They need you. There are no junior partners, and so you're right in it." During a period of intense rivalry between the Irish and Italian mafias in the city, Higgins prosecuted a number of underworld murders. Later (1970–73), he was a prosecutor for the United States Attorney's office in Boston.

Since the early 1960s, Higgins had been writing steadily and copiously in his spare time. Between 1961 and 1972 Higgins wrote ten novels, all described by the author as "pretty bad." Then, abandoning the "long Faulknerian sentences that not even I could understand" of his earlier work, he drew upon his intimate knowledge of the Boston underworld to give a sleazy authenticity to his first published novel, *The*

Friends of Eddie Coyle, a fast-plotted best-seller hailed as one of the best crime novels of the year.

Coyle, a small-time Boston crook, middle-aged, wary, and desperate, runs guns to a team of bank robbers while selling information to the cops to keep himself out of prison. In the end, his betrayals catch up with him, and he is "taken out" (executed), by one of his best friends, who is also an occasional assassin for the mob. "I didn't really invent Eddie Coyle," Higgins has said. "All I had to do is listen to the people I spend time with everyday—real people." Most critics were impressed by Higgins' sharp ear for criminals' idiom. His characters endlessly discuss their wives, their cars, their dental work and operations, but only in brutal slang and obscene euphemism do they plan their crimes or threaten one another. Reviewing the book in *Life*, Melvin Maddocks wrote of Higgins: "He can plot a whole book like one long chase scene. He can write dialogue so authentic it spits. He can catch character like a 'make' in a file of mug shots. And he can diagram double-crosses across his double-crosses." Other critics compared the author's command of the crime genre and its menacing language to that of Ernest Hemingway in his short story "The Killers."

The Digger's Game and *Cogan's Trade* share locale, style, and peripheral characters with *Eddie Coyle,* and followed that book into the best-seller lists. In *The Digger's Game* a part-time crook, more dangerous than he appears, evades a loan shark trying to kill him. *Cogan's Trade* recounts the fate of three amateurs who believe they can get away with robbing a mob-sponsored crap game. "Beneath the documentary exactitude of his lowlife landscape, Higgins writes of nothing less than the mechanisms that society creates in order to survive," wrote Clifford Ridley in his review of *Cogan's Trade.* "Higgins' society, to be sure, is a unique one—distrustful, incestuous, close-mouthed—and in *Cogan's Trade* he captures it again in the oblique, idiomatic, garrulous dialogue that has become his trademark. We hear a lot these days about the banality of evil and violence; Higgins understands it as well as anyone I know of." Roderick MacLeish (*New York Post,* April 9, 1974) noted certain similarities between the rambling Irish talk of Higgins and that of James Joyce. "Like James Joyce," wrote MacLeish, "Higgins plumbs and replumbs one geographical locale. His Dublin is the dark underside of Boston and its suburbs. Like Joyce, Higgins uses language in torrents, beautifully crafted, ultimately intending to create a panoramic impressionism."

As former government prosecutor (since 1974 he has been in private practice), Higgins followed the labyrinthine legal maneuverings surrounding the Watergate case and the resignation of President Richard Nixon with professional interest. Out of his own Washington experience came two books—a novel, *A City on a Hill,* and *The Friends of Richard Nixon,* non-fiction derived from a long article in the *Atlantic*—that marked a considerable departure from his previous work. Called by Christopher Lydon "the definitive novel of Washington at the staff level," *A City on a Hill* recounts the pressured lives of political staffers trying to activate a hopeless Democratic presidential campaign against the backdrop of Nixon's downfall. Higgins found obvious parallels between the chronic paranoia of the small-time hood and the fear infecting post-Watergate Washington. David S. Broder considered the book "an extraordinary piece of writing, in which Higgins employs his unerring gifts for recreating the tone and rhythm of politicians' talk to tell the entire story in dialogue." Other critics, lamenting his apparent abandonment of the Boston criminal milieu he had exploited so well in his first three books, were not comforted by *The Friends of Richard Nixon,* a lawyer's blow-by-blow, inside account of the Watergate trials. In the opinion of most reviewers, *The Friends of Richard Nixon* lacked analytical solidity and balance, but did provide what P. D. Zimmerman called "forensic savvy" and a "tipster's tour of the strategems that guided the cover-up."

Higgins returned to fiction with *The Judgement of Deke Hunter, Dreamland,* and *A Year or So with Edgar,* but most critics did not consider him to have regained his form until *Kennedy for the Defense.* Jeremiah Kennedy, a quickwitted Boston criminal lawyer, pragmatic but honest, moderates three worlds: the underworld of his petty criminal clients, a familiar one to Higgins' readers; the maze of the criminal justice system, through which Kennedy adroitly maneuvers; and his unusually happy home, which he strives to protect above all else. *Kennedy for the Defense* cut close to the bone of Higgins' own career, and for this reason was thought unusually convincing. Terry Curtis Fox noted in the *Village Voice* (April 7, 1980) that, for all Higgins' emphasis on the criminal mind, he has displayed "a consistently lawyerly point of view. . . . Indeed, what action there is [in his books] invariably occurs in the past tense—precisely the way it does in a lawyer's office. The concerns of his characters are lawyerly, too; they wish neither the solutions to mysteries nor the ideals of justice, but rather the practical resolution of a short-term personal problem."

The Rat on Fire is a profane comedy of manners about arsonists, slumlords, and fire marshals on the take. All dialogue, with the barest minimum of action—characters leave a van, enter a store or a coffee shop—*The Rat on Fire* reads much like a play. *The Patriot Game* investigates the underside of Boston city and church politics, with the protagonist, a tough federal agent, pursuing a mysterious IRA gunman. The plot is complex and somewhat implausible, but as Jonathan Yardley noted in the *Washington Post,* "plot is not and never has been Higgins's chief business. The manner and mores of the law and those who violate it are what most interest him, and what gives his novels their rich texture."

Higgins, since 1979 a columnist for the *Boston Globe,* was described by Thomas Collins in *Newsday* as having "the look of an interrogator about him, as though he has been in too many small rooms with too many sleazy characters who have done nothing but lie to him." His short stories, which cover much the same ground as his novels, have appeared in *Massachusetts Review, Esquire, Atlantic,* and *The Best American Short Stories 1973.* The author was married in 1965 to Elizabeth Mulkerin, with whom he had a daughter, Susan, and a son, John; he now lives in Milton, Massachusetts, with his second wife, Loretta Lucas Cubberly, whom he married in 1979.

PRINCIPAL WORKS: *Fiction*—The Friends of Eddie Coyle, 1972; The Digger's Game, 1973; Cogan's Trade, 1974; A City on a Hill, 1975; The Judgement of Deke Hunter, 1976; Dreamland, 1977; A Year or So With Edgar, 1979; Kennedy for the Defense, 1980; The Rat on Fire, 1981; The Patriot Game, 1982; A Choice of Enemies, 1984. *Non-fiction*—The Friends of Richard Nixon, 1975.

ABOUT: Contemporary Authors 77–80, 1978; Contemporary Literary Criticism 4, 1975; 7, 1977; 12, 1979; 18, 1981; Who's Who in America, 1983–84. *Periodicals*—Life February 18, 1972; March 12, 1972; National Observer April 1, 1972; New York Post March 16, 1972; April 6, 1974; April 9, 1974; New York Times April 10, 1974; March 14, 1975; February 6, 1981; New York Times Book Review March 30, 1975; March 2, 1980; February 12, 1984; Newsday April 25, 1973; Newsweek April 8, 1974; January 16, 1984; Washington Post March 20, 1975; April 14, 1982.

HINGLEY, RONALD F(RANCIS) (April 26, 1920–), British writer on Russian literature, politics, and history, was born in Edinburgh to Robert Henry and Ruth Esther (Dye) Hingley. He attended the Kingswood School in Bath; then, following his war service (1940–45), took his bachelor's and master's degrees in 1946 from Corpus Christi College, Oxford. In 1951 he received his doctorate in Slavonic and Eastern European Studies from the University of Lon-

RONALD HINGLEY

don. Four years later he became a university lecturer in Russian at Oxford; in 1965 he was made a research fellow, and in 1969 a fellow, of Oxford's St. Anthony's College, where he still teaches. Between 1959 and 1961 Hingley wrote a series of radio scripts on elementary Russian language instruction that were broadcast by the BBC. He married in 1953 and has seven children.

Hingley, whose command of Russian is exceptionally thorough, has written biographies of many of the major figures of modern Russian literature, has translated the complete works of Anton Chekhov for the Oxford University Press, and has published analyses, informed by his literary and historical studies, of the Russian temperament and modern Russian politics. Though not noted for groundbreaking scholarship, breathtaking insight, or revolutionary theses, Hingley's works are solid, thorough, and readable; his firm grasp of the language, literature, and history of modern Russia gives his biographies in particular both firmness and scope. His style, somewhat stolid in his early works, has over the course of more than two dozen books become light, fluid, and concise.

Hingley's first major work was the 1950 biography *Chekhov: A Biographical and Critical Study,* and it is Chekhov scholarship that still forms the backbone of his career. Offered as a corrective to the pervasive image of Chekhov as "a gentle, suffering soul," an "apathetic pessimist, obsessed to the exclusion of everything else with the futility of life," the book describes the doctor, playwright, and short-story writer as "an optimist, both in his writings and in his personal

life," who possessed a sense of humor, zest for living, and childlike freshness of observation that belies the standard Chekhov legend. Hingley also emphasized, for the reader in English, Chekhov's hundreds of short stories, which in his opinion have been unjustly neglected in favor of the plays.

Though praised for his "conscientious handling of sources," and thorough familiarity with recent Soviet criticism of Chekhov, Hingley was taken to task by reviewers put off by his uninspired narrative, which V.S. Pritchett called "pedestrian in manner and approach." The *Times Literary Supplement* critic thought Hingley's style too "dull and colourless" and the book's structure "altogether too formal and too mechanical" to "enable him to bring out with any liveliness or force of persuasion the fascination of Chekhov's personality." Nonetheless, *Chekhov: A Biographical and Critical Study* is now considered one of the standard short biographies of the writer and was issued in a revised edition in 1965.

In 1976 Hingley published *A New Life of Anton Chekhov,* drawing on previously unused literary and historical sources as well as Chekhov's own copious correspondence. *The Economist* hailed the new biography as "wonderfully illuminating . . . removing at a stroke—or rather in a succession of gleefully blood-letting stories—the ectoplasmic Hans Christian Andersen of the steppes, and substituting a wholly credible, almost wholly admirable, and very Russian man. [Hingley's book] is, in its scholarly way, a spectacular achievement." In spectacular disagreement was the *New York Times* reviewer, who called the author's style "both flaccid and jaunty," his critical judgments "venturesomely banal," and his psychological insights "full of self-congratulatory assumptions." Critics did agree, however, that *A New Life* covered "every nook and cranny of Chekhov's existence." In addition to the biographies, Hingley wrote on Chekhov in *Russian Writers and Society 1825–1904* and translated and edited the massive *Oxford Chekhov,* volumes one through nine.

Fyodor Dostoevsky and Boris Pasternak were also the subjects of full-length biographies by Hingley (Dostoevsky twice). The 1983 volume on Pasternak was especially well-received. Published hard on the heels of his colleague Guy de Mallac's exhaustive but rather wooden first biography of the Nobel-laureate poet and novelist, Hingley's pithier work concentrated on "the provocative asking of questions" and "sweepingly bold integrations of [Pasternak's] life, work, and age," to quote the *Times Literary Suplement,* making Pasternak's eccentricities, muddled behavior, and oblique resistance to the Khrushchev regime the book's main themes.

Pasternak was one of four poets—Osip Mandelstam, Anna Akhmatova, and Maria Tsvetaeva were the others—covered in one of Hingley's more original studies, *Nightingale Fever: Russian Poets in Revolution*. Here Hingley explored a characteristic Soviet problem: the conflict between the poet who "[cannot] stop singing regardless of the consequences" and the repressive policies of the state. The tragic lives of these writers—Mandelstam died on the way to a Soviet concentration camp; Tsvetaeva, in self-imposed exile, committed suicide; Akhmatova was persecuted and her husband murdered; Pasternak feared for his life during the Stalin and Khrushchev years—were summed up in Mandelstam's words: "And there is no hope/For heart still flushed/With Nightingale Fever."

In Russia, more than in many places, literature and politics are intimately connected. Hingley's literary research led him to write more general studies of Russian history, including *Nihilists; The Tsars: Russian Autocrats 1533–1917; The Russian Secret Police; Joseph Stalin: Man and Legend*; and *The Russian Mind*. Of these, *The Russian Mind* is his most important investigation into "what makes the Russian tick." Among the "peculiar features" of the national mentality, Hingley wrote, are the entrenched Russian propensity for broad sentimentality mixed with *vranyo*, the native form of blarney under which can be classified most official statements of the Soviet government; the Russians' ingrained secretism and strong feeling of national unity; and the national obsession with melodramatic confessions and penance, of which the most obvious examples are the show-trials at every level of organization from factory floor to state court. "[*The Russian Mind*] crackles, astonishes, baffles, and gives pause," wrote C. K. Davis in the *Christian Science Monitor*; "[Hingley] knows how to handle contradictions deftly. . . . He talks in degrees of group character and historical conditioning, not in nationalist absolutes. A non-Russian reader emerges from his book charmed and frightened, but if he has read carefully, not in a state of panic."

Currently Oxford University Lecturer in Russian, Hingley has also translated, with Max Hayward, Aleksandr Solzhenitsyn's *One Day in the Life of Ivan Denisovich*. He is a commentator on Soviet affairs for the *Sunday Times* and had published scores of articles in Russian-studies journals.

PRINCIPAL WORKS: Chekhov: A Biographical and Critical Study, 1950; Up Jenkins, 1956; Soviet Prose, 1959; Under Soviet Skins, 1961; (with T.J. Binyon) Russian: A Beginner's Course, 1962; The Undiscovered Dostoyevsky, 1962; (tr. with M. Hayward) Aleksandr Solzhenitsyn, One Day in the Life of Ivan Denisovich, 1963; (tr.) Abram Tertz, Fantastic Stories, 1963; (tr. and ed.) The Oxford Chekhov (9 vols.; in progress) 1965–; Russian Writers and Society 1825–1904, 1967; Nihilists, 1967; The Tsars: Russian Autocrats 1533–1917, 1968; (ed.) Modern Russian Reader, c. 1970; The Russian Secret Police, 1970; A People in Turmoil: Revolutions in Russia, 1972; A Concise History of Russia, 1972; Joseph Stalin: Man and Legend, 1974; (tr.) Anton Chekhov, Seven Short Stories, 1974; A New Life of Anton Chekhov, 1976; (tr.) Anton Chekhov, Eleven Stories, 1976; The Russian Mind, 1977; Dostoyevsky: His Life and Work, 1978; Russian Writers and Soviet Society 1917–1978, 1979; Nightingale Fever: Russian Poets in Revolution, 1981; Pasternak: A Biography, 1983.

ABOUT: Contemporary Authors, new revised series 7–8, 1969. *Periodicals*—Christian Science Monitor December 14, 1977; May 19, 1982; Economist May 11, 1974; May 22, 1976; June 9, 1979; New Statesman March 17, 1951; October 9, 1970; May 10, 1974; May 14, 1976; New York Review of Books June 10, 1976; New York Times Book Review June 20, 1976; September 9, 1979; December 10, 1981; New Yorker May 14, 1979; Times Literary Supplement February 2, 1951; October 16, 1970; June 14, 1974; March 12, 1982; August 26, 1983; Yale Review Spring 1980.

HOBAN, RUSSELL (CONWELL) (February 4, 1925–), American novelist and children's writer, was born in Lansdale, Pennsylvania, the only son and youngest child of Abram T. Hoban, a Russian immigrant and the advertising manager of the Philadelphia *Jewish Daily Forward*, and the former Jeanette Dimmerman. "The first two rules of etiquette I learned," he wrote in the *Third Book of Junior Authors*, "were never to cross a picket line and always to eat the union label on the pumpernickel for good luck." He was good at drawing, "and was expected to be a great artist when I grew up." After attending Temple University for a short time, he studied at the Philadelphia Museum School of Industrial Art from 1941 to 1943, when he began two years of service in the army. Hoban married Lillian Aberman in early 1944 and they lived in New York from 1945, where he worked as a commercial artist for magazines and advertising studios, eventually progressing to the post of television art director for the agencies Batten, Barton, Durstine & Osborne and J. Walter Thompson. After 1956 he was a freelance illustrator for ad agencies and for such magazines as *Time, Life, Fortune, Saturday Evening Post*, and *True*.

Hoban's career as a writer of juvenile books began in 1959 with *What Does It Do and How Does It Work?* He is perhaps best known in this

RUSSELL HOBAN

genre for his series of books for younger readers about the domestic adventures of Frances the badger and for a much loved novel, *The Mouse and His Child* (1967), which was described by Alex Hamilton in a 1975 interview as a "watershed" in Hoban's career. "Nobody is clear what category of classic it is, only that it is one. It is the fearful adventure through reality of a pair of wind-up toys, whom accident has made tramps, trying after more than they were wound up for. As they walk through the terrors, one of them always backwards, the key turns in the father's back like a knife in a wound." Eleven of the fifty-two children's books Hoban has produced through 1983, including all the Frances books, were illustrated by his wife Lillian.

A crisis in Hoban's life and career was precipitated by his move from Wilton, Connecticut, to London in 1969. Soon after his arrival in England with his family, his marriage broke up, and Lillian Hoban returned to the United States with their three daughters and one son. But Hoban found, as he said in 1974, that he "couldn't leave London. It had a lot to do with all kinds of things beyond needing a change, or my career, or anything like that, and for the first year after the breakup I kept trying to write, but couldn't get anything down on paper at all." In early 1971 he began work on his first adult novel, *The Lion of Boaz-Jachin and Jachin-Boaz.* The genesis of this book, in Hoban's own words, explains much about his method of writing in a new and, for him, more demanding genre: "I have always fancied the supernatural, like Oliver Onions, M. R. James, Sheridan Le Fanu, Arthur Machin, and I worked up some kind of start

after seeing a book on Mesopotamian art which had a lion—but not *the* lion—in it. I read up some Sumerian mythology and began to extrapolate some mythology of my own, expecting to get a story on a supernatural line, but nothing happened. It's funny, the way I write books— I'm not really capable of working up an idea on a theme, or planning out something with various themes, because there always is a specific thing which begins to work in me, and in this case it was some link between fathers and sons, which I had got into with *The Mouse and His Child* and now it was my own son, who was fifteen at the time, and angry at me. That seemed to put itself together with the idea of a lion which could be called out of the past by powerful feelings in a boy, and sent to hunt down his father. England became the place where I had really made contact with myself. I had written about cuddly animals and clockwork toys, but I had never attempted to use myself as a man, or my own experiences."

Kleinzeit, Hoban's second novel, concerns a successfully resolved crisis in the life of an unhappy, middle-aged advertising copywriter. The locale is London, an absurdly distorted place, described by Hoban as "a completely animistic world, where everything talks, the mirror talks to him, the hospital talks to him, Death talks." Most critics considered the book witty and inventive, and the *Times Literary Supplement,* in a highly favorable review, called it "clarity itself, . . . a very funny novel. . . . The fun comes partly from a delight in the misuse of words, partly from the indispensable ingredient of humor—incongruity."

Turtle liberation is the subject of *Turtle Diary,* in which a man and a woman, at first unknown to each other, come to realize a shared obsession with freeing giant loggerhead sea turtles from the London Zoo. The story is told in alternating chapters from the diaries of William G., a lonely, divorced man who lives in a dreary bed-sitter, and Neaera H., a successful writer of relentlessly anthropomorphic children's books—the popular "Gillian Vole" series—about which she herself is very sardonic. Victoria Glendinning thought the book "very intelligent and very funny, . . . most distinguished and memorable." Anthony Thwaite praised the author's style, "circumstantial, matter-of-fact, direct, yet apt to sidestep into the oddest connections and perceptions, so that pathos suddenly detonates into farce, and surrealist freewheeling is in a moment confronted with horror. . . . It's a marvellously funny and moving book, easy to read, hard to come to grips with, difficult to forget."

Reviewing *Turtle Diary* in *Newsweek,* P. S.

Prescott remarked that Hoban was showing "signs of becoming a cult writer" in Britain. The praise accorded the next novel, *Riddley Walker*, in that country was more extravagant than any American writer has received in years. The hero of the novel, which takes place in Kent about two millennia after a nuclear holocaust has obliterated civilization, is a twelve-year-old "Tel-Man," who had taken over from his dead father the duty of interpreting the handed-down ceremony of the traveling Punch-and-Judy show. Riddley tells his story in his own words, a language described by Hoban as "a worndown, broken-apart kind of English," the nuances of which the reader must struggle to learn as the novel progresses. Five and a half years and fourteen drafts were necessary before Hoban was satisfied with the book, which A. Alvarez called "an artistic *tour de force* in every possible way" and "an extraordinary achievement, comparable, in its way, to *Huckleberry Finn* itself." Penelope Lively considered the subject of the book to be "the human mind, its terrible and perhaps fatal duality, its capacity for salvation, its energy, its tragedy." She continued, "No review can do more than suggest the range and effect of this extraordinary book. It is *sui generis,* its inspirations both particular and diverse, its references legion, its craft remarkable—contributing to a whole that is vivid, compelling, and certainly unforgettable." Despite a generally favorable U.S. critical response, however, *Riddley Walker* achieved only very modest sales.

Pilgermann, a complex and allusive novel about the First Crusade of 1098, came about when a visit by Hoban in 1980 to a daughter in Israel made him realize, as he said in 1981, that "the Jewishness of me somehow seems to have been bypassed in the exploration of the depths of my being." Pilgermann is a German Jew whose pilgrimage in quest of truth ("the shock of Thing-in-itself, the enormity of Now") takes him to the Holy Land and its conflicting Jewish, Christian, and Islamic cultures. An eyewitness to the violence and brutality of the Crusades and himself a victim of anti-Semitism in his native Germany, Pilgermann is an Everyman figure, and his story is part allegory, part historical fiction. Every bit as ambitious in its conception as *Riddley Walker,* the novel shares with its predecessor what Joel Conarroe, in the *New York Times Book Review,* called "quirky brilliance," though its language is "more conventional, only occasionally twisting into a kind of exotic knottiness." Reviewers generally found *Pilgermann* less riveting than its predecessor—overly complex and weighed down with its burden of scholarship. Most conceded, however, that such comparisons were somewhat unfair—

Conarroe concluded: *"Riddley Walker,* after all, is miraculous; *Pilgermann* is merely remarkable."

Hoban married his second wife, Gundula Ahl, in 1975; they live with their three young sons in a Victorian house across from a playground on Eel Brook Common, Fulham, in southwest London. "I'm fifty-five years old," he said in 1981, "and in the last few years I've gotten to be good friends with my head. I see my psychiatrist daily, and I read him what I write. I think it probably works another way with other people than the way it works with me. There always seems to be something in my mind waiting to put something together with some primary thought I will encounter. It's like looking out of the window and listening to the radio at the same time. I am committed to what comes to me, however it links up." Hoban has continued to write juvenile books, sometimes producing as many as four in a single year. He leads a rather strictly regimented life, does not like traveling, and lists his recreations as short-wave listening and stones.

PRINCIPAL WORKS: The Lion of Boaz-Jachin and Jachin-Boaz, 1973; Kleinzeit, 1974; Turtle Diary, 1975; Riddley Walker; 1980; Pilgermann, 1983; Lavinia Bat, 1984; Charlie Meadows, 1984.

ABOUT: Contemporary Authors, first revision series 5-8, 1969; Third Book of Junior Authors, 1972. *Periodicals*—Atlantic August 1976; Encounter January 1981; Guardian March 24, 1975; New Statesman April 11, 1975; New York Review of Books October 19, 1981; New York Times November 1, 1981; New York Times Book Review March 21, 1976; June 28, 1981; May 29, 1983; November 27, 1983; Newsweek January 1, 1976; June 29, 1981; May 30, 1983; Observer March 23, 1975; People August 10, 1981; Publishers Weekly May 15, 1981; Times November 15, 1974; Times Educational Supplement October 31, 1980; Times Literary Supplement March 29, 1974; March 21, 1975; October 31, 1980; March 18, 1983; Village Voice July 8–14, 1981.

HOLLAND, CECELIA (December 31, 1943–), American novelist, was born in Henderson, Nevada, the daughter of William Dean and Katharine (Schenck) Holland. She enrolled at Pennsylvania State University in 1961, but at the end of the first year transferred to Connecticut College, where she specialized in European history, and received her B.A. in 1965. Holland was accepted for graduate work in European history at Columbia University, but dropped out of the program when her first novel, about the Norman invasion of England, written while she was still a student at Connecticut College, was accepted for publication. The book was pub-

CECELIA HOLLAND

lished in 1966, while she was working as a file
clerk at Brentano's Manhattan bookstore. At
twenty-two, already "established," she joined the
faculty of the Famous Writers School, then sev-
en months later went to Hollywood to work on
a script about the First Crusade that was never
produced. Since then, she has lived from the
earnings of her historical novels, which have
won both a popular following and critical acclaim, and have been appearing at the astonishing rate of about a book a year for nearly two
decades.

Holland's first novel, *The Firedrake*, established her immediately as one of the most promising, and certainly as the most precocious, of
current American historical novelists. Some reviewers made light of Holland's eleventh-
century chronicle, which ends with the battle of
Hastings in 1066, because of its stripped-down-
to-basics style, heroics, and emphasis upon action. But P. Albert Duhamel, in the *New York
Times Book Review,* found the action scenes
brilliantly realized. "The story is told," he noted,
"in lines as strong, with movement and color as
sure and flowing, as those of the tapestry [of
Bayeux]." The reviewer for the *Times Literary
Supplement* called the novel "an impressive effort, which conveys Holland's own excitement
over her period, . . . and in so far as such currently well-worn ground can be made to seem
brutally fresh, she shows an unusual skill and
imaginative power."

In *Rakóssy*, Holland shifted her scene to Hungary in the sixteenth century, to recount the
tragedy of a Magyar nobleman who forfeits his
life in a stand against Turkish invaders. The re-

viewer for *Time* remarked that "Holland writes
a spare, masculine prose. . . . She avoids the
stage-prop flummery that clutters so many historical novels. . . . The character and the story
have the ring of authenticity." Holland's third
novel, *The Kings in Winter,* which deals with
feuding clans in Ireland at the time of the Norse
invasion in the eleventh century, was praised
elaborately by Orville Prescott in the *New York
Times Book Review.* "She is adept in suggesting
in a few lines the tensions of dangerous times,"
he observed, " . . . no space is given to the details other novelists consider essential. . . . pure
narration, of a kind not critically fashionable for
years, is the essence of her appeal." The *Times
Literary Supplement* reviewer, who was equally
enthusiastic, concluded that Holland "belongs to
that small band of writers who can still show us
what distinction the historical novel can attain."
When the Sun Falls, of the following year, is
concerned with the thirteenth-century Mongol
invasion of Russia and Europe; and its emphasis
is once again upon passionate characters who become caught up in the complicated workings of
history.

Holland next published two historical novels
for children—*Ghosts of the Steppe* and *The
King's Road,* both of which drew critical praise.
Cold Iron, written under the pseudonym of Robert Stone Pryor, was a more unexpected book
from Holland, since it is not a historical novel
but a contemporary tale of the rock music scene
in California. Jay Cocks, in *Time,* called it a
"cool little novel . . . written with an obvious
insider's authority," but on the whole the reception of the book was restrained rather than enthusiastic. The reviewer for *Publishers Weekly*
observed that "the identity of the pseudonymous
author is supposed to be a secret, but we can say
that we think she writes better under her own
name."

In the same year, 1970, Holland published
Antichrist, about Holy Roman Emperor Frederick of Sicily. The book was praised by P. A. Duhamel and others for its management of large,
action-filled scenes, and for its sensuous pleasure
in the archaic and exotic. But some reviewers
felt that Holland's characterization of Frederick
was facile and simplistic. Yet in her novel of the
following year, *The Earl,* which centers upon
the tragedy of Fulk de Bruyère, Earl of Stafford,
in twelfth-century England, it was Holland's
skillful characterization that was singled out for
praise. What Audrey Foote found lacking in
Antichrist, she found very much present in *The
Earl.* "Miss Holland," Foote wrote in *Book
World,* "has been justly praised, though sometimes excessively, for her achievement in what
has been considered a male province, the depic-

tion of warfare. But this quiet convincing portrayal of a father's complex feelings toward a son, a subject not to be acquired by even the most conscientious academic researcher, is a more subtle triumph."

In an interview, Holland spoke of her method of selecting her subjects. "I never pick subjects which are too well-known," she said. "That would restrict my freedom. On the other hand, the historical facts provide the check points for my imagination. They're a way of finding out if I've really gotten a character right or not." *The Death of Attila* illustrates her method. Attila may be the title character, but he figures only at the fringes of the novel, which tests conflicting claims of loyalty of a young German, Dietric, and his Hun soldier friend Tacs. The book, however, received mixed reviews. Steven Marcus, in *Harper's*, felt that Holland attempted unsuccessfully to impose a modern consciousness on her historical characters, and Peter Ackroyd, in the *Spectator*, had a similar opinion. "[Holland] has managed to stir a little life into these old bones," Ackroyd wrote, "but she would have succeeded better if the characters had not behaved like the historical cardboard from which they came."

Holland's *Great Maria* shifts to yet another culture and time—that of England in the Caroline age, and at the same time she moves her viewpoint from her usual male one to that of the female title character. *Floating Worlds* was a bolder experiment still, since it is set not in the remote past but 4,000 years in the future, a time of interplanetary conflict. In general, reviewers felt that Holland lost much of her imaginative power in this lengthy and complex science fiction novel. Maria Hoffman remarked that Holland "has not succeeded in creating either a clearly delineated Future Earth or an understandable alien race"; and Mark Rose, in the *New Republic*, found the work filled with action but "empty of intellection." *Floating Worlds*, he remarked, "is little more than a space opera."

Two Ravens, an eleventh-century Icelandic saga, was well received, so much so that the critic for *Choice* concluded that Holland "remains beyond question one of the premier historical novelists of our time." *City of God*, concerned with Renaissance Rome, was praised by *Time's* reviewer, who remarked: "As usual, Holland, who writes refreshingly taut prose, dispenses with the ponderous plots and pageantry of the genre: her people matter much more than their costumes." In *Home Ground*, Holland once again departed from historical fiction. *Home Ground* is set at a present-day Northern California commune to which a woman returns, following the breakup of a ten-year relationship, to sort

out her life. The novel was considered able, but many reviewers felt that it lacked the excitement of her historical fiction. Holland's later work, *The Sea Beggars*, returns to the historical past to depict the tragic breakup of a family in sixteenth-century Holland during the spread of the Spanish Inquisition. The novel was praised not merely or its generous amount of action but also for its domestic realism.

In a profile of her in *Newsweek* in 1969, Holland was described as "a tall, talented, 25-year-old blonde . . . who, in a red velvet tunic and black, buckled boots, looks like a medieval page. [She] lives with three cats and six posters of The Doors' Jim Morrison in a secluded house near New Haven, Connecticut. [She] never works during the dead of winter because her office (the former garage) is too cold. [She] writes lyrics for local rock groups, . . . and desite her total immersion in the romantic past, is into everything current from street fights to the poetry of James Merrill." She had earlier lived for many years in California, and was once a member of a California commune. In 1969, she married Robert Rood, and has a daughter, Julie Ruth. Holland was visiting professor of English at Connecticut College in 1979, and the recipient of a Guggenheim fellowship for 1981–82.

PRINCIPAL WORKS: The Fire Drake, 1966; Rakóssy, 1967; The Kings in Winter, 1968; Until the Sun Falls, 1969; Ghost of the Steppe (juvenile), 1969; The King's Road (juvenile), 1970; Cold Iron (as Robert Stone Pryor), 1970; Antichrist, 1973; Great Maria, 1974; Floating Worlds, 1976; Two Ravens, 1978; City of God, 1979; Home Ground, 1981; The Sea Beggars, 1982; The Belt of Gold, 1984.

ABOUT: Contemporary Authors, new revision series 9, 1983; Who's Who in America, 1974–1975; Who's Who of American Women, 1974–1975. *Periodicals*—Book World March 22, 1970; September 19, 1971; Harper's March 1974; New Republic March 20, 1976; Newsweek February 10, 1969; New York Times Book Review January 15, 1967; January 28, 1968; Spectator October 22, 1977; Time August 17, 1970; April 9, 1979.

HOWARD, MAUREEN (June 28, 1930–   ), American novelist, was born in Bridgeport, Connecticut, the daughter of William L. and Loretta (Burns) Kearns, both of whom were of Irish descent. She was educated at local Catholic schools, and received her B.A. degree from Smith College in 1952. She worked in book publishing in New York City from 1952 to 1954, and in 1954 married Daniel F. Howard, an English professor, by whom she has a daughter, Loretta. Her husband taught at Williams and Kenyon col-

MAUREEN HOWARD

leges, but their life took them abroad at various times, particularly to London and Italy. Howard's first novel, *Not a Word About Nightingales,* was published in England in 1960 and in the United States in 1962, and brought her immediate attention.

Not a Word About Nightingales deals with a genteel professor of English, Albert Sedgeley, who goes abroad on a sabbatical year with his wife Ann. In Italy, he decides that his life is a "dry husk," and announces that he will remain in Italy. His wife returns to the quiet New England town, where she has a brief affair with the college's dean, while Albert sets himself up in a villa in Perugia, acquires an "upswept Garibaldi mustache," and a buxom mistress. The novel concentrates on the summer when Rosemary, the Sedgeleys' daughter, is sent (in a manner reminiscent of James' *The Ambassadors*) to bring the erring professor back home—which she does, his aspiration to be a "man of emotion and feeling" having proved to be short-lived. The reviewer for the *Times Literary Supplement* found the novel a charming but "lightweight" performance, but American critics were enraptured. "Everything about *Not a Word About Nightingales,*" Haskel Frankel remarked, "is a delight. The civility of its passions, a prose style, simple and clean . . . and a bitter sweet theme shot through with irony and subtleties all suggest the little British novel. It also suggests a writing talent to be watched and cherished." Martin Levin called it "a cool, subtly modulated novel." and Dorothy Nyren wrote that its "excellence lies in the nice calculation of its rate of irony to sympathy and in a fine sense of nuance and detail."

Bridgeport Bus, Howard's second novel, centers on Mary Agnes Keely, a thirty-five-year-old executive secretary in a Connecticut zipper factory, who surreptitiously reads French symbolist poets, and is in thrall to her widowed mother. Mary escapes to New York, to confront an assortment of dissarranged lives, including that of her roommate, Lydia Savaard. She has, in addition, an ill-fated affair with an art director who lives with his mother in Brooklyn, becomes pregnant by him, and later gives the baby up for adoption. Her personality, as one critic noted, "is splintered between reality and her self-defeating romanticism." Critics greeted *Bridgeport Bus* with enthusiasm but usually expressed reservations. Martin Levin found the book essentially a collection of vignettes, some of them superb, particularly the sequence dealing with Mary and Lydia Savaard. "Later," he wrote, "Miss Howard dredges into the memory of the protagonist for some mundane reminiscences of her cousin Sherry, a New York show girl. From here on, the novel loses a fluency it never quite regains." Daniel Stern agreed, commenting: "Sherry's persistent presence is never fully integrated in what is otherwise so fine a book. One hopes that next time Miss Howard will come to terms with structure. If she does, there is little she cannot do."

Howard's marriage ended in 1967, and the following year she married David J. Gordon, also an English professor. She taught English and creative writing at the New School for Social Research in New York (1967–68), and at the University of California, Santa Barbara (1968–69); and has subsequently taught at Brooklyn College, the New School, and Amherst College. She received a Guggenheim Fellowship for 1967–68, and during the same year was a fellow of the Radcliffe Institute. Her third novel, *Before My Time,* was nominated for a National Book Award. Using an unusual narrative method, by which the first half of the book is devoted to exposition, while the second comprises a series of four complete short stories, *Before My Time* follows Laura Quinn, a housewife in suburban Boston, who opens her home to Jim Cogan, the son of Bronx relatives. Two generations—the 1940s and the 1970s—collide, but by the end both Laura and Cogan know themselves somewhat better. He gives up the idea of running away from himself and his family, and Laura comes to accept herself and the loss of her youth.

Phoebe Adams noted that "the novel's distinction arises from the author's sharp, idiosyncratic vision and her delicate manipulation of an interlocked past and present." The reviewer for the *New Yorker* also called attention to Howard's subtle narrative strategies: "Miss Howard may be cavalier with niceties of plot (indeed, most chapters are simply character sketches, or 'stories within stories,' as she puts it), but her book is . . . full of moral intelligence, wit, and fresh insight into the way people live." Walter Clemons called Howard "subtle, oblique and precise." but was critical of the novel's construction. "The relationship between woman and boy," he wrote, "never gets fully dramatized. It remains a muffled theoretical 'given'—the peg on which the family stories are hung." Pearl Bell thought that the work depended too much on "stylistic virtuosity." "Laura and Jimmy," she remarked, "remain hazy and dim . . . One feels consistently cheated by the 'fine' writing, the artfulness of all those tentative ambiguities, the ornate fretwork of dissonance and dependence that registers so little thought and feeling about the ongoing war of American generations."

In 1977, Howard edited *Seven American Women Writers of the Twentieth Century,* and had a short play, *Songs at Twilight,* presented Off-Off-Broadway at the La Mama playhouse. In 1978, her memoir *Facts of Life* was published to glowing reviews, and was awarded the National Book Critics Circle Award. Like a number of other critics, the reviewer for *Harper's* magazine called *Facts of Life* a "worthy companion to Mary McCarthy's *Memories of a Catholic Girlhood.*" Alfred Kazin remarked: "Maureen Howard is a talented novelist who has never written anything so concentrated and properly disturbing as this memoir. . . . My first impression was of sheer novelistic skill. . . . She is a dogged snipper of the human heart who, despite her life with other breeds, retains a narrowly focused Catholic suspicion of enthusiasm, especially her own." Saul Maloff characterized *Facts of Life* as a "finely executed, sly, resonant memoir. . . . Howard is widely and deeply read, formidably intelligent, a striking stylist with a cast of mind both penetrating and sardonic—a witty and not seldom a deadly ironist." Howard's coming to terms with her Irish Catholic, Connecticut upbringing, particularly with her parents—her father, a county detective with a droll suspicion of intellect, and her mother, a culturally aspiring Smith graduate "before life caught up with her"—are handled with great finesse; and Howard's delicate balance of affection and judgment struck reviewers as the supreme triumph of the book.

With similar sensitivity and balance Howard's novel *Grace Abounding* explores the experience of Maude Dowd, an Irish Catholic widow of forty-three at the beginning, who lives in a big house in Connecticut with her fourteen-year-old daughter Elizabeth. In this section the widow seems lost in erotic daydreams and drained of will. Then, leaping ahead abruptly, she is shown in New York at fifty-three, in her marriage to Gilbert Lasser, a foundation executive. She works as a child psychotherapist, and fills her days with purpose. Still, all is not well. Her husband has too many problems of his own to pay heed to hers, and her daughter Elizabeth has forsaken her career as an opera singer for marriage and domesticity. Maude's "spiritual pilgrimage" seems to falter; but, as John W. Crowley remarked, "at this dark moment, as at her other times of need, grace is visited upon Maude. Her daughter starts to sing again . . . and her husband brings her equally miraculous comfort." Crowley called *Grace Abounding* a "spellbinding narrative" about Maude's effort "to retain some sense of identity in a discontinuous universe." Ada Long called attention to the book's "mysterious and complex integrity. It is a more concentrated work than any of Howard's previous books, and in its rendering of the characters a gentler and more compassionate one." Noel Perrin, however, thought *Grace Abounding* "a little short for its plot . . . [and it] does not quite come together at the end." In a similar vein, Peter Prescott remarked that Howard "introduces too many supporting characters and then feels obliged to follow them about as the principals fade from sight."

Maureen Howard lives with her family in New York City, teaches a writing seminar at Columbia University, and is a frequent contributor to the *New York Times, Washington Post, Yale Review, Hudson Review,* and other publications. In an account of herself published in the *New York Times Book Review* (April 25, 1982) Howard has commented on her persistent theme of a search for identity in a random world, and asked herself why she writes: "Because I enjoy it as my life," she concluded, "and with the hope that if I try again I will choose the right word or a tone, a gesture that will open the door of a closed room, connect to the world, give another some small revelation or unexpected delight."

PRINCIPAL WORKS: Not a Word About Nightingales, 1962; Bridgeport Bus, 1965; Before My Time, 1975; Facts of Life, 1978; Grace Abounding, 1982. As editor—The Penguin Book of Contemporary American Essays, 1984.

ABOUT: Contemporary Authors 53–56; Contemporary Literary Criticism 5, 1976; 14, 1980; Dictionary of Literary Biography Yearbook, 1983. Periodicals—America February 19, 1983; Book World October 10, 1982; Hudson Review Spring 1966; New Leader January 20, 1975; New Republic September 9, 1978; Newsweek September 25, 1978; New Yorker March 31, 1962; New York Times March 11, 1977; New York Times Book Review April 25, 1982; December 2, 1982; Saturday Review September 25, 1965; Time January 27, 1975.

*HRABAL, BOHUMIL (March 28, 1914–), Czech novelist and short story writer, was born in Brno, the son of a brewery manager. He received his law degree at the Charles University in Prague in 1946. During World War II and in the 1950s he held a variety of jobs and did not begin to make his living as a writer until the early 1960s. Hrabal's earliest work was strongly influenced by surrealism. In 1949 his first book was printed but not published. As a surrealist he was suspect with the authorities and had no recognized standing in Czech literature. By 1963, however, having published a well-received short story, *Perlička na dně* (Little Pearl on the Bottom), he became a popular writer. Some of his stories were filmed by the Czech "new wave" film makers and translated all over Europe and in the United States and Japan. Though these stories—full of paradoxes, incongruities, black humor—were "politically neutral," in A. French's phrase, "politically minded observers interpreted [them] as a gesture of escape from the socialist nightmare." One of his best known books was *Pábitelé* (The Crazies, 1964), the title a coinage by Hrabal to describe its characters—a group of humble but completely cheerful, liberated individualists who scorn conventional society and are in turn despised by it. Like American "hippies" of the same period, Hrabal's "crazies," French writes, "became a national type, setting a style for off-beat living."

Hrabal's international reputation is mainly based on one work, *Ostře sledované vlaky* (*A Close Watch on the Trains*, 1964), which was made into a highly praised film, *Closely Watched Trains*, and in the United States received an Academy Award as the best foreign film of 1968. Hrabal collaborated with the noted Czech film maker Jiri Menzel on the screenplay and later commented that he liked the film better than the novel because as a writer, "I rely basically on dialogue and the eye." The story of a young country boy on his first job as a railway dispatcher in the early days of the Nazi occupation, it is both warmly humorous as it recounts his pride in his new work, his naiveté, his sexual initiation, and deeply moving as he achieves maturity and martyrdom by heroically blowing up a German munitions train.

Popular as Hrabal was, his books were banned in Czechoslovakia after the Soviet invasion of 1969. His name reappeared only in 1975 when he was allowed to publish again but under various restrictions and constant official interfer-ence. The Western world has seen only one more of his works—a collection of his short stories, *The Death of Mr. Baltisberger*, characteristically slight and patternless, about the futility and meaninglessness of drab everyday life, but fascinating and original. Thomas Lask remarked, in the *New York Times Book Review*, that "Hrabal shows an off-beat, but original mind, a fey imagination and a sure hand in constructing his tales." It is a surrealist, Joycean approach to a world populated by people among whom Hrabal has spent a great part of his life: social outcasts, political anarchists, poets, boasters sitting over their mugs of beer, antiheroes of "great moments of history." Hrabal, an indefatigable storyteller, is one of them—their poetic voice. He creates a surreal world out of dreams and the density of small, apparently unimportant details which we tend to ignore or fail to understand. His stories build on the magic of his style to express absurd dimensions of life. The rambling narrative, mixing slang, humor, and a certain poetic spirit, reveals a disturbing reality hidden under the surface of everyday life and social hypocrisy.

WORKS IN ENGLISH TRANSLATION: E. Pargeter translated *A Close Watch on the Trains* in 1968; the screenplay *Closely Watched Trains* by Hrabal and Jiri Menzel was translated by Josef Holzbecher in 1971. Michael Henry Heim translated *The Death of Mr. Baltisberger* in 1975.

ABOUT: Columbia Dictionary of Modern European Literature, 1980; French, A. Czech Writers and Politics 1945-1969, 1982; Harkins, W.E. and P. Trensky (eds.) Czechoslovak Literature since 1956, 1980; Skvorecky, J. *Foreword to* A Close Watch on the Trains (Penguin ed., 1981) and *Foreword to* The Death of Mr. Baltisberger, 1975. *Periodicals*—New York Times Book Review October 5, 1975; Times Literary Supplement May 20, 1977.

HSIAO HUNG *See* XIAO HONG

HUGO, RICHARD (FRANKLIN) (December 21, 1923–October 22, 1982), American poet, was born in Seattle, the son of Franklin James and Esther Clara (Monk) Hogan. Hugo's father abandoned his adolescent wife and she in turn left her two-year-old son to be raised by his grandparents in the small Washington town of White Center. This dispossession marked Hugo for life; when his mother later married a man named Hugo, he adopted that name, perhaps as a means of taking on an identity.

Hugo grew up in an atmosphere of emotional and economic deprivation. His grandparents

°hrä´ bäl, bô´ hŏŏ mēl

RICHARD HUGO

showed little or no physical affection, and he later wrote that he never saw a man kiss a woman exept in movies. Moreover, Hugo was a child of the Depression. There was little money at home or in White Center, and Hugo experienced poverty as a constant degradation and humiliation. Years later, in "Letter to Levertov from Butte," he described this inheritance in terms that combine social conditions and personal experience:

> On the other hand
> I know the cruelty of poverty, the embittering ways
> love is denied, and food, the mean near-insanity of being
> and being deprived, the trivial compensations of each day,
> recapturing old years in broadcast tunes you try to recall
> in bars, hunched over the beer you can't afford, or bending
> to the bad job you're lucky enough to have.

Hugo joined the Army Air Corps in 1943. He was stationed in Italy for the next two years, flew thirty-five bombing missions, and returned home a first lieutenant with a Distinguished Flying Cross and the Air Medal. He enrolled in the University of Washington on the GI Bill, earning his B.A. in 1948 and his M.A. in 1952. It was there that Hugo came under the influence of Theodore Roethke, whom he described as "probably the best poetry-writing teacher ever." Roethke introduced Hugo to the poetry of Yeats, Hopkins, and Auden and to seventeenth-century poets like Herbert, Marvell, and Herrick. Hugo's career as a poet began in Roethke's classes.

Hugo's first book, *A Run of Jacks,* was published in 1961. Most of the poems in this austere volume are dense and knotty explorations of the grim countryside of the Pacific Northwest, its polluted rivers, ghost-like townspeople, and bored children. The book is marked by an op-

pressive grayness relieved only by images of colorful fish flashing through small streams. As Laurence Lieberman has suggested, Hugo, in his early work, shared with Wallace Stevens a belief that the greatest poverty "might be to live in a colorless world; the surest antidote to our impoverishment would be to restore radiance of color to the world by retraining the faculty of color perception."

Unfortunately, in *A Run of Jacks,* Hugo's metaphysical grayness clouded his vision and, despite some strong poems such as "Trout" and "Duwamish," the book is depressingly monotonous. In his next volume, *Death of Kapowsin Tavern,* Hugo relaxed his voice and expanded his range, but the tone is no less dour and the catalog of dusty Northwest towns no more inviting than in *A Run of Jacks.* Hugo once admitted in an interview in *Slackwater Review* that he was so concerned with the sound and rhythm of these two books that he did not pay much attention to meaning. As a result, many of the poems are difficult to penetrate and their allusions are obscure. Nonetheless, the books received considerable praise. Richard Howard wrote: "The regional strain in Hugo's apprehension of his subjects has grown so consistent with experience as to seem supremely general, universal, which is merely to say that by the end of his second book he had made his world exist."

Hugo wrote his first two books while working as a technical writer for the Boeing aircraft company in Seattle. In 1963 he resigned, and with his first wife, Barbara Williams (they were married in 1951), lived in Italy for a year. In the province of Apulia Hugo revisited the scenes of his World War II memories, and, as he describes it in his autobiographical essay *"Ci Vediamo,"* experienced an emotional epiphany. The work that resulted from this trip, *Good Luck in Cracked Italian,* begins to show a new openness and vulnerability in Hugo's sensibility. The poetry is less clotted, although his free-verse forms did not change. "In writing the poems of his third book," Michael S. Allen observed, "the tough masculine stance of such earlier poems as 'Duwamish' and 'Duwamish Head' began to fade as Hugo found in himself the more enduring toughness of the human heart." In "Docking at Palermo" Hugo compares his own guarded responses to the emotionalism of the Italians:

> For them, the gangplank'd down. For you
> a cheating cabby waits. Learn the names
> of streets or give them names to fight.
> You have five hours here. If here before
> with hate, you walk a street called war
> and beg a man who was a beggar then:
> now I have no gun, show me how to cry.

Upon his return to the United States, Hugo

was offered a position in the English department of the University of Montana. For the rest of his life he was a teacher of writing, mostly at Montana, but also for periods at the Universities of Iowa and Washington. He eventually became head of the creative-writing department at Montana.

Hugo's next two books confirmed his reputation as an important American poet and were nominated for National Book Awards. *The Lady in Kicking Horse Reservoir* and *What Thou Lovest Well Remains American* again describe passed-over towns and wasted lives in Washington and Montana, whose landscapes are *paysages moralisés* that reflect Hugo's psychological strivings. Jonathan Holden thought "Degrees of Gray in Philipsburg" from the earlier volume "has the beauty and stature of Stevens' 'The Idea of Order at Key West,'" but wondered whether the beauty of Hugo's lines "are appropriate to such bleak themes." The volume as a whole was highly praised; James Wright, in his review in the *American Poetry Review*, even called Hugo "one of the best poets alive, in any language I know." However, Dick Allen, in *Poetry*, while judging the collection "an exceptional one," made some reservations that Hugo's detractors have repeatedly echoed. He noted "a sameness of technique" and said that the book "is perhaps over-specific in its personal allusions, and sometimes forces meaning onto a subject not able to be so weighted."

What Thou Lovest Well Remains American contains no poem as powerful as "Degrees of Gray in Philipsburg," but it is more consistently forceful than its predecessor. In the *Dictionary of Literary Biography,* Bob Group wrote that with this book "the early Hugo form reaches perfection." One of the most memorable poems in the collection is "Goodbye, Iowa," the most frankly autobiographical piece Hugo had yet written. It examines a nervous breakdown he suffered in 1971 while teaching at the University of Iowa. According to Michael S. Allen in *We Are Called Human: The Poetry of Richard Hugo,* the collapse of Hugo's first marriage six years before had left a lingering aftershock. More importantly, Hugo had never surmounted the sense of worthlessness and inadequacy he felt as a child, and this sense left him unprepared to deal with the success that had suddenly come his way.

Hugo delved further into the roots of this psychological crisis in his next book, *31 Letters and 13 Dreams.* The first three poems analyze his nervous breakdown in some detail, using the form of letters addressed to friends. Some critics complained that the letters occasionally degenerated into prose, but most found Hugo's new voice engaging. The "dream" poems were more controversial. Some critics thought them appropriate complements to the letter poems, others found them inaccessible. Almost all the book's reviewers recognized Hugo's stylistic individuality: "The psychological quest for wholeness and the social discovery of personal connections," wrote Michael S. Allen, "combine to make *31 Letters and 13 Dreams* a hallmark in contemporary poetry, best understood from the twin perspectives of psychological quest and social discovery."

Hugo published two more books of poetry before his death from leukemia in 1982. *White Center* and *The Right Madness on Skye* did not really break new ground, but most critics considered the latter work a strong continuation of familiar themes. Reviewing Hugo's posthumously published collection, *Making Certain It Goes On,* Dave Smith summed up his poetic achievement: "He was looking for what he called the 'knowns' and, as if his readers were his companions, he was our guide to the permanent, passionate, not yet completely civilized, not entirely homogenized life where we might confront and survive degradation, shame and deterioration. . . . His form was right for what he wanted—intensity, immediacy, and verbal velocity, the panoramic and the telescopic. He made the poem a state of mind and a force field."

By the end of his life Hugo had accumulated many prizes and awards, including a Guggenheim fellowship, a Rockefeller Foundation creative writing grant, and the Theodore Roethke Memorial Prize. In 1977 he succeeded Stanley Kunitz as judge of the Yale Younger Poets series. In 1974 Hugo married his second wife, Ripley Schamm. In an obituary in *The Weekly, Seattle's Newsmagazine,* his friend William Stafford wrote that in his later years, "Hugo could no longer claim failure and loneliness."

PRINCIPAL WORKS: *Poetry*—A Run of Jacks, 1961; Death of Kapowsin Tavern, 1965; Good Luck in Cracked Italian, 1969; The Lady in Kicking Horse Reservoir, 1973; What Thou Lovest Well Remains American, 1975; 31 Letters and 13 Dreams, 1977; Selected Poems, 1979; White Center, 1980; The Right Madness of Skye, 1980; Making Certain It Goes On: Collected Poems, 1984. *Novel*—Death and the Good Life, 1981. *Non-fiction*—The Triggering Town: Lectures and Essays on Poetry and Writing, 1979.

ABOUT: Allen, M. S. We Are Called Human: The Poetry of Richard Hugo, 1982; Contemporary Authors, new revision series 3, 1981; Contemporary Literary Criticism 6, 1976; 18, 1981; Dictionary of Literary Biography 5, 1980; Holden, J. The Rhetoric of the Contemporary Lyric, 1980; Howard, R. Alone with

America: Essays on the Art of Poetry in the United States Since 1950, enlarged ed., 1980; Lieberman, L. Unassigned Frequencies: American Poetry in Review, 1964–77, 1977; Vinson, J. (ed.) Contemporary Poets, 3rd ed., 1980; Who's Who in America, 1982–83. *Periodicals*—American Poetry Review May/June 1973; Devil's Millhopper Spring 1983; Modern Poetry Studies Autumn 1978; New York Times October 26, 1982; New York Times Book Review February 26, 1984; Parnassus: Poetry in Review Spring-Summer 1978; Poetry May 1974; Slackwater Review (special Richard Hugo issue, 1978); The Weekly, Seattle's Newsmagazine November 10, 1982.

*HUSAYN, TAHA (November 14, 1889–October 28, 1973), Egyptian novelist, short-story writer, critic, and teacher personifies in many ways the trends and movements that have accompanied the development of modern Arabic literature in general. He may be considered its most significant figure to date. Born in an Egyptian village, he lost his sight at a very early age. A traditional Qur'an-school education led him to continue his studies at the Al-Azhar mosque-university in Cairo in 1902. The content of the curriculum and the attitudes of his teachers soon jarred with his enquiring and rebellious spirit and lively intellect and he moved to the newly founded secular Egyptian University (now Cairo University) where he obtained the first Egyptian Ph.D. degree ever awarded with a dissertation on a classical poet with whom he felt a close affinity, the blind Abū al-ᶜAlā' al-Maᶜarrī (973–1057). Husayn then pursued his studies in France, first at Montpellier and later at the Sorbonne. This and his earlier educational experiences are recounted in one of his major works, the three volumes of al-Ayyām (The Days, 1925, 1939, and 1967). After completing a dissertation on the great Arab social historian Ibn Khaldūn (1332–1406), he returned to Egypt in 1919 and began a career in both writing and university teaching. An irrepressible critic, he was a controversial figure for much of the rest of his life. Immediately before the 1952 revolution in Egypt he served for a short time as Minister of Education, and from the time of his retirement until his death he remained a major conservative cultural force.

Tāhā Husayn's autobiography, "The Days," takes pride of place among his works as a major contribution to the development of Egyptian fiction. Although documentary, it manages to seem fictional, both through the use of the third-person narration and also through a gentle sense of irony. These features (particularly strong in the first volume, less so in the other two), coupled with a lilting prose style, make his autobiog-

TAHA HUSAYN

raphy a work of major importance in the development of modern Arabic prose narrative. His contributions to fiction *per se* were significant in their own time but, as Ali Jad notes in a recent work on the Egyptian novel, few, if any, of his novels seem likely to survive as more than historical monuments. Of those, *Duᶜā' al-Karawān* (The Call of the Plover, 1941, translated as *The Call of the Curlew*) and *Shajarat al-Bu's* (The Tree of Misery, 1944) are the most accomplished.

Tāhā Husayn's impact on several generations of Arab intellectuals is considerable, ranging from studies of the heritage of classical Greece and Rome to numerous books and essays on Arab culture. Both *Fī al-Shiᶜr al-Jāhilī* (On Pre-Islamic Poetry, 1926), in which he advocated and applied a scientific critical method to the study of the texts of pre-Islamic poetry, and *Mustaqbal al-Thaqāfa fī Misr* (*The Future of Culture in Egypt*, 1938), in which he lays out a detailed program for the development of Egyptian education based on European models, were highly controversial at the time of their publication. Both by his own example and through teaching he managed to foster a new methodological rigor in the study of literature while still maintaining a deep love and respect for the masterpieces of the Arab literary heritage. The benefits of this fusion were evident among several of the next generation of critics, of whom Muhammad Mandūr (1907–1965) is the most notable.

The rapidity of political and cultural change in Arab societies in the final decades of Tāhā Husayn's life did not always meet with his approval. The very conservatism of this "dean of

Arabic letters" (as he is often termed) in the face of trends such as the use of colloquial language in works of literature and the movement of commitment which was so prevalent in the late 1940s and early fifties may indeed be a most accurate measure of the pace of development in the Arab world in recent decades. His works constitute a firm foundation for the study of Arabic literature.

WORKS IN ENGLISH TRANSLATION: The three volumes that comprise Tāhā Husayn's autobiography were translated into English over a forty-five-year period—*An Egyptian Childhood* by E.H. Paxton in 1932 (with a new edition in 1981), *The Stream of Days* by Hilary Wayment in 1943, and *A Passage for France* by Kenneth Craig in 1976. A.B. As-Safi translated *The Call of the Curlew* in 1980. Sidney Glazer translated *The Future of Culture in Egypt* in 1954.

ABOUT: Cachia, P. Tāhā Husain: His Place in the Egyptian Renaissance, 1956; Encyclopedia of World Literature in the 20th Century (rev. ed.) II, 1982; Hourani, A. Arabic Thought in the Liberal Age, 1962; Jad, A. Form and Technique in the Egyptian Novel, 1974; Safran, N. Egypt in Search of Political Community, 1961; Semah, D. Four Egyptian Literary Critics, 1974.

HUXTABLE, ADA LOUISE (1921–), American architecture critic, was born in New York City, the only child of Michael Louis Landman, a physician, and Leah (Rosenthal) Landman. Growing up on Manhattan's Upper West Side, she attended Wadleigh High School, received a B.A. in fine arts from Hunter College, and did graduate work in art and architectural history at New York University's Institute of Fine Arts. She was hired in 1946 as assistant curator of architecture at the Musem of Modern Art (MOMA).

The award of a Fulbright fellowship in 1950 (renewed in 1952) enabled Huxtable to spend two years studying in Milan. On her return she became a freelance writer of articles for specialized journals (including *Arts Digest, Interiors, Craft Horizons, Architectural Review,* and *AIA Journal*) and for the popular press (including the *New York Times Magazine*). She served for a decade as contributing editor of *Art in America* and *Progressive Architecture*; for a series of articles in the latter she was awarded a Guggenheim fellowship in 1958.

Huxtable's monograph on the contemporary Italian architect Pier Luigi Nervi—the subject of a traveling exhibit she organized for MOMA—was published in 1960 as the first volume in Braziller's Masters of World Architecture series. Allan Temko wrote that she "succeeds admira-

bly in showing how much 'passion' is possible in a philosophy which considers the best structural solution to be intrinsically the ideal answer to any problem of architecture."

Huxtable's second book, *Four Walking Tours of Modern Architecture in New York City,* was issued by MOMA in 1961. Her third, *Classic New York: Georgian Gentility to Greek Elegance,* was intended to be the first volume of a six-volume guide to the architectural history of the city. This plan was interrupted by her appointment in 1963 as the architecture critic of the *New York Times.* In creating the post, the *Times* became the first major newspaper in the nation to treat architecture as a subject worthy of sustained consideration by the public. Huxtable maintained that "the function of this broad kind of architectural criticism is educational; it must in many ways fill the gap that our schools have left so conspicuously vacant—the yawning chasm between the 'educated' man's perception and understanding of the man-made world around him."

Huxtable's devastating attacks on what she called "the four urban horsemen: expediency, obstructionism, stupidity, and greed" made her, according to Stephen Grover, "the delight of readers across the nation, an object of some awe in the architectural world, and perhaps the most powerful individual on the *Times*'s roster of critics—including the mighty reviewers of drama." Real estate developers, urban planners, land speculators, bankers, architects, and government officials found their schemes and reputations punctured by Huxtable's verbal swordplay (though, as Roger Jellinek noted, "her cautionary tales serve to educate readers rather than deride targets").

Many of Huxtable's articles in the *Times* were devoted to preservation, which she defines as "the retention and active relationship of the buildings of the past to the community's functioning present." In numerous cases her intervention forestalled the scheduled demolition of fine buildings and entire neighborhoods by developers eager to make a profit through new construction, at the cost of what Huxtable called "urbicide"—killing the unique characters of cities and towns and substituting "an all-American lookalike of gas stations, car salesrooms and drive-ins." New York City's Landmarks Preservation Commission was established in 1965 partly as a result of her opposition to "blind mutilation in the name of urban renewal." She also helped bring about the Presidential directive that ordered the General Services Administration to give local authorities control of historic buildings no longer needed by the federal government (among the buildings thus saved were the abandoned Custom House in lower Manhattan and the St. Louis Post Office). The director of New York's Office of Midtown Planning and Development called her "a very charming, feminine, quiet woman who's like a razor blade. . . . She has such a keen understanding of the politics, the money and the realities involved in any given situation that I can treat her as a peer. In that way she's alone among all architectural critics."

Some opponents have accused Huxtable of having no coherent rationale to justify her likes and dislikes and of advancing no theories of her own. Huxtable sees this as a virtue. The critic, she says, is "involved with the way people live and work and how they exist with good and evil in the most old-fashioned sense. You can't remove yourself from this simply to formulate abstract theories about the field. . . . Nothing is going to happen for good if we don't set it out in black and white and explain and interpret for the reader what is happening."

In the introduction to *Will They Ever Finish Bruckner Boulevard?*, a collection of her *Times* columns, Huxtable wrote: "People have been looking at the environment, as environment, for only a very short time. It has always been there, but it has finally been recognized as something that is terribly responsive to acts of will and judgment that have an endless impact on the state of humanity. . . . Esthetics is not some kind of optional extra or paste-on for pretty facades; it is the satisfaction of the needs of the body, the spirit, and the senses. . . . The art of design is an unavoidable part of every urban decision."

Will They Ever Finish Bruckner Boulevard? was published soon after Huxtable became the first recipient of the newly created Pulitzer Prize for distinguished criticism. Wolf von Eckhardt said in his review of the book: "With remarkably sure convictions, Mrs. Huxtable almost singlehandedly fills the void between the hubbub of urban construction and destruction and people's understanding of what it all adds up to. She lets us have these convictions with wit, erudition, and a swift sense of the truly relevant. There is obviously none like her." Jill Fischman wrote: "No mere aesthetician, Huxtable is profoundly aware of the mutual influence of social forces and physical forms, and she awakens the reader's political sense while educating his eye." A second collection, *Kicked a Building Lately?*, appeared in 1976. In his review, Lou Siegel described Huxtable's favorite themes as "support for diversity in style, preserving amenity in city life, retaining our architectural heritage as living

history—and opposition to unprincipled development, comprehensive planning, and the displacement of quality by commerce."

Huxtable's success made the previously ignored field of architectural criticism not only acceptable but prestigious. According to Lewis Mumford, writing in the *New Yorker,* "It wasn't until the *Times* got Huxtable that people began to pay attention to architectural criticism." The *Washington Post,* the *Chicago Sun-Times,* and the *Los Angeles Times* are among the major newspapers that were persuaded by her example to hire critics of their own. In 1973 Huxtable was named to the *Times'* editorial board, in which post she wrote a column for the Sunday edition and contributed unsigned editorials to the editorial page.

By the time Huxtable left the *Times* in 1981, the quality of urban life, once considered a matter of interest only to eccentrics, had become a national concern, with "an almost universal constituency," as Huxtable wrote in the introduction to *Kicked a Building Lately?* "People have learned to see and feel the city; they are consciously involved in the technology and esthetics and human effects of its buildings, spaces, and styles. These considerations have become—true test of relevance—political issues." The concept of neighborhood, she continued, is "evolving through the innovative use of a variety of legal, governmental, and architectural tools that never existed before. The standard of official construction has been raised light years beyond that of a generation ago, when the norm was unadulterated hack. . . . I measure success by the street-corner. My obsessions are now shared and my co-conspirators are everywhere."

In November 1981 Huxtable was awarded a MacArthur Foundation Prize fellowship, which guaranteed her an income for five years. Much of her research and writing since then has been devoted to a reevaluation and defense of modern architecture. In an article entitled "Is Modern Architecture Dead?" in the *New York Review of Books* (July 16, 1981), she wrote: "I have never been an apologist for the modern movement. My job, as a critic, has been to question a lot of the modernists' favorite received ideas and most cherished clichés. . . . As a historian, I was an unreconstructed partisan of periods and buildings consigned to oblivion. I never accepted the visionary, sanitized planning of modernism's neat division of life into segregated zones of activity. . . . The rejection of history led to the unthinking destruction of the historic urban heritage and the symbols and landmarks that anchor us to meaning and place; it dehumanized the environment and denied the continuity of culture." Nonetheless, she says, modernism was "an exhilarating and seductive campaign" that should not be asked to take the blame for all the social ills of the twentieth century.

Huxtable has been married since the 1940s to L. Garth Huxtable, an industrial designer, with whom she shares an apartment on Manhattan's Park Avenue. In addition to the Pulitzer Prize, she has received numerous honorary degrees and awards.

PRINCIPAL WORKS: Pier Luigi Nervi, 1960; Four Walking Tours of Modern Architecture in New York City, 1961; Classic New York: Georgian Gentility to Greek Elegance, 1964; Will They Ever Finish Bruckner Boulevard? 1970; Kicked a Building Lately?, 1976.

ABOUT: American Women Writers, 1980; Current Biography, 1973; Diamondstein, B. Open Secrets: Ninety-Four Women in Touch with Our Time, 1972; Torre, S. (ed.) Women in American Architecture: A Historic and Contemporary Perspective, 1977. *Periodicals*—Book World August 16, 1970; Christian Science Monitor April 9, 1969; November 11, 1973; Harper's Bazaar August 1972; House Beautiful November 1970; Library Journal October 15, 1970; January 15, 1977; February 1982; New York November 3, 1972; New Yorker December 17, 1973; New York Times May 5, 1970; September 26, 1973; January 2, 1975; March 13, 1977; September 29, 1977; December 30, 1981; New York Times Book Review April 24, 1960; July 12, 1970; Progressive Architecture March 1977; Wall Street Journal November 7, 1972.

*IDRIS, YUSUF (May 19, 1927–   ), Egyptian fiction writer and playwright, was born in Bairum, Sharqiva Province, according to his own words, "the point of contact between the Eastern Arab world and the Egyptian peasant Delts in which mingles a cocktail of folkloric cultures: Arab, Egyptian Coptic and Muslim." His father, Idris Ali, who had studied at Azhar University, was a specialist in land reclamation and had moved with his wife into a large house in the country. After a miscarriage, a hasty divorce and remarriage to the same woman, Yusuf was born. The first year of his life was plagued by grave infantile disease, but special care, particularly of the superstitious variety, allowed him to survive to become, as he writes, "the son of 'al-Ma'mour' which meant that I was more or less like the crown prince in a kingdom. Away from modern civilization we lived in a very big house with a vast garden and plenty of servants, those huge-breasted teenage peasant girls, who used to 'play' with me even offering me their female secrets . . . These people were actually the poorest stratum of Egyptian society, without home, family, or name."

YUSUF IDRIS

However, this idyll did not last long. In 1933, he was sent away by his father whom, Yusuf recalls, "I loved so much that sometimes I used to weep if I remembered him. With his big sunburned body, and his serious, wrinkled festures, he was the kindest and most loving man I ever knew." Ali Idris decided that his first-born son must be educated, but the nearest school was twenty-five miles away in the village from which Yusuf's family had originally come, and where his maternal grandmother still lived: "It was not just a distance for me, it was also a one-way journey. It took me away forever from my family and implanted me in a totally different atmosphere and community. From then on I had to live as a foreigner among foreigners, an orphan whose parents were still alive but totally unreachable . . . I did not feel it frequently, but at the times I did. I really felt that I must be the most miserable child on earth."

Not only was Yusuf far from his parents physically, but an economic gulf now separated him from the circumstances into which he had been born. His grandmother was poor, but not so poor that there were not twenty-five adults poorer than she who chose to accept the hospitality of her meager roof. Descriptions of his grandmother's hut may be read in many of Idris' stories, and especially in "House of Flesh" (1971) where a widow and her three daughters become accomplices in a sexual adventure with a blind Koran reciter. Descriptions of his grandmother, a harsh, cold woman, may also be read in many of his stories where he writes with obvious distaste for older women. Nor did school provide an escape for the lonely boy. The teachers were mean

°id´ ris, you sōof

and ridiculed him for the poverty of his attire, which Yusuf attributes to his mother's miserliness; every coin was carefully husbanded so that she might acquire more land to flaunt before her landless family. "In this ocean of ugliness and unfriendliness I was saved from sickness and death by a perpetual state of daydreaming: I dreamt of discovering, inventing, being rich, being mighty as a king or as a Count of Monte Cristo, being a magician or a musician." However, he never dreamt of becoming a writer, because he had not thought of writers as powerful or even influential. It may be that years later, when Idris finally became the one thing to which he had not aspired, he did after all retain his childhood dreams, for it is clear that once he had put pen to paper he considered his task to be vitally important: "In a constantly changing world, a writer is a major factor in revolution. He has a part to play in society. A writer differs from other people in that he is more impressionable, with keener sensitivity to his surrounding."

Since the boy was highly intelligent and there were few distractions from school work, he was academically successful and was accepted into the Egyptian University medical school, the preserve of the scholastic elite, in 1945, when the world was just beginning to recover from World War II. Egypt, still ruled by a corrupt monarchy, was occupied by British troops, and the Egyptian University campus was simmering with discontent. Idris threw himself into politics, espousing the nationalist cause within a Communist framework. He became executive secretary of the committee for the defense of students. Responsible for revolutionary publications, he also took part in several demonstrations and was imprisoned a number of times.

"While writing leaflets and revolutionary magazines I discovered very early in my life as a medical student that I was born to be a writer." In 1950 Idris wrote his first short story "A Song for Strangers" which was published in the literary journal Al-Qissa. Although the story became popular among students, he did not write again for a year, pursuing his medical studies instead. He graduated in 1952 and was appointed to the Kasr el Eini Hospital in Cairo. On July 23, 1952, in the middle of his first operation, he was told that the army, under the leadership of General Neguib, had just effected a bloodless coup d'état. Without further ado he handed over the scalpel to a colleague and rushed off to celebrate.

Ironically, within a month of the officers' revolution, relations between the Revolutionary Command Council and its erstwhile supporters the Communists had become strained. Thereafter, Idris tried to limit his political activities to carefully worded articles. In 1953 he became the literary editor of Ruz al-Yusuf. However, by 1954, with many others, he had begun to express openly his disappointment with Nasser, and he was jailed once again. During this period he joined the Communist Party, only to leave two years later. 1954 also saw the publication of his first collection of short stories, The Cheapest Nights, with an introduction by the world-renowned scholar Taha Hussain. This collection, and particularly the title story, which indicts overpopulation, vividly renders the dreams of a poor peasant as he returns home to the only entertainment he can afford. It established Idris as one of Egypt's leading writers, second only to established figures of the earlier generation such as Najib Mahfuz, Taufiq al-Hakim, Taha Hussain, and Yahya Haqqi. Between 1954 and 1958 Idris published five collections of short stories, a prolificness that he has not equalled since. In 1956 he wrote his first novel, A Love Story. And the following year, 1957, he wrote two one-act plays, "The King of Cotton" about peasant exploitation; and "Farahat's Republic" about petty despotism mixed with fantasies of the ideal, modernized society.

Idris continued to practice medicine until 1966. In the mid-fifties, he was appointed medical inspector in one of the poorest areas of Cairo. Out of this experience he has fashioned a number of stories that betray a deep sympathy for the exploited poor. In "Dregs of the City" Judge Abdallah suspects that the married woman he has employed as cleaning woman and concubine has stolen his watch. He ventures into the Cairo slums in search of his prey. He finds his watch; the woman loses her honor.

From 1960 to 1968 Idris was editor of the daily newspaper, al-Gumhuriya, publishing over 250 articles. During this period he reported on two major wars in the Arab world; the Algerian Revolution (1954–61) in which he participated for six months until he was wounded; and the 1967 defeat of Egypt by Israel. In 1966 Nasser awarded Idris the Order of the Republic. However, recognition by the Egyptian ruler did not blind Idris to the corruption that once again defiled the Egyptian government. Many intellectuals were challenging Nasser to answer for the '67 defeat, and in 1969 Idris wrote a play, "The Schemers," which was banned, and has never been performed. Despite the ban, Idris continued to publish stories and articles openly critical of the government. Perhaps this political disenchantment and also the mood of alienation that inspired much existential literature in the 60s played a part in the severe attacks of depression that afflicted him from 1966, and which have at times prevented him from writing. Since the early seventies he has published very little, although in 1973, after the October War, he joined the staff of *al-Ahram*, the daily Cairo newspaper.

Like many other Egyptian writers, Idris locates the real Egyptian in an economic stratum below that of the westernized bourgeoisie, and he writes of individuals and groups, sensitively exploring the values and exposing the tensions of people too often neglected by mainstream literature. In "The Shame" (1958), which takes place on a farmstead, a beautiful girl is suspected of an immoral encounter with the village Romeo. Her claims of innocence are rejected. She must submit to a physical test administered by the "veined, ugly, dry hands" of all the crones on the farm. Although she is proclaimed innocent, the vileness of the ordeal changes her and makes her "defiant, unflinching and unabashed." This condemnation of contemporary norms and values may be read throughout Idris' oeuvre, and especially in two of his novels, *The Taboo* (1959) and *The Sin* (1962). Women are victims, at first innocent but ultimately and inevitably, corrupted, since their patriarchal society cannot accept them as humans but must reduce them to sex objects.

It might well be that the contrast between the two lives he led as a child opened Idris' eyes and heart to the plight of the Egyptian poor. He has exploited the pain of his childhood to become the self-styled spokesman of Egypt's untouchables. He rips aside the veil of homogeneity and extracts individuals who eke out an existence attenuated only, it seems, by an unfailing sense of humor. However, Idris is not amused by the poverty and impotence of his people. Throughout his work he confronts again and again the question of power and powerlessness. And in his widely-acclaimed play *Farafir*, first performed in 1964, he experiments with notions of oppression, showing ultimately that the will to dominate is an instinct more entrenched than any other. This play was greeted with great excitement. Politically it was branded nihilist since it lauded the potential and righteous revolution fermenting in the hearts of the people, and yet provided no solution to their grievances. Nevertheless it was acclaimed a literary masterpiece of tragic force marking a significant stage in the development of the still new genre of drama. His scientific studies, particularly in nuclear physics, also led him to consider the kinetic, almost explosive nature of society, where the young are born to rebel against their elders. Yet this dynamism, too, has its limits: in an archsatire titled "The Miracle of the Age," Idris creates a superhumanly brilliant Tom Thumb who harnesses the forces of nature and propels himself into outer space to find a planet populated by clones of himself.

Idris displays great stylistic variety, experimenting with form in his prose fiction as in his drama. He has been important in the introduction of colloquial speech to Egyptian literature. Claiming that colloquial speech is acceptable only in dialogue, critics have charged him with failure to subject his work to sufficient control. But this spontaneity is the hallmark of his writing, the source of much of its power, projecting Idris into the vanguard of Arabic writers concerned with forging modern yet genuine Arabic literature. And it has often been said that Idris has taken up where the Modern School, known for its realist approach to literature, left off in the 1920s.

In autobiographical notes which he wrote in 1983 for *World Authors*, Idris says: "I was lucky I became a writer. But that is only a matter of luck. I was lucky that my childhood infused me with an irrepressible desire to be somebody, and to change, at least the world in which I had lived as a child." But he adds: "After thirty years of active writing and after thirty-three books I do not find that there is a great difference between the world against which I struggled, and the world today. But there is still a very great difference between the world of which I dreamt and the world in which I now live. Perhaps that is why I am still writing. Or, to be honest, that is why I feel that I have not begun to write."

WORKS IN ENGLISH TRANSLATION: Short stories by Yusuf Idris in English translation appear in D. Johnson-Davies' *Modern Arabic Short Stories*, 1967, his *Egyptian Short Stories*, 1978, and his *Arabic Short Stories*, 1983; also in R. Y. Ebierd and M. J. L. Young's *Arabic Stories East and West*, 1977, and in Roger M. A. Allen's edition, *The Eye of the Beholder: Tales from Egyptian Life from the Writings of Yusuf Idris*, 1978. A collection of his shorter writings was translated by Wadida Wassef as *The Cheapest Nights and Other Stories* in 1978.

ABOUT: Allen, R. M. A. *Introduction* to The Eye of the Beholder, 1978; Dictionary of Oriental Literature III, 1974; Encyclopedia of World Literature in the 20th Century (rev. ed.) II, 1982; Kurpershoek, P. M. The Short Stories of Yusuf Idris, 1981; Mikhail, M. Images of Arab Women, 1979. *Periodicals*—Guardian December 11, 1978; Journal of Arabic Literature 6, 1975; Middle East Journal 21, 1967; World Literature Today 55, 1981.

*IKE, (VINCENT) CHUKWUEMEKA (April 28, 1931–), Nigerian novelist, educator, and administrator writes: "Only a very detailed map of Nigeria stands any chance of showing

°e′ kā, cho͞o kwä mä′ kə

CHUKWUEMEKA IKE

Ndikelionwu, the town in which I was born on Nkwo market day, April 28, 1931, and to which my forebears migrated from the historical town of Arochukwu some centuries back. (My surname, Ike, is the shortened form of Ikelionwu, from which the town derived its name.) Known at various times as Umuchukwu, Aro-Omogho, Aro-Ndikelionwu, or Ndikelionwu, the town has held out for me a fascinating world different from the hybrid world of Nigerian cities, boarding schools and university campuses of Europe and America. A world of modest residential houses interspersed with farmlands over a wide expanse of fertile land. A world with a proud history, its own dialect of Igbo, spiced with wisdom-packed proverbs, its own customs, legal system, mores. A world in which you were your brother's keeper. . . . Little surprise that I have taken every available opportunity to return to it in my novels, as I do in real life. (*Toads for Supper, The Naked Gods, Sunset at Dawn, The Bottled Leopard,* and particularly *The Potter's Wheel* provide glimpses of this world.) I do so without apologies; that is the world in which most of my people live.

"My late father, Charles Chinwuba Ike (c. 1903–1974), was a most influential citizen of that world. (So is my mother, Dinah Mgbeke Ike, currently leader of Ndikelionwu women in church and civic affairs.) At various times church and school teacher, farmer, customary court judge, business man, councillor, civic and religious leader, and acclaimed for his intelligence, integrity, industry, fearlessness, and rigid Christian principles, he set out to ensure that I grew up into an educated, industrious, austere,

principled and upright Christian. Among other things, he forcefully separated me from my mother's breasts, as it were, and sent me to serve as domestic servant to a nephew of his. I owe much of what has become my philosophy of life to him, and his character traits have unavoidably permeated some of the characters in my novels.

"Government College, Umuahia (1945–1950) built upon the foundations laid by my parents. A very competitive school in those days, built by the British colonial government to serve the whole of Eastern Nigeria (including what was then Western Cameroon), it set out to impart sound western all-round secondary education to its handful of carefully selected students, emphasizing excellence, integrity, hard work, and fair play. It provided an ideal setting for the development of whatever literary talent I had, thanks to such excellent and inspiring masters as the versatile Australian, Charles Low—poet, playwright, and classical scholar. I edited my house magazine, served on the editorial board of the college magazine, and had the thrill of seeing myself in print for the first time in my life when my short story, 'In Dreamland,' appeared in the college magazine.

"On entering University College, Ibadan in October 1951 (for the London University B.A. degree program), I was invited to join the Magazine Club which published the *University Herald,* a highly regarded literary magazine. This boosted my interest in creative writing, and brought me in close contact with men and women who have since distinguished themselves as creative writers. I also served on the editorial board of a less prestigious but much dreaded student publication, the *Bug.* My short stories and articles appeared in the *University Herald,* the *University Voice,* the *Bug,* the *Christian Student.* Some were broadcast by the then Nigerian Broadcasting Corporation. I served on the Students' Representative Council, and had the privilege of representing the Student Christian Movement of Nigeria in international conferences/workshops held in five European countries. Eighteen months after graduation—during which period I taught in a girls' secondary school and served as the Honorary Organizing Secretary of the Student Christian Movement for Eastern Nigeria—I returned to Ibadan as a member of the senior administrative staff. My career as Assistant Registrar (Students) gave me an invaluable insight into the problems of Nigerian undergraduates, an insight which was to come in handy when the time came to write *Toads for Supper.*

"While at Ibadan, I married Adebimpe Olurinsola Abimbolu (on December 13, 1959).

Although Yoruba, she shared a similar tradition of a Government College (Queen's College) education, followed by University College, Ibadan, and leadership of the Student Christian Movement. A profuse reader, who has published widely in her professional field and is currently the University Librarian of one of the Nigerian universities, she has been my most honest and dependable critic. Thoughts of our son, Osita, born July 12, 1962, and his upbringing inspired me to write *The Potter's Wheel* and the novel I am currently tying up. (I wait to see what thoughts of me may inspire him to write! He appeared in print and won a prize for creative writing in primary school, and his secondary school, King's College, record has been no less impressive.)

"The period 1960–1971 which I spent on the pioneer staff of the University of Nigeria, Nsukka stands out as a very significant period in my life. During this period, I took time off to study the problems of higher education, in the U.S.A. and the U.K., through study visits and conferences and later for the M.A. degree of Stanford University. I attained the pinnacle of university administration, serving not only as the Registrar (or chief administrative officer) of the university for eight and a half years, but also as the chief executive responsible for reopening and managing the war-ravaged institution during the ten-month period (January–November 1970) immediately following the end of the Nigerian civil war. During this period also I had my first (and I pray my only) experience of a civil war, when we fought against oppression and ethnicity for thirty months in our short-lived Republic of Biafra. And, most importantly, I became a published novelist, *Toads for Supper* having been published in 1965 and *The Naked Gods* in 1970. My exposure to the academe and to a gruesome civil war during the period resulted not only in these two campus novels but also in *University Development in Africa: the Nigerian Experience* and *Sunset at Dawn*, both published in 1976 after I had left Nsukka.

"Some of my university friends were mad with me when *The Naked Gods* came out, considering my judgment on academics harsh. With two campus novels, and disenchantment with university professors, I left the academe in quest of fresh pasture. My eight years (1971–1979) in the turbulent, thankless and sensitive position of Registrar and Chief Executive of the multinational West African Examinations Council (W.A.E.C.) based in Accra, Ghana, saw the publication of *The Potter's Wheel* and the two books published in 1976 already referred to. The two novels which drew on the experience of my years in W.A.E.C. were published after I had left the Council. *The Chicken Chasers* I wrote in one month, at the rate of a chapter a day, working on it full-time in the quiet and pleasant atmosphere of A16, Patrice Lumumba Road, Airport Residential Area, Accra. *Expo '77* took three months, again working full-time, but this time in the hustle and bustle of Lagos.

"Each of my previous novels had taken years to write, as I could at the best of times spare no more than two hours (4–6 a.m.) of my hectic work schedule for creative writing. The prospect of writing many more novels if I made writing a full-time activity, coupled with the feeling that twenty-five years of public service at the senior level in present day Nigeria was ample enough, decided me against offers of full-time employment after my voluntary retirement from public service on July 1, 1979. I currently live in quiet Bauchi in Northern Nigeria, limiting my public service to part-time company directorships so as to devote maximum time to creative writing and related activities. From here I turn the searchlight not only on educational institutions, as I have done in most of my writing so far, but on other facets of Nigerian life."

The most prominent and widely acclaimed aspect of Chukwuemeka Ike's novels is their thoroughgoing humor, which prevails regardless of the seriousness of his books' subjects. His first novel, *Toads for Supper,* is the story of Amadi, an undergraduate who is engaged simultaneously to three women, of his expulsion by the university authorities, and of his efforts to clear his name. He is the hope of his village, the first Ezinkwo man ever to reach university, and at home he is treated with special consideration by his neighbors, who even build a new hut for his private study. The critic for the *Times Literary Supplement,* comparing Ike with Obi E. Egbuna and Nkem Nwankwo as novelists who "have explored the tensions and anomalies of village life in Nigeria," identified the theme of *Toads for Supper* as "the daily collision between modern urban fashion and tribal custom." He particularly praised the account of the profound relationship between Amadi and his father, Mazi, "who, though illiterate, is more than a match for him in argument. Mazi, a practical, honorable man, is given to lecturing his son in the small hours, and in these paternal homilies, oblique and unanswerable, Mr. Ike illustrates the conflict between the two generations with a wry poetry." Norman Shrapnel thought the novel "a bullseye for Nigerian writing. . . . Most of the way the tone is quiet, and the familiar clash between the tribal way of life and the new ideas is handled much more coolly, much less predictably, than the hardened reader will be accustomed to."

The Naked Gods concerns the savage, ruthless, and always comic intrigue to gain control of the vice-chancellorship of Songhai University. As Julian Symons described the fast-moving plot in the *Sunday Times,* "Bribes are offered, blackmail attempted, a witch-doctor consulted, as the struggle is played out between Professor Ikin who has only a B.A. and Doctor Okoro who possesses a slightly dubious Ph.D. . . . Social comedy of this kind written by an African is rare, and the eccentric note of the conversations has the right sort of feather-headed unreality." The *Times Literary Supplement* reviewer called *The Naked Gods* "shrewd multiracial comedy, laced with very tall tales which may be readily swallowed" and remarked that Ike's "style of humor is not unlike that of Evelyn Waugh, . . . while his attitude towards American diplomacy is as unfavorable as Graham Greene's." A bush chief, a powerful and impassive character, makes two brief but crucial appearances in the novel. His dominance of the action each time represented to the *Times Literary Supplement* reviewer "an important social attitude—a rooted conviction that fuss about things like vice-chancellorships and American influence is merely froth on the surface of life. However educated and powerful a man may become, he is always at the mercy of the common people, the 'illiterates,' the 'oral culture'—all those watchful eyes and eloquent rumors—with their magic, their ancestral spirits and their chosen chiefs." David Fletcher, however, seemed to object to the very idea of a Nigerian comedy appearing at the end of the bloody hostilities over Biafra; he "would have preferred" the novel "if [Ike] had allowed the characters to be a little sympathetic, a little deeper, instead of merely badly behaved puppets."

Village life is the focus of Ike's next novel, *The Potter's Wheel.* Obu is eight years old, the only son in a family of seven children, and outrageously spoiled by his mother, who is making up for the loss of face she suffered for years as the mother only of girls. Obu's father is also very proud of his son, who is an excellent pupil in school, but is determined to expose him to life's realities, and so sends him away from home as a servant to a fierce schoolmaster and his equally ferocious wife. The boy returns to his home almost wholly transformed into an obedient and considerate young man. The *Sunday Times* reviewer called the book a "simple but pleasing little comedy," adding that the "Victorian morality will hardly meet with the approval of those who support African or any other lib, but it makes a lively tale." *Sunset at Dawn* is a moving novel

about the tragic experience of the Biafran war. Set in that secessionist region of eastern Nigeria, it concerns Dr. Kanu, a university administrator and lecturer in medicine, who gradually becomes a valiant partisan of his new country's cause, and his wife, who is from the north of the country and hence initially hostile to that cause. The deaths of her husband and their son, and the experience of living in the village of her husband's people, turn her into a fervent Biafran, one of several profound changes that occur to characters in this novel. Norman Shrapnel remarked that *Sunset at Dawn* "puts the language to fullest use. . . . The remarkable thing about this book is the range of its impact, successfully fusing satire, horror, protest and sheer fun—a mix few writers would attempt, let alone hope to succeed in. It is rare to find such an unsentimental bite, and Ike provides an eloquent answer to those who still find it hard to accept that serious art and a powerful sense of absurdity can coexist." To Jill Neville, the novel, "though it tells a human story with skill and humor, is mainly interesting for its documentary mastery. This, no doubt, is what the war was really like seen through Biafran eyes." D.A.N. Jones wrote, "There are some very funny passages in this serious book, and Mr. Ike has managed to introduce them without being guilty of bad taste: the clashing tones of voice are more like life than art."

Most of Ike's books have been published only in Britain, by the Harvill Press, a house noted for its commitment to African literature, and by the paperback publishers Fontana. His novels are rich in their use of west African idiom, and he regularly appends a full glossary to each book, amusingly explaining each phrase used.

PRINCIPAL WORKS: Toads for Supper, 1965; The Naked Gods, 1970; The Potter's Wheel, 1973; Sunset at Dawn, 1976; The Chicken Chasers, 1980; Expo '77, 1980.

ABOUT: H. M. Zell and H. Silver (eds.) A Reader's Guide to African Literature, 1972; D. E. Herdeck (ed.) African Authors, 1973; J. Jahn et al. (eds.) Who's Who in African Literature, 1972. *Periodicals*—Guardian April 9, 1965; May 13, 1976; New Statesman May 14, 1965; Sunday Times May 24, 1970; September 2, 1973; Times Educational Supplement July 17, 1970; Times Literary Supplement April 8, 1965; June 18, 1970; July 9, 1976.

IRVING, JOHN (WINSLOW) (March 2, 1942–), American novelist, was born and raised in Exeter, New Hampshire, one of the three children of Colin F. N. Irving and Frances Winslow Irving. The older Irving was a teacher of Russian history and treasurer at Phillips Exe-

JOHN IRVING

ter Academy, one of the most prestigious of American prep schools. John Irving attended Exeter, where he excelled in English and history and was a champion wrestler, though he was not an outstanding student over all. Upon graduation, he chose to go to the University of Pittsburgh because it was strong in wrestling. Wrestling has been an important part of Irving's real life and his creative life. His characters are frequently wrestlers, and he often uses the terms of the sport as metaphors for larger ideas, likening the concentration necessary for writing to that required for winning at wrestling.

Outside of New England, Irving found himself outclassed as a wrestler, and the year at Pittsburgh was not successful. He returned home to attend the state university at Durham. A year there (1962–63) brought him to the realization that "anything I did except writing was going to be vaguely unsatisfying," and the next year he went off to study at the University of Vienna. Chosen by chance, because it sounded more exotic than the other possibilities, Vienna proved to be a fertile ground for him. A writer needs to travel to learn to notice, he told an interviewer. Removed "from looking with complacency at all the trivia of my surroundings—suddenly it made things not trivial anymore." Though he didn't write about Vienna at that time, the city was to appear repeatedly in his work as "a fictional realm," where he can freely imagine, unrestrained by the restrictions imposed by the reality of the familiar, everyday world.

Irving met Shyla Leary in 1963 and corresponded with her while he was in Europe. On August 24, 1964, they were married, and Irving

returned to the University of New Hampshire, receiving his degree *cum laude* in 1965. From there he went on to the Writers' Workshop at the University of Iowa, where he tended bar and sold pennants and souvenirs at college football games to support his family (a son, Colin, was born in 1964). He was awarded a Master of Fine Arts degree in 1967, and the family moved back East, to a converted barn in Putney, Vermont, where they still live. Irving taught English at a small local college and wrote his first novel, *Setting Free the Bears,* published in 1969. A picaresque tale of two university dropouts who hatch a plot to release the animals from Vienna's Hietzinger Zoo, the novel exhibits what were to become Irving hallmarks: Vienna, bears, what Anne Tyler called "manic high spirits" and "jaunty heroics," and an imaginative, complex, but tightly controlled narrative.

The next several years were spent in Vienna and in Putney while Irving worked on the screenplay of *Setting Free the Bears* and on his next novel. The Irvings' younger son, Brendan, was born in 1970. Irving returned to the University of Iowa as writer-in-residence (1972–75). In 1972, *The Water-Method Man,* for which Irving had received a Rockefeller Foundation grant, was published. *Book World* characterized it as an "ingeniously convoluted black comedy about a nonhero of epic ineptness." The nonhero, Bogus Trumper, is a graduate student at the University of Iowa, working on his dissertation and trying to cope with his failing marriage while an underground documentary is being made of his life. Abundant sex, with and without love, and a predilection for bathroom humor (the title refers to the treatment prescribed for Trumper's urinary infection) join the list of Irving characteristics. While again he was praised for inventiveness—his "ability to weave . . . the elements of Trumper's calamities into a rich, unified tapestry," as George Dickerson said—there were those who questioned the value of the exercise, like the *New Yorker,* which found the novel funnier than most but concluded that Bogus "ends up as a lovable soup-head telling us that life is just great."

What Jacob Epstein calls Irving's "celebration of the flesh" is prominent in his third novel, *The 158–Pound Marriage.* One of the four protagonists is the wrestling coach at a small New England college. The story tells of a *ménage à quatre* of two married couples and how the relationship works on each of the participants. Martin Levin was admiring, praising Irving's deft, hard-hitting style, his avoidance of "the ooze of a sloppier rhetoric," but other critics were less enthusiastic. *Publishers Weekly,* for example, felt that "Irving's conclusion seems to be that lust doesn't pay, but he's a long and sensual time getting there [in this] curious, well-written, perhaps angry novel that wallows in free-wheeling erotica while it points out that its practitioners will come to no good end."

Irving was thirty-six years old when the publication of his fourth novel, *The World According to Garp* (originally titled "Lunacy and Sorrow"), catapulted him into the small group of writers whose work achieves success commercially as well as artistically. His first three novels had earned him the reputation of a talented, "serious" writer. *Garp* made him a celebrity and so comfortable financially that he could retire in 1978 from Mount Holyoke College where he had taught since 1975 to devote all his considerable energies to writing. After *The World According to Garp* appeared in 1978, there were few readers who had not heard of T. S. Garp, the engaging, utterly human writer of great talent, an adoring, anxious father, a loving—though occasionally unfaithful—husband, whose vision of the world appears, from all evidence, to be close to Irving's own. The novel shot to the top of the best-seller lists, was nominated for a National Book Award, became a best-seller again when it was published as a paperback, and again when it was made into a movie. The paperback was awarded an American Book Award as the best paperback novel of 1979. Billboards, advertisements, and T-shirts across the nation proclaimed I LOVE GARP. Many people did and some didn't; no one who had read the novel remained neutral, however. Irving later remarked that this was the first novel in which he was creating characters he genuinely admired and cared for, which may account for the passionate responses it evokes. He started out knowing that he wanted to write about a mother and son, both strong individuals who would "test your love by being extremists," he told Barbara A. Bannon. "I always knew that as mother and son they would make the world angry at them. Each of them had to be assassinated because of the way the rest of the world would misunderstand them."

While reviewers praised the warmth, the humanity, and the readability of the story of Garp's life from birth to death and after ("as effortlessly readable as a pulp novel and as pointed as a Swiftian tract," said one), none of them failed to note the incidence of rape, mutilation, dismemberment, and violent death that exceeded anything Irving had yet provided. In the central tragic episode, one of Garp's children is killed; another loses an eye; Garp and his wife are seriously injured; and his wife's lover is emasculated in an automobile accident precipitated by Garp. The English novelist Margaret Drabble called the book "a bloody package"; nevertheless she had to read on. For William MacPherson, it is "a wonderful novel full of energy and art at once funny and horrifying and heartbreaking—an x-rated soap opera with grandeur—and immeasurably gratifying."

Garp's widespread popularity led some critics to question whether a book so successful commercially could be considered art. Joseph Epstein, while acknowledging that Irving and his readers take his work seriously, asked whether he should be "taken seriously by serious people." He scores the emphasis on the physical in Irving's work, the academic "game-playing" of the intricate plot constructions, the failure to investigate moral questions, and the "strained effort to be, simultaneously, adorable and gruesome." Irving's insistence on the importance of family relationships, that survival is possible only through living as purposefully and well as one can, led Epstein to conclude that the basis of Irving's appeal to such large audiences is his ability to "make his readers feel advanced in their views yet fundamentally sound in their emotions." Irving's heroes are fixed in adolescence, says Epstein, and Richard Gilmore agrees, accusing "Garp/Irving" of being "emotionally and intellectually both fixed forever at age seventeen."

Irving had ample opportunity to answer his critics; his success made him news beyond the confines of the literary pages, even to a cover story in *Time*. To the charges of excessive violence he replies that the news in any newspaper on a given day is of equal or surpassing violence, and that he uses violence for artistic reasons: in extreme situations—sexual or violent or whatever—people show themselves at their best and worst. His black humor is intended to make more bearable the events he describes. He is not a social novelist, nor does he believe it is the responsibility of the novelist to confront social issues. The novelist has an aesthetic responsibility to entertain. "I want to move you—" he told Larry McCaffery—"that's the important thing. . . . It's only bad art that's given soap opera a bad name. . . . I'm an artist, but I want to jerk tears." The novelist is obliged to write as clearly, as accessibly, as he can: "It's no triumph to be difficult to read or understand, in fact I think it's a triumph to be readable. I don't find that an aspect of commercialism but part of a writer's responsibility." Pointing out that art and entertainment are not contradictions, he deplores the obscurity of writing that requires the intervention of critics and academics for interpretation. In his own work, above all, he says that he strives for the "sense of movement and pace and rhythm" that he admires in the work of Dickens and of Günter Grass (both of whom, he points out, record violence). As for his work being auto-biographical, Irving says that while he *uses* things that have happened to him, he makes a distinction between the truth of the event and what the author as artist does with it. Wrestling, New England prep school background, Viennese experiences, or being a writer do not make Irving heroes Irving. "In the big matters, *Garp* is a novel about how perilous and fragile our lives can be. My life is neither perilous, nor has it been especially fragile."

Planned as a modern fairy tale, Irving's fifth novel, *The Hotel New Hampshire,* recounts the vicissitudes of Wyn and Mary Berry and their children, Frank, Fanny, John, Lilly, and Egg. Sustained by strong family bonds, tenacious courage, and dreams, they encounter sex, violence, rape, homosexuality, deformity, sudden death, and incest. By the novel's end, three Berrys are dead; one distances himself from life through cynicism; and the other two arrive at a degree of acceptance and affirmation. The title refers to the three hotels inhabited by the family: the first a converted girl's school in a New Hampshire prep school town; the second a Viennese fleabag, by day the workplace of a team of revolutionary terrorists, by night of a team of aging prostitutes; the third, in Maine, doubling as a rape crisis center and a resort hotel, the latter a fantasy maintained by the Berry children for the benefit of their blinded father.

As Irving had predicted, not everyone liked the new novel, though he himself thought it his best work to date. "Boring," "confusing," "a circus," and "nonsense" were some of the judgments. Robertson Davies credited Irving with writing originally, about themes that are important to him, but concludes that "they seem to boil down to a romantic insistence on the supremacy of passion and a desire for poetic justice." Scott Haller cited "unconsidered events, unexplained behavior, and anachronisms" that cost the reader's willing suspension of disbelief. Because the novel lacks the cause-and-effect characteristics of a true fairy tale, it is "missing the resonances that elevated *Garp* above 'an x-rated soap opera.'" Benjamin DeMott praised the "surprising narrative rhythms and a sharply distinctive tone," but questioned the rationale behind Irving's pairing of "the nightmare and sunshine." He managed it convincingly in *Garp,* according to DeMott, because he was showing how an artist converts experience into art, but here he found "a certain frailty in the book's emotional life," and that the author's jokiness tends to work against conviction.

An energetic writer, still in early middle years and with an impressive volume of work accom-plished already, Irving is in midcareer. In 1984 he was working in a new direction—a short novel, a love story, on the order of Turgenev's *First Love.* Irving received a National Endowment for the Arts fellowship in 1974–75, and a Guggenheim Foundation Grant in 1976–77.

PRINCIPAL WORKS: Setting Free the Bears, 1969; The Water-Method Man, 1972; The 158-Pound Marriage, 1974; The World According to Garp, 1978; The Hotel New Hampshire, 1981.

ABOUT: Contemporary Authors 25–28, 1977; Current Biography, 1979; Dictionary of Literary Biography 6, 1980; Miller, G. John Irving, 1982. *Periodicals*—Book World April 30, 1978; September 6, 1981; Commentary June 1982; Contemporary Literature Winter 1982; Critique 23: Number 1, 1981; MacLean's June 11, 1979; Mademoiselle February 1983; Modern Fiction Studies Summer 1981; New Republic April 26, 1980; Newsweek March 20, 1978; New York August 17, 1981; New York Times Book Review April 23, 1978; May 21, 1978; May 25, 1980; September 13, 1981; August 22, 1982; People December 25, 1978; Publishers Weekly April 24, 1978; Redbook November 1981; Time August 31, 1981; U.S. News & World Report October 26, 1981.

*IWASZKIEWICZ, JAROSLAV (pseudonym **Eleuter**) (February 20, 1894–March 2, 1980), Polish poet, essayist, playwright, and novelist, was born near Kalnik, Kievan Ukraine. His father, who died when the boy was eight, was the descendant of a noble family impoverished after the revolution of 1863. Iwaszkiewicz was educated at home and at Kiev University, where he completed his law studies in 1918. He also studied at the musical conservatory in Kiev. Early in his career he belonged to Karol Szymanowski's musical circle and wrote the libretto for Szymanowski's opera *King Roger of Sicily.*

After making his appearance as a poet in Kiev in 1915, Iwaszkiewicz moved at the end of World War I to Warsaw, where he became one of the founders of the literary group "Skamander." The group took its name from the title of its journal, *Skamander,* named for the son of Hector and Andromache, destined to restore the glories of Troy. Besides Iwaszkiewicz, its leaders were the young poet and critic Jan Lechon, and the poets Antoni Slonimski, Julian Tuwim, and Kazimiera Illakowicz. The Skamandrites were hopeful and energetic. They desired nothing but the chance to write of the universal joys and sorrows of mankind and to soar like the poets of other nations, free from the bondage of patriotic themes which seemed to shackle the poets of Poland.

Iwaszkiewicz's   first   volume   of   lyrics,

°ē väsh kje´ vich, ya´ ro släw

Oktostychy (Octaves), appeared in 1919. He was to publish over ten volumes of poetry. In contrast to the avant-garde trends of the age, his poetry has something of a classicist character. Western writers—Paul Valéry, Stefan George, Oscar Wilde, and André Gide—exercised an unmistakable influence on his poetry, which possesses great suggestivity of color and tone, a quality that Czeslaw Milosz describes as "exoticism, or, more accurately, a propensity for blending the cultures of Greece, of the Middle East, of Eastern and Western Europe." Experimenting with metrics, assonance, and dissonance, he produced an expressionistic poetry—especially in his *Dionizje* (Dionysiacs, 1922)—that was unique in Polish poets.

Turning to the short story, drama, and the novel, Iwaszkiewicz wrote several important early works—among them *Siedem bogatych miast niesmiertelnego Kosciej* (The Seven Rich Towns of the Immortal Kosciej, 1924) and *Ksiezyc wschodzi* (The Moon Is Rising, 1925). His best short stories are those included in the volume *Panny z Wilka* (Young Ladies from Wilk, 1933), which was translated into French. In the realm of romantic historical fiction he wrote *Czerwone tarcze* (Red Shields, 1934), about the twelfth-century Piast prince Henry of Sandomierz, with allusions to Poland's impotence during the years between the two world wars.

In the 1930s, as a result of the many pitfalls facing a writer on contemporary themes, Iwaszkiewicz was forced to seek material in the past. From this came two plays, the highly successful *Lato w Nohant* (*Summer in Nohant,* 1936), a series of scenes from the last chapter of the Chopin-George Sand relationship, and *Maskarada* (Masquerade, 1939), an improvisation on the final days of Pushkin's life. His last play (1959) was also based on an episode in literary history— *Wesela pana Balzaka* (The Wedding of Balzac), treating of the novelist's love affair with Countess Hanska.

All Iwaszkiewicz's writings were tinged with disillusionment, especially his novel *Pasje Bledomierskie* (The Passions of Bledomierz, 1938), but all are redeemed by their vitality and colorful style. His trilogy of novels, *Slawa i Chwala* (Fame and Glory, 1956–1962), presents the portrait of Polish society in the period from 1913 to the present. In these novels he deals with the great decline in culture and morals of the European intelligentsia. Other works include collections of short stories and translations into Polish of Rimbaud, Claudel, Gide, Tolstoy, and Chekhov. Editions of his collected poems appeared in Polish in 1952 and 1954.

In an assessment of modern Polish literature, Waclaw Borowy states that Iwaszkiewicz's "greatest strength is in his art of creating atmosphere and this he does at his best when he is painting the Ukraine, from which he came himself, as in the story 'The Feast of Autumn' or in the novel 'The Moon Is Rising.'" Borowy explains that Iwaszkiewicz's "The Lovers of Verona" and "Young Ladies from Wilk" describe love as a "fatal irresistible power, immeasurably enthralling but always accompanied by such degradations that its most fervid worshippers are happiest when they escape from it." Arthur Coleman also attests to the Strindbergian mistrust of women in Iwasziewicz's work and points to his short novels "The Teacher" and "The Mill on the Utrata" as examples of the theme of the unwholesome influence of women. Nevertheless, as Czeslaw Milosz writes, "he remained true to his belief in the ever-renewing and beneficent *élan* of Life." In a poem addressed to his wife, Iwaszkiewicz wrote of his work:

But you should know that often there were hours
When speech was strangled in my too narrow chest.
The world was far too beautiful to give my poems
Only to you. O my beloved,
I looked into unconfinable spaces,
I was transported by unconfinable feelings.
                                    —trans. C. Milosz

Iwaszkiewicz was a widely traveled man. He was often abroad as a state official in Paris, Copenhagen, and Persia. After 1945 he was a newspaper editor and head of many cultural organizations in Warsaw. He was president of the Polish Writers Union, editor of the respected and influential literary magazine *Tworczosc* (Creative Work), and an active participant in Poland's political life. In 1948 he won the Olympic Literary Competition.

WORKS IN ENGLISH TRANSLATION: Iwaszkiewicz's play *Summer in Nohant* was translated into English by Celina Wiencewska in 1942. A selection of his short stories is available in English translation in *Contemporary Polish Short Stories,* edited by A. Kijowski (1960) and in *Introduction to Modern Polish Literature,* edited by A. Gillon and J. Krzyzanowski (1964).

ABOUT: Cassell's Encyclopedia of World Literature 2, 1973; Columbia Dictionary of Modern European Literature, 1980; Encyclopedia of World Literature in the 20th Century (rev. ed.) II, 1982; Kridl, M. Survey of Polish Literature and Culture, 1956; Krzyzanowski, J. History of Polish Literature, 1978; Matlaw, M. Modern World Drama, 1972, Milosz, C. Postwar Polish Poetry, 1965; History of Polish Literature, 1969. *Periodicals*—New York Times Book Review June 5, 1938; Slavonic and East European Review 12 (1934); 15 (1936–37); World Literature Today 56 (Summer 1982).

*JABÈS, EDMOND** (April 16, 1912–),
French poet and aphorist, was born in Cairo of
Italian Jewish parents. His father had studied in
France, and determined that the boy would receive a French education—an option readily
available in the Egyptian capital, which in those
days boasted a cosmopolitan intelligentsia, deeply francophone and francophile. He attended
the Collège St.-Jean-Baptiste-de-la-Salle and the
Lycée Français in Cairo, then was sent to Paris
in 1930 to study literature at the Sorbonne, a
course he abandoned after a couple of years.
While in France he began a long correspondence with the French writer Max Jacob, whom
he has always claimed as a seminal influence on
his work and whose letters to him Jabès published in Egypt in 1945, the year after Jacob's
death. In 1935, having returned to Cairo, Jabès
married Arlette Cohen, whom he had met there
in late 1929.

During the 1930s and throughout World War
II he was active in the anti-Nazi cause, and
fought for a time alongside British troops in Palestine. Jabès had begun to write poetry, which
was published in magazines and by small presses
in Egypt and France. Although he came to know
several leading French writers, he was always a
figure apart, quite unaligned with any school,
explaining in a long interview with Paul Auster
in 1978: "I have always lived in the margins, so
to speak . . . even though my early poems were
very close to Surrealism and I had many friends
who were Surrealists. Éluard, for example, was
very eager for me to join the group, to participate actively in the movement. But I have always refused to join any kind of group. From the
very beginning I have felt that the risks a writer
takes must be taken alone. The idea of sharing
these risks is upsetting to me. Something very
important is taken away from you then, and as
far as I'm concerned, if there is no risk, there is
no writing."

In 1957, after the Suez invasion, life for Egyptian Jews became extremely precarious, and
Jabès was forced to leave Cairo, losing his culture, his home, and all his possessions. As Auster
noted, "He experienced for the first time the
burden of being Jewish. Until then, his Jewishness had been nothing more than a cultural fact,
one element in his life. But now that he had been
made to suffer for no other reason than that he
was a Jew, this cultural fact was transformed and
became all-important." Jabès settled in Paris,
where he has lived ever since. His major book of
poetry, *Je bâtis ma demeure* (I Build My Dwelling), a collection of most of his previously published work, appeared two years after his arrival
in France. An enlarged edition was published in
1975. Many of the themes and concerns devel-

EDMOND JABÈS

oped by Jabès in his later work are first evident
in *Je bâtis ma demeure*: the delineation of the
mystery of writing, of the unfathomable power
of words; the commanding of long-silenced
voices to sing:

The art of the writer consists in bringing words, little by little, to interest themselves in
   his books.

The poem has broken in the word the mirror
   which was distorting its image.

Sure of its road, prose differs from poetry just
   as a walker,
hastened along by his objective, differs from
   a dancer
intoxicated with never arriving.

Steve Light wrote of the sense summoned by
these poems of "yearning, the yearning to hear
the dead speak; the yearning to commune with
what has been lost; the yearning of a people, any
people, the Jews here; yearning for communion;
a yearning that is felt all the more because of the
extraordinarily *palpable* communion that Jabès'
books establish with their readers."

The predominant literary form in all of Jabès'
work is the aphorism, which enjoys a long and
respected history in French literature, though it
has, until recently, been out of favor for many
generations in English-speaking countries. In the
eight-volume *The Book of Questions,* his masterpiece, aphorisms form the basic structural units
of each part, giving the work a sense of fragmentation, of seemingly random assemblage, that is
an essential part of its determined strugggle for
wholeness and comprehension. The work's publication history is as follows: *Le livre des*

°jä bes´

questions comprises *Le livre des questions* (1963), *Le livre de Yukel* (1964), *Le retour au livre* (1965), *Yaël* (1967), *Elya* (1969), *Aely* (1972), *Et, ou le dernier livre* (1973), and *Le livre des ressemblances* (1976).

According to Jabès: "The story of Sarah and Yukel is the account, through various dialogues and meditations attributed to imaginary rabbis, of a love destroyed by men and by words. It has the dimensions of the book and the bitter stubbornness of a wandering question." Yet this tragic couple and their sadly thwarted love remain only "a kind of basic pretext" for the work as a whole, as the author explained to Auster: "*The Book of Questions* is based on the idea that we all live with words that obsess us. There is no question that highly emotional words such as 'death' or 'love,' for example, do not have precisely the same meanings for everyone. Behind these words we see our own stories of death and love. As for the story in the book, I simply wanted to point out the life and drama of this couple. It was not a question of telling the story of their lives, because in the end it wasn't their lives that interested me. . . . I am more concerned with interiority than description. It is the questioning around the story that gives the story its dimension." The ultimate aim of the book is the expression of the inexpressible, the naming of words that lie on the other side of speech. "We get to where we are going," Jabès remarked, "and then there is still this distance to cover. And a moment comes when you can no longer cover the distance; you get there and you say to yourself, it's finished, there are no more words. God is perhaps a word without words. A word without meaning. And the extraordinary thing is that in the Jewish tradition God is invisible, and as a way of underscoring this invisibility, he has an unpronounceable name. What I find truly fantastic is that when you call something 'invisible,' you are naming something, which means that you are almost giving a representation of the invisible. . . . There is a constant effacement, a constant peeling of layers, a stripping away of the name until this name becomes an unpronounceable name. . . . It is the very nature of my work, this constant questioning of things in order to say, finally, what is identity? What are we? What is the name? This name that we bear with us, what is it? . . . I don't presume to have any answers, I ask questions. If I give a special status to the question, that is because I find something unsatisfactory about the nature of the answer. It can never completely contain us. . . . I feel that answers embody a certain form of power. Whereas the question is a form of nonpower, one . . . that will be upsetting to power. Power does not like discussions. Power affirms, and it has only friends or enemies. Whereas the question is in between."

To Auster, Jabès' originality "lies in his ability to bring abstract ideas to life, to give them clear and palpable shape, and then to connect them to human concerns beyond the realm of mere literary theory. For all his sophistication and all the difficulties his work presents, Jabès is a poet with feelings so intense that they are bound to disturb." Yet the unremittingly oblique tone of all of the author's work has greatly irritated many of his English-speaking readers, even those favorably disposed to his themes. The reviewer of *Elya* in the *Times Literary Supplement,* for example, though admiring the book as a whole, admitted that it seemed "rebarbative: a sequence of inscrutable statements proffered by fictitious rabbis, on whose words the poet comments equally inscrutably. One is tempted to say that whereas [René] Char expanded the aphorism into poetry, M. Jabès had reduced poetry to the aphorism."

The French, however, with their inveterate fondness for nuanced intellectual exposition, have discerned a singular importance in all of Jabès' work. Maurice Blanchot, commenting on one of Jabès' key themes, "The homeland of the Jews is a sacred text in the middle of the commentaries which it has inspired," wrote: "The dignity of the exegesis is the importance accorded it by rabbinical tradition: to know that the written law, this nonoriginal text, must always be reprised by the voice that comments on it, reaffirmed by oral commentary which is not posterior to it, but contemporary with it, reprised yet not rejoined, in this disjunction which is the measure of its infinity." And Jacques Derrida, the principal structuralist critic, wrote that in *The Book of Questions* "a powerful and ancient root is exhumed, and on it is laid bare an ageless wound (for what Jabès teaches us is that roots speak, that words want to grow, and that poetic discourse *takes root* in a wound): in question is a certain Judaism as the birth and passion of writing. The passion *of* writing, the love and endurance of the letter itself whose subject is not decidably the Jew or the Letter itself. Perhaps the common root of a people and of writing. In any event, the incommensurable destiny which grafts the history of a 'race born of the book' onto the radical origin of meaning as literality, that is, onto historicity itself. For there could be no history without the gravity and labor of literality. The painful folding of itself which permits history to reflect itself as it ciphers itself. This reflection is its beginning." Criticism such as this, at least as dense and difficult as its ostensible object, has become almost a commonplace in French commentary on Jabès.

The author has made occasional trips outside France to read and discuss his work, notably a tour of the United States in late 1978. He became a French citizen in 1967, and has won the Prix des Critiques (1970), the literary prize of the Foundation for French Judaism (1982), and the Italian prize named for Pier Paolo Pasolini (1983).

WORKS IN ENGLISH TRANSLATION: Anthony Rudolf translated a small selection of the poems in *Je bâtis ma demeure* in 1979 under the title *A Share of Ink*. Six volumes of *The Book of Questions* have been published by Wesleyan University Press in Rosemarie Waldrop's translation: *The Book of Questions*, 1978, *The Book of Yakel* and *Return to the Book* in one volume, 1980, and *Yaël, Elya* and *Aely*, 1983.

ABOUT: Bénézet, M., Le roman de la langue, 1977; Blanchot, M., L'amitié, 1971; Derrida, J., Writing and Difference, 1978; Gould, E. The Sin of the Book: Edmond Jabès, 1984; Guglielmi, J., La ressemblance impossible: Edmond Jabès, 1978. *Periodicals*—New York Review of Books April 28, 1977; New York Times Book Review May 23, 1976; Times Literary Supplement July 19, 1974.

JACOBS, JANE (May 1, 1916–), American urbanologist and economist, was born in Scranton, Pennsylvania, the daughter of John Decker Butzner, a physician, and Bess Mary (Robison) Butzner. She got her first job, as a reporter for the *Scranton Tribune*, as soon as she graduated from high school. "I was so damn glad to get out of school," she recalled, "I couldn't even think of going to college." Moving to New York at the age of eighteen, she worked as a secretary and as a freelance writer and editor. During World War II she wrote articles on American architecture for the Office of War Information. She was married on May 27, 1944, to Robert Hyde Jacobs, Jr., an architect, with whom she had three children: James Kedzie, Edward Decker, and Mary Hyde. Her informal study of architecture with her husband enabled her in 1952 to become an associate editor of *Architectural Forum*.

Most of Jacobs' articles for the journal were investigations of the problems of major cities and of the public policies directed toward their solution. This research, some of which appeared in other periodicals and in her contribution to the volume *The Exploding Metropolis* (1958), culminated in the publication in 1961 of Jacobs' *The Death and Life of Great American Cities*, "the most important city planning document to be published in the sixties," according to Suzanne Stephens. The book was a lucid attack on professional urban planners, who, Jacobs said, are

JANE JACOBS

possessed of the same degree of insight into the actual workings of city life as the bloodletting physicians of the nineteenth century had into the actual workings of the human body. "As in the pseudoscience of bloodletting," she wrote, "just so in the pseudoscience of city rebuilding and planning, years of learning and a plethora of subtle and complicated dogmas have arisen on a foundation of nonsense." Jacobs traced the origins of this "intellectual dish of mush" to Ebenezer Howard, the English planner who sought to help the poor inhabitants of Victorian London by resettling them in meticulously arranged Garden Cities in the countryside. The legacy of these and other utopian schemes for social improvement was the idea, adopted without question by modern planners, that city dwellers, for their own good, must be kept away from the chaotic life of the streets and that densely populated areas must be rebuilt to give the remaining inhabitants prescribed quantities of open space and cleanliness, no matter what the cost in displaced families, ruptured neighborhoods, and taxpayer dollars. "Extraordinary governmental financial incentives have been required to achieve this degree of monotony, sterility, and vulgarity," Jacobs wrote.

Most of *The Death and Life of Great American Cities* was an exploration into "how cities work in real life, because this is the only way to learn what principles of planning and what practices in rebuilding can promote social and economic vitality in cities, and what practices and principles will deaden these attributes." Her conclusions were exactly the opposite of what conventional city planners assumed to be true.

She observed that vibrant urban communities— among them Boston's North End, San Francisco's Telegraph Hill, the Back-of-the-Yards in Chicago, and her own West Village in Manhattan—are areas characterized by diversity: of people (low-income and high-income), of use (residential and commercial), and of architecture (new and old). Where such diversity flourishes, she noted, the residents of a neighborhood form a network that keeps criminals out and makes the area socially and politically stable. The typical urban renewal project, by contrast, isolates people in anonymous high-rise buildings, where boredom and resentment fester. The result, Jacobs pointed out, is often a worse slum than originally existed. Many of the factors usually used by planners to identify slum conditions—density, for example—were shown by Jacobs to occur in healthy districts with low crime, disease, and mortality rates. Once a neighborhood is mislabeled a slum, she charged, bankers refuse to lend mortagage and rehabilitation money, and the area is marked for eventual destruction.

The Death and Life of Great American Cities, to quote Roger Jellinek, "terrorized the city planners by asserting that the good life was to be found in precisely what they abhorred: the apparent anarchy of the city street." The book was assailed by orthodox planners and by many liberals who regarded the government-funded slum-clearance scheme as a progressive method of improving the lot of inner-city dwellers. Other critics thought it sentimental and sensationalist, noting Jacobs' disregard for traditional techniques of scholarship. Many reviewers in the popular press, however, liked the freshness of Jacobs' thinking and the vigor of her writing style, which Lloyd Rodwin called "crisp, pungent, and engaging." "The great merit of Mrs. Jacobs' book," wrote Phoebe-Lou Adams, "is that she has looked at cities not as inanimate conglomerations of buildings but as the intricate working organisms that they really are: not as unsatisfactory substitutes for country life, but as necessary and valuable centers of human enterprise, experiment, and thought—of civilization, in fact . . . [It] is a fascinating book, and one of the few discussions of city life and problems that has ever been based on a sympathetic participation in them." Said Richard Sennett: "Although they scored numerous fine points in their attacks [on Jacobs], the planners never confronted her central argument: that community life is basically anarchic, that a workable neighborhood cannot be created by some central authority but grows out of the common experience of its inhabitants. . . . The intent of her mythmaking, and the unchallenged argument of her book, was

the value of anarchy; she was one of the first modern urbanists to advocate anarchy as *desirable* in the social life of city people."

As J. A. Kouwenhoven predicted, *The Death and Life of Great American Cities* proved to be "a book that will irresistibly overturn the preconceptions of generations of city planners." Adopted as required reading by schools of architecture and urban planning and published in several foreign-language editions, including Japanese, German, Spanish, and Czech, it was reissued as part of the Modern Library's series of modern classics. Jacobs herself told an interviewer in 1969 that the book had had little effect on public policy, but others have traced government acceptance of community participation in the planning process and the growing emphasis on the social and emotional needs of city dwellers directly to her work. In 1976 the United Nations Conference on Human Settlements endorsed the principles she had enunciated.

Jacobs left her job as senior editor of *Architectural Forum* in 1962 to continue her research, as well as her activism on behalf of threatened city neighborhoods, of which she calls herself "a fierce and rooted partisan." When, in the early 1960s, New York City planners decided to raze a fourteen-block section of her neighborhood and replace it with a high-rise development, Jacobs and her colleagues on the Committee to Save the West Village persuaded municipal officials to build a small-scale apartment project instead. In 1968 she led a vigorous campaign against the proposed Lower Manhattan Expressway. Although the campaign was successful, Jacobs was charged with inciting to riot during a protest demonstration and was convicted of disorderly conduct.

Jacobs' second book, *The Economy of Cities,* was another "amalgam of heresies" by the "Rachel Carson of the cities," according to George H. Favre. In it Jacobs set forth a theory of urban growth that contradicted centuries of received wisdom on the subject. Where most urban economists believed that cities are the outgrowth of agricultural settlements, Jacobs argued that, on the contrary, cities, as centers of trade, preceded farms, which were developed to supply the cities with food. The city, rather than being a parasitic user of rural resources, is the originator of new technologies and innovations by which the countryside prospers. The prosperity of the city itself is based upon its ability to take over the production of goods and services it previously imported and thereby to bring in new imports in a self-renewing cycle. To keep the cycle in motion, there must be a constant generation of new work to replace, refine, and expand on the "parent work"; this is achieved by maintaining a diversity of small, inefficient industries, all seeking through trial and error to create innovations, and in turn creating markets for yet more small industries.

Jacobs warned that the trend away from diversity and from "valuable inefficiencies and practicalities" in American cities doomed them to stagnation; urban renewal schemes without economic renewal merely hide temporarily the evidence of decay. The factors usually cited as the cause of urban ills—automobiles, pollution, decrepit housing—are in fact, she said, "symptoms of arrested development," because in a thriving city innovative entrepreneurs would develop new solutions to problems of transportation, energy use, waste disposal, and housing stock. Further, she insisted that ghetto areas cannot be saved by infusions of capital, whether government aid or private investment; there must first be "a multiplicity of small new departures" established into which capital can productively be fed—an unlikely situation, given the reluctance of bankers to take risks. Economic development, Jacobs wrote, is "profoundly subversive to the status quo." Groups with a vested interest in preventing diversity include well-established industries, their unionized workers, their investors, and the government, which derives much of its power from collusion with them.

Critical reaction to *The Economy of Cities* was both excited and cautious. It was pointed out that Jacobs is not a trained economist; had ignored current scholarship; had illustrated part of her argument with an imaginary city (though most of her examples were drawn from history); was biased in favor of cities and against agriculture; had not produced an adequate plan for dealing with urban problems; had paid insufficient attention to the roles of government, giant corporations, and capital; and did not take into account such factors in the growth of cities as location, climate, defense, available skills, and the effect of government policies of taxation and subsidy. "Her theory is put forth in a kind of vacuum in which cities grow or wane in accordance with her few simple rules," wrote Charles Abrams. "Influences on the growth and decline of cities, however, are not only multiple but change with times and conditions."

Despite these criticisms, most reviewers were impressed with Jacobs' insight and power of expression. Christopher Lehmann-Haupt said that she had developed a "radiant, harmonious and beautifully integrated theory" that "blows cobwebs from the mind." James Marston Fitch wrote that the book was "densely reasoned, rig-

orous in its clarity and economy, and absolutely brilliant for the new light it casts upon familiar, worked-over materials. It is, in short, that rare thing, an authentically innovative theoretical work. . . . Urban economic theory will henceforth be modified by this remarkable book." According to Asa Briggs, Jacobs "has one of the most independent minds on either side of the Atlantic. She also possesses what looks like unlimited intellectual curiosity and courage . . . Much of what she does say looks unbelievably obvious as soon as she has propounded her theories."

Shortly after publishing *The Economy of Cities* Jacobs moved to Toronto. Her third book was *The Question of Separatism,* based on the 1979 Massey Lectures that she delivered for the Canadian Broadcasting Corporation. She analyzed the possible advantages and disadvantages arising out of the proposed secession of the province of Quebec from Canadian federation and concluded that a peaceful secession might well be in the interests of all Canadians. Edgar Z. Friedenberg described the book as "a *tour de force,* the kind of force that expresses itself through restraint and precision, like a laser beam used with such exquisite care as not to insult the distressed body it is intended to relieve"—although this same tact, he felt, "limits the usefulness of her analysis" because it prevented her from criticizing the belligerencies of English Canada, and especially the federal government, toward Quebecois separatists. It was, he said, "a highly rational and reassuring work."

Jacobs' recent work on cities, published in *Cities and the Wealth of Nations: Principles of Economic Life,* attempts to show that cities, not nations, are the basic units of economic development. Economic prosperity, she argues, is the product of "import-replacement," a process by which a city evolves from an importer of goods to a manufacturer. Using numerous historical and modern examples, including Venice and Tokyo, she explains why unemployment can persist in a period of high prices, and argues that economic aid to distressed regions and countries is often wasted because the conditions for successful growth are not created. The general drift of her book, as Naomi Bliven noticed in a *New Yorker* review, "is totally at odds with the military kind of thinking that devises industrial strategies . . . and relies upon formal structures and will instead of ingenuity and spontaneity."

PRINCIPAL WORKS: The Death and Life of Great American Cities, 1961; The Economy of Cities, 1969; The Question of Separatism: Quebec and the Struggle over Sovereignty, 1980; Cities and the Wealth of Nations, 1984.

ABOUT: American Women Writers, 1980; Contemporary Authors 21–22, 1969; Current Biography, 1977; Political Profiles: The Kennedy Years, 1976; Torre, S. (ed.) Women in American Architecture: A Historic and Contemporary Perspective, 1977. *Periodicals*—Architectural Forum July 1969; Atlantic November 1961; July 1969; Christian Science Monitor November 9, 1961; June 26, 1969; Life June 29, 1969; New York Herald Tribune Books November 5, 1961; New York Review of Books January 1, 1970; February 19, 1976; November 20, 1980; New York Times April 18, 1968; May 1, 1969; New York Times Book Review November 5, 1961; June 1, 1969; New York Times Magazine May 25, 1969; New Yorker August 27, 1984; Progressive Architecture March 1977; Observer May 3, 1970.

CLIVE JAMES

JAMES, CLIVE (VIVIAN LEOPOLD) (October 7, 1939–   ), British journalist and essayist, was born in Sydney, Australia, the son of Albert Arthur James and Minora May Darke James. After attending Sydney Technical High School and Sydney University, he went to Britain for graduate work at Pembroke College, Cambridge, where he was president of Footlights, the theatrical society. James began his career as a song lyricist, producing several albums for the singer Pete Atkin, including "Beware of the Beautiful Stranger," "Driving through Mythical America," "Secret Drinker," "Live Libel," and "The Master of the Revels."

Since 1972, James has been a feature writer for the *Observer,* the venerable London Sunday newspaper. His reports on the general cultural scene, frequent book reviews, and regular television column are usually characterized by an acerbic wit, a fluent style, and a tendency to dislike almost everything. Much of the best of his writing on television is available in three books: *Visions before Midnight, The Crystal Bucket: Television Criticism from the Observer, 1976–79,* and *Glued to the Box.* Reviewing *The Crystal Bucket,* Peter Conrad called the author's persona as television critic one of "bluff (yet often preachy) plain speaking." An American critic, Richard Gilman, saw James' similarity to the film critic Pauline Kael "in many unpleasant ways. They have the same sort of viciousness, even sadism, the same more than ordinary interest in the scatological, the same itch to score off their material by exercises of wit. And both have turned to their account the 'trashiness' of so much of what they see by sharing it as a kind of joke with their readers."

As a literary critic, James possesses breadth of interest and, in T. J. Binyon's words, "a solid and individual critical personality." The first of his books to be published in the United States, *First*

Reactions: Critical Essays, 1968–1979, contained pieces on Edmund Wilson, John Berryman, Elizabeth Bishop, e.e. cummings, and D. H. Lawrence which had originally appeared in 1974 in his *The Metropolitan Critic;* television reviews from *Visions before Midnight;* and essays on Aleksandr Solzhenitsyn, W. H. Auden, Robert Lowell, and Raymond Chandler from *At the Pillars of Hercules.* The collection was generally well received by American reviewers; one critic described it as "packed with aggressive learning, wit, and flash—at times tediously so." T. R. Edwards saw the essays on prose writers as largely stylistic discussions, yet acclaimed the author as "a superb reader of poetry, one who knows that you 'read' not only with the eye and the mind but with the ear." Another collection of James' literary essays is *From the Land of Shadows,* which contains, besides articles on figures as disparate as Bernard Levin, Philip Larkin, and Gore Vidal, a substantial number of pieces on the work of contemporary Soviet dissidents— Solzhenitsyn, Sakharov, Bukovsky, and Zinoviev—"many of them," the publishers assert, "read in the original Russian." Binyon, a renowned scholar of Russian literature, remarked that James "doesn't so much parade his knowledge of Russian as double it ferociously round the square in full marching order until it collapses from exhaustion." Yet the author's "outstanding talent," he concedes, "is as a cicerone, guiding the ignorant traveler with patience, knowledge, and wit round some favorite literary edifice and communicating his own admiration of it to the goggling and fascinated visitor."

James is also well known as one of the few

modern practitioners of the neoclassical genre of narrative verse satire. Originally published in serial form in the *Observer,* then as books, his poems take aim at the broadest and most popular British targets: print and broadcast journalism in *The Fate of Felicity Fark in the Land of the Media*; authors, publishing, and criticism in *Peregrine Prykke's Pilgrimage through the London Literary World*; national politics in *Britannia Bright's Bewilderment in the Wilderness of Westminster*; and royalty and aristocracy in *Charles Charming's Challenges on the Pathway to the Throne.* As a verse satirist he is always good at irony and usually manages a competent imitation of the neoclassical mock-heroic strain, but his greatest technical accomplishment is a supple mastery of the rhymed couplet—ordinarily, even in many eighteenth-century hands, a stiff and unyielding form. Here, from *Britannia Bright,* is his hilarious and oddly prescient account of an appearance by Margaret Thatcher ("Margo Hatbox") before the Tory Party Conference in the autumn of 1976, nearly three years before she came to power as prime minister:

The audience made noises like *Niagara.*
A woman finely drawn as some *Tanagra*
Or *Dresden* figurine was now preparing
To give her kit of axioms an airing.
Her skin peaches and cream, her hair spun gold,
Cucumber-cool with eyeballs ice-cube cold,
She looked like the epitome of poise—
A schoolgirl twice as grown-up as the boys.

Another of James' ventures into verse satire was *Fanmail,* which consists of adulatory letters in various meters to his close friends in the London literary scene. Ian Hamilton complained of the relentlessness of "the self-mythologizing brio" when extended to book length: "the kind of racy hyperbole that can be chuckled over in a weekly magazine requires a more severe riposte when it pretends that its allure is built to last."

James' novel *Brilliant Creatures* is also a caricature of literary London. It contains several imitations of eighteenth-century literary conventions, including an ingenuous introduction and lengthy explanatory notes at the end, which accompany the picaresque story of Lancelot Windhover as he is corrupted by literary types in London and Los Angeles. Linda Taylor thought James' "sheer forcefulness . . . as overpowering, likeable, and ultimately unmemorable as ever."

Unreliable Memoirs is the author's recollection of his boyhood and coming of age in Kogarah, the suburban frontier between Sydney and the Australian outback. It is filled with jokes and self-deprecation, yet throughout recur motifs of sadness, hardship, and loss. David Bene-

dictus wrote, "He is both afraid that you will take him seriously, constantly warning you that what you are reading is a work of fiction—which it evidently isn't—and worried that you won't." Walter Clemons, however, in an American reaction to the autobiography, dismissed its humor as entirely juvenile and its writing as "blustering facetiousness."

In addition to having published works showing a passing acquaintance with such a large variety of literary forms, James is also frequently (some would say constantly) seen on British television. He has been an integral part of the popular series "Cinema," "Up Sunday," "So It Goes," "A Question of Sex," "Saturday Night People," and "Clive James on Television," and has made several specials and documentaries, including the segment on *Hamlet* in the series "Shakespeare in Perspective," "The Clive James Paris Fashion Show," "Clive James and the Calendar Girls," "The Return of the Flash of Lightning," and "Clive James Live in Las Vegas." Several British wags, including contributors to the satirical magazine *Private Eye,* have taken to calling him "Clive Jaws," in allusion to his purported long-windedness as well as, perhaps, to the famous shark's viciousness, voraciousness, and seeming ubiquity.

PRINCIPAL WORKS: *Verse*—The Fate of Felicity Fark in the Land of the Media, 1975; Peregrine Prykke's Pilgrimage through the London Literary World, 1976; Britanniaright's Bewilderment in the Wilderness of Westminster, 1976; Fanmail, 1977; Charles Charming's Challenges on the Pathway to the Throne, 1981. *Fiction*—Brilliant Creatures, 1983. *Memoirs*—Unreliable Memoirs, 1980. *Criticism*—The Metropolitan Critic, 1974; Visions before Midnight, 1977; At the Pillars of Hercules, 1979; First Reactions, 1980; The Crystal Bucket, 1981; From the Land of Shadows, 1982; Glued to the Box, 1982. *Travel*—Flying Visits, 1984.

ABOUT: Who's Who, 1983–84. *Periodicals*—Choice February 1981; Commonweal October 23, 1981; Current Biography 1984; Library Journal October 1, 1980; April 15, 1981; Nation May 2, 1981; New Republic March 21, 1981; New Statesman June 13, 1980; New York Review of Books April 2, 1981; New York Times Book Review November 9, 1980; February 15, 1981; Newsweek February 23, 1981; Observer June 19, 1977; Saturday Review September 1980; Times Literary Supplement April 25, 1980; May 8, 1981.

JAMES, P(HYLLIS) D(OROTHY) (August 3, 1920–), English mystery and crime novelist, was born in Oxford, the eldest of three children of Sidney Victor James, an income-tax officer with the Inland Revenue service, and Dorothy

P. D. JAMES

May (Hone) James. She grew up in Ludlow, Shropshire, and in Cambridge, where from 1931 to 1937 she attended the Cambridge School for Girls. Denied the opportunity to go to college— her parents could not afford it, and scholarships for women were few—she worked in a tax office, as assistant stage manager with the Cambridge Festival Theatre, and in a wartime food office. She was married on August 8, 1941, to Ernest Conner Bantry White, a physician. They had two daughters, Clare (born in 1942) and Jane (born in 1944)

For several years during World War II James raised the children alone while her husband served in the Royal Army Medical Corps. After his demobilization he was diagnosed as having a mental illness and entered the first of a series of psychiatric hospitals. The government refused to award him a disability pension, and James, then living with her husband's parents, took a clerk's job with the National Health Service in 1949. Going to school at night, she received diplomas in hospital administration and medical record-keeping and eventually became principal administrative assistant of the North West Metropolitan Regional Medical Board in London. Her husband died in 1964. She qualified as a senior civil servant in the Home Office in 1968 and was appointed to a post in the police department. In 1972 she transferred to the criminal policy department, where she became a specialist in juvenile delinquency.

Although James had nursed an ambition to write fiction since early childhood, the demands of supporting her family, raising her children, and caring for her invalid husband forced her to postpone any attempts at writing until she was in her mid-thirties. "I realized," she told Patricia Craig in an interview for the *Times Literary Supplement*, "that if I didn't settle down and get on with it, I would never be a writer; I'd end up telling my grandchildren that I'd always wanted to write fiction. And that would have been a dreadful failure in one of the most important areas of my life." She began writing in the early morning, before leaving for work. She decided to write a detective novel, she told Craig, because it "would have the best chance of being accepted" and because its "disciplined form" would help her to develop craftsmanship.

Cover Her Face, begun in 1959 and published in 1962, was a country-house mystery in the classical tradition of Dorothy L. Sayers, Margery Allingham, and Ngaio Marsh. Her detective, Adam Dalgliesh, a widower, combined the expertise and detachment of the police detective with a poet's sensitivity and was more fully developed as a character than the heroes of Sayers' and Agatha Christie's novels, who rely more on mannerisms. Dalgliesh returned in James' next three mysteries, *A Mind for Murder, Unnatural Causes,* and *Shroud for a Nightingale.* The critical reaction to these novels was mixed, but virtually all the reviewers identified James as a writer of unusual ability. H.R.F. Keating, writing in the *Times Saturday Review,* noted "the lifelikeness of her creations," her "marvellously sure hand" and "commonsensical decisiveness of moral judgment," adding: "Mrs. James's worlds are distinguished by the denseness of their texture. . . . I sometimes feel her books are to be compared with the music of Brahms."

Dalgliesh made only a minor appearance in *An Unsuitable Job for a Woman,* in which a novice detective named Cordelia Gray uncovers a revenge murder in the supposed suicide of a young man. The book was well received by James' already considerable body of readers and established her as the leading successor to Allingham and Sayers. The critics were less pleased with *The Black Tower,* which Newgate Callendar of the *New York Times* thought "slow-moving," but had nearly unanimous praise for *Death of an Expert Witness.* A reviewer in the *New Yorker* said that the disciple of the great mystery writers had become "their superior in almost every respect: a better, more sensitive writer, a more agile and teasing storyteller, a deeper, more clear-eyed observer of human nature, human fears, human drives and aspirations."

James' next book, *Innocent Blood,* was not a detective story at all but a "serious" crime novel about an adopted daughter who goes in search of her natural parents and discovers that they were responsible for the rape and murder of a child. Many of James' admirers were confounded by this change of direction. Julian Symons felt the novel and its characters "strikingly implausible," its plot "jarringly melodramatic." Paul Bailey, in the *Times Literary Supplement*, complained that James' device of having her overly erudite characters quote Shakespeare and Milton at every turn was "a short-cut to seriousness" and that her treatment of rape and murder "trivializes them with cleverness." Other readers felt that she had taken a risk and succeeded. The reviewer for the *Times* of London, noting that the book contained "imagery of flashing power," called it "a strong suspense story" in which the author delves into "that old, ever-new problem of nature and nurture, taking in the question of self-identity and ending with an exploration of the meaning of love." *Innocent Blood* was a best-seller, earning $1 million in the United States alone.

After this excursion James returned to the mystery form with another best-seller, *The Skull Beneath the Skin,* a Cordelia Gray story set in an island castle. James is also the coauthor, with Thomas A. Critchley, of *The Maul and the Pear Tree,* an account of a series of murders that actually took place in the East End of London in 1811.

As a mystery writer, James thinks of herself as "being more or less in the English classical tradition." Her plotting is solid but not overwrought; she does not construct elaborate puzzles in the manner of Agatha Christie. She is respected for the authenticity of her settings and the depth of her characterizations. Julian Symons, reviewing *The Skull Beneath the Skin* for the *New York Times Book Review,* wrote: "Even minor P. D. James characters are fully realized, given a pedigree, a school background and an attitude toward life. . . . It is the interplay of character that most concerns P. D. James, the lasting effect of a casual piece of cruelty, the deliberate rasping quality of a police interrogation, the moments of cowardice and betrayal that may mark an otherwise blameless life."

James' settings are built up detail by detail, with what one critic calls "a certain 19th-century ease." In many of her novels the sense of authenticity is derived from her first-hand knowledge of hospitals and similar institutions as well as of police procedure. The stabbing victim in *A Mind for Murder* is the administrative officer of a psychiatric hospital; the victim in *Shroud for a Nightingale* is a student nurse poisoned in a demonstration of forced feeding; *The Black Tower* finds Dalgliesh investigating a murder in a home for the incurably ill; and *Death of an Expert Witness* takes place in a forensic science laboratory.

In an article in the *New York Times,* James said that she often gets ideas for novels from locations, and that the careful evocation of background and atmosphere is essential to mystery novels, in which "the setting of the crime and the use of commonplace objects help to heighten by contrast the intruding horror of murder." She continued: "It is one of the paradoxes of the genre that it deals with that great absolute, death, yet deploys the trivia of ordinary life as the frail but powerful instruments of justice."

James has received awards from the British Crime Writers Association and the Mystery Writers of America and is a fellow of the Institute of Hospital Administration. She lives in South Kensington, London, and has a seaside home in Southwold, Suffolk. She belongs to the Church of England and intends her books to unfold moral issues as well as give pleasure in the reading. "Crime writers," she told an interviewer, "are as concerned as are other novelists with psychological truth and the moral ambiguities of human action," among which she mentioned "the idea that love can be a great deal more lethal than hate; and the fact that, in an extraordinary way, good may or may not come out of evil, but, paradoxically, evil much more often comes out of good."

PRINCIPAL WORKS: Cover Her Face, 1962; A Mind to Murder, 1963; Unnatural Causes, 1967; Shroud for a Nightingale, 1971; (with Thomas A. Critchley) The Maul and the Pear Tree, 1971; An Unsuitable Job for a Woman, 1972; The Black Tower, 1975; Death of an Expert Witness, 1977; Innocent Blood, 1980; The Skull Beneath the Skin, 1982.

ABOUT: The Author Speaks, 1977; Joyner, N. C. 10 Women of Mystery, 1981; Contemporary Authors, first revision series 21–24, 1977; Contemporary Literary Criticism 18, 1981. *Periodicals*—Christian Century May 16, 1984; Macleans June 30, 1980; Newsweek January 23, 1978; New York Review of Books July 17, 1980; New York Times July 18, 1979; September 12, 1982; August 25, 1983; New York Times Book Review December 11, 1977; April 27, 1980; June 5, 1981; October 29, 1982; Toronto Globe and Mail February 2, 1978.

JASTROW, ROBERT (September 7, 1925–), American physicist, author, and educator, was born in New York City, the son of Abraham Jastrow, a car salesman, and the former Marie Greenfield. As a student at Hunter College Elementary School in Manhattan, Jastrow won first prize at a science fair held at the

ROBERT JASTROW

American Museum of Natural History for his exhibit on "The Economic Potential of Cotton." He graduated at fifteen from Townsend Harris High School, a school for gifted students at that time associated with the City College of New York, and enrolled in a pre-medical program at Columbia University. There his interest shifted from medicine to biophysics and finally to theoretical physics, in which he won his B.A. in 1944 when only eighteen. Continuing at Columbia, he received an M.A. in physics in 1945 and a Ph.D., also in physics, with a dissertation on quantum mechanics in 1948. While in graduate school he was a lecturer in physics at Columbia (1944–47) and an instructor in the school of engineering at Cooper Union (1947–48).

During the academic year 1948–49 Jastrow was a postdoctoral fellow at the University of Leiden, in the Netherlands, where he continued studying under Dr. A. H. Kramer, the theoretical physicist who had been his mentor while on a visiting professorship at Columbia. After Leiden, Jastrow did further post-doctoral work at the Institute for Advanced Studies in Princeton and at the University of California at Berkeley, and in 1953–54 was assistant professor of physics at Yale where he won recognition for his studies in high-energy protons, known as the "Jastrow potential." In 1954 he became a consultant in nuclear physics at the U.S. Naval Research Laboratory in Washington, where his career in the space program began.

Though Jastrow began his work at the Naval Research Laboratory as a specialist in nuclear physics, he soon became involved in Project Vanguard, the first American effort to develop

an artificial satellite. In 1958, after the disintegration of the world's first satellite, the Soviet Union's Sputnik, Jastrow received worldwide attention with calculations proving that the satellite's booster rocket could not have landed on American territory, as the Soviets had maintained. Soon afterward Jastrow was asked to establish and head the theoretical division of the new National Aeronautics and Space Administration (NASA). An early contribution of that division was the discovery, based on observations made by a Vanguard satellite, that the earth is more pear-shaped than perfectly spherical. In 1959 Jastrow was appointed chairman of NASA's lunar exploration group, which planned many of the scientific investigations of the moon that were later undertaken in conjunction with the Apollo astronauts' moon landings.

In 1961, in order to take advantage of the scientific expertise concentrated in New York, Jastrow moved his NASA office from the Goddard Space Flight Center in Greenbelt, Maryland, and established the Goddard Institute for Space Studies near Columbia University, where he became adjunct professor of geophysics. Continuing as a professor of geology and astronomy at Columbia, he also took on the duties of professor of earth science at Dartmouth College in 1974. Under Jastrow's direction, the Institute for Space Studies has undertaken significant research on the origin of the solar system and the physics of the moon. It has also conducted investigations into the causes of weather phenomena, providing the groundwork for long-range weather and climate predictions.

In addition to his research, administration, and teaching activities, Jastrow has been a prolific author and editor of scientific works for scientists, students, and the public. He also edited the *Journal of Atmospheric Sciences* from 1962 to 1974. *Astronomy: Fundamentals and Frontiers,* a textbook he wrote with Malcolm H. Thompson, published in 1972, became the most widely used astronomy textbook in the country with new editions in 1974 and 1977.

Both on television and in print, Robert Jastrow has long been active in explaining space science and promoting the space program to the public. He is a frequent contributor to *Science Digest* and other popular magazines, writing on such subjects as "The Case for UFO's" (*Science Digest,* 1980), "The Space Program and the National Interest" (*Foreign Affairs,* 1972), and "Science and the American Dream" (*Science Digest,* 1983), in which he argued that the 1978 reduction in capital gains tax, by encouraging venture capital, would help keep America in the forefront of technological advance.

Many of Jastrow's articles are excerpts from or otherwise related to his concurrently published books. Thus the article in the June 15, 1978 *New York Times Magazine,* "Have Astronomers Found God?", coincided with his book *God and the Astronomers,* a brief, fifty-seven-page volume on the theological implications of the Big Bang Theory of creation, which he compared to the Biblical creation story. He returned to this theme in an interview in the August 6, 1982 *Christianity Today,* observing that "Astronomers now find that they have painted themselves into a corner because they have proven by their own methods, that the world began abruptly in an act of creation . . . as a product of forces they cannot hope to discover." A strong proponent of nuclear preparedness, Jastrow maintained in this interview that "the move for nuclear disarmament doesn't recognize the existence of evil," which is present in every society but "can take the reins of power" in a totalitarian state. In "The New Soviet Arms Buildup in Space," an article in the October 3, 1982 *New York Times Magazine,* he warned that the Soviet Union would soon be dominant in space unless Americans supported President Reagan's call for funding an American nuclear buildup in space.

Jastrow's first popular book, and the first volume in what became his major trilogy, evolved from a 1964 series of lectures he delivered on CBS-TV's Summer Semester. Titled *Red Giants and White Dwarfs: The Evolution of Stars, Planets, and Life,* the book deals with the origin and evolution of the universe (red giants and white dwarfs being older stars, in later stages of stellar development, than our sun), with a sweeping summary of events up to the dawn of life on earth and, finally, the appearance of humans. The book was generally praised for its clarity, accessibility, and style in popularizing complicated material. It was revised in 1971 and again in 1979 to include new information and photos obtained from NASA and Soviet space flights.

In 1971 Jastrow returned to Summer Semester with another series of lectures in which he extended his synopsis of cosmic history to speculate on technological advances of the twenty-first century. In print, he followed *Red Giants and White Dwarfs,* which concentrates on the astronomical prelude to life on earth, with *Until the Sun Dies,* which shifts the focus to the forces that have guided evolution and shaped Homo sapiens in his present form. Noting that Darwin's theory in the nineteenth century united humans to other animals, Jastrow calls his approach a new Darwinism which unites life on earth to life in the cosmos. Comparing his synthesis to a "natural religion," Jastrow notes that "like other religions, this one has a cosmology" (the scientific theory of the origin of the universe) and a "moral content" (in the "adversity and struggle" which he placed "at the very heart of evolutionary progress").

In effect, Jastrow views the whole history of the universe as a progression leading to the moment when, "Finally, man stands on the earth, more perfect than any other." Writing in the *New York Times Book Review,* H.S.F. Cooper called *Until the Sun Dies* "a sort of scientific rewriting of the Book of Genesis [which] shares the flaw of the Biblical acount: [the assumption] that we are somehow the culmination of creation." Unlike some anthropocentric cosmologists, however, Jastrow believes in the likelihood that other intelligent beings have evolved "in many parts of the universe"; and he foresees still higher forms to come as today's Homo sapiens, "the man of wisdom," becomes "the root stock out of which still more exalted beings must emerge."

It is a particular form of this further, future development of still more intelligent life that Jastrow takes up in *The Enchanted Loom.* After summarizing the astronomical and biological developments detailed in his previous two volumes, Jastrow concentrates here, as he puts it in the preface, on "how the brain evolved, the way it works, how it balances instinct and reason, what it is evolving into." Looking back, Jastrow sees the history of life as a flow "from the simple to the complex, from lower forms to higher, and always toward greater intelligence." Looking forward, he sees human intelligence enlarged and extended by the computer. Early in the book, after announcing that computers "have ushered in the Golden Age," he sets forth the vision with almost rhapsodic anticipation:

A bold scientist will be able to tap the contents of his mind and transfer them into the metallic lattices of a computer. Because mind is the essence of being, it can be said that the scientist has entered the computer, and that he now dwells in it. The machine is its body—a new form of existence. It seems to me that this must be the mature form of intelligent life in the Universe . . . [It] could live forever . . . [and] roam the space between the stars.

Explaining how this might come about, Jastrow foresees that if the present trend toward computer miniaturization continues, the machine's circuits will become as densely packed as the electrical systems in the human brain. If they could then be wired to work like the brain, says Jastrow, "man would be able to create a thinking organism of quasihuman power—a new form of intelligent life." He concludes that "the era of carbon-chemical life is drawing to a close on the earth and a new era of silicon-based life— indestructible, immortal, infinitely expandable—is beginning."

Like other reviewers, R. M. Restak in the *New*

York Times Book Review found Jastrow's vision thought-provoking but optimistic and imprecise in its view of computers' capabilities. In contrast, the noted evolutionist Stephen Jay Gould, conidering the book in the *New York Review of Books,* found Jastrow's idea of future intelligence possible and his argument "conceivably correct in outline." However, like H. S. F. Cooper in his review of *Until the Sun Dies,* Gould took issue with Jastrow's almost theological depiction of the entire history of life as an "inexorable and progressive march to increasing braininess; the carbon-to-silicon transition then simply completes a universal directionality." In fact, Gould notes, the fossil record reveals that "life is a ramifying bush with millions of branches, not a ladder." Gould also saw in Jastrow's argument "an unacceptable density of factual errors" in biological detail and an illogical association between biological and technological evolution. Like other reviewers, however, he found Jastrow's speculations thought-provoking and his presentation "eloquent"—a term that was also used by the *American Scientist* reviewer John A. Eddy. Expressing a common reaction to Jastrow's popular writing, Eddy said, "Jastrow is a clever teacher and a good explainer; while he sometimes oversimplifies we cannot care: he is such a good storyteller and puts us so at ease."

As a scientist Robert Jastrow has received the Columbia University Medal for Excellence in 1962, the Arthur Fleming Award for outstanding service in the United States government in 1964, the Columbia University Graduate Faculty's Alumni Award for Excellence in 1967, and the NASA Medal for Exceptional Scientific Achievement in 1968. He is a fellow of the American Geophysical Union, the American Association for the Advancement of Science, and the American Physical Society; a member of the International Academy of Astronautics, the Council on Foreign Relations, and the Leakey Foundation; and a member of the Cosmos, Explorers, and Century Clubs. In 1967 he married Ruth Witenberg, a former Israeli Army sergeant. They live in New York City.

PRINCIPAL WORKS: Red Giants and White Dwarfs, 1967; (with M. H. Thompson) Astronomy: Fundamentals and Frontiers, 1972; Until the Sun Dies, 1977; God and the Astronomers, 1978; The Enchanted Loom, 1981. *As editor*—Explorations of Space, 1960; (with A. G. W. Cameron) The Origin of the Solor System, 1963; (with M. H. Thompson) The Atmosphere of Venus, 1969.

ABOUT: Contemporary Authors, first revision series 23–24, 1977; Current Biography 1973; Who's Who in America, 1983–84. *Periodicals*—Christianity Today August 6, 1982; New York Post November 18, 1967; New York Review of Books April 15, 1982; New York Times May 19, 1961; New York Times Book Review October 2, 1977, March 7, 1982.

JOHNSON, DIANE (LAIN) (April 28, 1934–), American novelist and critic writes: "I was born Diane Lain, in Moline, Illinois, where my father was principal of the high school and my mother had been the art teacher. Thus I was surrounded by kindly and interested teachers, my parents' friends, and was expected to do well in school, which I did. Moline is a pleasant and small midwestern community, cold in winter, hot in summer (when we went to Michigan). Everyone knew you or your parents, and life was full of small pleasures, few excitements. One pleasure and excitement for me was to spend Saturdays in the local Carnegie Library, where I earnestly read at random from the shelves, or from lists of Great Books. The librarian put her foot down when I wished to read *La Dame Aux Camellias* and *Madame Bovary*.

"At seventeen I went to Stephens College, in Columbia, Mo., and studied there for two years. During that time I was changed from someone who thought she would be a painter, to an English major. It had not by then occurred to me that a writer was something you could be—I had imagined them all dead. Now I was given books by living writers! And I wrote stories, which people liked, just as they had liked my stories in elementary school and since.

"At the end of my second year I won a magazine contest (*Mademoiselle*) and went to New York—my first time east of the Mississippi. I found New York eye-opening but frightening; I went home, and married my boyfriend, and moved to California. There I got a job—to support him through medical school. I hated having a job, and exerted all my ingenuity in finding ways to be sent on special errands, to make a poster or buy supplies for the office party. I wished myself back in college, and luckily, after a year, I did enroll again in college, this time in Utah, where my husband was an intern. Also, at this time, I had my first baby, and became pregnant with the second, both born in 1956.

"After a year in Utah, my husband had to serve two years in the Air Force—in Sacramento, California. Then we moved back to Los Angeles, where I had two more babies and was divorced. My first novel was published then—in 1965. I had taken to novel-writing during the children's naps. I did not then think of myself as a novelist, but I was a serious writer.

"I had also been taking graduate courses at UCLA. Now, divorced, with the four little children, I went to England, where I worked on my

DIANE JOHNSON

dissertation and the book that became *Lesser Lives*, a biography published in 1972. I returned from England in 1968, remarried and moved to San Francisco, where I have been ever since. Since then I have also taught at the University of California at Davis."

———

Diane Johnson is the daughter of Dolph Lain and the former Frances Eloise Elder. She received her B.A. from the University of Utah in 1957 and her M.A. and Ph.D. from UCLA, the latter degree in 1968. Her fiction first began to attract attention with the publication of her third novel, *Burning*. Set in an expensive suburb of Los Angeles during the month of September, when everything is sere and flammable, it is the story of Bingo Edwards: "Except for being plain and a terrible housekeeper, she was a perfect wife. Cooked beautifully, sewed, was infinitely erudite on all subjects, was witty when she wasn't depressed." The various southern California adventures she endures, as well as the other self-obsessed, half-crazed characters, are described with deadpan irony leavened with a good deal of sympathy. "The literal holocaust," wrote J. R. Frakes, "threatens from page one, and when it finally roars . . . it comes almost as a relief. . . . Mrs. Johnson superintends this asylum with cool disdain and a remarkable neo-classic elegance of phrase, sentence, and chapter."

The Shadow Knows describes one week in the life of Mrs. N. Hexam, a woman who is "always walking along the edge of a knife" and whose unintentionally ironic voice—in the first person—dominates the novel. "Things haven't been going exactly well for me lately—not well at all, really—but we were safe, and we try to keep believing in love and harmony. But now I think we are going to be murdered. Just like that. It's not what you'd expect living quietly in North Sacramento." A. J. Solomon, calling this "a California Gothic novel," wrote of N. that she "is simultaneously liberated and enslaved, brave and cowardly, wise and foolish, attractive and repellent—in short, human." Roderick Nordell wrote, "As N. fantasizes herself into the detective-story world of an intimidating Famous Inspector, her efforts to explain her own and others' morally dubious behavior add a bit of consciousness raising to bizarre events. For N. is trying to be a whole person, but she is constantly being reacted to as a feminine stereotype. . . . Part of the suspense lies in whether this erring heroine will finally act according to her own best lights or to the self-image thrust upon her." N. herself says that "waiting to be murdered has given me you might say something to live for." Rosemary Dinnage praised the novel's "fast, free-wheeling accuracy of . . . style and moment-to-moment narrating, the absolutely confident representation, like fine bold draughtsmanship, of how feelings feel."

Lying Low, a psychologically complex account of four days in the lives of the four residents of a boarding house in northern California, was considered by Robert Towers to be "a nearly flawless performance, . . . a beautifully constructed, elegantly written book, delicate in its perceptions, powerful in its impact. . . . It is one of Diane Johnson's triumphs that she can capture and make interesting the sheer 'dailiness' of existence within a framework that could so easily lend itself to melodrama." P. S. Prescott wrote that she "nudges her story along entirely through her women's perceptions, jumping nimbly, restlessly among their thoughts, never lighting for long. She treats them lovingly, satirically, wittily all at once; it is a virtuoso performance, really a kind of balancing act that seems from the beginning impossible to sustain. But she does sustain it, using a prose tempo that is entirely her own and some amiable misanthropy: the men in this book are all useless, inadequate or deluded."

Johnson is well known and widely admired as a critic and essayist. Since the early 1970s she has written frequently for the *New York Times Book Review* and the *New York Review of Books*. The open-ended article format of the latter magazine seems especially congenial to her witty, discursive observations, and she is as comfortable handling trenchantly a single book as she is keeping a dozen in the air simultaneously.

Some of her best criticism was collected as *Terrorists and Novelists*, which Benjamin De-Mott called "jammed with good remarks." He praised in particular one of her most attractive qualities: the modest and unassuming brilliance of her perceptions. She "is nothing like a show-off. Her wit is unself-advertising, employed in the service of argument not dazzle: eagerness to wound, or to be cried up by fools as 'devastating,' or to adopt queenly social poses, nowhere disfigures her page. . . . The intelligence at work in the majority of the pieces is uncommonly flexible and sound-valued. . . . I was as often delighted as improved."

Her first extensive work of non-fiction was *The True History of the First Mrs. Meredith and Other Lesser Lives*, a biographical study (it was her doctoral thesis) of Mary Ellen Peacock Nicolls Meredith (1821–61), daughter of Thomas Love Peacock and first wife of George Meredith, a woman who "was argumentative and beautiful, and never let loose her hold on the imagination of the great novelist [Meredith]—even though she died early, and he had come to hate her, and rarely spoke of her after her death, and then told people she was mad." Very few indisputable facts about her subject's life have survived, and Johnson was accused by one critic of straying "across the border of biography into the province of fiction. . . . By a feat of biographical legerdemain 'artistic truth' has been substituted for literal." In general, however, the book was considered a tour de force. "She writes," remarked a critic in the *New Republic*, "with that kind of rare talent which combines research and romance without self-conscious pedantry." "*Lesser Lives*," according to another critic, "has the buoyant vitality of a book in which a writer has taken risks, and won." The book was nominated for the National Book Award in 1973.

In 1979 Johnson began work on a biography of the popular mystery writer Dashiell Hammett, whose life, she wrote, "apart from its particular qualities, was closely involved with the important things that have happened in this country in this century—the two World Wars, a tradition of violence, of political protest, the McCarthy era, detectives, Hollywood." Although she had the cooperation of Hammett's longtime ccompanion Lillian Hellman and access to Hammett's letters, the book, published in 1983, was judged disappointing by most reviewers. Partly this was the result of Johnson's deliberate effort to focus impersonally and objectively upon Hammett's life. Because she is herself a critic as well as a novelist, some readers expected more interpretation and analysis of Hammett's books. George Stade, for example, in the *New York Times Book Review*, wondered

" . . . what she thinks of them, although her few scattered interpretive remarks suggest that the novels have begun to fade a bit in her mind." Stade, however, admired her skills as a novelist, finding the biography "engrossing," and better "written and more shapely than its predecessors" (two other biographies of Hammett have been published in recent years). But Julian Symons, in his *Times Literary Supplement* review, suggested that the methods of the novelist which she used here did not serve Johnson well. He objected to passages in which Johnson attributes thoughts to Hammett and others who knew him. Though these are based on the letters, Symons found them "sentimental near-fiction." Lillian Hellman's choice of Johnson as Hammett's biographer makes her book the "authorized" biography, but, in Symons' judgment, it is not the definitive one.

Johnson has also worked in film and was coauthor with Stanley Kubrick of the screen adaptation of Stephen King's novel *The Shining* (1980). She was married to B. Lamar Johnson, Jr. in July 1953, and married her second husband, John Frederic Murray, a doctor, in November 1969. She has four children from her first marriage. She held a Guggenheim fellowship in 1977–78.

PRINCIPAL WORKS: *Novels*—Fair Game, 1965; Loving Hands at Home, 1968; Burning, 1970; The Shadow Knows, 1972; Lying Low, 1978. *Nonfiction*—The True History of the First Mrs. Meredith and Other Lesser Lives, 1972; Dashiel Hammett: A Life, 1983.

ABOUT: Contemporary Authors 41–44, 1979; Contemporary Literary Criticism 5, 1976. *Periodicals*—Best Sellers September 1, 1971; January 15, 1975; Book World September 5, 1971; December 22, 1974; November 26, 1978; Critique: Studies in Modern Fiction 16, no. 1, 1974; Nation June 14, 1975; November 11, 1978; New Statesman November 19, 1971; June 15, 1973; June 6, 1975; New York Review of Books November 2, 1972; February 20, 1975; November 23, 1978; New York Times Book Review September 5, 1971; December 31, 1972; December 22, 1974; November 19, 1978; July 15, 1979; October 31, 1982; October 16, 1983; New Yorker December 16, 1972; March 10, 1975; November 13, 1978; Newsweek October 25, 1971; December 23, 1974; October 16, 1978; Times Literary Supplement June 6, 1975; January 27, 1984; Working Women January 1983.

JOHNSON, LEMUEL (ADOLPHUS) (December 15, 1941–), Sierra Leonean poet and critic, was born in the city of Maiduguri in northeastern Nigeria, the son of Thomas Ishelu Johnson, an accountant for a British shipping firm, and Daisy Millicent Williams Johnson, a teacher; they were citizens of Sierra Leone,

LEMUEL JOHNSON

members of the Creole ethnic group (he calls them "Afro-Saxons"), descended from black freedmen who fought with the British in the American Revolution. He attended school in Freetown, Sierra Leone's capital—a "splendidly elitist British education," he has called it, which included much Latin and Chaucer. With his government's support, Johnson came to the United States in 1961 to train as an interpreter for the United Nations, but soon began his university education, taking a bachelor's degree from Oberlin College (1965), a master's from Pennsylvania State University (1966), and his doctorate from the University of Michigan (1969). He was a junior staff member of the Romance languages department at Michigan (1967–68), then of the English department (1968–70), before accepting a post at the University of Sierra Leone's Fourah Bay College in Freetown. In 1972, however, after only two years of teaching in his homeland, Johnson returned to a tenured post in Michigan's English department and has remained in Ann Arbor ever since.

Johnson's doctoral thesis, *The Negro as a Metaphor: A Study of Esthetic and Ethical Negativism in English, Spanish and French Literatures,* was quickly revised and published in 1971 as *The Devil, the Gargoyle, and the Buffoon: The Negro as Metaphor in Western Literature.* The theme of the study is the dehumanization of the black man throughout the West, his reduction into a moral and esthetic caricature of Western society itself. "In the attempt," the author writes in the preface, "to accommodate the suspicion that some element of human nature might lie

trapped in that blackness lie some of the most extraordinary scandals to which the human capacity to invent and to devise would be subjected. To the comic frightfulness of medieval inventions [about the nature of blackness] would be added the stimulating dynamism of renaissance curiosity and the ethnocentrism of pre- and post- nineteenth-century Darwinism. But in all this expanse of energy in English, Spanish and French literature there was much in deliberate sarcasm and enthusiastic inexactitude that was near surrealist in effect." The book surveys the rigid rejection of any notion of cultural relativism in all three literatures, then examines three chronicles by black poets of the interwar period: *The Weary Blues* (1926) by Langston Hughes, which he sees as a typical product of the Harlem Renaissance; *West Indies Ltd.* (1934) by the Afro-Cuban poet Nicolás Guillén; and *Cahier d'un retour au pays natal* (1939) by Aimé Césaire, which drew heavily on Haitian voodoo. These works "represent a coincidence of energies by which a race of erstwhile Africans, now inadequately Negroid and inadequately Caucasoid, sought to define itself in a world that was white and antithetical to human manifestations of blackness." The book is written in a bitter tone and its style is often extremely convoluted, but the author's passion is amply justified and his idea is original.

Johnson's poetry, in three volumes, constitutes a trilogy "spanning Sierra Leone Creole culture from the 1700s to the 1960s." *Highlife for Caliban* refers, in its title, to the Third World's standard interpretation of *The Tempest* as the primal myth of colonialism: Caliban's island is invaded, he is enslaved and forced to learn his oppressors' ways and language. The collection combines elements of African, European, and American culture; the poems thus display exotic imagery and evocative allusions in powerful language, often so intense the images grow surreal:

. . . black men
under stress
have
been shot, in proportion,
by three policemen
under stress some
in yarmoulkas some & others
in pork pie hats
others in soft hats
others constructing
hats under stress.

"The poetry burns and lives," wrote John Povey in an enthusiastic review, "with a grand antagonistic insolence. . . . But Lemuel Johnson as a poet becomes our witness, too, not only of a broken tragic environment but of a world where there is an infinite beauty: 'The river is full/ crested cranes fly banking against the moon.'

The eternal harmonies persist if only the poet's sardonic eye can encompass the 'rot at the Center.'"

Hand on the Navel consists, most importantly, of the title sequence of forty-six numbered poems, whose epigraph reads: "The Book of Corporal Bundu, Royal West Africa Frontier Force, who came back insane, and all those others who apprenticed our youth to an enchantment of sorcery and madness; and teased magic out of the fire of strange women singing of blue birds over the white cliffs of Dover. This then is a recording of memories and half-memories, of songs and half-songs,—and of half-lives." The persona is thus mad, and many of the poems are filled with hallucinatory images of futile bloodshed and racial incomprehension, as number XXIV:

we came across the face then
of a white man dead and,

his death too flippant,
we pried open his mouth

for with his tongue
we would coin a high joy

oh, to be pusillanimous in lust
by a high window

(a meticulous gentleman
in the small appetites of flies)

the hair a stark provocation
on the stinking rot of a bone!

the earth is a trenchant must
a banked bed of a skeletal sort

we came across the face
of a white man dead

beguiling a rainy season
by the arabian sea.

Elsewhere in the collection are poems showing a strong interest in classical myth, and in these the original mythic force is often left intact, as in "A Celebration in Istanbul," with its memorable epigraph, "No man alive today can know which side's dead men will win the war."

One reviewer commented on Johnson's "lyrical, often parodying style in which his vitality for the mystery of human life is mixed with his lament for human folly. The surface of his poems treats madness in a casual manner, but pervading and reverberating from the poems are cries of anguish and profound bitterness."

A Carnival of the Old Coast completes Johnson's poetic trilogy. Many of the poems here offer reconstructions of history, such as the beginning of the European slave trade in West Africa in 1498 and the founding of Freetown in 1792. The poet's own historical consciousness seems to have deepened, and he shows an increasing sensitivity to his own equivocal position as a West African with a rich heritage who has become part of mainstream, largely white, American culture. He has called this condition one of "ecstatic schizophrenia."

In August 1965, Johnson married Marian Yankson, a dental hygienist, who is also of Sierra Leonean Creole descent. They have a daughter and a son and live in Ann Arbor.

WORKS: *Poetry*—Highlife for Caliban, 1973; Hand on the Navel, 1978; A Carnival of the Old Coast, 1984. *Criticism*—The Devil, the Gargoyle, and the Buffoon: The Negro as Metaphor in Western Literature, 1971.

ABOUT: Who's Who Among Black Americans, 1977–78; Contemporary Authors 53–56, 1975. *Periodicals*—African Arts Spring 1974; American Book Review December 1978–January 1979; Choice September 1972; June 1974; December 1978; Journal of Modern Literature annual review 1974; Library Journal May 1, 1974; September 1, 1978.

JOHNSTON, JENNIFER (PRUDENCE)

(January 12, 1930–   ), Irish novelist and short story writer, was born in Dublin, the daughter of Denis Johnston, an eminent Irish playwright, and Shelagh Richards, a noted actress. She was educated at Trinity College, Dublin, is married with four children, and lives in Derry, Northern Ireland. Since 1972 she has published six novels, as well as some uncollected short fiction, and her work has been adapted for British television and radio. Her novels are arguably the most important body of work by an Irish woman writer of the last twenty years. Written with exemplary tact, they produce impressive emotional and cultural resonances within deceptively simple frameworks.

Four of her novels deal with the twilight of Anglo-Irish society. Set in various periods before and after the establishment of the modern Irish state, these novels review the cultural and physical decline of a once-powerful class. This theme has been an important and persistent one in Irish fiction, and has created a sub-genre unique to Irish fiction, the "Big House" novel. (Among the sub-genre's principal exponents are its founders Somerville and Ross, Elizabeth Bowen and William Trevor.) Jennifer Johnston's contribution to it is among the most resourceful and comprehensive to date. She is not, however, a cultural historian before she is a novelist, and it is the human drama being played out in the foreground that gives her work its character.

The importance of the theme of Anglo-Irish decline in Johnston's work may be seen in her

JENNIFER JOHNSTON

first novel, *The Captains and the Kings*. This simple, poignant story presents an unlikely relationship between the ailing, isolated scion of the Big House, Charles Prendergast, and Diarmid Toorish, a teenager from the local village. The relationship develops erratically, finally asserting itself when the youngster runs away from home rather than be sent to Dublin to learn shopkeeping. Mr. Prendergast, very much against his better judgment and despite his carefully cultivated antisocial demeanor, harbors the boy. His generosity gives rise to unfounded scandalous rumors, and Diarmid is reclaimed by his vulgar, pietistic family. Mr. Prendergast dies. The relationship was worthwhile but destructive. Class barriers were removed only to show the vulnerability of those who removed them. The Big House temporarily became an enabling agency, rather than the haunt of disabling memories. A chance for Diarmid (and a second chance for Mr. Prendergast) to live a little more abundantly came about spontaneously, only to be revoked by prejudice and malice. The relationship's unlikeliness gives it a precarious quality, and Johnston's convincing portrayal makes *The Captains and the Kings* a model on which her subsequent work is based.

In *The Gates,* written before *The Captains and the Kings,* an Anglo-Irish setting is again used to locate the author's interest in loyalty, continuity, and resilience. Minnie McMahon comes home from England to live with her decaying uncle in his decaying manor-house. Hoping to restore her family's fortune, she and her local boyfriend, Kevin, decide to sell the demesne gates. But Kevin absconds to England

with the proceeds of the sale, leaving Minnie and her uncle high and dry.

How Many Miles to Babylon?, published in the following year, is Jennifer Johnston's most ambitious novel. Set in the years 1914–15, it tells the story of an ill-fated friendship between two young Irishmen, the Anglo Alexander Moore and the native Jerry Crowe. The latter works for a time on the Moore farm, and his friendship with Alexander arises out of a shared passion for horses. This phase of the friendship is ended by Alexander's domineering mother. The second phase opens with the start of World War I, and the decision of both men to enlist. Alexander joins the army at his mother's command, which overcomes his own and his father's antipathy. Jerry joins for economic reasons, but also to gain experience of firearms to further his militant republicanism. The war is portrayed as squalid, dull, and cruel. Even at the front, circumstances and social distinctions combine to force Jerry and Alexander apart, until finally Alexander is ordered to command the firing squad detailed to shoot Jerry for desertion. Instead, Alexander shoots him on his own initiative, thereby assuring his own execution. The plot of this third novel is richer and more dramatic than those of Johnston's earlier books, and the note of doom that attends Alexander's and Jerry's friendship is sounded more sonorously than it was during her previous studies of friendships formed across social barriers. Although the range of *How Many Miles to Babylon?* is wider than that of its predecessors, the author still maintains her laconic, unobtrusive style and her uninsistent, economical narrative method.

With *Shadows on Our Skin* Jennifer Johnston forsook the terrain of her first three novels to deal with contemporary subject matter. The setting is depressed modern Derry. The author makes the transition to an urban setting and topical concerns with ease, perhaps because the novel's main plot line deals with another unlikely friendship, the relationship between a young southern Protestant schoolteacher, Kathleen Doherty (a name deliberately chosen, it seems, for its Catholic, native ring) and Joe Logan, a child of the Derry slums. Joe's dismal milieu, which includes his stunted parents and a brother in the Provisional I.R.A., is deftly depicted. His friendship with Kathleen, who is engaged to a British soldier serving in Germany, is blighted by the division between Irish society, and he is left without prospects.

In her fifth novel, *The Old Jest,* Jennifer Johnston goes back sixty years to the period when the modern Irish state was in its violent birth-throes, and once again places an unlikely relationship at the center of her narrative. Nancy Gulliver befriends a character whose real identity is revealed only towards the end of the novel and whom she calls Cass. Cass is on the run from the British army, and their friendship is temporary. Yet, given its brief time span (the novel is confined to August 1920) and its fugitive character, the relationship does produce an emotional bond, as we find when it is ended by Cass' coldblooded execution by the British army. Even if Nancy doesn't realize it yet, Cass' life and death mean that things will never be the same for her again, and underlining the change in Anglo-Irish fortunes is the fact that Cass is really a *declassé* landlord and ex-army officer.

In 1981 Jennifer Johnston's *The Christmas Tree*, marked a departure from her previous work, being less concerned with history than either of the two novels which immediately preceded it. Indirectly, however, it presents an enlargement of the author's frame of historical reference. Constance Keating's unlikely friend is Jacob Weinberg, a Polish Jewish writer and concentration-camp survivor. The heart of the novel deals with their affair, in itself an unusual circumstance in the unfashionably chaste world of Jennifer Johnston's fiction. The affair culminates in the birth of a child. No sooner does she give birth, however, than Constance learns that she has leukemia. She returns to her native Dublin to face her death, as though suddenly she now has a definite ambition—to die well. Her poignant fortitude is all the more affecting when we learn during the course of the novel that Constance hasn't managed to make much of her life. She has not been able to acquire the social graces typical of her class. She fails to graduate from Trinity College, Dublin, choosing instead to go to London to become a writer. But her writing doesn't prosper. Her one success is the affair with Weinberg, but even that is prevented from flourishing due to mortality's callous whim. Yet, it is important to Constance that her dying wish—to see Weinberg—be granted, just as it is important to her that a Christmas tree be trimmed, as usual. Ironically, Weinberg arrives for her Christmas Day death. Although *The Christmas Tree* is a good example of the author's deployment of limited resources, it is not one of her more impressive works.

Though of Anglo-Irish background, Constance rejects the mores of her class, leaving herself with only her innate humanity to keep her going—which it does, right to the end. Thus she is related to the other isolated, proud, tenacious members of Jennifer Johnston's fictional family. There is a gauntness about all these characters that is accentuated by the novels' laconic dialogue, slow narrative pace, and skeletal plots.

Within the various family homes of Jennifer Johnston's fiction the emotional atmosphere is decidedly chilly. Usually, it takes some unlikely person from outside the protagonists' class to enrich or reactivate their sense of life.

In Johnston's novels, hopeful friendships are usually extinguished, a conclusion which does not bode well for the possibility of cultural unity and rehabilitation that contemporary Ireland so plainly needs. Her work illustrates this need by placing it in the context of an uncontroversial, broadly based humanism. Numerous references to, and quotations from, Yeats reinforce this aspect of her writing. Her sympathetic portrayals of loneliness, old age, and adolescence have earned her work the respect of reviewers, as have her command of atmosphere and her uncluttered style. Anthony Burgess' encomium may stand for many: "This is a unique and perfect art, born of a time and place and temperament, not contrived against their grain. It represents no movement, and one can learn nothing from it except the ancient virtues of human concern and verbal economy."

PRINCIPAL WORKS: The Captains and the Kings, 1972; The Gates, 1973; How Many Miles to Babylon?, 1974; Shadows on Our Skin, 1977; The Old Jest, 1979; The Christmas Tree, 1981; The Railway Station Man, 1984.

ABOUT: *Periodicals*—Eire/Ireland 10, no. 3, 1975; New Statesman April 15, 1977; October 26, 1979; New Yorker May 12, 1980; New York Times Book Review March 26, 1978; March 16, 1980; Times Literary Supplement April 15, 1977; November 23, 1979; September 18, 1981.

JONES, MERVYN (February 27, 1922–), English novelist and journalist, writes: "I was born in London, twenty minutes' walk from where I live now. My father was Ernest Jones, the psychoanalyst, and my mother was a Viennese lady of varied gifts. I was sent to a (not very) progressive boarding school, where I did well in the subjects that appealed to me and failed abysmally in those that did not. In 1939 I went to the United States, as I supposed, for a short holiday. While I was in the 'World of Tomorrow' pavilion at the World's Fair, the war began, and for this reason I became a student at New York University instead of at Oxford, as intended. In addition to saving me from Oxford, NYU provided me with some enduring friendships and a valuable course on the modern novel given by Edwin Berry Burgum. I returned to England in 1941 and spent four and a half years in the Army, a period of enforced and prolonged boyhood; the last year was in India, a country that still holds

MERVYN JONES

endless fascination for me. I had never wanted anything but to be a writer, and I wrote my first novel by being the only British officer in India who did not sleep in the afternoon.

"A confused identity is an advantage for a writer. My European and American friends consider me to be English, and laugh when informed that I have not a drop of English blood. I can make a patrilineal claim to be Welsh, but my father had left Wales as a young man. I can also make a matrilineal claim to be Jewish, but my mother's family were the sort of Viennese people who had to be reminded of their Jewishness by Hitler. My most positive identification is that I am a Londoner; all my novels are set at least partly, and several of them entirely, in London. Although I am an insatiable traveler, and throb with excitement to find myself in Skoplje or Aligarh, I shout with joy when the sight of a tall red bus assures me that I am back in my native city.

"When I am asked why I became a writer, I often reply that it was because I couldn't do anything else. This answer, while it averts explanations that are either impossible or unnecessary, is truthful enough, since I am baffled (though intermittently fascinated) by the sciences, clumsy with my hands, and incapable of painting a picture or composing a tune if my life depended on it. Since my wife [Jeanne Urquhart] can do all the things that I can't, and believes that she could not be a writer, I need scarcely say that I am happily married. The English language is for me what liquor is for an alcoholic, and on any bright morning I would rather write something, be it an ephemeral article or a letter to a friend,

than nothing. I have given a great deal of my time to journalism, out of necessity—there have been only three years in my life when, through lucky chances, my novels have produced an adequate income—but on the whole with pleasure. I enjoy asking questions, meeting people such as reindeer herders or deep-sea divers, and acquiring scraps of diverse information; and, being a convinced Socialist and a man of strong opinions, I engage with zest in polemical journalism. I am glad to have worked for weekly journals that were congenial to me (four years on *Tribune,* two years on the *New Statesman*) and I left only because I am a natural free-lance and averse to sitting in offices. Still, facility in journalism is by slow degrees injurious to good writing, and if I had a son who wanted to be a writer I should advise him to earn his basic living as a carpenter.

"Graham Greene has said truly that all novels are failures, meaning that every novel is an attempt to grasp an ideal that hovers out of reach, and I regard my own novels with varying degrees of dissatisfaction. Some are as good as I could make them within the limitations of my talent, which is the most that any writer ought to claim, while others are worse than that. But a young writer should begin in the belief that he has the powers of Dostoyevsky, and this is not vanity, for it remains to be proved that he has not. As a writer like me grows older, he recognizes (unless given to wild self-delusion) that he is very far from being the equal of Dostoyevsky, and yet he must set this knowledge aside when in the act of writing, and imagine his novel as a work of genius. One thing is certain: anyone who reconciles himself in advance to writing a second-rate book will find that he has written a tenth-rate book.

"Since one book cannot be built upon another and experience confers no benefits on a writer— probably this is the essential difference between the arts and the sciences—I am beginning my latest novel at the age of sixty with the same anxious groping as my first. My compassion goes out to friends of my age in other professions who are contemplating the vacancies of retirement. It is struggle, at the necessary cost of failure, that preserves the sensations of youth."

———

Mervyn Jones is a novelist who over the past thirty years has steadily produced a number of books notable for their topicality and diversity of observation. Though modest about his literary achievements, he is a serious writer much concerned in his work with what he calls "the nobility and irony of idealism." His political convictions are firm but not dogmatic: "One doesn't write a novel to preach one's beliefs," he told Hugh Hebert in the *Guardian* in 1979, "but those beliefs are implicit in anything that has significance in literature." From his long experience in journalism and documentary writing, Jones has developed a narrative style that is simple (in the opinion of some critics "old-fashioned") and sensitive to the spirit of contemporary society. "If some of his work has the ephemerality of good journalism," Ian Scott-Kilvert writes, "he has never ceased to develop and he has always had something to say."

Jones' most ambitious novel is *Joseph*, a fictionalized biography of Joseph Stalin. Drawing from both research and Isaac Deutscher's masterly biography, Jones offers a sober and even-handed portrait. "By no means a work of idolatry," one critic observed, but "psychologically convincing." Unlike Hitler who, Jones told Hebert, was a totally evil force and therefore offers no historical problem, Stalin remains a mystery—"especially to someone like me who's been on the Left all my life. And the problem is, what the hell Stalin thought he was doing murdering all those people." More typical of Jones' work are his novels of working-class life *Holding On* and *Today the Struggle*, chronicles of English families trying to reconcile their left-wing idealism with the politics of trade unionism, the violence of Mosleyite fascism and the Spanish Civil War in the 1930s, the devastation of World War II, and the post-war challenges of the anti-nuclear movement and political terrorism in England and in Israel.

Like a latter-day Anthony Trollope, Jones' primary subject is "the way we live now." His best known novel is the apolitical *John and Mary*, filmed in 1969 with Dustin Hoffman and Mia Farrow, in which Jones describes a modern love affair with an almost clinical precision. Ian Scott-Kilvert asserts that "the most accomplished" of his books is *A Survivor*, a portrait of an ex-RAF officer turned novelist who finds success in his writing but remains a lonely man, unfulfilled in his quest for love. "How difficult it is to live," Jones has observed, is the subject of all his fiction. "If writing has a purpose, it is that some readers may find life a little easier or at least may understand the difficulties."

PRINCIPAL WORKS: *Fiction*—No Time to Be Young, 1952; The New Town, 1953; The Last Barricade, 1953; Helen Blake, 1955; On the Last Day, 1958; A Set of Wives, 1965; John and Mary, 1966; A Survivor, 1968; Joseph, 1970; Mr. Armitage Isn't Back Yet, 1971; Holding On, 1973 (U.S., Twilight of Our Day); The Revolving Door, 1973; Strangers, 1974; Lord Richard's Passion, 1974; The Pursuit of Happiness, 1975; Scenes from Bourgeois Life (short stories), 1976; Nobody's Fault, 1977; Today the Struggle, 1978; The Beautiful Words, 1979; Two Women and Their Man, 1982. *Non-fiction*—(with M. Foot) Guilty Men, 1957; Big Two: Life in America and Russia, 1962 (U.S., The Antagonists); Two Ears of Corn: Oxfam in Action, 1965 (U.S., In Famine's Shadow, 1967); (ed.) Kingsley Martin: Portrait and Self-Portrait, 1969; (tr.) Karol, K.S. The Second Chinese Revolution, 1974.

ABOUT: Contemporary Authors, new revision series 1, 1981; Vinson, J. (ed.) Contemporary Novelists, 1976; Who's Who, 1983–84. *Periodicals*—Guardian (London) July 9, 1979.

JORDAN, JUNE (MEYER) (July 9, 1936–), black American poet, novelist, essayist, writer of children's books, and editor, was born in Harlem, where she lived for two or three years until her parents, who were very devout people of Jamaican origin, moved to the Bedford-Stuyvesant section of Brooklyn. Here she grew up, fighting back when subjected to bullying and beatings by her father, Granville Ivanhoe Jordan, a postal clerk. Her mother, the former Mildred Maude Fisher, frequently worked as a private-duty nurse at night and many years later committed suicide.

June Jordan developed a love for words during her early childhood, and at the age of seven began writing poetry. After spending one year as the only black student at Midwood High School in Brooklyn, she attended (1950–53) the Northfield School for Girls, a private school in Massachusetts where her father hoped to prepare her for training as a doctor. Returning to Brooklyn, she commuted daily to Barnard College from 1953 to 1955 and during her sophomore year met Michael Meyer, a white senior at Columbia College whom she married in 1955. During the next academic year, she attended the University of Chicago and then, coming back to New York in 1956, studied for another year at Barnard but dropped out to devote herself to the writing of poetry.

By 1960, as she recounts in "One Way of Beginning This Book," an autobiographical piece prefacing the essays in her prose collection, *Civil Wars*, she and her husband were living in Queens and she was principally occupied with the care of their two-year-old son, Christopher David. She also continued with her poetry, made weekly trips to the Donnell Library in Manhattan, where she studied architectural books and journals and became acquainted with the writings of Buckminster Fuller, and after a while began to work as a free-lance journalist, forming friendships with black writers and political leaders in Harlem.

JUNE JORDAN

From 1963 to 1964 she served as assistant to Frederick Wiseman, who was producing *The Cool World,* a film that used actual teenagers from the streets of Harlem to portray characters in the novel by Warren Miller on which it was based. As a result of interviews with cast and crew members, June Jordan wrote a documentary entitled *Testimony,* which in turn secured her two assignments for the New York *Herald Tribune,* although the newspaper refused to print her article predicting the Harlem riots of 1964. During that summer, her husband, who was completing his graduate work in anthropology at the University of Chicago, wrote to inform her that he would not return, and the two were divorced in 1966. Also during the summer of 1964, she collaborated with Buckminster Fuller on an article, published in the April 1965 issue of *Esquire,* presenting a plan for the architectural redesigning of Harlem—a plan the editors of the magazine considered unrealistically utopian.

After working from 1965 to 1966 as a research associate and writer in the Technical Housing Department of Mobilization for Youth, in New York City, June Jordan joined the program of Teachers and Writers Collaborative in 1967 at the invitation of the educator Herbert Kohl. Together with Terri Bush, a white junior-high-school teacher, she started a Saturday morning creative-writing workshop for black and Puerto Rican children and teenagers. Beginning in East Harlem under the sponsorship of Teachers and Writers, the workshop moved in 1968 to the Fort Greene section of Brooklyn, where Terri Bush taught, and was eventually continued as an inde-

pendent program. Under the editorship of June Jordan and Terri Bush, a book of poems and short prose pieces by twenty-six of the young writers was published as *The Voice of the Children* in 1970. In that same year, June Jordan also edited *Soulscript: Afro-American Poetry,* an anthology presenting work by contributors to *The Voice of the Children* and by well-known black poets. Both collections were very favorably reviewed in major periodicals, and *The Voice of the Children* received the Nancy Bloch Memorial Award, while *Soulscript* was designated a Notable Book by the American Library Association.

Once again at the request of Herbert Kohl, June Jordan accepted a job in 1967 as a teacher of English at City College of New York, where she also directed the SEEK program (for disadvantaged students) from 1968 to 1969. This marked the beginning of a career in higher education that would include teaching positions at Connecticut College, Sarah Lawrence College (1969–1970, 1971–1974), Yale University (1974–1975), City College of New York again (1975–1976), and the State University of New York at Stony Brook, where she has taught since 1978 and is now professor of English.

During the later 1960s, she also began to read her own poetry at various schools and colleges throughout the United States. The Academy of American Poets sponsored her readings at the Guggenheim Museum and in the public schools of New York City and Minneapolis. Upon the death of Langston Hughes, the Academy recommended June Jordan to undertake a project he had begun in conjunction with Milton Meltzer. The result, published as a juvenile book in 1969, was *Who Look at Me,* a long poem based on twenty-seven paintings of black Americans by such artists as Charles Alston, Colleen Browning, Thomas Eakins, Winslow Homer, Eastman Johnson, Hughie Lee-Smith, Alice Neel, Ben Shahn, Symeon Shimin, John Wilson, and Andrew Wyeth. The poem's central theme of recognition is repeated in the closing lines: "Who see the roof and corners of my pride/ to be (as you are) free?/ WHO LOOK AT ME?" Zena Sutherland, praising the book in the *Saturday Review,* commented on the "passionate, bittersweet" quality of its language; and James A. Emanuel, in the *New York Times Book Review,* described the text as "an original, understated but intense poem" with many memorable lines.

June Jordan's novel *His Own Where* was written, as she states in *Civil Wars,* "as a means of familiarizing kids with activist principles of urban redesign or, in other words, activist habits of response to environment. I thought to present these ideas within the guise of a Black love story, written entirely in Black English—in these ways I might hope to interest teenagers in reading it." Reviewers in several periodicals praised the author for her depiction of the sixteen-year-old hero, Buddy Rivers, and for her artistic and effective use of language. In addition, *His Own Where* was nominated for the National Book Award, selected by the *New York Times* as one of the year's outstanding young adult novels, and named a Young Adult Notable Book by the American Library Association. Nevertheless, it was banned from public school libraries in Baltimore through the efforts of black parents apprehensive that it would undermine their children's motivation to master standard English. In response, June Jordan published several articles on this subject, arguing that Afro-Americans need to know both black and standard English culture.

Who Look at Me and *His Own Where* brought their author recognition as an exceptionally gifted writer of books for young people. She also received a Rockefeller Foundation Fellowship in Creative Writing for 1969–1970 and the Prix de Rome in Environmental Design, for which she was nominated by Buckminster Fuller, for 1970–1971. During her time at the American Academy in Rome, she planned to prepare a scenario for a film version of *His Own Where* and "to study alternative urban designs for the promotion of flexible, and pacific, communal street life," as she explains in *Civil Wars*. However, she returned to New York in mid-year to compile a manual on land reform in Mississippi, where she had traveled in 1969 gathering material for a *New York Times Magazine* article that appeared in 1970. When this manual was rejected for publication, she rewrote it as the still-unpublished novel, "Okay Now."

As a writer of children's books, she presented her "manifesto" in an article published in the October 1973 *Wilson Library Bulletin* under the title, "Young People: Victims of Realism in Books and in Life": "I will not write anything unless I can learn how to craft it into *usable*, good news, or *usable* information to interdict and humanely supersede the reality of some particular bad news." This has been the philosophy governing her other juvenile books: *Fannie Lou Hamer*, the biography of a woman from Mississippi who was active in black voter registration and established a cooperative farm; *Dry Victories*, a dialogue between two black boys who show the unfortunate parallels between the Reconstruction period and the Civil Rights era; and *New Life: New Room* and *Kimako's Story*, fiction books that offer creative approaches to environmental limitations.

As a poet addressing an adult audience, June Jordan has contended with the difficulties resulting from what she called "the universality of language" in a 1969 *Partisan Review* article. "The task," she wrote, "is to convert the most common, communizing tool of society into a distinctive, distinguishing vernacular and rhythm." In "Thinking About My Poetry," a 1977 essay reprinted in *Civil Wars*, she traces both her development as a poet and the literary influences on her work. Motivated by a childhood ambition to be "a great poet," she initially transcribed poems dictated by an inner voice and also devised exercises in technique for herself. Gradually moving beyond personal subject matter to cultivate a "collective voice" during the late 1960s, she shifted in the 1970s to a conception of herself as "one Black woman poet" striving "to be accurate about myself, and to force my mind into a constantly expanding apprehension of my political and moral situation." Whereas Shelley and Coleridge have remained lasting influences for June Jordan, she felt no affinity with the poets "pushed upon" her by her father during her childhood—the Biblical poets, Shakespeare, Edgar Allan Poe, and Paul Laurence Dunbar. In her early and middle twenties, she read the work of black poets, especially Margaret Walker, Robert Hayden, and Langston Hughes, adding to these the poetry of such women as Emily Dickinson, Jane Cooper, Adrienne Rich, Audre Lorde, Marge Piercy, Alice Walker, and Honor Moore during her late twenties and thirties. By the later 1970s, she had developed a "catholicity of interest" that included "white male poets" like Ted Hughes, Charles Simic, David Ignatow, and Charles Bukowski, and in her preface to *Passion* she claims kinship with Walt Whitman.

When *Some Changes,* June Jordan's first book of adult poems, appeared in 1971, Chad Walsh, in *Book World,* referred to her as "a prolific and uneven" but "powerful" poet. Jascha Kessler, writing in *Poetry,* commented on the "fine irony that manages to control her bitterness" and pointed out "the singer's sense of the dramatic" that enables her to "create her world" and "people it for us." *New Days: Poems of Exile and Return,* her second collection, contained a number of pieces deriving from her experiences in Rome, including the long "Roman Poem Number Five," which presents the speaker's reactions to the ruins of Pompeii. Honor Moore, reviewing the book for *Ms.,* observed, as Kessler also had done, that "she never sacrifices poetry for politics. In fact, her craft, the patterning of sound, rhythm, and image, make her art inseparable from political statement, form inseparable from content." *Things That I Do in the Dark* included "Who Look at Me" and poems from *Some*

Changes, New Days, and various periodicals. Hayden Carruth, in the *New York Times Book Review,* endorsed the "antiracist libertarian feminism" of nearly all the political poems, was "pleased by many, and deeply moved by some, of the love poems," and "impressed and enlightened by a few, but baffled by most, of the experimental poems." Reproducing "Sunflower Sonnet Number Two" in full, Carruth admired the poet's blending of "black idiom, her own voice and literary English." Saundra Towns, in the third edition of *Contemporary Poets,* found June Jordan's love poems to have "an underlying pessimism." This quality is evident in the final lines of the free-verse dramatic monologue, "From *The Talking Back of Miss Valentine Jones:* Poem #One":

what I wanted was
to braid my hair
bathe and bedeck my
self so fully be-
cause what I wanted was
your love
not pity
be-
cause what I wanted was
your love
your love.

With the publication of *Things That I Do in the Dark,* June Jordan was regarded by the *Virginia Quarterly Review* as belonging "in the front ranks" of women poets with Muriel Rukeyser, Adrienne Rich, Alice Walker, and Diane Wakoski.

Jordan's later volumes were seen by some reviewers primarily as a reflection of the influence of the black oral tradition. In its subject matter, which includes both personal relationships and such public concerns as feminism, racism, and police brutality, *Passion* resembles *Civil Wars.* Reviewing both volumes favorably in the *New York Times Book Review,* Darryl Pinckney characterized the chronologically-arranged essays, letters, journal entries, and lectures in *Civil Wars* as "a kind of autobiography of thought and feeling, the story of one individual's activism and search for community." Susan McHenry, in the *Nation,* observed that the book's "real subject . . . is power"; and Patricia Jones, in the *Village Voice,* emphasized its "faith in the necessity of change" and its concern with "the issue of self-determination," concluding that it shows "a fine mind at work."

Two productions of June Jordan's works have been presented at New York's Public Theatre, both of them directed by Ntozake Shange. In May 1979 Bernice Reagon and June Jordan collaborated in a performance of the latter's poetry called *In the Spirit of Sojourner Truth.* In April 1981 the New York Shakespeare Festival gave a staged reading of her first play, *The Issue,* which she described in *Civil Wars* as a drama "about freedom, police violence, and Black life."

June Jordan makes her home in Brooklyn and has been described in *Publishers Weekly* interviews as "a dynamic, outspoken personality" (1972) and as "the picture of composure," with "a manner slightly reserved" (1981). In recent years she has given poetry readings throughout the country, received several grants for creative writing, and served on the boards of various writers' organizations.

PRINCIPAL WORKS: *Poetry*—Some Changes, 1971; New Days: Poems of Exile and Return, 1974; Things That I Do in the Dark: Selected Poetry, 1977; Passion: New Poems, 1977–1980. 1980. *Essays*—Civil Wars, 1981. *For Children and Young Adults*—Who Look at Me, 1969; His Own Where, 1971; Dry Victories, 1972; Fannie Lou Hamer, 1972; New Life: New Room, 1975; Kimako's Story, 1981. *As editor*—Soulscript: Afro-American Poetry, 1970; (with Terri Bush) The Voice of the Children, 1970.

ABOUT: Contemporary Authors, first revision series 33–36, 1978; Contemporary Literary Criticism 5, 1976; 11, 1979; 23, 1983; Dallman, E. et al. (eds.) Woman Poet—The East, 1982; Rush, T. G., Myers, C. F., and Arata, E. S. Black American Writers Past and Present: A Biographical and Bibliographical Dictionary, 1975; Something About the Author 4, 1973; Vinson, J. (ed.) Contemporary Poets, 1980. *Periodicals*—Essence April 1981; Kalliope Fall 1981; New York Times Book Review November 16, 1969; November 7, 1971; October 9, 1977; August 9, 1981; May 8, 1983; Publishers Weekly February 21, 1972; May 1, 1981.

*KANE, CHEIKH (H)AMIDOU (April 2, 1928–), Senegalese novelist, was born in Matam, in eastern Senegal, near the Fouta River. His family called him Samba, a name usually given to the second son. His birthplace was in an entirely Moslem region, where the Koran was memorized by young Africans at a very early age. The Koran being "the word of God," its passages must be known literally without any omission or change, because Moslems believe that it is the true means of communication with God. A perfect communication is both an act of faith and allegiance. For Kane, Islam is "the religion of the heart." Until he was ten, he attended a Koranic school, where he studied the Koran and spoke only Pular, the language of six million African Peuls. At ten, he went to a French school, and after three years passed the C.E.P. examination (primary school diploma). He then attended secondary school in Dakar where he received a B.A. in 1948. Those years represented a transitional period during which he started to discover

°kan, shok am ē dōō

CHEIKH (H)AMIDOU KANE

the striking differences between African and Western cultures. In 1952, he went to Paris, where he obtained a license in law and philosophy and in 1959 a degree in management at the Ecole Nationale de la France d'Outre-Mer (National School of France Overseas). When he returned to Senegal, he was, successively: director of the Cabinet within the ministry of Industrial Development and Planning (1958–60), governor of the district of Thies (1960–61), and High Commissioner of Planning (1961–63). In 1961, he had published his famous narrative *L'Aventure Ambiguë (The Ambiguous Adventure)*, which, in 1962, won the Grand Prix Littéraire d'Afrique Noire d'Expression Française (Grand Prix for French-speaking Black Africa). Kane worked for UNICEF at Lagos, Nigeria (1963–67) and at Abidjan, Ivory Coast (1967–74). He was president of the Research Center for International Development, Ottawa, Canada (1974–76), and the chairman of Dakar Marine, in Senegal (October 1976–March 1978). In January 1981, he was appointed Senegal's minister for Industrial Development and Manual Trade, and has been minister of Planning and Cooperation since April 1983.

Despite the importance of his functions in Africa, abroad Kane is better known as a writer. Another paradox is that he is also considered to be a great novelist, although he has published only one book, *Ambiguous Adventure*. Kane's reputation reflects the exceptional importance of the book, the period it covers, and its time of publication. It was written during the 1950s, while Kane was studying in France, and Senegal was still a French colony. Many African writers

had successfully described, in poems, novels, dramas, and comedies, some of them autobiographical, the conquest of Africa by the Western powers and its subsequent partial and cultural subjugation. However, the confrontation between those two worlds was hardly ever expressed in terms of philosophical differences. In Senegal, this difference resulted, specifically, in a collision between the Western vision, which "conquered without being in the right," but brought the indispensable technological knowledge necessary to check the external world, and a Moslem Senegal, afraid of losing its God, its deep sense of the family as a unit, and its very soul.

This confrontation had two main stages: the first was physical and spiritual resistance against the conquerors; the second stage was a tortuous attempt to accept an alienating knowledge, without losing the faith. This synthesis process results in traumatic experiences for the Africans, who are fearful of being separated from themselves. Samba Diallo, the anti-hero of *Ambiguous Adventure,* expresses his dilemma this way: "I am not a distinct country of the Diallobé facing a distinct Occident . . . I have become the two. . . . There is a strange nature, in distress over not being the two." The statement is true not only of the Africans. In 1897 W. E. B. DuBois had clearly stated the ambiguity of the Afro-American: "One ever feels his twoness—An American, a Negro: two souls, two thoughts; two unreconciled strivings; two warring ideals in one dark body. . . . The history of the American Negro is the history of this strife, this longing to attain self-conscious manhood, to merge this double self into a better and truer." Later, DuBois went to Ghana, where he died, a Ghanaian citizen.

Ambiguous Adventure analytically questions the possibility of a philosophical synthesis of the two worlds of Senegal and the West. It is structured to reflect a thesis, antithesis, and synthesis. The first part has nine chapters. In the first six, Samba Diallo, who was chosen as heir by Thierno, the spiritual leader of the Diallobé, is completely immersed in the African world. The philosophical confrontation is nailed down to a simple and concrete reality: should the Senegalese send their children to the French school? The African world is not monolithic. While the Senegalese leaders are undecisive and worried, in their minds the masses have already opted for the new school. The Chief of the Diallobée, Samba's older cousin, is still undecided, as is the Knight, Samba's father. But the Great Royal Lady, the Chief's sister and real power, has made up her mind. The new generation must acquire the technology which paves the way to the future. In the last three chapters in this part, Samba is taken away from the Master's hearth and put in the French school. There he feels caught in a depersonalization cycle, although he perceives the convergence of Senegalese and Western philosophers.

In the first six chapters of the second part, Samba is immersed in France, that is, the antithetical world, which also is not monolithic. Chapters seven, eight, and nine see the return of Samba to Africa. Will he be able to make the synthesis, after his immersion in those two worlds? Demba, his rival, who had replaced him a long time ago, has succeeded Thierno, who is dead. Samba has lost his African faith and has not been able to replace it with any Western values. He is killed by the fanatical Fool, who considers him a traitor. Thus, his physical death follows his philosophical one. The solution offered in the final chapter is that the only place Samba's ambiguity can end is eternity, where all worlds become one. This ending may mean that the dilemma cannot be resolved as long as Senegal remains a colony, without any freedom of choice. Kane's choice of Samba, a practical peasant who was never consumed by his faith or the concept of death, indicates an attitude that is tolerant of the new trend.

Kane's silence as a writer, after the success of the book, is equally ambiguous. Whatever the strength of his personal beliefs, he has decided to be silent, while also opting to work diligently for the economic development of his country. This is probably the price to pay for an ambiguous synthesis. However, in his article "The African Writer and his Public" (1966), he indicated the path that Senegalese literature should take:

Our literature will only get its health back when writers are convinced that it is in Africa herself that they must look for these features of the 'human condition'—with the means Europe has inevitably endowed them with and whose effectiveness cannot be questioned. They must be as convinced as the Haitian, Jacques Stephen Alexis, that 'a great work is born from the dialectical conjunction of individual talent and the collective genius of the people.'

This is evidently the way it should be. Still, one cannot stop wondering whether Kane, still haunted by the emaciated face and frail body of his old master, did not for a long time, against logic and reason, feel guilty of having betrayed the inflexible faith and spirit of the ever-demanding Thierno, the incarnation of the old Africa.

WORKS IN ENGLISH TRANSLATION: *Ambiguous Adventure,* written originally in French, was translated into English by Katherine Woods in 1963 and re-issued in 1969 with an introduction by Wilfred Carter. Selections from Kane's work are included in Gerald Moore's

African Literature and the Universities, 1965, and in G. D. Killiam's *African Writers on African Writing,* 1973.

ABOUT: Brench, A.C. Writing in French from Senegal to Cameroon, 1967; Carey, W. Whispers from a Continent, 1969; Columbia Dictionary of Modern Literature, 1980; Herdeck, D.E. African Authors I, 1973; Mercier, R. and S. Battestini, Cheikh Hamidou Kane (in French), 1967; Who's Who in African Literature, 1972.

* * *

KATEB, YACINE *See* YACINE, KATEB

* * *

*KEDOURIE, ELIE** (January 25, 1926–), Iraqi-born British historian and essayist, was born in Baghdad, the son of A. Kedourie and L. Dangour. He was educated at the Collège A-D Sasson and the Shamash School in Baghdad. In his early twenties he enrolled in the London School of Economics and Political Science, earning his bachelor's degree there in 1950. After two years of graduate study at St. Antony's College, Oxford, he began his teaching career at the London School of Economics, where he has been, since 1965, professor of politics.

For three decades Kedourie has written on Middle Eastern politics, particularly as they have been perceived and formed in Britain, and several of his books have attracted international attention. His ability to describe contentious, tangled, and often bloody subjects "without advocacy or rhetorical color," in the words of his friend Saul Bellow, has won him a reputation as one of the most careful and fair-minded analysts of the contemporary Middle East.

Kedourie's first influential book, *The Chatham House Version, and Other Middle-Eastern Studies,* consists of a series of twelve essays dealing with such important topics as British control of Egypt, Lawrence of Arabia and the capture of Damascus, Palestine, pan-Arabism, the minorites under the Ottoman Empire, and the kingdom of Iraq. The title essay is an earnest attack on the ideas of Arnold Toynbee, from 1925 to 1952 director of studies at Chatham House, the London headquarters of the Royal Institute of International Affairs, who was perhaps the chief intellectual influence on the shaping of Britain's Middle East policy. According to Kedourie, the British position in the area was imperiled, then ruined, by a conventional support for the rights of the Arab majority, when it should have been based on satisfying nationalist aspirations within the individual states. British reviewers generally voiced alarm at such thor-

°ke dŏŏr´ē

oughly revisionist ideas, while acknowledging that these were being set forth with great intelligence and aplomb.

Another collection of essays, *Arabic Political Memoirs, and Other Studies,* may be taken as a continuation and complement of *The Chatham House Version.* The dominant theme of this collection is the failure in the Middle East, over the past century, of Western-inspired or Western-imposed constitutional models, and the concomitant development of traditional native autocracy into a Western-style statist absolutism. In Kedourie's view, the failure of constitutionalism is evident in the completely inappropriate nature of modern Middle Eastern representative institutions and political parties; the title essay considers the radical rhetoric and deep despair that developed in many leaders after the repeated failure of various constitutional experiments. G. E. Wheeler, describing the book as "a considerable event" and "an intellectual treat," also warned that it would offend established British sensibilities: "To those whom the author describes as the 'romantic Arabophiles' it will be largely, if not wholly, distasteful, although in the face of Professor Kedourie's formidable documentation they may experience some difficulty in making any effective rejoinder."

In the Anglo-Arab Labyrinth: The McMahon–Husayn Correspondence and Its Interpretations, 1914–1939 makes a full-length study of the misunderstanding and confusion underlying the genesis of modern Anglo-Arab relations. It gives an account of the important exchange of letters in 1915–16 (before the Balfour Declaration) between Sir Henry McMahon, British high commissioner in Egypt, and Husayn, Sharif of Mecca, which were thought by generations of Arabists to have in some way promised Palestine to the Arabs. The book follows the form of traditional diplomatic history, treating in one part the origins and nature of the correspondence, in another its "official historiography," in which the author exposes the many guilty men in the foreign and colonial offices who first misunderstood, then greatly exaggerated, Arab rights over the area. "No scholar," wrote a reviewer in the *Economist,* "—and certainly no diplomat—has ever worried so many facts (and fancies) out of official archives. His tenacious investigation is valuable for this alone." Douglas Dakin, while terming the second part of the book "highly entertaining," complained that Kedourie "has little to say about the ways in which decisions were reached or of the shifting background against which they were made. He seems to forget that the whole of history (and particularly diplomatic history) is strewn with untidy ends."

In Kedourie's typically wide-ranging collection of essays *Islam in the Modern World,* he returns to focus on several of the topics that have long occupied his special interest: the biographers of T. E. Lawrence, the surrender of Medina in 1919, the confluence of British and U.S. Middle Eastern policies, and the ways in which Western reformist ideas, applied in a Middle Eastern context, led not to increased popular liberty but to a despotic absolutism. In a finely argued article on contemporary Islamic fundamentalism, he discerns its main origins in the futile attempt by some Muslim leaders to inject into the Islamic political legacy a spirit of secular humanism and a desire for social renovation. The inevitable failure of these attempts, coupled with the severe economic deprivation attendant upon modernization, led directly to such reactionary movements as the Muslim Brotherhood in Egypt, Muammar Qaddafi's in Libya, and the Ayatollah Khomeini's in Iran, all of which are concerned, as Abbas Kelidar wrote, "to revive the original activism, the warrior spirit of early Islam, so that the objective conditions of their societies can be radically changed." Kelidar concludes his review by remarking that Kedourie "is now one of the world's most respected authorities on [modern Middle Eastern studies] and those concerned with it may either applaud or disapprove of his work, but they cannot ignore it."

Kedourie, who was elected a fellow of the British Academy in 1975, has also edited numerous books of essays by various authors, one of these, *Modern Egypt: Studies on Politics and Society,* with his wife, Sylvia Haim. Since 1964 he has been editor of the influential quarterly, *Middle Eastern Studies.* His marriage in 1950 to Haim, who was also born in Baghdad, has produced two sons and a daughter. He has frequently been visiting lecturer and professor at American and European universities.

PRINCIPAL WORKS: England and the Middle East: The Destruction of the Ottoman Empire, 1914–1921, 1956; Nationalism, 1960; Afghani and Abduh: An Essay on Religious Unbelief and Political Activism in Modern Islam, 1966; The Chatham House Version, 1970; Arabic Political Memoirs, 1974; In the Anglo-Arab Labyrinth, 1976; Islam in the Modern World, 1980. *As editor or coeditor*—Nationalism in Asia and Africa, 1971; The Jewish World, 1979; Modern Egypt, 1980 (with S. Haim); Towards a Modern Iran, 1980; Zionism and Arabism in Palestine and Israel, 1982; Palestine and Israel in the Nineteenth and Twentieth Centuries, 1982; The Crossman Confessions and Other Essays, 1985.

ABOUT: Bellow, S. To Jerusalem and Back, 1976; Contemporary Authors, revised series 21–24, 1977; new revision series 10, 1983; Who's Who, 1983. *Periodicals*—American Historical Review February 1977; Choice April 1968; July 1970; July–August 1981; Commentary September 1975; Economist March 21, 1970; March 20, 1976; Library Journal April 15, 1970; June 1, 1971; January 15, 1975; New Statesman June 19, 1970; New York Times Book Review July 25, 1971; Times Literary Supplement September 8, 1966; May 14, 1970; January 10, 1975; April 30, 1976; May 1, 1981; February 22, 1985.

KELLY, JAMES PLUNKETT *See* PLUNKETT, JAMES

KENNEDY, WILLIAM (1928–   ), American novelist, was born in Albany, New York. Of Irish Catholic background, he attended Albany's Christian Brothers Academy, and after graduating from Siena College in Memphis, Tennessee, and two years of service (1950–52) in the U.S. Army, he began a newspaper career in Glens Falls, N.Y. At one point in his career as a newspaperman, he left Albany to live in Miami and in San Juan, Puerto Rico, where he founded the *San Juan Star*, and met his wife, Dana. When his father fell ill, Kennedy returned to Albany, the locale of his subsequent fiction, to work fulltime as a writer. He has remarked that he finds "no limitations in Albany in terms of describing what America is all about. It has all the elements of the nation in microcosm—Presidential politics, national gangsterism, the foundation of capitalism. It is a place where you can find the grand themes of America played out in the everyday life of the city."

Kennedy's first novel, *The Ink Truck*, deals with a year-long guild strike at a city newspaper that settles into apathetic resistance by a handful of union activists. The central character, Bailey, a syndicated columnist, is now obsessed with harassing the company and will not admit defeat. He devises a plan to drain the printing ink from one of the company trucks, and from this point preposterous complications ensue. Shane Stevens characeized *The Ink Truck* as "a work of the imagination, inventive, circular and multilayered. . . . Kennedy has been able to confine his wickedly surrealistic imagination within a well-told tale. The result is a Dantesque journey through the hells of existence. The author, I am told, calls his novel 'a lustily metaphysical comedy.' Happily, it is exactly that . . . a fine debut by a writer of obvious talent and much promise." Generally, reviewers were divided between an admiration of Kennedy's verbal pyrotechnics and a suspicion that his fa-

© 1984 Thomas Victor

WILLIAM KENNEDY

cility revealed too little about his characters, who, as Dorothy Curley complained, exist, somewhat uncertainly, "between realism and farce." Reissued in 1984 after Kennedy's phenomenal success with *Ironweed*, it had, Anatole Broyard observed in an otherwise unfavorable review, "a special interest as a first novel, like a baby's first cry . . . though the book is little more than a bag filled with wind, Mr. Kennedy seems to have sharpened his skills with it."

Legs, the first in Kennedy's cycle of "Albany novels," is a fictional version of the life and times of the notorious bootlegger and gunman Jack "Legs" Diamond, who was killed in an Albany rooming house in 1931. W. T. Lhamon was impressed by Kennedy's "sustained verbal energy," and Peter Prescott commented that "Kennedy means to probe our peculiar American habit of reviling gangsters while pressing them for autographs. He cannot explain this ambiguity, perhaps because he shares it himself, but he attests to its existence. . . . It is a peculiarly seductive portrait and *Legs* is a very skillful story, full of bounce and wit." Other critics were less enthusiastic. The reviewer for the *Times Literary Supplement* noted that the novel has its share of "longueurs and detumescences, and as is the wont of stories told in flashes back, it lights up only in flashes," and questioned the ambiguous moral position of the novel's narrator, who is the gangster's lawyer: " . . . a morally and philosophically alerter fiction would certainly want more clearly to disown this narrator." As L. J. Davis suggested in another review, " . . . it is possible that Kennedy becomes somewhat more fond of his hero than is good for him."

Billy Phelan's Greatest Game, which continues the Albany cycle, deals with the kidnapping in 1938 of Charlie Boy McCall, sole heir of the McCall family, which runs the city's Democratic machine. One of the McCall brothers calls upon the journalist Martin Daugherty to quash the city's biggest story since the killing of Legs Diamond seven years earlier. Daugherty is, however, less important to the work than Billy Phelan, a part-time bookie and gambler who is pressed to finger the kidnapper or suffer the extreme displeasure of the McCalls. The situation results in an excursion through the city's low life, which has the tart, outrageous flavor of Kennedy's wit, and reveals his remarkable ear for barroom speech. Doris Grumbach wrote of the novel glowingly: "Most important for this new book, Kennedy's pitch is perfect. His is the true comic spirit, conveyed by a tumult of fierce and wonderful language. . . . Fighting, challenging and defending one another, profoundly Irish and equally profoundly American, the cast of *Billy Phelan* is, quite simply, a wonder—a magical bunch of thugs, lovers, and game players. No one writing in America today . . . has Kennedy's rich and fertile gift of gab. . . . Like his characters, he too is a wonder." But Peter Prescott complained of the novel's relative plotlessness. "The line of the narrative," he remarked, "would have been firmer if [Kennedy] had not been so distracted by the details, the anecdotes, the scraps of Albany lore and legend. . . . The pieces do not coalesce, the story does not really progress. We are left at the end with the impression of a great many shards thrown carelessly before us."

Although it had its enthusiastic admirers, *Billy Phelan* was a commercial failure. Kennedy himself described it as " not only not a best seller, it was a worst seller." As a result, he had trouble placing his next novel, *Ironweed.* Thirteen publishers rejected it, and it was only through the intervention of Saul Bellow, who had read and admired Kennedy's earlier books, that it found a publisher. When it was finally published to critical acclaim, the National Book Critics Circle Award, and the Pulitzer Prize for fiction in 1984, Kennedy responded: "I am now as much awash in critical magnanimity as I was bathed two years ago in insolvent obscurity. The nature of this new status is extreme pleasure, but also part of it is residual bewilderment at the causes of the previous condition." The novel follows Francis Phelan's odyssey through the soup kitchens, honky tonks, and flophouses of Albany on the last weekend of October 1938—the weekend of Hallowe'en and All Saints Day. Phelan, once the best baseball player ever to have come out of Albany, is now an alcoholic bum, who deserted his family (and whose son is Billy Phelan, of Kenne-

dy's previous novel). In his return to Albany, his past experience and his present mental states are recreated in haunting imagery that has an almost hallucinatory quality.

George Stade found in *Ironweed* a new and impressive disciplining of Kennedy's talents. Noting that its emotional focus is more powerful than that of earlier books, Stade commented: "for all the rich variety of prose and event, from hallucination to bedrock realism to blessed quotidian peace, *Ironweed* is more austere than its predecessors. It is more fierce, but also more forgiving." Robert Towers observed that "what [Kennedy] has written is a kind of fantasia on the strangeness of human destiny, on the mysterious ways in which a life can be transformed and sometimes redeemed. . . . Throughout the novel Kennedy plays with the contrast between sordid event and exalted illusion, between remembered past and threadbare present, between precise description and blunt colloquialism on the one hand and on the other a style so heightened as to become rhapsodic." William Pritchard remarked that "on occasion I felt the writing about the hero, and about Helen—the woman for whom Francis cares and whose own tale is important here—was grandiose, perhaps too ambitious." But he, too, regarded the novel as the finest work the author had yet done, and called Kennedy "an original and invigorating novelist . . . resourcefully assured in his command of language and place."

O Albany!, subtitled "Improbable City of Political Wizards, Fearless Ethnics, Spectacular Aristocrats, Splendid Nobodies, and Underrated Scoundrels," is an account of the city's variegated life, both past and present. *O Albany!* was described by Christopher Lehmann-Haupt as "part memoir, part history and part celebration of the Empire State's frowsy capital. . . . Mr. Kennedy sounds every note that his multioctaved voice can reach. . . . He is by turns reverent and cynical, boastful and defensive, angry and sentimental, wistful, witty and proud . . . " Thomas Fleming was impressed by the "nice blend of nostalgia and serious history" in the book, which he found entertaining and highly engaging. "In *O Albany!,*" he wrote, "William Kennedy sets out to prove his native city is 'centered squarely in the American and human continuum.' There is no question that he succeeds marvelously." In September 1984 the city of Albany honored Kennedy and itself in a four-day celebration featuring lectures, exhibitions, and walking tours; and New York State Governor Mario Cuomo proclaimed that Albany had "found its Homer in William Kennedy." While his achievement may not be of such epic proportions, Kennedy has indeed given his native city something of the dimensions of Joyce's Dublin and James T. Farrell's Chicago.

After years of relative neglect during which he supplemented his small earnings from his fiction with book reviewing, magazine article writing, and part-time teaching in the English department of the State University of New York at Albany, Kennedy emerged at last into his own in 1983. "Everything is reversed," he told a *New York Times* interviewer. "A while back I was so broke that I even applied to write speeches for an oil company. They didn't even bother to reply." He was appointed full professor with tenure at the State University that year, but shortly after received a MacArthur Foundation grant which enabled him to devote all his time to creative work. He remodeled his old house, where he lives with his wife and two children. (An older daughter is married and has one child.) He was co-screenwriter with Francis Ford Coppola of Coppola's lavish forty million dollar film *The Cotton Club* and in 1984 wrote screenplays of his earlier novels *Legs* and *Billy Phelan's Greatest Game*. Of his new life Kennedy says with characteristic candor: "Being unknown is difficult. This is easy."

PRINCIPAL WORKS: The Ink Truck, 1969; Legs, 1976; Billy Phelan's Greatest Game, 1978; Ironweed, 1983. *Non-fiction*—O Albany!, 1983.

ABOUT: Contemporary Authors 85–88, 1980. *Periodicals*—Book World October 5, 1969; May 18, 1975; Commonweal September 9, 1983; New Republic May 24, 1975; February 14, 1983; Newsweek, May 8, 1978; New York Review of Books March 31, 1983; New York Times, December 23, 1983; September 6, 1984; September 22, 1984; New York Times Book Review January 1, 1984; April 8, 1984; New York Times Magazine August 26, 1984; Saturday Review June 1978; Times Literary Supplement August 20, 1976; October 5, 1984.

KINGSTON, MAXINE HONG (October 27, 1940–), Chinese-American memoirist, writes: "I was born to be a writer, and have told stories and written stories as long as I can remember. In the midst of any adventure, a born writer has a desire to hurry home and put it into words. When looking at a flower or a landscape or a person's face, you want to capture its beauty forever by describing it. The way you celebrate and the way you praise and the way you mourn is to write a poem or a story or an article or a book.

"You can be a writer at any time. When I was a child, an artist told me that the tools of our trade—pencil and paper—are inexpensive. 'Pencil and paper are all you need,' he said. I was

MAXINE HONG KINGSTON

heartened and pass this fact on to you. You don't have to worry about talent. Writers need years—sometimes a lifetime—of practice. A good writer can write good books and never be recognized anyway. You have to have a great overview, and believe that if readers don't find your books in your lifetime they may find you someday. You don't want to be a fad but a part of literature forever.

"Now, practically, a writer, like everybody else in this world, has to figure out a way to make a living. There is a statistic that in the United States only one hundred writers can live on their book earnings. This means that most of us have to work at two jobs—writing and a paying job. The job for making money should be one that leaves you enough energy before day and at the end of the day and on weekends to write. I've worked at a paying job for about forty hours per week, and written for a minimum of twenty-five hours per week. The paying jobs I've had have been as a laundry worker, bookkeeper, tutor, typist, clerk, paper grader, insurance adjuster trainee, and teacher. When I was in college, I worked on the school newspaper and learned that one job that is not compatible with my writing is journalism, and I gave up the childhood idea of being a reporter.

"A writer should learn to live with few material needs. It has been a good lifeplan for me to save money, then quit the paying job, and give myself free time to write. My husband and I have both worked, saving one salary, and during the free year, I wrote my first book and he became an actor. I made no money on that practice book, and he worked in theaters that do not pay actors. I have had two free years, and they are two of the most important years of my life."

———

Maxine Hong Kingston is the eldest daughter of Tom Hong and the former Ying Lan Chew, immigrants who settled in Stockton, California in 1940, started a laundry business, and raised a family under the most trying of circumstances. A Cantonese dialect was spoken at home and the mother's fantastic "talk-stories" of rituals and events in China were a thread that kept the children tied to the homeland they had never seen. Kingston's parents were better educated than most members of their community, and Maxine was a particularly bookish child. She did well in school and won enough scholarships to attend the University of California at Berkeley, where she majored in engineering before switching to English. At Berkeley she met her future husband, Earll Kingston, an actor. They were married after graduation and have one son, Joseph, born in 1964.

Kingston's childhood is vividly and selectively recounted in her two books, *The Woman Warrior* and *China Men*. She appears in them as a moody, rebellious girl caught between the traditional Chinese culture of her parents and the American ways of her classmates and teachers. From this childhood conflict Kingston has fashioned an outlook that embodies the tensions of ethnic and personal identity. Yet to make the outward leap she has had to fuse autobiography with fact and fiction, history, and myth. As a result her books are almost unclassifiable, but as John Leonard said, "Whatever Maxine Hong Kingston is writing, it is certainly art."

The Woman Warrior: Memoirs of a Girlhood among Ghosts was published with little or no acclaim in 1976, but it won the National Book Critics Circle award for the best nonfiction book of that year. The "ghosts" of the subtitle are the pale Americans whose strange manners intrude on the enclosed Chinese community of Stockton: "social-worker ghosts," "teacher ghosts," and even "meter-reader ghosts." There are also the ghosts of dead relatives in China, the vestiges of an ancestral past that haunts the young Maxine in the present.

The Woman Warrior is divided into five sections, each centering on a representative Chinese or Chinese-American female in some sort of conflict. There is "No Name Woman," Maxine's aunt, who committed suicide in China after shaming her family by bearing an illegitimate child; Fa Mu Lan, the mythical woman warrior of the title who leads an army to victory over a tyrannous emperor; Brave Orchid, Maxine's pro-

digious and strong-willed mother, a woman warrior in her own right, but one who instinctively accepts the Chinese traditions of female subservience; Moon Orchid, Brave Orchid's fragile younger sister who gradually slips into insanity after coming to America; and lastly Maxine herself. The final chapter is a confrontation between the writer and her mother in which the adolescent Maxine finally but guiltily breaks free of Brave Orchid's domination.

There was scarcely a critic who did not find *The Woman Warrior* an important and powerful book, but different reviewers emphasized different things. Diane Johnson in the *New York Review of Books* saw *The Woman Warrior* chiefly as a feminist parable of "the service of maladjustment" that women perform for society. She placed Kingston's feminist preoccupations in a literary tradition that includes the Brontë heroines and Sylvia Plath. By contrast, Jane Kramer in the *New York Times Book Review* interpreted *The Woman Warrior* as a testament of the Chinese sensibility in a foreign land, or as a challenge to clichéd American notions of Chineseness. "It is a brilliant memoir," she said. "It shocks us out of our facile rhetoric, past the clichés of our obtuseness, back to the mystery of a stubbornly, utterly foreign sensibility." Kramer also pointed out the book's universality: "*The Woman Warrior* is about being Chinese in the way the *Portrait of the Artist* is about being Irish. It is an investigation of soul, not landscape."

Although published four years later, *China Men* was written more or less in conjunction with *The Woman Warrior*. It uses the same technique of fusing genres and has the same fierce, fixated tone, but the focus, as the title indicates, is on men, not women. *China Men* is similarly structured on individual life histories yoked together by a shared cultural inheritance and by the author's own questioning sensibility. The first man introduced is Maxine's father, whom she remembers cursing at women in a fit of sullen rage. From there Maxine tries to piece together his earlier life, from his days as a village schoolteacher in China to his condition as an embittered, misogynist immigrant in Stockton. (Eventually he acquires the laundry and becomes a hardworking family man.) Kingston then reconstructs the lives of her greatgrandfather and grandfather, who were lured by the promise of the "Gold Mountain" and ended up working as virtual slaves in Hawaii cane fields and on the transcontinental railroad. Other male figures appear, some ghostly, some mythic, some flesh and blood, all acting out paradigms of the Chinese or Chinese-American experience, and most "claiming America" in their own ways. The last China man is Maxine's younger brother, who finds himself, an American Oriental and pacifist, sent to Vietnam to wage war on other Orientals.

China Men was, if anything, greeted with even more acclaim than *The Woman Warrior*. Ann Tyler wrote in the *New Republic* that "it's every bit as compelling as its predecessor. It's a history at once savage and beautiful, a combination of bone-grinding reality and luminous fantasy." Frederick Wakeman, Jr., in the *New York Review of Books* considered *China Men* "less fanciful and flamboyant than her first book" and "a much more authoritative personal reflection."

Kingston discounts specific literary influences and says that her study of literature at Berkeley worked against her instincts as a writer. "It was all I could do to write these formal papers on literary criticism," she told *Mademoiselle* magazine. "I felt that if I stayed to get a master's degree it would *destroy* the writing." However, one book that has influenced her consciously is William Carlos Williams' *In the American Grain*. Williams's retelling of the American myth, his poetic adaptation of the facts of history, find their analogies in Kingston's two books. Kingston has also written essays for popular and educational journals and has published poems in the *Iowa Review*.

PRINCIPAL WORKS: The Woman Warrior: Memoirs of a Girlhood among Ghosts, 1976; China Men, 1980.

ABOUT: Contemporary Authors 69–72, 1978; Contemporary Literary Criticism 12, 1980; 19, 1981; Mainiero, L. (ed.) American Women Writers 2, 1980. *Periodicals*—Horizon July 1980; Mademoiselle March 1977; New Republic June 21, 1980; New York Review of Books February 3, 1977; August 14, 1980; New York Times February 12, 1977; June 3, 1980; New York Times Book Review November 7, 1976; June 15, 1980.

*KINOSHITA, JUNJI (August 2, 1914–), Japanese playwright and drama theorist, writes: "Until I left the University of Tokyo in 1939, I was studying Elizabethan drama, concentrating on Shakespeare, with the idea of becoming a scholar of the history of British theater. In those days the waves of militarism and Fascism that would become the Pacific War were already beating on the academic world. At the University of Tokyo there was a whole series of incidents. Many progressive professors were purged, and a retired vice-admiral took the post of the president of the university.

"As a young student around this time I came to feel that I should express my opposition to this

JUNJI KINOSHITA

trend directly, through drama, rather than through an indirect means like scholarship. Probably this was my main motive for becoming a dramatist. When I left the university in 1939 I was hired by a private university. While earning my living by lecturing there I wrote one long play and several short plays, with no hope of getting them published. My long play was based on an incident that had taken place on the southern island of Kyushu in the 1870s. This was just the time when the modern Japanese nation was being created, and the play treated the agony of young people beset by both progressive and reactionary trends. The short plays of this period were based on simplistic Japanese folk tales and were intended to explore the roots of mankind. Between 1939 and 1945 I was called up by the army on two occasions but each time was saved from conscription.

"In 1945 Japan surrendered and the war was over. The next year I revised my long play and published it, in 1947, under the title *Fūrō* (Turbulent Waves). My short plays found their way into publication one by one and were also performed on the stage. Among them was *Yūzuru*, which has been published in English as *Twilight Crane*. This play was first staged in 1949, and since then it has been performed more than 960 times with a single actress—the respected Yasue Yamamoto—taking the role of the heroine. *Yūzuru* has also been taken up on countless occasions by amateur drama groups and translated into more than ten languages. Ikuma Dan's operatic version has been performed both in Japan and abroad.

"I have now written over ten long plays and

°kē´ nō shē tă, yo͞on jě

dozens of shorter dramatic works, including plays for radio and television. I have been called a playwright with two different faces. One is that of the serious social playwright, as exemplified by, among others, *Fūrō*, mentioned above; *Ottō to yobareru Nihonjin* (A Japanese Called Otto), based on the Sorge espionage incident of 1941; *Okinawa*, a play depicting the struggle of the Okinawan people under the United States Occupation; and *Kami to hito to no aida* (Between God and Man), a drama about A-class war criminals at the Tokyo International Military Tribunal for the Far East and B- or C-class criminals at courts outside Japan. My other face is that of the folktale playwright creating easy-to-digest and unassuming works like *Yūzuru*. I myself have for a long time been wondering how I might unify these dual aspects.

"After the 1960s I became increasingly interested in classics and took part in experimental performances involving the recitation by actors and actresses of the *Heike monogatari*, a long historical tale set in twelfth-century Japan and originally transmitted orally by minstrels. I have also translated into the modern Japanese language classical Japanese literature from the eighth through the nineteenth centuries as well as fifteen plays of Shakespeare.

"My interest in the classics has, I think, helped me bring my dual aspects together. My most recent play is *Shigosen no matsuri* (The Meridian Rite), published in 1978. It is based on the *Heike monogatari* and depicts the struggle of two major clans at the hands of the Genji. In this play three styles—the twelfth century original, modern Japanese, and Shakespearean—are brought together and combined. There are two viewpoints: the microscopic one of warriors battling on the ground, and the macroscopic one in which the struggle is viewed from above. I also applied here the style of Nō and Kyōgen theater that originated in the fourteenth century, the style of seventeenth-century Kabuki, and the realistic staging of modern dramas. The actors and actresses were selected from specialists in each genre.

"The performance of *Shigosen no matsuri* was successful, and I think that play represents as well the fulfillment of my wish to combine the various devices I had been consciously and unconsciously concerned with since I first began writing serious drama. That was forty years ago, and I now believe that within me, as a playwright, one important cycle has been completed.

"Since last year [1980] I have been busy writing an autobiographical novel and preparing for my next play."

———

Since the early part of the twentieth century, the predominant dramatic style in Japan has been dictated by a movement known as "Shingeki," or the "new drama." This approach to the theater was primarily a rejection of the classical Japanese theatrical traditions of Nō and Kabuki and took its lead from the modern realistic drama of Europe. From its inception "Shingeki" has been uncertain of the proper direction for its energies, and without the inspirational lead of a handful of creative individuals, it is doubtful that the movement would have provided any works of lasting quality for the theater. "Shingeki" has been fortunate over the past four decades to have Kinoshita Junji as its foremost spokesman and creative author, for Kinoshita has been able to transcend the inherent limitations of the "Shingeki" concept of theater by bringing a sense of Japanese tradition back into the drama, while retaining a modern philosophical tone of inquiry that addresses vital social and moral questions of our society.

Though he is not formally classified as a Marxist playwright, Kinoshita shares many of the leftist concerns with the workings of history and the role of the individual. His finest plays have, in fact, blended a concern with historical development and a focus upon the heroic—or merely determined—individuals who have struggled to extract some meaning from the most chaotic of events. Many of Kinoshita's plays are set in moments of great upheaval: "Turbulent Waves" depicts the mortal struggles of a young man caught up in the clash between feudalistic conservatism and progressive modernism at the time of the Meiji Restoration in the 1870s; "A Japanese Called Otto" takes place in the difficult years leading to World War II; and *Between God and Man* focuses upon the responsibility of those who collaborated in the Japanese war effort.

At the same time that he examines the battered lives of these people standing at historical crossroads, Kinoshita maintains a persistent interest in the extra-historical, unifying qualities of the language spoken by the Japanese people throughout their history. Language to Kinoshita is the vehicle of culture, and the ability of the dramatist to transcend the barriers of time and create a "universal dialect" he considers one of the highest duties of his calling as an artist. In *Twilight Crane*, Kinoshita attempted to formulate a dramatic language composed of dialectical elements drawn from every part of Japan, while in "The Meridian Rite" he creates onstage a panoramic distillation of language by placing twelfth century minstrel priests alongside representatives from both classical and modern drama. His sense of pageantry, language, and history combine to make his theatrical writings the most interesting and influential of his time.

The success of plays such as *Twilight Crane* can be attributed as much to the quality of the writing and the universality of the theme as to the modern Japanese yearning for a sense of continuity amidst rapid, confusing social change. The story of a mysteriously beautiful woman who comes to aid a young man by spinning him strands of gold is familiar to every Japanese, and the ending, in which he betrays his promise not to glance at her while she works, remains moving for modern audiences who can still respond to the tragedy of trading moral values for the promise of material rewards.

Kinoshita's social conscience, and his refusal to gloss over central moral questions in Japan's modern history, work together to make *Between God and Man* a major literary and philosophical examination of war crimes—not only those committed by the Japanese military figures who were brought before the Occupation's tribunal, but also those in which all mankind is implicated. Japan's self-reflections about World War II have tended to be private and non-literary, and Kinoshita's play stands as one of the most frank and telling public literary statements about Japanese—and global—complicity in the multiple holocausts of the last half-century. Structured in two distinct but complementary parts, *Between God and Man* both questions our ability to judge one another in the segment on the war crimes trials, and demands in its second half that we all accept a measure of responsibility for whatever atrocities are committed in human society.

As Kinoshita himself suggests above, the many divergent concerns and interests in his plays, ranging from historical to contemporary to folk tale-style, are not easily brought together on the stage. "The Meridian Rite" is only one possible means of drawing these various motifs together, and the future of Kinoshita's work and of the modern Japanese theater as a whole will depend upon other experiments to bring some sense of unity to the many strains that make up the Japanese theatrical tradition. No playwright of this century, however, has made greater strides toward achieving such a unity than Kinoshita.

WORKS IN ENGLISH TRANSLATION: A. C. Scott's translation of *Twilight Crane* was published in his *Five Plays for a New Theatre*, 1956. *Between God and Man: A Judgment on War Crimes* was translated by Eric J. Gangloff, 1979.

ABOUT: Dictionary of Oriental Literatures I, 1974; Encyclopedia of Japan, 1984; Gangloff, E. J. *Introduction to* Between God and Man, 1979; Lang, D. M. A Guide to Eastern Literature, 1971. *Periodicals*—World Literature Today Spring 1980.

KIRSTEIN, LINCOLN (May 4, 1907–), American poet, novelist, critic, and authority on the dance, was born in Rochester, New York, the son of Louis Edward and Rose (Stein) Kirstein. In 1912 the Kirsteins moved to Boston, where his father was chairman of the board of Filene's, the department store. Kirstein was educated at Harvard University, from which he graduated in 1930. From an early introduction to ballet—a performance by Anna Pavlova during her 1924 American tour—Kirstein developed an enthusiasm for the dance that was to make him a major force, along with George Balanchine, in establishing ballet in America and founding the New York City Ballet. Kirstein has written important books, articles, and monographs on the dance, film, photography, and the arts. These include librettos for ballets (among them the highly acclaimed *Billy the Kid* for which Eugene Loring did the choreography), several major books on dance history, the iconoclastic *Blast at Ballet: A Corrective for the American Audience,* and studies of American painting, the sculpture of Gaston Lachaise and Elie Nadelman, and the photography of Walker Evans and Henri Cariter Bresson.

In 1927, while a Harvard undergraduate, Kirstein and a fellow classmate, Varian Fry, founded the brilliant literary quarterly, *Hound & Horn,* of which he was editor with Richard P. Blackmur, Bernard Bandler, A. Hyatt Mayor, Allen Tate, and Yvor Winters, and to which he contributed articles on the arts. Others who wrote for the magazine were Ezra Pound, who served as foreign advisor from 1930 to 1931, writing from his home in Rapallo, Italy, T. S. Eliot, Katherine Anne Porter, James Agee, Michael Gold, E. E. Cummings, Edmund Wilson, and Sean O'Faoláin. The aim of the magazine, initially subtitled a "Harvard Miscellany," was to introduce modernism to Harvard students. As Varian Fry wrote in the *Harvard Advocate* (Christmas, 1934): "I was an admirer of Joyce, Kirstein of Eliot. We had both read Gertrude Stein, looked at Picasso, listened to Stravinsky. They seemed to be important, and we felt that Harvard undergraduates ought to know more about them than they did. It was to hail the new and glittering world they and their influences were creating, and to bid farewell to the stodgy in the nineteenth century and its heavy hand on the twentieth, that I . . . wrote that first editorial." Kirstein's love for the ballet began to dominate his life from 1933 on, and in 1934, money for the *Hound & Horn* was diverted to establishing the School of American Ballet, and the magazine ceased publication.

Kirstein's first novel, *Flesh Is Heir,* was published in 1932, to mixed reviews. Fictionalized autobiography, it describes a sensitive young man, Roger Baum, in a variety of experiences—at boarding school, working in a stained glass factory in Boston that created windows for the Cathedral of St. John the Divine (as Kirstein did in 1925), traveling in Europe, where he saw a production of Balanchine's "The Prodigal Son" in 1929 and witnessed by chance the funeral of Diaghilev in Venice—through his first year at college. Reviewers attacked the hero's passivity and the static quality of the second half of the book but some commented favorably on the sensitivity of the writing and the freshness of the viewpoint—"one more voice in the rapidly swelling chorus of new writers who have grown dissatisfied with the novel of disillusionment and bitterness," the *Saturday Review of Literature* observed. Reviewing the novel when it was reissued in 1975, Arnold Goldman wrote in the *Times Literary Supplement* that the protagonist, Roger, is "consistently out of his depth," facing "menace," that is initially homosexual, then later heterosexual in nature. "In the key incident the girl prevents Roger from meeting Diaghilev . . . Diaghilev's power as a 'creator' is clearly linked to a benign homosexual force: the death of the god seems to leave the field to the uncreative heterosexuals. . . . There is no articulate development to Roger's character. . . . Though *Flesh Is Heir* is as unsatisfactory as its author says it is (in an afterword that is mostly apology) . . . it does link the 1920s stories of Robert McAlmon with James Purdy's *Malcolm.*"

It is as a poet that Kirstein has realized his gifts as a creative writer. His *Rhymes of a Pfc* was published in 1964, and republished in an expanded edition in 1966 and 1981 as *Rhymes and More Rhymes of a Pfc.* His personal experiences as a private in the army, where he was assigned to General Patton's Third Army and where, as arts and archives officer, he had the incredible good fortune to discover the location of the bulk of the art treasures looted by the Germans from all over Europe for the establishment of a museum for the Führer, are catalogued in his poems in roughly chronological order. The routine of army life, the high drama, the fear, the boredom, the tragedy are conveyed to the reader in a series of stark snapshots, with an acute ear for the vernacular of the speaker. He is at home in a variety of rhythms and meter that recall the poetry, as Richard Ellmann writes, of "Sir Henry Newbolt, Rudyard Kipling, and Robert Service . . . he has imitated their clanking hexameters, their obtrusive rhymes, and their archaisms and inversions. But in Kirstein the attitudes are much more reserved and guarded, and the irony more subtle, than in these earlier poets."

Kirstein's typical poetic voice, combining irony with toughness to convey a purely personal moment, joined with the male ritual obligatory in wartime, is seen in "Bath":

Bent benches, no lockers, nor nowhere near nozzles
   enough—
Still: stacked towel, fresh soap, fresh foamy warm intimate
   cream.
Disdain crutty layers of uniform wardrobe; husk off
Shoe, sock, shorts, shirt. High luxury's lathery dream

   Gargles hair-tonic tenor, brass baritone trill;
Life Buoy's lunatic tunes recollected from hymnbook, high
   school
   Slosh water by buckets. O brother. Slop, splash, and spill
All over crummy bifurcate buttock, soaked slick supple
   tool.
Athletes all, man or boy; at the least, what a sculptor
   might tease
Into classic athletic condition: life class, locker room:

Nudes in wet armor, a small-scale orgy of grandeur at
   ease
Or daft plastic mockup for votive historical doom.

Snap towel. Sting quirt. Rambunctiously prance, goose,
   gripe, grope.
Tank runs dry. Drain away all drear ordure, sud, sweat, and
   dirt.
Immaculate loons in raw hide, slicked hair, red ears
   rimmed in soap,
Strait-jacket us quick into stinky shorts, dead shoes, sodden
   shirt.

Of Rhymes of a Pfc, Paul Fussell wryly observed in the *Times Literary Supplement,* "Kirstein has no visible artistic pretensions and certainly no metaphysical ones. It would be funny and splendid if he should ultimately be recognized as the greatest poet of the Second World War." W. H. Auden connected Kirstein's work with that of Browning, Hardy, and Kipling, " . . . he learns how to write a dramatic monologue from Hardy and Browning, a fondness for complicated stanzas. . . . From Kipling . . . I think he got the idea of trying to let the G.I.'s speak in their own low—very low—style—and in this he is brilliantly successful, as Kipling was not." For Auden, *Rhymes of a Pfc* was, as a picture of World War II, "by far the most convincing, moving, and impressive book I have come across."

Lincoln Kirstein, whom *New York Times* art critic John Russell calls "one of the most valuable of living Americans," is presently at work on a "mammoth" autobiography, about which those who have seen it have predicted that "it may be to our time what *The Education of Henry Adams* and John Ruskin's *Praeterita* were to earlier generations." In 1941 Kirstein was married to Fidelma Cadmus, the sister of artist Paul Cadmus. He was elected a Fellow of the American Academy of Arts and Sciences in 1969, and has received many awards, among them the Freedom Medal in March 1984, for his contribution to the arts. His vast collection of dance memorabilia was given to the New York Public Library in 1961.

PRINCIPAL WORKS: *Novels*—Flesh Is Heir, 1932; For My Brother: A True Story by Jose Martinez/Berlanga as told/to Lincoln Kirstein, 1943. *Poetry*—Low Ceiling, 1935; Rhymes of a Pfc, 1964; Rhymes and More Rhymes of a Pfc, 1966, 1981. *Dance history and criticism*—A Short History of Theatrical Dancing, 1935; Blast at Ballet, 1938; The Classic Ballet, 1952; Movement and Metaphore: Four Centuries of Ballet, 1969; Thirty Years: Lincoln Kirstein's The New York City Ballet, 1979.

ABOUT: Auden, W. H. Forewords and Afterwords, 1973; Current Biography, 1952; Encyclopedia Americana, 1983; Hamovitch, M. B. *Introduction to* The Hound & Horn Letters, 1982; Lassalle, N., L. H. Silverstein, H. Simmonds (eds.) Lincoln Kirstein: A First Bibliography, 1978; Scannell, V. Not Without Glory: Poetry of the Second World War, 1976; Who's Who in America, 1982–83. *Periodicals*—New York Times Magazine June 20, 1982.

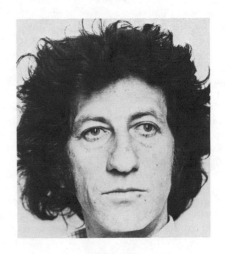

DANILO KIŠ

*KIŠ, DANILO (February 22, 1935–), Yugoslav novelist, short story writer, dramatist, essayist, and translator writes (in French): "My father, who was born in Hungary, studied at a commercial school in the home town of a certain Mr. Virag, who became, thanks to James Joyce, the celebrated Bloom of *Ulysses*. I believe that the political tolerance of Franz Josef II on the one hand, and my grandfather's desire to become integrated with the people among whom he dwelt on the other, prompted him to give a Magyar form to his young son's name. But there are many aspects of our family history that will always be obscure: in 1944 they were all, including my father, led off to Auschwitz. Among my maternal ancestors was a legendary Montenegrin hero who fought the Turks and learned to write at the age of fifty so that he could add the triumphs of the pen to those of his sword. Just so did the Amazon, for vengeance, cut off the head of the despotic Turk. This ethnic peculiarity, a union between Jews and Montenegrins, died out with me.

"At the time when anti-Jewish laws were enacted in Hungary, when I was four years old, my parents had me baptized in the orthodox Christian faith, thus saving my life. Until I was thirteen I lived in Hungary, working for wealthy country people. A disturbing sense of being alien, to which Freud applied the term

Heimlichkeit, was the inspiration of my earliest literary works; I wrote my first poems in Hungarian at the age of nine: one was about hunger, the other was a typical love poem.

"My childhood, and this sense of strangeness, became the subjects of my first three books: *Bašta, pepeo*, 1965 (*Garden, Ashes*), *Rani jadi*, 1970 (Precocious Sorrows) and *Peščanik*, 1972 (The Hour Glass). From my mother I inherited a taste for mingling historical fact and legend in my narrative, and from my father pathos and irony. My mother read novels until she was eighteen, at which point she realized, not without regret, that they are 'fabrications' and forswore them for ever. Her aversion for 'pure inventions' remains equally strong in me; this is why, as a prose writer, I separate personal experiences from documentary facts (see, for example, my novel *Grobnica za Borisa Davidoviča*, 1976 [*A Tomb for Boris Davidovich*] and the short stories in my book *Enciklopedÿa Mrtvih*, 1983 [Encyclopedia of the Dead]).

"In 1947 the International Red Cross helped my family to return to Cetinje in Yugoslavia— the home of my maternal uncle, a well-known historian, biographer and scholar of Njegoš, the Montenegrin poet-prince. In Cetinje I continued my education, began to write poetry in Serbo-Croatian, and translated Hungarian, Russian, and French poetry, primarily as an exercise in style and diction—I envisaged entering the profession of letters and becoming a poet. After taking my baccalaureat I enrolled in the University of Belgrade, where I was the first of my class to

*kēsh

receive a degree from the newly founded department of comparative literature. Working as a lecturer in Serbo-Croatian, I have lived in Strasbourg, Bordeaux, and Lille. At the moment [1983] I live in Paris.

"I was born in Subotica, a town on the Yugoslav-Hungarian border. I have been awarded the Yugoslav prize for the best novel of the year (1971) and in France the Grand Aigle d'or de la ville de Nice (1980) for my work as a whole."

—trans. H. Batchelor

The novelist Ernst Pawel considers Danilo Kiš "a quintessential product of Central Europe—not, to be sure, the heartland of kitsch, cafés, and castles on the Danube but of a Europe with a black night for the center. . . . " That "black night" was Kiš' traumatic childhood, echoed and re-echoed in his writings. Product of a marriage between a Hungarian-Jewish father and a Greek-Orthodox Christian mother, Danilo Kiš begins his autobiographical sketch by alluding to the ancestry of James Joyce's fictional Leopold Bloom. That character, son of a Hungarian Jewish immigrant who came to Dublin, married an Irish Catholic, and changed his name from the Hungarian Virag, meaning "flower" to Rudolph Bloom, later committed suicide. It was his father, however, Leopold Bloom's grandfather Lipoti Virag, who figures in the fantasy of the Circe episode of *Ulysses*. The haunting presence of the emigré parent also figures prominently in Kiš' first novel, *Bašta, pepeo* (*Garden, Ashes*). An intensely personal and subjective memoir of "a child without childhood," the book is a sensitive first-person account of the young narrator's search for "the proofs against my immortality." His memories of his mother are loving, but it is his eccentric father—the compiler of encyclopedic travel guides, a "messianic timetable" living only half in the world of reality, who dominates the book. The imagery of its title suggests its mood—a child's ability to imagine a garden in a real landscape of ashes. And the narrative itself, fragmentary as a child's memory, is strikingly evocative. "It is impossible to separate fact from fiction in this depiction of what must have been a childhood spent in the midst of financial impoverishment in Yugoslavia just prior to World War II," a reviewer writes in *World Literature Today*. "It is Kiš' subjective and poetic interpretations of these events with which he expresses the meaning of his youth."

A more ambitious work, hailed as a masterpiece in Yugoslavia where it was first published, was *Grobnica za Borisa Davidoviča* (*A Tomb for Boris Davidovich*). A collection of seven stories connected by the theme of "persecution and execution of human beings in the name of ideals and ideologies," it is a bitter and compelling yet restrained condemnation of Stalinism, although one of the most powerful of the stories, "Dogs and Books," deals with the persecution of Jews in medieval Italy. The hero of each story is a Jew, a revolutionary who suffers persecution for his beliefs. Written in a spare, almost journalistic, style, *A Tomb for Boris Davidovich*, Ernst Pawel writes, is "hagiography without the politics, compiled by an agnostic." Communism is recognized as a secular-religious faith which has failed and betrayed its followers, and the Jewish victims in these stories are "martyred apostles," victims of "the unholy alliance between dream and nightmare that turns men into commissars." Deliberately anachronistic, dispassionate in tone yet clearly passionate in conviction, Kiš (writes Zora Zimmerman in *World Literature Today*) "dissects the complex political postures of the revolution and its conspiracies and exposes pervasive nihilism."

A Tomb for Boris Davidovich enjoyed enormous success in Yugoslavia although it so shocked and offended Communist authorities that they claimed it was plagiarized—a charge Kiš easily refuted. He responded to his Communist critics in a non-fiction work "The Anatomy Lesson," published in Belgrade in 1978 but not translated into English. Here Kiš writes: "Nationalism is, above all, paranoia. In its collective form, it derives from fear, envy, and above all from a deficient sense of selfhood. Collective paranoia is the sum total of individual delusions carried to paroxysmal extremity." An emigré himself now, in 1983 Kiš was preparing another collection of short fiction, "Encyclopedia of the Dead," for American publication. The title story, a dream-allegory much in the spirit of Jorge Borges' fiction, is a first-person narrative by a Yugoslavian woman who discovers in a library an encyclopedia recording in infinite detail the lives of ordinary, otherwise unrecorded people. Here she reads the history of her father's life and discovers that in the *Encyclopedia of the Dead*, "history is the totality of the human condition, the entirety of ephemeral events. Because of this, every action, every thought, every breath, every peak elevation marked in the land register, every shovel scooping mud, every motion that went into clearing bricks from the ruins is noted."

WORKS IN ENGLISH TRANSLATION: *Garden, Ashes* was translated into English by William J. Hannaher in 1975, and *A Tomb for Boris Davidovich* was translated by

Duska Mikic-Mitchell in 1978. The story "The Encyclopedia of the Dead," in Ammiel Alcalay's translation, was published in the *New Yorker,* July 12, 1982.

ABOUT: Lukić, S. Contemporary Yugoslav Literature, 1972. *Periodicals*—Nation September 16, 1978; World Literature Today Summer 1977; Winter 1977; Autumn 1979.

FLETCHER KNEBEL

*KNEBEL, FLETCHER (October 1, 1911–), American journalist and novelist, writes: "Writers who remember vivid details of their childhood arouse my envy. Fred can recall his father's exact words when he rescued three-year-old Freddie from an overpowering wave at the seashore. Hannah's abundant recollection includes the precise fragrance of Aunt Clara's bosom, Uncle Harry's breath or Cousin Ed's dachshund. How come? Did they keep diaries, interview the combatants or inherit super memories and life-long kinesthetic imprints?

"Not me. Snatches of life before high school materialize in my memory like maimed survivors of some disaster stumbling out of smoke-shrouded debris. High school is clearer, a kind of unpleasant blur. From college I can remember distinct events, sounds and faces, but I suspect that all of them have been warped by that gift for embellishment and self-deception which I share with many of my fellow human beings. In short, I trust very little of what I recall of my first twenty years and place only moderate faith in the images of anything that occurred before this morning.

"I retain four strong impressions of childhood. First is the embarrassment I felt for being penalized by such outdated parents. My face flamed like a torch whenever I had to accompany such stodgy old-fashioned people in the presence of my peers. I used to walk several steps ahead or behind these naive unsophisticated specimens for fear someone would suspect us of a blood relationship.

"My second enduring impression is that a heavy pall of religiosity covered our home and those of our kinfolk. My father was a YMCA secretary, my mother the offspring of fundamentalist parents and they managed to saturate my childhood with more prayer and worship that I could accommodate. Up for membership in the Presbyterian Church at age fourteen, I was asked by a pre-induction examiner: "Do you believe in the divinity of Jesus Christ?" I snapped out a "no," thus flunking the theological loyalty test. I hoped this would spare me from initiation into the congregation, but to my dismay the elders winked at this heresy and took me in anyway. I do recall walking home that Sunday with my father, a tolerant sort. He said that I would come to embrace the concepts of God and divinity as matters of faith after I had lived and learned. I replied that the great question of God's existence or non-existence was wrapped in mystery and that no one on earth had a clue to the eternal truths, however loudly they might claim to the contrary. I have never varied that boyhood opinion over the decades. I'm just as much an agnostic now as then. Sorry, Pop.

"The third impression is of hedges, trees, long lawns and quiet avenues: suburbia. I lived only briefly in a city while growing up, never on a farm. Although born way back in 1911, my boyhood was shaped by the suburbs of New York, Chicago and Cleveland. In that sense, I'm a prototypical white middle-class product of the twentieth century, fashioned by the suburbs from which I took my ethics and my prejudices. I trace my life-long feeling of rootlessness to suburban living, for these verdant fringes of the cities are in essence Noplaceville. They lack the firm identity of towns or city neighborhoods. On the other hand, they are safe places to grow up in. I have very few fears, a boon for which I credit the security of suburban life as well as the security our family afforded.

"That's my fourth major impression from childhood, the sense of security with which my parents enveloped me. My father was a Texan, an open breezy, hearty self-made, self-educated

°kə nä´bul

jovial man despite his God-fearing ways. My mother, once an expansive beauty, became a cramped little soul who ran a spotless household and spent her latter days in psychic torment. In today's terms I'd guess that she was a creative, loving person who longed for independence and self-expression, yet was condemned to a woman's narrow role in the shadow of a highly successful, popular and dominating husband. Whatever their personal traits and problems, my parents never left me in doubt as to their love and support. The youngest by nine years of three boys, I was the lucky one. By the time I came along, my parents had jettisoned their theories of child-rearing and let me grow up with a minimum of supervision. I benefited by a nice mix of love, support, encouragement, trust and freedom.

"If my recollection of childhood scenes is hazy, not so my memory of my introduction to the lure of the written word. When I was a junior in high school my brother was a divinity student at Union Theological Seminary. Since he, a varsity swimmer and football player, had been my hero for years, I always did as he suggested. On his visits home, he brought me books to expand the mind. I read them all and fell in love with H. L. Mencken, the Baltimore sage and wordsmith, America's iconoclast of the twenties. I started writing at once, vowing to learn to handle the language as handsomely as Mencken did. Years later, as a newspaperman, I got to know Mencken quite well, covering several political conventions with him, drinking beer at his elbow, but never losing my admiration for his mastery of the language.

"I do not delude myself today about my talents. After thirty years as a journalist and twenty as a writer of fiction, I regard myself as a journalistic novelist, not a literary one. I can spin a good story with imagination, clarity, suspense and insight, but I am not a literary man in the sense that Joyce Carol Oates, a fellow resident of Princeton, is a literary woman or Paul Fussell, another Princeton friend, is a literary man. I enjoy the writing and reading of novels, but my life has many other interests—politics, travel, group psychology, sports, goofing about, films, holistic health and self-awareness exercises. Oh yes, and poker. In fact, I've just finished a novel for Doubleday called *Poker Game*."

Fletcher Knebel provides an accurate estimate of his stature by describing himself as a journalistic, not a literary novelist. A long career in newspaper work, most of it in the mazes of Washington politics, prepared him for the currently popular genre of the political-suspense thriller, where his depiction of behind-the-scenes action and his swift and direct writing style have won him wide readership. Mainly his subjects are government crises—imaginary but not incredible—such as the threat of nuclear war and a military takeover (*Seven Days in May*), the mental breakdown of a President (*Night of Camp David*), or terrorist movements within the United States (*Trespass*).

Twice at least in his writing career Knebel has stirred up the murky waters of Washington bureaucracy. In 1960, a few months after the publication of his and Charles W. Bailey's nonfiction account of the bombing of Hiroshima, *No High Ground,* in which the authors drew on unpublished documents in the archives of the Manhattan Project, the State Department suspended public access to material in its archives, citing specifically a series of newspaper articles on the 1945 Potsdam Conference by Knebel and Bailey in the Des Moines *Register and Tribune.* In 1964, in spite of Knebel's protests to a correspondent from Moscow's *Izvestia* that *Seven Days in May* was "a piece of fiction, pure and simple," the Soviet Ministry of Defense published a Russian translation of the novel with an introduction by Major General A. M. Shevchenko asserting that it was "profoundly realistic and politically timely." The novel was also the subject of a highly successful motion picture in 1964.

Knebel's relatively sheltered middle-class childhood and education (B.A. 1934, Miami University, Oxford, Ohio, with election to Phi Beta Kappa) were followed by early success in journalism even in the depths of the 1930s depression. He worked on newspapers in Coatsville, Pa., Chattanooga, Toledo, and Cleveland from 1934 to 1936, and in 1937 went to Washington as correspondent for the Cleveland *Plain Dealer*. After service as a naval officer in World War II, he joined the staff of Cowles Publications where he wrote for *Look Magazine,* the Des Moines *Register and Tribune,* and the Minneapolis *Star and Tribune* and also wrote a syndicated column, "Potomac Fever."

In 1964 Knebel decided "to shed the bonds of office routine" and "face a new challenge of the written word" by moving to Florida as a full-time independent writer. Producing on average a novel a year, Knebel did not change his professional writing habits. During the mid-1960s, however, he did re-examine and change many of his basic assumptions about American life. As he wrote in a candid article for the *New York Times Magazine* in 1974, "The Greening of Fletcher Knebel," he reversed his thinking on work ("Today I regard compulsive work as I do any other compulsive act—damaging to the psyche"), American technology ("blasphemies against ravaged nature"), and on life itself ("the range of my feelings, long suppressed, astounds me and I'm learning to trust those feelings"). The anti-war protests during the Vietnam campaign, ecology and human potential movements reshaped his thinking, and today he describes his political views as "conservative on finances, liberal on social welfare and human rights, and 'pay-as-you-go' humanitarianism."

In 1965 Knebel married the journalist Laura Bergquist, who died in 1982. From an earlier marriage in 1935 to Amalia Rauppius he has a son and a daughter and four grandchildren.

PRINCIPAL WORKS: *Fiction*—Night of Camp David, 1965; The Zinzin Road, 1966; Vanished, 1968; Trespass, 1969; Dark Horse, 1972; The Bottom Line, 1974; David Sulkin Cares!, 1978; Crossing in Berlin, 1981; Poker Game, 1983; (with Charles W. Bailey) Seven Days in May, 1962; Convention, 1964. *Non-fiction*—(with Charles W. Bailey) No High Ground, 1960.

ABOUT: Contemporary Authors, new revision series 1, 1981; Vinson, J. (ed.) Contemporary Novelists, 1976; Who's Who in America, 1983–84. *Periodicals*—Look, August 25, 1964; New York Times Magazine, September, 15, 1974.

*KOHOUT, PAVEL (July 2, 1928–   ), Czech playwright, poet, screenwriter, translator and theater and film director, was born in Prague and received his education at Charles University. After World War II, he joined the Communist Party and after the Communist takeover in 1948 he became one of the most prominent young intellectuals of the Party. In 1949–50 he was the cultural attaché in Moscow; in 1951–52 he was the editor-in-chief of a popular satirical journal; in 1953–55 editor of the official journal of the Czechoslovak army; and from 1955 to 1957 he worked with the state television. Since the late 1950s he has devoted himself exclusively to writing and occasionally to directing. Politically, Kohout went through a remarkable transformation. An orthodox Communist during the Stalinist era, he turned gradually more liberal, to become in the 1960s one of the leading reformists. During the Prague Spring of 1968 he was an active supporter of Alexander Dubček's concept of "socialism with human face." After the Soviet intervention of 1968, he refused to recant and

fell into disgrace with the authorities. He was prohibited from publishing and his works were removed from libraries. Expelled from the Party, in 1979, while on a trip abroad, he was stripped of Czechoslovak citizenship and forced to live in exile. Since then he has been active in the West primarily as a theater director and makes his home in Vienna where he received the Austrian State Award for European Literature in 1978.

Kohout entered Czech literature in early 1950s as a poet. His poetry, written mainly for the young, was regarded in official circles as model socialist realism, thanks to its one-sided ideological slant and stylistic simplicity. In the mid-1950s, however, during the first phase of the cultural thaw, he became the target of attacks from progressive critics who accused him of primitivism. Partly under the influence of these attacks, Kohout ceased to write poetry and embarked upon a career of a playwright. Prior to 1968 he had written eleven plays, and after his work was prohibited in his native country, he wrote eight additional dramas, primarily for foreign audiences. Since the late 1950s, numerous plays by Kohout have been performed in the West, where he is generally regarded, together with Václav Havel, as the leading Czech contemporary playwright. The Czech-born British dramatist Tom Stoppard paid him whimsical tribute in his play *Dogg's Hamlet, Cahoot's Macbeth*, in which a group of actors in an iron-curtain country perform *Macbeth* in a jabberwocky language, thereby driving the state police inspector mad.

In his native country, Kohout's position in Czech drama was not regarded as highly. Although his popularity with the audiences was considerable, leading theater critics were mostly negatively disposed towards his work. He was accused of technical virtuosity without substance, of effective but superficial treatment of topical problems, and even of commercialism and bad taste. Havel, who was also active as a theater critic in the early 1950s, wrote about Kohout's art: "We feel, figuratively speaking, as if the author were constantly peeping through the hole in the curtain at the audience and then, in response to the expression on our faces, manipulating from the background the destiny of his characters. Kohout does not hesitate to flirt with even the most questionable tastes of the spectator. At the same time, he experiments with the broadest possible scale of devices and with his dramatic exhibitionism creates the impression of trying to prove how rich his play is and with how much skill it has been written."

Kohout was troubled by the lack of response on the part of the intellectual elite. His stated

*kō hout͂, pä´ vel

goal was a dramatic art that would have universal appeal, pleasing "barbers as well as nuclear physicists." Kohout is neither an innovator, nor a creator of memorable characters and conflicts. His forte is an extraordinary understanding of the mechanism of the theater, and his works, when staged by an imaginative director, are usually an exciting experience. Kohout does not have a uniform style. He is an unabashed eclectic, using as his models such disparate authors as Chekhov, Pirandello, Brecht, Wilder, Beckett, and Pinter.

Kohout wrote his first play, *Dobrá píseň* (Good Song), as early as 1952. Very much like his poetry of this period, the play is burdened with socialist realism. It is a moralistic piece written under the influence of Kohout's wife's infidelity. His second period commenced with *Zářijové noci* (September Nights, 1956) and *Sbohem, smutku* (Goodbye, Sadness, 1957). These two plays were written under the influence of the post-Stalinist ideological crisis during which Kohout, like so many other of his contemporaries, suddenly realized the magnitude of the structural conflicts in Communist society. The two plays are set in a military milieu. "September Nights" is the story of a political officer who causes the demoralization of his regiment. The finger is pointed not at the man himself, however, but at the system that has promoted an individual to an unsuitable position because the criteria were not based on qualifications but on political considerations. "Goodbye, Sadness" aims also to deglamorize the army that occupied a privileged position in the official mythology. The most important play of this period was *Taková láska* (Such Love, 1958), which brought Kohout fame both at home and abroad. Using a deliberately melodramatic motif—an amorous triangle that ends with the suicide of a young girl who is betrayed by her lover—Kohout asserts the right of the individual to search for personal happiness. Another theme is the question of collective guilt on the part of a society that was indirectly implicated in the girl's death. The play was a radical departure from the socialist-realist tradition which upheld the sacrifice of the individual for the general interest. The social value of the young girl is admittedly small, yet the play virtually idealizes her romantic destiny, by implication rebelling against the two-dimensional rational world view into which Marxism degenerated after World War II, and against the cynicism and cruelty of the Stalinist era. Kohout also broke radically from the established structural norms. "Such Love" uses anti-illusionary techniques, reconstructing events in the form of a make-believe trial which takes place after the young woman's death, but she herself participates in the trial as one of the accused (and finally the only acquitted one).

In *Třetí sestra* (The Third Sister, 1960) Kohout attempted to create a microcosm of contemporary society by depicting the destinies of three daughters of a prostitute. The dead mother, who is made in the play a victim of the pre-war social order, begot each girl with a different man. The considerable differences in the ages of the sisters—seventeen, twenty-one, and thirty-four—are used by Kohout for the purpose of examining their different psychological makeups and political attitudes. The herione of the play is the "third," the eldest sister whose idealism contrasts with the self-centered attitude of the next eldest sister, and the frivolous naiveté of the youngest one. The play is developed by means of an elaborate, Brechtian apparatus, with its action, based on the belated search of the three girls for the anonymous fathers, resulting in numerous tragicomic situations.

In the early 1960s, Kohout became gradually overshadowed by a new generation of playwrights. After a very unsuccessful modern morality, *Říkali mi soudruhu* (They Called Me Comrade, 1961), in which he dealt with the moral disintegration of a once valuable man, he limited himself to stage adaptations of several novels, Jules Verne's *Around the World in Eighty Days* (1962), Karel Čapek's *Válka s mloky* (War with the Newts, 1963), and Jaroslav Hašek's *Debrý voják Svejk* (Good Soldier Švejk, 1963). These adaptations are among the best examples of Kohout's ingenuity in the creation of unexpected stage-effects. In 1967, one year before the Soviet intervention, Kohout made a comeback with *August August, august* (August August, the Clown), which was perhaps his most felicitous realization of his idea of a theater with a universal appeal. The play has several layers which can be appreciated by various audiences. The bulk of it is actually a sort of a circus show that features largely independent clownish routines. However, the fate of the protagonist, a clown named August, raises the show to a higher, metaphoric level. August is a quixotic individual who has a noble dream of becoming, at least for one day, an animal trainer. This ambition is skillfully used by the manager of the circus for the manipulation and exploitation of the clown until he is torn to pieces by wild beasts for the purpose of creating a sensational incident. The play has obvious political implications, denouncing the exploitative power of totalitarian regimes. It can be easily viewed, however, as a universal parable on the perennial conflict between the poor and the powerful, the idealists and the materialists.

After 1968, when Kohout's work was banned

in Czechoslovakia, he wrote several plays intended entirely for foreign audiences. They include the trilogy of one-acters titled collectively *Život v tichém domě* (A Life in a Quiet House): *Válka na třetím poschodí* (War on the Third Floor, 1970); *Pech pod střechou* (Bad Luck Under the Roof, 1973); and *Požar v suterénu* (Fire in the Basement, 1973). Each play has a different set of characters, yet they are linked thematically as well as stylistically and feature Kafkaesque situations that are developed in a manner of the theater of the absurd.

The most successful post-1968 work of Kohout is his full-length drama *Ubohý* (*Poor Murderer,* 1974). After its première in Vienna it was performed in a large number of West European cities. In 1976 it had a brief Broadway production. The play is derived from a short story by Leonid Andreyev but developed with the structural complexity typical of Kohout's earlier works. The action is set in a mental asylum in Russia at the turn of the century. A young actor, Kershentsev, has been committed to the asylum because of his *idée fixe* that he murdered his fellow actor and friend during the performance of *Hamlet.* Although he indeed had intended to commit the murder out of jealousy, in reality he collapsed just before the planned act. Nevertheless, he continues to believe that his friend is dead. The play consists of several intersecting time levels, flashbacks, and flashbacks-within-flashbacks as well as play-within-plays, that lead to a surprising finale. Rather than a study of insanity, *Poor Murderer* is a dazzling virtuoso piece whose success depends largely on the director's ability to unify its various levels and upon the acting skill of the protagonist. Another of Kohout's full-length dramas, *Ruleta* (Roulette, 1973), also an adaptation of Andreyev, is much less successful.

With the exception of stories for children, written in the late 1940s, most of Kohout's prose originated after 1968, and it contains either directly or indirectly political implications. Kohout lacks the verbal artistry of the most prominent contemporary Czech writers, and his ability to develop characters is also limited. Nevertheless, his narrative pieces are well structured and are hardly ever devoid of interest. He is relatively most successful when dealing with documentary or semi-documentary material. *Z deníku kontrarevolucionáře* (From the Diary of a Counterrevolutionary, 1969) is perhaps his most important work. It is a stylized autobiography that is developed in three separate narrative lines in which the author brings to light events and characters of the period from 1944 through 1968. The narrative includes some intimate situations, but by far the most interesting parts are the descriptions of historical events and Kohout's reaction to them. As a confession of a man who underwent a transformation from a hard-line Stalinist to a liberal reformist, the work is of considerable value, although it falls somewhat short of providing insight into the innermost psychological processes of the author. *Bílá kniha* (The White Book, 1970) is a parable on the ill-fated Prague Spring. Its central character, Adam Juráček (an obvious anagram on Alexander Dubček) discovers how to defy Newton's law of gravity. He levitates at will, and his proving that the impossible can be achieved totally befuddles the fossilized society that surrounds him. Written in a similar vein is *Nápady svaté Kláry* (The Ideas of Santa Klara, 1982) which is a satire on the narrow-minded rationalism of Communist society. *Katyně* (The Hangwoman, 1978) is a bizarre Orwellian story about a young girl who was chosen to become the world's first female executioner. Written in black humor, the novel contains some brilliantly repulsive passages. Especially effective are the painstakingly detailed descriptions of various methods of executions, and eyewitness accounts of famous executions in world history, that are skillfully incorporated into the narrative.

WORKS IN ENGLISH TRANSLATION: *From The Diary of a Counter Revolutionary,* Kohout's autobiography, was published in a German translation in 1969 and in an English translation from the original Czech by George Theimer in 1972. *The White Book,* with its long subtitle *Adam Juracek, Professor of Drawing and Physical Education at the Pedagogical Institute in K. vs. Sir Isaac Newton, Professor of Physics at the University of Cambridge,* was also first translated into German in 1970, with an English translation by Alex Page in 1977. *Katyne,* published in German in 1978, appeared in English as *The Hangwoman,* translated by Kaca Polackova-Henley in 1981. The play *Poor Murderer,* produced in New York in 1976, was published in 1975 in a translation by Herbert Berghof and Laurence Luckinbill, who played the leading role in the Broadway production.

ABOUT: Contemporary Authors, new revision series 3, 1981; French, A. Czech Writers and Politics 1945–1969, 1982; Goetz-Stankiewicz, M. The Silenced Theatre, 1980; Trensky, P. I. Czech Drama Since World War II, 1978. *Periodicals*—Encounter February 1984; Modern Drama September 1977; New York Times Book Review August 7, 1977; World Literature Today Spring and Autumn 1978, Summer 1979.

*KONRAD, GYÖRGY (April 2, 1933–),
Hungarian Jewish novelist and sociologist, was
born in Debrecen. His father, the owner of a
farm machinery shop, was able to provide a
comfortable living for his family during the hard
times of the 1930s. Konrád began his studies at
the elementary school of the renowned Debrecen Reformed College. The family's life took a
tragic turn in 1944 when the Germans occupied
Hungary and his parents were arrested. Fearing
that he and his sister would become victims of
the mass deportations going on in the region,
Konrád decided to find refuge with an aunt in
Budapest. Since Jews were forbidden to travel
by train, he took the money his father had hidden and bribed the local police to give them
passes to Budapest: "I was only eleven years old,"
Konrád says of this episode, "but I was already
an adult." The day after they left Debrecen,
June 6th, all Jews were deported, first to a ghetto
and then to Auschwitz, where all the women and
children perished, the men having already been
dispatched to the Ukrainian front as laborers.

GYÖRGY KONRAD

Konrád has spoken of the dangers he faced in
Budapest. During the Russian siege of the capital that winter, he experienced all the hardships
of war, the hunger and the constant threat of
death. Jews were packed twenty to thirty to a
room in apartment houses supposedly protected
by foreign embassies. He saw "a mountain of cadavers reaching up to the second floor" in the
courtyard of a ghetto hospital; "Hungarian Nazis
had just gone through the hospital with their machine guns." He faced death himself when Hungarian Nazis rounded him up with other
children to take them to banks of the Danube to
be shot; inexplicably, the officer in charge ordered them to be taken elsewhere at the last
minute. After Hungary's liberation in February
1945, not wanting to burden their aunt further,
Konrád and his sister returned to Debrecen to
live with an uncle, who was awaiting his family's
return: "After midnight, when he thought I was
asleep, he would smoke and he would weep, but
in a very disciplined way, so as not to wake me.
The sound of those masculine sobs coming from
a very strong man made a very strong impression on me." He enrolled at the Madách Gymnasium in Budapest in 1947 and graduated in 1951.
He then began advanced studies at the Lenin Institute, but transferred to the Loránd Eötvös
University; he published literary studies while a
student and completed a degree as a teacher of
literature in 1956.

Konrád's apprehensions about the course of
historical events in Hungary developed early. In
Debrecen, he had observed the disastrous political and social consequences of fascism and the
complex problems attending the establishment

of a new government. In Budapest, having
formed some ideas about the political situation
and the conflicting factions, he was, at fifteen,
"expelled from a youth organization for political
reasons: then came 1953, the thaw: I participated in the reform movement along with other
university students." He was a member of the
circle of György Lukács' students for a time before 1956. In the 1956 uprising, he writes, "I
even had a submachine gun which I never fired,
though it was there in my hand."

Konrád joined the faculty of the general gymnasium in Csepel, an industrial district on an island, in 1956. He joined the editorial staff of
Életképek (Life Scenes), but the publication
never appeared. After a long period of unemployment, in 1959 he became a caseworker for
juveniles and accepted a secondary position preparing editions of Tolstoy and Balzac for Magyar Helikon. From 1965 on he was a sociologist
at the Institute for Research and Planning for
City-Building and also worked for several years
at the Academy's Institute for Literary Scholarship. With Iván Szelényi, Konrád published a
book in 1969, Az új lakótelepek szociológiai
problémák (Sociological Problems in the New
Housing Development) and completed a longer
work in 1973, Településszerkezet—
társadalomszerkezet (Living Habitation—Social
Habitation), which was not published, as well as
essays in Valóság (Reality) that stirred wide interest with their proposals for reform.

In 1973, Konrád had his first collision with a
political system on guard against samizdat literature. In May, political police, thinking he had
smuggled a manuscript copy of Miklós Harasz-

°kōn´ rät, dyûŕ dē

ti's *Darabbér* (Piecework) out of the country, searched his apartment, seized his journal notes in the belief that they had found incriminating evidence, and held him under legal warning. He lost his position, and a publisher rejected his second novel, *A városalapító* (*The City Builder*), only to reconsider the decision later. Konrád has not held any position in Hungary since 1974, managing to live off royalties from works published abroad. He soon had another, even more serious run-in with authorities, which attracted considerable international attention. He had settled with Szelényi in a village about twenty-five kilometers from Budapest to write *Az értelmiség út ja az osztályhatalomhoz* (*The Intellectuals on the Road to Class Power*). Three weeks after its completion, the two authors were detained by the investigative section of the political police. Confiscating a large part of the manuscript, the police tried and failed to uncover any evidence of its circulation underground. The ensuing months were very difficult for them. Both authors were given the right to emigrate, which Szelényi exercised, eventually becoming a professor in Adelaide, Australia. Konrád remained in Hungary, working on his third novel, *A cinkos* (*The Loser*). When restriction on his travel was lifted, he accepted an invitation from the Exchange Board of the German Academy, West Berlin. Issued a passport granting him permission to return to Hungary, he traveled extensively in America and Europe, continued working on *The Loser,* and returned to Hungary after a year. Still a frequent visitor to the West, he always returns to his homeland, to maintain his professional integrity: "If he isn't forced to it, a writer should not emigrate, should not turn away from the risks of his profession. He must accept those risks and live with them; he must be free wherever he finds himself. After all, our freedom is not guaranteed by external conditions, by institutions. It exists first of all within ourselves." His view of literature further illuminates his commitment: "There are systems of morality that divide humanity into groups, approving the values of one group and rejecting those of others. Good literature never does this; it sticks up for humankind as well as for the individual human being. It voices, in other words, the morality of understanding."

In Konrád's first novel, *A látogató* (*The Case Worker,* 1968), a sensitive social worker in Budapest recounts his activities during a typical day as he tries to fulfill the needs of alcoholics, the indigent elderly, and abandoned and abused children, lunatics, every kind of human wreck. Based on Konrád's experiences, the novel "was born out of the feeling that I owe these people something." The lack of money and housing and the built-in shortcomings of the welfare bureaucracy itself prevent the case worker, named "T," from meeting the most basic requirements of his desperate clients. Frustrated and depressed, he becomes unmoved by the human detritus appealing daily for assistance. He describes his functions: "Actually, what I do amounts to nothing. I regulate the traffic of suffering, sending it this way and that, passing on the loads that pile on me to institutions or private citizens. But for the most part I wait and try to stop others from doing anything." The novel consists of descriptions, reports of scenes and situations, and frequent shifts in action. Its most developed episode involves Ferike Bandula, a pathetic five-year-old idiot whose parents have committed suicide; in a pure fantasy, the case worker relinquishes everything in order to assume total care of "this being who guzzles, pisses, and fiddles with himself." At the close of the novel, however, the protagonist holds out his arms almost Christlike toward human wreckage, saying "let all those come who want to; one of us will talk, the other will listen; at least we shall be together."

Though attacked in Hungary for its pessimism and for not allowing the "new society" the time to develop the modes to provide for its needy, the novel was widely praised for its realism and fresh narrative technique. It was favorably received in the United States. The critic for the *New York Review of Books* objected to the "monotony" caused by "violent, remorseless batterings of the feelings" and the "rhetorical seizures which spatter the reader with a hundred hot adjectives in a few sentences"; at the same time, he found "memorable" its "evoking of a 'case,' the brilliant, economical creation of a character in a trap." Writing in the *New York Times,* Irving Howe called it "a brilliant first novel" with which Konrád "strides to the forefront of contemporary European literature," gaining "its power from Konrád's gift for the vignette, the suddenly snapped picture, as if taken through a slightly over-focused camera."

His next novel, *A városalapító* (*The City Builder,* 1977), tells the story of a disillusioned middle-aged architect who presents the major developments of his life and four generations of his family's history in a series of ten interior monologues, in which past and present are interwoven through poetic principles of association and given direction by an essayistic structure, a technique intended by the author to extend the boundaries of the novel. Decades of Hungary's brutal history flash before the reader as the architect ruminates in the confines of the unnamed city he has helped to build. The architect, now disenchanted, concludes that socialism "is what we live in; it is what was and is—not a goal, a disaster, an ideal, a law, or an aberration, but an East European present tense, a neatly proportioned order, an unfolding drama, the power play of interests, endowments, self-delusions and self-exposures, trials and failures. . . . We don't know it but we lived it. We programmed a system and it programmed us."

In Hungary, Vilmos Faragó dismissed the architect's outlook as that of "a hopelessly bourgeois intellectual" who sees in Hungary's recent history only a change in course and not the class war that actually took place. The reviewer for the *Times Literary Supplement* considered the text "thin," and "the fabric so arbitrary that aphorismic platitudes rip through the surface." Susan Lardner, in the *New Yorker,* stated: "What held my attention through that first reading, arduous and intermittent though it was, was the Elizabethan extravagance of Konrád's style"; and American readers, she maintained, will find the novel's "most exotic aspect in the combination of a lavish metaphorical style with the structural forms and devices of classical rhetoric." Jascha Kessler, writing in the *New York Times Book Review,* claimed that Konrád perceives that the "intolerable evil inherent in our defective human condition" is what "spurs the revolutionist, and infuriates the utopian planner." Kessler viewed the architect's ruminations as "essentially an outcry against the hypocrisy and murderous careerism of state bureaucrats who live under terror from above, against the absurdities of utopian dictatorship and the utterly immoral pretension of speaking in the name of the people."

According to Konrád, his latest novel, *A cinkos* (*The Loser,* 1982), still unpublished in Hungary, expresses, in general, "the process by which people arrive at answers to questions of basic import, the ways in which they acquire practical wisdom." The hero, "who, unlike myself, has passed the severest tests of life" is, he says, "an independent Eastern European intellectual," a fifty-five-year-old official who is in a psychiatric hospital. This grandson of a celebrated Jewish merchant and scholar and son of a liberal land developer recollects the historical upheavals in Hungary from the nineteenth century through the aftermath of the 1956 uprising. He himself fights the fascists, serves in a labor battalion, and, captured by the Russians, is indoctrinated by them to become an agent in Hungary; there he participates in the Communist takeover in 1948–49, the 1956 uprising (the most violent episode in the novel), and then joins the dissident community. His involvement in the fate of his people is totally disastrous. For him, Communism had once been full of hope, "a metaphysical future, a second creation, the work of man replacing

God, the axis of all known human values—the thing we could accomplish together, . . . an open alternative to familiar oppression." Eventually, however, he abandons all the roles the system had seduced him to play; "the man of action," "the minutiae-loving pragmatist," and "the frivolous dissenter, too, who plays his well-practiced games with his old friends, the ministers." "A former Communist, I became," he avers, "an antipolitician. I am no longer interested in power, nor in counterpower . . . I was as ignorant about what I was selling as the man who hawks surprise bags at a fair—but at least he knows what he stuffed in the bag," and now "I am glad I am no longer a soldier, an activist, a political prisoner, a minister, a social scientist, or a dissident leader who proudly declares in Budapest what he would be tired of repeating in Vienna."

In his review for the *New York Times Book Review,* Richard Sennett found that, like Proust, Konrád employs remembrance, instead of external event, to build narrative details, but that the ingredients of his memories are different; instead of Proust's "dinner parties, shaded paths near the sea, longing and regret," Konrád's remembrances are of "prisons, psychiatric hospitals, fear and remorse." And yet, in Sennett's view, "it is the secret of Mr. Konrád's art that we experience these horrors, if not with Proustian pleasure, at least with the same compulsive interest." Sennett praised Konrad's "fusion of political vision and modernist technique" for producing "prose rich in texture and forceful in effect" and claimed that this work and that of other Eastern European writers affirm that the great time of literary experimentation introduced by Proust, Joyce, T. S. Eliot, and Gertrude Stein and seen as nearing its end is actually being cultivated in Eastern Europe "where literary modernism is officially forbidden or strongly disapproved."

Like *The Loser,* two of Konrád's major works of non-fiction have not been published in Hungary. *The Intellectuals on the Road to Class Power,* written with Szelényi, presents a theory of East European social structure that attempts to explain more adequately than Marxist ideology can the nature of "the new class oppression" present in those countries. Finding the proletariat the most oppressed economically and politically and the intelligentsia rising from the bureaucracy the dominant force, the authors examine the evolution of this new class of leaders in the light of their place in the social strata throughout history, in "market economies, under state monopoly, and in relation to rational distribution." Its reception was mixed. One critic found the writing verging on "opacity" at times and excessively dependent on the Hungarian experience but judged it "an elegantly argued thesis that has stood the first short test of time"; another believed its major weakness to lie in devoting too much attention to a secondary thesis, the history and significance of the rational distribution of resources. The reviewer for the *Library Journal,* however, praised it as "a provocative and possibly landmark book" for scholarly debate, especially "if it opens up questions of the role of intellectuals as a class in both East and West." *Antipolitics,* a series of essays, throws light on the political situation in Eastern Europe so inextricable from the East-West conflict and Soviet influence, especially Hungary, Poland, and Czechoslovakia, which Konrád views as a sub-bloc. Tracing the origin of the problems of the Yalta agreements—"What a dirty trick that was!" he says—and fearing the annihilation of the world, Konrád believes his part of the world can help reduce the danger by working toward the removal of power from the state and the creation among individuals of a sense of their capacity to influence events "through networks of friends" and to broaden spheres of their freedom for action. He makes a passionate plea for interaction among peoples rather than governments. Walter Goodman, in the *New York Times,* felt that "this deeply felt, lucidly written book should help Western intellectuals to break out of their own ideological categories and think more about real possibilities and real human beings."

Konrád was awarded the Herder Prize by the University of Vienna in 1984, and honored by the New York Institute of Humanities, the executive board of PEN American Center, and the New York Public Library in May 1984, on the eve of the publication of *The Loser.* He is working on a novel about an elderly couple living in a village.

WORKS IN ENGLISH TRANSLATION: Konrád's major writings have all had English translations. His novels were translated by Paul Aston—*The Case Worker,* 1974; and Ivan Sanders—The *City Builder,* 1977, and *The Loser,* 1982. Ivan Szelényi translated *The Intellectuals on the Road to Class Power,* 1979. *Antipolitics* was published in English in 1984.

ABOUT: Contemporary Authors 85–88, 1980; Contemporary Literary Criticism 4, 1975; New Republic February 14, 1983; New York Review of Books March 9, 1978; New York Times Book Review January 22, 1978; September 26, 1982; June 10, 1984; Times Literary Supplement January 31, 1975; October 14, 1983; World Literature Today 57, Summer 1983.

*KOPELEV, LEV (April 9, 1912–   ), Russian memoirist, essayist, and literary historian, writes (in Russian): "For as long as I can remember, political events and passions intruded into my life. I remember adults talking about war. We were living in a village near Kiev; we had company: the chief forester, the priest, the doctor. They spoke about the Germans and Austrians, the French and English; they argued, recounted, laughed; the ladies oohed and aahed, and Mother made me recite or sing: 'The German tsar is writing, writing, writing, he's writing to the Russian tsar, I will conquer all of Russia, I'll come live in your Moscow.' That song was taught to me by my nanny—Mother called her the 'bonne.' I shouted out this part, knowing that the adults liked it: 'Don't you worry, our Russian tsar, we won't give up Russia!' From nanny and pictures in magazines I knew that the Germans were fat 'sausage-makers,' in black spiked helmets, mean, cowardly, and stupid and that our brave, wise, and kind soldiers would soon 'chase them all the way back to Berlin.'

"That winter everyone kept saying that the Bolsheviks were coming, that they were bandits, looters, godless, that Lenin and Trotsky had sold Russia to the Germans. But the Germans came and it turned out that they were for the tsar, not the Bolsheviks, and their helmets were nothing like the ones in the pictures. Then I found out that they were honest, kind, strong, and neat. My new bonne, a German whom my mother called 'governess,' tried very hard to train my brother and me to be neat.

"After the Germans came the Petlurovtsy—the 'yellow-blues'—then the next winter, the Bolsheviks. In the spring, everyone was waiting for the whites. But when they came, they had a pogrom. We began to fear them, too. Power changed frequently in Kiev, and the flags, the wall posters, and the soldiers' uniforms kept changing. . . . With every change there was cannon and machine-gun fire. If the shooting came too close, my brother and I were taken into the cellar or the bathroom that had no windows. And each time there were fears: we were afraid of searches by the Cheka, afraid of the pogroms, of robbery, and executions.

"At school I became a Young Pioneer. I considered myself a Marxist-Leninist; for some time I was attracted by the slogans of the 'left opposition,' considered Trotsky Lenin's worthiest successor, helped print and distribute Trotskyite leaflets. I spent time in jail (ten days in April 1929) and attended several illegal secret meetings. But a year later I believed passionately in the necessity of 'great socialist construction,' proclaimed by Stalin; I believed that only accelerated industrialization and the immediate

°kō´ pel ev

LEV KOPELEV

unification of all peasants into large, rational collectives could save Russia from a world crisis and its multitude of imperialistic enemies, threatening it from the West and Far East. During 1930–34 I worked at a large factory in Kharkov manufacturing trains, tanks, and heavy tractors; I worked on the assembly line for a short time and on the factory newspaper for a long time. As a reporter, writer, and editor of propaganda leaflets, I participated in the grain hoarding of 1932–33; that is, in that senseless, cruel robbery of the peasants that led to mass starvation in the Ukraine.

"In 1930, barely eighteen, I married. Nadya Kolchinskaya was a true, fearless friend to me in the most difficult years (in 1956 we ceased being man and wife, but we remained friends). In 1933–34 we both entered Kharkov University, she to major in chemistry, I in philosophy. In 1935 we moved to Moscow with my parents and younger brother, also a student. She continued her studies at Moscow University, while I entered the Institute of Foreign Languages to study German. In 1938–41 I was a graduate student and instructor at the Institute of the History of Philosophy and Literature and defended my dissertation on 'Schiller's Dramaturgy and the Problems of the Revolution of 1789–93.' Nadya worked as a chemical engineer. We lived with my parents and brother in one room, which was eighteen square yards. In 1937 Maya, our first daughter, was born; Lena came in 1939, and we continued living together.

"The horrible famine of 1933 and the frenzied mass terror of 1936–38 elicited not only fear, but doubts in myself and my friends: was this the way to be living? Are the Party's policies really right, just, and wise? However, even ater the most tormenting doubts, we firmly believed 'my country right or wrong,' and that the Stalin regime with all its mistakes and flaws was still the lesser evil compared to Nazism or fascism. We continued to believe that despite the most grievous error and evil deeds—such as the partition of Poland, the union with Hitler, the attack on Finland—in the final analysis, we were building socialism and therefore helping our people and all humanity to find the road to eternal peace and eternal happiness.

"That was why on June 22, 1941, in the very first hour that I heard about the invasion by the German Army, I rushed to volunteer (I was exempt from military service because of my health and my work as a teacher). From August 1941 I was at the front, soon promoted to officer; 'propagandist among the enemy ranks,' I interrogated prisoners and defectors, wrote leaflets, agitated among German soldiers with the help of foxhole loudspeakers, and taught at the frontline school for POWs who agreed to become our propagandists or scouts. By 1945 I was a major. My attempts to mitigate the marauding and violence perpetrated by some of our men in East Prussia led to the charge: 'Propagandized bourgeois humanism and pity for the enemy . . . saved Germans and their property . . . calumniated the Soviet command.' In April 1945 I was arrested. The investigation lasted a long time; it was transferred to Moscow since many of my friends—both from the army and from Moscow—had written to the government on my behalf. The first trial in Moscow in December 1946 acquitted me, and I spent two months at liberty. But then the acquittal was overturned (my lawyer said that it was on Stalin's personal order), and in the fall of 1947 I was sentenced to ten years of imprisonment and five years of disenfranchisment.

"I was freed in 1954, but rehabilitated only in the fall of 1956, when I was allowed to live in Moscow once again. During 1957–60 I taught in the editorial department of the Moscow Polygraphical Institute; during 1960–68 I was a senior scientific worker at the Institute of Art History. In those years I wrote articles and books on the history of German literature and theater and also about some American and Czech writers. My books published in Russian include: 'Jarosalv Hacek and Soldier Schweik' (1957); a collection of essays and articles, 'The Heart Is Always on the Left' (1960); 'Goethe's Faust' (1962); 'Expressionist Drama' (1965); and 'Brecht—His Life and Work' (1966).

"In the spring of 1968 I was expelled from the

Party and fired from work because I appeared in the defense of arrested and unfairly convicted writers (Sinyavsky, Daniel, Ginzburg, Galanskov) and also because my article about the threat of 're-Stalinization' was published in an Austrian journal. I was no longer permitted to publish books, all my contracts were nullified. Occasionally, I managed to publish translations of Goethe, Brecht, Böll, sometimes under my own name, usually under a pseudonym. In the 1970s I began publishing articles and books abroad and continued to speak out in defense of unjustly persecuted people, who were beginning to be called 'dissidents' then, and naturally supported the great scientist and friend of humanity, Andrei Sakharov, whom my wife and I have the fortune to consider our friend.

"Therefore in early 1977 our phone was cut off and attempts were made to sever our mail connections with other cities and countries; first I and then my wife were expelled from the Writers' Union, which completely deprived us of any possibility to continue literary work. We received frequent invitations from German friends—the writers Heinrich Böll and Countess Marian Denhoff—and also from PEN of the Free German Republic and the German Academy of Language and Literature, which awarded me the Gundolf Prize in 1979. Each time we replied that we were willing to leave Russia only on the condition that we would be allowed to return. In 1980 Willy Brandt and Egon Bar obtained a promise from the Soviet authorities that we would be allowed to spend one year in the Free German Republic and then to return if we did not become involved in political activity. We accepted the condition and on November 12, 1980, we arrived in Cologne as guests of Heinrich Böll. We refused all interviews and public statements on political issues. But by the decree of the Supreme Soviet of the USSR of January 12, 1981, we were both stripped of Soviet citizenship.

"In May 1981 we became citizens of the Federal Republic of Germany. In the last two years we have spent time in many countries, including two long sojourns in the United States, where our oldest daughter, Maya, lives with her husband, Pavel Litvinov, our grandson Dima, and granddaughter Lara; they are Americans now. In May 1981 Cologne University awarded me an honorary doctorate and in October 1981 the Union of German Book Publishing awarded me their Peace Prize. Wuppertahl University has given me a research position which should lead to the publication of two series of books: 'Russia and Russians in German Literature of the Seventeenth to the Twentieth Centuries' and 'Germany and Germans in Russian Literature of the Seventeenth to the Twentieth Centuries.'"

—trans. Antonina W. Bouis

─────────

When Lev Kopelev visited the United States for the first time in 1981 he was received as a representative of all contemporary Soviet writers and intellectuals in exile. Like many of these, Kopelev's roots are planted so deeply in his Russian heritage that he can never reject his native land completely. Yet as an intellectual, a humanist, and a Jew, Kopelev can survive only in the Western world. He is known in the West for the volumes of his memoirs that have been translated into English, but in West Germany, where he and his wife and collaborator Raisa or Raya Orlova (whom he married in 1956) have lived since November 1980, he is also known as a scholar and literary critic—author of a major study of Russo-German literary relations (*Zwei Epochen Deutsch-Russischer Literatur vezuenhungen,* 1973).

Kopelev had not originally intended to publish his memoirs, preserving them mainly as a record for his children and grandchildren. At the urging of friends outside the Soviet Union, however, especially Ellendea and Carl Proffer, founders of the Russian-language publishing firm of Ardis, in Ann Arbor, Michigan, he published first *To Be Preserved Forever* (with a foreword by Lillian Hellman, who visited the Kopelevs in Moscow in 1966 and 1967), which covers the events of 1945–47—his arrest, trials, and imprisonment. "With his report," Heinrich Böll wrote in the foreword to the British edition, titled *No Jail for Thought,* "Kopelev puts the Soviet Army and the Soviet Union on trial; it is the report of a man accused who becomes the accuser because he has been charged with something that in terms of humanity and every socialist theory is axiomatic: of having spoken out against hatred, revenge, rape and looting." *The Education of a True Believer,* an account of Kopelev's life from 1917 to 1935, followed, and *Ease My Sorrows,* covering his life from 1947 to 1954, completed the trilogy, whose composite title is *One of Us.* The work is a record less of physical suffering than of the humiliating and demoralizing circumstances of life in a Soviet prison camp. Like his fellow prisoner Aleksandr Solzhenitsyn (whom he portrays sympathetically in *Ease My Sorrows* and who himself portrayed Kopelev as the idealistic Rubin in *The First Circle*), Kopelev experienced "a spiritual odyssey" of profound soul-searching only to discover the impossibility of reconciling Soviet "historical necessity" with his own "moral necessity." Distinguishing his memoirs from the many others being published by dissidents now living in the West is his good humor, what Herbert Gold calls "his Russian laughter at absurdity." Candidly self-critical, Kopelev has had, Gold remarks, a "hard-won victory" by becoming "with marvelous irony, just what the secret police had accused him of being—a humanist."

In collaboration with his wife, Kopelev is continuing his record with memoirs of famous people he had known in the USSR—Anna Akhmatova, Nadezda Mandelstam, Kornei Chukovsky, Eugenia Ginzburg, Ilya Ehrenburg, and others. A hearty, friendly, outgoing man, Kopelev has in recent years been active in international cultural affairs in spite of ill health. In September 1981, while a visiting senior fellow at the Russian Institute of Columbia University, he joined with a group of Soviet writers to hold a Moscow Book Fair in Exile at the New York Public Library. He then traveled throughout the United States assisted by a grant from the U.S. International Communication Agency. In 1982 Kopelev held a visiting professorship at Yale University and in 1983 he returned to the United States to urge American publishers not to boycott the annual International Book Fair in Moscow but to attend as a voice of protest. "It is always better to make a demonstration than to be silent," he told them, citing the example of the Solidarity movement in Poland.

WORKS IN ENGLISH TRANSLATION: *To Be Preserved Forever* (published in England as *No Jail for Thought*) was translated by Anthony Austin in 1977. Gary Kern translated *The Education of a True Believer* in 1980, and Antonia W. Bouis translated *Ease My Sorrows* in 1983. Raisa Orlova published her *Memoirs,* in Samuel Cioran's translation, in 1984.

ABOUT: Böll, H. *Foreword to* No Jail for Thought, 1977; Hellman, L. *Foreword to* To Be Preserved Forever, 1977; Who's Who in the Socialist Countries, 1978. *Periodicals*—American Educator Spring 1982; Guardian April 21, 1977; New York Review of Books October 13, 1983; New York Times July 29, 1977; September 8, 1983; New York Times Book Review September 18, 1983; Times (London) June 23,, 1977; Times Literary Supplement July 31, 1981.

KRAMER, HILTON (March 25, 1928–   ), American art critic, essayist, and magazine editor, was born in Gloucester, Massachusetts, to Louis and Tillie (Banks) Kramer. After receiving a B.A. from Syracuse University in 1950, he did postgraduate work in literature and philosophy at Columbia University (1950–51), the New School for Social Research (1950), Harvard University (1951), and the University of Indiana (1951–52).

© Thomas Victor

HILTOM KRAMER

Kramer began his career as an art critic in 1954 when he joined the staff of *Art Digest* magazine as a reviewer. From 1955 to 1961 he was managing editor, then chief editor, of *Arts Magazine,* which under his guidance evolved into one of the more scholarly and evenhanded of the popular art journals, supporting not only the dominant abstract trends but a range of realist artists as well. For a brief period he reviewed art and literature for the *Nation* (1962–63) and the *New Leader* (1964–65), but it was his long association with the *New York Times*—first as art news editor (1965–73) and then as chief art critic (1973–82), succeeding John Canaday— that established Kramer as one of the American art world's most influential commentators. As Lawrence Alloway noted in *Art in America,* "The *Times* critics take on more than an individual status; it is not 'Hilton Kramer says' but 'the Times says.'" In 1982 Kramer left the *Times* to found the *New Criterion,* a journal of conservative artistic and cultural opinion.

Although he is an immensely prolific reviewer and essayist whose interests extend to literature, philosophy, and current affairs as well as art, Kramer has written only one book to date, *The Age of the Avant-Garde: An Art Chronicle of 1956–72,* a selection of more than one hundred short gallery and museum exhibition reviews. Writing in what Roger Shattuck in the *New York Times Book Review,* calls "a flexible and potentially elegant prose," Kramer covers the century from 1855, when Gustave Courbet scandalized the Paris art world by defiantly mounting his own exhibition on the steps of the Exposition Universelle after his rejection by the

Exposition's jurors, to the beginning of wide-spread acceptance of Abstract Expressionism in the mid-1950s, with ventures into the artistic movements of the 1960s and 70s. The general thesis of the later reviews, set forth most clearly in the title essay, is that the avant-garde, which for a century acted as a refreshing and liberating influence in western art, has been absorbed into the very mainstream it challenged, and now functions as a repressive academy, restricting artists to the frantic search for the "new" at any cost.

The Age of the Avant-Garde confirmed Kramer's profound conservatism. In the *New York Review of Books,* James Ackerman noted that Kramer's essays are "consistently informative, acute, and helpful to the reader who wants some preparation for seeing an exhibition," but called him "for better or for worse, an academic art historian of a period that isn't art history." Unlike many of his colleagues who came of age in the 1950s, Kramer has not attached himself to any of the newer artistic movements or dogmas. Instead, he advocates an aesthetic firmly rooted in the tradition of Modernism, which in art can be defined as the line running from Picasso, Matisse, and the early-twentieth-century School of Paris to the Abstract Expressionists (with parallel developments in music and poetry). Those values typical of the best Modernist work—serious intellectual endeavor, persistent refinement of craft, and a sympathetic respect for the art of the past coupled with an authentic desire to revolutionize it—are those Kramer most often champions. David Littlejohn, in the *New Republic,* noted that much of Kramer's work "is an attempt to impress on the public attention the values of neglected artists, past and present—independent traditionalists, for the most part, men and women working in styles distinctly alien to those currently held in the highest regard."

Because of Kramer's great respect for history and tradition, in *The Age of the Avant-Garde* he has little sympathy for post-modern art, much of which he finds "alternately nasty and boring." He has no use for artists like Andy Warhol who ridicule the very possibility of "serious" art. Pop Art, Kramer says, is "a very great disaster" in which "an insidious facetiousness and frivolity could pass muster as an attitude of high endeavor." Similarly, he calls the experiments of the Conceptualists, Minimalists, and Neo-Dadaists of the last two decades "a carnival of rubbish in which artistic merit is no more important than its most cynical and grotesque simulacrum."

These attitudes have not endeared Kramer to more radical artists, especially the members of the contemporary New York avant-garde, whom he consistently refused to support in the pages of the *Times.* Calvin Tomkins, the author of *Off the Wall* (1980), a survey of the New York art scene of the 1960s, accused him of taking "the most advanced art as a personal affront." Kramer has responded to such attacks with acerbic wit, blasting not only what he views as bad art, but also those fellow critics who have in his opinion abrogated their responsibilities. In a December 1966 critical symposium, he described "the foggy glue" that passes for writing on the arts among critics who believe themselves "civic benefactors aiding local institutions."

Roger Shattuck described Kramer's own critical position as follows: "His most consistent and rugged stance is *against manipulation.* Artists should make art. They and everyone else should refrain from interfering directly with the public, the market, and the evolving traditions that permit an interchange. Critics should look long, investigate, inform, and have opinions—but never manipulate. . . . In a market rife with selling techniques Kramer stands for high-minded ideals." The jury of artists for the Sang Prize, awarded to Kramer in 1970 by Knox College in Illinois for excellence in fine arts criticism, wrote in their selection statement: "Mr. Kramer never draws attention to himself, but rather commits himself to shedding light on the topic. . . . He is uncorruptible and beholden to no one."

In leaving his position at the *Times* in April 1982 to edit the *New Criterion,* Kramer sought to establish a new forum, in his opinion long overdue, for scholarly, conservative criticism of the arts. Contributors have included Joseph Epstein, Norman Podhoretz, and Elias Canetti. Kramer's long essay "Postmodern: Art and Culture in the 1980s," in the magazine's first issue (September 1982), defended the values of Modernism against the anti-intellectual (New Left) movements born in the 1960s, whose aim, he claimed, was to "sever the link between high culture and high seriousness." While decrying the *New Criterion's* "philistinism in the defense of modernism," Leon Wieseltier, reviewing the journal in the *New Republic* praised Kramer's "lucidity" and noted that it is "in Kramer's contributions that the main themes of this [neoconservative] analysis of culture are best developed." Stepping outside the arena of art criticism, Kramer has also expressed his concern over what he views as the general intellectual and moral deterioration of our times. In a 1978 *Partisan Review* article he launched an assault on his political opponents, notably Gore Vidal and Garry Wills, who, he asserted, offer "nothing but attacks, and often vicious attacks, on the most elementary fealties of family life."

Kramer continues to be a frequent contributor to the *New York Times* and other periodicals. He has held academic positions at Bennington College, the University of Colorado, and Yale University, where he was a visiting professor at the School of Drama in 1973–74. He lives in Westport, Connecticut with his wife, the former Esta Leslie, whom he married in 1964.

PRINCIPAL WORKS: The Age of the Avant-Garde: An Art Chronicle of 1956–72, 1973; Brancusi, the Sculptor as Photographer, 1979.

ABOUT: Tomkins, C. Off the Wall, 1980; Vidal, G. The Second American Revolution and Other Essays, 1982; Who's Who in America, 1983–84; Who's Who in American Art, 1982. *Periodicals:*—Art in America, September 1981; New Republic, April 1982; New York March 19, 1984; New York Review of Books, February 7, 1974; New York Times, December 11, 1966; April 10, 1970; December 8, 1973; February 16, 1982; New York Times Book Review, January 6, 1974.

JANE KRAMER

KRAMER, JANE (August 7, 1938–), American journalist, is the daughter of Jessica (Shore) Kramer and physician Louis Kramer. She was born in Providence, Rhode Island, graduated Phi Beta Kappa from Vassar in 1959, and took an M.A. from Columbia University in 1961. Her first job as a reporter was with the Columbia neighborhood paper, *The Morningsider,* which she helped found; she then moved downtown in 1962 to write features for the *Village Voice* when that paper's politics were authentically leftist and its purview limited largely to Greenwich Village and its bohemian population.

Kramer's first book, *Off Washington Square: A Reporter Looks at Greenwich Village,* collected twenty-four of her short pieces for the *Voice* on such topics as the true geography of Washington Square Park, the self-described reformism of Ed Koch in his New York assemblyman days, the defense of Little Italy from the depredations of master builder Robert Moses, and the closing of the Bowery's famous Five Spot Club, haunt of jazzmen, poets, and action painters. These pieces, sharp and with a twist of sarcasm, displayed a whimsical detachment not entirely suited to the passionate and partisan *Voice*; in 1963 Kramer joined the *New Yorker*'s repertorial staff, where she has since remained. Under the tutelage of editor William Shawn, who more than anyone has shaped the present *"New Yorker* style," she quickly developed a flexible, smoothly surfaced prose. Most of her earlier work for the magazine was in the form of "profiles," from which she assembled her second, third, and fourth books; more recently she

has written regular reports form Europe. In 1967 she married the anthropologist Vincent Crapanzano; they have a daughter, Aleksandra, who has accompanied Kramer on most of her travels.

Her 1969 biography of the poet Allen Ginsberg, *Allen Ginsberg in America,* was originally published as a three-part series in the *New Yorker.* Not a literary study, the book instead placed Ginsberg, whom she described as "a disciplined artist and a thoroughly educated man," firmly in familial and social context, while making palatable the more unconventional aspects of his career (if not the scabrousness of his verse). Since then the poet and his work, even his homosexuality and his use of drugs, have been completely accepted into the mainstream; but at the time Ginsberg was still a figure of real controversy, retaining something of the air of a *tsaddik,* and Kenneth Rexroth, for one, complained that Kramer's biography had domesticated him. "Just as the Ginsberg of 10 to 15 years ago was a *hallucination publicitaire* of the news weeklies and picture magazines," wrote Rexroth, "so Jane Kramer's Ginsberg is a *New Yorker* Profile. This is a strange animal which resembles the window mannequins in Saks, the movie stars of the silents. . . . This is not really to put down [Kramer's book]. It is unquestionably written with affectionate sympathy and a large half measure of understanding. Perhaps deliberately [the book] is designed to domesticate Ginsberg, to smuggle him in to the glass-table breakfast nook. . . . There is nothing false about Miss Kramer's lovable Ginsberg, there's just a lot more to him than that."

While her husband was doing field work in

Meknes, Morocco, in 1968, Kramer lived with a Moroccan family for several weeks, gathering material for her third book, *Honor to the Bride Like the Pigeon that Guards Its Grain Under the Clove Tree*. In this short, wry tale, Kramer recounted the abduction of thirteen-year-old Khadija, whose virginity is her parents' major negotiable asset. Though Khadija is soon recovered, her virginity has been lost, and, afraid of losing her bride-price as well, the family embarks on an intricate scheme, ultimately successful, to snare a suitable husband. Kramer and Crapanzano appear in the book as the Hughs, Americans unable to comprehend the roundabout methods of local justice. "*Honor to the Bride* is an excellent example of the 'nonfiction novel,'" wrote Martha Duffy in *Time*. "The plot complications are as intricate as an arabesque. They entangle myriad relations, neighbors, judges, seers, and policemen, each sketched with a few vivid strokes, all involved yet laughing at the convoluted action. . . . Beyond its entertainment value, the book offers a remarkable glimpse into the personal lives of Arab multitudes; Arab attitudes toward justice, money, and women become apparent as one microcosm of society applies its energies to [its] dilemma." D. W. Littlefield added in *Library Journal*: "[*Honor to the Bride*] also reveals the grim brutality of the old system in which women were chattels to be sold to husbands who treated them like servants."

After several years reporting from Europe, Kramer returned to the United States. "I wanted—and needed—to look at America again," she wrote, "and it had seemed to me then that a cowboy's camp might be the proper place to start. A cowboy was, somehow, the most 'American' thing I could think of." The product of this desire was *The Last Cowboy*, which was serialized in the *New Yorker* in 1976. While writing it, Kramer spent several week in the Texas Panhandle with Henry Blanton (not his real name), the cowboy of the title, and his family. "Henry, in his own way, was different from the other cowboys," she wrote. "He had settled into his life, but he could not seem to settle for it. He moved in a kind of deep, prideful disappointment. He longed for something to restore him—a lost myth, a hero's West." The skilled foreman of a 90,000-acre cattle ranch whose owner had moved to Eaton Square in London, Blanton took his orders from a college-educated boy who knew nothing of the business and who thought nothing of going back on a private deal with him for a few cows. Blanton's resentful life became for Kramer "a parable of failed promise, and taught me more about America than I had ever hoped or wanted to discover."

In the *New York Review of Books*, Diane Johnson pointed out the advantages of Kramer's dealing with such familiar material in pseudo-fictional fashion. Kramer's non-fiction, she noted, is often indistinguishable in form from fiction; this allows the writer to claim journalistic verity while fashioning an emotionally satisfying narrative. "Hers is the touch of a satirist," Johnson wrote; "her writing, although admirably economical, can seem a bit as if she is working hard to keep powerful dramatizing and shaping impulses under control. *The Last Cowboy* is in fact so like a novel in many ways that it makes you wonder, as people have often wondered before, just why a work is or isn't one. . . . "

Kramer, whose own voice never intrudes obviously into her narratives, admitted in a 1980 interview that she approaches the writing of her profiles as she would a novel. She admired, she said, the novels of George Eliot for "the moral rigor of Eliot's world" and the novelist's concern with "the ethical dimensions of personal and social behavior"—which could be said to be Kramer's subject as well. The *Time* reviewer of *The Last Cowboy* likened Kramer's talent for the "selection of tactful though telling details" to that of Jane Austen.

Of all her books, *Unsettling Europe* showed, according to the critics, the deepest analytic intelligence. The book documented the lives of four families inhabiting a Europe, largely unknown in the United States, composed of vast numbers of migrant workers, refugees, displaced or returning colonials, and others simply out of step with the postwar economic miracles, the Common Market, and American-style consumerism. Kramer wrote of the problems of Yugoslavs forced by the lack of opportunity in their own land into economic exile as workers in Swedish factories; of Algerian *pieds noirs* getting by in an unfriendly Provence village; of formerly wealthy Ugandan Indians expelled by Idi Amin and living hand-to-mouth in London; and of old-line Italian Communists, confusedly watching the now complacent Party being absorbed by the ancient networks of patronage it was founded to combat. "[These Europeans] were unwelcome and unwanted," she wrote, "and merely by being themselves they managed to sabotage the image most other people held of Europe, but it was their labor and their various loyalties which had supported that image in the past, and which support it now—and all certainly have a lot to do with Europe's future."

"Whatever is description, evocation, significant detail, Jane Kramer does superbly," wrote Irving Howe in his review of *Unsettling Europe* for the *New York Times*. Howe did suggest, however, that the very smoothness of her style, her deliberate personal detachment, prevented Kramer from completely coming to grips with the intellectual issues her stories raised. "It is this style or manner that seems finally to limit Jane Kramer's book, and that is really a pity, since it is so good a book one keeps wanting it to be still better. There is a risk in not taking risks." Other reviewers were not so put off by the book's polish. "Kramer's . . . strategy compels us to examine the human consequences of migrations caused by politics or want or history or all these," Thomas Flanagan wrote in the *Nation*. "And she brings to her purpose a cool, and lean, deliberately uninflected style and an unerring sense of the ways in which meaning and significance can be established by the juxtapositions of telling detail." "The Invandrare," one of the segments of *Unsettling Europe*, won Kramer the Front Page Award for best magazine feature in 1977. In 1966 Kramer won an Emmy for her script for the television documentary *This Is Edward Steichen*; in 1968 she was named woman of the year by *Mademoiselle* magazine.

PRINCIPAL WORKS: Off Washington Square: A Reporter Looks at Greenwich Village, 1963; Allen Ginsberg in America, 1969 (U.K. Paterfamilias, 1970); Honor to the Bride Like the Pigeon that Guards Its Grain Under the Clove Tree, 1970; The Last Cowboy; 1978; Unsettling Europe, 1980.

ABOUT: Contemporary Authors 102, 1980. Periodicals—Christian Science Monitor July 17, 1967; Library Journal December 1, 1970; Nation May 31, 1980; New York Review of Books March 23, 1978; August 14, 1980; New York Times May 17, 1969; January 24, 1978; New York Times Book Review May 11, 1969; January 22, 1978; May 18, 1980; Time August 8, 1969; January 4, 1971; January 23, 1978; Village Voice September 4, 1969; Washingotn Post April 1, 1978.

*KROETZ, FRANZ XAVER (February 2, 1946–   ), German playwright, was born in Munich, the son of an official who worked in the Bavarian Treasury Department. Under the influence of his father, Kroetz first attended a business school, but dropped out to attend drama school in Munich in 1961 and later became a student at the Max Reinhardt Seminar in Vienna. Afterwards he engaged in a variety of occupations such as casual laborer, truck driver, nurse, and banana cutter. Today he lives on a farm in Kirchberg near Altenmarkt, Bavaria.

Kroetz's experiences as a drama student proved to be decisive for him as a playwright of Bavarian "Volksstücke" (folk plays). At the age of twenty-two he wrote a stage version of Gon-

FRANZ XAVER KROETZ

charov's *Oblomov* which was produced in 1968, to be followed by a peasant farce, *Hilfe, ich werde geheiratet* (Help, I am Getting Married) which set the tone for his later immersion in dialect and regional became topics. He became one of contemporary Germany's most prolific and vital producers of plebeian plays, mostly written in Bavarian dialect and always dealing with the world of the rural and urban proletariat.

Kroetz's literary models go as far back as Georg Büchner and Gerhart Hauptmann. His immediate predecessors and ideals are the Austrian Odön von Horváth and the Bavarian playwright Marieluise Fleisser who referred to him, shortly before her death, as "one of my sons." Kroetz was also influenced by certain popular aspects of Brecht's work whose message, however, he considered too optimistic. From Horváth and Fleisser, whose renaissance on the German stage occurred parallel with Kroetz's phenomenal stage successes in the early 1970s, he learned, as Heinz Ludwig Arnold writes, the dramatic use of "the discrepancy between what is said and what is meant; lack of language and dullness as areas of dramatic expression; the truthfulness of dramatic figures without speech and perspective; the function of the dialect; the understanding of the masses of suppressed people; the borrowed language of the so-called simpletons."

Kroetz's dramatic debut occurred in the years 1971 and 1972 when he wrote seven plays which, together with two earlier ones—*Wildwechsel* (Deer Crossing, 1968); *Heimarbeit* (Domestic Labor, 1969)—were produced simultaneously. Since then he has become one of the most frequently performed writers on

°krûtz, fränts ksä vär´

the German stage. In his dramatic style he is related to the contemporary playwrights Wolfgang Bauer, Martin Sperr, and the filmmaker Rainer Werner Fassbinder. But, as David J. Ward writes, "Kroetz's consistent use of an almost genuine Bavarian stage dialect, his uncompromising realism based on close observation, and, above all, his extremely laconic scenes give even his early plays a distinctive stamp."

Kroetz uses the classical Aristotelian elements of fear and compassion to dramatize the fate of his speechless, oppressed, and utterly intimidated victims of society. By revealing the origins of oppression, he sets the dramatic structure. His social analysis is derived from close observation rather than from political theory, a quality that gives his plays their freshness and originality and their complete lack of artificial didacticism. Kroetz's language has been compared with the language of naturalism. However, by stylizing and reducing his Bavarian stage dialect to the point of mannerism Kroetz makes it clear that he does not intend to render a photographic mimesis of "true folk scenes" but prefers to alienate an educated, well-read, and mostly urban audience with the sudden intrusion of an underprivileged consciousness that exists parallel to their own.

Kroetz's early plays know only one level of reality: the reality of those who are oppressed and without language and who in turn try to oppress one another. The best example for this muteness out of helplessness is documented in *Wunschkonzert* (Request Performance, 1971), a play without dialogue of a middle-aged woman who recognizes and plays the senselessness of her life to its suicidal conclusion. Similar passion plays of the mute and oppressed are *Männersache* (Men's Business), *Hartnäcking* (Stubborn), *Lieber Fritz* (Dear Fritz), *Stallerhof* (Staller's Farm), and *Geisterbahn* (Horror Show), all written in 1971 and 1972. In *Stallerhof*, the mentally retarded girl Beppi kills her child because her parents, the owners of the Staller farm, disapprove of her relationship with the foreman as being "unnatural" and "antisocial." In *Hartnäcking*, another love relationship is destroyed by the innkeeper parents of a cripple "because he is not a complete man anymore."

Under the influence of Brecht, Kroetz for a while experimented with the so-called "grand form," the traditional social drama. His involvement with the Communist Party (since 1971) also played a role in his choice of themes based on social ideas beginning with the adaption of two dramas by Friedrich Hebbel—*Maria Magdalena*, 1972; *Agnes Bernauer*, 1976. Only two of his own plays, however, *Globales Interesse* (Global Interest, 1972), and *Münchner Kindl* (Munich Lass, 1973) have a clear political message. After the experience with Hebbel which Kroetz did not deem very successful, he again turned to the "small form" with such plays as *Oberösterreich* (Upper Austria, 1972), *Das Nest* (The Nest, 1974), and *Mensch Meier* (Man Meier, 1976/77). As a new development the figures in these plays succeed in taking a stand against the forces of oppression (while the earlier ones remained completely passive). At the 1982 New York performance of *Michis Blut* (Michi's Blood, 1975) and *Request Concert,* the *New York Times* drama critic Frank Rich praised "the work of a playwright whose singular vision cannot be ignored. Mr. Kroetz, a leading figure in Germany's avant garde, is a chronicler of the modern industrial state's lowest, least articulate underclass, and he writes about these people with a spare, if violent, realism that is microscopic in its intimacy." In February 1984, reviewing an off-Broadway production of *Mensch Meier,* Rich described Kroetz's writing as "disconcerting" because it so vividly conveys "the panic of being an anonymous cog 'plugged into the circuit' of the mammoth industrial state." This family drama, while less grim than most of his plays, widens the scope of his indictment of modern society. "The Meiers' dehumanization," Rich wrote, "is attributed not only to their economic circumstances but also to the deadening values imposed by the mass culture of television and rock music." Two other plays by Kroetz have had off-Broadway New York productions: *Journey into Happiness* in 1983, and *Through the Leaves* in 1983 and again in 1984.

Kroetz has received several literary prizes, including the Suhrkamp-Dramatikerstipendium (1970); Ludwig-Thoma-Medaille of the City of Munich (1971); Fontanepreis, Kunstpreis Berlin (1972); Kritikerpreis Berlin (1973); Hannoverscher Dramatikerpreis (1974); Wilhelmine-Lübke-Preis (1975); Dramatikerpreis of the City of Mühlheim (1976).

WORKS IN ENGLISH TRANSLATION: *Farmyards and Four Plays*, 1976, has English versions of Kroetz's plays by Jack Gelber, Michael Roloff, Peter Sanda, and Carl Weber.

ABOUT: Blevins, Richard W. The Emergence of a Political Playwright, 1983; Cassell's Encyclopedia of World Literature, 1973; Columbia Dictionary of Modern European Literature, 1980; Encyclopedia of World Literature in the 20th Century (rev. ed.) II, 1982; Hoffmeister, Donna L. The Theater of Confinement, 1983. *Periodicals*—Modern Drama 4, 1981; New York Times October 7, 1984.

***KUNCEWICZ   (KUNCEWICZOWA),
MARIA** (October 31, 1897–), Polish novelist,
essayist, playwright, and author of children's
books, who writes in Polish and English, sends
the following sketch in English to *World
Authors*: "I was born in 1897 in Samara (now
Kujbyszew, U.S.S.R.) the last child of a Polish
couple, he a high school teacher of mathematics,
she a concert violinist *manquée,* both of them
the progeny of exiled fighters for Polish independence. At the age of three, as my parents settled in Warsaw, I returned to my ancestors'
homeland. Thus my early childhood was spent
in sharing the joys and agonies of reentry into a
paradise lost. Years of acclimatization followed;
I had to unlearn the classic Polish and its romantic inflections, a language my parents spoke. Instead, I learned the capital city's highbrow slang
and the provincial dialects practiced during my
father's consecutive assignments. In 1918, back
in Warsaw, I stood full of blissful expectation on
the threshold of the new era for Poland and humanity.

"The interlude between the two world wars
was the Poles' narcotic dream. Arts bloomed,
snobbery flourished, left-wing universalists
crossed swords with right-wing nationalists sipping drinks in a fashionable café, while intellectuals of all denominations indulged in witty
discussions with poets. Meantime, workers and
peasants tried through their deputies to vindicate their rights on the parliamentary scene only
seldom resorting to violence. A big port was built
on the Baltic; industries were encouraged by foreign capital, fertile land and the coal mines
promised lasting prosperity. No one mourned 'a
lost generation.'

"Travel in general—wanted and unwanted—
played an important part in my life. Owing to
my father's, the pedagogue, long school vacations, I visited early not only the Polish beauty
spots, but also Berlin, München, and Paris. For a
year I studied French literature at the University
of Nancy. At the time of my involvement with
music, I spent several months in Paris building
up a repertoire for a song recital of French im-
pressionists. The recital took place in Warsaw,
but, although the public response was encouraging, I decided to abandon musical ambitions in
favor of literature where, I felt, my self-
expression was more spontaneous. The daughter
of a *violiniste manquée* became *une cantatrice
manquée.*

"In 1921, I married a former colleague in a
pre-war political conspiracy, Jerzy Kuncewicz,
a science student turned lawyer and author, a
political activist on behalf of the Peasant Party,
of which he was one of the ideologists. The two
personal worlds did not blend easily, the more

MARIA KUNCEWICZ

so as my husband's family story was one of se-
date country dwellers, while mine was of all
kinds of migrants. In 1922, our son Witold was
born. To me the commonplace event assumed
the dramatic proportions of an initiation into nature's mystery. Unlike the customary triumph of
birthgiving, I felt the dread of the enigma I contributed to create. Never certain of what the
newcomer from some other world wished to say,
I refused to ignore the baby's cries. Also, since
that 'other world' meant the inside of my own
body, I, too, became an enigma to myself. The
horror came to an end once the baby shed it soulless mask and began to show human affection.
Told with great candor by my alter ego, Teresa,
the story bore the title *Przymierze z dzieckiem*
(Alliance with a Child, 1927). The unorthodox
treatment of the subject created much scandal
which, to my bewilderment, secured for me a
safe place on the literary scene. The critics
though, while praising the sharpness of perception, blamed me for using too many metaphors.
In due time, this exuberance was, I think, tempered, but metaphors are still serving my urge
to explore the unknown by way of analogy.

"Two more revelations I consider crucial in
my inter-war period: the discovery of the enchanted little town on the Vistula (Kazimierz),
where we built the house in which I am now
writing these words, and the death of my mother. The discovery resulted in a panorama of one
summer lived in a picturesque scene by two incompatible sets of people: the locals, a mixed
crowd of fishermen, small farmers and Jewish
shopkeepers existing on a minimum of maintenance, and a horde of bohemians, mainly paint-

ers, pupils of a beloved master,. a sort of modern Colas Breugnon. The contrast between the harsh daily toil and the misery of the native population on one hand, and on the other *plein air* studies, eccentric romances, the masquerades of the sleepwalkers under a late silvery moon when the tired poor were asleep behind their dirty little windows, made me write *Dwa Ksiezyce* (Two Moons, 1933), a review of social incongruities.

"In 1930, the death of my mother affected me in a way not dissimilar to the birth of my child; both facts forced me to accept man's incomprehensible origin and limit. In the novel *Cudzoziemka* (The Stranger, 1936), I described the last day of a woman who never came to terms with life. Raised in Russia by parents who belonged to third generation Polish political exiles, she was brought back to Warsaw by a patriotic aunt only to discover that she did not fit into the pattern. The alienation became complete when she married a man utterly indifferent to music, her all-consuming element. Critics attributed this work to the influence of Freud, whom, indeed, I have never read. The truth is that my stories are slices of my own life projected on a fictitious field of experience. The book is still alive on the international market.

"In the Polish thirties, much attention was paid to the 'man in the street,' the upcoming citizen of a democratic republic; thus the Warsaw radio commissioned me to write an appropriate cycle of scenes and dialogues. I called it "The Everyday of the Kowalski Family" (*Dni Powszednie Panstwa Kowalskich,* 1938). These radio talks soon assumed the form of a novel. Apparently, it was the first attempt at soap opera in Europe.

"In the autumn of 1939, after the Hitler–Molotov pact had eliminated the Polish state from the maps of Europe, my husband, son, and I left Poland in the wake of the official exodus—first to Paris, then London, where the Polish government in exile was finally established. My husband was given a post at the Polish Ministry of Information. Witold volunteered for the submarine service in the Polish Navy. I continued writing while also taking part in the writers' visits to the Polish units stationed in Scotland, composed mainly of escapees from the occupied country, survivors of the tragic September 1939 campaign. The émigré years in London turned my sensibility in two directions: nostalgia for the past, and bitterness of the present. The nostalgic trend brought forth "The Forester" (*Leśnik,* 1952), a novel set in an eastern province of Poland during and after the 1863 rising against Russia, a story based on my father's childhood memories. *The Conspiracy of the Absent*

(*Zmowa Nieobecnych,* 1946) reflects the bitter reality of war on two Polish fronts: the underground movement and the agony of everyday life at home, and official London of the ever-more-disillusioned émigrés.

"In 1955, following my son, who had miraculously survived the sinking of his submarine in the Arctic waters, I moved to the United States. My husband joined us soon after. Profiting by the Long Island construction boom, the men started work as masons, while I served for some time as domestic help. My next employment was at the New York Free Europe Radio Station where it fell to my lot to continue the Kowalski saga on the assumption that they, too, were émigrés, first in England, then America. This venture came to a brisk end in 1956, the year of the Gomulka successful resistance to the Soviets, followed by a cultural thaw. Formally assured that my texts would not be tampered with, I accepted the offers of Warsaw publishers to produce my new work and reprint the old. As a result, the 'Polish Desk' in Münich ordered New York to stop employing me. But my books, translated into English, kept on appearing in London and in New York, as well as being published in other languages—French, Spanish, Italian, Dutch. Since my husband prospered as a building contractor at West Point, we moved to Manhattan where I undertook the editing of an anthology which I called *The Modern Polish Mind.* To this period also belongs the novel *Gaj oliwny* (The Olive Grove, 1961), inspired by the aftermath of the *maquis* in the south of France still vibrant with xenophobia and inner strife. I wrote it both in English and Polish.

"In 1960, we became naturalized Americans. This serious step was facilitated by the fact that the United States does not require new citizens to relinquish their former nationality, a liberty Great Britain had refused. In 1963, we moved to Chicago where, for the subsequent seven years, I taught as a guest professor of Polish literature at the University of Chicago. Despite my humanistic studies, once, at the universities of Krakow and Warsaw, I had to work hard to modernize my knowledge and adapt it to the mentality of the American students. Somehow these difficulties were overcome, and till this day my Chicago years remain among the happiest in my memory. During summer vacations we journeyed to Canada and Spain, but also to Poland which I had revisited for the first time in 1958 traveling on a flimsy identification document delivered by the Cunard Lines. Our house in Kazimierz survived the occupation, and my compatriots welcomed me. In British Columbia I wrote "Tristan 1946"—an echo of the years spent in Cornwall between 1943–46. This novel, too, I wrote both in English and Polish. Particulars of all these literary and social endeavors can be found in my two volumes of autobiography, *Fantomy* (Phantoms, 1972) and *Natura* (Nature, 1975).

"This is a sketchy summary of a very long life, written at a time when my remaining energies go to completing *Przezrocza* (Slides—Italian Notes), a cycle on the same autobiographic lines, but confined to Italy where I spent the last eight winters witnessing many a historical development, observing changes in customs and thought. Some critics in France and England voiced uncertainty as to what literary kind my books represented. Reportage? Fiction? Essay? *Vie romancée?* The same doubts were echoed in Poland after my last performance, 'Fantasia alla Polacca'—a fantasy on the early work and life of the Polish modernist, Stanislaw Przybyszewski. It is now November 1982. Our park displays the golden extravagance of the Polish birches and oaks while we, Polish people, stand queuing for bread and a whiff of hope that 'Poland was not yet lost.'"

Born in Russia, Maria Kuncewicz has lived the greater part of her productive life outside her native Poland and much of what she has written focuses on themes and persons outside that country. Initially hailed for her capacity to portray "the soul of a woman" and for her lingering attention to detail, she soon came to be admired for the charm of her narrative, her short, carefully chiseled episodes, and her gift of personal observation and description. Today she is considered to be the voice of her generation. The personal itinerary which has given her special insight into the "loneliness and grandeur of exile" has also led her to be seen by Czeslaw Milosz as one of "the most 'Western' among her Polish contemporaries." Over a period of decades she has written prize-winning novels that deal with confrontations arising from the alienation of the individual, and from conflict between those-at-home and those-abroad. She expresses her thoughts through description, plot, and lapidary character development. Breaking with formal convention, she will upon occasion address her readers directly, letting them in on the secrets of her writing-craft.

Several of Kuncewicz's works are well known among English-language readers. *The Forester* is a capacious novel of religious and communal strife, describing a middle-class Polish family in the 1860s when Poland was fighting for national survival. *The Stranger* is a subtle yet powerful attempt to probe a complex personality, the plot

developed within a single day. It is one of the best and most interesting psychological novels ever written in Polish. Her war-time writing was greeted with enthusiasm. In *Conspiracy of the Absent* she treats the German occupation of Poland and the life of Polish exiles in England "with an ear for poetry, a mind for irony, a stomach for terror, a spirit unwilling to relinquish essential truths," Virgilia Peterson wrote.

During the 1940s and '50s Kuncewicz joined many othe Polish émigré writers in working for the international writers' organization PEN. She helped to establish the Centre for Writers in Exile, which still has branches in London and New York. Following her retirement from the University of Chicago in 1964, Kuncewicz returned to her home in Kazimierz, near Lublin. Highly esteemed by her countrymen, she has seen the books she wrote abroad published in her homeland; while new editions of her pre-war books are reissued by Warsaw publishing houses. Fellow-exile and critic Alexander Janta calls Maria Kuncewicz "probably the finest woman writer now at work in Polish letters."

WORKS IN ENGLISH TRANSLATION: Novels by Kuncewicz in English translation include *The Stranger*, by B.W.A. Massey, published with an introduction by the English novelist Storm Jameson, 1944; *Conspiracy of the Absent*, by Maurice Michael and Harry C. Stevens, 1950; *The Forester*, by Harry C. Stevens, 1954. Kuncewicz translated her own novel *The Olive Grove* in 1963. Among her works of non-fiction available in English are *Polish Millstones*, in Stephen Garry's translation, 1942; and *The Keys: A Journey Through Europe at War*, by Harry C. Stevens, 1946. A translation of her story "A Turban," by G. Maciuszko, is included in *Ten Contemporary Polish Short Stories*, edited by Edmund Ordon, 1958. Kuncewicz herself edited two collections in English: *Modern Polish Poetry*, 1943, and *The Modern Polish Mind*, 1962.

ABOUT: Columbia Dictionary of Modern European Literature, 1980; Contemporary Authors 1, 1975; Encyclopedia of World Literature in the 20th Century IV, 1975; Jameson, S. The Writer's Situation and Other Essays, 1950; Milhailovich, B.D. Modern Slavic Literatures, II, 1976; Milosz, C. the History of Polish Literature, 1983. *Periodicals*—Polish Perspectives July 1960; October 1967; Polish Review Winter 1972; Queens Slavic Papers I, 1973.

---

*KÜNG, HANS (March 19, 1928–   ), Swiss theologian, was born in Sursee, on Lake Sempach in the canton of Lucerne, the eldest of six children of Hans Küng, a prosperous shoe merchant, and Emma Gut Küng. He has recalled that his family life was one of "traditional Catholic piety." He took a degree in humanistic studies

°koõng, häns

HANS KUNG

from the gymnasium in Lucerne, then was sent
to Rome to study at the Jesuit-run Pontifical
Gregorian University, from which he received
licentiates in philosophy in 1951 and theology in
1955, the year after his ordination to the priesthood at the Jesuit Church of the Gesù in Rome.
In 1957 he took his doctorate in theology from
the Catholic Institute at the Sorbonne in Paris;
he also studied in Berlin, Amsterdam, London,
and Madrid. After two years of pastoral work in
Lucerne, he was appointed assistant in dogmatic
theology at the University of Münster, West Germany, then in 1960 was elected *Ordinarius,* or
professor, at Tübingen, the renowned university
of Kepler, Hegel, and Schelling, in whose school
of theology Philipp Melanchthon, the first Lutheran apologist, taught in the sixteenth century.
In 1963 Küng was made professor of dogmatic
and ecumenical theology and became the first
director of the Institute for Ecumenical Research. He was appointed by Pope John XXIII
as *peritus,* or official theologian, at the Second
Vatican Council, convoked in October 1962.

Küng's dissertation formed the substance of
his first book, an epochal study of the eminent
German Protestant theologian Karl Barth,
*Rechtfertigung: Die Lehre Karl Barths und eine
katholische Besinnung (Justification: The Doctrine of Karl Barth with a Catholic Reflection).*
Küng argued that Barth's position on justification—the Lutheran view that the sinner can win
divine salvation by means of faith alone—does
not diverge from the Catholic doctrine on salvation as enunciated by the Council of Trent during the Counter-Reformation. This ecumenical
argument shocked many conservatives in Rome,

and a dossier was begun on Küng by the Sacred
Congregation for the Doctrine of the Faith, the
venerable Vatican institution that was formerly
and in some quarters is still popularly known as
the Roman Inquisition. Barth, for his part, contributed an introduction to the book, highly approving its author's ecumenical spirit: Küng, in
his words, is "a true Israelite, in whom there is
no guile."

Küng's hopes for the Second Vatican Council
were stated in *Konzil und Wiedervereinigung:
Erneuerung als Ruf in die Einheit (The Council,
Reform, and Reunion).* Here he adumbrates for
the first time his views on infallibility, asserting
that the church has in fact erred on several occasions, and he argues for a thorough reform and
renewal of Roman Catholicism. This can be best
accomplished, in his view, by granting broader
powers to the bishops and thereby limiting those
of the Roman Curia; by encouraging a certain
latitude in liturgical observance and use of the
vernacular whenever possible; and by maximizing freedom of discussion within the church,
starting with the reformation or even abolition
of the notorious Index of Prohibited Books. He
also suggests a fresh examination of the questions
of papal infallibility and clerical celibacy, and of
church laws relating to marriage. His conclusion
expresses the hope that "if Catholics carry out
Catholic reform and Protestants carry out Protestant reform, both according to the Gospel image, then, because the Gospel of Christ is but
one, reunion need not remain a utopian dream.
Reunion will be neither a Protestant return nor
a Catholic capitulation, but a brotherly approach from both sides." The book elicited high
praise from many Protestant ecumenicists but
mostly angry bewilderment from conservative
Catholics.

At a news conference in early December
1962, shortly before the council ended its first
session, Küng expressed the opinion that the session had "changed the atmosphere of the whole
church." He accorded most of the credit for this
to John XXIII, of whom he has always spoken in
the highest terms, as "a real pastor, not overly
progressive, leading quietly and a little joyfully."
His work during the years immediately following was a clarification of his views on the
changes occurring in his church. *Strukturen der
Kirche (Structures of the Church)* attempted a
liberal explication of Catholic dogma in an ecumenical light; *Kirche im Konzil (The Council in
Action: Theological Reflections on the Second
Vatican Council)* examined the conciliar accomplishments from a theologian's perspective; *Die
Kirche (The Church)* and *Wahrhaftigkeit: Zur
Zukunft der Kirche (Truthfulness: The Future of
the Church)* both tried to read the future of the

church in as progressive a light as possible, as if the Curia and its conservative apologists had completely internalized the council's reforming spirit. They had, of course, done no such thing, and Küng's greatest battle had only just begun.

He found himself deeply embroiled in controversy on the publication of *Unfehlbar? Eine Anfrage* (*Infallible? An Inquiry*), in which he begins by citing a lengthy list of errors of fact and doctrine in ecclesiastical pronouncements over many centuries, including the well-known condemnations of liberalism and democracy by Pius IX in 1864 and of ecumenism by Pius XI in 1928. The church has often failed in its duty to interpret the Gospel anew in every age in keeping with the human knowledge available. John XXIII had at last, in Küng's view, returned to the early idea of the church as *semper reformanda*, always in the process of restating its truths and redefining its structures. The mysterious power over truth claimed by popes since the promulgation in 1870 of the doctrine of papal infallibility was far too final, concrete, and legalistic to be accepted any longer. The Sacred Congregation for the Doctrine of the Faith, beginning in the early 1970s, repeatedly summoned Küng to be confronted with the charges brought against him by conservatives throughout the Curia. He repeatedly defied each summons, at first claiming he had no time, then, more seriously, challenging the basic fairness of curial procedures in such matters. "The norms" of the congregation, he wrote on June 21, 1971, to its prefect, Franjo Cardinal Šeper, "must, unfortunately, still be characterized as inquisitorial and discriminatory." In the same tone, he posed a crucial question in an article published in July 1973: "What all these practices in the Palace of the Holy Office, which have done the credibility of the Catholic Church and its theology incalculable damage, have to do with the Gospel of Christ is asked about today no longer only by the readers of Dostoevsky's *Karamazov* but also by many bishops and even not a few Roman curialists."

Roman attacks on Küng abated in February 1975, when Cardinal Šeper wrote him that the proceedings against him would be "ended for now," but only two days later the German Bishops' Conference issued its first statement against his new book, *Christ sein?* (*On Being a Christian*), the 720-page apologia that is widely regarded as his most influential work. Küng considers the book to be "a guide in the present difficult situation of Church and society, . . . so to speak, a positive counterpart to my book on infallibility."

He wrote it not because he "thinks he is a good Christian, but because he thinks that being a Christian is a particularly good thing." The book's highly systematic structure and many pages of closely reasoned exegesis are leavened, for the general reader, by Küng's characteristically lucid style and by a pervasive sense of the great generosity of the endeavor. Werner H. Kelber, in a typical Protestant reaction, called the book a "stupendous achievement" and "cause for rejoicing without end," especially praising the author's "rare mastery over biblical criticism and New Testament theology, philosophical and historical theology, church history and ethics, and the history of religion and cultural history. The result is a composition of systematic coherence and intrinsic plausibility."

Existiert Gott? (*Does God Exist: An Answer for Today*) is intended by Küng to be "mutually complementary" with *On Being a Christian*. It is hardly shorter, and no less rigorous, than its predecessor. "The important thing for me," he writes in introducing the book, "was to set out as lucidly and consistently as possible the meaning of belief in God in its totality, even if in some particular questions this meant pointing to different ways of thinking, rather than producing ready-made solutions." Küng's first aim in the book, according to Fr. Leonard Swidler, an American priest much involved in the ecumenical movement, is to establish "a solid basis for human knowledge in a critical rationality founded on an act of basic trust in the meaningfulness of reality." His approach to the fundamental question of nihilism is to place "the discussion within the historical framework in which the modern manifestation of atheism developed from the Age of Enlightenment and then especially the nineteenth century forward, dealing sympathetically with all significant figures involved in modern atheism, particularly Feuerbach, Marx, and Freud." Elsewhere, Swidler wrote that "in Küng the reader has a guide not only of complete integrity, but also of extraordinary breadth and depth of knowledge and great clarity of expression. The book analyzes thoroughly and sympathetically many of the pertinent thinkers from Descartes to the present." Swidler is the editor of the best account in English of Küng's long-running argument with Rome, *Küng in Conflict*, which includes all the important letters and statements of the two sides.

In August 1978, in a statement to a newspaper on the death of Paul VI, Küng expressed how grateful he was to the late Pope "that through all the years he held his protective hand over me," shielding him against his enemies in the Curia. The Polish cardinal, Karol Wojtyla, who eventually succeeded Paul as John Paul II, quickly proved to be not only a man of great charisma but also a stern moralist, a conservative theologian, and severe disciplinarian. The "fraternal criticism" directed by Küng to the Pope one year after his election, and published in many newspapers throughout the world, seemed to many observers to precipitate decisive action by the Curia, probably at papal urging. Just before Christmas 1979 the Pope promulgated a Congregation ruling which said, in part, "Professor Hans Küng, in his writings, has departed from the integral truth of Catholic faith, and therefore he can no longer be considered a Catholic theologian nor function as such in a teaching role." Küng was quickly stripped by the German bishops of the *missio canonica,* the approval granted all official Catholic theologians, and was removed from the Catholic theological faculty in Tübingen. He was, however, kept on by the university as professor of theology and retained the directorship of the ecumenical institute which he helped form.

Küng's visit to the United States in December 1981 was a great success. In a speech to thousands of reformist Catholics in Chicago he stated, "Very many of us, not by our own will, feel something like the loyal opposition within the church, loyal opposition which, without illusions but with a readiness for dialogue, seeks to plead for more sincerity, frankness, pluralism, and tolerance within the Catholic Church." In an interview before leaving the city, he remarked, "I tried to avoid becoming a leader of the opposition, but I do not care so much anymore."

Küng lives in a house in the hills above Tübingen. He has published twenty-nine books in the last twenty-three years, many of which have been translated into a dozen languages—a record that can have been equalled by few theologians in history. In addition to his native German he is fluent in English, French, Italian, Spanish, and Dutch, and has a thorough command of Latin, Greek, and Hebrew. He is extremely fond of classical music, and is an avid swimmer and skier.

WORKS IN ENGLISH TRANSLATION: The Council, Reform, and Reunion (tr. C. Hastings), 1962 (U.K. The Council and Reunion); That the World May Believe: Letters to Young People (tr. C. Hastings), 1963; The Council in Action: Theological Reflections on the Second Vatican Council (tr. C. Hastings), 1963 (U.K. The Living Church, 1963, The Changing Church, 1965); Justification: The Doctrine of Karl Barth with a Catholic Reflection (tr. T. Collins, E. E. Tolk, D. Granskou), 1964; Structures of the Church (tr. S. Attanasio), 1964; Freedom in the World: Sir Thomas More (tr. C. Hastings) 1965; The Church (tr. R. and R. Ockenden), 1967; Truthfulness: The Future of the Church (tr. E. Quinn), 1968; Infallible? An Inquiry (tr. E. Quinn), 1971; Why Priests? A Proposal for a New Church Ministry (tr. R. C. Collins), 1972; On Being a Christian (tr. E. Quinn), 1975; Freud and the Problem of God (tr. E. Quinn),

1979; Does God Exist: An Answer for Today, 1980; The Church—Maintained in Truth: A Theological Meditation (tr. E. Quinn), 1980; Eternal Life? Life After Death as a Medical, Philosophical, and Theological Problem (tr. E. Quinn), 1984.

ABOUT: Duggan, G. H., Hans Küng and Reunion, 1965; Häring , H. and Kuschel, K.-J., Hans Küng: His Work and His Way, 1980; Nowell, R. A Passion for Truth: Hans Küng, a Biography, 1981; Swidler, L. (ed.) Consensus in Theology? A Dialogue with Hans Küng and Edward Schillebeeckx, 1980; and Küng in Conflict, 1981; Contemporary Authors 53–56, 1975; Current Biography, 1963. *Periodicals*—America September 22, 1979; July 19–26, 1980; Christian Century September 13, 1978; Christian Science Monitor April 3, 1980; Commonweal November 24, 1978; May 9, 1980; November 7, 1980; Chicago Tribune November 29, 1981; New Republic July 21 and 28, 1979; November 8, 1980; New York Review of Books February 7, 1980; June 14, 1984; New York Times July 9, 1973; July 10, 1973; February 21, 1975; February 25, 1975; October 12, 1975; May 23, 1976; December 19–23, 1979; December 30, 1979; December 31, 1979; January 28, 1980; February 1, 1980; November 15, 1980; December 13, 1981; New York Times Book Review December 19, 1976; July 22, 1979; Publishers Weekly September 26, 1980; Saturday Evening Post April 1977; Time August 21, 1978; January 21, 1980; Times Literary Supplement July 24, 1981; Toronto Globe and Mail September 27, 1974; April 30, 1977; October 25, 1980; Wall Street Journal September 22, 1980.

*KUZNETSOV, ANATOLY VASILYE-VICH (pseudonym **A. Anatoli**) (August 18, 1929–June 13, 1979), one of the better-known contemporary Soviet expatriate authors, has come to be identified with a single book, the documentary novel *Babi Yar.* He was born in Kiev of a Ukrainian mother and a Russian father and grew up on the outskirts of the Ukrainian capital, near a ravine that would one day become notorious as "Babi Yar." Kuznetsov's early years in the Ukraine were uneventful. He graduated from the Gorky Institute of Literature in Moscow, but worked as a laborer before undertaking a writing career. After serving as a carpenter and bulldozer operator in the Kakhova hydroelectric plant and as a construction worker during the building of the Irkutsk plant in southwestern Siberia, he began to write of his experiences.

Kuznetsov contributed to the factory newspaper in Kakhovka, but his first significant published work, short narratives, appeared in the newspaper *Pionerskaya Pravda* in 1946. Thereafter he seemed to pursue a fairly conformist career as a rising man of letters. He became a member of the Communist Party in 1955, and in the late sixties was assigned to the editorial

°kōoz net′ zof, ä′ nya tôl ē

panel of the youth periodical *Yunost*. In 1957 he published the first work that won him a measure of recognition, *Prodolzhenie Legendy: Zapiski Molodogo Cheloveka* (Sequel *to* a Legend: Notes of a Young Man), a novel-like account of his Siberian experiences. From 1959 to 1969, he was a member of the Soviet Union of Writers. Before his defection from the Soviet Union in 1969, he had won three literary competitions in Moscow and the Ukraine and was considered a writer of promise. Three of his novels appeared in the early sixties: *Bienie Zhizhni* (The Pulsation of Life) in 1961, *Selenga*, in 1961, and *U Sebia Doma* (At Home), in 1964. In 1966 the first published version of *Babi Yar* appeared serially in a heavily censored form in *Yunost.*

By his own account, Kuznetsov abandoned his native land in 1969 for a number of reasons, but chiefly because of the censorship of *Babi Yar*. While in London on a trip subsidized by the Soviet Writers Union for the ostensible purpose of conducting research on Lenin (who had spent some time in London in 1902), Kuznetsov eluded his Soviet escort and asked for political asylum. He remained in England until his death of a heart attack in 1979, publishing an uncensored edition of *Babi Yar* and other works and, from 1974 to 1979, serving as chief correspondent for Radio Liberty, which beamed programs to the Soviet Union.

A comparison of Kuznetsov's early *Sequel to a Legend* with *Babi Yar* reveals a striking contrast between the establishment novelist of the forties and fifties and the expatriate whom the Soviets denounced as a traitor and betrayer of his motherland. In the *Sequel,* the first-person narrator recounts his travels on the Trans-Siberian railroad enroute to the Bratsk Power Station. He has completed his schooling and has learned of a rosy "legend" concerning the easy life awaiting him far in the east. The early portions of the narrative are devoted to the exchanges between the narrator and his fellow-travelers. After five days, the narrator reaches Irkutsk and finds employment as a concrete worker. He writes to his friend Victor back home and talks of Una, also at home, whom he loves. His labors become so terrible a burden that he wishes to return to Moscow, but he is dissuaded by a fellow-worker. He falls ill and winds up in the hospital. In time, he recovers and exults over his share in the successful damming of the Angara river and the completion of the Irkutsk power station. His narration ends on a note of triumph which proclaims the virtue of work through adversity for the greater glory of socialism and the USSR. The tone of the *Sequel* is positive and exuberant. The details of the narrator's trials are rendered realistically, but the emphasis throughout the account

and at the end is on the value of the enterprise. *Sequel,* immensely successful, was dramatized and produced on the Moscow stage in 1961.

Babi Yar was another matter entirely. It had its own pre-and post-exile publishing history, as well as a vast secondary biographical and critical literature. On more than one occasion, Kuznetsov told of the background of what he called his "document in the form of a novel." He remembered very well the German take-over of Kiev on September 19, 1941, when he was twelve. Stalin had promised to fight for the city, but it was in fact abandoned with practically no resistance. After a period of rapine and looting, the victorious Germans consolidated their control, rounded up the city's Jews, and massacred and buried them in the Babi Yar ravine. During the next two years, they also slaughtered countless Ukrainians and Russians and likewise interred them in the ravine.

After the war, Kuznetsov met Yevgeny Yevtushenko at the Gorky Institute of Literature and the Kakhovka hydroelectric plant, where both were employed, and both writers visited the Babi Yar site. Yevtushenko wrote his celebrated "Babi Yar" poem in 1961 and was attacked widely and furiously in the Soviet Union for identifying the Kiev Jews as the principal sufferers at the hands of the Germans. Five years later, Kuznetsov published his documentary novel, with significant portions cut by the censor. Reviewing the English translation of this book, George Feifer, in the *New York Times Book Review,* observed that by allowing the novel to appear in print, the Soviets acknowledged that an error had been made in hiding the fact that Jews had been the Nazis' chief victims. Feifer identified the work from a literary point of view as "less than brilliant," though he underlined its importance as containing "the truth." He noted that Kuznetsov uses some literary devices originated by John Dos Passos (such as reproducing newspaper headlines) but not as effectively. Feifer revealed finally that Soviet reviewers reacted to Kuznetsov quite differently from the way they reacted to Yevtushenko, lauding Kuznetsov for courageously and forthrightly treating a too-long-hidden subject. Feifer predicted that his book would be remembered in this light, rather than on strictly literary grounds as a work of art.

At the time of the 1966 publication of *Babi Yar,* Kuznetsov addressed the youth of the Soviet Union, asserting that his chief aim in writing the book had been to remind them that the "Fascist mentality" responsible for the murderous outrages on the outskirts of Kiev was still active in the world, actually and potentially. He appealed to them to see that the earth would survive and that the crime of Babi Yar would not be permitted to happen again. But in the course of the next three years, Kuznetsov grew increasingly disaffected with the Soviet Union, and the 1969 he planned his own defection in London. Assuming the pseudonym of A. Anatoli he published a more complete edition of his novel, with all the censored material restored. The definitive *Babi Yar* of 1970, much larger than the 1966 volume, contains the original censored text, plus the censored passages now restored, and additional material that Kuznetsov asserted he added on his own between 1967 and 1969. He was later challenged on the validity of this added material, which he argued was entirely legitimate and not "made up" for the occasion.

In an article in the London *Sunday Telegraph* of August 10, 1969, entitled "Why I Left Russia," Kuznetsov disclosed that most Russian writers are at the mercy of the KGB, the secret police, except those who actively cooperate with them. And since he objected to the censorship of *Babi Yar*, to the suppression of the Czechoslovaks, and to other aspects of Soviet policy, he decided to go into exile. He refused to act as an informer for the KGB and so became *persona non grata*. He now regretted not having had the courage to accept the invitation of Alexandr Solzhenitsyn to lend his name to an expression of dissent. As part of his plan to escaping to the West, he related, he made a pretense of agreeing to act as an informer—at the expense of Yevtushenko and others. Thus, he was permitted to travel to England, supposedly to conduct his Lenin research.

In four public letters from London, Kuznetsov explained even more definitively his reasons for leaving Russia. He argued that it was impossible to write unfettered and uncensored in the Soviet Union and he asked the Russian government not to harass members of his family for his staged flight and defection. Furthermore, Kuznetsov disavowed all of the writing he had done in Russia as a fake and sham, heavily censored as it had been to conform to absolutist Leninist doctrine. Now, as A. Anatoli, he would be able to write as he wished. In a letter to the Central Committee of the Communist Party, Kuznetsov rejected Marxist-Leninist dogma, calling it corrupt and inefficient, and withdrew from membership in the Party. In a final letter to the Union of Soviet Writers, he said: "I have come to realize the utter falsity, stupidity, and reactionary nature of Socialist realism," and asked to be relieved of membership in the union.

Babi Yar, like the constituent novels of Dos Passos' *USA*, is fictionalized reportage told in the first person, using names of real people and places, with periodic interludes indentified as "A Word from the Author," brief editorial commentaries. The restored portions of the original work not surprisingly reflect negatively on the Soviet state. In even greater detail than in the earlier version, the expanded book shows the partiality of the Ukrainians for the invading Germans and their hatred of Stalin. One of the restored passages, for example, records the significant anonymous placard reading: "Jews, Poles, and Russians are the bitterest enemies of the Ukraine." One of the chief incidents of the German occupation of Kiev, narrated in detail in the uncensored version, is the destruction of the "Kreshchatik," the city's principal square. The official Soviet position had held the Germans responsibile for the devastation, but the uncensored *Babi Yar* attributes it to the Russians themselves.

In both the censored and restored sections of his work, Kuznetsov details the characteristically efficient German rounding-up and destruction of Kiev's Jews. He reports his own grandfather's barely suppressed gleeful excitement over the mass arrest of the Jews—a reflection surely of the legendary Ukrainian anti-semitism—but he reports too his grandfather's horror when he learns of the ultimate fate of the Jews. According to Kuznetsov, prior to the German occupation of the city, the official Russian propaganda, not unrelated to the Hitler-Stalin pact, had not revealed Hitler's enormities, and as a result the Jews had not expected to be massacred. The final sentences of the uncensored version restore Kuznetsov's parting admonition to his fellow-countrymen—and really to the entire world—an admonition that the Soviets had naturally chosen to suppress: "I wonder if we shall ever understand that the most precious thing in this world is a man's life and his freedom? Or is there still more barbarism ahead? With these questions I think I shall bring this book to an end."

The critical reception of the censored edition was mixed but basically favorable. Oleg Ivsky, writing in the *Library Journal,* called attention to the unevenness of the narrative and, by implication, points to the heavy hand of the censor: "Kuznetsov's claim to actual and factual historical truth places an additional burden on his narrative. Judged as fiction by the usual literary standards, it deserves every praise as a highly competent professional work, deeply felt and deeply moving, compassionate, ironic and horrifying, but never despairing . . . distorts the overall picture in the interests of Party line and Socialist Realism."

Four years later, Ivsky wrote more favorably

of the uncensored, revised novel: "There is an immense improvement [in this revision]; this is the true story of the time and place. . . . Its veracity cannot be questioned; Kuznetsov's feeling for atmosphere and dialogue rings true." An unsigned review of this version, in the *Times Literary Supplement*, expressed mixed feelings about the revision, questioning particularly the material added to the text between 1967 and 1969: "Although Kuznetsov lacks the psychological and philosophical depth of Solzhenitsyn, he has the Russian gift for immediate physical detail, and many scenes, both horrifying and at times grotesquely humorous, come across with great vividness. . . . It is rather a pity that Kuznetsov has not been content simply to restore his whole text but has also added, in square brackets, many new passages which tend to be shrilly anti-Soviet and detract from the natural force of the terrible story."

In sum, Kuznetsov cannot be considered a major novelist, like Solzhenitsyn, for example, although *Babi Yar* is certainly an important book. By his own admission, it it not so much a novel as a documented narrative, a cinematized history. (In 1981 the English writer D.M. Thomas used large sections of it in the harrowing conclusion of his own sensational and controversial novel *The White Hotel*.) Kuznetsov wrote other works, some traditional fiction, other semi-autobiographical renderings of his own experiences. He also produced volumes of short stories and several motion picture scenarios.

WORKS IN ENGLISH TRANSLATION: The Russian-censored version of *Babi Yar: A Documentary Novel* was translated into English by Jacob Guralsky in 1966. The restored, complete text, in David Floyd's translation, was published as *Babi Yar: A Document in the Form of a Novel* by A. Anatoli in 1970. An earlier work, *Sequel to a Legend*, was published in 1959 in Moscow in an English translation by R. Bobrova.

ABOUT: Columbia Dictionary of Modern European Literature, 1980. *Periodicals*—Hudson Review Summer 1971; Library Journal April 1, 1967; April 1, 1971; New York Review of Books June 15, 1967; New York Times June 15, 1979; New York Times Book Review January 15, 1967; April 9, 1967; Saturday Review January 23, 1971; Times Literary Supplement November 27, 1970.

*LACAN, JACQUES (April 13, 1901– September 9, 1981), French psychoanalyst, was born in Paris of middle-class parents, Alfred Lacan and Emilée Baudry. His early education was conducted at Jesuit schools; he later entered medical college and then trained as a psychia-

°lä cäN´

JACQUES LACAN

trist, delivering his first professional paper in 1926. His most influential teachers, other than the primary texts of Sigmund Freud, were Georges de Clérambault and Henri Claude, both of whom had been instrumental in disseminating Freud's ideas in France. There, as in other countries, Freudian thought encountered strong resistance, both because of its Germanic origin (a special problem in France after World War I) and because of its pervasive emphasis on sexuality. But Lacan kept aloof from such squabbles, demonstrating early, as his subsequent career would prove, that he always took his own way.

Lacan's doctoral dissertation, "On Paranoiac Psychoses in their Relations to the Personality," first published in 1932 and reissued in 1975, is a more or less conventional extension of Freud's early work on paranoia, especially the famous essay on the case of Dr. Schreber (1911). But the dissertation already shows two original elements in Lacan's approach: his difficult, convoluted writing style (which would later become as notorious as his ideas) and his persistent interest in severe mental disorders like paranoia and schizophrenia, with which orthodox psychoanalysis has had little to do. In the late 1920s and early thirties, Lacan was also loosely associated with an avant-garde group of psychoanalysts calling themselves L'Evolution psychiatrique (Psychiatric Evolution), centered at the Hôpital Sainte-Anne in Paris. These young psychiatrists sought to establish links between their profession and other contemporary movements, such as surrealism and existentialism. Lacan painted and wrote a few poems, but by 1933 he seems to have gone his own way again.

Information on Lacan's early years is sketchy; indeed, throughout his life he endeavored to maintain his privacy. In the professional sphere, however, Lacan reveled in controversy, which surrounded him from the mid-1930s till his death. His early fame derived more from his activities as a teacher and lecturer than from his publications; before the early 1950s, in fact, he published remarkably little. The most notable of his early papers is the short essay on the "Mirror Stage," the first version of which was delivered at the Fifteenth International Psychoanalytic Congress at Marienbad in 1936. This is the earliest statement of what would become the central concept in Lacan's thought, his most important contribution to Freudian psychology and his most striking divergence from orthodox Freudianism. Lacan revised his concept of the Mirror Stage frequently throughout his career, restating it many times; its briefest summary is found in "The Mirror Stage, Source of the I-Function, as Shown by Psychoanalytic Experience," a paper read before the Sixteenth International Congress at Zürich in 1949, published that year and reprinted in his *Ecrits.* Already in the 1936 paper, however, the basic outlines of the concept are clear.

The mirror stage begins at the moment when, catching sight of its reflection in a mirror or by some other means, a child first becomes aware of the existence of its own body as an entity distinct from private consciousness. Prior to the moment, the child has had no sense that it and its mother's breast, for example, are separate objects, that the child's mouth is other than the source that gives it nourishment. The child will continue to dwell for some time in what Lacan calls the "imaginary order," a state of non-differentiation, or ceaseless interchange, between the internal and the external, the self and the other. Even at the mirror stage, the child (which does not yet have full control over the members of its body) regards its image as part of itself, as the world is; but the mirror stage marks the beginning of a sense of self, the first step in the formation of what will later be an "ego."

The concept of the mirror stage illustrates some of the far-flung intellectual influences which Lacan brings to bear on Freudian thought. In its basic structure, the mirror stage follows Freud's understanding of narcissism, as laid down in such essays as "On Narcissism" (1914) and "The Economic Problem of Narcissism" (1924): the child can understand the otherness of the world only narcissistically, by identifying itself with the other and thereby incorporating it. The ego, according to Freud, will continue to build itself up in layers of such narcissistic identifications. But Lacan participated in the renewal of interest in Hegelian phenomenology that swept France in the 1930s, stimulated by Alexandre Kojève's famous series of lectures at the Ecole des Hautes Etudes between 1933 and 1939, which Lacan attended. By proposing that the child's first recognition of selfhood is grounded in an experience of otherness—that the self begins in bifurcation, itself and other simultaneously—Lacan imports into Freudian psychology a definite Hegelian element, reminiscent of the interaction of the Master and the Slave in Hegel's *Phenomenology of Mind* (1807).

The most significant Lacanian modification of Freudian theory, however, is Lacan's frequent recourse to the linguistics of Ferdinand de Saussure (1857–1913). The fundamental tenet of Saussurean linguistics is that language is not a system of absolute values but one of differences; signs are distinguishable from one another not on account of their separate references to things in the world, but solely because they are different, either aurally or visually, within the linguistic system itself. The sign, furthermore, is a double structure, composed of the linkage between a signifier (*signifiant*) and a signified (*signifié*); the sign is purely "arbitrary," in that it is motivated by nothing in the object to which it may be taken to refer. The signified is not an object but a concept; it is therefore also a signifier which can be linked to another signified, forming a chain of signification which in its totality constitutes the linguistic system.

The child before the mirror forms a Saussurean sign: the child is the signifier which "means" its signified image. So far, however, because the child is still in the imaginary order, it had not yet recognized difference; it still regards itself and its image as part and parcel of the same thing. Difference arrives in the person of the father, who brings with him the paraphernalia of the Freudian Oedipus complex, recast in Saussurean terms. The father inserts himself between the imaginary union of the child and its mother; he turns it from a dyadic (two-termed) into a triadic (three-termed) relation, thereby opening up the closed system of the sign to the full play of linguistic differences. The child's desire for its mother is repressed; desire enters the unconscious, which structures itself, in Lacan's most famous phrase, "like a language." Lacan never claims that the unconscious *is* a language, composed of words; rather, he maintains that the structure of unconscious desire and the structure of linguistic signification are analogous. The child is introduced to language and desire in the same gesture; signs signify the absence of their referents, just as desire signifies the absence of its object. Prior to the entry of the father, the child cannot properly be said to "desire" its mother, since it imagines itself one with her. But when the mother is forbidden, desire arises as an unconscious signifier.

The father thrusts the child into the second of Lacan's three "orders," the symbolic, in which the imaginary unity of signifier and signified (mouth and breast, body and reflection) is ruptured forever. Because the child cannot identify itself with the father as it once did with the mother—and, in the mirror stage, with its own image—it constructs a symbolic Father who is neither imaginary nor "real" (Lacan's third and vaguest "order," corresponding generally to those objects in the world to which the self attributes significance). The child may or may not have a real father in order to construct a symbolic one; the symbolic Father is a function, a place, which the child supposes it can someday perform or occupy. This Father is permanently absent, only signified and never possessed; he is the Other, the Law (Lacan has several shifting names for him), the endlessly receding principle of language and human society. Having now entered the symbolic order, the child recognizes—belatedly, according to the Freudian scheme of *Nachträglichkeit* ("deferred action")—that it was there all along without knowing it, even in regard to its own mirror image. So it finds a gap, a difference, within itself, which it will attempt for the rest of its life to fill.

This summary of Lacan's major conceptual structures has been culled from a number of essays published over many years; Lacan never wrote a comprehensive introduction to his thought, and he was continually adjusting and altering his expressions till the end of his life. To make matters worse, his style, cryptic to begin with, grew steadily more elusive as time went on. As Stuart Schneiderman reports, Lacan once told a television interviewer that on no account would he reduce the opacity of his style, even for a mass audience: "My discourse," he said, "is for those who are not idiots." It has often been questioned whether the real idiots are not those who claim to have found breathtaking profundity in a perverse obfuscation of the commonplace. Nevertheless, the general thrust of Lacan's work—its strict adherence to Freud combined with heavy doses of Hegel and Saussure—made him the foremost psychoanalytic innovator of the mid-twentieth century and an extremely controversial figure.

Lacan's early fame grew from his lectures; he was a hypnotically charismatic speaker, especially when he commented on Freud's texts. In 1951 he began a series of yearly seminars, first at Sainte-Anne and after 1963 at the Ecole Normale Supérieure, which continued till his death and attracted steadily more students, over a thousand per session in his last years. This success was achieved despite Lacan's numerous idiosyncrasies—such as his policy of never speaking directly to his students, and his habit of falling inexplicably silent, sometimes for fifteen minutes. The texts of his seminars, transcribed by students as Saussure's had also been, make simpler reading than Lacan's highly condensed written works, though the Lacanian Bible remains the monumental *Ecrits* of 1966, which contains his principal writings over thirty years, each with a short new introduction.

Lacan stirred up controversy, however, in more than just the theoretical realm. He had joined the orthodox Société psychanalytique de Paris (Paris Psychoanalytic Society) in 1934 and became a full member in 1939; but in 1952, he and his colleague Daniel Lagache broke from the older society to found a new one, the Société française de la psychanalyse (French Society for Psychoanalysis). The issue was one of psychoanalytic practice: Lacan maintained, contrary to orthodoxy, that the relationship between analyst and analysand should be regarded, in a Hegelian sense, as dialectical. The analyst cannot remain utterly aloof from his patient; he, too, is a subject, and he must analyze not only the patient's transference—the therapeutic shifting of emotional focus from others in the patient's life to the analyst—but also his own countertransference—the prejudices and blind spots that influence the analyst's attitude toward the patient—if the dialectic is to be fruitfully maintained. As was his wont, Lacan called upon the early Freud to support him; he cited the case history of Dora (1905), in which Freud admits that his own preconceptions had impeded the analysis and perhaps even bungled it.

The argument over psychoanalytic technique led directly to the *Discours de Rome* (Rome Discourse), addressed to the first meeting of the schismatic new society in 1953 and published in 1956. It is the closest Lacan ever came to a systematic exposition of his ideas, and it immediately became the manifesto of the society, despite the virtual impenetrability of its style. After 1953, Lacan emerged rapidly into intellectual prominence; not only did his seminars attract increasing crowds of analysts in training, but he also became an important influence on French intellectual life in various fields. The foremost contemporary thinkers read and listened to him, including the Marxist theoretician Louis Althusser and the historian Michel Foucault. This attention, however, did Lacan and his disciples little good in official circles. At the

Eighteenth International Psychoanalytic Congress in 1954, Anna Freud herself spoke out against the heretics, and at the Nineteenth Congress, two years later, the Société Française was excluded from international membership. The final turn of the screw was given in 1963, when it was declared that no member of the French Society would be allowed to join the International Association until Lacan had been removed from the Society's roster of training analysts.

This was done, and again Lacan was on his own. He moved from Sainte-Anne to the Ecole Normale and founded the Ecole Freudienne (Freudian School). Students still flocked to him, but he had no official affiliations beyond those he arranged for himself. Like Otto Rank, Wilhelm Reich, and many others before him, Lacan had been driven from the psychoanalytic fold because his innovations, which some have regarded as the mark of his genius, were seen as lunacy by the establishment. Lacan's case is unusual, however, in that though his intellectual impact derived from the modifications he made to Freudian theory, his official expulsion was motivated by the rumor that he had drastically altered orthodox practice. The primary charge against him in 1963—it has remained the most controversial feature of Lacanian analysis ever since—was his tampering with the traditional fifty-minute psychoanalytic hour.

There is no evidence that, especially in his early years, Freud prescribed an hour as the daily time to be spent with each patient; nor is there firm precedent for reducing the time by ten minutes. But long before 1963, possibly under the influence of college timetables, fifty-minute consultations had become standard practice. Lacan introduced the "short session," sometimes as brief as five minutes. Unlike orthodox Freudians, who contract to spend fifty minutes with their patients no matter how the patients use that time, Lacanian analysts reserve the right to end the session whenever they choose, abruptly and without warning. The advantage of the short session, according to Lacan, is twofold: it compels the patient to forgo evasions and come to the point, since he has no idea how short his time may be; and it saves the analyst the trouble of listening to irrelevancies, since he can simply end the proceedings when he get bored. Critics of the technique, however, argue that it is nothing more than self-indulgent rudeness.

The future of Lacanian analysis, both as theory and as practice, remains uncertain. At Lacan's death, there were reportedly about 5,000 Lacanian analysts in France, most of them in Paris; but the impact of Lacanian techniques on psychoanalysis in other countries has so far been slight. On the theoretical side, there is little doubt that, for all their murkiness, Lacan's essays on Freud count among the most incisive and thought-provoking psychoanalytic commentaries of the last fifty years. His numerous discussions of Freud's early works, reconsidering them in the light of Saussurean linguistics, have notably contributed to the study of Freud as a philosophical-literary figure, rather than simply the inventor of a therapeutic technique. In the Rome Discourse, Lacan declared his intention of launching a "return to Freud"; psychoanalysis, he said, had become a parody of itself, twisted out of recognition by too many slight tamperings with Freud's original doctrines. Toward the very end of Lacan's life, in 1980, he dissolved his own Freudian School and instituted a new group, the Cause Freudienne (Freudian Cause), for the same reason: the Freudian School, he explained, had lost track of its original aims in "deviations and compromises," and yet another "return to the true Freud" was called for. This fidelity to Freud, the continual rereading and reinterpretation of the founding texts of psychoanalysis, characterized Lacan's work throughout his career. He was, in a sense, the preeminent literary critic of psychoanalysis, and it seems likely that his most lasting influence will be felt not in psychoanalysis at all, but in the neighboring fields of literary and historical studies.

Whatever the future of Lacanian analysis, Lacan's writings have already had an international impact on those other disciplines. Lacan's constant emphasis on the linguistic structure of the Freudian unconscious, on the mind as a system of signification, made him attractive to students of literature from an early date, even before his major works had been translated. Lacan himself showed a lifelong interest in literature—his seminar on Poe's "Purloined Letter," among the first of Lacan's works to be translated into English, is a case in point—and Lacan's teaching, like Freud's, has proved easily adaptable to literary-critical purposes. Though there is no doubt that Lacan was, as John Forrester has called him, "the most original psychoanalyst since Freud," the durability and value of his contributions to his own and other fields will continue to be questioned for years to come. His works exhibit the primary traits of his life: uncompromising, self-willed, often perverse and sometimes self-defeating, he went his own way and dared others to follow him. Only the long run can decide how many will choose to do so.

WORKS IN ENGLISH TRANSLATION: Lacan's writings have been collected and translated in *The Language of the Self: The Function of Language in Psychoanalysis*, by A. Wilden, with notes and commentary, in 1968. A selection from *Ecrits,* Lacan's basic work, was translated by Alan Sheridan in 1977, with notes and bibliographical references. Sheridan also translated *The Four Fundamental Concepts of Psychoanalysis,* edited by J. A. Miller, in 1977.

ABOUT: Balmary, M. Psychoanalyzing Psychoanalysis, 1982; Clement, C. The Lives and Legends of Jacques Lacan, 1983; Davis, R. C. (ed.) The Fictional Father: Lacanian Readings of the Text, 1981, and Lacan and Narration, 1984; De Waelhens, A. Schizophrenia: A Philosophical Reflection on Lacan's Structuralist Interpretation, 1978; Gallop, J. The Daughter's Seduction, 1982; Laplanche, J. Life and Death in Psychoanalysis, 1970; Lemaire, A. Jacques Lacan, 1977; Mitchell, J. and Rose, J. (eds.) Feminine Sexuality: Jacques Lacan and the Ecole Freudienne, 1983; Muller, J. P. and Richardson, W. J. Lacan and Language: A Reader's Guide to Ecrits, 1982; Roustaing, F. Dire Mastery: Discipleship from Freud to Lacan, 1982; Schneiderman, S. (ed.) Returning to Freud: Clinical Psychoanalysis in the School of Lacan, 1980; Schneiderman, S. Jacques Lacan: The Death of an Intellectual Hero, 1983; Smith, J. H. and Kerrigan, W. Interpreting Lacan, 1983; Stanton, M. Outside the Dream: Lacan and French Styles of Psychoanalysis, 1982.

LAHR, JOHN (HENRY) (July 12, 1941–   ), American biographer, theater critic, and novelist, writes: "A writer is someone for whom writing is harder than for other people. In front of my typewriter is a card saying: ENJOY IT. I enjoy having written much more than I enjoy the solitude and sweat of getting things right on the page. But my gift, if I have any, is perseverance and discipline. I don't know when exactly the notion of being a writer took shape in my life. But it was late, not until my mid-twenties that all my dabbling with words as editor of the high school yearbook and reporter on the *Yale Daily News* began to look to me like a calling. My mother, worried about my vocation, had me tested and the results, in order of aptitude, were Public Relations, Advertising, and Writing. The latter was a non-starter as far as my father [the comedian Bert Lahr] was concerned. His advice was to get a job in advertising where I could make the big bucks and cash in on the contacts he'd expected me to make at Yale. (Dad didn't take any interest in my writing until an essay was published in a slick magazine that cost $1.25.)

"Four events stand out in my mind as turning points. In the summer of 1962, I worked as a reporter on the *Miami Herald.* It was a thrilling summer—earning my by-line, covering murders and fires, making the friendship of an outstanding foreign correspondent Al Burt who thought I had talent and really worked hard with me on

JOHN LAHR

writing. The last piece I wrote that summer was a full-page story about being the son of a clown. It was called "Notes on a Cowardly Lion"; and seven years later, that would be the title of my first book. The experience on the *Herald* gave me a certain cachet at Yale where I was starting my senior year: and when the editors of the *Yalie Daily* were looking for someone to go to Mississippi and cover James Meredith's attempt to integrate Ole Miss, I was their man. I won the Yale writing prize for that series of stories, but my literary ambitions were still vague. At Worcester College, Oxford, where I spent 1963–1965 under the tutelage of Christopher Ricks, I began to understand that it was possible to have a life somehow in literature. Just how, I wasn't sure. It was in England that I met and married Anthea Mander, whose editorial skill and adamantine will helped me to be what I barely had to courage to admit to myself I wanted to be: a writer of books.

"My adult life has been spent unlearning the assumptions of celebrity with which I grew up, and mastering the insecurity borne of a negligent and aloof father. Bert Lahr was a great clown and an absent parent. I loved him dearly on his terms but paid a price for it. One way or another my writing has been an attempt to understand my past and work out a more humane life beyond the tyranny of stardom. *Notes on a Cowardly Lion* was a way of knowing and of mourning my father. My criticism too acknowledged a theatrical past I shared through him and was proud of. But the self-aggrandizement of criticism, the frivolity of the scene, and finally the stricture of the formalized critical language began to wear me down. I wanted to extend my writing; and I couldn't in the endless repetition of weekly deadlines. During the summer of 1970, I wrote the first half of *The Autograph Hound* in five weeks and spent the rest of the year finishing it. The novel liberated me from the gravity of critical language and allowed me to be more myself in print. *The Autograph Hound,* which is about fame, is also about being a critic, the predicament of getting one's energy from others. *Hot to Trot,* my second novel, examined the absurdities of the appetite for status, success and the spirit of aggrandizement which was the ruling ethic of the Lahr household. If the content owed something to my past, so did the style which aspired to be a kind of literary vaudeville and to corrupt an audience with pleasure.

"Since 1975, I have lived away from America where I can concentrate solely on my family and my work without the constant pressure of going public. It is hard being a stranger, but it's healthy. Outside of American society one gets a much clearer view of it, and also oneself. And without any favor to curry and nothing to lose, words don't have to be minced. One can be free, and therefore dangerous. The old panics and pressures no longer seem relevant abroad. Work is now just part of a life, not the reason for it. Sometimes I think of throwing it all in and learning medicine or doing something that would take me out of my room. But these follies attack every writer in his struggle to make sense of the chaos of his mind. What I really want is to keep growing in my life and in my craft. 'Writing,' Simenon said, 'is a vocation of unhappiness.' I agree. But what I've learned is that you needn't extend that unhappiness to life itself."

John Lahr wanted his biography of his father to be as fine as it could be, because "if I blow it, it won't get done again." The book was begun as a short story when he was at Yale, grew in scope during his two years at Oxford, and he began intense work on it upon his return to the United States. It was very well received. *Variety* found it "sensitive, perceptive, moving and memorable. . . . It's both a touchingly human document and an authoritative work of theater historiography . . . [and] a broad but accurate account of the evolution of public comic taste in the twentieth century." Harold Clurman noted, "Some of the descriptions of his father's performances he could not have seen . . . are often more telling than those by reviewers who did see them. The past becomes present in this biography, so that we come to know and understand the actor as clearly as the man."

Lahr was professionally involved in theater history and commentary from the late 1960s, as instructor at New York's Hunter College (1967–68), literary adviser to the Repertory Theater of Lincoln Center (1969–71), and theater editor for Grove Press (1969–71). He was also a frequent contributor to Grove's *Evergreen Review,* and the essays in his second book, *Up Against the Fourth Wall: Essays on Modern Theater,* come from that magazine. For Martin Esslin, the essays "add up to a valuable introduction to the contemporary American theater, with a heavy emphasis on the avant-garde and underground movements. . . . [They] are distinguished by the breadth and depth of the intellectual world their author inhabits." Foster Hirsh thought that the essays, "in their staunchly anti-establishment posture, . . . parallel the theatrical revolution which they chronicle," yet added that "Lahr's belief that radical theater can compete with other modern art forms and that it can educate and improve is refreshing yet somehow naive."

Astonish Me: Adventures in Contemporary Theater is another collection of essays with a somewhat wider scope. In addition to discussion of the works of Harold Pinter, Joe Orton, and Heathcote Williams, the book also offers an analysis of football as theater, and even an appreciation of Tina Turner's singing as myth.

During the 1970s, Lahr became engrossed in the career of Joe Orton, the iconoclastic bad boy of the English theater of the 1960s and author of *Entertaining Mr. Sloane* and *Loot.* He edited Orton's *Complete Plays* in 1975 and wrote an authorized biography, *Prick Up Your Ears.* Some critics found the book voyeuristic, primarily because of its dwelling on the seamy, violent end of Orton's life. Ben Sonnenberg accused him of writing "the murder of Orton more than the life. Orton is shown as the Doomed Artist, his lover, Kenneth Halliwell, as the Fatal Man, and together they form the stereotype of the Tragic Marriage. Lahr throughout is the Reliable Narrator: self-effacing, obtuse, almost proud he is dull." Yet Alan Ross considered it "a full, well-documented biography, decently illustrated, and leaving nothing out. It is eminently readable, in turns entertaining, revealing and very sad." Walter Clemons also praised Lahr for "unexpected feats of imaginative sympathy and critical discrimination." Unfortunately for the book, Orton's reputation as a theatrical innovator was on the wane well before its publication.

By many estimates, Lahr's most assured work of biographical criticism is *Coward the Playwright.* As a subject for Lahr's attention, Noel Coward would seem very far removed from radical or experimental theater, yet he sees the plays as expressing "the metaphysical exhaustion behind the twenties binge." In Coward's characters there is the suggestion of the moral void: "Unlike their plot-heavy antecedents, Coward's characters live comparatively plotless lives. Although Coward's comedies are well-made, the life they depict has lost its thru-line." There is a great deal of concentration here, as there was in the book on Orton, on the subject's homosexuality. Nicholas Shrimpton noted that Lahr "sees homosexuality as an end as well as a means, a covert topic implicit in the plays," yet concluded that the biography "seems to me to miss the heart of Coward's achievement (in the end, indeed, it is driven back on to the conventional praise of him as an all-round 'phenomenon')."

Lahr's two novels, *The Autograph Hound* and *Hot to Trot*, received mixed critical receptions. Studs Terkel was enthusiastic about the former: "In a wild, hilarious and ultimately terrifying work, John Lahr has created a new Everyman." The central character is a busboy, who lives vicariously in the celebrities he pursues. "Lahr's book may be the comic epitaph for an epic in which the plastic face of Somebody Famous replaces the faceless face of Nobody." Crawford Woods, however, found it "an experimental comic novel graceful in many of its moods but diminished by its methods." Anatole Broyard described *Hot to Trot*, a wildly profane story of a calamitous love life, as happening "in short takes, cinematic spatters, as if life had hit the fan. The author has inherited his father's sense of timing." Philip French wrote: "Formally the novel is like a movie of a few years back that follows Godard's dictum about believing in a beginning, a middle and an end, but not necessarily in that order." He considered the book, despite "the relentlessly scatological tone and the obsessive concern with sex [to be] technically . . . immensely accomplished, indeed something of a tour de force. But the form only partially conceals the fact that we learn surprisingly little about the times or about the real source of [the hero's] problems."

Lahr's mother was the former Mildred Schroeder. On August 12, 1965, he married Anthea Loveday Veronica Mander; they have a son, and now live in North London. He won the George Jean Nathan Award for theater criticism for 1968–69, and also in 1969 shared with John Hancock an award of $10,000 from the American Film Institute for the filmscript "Sticky My Fingers, Fleet My Feet."

PRINCIPAL WORKS: *Novels*—The Autograph Hound, 1973; Hot to Trot, 1974. *Non-fiction*—Notes on a Cowardly Lion: The Biography of Bert Lahr, 1969; Up Against the Fourth Wall, 1970; Astonish Me, 1973; (with J.

Price) Life-Show, 1973; Prick Up Your Ears: The Biography of Joe Orton, 1978; Coward: the Playwright, 1982; Automatic Vaudeville: Essays on Star Turns, 1984. *As editor*—Show-Case One, 1970; Grove Press Modern Drama, 1975; The Complete Plays of Joe Orton, 1975.

ABOUT: Contemporary Authors 25–28, 1977. *Periodicals*—Atlantic December 1969; Christian Science Monitor November 28, 1969; February 28, 1973; Harper's November 1969; November 1970; Nation December 7, 1970; November 11, 1978; New Republic December 20, 1969; New Statesman October 6, 1978; New York Review of Books March 22, 1973; October 11, 1979; New York Times Book Review November 23, 1969; September 20, 1970; March 4, 1973; December 17, 1978; March 25, 1984; Newsweek November 24, 1969; March 12, 1973; November 27, 1978; Saturday Review November 15, 1969; Saturday Review of the Arts February 1973; Times Literary Supplement November 9, 1973; October 6, 1978; October 1, 1982; May 28, 1976; Variety November 26, 1969.

*LANDOLFI, TOMMASO (August 9, 1908– July 9, 1979), Italian short story writer, novelist, poet, dramatist, and critic, was born in Pico Farnese, in Frosinone province. From his youth he spent a great deal of time in Florence, eventually taking a degree in letters from its university, where he began his lifelong study of foreign languages, especially Russian, German, and French. Introduced to the Italian poetic movement of "hermeticism" (a term derived from the third-century writer on mysticism Hermes Trismegistus and adopted by early twentieth-century poets and critics to describe a highly metaphoric and often difficult poetry), he came to know well most of the younger hermeticists— he was a near-contemporary at university of Carlo Bo, Mario Luzi, and Leone Traverso; and his earliest published stories appeared in the hermeticist reviews *Campo di Marte* and *Letteratura*. Although he was not a political writer, several of his early works were considered to contain anti-Fascist allusions, and he was imprisoned for a time just before World War II. Upon his release he began to live in a withdrawn, hermitlike fashion, alternating between Pico, Florence, and Rome. Over the course of the next four decades he produced about twenty major books, but always remained resolutely hidden from the public eye.

The seven stories in *Dialogo dei massimi sistemi* (Dialogue of the Greater Harmonies, 1937) formed Landolfi's first published work. The title story shows an already evident fascination with language: a man is amazed, then exasperated, and finally undone by the realization that he has composed three of his very rare po-

°län dôl´ fē, tō mä´ sō

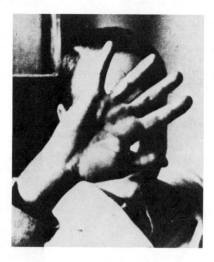

TOMMASO LANDOLFI

ems in a strange language which he has imperfectly learned, then partly forgotten, and which, he discovers during the course of the story, does not even exist. The critic Pietro Pancrazi in an early review recognized the complex nature, at once poetic and ironic, of Landolfi's vision, as well as the astonishing maturity of his first book and the novelty of his apparently archaizing style. He quickly followed this success with others: the six stories, five dialogues, and a fable of *Il mar delle blatte* (The Sea of Cockroaches, 1939), the book that aroused the particular ire of Mussolini's censors, and his first novel, *La pietra lunare* (The Moon Stone, 1939), a strange tale of the boy Giovancarlo's ruined love for Gurù, a tender girl with a profound knowledge of nature who has goat's feet. Landolfi's characters often have a particular rapport with nature and animals, but the spiders, rats, snakes, cockroaches, tapeworms, and apes that inhabit his world may be just as often the focus of the author's (and the reader's) morbid attention and disgust.

Le due zittelle ("The Two Old Maids" published in Italian in 1945, but written in 1939) has remained one of Landolfi's most admired novellas. Wickedly funny, imbued with a distinctly anticlerical tone, it recounts the story of two elderly sisters who discover, to their horror, that their beloved monkey has been slipping out of the house at night to say Mass by himself in the convent next door. Their consternation leads to much arch discussion on the nature of sin, the suffering of the animal world, and the absolute unwillingness of those in power—represented by a fat and complacent monsignor—to understand any occurrence at all out of the ordinary.

Landolfi's gift for narrative was subordinated, ever more frequently as his talents developed, to a kind of diaristic notation, difficult and oblique like most interior monologue. His characters tend increasingly to be unsatisfied—unable to express love, to find faith, or even choose the right words for their thoughts. In *Cancroregina* (1950; translated by M. Caetani under the same title), a rare foray into the genre of science fiction, we read the diary of a pilot, long lost in space, who agonizes over the aptness of his words and phrases even though he knows he is the only one who will ever read what he writes. Apart from the historical novella *Ottavio di Saint-Vincent* (1958), about imposture and reality in pre-Revolutionary France, most of Landolfi's later works tended to be short, slender of plot, and filled with word-play. These included the stories in *Se non la realtà* (If Not Reality, 1960), *Racconti* (Stories, 1961), *In società* (In Society, 1962), and *Racconti impossibili* (Impossible Stories, 1966). He twice published what amounted to literary journals, although in these the diaristic "I" is by no means to be entirely identified with Landolfi himself. These books, *Rien va* (Nothing Goes, 1963) and *Des mois* (A Few Months, 1967), were highly praised for their stylistic innovation, but were also felt to be somewhat inaccessible.

In common with most other members of the literary avant-garde, Landolfi made no attempt to attract any wider audience. Even his titles seem intentionally mystifying: the above-mentioned diaries were entitled in French, as was his 1953 novella *La biere du pecheur* (in which *biere* may mean "beer" and "bier" and *pecheur*, "fisherman" and "sinner"); *Le labrene* (1974), the title of one of his last collections, is a word meaning "geckoes" borrowed from a provincial French dialect—an uncommon word in French and one almost unheard-of in Italian. One of the literary modes most frequently employed in his later years was the *elzeviro*, or short sketch. Fifty of these were collected as *Un paniere di chiocciole* (A Basket of Snails, 1968), and another fifty appeared as *Del meno* (At Least, 1978). From the mid-1970s the publishing house of Rizzoli has been bringing out a uniform edition of Landolfi's complete works.

His dramatic writings were few and considered rather recondite in style. *Landolfo VI di Benevento* (1969), a poetic drama in six acts, takes place in the eleventh century; *Faust 67*, on which he collaborated with Goffredo Parise, has "No One" as its protagonist. The latter enjoyed a short theatrical run in May 1969. His poetry is actually only an experimental episode in his literary career. The 301 poems in *Viola di morte* (Viola of Death, 1972) were all written within the course of a year; the 131 of *Il tradimento* (The Betrayal, 1977) were similarly restricted in their circumstances of composition. Both collections resemble the diaries in form, though the dominant theme is not so much the connection between writing and living as it is between life and death, between "I" and God. His literary criticism is collected in one volume, *Gogol a Roma* (Gogol in Rome, 1971), consisting of previously published reviews and comments, all from the 1950s, on many European writers, particularly Russian and French.

Landolfi is often spoken of with Carlo Gadda as a major figure in modern Italian prose; Franz Kafka's surreal terror and James Joyce's linguistic fecundity are both cited as influences on his development. He is one of the best-known translators into Italian from Russian; in his anthology, *Narratori russi* (1948), of which he was editor and principal translator, he took upon himself the major figures; Pushkin, Gogol, Turgenev, Tolstoy, Dostoevsky, Chekhov, and Bunin. He was also the translator of some of the works of E.T.A. Hoffmann, Hugo von Hofmannsthal, and Prosper Mérimée.

Landolfi won all the major Italian literary awards at least once: the Viareggio prize in 1958 and 1977, the Campiello prize in 1964 and 1974, the Bagutta prize in 1964, and the Strega in 1975 for the thirteen tales collected in *A caso* (By Chance), as well as several other prizes.

Of Landolfi's private life almost nothing is known. He was only rarely photographed, almost never interviewed; he granted a rare interview on television in the 1960s in which he seemed to be talking, quietly and ironically, to himself alone. The critic Gianfranco Contini wrote: "He is the only contemporary writer to have devoted a minute care, worthy of a romantic dandy . . . to the construction of his own 'personage': nocturnal, of an extravagant exceptionality, a wastrel and an inveterate gambler; a personage who has been introduced and even paraded constantly in the works, particularly in the more recent pages of diaristic posture." He was reported to have consigned his manuscripts in mysterious appointments to emissaries from his publishing house. Journalists printed imaginary interviews with him. He forbade any of his publishers to print any photo, blurb, or biographical sketch in his books. Yet he was occasionally able to poke fun at such eccentricities. In the story "Premio letterario" (Literary Prize) from the collection *Del meno* he examined the image that others had made of him, singling out those aspects of his reputation that exerted a force as much symbolic as mysterious. In the apt opinion of Alberto Moravia, who considered

Landolfi the most original writer of his generation, "There is a certain identity between him and his style."

Landolfi's death, from a severe attack of emphysema, occurred in a clinic in Rome. (He had been seriously ill for several years.) So great was his passion for secrecy that the event was not discovered, even by the redoubtable Roman press, until the following day.

WORKS IN ENGLISH TRANSLATION: *Cancroregina* was translated by M. Caetani in his *Anthology of New Italian Writers* in 1950 and in 1971 by Raymond Rosenthal in *Cancerqueen and Other Stories;* Rosenthal and Wayland Young translated *Gogol's Wife and Other Stories* in 1963, which includes "The Two Old Maids" and "Dialogue on the Greater Harmonies."

ABOUT: Bernabò Secchi, G. Invito alla lettura di Tommaso Landolfi, 1978; Columbia Dictionary of Modern European Literature, 1980; Contini, G. Letteratura dell'Italia unita, 1968; Ghetti Abruzzi, G. L'enigma Landolfi, 1979; Pacifici, S. The Modern Italian Novel from Pea to Moravia, 1979; Pancrazi, P. Scrittori d'oggi 4, 1946; Sanguineti, E. in I contemporanei 2, 1975.

*LAO SHE** (pseudonym of **Shu Ch'ing-Ch'in or Shu She-Yü**) (February 3, 1899–August 24, 1966), Chinese novelist, short story writer, and dramatist, was born in Beijing (Peking) to a Manchu family. His father was a foot soldier in the city guard, trying to feed a family on his monthly pay of three ounces of silver. He died before Lao She was two years old, fighting against the allied international forces of the six invading countries during the Boxer Rebellion. The family lived on the mother's meager earnings, and Lao She became well-acquainted with slum life in Beijing, the rickshaw pullers, coolies, policemen, craftsmen, peddlers, street musicians, and prostitutes. He recalled in a memoir that his mother "stopped at no sacrifice for her son to get on in the world." After graduating from a teacher training school in 1918, Lao She started to work, first as a teacher and then as an inspector of education, a post which gave him a chance to get a close look at the government corruption prevalent under the war lords.

In 1924 Lao She went to England as a Chinese language instructor at London University's School of Oriental and African Studies. There he started his wide reading in English fiction, and launched on his literary career with two novels that show the influence of Charles Dickens—*Laozhang Di Zhexue* (Lao Zhang's Philosophy, 1925), with its villainous schoolmaster modeled on the sadistic Wackford Squeers of

°lou shē

Nicholas Nickleby; and the broadly farcical *Zhaozi Yue* (So Says Zhao, 1926), which C. T. Hsia calls "the first serious comic novel in modern Chinese literature." A third novel, *Er Ma* (The Two Mas, 1929), dealing with Anglo-Chinese relations, "clearly invites comparison with *A Passage to India*," Hsia writes.

In 1929 Lao She started on his journey home by way of France, Germany, and Italy, stopping to teach in Singapore; he arrived in Shanghai in 1930. Teaching Western literature in various universities, he continued to write. *Mao cheng Ji* (1932, translated as *City of Cats* and *Cat Country*), and *Lihun* (*Divorce*, 1933), are products of this period. The former is a fable, set on Mars, while the latter, using the urban poor of old Beijing as background, is a satire on the small bureaucracy and the sickness of Chinese society in general. But these tales and others were only early efforts leading to his first major work *Lo-t'o Hsiang-tzu* (*Camel Hsiangsi*, 1936, also translated as *Rickshaw Boy*).

"Camel" Xiangzi, a poor but honest Northern lad, sees in owning his own rickshaw a symbol of the independence that he is determined to achieve. He is repeatedly thwarted. First his rickshaw is lost when he is drafted into the army. He escapes from the barracks taking with him three camels (hence his nickname), which he sells for a pittance. He works harder than ever, first on a rented rickshaw, then as a private rickshaw puller for a professor with radical associations. His savings are extorted by the rapacious police when the professor's house is raided, and he has to go back to work again for the rickshaw owner Liu. Fate intervenes in the shape of Liu's daughter, called "tiger" after her temperament, who seduces Camel and eventually tricks him into marriage. Although Camel pulls his own rickshaw now, he is unhappy with his nagging wife. When she dies in childbirth, he has to sell everything to pay the funeral expenses. Back where he started from, he goes in search of Xiao Fusi, a neighborhood girl who supports her family as a prostitute, in the hope of marrying her and making a new start. When he finds out that she has hanged herself, he loses the will to strive and sinks into degradation, survivng from day to day as a petty thief and loafer. In the dying old paupers huddled on street corners he foresees his own end.

With its portrait of Camel's futile struggles, the novel is a panorama of slum life in old Beijing, a harsh social indictment and, on a deeper level, an inquiry into the perennial problem of man and his fate. The ending conveys the author's negative attitude toward the individual's lone efforts to raise himself. Just as Dickens had influenced his earlier works, there is an affinity between this novel and Thomas Hardy's novels of fate, especially, as C. T. Hsia suggests, *The Mayor of Casterbridge*. The novel, undoubtedly one of the most important Chinese novels of the 1930s, enjoyed wide popularity in the Western world. The unauthorized translation, *Rickshaw Boy,* by Evan King in 1945, a Book-of-the Month Club selection, was hailed as a masterpiece, "a various and brightly colored tale . . . despite its tragedy, a heartening and beautiful story" (A. C. Spectorsky in *Book Week*) and as a "sad, brave, unglamorized novel . . . just the kind of book that is best suited to the education of the intelligent reader who wants to acquire both a sensible emotional appreciation of the ordinary men and women [of China] and a thorough comprehension of their humanity and their essential invincibility" (Richard Watts, *New Republic*). Lao She himself, however, repudiated the translation because the original novel had been altered to give the story a happy ending.

Lao She's other works of the 1930s included a collection of "hastily exacted stories" called *Ganji* in 1934 and other short fiction, mainly scenes from slum life in old Beijing, full of humor and satire, exuding at the same time a deep love for the lowly people he knew so well. With the outbreak of the Sino-Japanese war in 1937, Lao She move to Wuhan, then to Chongqiing. Because of his respected position and wide associations with writers of different sympathies, he was chosen to head the Chinese Writers' Anti-Aggression Association in 1938. During the war, Lao She threw himself wholeheartedly into cultural activities, dashing off much writing to boost the war effort—plays, poems for recital, scripts for traditional and popular art forms—all fired with intense patriotic fervor. His ambitious trilogy *Sishi Tongtang* (Four Generations Under One Roof, 1944–50), traces the fortunes of several households under the Japanese occupation and studies the effect of the war on the national character. In 1946 Lao She visited the United States at the invitation of the State Department, lecturing, writing, and supervising the translation of his own works.

He left for his homeland in 1949, immediately after the founding of the People's Republic, and became actively involved in the reconstruction of his country's cultural life. In spite of his many engagements in cultural affairs at home and abroad, he continued his writing. Prominent among the works of this period are the plays *Longxu Gou* (*Dragon Beard Ditch,* 1951), and *Chaguan* (*Tea House,* 1957). The first depicts the happy changes that take place in a slum after the liberation, while the latter is a vast panorama of life in Beijing from the turn of the century up to the end of World War II. It presents in grand strokes, with perceptive insights, the many facets of life in China from the last days of the Qing dynasty to the first republic, the chaos of the war lords, and finally the explosive domestic situation after the war—all these seen through the patrons of a tea house and the changes in their lives. *Tea House* is firmly established as one of the landmarks of the new Chinese drama, and in its revival in 1979 by the People's Art Theatre it played to capacity audiences. Subsequently *Tea House* was widely acclaimed on a European tour in the early 1980s, and was produced in New York by the Pan Asian Theater in March 1983.

Among modern Chinese writers, Lao She is outstanding for his deep understanding of and love for the downtrodden and underprivileged, particularly the urban poor of old Beijing. He was adept at catching the nuances of the Beijing vernacular and the mannerisms of the old inhabitants. His wit and humor, his satire of social evil and human failings, combined with expert handling of local color, make his work stand out as a unique portrayal of the Chinese scene and the Chinese character. An abiding love for his country and his people permeates his life and writings. "I apply the lash," Lao She wrote, "but never go to extremes." His criticism is mild, but, as the Chinese writer Mao Dun says, "under the raillery and rant, we can feel his serious attitude toward life, his sense of justice, his tenderness and, above all, his deep love for his country." In view of all this, it is particularly tragic that he should have died by his own hand during the early days of the "cultural revolution."

WORKS IN ENGLISH TRANSLATION: Apart from Evan King's 1945 version, *Rickshaw Boy*, published in a new translation as *Rickshaw* by Jean M. James in 1979, and again in Shi Xiaoqing's translation as *Camel Xiangzi* in 1981, a number of Lao She's other works are now available in English. These include King's translation of *Li-hun* as *Divorce* in 1948, also repudiated by the author, and a new translation by Helena Kuo in the same year as *The Quest for Love of Lao Lee*. Another novel of 1936, *Niutian Zizhuan*, was published as *Heavensent* in 1951 by an unidentified translator. Of Lao She's plays, *Lungxu Gou* was translated as *Dragon Beard Ditch* by Liaio Hung-ying in 1956, and *Chaguan* as *Tea House* by John Howard-Gibbon in 1980. Excerpts from *Mao Cheng Ji* were translated as *City of Cats* by James Dew in 1964 and the work in its entirety by William A. Lyell, Jr. as *Cat Country* in 1970. An abridgement of his trilogy *Sishi Tongtang t'ang* was translated by Ida Pruitt, with Lao She's assistance, in 1951 as *The Yellow Storm*; and he collaborated with Helena Kuo in 1952 on a translation of a novel that had not until then been published in China, *The Drum Singers*. *Ma Hsien Sheng Y'u Ma Wei* was translated as *Ma and Son* by Jean M. James in 1980. *Cheng*

Hung Chi Hsia was translated as *Beneath the Red Banner* by Don J. Cohn in 1982. English translations of his short stories have been published in many anthologies including two collections edited by C. C. Wang—*Contemporary Chinese Stories*, 1944, and *Stories of China at War*, 1946—George Kao's *Chinese Wit and Humor*, 1946; Chia-Hua Yvan and Robert Payne's *Contemporary Chinese Short Stories*, 1946; Gene Hanrahan's *50 Oriental Stories*, 1965; W. J. F. Jenner's *Modern Chinese Stories*, 1970; and W. J. and R. I. Meserve's *Modern Literature from China*, 1974.

ABOUT: Biographical Dictionary of Republican China, 1967–1971; Buxbaum, D. and F. W. Mote, Transition and Permanence: Chinese History and Culture, 1972; Dictionary of Oriental Literature I, 1974; Encyclopedia of World Literature in the 20th Century IV, 1984; Hsia, C. T. A History of Modern Chinese Fiction, 1971; Kao, G. Two Writers in the Cultural Revolution, 1979; Munro, S. R. The Function of Satire in the Works of Lao She, 1977; Prusek, J. (ed.) Studies in Modern Chinese Literature, 1964; Slupski, Z. The Evolution of a Modern Chinese Writer, 1966; Vohra, R. Lao She and the Chinese Revolution, 1974. *Periodicals*—Chinese Literature 4, April 1970; 11, November 1978; China Quarterly 8, October–December 1961.

*LAPOINTE, PAUL-MARIE (September 22, 1929–   ), Canadian poet and journalist, was born in Saint-Félicien, Quebec, near Lac Saint-Jean in the forest country 150 miles north of Quebec City. He was educated at the Séminaire de Chicoutimi during the final years of World War II, then at the Collège Saint-Laurent in Montreal. He studied architecture at the École des Beaux-Arts for a year (1947–48) before beginning a long career as a journalist. Lapointe served on the staffs of *L'Événement-Journal* from 1950 to 1954 and *La Presse* from 1954 to 1960; with Jean-Louis Gagnon he founded *Le Nouveau Journal* in 1961, and he was chief editor of *Le Magazine Maclean* from 1964 to 1968. Since 1968 he has been employed by Radio-Canada, currently as director of the news and public affairs service of the French-language radio network.

Lapointe wrote most of the hundred-odd poems in his first collection, *Le Vierge incendié* (Virgo in Flames, 1948), in one three-week period of intense experimentation with automatic writing. The daring imagistic freedom of many of these poems, which are often disposed as compact blocks rather than in the manner of free verse, is entirely evocative of Paul Éluard and Les Automatistes:

syrinx charmer of grass snakes   paradoxical saw-toothed flute   reedy satyr   feverish eel   o shaggy with love fascination of veins in the streams of running gas   paper snakes of rhythm and Bacchus imprinted

°lä pwaNt´

on temples through
the balls of the feet   sea urchins in aquariums   spiky
hair full of slugs and the sea's rollers   barnacles
gulls   hippocampi

—trans. D. G. Jones

Others among these early works, however, are more conventional in their form and far more pointed and political in their frame of reference:

In the orchards
the noonday monsters forgot us
because they were blind
or could no longer sniff us out

So we set forth to lay hold
of the crystal future
the castle gleaming with every hope
streaming like watered silk

And already the most nimble
sprung from their furry hide-outs
the hundred-limbed monkeys
and the whole troop
we went running one after the other
single file we are free

But an invisible vulture
unsuspected
swallowed subito the snake

—trans. D. G. Jones

Both strains are evident throughout the poet's subsequent career. Pierre Nepveu called *Le Vierge incendié* "one of the craziest, most excessive books in our literature," and D. G. Jones described the poems as revealing "an exuberant delight in language and a spontaneous mixture of ironic irritation and lyric affirmation. Organized in associational clusters, they increasingly abandon conventional form and syntax. In both form and theme, they were entirely new in Quebec literature."

The same year he published his first book, Lapointe wrote a sequence of poems, *Nuit du 15 au 26 novembre 1948* (Night of the 15th to the 26th of November, 1948), which remained unpublished until 1969. This is a cry of protest against the repressive reaction of the Quebec provincial government to the neosurrealist manifesto of Paul-Émile Borduas, *Refus total* (Total Refusal), in which the painter and his confreres rejected both the traditional, stultified Quebec culture and the new culture promised by modern technology. Lapointe published no poetry from 1948 until 1960, when *Choix de poèmes—arbres* (Choice of Poems—Trees) appeared. Along with his 1964 collection, *Pour les âmes* (For All Souls), these poems represent little appreciable stylistic advance on those of his first book, but are less angry and rejectionist in tone and reflect his positive view of the new, more hopeful sociopolitical climate just beginning to prevail in the province. When his first three works were published together as *Le réel absolu: poèmes, 1948–1965* (The Absolute Real, 1971),

Lapointe was immediately recognized by the generation younger than his own as an important stylistic and thematic precursor. This retrospective volume won the David prize and the Canadian Governor General's award.

Many of the poems in *Tableaux de l'amoureuse* (The Lover's Canvases, 1974) reflect Lapointe's intense commitment to social justice. The Vietnam War, in particular, was frequently a source of anguish for him, as it was for most Canadians, and the focus of some of his best poems, such as "Mission Accomplished":

death's lanterns at sea
at dawn
in a flat calm
phosphorous hedgehogs send up yellow signals to
    the bombardiers who return
smooth as the decks for landing
are the shattered villages
the servomechanism is merely memory
and pure serenity the metal

—trans. D. G. Jones

Lapointe's more recent work has tended to return to the disjunctive automatism of the block-poems in *Le Vierge incendié*. The poems in *Bouche rouge* (Red Mouth, 1976) celebrate, highly abstractly, the eternal feminine and discourse on the accompanying drawings of his illustrator, Gisèle Verreault. The thousand pages of *Écritures* (Writings, 1979) represent a deconstructionist's dream: all the writing is deliberately meaningless, incoherent, and anti-interpretational; only the individual words themselves are important, not their references, associations, or contexts. One surrealist's homage to another is *Tombeau de René Crevel* (Tomb of René Crevel, 1979), which consists entirely of arbitrarily arranged segments from the work of Crevel—a minor French poet whom Lapointe claims as a major inspiration.

WORKS IN ENGLISH TRANSLATION: Lapointe's best-known earlier poems (from all collections through *Tableaux de l'amoureuse*) are available in English in a collection entitled *The Terror of the Snows,* 1976, translated by D.G. Jones. Selections from his work also appear in J. Glasscoe's *The Poetry of French Canada in Translation,* 1970.

ABOUT: Canadian Writers: A Biographical Dictionary, 1967; Fisette, J. Le Texte automatiste, 1977; Major, J.-L. La Nuit incendiée, 1978; Nepveu, P. Les Mots à l'écoute, 1979; Oxford Companion to Canadian Literature, 1983. *Periodicals*—Choice July–August 1977; Ellipse no. 11, 1972; Library Journal October 15, 1976.

*LAQUEUR, WALTER (May 26, 1921–　),
German-born historian, journalist, and novelist,
writes: "Born in Breslau, then part of Germany.
Family—middle middle class, very assimilated,
some branches were converted in nineteenth
century. (Learned to my surprise the other day
that I am related by marriage to the Lev
Nikolaevich Tolstoy family). Uncles, great-
uncles, etc., were merchants, physicians, historians, art dealers, philosophers—my maternal
grandmother belonged to the Cassirer clan.
Graduated from high school-junior college
('gymnasium') in early 1938, went to Palestine.
Was the youngest student at Hebrew University
at the time, also the first dropout. During the
next five years I was a member of a kibbutz,
where I married [Barbara Koch], aged nineteen.
From 1944 to 1953 journalist in Jerusalem—
most interesting period—covered also to some
extent events in other Middle Eastern countries.
Went to London in 1953 but kept ties with Israel
(teaching each spring at Tel Aviv University). In
London I founded the periodical *Survey*, which
still exists; became in 1964 director of Wiener
Library and Institute of Contemporary History
and editor of *Journal of Contemporary History*.
Began to teach in U.S. in 1956 on a part-time basis despite absence of B.A., M.A., Ph.D. and other such degrees. Was not a good teacher in the
beginning, C- at best, and wonder why anyone
kept me. Improved over the years to B standard.
For the last twenty years I have been commuting
between Europe and the U.S. but since 1970 I
have lived most of the time in Washington. I am
head of the Research Council of CSIS, Washing-
ton-based think tank. We have two daughters
and three grandchildren. I have written articles
and books in German, Hebrew and English, but
for the last twenty years only in English.

"My main interest for a long time was in political and intellectual history and current international affairs (Europe, Soviet Union, U.S. foreign
policy). My best books in these fields are probably *Young German* and *Guerrilla*, but I may not
be the best judge. I began to write a novel while
I lived in the kibbutz, continued to work on it in
later years but did not think of publishing. In between my historical and political work (and administration, public speaking, consulting, public
relations, fund raising, etc., etc.) I wrote and
published some short autobiographical pieces
('Homecoming,' '1938—a Memoir,' 'Utopia Plus
Twenty') and also some travelogues (mainly
about the Soviet Union) which later appeared in
a collection of essays *Out of the Ruins of Europe*.
Attained a certain reputation as commentator
and pundit on international affairs, but also
learned the lesson that being right prematurely
is not conducive to enchancing one's popularity.

WALTER LAQUEUR

"I began again to write a novel in the late
1970s notwithstanding skepticism on the part of
friends and publishers, partly out of boredom
with conventional political science and history,
partly because I had become less self-conscious
("serious scholars do not write fiction"), partly
because with advancing age one does not really
care that much what critics will say. Above all,
I thought that I should try to describe the fate
of a group of people (whom I knew well) during
a certain period, broadly speaking my own life
time, and that this could be done best in a fictional (or semifictional) way, a *roman à clef*.
Thus I came to write *The Mississing Years* and
its sequel *Farewell to Europe*. Looking back I
am not unhappy with the result. I regret that I
stuck too closely to fact; there are too many didactic interludes, too much history, too little personal impression and feeling. I learned from my
mistakes, I shall try to do better next time."

In his preface to *Out of the Ruins of Europe*,
Walter Laqueur described the awakening of his
interest in twentieth-century history. On guard
duty one day in a kibbutz in Palestine in 1942,
among peaceful surroundings, he recalled, by
striking contrast, the devastation in Europe
which he had so narrowly escaped and concluded that "having been the plaything of historical
forces over which there was seemingly no control, I might one day soon at least try to comprehend the events which had led up to that sudden
and altogether inexplicable catastrophe." In the
judgment of his peers, Laqueur's lack of formal

°lä kûr´

academic training has in no way diminished the value of his work as a historian. Indeed, a fellow historian of the Holocaust, Terrence Des Pres, wrote in the *New Republic* in 1980 that this circumstance is "his special strength," because combining scholarship with eyewitness experience and a varied career in journalism, Laqueur "has turned his condition of exile to the pursuit of practical knowledge, with the fortitude of a mind that knows its job to be endless and knows, as theorists do not, that the last word can never be spoken." Like the hero of his novels *The Missing Years* and *Farewell to Europe,* Laqueur the historian is a modern Everyman who witnesses and records the major crises of the modern world—the collapse of the German Republic, the growth of Nazism, the Holocaust, the growth and spread of terrorist and guerrilla movements, the emergence of the state of Israel, and the developing crises in the Middle East.

Laqueur's earliest historical writing set a course that he has followed steadily. *Communism and Nationalism in the Middle East* was a pioneering work in the the study of nationalist movements in the contemporary Arab world, Turkey, and Israel. In subsequent books he has surveyed the Arab-Israeli conflicts of recent years with authoritative scholarship and, reviewers agree, remarkable objectivity. His *History of Zionism,* for example, was praised for its balance and candor. Only at the end of this very long book, the *Economist* observed, "does he allow himself an apologia for Zionism." Even when writing on the emotionally charged subject of the Holocaust and the failure of the Western Allies to act in time to save millions of lives (*The Terrible Secret*), Laqueur presented a dispassionate analysis of a tragically complex situation. "The evil nature of Nazism was beyond their comprehension," he wrote, although he offers in that book massive evidence that the leaders of the democratic world had been informed of the enormity of Hitler's "Final Solution." As a reviewer in *Time* observed: "The author is not a man to dwell in the conditional: those who might have been saved are gone, and Laqueur is more interested in first causes than in lamentations."

Emerging as a novelist somewhat late in his career, Laqueur traced, through the life of a German-Jewish doctor, the history of a twentieth-century man of intelligence and good will. In *The Missing Years* his protagonist reviews his life from the relatively peaceful days of the Weimar Republic through the horrors of the Nazi years and his family's ultimate escape to Switzerland. In *Farewell to Europe* this same character sees his family separated—his wife dead, one son embroiled in the Zionist struggle for an Is-

raeli state, the other in California where the now aging father joins him only to witness new crises and challenges to his traditional values. Though these two novels lack the authority for which his histories are noted, they confront the major issues of the age with immediacy and sympathy, with what Christopher Lehmann-Haupt described as "a quiet ring of authenticity that only the best of historical writing achieves."

PRINCIPAL WORKS: Communism and Nationalism in the Middle East, 1956; Young Germany, 1961; Russia and Germany, 1965; The Road to War, 1967 (U.S. The Road to Jerusalem); Europe Since Hitler, 1970; Out of the Ruins of Europe, 1971; Zionism: A History, 1972; Confrontation: The Middle East War and World Politics, 1974; Weimar: A Cultural History, 1918–1933, 1974; Guerrilla, 1976; Terrorism, 1977; Germany Today: A Personal Report, 1984. *Novels*—The Missing Years, 1980; Farewell to Europe, 1981.

ABOUT: Laqueur, W. Out of the Ruins of Europe, 1971; Who's Who, 1983; Who's Who in America, 1983–1984. *Periodicals*—New Republic May 10, 1980; Time March 2, 1981.

LASCH, CHRISTOPHER (June 1, 1932–   ), American historian and social critic, was born in Omaha, Nebraska. He is the son of Robert Lasch, a journalist and editorial writer for the *Omaha World Herald,* and Zora (Schaupp) Lasch, a professor of philosophy. Lasch studied history at Harvard University, where he won the Bowdoin Prize and graduated summa cum laude. He earned an M.A. in 1955 and a Ph.D. in 1961 from Columbia University; in 1956 he married a fellow Columbia student, the potter Nell Commager, the daughter of historian Henry Steele Commager. After teaching at a number of colleges, including the University of Iowa (1961–66) and Northwestern University in Chicago (1966–70), Lasch joined the history faculty of the University of Rochester in New York where, since 1979, he has been Don Alonzo Watson Professor of History.

In 1962 Lasch published his first book, *The American Liberals and the Russian Revolution;* it revealed his early and abiding concern with the contrast between radical and liberal (usually a denigratory term in Lasch's vocabulary) politics, but it received little critical attention. However, his second work, *The New Radicalism in America 1889–1963: The Intellectual as a Social Type,* established him as an important and original thinker. An unconventional history of social reform in the United States, *The New Radicalism* did not, for the most part, chronicle the gritty particularities of party meetings, polit-

CHRISTOPHER LASCH

ical programs, and the like; instead, using "an imaginative composite of social history, depth psychology, and textual analysis," according to *Time* magazine, Lasch examined the lives and writings of the "new radicals"—those intellectuals of this century primarily concerned with "the improvement of the quality of American culture as a whole, rather than simply a way of equalizing the opportunities for economic self-advancement." As examples of such figures Lasch discussed, among others, Jane Addams, the pacifist and social worker; the feminist Mabel Dodge Luhan; Randolph Bourne, an early advocate and hero of youth revolt; and Lincoln Steffens, whose disillusionment with the internal failures of progressivism forced him, like many of his generation, toward an even more ineffectual, if seemingly more rigorous, communism. Lasch also tackled the anti-intellectual radicalism of the present day, as seen most clearly in the work of Norman Mailer, in which, Lasch wrote, "the body of ideas and assumptions which I have called the new radicalism achieved some kind of final and definitive statement. The confusion of power and art, the effort to liberate the social and psychological 'underground' by means of political action, the fevered pursuit of experience, the conception of life as an experiment, the intellectual's identification of himself with the outcasts of society—these things could be carried no further without carrying them to absurdity."

The New Radicalism in America provided not only an original perspective on the early strength and gradual decline of utopian reformism, but also an excellent introduction to the intellectual and literary ancestry of the New Left

and the nascent youth counterculture of the 1960s. "Only a literary shotgun marriage could unite such diverse partners as Jane Addams and Norman Mailer," wrote the critic for *Newsweek*. "With this study of intellectuals as a 'subculture,' a 'social type,' a 'status group,' Lasch has written an important and engrossing contribution to a complex and elusive subject." Daniel Aaron, writing in the *New York Times*, was most impressed with "the insights, casually dropped and often brilliantly phrased, that illuminate a person or a period, and the almost novelistic way in which Lasch makes use of published and unpublished material. . . . He discerns the sentimentality and suppressed violence, the fantasies drawn from boys' fiction and popular romance which 'the new radicals brought to experience' . . . his book can be read as a treatise on the fate of intellectuals who forsake the role of criticism and who sacrifice moral and intellectual imperatives to the hopes of the future."

Increasingly, the mortgaging of the future due to the loss of contemporary moral and intellectual rigor became Lasch's primary concern; he gradually turned from social history to outright social criticism. At the same time his politics, which had seemed firmly, though not slavishly, of the left, began an unusual shift toward what several critics would eventually call "reactionary" positions. The five essays *The Agony of the American Left* analyzed the fragments of the mid-60s left—militant black and student movements, Marxists, peaceniks, and even conventional liberals—noting repeatedly that without a unified party, a common radical theory, and a rational program of political action the left was doomed to continuing ineffectuality. Though earnest, his tone showed a detachment from the immediate passions of radical politics; he was "as critical of his friends as of his enemies," wrote one critic: "this is a real contribution to these times of rhetorical overkill on the Left." *The World of Nations*, a collection of eighteen lectures, reviews, and short articles written over a fifteen-year period, covered a miscellany of subjects, including foreign policy, feminism, the family, and conservative reforms. At the end of one essay Lasch called for a new assessment of "the long tradition of conservative criticism of modern culture that has too often been ignored by the left."

Haven in a Heartless World: The Family Besieged attempted just such a conservative cultural critique. In this book, Lasch's objective was not a study of the family per se, but an attack on the divisive opinions of "experts" on the family, from Freud to R. D. Laing to the bureaucrats behind the vast state-run programs that have a crucial impact on familial structure. At the same time Lasch presented his own analysis (gleaned from recent work in family psychology) of how this body of expert but often erroneous opinion, when absorbed by the family itself, results in a degenerating psychodynamic in which narcissistic parents, following the vagaries of the latest social theory, no longer can provide stable moral, emotional, and intellectual models for their children. Surprisingly, Lasch paid little attention to the effect on the family of changing socioeconomic forces, as would be expected from a writer so familiar with Marxist theory. "He does not," wrote Marshall Berman in the New York Times, "really integrate his Freudian and Marxian analyses, and they sometimes appear to cancel each other out." Reviewers expecting a well-reasoned, orderly critique were disappointed; Haven in a Heartless World, most agreed, was a lurching, emotional rant against what Lasch called "the guardians of public health and morality," and, more generally, "the psychopathology of our society." Wrote Berman: "Lasch's lucid thoughts will suddenly become murky, his complexity dreadfully simple, his critical balance will be swept away by eruptions of rage and despair. As a result, Haven in a Heartless World is one of the strangest and most disturbing books to have appeared in years."

No one was more surprised than Lasch when his next book, The Culture of Narcissism: American Life in an Age of Diminishing Expectations, became a best-seller in 1979. (In an interview in People, certainly the magazine most identified as pandering to the narcissistic proclivities of Americans, he said that he thought the book "difficult, even forbidding.") The author, in tones of scholarly despair, described in detail "a way of life that is dying—the culture of competitive individualism, which in its decadence has carried the logic of individualism to the extreme of a war of all against all, the pursuit of happiness to the dead end of a narcissistic preoccupation with the self." As Lasch argued, unfettered consumer capitalism, coupled with the self-consciousness engendered by the intrusion of experts into every area of private life, was largely responsible for this condition, which has reached its highest development in the United States. "The values associated with the work ethic—delayed gratification, self-sacrifice, thrift, and industry—no longer enjoy wide play," he told People. "The stress is now on the legitimacy of immediate gratification. . . . The new value system has shifted from Horatio Alger to the Happy Hooker." Far from signaling an increase in the perception of self-worth, Lasch claimed, rampant narcissism is an indication that men and women are experiencing "their inner impulses as intolerably urgent and menacing."

As a profoundly conservative psychological critique of an entire culture, The Culture of Narcissism offered little in the way of therapy. Though Lasch made occasional mention of "the signs of new life in the U.S."—which in 1979 probably referred to the rise of neo-conservatism in politics and religion, though he also referred to so-called "communities of competence," by which he evidently meant centers of self-help populism that slip through the cogs of the bureaucratic machine—he provided no program for regaining the solid old values. "In America you're supposed to come up with the answers, like a diet formula," he told the New York Times, "but I have no easy solutions. My book is not doomsaying, but exposing a condition."

Popular journals such as Time, Newsweek, and People itself seemed to find Lasch's arguments convincing, even obscurely flattering, as did those who bought the book. "He has brilliantly performed the first job of a social critic," wrote Newsweek, "by prompting us to look at our reflection—shorn of vanity." Historical scholars, however, questioned the validity of the book's central premise that contemporary American culture is singularly decadent. In the Times Literary Supplement Galen Strawson pointed out a basic flaw in the author's reasoning. "[The book] is everywhere undermined by a failure to take account of the constant elements in human nature and culture, to appreciate how little is really new. And in its melodramatization of the uniqueness of our spiritual condition today, it doubtless both appeals to and, perhaps, reveals, a narcissistic inability to feel oneself part of a historical stream."

Lasch lives with his wife and teen-aged children in Avon, New York, near Rochester; they summer in Pittsford, New York.

PRINCIPAL WORKS: The American Liberals and the Russian Revolution, 1962; The New Radicalism in America, 1889–1963: The Intellectual as a Social Type, 1965; The Agony of the American Left, 1969; The World of Nations, 1973 (published as World of Nations: Reflections on American History, Politics, and Culture, 1974); Haven in a Heartless World: The Family Besieged, 1977; The Culture of Narcissism: American Life in an Age of Diminishing Expectations, 1979; The Minimal Self: Psychic Survival in Modern Times, 1984.

ABOUT: Contemporary Authors 73–77, 1978; Who's Who in America, 1983–84. Periodicals—Book Week June 27, 1965; March 16, 1969; Commentary July 1969; April 1979; Nation, June 23, 1969; February 17, 1978; January 27, 1979; New Republic February 18, 1979; New York Review of Books February 23, 1978; New York Times Book Review June 13, 1965; September 30, 1973; January 15, 1978; January 14, 1979; April

15, 1979; May 25, 1980; October 28, 1984; New Yorker August 27, 1979; Newsday March 22, 1968; Newsweek May 17, 1965; January 22, 1979; People July 9, 1979; Time January 8, 1979; Times Literary Supplement July 4, 1980.

LAUGHLIN, JAMES (October 30, 1914–), American publisher, editor, and poet, was born in Pittsburgh, Pennsylvania, the son of Henry Hughart and Marjory (Rea) Laughlin. An heir to the Jones-Laughlin steel fortune, Laughlin was the great-grandson of James Laughlin, a Calvinist immigrant from the north of Ireland who came to America in the nineteenth century and sold crockery as a traveling peddler before founding an iron foundry in Pittsburgh. James Laughlin IV was raised in Pittsburgh in an affluent home where there was no particular interest in literature. He studied at several preparatory schools—at Le Rosey in Rolle, Switzerland in 1928; the Eaglebrook School in Deerfield, Massachusetts in 1929; and the Choate School in Wallingford, Connecticut from 1930–1932. Laughlin's interest in literature was awakened at Choate, encouraged particularly by two teachers, Carey Briggs and Dudley Fitts, the poet and translator. He wrote for and helped to edit the Choate literary magazine, and before entering college published a prize-winning story, "Salle d'étude," in the May 1933 issue of the *Atlantic Monthly.*

Laughlin entered Harvard University in 1934, but in the middle of his sophomore year, reacting to the "stuffy" atmosphere of the university (the reigning figure in the English department at that time, the poet Robert Hillyer, would leave the room if someone mentioned T. S. Eliot or Ezra Pound), he took a leave of absence to wander in Europe. In Salzburg, a French professor introduced him to Gertrude Stein, whom he visited at her country house at Bilignin, France. For a month Laughlin stayed with Stein and Alice B. Toklas, and prepared press releases for Stein's forthcoming American lecture tour, translating her memoranda in "Steinese" into English. Laughlin found Stein a "charismatic" personality, inclined to "megalomania," and after sensing that their personalities were incompatible went to stay in Paris. There, making use of a letter of introduction from Dudley Fitts, he wrote to Ezra Pound, asking if he might see him. Pound wired, encouragingly, "Visibility high," and Laughlin soon joined the Pounds in Rapallo, Italy.

At Rapallo, Laughlin became an informal student at Pound's one-man "Ezuversity," where studies consisted of having lunch with Pound

JAMES LAUGHLIN

and his wife, joining them for mountain walks, dining with them, and listening to Pound's monologues on economics, social credit, and literature. Pound read Laughlin's stories and plays, editing them stringently, and after six months advised that instead of becoming a poet Laughlin should make himself useful to others by becoming a publisher. Laughlin returned to the United States, and resumed his studies at Harvard, where he began printing books. New Directions, later the New Directions Publishing Corporation, was founded by Laughlin while he was still an undergraduate. Pound arranged for him to edit a literary section, "New Directions in Literature," in Gorham Munson's magazine *New Democracy,* contributors to which included Pound himself, William Carlos Williams, E. E. Cummings, T. S. Eliot, Marianne Moore, and Henry Miller; and in 1936 Laughlin decided to "put all this good material together" in *New Directions in Prose and Poetry,* the first of forty-three volumes in one of the most distinguished series in American publishing history. With money furnished by his father, Laughlin traveled across the country by car, persuading bookstores to buy a copy or two—an undertaking that for years involved operating at a loss. Laughlin has estimated that for over twenty years, before beginning to realize a profit, New Directions lost $250,000.

After receiving his B.A. degree from Harvard in 1939, Laughlin transferred his publishing operations to the barn of a house in Norfolk, Connecticut. Later he opened a New York office, which has changed its location several times and is situated today in Greenwich Village. Although subsisting on a marginal budget, and able to offer authors only the most meager advances, Laughlin achieved remarkable successes as a publisher of experimental or avant-garde writing. Among others, New Directions has published Ezra Pound, Dylan Thomas, Kenneth Rexroth, Nathanael West, Thomas Merton, Vladimir Nabokov, Djuna Barnes, John Hawkes, Gary Snyder, Lawrence Ferlinghetti, Robert Creeley, James Purdy, Frederico Garcia Lorca, Boris Pasternak, Jorge Luis Borges, and Yukio Mishima.

The story of how Laughlin attracted a galaxy of major writers to New Directions has been told in Donald Hall's account in the *New York Times* (August 23, 1981), and in Robert Dana's interview with him in the *American Poetry Review* (November/December 1981). Laughlin achieved his phenomenal success partly by listening to brilliant advisers, and by being a step ahead of the public, which eventually caught up with him and bought his books. Although best known as a publisher and editor, Laughlin is also the author of some six collections of poems. The poet and translator Robert Fitzgerald collected a sampling of Laughlin's poetry, *In Another Country: Poems 1935–1975,* and in his introduction speaks of the poems as being distinct, unique, "utterly clear, stained by no muddiness." Sometimes informed by "bitter knowledge" or by "lyrical joy," he went on, they have the "precise" quality of "classical epigrams." Reviewing the book in the *Nation,* Hayden Carruth said of the title poem that "in its apparently small, simple narrative it gathers and condenses all of modern poetic technique, considered as the instrument of sensibility." Denise Levertov called Laughlin "an exquisite and distinctive stylist," which seems a fair assessment of the delicacy of Laughlin's effects, the peculiar candor of his voice. Laughlin is modest about his poetry, which he once said is "very light; it's sentimental, it deals with no great subjects."

Laughlin has been president of Intercultural Publications, Inc. (1952–1969); a trustee of the Allen-Chase Fund, the Merton Legacy Fund, and the Rosenbach Foundation; and served on innumerable committees. He has also been visiting professor at the University of California, San Diego (1974) and at the University of Iowa (1981). Laughlin's many honors include Chevalier of the Legion of Honor, awarded for publishing translations of French literature, D. Litt. degrees from Hamilton College (1969) and Colgate University (1978), and the Distinguished Service to the Arts award from the American Academy of Arts and Letters (1977).

Laughlin married Margaret Keyser in 1942,

but the marriage ended in divorce in 1952; in 1957, he married Ann Clark Resor. By the first marriage, he has a son and daughter, Paul and Leila; by the second two sons, Robert and Henry. He is an ardent sportsman and with the photographer Helene Fischer has published a book on skiing resorts in America (*Skiing: East and West,* 1947). He has long been associated with the Alta Skiing Lodge, at Alta, Utah, and since 1950 has been president of the Alta Ski Lifts Company.

PRINCIPAL WORKS: Some Natural Things, 1945; Report on a Visit to Germany, 1948; The Wild Anemone and Other Poems, 1957; Confidential Report and Other Poems, 1959 (retitled Selected Poems, 1960); The Pig, 1970; The Woodpecker, 1971; In Another Country: Poems 1935–1975, 1978; (with Kenneth Patchen) What Shall We Do Without US?, 1984. *As editor*—New Directions in Prose and Poetry, 43 vols., 1936–1981; Poems from the Greenberg Manuscripts: A Selection of the Works of Samuel B. Greenberg, 1939; Spearhead: Ten Years' Experimental Writing in America, 1947; (with Hayden Carruth) A New Directions Reader, 1964; (with Naomi Burton and Patrick Hart) The Asian Journal of Thomas Merton, 1974.

ABOUT: Contemporary Authors, first revision series 21–24, 1977; Current Biography 1982; Vinson, J. (ed.) Contemporary Poets, 1980; Who's Who in America, 1982–83; Who's Who in the World, 1974–75. *Periodicals*—American Poetry Review November/December 1981; Choice January 1979; Nation December 23, 1978; New York Times Book Review February 25, 1973; August 23, 1981; February 28, 1982; Paris Review Fall 1983; Publishers Weekly March 11, 1983; Village Voice October 23, 1978; Washington Post December 20, 1978.

*LEIBER, FRITZ (REUTER, JR.) (December 24, 1910–), American novelist and short story writer, author of science fiction, supernatural horror, fantasy adventure, and psychological stories and novels, writes: "I was born in Chicago, Illinois, and mostly educated there: four years at the University of Chicago (third year Phi Beta Kappa), leading to the degree of Bachelor of Philosophy in the biological sciences; one year at the General Theological Seminary, NYC; one year graduate studies at Chicago.

"My parents were Shakespearean actors, touring their own company 1920–35. My father starred in several silent films and was a recognized character actor in talkies the last fifteen years of his life. I acted with them for two seasons. I was regularly employed for seventeen years during the first half of my life: one year instructor in speech and drama at Occidental College, Los Angeles; four years writer-editor for Consolidated Book Publishers, Chicago;

°lē′ bə

FRITZ LEIBER

twelve years associate editor of *Science Digest* magazine; more recently I taught at the Clarion Science Fiction Writing Workshop during its first three summers.

"Four big cities in or near which I resided successively shaped me: Chicago, New York, Los Angeles, and San Francisco. Four playwrights strongly influenced me: Shakespeare, and John Webster, Henrik Ibsen and Ingmar Bergman. In science fiction I owe much to H. G. Wells, Olaf Stapledon, and the chiefly American modern science-fiction writing community: Heinlein, Clarke, Asimov and Judith Merril. In supernatural horror I am principally indebted to Edgar Allan Poe, H. P. Lovecraft, and the modern British ghost story tellers: M. R. James, Algernon Blackwood, Arthur Machen, Lord Dunsany, H. Russell Wakefield. My essays have been chiefly in this field: 'Terror, Mystery, Wonder,' 'Monsters and Monster-Lovers,' 'A Literary Copernicus,' and 'Through Hyperspace with Brown Jenkins,' the last two being studies of Lovecraft.

"Four persons have specially influenced me: Jonquil Stephens, British poet and writer, our marriage lasting thirty-three years; our son Justin, professor of philosophy at the University of Houston and author of the scientific romance *Beyond Rejection*; Lovecraft, with whom I corresponded intensively for three months before his death; and Harry Fischer, the friend who invented the characters of Fafhrd and the Gray Mouser, heroes of my 'Swords' Saga.

"My chief and some of my minor concerns in writing fiction, mostly involve science and the weird-supernatural, but in general follow the fantasy trail that curves and zigzags between imagination and fancy."

Fritz Leiber is the son of the actor Fritz Reuter Leiber, Sr., and the former Virginia Bronson. His paternal grandfather had come to the United States from Germany after the revolutions of 1848 and later served as captain in the Union Army during the Civil War. Leiber grew up in theatrical surroundings. He described the years of touring with his parents as filled with "memories redolent of grease paint, spirit gum, curling colored gelatins of flood- and spot-lights; and of actors and actresses; wonder-world in reminiscence."

Leiber's writing career has been beset by recurrent "dry spells," as his critics have called them. He himself speaks of "four chief bursts of creativity, triggered off by the Second World War, the nuclear bomb, the sputniks, and the war in Vietnam. I'm glad I've been able to react to those dreadful stimuli with laughter as well as fears." "His interest in fiction," according to Leiber's friend Judith Merril in one of the most extensive critiques of his work, "had started at college, where most of the time left over from his education in Utopian Socialism, pacifism, fencing, and chess . . . was devoted to long literary correspondences. The most significant of these were with H. P. Lovecraft (and other members of the Lovecraft Circle) and with his friend Harry Fischer, of Louisville." To Lovecraft's influence are due his early forays into witchcraft and the supernatural, the novels *Conjure Wife* (dramatized for television and then as a feature film, *Burn, Witch, Burn!*) and *Gather, Darkness!*, whose first publications were in the magazines *Unknown* and *Astounding*, respectively. From Henry Otto Fischer he received the inspiration for one of his most successful series, the heroic fantasies featuring the diminutive but powerful Grey Mouser and Fafhrd, the seven-foot giant from the north. Leiber's "Swords" series, including the novels *The Swords of Lankhmar, Swords and Deviltry*, and *Swords Against Death* and the story collections *Two Sought Adventure, Swords Against Wizardry*, and *Swords in the Mist*, concern the triumphant adventures of these two intrepid figures and have achieved great popularity among readers favoring heroic fantasy. "Leiber's sense of pace," wrote Sam Moskowitz of this saga, "rich background detail, taut battle scenes, fine characterization, fascinating supernatural elements, together with his extraordinary talent for weaving tasteful humor throughout the entire fabric of his story—a talent unsurpassed by any living fantasy writer today—make this a classic fantasy."

These two subgenres of science fiction, however, are not the only areas in which Leiber is considered a master. His following, according to Merril, "includes the entire spectrum of the curious multigenre currently known as 'science fiction': the weird-and-macabre, whimsical and 'heroic' fantasy, hardware-sci-fi, sociological speculation and political satire, psychological symbolism and *avant-garde* surrealism." Yet it is this very variety that, some feel, has prevented Leiber from achieving the general recognition accorded such other science-fiction pioneers as Robert Heinlein, Ray Bradbury, and Arthur C. Clarke.

Other memorable novels by Leiber include *The Green Millennium* a disquieting tale, published in the McCarthy era, of a government controlled by organized crime and a populace kept subdued by various sexual diversions; *Destiny Times Three*, a complex exploration of simultaneously existing worlds; and *The Wanderer*, which according to Moskowitz "was intended to be the definitive world-doom story, told in alternating vignettes of various stratas of society."

Leiber's style has often been called theatrical. "In the television age," wrote Merril, "an audience of viewer-readers responds warmly to the specifically (and increasingly) theatric quality of his work: everything he writes has as much of the stage as the page in it." Another critic wrote, "Leiber writes *plays* rather than stories, even in his fantasies. His works are scripts, acted out by characters in settings suited to a restricted theatrical stage (in *The Big Time*, one room throughout)."

Leiber has received every honor and award the field of science fiction can offer, including the Hugo Award for best novel in 1958 and 1965, for best novella in 1970 and 1971, and for best novelette in 1968. The Science Fiction Writers of America Nebula Award was his twice, in 1968 for the often-anthologized story "Gonna Roll the Bones" and in 1971 for "Ill Met In Lankhmar," another instalment of the Grey Mouser-Fafhrd series. Leiber, who at six feet four inches is usually taken to be his own model for the giant Fafhrd, married Jonquil Stephens, a writer of British extraction whom he met at the University of Chicago, in January 1936. She died in September 1969. He gave his credo as a writer in his "Introduction" to Angus Wells' British compilation, *The Best of Fritz Leiber*: "All I ever try to write is a good story with a good measure of strangeness in it. The supreme goddess of the universe is Mystery, and being well entertained is the highest joy." About his future literary production he is adamant. "I hope to write better [stories]. I'll never stop writing. It's one occupation in which being crazy, even senile, *might* help."

PRINCIPAL WORKS: *Novels—Scientific romances*: Gather, Darkness, 1943; Destiny Times Three, 1945; The Green Millennium, 1953; The Big Time, 1958; The Silver Eggheads, 1959; The Wanderer, 1964; The Night of the Wolf, 1966; A Specter is Haunting Texas, 1968. *Supernatural thrillers*—Conjure Wife, 1943, You're All Alone, 1950; Our Lady of Darkness, 1977. *Fantasy adventure*—Tarzan and the Valley of Gold (authorized by Edgar Rice Burroughs, Inc.), 1966; Swords in the Mist, 1968; Swords Against Wizardry, 1968; The Swords of Lankhmar, 1968; Swords and Deviltry, 1970; Swords Against Death, 1970; Swords and Ice Magic, 1977; (with Justin Leiber) The Mystery of the Japanese Clock, 1982; (with others) Quicks around the Zodiac, 1983; The Ghost Light, 1984. *Short stories*—Night's Black Agents, 1947; Two Sought Adventure, 1957; The Best of Fritz Leiber, 1974; Night Monsters, 1974; The Book of Fritz Leiber, 1974; The Second Book of Fritz Leiber, 1975; The Worlds of Fritz Leiber, 1978; Heroes and Horrors, 1978; The Change War, 1978; Ship of Shadows: Six Award Winning Stories, 1979.

ABOUT: Dictionary of Literary Biography 8, Pt. 1, 1981; Frane, J. Fritz Leiber: Starmont Reader's Guide 8, 1980; Moskowitz, S. Seekers of Tomorrow, 1967; Smith, C. C. (ed.) Twentieth Century Science Fiction Writers, 1981; Tymn, M. B. Horror Literature, 1981; Vinson, J. (ed.) Contemporary Novelists, 1982. *Periodicals*—Magazine of Fantasy and Science Fiction July 1969.

LELCHUK, ALAN (September 15, 1938–), American novelist, writes: "I grew up in the Brownsville section of Brooklyn in the 1940s, home turf for characters and figures like Alfred Kazin and Bugsy Siegel, Meyer Schapiro and Meyer Lansky, among others. And I came to know and cherish the neighborhood as well as any country boy knew his barn and dirt road: the concrete schoolyards and parks (Lincoln Terrace, Betsy Head), the streets and vacant lots (used for punchball games), the soda fountains and our boulevards (Pitkin Avenue, Eastern Parkway). Not to mention the public schools— Winthrop Junior High, Jefferson High, Brooklyn College—where one received an education in democratic give-and-take as serious as any formal study in melting pot pluralism. The hustling streets and schools of Brooklyn gave me a taste for adventure, an appetite for experience, that has stayed with me and shaped my work.

"My family, a torn one emotionally, fueled my interior world of emotions and imagination. My father was an unrepentant Communist and strong Zionist who had emigrated to America from Russia at age seventeen, after his father had had his head lopped off by a marauding Czarist commander during the chaotic days of the Russian Revolution. Emigrated in body only,

ALAN LELCHUK

to be sure, leaving his soul, along with his brothers and sisters, in Russia, a country he yearned for through the rest of his days. Once indeed he tried to return, putting all of us, my mother, eight-year-old sister, and one-year-old son (me), on an ocean liner bound for Russia; my sister however was afflicted with a severe ear infection, forcing us to put her in the hospital—against my father's wishes—until she healed. That week Germany invaded Poland, Sept. 1939, starting World War II, and we never made the trip. Hence I grew up an American boy, rather than Russian, and I have been forever partial to earaches.

"From my father I inherited a bad temper and early chess skills (gone now), a passion for foreign movies (on Sundays he took me regularly to the old Stanley Theater in Manhattan to see Russian and Chaplin movies) and affection for books; because of him I developed a robust resentment against tyrannical authority. My mother was an unschooled woman of great warmth and splendid common sense, and early on she inspired in me a feel for self-reliance and independence, granting me, for example, her blessing to hitchhike to Mexico when I was sixteen, and the next year, to sign on for the first of several trips, to Africa and Europe, with the Norwegian Merchant Marine. (You needed to be only age sixteen with them, and possess an American passport, to be a *dekksgutt* on freighters.) From my parents' intense battles I gathered an early appreciation of family turmoil and intensity, and faced a testing in my teenage years which I believe has served me well through the years. Such tests are useful for budding writers, it

seems to me; witness [Isaak] Babel, a favorite writer. So long as one passes the tests and moves on, rather than spending one's life in breakdown and bereavement.

"In Brooklyn College in 1955 another important event occurred when I began attending the literary meetings of the night school magazine, *Nocturne*. For there I encountered a group of older students who began my literary education. When Heinz B. assigned me *Look Homeward Angel* and *Of Human Bondage* to read, and then quizzed me severely about them, or when David B. or Art E. read one of my own juvenile stories and carefully criticized it to shreds, I listened, and learned, about writing, reading, arguing. I listened, to be sure, in part because they carried the right credentials—veterans of wars, romances, chaotic lives—and in part because they spoke with clarity and good sense and love of writing, and avoided obscure jargon or pretentious attitudinizing. It was Boroff, Art, Heinz, and a few others who showed me that adventure could happen on the page as well as on the motorcycle. (In 1978 I dedicated my third novel, *Shrinking*, to that band of friends.)

"Though I grew up on the sidewalks of Brooklyn, my mother saw to it that every summer we journeyed to the mountains of upstate New York. And now, in my forties, I still try to live that way, in city and in country. In New Hampshire I experience the slow beautiful routines of country life, where birds and trees and hills and changing sky dominate the landscape, and allow one's imagination to roam in peace, in quiet pleasure. In cities like Cambridge, Jerusalem (where I have spent four of the last five springs), Amherst, I enjoy walking the streets, hearing the new lingos, seeing the latest fashions, searching out the new vibrations. That is, I look for my senses to be assaulted with the latest noises in the cities, so that I can go back home and, in retreat, take stock of the sounds. In this way I try to cope with one of the great problems of being a writer: living, experiencing. Or how to stay awake in life, rather than in words alone. For though a good many of my comrades seem to believe in the power, if not supremacy, of the word alone, I take an old-fashioned view of this, for my fiction. I still think of words as vehicles, as means, to deeper ends—characters and their passions, stories and their consequences, places and their resonances."

———

Alan Lelchuk is the son of Harry Lelchuk and the former Belle Simon. He took his B.A. from Brooklyn College in 1960 and his M.A. from Stanford University in 1963. After a year of graduate study at the University of London (1963–64), he earned his Stanford Ph.D. in 1965. He joined the staff of Brandeis University in 1966 as assistant professor of English and became writer in residence in 1978.

American Mischief, Lelchuk's first novel, appeared in a blaze of publicity: it gained a hefty paperback sale, became a Book of the Month Club selection, and even prompted Norman Mailer, incensed that one of the novel's minor characters—a famous writer bearing his name—is murdered by the hero, publicly to threaten Lelchuk with physical violence. The subject of the 500-page novel is student activism in Cambridge, Massachusetts. The first two sections, "Family Talk" and "Barricade Anxiety," concern the dean of Cardozo College, first in an attempt to justify his hedonistic and exploitative life, then in another attempt (equally unsuccessful) to dissuade a group of students from occupying a campus museum. The museum is destroyed amid much violence, including a surprising amount of defecation, and the final section, "Gorilla Talk," is the narrative of Lenny Pincus, student of literature and tragic radical militant.

The book elicited opposite reactions, strongly positive and negative, sometimes from the same critic. J. A. Avant thought it "powerful and authoritative, . . . [perhaps] the first successful visionary novel of the new American left." "Lelchuk," Avant went on, "places his radicalism within a rigorously constructed social and literary context; as literature, [the book] is a conscious act of devotion to *The Possessed* [Dostoevsky's antiradical novel], and pays clear homage to other writers, especially Mailer, whose influence early on threatens to dominate the book." Eliot Fremont-Smith wrote that *American Mischief* "has genuine literary and intellectual quality. . . . It turns out to be, among other things, good and bad, immensely repetitive and boring, . . . clever, funny, and fashionable. . . . Lelchuk is a writer gifted with intelligence, wit, [and] daring." Yet the reviewer for *Time* compared Lelchuk to "a gratuitous looter in a cultural disaster area" and Joseph Epstein called the book "slipshod and disappointing" and "as botched a piece of literature as has come along in some while." Phoebe Adams wrote, "The sexual and cloacal detail is interminably explicit; the both-your-houses conclusion, a self-righteous banality."

Lelchuk's second novel, *Miriam at Thirty-Four*, appeared eighteen months after *American Mischief* and is about half as long. Also set in Cambridge, it tells the painful story of Miriam Scheinman, a photographer, mother,

and imperfectly liberated woman, of her three lovers and many brief affairs, and of her self-inflicted humiliation and destruction. Some of the critical reaction was negative, even strongly so. Bruce Allen considered the novel "a sour, nasty rap at the women's movement" which "has some drama (melo-, mostly) but suffers from overabundant witty chat [and] 'meaningful' consciousness-baring." Sara Blackburn complained that Miriam and the other characters are presented "in only one dimension—the sexual" and in so doing, Lelchuk "has at once sensationalized and trivialized the culture and character whose life he means to illuminate." Benjamin DeMott, on the other hand, while noting "sensationalism" and "evasions of moral analysis" in the book, found "fine control and compassion" in Miriam's characterization as a woman discovering her true self: "And because of the impressive authority of the author's performance, we, as readers, are inside the thunderclap of rebirth, taking the full enveloping force from within." The indomitable Miriam "reborn" at forty-two is the subject of a sequel, *Miriam in Her Forties*. Older and wiser, this Miriam, Mary Catherine Bateson writes, "is not a model or an ideal, but it is precisely for her individuality that we admire her most."

One of Miriam's lovers is a painter who at one point lashes out at the pietism, obtuseness, and selfishness of all critics of his work. Like him, the hero of the 564-page *Shrinking: The Beginning of My Own Ending*, Lionel Solomon, a teacher at a college near Boston, is a writer much reviled by imperceptive critics. He has a comfortable life, including a farm in New Hampshire, but is driven insane by a woman who insinuates herself into his bed and life, then belittles him in an article for a national magazine. R. S. Spitz considered the novel, which is in the form of a letter from Lionel to his psychiatrist, "a discordant étude of one man's madness orchestrated by greed and desire. . . . a confusing, often brilliant work that is too grandiose in scope to command the force or the focus necessary to substantiate any one of its many subplots." The novel's fragmentary quality was criticized by Robert Towers, who thought that apart from the sections dealing with the opportunistic woman, *Shrinking* "is an enormous catchall, made up of diatribes against critics and against stylistic distinction (here called 'pretty writing'), . . . letters to dead and absent friends, . . . a fantasy involving Erik Erikson, transcripts of creative writing classes, and remembered episodes from Solomon's Brooklyn childhood. The last—despite the familiarity of the material—are the most interesting and authentic sections of the book." John Leonard, however, admired the "interesting counterpoint between the devices of art and psychiatry" in *Shrinking*.

A recipient of a MacDowell Colony fellowship in 1969, Lelchuk also held a Guggenheim fellowship in 1976–77.

PRINCIPAL WORKS: *Fiction*—American Mischief, 1973; Miriam at Thirty-four, 1974; Shrinking, 1978; Miriam in Her Forties, 1983. *As editor*—(with Gershon Shaked) Eight Great Hebrew Short Novels, 1983.

ABOUT: Contemporary Authors, new revision series 1, 1981. *Periodicals*—Atlantic March 1973; October 1974; Library Journal December 1, 1972; October 15, 1974; May 1, 1978; New York Review of Books February 8, 1973; New York Times Book Review February 11, 1973; November 17, 1974; May 21, 1978; May 15, 1983; Saturday Review February 17, 1973; November 16, 1974; June 24, 1978; Time February 26, 1973; Times Literary Supplement June 20, 1975.

JOZSEF LENGYEL

*LENGYEL, JOZSEF (August 4, 1896–July 12, 1975), Hungarian novelist and short story writer, was born in Marcali, Somogy County, into a well-to-do family. He completed his university studies in the liberal arts in Budapest and Vienna and participated in the workers' demonstration on May 23, 1912. During the early years of World War I, he joined the anti-military movement led by Ervin Szabó; in 1918 he became a founding member of the Hungarian Communist Party and helped to edit *Vördös Újság* (Red Newspaper) and *Ifjú Proletár* (Young Proletar) under the short-lived Hungarian Soviet Republic headed by Béla Kun. Arrested in February 1919 along with Communist leaders, he began long years of exile in Vienna, Berlin, and finally Moscow, where he emigrated in 1930 at Kun's urging. He was for many years an editor and contributor to *Sarló és Kalapács* (Hammer and Sickle), the literary journal of Hungarian émigrés. His first novel, *Visegrádi utca* (Visegrad Street), was published in Moscow in 1932. Kun and his followers were imprisoned at the end of 1937 during the Stalinist purges; Lengyel was also arrested in February 1938. After three years of relentless interrogation, he was sent to a labor camp in Morilsk, Siberia; he was eventually released and exiled to Deleb, Siberia. Rehabilitated in 1955, he returned to Hungary, where, at age fifty-eight, after an absence of thirty-six years, he set about establishing a literary reputation in his homeland. He eventually received several awards, including the Kossuth Prize in 1963.

Lengyel's first work, published in 1957 after his return to Hungary, was a revised version of *Visegrád Street*. An account of the Communist leaders' actions in the Hungarian revolution, the novel employs the technique of "historical reportage," which seeks to convey factual information instead of fictional effects. Nevertheless, as critics quickly noted, the characters are distinct living personalities. According to András Diószegi, the major artistic significance of the novel lies in "characterizations based on modern, intellectual, and psychological elements." As is increasingly true in his fiction from the mid-1930s on, Lengyel stresses the need for the protagonists to preserve their integrity under the enormous moral pressures circumstances impose on them. Besides establishing ethical struggle as one of his major themes, the novel uses a narrative mode that becomes a permanent feature of his style. As Diószegi points out, instead of being the spectator-narrator of past events, Lengyel composes like a film director; he preserves a chronological plot but freely introduces pictures that serve his message, sometimes presenting the characters "through closeups, sometimes from the distance of ten years" and frequently utilizing "the montage and the acceleration and dissolving" of cinematography.

Prenn Ferenc hánytatott élete, avagy minden tovább mutat (Prenn Drifting) appeared the following year. To the psychological characterization and events drawn from personal experiences Lengyel adds the attributes of the picaresque as he delineates the adventures of Prenn, a military deserter freed from prison by the revolution. His use of a ruffian as a hero was a significant departure from the idealized hero required by schematism, a change welcomed by readers of the time. Prenn's spiritual redemption

°län´ gyel, yō´ zef

under the impact of revolutionary humanism is closely interwoven with the individual fortunes of other revolutionaries, including the leaders of the movement, as he shoulders greater responsibility for events within the organizational apparatus of the Communist Party. When the revolution fails, inhumanity once again prevails, and Prenn wanders alone, lacking the strength to support the revolutionary ideal any longer. According to Diószegi, the artistic success of the novel lies in its compact style, "its film-like swiftness of scene changes, wide tableaus and close-ups, its absorption in psychology, and its development of the intellectual aspects of a worker's personage."

Two collections of short stories, *Igézö* (*The Spell*, 1961) and *Elévült tartozás* (A Discharged Debt, 1964), introduced into Hungarian literature portrayals of the trials endured by exiled Hungarian Communists under the Stalin personality cult in the Siberian labor camps. These works, which place Lengyel among the best short story writers in modern Hungarian literature and invite favorable comparison with Solzshenitsyn's fiction, are commonly grouped in three classes, depending on the extent to which Lengyel's imagination shapes his recollections: (1) those like "Elejétöl végig" (*From Beginning to End*), a memoir, and "Út épül" (A Road Is Built), a sociographic piece, that present Lengyel's own experiences within a short story augmented by recollections and documents; (2) those like "Reggeltöl estig" (From Dawn to Night) and "Sárga pipacsok" (Yellow Poppies) that mesh documentary details with elements of the short story and often contain a personal lyrical tone; and (3) those like "Igézö" (The Spell) and "Kicsi, mérges öregúr" (The Angry Little Old Man) that are genuine short stories exploring characters' dilemmas or presenting thought parabolically. Generally, Lengyel's stories try to comprehend a society that betrayed communist ideals and shattered the dreams of the revolution. It is the world of false arrest, painful grilling, and stultifying imprisonment, sometimes followed by liberation and re-imprisonment. Most of the stories deal with the struggle to obtain food, the drive to survive the physical and spiritual threats of the camp with integrity. "From Beginning to End" traces the consequences endured by the victims of Stalin's purges from fabricated charges to vicious interrogation and years of slave labor. "The Spell" and "Angry Little Old Man" are two of the best. The first probes the conflict between good and evil among men forced into isolation and enslaved by their surroundings, but sustained by their hanging on to life, demonstrating the power of ordinary men to act selflessly. "Angry Little

Old Man" testifies to the indestructability of the human spirit through the actions of an apolitical and remote professor who develops the capacity to act morally under the threat of death. Rather than confess to a false accusation, he gives up his life, thinking not of himself but of his fellow prisoners and the temporary relief his self-sacrifice will bring to their horrible lives.

Two short novels, *Újra a kezdet* (Beginning Anew, 1964; translated as *The Judge's Chair*) and *Trend Richárd vallomásai* (The Confessions of Richard Trend, 1964; originally *Ante apud., ultra, trans*) are concerned with the period just before the liberation of prisoners from the labor camps in 1945. The former is an especially effective presentation of the thoughts of four prisoners as they look to the future and evaluate their situation. One is prepared for any sacrifice that life may demand of him; another is willing to give up his life even if that act is without any meaning at all. Prenn, the former revolutionary, is lost in the desire to satisfy his private pleasures. István Banicza, his student and the central character, stands ready to sacrifice his life for his fellow man, but he faces the connection between morality and action with greater depth than the others; he accepts the responsibility to act, even if it means his life, but he wants to know the value of his act within the purposes of revolution.

One of Lengyel's novels, *Szembesítés* (*Confrontation*, 1973), has been published only in English. Two friends in the Hungarian underground, one on the staff of the Hungarian Embassy in Moscow (again István Banicza from *Prenn Drifting* and *The Judge's Chair*) and the other named Lassú, just freed from a labor camp, try to account for the appalling legacy of Stalinism. Lassú, who finds Stalinism to be worse than Nazism because it eliminated comrades-in-arms and calls his time in the labor camp similar to "a thousand-and-one St. Bartholomew's nights," sets two conditions to his faith in the strength of the Communist system: a complete disclosure of what had happened and the absence of a small ruling clique at the top. He speaks of the need for the scalpel rather than bandage; he emphasizes the need for speaking out and for questioning the omnipotence of dictatorship as an essential step in the evolution of society toward a proletarian democracy. In the end, neither protagonist can decide what made the purges possible, whether it was something in Stalin himself or a flaw in Leninist ideology. The reviewers in the *Times Literary Supplement* and the *New York Times Book Review* both considered the novel to be a significant work but not a distinguished piece of writing. The latter called it "an honest, decent workmanlike and estimable book—but also a terribly weary one," finding real life in Lengyel's descriptions of moments that reveal Lassú's inner struggles rather than in the debate between the two characters.

His other important books, most of them published in the 1970s, are a volume of expressionistic poems written in his early years, an account of his visit to China in the summer of 1960, three volumes of tales and dialogues, and a memoir of his years of exile in Vienna.

WORKS IN ENGLISH TRANSLATION: Ilona Duczynszka has translated into English the following works by Lengyel: *The Spell* and *From Beginning to End,* 1966; *Prenn Drifting,* 1966, and *The Judge's Chair,* 1968. *Confrontation* was translated by Anna Novotny, 1973. Duczynszka also translated a collection of his short fiction, *Acta Sanctorum and Other Tales,* 1970.

ABOUT: Columbia Dictionary of Modern European Literature, 1980; Contemporary Authors 85–88, 1980; Tezla, A. Hungarian Authors: A Bibliographical Handbook, 1970. *Periodicals*—Books Abroad Spring 1973; Summer 1975; Winter 1975; Encounter May 1965; New York Times Book Review April 14, 1968; March 24, 1978; Times Literary Supplement January 21, 1965; April 28, 1972; December 21, 1973; November 20, 1977.

*LENZ, SIEGFRIED** (March 17, 1926–   ), German novelist, short story writer, dramatist, and essayist, is the son of a civil servant in the town of Lyck, in the Masurian region of East Prussia. In his autobiographical essay *Stimmungen der See* (Moods of the Sea, 1962), he narrates how he went to school "by boat in summer, by sled in winter" and how he helped to "reinforce the Baltic Fleet under a man named Hitler thus becoming a witness of the Great Flight and Fall." Ater the war Lenz studied philosophy, English literature, and literary history in Hamburg and became a journalist. In 1950 he was the editor of the cultural section of the Hamburg daily *Die Welt.* In 1951, after joining the famous "Gruppe 47" writers' association, he turned to creative writing. His first novel *Es waren Habichte in der Luft* (Hawks Were in the Sky, 1951), impressed the critics with its symbolic representation of persecuted man. It is the story of a Finnish teacher during World War I who, despite his disguise as a gardener, is recognized and assassinated by his Communist adversaries. Lenz received the René Schickele Prize for this first novel. On the occasion of another prizewinning ceremony in Bremen (1962) Lenz confessed his admiration for the works of Faulkner, Camus, Hemingway, and Dostoevsky. In his acceptance speech entitled "On the Gloomy Relationship between Language and Power," he

SIEGFRIED LENZ

acknowledged the obligation of the writer to defend his language against power: "The writer acts by revealing something: a common need, common passions, hopes, joys, or a common threat." In the novel *Duell mit dem Schatten* (Duel with a Shadow, 1953), the story of a German colonel who has abandoned his driver in the desert during the African campaign of 1943, the guilt of the war generation is pitted against the haunted innocence of their offspring: while the colonel is driven back to the scene of his failure and perishes there, his daughter who accompanies him is led back to life.

A collection of Masurian stories under the title *So zärtlich war Suleyken* (So Tender Was Suleyken, 1955) established Lenz's reputation as careful observer and skillful narrator of the people and their world of the now vanished Masurian culture. The collection consists of fairy tales, anecdotes, and picaresque stories with a unique combination of Prussian, Polish, Brandenburgian, and Russian elements. *Der Mann im Strom* (The Man in the River, 1957) is a satirical novel of an aging diver who tries to falsify his identity papers in order to keep his job, and his daughter who is seduced by a young man who also cheats his way through life. The sports novel *Brot und Spiele* (Bread and Games, 1959) tells the tragic story, anticipated in the short narrative "Der Läufer" (The Runner), in Lenz's collection of "tales of our time" entitled *Jäger des Spotts* (Hunters of Scorn, 1958), of a long distance runner and public idol who does not live up to his fame and experiences "the lesson of defeat" by collapsing just before the finishing line. In his novel *Stadtgespräch* (*The Survivor,* 1963), Lenz

°lents, zēk′ frēt

assumes a dual narrative position to represent the dilemma of a Norwegian resistance fighter who, during the German occupation, has to choose between self-sacrifice and the sacrifice of innocent hostages.

Lenz's most famous novel is undoubtedly *Deutschstunde* (*The German Lesson*, 1968), which deals with the suppression of artistic freedom during the Hitler regime. The youthful narrator is required to compose an essay on the "Joys of Duty" while incarcerated in a reform school. Thus he remembers the obsessive dedication to duty of his father, a policeman, charged in 1943 with the supervision of his friend and life saver, the Expressionist painter Nansen (which could be a pseudonym for Nolde or Barlach). The policeman's unyielding sense of duty destroys the artistic existence of his friend. "Duty" thus turns from a positive affirmation into mindless inhumanity. Like *The German Lesson,* the novel *Das Vorbild* (*An Exemplary Life,* 1973), is filled with colorful portraits of contemporary characters with their foibles, idiosyncrasies, and ultimately poignant vulnerabilities. Once again a pedagogical goal turns into a revelation of the human condition: three editors of a school reader meet in a Hamburg hotel to choose an "exemplary life" as a role model for its final chapter. While they move from one unlikely example to the other, each one of them discovers his own failure to set a positive example during his lifetime.

In the novel *Heimatmuseum* (The Heritage, 1978) the narrator delves deeply into his own past in a work of restoration and preservation, an anecdotal, folkloric, and historical archive of the vanished culture of his Masurian province, which was wholly incorporated into Poland at the end of World War II. The argument of the book—that the creative individualism of regional Germany was swamped by a centralized ideology proclaiming the very values of "Heimat" it was virtually destroying—is expressed by the journalist Conny who sees the ideological perversion of the concept of "Heimat" by the Nazis as follows: "There are some things that cannot remain innocent, and one of them is a museum of local history. At its best, it fosters sentimental stupidity. At its worst, it plays straight into the hands of the ethnic-purity boys." Consequently Zygmunt, the main character, sets fire to the new museum of local history erected after the war in West Germany once he discovers that a former Masurian Nazi has been made chairman of the museum association. S. N. Plaice in his review of *Heimatmuseum* compared the novel with Thomas Mann's *Doctor Faustus.* This seems exaggerated as far as format and style are concerned. An analogy to another modern classic, however, Gunther Grass' *The Tin Drum,* appears much more logical in the sense that Lenz's novel, like Grass', managed to put a former province of German culture on the literary map forty years after it had ceased to exist. In his collections of short stories under the titles *Der Geist der Mirabelle* (The Spirit of the Yellow Plum, 1975) and *Einstein Überquert die Elbe bei Hamburg* (Einstein Crosses the Elbe near Hamburg, 1977), Lenz once more proves himself a master of imaginative realism and occasional flashes of critical commitment when he lets, for example, an eponymous couple on their eighth wedding aniversary find out more about each other than they bargained for—"Herr und Frau S. in Erwartung ihrer Gäste" (Mr. and Mrs. S. Awaiting Their Guests). In "Die Wellen des Balaton" (The Waves of Balaton) a prosperous couple from Bremen and an impoverished one from the German Democratic Republic meet in a brief and fruitless encounter full of misunderstandings. "Achzehn Diapositive" (Eighteen Slides) is a masterly exploitation of a modern social ritual: the host showing slides to a bored group of guests reveals the hidden tensions that exist between the participants of the dull party. "Die Augenbinde" (The Blindfold) is a savage and eerie allegorical comment on the leveling processes to which society subjects its members. In "Die Schmerzen sind zumutbar" (The Pains Are Tolerable) a military dictator voluntarily undergoes a series of tortures which have been applied by his henchmen to his suppressed people. When Lenz's novel *Der Verlust* (The Loss, 1982) first appeared in Germany, it met with faint praise. The story of Ulrich Martens (a footloose bachelor in his forties who, when struck down, is making his living as a highly articulate coach-tour guide in a large German city), appears mildly mawkish, and it suffers from various irrelevancies: Lenz's determination to make room for all his anecdotes finally results in clutter. "His style," as one critic put it, "seems to be on the wane, spoiled by an admixture of banality and mannerism."

Although Lenz is better known for his radio plays, his stage drama *Zeit der Schuldlosen* (Time of the Guiltless, 1962) also evoked considerable discussion. A volume of essays entitled *Beziehungen* (Relationships, 1970) deals with social and literary questions. So does *Elfenbeinturm und Barrikade* (Ivory Tower and Barricade, 1982).

WORKS IN ENGLISH TRANSLATION: Michael Bullock translated two of Lenz's novels into English—*The Lightship,* 1964, and *The Survivor,* 1965. Also available in English translation are *An Exemplary Life,* by Douglas Parmee, 1964, and *The German Lesson,* by Ernest

Kaiser and Eithne Wilkins, 1971. *The Heritage*, translated by Krishna Winston, was published in 1981.

ABOUT: Cassell's Encyclopedia of World Literature, 1973; Contemporary Authors 89–92, 1980; Columbia Dictionary of Modern European Literature, 1980; Encyclopedia of World Literature in the 20th Century IV, 1978; Murdoch, B. and Read, M. Siegfried Lenz, 1978; *Periodicals*—German Life and Letters 19, 1966; Seminar 13, 1977.

LERNER, GERDA (April 30, 1920–), American historian, was born in Vienna, the daughter of Robert Kronstein and the former Ilona Neumann. She managed to complete, with academic distinction, her secondary education before fleeing Austria just prior to World War II; "a good part of my family," she has said, perished under the Nazis. She arrived in America in 1939, and two years later married Carl Lerner, a film editor. Over the next two decades Gerda Lerner helped raise their son and daughter while learning about her new country, having become an American citizen herself in 1943. "I read and studied history intently," she said in an interview in 1962, "and I found that apparently men alone had made the country. I dug deeper and discovered that, actually, women had made great contributions for which men would have gotten into the history books, but which were overlooked just because they were women. . . . A highly significant point is that women's contributions have always been to the general good, not just to benefit themselves."

In the autumn of 1962, Lerner gave a course, "Great Women in American History," at the New School for Social Research in New York. It was well attended and stirred much discussion; in retrospect it may be seen as an intellectual impetus to the second wave of American feminism, just beginning in the early 1960s. The course was revised and presented the following year over a Manhattan radio station. Lerner was all the while studying at the New School for her bachelor's degree, which she received in 1963. She then pursued graduate work in history at Columbia University, earning her M.A. in 1965 and her Ph.D. in 1966.

Lerner's doctoral dissertation, with only slight changes, was published as *The Grimké Sisters from South Carolina: Rebels Against Slavery*. It tells the story of the rise of Angelina Emily and Sarah Moore Grimké from their rich, complacent Charleston beginnings to national renown as Northern abolitionists and champions of women's rights. Despite a somewhat sour reception from a few male historians, the book was generally praised for the rich circumstantiality

GERDA LERNER

which Lerner brought to the lives of the nearly forgotten sisters. The *Choice* reviewer called it "conscientious and well researched," particularly admiring the author's obvious interest in her subjects and her "narrative sense."

Lerner's anthology *Black Women in White America: A Documentary History* was immediately hailed as a landmark in black studies, courses in which were then just beginning to be widely offered. The American women, mostly black, who were responsible for the many letters, articles, speeches, and statements gathered in the book, included not only such well-known figures as Harriet Tubman and Sojourner Truth but also Susie King Taylor, a nurse in the Union Army; Maria L. Baldwin, a pioneer teacher; and Maria Stewart, an early militant feminist. Alden Whitman wrote, "The gallery is large and impressive. It ranges from women in slavery, to freedwomen, to sharecroppers' wives, to women of relative privilege. Reading these women, I was impressed by their unquenchable fire and dignity. . . . However much this may be a book for blacks it is even more a book for whites. If whites are to know blacks and to join with them in seeking a just and polycultural American society, whites had better discover from the blacks themselves the nature of the black experience. A significant portion of it is here in Dr. Lerner's exemplary book." In an interview on the eve of the book's publication, Lerner remarked that in her readings in American history she had been impressed by the neglect of black women's contributions—scholars specializing in black and feminist history had even maintained there was no source material on black women. She also be-

came interested, she said, in "the parallels between the history of black and white women. It's
simply that both black and white women live in
a society in which the positions of decision making, power, rank, and high status are firmly held
by men. This has affected the way in which
women experience life. . . . Many of my colleagues think women's history is an unimportant, exotic specialty. But I'm not concerned
with critics. They had it their way all this time.
Now it's our turn."

Another feminist anthology compiled by Lerner, *The Female Experience: An American
Documentary,* may be seen as a complement to
the preceding book. The words of women from
colonial times to the present, commenting on
their condition, are arranged in topical divisions;
more than half the documents were never before
published. Adrienne Rich wrote that Lerner's introduction, and her analytical essays preceding
each of the book's sections, "are essential reading
for those who want to grasp the shifts in perspective created by a woman-centered historiography. They crystallize what the documents
themselves reveal: the nature and structure of female historical experience." Quoting one of the
author's most important statements—"There
comes a moment in woman's self-perception
when she begins to see man as 'the other.' It is
this moment when her feminist self-
consciousness begins"—Rich remarked,
"Compressed in this brief paragraph is a process
we discover in the texts; . . . Lerner traces feminist consciousness from such individual moments of recognition through more or less
isolated refusals of traditional female status to
collective self-consciousness, the building of female community."

Twelve essays written since 1969 comprise
*The Majority Finds Its Past: Placing Women in
History.* Among the topics Lerner considers are:
how to define women as a distinct group in society; how useful to the study of history is the idea
of women's oppression; and how to assess the importance of race, class, and sex as historical factors. She also has strong views against
"compensatory" history, which concentrates on
"notable" individual women while resolutely ignoring the mass, and "contributory" history,
which focuses on female contributions to male-
dominated society. The *Choice* reviewer commented, "What makes these diverse pieces a coherent whole is Lerner's desire to illuminate
what was until recently a neglected area of historical inquiry. As such, this is an important book
that all American historians must read for the
question it raises about the scope and method of
American social history."

Lerner's non-historical writing includes a novel about Austria, *No Farewell,* a screenplay for
Black Like Me, and *A Death of One's Own,* a
poignant account of her and her husband's valiant eighteen-month struggle against the incurable brain tumor that caused his death in August
1973.

From 1968 to 1980, Lerner was a much-
admired history professor at Sarah Lawrence
College, Bronxville, New York. Since 1980 she
has held the Robinson-Edwards chair in history
at the University of Wisconsin in Madison. She
is a frequent lecturer at campuses throughout
the United States, is closely involved in the creation and preservation of several archives of
women's history, and in 1981–82 was president
of the Organization of American Historians.

PRINCIPAL WORKS: The Grimké Sisters from South Carolina, 1967; The Woman in American History, 1971; A
Death of One's Own, 1978; The Majority Finds Its
Past, 1979; Teaching Women's History, 1981. *As
editor*—Black Women in White America, 1972; The
Female Experience, 1976. *Fiction*—No Farewell,
1955.

ABOUT: Contemporary Authors 25–28, 1977.
Periodicals—Book World April 16, 1972; Choice Feb-
ruary 1968; September 1972; July-August 1977; March
1980; Journal of American History June 1968; June
1983; Library Journal September 1, 1967; May 1, 1972;
March 1, 1977; July 1, 1978; October 1, 1979; New
York Post September 17, 1962; New York Review of
Books September 15, 1977; New York Times April 8,
1977; January 5, 1981; New York Times Book Review
March 20, 1977; August 6, 1978; Saturday Review May
6, 1972; Virginia Quarterly Review Summer 1972;
Washington Post April 16, 1972.

*LEROUX, ETIENNE (June 13, 1922–   ),
South African (Afrikaans) novelist, writes: "To
date I have written eleven novels; several sketches, short stories, essays etc. published in book-
form. I am now sixty-one and I am not quite sure
what the future holds for me. I always seem to
be involved in some controversy or other with
every novel published in my country. For the
foreign reader the abovementioned controversies would be inexplicable. If they have no
knowledge of the South African scene, this particular part of Africa, then it will not make sense
to them that one of my books was banned. I have
just written a rather vicious satire, called 'Our
Hymie.' It went a peaceful way and caused great
concern neither to the left or the right. I am now
threatened by younger writers who would love
to see me as a G.O.M. [Grand Old Man]—which
I am not.

"As a writer I am quite unpredictable. I have

°la r$\overline{oo}$´ , ā tyen´

been accused of being an escapist in the sense that most of my novels were based on the empirical mysticism of Jung. I dabbled with the mysteries of the Kabbala, alchemy, demonism, vampirism, and all other manifestations of the living dead. Activists accused me of taking the blind eye of Tiresias to look into the vague future and not into the present state of our unfortunate country. Nowadays I take a very close satirical look at the local scene.

"I was born on the thirteenth of June, and I am a typical Gemini. This duality haunts me to this day—in my writing and in my whole makeup. The town of my birth is called Oudtshoorn and it was the mecca of the ostrich feather boom of those years when farmers became millionaires overnight and spent their money with abandon and with a vulgarity that was quite fascinating. (I mean: hiring a train to bring Tivoli-girls from Cape Town to dance for them in their own theatre; washing their horses with champagne; lighting their cigars with five-pound notes; building turn-of-the-century mansions with turrets, cellars, balconies, and stuffing these edifices with unbelievable kitsch, etc.). Most of them went bankrupt after the boom but they survived the catastrophe because they happened to be excellent farmers.

"In my pre-teen years I experienced the naughty twenties at a very impressionable age. I was a great looker on, but I also had a wayward aunt and a cousin or two who initiated me in this strange world of the flappers and the Charleston and the Black Bottom and jolly sex. The previous wars: the Anglo-Boer War, the 1914–18 war, were so many legends with so many impeccable heroes. It was not a reality; but the Great Flu was ever present.

"In this complete isolation I had a rage to read and I wrote all my novels, short stories and essays here. I subscribed to all possible literary magazines within my budget: the *Hudson Review,* the *Sewanee Review,* the *Evergreen Review,* the *Partisan Review,* the *London Magazine,* *Horizon,* the *Kenyon Review, Perspectives,* the *Times Literary Supplement,* etc., etc., etc. I also discovered great writers like Nathanael West when he was ignored in the U.S.A. I came under the spell of the vernacular of Hemingway, but I also fell a victim of the mandarin style of Virginia Woolf. *The Great Gatsby* overwhelmed me, and I still consider it as one of the best novels ever written. I knew the American scene in the fifties-sixties, as well as writing in France, Italy, Germany, and England during the war and postwar.

"And then I came under the spell of Jung.

"I seem to write my books in trilogies. That is the magic number.

"Graham Greene and Paul Theroux are personal friends. I admire their works greatly, and I consider them as two of the best writers alive and kicking.

"Unlike generals, most serious writers do not fade away: they die.

"It is presumptuous to say that I in my small way am not prepared to fade away, but that I hope to die so that I can haunt you one day."

———

Etienne Leroux was the only son of Stephanus Petrus Le Roux, a farmer, politician, and one-time minister of agriculture, and the former Elizabeth Scholtz. He received his secondary education at Grey College, Bloemfontein, and took his University of Stellenbosch B.A. in 1942, his LL.B. in 1944. Probably his country's best-known Afrikaans-language novelist, Leroux has for several years been the focus of a burgeoning industry in South African university dissertations. His eleven novels, which he divides into at least three trilogies, have become progressively more allegorical, mythological, and dense—he has often been accused of obscurity. Although he is credited with helping to alter the pastoral, patriotic, and puritanical tone of the traditional Afrikaner novel, he has not—nor has any Afrikaans-language prose writer—ever created the kind of clear-eyed parables of his tyrannical, white-supremacist society that his Anglophone compatriots have produced in such abundance—one thinks, first of all, of the works of Nadine Gordimer and J. M. Coetzee. He is, perhaps in consequence, known in English-speaking countries only for one of the trilogies—the second, entitled *To A Dubious Salvation,* which comprises novels published first in Cape Town from 1962 to 1966. This trilogy appeared in a one-volume paperback edition in 1972.

Sewe dae by die Silbersteins (*Seven Days at the Silbersteins,* 1962) is the story of Henry Van Eeden, a young, highly impressionable South African, who is one party to an arranged marriage. He has never met Salome Silberstein, his fiancée, and does not see much of her during the week he spends on her parents' estate, but what he is shown of their endlessly, hollowly festive life becomes, in Leroux's handling of it, a heavily symbolic, surreal, and violent allegory of contemporary Cape Dutch life. The symbolic irony, however, frequently becomes so attenuated that, as S. K. Oberbeck remarked, "most South Africans will have a hard time recognizing" the world described as their own. Yet he concluded that the book "ominously evokes the yawning void in South African life, the slightly frantic efforts of a precariously enthroned hierarchy to shut out the darkness."

In *Een vir Azazel* (*One for the Devil,* 1964) eighteen years have passed since young Henry's visit to the Silbersteins. Salome has died, and her child, Adam Kadmon, is a giant who is suspected of murder. The main character in this novel becomes Detective Sergeant Demosthenes H. de Goede, who, though he never proves the boy's guilt or innocence, engages in a great deal of ironic and erudite conversation about the Jungian ideas of myth and dream, the collective unconscious, and collective guilt. The reader learns in this novel about Welgevonden, an agrarian society which is an uneasy amalgam of Nordic, Semitic, and African cultures. To C. R. Larson, this book, "even more than its predecessor, reads as if it were an allegory of an allegory": it is "undoubtedly," he feels, this obscurity "which has prevented Leroux's works from being banned in his native country." Yet within the author's treatment of Welgevonden and its inhabitants, Larson concludes, "are the myths and dilemmas of South Africa's withdrawal into what has become a valueless and impersonal society completely out of touch with reality."

The third novel in the trilogy, *Die derde Oog* (*The Third Eye,* 1966) continues to focus on de Goede, who now holds the rank of captain in the Criminal Investigation Department of the Secret D Service. He is assigned ostensibly to track down the infamous tycoon Boris Gudenov, but his real assignment, he is told, is "to wander down into the Unknown, the psychic substratum, . . . to free the world from a corrupting monster that has appeared out of the darkness and seized on our understanding; you are going to free man himself." This novel is no less allegorical than its predecessors, its many characters no less bizarre and apparently symbolic. As usual, critical opinion was sharply divided: to James Fenton it was "a very muddled and confusing book, from which little may be concluded"; Jack Kroll thought it a "beautifully detailed story . . . a vision of our chaotic time that is diamond-bright, clear as crystal, pulsing with urgent intellectual energy."

18–44 (1967), the first novel of Leroux's third trilogy, is the only other of his major works to appear in English. (The other books in this trilogy are entitled *Isis, Isis, Isis* [1969] and *Na'va* [1972].) This is the story of Y, the forty-four-year-old narrator, his wife, aunt, mistress, and an eighteen-year-old girl who writes to him; his neat, self-contained world is reduced to ashes by the novel's end. Although Leroux's language here is characteristically symbolic, even oblique, and his tone allegorical, this book seems to explore, in J. M. Carroll's words, "psychological and introspective depths in place of the crowded, rococo, outgoing, sociological excitement" of the preceding three works. This relative lack of comment on societal realities suggests that Leroux aims at describing "a universe far greater" than the novel's apparent setting in contemporary South Africa.

Leroux has been much honored in his country. His fiction has twice won the coveted Hertzog prize of the South African Academy for Arts and Sciences: in 1964 for *Sewe dae by die Silbersteins* and in 1979 for *Magersfontein, o Magersfontein!* The latter novel, based on a famous battle during the Boer War, was described by the author as "an experiment in irony and satire in a contemporary medium." It was banned by the central government in 1978, two years after its publication, and thus won the Hertzog prize as a forbidden book. The ban was lifted in 1981. In 1978 the University of Natal, a segregated, English-language institution, awarded Leroux an honorary doctorate of letters.

In 1948, Leroux married Renée Malherbe, a painter, by whom he had two daughters and a son. They divorced in 1969, and the following year he married Elizabeth Joubert, a pianist. Since 1946 he has lived and farmed in Koffiefontein, in the southwestern part of the Orange Free State, the Boer heartland. He habitually writes—"under tremendous stress," he says—only from January to April; farming takes up his entire attention the rest of the year.

WORKS IN ENGLISH TRANSLATION: Charles Eglinton translated *Seven Days at the Silbersteins* in 1967 and *One for the Devil* in 1968. *The Third Eye* was translated in 1969; these three novels were collected into a one-volume edition with the title *To a Dubious Salvation* in 1972. Cassandra Perry is the translator of *18–44,* 1972.

ABOUT: Contemporary Authors, new revision series 2, 1981. *Periodicals*—Best Sellers September 1, 1967; April 15, 1968; September 1, 1972; Choice April 1973; Library Journal August 1967; March 15, 1968; April 1, 1969; July 1972; National Review October 17, 1967; October 27, 1972; New Republic September 16, 1967; September 16, 1972; New Statesman December 12, 1969; New York Times Book Review September 24, 1967; New Yorker November 18, 1967; July 22, 1972; Newsweek September 11, 1967; April 28, 1969; Saturday Review May 4, 1968; Times Literary Supplement January 8, 1970.

*LE ROY LADURIE, EMMANUEL (BERNARD) (July 19, 1929–), French historian, was born in Les Moutiers-en-Cinglais, in the Norman department of Calvados, the only son of Jacques Le Roy Ladurie, a well-to-do farmer, a Catholic conservative, mayor of Les Moutiers, and Vichy minister of agriculture for six months

°lə rwä´ lä dü rē´

EMMANUEL LE ROY LADURIE

in 1942 before going over to the Resistance. His mother was the former Léontine Dauger. He attended the Collège Saint-Joseph in Caen, the renowned Lycée Henri-IV in Paris (from which he was expelled for a prank), and the Lycée Lakanal in the suburb of Sceaux, obtained his *agrégation* in history from the prestigious École Normale Supérieure, and the degree of *docteur ès lettres,* France's highest earned degree, from the Faculty of Letters of the University of Paris. After teaching at the Lycée de Montpellier (1953–57) and at the university in that city (1960–63), he became director of studies at the École Pratique des Hautes Études (from 1965). Since 1970 he has been teaching and research professor of geography and social sciences at the University of Paris VII, and professor of the history of modern civilization at the Collège de France (from 1973). He also held for three years (1957–60) a research post at the C.N.R.S., the National Center for Scientific Research.

Le Roy Ladurie has become the most widely known of the second generation of *annalistes,* a group of historians named after the journal *Annales,* founded in 1929 by Marc Bloch and Lucien Febvre. The *annalistes* aim at revitalizing the writing of history by means of sensitive recourse to documentary and quantitative evidence, often from diverse fields, and they are usually contrasted with the practitioners of *l'histoire événementielle,* the traditional diplomatic or political narratives still frequently encountered elsewhere in Europe and in the United States. The imaginative use of primary sources has always been the forte of Le Roy Ladurie and his colleagues; he has been an editor of *Annales* since 1967.

His first book, *Les Paysans du Languedoc* (*The Peasants of Languedoc,* 1966), was an adaptation of his doctoral thesis. Every conceivable aspect of the lives of the peasants of this region of southern France from the late 1400s to the early 1700s is explored in this work, which is primarily based on a minute study of the volumes recording the *taille,* the comprehensive tax levied until the French Revolution on all non-noble property. Fredric Cheyette called the book "one of the five or six finest products of the *Annales* school of social history. It is not only a monumental demonstration that peasants do indeed have a history that can be known, but also an exemplary presentation of the historical method the *Annales* has long advocated: quantitative, serial history; psychohistory; history of group attitudes; history of material culture; history of climate; history of diet."

Le Roy Ladurie then turned to a topic no less vast, one rarely treated systematically, and one seemingly made to order for his historiographical method. *Histoire du climat depuis l'an mil* (*Times of Feast, Times of Famine: A History of Climate since the Year 1000*) considered the evidence from sources as disparate as parish records, the study of radioisotopes, and dendrochronology to chart with obviously painstaking accuracy the subtle fluctuations of European and even world climate over the last millennium. Although its highly technical text, nineteen appendixes, and detailed notes may daunt the general reader, the book nevertheless amply displays the author's characteristic style, described by Philip Morrison as "readability, warmth, and [a] constructively skeptical tone." Morrison added that the book is "the product of a genuine historian, who knows the strengths and the limitations of how we learn from our fragmentary record of the past."

In 1975 *Montaillou, village occitan de 1294 à 1324* (*Montaillou: The Promised Land of Error*) became almost a household name in France and has been generally acknowledged to be a masterpiece of ethnographic history wherever it has been published. It is the story of a village in the upper Ariège region of extreme southern France during the early fourteenth century, told in the words of the inhabitants themselves. They were followers of the Cathar or Albigensian heresy, and were minutely investigated by Jacques Fournier, bishop of Pamiers and later Benedict XII, pope at Avignon, who kept a meticulous and voluminous record, now preserved in the Vatican Library, of their testimony before his Inquisition court. Le Roy Ladurie calls Fournier "a sort of compulsive Maigret, immune to both supplication and bribe, skillful at worming out the truth (at bringing the lambs forth, as his victim said), able in a few minutes to tell a heretic from a 'proper' Catholic—a very devil of an Inquisitor, according to the accused. . . . The whole Pamiers Inquisition Register bears the brand of his constant intervention. This is one of the reasons why it is such an extraordinary document." Keith Thomas thought *Montaillou* a "magic" book, "superbly invigorating and original. . . . It is the first wholly successful attempt to write the total history of a small community with as much regard for the mental attitudes of the inhabitants as for their social and economic situation." Lawrence Stone made the extraordinary comment that the author brought "the Middle Ages to life in a way that has probably never been achieved before by any historian."

Le Roy Ladurie held his international readership in 1979 with *Le Carnaval de Romans* (*Carnival in Romans*), a book which marked his debut as an urban historian. It is a portrayal of the popular culture and the class and religious conflict of early modern France, focusing on the complex events surrounding the massacre on February 15–16, 1580, in Romans, a small city west of Grenoble, of a band of artisans and their leader. The author, in his foreword, characterizes his study as "a deep probe into the geological stratifications of a dated culture" and an elucidation of the "urban dramas" of the Renaissance, Reformation, and Catholic Counter-Reformation. As always, he is scrupulous in his inferences from his sources, and so the book is not easy to read, but Theodore Zeldin saw "a lively, humane spirit" behind the erudite academic: "The interest of this book for the general reader is that it . . . offers a taste of what people were like, what they cared about, how they behaved in daily life."

Le Roy Ladurie's other major works include: *L'Argent, l'Amour et la Mort en pay d'Oc* (*Love, Death, and Money in the Pays d'Oc*), an analysis of the eighteenth-century novella *Jean-l'ont-pris*, described by the author as "a *summum* of Occitan culture and literature in the seventeenth and eighteenth centuries"; the two volumes of collected essays in *Le Territoire de l'historien* published in 1973 and 1978 (*The Territory of the Historian* and *The Mind and Method of the Historian*); the two volumes, in collaboration with Michaël Morineau, of *Histoire économique et sociale de la France* (*The Economic and Social History of France*); and volume three of *L'Histoire urbaine de la France* (The Urban History of France). In 1983 he turned his attention to the peasants of Gascony with *La Sorcière de Jasmin* (Jasmin's Witch), based on the nineteenth-century poet Jacques Jasmin's story of witchcraft in a sixteenth-century Gascon village.

In 1949, upon entering the École Normale Supérieure, Le Roy Ladurie, who had at one time considered joining the priesthood, became a devoted and, by his account, nearly fanatical member of the French Communist Party. His effort to recreate the period and to explain his seven-year allegiance to what he now sees as an illiberal and repressive organization resulted in *Paris-Montpellier, PC–PSU, 1945–1963* (1982), which is at once a personal memoir of a political pilgrimage and a careful work of history. The book has received much critical attention in Paris, where Le Roy Ladurie has become a highly influential intellectual—frequently appearing on state television and in the pages of *Le Monde*, *L'Express*, and *Le Nouvel Observateur*, an apparently sure candidate for the Académie Française, and a member of President François Mitterand's intimate circle. Yet he is interesting above all as a gifted interpreter of history, a discipline which, he wrote in a 1977 essay in *Daedalus*, "answers both an individual and a collective need for serious thought; it answers a curiosity, a desire; it answers the search for pleasure in reading (for the reader), and often for pleasure in writing (for the writer of history). In this sense, the decor and the display are as important as the merchandise, and the style as important as the thought, from which it is indeed inseparable, and whose validity it upholds with its pertinence and its impact."

Le Roy Ladurie married Madeleine Pupponi in July 1955; they have a daughter and a son. He is a chevalier of the Legion of Honor.

WORKS IN ENGLISH TRANSLATION: English translations of Le Roy Ladurie's major works include *Times of Feast, Times of Famine,* by Barbara Bray, 1971; *The Peasants of Languedoc,* by John Day, 1974; *Montaillou* also by Bray, 1978; *Carnival in Romans,* by Mary Feeney, 1979; *The Territory of the Historian,* 1979, and *The Mind and Method of the Historian,* 1981, by Ben and Siân Reynolds; and *Love, Death, and Money in the Pays d'Oc,* by Alan Sheridan, 1982.

ABOUT: International Who's Who, 1981–82; Who's Who in France, 1983–84. *Periodicals*—Current Biography 1984; Economist January 20, 1973; June 3, 1978; Encounter September 1978; February 1980; November 1980; December 1981; Guardian May 24, 1979; June 3, 1979; March 28, 1982; Library Journal November 1, 1974; New Statesman January 26, 1973; June 9, 1978; June 13, 1980; New York Review of Books October 12, 1978; November 8, 1979; New York Times Book Review November 4, 1979; December 12, 1982; Science September 15, 1972; Scientific American February 1972; Times Literary Supplement July 2, 1982; Washington Post August 20, 1978; November 4, 1979; December 19, 1982.

LEVINE, NORMAN (October 22, 1924–   ),
Canadian poet, novelist, and short story writer,
writes: "My parents, as young adults, came from
Poland to Canada in the early 1920s, and settled
in Lower Town, Ottawa. In those days the place
was like a village, made up of European immigrants (mostly Jews) and native Canadians
(mostly French). It was a working-class area.
Fruit peddlers and rag peddlers rode, slowly,
through the streets in wagons (sleighs in winter)
being pulled by old horses. There were several
large Catholic churches and two synagogues.
There was (and still is) the open market where
the farmers came in with their produce. While
away from the market: the second-hand clothing
stores, the pawnbrokers, the French Canadian
schools, bakeries, butchers, and the corner stores.
Priests and nuns were a common sight. As were
men with long beards in the market. . . .

"I grew up in this rich human atmosphere.
But at the time all I wanted to do was to get out.
I did get out when I was eighteen. The Second
World War was on. I joined the RCAF. And, af-
ter training in Western Canada, went over to
England, as a Pilot Officer, at the start of 1944.
And eventually flew with a Lancaster Squadron
based at Leeming, Yorkshire.

"After the war I returned to Canada and went
to McGill University in Montreal as a veteran. In
the summers I worked as a tutor, to three Guate-
malans and one French Canadian, in a country
house, in Ile Aux Noix, by the Richelieu river.
Another summer, in an iron mine in Northern
Ontario, at Wawa. I also had some verse published while an undergraduate and finished a
first novel. My Canadian publisher (to be) after
reading the novel said that I needed to find an
American or a British publisher. Then he would
take copies for the Canadian market.

"I decided to go to England (in the summer
of 1949) partly for personal reasons—I met an
English girl at McGill and she was going back to
England after graduating. Perhaps because of
the wartime experience—not the flying, but because of seeing how the English civilian population behaved during the war. And partly
because English literature was what I was
brought up on. I spent the first two winters in
London, the summers in St. Ives, Cornwall. During this time I lived a kind of bohemian life with
other young hopefuls who had come from different parts of the English-speaking world and
wanted to be writers or painters. When the novel
was accepted, I married, began a family (three
daughters), and moved to Cornwall. And apart
from moving around to different parts of England during the next few years (London, Brighton, Devon, Sussex), I have lived for more than
thirty years in St. Ives.

NORMAN LEVINE

"I was fortunate to be in St. Ives—especially
those early years (1949, the 1950s, and the early
1960s) because next to London, St. Ives was then
the center of British painting. And my friends
were the painters I first met there: Peter
Lanyon, Francis Bacon, Alan Lowndes, Terry
Frost, Patrick Heron. Of all these the one who
influenced me most, as a writer, was Francis Bacon. It was through conversations with him, over
the years, that I began to feel much freer in my
work. And the first book to show this is the novel
From a Seaside Town.

"These have been the main sources from
which my writing has come: Lower Town, Ottawa . . . McGill . . . the iron mine in Northern
Ontario . . . Ile Aux Noix . . . different parts
of England, but especially St. Ives . . . married
life . . . and running through them all is the
feeling of not belonging to the place I happen to
be in—but quite happy, for a while, to be there.
My wife died in 1978. And since 1980 I have
lived mostly in Toronto and some of the time in
St. Ives."

————————

Norman Levine, the son of Moses Mordecai
Levine and the former Annie Gurevich, attended Carleton College in Ottawa as well as McGill
University in Montreal, from which he graduated with honors in 1948 and took an M.A. the following year. At McGill he won the Peterson
Memorial Prize in literature and the Chester
McNaughton Prize for creative writing, and was
also editor-in-chief of *Forge,* the university literary magazine.

His first two books were collections of poetry, *Myssium* and *The Tight-Rope Walker*. Undoubtedly the best known of his poems is "Crabbing," which was included in both the 1954 revision of Bliss Carman's *Canadian Poetry in English* and in A.J.M. Smith's compilation, *The Oxford Book of Canadian Verse* (1960). A sensuous description of a day spent on a coastal crabbing boat, the poem's heavily alliterative scansion is strongly reminiscent of Old English verse.

The first book by Levine to attract wide public notice was *Canada Made Me,* a bitter memoir of a writer's return to his home in Canada after years as an expatriate in England. The narrator's travels through Montreal, Ottawa, and the West comprise a journey of recognition and rejection. His Canada is seen as, in one critic's words, "vulgar and careless, a shoddy world of dingy restaurants filled with blank-eyed girls and leather-jacketed youth. Blobs of chewing-gum stuck underneath the table signal the return to Canadian life. . . . The total effect of the book is that of a nightmare, where brilliant particles of realistic reporting whirl into a grotesque reprise. . . . A memorable book, . . . it reflects the shock, stimulus, elation, and despair roused in a sensitive observer by this nation."

Levine's several collections of short fiction began with *One Way Ticket,* which included a novella and eight stories set in various parts of Canada and England, treating the summer and winter seasons at a Cornish seaside resort, an isolated mining community in the back country of Ontario, and a young Canadian family living in considerable poverty in the English countryside. The last situation was used again by Levine in "I'll Bring You Back Something Nice," a story that was his contribution to his anthology, *Canadian Winter's Tales*. A young Canadian writer, living in conditions approaching squalor with his English wife and two daughters in an unattractive part of rural England, goes to London to raise some money to pay an overdue electricity bill. While there he goes to an unexpected reunion with some of his old McGill classmates, all now well-heeled businessmen working in Britain, and ends by begging money from some of them.

Inherent in most of Levine's stories, including those in the evocatively titled collection *I Don't Want to Know Anyone Too Well,* is what the *Times Literary Supplement* reviewer called "a studiously fostered sense of natural reserve. The intention here is not to tease, but to instil in events modestly stated a real sense of depth by using what amounts to a kind of extended meiosis, thus causing the reader to take a closer interest in occurrences which, in other hands, would have served as little more than fictional kinetics: as a means to push the story along from beginning to end." Many of Levine's stories express a pervasive nostalgia, more fond than regretful; events and people once so immediate have become strangly irretrievable. "A minor incident," said the *Times Literary Supplement* reviewer, "distanced by a brief description of the intervening circumstances, [is] recalled during a return to the place or the people concerned. . . . It's a masterly and greatly rewarding touch, scarcely ever overplayed; and despite his reliance on the art of exclusion, Mr. Levine is never prevented from endowing the stories with a gentle humor, or an atmosphere of sympathetic concern."

Levine was called "a very good but not an inventive writer" by Victoria Glendinning in her review of the dozen stories in *Thin Ice*. His "gift is for a peculiar, very personal kind of reportage. When one turns to his new fiction . . . the 'personal' seems a bit of a stranglehold. His experiences are recycled: scraps of dialogue, anecdotes, descriptions from *Canada Made Me* recur in the stories, transposed but not transformed." Jonathan Steffin considered the stories "starkly elegant. . . . It is distances which obsess Levine—between places, between people, between past and present. . . . [He] escaped from the Jewish immigrant community of Lower Town, Ottawa, only to find that it is still where he belongs. . . . This crumbling world, and its pervasive persistence in memory, is beautifully evoked, as is the London of the postwar generation."

Levine married Margaret Payne in January 1952; they have three children. He was resident writer at the University of New Brunswick in 1965–66 and won a fellowship from the Canada Council in 1959 and its arts award in 1969 and 1971. He was also the subject of a Canadian Broadcasting Company's film, *Norman Levine Lived Here* (1970) and of the British Broadcasting Corporation's *Norman Levine's St. Ives* (1972).

PRINCIPAL WORKS: *Poetry*—Myssium, 1948; The Tight-Rope Walker, 1950; I Walked by the Harbour, 1976. *Short stories*—One Way Ticket, 1960; I Don't Want to Know Anyone Too Well, 1971; Selected Stories, 1975; Thin Ice, 1980. *Novels*—The Angled Road, 1952; From a Seaside Town, 1970. *Non-fiction*—Canada Made Me, 1958. *As editor*—Canadian Winter's Tales, 1968.

ABOUT: Contemporary Authors, first revision series 73–76, 1978; Literary History of Canada 2 and 3, 1973; Supplement to the Oxford Companion to Canadian History and Literature, 1973. *Periodicals*— Daily Express London October 22, 1952; New Statesman

Christmas issue, 1958; Time Magazine January 7, 1959; Spectator December 1, 1961; Canadian Literature, Spring 1962; Times Literary Supplement December 3, 1971; Canadian Literature Autumn 1976; Sunday Times London March 29, 1980; New Statesman February 15, 1980; Times Literary Supplement March 14, 1980.

ENRIQUE LIHN

*LIHN, ENRIQUE (September 3, 1929–   ), Chilean poet and novelist, was born in Santiago. His parents were Enrique Lihn Döll and Maria Carrasco. He attended secondary school at the Liceo de los Padres Alemanes, and then enrolled in Santiago's Institute of Fine Arts. He never graduated, but spent several years studying literature on his own and the art of drawing and painting under the guidance of master impressionist Pablo Burchard. According to his own testimony, Lihn worked hard at becoming a painter, never being quite convinced that he had real talent. Instead, he became a self-taught teacher of literature specializing in the theories of the French avant-garde. The writings of Chile's three great poets of the twentieth century—Gabriela Mistral, Vicente Huidobro, and Pablo Neruda—had a deep and lasting impact on the young Lihn. These influences came in different ways and degrees. In Huidobro he valued the uncompromising search for a poetic language beyond the rhetorical restrictions of Rubén Darío and his Modernist School. Lihn understood and shared Huidobro's attempt to create a poetic discourse based on imagery and sound and devoid of objectivism and sentimentality. Huidobro was read by young poets of Chile as the representative of "grace," while Neruda and his surrealistic *Residence on Earth* stood for "gravity" in the nomenclature proposed by Simone Weil. But it was Mistral who attracted Lihn the most. He sympathized with her philosophical consideration of the existential condition of man in Spanish America, although he eventually drew away from her religious symbolism. Lihn eloquently expressed his personal devotion for Mistral in his "Elegía a G.M." (*La pieza oscura* [Dark Room], 1963).

The tradition of Chilean baroque poetry was coming to an end when Lihn published his first book, *Poemas de este tiempo y de otro, 1949-1954*, in 1955. Yet certain elements of his early poetic structures can be traced back to Neruda, specifically his nostalgic love monologues, heavily sensual and functionally dependent on the use of leitmotif. On the other hand, other characteristic traits of the early Lihn, such as his eccentric explosions of anger in the middle of lyrical statements, seem to echo Nicanor Parra's *Antipoems*. In spite of these possible influ-

ences, Lihn maintained a fiercely independent position in regard to established Chilean poets. Instead, he sought an alliance with the so-called "objective" poets of his own generation and with outsiders. He was attracted by Gonzalo Rojas, at that time an obscure professor of literature in Valparaíso, of whom Lihn writes: "Rojas is objective because he plays with sound and sense in poems (which allow him to experiment with significant elements). These poems at time imitate the expositive and persuasive power of oratory. Such poetry shows a productive and creative relation with rhetoric. The use of intertextualism for the sake of hyperbole interests me."

In the early 1940s Lihn had been close to Rojas' mentors, the founders of the surrealistic *Mandragora* group, but he never identified himself completely with their brand of nihilism. Anarchy appealed to him, but he was also drawn to the rigorous banality of courtly poetry in the Provençal tradition. He produced fascinatingly incongruous glosses on Spanish Renaissance poets in the manner of the *trovar clus*.

The publication of *La pieza oscura* in 1963 established Lihn as the most promising poet of a generation that strongly challenged the aesthetic principles of the neo-realist writers of the 1940s as well as the militancy of Marxist followers of Neruda. Official critics, however, remained doubtful and distant. What disturbed and intrigued them was the realization that Lihn was proposing a discourse closely related to pastoral poetry of the Spanish Golden Age at the same time as he was destroying it by exposing his literary characters as schemers in the art of self-destructive debauchery. His lovers confronted

°lēn, ăn rē` kā

each other with brutal sarcasm. The poet's exquisite speculations usually came to an abrupt end amidst expressions of gross violence. These lovers appeared to become doubles of themselves, striving to possess others as artifacts symbolic of uncontrollable passion. In his prologue to *La pieza oscura*, art and literary critic Jorge Elliot wrote: "The great magic of Lihn's poetry lies for me, his reader, not so much in 'the music of his ideas' as in the underground murmur, subjective, sub-sexual, sub-desire, that runs through it. It gives us fear, like the murmur that precedes an earthquake, passes and destroys nothing, but leaves the heart troubled. Life pressing against our throats, the body trembling, anguish fills all our desires. As Lihn himself says: 'It's impossible to tell tears from sweat in two dry mouths struggling with each other.'"

To every student of Chilean poetry at that time it was obvious that Lihn was making a major poetic statement in a language that was playfully conversational but concealed a sharp and basic social criticism. His brand of humor, his heavy-handed satire, a sort of mocking oratory, brought Lihn closer to Parra. In *La pieza oscura,* the poet is a disenchanted fellow who comments on bourgeois habits and conventions with the sententious tone of a student of philosophy. The cumulative effect of his moral-amoral contradictory discourse is one of sad pessimism. The statements are brief and to the point; most speculations are illustrations by graphic descriptions of bodies in distorted motion, finishing nearly always with crude expletives.

Lihn has told of the time when he collaborated with Parra in the production of a pseudo-newspaper called *Quebrantahuesos* (Bonebreakers), privately circulated among friends. It was a dadaist enterprise in which poets contributed by pasting clippings of headlines in creative disorder. Huidobro, of course, had anticipated them. But Parra, Lihn and friends added a new element to these collages. Their sick type of humor revealed a very angry social commitment which brought them close to a Marxist position. Incidents that had to do more with personal life than with ideological attitudes drove them away from militancy. There was in Parra and Lihn a clear feeling of distaste for Neruda's total adherence to party discipline. Parra indeed eventually came to identify himself with the USA yippies. Lihn spoke forcefully against militancy.

In a poem such as "Zoológico" Lihn assumes the image of an eccentric, disillusioned, funny moralist who complains against the "cost of living" in terms that cleverly imply not only "living" in this world but in the world beyond as well.

What is your little story compared to your history?
Here you have life in its only form: the moment you live, tomorrow.
As for the rest, memory deceives you, only the earth remembers what is alive.
This tree's new leaves remember the old leaves, however, observe in what manner.
And it feels good walking by your side, on the earth's side that makes our heart speak for it, without rest in an old language jeweled with commonplaces . . .

and I'm the serpent, almost invisible in its glass cell, in the most somber corner in the park, alien to the curiosity it awakens, alien to earth's interests, its stepmother;
I'm this insensible lover of himself sleeping astutely while everything awakens.

—trans. F. Alegría

In 1958 Gonzalo Rojas initiated a series of literary encounters at the University of Concepción, in southern Chile, which have since grown in significance. Beginning as a symposium with a loose format in which writers discussed questions of literary theory and practice in the context of pressing social and political problems, it developed into a confrontation between the Chilean literary establishment and the young exponents of anti-poetry and surrealism. Neruda was present as a venerable figure to be respected but not worshiped blindly. Neither Parra, Lihn, nor Rojas made any allusions to Neruda, but it was obvious that they had come to challenge the concept and practice of political poetry. Shortly after this meeting and encouraged by its success and wide media coverage, Rojas called for a larger one, this time inviting representatives from most American countries. From the United States came beat poets Allen Ginsberg and Lawrence Ferlinghetti, from Cuba Alejo Carpentier, Ernesto Sabato from Argentina, Carlos Fuentes from Mexico, Jose María Arguedas from Peru, and many others. Lihn's contribution to these meetings reaffirmed his position as the leader of a non-aligned group of young poets marking the transition which signified the end of the Huidobro–de Rokha–Neruda predominance in Chilean poetry. The books that Lihn published after the University of Concepción meetings gave definite form to an ideological position which, moving further and further away from militant Marxism, placed him closer to an independent left represented by writers such as Cisneros in Peru, Dalton (his late period) in El Salvador, Sabines in Mexico. Of this period Lihn wrote: "These publications answered the need to sustain a strategy for an open type of realism which would liberate Marxist writers from the ghost of traditional social realism. It was the time of the thaw. In Chile, a generation of Marxist writers had reached mature age when the thaw gave them one more reason to separate themselves from dogmatic, Stalinist cadres of the old guard."

Lihn's poetry has been described in diverse and at times contradictory ways. To one critic it was "Gothic romanticism," to another "an attempt to uncover the hidden madness and emotional turbulence of a society that has surrendered its institutions and conventions to state and individual violence." One thing was clear: Lihn's voice had become unmistakably his own; his structural devices had no parallel in Chilean poetry. Here was a technique based on superimposed images distorting situations which the reader identifies as daily routine. The poet eliminated the necessary link relating poetic discourse with expected reactions to emotional contents. This structure of chaos brought to mind Picasso's early forms of Cubism. Reality is seen through a sharp, rationally unreliable prism that makes persons and objects appear in an absurd context. The movement of images follows an unplanned course originating in poetic experience, not in an objective perception. The reader guesses that the poet is working with scraps of memory which have a significance accessible only to him. Such memories function on two levels of reality. One is the world of fantasy and impressions of childhood and adolescence; the other is the experience of love expressed in pastoral terms but full of allusions to sexual activity leading to anger and physical violence.

Al bello aparecer de este lucero (At the Beautiful Arising of This Star, 1983) marks a culminating point in Lihn's literary career. His poetry is essentially lyrical, but dependent on rhythms of speculative and persuasive prose. There is a tone of subdued skepticism here, replacing the brashness of his previous nihilistic statements. Lihn is in complete control of the complex structue of texts and intertexts. As usual, lovers lose their individuality in a form of purposeless violence, but now they regain it in a dialectic affirmation of the power of poetry over the power of death. The poet continues to carry on a dialogue with characters of another age and civilization who proclaim the unreality of being while they extol the asphyxiating opulence of love conceived as a dream. Lihn, the troubadour without hope in a world of ghettos and capitalistic jungles, begins to consider language an artifact of destruction. He writes of Occidental culture as a devastated kingdom, violated in wars characterized by indiscriminate extermination, a prestigious ruin to be sung with nostalgia and remorse.

Lihn's poetry affirms and denies itself endlessly in a dialectic that has no solution. He wanders among the labyrinths of a decadent world, seeking an impossible metamorphosis: a survival in that part of himself which has conquered love in the possession of a loved object. The possession

has the persistent rhythm of the sea, holding and abandoning its prey. Life and death engage in an unresolved duel. Lihn points to a supernatural deceit that man can never unriddle. One poem expresses this philosophy of hope and despair better than any other, "The Star with Two Names the Name of Two Stars":

"We have, and they're twin images,
the pain of love that's being born
–Venus, the morning star–
and the pain of the evening star
the other Venus who is dying
Not two images [ay!] but one planet
christened with different names
at once, thus wandering and fixed.

Great whore of a
    dawn you're titillating
while I've gone and lost my head
How could you eclipse yourself?
To think a change of adjectives
and hours enough to make the difference

Venus you'll never think
you're other, though you are
    you by accident
you're blinding me with the light it had
instead of one star I see two:
light of dawn light of dusk
distinguishable since they're the same:
love and lovelessness in love."

—trans. John Felstiner

Lihn's anti-novels—*Agua de arroz* (Rice Water, 1964), *Batman en chile* (1973), *La orquesta de cristal* (The Crystal Orchestra, 1976), and *El arte de la palabra* (The Art of Speaking, 1981)—are highly complex experiments in which the narrator parodies himself in an effort to destroy his own narrative and to sustain only the language which becomes object and subject at the same time. Humor is the key element that provides reality to his characters and situations. Like Hector Libertella in Argentina, Lihn uses parody for parody's sake, without the social connotation implied by Manuel Puig or Luisa Valenzuela.

Abhorring eloquence and dogma of any kind, disregarding traditional divisions of genres, intent on creating situations, employing a sophisticated form of dramatic monologue, Lihn has attained a high place among present innovators in Latin American poetry. Like the best exponents of the Latin American fiction he prefers to report as a chronicler of unheard of happenings. His verse, although lengthy and oratorical in appearance, is always rhythmical and painstakingly constructed. He has been successful in organizing a system of metaphors to suggest that the true quest of a poet is poetry itself. If there is a dilemma in his poetry, Lihn has chosen not to disclose it. It is a mystery that deepens and enriches his work.

WORKS IN ENGLISH TRANSLATION: Selections from *La pieza*

oscura and *Poesia de paso* were translated by William Witherup and Serge Echeverria as *The Endless Malice* in 1969. Dave Olipant published a translation, *If Poetry Is to Be Written Right,* in 1977, and Patricio Lerzundi collected *The Dark Room and Other Poems,* with translations by Jonathan Cohen, John Felstner, and David Unger, in 1978.

ABOUT: Contemporary Authors 104, 1982; Foster, D. W. Dictionary of Contemporary Latin American Authors, 1975; Lerzundi, P. *Introduction to* The Dark Room and Others Poems, 1978; Review 23, 1978. *In Spanish*—Cortinez, C. and Lara, O. (eds.) Poesía Chilena, 1966; Lastra, P. Conversaciones con Enrique Lihn, 1980.

LODGE, DAVID (January 28, 1935–   ), English novelist, critic, and scholar, writes: "I was born in south-east London, where, apart from periods of 'evacuation' in the war, I grew up. My father was what used to be called a 'dance-band' musician. His grandmother was Jewish. My mother's father was an Irishman and her mother was Belgian. This has always seemed to me a good genetic mix for a writer. Because my mother was Catholic, I received a Catholic education; later I married a Catholic girl whom I met at university. I am still a practicing Catholic, of liberal theological views. I am an only child—a rather unusual circumstance for a Catholic—but have three of my own.

"I belonged to the first generation in Britain to benefit from free secondary and college education. In my seventeenth year I went from my state-assisted Catholic 'grammar-school' to University College London, where I took a first class degree in English in 1955. I then did two years' national service in the Royal Armoured Corps, during which I started my first novel, *The Picturegoers,* published in 1960, and acquired the raw material for my second, *Ginger, You're Barmy.* From 1957–59 I did graduate work at University College London, writing a monster 700-page master's thesis on the Catholic novel. In 1959 I married [Mary Frances Jacob] and in 1969 was appointed to an assistant lectureship at the University of Birmingham, where I have been ever since, climbing gradually up the academic ladder until, in 1976, I acquired my present title, Professor of Modern English Literature. My scholarly work has been mainly concerned with the nineteenth and twentieth century novel, and with literary theory. My most recent books have been strongly influenced by European structuralism. I have made a conscious effort to combine two activities many people consider incompatible—academic criticism and writing novels—producing books of each kind in alter-

DAVID LODGE

nation. I like to think that as a novelist I am a more self-conscious craftsman by virtue of my critical skills, and that my criticism of fiction benefits from my experience of writing it.

"In 1964–65 I held a Harkness fellowship to study American literature, and traveled widely in the United States with my wife and family. It was a liberating, life-enhancing year that I shall never forget, and never cease to be deeply grateful for. In 1969 we went back to America for six months, to Berkeley, where the student revolution was at its height, and where I got some of the background for *Changing Places.* This was my first really successful novel. It won two small but prestigious prizes—the Hawthornden Prize and the *Yorkshire Post* Fiction Prize— and has been translated into Spanish, Czech, Japanese, and Hebrew; though, to my great disappointment, and in spite of being something of a cult book among American academics, it has never been 'properly' published in the United States (the Penguin edition is available there). My most recent novel, *How Far Can You Go?,* won the Whitbread awards for Novel of the Year and Book of the Year, 1980—a double prize worth £5,000.

"My wife works as a teacher and personal counselor in a Catholic comprehensive school (i.e. high school). My daughter Julia studied biology at Southampton University, and my elder son Stephen went to Cambridge to read natural sciences. I am rather pleased my two older children have specialized in science as I learn from them, and am relieved of the duty of having to help them with their work. My youngest child, Christopher, is mentally handicapped, though not too severely, and is the happiest person I know. He would like to be a cook, and can already produce excellent shortbread cookies unassisted.

"I lead a full and busy life, and am something of a workaholic. I do a full teaching load at the University of Birmingham and supervise graduate theses. I do a good deal of book reviewing for journals like the *Times Literary Supplement* and the *New Statesman*. I broadcast occasionally on radio and take part in TV programs about books and the arts. I travel abroad on lecture tours and to attend conferences. In the past few years I have visited Italy, Norway, Switzerland, Israel, and Turkey, and have been three times to America, most recently as short-term Visiting Fellow at Princeton. I like the combination of business and pleasure these trips afford. I have never quite mastered the art of taking a vacation."

In an essay on Kingsley Amis in *Language of Fiction,* David Lodge praises his fellow novelist for focusing "in a very precise way a number of attitudes which a great many middle-class intellectuals of the post-war period find useful for the purposes of self-definition." The same observation might apply to Lodge's novels, which he describes as belonging "to a tradition of realistic fiction (especially associated with England) that tries to find an approximate form for, and a public significance in, what the writer has himself experienced and observed." Lodge has drawn upon his own experiences as a struggling student from a lower middle-class background, as an army draftee, an academic, a Catholic, a husband and father. His novels are often satirical, but Lodge's wit is genial, inclining toward parody and farce. In 1980, with *How Far Can You Go?* (U.S. *Souls and Bodies*), he dealt with the subject of Catholic doctrine. Although ostensibly a comic novel, *How Far* is a serious attempt to explore the reactions of contemporary Catholics to the radical changes within their church since the second Vatican Council, and has a note of moral urgency lacking in his earlier work. Lee Anne Schreiber, reviewing it in the *New York Times,* called Lodge "forthrightly didactic" for introducing a disquisition on Catholic doctrines of sexuality, but she defended this section as "one of the most cogent explanations of church doctrine to the found in or out of fiction. And certainly the wittiest." His academic novels, *Changing Places* and *Small World,* are closer to satiric farce than pure wit. Both deal with the transatlantic adventures of a new breed of college professor of English literature—an extroverted American, Morris Zapp, and a mousey Englishman, Philip Swallow. In *Changing Places,* subtitled "A Tale of Two Campuses," they literally exchange professorships, exposing Zapp to the red-brick university of welfare-state England of 1969 and Swallow to the often literally explosive American university of the same period. These characters reappear a decade later in *Small World,* international travelers, inveterate scholarly meeting-goers (with sidetrips to the porn shops of London and Amsterdam), mainly now involved in the crises of late middle-age sex—hence its subtitle, "An Academic Romance." Both novels have won Lodge a devoted readership among transatlantic academics, but they tend to disarm rather than excite the critics.

The young hero of Lodge's early novel *The British Museum Is Falling Down* is struggling to complete a doctoral dissertation on "The Structure of Long Sentences in Three Modern English Novels." Absurd though the subject is, it reflects Lodge's preoccupation as a literary critic with the structure of language. As a novelist and a teacher of literature, he is concerned both with the theory and practice of literature. Noting that fiction lacks a "poetics" and is often relegated to a sub- or non-literary status in the critical hierarchy, he has explored formalist criticism and the work of the European structuralists Saussure, Jakobson, Derrida, and Barthes to find "a single way of talking about novels, a critical methodology, a poetics or aesthetics of fiction." In *Language of Fiction* and *The Novelist at the Crossroads* he analyzed a number of nineteenth- and twentieth-century novels in an attempt to define the nature of realism in the modern novel. In *Modes of Modern Writing,* using a distinction first made by Roman Jakobson, he tested some of his definitions by noting the linguistic oscillations in modern literature between the metaphoric (based on similarity or analogy—i.e. the symbolic poetic) and the metonymic (based on sequence and contest—i.e. the realistic). The result, Terence Hawkes wrote in the *Times Literary Supplement,* was "a bold, incisive essay which, with admirable lucidity, offers its readers a brilliantly honed and deftly applied analytical tool." In *Working with Structuralism* Lodge applied structuralist principles to the contemporary English and American novel. His flexible approach to literature allows him to translate the arcane mysteries of structuralism into a working system that can form the basis of an educated but non-specialist reading of literature. Graham Hough, in the *Times Literary Supplement,* describes his achievement as "admirably lucid exposition of some of the more manageable bits of current linguistic and semiotic thinking."

PRINCIPAL WORKS: *Novels*—The Picturegoers, 1960; Ginger, You're Barmy, 1962; The British Museum Is Falling Down, 1965 (U.S. Vatican Roulette, 1968); Out of the Shelter, 1970; Changing Places, 1975; How Far Can You Go?, 1980 (U.S. Souls and Bodies); Small World: An Academic Romance, 1984. *Criticism*—Language of Fiction, 1966; The Novelist at the Crossroads, 1971; The Modes of Modern Writing: Metaphor, Metonymy and the Typology of Modern Literature, 1977; Working with Structuralism, 1981.

ABOUT: Contemporary Authors, first revision series 17–20, 1976; Vinson, J. (ed.) Contemporary Novelists, 1976; Dictionary of Literary Biography 14, 1983; Who's Who, 1983–84. *Periodicals*—The Month February 1970; Times Literary Supplement January 13, 1978; June 26, 1981; March 23, 1984.

AUDRE LORDE

LORDE, AUDRE (GERALDIN) (February 18, 1934–), American poet and memoirist, was born in New York City, the daughter of Frederic Byron Lorde, a real estate broker, and the former Linda Belmar, both immigrants from the West Indies. After graduating from Hunter College High School, she received a bachelor's degree from Hunter College in 1959 and a master's degree in library science from Columbia University in 1961. The following year she married Edwin Ashley Rollins, an attorney; they had a daughter and a son, and were divorced in early 1970. After two years of library work in Mount Vernon, New York, Lorde taught from 1966 to 1968 at the Town School in New York. She then spent a year as poet in residence at Tougaloo College in Mississippi before beginning to teach English at the City University of New York, first at Lehman College (1968), then at City College (1969), John Jay College (1970–81), and finally at her alma mater, Hunter College (from 1972), where she has been professor of English since 1981.

Lorde has been writing poems since the early 1950s, and has produced a half-dozen major collections of her verse since the appearance of *The First Cities* in 1968. It is difficult to speak of the development of her poetry, since in its sureness of tone and maturity of vision her work has seemed whole and *sui generis* from the very beginning. "Coal" gave its title to a retrospective collection published in 1976, but the poem itself dates from 1962, and demonstrates that at the time of its composition the author was aware of the possibilities of her medium of expression.

. . . Some words live in my throat
breeding like adders. Others now sun
seeking like gypsies over my tongue
to explode through my lips
like young sparrows bursting from shell.
Some words
bedevil me.

Love is a word, another kind of open.
As the diamond comes into a knot of flame
I am Black because I come from the earth's inside
now take my word for jewel in the open light.

Learning the limits of that power has naturally been a time-consuming process. As a black woman, a feminist, a mother, and a lesbian, she has usually managed to avoid any strident or doctrinaire tone in her work, continually aware of the risks run in treating the objective world of pain, repression, and deprivation: "unless I learn to use/the difference between poetry and rhetoric/my power too will run corrupt as poisonous mold/or lie limp and useless as an unconnected wire."

In addition to her constant attention to terseness and minuteness of observation, Lorde has always been quick to use humor wherever she could find it. She is generally considered one of America's best urban poets, adept at showing the individual human face behind much apparently general suffering. "When the Saints Come Marching In," from the collection *Cables to Rage,* suggests a surprising resolution to urban violence and alienation:

. . . I expect some new religion
to rise up like tear gas
from the streets of New York. . . .

The high priests have been ready and waiting
with their incense pans full of fire.
I do not know the rituals
the exhaltations
nor what name of the god
the survivors will worship
I only know she will be terrible
and very busy
and very old.

Feminist themes have been prominent in Lorde's work virtually from the start, and during the 1970s they came to the fore. "Black Mother Woman," out of the collection *From a Land Where Other People Live,* for which Lorde was nominated for the National Book Award of 1973, is a stark statement of a strong mother's influence on the molding of an even stronger daughter:

I cannot recall you gentle
yet through your heavy love
I have become
an image of your once delicate flesh
split with deceitful longings. . . .

But I have peeled away your anger
down to the core of love
and look mother
I Am
a dark temple where your true spirit rises
beautiful
and tough as chestnut
stanchion against your nightmare of weakness
and if my eyes conceal
a squadron of conflicting rebellions
I learned from you
to define myself
through your denials.

She has also, from the early 1970s, been writing candidly of her love for women, and by now is able to do so with grace, depth, purity, and no dissembling. Her profound concern over the mindless violence that daily affronts women, especially black women, is expressed in one of her most powerful recent works, a long poem entitled "Need: A Choral of Black Women's Voices," in which she speaks the minds of two hundred women:

Dead Black women haunt the black maled streets
paying the cities' secret and familiar tithe of blood
burn blood beat blood cut blood
seven year old child rape victim blood blood
of a sodomized grandmother blood blood
on the hands of my brother blood
and his blood clotting in the teeth of strangers . . .
why is it our blood
that keeps these cities fertile?

Lorde's own selection of her most important work has been brought together in a major retrospective collection, *Chosen Poems Old and New,* which shows her, first and foremost, as an engaged poet, shunning isolation and demanding attention for her continual attempt to voice the political and social realities of her life. In this attempt she is, Rosemary Daniell has written, "refreshingly removed from the pale frozen works of many poets, who appear immobilized by the image of themselves as poet. Instead, she is a poet of her time, her place, her people."

As a prose writer, Lorde is best known for two works, *The Cancer Journals* and *Zami: A New Spelling of My Name.* The former book is the frank and painful account, sometimes day-by-day, of what it means to have a mastectomy. She describes her reasons for writing the book, and its entire compass, in an introduction of searing eloquence: "I do not wish my anger and pain and fear about cancer to fossilize into yet another silence, nor to rob me of whatever strength can lie at the core of this experience, openly acknowledged and examined. For other women of all ages, colors, and sexual identities who recognize that imposed silence about any area of our lives is a tool for separation and powerlessness, and for myself, I have tried to voice some of my feelings and thoughts about the travesty of prosthesis, the pain of amputation, the function of cancer in a profit economy, my confrontation with reality, the strength of women loving, and the power and rewards of self-conscious living." This book, unlike many that treat the same subject, is not at all in the "self-help" or "inspirational" vein; rather, we can read on nearly every page, in Adrienne Rich's words, "grief, terror, courage, the passion for survival and for more than survival."

Zami is the story of Lorde's insulated childhood and tumultuous coming of age. It is dense with specific memory, sensual detail, and carefully chosen, apt imagery, and conveys the feeling of living in such places as Harlem in the late Depression and Greenwich Village during the 1950s. The book's "personal honesty and lack of pretentiousness" were praised by Rosemary Daniell, because they bespeak "the evolution of a strong and remarkable character." Admirers of Lorde's prose may hope for a sequel to *Zami,* which concludes in 1960.

Lorde has been an active member of writers' organizations and of state and federal arts councils, and is on the editorial boards of *Chrysalis, Black Box,* and *Black Scholar* magazines. She has lived for many years on Staten Island.

WORKS: *Poetry*—The First Cities, 1968; Cables to Rage, 1970; From a Land Where Other People Live, 1973; New York Head Shop and Museum, 1974; Coal, 1976; The Black Unicorn, 1978; Chosen Poems Old and New, 1982. *Prose*—The Cancer Journals, 1980; Zami, 1982.

ABOUT: Contemporary Authors, revised series 25–28, 1977; Contemporary Literary Criticism 18, 1981; Contemporary Poets, 1980; Evans, M. (ed.) Black Women Writers (1950–1980): A Critical Evaluation, 1984; Tait, Claudia (ed.) Black Women Writers at Work, 1983; Who's Who in America, 1983–84. *Periodicals*—Best Sellers November 1976; January 1979; Choice September 1975; November 1976; March 1979; Commonweal November 25, 1977; Library Journal September 1, 1975; June 15, 1976; October 1, 1978; June 15, 1982; Ms. September 1974; January 1979; February 1983; Nation December 23, 1978; Ne-

gro Digest September–October 1968; New York Times
Book Review September 29, 1974; September 7, 1975;
December 19, 1982; Poetry February 1977.

McCLURE, JAMES (HOWE) (October 9,
1939–   ), South African-born detective-story
writer and journalist, was born in Johannesburg,
the son of James Howe McClure, an army officer, and the former Isabella Cochrane. Educated
in South Africa, McClure worked for a time
(1958–59) as a commercial photographer, then
as an English and art teacher in a boys' school
in Pietermaritzburg (1959–63), before beginning his journalistic career. He was a reporter for
three newspapers in Natal, the province on the
Indian Ocean, from 1963 to 1965, then got a job
in Britain on the Edinburgh *Daily Mail,* from
which he soon moved south to Oxford to a series
of editorial positions on the *Mail* and the *Times.*
After his crime novels had attained an international readership, he retired from the world of
full-time journalism in 1974, by which time he
was deputy editor of the Oxford Times Group.

McClure's several police fictions—about one
a year has been published since his first book,
The Steam Pig—are set in South Africa, usually
in the small Boer city of Trekkersburg. His heroes are Lieutenant Tromp Kramer of the Trekkersburg Murder and Robbery Squad and his
Watson, Bantu Detective Sergeant Mickey
Zondi. The delineation of their relationship
through the novels, hesitant, suspicious, yet respectful and intensely loyal, is one of the things
McClure's admirers like most about his work;
another is his deft yet scathing satire of South African life. One reviewer commented on his
"sharp imaginative response, evoking offices,
streets, homes, native townships with never a
threat of a purple passage, and etching a hundred shades of social and professional hierarchies, temperament, prejudice in blacks and
Afrikaners and British Colonials without ever
telling us what we should think of them." Another critic, acknowledging almost in passing the
sharpness of the writing and the craftiness of the
plots, also praised "above all, a wonderfully well-
calculated attitude to the great South African
bugbear, never overtly damning, never loading
the scales either way, and all the more a condemnation for that." The Kramer-Zondi series,
in addition to *The Steam Pig,* consists of *The
Caterpillar Cop, The Gooseberry Fool, Snake,
Rogue Eagle, The Sunday Hangman,* and *The
Blood of an Englishman.* He has also published
one crime novel set in England, *Four and Twenty Virgins,* which a critic dismissed as "frankly
unsuccessful."

JAMES McCLURE

McClure spent many months of research
among the police in the port city of Liverpool on
a major work of non-fiction, *Spike Island: Portrait of a Police Division.* This 533-page book is
an intense scrutiny of "A" Division, the smallest
of the largely independent territories comprising
the patrol area of the Merseyside Police. The
division, nicknamed Spike Island, is
"superimposed upon innermost Liverpool, and
has been described by one of its officers as 'a sort
of Band Aid stuck over where they ripped the
heart out.' . . . The inner-city area of Liverpool
is today one of the most wretched in Western
Europe, just as it was more than a century
ago. . . . It was also said to have the country's
worst law-and-order problem. . . . 'A' Division
took the brunt of the increase in violence and
disorder, and the Chief Constable warned that,
if things did not improve considerably, the city
centre might need 'an army of occupation' by
1980." The book studies every area of police responsibility and is full of anecdotes and long, often colorful quotations from police officers
themselves. Transcribing the many hours of tape
recordings alone took three months. McClure's
style is typically controlled, noncommittal, essentially journalistic; it nevertheless reveals
much of the overt racism and the extreme but
hidden violence for which the British police
have become notorious, as well as McClure's respect for a bunch of overworked men and wom-
en who are doing a very nasty job—though not
by American urban standards a particularly
dangerous one. The book, in the words of Laurie
Taylor, "provides a wholly credible sense of the
pointless nastiness of much of the crime and de-

viance in this tatty urban scene; a tight close-up on a long list of social problems which, although created by factors well outside any police jurisdiction, are nevertheless gratefully passed over to them for solution. Small wonder that this compelling book can bring no promise of improvement; only news of the precariousness of the present efforts at containment."

In January 1962, before leaving South Africa, McClure married Lorellee Ellis. They have two sons and a daughter and live in Headington, a suburb of Oxford.

WORKS: *Fiction*—The Steam Pig, 1971; The Caterpillar Cop, 1972; Four and Twenty Virgins, 1973; The Gooseberry Fool, 1974; Snake, 1975; Rogue Eagle, 1976; The Sunday Hangman, 1977; The Blood of an Englishman, 1980. *Non-fiction*—Killers, 1976; Spike Island, 1980.

ABOUT: Contemporary Authors 69–72, 1978. *Periodicals*—Best Sellers July 1, 1973; June 15, 1974; Library Journal November 1, 1972; July 1973; July 1974; March 1, 1976; September 15, 1980; November 1, 1980; New Republic July 26, 1976; June 28, 1980; February 7, 1981; New York Times Book Review October 22, 1972; July 1, 1973; June 13, 1976; August 24, 1980; February 1, 1981; Saturday Review October 28, 1972; Times (London) November 6, 1975; August 4, 1977; April 12, 1980; July 10, 1980; Times Literary Supplement October 29, 1971; October 13, 1972; September 1, 1974; December 19, 1975; November 12, 1976; April 18, 1980; July 25, 1980.

McCULLOUGH, COLLEEN (June 1, 1937–), Australian novelist, was born in Welling, New South Wales, Australia. Her father, James McCullough, an Ulster Orangeman, immigrated to Australia in the 1920s; his wife was a New Zealander of Irish Catholic and Maori ancestry. In an interview, McCullough has described her father, a sugar cane cutting contractor, as "tightfisted," "cold," and "disinterested in his family." His work in the sugar cane country caused him to be away from the house much of the time, and McCullough found paternal substitutes in her mother's nine unmarried brothers, most of whom lived with them at various times during the 1930s and 1940s. Raised mainly in Sydney, McCullough attended a convent school for twelve years. After graduating from Holy Cross College, she enrolled at the University of Sydney with the intention of becoming a physician; but was forced to withdraw by her father, who opposed medical careers for women. For a time she worked in the Australian outback as a librarian and schoolteacher; then returned to the University of Sydney to complete a bachelor's degree as a medical technician, specializing in neurophysiology.

COLLEEN McCULLOUGH

McCullough emigrated to England in 1963, at the age of twenty-six and for four years cared for epileptic and retarded youths at the Hospital for Sick Children in London. In 1967, she came to the United States, at the invitation of the chairman of the department of neurology at Yale University's School of Medicine, to manage their neurological research laboratory—a position she held from 1967 to 1976. In her spare time she wrote her first novel, *Tim. Tim* enjoyed a respectable sale, but following the phenomenal success of *The Thorn Birds* was reissued in paperback, and sold in vast numbers (700,000 copies). Its reissuing also coincided with the release of Michael Pate's film adaptation of *Tim*, which starred Piper Laurie and Mel Gibson.

Set in a suburb of Sydney, *Tim* tells the unusual story of a relationship between a middle-aged woman—an unmarried mining-company executive—and a young laborer who has the face and body of an Adonis but whose mental faculties are those of a child. They are drawn to each other, and marry at the end. *Tim* was not widely reviewed, but those reviews it did receive were favorable. The critic for *Booklist* remarked that it was written with "an affecting honesty," and the reviewer for *Publishers Weekly* called it "accomplished, sensitive, and wise." Margaret Ferrari, in *America*, noted that "its language is clear and direct, full of colorful Australian slang. McCullough's feeling for character . . . is compassionate . . . concise. Her delicacy is perfectly suited to the story. *Tim* is a warm book to read, reassuring about goodness in human nature and about the power of love to overcome worldly obstacles and to make us care more for another person's interests than for our own."

McCullough began writing *The Thorn Birds* in June 1975, in the aftermath, she has said in an interview, of an unhappy love affair. After returning from work at the Yale laboratory, she worked on the novel every evening until dawn, often producing 15,000 words at a sitting. *The Thorn Birds* went through ten drafts in as many months, and upon completion was accepted enthusiastically by Harper & Row, which touted the large, multigenerational novel as "an Australian *Gone With the Wind*." *The Thorn Birds* soared immediately to the top of the best-seller list, eventually selling more than ten million copies in the United States alone. It also made publishing history when paperback rights were sold for $1,900,000 in 1977, setting a record. *The Thorn Birds* came again into prominence when a film version was presented on network television as a mini-series, beginning on March 27, 1983. The ten-hour chronicle, aired on four consecutive nights, starred Richard Chamberlain, Rachel Ward, and Barbara Stanwyck.

The Thorn Birds focuses on the Cleary family in the course of three generations, spanning the years from 1915 to 1965. It begins in New Zealand as Paddy Cleary, a down-on-his-luck stockman, and his wife, Fee, endure back-country hardship. In time Cleary is summoned by his wealthy, aging sister, Mary Carter, to run—and eventually to inherit—Drogheda, her vast sheep station in New South Wales, Australia. Here Young Meg Cleary, the novel's heroine, first meets the handsome, ambitious young priest Father Ralph de Bricassart. Many complications ensue as the two are divided during the course of their lives, yet manage briefly to find a consummation of their sexual attraction to one another. The panoramic novel ends with the death of Cardinal de Bricassart, and with Meg's recognition that her frustrated love for him has been both the pain and the enrichment of her life.

Charles Nicol called *The Thorn Birds* "honest, earnest, well-written, and tolerably interesting," and noted that, with its domestic details and concerns, it was a novel "by a woman . . . for women." Christopher Lehmann-Haupt commented that it "satisfies the need for . . . popular escape fiction. It is nothing . . . if not good old-fashioned story-telling." Amanda Heller, however, complained that the book was "awesomely bad. . . . The dialogue is leaden . . . the characters are mechanical contrivances." Walter Clemons remarked that *The Thorn Birds* "offers big, simplified emotions, startling coincidences and thumping hammer blows of fate"; and Steven Kroll charged that despite its impressive scope, it "lacks any real dimension." Webster Schott summed up the novel by remarking that McCullough's

"memories of Australia and her imagination never run dry. She reads easily. Her characters are credible, if interchangeable . . . and if we read fiction to fill the boring spaces left by reality, then *The Thorn Birds* fits our needs. It runs like a dream factory."

With the publication of *The Thorn Birds*, McCullough at first went ahead with her plans to begin training as a nurse at St. Bartholomew's Hospital in London. In mid-1977, however, she postponed her schooling to embark on an international publicity tour for the book; and by its end abandoned the idea of nursing, explaining in an interview: "I don't believe a patient would appreciate the idea of having a millionaire nurse carrying the bedpan." Instead, she returned to her typewriter to write a third novel, *An Indecent Obsession*. Although wholly unlike *The Thorn Birds*, this book also became an immediate best-seller, and earned a seven-figure prepublication fee for paperback rights. It is set in the mental ward of a military hospital on a tropical Pacific island at the end of World War II. Ward X, the "troppo" ward for soldiers who have broken under the stresses of jungle warfare, is presided over by its nurse, Honour Langtry, who finds the delicate equilibrium of the ward disturbed by the appearance there of a new patient. Complications lead to a gruesome murder, with homosexual overtones, and Honour Langtry, choosing duty over desire, decides to devote her life after the war to caring for the mentally ill.

Reviews of *An Indecent Obsession* were harsh. Alexandra Johnson remarked: "The plot, centering on the conflict between Wilson and a blackmailing bisexual, creeps on with eye-rolling tedium . . . Worst, though, is the heroine Honour Langtry, a damp souled Florence Nightingale." Carol Rumens commented that "McCullough touches on some interesting areas of ambiguity: between sane and insane, hetero- and homosexual . . . male and famale attitudes to sex, but fails to explore them in depth. . . . [Her] narrative is often slow, plodding and short on surprise. The argument between love and duty becomes increasingly banal after the climax of Luce's death." Joanne Greenberg found Honour Langtry a "colder" character than McCullough had probably intended her to be, and questioned whether she had really found self-understanding at the end.

Colleen McCullough is an enthusiastic cook, and has published *Cooking with Colleen McCullough and Jean Easthope*—a guide to Australian cuisine. She lives on Norfolk Island, about 1,000 miles off the east coast of Australia—a small, secluded place that has no telephones or television.

Because there are no typewriter repair shops in the island, she has equipped her office with a dozen electric typewriters. In an interview in the *New York Times* in November 1981, she spoke of plans for a new book. "I'm going to have a bash at a biography this time," she said. "It will be about an English woman now in her late sixties who flew Spitfires in World War II and has led an equally fascinating life since."

PRINCIPAL WORKS: Tim, 1974; The Thorn Birds, 1977; An Indecent Obsession, 1981. *Non-fiction*—Cooking with Colleen McCullough and Jean Easthope, 1982

ABOUT: Contemporary Authors 81–84, 1979; Current Biography, 1982. *Periodicals*—America August 10, 1974; Commonweal July 22, 1977; Harper's July 1977; New York Times Book Review April 21, 1974; May 8, 1977; October 25, 1981; Publishers Weekly March 7, 1977; Saturday Review October 1981; Times Literary Supplement December 11, 1981.

JOSEPH McELROY

McELROY, JOSEPH (August 21, 1930–), American novelist, writes: "My mother and father gave me a typewriter for my eighth birthday and I got right at it, as I remember, inventing stories about Mexico, where I'd never been, and about automobiles personified with real feelings. Later on, I devoted much of my writing energy to remembering what had happened during my earlier life (doing so partly through invention). I grew up in Brooklyn Heights, where the view of New York harbor often seemed to me as much the setting for our roller-skate hockey and stickball as were our quiet streets long before the Heights got to be known as a smart place to live. I was an only child, independent and busy with friends. At seven I took the subway alone one stop to Wall Street to have lunch with my father; at nine I was permitted to go to the World's Fair once alone. My parents were generous and highly intelligent, also very social.

"One thing that started me thinking about people was the difference between my parents' families. My father's were fairly poor for years, lived in Brooklyn, were affectionate and possessive; my grandmother was from Georgia, a charmer, dependent on my father; I recall her slow accent and that of her two ubiquitous sisters, also widowed young (though not remarried), each with an only and unmarried daughter; and I recall discovering genteel differences between Christian views and southern thinking. My father became an elder in the Presbyterian church. He went to Harvard on scholarships, studied chemistry, was a natural teacher, wound up a stockbroker who worked too hard

and was beloved by his rich clients. He and I took walks on the Brooklyn docks on Sundays; we played word games; he loved to quote Emily Dickinson and Shakespeare. I see him standing in front of museum exhibits longer than I wanted to. I see him sick in bed listening to the news of FDR's death on a radio he had purchased for Willkie campaign headquarters. My father had been a champion lacrosse player but had a heart condition that kept him out of the War. He died when I was fifteen. That was when I could have used a sister or a brother.

"My mother's family were well-known Democrats in New Jersey; her father, Rulif Lawrence, was a judge; her mother, whose family ran a newspaper for generations, managed a strict, entertaining Victorian home, ran for state senate, served on the prison board, wrote fascinating letters, traveled widely, and when I visited Freehold (which to me, a city kid, was my second hometown) took me to afternoon movies and to visit the jail. My mother told of playing the violin for death-row inmates in Trenton. She taught music, studied at Fontainebleau, saw that I had lessons on several instruments, played the piano for me to sing, could have been a first-class performer but chose another life. She was a great, vivacious lady, doubted herself when she became a young widow and therefore was somewhat dubious about my being a writer; feared for me, feared to be possessive; loved me more than she was able to show.

"I went to good private schools—Brooklyn Friends, where I skipped fifth grade and in seventh fell in love with grammar; and Poly Prep, where I studied Latin for four years and felt younger than my classmates. I tried with little success to act in plays at Williams College. I shipped on a Coast Guard weather cutter and on the mid-Atlantic patrols understood for the first time the hugeness of the sea. I taught English at the University of New Hampshire, very nearly settled there; finished a Columbia Ph.D., gave myself permission to write a novel. In 1961 I married Joan Leftwich in London, her home. She is a gifted designer and colorist who has been reluctant to see herself as making art. She is a brilliant, witty, remarkable person; I lived with her for twenty years. In 1967 our daughter Hanna was born, and I was present. Joan's father was an orthodox Jew, a poet and translator of Yiddish; her mother was born in Poland, a strong, humorous woman whose spoken Yiddish was richer than anything I had heard in New York. I very nearly settled in London, lived there for a while. New York, which I will always leave, remains my obstacle, quest and inspiration.

"I have taught at several universities here and abroad; my home job since 1964 has been at Queens College. All that's said against teaching as a living for a novelist is true enough. I mean the passion squandered talking, the spirit spent preparing to explain Act III, scene iv or "Out of the Cradle Endlessly Rocking" so that the students won't feel merely lectured at. And I'm sure I could have prospered in diplomacy or a wild game preserve. But teaching has given more than it has taken; has helped me think, brought me friends, provided a livelihood averaging in actual weeks including fall and spring terms almost half the year off; has proved Mark Van Doren's truth that a teacher must want to talk and must want to be loved.

"My books celebrate having to put the world together all over again every day. That process is my only sanctuary, though places have often come close—New England, New Mexico, Chartres—as have many people to whom I have become deeply attached."

In 1979 Joseph McElroy told an interviewer that early in his writing career he had rejected "a packaged, settled sort of well-behaved fiction" in order to give his consciousness "free play, room to jump, to wander, to sweep." He has kept to that resolve at the sacrifice of easy popularity and general critical acclaim. Even his most devoted readers—a small but highly discriminating group—find him sometimes "over-ingenious" and always demanding. But they also find his work unfailingly brilliant and, in spite of, or possibly because of, the challenges to the reader's concentration, emotionally and intellectually rewarding. For all the intricate structure and obscure allusiveness of the novels, they measure up to the standards McElroy sets for himself: "I like to think of my books as being true rather than literary in some artificial sense. And I think that my books, up through *Lookout Cartridge* anyway, tried in a sane more than a paranoid way to create a collaborative network which human experience is. We can never know enough in order totally to understand it, but it is there as some kind of mysterious network."

The earlier novels are not only "sane," but do indeed explore "the mysterious network" of totally human experience. The first of these, *A Smuggler's Bible,* may strike the hasty reader as fiction of the absurd, but on closer examination it emerges as a lucid and moving study of human love, especially of a son's deepening perception of his relationship to his father. It is also witty, erudite, and a razor-sharp satire of American academic life. The structure seemed to some reviewers eccentric and contrived, the central metaphor of the eponymous "bible" (a box designed to look like a Bible in which smugglers conceal their booty) forced. Nevertheless, it serves as a solid frame for McElroy's—and his protagonist's—attempts to explore the hearts of his characters in striking scenes that range from Brooklyn Heights to a New England college campus to England and Greece. Its eight parts—separate manuscripts centering on the author-protagonist's perceptions of a single character or group of related characters—is a fragmentary bible recounting his genesis and life history and gradually reconstructing his past. McElroy, V. R. Yanitelli wrote in a review, "may just be guilty of smuggling a spiritual *Weltanschauung* past the reader's unsuspecting nose."

Subsequent novels have had a similar response from reviewers—complaints that they are "exhausting," overly-erudite, unreasonably demanding, invariably balanced with admissions that they offer "real rewards." Even as vehement a nay-sayer as Paul Wagner—writing that *Hind's Kidnap*'s wordplay, "time-disjuctions and mind-wrenching flashbacks . . . bored the hell out of me"—conceded that McElroy "is a writer of undisputable intelligence and wit." In this second novel, subtitled "A Pastoral on Familiar Airs," McElroy transforms the conventional genre of detective story (an investigation into a long-forgotten disappearance of a little boy) into a sensitive and probing journey into the self of the protagonist who is obsessed with tracking down the mystery. An even more obscure mystery—the suicide of the narrator's neighbor—is the subject of *Ancient History.* The ingenuity of the plot, however, is less impressive than its sly humor and vivid New York scenes. Stephen

Donadio wrote in the *New York Times Book Review*: "*Ancient History* succeeds in repossessing the lost world of the forties and fifties, and in locating that world in a continuum which embraces the present. Unfailingly interesting, conceived with high intelligence, lucidity and wit, Mr. McElroy's third novel compels respect; but it is a difficult and disorienting book."

Lookout Cartridge moved into even more oblique mysteries, evoking reviewer George Stade's comparison of the novel to Robbe-Grillet for its detachment, Pynchon for its symbolism drawn from science and technology, Dostoevsky and Michel Butor for its radical uses of mystery story conventions, and Norman Mailer for its fascination with power and violence. The narrator and central character, whose name is Cartwright, is making a film in England, and film provides a rich imagery of illusion and reality, art and technology. Working not unlike the typical sleuth of contemporary detective fiction, Cartwright—whose mind, like a cartridge, is ready for the trigger and the inevitable concussion—attempts to track down the elusive mystery of the theft of his film and the more ominous threat to his daughter's life. "For all its technical brilliance," Stade writes, "its unremitting intelligence, for the rich complexity of the homologies and analogies between its systems and the fearful times we live in, *Lookout Cartridge* is the rarest kind of achievement."

Given McElroy's fascination with science and technology, it is not surprising that he should have moved on in *Plus* to what appears to be science fiction—with a disembodied human brain orbiting the earth as part of a solar energy project. Again this short and densely complicated novel resists classification into a genre. "What I had in mind," McElroy told an interviewer, "was a more transcendent, visionary, even simple book. While the book arises out of materials that are scientifically observable, it is more inclined toward the visionary or the religious." No amount of technology can permanently obscure the human brain's humanity nor its capacity for growth, and this brain (named Imp Plus) begins to remember and grow: "His thoughts on sunlight had come between those missed transmissions, but if Earth had overheard, Earth made no comment. Imp Plus felt he missed the point. But something was more. He remembered being thirsty; it had been a growing absence across something of him and he wanted it to give a little and slide and spread and be cool which was not the same as wet. But now this other something that was more, burned, but not through the window and not with thirst, for he only remembered thirst. He was reaching back from as far as he was near. Reaching also to those points from

which he reached back. Points also which came into being by his reaching." The reading of *Plus*, as Michael Wood observed in his review, is "extremely hard work," but worth the labor: "If I say that this icy-sounding fantasy is actually very moving, I shall perhaps give a sense of McElroy's achievement . . . its major implication may help us home from the apocalypse: Humanity is not what we've lost, it is what we grimly hang on to, even when we're not persuaded that it's still there."

The son of Joseph Prince and Louise (Lawrence) McElroy, Joseph McElroy received his B.A. from Williams College in 1951 and an M.A. (1952) and Ph.D. (1961) from Columbia University. After two years of service in the U.S. Coast Guard, he began his teaching career at the University of New Hampshire (1956–62). Currently Professor of English at Queens College of the City University of New York, he teaches literature and creative writing workshops. He has also been visiting professor at Johns Hopkins, Columbia, and New York University. He has received grants from the National Endowment for the Arts, the Rockefeller and Ingram Merrill foundations, and the National Academy of Arts and Letters.

PRINCIPAL WORKS: A Smuggler's Bible, 1966; Hind's Kidnap, 1969; Ancient History, 1971; Lookout Cartridge, 1974; Plus, 1976; Ship Rock, a Place, 1980.

ABOUT: Cherner, Anne Joseph McElroy, an interview, 1979; Contemporary Authors, first revision series 17–20, 1976; Contemporary Novelists, 1982; Who's Who in America, 1983–84. *Periodicals*—Chicago Review 30, Spring 1979; Library Journal October 1, 1969; New York Times Book Review May 30, 1971; February 2, 1975; Tri-Quarterly 34, 1975.

McEWAN, IAN (June 21, 1948–   ), British novelist, short story and screen writer, was born in Aldershot, England, the son of David and Rose (Moore) McEwan. He attended the University of Sussex, where he received a B.A. in 1970, and the University of East Anglia, where he received an M.A. in 1971. McEwan began writing short stories in 1970, and by 1973 had received an Arts Council Award. His first book, consisting of eight short stories entitled *First Love, Last Rites*, was published when he was twenty-seven and won the Somerset Maugham Award. The stories in the collection characteristically present sexual fantasies in a style that has the circumstantial lucidity and strangeness of a dream. "Conversation with a Cupboard Man" concerns a young man so withdrawn that his world is no larger than the closet in which he masturbates.

IAN McEWAN

In "Butterflies," a boy in a large industrialized city exposes himself to a small girl and than drowns her in a polluted canal.

First Love, Last Rites received exceptionally favorable reviews in England. Julian Barnes wrote that the book "marks the debut of a talented and genuinely imaginative writer," and Jonathan Raban remarked that *First Love* "is one of those rare books which strike out on a new direction in current English fiction." Critical response in the United States was divided. Robert Phillips was impressed by the book, calling it "perhaps the most remarkable collection of stories since William Trevor's *The Day We Got Drunk on Cake*. But J. D. O'Hara was hostile: the tales, he wrote, "are essentially only Roald Dahl with a double dose of sexual explicitness and perversity. This is pandering, not writing, it is done with ability and intelligence, which makes it all the more dismaying."

First Love, Last Rites was followed by McEwan's first novel, *The Cement Garden*, whose bizarre plot concerns the attempt of four children to conceal their mother's death by burying her in the cellar of the house in a trunk, which they cover with fresh cement. During the hot summer, however, the cement cracks and a smell of corruption rises through the house. In the meantime the reader observes the children. The youngest, six-year-old Tom, dresses up as a girl and eventually takes to a cot where he becomes an infant. Fifteen-year-old Jack daydreams and is discovered having sexual intercourse with his older sister Julie. As one critic remarked, "the family structure collapses inwardly, implodes."

The Cement Garden was reviewed extensively in both England and the United States and was regarded generally as an astonishing performance. Blake Morrison wrote in the *Times Literary Supplement* that the novel "should consolidate Ian McEwan's reputation as one of the best young writers in Britain today"; and Richard Holmes, although expressing some reservation about McEwan's "artistic intentions," concluded that "certain scenes . . . show the touch of real fictional genius, an absolute precision and economy of intended effect." In America, the critic for the *Nation* called the work "a splendid first novel . . . a seamless book . . . careful and shimmering with macabre imagining." Robert Towers, in the *New York Review of Books,* commented that *The Cement Garden* "is in many ways a shocking book, morbid, full of repellent imagery—and irresistibly readable. . . . As in [his] short stories, the effect achieved by McEwan's quiet, precise, and sensuous touch is that of magic realism." The reviewer for the *New Yorker,* however, tended to regard the novel as a mere stylistic exercise, and Anne Tyler, in the *New York Times Book Review,* found the novel's characters too unattractive to evoke her interest.

McEwan's second volume of short stories, *In Between the Sheets and Other Stories,* is more surrealistic than his first. The title story deals with a man whose daughter brings home as her lover a three-foot six-inch lesbian dwarf named Charmian, and "Psychopolis," a haunting, memorably evoked story, captures the sense of Los Angeles as an "unreal" city, inhabited by the lost and the sexually estranged. "Pornography," set in London, concerns a pornography dealer who is castrated by two nurses whom he has infected with gonorrhea. Paul Bailey called the collection "every bit as good as its predecessor . . . which invoked comparisons with Angus Wilson [and] Jean Rhys. His stories are resonant and frightening because they are totally original." Caroline Blackwood, however, found the stories "nasty, deliberately unbelievable . . . contrived"; and Hermione Lee complained that "there is an air of mere games-playing about these neo-Gothic pieces." Julian Moynahan reviewed the book severely, remarking that "behind the play with such currently fashionable motifs are unmotivated behavior, plotlessness and indeterminancy of meaning. It is difficult to find or even surmise a serious talent seriously employed."

In 1980, McEwan published in England a collection of his plays for British television entitled *The Imitation Game: Three Plays for Television.* "Jack Flea's Birthday Celebration," the first work in the trilogy, is about a birthday party for a character named David, who is writing a novel about a young man whose mother puts him in a play pen and gives him a baby's bottle. It is revealed during the party that the novel reflects David's relationship to his mother. "The Imitation Game" centers upon a young woman who is the victim of male chauvinist attitudes in the British intelligence service during World War II. The play, in McEwan's words, is "fuelled by the conviction that social oppression has more to do with sex than with class." The abstract and intellectual third play, "Solid Geometry," adapted from McEwan's story of the same title, became celebrated when the chief executive of the BBC refused permission to broadcast it. The incident was widely discussed in the British press, and gave McEwan a reputation as an *enfant terrible*.

McEwan lived up to that reputation with his screenplay of *The Ploughman's Lunch* which became a highly acclaimed film, directed by Richard Eyre, in 1983. Its title gives no clue to this bitter, strictly contemporary story of an opportunistic and conscienceless young journalist who rises to prominence in his profession with a book that celebrates the 1956 Suez War and sees the culmination of his own brand of politics in the uneasy celebrations that followed the Falklands War. McEwan himself has written candidly, in the *Times Literary Supplement* (November 18, 1983), of the need "for the British cinema to develop its own distinctive qualities, drawing where necessary on our strong literary and theatrical traditions, and transforming them in the process to meet the requirements of film making. If a 'literary' cinema is one which takes its writers seriously . . . and if directors were sufficiently respectful towards writers to make no changes in these scripts without their agreement, then I am for such a cinema."

McEwan's *The Comfort of Strangers*, which depicts an English couple on vacation in an unnamed European city has the dreamlike quality and sexual perversity of his earlier writing. Richard P. Brickner, in the *New York Times Book Review*, described *The Comfort of Strangers* as "a nightmare . . . conceived by a Harold Pinter, descended from a Henry James." Although impressed by the novel, Brickner faulted it for its "careless overdose of perversity," and other reviewers objected to McEwan's "ingenious disregard for the usual proportions of human emotions and human behavior." Eliot Fremont-Smith, in particular, found the novel unclear and only partially realized. "What clearly was thought through, and worked on," he remarked, "was elegant and restrained prose style."

Ian McEwan resides in London but has traveled widely in Europe and been a writer-in-residence at the University of Iowa Writers'

Workshop. He is regarded as one of England's most promising young writers, and his work is eagerly anticipated by those who cannot decide whether his admired prose style is merely a vehicle for adolescent fantasies, or whether his is one of the notable talents of contemporary literature.

PRINCIPAL WORKS: *Novels*—The Cement Garden, 1978; The Comfort of Strangers, 1981. *Short stories*—First Love, Last Rites, 1975; In Between the Sheets and Other Stories, 1979. *Drama*—The Imitation Game, 1980.

ABOUT: Contemporary Authors 61–64, 1976; Contemporary Novelists, 1982; Dictionary of Literary Biography 14 (Part 2), 1983. *Periodicals*—American Book Review November-December, 1982; Commonweal November 7, 1975; Critical Quarterly Autumn, 1983; Encounter June 1975; Esquire July 1981; Guardian October 8, 1981; New Statesman January 20, 1978; September 29, 1978; New York Times Book Review, September 28, 1975; November 26, 1979; Times Literary Supplement May 16, 1975; September 28, 1978; January 20, 1979; Village Voice, July 15, 1981.

MACLEAN, SORLEY (SOMHAIRLE MACGILL-EAIN) (October 26, 1911–),

Scottish poet. The poet and critic Robin Fulton writes: "Sorley Maclean was born on the Isle of Raasay and educated at Portree, Skye, and Edinburgh University (1929–1933). He went into school teaching, but at the outbreak of war he volunteered and served in Libya and Egypt. Seriously wounded on the last day of the Battle of Alamein, he spent nine months in hospitals before returning to Edinburgh, where he taught at Boroughmuir School until 1956. He then returned to his native ground as headmaster of Plockton High School, Wester Ross. On retirement from teaching he succeeded Robert Garioch as writer in residence at Edinburgh University (1973–1975), after which he spent a year as Resident Bard at Sabhal Mor Ostaig, the Gaelic College on the island of Skye. He was been awarded a LL.D. by Dundee University, a D. Litt. by the National University of Ireland, and a D. Litt. by Edinburgh University.

"In his book *Scotland* (1971), Douglas Young declared that 'the best poetry written in our generation in the British Isles has been in Scottish Gaelic, by Sorley Maclean.' Over the last four decades or so Gaelic readers have continued to hold Maclean in high esteem, and over the last two decades an increasing number of English-speaking readers have come to understand at least some of the reasons for Maclean's uniqueness. He published some poems first along with Robert Garioch in a booklet called *17 Poems for 6d*, in 1940, but the breakthrough, for both Ma-

°mə klān

SORLEY MACLEAN

clean as a poet and modern Gaelic poetry as a
whole, came in 1943 with the publication of
Dàin do Eimhir agus Dàin Eile.

"Formally, the poems, or songs, to Eimhir
showed rhetorical procedures which meant little
to English poets of the time, but in their handling of imagery (for which Maclean had
learned something from Donne and Yeats) and
in their personal confrontation with the contemporary world they spoke with an urgent and
present voice. The personal aspect was crucial,
for we can see in these poems two areas or levels
of experience which were both very pressing for
the poet. One area was private: an intense and
unhappy love-affair. The other was public: an
agonized response to the events of the mid- and
later 1930s in Europe, especially to the Spanish
Civil War. These two strands coalesce and pull
apart with a strength of passion and hard intellect that give the poetry a vigor it would be difficult to match in English poetry of the time.
Poem 19 indicates one pole:

I've built you a tall monument
on the crumpling mountains of our time,
yet this is a memorial
that men will speak of when you're dumb
and though i lose you, and another
enjoy you to his every wish
you'll blaze and glitter in my songs
after the setting of your flesh.

The other pole can be seen in Poem 32:

Let me lop from my verse every grace
shed by the lustre of your face,
and let it learn the economy
of Liebknecht's death and slavery:
let me burn away each leaf
that grew joyfully from my grief.

And let me hammer the people's wrongs
into the iron of my songs.
—trans. Iain Crichton Smith

"The intensity that informs Maclean's shorter
lyrics strikes us also in his longer poems, of which
the most admired are perhaps 'The Woods of
Raasay' (1940), 'Hallaig' (1954) and 'Elegy to
Calum I. Maclean' (1968). The first of these employs the woods as a symbol:

The wood of Raasay,
my dear prattler,
my whispered reason,
my sleeping child.

The local, personal references come in the middle of the 223-line poem, preceded and followed
by a conjuration of the symbols offered by the
wood, an abundance almost too complex to trace
in detail. It is this abundance that is felt behind
the bafflement of the closing stanzas:

There is no knowledge of the course
of the crooked veering of the heart,
and there is no knowledge of the damage
to which its aim unwittingly comes.

There is no knowledge, no knowledge,
of the final end of each pursuit,
nor of the subtlety of the bends
with which it loses its course.
—trans. S. Maclean

"The 217-line elegy for his brother Calum
(himself a notable Gaelic scholar), with its traditional opening—

The world is still beautiful
though you are not in it,
Gaelic is eloquent in Uist
though you are in Hallin Hill
and your mouth without speech.

—shows the remarkable extent to which Maclean could use the form of the panegyric to celebrate both his brother's life and the Gaelic
world.

"In that world, history is very much alive: a
sense of family and ancestry is vivid. It was quite
in character for Maclean to explain, as he once
did in a *Radio Times* interview, that 'the house
I live in, in Braes in Skye, once belonged to my
great, great, great-grandfather on my mother's
side.' The history through which those families
descended was often harsh: socially and politically such a heritage can give rise to anger and
despair, while in the arts it has at times led to a
crippling nostalgia. The precarious future of the
Gaelic language has served to focus a wide range
of anxieties. In order to reach a wider readership
the Gaelic poet has to supply (as Maclean has
done for most of his poems) a line-by-line English rendering, and translation faces almost in-
surmountable obstacles: formal patterns resist

copying, and many Gaelic words have historical and literary resonances for which English parallels are lacking. In *Dàin do Eimhir* No. 55 the poet exclaims:

I cannot see the sense
of writing in a dying tongue
now that Europe, raped and torn,
moans behind my song . . .

Yet, despite this painful knowledge, Maclean's response is positive. John MacInnes has remarked that Maclean was able 'by sheer intellectual and poetic power, to transmute the conflicts of the Gaelic-English relationship into opportunity. . . .'

"Perhaps the best short account of this aspect of Maclean's work is Iain Crichton Smith's introduction to his translation of the main part of *Dàin do Eimhir* in 1971. This book, along with the Sorley Maclean issue of *Lines Review,* edited by Robin Fulton, coincided with and helped to foster an interest in Maclean beyond the confines of his Gaelic readership. Smith's introduction concludes: 'It seems to me that here in process of formation we have a new kind of Highland consciousness. . . . It is astonishing that a Highlander brought up in such a narrow world (though broadened by a liberal education at Edinburgh University) should not have succumbed in the furnace of Communist ideology, a love affair of great intensity, and a cause demanding decision of poets and artists. It is precisely this creative confusion which produced the poetry: one feels that no other combination of factors would have been enough. It produced a union of the sophisticated and the primitive, of the intelligence and passions, which is quite unique in Gaelic literature. It probably will not happen again in the conceivable future. That it should have happened at all seems little short of miraculous.'"

In August 1981, in celebration of Maclean's seventieth birthday, the National Library of Scotland mounted an exhibition documenting his life and work. Reporting on that occasion for the *Times Literary Supplement,* James Campbell wrote that following the death of Hugh MacDiarmid, "Maclean is regarded today as Scotland's greatest living poet." Thanks to his public readings in England, Europe, Canada, and the United States (he reads in Gaelic but also recites an English translation for his audiences), Maclean has won a following outside his native land.

WORKS IN ENGLISH OR ENGLISH TRANSLATION: (with R. Garioch) 17 Poems for 6d, 1940; (with others) Four Points of a Saltire, 1970; Poems to Eimhir (trans. I. C. Smith), 1971; Spring Tide and Neap Tide: Selected Poems 1932–1972, 1977.

ABOUT: Cassell's World Literature, 1973; The Pleasure of Gaelic Poetry, 1982. *Periodicals*—Lines Review 34 (1970); Listener September 2, 1971; Scottish International Review May 1970, December 1971; Times Literary Supplement September 9, 1977, August 21, 1981.

McMAHON, THOMAS (ARTHUR) (April 21, 1943–   ), American novelist and scientist, was born in Dayton, Ohio, the son of Howard Oldford McMahon, an atomic physicist, and the former Lucille Nelson. He received his bachelor's degree from Cornell University in 1965, his doctorate from the Massachusetts Institute of Technology in 1970. He has worked since then at Harvard University, where he has been since 1977 the Gordon McKay professor of applied mechanics and professor of biology.

McMahon has undertaken a good deal of research in his somewhat rarefied scientific field, biomechanics, especially on the application of physics to medicine and biology; he has published several articles in specialized journals and in the popular magazines *Science* and *Scientific American.* No book on biomechanics or its practical applications has yet come from him, but he has published two novels, each quite different from the other in subject matter, that reflect a scientific approach to life in both their narrative technique and choice of characters.

Principles of American Nuclear Chemistry is the narrative of Timmy MacLaurin, a troubled young scientist. When he was thirteen he accompanied his father, Harold MacLaurin, "Ph.D., physicist, fluid mechanicist, potential scientific clairvoyant, adulterer," from Cambridge, Massachusetts, where he was a researcher at MIT, to Oak Ridge, Tennessee, and thence to Los Alamos, New Mexico, where he became one of the key American scientists involved in developing the atomic bomb. Timmy is fascinated by Maryann, his father's mistress, and his narrative is both an attempt to recall in detail her power over him and to recreate the atmosphere of friendly cooperation "outside of the constraints of national distinctions to make war impossible and peace bountiful." But the explosion of the bomb and its subsequent use against the Japanese changed everything and killed the ideal. "It didn't happen. The end of an idea, the proof of its fallacy, would leave people in something very much like mourning for a period, as if it were a true death. This was because everyone's heart was in the project so much that he counted his own personal fortune in the population of ideas

THOMAS McMAHON

which, taken as a whole, would say true things: in this respect it was a period of great selflessness. The death of a beautiful but impractical idea . . . diminished the total hope, diminished each individual hope." W. B. Hill called *Principles* "a strangely impressive novel, one that haunts the mind. . . . [Here] we have adolescence in strange surroundings, scientific absorption, the breaking up a boy's world—all told with notable skill." L. L. Barrett wrote, "Beyond lost innocence the book is about a problem that troubles the age—a sense of having pursued wrong priorities too hotly, an awareness of the neglect of life and love that results."

McKay's Bees tells of Gordon McKay, a wealthy and energetic Bostonian entrepreneur and, incidentally, endower and namesake of the chair held by McMahon at Harvard. In 1855 he leads an expedition to Kansas, where he plans to become even richer practicing scientific apiculture. Among the other main characters in the book are Catherine, his wife, and her brother Colin, who are incestuously involved with one another; Bernadette Blennerhasset, a crippled young woman with whom Colin falls in love; William Sewell, a passionate amateur entomologist; and Louis Agassiz, the renowned professor of natural history at Harvard and Charles Darwin's chief American opponent. Using a technique compared by some critics to E. L. Doctorow's in *Ragtime,* McMahon introduces other historical characters into brief episodes: John Brown splits the skull of a slaveowner; Abraham Lincoln reads *Aesop's Fables* to one of his son Willie's friends in the presence of his son's dead body; Stephen Foster dies in poverty

and obscurity. The novel tells the story of the principal characters' adventures in careful detail, with special attention given to scientific description. The exact method of making a daguerreotype takes up several pages; several more, in many parts of the book, are devoted to how the bees are cared for and the characteristics of the various diseases that afflict them. Colin spends a great deal of time designing and building a "hydraulic funicular" for Bernadette to carry her up the stairs of her house. His satisfaction at his final success is recounted in a passage typical of many in the book: "When the funicular was finished, Colin rode it to the top of the stairs, and although the ascent was a trifling dozen or so feet, the sense of rising with no effort was exhilarating. The only sound which betrayed the machine's vertical progress came from the centrifugal weights of the speed governor, which made a faint whir like the clockwork of a music box. With the counterweight in balance, he found that as little as two cycles of the pump handle would provide sufficient force to carry the car to the top at a dignified speed. A similarly modest valving of water would allow it to glide back down. The car ascended or descended in accordance with the principle of buoyancy, a buoyancy which was always under the control of the operator. It was like a bubble rising from the bottom of a lake, but it was a bubble which was prepared to go back down again when commanded." McMahon's accomplishment in this novel lies in the blending of many such passages into a conventional historical saga; neither the scientific description nor the more mundane accounts of his characters' loves and lives seem out of place side by side. Patricia Goodfellow called *McKay's Bees* "an authentic portrait of the building of America. . . . Spare as a film script, but riveting, the novel becomes an orchestrated prologue to the present." Edmund White, however, while admiring the scientific tone and the vividness of the historical vignettes, complained of a static narration: "The people do not develop or change. If a climax does occur . . . it takes place off stage, between chapters. Numerous subplots are generated, but they seem to go nowhere. Indeed, this brief novel reads somewhat like the précis of vast epic."

McMahon married Carol Ehlers in June 1965; they have a son and a daughter.

PRINCIPAL WORKS: *Fiction*—Principles of American Nuclear Chemistry, 1970; McKay's Bees, 1979.

ABOUT: Contemporary Authors, first revision series 33–36, 1978. *Periodicals*—Best Sellers August 1, 1970; October 1979; Christian Science Monitor October 1, 1970; August 15, 1979; Library Journal July 1970; Au-

gust 1979; Life July 24, 1970; Nature April 2, 1970;
New York Times Book Review August 23, 1970; August 19, 1979; New Yorker November 7, 1970; August
20, 1979; Newsweek September 24, 1979; Time August
24, 1970; Virginia Quarterly Review Autumn 1970.

McMURTRY, LARRY (June 3, 1936–),
American novelist, was born in Witchita Falls,
Texas, the son of William Jefferson and Hazel
Ruth (McIver) McMurtry. His father was a Texas rancher, as his ancestors had been for several
generations, a prosperous cattleman clan described by McMurtry in his book *In a Narrow
Grave.* McMurtry grew up and attended high
school in Archer City, near Witchita Falls. At
North Texas State College, where he received his
B.A. in 1958, he wrote over fifty "appalling" stories, he told an interviewer, before he began to
draw on his cowboy background. When he received his M.A. from Rice University, in Houston, in 1960, he had already finished a draft of
his first novel, and partly on the strength of this
work was awarded a Wallace Stegner fellowship
for creative writing when he did additional
graduate work at Stanford University. In 1964–
65, he had a Guggenheim fellowship. In the early part of his career, McMurtry taught creative
writing at Texas Christian University (1961–62),
Rice University (1965), George Mason College in
Virginia (1970), and at the American University
in Washington, D.C. (1970–71). Since then he
has lived, without academic commitment, as a
novelist and free-lance writer.

McMurtry's first novel, *Horseman, Pass By,*
written while he was still in his early twenties,
received the fiction award of the Texas Institute
of Letters and was adapted as the film *Hud,*
which received an Academy Award. It is narrated in the first person by a seventeen-year-old
boy whose personal experience captures the
passing of the old, mythic West and the coming
into being of the new. Two men, with representative qualities, are particularly important to
him—his grandfather, Homer Bannon, the old-
time rancher whose herd is destroyed in an epidemic and who himself dies at the end, and Homer's stepson Hud, arrogant and amoral, who
symbolizes a tawdry, diminished present. On the
verge of manhood, young Lonnie, the narrator,
leaves the ranch, but has no place to go. Without
being sentimental, the novel is mutedly poignant
and, as reviewers were quick to note, reveals an
acute sense of Texas character and idiomatic
speech.

Many of the same qualities that marked
Horseman, Pass By as an exceptional first novel
were also present in McMurtry's second one,

LARRY McMURTRY

Leaving Cheyenne—a downbeat lyricism, wry
realism, and finely attuned ear for the texture of
regional speech. But *Leaving Cheyenne* deals
with a much longer time span than the spare,
concentrated *Horseman, Pass By.* It is narrated
by three of its principal characters, each of
whom takes the reader part of the way through
the tale. Two friends, Gideon and Johnny, are attracted to Molly, but she eventually marries a
third man, Eddie. Instead of having children by
him, she has a son by Gideon and one by Johnny,
and both sons of her lovers die in World War II.
Critics found McMurtry's novel superior in
many respects to his first, and more deeply felt.
"It is McMurtry's . . . farewell," Raymond
Neinstein commented, "to an admired generation that has almost entirely passed into myth;
and it is perhaps the mythic dimension of the
novel, its quality of folklore, that [most] capti-
vates the reader." *Leaving Cheyenne* was subsequently adapted by Sidney Lumet into the film
Lovin' Molly.

Like his earlier books, McMurtry's third novel, *The Last Picture Show,* also became a Hollywood film. McMurtry himself collaborated as
screenwriter with Peter Bogdanovitch, whom
the movie established as an important young director. *The Last Picture Show* differs from Mc-
Murtry's previous novels in that it seems sharply
hostile to its Texas small town setting and characters, and it employs elements of "dark humor"
in its exposure of the characters' unfulfilled lives.
It deals with a youth, Sonny Crawford, in his last
year of high school, and his sexual rites of passage. Sex is the only diversion the "dusty, dry,
wind-scraped" town of Thalia has to offer; but,

characteristically, the experience is either meaningless or grotesque. At the end Sonny returns to an ephemeral relationship with Ruth, who is old enough to be his mother and is the wife of the high school football coach, a latent homosexual. W. J. Jack found the novel effective at times, but felt that McMurtry relied too much on stock types. "The whole," he wrote, "is not as satisfying as the parts. . . . Sonny finally becomes almost mute, victimized by a too-contrived story line."

The Last Picture Show is in some ways complementary to McMurtry's *In a Narrow Grave: Essays on Texas*, a collection of acerbically witty articles on contemporary Texas life. In a particularly amusing essay, McMurtry comments on the provincialism of the state's cities, especially Houston and Dallas; but the finest piece is concerned with the ancestral clan of the McMurtrys, huge land owners who, by his youth, had become an anachronism. The contrast between an expansive, mythic Texas past and a constricted present also informs the next three novels McMurtry wrote, which have been called his "urban trilogy." These novels treat characters uprooted from the land, and unable to find a sense of purpose or identity in Texas' modern cities. The first, *Moving On*, an anatomy of a failed marriage, shows a young Texas couple, Jim and Patsy Carpenter, from a well-to-do background, who pursue aimless and banal lives. While acknowledging McMurtry's exceptional gifts for dialogue and social observation, almost all of the reviewers complained of the novel's excessive length of 800 pages. Elroy Bode remarked that "Jim and Patsy are never quite interesting enough to make the reader care about them. . . . They become faceless through McMurtry's massive overwriting of their lives. . . . He gives the reader enormous amounts of information rather than groping toward a personal truth."

All My Friends Are Going to Be Strangers is much shorter, and on the whole more successful. It follows a young novelist from Texas to California and back again, as he searches for meaning in the sexual revolution and the "new" Texas, and ends with his apparent suicide. Walter Clemons called the novel "a lively, talented piece of work, with McMurtry's particular blend of laconic funniness and openheartedness." A number of reviewers praised the work—including Martha Duffy, who described it as "acute, elegaic, funny and dangerously tender." Reed Whittemore, who believed that it floundered in its sexual obsession, remarked "constantly we are treated in the novel to fine but ephemeral insights, then taken back to bed." *Terms of Endearment*, which concludes the trilogy, also

drew mixed reactions. Dorothy Rabinowitz praised it for its literacy and wit, and other reviewers were impressed by the novel, or at least its main part, as an engrossing comedy of modern-day Southwestern manners. But many reviewers were critical of the book's structure, by the incongruity between the extremely lengthy early and the brief final part, which seemed tacked on and wholly different in tone. Nor, to reviewer Robert Towers, did McMurtry manage to develop a clearly focused theme. In 1983 *Terms of Endearment* was adapted into a film of the same title, which enjoyed a considerable box-office success and won four "Oscars" from the Academy of Motion Picture Arts and Sciences in 1984 (best film of the year, best director, best actress, and best supporting actor).

Following the "urban trilogy," McMurtry has explored the theme of modern loneliness from a variety of perspectives. *Somebody's Darling* is a Hollywood novel centering upon Jill Peel, a young film director whose personal life is less under control than her professional one. A number of reviewers were impressed by the naturalness and charm of the novel's opening, narrated by Joe Percy, an aging roué whose affection for Jill is unwavering. But the later sections, narrated by Owen Oarson, her sometime macho lover, and by Jill herself, seemed a falling off. Brina Caplan observed that McMurtry relies on rapid-fire humor at the expense of "fully dimensional portraits. . . . As a result his novel trades away substance for speed, a costly bargain."

McMurtry's later novels include *Cadillac Jack* and *The Desert Rose*. *Cadillac Jack* is a partly comic account of a huge ex-bulldogger on the rodeo circuit who has taken to traveling about in his pearl-colored Cadillac to trade in antiques and collectibles, in the course of which he meets an assortment of eccentries and shares the beds of a number of women. Although reviewers found the novel ingratiating, with McMurtry at his best in delineating peripheral characters, they tended to fault it for a lack of direction and a shadowy theme. *The Desert Rose* concerns a thirty-nine-year-old showgirl in Las Vegas who finds that she is now "over the hill." Reviews were in many cases favorable. Steve Tesich praised the novel's "sweet smell of humanity and realism," and was moved by McMurtry's depiction of the central character, Harmony, who wears eye patches to close out Las Vegas' bright, fantasy nights, "depriving herself of one of her senses in order to make sense of life."

A key figure in contemporary Texas fiction, McMurtry lives in Washington, D.C., where he owns a rare-book shop, Booked-Up, in the Georgetown section. In 1959, while a graduate student, he married Josephine Ballard, and by the marriage, which ended in divorce in 1965, he has a son, James Lawrence. A versatile, energetic man, McMurtry says that he writes fiction in the morning, and "piddles" in his rare-book shop in the afternoon. In addition to his novels, he has reviewed numerous books for such publications as the *Houston Post, Washington Post,* and *New York Times.* He has also written an unproduced screenplay about "the end of the West," and extensive film criticism. In an interview, he has told of watching films, one after another, around the clock.

PRINCIPAL WORKS: Horseman, Pass By, 1961; Leaving Cheyenne, 1963; The Last Picture Show, 1966; Moving On, 1970; All My Friends Are Going to Be Strangers, 1972; Terms of Endearment, 1975; Somebody's Darling, 1978; Cadillac Jack, 1982; The Desert Rose, 1983. *Non-fiction*—In a Narrow Grave: Essays on Texas, 1968.

ABOUT: American Novelists Since World War II, 1978; Contemporary Authors, new revision series 7, 1969; Contemporary Novelists, 1982; Current Biography, 1984; Encyclopedia of World Literature 4, Supplement, 1975; Peavy, C.D. Larry McMurtry, 1977. *Periodicals*—Book World June 21, 1970; New Republic April 1, 1972; New York Review of Books October 19, 1975; New York Times Book Review November 13, 1966; November 19, 1978; November 21, 1982; November 23, 1983.

McNEILL, WILLIAM H(ARDY), (October 31, 1917–), American historian, writes: "I was born in Vancouver, Canada on 31 October 1917. This was an unusually auspicious date in the eyes of my father, who, as a professor of church history, knew that it exactly marked the 400th anniversary of the event that started the Lutheran Reformation. In terms of my own lifetime, however, it is perhaps more significant that my birth anticipated the Bolshevik revolution by one week. As a young academic my father moved from Vancouver to Chicago (to finish his Ph.D.), to Kingston and Toronto, and then back to Chicago in 1927. My earliest memories are therefore of Canada, but from the age of ten Chicago has been my home. I grew up in the Hyde Park community adjacent to the University of Chicago campus and stayed home during my college years, when the depression combined with the charismatic figure of its president Robert Maynard Hutchins to give the University of Chicago a special tone and quality.

"I had a good education there, thanks to the systematic way the survey courses touched on all fields of knowledge and to the philosophical awareness that pervaded the campus as a result

WILLIAM H. McNEILL

of Hutchins' advocacy of 'Great Ideas.' In 1939 I went to Cornell to complete a Ph.D. under Carl Becker, but was drafted into the army in 1941 and came back to finish my thesis only in 1946–47. In between I had many diverse experiences in the ranks of the army, serving as private in Hawaii in 1942, as battery officer at various posts in the Caribbean in 1943, and as assistant military attaché to Greece from 1944–46.

"My first book, *Greek Dilemma: War and Aftermath,* summarized the wartime disasters that afflicted Greece, and was based almost entirely on oral testimony I had accumulated as assistant military attaché. I wrote it in thirteen days just before my marriage to Elizabeth Darbishire, whom I had met in Athens. Working to a deadline has always seemed sensible to me, but this represents an extreme I have never subsequently matched.

"In 1947, after completing my Ph.D. at Cornell, I returned to the University of Chicago as an instructor and have remained there since. From time to time I held appointments that allowed me to work abroad. In 1950–52, for example, I was in London where I wrote a book on the grand alliance of World War II under the aegis of Arnold J. Toynbee. This appeared in 1954 as *America, Britain and Russia: Their Cooperation and Conflict 1941–46.* Thirty years later (1980–81) I was Eastman Professor at the University of Oxford, and while there was able to complete another book, *Pursuit of Power: Technology, Armed Force and Society since A.D. 1000,* published in 1982.

"Between whiles some sixteen other books came from my typewriter. Some were textbooks for use in colleges and schools; but most were aimed at the ever-elusive 'educated reader,' i.e. were written to answer questions that seemed important to me. The principal book of my career was *The Rise of the West: A History of the Human Community.* It won the National Book Award for history in 1964 and sold more copies than anything else I have ever written. This was a history of the world, and, despite the title, managed to escape Europeo-centric bias more completely than its predecessors by recognizing that before 1500 other civilizations held primacy within the ecumene. My organizing ideas for *The Rise of the West* derived from cultural anthropology as taught by Robert Redfield at Chicago in the 1930s though, of course, other influences also played upon my mind, notably that of Arnold J. Toynbee.

"More recently, I have become concerned with ecological constraints on the cultural autonomy my anthropological training had emphasized. This was largely due to work I did to prepare a book, *Plagues and Peoples,* that analyzed the impact of infectious disease fluctuating on human societies. About half of my books have focused on Europe and modern Greece rather than on the whole globe. My main concern here has been to understand the differences between east and west within Europe— differences illustrated by the rapid breakup of traditional Greek peasant society in my own lifetime as well as by long standing contrasts between the history of Russia and other orthodox lands and that of France and England. My views on these matters are most concisely set forth in two books: *Venice: the Hinge of Europe, 1081–1797* and *The Metamorphosis of Greece since World War II.*

"Writing comes relatively easily to me, but the supportive ambience of the University where I have worked and of my family has made a more or less uninterrupted flow of books possible across the past thirty-five years. It is a great privilege to be paid a salary for doing what one likes; and that has been my good fortune throughout my career."

William H. McNeill is the son of Professor John Thomas McNeill, a church historian, and the former Netta Hardy. He was a history major as a Chicago undergraduate, and his M.A. thesis, awarded in 1939, was a structural comparison of the histories of Herodotus and Thucydides. For his Ph.D. he studied the influence of the potato on Irish history.

He began his impressive list of publications in 1947 with *Greek Dilemma: War and Aftermath,* a history of World War II, liberation, and the civil war as they affected Greece from 1940 to 1946, based on his firsthand wartime experiences in the country. Appearing at the time the Truman Doctrine was promulgated, it was praised for objectivity and craftsmanship. Leigh White called it "the most useful study of the Greek tragedy this reviewer has read" and J. S. Roucek, "the best and most up-to-date treatment . . . available to the English-reading public." McNeill returned to modern Greek history several times in his career. For the Twentieth Century Fund he coauthored, with his wife and Frank Smothers, *Report on the Greeks,* and was sole author of *Greece: American Aid in Action, 1947–1956;* his monograph *Greece: A Permanent Crisis* (1951) was published by Foreign Policy Reports. Finally, he wrote *Metamorphosis of Greece since World War II,* which the *Choice* reviewer called "an informed and sociologically oriented history of sweeping scope and clarity" and "essential reading for an understanding of modern Greece."

John Keegan considers McNeill "a prodigy among living historians. . . . Almost any subject acquires, in [his] hands, a largeness and sweep more timid men would shrink from giving it." His two world histories are generally considered, at least in scope, his most considerable achievements. *The Rise of the West: A History of the Human Community* studies, in more than 800 pages, the three major eras of human development—the Middle Eastern dominance to 500 BC, the Eurasian balance to AD 1500, and the ascendancy of the West since then. "This is," wrote Hugh Trevor-Roper, "not only the most learned and the most intelligent, it is also the most stimulating and fascinating book that has ever set out to record and explain the whole history of mankind. . . . His scholarship is impressive alike in its range and in its exactitude, and yet it never overpowers his thought." *A World History* covered the same historical eras as its predecessor in little more than half its length. The book was intended primarily as a college text, and its compression of more than six thousand years of human history was accomplished, according to Dennis Sciama, "with superb humaneness and erudition." Yet Geoffrey Barraclough considered the book's structure to be "basically mechanistic" in its emphasis on the primacy of technological change: McNeill "is a convinced 'diffusionist,' for whom all civilizations arose through stimuli offered by events occurring far away in Mesopotamia. . . . This view leads inexorably to a pattern of world history of which the central fact is the rise to predominance of the West. . . . I only wish his history had been a little more tentative and 'open-ended,' less concerned to provide water-tight answers than to suggest the problems and ambiguities inherent in human society." *The Contemporary World,* another large-scale history, was described by its publishers as concentrating "upon the two great changes in human affairs during the past fifty years: (1) urbanization and (2) the experience of war mobilization and peacetime defense planning." F. E. Hirsch called the book "intriguing because of the emphasis he places on the global view and on other important aspects often overlooked by conventional textbook writers. While his coverage of political events is uneven and rather colorless, he does offer brilliant cultural vistas." McNeill's other essays in "universal history" are *The Ecumene: Story of Humanity* and *The Shape of European History.*

The confidence and brio with which McNeill accomplished histories of the widest possible scope were also applied to his treatment of smaller subjects. His first specialized study of this kind was *Europe's Steppe Frontier, 1500–1800,* "a broad analysis," according to the publishers, "of the historical process whereby these thinly occupied grasslands were partitioned between the three great empires of Russia, Austria, and Turkey and then incorporated into the respective bodies-social of these states." To Geoffrey Barraclough, the book "impressively demonstrates the impact of the open frontier on European history in its formative period. [Its] first merit . . . is his dispassionate examination . . . of the reasons for the progressive Turkish failure. The second is his freedom from the nationalist preconceptions which . . . have distorted the history of the area and made it virtually impossible to review it as a whole."

McNeill's aim in *Venice: The Hinge of Europe, 1081–1797* was, he wrote in the introduction, "to describe the ebb and flow of styles and skills across southern and eastern Europe between the eleventh and the eighteenth centuries." This was another area where national and religious prejudices had hitherto prevented balanced, objective assessment; in McNeill's words, "Existing historiography is recalcitrant to the scale of vision attempted here." David McNeil adjudged the author "a master of isolating the essential factor, the dominant trend, the ultimate consequence"; he called the book "macro-history at its best."

The theme of *Plagues and People* is the impact of epidemics on the development and decline of civilizations or, in McNeill's words, "the interaction of human populations and micro-parasites." An admittedly speculative book, it proposes, in the words of the *New Yorker* reviewer, "that the course of human history . . . has been decisively shaped by the arbitrary forces of epidemic disease—smallpox, measles, influenza, typhoid fever, tuberculosis, yellow fever, dysentery, malaria, plague, cholera. This is a fascinating hypothesis, and one that lights up some of the darker corners of other theories of history." Peter Stoler wrote, "McNeill is usually convincing, though his originality is demonstrated less through the use of new research than through the application of an unexpected point of view."

McNeill's encounter with the sober, somewhat static field of military history produced *The Pursuit of Power: Technology, Armed Force, and Society since AD 1000,* which argues that the warrior, the tools and techniques he used and adapted, and the political and social relationships he fostered were central rather than peripheral historical forces, an argument at odds with what "the fast men on the inside track of scholarship have been insisting these last two hundred years," in John Keegan's words. Despite several severe methodological criticisms, Keegan felt that the book "is nevertheless a magnificent achievement, a soaring work of scholarly imagination, by far the most interesting study in the field of military history that this reviewer has read in many years and a book certain to become a focus of debate among historians of all specialties for years to come."

Among McNeill's many other books, the most important are his editorship of the ten volumes in the series, *Readings in World History* (1968–73), and the collection of his lectures on *The Human Condition: An Ecological and Historical View,* an attempt at ecological history that J. H. Hexter called a "remarkable tour de force." He has contributed chapters to numerous books by others, and has regularly published articles and book reviews in scholarly journals.

McNeill and his wife, Elizabeth Darbishire, whom he married in 1946, have two sons and two daughters. He began his long teaching career at the University of Chicago as an instructor in 1947, and in 1982 retired as the Robert D. Millikan Distinguished Service Professor of History, a chair he had held since 1969. He has been visiting professor at the University of Frankfurt (1956), John H. Burns Distinguished Visiting Professor at Hawaii (1980), and the George Eastman Professor at Oxford (1980–81). Over the years he has held grants from the Fulbright, Rockefeller, Ford, Carnegie, Macy, and Guggenheim foundations, and has been associated in various capacities with the American Historical Association.

PRINCIPAL WORKS: Greek Dilemma: War and Aftermath, 1947; (with E. D. McNeill and F. Smothers) Report on the Greeks, 1948; History Handbook of Western Civilization, 1953; America, Britain and Russia: Their Cooperation and Conflict, 1941–46, 1953; Past and Future, 1954; Greece: American Aid in Action, 1957; The Rise of the West: A History of the Human Community, 1963; Europe's Steppe Frontier 1500–1800, 1964; A World History, 1967; The Contemporary World, 1967; The Ecumene: Story of Humanity, 1973; The Shape of European History, 1974; Venice: The Hinge of Europe, 1081–1797, 1974; Plagues and Peoples, 1976; The Metamorphosis of Greece since World War II, 1978; The Human Condition: An Ecological and Historical View, 1980; The Pursuit of Power: Technology, Armed Force, and Society since AD 1000, 1982; The Great Frontier, 1983; (with Marilyn Robinson) The Islamic World, 1983. As editor—Lord Acton's Essays in the Liberal Interpretation of History, 1967; Readings in World History, 1968–1973; (with R. S. Adams) Human Migration: Patterns and Politicies, 1978.

ABOUT: Contemporary Authors, new revision series 2, 1981. Periodicals—America February 4, 1984; American Historical Review December 1983; Annals of the American Academy July 1947; Choice March 1979; Christian Science Monitor August 8, 1963; Current History July 1954; Isis March 1984; Journal of Modern History March 1984; Library Journal April 15, 1968; Nation July 3, 1954; New Republic September 22, 1979; New Yorker October 18, 1976; September 12, 1983; New York Review of Books May 16, 1974; January 20, 1983; New York Times May 11, 1947; May 2, 1954; New York Times Book Review October 6, 1963; May 21, 1967; August 12, 1979; October 19, 1980; November 28, 1982; Saturday Review August 24, 1963; June 10, 1967; Scientific American September 5, 1967; Time November 22, 1976; Times Literary Supplement November 2, 1967; November 11, 1977.

*MAHFUZ (ABDEL AZIZ AL-SABILGI), NAGUIB (December 11, 1911–   ), Egyptian novelist and short story writer, writes (in Arabic): "My childhood was a perfectly normal one: I grew up with two parents who lived a quiet settled life together and in my love for them and my respect for our family was a degree of awe and reverence that colored my whole childhood, of which they were the central reference-point. I was utterly unlike those children, to be sure, who rebel against fathers or mothers, or who feel the need to defy their families. During my secondary school years I read a great deal, going right through Clarity and Rhetoric by al-Jahiz (died 869), The Unique Necklace by Ibn Abd Rabbihi (died 940), and other works in the Arabic encyclopedic tradition. I can remember using phraseology borrowed from them in my own compositions and amazing my Arabic teachers. Every Friday a friend and I used to go to the

° ma fōoz, nä jëb´

NAGUIB MAHFUZ

Olympia Cinema to see adventure films; and when we came out we'd go to Muhammed Aly Street and buy the novels the films were based on, so that we could live all over again the mood of action—the thrills—that the movie heroes had aroused in our boyish imaginations.

"Then I went to university (1930). When I enrolled in the philosophy department, it was my intention to make myself like the great intellectuals I so much admired, Taha Husayn, Abbas Mahmud al-Aqqad, and Salama Musa. Had I realized from the outset that literature would gradually infiltrate my very soul, I'd have enrolled in the departments of French, English, or even Arabic literature. It was only after I had been graduated, however (1934), and decided to register for studies leading to a master's degree, under Shaykh Mustafa Abd-el-Raziq, in the field of Sufism and Islamic philosophy, on which I had already published a few articles, that I began to feel the itch to become a writer. At that point I sat down to study literature systematically, century by century, without concentrating on any one literary tradition to the exclusion of others, thus treating the whole process as world literature, rather than as a series of discrete, individual traditions among separate peoples, confining myself only to accepted classics, starting with the modern period and working backwards. From about 1936 I therefore began to read realistic and naturalistic fiction, including the analytical short story, then explored such recent new departures as the expressionism of Kafka, the stream-of-consciousness realism of Joyce, and the annihilation of time in Proust.

"The major Egyptian influence on my

thought was the Fabian intellectual Salama Musa, who channelled my ideas into two directions: science and socialism. My early historical novels seem to me even now to show heavy traces of philosophical training: *Radubis* (1943) shows some of it, for example, as had *Mockery of the Fates* (1939), the fourth novel I wrote and the first published, where the title itself is a complex philosophical allusion. Before I published these two early novels, I had written and published a number of short stories likewise bearing on philosophical issues. The only *littérateur* of the older generation to take an interest in my earliest fiction, Salama Musa, read the three novels I wrote during this period and told me that I had talent, but wasn't really ready for publication as a novelist. When he read through my manuscript of *Mockery of the Fates,* however, he approved, and published it complete and unabridged in *The New Magazine.*

"When I chose writing as my career, the decision was irrevocable. There was no question of simply trying one thing instead of something else, with a view to giving it up if something more appealing came along. It was a choice for life, from which I could never turn back, only carry on and persevere, whatever the consequences. I saw writing as a responsibility not unlike marriage, where a man produces children who impose upon him an indissoluble bond, from which he cannot back out or retreat. A man cannot abandon or disown his own children.

"Among the fundamental sources that I drew upon as an artist, it is the experience of political emotions—feelings and reactions—that is the most important. I can be even more explicit: politics, faith, and sex are the three poles around which my works revolve, and of the three, politics is by all odds the most essential, to the extent that none of my books is without political dimension. As for sex, it is one of those subjects, along with politics and faith—as well as crime, love, and so on—that cannot be ignored, but must, in any literature that is worthy of the name, be treated seriously. A novel may begin as a mere feeling—an idea or an imagined situation—occurring in the writer's mind long before he actually sits down to compose his novel. For a year, or even twenty, this feeling, idea, or situation may occasionally return to haunt him, until at last the day dawns when he recognizes that it has finally come to fruition, is matured, ready, and longing to emerge. Nearly everything I have written has been the result of study, meditation, and planning before I sat down to write, the only exceptions being the short story collections *Under the Shelter* (1964), *Story with No Beginning and No End* (1971), and *Honeymoon* (1971), which I embarked upon impelled by sheer emotional reaction.

"My novels are not sad by intention. I am, however, a melancholy man, from a generation that has felt whelmed in sadness even at moments of joy, a generation in which only the indifferent and the rich—never the popular classes—have been able to hold on to a kind of happiness. It is therefore not strange for us to write sad stories. It would be odd for us, on the contrary, if we wrote happy ones.

"If I have the sense that I have achieved everything I set out to do in my life as a *littérateur,* it is the same sense of achievement a man feels who has been successful at marrying in order to have children. Though he may have imagined once that those children of his would one day become great leaders or unique geniuses—no less!—and though one is now a third-rate writer, another has never finished his education, and the third is only a country doctor, he is completely content with them, the mediocre outcome of his dreams having in no way diminished his love for them or his own sense of fulfillment. That is how I feel about the things I have written. And when I make this declaration I am not trying to show false modesty or to deny whatever stature my novels may have, only to be as honest and straightforward as I can."

—trans. Roger Allen

The youngest of four children, Naguib Mahfuz spent the first six years of his life in the Gamaliya, a picturesque medieval quarter of Cairo that is the setting for portions of several of his books, especially those published between 1945 and 1960. His schooling began when he was four. At fifteen, over the protests of his family, he took up the study of philosophy. His first articles were published when he was only seventeen, and a dozen more followed during his undergraduate years, on subjects ranging from social issues to the Bergsonian theory of laughter. By 1936, having spent a year working on an M.A., Mahfuz had decided to become a professional writer and was fortunate in finding a post, as Secretary of Fuad I (later renamed Cairo) University, that would support an otherwise impoverishing vocation.

His attention initially turned from articles (thirty-five published by mid-1937) to short stories, of which a first collection was to appear in 1944, in a volume cunningly described by its publisher as the "second edition" of a work issued in 1938. Twenty-seven stories from the prewar period remain uncollected. In 1939, having written and discarded three others, he published his first novel, *Mockery of the Fates.* In the same year he entered the government bureaucracy, where he was to be employed for the next thirty-five years, taking up a post in the Ministry of Wakfs (Mortmain Endowments) that he was to hold until 1954. A second novel, *Radubis,* was published in 1943 and a third, *The Struggle for Thebes,* published in 1944, established the beginning of his reputation when an enthusiastic reviewer recommended free distribution of copies to every Egyptian household.

With three historical romances behind him, however, Mahfuz now embarked on a different kind of venture, a series of eight novels that was to culminate in the Cairo Trilogy, the work that would make him famous throughout the Arab world. Of the five novels preceding the trilogy—*New Cairo* (1945), *Khan el-Khalili* (1946), *Midaq Alley* (1947), *Ignis Fatuus* (1948), and *The Beginning and the End* (1949)—only *Midaq Alley* has as yet been published in English. Taking its name, like many other Mahfuz novels, from a real locale, a cul-de-sac in the Gamaliya, *Midaq Alley* typifies even in its title his concern during this period with the "traditional" urban lower and lower-middle classes, their conservative way of life, and its ultimate fragility. Other Egyptian novelists had written books about single social issues, but in the works leading up to the trilogy Mahfuz expands the scope of the novel to include the whole of what is almost a national *morale.* Before its crowning achievement could be published, however, this period to productivity was brought to a halt by the Revolution of July 1952. Mahfuz stopped writing, though the successful republication of *New Cairo* as *Scandal in Cairo* in 1953 may have suggested that his readership had not disappeared. In 1954 he left the Ministry of Wakfs to take up an appointment as Director of Censorship in the Arts Bureau; and it was only at this point, more than two years after its completion, that the first volume of the trilogy began to appear, that same year. It would be three more years before the entire shape of the whole trilogy would be known.

Bayn al Qasrayn (published serially 1954–56, in book form in 1956), *Qasr al-Shawq* (1957), and *Al-Sukkariya* (1957) trace the life of a family from 1918 to 1944, taking change—biological, political, and social—as their central theme. To a novelistic mode that is identified with a line traceable from Balzac and Dickens through Tolstoy to Galsworthy and Bennett (with all of whose major works he is, of course, familiar), Mahfuz makes additions that identify him as a modern Arab. Dialogue is arranged almost theatrically and stream-of-consciousness is used to reinforce a point of view that treats all the major characters with nearly equal intimacy. The result is an astonishing evocation of the "feel" of Cairene life, especially the quality of its most characteristic emotions: the anxiety and nostalgia that accompany all sympathy when it is sufficiently intense, the loves and hatreds inevitable in a society where passion, not mere profession, is a major root of identity. The trilogy is the first modern literary monument to that ability to "read character"—that alertness to mood and temperament—for which the Arabs are famed; and the response to it within the Arab world was to make it a classic almost from the moment of its completion. Its reception was perhaps not unassisted by the fact that it could also be seen as a triumphant assertion of Egyptian identity in the aftermath of the Tripartite Aggression of 1956. Mahfuz was given an Egyptian State Prize.

The trilogy had actually been completed in its entirety in April 1952, two months before the July Revolution. "The world I have made it my mission to describe," he told Philip Stewart, one of his translators, "had disappeared," and he had in fact written nothing since but one short story.

When a new novel, *Awalad Haratina,* appeared two years later (1959), however, it aroused such a furor in serial form that it was banned from publication as a book in Egypt, though an edition was published in Beirut in 1967, and it has appeared in English (1981) under the title *The Children of Gebelawi.* Marking a kind of resurrection for Mahfuz, *The Children of Gebelawi* is nothing less than an allegory of the religious, social, and political history of mankind. Each of its five sections represents an era in the life, simultaneously, of a typical Cairene hara—the kind of crowded, physically confined, and socially self-contained community that typified any lower-class quarter two or three generations ago—and in the history of the human race. The book consists of five stories, four of which retell, in effect, the stories of Adam, Moses, Jesus, and Mohammad, while the fifth suggests Mahfuz' own vision of the present, in which the latest in a series of squalid *mafiosi* dominates a demoralized and disculturated populace whose only hope for a decent life would appear to reside in the recovery of some lost magical formula. Such a vision, founded equally on realism and compassion, could hardly have pleased either the religious or civil authorities of the time and the book remains under ban. As a censor himself, Mahfuz is unlikely to have been unaware of the challenge he was issuing, even disguised by allegory and serial publication. He left his post as Director of Censorship in the Arts Bureau the same year, to be appointed Director of the Foundation for the Support of the Cinema some months later.

This period which began with *The Children of Gebelawi* and ended with the June War of 1967, came to include not only six more novels and two collections of short stories, but a spate of articles as well. The six novels of this period after *The Children of Gebelawi* all center at one level on the question of adjustment to the July Revolution, which Mahfuz attempts to evaluate less in terms of the destruction it made of the old regime than of its own premises to fulfill constructive ideals; like *The Children of Gebelawi*, all make some use of allegory, though their settings are not the "traditional" quarters of his earlier work, but the hotels, restaurants, nightclubs, offices, and flats of the urban middle class. A partial exception to this generalization is the first of the series, *The Thief and the Dogs* (1961), of which the protoganist is a convicted burglar whose alienation has moral, social, political, and even topographical dimensions.

The Thief and the Dogs' successors during this period—*Autumn Quail* (1962), *The Path* (1964), *The Beggar* (1965), *Small Talk on the Nile* (1966), and *Miramar* (1967)—transfer the same theme of alienation to contexts that, in appearance, at least, are more "respectable," though it might be noted in passing that no one of Mahfuz' mature novels is without at least a glimpse of the *demi-monde* or a suggestion of violence. The world described in these book is that of bureaucrats and professionals, the world that Mahfuz had come to know during the course of his own government career. In each case the protagonist is either destroyed by the circumstances of his alienation or makes an accommodation to it, though this accommodation may often be either merely ironic, promised, or, as it were, transcendental. Mahfuz would appear to have been among the first to recognize that, once having cleared away the old regime, the July Revolution had little further sense of direction. Certainly these novels as a whole reflect a mood that is almost nihilistic and was thoroughly characteristic of the times.

Miramar, the last of the series, which was published in English in 1978, is, in effect, a distillation. Like *The Children of Gebelawi*, it is set in a single confined locale and is divided into five narrative sections, four centered on the personalities of four different characters and a fifth to bring matters up to date. Of the seven main characters who enter the story, all are alienated and none is without a representative function that approaches the allegorical. Published on the eve of the 1967 war, *Miramar* was a courageous statement at the time, voicing a disenchantment that found ready echoes everywhere, the more so as it is enlivened throughout with the desperate humor that is so much to the Egyptian taste.

After the war it was made into a successful film and was later adapted into a television series.

The shattering effect of the June War is visible even in the form of Mahfuz' next works. Between 1967 and 1971 he produced four collections of short stories, three of which, as he notes in the autobiographical statement quoted above, he wrote "impelled by sheer emotional reaction." Frequently brutal and enigmatic, dream-like or surreal in their settings, these stories seem to constitute a kind of *Guernica*, an agonized outcry against what had been done to Egypt and the weaknesses that had made it possible. Their meaning was not always readily understood; and Mahfuz was accused of writing "riddles." When his next novel, *Mirrors,* appeared in 1971, it was no less puzzling: a series of fifty-five narrative character sketches, each only one or two pages long, arranged in alphabetical order according to the name of the character described.

In Egypt *Mirrors* has not been well received. Abroad, however, it has been better regarded and it was translated into English in 1977. Certainly no other Egyptian writer has sought, much less ingeniously succeeded at, what Mahfuz achieves in *Mirrors*, for it is little less than a miniature *comédie humaine* spanning the years from before 1919 to 1971. While the "mirrors" that reflect the narrator's character likewise reflect every major event in Egyptian history during those years, Mahfuz also records, in particular, the qualities of feeling and intellect that typified the generations before the Revolution.

Implicit in *Mirrors* are what seem to be Mahfuz' own fundamental convictions—that religion is appropriately a framework for contemplation, not action; that morality is defined by politics, not religion; that politics is thus a central determinant of an individual's interior life; and that as such it is a better key to the psyche than sex or religion, both of which represent our mere comprehension of the limits of biological destiny, while politics stands for the most human activity possible to a civilized man. In political frustration Mahfuz sees what has been the fate of Egypt—and most of the rest of the world—in the twentieth century. It is this vision, intensely Mediterranean, that continues to bring him an audience of the hopeful throughout the Middle East, as well as a popular readership.

In 1969 Mahfuz had left the Foundation for the Support of the Cinema and became a consultant to the Ministry of Culture, with offices in what had formerly been two private houses. In 1972 he retired at last from the bureaucracy, publishing his twentieth novel the following year. The ensuing decade saw the publication of seven more novels and novellas and six collections of short stories, an extraordinary outpouring, much of it experimental, that still awaits critical evaluation. Representative of this latest epoch in his career is *Wedding Song* (1981), an ironic tale of novella length that contrasts the often absurd idealism of a young playwright with the corruption of his elders in the world of the theater, a world that Mahfuz knows well not only from his ten years as Director of the Foundation for the Support of the Cinema, but also from having worked in the field as a screenwriter; no fewer than sixteen of his novels have been made into films. The story is told through four overlapping first-person narratives, a technique foreshadowed in *The Children of Gebelawi* and recurrent in his work from *Miramar* onward.

Mahfuz' premier role in Arabic literature remains assured. It is inconceivable that any novelist writing in Arabic for the next several generations will not owe something to his work. He himself has continued to restrict his themes and techniques to those things he knows best, pursuing his own literary and intellectual goals with a single-minded devotion that few writers can equal. His books, even the earliest, are constantly reprinted, to the extent that at no time is more than a tiny fraction of his enormous achievement over nearly half a century unavailable to the public. If only because of his impact on the Arab world, Mahfuz must be considered an author of international import. It is a pity that so little of his work has as yet been published in any language other than his own, for the rest of the world is thus deprived of the privilege of attempting to understand a writer who, more than any other now living, has set himself the mission of forging what he feels to be still an uncreated conscience.

WORKS IN ENGLISH TRANSLATION: English-language readers know Mahfuz' work best through his novel *Midaq Alley*, translated by Trevor Le Gassick and published in Beirut in 1966 and in London in 1975. Other novels available in English are Roger Allen's translation of *Mirrors*, 1977; *Miramar*, translated by Fatma Moussa-Mahmoud, edited and revised by Maged el Kommos and John Rodenback, with an introduction by John Fowles, 1978; and Philip Stewart's translation of *Children of Gebelawi*, 1981. Further translations of novels by Mahfuz, including *Wedding Song, The Thief and the Dogs, The Beginning and the End,* and *Autumn Quail,* are scheduled for publication by the American University in Cairo Press. An anthology of Mahfuz' short stories, *God's World,* translated with an introduction by Akef Abadir and Roger Allen, was published in 1973.

ABOUT: Allen, R. The Arabic Novel: An Historical and Critical Introduction, 1982; Cassell's Encyclopedia of World Literature III, 1973; Dictionary of Oriental Literatures III, 1974; Encyclopedia of World Literature in the 20th Century (revised ed.) 2, 1982; Jones, M. and H. Sakkut, Najib Mahfuz: A Bibliographical Study, 1973; Ostle, R. C. Studies in Modern Arabic Literature, 1976; Peled, M. The Literary Works of Najib Mahfuz. *Periodicals*—Times Literary Supplement September 25, 1981.

*MAHON, DEREK (1941–   ), Irish poet, was born in Belfast, Northern Ireland. He was educated at Trinity College, Dublin, graduating in 1965 with a degree in English and French. Mahon has lived and worked in the United States, Canada, France, England, and Ireland and has held a variety of positions, including that of writer-in-residence at the New University of Ulster at Coleraine, Co. Antrim, cultural affairs editor for *Vogue* magazine, poetry editor of the *New Statesman,* and script writer and producer for the BBC in London. Currently he is a free-lance screenwriter, specializing in the adaptation of novels (of Jennifer Johnston, Brian Moore, and Elizabeth Bowen, among others).

Since the publication of his first book, *Night-Crossing,* in 1968, Mahon has been recognized in Ireland and England as one of the outstanding poets of his generation. "Few other poets," says the critic Adrian Frazier, "can admit so much of the world into a poem, and still compose it in a form both intimate and elegant, urbane and profound." Another critic refers to his "compelling independence of voice and vision; the elegant mastery of craft that marks everything he writes; a range of imaginative commitments that link him not only to major Irish poets of the preceding generation like Louis MacNeice and Patrick Kavanagh but also with Auden, with Lowell, with the Matthew Arnold of 'Dover Beach' and the Wallace Stevens of 'The Idea of Order at Key West.'"

Mahon's first three books—*Night-Crossing, Lives,* and *The Snow Party* (revised and augmented by new work in the 1979 collection, *Poems 1962–1978*)—show him marking off, then working and re-working the ground of his central preoccupations. Chief among these are a sympathetic feeling for the victim, spreading to a sympathy for what is marginal in the human or non-human world; involvement with his native North of Ireland; a sense of impending apocalypse (he has been called "the Dean of Poems on World Destruction"); the mundane and trivial as occasions of celebration and restoration.

Mahon's sympathy for the outsider, the vic-

°män

DEREK MAHON

tim, the scapegoat appears in many early poems, for example in "Van Gogh in the Borinage":

Shivering in the darkness
Of pits, slag heaps, beetroot fields,
I gasp for light and life
Like a caged bird in springtime
Banging the bright bars.

"The Death of Marilyn Monroe" composes an emblem of the dead star, a cautionary, contemporary icon of her career:

If it were said, let there be no more light,
Let rule the wide winds and the long-tailed seas,
Then she would die in all our hearts tonight—
Till when, her image broods over the cities
In negative, for in the darkness she is bright,
Caught in a pose of infinite striptease.

This instinctive sympathy for the unfortunate other appears, above all, in the climactic poem to *The Snow Party,* "A Disused Shed in Co. Wexford." This poem rises out of its plain occasion—mushrooms growing in an abandoned shed—to become an outburst of compassion for all condemned, abortive lives:

They are begging us, you see, in their wordless way,
To do something, to speak on their behalf
Or at least not to close the door again.
Lost people of Treblinka and Pompeii!
'Save us, save us,' they seem to say,
Let the god not abandon us
Who have come so far in darkness and in pain.
We too had our lives to live.
You with you light meter and your relaxed itinerary,
Let not our naive labours have been in vain!

Mahon's tense involvement with his native territory has always been one of vexed ambivalence, source of distress and self-questioning. The early "Glengormley" and "The Spring

Vacation" suggest the outline of the relationship—the poet poised uneasily between rejection and acknowledgment, recognizing the diminished, fallen condition of his home and the inescapable fact that "By/ Necessity, if not choice, I live here too." Able to adjust to this fact, he is nonetheless unsparing in his anatomy of the dark side of the Northern spirit:

We could all be saved by keeping an eye on the hill
At the top of every street, for there it is,
Eternally, if irrelevantly, visible—

But yield instead to the humourous formulae,
The hidden menace in the knowing nod.
Or we keep sullen silence in light and shade,
Rehearsing our astute salvations under
The cold gaze of a sanctimonious God.

In later poems like "Afterlives," "Rage for Order," and "The Last of the Fire Kings," this involvement has been knotted by the even more disastrous circumstances of Northern Ireland since 1968. Seeing, after an extended absence, Belfast transformed "by five years of war," the poet's response is one of helpless regret:

But the hills are still the same
Grey-blue above Belfast.
Perhaps if I'd stayed behind
And lived it bomb by bomb
I might have grown up at last
And learnt what is meant by home.

Elsewhere he questions his own being as a poet "far from his people" in the midst of such turmoil ("the fitful glare of his high window is as/ nothing to our scattered glass."). Or he says he is "Through with history" and will escape its bleak, violent cycles, realizing how this wish sets him apart, again, from "his people," and how this "fire-loving/ People, rightly perhaps,/ Will not countenance this"

Demanding that I inhabit,
Like them, a world of
Sirens, bin-lids
And bricked-up windows.

For all his sense of apartness, Mahon's imagination seems at root a border condition, a sensibility at civil war with its own state. The North, spoken or unspoken, is at the heart of all he writes.

It is his sense of the dead-endness of the facts of life in Northern Ireland that fuels Mahon's most expansive philosophical view of the world—seeing the civilization we have evolved and inhabit as doomed by its own reprehensible or stupid excesses. Beginning with *Lives,* poems such as "Entropy," "Going Home," "Matthew V. 29–30," "Beyond Howth Head," "The Antigone Riddle," or "The Banished Gods" are poems, as one critic has said, "of final definitions." They cast a cold, ironic eye on the mindless and heartless Western culture of acquisitive well-being, the culture of technological knowhow and biological indifference:

Elocution, logic, political science,
Antibiotics, do-it-yourself,
And a plover flops in his oil-slick.

"Rehearsing for the fin-de-siècle," the poet, his mordant authority salted by laconic wit, composes "Gruff Jeremiads to redirect/ Lost youth into the knacker's yard/ Of humanistic self-regard." Pollution is a common condition, his own poetic dialect an attempt to keep the language clean, "an eddy of semantic scruples/ in an unstructurable sea."

Out of this nightmare of history Mahon's imagination wakes to the saving grace of the quotidian, the brief consolatory glitter of "the mute phenomena." In a world where transcendence is a lost cause, the immanent may offer a hint of salvation, for "God is alive and lives under a stone," and "thought is a fondling of stones/ And wisdom a five-minute silence at moonrise." There is, as he explains in "The Mayo Tao," "an immanence in these things/ which drives me, despite/ my scepticism, almost/ to the point of speech." In "The Snow Party" he can find such momentary solace not in the natural but the social world. Here he places in counterpoint the savage atrocities of history ("Thousands have died since dawn/ In the service/ Of barbarous kings") and the civil decencies of the gathering in seventeenth-century Nagoya to which the poet Bashō is invited:

There is a tinkling of china
And tea into china;
There are introductions.

Then everyone
Crowds to the window
To watch the falling snow.

Mahon's whole work (Beckett and Bashō among the influences on its austerity and with) honors the desirable human aspiration toward such decencies, as well as mourns, in most of life, their loss.

The unflagging discipline of Mahon's poetic style sanctions and lends real authority to the values implicit in his verse. His work has been marked from the beginning by a commitment to decisive stanza forms and the habit of rhyme. These are signs of his scrupulous struggle to find some order in experience. His early work is characterized by technical refinement, as may be seen in "In Carrowdore Churchyard," an elegy for Louis MacNeice:

Your ashes will not fly, however the rough winds burst
Through the wild brambles and the reticent trees.
All we may ask of you we have. The rest
Is not for publication, will not be heard.

Maguire, I believe, suggested a blackbird
And over your grave a phrase from Euripides.
Which suits you down to the ground, like this churchyard
With its play of shadow, its humane perspective.

The stanza is a fluid, steady movement between sentences, showing the supple activity of the poet's intelligence as he sorts meticulously among the elements of this experience. Mahon's later work abounds in fairly strict stanza forms, from the spare three-liners that carry many of the best poems in *Lives* and *The Snow Party,* to the speedy double quatrains of his translation of François Villon. (Mahon's internationalism deserves some mention here: it is a rarity among Irish poets to find the breadth and ease of reference that characterize his work, visible especially in the translations and adaptations—from Villon, Jaccottet, Corbière, Rimbaud, Nerval, Brecht, Cavafy.) The buoyancy and speed of his stanza forms owe less to the Irish master of stanzaic form, Yeats, than they do to Auden and Marvell. Dense and elegant, his rhythms are responsive to the urgency of speech, beyond purely metrical considerations.

The poems in Mahon's 1983 volume *The Hunt by Night* reaffirm the fidelity to craft visible in the revisions and new work of *Poems 1962–1978.* They also serve as a summary of many of the virtues—substantive and stylistic—which distinguish the earlier work. The speaker in "Ovid in Tomis," for example, is at once victim, outsider, and poet-philosopher who exists in a post-historical state of mind, concentrating on "the infinity/ Under our very noses—/ The cry at the heart/ Of the artichoke,/ The gaiety of atoms." The rich mixture of the poet's relationship with Northern Ireland also reappears—astringent, elegiac, and celebratory as ever—especially in "Derry Morning" and "North Wind: Portrush."

A few poems about paintings in *The Hunt by Night* pay tribute to a particular influence on Mahon's imagination (present in his first book in the poems about Van Gogh and the great forger Van Megherem) and on what he values in his own vocation: how a painting such as De Hooch's *Courtyards in Delft,* for example, casts "Oblique light on the trite" and celebrates "the chaste/ Precision of the thing and the thing made." This loving attention to detail is Mahon's alternative to the belligerent ideologies of the historical world.

Among modern poets it is Mahon's special genius to be able to offer such moral lessons without didactic or self-important rhetorical gesture. His poems, charting as they do a coherent, maturing meditation on our world, make without sentimentality that offering of the self that is true speech: in their precision, perception, and modesty, they command our attention.

PRINCIPAL WORKS: Night-Crossing, 1968; Lives, 1972; The Snow Party, 1975; Poems 1962–1978; Courtyards in Delft, 1981; The Chimeras (translations from Nerval), 1981; The Hunt by Night, 1983.

ABOUT: Brophy, J. D. and Porter, R. J. (eds.) Contemporary Irish Writing, 1983; Brown, T. Northern Voices: Poets from Ulster, 1975; Dunn, D. (ed.) Two Decades of Irish Writing, 1975; The Macmillan Dictionary of Irish Literature, 1980. Periodicals—Eire-Ireland 16, 1981; 18, 1983; Times Literary Supplement February 15, 1980; February 18, 1983; October 19, 1984.

VLADIMIR MAKSIMOV

*MAKSIMOV, VLADIMIR (EMELYAN-OVICH) (September 12, 1930–), Russian writer of fiction, drama, and political commentary, was born in Moscow to working-class parents. His father was arrested in 1933 and disappeared. He spent the years 1945–50 in a children's labor colony, where his name was changed from the original Lev Alekseevich Samsonov. Upon finishing trade school Maksimov worked as a mason at construction sites in the northern Soviet Union, and explored for diamonds. From 1952 he worked in the Kuban as a journalist.

In 1956 Maksimov published his first collection of poetry Pokolenie na chasakh (A Generation Keeping Watch). At the end of the 1950s he moved to Moscow, the literary center of the country. Konstantin Paustovsky included his story "My obzhivaem zemlyu" (We Tame the Land) in the 1961 collection Tarusskie stranitsy (Pages from Tarusa). The story "Zhiv chelovek" (A Man Survives) appeared in the journal Oktyabr (1962), bringing the author widespread recognition. It was followed also in Oktyabr by the stories "Iskushenie" (Temptation), "Dusya i nas pyatero" (Dusya and the Five of Us), "Sashka" (all 1964, no. 2), the play Pozyvnye tvoikh parallelei (The Call Signs of Your Position; 1964, no. 2), and the longer story "Stan za chertu" (Dare to Cross the Line; 1963, no. 2).

Maksimov served on the editorial board of Oktyabr from 1964 to 1968, when he resigned in protest at the Soviet invasion of Czechoslovakia. The novels Sem dnei tvoreniya (The Seven Days of Creation, 1971) and Karantin (Quarantine, 1973) appeared in Frankfurt-am-Main. They were nonetheless distributed via the clandestine channels of samizdat and became widely known within the Soviet Union. In June 1973 Maksimov was expelled from the Writers' Union, and in 1974 was forced to leave the country. In that same year his novel Proshchanie iz niotkuda (Farewell from Nowhere) appeared in the West German emigré journal Grani. Maksimov now lives in Paris with his wife Tat-

yana (Plotoratskaya) and their daughters. He is editor-in-chief of the journal Kontinent, one of the most authoritative and best known Russian emigré periodicals. Of his own writing Maksimov has published in Kontinent not only fiction, but also pointed political and social commentary.

Maksimov's work falls into two periods. The first is characterized by his attempt to express himself within the limits of socialist realism, avoiding as far as possible any conflict with official dogma. Nevertheless his heroes (homeless child, escaped convict, vagrant) never quite fit into the framework of socialist realism, with its insistence on positive example, because of their social condition. Their very existence speaks of problems in the society which is "building Communism," of the many people who, cast aside by life, are not involved in the "great historical project." But while sympathizing with his heroes and bringing them to the point of blind, unreasoning rebellion, Maksimov as a rule defeats them and so seems to be on the side of official, poster optimism. The story "Sashka" is the lone exception. The homeless youth Sashka avenges his friend, a known thief, by killing the police agent to whom through inexperience he had accidentally betrayed the friend. The story is written with obvious sympathy toward the youth.

In short, the rebellion of Maksimov's heroes generally ends in their defeat, or else in the triumph of the idea of the "positive whole" (by which negative elements are admissible if ultimately outweighed in an overall positive impression). In the name of this idea Maksimov has

°mak see´ môf, vlä dē mēr

sacrificed not only his heroes, but on one occasion, himself. In 1963 he published a short article in *Oktyabr* entitled "Estafeta veka" (Passing the Baton) in which he glorifies the Communist Party and socialist realism. However, when he resigned from *Oktyabr* in 1968 over the events in Czechoslovakia, a new period in Maksimov's literary career began.

The Seven Days of Creation is a novel written in the spirit of the family chronicle, a genre widely represented in the literature of socialist realism. But insofar as the message of Soviet family chronicles is the singular strength and harmony of the Soviet working-class family thanks to the new socialist morality, Maksimov's novel flatly contradicts it. (Nevertheless, from a purely stylistic point of view, *The Seven Days of Creation* continues their tradition of epic realism.) Maksimov believes that a strong, harmonious family cannot form around a man who lives by Marxist ideology, whose destructive power lies in its absolute inhumanity. The main character of the novel, the old Bolshevik and former commissar Pyotr Vasilyevich Lashkov, gradually becomes convinced that his whole life has been a series of mistakes and delusions. He has been a bad husband, father, and grandfather, separated from those nearest him by a longstanding lie, by an ideology which is hostile in its essence to the feeling of love and which fosters not intimacy but alienation.

To judge from changes in tone and emphasis during the course of the novel, Maksimov apparently hoped to see it published in the Soviet Union when he began work on it. As he gradually renounced this possibility, the theme took on a sharper and sharper edge. In the chapter devoted to Vadim Lashkov, grandson of Pyotr Lashkov and a talented actor who has been confined to a psychiatric hospital without medical justification, the novel as denunciation reaches its apogee. It is possible that Maksimov drew on his own experience in describing a psychiatric hospital where he was once himself confined eight months for carrying false identity papers.

The novel *Quarantine* is stylistically more unified and ideologically more subtle than its predecessor. In it Maksimov employs an extremely complex symbol: a train, which has been stopped outside Moscow because it is traveling from Odessa, where a cholera epidemic is raging. The train is ringed by soldiers. In telling the stories of the passengers, who include well-known Moscow intellectuals as well as simple, ordinary people, Maksimov creates an image of Soviet Russia—"surrounded," isolated, full of hopes and fears, hating and loving, self-satisfied and self-sacrificing, blindly cruel and compassionate,

inured to sin and passionately seeking salvation. The narrative structure of the novel is complicated, as well, with long digressions, historical scenes, monologues, and symbolic descriptions.

The novel *Kovcheg dlya nezvannykh* (*Ark for the Uncalled*, 1979) deals with the artificial settlement of the Kurile Islands after they were seized from Japan. Many people die in the very first days during a volcanic eruption. The land itself will not accept the new inhabitants. An artificial paradise is impossible—such is the leading idea of the novel. Maksimov again provides a broad social cross-section, ranging from Joseph Stalin at the top to homeless vagabonds. The central character is Captain Zolotaryov, who has been placed in charge of the fishing industry in the Kuriles. Realizing that the Kremlin will not forgive him the catastrophe caused by the volcano, Zolotaryov kills himself. His suicide is made to bear witness to the phantasmagorical nature of a society that is spiritually sick or even criminal. Maksimov argues that in the final analysis all Soviet citizens are social discards—those who, caught up in Stalin's terror, are thrown overboard from the ship of life, those who are exalted by it to the top of the hierarchical ladder, and those who swarm over its lower rungs in eternal fear of Soviet "justice."

In all these novels of the second period, the church is the only counterweight to the absurdity of a Sovietized society, in the sense that it alone is a source of truly authentic being. In a Christianized world the problem of alienation does not exist; what does exist is the problem of the fall from Grace, where a man is cast aside not by society but by God. Man fears this rejection most of all, according to Maksimov, and it is the source of the religious feeling which lives in him unconsciously and draws him to God. In *Quarantine* God is present among the passengers in the person of Ivan Ivanovich Ivanov (the Russian equivalent of John Doe), and everyone needs him and seeks his help. The old Bolshevik Pyotr Lashkov in *Seven Days of Creation* comes to the idea of God. In *Quarantine* that hardened butcher Joseph Stalin begs forgiveness of Christ, and in the chapter "The Transformation of a Quiet Seminarian" Maksimov provides, as it were, a continuation of Dostoevsky's "Legend of the Grand Inquisitor" from *The Brothers Karamazov*. But where Dostoevsky's Christ forgives the Inquisitor, Maksimov's refuses to forgive so great a sinner as Stalin. It is interesting to contrast Maksimov's interpretation of Stalin in *Quarantine* and in *An Ark for the Unchosen*. If the former proceeds by metaphysical analysis and so is closer to Dostoevsky, the latter proceeds by an accumulation of psychological and material detail which serves to discredit Stalin, and so is closer to Tolstoy in his treatment of Napoleon in *War and Peace*.

The novel *Farewell from Nowhere* is autobiographical. Maksimov portrays himself in the character of Vlad Samsonov. He recounts his wanderings through southern Russia, his job in a brick factory, an unsuccessful attempt to publish his first book, and much more. In part he returns to the themes of his "Soviet" prose, but the observation of social types and institutions is much sharper and more in accordance with reality. A continuation of *Farewell from Nowhere* is *Chasha ya rosti* (Cup of Broth, 1981–82). In describing his rise to fame and subsequent break with the regime, he again returns to "Soviet" themes.

An internal conflict of Maksimov's finds expression in both these autobiographical novels. On one hand there is a thirst for universal brotherhood, a longing for unity and all-embracing love, which in fact lie at the foundation of Maksimov's Christian ideal. But on the other hand there is a lack of submissiveness, of tolerance, which are no less Christian virtues. Hence the demand in these novels is for moral perfection as an abstract imperative, not as something strictly required of oneself. Vlad Samsonov hates and despises the system, while trying at the same time to compromise with it, and does not sense how damaging this is to his moral position. A general hatred of falsity that is not combined with self-criticism leads to a cult of personal anarchism, which, together with the feeling that others have wronged him, results in an essentially very dangerous state of mind— the notion that all is permitted. When it comes to making moral demands on himself, Vlad Samsonov's capacity for self-analysis disappears, giving way to a very ordinary craving for alcohol.

Maksimov has written a number of plays based on motifs from his stories, and has adapted Dostoevsky's *The Possessed* for the screen. In his political commentary written for *Kontinent*—"Saga o nosorogakh" (The Rhinoceros Saga), "Oni i my" (They and We), Maksimov sharply criticizes Western cultural figures and liberal intellectuals for their sympathy toward the Soviet regime and socialist ideals. Identifying the Soviet regime with Hitler's fascism, he categorically opposes any compromise with it. Maksimov shares Solzhenitsyn's opinion that Soviet Communism is in no way a peculiarly Russian phenomenon, but is capable of spreading to any country where faith in "democratic socialism" gives it an opening. This and related points are currently the subject of sharp debate in the emigré press.

WORKS IN ENGLISH TRANSLATION: Excerpts from Maksimov's writings are translated in M. Scammell's *Russia's Other Writers*, 1971; and in C. and E. Proffer's *The Ardis Anthology of Russian Futurism*, 1980. His novels in English translation are *Quarantine*, by Michael Glenny, 1973; *A Man Survives*, by Anselm Hollo, and *The Seven Days of Creation*, both 1975; *Farewell from Nowhere*, by Michael Glenny, 1979 and *Ark for the Uncalled*, 1985.

ABOUT: Ben-Amos, D. and K. Goldstein (eds.) Folklore: Performance and Communication, 1975; Brown, D. Soviet Literature since Stalin, 1978; Columbia Dictionary of Modern European Literature, 1980; Contmeporary Authors 104, 1982; Hosking, G. Beyond Socialist Realism, 1980; International Who's Who, 1983–84; Slonim, M. Soviet Russian Literature, 1977. *Periodicals*—Encounter June 1974; Journal of Russian Studies 36, 1978; Publishers Weekly April 30, 1979; Times Literary Supplement February 22, 1985.

MALOUF, DAVID (March 20, 1934–   ), Australian poet and novelist, writes: "I was born and grew up in Edwardian England, a fact that has somehow got itself recorded in the real world as Brisbane, Australia, in 1934. I mean by this that until the war ended, when I was eleven years old, I lived in a green, subtropical weatherboard city of mango trees, cannas and giant weeping figs that still thought of itself as being a stone's throw from London at the height of the empire. We ate English food—huge roasts with potatoes and boiled puddings (it took the Americans when they arrived to tell us that we could also eat steak); we wore ties and jackets even in hottest February; we read English books, sang songs about 'old father Thames,' and generally lived as if real conditions were illusory and what was most significant came to us by some other means than through the senses. Brisbane existed simultaneously on both sides of the planet and was at once shabbily, earthily actual and utterly unreal. An awareness of this was general, but if others of my generation felt it they have not found it necessary to record the fact. Brisbane still seems to me to be the strangest and most exotic place I know and most of what I have written is set there or springs from its paradoxical nature. During the war it was a garrison city. General MacArthur had his headquarters in a city hotel and a large part of the population was suddenly American—much of it black.

"My father's people came from Lebanon. My grandparents migrated in the 1880s to escape a massacre and all my father's brothers and sisters were born in Brisbane and had taken pains (as most first generation migrants do) to lose all their cultural baggage. My grandfather spoke little English, but neither my father nor any of

DAVID MALOUF

his brothers and sisters spoke anything else. My mother's family was from London. They moved in 1913 from a big, four-storeyed house in New Cross to a tent on the goldfields at Mount Morgan. It was part of the reticence practiced by my mother's people that I did not discover why till the last of her sisters was dead: they had lost all they had in a bank-crash in 1912. They were Portuguese Jews of a grand kind (an ancestor was Daniel Mendoza the boxer, a friend of Byron) and none of them, I think, ever really made the crossing. This affected the rituals of the house I was brought up in, a big weatherboard with verandahs, very tumbledown but with the remains of a tennis-court and garden, and made me aware always of another and alternative place from which all things in our world derived and on which they still depended. It also made me feel that my being who I was, and where I was, had in it a large element of the accidental; even the language I spoke was a chosen one— though it was the only one I would ever know. It was this language, English, spoken locally, but also spoken in that other and realer world on the other side of the globe, that held our life together. In it all the contraries were explained and made whole. This is an adult's perception, of course, but a child might very well have felt it and understood. Language has always been important to me. It was the names of things as much as their shape or smell or colour that excited me, even as a child. I always knew that naming things was a kind of magic that gave them a different and perhaps more manageable form.

"Brisbane is an easy, outdoors place with no winter, and my father was a professional sports-man, boxer and footballer. My sister and I could swim before we could walk and our lives were led in real weather and among plants, trees, animals that were local; but the ideas we were presented with, and all the social and cultural forms that grew out of them, came from elsewhere. This situation and the confusions it produced may not be ideal—they were deeply colonial— but they are at least complex and demanding. I have always written, I think, out of this early sense of seeing and feeling in one hemisphere and reading in another, or of doing both at the same time, and from the oddness of being plainly neither Anglo-Saxon nor Celtic in a place that was in those days ninety-five percent either one or the other. I felt strongly the tug between family style or temperament, and my education in a world that was British to its boot-straps. This too was demanding and useful. I read avidly, developed an early passion for music, did well at Grammar School and better at university, began to write poetry, and after a couple of years of teaching, and another year of drifting, went to Europe in 1959 and stayed there, working as a teacher in London and the North of England, till 1968. Back in Australia I taught English at the University of Sydney and eventually gave up in 1978 to spend part of each year in Brisbane and part in a small village in southern Tuscany."

―――――――

David Malouf was educated at Brisbane Grammar School (1947–50) and the University of Queensland in that city (1951–54), from which he earned a B.A. with honors in English. He first became noticed in his native country as a poet. "Interiors" was the title of his section in *Four Poets*, a volume comprising the work of a Brisbane-based group of young poets that included Judith Rodriguez, Rodney Hall, and Donald Maynard. Some of Malouf's continuing thematic preoccupations are first evident here— his Australian childhood, the strangeness of the country, his family, dreams and their meanings, and his fascination with European culture.

His first collection, *Bicycle and Other Poems* (published in the United States, with some changes, as *The Year of the Foxes and Other Poems*), showed the maturity and assurance of his voice. Northern Australia is described as a threatening, miasmic wilderness in "Letter from North Queensland: 1892":

Equivocal land: the coastline
dips south from mangrove swamp to a

blinding surface
of salt, the sea begins; though where precisely
is a point on which our maps fail to agree. . . .
And nothing is real, or what it seems: the
    lizards'

papery dry wings
rattle like hail; pale orchids,
birdlike, parasitic, take their flight
like angels, subtly abroad in empty rooms, their perfume
teasing our hearts with
    Paradise;
trees rooted in earth and water feed on dew.

We dream of England, home. Under the net
    our sleep's a cool blue portico
of air, ionic glades—trees gravel water under
    one
law established, quiet like the snow . . .

Neighbours in a Thicket consists of thirty-six "essentially meditative poems," in Thomas W. Shapcott's words, "poems of exploration rather than arrival, and their starting point is always a fine awareness of the past as being something as immediate and contemporaneous as the present. This capacity to respond to time laterally rather than chronologically makes Malouf unique among Australian poets in that it enables him to transcend issues of cultural identity and assertion, issues that have been of dominant concern in so much Australian writing. Malouf's sense of region is intense and sharply visual. He is thus the most European, yet one of the most regional, of contemporary Australian poets."

Malouf's next two books of poetry are both very short. *Poems 1975–76* is dominated by two sequences, of which the more notable is "Twelve Nightpieces," filled with carefully surveyed dreamscapes. *First Things Last* showed the poet's habitual themes taking on even greater resonance and refinement. As Fleur Adcock wrote in a review of this book, "Malouf's powerful imagination allows a certain amount of surrealism, without too much self-indulgence. He uses a variety of fairly free verse forms, including prose-poetry, while retaining a commitment to normal syntax. He can be playful, and his obsession with the visual sometimes carries him away into digressions, but he is a serious poet concerned with serious things."

To Adrian Mitchell, Malouf's is "a fiction characterized by cool deliberation and meticulous craftsmanship." *Johnno*, his first novel, is the story of the growing into manhood of two Brisbane youths, the narrator Dante, "well-brought-up" and sensitive, and Johnno, a violent, disturbed boy whose wildness and unconventionality attract his friend. Judith Rodriguez remarked that the narrator's fascination with Johnno slights potentially interesting minor characters; to her, the novel's strength "is the richly evoked presence of Brisbane before and after the War, and of the War itself in the imaginative life of Dante." Frank Pike, praising both these aspects of the novel, thought it as a whole rather less successful; in particular, "the specially

Australian significance of Johnno's Weltschmerz remains as elusive as the Australian Dream mentioned on the dustjacket. Nevertheless no geographically conditioned insights are necessary."

An Imaginary Life is a powerfully evocative novel about the sad, introspective exile of the Roman poet Ovid among the barbarian Getae in the village of Tomis on the Black Sea. The poet's encounter with a feral child, raised by wolves, is drawn, in Malouf's words, "from J.M.G. Itard's painstaking observations of Victor, the wild boy of Aveyron." The secondary characters are much more fully realized here than in *Johnno*. To Rodriguez the novel is "an enormous advance in Malouf's skill. The prose is of richly distinctive poetic quality. As with many cherished novels, the voice outlasts in the mind the happenings which call it into existence, but not the area in which it re-echoes, of conjecture about civilization and destiny." Adrian Mitchell, however, thought the novel's concerns "poetic, not moral, and while it is a book of considerable intelligence and skill, the studied elegance of its style betrays it, for the precious writing becomes brittle rather than refreshing."

Malouf's fiction has become, according to several critics, progressively more difficult and oblique. *Child's Play* is a story narrated by a terrorist, who may or may not have been invented by the novel's main character, a famous writer who in his work "flirts with destructive passions—madness, perversion, the flight into illness" in order to create in his fiction "a delicate balance between moral strictness and a disarming openness to the destructiveness of things."

Alan Brownjohn considered that *Fly Away Peter* "reads like an exercise in studied elusiveness." Set on the Queensland coast in 1914, it is the story of Ashley Crowther, a wealthy landowner who sets up a bird sanctuary which he peacefully enjoys with a neighbor, Imogen Harcourt, like him an immigrant to Queensland, and his young assistant, Jim Saddler, who must leave for the trenches in the course of the novel. Brownjohn felt the war scenes to be "much the finest in *Fly Away Peter*: men passing down the slope from fields where peasants continue to till the ground and birds continue to sing, to enter that labyrinth of mud, rats and twitching bodies from which they will never return, or never return the same." Yet because of Malouf's reticence about stating his messages clearly, the nature of this Australian allegory is lost on the reader; to Brownjohn, the book finally "skirts the issues and hides behind the flimsy gauzes of the poetic novel."

Malouf has received several Australian literary awards, including the gold medal of the Aus-

tralian Literature Society (1974), the Grace
Leven prize for verse (1974), the James Cook
award (1975), and the New South Wales Premier's prize for fiction (1979). In 1978 he held
a fellowship awarded by the Australia Council.

PRINCIPAL WORKS: *Poetry*—"Interiors" *in* Four Poets,
1962; Bicycle and Other Poems, 1970 (U.S., Year of the
Foxes, 1979); Neighbours in a Thicket, 1974; Poems,
1976–77, 1977; First Things Last, 1980; Selected Poems, 1981. *Fiction*—Johnno, 1975; An Imaginary Life,
1978; Child's Play *with* Eustace and the Prowler, 1982;
Fly Away Peter, 1982; Harland's Half Acre, 1984; An-
tipodes, 1984.

ABOUT: Oxford History of Australian Literature, 1981;
Contemporary Novelists, 1982; Vinson, J. (ed.) Contemporary Poets, 1980. *Periodicals*—Australian Book
Review December 1980; Library Journal March 1,
1978; June 1, 1979; New Republic May 13, 1978; New
Statesman September 15, 1978; New York Times Book
Review April 23, 1978; October 14, 1984; Quadrant
October 1976; Times Literary Supplement April 9,
1976; September 22, 1978; January 29, 1982; May 21,
1982; October 15, 1982; February 8, 1985; World Literature Today Winter 1980.

DAVID MAMET

*MAMET, DAVID (November 30, 1947–),
American dramatist and screenwriter, was born
in Flossmoor, Illinois, the son of Bernard, a labor
lawyer, and Lenore (Silver) Mamet, a teacher of
retarded children. Of Russian and Polish ancestry, Mamet spent his early childhood in a Jewish
neighborhood on Chicago's South Side. When
his parents divorced in the late 1950s, Mamet
moved with his mother to nearby Olympia
Fields. He completed his secondary education at
Rich Central High School and at the private
Francis W. Parker School in Chicago before enrolling at Goddard College, Plainfield, Vermont,
in 1965.

Even before Mamet studied drama, acting,
and dance at Goddard, he had been exposed to
a variety of experiences that developed his keen
ear for spoken language as well as his sense of
theater and influenced the style, structure, and
subject matter of many of his plays. As a child,
according to Richard Christiansen (*Chicago
Tribune*), Mamet read voraciously, studied piano, and "learned complex children's rhymes
from a recording produced by the Internatinal
Society for Semantics." Semantics was a particular passion of Mamet's father, and he encouraged his son's interest in words and precise self-
expression.

Mamet's first experience of the theater came
while he was still in high school working as a
backstage volunteer at Chicago's Hull House
Theater. There he was exposed to productions of

plays by Beckett and Pinter, writers whose influences on his own work he has acknowledged.
Later, during a vacation from Goddard, Mamet
became a busboy at Second City, Chicago's renowned improvisational comedy cabaret. Characteristics of the Second City style can be seen
in Mamet's penchant for the short scene, frequently featuring interaction between two characters. A series of such brief scenes forms the
basic structure of many of his plays. Mamet has
also acknowledged the importance of the
rhythms of speech and action he found in Second City performances in shaping his own dramatic style and language. Finally, though
Mamet has tended to downplay their importance, a series of odd jobs he undertook in the
early 1970s introduced him to the speech and
behavior of a cross-section of the American work
force. Between periods of teaching, acting, writing, and running his own theater company, Mamet worked as a window washer, taxi driver,
short-order cook, in truck and canning factories,
and for a real estate agency—which last experience he drew upon for his play *Glengarry Glen
Ross*. He also spent a year in the merchant marine, the subject of his one-act play *Lakeboat*.

Primarily, however, from his days at Goddard
till now, Mamet's has been a life in the theater
and, more recently, films. Apart from having become one of the foremost American playwrights,
he has taken turns at many of the other arts,
crafts, instructional, and managerial positions involved in creating theater. His first play, *Camel,*
a revue, was written to satisfy a requirement toward his B.A. in English, which he received
from Goddard in 1969. Before graduating, he

° mam´ it

took a year off and enrolled as an acting student at Sanford Meisner's Neighborhood Playhouse in New York City, where he became well-versed in the tenets of Stanislavsky. During that time he worked nights and subsequently served as house manager at the Sullivan Street Playhouse for the long-running musical *The Fantasticks.*

After graduating from Goddard, Mamet tried his hand at acting on a tour of New England straw-hat theaters. Though he was to continue acting for some time after, Mamet readily admits that as a performer he was "terrible." The following year he accepted a position as an instructor in acting at Marlboro College, Vermont, where he wrote *Lakeboat* (1970), and in 1971 he returned to Goddard as an acting teacher. Mamet organized the St. Nicholas Theatre Company in its earliest incarnation with students from his Goddard classes, principally Steven Schachter and William H. Macy. A few years later, having begun to make a name for himself as a playwright in Chicago, he reconstituted the St. Nicholas company (1974), serving as its first artistic director. While teaching at Goddard, Mamet continued writing—scenes and short plays composed primarily, he suggests, to provide material for the students in his acting classes. One of these, *The Duck Variations,* was performed by the Goddard St. Nicholas company in 1972 and staged by the Body Politic Theater in Chicago in the fall of that year. It gave Mamet at age twenty-four his first recognition as a playwright of promise.

In *The Duck Variations* two elderly Jewish men sit on a park bench facing a lake and, in a series of fourteen vignettes, discuss the habits and fate of ducks and other topics. A great deal of humor emerges from the characters' anthropomorphic view of their subject and from the discrepancy between the tone of assurance in their voices and their underlying ignorance of much that they debate. Gradually, however, a portrait emerges of two men near the end of their lives needing friendship, fearing loneliness and death, each asserting his self-worth through the scoring of verbal points. Ted Kalem of *Time* saw Pinter's influence in the characters' "wearing word masks to shield feelings and defying communication in the act of communicating." But others saw an original voice at work as well.

In 1973 Mamet moved back to Chicago to concentrate on his writing, supporting himself in the meanwhile with a variety of temporary positions including some acting. Two works, *Mackinac,* a children's play, and *Marranos,* set during the Inquisition, received stagings. Then in June of 1974, the Organic Theater Company

produced *Sexual Perversity in Chicago.* The play's reception was excellent, and it won for Mamet the Joseph Jefferson Award as Chicago's best new play of the year. Two years later Mamet's prestige as a regional dramatist received national confirmation when a double bill of *The Duck Variations* and *Sexual Perversity in Chicago* opened on June 16, 1976 at New York's Off-Broadway Cherry Lane Theatre and ran till the following April. At the end of the 1975/76 season Mamet received the *Village Voice* Obie Award as "Best New Playwright" for *Sexual Perversity* and *American Buffalo,* which was produced off-Broadway in January 1976.

Sexual Perversity in Chicago, like *The Duck Variations,* moves through a series of brief episodes, most of them dialogues. The play explores the sexual attitudes and behavior of four young single people over one summer in the bars, bedrooms, and other mating grounds of Chicago. *Sexual Perversity* succeeds on one level as hilarious satire on sexual misapprehension among supposedly knowledgeable members of a liberated generation. But Mamet's purpose is deeply serious as he charts the destruction of a potentially loving relationship between Danny Shapiro and Deborah Soloman. They meet, move in together, and make some progress toward knowing and accepting each other as individuals. But Danny and Deborah are finally unable to overcome their misconceptions and fears of each other as male and female or to relinquish their sex roles. Contributing in no small way to their eventual breakup are the proddings of their respective friends, Bernie and Joan, two hostile veterans of the sexual wars. Bernard Litko, particularly, is one of Mamet's ripest creations, a superb type of macho sexuality by turns funny, pathetic, repellent, and frightening in his misogyny.

Mamet's gift for language, for recreating in dramatic form the vocabulary, rhythms, and idiosyncrasies of everyday American speech, has been widely praised. Wrenched syntax, repetitions, redundancies, pauses, truncated sentences, the odd word used inappropriately by a character in the grip of emotion, incongruously heightened diction, staccato exchanges interrupted by extended outbursts, the liberal use of obscenities—components such as these are characteristic of Mamet's early plays, especially *American Buffalo.* However, the playwright has moved toward a greater formality and economy of language in many of his later works, and the larger truth is that Mamet has sought for each of his plays a style appropriate to its characters, themes, and milieu.

In interviews Mamet has endorsed an interpretation of the action of *American Buffalo* as a

kind of metaphor for the American business ethic: "There's really no difference between the
lumpenproletariat and . . . the lackeys of business . . . ," he told Richard Gottlieb in the *New
York Times.* "Part of the American myth is that
a difference exists, that at a certain point vicious
behavior becomes laudable." Certainly much of
the mode of the play is rooted in this perception.
The milieu of *American Buffalo* is a Chicago
junk shop inhabited by three petty crooks, cast-
offs of society: Don, the owner, Walter Cole, called Teach, his friend and "business associate,"
and Bob, a young junkie who serves as Don's go-
pher, surrogate son, and, possibly, lover. The action of the play turns on the planning of a
robbery and the consequences for the three men
when the plan fails. Although the burglary is
thwarted and violence erupts over an apparent
betrayal, the play ends with a revelation that
brings Don and Bob closer together and exposes
Teach's pitiable vulnerability. The success of
The Duck Variations and *Sexual Perversity in
Chicago* enabled Mamet to get a Broadway
showing for *American Buffalo,* where it opened
on February 16, 1977. Although some notices
were negative, most were very favorable and,
despite a short run, *American Buffalo* went on
to win the New York Drama Critics Circle
Award as "Best American Play of the Year."

Neither the satiric possiblities realized in having petty thieves identify with respectable businessmen, nor the oft-praised virtuosity of
language can alone explain the success of the
play. Since its first Broadway production
American Buffalo has been presented in regional
American theaters, by Britain's National Theatre in 1978, in Europe, and in two major reviv-
als in New York, off and on Broadway (1981 and
1983, each of these directed by Arvin Brown
with Al Pacino as Teach). In 1977 critics were
preoccupied by Mamet's language, held by the
play's bleak vision and the menace in Robert
Duvall's Teach, and generally disappointed by
the lack of action in Mamet's first full-length
stage work. By 1983 Benedict Nightingale represented many when he proclaimed in the *New
York Times* that *American Buffalo* had proved
its "durability and resilience . . . revealed more
of itself, shifted, modulated, grown. . . . Mr.
Mamet isn't simply a latter-day Dreiser, yearning to trim the capitalist jungle. What really interests him . . . are the shadowy, elusive
frontiers between business and friendship, greed
and altruism . . . evil and good."

Nineteen seventy-seven was an *annus
mirabilis* for Mamet. In addition to earning recognition for *American Buffalo* he added several
new plays to his canon. Chicago saw productions
of *The Woods, The Water Engine: An American*

Fable, and *A Life in the Theatre,* and the latter
two were also introduced in New York late in
that year. Mamet also completed a year as a CBS
fellow in playwriting at Yale where the prestigious Yale Repertory Theatre staged two additional short works, *Reunion* (first seen in
Chicago, 1976) and *Dark Pony.* The American
actress Lindsay Crouse appeared in the Yale
twin-bill; on December 21 she and Mamet were
married. For his sustained contributions to the
American theater Mamet received a 1977/78
Outer Critics Circle Award.

A Life in the Theatre, produced off-
Broadway in 1977, was a popular success. Mamet wrote his "sad" comedy as an affectionate
tribute to actors whom he has called
"misunderstood" and "the only essential
component" of the theater. The two characters
in the play are an aging traditionalist actor and
a blunt, unromantic young actor, eager to learn
his craft and perfect his art. As they move
through a series of twenty-six scenes representing and parodying moments from actual performances, we witness the older man's decline and
the younger's rise in the profession, and the unfolding of the play's theme of the ephemeral nature of theater and the reality that most actors
spend most of their lives acting in poor plays. A
public television production of the play was
broadcast in June 1979.

Critical opinion on *The Water Engine* in its
New York Shakespeare Festival production
(winter 1977/78) was divided. Negative response focused on the work's origins as a radio
play and found it a thin melodrama barely altered by theatrical staging. At its most basic level
The Water Engine is a play about human communication. We hear private conversations,
public speeches, gossip, phone calls, lectures, an-
nouncements, and we are made aware of the
uses of the mails, the press, and other media.
Principally though, the work is about the
achievement of progress through the communication of ideas. The play is set in 1934 and meant
to be enacted in a radio studio at the time of Chicago's Century of Progress Exposition.

Except for the one-character sketch, *Mr.
Happiness,* written as a curtain-raiser for the
Broadway run of *The Water Engine,* Mamet's
next New York offering was *The Woods* in a
New York Shakespeare Festival production in
April 1979. It charts the disintegration of the relationship between two lovers after a night spent
together in a cabin in the woods. While the work
had its staunch supporters, including Richard
Eder and Terry Curtis Fox of the *Village Voice*
("as good a play as any written by an American
in the past ten years"), most critics found it a fail-

ure, citing sketchy characterization, heavy-handed symbolism, and, above all, an excessively mannered language riddled with monosyllables, repetitions, interrogatives, and stilted syntax. A New York revival of the play in 1982, directed by Mamet himself, was no more enthusiastically received. An even greater critical failure came in May of 1979 with the world premiere in Chicago of *The Lone Canoe*. Mamet's drama with music (by Alaric Jans) was based on the disappearance in the Canadian north of the nineteenth-century explorer, Sir John Fairfax. Richard Eder commented on the growing tendency of Mamet to pare down his language: "Here, though, the spareness is empty and forced, becoming a kind of grandiloquence in reverse. And the sentiment is inflated and operatic."

For the next three seasons while Mamet devoted much of his time to the writing and filming of two screenplays, New York saw only a series of minimal one-act dramas from him (outside of a turn at directing *Twelfth Night* for Circle Repertory in 1980 and the *American Buffalo* revival in 1981). The most significant of these short plays were *Reunion* and *Dark Pony* with a third sketch, *The Sanctity of Marriage*, added to the evening's bill at the Circle Repertory Theatre October 1979.

Of Mamet's two produced film scripts, for *The Postman Always Rings Twice* (1981) and *The Verdict* (1982), the latter was by far the more favorably received and won for Mamet a Motion Picture Academy Award nomination. Based on the novel by Barry Reed and directed by Sidney Lumet, *The Verdict* is about the self-redemption of a failed Boston-Irish lawyer who takes on corrupt forces within the church, the medical profession, and the law and beats them in court. David Mamet's screenplay was called "strong on character, on sharp and edgy dialogue, on the detective-story suspense of a potent narrative" by *Newsweek*'s Jack Kroll. Constructing narrative for two films has had an admitted effect on Mamet the dramatist. In an interview shortly before the New York premiere of *Glengarry Glen Ross* he said, "the older I get, the more in love I get with traditional aspects of dramaturgy. Working on screenplays has taken me in that direction. You'd better tell a story and make it pay off, or you have nothing."

Mamet's 1982 drama, *Edmond*, though constructed from brief episodes—in performance twenty-three scenes in seventy-five minutes—has a sequential narrative that tracks the spiritual journey of its title character. Edmond, a respectable middle class businessman dissatisfied with life and his marriage, leaves home to dis-cover where he "belongs." The play follows his descent into Manhattan's underworld where, after a series of degrading and violent confrontations, he is left with little except a sense of liberation in being able to declare his prejudices, chiefly against blacks and homosexuals.

Edmond was first performed in June of 1982 at Chicago's Goodman Theater where Mamet has been playwright-in-residence and associate artistic director since 1978. (He resigned from the St. Nicholas company in 1976.) The Goodman production opened to mixed reviews in New York on October 27 at the Provincetown Playhouse. Frank Rich in the *Times* felt "the author's ear has gone tone-deaf, and his social observations have devolved into clichés." But many critics, despite reservations, saw in *Edmond* a re-affirmation of Mamet's talent. John Simon in *New York* thought it "probably [his] best play in a long time" and Michael Feingold in the *Village Voice* said, "for all its waywardness and eccentricity . . . its fumblings for the abstract, *Edmond* states the problem of our lives . . . with considerable power." For *Edmond* Mamet received his second Obie Award.

His next work, *Glengarry Glen Ross*, had its world premiere in London at the British National Theatre in September of 1983, and, in a Goodman Theater production, opened in New York on March 25, 1984. Critical reaction on both sides of the Atlantic was almost unanimously favorable, and many hailed the play as Mamet's finest work to date. In London it won the Society of West End Theatres Award (the equivalent of Broadway's "Tony") as the year's best play. American honors included the 1984 Pulitzer Prize for drama and the New York Drama Critics Circle award for the best play of that year. The world of business which Mamet indicted as the enemy of progress in *The Water Engine* and satirized obliquely in *American Buffalo* returns as principal target in *Glengarry Glen Ross*. We are introduced to a group of salesmen, dealers in worthless tracts of Florida land with picturesque names, engaged in a cruel sales competition—top man to win a Cadillac and access to premium "leads" on prospective buyers, bottom two men to be fired. The play delivers a blistering attack on American enterprise, on a system where the success of the sale is more important than the quality of the product. Its staying power as drama, however, lies more in Mamet's achievement in generating empathy and a kind of admiration for a group of desperate men who sell their souls to steal other men's dreams.

Michael Billington, reviewing the London production for the *New York Times*, located the play's strength and complexity in its tone of "moral neutrality." It "presents its salesmen both as professional word-spinners trying to deprive gullible buyers of their savings and as victims themselves of a merciless cutthroat system." Others found a new level of mastery in Mamet's racy stage idiom, an exhilarating blend of caustic humor and obscenity, of the salesman's glib art of persuasion and his unmasked invective under fire. Structurally *Glengarry Glen Ross* may prove in time to have been a transitional play for Mamet, pointing toward a more sophisticated dramaturgy in subsequent works.

Along with Sam Shepard and Lanford Wilson, David Mamet remains preeminent among the generation of American dramatists who came to prominence in the 1970s. He has "specialized in plays of minimal plot, where the interaction of the characters—through dialogue—tells a story far broader than the limitations of a narrative will often allow," summarized David Blum in a 1982 *Wall Street Journal* piece. But Mamet's emphasis on dialogue at the expense of other components of drama has been perceived as the source both of his virtues and his weaknesses. Many critics have echoed the praise of British reviewer Robert Cushman ("Nobody alive writes better American"). Others have expressed disappointment over Mamet's failure to integrate his distinctive language into more conventionally plotted plays of full length, replete with scenes of externalized action involving characters in multiples greater than two. In his more recent work Mamet has, in fact, begun to embrace more traditional elements of the drama. Still, he has already created a body of work noteworthy not only for its verbal brilliance—poetic, witty, and revelatory on its own terms—but for its sensitivity to personal relationships even in the harshest of settings, and for its exploration of the myths that drive and frustrate Mamet's gallery of American characters.

Mamet and Lindsay Crouse, who have a daughter, Willa, born in 1982, maintain two residences, a small farm in Cabot, Vermont, where Mamet retreats, raises ducks, and in summer runs an acting school, and an apartment in the Chelsea section of Manhattan. He returns to Chicago periodically for his work with the Goodman Theater. He has also written a number of children's plays such as *The Poet and the Rent*, 1974, and *The Revenge of the Space Pandas*, 1977, and a children's book, *Warm and Cold*, 1984, as well as occasional journal articles on drama and theater. Other short plays include *Squirrels*, 1974; *All Men Are Whores*, 1977; *Shoeshine*, 1979; *A Sermon*, 1981; *Five Unrelated Pieces*, 1983; and *The Disappearance of the Jews*, 1983.

PRINCIPAL WORKS: *Plays*—American Buffalo, 1977; A Life in the Theatre, 1978; The Revenge of the Space Pandas or Binky Rudich and the Two-Speed Clock, 1978; Sexual Perversity in Chicago and The Duck Variations, 1978; The Water Engine: An American Fable and Mr. Happiness, 1978; Reunion and Dark Pony, 1979; The Woods, 1979; Lakeboat, 1981; Edmond, 1983. *Other*—Warm and Cold (juvenile), 1984.

ABOUT: Bock, H. and A. Wertheim (eds.) Essays on Contemporary American Drama, 1981; Contemporary Authors 81–84, 1979; Contemporary Dramatists, 1982; Current Biography, 1978; Encyclopedia of World Literature in the 20th Century, 1983; Kiernan, R.F. American Writing Since 1945: A Critical Survey, 1983; King, K. Ten Modern American Playwrights; an Annotated Bibliography, 1982; Twentieth-Century American Dramatists (Dictionary of Literary Biography), 1981; Who's Who in America, 1982–83; Who's Who in the Theatre, 1981. *Periodicals*—Chicago Tribune Magazine July 11, 1982; Decade—Promotional Issue, 1978; Harpers May 1978; Hollins Critic October 1979; Horizon November 1977; Kansas Quarterly 1980; Modern Drama September 1981; New Times November 25, 1977; New York April 9, 1984; New York Times February 13, 1977; August 21, 1977; December 4, 1977; January 15, 1978; March 12, 1978; October 24, 1982; March 28, 1984; Other Stages November 4–17, 1982; Performing Arts Journal 15, 1980; Time July 12, 1976; Village Voice July 5, 1976; Wall Street Journal June 11, 1982.

*MAMLEYEV, YURI (December 11, 1931–), Russian novelist, short story writer, and essayist, writes: "I was born in Moscow, USSR. My father, a professor of psychology, died in Stalin's concentration camp. In 1955 I graduated from the Moscow Forestry Institute and thereafter I worked as a teacher of mathematics in various schools. However, my real interest was in literature. Soon after the death of Stalin I moved into the non-conformist society and circles. I became a non-conformist writer and during the sixties and early seventies participated in the non-conformist movement in Moscow. During this period, I wrote two novels, about one hundred stories, a book of poems, and works on metaphysics. It was impossible to publish these in the Soviet press for my writings deviated from the standards of Soviet arts. My works were circulated in the *samizdat*. Non-conformist art in the late fifties and the sixties became known to a wider public by *samizdat* publications and by private showings and readings in apartments. Many literary schools and groupings sprouted up, forming associations—circles. Reading was my favorite kind of contact. I usually read my stories in private apartments, including my own, with up to fifty people present.

"In 1973 I was married to Farida Maria Abi-

°mäm lä´ yev, yu´ rē

YURI MAMLEYEV

dova who helped me greatly in my uneasy way of life as a non-conformist writer. She has always stayed with me in our attempt to secure our independence and in this she has followed a tradition of the wives of many Russian writers. In 1974 we emigrated from the USSR, and in 1975 came to the USA. Since coming to the USA, many of my writings have been published in Russian, English, French, German and Dutch. During the 1976–77 academic year, I taught Russian literature at Cornell University. Since 1977 I have been a freelance lecturer. Since 1979 I have also been a library assistant at Cornell University Libraries. In 1980 my wife and I became American citizens.

"My first book in English, *The Sky Above Hell,* was published in the end of November 1980, and subsequently I became a member of the American PEN Center. In 1981–82 I participated in the International Congresses of Psychoanalysis and Culture in New York and Paris. Some critics, in the West as well as in Russia, consider my prose as belonging to 'metaphysical realism.' Often I used in my writings this method: to begin with the internal potential of the human soul and bring it to external expression. Such a method includes penetration into hidden realities, abysses of the human soul and its secret recesses. Because of this penetration my stories on the surface seem 'surrealistic' or even 'fantastic': the greatest 'fantasy' lies in our hidden potential which I bring to the level of human behavior. In other words, it is not 'fantasy' but the revelation of a deeper level of reality. In addition, I try to describe that which lies obviously beyond the limits of our world. Subsequently,

my works do not belong to 'usual realism' but by using special knowledge, experience and intuition I create some kind of 'synthetic realism' which includes a display of several levels of reality. This includes the level of ordinary life as well as other levels ranging from paradoxical and extreme situations to metaphysical, cosmological and esoteric phenomena. These are reflected in the themes of my stories and novels: from the attempt to display the psyche and inner world of some non-human beings to the description of a killer's life in the family of his victim.

"Some critics here, in the West, wrote that in my prose I concentrate excessively on the dark and evil side of life. I think that the darkness is not my fault but the fault of this world. I simply reflect it and penetrate into its deepest levels. Cosmological darkness is a sign of our times. Indeed we live in Kali-Yuga (in terms of Hinduism), i.e. in the darkest cosmological cycle. In our present state, we are almost completely cut off from our sources of immortality. This alone is enough for calling our age the darkest age of humanity.

"Moreover, if I describe, as one well-known American writer said of me (see *Epoch,* Fall 1980), the earth turned into hell, it doesn't mean hell hasn't some secret and mysteriously positive sides. All kinds of existence have positive sides (although not very often secret ones). In an esoteric sense there are positive sides even in my most monstrous heroes, but these sides are hidden behind the smoke of hell and laughter of devils. At least, my underground readers in Russia felt this way. Also, they felt that to unveil evil (even cosmological evil) is not evil itself.

"However, in my opinion, some hope exists. In certain of my past and present works I try to show a more obvious balance."

Emerging during the cultural "thaw" that followed the death of Joseph Stalin in 1953, Yuri Mamleyev was one of a number of young Soviet writers who rejected Socialist Realism for a genre that the dissident writer Andrei Sinyavsky has called "fantastic realism," actually a revival of a tradition established by nineteenth-century Russian writers such as Gogol and Dostoevsky. As Peter Lewis describes his work: "Mamleyev's characteristic fusion of grand guignol and farce creates a nightmare world presenting the Soviet Union as a monolithic madhouse." Inevitably such writing could flourish only in the underground *samizdat* press, but there Mamleyev found a large appreciative audience for his novels and short stories.

It was not until five years after his emigration

to the United States that Mamleyev became known to the English-speaking public, and to date only a fraction of his work is available in English. He has continued to write for a Russian-speaking public, however, in publications of the Russian emigré press in France. A number of his stories and essays have also been translated into French, German, and Dutch. Mamleyev's reputation primarily rests on *The Sky Above Hell,* a collection of his short stories and one novella, "Shatuny." These bizarre, shocking yet also often grimly funny stories provoke reader reactions that range from disgust to awed admiration. Mamleyev's surrealist-nightmare world is obsessed with sexual perversion, brutality, and madness, but it also emerges as his vision of the Soviet Union. "The author's view of Soviet life is obvious," Anatoly Liberman writes. "He describes a society dominated by senseless violence in every form conceivable; this society is so bad that it cannot even be slandered; its inmates and masters are at best impotent, but usually they are dangerous perverts." Yet Mamleyev is also curiously metaphysical and mystical, portraying the world as horror precisely because it has lost all its religious and spiritual values. Oddly, but significantly, James McConkey detects a parallel to the stories of Flannery O'Connor—the mixture of "humor and violence in the service of metaphysical principles." His characters are so depraved that they can not recognize that the vacuum in which they live is hell and that they are the damned. "The underlying vision is religious," McConkey writes. "The comedy of this book is deadly serious."

The filthy clinic where his story "The Last Trace of Spinoza" takes place—where "doctors and nurses alike are struck with thoughts so ridiculous, so inappropriate, that they are more likely to be afraid of themselves than of their decomposing clients"—is a none-too-thinly disguised Communist state. And the obese, gluttonous woman doctor, having an affair with a patient who is convinced that he is Spinoza reincarnated, believes that "the more she saw the world and herself as meaningless, the closer she was to God and the truth about Being after death." In other stories in *The Sky Above Hell* a woman turns into a fox and castrates her lovers who thereupon become generals in the Russian army; a sexually naive young man accused of rape is condemned to death; a hit-and-run truck driver who has killed a child is adopted and idolized by his victim's family. And in the short novel "Shatuny" the central character is a psychopathic killer whose "huge, convoluted and wrinkled face was totally alienated, sunken in on itself. For the owner of this face, the world did not exist," and another character hates children "because in all the world he recognized only his own naked licentiousness, which enveloped the globe like huge elephant ears."

Grotesque and even repulsive as Mamleyev's fiction is, it is compelling and challenging. The Russian-language scholar George Gibian suggests the questions it raises and he implicitly answers them: "Can events that would be disgusting in real life be turned into eloquently artistic creations? Quite apart from what he is saying about our historical epoch, is he hinting at dim occult forces beyond the scope of the human intellect's unaided perceptions? At their best, however, Mamleyev's stories suggest arresting meanings that are not quickly forgotten."

WORKS IN ENGLISH TRANSLATION: *The Sky Above Hell and Other Stories* was translated by H. W. Tjalsma in 1980. Short stories by Mamleyev in English translation have been published in the journals *Epoch* (Spring 1978, Spring–Summer 1980) and *Annex* 4 (1982).

ABOUT: Contemporary Authors 85–89, 1980. *Periodicals*—Epoch Fall 1980; New Leader December 15, 1980; Russian Language Journal Winter–Spring 1982; Times Literary Supplement May 6, 1977; May 15, 1981; World Literature Today Spring 1981.

*MANGIONE, JERRE GERLANDO (March 20, 1909–   ), American memoirist, novelist, and social historian, writes: "I was born in Rochester, New York of immigrant Sicilian parents, the eldest of four children who grew up in a working-class neighborhood of Jews, Poles, and other Italians—the neighborhood that became the setting of my first book, *Mount Allegro.* English was forbidden in our home—for reasons of love. Fearful of losing communication with their children, my parents insisted we speak with them in Sicilian. My feelings as an outsider may have begun with that edict and were probably confirmed by the taunts of my ethnic gangmates who would not accept me until they had reduced my baptismal name of 'Gerlando' to 'Jerry.' Before long it became apparent that I was doomed to live a double life: the one thrust upon me by the Old World customs and values of my Sicilian relatives, and the other I experienced on the street and in the classrooms. From my public school teachers I acquired Horatio Alger notions of free will and free enterprise that were diametrically at odds with my relatives' staunch faith in the power of destiny.

"There was a third life, the secret one, that was fuelled by piles of books from the public library (mostly fiction) which I read clandestinely in deference to my mother's belief that too much reading could drive a person insane. The intensi-

°man jyō´ nē, je´ rē

JERRE GERLANDO MANGIONE

ty of my inner life blinded me to the richness of my Old World heritage and promoted the unspoken resolve to live among 'Americans' (I wasn't quite sure what they were) without feeling like an imposter. Above all, it gave birth to my obsession to become a writer. Writing became fixed in my mind as an avenue for assertion and self-discovery, an escape into a more compatible world where my introverted nature might be less of a liability.

"My shyness did not prevent me from going public with the determination to become a writer. In high school I won my first literary prize, a Baldwin apple from the orchard of an English teacher, and I became editor-in-chief of the school weekly. Despite the burden of too many part-time jobs, the years at Syracuse University were frenetically devoted to proving to peers, teachers, and myself that I could be a writer. On graduation in 1931 (perhaps the most depressed year of the Great Depression) my campus activities as journalist, columnist, and editor won me a job on the editorial staff of *Time* magazine. But my elation was short lived. Insisting that 'the less you know about a subject the better you can write about it,' Henry Luce assigned me 'Business and Finance,' about which I knew nothing and cared less. Within weeks *Time* and I parted company (an imprudent decision on my part), and I was plummeted into the maelstrom of the nation's collapsed economy.

"Like thousands of other Americans appalled by the paradox of mass privation in our land of plenty, I rapidly developed an acutely aware social conscience and joined the impassioned chorus of critics attacking the nation's status quo

and the spread of fascism. In liberal and radical magazines, for little or no pay, I expressed my concerns with articles, book and theater reviews, and satiric sketches (much later I was to indulge in my love for satire with a book of single-sentence fables, *Life Sentences for Everybody*), all the while barely maintaining myself with jobs for which I was absurdly unqualified.

"In 1936, two years after I had finally landed a job I liked in a publishing house, I made a somewhat reckless journey to Mussolini's Italy, not only to observe fascism in the flesh but also to assuage my curiosity about my Sicilian roots. On my return, I left the circumscribed world of book publishing and went to Washington, D.C. to help administer the WPA Federal Writers' Project, the New Deal's unique experiment in collective writing on a national scale. I was to work for the Federal government in various capacities during the next ten years.

"By then the bond with my Rochester Sicilian relatives had, unexpectedly, become stronger rather than weaker. Distance had provided me with the objectivity to appreciate their Old World qualities and cherish them as a natural source of psychic energy. Partly to record a past I had no wish to lose, and partly to write of Sicilians as I knew them, not as they were—and are—misrepresented, I made them the subject of a narrative memoir, *Mount Allegro,* in which I cast myself in the role of observer-participant, a role suited to the introvert-extravert personality I had become. In varying degrees the same technique was adopted for my other major works.

"The only two novels I have published so far, *Night Search* and *The Ship and the Flame* (I keep rewriting the manuscript of another every few years), are written in the third person with a deliberate sense of drama. While they make no attempt to involve the persona of the reader with my own, as happens in the first-person nonfictional works, they are probably more revelatory of my metaphysical self than anything else I have written. A British critic thrilled me by characterizing *Night Search* as 'a philosophical thriller.'

"In the belief that many a would-be writer has fallen by the wayside by becoming a teacher too early in life, I avoided the academic world until 1961 when I joined the University of Pennsylvania. The majority of my books were produced there during my tenure as director of its writing program and professor of American literature. Writing continues to be my raison d'être."

In 1980 the University of Pennsylvania awarded Jerre Mangione an honorary Doctor of

Letters degree with a citation that read in part: "Mangione has recorded the uniquely varied experiences of a lifetime in novels, autobiography, and social history." Those experiences have a special timeliness in an age that is at last beginning to recognize the importance of the two areas in which Mangione has done his major work—ethnicity and the cultural and social effects of the depression of the 1930s. As a recorder of his discovery of his Sicilian heritage, and as a historian of the Federal Writers Project of the New Deal, Mangione has made an important contribution to America's knowledge of itself.

Mount Allegro, Mangione's first book, was published in 1943 at a time when the Italian image in America was largely shaped by gangster films and lurid newspaper reports that linked "Sicilian" with "Mafia" and "Blackhand" and isolated the Italian-American both socially and psychologically from mainstream society. Mangione's warm and sensitive account of his own boyhood in the Rochester neighborhood he describes in *Mount Allegro* did much to dispel that image. "A combination of folklore, sociology, portraiture and drama all rolled into one," as Louis Adamic described it, *Mount Allegro* became a landmark ethnic study. It has had a curious publishing history. Written and accepted for publication by Houghton, Mifflin as a non-fiction memoir, it was first published as fiction (Mangione simply changed the names of his real people into fictitious ones) because the publisher thought it would sell better. In 1952 it was published as non-fiction by Alfred Knopf with an introduction by Dorothy Canfield Fisher; in 1963 it appeared in Hill and Wang's American Century series; in 1972 Crown published it for the young adult market; and in 1981 Columbia University Press published it with an introduction by the sociologist Herbert J. Gans who called the book "a classic of American ethnic literature, as relevant to the students of American literature as to those of ethnicity and social history." In this latest edition Mangione added an appendix noting the disappearance of his native community in the spreading urban blight of recent years: "Mount Allegro no longer exists as a neighborhood," he wrote.

Mount Allegro opens with a child's wish for assimilation in the New World—"When I grow up I want to be an American ." This marks the beginning of Mangione's search for identity and a home. American-born, he was nevertheless haunted by his Sicilian heritage and his love for his large immigrant family. The result was a divided, but not a troubled, life. Whatever conflict he felt between the two cultures was eventually resolved. Resuming his memoirs in *An Ethnic at Large,* Mangione described his coming of age during the depression, his encounters with artists and eccentrics in Greenwich Village, with communists in the John Reed Club, his enlightening but frightening visit to fascist Italy in 1937, his experiences with the Federal Writers Project, and his work with interned "enemy aliens" during World War II.

Mangione's Italian roots remained strong. He described a postwar visit to his relatives and his search for the "Sicilian soul" in *Reunion in Sicily,* a humorous and candid book that is part travel book, part political report, and part memoir. In 1965 he returned to Italy to visit Danilo Dolci, the social reformer who was called "the Gandhi of Sicily." After spending six months with Dolci, Mangione wrote *A Passion for Sicilians: The World Around Danilo Dolci,* a book Luigi Barzini judged "readable, accurate and reliable" as a report on Dolci, and other reviewers admired for its skillful writing. "I have learned much from it," Kay Boyle commented. "Its simplicity, its untroubled respect for truth could serve as a model for some time to come for the particular kind of writing problem with which Jerre Mangione was faced."

Mangione's American self has found its expression in his detailed and authoritative history of the Federal Writers Project (1935–1943), *The Dream and the Deal.* A "personal public history," as Daniel Aaron described it in *American History* (June 1973), the book reflects the author's own experiences and observations. Controversial, target of political sniping, and victim of its own inefficiency and internal squabbles, the project nevertheless provided desperately needed work for writers (among them Saul Bellow, Ralph Ellison, Richard Wright, and John Cheever) and produced many important books, including collections of folklore, archives of American social history, and regional and state guides that, periodically updated, remain definitive. Even in this heavily documented study Mangione retained his lively anecdotal style and produced a book that, Aaron writes, "looks behind the bare statistics and figures out the 'arithmetic' of human costs and dividends."

Professor (now emeritus) of English at the University of Pennsylvania, Mangione has received Fulbright, Guggenheim, and NEH fellowships. In 1971 the Italian government named him *Commendatore* and in 1982 the Italian Historical Association gave him a special award for "distinguished service to the Italian-American community." Since 1981 he has been engaged in a large-scale study of the Italian-American experience following the great migration that began in 1880, surveying its historical, sociological, cultural, and economic developments over the next century.

Mangione has been described as "a lithe, elegant man whose fine nose, high forehead and almond-shaped eyes and sometimes knowing quiet smile give credence to the theory that Etruscans once made up Sicilian civilization. In 1957 he married Patricia Anthony, a painter. They live in Philadelphia.

PRINCIPAL WORKS: Mount Allegro, 1943; Reunion in Sicily, 1950; A Passion for Sicilians: The World Around Danilo Dolci, 1968; America Is Also Italian, 1969; The Dream and the Deal: The Federal Writers Project, 1934–1943, 1972; Mussolini's March on Rome, 1975; An Ethnic at Large, 1978. *Fiction*—The Ship and the Flame, 1948; Night Search, 1965; Life Sentences for Everybody (fables), 1966.

ABOUT: Contemporary Authors, revised series 15–16, 1975; Current Biography 1943; Who's Who in America, 1982. *Periodicals*—Il Caffe July–August 1982; Italian Americana 7 (Fall/Winter 1981); New York Times Book Review August 6, 1978; Today (Philadelphia Inquirer) April 15, 1973, January 26, 1975; Upstate New York (Rochester Democrat and Chronicle) March 4, 1973.

*MAO DUN** (also rendered as **Mao Tun,** pseudonym of **Shen Yan-bing,** formerly **Shen Yen-ping**) (July 4, 1896–March 27, 1981), Chinese novelist, social and literary critic, editor, translator, and Communist bureaucrat, was born in Tongxiang, Zhejiang Province, into an upper-class family. Both he and his brother were encouraged by their father to study Western technology, but like many young people of the time, their interests were in social science and literature. While his brother Shen Zemin later became an important member of the Communist Party, Shen Yan-bing emerged as a major writer whose prestige in the intellectual circles was such that he was made Minister of Culture in his later years.

After attending middle school in Hangzhou and Nanjing, Shen went to Beijing (Peking) at the age of seventeen to attend classes at Beida (Peking University). He did not graduate. After three years in college he was compelled for financial reasons to return south to Shanghai to work at the Commercial Press, then China's largest publisher, as a proofreader. The job afforded him opportunities for learning, and he soon developed an interest in literature and foreign languages. His writings and translations began to appear in *Xuesheng Zazhi* (Student Magazine) and before long he was promoted to editor at the Commercial Press.

By the time he was twenty-four, already a well-known author, he had become acquainted

with young writers of the May Fourth movement. Together with such writers as Zhou Zuoren, Zheng Zhenduo, Ye Shengtao, Xu Dishan, and a few others, he founded Wenxue Yanjiu Hui (Society for the Study of Literature), which was to become one of the two most influential forces in the development of modern Chinese literature, the other being Chuanzao She (the Creation Society), headed by Guo Moruo. The focal point of the rivalry between the two may be summarized as a debate on the purpose of literature: whereas the former advocated "literature for life's sake," the latter believed in "literature for art's sake."

Soon after, Wenxue Yanjiu Hui succeeded in taking control of *Xiaoshuo Yuebao* (Story Monthly), published by the Commercial Press, and transformed a popular fiction magazine into a journal of serious literature with Shen as its editor. Launched in a new format in January 1921, it exerted great influence in shaping the future of Chinese literature. It was through this magazine that foreign authors such as Tolstoy, Chekhov, Balzac, Flaubert, Zola, Byron, Keats and Shaw were introduced to Chinese readers. In fact, Shen's enthusiasm for Western literature was such that he was later to found the magazine *Yiwen* (Translated Literature) with Lu Xun (Lu Hsün) in 1934.

In 1923, Shen relinquished the editorship of *Xiaoshuo Yuebao* to become more active in politics. It is not clear exactly when he joined the Party, but in this year he was elected a member of the executive committee of the plenary session of the Communist Party, Shanghai branch. He also taught at Shanghai College, a training ground for Marxists, where he made friends with Chen Duxiu, founder of the Chinese Communist Party.

He left Shanghai for Guangzhou (Canton) in 1926 under the Party's instruction to participate in the work of the propaganda department of the Guomindang (Nationalist Party) in the spirit of cooperation of the two parties for the success of the Northern Expedition. He followed the victorious National Revolutionary Army to Wuhan and was appointed editor-in-chief of *Minguo Ribao* (National Daily), an official organ, but he soon became disillusioned with Chiang Kai-shek's leadership and broke with the Guomindang. His disappointment with his experience in the national revolution resulted in three novellas: *Huanmie* (Disillusionment), *Dongyao* (Vacillation), *Zhaiqiu* (Pursuit), which were serialized in *Xiaoshuo Yuebao* starting in 1927 and were published as a trilogy under the title *Shi* (Eclipse). The trilogy attracted a great many readers, especially among the young and

°mou doon

the educated, but was attacked by both the leftist writers and members of the Creation Society as "antiproletarian," "unwarrantedly pessi-0D mistic." It also marked the first time he used the pen-name Mao Dun (which means "contradiction"). His reputation as a revolutionary writer was restored, however, by the publication of his second novel *Hong* (Rainbow), in 1930, a fictional account of students' involvement in the May Fourth and May Thirtieth patriotic movements.

After a two-year stay in Tokyo he returned to Shanghai in 1930 to be active again in politics. Together with Lu Xun, Qu Qiubai and other writers he founded the League of Left-Wing Writers, a Communist-front organization that was to last till 1936 when it was dissolved after a quarrel had developed among writers over two slogans responding to Japanese aggression. Zhou Yang, representing the Party, favored "Literature for National Defense," whereas Lu Xun, as leader of a group of free-spirited writers, advocated the "People's Literature for National Revolutionary War." Mao Dun sided with Lu Xun in the end. The quarrel was soon forgotten, however, in the interest of unity. The few years immediately before this episode had been Mao Dun's most productive period. Well-known stories such as "Spring Silkworms," "Autumn in Guling," "The Lin Family Shop" were all written then. But it was his third novel *Ziye* (*Midnight*), published in 1933, that firmly assured his place in modern Chinese literature. *Ziye* is an impressive study of the complex life of Shanghai's business world, detailing the ups and downs of an enlightened capitalist who is caught in the struggle between his patriotism and his distaste for Communist-led strikes.

The year 1936 also saw another achievement of Mao Dun's: the editing and publishing of the anthology *Zhongguo di Yir* (One Day in China), a collection of 469 autobiographical pieces written by people from all walks of life recording their experience on one particular day, May 21, 1936. Not a few young contributors were thus inspired to pursue careers in writing.

After the Sino-Japanese War broke out in the summer of 1937, Mao Dun in the next few years traveled to many places, including Wuhan, where he started the magazine *Wenyi Zhendi* (The Literary Front); Hong Kong, where he edited the literary page of the newspaper *Libao*; Xinjiang, where he served as a dean at Xinjiang University; and Yanan, where he lectured at the Lu Xun Institute of the Arts. He settled in 1942 in Chongqing, China's wartime capital, serving under Guo Moruo, his old adversary, in the government, again in the spirit of cooperation between Nationalist and Communist parties. In 1945, he completed a play, *Qingming Qianhou* (Before and After the Qingming Festival), his only attempt at playwriting and his last major creative effort.

Soon after the war had ended, Mao Dun returned to Shanghai. In 1946, he was invited to visit the Soviet Union with his wife and wrote a favorable report upon his return the next year. He again went to Hong Kong in 1948, where he started *Xiaoshuo Yuekan* (Fiction Monthly), and when liberation came in 1949, he found himself in Peking attending the All-China Congress of Writers and Artists with many other leftist writers. An All-China Federation of Literary and Art Workers was born out of this conference with Guo Moruo as its chairman and Mao Dun vice-chairman. Having reached the top of the literary hierarchy in the Communist bureaucracy, he became head of the Writers' Union the next year. Loaded down with bureaucratic chores, by then he had ceased to function as a creative writer. Soon afterwards, he was appointed Minister of Culture by Chairman Mao.

Despite his official duties, Mao Dun continued his involvement with literary affairs. He was the founding editor of *Renmin Wenxue* (People's Literature), China's most important literary journal in 1951, and of the new *Yiwen* (Translated Literature) in 1953. In 1951 he also started the monthly *Chinese Literature*. Although its editor-in-chief in name only, he lent his prestige to the only literary journal read regularly by Western readers. He had thus achieved two goals in his career as a writer-translator: to introduce Western literature to Chinese readers, and to introduce Chinese literature to Western readers. During Mao Zedong's anti-Rightist campaign in 1957, shortly after the "100 flowers bloom" period, he was criticized for his outspokenness. In 1964, he was dismissed as Minister of Culture in connection with ideological attacks leveled against the film "The Lin Family Shop" which was based on his story. As its author, Mao Dun was accused of showing undue sympathy for a petty bourgeois shop-owner. He, however, survived the Cultural Revolution without suffering the personal indignities inflicted on other writers such as Ba Jin and Lao She.

Mao Dun died an honored man, carrying with him many official titles. Perhaps the greatest honor bestowed on him in his retirement was a request to write his memoirs, which were subsequently serialized in the Party publication, the quarterly *Xinwenxue Shiliao* (Historical Materials on New Literature). Since its inception in 1978, every issue of *Xinwenxue Shiliao* has carried a detailed chapter of Mao Dun's literary (and political) life. Unfortunately he did not finish the memoirs before his death.

WORKS IN ENGLISH TRANSLATION: Mao Dun's novel *Midnight* was translated into English by Hsu Menghsuing in 1957; Sidney Shapiro translated *Spring Silkworms and Other Stories* in 1956.

ABOUT: Biographic Dictionary of Chinese Communism, 1921–1965, 1971; Biographical Dictionary of Republican China, 1981; Cassell's Encyclopedia of World Literature, 1973; Dictionary of Oriental Literature I, 1974; Gálik, M. Mao Tun and Modern Chinese Criticism, 1969; Goldman, M. (ed.) Modern Chinese Literature in the May Fourth Era, 1977; Hsia, C. T. A History of Modern Chinese Fiction, 1971; Lai, M. A History of Chinese Literature, 1964; Prusek, J. Three Sketches of Chinese Literature, 1969; Yang, W. and N. K. Mao, Modern Chinese Fiction, 1981. *Periodicals*—Chinese Literature 2, 1979; 3, 1979; Chinese Quarterly 19, 1964; 20, 1964; Literature East and West 12, 1968; Review of National Literatures 4, 1975.

MAO TUN See MAO DUN

*MARECHAL, LEOPOLDO (June 11, 1900–June 26, 1970), Argentine poet, novelist, and dramatist, was born in Buenos Aires, the son of Alberto Marechal and the former Lorenza Beloqui. Marechal's father was a mechanic and the poet grew up in working class surroundings. After graduating from the Escuela Normal de Profesores "Mariano Austa" in Buenos Aires in 1922, Marechal embarked on a teaching career that was to last most of his adult life. In the same year he published his first book of poems, *Los Aguiluchos* (The Eaglets), an immature effort that he later described as a part of his literary "prehistory."

The 1920s was a decade of intense literary activity in Argentina and two magazines, *Proa* and *Martin Fierro*, were in the forefront. Marechal was soon publishing and editing in both reviews and he became a leading member (another was Jorge Luis Borges) of the "Martinfierrismo" and "ultraismo" movements. Both groups sought to rejuvenate Argentine literature by replacing outmoded realism with techniques and attitudes borrowed from European modernism. The outcome of Marechal's involvement with the avantgarde was his first important book, *Días como flechas* (Days Like Arrows, 1926).

In an interview in the Argentine magazine *Mundo Nuevo* in 1967, Marechal said that *Días como flechas* was written in the heat of battle, and the metaphoric abundance of these poems has a polemical edge (the *ultraístas* advocated

the centrality of metaphor in all lyric poetry). Despite the youthful aggressiveness of the style, Marechal's thematic concerns are mature and amply conceived. A critic in another Argentine magazine, *Sur*, wrote that in the poems of *Días como flechas*, "the images most clearly linked to the senses contain a transcendency within themselves. They are either united by a glorification of the spirit or intertwined by an anguish that gives voice to the eternal fears of the human soul in the face of the growing indifference of the world and of life."

In the poetry that followed *Días como flechas* Marechal moved away from his heavy reliance on metaphor to more controlled and traditional verse forms. *Odas para el hombre y la mujer* (Odes for Man and Woman, 1929) is a transitional work that earned Marechal the first municipal poetry prize in Buenos Aires. His next book, *Laberinto de amor* (Labyrinth of Love, 1936), completed the transition; it is a long poem in paired alexandrines dealing with the conflict between divine and human love.

In 1937 Marechal published what is generally considered his finest work in verse, *Cinco poemas australes* (Five Southern Poems). This book, writes F. Díez Rejón, "leaves things and their beauty aside and converts itself into a work of controlled ardor and movement, a rhetorical wisdom which does not disfigure the lyrical content. The five poems form a special elegy where the recovery of the time of childhood defines places and men. Spiritual realities are situated in the real world that surrounds us." In "Gravatación de Cielo" (Heaven's Gravity), the poet describes a lost state of grace that is in the background of much of his work:

I recall an age hidden among flowers:
it has left on my tongue a deep
   taste of paradise.

Marechal won the Buenos Aires poetry prize again for his two following collections, *El Centauro* (The Centaur, 1940) and *Sonetos a Sophia* (Sonnets to Sophia, 1940). These books continued his exploration of traditional themes in traditional stanzas and meters.

By the 1930s Marechal's poetry had taken a markedly theocentric turn. This was the result of a spiritual crisis that he underwent after returning from his second trip to Europe in 1929. On his first trip in 1926 Marechal had mainly contented himself with the bohemian life in Paris, but now he began an intensive study of Greek philosophy and the Fathers of the Church. When, back in Buenos Aires, a friend suffered a serious illness, the crisis that had been building in him broke out, and Marechal returned to the strict Roman Catholicism that he had abandoned as a child.

°mä´´ rä skäl´, lä´´ ō pōl´ dō

Marechal began to write prose fiction during this spiritual crisis. In the *Mundo Nuevo* interview he explained how he experienced a need to translate "a series of lived experiences and ontologies that did not appear in current poetic forms, (usually lyrical or subjective), but which formerly figured prominently in traditional poetic forms such as the epic poem (primarily objective). In reality, my leap was not from poetry to the novel, but from the lyric genre to the epic genre, and I made it when I understood that the novel (a very modern genre) is the natural outcome of the epic poem."

The novel that Marechal finally published in 1948 has taken its place, along with others by Miguel Angel Asturias and Alejo Carpentier, as one of the key works of Latin American fiction of the decade. *Adán Buenosayres* (Adam Buenosayres) is a long, difficult, and at times confusing book, but its influence on Julio Cortázar and other writers of the "boom" generation of the sixties has been profound. The narrative follows a young Argentine poet in the 1920s, Adán Buenosayres, as he explores his patronymic city in search of a beloved, in company with three or four intellectual and literary friends. To this meagre plot are added complex authorial techniques which reflect the unstable nature of reality that Marechal sees as a condition of twentieth-century civilization. In the prologue the author, "Leopoldo Marechal," tells of his acquaintance with the now deceased Buenosayres and of his reading of two autobiographical manuscripts by his friend. These manuscripts appear as the last two sections of the novel; the first five sections are Marechal's third-person accounts of Buenosayres, his companions, and their compulsive conversations. Thus, levels of reality and illusion play against each other to create a purposeful uncertainty and ambiguity. Despite his avant-garde style, Marechal was able, as Martin Seymour-Smith put it, to "characterize Buenos Aires more fully than any 'socially aware' writer."

Despite its historical importance, *Adán Buenosayres* received scant critical attention upon its appearance. The reason for this neglect was largely political. In 1945 Marechal had become attracted to the right wing politics of General Juan Domingo Perón, and when Perón won the presidency the following year Marechal was rewarded for his support with various educational and cultural posts in his administration. For this association he was ostracized by the leftist intellectuals of Buenos Aires and the ostracism only became deeper when Perón fell from power in 1955.

It was also during the Perón years that Marechal met and married his second wife, the former Elbia Rosbaco, who was to be the inspiration for much of his later poetry. They met in 1947, shortly after the death of his first wife, and were married three years later. Marechal's greatest tribute to "Elbiamor" is the section called "La Erótica" in his *Heptámeron* (1966):

> Elbialove, they say
> I only sing to women in the form of numbers,
>   that your eulogy is like a babe
> that cannot be born.
>   Leave them to their world, and let them
>   leave us,
> me in the mine of your grace,
>   you in your poet's equator,
> Elbiallsilence
> and elbialovingly unsung.

> ("To Elbialove unsung,"
> trans. Patrick Morgan)

In *Heptámeron,* writes F. Díaz Rejón, "Marechal embraces the great themes of man on which the poetic and the metaphysical have always turned. . . . [The poems are] treated with a disconcerting lyrical audacity and a great intellectual rigor which does not exclude touches of the transcendent humor so characteristic of his works in prose."

In the 1950s Marechal began writing plays, only a handful of which have been performed or published. The first was *Antígona Vélez* in 1951, but perhaps the best-known is *La batalla de José Luna* (The Battle of Jose Luna, 1967). Marechal's dramas are generally less admired than his fiction and poetry, but *La batalla de José Luna,* a comic allegory of the battle between Light and Darkness in a district of Buenos Aires, does demonstrate his ability to translate theological concerns into human dimensions.

Probably the most significant work of Marechal's later years is his novel *El banquete de Severo Arcángelo* (The Banquet of Severo Arcángelo, 1965), for which he won the recently instituted Forti Glori Prize. It was written in the period after the fall of Perón, when Marechal was forced into retirement by the new government and faced proscription by the victorious anti-Peronists. Yet the appearance of the novel, which is shorter and more tightly controlled than his first, restored his fortunes. Once again "Leopoldo Marechal" appears as a minor character who claims to have come into the possession of a manuscript, which in this case comprises the bulk of the novel. The manuscript has been written by one Lisandro Farías, and it tells of his involvement, as a chosen "guest," in the bizzare preparations for a banquet to be given by a rich and mysterious industrialist, Severo Arcángelo, at his estate on the outskirts of Buenos Aires. Echoes of the Last Supper and references to the thirty-three years of Christ (there are thirty-three guests at the banquet and thirty-three chapters in the book) evince the theological and ontological intentions of the novel, but its ultimate meanings are typically elusive. However, it seems clear that Marechal is painting a grim picture of the modern world, where man, according to the interpretation of Kessel Schwartz, "is a self-satisfied victim of mechanization."

Some readers complained that the vigorous, poetic prose of *Adán Buenosayres* was not carried over to *El banquete de Severo Arcángelo*. The same criticism could be made of Marechal's last novel, *Megafón, o la guerra* (Megafón, or, War, 1970), a much simpler work that describes the rise and fall of a modern Argentine folk hero, warrior, and prophet. Critics have found little reason to subject this novel to the kind of analysis that has been bestowed on *Adán Buenosayres* and *El banquete de Severo Arcángelo,* and it is on those two books and his poetry that Marechal's reputation rests.

WORKS IN ENGLISH TRANSLATION: Selections from Marechal's poetry in English translation are published in Dudley Fitts' *Anthology of Contemporary Latin America Poetry* (1942) and in José Donoso's *Tri-Quarterly Anthology of Contemporary Latin American Literature* (1969).

ABOUT: Andres, A. (ed.) Palabras con Leopoldo Marechal, 1968; Armiño, M. (ed.) Parnaso: diccionario de la literatura 1, 1972; Brushwood, J. S. The Spanish American Novel, 1975; Encyclopedia of World Literature in the 20th Century 4, 1975; Foster, D. W. (ed.) Modern Latin American Literature 2, 1975; Guillermo, E. Quince novelas hispanoamericanos, 1971; Schwartz, K. A New History of Spanish American Fiction 2, 1971; Seymour-Smith, M. Guide to World Literature 3, rev. ed., 1975; Squirru, R. Leopoldo Marechal, 1961; *Periodicals*—Sur July 1939; Mundo Nuevo no. 18, 1967.

*MARQUES, RENE (October 4, 1919–March 22, 1979), Puerto Rican playwright, short story writer, and essayist, was born in Arecibo, on the northern coast of Puerto Rico. Although his parents were also born there, his grandparents had emigrated from Mallorca and the Canary Islands. They were farmers, and Marqués spent his early years in their home. This agrarian background influenced his personality and writing. Another influence, that of the poet Doña Padrina Padilla de Sanz, a relative whose home was a meeting place for writers and artists, nurtured his passion for Puerto Rican independence.

He attended the College of Agriculture and Mechanical Arts in Mayagüez, received his agronomy degree in 1942 (when he married Serena Valesco, whom he divorced fifteen years later), and worked for the Department of Agri-

culture for two years. Marqués' interest in literature, however, prevailed. His first work, *Peregrinación,* a collection of poems, was published in 1944.

In 1946 he went to Spain to familiarize himself with the contemporary Spanish theater and to study literature at the University of Madrid. Influenced by the philosophy of Miguel de Unamuno, he also wrote his first plays there: *El hombre y sus sueños* (Man and His Dreams, 1946, published two years later in *Asomante*) and *El sol y los Mac Donald* (The Sun and the MacDonalds, 1947). In 1947 he returned to Puerto Rico. Supporting himself by working for his father-in-law, he began his literary career with reviews and criticisms for *El mundo* and *Asomante*. Also in 1947 he founded and directed Pro Arte de Arecibo, and soon began to write regularly for the *Diario de Puerto Rico.*

Awarded a Rockefeller Foundation grant, Marqués came to New York for a year in 1949 to study playwriting at Erwin Piscator's Dramatic Workshop, and at Columbia University. It was for a university course that he wrote his only play in English, *Palm Sunday* (1949), a dramatization of the Easter 1937 Ponce massacre.

On returning to Puerto Rico in 1950, he worked for the Department of Education, becoming the director of the editorial unit of its Division of Community Education. Aside from affording him scope to pursue his literary interests, this work gave him experience in filmmaking. Other activities of this period include his founding of the Experimental Theater of the Ateneo (1951), which he directed for the next three years while serving as secretary of the Puerto Rican Ateneo board of directors, and his founding of the Book Club of Puerto Rico (1959, with Eliezer Curet Cuevas).

But as the large volume of fiction and drama he produced in those years suggests, Marqués spent much of his time writing: *Juan Bobo y la Dama de Occidente* (Juan Bobo and the Lady of the Occident, 1955), *Otro día nuestro* (Another Day of Ours, 1955), *La muerte no entrará en palacio* (Death Shall Not Enter the Palace, 1956), *La víspera del hombre* (The Eve of Manhood, 1957), *Los soles truncos* (Maimed Suns, 1958), *Un niño azul para esa sombra* (A Blue Child for that Shadow, 1958), and *Cuentos puertorriqueños de hoy* (Modern Puerto Rican Short Stories, 1959).

Almost all of these deal with rural subjects, and they reflect the interests, articulated in Marqués' many essays, that were to preoccupy him throughout his life. Foremost among these are nationalism and a love for the land. He was a passionate advocate of Puerto Rican sovereignty: atypically, the characters in *Palm Sunday* are two-dimensional, villains and heroes, here dramatizing Marqués' anti-American bias. Another recurrent theme in his drama and fiction is that of guilt and self-destruction: in *El sol y los Mac Donald,* another early play, it is flagrantly portrayed in the incestuous feelings of Gustavo for his sister and in the relationship of Ramiro and his mother.

Marqués' pervasive agrarian sympathy is expressed in all his writings. It is explicitly dramatized in the best-known and probably the best of his plays, *La caretta* (*The Oxcart,* 1951), a tragedy about an old *jíbaro* (peasant) and three generations of his family. With much local color as well as pathos and humor, it portrays the gradual loss of their dreams after uprooting themselves from the land to move, first to San Juan and then to the Bronx. Alienating themselves from their heritage, they yearn for urban materialism. "Of course, it'd be easier up there," Luis says, thinking of New York. "They say there's plenty o' work. They pay good. An' the poor man's as good as the rich." Their dreams are quickly shattered amidst the horrors of city slum life. The irony of the family's alienation is underlined as Luis is told, after repeated unemployment when he finally finds a job as a gardener: "You came to the city to get away from the land. And now the land helps you out right here in the city."

The Oxcart was the first modern Puerto Rican drama produced in Europe (as it was in mobile outdoor productions in New York). Marqués attended its premiere at the National Theater María Guerrero in Madrid in 1957. That year he also traveled to Palma de Mallorca to meet his father's family, and then he went to New York. There, with the help of a Guggenheim award that had been granted him in 1954, he spent much of the year writing his first novel, *La Víspera del Hombre,* whose protagonist, Pirulo, is an adolescent from the Canary Island mountains who leaves home to make his way in Arecibo. The novel symbolically portrays the emergence of Puerto Rico into maturity and national sovereignty.

Though Marqués was to return to writing novels, he was more successful with his short stories. The six published as *Otro día nuestro* (Another One of Our Days, 1955), like his other stories, are characterized by skillful narrative. Unified by the emotion of nationalism, they are sharply focused, incidents are dextrously arranged, and a single atmosphere pervades each story—skills honed in the theatrical works that constitute the major part of Marqués' writings.

Marqués' drama is characterized by his use of modern theatrical techniques as well as realistic dialect and slang. This is especially true in later plays, such as *La muerte no entrará en palacio* and *Un niño azul para esa sombra.* Although these are nationalistic protests, they transcend the oversimplified portrayals of propaganda and present tragic human conflicts. Donald Shaw wrote of *La muerte no entrará en palacio*: "Marqués, with great technical resourcefulness, strives to conciliate belief in his duty as a 'committed' writer with pressure from his artistic conscience to aim at a work in one of the highest universal categories." Elsewhere, as in *La casa sin reloj* (The House Without a Clock, 1961), Marqués dramatizes nationalistic views in a humorous vein. In *Los soles truncos,* a Chekhovian tragedy about three elderly sisters, atmosphere is sustained by folklore and classical music, and symbolism is heightened by lighting effects. This play, a dramatization of one of Marqués' own short stories, was his contribution to the first Festival of Puerto Rican Theater (1958).

Most of his last works are dramatic. In 1965 he wrote *Mariana o el alba* (Mariana or the Dawn), which received its premiere at the Eighth Puerto Rican Theater Festival in San Juan that year. His *Sacrificio en el Monte Moriah* (Sacrifice on Mount Moriah, 1969) was first performed at the Puerto Rican Theater Festival in 1970. That year he also wrote the two plays *David y Jonatán* and *Tito y Berenice.* In 1971 appeared his oratorio, *Via crucis del hombre puertorriqueño.* He also published two collection of essays in these years, *Ensayos 1953-1966* (1966) and *Ensayos 1953-1971* (1971). His second novel, *La mirada* (The View), and a third collection of short stories, *Inmersos en el silencio* (Immersed in Silence), were published in 1976.

René Marqués died of a liver ailment in San Juan on March 22, 1979.

WORKS IN ENGLISH TRANSLATION: Marqués' tragedy *La caretta* was translated as *The Oxcart* by Charles R. Pilditch in 1969.

ABOUT: Encyclopedia of World Literature in the 20th Century (rev. ed.) III, 1983; Foster, D. W. and Foster, V. R. (eds.), Modern Latin American Literature, 1975; Martin, E. J. René Marqués, 1979; Pilditch, C. R. A Study of the Literary Works of René Marqués from 1948 to 1962, 1966. *Periodicals*—Symposium Spring 1964.

*MARSE, JUAN (January 8, 1933–   ), Spanish novelist, was born Juan Fonseca and was immediately adopted by the Marsé family, his mother having died at his birth. His early years were spent between Barcelona and two towns of the nearby province of Tarragona: Sant Jaume

°mär sä´, hwän

JUAN MARSE

del Domenys and Arboç del Penedés. His schooling was minimal, as he tells us himself: "I was a
poor student and at the age of thirteen, with my
father in prison, [for political activities], I left
school (in which I had learned nothing) and began an apprenticeship in a jewelry workshop in
the Gracia neighborhood, where I lived (and
where I have returned to live today)." By the late
1950s he was writing short stories and in 1961
published his first novel, *Encerrados con un solo
juguete* (Locked in with a Single Toy). As a result of these publications the young author found
his way into the literary circles of Barcelona, establishing friendships with other emerging writers such as Manuel Vázquez Montalbán and Luis
Goytisolo. At the same time the publication of
his first novel brought him into contact with the
major figures of the Catalan literary world: Carlos Barral, José María Castellet, Jaime Gil de
Biedma, and Gabriel Ferrater.

Soon afterward Marsé left Barcelona for Paris,
going into a self-imposed cultural exile common
among artists and writers of the fifties and sixties. There he continued to meet and be influenced by established figures of Spanish
intellectual life: Juan Goytisolo, Antonio Saura,
Manuel Tuñón de Lara, Jorge Semprún, among
others. Marsé worked in the laboratories of the
Pasteur Institute, specifically in the department
of cellular biochemistry of the Nobel Prize winner Dr. Jacques Monod. From this job he moved
on to work in film production, where he formed
his friendship with Roberto Bodegas, today a
well-known director. This second employment
influenced Marsé's future more than his work in
science, and he has since been involved in film

writing, most recently in the script for the adaptation of his own novel, *Ultimas tardes con
Teresa* (The Last Evenings with Teresa).

Throughout the 1960s Marsé continued to
write and find ways to support himself (continuing in the film world and also taking on a job as
a publicity agent) until 1970, when he began to
earn his living solely as a novelist and journalist.
His novels, seven to date, have been very much
in the mainstream of the evolution of Castilian
prose. Marsé has never written in Catalan; and
though his works always deal with the Catalan
world, and though he feels the influence of certain Catalan writers (the novelist Josep Pla is the
most notable example), his modes of expression
and style are much more in line with the Castilian peninsular-oriented literature than with the
more European tradition of modern Catalan
narrative.

In 1965, with his third novel, *Ultimas tardes
con Teresa*, Marsé won the nation's most coveted
narrative prize, the *Premio Biblioteca Breve* (he
had already been the highest vote-getter for this
prize with his first novel in 1960, but he did not
receive a majority and therefore no prize was
given that year). *Ultimas tardes . . .* is of major
importance for Marsé's literary growth and also
for the evolution of the Spanish novel in general,
for it is one of the first works to follow the new
subjectivist direction established by Luis Martín
Santos with *Tiempo de Silencio* (Time of Silence) in 1962. (Martín Santos, generally considered the finest literary mind of post-war Spain,
died in 1964.) The Peruvian novelist Mario Var-
gas Llosa termed *Ultimas tardes . . .* "a sarcastic explosion in the Spanish modern novel," and
in this explosion the reader finds the creation of
a fine-tuned irony that was to become Marsé's
trademark in this novel and its sequel, *La oscura
historia de la prima Montse* (The Obscure Story
of Cousin Montse, 1970). These two novels depict and deride the class structure which is so evident in everyday Barcelona life, with its accent
on material wealth and Catalan/non-Catalan origins. And within the highly ironic context of the
novels' approach, Marsé created two sets of characters who are among the most memorable in
contemporary fiction: the upper class Teresa and
Montse and their less wealthy male counterparts,
Manolo and Paco. Manolo is actually the sexual
partner for both female protagonists, reappearing in the second novel, but the character/
narrator Paco J. Bodegas is also a major creation
in Marsé's narrative evolution. In these two
works nothing is sacred as Marsé attacks the political and social hypocrisy of all members of the
society he lives in. Only Montse, the protagonist
of *La oscura historia . . .* , is saved from his irony, and perhaps her suicide represents the fail-

ure of truly disinterested altruistic activity in the modern world.

In 1973 Marsé won the International Novel Prize of Mexico with *Si te dicen que caí* (translated as *The Fallen*), by far his most powerful work. The title is an ironic usage of a line from the Falangist Hymn "Cara al sol" and the work, which narrates the tragic and picaresque events which immediately followed the Civil War, is a radical departure from the ironic and sarcastic critiques of contemporary bourgeois Catalan society which had been the focal point of his previous novels. After three years of battling with censorship, *Si te dicen que caí* was finally published in Spain and immediately became the nation's number one best seller. This success was due not so much to the vivid thematic presentation as to the radically new novelistic structure of the work, a series of narrations within narrations and imaginative sequences which made for a difficult but fascinating literary presentation.

Marsé won another prestigious prize in 1978, the *Planeta*, for his curious novel *La muchacha de las bragas de oro* (translated as *Golden Girl*). This work, often misunderstood, constitutes a kind of literary aside, and is doubly experimental. It is an attempt at a Jamesian creation of author/narrator/reader reality play, and at the same time is a burlesque of the memoirs of one of Spain's leading "Falangist turned liberals," Pedro Laín Entralgo. Those who are unaware of the intentions, stylistic or thematic, of the work are skeptical of its literary value, but more studied critical approaches are slowly placing the novel in its correct perspective. This novel, as in the case of *La oscura historia . . .* and *Ultimas tardes . . .* , was later adapted for the screen.

Un día volveré (One Day I Will Return), published in 1982, is a return to the confused and violent world of the earlier post-war period. Though the action takes place in the late 1950s it is based on earlier historical and emotional constructs. Perhaps what is most interesting in this novel, and in all of Marsé's novels for that matter, is the constant reappearance of all types of literary phenomena from previous works. The constant intertextual play among Marsé's various novels creates a solid continuous narrative which flows from 1957 to the present. At times this intertextuality is thematic, at times stylistic, but it is a basic factor in the constant evolution of the author's prose creation and is achieved without isolating him from his public. Though there exists a constant return to the self as previous author in his works there is, at the same time, a constant and evolutionary reflection upon the society, literary and nonliterary, in which the author lives.

WORKS IN ENGLISH TRANSLATION: Helen R. Lane has translated two of Marsé's novels—*The Fallen,* 1979, and *Golden Girl,* 1981.

ABOUT: Columbia Dictionary of Modern European Lterature, 1980; (in Spanish) Sherzer, W. M. Juan Marsé, 1982. *Periodicals*—Journal of Spanish Studies: Twentieth Century 3, 1975; Modern Language Notes 95, 1980; New York Times September 8, 1981.

MARTY, MARTIN E(MIL) (February 5, 1928–   ), American theologian and historian writes: "Childhood in a small Nebraska town where people were either of my kind, Lutheran, or their kind, Catholic—with blacks and Jews ninety miles away in Omaha—provided a mental landscape that has never left me. It also helped create a cocoon around those of us who lived there, snugly and sometimes smugly. Our practices and our truths sufficed, and were unchallenged.

"I have chosen to live my adult years in metropolitan settings, chiefly in Chicago. The chaos of its business and politics finds little ordering for a religious scholar in a secular pluralist school like the University of Chicago, where I follow my vocation. It delights me to know that never does the fact of ordination to ministry or the ownership of a clerical collar back home give privilege. If anything, it forces one to be more reflective and articulate, not less so. Living between the cocoon and the metropolis has served as a kind of metaphor for the intellectual problem, and the political one, too, that has most interested me: integrity of faith and pluralism. I have been repelled by civil people who are not committed and committed people who are not civil. Yet the historian finds few models of groups, be they national or religious, who learned how to hold to what they believed and also to have an empathic understanding of others. Call it the problem of the One and the Many, in theology and in public philosophy; it is my favorite theme.

"Of course, in the modern world of writing and scholarship one has to step back further and argue the case for religion itself. This seems bizarre. Over eighty percent of the people in the world are listed in the encyclopedias as being in religious camps. More people kill others over religio-cultural tribalism than anything else these days. Many of the most tense issues in our society are determined by religion. Yet in the academic and literary worlds many underestimate the power of faith, perhaps because so few of us regard ourselves as having it or recognizing it when we see it. I have found that over cocktails or in committee it is very easy to move conversa-

MARTIN E. MARTY

tion from apathy about religion to disdain for it to sudden animation: things spiritual easily become preoccupying.

"The vocation to which I refer combines teaching, editing, and lecturing. The heart of my calendar and calling is in the graduate seminar classroom where through the years well over fifty students and I have explored the meanings of 'modern'—my title is professor of the history of modern Christianity. I grow from what they find. At the same time, since 1965, I have been book review editor and columnist for *The Christian Century,* another ecumenical and pluralist crossroad. Lecturing has taken me to over 500 campuses. This has given me an unparalleled chance, for an historian, to get to archives, to see traditions in action.

"The themes of my books have ranged from the intimate to the vast. Some of them give evidence that I have been a minister, have sat with people at three A.M. when the candle is low and life is going. Others find me pursuing specialties about religious history. What determines the choice of topic? A game I play. I am trying to go through life never having written an unsolicited article or book. Gifted editors and publishers who know something of my scope ask for a book, article, or lecture on a subject. This forces me always to study something fresh. It has greatly enlarged my repository of options and themes. My religious commitment, which is Christian, is not of a sort that leads me back to the cocoon or to tribalism. It is of the expansive sort, which wants to see grace bounced into a fallen world, suffusing it with at least a pale light. At the same time, if one goes deep enough into 'exclusive' Chris-

tianity one comes to the 'universal' point at which in many respects we reach motifs of a common humanity.

"I have to mention the influence of a strong family life. My first wife and I enjoyed extended family, with permanent and temporary foster children added to our own four. Her death by cancer left me more porous to human suffering and, I hope, more sympathetic. A second marriage is also a sign of 'new creation,' as Christians call it.

"For the future? I project a four-volume work on Modern American Religion, interspersed with some shorter projects. What they are about depends upon what the editors ask for, and how the Spirit moves."

———

Martin E. Marty was born in West Point, Nebraska, the son of Emil A. Marty, an elementary school principal, and the former Anne Louise Wuerdemann. From the age of four he was aware of a vocation to the Lutheran ministry; he attended Concordia High School and Concordia Junior College in Milwaukee, then Concordia Seminary in St. Louis, where he edited the *Seminarian* and from which he took his B.A. in theology and church history in 1949 and his B.D. in 1952. His master's degree in sacred theology (S.T.M.) was conferred by the Lutheran School of Theology in Chicago (1954) and his Ph.D. in intellectual and religious history, by the University of Chicago (1956). His doctoral thesis was published in 1961 as *The Infidel: Freethought and American Religion.*

Marty's active career in the ministry extended from 1950 to 1963. He served in churches in the Washington, D.C., area and in the Chicago area, and was the founding pastor in 1957 of the Church of the Holy Spirit in Elk Grove, Illinois. He was also from 1956 an increasingly prolific religious journalist and commentator and a contributor to dozens of publications, especially the liberal weekly *Christian Century,* of which he has been associate editor since 1958. He has also been widely published in Catholic and secular magazines, and for a time was a member of the board of directors of the weekly *National Catholic Reporter.* He resigned his pastorate in 1963 on assuming a professorship of the history of modern Christianity at the University of Chicago Divinity School. Since 1978 he has held the Fairfax M. Cone Distinguished Service chair.

Marty's reputation as a defender of ecumenical values rests as much on his two dozen major books as on his writing for periodicals. His first two books are still considered to be among his best. *A Short History of Christianity* traces the continuing tension through the ages between the ideal and the reality of the faith. It was welcomed by W. S. Hudson as "thought-provoking" and "a means of introducing a growing group of earnest inquirers to the life of the church"; and G. R. Kelly wrote that Marty's "vigorous, witty style completes the intended appeal for the general reader without sacrificing depth." *The New Shape of American Religion* is, according to the author's preface, "a call for a cultural ethic for American Protestantism" which includes "an analysis of the new shape of American religion against the background of the past" and suggests "resources and strategy for reshaping Protestantism in a new cultural situation." T. B. Douglass called the book "pungent and provocative" and "of first-rank importance for American Protestants." Gabrial Vahanian felt that Marty's "proposals generally consist of a return to the sources—Biblical faith and classical Protestantism. Concretely, they center in the necessity of a theological renascence which, for the sake of our present world, would clarify the Biblical meaning of God, man and community."

Varieties of Unbelief marked Marty's transition from religious journalist to historian of religion. The book, which evolved from the 1963 Walter Rauschenbusch lectures at the Colgate-Rochester Divinity School, attempts to discuss and distinguish among the various kinds of secular, syncretistic, and institutional unbelief and to show how pervasive unbelief is in contemporary everyday life. K. L. Woodward thought it a "comprehensive, complex and demanding study," and Thomas Merton remarked that it "quietly and devastatingly makes a few really dreadful points about American religion—but Dr. Marty never departs from that tolerance and openness which, though they may seem to permit a certain religious and moral inauthenticity among us, remain nevertheless a genuine source of hope for . . . rational dialogue."

A more historical approach to understanding American religion characterized Marty's next two major books. *The Modern Schism: Three Paths to the Secular* argues that the secularizing trend that began early in the nineteenth century in Britain, America, and Western Europe can be best understood as schism and that each of those areas exhibits a recognizably secularistic, schismatic style. *Religious Empire: The Protestant Experience in America*, which won the National Book Award for philosophy and religion, traces the "tragic" influence on U.S. history of the early settlers, mostly white Anglo-Saxon Protestants, and their self-proclaimed divine mission to create an empire.

Protestantism and *A Nation of Behavers*, on the other hand, are more like sociological surveys of the often strange terrain of modern U.S. religious life. The former book, attempting to do justice to the diversity of American Protestantism, identifies adherents by geographical, cultural, ethnic, and economic distribution, describes their worship, and identifies their various contributions to the Protestant American ethos. *A Nation of Behavers* explores all forms of American belief, from the "mainline religions" (Catholicism, Lutheranism, Episcopalianism, Judaism), through Evangelicalism, Fundamentalism, and Pentecostalism, to the various new religions (many Asian in origin), "ethnic religion," and "civil religion." This book encountered a very mixed reception, with one reviewer calling it an "intriguing essay" and another "replete with sociological and theological jargon." D. M. Kelley expressed the opinion the Marty's works in general "are just a little facile, . . . a little 'surfacey.' I sometimes wish he would write half as much and twice as deep." This kind of complaint was not shared by Michael Kamman, reviewing Marty's *Pilgrims in Their Own Land: 500 Years of Religion in America*. Although he regretted the book's failure to confront issues of current religious controversy, Kamman judged the book "the most engaging one-volume history of American religion we now have . . . amazingly thorough, especially in view of its brisk pace."

Among the best received of Marty's more recent works is *The Public Church: Mainline-Evangelical-Catholic,* a study of the development of a new constellation of religious believers in the United States whose distinguishing feature is a refusal to make the old fundamentalist-authoritarian choice, defined by David Hollenbach as "between committed faith and responsible participation in the give and take of a pluralist world." That reviewer called the book "a stimulating, sobering and challenging portrayal of the signs of pain and hope which mark the public face of the American churches in the early 1980s." J. N. Hartt thought it "full of shrewd assessments of the religious situation in contemporary America—particularly when Mr. Marty deals with the flight to private religious experience so characteristic of revivalistic piety and with the growth of 'incivility' in discourse with religious adversaries and in characterizations of them."

Marty's marriage to Elsa Schumacher in 1952 lasted nearly thirty years, ending with her death in 1981. He holds nearly two dozen honorary degrees from various U.S. educational institutions and has been elected a fellow of the American Academy of Arts and Sciences and the Society of American Historians.

PRINCIPAL WORKS: A Short History of Christianity, 1959; The New Shape of American Religion, 1959; The Improper Opinion, 1961; The Infidel, 1961; Baptism, 1962; The Hidden Discipline, 1963; Second Chance for American Protestants, 1963; Church Unity and Church Mission, 1963; Varieties of Unbelief, 1964; (with others) What Do We Believe?, 1968; The Search for a Usable Future, 1969; The Modern Schism, 1969; Righteous Empire, 1970 (National Book Award); Protestantism, 1972; You Are Promise, 1973; The Fire We Can Light, 1973; The Pro and Con Book of Religious America, 1975; A Nation of Behavers, 1976; Religion, Awakening and Revolution, 1976; The Lord's Supper, 1977; Baptism, 1977; The New Shape of American Religion, 1978; (with others) Religion in America, 1950 to the Present, 1979; The Lord's Supper, 1980; Where the Spirit Leads, 1980; Friendship, 1980; The Place of Bonhoeffer, 1981; By Way of Response (autobiography), 1981; The Public Church, 1981; (with Kenneth Vaux) Health/Medicine and the Faith Traditions, 1982; (with William James: 1842–1910) The Varieties of Religious Experience, 1982; (with Martin Luther: 1483–1546) The Place of Trust, 1983; Health and Medicine in the Lutheran Tradition, 1983; (with others) Faith and Ferment, 1983; (with Kathy Lowe) Opening Eyes and Ears, 1983; A Cry of Absence, 1983; The Word, 1983; Pilgrims in Their Own Land: 500 Years of Religion in America, 1984; Being Good and Doing Good, 1984.

ABOUT: Contemporary Authors, first revision series 5–8, 1969; Current Biography, 1968; Who's Who in America, 1982–83; Stewart, John, The Deacon Wore Spats, 1962. Periodicals—America March 7, 1964; January 4, 1969; February 22, 1969; July 22, 1972; October 30, 1976; April 25, 1981; February 5, 1983; October 6, 1984; Catholic World July 1960; Christian Century May 27, 1959; December 30, 1959; July 8, 1964; February 3, 1965; September 10, 1969; November 26, 1969; February 17, 1971; November 15, 1972; January 26, 1977; July 29, 1981; February 22, 1982; February 16–23, 1983; March 2, 1983; August 31– September 7, 1983; August 29–September 5, 1984; September 26, 1984; Commentary May 1969; Commonweal January 8, 1965; March 28, 1969; February 13, 1970; May 27, 1977; January 28, 1983; Criterion Summer 1963; Spring 1967; Journal of Religion July 1960; Journal of the American Academy of Religion March 1984; Library Journal April 15, 1959; October 15, 1964; October 1, 1970; October 1, 1971; June 1, 1972; December 15, 1976; May 15, 1981; Nation April 16, 1960; New York Herald Tribune Book Review July 12, 1959; New York Review of Books October 28, 1976; New York Times Book Review March 15, 1970; March 14, 1971; April 19, 1981; June 17, 1984; People Weekly November 14, 1983; Saturday Review January 4, 1969; May 10, 1969; February 6, 1971; January 1, 1972; Theological Studies March 1984.

MASSIE, ROBERT K(INLOCH) (January 5, 1929–   ), American biographer and memoirist, was born in Lexington, Kentucky, the son of Robert Kinloch Massie, founder of a boys' school

ROBERT K. MASSIE

near Lexington, and the former Mary Kimball. He studied American history at Yale (B.A., 1950), then modern European history as a Rhodes scholar at Oxford (B.A., 1952). Following service as a lieutenant junior grade in Naval Intelligence after Oxford (1952–55), Massie found work as a journalist, first in 1955 as private secretary to Paul C. Smith, who was trying to resuscitate the Collier's magazine empire, then as research assistant to the magazine's chief writer, Theodore H. White. When Collier's closed down in 1956, Massie got another job almost immediately as a book reviewer on Newsweek where he stayed until 1962. Before becoming a full-time freelance writer in 1965, he also worked on the staffs of USA-1 magazine (1962) and the moribund Saturday Evening Post (1962–65).

In December 1954, Massie married Suzanne Rohrbach, the daughter of a Swiss diplomat, graduate of Vassar, and an employee of Life magazine. Their eldest child and only son, who bears his father's name (they also have two daughters), was diagnosed at the age of five as suffering from classical hemophilia, most likely acquired as a result of spontaneous chromosomal mutation in his mother. The Massie family's struggle to understand the boy's disease is the subject of Journey, a gripping, passionate book jointly written by mother, father, and son. The book comprises both an etiology of "one of the most mysterious and malicious of the genetic chronic diseases" and a series of painful vignettes of family and individual suffering, the latter parts all by Suzanne Massie. Her anger at the medical callousness she encountered over many years pervades the book. She writes of "the sullen anger, the mutinous rage, that grows in the helpless," of how she was continually "seared by the lack of understanding, the lack of compassion—yes, the cruelty—that comes from the rigid and arbitrary rules practiced in some of the best hospitals we have." The authors' preface describes the disease's deep imprint on their lives and poses an arresting question: "For eighteen years hemophilia has dominated our lives. It has molded our relationships with people and our attitude toward the world. . . . We have learned to look directly at illness and to ask ourselves, Who is the more seriously handicapped—the child trying to lead a normal life despite his defects or the physically healthy person who is unable to accept him? In a world whose moral disabilities are far greater than its physical imperfections, the question deserves thought." By the time of the book's publication, young Bob Massie, though not cured of his disease, was in stable enough condition to function successfully as a full-time student at Princeton.

Massie's first article on hemophilia was written for the *Post* in 1963. He prepared a short ancillary historical sketch, which did not in the end appear with the article, on "the most famous hemophiliac of all," the Tsarevich Alexis, heir to the Imperial Russian throne. Massie's interest grew in the fall of the Romanov dynasty, for he soon began work on the book that was to become *Nicholas and Alexandra,* one of the most popular historical studies ever published. The book is not only a succinct, dramatic account of the sweeping historical events that engulfed Russia and its ruling family; it breaks new historical ground by taking a fresh, more informed look at the pivotal drama at the core of the epochal occurrences: that Empress Alexandra, "in an effort to deal with the agonies hemophilia inflicted on her son, . . . turned to Gregory Rasputin, the remarkable Siberian mystagogue. Thereafter, Rasputin's presence near the throne—his influence on the Empress and, through her, on the government of Russia—brought about or at least helped to speed the fall of the dynasty." The author is also revelatory in pointing out the tsar's and tsarina's struggle to hide from all the world the truth of their son's affliction, and their preoccupation with so "un-Russian" a disease, which he—along with other European royal heirs—had inherited from his great-grandmother, Queen Victoria. The book was a general critical success: S. J. Laut called it "intimate history at its magnificent best"; Robert Payne remarked that "for perhaps the first time we meet the actors in the drama face to face in their proper setting."

After many years of travel and research, Massie produced his next biography, *Peter the Great: His Life and World,* a massive yet eminently readable book of more than nine hundred pages, crammed with significant detail, about the powerful career of Russia's first modern ruler. Among other historical set-pieces, the author recounts the rise of the titanically energetic Peter to imperial power, his arduous construction of St. Petersburg, "a city built on bones," his opening of his country to Westernizing influences, and his brutal execution of the Streltsy, the conservative and rebellious Muscovite boyar-merchant class. Massie's lucid narrative style was once again greatly admired by the critics. Walter Clemons called him "a clear, entirely unpretentious master of narrative history. . . . Massie's biography may draw adverse comment because he suspends conclusive judgment. He is bewitched by Peter. What he offers is the story, detailed and urgently readable, of a very complicated man." Linda Ganz termed the book "a sympathetic appraisal of Peter's accomplishments, although there is little information of how his reforms affected ordinary Russians. The lives of the aristocracy are explored, however, and the changes wrought upon them emphasized. This lengthy and informative book reads like a novel full of romance and intrigue."

Massie has also written a lengthy introduction to an interesting book of photographs, *The Last Courts of Europe: A Royal Family Album 1860–1914,* the picture research for which was done by his collaborator, Jeffrey Finestone. Though he has spent most of his professional life studying the lives of autocrats, Massie still finds the institution of monarchy richly fascinating: "Monarchy has many facets, some boldly clear, others less so. Certainly it consists in a family of people, singled out at birth, struggling through the experiences of private and public life to behave themselves and do their duty. But it is also an institution of government which provides a nation with stability and continuity, and which cannot be pressured or bought."

PRINCIPAL WORKS: Nicholas and Alexandra, 1967; (with Suzanne R. Massie) Journey, 1975; Peter the Great, 1980; (with Jeffrey Finestone) The Last Courts of Europe, 1981.

ABOUT: Contemporary Authors 77–80, 1979; Who's Who in America, 1983–84. *Periodicals*—American Historical Review October 1981; Best Sellers September 1, 1967; September 1975; Choice January 1981; Christian Science Monitor August 17, 1967; October 15, 1980; Commentary December 1980; Critic February 1981; Harper's October 1967; Horn Book October 1975; Library Journal July 1967; September 15, 1980; New Republic December 27, 1980; New York Review of Books March 19, 1981; New York Times Book Review August 20, 1967; May 11, 1975; November 2,

1980; Newsweek August 28, 1967; May 26, 1975; October 20, 1980; Observer January 14, 1968; Saturday Review October 7, 1967; October 1980; Time August 18, 1967; May 19, 1975; November 10, 1980; Times Literary Supplement April 24, 1981.

ANA MARIA MATUTE

*MATUTE, ANA MARIA (July 26, 1926–   ), Spanish novelist and short story writer, was born in Barcelona, the second of five children of a Catalan industrialist. Because of her father's business, the family had to divide its time between Madrid and Barcelona, spending summers in Mansilla de la Sierra, a small town located in Old Castile. Barcelona and Mansilla have both served as settings for her fiction, but not one of her works takes place in Madrid, a city where she has always felt ill at ease. The outbreak of the Spanish Civil War, in July 1936, a few days before her tenth birthday, shattered what until then had been a happy childhood.

In spite of having discovered a brutal reality, she continued to hold on to her private world of fantasy. When the fighting ended, she resumed her secondary school studies, but two years later, in 1941, she abandoned them to devote herself to writing, painting, and music. Her first published work was a short story which appeared in a Barcelona magazine when she was only sixteen. The following year, 1943, she decided to devote herself exclusively to literature. The prevailing conditions in Spain were far from ideal for someone about to embark on a literary career: an indifferent public, censorship, repression. Like other young writers of her generation, Matute was motivated to write by a need to denounce the injustice of Spanish society. Though she had already published several novels (one of which received the Premio Planeta in 1954) and two collections of short stories, her reputation as a writer did not become firmly established until the late 1950s. Between 1958 and 1960, she won Spain's three most prestigious literary awards— the Premio de la Crítica, the Premio Nacional de Literatura, and the Premio Nadal—which brought her recognition as one of the leading new novelists. The resultant publicity drew foreign attention, and numerous translations of her works began to appear. This enabled her to travel extensively throughout Europe during the 1960s. In 1964 she visited the United States for the first time, lecturing at various colleges and universities. She returned to this country as a visiting professor at the University of Indiana (1965) and later at the University of Oklahoma (1969). Boston University owns a collection of her original manuscripts. She is a corresponding member of the Hispanic Society of America.

Matute married in 1952 and has one son. She was divorced in 1963, and lives in Barcelona.

Even though she had already published a novel in 1948, Matute forms part of a group of writers whose first novels did not appear until the following decade, in the majority of cases in the mid-1950s. Born between 1925 and 1931, these writers were not old enough to participate in the Civil War, but they experienced it as children. For most of them, including Matute, it was a traumatic event. Ideologically, they shared certain common traits: solidarity with the oppressed and the downtrodden, a critical attitude toward Spanish society, and a desire for social change. Their sympathies lay with those who had lost the war rather than with the victors. Most of the novelists of her generation came under the influence of *objetivismo* ("objectivism"), an outgrowth of the French "new novel" or *nouveau roman,* which emphasized concentration on external reality: words, actions and, above all, descriptions of objects, in the hope of achieving scientific exactness. Some of the objectivist writers were also drawn to social realism, which, along with objectivism, was one of the dominant tendencies in Spanish fiction throughout the 1950s and well into the following decade.

While Matute's novels from 1955 on reveal an increasing degree of social consciousness, as well as some objectivist influences, her individual style and techniques have remained basically unchanged. A highly subjective writer, often drawing on autobiographical sources, she has always inclined toward lyricism and fantasy. Even in her longer narratives, where realism predominates, her language remains richly poetic, with

°mä to͞o′ tä

vivid images and abundant rhetorical figures. Of all the novelists writing in Spain today, she is perhaps the one who comes closest to creating a coherent, personal world.

Matute's first published novel, *Los Abel* (The Abel Family, 1948), revolves around one of the recurrent themes in her work: the Cain and Abel myth, which may be interpreted as a symbolic representation of the Civil War. Other themes already present in this early novel—the world of childhood and adolescence, social injustice, loneliness, incommunicativeness, and alienation—reappear in her subsequent fiction. *Pequeño teatro* (Little Theater) was written when she was seventeen, but did not appear in print until 1954. By subtly utilizing one of her favorite literary devices—the puppet theater as a metaphor for life—she manages to expose the narrow conformity and hypocrisy of small-town life. Although the novel won the Premio Planeta (now Spain's most richly endowed literary prize), it has never found favor with Spanish critics or readers. *En esta tierra* (In This Land), a rewritten version of an earlier censored novel entitled *Las luciérnages* (The Fireflies), was published in 1955. It is the first of her novels to be located in a definite period of time, the Spanish Civil War. While not one of her better efforts, it anticipates many of the political and social themes developed in her later novels. *Fiesta al noroeste* (Celebration in the Northwest), a novella which again makes use of the Cain-Abel motif, remains one of her best works. Written early in her career, it won the Premio Café Gijón in 1952, but was not published until 1959.

Los hijos muertos (*The Lost Children*) is a monumental novel in which the Civil War serves as a background. Over 500 pages in length, it was published in 1958 and won the Premio de la Crítica, an unendowed but highly coveted prize awarded by the critics. The following year it was "officially" honored with the Premio Nacional de Literatura. Generally considered to be her finest work to date, it presents a broad social panorama, in which the victors as well as the vanquished are portrayed in nonpartisan fashion. The novel focuses on two generations of children and adolescents, while at the same time tentatively exploring the underlying causes of the conflict which divided Spain. The dominant message of the novel is the futility of war.

Primera memoria (translated in England as *Awakening* and in the U.S. as *School of the Sun*), which won the Premio Nadal and was published in 1960, is the initial volume of a trilogy entitled *Los mercaderes* (The Merchants). Set against the background of the Civil War, the novel is centered on an adolescent girl and her emotional problems. On a deeper level, it is a study of war and its causes. Together with *Los hijos muertos,* it remains a favorite of critics who consider it one of Matute's most significant novels. The fortunes of some of the original characters continue to be traced in the two subsequent volumes, *Los soldados lloran de noche* (The Soldiers Cry by Night, 1964) and *La trampa* (The Trap, 1969), which carry forth the action up to the late 1960s. The trilogy thus spans three decades of Spanish history marked by ideological clashes, class-inspired antagonisms, violence, and the imposition of an authoritarian regime, as well as by profound social and economic changes. Though there is no continuity of plot from one part to the next, it derives its unity from its theme and intention. The "merchants" of the title does not refer to any specific social group, but rather to all those individuals who unscrupulously exploit others. While its central idea is the opposition between materialism and idealism, the trilogy contains many of Matute's characteristic, obsessive themes. In a later novel, *La torre vigía* (The Watchtower, 1971), she changed directions and chose a medieval setting. Despite the temporal exoticism, the numerous chivalric motifs, and the archaic linguistic elements, the thematic constants found in her previous narratives have not disappeared.

The major themes of her novels also resurface in Matute's short stories, albeit with an even greater emphasis on childhood, adolescence, loneliness, estrangement, and cruelty. Lyricism and fantasy play a far more important role in her short stories than in her novels. *Los niños tontos* (*The Foolish Children,* 1956) is a collection of brief poetic sketches about strange children—invariably misunderstood, rejected, or unloved—who inhabit private imaginary worlds. *El tiempo* (Time, 1957) consists of previously published stories on a variety of subjects, loosely linked together by the theme of time viewed as a destructive force. Like *Los niños tontos, Historia de la Artámila* (Tales of Artámila, 1961) shows a greater thematic and stylistic unity. It comprises twenty-two stories, all of which share a common setting: the mountain village in which Matute spent her summers as a child. Mostly melancholic in tone, many of the stories emphasize the incompatibility between illusion and reality. *Tres y un sueño* (Three and a Dream, 1961) contains three independent tales of lonely children who take refuge in a fantasy world where realism and magic merge. *El arrepentido* (The Repentant One, 1961), with its stress on the social and economic factors which led to the Civil War, reflects the author's growing historical awareness. Fantasy and social preoccupations continue to be very much in evidence in *Algunos muchachos* (A Few Kids, 1968), a collection in which she reaches maturity as a short story writer. Matute has also written autobiographical sketches, essays, and juvenile fiction.

While some critics, especially Spanish ones, continue to believe that her style is marred by rhetorical excesses, many believe that she is one of post-Civil War Spain's most important writers of fiction.

WORKS IN ENGLISH TRANSLATION: *Primera memoria* was published in the U.K., in J. H. Mason's translation, as *The Awakening*, 1963, and in the U.S. as *School of the Sun*, translated by Elaine Kerrigan, also 1963. In 1965 Joan MacLean translated *The Lost Children*. A translation of Matute's story "The Foolish Children" was in *Texas Quarterly* 4, 1961, and another story, "A Wounded Generation," was published in the *Nation*, November 29, 1965.

ABOUT: Columbia Dictionary of Modern European Literature, 1980; Contemporary Authors 89–92, 1980; Díaz, J.W. Ana María Matute, 1971; Encyclopedia of World Literature in the 20th Century (rev. ed.), 1983; International Who's Who, 1983–84; Jones, M.E.W. The World of Ana María Matute, 1970; Library of Literary Criticism: Modern Romance Languages, 1967; Weitzner, M. The World of Ana María Matute, 1970. *Periodicals*—New Statesman October 27, 1967; Times Literary Supplement December 28, 1967; October 8, 1971.

*MEDVEDEV, ROY A(LEKSANDROVICH) (November 14, 1925–), Soviet historian, was born in Tbilisi, the capital of the Georgian SSR, the son of Aleksandr and Yulia Medvedev. He was educated at Leningrad State University and the state Academy of Pedagogical Sciences, and holds a doctorate of philosophy. He began his career as a history teacher in a secondary school in the Urals (1951–53), then became director of a similar school in the Leningrad region (1954–56). For the next two years he served as deputy to the editor-in-chief of the state's publishing house for pedagogical literature, which in 1960 put out his first book, a study of a pilot project on vocational education for schoolchildren. For a decade (1960–70) he was a department head in the Research Institute of Vocational Education, attached to the Academy of Pedagogical Sciences. Medvedev was a longtime member in good standing of the Communist Party, but when *Faut-il réhabiliter Staline?* (Must We Rehabilitate Stalin?, 1969, translated by François Oliver from the unpublished Russian original) appeared in the West, arguing for greater openness in the Soviet system, his party membership was revoked and he lost his job.

In 1970 the molecular biologist Zhores Medvedev, Roy's twin brother and a leading dissident, was imprisoned in a psychiatric clinic for nearly three weeks by state authorities. Like his brother, he had published a book abroad the year before: *The Rise and Fall of T.D. Lysenko* (1969), the first Soviet account of the extent to which ideology perverted scientific inquiry in the USSR from the 1920s to the 1960s. Roy Medvedev led a successful international campaign for his brother's release, and they then collaborated on *A Question of Madness,* an hour-by-hour account, told by each brother in alternating chapters, of the nineteen-day involuntary incarceration. The book's publication abroad provoked a highly unusual and lengthy statement in *Izvestia* that there was no truth to charges that the state was imprisoning political dissidents in psychiatric hospitals.

The original manuscript of Medvedev's *Let History Judge: The Origins and Consequences of Stalinism* was confiscated by the KGB in a raid on Medvedev's Moscow apartment, but a copy of it had already reached the West, where it was published in 1971. The book chronicles Stalin's origins, his gradual emergence from Lenin's shadow, and his rise to absolute power; the growth of Stalinism and the personality cult; and the consequences of the mass state terror of the 1930s. Merle Fainsod called it a "magnificent study," but claimed that it is at pains "to exculpate the Leninist legacy and to blame all the sins of Stalinism on Stalin himself." Harrison Salisbury thought the book possessed "the assured detail of an 'insider's story.' . . . What is most exciting about it is that Medvedev is doing all this as a Russian, as a Marxist, and that he is giving us Stalin and Russia *from the inside.* We have never quite seen it like that before." Many reviewers complained, however, that the figure of Stalin presented in the book is too "consciously demonic," as one put it, and that his motivations are not satisfactorily explored.

On Socialist Democracy was originally written for *samizdat* (underground) circulation in the USSR in 1970–71 and was published in Russian in Paris in 1972. In it, Medvedev attempts a full-scale and always positive critique of the Soviet system, again attacks Stalinism as Marxism gone wrong, and reiterates his faith in Lenin and Leninist ideals. His idea of Leninism was described by Roger Jellinek as "Jeffersonian, decentralized, unmanipulative, and sweetly reasonable," a position which infuriated his more conservative anti-Communist reviewers. Jane Majeski maintained that democracy was, for the author, only a means to an end, which she described as "governmental efficiency and the upholding of the Soviet Union's global position."

°med vād´ yef

Stephen F. Cohen held, however, that the book was of quite exceptional importance: "Other Communists have argued for authentic democratization, but none has made the case so fully and systematically in the context of everyday Soviet reality as Medvedev."

The Medvedev brothers collaborated again on *Khrushchev: The Years in Power,* which covers the former first secretary's rise from obscurity to total authority, and analyzes the failure of his policies, especially his disastrous agricultural program, that led to his downfall in 1964. Joshua Cohen characterized it as a "fair-minded, incisive account. . . . By analyzing Khrushvhev's difficulties in power, . . . the authors have initiated a discussion of the complex political inadequacies of the Soviet system—in contrast to the usual focus on abuses of power and outright crimes." Roy Medvedev also wrote *Khrushchev,* a more general and balanced biography, free of the extensive agricultural commentary of the earlier volume.

Zhores Medvedev had his passport annulled and his citizenship revoked—the latter penalty is strictly prohibited by the Soviet constitution—while on a visit to Britain in 1973, and has lived there ever since. Roy Medvedev has continued to live in Moscow and, in the face of repeated warnings by the KGB, has continued to write his books of revisionist analysis, which have continued to be published in the West. *Problems in the Literary Biography of Mikhail Sholokhov* considers the possibility that Sholokhov, the country's favorite official novelist, was not the author of the great patriotic novel *And Quiet Flows the Don. Philip Mironov and the Russian Civil War,* on which Medvedev collaborated with Sergei Starikov, examines the career of Mironov, a Red Army commissar who was shot for criticizing the new Bolshevik regime's policies toward the peasantry. *The October Revolution* attempts a Marxist but non-Soviet analysis of the epochal events of 1917. *On Stalin and Stalinism* is a further study of Stalin's enduring impact on Soviet society. *Nikolai Bukharin: The Last Years* gives an account of the career of the great ideologue, rival of Stalin, and favorite of the people from 1929 until his execution for treason in 1938. In *All Stalin's Men* Medvedev culled the memoirs and his own knowledge of six top leaders of the Soviet Union in the Stalin era—Voroshilov, Mikoyan, Suslov, Molotov, Kaganovich, and Malenkov—with the purpose of showing, he writes, that "democratic mechanisms and institutions must be created in the Soviet Union that will ensure that people like Stalin and most of those around him can never again hold power or assume control of the country." *On Soviet Dissent* is a reprinting of a series of interviews Medvedev

gave to the Italian journalist Piero Ostellino. *An End to Silence: Uncensored Opinion in the Soviet Union* reprints, with commentary by Stephen F. Cohen, articles from *Political Diary,* a *samizdat* journal edited by Medvedev from October 1964 to March 1971. Medvedev has also edited two volumes of *The Samizdat Register* (1977, 1981), comprising a group of articles originally published in the *samizdat* journal *XX Century.*

In January 1983, at the outset of the Yuri Andropov regime, Medvedev was given a formal warning by the deputy prosecutor general of the USSR to cease his "political lampooning" or face criminal charges. "I told him," the historian related shortly afterwards to Western journalists, "'If I have been breaking the law for twenty years, you ought to put handcuffs on me right away and take me off to jail.'" Then, in an extraordinarily brave and forthright statement which was printed in many Western newspapers, Medvedev defined his work as that of "a citizen struggling to see his country live at peace with the world, flourishing in democracy and socialism." He went on to speak at length about the difficulties he faces as a Soviet historian:

"Unfortunately, it is difficult to be a historian and chronicler in a country where a vast number of political and felonious crimes in recent years have been committed by the people in power, and where corruption and abuse of power have penetrated deeply into many areas of party and state activity, not excluding the judicial system, the procuracy, and the KGB.

"It is difficult to be a political writer in a country where the constitution requires all citizens to work toward strengthening the authority of the state, but where many of those in the highest positions of state leadership care little, abusing their power for personal gain or for the removal of rivals and critics. The interests of the state, of socialist society, and of the people are of far less concern to these people than their personal interests and privileges.

"In a country such as the Soviet Union, an honest historian often has to step forward not only as a researcher but also as an investigator and judge, and to express moral and political opinions, regardless of whether these are in accord with the views of the existing government. I am little troubled as to the value attached to my work by the prosecutor or the KGB. Any honest and independent historian should be concerned with only one thing—the search for truth."

Writing with such candor of the Soviet government, Medvedev has inevitably come under ever-tightening restrictions. In February 1984 police guards were stationed in front of his apartment and Westerners were barred from visiting him. He was not, however, arrested and continued to go about freely and receive Soviet visitors.

Medvedev married Galina A. Gaidina in 1956; they have one son.

WORKS IN ENGLISH TRANSLATION: *All Stalin's Men*, translated by Harold Shukman, was published in 1981. Other translations of Medvedev's works include Colleen Taylor's *Let History Judge,* 1971; Ellen de Kadt's translation of Roy and Zhores Medvedev's *A Question of Madness,* 1971, and *On Socialist Democracy,* 1975; Andrew P. Durkin's translation of Roy and Zhores Medvedev's *Khrushchev: The Years in Power,* in 1976; and Brian Pearce's of Roy Medvedev's *Khrushchev* in 1983. His earlier *Problems in the Literary Biography of Mikhail Sholokhov* was translated by A. D. P. Briggs in 1977, and Guy Daniels translated Medvedev and Starikov's *Philip Mironov and the Russian Civil War* in 1978. In 1979 two books were translated: *The October Revolution,* by George Saunders, and *On Stalin and Stalinism* by Ellen de Kadt. Briggs also translated *Nikolai Bukharin* in 1980. *On Soviet Dissent* was translated from an Italian version by W. A. Packer in 1980, and Saunders translated the articles from the *samizdat* journal as *An End to Silence* in 1982.

ABOUT: Contemporary Authors 81–84, 1979; International Who's Who, 1981–82. *Periodicals*—American Historical Review December 1972; Book World November 28, 1971; January 2, 1972; Christian Science Monitor January 6, 1972; Commentary January 1972; June 1972; February 1977; Current Biography September 1984; Economist November 27, 1971; March 25, 1972; November 8, 1975; Nation December 31, 1977; June 4, 1983; April 14, 1984; National Review August 1, 1975; May 16, 1980; New Republic November 12, 1977; New Statesman December 17, 1971; April 4, 1972; May 6, 1977; New York Review of Books February 10, 1972; April 17, 1980; April 28, 1983; New York Times January 20, 1983; February 24, 1984; New York Times Book Review November 28, 1971; December 26, 1971; July 13, 1975; July 9, 1978; December 30, 1979; November 16, 1980; February 7, 1982; Saturday Review November 20, 1971; January 8, 1972; September 17, 1977; Times Literary Supplement January 7, 1972; September 30, 1977; December 16, 1977; April 11, 1980; November 6, 1981; April 1, 1983; March 23, 1984.

NICHOLAS MEYER

MEYER, NICHOLAS (December 24, 1945–), American novelist, screenwriter, and film director, was born in New York City to Bernard C. Meyer, a psychoanalyst and biographer, and Elly (Kassmann) Meyer, a concert pianist, who died of cancer when Nicholas Meyer was fourteen. During his mother's illness he became an obsessive filmgoer. At thirteen, with his father's help, he produced his own 8mm version of Jules Verne's *Around the World in 80 Days.* After graduating from Fieldston School, in the Bronx, he entered the University of Iowa as a theater and film major, received his B.A. in 1968, and returned to New York to work for Paramount Studios as a publicist and then for Warner Brothers as a script reader. Failing to find a market for six screenplays he wrote in his spare

time, he turned out an account of the publicity campaign for Paramount's *Love Story* (*The Love Story Story,* 1971) and with the proceeds moved to Los Angeles, where he wrote the screenplays for the television movies "Judge Dee" (1974) and "The Night That Panicked America" (1975), based on Orsen Welles' radio adaptation of H.G. Wells' "The War of the Worlds."

In 1974, Meyer published two novels. The first, *Target Practice,* a detective story about American prisoners of war, won the Mystery Writers Guild Award but received little notice. The second, *The Seven-Per-Cent Solution,* researched and written during the six-month screenwriters' strike in 1972, was one of the biggest publishing successes of the year, receiving a massive promotional campaign; it was forty weeks on the best-seller list, and won the Gold Dagger Award of the British Crime Writers Association. *The Seven-Per-Cent Solution* was an ingenious pastiche of A. Conan Doyle's eternally popular Sherlock Holmes stories. The book had its genesis in a remark by Meyer's father that psychoanalysis and detective work have much in common. Meyer's Holmes is a paranoid cocaine addict tricked by the loyal Dr. Watson into visiting his Viennese contemporary, Sigmund Freud, for a cure; the two geniuses, applying their analytic methods by turns, rescue a kidnapped heiress and foil a plot by German munitions makers, thus delaying World War I. Holmes purists were horrified, but the general public liked the combination of Victoriana, psychoanalysis, and cocaine. "In a field replete with pastiche," wrote E. F. Palencia in *Library Journal,* "Meyer succeeds because of a superior ear for Conan Doyle's style, a gentle sense of fun, and a talent for plot that few of [Doyle's] imitators have possessed." Newgate Callendar, crime fiction reviewer for the *New York Times Book Review,* called it "an amiable conceit, amiably written."

Meyer's screenplay for the 1976 film version of *The Seven-Per-Cent Solution* was nominated for an Academy Award. His second Holmes pastiche, *The West End Horror,* about a double murder in the London theater world, gave readers the pleasure of hearing Holmes and Watson converse with such luminaries as George Bernard Shaw, Oscar Wilde, W. S. Gilbert and Arthur Sullivan, Bram Stoker, Henry Irving, Ellen Terry, and Richard d'Oyly Carte. Newgate Callendar found it somewhat too formulaic, but concluded, "If Meyer has never really hit the Holmesian essence, he has made a brave try. *The West End Horror* is a pleasant entertainment." The author attributes the popularity of both his Holmes books to his abilities as a parodist. "On the basis of these books, I can't take myself remotely seriously as an artist. But as a forger, I was very good."

Meyer sold his next screenplay, *Time after Time,* on condition that he be allowed to direct it as well. Based on a novel by Karl Alexander, a classmate at the University of Iowa, *Time after Time* brought H. G. Wells, the science-fiction writer and social reformer, to twentieth-century San Francisco in search of Jack the Ripper, who had escaped justice in Wells' time machine. The movie, wrote Jean Vallely in *Rolling Stone,* "was remarkably free of problems endemic to filmmaking and first-time directors." Released in 1979, it was a surprise hit and confirmed Meyer's reputation as a *Wunderkind.* The film won the Grand Prize of the Avoriaz Film Festival and the screenplay award of the Academy of Science Fiction, Fantasy, and Horror Films.

Meyer describes what he does as "relief pitching"—taking an idea that has originated with someone else and developing its potential. After two years of trying to find a producer for his screenplay *Conjuring,* based on the novel *Fifth Business* by the Canadian writer Robertson Davies, he was invited by Paramount to direct the second *Star Trek* movie. The first one, released in 1979, had been considered something of a disappointment, with too much emphasis on expensive special effects. Meyer's sequel, subtitled *The Wrath of Khan,* was a more literate film, filled with ruminations on aging and the inevitability of death. It broke all box-office records on its release in the summer of 1982.

In an interview after the opening, Meyer told Stephen Farber of the *New York Times,* "I had a very unhappy childhood, and my life was saved by art in various forms. I still feel that the purpose of art is to give you the courage to face life. It gives you a transfusion, pours blood into your veins, so you can go out and do battle."

It is Meyer's custom to alternate writing and directing. His 1977 novel *Black Orchid,* written in collaboration with another University of Iowa classmate, Barry J. Kaplan, was moderately successful and was for a time due to be adapted by Meyer for the screen. *Confessions of a Homing Pigeon,* published four years later, received lukewarm reviews.

In 1982 Meyer was invited by the ABC Television network to direct a projected four-hour, two-part film of Edward Hume's screenplay *The Day After,* depicting a nuclear attack on an American city. The project was so formidable and forbidding that several other directors had refused it. Meyer described his initial reaction in an article in *TV Guide*: "I cannot live with myself if I don't make this movie. How often do you get the chance to put your work in the service of your beliefs? In my business, not often. If this film could sober the world and slow the pace with which we seem determined to turn our planet into a nuclear porcupine, then I guess I'm signing up, no matter what lists my name appears on." As Meyer anticipated, advance reports on the sensational and controversial nature of the film turned it into a political, as well as a larger, moral and ethical, issue. Following its showing on November 20, 1983 (cut to a three-hour, one-part film), to one of the largest viewing audiences on record, ABC broadcast a panel discussion, with Henry Kissinger, Elie Wiesel, William F. Buckley, and Carl Sagan among the panelists. In view of the excitement caused by *The Day After* (public debates, newspaper editorials, special preparatory classes in schools all over the country), its reception was inevitably somewhat less dramatic than its anticipation. Nevertheless, it was received as a landmark undertaking in television and was nominated for an Emmy in 1984.

Meyer continued to seek a backer for *Conjuring.* "I don't look too far into the future," he told Farber. "The world seems to be going to hell very fast. My one ambition is to see *Conjuring* in the theaters before we're all cinders." He has received the Anne Radcliffe Award of the Count Dracula Society for contributions to literature.

PRINCIPAL WORKS: *Fiction*—Target Practice, 1974; The Seven-Per-Cent Solution; Being a Reprint from the Reminiscences of John H. Watson, M.D., 1974; The West End Horror: A Posthumous Memoir of John H. Watson, M.D., 1976; (with Barry J. Kaplan) Black Orchid, 1977; Confessions of a Homing Pigeon, 1981. *Screenplays*—Judge Dee (television), 1974; The Night That Panicked America (television), 1975; The Seven-Per-Cent Solution, 1976; Time after Time, 1979. *Nonfiction*—The Love Story Story, 1971; *Films*—Time after Time, 1979; Star Trek II: The Wrath of Khan, 1982.

ABOUT: *Periodicals*—Playboy September 1980; Publishers Weekly November 21, 1977; New York Times September 23, 1979; June 27, 1982; Rolling Stone November 15, 1979; September 2, 1982; TV Guide November 19, 1983.

MICHAELS, LEONARD (January 2, 1933–), American short story writer and novelist, was born in New York City, the son of Jewish immigrants, Leon and Anna (Czeskies) Michaels. In 1949 he entered New York University, where he received his B.A. in 1953; he has an M.A. (1956) and Ph.D. (1966) in English from the University of Michigan. Michaels began writing fiction as a graduate student, and in an interview speaks of having written a novel at that time which he "incinerated." His short stories published in a variety of journals brought him early recognition, but he decided to complete his doctorate and take up a teaching career, since he felt that he would never be able to make a living as a writer. Michaels taught in the English department at Paterson State College, in New Jersey, in 1961–62, and at the University of California at Davis in 1966–68. He received an award for fiction from the National Foundation for the Arts and Humanities in 1967, and a Guggenheim fellowship in 1969—the same year in which he completed his doctorate, published his first collection of short stories, *Going Places,* and became professor of English at the University of California at Berkeley, where he has remained.

Going Places, a collection of oblique, visceral, and rather Kafka-esque tales, brought Michaels to national attention, and was nominated for the National Book Award for 1969. Denis Donoghue called *Going Places* "a brilliant book," and noted the impersonal and violent sense of life conveyed by the tales. "Michaels drives his language hard," he commented. "He writes in a high rush, the sentences tormenting each other . . . as if nothing short of annihilation could suffice. . . . In several stories I was reminded of John Hawkes' *The Lime Twig*, an essay in modern Gothic which perhaps marked for Mr. Michaels the possibilities of the genre." Ronald Christ captured the quality of Michaels' stories well when he compared them to unsettling dreams. "His stories," he remarked, "present a weirdly heightened world where simple acts and feelings are

LEONARD MICHAELS

translated into nightmarish reality by means of a distinctive style that gives substance to humorous, horrifying whimsy . . . a rare talent in perfect control of its power." Some reviewers, however, expressed dissatisfaction with the collection. Joyce Carol Oates commented that "story after story resolves itself in comic violence, fights or self-annihilating tricks. . . . Charming though the bizarre antics may seem in the first few stories, they become largely tedious and unconvincing as the volume goes on. . . . Michaels shows the influence of Malamud, but most obviously that of Donald Barthelme and Philip Roth. His own whimsical, antic style needs something harder behind it, something less arbitrary and less cartoon-like, if it is to create fiction in proportion to his obvious intelligence."

Reflecting the prestige of his early work, Michaels received a fellowship from the National Endowment for the Humanities in 1970, and an award for fiction from the American National Academy of Arts and Letters in 1972. In 1975 he published his second collection of stories, *I Would Have Saved Them If I Could,* reviews of which were generally favorable. Paul Zweig called it "one of the outstanding works of fiction of the year." "Although one senses," he remarked, "the hovering of recent literary kin—Burroughs, Barthelme, perhaps Roth—these stories are more nearly poems, with a tightly reasoned quality." Comparing Michaels to Kafka and Borges (both of whom make appearances in the book), Thomas R. Edwards commented that "Michaels works on a small scale, but his effects are clean and incisive. I know of few writers who can so firmly articulate intensity of feeling with the musculature of cool and difficult thinking." Other critics found *I Would Have Saved Them If I Could* a more fragmented and less effective collection than his first. Amanda Heller observed that "to some extent, the book's effects are simply flashy. One piece pays homage to Borges so efficiently that there's hardly any Michaels in it. Others wield a powerful, manic prose that extorts attention by brute force." Robert Phillips confessed to "a blindness to many of the merits of Leonard Michaels' highly-praised second story collection. To begin with, Michaels' first collection was unquestionably stronger. Except for that volume's tricky sexual fantasies (Michaels writes perhaps too exclusively about sex), the stories often succeeded . . . they succeeded because Michaels had stories to tell. In the new book we are given revelations, jottings, successions of sins, perversions, and violence— all of which do not necessarily constitute a good short story." Irving Howe also faulted Michaels for his minimal narrative and characterizations. "Mr. Michaels," he observed, "writes two kinds of stories: 'American-Jewish,' flauntingly bold and inauthentic, and a Borges-like stringing together of two or three paragraph sketches, vignettes, and reflections, featuring Marx, Freud, Trotsky, Nietzsche, Byron, Hegel, Dostoevsky, and other star players. This later group of pieces I found impossible and incomprehensible. I think that Mr. Michaels' [reductionist technique] . . . relieves him of responsibility for regarding his characters as, perhaps, human beings."

The most noted and widely discussed of Michaels' books has been *The Men's Club,* his first novel, which depicts a group of middle-aged men who gather at a house in Berkeley to "talk out" their lives and marital-sexual discontents. The session leads to inarticulate frustration, wolfish howling, and the destruction of furniture. The book was inspired by a real life experience—a group of men, Michaels among them, who met regularly for over a year to express their feelings and problems to each other. "Meeting after meeting," Michaels told an interviewer, "I found myself profoundly concerned about the unhappiness of a man whom I hardly knew." The incidents in *The Men's Club,* however, are imaginary; he makes clear that his aim was to write fiction not gossip. Like Michaels' other fiction, *The Men's Club* is partly comic and wholly horrifying. David Evanier, who compared *The Men's Club* to *The Iceman Cometh* and *That Championship Season,* commented that "nothing in Michaels' two previous books of short stories . . . prepares . . . for the relentlessly dark and brilliant strength of these

pages. Here is a middle-aged predatory Berkeley inferno of loss and chaos." Robert Towers noted that "the shifting of his fictional scene from New York to the Bay Area has been good for Mr. Michaels' art. There is a new expansiveness, an ease, in the writing of *The Men's Club* that distinguishes it from the rather twitchy and abrasive qualities of the short stories. . . . The literary influences so evident in the stories have now been largely assimilated." Other reviewers, however, argued that Michaels' male characters were undifferentiated. Anne Tyler called them "poorly characterized," with voices and complaints sounding exactly the same. He fails, the reviewer for the *New Yorker* commented, "to provide seven faces with seven voices, and the whole cast seems no more than one married misogynist split seven ways."

In addition to his fiction, Michaels, with Christopher Ricks, edited a large (over 600 pages) and lively compilation, *The State of the Language,* an anthology of essays on the use of English—from prison argot, the special vocabularies of feminism, homosexuality, and Black English to the language of computers, book reviewing, psychotherapy, and California. Michaels lives in the Berkeley hills, in a house that looks out over San Francisco Bay. He has been twice married, first to Priscilla Drake Older (1966), from whom he is divorced, and then to Brenda Lynn Hillman (1976). He has two children by his first marriage (Ethan and Jesse), and one (Louisa Alice) by his second. Michaels lists as the writers who have most influenced him Saul Bellow, Wallace Stevens, and the Russian Isaac Babel—Bellow's novels for "their deep rhythms and paragraphs of dense, multitudinous apprehension," and Stevens' poetry because "Stevens' words are intrinsically good." Of Babel he writes simply: "I never talk about his work." Of his own writing Michaels says: "I have the worst possible habits as a writer. I can't write page two until I'm satisfied with page one, so I rewrite page one twenty-five times, then page two, and meanwhile I'm dying to get to page thirty. What I publish is usually pretty thin and ecologically sound, but the paper I waste getting to it is equivalent to a small forest."

PRINCIPAL WORKS: *Fiction*—Going Places, 1969; I Would Have Saved Them If I Could, 1975; The Men's Club, 1981. *As editor*—(with C. Ricks) The State of the Language, 1979.

ABOUT: Contemporary Authors 61–64, 1976; Contemporary Literary Criticism 6, 1976; 25, 1983; Who's Who in America, 1983–84. *Periodicals*—Atlantic April 1969; Book World March 30, 1969; Commonweal November 7, 1975; Harper's September 1975; New Republic May 2, 1981; New York Review of Books November 13, 1975; July 16, 1981; New York Times Book Review August 3, 1975; April 12, 1981; August 9, 1981; Saturday Review April 2, 1969; Times Literary Supplement October 16, 1981.

*MŇAČKO, LADISLAV (January 29, 1919–), Slovak writer and journalist, was born in Valašské Klobouky, Czechoslovakia. After World War II, he entered the Communist Party and became one of the leading propagandists for the Marxist cause. After the Communist takeover in 1948, he became the editor-in-chief of the official journal of the Slovak Writers' Union, *Kulturný život*. He established his reputation at first as a journalist. In his writings he dealt with various domestic problems which he approached from a Marxist point of view, but in some of them he exhibited independent critical opinions. Widely read were his travelogues from distant foreign countries to which he was sent as an official reporter (Albania, China, Vietnam). Among them are *Albánská reportáž* (Reportage from Albania, 1950); *Daleko je do Whampoa* (It Is Far to Whampoa, 1948); and others. His report on the trial of Adolf Eichmann in Israel was published in 1961.

As a fiction writer, Mňačko entered the Czechoslovak literary scene with *Smrt' sa volá Engelchen* (*Death Is Called Engelchen,* 1960). The work was translated into numerous languages and also adapted for a film. On the whole, it is a fairly conventional anti-Nazi resistance novel, which describes the fate of a partisan unit in the final months of World War II. The unit is a motley of Czech, Slovak, Yugoslav, and Russian men and women. What distinguishes the novel from other works dealing with the same theme that were written in Czechoslovakia after World War II is Mňačko's seemingly deliberate avoidance of turning the work into political propaganda. The members of the unit are far from cardboard socialist realist heroes. In spite of the fact that their activities sometimes border on the spectacular, they are portrayed as frequently flawed individuals who can become senselessly cruel and morally corrupt. This work was seemingly patterned upon Hemingway's *For Whom the Bell Tolls,* but the novel falls short of its model, especially in the portrayal of intimate relations that tend to be either excessively sentimental or plainly uninteresting.

In the 1960s, Mňačko became one of the leading reformists. While he continued to profess a Marxist world view, he was increasingly critical of the regime's rigidity, incompetence, and disregard for human values. Due to his popularity,

the regime at first tolerated Mňačko's views, but in 1967, when he publicly criticized the East European policy towards Israel, he was expelled from the Party, and stripped of his citizenship while abroad. In 1968 he was allowed to return to Czechoslovakia and reinstated in the Party, but after the Soviet intervention, he left the country and has been living mainly in Austria and Israel.

His most important reformist work was *Oneskorené reportáže* (Tardy Reportages, 1963). The work is a collection of eleven independent short stories in which the author deals with the excesses of the regime during the Stalinist era. However, the political message of the work is enhanced by the implication that the outrages of the police-state remain not only unpunished, but unredeemed by an honest rehabilitation of the victims. Mňačko's most ambitious pre-1968 work was *Ako chuti moc* (*The Taste of Power,* 1966). The novel was never published in Czechoslovakia, and only excerpts appeared in the literary journal *Plamen*. Written originally in Slovak, it was published first in German translation, and subsequently in English. It describes the life of a top government official, from his youth to his premature death, as a slow process of moral and physical disintegration. In his youth a sometimes impetuous but essentially good-natured, idealistic, and courageous man turns gradually into a corrupt, cruel, and cowardly Party monster. Mňačko leaves no doubt about the reasons for his moral downfall—the political system that entrusted him with enormous power which he was incapable of controlling. The author insisted on the documentary nature of the individual episodes which include some horrifying examples of corruption behind the iron curtain. Max Hayward considered it "the best portrait so far drawn of *homo stalinensis* and it shirks nothing in its explicit and clinical examination of a peculiarly insidious form of tyranny . . . [with] an almost textbook quality for anyone interested in the mechanisms of totalitarian politics!" The work, however, does not rise above a rather obvious *roman à thèse,* lacking particularly psychological insight and verbal artistry.

Less politically oriented are *Dl'ha biela prerušovaná čiara* (The Long White Interrupted Line, 1963), *Kdie končia prašné costy* (Where the Dusty Roads End, 1963), *Rozprával ten Kapitán* (What the Captain Told Me, 1965). These works are loosely structured travelogues which contain a mixture of impressionistic, lyrically colored descriptions, and socio-political observations on life in the East as well as the West.

After his second exile and since 1969, Mňačko

°nāk´ ō, lä´ dyē släf

has written several works, that have been published either in Czech emigré publishing houses, or in foreign languages, primarily English and German. *Sedma noc* (*The Seventh Night*, 1968) is an account of the first week of the Soviet invasion of Czechoslovakia of 1968, which is interspersed with the author's reminiscences of historical events during the previous twenty years. It is perhaps the most sustained of Mňačko's attempts to present an objective evaluation of Marxist ideology in practice. *Agresori* (The Aggressors, 1968) deals with the Israeli-Arab conflict, with a strong pro-Israel bias. To the journalistic genre belongs also *Hanoi* (1973). Mňačko's most important post-1968 fictional work is *Súdruh Munchhausen* (Comrade Munchhausen, 1972), a Swiftian satire on the Czechoslovak communist regime. In this work it appears that Mňačko abandoned ultimately all his Marxist sympathies. It is an invective against Communism so venomous that perhaps only an ex-believer would be capable of writing it. The system is shown as irreversibly corrupt, inefficient and, above all, monstrously stupid. The satire consists of a description of a trip by a left-wing Western reporter who runs again and again into the most absurd situations imaginable. The pattern of the narrative, numerous independent episodes, lies in the development of an initially plausible situation into a grotesque hyperbole. Of less significance in *Udalost'* (Happening, 1970).

Without exception, the work of Mňačko is politically motivated. His coming to terms with the Marxist ideology runs through his entire writing career, and even in pieces which do not ostensibly deal with ideological matters, one can always feel the author's prime concern. Mňačko is, first of all, a journalist and the journalistic technique is reflected even in his fictional works. Almost all his works are written in the first person with the narrator being always less important as a character than as an observer. As a journalist, Mňačko ranks among the best that have ever come from eastern Europe. His fiction, however, is devoid of all poetry and its stylistic shortcomings are glaring. The American journalist Harry Schwartz wrote in 1969: "He was his nation's most celebrated journalist, enjoying a prestige comparable to that of, say, James Reston or Walter Lippmann, though his writing was more often in the traditions of Richard Harding Davis and the muckraking of Upton Sinclair."

WORKS IN ENGLISH TRANSLATION: Three of Mňačko's novels have been translated into English—*Death Is Called Engelchen* by George Theiner in 1960, *The Taste of Power* by Paul Stevenson in 1967, and *The Seventh Night* (translator not identified) in 1969. A brief excerpt from *Death Is Called Engelchen* is published in *The Linden Tree: An Anthology of Czech and Slovak Literature 1890–1960*, edited by M. Otruba and Z. Pešat, 1962.

ABOUT: Columbia Dictionary of Modern European Literature, 1980; Encyclopedia of World Literature in the 20th Century IV, 1975; French, A. Czech Writers and Politics 1945–1969, 1982; Hayward, M. *Foreword to* The Taste of Power, 1967; Modern Slavic Literatures (Library of Literary Criticism, II), 1976; Schwartz, H. *Foreword to* The Seventh Night, 1968. *Periodicals*—New York Review of Books June 19, 1969; New York Times Book Review September 10, 1967; Times Literary Supplement June 5, 1969.

*MODIANO, PATRICK (July 30, 1945–   ), French novelist, was born in Boulogne-Billancourt, a suburb of Paris, the son of Albert Modiano, a businessman, and Luisa Colpeyn Modiano, who had been an actress. He was educated at the prestigious Lycée Henri-IV in Paris, but did not attend university. Since his early twenties he has been a published novelist, widely read and critically praised; he has won nearly all the major French literary prizes.

Modiano is fascinated by the past, and by the imperfect selectiveness of memory, our ability to recall that past. He is best known for his early work: novelistic treatments of the dark, fearful lives led by Jews under the German occupation of France during World War II. Francis Steegmuller has remarked on the astonishing fact that the author, who was born after the end of that period, "should succeed in evoking, as almost no one has who lived through it, its frightful paradoxes. His characters [in these early books] are chiefly the Nazi occupiers and their French and international hangers-on; the Résistants are the mice they betray and catch." Steegmuller calls Modiano "the Graham Greene of the Occupation."

La Place de l'Étoile (1968) begins with an epigraphic anecdote explaining the grim pun of the title. A German officer, a member of the Nazi army of occupation, approaches a man on the streets of Paris in June 1942. "Pardon me, monsieur. Where is the Place de l'Étoile?" [The Place of the Star is a famous crossroads in Paris.] The man, without a word, points to the left side of his chest. The novel consists of the vivid, terrifying, yet strangely disconnected memoirs of a Jew, unidentified except for his family name, Schlemilovitch. The experiences he recounts run the gamut of Jewish stereotypes, in Steegmuller's words, "from situations of caricatured humility and self-analysis, through distinction in scholarship and finance, to grim scenes of persecution

°mō dē ä´ nō

PATRICK MODIANO

and extinction." Real characters of the period, including Pierre Drieu la Rochelle, Robert Brasillach, Guillaume Apollinaire, and Max Jacob, join the characters invented by the novelist. *La Place de l'Étoile* won the Félix Fénéon and Roger Nimier prizes.

Modiano's next two novels explored similar historical ground. *La Ronde de nuit* (1969, *Night Rounds*) strongly attacks the literature and legends—largely self-serving lies—surrounding the Occupation; *Les Boulevards de ceinture* (1972, *Ring Roads*) is the story of a young Jewish boy's search for his missing father in the outskirts of wartime Paris and his discovery of the criminal underworld that flourished there. This novel won the French Academy's Grand Prix du Roman.

In 1974, Modiano wrote, with the film director Louis Malle, the script for *Lacombe Lucien*. The film, released the same year, has ever since been recognized as a classic narrative of collaboration and betrayal and a stark portrait of the Fascist sensibility. The fact that the hero is a simple country boy, typical in many ways of millions of his compatriots, seemed strongly to reinforce the impact of the film on the modern French consciousness.

Villa triste (1975), which won the lucrative Booksellers' prize the year after its publication, is a further exploration of the imperfectness of memory. An unnamed narrator, a man of ambiguous nationality, fled Paris at the height of the Algerian terror in the early 1960s and came to a resort town on the French side of Lake Geneva. In his narrative he attempts, some fifteen years later, to recreate this summer in detail. He

has a fear, never fully identified, which becomes for the reader the most interesting part of his narrative, overshadowing his rather nostalgic observations about the past. Quite near the end we learn he is Jewish; he speaks of how his hotel room reminds him of the transient Parisian rooms quit hastily, in cold fear, only a step ahead of the Gestapo. He is clearly too young to have witnessed such flights firsthand, but the exploding bombs and the heavy police presence throughout Paris (in the early 1960s) force him to revert to his people's common memory: "I was dying of fear . . . and I had chosen this place of refuge because it was situated five kilometers from Switzerland." *Villa triste* has some entertaining minor characters and several grandly comic scenes involving an "elegance competition" at the resort and the complicated stratagems of several of the entrants.

Livret de famille (Bridal Book, 1977) is among Modiano's most mystifying works. The narrator, as usual an anonymous, rather anxious young Jewish male, describes fifteen episodes from his life, in no particular rational or chronological order, from the time of his parents' marriage through his own adolescence and early manhood. His experiences exactly echo in many respects what we know of Modiano's own life, yet it is impossible to tell whether the book is autobiography or fiction. "One cannot presume to say," wrote Steegmuller, "that Patrick Modiano has deliberately set out to make himself, in his books, a man of mystery; yet in *Livret de famille* conjecture constantly takes over. The many dates confuse; the internationalism and the exotic names are kaleidoscopic. . . . But just as one cannot presume, one cannot complain. So excellently recounted, so vivid, are the great majority of the episodes, that the book as a whole escapes the schematic mold its title and the opening pages had led one to apprehend. The sometimes irritating mysteriousness of it all may well be a key to that success."

The hero-narrator of *Rue des Boutiques Obscures* (Street of Unlit Shops, 1978) is attempting, some time after the end of World War II, to piece together his past: a severe shock in the early war years has left him a selective amnesiac. The title is the name of a street in Rome where he may have lived, and an international cast of minor characters all try to aid him in recovering his memory and his identity. John Weightman considered that Modiano had this time made "too mechanical a use of his theme." In the case of this narrator, he continued, the author "seems to have made the elementary mistake of supposing that, in the absence of a definite identity, blankness will do; or perhaps he has just worked out his first vein and needs to find another." Despite this British reservation, the novel was popular in France with critics and the public, and won the Goncourt prize, the country's most exalted literary award.

In *Une Jeunesse* (A Youth, 1981), Odile, thirty-five years old and married to Louis, who is the same age, poses an hypothesis with which readers of Modiano will be thoroughly familiar: "How strange it would be if children knew their parents as they were before their birth, when they were not yet parents but simply themselves." What Louis and Odile get, instead, is the chance to be rejoined to their own past, and the author's recreation of their life in the Paris of the early 1960s is presented in typically precise and economical detail. Yet this past, as it becomes recreated, verges always toward the uncertain, the equivocal, and the imaginary, as if it were, indeed, the future. John Sturrock described the novel as "spare and stage-managed" while admiring it as "exceedingly clever [and] well made": "It is never certain just who the characters are in this novel, or why they do what they do. . . . New lives, or new identities, constantly beckon in Modiano's enjoyably ambiguous plots, which do not try too hard to be definitive: these, we can assume, count among life's possibilities, but no more."

Modiano married Dominique Zehrfuss in September 1970; they have two daughters. In 1976 he published a book-length interview with Emmanuel Berl (1892–1976), eminent journalist (founder of *Marianne* and editor of *Les Pavés de Paris*), admirer of Anna de Noailles, husband of the *chanteuse* Mireille, and neighbor, in the Palais Royal, of Jean Cocteau and Colette. Subjects covered include Berl's impressions of French life before World War I, the sociopolitical landscape of French journalism, and, most pointedly and especially, the place of Jews in French society.

WORKS IN ENGLISH TRANSLATION: Three novels by Modiano have been translated into English: *Night Rounds* by Patricia Wolf in 1971, *Ring Roads* by Caroline Hillier in 1974, and *Villa Triste*, also by Hillier, in 1977. Sabine Destree translated the screenplay *Lacombe Lucien* in 1975.

ABOUT: Who's Who in France, 1983–84; Contemporary Authors 85–88, 1980. *Periodicals*—New Statesman May 31, 1974; March 11, 1977; New York Times October 21, 1975; New York Times Book Review March 15, 1971; Observer March 26, 1972; July 21, 1974; Times Literary Supplement December 4, 1969; May 5, 1972; December 12, 1975; July 15, 1977; October 27, 1978; May 5, 1981.

*MOJTABAI, A(NN) G(RACE) (June 8, 1937–), American novelist, writes: "My maiden name was Alpher. I tend to think of that as one of the primordial names, for I have a cousin, Ralph Alpher, who, as a graduate student in physics in the 1940s, was a signatory—indeed, the first signatory—to a decisive formulation of the 'Big Bang' theory of the origin of the universe. I have never seen the document, but, the way the family tells it, the paper was signed 'Alpha, Beta, Gamma'—for Ralph Alpher, Hans Bethe, and George Gamow.

"I come from a family with some intellectual pride, and with a great love and facility for music. My parents were lawyers. My father's first training was in chemistry, and he subsequently put his double expertise to work by becoming a patent attorney. The paradigm of good writing which he has always held up to me is that of the patent specification: clarity and distinctness, a prose of utter transparency. My sister is a painter, who has taught me how to look attentively at things, how to look contemplatively, and not just for use.

"My father was the least musical member of his family, although he, and all the rest of us, have a tremendous love and reverence for music. Music, to me, is the highest, purest, most rigorous of the arts. I aspire to music in what I write, but, necessarily and continually, fall short of that standard. Prose fiction has always seemed to me to be a low, mixed, mimetic form. I prefer music, myth, poetry—in that order. My writing has been likened to a process of dissection. Layer after layer, the soul of the character is laid bare—so goes the formulation. There is some truth in this. In any event, dissection has been my method of investigation from an early age. My parents were not very religious, but there was considerable hocus pocus and inconsistency in their accounts of death. The subject of death left me curious and anxious, so I began collecting dead animals, bringing them into the house, and opening them up to have a look.

"I was tracked for a scientific career from the time I started high school, and spent two summers interning at the Jackson Memorial Laboratory for cancer research in Bar Harbor, Maine. Two of my fellow students from that group are already Nobel laureates. In high school, I was also placed among the slow students in English, for I disliked Dickens. To fail to appreciate Dickens was a sure sign of a deficient literary sensibility. Actually, Kafka was the only novelist I enjoyed reading, and I think of him more as a writer of parables and myths, than of novels.

"My own books are novels only by courtesy. I write 'novels' to recreate the form, or—since it

°much tä bī ´ ē

A.G. MOJTABAI

is the loosest of forms—to stretch the form to its limits. My methods are strange: I work backwards from the ending. I usually begin with a haunting final image—a recognition scene— and proceed by unpacking the implications of that image as I go. Looking back over my books, I am struck by the prevalence of images of separation in them. In *Mundome:* Richard presses himself against a silent door. In *The 400 Eels of Sigmund Freud,* Naomi studies the photographs of a student no one could ever abide, noticing his separateness and the fact that no one has been able to put a name to this picture. In *A Stopping Place,* there are multiple images of fences, dividers: Aleem pressing his hand against the wire mesh of the airport fence as Tom walks away; Kate leaning far over the rail of the departing ship, as her husband waves from shore, the shore beginning to recede; Meena standing at the railing of her porch, reading Nirmal's last letter; Nirmal walking on to meet his death, the last, the great, divider. In *Autumn,* though, the last scene is of Will calling out: 'Hello? Hello . . . I'm here.' It is a cry of broken connection, a reaching out, which is, I think, an improvement.

"As a Jew, who married a Muslim, and now is drawn closely to Roman Catholics working in the peace movement, I do not believe in most of the social divisions which we create for ourselves—whether religious, national, gender or age-related. The emphasis on separation in my work has never been intended to reinforce existing divisions, but to dramatize the pity and the waste of these divisions, the narrowings and stultifications of self, due to the artificial boundaries we impose upon ourselves."

A. G. Mojtabai was born in Brooklyn, the daughter of Robert and Naomi Alpher. She graduated from Antioch College in 1958 with a B.A. in philosophy, married Fathollah Mojtabai two years later, and moved with him to Iran. Their two children were born there, but the marriage ended in divorce and Mojtabai returned to the United States with her daughter, Chitra. From 1966 to 1968 she lectured in philosophy at Hunter College, earning her M.A. in philosophy from Columbia in 1968. For the next two years she worked as a librarian at Columbia's Graduate School of Business and she received her M.L.S. in library service in 1970. From 1970 to 1976 she was a librarian for the City College of New York, and it was during this period that she completed her first novel. After contacting A. Alvarez, a British critic whose work she admired, Mojtabai sent him the manuscript, and he in turn made criticisms and gave her the name of a literary agent. Thus was *Mundome* brought to light.

Mundome was published to great critical acclaim and it is still the best known of Mojtabai's novels. It is a brief, elliptical, and unsettling account of a descent into madness. The book's narrator, Richard Henken, is an archivist in a dusty Manhattan library. At the novel's beginning, his seriously disturbed sister, Meg, has just returned from twelve years of institutionalized care. The rest of the novel traces Richard's gradual breakdown as he attempts to restore Meg's mental health and only damages his own. In the final sections it is hard to sort out Richard's observations of reality from his hallucinations, and the reader is left with some profound ambiguities: has Richard somehow caused Meg's insanity? Does Meg even exist, or is she a figment of Richard's imagination? Is Richard a figment of Meg's imagination? These puzzles intrigued the book's reviewers. Timothy Foote, in *Time,* wrote that "the book erupts with dramatic clues that flare backward and forward through the narrative like thin, ignited trains of gunpowder," and Jonathan Yardley said, "rarely has [madness] been so affectively—indeed devastatingly—employed as in this novel." Mojtabai was also praised for her precise, lapidary prose. The only complaint that some reviewers voiced was that *Mundome* was so concise and controlled that it seemed a little bloodless or claustrophobic.

Mojtabai's next novel, *The 400 Eels of Sigmund Freud,* was loosely based on her adolescent experience of the Jackson Memorial Laboratory. It concerns a group of high school students interning in scientific research for one summer at an experimental institute called the Four Winds. The students are a picked lot and expectations are high on both sides. "It's going to be a beautiful summer," one of their supervisors tells them, but before long the communal spirit succumbs to the neuroses of the adult supervisors and the same ominous sense of fate that was central to *Mundome.* Exacerbating the tension and precipitating the novel's crisis is Isaiah Yettman, an acne-ridden iconoclast from Brooklyn whose contant nay-saying mocks the scientific humanism on which the Four Winds is supposedly based.

The 400 Eels of Sigmund Freud was not as highly praised as *Mundome* had been. A minority of critics, like Doris Grumbach, considered the book "fine, intelligent, and moving," and there was much praise for Mojtabai's stylistic control. But the consensus seemed to be that Mojtabai failed to put her more complex plot and larger cast of characters into any kind of synthesis. Michael Wood's was a fairly representative voice when he said in the *New York Review of Books,* "The writing is good enough to create a final dissatisfaction with the novel, which seems to promise more than it gives. Looking for emblematic truth by means of concrete occasion, A. G. Mojtabai ends up with a beautifully caught occasion which is slightly too concrete to carry any distance beyond itself. . . . It is not enough to make an emblem, it makes only a delicate story rather thinly clothed in implications."

Mojtabai drew on her years in Iran and Pakistan for the background material of her third novel, *A Stopping Place.* As different from *The 400 Eels of Sigmund Freud* as that novel was from *Mundome, A Stopping Place* deals with broad cultural issues of East and West and remains Mojtabai's longest, most ambitious book to date. The plot revolves around the theft of a holy moslem relic in the early sixties and the Pakistani civil servant assigned to recover it. Two Americans, a young wife married to an Iranian embassy attaché and a frustrated poet on a lecture tour, are drawn into this turbulent atmosphere in ways not entirely clear. Indeed, the major criticism of *A Stopping Place* was that Mojtabai did not successfully integrate the intersecting paths of her principal protagonists into a unified whole. There was general agreement that the large-scaled, historical portrait that she was attempting did not suit her talents particularly well. Julian Moynahan wrote, "Mrs. Mojtabai is best at showing the lonely, beset individual enduring unsupported the ordeal of his—or her—life" and considered her "not invariably successful at interweaving plot line and intertwining private lives with public scenes and issues." Still, Mojtabai's continued exploration of isolation, alienation, and oppression within human relationships lent the novel a strong thematic, if not stylistic, coherence. "At the book's core," wrote Daphne Merkin, "as in Mojtabai's earlier novels, is a perception of humankind as utterly lonely, adrift in individual consciousness."

In *Autumn* Mojtabai returned to the small-scaled canvas of her earlier work, but the story line was no more to be predicted than any of her others had been. The protagonist is Will Ross, a retired accountant whose wife of forty years has died shortly before the novel opens. Little of outward significance occurs in the few days covered by the action. Will bumbles around his house in Maine, talks to his absent wife, has a brief, unsatisfying affair with a neighboring widow, and generally tries to deal with his grief and his life as best as he can. Surprisingly, for all the bleakness of Will's situation, he achieves a stronger sense of spiritual wholeness than most of Mojtabai's other characters, perhaps because, as Benjamin De Mott suggested in his review, he evinces "the moral rightness of reserve." Yet the depiction of isolation and emptiness remains central to *Autumn,* and De Mott extolled the novel for its intense concentration on loneliness: "The novelist moves with the feeling, wherever it leads, stands inside it catching its weather, making one sense the currents, the back eddies of loneliness. It seemed to me at times, reading *Autumn,* that no one I had previously read had been as patient or keen or unsentimental as Mrs. Mojtabai about the matter of loss."

Autumn received very favorable reviews, but there were some dissenters, notably Peter S. Prescott in *Newsweek.* He thought Will Ross merely dull and that the story "reads as if it had been diagrammed by a professor who had spent a lot of time thinking about what fiction should be." What Prescott seemed to be objecting to was Mojtabai's inhabiting a literary terrain not her own, her purposely taking on a subject far removed from her experience. ("As a good theorist should," said Prescott, "she goes where the difficulty is.") Certainly Mojtabai does not tread the same ground from novel to novel, although some of them do have autobiographical elements. Yet other critics have seen this tendency as a strength rather than a weakness, and Mojtabai, at any rate, is unperturbed by the lack of consistency in her subject matter. In a 1982 interview in *Publishers Weekly* she explained her practice succinctly: "In each novel I take a different problem and a different form, and I work on different things. I write what I have to."

A. G. Mojtabai was Briggs-Copeland Lecturer in English at Harvard from 1978 to 1983. She received a Guggenheim fellowship for the year 1981–1982 and a fellowship from the Radcliffe Institute for the years 1976–1978. In addition to her fiction she has published criticism in the *New York Times Book Review* and the *New Republic* and has lately turned to journalism. Her account of nuclear disarmament protests in Amarillo, Texas appeared in *Working Papers,* July/August, 1982.

PRINCIPAL WORKS: Mundome, 1974; The 400 Eels of Sigmund Freud, 1976; A Stopping Place, 1979; Autumn, 1982.

ABOUT: Contemporary Authors 85–88, 1980; Contemporary Literary Criticism 5, 1976; 9, 1978; 15, 1980; Mainiero, L. (ed.) American Women Writers 3, 1981. *Periodicals*—Critique December 1978; New Republic December 29, 1979; New York Review of Books June 10, 1976; New York Times Book Review November 18, 1979; August 8, 1982; Newsweek September 13, 1982; Publishers Weekly July 30, 1982; Sewanee Review Summer 1974; Time May 20, 1974.

© 1985 Thomas Victor

N. SCOTT MOMADAY

MOMADAY, N(AVARRE) SCOTT (February 27, 1934–　), American poet, novelist, memoirist, writes: "I often wonder what it would be like to be a full-time writer. I have written several books of various kinds, a novel, an autobiographical narrative, books of poems, an evocation of the Plains Indian culture, etc. But in each case the writing was secondary, or at least additional, to other occupations. I happen to be a teacher and a graphic artist as well as a writer. I have to juggle my energies, but it is what I want; I like working in different fields, and I would be unwilling, I think, to give up one for another. I find great satisfaction in going from the typewriter to the easel to the classroom, and then, in my recreational hours, to cook (I am fond of cooking ambitious soups and stews), to pursue my interests in archery, swimming, and horsemanship, and to travel. There is an ancient nomadism in my blood. I dearly love to pick up and take off for sights as yet unseen, for the near and far corners of the earth. I have seen much of the world, and I have been glad to see it. I want to see more.

"I first thought of being a writer when I was a very young boy. I was fortunate to have excellent and immediate examples of creative accomplishment. My mother wrote the juvenile classic *Owl in the Cedar Tree.* My father was one of the best American Indian artists of his time, a watercolorist who remarkably improved his expression to the end of his life.

"If I remember rightly, my first published work was a poem included in the pages of a small and now defunct literary journal. There was something about seeing my words in print that mattered to me greatly. It made a certain

difference in my life, and I knew from that moment that I had to have more of the same. I had, in an instant, suffered an addiction. One of the great men I have been privileged to know was Yvor Winters, a teacher, poet, and critic I worked with as a student at Stanford University. He admonished me on more than one occasion to 'write little and write well.' It seems to me good advice, and I have tried to follow it.

"Mythology has great appeal for me. At the moment I am writing a book that is essentially the extension of an American Indian myth. My favorite of my books, *The Way to Rainy Mountain,* is, as some readers have been kind enough to say, an example of the way in which poetry, myth, history, memoir, and graphic art can come together in a whole and expressive statement. I want to go further in the exploration of myth, to understand and indicate as well as I can how myth informs literature, even contemporary writing, even—or especially—my own. I have become deeply curious about the relationship between graphic imagery and language. A number of my paintings and etchings have incorporated calligraphy into the picture plane. I have illustrated books, and I want to illustrate more books.

"Some people have said to me, 'you must have a good deal of energy to pursue all of these interests and enthusiasms and commitments.' And I reply, 'I feel that I have more stamina than energy; I would like to have more energy than I have. But I like even better to have the strength to persist in my work, sometimes doggedly, sometimes beyond my energy. And I am the father of four daughters. I feel that I am a very rich man.'"

An eloquent spokesman—as poet, novelist, and memoirist—of the Kiowa Indian culture of the American Southwest, N. Scott Momaday was born in Lawton, Oklahoma. His father was Alfred Morris Momaday, a school teacher and highly regarded Indian artist; his mother, also a teacher and the author of books for young adults, was the former Natachee Scott, of mixed Indian and white descent. Her ancestors included Samuel Scott, a member of the Virginia House of Burgesses, and Charles Scott, a Revolutionary War general and the fourth governor of Kentucky. In 1935 the Momadays moved to Arizona, where Alfred worked for the Bureau of Indian Affairs, and then taught at the day school at Jemez Pueblo. After attending schools on Navajo, Apache, and Pueblo reservations in the Southwest, Scott Momaday was sent to the Augusta Military Academy in Virginia to complete his last year of high school. Upon graduation, he enrolled at the University of New Mexico, receiving his B.A. degree in 1958. For a year he taught school at the Jicarilla Apache reservation, before entering Stanford University as a graduate student in literature. There he won a series of awards—the university's Creative Writing fellowship in poetry, the John Hay Whitney fellowship, and the Wilson Dissertation fellowship. He obtained his M.A. in 1960, and his Ph.D. in 1963. His dissertation, an edition of the poems of Frederick Goddard Tuckerman, was published in 1965 by the Oxford University Press.

Momaday joined the faculty of the University of California at Santa Barbara in 1963. In 1966–67 he was a Guggenheim fellow at Harvard University, after which he returned to Santa Barbara as associate professor. In 1969 he became professor of English at the University of California at Berkeley, where he taught creative writing and a popular course in American Indian literature and mythology. Since 1973 he has been professor of English at Stanford; and at various times has been visiting professor at the State University of Moscow, Idaho (1974), and at Columbia University and Princeton University (both in 1979).

Momaday's first book, the novel *House Made of Dawn,* which received the Pulitzer Prize for fiction, deals with an American Indian who returns from combat duty in World War II to experience the anguish of his belonging neither to the reservation world, where he grew up, nor to the technological society of Los Angeles, where he goes to find work. After a series of experiences that include a murder and subsequent imprisonment, he returns to the reservation where he sets out alone on a grueling footrace, an ancient tribal ritual, in which, with lyric effect, he has a vision of the nobility and heroism of the In-

dian past. The reviewer for *Publishers Weekly* described *House Made of Dawn* as "a brilliant performance . . . a beautiful and moving tale, one of the finest first novels to come along recently." Marshall Sprague found it "as subtly wrought as a piece of Navajo silverware," and was impressed by the quality of "wonder and revelation" in the book. William James Smith felt that Momaday's evocative style "gets in the way of . . . content. [His] characters are all bemisted by words. . . . His hero does not come through at all, but the incidental characters manage to assert themselves with an intermittent vividness that suggests a much more interesting novel behind that unfortunate veil of literature in front of them."

The Way to Rainy Mountain, published a year after *House Made of Dawn,* is a slender volume which records the rise and fall of the Kiowa culture. Each set of facing pages contains three paragraphs, in three different styles of type. The first paragraph is concerned with old Indian legend; the second with the historical circumstances of the Kiowas in the nineteenth century; the third with Momaday's own sense of what this history means to him. By the end all three concerns become fused. Phoebe-Lou Adams called the book "beautifully written, full of gentleness and dignity," and Charles L. Kenner was struck by Momaday's evocation of his people and their land "in a prose that is close to poetry." The reviewer for the *New Yorker* characterized the book as "an act of ancestral piety," and called the tribal material fascinating, but thought the work came perilously close to "sentimentality and a kind of Fenimore Cooper nostalgia."

Momaday's poetry was first gathered together in a slender volume, *Angle of Geese and Other Poems* in 1974, and was praised by many reviewers. Robert R. Shaw remarked that "the Indian background seems basic to Momaday's poems, providing not merely decorative bits of local color but the perception of cosmic harmony upon which they are founded. They are all written by a man who 'stands in good relation to the earth.' Even in those poems that lack overt Indian content Momaday casts a knowing eye upon the uncalculated but beautifully balanced patternings in nature." David Bromwich agreed entirely, commenting that Momaday "is a good descriptive writer because his ear is so wholly at the command of his eye. . . . He has mastered a tense and dignified language that would be incapable of preening." *The Gourd Dancer,* a second collection, was also well received. The reviewer for *Choice* noted that the poems, whether written in an iambic meter, short-line free verse, or in paragraph-poetry, were "fresh, original, and direct." Paul Ramsey, in the

Sewanee Review, preferred the Indian poems in paragraphs, "which have a wonderful freshness of rhythmical movement, an exact rightness as celebration of courage and labor and of mysterious beauty in the world."

Momaday's *The Names* is a memoir of his early life as a reservation child, and a homage to his Indian ancestors. Edward Abbey remarked that he "takes us, through sympathy, empathy, and imaginative feeling, deep into the interior of places and a people. . . . The tone of the whole is inescapably elegaic." Richard Nicolls called the book "subtle and beautifully rendered . . . a celebration of individual life, of one's people, and of the 'human spirit, which endures.'" Judith Pheron, however, thought that the connections Momaday makes with his ancestors were "strained and static, too intent on endowing the past with dignity. Ironically, it is his experience of discontinuity and contingency, his childhood spent largely as an outsider, that is made to come most alive."

Momaday is the only American Indian to date to have received the Pulitzer Prize. In 1959 he married Dorothy Gaye Mangold, and by the marriage, which ended in divorce in 1973, he is the father of three daughters, Cael, Jill, and Brit. He has since married Regina Heitzer, by whom he has another daughter. He has received numerous honors, including an American Academy Award in 1970 and a Western Heritage Award in 1974.

PRINCIPAL WORKS: House Made of Dawn, 1968; The Way to Rainy Mountain, 1969; Angle of Geese and Other Poems, 1974; The Gourd Dancer, 1976; The Names: A Memoir, 1976.

ABOUT: Contemporary Authors 25–28, 1971; Current Biography 1974; Who's Who in America, 1983–84. *Periodicals*—Commonweal September 20, 1968; Harper's February 1977; New Yorker May 17, 1969; New York Review of Books February 3, 1977; New York Times Book Review June 9, 1968; June 16, 1974; March 6, 1977; Saturday Review June 21, 1969; Sewanne Reviews April 1975; July 1977; Times Literary Supplement May 22, 1969.

MOORCOCK, MICHAEL (December 18, 1939–), English science-fiction writer writes: "I was born in London at the end of 1939 and most of my early memories are connected with air-raids. I grew up playing amongst the bombsites, which were quickly overgrown with weeds and wild-flowers, and in ruined houses. For me it was a tremendously romantic time and sometimes I suspect that my penchant for landscapes of ruins is purely nostalgic, an attempt to recap-

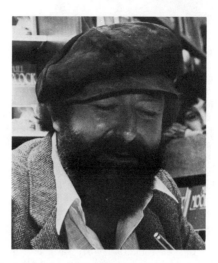

MICHAEL MOORCOCK

ture the pleasure I knew as a child. I was an indiscriminate reader from a very early age and can scarcely remember a time when I wasn't reading. Perhaps because of the War, or perhaps simply because there were not a lot of books around me, I missed most of the children's stuff and was probably too far gone by the time I was at school and was told what was and wasn't suitable for me. I read George Bernard Shaw as cheerfully as I read Edgar Rice Burroughs and E. Nesbit gave me as much pleasure as Dickens, but it was Burroughs' fantasies which led me to read similar books in the same genre (though I read very little science fiction as such) and found, by the time I was ten or eleven, that I had a talent for producing stories and publishing them in my own magazines (at one point I had a small empire of amateur magazines, typed and illustrated on mimeograph stencils, with titles like *Burroughsiana, Book Collectors News,* and *The Rambler*). I left school at fifteen, worked as an office boy for a firm which allowed me unlimited duplicating facilities, and by the time I was sixteen was publishing regularly in a juvenile magazine called *Tarzan Adventures* which reprinted the Tarzan comic-strip and ran original text articles and fiction.

"Probably because I was prepared to work for low wages I was soon asked if I'd like the job of editor of *Tarzan Adventures.* By the time I was seventeen I was a fully-fledged professional writer and editor and have earned my living in this way ever since. Originally I worked for popular magazines, more or less the same as the U.S. fiction pulps. I worked almost entirely to commission, which is how I came to write fantasy stories for the British commercial SF magazines long after I'd lost interest in the genre as such. Boredom and impatience with conventions made me want to try to ring changes within that genre and gradually, with no particular ambition to win myself the reputation, I became identified with both the literary avant-garde and so-called New Wave science fiction. Again any innovations I was responsible for came as a result of curiosity and boredom rather than any intellectual will to change.

"By the time I was asked to edit the magazine *New Worlds* I had begun to take a more aggressive interest in the literary possibilities of the SF genre. It offered a range of metaphor and structural techniques, as well as a fresh vocabulary, and I hoped to encourage other authors to explore the genre and take what was good from it for their own purposes. Eventually I financed the magazine mainly with my own money, by writing generic fantasy books for which I had a tremendous facility. I often regret that I've lost that facility, when I could produce a perfectly satisfactory book within three days and get as much money for it as a novel which took perhaps a year or more to write. Those books, most of which were produced in the sixties when the magazine was running, have continued to be my bread and butter and my only regret about having produced so many is that they tend to overshadow what I think of as my 'serious' books, though I'm not in any sense ashamed of them. They're better than most examples of their genre.

"I think my commercial experience gave me a broader range of techniques than most authors these days have at their disposal and these in turn led me to explore fresh narrative forms. My favorite 'experimental' work (of my own) is the Jerry Cornelius tetralogy which pretty much abandoned 'plot' without, in my view, losing any narrative tensions. 'Plot' is there to be found by anyone looking for it, but it's a sort of optional extra which I threw in along the way. Most recently my experiments have been less obvious, as with the narrative techniques in *Byzantium Endures* and *The Brothel in Rosenstrasse,* which are set primarily in the past but are not in the accepted sense 'historical' novels, since they form part of a whole, the final volumes of which will be set entirely in the present. My first large series was generic fantasy and contains about thirty interlinked books, but most of my work links in with it in one way or another and in my own mind I sometimes feel I'm writing a single gigantic novel. This is probably what gives my work an over-all coherence, even when I write in very different modes. Each book will pick up and explore themes from previous books, fre-

quently using devices learned either from Victorian fiction or from science fiction, and I'll frequently write a minor book in a particular mode in order to learn how to solve technical problems which I anticipate in more ambitious books. This sometimes still leads me occasionally to write in a simplified, even crude, style and consequently to puzzle critics whose training enables them to recognise the quality of language but not the quality of narrative construction. I suppose if I wrote under a batch of pseudonyms (which legend used to say I did) I would present a less confusing image. As it is I've become used, over the years, to reading how my fiction goes through 'good' and 'bad' cycles. Needless to say, I believe this to be a misconceived way of reading my work. It could be true that I'm facile and lazy and that this frequently shows in books which I don't take as seriously as others; but in my view some subjects don't demand as much hard work, and I see little point in wasting energy on something which is designed primarily as an entertainment for the reader and a minor experiment in narrative technique for me. Over the years I've made some attempt to subtitle books (some are 'tales,' some 'romances,' some 'fables' and a very few are 'novels') as a clue to my regular readers, but that's about as far as I'm prepared to go. I'm currently at work on the sequence which began with *Byzantium Endures* and whose narrator was a minor character in the Cornelius sequence. This is my own attempt to deal with the Holocaust and will take me up to my own time. Thereafter I shall mainly be writing stories set between 1940 and the present-day and drawing much more closely on direct experience."

Michael Moorcock was born in Mitcham, a Surrey suburb of London, the son of Arthur and June (Taylor) Moorcock. He edited *Tarzan Adventures* from 1956 to 1958, worked for the Sexton Blake Library from 1959 to 1961, then for a while wrote and edited political material for the Liberal Party. He first became well known when he took over the editorship of *New Worlds* in 1964; during the next decade he turned it into what many consider the most exciting and innovative science-fiction magazine of its time. In addition to his own work, he published that of such writers as Brian Aldiss, J. G. Ballard, Samuel R. Delaney, Thomas M. Disch, and Harlan Ellison. It is no exaggeration to say that the international reputation of these writers, like that of Moorcock himself, started in the magazine.

This decade was also Moorcock's most prolific

period. He produced dozens of fantasy novels, the majority of which are grouped into series: there are eight novels in the "Elric" series, three in the "Michael Kane" series, four in the "Runestaff" series, seven in the "Corum" series, two each in the "Karl Glogauer," "Eternal Champion," "Oswald Bastable," and "Castle Brass" series. Those which have proved most popular, however, are the five books in the "Dancers at the End of Time" series and his "favourite 'experimental' work," as he says above, the stories and novels in the "Jerry Cornelius" series. These are *The Final Programme* (1968), *A Cure for Cancer* (1971), *The English Assassin* (1972), *The Lives and Times of Jerry Cornelius* (1976), *The Cornelius Chronicles* (1977), and *The Condition of Muzak* (1977). Angus Wilson thought the Cornelius series among "the most ambitious, illuminating, and enjoyable works of fiction published in English since the last war."

"What is Jerry Cornelius?" asks Ron Kirk in a review of *The Lives and Times.* "A hero for our time, a man without qualities or with all of them—which amounts to the same thing ('In times like these any thing was possible and nothing was likely'). His loyalties are partly given to the shadowy Time Centre, an organization dedicated to knitting up the ravelled web of time, ironing out bulges in the seamless garment. His missions take him to scores of possible twentieth centuries, unruly and catastrophic, but none more so, I am sure, than Mr. Moorcock's view of Original Reality."

Angus Wilson, in his review of the series, likened Moorcock to some of fiction's highest paragons, calling him "a master of narrative and he never does less than tell a good story: for this reason he has been compared to Joyce Cary and to Chandler. But he is also a master of fictional play with the reader; hence he has been compared to Bernard Shaw and to Ronald Firbank. But as striking as either of these gifts is his exact ear for nuances of speech and particularly for the language of popular fiction, newspapers, high class magazine ads, and so on. He is, in fact, a splendid and subtle parodist. In all this I see him as the heir of Dos Passos and his neglected epic of the USA. And, like Dos Passos, he is that rare thing for England: an urban romanticist, a poet of London street life, of Notting Hill's slums and carnivals and markets. . . . Best of all are Mr. Moorcock's characters, beautifully observed and exaggerated both in appearance and speech."

Having turned away from science fiction ("If I've had any radical influence on SF," he said in 1978, "it's largely because I sort of hate it"), Moorcock has produced more of the fiction he

calls "experiments." Among these are *Gloriana, or the Unfulfill'd Queen* (1978), a Spenserian fantasy which takes place in what Alastair Fowler called "the Elizabethan court of some other time line than ours. . . . The heroine is a discontented giantess . . . who vainly searches for fulfillment in polymorphous sexual adventures and orgies with a seraglio of monsters."

Byzantium Endures (1981) is the first novel of yet another Moorcock series. Richard Rayner called it "massively ambitious, an attempt to combine the eighteenth-century epic, as practised by Fielding and Smollett, with modern psychology and history." It is narrated by the disreputable, Russian-born Colonel Pyat, who is a minor character in the Cornelius Quartet, and deals with his adventures in Czarist Russia up to the time of the Revolution. Penelope Lively thought the book "long, complex, richly peopled, as confusing, turbulent and intense as the events it describes," and Brian Martin called it "a brilliantly described, masterfully researched account of the Ukraine's suffering, marred only by touches of fantasy attributable not to Pyat but to his creator." In 1984 Moorcock continued Pyat's outrageous adventures with *The Laughter of Carthage,* a story of "gargantuan sweep and hubristic excess," as Valentine Cunningham described it.

Moorcock married Hilary Bailey in September 1962. They have two daughters and a son. The Moorcocks lived for several years in a somewhat dilapidated house in Ladbroke Grove in the Notting Hill area of London. So accessible did he become to his many fans and others that he was called "The Oracle of Notting Hill Gate." He now lives in the borough of Fulham, in London's southwest. He dislikes literary lionization of any sort: "It may be infantile," he remarked in 1982, "but I do feel apart from the establishment. I just don't like being the respectable figure at a literary festival. I tend to get blind drunk and pass out." For a time he was also active in the world of popular music, as a member of the band Hawkwind and as a composer of songs for other groups. Yet his literary efforts have always dominated his life, and today he does little but write. "I justify my fiction for rather pious reasons," he remarked in 1978. "I *do* think everyone should contribute a bit to mutual understanding and tolerance. I write for that reason. I guess I'm an idealist and an old-fashioned humanitarian. I believe it's worth writing in that tradition. The fantasies I write have always got a moral. Perhaps it's as simple as 'Be decent to one another.' But I can't sit at a typewriter and hand out lies. One needs hope, realistic hope. I try to confirm people's resistance to cynicism. Maybe it's naive. . . . "

PRINCIPAL WORKS: Using the pseudonyms William Barclay, Michael Barrington, Edward P. Bradbury, and James Colvin in addition to his own name, Moorcock has published more than a hundred novels and edited numerous collections of science fiction. Many of his novels belong to ten "series" entitled "Elric," "Michael Kane," "The History of Runestaff," "Jerry Cornelius," "Karl Glogauer," "Corum," "The Eternal Champion," "Oswald Bastable," "Dancers at the End of Time," and "Castle Brass."

ABOUT: Bleiler, E. F. (ed.) Science Fiction Writers, 1982; Carter, L. Imaginary Worlds, 1973; Dictionary of Literary Biography 14, Pt. 2, 1983; Searles, B. Reader's Guide to Science Fiction, 1979; Smith, C. C. (ed.) Twentieth Century Science Fiction Writers, 1981; Wollheim, D. A. The Universe Makers, 1971. *Periodicals*—Encounter November 1981; New Republic June 15, 1974; New Statesman April 4, 1969; May 18, 1973; June 18, 1976; New York Times Book Review April 5, 1970; May 19, 1974; April 25, 1976; Times Literary Supplement November 9, 1973; October 10, 1975; June 3, 1977; June 30, 1978; June 20, 1980; July 3, 1981; September 23, 1983; September 7, 1984.

© 1985 Thomas Victor

TED MORGAN

MORGAN, TED (March 31, 1932–), American biographer and journalist, was born Sanche de Gramont in Geneva, Switzerland, the son of Gabriel Armand de Gramont, Count de Gramont, a diplomat, and the countess, the former Mariette Negroponte. He spent much of his youth in the United States, when his father was stationed in Washington, and after a year at the Sorbonne entered Yale University, earning his bachelor's degree with highest honors in 1954. He took a master's degree in journalism from Columbia the following year. In 1956–57 he served in Algeria as a lieutenant in the French Army, but by 1958 had begun working in New York City, first as a reporter for the Associated Press (1958–59), then as reporter and Paris correspondent for the *New York Herald Tribune* (1959–64). Gramont won a Pulitzer Prize in 1961 for local reporting, and was seriously wounded in 1962 covering the war over the secession of Katanga.

Gramont became a freelance writer when the *Herald Tribune* closed in 1964. He had already published two well-received books, the first of which was *The Secret War: The Story of International Espionage Since World War II*. Here he compares United States and Soviet intelligence structures, describes the careers of "master movers and workers" in espionage like "Wild Bill" Donovan, Allen Dulles, Rudolf Abel, and Gary Powers, and analyzes what were at the time prime examples of contemporary espionage: the Rosenberg case, the Bay of Pigs disaster, and the downing of the U-2 spy plane. The book was described by Oliver Pilat as "factually satisfactory and often romantic." Pat Frank called it "the most exciting, comprehensive, and authoritative book on modern espionage ever published."

De Gramont's next four books in English were on French topics. He edited and translated a one-volume American edition, called *The Age of Magnificence,* of the monumental memoirs of the Duc de Saint-Simon, principal chronicler of life at the court of Louis XIV. *Epitaph for Kings* is a study of the *ancien régime* in which the author describes the events of 1789 "not as the start of a revolutionary era, but as the end of the longest continuous form of government in French history." The "complexity of . . . events" leading to the Revolution is thoroughly analyzed: "the path of decline is strewn with clues," the author writes. *The French: Portrait of a People* is, in one critic's words, "a clever, acidulous study" of de Gramont's compatriots which seeks to explain, according to the book's publishers, "why the French are admired, detested, misunderstood, and unique." Although generally praised for its witty fluency of style, *The French* was also attacked as ungenerous: "In evident haste," complained John Hess, "de Gramont has thrown together a vast ragbag of dubious data, tasteless anecdote, and pointless epigram. There is no apparent order in his chapters." *Lives to Give,* de Gramont's only published novel, is the grim story of four leaders of the French Resistance who have been captured by the Gestapo. The novel's business is to discover, amid lurid descriptions of torture, which of the four betrayed the others.

In 1973, de Gramont, by then a successful writer of independent means living comfortably in Morocco, decided to return to New York in order to establish residency for United States citizenship. He describes this decision and its consequences in *On Becoming American,* which received much more attention, by no means all of it favorable, than any of his previous books. Having chosen at the outset as a new American name the "forthright and practical, incisive and balanced" Ted Morgan (an anagram of de Gramont), he then spends little time in his book on autobiography; most of it is a paean to American virtues and values, with sections on immigrants and immigration, American history, and contemporary life. Although many critics described the book as "lively" and "well-written," nearly all objected to two prominent aspects of it: Morgan's failure to see his great material advantages over the immigrants of the past he constantly compares himself to, and his uncritical acceptance and lavish praise of virtually every aspect of American life. Henry Fairlie called the book "shallow," "lightweight," and "unlikable": "From the sunshine of Morocco to the sunshine of California is not the obvious way of knowing what it means to be American. [Morgan] seems to think that changing his name reflects the same experience as a Ukrainian Jew changing his name on arrival at New York harbor. This is not foolish; it is offensive." There is "about this book," writes Jane Larkin Crain, "a regrettable tendency toward breezy and reductive formulations that undermine its ultimate seriousness. . . . Morgan seems to have borrowed his attitudes and assumptions wholesale from shopworn conventional wisdom, making jejune and facile pronouncements on matters of weight and controversy." Other critics complained of a lack of depth in Morgan's treatment of his new country. "The man," wrote F. E. Hoxie, "who has written a book which the dust jacket promises will tell us 'what it means' to be an American doesn't seem to have talked with anyone outside of Palo Alto and New York City's Upper East Side."

The minutiae of W. Somerset Maugham's ninety-one years are thoroughly covered in Morgan's *Maugham,* published in 1980. Greatly praised for the thoroughness of its research and documentation, the book even won, upon its completion, the somewhat reluctant approval of the Maugham estate as an authoritative biography. British reviewers were quick to point up what was for them a glaring anomaly: this book on one of the most British of British writers was written by a French-born American for an American audience. Victoria Glendinning noted, in the *Times Literary Supplement,* Morgan's "occasional wild flights of fancy" and his "innocence and unfamiliarity": "He is an Ameri-

can, and English social history is a minefield. Behavior or circumstances that he finds extraordinary or noteworthy are very often, in context, neither." American reviewers were more favorable, although Paul Fussell, for one, found the biography digressive and repetitious and others complained of its massive length. Nevertheless, there was general agreement that Morgan had covered Maugham's long and crowded life with thoroughness and considerable sensitivity. Especially detailed on such matters as Maugham's stammer (on which Morgan indulges in much psychological speculation) and his homosexuality, *Maugham* brought together for the first time a wealth of material that will prove of value to future students of his work. As Keith Cushman wrote in the *Library Journal:* "Someone may come along to write a trimmer, shapelier life; but even when that book appears, this one will remain the authoritative biography."

Churchill: Young Man in a Hurry 1874–1915 is the first installment of a multivolume biography of the greatest modern Englishman, the other full-scale treatment of the life being the official biography begun by Randolph Churchill and continued since his death by Martin Gilbert. Morgan makes constant use of the official biography, particularly the documentary "companion volumes," prepared by a team of experts, which accompany each installment. The breadth of documentation is thus considerable as he follows Churchill through his first forty-one years, up to and including the disastrous blunders committed during his tenure as First Lord of the Admiralty, his resignation from the Asquith government, and departure for the trenches in France. The book was generally praised as "vivid and pleasurably written" with a "sense of pace" and "telling and witty detail," in the words of two reviewers, but several others discerned little substance to the life beyond its obvious concern for circumstantial detail. Peter Stansky called it "a surprisingly unreflective biography, without a particular focus or point of view . . . no more than an intelligent chronicle." J. A. Turner was much more harsh, terming it "one of the least satisfactory political biographies to appear in recent years" and criticizing the extent of the author's dependence on the companion volumes to the official biography.

A collection of Morgan's short pieces, *Rowing Toward Eden,* published in 1981, consists of a series of remembered moments unconnected by any strong autobiographical thread. Morgan makes this clear in his introduction: "We think that our life is an even progression of days, soldiers in single file marching in step, but when we listen for the beat it fades out of hearing. We have shafts of memory between dark spaces, so that life remembered takes on the featues of an archipelago, mostly submerged, with points of land rising up above the sea's surface. Such points of land make up the episodes in this book."

Morgan has been twice married and twice divorced; he has two daughters from his second marriage. He lives on New York's Upper East Side.

PRINCIPAL WORKS: *Non-fiction*—The Secret War, 1962; (ed. and trans.) The Age of Magnificence, 1963; Epitaph for Kings, 1968; The French, 1969; The Way Up: The Memoirs of Count Gramont, 1972; The Strong Brown God: The Story of the Niger River, 1975; On Becoming American, 1978; Maugham, 1980; Rowing Toward Eden, 1981; Churchill 1874–1915, 1982. *Fiction*—Lives to Give, 1971.

ABOUT: Contemporary Authors, new revision 3, 1981. *Periodicals*—American December 20, 1969; May 17, 1980; Antioch Review Fall 1978; Atlantic September 1969; Best Sellers September 1, 1969; April 1, 1971; July 1978; Book World March 24, 1968; August 24, 1969; April 4, 1971; March 26, 1978; March 2, 1980; Christian Science Monitor February 21, 1968; March 11, 1971; March 29, 1978; April 2, 1980; Critic November 1969; Economist May 3, 1980; Library Journal April 15, 1962; September 1, 1969; April 15, 1971; February 1, 1976; February 15, 1978; February 1, 1980; January 1, 1981; June 1, 1982; New Republic March 8, 1980; New Statesman December 5, 1975; New York Herald Tribune Books May 20, 1962; New York Review of Books July 15, 1982; New York Times Book Review August 5, 1962; March 24, 1968; August 17, 1969; February 28, 1971; April 1, 1976; April 2, 1978; March 9, 1980; February 8, 1981; June 13, 1982; New Yorker September 13, 1969; February 16, 1976; Newsweek February 9, 1976; April 3, 1978; Saturday Review May 19, 1962; March 23, 1968; September 20, 1969; July 3, 1971; February 1, 1978; June 1982; Time March 1, 1968; September 12, 1969; March 22, 1976; March 20, 1978; March 10, 1980; August 16, 1982; Times Literary Supplement April 25, 1980; June 17, 1983.

MORRIS, DESMOND (JOHN) (January 24, 1928–   ), British ethologist, writes: "I grew up in the Wiltshire countryside in southern England, surrounded from an early age by animals of all kinds. My father was an author of children's fiction and the sound of incessant typing in the house is one of my earliest recollections. I was able to type almost before I could write and was soon hard at work producing vast quantities of appalling, youthful poetry.

"In my teens I became passionately involved in the surrealist movement and began painting and exhibiting in the late 1940s. My first London

DESMOND MORRIS

exhibition was held in 1950 but by this time my other great interest—in animal behavior—was asserting itself and I obtained a degree in zoology from Birmingham University in 1951. I then moved to Oxford to join a research group studying comparative ethology, under Niko Tinbergen, one of the founding fathers of this new discipline. There I obtained my doctorate and wrote many scientific papers on the reproductive behavior of fish and birds. At the same time I was writing surrealist scripts for films and continuing to exhibit my paintings.

"In 1956 I moved to the Zoological Society of London as head of a newly formed TV and Film Unit, to make television programs and animal behavior films. There I was able to combine my two major interests—art and animals—in a study of the picture-making behavior of chimpanzees, and published the results in my first serious book *The Biology of Art*, in 1962. After three years of film-making, I was appointed Curator of Mammals at London Zoo and spent several years compiling a reference work called *The Mammals, A Guide to the Living Species*. I also wrote and edited other books on animals during this period and established a behavior research group at the zoo. It was during this time that I took the major step of applying my ethological methods to studying the human animal. Although it had not been deliberate, there seemed to have been a long sequence building up to this. I began with studies of fish in the early 1950s, then moved on to birds, then mammals, ending up with our closest relatives, the great apes. It was only one more step to turn my attention to human beings and this I did with my 1967 book called *The Naked Ape*. It was written in an intense burst of activity, in less than four weeks, and its impact after it was published astonished me. From my zoologist's standpoint it seemed perfectly natural to study humans as animals— for that is what they are—but to others it seemed a perverse and even shocking way of approaching our 'sacred' species. Some saw it as an insult to the dignity of mankind, but to me, with my lifelong love affair with the animal world, no praise could be greater than to call people animals. I should not, perhaps, have been surprised as the pomposity and self-deception I was uncovering in certain human beings, who expressed their outrage at being discussed in animal behavior terms, and I did expect a few high priests to complain, but I did not anticipate the worldwide interest in what I had to say.

"At the time of the publication of *The Naked Ape* I had left the London Zoo and had returned to my other great passion—the world of art. I was Director of the Institute of Contemporary Arts in London when the overnight success of the book caught me unawares. I realized that, for the first time in my adult life, I could dispense with office work and devote myself entirely to writing and painting. My reaction was to move to the Mediterranean with my wife, where we set up homes in Malta and Cyprus. I continued to paint and produce more books on human behavior in the late 1960s and early 1970s, but in 1973 I returned to Oxford University to undertake a major research project in human behavior patterns. There I wrote *Manwatching* and *Gestures,* and with a team of research workers visited twenty-five countries, analyzing variations in human behavior. I also began a long-term study of archaeo-aesthetics—an investigation into the origins of human art—and became increasingly involved in archaeology.

"During recent years I have written a light-hearted autobiography called *Animal Days,* dealing with my earlier years as an ethologist, and a science fantasy based on my paintings, called *Inrock.* I have also made a special study of human sporting activity, looking at the parallels between ancient hunting patterns of primeval man and the modern pseudo-hunting patterns of professional sports. My findings were published in a book called *The Soccer Tribe.*

"My writing career can be summed up as fifteen years devoted to studies of the behavior of other animals (1952–1967) followed by fifteen years devoted to studies of the human species seen as another fascinating kind of animal. All through this, at a more private level, I have maintained my obsession with the visual arts, especially the surrealist and the fantastic. In my scientific work I attempt a ruthless objectivity; in the arts, I pursue, as an antidote, an intense subjectivity. The combination gives me a balance but leaves me with a constant feeling that there are not enough hours in the day. My weakness is that I have always attempted to do too much; my strength is that I have never, ever been bored."

————

Desmond Morris was born in the village of Purton, near Swindon, Wiltshire, the son of Harry Howe Morris and the former Dorothy Marjorie Fuller Hunt. He was educated first at Dauntsey's School in Wiltshire, then fulfilled his two years of National Service and was nearly twenty-one when he enrolled at Birmingham University. His mentor there, the zoologist Peter Medawar, encouraged him to continue his studies under Nikolaas Tinbergen at Oxford. He took his D.Phil. in 1954; his thesis, *The Reproductive Behaviour of the Ten-Spined Stickleback,* was the first of his many published books.

Morris remained at Oxford for two years of postgraduate research into bird behavior, then became the founding host of "Zootime," a popular animal show on the Independent Television Network produced by Granada Television in association with the Zoological Society of London, whose film unit he led. The most discussed of his discoveries on the program was Congo, a young chimpanzee who developed a knack for abstract painting and whose "work" was exhibited in 1957 at the Institute of Contemporary Arts in London. Morris wrote *The Story of Congo* for children, and the chimp's case was the centerpiece of *The Biology of Art: A Study of the Picture-Making Behaviour of the Great Apes and Its Relationship to Human Art.* "The aim of this book," he wrote in the introduction, "is to gather together for the first time and analyse all the known information concerning this new biological source of material and then . . . to re-examine briefly the development of human art in an attempt to establish a set of biological principles of aesthetics." The art critic Emily Genauer called the book "serious and thoroughly absorbing," and wrote that its conclusions, "from a biological instead of the usual historical, sociological or critical points of view, are not only real but staggering."

From 1959 to 1967, Morris was the London Zoo's curator of mammals. In this position he was responsible for many innovations and improvements in the animals' environment; he wrote a number of juvenile books during this period. With his wife, the former Ramona Joy

Baulch, an Oxford University history graduate whom he married in 1952, he wrote the popular series *Men and Snakes, Men and Apes,* and *Men and Pandas.* He was also editor, with Caroline Jarvis, of the London Zoo's *International Zoo Yearbook* from 1959 to 1962 and edited a collection of essays by others, *Primate Ethology,* in 1967.

In that year Morris published his best-known book, *The Naked Ape: A Zoologist's Study of the Human Animal,* a project he had been planning for several years, in which he intended to force readers to examine the "thesis that we are still subject to the basic laws of animal behavior and must recognize this in order to survive." He concentrates "on those aspects of our lives that have obvious counterparts in other species: such activities as feeding, grooming, sleeping, fighting, mating and care of the young. When faced with these fundamental problems, how does the naked ape react? How do his reactions compare with those of other monkeys and apes? In which particular respect is he unique, and how do his oddities relate to his special evolutionary story?" The book was an enormous popular success in nearly all the twenty-five countries where editions appeared, but many scientists expressed harshly skeptical opinions in reviews. G. G. Simpson called it "bad zoology and inept biology. . . . Most evolutionists, geneticists, and anthropologists will feel that he overemphasizes genetic controls and underemphasizes the fact that a loosening of such controls, a broadening of genetic reaction ranges, is a fundamental element in the origin of this non-ape." Ronald Singer granted that "the author's attempts to startle and dismay the reader by his interpretations are, in a sense, stimulating and often thought provoking, but he must be taken to task for anatomical and physiological nonsense. . . . He has introduced some novel and challenging ideas and speculations. . . . I believe that a more accurate subtitle could be 'speculations on man's ethos based on the studies of other animals.'" Peter Williams hoped the book "could become a useful social antidote, in the sense of bringing meaning once more to actions that have become meaningless in the sexy-permissive, swinging Britain of the late 1960s. . . . Dr. Morris has written a lively and provocative book, and I for one am happy to forget its limitations in return for this new, if incomplete, view of myself."

Newly wealthy from the unexpected success of *The Naked Ape,* Morris abruptly quit his new position as executive director of the Institute of Contemporary Arts and moved to Malta to write and paint. *The Human Zoo,* a sequel to the previous book, propounded the thesis that the abnormal patterns of behavior experienced by captive wild animals are related to those exhibited by urban human beings: like a caged animal, the urban human may engage in meaningless activities, unnatural forms of sexual behavior, and exaggerated ways of controlling unnatural stimuli. This book also had more than its share of angry critics. R. A. Hinde, for one, acknowledged Morris' "serious intent—to help us to take a new look at ourselves, not against the backdrop of our accepted culture, but against the wider vistas of our biological heritage," but advised the general reader to "take care. Science for the non-specialist is full of pitfalls and Morris gives [the reader] practically no help in distinguishing between established fact and flights of fancy. This is a cardinal sin, and one which carries great danger. . . . Finally, it is sad that Morris never really dips below the surface." Nikolaas Tinbergen attempted to allay scientists' anxieties over his protégé's apparently sensationalizing methods: "The specialist who grumbles because he disagrees with interpretations, generalizations, or oversimplifications is not quite fair; what Morris is trying to do is to shock people into an awareness of our ignorance of ourselves. In this he certainly succeeds and I find it an important social service; it is a step in the important social process of cutting ourselves down to size."

Morris' next book, *Intimate Behaviour,* is a study of a basic form of communication, physical-contact behavior among human beings. He believes that such behavior is central to our existence, that its roots are formed around the time of birth, and that its absence forces a human to seek out the substitute, sham intimacies of our culture. Minutely described human sexual behavior occupies once again the very center of the author's attention. Alex Comfort thought this "a much better book" than Morris' previous two, and "timely, because it not only inculcates the cross-biologic viewpoint but deals with a number of our hangups in relation to the expression of our emotions, of which we are becoming increasingly aware." *Manwatching: A Field Guide to Human Behavior* describes and categorizes virtually every conceivable form of human action and behavior, innate and learned, and usually illustrates each category with photographs that are often striking. According to the author's introduction, it is "a book about actions, about how actions become gestures, and about how gestures transmit messages. As a species we may be technologically clever and philosophically brilliant, but we have not lost our animal property of being physically active; and it is this bodily activity that is the primary concern of the man-watcher."

With coauthors Peter Collett, Peter Marsh, and Marie O'Shaughnessy, Morris next published *Gestures: Their Origins and Distribution,* a three-year study of twenty symbolic gestures and their variants in forty locations in twenty-five countries, sponsored by the Guggenheim Foundation. The book delighted most critics. The *Economist* reviewer thought it "erudite and exact but wonderfully entertaining," Kay Larrieu called it "a pioneering effort toward the eventual establishment of a semantics of gesture," and Elizabeth Peer remarked that *"Gestures* is one of those rare scholarly books, that, by raising more questions than it answers, leaves the reader ravening for further explorations."

Morris' autobiography, *Animal Days,* is an amusing account of his forebears, youth, education, and career up to his departure from the zoo for the ICA. The book is mainly a series of connected anecdotes, long and short, which sometimes allow the reader to see unfamiliar sides of such famous scientists as Tinbergen, J.B.S. Haldane, and Karl von Frisch. The central characters, however, are invariably the animals, and Morris' central point, in Michael Schuyler's words, is that "we should be concerned that we are 'humanizing' animals, especially in zoos, to such a degree that they can no longer function in their native environment, preferring human company to that of their own kind." Walter Goodman likened the book to "a visit with an engaging raconteur who has spent his life in a fascinating field."

Since 1973, Morris has been a research fellow of Wolfson College, Oxford, a relatively new research foundation, and has been again working closely with Tinbergen's animal behavior research group in the university's zoology department. He has continued to paint in the surrealistic style, and has had several exhibitions of his work. He and his wife have a son, born in 1968, and divide their time between their home in North Oxford and a twenty-seven-room villa in Attard, Malta.

PRINCIPAL WORKS: The Reproductive Behaviour of the Ten-Spined Stickleback, 1958; Introducing Curious Creatures, 1961; The Biology of Art, 1962; The Mammals, 1965; The Naked Ape, 1967; The Human Zoo, 1969; Patterns of Reproductive Behaviour, 1970; Intimate Behaviour, 1971; Manwatching, 1977; The Soccer Tribe, 1981; The Book of Ages, 1984. *Autobiography*—Animal Days, 1979. *Juvenile*—The Story of Congo, 1958; Apes and Monkeys, 1964; The Big Cats, 1965; Zootime, 1966; Inrock, 1983. *As coauthor*—Men and Snakes, 1965; Men and Apes, 1966; Men and Pandas, 1967; Gestures, 1979.

ABOUT: Current Biography, 1974; Contemporary Authors 45–48, 1974; Who's Who, 1984; Who's Who in America, 1983–84. *Periodicals*—Best Sellers December 15, 1969; Book World October 12, 1969; February 27, 1972; Economist September 27, 1969; December 31, 1977; May 26, 1979; Library Journal July 1980; Natural History February 1980; January 1970; New Republic September 10, 1962; February 3, 1968; April 20, 1968; New Statesman October 13, 1967; September 26, 1969; May 15, 1970; October 15, 1971; May 18, 1979; Newsweek August 6, 1979; August 4, 1980; New York Herald Tribune Books August 12, 1962; New York Times Book Review February 4, 1968; November 30, 1969; May 5, 1972; November 13, 1977; August 10, 1980; Observer September 28, 1969; October 10, 1971; Saturday Review February 17, 1968; March 4, 1972; Science April 7, 1967; March 22, 1968; Science Digest February 1984; Time January 16, 1978; Times Literary Supplement December 30, 1965; June 23, 1966; November 9, 1967; October 30, 1969; January 27, 1978; December 7, 1979.

MORRIS, WILLIE (November 29, 1934–), American journalist, memoirist, and novelist, was born in Jackson, Mississippi, the son of Henry Rae Morris, a bookkeeper, and Marion (Weaks) Morris. He spent his childhood from the age of six in Yazoo County, on the edge of the Mississippi Delta country, then attended the University of Texas, where he wrote a good deal of what he later termed "Wolfean prose" for the *Daily Texan,* earning his bachelor's degree in 1956. He won a Rhodes scholarship and spent three years reading modern history at New College, Oxford University.

In 1960, Morris was hired by his "mentor and comrade" Ronnie Dugger to become editor of the *Texas Observer,* a crusading political weekly published in Austin. The magazine enjoyed a respectable circulation and was a never-ending source of exposés in the spectacularly corrupt world of Texas oil-based politics, but the fledgling journalist found the pace and the lack of support staff too taxing, and he resigned in 1962. After a brief sojourn in graduate school at Stanford University, he moved to New York City, where in 1963 he landed an editorial job on *Harper's* magazine. During his nine years there, the last four as editor-in-chief, the country's oldest magazine grew in circulation and prestige, publishing some of the best work of such writers as Norman Mailer, William Styron, Larry King, and David Halberstam. He resigned from *Harper's,* along with virtually his entire staff, in March 1971, after a long dispute with John Cowles, Jr., the principal owner. He later called his time as a magazine editor "an unhappy experience . . . I had given too much of myself to someone else's property, and to their caprices about it."

Two of Morris' best-received books of reportage, *North Toward Home* and *Yazoo: Integra-*

tion in a Deep-Southern Town, were published while he was at Harper's, the latter appearing in its entirety in the magazine. North Toward Home is a young man's autobiography which, although it says "something about belonging in America" and about the marked differences in life-styles in Mississippi, Texas, and Manhattan, is most interesting as a book, as Morris describes it in his introduction to Yazoo, "about myself and about the people I had grown up among in Yazoo." The Mississippi section of the book, which received much higher praise than the other two, "deeply disturbed the town," and later, when several return visits were required to measure the effects of school desegregation, he felt a strong ambivalence about going back: "Since my town is the place which shaped me, for better or worse, into the creature I now am, since it nurtured me and gave me much of whatever sensibility I now possess, since it is a small Deep-Southern place where the land and the remembered places have changed very little, where the generations come and go in the context of these common and remembered places and amidst the same drawn-out seasons, where mortality itself grips and maddens one's consciousness in the missing faces . . . I knew, as I had known for some time, that going back for me, even more than exposing myself in some new notoriety, would bring the most intense emotional pain." He soon abandons such romantically painful notions, and his portrait of his town, its white and black residents in the grip of rapid social change, is remarkable for its clear-eyed optimism. As Geoffrey Wolff wrote, Morris "suggests a potential community of Southern blacks and whites, a community bound tight for having shared ancient griefs and exhaustions, a community of many, many shared values and instincts."

Morris' other works of non-fiction focusing on the South include Terrains of the Heart, and Other Essays on Home, a collection of pieces, for the most part previously published, on the themes of home and homecoming, a book commissioned by the Yoknapatawpha Press of Oxford, Mississippi, and The Courting of Marcus Dupree, about the discovery (and exploitation) of a black high-school football star from Philadelphia, Mississippi, who was born "one month less a day" before three young white civil-rights workers were murdered in his town.

A decade of close friendship with the novelist James Jones, Morris' near neighbor in Sagaponack, near Bridghampton, Long Island, is the subject of what many consider his best book, James Jones: A Friendship. He acknowledges at the start that "the two great presences in my whole life were my mother . . . and my friend Jim Jones," and intends the book, begun shortly

after Jones' death from congestive heart failure in 1977, to be "an illumination of a friend, and perhaps of myself and others of us, and I hope it tells something about writing, especially about being a writer in America." The result is a revelatory portrait of one of the most aloof and mysterious of contemporary American writers. Although the two men met only in the mid-1960s, after Jones' return to the United States from his long exile in Paris, and although Jones was fifteen years Morris' senior, the two became "like brothers": "Beneath the rough exterior was a profoundly cultured and sophisticated man, a student of literature, history, art, music. He . . . had, too, an almost religious dedication to his work. Up until two days before he died he would be talking into a tape recorder about his novel. Even with the final collapse of his body he was the sanest man I ever knew. He was, in the truest and best sense, an old-fashioned man. He and his work were all of a piece; I never knew anyone who was more like his own writing, so attuned to the deep, informing spirit of it." Much of the book adopts this tone of intense admiration, a trait some critics—especially those unfriendly to Jones' work—found objectionable, yet the memoir was generally judged, in one critic's words, "anecdotal and affectionate, witty and wise."

Morris' only published venture into fiction, The Last of the Southern Girls, was accounted only a partial success. It tells the story of Carol Hollywell, an Arkansas debutante (said to be modeled on Barbara Howar), who arrives in Washington to seek her fortune in 1957. Her rise to prominence and her romances, especially with an idealistic congressman, are drily detailed, yet the moral is the familiar one that ambition feeds only upon itself and successful politicians use up everyone in sight. Critics found the story "great fun" with "fine dialogue," yet felt the author "has difficulty weaving expository material into his story" and had produced, in the end, nothing of any excitement. "It doesn't offend," wrote the reviewer for the New York Times Book Review, "it doesn't astonish. It doesn't bore; it doesn't enthrall. . . . The risk was negligible. And the significance also."

Morris married Celia Ann Buchan, a Texan, in August 1958; they have a son. He still lives in the Hamptons year round, and continues to consider himself a product of New York City and the South, "the two places in America that more than any others are the nation writ large, as many an exile has finally discovered." "I go back to the South," he writes in Yazoo, "physically and in my memories, to remind myself who I am, for the South keeps me going; it is an organizing principle, a feeling in the blood which pervades my awareness of my country and my civilization, and I know that Southerners are the most intensely incorrigible of all Americans. In the end, being what I am, I have no other choice; only New York could raise the question. When I am in the South and am driven by the old urge to escape again to the city, I still feel sorry for most of my contemporaries who do not have a place like mine to go back to, or to leave."

PRINCIPAL WORKS: *Non-fiction*—North Toward Home, 1967; Yazoo, 1971; James Jones, 1978; The Ghosts of Ole Miss and Other Essays, 1981; Terrains of the Heart, 1981; The Courting of Marcus Dupree, 1983. *Fiction*—The Last of the Southern Girls, 1973. *Juvenile*—Good Old Boy, 1971. *As editor*—The South Today, 100 years After Appomattox, 1965.

ABOUT: Contemporary Authors, revised series 17–20, 1976; Current Biography, 1976; King, Larry The Old Man and Lesser Mortals, 1974; Who's Who in America, 1983–84. *Periodicals*—America November 13, 1965; December 9, 1967; Atlantic June 1971; Best Sellers November 15, 1967; Book World October 15, 1967; Choice November 1971; October 1973; Christian Century October 25, 1967; November 17, 1971; Christian Science Monitor November 16, 1967; March 25, 1971; May 20, 1971; Commonweal October 26, 1973; Library Journal August 1965; September 15, 1967; June 1, 1971; May 15, 1973; October 15, 1978; Nation July 2, 1973; October 28, 1978; New Republic November 18, 1967; May 10, 1973; November 25, 1978; New York Review of Books December 21, 1967; September 2, 1971; New York Times Book Review October 22, 1967; May 16, 1971; May 20, 1973; December 17, 1978; December 18, 1983; New Yorker June 2, 1973; Newsweek November 6, 1967; March 15, 1971; May 10, 1971; Reporter November 30, 1967; Saturday Review January 13, 1968; June 5, 1971; Texas Observer November 16, 1962; Time May 10, 1971.

MORRISON, TONI (February 18, 1931–   ), American novelist, was born Chloe Anthony Wofford, in Lorain, Ohio, a steel town twenty-five miles west of Cleveland. She is the daughter of George and Ramah (Willis) Wofford, and the second of their four children. After graduating with honors from high school in Lorain, in 1949 she enrolled at Howard University in Washington, D.C. There she devoted much of her free time to the Howard University Players, a campus theater company, often appearing in its productions, and in the summers she traveled throughout the South with a repertory troupe made up of faculty members and students. At Howard she also met and married Harold Morrison, an architecture student from Jamaica, by whom she has two sons, Harold Ford and Slade Kevin. Morrison received her B.A. from Howard in 1953, and went on to do graduate work in English at Cornell University, where she wrote her

TONI MORRISON

thesis on Faulkner and Virginia Woolf and received her M.A. in 1955.

Morrison was instructor in English during 1955–57 at Texas Southern University, at Houston, and then taught in the English department at Howard. There, among others who came to prominence in the 1960s, she met Amiri Baraka (LeRoi Jones) and Andrew Young. Her students included Stokeley Carmichael and Claude Brown, who showed her his manuscript of *Manchild in the Promised Land*. In 1964 she resigned from Howard, and, following her divorce, moved with her children to Syracuse, New York, to take a job as a textbook editor with a subsidiary of Random House. After eighteen months, she was transferred to the New York headquarters of Random House, where she edited books by such black authors as Toni Cade Bambara and Gayl Jones. In 1970 her novel *The Bluest Eye* was published.

The Bluest Eye, set in the black community of a small Ohio town, chronicles the experience of the Breedlove family, who have traveled from the South to the Midwest, confronting a loss of purpose and identity in their lives. The story centers, particularly, upon twelve-year-old Pecola, who fantasizes that she will be given blue eyes, like Shirley Temple, the adored white child of films. She is, instead, raped and impregnated by her father, and at the end driven to madness. *The Bluest Eye* was received by reviewers as a striking first novel by a distinctive prose stylist. John Leonard described Morrison's prose as being "so precise, so faithful to speech and so charged with pain and wonder that the novel becomes pure poetry"; and Raymond Sokolov called the novel a lyrical story pitched in "a private tone, the tone, as it were, of black conversation."

Morrison's second novel, *Sula*, was nominated for the National Book Award in 1974 and was an alternate selection of the Book-of-the-Month Club. It deals with two black women, the sensual and morally rebellious Sula Peace, and Nel Wright, who marries, bears children, and is at last conscious of something missing in her life of coventionality. By the end, Sula and Nel seem like the contrasting and irreconcilable parts of a single self. Jonathan Yardley was particularly struck by Morrison's evocation of the life of a Midwestern town. "Morrison is not a Southern writer," he remarked, "but she has located place and community with the skill of a Flannery O'Connor or Eudora Welty." Many reviewers were impressed by Morrison's depiction of the sensual Sula, but some others demurred. The reviewer for the *Times Literary Supplement*, for example, felt that Sula is "left on the level of allegory in her growing up, her effect on the village and particularly at her death." Sara Blackburn noted a certain constriction in Morrison's envisioning of the tale, which "refuses to brim over into the world outside its provincial setting. . . . Toni Morrison is far too talented to remain only a marvelous recorder of the black side of provincial American life. If she is to maintain the large and serious audience she deserves, she is going to have to address a riskier reality than this beautiful but . . . distanced novel."

In her next novel, *Song of Solomon,* Morrison exceeded anything she had yet done, and was catapulted to national prominence. The novel received the National Book Critics Circle Award for 1977 and was a main selection of the Book-of-the-Month Club—the first novel by a black writer to be chosen since Richard Wright's *Native Son* in 1949. *Song of Solomon* details the life of a black family with the strange surname of Dead. Macon Dead, the patriarch of the clan, is obsessed by the idea of material advancement, and owns a large amount of real estate, while his estranged sister Pilate, somewhat like Sula, is an outcast and rebel, associated with the sensual, the inward, and the non-rational. Macon Dead, Jr., known as Milkman, is the inheritor of a complex family conflict that is also a conflict of black identity; and later in the novel he sets out on a "mythic" journey to discover his origins in the South. What he discovers is that the buried "humanity" of the family's past is his real treasure; the discovery sets him free and redeems him into life.

Song of Solomon received many favorable reviews, some of which cited the work as the most important novel by a black writer since Ralph Ellison's *Invisible Man.* "Mining black American folklore, mysticism, and mythology," Earl Frederick wrote, "the novel dazzles like a daydream." Frances Taliafero called *Song of Solomon* Morrison's most ambitious work, stunning in execution and effect. "The familiar framework of [initiation]," she commented, "supports a novel of amazing richness. Enchantment and practicality are inseparable, myth and symbol . . . perfectly compatible. . . . *Song of Solomon* is a fine title for this novel of wisdom and sensuousness, eccentrically combined." Susan Lardner, however, noted "problems" in the work—particularly the character of Guitar Baines, who she felt fails to become intelligible; and Vivian Gornick considered the mythic journey manipulative, "with the characters acting to fulfill the requirements of . . . structure. Once this happens, the plausibility of Milkman's search . . . begins to disintegrate. . . . It seems to me that the source of the artistic troubles in *Song of Solomon* lies with Morrison's choice of Milkman as protagonist—instead of one of the women in the book [who have been more powerfully imagined]. Milkman never really comes to life."

Morrison's *Tar Baby* is cast in the form of allegory. It begins on a French island in the Caribbean, at the home of a wealthy Philadelphian named Valerian Street. Valerian and his wife Margaret, who are white, have black servants, including a couple named Sydney and Ondine, whose light-skinned daughter Jadine has been educated by Valerian at the Sorbonne. A beauty and model, a showpiece of Valerian's creation, Jadine has little relation at all to her black heritage. The edgy tranquility of the house is then suddenly disrupted by the appearance there of a young runaway black man, Son, who suggests a primitive black past. The remainder of the novel, in which Jadine and Son attempt to come together but finally cannot, explores the cultural division created by white society between black men and women.

Although *Tar Baby* received a number of favorable reviews, with some critics calling it a brilliant novel of ideas, others expressed reservations or concluded that the book did not succeed at all. Wilfred Sheed considered it Morrison's weakest book. "With *Tar Baby*," he wrote, "Morrison has attempted to hitch . . . a bucking bronco of a theme onto a comedy of manners, and they're an odd pair. No sooner have we set up the thrumming poetry, the animistic sense that clouds and trees are onto something big, than we are exchanging persiflage with some desiccated white folks and their gelded black retainers in a gingerbread house in the Caribbean. The contrast, to put it temperately, is heavy-handed." Webster Schott observed that there was much that "is good, sometimes dazzling" in the work, but objected to Morrison's handling of the white couple as racial stereotypes, too obviously manipulated for the sake of delivering political messages. Somewhat similarly, Brina Caplan remarked: "Undoubtedly, *Tar Baby* is successful [as a novel of ideas] . . . but it remains teasingly deficient as a novel of character. Because the primary function of Morrison's characters is to voice representative opinions, they arrive on stage vocal and higly conscious, their histories symbolically indicated or merely sketched."

In addition to her writing and her work as an editor at Random House, Morrison is in demand as a lecturer on modern black and feminist literature. She has at various times held academic posts: associate professor at the State University of New York at Purchase in 1971–72; visiting lecturer at Yale University, 1976–77; and visiting lecturer at Bard College in 1983–84. In 1984 she was appointed to an Albert Schweitzer chair at the State University of New York at Albany. In a cover story on her in *Newsweek* magazine, Morrison revealed how remarkably busy and versatile her life has been—as a "working mother," novelist, editor, and lecturer. She owns a four-story house near Nyack, New York, which she bought after the success of *Song of Solomon,* and keeps an apartment in Manhattan.

PRINCIPAL WORKS: The Bluest Eye, 1970; Sula, 1974; Song of Solomon, 1977; Tar Baby, 1981.

ABOUT: American Women Writers 3, 1981; Contemporary Authors, first revision series 29–32, 1978; Contemporary Novelists, 1982; Current Biography, 1979; Dictionary of Literary Biography 6: American Novelists Since World War II, 1980; Evans, M. (ed.) Black Women Writers (1950–1980): A Critical Evaluation, 1984; Living Black American Authors, 1977. *Periodicals*—Atlantic April 1981; Book World February 3, 1974; March 22, 1981; Nation November 19, 1977; New Republic March 21, 1981; Newsweek March 30, 1981; New York Times Book Review December 30, 1973; September 11, 1977; April 30, 1981.

*MUJICA LAINEZ, MANUEL (November 11, 1910–April 21, 1984), Argentinian poet, novelist, and short story writer was born in Buenos Aires to an aristocratic family of old Argentinian lineage. His education followed the customary

course of men of his class: trips and prolonged residences in France and England, cultural bilingualism, journalism and literature in the midst of wealth and aesthetic refinement. Further, he worked for many years as art critic of the important conservative daily *La Nación.* After Perón's fall in September 1955, Mujica Láinez was Director of Cultural Relations for the Ministry of Foreign Relations for three years. He was a member of the Argentinian Academy of Letters, an honor not shared by any other fiction writer. Recipient of several national and municipal awards, he was accorded national homage shortly before his death.

Mujica Láinez cultivated practically all of the literary genres in his forty-three books, but above all he is regarded as an accomplished storyteller. Apart from his two volumes of poetry, a volume of essays, and two biographies of "gauchesco" poets (1936–1948), his *oeuvre* chiefly consists of short stories—*Aquí vivieron* (They Lived Here, 1949), *Misteriosa Buenos Aires* (Mysterious Buenos Aires, 1951), *Crónicas reales* (Royal Chronicles, 1967), *El escarabajo* (The Black Beetle, 1982), *Un novelista en el Museo del Prado* (A Novelist at the El Prado Museum, 1984)—and novels—*Don Galaz de Buenos Aires* (Don Galaz of Buenos Aires, 1938), *Los ídolos* (The Idols, 1953), *La casa* (The House, 1954), *Los viajeros* (The Travelers, 1954), *Invitados en El Paraíso* (Guests at The Paradise, 1957), *Bomarzo* (Bomarzo, 1962), *El unicornio* (*The Wandering Unicorn,* 1965), *De milagros y de melancolías* (About Miracles and Melancholy, 1968), *Cecil* (Cecil, 1972), *El laberinto* (The Labyrinth, 1974), *El viaje de los siete demonios* (The Trip of the Seven Demons, 1974), *Sergio* (Serge, 1976), *El gran teatro* (The Great Theatre, 1979).

Like Proust, Mujica Láinez is considered to a great extent the chronicler of his nation's upper class. He reviewed Argentinian history from the mythical past, through the golden years at the end of last century, to the beginning of the present, in order to show its present decadence in the midst of industrialization and new millionaires totally devoid of a sense of tradition and principles. Ironic and skeptical, he drew a dynamic portrait of the decadence of the ruling Argentinian class and not a mere lifeless chronicle. His novels and short stories about Buenos Aires have a cyclical aspect; several of their characters appear in different books, highlighting the continuity of a way of life. This is well exemplified in the best novel of this cycle, *La casa* (The House). In later books, Mujica Láinez abandoned the Argentinian scene and shifted to the Italy of the Renaissance, to imaginary medieval European kingdoms, showing remarkable pow-

°mo͞o hē´ kä lä näs´

ers of reconstruction and even of literary archeology. But this change is only geographical and
historical because the spiritual and psychological
climate is very similar to his former creations.
His two novels translated into En-
glish—*Bomarzo* and *The Wandering Unicorn*—are the most accomplished samples of this
"second cycle" of his narrative.

Bomarzo (1962), the basis of Alberto Ginas-
tera's opera of the same name, is the voluminous
biography of the physically deformed Pier
Francesco Orsini, Duke of Bomarzo, who, from
his twentieth-century study, re-creates his own
past in a Renaissance court complete with
princes, *condottieri,* jesters, and artists. With detailed prolixity Mujica Láinez narrates the adventures of the protagonist, magically bringing
to life the Duke's fantastic park full of grotesque,
gigantic stone figures that embody his tormented soul. He introduces historical, literary, and artistic personalities of the times, such as
Paracelsus who cures the Duke; Benvenuto Cellini who gives him a ring; Lorenzo Lotto who
paints his portrait; Michelangelo who rejects a
commission but recommends his friend del
Cuca; Miguel de Cervantes who saves the Duke's
life at the battle of Lepanto; Charles the Fifth
the great Spanish Emperor who knights him;
and even the pirate Barbarossa who has some
dealings with the Duke. The descriptions at the
beginning of the novel are perhaps the finest—
Pier Francesco humiliated and scorned by his
brothers; his confinement with a skeleton; the
moment when his father notices him and caress-
es him slightly with one finger; and his chats
with his grandmother. In *Bomarzo* the reader attends the birth of the Duke, views the fall of the
house of Medici, the arrival of Charles the Fifth
in Naples, everything—the historical and the
imaginary, the veridical and the fictitious—
assembled in a narrative in which the grandiose
and the ridiculous, the comic and the dramatic
are always present.

El unicornio (*The Wandering Unicorn,* 1965)
is the story of a medieval knight from birth until
death. This story is a pretext for the evocation of
a world in which, according to Mujica Láinez,
"men accepted only what was unusual as if it
were habitual" and in which familiarity with the
supernatural conferred upon life a touch of magnificence. The novel is somewhat wordy, achieving its best effects in descriptive passages. In
later books—*Crónicas reales* (Royal Chronicles)
and *El viaje de los siete demonios* (The Trip of
the Seven Demons)—Mujica Láinez created a
panorama, both historical and satirical, of Europe as the center of modern culture.

Manuel Mujica Láinez wrote of himself: "I
was and I am terribly timid. I had to confront
the social group to which I belonged and whose
values I did not share. I was neither interested
in the ranch nor in cattle; their only attraction
for me was literary. I disliked sports; I was not
machista; I was not strong. I loved literature and
beautiful things. I loved merriment and pleasure. I detested the somber character of the Argentinian males. I had few weapons to defend
myself: the boldness of timidity, my imagination
and my irony. With these I defeated the
dragon."

WORKS IN ENGLISH TRANSLATION: Gregory Rabassa translated *Bomarzo* in 1969. *The Wandering Unicorn* was
translated by Mary Sitton in 1984.

ABOUT: Contemporary Authors 81–84, 1979; Encyclopedia of World Literature in the 20th Century 4, 1975;
Foster D. W. and V. R. (eds.) Dictionary of Contemporary Latin American Authors, 1975; Foster, D. W. and
V. R. (eds.) Modern Latin American Literature 2,
1975. *Periodicals*—Books Abroad 43, 1969; 44, 1970;
49, 1975; Hispania 59, 1976; Latin American Literary
Review 1, 1973; New York Review of Books February
10, 1972.

*MULISCH, HARRY (July 29, 1927–   ),
Dutch novelist, poet, playwright, essayist, and li-
brettist, was born in Haarlem. His father was
born in Gablonz, then in Austria, now in Czechoslovakia. His mother, Alice Schwartz, was born
in Antwerp, of German and Austrian Jewish parents. They met in Holland, where Mulisch grew
up as "a descendant of an international potpourri of nomads." Though he has made of the
Dutch language his home, and lives permanently in Amsterdam, he is very much a citizen of
Europe.

Mulisch's parents divorced when he was nine
and he remained in Haarlem with his father who
worked there for Jewish bankers. When these
had to flee at the onset of World War II,
Mulisch's father became personnel director of a
bank under German control, while his mother
worked for the Jewish Council in Amsterdam.
Her mother and grandmother died in the Sobi-
bor camp. At the end of the war it was his father
who was sent to a concentration camp. "It isn't
so much that I went through the war, I AM the
Second World War," says Mulisch. Much of his
work is influenced by the ambiguous two-
sidedness of his childhood loyalties.

°mŏŏl´ ish

HARRY MULISCH

At first fascinated by physics, his studies in this field were interrupted by the war and he began to write. His first novel, *Archibald Strohalm,* received a literary prize in 1951. From then on his phenomenal output and eight more prizes have made him one of the rare Dutch authors who have been able to live from their writings. His first international success came with the novel *Het Stenen Bruidsbed* (*The Stone Bridal Bed,* 1959). The title refers to the city of Dresden to which an American bomber-pilot, instrumental in its ruin, returns in the fifties. Classical in structure, the novel is a study in guilt, at once highly contemporary and yet constantly referring to Homeric times. This historical sense and ability to see contemporary events from an impartial perspective, the highly civilized sensibility and yet awareness of the fundamental barbaric ground of human nature, characterize much of Mulisch's writing. In his play *Tanchelijn* for instance, the life of a Flemish heretic is treated on a vast canvas of excessive barbaric splendor, while his eyewitness accounts of the Eichmann trial, his humorous sketch of the Provo movement, and report on a visit to Cuba are those of a political observer of the sixties. His position remains that of a neo-liberal, a leftist without a party, a pacifist involved in the antinuclear arms movement.

Mulisch married, when he was forty-four, Sjoerdje Woudenburg, twenty-one years his junior, by whom he has two daughters. In the seventies his interest inevitably turned to the women's question with a highly popular novel, *Twee Vrouwen* (Two Women, 1975). Straight-

forward in style, it is a story of love between two women told in the first person by one of them. The necessity of a man's intervention to give them a child develops into a fatal triangle. The film version, with Bibi Andersson and Anthony Perkins, was shown at the Cannes Film Festival in 1979.

His latest success and perhaps most universal in appeal is the novel *De Aanslag* (*The Assault,* 1982). It sold 200,000 copies within a year, a record for Holland, and was translated into German, French, Norwegian, Czechoslovakian, and other languages. The popularity of this book is perhaps due to its direct, simple style and cleverly unfolding plot which reveals all the intricate details of an event which took place in 1945, during the last winter of the war. Perhaps no country is still haunted by the Occupation as much as Holland. Obsessed with a Calvinistic need to classify people and events as "right" or "wrong," a continuous reevaluation still goes on. Mulisch sets his story in a typical middle-class Dutch setting, where a typical family in Haarlem is victimized by a senseless act of violence. A young survivor, Anton Steenwijk, is confronted throughout his life against his will with various characters that reveal new facets of this event which he has been trying to forget. As in a whodunit, one waits to find someone to blame, but there is no one. Only human nature and its emotional responses exist, Mulisch seems to say, and quoting Homer he proposes " . . . what one remembers are not the soldiers fighting, but the image of nature—and that goes on existing." Fond of metaphor, Mulisch continuously enriches his story-telling with flights of fancy that make the book readable on many levels. As a national writer, his point of view is definitely related more to the humanist tradition of Erasmus or Spinoza than to Calvinism, but his affinity for myth and for the illogical ground of history places him at the center of European thought of the second half of the twentieth century. In his vast most recent work, *De Compositie van der Wereld* (The Composition of the World, 1985), he attempts to coordinate his philosophical and imaginary views in an all encompassing system based on the harmony of the musical octave.

WORKS IN ENGLISH TRANSLATION: Adrienne Dixon translated *The Stone Bridal Bed* in 1962 and *Two Women* in 1980. *The Assault* was translated in 1985 by Claire Nicolas White, who also translated one of Mulisch's nine volumes of poetry, *Wat Poezie Is* as *What Poetry Is* in 1982.

ABOUT: Columbia Dictionary of Modern European Literature, 1980; Contemporary Authors, revised series 9–10, 1974; Meijer, R. P. Literature of the Low Countries, 1978. Periodicals—New Statesman October 5, 1980; Observer October 5, 1980; Times (London) November 27, 1980; Times Literary Supplement October 3, 1980.

*NAGEL, ERNEST (November 16, 1901–), American philosopher, was born in Nové Město, a town northeast of Bratislava in present-day Czechoslovakia, the son of Isidor Nagel, a shopkeeper, and the former Frida Weisz. He came to the United States with his family at the age of ten, and became a naturalized citizen in 1919. Nagel received his bachelor's degree from City College in 1923 and his master's and doctorate in philosophy from Columbia University (1925 and 1931, respectively). He taught science and mathematics in the New York City public school system from 1923 to 1929, while earning his graduate degrees. Except for one year (1930–31) teaching philosophy at City College, he spent his entire academic career at Columbia, as full professor from 1946, and as the John Dewey professor of philosophy from 1955 to 1966. Since 1970 he has been university professor emeritus.

Nagel was termed by the editors of his festschrift, Philosophy, Science, and Method (1969), "one of this generation's most distinguished philosophers of science and one of its most effective spokesmen for scientific naturalism. [These] are intimately connected, for he believes that the methods and results of science vindicate the spirit of classical naturalism, and that modern naturalism is intolerably thin when it is not informed by considerable familiarity with those methods and results. Nagel therefore insists that theorists of knowledge should carefully examine the logic of science; and . . . that the conclusions and self-corrective methods of science lend support to social and political liberalism."

His first important publication was a textbook, written with Morris R. Cohen, that proved to be a classic in its field. Introduction to Logic and Scientific Method was many times revised and reprinted. The authors recognized that although nearly all texts in logic before theirs closely followed, in format and even in examples used, the standard set by Aristotle's Organon—"terms, propositions, syllogisms and allied forms of inference, scientific method, probability and fallacies—there is a bewildering Babel of tongues as to what logic is about." They define logic as "concerned with the question of the adequacy or probative value of different kinds of evidence" and as "the autonomous science of the objective though formal conditions of valid inference." Their text had high aims: "the realistic formalism of Aristotle, the scientific penetration of Peirce, the pedagogical soundness of Dewey, and the mathematical rigor of Russell—this was the ideal constantly present to the authors." In a benedictory review of the book, John Dewey, then perhaps the greatest living American philosopher, called it "solid [and] genuinely modern. . . . For the first time, as far as I am aware, it unites in a textbook the revisions and additions of competent thinkers in the logical field with an exposition of the traditional Aristotelian logic and with an effective critical restatement of the traditional 'inductive' logic of Mill. The task of bringing about such a union within the compass of a textbook is extraordinarily difficult."

Like most philosophers, Nagel has opted for the article as the preferred means of communication in his field. His first major collection of previously published essays was Sovereign Reason and Other Studies in the Philosophy of Science, published in 1954, sixteen carefully argued pieces, many of them from the 1930s, which are unified by four main themes: (1) the relation of abstract scientific theory to ordinary experience; (2) the revision of classical metaphysical assumptions about the nature of reliable knowledge; (3) the expendability of any metaphysical system that pretends to encompass all the sciences; and (4) the way in which scientific research has affected established modes of thinking, and produced new ones. The author concentrates in several of the essays on analyzing the contributions to the philosophy of science of such influential philosophers as Peirce, Whitehead, Russell, and Brand Blanshard. Robert Palter wrote that "Nagel's strictures always illuminate by challenging us to reconsider any settled opinions we may have formed about the philosophies he is discussing."

Nagel's other compilations of related articles are Logic Without Metaphysics, a companion collection to Sovereign Reason, and Teleology Revisited and Other Essays in the Philosophy and History of Science. The latter collection, eloquent testimony to the author's continuing vigor as a philosopher a decade after his retirement, comprises his response to the growing skepticism about the logic of scientific inquiry and even the concept of scientific method itself. Nagel terms himself "an unreconstructed empirical rationalist, who continues to believe that the logical methods of the modern natural sciences are the most effective instruments men have yet devised for acquiring reliable knowledge of the world and for distinguishing warranted claims to such

°nä´ gel

knowledge from those that are not." Several of the essays "deal explicitly with the challenge from the 'new philosophy of science,' which has cast doubt on the possibility of acquiring reliable knowledge through scientific enquiry." He examines current misconceptions about the "old philosophy of science" and its exponents, and places in perspective the challenges from such philosophers of science as Thomas Kuhn, Paul Feyerabend, and Karl Popper.

Nagel's one extended text in his field is a lengthy and rigorous one—*The Structure of Science: Problems in the Logic of Scientific Explanation*. It constitutes a summation of his particular, somewhat traditional way of looking at scientific enquiry, and is, in his words, "an examination of logical patterns exhibited in the organization of scientific knowledge as well as of the logical methods whose use (despite frequent changes in special techniques and revolutions in substantive theory) is the most enduring feature of modern science." J. J. C. Smart praised the author's "lucidity and dispassionateness. He is indefatigable in extracting the grains of truth that may perhaps reside in the most far-fetched philosophical views." The reviewer for the *Times Literary Supplement* also called the book a summary: "Not only does it sum up Professor Nagel's own contribution to the understanding of the workings of science, but it also brings together into one connected whole a tradition of philosophic enquiry into the sciences. . . . Broadly speaking, the author sees a physical theory as a logical or mathematical calculus, partially interpreted, on one side, . . . in terms of experimentally defined concepts, and on the other in terms of some model, in which our picture of the workings of nature is expressed. This is not a new idea, but what distinguishes Professor Nagel's account is the detailed working out of the implications of this account."

Perhaps the most widely known of Nagel's works is the short explanatory book he wrote with James R. Newman, *Gödel's Proof*. This is still the best nontechnical account of Kurt Gödel's celebrated paper of 1931 which challenged the belief, until then widely held in philosophical circles, that the theorems of mathematics could all be deduced from a set of axioms with the sole help of principles of logic. The paper, in the authors' words, "presented mathematicians with the astounding and melancholy conclusion that the axiomatic method has certain inherent limitations, which rule out the possibility that even the ordinary arithmetic of the integers can ever be fully axiomatized. What is more, it is impossible to establish the internal logical consistency of a very large class of deductive systems . . . unless one adopts principles of

reasoning so complex that their internal consistency is as open to doubt as that of the systems themselves." The reviewer for the *Times Literary Supplement* wrote, "Though *Gödel's Proof* is even more abstract than the beliefs it calls in question it has convinced those who are able to follow it. . . . Mr. Nagel and Mr. Newman succeed in making clear the background of the problem, the basic structure of the demonstrations, and the core of the conclusions."

Nagel has been an active member of all the major philosophical organizations, and over two decades was editor of three influential philosophy journals: *Journal of Symbolic Logic* (1939–45), *Journal of Philosophy* (1940–56), and *Philosophy of Science* (1956–59). He has twice been a Guggenheim fellow (1934–35; 1950–51), and has received several honorary doctorates, including one each from the City University of New York (1972) and Columbia (1971).

Nagel married Edith Haggstrom, a physicist, in January 1935. They have two sons.

WORKS: On the Logic of Measurement, 1932; (with Morris R. Cohen) Introduction to Logic and Scientific Method, 1934; Principles of the Theory of Probability, 1939; Sovereign Reason, 1954; Logic without Metaphysics, 1957; (with James R. Newman) Gödel's Proof, 1958; The Structure of Science, 1961; Teleology Revisited, 1979.

ABOUT: Contemporary Authors 93-96, 1980; Morgenbesser, S., Suppes, P., and White, M. (eds.) Philosophy, Science, and Method, 1969. *Periodicals*—American Political Science Review March 1955; American Sociology Review August 1961; Choice December 1979; Ethics January 1955; Journal of Philosophy April 12, 1934; April 12, 1962; Nation May 2, 1934; June 10, 1961 New Republic November 29, 1954; New York Times January 2, 1955; Saturday Review February 5, 1955; Times Literary Supplement November 1, 1934; May 26, 1961.

*NAGY, LASZLO (July 17, 1925–January 30, 1978), Hungarian poet and translator, was born in Felsöiszkáz, a small village not far from Lake Balaton. His parents, frequent subjects of his poems, were peasants who constantly struggled to hold on to their land to support their four children. His mother's story-telling and drawing skills deeply influenced Nagy's development. His intimate relationship with nature provided him with a vast store of imagery for use in his poetry. He was, he remarked, raised "among tales and ballads, in the enchanting, command-

°näj, läs´ lō

LASZLO NAGY

ing rhythms and in the Niagara of the songs of winter festivity that assailed the house." His half-wild life in the fields ended abruptly at age ten when osteomyelitis lamed his left leg.

During his early schooling Nagy excelled only in penmanship, spelling, and drawing. Later, he and two sisters attended school in nearby Pápa, where their grandmother, at great financial sacrifice to her and his parents, moved to make a home for them. Interested in the graphic arts, Nagy really wanted to become a painter but was already translating Heine and versifying on his own. In 1941 he entered the Business School of the Reformed College in Pápa but often neglected his studies to paint in the city's outskirts. As the Soviet Army drove the Germans from the area, he watched a large part of his village burn down and helped bury the dead by the wagon load. "After I threw the handgrenades left behind," he stated, "I planted poppyseed with my mother, and I said peace has come and I shall go back to school." He participated in the student reform movement and graduated in 1945. The poems he wrote at this time expressed his love of nature and animals, described the hard life of the peasant, and revealed an early obsession with the paradox of life and death as well as doubts about the existence of God.

Feeling stifled by village life, he went to Budapest in the fall of 1946 to study graphic arts at the College of Industrial Design but soon left it for a people's college then being established. He was swiftly caught up in the current optimism about the social and economic justice that socialism was extending to workers and peasants. He finally decided to become a poet instead of

an artist, because, he said, "verse is more lively and can immortalize a place, a feeling, an event with a few motions." Seven of his poems were published in the Christmas 1947 issue of *Valóság* (Reality). At the college he and Ferenc Juhász, who was also to become a noted poet, vowed to create a new kind of poetic language for their country. Both later entered the Attila József College to study Hungarian literaure, philosophy, and sociology, but left it when they found the courses meaningless.

His book of poems *Tünj el, fájás* (Vanish, Pain) appeared in 1949; many of the poems celebrated the lives of workers and peasants amid increased industrialization and the establishment of agricultural cooperatives after the Rákosi government came to power in 1948; some experimented with the versification of seventeenth-century Hungarian love songs. *Tüzér és rozs* (Gunner and Rye), published in 1951, contained thirty-two poems. Those praising Stalin, the Soviet Army, and Communism were omitted from later collections. Shortly afterward, he spent eighteen months in Bulgaria learning the language and translating extensively from that country's folk literature; this activity prepared him for the use of folklore and ballad measures in his later poetry. When he returned to Hungary, he was distressed by the conditions the Communist regime had created. Years later he said of this time: "On my return I was shocked: the nation was impoverished, agriculture was in ruin, private farms were plundered. . . . I saw a sad, tragic, ruthless exploitation. The drama of 1956 began at this time." The poems expressing this deep betrayal of the humane ideals of socialism by the country's political leaders were not published until 1953, in the periodical *Csillag* (Star). His response is best expressed in "Gyöngyszoknya" (Skirt with Pearls) written in 1953, the first to manifest his talent for the long poem and flowing imagery. The poem attacks the deplorable situation through images of a hail storm and superstition. A powerful woman with a skirt of pearls comes driving a wagon above the wheat fields. During a hellish dance she casts her pearls to earth and destroys the crop. At the close, a lone man appears; undefeated by the horror before him, he vows to start anew. Nagy stated that he wrote the poem and others like it "to save my self-respect and poetic integrity."

In 1952 he married Margit Szécsi, also a poet. He became a staff member of *Kisdobos* (Drummer Boy), a children's magazine. To his great personal anguish, he did not participate in the 1956 uprising. Later, this failure became the subject of a soul-searching poem, "A falak négyszögében" (Squared by Walls):

Couldn't you have died,
or at least bled,
instead of pacing the floor
stunned with despair?
You kept clear of the trouble:—
bullets, armoured tracks, emblazoned
girl's screams. Not for you the broken
wheels, scattering rooftiles,
grim gangs of working lads,
and soot-brindled petals.
You did not spill one drop
of blood, and when it stopped,
you had only gone gray and mad.

—trans. Tony Connor and George Gömöri

Several more books of his poems appeared before the 1956 uprising, but afterward, except for a collected edition, 1944–1956, only his translations were published in book form, and for several years even public recitations of his poems were discouraged because they expressed pessimism about the future of Hungary. Nagy considered the late 1950s to be the most painful years of his life, when he was charged with financial trickery and even physically assaulted in Sofia by a countryman because he had "blood on his hands." His poems had attracted critical attention from the very beginning, and though reviewers generally saw the maturity of his artistry and placed him in the forefront of the new poets, they regretted that his poems were little concerned with the life around him and pessimistic in outlook, literary attributes at the center of debates during the time of schematism. However, once schematism became passé and his *Himnusz minden időben* (Hymn for Anytime) appeared in 1965, his poems, as he himself stated, "received their due, even though I did nothing in their behalf, did not campaign, did not abase or sell out anything for myself." In the 1960s, he broke out of his private world and developed a wide circle of literary friends, participating in many literary evenings and recording readings of his poems, many of which were set to music. He became picture editor of *Élet és Irodalom* (Life and Literature) in 1959, a post he held until his death.

Nagy's shock at the deplorable conditions he found on his return from Bulgaria caused a striking change in his concept of poetry and his view of existence and inspired a rich period of creativity between 1954 and 1956. Rebelling against the prevailing doctrine that the duty of poetry is to serve society along the lines predicated by socialist realism, he dealt increasingly with the subjects of love and nature and questions of ultimate concern to mankind generally: life and death, pleasure and pain, love and loneliness, and infinity. The personal tone diminished and his world view came to the fore, especially his distress at current threats to human existence and the natural world, and the degeneration of

ethical norms. As he reached out for the human community, his poetic line became longer and more complex, and his poems, using mythical and folkloristic images without their traditional associations, conveyed archetypal patterns of human behavior and situations, often fluctuating between hope and despair about the prospects for human happiness. Such was especially true of the poems the critics called "long songs," among them "Vasárnap gyönyöre" (The Bliss of Sunday, 1955), a poem celebrating the simple pleasures of the workingman's holiday and voicing the confidence that mankind will never surrender the pleasures and humaneness of this day. In the first half of the 1960s, he wrote even longer poems, dynamic in character and often tragic and angry in tone. In "Menyegzö" (Wedding), written in 1964, the Bride and Groom represent the archetypal opposition between the new and the conventional and defy the established canons by contrasting the couple's spiritual dignity and the sensual pleasures of the guests. Based on his direct observation of a wedding ceremony in Bulgaria, the poem, according to Nagy, "opposes deterioration and destruction, every power to revoke in behalf of the young." Although often despairing at the fact that poetry had not been able to prevent "the murderous twentieth century" from happening, he nevertheless found some personal significance in his poetic activity at this time. In "Ki viszi át a szerelmet" (Carrying Love, 1965), he felt that creativity gave meaning to his struggles with life, especially in preserving human love:

When my life has sunk for good
who will battle that deadly bird?
whose mouth will be strong enough to bear
foundering Love to the farther shore?

—trans. Tony Connor and George Gömöri

The poems written from 1967 to 1972 were still filled with sadness and concern for the human condition. He did not think humanity would improve: "Many old troubles can be repaired with the tools of civilization, but perhaps we are living in such a historical state that mankind cannot see a comforting future." Although he believed that education can elevate mankind from an animal state, he asked: " . . . what kind of humanity is it that can tolerate the inhumanity present in the world?" During this same period, he began to write prose poems. Among them, "Vértanú arabs kanca" (The Martyred Arabian Mare) is an especially telling depiction of human cruelty. The white mare is beaten to death by drunken field workers, and Nagy's father flays her aborted black colt, the entire experience leaving the poet powerless to find consolation for the horror he witnessed: " . . . we were all soiled and moved along repentant. And there is no end, can be no end to the road: we move through the night to the end of time. I in front with a hurricane lamp, in man-high frost."

A new, quite prolific period began after 1973. Although he wrote playful and humorous poems using strokes of irony, he remained skeptical about human potential for good: "Our century nearing its end proves that these couple of decades demanded more victims than, say, from the Mohács Disaster [1526] to the beginning of the twentieth century. This is tragic; it shows that . . . thoughts of defending humankind have not advanced very far. Human greed, the desire to slaughter for material goods—this must all be eradicated from human history. When someone hopes for all this without fear, that is suspect to me. One cannot be idly hopeful of mankind's goodness. Mankind must be made better, and we can achieve successes in this way. This is the work of the poet and more broadly of human beings who serve the intellect."

Nagy considered his translations of poetry to be an integral part of his life's work. They were at the center of his activity in the 1960s, when he translated nearly thirty thousand lines, saying "they remind me of my troubles, joys, and concerns." In addition to the folk poetry of Bulgaria and the Balkans, he translated from the works of Spanish, Canadian, Yugoslavian, Swedish, German, Bulgarian, Roumanian, Polish, South American, Russian, ancient Chinese, French, and English poets. Among them are Arthur Rimbaud, Guillaume Apollinaire, William Butler Yeats, Gregory Corso, Dylan Thomas, and Federico García Lorca, the latter two clearly influencing Nagy's own poetic development. Entitling one of his books of translations Darázskirály (Wasp King), he explained that "like the wasp with the honey, the translator steals the sweetness of the foreign spirit. These violent thefts do not harm anyone; people gladly accept these aggressions, especially those of a small country."

A year before his death, in answer to an interviewer's question, he summarized his attitude toward life: "Hope? we can do nothing more than what we, especially the humanists, have been doing all along, to continue as the warriors, partisans, and secret advocates for a better lot. We must not give up hope; after all, it is only hope that helps us to break out of the greatest tragedies and catastrophes, the afflicted masses to rise from them. At the same time, let's also exercise the right to doubt; this is the motor that drives our creative work. We must look critically at our work and that of others. We must constantly do better. This is our purpose."

Nagy received many awards: the Attila József Prize in 1950, 1953, and 1955, the Kossuth Prize in 1966, the Golden Laurel of the International Poets' Festival (Yugoslavia) in 1968, the International Botev Prize (Bulgaria) in 1976, and the Endre Ady Memorial Award in 1977. In final tribute, hundreds attended his funeral, with groups singing folk songs and some of his own lyrics. In March 1984 his home in Felsöiszkáz was dedicated as a national monument.

WORKS IN ENGLISH TRANSLATION: Selected poems by Nagy, 1953–1971, were collected and translated into English by Tony Connor and Kenneth McRobbie, 1973, with the title *Love of the Scorching Wind.* Translations of other poems, some short prose pieces, and an interview are published in Albert Tezla's *Ocean at the Window: Hungarian Prose and Poetry since 1945,* 1980. There are also selections of his poems in English translation in Miklos Vajda's *Modern Hungarian Poetry,* 1977.

ABOUT: Columbia Dictionary of Modern European Literature, 1980; Tezla, A. Ocean at the Window, 1980. *Periodicals*—New Hungarian Quarterly Winter 1978; Times Literary Supplement March 15, 1974; World Literature Today Autumn 1978.

NATHAN, LEONARD (EDWARD) (November 8, 1924–   ), American poet, critic, and translator, writes: "I was born in Los Angeles, California, grew up there, served in the U.S. Army during World War II, and afterwards attended the University of California at Berkeley. I'm married and have three children, all now on their own. I haven't a glimmer as to why in early adolescence I decided to become a poet. My family was not bookish. Nobody I knew as a boy had any notion of what a poet was, let alone that poetry was an available calling. But for me, it was that calling or nothing. A kindly high school teacher—himself a writer—gave me a book on traditional prosody; perhaps this is why I have clung to a certain formality when so many other poets of my generation have moved toward the open and free styles.

"Six years teaching at Modesto Junior College got me close to the country and far enough away from the University, where everybody was a poet and it was hard to hear oneself under the echoes of Yeats, Eliot, Pound, Stevens and Auden (Williams and Olson hadn't quite made it West yet and the Beats were only beginning to be heard). When I did come back to the University, I came back to a department, Rhetoric, in which the human voice was taken seriously. Ever since I have worked toward a poetry in which voice, the sound of someone talking to others, was central. But I also wanted this voice to possess an eloquence that lifted it above con-

LEONARD NATHAN

versation. In this, I never betrayed that primer on prosody that still had faith in the idea that poetry ought to be more memorable than ordinary discourse. My ideal, then, is to blend the immediacy of actual speech with the formality of a special occasion. I believe in this—that I have shared a common aim with some of the poets of my generation: Howard Nemerov and Maxine Kumin, for example, different as they are. And the slightly older poets I have admired— William Stafford, Theodore Weiss, Josephine Miles, and Karl Shapiro, to name a few—have aimed, it seems to me, at much the same effect.

"But unlike some of these, I have never found (to my own ear) a steady voice, developing but recognizably the same from poem to poem, book to book. I always surprise myself a little with what comes next, a fact which I have, in bad moments, attributed to lack of character; in better moments, to a refusal to repeat myself. Still, like other, steadier poets, I have obsessions that persist in whatever I do: persistence itself, for example, that minor courage within the grasp of non-heroes. The other-worldliness of this world has been an obsession of mine. So too has been communication, both in its difficulty and in its amazing power, that moment when everything seems to come together right. These obsessions have, of course, been partly shaped by the great social movements of the time, though these tend to enter my work indirectly. And underlying all these obsessions has been a deeper one: to see things whole, if only momentarily so.

"I've never regretted my calling, though its rewards aren't always visible. Nor have I ever regretted working as a teacher, an occupation no

more dangerous to writing poetry than any other. There are characteristically bad poems written by academics; but there are characteristically bad poems written by truck drivers and saints. Teaching demands a certain clarity, good hearing, and persuasiveness. I would like my poems to have these characteristics too, as well as another associated with teaching: subjects that matter beyond the narrow range of the personal.

"I share the common view that poetry is somehow expressive of the poet. But I also am convinced that mere expressiveness is self-serving or futile unless *what* is expressed applies to the human condition and can be communicated in a language that transcends the poet's private experience. I believe I'm talking here about truth or, at least, the truth available to poetry: the unique quality of sharable lives. Some currents of contemporary thought tend to cast doubt not only on the possibility of communicating such a truth, but on the very existence of that truth itself. I cling to the old belief that the poet's task is to find true relations between the personal and the public, relations that, tested by time and rereading, hold up. And in this, I am still a child of that primer, a gift from a teacher who thought there was still something worth passing on from the past, including the craft of saying well what needed saying."

———

Leonard Nathan is the son of Israel and Florence (Rosenberg) Nathan. He studied at Georgia Institute of Technology and U.C.L.A., but earned his B.A. from Berkeley in 1950, graduating summa cum laude. From Berkeley Nathan also earned his M.A. (1952) and Ph.D. (1960). Except for two years in the Army during World War II, Nathan has spent almost all his life in California. He married Carol Gretchen Nash in 1949 and has been a professor of rhetoric at Berkeley since 1960.

Nathan's work, as he admits, does not have a consistent "voice," but is marked by precision, polish, and formality. These qualities are very much in evidence in *Glad and Sorry Seasons*, Nathan's second book and the first to be issued by a major publisher (Random House). Most of the poems in this collection are in strict iambic meter and many are in rhymed quatrains. The subjects are conventional—love, nature, family and history. The tone is more sorrowful than glad and conveys the rueful wisdom of a middle-aged poet. John R. Cooley, a critic not charitable to Nathan's formalism, remarked on the autumnal mood of the book and thought that some of the poems rose to an intensity unusual for him.

The Day the Perfect Speakers Left, was Nathan's next collection. The title poem in particular, a strange apocalyptic piece that was singled out for praise by most reviewers, seemed to encapsulate Nathan's dark premonitions about the state of civilization in the late sixties. To George W. Nitchie in *Shenandoah,* the collection seemed a crystallization of a certain type of poetic utterance: "Uncluttered and unpretentious, it has some fairly standard virtues—wit, coherence, compassion—but also an altogether remarkable capacity for transforming fable or dream or anecdote into something as simple and mysterious as a geode." Other reviewers emphasized the poise and elegance out of which Nathan created a "poignant complexity of mood" (*Malahat Review*). But, as usual, some critics saw Nathan's poise and elegance as just the problem. Peter Schjeldahl, for instance, praised the title poem for what he considered its uncharacteristic depth and feeling, but said that too many of the others were "supercilious in a way that invites disbelief, seeming to speak of grave things but meanwhile insisting on their layers of stylish glitter."

Nathan's detractors made the same kind of criticism about his next volume, *Returning Your Call.* In this book Nathan moved away from his usual iambic line to a looser, more personal manner of utterance. Some critics were heartened by this development; John R. Cooley thought Nathan's voice "more direct, less given to cleverness than previously." Nevertheless, many of the poems were metrically regular and their formal sophistication was no less apparent. What was perhaps new for Nathan was the emphasis on explicitly political themes, such as the atrocities of the war in Vietnam and the legacy of slavery. Indeed, D. M. Thomas considered the book "a compendium of contemporary American guilts," yet these political poems were balanced by love poems, verse satires, and meditative lyrics. One of the most widely praised poems in the book was "Breathing Exercises," which struck some critics as a sign of a new openness and daring in Nathan's sensibility. Here the poet's gift for parody is turned on himself:

If somebody screws your mouth shut, whistle
Through your nose. For God's sake, keep breathing.

Inhale fifteen seconds, thinking
OM, hold ten, exhale fifteen.

Grandpa scares me holding his breath.
His last address was an oxygen tent.

For Hayden Carruth such poems were "tough and humorous, pragmatic and existential." William Logan disagreed. "Most of the verse in this book has little to say," he wrote, "or no way to express itself beyond its postures." Yet Logan's harsh review in *Poetry* was not typical. *Returning Your Call* is one of Nathan's most esteemed books, and it was nominated for a National Book Award in 1975.

In his most recent books, *Dear Blood* and *Holding Patterns*, Nathan has moved closer to the human voice in poems concerned with people as much as with ideas. Yet this movement has been balanced by a counter-movement towards even greater compression. The result, in many cases, has come close to Nathan's ideal of a blend of "the immediacy of actual speech with the formality of a special occasion." For the most part, critics have taken kindly to these later efforts. Observing the compression in *Dear Blood,* a reviewer wrote in *Publishers Weekly,* "What is most remarkable about Nathan is that he crams epic themes into simple lyrics."

In addition to his thirteen books of poetry (some privately printed), Nathan has translated several volumes of Hindi and Swedish verse. He has also contributed essays and reviews to various journals, and his study of Yeats' drama was published by Columbia University Press in 1973.

PRINCIPAL WORKS: *Poetry*—Western Reaches, 1958; Glad and Sorry Seasons, 1963; The Matchmaker's Lament and Other Astonishments, 1967; The Day the Perfect Speakers Left, 1969; Flight Plan, 1971; Without Wishing, 1973; Coup and Other Poems, 1975; The Likeness: Poems Out of India, 1975; Returning Your Call, 1975; The Teachings of Grandfather Fox, 1976; Lost Distance, 1978; Dear Blood, 1980; Holding Patterns, 1982. *Translation*—Modern Hindi Poetry (V. N Misra, ed.), 1965; First Person, Second Person (poems) by Ageyeya, 1971; The Transport of Love: The Meghaduta of Kalidasa, 1976; Songs of Something Else (poems) by Gunnar Ekelöf, 1982. *Criticism*—The Tragic Drama of William Butler Yeats: Figures in a Dance, 1963.

ABOUT: Contemporary Authors, new revision series 7, 1982; Vinson, J. (ed.) Contemporary Poets (3rd ed.), 1980; Who's Who in America, 1983–84. *Periodicals*—Georgia Review Fall 1983; Malahat Review October 1969; New York Times Book Review April 4, 1976; Poetry January 1971; July 1977; Publishers Weekly January 11, 1980; Shenandoah Autumn 1969; Times Literary Supplement June 11, 1976.

NEAL, LAWRENCE (LARRY) P. (September 5, 1937–January 6, 1981), black American poet, essayist, and dramatist, was born in Atlanta, Georgia, the son of Woodie and Maggie Neal, who moved their family to Philadelphia when he was a child. There Neal, who had four brothers, attended a Roman Catholic high school, and in 1957 entered Lincoln University, near Philadelphia, where he won two literary prizes and

earned a B.A. in 1961. While doing graduate work in folklore at the University of Pennsylvania, where he completed an M.A. in 1963, he started to write, lecture, and participate in black community affairs.

After becoming a regular contributor to the *Liberator* magazine, of which he served as arts editor during the mid-1960s, Neal went on to publish poems, theater reviews, and articles on black literature, music, and aesthetic theory in a variety of black periodicals, including *Ebony, Negro Digest* (later *Black World*), *Black Theatre, Black Scholar, Journal of Black Poetry*, of which he was a contributing editor, *Black Dialogue, Umbra, Freedomways, Pride*, of which he was an editor, and *The Cricket*, a journal of black music that he co-edited with LeRoi Jones (later known as Imamu Amiri Baraka) and A. B. Spellman. During the late 1960 and early 1970s, Neal also contributed essays on subjects of interest to blacks to *The Drama Review* (formerly *Tulane Drama Review*) and *Partisan Review* and reviewed several films and plays on black themes for the *New York Times*.

Having worked with LeRoi Jones in 1965 to establish the government-funded but short-lived Black Arts Repertory Theatre in New York City, Neal took a position as an instructor in English at City College of New York (1968–69), and continued his academic career as writer-in-residence at Wesleyan University (1969–70) and as a fellow at Yale University (1970–75). He received a Guggenheim Fellowship for the study of contemporary Afro-American culture in 1971–72, held a chair in humanities at Howard University, and lectured on literary topics at various colleges and universities. Neal, who was also educational director of the New York Black Panther Party, eventually made his home in Manhattan with his wife, the former Evelyn Rodgers of Birmingham, Alabama, and their son, Avatar.

Together with LeRoi Jones, John Oliver Killens, John Henrik Clarke, Don L. Lee, and Hoyt Fuller, Neal was one of the principal organizers and spokesmen of the black arts movement of the 1960s and early 1970s. His influential essay, "The Black Arts Movement"—originally published in *The Drama Review* (summer 1968) and later reprinted in *The Black American Writer (ed.) C. W. E. Bigsby,* and in *The Black Aesthetic* (ed.) Addison Gayle, Jr.—presented a manifesto: "Black Art is the aesthetic and spiritual sister of the Black Power concept. As such, it envisions an art that speaks directly to the needs and aspirations of Black America. In order to perform this task, the Black Arts Movement proposes a radical reordering of the western cultural aesthetic. It proposes a separate symbolism, mythology, critique, and iconology."

Black Fire: An Anthology of Afro-American Writing edited by Jones and Neal appeared in 1968. This collection of essays, poems, short stories and plays by more than seventy black writers included several contributions by Neal—four poems, a short story, and a lengthy afterword presenting the radical black aesthetic position. Rejecting "the dead forms taught most writers in the white man's schools" and stressing that "the key to where the black people have to go is in the music" of their culture, Neal's afterword concluded that "the poet must become a performer, the way James Brown is a performer— loud, gaudy and racy. He must take his work where his people are: Harlem, Watts, Philadelphia, Chicago and the rural South . . . We must make literature move people to a deeper understanding of what this thing is all about, to be a kind of priest, a black magician, working juju with the word on the world."

Reviewers were generally in agreement on *Black Fire*. Edward Margolies, in *Library Journal*, considered the writing "shoddy" and felt that, "although some of the essays contain good insights, and a few of the stories and plays a certain power (the poems with rare exceptions are very poor), they generally all fall apart in embarrassing, adolescent, pedantic, and hysterical race-war ravings of revenge and retribution." Peter Berek, in *Saturday Review*, found this "polemical" anthology to be "newsworthy and instructive" by virtue of its "ambitions," but stated that "the expression never achieves the precision and control which are the hallmarks of successful art." The views of these critics were shared by Jack Richardson in the *New Yorker*. Although more favorable in his assessment of the book as a source of "social documentation" and as a "compendium of most of the most important revolutionary Black writers" of the 1960s, Samuel J. Sackett, in *Negro American Literature Forum* (now *Black American Literature Forum*), judged the contents to range "in quality from embarrassingly amateurish to profoundly powerful."

Neal's concern with black music was expressed in *Trippin': A Need for Change*, a short book that he wrote in 1969 in collaboration with LeRoi Jones and A. B. Spellman. He also continued to expound militant political and social ideas in two essays included in books edited by Floyd B. Barbour: Neal's "Black Power in the International Context" appeared in *The Black Power Revolt* (1968), and his "New Space/ The Growth of Black Consciousness in the Sixties" was published in *The Black Seventies* (1970). By 1976, however, a shift to a more moderate aesthetic stance was discernible in the chapter on "The Writer as Activist—1960 and After," that he wrote for *The Black American Reference Book.* Advocating "craftsmanship and study" as essential for the attainment of "artistic integrity," Neal asserted that "literature can indeed make excellent propaganda, but through propaganda alone the black writer can never perform the highest function of his art: that of revealing to man his most enduring human possibilities and limitations."

During the late 1960s and early 1970s, poems by Neal appeared in numerous anthologies, among them *For Malcolm* (1969), edited by Dudley Randall and Margaret G. Burroughs; *The Black Poets* (1971), edited by Dudley Randall; *New Black Voices* (1972), edited by Abraham Chapman; and Stephen Henderson's *Understanding the New Black Poetry* (1973). In 1969 Neal published *Black Boogaloo: Notes on Black Liberation,* a small volume of his own poems with a preface by LeRoi Jones, and in 1974 he collected his poetry of the preceding ten years in a second book entitled *Hoodoo Hollerin' Bebop Ghosts.* Reviewing this work for *CLA Journal,* Harry L. Jones found its strengths to lie in the "Afro-American locales," especially in Neal's affectionate treatment of Harlem; in the prevalence of black music as a subject, for "Neal manages to evoke the lyrical life of an era when music was life and love and death"; and in "the nostalgia and the eroticism" of the poems. For Jones, the weakest pieces in the collection were those "attempting to link the Afro-American to . . . Africa and the Caribbean."

As Nathan A. Scott, Jr., pointed out in the *Harvard Guide to Contemporary American Writing,* Neal was influenced by Langston Hughes and Sterling Brown, who emphasized the creation of distinctively black poetry out of black speech, music, and folk tradition. Neal's poems are populated by such political leaders as Malcolm X and Marcus Garvey, who are given almost mythic status, by black urban folk-heroes like Shine and the Signifying Monkey, and by a large number of well-known black jazz musicians. Analyzing Neal's style, Theodore R. Hudson, in the third edition of *Contemporary Poets,* mentioned his "conversational . . . tone," his "technical effects . . . suggestive of jazz music," his "deft and clear" but sometimes "ethnocentric" imagery, his propensity for cataloguing, and his use of free verse. "Harlem Gallery: From the Inside" begins with a description—"The bars on Eighth Avenue in Harlem/ glow real yellow, hard against formica/ tables"—and ends with a long list of the "wandering ghosts and Harlem saints" referred to directly after the opening lines. Musical effects of different kinds are present in "Kantu," which simulates the rhythms of African drums,

and in "Don't Say Goodbye to the Pork-Pie Hat," which evokes the jazz styles of black American musicians.

Of the plays written by Neal—which include *The Suppression of Jazz* (1970) and a musical entitled *Kansas City Stomp Down*—at least two were performed publicly in New York City: *The Glorious Monster in the Bell of the Horn,* a lyric drama portraying black artists and middle-class characters just prior to the bombing of Hiroshima, and a reading by the Frank Silvera Writers' Workshop of the Harlem Cultural Council in May 1976. *In an Upstate Motel,* a play about a professional killer and his girlfriend who go into hiding after bungling a murder, was presented by the Negro Ensemble Company after Neal's death in 1981. Reviewing this production in the *New Yorker* in April of that year, Edith Oliver found it "depressing" both in subject matter and in quality, for Neal had not been able "to rewrite and edit a script that surely needed more work."

In January 1981, while attending a theater workshop at Colgate University in Hamilton, New York, Neal suffered a fatal heart attack. During the period shortly before his death, he had served as executive director of the District of Columbia Commission on the Arts and Humanities (1976–78) and had written both a screenplay about Zora Neale Hurston and an introduction to her work, as well as a jazz series for WGBH-TV in Boston and a film script about musical improvisation for Clark College in Atlanta. At the time of his death, he had nearly finished a book on the development of black consciousness during the 1960s. Posthumously, in March 1981, Neal was one of thirteen recipients of the Before Columbus Foundation's second annual American Book Awards, which were established to honor literary accomplishment by members of diverse ethnic groups.

PRINCIPAL WORKS: *Poetry*—Black Boogaloo: Notes on Black Liberation, 1969; Hoodoo Hollerin' Bebop Ghosts, 1974. *Essays*—The Black Arts Movement, 1968, *in* Bigsby, C. W. E. (ed.) The Black American Writer, 1969, *and* Gayle, A. (ed.) The Black Aesthetic, 1971; Black Power in the International Context *in* Barbour, F. B. (ed.) The Black Power Revolt, 1968; New Space/ The Growth of Black Consciousness in the Sixties *in* Barbour, F. B. (ed.) The Black Seventies, 1970; The Black Contribution to American Letters: Part II, The Writer as Activist—1960 and After *in* The Black American Reference Book, 1976. *Non-fiction*—(with Imamu Baraka [LeRoi Jones] and A. B. Spellman) Trippin': A Need for Change, 1969. *As editor*—(with LeRoi Jones) Black Fire: An Anthology of Afro-American Writing, 1968.

ABOUT: Arata, E. S. More Black American Playwrights: A Bibliography, 1978; Arata, E. S. and Rotoli, N. J.

Black American Playwights, 1800 to the Present: A Bibliography, 1976; Contemporary Authors 81–84, 1979; 102, 1981; Hatch, J. V. and Omanii, A. (eds.) Black Playwrights, 1823–1977: An Annotated Bibliography of Plays, 1977; Hoffman, D. (ed.) Harvard Guide to Contemporary American Writing, 1979; Rush, T. G., Meyers, C. F. and Arata, E. S. Black American Writers Past and Present: A Biographical and Bibliographical Dictionary, 1975; Vinson, J. (ed.) Contemporary Poets, 1980. *Periodicals*—Bookman's Weekly January 26, 1981; CLA Journal December 1976; Library Journal July 1968; Negro American Literature Forum (now Black American Literature Forum) 1974; New York Times January 9, 1981; March 2, 1981; New Yorker December 7, 1968; April 27, 1981; Saturday Review November 30, 1968.

ÁGNES NEMES NAGY

*NEMES NAGY, ÁGNES (LENGYEL) (January 3, 1922–   ), Hungarian poet, essayist, and author of books for children, writes (in English): "I was born in 1922 in a family of intellectuals. My father was a lawyer, my ancestors were mainly lawyers and Calvinist pastors. I finished my secondary-school studies in 1939. Further studies at the University of Budapest brought qualifications as a secondary-school teacher. I began publishing poems after the war, in 1945; from 1949 onwards, for about ten years, I was not allowed to publish, due to the cultural policies of the 'personality cult' of the 1950s. I worked on the staff of a pedagogical review and also as a teacher. Since 1958 I have made my living from writing and translations; recently I have been giving lectures at the university as well.

"The place of my intellectual birth was not simply Budapest. It was a secondary school, an exceptionally good school, a Calvinist *Gymnasium* for girls, with very high standards, wide horizons, and a renowned poet at its head as director [Lajor Áprily]. There, in the well-equipped classrooms and the luxuriant park, I learnt that literature and sports were great things, the community of humans bursting with goodwill, and virtue always received its just reward. What followed, however, did not quite bear this out. What followed were the university—and the war. The war, this unavoidable, fundamental experience of my generation, influenced and still influences our attitude, our writings. I do not claim to have possessed what is called a 'world-view' then, nor an articulate political credo. I simply disliked the war and disliked the Nazi slogans. With my young companions—some of them writers—I tried to do something, anything, in the given situation, which was mostly hiding the persecuted, with success at one time, failure at another. It was strange stepping from a well-protected, comfortable middle-class existence straight, as it were, into history. Later the Germans occupied the country and the front was drawing near, and during the siege of Budapest, which lasted for a month and a half, the Russians fought their way against the Germans inch by inch. The inhabitants lived in cellars; so did my husband and I, under false names, hiding from Nazi raids. Then my husband was taken prisoner of war, and only after his return did we begin our literary activities.

"Together with a group of young writers we founded a periodical called *Újhold* (New Moon). Its editor was my husband, Balázs Lengyel, an essayist and critic. The review was suppressed in 1948, the year of the Communist takeover; its charter was withdrawn. We, and other writers, did not fulfill the requirements of current literary policies, and were barred from literature. A period of silence ensued. After 1956 my husband was imprisoned, fortunately only for a short time. Then the slow process of the 'thaw' began, and silenced writers and poets began to be published again.

"There is no trace in my poems of what I have just described. No trace? Really? On the contrary, my poems, my writings are full with historical and personal experiences. It is just that there are experiences, for instance of the war, which are, I think, almost non-anthropomorphic, elemental, and inarticulate. No poem can rival such experiences, since, as I wrote in an early poem, the throat is narrower than the cannon. Poetry, however, is all the more suitable for conveying, or eliciting through motifs, metaphors, and suggesting through emo-

°nem´ ās näj

tion, that which cannot be told in any other way. Besides, there is a domain of the human psyche which I cannot disregard and which I call the wave-band of unnamed emotions. Each and every day of ours is full of such strong yet unlabeled emotions; when the tourist reaches the hilltop and looks around, when the gardener points his finger at a tree and says 'it's an alpine maple,' when an old woman wipes a red Jonathan apple until it shines—they all recite a poem of themselves, one made up of nameless emotions. Always, there is something behind something, and these nameless things are there, in the unconscious, waiting to be called forth. After all, ever since Rimbaud, it has been a major tendency of modern poetry to express and uplift into a poem these fringe phenomena of the psyche. With what modulations and by what means—that is the concern of the poet.

"It is *objects* in the first place which help me in my search for this other dimension. Let me add that when Hungarian critics describe my work, they usually attach two adjectives to it: 'humanist' and 'objective.' As for 'humanist,' it needs no explanation (though the word has taken on a special meaning in Central Europe). The word 'objective' refers both to an objective poetic tone and to my strong attachment to objects—I find great expressivity in them. I truly believe that objects and phenomena carry some hidden 'news' in themselves; a leaf, a coffee-cup, a torrent of rain, or even a statue and myth of an Eyptian pharaoh, dead for three thousand years, is able to convey volumes of information about the 'other face' of the world—or at least about ourselves. Without knowledge of this other face we are blind, doomed.

"The poet works, I believe, between two silences. On one side there is the loudness of the fatal crises of the world, which silences him; on the other, the barely audible, hidden stammering of the unknown, the inner nameless. I am searching for the narrow band through which I can speak."

———

Nemes Nagy's first book of poems, *Kettös világban* (In a Dual World, 1946), was welcomed by reviewers. István Vas, himself a recognized poet, spoke of the austerity of her verse and the tension between "passion and intellect, reality and abstraction, life and philosophy" sustaining it. Her Donne-like imagery, he wrote, "distills the essentials of reality to create its essence" in order to offer "more reality, life, and experience" to the reader. "Actually," he said, "reality so inundates [her] poetry that she does not have the time to engage a part, a movement,

or an event at length. Her most comprehensible images are unbelievably condensed." He concluded: the eighteen poems "are already startlingly accomplished, and it is difficult to imagine what the continuation of this beginning can be."

A victim of the "szilencium," she could not publish her next book of poems, *Szárazvillám* (Heat Lightning), until 1957. Reviewers quickly noted the small number of poems in the volume, regarding her composition of only two or three poems annually as evidence of her careful craftsmanship. László Kardos called the "severely fashioned" poems "vehicles of unyielding artistic attention and noble aspiration. . . . The more hidden turbulence, the concealed flourishes, the secretly weathered experience of the soul, and the barely revealable connections between humanity and the world are voiced sufficiently clearly, sufficiently candidly." To him, the "harmonically surging rhythms" and "fully resounding rhymes" were, "in a curious way, the attire of an anguished nerve, of an imagination constantly beating between fears, of a wary and already hopeless soul." Kardos regretted that Nemes Nagy was "withdrawn and locked into alien doubt and mistrust" and disregardful of the "prospects of a new life" opening before her. György Rónay, on the other hand, emphasized that she loves reality too much "to let it slip from her hands" and that "she does not want to engulf herself in the night but to divide the light from the darkness." This disagreement about her attitude toward life has persisted among Hungarian critics.

The poems in these two books established her verse techniques and her search for a value-based relationship with reality. Convinced that World War II had brought about the collapse of morality, Nemes Nagy is tormented by doubts about the worth of human existence and employs the creative act of poetry itself to seek an order on which to construct a value system that will reduce the existential nothingness she finds in life. Poems in both volumes reveal the depth of her despair at the human condition. "A reményhez" (To Hope) holds man responsible for every evil he commits; "A bün" (Crime) rejects the notion that serving the common good gives man "a letter of defense" against his iniquities. "A szomj" (Thirst) claims love is without hope, and "Hadijelvény" (Military Emblem) maintains that reflection offers enlightenment but delivers only despair to humanity. This bleakness of outlook continues in "Heat Lightning." "Trisztán és Izolda" (Tristan and Isolde), a picture of an "egg-shell life," describes her personal experiences with the horrors of war, including the burying of the dead with a pick-axe, the crime and punishment of it all making her retch. In "Patak" (Brook), she wonders where God has fled and what made possible the destruction of the moral order that had existed for two thousand years: "How can I quench my keen thirst,/And forgive the unforgivable?" and in "Kiáltva" (Crying Out) she pleads: "Lord have mercy on me, I no longer believe in you." In the depth of her despair and dislocation, she often raises doubts about the value of life and then, as in "Eszmélet" (Consciousness), she finds hope in the rational faculty of man. Despite this ambivalence, Nemes Nagy presses forward in her quest for a new moral order, and declares that her poetry, its very processes, will lead her to a new set of durable values:

between morality and terror,
or else in immoral terror,
my craft, for all that, it's you
that measures, that's beyond measure,

even if convulsively, but like a clock
that taps out illusory rhythms despite
its equable tick-tick—nonetheless
you divide the light from the night.
                    —"To My Craft," trans. Bruce Berlind

When her third book of poems, *Napforduló* (Solstice), appeared ten years later, a reviewer defended Nemes Nagy against the recurring charge that her "obstinate withdrawness" is inadequate for the "wholeness of life": "she simply does not cast the spotlight on her human connections or the autobiographical details of her personal life. This occurs because of a very carefully thought-out *ars poetica*. She wants to enclose only a 'little pail' from the endless ocean of reality ('Formátlan,' Shapeless), because she feels that at a time of unprecedented differentiation in the sciences, she cannot suddenly undertake a wide and deep examination of totality. She does not renounce esteem for the rational, for the mind—for creating order with the help of the intellect amidst the confusion of experiences; she simply feels her achievable responsibility to be the ordering of the parts, instead of the examination of the whole." This reviewer concluded: "I do not think a Marxist critic recommending Ágnes Nemes Nagy's *ars poetica* to a beginning poet would ever crop up. But of the standard attained by the poetry in *Solstice,* one must speak with due recognition of a significant artistic achievement."

The intellectualism of her verse was also singled out for attention. János Bányai particularly commented on thought as the true activator of her poetry: "She is stimulated not by the pure fact of the emotions, visions, and the current of feelings pouring into images but by the emotion of thought—by the compulsion to think . . . we exist in spite of a 1001 problems and we have a 1001 reasons to pose the question repeatedly, stubbornly: why are we here? Of course, this human situation has to be felt, but we have a vital reason to break the omnipotence of the emotions and *feel with our minds.* This paradox is the basis of the poet's intellectualism." Nemes Nagy herself stated that her poems "take on the mood of intellectuality, the mood of the intellectual faculty."

Many of the poems in this book depart significantly from the despair and alienation present in the earlier works. Béla Pomogáts believes that the poems reveal her catharsis: "Until now [she] lived amidst the complex rhythms of acceptance and rejection; sometimes she felt herself to be a stranger, sometimes competent; sometimes she accepted the fundamentals of human fate, sometimes she rebelled against them. Now her tragic conflicts are subsiding; she experiences her situation and fate with peace and dignity." Tragic feelings persist in poems like "Szobrok" (Statues), a bitter expression of impotence in the face of mankind's helplessness and a cosmic indifference to the human condition, and in "Madár" (Bird), in which pain has become essential to the sustenance of life; but nevertheless, she is finding her way out of the morass of despair. Now the transcience of life, the inevitability of death does not overwhelm her in "A lovak és az angyalok" (The Horses and the Angels); instead, as a critic observed, she "renders palpable . . . the elusiveness of time's passage, plugs into the live circuit of life's continuity, and the multi-shaped alterations break toward inevitable permanence." The verse cycle "Ekhnáton" (Akhenaton) is an especially dramatic attempt on her part to begin anew this search for sustaining values through the mythical figure of a man who, as she puts it, "sees for the first time"—ethical principles that will again permit the existence of belief and justice—and creates a god who will console humanity for suffering and once again make love and justice available to human kind:

I must do something still undone:
I must deal with pain.
I ought to make a god
to sit on high seeing all.

The desire is no longer enough,
I must build a solid sky.
So, Almighty, take my shoulder,
I'll help you rise, and as you limp
to your throne, lean on some cherubs.
Don't worry, I shall clothe you,
so the night won't see you naked.

I fasten suffering around your neck
like a circlet of blood appearing,
and make my love of plants your warm cape.

In your bejeweled heart I settle this:
I always strive for justice.
    —"From the Notes of Akhenton," trans. Enikö Molnar
                                    Basa and Maxim Tobory

The first collected edition of her poems was published in 1969 with the title *A lovagok és az angyalok* (The Horses and the Angels); the second in 1981 under the title *Között* (Between), which included her first prose poems. In the 1970s she turned increasingly to the writing of essays on literature, among which those on the lyric poem are especially noteworthy. These essays have been published as *64 hattyú* (64 Swans, 1975) and as *Metszetek* (Engravings, 1981). Her poems for children, an effort on her part to modernize the genre, are extremely popular with both children and adults, especially those concerned with the delightful seventy-year-old "Bors néni," in *Bors néni könyve* (Aunti Bors's Book, 1978). She has also translated widely from the lyric poetry of the past and present, the works of the French classical authors, and, among others, from Rilke, Brecht, and Dylan Thomas. A selection of her translations was published under the title *Vándorévek* (Journeyman Years, 1964). She received the Baumgartner Prize in 1946 and the Kossuth Prize in 1983.

WORKS IN ENGLISH TRANSLATION: Bruce Berlind translated Nemes Nagy's *Selected Poems,* 1980. English translations of individual poems are also included in Miklos Vajda's *Modern Hungarian Poetry,* 1977, and in Albert Tezla's *Ocean at the Window: Hungarian Prose and Poetry since 1945,* 1981, which also contains an interview with her done in 1967.

ABOUT: Tezla, A. Ocean at the Window, 1981. *Periodicals*—New Hungarian Quarterly Winter 1979.

NEWLIN, MARGARET (RUDD) (February 27, 1925–   ), American poet and critic, writes: "Angry voices. The sound of scuffling. Banshee shrieks, doors slamming, and at last the heavy outer door of the apartment closing with a metallic thud. The child in her room, sobbing, knowing that her father had stormed off once again to stay at his club, knowing too, that at any moment the molten anger of her mother would descend on her. It was all the child's fault, the mother would scream.

"No wonder, many years later, I felt quite at home trying to make sense of Blake's wailing shrieking protagonists! Not all of my childhood was like this, of course, although enough of it was that in retrospect it colors and possibly distorts the whole. Even in the womb I was a trouble to my beautiful disturbed mother and was removed by caesarean section at seven months. The eldest girl in an Irish family of nine children, my mother did not want a child of her own. She wanted, as she said, to be 'Queen Bee.' But my father, also of Irish background, insisted.

MARGARET NEWLIN

"I was cared for by a German nurse until I was nine. She was a buffer of sorts, as was Gran'pa Rudd, who lived in a Manhattan hotel in winter, but came with us in the summer to a rented house in Pine Orchard, Connecticut. There, ashamed, I think, to have Gran'pa witness her hysteria, my mother subsided, and seemed almost content. And when my father arrived on weekends, they often went dancing at the country club. I learned to swim and ride, and I would spend long hours on the rocky point watching Gran'pa fish. When peaceful, my mother could whistle like a bird or a cheeky boy, and had a lovely singing voice.

"Outwardly I was privileged. Wonderful books, clothes from Tot's Toggery and Best's, excellent schools. I went riding at the armory and ice skating in Central Park. I did well at the Brearley despite my mother's taunt that I would never be more than mediocre. I won first prize in the Junior Division of a National Photography Salon. I remember the feeling of power and joy when I wrote my first poem at the age of eleven. My father would take me on Sundays to visit great-uncle James McGraw, founder of McGraw-Hill where my father was a vice-president. Uncle James looked just like God, and received in bed. I remember a distinct feeling of irritation when he pontificated—'Pegg-eh . . . one day . . . you . . . will have . . . a book.'

"My war-time activities were not in the least heroic. As a schoolgirl I rolled bandages and knitted, very badly, balaclava helmets. Later, I helped out at an officers club. I was accepted as a Conover model, but nothing much came of it, since I was ready to go to college. At Bryn Mawr, recovering from the after-effects of anorexia, in a serene atmosphere where accomplishment was taken for granted, I thrived. I was grateful for the encouragement and approval of my teachers, and both Katherine McBride, president of Bryn Mawr, and Leonora Speyer, a Pulitzer prize poet, befriended me during these years and after. In my senior year I won both of the important writing prizes, one for my honors essay on T. S. Eliot, the other for a group of poems, judged by a committee headed by Marianne Moore. 'Content valuable for living rather than stunt performance' was Miss Moore's criterion, and she praised my entry for 'undisguise, with restraint.' On the more frivolous side, I was a finalist in *Vogue*'s Prix de Paris, but, to my mother's chagrin, I eschewed the obligatory Condé Nast festivities, so did not win.

"It is hard to telescope the flavor and excitement of my years abroad. I went, in '47, to the first post-war Shakespeare summer school, planning to stay six weeks in England. In fact, I stayed eight years, with the exception of two separate—(one in teaching and one in Admissions)—one semester jobs at Bryn Mawr, summoned by cable by Miss McBride who seemed to know clairvoyantly when my funds might be low. Two AAUW fellowships and one from the American Philosophical Society enabled me to work at Reading and Oxford on my Ph.D. thesis, a study of Blake and Yeats. During visits to Dublin, Mrs. Yeats, the poet's widow, was extraordinarily kind, not only giving an unknown young American access to all sorts of diaries and papers, but also providing her with warm slippers and a tray of lunch when days, as they often were, proved wet. I sat, undisturbed, in Yeats' black chair at his huge refectory work table. Hard by stood the shining chest in which he stored his 'barbarous words.'

"When I had completed the thesis, I was granted the degree. Herbert Read, who was my external examiner, but had declined to come down from Yorkshire to examine me since he had no reservations, told me to send the m.s. along to him at Routledge & Kegan Paul, where with magical alacrity it was accepted. In Oxford Blackwell displayed in its window not one but several copies of *Divided Image*. Adding to the sense of dream, the reviews were prompt, serious and good. Routledge gave me an advance so that I could stay in England and start work on a second book which appeared in '56 as *Organiz'd Innocence: The Story of Blake's Prophetic Books*.

"By this time I was back in the USA. My parents insisted that I live at home, but it didn't work out. Although he gave my mother diamonds and mink, my father still had not gotten

her the treatment she so obviously needed. Even after she tried to choke me, all he would say was 'When the time comes, I will do something.' The time never came. She had a stroke at age sixty-six, and he was dead three years later. She lived ten more years and was my responsibility. This was not easy, but by then I was married and was enormously happy. Nicholas Newlin, a Philadelphia gentleman, witty, urbane and civilized, was seventeen years my senior. He was chairman of the English department at Washington College where I had accepted a teaching post in the fall of '55. By spring we were married and our first son, Jamie, arrived nine months and one day after the wedding. Three more sons—twins David and Robin, and Tom, arrived in record time.

"Poetry had gone underground for more than fifteen years, perhaps from too much academia. My husband feared that marriage might further kill whatever it was that made me write poetry. Instead it seemed to free it. By '69–70, the sabbatical year we all spent in Oxford, I had enough poems for a slim volume, which was published as *The Fragile Immigrants* by Carcanet Press. This was followed in '73 by *Day of Sirens*. At home, Ardis wanted to publish my two English volumes in a collected edition along with a new book, *The Snow Falls Upward*. I received my author's copies a short time before my husband's unexpected heart attack and death on July 16, 1976, twenty-one years to the day from the day we had met. He did not know that the book would receive a NBA nomination in '77, despite the fact that it was the first book I had published in the USA.

"Each poem in *The Book of Mourning* was like squeezing out a drop of heart's blood, but it was necessary to me and apparently a help to others. Although some cannot handle the subject matter, I have received letters and response to this book way beyond anything else I have written. Since Nick's death, I have seen our four boys through college. I swim a lot, and have exhibited drawings and paintings. One show, at Drexel, combined my books, some drawings and paintings, and manuscripts. Animals are very important to me. Four cats stretch out around the wood burning stove in the kitchen, and two dogs. Fingall, our ten-year-old goldfish, sickened and died recently, and three tiny new fish dart in the gurgling tank. A field mouse lives in a room upstairs and accepts gourmet meals. I have raised wild birds and rabbits.

"In 1980 I received an Honorary D.Litt. from Washington College. I was asked to give their convocation address the following autumn. I compared the teaching of young unknown students to my hilarious touching experience bringing up five Flickers, or Golden-shafted Woodpeckers. I suffer from stage fright, but for my pains I received a standing ovation. I had to flap my arms like wings in order to get away!"

The late Louis Untermeyer wrote of Margaret Newlin's poetry: "Although her craftsmanship is impressive, it is the sensibility which penetrates and pervades." That same sensibility pervades her critical essays and the two books she published under her maiden name of Margaret Rudd. The first of these, *Divided Image,* is a comparative study of Yeats and Blake. Yeats, who had collaborated on an edition of William Blake's poetry and illustrations, was much influenced by the eighteenth-century poet, but it is Rudd's thesis that Blake was a genuine mystic while Yeats achieved only "the attitude of the magician," and "magic is antithetical to mysticism." Taking her title from Blake's "First Book of Urizen," ("Eternity shuddered when they saw / Man begetting his likeness / On his own divided image") and acknowledging in her introduction that her approach was "frankly Christian," Rudd offered a series of original and controversial readings of both poets. "Her method," Rex Warner observed, "reminds one more of the inquisitorial and dogmatic elements in Christianity than any other"; and the *Times Literary Supplement's* reviewer, while judging her case "ably argued" and a valuable contribution to Blake and Yeats studies, nevertheless thought her book "vitiated by her determination to see Yeats as a 'spoilt' Blake." A reviewer in *The Tablet,* however, judged that its main value was not in its conclusions, which were based largely on speculations, but in the speculations themselves: "We are continually delighted by the flashes of insight which her eager exploring mind gives off; and they may be more valuable than the precisions of a more mature mind, blunted with too long use."

Organiz'd Innocence (its title taken from a note Blake wrote in his manuscript of "The Four Zoas"—"Unorganiz'd Innocence is An Impossibility / Innocence dwells with Wisdom, but never with Ignorance") was a less tendentious but equally personal and original book. For this study of Blake's prophetic books—"The Four Zoas," "Milton," and "Jerusalem"—she had read widely in the massive canon of Blake scholarship, but rejected the "heavy machinery of scholarship" for an approach she frankly described as "in many ways unorthodox." For her these poems "tell, like all epics and myths, a very wonderful story about unusual human events of the spirit" and document "Blake's own psycho-

logical drama"—his marital difficulties, his sometimes stormy relationship with his patron William Haley, his spiritual crises. Again critics found her work dogmatic but stimulating and full of insight.

The truly distinctive mark of most of Margaret Newlin's writing, both in poetry and in literary criticism, is her feminine sensibility. She is a sensitive and perceptive reader of other women's poetry, as her essays on Sylvia Plath, Marianne Moore and H. D. demonstrate. On Plath, for example (in "The Suicide Bandwagon," *Critical Quarterly,* Winter 1972) she takes issue with A. Alvarez, who found Plath the quintessential "extreme" poet—one of a large number of contemporary poets, men and women alike, whose pursuit of "inner violence" leads to depression, mental breakdown, and often suicide. Newlin's reading of Plath rejects this view, finding that her poetry operates "on the level of praise, not nihilism," and that her "flirtation with death" was not a morbid obsession but "an authoritative voice . . . of ordinary human life as it glimmers, fades, endures from day to day, year to year, century to century." Comparing her to Rilke as a poet who wrote without self-pity, she found that "Sylvia Plath accepted the lure of death as a final answer to what she wanted to know."

Drawing upon her correspondence with Marianne Moore, Newlin gave thoughtful consideration to the probably unanswerable question, "Would the claims of domesticity really have stolen from their [i.e. women's] poetic gifts?" in an essay "'Unhelpful Hymen!' Marianne Moore and Hilda Doolittle" (*Essays in Criticism,* July 1977). Here she effectively refutes Robert Graves' curious assertion that women are not great poets because they can so freely release their emotions in tears. H. D.'s turbulent emotional life and her poetry, to be sure, reflect the conflict "between the demands of poetry and those of love." But in Moore, who renounced marriage and wrote of her emotional life with restraint, even reticence, Newlin finds an interesting ambiguity and cynicism about "the ritual of marriage" (she cites Moore's poem "Marriage"—"Unhelpful Hymen! / a kind of overgrown cupid") and her deep and sympathetic interest in marriage, domesticity, and motherhood. She has for evidence some of Moore's letters, which express a warm interest in Newlin's own marriage and children.

Certainly "the claims of domesticity" have enriched Newlin's own poetry. In lyrics that are deceptively simple and forthright, she has written intimately and eloquently of the joys and pains of marriage and motherhood. It is a deeply personal poetry, often—especially in her poems on her mother's long dying and their love-hate relationship and of her grief at her husband's sudden death—tragic. In "Twelve Years" (from *Day of Sirens*) she writes of her mother:

She's bedridden and mute.
I'm all that's left to visit,
Rinse her clothes.
Twelve dozen months I've chattered cheerfully.
Unthinkable to bring up old scores now.

And in *The Book of Mourning* she remembers with both anguish and joy her happy marriage, writing in "Words"—

. . . Words fail
They stick in the throat.
In the gut.
They are a belly full
of stillborn babies.

And in "The Airy Bedroom"—

Of all the farm's
Rooms this surely is the heart.
It is here I would like to die,
Still missing the touch of your toes and your back,
Still wearing your wedding ring.

Much as Newlin cherishes home and family, there is a hard core of realism even in her most subjective poems. In "Occupation: Housewife" (from *The Fragile Immigrants*), the sensitive woman-voice seeks "some ghostly confirmation of myself"—

I should not need dead 'yeas' to know
That what I give,
What child must teach his child,
Must win election over holocaust.
It will not help to whimper like Cassandra.

And she finds consolation in the aesthetics of the kitchen ("Wishing for Vermeer, Breughel")—

Get to your cooking, girl!
Tear up that still-life in the wooden bowl—
Those wrinkled spinach darks and lettuce pales.
Drizzle the mushroom umbers, taupes,
With acid red and green-gold oil.
Here is an abstract that should go down well!
Stop fretting for a radiance out of time.

In the later poems of *Day of Sirens* Newlin is uneasily aware of the violence and brutality of the outside world impinging upon her sheltered family life. On a bland college campus where students have long hair and smoke "grass," she recalls wryly a movie image—"None of the profs behave like Burton / None of the wives look much like Liz," but movie violence turns to grim reality in "The Day of the Sirens," when a fugitive young couple—"A Bonnie and Clyde pair / Wanted in four states / Hold up longside our river" in a shoot-out with the police. A child is murdered, a policeman is shot, a farmer is

crushed by his tractor, the family dog is killed by a hit and run driver.

In *The Snow Falls Upward,* her collected poems 1963–75, nominated for a National Book Award in 1977, a family Thanksgiving dinner expands into a moving war protest. She writes an elegy on the death of a hamster and in a cycle "Of Birth, Of Death" she celebrates the young lives of her sons and laments the death of her father. Of these poems Untermeyer wrote: "She flinches at nothing; she doesn't try to cajole the reader . . . Sometimes the poem is wryly deadpan, sometimes grim-gayley ironic, sometimes emanating sheer horror, the more shocking because it is so quietly casual."

PRINCIPAL WORKS: *Prose* (as Margaret Rudd)—Divided Image: A Study of Blake and Yeats, 1953; Organiz'd Innocence: The Story of Blake's Prophetic Books, 1956. *Poetry* (as Margaret Newlin)—The Fragile Immigrants, 1971; Day of Sirens, 1973; The Snow Falls Upward: Collected Poems, 1976; The Book of Mourning, 1982.

ABOUT: Contemporary Authors, new revision series 1, 1981.

NICOLSON, NIGEL (January 19, 1917–   ), British editor, biographer, historian, and architectural critic, was born in Ebury Street, London, the second son of Harold Nicolson, diplomat, member of Parliament, biographer, and diarist, and Victoria Mary ("Vita") Sackville-West, poet, novelist, biographer, expert gardener, close friend of Virginia Woolf, and the model for the title character in Woolf's *Orlando.* He attended Eton and Balliol College, Oxford, and served in the Tunisian and Italian campaigns during World War II as a brigade intelligence officer with the Grenadier Guards. In 1947, with George Weidenfeld, Nicolson founded the publishing firm of Weidenfeld and Nicolson Ltd., which has since become one of the most successful houses in Britain. A Conservative, he contested the Parliamentary seats of Leicester Northwest (1950) and Falmouth and Camborne (1951) before winning election in February 1952 from the constituency of Bournemouth East and Christchurch. He sat in Parliament until September 1959, becoming particularly known as a spokesman on international issues: he was a notably outspoken opponent of the Anglo-French invasion of Suez in 1956. In *People and Parliament,* a response to the severe criticism he had received within his deeply conservative constituency over his opposition to capital punishment and the Suez campaign, he unstintingly advocated principle, integrity, and freedom of judgment. "I see as much danger as advantage," he wrote, "in a member's subservience to his party. For a time it may be a convenience, and an aid to steady government. In the end it can only lead to the impotence of Parliament itself." This argument did not satisfy his most influential constituents, and he soon resigned his seat. He was chairman of the executive committee of the United Nations Association from 1961 to 1966.

Nicolson's first published work was a two-volume history of his regiment's exploits in World War II, *The Grenadier Guards in the War of 1939–1945*. He wrote the first volume, "The Campaigns in North-West Europe," with a collaborator, Patrick Forbes, and the second, "The Mediterranean Campaigns," entirely on his own. The work was regarded as well written and lucid by the standards of military history, but sold only a modest number of sets; it was one of the few of Nicolson's own books not published by his firm.

As an editor, Nicolson first distinguished himself by assembling and publishing his father's *Diaries and Letters*. Sir Harold was unable, at the end of his life (he died in 1968), to attend to their publication, so his younger son took up the work. The three volumes cover the period 1930–62; the editor considers them "of historical importance in the picture they give of literary, political and social London in the 1930s. But they also form the portrait of a marriage." Nicolson's fascination with the details of his parents' lives is everywhere evident in the careful editorial arrangement and annotation of the mass of material presented, which for all its length represents actually only one-twentieth of the quantity of the original sources. Reviewers praised the editor as much as the diaries' and letters' author. Philip Magnus thought Nigel Nicolson "outstandingly successful in imposing shape upon a formidable mass of material, and he has launched a work of historical significance, deep human interest and literary art." The diaries, he concluded, "deserve . . . to rank alongside those of Saint-Simon, John Hervey and Charles Greville." The *Times Literary Supplement* concurred, adding that "affection and objectivity have gone to the editing of this volume and have created, from the formidable mass of material, a work with a shape and with a deep personal as well as a public interest."

Nicolson's other major editorial endeavor was *The Letters of Virginia Woolf*, which appeared in six volumes from 1975 to 1980. The editorial quality of each volume was critically highly regarded, as highly as any of the multitude of other contributions to the study of Bloomsbury and its participants. Woolf's letters' graceful readability was enhanced by a self-imposed editorial reserve, a marked reluctance to interfere with the continuity of the work. "We do not wish," wrote Nicolson in the preface to volume two, "to produce an edition of her letters in which a few lines of her text struggle, page after page, to keep afloat on a sea of footnotes. While that might be editorially impressive, it would destroy her fluency. . . . We are consoled . . . by the certainty that Virginia herself would have thought it foolish to subject her letters to feats of editorial archaeology."

In 1937, while still an Oxford undergraduate, Nicolson became the sole owner of the Shiant Islands, off the coast of Lewis and Harris Islands in the Outer Hebrides. When he began casting about for a subject for his first biography, an earlier outlander owner of Lewis and Harris appealed to him as a kind of kindred spirit. This was the genesis of *Lord of the Isles: Lord Leverhulme in the Hebrides*, the story of William Hesketh Lever, first Viscount Leverhulme, who "made a fortune by manufacturing and selling soap on a scale unequalled by any man before him." He decided, in 1918 at the age of sixty-six, to buy Lewis and Harris, the northernmost of the Hebrides, "and arrest their decline," but after his death in 1925, having spent well over a million pounds on his purchase, "almost nothing of permanent value to the inhabitants remained. . . . The social evils that he had determined to remedy were only aggravated by his intervention." The book is written in a lively style, and is, in the author's words, the "portrait of a man in the last years of his life, when convinced by almost uninterrupted success that no achievement was beyond his powers, he at last found himself confronted by a major failure."

Alex: The Life of Field Marshal Earl Alexander of Tunis was for Nicolson a chance to review once again the final years of British military prowess and to write about one of the war's greatest heroes, Harold Alexander, often styled "Alexander Africanus," Montgomery's commander in chief at Alamein, later governor general of Canada (1946–52), and minister of defense in Churchill's second government. Nicolson saw him first in 1942, at the very moment of his triumphant victory over the Germans, and then and there "conceived the ambition to write his life." Alexander, he writes in his preface, "was a man whom it would not be easy to know, and what made it difficult were his most obvious traits, his modesty and his reserve. How, I asked myself, could a man of so gentle a nature have chosen the life of a professional soldier? And how could a soldier apparently so undemonstrative have risen to the highest rank of field command, and gained the confidence and affection of a million men of mixed nationality who marched on his orders to possible death?" The book was highly praised and very popular; its author's similarity in background and career to its subject was seen as a distinct advantage. Nicolson, wrote the reviewer for the *Economist,* "has risen to the heights necessary to describe one of the towering figures of both recent world wars, who was nevertheless a man of retiring spirit and disarming modesty."

Nicolson's most popular work as a biographer, and the book for which he has become best known, is *Portrait of a Marriage.* Shortly after his mother's death in 1962, while searching as her executor through her carefully ordered papers, he "came upon a locked Gladstone bag lying in the corner. . . . I cut away the leather from around its lock to open it. Inside there was a large notebook in a flexible cover, page after page filled with her neat pencilled script. . . . It was an autobiography written when she was aged twenty-eight, a confession, an attempt to purge her mind and heart of a love that had possessed her, a love for another woman, Violet Trefusis." This manuscript, dated July 23, 1920, forms the cornerstone of this warm memoir of two extraordinary people who managed to sustain a marriage through five decades despite marked sexual incompatibility and continual extramarital love affairs. It was, according to their son, "the strangest and most successful union that two gifted people have ever enjoyed." "The marriage succeeded because each found permanent and undiluted happiness only in the company of the other. If their marriage is seen as a harbour, their love affairs were ports of call. It was to the harbour that each returned; it was there that both were based." A few reviewers expressed mistrust, one seeing "no reason why we must now indulge this family's romantic myth-making about itself." Most, however, admired the book as well as its author's intelligence, honesty, and finely expressed sense of filial piety.

With *Mary Curzon* Nicolson had a subject very different from his earlier works. The biography is the near-fairy tale of a beautiful, rich, young American heiress, Mary Victoria Leiter, who in 1895 married George Nathaniel Curzon, a British aristocrat whose political star was rising fast. Three years later she became Vicereine of India, "the highest position which any American, man or woman, has ever held in the British Empire." "Proud and reserved as she was," writes Nicolson of his subject, "she was never contemptuous or austere. American she remained at heart, but through her husband she came to respect the British. She wanted, deserved and fulfilled a great role in life, and her

enjoyment of it was earned by her sustained effort to survive its tribulations." Several reviewers expressed dissatisfaction at the slightness of the book. One called it of "limited value, . . . overly sympathetic, . . . focused on the flowers, frills and parties of Mary's social life. [It] slights Mary's influence on important decisions governing people's lives." Another felt Nicolson was "unable, amid the swirl of party lists in his early chapters, to bring her to life."

Nicolson has produced the texts to two influential books of domestic architecture in the grand manner. *Great Houses of Britain* looks at thirty-nine widely scattered country estates and takes as its chief emphasis "the continuity of family and taste. The people who could afford to build such houses formed a very small circle. They all knew each other, and their children intermarried down the generations." He sees all the money and time expended on the preservation of old buildings in Britain well worthwhile; the houses "are not replaceable; they form collectively Britain's greatest contribution to the visual arts." *Great Houses of the Western World* accords a very similar treatment to thirty-six houses in Europe and America. The author sees this book as "an architectural anthology, not a guide to homes. It illustrates how Europeans changed their manner of building through some six hundred years, how each country acquired an individual style and influenced the style of others, and how the continent as a whole gave something of permanent architectural value to America. It traces the development of sophisticated housing seen through thirty-six examples of the best." Both books, with their many sumptuous photographs, achieved great popularity in the genre, perhaps because, as the author supposes, of the "insatiable human interest in how other humans live or have lived."

In 1953, Nicolson married Philippa Janet Tennyson d'Eyncourt, the daughter of a baronet. They have a son and two daughters, and were divorced in 1970. Nicolson lives in Sissinghurst Castle, Kent, the Tudor and Elizabethan manor bought by his parents in 1930 and rescued from virtual ruin. He is a fellow of the Royal Society of Literature and of the Society of Antiquaries; he is a keen amateur archaeologist. He was awarded an M.B.E. in 1945 for meritorious wartime services.

PRINCIPAL WORKS: *Biography*—Lord of the Isles, 1960; Alex, 1973; Portrait of a Marriage, 1973; Mary Curzon, 1977. *History*—The Grenadier Guards, 1939–45, 1949. *Politics*—People and Parliament, 1958. *Architecture*—Great Houses of Britain, 1965, rev. ed., 1978; Great Houses of the Western World, 1968. *Travel*—The Himalayas, 1975. *As editor*—Harold

Nicolson, Diaries and Letters 1930–62, 1966–68; Letters of Virginia Woolf, 1975–80.

ABOUT: Who's Who, 1983–84. *Periodicals*—American Historical Review October 1967; Atlantic November 1966; December 1973; Best Sellers July 15, 1967; November 1, 1968; June 1, 1973; Book Week December 18, 1966; Book World July 21, 1968; December 8, 1968; Choice November 1966; February 1967; September 1973; June 1978; Christian Science Monitor November 17, 1966; August 10, 1967; August 1, 1968; May 16, 1973; Commonweal December 2, 1966; December 29, 1967; Economist December 25, 1965; October 8, 1966; September 30, 1967; August 31, 1968; December 28, 1968; March 31, 1973; October 27, 1973; October 29, 1977; Harper's January 1967; July 1967; Library Journal November 15, 1965; November 1, 1966; May 15, 1967; June 15, 1968; November 15, 1968; May 1, 1973; October 15, 1973; November 15, 1977; Nation April 3, 1967; National Review May 2, 1967; New Republic November 12, 1966; June 17, 1967; February 4, 1978; New Statesman October 7, 1966; October 13, 1967; August 30, 1968; March 30, 1973; October 26, 1973; New York Review of Books March 23, 1967; August 3, 1967; November 15, 1973; New York Times Book Review November 27, 1966; June 11, 1967; July 28, 1968; December 1, 1968; October 28, 1973; January 8, 1978; New Yorker December 18, 1965; November 19, 1966; September 9, 1967; Juy 27, 1968; October 29, 1973; Times Literary Supplement December 30, 1965; October 13, 1966; October 5, 1967; August 29, 1968; December 12, 1968; March 30, 1973; November 30, 1973; November 11, 1977; Virginia Quarterly Review Spring 1967; Winter 1968.

ROBERT NISBET

NISBET, ROBERT ALEXANDER (September 30, 1913–), American sociologist and social critic, was born in Los Angeles. He attended the University of California at Berkeley, where he earned a B.A. in 1936, an M.A. in 1937, and a Ph.D. in 1939. During these years, the most important influence on Nisbet's intellectual growth was Frederick Teggart, professor of Social Institutions at Berkeley. From Teggart, Nisbet learned to think of history as a conflict of "idea systems," and more specifically, the "historical conflict between traditionalism and modernism," which came to serve him as "both philosophy of history and framework of analysis."

While still a graduate student, Nisbet became intrigued by the writing of the great eighteenth- and nineteenth-century European conservatives, including Louis de Bonald, Joseph Marie de Maistre, Edmund Burke, Ludwig von Haller, Georg Frederich Hegel, and somewhat belatedly, his favorite, Alexis de Tocqueville. Nisbet's doctoral thesis, "The Social Group in French Thought" (1939), explored the conservatives' analysis of the French Revolution and its political after-

math, particularly its destructive effect on traditional authority. Years later, Nisbet explained the fascination that conservative thought has held for him throughout his career. "These works told me things about the nature of power and society that I had not gotten from my more or less conventional education as an undergraduate," he wrote in the introduction to *Tradition and Revolt.* In their attacks on modern society, the conservatives gave him new perspectives on its "physiognomy," particularly the penetration of the state into society, the decline of community and rise of individual alienation, and perhaps most profoundly, the recognition that change is not necessarily for the good. The central preoccupation of Robert Nisbet's work thus became and has remained the classic sociological distinction between *gemeinschaft* and *gesellschaft*: the contrast between traditional pre-industrial society, which anchored the individual within a dense hierarchy of family, church, and community loyalties, and the modern industrial social order, which pits the isolated individual against an all-powerful state.

Nisbet's first major book, *The Quest for Community,* represents an elaboration of his doctoral research along these same lines. He shows that in order to command its citizens' total obedience and dedication, the modern nation state has systematically eliminated the competing ties of "intermediate associations" such as the family and church, so as to intrude its power into every aspect of social life. This "triumph of the political relationship and of man's political status over all other relationships and statuses in society" has been a source of profound social dislocation and political upheaval in the twentieth century. Shorn of the security provided by non-political associations, the modern masses have been easy prey to the "total" ideologies of left and right. As a corrective, Nisbet calls for a more pluralistic state that will simultaneously withdraw from its citizens' private lives and foster their participation in meaningful intermediate associations.

In perhaps his most famous work, *The Sociological Tradition,* Nisbet extends the "quest for community" into another dimension: sociology itself. Like the political conservatives of their era, the founders of sociology, men such as Karl Marx, Alexis de Tocqueville, Georg Simmel, Max Weber, and Emile Durkheim, were concerned with the decline of the traditional community. Their attempts to understand and analyze the conflicts between traditional and modern values in their own society laid the foundations of modern sociology. Nisbet writes:

What sociology, at its best and most creative, has done is to lift these conflicts from the currents of ideological controversy in which they made their appearance during the age of the industrial and democratic revolutions and to convert and refine them . . . into the problems and concepts that today give sociology its unique position in the understanding of not only the development of modern Europe but of the new nations that are now undergoing some of the same kinds of social change that were still vivid in Europe and the United States two generations ago.

Specifically, Nisbet identifies five oppositional concepts in nineteenth-century sociology that still form the "unit ideas" of the modern discipline: community/society, authority/power, status/class, sacred/secular, and alienation/progress. In the way they developed these unit ideas, Nisbet argues, the founders of sociology—with the exception of Marx and Herbert Spencer—betrayed a concern for the loss of community and a distrust of modernity quite similar to the views expressed by the political conservatives of their time. Disputing the conventional notion of sociology as forward-looking, Nisbet stresses the conservatism of its founders. This is the paradox of sociology, he concludes: that "although it falls, in its objectives and in the political and social values of its principal figures, in the mainstream of modernism, its essential concepts and its implicit perspectives place it much closer, generally speaking, to philosophical conservatism."

In *Social Change and History,* Nisbet took on yet another central aspect of the sociological tradition: the use of metaphors of growth and development to explain social change. After reviewing metaphors of change from the Greeks to Herbert Spencer, Nisbet moves to the real point of his book: the critique of developmental-ism, functionalism, and neo-evolutionism in modern sociology. Strenuously objecting to the idea that societies have some sort of developmental "essence" or inborn predisposition to evolve according to universal laws of growth, he argues that such a conflation of the process of historical change and the growth of the biological organism represents a serious abuse of the metaphor and dangerously flawed intellectual premise. Historical forces, not biological imperatives, are the key to understanding social change. "We shall not find the sources of change in society through efforts which seek to deduce it as a fixed property of social structures," he writes.

In later works such as *The Twilight of Authority* and *The History of the Idea of Progress,* Nisbet has ventured even more deeply into the realm of social criticism. He portrays the twentieth century as a "twilight age," an epochal era of disillusionment and social anarchy that threatens to fulfill the conservatives' predictions about the dire consequences of modernity. The prevailing "atmosphere of guilt and loss of meaning or purpose in the West" is nowhere better illustrated than in the widespread intellectual assault on the concept of progress that, according to Nisbet, is the foundation of Western civilization. The only hope—and Nisbet sees it as a slim one—is a profound revolution in values that will restore what he terms a "new laissez faire," a nation state that fosters political and social pluralism. As he wrote in 1968: "A genuine philosophy of freedom is inseparable from some kind of pluralism: it is inseparable from a distinction between state and society."

At a time when many sociologists place increasing faith in quantitative methods and mathematical modeling to make their discipline more scientific, Nisbet has steadfastly maintained sociology's kinship with the humanities. In "Sociology as an Art Form," which he published as an article in 1962 and expanded into a book by the same title in 1976, Nisbet makes the case for the similarities between sociology and art. In the preface to the book, he states that while writing *The Sociological Tradition,* it struck him that "none of the great themes which have provided continuing challenge and also theoretical foundation for sociologists during the last century was ever reached through anything resembling what we are today fond of identifying as 'scientific method.'" Believing that there is a "basic unity of the creative act," he argues that the real difference between sociology and art lies in the mode of verification, not the "underlying act of discovery or illumination or invention." Thus Nisbet is very critical of what he terms scientism, or "science with the spirit of discovery and creation left out."

Not surprisingly, many younger sociologists chafe at Nisbet's conservatism. Jerome Himmelstein, in a review of *The History of the Idea of Progress,* accused him of "intellectual schizophrenia"; on the one hand, Nisbet portrays the idea of progress as the cornerstone of Western civilization; on the other, he condemns its social consequences. Himmelstein concludes that Nisbet's work "reflects the dilemmas of conservative thought in general in the late twentieth century." These dilemmas are reflected again in Nisbet's *Prejudices: A Philosophical Dictionary,* a collection of brief essays on topics beginning (alphabetically) with Abortion and ranging over the spectrum of social thought with entries as diverse as Alienation, Boredom, and Creationism to Technology and War. Tackling the most challenging issues of modern times, Nisbet claims that he writes in the spirit of Edmund Burke, seeking not to refute "general" prejudices but to discover their "latent wisdom." In the process Nisbet produced a lively, controversial, and eminently readable book which epitomizes his long career and characteristically antagonized his critics while it delighted his admirers.

Controversial as it is, Nisbet's work exemplifies the contribution that rigorous, well-written scholarship can make to both academic and popular discourse. The breadth of his intellectual grasp and the clarity and elegance of his writing style have made him much admired by his peers, even when they disagree with his conclusions. "For the past twenty-five years," writes Joseph Gusfeld, "Professor Nisbet has combined an understanding of political philosophy and history with the analysis of the major issues which have preoccupied sociologists in their efforts to provide an intellectual perspective toward modern societies. Almost alone among us, he has had the knack and the wisdom to see how the persistent issues of political philosophy have been recast by sociological analysis and to place the description of modern society in the context of those abiding issues."

Nisbet joined the faculty of the University of California at Berkeley in 1939, then (following Army service in World War II), he moved to the University of California at Riverside in 1953, where he remained until 1972. After a brief time at the University of Arizona, he was Albert Schweitzer Professor of the Humanities from 1974 until his retirement in 1978. Nisbet is now a resident scholar with the American Enterprise Institute in Washington, D.C. He has also been a visiting professor at Columbia University.

PRINCIPAL WORKS: The Quest for Community, 1953; Human Relations in Administration, 1956; Contemporary Social Problems, 1961; The Sociological Tradition, 1967; Tradition and Revolt: Historical and Sociological Essays, 1968; Social Change and History, 1969; The Social Bond 1970; Western Theory of Development, 1970; The Degradation of Academic Dogma, 1971; The Social Philosophers, 1973; The Sociology of Emile Durkheim, 1975; The Twilight of Authority, 1975; Sociology as an Art Form, 1976; A History of Sociological Analysis (with T. Bottomore), 1978; The History of the Idea of Progress, 1980; Prejudices: A Philosophical Dictionary, 1983.

ABOUT: *Periodicals*—American Journal of Sociology 75, 1969-70; 82, 1976; American Sociological Review 32, 1967; New York Times Book Review October 31, 1976; Social Forces 60, 1981.

***

*NIZAN, PAUL-IVES (February 7, 1905–May 23, 1940), French novelist, journalist, essayist, and translator, was born at Tours, France, the son of Pierre Nizan, a railway engineer, and his wife, Clémentine Metour. After attending the lycée at Périgueux, he entered the Lycée Henri IV in Paris at age eleven, where he distinguished himself as a brilliant student and where he met Jean-Paul Sartre, a fellow student, who became his lifelong friend. Both moved to the Lycée Louis-le-Grand in 1922 and to the Ecole Normale Supérieure in 1924. Despite Sartre's envy of Nizan's greater facility in writing, the two were close companions and were often mistaken for each other because of a remarkable physical resemblance. In a retrospective view written many years after Nizan's death and designed to serve as a preface to Nizan's *Aden-Arabie,* reissued in 1960, Sartre characterizes the young Nizan as gentle in manner, yet intellectually aggressive: "I never saw him frown or heard him raise his voice; he would fold his hands and would become engrossed in studying his nails, while he let loose his violence with an imperturbable demeanor that was both sly and misleading."

In common with many young people in the 1920s, both radicals and traditionalists, Nizan searched for new values. He was associated with a group of philosophy students who sought reforms in a number of disciplines, including philosophy, psychology, and religion. Perhaps to settle his intellectual turmoil, he went to Aden from October 1926 to May 1927 as a tutor to the son of Antonin Besse, the colony's most prominent businessman. His stay there produced an important early book, *Aden-Arabie* (1931). W. D. Redfern notes that the work "has a tripartite structure: an initial spate of the young man's prefabricated images, followed by his journey out which ends in bitter disillusion, and finally his return home filled with new and radical

°nē zäN´

resolve." In this pamphlet he attacks the Ecole Normale Supérieure, which, he thought, did not teach its students to face the plight of their fellow human beings. Though he has only praise for Lucien Herr, the late principal, who introduced Marx and Hegel into the curriculum for the first time, he does not admire his successor, Gustave Lanson. He poses the question as to how one can best counter the effects of such an education and concludes ironically that one should imitate ordinary people by plunging into such human activities as drinking, sex, and friendship. In a scornful tone typical of most of the book, he mocks the capitalist Mr. C., his employer Besse transformed, as an "incomplete man . . . faithfully preserving the remnants of a sentimental adolescence troubled by the taste for glory and a sort of poetic ambition." He notes the sterility of life among the European colonialists, commenting that their sole motive for existence is economic, and he finds it ridiculous to discuss the arts or social questions in this environment. Redfern suggests that Nizan's attack on Besse was at least partially prompted by the fact that Nizan almost accepted an offer of permanent work in Besse's organization, before recoiling from the prospect of joining the wrong side. Nizan concludes the book that Tillie Olsen has called "fierce, brilliant, rash, mixed up, unjust" by observing that he is, after all, an outsider in Aden and had best confine his reforming activity to Europe.

Upon his return to France in 1927 Nizan married Henriette Alphen, by whom he had two children, born in 1928 and 1930. In 1927–28 he also joined the French Communist Party, of which he had briefly been a member in 1926. Both his marriage and his political affiliation separated him from Sartre. In 1929 he received his degree in philosophy, and after performing his military service he taught philosophy in 1931–32 at the lycée in Bourg, a provincial town whose conservative residents were scandalized by his political activities. He attempted to unionize town workers, and in the legislative elections of 1932 he ran unsuccessfully as the official Communist Party candidate. He then returned to Paris, where he helped to organize the "Workers' University," in which he also taught. From 1929 until his death he championed the Marxist-Leninist cause in numerous journals.

Though he had earlier, in *Aden-Arabie*, attacked his former teachers, in his 1932 pamphlet *Les Chiens de garde* (*The Watchdogs*) he launches an all-out war against the professors of philosophy, who, through their stance of detachment, frustrate the young in their search for an integrated life that does not separate the intellect from the body. Of this book André Gide said in his *Journal* that, though he found it repetitive and obvious, he read it with great interest, for he believed it to be a "sign of the times," a clear indication that "games are out, even if they are games of intellect." Nizan asserts: "It is about time we laid to rest the old notion that the philosophers are cut off from everything and everyone. . . . Every philosophy, however far removed it may seem from the workaday world, possesses a temporal and human significance." He characterizes these philosophers as preferring their own "spiritual comfort, and the mundane guarantees of this comfort, to dealing with ugly human problems," and, in an extended metaphor that is typical of his style, he pours sarcasm on them for their smugness: "And so they fold their arms and relax in the warm serenity of the Sabbath. No more work on the agenda. The tranquility of the seventh day. . . . But for some men Sunday is still a long way off." Bourgeois philosophy has nothing to offer the common man, for its assertion that salvation lies within directly contradicts the common man's experience of life. Nizan wants commitment and involvement in the contemporary scene. In *Les Chiens de garde* he introduces the concept of engagement in its modern sense, as well as the idea that abstention is also choice.

Nizan's three novels—*Antoine Bloyé* (1933), *Le Cheval de Troie* (*The Trojan Horse*, 1935), and *La Conspiration* (Conspiracy, 1938)—all illustrate his view that a great work of literature should be an accusation and an instrument of knowledge. The writer should have the will "to face reality, however hard, however disagreeable it may be." One such reality is his obsession with death, which some critics claim dominates his work.

Sartre, who regarded *Antoine Bloyé* as an important autobiographical statement, said that the main character, Bloyé, represented both Nizan and his father; according to Redfern, Nizan both tries to get into his father's shoes and to explain his own options. This novel is "a double indictment, of an age (1864–1927) and of a man." Bloyé, a railway engineer, is seen as a man who passes his life more dead than alive because he has cut himself off from his working class origins, much as Nizan's father, who rose to the position of railway engineer, had cut himself off from his proletarian and Breton farming origins. The novel traces the life of Bloyé from cradle to grave, illustrating through frequent authorial comment the estrangement of Bloyé from all that is vital and his substitution of extraneous values for real ones. A young man from a poor working-class background, Bloyé decides to marry a young woman of the petty bourgeoisie, though he is in love with another woman, when he perceives that an advantageous match may help him rise socially. Gradually becoming a member of the railroad's managerial staff, he goes over to the side of those who give rather than receive orders. In an impassioned vein Nizan generalizes the experience of his character: "Will man never be more than a fragment of a man, alienated, mutilated, a stranger to himself?" Bloyé devotes little time to either love or marriage, but an unexpected bond develops between him and his wife from their mutual concern for their invalid daughter, a bond that dissolves when the child dies. When his son is born, Bloyé thinks suddenly, "'My son will avenge me.' For Antoine is a man with scores to settle, a man who has not enjoyed life to the full, who knows that he will never himself get even with life." Bloyé attains the post of "manager of the shops," but during World War I he is forced to accept a much less important job after defective munitions accidentally pass through his plant. This is the beginning of the end for him, and he spends his remaining days privately acknowledging his failure.

A high point in Nizan's life was a trip to the Soviet Union as a delegate to the 1934 Soviet Writers' Congress. He stayed a year, obviously impressed with what he saw, but he never composed panegyrics on the Soviet Union as did many communist writers in the 1930s. His intense activity as a journalist did not preclude other creative efforts. He translated Dreiser's *An American Tragedy* (1933); wrote *Le Cheval de Troie*, which contains a portrait of Sartre as the intellectual Lange; a popularization of his favorite classical philosophers, Democritus, Epicurus, and Lucretius, *Les Matérialistes de l'antiquité* (The Materialists of Antiquity 1936); and adapted Aristophanes' play *The Acharnians* (1937).

In *La Conspiration*, which won the Prix interallié (Interallied Prize), he depicts a group of young intellectuals, modeled on the young philosophers' group that he had known at the Ecole Normale, who rebel against their bourgeois background as they pass from adolescence to maturity. Rosenthal, one of the main characters, manipulates the other members and "organizes a tiny network of industrial and military espionage, in order to contribute, he hopes, to Soviet strategy." He incites a former schoolmate to steal secrets from the army, seduces his own brother's wife, and finally commits suicide. Pluvinage, the group's "odd-man out," is discovered to be a police spy when an older friend of the group is arrested on sedition charges. Laforgue agrees to steal industrial secrets from his father's engineering firm. When he realizes that Rosenthal never used the information, he is shocked into a growing awareness of the differ-

ence between aspiration and accomplishment. Following his recovery from a serious illness, he experiences a sense of renewal and becomes the one real "survivor" of the group. This work shows, in Redfern's view, how great a loss Nizan's premature death was, for its "complexities correct the dogmatism Nizan often slipped into in his polemical writings, . . . [it] proves in action how public and private lives intermingle and influence each other, yet it does not pretend that there is any final solution to their dialectical struggle."

Ironically, this novel contributed to the near-obliteration of Nizan's name in the years following his death. Henri Lefebvre, a member of the young philosophers' group at the Ecole Normale and a former friend of Nizan's, was outraged at the "distortions" of fact in this work and regarded it as evidence that Nizan himself was a police informer. The French Communist Party, from which Nizan resigned following the Soviet-Nazi Pact of 1939, denounced him as a police spy and continued to circulate rumors of his treachery during the post-war period, but produced no evidence against him when a group of writers led by Sartre challenged them to do so. Shortly after Nizan resigned from the Party, he was drafted into the French Army, but was excused from combat because of defective vision. In 1940, while serving as an interpreter and translator with the English forces at Dunkirk, he was killed by a stray bullet. An English soldier on his way to a prisoner-of-war camp hid Nizan's manuscripts, including the nearly completed sequel to *La Conspiration*. They were never recovered. Since 1960, his life and works, particularly his three novels, have aroused considerable interest.

WORKS IN ENGLISH TRANSLATION: Paul Nizan's work is best known to English-language readers through Joan Pinkham's translation of *Aden-Arabie*, published in 1968. Charles Ashleigh translated *The Trojan Horse* in 1937. *The Watchdogs: Philosophers and the Established Order* was translated by Paul Fittingoff in 1971.

ABOUT: Brochier, J.-J. (ed.) Paul Nizan, intellectuel communiste, 1967; Cohen-Solal, A. Paul Nizan: Communiste impossible, 1980; Columbia Dictionary of Modern European Literature, 1980; Fé, F. Paul Nizan un intellettuale comunista, 1973; Ginsbourg, A. Nizan, 1966; Ishaghpour, Y. Paul Nizan, 1980; King, A. Paul Nizan écrivain, 1976; Leiner, J., Le Destin littéraire de Paul Nizan, 1970; Ory, P. Nizan: Destin d'un révolté, 1905–1940, 1980; Redfern, W. D. Paul Nizan: Committed Literature in a Conspiratorial World, 1972; Sartre, J.-P. Situations, IV, 1964; Schalk, D. The Spectrum of Political Engagement, 1979. *Periodicals*—Horizon June 1947; Romanic Review December 1967; May 15, 1981; New York Reveiw of Books November 15, 1973; New York Times Book Review June 23, 1973; Times Literary Supplement September 30, 1965; May 15, 1981.

NORRIS, LESLIE (May 21, 1921–), Welsh poet, short story writer, editor, playwright, and translator of medieval Welsh verse, writes: "Merthyr Tydfil, in Wales, was the very first town in that small country. Before the early years of the last century, Wales was a land of small villages, with its own language and culture, and ancient and noble literature. But a combination of coal and iron ore changed all that. In a few years an idyllic village at the foot of Brecon Beacons, a place that Defoe thought the most beautiful in Britain, had become the biggest steel-producing town in the world. The first steam engine ever to run on rails was invented there. As a child I could see the tracks on which it had made that prophetic journey. The foundries lit the sky at night for miles around; the Industrial Revolution was born there. Men flocked to work there from the farms and villages of Wales, from the West Country, from the impoverished small conurbations of Spain and Italy. It was like the Klondyke. George Borrow thought it looked like a vision of Hell. A curate in one of Trollope's novels, on learning that he was to be sent to Merthyr Tydfil, fainted. It was at once a place of immense riches and the worst poverty. The houses were built without regard for beauty or comfort. Epidemic disease was commonplace. Policemen walked the streets in pairs for safety. But in the big houses people spoke of painting and drama. Lady Charlotte Guest, wife of the great ironmaster, labored with her team of scholars to complete her translation of *The Mabinogion,* greatest of Celtic prose works. After its first wild and heady days, the town settled a little, grew less wild, smaller even. Heavy industry moved to the ports, many families left to live in Cardiff or Swansea, or Pittsburgh or Philadelphia. When I was born there some years after the first World War, the great days were over and the town had begun to sink into a place of unemployment and despair that were to last for almost twenty years. Such contrasts, I was always aware of them. I saw very early a rural and beautiful heaven and an urban hell.

"My father came late to the town. He was born in the 1890s in Cardiff and moved to Merthyr Tydfil with his family in the early years of this century, while he was still a boy. My mother's family had come from a farm, remote and idyllic, in the hills behind Llandovery. They remained farmers and horsemen, living on the side of the mountain. Fifty years has seen my father's family scattered all over the world. Of my paternal grandfather I recall only that he was small and plump. As he sat in his wooden armchair he played his accordion, a small octagonal instrument. He was not Welsh. He might have come

LESLIE NORRIS

originally from England, although an old man who knew him told me that he was Norwegian.

"I went to a village school not far from the farm. I was brilliantly taught there, by a young man who educated our senses. We saw sharply, knew the surfaces of wood and metal, understood the nature of living things. Early on I was made to recognize the miraculous nature of the world. In essence all my work has been an attempt to recreate and define that miracle.

"I wrote poetry as a child and have never stopped, but prose is, comparatively, a recent development for me, although I had written many critical and academic pieces. I wrote my first short story at a time when poems were not happening for me very often, and I enjoyed the experience so much that I've continued. The short story was very popular when I was young and I read many of the great masters. It suits me very well, being like the poem an art of selection. And I'm constantly surprised by what happens in my stories. My task is to make a world of such balance and clarity, in which things are clearly visible and palpable, that when my people walk into it they already exist, walking and talking and making things happen. It seems to me that I am mainly a maker of these small alternative worlds, which succeed only to the extent that I remain a passionate and non-judging observer of the great world about me. That, I think, is true of every writer. And to that extent my work is autobiographical. I normally write of places I know. But the men and women who inhabit my little worlds, they continually surprise me. They are nothing to do with me. I'm glad they are mysterious in this way."

While making his home today in Chichester, Sussex, Leslie Norris has for nearly two decades spent part of each year in Wales, at his cottage near Llandysul. Born in Merthyr Tydfil in Mid-Glamorgan, he attended elementary and secondary schools there and then served in the Royal Air Force during World War II. He published two poetry collections in the forties for which he received early recognition and, after matriculating at Coventry College and the University of Southampton, embarked on a career of college teaching—and nearly fifteen years of silence. *The Ballad of Billy Rose,* probably his most popular, certainly his most anthologized, poem broke this silence in 1964 and Norris has maintained considerable creative activity since then. Having taken out time in the seventies and eighties to teach poetry at the University of Washington and at Brigham Young University, he is now a full-time writer.

Norris describes the scope of his technique as embracing formal patterns, free verse, and invented forms, sometimes exploring verbal patterns, very often breaking from a specific remembered incident into a general poetic exploration. His poems are for the most part written in traditional stanzaic forms, usually without rhyme. Perceiving himself to be a Jungian poet, he "bring[s] up the images from some unknown source." Poetry as *anamnesis*—recreating, rather than describing—is the task that the poet has set for himself.

It was his collection *Finding Gold* published in 1967 that brought him to the sustained attention of the critics once again. Here he makes use of his own past in order to deal with current situations. Demonstrating, as John Fuller writes, that "moments of visionary illumination may well occur" in a cinema or on the football field, he "communicates a real sense of life endured, of the flux tamed."

His poetic voice, subtly modulated, is full of love for his native Wales, the rhythms of its ancient language, the lives of its people—great and small—from their homes on green farms and in isolated villages, through the seasonal and diurnal changes. His homely elegies range in tone from regret or quiet sadness to rough compassion. One short poem provides the flavor of some of his work, "both an elegy for the world in decay and a celebration of its perpetual renewal" as Roland Mathias describes it:

Moving into fall, I give my body rest
After heady summer. The hills turn early blue,
    The rivers are rising.

Yesterday, winds from the untempered north
Put me shutting windows. At night I closed my eyes
    On the last of summer.

I have set the fire, collecting the slight
Twigs. Spent as leaves, I watched my fallen hands,
    The bark hardening.

Throughout his career critics have spoken of Norris' neat, vivid, piercing observation. James Finn Cotter observes that he "writes fine poems about ordinary people. Many good poems communicate an inner feeling of life close to the earth. Norris surprises his readers with his firm grip on mortality and the things of this world." Another critic wrote of his vision "encompass[ing] acceptance and understanding; it is this stance and his eye for detail and the meaning of that detail, that reassures and makes the reader pay attention." A third has acclaimed his ability to "conjure common observation into his own idiosyncratic mode."

In *Ransoms* Norris invokes the spirit of the eminent twentieth-century Anglo-Welsh poet, Vernon Watkins (1906–67). "A True Death," included in this collection, originally appeared in the memorial volume for that poet which Norris edited, a significant edition both biographically and critically. He has compiled a second homage volume in memory of the poet Andrew Young and has also written *Glyn Jones,* a critical work of distinction in the Writers of Wales Series. Norris' short stories have appeared in *Atlantic Monthly, Esquire, New Yorker, Sewanee Review,* and *Short Story International.* A major gathering of these, entitled *Sliding,* appeared in 1976 to enthusiastic reviews and was awarded two major prizes.

Like most twentieth-century Anglo-Welsh poets, Leslie Norris is a professional man: a college lecturer for much of his mature life. In using English as his medium, he has resorted to what has been the speech of the professional community for the greater part of four centuries. Edward Lucie-Smith has remarked on "a rhythmic litheness allied to an unforced purity of diction, a chastened but natural mode of speech," and Roland Mathias praises "a style which in its limpidity, clarity, and latent force carries the simple, the anecdotal, even the common, experience and give it an unexpected memorability." It is this capacity to make his work accessible without cheapening the experience of the poem or blunting its delicacy that is arresting.

Norris' retrospective anthology *Walking in White Fields* brings together a selection of poems from three earlier volumes, *Ransoms; Mountains, Polecats, and Pheasants, and Other Elegies;* and *Water Voices,* together with two new poems. Michael J. Collins has written of this anthology: "The rhythms, quiet and conversational, are tightened at appropriate moments with remarkable effectiveness. His subtle grooming makes the poems here moving and effective, and they bring us, through their portraits of particular people and their re-creations of the natural world, to a richer appreciation of our own lives and the world in which we live them."

PRINCIPAL WORKS: *Poetry*—Tongue of Beauty, 1941; Poems, 1946; The Ballad of Billy Rose, 1964; The Loud Winter, 1967; Finding Gold, 1967; Curlew, 1969; Ransoms, 1970; His Last Autumn, 1972; Mountains, Polecats, Pheasants and Other Elegies, 1973; Stone and Fern, 1973; Wthan Moonfields, 1973; The Dove and the Tree, 1973; At the Publishers', 1976; Ravenna Bridge, 1977; Islands Off Maine, 1977; Merlin and the Snake's Egg, 1978; Hyperion, 1979; Water Voices, 1980; Walking the White Fields: Poems 1967–1980, 1980. *Criticism*—Glyn Jones, 1973. *Short stories*—Sliding and Other Stories, 1976. *As editor*—Vernon Watkins: 1906–1967, 1970, Andrew Young: Remembrance and Homage, 1978; The Mabinogion, translated by Lady Charlotte Guest, 1980.

ABOUT: Authors of Wales Today, 1972; Contemporary Authors 11–12, 1965; Contmeporary Authors, Permanent Series 1, 1975; Contemporary Literary Criticism 14, 1980; Vinson, J. (ed.) Contemporary Poets, 1970; Contemporary Poets (2nd ed.) 1975; (3rd ed.) 1980; International Authors and Writers Who's Who, 1982. *Periodicals*—Anglo-Welsh Review 1972; Encounter April 1974; The Hudson Review Summer 1981; London Magazine June 1967; November 1974; New Statesman June 7, 1974; New York Times Book Review October 24, 1976; April 30, 1978; Poetry May 1972; Poetry Review Summer 1967; Poetry Wales 1972; Priapus 1972; Punch April 5, 1967; Sewanee Review Winter 1981; World Literature Today Autumn 1981.

NOVA, CRAIG (July 5, 1945–), American novelist, was born in Los Angeles, the son of Karl Nova and the former Elizabeth Sinclair. He graduated from the University of California at Berkeley with honors in 1967, then took a master's degree in fine arts from Columbia University in 1969. He has held numerous jobs but pursued no career other than writing.

Nova began his career as a novelist of the American counterculture of the late 1960s and early seventies—one of the many disaffected young writers who expressed their rage and—in the view of some of their older critics—their confusion, in an era of radical social change, war in Southeast Asia, and national and international violence and terrorism. They produced a literature that was intended to disturb, shock, and even undermine the prevailing establishment culture. A representative example is Nova's first novel, *Turkey Hash,* the story of Niles Cabro, a hopeless petty hustler, a denizen of the Los Angeles countercultural underworld. He gradually

CRAIG NOVA

goes violently insane, abetted by a similarly unsavory urban crew: his fellow small-time con men, drug addicts, rodeo hangers-on, horse thieves, and his family: Hawkeye, Burned, and Sis. All the novel's characters are rootless, alienated, and miserable, though only Niles, fleetingly, possesses the intelligence to realize it. J. G. Bowles considered this first novel "in the end, oddly unmoving," although he acknowledged that "Nova is a fine writer. . . . His characters appear both real and surreal as they act out strange rituals and plot insane acts. His handling of pace and dialogue is superb, and the writing in general has the feel of a polished hand." G. A. Foster, on the other hand, considered the inarticulate anomie of the antihero a real failing in the book: "the author . . . has nothing to say. We get only glimpses into the main character's motivation, but no understanding of his passions. This first novel has a sterile aura of noncommunication about it."

The Geek, Nova's second novel, is set almost entirely on the Greek island of Samos and recounts the disintegration of Boot, an alcoholic American resident. His misadventures begin with his discovery of a girl's corpse on the beach and his subsequent difficulties in disposing of his find. He is treated with a mixture of bare tolerance and deep suspicion by all of his neighbors, who include a powerful opium smuggler. After an only partly satisfying affair with Mara, a querulous, imperious American, he becomes attached to a small traveling carnival which includes among its attractions a geek, a very dirty man with a "soft and mild and reassuring" gaze who bites off and eats the heads and feet of live chickens. At the end of his story, Boot becomes the carnival's second geek. "His gaze was distant and steady, since he was now safe, in league with everything he had despised, having found immunity by relinquishing all that had made struggle necessary: honor, character, word, anger." Robert Bonazzi observed that it was "the ongoing interest of the story, not the straining for significance, that impresses. . . . The plot is engaging, and the not always conventional style has its witty and insightful delights." Michael Wood found "something too cryptic about a lot of the novel's transactions, a suggestion of dialogue out of Henry James shifted to a dusty taverna, and . . . the writing keeps reaching for effects that are more than a little lurid. But the blending of emblematic and literal truth . . . is remarkable. . . . *The Geek* [is pitched] somewhere between reality and nightmare." The novel is accompanied by eighteen evocative, erotic drawings by Brad Holland, whose illustrations appeared for several years in the *New York Times*.

Stargell, the narrator of Nova's third novel *Incandescence*, is a harried, wise-cracking New Yorker ("a resourceful survivor," as one reviewer describes him), another antihero who witnesses his world collapsing around him. Fired from his job at a think tank "because I used the computer to play the horses," he is forced to borrow money at exorbitant interest from the Barber, his neighborhood loan shark, in order to please his Greek-born wife, Enid, a deeply depressed woman made psychotic by constant exposure to American television. The arrival of his macho Greek father-in-law, a retired colonel in search of something American to sell in Greece, sets Stargell to thinking that he may be able to strike it rich and thereby avoid getting killed by the Barber's hit men. The two relatives find no success in their respective goals, however, amid one night's frantic dashing around New York City and meetings with a large number of grotesque characters. In Nova's world of *Incandescence* the sinister and the ludicrous are converted into the near-normal, while his antihero searches for "incandescence"—moments of insight into the meaning of living: " . . . the fun-house spin. You'd feel the blood jump then, Jack. That's when you'd know your skin was filled with magic ." He has such moments, but they are communicated to the reader as absurdist ironies rather than epiphanies. One reviewer called *Incandescence* an "urban picaresque" adventure, remarking that while Stargell's "individual adventures are vividly rendered, they never coalesce into a very organic plot." Nova's intensely drawn minor characters, Tim O'Brien wrote, "begin to seem like links on a chain, identical in

their tough-guy fatalism, their world-weary lingo, their antic behavior. This sense of repetition also infects the events of the novel, which become variations on the same slapstick joke."

Having won his reputation as an eccentric but articulate spokesman for the malaise of the 1970s, Nova was watched with interest by critics to see whether he would develop a new and equally effective voice in the 1980s. In 1982 he apparently found that voice with *The Good Son*. Retaining the perverse wit and bitter irony of his earlier work, Nova added a new dimension of seriousness in this long family novel. Jim Crace, in the *Times Literary Supplement*, described the book as a restaging of "*King Lear* on the banks of the Delaware River in the 1950s." It is the story of a wealthy patriarch who must learn, like Lear, "that children are not private property to be bought and sold like real estate." Nova employs an ambitious and challenging structure, involving eight different narrators—father, mother, son, the two women in the son's life, the sister of one of those women, the family chauffeur, and the local deer poacher. Nevertheless, he produces an integrated and coherent book. Crace was impressed with both its structure and its "imaginative flair," but he objected to the unnecessarily complex sentences, overlong and burdened with parentheses. In the *New York Times Book Review*, however, novelist John Irving found it "almost without fault," written with "consistent grace . . . a narrative of momentum and of linear clarity . . . [with] characters of great, outward bravery and of heartbreaking inner need."

Nova, who lives in Manhattan, has won, in 1971 and 1975, fellowships from the National Endowment for the Arts and, in 1977, a Guggenheim fellowship. *Turkey Hash* won the Harper-Saxton prize in 1971.

PRINCIPAL WORKS: *Fiction*—Turkey Hash, 1972; The Geek, 1975; Incandescence, 1979; The Good Son, 1982,

ABOUT: Contemporary Authors 45–48, 1974 and 2NR, 1981; Contemporary Literary Criticism 7, 1977. *Periodicals*—Library Journal August 1972; December 1, 1975; February 1, 1979; New Statesman December 3, 1976; New York Review of Books June 10, 1976; July 19, 1979; New York Times Book Review October 29, 1972; December 21, 1975; February 11, 1979; October 3, 1982; Newsweek March 12, 1979; Saturday Review December 23, 1972; February 17, 1979; Times Literary Supplement February 4, 1983; Village Voice November 3, 1975; Virginia Quarterly Review Winter 1973.

NOZICK, ROBERT (November 16, 1938–), American philosopher, was born in Brooklyn, New York, the son of Max Nozick, a manufacturer, and the former Sophie Cohen. He grew up in the Brownsville and East Flatbush sections of Brooklyn, attended public schools, then entered Columbia University where, he notes at the beginning of his second book, he sorely tried his parents' faith in him by pursuing a "meandering academic way (which included failing five courses . . . three of them in philosophy)." He took his A.B. in 1959, then went for graduate work in philosophy to Princeton University, where he performed brilliantly, earning his M.A. in 1961 and his Ph.D. in 1963. A member of Princeton's philosophy faculty until 1965, he then taught at Harvard (1965–67), Rockefeller University, New York City (1967–69), and finally again at Harvard, where he has been professor of philosophy since 1969.

ROBERT NOZICK

Nozick has published only two books, but they have been brilliant and controversial enough to place him in the front rank of contemporary ethical and political philosophers. A committed socialist until graduate school, he is now a libertarian capitalist, and his first book especially gave libertarianism—a political doctrine maximizing individual freedom and minimizing the state's functions and perquisites—a much-needed modern defense and justification.

Anarchy, State, and Utopia, which won the National Book Award for philosophy and religion in 1975, takes as its central concern "the nature of the state, its legitimate functions and its justifications, if any." The subject of anarchy, equated by the author with Locke's "state of nature," is dealt with summarily. The dominant arguments and conclusions are that the "minimal state, limited to the narrow functions of protection against force, theft, fraud, enforcement of contracts, and so on, is justified; that any more extensive state will violate persons' rights not to be forced to do certain things, and is unjustified; and that the minimal state is inspiring as well as right." Two applications of these conclusions are also discussed at length: "the state may not use its coercive apparatus for the purpose of getting some citizens to aid others, or in order to prohibit activities to people for their *own* good or protection." Finally, perceiving that "the idea, or ideal, of the minimal state [may] lack luster. Can it thrill the heart or inspire people to struggle or sacrifice? Would anyone man barricades under its banner?" Nozick turns to "that preeminently inspiring tradition of social thought," utopian theory. "What can be saved" from this congeries of inspirational speculation, he finds, "is precisely the structure of the minimal state." Throughout the book the author is in-

sistent that he is not presenting "some sort of political tract." "It is a philosophical exploration of issues, many fascinating in their own right, which arise and interconnect when we consider individual rights and the state." He expects that many will utterly reject his views as "apparently callous toward the needs and suffering of others. I know that reaction; it was mine when I first began to consider such views. With reluctance, I found myself becoming convinced of (as they are now often called) libertarian views. . . . Over time, I have grown accustomed to the views and their consequences, and I now see the political realm through them." He recognizes, but is not much bothered by, the "narrow and rigid . . . bad company" his views force him to keep—perhaps an allusion to the illiberal policies of the Libertarian Party of the United States. He also ruefully sees "the fact that most people I know and respect disagree with me."

Anarchy, State, and Utopia was received by critics with about an equal measure of admiration and consternation. Peter Singer wrote, "Political philosophers have tended to assume without argument that justice demands an extensive redistribution of wealth in the direction of equality; and that it is a legitimate function of the state to bring about this redistribution by coercive means like progressive taxation. These assumptions may be correct; but [now] they will need to be defended and argued for instead of being taken for granted." Steven Lukes, calling the book "brilliant and strange" but its methods and conclusions "absurd," considered that "the central flaw in [Nozick's] arguments is the abstraction of the individualism they presuppose. . . . This abstract individualism . . . is a distorting lens which satisfies the intellect while simplifying the world." Lukes urged a comparison of Nozick's book to another American classic of modern political philosophy, John Rawls' *A Theory of Justice* (1971)—"to the considerable advantage of the latter."

Nozick wrote *Philosophical Explanations* over a four-year period: most of the first draft in Jerusalem in 1976–77 while on leave from Harvard; the rewriting, expansion, and completion in 1979–80, during another sabbatical. Impelled by familiar philosophical problems—on the meaning of life, on the existence of objective ethical truths and free will, on the nature of self-identity, and on the limits to knowledge and understanding—he considers in turn questions of metaphysics (the identity of the self, why there is something rather than nothing—what Heidegger called "the fundamental question of metaphysics"), of epistemology (knowledge, skepticism, types of evidence), and of value theory (free will, punishment, ethical foundations, and philosophy's connection to the meaning of life).

Producing a 752-page book of exceptional complexity on such deep subjects required in Nozick "the most extensive flights of philosophical fancy. That I take such flights sometimes strikes me as absurd, anyway. Isn't it ludicrous for someone just one generation from the *shtetl*, a *pisher* from Brownsville and East Flatbush in Brooklyn, even to touch on the topics of the monumental thinkers?" He then undercuts this striking note of modesty: "Even the monuments themselves, so serenely in command of culture and intellect, must have been children once and adolescents—so they too are immigrants to the realm of thought." A healthy distrust of organized philosophy—which he calls, somewhat tendentiously, "coercive philosophy"—permeates the book. "Why are philosophers intent on forcing others to believe things? Is that a nice way to behave toward someone? I think we cannot improve people that way. . . . The valuable person cannot be fashioned by committing philosophy upon him." To this coercive attitude Nozick opposes a kind of philosophy "not directed to arguments and proofs: it seeks explanations. The philosophical goal of explanation rather than proof not only is morally better, it is more in accord with one's philosophical motivation. Also it changes how one proceeds philosophically." "The view of philosophy," Nozick concludes, "as philosophical explanation is put forth here as a tentative hypothesis, designed to encompass much of the actual historical activity of philosophers while demarcating a legitimate and important task. . . . In contrast,

the view that philosophy is the theory of self-evident fundamental principles and their consequences, for example, seems neither to be self-evident nor derivable from such." This, as several critics have noted, is nothing less than a new way of "doing philosophy."

That Nozick addressed such a formidable book, concerned with the most basic philosophical problems, to the general reader as well as to his philosophical colleagues occasioned wonderment among many of those colleagues. "It is unsurprising," wrote Alasdair MacIntyre, "that philosophy has become ingrown, and that while John Stuart Mill and William James felt able to address the general educated public on the central problems of philosophy, Professor X now writes for Professor Y." For Bernard Williams, Nozick's campaign against "coercive" proof is "fine and good" in its recommendation that philosophers "entertain ideas in a patient and imaginative manner. . . . It is not the most creative approach in philosophy to shoot an idea out of someone's hand as soon as he picks it up." Yet Williams rejected the book's general findings because of the last part's lack of focus: "I think that the part of this book that is about value is utterly misconceived, and that the whole enterprise of approaching the problems in this abstract way, virtually unrelated to human psychology or society, and assuming ill-defined and suspect notions or spiritual superiority, is a large error." M. F. Burnyeat thought the hundred-page chapter on knowledge and skepticism "really is what the whole aspires to be: a major work of twentieth-century philosophy," yet also sharply criticized the 350-page section on value as "a complete disaster: vapid, tedious, embarrassingly pretentious. It is a long time since a professional philosopher undertook to say so much and succeeded in saying so little."

Nozick married Barbara Claire Fiere, a teacher, in August 1959. They have a daughter and son, and were divorced in 1981. Since 1971, Nozick has been a member of the editorial board of the scholarly journal, *Philosophy and Public Affairs*. He lives in Cambridge, Massachusetts.

PRINCIPAL WORKS: Anarchy, State, and Utopia, 1974; Philosophical Explanations, 1981.

ABOUT: Contemporary Authors 61–64, 1976; Current Biography 1982; Who's Who in America 1982–83; Wintle, J. Makers of Modern Culture, 1981. *Periodicals*—America July 19, 1975; American Scholar Summer 1982; Choice March 1975; January 1982; Commentary September 1975; September 1982; Commonweal November 7, 1975; January 15, 1982; Economist February 22, 1975; Harper's March 1975; Library Journal January 15, 1975; November 1, 1981; National Review July 4, 1975; New Republic April 26, 1975;

October 7, 1981; New Statesman March 14, 1975; New York Review of Books March 6, 1975; February 18, 1982; New York Times Book Review May 11, 1975; September 20, 1981; New York Times Magazine December 17, 1978; Newsweek March 31, 1975; Times Literary Supplement January 19, 1975; October 15, 1982; Yale Review Spring 1982.

OKARA, GABRIEL IMOMOTIMI GBAINGBAIN (April 21, 1921–), Nigerian poet and novelist, was born in Bumoundi, Rivers State, eastern Nigeria. His parents were Christian, and his father an Ijaw chief. After a local grammar school, Okara's secondary education began at Government College, Umuahia, which the young Chinua Achebe, the novelist, was later to attend. Okara's schooling was interrupted by World War II. He finished at Yaba Higher College, where he passed the Senior Cambridge Examinations with an A in art. Early on, he showed a deep interest in philosophy, music, and literature, in which he read widely. His chief passion, however, was art. He painted in water colors, which he studied with one of Nigeria's great artists, Ben Enwonwu. After a brief stint teaching school, Okara studied bookbinding and went to work in Lagos as a bookbinder for the Government Press. It was at this time, according to Theo Vincent, that he began to read seriously in English literature, from the romantic poets to Hopkins, Dylan Thomas, and Eliot. Okara came to the United States in 1956 and he studied journalism at Northwestern University. Since his return to Africa, he has moved between the publishing business and the cultural wing of the civil service, working in both broadcasting and the government information service. During the Nigerian Civil War, he took the side of Biafra, and he and Achebe traveled in the United States in 1969 giving lectures on the Biafran cause. Okara is now head of the Rivers State Cultural Center in Nigeria. One of the most prolific and widely anthologized of African poets, it comes as a surprise to learn that he has published only three slim books: a volume of poems, *The Fisherman's Invocation,* and a novel, *The Voice.* His *Poems 1957–1972* was published in Nigeria in 1973. In his introduction to the poetry, Theo Vincent explains that Okara has written thousands of poems, as well as short stories and radio plays. Because of an early carelessness with manuscripts—he was then content to read to audiences—and because of the later tragedy of the Biafran Civil War, almost his entire *oeuvre* has been lost. The poems that have been collected in *The Fisherman's Invocation* are among those that have been most anthologized and would seem to assure him a permanent place in the literature of Africa.

GABRIEL OKARA

Okara's novel, *The Voice,* was initially received with mixed reviews. Arthur Ravenscroft, in his introduction to the 1970 edition, says that earlier critics objected to the strange use of language and the naive symbolism. Some saw in it a reference to Amos Tutuola, his fellow Nigerian novelist; Ravenscroft himself does not share this view but regards *The Voice* as "one of the most memorable novels to have come out of Nigeria." The story concerns a young student, Okolo (the name means "The Voice"), who has just returned from abroad to his village of Amatu. Amatu's chief is Izongo, traditionalist, conservative, and cruel. Okolo begins his query and his quest with Izongo, "Do you have *it*?" Of course, Izongo doesn't have "it," nor do other members of the establishment. Okolo then exiles himself to the neighboring town of Sologa. On his way, he is accused of seducing a girl-bride, but is later absolved. At Sologa, he encounters the Big One, Izongo's counterpart, whom everyone serves. Okolo ends up in the lunatic asylum where he is rescued by the girl-bride. He returns to Amatu where Izongo has him set adrift in a canoe.

The critics are divided on the merits of this thinly disguised political and moral fable. Among its promoters are Ravenscroft and Eustace Palmer, who invokes the entire literary tradition to elucidate the technical innovations of the novel, including Bunyan, the author of *Everyman,* Chaucer, Shakespeare, Cervantes, Kafka, Eliot, Armah, Camara Laye, among others. The critics in the opposite camp seem to stand on firmer ground. They see the novel's merits as largely an experiment in language, an effort to transfer the idiom of the Ijaw language to English. Comparing Okara's efforts with those of Achebe, Chinweizu *et al.,* the authors of *Toward the Decolonization of African Literature,* remark: " . . . whereas Achebe tries to convey the idiom and tone of Igbo rhetoric . . . , Okara focuses more on arranging his English words according to the Ijaw syntax. To those familiar with the problems of translation it might not come as a surprise that Okara's results do not work. For the strategy of translation is not to reproduce word for word with the aid of a dictionary, but rather to discover and use *idiomatic equivalents* between two languages, and to invent equivalents where none are available." Another objection to the novel is its pessimistic, if not nihilistic, philosophy. In a 1964 taped interview with the Jamaican writer Andrew Salkey, Okara rejects this pessimistic reading, observing that though Okolo dies, his search for "it," that is, for the meaning of life in Nigeria and in the universe, does bear fruit. The current consensus seems to be expressed by O.R. Dathorne in *African Literature in the Twentieth Century:* "The book therefore remains only an idea; within the framework of a novel there is little motivation for the search and what little incident there is, is insignificant in itself and rigidly yoked to symbolism."

Few would dispute Theo Vincent's remark in the introduction to *The Fisherman's Invocation* that the publication of the selected poems "can be justifiably referred to as a monumental contribution to African literature." Vincent is equally persuasive in arguing that Okara's greatness as a poet lies precisely in linking the techniques of traditional African oral poetry with those of the European modernists: " . . . the many influences on him, foreign and traditional African, blend and do not obtrude in his writings." The critics generally see a progression of concerns and techniques in the poetry. There are the love poems; there are what Dathorne calls the early Negritude poems, such as "Spirit of the Wind." There are the war poems that grew out of the civil war. And there are the clash of culture poems which mark his mature work, emphasizing the conflict between traditional values and modern civilization. Okara is especially equipped by both temperament and skill to reconcile these opposites. In the mature poems, such as "Piano and Drums," "The Call of the River Nun," "To Paveba," and "One Night at Victoria Beach," Dathorne in a close reading shows how their magic comes from what he calls reorganization of the language of the public poem. "It is the ease of the songster that makes him such a satisfying poet," Dathorne concludes.

PRINCIPAL WORKS: *Poetry*—Poems 1957–1972, 1973; The Fisherman's Invocation, 1978. *Novel*—The Voice, 1964, 1970.

ABOUT: Chinwezu, O. Jemie, I. Mandubuike, Toward the Decolonization of African Literature, I, 1980; Contemporary Authors 105, 1982; Dathorne, O.R. African Literature in the 20th Century, 1976; Encyclopedia of World Literature in the 20th Century IV, 1975; Goodwin, K. Understanding African Poetry, 1983; Herdeck, D.E. (ed.) African Authors, 1973; Palmer, E. An Introduction to the African Novel, 1972; Popkin, M. (ed.) Modern Black Wriers (Library of Literary Criticism), 1978; Ravenscroft, A. *Introduction to* The Voice, 1970; Vincent, T. *Introduction to* The Fisherman's Invocation, 1978. *Periodicals*—Pan-African Journal 4, 1971.

*ONDAATJE, (PHILIP) MICHAEL (December 9, 1943–   ), Canadian poet and novelist, was born in Ceylon, where his family had lived for several generations, the son of Mervyn and Doris Gratiaen Ondaatje. He was sent to Dulwich College, an English public school, at the age of eleven, then attended Bishop's University in Quebec, and took his B.A. from the University of Toronto and his M.A. from Queen's University, Kingston, Ontario. From 1967 to 1971 he taught at the University of Western Ontario in London, and since 1971 he has been a member of the English Department of Glendon College of Toronto's York University.

Poems by Ondaatje were included in Raymond Souster's landmark anthology *New Wave Canada: The New Explosion in Canadian Poetry* (1966). The following year he published his first collection, *The Dainty Monsters,* which is, at its best, a witty modern bestiary with a fine sensitivity to animals, both domestic and mythological, and deft touches of surreal absurdity. His vision of the suburban peaceable kingdom in "Over the Garden Wall" has its built-in limitations:

. . . the infamous camel
would look profound in a felt hat,
pigs could trot, cherub white,
down the high streets,
leopards in a two-seater
would be star-spangled roués.

Yet in spite
of warnings by Daphne du Maurier,
we find the 'potamus barred from public swimming pools,
and a vulture calmly resting at a traffic light
would undoubtedly be shot, very messily,
by the first policeman who spotted him.

Other poems describe the bloody dreams of the much-fondled family dog, the "polemic bones of centaurs" that may be found in Toronto after the spring thaw, and a dragon with "an extinct burning inside" so unfierce that the whole family one day discovers it "trapped, tangled in our bad-

°än dät´ yē

MICHAEL ONDAATJE

minton net." Domestic pigs also figure largely in this collection, as well as in Ondaatje's other books. He has for several years raised hogs on his farm in northern Ontario, and is even credited with the invention, in 1975, of the Dragland Hog Feeder.

The collection *Rat Jelly* demonstrated, in the opinion of most critics, a maturing of Ondaatje's technique. His richest subject, and the one he turns to most often, is still domestic irony, present in countless forms in these poems, even in the gruesome title piece:

See the rat in the jelly
steaming dirty hair
frozen, bring it out on a glass tray
split the pie four ways and eat
I took great care cooking this treat for you
and tho it looks good to yuh
and tho it smells of the Westinghouse still
and tastes of exotic fish or
maybe the expensive arse of a cow
I want you to know it's rat
steamy dirty hair and still alive

(caught him last Sunday
thinking of the fridge, thinking of you.)

The first of Ondaatje's books to be published in the United States was *The Collected Works of Billy the Kid* in 1974, which had won the Governor General's award after it appeared in Canada in 1970. The work is divided into sixty-eight sections, some of which are lyric poems, others virtual short stories, all interspersed with ballads, tall tales, photographs, and the hero's wholly fictitious meditations on nature and violence. Ondaatje does not intend a reconstruction of the true life of Billy, or William Bonney, but rather seeks to explore the basic conflict between na-

ture and civilization. Both poetry and prose are permeated with the author's strongly visual imagination, as in the imaginary exhumation of the Kid, all bone and metal:

Imagine if you dug him up and brought him out. You'd see very little. There'd be the buck teeth. Perhaps Garrett's bullet no longer in thick wet flesh would roll in the skull like a marble. From the head there'd be a trail of vertebrae like a row of pearl buttons off a rich coat. . . . And a pair of handcuffs holding ridiculously the fine ankle bones. (Even though dead they buried him in leg irons.) There would be the silver from the toe of each boot. His legend a jungle sleep . . .

Reviewers in the United States acclaimed the book almost as highly as their Canadian counterparts had done. It is through the poet's "special sensitivity to light and color, movement and sound," in Karyl Roosevelt's words, "that the deserts of Texas, Arizona and New Mexico begin to breath hotly in our imaginations. The slow, sensuous unravelling of these violent lives is filtered through the monochromatic desert light."

Coming through Slaughter, a work entirely in prose, attempts the selective recall of another historical character. A disparate mélange of archival material, interviews, fictional sketches, and even three "sonographs" of dolphin sounds reimagine the life of the black cornetist Charles "Buddy" Bolden, one of the fathers of jazz, who went mad in 1907 while playing with a marching band in New Orleans and spent the last twenty-five years of his life in East Louisiana State Hospital. The "Slaughter" of the title refers only to a town Bolden passed through while being taken to the hospital. Anatole Broyard thought the book filled with "pretentious writing, . . . self-conscious and arty," but the reviewer for the *New Yorker* felt the collage-like effect was successful: "We understand the slow, ceremonial sense of time peculiar to New Orleans, we see the leaking colors of the houses and streets, and we feel the brilliant pressures of the music. But the book really works when Bolden begins to go mad and Ondaatje moves right inside his head."

Ondaatje's poetry first appeared in the United States in the retrospective collection *There's a Trick with a Knife I'm Learning to Do: Poems 1963–1978,* which contains selections from *The Dainty Monsters* and *Rat Jelly* plus a new section entitled *Pig Glass,* comprising poems composed between 1973 and 1978. The Canadian reviewer Douglas Barbour described the newer poems as ranging "far and wide, traveling the world with the poet, and moving back and forward in time with his seeking mind and heart." The "trick" of the title is, to Barbour, "to cut right to the bone and leave no obvious scar. But make sure the cut remains, raw and necessary as skin. Ondaatje is not just learning the trick; in his best poems he shows he is an accomplished practitioner of the art." Reviewers in the United States, however, were not nearly so enthusiastic in their reception, and Ondaatje has not so far won the reputation in the United States that the size of his Canadian audience would suggest he deserves.

Ondaatje is married and has a daughter and a son. He has also published a critical study of the Canadian poet Leonard Cohen and is the editor of *The Broken Ark,* a collection of animal verse, and *The Long Poem Anthology.* He has directed several films, including *Son of Captain Poetry,* (1971), on the Canadian concrete poet bp Nichol; *Carry on Crime and Punishment* (1972); and *The Clinton Special* (1974), about Theatre Passe Muraille's *The Farm Show.*

WORKS: *Poetry*—The Dainty Monsters, 1967; The Man with Seven Toes, 1969; The Collected Works of Billy the Kid, 1974; Rat Jelly, 1973; There's a Trick with a a Knife I'm Learning to Do, 1979. *Prose*—Leonard Cohen, 1970; Coming through Slaughter, 1976. *Non-fiction*—Tin Roof, 1982; Running in the Family, 1984. *As editor*—The Broken Ark, 1971; Personal Fictions, 1977; The Long Poem Anthology, 1979.

ABOUT: Lee, D. Savage Fields, 1977; Contemporary Authors 77–80, 1979; Vinson, J. (ed.) Contemporary Poets, 1980. *Periodicals*—Atlantic November 1974; Best Sellers August 1977; Canadian Forum December 1976–January 1977; June–July 1979; Choice February 1975; September 1977; October 1979; Hudson Review Autumn 1983; Library Journal December 15, 1974; April 1, 1977; April 1, 1979; Nation May 19, 1979; New York Times Book Review October 17, 1974; April 24, 1977; September 2, 1979; New Yorker May 9, 1977.

*ORKENY, ISTVAN (April 5, 1912–June 24, 1979), Hungarian short story writer, novelist, and dramatist, was born in Budapest. His father, the owner of a successful pharmacy, gave his son all the advantages that money could bestow, including schooling at the highly esteemed Piarist Gymnasium and stays of two years in France and one year in England. By the time Örkény was eighteen, he had mastered German, English, and French. To suit his father, he took a certificate in pharmacy and then a degree in chemistry, but eventually he chose to pursue a literary career. His first three stories appeared in a short-lived periodical in the mid-thirties to indifferent notices; but "Tengertánc" (Dance of the Ocean), published in 1938 and included in a 1941 collection of his stories, was singled out by Antal Szerb as being more than promising. Surreal and grotesque, the story attacked Nazism through a portrayal of lunatics who break out of their locked cells and seize control of a city with the help of

ISTVAN ORKENY

imbeciles, eccentrics, and various kinds of freaks.

The war interrupted his literary career. Called into service, he was stripped of his reserve rank in the army because of his Jewish descent—although he was a practicing Catholic at the time—and ordered to serve in a labor battalion on the Russian front. His war experiences profoundly affected his lifeview and later literary development. Captured after six months, he spent five years as a prisoner of war. He recorded the life in the camp on bits of wrapping paper and published two realistic accounts of his experience after his return to Budapest at the end of 1946. *Amíg idejutottunk . . . Magyarok emlékeznek hadifogságban* (Until We Got Here . . . Hungarians Recollecting in Captivity, 1946) describes how the war and imprisonment altered the outlooks of several prisoners; *Lágerek népe* (People of the Camps, 1947) is a documentary account of the prisoners' lives. He also wrote *Voronyezs* (1948), a play expressing the desire to survive imprisonment and to probe fairmindedly the circumstances that caused the deaths of so many thousands. His five years in the camp made him acutely conscious of the bond existing between human beings on the basis of "individual memories, passions, longings, and sufferings" each person possesses. This feeling of humanity provided, according to Örkény, the source of inspiration from which all his writings flow.

Örkény's literary development significantly reflected the aesthetic doctrines imposed on writers by the Rákosi regime after it came to power in 1948. He supported the principles of

°ôr kā´nē, isht´vän

socialism and adopted socialist realism because he believed that the sacrifice of his individuality was a price worth paying to achieve a better future for his people. Later, in the 1960s, critics noted that his writings during this period, especially from 1950 to 1952, were marred by optimistic portrayals of Hungarian society and that as his critical sense lessened so did the vitality and vigor of his style. Instead of nurturing the humor and disharmonies of the grotesque that had begun to appear in his writings, Örkény fell back on the anecdotal form of narration. According to some present-day critics, his continuing effort to discover his individuality was, however, reflected in *Ezüstpisztrang* (Silver Trout, 1956), in which most of the sketches reveal his struggle against demands of the anecdotal mode. While many other writers of his generation chose to be silent during this time, Örkény's career flourished; he published, among others, several books of short stories, some novels, and a play. His compliance, however, did not completely spare him the wrath of the official arbiter of literary policy, József Révai, who called the short story "Lila tinta" (Purple Ink, 1952) "rotten and untrue" because it appeared to sanction prostitution and represented a return to the stories Örkény wrote after his return from the war. Many years later in an interview, Örkény said about his writings of this period: "I experienced successes, and it is most dangerous for a writer to be applauded for what isn't any good."

The 1956 uprising radically reversed his fortunes. Because of his allegiance to the Rákosi policies, he was not permitted to publish, not even to translate or to correct proofs for a livelihood; instead he was forced to work as a chemist in a factory for five years. And yet, in his view, the years of silence imposed on him from 1956–66 were indispensable to his literary development; it was a time "to look myself in the eye, to evaluate what was inside me: my strengths, talents, propensities, and delights." In addition, he viewed the post–1956 period as one in which authors gained the freedom to follow their personal literary inclinations: "Self-abandon, literary experimentation, and artistic playfulness were again enfranchised after a time during which increasingly severe deliberateness had grown so terribly conscious that in the end it completely erased the author's soul from his written work."

Abandoning realism, he revived the "somewhat playful, bantering, chaffing, grotesque voice" of his early twenties. The tragic events of the twentieth century had, in his eyes, demolished the nineteenth century's "monstrous certitude" that it could solve all problems and that morality so permeates life that "sin, obsceni-

ty and vileness, and the dark powers of instinct are foreign to it." The events of his own lifetime made him aware that "our every movement is ambiguous and we risk falling flat on our faces with every step we take"; they swept away two thousand years of moral beliefs: "The word 'Auschwitz' blows the books and all they represent off my walls. And so do 'he was executed,' 'he was detained,' and 'he hit the ground.'"

From this time on, he used the outlook and modes of the grotesque to grasp the essence and contradictions of his times. Calling it the act of "making the improbable probable," he described his own form of the grotesque as containing "a little Ionesco (particularly the precedence given to the absurd and to thought), a little Giraudoux (with view to poetical qualities), and a little Kafka (in the sense of the tragic)." In his view, the purpose of the grotesque is not simply to provide answers in the manner of traditional literature, but to compel readers to confront their illusions. On one occasion he declared: "Death to the period! Long live the question mark!" Unlike the absurdists in the West, he did not view life as "absurd, hopeless, and unbearable." To him action was the only hope amid the contradictions and paradoxes of life: "I believe in acting man; in general I believe in the life-saving quality of action, even though I well know that our individual lives end in death; after all, this is our doom biologically. I even believe in futile action, because it, too, gives us something subjective; and here I am similar to the writers of the absurd. Camus writes . . . that there is a moment when Sisyphus must imagine he is happy." Örkény's belief in action becomes grotesque "in the sense that one must act even when action is meaningless, futile."

From 1966 on, the grotesque dominated his writings. In addition to stories, two short novels appeared, both quickly adapted as plays in Hungary and later abroad. *Macskajáték* (Catsplay, 1966), portraying a love triangle, becomes grotesque because the lovers are in their sixties. The sixty-two-year-old Mrs. Orbán, still capable of a grand passion, faces the prospect of renewed loneliness at the loss of her lover but, refusing to surrender, prepares to begin anew. Vercors, who translated the play for the French stage, calls Mrs. Orbán "One of those characters whose perfection is the guarantee of their immortality, on par with Célimène in *Le Misanthrope* or Kate in *The Taming of the Shrew*." *Tóték* (*The Toth Family*, 1967), another effort to give the grotesque larger scope, is more bitter in its humor. The members of the family, including its head, Lajos Toth, kowtow to every wish of the convalescing commanding officer of their son, no matter how unreasonable it is, no matter how much it may upset the normal course of their life, in the hope that the officer will, on his return, protect the life of the son from combat (only the mailman and the reader know the son is already dead). The theme of the oppressor and the oppressed, who accommodate themselves to the oppressor, is brought home through the comical activities the officer forces on the family and through the inhumanity of war present in his grotesque behavior. In the end Mr. Toth does rebel and chops the major into four pieces with the giant paper cutter he had constructed on the major's orders to expedite the assembling of cardboard boxes during the night for additional family income.

In 1968 *Egypercesek* (One-Minute Stories) appeared, a genre of the short story Örkény himself created on the basis of the writings of Jules Renard and two Hungarian authors, Frigyes Karinthy and Dezsö Kosztolányi. Ranging in length from just a few lines to several pages— and first appearing in *Ezüstpisztrang* (Silver Trout, 1956)—these stories are stripped of all narrative detail Örkény considers superfluous, leaving "on one side, the minimum of communication on the part of the author; on the other, the maximum of imagination on the part of the reader." He attempts to "strike only those notes to which we commonly respond. . . . I would try to call forth certain resonances; I particularly tried to hearken to these resonances within myself in the hope that others will vibrate to them sympathetically." Claude Bonnefoy connected the one-minute stories to the prose poem, the tale, the satire and noted that the "seriousness and ridicule, humor and tragedy are so intermingled in them that we are forced to laugh with tears in our eyes." "Havas tájban két hagymakupola" (Two Cupolas in a Snow-Covered Landscape) is one the most shocking. The title suggests an idyllic scene, but it recounts the hanging of a Russian woman in the presence of her little daugher, who giggles at the sight of her mother swaying in the wind and is attracted by the Leica being used by the army photographer to record the event for the archives. "In memoriam K.H.G." (In Memoriam Professor G. H.K.), which Örkény thought one of his best writings, is an outstanding expression of his black humor:

Professor G. H. K. was digging a hole in which to bury the carcass of a horse.
"Hölderlin ist ihnen unbekannt?" he asked the German guard.
"Who's he?"
"The author of *Hyperion*," explained the professor, who dearly loved to explain. "The greatest figure in German Romanticism. How about Heine?"
"Who are *these* guys?" asked the guard.
"Poets," said the professor. "Surely you have heard of Schiller?"

"Sure I have," said the guard.
"How about Rilke?"
"Him too," said the guard. Reddening with rage, he shot the professor.

—trans. Carl Erickson

Örkény remained a passionate experimenter searching for fresh ways to stir readers to the thoughtful confrontation of contemporary issues. In *Pisti a vérzivatarban* (Stevie in the Blood Storm, 1969), a play portraying an effort to be born and live in a bearable way made futile by circumstances outside the chief character's control, he provides the barest plot augmented by episodes sometimes tragic, sometimes comical that take on wholeness in the spectators' minds as shaped by the personal experience of each. In another play, *Vérrokonok* (Kinsmen, 1974; translated as *Blood Relations*), which he believed his best, Örkény develops the question of what force actually determines the true nature of the individual in the context of a family whose every member works for a railroad that consumes their lives and who are, according to him, happy to give their energies and even at times their lives in the service of a cause. The play *Kulcskeresök* (Searchers for the Key, 1976) shows the circumstances that foster the illusion of self-justification and lead men to cope with their failures by falsely calling them heroic. In this work the pilot of a passenger plane misses the runway but comforts himself with the thought that he maneuvered the plane around a little ditch.

Rózsakiállítás (*The Flower Show*, 1977), a short novel representing a momentary return to realism but still touched in places by the absurd, delineates the effort of a television producer to capture on film the last breath of three characters who are dying. Prompted by a television program on death and dying that he had watched in a hotel room in New York, Örkény sought through this work to bring the question of death into open discussion in Hungary, a subject on which, he said, "no instruction, support, and guidance are given."

Örkény lived to see his books become bestsellers and his plays performed to full houses. He was awarded several literary prizes in Hungary and received the 1970 Grand Prize for Black Humor in France for *The Toth Family*, first performed in Paris in the fall of 1968. It was performed in the United States in 1977 at the Arena Theater in Washington, D.C. *Catsplay* had a brief New York production in 1979.

WORKS IN ENGLISH TRANSLATION: Two of Örkény's plays, *The Flower Show* and *The Toth Family*, were translated into English by Michael Henry Heim and Clara Gyorgyey, published in one volume, 1982. Excerpts from *Catsplay*, translated by M. Kuttna, appeared in

New Hungarian Quarterly, Winter 1971. Selections from his *Egypercesek* (One-Minute Stories) are translated by Carl Erickson in Albert Tezla's *Ocean at the Window: Hungarian Prose and Poetry since 1945,* 1981.

ABOUT: Contemporary Authors 103, 1983; McGraw-Hill Encyclopedia of World Drama IV, 1984; Tezla, A. Ocean at the Window, 1981. *Periodicals*—New Hungarian Quarterly Spring and Winter 1981; New York Times February 1, 1976; February 23, 1976; July 27, 1977.

*PACHECO, JOSE EMILIO** (June 30, 1939–), Mexican poet, novelist, short-story and screen writer, literary critic and translator, was born in Mexico City, a child of the middle class. His earliest writings (at the age of six) were continuations of stories he had read or movies he had seen. His mature work—especially *Las batallas en el desierto* (The Battles in the Desert, 1981, set in Mexico City in the 1940s)—often echoes those early years and the then-prevailing cultural values, mainly those typified by media heroes and consumer goods "Made in USA." Although he studied law and philosophy at the National University (UNAM) in Mexico City, Pacheco's main energies were always devoted to literature. As a student he wrote plays and edited several university journals. In later years he edited the Colegio de México's critical review *Dialogos,* the cultural supplements to the newspapers *Excelsior* and *Novedades,* and "La cultura en México" for the weekly magazine *Siempre,* as well as an anthology of nineteenth-century Mexican poetry—*La poesía Mexicana del siglo XIX,* 1965, and a two-volume anthology of modernist poetry, *Antología del Modernismo 1884–1921,* 1970.

A versatile writer who has worked successfully in many literary genres, Pacheco combines, in both his poetry and prose, a mixture of social protest in the tradition of much contemporary Latin-American literature and a seemingly rarified exoticism—a fascination with cultures of the ancient past, the symbols and rituals that transcend time and history, the paradoxical continuity of the past in the present. He first established his name as a creative writer with the two short stories published in 1958 as *La sangre de Medusa* (The Blood of Medusa), followed in 1963 by a larger collection in the well-received *El viento distante* (Wind from Afar). Both books testify to the strong influence of Jorge Luis Borges' surrealism. In *El viento distante,* for example, a deceptive simplicity of language renders more concrete the imaginary world Pacheco implicitly compares with the absurdities and hor-

© 1985 Layle Silbert

JOSE EMILIO PACHECO

rors of what we call reality. One story—"Parque de diversiones" (Amusement Park)—tells of two pupils whose comportment so displeases their biology teacher that she feeds them to carnivorous plants in the botanical garden, much to the interest of their classmates. The story begins with a quotation comparing life and death to a labyrinth and concludes with a madman-architect's project for a park within a park within a park, ad infinitum. The last several sentences of the tale are identical to those with which it begins, bringing us back to the start of the labyrinth.

The dedication of *El viento distante* to Carlos Fuentes, Pacheco's editorial collaboration with Octavio Paz on *La poesía en movimiento* (Poetry in Motion, 1966), and the explicit recognition by Paz of the younger writer's talents heralded Pacheco's sharper awareness of contemporary social and political problems. Characteristic of that awareness is his novel of 1967, characterized by the *Oxford Companion to Spanish Literature* as "technically brilliant," *Morirás lejos* (You Shall Die Far From Home), where an astonishing vision of past and present reveals itself, made all the more complex by speculations on the meaning of reality and by the "Chinese boxes" motif familiar from his earlier work. Here a deceptively simple linear plot is transformed into a series of historical episodes dealing with the persecution of the Jews. These are counterpointed with scenes in modern times that have mysterious parallels to Nazi Germany. The story is open-ended; the reader is called upon to draw his own conclusions, which may range from common-sense identification of a real war criminal in a real world to a retreat into solipsism.

°pä chä´ kō

Carlos Fuentes observes that *Morirás lejos* marked a new stage in the growing cosmopolitanism of Latin American novelists. Never before had the theme of the ancient Roman and modern German holocausts been dealt with in Latin American fiction. Luis Leal makes the equally telling point that Pacheco's novel is a qualitative advance in the development of the Latin American "new novel": a creative synthesis between the traditions of "vanguardism" and "indiginism." Leal writes: "The action, which takes place in the minds of the characters living in Mexico City, is of interest not because it gives the novel a Mexican setting but because in the process it makes the capital of Mexico part of the international scene, both in time and space." Pacheco's aspirations for the novel are revealed by his comment near the end that it was intended as a "modest attempt to assist in assuring that the great crime is never repeated."

Some of Pacheco's best poetry was written in the turbulent decade of the sixties and published first in 1963 as *Los elementos de la noche* (Elements of the Night). *Elementos* revealed a new facet of his talent, demonstrating a mastery of form and versification, and the use of unorthodox typography. As Thomas Hoeksema points out, Pacheco's "Apollonian discipline" led Octavio Paz to characterize him as a "lake." The calm, reflective side of the poet's nature is balanced, however, by anguished concern about the eternally recurring cycle of the world's destruction—a current running just below the surface of formal restraint. The place of the poet in such a world is set forth in "Arbol entre dos Muros" (*Tree Between Two Walls*). There is no salvation from the transitoriness of this life, which is like a tree between two walls, or the sun which shines between the night just past and the night to come. But if all existence terminates in night, its brevity in the perspective of eternity makes it akin to lightning: the poet may be "the grove of trees / in which the thunder entombs its rumble." The long poem *El reposo del fuego* (The Repose of Fire, 1966) exhibits in exemplary fashion Pacheco's balance of the Apollonian and Dionysian forces. The formal structure—three sections of fifteen poems each—works in counterpoint to the author's recurrent theme of the distant or mythic past preserved in the present. In a world of eternal Heraclitan flux, he seeks a principle of permanence within change, within the fire itself which is not only the incarnation of change but also the essence of creativity

Pacheco's most successful and widely translated book, *No me preguntes como pasa el tiempo* (*Don't Ask Me How the Time Goes By*) consists of poetry written between 1965 and 1968. Its publication in 1969 won the author the National Poetry Prize of that year. The book clearly reflects the poetic "minimalist" tendencies of Samuel Beckett, whose *Comment c'est* (*How It Is*) Pacheco had translated in 1966. The sheer profusion of poetic forms used in *Don't Ask Me*—fables, traditional long and short poems, a bestiary, haikus—can be bewildering. Yet the text never loses itself in abstraction, and the note of urgent concern about the human condition is strong. Aptly described by one reviewer as "the poet as archaeologist," Pacheco writes in his collection of 1973 *Irás y no volverás* (You Shall Go and Not Return) of such varied themes as the ruins of the Great Temple of the Aztecs in Mexico City, the ephemeral quality of life, inspired by places like Urbana, Illinois, a delightful spoof on the decorative poetry of his contemporary Montes de Oca, and a shockingly macabre antiwar poem, "For Vietnam." He again vividly evokes Mexico's ancient past in *Islas a la deriva* (Islands Adrift), a collection of poems written between 1973 and 1975, published in 1976.

The poet as archaeologist is also in evidence in the mixture of poetry and prose published in 1980, *Desde entonces* (Until Then), which returns to many of Pacheco's familiar concerns—Heraclitus, the ancient civilization of Mexico, reflections on insects and animals. The tone is generally lighthearted, but abrupt changes often shock the reader. Yet there is more humor here than in previous collections—as in the brief epigram about the "Ultraist" writers who pride themselves on their unintelligibility, or in the several paragraphs of "Shopping Center," which bemusedly compare modern men with ants who perish while wallowing in the honey whose attraction they cannot resist.

During the brief period from 1970 to 1976, when the Mexican government, under Luis Echeveria, took measures to bring new creative talent into the moribund Mexican film industry, Pacheco tried his hand at screen writing. With the director Arturo Ripstein he wrote scripts for *El castillo de la pureza* (The Castle of Purity, 1972), *El santo officio* (The Holy Office, i.e. the Spanish Inquisition), and *Fox Trot* (1975). The reviews were favorable, citing the script of *El castillo* as "a model of precision and rigor" and "the best Mexican film of the year." *El santo officio* returned to the theme of anti-Semitism in *Morirás lejos* but set the tragedy in Mexico instead of Spain.

Pacheco has translated many poets, ranging from those in *The Greek Anthology* to Rimbaud, Rexroth, Auden, Seferis, and Cavafy. He calls his translations "approximations," meaning that he has "taken over" the work of other poets in order to produce not an academic, literally faithful translation, but a re-creation of the original, intended to be read as a Spanish poem in its own right. His translations are collected in *Tarde o tremprano* (Sooner or Later, 1980), which also includes many of his original poems.

Pacheco has often lived abroad—as visiting professor in Toronto, New York, Urbana, Illinois, and at the University of Essex in England. He makes his permanent home in Mexico City with his wife, Cristina, a journalist, and their two daughters. He has received many honors, among them the Enrique Lihn Prize for poetry in 1966, the Magda Donato Prize in 1968, the National Poetry Prize in 1969, a Guggenheim fellowship in 1970, and the Xavier Villarrutia Prize in 1973.

WORKS IN ENGLISH TRANSLATION: English translations of Pacheco's writings include *Tree Between Two Walls*, by Edward Dorn and Gordon Brotherston, 1969; *Don't Ask Me How the Time Goes By*, by Alastair Reid, 1978; and *Signals from the Flame*, a selection of his poems, collected and translated by Thomas Hoeksema, 1980. Pacheco's lectures given at the University of Toronto on Francisco Xavier Clavijero and the "national culture" of Mexico in the eighteenth century, were published as *The Lost Homeland* in 1976.

ABOUT: de Báez, Y. et al. Ficción y historia; la narrativa de José Emilio Pacheco, 1979; Diccionario de Escritores Mexicanos, 1967; A Dictionary of Contemporary Latin American Authors, 1975; Fernández Moreno, C. (ed.) Latin America in Its Literature, 1980; Forster, M. H. (ed.) Tradition and Renewal, 1975; Handbook of Latin American Studies, 1982; Hoeksema, T. *Introduction to* Signals from the Flames, 1980; International Authors and Writers Who's Who, 1976. *Periodicals*—Hispania May 1983; Latin American Literary Review Fall–Winter 1974; Spring–Summer 1982; Latin American Literature and Arts Review May/August 1981; Times Literary Supplement June 18, 1970; October 12, 1973.

PA CHIN *See* BA JIN

*PALM, GORAN (JOHAN SAMUEL) February 3, 1931–   ), Swedish poet, social and literary critic, editor, and translator, was born in the university town of Uppsala, the son of Samuel P. Palm, a minister, and the former Valborg Ekman. He grew up in Uppsala and Falun and attended Uppsala University, where he received an M.A. degree in 1956. Even as a *gymnasium* student, he attracted attention for his analytical insight into modern poetry, and it was as a critic that he first became professionally active, editing and writing for the literary magazine *Upptakt* (Anacrusis) from 1955 to 1958. Palm also contributed essays and articles to *Bonniers*

GORAN PALM

Litterära Magasin (Bonnier's Literary Magazine)and *Ord & Bild* (Word and Image) as well as *Expressen* (The Express) and other newspapers. On the basis of such work, he became known for a clear and energetic style, for careful research of his subjects, and for a presentation that was fresh and unlabored. Ake Runnquist writes: "These qualities made him one of the Swedish presses' most noted reviewers and polemicists." Palm took an early interest in neglected areas and authors; and he approached simple things with the same calm as difficult ones.

His first collection of poems, entitled *Hundens besök* (The Dog's Visit), was published in 1961. The title poem refers to an experience he had on a trip he took to Spain to write.

In the morning heat I sit in the square,
shy and alone, with a book by Unamuno
that may possibly afford appetite for lunch,
when I get an unexpected visit; I who never get visits.
A yellow-brown dog with fox ears heads my way
—trans. Verne Moberg

The visit was, Palm felt, after all a meeting: without content or depth, granted, but a bit of fellowship. "It happens that reality, the impure dog, visits us. And we have no choice. It is from the 'impure' human encounter, not out of solitude . . . that we acquire our identity and our knowledge of self and existence, what writes the blank page full." In a kind of anxiety state, Palm fled Spain for the sense of community at home in Sweden.

In his early criticism he expressed displeasure with "the old, metaphysical, aristocratic modernism," mentioning such poets as Ezra

°päm, yû´ rän

Pound and the Swedish imagist Erik Lindegren. The modernists were too rigid, idyllic, and removed from the world, talking of "Culture" with a capital *C. Hundens besök* contained the poetic manifesto, "Megafonen i poesiparken" (The Magaphone in Poetry Park), an ironic attack on the modernists of the fifties, and in several prose pieces he criticized current poetic conventions. "The culture's experiences of horses has become minimal, but out there on the hills and dales of poetry we still see ten horses for every tractor." Palm argued for poetry that would reflect social realities and everyday life with a language that could be understood by all. He wrote: "You look for poems that capture something of the impetuous, noisy, abrupt rhythm of the modern world but find that the majority of poems—however experimental they may be otherwise—are remarkably *slow,* elegiac, that their rhythm is regular and seldom interrupted, as if they'd been created on a quieter globe, without cars."

As an alternative Palm proposed simple, direct language to get relevant messages across to a maximum number of readers. Indeed, *Hundens besök* was welcomed as personal and original, representing a new direction in Swedish poetry. Critics commented on the unadorned form of some of the poems, approaching prose, and the forthright reasoning, immediately accessible to its readers. This new style of poetry writing, now produced by a number of Swedish writers, was the following year dubbed *nyenkelheten* (the new simplicity) by Lars Bäckström, one of its leading exponents. The idea of "new simplicity" gained importance in the following years in discussions of poetry, but Palm himself questioned the label: "Personally I've always paused at the designation, for the simple reason that it's always complicated experiences that make me write."

His next collection, *Världen ser dig* (The World Sees You, 1964) enlarged on the concept of new simplicity, including one little poem (an entire section in the book) that, according to Tom Hedlund, became "perhaps the most well-known example of opposition to a poetic convention overburdened with symbol":

The Sea
I stand beside the sea.
There it is.
There's the sea.
I look at it.
The sea. Uh-huh.
Just like at the Louvre.

—trans. Verne Moberg

The book is dominated by the long, thirty-five-page poem "Själens furir" (The Soul's Sergeants), a kind of tragicomedy with autobiographical analysis. The poet's sergeants (*furir* in Swedish,

also suggesting *furier* or furies) embody authoritarian force, tradition, language, inner voices, conscience, and anticonscience. The poem has been described as an intimate sermon or one-man theater, with clear dramatic parts and elements of dialogue, narrative, reportage, summary, self-criticism, outburst, audience questioning, rhetoric, personal confession, slogan, current events, and quoted radio commentary. The reader is drawn into the poem ("But you must have a name . . . ?" "You who are reading this . . . "), and the poet is simply himself, not an abstract presence.

Although Palm has been critical of traditional poetry and takes great liberties in his language, "it is not a question of anti-poetry," according to Karl Erik Lagerlöf. His language is "strongly rhythmical and in every sense 'singing.'" Many elements of his poetry seem new, but he also reflects tradition. In "Själens furir," for example, one passage contains recurring iambic octameter, a form familiar to Swedes from Runeberg's "Tales of Ensign Stal." In his poetry Palm often works with synonyms, exhortations, repetition, variation. He believes in the long poem and also in mixing genres. He has said he is especially fond of "impurer" kinds of art: the novel-essay, film-theater, or poetry that is musical prose.

One critic has commented on a dualistic quality in Palm's writing personality, with a dayside (the rational moral critic) and a nightside (the depressive mystic, searching for reality that words cannot capture). Others have suggested the self-contradiction involved in the contrast between his fear of silence, his despair that reality is impossible to articulate (e.g. the poem "Bokstäverna före A och efter Ö," The Letters Before A and After Ö), and his insistence that reality *must* be expressed though older poetry failed to do so ("Megafonen i poesiparken").

Världen ser dig was Palm's temporary farewell to poetry; after it he published three collections of political essays that attracted much attention in the late 1960s, including *En orättvis betraktelse* (An Unjust Observation, translated as *As Others See Us); Indoktrinering i Sverige* (Indoctrination in Sweden, 1968); and *Vad kan man göra?* (What Can One Do?, 1969). The first of these stirred intense controversy, with its depiction of highly industrialized countries from the perspective of the poor countries; the title's "unjust observation" (or sermon or reflection) is an admission of the author's bias—and a questioning of the "objectivity" of traditional Western views. In *Indoktrinering i Sverige* he argued that the selection of facts in mass media, schoolbooks, etc., onesidedly favored Western, nonsocialist interests. *Vad kan man göra?* was a kind of handbook for activists, with articles, poems, sketches, assemblages of statistics, and historical data, offering many suggestions for action. His literary mission, Palm has said, is political: "To describe and point out the same thing that other socialists are describing and pointing out, in such a striking, personal, or captivating way that many readers can experience it as if it had never been described or pointed out before."

A major figure on the Swedish left by the end of the sixties, Palm was criticized (by Jan Myrdal and others) when it became known that he was interested in the psychology of Arthur Janov and in psychotherapy. His psychoanalytic interests, along with ongoing political commitments, are reflected in the little collection of small prose poems entitled *Varför har nätterna inga namn?* (Why Do the Nights Have No Names?, 1977), an engaging expression of the "nightside" Palm and a dynamic confrontation between his relativism and his ideological criticism.

Applying his talents to Swedish political issues in a more direct fashion, Palm deliberately kept a low literary profile for a time as he took a factory job with the Swedish telephone company L. M. Ericsson, in their plant in south Stockholm. The result of his experience as a fulltime worker (and a diligent diarist in the evening) are the two volumes *Ett år på LM* (One Year at L. M. Ericsson, 1972) and *Bokslut på LM* (The Balance Sheet on L. M. Ericsson, 1972), in which he set out to present a realistic picture of some Swedish workers and their environments and to question the basic organizational forms of work in Sweden today. The books were read widely and elicited major debate in the press and media. After this investigation of Swedish working conditions, Palm returned to a poetry project that was his largest to date. When his daughter complained about the dreariness of her schoolbooks, he elected to write *Sverige an vintersaga* (Sweden—A Winter Tale), volume I of which was published in 1984, a verse epic in several volumes constituting a panorama of Swedish history and landscape, legends and present-day life, individuals and society. Here he tells modern "winter tales" (e.g. about the woman who died in the Bingo Hall, annoying everybody by holding up the game) but also old historical stories with an up-to-date political perspective. Then, like modern day Nils Holgersson, he sets off on a journey around Sweden, seeing what is happening with his own eyes and sometimes others'. The poem of several hundred pages was composed in blank verse, as the author felt prose presented "too little resistance." "The winter tales I tell are familiar, told many times. When the verse enters in, the story becomes new again." Initially he tried to rhyme, as did Heinrich Heine and Wolf Bier-

mann in "Germany, A Winter Tale," but the rhyme ran away with the plot. "Blank verse worked better . . . made it tempting to write about Sweden again." With this form Palm was searching for a new start. As he told a reporter, "I can't just do a new version of *Indoctrinering i Sverige.*"

Critics have noted in Palm's work the influence of a number of modern Swedish writers who have emphasized themes of loneliness and isolation—the poet and novelist Dan Andersson, Sweden's major modernist poet Gunnar Ekelöf, the folk poets Nils Ferlin and Birgir Sjöberg, the philosophical poet Bertil Malmberg—and of at least one American writer, the poet Theodore Roethke. Palm himself has translated into Swedish works by Rudyard Kipling, Ezra Pound, and (with Jan Kunicki) the Polish poet and playwright Tadeusz Rózewicz.

From 1978 to 1979 Palm served as chairman of Författarförlaget, the Authors' Cooperative Publishing House, in Stockholm (where he has lived since the sixties). Since 1979 he has also chaired Föreningen Liv i Sverige (the Life in Sweden Association), producing books by "ordinary" Swedes, written in collaboration with professional authors. Palm was awarded the literary prize from the newspaper *Aftonbladet* in 1964 and the Aniara prize from the Swedish libraries in 1977. For some years he was married to the former Tora Cederberg, a Swedish translator, with whom he has joint custody of an adopted daughter Måna. He has traveled in Spain, Guinea-Bissau, Hungary, and Tunisia.

WORKS IN ENGLISH TRANSLATION: Verne Moberg translated *En orättvis betraktelse* into English in 1966 as *As Others See Us.* Palm's writings on the L. M. Ericsson Company were translated as *The Flight from Work* by Patrick Smith in 1977. The poem *Själens furir* was translated as "The Sergeant" by Siv Cedering Fox in 1972.

ABOUT: Columbia Dictionary of Modern European Literature, 1980; Contemporary Authors 29–32, 1978.

PARSONS, TALCOTT (December 13, 1902– May 8, 1979), American sociologist, was born into a liberal academic family. He grew up in Colorado Springs, Colorado, where his father, Edward Smith Parsons, taught English at Colorado College, then moved in his teens to New York City, where he attended the experimental high school attached to Columbia University. Both his parents held liberal political views; his mother, Mary Ingersoll Parsons, was a suffragist, and his father, who was an ordained Congregationalist minister as well as an English professor, adhered to the "social gospel," a liberal Protestant reform movement aimed at ameliorating the social ills caused by rapid industrialization.

In 1920, Parsons went to Amherst College to study biology and philosophy in preparation for a medical career. Then in his junior year he took a course with Walter Hamilton on "institutional economics," a kind of political economy approach pioneered by Thorstein Veblen. Hamilton's attempts to relate economic behavior to its social context fascinated the young Parsons, so when an uncle offered to send him abroad after graduation, he decided to go to the London School of Economics and study political economy. At the LSE, Parsons worked with a group of brilliant political economists, including R. H. Tawney, L. T. Hobhouse, and Harold Laski. But the professor who intrigued him most was Bronislaw Malinowski, the leader of the new functionalist school of anthropology. Using psychoanalytic concepts, Malinowski emphasized the function of social customs in regulating instinctual behavior. He envisioned institutions such as the family and clan as an interlocking social system that patterned the individual's interaction with the environment in productive ways, a line of analysis Parsons would later pursue in his own work, albeit in far more theoretical terms.

Although still undecided about pursuing an advanced degree, Parsons decided after a year at the LSE to go to the University of Heidelberg for further training. There he got his first systematic introduction to social theory and began his life-long fascination with the work of Max Weber. The great German sociologist had been dead only a few years, and a dedicated "Weber circle" at the university kept his influence alive. Interested in the analysis of capitalism as a social system, Parsons decided to write a thesis reviewing the work of Weber, Karl Marx, and Werner Sombart.

After passing his orals in 1926, Parsons returned to the United States to teach economics at Amherst and finish his doctoral thesis. His work soon attracted the attention of Harvard, where he became an instructor of economics in 1927. In that year he married Helen Bancroft Walker, a research worker. They had three children. During his first years at Harvard, Parsons finished his thesis and completed a translation of Weber's *The Protestant Ethic and the Spirit of Capitalism,* published in 1930, making this work accessible to an American audience. Increasingly frustrated with the inability of classical economic theory to account for the social determinants of economic behavior, he became more and more interested in sociology. When

Harvard decided to establish a sociology department in 1931, Parsons accepted an instructor's position in it. Here he began the theoretical work that would make him the most influential American sociologist of his generation.

Parsons' work is usually divided into three major phases. The first, spanning the late 1920s and 1930s, culminated in his first major work, *The Structure of Social Action,* which established a framework for analyzing both the objective and subjective meanings of human behavior. In the second phase, Parsons moved from a focus on the individual "unit act" to the social system in which it occurred. The major works of this period, *Toward a General Theory of Action* and *The Social System,* set forth a theoretical schema for analyzing the structure and function of social behavior: hence Parsons' identification as a "structural-functionalist." Yet he eventually grew dissatisfied with the static quality of functionalism, and in the third and final phase of his work, beginning in the 1960s, developed a comparative, "neo-evolutionist" theory of social change.

The foundation of Parsonian theory was laid in *The Structure of Social Action,* which set forth his "voluntaristic theory of action." In this book, he addressed a problem that had concerned European theorists for almost a century: if objective, impersonal social forces determine human behavior, how can any individual action be seen as the product of subjective choice or free will? Positivists had resolved the problem simply by ignoring the subjective or non-rational aspects of behavior; idealists took the opposite approach, insisting that only the subjective meanings of an action had real significance. Reviewing the efforts of four major theorists—Alfred Marshall, Vilfredo Pareto, Emile Durkheim, and Max Weber—to grapple with this problem in terms of the social determinants of economic behavior, Parsons arrived at his own analytical approach. Objective reality, he reasoned, does indeed set constraints upon human action; the individual has to adapt to his particular material environment in order to survive. But even the most constrained of economic situations offers a range of behavioral options; here is where the element of choice enters in. The actor interprets his situation in terms of subjective factors—values, norms, preferences, and the like—that shape his conception of desirable means and ends. This normative orientation leads him to choose one option over another. Thus any human action has both an objective and subjective meaning, which a general social theory must incorporate. Parsons later christened his approach "analytical realism," signifying his belief that facts have no meaning outside the specific conceptual framework in which they are interpreted.

The Structure of Social Action was not well received by American sociologists in the late 1930s. The "Chicago School," which practiced a very pragmatic "microsociology" of urban problems, dominated the field, and its narrowly empirical, inductive methodology was the very antithesis of Parsons' bold theorizing. Many sociologists regarded his advocacy of European theoretical sociology as both unscientific and unpatriotic. Perhaps due to this unenthusiastic response, Parsons grew closer in the 1940s to scholars outside his own discipline. In 1946, he left the sociology department to establish a new Department of Social Relations at Harvard with psychologists Gordon Allport and Henry Murray and anthropologist Clyde Kluckhohn. The same year he decided to expand his long-standing interest in Freudian theory by enrolling in the Boston Psychoanalytic Institute for formal training.

Parsons' new interdisciplinary interests resulted in the publication of two major works, *Toward a General Theory of Action* and *The Social System,* which established the structural-functionalist paradigm that would inform his work for the next decade. In this phase of his theoretical development, Parsons moved beyond the individual act that concerned him in his previous work to the social context in which it occurred. His aim was a grandiose one: to devise an analytical framework that could be used to interpret all facets of human behavior.

At the heart of Parsons' intellectual enterprise was the question: how did the seemingly random multiplicity of individual actions coalesce into a cohesive social order? To answer this question, Parsons first identified four different "action systems" or dimensions of human behavior—the biological organism, the individual personality, the social structure, and the cultural tradition— and specified the social mechanisms that linked them into a unified system. "Sociologizing" Freudian theory, Parsons posited that through a socialization process, occurring primarily within the family, the individual "introjected" the basic cultural values or "norms" of a given society. The social structure then provided institutionalized interactions that directed the socialized behavior into productive channels. Thus individual and collective behavior functioned to reinforce the social structure and vice versa.

Within this general framework, Parsons further explored the dynamics of social interaction and devised a schema to categorize individual exchanges or unit acts, specifying the larger "functional imperatives" that they must serve in order for the social system to be maintained. His famous "AGIL schema" summarized these imperatives: *adaptation,* the acquisition and distribution of material resources; *goal-attainment,*

the mobilization of social resources necessary to accomplish the system's ends; *integration,* the creation and maintenance of social cohesiveness; and *latency,* the management of emotional energy through tension release and collective ritual.

The AGIL schema, the pattern variables, and the processes of socialization and social control linking the four action systems formed the basic elements of Parsons' structural functionalism. In succeeding works, he applied this analytical framework to a variety of topics, most notably the family and the economic system. In *The Family, Socialization, and Interaction Process,* which he wrote with Robert Bales and several others, Parsons interpreted the child's development in terms of the AGIL schema. In *Economy and Society,* written with Neil Smelser, he analyzed economic theory as "a special case of the general theory of social systems."

Parsons' work in the 1950s firmly established him as the leading American sociologist of his generation. For varied reasons, post-war sociologists proved more receptive to theory building than had their predecessors. By then, students trained by Parsons at Harvard in the '30s and '40s, including Robert Merton, Wilbert Moore, and Kingsley Davis, had established their own careers, thereby extending his influence to institutions across the country. Due to its interdisciplinary breadth, Parsons' work also found a wide audience in other fields, particularly anthropology, history, and political science. Yet even at the height of his influence, Parsons had his critics, among them C. Wright Mills, David Lockwood, and Ralf Dahrendorf. In the late 1950s, theoretical challenges to Parsons' structural functionalism began to proliferate. In addition to recurrent protests about Parsons' convoluted, obscure writing style, criticisms centered on his theory's inability to explain social conflict and change. If the parts of the social system always functioned to produce integration, critics asked, how did structural changes ever occur? Structural functionalism, they concluded, was simply too static in its conception to account satisfactorily for social change.

In fact, Parsons was the first to admit that his theory was not sufficiently developed to permit him adequately to conceptualize social change. Prompted by his own dissatisfaction with functionalist theory, as well as the criticisms of others, he turned his atention in the 1960s to a consideration of change, and modified his model of the social system to make it more dynamic. The result was a neo-evolutionist approach explicated in his major works, *Societies: Evolutionary and Comparative Perspectives* and *The System of Modern Societies.*

A major influence on Parsons' third and final stage of development was the "cybernetic" or information theory then being developed in biology. Simply put, cybernetic theory analyzed the "feedback" processes by which information was used to regulate energy expenditure, as in the brain's regulation of other bodily systems. Along similar lines, Parsons posited a hierarchy of energy flow and informational control linking the four action systems. Energy flows from the biological organism upward, control flows from the culture downward. Disruptions of either the energy flow or the informational control would then force the system to change.

Envisioning the social system as a kind of super-organism capable of variation and evolution, Parsons argued that societies adapted most successfully to changing environments when the elements of their social systems became more differentiated. In other words, the more specialized, and thereby distinct from one another, the family, economy, and polity became, the more likely the society was to solve basic problems of existence. Western European society, having passed through successive industrial, democratic, and educational "revolutions," had the most differentiated social system, he concluded, and thus had been able to adapt most successfully to its environment.

Parsons' neo-evolutionist theory did little to dispel his reputation as defender of the status quo, yet his work left an indelible mark on American sociology. The terminology and analytical concepts he used to formulate his theory—terms such as norm, role, and socialization—became part of the basic idiom of sociology. Moreover, his work legitimated a concern with social theory that remains central to the field's intellectual agenda.

Parsons retired from Harvard in 1973, and seemingly unperturbed by his critics, continued to expand and refine his theory. In May 1979, he traveled to Heidelberg to attend a celebration in honor of the fiftieth anniversary of his doctoral degree. After the ceremony, he went to Munich to give a series of lectures. There, on the evening of May 8th, he suffered a stroke and died at the age of 76.

PRINCIPAL WORKS: The Structure of Social Action, 1937; Essays in Sociological Theory Pure and Applied, 1949, rev. ed., 1954; (with E. Shils and others) Toward a General Theory of Action, 1951; The Social System, 1951; Working Papers in the Theory of Action, 1953; (with Robert Bales and others) Family, Socialization, and Interaction Process, 1955; (with Neil Smelser) Economy and Society, 1956; Structure and Process in Modern Society, 1960; (with Edward Shils and others) Theories of Society; Societies: Evolutionary and Comparative Perspectives, 1966; Sociological Theory and Modern Society, 1967; The System of Modern Societies, 1971.

ABOUT: Bourricand, F. The Sociology of Talcott Parsons, 1974; Current Biography, 1961; Hamilton, P. Talcott Parsons, 1983; International Encyclopedia of the Social Sciences 18, 1979; Mitchell, W. Sociological Analysis and Politics: The Theories of Talcott Parsons, 1967; Rocher, G. Talcott Parsons and American Sociology, 1974.

*PASINETTI, PIER MARIA (June 24, 1913–), Italian novelist and journalist, sends the following sketch: "Pier Maria Pasinetti was born in Venice, the son of Carlo Pasinetti and the former Maria Ciardi. His father was a prominent physician in Venice and his mother belonged to the Ciardi family of painters. His brother was Francesco Pasinetti (1911–1949), the pioneering film critic and historian, director and screen-writer. Pasinetti followed the regular course of studies in his native Venice, from elementary to secondary school, receiving his *maturitá classica* in 1930 at the Liceo Marco Foscarini. Between 1933 and 1935, Pasinetti studied English at Oxford and visited Ireland to do research for his dissertation on James Joyce, with which he took the degree of Dottore in Lettere at the University of Padua in 1935. In September of that year he first came to the United States, having won an Italian exchange fellowship to Louisiana State University, where he took an M.A. in English and had the good fortune of being in close contact with the founders and editors of the *Southern Review,* Robert Penn Warren, Cleanth Brooks—in which some of his very early stories appeared in English translation. Already captivated by American life, people, and landscapes, Pasinetti managed to prolong his stay by receiving a new scholarship at the University of California at Berkeley, where he spent the academic year 1936–37 as a graduate student in English. Back in Italy, he pursued his literary and journalistic activities by contributing to daily newspapers and magazines as he had done since the age of eighteen. In 1938, on yet another scholarship, he went to Berlin to acquire fluency in German. Here he witnessed, among other things, the pogrom of November 1938, a decisive experience that is also reflected in his novel *Venetian Red.* From 1939 to 1941, he was also active in the editorial offices of film and literary magazines in Rome, and in 1941 he was sent to the University of Göttingen as Italian lecturer, where because of his transparent moral and political views his situation was not without danger. In September of 1942 he received with

°pä´´ sē net´ tē, pir

PIER MARIA PASINETTI

enthusiasm an appointment to the University of Stockholm, where he stayed for the duration of the war. The experience in a neutral country with its possibility of contacts in all directions, and the unfolding of world events were a definitive, disillusioning test of the idea then entertained by many idealists of the European conflict as a war of basic human principles that transcended national ties. While still in Stockholm, Pasinetti received an offer to teach at Bennington College in Vermont, and after a seventeen-day crossing from Jöteborg to Philadelphia he reached Bennington in February of 1946 and taught there until June 1947. Following the example of other writers of fiction, he decided on an academic career, and to acquire the proper credentials he spent the years between 1947 and 1949 at Yale, where he received the first Ph.D. in comparative literature, under the direction of René Welleck. His dissertation, ' Life for Art's Sake: Studies in the Literary Myth of the Romantic Artist,' received the John Addison Porter prize for that year. In 1949 he accepted the offer of an assistant professorship at the University of California at Los Angeles, where he started the program in the humanities–world literature, mainly intended for non-specialists, i.e. for students not majoring in one of the literary disciplines. For many years, Pasinetti's basic course was a requirement for all theater arts majors and for the instructor it proved also to be a very valuable learning experience. Pasinetti has taught at UCLA ever since, though not uninterruptedly, and is still a professor of Italian and comparative literature there.

"Pasinetti has often declared, in interviews and elsewhere, that he considers his literary aptitudes to be a natural consequence of his heritage, being the son of a doctor and of a mother who belonged to a distinguished family of painters. Never did he and his brother Francesco doubt that the transportation of experience into some form of art was the most relevant, practical, and enjoyable of all possible occupations. His father had a taste for imitation and mimicry, which he applied to his large clientele and circle of friends; to this day, the novelist Pasinetti maintains that his father was, in this sense, one of his early sources. When he was a child, his mother wrote fairy tales in dramatic form, and had him and his brother perform them with other children wearing costumes sewn by her and her friends. For years, his and Francesco's taste for invention found a basic outlet in puppet shows, which they produced according to fairly strict patterns: a bloody tragedy on vague aristocratic backgrounds was followed by a farce with characters taken from life, indeed often from their immediate surroundings; the originals might be invited to watch themselves turned into marionettes and uttering lines which had been caught from their very lips and considered worthy gags for those comic *canovacci* [plays with improvised dialogues]. From the age of ten, Pasinetti was particularly infatuated with Dickens; there followed a less decisive infatuation with Pirandello's plays. But Pasinetti's readings had greater variety, including treatises found in his father's library, particularly one on mental diseases. He wrote incessantly even as a teenager."

––––––––

Pasinetti's first published fiction in book form was a collection of three novellas entitled *L'ira di Dio* (The Wrath of God, 1942). One of the three stories, "Storia di famiglia" (Family History), had been published in English translation in the *Southern Review* in 1939, and also appeared in Edward J. O'Brien's annual anthology of the best short stories of 1940. There was a long interval before the publication of Pasinetti's first novel, *Rosso veneziano* (*Venetian Red*). In that period he was busy with his varied academic and journalistic career, and of course with the composition of that first novel. The history of *Venetian Red* was rather curious. When it first came out in Italy in 1959, for various reasons it passed largely unnoticed. In the meantime, however, the Italian manuscript of the book was read at Random House; on the basis of that manuscript a contract was offered to the author with the advice that he translate the novel himself, which he did by dictating into a tape recorder. Hailed by such publications as the *Saturday Re-*

view, *Time*, the *New Yorker*, the novel's reputations somehow bounced back to Europe, where a French translation (from the English text) had considerable success. This set of circumstances contributed to the confusion regarding the nationality of Pasinetti, which may have been perpetuated by the subject matter of Pasinetti's next two novels, *La confusione* (1964; published in revised form in 1980 as *Il sorriso del leone* [*The Smile on the Face of the Lion*] and *Il ponte dell'Accademia* [1968, *From the Academy Bridge*]), which in their very different ways present situations and characters belonging to a composite society in which transatlantic jet flight are routine. With all that, the major characteristic of Pasinetti's fiction undoubtedly remains the attention to and exploration of his Venetian roots. This, of course, was already true of his first novel, the story of the Partibons, a proud and well-to-do Venetian family on the eve of World War II, *Venetian Red*, which was described by one reviewer as "a world of mystery and a search, of love in every form . . . a novel which offers the reality of pleasure and the pleasure of reality." R. W. B. Lewis, in the *Saturday Review*, wrote that *Venetian Red* "suggests how the novel can still offer a meaningful and thoroughly engrossing form of life, even in our present moment of dislocated sensibility. What emerges . . . is not only a family portrait but a profoundly meaningful action." The *London Times Literary Supplement* called it "an excellent book . . . with its minute observation of Italian life and customs, its humor and biting Latin asides, its regionalism and yet its wider, more general application, it is a work of art." A kind of pendular motion between Venice and America is evident in *The Smile on the Face of the Lion*, in which Bernardo Partibon, moving on from *Venetian Red*, now an art dealer in America, tries to re-establish his family roots. According to Robert Maurer in *Book Week*, the novel "is worth reading and rereading—the work of a mind that perceives and distinguishes, of a literary talent that is already a major one," and Helene Cantarella in the *New York Times Book Review* called it "a paean of praise for the enduring strength and indestructible spirit of Venice and its women." In the novel that followed, *From the Academy Bridge*, a considerable part of the action takes place at a mythical institute for language and communication studies on the West Coast. Like many other novelists from Balzac to Faulkner, Pasinetti has several of the same characters appear in different novels, though each of his books is self-contained and the series does not constitute a "saga" in the traditional sense. *Domani improvvisamente* (*Suddenly Tomorrow*) and *Il Centro* (The Cen-

ter) are somewhat different in tone from Pasinetti's previous novels. The satirical element in his depiction of modern computerized society characterizes these two works, and the *Times Literary Supplement* describes him as a moralist, but feathery light in his treatment of iniquity, eccentric in his choice of villains and heroes, and funny with an intellectual zaniness that tempers indignation, though the latter ends on a serious, indeed tragic note. Again to quote from the *Times Literary Supplement*, "Pasinetti's writing is strong enough to appear totally easy, relaxed and casual, his feelings are passionate enough to be camouflaged in coolness and lightness." Pasinetti's latest novel, *Dorsoduro* (1983), named for one of the six districts of Venice, marks a full return to the Venetian setting; indeed, its narrator, Giorgio Partibon, now in his sixties, was one of the youthful protagonists of *Venetian Red*, and also appeared in *From the Academy Bridge*. *Dorsoduro* is largely Giorgio's evocation of a time (1926–29) when he was a child; in the novel, individual situations and events ranging from the deeply moving to the hilarious are seen within the framework of a crucial historical period. From the point of view of content, Pasinetti had been particularly praised for his ability to see the reflection of historical forces on the destiny and emotions of individuals, the analysis of which is the most important facet of his novels. No less characterizing is Pasinetti's language, which has been described by Lowry Nelson, Jr. as a "sinuously intellectual but direct spoken language that is unrivaled in modern Italian literature."

WORKS IN ENGLISH TRANSLATION: Venetian Red, 1960; The Smile on the Face of the Lion, 1965; From the Academy Bridge, 1970; Suddenly Tomorrow, 1972; Dorsoduro, 1983.

ABOUT: Columbia Dictionary of Modern European Literature, 1980; Contemporary Authors 73–76, 1978; Curley, D. N. and A. (eds.) Modern Romance Literature (Library of Literary Criticism), 1967. Periodicals—Italian Quarterly Spring 1964; New York Times Book Review February 14, 1965; Saturday Review May 18, 1960; Times Literary Supplement June 30, 1961.

PELIKAN, JAROSLAV (JAN) (December 17, 1923–   ), American historian, was born in Akron, Ohio, the son of the Rev. Jaroslav Jan Pelikan, a Lutheran minister, and the former Anna Buzek. His paternal grandfather was bishop of the Slovak Lutheran Church in the United States, a sect well known for its devotion to learning. He spoke of his early education in an

JAROSLAV PELIKAN

interview in 1981: "I went to what was, in effect, a German *Gymnasium* in Indiana, where we started Latin and German and Greek in our high-school years and started Hebrew in our first college year. I learned Syriac as a consequence of learning Hebrew, and by the time I was eighteen I had these languages and, thanks to the advantage of coming from a Slavic home, had the Slavic languages as well." He knew he would be a scholar even as a teenager. After graduating from Concordia Junior College in Fort Wayne, Indiana, he pursued joint studies at Concordia Seminary in St. Louis and the University of Chicago, earning in 1946 a B.D. from the former and a Ph.D. from the latter. He was also ordained a minister in the Lutheran church.

Not only his career but even its principal goal was apparent to Pelikan virtually from the start: he would write a comprehensive history of the Christian church. His mentor—he called him his *Doktorvater*—at Chicago was Wilhelm Pauck, an authority on the Reformation, who had himself been the pupil of Adolf von Harnack, author of the multivolume *History of Dogma* (1886–89), one of the earliest and most influential applications of modern methods of research to the enormous array of Christian primary sources. Pelikan saw that in this century the severe social dislocation produced by two world wars had interrupted the work of updating doctrinal history; no one, in short, had followed Harnack's example. "I began thinking," he recalled in 1979, "about this missing generation, and wondered if I might just be the one to try it." He wrote an eighty-four page prospectus for the project in 1950—he had already been gathering

information for years—and eventually had his plans accepted by the University of Chicago Press. Pelikan molded many of the courses he taught around the project. "When I've given lectures, or done research for papers, books, or lectures, or directed dissertations—done any of the things a scholar does—I've always had metaphorical boxes to put information in." With his customary self-deprecating wit, he called this practice, "carrying out my private education in public." Doctrinal history had become "a cause, a passion, and a mission."

During the two decades of preparation for his life's work, Pelikan published extensively—managing, in fact, to squeeze into those years practically an entire lifetime of scholarly labor. He was general editor of the first thirty volumes of the fifty-five-volume English translation of Luther's complete works, a project that began publication in 1959, and he contributed to the series a volume of introduction to the reformer's exegetical writings, *Luther the Expositor.* His other books of the period show his command of the dialectics of the Lutheran Reformation (*From Luther to Kierkegaard; Obedient Rebels: Catholic Substance and Protestant Principle in Luther's Reformation;* and *Spirit Versus Structure: Luther and the Institutions of the Church*), a sure knowledge—second to none among modern scholars—of patristics, the writings of the church fathers (*The Shape of Death: Life, Death, and Immortality in the Early Fathers; The Light of the World: A Basic Image in Early Christian Thought; The Finality of Jesus Christ in an Age of Universal History: A Dilemma of the Third Century;* and *Development of Christian Doctrine: Some Historical Prolegomena*), as well as a sympathetic understanding of the problems facing the Roman Catholic Church both before and after the Reformation, notably evident in *The Riddle of Roman Catholicism,* published in 1959, which was called "the most talked-of Protestant book of the season" by the Protestant review *Christian Century* and by the Catholic *Commonweal* "an honest, often searching exploration of doctrinal differences and . . . the best fruit of the new American encounter between Protestant and Catholic thought." These books, with their straightforward, unmannered style, profound learning, and civilized good humor seem in retrospect carefully spaced stepping stones leading to the magnum opus.

Pelikan's life's work finally began to take published shape in 1971. The first volume of *The Christian Tradition: A History of the Development of Doctrine* was entitled *The Emergence of the Catholic Tradition (100–600),* and for the first time posited Pelikan's often-repeated definition of doctrine as "what the church of Jesus Christ believes, teaches, and confesses on the basis of the word of God." He added, however, that doctrine was "not the only, not even the primary, activity of the church." The book comprises a thorough summary of the trinitarian and christological disputes resolved in the early ecumenical councils, which produced a fundamental agreement on what constituted the orthodox Catholic faith. The second volume, *The Spirit of Eastern Christendom (600–1700)*, focuses on the divisions between Eastern and Western Christianity, beginning with the iconoclastic controversy and proceeding through the Great Schism and the last flowering of Byzantine Orthodoxy. Volume three, *The Growth of Medieval Theology (600–1300)*, which opens with a thirteen-page list of primary sources, is one of the first clear accounts of an immensely complex and disputatious period. Referring to the whole project, Pelikan remarked in 1981, "My interest, because it extends across periods and across a variety of themes, is in how the tradition received is reinterpreted and applied. It is really the relationship between continuity and change. . . . There is really no institution in Western culture besides the church where we have this kind of laboratory, on this scale, for the study of change and continuity. If I have a motto or slogan, it comes from Goethe's *Faust*: 'What you have received as an inheritance from your fathers, you must possess again in order to make it your own.' I'm interested in how that has been done in the Christian tradition." Pelikan plans a fourth volume, "Reformation of Church and Dogma (1300–1700)" and a fifth on the modern period, "Christian Doctrine and Modern Culture (since 1700)." All volumes so far have received the effusive praise of theologian reviewers, normally a testy and contentious group. "I have found," Pelikan once wrote, "that liturgics is better than adrenalin for raising blood pressure."

Other editorial productions by Pelikan include the five-volume *Makers of Modern Theology*, the three-volume *Twentieth Century Theology in the Making*, and collections of the sermons of St. John Chrysostom and St. Augustine of Hippo. He also edited the *Festschrift* for Wilhelm Pauck, *Interpreters of Luther* (1968). From 1978 he has served on the editorial board overseeing the Yale edition of the complete works of Erasmus.

After teaching church history at Valparaiso University (1946–49) and Concordia Seminary (1949–53), Pelikan was appointed professor of historical theology at the University of Chicago (1953–62). He has been at Yale since 1962, first as Titus Street professor of ecclesiastical history at the Yale Divinity School, and from 1972 as Sterling professor of history and religious studies in the university's department of history. His administrative posts at Yale have included director of graduate studies, dean of the graduate school, chairman of medieval studies, and chairman of the publications committee of the university press. He regularly teaches both graduate seminars in his own field and the freshman introductory course in Western civilization, popularly known as "Plato to NATO." He has always had a clear idea of the nice separation between the sacred and secular in his academic life: "In my own field of the history of Christian thought, I am, as a Christian, pleased if a student, through his research or perhaps even through mine, receives the grace to decide to take up residence in the household of faith, if he learns to eat at its banquet table and to die in its family circle. But as a historian . . . all I can require of such a student is that he give me an accurate description of the furniture."

Pelikan married Sylvia Burica in 1946 and they have two sons and a daughter. He lives in Hamden, a suburb of New Haven, travels all over the world to deliver about a dozen lectures a year, but confesses himself happiest in the library, where he can work at his own impressive speed. He has received many book awards from both Protestant and Catholic organizations, and more than fifteen universities have conferred honorary degrees on him.

PRINCIPAL WORKS: From Luther to Kierkegaard, 1950; Fools for Christ, 1955; The Riddle of Roman Catholicism 1959; Luther the Expositor, 1959; The Shape of Death, 1961; The Light of the World, 1962; Obedient Rebels, 1964; The Finality of Jesus Christ in an Age of Universal History, 1965; The Christian Intellectual, 1966; Spirit Versus Structure, 1968; Development of Christian Doctrine, 1969; Historical Theology, 1971; The Christian Tradition, 1971 to date; The Spirit of Eastern Christendom, (600–1700), 1974; The Shape of Death, 1978; The Growth of Medieval Theology (600–1300), 1978; Reformation of Church and Dogma (1300–1700), 1983; Scholarship and its Survival, 1983; The Vindication of Tradition, 1984. *As editor*—Luther's Works, 1959–70; Makers of Modern Theology, 1966–68; The Preaching of Chrysostom, 1967; Interpreters of Luther, 1968; Twentieth Century Theology in the Making, 1969–71; The Preaching of Augustine, 1973.

ABOUT: Contemporary Authors, new revision series 1 (1981); International Who's Who, 1981–82. *Periodicals*—New Yorker February 2, 1981; New York Review of Books May 20, 1971; September 2, 1971; May 3, 1979; New York Times January 2, 1979; New York Times Book Review September 30, 1984; Yale Review Winter 1971.

*PENNA, SANDRO (June 12, 1906–January 21, 1977), Italian lyric poet, has for forty years been considered in his homeland a poet of the first importance, yet has found almost no audience abroad. The delicacy of his verse makes it extremely difficult to translate: his simple, restrained language, mastery of rhyme and restrictive verse forms, and his classical tone all lose their vitality when not in Italian. His theme is almost invariably homosexual love, or more specifically pederasty, yet his poems are never prurient; their true subject is the sensibility of the poet himself. "My only work," he said in an interview in 1960, "is represented by a group or cluster of short poems which during my no longer brief life have spontaneously flowered, as if by their own force. I never sought to publish them, not from modesty (false modesty), but only because I felt in part a hostile climate among the literati, and in part because I was sure also of their unpopularity."

Penna was born in Perugia, the son of a shopkeeper. After a wandering, restless youth he concluded his irregular studies by getting a diploma in accounting. He worked for some time while a young man as a bookstore clerk in Milan, then moved in 1929 with his mother to Rome, a city he came to love deeply and where he lived the rest of his life. He always chose work that was disparate and desultory—proofreader, substitute teacher, door-to-door salesman—so as not to deplete his spiritual stock.

Also in 1929, Penna began to send his poems to Umberto Saba (1883–1957), a well-known poet, who reacted immediately with appreciation and help. A volume was ready for publication by 1936, but the preeminent lyric poet of the time, Eugenio Montale, in his role as literary arbiter, advised against bringing it out then, believing that most of the poems were liable to be censored. Yet when Parenti, a Florentine house, published *Poesie* (Poems) in 1939, the critical response was overwhelmingly positive. One review in particular, by the influential critic Sergio Solmi in *Circoli,* established the critical standard by which Penna's poetry would be judged for a generation. Solmi praised the poems' lucid simplicity, their classical "grace," their wholly physical adherence to the representative world. "He appears to be only what he is, as do the things of nature."

Penna has always been seen in this way as a case apart, a natural being, genius *sui generis.* He is not customarily identified with the hermeticists, the prevailing school when *Poesie* was published. The critic Gaetano Mariani describes Penna as "an island" in twentieth-century poetry, and writes of the difficulty of inserting his lyric in any current, school, or group. Some crit-

SANDRO PENNA

ics, however, such as Giuseppe De Robertis, have pointed to his stylistic similarities with hermeticism—to the basic and unrhetorical quality of his language, to "the speed and deftness of his transitions," and to his "knowing how to join an apparent clearness with a substantial obscurity." An interesting tension is everywhere in Penna's work. His meter and syntax, apparently traditional, are actually subtly disarranged. His account of an experience, of something seen, may be heavy with sadness and alienation, yet the poetry is exalted by a natural, almost effortless lightness.

Penna contributed to numerous journals and little magazines both before and more frequently after his first book's success; these included *Letteratura, Campo di Marte, Corrente, Frontespizio, L'Ambrosiano, Poesia, Il Mondo, La Rassegna d'Italia, Botteghe oscure,* and especially *Paragone.* His second slender book, *Appunti* (Notes), was enthusiastically received in 1950.

A new generation's appreciation of Penna began in 1956 in the pages of *Paragone,* after the appearance of his third book, *Una strana gioia di vivere* (A Strange Joy of Living), which won a one-third share of the Viareggio prize in 1957. Pier Paolo Pasolini (1922–75), an old friend of Penna's, was at that time coming to be well known in Italy as a poet, playwright, and discerning critic, and later became internationally famous as a film director. He attempted to disperse the atmosphere of delicate superficiality and biased judgment in which he felt readers had enveloped Penna and his work. To Pasolini, Penna's was "an ineffable poetry, critically impalpable." "For him we ought to suspend all critical judgment," he wrote, "as well as whatever psychological, ideological, and moral judgments might be behind stylistic analysis." We would then "be stopped short by a kind of unrelated consciousness of his value. Of his grace." This rare quality of natural "grace" is a commonplace of most criticism of the poet.

The 1950s was Penna's most prolific decade. The *Poesie* of 1957 was a compilation of all his published and unpublished poems, and was followed by yet another book, *Croce e delizia* (Suffering and Delight), in 1958. The impressionistic and evocative lyricism of the early poems had taken on a more mature and sadder voice, which was still devoted to exploring the love of the senses: "Perhaps youth lies only in this / perpetually, and unrepentantly, to love the senses." His locales are ordinary—streets, houses, stations, schools, taverns—yet infused with either the delirious joy of illusion or the anguish and sadness of exclusion and alienation.

Under the April sky my peace
is uncertain. The clear greens now move
under the wind at their caprice . . .
Boys run on the grass, and it seems
that the wind scatters them. But only
my heart is scattered: what remains is a vivid
flash (oh youth) of their
white shirts patterned on the green.

("The Balcony")

Many critics have noticed the abstract qualities of the boys in Penna's poems. They usually have no faces, no personalities, no particularities, but exist only in glimpses, gestures, visions of real or imagined happiness; they are mainly the occasions of the poet's love of life and its "gentle dream": "The world seemed to me a clear dream, / The life of every day a legend."

Tutte le poesie (Complete Poems), a restructuring by Penna of his complete works along with a few brief accompanying notes, appeared in 1970 and won the Fiuggi prize; it gave critics and readers a complete view of his poetic evolution. His only work in prose, *Un po' di febbre* (A Slight Fever, 1973), was a collection of essays and articles on diverse subjects, some published before the war and others written since and there published for the first time.

The last years of Penna's life were spent in increasing ill health and poverty. Accompanied only by his German shepherd dog and unknown to most of his neighbors, he lived in a dingy and chaotic sixth-floor apartment in the house he had always occupied near the Tiber. In early 1974 a group of writers, among them Natalia Ginzburg and Goffredo Parise, made a public appeal in *Il Messaggero* for funds to alleviate Penna's "extreme indigence." The ten million lire raised for him reportedly made little difference in his living conditions. His last volume of poems, *Stranezze* (Oddities), was published in 1976 by Garzanti, which also brought out in 1973 a popular edition of his works. He gave frequent interviews to popular journals, in which he delighted in making dismissive remarks about his literary contemporaries and friends. One such, by a bizarre coincidence, was published in *Il Messaggero* the day of his death, which occurred in his apartment, from heart failure. His final illness prevented him from accepting in person the Bagutta prize, which he was awarded for *Stranezza* only a week before his death.

WORKS IN ENGLISH TRANSLATION: The only volume of Penna's verse in English translation—by W. S. Di Piero—is *This Strange Joy*, 1982. Selections from his poems are in C. Golino's *Contemporary Italian Poetry*, 1962, 1977, and L. Lind's *Twentieth Century Italian Poetry*, 1974.

ABOUT: De Robertis, G. Altro Novecento, 1962; Manacorda, G. Storia della letteratura italiana contemporanea, 1967; Mariani, G. *in* I contemporanei 3, 1969; Pacifici, S. A Guide to Contemporary Italian Literature, 1972; Pozzi, G. La poesia italiana del Novecento, 1965. *Periodicals*—Paragone no. 76, April 1956; Circoli 1, 1939.

PERRIN, NOEL (September 18, 1927–), American essayist, writes: "I was born in New York City, where my father was in the advertising business (and his father a teacher at City College, and *his* father a lawyer). For the sake of their two children, my parents moved to one of the comfortable Westchester suburbs. There, at around fifteen, two thoughts struck me which have largely determined the rest of my life. One was that I could walk fifty miles in any direction except east—Long Island Sound was there—and almost never be out of sight of a house. The other was that my suburb didn't seem real. It was a place where people of a certain income level lived, when they had jobs in the city and wanted to be near a country club, but they were really from Ohio or Texas, and that was where they would return when they retired from the bank or the mattress company. It took me a long time to act on these perceptions, and meanwhile I got a typical upper middle-class education, culminating in two years of graduate study at Cambridge University in England. I worked for a few years in and around New York—as a copy boy on the *Daily News*, as an editor of a trade magazine. I began to publish in the *New Yorker*.

"Then in 1959 the main part of my life began. I took a job teaching at Dartmouth, and soon thereafter bought an old farm in Vermont. I still

NOEL PERRIN

teach part-time at Dartmouth (nowadays environmental studies about as much as American literature), and I still have the farm. For twenty years I have edged steadily closer to being a farmer, without ever quite becoming a 'real' one. With no conscious planning on my part, my writing has turned out to be of three kinds, all nonfiction. Rural essays have dominated. These have ranged from the severely practical (if you were to buy a pamphlet on how to make maple syrup, I would be quite likely to have written it) to the downright meditative. What amused me most was a column I wrote for a while for an urban magazine, interpreting rural mores for a city audience.

"Totally unconnected with this, and reflecting the remaining split in my own life, I like to write about books. I do a fair amount of reviewing. *Dr. Bowdler's Legacy* was a history of expurgated books. I have devoted a good deal of time to authors I thought undervalued, notably the novelist James Gould Cozzens and the great *New Yorker* essayist Joseph Mitchell. I have a slow-paced column called 'Rediscoveries' in *Book World* of the *Washington Post,* in which I write about almost-forgotten authors who shouldn't be—and occasionally I assist in getting one back into print. Once in the British Museum I stumbled on a totally forgotten and very funny novel about the Revolution, called *The Adventures of Jonathan Corncob, Loyal American Refugee.* It came out in 1787. That one I edited myself for its first American publication in 1976.

"Finally I do a certain amount of environmental journalism—started back in the early sixties before I even knew there *was* such a genre. It's

hard work because it takes so much research—much more fun to spin out a rural essay out of what one has simply lived, or observed. It also leaves one open to charges of elitism. But it took an elite group—in fact, two: one of scientists and one of politicians—to lead us into environmental catastrophe; it certainly was no conscious choice of the people to have acid rain or nuclear plants or the danger of no ozone layer. So there may be an argument for an elitist effort to help get us back out."

————

Noel Perrin is the son of Edwin Oscar Perrin and the former Blanche Chenery. He earned his B.A. at Williams College (1949), his M.A. from Duke University (1950), and the degree of M. Litt. from Trinity Hall of Cambridge University in 1958. He served as an artillery officer in the Army in 1945–46 and in Korea in 1950–51 and won the Bronze Star. Perrin taught English at Woman's College of the University of North Carolina at Greensboro (1956–59), and has been at Dartmouth since 1959. Called "Ned" by his friends, Perrin has for more than two decades been recognized by Dartmouth students as among the least doctrinaire and most amiable of their teachers. His long involvement with his farm in Thetford Center, Vermont, across the Connecticut River from Hanover, a small New Hampshire town completely dominated by Dartmouth, is one reason for his rare ability to keep collegiate tensions and departmental infighting at arm's length.

His first book, *A Passport Secretly Green,* is a slender volume of twenty-one essays, thirteen of which had been previously published in various magazines. Some deal with his experiences in England, some treat America, and one uncharacteristically angry piece discusses the threat of nuclear war. J. C. Pine praised Perrin's "genuine knack for putting his finger on what is human and significant in everyday life," and J. A. May wrote, "The essence of Mr. Perrin's humor is delight. Delight at the humanity of humans. Delight at their variety. Delight at their freshness. Delight in the English language. Not a wild delight, not a simpering delight, but a toughly gentle and sardonic delight."

The twenty country pieces in *First Person Rural: Essays of a Sometime Farmer* were critically well received, though reviewers differed as to whether Perrin's strongest essays were those of metaphysical or practical bent. Christopher Andreae thought him "best when factual. On making fences, buying a pick-up truck, coping with last year's frantic supply of sweet maple sap, purchasing a chain saw, raising two sheep, sugar-making: on such matters this ex-New Yorker turned full-time Vermonter manages a rare combination of the fascinating and informative." To J. N. Baker, however, "the best essays are less practical: they dabble in the metaphysics of country life. In 'Tell Me, Pretty Billboard,' Perrin, an unofficial consumer-rights crusader, conducts imaginary conversations with roadside signs and supermarket packages. . . . 'Old MacBerlitz Had a Farm' is a funny piece about the international variants in animal talk. . . . In 'The Other Side,' Perrin speculates that most New Yorkers who move to Vermont to escape sanitation slowdowns, invasions of privacy and traffic noise would flee back to the city in six months when confronted with rat-infested garbage dumps, myopic deer hunters and throbbing snowmobiles."

The critical response to *Second Person Rural: More Essays of a Sometime Farmer* was even more enthusiastic. Comparing this book with its predecessor, L. B. Hodges found "fewer pieces on how to do various farm chores and more on the 'differences between the city and the country and especially differences in psychology.'" Maria Lenhart called the essays "astute and amusing observations about rural life, especially as it affects and is affected by nonrural people. . . . *Second Person Rural* casts an unromantic eye on the realities of country life; there is little about wildflowers and trout streams and a good deal about chain saws, stone removal, and butchering lambs. There is also a lot about behavior—both the animal and the human kind." With *Third Person Rural: Further Essays of a Sometime Farmer,* Perrin announced his total conversion to rural life: "I am so deeply into rurality that my own childhood conditioning has almost been overcome." Perrin's other writings on country living are in *Vermont in All Weathers* and in a how-to book, *Amateur Sugar Maker.* He has been a regular contributor to the *New Yorker* and to such rural magazines as *Vermont Life, Country Journal,* and *Horticulture.*

The first scholarly study published by Perrin was *Dr. Bowdler's Legacy: A History of Expurgated Books in England and America,* a study of bowdlerizing and the Shakespearean editor whose name was given to the practice. The book is full of examples of expurgation committed by Thomas Bowdler and his fellow bluenoses, which one critic felt led to "tiresome reading," but the *New Yorker* reviewer thought the book "delightful reading, if touched with that streak of melancholy which accompanies any record of human folly." This reviewer also thought Perrin "most engrossing when he describes the formidable eccentrics who devoted themselves to this

pursuit, particularly the Bowdler family itself, and the Rev. Mr. James Plumptre, who felt it his mission to divert the whole course of English literature into purer channels."

Giving Up the Gun: Japan's Reversion to the Sword, 1543–1879 is a brief history of the period covering more than 250 years when Japan voluntarily renounced the production and use of military firearms. Originally a shorter essay appearing in the *New Yorker,* the book was expanded into what R. A. Sokolov called "an elegant monograph, magnificently illustrated with a wealth of Japanese prints that depict old-fashioned samurai and Japanese riflemen, sometimes both fighting together in the same battle." Ron Anderson wrote that the book is "as tight and elegant as a *haiku.* . . . Perrin's ample research shows several reasons for the gradual abandonment of the gun after the Japanese had used it domestically and in international conflicts for over a hundred years. These reasons can be summed up in three categories: samurai honor, local geography, and personal aesthetics. . . . Because of its subject matter, *Giving Up the Gun* might be considered a book of limited interest, which would be unfortunate, for Perrin's work is so crisp and interesting and so loaded with background information and revealing anecdotes that the whole peculiar episode it describes jumps to life from its pages."

Perrin married Nancy Hunnicutt in 1960; they have two daughters.

PRINCIPAL WORKS: *Essays*—A Passport Secretly Green, 1961; Vermont in All Weathers, 1973; First Person Rural, 1978; Second Person Rural, 1981; Third Person Rural, 1983. *History*—Dr. Bowdler's Legacy, 1969; Giving Up the Gun: Japan's Reversion to the Sword, 1543–1879, 1979.

ABOUT: Contemporary Authors, first revision series 13–16, 1975. *Periodicals*—Christian Science Monitor March 13, 1961; November 20, 1969; August 23, 1978; November 10, 1980; Chronicle of Books and Arts August 6, 1979; Library Journal February 1, 1961; September 15, 1969; November 1, 1980; New Republic June 9, 1979; Newsweek September 22, 1969; August 7, 1978; New Yorker October 25, 1969; New York Review of Books October 11, 1979; New York Times Book Review November 9, 1969; July 23, 1978; July 15, 1979; October 26, 1980; January 8, 1984; Saturday Review March 11, 1961; October 14, 1978; Sciences September 1979.

*PILINSZKY, JANOS (November 27, 1921– May 16, 1981), Hungarian poet, was born into a well-educated middle-class family in Budapest; his father was a lawyer. After obtaining his diploma from the Piarist High School, he studied

°pil inz´ skē, yä´ nosh

JANOS PILINSZKY

law at the University of Budapest, but after a
time, he specialized in Hungarian literature and
the history of art; he began work on a dissertation on Jenö Péterfy, the influential nineteenth-
century essayist and critic, but never completed
requirements for a doctor of philosophy. In 1941
he became an assistant editor of Élet (Life), a
weekly of the St. Stephen Society, a post he held
until he was called into the army in the fall of
1944. During this time he contributed many articles to the periodical, mostly unsigned reviews
of books, films, and plays. He also published
some poems from 1941–42, not only in Élet but
in such eminent journals as Ezüstkor (Silver
Age), edited by the noted author and critic
István Sötér, Magyar Csillag (Hungarian Star), a
continuation of the influential Nyugat (West),
edited by the poet Mihály Babits, and Vigilia
(Vigil), a highly regarded voice of Catholic intellectuals. His army unit was ordered to duty outside Hungary in February 1945 and arrived in
Harbach, Germany, after several weeks of travel. His experiences of concentration camps, prisoners of war, and other horrors in Germany
deeply affected his view of human life and his
religious beliefs. Because of illness, he performed field work until the end of the war and
did not write anything until after he returned to
Hungary in November 1945.

He immediately became active in literary life
in Budapest, did some work for radio, mainly
translations for broadcast, and joined the
Írószövetség (Writers Federation). He served as
an editor of Újhold (New Moon), which was
staffed by young writers attempting to advance
the modern literary trends that had developed

in Hungary between the two wars. Pilinszky
published only a poem and a translation of an extract from Hoffmanstahl's play Elektra in this
periodical, but his verses appeared frequently in
other journals, including several in Vigil in 1949.
The poem "Trapéz és korlát" (Trapeze and Parallel Bars), first published in Ezüstkor in May
1946, provided the title for his first book of poems, which appeared in 1946 and received the
Baumgartner Prize in 1947. Five of his poems
were published in 1948 in Négy nemzedék
(Four Generations), a landmark anthology of the
time.

His active literary life, like that of so many of
his contemporaries, was abruptly cut off by the
Communist takeover in 1948 and his refusal to
follow the dicta of schematism. The more liberal
policies instituted after the 1956 uprising enabled him to resume his literary activities. In
1957 he began his long service as an editor of Új
Ember (New Man), a Catholic weekly; in 1958
he published Aranymadár (Golden Bird), a book
of verse tales, and in 1959 his second book of poems, Harmadnapon (On the Third Day). From
this time on his works appeared quite regularly,
especially after the publication of his first collected edition, Nagyvárosi ikonok (Big City
Icons), in 1970. When criticized for the small
number of his poems, he replied: "It doesn't matter how many times a bird beats its wings, what
counts is that he takes flight."

The poems in "Trapeze and Parallel Bars" reveal the enormous impact of the troubled times
and the war on Pilinszky's moral world. Composing confessions and self-portraits without
particularizing them excessively with personal
details, he paints a stark and lonely private
world, one of utter isolation and alienation.
Sparse, distilled lines present him as abiding in
a world of utter futility and suffering the agony
of one turned into an outcast by his experiences.
In "Tilos csillagon" (I Was Born on a Forbidden
Star), he pleads: "I did not desire to be born, /
the void bore me, suckled me, / love me darkly,
fiercely, / like the bereaved the dead." The essentials of his outlook are poignantly expressed
in "Halak a hálóban" (Fish in the Net), one of his
most important poems:

We thrash about in a net of stars,
fish dragged to the shore;
our months gape into nothingness,
snapping dry void.
The lost element, whispering,
calls us in vain.
Among sharp-edged stones and pebbles
gasping for air
We must live and die against one another.
Our hearts tremble.
Our struggles wound
and strangle our brother.
Not even an echo answers

our voices, each outshouting the other;
We have no reason to fight and kill
yet do it we must.
We atone yet our atonement
is no punishment;
no suffering can redeem
us from our hells.
We thrash about in an enormous net
and at midnight perhaps
we shall be food on the table
of a mighty fisherman.

—trans. Peter Sherwood

This sense of the meaninglessness of life, the struggle for existence, the compulsion of human beings to destroy each other, and the conviction that even suffering cannot lead to atonement are aspects of Pilinszky's thought that received constant refinement throughout the remainder of his creative life.

The poems he wrote from 1946 to 1958, published in *Harmadnapon,* become less personal, and the major ones universalize Pilinszky's fate by associating it with the suffering of all humanity under the impact of his experience with the concentration camps in Germany. In them religious symbols of the passion of Christ abound; resurrection is sought, and apocalypse looms in a world bereft of moral bases, a place of utter desolation and alienation. The moral turpitude of fascism, its bestiality and its stripping every shred of human essence from life, leads him to a cosmic treatment of present reality. The crucifixion of Christ is used as a symbol in the execution of a prisoner in "Ravensbrücki passió" (Passion of Ravensbrück, 1959):

He steps out from the others.
He stands in the square silence.
Prisoner's dress and convict's head
flicker as on a screen.

He is terrifying alone.
Even his pores are visible.
Everything about him is so huge,
Everything about him is so tiny.

And that is all. The rest,
well, the rest was simply
that he forgot to cry out
before slumping to the ground.

—trans. Peter Sherwood

The crimes against humanity are those of all humankind, and there is no atonement for them; the struggle between belief and hopelessness takes place in the sight of a God who knows there is no escape from sinfulness, a view developed in "Jelenések VIII.7" (Revelations VIII.7). These poems, a reviewer wrote, point to "the mystery of resurrection . . . but of the kind of human being whose sores from the nails have not healed and whose soul continues to bear its terrible wounds." "Apokrif" (Apocrypha) dramatically interweaves Pilinszky's thoughts about the war

and the death camps with a vision of universal suffering in three brief scenes of a prisoner leaving one of the camps and arriving at home a total stranger after his Calvary, unable to shed his loneliness or to speak the language of those who had not shared his alienation.

In the 1960s Pilinszky began to experiment with new forms to express his fundamental loneliness and alienation, among them an oratorio called *Rekviem* (Requiem, 1970), and also wrote many essays, including a number that illuminated his concepts of the function of poetry, thus adding vastly to the understanding of the character of his poetry. The essay "A 'teremtö képzelet' sorsa korunkba" ('Creative Imagination' in Our Time, 1970) reveals the religious basis of his *ars poetica.* According to Pilinszky, original sin not only dimmed the human intellect and predisposed the human will to violence; it also infected the human imagination so that it has difficulty in carrying out its natural function of consummating the incarnation of the world's reality. The creative imagination, he believes, has mistakenly turned to "the uncertainty of submission, 'with downcast eyes.'" Poetry—indeed all art—is, he is convinced, the instrument of the "imagination's morality," and its purpose is to restore the reality and incarnation of creation, to obtain some glimmer of an attainable experience of a now vanished moral world.

The publication of *Nagyvárosi ikonok,* which included the preceding works, heralded his most prolific period of creativity. The poems reevaluating the tragic past of the prison camps are characterized by some modifications in his earlier concepts of morality, and they are quickly followed by *Szálkák* (Splinters, 1972) and *Végigfejlet* (Dénouement, 1974). These works reveal some movement toward an inner peace. The horror lessens; though still marked by pain and doubts about the possibility of atonement, they show an emerging relationship between humankind and God. As one critic points out, God now becomes "a participant in the insoluble dialogue between birth and death, the principle of the irresolvable and never-to-be-resolved enigma. The principle of the union between man and God—and the final word of every single human being in this union is an ever simpler silence," a movement toward harmony suggested by "Fokról-fokra" (Step by Step).

Pilinszky's four experimental plays, all written in the early 1970s and included with the lyric poems in *Végigfejlet,* are allegorial, resemble mystery and morality plays in design, and are concerned with human loneliness and suffering; but they are difficult to understand and, critics generally agree, do not equal the artistry and power of his lyric poems; Of them, *Elöképek* (Tableaux Vivants, 1974) is often considered to be an especially effective portrayal of the universal horror of the concentration camps.

Pilinszky also published a collection of tales for children and *Beszélgetések Sheryl Suttonal* (Conversations with Sheryl Sutton, 1977), a valuable source for his ideas that grew out of his conversations with a black American actress.

Beginning in the early 1960s, he traveled abroad frequently. In 1963 he made his first visit to Paris, at the invitation of Pierre Emmanuel; in 1968, on the hundredth anniversary of Baudelaire's death, he gave a reading of his own poems at the Petit Odéon in Paris. In 1969 he participated in a festival of poets in London; in 1970 he spent six months in Paris as a guest of Gabriel Marcel. He held a reading of his poems in Canada in 1972 and was named a member of the Bavarian Academy of Fine Arts in 1973. His own country honored him with the Attila József Prize in 1971.

WORKS IN ENGLISH TRANSLATION: Two volumes of Pilinszky's poetry are available in English translation: *Selected Poems*, translated by the English poet Ted Hughes and Janos Csokits, 1976, and Peter Jay's translation of *Crater: Poems 1974–1975*, 1978. Selected poems, in Peter Sherwood's translation, an essay "Creative Imagination in Our Time," and an autobiographical sketch are in Albert Tezla's *Ocean at the Window: Hungarian Prose and Poetry Since 1945*, 1981.

ABOUT: Columbia Dictionary of Modern European Literature, 1980; Contemporary Authors 104, 1982; Encyclopedia of World Literature in the 20th Century IV, 1975; Gomöri, Z. Polish and Hungarian Poetry 1945–1956, 1966; Hughes, T. *Introduction to* Pilinszky's Selected Poems, 1976; Tezla, A. Ocean at the Window, 1981. *Periodicals*—New Hungarian Quarterly Spring and Winter 1981.

PINSKY, ROBERT (NEAL) (October 20, 1940–   ), American poet and critic, writes: "I was born in Long Branch, New Jersey, a decayed seashore resort town, where I went to the same schools as had been attended by both my parents, and many of my uncles, aunts and cousins. My grandfather for many years owned the Broadway Tavern in Long Branch. My father has been an optician there since he graduated from Long Branch Senior High School. (Voted the best-looking boy, and best dancer in his class: he was also a local athlete of some note.) Before her family settled in Long Branch, my mother as a child lived all over the country. She was born in Arkansas, and has happy memories of Oregon. She taught me to read and, by example, to read

ROBERT PINSKY

with considerable hunger. My family practiced an unpredictable, rather secularized version of Orthodox Judaism, from which I drifted effortlessly far away at thirteen.

"In grammar school and junior high I did very poorly. In the eighth grade, I was placed in what was known as 'the bad class.' After a poor record in high school (the only thing I did at all well was play the saxophone) I went to Rutgers, where I succeeded better, and then to Stanford, where I learned a large part of what I know from Yvor Winters, becoming his devoted student—but not ever quite, even in the first intensity of discovery, 'Wintersian.' The most important thing Winters did for me, I think, was to open up the sixteenth and seventeenth centuries in a way that broke the spell of Eliot's essays.

"I was married to Ellen Jane (Bailey) Pinsky on December 30, 1961. We have three daughters. From 1968 to 1980 I taught at Wellesley College, where my close friends and colleagues included the poets Frank Bidart and David Ferry. I have also taught at the Universities of Chicago and Harvard. I now teach at Berkeley, where I have renewed an old student-days friendship with the poet Robert Hass.

"My deepest attachment to writing is physical, an attraction to the sounds of lines, consonants, syllables, retards and quickenings. After that, what I prize most may be a quality of surprise: the upsetting of expectation, a sense of diversions and fresh jokes or gulfs, a fable-like sea of feeling under every innocent surface. These interests—in the musical side of writing, and in setting up ideas in order to break them or vary them as rapidly as possible—may hark back to my first, frustrated ambition to be a glorious jazz musician."

Robert Pinsky is the son of Milford Simon Pinsky and the former Sylvia Eisenberg. He earned his Rutgers B.A. in 1962, his Stanford Ph.D. in 1966. Before going to Wellesley, he taught for a year (1966–67) at the University of Chicago. He is at present a professor of English at Berkeley. Pinsky's first book of poetry, *Sadness and Happiness,* appeared as part of the new Princeton Series of Contemporary Poets. The *Choice* reviewer called Pinsky's "a neoclassical temper. His poems are aggressively controlled, rhymed and patterned, given to wit, fancy, urbane observation." William Pritchard commented that "it is the measuring and measured quality of this poetry that is freshly attractive; matters of feeling, weighing, choosing among alternatives become the real subject of Mr. Pinsky's concern." Pritchard called the collection as a whole "a distinguished accomplishment, remarkable for its daring and its poise—indeed the best work by any younger poet within recent memory." Louis Martz also considered Pinsky's a thoroughly new and compelling voice, "the most exhilarating new poet that I have read since A. R. Ammons entered upon the scene. He has a crisp, unfaltering technique, a firm grip on images, a sense of humor, and above all, something to say. . . . The whole of the modern world is for Pinsky a region where the soul, yes the Soul, has to face its mysteries; and the outer conditions for him are no worse or no better than they ever were for any generation." Pinsky, concludes Martz, "points a way toward the future of poetry."

The Situation of Poetry: Contemporary Poetry and Its Traditions is a collection of essays on contemporary poetry and its romantic and modernist past. Pinsky, according to the publishers, "isolates certain persistent ideas about poetry's situation relative to life and focuses on the conflict the poet faces between the nature of words and poetic forms on one side, and the nature of experience on the other." His examples range from Keats and John Clare to the protomodernists Stevens and Williams, and he also considers such poets as Ammons, Ashbery, Bogan, Ginsberg, Lowell, Merwin, and O'Hara. The *Choice* reviewer called the book "appropriately genial, wide-ranging, and observant; descriptive rather than prescriptive" and Pinsky's commentaries "compellingly sound and informed." David Bromewich, however, denied that *The Situation of Poetry* is "a sober work of literary history or literary criticism;" it is instead "intelligent propaganda for one kind of poetry, the kind that Mr. Pinsky happens to write. In violation of a cherished American privilege he does not stop to praise his own work. But any reader who knows the best of Mr. Pinsky's shorter poems, or his delicate long poem 'Sadness and Happiness,' will see that by his own canons of taste he might have awarded himself fairly high honours."

Pinsky's second volume of poems, *An Explanation of America,* is an attempt to grasp the whole complexity of the United States in poetry's concentrated essence. Lynn Emanuel called it a surprisingly "calm book about America and its 'love of death,' its deceptions, its politics and possibilities. . . . From the beginning the reader is made to understand that the explanation is not a mirroring of reality: there is no celebration of local color or simple political sentiment. The book is, instead, a long meditation on origins and lineage; it is about how a writer constructs his own country and it is a wise, sober work." The extended title poem seemed to Michael Hamburger "to defy not only all the dominent trends in contemporary poetry but all the dominant notions . . . of what is to be expected of an American poet. . . . The meaning of America . . . as it emerges from the poem as a whole is also contrary to dominant notions and prejudices. . . . Pinsky's seemingly anachronistic meter serves his difficult and subtle purpose by slowing down the movement of his poem . . . and preventing us from jumping to premature conclusions. For related reasons his poem is memorable as a whole, rather than for any purple passage or punch line that would invite quotation as a summary of the poem's 'message.'" Fred Moramarco was struck by "the persistent specificity of the [title] poem, and by his ability to flesh out an aphorism with illustrative images. . . . While 'explaining' America in its immense and contradictory variety may be beyond the pale of any poet's range these days, Pinsky comes as close to capturing a contemporary sense of both the idea of America and the kaleidoscopic images which reflect its reality as anyone is likely to for some time."

Pinsky has been visiting lecturer at Harvard and Hurst professor at Washington University, St. Louis. He has been poetry editor of the *New Republic* since 1978. He won an Artists award from the American Academy of Arts and Letters in 1979 and the Saxifrage prize in 1980. He held a Guggenheim fellowship in 1980–81.

PRINCIPAL WORKS: *Poetry*—Sadness and Happiness, 1975; An Explanation of America, 1979; History of My Heart, 1984; *Prose*—Landor's Poetry, 1968; The Situation of Poetry, 1977.

ABOUT: Contemporary Authors, first revision series 29–32, 1978; Dictionary of Literary Biography 1982; Who's Who in America, 1982–83. *Periodicals*—America May 28, 1977; Choice May 1976; June 1977; Library Journal July 1979; National November 13, 1976; September 3, 1977; January 26, 1980; New Statesman September 28, 1979; New York Times Book Review April 4, 1976; February 20, 1977; May 4, 1980; April 8, 1984; Times Literary Supplement June 11, 1976; July 8, 1977; January 18, 1980; World Literature Today Spring 1980; Yale Review Autumn 1976.

PLANTE, DAVID (ROBERT) (March 4, 1940–   ), American novelist, writes: "I was born in the same bed in which I was conceived, in a small, Franco-American, working class parish in Providence, Rhode Island. My father [Anaclet Joseph Plante] was forty-three years old, my mother [Albina Bison Plante] thirty-nine at the time of my birth. I was their sixth son; one more son, two years later, was born. Then there were two miscarriages, and my mother often wondered if one might have been a daughter. My father worked in a factory which manufactured industrial files. My mother worked at home.

"This is an early memory: of my mother or father preparing me for bed, I standing on a chair while she or he undressed me, and I hearing a quiet, tired voice telling me to raise a foot, turn around, put out an arm, and the feeling coming over me that their tiredness was total, and that I must do exactly as I was told. My parents worked very hard for me, for my family.

"I went to the parochial grammar school, Notre Dame de Lourdes, where I was taught by French Canadian nuns, les Mères de Jésus-Marie. We had classes in French in the morning, in English in the afternoon. The pastor of the church, Monsieur le Curé, could not speak English. We sat in terror in the classroom when, every month, he came in to hand out our report cards. We had to bow before him before we reached out for the card. And we had to stand and bow, too, every time we were called on in class by a nun to answer a question. In the French classes, we learned how French martyrs had been tortured and killed by Indians (the Indians heated up tomahawks till they were white hot and pressed them to the naked flesh of the missionaries), and we thought we, too, would one day be captured and tortured because we were Catholics and loved God. This caused worry in me, because I knew that my family, from my father's side, was part Indian. My great-grand-mother was a Blackfoot. I thought that if I were ever captured by Indians, I would say, 'I am an Indian too.' Except I didn't know any Indian language, and had no way of proving I was Indian. My mother, not my father, helped me by teaching me an Indian word. She wrote it out so I, too, could learn to write it. I remember it till this day: 'Chauggaug agaugmanchaugagaug-chabunagungamaug.' It is the name of a lake in Western Massachusetts. Luckily, I have never had to use it.

DAVID PLANTE

"For high school, I went to La Salle Academy and was taught by Christian Brothers. For college, I went to Boston College, and was taught by Jesuits. In 1959, I went to the University of Louvain, in Belgium, to study for a year. I studied French Literature and some philosophy. That year, I was in an automobile accident, outside Paris, in which a friend from the university was killed. His name was Tom, and I often think that, not Tom, but I died, and, not I, but Tom is alive.

"When I got back to America, I lived in New York for a while, and helped research and write up on men's barbershops, foreign language newspapers, ethnic churches, bookshops for a guide to New York, called *Hart's Guide to New York*. I left long before the book was published. I went to Boston, and taught English to foreign students at the Boston School of Modern Languages. Then I taught French to young American students at Danvers Preparatory School, in Danvers, Massachusetts. All the while I was writing short stories and novels.

"In 1966, I came to London, where I am resident. I go often to France, Italy, and Greece. Being out of America has helped me to write about America.

"I have another twenty novels to write before I die."

David Plante's novels are primarily concerned with family life, or more particularly sibling life, and the process of maturation. *The Ghost of Henry James*, his first, studies in sixty-seven short chapters of oblique dialogue the relationship between four brothers and a sister who wander between Boston, New York, London, and Rome, chronically unhappy and disillusioned with themselves, each other, and practically everyone else they encounter. "The events," wrote J. A. Avant, "—mysterious deaths, homosexual incest, etc.—have no meaning except in that they further the book's skillfully created tone, which is wonderfully eerie and perverse. The characters, about whom we never really learn anything, don't develop, as far as we can tell; they simply become absorbed into the bizarre atmosphere. One enjoys this novel, but it is really nothing but shades and nuances." Jonathan Raban thought the novel "splendidly intelligent and ambitious. . . . Everywhere there are subtly managed echoes of James. . . . James's ghost broods over the book; an unattainable ideal, both of a state of fiction and of a state of fully realized relationships."

Slides is virtually a mirror image of the previous novel. Once again, sixty-seven impressionistic chapters attempt to delineate the relationship among five extremely self-absorbed Americans in their twenties. As a kind of touchstone, this novel uses Nathaniel Hawthorne's *The Marble Faun* much as the earlier one used Henry James. Anthony Bailey considered that Plante's descriptions of sexuality "possess an honest and moving precision," and Jonathan Strong, remarking that "puritanical guilt still operates in the minds of these young people," observed, "This is no novel of communal love. In that sense it is an honest novel, because no love comes free. But Plante never lets us understand why his five characters are so obsessed with and disturbed by their emotional relations, and therefore it is also a disappointing book."

Plante's next three novels grew increasingly experimental in form. *Relatives* is a chronologically arranged series of short dialogues in which several characters, according to Thomas LeClair, "talk and talk and talk 'to extend themselves until they reached the edges of a sustaining context,' but the context achieved at the end of the novel has no more significance to the reader than a fence around a dreary house of mirrors." *The Darkness of the Body* was felt by some critics to be even more oblique. Valentine Cunningham complained of Plante's "persistent vagueness about people and places— the refusal to specify which cities or countries are being lived and loved in, on grounds that it's

the inner topography that matters." The *Times Literary Supplement*'s reviewer found the characters' behavior "childishly perverse and many of the metaphysical passages of reflective description seem hopelessly inflated." *Figures in Bright Air* was described by Susannah Clapp as abandoning "even the intermittent verisimilitude of his previous books; it describes in long and excited swirls of prose the kind of fictions people use to describe themselves and their relations with others—and the implications of writing fiction." Plante was described by Neil Hepburn as "a literary Gawain bent on rescuing the English novel from durance vile [he means from naturalism]. And an appallingly lonely and dangerous business it must be: there are few enough in England willing to allow justice to his cause, let alone to encourage him in it. Its sponsors, living and dead, are all abroad, where they harbour the strangest notions about what the novel, given its liberty, will do for us all."

The saga of the Francoeur family occupies Plante's next three novels, *The Family*, *The Country*, and *The Woods*. The narrator in each is Daniel, the sixth of seven sons, who describes a world, in Mary Gordon's words, "of silence, of baffled and balked love, of pain borne stoically, of Indian cruelties and natural ties, of French Catholic pieties and the bleak light of failed New England cities." These novels mark a clear shift in Plante's writing away from antinaturalistic experimentation toward the minute descriptions of the inner workings of a family and a character he knows very well. J. B. Hemesath praised *The Family* for its realistic and positive descriptions of family life and of the city; Anne Stevenson thought it "a meticulous laying bare of what must be raw experience. . . . It is Daniel's adolescent sensitivity we follow as it widens into an understanding of the complicated yet narrowly innocent relationship between his mother, Reena, and his father, Jim Francoeur— as, in turn, their relationship is strained by the difficult love and need for independence of their sons."

In *The Country* Daniel is a grown man, returning from England, where he is a writer, to see his mortally ill father and attend to his mother, who is going insane. "The madness of the one Francoeur woman," in Mary Gordon's view, "is the crack in the dark rock that is the foundation of the family. Madness, like language, laughter, hope, are associated in this novel with the female, and the relentless attempts of the family men to push these elements out of their lives lead, in the view of Daniel, the narrator, only to insanity and sorrow."

Daniel Francoeur is a college freshman in *The*

Woods, a series of three interconnecting stories, and his intense, adolescent self-absorption is at the book's very center. "He closed his eyes. He was aware of so much, and it all escaped him. With his eyes closed, he felt his head expand, and it seemed to him he didn't have a body. He was aware of so many things." The book recounts Daniel's strange half-affair with an older woman and his attempt to reconcile his embryonic pacifism with the militaristic views of his elder brother, a Marine officer. Edith Milton called it "a very short and very dense novel. And it has its faults. It could be accused of lacking resolution, of being elliptical to the point of being obscure, of indulging a hero so passive that next to him Oblomov would look like an activist. But it is also a brilliantly original work, intense, illuminating and compelling. Eccentric enough to be beyond the pale of most critical judgment, its virtues are certainly worth considerably more than its faults."

Plante's *Difficult Women: A Memoir of Three* is a personal and intimate memoir of his friendship with Jean Rhys, Sonia Orwell, and Germaine Greer, all women he met in London and all of whom, while making demands on him, also gave him vital insights into his own artistic and emotional development. The most poignant portrait is of the frail, alcoholic, dying Jean Rhys whom he assisted in the composition of her autobiography, *Smile Please* (1982). He frankly exploited the literary associations offered him by George Orwell's widow Sonia. "Here," Lorna Sage writes in the *Times Literary Supplement*, "Plante's self-interest becomes creepily obvious." And in his relationship with the aggressive and "unpredictable" Germaine Greer, he explored his own homosexuality. Controversial, painfully candid, but always fascinating, Plante "neither distorts his subject nor pushes his prose out of shape," Vivian Gornick writes in the *New York Times Book Review*; "it only indicates the source of his engagement and reveals his wholly admirable ability to convert necessity into virtue by bringing these extremely interesting women to brilliant, mythic life."

PRINCIPAL WORKS: *Fiction*—The Ghost of Henry James, 1970; Slides, 1971; Relatives, 1972; The Darkness of the Body, 1974; Figures in Bright Air, 1976; The Family, 1978; The Country, 1981; The Woods, 1982; The Foreigner, 1984. *Non-fiction*—Difficult Women: A Memoir of Three, 1983.

ABOUT: Contemporary Authors, first revision series 37–40, 1979; Contemporary Literary Criticism 7, 1977; Dictionary of Literary Biography Yearbook, 1983. *Periodicals*—Book World November 1, 1970; Harper's January 1983; Library Journal August 1970; August 1971; June 1, 1978; Listener February 7, 1974; April 1, 1976; New Republic October 7, 1981; October 11, 1982; New Statesman March 13, 1970; March 12, 1971; February 1, 1974; April 2, 1976; March 13, 1981; New York Review of Books November 5, 1970; August 17, 1978; November 19, 1981; December 16, 1982; New York Times Book Review November 29, 1970; August 22, 1971; October 20, 1974; July 2, 1978; October 4, 1981; August 15, 1982; January 16, 1983; October 7, 1984; Spectator April 10, 1976; Times Literary Supplement March 19, 1970; April 16, 1971; February 1, 1974; April 28, 1978; March 13, 1981; January 29, 1982; February 25, 1983.

PLUNKETT, JAMES (JAMES PLUNKETT KELLY) (May 21, 1920–   ), Irish novelist, dramatist, and short story writer, son of Patrick and Cecilia (Cannon) Kelly, was born in Dublin, a city whose contemporary history and physical location permeates all his work.

Educated at the Christian Brothers school, Synge Street, and at the College of Music, where he studied the violin, Plunkett's first job was as a clerk for the Dublin Gas Company. Following his father's example, he became active in the Irish Trade Union movement, and was employed as an officer of the Workers' Union of Ireland under James Larkin, one of the heroes of Irish labor and an embodiment of historical potential as portrayed by Plunkett in his first novel, *Strumpet City*. Plunkett held his union post from 1945 to 1955, leaving it to take a position in the drama department of Radio Eireann (Ireland's national radio service). This post strengthened the interest he had shown in radio drama in the early fifties, when he successfully adapted some of his short stories ("Dublin Fusilier," "Mercy") for the medium. His greatest success as a radio dramatist came in 1954 with a production of *Big Jim*, a play about James Larkin, which he subsequently rewrote for the stage and entitled *The Risen People*. This play had a successful run at the Abbey Theatre, Dublin, in 1958.

Plunkett moved from radio to television drama production with the inauguration of an Irish television service in 1960, and has continued to work there since as a producer. He has written a number of television plays, and his *The Gems She Wore: A Book of Irish Places* arose out of a television travelogue that he wrote and produced. Plunkett's work as a dramatist is seen to best advantage in *The Risen People*, which in its depiction of Irish life recalls the work of Sean O'Casey. Plunkett's main contribution to recent Irish writing, however, is his prose fiction.

This medium has given him an international audience: *Strumpet City* and his second novel, *Farewell Companions*, were best-sellers, the former selling particularly well in England and

America. Both novels are consolidations of material and themes previously treated in his writing. The historical background of *The Risen People* provides the *milieu* for *Strumpet City,* while "the world of small salaries" depicted in the early short stories collected in *The Trusting and the Maimed* provide the basis for Plunkett's second novel.

The author has described *Strumpet City* as "a picture of Dublin in seven years, 1907 to 1914. . . . Joyce wrote about the lower middle class, and O'Casey about the slums of the period. I was concerned with finding a form in which all the elements would fit." The novel is certainly panoramic, depicting suburbs and inner city with loving fidelity. The climactic event of those years, the strike and lockout of the Dublin Transport workers in 1913, is the action's centerpiece—this event marked the literary conscience of the time, as Yeats' "September 1913" records. Plunkett responds to Yeats' refrain "Romantic Ireland's dead and gone" by presenting a naturalistic account of working-class Dublin life, and by elevating James Larkin's tenacious and resourceful leadership of the strike to heroic status. The novel is the author's most complete statement of his secular, populist socialism.

No doubt the fact that Plunkett was drawing on his father's experiences in *Strumpet City* is one reason why the working-class sections of the novel are so touching and persuasive. Their impact, however, is diminished by the novel's panoramic ambitions. The suburban, middle-class interludes seem stagey and pallid, and while they offer a wider view of Irish impoverishment, alienation and heartbreak, they do not possess the compelling interest of their working-class counterparts. Also crucial to the novel's moral view is Plunkett's portrayal of the Church as an institution that fails to perform its spiritual and social responsibilities.

The criticism that *Strumpet City* is less than the sum of its parts and that its panoramic conception results in an episodic structure may be applied even more justly to *Farewell Companions.* To some extent, all of the characters in Plunkett's first novel are victims of history. Now, however, the world has moved on a generation and Plunkett speaks of his own world between the end of the Irish Civil War (1923) and the start of World War II. Within the frame, however, there is only simple, poignant personal time measured not by momentous historical events but by difficult personal decisions. Tim McDonagh, the protagonist, is brought to rediscover "the childhood truth" at the end of the novel: that "there was a thief unceasingly at work in the world who made use of love to break

the heart." Although this conclusion is reached after Tim's heart has been broken, it also crystallizes the mood of constraint, frustration and discouragement in which Tim and his two pals, Brian and Des, grow up. And as though to give conclusive expression to that mood, the novel ends up with the friends' dispersal. Hence the title, which is also a phrase from a ballad about Robert Emmet (executed in 1803), the darling of romantic Ireland, an echo which draws attention not only to the novel's ballad-like simplicity and plaintiveness, but also to Plunkett's sense of the death of romance as a literary form applicable to contemporary Ireland.

Typically, however, Plunkett's good-natured, fair-minded approach to his material leads him to consider it from various angles. In *The Gems She Wore,* he remarks: "Despite its tensions and its tragedies, Dublin was a good city to grow up in." Similarly, in *Farewell Companions,* the three youngsters are not entirely immured in an unpromising environment, but can respond to natural landscape, particularly the Dublin mountains—"They are very beautiful, those mountains," Plunkett wrote in *Gems,* "much more to me than mere landscape."

Less successful, however, is the character of O'Sheehan, who calls himself Oisín (an Irish accent pronounces the names alike), the mythological character who was transported to Tír na n-Og (the Land of Youth). When he returned after an interval of a hundred years, he found Ireland Christianized, much to his disgust. O'Sheehan, extravagantly well-versed in ancient Irish lore and legend, and disposed to timetraveling, expresses in his rhapsodic speeches a colorful and authentically Irish alternative to dull contemporary cultural and moral norms. His eccentricity and isolation in *Farewell Companions* suggests that he is serving Plunkett's objectives rather than the other characters' needs. Instead of identifying with this lively embodiment of cultural tradition, the trio of youngsters repudiate it. Brian and Des join the Royal Air Force at the outbreak of war, echoing the close of *Strumpet City,* where Fitz, the defeated striker, is last seen bound for the trenches of World War I. More shockingly, Tim decides to become a priest, which under the circumstances represents not only a definitive break with the past but an attempt to become immune to time.

The success of Plunkett's novels has overshadowed his short stories, which he had been writing for twenty-five years before tackling the longer form. It may be, indeed, that his novels are episodic because they are conceived by a short story writer. In fact, *Farewell Companions,* considered structurally, seems to owe something to the technique of using one set of characters for a number of stories, as shown in *The Trusting and the Maimed*. One important feature of Plunkett's stories is that they relocate Dublin on the Irish literary map. Thanks to the stories of Sean O'Faolain and Frank O'Connor, Ireland in literature had become a largely non-metropolitan place. Although Plunkett's stories hardly rival Joyce's *Dubliners* in texture or finesse, they do communicate some of the emotional negation and spiritual poverty that made Joyce's stories so striking. Occasionally, the stories employ Joycean narrative style, but in general the resemblances are thematic. With minor exceptions, Plunkett's Dublin stories depict the unpromising lives of shabby clerks and the pitiable existence of slum children. His treatment of material from the latter category (in such stories as "Weep for our Pride," "The Half-Crown" and "Janey Mary") is distinguished by the strength of the sympathy extended to the victims. The indignity of poverty is expressed by an imagination fully attuned to its gratuitousness and its inevitability.

Their undoubted humanity, their tacit but earnest moral sense, and their crucial attachment to Dublin past and present (past represented in "Mercy" and "Dublin Fusilier") assure Plunkett's stories a place in the history of the form in Ireland. Their importance, however, is due to their sensitivity to social and cultural conditions, and not to their artistic accomplishments. Almost all are hampered by structural awkwardness; their naturalism has an obtuseness about it; they are strangely deficient, for the most part, in their rendering of Dublin talk.

James Plunkett is not among the first rank of Irish writers of his generation. Nevertheless, his work has helped to establish a body of contemporary Irish writing that is commercial but genuinely involved with Irish life. His fidelity to place is a further mark of his integrity, and his life and work support his claim "that nothing much happens to a writer after the age of twenty or so that will affect his work."

Plunkett married Valerie Koblitz in 1945; they have four children. His home is in Dublin.

PRINCIPAL WORKS: The Trusting and the Maimed, 1959; Strumpet City, 1969; The Gems She Wore, 1972; Farewell Companions, 1977; Collected Short Stories, 1977; The Risen People, 1978.

ABOUT: Contemporary Authors 53–56, 1975; Cahiers Irlandais 1, 1976; Dictionary of Literary Biography 14, 1983.

PORTER, ANDREW (BRIAN) (August 26, 1928–   ), South African-born music critic and translator was born in Cape Town, the son of Andrew Ferdinand Porter and the former Vera Sybil Bloxham. He received his primary education at the Diocesan College, Rondebosch; while still a schoolboy he accompanied the cellist Albert Coates at rehearsals and played continuo during his performances. He was organ scholar at University College, Oxford—the organ scholar's chief duty is to play at college chapel services—from 1947 to 1950, while reading English. As a student he contributed occasional reviews of Oxford musical events to the *Manchester Guardian*, and soon after receiving his bachelor's degree began his career as a critic. He was part-time assistant in turn to Desmond Shawe-Taylor on the *New Statesman*, to Frank Howes on the London *Times*, and to Richard Capell on the *Daily Telegraph* before being hired in 1955 as the first music critic of the *Financial Times*. It was on that paper, with considerably more space allotted him and a staff of five assistants, that Porter developed his distinctive style—magisterial yet personal, unhurried and discursive, and always careful to respect the integrity of the work under discussion. "My interest," he wrote in 1978, "is usually in the work itself, in what it has meant and what it can mean, and then in the details of individual performances insofar as they illumine or fail to illumine the composer's intention and meaning."

In 1972, Porter accepted the invitation of William Shawn, editor of the *New Yorker*, to become music critic of that magazine for one season. He went back to England the following year as a visiting fellow of All Souls College, Oxford, but returned to the *New Yorker* in the autumn of 1974. A critic's position on the venerable weekly represented the ideal critical environment: "I was invited, encouraged, to attempt a kind of criticism for which the British press had ever less space—part descriptive chronicle, part essay in which a particular performance may be viewed as the latest addition to the long history of a work and, more personally, to a critic's experience of it."

Porter's reviews for the magazine have been collected into several books. The first, *A Musical Season*, contained the results of his first year's stint as music critic and included, besides a great deal of space devoted to his often-remarked interest in opera performances, a considerable number of well-informed critiques of composers, conductors, directors, and choreographers, and of various performers—singers, instrumental soloists, and dancers. "He is not above being digressive," wrote Louis Snyder, "but he does not have a permanent chip on his shoulder. Besides,

ANDREW PORTER

it would be a mistake to imagine that *A Musical Season* is limited to dry recapitulation of past concert and operatic events. [He] has some shrewd, practical observations to make about the American music scene." John Yohalem concurred: "He makes it all fascinating. At these descriptions the music-lover longs to hear things that never appealed to him before. Porter is thus especially good on recent compositions, music of increasing popularity but still strange and fearsome to much of the public. . . . For the devotee of opera, ballet, modern music and, to a lesser degree, symphonic style, chamber styles, and lieder, Porter is, in tranquillity, a well-stocked curiosity shop of information you always wanted to know or never knew existed about your favorite objects of art." Similarly enthusiastic notices greeted *Music of Three Seasons: 1974–1977* and *Music of Three More Seasons.*

In practicing what he calls "my own chosen sideline"—translating operas into English—Porter has firmly staked out his position on a subject of longstanding disagreement among opera lovers. In 1978 he wrote of "my repeated insistence that when music with words is performed, those words should be comprehended; that when operas are sung in a foreign tongue, librettos with translations should be available in advance; that in the concert hall text, translations, and light to read them by should be provided. A concern for the whole meaning of a composition, not just voice fancying, is at the base of this." His translation of Wagner's *The Ring of the Nibelung* was commissioned by the English National Opera and performed and recorded by them and other

companies; it appeared in lavishly illustrated book form in 1976. He has also published his English version of Wagner's *Tristan and Isolde.* Critics have generally considered his among the best of the many English translations of Wagner that have appeared over the past century, and have particularly praised his respect for the literary as well as the singing qualities of Wagner's librettos. In addition to other translations from the German—works by Handel and Haydn, Mozart's *The Magic Flute* and Strauss' *Intermezzo*—he has also extended his translating efforts to Italian opera, where performances in English are rarer and the literary quality of the librettos far more variable. He has translated works by Rossini, Mozart's *Lucio Silla,* and *La Forza del Destino, Don Carlos, Otello,* and *Falstaff* by Verdi.

Porter's chief scholarly interest has long been the operas of Verdi. His most important discovery, in the library of the Paris Opéra, was the full original version of *Don Carlos,* which had been composed in 1867 for that house and lost for more than a century. He was on the editorial executive committee of the *New Grove Dictionary of Music and Musicians,* and wrote the 1980 edition's thirty-page entry on Verdi. This article, especially its section entitled "Composition, Style," was the subject of a scathing attack by the pianist and musicologist Charles Rosen in a generally favorable review of the *New Grove* in the *New York Review of Books.* Porter's treatment of the technical aspects of Verdi's music, according to Rosen, is "filled with mistakes of analysis . . . of so elementary a nature that it is astonishing to find them in a musical encyclopedia of such high standards." The critic detailed these errors at considerable length, adding further blame for Porter's alleged failure to include any "convincing assessment of Verdi's relation to his contemporaries." Readers who sensed that the attack by Rosen was motivated, at least in part, by the spleen endemic among critics were perplexed when, far from initiating a long polemic on Verdian musicology, the review and its many allegations of error elicited no immediate response from Porter.

Among Porter's contributions to music criticism may be cited his innovative editorship of *Musical Times* from 1960 to 1967 and his regular contributions to the magazines *Opera* and *Gramophone.* He was a founding member of the editorial board of the review *19th Century Music* (1977) and founding editor of the newsletter of the American Institute of Verdi Studies (1976). He was named Ernest Bloch lecturer at the University of California at Berkeley in 1980–81 and has also undertaken some teaching at the City University of New York.

works: *Criticism*—A Musical Season, 1974; Music of Three Seasons: 1974–1977, 1978; Music of Three More Seasons, 1981. *As translator*—Wagner's Ring, 1976; Wagner's Tristan and Isolde, 1981.

about: Contemporary Authors 53–56, 1975; The New Grove Dictionary of Music and Musicians, 1980; Who's Who in America, 1983–84. *Periodicals*—Choice April 1977; May 1979; Christian Science Monitor July 17, 1974; Commentary October 1974; Library Journal June 15, 1974; January 1, 1977; November 1, 1978; Music Library Association Notes June 1979; New Republic September 21, 1974; December 2, 1978; New York Review of Books May 28, 1981; August 31, 1981; New York Times Book Review July 7, 1974.

CHAIM POTOK

*POTOK, CHAIM (February 17, 1929–), American novelist and historian, was born in the Bronx, the eldest child of Benjamin Max Potok, a jeweler and watchmaker, and Mollie (Friedman) Potok. Potok's parents were Jewish immigrants from Poland, and their son's upbringing was very Orthodox if not quite Hasidic. That upbringing has been the inspiration for each of Potok's five novels; all are set, in whole or in part, in Orthodox Jewish communities in Brooklyn and the Bronx during the thirties, forties, and fifties. "Just as Faulkner came from the South," he told Philadelphia's *Inside* magazine in 1981, "I came from Jewish Orthodox. And writers who write seriously, write about what they know best. This is what I know best."

As a child, Potok attended yeshivas, studied the Talmud, and observed the rituals of Orthodox Judaism, but artistic impulses were pulling him in another direction. Like the hero of *My Name Is Asher Lev*, Potok had a precocious talent for drawing and painting which his parents could not comprehend. In his community, he told *Newsday* in 1982, the arts were considered "at best a waste of time and at worst an act of sinfulness." Before long, however, young Potok had switched his allegiance from painting to writing, which was "less an attack on Jewish religious tradition than painting since the written word and sacred texts are the basis of Judaism."

The immediate impulse behind Potok's writing was his chance discovery of Evelyn Waugh's *Brideshead Revisited* when he was fourteen or fifteen. It was the first serious adult novel he had read and it changed him. "I found myself inside a world the merest existence of which I had known nothing about," he told *Newsday*. "I lived more deeply inside the world in that book than I lived inside my own world, for the time it took me to read it." For the next five years, Potok filled his spare time with the study of such masters as Hemingway, Faulkner, Joyce, and Mann,

°pō´ tok, hī´ em

and with his own apprentice writing. Inevitably, he moved further from the fundamentalist beliefs of his parents.

At Yeshiva University Potok majored in English and graduated summa cum laude in 1950. By the time of his senior year he had abandoned Orthodoxy completely, thus making himself more than ever an exile from the world in which he had grown up. Potok continued his education at the Jewish Theological Seminary of America, a Conservative institution in upper Manhattan which permitted a more broad-minded, historical approach to Judaic studies than he had yet known. In 1954 Potok received an M.A. in Hebrew literature from the seminary, as well as his rabbinical ordination (although he has never worked as a "pulpit rabbi").

In the following decade Potok worked variously as national director of the Conservative movement's Leaders Training Fellowship, as a chaplain with the United States Army in Korea, and as a teacher at the University of Judaism in Los Angeles and the Jewish Theological Seminary. He also found time to earn a Ph.D. in philosophy from the University of Pennsylvania (granted in 1965), with a dissertation on "The Rationalism and Skepticism of Solomon Maimon." Perhaps the most significant of these experiences was the time spent with Jewish and Christian soldiers in Korea from 1955 to 1957. Potok would later draw on that experience in his most mystical work, *The Book of Lights*. And it was in Korea that he wrote his first novel, a Hemingwayesque account of army life which was almost but not quite accepted for publication. Yet that book spawned another, which, reworked and trimmed-down, in 1967 became *The Chosen*.

The Chosen received generally favorable if not over-enthusiastic reviews; like many a first-published novel, it had its share of technical flaws, duly noted by the critics. But it was an immediate best-seller and it remains Potok's most popular book. The simplicity of the story may account for part of its appeal. It concerns the friendship and rivalry of two Jewish boys in the Williamsburg section of Brooklyn in the late forties. One, Danny Saunders, is the son of a respected and powerful Hasidic rabbi whose spiritual mantle Danny is expected some day to inherit; the other, Reuven Malter, the son of a mild Orthodox scholar, is at ease in the secular world which Danny secretly wishes to enter. The tensions between traditionalism and modernism, faith and doubt, no less than the characteristic New York setting that embodies them, are thus established from the start of Potok's work. Potok has continued to explore these tensions in a more complex and less schematic fashion, but *The Chosen* retains its peculiar freshness. It was turned into a successful film in 1981, starring Rod Steiger and directed by Jeremy Cagan. Potok himself wrote the screenplay.

The Promise, which Potok originally conceived of as the second half of *The Chosen*, follows the two protagonists of that novel into young adulthood. Danny Saunders, whose fascination with Freudian psychology in *The Chosen* had lured him away from the faith of his father, earns a doctorate in psychology at Columbia and begins clinical work with a difficult test case, while Reuven Malter studies for his rabbinical ordination and confronts the task of reconciling modern textual criticism (and his own humanistic outlook) with the writings of the Talmud. In each case the conflict is as much inner directed as outer and centers on existential questions of Jewish and personal identity. This pattern recurs in all of Potok's fiction.

Many critics thought that *The Promise* was burdened with the same flaws as *The Chosen* (e.g., wordiness, inadequate dramatization), yet lacked the earlier novel's corresponding freshness. Others, however, while conceding weaknesses in Potok's craftsmanship, praised the novel for its depth and seriousness. Hugh Nissenson, in the *New York Times Book Review*, thought *The Promise* "a better book" than *The Chosen* because of the greater complexity of its theological conceptions. Nissenson analyzed those conceptions with some perspicacity. "On the deepest level," he wrote, "*The Promise* is about Jewish identity. Each character tries to define himself in relation to Jewish tradition. This

is never a parochial concern because of Potok's heightened awareness that this is the greatest gamble of all: a people who have wagered their existence throughout history on the promise made by God to Abraham that they will be self-conscious agents of redemption. Nor does it make any difference, Potok implies, whether the assumption is true or not. The wager has been made."

With *My Name Is Asher Lev*, Potok's technical facility seemed to have caught up with his artistic ambitions, or so was the opinion of many of the book's reviewers. In *Saturday Review*, Robert J. Milch wrote that Potok's Jewish concerns, "though just as pronounced as in the previous novels, are not defined by a superior auctorial voice but progressively define themselves in the course of the ongoing revelation provided by action and character."

The story is narrated by Asher Lev, the only child of devout Hasidic parents living in the Crown Heights section of Brooklyn, who is possessed of (and possessed by) an enormous talent for painting and drawing. This talent scandalizes his father (painting contravenes the second commandment, "Thou shalt not make unto thee a graven image"), pains his mother, and brings turmoil and confusion on the boy himself. A wise rabbi intervenes, however, and sends the adolescent Asher to study with the great abstract painter and sculptor (and non-believing Jew), Jacob Kahn. Asher's art increasingly alienates him from his parents, as he goes to college, has his first gallery show, and studies the masters in Europe for a year. The final break comes over the unveiling of his masterpiece, "Brooklyn Crucifixion," which, in employing the taboo imagery of Christ's death, causes his parents unspeakable anguish.

Guy Davenport thought the novel was written "with deepest and total understanding," and called it "little short of a work of genius." David Stern disagreed. Writing in *Commentary*, a magazine that has generally been hostile to Potok's work, Stern complained that Potok's "portrait of the artist" was "without distinction" and that his descriptions of Asher Lev's paintings were "banal and sentimental." More seriously, Stern took exception to what he considered Potok's assumption of "the impossibility of existing in both the religious and the secular spheres—an assumption whose net effect amounts in the end to a kind of apology for assimilation. The schizophrenic trap of living a double life and of speaking in two, often exclusive languages—the subject of all of Potok's novels—is precisely what he has been most unsuccessful either in depicting or in attempting to resolve."

In the Beginning is set in the familiar territory of the Bronx and once more concerns an intelligent, sensitive Orthodox protagonist who must accommodate himself to the modern world as he makes his way into adulthood. The particular challenge that David Lurie faces is that of secular Bible scholarship. David realizes that such scholarship has often been used as a weapon against Jews, yet, to the chagrin of his strictly orthodox father, he moves into that arena as a means of interpreting Jewish tradition from a modern vantage point. A larger conflict, and a new one in Potok's work, is that of anti-Semitism in general. From David's schoolboy sufferings at the hands of a bigoted street-bully to his pilgrimage to the Bergen Belsen concentration camp two years after the war had ended, anti-Semitism informs David Lurie's understanding of Judaism.

In the Beginning was treated with respect by most critics, with scorn by a few. Among the former was Michael Irwin, who wrote in the *Times Literary Supplement,* "Chaim Potok has remarkable gifts of recall. He catches beautifully the atmosphere of a family party or a school quarrel. Rarer than this is the skill with which he shows how what a child learns and what it experiences are fused and transformed by the imagination. As an evocation of a religious childhood *In the Beginning* is impressive." Daphne Merkin, on the other hand, dismissed Potok's fourth book as "an all-but-negligible variation on the theme of his first three" and as a falsification and sentimentalization of Orthodox Judaism. Her article in *Commentary,* "Why Potok Is Popular," remains the most unsympathetic assessment of the author in print.

Potok's *The Book of Lights,* ranges further afield than his earlier works—there are extended sequences in Korea and Japan—but the protagonist is very much in the line of Potok's other heroes. Gershon Loren is a young New York rabbi who finds in the mystical Kabbalah an affinity with his own spiritual needs that the more practical Talmud does not offer. In a restless search for religious enlightenment, Gershon travels to post-truce Korea as an Army chaplain and makes frequent excursions to Japan. He is later joined by his friend Arthur Leiden, an American Jew ridden with guilt over the part his father (a well-known physicist) played in the creation of the atomic bomb. In these "pagan" lands untouched by Judaism, Gershon contemplates the presence of God in a new and strange light, while Arthur attempts to expiate his guilt at the places of the bomb's destruction.

The Book of Lights struck some critics as Potok's darkest, most somber work; it was certainly his most ambitious. Johanna Kaplan, in the *New York Times Book Review,* called it "powerful, controversial and enigmatic." Potok himself has described the novel as a culmination of his work. As he said in *Inside* magazine, "This is where the others were leading me, I guess."

At the suggestion of his editor at Knopf, Potok undertook a personal history of the Jews before beginning *The Book of Lights. Wanderings: Chaim Potok's History of the Jews* was a lavishly illustrated and, for the most part, well-received volume which successfully combined scholarship and readability. Potok's other non-fiction includes articles for the periodical press, his screenplay for *The Chosen,* and editorial work on the new translation of the Hebrew Bible by the Jewish Publication Society of America, an organization he has served since 1965.

Chaim Potok lives in Merion, Pennsylvania, a suburb of Philadelphia, with his wife, Adena (Mosevitsky) Potok, a psychiatric social worker. They were married in 1958 and have three children, Rena, Naama, and Akiva. The Potoks also have an apartment in Jerusalem.

In interviews and in articles, Potok appears as a deeply serious man with a professorial manner, passionately committed to his own beliefs. In a 1978 interview in *Christianity Today,* he summed up his philosophy: "I would prefer to say that the universe is meaningful, with pockets of apparent meaninglessness, than to say it is meaningless with pockets of apparent meaningfulness. In other words I have questions either way. I see it as my task to attempt to infuse with sense those elements that make no sense."

PRINCIPAL WORKS: *Fiction*—The Chosen, 1967; The Promise, 1969; My Name Is Asher Lev, 1972; In the Beginning, 1975; The Book of Lights, 1981; Davita's Harp, 1984. *Non-fiction*—Wanderings: Chaim Potok's History of the Jews, 1978.

ABOUT: Contemporary Authors, first revision series 17–20, 1976; Contemporary Literary Criticism 2, 1974; 7, 1977; 14, 1980; Who's Who in America, 1983–1984. *Periodicals*—Christian Century May 16, 1984; Christianity Today September 8, 1978; Commentary October 1972; February 1976; March 1982; Current Biography May 1983; Inside Winter 1981; New York Times Book Review April 30, 1967; September 14, 1969; October 19, 1975; October 11, 1981; Newsday November 15, 1982; Publishers Weekly April 3, 1967; May 22, 1978; Saturday Review April 15, 1972; Times Literary Supplement April 9, 1976.

*POULET, GEORGES (November 29, 1902–), Belgian literary critic, was born in the village of Chênée, in the Ardennes, the son of

°po͞o lä´

Georges François Poulet and the former Anne Lion. He studied law at the University of Liège, receiving his doctorate in that subject in 1925. By that time, however, he was convinced that literature would be his life's work, and he earned a Ph.D. in literary studies from Liège in 1927, the year before he took up a post in the department of French at the University of Edinburgh, Scotland, where he remained for twenty-three years, eventually becoming professor of French. He has also taught at Johns Hopkins University (1951–57), and ended his full-time teaching career at the University of Zürich, Switzerland (1957–73). Since the mid-1970s he has lived in Nice, on the French Riviera, and has often lectured at the university there.

"More than any other," wrote Paul de Man, "the criticism of Georges Poulet conveys the impression of possessing the complexity and the scope of a genuine work of literature, the intricacy of a city which has its avenues, its dead-ends, its underground labyrinths and panoramic lookouts." Poulet's "meditation" has taken "the whole of Western literature for its theme." His principal method, which he has greatly refined over the years, is to search, in the study of a writer, for the "point of departure," an experience, in de Man's words, "that is both initial and central and around which the entire work can be organized." Poulet was using the term as early as 1924, when, in an essay on Henri Bergson, he defined it as "a kind of postulate located in the character of the protagonist as well as in the setting of the future action." In essay after essay, over the next six decades, he developed the psychological and subjective nuances of this critical position. "I want at all costs," he has written, "to save the subjectivity of literature."

Poulet's chief critical monument is the massive *Études sur le temps humain,* a four-volume work of which the first two have appeared in English translation. Volume one, *Études sur le temps humain* (1949, *Studies in Human Time*), comprises separate essays on most of the giants of classical French literature: the philosophers Montaigne, Pascal, Descartes, Diderot, and Rousseau; the dramatists Corneille, Racine, and Molière; the nineteenth-century masters de Vigny, Flaubert, Baudelaire, Gautier, and Valéry; and Proust, the intensive study of whose works has occupied Poulet for many years. The American edition contains a special appendix, "Time and American Writers," which treats in somewhat briefer fashion all the great nineteenth-century American poets and novelists, plus James and Eliot. The book was originally published in French in Edinburgh, then was reissued in Paris to great critical acclaim, winning the Sainte-Beuve prize. René Wellek wrote, in a review of the American edition, that the book is "the achievement of an original mind who sees things directly, penetratingly, from a new point of view as things have never been seen before."

Volume two, *La Distance intérieure* (*The Interior Distance,* 1952), comprises essays on Marivaux, Balzac, Hugo, Musset, and Mallarmé, among others. In his preface, Poulet describes the subjectivity implied by his critical method. Interior distance, he writes, "separates me from, or draws me closer to, that which I am able to think. For all that I think is in myself who think it. The distance is not merely an interval; it is an ambient milieu, a field of union. . . . Objectively, literature is made up of formal works the contents of which stand out with a greater or lesser clarity. . . . Subjectively, literature is not at all formal. It is the reality of a thought that is always particular, always anterior and posterior to any object; one which, across and beyond all objects, ceaselessly reveals the strange and natural impossibility in which it finds itself, of ever having an objective existence." Such dense and exalted language, almost vatic in its intensity, is characteristic of Poulet; an existential tone of anguished uncertainty inhabits the whole of his work and expresses, in de Man's opinion, "a constant solicitude for literary survival." This volume won the Grand Prix de la Critique Littéraire and the French Academy's Durchon prize in philosophy.

Poulet continued the series with *Le Point de départ* (The Point of Departure, 1964), a consideration of Bernanos, Char, Éluard, Perse, and Sartre, among other writers, and *Mesure de l'instant* (Measure of the Moment, 1968), which covers some of the same writers as the earlier volumes, plus such contemporaries as Julien Green. He has latterly turned more and more to the study of modern writers: he notes that in the novels of Green, for example, "there always comes a moment in which consciousness and happiness, self-awareness and sensation are mysteriously joined in an experience which is the point of departure, the apogee, or even the endpoint of their history."

Among his other works is *Les Métamorphoses du cercle* (*The Metamorphoses of the Circle,* 1961), an examination of the persistent recurrence of the circle as emblem of the elusive mysteriousness of the universe, considering the works of Pascal, Balzac, Flaubert, Baudelaire, and the Americans Poe, James, and Eliot. Wallace Fowlie considered Poulet's language "a ceaseless effort to reach an identification with the conscience of the writer he is studying. It is a struggle to bring about some closeness between the writer's language and the critic's. In these studies . . . the critic . . . ends by prolonging the thought of the writer. He yearns to live in the life of the writer. And yet the critic's writing is never an empty echoing of the novelist or the poet. It is a deepening of the original work, a contemplation of the entire expanse of the work, and precisely that kind of contemplation that the writer himself never enjoyed." *L'Espace proustien* (*Proustian Space,* 1963) is a short, difficult book about *À la recherche du temps perdu* which sees the novel not only as a search for lost time but as, even more essentially, an attempt to reintegrate, reformulate, and reinvent, by means of the intermittent character of memory, the fragmented nature of exterior and interior space. A considerable number of pages are devoted to the differences between Proust's idea of space and that of Bergson, a writer with whom he has often been compared.

Poulet's other works include: *La Conscience critique* (The Critical Conscience, 1971), essays on a dozen contemporary literary critics; *Trois essais de mythologie romantique* (Three Essays on Romantic Mythology, 1971), on Nerval, Gautier, and French romantic poets in general; *Entre moi et moi* (Between Me and Me, 1977), on the works of Henri Michaux, Claudel, Valéry, and Mallarmé; and *La Poésie éclatée* (Exploded Poetry, 1980), a side-by-side study of Baudelaire and Rimbaud. His *festschrift, Mouvements premiers* (First Movements, 1972), presented him on his seventieth birthday, consists of twenty-one articles on diverse subjects by some of the world's most eminent critics, including Jean Starobinski, J. Hillis Miller, Marcel Raymond, and Paul de Man.

A succinct summary of the author's critical method and its rewards was offered by his translator, Elliott Colemen. Poulet reads French literature, in Coleman's words, "in the light of man's changing concepts of mortal time. . . . [He] conceives the essential effort of the critic to be that of discerning the total meaning of a writer's work by paying attention to his sense of man's temporality and place. Once this is understood, in relation to all other human activity, then the philosophic temper of the literature of a time is seen as vitally determining the way life will take. The work of an artist can be penetrated and can penetrate us, unhindered, only if we are led to a view of the center of it, where the generative power is imparted. Without this second sight, works of art can hardly be seen or known at all."

WORKS IN ENGLISH TRANSLATION: English translations of Poulet's writings by Elliott Coleman include *Studies in Human Time,* 1956; *The Interior Distance,* 1956; (with C. Dawson) *The Metamorphoses of the Circle,* 1967; and *Proustian Space,* 1977. Francoise Meltzer translated *Exploding Poetry,* 1984.

ABOUT: Columbia Dictionary of Modern European Literature, 1980; Contemporary Authors 13–14R, 1975; de Man, P. Blindness and Insight, 1971. *Periodicals*—Comparative Literature Studies June 1973; Criticism Winter 1974; Poetry March 1960; April 1968; Times Literary Supplement February 19, 1960; Virginia Quarterly Review 43, 1967; Yale Review Autumn 1956.

---

*PUIG, MANUEL (December 1932–), Argentinian novelist, was born in the provincial town of General Villegas where he spent his childhood and received his elementary education. In 1946 he was sent to Buenos Aires to an American boarding school. He had begun learning English in 1942 in order to enjoy more thoroughly the American films that he and his mother saw every afternoon. Within a year the boy was first in his class, and had switched his interest from American movies to books—Gide, Hesse, Huxley, Sartre— as well as essays in psychology and French and on Italian films. *Quai des orfevres* (Quay of the Goldsmiths), a film directed by Clouzot, revealed to him what was really his vocation: to be a film director. Toward that end, he began studying French and Italian and improving his English. In 1950 Puig registered at the School of Architecture of the University of Buenos Aires but "couldn't stand [it]"; so he shifted to philosophy. In 1955 he received a scholarship for travel to Italy, to attend a film school which, in turn, proved to be a big disappointment. He traveled to Paris, then to London, where he survived by giving Spanish and Italian lessons as well as by washing dishes at a theater restaurant.

At this time, Puig began writing film scripts, continuing to do so in 1959 when he moved to Stockholm. A year later, back in Argentina, he began working as assistant director in the Argentine movie industry. After a short sojourn in his native country, he moved to New York City to experience Broadway musicals while working for Air France at Idlewild (now Kennedy) Airport. In 1965 he finished his first novel, which he had begun in 1962 in Buenos Aires but which was not to be published for three years due to problems of censorship and lack of vision on the part of the publishers. Manuel Puig considers these years (1963–65), along with those of his childhood (1940–43), to be the best years of his life. This was because he was able to work freely, without having to please anybody, with no deadlines, expressing himself in his own terms. Finally, in 1968 *La traición de Rita Hayworth* (*Betrayed by Rita Hayworth*) was published in Buenos Aires. The next year *Boquitas pintadas* (*Heartbreak Tango*) became an instant best-

*poy ēg´, mä nwel´

MANUEL PUIG

seller which, in turn, reawakened interest in the first novel.

Betrayed by Rita Hayworth, selected as one of the three best foreign novels of 1968–69 by a group of French critics of the Parisian daily *Le Monde,* examines the narrow world of alienated human beings who find refuge in the massive consumption of movies and soap operas. Like *Hopscotch* by Julio Cortázar (filmed by Antonioni as *Blowup,* 1966) or *One Hundred Years of Solitude* by García Márquez, *Betrayed* is the kind of text that implicitly questions the reality of the novelist's own creations. In fact, *Betrayed* even questions its own narrative format. Puig examines in this novel the limited world of the petit bourgeoisie and of the blue-collar Argentinians, all creatures who feel alienated, seeking refuge in movies and in serialized stories. The book was considered to be an attack on the stratified and conventional realism of the traditional novel and also on the cultural foundations of the experimental and avant-garde novel with Puig engaged in a task of demythifying today's Argentinian conventions. The novel takes place in a provincial town, depicting the life of a nuclear family, their relatives and friends, between the years of 1933 and 1948. Uniting these people, apart from their family ties and their love for each other, are their mental horizons. All of them live in an alienated world. They evade reality through movies, best-sellers, or sex. All share the same obsession: unwillingness to accept their own mediocrity. Puig presents this dark portrait with light humor and fantasy, creating a counterpoint of voices through which he plays with the mediocrity of his characters. Nar-

ration, as it is usually understood, is nonexistent in this novel since every page of it is dialogue (without annotations), interior monologues, entries of personal diaries or letters. To a certain degree—as critics have pointed out—*Betrayed* has the structure of a thriller, because only at the end is the reader given all the clues to understanding the family chronicle. The result is a sort of narrative fiction with strong psychoanalytical depths—obsessive behavior, neuroses, and family taboos. Puig uses sexual frustration as his principal literary tool for the task of demolition both on the individual as well as the social level. It should be noted that a good portion of the novel takes place during the years in which Juan Perón was climbing to power, bringing about the most extreme changes in modern Argentinian history. *Betrayed* portrays the resentment and frustration of the entire Argentinian people. There is no specific intention of political denunciation, but the novel provides the socio-political context against which are projected the mentality, the prejudices, the feelings, and the dreams of the characters. At another level, *Betrayed* is a record of the oral language spoken by a very definite segment of the Argentinian people during a period of the country's history. If the emotional and even the imaginative alienation of the characters is shown through their way of elaborating fables out of books or movies, their everyday speech demonstrates how deep the roots of that alienation have gone, because it is a tissue in which is imbedded the contemporary language of serialized novels, popular biographies, soap operas, movie subtitles, plus the rhetoric of the politicians and the pseudo-intellectual utterances of journalists. In sum, Puig's characters speak nothing but clichés, and they act through imitation of the social and erotic patterns they see in the American films, motivated only by evanescent pop fashions.

Heartbreak Tango (1969), Puig writes, "is a *feuilleton* [serialized novel] in which, without dismissing the stylistic experiments of my first novel, I try a new format of popular literature." In fact, he was trying to condition his readers to read each chapter as if these were entries or episodes of a serialized story. But nothing could be more different from the traditional *feuilletons,* such as Dumas' *The Count of Monte Cristo* or Sue's *The Mysteries of Paris,* than the Argentinian novel, which is, in reality, a parody of that kind of adventure story. The first and the last entries in the novel are newspaper obituaries of the protagonists of the story. Their lives are unfolded through intimate letters, meditations, dialogues, religious confessions, prayers, objective descriptions, and synchronic episodes in which each character is studied at a given time engaged in a common situation. Nevertheless, the major interest of the book resides in the clichéd speech used by the characters, a speech canonized by the mass media, a euphemistic kind of language which abhors calling things by their rightful names. Thus "tuberculosis" becomes "that highly contagious sickness," sexuality is reduced to silences and, in general, language becomes symbolic, representing that which is ideologically permissible. Otherwise, society will chastise the trespasser. *Heartbreak Tango's* purpose is to create a kind of highly fictional narrative which accounts for the abundant number of characters and incidents which involve them. But *Heartbreak Tango* does not make concessions to the cheap sentimentalism characteristic of the European *feuilleton* or the soap opera. It presents the reader with a veridical story, with credible circumstances and characters and with a narrator who limits himself to describing the characters' acts, transcribing their conversations and letters, inviting the reader to be an active participant in the story, as well as a judge of his characters.

Manuel Puig's third novel, *The Buenos Aires Affair* (1973), proves in its subtitle—*Novela policial (A Detective Novel)*—that the Argentinian author was again aiming at utilizing a popular literary form deeply rooted in the collective subconscious. But although there are three corpses, a kidnap, a rape, and a police investigation of sorts, the novel is more a psychoanalytic study of its two leading characters, and a parody of their way of life. Again, as in the two previous novels, it is on the linguistic level that Manuel Puig is most successful. Introducing each chapter of this book is an epigraph from a Hollywood film of the 1930s and '40s in which the leading lady (always a sex symbol) voices clichés which convey the meaning of the chapter. The book again is "narrated" through several different techniques and styles which are always parodic: visual descriptions, fictitious interviews, journalistic pieces, interior monologues, footnotes (as in Borges), dialogues with a silent interlocutor, a police shorthand crime report are some of the devices used by Puig to mirror the violent atmosphere encountered by him upon his return to his native Argentina. As might be expected, Puig's fellow countrymen welcomed neither him nor his book. The latter was considered too negative and too destructive and was rejected by the public. The Argentina of military dictatorship and of guerrillas refused to recognize itself in the ugly portrait drawn by the author.

With *El beso de la mujer araña* (*The Kiss of the Spider Woman*, 1976), Manuel Puig's narrative achieved an unusual concentration at several levels: the drama is polarized between two male protagonists —Molina, the homosexual, and Valentín, the *guerrillero*, the political prisoner; it takes place in a small jail cell shared by the two men and progresses chronologically from the present on. The temporality of the novel is linear, and the narration is accomplished through fewer "voices" than the other novels: fundamentally dialogues, police reports, thoughts, footnotes plus straight narration of the plots of American movies given by Molina while chatting with his cellmate or while daydreaming. This technique, cleverly sustained throughout the novel, permits the reader to get to know the characters without the mediation of the narrator. The different "voices" that the narrator assumes serve to introduce the reader to the fictional fabric of the novel. In this way the verisimilitude of the narration is reinforced; the story is developed from the point of view of its actors who also speak about themselves. The reader is drawn close to the story because it reads like a *confidential* report and, at points, even like an autobiography. At the same time, the absence of an explicit narrator, and the presence of such a great degree of objectivity and impersonality create a disturbing ambiguity, intensifying the reader's partial knowledge of the characters. Episodes of silences of the characters are highlighted by ellipses (. . .), with three lines of periods marking more prolonged interruptions. The characters really seem to be narrating themselves. The footnotes provide "non-narrative" material attributable to the author and juxtaposed to the fictional text. At first glance this discourse can be considered exterior to the fictional text because of its "scientific" quality. In fact, the footnotes are documentary evidence offered the reader by somebody who takes seriously what is being developed in the fictional discourse. They provide a synthesis of the current state of the diverse problems—homosexuality, Nazism—totally without relationship to the fate and conduct of the characters. The reader must establish his own interpretations. The commentaries in these footnotes are cold, analytical, impersonal; they do not seem to emanate from a narrator but from somebody totally alien to the fictional world. They never allude directly to the fictional characters; they appear entirely devoted to imparting information. However, this essayistic synthesis which seems so alien to the story is in reality a valuable complement of it.

Another narrative procedure used by Puig in this novel is the *bolero*. The verses of these popular musical compositions have a mystifying character: they lend credibility to what is said. Puig's characters find in them "a lot of truth" because they are "naked and real as life itself" since "they reproduce the daily happenings of life." Externally this novel has two parts, with eight chapters in each. The last chaper of the first part is an exceptional one, since it interrupts the predominant narrative mood and is formulated as a penitentiary report. Here again Puig is reaching to another form of communication. In this way, like many other Spanish-American writers, he is modifying narrative language, ironically displacing accepted narrative conventions. The existential balance of this novel is neither more nor less desolate than in Puig's other novels, although perhaps one should consider it more devastating because it seems to frustrate an option not alluded to in former books: that of revolutionary action. But Puig says nothing about the possible success or defeat of Valentín's political friends. At the end, Valentín is tortured by the police, but he does not give up. His final delirium is a way of *not* making a pronouncement, thus leaving the situation open-ended and the reader free to chose an answer.

Maldición eterna a quien lea estas páginas (Eternal Curse on the Reader of These Pages, 1980), originally written in English, is a novel that takes Puig's narrative discourse to surprising consequences. It narrates the story of two lonely people—a sick old Argentinian gentleman and his American male nurse, both vexed by guilt and the lack of the female presence which they have either longed for or rejected or lost forever. Their dificulty in finding ways to trust each other, to develop a friendship, and to love each other, is initially the subject. During this search each reveals himself to the other, to himself and to the reader. The major interest of this book is twofold: on the one hand, the reader can admire how Puig works with a new kind of material—American everyday life—through Larry, the nurse. On the other hand, the reader can admire Puig's linguistic virtuosity, since the whole novel is told through nonannotated dialogues. But, as the novel progresses, the dialogues do not follow any apparent rational order, so that the reader begins to wonder if he/she is really confronted with two interlocutors, or perhaps only with one who is engaged in dialogue with an imaginary other.

Sangre de amor correspondido (Blood of Requited Love, 1982) takes its readers to a new locale within Puig's fictional world. This novel takes place in a small rural town in Brazil. In a desolate and rough present, a lost past emerges, a golden age—the lustful youth of the characters. But, little by little, that Arcadian past begins to fracture. The reader discovers that this is not a love story, but a tale of the masks, transfigurations and metaphors with which remembrance covers (and dis-covers) the conscious memory of adults. The novel ends with a simultaneous hedonistic celebration of adolescence and an elegy of that period together with an implacable study of the fictions that the adults interpose between past and present, between solitude and the necessity for love.

Beneath the disguise of *pop* literature, Manuel Puig has built an elaborate kind of narrative in which each element functions in perfect agreement with the total structure of which it is a part. He has published two other books: one, a novel—*Pubis Angelical,* 1979 (Angelic Pubis) and the other, two plays under the title *Bajo un manto de estrellas,* 1983 (Under a Star's Clock). None of these has been translated into English. Puig has left Argentina and presently spends his time both in New York City and in Brazil where his family now lives. He translates most of his own works into English and also writes in that language.

WORKS IN ENGLISH TRANSLATION: Betrayed by Rita Hayworth, 1970 (trans. S.J. Levine, 1984); Heartbreak Tango, 1973; The Buenos Aires Affair, 1976; The Kiss of the Spider Woman, 1979 (trans. T. Colchie, 1984); Eternal Curse on the Reader of These Pages, 1982; Blood of Requited Love (trans. J.L. Grayson), 1983.

ABOUT: Contemporary Authors, new revision series 2, 1981; Forster, D.W. (ed.) Modern Latin American Literature II, 1975; Forster D.W. and V. (eds.) Dictionary of Contemporary Latin-American Authors, 1975; MacAdam, A. Modern Latin American Narratives: the Dreams of Reason, 1977. *Periodicals*—American Hispanist, 2, 17 (April 1977), 11–12; Georgia Review, 29 (1975), 95–114; Latin American Literary Review, 2, 3 (Fall–Winter 1973), 45–53; 3, 5 (Fall–Winter 1974), 137–141; 4, 9 (Fall–Winter 1976), 22–28; Modern Language Notes 97, 2 (March 1982), 411–421; New York Times Book Review December 16, 1973; September 5, 1976; April 23, 1979; July 4, 1982; September 23, 1984; Review 72, 4–5 (1971–1972), 49–51; 52–55; 57–64; Review 73 (1973), 46–48; 49–54; Symposium Spring 1978, 15–24; Times Literary Supplement September 21, 1984; Translation I–II, 2 (1974), 32–41.

*QIAN ZHONGSHU (also rendered as Ch'ien Chung-Shu), (November 21, 1910–), Chinese novelist, essayist, and literary critic, writes to *World Authors* of himself that "both as a writer and as a scholar, I have always been content to cultivate my pocket handkerchief garden and plough my lonely furrow." The "garden," as a matter of fact, includes the novel, short stories and essays, and literary criticism which covers both Chinese and Western studies.

Born in Wuxi to a literary family, Qian Zhongshu's early education combined classical scholarship, which was a tradition in his family, with the newly instituted modern style of school-

*chē yen jŏong shŏo

QIAN ZHONGSHU

ing. He entered Qinghua University in 1929, where he distinguished himself by his wit, critical acumen, and prodigious memory. Before his second year was over, he started to publish literary articles. On graduation, he returned to Shanghai to teach at a private college, pursuing his literary studies all the while. It was in this period that he married Yang Jiang, also a writer and scholar. In 1935 the couple went to Oxford, where Qian studied English literature and earned his B. Litt. degree in 1937; they spent the next year, 1937–38, in France. Qian returned to China in the summer of 1938, to teach English language and literature at the South-West Associated University, in the border province of Yunnan, the greater part of the mainland being occupied by the Japanese. He then spent the years 1941–45 in occupied Shanghai, where the couple eked out a living, Qian by teaching and Yang by writing plays. It was at this period that Qian started writing fiction.

Weicheng (*Fortress Besieged*) appeared in print immediately after the war, first as a serial in a literary quarterly, then in book form in 1947. It immediately became a great success. Using the war years as a background, the action of *Fortress Besieged* shifts between Shanghai and the unoccupied interior, but transcends the local scene to present the progress of a "modern," "intellectual" Everyman is the story of Fang Hong Chien's journey to the interior, a journey that is both geographical and psychological. The novel opens with his sea trip back from France to Shanghai, then to his home town (presumably Wuxi), then his journey to the interior (probably Hunan) to work in a bogus university where he

is trapped into marriage, and then back to Shanghai via Hongkong when his contract is not renewed. The story ends in Shanghai in an ugly domestic quarrel, mirrored in its title, drawn from a French proverb that marriage is a besieged fortress where "those inside want to get out, and those outside want to get in."

Fortress Besieged is many things at the same time. It is a picaresque novel with perceptive insights into the prevalent confusion and corruption of Chinese society on the eve of the occupation. It is a gradual unveiling of the protagonist, his lack of judgment, his moral cowardice, his inability to come to grips with reality; he starts out with hopeful prospects and ends up a dismal failure without attaining self-knowledge. Fang has been said to be the first anti-hero in contemporary Chinese fiction. The novel is a satire on manners, the bumbling father with his endless sermonizing, the hoax of a professor who sells medicine on the black market, the pompous chairman of the Chinese department with his sex-starved wife. Using the besieged city as a symbol, it is a fable going beyond courtship and marriage to comment on the futility of human endeavor and the vanity of worldly pursuits. Qian himself avows in the original preface that "in this book I intended to write about a certain segment of society and a certain kind of people in modern China. In writing about these people I did not forget that human beings they were, still human beings with the basic nature of hairless, two-legged bipeds." *Fortress Besieged* is, in effect, a philosophical novel, sometimes hilariously comic, often darkened with pessimism, commenting on the petty, the ineffective, the mean and the cowardly or the downright stupid in human nature. The artist spares nothing in his merciless probing, while the whole is permeated with a deep understanding and pity, a profound reflection on the human condition.

Acclaimed by C. T. Hsia as "the crowning achievement of modern Chinese literature," by 1982 *Fortress Besieged* had been translated into English, Russian, Japanese, and German, although, as David Hawkes writes, considering the "dandyish style, wit and word-play . . . probably only the author himself could have done it [the English translation] successfully." In his short stories, notably *Mao* (Cat) and *Linggan* (Inspiration), collected in 1946 in *Ren, Shou, Gui* (Men, Beasts, and Ghosts), Qian is gleefully, sometimes wickedly, satirical, while surveying the world of "featherless bipeds" regardless of whether they are would-be fashionable hostesses or would-be immortal bards, from the standpoint of immeasurably superior intelligence. Only in one of the stories, *Jinian* (*Souvenir*), is satire muted in the face of an ironic fate which seems to hold all poor "featherless bipeds" in its grip.

Qian is also a notable literary critic. Theodore Huters writes: "Qian has produced noteworthy work of greater variety than anyone else in modern China. His criticism demonstrates a phenomenal control over the entire corpus of traditional literature as well as knowledge of European literature that would put many Western scholars to shame." *Tan Yi Lu,* completed in the 1940s, is a series of essays, or as Qian himself calls them, "Causeries on Poetry," mainly relating to traditional poets and poetry, which is now being prepared for a new edition. Other essays were collected in 1941 in *Xie Zai Rensheng Bianshang* (Written on the Margin of Life).

Qian's *Guanzhui Pian* (Partial Views on Ideas and Letters), a mammoth work of more than one million words, on which he has worked for the last twenty years, was published in Beijing (Peking) in 1979–80. It focuses on ten of the classics of Chinese literature, but goes beyond Chinese historical-literary studies to encompass general cultural issues. The publication of the book has been regarded as a major event in scholarly circles. It is a mine of learning that in breadth and scope could find its modern Western counterpart only in the work of René Wellek or Eric Auerbach, to whom Qian has been compared. "There are few people alive," Huters writes of Qian, "who can match his erudition."

After the liberation of China in 1949, Qian and his wife taught at Qinghua University in Beijing until 1952 when the couple, along with other distinguished scholars, were transferred to the Institute of Literature, now part of the Chinese Academy of Social Sciences. *Song Shi Zuan Zhu* (Selected Sung Poetry with Annotations), published in 1958, is a product of this period, along with a number of essays in literary scholarship. A patriot who refused an offer to go abroad on the eve of liberation, in order "to stay around and do my bit" for his war-ravaged country, Qian has weathered all the political upheavals of the last three decades with his personal integrity untouched. Since the removal of the Gang of Four and the opening up of China to Western visitors, Qian has become a legendary figure, and his works are extensively commented on at home and abroad. Both *Fortress Besieged* and *Guanzhui Pian* have become the subject of study in Chinese universities. Since 1982 Qian Zhungshu has been a vice-president of the Chinese Academy of Social Sciences. When he visited the United States in 1979 as a member of the delegation from the Chinese Academy, Jonathan Spence described him as "sardonic, erudite, elegant, purveying a sense of slightly world-weary charm, and quite delighted at his own survival."

In 1984 Howard Goldblatt published his English translation of Yang Jiang's memoir of the difficult years of the Cultural Revolution when she and her husband were sent to separate "re-education schools"—*Six Chapters from My Life "Downunder"*—a book that, Judith Shapiro wrote in the *New York Times Book Review,* "faithfully expresses the ethos of an older generation of Chinese intellectuals, very different from their often openly disillusioned children . . . marked by the dignity, absence of recrimination, deep love of country and fatalism typical of her generation."

WORKS IN ENGLISH TRANSLATION: *Fortress Besieged* was translated by Jeanne Kelly and Nathan K. Mao in 1980, and Qian's short story "Souvenir" (*Jinian*) appears in *Modern Chinese Stories and Novellas 1919–1949,* edited by J. S. M. Lau, L. O. Lee, and C. T. Hsia in 1981. Several of his literary essays written in English on China in the English literature of the seventeenth and eighteenth centuries were published in the *Quarterly Bulletin of Chinese Bibliography* in 1940 and 1941. A bibliography of his works in Chinese appears in Theodore Huter's book on him in the Twayne World Authors Series listed below.

ABOUT: Dictionary of Oriental Literature I, 1974; Hsia, C. T. A History of Modern Chinese Fiction, 1971; Huters, T. Qian Zhongshu, 1982; Mao, N. K. Introduction to Fortress Besieged, 1980; Spence, J. Introduction to Young Jiang's Six Chapters from My Life "Downunder," 1984; Yang, W. L. Y. and N. K. Mao, Modern Chinese Fiction, 1981. *Periodicals*—Journal of Asian Studies May 1978; New York Review of Books April 17, 1980; New York Times Book Review November 25, 1984; Times Literary Supplement June 27, 1981.

*RABAN, JONATHAN (June 14, 1942–), British essayist and travel writer, was born in Fakenham, Norfolk, the son of the Reverend Peter Raban, an Anglican vicar, and the former Monica Sandison. He earned his bachelor's degree from the University of Hull in 1963, and stayed on there for two years of further study. At first he pursued an academic career as assistant lecturer in English literature at the University College of Wales at Aberystwyth (1966–67), then in a similar post at the University of East Anglia at Norwich (1967–69). Since 1969 he has been a full-time writer and resident of London.

The first of Raban's books to gain wide attention was *Soft City,* a description of contemporary life in London, New York, and Cambridge, Massachusetts. The adjective in the title describes the sense or impression created by living in a great city, "as real, maybe more real than the hard city one can locate on maps, in

°rə bän´

JONATHAN RABAN

statistics." Some reviewers were put off by the book's mixture of elements—personal reminiscence combined with anthropology, urbanology, literary criticism, and even a short story. Richard Sennett called it "the first good picture of the quiet, rather private world of London's middle-class young. . . . This book is both a concrete critique of a certain life style and an intellectual product of it." The reviewer for the *Economist* remarked that *Soft City* "has easily discernible . . . nuggets of solid base metal that deserve being struck into the coinage of planners, politicians, and all urban dwellers."

Fourteen weeks spent traveling in the small oil sheikhdoms of the Persian Gulf—Qatar, Bahrain, Abu Dhabi, and Dubai—as well as in Egypt, North Yemen, and Jordan, resulted in *Arabia: A Journey through the Labyrinth.* Raban disarms his reader by disclaiming at the outset any interest in the traditional Arab life of the desert, Arab-Israeli politics, the Islamic religion and legal code, or international petroeconomics. "He is determined," in Tamar Jacoby's words, "to describe only what he happens to see, and to make no moral judgments." "Nevertheless," observed Edward Hoagland, "by being himself, in an outpouring of quicksilver observations—of camel-necked dhows, of Yemeni dirks worn at the waist like codpieces—he has produced within these limits a delicious travel book, quite apart from its timely significance. . . . [He] has a sharp tongue, on occasion . . . and, at his brilliant best, he is the most valuable traveler Britain or America has sent to the Persian Gulf in thirty years." Noel Perrin thought that *Arabia* took Raban up "in one

bound . . . into the company of T. E. Lawrence, Sir Richard Burton, Charles Doughty, and Freya Stark." The book's "high quality . . . stems partly from its style, which can be described as a sort of English Truman Capote: vivid, funny, accurate, full of hyperbolic wit and outrageous metaphor; no reticence at all." Equally striking, Perrin writes, "is the author's ability to make an instant connection with virtually any human being whomsoever. It is typical of him that almost as soon as he arrived in Sana, a non-Western city if there ever was one, he wanders into a 'cafe' consisting of a corrugated iron roof supported by a pile of rocks. Three Yemenis are sitting at a table chewing the drug called qat and playing cards. About a minute later there are four people playing cards, chewing qat, and exchanging confidences. I would guess that a week later Mr. Raban knew more about the inner life of Yemen than many Yemenis do."

Old Glory: An American Voyage is an Englishman's journey down the Mississippi River, from St. Paul to the Louisiana bayous. The adventure had its origins in Raban's childhood, when at the age of seven he first read *Huckleberry Finn* and imagined the narrow Norfolk stream running beside the vicarage as the mighty American river: " . . . if I concentrated really hard, I could see the Mississippi there. First I had to think it twice as wide, then multiply by two, then two again. . . . The rooftops of Fakenham went under. I sank roads, farms, church spires, the old German prisoner-of-war camp, Mr. Banham's flour mill. I flooded Norfolk; silvering the landscape like a mirror, leaving just an island here, a dead tree there, to break this lonely, enchanted monotony of water. It was a heady, intensely private vision. I hugged the idea of the huge river of myself. I exulted in the freedom and solitude of being afloat on it in my imagination." The author's ease with strangers, as well as his indubitable foreignness, helped him get on with Americans of the most disparate backgrounds, and he has included deft descriptions of nearly all his chance encounters in all their individuality. As Noel Perrin confessed, "There are at least 300 portraits in this book; of them, probably 150 are of people belonging to types that I myself have never been able to break through and really talk to. Like a Yemeni reading *Arabia,* I have the uneasy feeling that this fellow knows my country better than I do." Paul Fussell, however, objected to *Old Glory's* "tedious structure," and particularly to the author's governing theory, stated early in the book: "The book and the journey would be all of a piece. The plot would be written by the current of the river itself." Fussell wrote, "The pattern—alone on the river by day, ashore chinning with 'characters' by night—is unvarying, and the repeated alternation finally grows wearisome."

Raban is the author of several books of literary criticism, including a study guide for *Huckleberry Finn,* and works on modern fiction and poetry. He has also written television plays for BBC-TV and radio plays for BBC Radio 3. He is a fellow of the Royal Society of Literature and a member of the Society of Authors.

WORKS: The Technique of Modern Fiction, 1968; Huckleberry Finn, 1968; The Society of the Poem, 1971; Soft City, 1974; Arabia, 1979; Old Glory, 1981. *As editor*—Robert Lowell's Poems: A Selection, 1974.

ABOUT: Contemporary Authors 61–64, 1976. *Periodicals*—Christian Science Monitor October 16, 1974; December 3, 1979; November 9, 1981; Economist March 16, 1974; October 24, 1981; Encounter April 1974; February 1982; Nation September 26, 1981; National Review June 27, 1980; March 19, 1982, New Republic October 20, 1979; October 28, 1981; New Statesman January 25, 1974; New York Review of Books April 17, 1980; November 19, 1981; New York Times Book Review November 10, 1974; October 14, 1979; September 6, 1981; June 6, 1982; New Yorker March 10, 1980; Newsweek October 8, 1979; October 5, 1981; Saturday Review September 1981; Times Literary Supplement March 22, 1974; October 23, 1981.

KARL RAHNER

*RAHNER, KARL (March 5, 1904–March 29, 1984), German theologian,was born in Freiburg im Breisgau, in what is now West Germany, the son of Karl Rahner, a Latin teacher, and the former Luise Trescher. After a somewhat mischievous childhood, he grew serious about his studies, and while still in his teens followed his elder brother Hugo, who later became world-famous as a church historian, into the Society of Jesus. He plunged with vigor into the lengthy study of theology, philosophy, and spiritual discipline characteristic of that most rigorously intellectual of religious orders, and after spending ten years at various seminaries in Germany, Austria, and Holland, was ordained a Jesuit priest in 1932. Although he pursued graduate work in philosophy at the University of Freiburg under the direction of the stern neo-Thomist Martin Honecker, he was most influenced there by the lectures of Martin Heidegger, the eminent existentialist metaphysician, who had at one time been a Jesuit seminarian. Rahner remarked in 1967 that Heidegger's "style of thinking and of investigating" was the most valuable influence on his developing career.

After taking his doctorate in theology in 1936 from the University of Innsbruck—Honecker had rejected his dissertation in philosophy at

Freiburg—Rahner remained in that Austrian city to teach in a Jesuit college until the institution was closed by the Nazis in 1939. He spent the war in Vienna as an instructor in pastoral theology, and afterwards taught theology at a Jesuit college near Munich. He was eventually in 1949 elected to a professorship in dogmatic theology at Innsbruck, where he remained until returning to Munich in 1964 as professor of the philosophy of religion. In 1967 he assumed the chair of dogmatic theology at Münster. He was emeritus professor from 1971 until his death. Rahner spent his last years in a Jesuit college in Innsbruck, where he died at the age of eighty.

Rahner was named by Pope John XXIII as a *peritus,* or official theologian, at the Second Vatican Council, which convened in 1962. He was by that time coming to be internationally known as a profound, somewhat cautious, rigorously orthodox, yet intellectually comprehensive Catholic theologian. His central interest had always been the formulation of a present-day interpretation of Thomism—the basic Catholic theology postulated by St. Thomas Aquinas in the thirteenth century. Although he is considered an important force in the ecumenical movement, he was careful not to seem a controversialist. His many books and essays have treated topics as diverse as Christology, the Trinity, Christian ethics, death and the afterlife, and evolution; yet he generally steered clear of the politically fraught questions of church structure and papal preogative that have beset and divided the Catholic church in the postconciliar era. He sometimes was the focus of attacks by right-wing and reactionary Catholics, though rather less frequently than several of his brother theologians. In Timothy F. Lull's words, he always was a contemporary Catholic theologian who knew "how to stay out of trouble."

Rahner's rejected philosophy thesis formed the basis of his second book, *Geist in Welt: Zur Metaphysik der endlichen Erkenntnis bei Thomas von Aquin* (*Spirit in the World*). It was an immediate success, and has been widely translated and reprinted many times since its original publication. The work explains Aquinas' philosophy of knowledge in a transcendental, existential light: Rahner rejects the Platonic dualism of traditional Catholic philosophy, turning to a theory very close to Heidegger's notion of man as being ineluctably "thrown" into the world. For all his spirituality, man is thoroughly bound up with the material world, and always will be. In Thomas Sheehan's words, "Rahner's attack on Platonic Christianity and its bloodless desire for the angelic is thorough and uncompromising, . . . his position is in fact more consonant with the Judaeo-Christian promise of resurrection of the body than is the Greek doctrine of immortality of the soul." The book constitutes the philosophical underpinning of much of Rahner's subsequent work in theology.

Sendung und Gnade (*The Christian Commitment*), published in 1959, has become one of the most influential of Rahner's books. It consists of seven essays on the Christian life that "illuminate," in the words of one reviewer, "the practical problems confronting any Christian living in the world." Among the subjects treated are the order of redemption within the order of creation, the nature of eucharistic devotion, and the individual believer's significance in terms of redemptive history. Most commentators praised the originality of Rahner's ideas; the reviewer for the Protestant *Christian Century* termed the book "an instance of twentieth-century Catholicism at its best."

Rahner always wrote as much for his fellow clerics as for the laity. Among the most useful of modern manuals on the priesthood is *Einübung priesterlicher Existenz* (*The Priesthood*), which is in the main a reflection on St. Ignatius of Loyola's *Spiritual Exercises*. R. M. Liddy called it "an introduction into the mystery of the Christian life and the priesthood. Everything is focused on the experience of the Spirit, God's direct and loving dealing with his creatures, in a way not often adverted to in Catholic theology." The essays in *Glaube, der die Erde liebt* (*Everday Faith*), on the other hand, are much simpler and more meditative in tone, and are directed primarily at a lay audience. The reviewer for *Christian Century* felt that the popular style of these essays did not dilute their "theological substance" and that they "speak meaningfully to Catholic and non-Catholic alike." Kenneth Becker wrote, "Especially in the more meditative essays, one finds the deep sincerity of trust and love and searching that have inspired Rahner's more technical theological studies." Rahner was also the author of numerous short popular monographs on various theological and meditational subjects. These include *On Prayer* (1958), *Ignatius of Loyola* (1978), *A World of Grace* (1980), and *The Courage to Pray* (1981).

A comprehensive view of Rahner's theology may be found in *Grundkurs des Glaubens: Einführung in den Begriff des Christentums* (1976), *Foundations of Christian Faith: An Introduction to the Idea of Christianity*). "I do not intend," wrote the author in introducing his subject, " . . . simply to repeat what Christianity proclaims after the manner of a catechism and in the traditional formulations, but rather, to the extent that it is possible in such a short essay, I shall try to reach a renewed understanding of this message and to arrive at an 'idea' of Christianity." His painstakingly thorough reflections on the most central Christian tenets comprise this weighty volume: man's relation to the absolute mystery of God, the Trinity, revelation and salvation, the nature and meaning of Christ, the importance of the church, the Christian life and the sacraments, and eschatology. Martin Marty wrote that a serious audience should try to "wrestle" with this difficult testament: "The patient pursuer will here learn much about how Christian trackers of the divine name in our time speak of the transcendent, look for signs of the sacred in human response, and regard both the church and the surrounding world. Reflective believers can use Father Rahner's system as a checkpoint for their own viewpoints and, at the very least, will learn why he has provided foundations for the men and women who teach their ministers and priests."

Notwithstanding his many lengthy and successful books, Rahner's preferred mode of exposition throughout his career was the essay. Since 1954 he published twenty volumes, comprising hundreds of short pieces, entitled *Schriften zur Theologie* (*Theological Investigations*). From the first volume, *God, Christ, Mary and Grace*, to the last, *Concern for the Church*, the series has ranged as widely as possible among those topics of central interest to Christians. He was also the prime collaborator in the ten-volume *Lexikon für Theologie und die Kirche* (1957), later retitled *Sacramentum Mundi: An Encyclopedia of Theology* published in six volumes in 1969.

Rahner's gentle approach to the divisive question of papal infallibility may be seen in the last volume of *Theological Investigations.* He tells of a dream he had in which, in the near future, a pope discusses his own infallibility with representatives of other Christian churches. The congenial pontiff promises his "dear brothers" to be extremely careful about exercising the doctrine in the future—indeed, he fosters the impression that he might never use it again. The attending clergymen, most impressed by this genuinely ecumenical statement, are on the point of reuniting with Rome when Rahner wakes up. He recounts the dream to a friend, who says it is a nice idea but highly unlikely to happen. Rahner's response "summed up," according to Thomas Sheehan, "simply and clearly, the spirit that has kept him working for over forty years. Yes, he agreed, 'but we may dream and hope.'"

WORKS IN ENGLISH TRANSLATION: All of Karl Rahner's major writings have been translated into English. These include *Spirit in the World,* translated by William V. Dych in 1968; *The Christian Commitment,* by Cicely Hastings in 1963; *The Priesthood,* by Edward Quinn in 1973; *Everyday Faith,* by W. J. O'Hara in 1968; William V. Dych's *Foundations of Christian Faith: An Introduction to the Idea of Christianity* in 1976; *Theological Investigations* by David Bourke, in 20 volumes, 1962–79. A one-volume edition of *Sacramentum Mundi: An Encyclopedia of Theology* was published in English as *The Encyclopedia of Theology* (with revisions) in 1975. Gerald A. McCool's edition of *A Rahner Reader* in 1975 is probably the best among the several introductory collections of his work. Rahner's short, devotional *The Love of Jesus and the Love of Neighbors,* the last of his books published in his lifetime, was translated by Robert Barr in 1983.

ABOUT: Bacik, J. J. Apologetics and the Eclipse of Mystery, 1980; Contemporary Authors 109, 1983; Fabro, C. La svolta antropologica di Karl Rahner, 1974; Kürschners Deutcher Gelehrten-Kalender, 1983; Granfield, P. Theologians at Work, 1967; McCool, G. A. (ed.) A Rahner Reader, 1975; Reinisch, L. (ed.) Theologians of Our Time, 1964; Roberts, L. The Achievement of Karl Rahner, 1967; Sheehan, T. Karl Rahner: The Philosophical Foundations, 1984; Tallon, T. Personal Becoming: Karl Rahner's Christian Anthropology, 1981; Vorgrimier, H. Karl Rahner, 1966; Walsh, M. J. The Heart of Christ in the Writings of Karl Rahner, 1977. *Periodicals*—America May 9, 1964; November 7, 1964; February 6, 1965; January 1, 1966; October 22, 1966; November 12, 1966; February 10, 1968; November 16, 1968; July 21, 1973; June 7, 1975; May 29, 1976; March 19, 1977; May 6, 1978; March 14, 1981; Catholic World July 1960; Christian Century November 2, 1960; November 27, 1963; February 24, 1965; November 10, 1965; January 11, 1967; September 4, 1968; January 29, 1969; October 15, 1969; April 20, 1977; November 16, 1977; October 25, 1978; August 13–20, 1980; November 18, 1981; Commonweal February 28, 1964; October 30, 1964; February 26, 1965; February 25, 1966; June 20, 1969; August 10, 1973; October 27, 1978; May 21, 1982; Critic December 1964–January 1965; February 1966; October 1968; November 1969; May–June 1975; October 1980; Library Journal February 15, 1964; October 1, 1964; April 1, 1966; May 1, 1968; July 1973; February 15, 1978; September 1, 1979; Lutheran Forum Spring 1982; New York Review of Books February 4, 1982; New York Times April 1, 1984; New York Times Book Review January 3, 1965; March 12, 1978; Time December 14, 1962; Times Literary Supplement May 12, 1966; May 4, 1967; October 26, 1967; September 6, 1974; September 3, 1982.

RAINE, CRAIG (December 3, 1944–), British poet, was born in Bishop Auckland, County Durham, the son of Norman Edward and Olive Marie Raine. He had a conventionally middle-class, Roman Catholic upbringing, attended Barnard Castle School, and went up to Exeter College, Oxford, to read English, earning his B.A. in 1966 and his B. Phil., a graduate degee, in 1968. He has continued to live in Oxford, teaching English at Christ Church. He has also worked as consulting editor for Faber & Faber, the London publishers, as books editor of the *New Review,* and occasionally as poetry reviewer for the *New Statesman* and other magazines. His major enterprise, however, has been writing poetry, and his small body of distinctive lyrics has led several influential critics to place him in the highest rank of the poets of his generation.

Raine's work is famous for the sharpness, ingenuity, and fecundity of its images, which often engender in the careful reader an authentic shock of discovery. Thematic values and formal refinement seem always to be of secondary importance; overt emotionalism and analytical exploration are almost never encountered. James Fenton has referred, in this connection, to Raine's "phenomenological style": "During the contemplation of his subject [he] deliberately rejects certain modes of consciousness. . . . The only activity is that of a free contemplation, without ulterior motive, eager if anything for the most improbable discoveries." Some, however, have branded the poetry as mere verbal dexterity, or, worse, as heartless cleverness of a particularly disreputable Oxonian sort. John Carey, alluding to this verbal sharpness, called him "immensely talented but unerringly rebarbative"; Fenton commented on the "startlingly repulsive effects" sometimes created by Raine's "penchant for the outrageous image."

The eighty-four pages of *The Onion, Memory,* Raine's first collection, contained some material that had already been published in *Poetry Introduction 4,* part of the respected Faber series. Critics who perhaps expect overt emotionalism in the verse they admire were disappointed: the *Choice* reviewer lamented the collection's lack of "clarity of emotion" and "clarity of thought." Alan Brownjohn, who seemed not to like the book as a whole, admired only the "three or four poems where the poet himself manages to emerge." Derek Mahon, while rating the collection somewhat more highly, found the title poem "the one moving poem in the book, and the most achieved." In it, the poet visits his ex-wife. "Divorced, but friends again at last,/we walk old ground together." They pass the day in a friendly manner. Outside, "the trees are bending over backwards/to please the wind." As she sews, he slices onions.

It is the onion, memory,
that makes me cry.

Because there's everything and nothing to be said,
the clock with hands held up before its face
stammers softly on, trying to complete a phrase—
while we, together and apart,
repeat unfinished gestures got by heart.

And afterwards, I blunder with the washing on the line—
headless torsos, faceless lovers, friends of mine.

"Here, at last," wrote Mahon, "is the human face," and the sharpness of the scene of loss is indeed highlighted by the sharpness of the images. In John Osborne's opinion, *The Onion, Memory*, in "brilliance of figurative invention, . . . is a book of poems unrivalled in this country since Sylvia Plath's *Ariel*."

A Martian Sends a Postcard Home, which followed Raine's first collection by a year and was received even more enthusiastically. The title poem won the Prudence Farmer award as the best poem published in the *New Statesman* during 1978, and is a good introduction to the rest of the volume. A Martian's innocent eye surveys the Earth's great beauty, strangeness, and variety.

. . . Mist is when the sky is tired of flight
and rests its soft machine on ground:

then the world is dim and bookish
like engravings under tissue paper. . . .

In homes, a haunted apparatus sleeps,
that snores when you pick it up.

If the ghost cries, they carry it
to their lips and soothe it to sleep

with sounds. And yet, they wake it up
deliberately, by tickling with a finger. . . .

At night, when all the colours die,
they hide in pairs

and read about themselves—
in colour, with their eyelids shut.

Fenton's comment on this poem is most telling: "The Martian's point of view is a useful fiction,

but it is not unlike the poet's own, which always insists on presenting the familiar at its most strange. The misunderstandings, appropriately enough for an Oxford poet, are like riddles in the Anglo-Saxon mode. Once solved, they do not lose their interest." And even easy-to-solve kennings have a retentive quality, such as the opening image of a poem about the impersonality of death, "In the Mortuary":

Like soft cheeses they bulge
sideways on the marble slabs,

helpless, waiting to be washed. . . .

John Bayley, reviewing the collection, dissented from the critical consensus in holding that Raine's poems that "display feeling" are not his strongest ones; they are best when an "absence of sentiment" is conjoined with an "absence of the poetic." He makes much of the poet's particularity: "His poems don't sound like those of any contemporary, . . . and they frequently pull off the really difficult feat of not sounding like 'poetry' at all, but just seeming a very clear way of saying something arresting." At their best, they "draw attention not to themselves but to an unfamiliar pleasure of familiar consciousness." And from his great familiarity with modern Russian poetry, Bayley draws an illustrious comparison: "the closest parallel to Raine's kind of inspiration seems to me the youthful Pasternak, who . . . verbalized perceptions with the same style of lens and focus. . . . All ingenuity in poetry is a hit-or-miss affair. When Raine's works, it puts us in new touch with life as unexpectedly and joyfully as the early Pasternak did, or the young Betjeman, but when it does not quite come off it seems like a closed circuit on a cassette, fixed up for the private pleasure of cronies."

Craig Raine was married in 1972 to Ann Pasternak Slater, a university teacher. They have a daughter.

PRINCIPAL WORKS: The Onion, Memory, 1978; A Martian Sends a Postcard Home, 1979; A Free Translation, 1981; Rich, 1983.

ABOUT: Contemporary Authors 108, 1983; Vinson, J. (ed.) Contemporary Poets, 1980. *Periodicals*—Choice June 1979; November 1980; Encounter November 1978; August–September 1980; New Statesman June 23, 1978; October 20, 1978; December 14, 1980; Times Literary Supplement June 20, 1978; January 4, 1980; February 5, 1982; October 19, 1984.

*RECHY, JOHN (FRANCISCO) (1934–   ),
American novelist, was born in El Paso, Texas,
the son of Roberto Sixto Rechy and the former
Guadalupe Flores. He earned a B.A. at Texas
Western College in El Paso and then for a while
attended the New School for Social Research in
New York City. He also served a tour of duty in
the U.S. Army, mostly in Germany.

Rechy published several journalistic pieces in
Evergreen Review during the early 1960s; one
of them formed the basis of his first novel, *City
of Night,* which remains by far his best known
and most original and controversial work. In a
tone of careless fury reminiscent of Jack
Kerouac, it describes the cold, violent, and loveless lower depths of urban American homosexual
life, as witnessed by an anonymous hustler who
wanders from place to place and encounters everywhere only unhappiness, fear, and misery:
"Later I would think of America as one vast City
of Night stretching gaudily from Times Square
to Hollywood Boulevard—jukebox-winking,
rock-n-roll-moaning: America at night fusing its
dark cities into the unmistakable shape of
loneliness." A largely hostile critical reception
greeted the book; Robert Gutwillig claimed it
was "not a novel. . . . There are no characters,
only caricatures; no action, only frenzy; no plot,
only episodes; no discovery, only evasion; no
themes, only posturing; and no ideas, only
sentimentality." Granville Hicks, however, admired the strong impression the novel gives "of
obsessed behavior . . . in a harsh and often nasty world. . . . Rechy's style, though it can be
tiresomely exclamatory, is usually controlled
and quietly forceful. . . . He is more than a
good reporter, for he has touched his materials
with the imagination and the craft of a writer."

The author attempted in three remarkably
similar subsequent novels, *Numbers, This Day's
Death,* and *The Vampires,* to reproduce the
succès de scandale his first book had created. All
concern the anonymous self-gratification and ultimate sterility prevalent in Rechy's version of
the homosexual subculture. They were moderate
commercial successes, but were resolutely ignored by the critical establishment. *The Fourth
Angel,* however, marked what Simon Karlinsky
called "an entirely new departure" for Rechy. It
is the story of four Texas teenagers, rejects of
American culture, and of how, amid much drug-
taking and violence, they come to understand
that they are outsiders. Karlinsky remarked that
the book was "written with an intensity and a
driving originality" and that we "meet a different and more interesting John Rechy in this
book, one with newly sharpened powers of observation and an expanded emotional range.
Where he used to go in for rubbing his readers'

JOHN RECHY

noses in *Mondo Cane* pseudo-revelations, he now
takes them on a tour of his juveniles' believably
constructed private hell."

*The Sexual Outlaw, a Documentary: A Non-
fiction Account, with Commentaries, of Three
Days and Nights in the Sexual Underworld* takes
as its premises the ideas that "public sex is revolution, . . . the greater the repression, the greater the defiance" and that the promiscuity and
exhibitionism of the sexual outlaw result from
his "being forbidden by law to seek out a sexual
partner." The book is a mélange of interviews,
news clippings, exhortations, and Rechy's characteristic scenes of anonymous sexual encounters. Alix Nelson called the book "actually an
intelligent, persuasive, and, in its way, heartbreaking manifesto for abolishing all prohibi-
tions against acts between consenting adults.
And here and there, punctuating Rechy's assurance that sex in the streets is 'our noble revolt,'
a small, painful light breaks where no sun shines:
'Perhaps it will turn out to be the straight world's
ultimate revenge. A loveless sacrifice of all human contact.' You can read Rechy's book either
way."

With *Rushes* in 1979, Rechy returned to the
fictional depiction of the homosexual underworld—in this case, the desolate ambience of a
sadomasochistic bar. Throughout the novel, a
great deal of religious imagery is attached to
some very profane behavior. Darryl Pinckney,
in a lengthy review, described the book's many
characters as "deliberately contrived, scarcely
more than vessels for Rechy's reflections. They
are seen from the inside, but not profoundly.
There is so much on Rechy's mind—the nature

of masculinity, the fascination of the 'sex-hunt,' the tyranny of beauty, the dread of aging, attitudes toward women and transvestites, violence and subjugation, the poverty of feeling. Delineation of character is thus secondary, resulting in the kind of writing Mary McCarthy once called ventriloquism." The novel's menace and power, he continued, depend "on a saturation of mood, on a voluptuous concentration of place. Everything is meticulously described and therefore aggrandized: the arcane rituals, the bodies, the styles, the urgent yearnings, the growling music, the bar's squalor. Everyone is trapped by need." David Taylor praised *Rushes* as "a triumph of dramatic skill. The horror of his infernal cult is fully realized, but often only in spite of the overrich language. At times it is as if one of his characters had become the author, seeking in a straining lyricism to justify the horror or to blur the distinction between beauty and ugliness, pleasure and pain, heaven and hell."

Bodies and Souls, set in Los Angeles, focuses on a trio of runaways whom the author calls "lost angels" and their life in the "city of scarred beauty." Their narrative is interspersed with short scenes describing the lives of other Angelenos, who are almost uniformly repulsive, selfish, and shallow. The lost angels are required by the author to bear the weight of allegorical comparison with Satan and his cohorts, a weight that is simply too heavy for them and their thin story. The main characters, according to Alan Cheuse, "don't even profit from comparison to the characters in *Rebel Without a Cause,* a film to which allusions abound in these pages. But Mr. Rechy's customary power at depicting raw lives with a kind of brute lyricism stands him in good stead here, as does his talent for sketching scenes of Los Angeles itself." Near the novel's conclusion is a scene of highway mass carnage for which Los Angeles is world-famous.

Rechy lived for many years in his native El Paso, close to his mother. After her death, in 1970, he moved to southern California, where he lives near Hollywood Boulevard and teaches creative writing at institutions in the area, including UCLA, USC, and Occidental College.

WORKS: *Fiction*—City of Night, 1963; Numbers, 1967; This Day's Death, 1969; The Vampires, 1971; The Fourth Angel, 1974; Rushes, 1979; Bodies and Souls, 1983. *Nonfiction*—The Sexual Outlaw, 1977.

ABOUT: Contemporary Authors, new revision series 6, 1982; Contemporary Literary Criticism 1, 1973; 7, 1977; 14, 1980; 18, 1981; Dictionary of Literary Biography Yearbook, 1982; R. Gilman, The Confusion of Realms, 1969; J. A. Martinez, Chicano Scholars and Writers, 1979; Moore, H. T. (ed.) Contemporary American Novelists, 1965; Vinson, J. (ed.) Contemporary Novelists, 1976; Who's Who in America, 1982–83. *Periodicals*—American Book Review June 1980; Atlantic August 1963; Chicago Review nos. 2–3, 1964; Nation June 29, 1963; January 5, 1974; New Republic September 14, 1963; New Statesman February 2, 1973; New York Herald Tribune Books June 9, 1963; New York Times Book Review June 30, 1963; January 14, 1968; April 3, 1977; July 17, 1977; Februay 17, 1980; July 10, 1983; Saturday Review June 8, 1963; Time June 14, 1963; Times Literary Supplement September 11, 1970; August 11, 1978; Village Voice August 22, 1977; October 3, 1977; March 3, 1980.

*RICHTER, HANS WERNER (November 12, 1908–), German novelist, author of children's books, radio playwright, essayist, editor, and founder of the famed "Gruppe 47," writes (in German): "What an author has to say is essentially in his books. My novels and stories are never purely autobiographical, but the great themes that have preoccupied me in my life and, to a large extent, make up my life, have gone into my books. When I am asked where I come from, I could answer with a book title that reads 'Geschichten aus Bansin' (Stories from Bansin). I was born in Bansin, a fishing village on the Baltic Sea, in Pomerania, which today belongs to Poland. I have never quite lost my Pomeranian accent although I left little Bansin early on, at the age of nineteen, to move to big Berlin. As a matter of fact, this Pomeranian accent does not bother me in the least, rather to the contrary. I fall into it quite easily and even stress it when I tell stories from my childhood and early youth, that is 'Stories from Bansin.'

"In Berlin I learned the bookdealer's trade from scratch. Thus, the tie to literature was fastened strongly early in my life. Yet what preoccupied us young people in those years from 1929 to 1933 most of all, what literally made us spin, was politics. Because of the rise of National Socialism we were driven further and further to the left. I joined the Communist Party, participated in hall fights, demonstrations, and street battles, lost my job and, in November 1932, was expelled from the Communist Party because of my Trotskyism. Like so many of my friends, I considered Hitler's 'seizure of power' to be unlikely, too. In order to live during the great crisis, I became a street singer in Berlin without abandoning my participation in the political discussion. In the fall of 1933 I went to Paris together with a girlfriend who wanted to continue her studies there in order to avoid political persecution. Life in Paris soon turned bleak and hopeless; we were poor and, with my emigré friends, lost ourselves in endless discussions on Marxism,

°riK´ tə

HANS WERNER RICHTER

National Socialism, and the possibilities of resistance. From where we were, nothing, absolutely nothing, could be accomplished. So I decided one day to return to Germany despite all the dangers. Only now, fifty years later, have I written something about this period, in my novel *Ein Julitag* (A Day in July, 1982).

"And I had the good experience that—while writing such a book—the recollection of images, scenes, and conversations came about as if by itself. However the question whether one can also recollect feelings remained open to me. But back to Berlin under the Nazis. I became a bookdealer once again and remained one until I was drafted into the Wehrmacht in April 1940. I experienced the war as a soldier, and I survived it. In November 1943 I was captured by the Americans in Italy and brought to the United States, first to Camp Ellis, Illinois, later to Fort Kearney, New Jersey.

"War, captivity, and the post-war era became the great topics of my generation, a generation uprooted by the war. My books, *Die Geschlagenen* (*Beyond Defeat*, 1949) and *Sie fielen aus Gottes Hand* (*They Fell from God's Hands*, 1951) talked about this generation and to this generation. I tried to juxtapose moral and spiritual power with the power of violence. I wanted to show how the incitement of the masses as well as terror had operated in a diabolical manner. For only by understanding this terrible operation could a way toward the humane coexistence of people be found.

"Fort Kearney, the prison camp sixty kilometers away from New York City, on the Atlantic Coast, turned the bookdealer and former soldier into Hans Werner Richter, the writer. First against my volition altogether. I wanted to go home, but I had to stay in order to contribute to the newspaper for war prisoners, *Der Ruf—Blätter für deutsche Kriegsgefangene* (The Call—Paper for German Prisoners of War [1945–1946]); and this newspaper represented the thesis that all Germans were collectively guilty. This was not my thesis. I became aware that all of us were losers, even those of us who had been against the Nazis. If I wanted to do something for the development in Germany, I could only represent the interests of the losers. We had to build up our own case, conceivably in opposition to the occupying forces.

"When, in April 1946, I was released from captivity to go to Bavaria, I tried to accomplish my self-assigned task by publishing a journal. Together with Alfred Andersch I edited a new *Ruf*, now appearing in Germany (August 1946–April 1947): *Der Ruf—Unabhängige Blätter der jungen Generation* (The Call—Independent Paper of the Young Generation). Around this journal and in its pages, those authors were gathering who wanted to help build a free democratic Germany, who pleaded for the freedom of art and the freedom of criticism, and who did not shy away from the conflict with the occupation force. At the time, however, all criticism of the armies of occupation was forbidden. The military government decided to prohibit the *Ruf*, and Alfred Andersch and I were forced to leave the *Ruf* to someone else. Yet we did not give up our goals. I kept working on the concept of a new literary periodical, *Der Skorpion*, and in September 1947 I invited the contributors of *Ruf* to a meeting in Bannwaldsee near Füssen. I was determined to keep this circle together; we stayed in Bannwaldsee for three days.

"Almost every one of the authors had brought along a manuscript. Nothing was more natural than for everyone to read from his manuscript and for the others to judge it spontaneously. Thus the rules of the game and the style of the gatherings of Group 47 were found. As for the periodical *Der Skorpion*, I only managed to come out with a so-called zero-issue, a trial issue of only one hundred copies. Because we had no license, the periodical could not really be published in the first place. Instead, Bannwaldsee had become the birthplace of Group 47. For the next thirty years I would invite my friends to these gatherings year after year, widening their circle carefully. They were always young, unknown authors who had not yet published anything. I left out prominent writers, for instance those of the twenties, whether they had emigrated or not. I was all too convinced that this was our own cause, the cause of a new generation and of a different mentality. As the years went by, the situation changed once again: I and the friends of my generation were now the older who discovered a new mentality among the younger. Group 47 was able to integrate three generations of writers. It is not for me to judge the significance of Group 47 for German postwar literature. Even if I wanted to, I would not succeed. It is hard for me to evaluate its influence, its emanation, and its power of attraction. From my own point of view it would be altogether much too subjective. But what I can and perhaps also must explain is this: why did I give up Group 47, why did I consider its task and its existence to be limited in time? Well, it corresponds to my conviction. Can one imagine—and I ask to be forgiven for this comparison—that movements like 'Sturm und Drang' or 'Junges Deutschland' or even Fontane's 'Unter dem Tunnel' would have existed for over thirty years and thus outlived their own era? I consider it impossible.

"I once wrote down some recollections of the meetings of Group 47 for Bavarian and North German Broadcasting. On the occasion of my seventieth birthday this text was incorporated into the volume *Hans Werner Richter und die Gruppe 47* (1979), which also includes contributions by a number of friends from Group 47, among them Ilse Aichinger, Alfred Andersch, Heinrich Böll, Günter Grass, Wolfgang Hildesheimer, Walter Jens, Siegfried Lenz, and Martin Walser. At some point all of them—and how many others besides!—read in Group 47 for the first time and, from then on, almost every year.

"As you grow older, you begin to collect honors if all goes well. Thus I even became a Doctor (honoris causa) and a Professor at the age of seventy. In reality, I remained what I had always been since those days in the prison camp at Fort Kearney: a writer. Once the time of Group 47 was gone, I returned to this main profession of mine with even greater involvement. The story, 'Die Flucht nach Abanon' (The Escape to Abanon), appeared in 1980, the novel *Die Stunde der falschen Triumphe* (The Hour of False Triumphs) in 1981, and yet another novel, "*Ein Julitag* (A Day in July) in 1982. There are people who say that these are my best books."

—trans. Tamara S. Evans

Hans Werner Richter is a prominent representative of the first generation of post-World War II German writers who began to write in a literary era that was termed "Kahlschlag" (complete deforestation) by one of them (Wolfgang

Weyrauch), and that is characterized by what another one (Wolfdietrich Schnurre) called "Auszug aus dem Elfenbeinturm" (exodus from the ivory tower). In his novel *Linus Fleck oder Der Verlust der Würde* (Linus Fleck or The Loss of Dignity, 1953), Richter draws a vivid portrait of those days of great hopes and meager beginnings.

Richter is renowned above all as the foremost organizer, manager, and editor of early post-war German literature. As a literary scout, discoverer of new talents, and promoter of young and inexperienced authors, Hans Werner Richter had no peer. No wonder that his own literary production, which is considerable, remained somewhat in the shadow of his role as the undisputed leader of Group 47. Literary critics have pointed out that his first novel, *Die Geschlagenen,* is also the first critical account of World War II written by a German soldier. Richter's style has been described as laconically realistic, "a kind of verismo"; critics also noted the tendency of Richter's narrative technique toward superficiality and banality in such novels as *Sie fielen aus Gottes Hand, Spuren im Sand* (Tracks in the Sand, 1953), and the above-mentioned *Linus Fleck.*

The power of Richter's first novel was determined by the intensity of his personal war experiences and the enthusiasm of a young writer determined to change the literary face of Germany. That he indeed succeeded is due less to his own literary work than to his invaluable contribution as an unsurpassed judge and connoisseur of literature and its authors as well as to his efforts to establish a dialogue between authors and critics. By 1966 younger writers, including the Austrian Peter Handke, were dismissing Gruppe 47's founders as "the old guard of modern German literature" and challenging both their political and their literary relevance. Reexamining his own political thinking in *Briefe an einen jungen Sozialisten* (Letter to a Young Socialist) in 1974, Richter defended his break with Stalinism (he had been expelled from the German Communist Party in 1932 for Trotskyism), his support of the moderate Social Democratic Party, and his criticism of the East German Democratic Republic as a dictatorship. In the position now of a kind of "grey eminence" in modern German literature, he remains celebrated as "the founding father" of Gruppe 47 and a sensitive register of the turbulent history of German politics in modern times.

WORKS IN ENGLISH TRANSLATION: Two novels by Richter have been translated into English—*Beyond Defeat* (U.K. *The Odds Against Us*) by Robert Kee, and *They Fell from God's Hands,* by Geoffrey Sainsbury, in 1956.

ABOUT: Cassell's Encyclopedia of World Literature, 1973; Contemporary Authors 97–100, 1981; Columbia Dictionary of Modern European Literature, 1980; Demetz, P. Postwar German Literature, 1970; Penguin Companion to European Literature, 1969; Wilkinson, J. The Intellectual Resistance in Europe, 1981. *Periodicals*—Times Literary Supplement November 9, 1974; October 16, 1981.

*RICOEUR, PAUL (February 27, 1913–), French philosopher, was born in Valence, a small town in south-central France. His father, Jules, a professor of English at the Lycée, was killed in World War I only a few months after Paul's birth. His mother died two years later and Paul and his sister, Alice, were raised by his paternal aunt, Adèle Ricoeur, in Rennes. His sister, to whom he was very attached, died in 1935. After receiving his *Licence ès Lettres* from the University of Rennes in 1933, Ricoeur taught philosophy in the lycée of Saint-Brieuc. In 1935, he prepared for the *agrégation* (a competitive examination for a permanent teaching position) which he successfully completed the same year. He then married his long-time friend Simone Lejas. After a year of obligatory military service at the military school at St. Cyr, during which he was commissioned a reserve officer, he taught at the lycée in Lorient for two years before being mobilized for World War II. His first son, Jean-Paul, was born in 1937 and a year later another son, Marc, was born.

With the rapid defeat of the French army in May and June of 1940, Ricoeur was captured and sent to a German POW camp in northern Germany where he spent the next five years. During these years, he and his fellow prisoners organized a 'university within the walls' of the camp and Ricoeur taught philosophy. He was also able to obtain a copy of the German philosopher Edmund Husserl's influential book *Ideen,* which he translated into French, using a miniscule hand writing in the margins of the book. His daughter, Noelle, was born only a few months after his capture, and so he didn't see her until she was five. After the war, he taught at a small Protestant school, Collège Cevenol, in the central mountains south of Lyons. In 1948, he was named professor of the history of philosophy at Strasbourg. In 1956, he was called to the Sorbonne in Paris. Two more sons, Olivier and Etienne, were born during this period.

In addition to his translations of Husserl, Ricoeur published books on Karl Jaspers and Gabriel Marcel after the war. His first major work, *Le Volontaire et l'involontaire* (*Freedom and Nature: The Voluntary and the Involuntary*), published in 1950, was his doctoral thesis. It is a

PAUL RICOEUR

phenomenological study of freedom and action in which he rejects Sartre's absolute freedom in favor of a dialectical relationship between freedom of action and the involuntary aspects of our experience. This study of freedom was complemented ten years later with *L'Homme faillible* (*Fallible Man*), in which Ricoeur shows how the possibility of evil is inscribed into the structure of human action. A second book, published the same year, *La Symbolique du mal* (*The Symbolism of Evil*), is a hermeneutic interpretation of the symbols of evil, such as stain, burden, errancy, bondage, etc. and the myths of the beginning of the world which are the first interpretations of these symbols. This book in particular established Ricoeur's reputation among theologians for whom he has been a major influence in the theory of interpretation. This book also represented a decisive reorientation in his method from the Husserlian model to a hermeneutic model. A collection of his essays on history, particular philosophers, phenomenology, and politics written during this period was published as *Histoire et Vérité* (*History and Truth*).

Ricoeur's interest in symbols was extended in 1965 from religious symbols to the whole field of symbolism opened up by Freud. His massive *De l'interpretation: Essay sur Freud* (*Freud and Philosophy*) was at once a reading of Freud, an interpretation of Freud, and a long analysis of the epistemology of psychoanalysis. One of his major theses in this book is that the "archeology of the Self" represented by Freudian psychoanalysis calls for a complementary "teleology of the Self" along essentially Hegelian lines. This book, and many articles published in France and

°rē kûr´, pôl

the United States on psychoanalysis, made Ricoeur one of the foremost figures in the philosophy of psychoanalysis. In 1968 he published a collection of his articles on hermeneutics, psychoanalysis, and biblical interpretation under the apt title *Le Conflict des interpretations* (*The Conflict of Interpretations*).

A man of peace and reconciliation, an academic and intellectual, he nevertheless found himself thrust into the public arena because of his convictions. In the late 1950s he wrote and spoke out against French policy in Algeria and participated in demonstrations against the Algerian War. Later, Ricoeur and one of his colleagues left the prestige of the Sorbonne in 1967 to go to the newly-founded branch of the University of Paris in Nanterre, a working class suburb west of Paris. He had written many articles on the need for reform in the French university system, and he believed that at a new university he would have a closer rapport with his students and that there would be a greater chance for innovation. The student riots and workers' strikes of 1968 left Nanterre untouched, but it became the focal point in 1969-70 of the remnants of the disorders. By this time Ricoeur had been elected *Doyen,* a position which is in some respects like the dean of an American university, and in other respects more like the president. The situation at Nanterre progressively deteriorated to the point that bands of *enragés* (angry and politicized students and other youths who had participated in the political demonstrations of 1968) were roving the campus. Students and faculty, including Ricoeur, were attacked. This led to a three-day confrontation between students and police which caused enormous damage to the buildings and interiors of the almost new university. Ricoeur, disillusioned and in poor health, resigned his position and took a three-year leave from the French university. He taught at the Catholic University of Louvain in Belgium and accepted the John Nuveen chair at the University of Chicago, from which he had received an honorary doctorate in 1967. From 1970 until his retirement in 1983, Ricoeur divided his time between Paris and Chicago.

In 1975, he published a book on metaphor, *La métaphore vive* (*The Rule of Metaphor*), in which he reviews the history of metaphor, including recent French and American theories, and he develops and defends his own theory of metaphor. In 1978 a historical anthology of his work, *The Philosophy of Paul Ricoeur*, was published in the United States. Three years later, a collection of his most recent articles on hermeneutics was published with the title *Hermeneutics and the Human Sciences.* During this period, Ricoeur's interest shifted from general hermeneutic theory and metaphor to the problem of narrative writing. The first volume of a two-volume work, *Temps et Récit* (*Time and Narrative*), was published in 1983. In this work, he brings together St. Augustine's study of time with Aristotle's account of narrative plots in the *Poetics.* The outcome of this confrontation leads to a theory of narrative which is tested against contemporary theories of history. The second volume will test his thesis against theories of fictional narrative and the phenomenology of time. Ricoeur's thesis, which joins time and narration, is that "time becomes human time to the extent that it is articulated in a narrative manner; in return, narrative is meaningful to the extent that it sketches the traits of temporal experience."

Ricoeur's method is typically a dialectic between positions which are usually taken as mutually exclusive. His long experience as a professor of the history of philosophy has taught him that all of the great philosophers have something of the truth, but not all of it. So his task is to see whether a dialectic between opposing positions can capture the contributions of each without falling into a lazy eclecticism. Since absolute truth is unattainable, we are ineluctably left with a "conflict of interpretations." The task of philosophical hermeneutics is, he says, "a true arbitration among the absolutist claims of each of the interpretations."

WORKS IN ENGLISH TRANSLATION: Charles Kelbley translated two books by Paul Ricoeur into English in 1965, *Fallible Man* and *History and Truth.* In 1966 Erazim Kohak translated *Freedom and Nature.* Additional translations include: *Husserl: An Analysis of his Philosophy,* by Edward G. Ballard and Lester Embree, 1967; *The Symbolism of Evil,* by Emerson Buchanan, in 1967; *Freud and Philosophy,* by Denis Savage, 1970; *The Conflict of Interpretations,* by Don Ihde, 1974; *Political and Social Essays,* by David Stewart and Joseph Bien, 1974; *The Rule of Metaphor,* by R. Czerney, 1977; *Essays on Biblical Interpretation,* ed. by Lewis Seymour Mudge, 1980; *Hermeneutics and the Human Sciences,* by John B. Thompson, 1981; *Critical Hermeneutics,* by John B. Thompson, 1981; and volume I of *Time and Narrative,* by K. McLaughlin and D. Pellauer, 1984. Charles Reagan and David Stewart have translated and edited selections from his writings as *The Philosophy of Paul Ricoeur,* 1978; and lectures given in English by Ricoeur at Texas Christian University in 1973 were published in 1976 as *Interpretations Theory: Discourse and the Surplus of Meaning.*

ABOUT: Contemporary Authors 61–64, 1976; Bourgeois, P. Extension of Ricoeur's Hermeneutic, 1973; Ihde, D. Hermeneutic Phenomenology: The Philosophy of Paul Ricoeur, 1971; Rasmussen, D. Mythic-Symbolic Language and Philosophical Anthropology, 1971; Reagan,

C. (ed.) Studies in the Philosophy of Paul Ricoeur, 1979; Who's Who in France, 1983-84. *Periodicals*—Dissent July–August 1970; Journal of the American Academy of Religion December 1983; Modern Age Spring 1983; Modern Language Notes December 1981; December 1983; Philosophy Today 1972; 1973.

*RIMANELLI, GIOSE (November 28, 1926–), Italian-American novelist, essayist, journalist, and critic was born in Casacalenda, Molise, Italy, to an impoverished family. He has sent the following sketch to *World Authors*: "Vincenzo, his father, was the son of Seppe who worked in the sewers in St. Paul, Minnesota. His mother, Concettina Minicucci, a Canadian citizen, was the daughter of Tony 'Dominick' Minicucci, sired in 1863 in New Orleans by a sailor from Casacalenda who became a justice of the peace during the Reconstruction period (1867–1910), a witness to the slaughter of eleven Italian immigrants of 1891 which has passed into the annals of the history of the emigration under the title 'The Lynching of New Orleans' (Tony 'Dominick' is the central character in the novel *Una posizione sociale*). At the age of ten he was sent to the seminary at Ascoli Satriano, in the Puglie, by his mother who wanted him to become a priest. She probably thought that by so doing she would assure her son's fate along a certain direction in a world that offered few life-alternatives. At the seminary he studied not only the Scriptures and Latin, but also Greek, Provençal, French, Hebrew. On his own he translated the French symbolists, Rimbaud, Verlaine, Apollinaire. He also began his first exercises in writing. However, he left the seminary in 1940, rejecting the ambience and definitively renouncing the priestly vocation. The short story 'Il Pretino' (The Fledgling Priest) published in *Il Mondo* in 1956, is a transcript of this event.

"Between 1941 and 1942 he lived in a state of uneasiness, maceration, and mortification, in the family and in the town. It was a bleak, black year during which his intolerance of his situation incubated, matured and led to his flight. In 1943, in fact, hitchhiking on a German lorry he arrived in North Italy where, as a lost and confused youth without a precise political consciousness, he was sucked into the vortex of the fratricidal war. He was forcibly recruited into the army of the Republic of Salò and underwent a terrible adventure of soldiering on the mountains of Val Sesia and of Val Camonica, until he became a prisoner of war of the Allies. In the concentration camp of Coltano, near Pisa, he met the American poet Ezra Pound who was, at that time, detained by the Allies as a war crimi-

GIOSE RIMANELLI

nal. At Cava dei Tirreni he managed to escape from the sealed freight cars of the train that would have taken him to Africa and from there made his way on foot to Casacalenda, where his mother had been mourning him as dead. It was 1945. But he remained only for a short time in Casacalenda, where he conceived and wrote the first drafts of the novels of his youth—*Tiro al piccione* (*The Day of the Lion*) and *Peccato originale* (*Original Sin*), just long enough to understand that he had become a stranger in his own house, his own ambience. In fact 1946 was the year when he began his wanderings all over Italy and Europe, hitchhiking and secretly boarding freight cars, as an aspirant reporter, as a student, as a man desirous of experiencing the world. He settled down in Paris (after having roamed about in Switzerland, Holland, Germany, Sweden, Lapland) earning his keep as a jazz musician. Here he audited the lectures of the philosopher Gaston Bachelard at the Sorbonne, made the acquaintance of Sartre, Camus, Boris Vian, and the linguistic circle around André Martinet. He returned to Rome in 1947 where he met the writer Francesco Jovine, his fellow-countryman, to whom he became attached in a bond of fraternal friendship.

"His Roman sojourn was marked by poverty, loneliness, and a fervor born of desperation. He took up residence, as it were, in the National Library where he wrote graduation theses for a few lire with a sandwich thrown in. But in the meanwhile in Rome, where he audited the lectures of N. Sapegno and G. Ungaretti at the University and where he made the acquaintance of writers such as Corrado Alvaro, he wrote his first

°rē´´ mä nel´ lē, jyo´ sä

articles for *La Repubblica*. His friends were few: F. Jurlo, the painter; Roberto Ruta, the sculptor; Ugo Moretti, the writer; all personages who were to mark important moments of his life.

"In 1949, in Rome, he met Cesare Pavese who read the manuscript of *Tiro al piccione,* intuited its importance and included it in Einaudi's *I Coralli* series. It was scheduled for publication together with Jovine's *Terre del Sacramento* which Rimanelli had typed at the author's dictation. But Jovine died in 1950 and Cesare Pavese committed suicide, in consequence of which the publication of *Tiro al piccione,* urgently pressed by Pavese, was boycotted. Meanwhile he continued his wandering life: Argentina, Brazil, Columbia, Greece, Israel; among others, he made the acquaintance of Pablo Neruda. In 1952 he elaborated the first draft of the novel titled *Una posizione sociale* (A Social Position). At the suggestion of Carlo Ponti and Mario Soldati, whom he got to know in Stockholm, he also began to write movie scripts. Thus were born *La lupa* (The She-Wolf) for Mai Britt (based on the short story with the same title by Verga) and *Suor Letizia* (Sister Letizia) for Anna Magnani.

"The year 1953 found him visiting his parents in Canada, where he wrote pieces for RAI, the Italian national radio and TV network. He was also director of the Italian language newspaper *Il cittadino canadese* in Montreal for a brief period. Meanwhile in Italy, at the urging of Vittorini, Mondadori published *Tiro al piccione.*

"Subsequently he traveled through the immense length and breadth of Canada, on occasion adapting himself to the hard work of tobacco picker. He crossed over the border to the United States, moving southward, and in New Orleans, Louisiana, he visited the house on Ursuline Street in which his mother's father was born. He also did research on the slaughter of the Italians in 1891, utilizing some of the material thus gathered in the second and definitive draft of *Una posizione sociale.* In 1954 he returned to Italy and was engaged as a reporter by the *Gazzetta del Popolo* of Turin. He wrote about his Canadian experiences in *Biglietto di terza* (Third Class Ticket) published in 1958. In 1955 he married Liliana Chiurazzi, by whom he had two sons, Marco and Michele, and from whom he was later divorced. He established a fixed residence in Rome and worked as a journalist and as a writer of movie scripts. He wrote the play *Tè in casa Picasso* (Tea at Picasso's) and the ballet *Lares,* both works inspired by Pablo Picasso whom he had come to know in Vallouris. This was also the year when, owing to a mysterious combination of circumstances and against his will, he began his collaboration with the Roman weekly *Lo*

Specchio (The Mirror) for which he wrote a literary column under the pseudonym A. G. Solari in which he satirized the Italian literary world with its prizes, its trendy drawing rooms, its mafioso structure. When his true identity was disclosed, he collected his essays in a single volume under the title *Il del furbo* (The Sneak's Craft) in 1959. It was tantamount to signing his own death sentence with the power élite that ruled over the Italian literary scene. In this same year, his novel *Una posizione sociale* was published. It also contained a record cut by the Lambro Jazz Band of Milan, with music written by himself and the Italo-American Pasquale Miozza, at a time when for Italians jazz was still a novelty awaiting discovery.

"It was at this point that he decided on self-exile to the United States, turning his back on Italy and his own family. He left after a fleeting visit to Molise. In the United States he went from one university to another as a professor of Italian literature and as a lecturer, until he settled down, temporarily, at Yale University. This was the year 1962 when he divorced his first wife and married Bettina Quatran, a student in one of his courses. But even this marriage, from which was born his third son David, was destined to fail in the passage of time. This was a time of estrangement, of continuous displacements from one American city to another, of secret industriousness, of a fatiguing appropriation of new realities and new languages, of a re-immersion in life and of comeback as a writer: thus came into being numerous novels in English and Italian almost all of which are still unpublished, essays on American and Canadian literature.

"In 1967 he brought out in Italy collections of his whimsical poems *Carmina blabla* and *Monaci d'amore medievali* (Medieval Monks of Love). This was also the year when he wrote a lengthy novel, still unpublished, titled *La Macchina paranoica* (The Paranoid Machine) in which he portrayed the existential agitated and unsettled condition of contemporary man. In 1968, in Italy, he published *Tragica America* (Tragic America), a collection of essays on the multiple aspects of present-day American society. In this same year he transferred to the State University of New York at Albany, New York, as tenured professor of Italian and comparative literature.

"During this time he also wrote other poetic works in English including a book of visual poetry for children, *Poems Make Pictures Pictures Make Poems* (1971). The year 1972 saw the publication of the novella "Shortage" in *La Tribuna* of Montreal as well as the publication in *Change,* a Paris journal of linguistic studies, of the first chapter of a French translation of *Graffiti*, the novel written in 1967, extracted from the vaster corpus of *La Macchina paranoica*. These were years marked by intense industriousness, but also years of maceration, bitterness, agony, deriving not only from his problematic and unquiet nature but also from the difficulties of his conjugal relations, from his rejection of the exile world, from his self-feeling as a stranger, from the frustration of his dreams as a writer, from his alienation from the reality of the academic world. In fact the key events of these years were the separation from his second wife with the consequent divorce and the first draft of a new novel, 'The Academics' (later re-written with substantial changes in its structure under the new title 'The Anaconda Journals') in which he reveals his hallucinating experiences in the groves of Academe.

"In 1976 he revisited Italy and the Molise region, where he experienced the sensation of a rebirth after death. In this same year he became a contributor to the Milan daily *Il Giorno*, a collaboration which was to last for several years.

"In the following year the publisher Marinelli brought out his novel *Graffiti*. For Rimanelli it was a fundamental and significant event in his life because he re-discovered his Molisian roots. And in a vast autobiographical novel, *Molise Molise*, his last work published by the same firm in 1979, he viewed his life as a myth-symbol of the great journey in the world, of growth of return."

"*Brioso*, inquisitive, and always engaging," Thomas G. Bergin writes, "Rimanelli has had a career more unusual than most men." The two novels by which English-language readers best know him, *The Day of the Lion* and *Original Sin*, trace in graphic detail his early years and the struggles of his family to survive in the poverty and disruption of Italy during the last days of Fascism. *The Day of The Lion* (its title is an ironic quotation of Mussolini's aphorism: "Better to live one day as a lion than a hundred years as a sheep") is dedicated to the memory of the Italian writer Francesco Jovine and "to the stranger, a workman in Cava dei Terreni, who, in early June 1943, took me into his home and thus saved me from further hardships." That real-life rescue is the turning point in the novel in which the young first-person narrator describes the horrors of the war in Italy, a war in which, as one character observes, "you die piecemeal." The boy's experiences—his adolescent love affairs, his first direct encounters with death in battle, his conva-

lescence from severe wounds, and his return to a ravaged but still loving family—are told in an impressionistic style that Taliaferro Boatwright described in a review as "reminiscent of Céline and Stendhal." The book was widely praised for its stark power and its realism. Its successor, *Original Sin*, in which the now desperately poor family at last finds refuge in Canada, was even more terrible in its realistic detail: "A tale of bitter irony and recurrent violence, and a tale well told," Bergin wrote in the *Saturday Review*, "for all its melodramatic elements, a true one."

Rimanelli's work as a critic includes, in addition to his many Italian writings, his edition (co-editor Roberto Ruberto) in 1966 of a collection, *Modern Canadian Stories*, to which he contributed a long and scholarly introduction on the history of Canadian literature that the Canadian writer Earle Birney called "as original and insightful a piece of writing as any of the stories that follow." He has also written an essay on Cesare Pavese, "Pavese's *Diario*: Why Suicide? Why Not?" published in *Italian Literature: Roots and Branches*—a *festschrift* for the Italian-language scholar Thomas G. Bergin which Rimanelli co-edited with Kenneth John Atchity in 1975.

WORKS IN ENGLISH TRANSLATION: Ben Johnson translated both *The Day of the Lion* (1954) and *Original Sin* (1957).

ABOUT: Columbia Dictionary of Modern European Literature, 1980. *Periodicals*—Books Abroad January 1967; Canadian Modern Language Review March 1967; Times Literary Supplement December 1, 1972; October 31, 1975; World Literature Today Winter 1981.

---

*ROBLES, EMMANUEL (May 4, 1914–), French novelist and dramatist, writes (in French): "I was born in Oran, Algeria. My father, a mason, and my mother, a washerwoman, were both of Spanish origin, their parents having emigrated from Malaga and from Grenada. I did not know my father, who died in December 1913 in Casablanca, where he had gone to work on the construction of a military hospital. I have described my childhood, which was difficult although brightened by my mother's affection, in *Saison violente* (Violent Season), the only autobiography I have so far written. After receiving my primary school education I attended Ardaillon College, thanks to a scholarship without which I could not have continued studying. In 1931 I entered the Ecole Normal in Algiers, and then the Faculty of Letters before being drafted for military service. In September 1937, when I

EMMANUEL ROBLES

was serving in the air force, I met Albert Camus. He was then directing rehearsals of the comedy *La Celestine,* with Fernando de Roja in the role of Calixte. My friendship with Camus grew out of our common passion for the theater and for Spain.

"During the period immediately preceding the war I became a member of the group led by Camus that was later known as the 'School of Algiers.' Although my period of miltary service ended in September 1939 I was [appointed to] the staff of a general officer as a translator. Nevertheless, in March 1940 I asked to be transferred to an air force batallion, and that was how I found myself, before the defeat of June 1940, on a military airbase in eastern Algeria. The enormous infestation of mosquitos there, though less redoubtable than Hitler's tanks, caused many deaths from malaria in our little unit.

"By this time I had already published two novels: *L'Action,* and *La Vallée du paradis* (The Valley of Paradise), which appeared in serial form in the *Soir Republican,* a journal directed by Camus. I had taken the pseudonym of Emmanuel Chênes. After my discharge from the army I became a teacher. I had just married, and in the tranquility of an Algerian village I took up my pen again to write the novel *Travail d'homme* (*The Angry Mountain*), which must have appeared in 1943, after the English-American invasion of North Africa on November 8, 1942. I was employed by the Allied intelligence services as a Spanish translator, and then became a war correspondent reporting on the invasion of Corsica and the advance through southern Italy at the time of the battle of Monte

Cassino. After the liberation of Paris I was recalled by the Ministry of the Air Force, but the bomber in which I was traveling crashed in flames. Four people died in the accident, including Colonel Chopin, commander of the French air force in Syria. My only loss in this accident was my war correspondent's notes which, under the circumstances, was not serious. I was sent on a mission to Great Britain, and then to Germany, and I followed those troops that were sent in haste to the notorious bridge at Remagen.

"Once the war and all this work had finished I was sent, before my demobilization, to South America to report on the test flight of hydroplane Laté 631, which crashed in Uruguay at Rochas Lake killing two people. After my discharge in April 1946 I attempted to live in Paris with my wife and young son, but nostalgia for the sun made me return to Algeria, where I became the literary critic of Radio Algiers. There I wrote my play *Montserrat* and my novel *Les Hauteurs de la ville* (City Heights), which each won a prize and whose success in France and in other countries allowed me to continue working without material hardships. At just that time my wife and I had a daughter.

"At that time I traveled a great deal as a reporter, and when the war for the liberation of Algeria began I was in Mexico working with Luis Bunuel on the screenplay of my novel *Cela s'appelle l'aurore (Dawn on Our Darkness).* On my return to Algeria I became one of the founders of the Federation des Libéraux and a contributor to the movement's journal, *Espoir Algerie.* In 1957 a bomb destroyed the printing house at which the journal was printed. This was the work of the hit men employed by powerful members of the colonial faction, the future supporters of the OAS, who opposed our work for a new Algeria, freed of colonial rule, in which all communities would enjoy equal rights and responsibilities. The accidental death of my sixteen-year-old son in April 1958 forced my wife and me to return, at least temporarily, to Paris. The tragic course of the fighting in Algeria, especially after the OAS entered the conflict, kept us in France where danger still followed us.

"I continued to write for the theater, and then for television, without neglecting my work as a novelist, or conferences that took place in the United States, Canada, South America, and elsewhere. Since the death of my wife in 1974 I have divided my time between traveling and quiet intervals of study, making myself a living example of a saying of Camus': 'There is a time to live, and a time to bear witness to life.' I feel more than ever face to face with myself and with the puzzle of a world that we must all try to make more just, more human and, in a word, more habitable."

—trans. H. Batchelor

In the judgment of the French scholar and critic Henri Peyre, Albert Camus and Emmanuel Roblès are "the two most important writers to have come from French Algeria in this century." But in contrast to Camus' international fame, Roblès is relatively unknown to English and American readers. His play *Montserrat,* adapted by Lillian Hellman who also directed it, had a brief run on Broadway in 1949, but his fiction, though a considerable amount of it is available in English translation, remains largely unknown. In France, however, Roblès is ranked not only with Camus but with Sartre and Malraux as a writer of profound moral and intellectual significance. He has received many honors (including the Prix Femina in 1948 for *Les Hauteurs de la ville,* the Prix Populiste in 1945 for *Travail d'homme*), membership in the Goncourt Academy, and in 1963 he was elected Chevalier of the Legion of Honor. Nevertheless, perhaps because of his refusal to commit himself to any ideological or political philosophy (his thinking comes close to Existentialism but he is not an existentialist), his use of traditional literary techniques and conventional forms, and his fundamental romanticism, Roblès remains outside the mainstream of current literature.

Dominating Roblès' work is the theme of the man of good will struggling to find meaning in a world torn by war and madness. Erotic but also romantic love—an intimate relationship with a devoted and sympathetic woman—is at once his salvation and his tragedy: a salvation because it offers him the values he cherishes, a tragedy because the circumstances of life in the modern world frustrate and sometimes destroy the relationship. Often the Roblès hero sacrifices his life for his vision of beauty and love. And where he survives, it is only with the knowledge that, as he writes near the end of his novel *Vesuvius,* "there is a tragic side to happiness, and . . . it can never be wholly innocent."

Roblès' first major literary success came with his novel *Cela s'appelle l'aurore (Dawn on Our Darkness)* in 1952. Translated into fifteen languages and filmed by Luis Bunuel, the novel is set in a poverty-stricken town in Sardinia, where the author had served during World War II. A doctor leaves his wife and his comfortable life in Naples to serve a primitive and exploited community where he falls passionately in love with a young widow and faces a crisis of loyalty and duty when he shelters a fugitive murderer. "The dismal atmosphere of the least attractive parts of Sardinia, the savagery of the peasants untouched by charity or by obedience to the law, the tragedy of the doctor as he realizes that he is being forced to fight with his back to the wall, alone against fate and society, are as powerfully rendered as they are in any novel of Julien Green, of Graham Greene, and even of William Faulkner," Henri Peyre wrote. Maurice Faure called the book "a hymn to woman," celebrating the redemptive power of love even in sordid surroundings. Faure's description would apply equally well to *Printemps d'Italie* (Italian Spring, 1970), a love story set in German-occupied Italy in World War II. In it, French reviewer Yvan Audouard commented, "I found again the enchantment that years earlier I had felt in Hemingway's *A Farewell to Arms.*" War-ravaged Italy, this time Naples, was the scene of the earlier and better known novel *Le Vesuve* (1961). Here, played against the background of the bombed and demoralized city and a smoldering eruption of the nearby volcano, a French army officer recuperating from a severe wound has an idyllic love affair with a beautiful but strangely aloof woman. Although in the end they marry, they both learn bitterly that in a world gone mad the struggle for happiness must end at best in compromise and even sometimes in despair. Yet the ideal of love remains; the conscious struggle itself, as Fanny Landi-Bénos, a longtime friend of Roblès, writes, marks the "roblèsien" hero, constitutes "the supreme dignity of mankind," and allows always for the possiblity if not the fulfillment of hope.

The most dramatic "roblèsien" hero is Montserrat, a Spanish officer in Venezuela in 1812 who defies his commander to protect the native insurrectionist leader Bolivar. Inspired by his own Spanish background, Roblès found in this historical figure a symbol of the tragic lot of Europe under Fascist domination. Suspected by his commanding officer, the ruthless and cynical Izquierdo, Montserrat is subjected to the most terrile of tortures: he is confronted with a group of innocent hostages and told that they will be executed one by one if he does not reveal Bolivar's whereabouts. One by one they are led off to death as Montserrat watches. His own fate is inevitable, but before he dies he learns that Bolivar has escaped and that his dreams of liberation from Spanish tyranny have some hope of realization. A stark and grim tragedy, *Montserrat* was acclaimed at its first production in Paris in 1949 and has subsequently been produced in forty-five countries and in twenty-three languages, including Chinese, Japanese, Yiddish, and Afrikaans. The American director Harold Clurman staged a Hebrew production for the Habimah company in Israel. In its English language version, however, the play has not fared well. Lillian Hellman's adaptation, which Clurman called "an honest attempt to capture the spirit of the original play," but others, like James A. Kilker, considered to be "unfaithful to the spirit of the play," followed Roblès' plot and dialogue but omitted some of the longer philosophical passages. Nevertheless, American and later British audiences found it slow-moving and "talky," and it ran for only sixty-five performances on Broadway. It has subsequently been revived in several off-Broadway productions and filmed for educational television. Hellman herself attributed its failure not to the adaptation but to her directing and casting of the play: "I not only cast the play with a kind of abandoned belief that good actors can play anything, but I directed it in a fumbling, frightened way . . . " she wrote in her memoir *Pentimento* (1973). According to one of her biographers, Richard Moody: "She tried to make a revolutionary document out of a play that was primarily concerned with moral issues and with an existentialist hero who knew exactly why he must die."

WORKS IN ENGLISH TRANSLATION: Lillian Hellman's adaptation of *Montserrat* was published in 1950. Three later plays by Roblès: *Porfirio* (1953), *L'Horloge* (The Clock, 1965), and *Plaidoyer pour un rebelle* (Case for a Rebel, 1966) were translated into English by James A. Kilker in 1977. Roblès' first book to appear in English was his third novel, *Travail d'homme* (1943) which was translated by Dorothy Bolton in 1948 as *The Angry Mountain*. Also available in English are the novels *Dawn on Our Darkness,* translated by Thérèse Pol, 1954; *Flowers for Manuela,* in 1956, a translation by Joyce Emerson of *Federica* (1954); *The Knives,* 1958, Geoffrey Sainsbury's translation of *Les Couteaux* (1956); and *Vesuvius,* 1970, translated by Milton Stansbury from *Le Vesuve* (1961). Roblès himself has translated into French a number of Spanish writers, including Ramon Sender and Garcia Lorca.

ABOUT: Astre, G.A. Emmanuel Roblès ou l'homme et son espoir, 1972; Contemporary Authors 81–84, 1979; Columbia Dictionary of Modern European Literature, 1980; Depierris, J.L. Entretiens avec Emmanuel Roblès, 1967; Kilker, J.J. Introduction to Three Plays by Emmanuel Roblès, 1977; Landi-Bénos, F. Emmanuel Roblès ou Les raisons de vivre; Peyre, H. Afterword to Roblès' Vesuvius, 1970; Rozier, M.A. Emmanuel Roblès ou la rupture du Cercle, 1973. Periodicals—Kentucky Foreign Language Quarterly 1964; Livres de France February 1965; Simoun December 1959.

RODRIGUEZ, JUDITH (GREEN), (February 13, 1936–), Australian poet, writes: "I was born Judith Catherine Green, in Perth, Western Australia. My mother Dora Spigl Green came of a Russian Jewish family—she was the second child born in Australia—and had trained as a teacher; my father Gerald Green, who had migrated from England when he was twenty, was working his way up in the Australian Electrolux organization. From four till twenty-four I lived in Brisbane, Queensland, and went to Ascot State School, Brisbane Girls' Grammar School and the University of Queensland, ending with first class Honours in English Language and Literature. My mother's values, although she had rejected Judaism and my brother and I were brought up Anglicans, were very Jewish in that education was the great good she sought for her children; and I was taught to compete in swimming (didn't like it), music (a permanent love and Spigl family tradition), and art (won prizes, might have been an artist except my mother had inculcated a respect for the salaried life).

"I wrote poems from when I was eight, parodies and lyrics about Beauty and Truth (predictably) for the school magazine; and had my first acceptances from literary magazines in 1959 (*Meanjin Southerly* and *Australian Letters*). After graduating (1957) I first taught, then lectured for a bit at the University of Queensland, then won the Walter and Eliza Hall Travelling Scholarship to Cambridge, England. At Girton College there I won Firsts (easier than Queensland) but this period was unhelpful except that I traveled very widely in Europe and the Levant. I turned down a job at the University of St John's, Newfoundland (too cold) and instead lectured for two years at the University of the West Indies at Kingston, Jamaica, where I met and married Colombian Fabio Rodriguez (1964) by whom I have four children. I wrote very little, however, till we returned to Australia after a few years teaching English to foreigners and lecturing at Colleges of Education in London; the culture shock of re-entering Australia stimulated me, partly to protest.

"In 1962 David Malouf and I—we traveled a great deal together, especially in Greece, Austria and Italy—got together (by post) with Rodney Hall and and Donald Maynard to put our *Four Poets* (Cheshire, Melbourne). My section was called "A Question of Ignorance." My books of poetry after this are *Nu-Plastik Fanfare Red, Water Life* (with my own linocuts, as also the following two books), *Shadow on Glass, Mudcrab at Gambaro's,* and *Witch Heart. Mrs Noah and the Minoan Queen,* my anthology of women poets of my generation in Australia, is to come out this year from Sisters Publishing.

JUDITH RODRIGUEZ

"Since 1969 I have taught in the Department of English at La Trobe University, Melbourne, and also taught creative writing classes for many institutions throughout Australia. I was Poetry Editor for *Meanjin Quarterly* from 1979 to 1982. I have held writing fellowships from the Australia Council for the Arts in 1974, 1978 and 1983. *Water Life* won the inaugural South Australian Government Biennial Prize for Literature and *Mudcrab at Gambaro's* the PEN/Peter Stuyvesant Prize for Poetry in 1981. I have read my poetry and talked on Australian Literature at various overseas universities and other venues in New Zealand, U.S.A., Canada, Sweden, Denmark, Germany, France, Italy and Yugoslavia. Since 1974 I have worked at printmaking (linocuts), mainly for book decoration; there have been four exhibitions of my work since 1978.

"Fabio Rodriguez and I divorced in 1980 and I married the writer Thomas Shapcott in October, 1982. I find feminist literary circles the most stimulating in discussion. The fellowship of women artists is the great gift of the seventies— my growing-up lacked visible contemporary models of women's achievement. However, I was fortunate in the early criticism of John Manifold, and of my contemporaries David Malouf and Rodney Hall. More recent stimulus has been from Siv Cedering (a New York writer), Robyn Archer (an Australian stage performer) and Emily Hope (artist and writer); also from women's enterprises such as Salon A-Muse, Melbourne, and Sisters Publishing. Especially at a time when education's wings are being clipped, the new things and encouragement have to be sought out. I find teaching and writing divide my life—I am sure it should not, ideally, be that way; there have been moments when they added up.

"I write poetry to live more fully."

_____

Judith Rodriguez' first poems in *Four Poets* have been characterized by her husband, Thomas W. Shapcott, as displaying "a vigorous manipulation of language (barely kept in check by the formal lyricism of the time) to serve the ends of immediacy and directness of expression." Upon her return to Australia after an extended sojourn in Europe and Jamaica, however, her published work showed new depth and sophistication. *Nu-Plastik Fanfare Red and Other Poems* contained several poems distinguished by a voice of passionate commitment. Others from the collection show a sure grasp of colloquial idiom tinged with irony, as in "She Speaks," from the four-poem sequence "My Grandmother":

I used to think
it would be sinful to complain, my dear,
of being old; and then Queen Mary said
it was a perfect nuisance! if she thought
it right to say so, then perhaps I may.

Shapcott described the poems in this collection as "imbued with a warm female sharpness— precisely observed moments and objects and responses, place rather than time, people through things, humanity through attitudes. Her tone had become clipped, never sloppy; her poems as tight-packed as a larder full of preserves. She had found a way with language to contain her wide experience and range of interests."

Water Life was the first of Rodriguez' poetry collections to be accompanied by her own linocuts, some of which illustrate the poems directly, while others partake only of the general watery theme. A note of firm self-assurance echoes throughout this book; she seems able to look at herself and even aspects of her career with a sunny irony untinged by anger or remorse, as in "Occasion for Elegy":

That was your gibe: I was waiting
for people I knew to die
so as to agonize elegies
and monkey with memory;

but that was when I was younger.
Now I'm near forty, I'm wary
of the body all booby-traps
and the world-wide cemetery,

reminiscence slippery as rot
and loyalty much like libel,
compassion that gobbles down horrors
and suffering worse than I feel.

Shapcott considered that *Water Life* "summed up not only stages in the poet's own intellectual and emotional development, but that of a generation of women, and in ways directed to growth and celebrative instincts rather than rejection and self-immolation." The critic for *Choice* remarked of the poems: "These are the honest scenes of a decent, unexaggerated world. Some of the best moments are neat self-revelation by a lively woman who 'malingers and charms in fits and starts, dies daily,' affable but with an edge of sharpness. This is an attractive book, full of calm, competent studies of a woman's world, the images always appealing more to the eye than to the ear." Christopher Pollnitz, however, writing in *Southerly,* suggested that "few of her poems satisfy as wholes. *Water Life* is a versatile volume. Rodriguez writes well in short bursts, about domestic and suburban scenes, poetry and poets, animals and politics. Unfortunately the versatility invades individual poems in the form of the failure to maintain a stable mode of address to the reader."

In Rodriguez' collections, *Shadow on Glass Mudcrab at Gambaro's* and *Witch Heart,* Shapcott suggested, "the combination of song-flow and mind-stress [has] fully cohered. . . . She is in many ways the most exciting and explorative of the 'Brisbane Octopus' generation, her work providing the sense of an intellect—and a female strength—in course of liberation and growth." Chris Wallace-Crabbe wrote that *Mudcrab at Gambaro's* "is surely the arena where Judith Rodriguez comes into her own as a maker of distinction." The collection seemed to him "restlessly rooted in the domestic, the passionate and the grittily audibly factual. The poems in the book's second half "chart and bear witness to a new, intimate relationship. . . . They point resolutely toward the private life, while using the linking, even repetitive metaphor of the mudcrab to signal both a private bond and the literary antecedent of Robert Lowell's dolphin, itself alluded to in one poem . . . the poems celebrate the common life, its jiggers and whatnots, but also do new things with that stubborn customer, language."

Most of Rodriguez' major collections have been published by the University of Queensland Press, which Les Murray has called "the runaway success story of Australian poetry publishing." In addition to the awards she lists above, she has received the South Australia Government prize (1978) and the Artlook Victorian prize (1979).

PRINCIPAL WORKS: "A Question of Ignorance," *in* Four Poets, 1962; Nu-Plastik Fanfare Red and Other Poems, 1973; Water Life, 1976; Shadow on Glass, 1978; Mudcrab at Gambaro's, 1980; Witch Heart, 1982.

ABOUT: Vinson, J. (ed.) Contemporary Poets, 1980. *Periodicals*—Australian Book Review December 1980; Choice November 1977; Library Journal August 1977; Quadrant October 1976; Southerly no. 4, 1977.

ROREM, NED (October 23, 1923–), American composer, memoirist, and writer on music, was born in Richmond, Indiana, of a Quaker family. He grew up in Chicago where he spent two years at the Music School of Northwestern University before transferring to the Curtis Institute of Music in Philadelphia. After two summers of study at Tanglewood, he took his B.A. (1946) and M.A. (1948) at Juilliard School of Music in New York. In *An Absolute Gift* he writes that Juilliard taught him little about music because "for a full degree at Juilliard one took nonmusical courses. Having passed the entrance exams with flying colors, I wasn't required to attend musical classes except in piano and composition. What I therefore recall most clearly of that illustrious school in 1946–47 are studies in sociology, American history, physical education, and, yes, hygiene." Rorem was also influenced by his association with the American composer Virgil Thomson as student and music-copyist.

From an early age Rorem was attracted to French traditions in both music and literature, and in 1949 he left the United States for an extended stay abroad, first in Morocco and then, through the early 1950s, in Paris. There he made the acquaintance of many people important in France's cultural life who came later to figure in his published diaries and essays, among them Jean Marais, Julien Green, Julius Katchen, Francis Poulenc, Nadia Boulanger, and his close friend the Vicomtesse Marie Laure de Noailles.

In 1966 Rorem's first book, *The Paris Diary,* was an immediate *succès de scandale.* His undated diary jottings reveal a persona obsessed with social climbing, drinking, and sex. The book is loosely structured, with few points taking more than two paragraphs to develop. Its special characteristic is its liberal use of aphorisms: "Paris today is a city asleep. And loudly snoring"; "It's harder to maintain a reputation for being pretty than for being a great artist"; "Is a fugue the pointless conversation of persons in too-perfect agreement? Or someone talking to himself?"; "Composition is notation of distortion of what composers think they've heard before. Masterpieces are marvelous misquotations"; "The twelve-toners behave as if music should be seen and not heard." A number of readers found *The Paris Diary* repulsive because of Rorem's candid remarks about his acquaintances and his obsession with his own looks and sex life. Rorem later

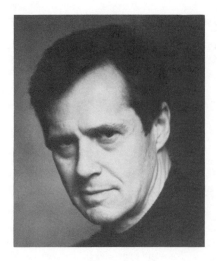

NED ROREM

expressed some indignation over this kind of re-action, writing that when *The Paris Diary* was published, Harold Acton, "who loathed it, " asked: " . . . what have such horrors as crabs, piles, and bedbugs to do with musical inspiration and 'the crushing necessity to be an artist'?" To which Rorem responded: "How should I know? I'm the artist, he's the esthete" (*An Absolute Gift*). In Robert Phelps' preface to the diary, Rorem is termed "an earnest narcissist" and Rob-ert Mazzocco, in *New York Review of Books* saw Rorem as "a Columbus of the looking-glass."

The *New York Diary* followed in 1967, open-ing with an assertion that "it's not that I'm more self-involved than other people, I'm just more free about showing it." His sense of freedom in this book leads to extended sections on his "compulsion to drink," the "anonymous carnality" of a Manhattan homosexual bath-house, and his experimentation with mescaline. He looks back occasionally on his own past with surprise: "To think I used to introduce myself by enclosing half-naked pictures in letters to people I'd never seen!" In both diaries Rorem's irre-pressible pleasure with himself seems unforced and engaging, resulting in a kind of blithe cheer-fulness at unexpected moments. He concludes *The Paris Diary* by noting, "Alas, I am hap-py! . . . I eat, with good appetite, sleep and screw well when not working well, and am, as they say, *appreciated*. And so, though the style was always tragic, larger than life, today I'm happy, alas!"

Rorem's later books exemplify his principle that "I am a composer who also writes, not a writer who also composes" (*Critical Affairs*).

Generally compiled from magazine articles in-terspersed with new "diary" material, these vol-umes vary in quality from chapter to chapter and have reached a somewhat smaller audience than the first two books. Yet they contain many fine things. His essay on "The Beatles," first pub-lished in the *New York Review of Books,* repub-lished in *Music and People,* and again republished in *Setting the Tone,* is characteristic of Rorem at his provocative best ("I never go to classical concerts any more, and I don't know anyone who does"). The essay traces what Rorem sees as the deterioration of the tradition of American serious music and its performance ("most modern song specialists have awful voices and give vanity concerts for invited guests"). His warm appreciation for the Beatles' genius should be read in the light of a later essay, the hostile "Against Rock" (*Critical Affairs*), which takes as its starting point the Rolling Stones' album *Sympathy for the Devil*: "The Stones are fake simple, without gift."

"Ezra Pound as Musician" (*Music and People,* reprinted in *An Absolute Gift*) is important be-cause Rorem's expertise as a professional musi-cian enables him to judge what in Pound's writings about music shows genius and what shows ignorance: "A cultured and imaginative lay-genius like Pound can insist on learning the hard way (i.e. on his own) what a trained profes-sional was quite simply taught at school and takes for granted" (*Music and People*). He feels that, despite its obvious amateurishness, Pound's opera *Le Testament* "is of geniune and haunt-ingly unclassifiable beauty."

In "Making Miss Julie" (*Music and People*), Rorem presents a view of his own compositional process—struggle, revision, and stress—by de-scribing his composition of the opera *Miss Julie,* based on Strindberg's play. After hearing a re-cording of Benjamin Britten's *War Requiem* during this period, he says disarmingly of him-self, "What after that am I but a midget!" Though the New York City Opera production of *Miss Julie* was received respectfully, it was not a popular success and Rorem termed it a "soap opera of sound effects smeared on a European classic" (*An Absolute Gift*). Other important in-formation about Rorem's compositional process can be found in the seven lectures he gave at the University of Buffalo in 1959 and published in *Music From Inside Out*. In one of these, "Writing Songs" (also printed in *Setting the Tone*), Rorem gives the reader some insight into his own working methods: choosing a text ("the only poems I've ever really 'understood' are those I've put to music"), then joining verbal prosody, musical tessitura, rhythm, and accom-paniment in order to achieve a work "of greater magnitude than either text or music alone."

Recognized as one of the best living composers of art songs, Rorem has also written ballets, incidental theater music (including settings for plays by Sean O'Casey and Tennessee Williams), chamber and instrumental music, and symphonies that have been performed by major artists and orchestras in the United States and in Europe. Almost all his musical compositions, his songs in particular, have literary origins. The poets he has set to music range from Tennyson, Browning, Christina Rossetti, and Emily Dickinson to W. H. Auden, John Ashbery, Marianne Moore, Howard Moss, Theodore Roethke, and Wallace Stevens—all in songs notable for their sensitivity and careful workmanship. "I've set just about everything but the telephone book to music," he told an interviewer in 1968.

Rorem's prose style is generally vivid, but its effect is occasionally weakened by idiosyncratic syntax ("Music is *so much* about he who performs it" [*Critical Affairs*] and "Yet I still pursue the longed-for pursuers whom I'm certain could have given me that which is never given" [*Setting the Tone*]). His later diaries are concerned less with sex and alcohol (he no longer drinks) and more with music and his long term-relationship with JH (James Holmes). These later diaries are just as important to Rorem's achievement as an author as his earlier ones, although some reviewers have found them chatty and discursive to the point where (as Ben Sonnenberg wrote in the *Nation* of *An Absolute Gift*) they read "more like spoken than written prose, but less like conversation than like talk on a 'serious' talk show."

Rorem has been awarded a Fulbright fellowship twice (in 1957 and 1978), three Ford Foundation grants, two Guggenheim fellowships (1957 and 1978), and an award from the National Institute for Arts and Letters (1968). *Critical Affairs* received the ASCAP–Deems Taylor Award, as did *The Final Diary*. In 1979 he was elected a member of the American Academy and Institute for Arts and Letters. He received the Pulitzer Prize in 1976 for his orchestral composition, *Air Music*. In 1980 he was appointed co-director of the undergraduate composition program at the Curtis Institute. In the early 1980s he contributed frequently to *Opera News, Christopher Street,* and other periodicals. Rorem lives in New York City.

PRINCIPAL WORKS: The Paris Diary of Ned Rorem, 1966; The New York Diary, 1967; Music From Inside Out, 1967; Music and People, 1968; Critical Affairs, 1970; Pure Contraption, 1973; The Final Diary, 1974; An Absolute Gift, 1978; Setting the Tone, 1983.

ABOUT: Contemporary Authors, first revision series 17–

20, 1976; Current Biography, 1967; Ewen, D. (ed.) Composers since 1900, 1969; Who's Who in America, 1982-83. *Periodicals*—Advocate March 31, 1983; High Fidelity/Musical America September 1974; Keynote May 1980; Nation June 17, 1978; New York Review of Books September 8, 1966; New York Times May 1, 1983; New York Times Book Review November 17, 1974; July 17, 1983; Newsweek December 23, 1968; Opera News December 8, 1973.

ROSEN, CHARLES (WELLES) (May 5, 1927–   ), American musicologist and pianist, was born in New York City, the son of Irwin Rosen and the former Anita Gerber. Showing prodigious talent at the piano at a very early age, he was enrolled at the Juilliard School of Music when only six. The following year he played for the famous pianist Leopold Godowsky, who expressed astonishment at the boy's pianistic facility and assurance. Rosen left Juilliard at the age of eleven to study with the renowned piano teacher Moritz Rosenthal, who had been a pupil of Liszt. Along with his music studies, he attended Princeton University, from which he graduated summa cum laude just after his twentieth birthday; he then took a master's degree (1949) and doctorate (1951) in French literature. Once his doctoral work was completed, Rosen began his performing career, and over three decades has established a solid reputation as a sensitive interpreter of the classical, romantic, and modern piano repertories. His special emphasis, reflected in his current performing habits and in many recordings, has been on the music of Beethoven, but he has also been invited by modern composers to record their works (Igor Stravinsky's *Movements for Piano and Orchestra,* Elliot Carter's *Double Concerto,* and Pierre Boulez' complete piano works).

As a writer on music, Rosen is fluent in his style, persuasive in his criticism, and technically demanding. His first book, *The Classical Style: Haydn, Mozart, Beethoven,* is no mere survey of music from the classical period, but "a description of its language." He holds to what he calls "the old-fashioned position . . . that the musical vernacular can be best defined in terms of the achievements of the period's three major figures. Rosen does not share the common belief "that the greatest artists make their effect only when seen against a background of the mediocrity that surrounded them," but suggests instead that a work of music sets its own terms. The book's structure follows the development of different genres in the work of each composer: the concerto, string quartet, and comic opera for Mozart; the symphony and string quartet for Haydn; the symphony and various styles of pi-

CHARLES ROSEN

ano music for Beethoven. *Opera seria* is accorded separate treatment. The book's technical argument—as well as, to a lesser extent, its critical one—depends on a great number of musical examples, which have undoubtedly restricted its readership. Its aim, however, is much more general: to show that "the music of the classical period, like the painting of the High Renaissance, still provides today a standard by which the rest of our musical experience is judged." *The Classical Style* was generally well received by music critics. Robert Lilienfeld, though critical of Rosen for being "abstract, elusive and allusive," contended that the book "does represent something new—a serious attempt to import into music the categories and the rhetoric of literary and art criticism." E. T. Cone called the book "a first-rate job. What he demonstrates, by example after example, is the way the three great composers developed a musical language characterized by 'the symmetrical resolution of opposing forces.' . . . [Rosen's] emphasis on the dramatic nature of the classical style is by no means new, but I can recall no discussion that so amply explains, by musical illustration, exactly what is meant." *The Classical Style* won the National Book award for musicology in 1972 as well as the Deems Taylor award from ASCAP.

Rosen's contribution to the Modern Masters series, the short critical biography *Arnold Schoenberg,* was also criticized as "musicologically inbred." Louis Snyder complained, "This is a book for specialists, rather than for seekers of the key to the composer's basic, world-sweeping innovations." "Who except musicians," asked Robert Craft, "will be able to follow Mr. Rosen's exposition of Schoenberg's serial system, though this is admirably lucid as well as free from the diagrammatic and numerical sigla that limit to initiates the readership of most new publications on the subject?" Yet Craft then declared at length his admiration for the book, calling it "one of the most brilliant monographs ever to be published on any composer, let alone the most difficult master of the present age. It is also the first essay on Schoenberg that is beyond partisanship, as well as the first to place him in the perspective of four centuries of European music."

Sonata Forms is a formidable attempt at a historical and stylistic analysis of the sonata, which, Rosen writes, ever since it "was defined by theorists in the second quarter of the nineteenth century on the basis of late eighteenth- and early nineteenth-century practice, has been the most prestigious of musical forms." He wants "to see what can be salvaged of the traditional view of" the form. "Its insufficiencies, its absurdities, even, have become steadily more glaring." The term is used today by musicologists about eighteenth-century works "only prudently, skeptically, half-heartedly, and with many reservations, spoken and unspoken." Yet Rosen believes we still need the term for an understanding of the classical and later periods. His use of the plural in the title reflects his belief "that what was eventually to become the canonic type of sonata form developed along with other forms, which influenced each other and were, in fact, interdependent." The opera aria and concerto forms are also extensively considered: without them "the history of sonata forms is quite simply unintelligible." The problem, however, of defining the form in its classical (eighteenth-century) manifestation is immense. "It is very dubious that a unique sonata form can be so defined even for a single decade of the late eighteenth century. . . . If a form 'changes,' it is not clear when it would be useful to consider it the same form, although changed, and when we must think of it as a new form altogether. . . . There is no biological continuity among sonata forms, and there are many sonatas more closely related to concertos, arias, and even fugues than to other sonatas." One reviewer, Joseph Kerman, thought the "reconstruction of sonata forms will probably cause . . . much raising of eyebrows (and clenching of fists) in music-theoretical circles." Kerman also commented on the "plenitude of music examples that is without precedent in book publishing, as far as I know: more than half of this book consists of music." Another critic praised the book "for its clarity and rational flow." "There is no other work comparable to this in English," wrote the reviewer for *Choice.*

Romanticism and Realism: The Mythology of Nineteenth-Century Art, on which Rosen collaborated with Henri Zerner, professor of fine arts at Harvard and curator of prints at the Fogg Museum of Art, represents, in its primary concern with visual art, a departure in subject matter from his previous books. Five of the book's eight essays were jointly written reviews, originally published in the *New York Review of Books,* of art exhibitions or books; these, and the other, separately written, essays were then carefully edited to form a running argument concerning the supposed polarity in the nineteenth century between official or academic and avant-garde art. The authors describe and explore many links between the two isms of their title. In romanticism they find, in Marina Vaizey's words, "two distinct tendencies interlocked—art for art's sake, which involved the gradual demotion of such genres as history painting, and a new realism based on the belief that nature and natural forms were capable of being intrinsically expressive. The crucial bond between romanticism and realism was the gradual excision of subject matter as a primary concern in painting. If the romantics used a technique of alienation, making the ordinary strange, the realists made the familiar familiar." Vaizey termed the book "itself a sketchy yet highly wrought work of art."

Rosen lives in Manhattan, in the same apartment in which he grew up, and performs and lectures widely. He was Ernest Bloch lecturer at Berkeley in 1977 and Charles Eliot Norton professor of poetry at Harvard in 1980–81. He holds honorary degrees in music from Trinity College, Dublin, and Leeds University, and is a member of the National Academy of Arts and Sciences.

WORKS: The Classical Style, 1971; Arnold Schoenberg, 1975; Sonata Forms, 1980; (with Henri Zerner) Romanticism and Realism, 1984.

ABOUT: Who's Who in America, 1983–84. *Periodicals*—Art in America Summer 1984; Choice February 1976; December 1980; Christian Century October 22, 1975; May 30, 1984; Christian Science Monitor March 24, 1976; Library Journal May 15, 1971; January 15, 1976; April 15, 1980; December 15, 1983; Music Library Association Notes March 1981; Nation December 6, 1971; National Review January 23, 1976; New York Review of Books September 18, 1975; October 23, 1980; New York Times Book Review May 23, 1971; December 28, 1975; December 21, 1980; April 1, 1984; Times Literary Supplement April 16, 1971.

ROSSNER, JUDITH (March 31, 1935–), American novelist, was born in New York City to Joseph George Perelman and the former Dorothy Shapiro. She attended Taft High School and spent three years at City College, dropping out in 1955 to marry Robert Rossner, by whom she had two children. Although she divorced Rossner in 1972 she has retained his name; in 1979, she married Mordecai Persky. She has lived in New York City all her life, originally in the Bronx and later in Manhattan.

Rossner's first three novels, *To the Precipice, Nine Months in the Life of an Old Maid,* and *Any Minute I Can Split,* established her distinctive style and preoccupations, but they are tentative, flawed performances that attracted little critical attention and sold poorly. Her fourth novel, *Looking for Mr. Goodbar,* enjoyed tremendous popular and critical success, however, and was made into a noteworthy film; it led to the re-issue of her out-of-print earlier works and the general reassessment of her talent. It also brought her financial independence, the opportunity to give up her job (while writing the novel she worked as a secretary in a methadone clinic), and a not entirely welcome amount of publicity, including a television interview with Barbara Walters.

Looking for Mr. Goodbar tells the story of Theresa Dunn, an outwardly respectable Catholic schoolteacher, who spends her nights cruising Manhattan singles' bars. The novel begins with Theresa's murder by a man she had picked up for casual sex; in flashbacks, Rossner then examines the complex of causes—parental oppression, religious guilt, urban anomie—that led her to this violent, scandalous end. *Looking for Mr. Goodbar* was inspired by the highly publicized case of Roseann Quinn, who had been murdered on Manhattan's Upper West Side, not far from where Rossner was then living. But critics were quick to recognize that the novel was more than a piece of sensational pseudo-journalism. It is a serious, sympathetic examination of a contemporary woman in a desperate situation, told in the crisp, restrained prose that has become Rossner's trademark. "A complex and chilling portrait of a woman's descent into hell . . . full of insight and intelligence," C. E. Ringler wrote in the *New York Times Book Review.* Rossner told an interviewer in 1976 that she had not been especially interested in Quinn's murder when she first read about it. But some weeks later, recuperating from injuries she had received in an automobile crash, she began to give it serious thought. "When we have accidents, we say 'I did this to myself,' and I was wondering whether I had done this to myself. That was the entry into the story for me." Although the novel was well

JUDITH ROSSNER

received by feminists, it was not intended as a feminist work. "The movement by definition," Rossner has said, "does not deal in ambiguities whereas a novel by definition does."

Women driven to extremes had formed Rossner's principal theme all along. *To the Precipice* centers on Ruthie Kossoff, who marries a millionaire but still loves her impoverished childhood sweetheart; Beth, the narrator and heroine of *Nine Months in the Life of an Old Maid,* inhabits a crumbling Gothic mansion with her deranged sister and half-brother; and *Any Minute I Can Split* begins when Margaret, pregnant and naked, steals her husband's motorcycle and flees from him to join a commune. In retrospect, these early efforts look like preliminary sketches for *Mr. Goodbar*: far-fetched, improbably motivated, and sometimes clumsily written, they nevertheless display an abiding concern with the psychology of women struggling to bear the pressures of modern life.

Rossner's next two novels, *Attachments* and *Emmeline,* won widespread critical acclaim but failed to equal the popularity of *Mr. Goodbar.* They represent, however, notable improvements in subtlety and technical polish. *Attachments* offers Rossner's most bizarre situation so far: a woman in love with a pair of Siamese twins, who persuades a friend to marry one of them so she can marry the other. The resulting ménage provides several opportunities for the description of sexual gymnastics; but, again, the sensationalism of *Attachments* is only superficial. As Rossner told an interviewer, the novel is really about "how people marry symbols and then discover that they have to deal with realities. And it's

about friendships. The Siamese twins are part of but not the whole story." For novelist Jerome Charyn, writing in the *New York Times Book Review,* the theme of the novel was less attachments (literally of the twins, figuratively of their relationship with two women) than the deeply felt loneliness of women in the quest "for identity through sexual power and lust." He writes: "A kind of demon has caught Rossner. God knows, she must have torn bits of herself into the book . . . the writer moving closer and closer to that edge where metaphors aren't simply games of play, where language begins to hurt." Far less enthusiastic, however, was *Newsweek*'s reviewer, who dismissed *Attachments* as "mawkish fantasy, implausible and plain embarrassing."

Emmeline, like *Mr. Goodbar,* is based on a real-life case, that of a nineteenth-century New England girl who falls in love with her own illegitimate son. The heroine and her predicament are typically Rossnerian, but the novel's historical setting and somber, brooding tone mark it as an ambitious advance beyond Rossner's previous work. By this time, Rossner's characteristic preoccupations were public knowledge: she was led to write *Emmeline* by a phonecall from a stranger, referring her to a ninety-year-old woman who as a child had known the real-life Emmeline, then in old age herself. Rossner also had learned that her famously outré subject matter tended to discourage many potential readers; in *Emmeline,* she focuses more on the tangled psychology of the story and less on its simple shock value. "You have to kind of gentle down readers," she told *Publishers Weekly,* "if you're using a subject like this."

In her seventh novel, *August,* Rossner achieved a combined critical and popular success almost as great as that of *Mr. Goodbar.* Her most serious novel so far, *August* tells the alternating stories of Dawn Henley and Dr. Lulu Shinefeld—the one a dangerously troubled teenager, the other a fortyish Manhattan psychiatrist to whom Dawn is sent for treatment. The title refers to the month when, traditionally, psychiatrists go on vacation—leaving their patients, somehow or other, to fend for themselves. But the title is symbolic, too, since the novel's deepest concern is with the convoluted attachments that form between analyst and analysand, attachments which exist only so they can eventually be broken. In *August,* Rossner's interest in psychology turns back on itself, exploring the forum—the analytic session—where psychology becomes its own subject. There are sensational details in the novel, such as Dawn's lesbian "parents," but they are handled with new restraint and tact; and the style is, as one reviewer remarked, "sparse almost to deprivation." As Eva Hoffman observed, "*August* is a phenomenon of some interest, for it represents what may be the ultimate step in the marriage of Freud and fiction—the attempt not to talk *about* analysis, but to replicate it in a novel." Each new novel by Judith Rossner has marked a step forward, and in *August* she moves to a higher plane altogether.

PRINCIPAL WORKS: To the Precipice, 1966; Nine Months in the Life of an Old Maid, 1969; Any Minute I Can Split, 1972; Looking for Mr. Goodbar, 1975; Attachments, 1977; Emmeline, 1980; August, 1983.

ABOUT: Authors in the News II, 1976; Contemporary Authors, revised edition 19–20, 1976. *Periodicals*—Harper's September 1983; Hudson Review Winter 1983/84; Ms. September 1983; New York Times Book Review June 9, 1975; September 18, 1977; November 6, 1983; July 24, 1983; Publishers Weekly August 22, 1980; Time July 7, 1975; Times Literary Supplement November 4, 1983.

THEODORE ROSZAK

*ROSZAK, THEODORE (1933–   ), American social philosopher, educator, and fiction writer, has only sparingly revealed his personal history. Born in Chicago to Blanche and Anton Roszak, he was raised as a Roman Catholic. His father was a cabinetmaker. After earning a B.A. from the University of California at Los Angeles in 1955, Roszak received a doctorate from Princeton University. From 1959 to 1963 he was a history instructor at Stanford University; he took a year's leave in 1964 to edit a pacifist journal, *Peace News,* in London, then joined the faculty at the California State University at Hayward, where he is now a professor of history and chairman of the university's History of Western Culture program. Beginning in the late 1960s, he began publishing regularly in the *Nation, Atlantic,* and other journals.

In 1968 Roszak edited *The Dissenting Academy,* a collection of eleven essays by noted educators in the social sciences and humanities—among them Noam Chomsky and S. M. Rosen—that sharply criticized the plummeting educational standards of the modern university and the slack social consciousness of most academics. In his own contribution Roszak characterized contemporary instruction in the humanities as beset by "mindless collaboration on the one hand and irrelevant research on the other," with professors and texts offering little more than "pedantry." A few critics saw in this collection yet another example of academics biting the hands that feed them, but others found it cogent and penetrating, though it failed to suggest any constructive alternatives to the present system of higher education. Neil Compton

in the *Nation* expressed a further reservation: "I must confess that the cumulative effect of many (not all) of the essays was to arouse fears that disillusion with orthodox scholarly methods is driving some academics close to a dangerous irrationalism." (For many critics, Roszak's subsequent work is an embodiment of this trend.) Read not as analyses of currently pressing problems but as historical documents, the essays seem a product of the shrillness of the time—the radical student movement was at its height, as was Pentagon control of social science research monies. Yet the limiting and abuse of academic freedom, major concerns in these works, are again hotly debated topics in the universities.

The timely appearance of the best-selling *The Making of a Counter Culture: Reflections on the Technocratic Society and Its Youthful Opposition* in 1969 established Roszak as the principal explicator of the social disaffection of the young. The book itself, however, after the first section, has relatively little to do in detail with student rebellion, hippies, or the generation gap, though Roszak heartily approved of all these, in fact, hailed them as the harbingers of "the radical discontent and innovation" that "might transform this disoriented civilization of ours into something a human being can identify as home." Rather, in a smooth, catchy prose that occasionally aspired toward the oracular, Roszak scathingly attacked what he perceived as the mortal deficiencies of modern society— primarily the scientific-industrial control of an increasingly spiritless culture. "The capacity of our emerging technocratic paradise to denature the imagination by appropriating to itself the

°rō´ zāk

whole meaning of Reason, Reality, Progress, and Knowledge," he wrote, "will render it impossible for men to give any name to their bothersomely unfulfilled potentialities but that of madness. And for such madness, humanitarian therapies will be generously provided." To counter this dystopian vision Roszak offered a deliberately Romantic model of culture based in part on the social/psychological theories of Herbert Marcuse and Norman O. Brown, the transplanted mysticism of Allen Ginsberg and Alan Watts, and the shamanistic lore of the American Indians, all of which, he maintained, was embodied in embryonic form by dissenting college youth. Wrote Roszak: "There must be a new culture in which the non-intellectual capacities of the personality—those capacities that take fire from visionary splendor and the experience of human communication—become the arbiters of the good, the true, and the beautiful."

Critical reaction to this book was mixed, as it has been to all of Roszak's work. The *New York Times* called *The Making of a Counter Culture* "reasonable in tone, scrupulous in its qualifications, [and] prudent in its reservations." *Newsweek* reviewer Robert A. Gross considered it "the best guide yet published to the meaning of youthful dissent not only in the U.S. but throughout the world's advanced industrial societies," though he was disappointed by Roszak's "rhetorical call for a 'magical' subjective approach to reality" and his "repetitious, eventually numbing attack on the scientific world view." Roszak's forthright attack on the "experts" smacked to others of simplistic finger-pointing and fashionable anti-intellectualism. Margaret Mead, writing in *Critic*, found Roszak's reasoning fundamentally flawed: "What is . . . most horrifying about this book is its total lack of scale. . . . One would think we were a tiny society of some few thousand people, who had been led astray by these new inventions, the water wheel, the plough, and the sail, and who could be easily recalled to a life of simple meditation, while those who have enough to eat could afford to feed the devout observers in their midst. . . . Finally, the book is absurdly culture bound, looking for salvation within the Western world—with a few badly assimilated bits of Zen." *The Making of a Counter Culture* had sold some 400,000 copies by the mid-1980s and was nominated for a National Book Award.

Roszak's next projects were two anthologies of scholarly protest: *Male/Female: Readings in Sexual Mythology and the Liberation of Woman* (with his wife Betty), and *Sources: An Anthology of Contemporary Materials Useful for Preserving Personal Sanity While Braving the Great Technological Wilderness.* In 1972 he published

Where the Wasteland Ends: Politics and Transcendence in Post-Industrial Society, written on a grant from the Guggenheim Foundation. Essentially an extension of the ideas articulated in his second book, *Where the Wasteland Ends* concentrated particularly on "the odd psychology" of science and "its role in contemporary life. Science is not, in my view, merely *another* subject for discussion. It is *the* subject." Comparing his vision to that of the visionary William Blake, Roszak saw "in the steady advance of science and its machines a terrifying aggression against precious human potentialities—and especially against the visionary imagination," which "has been exiled from our culture." Convinced that there is "a strange new radicalism abroad which refuses to respect thought and value, which insists on making the visionary powers a central point of critical reference," Roszak offered as a paradigm of societal revolution the "apocatastasis": the Gnostic restoration of the misled soul to reillumination. He saw this spiritual reawakening spreading from disaffected youth to middle-class Californians experimenting with yoga, tai-chi-chuan, and astrology. Though most technocrats, wrote Nicholas Wade in *Science*, would find Roszak's line of reasoning unrealistic and his proposed solution to overweening technology bizarre at best, "to dismiss [his book] simply because of its poetic element is to do just what Roszak is complaining of."

The author's *Unfinished Animal: The Aquarian Frontier and the Evolution of Consciousness* was a survey of recent popular mysticism, while *Person/Planet: The Creative Disintegration of Industrial Society* was an attempt to identify the political right of the individual to "authentic personhood" with the collective, ecological "rights" of the entire planet. Though different in angles of attack, much the same message was purveyed in these as in the earlier books: to save itself humanity must loosen the grip of reductive rationality and embrace the Old Gnosis, the pagan spiritual symbiosis with nature. Pete Hamill found the version of that thesis propounded in *Unfinished Animal* "encased in a long, windy sermon of a book, loaded with hyperbole, written in the mystically distracted style of the hippies Roszak once so admired. But the basic message is straight out of the old-time religion: Ye Must Be Born Again."

Roszak answered all "hasty and prejudicial" criticisms of his interest in New Age spiritual projects in his introduction to *Person/Planet*: "One must discriminate between the authenticity of the needs people express and the inadequacy of the material that may be offered to meet those needs. For to use the sins of charlatans as an excuse to mock the spiritual and moral needs of people is no better than to despise hungry people for eating the adulterated food that scoundrels have sold them. This is a cruel and senseless line of criticism—one that I suspect could only be taken by those whose real intention is to enforce an even tighter censorship upon our personal and transcendent longings." But few important, much less officially sanctioned, critics of politics or society have taken his later works seriously enough to support or rebut his claims at length.

Roszak is also the author of *Pontifex,* a morality play about youthful revolution, and *Bugs,* an implausible science-fiction novel described by the author as concerning "terror in the computer age." Neither has received the critical attention accorded his other works. He is married and has one child.

PRINCIPAL WORKS: The Making of a Counter Culture: Reflections on the Technocratic Society and Its Youthful Opposition, 1969; Male/Female: Readings in Sexual Mythology and the Liberation of Woman, 1969; Sources: An Anthology of Contemporary Materials Useful for Preserving Personal Sanity While Braving the Great Technological Wilderness, 1972; Where the Wasteland Ends: Politics and Transcendence in Post-Industrial Society, 1972; Unfinished Animal: The Aquarian Frontier and the Evolution of Consciousness, 1975; Person/Planet: The Creative Disintegration of Industrial Society, 1978. *Drama*—Pontifex: A Revolutionary Entertainment for the Mind's Eye Theater, 1974. *Fiction*—Bugs, 1981. *As editor*—The Dissenting Academy, 1968;

ABOUT: Contemporary Authors 77–80, 1979; Current Biography, 1982; Who's Who in America, 1983–84. *Periodicals*—America November 29, 1975; Christian Science Monitor February 19, 1970; Critic January 1970; Denver Quarterly Winter/Spring 1974–75; Nation September 4, 1976; New Scientist March 4, 1971; New York Times Book Review September 7, 1969; November 30, 1975; Newsweek September 15, 1969; Saturday Review September 23, 1972; Science December 1, 1972; Time September 11, 1972; Times Literary Supplement April 16, 1970.

*ROUECHÉ, BERTON (April 16, 1911–   ), American journalist and novelist, was born in Kansas City, Missouri, the son of Clarence Berton Roueché, a business executive, and Nana Marie (Mossman) Roueché. Roueché attended the University of Missouri, graduating with a Bachelor of Journalism degree in 1933. The following year he became a reporter for the *Kansas City Star,* moving on to the *St. Louis Globe-Democrat* in 1941, and to the *St. Louis Post-Dispatch* in 1942. In 1944 he joined the

BERTON ROUECHÉ

staff of the *New Yorker,* where he has remained ever since.

Roueché made his reputation in the late forties and early fifties with a series of articles appearing in the *New Yorker* under the rubric "Annals of Medicine." These were case histories turning on something unusual or unaccountable in the symptoms of a particular malady and the circumstances surrounding it. Typically, the narratives began with the sudden illness of a person or people (whose social milieus and occupations were concisely sketched in), included a middle section of medical exposition, and concluded with the mystery solved and the disease diagnosed by the painstaking efforts and deductive reasoning of the doctors and medical professionals involved. Thus, without sacrificing scientific accuracy, Roueché was able to construct suspenseful narrative out of the circumstances of disease and dysfunction. A representative example is the title piece of Roueché's first collection of medical journalism, *Eleven Blue Men and Other Narratives of Medical Detection.*

"At about eight o'clock on Monday morning, September 25, 1944," Roueché begins, "a ragged, aimless old man of eighty-two collapsed on the sidewalk on Dey Street, near the Hudson Terminal." A policeman bending over the man discovers that this is not an ordinary Bowery drunk: "The old man's nose, lips, ears, and fingers were sky-blue." The sick man is taken to the Beekman-Downtown Hospital, where, by noon, eight other old men from the area in similar states of collapse are brought in. "The entire body of one, a bony, seventy-three-year-old con-

° roo shā´

sumptive named John Mitchell, was blue." Two epidemiologists from the New York City Department of Health, Drs. Morris Greenberg and Ottavio Pellitteri, begin their investigation that afternoon. They learn from the stricken men (all but one of whom recovered), that they all had eaten breakfast in the same cheap cafeteria. Their first hunch is gas poisoning, but, as Dr. Pellitteri explains, "there didn't seem to be any of the headache and general dopiness that you get with gas." The two epidemiologists then narrow down the cause to food poisoning, and their suspicions are confirmed the next day, when Dr. Pellitteri goes to the cafeteria (by then closed by the Bureau of Food) to interview the cook. It emerges from the interview that a handful of salt thrown into a batch of oatmeal the previous day (all the sick men had eaten oatmeal) contained a small amount of sodium nitrite, which looks and tastes like table salt but is actually a fairly powerful poison. The results of the bloodtests done on the men and the food samples taken from the cafeteria are positive: both contain sodium nitrite. Yet one puzzle remains, which Roueché withholds till the last paragraph: of all the customers who ate oatmeal in the cafeteria that morning, why did only these eleven become sick?

With *Eleven Blue Men*, Roueché set the pattern for a series of books on medicine that were to follow: *The Incurable Wound and Further Narratives of Medical Detection, A Man Named Hoffman and Other Narratives of Detection, The Orange Man and Other Narratives of Medical Detection,* and *The Medical Detectives.* Indeed the formula in these books is essentially unchanging, yet few critics have complained of repetitiousness. The extraordinary variety of the diseases Roueché traces (leprosy, amnesia, and "pseudocyst of the pancreas and carotenemialycopenemia," to name a few) and the suspense he generates with each case almost invariably sustain the reader's interest. One criticism that has been made, however, is that the selectivity of Roueché's materials tends to glamorize the medical world. Unquestionably the heroes of these books are the epidemiologists and public health officials who trace dangerous diseases back to their microbial sources. Yet Roueché's accuracy has always been unimpeachable, and at the least most critics would agree with the *Publishers Weekly* reviewer who said of *The Orange Man*, "Once again, Roueché's *New Yorker* pieces on 'medical detection' make a superbly readable book." Roueché has received the Albert Lasker Medical Journalism Award, once in 1950 for "The Fog" (one of the essays in *Eleven Blue Men*), and again in 1960 for *The Neutral Spirit, a Portrait of Alcohol.*

After a lapse of ten years (following *The Delectable Mountains and Other Narratives*), Roueché turned his attention once more to nonmedical subjects with *What's Left: Reports on a Diminishing America.* The eight "reports" described such unspoiled places as the Islandia Keys off the coast of southeast Florida and the Big Thicket swamp in east Texas. As the title indicates, an ecological slant runs throughout the book, for the threat of industrial exploitation hangs over most of the wilds that Roueché writes about. Once or twice he admits to feeling "a kind of rage" at the thought that these places "might not always be here to be seen," yet his tone remains characteristically calm and understated.

What's Left received generally favorable reviews. Robert W. Stock, in the *New York Times-Book Review*, thought most of the book "informed by a devoted admiration of the natural world and a firm dedication to the importance of keeping it natural." Yet Stock also voiced a complaint that has been raised more than once against Roueché: that his magazine work is "somehow diminished" when gathered together between hard covers. "Read in one sitting," he said, "the first-person tales, with all their endless celebration of minutiae and their too-honest conversational reportage, are apt to pall."

The River World and Other Explorations was a more miscellaneous collection than *What's Left.* Among its thirteen essays were an account of a trip down the Mississippi by towboat, a profile of an over-worked general practitioner in Jal, New Mexico, and three articles about food (apples, garlic, and bananas). At the core of the book, in the opinion of Benjamin DeMott, writing in the *New York Times Book Review*, was "a celebration of the unbeaten path (the backwater community or enterprise that has somehow escaped the processes of urban homogenization) and the homely pleasures (plain, hearty meals after physical labor, landfalls after hard passages, straightforward talk with folks unburdened with convoluted consciousness)." Yet DeMott's review was not sympathetic. He strongly objected to what he considered Roueché's reductive "Good vs. Evil parables" contrasting the virtues of country life with the vices of the city, and he thought that, technically, the pieces here were not quite as successful as Roueché's medical reporting. But other reviewers had no such reservation. Peter Stoler, of *Time*, wrote, "no subject seems beyond the interest of Berton Roueché," and he praised particularly this passage from the title piece: "The river was unmistakably the Mississippi now. It stretched a mile wide and infinitely on ahead. In the thin white early-morning light, it might have been a lake. But the banks were still riverbanks—sandbars and willow flats, willow slopes and high cottonwood bluffs."

Two of the essays in *The River World* were reprinted with different titles in *Special Places: In Search of Small-Town America,* probably Roueché's most highly praised book to date. Most of the seven towns portrayed are solidly middle American and share common attitudes and features, but each, as Roueché shows, has its own distinctive character and customs. They range from Stapleton, Nebraska, with a population of 303, where there is no crime and the high school marching band practices every day on Main Street, to Hope, Arkansas, population 10,290, where, in 1980, the world's largest watermelon was grown (it is listed in the *Guinness Book of World Records*) and where magnolias adorn every yard, park, and cemetery. Yet the book is not simply a paean to rural life. The familiar complaints of small town America are here too, such as those Roueché hears from the teen-ager in Welch, West Virginia whom he picks up hitchhiking. "The only trouble here is there isn't nothing to do," the boy tells him. "There isn't no place you can go with a girl and park. Where you can be alone. What you have to do is go all the way out to the movie at Kimball—to the drive-in."

In his review in the *American Scholar,* James Kaufman praised Roueché for his "ability to convey so clearly what small-towns are really like." Roueché, he wrote, gets "beneath the high-contrast surface matter to those deeper, grayer areas in which most of life is lived. He manages more often than not to find what is truly typical, to find the rhythm of a place, to replace generalizations and myths with things more substantial." His only criticisms concerned the selectivity of the material—specifically, that Roueché's "small-town folks are a little too homogeneous," and that he does not "visit any towns where the other-side-of-the-tracks style of life is dominant." But such objections, Kaufman said, "slide away in view of the quality of Roueché's writing and perceptions."

In addition to his dozen-odd volumes of nonfiction, Roueché has written four suspense novels. *Feral,* which concerns some rather undomestic cats on the loose in rural Long Island, is perhaps the most successful and alarming of the four. The *Times Literary Supplement* called it "a very nasty little fable indeed," and a reviewer for the *New Yorker* said, "the low-keyed narrative has the satisfying, precise pace and the regular, resounding jolts of a grandfather clock."

Berton Roueché is married and lives in Amagansett, Long Island. He and his wife, Katherine Eisenhower Roueché, have one son, Bradford.

William Shawn, his editor at the *New Yorker,* has remarked on Roueché's "blithe indifference to publicity, celebrity, and social glamour." Certainly Roueché's personality rarely if ever intrudes on his work. But like the man himself, Shawn said in his introduction to *Special Places,* "his writing is unhurried, quiet, peaceable, warm."

PRINCIPAL WORKS: *Journalism*—The Greener Grass and Some People Who Found It, 1949; Eleven Blue Men and Other Narratives of Medical Detection, 1953; The Incurable Wound and Further Narratives of Medical Detection, 1958; The Delectable Mountains and Other Narratives, 1959; The Neutral Spirit, a Portrait of Alcohol, 1960 (*also published as* Alcohol, its History, Folklore and its Effects on the Human Body); A Man Named Hoffman and Other Narratives of Medical Detection, 1965; (U.K. Dossier of Medical Detection); Annals of Epidemiology, 1967; Field Guide to Disease: A Handbook for World Travellers, 1967; What's Left: Reports on a Diminishing America, 1969; The Orange Man and Other Narratives of Medical Detection, 1971; Desert and Plain, the Mountain and the River: A Celebration of Rural America, 1975; The River World and Other Explorations, 1978; The Medical Detectives, 1980; Special Places: In Search of Small Town America, 1982. *Fiction*—Black Weather, 1945 (*also published as* Rooming House); The Last Enemy, 1956; Feral, 1974 (U.K. *The Cats*); Fago, 1977. *As editor*—Curiosities of Medicine: An Assembly of Medical Diversions, 1552–1962, 1963.

ABOUT: Contemporary Authors, new revision series 1, 1981; Who's Who in America, 1983–84. *Periodicals*—American Scholar Winter 1982/83; New York Times Book Review June 20, 1965; July 6, 1969; January 21, 1979; July 25, 1982; New Yorker November 11, 1974; Publishers Weekly June 21, 1973; Time November 27, 1978; Times Literary Supplement September 26, 1975.

ROVERE, RICHARD H(ALWORTH) (May 5, 1915–November 23, 1979), American journalist and political commentator, was born in Jersey City, New Jersey, the son of Louis Halworth and Ethel (Roberts) Rovere. His father, an electrical engineer, moved the family to New York City, where Rovere attended public schools before entering a preparatory school in Stony Brook, Long Island. In 1933, Rovere entered Bard College, Annandale-on-Hudson, where he edited the campus newspaper, the *Bardian,* and was awakened to political activism. Like many of his contemporaries, he gravitated toward Communism; and in his memoirs described himself at that time as a "Marxist-Leninist with only a sketchy reading of Marx and an even sketchier one of Lenin." He attended party meetings, but never became a member of the Communist Party.

After receiving his B.A. degree from Bard in 1937, Rovere became an associate editor at *New Masses*; but in 1939, disillusioned by the Soviet pact with Nazi Germany, he resigned from the magazine. He was assistant editor at the *Nation* until 1943, when he joined the staff of *Common Sense*. In 1944, he began to contribute political profiles to *Harper's* magazine, and in the same year he became the *New Yorker's* regular columnist on American politics. His first book, *Howe & Hummel: Their True and Scandalous History*, an enlargement of a series of four *New Yorker* profiles entitled "89 Centre Street," was a partly humorous investigation of two notorious New York shyster lawyers. The reviewer for the *New York Times* called the book a recreation "with discernment and wit . . . of one of the most raucous periods in the history of the main chance in America." Other reviewers noted that Rovere's polished style epitomized "the *New Yorker* school of writing."

The General and the President, & the Future of American Foreign Policy, written three years later in collaboration with the historian Arthur Schlesinger, Jr., related the events surrounding Truman's recall of General Douglas MacArthur from his command in Korea. The *Chicago Sunday Tribune* called the book a "masterful piece of work" in its appraisal of General MacArthur's career, and its elucidation of the implications of the controversy for American foreign policy.

Rovere's next book, *Affairs of State: the Eisenhower Years*, was a collection of forty-one pieces, mostly written for the *New Yorker*, covering the years 1950–56. The book did not aim to be a formal history, but described many of the people who surrounded the President, and a number of the events of the time. Vice President Nixon, adroit in the use of modern advertising and public relations methods, was regarded as having "set the political style of the Eisenhower Administration." In "Trial Balances," Rovere compared Eisenhower to Truman in his "standard-American personality." "Both," he pointed out, were "essentially unideological, unintellectual, intuitive pragmatists, and feeble verbalizers." In summing up, however, Rovere concluded that Eisenhower had been a better President than might have been expected, having strengthened the Western alliance and kept the United States from becoming mired in overseas wars.

Rovere's most popular work was *Senator Joe McCarthy*, written two years after the Senator's death. *Time* magazine called Rovere's treatment of McCarthy "remarkably well-balanced and even-tempered . . . To Rovere himself, McCarthy remains 'in may ways the most gifted

demagogue' in U.S. history, with 'access to the dark places of the American mind.' But he was no totalitarian. . . . Anything but a conformist, he attacked the Army, the Protestant clergy, the press, the two major political parties. He was, says Rovere, 'closer to the hipster than to the organization man.'" *Senator Joe McCarthy* is a study of an enigmatic personality whose downfall was brought about by his failure of conviction in his own demagogic mission.

By the late 1950s, Rovere was established as one of the country's most respected political journalists. In addition to his "Letter from Washington," begun in the *New Yorker* in 1958, he contributed to a number of other publications; was a contributing editor of *Harper's* (1948–54); American correspondent for *Spectator* (1954–62); and a member of the board of editors of *American Scholar* (1958–67). He was also associate professor of American civilization at Columbia University (1957–59), and lecturer at Yale University (1972–73). Rovere's wide-ranging interests were reflected in The *American Establishment and Other Reports, Opinions, & Speculations*, which included perceptive studies of Justice Holmes, Ezra Pound, and George Orwell, as well as pieces on Arthur Vandenberg, Harold Ickes, and Wendell Wilkie. In his review in the *Saturday Review*, Granville Hicks found in the book's style "the mind of a fine journalist who is no less a man of letters because he happens not to write poetry or fiction."

Rovere's other books of the 1960s were *The Goldwater Caper* and *Waist Deep in the Big Muddy*. William Barrett wrote of *The Goldwater Caper*, a retrospective look at the Goldwater presidential campaign of 1964, that although Rovere showed genuine sympathy with Goldwater as a man, "the net effect of this judicious reporting is the most deadly portrait yet painted of the whole Goldwater movement." Rovere's analysis of Goldwater was that he was two men at once—a charming, modest, uncomplicated man committed to the values of his region, and the creature of ghost-writers and lieutenants whose statements issued in his name created a conflicted sense of who he was and what he represented. In *Waist Deep in the Big Muddy: Reflections on United States Policy*, written just before the 1968 election, Rovere examined the foreign policy leading up to American involvement in Vietnam, which he found "unconscionable." A slender volume of sustained analysis, *Waist Deep in the Big Muddy* was Rovere's most personal book on political affairs.

Arrivals and Departures; a Journalist's Memoirs was a collection of pieces, some autobiographical, from different periods of Rovere's career. Reviewers tended to find the book modest, without revealing very much about Rovere personally, but noted in it the qualities that Rovere exemplified—a personal unpretentiousness, decency, and steady judgment "unswayed by the passion of the moment." *Final Reports,* subtitled "Personal Reflections on Politics and History in Our Time," a collection of Rovere's unpublished pieces, appeared posthumously. It included an hilarious description of Harry Truman's whistle-stop campaign against Thomas E. Dewey, further commentary on Senator McCarthy, on the Vietnam war, and a profile of John F. Kennedy. In a foreword, Arthur Schlesinger, Jr. wrote of Rovere's work: "I don't think that any one of the writers of my generation recorded the dying fall of history with such verve and at the same time reflected on it with such dispassion and elegance." A slight, scholarly-looking man, Rovere kept aloof from the active center of politics. His "Letter from Washington" column was written in New York, but he made trips to Washington as needed. Rovere married Eleanor Alice Burgess in 1941, and they had three children, Ann Megan, Richard Mark, and Elizabeth. The Roveres divided their time between their house in Rhinebeck, New York, and an apartment on West 44th Street in midtown Manhattan, within walking distance of his office at the *New Yorker*. When Rovere died of emphysema at the age of sixty-four, his long-time editor at the *New Yorker,* William Shawn, commented on him to the *New York Times*: "Richard Rovere was among the fairest, most nearly objective, most brilliant writers on American politics. He wrote with tremendous skill, with care, with humor, with style. . . . He brought an extraordinary clarity of mind to bear on complex situations and made them comprehensible."

PRINCIPAL WORKS: Howe & Hummel: Their True and Scandalous History, 1947; (with Arthur M. Schlesinger, Jr.) The General and the President, & the Future of American Foreign Policy, 1951 (reprinted as The MacArthur Controversy and American Foreign Policy, 1965); Affairs of State: the Eisenhower Years, 1956; Senator Joe McCarthy, 1959; The American Establishment and Other Reports, Opinions, & Speculations 1962; The Goldwater Caper, 1965; Waist Deep in the Big Muddy; Reflections on United States Policy, 1968; Arrivals and Departures: A Journalist's Memoirs, 1976; Final Reports, 1984.

ABOUT: Contemporary Authors 49–52, 1975; Current Biography, 1977; Who's Who in America, 1978. *Periodicals*—Atlantic December 1951; April 1965; Commonweal November 30, 1951; June 29, 1962; Current History August 1956; Harper's July 1968; Newsweek November 29, 1976; New Republic May 7, 1956; New Yorker June 27, 1959; New York Times August 24, 1947; March 14, 1956; June 23, 1968; November 24, 1979; New York Times Book Review February 19, 1984; Saturday Review August 30, 1947; May 26, 1962; April 7, 1956; Time July 13, 1959.

*RUSHDIE, (AHMED) SALMAN (June 19, 1947–   ), Indian novelist, was born in Bombay to an affluent middle-class Moslem family. His paternal grandfather was an accomplished Urdu poet; his Cambridge-educated father, he said in an interview in 1983, is "a very literary man, a student of both Arabic and Persian literature and of Western literature"; his mother, he continued, "was the keeper of the family stories. She has a genius for family trees; forests of family trees grow in her head, and nobody else can possibly understand their complexity." He was sent at the age of fourteen to Rugby School in England, and when he was seventeen his family moved from Bombay to Karachi, Pakistan. In 1965, just before going up to Cambridge, he visited his parents in their new home. It was a time of war between India and Pakistan, and the necessity to choose sides, he now feels, "really did partially derange me. . . . In the end my parents more or less forcibly threw me on a plane to England."

After Cambridge Rushdie remained in Britain, working for a time as an actor, then as a copywriter. His first novel, unpublished—he calls it "a total, appalling blunder"—is the story of a Pakistani holy man "who has a huge following, and a group of businessmen, generals, politicians, millionaires . . . use him as a kind of front for a political takeover." His first published book, *Grimus,* though set in the present, has many of the characteristics of science fiction. The hero, a rather dejected American Indian called Flapping Eagle, has been immortal for some seven centuries because he drank an elixir given him by a peddler who may (or may not) have been God. His protracted quest for truth forms the essence of the book; the people he meets along his way, much of its interest. Reviewers were unanimous in praising the author's confident displays of wit and marked ability to control the ingenious convolutions of his story. David Wilson, however, posed the question of "whether his dryly entertaining intellectual conceit is anything more than an elaborate statement of the obvious decked out in the mannerisms of Oxford philosophy."

With *Midnight's Children* Rushdie amply fulfilled the promise of his earlier novel. Very long, complex, and wholly original in tone and rhythm, it is the narrative of Saleem Sinai, who

SALMAN RUSHDIE

in 1977, in the novel's present, is the dying owner of a Bombay pickle factory. In order to recount the story of his life, he must begin in 1915, with the first glimpse his grandfather, a Heidelberg-trained Indian Moslem physician, had of his grandmother. He continues the family's history through the decades of social and political ferment leading to the stroke of midnight on August 15, 1947, the moment of India's independence and of Saleem's birth. From this point, a hundred densely printed pages into the novel, the story must encompass the lives of the one thousand and one children born between that midnight and one a.m.: they are midnight's children, "every one of whom was, through some freak of biology, or perhaps owing to some preternatural power of the moment, or just conceivably by sheer coincidence (although synchronicity on such a scale would stagger even C. G. Jung), endowed with features, talents or faculties which can only be described as miraculous." It is Saleem, the first-born of the group, who has "the greatest talent of all—the ability to look into the hearts and minds of men." "If I seem a little bizarre," he says, "remember the wild profusion of my inheritance." He finds at the age of ten that he is in telepathic communication with the five hundred eighty-one disparate and far-flung survivors—India's high infant-mortality rate does not spare even these exceptionally gifted children—and organizes them into the Midnight Children's Conference, whose meetings he convenes every evening from afar. Saleem's loquacious, easily diverted narrative is equally apt at describing his middle-class childhood in teeming Bombay, the eventful lives

of his numerous relatives, the developing stories of many of the children, his family's move to Pakistan and life in that militaristic country, and the contemporary political histories of Pakistan, India, and Bangladesh. The novel's principal message is a serious, though ironic, condemnation of the statism, corruption, and tyranny rife on the subcontinent, yet, as Robert Towers notes, "One must not underestimate the novel's playfulness, its absurdities, its highjinks—elements that continuously undercut the despair of its political vision." All critics noted the sheer monumentality of Rushdie's fiction, his extraordinary ability to create an evidently finished and dextrous work of art out of the most heterogeneous, sprawling, and untidy parts. *Midnight's Children* won the Booker-McConnell prize, Britain's most coveted literary award.

Shame appeared remarkably soon after its dazzling predecessor. The setting is a country "not quite Pakistan"; the narrator seems often to be, quite overtly, Rushdie himself. By artful indirection, using nothing like linear narrative style, and with many asides on history, politics, and literature, he tells "a sort of modern fairy tale" concerning several remarkable people whose lives exemplify honor, shame, and shamelessness. The most central of these are two archrivals for supreme power in their country— General Raza Hyder, an Islamic fundamentalist, an unimaginative man of rigid honor who eventually assumes dictatorial control; and Iskander Harappa, a rich, Westernized, debonair demagogue, an elected prime minister who is overthrown, brought to trial, and hanged by Hyder. Their extensive stories, chock full of suggestive incidents and bizarre details, closely parallel the real-life tragedy of modern Pakistan and the successive regimes of Zulfikar Ali Bhutto and Gen. Mohammed Zia ul-Haq. Yet it is the women of their families who come to dominate both the novel and the narrator's vision of its meaning: "I had thought before I began that what I had on my hands was an almost excessively masculine tale, a saga of sexual rivalry, ambition, power, patronage, betrayal, death, revenge. But the women seem to have taken over; they marched in from the peripheries of the story to demand the inclusion of their own tragedies, histories, and comedies, obliging me to couch my narrative in all manner of sinuous complexities, to see my 'male' plot refracted, so to speak, through the prisms of its reverse and 'female' side. It occurs to me that the women knew precisely what they were up to—that their stories explain, and even subsume, the men's." Indeed, the obsessive and terrifying aspects of the women's stories—all of which also exemplify the novel's title—remain longest in the reader's memory. "Repression," the narrator continues, "is a seamless garment. A society which is authoritarian in its social and sexual codes, which crushes its women beneath the intolerable burdens of honour and propriety, breeds repressions of other kinds as well. Contrariwise, dictators are always—or at least in public on other people's behalf—puritanical. So it turns out that my 'male' and 'female' plots are the same story, after all."

Midnight's Children, in the extravagance of its invention, reminded some critics of the works of Gabriel García Marquez; its deft use of allegory and wide scope made others think of Günter Grass. Robert Towers compared *Shame* to "those unclassifiable works in which certain writers of the eighteenth century excelled—Swift in *Gulliver's Travels,* Voltaire in *Candide,* Sterne in *Tristram Shandy.* The genius of these not-quite novelists expresses itself in a taste for absurd juxtapositions, for fantastic happenings, for the physically grotesque, for mockery and parody, for sexual innuendo and, on occasion, scatology. Often their talents are put to the service of satire. Salman Rushdie, it seems to me, is very much a latter-day member of their company."

WORKS: Grimus, 1975; Midnight's Children, 1981; Shame, 1983.

ABOUT: Contemporary Literary Criticism 23, 1983. *Periodicals*—Washington Post Book World March 15, 1981; Commonweal September 25, 1981; Encounter February 1982; January 1984; Hudson Review Spring 1984; Nation December 10, 1983; New Republic May 23, 1981; December 5, 1983; New Statesman May 1, 1981; New York Review of Books September 24, 1981; December 8, 1983; New York Times Book Review April 19, 1981; November 13, 1983; New Yorker July 27, 1981; Newsweek April 20, 1981; Publishers Weekly November 11, 1983; Times Literary Supplement February 21, 1975; May 15, 1981; September 9, 1983; Village Voice Literary Supplement November 1983.

RUSSELL, JOHN (January 22, 1919–), British art critic and translator, was born in Fleet, England, the son of Isaac James Russell and Harriet Elizabeth Atkins Russell. He was educated at St. Paul's School and Magdalen College, Oxford. After leaving university he worked for a time (1940–41) as an honorary attaché at the Tate Gallery, then served as a junior officer in the Ministry of Information (1941–43), and ended his war service in the Admiralty's Naval Intelligence Division (1943–46). By 1945 Russell was a regular contributor to the London *Sunday Times.* He served on that paper's staff as art critic from 1949 to 1974, at which time he accepted the offer to join the art criticism staff of the *New York Times.* In 1982, on the resignation of Hilton Kramer, he became the newspaper's chief art critic.

Many veteran observers of the *Times* contend that Russell is the most distinguished art critic the paper has had, whose wide range of interest is matched by a pungency and facility of expression and informed above all by a pervasive, natural wit. Russell was internationally noted for these qualities long before he came to work in New York; indeed, they are evident in his first book of art criticism, *British Portrait Painters,* regarded today as the best one-volume study of a well-regarded but little-understood British specialty. The book is a complete history of British portraitists from the time of Nicholas Hilliard in the sixteenth century through the peak of the genre in the work of Joshua Reynolds and Thomas Gainsborough to Lawrence Gowing, Henry Lamb, and the protean Augustus John in our own century. Throughout the book Russell's judgments are straightforward, precise, and surprisingly modern. "Reynolds alone," he wrote, "among British artists gains nothing by editing. His work is inestimably more impressive in its totality than in any of its items. Throughout a long and unbroken career he was able so to renew the sources of his inspiration that his work comes to resemble a vast convoy of intelligence, beauty, rank and power, as fecund and various as the age which produced it."

Russell's other major large-scale study in book form is *The Meanings of Modern Art* (largely written in 1974; first published as a whole in 1981). The work is grounded in two beliefs: "One is that in art, as in the sciences, ours is one of the big centuries. The other is that the history of art, if properly set out, is the history of everything." The author takes as his models such books as Bertrand Russell's *Our Knowledge of the External World,* Lytton Strachey's *Landmarks in French Literature,* and Maurice Baring's *An Outline of Russian Literature,* examples of "the democratic Enlightenment that came into being in Victorian times and was a force for good at least until the outbreak of World War I. It had to do with the notions of self-help and of adult education, but it also had to do with a moral obligation that was felt by many good writers, even if they did not always put it into words. It was a point of honor with these writers to make the best of themselves available to the largest possible public at the lowest possible cost. . . . These books had . . . an element of covert autobiography. Their authors wrote as men made and marked by what they were writing about." This very English sense of obligation in sharing the intellectual wealth, as well as a complete absence of snobbishness or the standard *de-haut-en-bas* attitude of many art critics are the qualities that distinguish this work from many another of its type. Russell attempts a fair account of every artist he mentions, dismisses no one, and saves his most intensive analysis for those he believes are best. "In art, as in most other things, I hold with what André Gide once said: 'The world will be saved by one or two people.'" Tim Hilton called *Meanings of Modern Art* a "large, affable book . . . that relates the main movements of our century (mentioning hundreds of artists on the way, from Manet to Frank Stella and Nancy Graves) with much ease and a remarkable freedom from contention."

Much of Russell's work in book form has been devoted to short monographs or introductions to selections from artists' work. Among the most acclaimed of these is *Max Ernst: Life and Work,* a lengthy and copiously illustrated critical biography of the surrealist master. Russell draws "continually upon notes taken during conversations with Max Ernst himself, who was still very much alive at the time of the book's composition." The artist, Russell concludes, is "profoundly and unalterably European. He allies, that is to say, a maximum of private involvement to a maximum of detached curiosity. He judges ideas on their merits, excluding none of them *a priori.* . . . He is without prejudice; and he has yet to be faced with a situation with which he cannot deal on his own terms. Public events have dealt with him brusquely, often enough; but he has never allowed them to inflict upon him the wounds which, in the case of many of his contemporaries, amounted to a lasting mutilation." Other monographs by Russell have considered such artists as Braque, Henry Moore, Ben Nicholson, Edouard Vuillard, and Francis Bacon.

Like most of his fellow art critics, Russell is an inveterate traveler. Among his earliest books are two travel guides—*Shakespeare's Country* and *Switzerland*—and his familiarity with the treasures of foreign cities has led to other books on Paris, the state museums of Berlin, the palaces of Leningrad, and Turner in Switzerland. He also wrote a historically and sociologically apt introduction to a massive history of Buckingham Palace and the monarchs who made their several additions to its architecture and its art collections.

During the 1950s and sixties, Russell published a considerable number of translations of French novels by modern authors of note, including André Gide's *Oedipus and Theseus* (1950), Gilbert Cesbron's *Saints in Hell* (1953), Roger Nimier's *The Blue Hussar* (1953) and

Children of Circumstance (1954), and Roger Martin du Gard's *The Postman* (1957). He is also the translator of Claude Lévi-Strauss' *Tristes Tropiques* (1961; called *A World on the Wane* in its British edition) and of the *Correspondence, 1899–1926* (1952) between André Gide and Paul Claudel.

Russell has written occasionally on music, notably a biography of Erich Kleiber (1956). His employment with the *Times* has led to some unusual and memorable assignments, such as his reports from Dallas during the Republican Convention of 1984, in which he was able to quote from W. E. Gladstone and J. B. Priestley while conveying the understanding of a surprising amount of American political reality. He has been married three times, divorced twice, and has a daughter by his first marriage. He was named a Commander of the British Empire in 1975.

PRINCIPAL WORKS: Shakespeare's Country, 1942 (rev. ed. 1961); British Portrait Painters, 1944; From Sickert to 1948, 1948; Switzerland, 1950 (rev. ed. 1962); Erich Kleiber, 1957; Braque, 1959; Paris, 1960; Oskar Kokoschka, 1962; Francis Bacon, 1964; Seurat, 1965; Max Ernst, 1967; Henry Moore, 1968; The World of Matisse, 1969; Edouard Vuillard, 1971; Francis Bacon, 1971; The Meanings of Modern Art, 1981.

ABOUT: Contemporary Authors 13–16R, 1975; Who's Who 1983–84; Who's Who in America 1983–84. *Periodicals*—Times Literary Supplement March 19, 1982; Washington Post October 1, 1969.

*SABATO, ERNESTO (June 24, 1911–), Argentinian novelist and essayist, writes (in Spanish): "I was born on June 24, 1911 in a rather small town [Rojas] in the province of Buenos Aires which until 1870 was a fortified outpost in the fights against Indians. Slightly transposed, this fort appears in my novel *On Heroes and Tombs* as 'Capitán Olmos.' In that town I received my secondary education, afterwards being sent to continue secondary studies in La Plata, capital of the Buenos Aires Province and a university town. Curiously, my first calling was painting. I say curiously, because I have returned to it during these last years. But I also began to write from very early in my life. As a child and adolescent I was an extremely timid and introverted boy with serious psychological problems, for one, somnambulism. My dark inner self found a serene order in mathematics, which explains why I then chose to study physics for my Ph.D. However, with my enrollment at the University, there began a tumultuous epoch in my life. I first joined anarchist groups, then

°sä´ bä to´

ERNESTO SABATO

the Communist Party, remaining in the latter for five years until finally breaking with it because of the Stalinist crimes and trials.

"This constituted my first spiritual crisis, the second taking place when I abandoned my scientific career. Upon finishing my Ph.D., I was awarded a fellowship to work at the Curie Laboratory in Paris. It was there that my second spiritual crisis began. I came to feel that science was ominous for the future of mankind and that technology inexorably led to alienation. Therefore, I turned toward art, and established connections with the Surrealist group in Paris. During the day I worked in atomic radiation, spending my evenings with the Surrealists, as if an honest housewife became a prostitute at night. I felt that my former life had come to an end and that I was going to find my (painful) destiny in that which had been my earliest inclination—art. During that time in Paris I began writing my first novel, 'The Silent Fountain,' which, although never published, provided some elements that many years later were incorporated into *On Heroes and Tombs.* I developed a passion for painting, as well as a close friendship with the Spanish Surrealist painter Oscar Domínguez, who was one of the first to encourage me to paint after seeing some of my charcoal sketches. With this friend, who committed suicide after the war by cutting his veins, we invented the doctrine of 'lithochronism' or 'time petrifying,' which André Breton discussed in some of his essays. Surrealism left a deep imprint in me, and very probably my 'Report on the Blind' cannot be explained without taking it into consideration. After Paris I spent a couple of

months at MIT, Cambridge, Massachusetts, where I worked on cosmic rays and relativity, finally to return to my university position at La Plata. But deep within me my abandonment of science had been already decided at that point, even though it was a very costly decision. Once in La Plata, I began to publish my first essays in *SUR* because I was too abashed to publish my fictional works; the transition would have been overly spectacular. How could I teach relativity and yet publish novels? Robert Musil did it, but my timidity was stronger than the example of my illustrious forebear.

"In 1943 I decided to give up everything. So Matilde, my little son, and I went to live in the mountains of Córdoba's Province, in a little hut (rancho) without electricity or any other civilized comfort. There we spent a year, enduring a very cruel winter with temperatures falling to 15° C below zero, with no heat whatsoever. During that year I wrote my first book, *Uno y el Universo* (Oneself and the Universe), a sort of philosophical 'bilain' [balance sheet] of my life. That book, first published in 1945, marked the end of my life as a scientist. Upon my return to Buenos Aires, I had to work on odd jobs in the most unlikely occupations merely in order to exist. In 1948 I published my first novel, *El túnel* (The Tunnel), and I was lucky enough to win praise from Albert Camus, at that time Gallimard's reader of Spanish books. This accounts for the book's immediate translation into French, and when published in English, in 1951, under the title *The Outsider,* I was lucky again; Thomas Mann wrote encomiastically about it in his *Diary*. The remainder of my life is better known. There appear other books of essays and two other novels, i.e. *Sobre heroes y tumbas* (*On Heroes and Tombs*) in 1961, and *Abaddón, el Exterminador* (Abaddon, the Destroying Angel) in 1974. This latter novel won, in its year of publication in Paris (1976), the award for the Best Foreign Book of the Year (Prix du Meilleur Livre Etranger).

"In all the years of my life I have always struggled against all types of dictatorships, be they from the right or from the left. I fight for a society built on the basis of freedom and justice, not believing in freedom without social justice, because freedom then becomes apocryphal for the majority of the people. Nor do I believe in social justice without freedom, because then economic slavery is replaced by slavery to the one party. Similarly, I have written incessantly against the alienation and 'robotization' of man in contemporary society, on both sides of the Iron Curtain. My philosophical position is, thus, a 'personal' existentialism, a defense of man against any type of alienation, be it economic (the one that Marx discussed), or technologic, with its effects equally upon supercapitalism and supersocialism. As Berdyaev has said: both kinds of societies are abstractions which disregard the man of flesh and blood; in both societies the human being is alienated. In this dreadful total crisis which affects the whole of mankind, the solution has to evolve from the community of human beings in its entirety, not from social machines."

—trans. A. Dellepiane

To become acquainted with Sabato's novels, one first should acquire a general knowledge of the ideas he expressed in his essays, since the fiction and discursive prose of this widely read significant figure of Hispanic letters form a continuum. His essays and novels emanate from a single system of obsessive ideas. Sabato is basically a thinker who (like Sartre) requires the medium of imagination afforded by the novel, which Sabato regards as the only literary form (apart from drama) in which reality can be seen alive. In Sabato's hands, however, the novel is closer to metaphysics than to literature. Hence, when discussing his novels, reference should be made to those essays in which Sabato has made explicit the thoughts which are illustrated in a given novel.

In the essays *Ombres y engranajes* (Men and Gears, 1951), for example, he had stated that "the fundamental fact is *man with man*" because Sabato is preoccupied by the "reification" (*cosificación*) of man, by the "dehumanization of humanity" enslaved to the "Great Machine" and to the impersonal "Government-Master." He is persuaded that by searching deep inside himself to construct his novels, he can find answers to those basic existentialist questions which he has posited since his very first book, *Uno y el Universo* (1945). Another collection, *El escritor y sus fantasmas* (The Writer and His Ghosts, 1963) is Sabato's most engaging book of essays devoted solely to discussion of literary creation and the making of the novel. The book is divided into three parts—a "Preliminary Interview," "Literature and the Arts in Today's Crisis," and "Variations on the Same Theme." It was published a year after *On Heroes and Tombs,* primarily in order to explain Sabato's views on that novel, as well as to clarify certain concepts lightly used—that of realism, for instance. Furthermore, he wished to counsel young writers by describing to them his own experience, searches, doubts, and agonies. Ostensibly paradoxical and epigrammatic formulas, with which he sums up his thought in powerful endings, are characteristic of his writing. Sabato sees the novel as a uni-

verse, as a reality emanating from an "I" that is a synthesis of the subjective and the objective. He perceives the artist as the "unique" human being, able to escape the influence of contemporary "technolatric" civilization by becoming "a mixture of masculine consciousness and reason, and feminine unconsciousness and intuition" (*Heterodixia*, 1953). For Sabato the novel is "an inquiry into man," and contemporary literature "constitutes an effort to elucidate the meaning of life; it is an ethical and metaphysical literature" which "shuns ornamentation and rhetoric" because "nothing is said in vain." Having thus defined his own brand of literature, Sabato formulates his "Poetics of the Novel," which amounts to a characterization of today's state of the genre. This new departure in Hispanic letters fertilized a genre that many considered exhausted. The "Variations" on this theme lead him to discuss the French *nouveau roman,* the relation of authors and characters, techniques, playful and serious literature, social realism, the nature and problems of Argentinian literature. He devotes long and illuminating pages to Borges and to the need in his country for a "problematic" literature, deeply metaphysical in accordance with Argentines' congenital feeling of transitoriness and finiteness. "The Writer and His Ghosts" is a polemic book (like all of Sabato's work) equally useful for the specialist and the average reader, which not only explains his thesis (with the addition of quotations from about thirty international authors), but one in which Sabato answers possible objections and hypothetical opponents. The latest book of essays, *Apologías y rechazos* (Apologies and Rejections, 1979), collects seven essays of which four are of special interest because they discuss contemporary cultural and political problems of Argentina. Sabato not only analyzes facts, persons, and circumstances but offers the fundamentals of a praxis, a testimony and a brave denunciation stemming from the very center of the recent sad and cruel Argentinian reality. His essays demonstrate the broad gamut of this author's interests, his iconoclasm, complexity, and richness.

Among his novels, *El túnel (The Outsider,* 1948) is a confessional story of an apparent crime of passion told by Castel, the perpetrator and narrator, from prison, any description of the external world and of the other characters being practically non-existent. The story is unfolded from the dénouement backward, in an internal search for understanding of the crime. Thus the focus is on the dark world of the unconscious, whose dreams, premonitions, and inexplicable certitudes are made sharper by the protagonist's implacable analytical lucidity. The stark language is the formal expression of the tunnel of the original Spanish title, of Castel's solitude and strangeness. The title is also an anticipation of the final realization that Castel reaches in his cell: that of living in a tunnel, of himself. Sabato shows his capacity to create an unforgettable morbid character, whose mental process totally absorbs the reader—a character for whom "nothing makes sense . . . Is it that our life is going to be nothing but a series of anonymous cries in a desert of indifferent planets"? It is evident that Sabato is confronting his reader with the same infinite and obsessive existential search already launched in his essays. The dark labyrinth of Castel's mind is to become more confused by his lover, an enigmatic young woman whose gaze seems to come "from other times," married to a blind man, seemingly involved in an adulterous affair with a cousin and perhaps with other men, melancholic, sensitive, unhappy with her present and without hope for the future, features that, of course, have endeared her to Castel. She awakens a violent, jealous Oedipal love in Castel, and although they physically consumate it, he is unhappy because he is not looking for carnal fulfillment but for an absolute and total communion that escapes him. One cannot ascribe his crime to jealousy, which is but one of the avenues of his tunnel of incommunication, similar to his irrational hatred of groups and of the blind, his hopelessness and his fear of women. Beyond its uncomplicated but suspenseful basic plot, *The Outsider* can be read as a pessimistic allegory of the human condition, as "a fictionalized statement of the theses set forth by Sabato" in "Men and Gears." "Viewed as a statement of total isolation, *El túnel* is in the mainstream of twentieth-century existentialism," H.D. Oberhelman writes. *The Outsider* has become a classic of contemporary Argentine narrative and continues to be read with the "absolute absorption" granted it by Graham Greene.

Sobre héroes y tumbas (*On Heroes and Tombs*, 1961) presents a wider fictional world than *The Outsider,* and a greater variety of languages and techniques. The characters' subjectivity, captured in depth, goes hand in hand with the display of different psycho-social, historical, cultural, and symbolic levels to convey a vast mural of modern Argentina. Nevertheless, the book has a universal appeal because its interest rests upon its timeless examination of the human condition (which Sabato had minutely analyzed in his earlier essays). A scrupulously structured book, *On Heroes* stitches together Sabato's speculative thinking and imaginative gifts. Its four parts are something of a puzzle, fragments told from differing points of view, the synthesis to be made by the reader. The book was conceived as a vast verbal symphony, intended to translate into fiction the "I" and the "Id," the human being and his masks as well as the collective mind of a nation, its present and past heroes and its history (tombs). It starts by announcing, in a two-paragraph journalistic report, that on June 24, 1955, Alejandra Vidal Olmos, the last descendant of a prominent but faded Argentinian family, shot her father, Fernando, and then set fire to herself and him. The report also tells us that Fernando has left behind a wild "Report on the Blind" that suggests a "sinister" and "obscure" explanation for this immolation. Coincidentally, a few days prior to this tragedy, the Argentinian Navy had tried to dislodge Perón from power and Buenos Aires was bombed. Later on, the angry mob of Peronists sets fire to the oldest churches of the city and loots them—a violent and fateful counterpoint to the incestous couple's fate and to the "Report." To try to summarize the plot would be futile. Suffice it to say that there is a fatal love story (that of Alejandra and Martín), the history of her patrician Argentinian family, a seemingly incestuous relationship with her father Fernando expiated through fire, the frustrated suicide of Martín, and his subsequent hopeful journey to the future.

As a simultaneous counterpoint to this narrative, Sabato has interpolated—in the first and fourth parts—the poetic saga of General Lavalle, a foe of the Rosas dictatorship of last century. In his search for the roots of history, Sabato is attempting to deliver not only today's Argentina, but also yesterday's. The famous "Report on the Blind," the third part of the novel, a complete literary work in its own right, is an hallucinatory objectification of a superreality. In it there are no frontiers between the exterior-objective world and the interior-subjective one; there is no division between the dream state and wakefulness, between hallucination and sanity, insanity and wisdom. In the "Report" (as in surrealist philosophy) those mysterious states of insanity and nightmare are precisely the ones that awaken the character to a better understanding of his internal reality while, at the same time, revealing new and unsuspected facets of an ampler and richer external truth even though this proves to be more gloomy and fatal. Fernando's descent to the sewers of "The Sect" is a mystical, but sacrilegious one, a form of cognition, a supreme knowledge of himself and, through this, an ultimate knowledge of the inscrutable designs of existence. Apart from its artful construction, the gravity center of *On Heroes and Tombs* is to be found in its episodic and conceptual richness which turns the novel into a sort of compendium. And it was this "monster novel," John Butt wrote, which placed Sabato "in the category of major novelists of the twentieth century."

In Sabato's essays a major theme is the fragmentation of human experience between the rational and the irrational, both to be explored at the same time. This theme compelled him to create a fictional world that precisely reflects the paradoxical nature of life in his novel *Abaddón, el Exterminador* (Abaddon, the Destroying Angel, 1974), called by one critic a "gnostic eschatology," a search to apprehend the existential truth about man and his destiny in the universe. But in this latest novel (awarded the coveted Great Honor Prize by the Argentinian Society of Writers), the initiatory trip is done by the author himself, Sabato, just as another character in the novel, and "like the others, all emanating from the artist's soul, as a mad hero who will cohabit with his own *desdoblamientos* [double]. But not gratuitously. Oh, no. God help me, but in order to see if in this way one can penetrate deeper into the great mystery." Sabato has become his own propitiatory victim to demonstrate that the sinister prophecies of *Apocalypse* 9:11 are about to become a reality, the end of a materialistic civilization brought about by Abaddon, the Beautiful Demonic Angel; mankind to be renovated through annihilation. Sabato has faith in a new cosmogonic beginning for man that will reestablish the divine order. In Sabato's artistic process each new novel has developed on the basis of the preceding one in an almost incestuous process, to the point that Sabato, like Castel in *The Outsider,* is trapped in *Abaddon,* thus permitting the readers to peep into Sabato's laboratory, into his bloody combat with literature. Sabato appears in *Abaddon* as Sabato-character, under his complete name, or under the initial S. The former seems to designate the writer mixed in the plot as one of the most delirious characters (which prevents the reader from considering such character autobiographical). The latter depicts Sabato's own temperamental ego, with his ghosts and occult tenets, constantly voicing his personal obsessions. On still other occasions he is called the "Maestro," evidently the alchemist of all those transformations of his personality. But there is still another elusive character, R, the very depths of the writer's personality who appears in critical moments of the novel. This "double," who presides over the entire novel, is seldom mentioned, and then, in a very imprecise manner. The choice of the letter "R" could refer to Sabato's native town of Rojas or possibly to rebirth, rediscovery, remembrance, words not solely meaningful in the novel's context but a key to the comprehension of the novel and, in general, of those obsessions presented in the "Report." In broad terms, the subject of *Abaddon* is not only the fragmentation of reality presented in terms of the conflict between opposites, but the necessity of harmonizing these opposites. *Abaddon* is Sabato's "Summa," but with a novel turn: the author himself is questioned, satirized, vexed, and forgiven by his own torturer-characters, even provided with an excruciating *via cruxis*, the book thus being both a catharsis and an exorcism of Sabato's personal ghosts. Some judge *Abaddon* as a "metanovel," "the novel of the novel"; others perceive it as "a project" or as "a masterpiece's dossier" of "extravagant and innovative nature," "a polemic and lacerating call to attention." It seems judicious to conclude in Raymond Souza's words that "[w]hat Sabato has done is to offer a great deal of himself. Some will question the novel's egocentricity and unconventional form, others will applaud its openness and emotional power, few will be unmoved by the anguish it reveals. . . . "

Ernesto Sabato is the son of Francisco Sabato and Juana María Ferrari, a northern Italian middle-class couple who emigrated to Argentina at the end of last century and operated a flour mill in the provincial town of Rojas, where the writer was born. He married Matilde Kuminsky-Ritcher, whom he met and eloped with during his student years at La Plata. There are two sons: Jorge Federico and Mario. Sabato, a man of formidable personality, sharp features, piercing eyes, and an almost pathologic sensitivity, has lived for many years in Santos Lugares, a proletarian suburb of Buenos Aires, in an old labyrinthine house whose garden he lovingly tends. Due to a gradual loss of sight, presently he divides his time between painting and writing short stories for his grandchildren, but, as always, he is ever-present in debating his country's issues as "the aged literary hero," "the idol of the country's young" as E. Schumacher observed in the *New York Times.* Sabato has extensively lectured at universities and learned institutions throughout Latin America and Western Europe, as well as in Poland, Czechoslovakia, Hungary, the British West Indies, and in the major American universities from coast to coast. He is Chevalier de l'Ordre des Arts et des Lettres of the French Republic, and has been distinguished with awards in Italy and West Germany. In his own country he was the first recipient of the highest official prize, the National Consegration Award, reserved for personalities in the creative and/or scientific fields who have contributed to the cultural heritage of the Argentinian Republic.

WORKS IN ENGLISH TRANSLATION: Two of Sabato's novels are available in English—*El túnel,* translated by Harriet de Onís in 1950, as *The Outsider,* and *Sobre heroes y tumbas,* translated as *On Heroes and Tombs* by Helen R. Lane in 1981.

ABOUT: (in Spanish) Dellepiane, A. Sabato el hombre y su obra, 1968; Foster, D.W. Currents in the Contemporary Argentinian Novel: Arlt, Mallea, Sabato and Cortázar, 1975; Hayden, R. L. An Existential Focus on Some Novels of the River Plate, 1973; Oberhelman, H.D. Ernesto Sabato, 1970. *Periodicals*—Books Abroad Summer 1946; Spring 1947; Spring 1952; Summer 1952; Forum for Modern Language Studies 15, 1979; Graduate Studies in Latin America (Lawrence, Kansas), 1974; Hispania, 1965; 1967;1968; 1969; 1972; Modern Language Notes, March 1968; Newsweek, September 21, 1981; New York Herald Tribune May 14, 1950; New York Review of Books September 22, 1981; New York Times July 24, 1981; November 15,. 1981; New York Times Book Review July 26, 1981; Romance Notes 10, 1968; 14, 1972; 1981; Times Literary Supplement, August 6, 1976; August 13, 1982.

SAGAN, CARL (EDWARD) (November 9, 1934–), American astronomer, exobiologist, and science writer, was born in the Bensonhurst section of Brooklyn to Samuel Sagan, a garment cutter and later foreman in a clothing factory, and Rachel Molly (Gruber) Sagan. Encouraged by his parents to read and develop a "sense of wonder," Sagan showed an early interest in astronomy and the possiblity of life on other worlds. At the age of ten or eleven, he devoured Edgar Rice Burroughs' Mars novels, and later discovered science-fiction magazines—notably John Campbell's *Astounding Science Fiction*—and the works of Jules Verne and H. G. Wells. In 1951, aged sixteen, Sagan graduated from Rahway High School in New Jersey and entered the University of Chicago, then renowned for instruction in the physical sciences; Nobel prize winners Harold Urey and Enrico Fermi and future winner Subrahmanyan Chandrasekhar taught there. On a series of scholarships, including grants from the National Science Foundation, Sagan earned a B.A. with special honors in natural sciences in 1954, an S.B. in physics in 1955, and an S.M. in 1956. During the summer of his freshman year he assisted the eminent geneticist Hermann J. Muller in his investigations of the effect of radiation on genetic mutation. Sagan's first published paper, "Radiation and the Origin of the Gene," was accepted by the journal *Evolution* in 1956, and his doctoral thesis, "Physical Studies of Planets," written under planetologist Gerard Kuiper, earned him a Ph.D. from the University of Chicago in 1960.

For the next several years Sagan made his mark as a theorist in the burgeoning field of planetary studies, then being revolutionized by the recent findings of radiotelescopes and unmanned space vehicles. Sagan contributed pioneering studies of the surface of Venus: he was the first to claim that the surface of the planet was far hotter than the hottest terrestrial desert, and originated the idea of "terraforming" the arid world by introducing algae into its upper atmosphere to absorb carbon dioxide and produce oxygen and organic materials. He also studied the climate and seasonal color changes of Mars, and the problem of microbial contamination of spacecraft. In 1961 he collaborated with W. W. Kellogg on his first book, *The Atmospheres of Mars and Venus*.

The possibility of extraterrestrial life, both in and beyond the solar system, continued to fascinate him. In 1962 Sagan sent a paper he was writing on radio contact with extrasolar civilizations to the Russian astronomer I. S. Shklovskii. Their correspondence eventually turned into a collaborative book, *Intelligent Life in the Universe*, based on an original Russian text by Shklovskii and copiously annotated by Sagan. Still considered the definitive work in the field, *Intelligent Life in the Universe* begins with a succinct review of what was currently known of planetary and biological evolution, and then embarks on increasingly heady speculations as to the likelihood, distribution, and technological level of alien civilizations, and how they might be contacted. The latter half of the book, with its serious discussion of what was up to then considered pure science fiction, is the most controversial, as it is based completely on conjecture and statistical inferences, but it is also, to quote Philip Morrison (*Scientific American*), "a most readable and quite complete example of the new genre of this protoscience [exobiology], so close to the edge of fiction and yet so plainly potential fact."

While a visiting professor at Stanford University in 1962, Sagan worked with another Nobel laureate, biologist Joshua Lederberg. Sagan did a series of sophisticated variations on the classic Stanley Miller-Harold Urey experiment, which in 1953 showed that basic organic materials could have been created spontaneously on the primordial earth. Sagan's results confirmed his belief that terrestrial life originated on earth, and not, as some astronomers and biologists (most recently, Francis Crick) have suggested, from an extraterrestrial spore or seed. As an astronomy professor at Harvard University (1962–67) and a member of the Smithsonian Institution's Astrophysical Observatory, also in Cambridge, Massachusetts, he continued his observations of the planets. In 1968 he became Duncan Professor of Astronomy and Space Science at Cornell University, and headed the university's Laboratory for Planetary Studies.

Sagan's close association with NASA, which

led to his first real public exposure, began when he was asked to join the group formulating sterilization procedures for the Apollo Program and the Mariner flights. Later he was a principal member of the groups of scientists preparing for the Mariner, Pioneer, Viking, and Voyager programs. Sagan, who views himself as an "intellectual gadfly," functioned, particularly on the Viking team, which devoted much effort to the search for life on Mars, as a passionate advocate for "ideas at the boundaries of the plausible." In so doing, he aimed to push his more conservative colleagues to disprove—or maybe prove—his theories.

The same eclectic imagination and challenging attitude was revealed in Sagan's increasingly popular series of science books, beginning with *The Cosmic Connection: An Extraterrestrial Perspective.* In three main sections, Sagan describes the history and scale of the universe (to provide, in his words, "a sense of cosmic perspective"), outlines the history of the solar system, and finally describes how extraterrestrial civilizations might be contacted by radio. In his *Time* magazine review, John Wilhelm wrote: "Sagan happily created scientific scenarios in terms of possibility, rather than strict probability. . . . [His] purpose is nothing less than to refocus man's perspective about his place in the great chain of being." *The Cosmic Connection* was notorious for reproducing on its cover a plaque, designed by Sagan and his second wife, artist Linda Salzman, that was sent out of the solar system on Pioneer 10. As the plaque included, along with other scientific information, a detailed drawing of a naked man and woman, many readers evidently bought the book expecting to enjoy an unlikely combination of science and sex. To promote his book Sagan made the first of what became regular appearances on television talk shows. He proved to be a born explainer whose obvious, even boyish, enthusiasm for science and personal charm came over well on television.

In *The Dragons of Eden*, Sagan left space science completely to examine informally the evolution of human intelligence. Among the specific subjects he touched upon were the differing abilities of the right and left brain, the nature of dreams, the retention of reptilian and lower mammalian brain structures and their influence on human behavior, and our (perhaps genetic) fear of dragons. Sagan's overarching metaphor was that of the Garden of Eden and the expulsion of Adam and Eve, which, he claimed, provides a useful mythic framework for understanding aspects of human evolution. Although, according to Roger Bingham, writing in *New Scientist*, many critics in the scientific press saw the book as "little more than a clever piece of synthesizing, which drew heavily on the work of other specialists and contained very little original thinking (together with some unfortunate errors of fact)," the book was a bestseller and won the 1978 Pulitzer Prize for non-fiction. Raymond Sokolov wrote in *Newsweek*: "We live in a period rich in scientific discovery and poor in science writing. . . . Non-scientists can be particularly grateful, then, that a scientific popularizer of high caliber has turned his mind to the significant, currently hyperactive field of brain research." Stephen Toulmin, writing in the *New York Review of Books*, called Sagan "a true 'natural philosopher'" whose book "is an antidote to much of the recent controversy about human evolution. His style and manner have a certain briskness and astringency, an alkalinity perhaps, which came pleasantly to the reader. . . . One important virtue of a book like Carl Sagan's is the contribution it makes toward reconciling the parochially human and the cosmological perspectives."

In 1978 Sagan and five collaborators—Timothy Ferris, radio astronomer Frank Drake, Jon Lomberg, Sagan's wife Linda Salzman Sagan, and his future third wife, writer Ann Druyan—published *Murmurs of Earth*, an account of their development of the phonograph record sent into interstellar space on the Voyager spacecraft. By far the most complex attempt to communicate with extraterrestrial intelligences, the record includes more than 100 audio-encoded photographs, greetings from global dignitaries in fifty-four languages, and a selection of the world's music.

Critics found Sagan's next book, *Broca's Brain: Reflections on the Romance of Science*, a wide-ranging collection of essays originally published in *Esquire, Atlantic, Smithsonian, Playboy,* and other magazines, irritatingly uneven. Robert Jastrow (*New York Times Book Review*) warned that the reader "must pick his way through a mixture of sense and nonsense," but that "[the book's] flaws are almost as interesting and amusing as its virtues." Richard Berendzen noted in *Science* that "for the nonspecialist, the book will be frustrating reading. . . . But if the reader can make it through, this curious volume can answer old questions, raise new ones, open vistas, become unforgettable. . . . The book's title may be *Broca's Brain*, but its subject is Sagan's."

In the late 1970s Sagan initiated his most ambitious popular project, the thirteen-part television science series *Cosmos*. Starring Sagan himself as seasoned guide to the wonders of the universe, *Cosmos* was produced by Sagan's own production company, Carl Sagan Productions, Los Angeles' KCET television station, and Public Television. It first aired in mid-1980. Scientifically accurate, thought-provoking, and spectacularly visual—ample use was made of the latest tricks of matte cinematography and computer graphics—*Cosmos* was also seriously overproduced. Sagan's deliberate and emphatic lecture style, though not as pedagogical as Jacob Bronowski's in *The Ascent of Man,* an earlier science series, contrasted with the fast-paced visual effects. Reviewers parodied his vocal mannerisms ("Bill-yuns and bill-yuns of stars," and so on) and objected to endless shots of Sagan piloting his "spaceship of the mind" through the cosmos. Despite its flaws, the series was widely watched and established Sagan as the country's most visible scientist. Sagan's accompanying book, also titled *Cosmos* headed non-fiction bestseller lists for months after the series ended. James Michener called the book "a highly personal . . . clearly written, [and] imaginatively illustrated summary of [Sagan's] geological, anthropological, biological, historical and astronomical ruminations about our universe."

Even at the height of Sagan's popularity as a "science entertainer," some members of the scientific community were criticizing him for venturing into areas beyond his competence, and, with such big-budgeted efforts as *Cosmos,* drawing attention and funds from the more serious but unglamorous work of lesser-known researchers. Roger Bingham noted that while there was "an element of truth in this," there was "also a considerable amount of sour grapes." Sagan has since embarked on other nonscientific enterprises: in 1981 he signed a contract to write a novel on extraterrestrial contact for Simon and Schuster (scheduled to be published in 1984), and also in 1981 opened The Cosmos Store, a Los Angeles-based publishing company specializing in science materials. In November 1983 he was a panelist in a televised discussion (with Henry Kissinger, William Buckley, Elie Wiesel, and others) on nuclear war that followed the ABC television film *The Day After.*

Sagan, who has published some 300 scientific papers, is a member of more than a dozen scientific societies and has won a number of important awards, including the NASA Medal for Exceptional Scientific Achievement, the Joseph Priestley Prize "for distinguished contributions to the welfare of mankind," and the John W. Campbell Memorial Award. Of the inquisitive habit of mind he encourages in his writings, Sagan says: "It's clear that there's not a society on the planet today which is working as cultures will need to work 100 years from now in order to be in existence then. How do we get from here

to where we want to go? By challenging everything."

PRINCIPAL WORKS: (With W. W. Kellogg) The Atmospheres of Mars and Venus, 1961; (with I. S. Shklovskii) Intelligent Life in the Universe, 1963; (with Jonathan Leonard) Planets, 1966; Planetary Exploration: The Condon Lectures, 1970; (coeditor) UFOs: A Scientific Debate, 1972; (contributor) Mars and the Mind of Man, 1973; (contributor) Life Beyond Earth and the Mind of Man, 1973; (editor) Communication with Extraterrestrial Intelligence, 1973; The Cosmic Connection: An Extraterrestrial Perspective, 1973; Other Worlds, 1975; The Dragons of Eden, 1977; (with F. D. Drake et al.) Murmurs of Earth, 1978; Broca's Brain, 1979; Cosmos, 1980.

ABOUT: Contemporary Authors 25–28, 1977; Current Biography, 1970; Who's Who in America, 1983–84; American Men and Women of Science, 1983. *Periodicals*—New Scientist January 17, 1980; New York Review of Books June 9, 1977; New York Times Book Review June 10, 1979; January 25, 1981; New Yorker June 13; June 20, 1976; Newsweek June 27, 1977; Science July 6, 1979; January 8, 1982; Scientific American October 1966.

*SAID, EDWARD W(ILLIAM) (November 1, 1935–   ), Palestinian-American literary and social critic, was born in Jerusalem, then part of the British mandate of Palestine. His parents, William A. Said, a businessman, and Hilda (Musa) Said, were Episcopalians. With the creation of Israel in 1948, the Saids moved to Cairo, where Edward was expelled from his proper English prep school for participating in student demonstrations. In the United States, he earned an A.B. from Princeton in 1957 and a doctorate in English literature from Harvard University in 1964.

Though Said has since attained some national prominence for his passionate espousal of the Palestinian cause and his scathing attacks on Western Orientalists, he began his career conventionally, as a tutor of history and English literature at Harvard. In 1960 he moved to Columbia University, where he became professor of English and comparative literature in 1970, at the age of thirty-three. His first major publication, *Joseph Conrad and the Fiction of Autobiography,* an expansion of his doctoral thesis, was a study of the close relationship between Conrad's personal history, as revealed in his letters, and the themes of his short fiction. "The accurate grasp of someone else's concerns is never an easy matter," Said wrote of his difficulties in analyzing Conrad's copious and unsystematic correspondence. "Pain and intense effort are the profound keynotes of Conrad's spiritual history,

°sī èd´

EDWARD SAID

and his letters attest to this." They also, in Said's view, attest to the writer's "creation of a public personality that was to camouflage his deeper and more problematic difficulties with himself and with his work." The letters reveal that Conrad "believed that his life was like a series of short episodes (rather than a long, continuous, and orderly narrative) because he himself [was] so many people, each living a life unconnected with the others. . . . Hence, it was natural for him to express himself more effectively in shorter works" in which "the inner dynamics of Conrad's letters seem to be paralleled especially closely."

Said's analysis of Conrad, clearly influenced by French philosophy and modernist critical theory (he was already one of the most able practitioners of a modified structuralism in the United States) was, according to the *Choice* reviewer, "a brilliantly elaborated patterning of the energies and conflicts that lie beneath the surface of Conrad's rhetoric. Marred in execution only by sometimes gratuitous references to phenomenological and existentialist philosophy and by occasional passages of stylistic virtuosity, the book is an important addition to Conrad criticism. It is also valuable as a sophisticated and powerful example of psychological criticism." Said's interest in Conrad—who, like him, was an expatriate writer inhabiting several conflicting linguistic and cultural worlds at once—was to lead naturally to a more general preoccupation with the effects of individual and social contexts on literary interpretation (Conrad's stories are often presented by a "tale-teller" who filters the narrative through his own sensibility) and with the

problem of Western misunderstanding and domination of the East.

Beginnings: Intention and Method was written partly on a grant from the Guggenheim Memorial Foundation (1972–73). Rather hermetic to the casual reader in its dependence on the critical methods of Maurice Merleau-Ponty, Michel Foucault, and Roland Barthes, *Beginnings* explored the self-conscious complexities of initiating a work of literature or scholarship. In his preface, Said outlined his central thesis. "When one actually begins to write, a complex set of circumstances obtains that characterizes the beginning enterprise. In language, therefore, writing or thinking *about* beginning is tied to writing or thinking *a* beginning. A verbal beginning is consequently both a creative and a critical activity, just as at the moment one begins to use language in a disciplined way, the orthodox distinction between critical and creative thought begins to break down." In this light Said examined the fiction of Conrad, Marcel Proust, Jorge Luis Borges, Thomas Mann, and Charles Dickens, with substantial sections on the pseudo-fictional case studies of Sigmund Freud, the critical system of Michel Foucault, and the cyclical meta-history of Giambattista Vico.

Richard Kuczkowski found the book "rich and fascinating despite needless obscurity and graceless jargon." He praised Said's "impressive learning" as it was applied to the problem of "how forms like the novel and concepts like text are forms of beginning and being in the world." Robert Towers described this same elaborate erudition more negatively as "a fantastically structured armoring that bristles at every point with a fashionable virtuosity" and merely revealed "the domination of literature by system and little that is useful in the way of practical criticism."

At the end of his last chapter, Said, calling for fresh beginnings in several areas of literary scholarship, pointed out the need to investigate "the question of the cultural domination of one intellectual or national domain over another," a study "to which I hope our moral will shall be equal." Said himself next undertook such an investigation, which was to provoke a major and unusually heated scholarly controversy.

For several years, Said has written, he read widely in Orientalist texts; that is, the writings, historical and contemporary, of Western scholars on the languages, literature, customs, and politics of the Orient (in his definition, primarily the present Middle East). But it was not until the defeat of the Arabs in the Six-Day War of 1967 and the subsequent emergence into world politics of the Palestine Liberation Organization that Said found his own political position on the Middle East—previously ill-defined and repressed—and undertook a form of scholarly political action against traditional Orientalists. Said conceived the thesis, elaborated in *Orientalism,* that Orientalism as a scholarly discipline acted in the past, and in the United States still acts, "as the corporate institution for dealing with the Orient—dealing with it by making statements about it, authorizing views of it, describing it, by teaching it, settling it, ruling over it—in short, Orientalism as a Western style for dominating, restructuring, and having authority over the Orient." In other words, Orientalism was and is the intellectual arm of Western imperialism. "So authoritative a position did Orientalism have [during the British and French colonial periods] that I believe no one writing, thinking, or acting on the Orient could do so without taking account of the limitations of thought and action imposed by Orientalism," Said continued; "because of Orientalism the Orient was not (and is not) a free subject of thought or action." Said also attempted to show that "European culture gained in strength and identity by setting itself off against the Orient as a sort of surrogate and even underground self"—an idea seemingly derived from Conrad's story of an alter-ego "The Secret Sharer" and expanded from the interpersonal to the intercultural.

The book was widely reviewed and excerpted in the popular press, but few scholarly reviewers, most of them Orientalists themselves, were willing to take Said's thesis at face value (though many agreed with T. M. Greene that "simply as an anthology of overbearing observations, analyses, and 'explanations' of non-European cultures, this book makes for painful reading"). Said's tone—passionate, angry, sarcastic—was often cited as evidence of his partisanship, and the accuracy of his scholarship was also called into question, most notably in a lengthy *New York Review of Books* article by Bernard Lewis. In his book, Said had attacked Lewis as a modern example of all that was biased in Orientalism; Lewis retorted with a point-by-point refutation of the book's factual bases and suggested that Said's attack on Orientalists, which Lewis claimed was poisoning the atmosphere of free inquiry in the field, was really symptomatic of a resurgent political and religious animosity of Arabs toward the West. "Lewis's verbosity scarcely conceals both the ideological underpinnings of his position and his extraordinary capacity for getting everything wrong," Said replied in the same journal. "He proceeds in his usual mode by suppressing or distorting the truth and by innuendo"—contentions which Lewis, in his rebuttal, simply turned back on Said. More even-tempered were the observations of Oleg Grabar, a professor of Islamic art at Harvard, who wrote that the anti-Orientalist movement that Said in part inspired "obviously corresponds to something which is deeply rooted in the minds of many young and not-so-young scholars from the Muslim world and it cannot be answered simply by pointing out factual errors or willful misunderstandings."

Though not (as of 1980) a member of the PLO, Said is a member of the Palestine National Council, a consultative body affiliated with that organization, and has met publicly with PLO leaders. He has written a number of articles critical of Israeli policies and supporting the creation of an independent Palestinian state, and his two books, *The Question of Palestine* and *Covering Islam,* dealt very directly with contemporary political issues. As an historical overview of Western and Zionist prejudice against Arabs, and particularly Palestinians (who have been depicted, he wrote, as "synonomous with trouble—rootless, mindless, gratuitous trouble"), *The Question of Palestine* was generally accepted as accurate, even moving. There was, however, considerable debate over Said's analysis of recent political events, including the Camp David accords and the de facto annexation of the West Bank and Gaza by Israel. According to Terence Smith, Said described Camp David as "a cynical cover for sustained and indefinite Israeli domination [of the West Bank], underwritten by the U.S. and Egypt." Again, Said was accused of offering what was, in essence, a nationalist tract in the guise of evenhanded political analysis. In an otherwise sympathetic review, Nicholas Bethell wrote: "Both the quality of the book and the strength of the author's case are marred by inconsistency. The style is sometimes incisive, sometimes repetitive and rambling. The political approach is sometimes gentle, sometimes furious. He makes a conciliatory statement, then contradicts it with a hawkish statement." Nonetheless, Bethell hoped that "supporters of Israel will read this book and emerge from it, as I did, with a feeling of sympathy for the dispersed Palestinian people."

Likewise, *Covering Islam* was meant as a corrective to the distorted picture of the Muslim world perpetuated by the mass media, particularly television. Said cited American coverage of the Iranian revolution as the most clearcut recent case of media inflation and misperception exacerbating what was already a debacle for American interests into an ideological war. He pointed to academic experts "in the service of power" as the principal suppliers of willful misinformation to the press. Because of this, Said wrote, Islam is now perceived as "a kind of scapegoat for everything we do not happen to like about the world's new political, social, and economic patterns." In his *New Republic* review, Leon Wieseltier disagreed. "[Said's] book is really nothing more than the application to the Arab question of the most tired cliché of political criticism, which is that the real problem is the media. . . . The tyranny of the [Iranian] mullahs is detested [by Americans] not because it is Islamic, but because it is wrong."

Said's *The World, the Text, and the Critic* gathered a selection of the author's literary essays of the past fourteen years on such figures as Jonathan Swift, Ernst Renan, Conrad, Foucault, Jacques Derrida, and Raymond Williams, and on such problems as the effect of culture and ideology on literary theory. Perhaps relieved at not having to take a stand on some highly charged political issue, most reviewers had nothing but praise for Said's critical acumen. "No critic writing today can match Said for range of ideas and intensity of argumentation," wrote Alexander Gelley in *Library Journal*, while to Denis Donoghue of the *New Republic* these essays revealed "a remarkably sharp intelligence" that forces the reader "to face questions and possibilities that literary theorists on the whole prefer not even to raise." Irvin Ehrenpreis, however, in *New York Review of Books*, judged *The World, the Text, and the Critic* "a disconcerting example of a rational position sapped by alarming faults." He challenged Said's accuracy in his readings of Plato, Swift (Ehrenpreis is the author of a major biography of Swift), Renan, and even Conrad, writing: "As a practical and theoretical critic of literature, Said sacrifices accuracy and good sense to self-indulgent carelessness." The strength of the book, Ehrenpreis noted, was in its discussion of European Orientalism where "Said sets fresh and important vistas before us"; its weakness derives "from the inadequacies of his knowledge and method."

Said, currently Parr Professor of English and Comparative Literature at Columbia, has been a visiting professor at Princeton, Johns Hopkins, Harvard, and Stanford universities. *Beginnings* was awarded the first annual Lionel Trilling Award by Columbia; *Orientalism* was a runner-up for the National Book Critics' Circle Award for criticism. Said married Mariam Cortas in 1970; they have two children, Wadie and Najda. Of his status as a politically committed Palestinian teaching at an American university, Said told the *New York Times*: "I know I'm not easily classified. I'm a Palestinian on the one hand, and I'm part of the most Establishment world possible. My appearance is, judging from what people say, eminently respectable; yet I am sometimes with people who would be deemed dreadful. When you stop worrying about who you are and

what you ought to be doing, going from one role to another, from one life to another, from one personality to another, it becomes extremely inspiriting. I would say that is what humanism is all about."

PRINCIPAL WORKS: Joseph Conrad and the Fiction of Autobiography, 1966; Beginnings: Intention and Method, 1975; Orientalism, 1978; The Question of Palestine, 1979; (ed.) Literature and Society, 1980; Covering Islam, 1981; The World, the Text, and the Critic, 1983.

ABOUT: Contemporary Authors, revised series 21–24, 1977; International Who's Who, 1983–84. *Periodicals*—American Scholar Autumn 1979; Canadian Forum November 1981; Choice March 1967; June 1983; Library Journal November 15, 1975; New Republic December 15, 1979; September 23, 1981; April 18, 1983; New Statesman January 26, 1979; New York Review of Books March 8, 1979; June 12, 1980; May 27, 1982; June 24, 1982; August 12, 1982; January 19, 1984; New York Times February 22, 1980; New York Times Book Review, December 21, 1975; February 18, 1979; January 20, 1980; July 26, 1981; February 27, 1983; Times Literary Supplement May 4, 1984; Yale Review Summer 1979.

SALE, ROGER (August 19, 1932–   ), American critic, writes: "Like most others, as I was growing up I assumed that writers were poets, novelists, dramatists. So much so that I was for a long time puzzled by a figure like Dr. Johnson, called a 'great writer,' yet the author of an unreadable play, a handful of poems, and a moralizing romance. Thus, if I were going to be a writer, I would write fiction, which I did, very badly. So I was not going to be a writer. An academic, a teacher, a critic, yes, but not a writer.

"Teaching at Amherst, starting right out of graduate school twenty-six years ago, helped change that. People referred to others as writers even if they wrote nothing more than assignments, or suggestions for classes. A friend once called a memo I wrote to a class 'a good piece of writing.' By the time I came to the University of Washington in 1962, though I had written only a handful of reviews and essays, I was pretty clear I would be a writer, and write no poems or novels. I was also lucky, because having some steady reviewing jobs meant I worried less about being an academic writer, about writing as my colleagues were. I also was free to teach a large variety of courses, ranging from the Bible to the Renaissance and nineteenth and twentieth century fiction, which meant I was seldom called upon to have a 'field,' to be a specialist.

"With this background and these lovely working conditions, it was hard not to have fun writing. Especially in the earlier years, writing came

ROGER SALE

slowly; for a long time I would take a third or fourth version home to my wife, asking her to read it, calling it a rough draft. Good that I did, since she was a tough reader; no telling how many versions the Lawrence chapter in *Modern Heroism* went through before she was finally satisfied. That too was fortunate, of course, since after a while I began to be able to anticipate her and other people's responses, and actually begin to be able to get it close to finished by myself.

"As to what writing is for me: a way to find out what I think, where I live, how I love what I do love—'just like a novelist,' I might have said, except by the time I knew this I no longer fretted not being a novelist. One sabbatical left me free to start a history of Seattle I had long dreamed of attempting, another gave me a year in England to walk the landscapes from whence came some of our great children's books, another coming up soon will let me haunt some more of those landscapes and start a book on the history of feelings and places in English literature. I seem to find little that I say I must write, or write about, but much that seems absorbing and baffling and fun once I get into it. So I write about Seattle's professional basketball team, and its race track; about contemporary fiction and children's books when called upon; I get to spend any spare time in the next few months writing about Spenser for the first time in years, and about the culture of my childhood. And in a given teaching year, a large amount of my writing is comments on student papers; whenever I began to realize that that too was writing, it too became a challenging pleasure, because it too is making words out of not words.

"As the years remaining just begin to seem limited, I sometimes wonder if there is something I will later regret not having done. No doubt there will be, but I know a writer makes the subjects, even those which seem to demand the writer's attention. For years I have contemplated a handbook to the Bible, something like an *Oxford Companion,* because I would like someone else to have done one. If time adheres with place and place with choosing, then maybe. But then, maybe something else. Part of the fun is the not knowing."

———

Roger Sale was born in New Haven, Connecticut, the son of William M. Sale, Jr., a teacher, and the former Helen Stearns. He received his B.A. from Swarthmore College in 1953 and his M.A. and Ph.D. from Cornell, the latter degree in 1957. In the same year he began six years of teaching at Amherst College. He has taught at the University of Washington at Seattle since 1962, as professor of English since 1970.

His first widely discussed book was *Modern Heroism: Essays on D.H. Lawrence, William Empson, and J.R.R. Tolkien.* The three subjects are, in Sale's words, "historians of the Myth of Lost Unity," which he describes as a belief that the world was at one time unified and whole but that it has in recent times begun to disintegrate, and that hence the human condition is now one of alienation and loss. Lawrence, Empson, and Tolkien are heroic because they accepted the major features of this myth, though Sale sees them as defying its implications. They help to release us "from the tortured consciousness in which we live," so we may "rise to some human but seemingly seraphic state where life is as it has always been, but replete with forgotten possibilities."

Critical opinion was divided about this book. Derek Willard thought the essay on Empson the best: it "documents [his] contributions to literary criticism and places him in relation to other framers of modern literary interpretation. . . . The book is not merely a reaction against something, but a guide to recovering human possibilities that we thought were lost to us." Keith Cushman wrote that Sale's "rather loose notion of 'modern heroism' fits practically any old modern writer," and that "the interpretation of Empson—criticism of criticism—is genuinely exciting: it's hard to think of a better analysis of this difficult writer. . . . A lively and engaged mind is clearly in evidence throughout this book." Herbert Leibowitz thought the treatment of Empson "overingenious," but the piece on Lawrence "a brilliantly lucid guide to [his] artistic growth." The reviewer for the *Times Literary Supplement* found the Lawrence essay "intelligent if unoriginal," the other two "distinctly inferior. . . . Professor Sale has most of Empson's faults without his cardinal virtue—the gift of close analysis, a gift underrated in this account of Empson's achievement. They share a colloquial style, . . . a deliberate whimsicality, . . . and, worst of all, critical night falls with an Empsonian suddenness in some of these pages."

In *Fairy Tales and After: From Snow White to E. B. White,* Sale discusses his favorite children's writers in a set of discrete appreciative essays with little overall coherence. The "classic successes" for Sale among these writers are Charles Perrault, the Grimm brothers, Lewis Carroll, Beatrix Potter, Rudyard Kipling, L. Frank Baum, and E. B. White, among others. Some authorities on children's literature seemed quite delighted that an authentic literary critic was at last paying attention to their field: "The publication of this book," wrote Francelia Butler, "by an Ivy-League press is of historic importance to the field of children's literature because it aids greatly in establishing the legitimacy of a field which still is ignored by most scholars in English departments." Earl Rovit disliked the book, finding it "remarkably tepid. . . . For the most part, Sale's examination consists of plot summary, some recourse to biography, more than a little belaboring of the obvious, and occasional flashes of genuine insight." Denis Donoghue, however, saw in *Fairy Tales and After* a significant link to the author's earlier book: "Mr. Sale is concerned to preserve those values that were once available, he believes, to the whole society but now only to a nonchalant minority, the children who entertain unofficial values and delight in their freedom. . . . He insists that 'children's literature is one of the glories of our more recent literary heritage'—a stuffy sentence in a book that is rarely stuffy. The motive of Rumpelstiltskin, he maintains, is 'the great traditional motive of fairy tales, to triumph over our deepest fears with our deepest desires.' This is the point at which the continuity between *Modern Heroism* and *Fairy Tales and After* becomes clear." Alison Lurie thought that because the book "is so personal, every reader will probably have some quarrel with it. . . . When Sale writes about the books he loved as a child, though, he is interesting and very engaging; he is a constructive rather than a destructive—or a deconstructive—critic. In this era of self-conscious and abstruse (often obtuse) textual analysis, his air of wondering and grateful appreciation, his concern for the writer's intention, and his willingness to use the word 'I' seem most attractive."

Sale has been from the mid-1960s a frequent contributor of book reviews to such publications as *Husdon Review, New York Review of Books,* and *New Republic.* A collection of twenty-two of these previously published pieces is *On Not Being Good Enough: Writings of a Working Critic,* which considers work by such writers as Norman Mailer, Bernard Malamud, Dashiell Hammett, I.F. Stone, Kurt Vonnegut, Hugh Kenner, Lionel Trilling, Marvin Mudrick, Jane Jacobs, Lewis Mumford, and Buckminster Fuller. Sale is "one of the most consistently readable critics around," wrote Mark Shechner, "and his collection is as good a lesson on the reviewer's craft as anything I know. The special flavor of this critic's writing comes . . . from the quality of his voice, the personality he brings to the job. He is an eager, skeptical, affectionate reader whose response to books is personal and immediate."

Sale married Dorothy Young in 1955; they have two children and live in Seattle.

PRINCIPAL WORKS: Reading Spenser, 1968; On Writing, 1970; Modern Heroism, 1973; Seattle Past to Present, 1976; Fairy Tales and After, 1978; On Not Being Good Enough, 1979; Literary Inheritance, 1984.

ABOUT: Contemporary Authors, first revision series 21–24, 1977. *Periodicals*—American Scholar Autumn 1973; Choice December 1978; Christian Science Monitor February 12, 1979; Library Journal December 1, 1972; December 15, 1978; July 1979; Library Quarterly October 1979; Michigan Quarterly Review, 1978; Nation November 11, 1978; New Republic October 14, 1978; September 15, 1979; New York Review of Books March 8, 1979; November 8, 1979; New York Times Book Review July 29, 1973; November 19, 1978; October 7, 1979; New Yorker December 4, 1978; Times Literary Supplement July 27, 1973.

SANDEL, CORA (pseudonym of **Sara Fabricius**), (December 20, 1880–April 3, 1974), Norwegian novelist and short-story writer, was born in Kristiana (now Oslo). Her father, Jens Schouw Fabricius, was a navy captain and the family was identified with the upper class. They made a dramatic move when she was twelve, leaving the southern capital for the far-northern port of Tromsø. Here, well above the Arctic Circle, Cora Sandel spent her adolescence. Tromsø awed her with its glittering natural beauty, yet she felt stifled by the extreme winter cold and isolation. Sandel nurtured the dream of becoming an artist and as a young adult was given the opportunity to study with Harriet Backer, one of Norway's finest painters. In 1905 she left home for further studies in Paris. A planned six-month stay became instead a fifteen-year residence.

CORA SANDEL

Sandel's intimate knowledge of Paris in the years around World War I left its mark upon her writing, as did the powerful experience of life in northern Norway. Nowhere are these places more realistically depicted than in her celebrated Alberte trilogy.

Like many women writers of past generations, Sandel did not make her debut until quite late. She was well into her forties when her first book appeared in 1926. Her commitment to literary expression developed gradually and was impeded by competing commitments, first to painting and then to her family. In 1913 she married the Swedish sculptor Anders Jönsson; in 1917 their son Erik was born. After moving to Sweden in 1921, she and Jönsson parted company, and they were divorced in 1926. Economic necessity helped crystallize her ambitions and she now began writing in earnest. For inspiration, she turned to the novels of Colette, one of which (*La vagabonde*) she later translated into Norwegian.

Alongside work on the Alberte narrative, Sandel in the 1920s produced a number of short stories for the Norwegian press. She took the pen name Cora Sandel in an attempt to preserve her privacy and used it tenaciously throughout the rest of her life. So thoroughly did Cora Sandel become her public identity that all literary histories, critical studies, and reprinted editions refer to her under this name.

At the center of Sandel's production stands the Alberte trilogy, her most impressive work. The volumes were published at fairly long intervals: *Alberte og Jakob*; (Alberta and Jacob) in 1926; *Alberte og friheten* (Alberta and Freedom) in 1931; and *Bare Alberte* (Alberta Alone). Each

volume focuses on a critical period in Alberte's life; the years in between are largely ignored. Presenting as it does the struggles of a woman to define her creative and personal roles, the trilogy both fits into and extends the tradition of novels of artistic development. That it is a woman whose path to self-confidence and accomplishment we follow is most significant. The expectations placed upon Alberte and the obstacles to her self-realization prove time and again to be interwoven with the fact of her sex. With this psychologically apt, carefully crafted portrait of the emerging artist, Cora Sandel documented important new realms of female experience. Although Alberte's story has points in common with Sandel's own life, the novels cannot be characterized as autobiographical. What Sandel has done is to adopt an aesthetic stance similar to the one she allows her heroine to discover. Barbara Wilson describes this as "a feminist aesthetic, a way of writing about her own life, using her experiences for literature."

Alberte Selmer freezes outwardly and inwardly as a young woman in northern Norway. Unlike her brother Jakob she receives no intellectual encouragement and has no opportunity to escape either the tyranny of the marriage market or the suffocating stuffiness of their provincial environment. Jakob goes off to sea and Alberte sinks into suicidal despair. But eventually, Alberte, too, makes her way out into the world. In Paris she finds the freedom for which she has so intensely longed; however, this freedom is negatively, rather than positively, defined—"free from that which she did not desire and no clue as to what she should do with herself." Alberte has landed in a flock of foreign artists and she moves through the days haunted by financial worries, starving emotionally as well as physically. Only scribbled scraps of paper flung helter-skelter into a suitcase hint of her creative promise. The birth of a child and frustrating years spent in hapless domesticity further delay the blossoming of her talent. When Alberte at long last has welded the scraps of paper into a manuscript, she sets out, by herself—"to tell some truths." This mission transforms Alberte from a passive into an active individual. Virpi Zuck asserts: "Although alone, Alberte is not lonesome; she has left the deceptive security of a family for the uncertain but rewarding involvement in human liberation."

Sandel's psychological portraits are always attuned to social and economic status. From her years in Paris Sandel knew first-hand the pain of poverty and as the motto for her next novel borrowed a quotation from Swedish author Hjalmar Söderberg: "Poverty is terrible. Of all the so-called external misfortunes, it is probably the one that most deeply affects us internally." Katinka Stordal, the main character in *Kranes konditori* (*Krane's Café*, 1945), is viewed by many critics as a variation of the Alberte character. The works are, however quite different. In *Kranes konditori* the time frame is compressed to two days and the setting to a single spot—a café in a small town in northern Norway. Here Katinka Stordal verbalizes a severe depression and rebels against her slave-like life as mother and struggling seamstress. All the individuals central to her life visit the café. The result is an unmasking of social conventions and human frailties. Technically, this novel is a triumph. The composition incorporates elements of the drama and the text displays the author's expert control of both the narrative tone and the multiple levels of eavesdropping on which the narrative is based.

The last novel, *Kjøp ikke Dondi* (Don't Buy Dondi, 1958, translated as *The Leech*), is an experiment with modernistic form. It borders even more closely on the dramatic and uses dialogue to construct the main action retrospectively. The work is also more pessimistic, particularly with regard to the female characters. This may be due, Norwegian critic Janneken Øverland suggests, to the distance which Sandel places between herself and the fictional material. The spark of personal engagement, of sympathy, which flows through Sandel's other writing seems here to be missing.

Although acknowledged to be of high quality, Sandel's short stories have been overshadowed by her novels. In fact, her production in this genre alone earns her a lasting place in contemporary literary history. Her precise style and mastery of irony and humor produce a sparkle and depth which are splendidly communicated in the story format. Sandel published five short story collections; four of them share central themes: *En blå sofa og andre noveller* (A Blue Sofa and Other Stories, 1927); *Carmen og Maja og andre novellar* (Carmen and Maja and Other Stories, 1932); *Mange takk, doktor* (Thank You Very Much, Doctor, 1935); and *Figurer på mørk bunn* (Figures Against a Dark Background, 1949). Other of her stories were gathered from periodicals by Steinar Gimnes and published in 1973 under the title *Barnet som elsket veier* (The Child who Loved Roads).

The search for freedom runs through many of these stories. People are held in place like flies stuck to flypaper, as Steinar Gimnes points out; and not a few of the characters puzzle over a strategy for this "difficult life of ours." Sometimes individuals manage to pull away. Movement, dance, rhythm are important signals of emerging personal autonomy. Sandel often juxtaposes purposeful individuals and those without direction. The contrast may also be expressed as efficient/impractical; sturdy/vulnerable; male/female. Another critic, Janneken ØOverland, posits the overarching label "power and powerlessness." Most often it is women who are portrayed as powerless, vulnerable, and passive. Perhaps the most striking illustration is provided by the story "Mange takk, doktor" (Thank You Very Much, Doctor), where a young woman artist undergoes an abortion and discovers that she is not in control of her own body.

Cora Sandel felt a special affection for animals and the reader will note references to them throughout her work. The vulnerability and dependency of animals in their relationship with human beings awakened a sympathy within Sandel; this sympathy can be compared to that with which she examined the weak and defenseless among humans. The earliest published pieces from her hand were turn-of-the-century sketches for *Dyrenes Ven* (The Animals' Friend), among them a description of captured polar bears awaiting shipment out of Tromsø harbor. Compassion for animals forms the unifying thread in the story collection of 1945, *Dyr jeg har kjent* (Animals I Have Known).

From the outset Cora Sandel won high praise for her superb writing style and skillful use of psychological realism. More recently, critical attention has focused on her penetrating analyses of female experience and on the social and political implications of her art. Sandel's contributions to both literary form and subject place her among the best of Scandinavia's modern writers. Her reputation continues to grow internationally. With her Alberte novels in particular, Cora Sandel inspires new generations of readers and writers.

WORKS IN ENGLISH TRANSLATION: Elizabeth Rokkan translated the following novels by Cora Sandel—*The Leech*, 1960; *Alberta and Jacob*, 1962; *Alberta and Freedom*, 1963; *Alberta Alone*, 1965; and *Krane's Café*, 1968. The Alberta trilogy, in Rokkan's translation, was re-issued by Ohio University Press in 1983, and in paperback by the Women's Press. A one-volume edition of the trilogy was published as *Alberta Alone* in 1966, and a selection of her short stories translated by Barbara Wilson is scheduled for publication in 1985. Translations of Sandel stories will also be found in The New Review 3 (November 1976); The Norseman 7, no. 1 (1949); The Norseman 10, no. 2 and no. 6 (1952); The Norseman 14, no. 6 (1956); The Norseman 15, no. 5 (1957); The Norseman 16, no. 6 (1958); Scandinavian Review 23, no. 3 (1935).

ABOUT: Cassell's Encyclopedia of World Literature, 1973; Columbia Dictionary of Modern European Literature, 1980; Hunt, L. C. *Introduction to* Alberta Trilogy, 1983; Seymour-Smith, M. Who's Who in Twentieth Century Literature, 1976; *Periodicals*—Backbone 3, 1981; The Norseman 1949; 1957.

*SANTOS, BIENVENIDO N(UGAI)

(March 22, 1911–   ), Philippine-American novelist, short story writer, and poet, wrote to *World Authors* in 1981: "A native of the Philippines I learned English early from American and Filipino teachers, fell in love with the language, the sweetness and the melody of it, and somehow managed over the years to have some sort of meaning in what I wrote come through the music of its sounds. As the son of a public works foreman who knew only two English words, 'roads' and 'bridges,' I felt it quite an achievement when I became a teacher of English. Soon I became more enamored of the language and wrote furiously in the manner of Edgar Allan Poe, Henry Wadsworth Longfellow, and Washington Irving whose works were fed to us in abundance by our American mentors. In the fall of 1941, the Philippine government sent me to the United States to learn more of it. I stayed on for the duration of World War II, close to other Filipinos in the United States, taxi drivers, students, menials, factory workers, whose stories I have been writing about since then, their dilemmas in loyalties and identities, their confusions and confessions.

"On my return to the Philippines after liberation, as we called the surrender of the Japanese and their departure from the islands, I taught school, wrote and published poems, stories, essays, plays. Without intending to, I became a college president, but 'abandoned' the presidency for a Rockefeller Foundation fellowship to study and write a novel at the Writers Workshop in the University of Iowa. I brought my wife and ten-year-old son with me. We lived in a quonset hut on Riverside Drive in Iowa City where I struggled through the first draft of a first novel while my wife went to graduate college and my son to parochial school. The novel I was writing won for me another year of Rockefeller Foundation support. Another novel, *The Volcano*, followed soon after *Villa Magdalena* and got me a Guggenheim Foundation fellowship. With my wife and son I traveled around the world. Back to my country, I received the government's highest award, the Republic Cultural Heritage Award in Literature. My two novels were published almost simultaneously the same year, 1965.

"The following year the University of Iowa

BIENVENIDO SANTOS

took me back, this time as a member of the faculty in the Writers Workshop under a Fulbright Exchange professorship. I have been in the United States since then except for one year, 1969, when my wife and I returned to the Philippines, for good, we thought, until we realized that great unrest, often bloody, was brewing in college campuses, including the university where I was Vice President for Academic Affairs. I found myself in the middle of confrontations which I did not relish because, among other things, I had very little time or no time at all for my writing.

"So I returned to the University of Iowa, taught for two more years and in the summer of 1972, my wife and I were again on the move, back to the Philippines for good as we always thought every time we came home. This time we got as far as San Francisco where we found ourselves stranded because martial law had been declared in the Philippines. My novel *The Praying Man*, scheduled for publication late that year, was censored by the martial law government. Things looked pretty grim and worsened as time went on. So my wife and I started looking around for work. Soon we realized that we were too old for sunny California standards.

"Fortunately, before our funds ran out, I found work as Distinguished Writer in Residence at Wichita State University in Kansas, where I have been since 1973.

"For the first time in eleven years I was in the Philippines in November 1981 to bury my wife of forty-seven years at the foot of the volcano where we had built a house some thirty years ago. The newspapers and magazines were filled

° sän´ tōs, byen´ ven ē´ dō

with stories of my bitter-sweet homecoming. I had come with the body of my wife and returned to this country with clippings, quite an unfair exchange.

"My novel *The Praying Man,* censored in the early phase of martial law, will be published in full and unexpurgated in 1982 in Manila. I have just accepted an offer from the Ohio State University in Columbus to teach as visiting writer this fall, after which, I shall take a brief vacation at the foot of Mount Mayon, return to Colorado where I have a place, resume work on another novel and keep writing in between trips abroad mostly to the Philippines where I intend to live eventually. After all, 'all exiles want to go home. Many of the old Filipinos in the United States . . . never return, but in their imagination they make the journey a thousand times, taking the slowest boats because in their dream world time is not as urgent as actual time passing, quicker than arrows, kneading their flesh, crying on their bones. Some fool themselves into thinking that theirs is a voluntary exile, but it is not. The ones who stay here to die know this best. Their last thoughts are of childhood friends, of parents long dead, old loves, of familiar songs and dances, odors of home like sweat and sun on brown skin or scent of *calamondin* fruit and fresh papaya blossoms' (Preface to *Scent of Apples*)."

Like the characters in his delicate, straightforward, and deeply felt short stories, Bievenido Santos lives in two worlds: "the Philippines, land of my birth; and the United States, sanctuary, a second home," as he wrote in dedicating one of his books to his wife. Both in his fiction and in his poetry Santos ranges over his early life in his beautiful but impoverished native land, his years of wartime exile in the United States, and his return to his country devastated by war and political unrest. His tone is elegiac, Leonard Casper writes. "It is the sound of endurance, denying that it must drop into silence unheard"—

My father's wound was deep
Stretched through the ends of earth
Tortuous like many rivers
Thus waited for my birth.

("Father and Son")

His characters, like the wounded stag of the title poem of one of his collections, are hurt, trying to come to terms with their loneliness and grief, resolute in their determination to survive with dignity. Thus he both embraces and transcends the Philippine experience and speaks of the human condition in terms that are moving and significant to all readers. With the publication in the United States of *A Scent of Apples* in 1980, Santos finally achieved national recognition. Reviewing that volume in the *New York Times,* Maxine Hong Kingston wrote: "He ought to be read by more of the general public and his work should make its way into the mainstream of American literature."

PRINICPAL WORKS: *Poetry*—The Wounded Stag, 1956. *Stories*—You Lovely People, 1955; Brother My Brother, 1960; The Day the Dancers Came, 1967; Scent of Apples, 1980; *Novels*—Villa Magdalena, 1965; The Volcano, 1965.

ABOUT: Bernad, M. A. Bamboo and the Greenwood Tree: Essays on Filipino Literature in English, 1961; Casper, L. New Writing from the Philippines, 1966; Contemporary Authors 101, 1981; Murphy, R. (ed.) Contemporary Poets, 1970. *Periodicals*—New Writers May 1976; New York Times Book Review March 18, 1982.

---

*SASTRE, ALFONSO (February 20, 1926–), Spanish dramatic theorist and playwright, was born in Madrid, the son of a conservative, middle-class family. He was ten years old when the Spanish Civil War erupted in July 1936, and the bombings, hunger, and other sufferings he experienced as a child in the besieged capital, as well as the fierce repressions carried out against the vanquished by the victorious Franco regime, had a profound effect on the future writer. After completing his secondary education at the Instituto Cardenal Cisneros (Madrid), Sastre entered the University of Madrid, where he studied literature and philosophy. In 1945, while still a student, he helped found Arte Nuevo, an experimental theater group that aspired to revitalize the stagnant Spanish stage. Though Arte Nuevo ceased to exist after approximately two years without having changed the course of Spanish theater, it anticipated a major development which would soon take place in Spain: the emergence of a serious theater with a deep concern for social issues. In 1950 Sastre and the critic José María de Quinto (a former companion of Arte Nuevo) issued a manifesto announcing the formation of Teatro de Agitación Social (T.A.S.), a dissident theater group which the censors did not allow to evolve beyond the project stage. Sastre transferred to the University of Murcia in 1953, obtaining a licenciate in philosophy that same year. His involvement with the theater, however, remained strong not only as a dramatist but also as an essayist and theorist. As early as 1948 Sastre began publishing numerous essays attacking the escapist trivia which dominated the Spanish stage dur-

°säs´trä

ing the decade following the Civil War and called for the reform of all aspects of theatrical life. Eventually he developed a theory of theater as an instrument for the transformation of society in many of the essays later collected in his books *Drama y sociedad* (Drama and Society, 1956), *Anatomía del realismo* (Anatomy of Realism, 1965), and *La revolucion y la crítica de la cultura* (Revolution and Criticism of Culture, 1970). In 1960 Sastre and Quinto founded yet another dissident theater organization, the Grupo de Teatro Realista (G.T.R.). Designed to explore the different possibilities of realism, it staged three works by Pirandello, Carlos Muñiz, and Sastre himself. Financial pressures and censorship forced the G.T.R. to discontinue its activities after one season.

Despite being acclaimed as an outstanding dramatist, Sastre has had little commercial success in his own country. Not only has he encountered the usual economic barriers, but during the Franco dictatorship, which lasted until 1975, many of his plays were prohibited owing to their controversial themes. As a result of his increasing political radicalization, he was prevented from having all but one of the dramas he wrote after 1961 performed or published in Spain until the termination of Franco's rule. An outspoken critic of the dictatorship, Sastre was arrested on several occasions for his political activities, the last time in late 1974, when he was imprisoned for eight months in connection with a bombing allegedly carried out by Basque separatists.

Throughout his career Sastre has defended the social mission of the dramatist, while at the same time categorically rejecting propagandistic theater. From the very beginning he has attempted to fuse an existentialist concept of the world with a commitment to man's social improvement. Since approximately 1960, he has placed the primary emphasis on the social dimension of life; yet Sastre's Marxism, which did not fully crystalize until then, is never free from existential preoccupations. In his continuing search for effective theatrical forms, tragedy and realism remain as the theoretical foundations of his dramaturgy. Just as he has felt the need to go beyond Aristotle's concept of tragedy, his view of realism is broad and flexible. The recurrent themes in Sastre's theater are freedom and revolution, as well as a constant protest against injustice, human exploitation, the threat of nuclear warfare, and torture; but he also focuses on individual problems such as guilt, moral responsibility, the fear of death, and anxiety regarding one's own destiny. There is a great deal of violence—murders, executions, suicides, torture—in Sastre's theater. Though these manifestations of violence are played out on a personal level, they have broad social significance. Faced with the problem of censorship, many of his plays are set in exotic places, but the audience is aware that he tends to place his characters in limited situations destined to end tragically.

The diversity of his adaptations attests to his broad literary background: Euripides' *Medea*, Ibsen's *The Lady from the Sea*, Strindberg's *Creditors*, Langston Hughes' *Mulatto*, O'Casey's *Red Roses for Me*, Sartre's *No Exit, The Respectful Prostitute*, and *The Condemned of Altona*, as well as Peter Weiss' *Marat/Sade*. Most of these adaptations, in addition to others which were not staged, were completed during the 1960s, when Sastre found it almost impossible to have any of his own plays performed in Spain. Among the foreign dramatists who have influenced him most are Brecht, Sartre, and Peter Weiss. Drawing upon Spanish theatrical tradition, he has assimilated elements not only from Golden Age drama but also from more recent forms such as the *esperpento*, a type of grotesque farce created in the 1920s by Ramón del Valle Inclán.

Sastre's dramatic output may be divided into three periods or phases. The plays of the first period are four experimental one-act pieces which represent his contribution to Arte Nuevo, the youthful theatrical group he helped found in 1945: *Ha sonado la muerte* (Death Has Sounded, 1946), *Uranio 235* (Uranium 235, 1946), *Cargamento de sueños* (Cargo of Dreams, 1946), and *Comedia sonámbula* (Sleepwalking Play, 1947). This last play, as well as the first one, were written in collaboration with Medrado Fraile. Pessimistic in tone, all four works are cast in an avant-garde mold with surrealist and symbolist ingredients. While they are ineffective as drama, these early plays contain themes which reappear in Sastre's later works: the terrors of war, the lack of communication between successive generations, and the painful awareness of time.

After his Arte Nuevo experimentations, Sastre's increasing consciousness of the social and political potential of drama has led him to turn his attention to what he has termed "the great theme of the revolutionary transformation of the world." The plays of his second period were written between 1950 and 1962. Rejecting the avant-garde techniques of his earlier plays, Sastre became a staunch defender of realism and of a theater of commitment. His career as a dramatist did not begin definitively until 1953, when *Escuadra hacia la muerte* (Condemned Squad), an anti-war drama written the previous year, was staged in Madrid by a university group. Prohibited after only three performances because military authorities saw it as an attack on their profession, the play focuses on the members of a condemned squad who rebel against and kill their tyrannical leader only to discover the futility of their action. Despite the prohibition order, Sastre's reputation as a major young dramatist was established with *Escuadra hacia la muerte*. Other notable plays of this period are: *La mordaza* (The Gag, 1954), an allegory against censorship; *Muerte en el barrio* (Death in the Neighborhood, 1955), a drama of collective guilt in which angry neighborhood residents murder a doctor whom they hold responsible for the death of a child; *Guillermo Tell tiene los ojos tristes* (*Sad Are the Eyes of William Tell*, 1955), an attempt to portray the legendary hero as a tragic symbol of the sacrifice of the individual in the revolutionary process; and *La cornada* (*Death Thrust*, 1960), a study of exploitation set against the background of the world of bullfighting. Of these four plays, only *La mordaza* and *La cornada* managed to receive the censors' stamp of approval, and both enjoyed successful runs in Madrid.

Even though Sastre evolved toward a theater of social commitment around 1950, he occasionally wrote asocial dramas dealing with personal frustration until 1956. Like his early vanguard efforts, *Ana Kleiber* (*Anna Kleiber*, 1955), *La sangre de Dios* (The Blood of God, 1955), and *El cuervo* (The Raven, 1956) constitute experiments in dramatic form.

Sastre's epic plays, all of which were banned for performance as well as for publication, constitute the third phase of his dramaturgy. In the late 1950s he began studying the dramatic theories of Brecht, and a few years later proposed a new theater derived from the German writer's experimentations but surpassing them. Sastre calls his type of epic drama a *tragedia compleja* ("complex tragedy"). According to the playwright, it is a neo-tragic form that attempts to transcend Aristotelian or "simple" tragedy, the anti-tragic Brechtian drama, and the nihilism of the avant-garde or of the *esperpento*. *Asalto nocturno* (Nocturnal Assault, 1959) marks the transition from Sastre's second period to his post-Brechtian phase. The play has a contemporary setting and theme, as do *El banquete* (The Banquet, 1965), *La taberna fantástica* (The Fantastic Tavern, 1966), and *El camarada oscuro* (The Dark Comrade, 1972). The latter play spans a period of Spanish history from the Barcelona of 1902, with its revolutionary ferment, to present-day Madrid. In *La sangre y la ceniza* (Blood and Ashes, 1965) and *Crónicas romanas* (Roman Chronicles, 1968), Sastre uses a historical setting in his attempt to find an effective theater based on epic principles. Beginning with *La sangre y la ceniza*, Sastre ceased writing plays with the Spanish commercial theater in mind and began

concentrating his efforts on the experimental groups (some of them highly professional) which function outside that system.

In addition to hundreds of essays and some thirty plays to date (including two works for children and a radio drama), Sastre has also written a biography of Miguel Servet (the sixteenth-century Spanish theologian and physician who, after having escaped from the Inquisition, was tried and burned at the stake on Calvin's order, and who is also the protagonist of *La sangre y la ceniza*), a novelette, short stories, and poetry. One of his most recent publications is *Crítica de la imaginación* (Critique of the Imagination, 1978), a study of creativity and the imagination.

Sastre is one of the major figures of the contemporary Spanish theater. The fact that he has found only limited commercial success in his own country has not prevented him from attracting attention at home and abroad. His plays have been translated into a number of languages and performed in many European and Latin American countries. Even though censorship has been lifted and a democratic government established in Spain, Sastre remains an essentially underground playwright.

WORKS IN ENGLISH TRANSLATION: Several of Sastre's plays have been translated (mainly by L. C. Pronko) and published in drama anthologies. These include: "Pathetic Prologue," in *Modern International Drama* 1, 1960; "Anna Kleiber" in R. W. Corrigan's *New Theatre of Europe*, 1962; "Death Thrust," in Corrigan's *Masterpieces of the Modern Spanish Theatre*, 1967; "Condemned Squad," in M. P. Holt's *The Modern Spanish Stage*, 1970; and "Sad Are the Eyes of William Tell," in G. E. Wellwarth's *The New Wave Spanish Drama*, 1970.

ABOUT: Anderson, F.F. Alfonso Sastre, 1971; Columbia Dictionary of Modern European Literature, 1980; Encyclopedia of World Literature in the 20th Century IV, 1975; Holt, M.P. Contemporary Spanish Theater, 1949–1972, 1973; McGraw-Hill Encyclopedia of World Drama, 1983; Matlaw, M. Modern World Drama: An Encyclopedia, 1972. *Periodicals*—Tulane Drama Review 5, 1960.

SCHAPIRO, MEYER (September 23, 1904–), American art historian, was born in Shavly, Lithuania, the son of Nathan and Fanny Adelman Schapiro. With his family he came to the United States at the age of three, and became a naturalized citizen in 1914. For his entire academic career he has been associated with Columbia University, from which he received his bachelor's degree (1924) and his doctorate (1931), and where he taught art history from 1928, as full professor from 1952 and as emeritus

MEYER SCHAPIRO

professor since 1973. Schapiro has held each of
the major international art history lectureships,
including the Norton professorship at Harvard
(1966–67) and the Slade professorship at Oxford
(1968), and has lectured at the Warburg Institute in London (1947, 1957) and the Collège de
France in Paris (1974). Perhaps his greatest impact as a teacher, however, was achieved during
his long tenure (1938–52) as lecturer at the New
School for Social Research in New York City,
where he introduced thousands of students to art
history.

In common with many of the greatest art historians, Schapiro has made his mark by means
of articles and short monographs rather than
full-length books. Few of his works have been directed at the general public, and all display the
encyclopedic knowledge of whatever subject he
addresses that made him a legend in his field.
William Phillips and Alfred Kazin, in their
memoirs of New York literary and intellectual
life from the 1930s and forties, both refer to
Schapiro's apparently total recall of everything
he has ever read. James Breckenridge, remarking on Schapiro's failure to produce any book-
length publication, wrote that "he is clearly un-
suited by temperament, by genius, to the pace
of book-length writing. His thought is too dense
and compact, his arguments too tight, his evidence too wide-ranging. At any length greater
than fifty pages, it would become unbearable."
The most influential and enduring of
Schapiro's articles have been collected in three
volumes by the publisher George Braziller. They
are reprinted essentially as they were originally
published, with only minimal updating. The

first collection, *Romanesque Art,* published in
1977, consists of eight pieces, mostly from the
1930s and forties, including two seminal survey
articles, "On the Aesthetic Attitude in Romanesque Art" and "On Geometrical Schematism in
Romanesque Art," plus groundbreaking studies
of the Romanesque sculptures at Moissac, Souil-
lac, and Rodez. Many of the articles, in fact,
grew out of Schapiro's doctoral dissertation,
which studied the twelfth-century portal and
capitals in the abbey church at Moissac in south-
central France. Robert Cahn thought that the articles as a whole "point ultimately to a refinement of our understanding of the style as a
totality" and remarked further that the essays
are "in addition, model demonstrations of methodological approaches open to the art historian."
The second volume of Schapiro's selected papers is *Modern Art: 19th & 20th Centuries,* fourteen essays conveying his mastery of an area of
art far removed from his original field. Most
range from the 1940s and fifties, and include
three on Cézanne, one each on Courbet, Van
Gogh, Seurat, Picasso, Chagall, Gorky, and Mondrian, and three lengthy analyses of the nature
of abstract art. Schapiro was an early admirer of
Cézanne, superficially the least attractive of the
Postimpressionists, and his introduction to the
portfolio *Paul Cézanne* sees the artist as a genius
apart from his contemporaries, one whose
achievement possesses "a unique importance for
our thinking about art. His work is a living proof
that a painter can achieve a profound expression
by giving form to his perceptions of the world
around him without recourse to a guiding religion or myth or any explicit social aims. . . .
The purely human and personal . . . are a sufficient matter for the noblest qualities of art. . . .
The secular culture of the nineteenth century . . . was no less capable of providing a
ground for great art than the authoritative cultures of the past." This volume won the National
Book Critics Circle award for criticism.

The most popular and widely reviewed volume of selected papers was the third, *Late Antique, Early Christian and Medieval Art.* These
twenty-two articles, from the 1940s to the early
1970s, cover a period of nearly a thousand years.
Schapiro starts the introduction with a basic and
challenging assumption: "that religious art, like
religious cult, is not just an expressive representation of sacred texts and a symbolizing of religious concepts; it also projects ideas, attitudes
and fantasies shaped in secular life and given
concrete form by imaginative, I may say, poetic
minds. . . . The habitual concentration of
scholars on the sources of imagery in religious
texts has led them to neglect or underestimate
the importance of the interactions of religious

and secular life for interpreting that art." With this interpretative principle firmly in mind, he ranges widely in the ancient art, both Christian and Judaic, of many times and places, studying the Joshua Roll, the Maximianus Throne, and the Glazier Psalter as examples of "the relations between religion and the contemporary state"; the famous early Italian Flagellation of Christ from the Frick Collection exemplifies "the spontaneous response of a suffering people to a crisis during a civil war"; and several other art objects, including the Ruthwell Cross and the Mérode Altarpiece, evince "the emergence of the vernacular, the folkloric and rationalistic conceptions in the art of the Northern peoples, with a new concreteness of fantasy." Breckenridge held that the author's "concern with the interplay of secular and religious art and thought forms a golden thread that makes this collection more than the sum of its parts, and more than a reference work for specialists." At least one further volume of selected papers is in preparation.

Another monograph of high note in Schapiro's career is *The Parma Ildefonsus: A Romanesque Illuminated Manuscript from Cluny and Related Works*, which treats a very important but little-studied manuscript composed at the Abbey of Cluny about the year 1100 "in which the Italo-Byzantine style and a Germanic variant of the native Romanesque occur together." Apart from its own high intrinsic quality, the work is important "as evidence of the otherwise scarce manuscript art of the greatest monastic center in Western Europe at a moment of intense stirring in art, when monumental stone sculpture was revived in Burgundy and in the Cluniac order at large and a new architecture was created." *Words and Pictures: On the Literal and the Symbolic in the Illustration of a Text* comprises four speculative articles: on the artist's reading of a text, on the theme of state and the theme of action, and on the frontal and the profile as symbolic forms. The general theme of the articles is "to bring out the interplay of text, commentary, symbolism, and style of representation in the word-bound image."

In 1928, Schapiro married Lillian Milgram, a physician; they have a son and a daughter.

WORKS: Van Gogh, 1950; Paul Cézanne, 1952; The Parma Ildefonsus, 1964; Words and Pictures, 1973; Romanesque Art, 1977; Modern Art, 1978; Late Antique, Early Christian and Medieval Art, 1979.

ABOUT: Contemporary Authors 97–100, 1981; Kazin, A. Starting Out in the Thirties, 1980; Phillips, W. A Partisan View: Five Decades of the Literary Life, 1984; Who's Who in America 1983–84. *Periodicals*—Choice September 1977; June 1980; Commentary August 1980; Current Biography July 1984; Library Journal May 1, 1977; October 1, 1979; New York Review of Books May 12, 1977; New York Times Book Review February 24, 1980.

* * *

SCHUYLER, JAMES MARCUS (November 9, 1923–   ), American poet, novelist, and playwright, was born in Chicago. His family moved East during his infancy and lived in Buffalo and East Aurora, New York, and in Washington, D.C. His father, Marcus James Schuyler, was a newspaperman. His parents divorced when he was a young child, and his father died relatively young. His mother, Margaret Daisy Connor Schuyler Ridenour, died in her eighties. She often appears, described both with affection and irritation, in Schuyler's poetry.

Schuyler attended Bethany College in West Virginia from 1941 to 1943, and served in the Navy during World War II. He spent several years in Italy, where he attended the University of Florence from 1947 to 1948. When he returned to the United States, he settled in New York City (where he lives today in the Chelsea Hotel) and met the poets of the New York School: Frank O'Hara, John Ashbery, and Kenneth Koch, who influenced his poetic technique and, especially, his approach to poetry, which has been described simply as the desire to "see and say things as they are." During the 1950s and '60s, Schuyler was also active in the art world: a member of the staff of the Museum of Modern Art in the Department of Circulating Exhibitions from 1955 to 1961, and associate editor of *Artnews* magazine for ten years. When asked why he gave up editing, he replied that he found himself becoming repetitious. Schuyler's concern for not repeating himself is apparent in his poetry and in his highly original novels. He has, however, been consistently preoccupied with certain themes: love, friendship, homosexuality, loneliness, "life's unrelenting hardness," flowers, architecture, and the weather. He paints the scene around him, urban or rural, with such telling realism that comparisons between his technique and that of a painter have often been made.

Schuyler's vantage point is highly personal; his poetry lacks philosophical or political argument. Howard Moss, who Schuyler says has written "of my work very perceptively," observes that "he is not a poet of great ideas, of grand gestures, or of psychological insight (except in passing)." The title poem of *The Morning of the Poem* (which won the 1981 Pulitzer Prize in poetry) is a sixty-page monologue whose style is typical of his work. "His subject matter, ostensible and real, is

© 1985 Thomas Victor

JAMES SCHUYLER

the flux of everyday life," Moss writes. "But what are merely grocery lists in other hands are transformed into sacred objects in his. By writing so well, he justifies a subject and a method—this-is-my-life, and I'm-telling-it-like-it-is. It is not secret by now that, taken in tandem, they can be one of the great gifts to tedium devised by the human mind. Though Schuyler belongs to a convention, he lets us know what it is by transcending it."

Among poets other than those of the New York School who have influenced Schuyler are Whitman, D. H. Lawrence, Boris Pasternak, Elizabeth Bishop, and Marianne Moore. He especially admires Wallace Stevens and W. H. Auden, the latter a friend of many years whom he eulogized in a poem, "Wystan Auden" in *The Morning of the Poem.* Although he had been writing poetry himself since the age of twenty-five—he had originally set out to be a short-story writer under the inspiration of John Cheever and John O'Hara—Schuyler did not publish any poetry until 1960. His first "real" collection ("real" in that it was published by a trade publisher) was *Freely Espousing: Poems,* which won him a small but admiring audience who found in this lyric poetry, as Guy Davenport writes, "a new Romanticism . . . a new subjectivity." With *The Crystal Lithium* of 1972 and *Hymn to Life,* published two years later, both with jackets designed by his friend the landscape painter Fairfield Porter, Schuyler became recognized as a significant voice in American poetry, "a limited but exquisite poet, distinguished from his confrères of the New York School by a meticulous, [W. C.] Williams-like devotion to the

physical world," observed the *Virginia Quarterly Review.* Within its deliberately limited range—"the minutiae of daily life"—the poems "constitute paradoxically a transcendental poetry without the divine term," David Shapiro wrote in *Poetry.* Stephen Spender noted (in the *New York Review of Books*) that they were like "a sensitized plate held up to a real landscape, transforming the objects actually there into poetry and creating form which is dictated by the rhythms of the sights and sounds actually present." Schuyler's real landscape is usually New England, Eastern Long Island, or Canada, and characteristic of his power to evoke the sights and sounds of a scene is a passage from a poem in *The Crystal Lithium*:

A wonderful freshness, air
that billows like bedsheets
on a clothesline and the
clouds hang in a traffic jam: summer heads home.   Evan-
geline,
our light is scoured and Nova
Scotian and of a clarity that
opens up the huddled masses
of the stolid spruce so you
see them in their bristling
individuality.

("Light from Canada")

Although he has been mentally ill and hospitalized many times—a subject of a number of his poems—it is Schuyler's sense of pleasure in his experiences that his poetry best communicates: delight in the everyday and familiar, in friendships, in natural landscapes.

The Morning of the Poem, which many consider to be Schuyler's "masterpiece," has been compared to Kenneth Koch's long poems, particularly for its digressiveness. Vernon Shetley, in the February 1981 *Poetry* magazine, remarked that "where Koch's scattershot tours-de-force seem to be one continual crescendo, Schuyler avoids climax altogether. There is little beginning, hardly an end, and in between no structure, only more writing of engaging good humor and sense." Schuyler's long title poem is a rich tapestry, an autobiographical memoir full of interesting scenes, thoughts, memories, dialogues, incidents. "Its method is the free fall of recollection," Denis Donoghue wrote of the poem.

. . . I
Begrudge that far-off island in Penobscot Bay,
mossy walks and Twin Flower
Corner, icy swims in early morning off pebble
beaches, the smell of juniper
Where my dead best friend will always walk
beside me, stride ahead of me.
"When I walk with you, all I see is the heels
of your sneakers": were
You buried in your sneakers? Of course not,
though in a tender joke you were:
A nosegay tossed on the coffin: but this is not

your poem, your poem I may
Never write, too much, though it is there and
needs only to be written down
And one day will and if it isn't it doesn't matter:
the truth, the absolute
Of feeling, of knowing what you know, that is
the poem, . . .

Candid and explicit on his sex life, his illnesses, his suicidal tendencies, the poems nevertheless reveal humor, a life-celebrating quality that one reviewer described as "an amalgam of joy and sorrow." Unorthodox as their subject matter may seem, they are in the spirit and tradition of English romantic poetry. As Tom Simmons wrote of *The Morning of the Poem* in the *Christian Science Monitor*: "For Schuyler the lure of tradition is strong; the desire for a compassionate divine spirit, for reasoned wisdom, for ultimate salvation within an orthodox framework brings a difficult but valuable tension to his poems."

James Schuyler's novels are an acquired taste. Dialogue is central to them, plot and characterization almost nonexistent. The characters in *A Nest of Ninnies*, which he wrote in collaboration with John Ashbery, are so shallow and their conversation so superficial that the novel has an almost surreal quality. Concerned with the lives of two suburban couples whose banal reactions to their travels in Florida, Europe, or the local shopping plaza are recorded in satirical and linguistically playful detail, the novel was described by Auden (in the *New York Times Book Review*) as a mixture of the pastorals of Theocritus with Ronald Firbank and P. G. Wodehouse, depicting "an imaginary Garden of Eden, a place of innocence from which all serious needs and desires have been excluded." Auden predicted that the book was "destined to become a minor classic," but other reviewers found it pointless and exasperating.

Schuyler's later novel, *What's for Dinner?*, is another tour de force in that, although the characterization is totally external, the reader comes to care about the people in it, particularly the alcoholic heroine Charlotte, or Lottie, Taylor. We know only what has been said, and the dialogue is often silly or superficial, and yet, as one reviewer observed, the characters have voices and "the consistency found in life." Part of the novel takes place in a hospital for the mentally ill and the other half in the outside world. Schuyler moves back and forth from one to the other. Lottie is our connection between these two worlds since she is visited by and talked about by those outside the hospital: her husband and friends. She is trying to understand why she drinks and wants to break the habit, despite a tremendous urge to keep on drinking. There seems to be very little difference between the people inside the institution and those living "normal" lives. If there is any difference, the mentally ill patients often appear to be "saner"; certainly they are more honest and open with each other. Whatever cruelties they perpetrate are out in the open, rather than hidden and devious, as illustrated by the plotting widow, Mag Carpenter, who is having an affair with Lottie's husband Norris and wants to steal him form Lottie; or the Delehantey twins, stealing money from their mother in order to get high on marijuana. However Schuyler feels about his characters, he does not judge them. His is a live-and-let-live nature and this is part of the appeal of his work.

Schuyler has written two plays that have been produced in off-Broadway theaters—*Unpacking the Black Trunk,* written in collaboration with Kenward Elmslie, and *Shopping and Waiting*. He has also collaborated with the writer and composer Paul Bowles on *Picnic Cantata,* which has been recorded by Columbia. Unlike many of his fellow poets, he does not teach, and only rarely gives poetry readings. In addition to winning the Pulitzer Prize for poetry in 1981, he has received many other honors, including the Longview Foundation award (1961), the Frank O'Hara prize (1969), a National Institute of Arts and Letters award (1976), and two grants from the National Endowment for the Arts (1971, 1972). In 1981 he was a Guggenheim fellow.

PRINCIPAL WORKS: *Poetry*—Salute, 1960; May 24th or so, 1966; Freely Espousing, 1969; The Crystal Lithium, 1972; A Sun Cab, 1972; Hymn to Life, 1974; The Fireproof Floors of Witley Court: English Songs and Dances, 1976; Song, 1976; The Home Book: Prose and Poems 1951-1970 (ed. Trevor Winkfield), 1977; The Morning of the Poem, 1980; Collabs (with Helena Hughes), 1980. *Novels*—Alfred and Guinevere, 1958; A Nest of Ninnies (with John Ashbery), 1969; What's For Dinner?, 1978. *Plays*—Presenting Jane, 1952; Shopping and Waiting, 1953; A Picnic Cantata (with Paul Bowles), 1955; Unpacking the Black Trunk (with Kenward Elmslie), 1965.

ABOUT: Contemporary Authors 101, 1981; Dictionary of Literary Biography 5, 1980; Magill, F. (ed.) Critical Survey of Poetry 6, 1982; Moss, H. Whatever Is Moving, 1981; Oxford Companion to American Literature, 1983; Vinson, J. (ed.) Contemporary Poets (2nd ed.), 1975. *Periodicals*—American Book Review November-December 1980; Christian Science Monitor May 12, 1980; New York Review of Books September 20, 1973; October 11, 1979; August 14, 1980; New York Times Book Review November 2, 1980; April 18, 1980; Poetry July 1973; February 1981; Times Literary Supplement June 19, 1981; Virginia Quarterly Review Winter 1973.

*SEIFERT, JAROSLAV (1901–), Czechoslovak poet, was born in Prague to working-class parents. He became a journalist and poet as a very young man, and during the first Czechoslovak republic (1918–38) edited various Communist Party publications. He has always been a man of the progressive left, and his first two collections of verse, *Město v slzach* (City in Tears, 1921) and *Samá láska* (Only Love, 1923), specifically expressed the sharp longing among the younger generation for the promise of the Soviet revolution to be fulfilled. "Aiming to depict the workers' world," wrote Alfred French, "he wrote in their language and brought the form of poetry close to that of ordinary speech." A trip to the Soviet Union in 1925, however, dampened his enthusiasm for Communism. He was expelled from the party and became a Social Democrat in 1929.

Much of Seifert's work after 1925, like that of many of his contemporaries, was greatly influenced by Dada and then by surrealism. A whole generation of Czech poets, in Roger Scruton's words, "hoped to cure themselves of Germanic and Austrian influence through a dose of modernism and Paris." Seifert's chief foreign literary influences were Guillaume Apollinaire, Paul Éluard, and Francis Ponge; a whimsical humor very like theirs finds abundant expression in his poetry collections *Na vlnách TSF* (On Radio Waves, 1925) and *Slavík zpívá spatně* (Nightingale out of Tune, 1926). Life as it appears in these poems "had shed," according to French, "all devotion to lost causes and unattainable absolutes: it was a dialogue between people uncommitted to the salvation of the world, a game of tennis in which the stakes were trivial and the rules agreed, a modern carnival signifying nothing but itself, a parlour game featuring the witty gesture and the amusing paradox."

Rebelling against "Poetism," the self-conscious and mannered word plays of Dadaist poetry, Seifert changed course again in the 1930s. In *Jablko z klína* (An Apple from the Lap, 1933) and *Ruce Venušiny* (Arms of Venus, 1936) the dominant theme is love; the poet's style has a direct, unaffected sincerity. Traditional forms occur frequently; there are few images and no symbols, and his language is more simple and colloquial than ever. In a review of *Jablko*, F.X. Šalda, the most eminent Czech critic of the day, wrote in 1933 of Seifert: "Today his spirit is undivided, removed from all the restlessness of passions and problems; it has been healed and inwardly unified. A singular wholeness, simplicity, fluency, and, above all, a singular peace . . . lie like a dusting of pollen over his new book. . . . He speaks in the calmest of tones about the miracles of life and death, as if he were

JAROSLAV SEIFERT

recounting a conversation between neighbors over the garden fence."

The Nazi menace galvanized Seifert, as it did the rest of his countrymen. *Zhasněte světla* (Turn out the Lights, 1938) is full of nervous, edgy poems about a nation threatened with annihilation—a threat the Germans carried out the following year. The title poem from that collection is one of the poet's most famous. It refers to the general mobilization and its accompanying blackout proclaimed in Prague in September 1938, when war seemed just about to break out:

Put out the lights! Hush, lest a word should start
The tears that dew my lashes. Be all said
Softly, without self-pity, in the heart:
How great, how great a light it shed,

This night when universal darkness fell,
And each man crouched his own clan roof-tree under!
I know, I know, this time we should do well
To hear and heed the thunder.

—trans. A. French

Only one book by Seifert, *Světlem oděná* (Arrayed in Light, 1940), a series of poetic tributes to the city of Prague, was allowed to be published during the Nazi occupation. Immediately after the liberation he brought out *Přilba hlíny* (Helmet of Clay, 1945), celebrating the Czechs' heroic resistance to the Nazis during the 1945 Prague Uprising.

The Communist usurpation of power in Czechoslovakia in 1948 brought in a regime not at all friendly to writers of independent views. A series of poems by Seifert in 1950 honoring the 130th anniversary of the birth of the village and rural novelist Božena Němcová, a greatly revered woman writer of the classic period of

°sī ´fert

Czech literature, earned him the enmity of official critics. He was denounced by younger Marxists, hard-line favorites of the establishment, as a proletarian poet who had "turned against his own class." "He was silenced," wrote Alfred French, "and his name appeared only in the mouths of those who abused him." He turned to writing children's literature, a genre to which his direct, simple sytle well suited him. One of these efforts, *Maminka* (Mother, 1954), has become a classic of Czech literature, epitomizing, as French wrote, "a whole trend of literature away from the monumental to the humble; from public themes to private; from the pseudoreality of political slogans to the known reality of Czech home life which was the product of its past."

Seifert's reputation was sufficiently rehabilitated in the period of thaw that followed Stalin's death for him to be able to make a memorable speech to the congress of the Writers Union in April 1956. In chilling tones, he demanded respect for the old idea that the writer is the very conscience of the nation. "I am afraid we have not fulfilled this role for many years—we have not been the conscience of the many; we have not even been our own conscience. . . . If an ordinary person is silent about the truth, it may be a tactical maneuver. If a writer is silent, he is lying." He further demanded that public apologies be issued to all writers silenced since 1948 and that they be invited to return to public life. His speech had little immediate effect beyond infuriating the establishment, but the poet was from that time onward generally regarded as the dean of Czech letters, a man from the old days whose contemporaries were almost all dead, who could always be counted on to speak the truth.

A few slim volumes of verse appeared in the mid-1960s, including the sequence *The Casting of Bells* (1967). Seifert was in the forefront of the drive among writers to support the liberalization and de-Sovietization of the regime, a national movement that led to the catastrophic Warsaw Pact invasion of Czechoslovakia in August 1968. The following October, in a feeling of desperation, the Writers Union elected Seifert president to replace the exiled Eduard Goldstücker. "I can still see him," recalled Milan Kundera sixteen years later. "He already had great difficulty walking, with crutches. And—perhaps because of that—there in his seat he seemed like a rock: unmoving, solid, firm. It consoled us to have him with us. This little nation, trampled and doomed—how could it possibly justify its existence? There before us was the justification: the poet, heavy, with his crutches leaning against the table; the poet, the tangible expression of the nation's genius, the sole glory of the powerless."

The Writers Union was disbanded late in 1969, and another period of repression descended on Czechoslovakian writers. Seifert's poems appeared occasionally in *petlice* (padlock) editions, a clandestine form of publishing comparable to *samizdat* in the Soviet Union. They also appeared abroad. *Morový sloup* (*The Plague Monument*, 1977) was published in Czech by the émigré publishing house Index in Cologne, West Germany. It is a single, long poem, divided by number into constituent lyrics. The monument of the title, erected by the people of Prague soon after the end of the Thirty Years War in thanksgiving for deliverance from the plague, "seems to represent," according to William E. Harkins, "a great and terrifying image of the unity of Czech fate and Czech history, bringing together past and present, and symbolizing a destiny for the land which is external to it yet which can neither be dealt with nor avoided, the land of a small people eternally invaded, occupied, and encroached upon. This harsh fate can only be evaded, and this only for a time." The hopelessness of the poem, as well as its political pointedness, represent something new in Seifert's work:

Don't let anybody con you into thinking
the plague here is over.
I've seen a lot of coffins
coming through this very gate
and it's not the only way in.

The plague still rages and the doctors
have apparently taken to calling the sickness
by different names, in order to prevent panic.
It's still the same old death though,
nothing else,
and so contagious
not even the smallest creature can escape.
—trans. L. Coffin

At about the time this book was published in Germany, Seifert was among the several hundred Czechoslovak intellectuals who were signatories of Charter 77, a manifesto protesting the suppression of human rights in their country.

On October 11, 1984, the Swedish Academy announced that Jaroslav Seifert had won the Nobel Prize for literature for 1984, the first of his countrymen to be so honored. A part of the academy's citation read: "He conjures up another world than that of tyranny and desolation—a world that exists beyond here and now, although it may be hidden from our view and bound in chains, and one that exists in our dreams and our will and our indomitable spirit. His poetry is a kind of maieutics—an act of deliverance." Seifert, who had been hospitalized for years with heart disease and diabetes, was reported by the Swedish ambassador to be "overjoyed" at the news. His wife, Marie, to whom he has been married since 1928, confessed to mixed emotions that are widely shared by those familiar with her husband's work. "I would be happier," she said, "if he were healthy. He is traveling from hospital to hospital. Of course he will be glad. Had it only come twenty years sooner!" Their daughter, Jana Seifertova, was the only person permitted to attend the prize-giving in Stockholm in December 1984. Her husband, Daribor Plichta, who has served for years as the poet's secretary, was denied permission by the regime to accompany her.

WORKS IN ENGLISH TRANSLATION: With the announcement of the Nobel award English translations of Seifert's works were in immediate demand, but little had been available before 1984. In 1982 E. Osers' translation *The Plague Column* was published; it appeared in L. Coffin's translation as *The Plague Monument* in 1984. P. Jagasich and T. O'Grady translated *The Casting of Bells,* 1983. Also available are *Russian Bliny,* translated by M. Suino, 1983; and E. Osers' *An Umbrella from Piccadilly,* 1984. Selections from Seifert's poetry are in *The Linden Tree: An Anthology of Czech and Slovak Literature 1890–1960,* edited by M. Otruba and Z. Pesat, 1962.

ABOUT: Columbia Dictionary of Modern European Literature, 1980; Encyclopedia of World Literature (rev. ed.) IV, 1984; French, A. The Poets of Prague: Czech Poetry between the Wars, 1969; French, A. Czech Writers and Politics 1945–1969, 1982; Ivask, I and G. von Wilpert, World Literature Since 1945, 1973; Modern Slavic Literature: A Library of Literary Criticism 2, 1976; Novak, A. Czech Literature, 1976; Penguin Companion to European Literature, 1969. *Periodicals*—New York Review of Books November 22, 1984; New York Times October 12, 1984; October 15, 1984; December 20, 1984; Times Literary Supplement February 24, 1984; October 26, 1984.

SENNETT, RICHARD (January 1, 1943–   ), American sociologist and novelist, was born in Chicago, the son of Maurice and Dorothy Sennett. He took his bachelor's degree summa cum laude from the University of Chicago in 1964 and pursued study in sociology at Harvard, receiving his doctorate in 1969. He was briefly assistant professor of sociology at Yale (1967–68), then directed the Urban Family Study in Cambridge, Massachusetts (1968–71), and since 1971 has been a member of the sociology faculty at New York University, holding the rank of full professor since 1973.

Although barely in his forties, Sennett has for more than a decade occupied a place in the front rank of American sociologists. He began his career—characteristically for a social scientist—analyzing raw data to arrive at social theories, but he has become an eloquent and persuasive moralist of the left, rather little concerned with

RICHARD SENNETT

digging up the "hard evidence" of social interaction that attracts his colleagues. "Not for Sennett," according to J. S. Allen, "the dreary graphs and statistics, the inflated trifles, the barbarous abstractions that squeeze the life out of so much scholarship. Sennett traffics in tales of human feeling, taken from both life and fiction and embellished by excursions into history and theory."

After editing and contributing essays to two anthologies of urban sociological criticism, *Classic Essays on the Culture of Cities* and *Nineteenth-Century Cities* (edited with Stephan Thernstrom), Sennett published two books on the nature of city life and the various ways it affects urban dwellers. *Families Against the City: Middle Class Homes of Industrial Chicago, 1872–1890* examines the lives of 12,000 residents of Union Park, a Chicago suburb, at the end of the last century in order to answer a basic question: What was the role of an individual's family in his or her adjustment to the urban, industrial order? Although several sociologists, reviewing the book, sharply questioned elements of the author's methodology, most reviewers admired the energy of his speculations, one calling the book "one of the best recent descriptions I have read of the city as a powerful agent of social change," and another, "a historical base line against which contemporary middle-class family patterns may be examined." The theoretical basis of this book served as underpinning for Sennett's arguments in *The Uses of Disorder: Personal Identity and City Life,* in which he asserts that the development of personality in America produces rigid attitudes that generally stifle further personal growth. For most Americans, equality has come to signify "the dignity of sameness" and has given rise to ideals of "purified identity" and strict civic order. Sennett's visionary city would thrive and function on, in the publishers' words, "anarchy, diversity, and creative disorder" which would "bring into being adults who can openly respond to and deal with the challenges of life." Kenneth Keniston called the book "the best available contemporary defense of anarchism. . . . Like all anarchists, Sennett is an optimist about human nature, and is convinced that post-affluent 'adulthood' will permit ideally anarchic cities where immediate self-interest alone will suffice to create livable communities. However questionable this faith, the issues [he] raises are fundamental and profound. His book is utopian in the best sense—it tries to define a radically different future and to show that it could be constructed from the materials at hand." *The Uses of Disorder* seems in retrospect a product of the visionary euphoria prevalent in some quarters during the 1960s.

In *The Hidden Injuries of Class*, written with Jonathan Cobb, Sennett examines the social attitudes of one hundred and fifty blue-collar workers from the Boston area. Awareness of social class is considerably less common in America than in other industrial societies, and a salient point evident throughout the interviews and the authors' interpretation of them is that, in L. S. Kaplan's words, "the individuals take onto themselves the burden of responsibility for their situation, while in truth it is the external 'burden of class.'" Norman Birnbaum thought the book "an exercise in secular prophecy. . . . The middle class, no less than the working class, is crippled by the pursuit of success. The authors' plea for fraternity, for a genuine egalitarianism, is moving."

Sennett puts history at the service of social theory in *The Fall of Public Man*, an analysis of the imbalance that now exists between public and private life. In his view, public life at its most noble and beneficial flourished during the eighteenth century in the capital cities of Europe, and he traces its decline through the industrial, revolutionary nineteenth century as the institutions and rituals of public life gave way before a rampantly inward-looking culture. Just as he argued in *The Uses of Disorder* for more creative anarchy and disorder in our community relationships, so here he advocates a greater degree of impersonality in public life. Richard Todd thought Sennett's thesis "particularly weak in its insistent view of the history of public life as a study in steady decline. . . . In dealing with the present he makes relatively scant use of evidence, perhaps because its abundance and con-

trariety would play hob with his thesis." Robert Lekachmen bemoaned the inability of the author's "usually graceful literary style" to keep up with his complex and subtle argument, but concluded that he had "seldom read a serious work of social theory that explains as much contemporary experience as Sennett's volume does."

Authority, the first of four projected volumes on the social sources of emotion, is a demanding meditation on a social phenomenon that most people fear and distrust even while being simultaneously attracted to it. Max Weber held that we accept only that authority we perceive to be legitimate, but Sennett believes that now "we feel attracted to strong figures we do not believe to be legitimate." This has given rise to a society of "disobedient dependence" on authority, one "held together by its disaffections." The moral legitimacy conferred today on suffering has created a new demand for acknowledgment: "The ennobling of victims means that in ordinary middle-class life we are forced constantly to go in search of some injury, some affliction, in order to justify even the contemplation of questions of justice, right, and entitlement in our lives." The "autonomous person" is the one who refuses the comfortable "seduction" of authority, who "disrupts the chain of command"—a reassertion of the anarchistic impulse at the heart of Sennett's philosophy. Two of the book's principal reviewers, Elizabeth Fox-Genovese and J. S. Allen, thought the treatment of the complex subject far too brief and unsatisfying. "The social scientist as moralist," wrote Allen, " . . . has here allowed himself too free a rein. Leading us into a roughly mapped field, Sennett identifies varieties of authority and resistances to it, ruminates fitfully, and then quits the scene, leaving us intellectually unsatisfied and uncertain of the way out."

Sennett has also written novels. *The Frog Who Dared to Croak* uses a mélange of diary entries, correspondence, oblique narrative, and public speeches to sketch the career of Tibor Grau, a Hungarian Jew, a Communist philosopher, and a homosexual—a man deeply learned in the art of political and personal survival. Grau bears a close resemblance to György Lukács, the Hungarian Marxist philosopher and literary critic, who has long been a focus of ideological controversy on the left. This principal character, whose narrative makes up much of the novel, starts out as "a cipher or allegorical figure," in Michael Wood's words, but "becomes a complicated and melancholy character of some depth."

Grau's inner life, music critic Edward Rothstein observed, "is shaped by outer tyrannies," the political pressures of Eastern European

Communism. In *An Evening of Brahms,* Sennett's second novel, he "turns his attention to the heart of another sort of inner life—the struggle with music." An amateur cellist himself, Sennett makes his hero a gifted cellist who reviews his brief marriage to a pianist killed in a traffic accident. Counterpointing this unhappy contemporary romance in a series of interwoven lectures is the stormy romance of Brahms and Clara Schumann. As a novel, *An Evening of Brahms* is flawed. Rothstein finds its style "self-consciously lyrical," and its pace and plot "often awkward." But Rothstein was impressed by Sennett's "sophisticated sensibility about music." Where, in *The Fall of Public Man* he offered "a traditionally liberal critique of the world of capitalism," *An Evening of Brahms* is a critique of another "tyranny," the bourgeois family, the crises of private life where music is the true liberating force. Christopher Lehmann-Haupt, reviewing the book in the *New York Times,* wrote: "If *The Frog Who Dared to Croak* achieved a semblance of life with its clever pastiche of letters and memos, then this new novel surpasses it in rendering the documentary lifelike. Music is the medium through which Alexander Hoffmann [the cellist] transmutes intellection into feeling, and in passage after brilliant passage of musical analysis Mr. Sennett creates a simulacrum of the living."

PRINCIPAL WORKS: Families Against the City, 1970; The Uses of Disorder, 1970; (with J. Cobb) The Hidden Injuries of Class, 1972; The Fall of Public Man, 1977; (with A. Touraine, T. B. Bottomore, et al.) Beyond the Crisis-Society, 1977; Authority, 1980. *Fiction*—The Frog Who Dared to Croak, 1982; An Evening of Brahms, 1984. *As editor*—Classic Essays on the Culture of Cities, 1969; (with S. Thernstrom) Nineteenth-Century Cities, 1969; The Psychology of Society, 1977.

ABOUT: Who's Who in America, 1982–83; Contemporary Authors 73–76, 1978. *Periodicals*—American Journal of Sociology March 1971; Annals of the American Academy March 1971; Atlantic February 1977; Commentary May 1971; December 1972; April 1977; September 1980; Commonweal February 5, 1971; September 26, 1980; Journal of American History March 1971; Library Journal May 15, 1970; July 1970; September 15, 1972; December 15, 1976; May 15, 1980; June 1, 1982; Nation November 22, 1980; July 24–31, 1982; New York Review of Books April 14, 1977; October 23, 1980; August 12, 1982; New York Times May 14, 1984; New York Times Book Review September 6, 1970; November 26, 1972; July 13, 1980; June 27, 1982; May 27, 1984; New Yorker December 23, 1972; May 12, 1980; Newsweek July 20, 1970; May 5, 1980; Psychology Today May 1980; Saturday Review July 4, 1970; January 8, 1977; June 1980; Time September 6, 1982; Times Literary Supplement October 29, 1982.

*SHALAMOV, VARLAM TIKHON-OVICH (June 18, [NS: July 1] 1907–January 17, 1982), Russian poet and fiction writer, is often compared to Alexander Solzhenitsyn as a chronicler of life in the Soviet Gulag, or forced-labor prison camps. He was born in the city of Vologda, in the northeastern section of what is now the Soviet Federated Socialist Republic. He was imprisoned by Soviet authorities on two separate occasions. In 1929, after three years as a law student at the University of Moscow, he was arrested on an undisclosed charge and placed in a camp in "Solovki" (the Solovetsky Islands, in the White Sea near the Finnish border). Released after a term of three or five years (accounts of the duration of the sentence vary), he pursued a career as a writer of fiction, verse, and criticism, only to be re-arrested in 1937, again for no acknowledged reason, at the beginning of Joseph Stalin's Great Purge. Shalamov's second sentence of five years in the gold-mining camps of the northeastern Siberian area of the Kolyma river basin grew to seventeen years before he was finally freed in 1954. The original sentence had been extended "until the end of the war," and in 1943, it was increased by ten more years as a result of Shalamov's reported praise, as a "classic of Russian literature," of the expatriate author, Ivan Bunin, winner of the Nobel Prize for literature in 1933 but a proclaimed enemy of the Soviet state.

Returning to Moscow a few years after his official release, Shalamov resumed his literary career, concentrating on poetry, and publishing, in the two decades before his death, five volumes of verse. More significantly for his foreign reputation, he also wrote a series of semi-documentary narratives about life in the Kolyma camps, entitled eventually *Kolymskie Rasskazy (Kolyma Tales),* practically all of which remain unpublished in the Soviet Union to this day. Shalamov circulated these stories to friends in the form of "samizdat," or underground literature published by its author. Fewer than six of them appeared in print in the Soviet Union in the early 1960s during the premiership of Nikita Khrushchev, who sought to expose the enormities of Stalin's regime. Some of the tales appeared in Europe in French, German, and Italian translation in 1967 and 1969. Some were published periodically from 1969 to 1975 in Russian in the New York emigré magazine *Novy Zhurnal* (New Review), and some, also in Russian, in 1970, in another emigré periodical, *Grani* (Borders), in Frankfurt. In 1978, 103 of the stories, almost all that Shalamov is known to have written, were published in Russian in London. In his later years, in order to gain readmission to the Russian Writers Union and thereby

°shä lä´ môv, vär läm´ ti kô´nô vich

avail himself of its medical and pension benefits, Shalamov found it expedient to repudiate the Kolyma narratives and to protest against all foreign publication of them, whether in Russian or in translation. For the same reason, in 1972, he composed a formal, obligatory statement for the Soviet journal, *Literaturnaia Gazeta* (Literary Gazette), in which he rejected the tales as "no longer topical."

Somewhat rehabilitated, Shalamov lived out his last years in nursing homes in poor health, suffering from an assortment of ailments, including blindness and deafness. His death, on January 17, 1982, was attributed to "heart failure." His last wish, to be buried in accordance with the rites of the Russian Orthodox Church, was denied him by the Writers Union.

Shalamov's reputation in the English-speaking world rests almost entirely on his tales of life in the Kolyma Gulag, fifty-four of which have been translated by John Glad. Less well-known than Solzhenitsyn's accounts of roughly similar experiences, these understated renderings of the horror of Stalin's labor-prison system constitute a powerful record of human tragedy and suffering and sheer visceral instinct for survival. In the two volumes to date, Glad has arranged the tales under his own headings. Most of the stories are brief, some mere fragments. In some, the author is a first-person narrator, in others, a semi-detached observer. In the most memorable, there are unmistakable Chekhovian qualities of understatement, anecdotal form, an apparent lack of art or contrivance, a tone of faint and refined irony. The landscape is stark, the action and characteriztion unembroidered.

"Noch'ui" (In the Night) depicts two *zeks* (or camp prisoners) undressing buried corpses to take their underwear. "V Bane" (In the Bathhouse) is low-key Dante. Prisoners shun the baths because they almost invariably find their clothes and meager possessions stolen when they come out. In "Poslednii Boi Maiora Pugacheva" (Major Pugachov's Last Battle), one of the best tales, the major, imprisoned in the Gulag for having been captured by the Germans during the War, vainly attempts to escape from his camp, and ends by shooting himself in the mouth. In "Po Lend-Lizu" (Lend-Lease), bull-dozer-tractors, part of America's wartime assistance to the Soviets, are used to dislodge the frozen corpses of convicts buried in mass graves. "Vykhodnoi Den'" (A Day Off) shows us the anguish of Zamiatin, one of the convict-priests, who is reduced to eating the flesh of a recently killed dog. The protagonist of "Vas'ka Denisov, Pokhititel' Svinei" (Vaska Denisov, Kidnapper of Pigs), is pictured fleeing with a suckling pig,

which he proceeds to eat raw, even as he is being apprehended. In "Prokazhennye" (The Lepers), Shalamov describes the bizarre "marriage" of a leprous convict and a nurse who contracts his disease. "Zhenshchina Blatnogo Mira" (Women in the Criminal World), one of the longer narratives, is an archetypal recounting of the plight of female convicts—their subservience to the men, their roles as sexual merchandise, their vulnerability to venereal infection. "Zelenyi Prokuror" (The Green Procurator), the longest of all the stories, contains a running history of the Gulag as a whole, as well as of the Kolyma camps. "Suka Tamara" (Tamara the Bitch) is a poignant narrative of the "execution" of a favorite camp dog. "Nadgrobnoe Slovo" (An Epitaph) begins with the line, "They all died," and then proceeds to identify the particular deaths of a number of Shalamov's fellow-convicts. In the last story, "Grafit" (Graphite), the narrator explains how every corpse is marked with a pencil, for the graphite of a pencil will outlast any other means of identification.

It is both instructive and inevitable to speak of Solzhenitsyn and Shalamov together as Gulag historians, but in fact there are significant differences between the men and their work. Solzhenitsyn, eleven years younger, made his first impact on the reading world during the anti-Stalin "thaw" under Khrushchev with the publication of *Odin den' Ivana Denisovicha* (*One Day in the Life of Ivan Denisovich*), in 1962. This novel, like its successor, *V Kruge Pervom* (*The First Circle*), published abroad in 1968, was based on Solzhenitsyn's experiences as a prisoner from 1945 to 1956. In 1974, with an international reputation earned largely by the foreign publication of his books and protesting bitterly against the Soviet censorship, he left the Soviet Union on request, settling eventually in the United States. During the composition of his massive *Arkhipelag Gulag, 1918–1956* (*Gulag Archipelago, 1918–1956*), published in three installments from 1973 to 1976, he discovered that Shalamov had preceded him in the camps and had, moreover, written about them. Solzhenitsyn offered to collaborate with Shalamov, but the older man refused, most likely because he was ill and no doubt also because his literary conception and rendering of the prison years were different from Solzhenitsyn's. Nevertheless, Solzhenitsyn recognized the precedence and excellence of Shalamov's narratives. "Shalamov's experience in the camps," he wrote, "was longer and more bitter than my own, and I respectfully confess that to him and not me was it given to touch those depths of bestiality and despair toward which life in the camps dragged us all."

The contrast between the two camp veterans

is well drawn by Geoffrey Hosking in two reviews of Glad's edition of the tales. Solzhenitsyn's volumes, says Hosking, are epic, continuous, moralistic, almost optimistic in their suggestion that suffering ennobles and that a kind of good can emerge from the frightful camp experiences. By contrast, Hosking writes, Shalamov's account is discontinuous, not part of a larger epic canvas. Indeed, it consists of whatever any editor wants to make of the discrete short narratives. Solzhenitsyn has seen to the arranging, editing, and publishing of his records; Shalamov has left others to take care of these matters. Moreover, Shalamov points no obvious morals in his tales, nor does he suggest that suffering is redemptive. There is little to lift the spirit in the reading of the Kolyma stories. Here is what we suffered, Shalamov tells us; here is the minimal human state that we were reduced to, and here are some of the results of our suffering—and no more. Hosking offers a comparison: Solzhenitsyn is to Shalamov as Tolstoy is to Chekhov. The analogy is not exact, but it seems essentially correct.

In his review of Glad's first volume of translations, Irving Howe identifies Shalamov as a writer of "purity," Solzhenitsyn, of "power." In contradistinction to Solzhenitsyn, with his expansive "proclamations," Shalamov deals in "economical snippets." Solzhenitsyn is to Howe "apocalyptic" and "dogmatic," while Shalamov is neither. Howe, too, points to the Chekhovian characteristics of the Kolyma tales, but observes that they also contain echoes of Isaac Babel. Shalamov speaks with what seems to Howe to be a voice "beyond bitterness." And Howe continues: "Anger and grief have long ago exhausted themselves. What remains is the determination, perhaps beyond explanation, to get things straight for whatever record may survive."

George Gibian shows that Shalamov combines the stylistic traits of Ernest Hemingway and Isaac Babel: "He does not analyze the states of mind, or render the thoughts, of his characters. His narration is laconic, understated, like the reports of a camera or microphone—with occasional ethnographic explanations of camp life, and death, added for the benefit of the uninitiated reader—and he has a fine eye for gestures." Gibian finds Shalamov "more self-restrained" than Solzhenitsyn, while also exhibiting "artistic concentration and intensity." Gibian concludes: "Flaunting artlessness, Shalamov may indeed possess the greater art."

Among the few critics to offer merely qualified praise of Shalamov's art is Jay Martin, who argues that Glad does Shalamov no favor by comparing him to Chekhov. He cannot rank with Chekhov, in Martin's judgment, and no wonder, considering the conditions under which he lived and later wrote. What we have in the tales, according to Martin, are too often "ragged fragments—scribbles—like the graphite scrawls on the plywood identification tags of the dead bodies in the camps." John Bayley observes that the tales are of uneven quality. Some of the shortest, which have the least literary merit, are nevertheless most significant for their documentary value. The best stories—he calls "In the Night" a "masterpiece"—are evocative of Chekhov, Bunin, and Babel. Stephen Miller calls attention to Shalamov's fierce determination to survive, when most of his fellow-convicts were shot or died in captivity. He adds, however, that the author's survival was undoubtedly due, in part at least, to his having become a para-medic, a fact reflected in a number of the narratives. He refers to Shalamov's own observation that survival was often a matter of luck, and that most of those who did in fact survive had learned to adapt themselves to the most intractable conditions of life. The priest-convicts and other devoutly religious prisoners were the first to perish because they were the least able to compromise. David Evanier pictures Shalamov following Kafka's lead and joining André Schwarz-Bart, Solzhenitsyn, Anatoly Kuznetsov, and Elie Wiesel as an artist-witness to man's degradation. Shalamov renders not only the sadism of the jailers and guards, but also the "spiritual dullness" of the prisoners. Shalamov's work, he concludes, shows a "convergence of the artist's eye with the most desolate images of what man has done to man [that] produces a work of art so fine and pure as to confound the devil."

In "A Day Off," Shalamov identifies what it was that helped to keep him alive—his passion for literature, particularly poetry:

I know that everyone has something that is most precious to him, *the last thing that he has left,* and it is something which helps him to live, to hang onto life of which we were being so insistently and stubbornly deprived. . . . My *last thing* was verse—everything else had long since been forgotten, cast aside, driven from memory. Only poetry had not been crushed by exhaustion, frost, hunger, and endless humiliations.

Such a statement takes on ironic overtones in light of Shalamov's literary activity and reputation after his rehabilitation. Since his prose was interdicted, he resorted to poetry almost exclusively; and when Soviet critics wrote of him at all, it was as a poet.

In his "memoir" entitled *Bodalsia Telenok s Dubom* (*The Oak and the Calf,* 1975; English translation, 1978), Solzhenitsyn tells us how he attempted unsuccessfully to see into publication in *Novy Mir* (*New World*), a relatively liberal Soviet periodical, some of Shalamov's poems.

These works, in which Shalamov spoke openly of his life in the Kolyma camps, Solzhenitsyn had read for the first time in "samizdat" in 1956, "trembling as I recognized a brother! One of the secret brothers of whose existence I knew beyond doubt." Soviet criticism of Shalamov's poetry generally makes him out to be a "nature poet" essentially, one addicted to scenes of the taiga and tundra of the "extreme north."

L. Levitzkii, in writing of Shalamov's poems in *Ognivo* (Embers, 1961) observed that in such a poem as "Memory," the poet is obviously doing more than describing external nature alone. More particularly, he is alluding to some arduous experiences in the north: "If you are able to work the ax and the saw perfectly/The memory of past joy will remain in the muscles of the body./ These long-forgotten, precise movements are like a flow/Of a poem which is recited by heart." In his critique of Shalamov's second book of verses, *Shelest List'ev* (Rustling of Leaves, 1964), Levitzkii notes, with sympathy, that Shalamov's career as a published poet did not begin until he was more than fifty years old. He quotes from one of the poems to this effect: "Poetry is the business of the greyhaired,/It is not for boys, but for men,/Of those wounded, not young/Those who are covered with seams of wrinkles."

Beyond the criticism of his verse, there has been scant attention paid to Shalamov in official Soviet publications. Biographical accounts are almost non-existent. In 1975, a brief biographical-critical paragraph appeared in *Kratkaia Literaturnaia Entsiklopediia* (*Shorter Literary Encyclopedia*), written by Leonid Chertkov, a former fellow-convict in Kolyma who later emigrated from the Soviet Union. Chertkov refers to Shalamov's having been "unlawfully repressed" in 1937 and renewing his literary work, "mainly as a poet," after rehabilitation. Chertkov identifies Shalamov as a translator of Bulgarian, Kazaghstanian, Chuvashian, and Jewish poetry; a literary critic; and a writer of short stories "which distinguish themselves by heightened emotionalism and laconism." As a poet, he exhibits "a precise selection of words, controlled poetic means, and rhythmical variety."

Although Shalamov and Solzhenitsyn endured similar hardships, their reputations as writers are strikingly different. Whether or not he was a finer, more sensitive writer, as Howe and others contend, Shalamov can hardly be expected now to achieve Solzhenitsyn's kind of renown. In 1980, Robert Smith called Shalamov "perhaps the greatest living Russian writer," an encomium repeated by Glad in his foreword to *Graphite*. The appearance of the remaining Kolyma stories in English and in other languages is likely to confirm Shalamov's stature as one of the first, and possibly the finest, of the Gulag memorialists.

WORKS IN ENGLISH TRANSLATION: John Glad's English translations of Shalamov have been published as *Kolyma Tales* (1980) and *Graphite* (1981).

ABOUT: Columbia Dictionary of Modern European Literature, 1980; Conquest, R. Kolyma, The Arctic Death Camps, 1978; Glad, J. *Foreword to* Kolyma Tales, 1980, *Foreword to* Graphite, 1981; Lindstrom, T. S. A Concise History of Russian Literature from 1900 to the Present, II, 1978; Solzhenitsyn, A. I. Gulag Archipelago, 1973–1976, The Oak and the Calf, 1975. *Periodicals*—American Spectator September 1980; Dissent Summer 1974; National Review December 12, 1980; New Leader April 7, 1980; New Republic September 27, 1980; New Statesman July 18, 1980; New York Review of Books August 14, 1980; New York Times Book Review March 9, 1980; Survey Spring 1979; Times Literary Supplement October 17, 1980.

*SHANGE, NTOZAKE (October 18, 1948–), American dramatist, poet, and novelist, writes: "I was born down the street from where I lived in Trenton, New Jersey. My mother, Eloise Owens Williams, truly believed she could not have children: so I was quite a surprise. My father, Paul T. Williams. M.D., practiced general medicine on the first floor of our house. We lived in a section, now demolished, called East Trenton, where most black people lived. I was comfortable there in a tiny old-fashioned house that actually had a dumbwaiter my sisters and I used to play tea party with. We were visited by many, many black people; due to the fact that hotels wouldn't accept us, we stayed in people's homes. This was true of Robeson, DuBois, Dizzy Gillespie, and Duke Ellington, all of whom graced our doorway.

"But, this world was quickly interrupted by my father's induction into the United States Air Force as a Captain during the Korean War. Then, we moved from one base to another: New York, Alabama. I remember the MP's at the gates, everytime we came from the grocery store. I remember, too, watching Howdy Doody and the McCarthy hearings. Eventually, from this, also segregated, experience (all black officers lived in the same barracks), we moved to St. Louis where my father completed his residency in surgery at Homer G. Phillips Hospital, another segregated institution. We lived across the street from my school, Clark School, which was within a block of the Cabanne Branch Library I write about so often. Our street, Windermere Place, was a marvel. Haitians, East Indians, Puerto Ricans, Cubans, prize-fighters, Chuck

°shang´ gä, en tō zä´ kē

NTOZAKE SHANGE

Berry, and some white people all lived together. It never occurred to me that the world wasn't multi-cultural or that white folks hated us until I was designated 'gifted' by the Board of Education. And off I went to be the one of five black children in a working-class neighborhood far from my lovely bilingual street and friends who would never think to call me 'nigger.'

"Somehow or another we ended up in Lawrenceville, New Jersey, by the time I was thirteen. Those were not happy years for me. I don't care to think of them: the loneliness of a suburb after the black bustle of St. Louis. Yet, going to Barnard College soothed some of that pain and heightened my intellectual skills to the extent that I was afraid of no idea: not racism, sexism, or imperialism. In the Black Power movement, the movement against the Vietnam War, and in my poetry, I first started to read with the Young Lords Party, I found a path from which I have strayed very little to date.

"Teaching Women's Studies at Sonoma State College in Cotati, California, with J. J. Wilson was a godsend. Just as dancing with Halifu, Raymond Sawyer, and Ed Mock were gifts. My poetry grew. I grew. I moved to New York where I stayed for seven years instead of the six months I'd intended. Mr. Joseph Papp and the New York Shakespeare Festival changed all that with the production of *For Colored Girls. . . .* But, I have a little too much of Missouri left in me to battle Manhattan: too much Lawrenceville to handle Hollywood. So I live here, in Houston, where I am raising my daughter, Savannah, writing, building installation pieces, planting flowers, weaving, and being left to be whoever I am without being recognized in the grocery store. That's quite enough for me. In between trips to La Habana and Managua, where I have many artist friends, I mostly send pictures of the baby and talk on the phone a lot. I am a strange sort of hermit, I guess: wanting contact, but craving solitude. But, that's what makes me write poems, too."

———

For the first twenty-three years of her life, Ntozake Shange's name was Paulette Williams. Her childhood, which she describes above, was privileged. She graduated from Barnard College in 1970 with a bachelor's degree in American studies and took a master's degree in the same subject in 1973 from the University of Southern California. The epochal event of her early maturity was her renunciation of her "slave" name in 1971 on a beach in California. Of the elements of her new "African" name, "Ntozake" has been reported as meaning, cryptically, "she who comes with her own things"; "Shange," which refers to the gait of lions, was the name of the man she was living with at the time. She has been married twice.

The almost undeviating mood of Shange's writing is racial and sexual rage. "I write about pain," she has said. "Apathy stops me up. I think I write choppy prose, but the very choppiness of the prose releases my poetry." Even her greatest admirers would probably agree that "choppy" is a fair description of the tone of much of her work, both poetry and prose, but they would claim that *what* she is saying is more important than *how* she says it. Such "poetic" or "formal" considerations as meter, structure, rhythm, phrasing, and syntax are alien to her work, which, for all its intermittent power, often seems hasty, unfocused, unrevised.

Shange is best known for the theater piece—she called it a "choreopoem"—*For Colored Girls Who Have Considered Suicide/When the Rainbow Is Enuf* (1976). She describes the work in the introduction to the published text as "the words of a young black girl's growing up, her triumphs and errors, [her] struggle to be all that is forbidden by our environment, all that is forfeited by our gender, all that we have forgotten." Seven actress-dancers enact these rites of passage, "movin from Mama to whatever was out there," describing the terrors of rape, abortion, "lovers" who abuse them, and a general, all-pervasive discrimination, arriving finally at an affirmation of their dignity and identity as black women.

Ever since I realized there waz someone callt
a colored girl and evil woman a bitch or a nag

i been tryin not to be that & leave bitterness
in somebody else's cup.

During its seven-month off-Broadway run,
produced by Joseph Papp's New York Shakespeare Festival and an auspicious move to
Broadway, most theater critics remained enthusiastic about *Colored Girls* (the piece's customary nickname): "a compelling cry of anger,"
they called it, "a howling protest," "a gripping
celebration of pain, dignity, and triumph,"
"vivid and authentic."

In 1977 Papp produced Shange's next theatrical effort, a "poemplay" (again her term) entitled *A Photograph: A Study of Cruelty* (another
version, *A Photograph: Lovers in Motion,* appeared two years later), which examines the unhappy lives of a black couple, a blithe dancer,
and a bitter photographer. The general critical
view of this piece was that the dramatic structure required by the story was not well served by
the disjointed vignettes that delineate the characters. These "perceptions," in Richard Eder's
words, "are made to do the donkey-work of
holding up what attempts to be a whole dramatic structure, and they fail." The experience of
being black is the theme of another theater
piece, *Spell No. 7*, also produced under the auspices of the New York Shakespeare Festival.

Shange's novel *Sassafrass, Cypress & Indigo,*
published in 1982, the result of eight years of
work, has the same title as a novella she published in 1976 with a small feminist press in California. "The novella," she explained in an
interview in 1982, "is a little bitty story about a
woman whose parents are dead; I wrote it in the
form of poems. In the new book the mother is
a major character, I wrote it the way people usually write prose, and it's about all the different
ways black people choose to live. That's what's
nice about fiction, you can change it if you don't
like it." The novel's title is the names of three sisters, the children of a weaver in Charleston,
South Carolina, who wants only to see her
daughters happy, settled, and comfortable. The
author describes their childhood at length, then
their development into women of strength and
independence. Her narrative is densely interspersed with italicized poetry, recipes, charms,
letters, and even newspaper writing (theater
criticism), all of which, according to one reviewer, "seems to be nothing less than an attempt to
capture the essence and the glory of black
culture." Cypress becomes a dancer, along the
way abandoning her training in classical ballet
to join an Afro-American dance troupe. Sassafrass becomes a weaver like her mother and falls
in love with a musician who is a former convict
and junkie. Indigo becomes a violinist, as well as

a conjuror and radical feminist. Susan Isaacs asserted that the novel contains several well-
written passages of deep feeling, especially those
describing childhood, but as the sisters' "world
begins to widen, the writing starts to deteriorate.
When the sisters leave the protection of their
mother—the best-drawn character in the
book—they drift into relationships so banal they
seem no more substantial than mist over a red-
wood hot tub." This last simile refers to the
heavy use in the book of trite and unspecific California English: "Sassafrass was so full of love
she couldn't call anybody anything without
bringing good vibes from a whole lot of spirits
to everything she touched." Such statements are
made without irony and are not intended to define character; they are a dead weight in the
novel. Isaacs remarks of the statement cited
above that it "would not have been credible even
in Haight-Ashbury in 1967."

Shange has also published two collections of
poetry. In 1980 she saw presented, again at the
New York Shakespeare Festival, her adaptation
of Brecht's *Mother Courage and Her Children.*
Her version featured a black cast and is set during the American Civil War.

PRINCIPAL WORKS: *Drama*—For Colored Girls Who Have
Considered Suicide/When the Rainbow Is Enuf, 1976;
Negress, 1977; A Photograph: A Study of Cruelty,
1977; Where the Mississippi Meets the Amazon, 1977;
From Okra to Greens, 1978; Spell No. 7, 1979; Boogie
Woogie Landscapes, 1980; Mouths, 1981; Three
Pieces: Spell No. 7/A Photograph: Lovers in Motion/
Boogie Woogie Landscape, 1981. *Poetry*—Nappy
Edges, 1978; A Daughter's Geography, 1983.
Fiction—Sassafrass, Cypress & Indigo, 1982; Betsy
Brown, 1985.

ABOUT: Contemporary Authors 85–88, 1980; Contemporary Literary Criticism 8, 1978; Current Biography,
1978; Who's Who in America, 1983–84.
Periodicals—Booklist November 15, 1976; Choice November 1977; Library Journal June 1, 1977; September
1, 1978; New Leader July 5, 1976; New York Times
June 16, 1976; December 16, 1977; June 8, 1979; July
22, 1979; New York Times Book Review September
12, 1982; September 19, 1982; New Yorker June 14,
1976; August 2, 1976; January 2, 1978; Newsday August 22, 1976; Publishers Weekly May 3, 1985; Village
Voice August 16, 1976.

SHAPIRO, DAVID (JOEL) (January 2,
1947–), American poet and critic, was born in
Newark, New Jersey, the son of S. Irving (a physician) and Fraida (Chagy) Shapiro. A precocious child, he performed as a violinist with the
New Jersey Symphony and other orchestras, and
at sixteen played violin under Leopold Stokow-

DAVID SHAPIRO

ski. By the age of thirteen he was also writing and publishing poetry, attracting such attention, in fact, that at fifteen he was the recipient of the Gotham Book Mart Avant-Garde Poetry Award. Shapiro enrolled at Columbia College, in New York, in 1964, and in 1965, while still a freshman, received the Breadloaf Writers Conference Robert Frost fellowship, and had his first volume of poetry, *January: A Book of Poems*, published. The jacket of the book carried endorsements ("remarkable," "fresh," "brilliant") from an array of well-known writers including Kay Boyle, Dudley Fitts, Kenneth Rexroth, and Jack Kerouac. Although a number of critics found the poems derivative of an established modernist, and particularly Dadaist, tradition, it was generally felt that Shapiro showed unusual promise. X. J. Kennedy, in the *New York Times Book Review*, remarked that "though *January* isn't a book so sensational as [the endorsements on the book's jacket] might suggest, neither is it inferior to most other work produced by the current Manhattan-centered school of John Ashbery and Kenneth Koch. . . . Shapiro has [their] fondness for vanishing connectives, and quick shifts in points of view; for ambiguity, false naiveté and studied carelessness. But he has more innocence, recklessness and passion in him." Two years later, while still in his teens, Shapiro received the Ingram Merrill Foundation fellowship for poetry.

A self-styled "fellow-traveler of the S.D.S.," Shapiro was embroiled in the student riots at Columbia in April 1968. He achieved national notoriety for the photograph of him (in *Newsweek*, October 13, 1969) "occupying" President Gray-son Kirk's office chair while puffing on one of Kirk's "liberated" cigars. Yet by graduation, much was apparently forgiven, since Shapiro received his B.A. degree magna cum laude and was awarded Columbia's prestigious Kellett fellowship for study at Cambridge University in England. Making his sweep of honors complete, he also received the Book-of-the-Month Club fellowship for creative artists during the same year. In 1969, while at Cambridge studying Greek tragedy and English literature, Shapiro published his second volume of poetry, *Poems from Deal*. John Koethe, in *Poetry* magazine, called *Poems from Deal* "a real advance over his first [book]—it is a collection of twenty-seven good poems instead of the dazzling but a little unsatisfying *tour de force* of the earlier. He has an incredible mastery of the language and an ear sensitive to every nuance of idiom and rhythm. . . . The essence of Shapiro's poetry is musical, for the poems seem to flow in a continuous wave which the poet gently modulates rather than consciously orders." Other reviewers praised *Poems from Deal*, but some tended to view the poems as brilliant exercises. Herbert Leibowitz conceded that Shapiro possessed "a trained sensibility and deft technique," but found the book "mannered" and "too clever for its own good." There is an undeniable element of precocity in these early poems:

When I was sixteen, disgusted
With everything except their abstractions
I qualified as a virtuoso
But my bow was (speedily) flung away.
My story is the reverse of amber
Which usually includes flies and straws
Though it is a rare element itself.
My childhood was insignificant
Though it seems to perpetuate
The most curious mind-dazzling facts:
The desire to burst was pure masochism.
There lies a spoon in outer space
Waiting to be used by me for breakfast.
　　　　　　　—from "In Memory of Your Body"

In 1970 Shapiro received a B.A., with first-class honors, from Cambridge University, and in April of that year married Jean Lindsay Stamm, a designer. He returned to New York City where, at the Bedford-Stuyvesant Children's Museum at Lincoln Center, he taught and studied writing done by children; and, with Kenneth Koch, in 1968 he edited *Learn Something, America*, a collection of the writings produced by these children. He has also edited, with Rod Padgett, the six-hundred page *An Anthology of New York Poets*. Its quality was suggested by the reviewer for *Publishers Weekly*, who remarked that "some [of those included], notably Kenneth Koch, John Ashbery, the late Frank O'Hara . . . already are well known for their poetry. If there's an overriding influence in this huge anthology, it's Allen Ginsberg-cum-William Carlos Williams-cum-Whitman—with a tipsy bow perhaps to Baudelaire and Rimbaud. Good things turn up in this cool cornucopia."

Shapiro's third book of poems, *A Man Holding an Acoustic Panel,* was published in 1971, and was nominated for the National Book Award for poetry. Reviewers were of different minds about the book, some praising Shapiro's brilliant technique and virtuosity, others objecting that his surrealism was too insistently obscurantist. The reviewer for the *New York Review of Books* characterized the book concisely by noting that "in the poems that reveal [Shapiro] most clearly, his method parallels Barthelme's in prose—ransacking the mind's attics and making improbable arrangements of the tatty, unseasonal stuffs shelved away there. . . . [The] process of assemblage is Dadaistic but in a most refined and civilized fashion. . . . Some of the poems are more conventional, but the essential unpredictability remains, a faintly eerie playfulness and an impressive *déreglement* of the familiar" as his poem "Flowers of the Mediterranean" illustrates:

Out of the car so old it is growing mushrooms, you emerge
    with a
vivarium to say: Here are anemones laid at leisure and
    daisies
in an inch of earth.

Figs and olives making insignificant profits. And these
    are vegetables
in a basin called a port. Fish in frenzy, open to the sky.

I overlooked the apples, the authentic apples being
    the "little
apples." Here are giant fennel renewing in a radical way.
    And
here's the squirrel, expecting to be fed.

The squirrel jumps on the customer, actually tasting
    him, locked
onto his chest. The Food and Health people are taking
    inventories
of this squirrel atrocity.

We could only sketch it. An island does not work.
    Delos didn't produce (much).

In 1972 Shapiro became an instructor in the English department at Columbia, and in 1973 assistant professor. In 1973, too, he published *The Page-Turner,* a gathering of his latest poems, which Peter Meinke, in the *New Republic,* described as "surrealistic, almost Dadaesque, highly polished." Jerome J. McGann, in *Poetry,* called *Page-Turner* a subtle and impressive performance. "Poems deliberately echo, even quote from, each other," he wrote, "and a crazy order constantly floats to the surface [only to dissolve again]." Brian Swan, who was less impressed,

complained that "Shapiro's fourth book is uncritical in its acceptance of what bubbles up. . . . There is little felt pressure; . . . the words that want to be a poem remain a 'dream diary.'"

Shapiro received his Ph.D., with distinction, from Columbia in 1974, and since then has been honored with numerous fellowships and awards. These include a Creative Artists Public Service fellowship (1974), the Morton Dauwen Zabel Award from the American Academy of Arts and Letters (1977), and a grant from the National Endowment for the Humanities (1978). In 1978 he published a new volume of poetry, *Lateness,* which Harold Bloom called "his fifth and so far the best of his books." Bloom noted that Shapiro was still "working through the complex influence of Ashbery," and remarked on "the struggle in the poems between Shapiro's very individual temperament with a poetic inheritance he loves almost too well." Reviews were generally quite favorable, although reservations of one kind or another were expressed. Vernon Shetley observed that "even sympathetic critics seem to find David Shapiro's poetry intermittently dazzling but fundamentally obscure and obscurantist, a sort of disjunctive hijinks or cartoon anarchy. . . . Too often he seems more bent on avoiding expected methods of continuity and development than on devising new ones; great energy is expended and little headway gained. Yet if these poems produce more heat than light, there is real imagination in them nevertheless." Music, like painting, informs many of the poems which he appropriately describes as "the house of music splashed with ink." It is the central metaphor of the long poem "The Devil's Trill Sonata," which begins:

As Aeschylus puts it
In Frag. 351: Let us say what comes to our lips, whatever
    it
may be; or perhaps, Let's say what's on
the tip of our tongue.

As Achilles put it to Apollo,
You have made a fool of me.

It was with some interest
I noticed the violin back in its case
of itself, was playing the piece
correctly, and with almost
no trepidation of the string!
It played along and is playing
by and of and for itself—

The persistent association of Shapiro with John Ashbery was highlighted again in 1979 when Shapiro published his critical study *John Ashbery: An Introduction to His Poetry.* As John Unterecker observed in his Foreword to the volume, this was not intended as a conventional introduction for readers seeking explanations of Ashbery's complex and often obscure poetry:

"His [Shapiro's] approach is unorthodox. His insights into the ways a major contemporary poet organizes his art give us a sense not just of the techniques used by Ashbery but of a structural aesthetic drawn on by a whole generation of poets, painters, musicians, and sculptors." The book is as interesting for its expression of Shapiro's own aesthetics as it is for its study of Ashbery. "Incoherence" and "randomness," qualities of the poetry of both men, are the essence of modern experience, and, Shapiro writes: "One of the central functions of an 'abstract' poetry is to be aware of itself as non-discursive palpability. Such poetry is involved in particularity without a stable ground. That is the 'meaning of meaninglessness,' and Ashbery's poignant privacies affirm our elaborate sense of the certainty of uncertainty." Modern art, like modern poetry, is atomistic, but because the arts are "cross-stimulating," they are also unifying and essentially structured. In an essay called "Poets & Painters: Lines of Color," written for the catalogue of an exhibit of contemporary paintings and poems at the Denver Art Museum in late 1979, Shapiro offered a striking analogy of the relationship: "Once, in a dream, I requested an insight from my mother as to the practice of poetry in Paradise. In the dream, I was scrutinizing the surface of a lake. The poem of Paradise would presumably float to the surface very much the way answers floated to the top of a toy mystic ball sold in my childhood for use at parties. Straining with some anxiety to glimpse the poem, I was surprised and frightened when a series of colored lines floated to the top of the lake and revealed that poetry may be a form of painting. This dream seems a parable of the union of art and language."

Shapiro contributes frequently to magazines and journals, and has many-sided interests. In the 1970s he was an editorial associate for *Art News* and art critic for *Art in America,* the *New Yorker,* and other magazines; and he is a violinist and composer, as well as a skillful translator from the French. Considered today, along with Kenneth Koch and John Ashbery, one of the best known of the "New York Poets, "he has taught, as a visiting professor, at William Patterson College, Cooper Union, and Princeton, and makes his home in New York City.

PRINCIPAL WORKS: *Poems*—January: A Book of Poems, 1965; Poems from Deal, 1969; A Man Holding an Acoustic Panel, 1971; The Page-Turner, 1973; Lateness, 1978. *Prose*—John Ashbery: An Introduction to His Poetry, 1979. *As editor*—(with K. Koch) Learn Something, America, 1968; (with R. Padgett) An Anthology of New York Poets, 1970.

ABOUT: Contemporary Authors, revision series 15–16, 1975; The Reader's Adviser I, 1974; Vinson, J. (ed.) Contemporary Poets, 1980; Who's Who in America: 1980–81; The Writer's Directory 1982–84. *Periodicals*—Hudson Review Autumn 1969; Library Journal August 1965; January 15, 1974; New York Review of Books June 3, 1965; December 16, 1971; New York Times Book Review November 15, 1970; Poetry October 1970; January 1973; October 1974; July 1979; Sewanee Review July 1978.

SHEN YAN-BING *See* MAO DUN

SHILS, EDWARD ALBERT (1910–), American sociologist, was born in Springfield, Massachusetts, of German-Jewish ancestry. The family moved to Philadelphia, where Shils attended the University of Pennsylvania, taking a B.A. in 1931. Shils' fascination with intellectuals and politics dates back to his youth in Philadelphia. He recalls as a boy of ten being taken to see the Middle Eastern antiquities at the University of Pennsylvania museum, and noticing that many of the originals were in Berlin; thus began his interest in German culture. Shils began to read widely in European literature and politics, and was struck by the question, "Why did the writers, historians, philosophers and other intellectuals, some great and all interesting, feel such revulsion for their own societies, for the institutions through which they were ruled and the persons who ruled them?" (*Intellectuals and the Powers*).

The political climate of the 1930s furnished new and more urgent sociological questions for the young Shils. He wondered, for example, "how, despite the demoralizing influence of the Depression, great numbers of persons remained attached to their society" (*Center and Periphery*). He was also concerned about the rise of Fascism and Marxism as rivals to the liberal-democratic political traditions of the West. After a brief stint as a social worker in New York City and Chicago, in 1933 Shils began to take graduate courses at the University of Chicago, where he began the formal study of sociology. Although no longer the unchallenged center of the American discipline, the Chicago sociology department in the mid-1930s was still very impressive; following the work of Robert Park and his colleagues, Shils focused on the study of "primary groups": the basic units of society such as the family, gang, and neighborhood where the individual's loyalty to collective values was forged.

During his early years at Chicago, Shils con-

EDWARD SHILS

centrated primarily on political groups, doing field work among Nazi and nativist groups and reading Communist newspapers. After the United States entered the war, he conducted studies of German and American soldiers to probe the role of primary groups in the military. Teaching first at the London School of Economics, then at the University of Chicago, Shils had done considerable work on the dynamics of primary groups by the late 1940s, but still felt unsatisfied with the level of his analysis; as he put it, "the ties which bound those primary groups to the larger structure remained obscure to me" (*Center and Periphery*).

Shils' collaboration with the distinguished American sociologist Talcott Parsons supplied the larger analytical perspective he was missing. In 1949, Shils went to Harvard to spend a year working with Parsons and a small group of Harvard faculty on a new theoretical agenda for the social sciences. Parsons, whose first book, *The Structure of Social Action* (1937), had introduced European-style grand theory to American sociology, was now intent upon building a conceptual framework for the study of all forms of human activity. Together, Parsons and Shils wrote a long essay, "Values, Motives, and Systems of Action," which appeared in *Toward a General Theory of Action*, attempting systematically to link personality, culture, and social structure. In their schema, culture, which they defined as "ways of orienting and acting . . . embodied in meaningful symbols," provides the vital mediator between the individual and the society. Collective values and norms, which are transmitted chiefly by primary groups, act to

pattern individual needs and behavior into a coherent and meaningful whole.

Working within this structural-functionalist framework, Shils proceeded over the next two decades to pioneer the field of "macrosociology," as the large-scale study of society came to be called. He has been particularly concerned with the problem of social integration, or "the constitution of the parts of society into a whole society" (*Center and Periphery*). Taking issue with the scholars of the neo-Marxist Frankfort School, who portray modern industrial "mass society" as much more atomistic and alienated than the traditional preindustrial world, Shils emphasizes the new forms of integration made possible by the higher educational achievements, mass communication, and democratic political forms associated with modernization. "As I see it, modern society is no lonely crowd, no horde of refugees fleeing from freedom," he wrote in 1957. "It is no *Gesellschaft*, soulless, egotistical, loveless, faithless, utterly impersonal and lacking in integrative forces other than interest or coercion. It is held together by an infinity of personal attachments, moral obligations in concrete contexts, professional and creative pride, individual ambition, primordial affinities, and a civil sense which is low in many, high in some, and moderate in most persons" (*Center and Periphery*). His numerous articles on cultural authority and institutions, intellectuals, ideology, and science aimed to show the manifold processes by which modern societies achieve social integration. As such, Shils sees his work as a corrective to left-wing intellectuals who deny the potential for human dignity and improvement in modern capitalist nations.

Central to Shils' work has been the distinction between the "center and the periphery," the title of perhaps his best known article. Every society, he argues, has a cultural center where its essential values, beliefs, and symbols reside. This central value system informs the various subsystems of the social system, e.g. the family, the economy, the institutions of education and politics. But the consensus created by these overlapping subsystems is no means complete; "dissensus" always exists in a society, no matter how well integrated it is. It is precisely the ability of the center "to spread a cover of consensus around itself and over the entire society" that fascinates Shils (*Center and Periphery*).

In Shils' analysis, symbol and ritual are critical components of the process of creating consensus. In "The Meaning of the Coronation," which he wrote with the British sociologist Michael Young, Shils explores how the ritual surrounding

Elizabeth II's coronation in 1953 allowed the war-weary English to revitalize their commitment to the nation's collective value system. Ordinary citizens, Shils and Young argue, have moral values, but they are routinely expressed only in the concrete situations of everyday life. So there remains a longing for more intense spiritual experiences, especially in times of crisis, that only solemn rituals can provide. Thus the masses of Britons who celebrated Elizabeth's coronation eagerly participated in that "great act of national communion" as a means of affirming the nation's central value system (*Center and Periphery*). Ordinary citizens may occasionally immerse themselves in "the sacred," but only a small minority of intellectuals have "an unusual sensitivity to the sacred, an uncommon reflectiveness about the nature of their universe and the rules which govern their society," Shils writes in *The Intellectuals and the Powers*. By producing works of art, literature, and history, intellectuals play a vital role in generating and maintaining the central value system. At the same time, their devotion to ultimate truth can make them enemies of authority. Thus Shils sees a permanent tension between "the intellectuals and the powers" in modern societies.

Nowhere is the potentially destabilizing power of the intellectuals more evident than in their propensity to develop ideologies. An ideology, as Shils defines it, is a total system of belief that unites its followers in opposition to the prevailing value system. Ideologies are most likely to arise in periods of rapid change, when traditional values cannot order new social realitites, thus leaving people ripe for conversion to new points of view. Although Shils believes that ideological movements are an unavoidable aspect of modern life, he is nonetheless profoundly suspicious of ideological or "alienative" politics such as Fascism or Marxism, which he believes foster dangerous extremism. Along with other liberal academics of his generation, he has openly hoped that the "age of ideological politics" has come to an end.

As a bulwark against ideological extremism, Shils looks to the standards and institutions of science, whose spirit he sees as "alien to ideology." He admits that the social sciences may have incorporated some ideological points of view, but "insofar as [they] have been genuinely intellectual undertakings with their own rules of observation and judgment, open to criticism and revision, they have not been ideological and are in fact antipathetic to ideology" (*The Intellectuals and the Powers*). In his long and fervent support for academic freedom (he was an outspoken critic of McCarthyism in the 1950s) and his editorship of *Minerva*, a journal dedicated to the study of science and scientific institutions, Shils has attempted to counter ideological politics by championing a value-free notion of the social sciences.

Shils' impassioned defense of liberalism and hatred of Marxism have not endeared him to the younger, more radical generation of sociologists who came of age in the turbulent 1960s. Critic Steven Lukes describes him as a "paradigm of what [Antonio] Gramsci called the 'traditional intellectual,'" that is, one who devotes his scholarly labor to legitimating the dominant political order. As Lukes correctly observes, Shils' academic career has been devoted to justifying his own liberal democratic vision of modern society. But one need not share Shils' political views to appreciate his contributions to sociological theory, which James Stoltzman describes as "the rescue of the classical consensual view of society from its current state of disrepute by fusing it with tenets derived from the conflict framework." This "wayward Parsonian," as Stoltzman describes him, has produced a fascinating body of work on culture, science, and ideology that transcends the political climate in which it was produced.

PRINCIPAL WORKS: (with T. Parsons) Toward a General Theory of Action, 1951; The Torment of Secrecy, 1956; Selected Papers of Edward Shils: vol. 1, The Intellectuals and the Powers, vol. 2, Center and Periphery: Essays in Macrosociology, 1975, vol. 3, The Calling of Sociology, 1980; Tradition, 1981.

ABOUT: *Periodicals*—American Journal of Sociology 84, 1978; American Scholar Spring 1982; British Journal of Sociology 25, 1974; Times Literary Supplement July 23, 1982.

*SHKLOVSKY, VIKTOR BORISOVICH

(1893–December 14?, 1984), Russian critic, wrote (in Russian) in 1983: "I was born in Petersburg at the end of the last century. It was winter. The streets were clean and snowy. The buildings were still modest in size and had only two or three stories. People got to the other side of the Neva by crossing the ice. When spring came and the ice melted, steamboats and barges made their appearance. Up the Neva came boats with high prows, no different from the boats that plied the river during the time of Peter the Great. It was 1893 and nothing, as they used to say in old-fashioned novels, seemed to indicate that great changes were in the offing. It was the end of the nineteenth century. My nurse read me fairy tales and the novels of Jules Verne.

"I was the fourth child in a big Jewish family. My father had been studying to be a rabbi, but

°shklôf´ ske

VICTOR SHKLOVSKY

he left the community and moved to another city. He taught mathematics at a private school. My mother, Latvian by birth, looked after the children. We were poor. I knew that if you ate soup without having any bread, you'd still be hungry. Like my brothers, I was baptized in the Orthodox faith. We had many books on religion at home. The famous preacher Ioann of Kronstadt was somehow distantly related to my mother. But I was reading books on sectarianism and heresies. At the age of fifteen—in 1908—I entered a short-story contest being held by the journal *Vesna (Spring)*. My story, with its considerable sacrilegious elements, got published.

"I was not a good student. I went from school to school, always being told the same thing: that I was a capable lad who didn't apply himself. My mother gave up on me. I did finish school, though. At graduation, it was suggested that I enter the St. Petersburg Theological Seminary. Instead, I went to Petersburg University. I enrolled in the Department of Philology. By that time, I had lost interest in sculpture. I was doing a lot of writing and working on what I then took to be literary theory.

"It was the beginning of the twentieth century. Moscow and Petersburg echoed to the sound of the Futurists—Mayakovsky, Khlebnikov, Kamensky, the Burliuk brothers, the painters Larionov and Goncharova. I listened to their poetry and took part in their poetry evenings. I was writing my first book, *Voskreshenie slova* (Resurrection of the Word). In sixteen pages, I demonstrated that contemporary literature had come to a dead end. Words had lost their vitality and become automatic. Futurism was restoring

to literature a sense of life, a feeling for the word/thing that it had lost. Art was returning to its sources and being reborn. The book came out in 1914. I ran it off myself at a printing firm that had previously published only calling cards. I was friends with Mayakovsky, Khlebnikov, Tatlin, Malevich, Chagall. They were great men. But so was the time in which they lived.

"When I entered the university, the old professors asked me why I had chosen philology. And I answered: because I want to do away with the old-fashioned, academic study of literature. At the university I quickly found kindred spirits. I got to know a circle of philologists who felt that the old methods did little to promote an understanding of literature. We organized Opoyaz (Society for the Study of Poetic Language) and in 1916 we published our first collection. We wrote about the self-value and autonomous quality of literature. We wrote that so-called 'form' is actually the content of literature, that students of literature should study the structure of the work—how it is 'made.' Opoyaz grew, attracting more and more new people. The 'formal' esthetic kept gathering strength, but at that point I gave up my studies and volunteered for service at the front. I fought in the Ukraine against the Germans. I commanded an armored division and was even awarded a Cross of St. George. I was also writing articles.

"Now my old articles—'Art as Device,' 'How *Don Quixote* Is Made,' '*Tristram Shandy* and the Theory of the Novel'—are being translated into numerous languages and republished just as they were originally written. Not, of course, because they are flawless, but, I think, because just as we write with a pencil, so time writes with us. Apparently we did do away with the old academic approach to literature. Among the members of Opoyaz were such scholars as Tynyanov, Eikhenbaum, Zhirmunsky, and Tomashevsky; we worked with Roman Jakobson, who carried our ideas into structuralism.

"Then came the Revolution. I took part in it and helped capture the Admiralty. Then, as a representative of the provisional government, I went to northern Persia and fought there. But I soon returned to Petrograd and kept writing. I have always worked a lot. I have published a lot. I simply kept writing, without thinking about the possible consequences, and that is no doubt why I left Russia in 1921, why I found myself going across the Gulf of Finland on the ice. I lived in Germany. I got ready to take part in the revolution that was imminent, and I wrote two books—*Sentimental'noe puteshestvie* (1923, *A Sentimental Journey*) and *Zoo, ili pis'ma ne o ljubvi* (1923, *Zoo, or Letters Not About*

Love)—which I still consider my best books. But the revolution in Germany never came. Gorky and Mayakovsky helped me get back to Russia. I settled in Moscow, where I seemed to have gotten a firmer grip on myself. I published my articles *O teorii prozy* (1925, 1929, Theory of Prose) and I worked in films. Two films for which I wrote screen plays [in 1926 and 1927] are still in circulation. I worked with L. Kuleshov, V. Budovkin, A. Romm. I knew Eisenstein well and wrote a book about him many years later [1973].

"Tolstoy was once asked what he wanted to say in *Anna Karenina*. He replied that in order to answer that question, he would have to write the entire novel all over again. It is hard to tell my life all over again, even harder with my books. I do not repudiate my past, though my frequent arguments with myself occasionally degenerate into a quarrel. Life is kept in motion by contradictions. Only boulders, being lifeless, stay put.

"Here I am now—ninety years old. That age somehow crept up on me. I haven't stopped working. It won't be long now until the publication of my new book, which has the same title as the book I published in my youth—'Theory of Prose.' During the time that has passed since its appearance in 1925, I haven't stopped thinking, and my book has grown from the old one as a tree grows from a seed."

—trans. Richard Sheldon

———

Viktor Shklovsky began his career as a Futurist. Strongly attracted by the poetry of Mayakovsky and Khlebnikov, he enthusiastically joined their crusade against the tenets of Realism and Symbolism. In the process, he wrote a booklet called "Resurrection of the Word," 1914, which is usually regarded as the cornerstone of the movement that became known as Russian Formalism. Shklovsky showed the booklet to the eminent Baudouin de Courtenay, who introduced Shklovsky to his most brilliant linguistics students, Lev Yakubinsky and Evgeny Polivanov. They were tired of analyzing ancient texts and intrigued by the possibility of applying their techniques to the language of Futurist poetry. These students formed the nucleus of Opoyaz. Before long, their interest in the language of Futurist poetry broadened into an interest in the specific nature of verse language as a whole. Collections of their articles were published in 1916, 1917, and 1918.

The collection published in 1919 contained Shklovsky's seminal articles "Art as Device" and "The Connection between Plot Devices and General Stylistic Devices." In these two articles, Shklovsky enunciated the theoretical principles which laid the foundation for the Formalist school of criticism. His interest had by now shifted to prose. He had learned from the studies of Aleksandr Veselovsky that a work of literature can be effectively analyzed as a discrete formal entity. Now he set out to rescue literature from all the critics who insisted on treating it as a mirror of society or of the author's life. Rejecting the conventional dichotomy of form and content, he substituted the dichotomy of form and material. Then he insisted that a work of literature, in all its component parts—hero, plot, motif, etc.—is form and only form. In one of the provocative formulations for which he was famous, and upon which he was frequently criticized by his Marxist foes, he proclaimed, "A work of literature does not exceed the sum of its stylistic devices." He used the term "material" to describe all the events and experiences out of which the writer fashions literature. Once such material is converted into literature, it loses its status as factual information and becomes part of a verbal entity that needs to be studied as one would study a watch: to see how it is made and what makes it effective.

Effective literature is that which restores outworn words, objects and genres to perceptibility. To describe that process, Shklovsky coined two terms that subsequently gained wide currency: estrangement (*ostranenie*) and obstructed form (*zatrudnennoe postroenie*). Estrangement includes all the techniques by which a writer renders his material unfamiliar, such as the use of a peculiar narrative viewpoint (a child or a horse); obstructed form refers to the process by which a writer dismantles his material and arranges it into arresting verbal patterns.

Finally, in his article on the philosopher and critic Vasily Rozanov in 1921, Shklovsky completed his theoretical edifice with a new hypothesis about the dynamics of literary history that drew upon his theory of perception. At any given time, literary forms exist in a complex hierarchy. As a dominant form ceases to elicit perception, it is replaced by one of the peripheral forms in the hierarchy. In other words, a major new writer draws primarily not from his major predecessor, but from minor genres and writers in the literary stockpile of the time. As Shklovsky phrased it, "In the history of art, the legacy is transmitted not from father to son but from uncle to nephew."

These ideas contributed substantially to the revolution in the arts that had gotten under way in Russia well before 1917. Throughout a decade convulsed by world war, revolution, and civil war, groups of poets, painters, theater directors, prose writers, and critics sat in the freezing rooms of besieged Petrograd and passionately discussed the new ideas that filled the air. Shklovsky periodically vacated such rooms to fight. He fought in the Ukraine under the Czar and in Persia under the provisional government. After the October Revolution, he joined an underground group working to restore the Constituent Assembly; then he fled to the Ukraine to escape arrest, returning to Petrograd early in 1919 after being exonerated of those charges. For the next two years, he propagated the doctrines of Formalism in countless articles and lectures, working with special intensity as mentor to a brilliant group of young writers who called themselves the Serapion Brothers. Then, in 1922, the charges against him were revived and he fled abroad, settling in the large Russian colony that had formed in Berlin after the Revolution.

Life in Berlin depressed Shklovsky. Forgiven his past sins by the Soviet government, he returned home in the fall of 1923 and resumed his ties with the Serapion Brothers, the Formalists, and the Futurists. By now, the Futurists had reorganized under the name of LEF, Left Front of the Arts, which advocated an art more oriented toward the demands of the epoch. While still in Berlin in 1923, Shklovsky had published an article on Charlie Chaplin and a book on literature and cinematography, where he applied his theories about literature to the new medium. Now he plunged into film work, beginning an important new phase of his career. He worked closely with the important film directors of the twenties, especially Eisenstein, whose theories of montage owe something to Shklovsky's influence. He wrote theoretical articles about the cinema, reviewed films, and wrote scenarios, some of which have become classics. At the same time, he came under increasing pressure to abandon his Formalist ideas, viewed by the authorities as totally incompatible with the doctrines of Marxism. All the travails that Shklovsky endured during a decade of world war, revolution, civil war, exile, and suppression are brilliantly set forth in the experimental prose of his three documentary novels: *Sentimental Journey; Zoo, or Letters Not About Love,* and *Tret'ja fabrika* (1926, *Third Factory*).

During the late 1920s, after the inauguration of the first five-year plan and the collectivization of agriculture, the Party imposed tight controls on literature and brought to heel those unorthodox writers known collectively as "fellow travelers." By then, Shklovsky had already modified his approach. His work in films, changes in

Russian tastes for literature, and pressure from the Marxist critics combined to push him in new directions. As a member of LEF, he abandoned his early insistence on intricate forms and on irony. Invoking his theory of perception, he asserted that the new Russian reader had ceased to respond to these forms and now preferred factual literature. Accordingly, he led the exploration and refinement of such genres as the newspaper article, the *feuilleton,* and the sketch—the forms that would dominate the Russian literary scene during the 1930s. He retained his much maligned dedication to formal analysis, but he enlarged his scope to include the impact of society on the formation of literature. This new orientation is reflected in two books that he published at the end of the decade: *Mater'jal i stil' v romane L'va Tolstogo 'Vojna i mir'* (Material and Style in Lev Tolstoy's Novel *War and Peace,* 1928) and *Matvei Komarov* (1929).

Under increasing pressure from Marxist critics, Shklovsky modified his Formalist views by enlarging his studies to embrace more popular genres, but he never abandoned his major critical principles. In 1930, he published his much-discussed article "A Monument to Scientific Error," which has been widely misinterpreted as his unconditional surrender to the Party's demand for orthodoxy in art. In fact, this article takes the position that the charges against the Formalists apply only to the initial stage of their development. Shklovsky argues that after 1924, the Formalists evolved a more sophisticated approach to literature that includes recognition of social and economic factors. He concludes the article by flatly refusing to declare himself a Marxist. Despite his stubborn refusal to make a complete capitulation, Shklovsky was able to remain active during the thirties. He continued his work in films and wrote books on Pushkin, Mayakovsky, and a series on historical figures.

During World War II, Shklovsky worked as a war correspondent, covering the Soviet occupation of eastern Poland in the fall of 1939 and various sectors of the front through 1943. These articles appeared in book form in 1944 under the title *Vstreči* (Encounters). In 1944, he worked as a consultant to Eisenstein during the filming of *Ivan the Terrible.* Shklovsky's only son, Nikita, was killed in the final months of the war. In 1946 the brief respite granted to writers during the war came to an end; a strident campaign against "servility to the West" and "cosmopolitanism" got under way. As a recognized authority on, and admirer of, Western literature and as a Jew, Shklovsky was in jeopardy and between 1948 and 1953 published almost nothing.

With the "thaw" in Communist Party control

after Stalin's death, Shklovsky resumed publishing. But even then his book on Dostoevsky (an author virtually tabooed in the Stalin era), *Za i protiv* (Pro and Contra, 1957), was delayed by the censors during the reactionary period after the Hungarian revolution, and its favorable reception in the Soviet Union was soon followed by official denunciation. In the West, however, it received an enthusiastic response from many critics, among them Roman Jakobson. Two years later, in 1959, Shklovsky published his critical masterpiece, *Xudožestvennaja proza: Razmyšlenija i razbory* (Artistic Prose: Reflections and Analyses), re-establishing himself as a masterly comparatist with discussions of Shakespeare, Boccaccio, Cervantes, Fielding, Sterne, and Dickens, along with Russian writers such as Tolstoy, Chekhov, and Sholokhov. In a 1966 edition he added chapters on Gogol, Pushkin, and Dostoevsky, changing the title to *Povesti o proze: Razmyšleni i razbory* (Facts about Fiction: Reflections and Analyses). During the same period (1963) he published his monumental biography of Tolstoy, which has been widely translated; and in 1970, at the age of seventy-seven, he published *Tetiva. O nesxodstve sxodnogo* (Bowstring: On the Dissimilarity of the Similar) in which he moves far beyond the confines of the individual text into a sort of meditation on the essence of literature. Peter Demetz, in *Die Zeit*, regretted only that the German translation had been abridged, while the reviewer in the *Times Literary Supplement* described it as "the champagne of criticism."

During the 1960s Shklovsky also began collecting his memoirs, sections of which were published in the journal *Znamja* (Banner) and collected in book form as *Zyli-byli. Vospominanija* (Once Upon a Time) in 1964. On his seventieth birthday, now the author of more than fifty books and some two dozen screenplays, he received long overdue recognition in his own country with the award of the Red Banner of Labor. In the late 1960s he was finally allowed to go abroad—to West Berlin, where he had spent several unhappy months as an emigré in the early 1920s. In 1972 he read a paper on Dostoevsky at the International Dostoevsky Conference in Venice, and in 1973 he made his first trip to England to receive an honorary degree from the University of Sussex. During the 1970s programs based on his memoirs and his book on Tolstoy were shown on Soviet television, and in 1973–74 he was honored by the publication of a three-volume edition of his collected works. Of his seminal work during the 1920s, however, nothing except a sanitized version of *Zoo* was included. If ever conditions in the Soviet Union permit a more objective assessment of early

twentieth-century literature, Viktor Shklovsky will be recognized as a central figure of that period. The revolution which he led against hackneyed language, form, and thought, strenuously resisted though it was, has made a lasting contribution both to Russian and world culture.

WORKS IN ENGLISH TRANSLATION: English translations of Shklovsky's critical writings include "Art as Device," in *Russian Formalist Criticism*, edited by L. T. Lemon and M. J. Reiss, 1965; "The Connection between Plot Devices and General Stylistic Devices," in *Russian Formalism*, edited by S. Bann and J. Bowlt, 1973; and articles on Sterne, Pushkin, and Bely in *Review of Contemporary Fiction*, 1981–1983. His book *About Mayakovsky* was translated by Lily Feiler in 1940, reissued as *Mayakovsky and His Circle*, 1974. Richard Sheldon translated his novelized autobiography *A Sentimental Journey*, 1970, and his novels *Zoo, or Letters Not About Love* (presumed to be based on his relationship with the Russian-born French writer Elsa Triolet), 1971, and *Third Factory*, 1977. Sheldon also published *Viktor Shklovsky: An International Bibliography of Works by and About Him*, 1977. Olga Shartse translated his *Lev Tolstoy* in 1978, and a translation of *Eisenstein* appeared in 1973.

ABOUT: Bann, S. and J. Bowlt, Russian Formalism, 1973; Bennet, T. Formalism and Marxism, 1983; Columbia Dictionary of Modern European Literature, 1980; Erlich, V. Russian Formalism: History, Doctrine, 1955, 1975; International Who's Who, 1982–83; Lemon, L. T. and M. J. Reisse, Russian Formalist Criticism, 1965; Matejka, L. and K. Pomorska, Readings in Russian Poetics: Formalist and Structuralist Views, 1971; Medvedev, P. N. and M. M. Bakhtin, The Formal Method in Literary Scholarship: A Critical Introduction; Pomorska, K. Russian Formalist Theory and Its Poetic Ambience, 1968; Thompson, E. M. Russian Formalism and Anglo-American New Criticism 1971. *Periodicals*—New York Times December 20, 1984; Russian Literature Tri-Quarterly, Winter 1972; Slavic Review March 1975; Slavic and East European Journal Spring 1968; Times Literary Supplement October 15, 1971.

SHU CH'ING-CH'IN *See* LAO SHE

SHULMAN, ALIX KATES (August 17, 1932–), American novelist, writes: "I was born in a suburb of Cleveland, Ohio, a place where traditional sex roles were so deeply ingrained as to constitute a kind of destiny. By the middle of high school, seeing my friends fast rushing to become housewives and mothers as soon as possible after graduation, I began to wonder how to escape our collective destiny for a life of my own choosing. What life? I had no idea; and without an understanding of how our destiny arose I

ALIX KATES SHULMAN

could hardly hope to evade it. Still, I dreamed. During my college years in Cleveland, I became a serious student—of history, literature, philosophy—and came to believe that if I were ever to fashion my own life, it would have to be outside the midwest. Upon graduation from college at twenty, I left Cleveland for New York City, enrolling in the Graduate School of Columbia University to study philosophy.

"I soon discovered that the pressures I fled were not restricted by geographical boundaries. The following year I married a graduate student; I began working at a number of jobs from bank clerk to research assistant to encyclopedia editor; I divorced, remarried, had two children. Although I continued to do free-lance editorial work while my children were small, I came increasingly to feel that by electing to have children I had given up, however reluctantly, the possibility of any large alternative satisfactions in my life.

"Nevertheless, as soon as both children entered nursery school, leaving me with two and a half 'free' hours a day, I began writing stories. In 1967 I became involved with the fledgling women's liberation movement in New York City. Those were heady times: a new generation was ardently questioning traditional social and political values in every quarter of American society. The radical feminist ideas we were developing in our small discussion groups gave me an understanding of my life and society that fueled my writing and ultimately, by giving me both a subject and an audience, enabled me finally to create a life of my own choosing.

"In my fiction I have tried to portray some of

the prototypical predicaments facing American women in our time, with their many contradictions and binds. *Memoirs of an Ex-Prom Queen,* my 1972 comic novel about coming of age in the fifties, depicts the impossible fate of a white, middle-class midwestern girl who grows to womanhood trying to be everything an ideal woman was expected to be before the women's movement—sexy prom queen, beautiful wife, devoted mother. But nothing works out as expected. *Burning Questions* is the story of another kind of woman, a self-styled rebel whose political awakening in the late sixties transforms her. At once a political and historical novel, spanning four decades including the activist sixties and the backlash seventies, *Burning Questions* attempts to portray the important changes in women's lives and consciousness wrought by contemporary feminism.

"In *On the Stroll* I tried to capture two more prototypes of the ongoing female predicament among the contemporary range of possibilities: the shopping-bag lady, wandering homeless through the streets, and the teenage runaway, prey to all the dangers of the city. Of course, homeless women, young and old, have always been among us, but I think it is only recently that the images of the runaway and the bag lady—alone, poor, abandoned, yet somehow survivors—have entered contemporary consciousness as powerful symbols of what many women fear may lie in store for them at a time when traditional family supports for women and children are fast disappearing. In my novel I tried to explore the meaning and reality behind those symbols."

Alix Kates Shulman is the daughter of Samuel S. and Dorothy Davis Kates. She graduated from Bradford Junior College in 1951 and from Western Reserve University in 1953. She did graduate work in philosophy at Columbia (1953–55) and in mathematics at New York University (1960–62). She took an M.A. in humanities from N.Y.U. in 1978. In the late 1960s she was a founding member of Redstockings, an early radical feminist group. She now lives with her family on Washington Square in Greenwich Village, New York City.

Shulman's first novel, *Memoirs of an Ex-Prom Queen,* had a considerable underground reputation in feminist circles even before it was published. It is the story, told in the first person, of Sasha Davis and her passage through the perilous shoals of childhood and young adulthood. Lucy Rosenthal called it "a break-through book, innovative both in its rendering of the feminine experience and in its quite perfect marriage of thesis to art." It catalogs and dramatizes in a careful, humorous, yet essentially serious way the entire list of feminist complaints about female subjugation by acculturation in Western society. P. S. Prescott wrote that it "suggests a pattern imposed by the way we live and learn, by the values prepubescent girls learn to cherish: 'Boys are taught it is weak to need a woman, as girls are taught it is their strength to win a man.'" To Rosenthal the book's strength as an exemplar lies in the fact that "a woman can read it with the keen pleasure and astonishment that come from seeing what one believed were her own private thoughts and secret experiences set down on paper." Marylin Bender, however, considered that Sasha as "female victim" was "too much of a pushover." "When she boasts, at twenty-four, of having surpassed her own record of a lover for every year of life, poignancy evaporates. Yes, sisters, the struggle has been hard and unequal. But must you give up so easily?"

Burning Questions is about Zane, who shares much of Sasha's middle-class, middlewestern background and many of her feminist problems, but is considerably more conclusive in her analysis of her plight, and experiences a convincing rebirth as a self-respecting feminist by the end of her story. "It is bliss," wrote Angela Carter, "to read a novel in which the heroine is a better, nicer, wiser and kinder person after having come to consciousness as a woman (though this is usually true in real life), and one in which that coming to consciousness has nothing to do with the quality of her orgasms but everything to do with the quality of her rationality." For Alden Whitman, the novel is sustained by the "intensely lifelike creation of Zane, a woman who chooses to join up with history in the form of feminism without losing her new-found identity as a woman and a person." The book elicited some very unfavorable reviews as well, notably one by Pearl K. Bell, who thought it "almost tempting" to read it as "hilarious caricature, sly mockery of the radical feminist dedicated to a fault. But . . . it is all straight from the heart, sentimental, doctrinaire, and intellectually preposterous . . . the sort of tract that could set back the cause of women's equality some fifty years and more. All unwitting, Mrs. Shulman has invented a heroine so irredeemably self-absorbed and simpleminded, so resentful and credulous, that she reinforces precisely those myths about women that she set out to demolish."

Three poor, lonely, tired characters form the core of Shulman's third novel, *On the Stroll*: an elderly bag lady called Owl, a sixteen-year-old runaway called Robin, and the pimp, Prince, who picks up Robin as she gets off the bus from Boston and "turns her out" as a "ho" who is "on the stroll"—the latter a slang term for Manhattan's 42nd Street and the area surrounding the Port Authority bus terminal. Owl is Shulman's most memorable fictional creation, a deeply pathetic woman who keeps her entire life by her side arranged (or disarranged) in a series of shopping bags. "What should she do with this burdensome treasure, this monument to her life? . . . For what had she stalled her death if she couldn't pass them on, share their meaning, see one face light up with understanding looking into her bags?" She feels on first seeing Robin that the girl must be a reappearance of her daughter Milly, who rejected her years before, and she dedicates her life to rescuing her, making her her spiritual heir. Anatole Broyard thought this "a selfless, careful and satisfying book" which is saved from "bathos, or a documentary earnestness" only by the author's skill at character delineation. Mary Cantwell made the point, applicable to Shulman's other novels, that "what actually happens" in the book "is comparatively unimportant. The plot is sufficient to give Mrs. Shulman's story a shape, but the book's strength lies in its portraits of Prince, Robin and Owl and the evocation of the blasted landscape through which these wanderers move." Yet some reviewers found the novel's feminist assumptions unconvincing. "But what is it all about?" asked Mary Kathleen Benet. "The tone is dispassionate, didactic; here is no Dickens or Zola, indicting society for allowing such things to happen. Even Shulman's feminism, her previous crusade, is muted here: it just goes without saying that in the past of each of these unhappy characters is a brutal or irresponsible man. Original sin is firmly located in the male psyche, but she doesn't insist on the fact, merely treats it as if we have known it all along." To Benet, the novel "remains a miscellany, never unified by passion, pathos, or a compelling point of view."

Shulman has written several juvenile and non-fiction books, most notably *To the Barricades: The Anarchist Life of Emma Goldman,* and is the editor of two volumes of Goldman's selected writings and speeches. She is a frequent essayist and reviewer on feminist themes, and has taught fiction at various academic institutions, including New York and Yale universities.

PRINCIPAL WORKS: *Novels*—Memoirs of an Ex-Prom Queen, 1972; Burning Questions, 1978; On the Stroll, 1981. *Non-fiction*—To the Barricades: The Anarchist Life of Emma Goldman, 1971; (ed.) The Traffic in Women and Other Essays by Emma Goldman, 1970; (ed.) Red Emma Speaks: Selected Writing and Speeches by Emma Goldman, 1972. *Juveniles*—Bosley on the Number Line, 1970; Awake or Asleep, 1971; Finders Keepers, 1971.

ABOUT: Contemporary Authors 29–32, 1978; Contemporary Literary Criticism 2, 1974 and 10, 1979. *Periodicals*—Atlantic May 1978; Book World May 14, 1972; Harper's August 1978; Library Journal February 15, 1972; April 15, 1978; Nation April 15, 1978; New Republic May 13, 1972; New York Times September 16, 1981; New York Times Book Review April 23, 1972; March 26, 1978; September 27, 1981; New Society June 21, 1979; New Yorker April 10, 1978; Newsweek May 1, 1972; Saturday Review May 20, 1972; Times Literary Supplement July 1, 1983.

SHU SHE-YÜ *See* LAO SHE

L. E. SISSMAN

SISSMAN, L(OUIS) E(DWARD) (January 1, 1928–March 10, 1976), American poet, essayist, and advertising executive, was born in Detroit, Michigan, the son of Edward James Sissman, an advertising man who was in the field of commercial art, and the former Marie Anderson, described in a poem by Sissman as having been at one time an actress and stage performer and then a pianist. Because he was much younger than his half brother, Sissman was brought up as an only child, reading widely and developing what were to prove lifelong interests in cars, military history, and machinery of all kinds. After winning the National Spelling Bee in Washington at the age of thirteen and then becoming a temporary Quiz Kid on national radio at fifteen, he graduated from a private school in Detroit in 1944 and entered Harvard University at the early age of sixteen. Rusticated from Harvard for disciplinary reasons in 1946, Sissman collaborated with a group of college friends a year later in the founding of *Halcyon,* a short-lived literary magazine. When he returned to the university, he was encouraged in his poetic efforts by his teachers, John Ciardi, Andrews Wanning, and Theodore Morrison. His first, brief marriage in 1948 was followed in 1949 by graduation cum laude from Harvard as Class Poet and recipient of the Garrison Poetry Prize.

For the next three years, Sissman worked in New York City publishing houses—first as copy editor at Prentice-Hall, then as production manager for A. A. Wyn (now defunct)—but he decided to return to Boston, of which he considered himself an "adoptive son," and settled there permanently. After serving on John F. Kennedy's senatorial campaign staff in 1952, he began a highly successful career in advertising, moving from the firm of John C. Dowd (1953–

56) to Kenyon & Eckhardt (1956–72), where he held the positions of senior writer and supervisor and later creative vice-president, and finally to Quinn & Johnson, where he was creative vice-president from 1972 until the end of his career. As an advertising man, he wrote copy and designed campaigns for banks and insurance companies, as well as for civic and charitable organizations, winning an award in 1969 for his publicity promoting a Cardinal Cushing Charity Fund event. In 1958 he began a happy marriage to Anne Bierman, and the couple, who had no children, eventually made their home in the suburb of Still River, Massachusetts.

Having failed to publish any poetry during the four years following his graduation from college, Sissman gave up writing verse for the next ten years. In 1963, at the age of thirty-five, he decided "it was then or never" to make a serious attempt at producing and publishing his work. Beginning with short nature poems, he progressed to sonnets, sonnet sequences, and longer poems, increasingly using personal experiences as his subject matter. Describing the development of his individual style in October 1970 in the *Writer,* Sissman characterized his tone as "dry, amused, analytical. . . . The style made use of impacted bits of diction—sharp and smooth edges of language thrown together in such a way as to create a fresh impression of sound. . . . To this I added dialogue, mimicry of sounds, parody of and allusion to other poets of every period." In the second edition of *Contemporary Poets,* he further defined his poetic intentions: " . . . I write traditional, scanning, stanzaic verse, with special emphasis on iambic pentameter and the couplet. My poems tend to be long, segmented, exceedingly specific evocations of my time and place; I hope to achieve some sort of universality by wedding colloquial, allusive contemporary language to traditional form. I experiment both with language and with time sequences and often invent words based on existing roots."

In shaping his own poetic voice, Sissman, while much impressed by Yeats and Eliot, took Auden as his principal model. His essay on Auden, included in his collection *Innocent Bystander,* relates that the Harvard undergraduate felt a kinship of interests with the older poet, was fascinated by his subject matter, and admired both his mastery of traditional forms and his versatility of style. Other early influences on Sissman, mentioned in his statement for *Contemporary Poets,* were Shakespeare, Milton, Donne, Herbert, and Pope. In addition, "The Constant Rereader's Five-Foot Shelf," an essay in *Innocent Bystander,* lists a large number of favorite poets whose work Sissman periodically reread, including Dryden, Swift, Gay, Blake, Wordsworth, Coleridge, Keats, W. S. Gilbert, Hopkins, Cummings, Stevens, Ransom, Hart Crane, Robert Lowell, and Philip Larkin.

In 1964 Sissman began to publish his poems in the *New Yorker,* where fifty-one of them eventually appeared. His verse appeared in other magazines as well, including *Harper's* and the *Atlantic.* In 1969 his literary career expanded to include the writing of book reviews for the *New Yorker,* and the next year he started contributing to the *Atlantic* a monthly column, "The Innocent Bystander," containing personal reminiscence, social and political observation, and literary commentary. The *New Yorker* obituary later stated that these reviews and essays "showed wide reading, a crisp fund of unexpected information, an avidity for the mundane, an even temper, and a truly benevolent nature." This productive period also saw the appearance of three volumes of poetry in rapid succession—*Dying: An Introduction* in 1968, *Scattered Returns* in 1969, and *Pursuit of Honor* in 1971—to be followed in 1975 by a selection of essays published in book form as *Innocent Bystander: The Scene from the 70's,* with an introduction by John Updike.

Dying: An Introduction brought academic honors and public attention. Sissman was awarded a Guggenheim fellowship in 1968 and a grant from the National Institute of Arts and Letters in 1969, and he became Phi Beta Kappa Poet at Harvard in 1971. In 1969 an issue of *Business Week* carried an article about him entitled "Poet Doubles as an Adman," with a very similar piece

appearing the next month in *Newsweek* under the heading, "Boston's Adman-Poet." Placing him in the tradition of Whitman, William Carlos Williams, Edgar Lee Masters, and Wallace Stevens, American poets who also worked in business or the professions, the *Business Week* profile quoted Sissman as saying, "My mind is compartmentalized, and I separate my careers."

The title poem of his first published volume describes a harrowing personal experience that was to color his daily existence and his writing for the rest of his life. Diagnosed in 1965 as having Hodgkin's disease, a cancer of the lymph nodes, Sissman was at one time believed to be cured, but a recurrence in 1969 ultimately proved fatal. In "A Little Night Music: The Curvature of the Earth," the first of two essays on this subject originally published in the *Atlantic* in 1972, he recalled his initial response to the news of his illness: "Somehow, my personal home demonstration of the fleetingness of life redoubled my perception and enjoyment of its mutant shapes and shadows. Instead of a curtain falling, a curtain rose." This renewed appreciation of the world, which led to increased literary activity, was expressed in the last lines of "Dying: An Introduction":

Through my
Invisible new veil
Of finity, I see
November's world—
Low scud, slick street, three giggling girls—
As, oddly, not as sombre
As December,
But as green
As anything:
As spring.

By 1971, however, as Sissman wrote in "A Little Night Music: A Tangential Line," "the stoic mask had gone": "I have been looking down at the curvature of the earth, at the trajectory of my life and death, from a new perspective: from the perspective of a tangential line lifting, straight as a contrail, away from the earth and myself and all the other things and people." Contrasting Sissman with confessional poets like Sylvia Plath and Anne Sexton, Daniel Hoffman, in the *Harvard Guide to Contemporary American Writing,* has called him an autobiographical poet who treated illness and death with "perspective, detachment, humor."

Sissman's wit frequently manifested itself in literary allusion, as in his paraphrase of three lines from Wordsworth's "Composed upon Westminster Bridge": "This Sally now does like a garment wear/The beauty of the evening; silent, bare,/Hips, shoulder, arms, tresses, and temples lie. . . . " Anthony Hecht, reviewing *Dying: An Introduction* for *The Hudson*

Review, praised the effectiveness of this "Wordsworthian adaptation," which is part of "In and Out: A Home Away from Home, 1947," as well as the "wonderful and eloquent coherence" of the entire volume. However, reviewers like James Atlas and Jim Harrison objected to the traditional settings and style of the poems. Discussing *Scattered Returns* shortly after it was published, Atlas, in *Chicago Review,* again criticized Sissman's "literary posture," although he gave high praise to such individual poems as "A War Requiem" and "Patrick Kavanagh: An Annotated Exequy." Attacked by Steven Aronson, in *Poetry,* for the "urbane" personality and life-style it revealed, *Scattered Returns* was, on the other hand, commended by X. J. Kennedy, Walter Arnold, and others for its detailed depiction of people, places (mainly in Boston and New York), and the recent past. Duane Schneider even predicted "that someday Sissman will be considered one of the truly outstanding poets of our times" (*Library Journal*).

Pursuit of Honor received a number of favorable notices after its publication. Richmond Lattimore praised Sissman's prosody and content: "He has memories, scenes, stories, people, and he has the language for them" (*Hudson Review*). Marvin Bowers, in *Modern Poetry Studies,* admired Sissman's sometimes abstruse vocabulary and his craftsmanlike use of meter, assonance, alliteration, puns, hyperbole, and understatement, while Robert Regan cited "The Big Rock-Candy Mountain" in particular as a "human, compelling" work (*Library Journal*).

Not long after Sissman died in Boston in 1976, at the age of forty-eight, his unpublished verse began to appear in the *New Yorker,* the *Atlantic,* and the *Times Literary Supplement.* His collected poems were published in 1978 under the title *Hello, Darkness,* with a preface by Peter Davison, who described Sissman as "a long, slightly lopsided man, grave, formally dressed, extremely courteous, even owlish." The volume reproduced the texts of the first three books of poetry and added a posthumous section consisting of poems written mostly "between 1970 and the cessation of poetic capability" at the end of 1974.

Hello, Darkness occasioned a reassessment of Sissman's work, resulting in a new appreciation both here and in England. Accounting for Sissman's mixed critical reception during his lifetime, Hilton Kramer, in an admiring *New York Times Book Review* column, pointed out that "in neither his style nor his choice of subjects did Sissman conform to prevailing literary fashions." William H. Pritchard, reviewing *Hello, Darkness* for the *Times Literary Supplement,* noted that "Sissman's wryly intelligent hu-

mour . . . looked formally old-hat and insufficiently national or global in its aspirations" to many young people during the 1970s. Moreover, as Julian Symons remarked in his *Times Literary Supplement* review of the British edition of *Hello, Darkness,* "the confessional nature" of much of the poetry of the 1960s and the "general American tendency towards a loosening of forms . . . found no echo in his writing." In answer to Sissman's detractors, X. J. Kennedy stated, in *Parnassus,* that he used commercial names in his poems ironically, "as emblems of our culture," and, in his essays, deplored "whatever is slick, amoral, and shoddy." Furthermore, in a *Sewanee Review* article presenting the merits of Sissman's "middle-class nostalgia," D. E. Richardson observed that he was unusual in writing during the 1960s "poems that are really frank about bourgeois origins."

Sissman's personal courage and detached poetic treatment of his illness won praise from all these commentators, as well as from John Updike, writing in the *New York Times Book Review.* The last three poems in *Hello, Darkness*—"Homage to Clotho: A Hospital Suite," "Cancer: A Dream," and "Tras Os Montes"—have been considered especially remarkable. While acknowledging some flaws in Sissman's earlier style, Updike found that these final poems "grapple the unthinkable and the unbearable into bright, firm form."

PRINCIPAL WORKS: *Poetry*—Dying: An Introduction, 1968; Scattered Returns, 1969; Pursuit of Honor, 1971; Hello, Darkness: The Collected Poems, 1978. *Essays*—Innocent Bystander: The Scene from the 70's, 1975.

ABOUT: Contemporary Authors 21–24, first revision series, 1977; Contemporary Literary Criticism 9, 1978; Dictionary of Literary Biography 5, 1980; Hoffman, D. (ed.) Harvard Guide to Contemporary American Writing, 1979; Vinson, J. (ed.) Contemporary Poets, 1975; Who's Who in America, 1976–77. *Periodicals*—Atlantic May 1976; Business Week September 20, 1969; New England Review 1978; New York Times March 11, 1976; New York Times Book Review July 3, 1977; May 14, 1978; New Yorker April 5, 1976; Newsweek October 13, 1969; Parnassus Fall/Winter 1979; Sewanee Review Winter 1981; Times Literary Supplement July 28, 1978; October 24, 1980; Yale Review Spring 1979.

*SJOSTRAND, OSTEN (June 16, 1925–   ), Swedish poet and essayist, was born in Gothenburg. Robin Fulton, Sjöstrand's translator and editor, writes: "His father Oscar Sjöstrand, was a schoolteacher turned publisher and a man of considerable artistic and philosophical interests.

°shō´ stränd, ō´ sten

OSTEN SJOSTRAND

Leaving school in 1947, Sjöstrand attended lectures at Gothenburg University without taking a degree, but by this time he was already acquainted with literary circles, in Copenhagen as well as in Sweden, and was beginning his life's work as a writer. As readers with hindsight we can see that aspects of his earlier life which were to be important for his writing must include the following: his friendship with Professor Hans Pettersson, who stimulated his scientific interests, especially in oceanography; his early familiarity with the coastline landscapes of western Sweden; his discovery of French poetry and music, which inspired him to write himself; his marriage in 1949 to the author Ella Hillbäck (1915–1979) which ended in 1974 (he married Eva Furusjö in 1979); and his joining the Catholic Church in 1953.

"The influence of his travels is also evident in his poetry, for although for much of his adult life his home has been Stockholm, he has journeyed extensively in southern Europe: France, Italy, Greece, Yugoslavia, Turkey, Romania, Spain. His knowledge of the life and arts of such countries not only gave him material for the work he contributed to Swedish radio and a wide range of periodicals, but also in the long run gave him special qualifications for the positions which he came to hold from the mid-1970s onward. The most important three of these dating from 1975 are: membership in the Swedish Academy (he took over Pär Lagerkvist's chair), membership in the Nobel Committee of the Swedish Academy, and the editorship of Artes, a bimonthly magazine sponsored by the three academies and devoted to literature, art, and music. He has also

been actively involved in the Alliance Française, the Association Franco-Nordique pour les Echanges Littéraires, the Swedish National Committee for Cultural Cooperation in Europe, and the Confidencen Rediviva.

"Among his musical interests special mention should be made of his opera translations (including Gluck's Iphigenia in Aulis and Alceste, and Stravinsky's The Rake's Progress) and of the works on which he has collaborated with the Swedish composer Sven-Erik Bäck—Gästabudet (The Banquet), In Principio (In the Beginning), and I det yttersta (At the Outermost Edge). Among honors special mention should be made of his winning the Bellman prize in 1967.

"Sjöstrand's literary production has now reached considerable proportions, especially when we include his essays, translations, anthologies, and editorial work. His most personal and original work is of course his poetry. A 'Collected Poems' in 1958, Dikter 1949–55, gathered his earlier work; a selection in 1970 Ensamma stjärnor, en gemansam horisont (Lonely Stars, a Common Horizon) then gave a more up-to-date if selective view of his work into the late 1960s; and then a more substantial selection appeared in 1981, covering the years 1949 to 1979. The eleven individual volumes he has so far published range from unio in 1949 to Strömöverföring (Power Transmission, 1977).

"Perhaps the richest collection, one that most fully embodies his concerns up to the mid-1960s, and certainly may best serve the new reader, is I vattumannens tecken (In the Sign of Aquarius, 1967). The reader will sense how Sjöstrand's life-long interests in music and science and religion all contribute to his individual way of responding to, searching into, and making poetry out of his personal encounters with some very fundamental and traditional human dilemmas.

"Music, for instance, has been important to his poetry in many ways, most important of all being the manner in which a sense of rhythm is basic to the initial processes of writing. In an essay called 'What can a poet today learn from music?' collected in Fantasins nödvändighet (The Necessity of Imagination, 1971), he explains how he cannot regard rhythm as an exclusively musical element: 'rhythm touches something utterly secret within us, at the deepest personal level . . . the struggle between faith and doubt, the paradoxical meeting of opposites, can be resolved only through rhythm; through an underlying wordless rhythm.'

"His interest in science has not only provided him with ways of thinking about language, as we can see from his essay 'Have words lost their meaning in our time?,' collected in Världen ska-

pas varje dag (The World is Created Every Day, 1960), but, more important, it has contributed a fruitful dimension to his thoughts about human history. Staffan Bergsten has described such a dimension in this way: ' . . . for Sjöstrand the dematerialising of the world picture of physics has helped to open the door to such previously excluded guests as mysticism, religion, and metaphysics. In his search for images and symbols which can mediate this new unified view he has reached back to the past for intuitions and doctrines which proclaimed, in harmony with the knowledge and speculation of their time, the mutual connection and inner correspondence of man and nature. . . . '

"A deeply experienced religious sense can hardly be labelled as an 'interest' and clearly the work of a poet with such a sense is influenced by it at a very basic level: but as far as Sjöstrand's Catholicism and the way in which it has guided and stimulated much of his creative work are concerned, there is at least one aspect which can be mentioned, however briefly. That is his fascination with the syncretic and evolving nature of Catholicism: Christianity did not merely replace earlier religions but subsumed them and has shown a capacity not just to survive but to develop, like a continuing *opus* or process. The manner in which such a fascination can then give potency to things seen, thus transmuting them into poetic images, can be observed in such a remark of Sjöstrand's as the following, referring to the ancient buildings in Rome: they are 'like a palimpsest: a parchment or tablet which has been used over again, without the letters having been fully erased, so that you can still read the inscriptions from various periods. . . . One literally treads through the centuries, even in a religious sense, and it is impossible not to notice the enormous variety, multiplicity, and difference; yet in religious terms there is an overall unity—a useful *collected* human experience.' (From the conversation with Lief Sjoberg printed in *Poetry East.*)

"The range of reference, geographical, historical, and intellectual, drawn upon by Sjöstrand is considerable: it is wider and deeper than that which most other contemporary Swedish writers are able or wish to draw upon (although one could name some exceptions, such as Gunnar Ekelöf and Kjell Espmark). For that reason alone his work has never fitted the kind of literary categories which from time to time have been current in Swedish literary life: this could well have delayed recognition but, on a level more important than that of literary politics, his work has been in touch with sources and ideas that cannot but be regarded as central to a European tradition and in the long run such a writer is bound to be regarded as much less of an outsider than those of his contemporaries who, by cultivating more partial or peripheral interests, achieved more immediate but also more temporary (perhaps merely temporary) recognition.

"And because Sjöstrand draws on such a rich field of reference and association, there is clearly much exploration waiting for the new reader. Yet there is a vital sense in which this exploration belongs to the background, for both the poet and his readers: the best of Sjöstrand's work has a new and personal music which subsumes and surpasses whatever we can say about its sources. The journeys in his poems are his own spiritual journeys, and we get a strong feeling of the poems living on his nerve-ends. His simplest images, wherever they originate, can appear with all the more concrete vividness for their being invested with a compulsive sense of not owing their existence simply to what we see of them, however clearly."

WORKS IN ENGLISH TRANSLATION: Östen Sjöstrand's principal English translator and editor is the poet Robin Fulton, who translated *The Hidden Music* in 1975. Selections from his work appear in *Modern Swedish Poetry in Translation,* edited by G. Harding and A. Hollo, 1979.

ABOUT: Bergsten, S. Östen Sjöstrand, 1974; Columbia Dictionary of Modern European Literature, 1980. *Periodicals*—Mosaic 4 1970; Poetry East 1980; World Literature Today 55 1981.

*SKVORECKY, JOSEF (September 27, 1924–), Czech novelist, short story writer, and scenarist, writes: "I was born in Náchod, Bohemia, Czechoslovakia. My father was a bank clerk and chairman of the local Sokol Gymnastic Association, a patriotic organization. Consequently he was arrested and jailed by both the Nazis and the Communists. I graduated from the local *realgymnasium* in 1943, worked for two years in the Messerschmitt factories in Náchod and Nové Město under the *Totaleinsatz* scheme, then was drafted into the *Organisation Todt* for trench-digging duty, from which I defected in January 1945. For the remaining months of the war I worked in a cotton mill.

"After the war I studied for one year at the Medical Faculty of Charles University in Prague, then at the Philosophical Faculty from which I graduated in 1949, and received a doctorate in American philosophy in 1951. In 1950–51 I taught at the Social School for Girls in Hořice v Podkrkonoší, then did two years of military service with a tank division stationed in the Mladá military camp near Prague—the camp

°shquǒr et´ ske

JOSEF SKVORECKY

where the Soviet army of Occupation has its headquarters now. From 1948 I was a member of the Prague underground circle of Jiří Kolář, the avant-garde artist and poet; other members included Bohumil Hrabal (author of *Closely Watched Trains*); Jan Rychlík, the composer and author of the first Czech book on jazz theory; Věra Linhartová, the experimental fiction writer; and Jindřich Chalupecký, the theoretician of modern art. As a member of this circle, and as a frequent visitor at the meetings of the semi-illegal Prague surrealist group in the apartment of the painter Mikuláš Medek, I became known to the non-establishment *littérateurs* of the early '50s.

"The first novel (my third) I offered to a publisher, *The End of the Nylon Age,* was banned by the censors before publication in 1956. After my second novel had come out in 1958—*The Cowards,* written ten years earlier—I was fired from my editorial post on the magazine *World Literature.* The book was banned and seized by the police; the editors responsible for it were dismissed—including the editor-in-chief and the director of the Čs. Spisovatel Publishing House; the affair developed into a major literary scandal and was used as a pretext for one of the most extensive purges of the Prague intellectual community.

"However, the political climate was changing slightly, and after five years I was able to publish *Legenda Emöke,* a novella which, though criticized by the Party, became one of the major publishing successes of the mid-'60s. Nevertheless, I continued to be closely watched and, for example, was not admitted to the Czechoslovak

Writers Union until 1967 and then only through a back door: I was elected chairman of the Translators' Section, and as such was automatically coopted. In 1968 I became a member of the Central Committee of the Writers Union, and earlier also a member of the Central Committee of the Film and Television Artists Union.

"My last novel to be published in Czechoslovakia was *Miss Silver's Past* (1968—rejected in 1967 by the director of the Mladá fronta Publishers who had replaced his purged predecessor), the second printing of which (80,000 copies) was ordered destroyed in 1970, together with the plates of another novel of mine, *The Tank Corps.* In the '60s I collaborated with some major Czech film directors of the New Wave. A script I had written with Miloš Forman (director of the films *One Flew Over the Cuckoo's Nest* and *Hair*), entitled *The Jazz Band Has Won,* was personally banned by the then President of the Republic, Antonín Novotný, because it was based on my short story 'Eine kleine Jazzmusik,' itself banned two years earlier, together with the whole first issue of the 'Jazz Almanach.' For Oscar-winning Jiří Menzel (*Closely Watched Trains*) I wrote two scripts which Menzel made into successful feature comedies: *Crime in a Girls' School* and *Crime in a Night Club.* For Evald Schorm I wrote *End of a Priest,* which represented Czechoslovakia at the Cannes Film Festival in 1969 and is in distribution in North America.

"I received two literary awards in Czechoslovakia: in 1965 the Annual Prize of the Czechoslovak Writers Union for Best Translation, for William Faulkner's *A Fable* (translated in collaboration with P. L. Doružka), and in 1967 the Annual Prize of the Publishing House of the Czechoslovak Writers Union for the Best Novel, for *The End of the Nylon Age*—the book first banned in 1956 which finally came out after eleven years; sixteen years after I had written it.

"After the Soviet ambush in 1968 I and my wife, Zdena Salivarová, a singer, actress (the film *The Party and the Guests*), and novelist (*Summer in Prague*), left for Canada where I eventually became Professor of English and Film at the University of Toronto. In the ten years I have spent in Canada I have written and published more works of fiction and non-fiction than in the twenty years of my writing life in Czechoslovakia. Together with my wife I also founded a Czech-language publishing house, the Sixty-Eight Publishers Corp., which started operations in 1971 and has to date published more than seventy books by such leading Czech authors, living both in exile and at home, as Milan Kundera (*The Joke; The Farewell Party*), Václav

Havel (*The Memorandum*), Ludvík Vaculík (*The Guinea Pigs*), Pavel Kohout (*Poor Murderer, The White Book*), Heda Kovályová and Erazim Kohák (*The Victors and the Vanquished*), and many others. My own book, *The Bass Saxophone* was described by at least two critics as the best fiction on jazz ever written.

"In Canada I received a Canada Council Senior Arts Grant during the tenure of which I wrote a novel, *An Engineer of Human Souls*. In the U.S.A. I was elected Honorary Member of the Mark Twain Society in 1975 for my novel *Miss Silver's Past*. In West Germany my radio play *The New Men and Women* was nominated 'Play of the Month' in June 1978. In 1980 I received the Neustadt International Prize for Literature, and in the same year I was appointed Fellow of the John Simon Guggenheim Memorial Foundation for writing a novel about Antonín Dvořák's American sojourn, *Scherzo capriccioso*. I finished the novel in 1982."

Josef Škvorecky, who writes in both his native Czech and in English, began his literary career as a translator of American writers (Henry James, William Faulkner, Ernest Hemingway, Ray Bradbury). American culture figures in his first published novel *Zbabělci* (translated as *The Cowards*) in which Danny Smiricky, his young hero-narrator, much influenced by American films and jazz, observes the farcical but ultimately tragic efforts of provincial officials in his small town to play the local Communist sympathizers against the Nazi occupation forces. In spite of his own defiance of the Communist Party, Škvorecky continued to write and publish. By the mid-1960s he was an influential literary figure in Czechoslovakia, widely admired not only for his novels but also for his short stories, his writings on jazz, and his detective stories. His non-fiction book, *Nápady čtenáře detektivek* (1965) was a critical study of the detective-story genre.

Although several of Škvorecky's short stories were translated into English during the 1960s, he remained little known outside his own country until the publication of *The Cowards*. Hailed in the *Times Literary Supplement* as "a major Czech novel," the book was a moving and dramatic record of the profound social pressures exerted by the U.S.S.R. on the nations occupied by Soviet troops. *Miss Silver's Past* was a scathing satire on the Czech publishing world, which cynically conformed to Communist Party pressure. His *Emöke*, with its portrait of a ruthless and opportunistic Czech schoolteacher, was published with *The Bass Saxophone*, another novella in

which jazz itself (and the young hero's longing for a bass saxophone to play in a small jazz orchestra) becomes a metaphor for human freedom and the desire for self-realization.

The jazz-loving Danny Smiricky, now middle-aged and a professor of English at a college in Toronto, reappears in *The Engineer of Human Souls* (a term used by Stalin to describe writers). The formidable subtitle, *An Entertainment on the Old Themes of Life, Women, Fate, Dreams, the Working Class, Secret Agents, Love and Death*, sets the tone for this sprawling, witty, yet fundamentally serious novel. Danny's past— his youthful encounters with the Nazis in Czechoslovakia, his love affairs, his experiences with his fellow emigrés—and his present life mingle in flashes of scenes, "almost an embarrassment of riches," Robert Towers wrote of it. Its variety, what Eva Hoffman calls "its playful inventiveness," gives *Engineer* a breadth of vision far beyond its subject matter. A "novel of ideas," in perhaps the old-fashioned sense of the phrase, the book is both Škvorecky's own story (he says that Danny "is an autobiographical figure, a mix of reality and wish-fulfillment") and, as D. J. Enright describes it, "a Bible of Exile."

Škvorecky's prose style is poetic and evocative, consisting of long sentences with, Russell Davies writes in the *Times Literary Supplement*, "clauses suspended into infinity while huge parentheses rumble by." It communicates both the nostalgia and the bitterness of a writer who has seen his native country suppressed by an alien totalitarian force. "To me," Škvorecky wrote in a foreword to the English translation of *The Bass Saxophone*, "literature is forever blowing a horn, singing about youth when youth is irretrievably gone, singing about your homeland when in the schizophrenia of the times you find yourself in a land that lies over the ocean, a land—no matter how hospitable or friendly—where your heart is not, because you landed on these shores too late."

WORKS IN ENGLISH TRANSLATION: English translations of Joseph Škvorecky's novels include *The Cowards* by Jeanne Němcová (1970), *Miss Silver's Past* by Peter Kussi (1970), *The Bass Saxophone* by Kaca Polaskova-Henley (1977) and *The Engineer of Human Souls* by Paul Wilson (1984). His personal history of the Czech cinema of the 1960s, *All the Bright Young Men and Women* (1971), was written in both Czech and English. *The Mournful Demeanour of Lieutenant Boruvka*, a collection of Škvorecky's short stories, was translated by Rosemary Kavan, Kaca Polackova, and George Theiner in 1973. His short stories are also included in *Czech and Slovak Short Stories*, edited by J. Němcová, (1967), and *New Writing in Czechoslovakia*, edited by G. Theiner (1969).

ABOUT: Columbia Dictionary of Modern European Literature, 1980; Contemporary Authors 61–64, 1977; Encyclopedia of World Literature in the 20th Century IV, 1975; French, A. Czech Writers and Politics, 1945–66–69, 1982; Liehn, A. J. The Politics of Culture, 1972. *Periodicals*—Dissent September–October 1970; New York Review of Books November 19, 1970; September 27, 1984; New York Times June 5, 1983; July 23, 1984; August 9, 1984; New York Times Book Review August 19, 1984; Publishers Weekly June 22, 1984; Times Literary Supplement June 23, 1978; World Literature Today Autumn 1980.

SMITH, MARTIN CRUZ (MARTIN WILLIAM SMITH) (November 3, 1942–), American novelist, was born in Reading, Pennsylvania, the second child of jazz saxophonist John Calhoun Smith and singer Louise Lopez Cruz Smith, an Indian activist of mixed Hopi-Yaqui ancestry. Smith's childhood was spent in Reading and the reservation areas of New Mexico. Despite his parents' hopes that he would study music, he went to the University of Pennsylvania to study sociology. Having failed statistics, Smith graduated in 1964 with a degree in creative writing. He supported himself after college with a variety of writing jobs—reporter for the *Philadelphia Daily News*, stringer for the Associated Press, editor of action and sex stories (many of which he wrote himself under such pseudonyms as Simon Quinn, Jake Logan, Martin Quinn, Nick Carter) for Magazine Management, publishers of macho magazines—and even a stint as a Good Humor ice-cream man.

Smith left Magazine Management in 1968, the year he married a fellow University of Pennsylvania student, professional chef Emily Arnold. Writing pseudonymously, he began churning out dozens of paperbacks, mysteries, Westerns, action-adventures, even the occasional sex novel. He earned a meager living—Smith claims to have bounced thirty-seven checks in one month—but, as he has said, "Paperbacks are the place to learn the craft. . . . I wrote an awful lot under tremendous presssure. I learned to write constantly, to simplify the narrative, to throw out the adjectives."

Though formulaic, these novels were not merely hackwork. Smith's first, *The Indians Won* (under the name Martin William Smith), a revenge fantasy in which the Indians, having won the wars of 1876, are ready to attack the present United States, drew verisimilitude from his own boyhood experiences. Two of his suspense series attracted some critical attention and showed Smith's ability to turn solid research into an unusual feeling for exotic worlds: the "Inquisitor" series (*His Eminence Death, Nuplex Red, The Last Time I Saw Hell*, etc., all under

MARTIN CRUZ SMITH

the name Simon Quinn), featuring Francis Xavier Kelly, a modern-day executioner for the Vatican's (now abolished) Holy Office of the Inquisition; and two mysteries centered on the New York gypsy subculture, *Gypsy in Amber* and *Canto for a Gypsy*. Of the latter books, Newgate Callendar wrote: "Roman Grey, the antiques dealer who is the hero of Smith's series is to the gypsy world what Harry Kemelman's David Small is to Judaism. Both solve crimes that confront them; both are walking encyclopedias about their people and their way of life and thought. And all this is not supererogatory; it is germane to the mystery at hand and helps to solve it. . . . Smith is a smooth operator. He plots well, maintains tension, and creates believable characters. There is an underlying menace in his books that hints at the racial subconscious."

Smith's first commercial success was *Nightwing* (1977), a grisly supernatural thriller with an Indian background. Hopi deputy Youngman Duran's only friend on the reservation, ancient medicine man Abner, decides to end the abuse of the Hopi by whites and Navajos by destroying the world with an elaborate spell. Duran, no believer in the old ways, pays little heed until he has to investigate a series of gruesome and inexplicable murders, beginning with Abner's own. With the help of an obsessed medical investigator and Duran's lover, a white woman, he discovers that a horde of vampire bats are not only responsible for the killings but are spreading a plague epidemic that could drive man from the Southwest. To end the threat Duran is forced to confront his own Indian identity;

in saving the present world he sacrifices the Hopis' last chance for revenge and renewal. According to Walter Clemons, writing in *Newsweek,* Smith enlivened yet another example of the disaster novels so popular at the time with "a fresh locale, arresting social detail about whites and Indians and a truly sickening ability to portray death in desert country. . . . The wipe-out of human life in the Western desert is averted, but the possibility seems very real: the bats and fleas have much greater vitality than the human characters. The leathery rustle of wings becomes unnerving; the activity of fleas under a microscope provides one of the book's best scenes. An imperfect thriller, *Nightwing* is a nightmare of natural history." *Nightwing* was nominated for an Edgar by the Mystery Writers of America and was later made into a mediocre film.

The royalties from *Nightwing* allowed Smith to continue work on *Gorky Park,* a novel he had been researching for five years. Originally inspired by a *Newsweek* article on the Soviet forensic pathologist M. M. Gerasimov, a specialist in recreating the faces of long-dead murder victims, the book was to follow the partnership of an American and a Russian detective in Moscow. But a two-week research trip to the USSR in 1973, during which he spent a scant five days sketching locations in the capital, inspired Smith to use only a Russian hero, to the dismay of his publisher, G. P. Putnam and Sons. That his story would be told from the Russian perspective was, however, the essential innovation that was to make *Gorky Park* a best-seller. Smith checked his own impressions of Soviet life against the recollections of several Russian emigrés, and used New York libraries to fill in other details. Heavily promoted by Random House, the publisher Smith selected after buying back the rights from Putnam, *Gorky Park* sold some 100,000 copies within a few months of its publication in 1981.

Most reviewers agreed that with *Gorky Park* Smith left the realm of the hack novelist to join the ranks of such British masters of the stylish novel of intrigue as John Le Carré, Eric Ambler, and Len Deighton.Peter Andrews wrote in the *New York Times Book Review,* "Just when I was beginning to worry that the large-scale adventure might be suffering from a terminal case of the Folletts, along comes *Gorky Park* . . . , a book that reminds you just how satisfying a smoothly turned thriller can be. Mr. Smith fulfills all the requirements of the adventure novel and then transcends the genre." Moscow police inspector Arkady Renko, Smith's protagonist, is nonetheless cast directly from the classic mold of the heroes of such books. He is singularly honest, a craftsman in his field, and at the deepest level

an idealist; inevitably he ferrets out the truth, but, enmeshed in a dishonest system and beset by professional and personal betrayals, he is nearly crushed for his efforts. As Renko follows the trail of a very un-Russian murderer who has left three bizarrely mutilated bodies in Moscow's Gorky Park, he gradually discovers that he is being used as a pawn by the KGB, the FBI, and Osborne, a wealthy American fur dealer who is a personification of capitalist corruption. Smith's narrative drive, skillful characterizations, and convincing portrait of life in the Soviet capital outweighed, for the majority of critics, the book's unlikely plot twists and disappointingly conventional ending—a bloody shootout between Renko and Osborne on Staten Island. On the whole, wrote John Dunlap in the *American Spectator,* "Mr. Smith's dramatic stitching is astonishing plausible—neatly tailored to the grim reflections of Solzhenitsyn and the grimly hilarious observations of Voinovich. It takes quite an imaginative leap, but, given the suppleness of the human spirit and the imbecility of the police state, a character like Chief Investigator Arkady Renko follows. . . . In a totalist police state, the ordinary policeman is no less oppressed than the hapless citizen, and one of the minor feats of *Gorky Park* is that it exposes—incidentally and therefore powerfully—the very core of the totalitarian social order: a system that tacitly encourages its captive people to hate each other."

Unsurprisingly, *Gorky Park*'s worst review appeared in the Soviet press. Kirill Senin, writing in *Literaturnaya Gazeta,* sarcastically referred to the novel as "rubbish," which, were it presented to a Moscow publishing house, would cause the author to be "shove[d] out by the scruff of his neck, even at the risk of subsequent explanations to the police." An effort to subvert detente, Senin claimed, was behind *Gorky Park*'s expensive promotional campaign and reviewers' efforts to raise the novel "to the top of the American literary Olympus." Continued Senin: "Portraying Osborne as a complete scoundrel, Martin Cruz Smith discredits all supporters and friends of detente. This, apparently, was what appealed to the bosses of the book business—and hence the uncontrolled publicity boom around an empty space."

Smith currently lives in New York City with his wife and three children. *Gorky Park* was made into a film by Michael Apted and released in 1983.

PRINCIPAL WORKS: (As Martin William Smith): The Indians Won, 1970; Gypsy in Amber, 1971; Canto for a Gypsy, 1972; The Human Factor, 1975; (as Simon Quinn): His Eminence, Death, 1974; Nuplex Red, 1974; The Midas Coffin, 1975; Last Rites for the Vulture, 1975; The Last Time I Saw Hell, ca. 1975; (as Martin Cruz Smith): Nightwing, 1977; The Analog Bullet, 1978; Gorky Park, 1981; Stallion Gate, 1984.

ABOUT: Contemporary Authors, new revision series 6, 1982; Contemporary Literary Critics 25, 1983. *Periodicals*—American Spectator September 1981; New York Review of Books June 11, 1981; New York Times November 10, 1981; New York Times Book Review, January 21, 1973; September 7, 1980; April 5, 1981; May 3, 1981; Newsweek December 5, 1977; May 25, 1981; People May 25, 1981; Publishers Weekly March 20, 1981; Time March 30, 1981.

© Thomas Victor

RED SMITH

SMITH, RED (WALTER WELLESLEY)

(September 25, 1905–January 15, 1982), American columnist and sportswriter, was born in Green Bay, Wisconsin, the second of three children of Walter Philip Smith and the former Ida Richardson. His father owned a wholesale produce and retail grocery business. As a child, Smith camped, hiked, and fished, developing a lifelong love of the outdoors. Although he was not an athlete, he became a devotee of sports and an avid fisherman; his favorite spectator sport was horse racing.

Smith majored in journalism at the University of Notre Dame and after graduating in 1927 worked for the Milwaukee *Sentinel* as a reporter. He then became copyeditor, and ultimately sportswriter on the St. Louis *Star,* where he remained until 1936, when he moved to the Philadelphia *Record* as sports columnist with his own byline. Smith's columns for the *Record* brought him to the attention of the New York *Herald Tribune,* for which he began writing a column, "Views of Sports," in 1945. Syndicated in more than ninety newspapers, he became, after the death of Grantland Rice in 1954, the most widely read sportswriter in the United States. The column survived the demise of the *Herald Tribune,* and in 1971 Smith joined the sportswriting staff of the *New York Times* for which he wrote four, and then three columns a week until a few days before his death. He was also a contributor to some of the country's leading magazines, including *Sports Illustrated,* the *Saturday Evening Post,* and *Collier's.*

Smith, who was one of the most literate of American sportswriters, collected his columns into several books. His prose style was the work of a man who insisted that he wanted only to be "a newspaper stiff" but wrote with the passion and dedication of an inspired poet. "What made him famous," Wilfrid Sheed observed in a review of his last book, *To Absent Friends,* "was his phrasing. In Smith's world, coaches didn't just tear their clothes, they rent their haberdashery;

his team not only overwhelmed their opponents but occasionally underwhelmed them or just plain whelmed them." His readers included people with no interest in sports who appreciated his wit and style. Some of his columns have been used in college English courses as models of clear, graceful writing, and he served on the advisory board of the *American Heritage Dictionary.*

Essentially a storyteller (John Leonard wrote that Smith "was to sports what Homer was to war"), Smith respected his craft. "Sports is not really a play world," he said. "I think it's the real world . . . games are a part of every culture we know anything about. . . . It's no accident that of all the monuments left of the Greco-Roman culture, the biggest is the ball park, the Colosseum, the Yankee Stadium of ancient times. The man who reports on these games contributes his small bit to the record of his time." Dave Anderson, Smith's sportswriting colleague on the *New York Times,* considered integrity his "most important attribute"—citing his demand in 1980 for a boycott of the Moscow Olympics because of the Soviet Union's invasion of Afghanistan. Unlike some of his contemporaries, however, Smith shunned the prophetic-professorial role. He took sports seriously but not solemnly: "I'm just writing about games that little boys play." Nevertheless, his sports column often had the sting of the moralist-satirist. In a piece on the cheating scandal involving the All-American Soapbox Derby in 1973, written at the height of the national scandal of Watergate, Smith moved smoothly from Nero's bribery and intimidation of competitors in the Roman games to the current political scene: "There is little enthusiasm in this corner for moralizing, yet it is hard to shake off a suspicion that our national preoccupation with winning leads to many excesses. . . . We have had painful reminders of the tragic effects of a victory-at-any-cost attitude in an election campaign. Now we see what it can do to children."

In 1976 Smith won the Pulitzer Prize for "Distinguished Commentary," the committee praising his work as "unique in the erudition, the literary quality, the vitality and the freshness of viewpoint." He had earlier (1956) received the Grantland Rice Memorial Award for outstanding sportswriting. He was a small man, who described himself as "a seedy amateur, with watery eyes behind glittering lenses, a retiring chin, a hole in his frowzy haircut." A chain smoker, he was known for his quick movements and his taste for sports jackets. Warm and generous, he always had time for young would-be sportswriters, dispensing stories and advice freely. Recalling his own long career in what proved to be his last column for the *Times*, "Writing Less—and Better," he pointed out that he had, in earlier days, written seven columns a week: "Between those jousts with the mother tongue, there was always a fight or football match or ball game or horse race that had to be covered after the column was done. I loved it."

Smith was married twice—in 1933 to Catherine Cody, who died in 1967, and in 1968 to Phyllis Warner Weiss. He had two children by his first wife. His homes were in New Canaan, Connecticut, and Martha's Vineyard.

PRINCIPAL WORKS: Sports Stories, 1949; Out of the Red, 1950; Views of Sport, 1954; Red Smith on Fishing Around the World, 1963; The Best of Smith, 1963; Strawberries in Wintertime, 1974. *As editor*—Press Box: Red Smith's Favorite Sports Stories, 1976; The Red Smith Reader, 1982; To Absent Friends, 1982.

ABOUT: Current Biography, 1959; Contemporary Authors 77–80, 1979; Who's Who in America, 1980–81. *Periodicals*—New York Review of Books September 23, 1982; New York Times, January 16, 1982; Newsweek April 21, 1958; Time May 15, 1950.

*SOLOUKHIN, VLADIMIR (ALEKSEYEV-ICH) (June 14, 1924–), Soviet Russian fiction writer, poet, and essayist, was born to a peasant family in the village of Alepino in the Vladimir district. After finishing technical school, he served in the Soviet Army from 1942 to 1946, when he entered the Gorky Institute of Literature. In 1951 he began work as correspondent and essayist for the magazine *Ogonyok*. The fol-

VLADIMIR SOLOUKHIN

lowing year he joined the Communist Party and since 1967 has been chief editor of the journal *Molodaya Gvardia*.

Soloukhin's first publication dates from 1946, when a poem appeared in the newspaper *Komsomolskaya Pravda*. His early poems show the influence of Svetlov, Simonov, Lugovskoy, and the lyrical poetry of the World War II era. Strangely enough, there is comparatively little reflection of the war in his poetry of this period. He clearly preferred the themes of love and nature. The early love lyrics reveal the main qualities of Soloukhin's poetic persona: he is generally the passive victim of his beloved, who torments him and discards him, but whom he dreams of seeing again anyway. Nature, by contrast, is mother and friend, a healer of his suffering and pain. Nevertheless, the theme of tormentor and victim carries over into the nature poetry, where man is the tormentor and nature the victim. In one poem people are stripping the unripe fruit from a roadside apple tree. The tree addresses them as follows:

Leave at least one apple
to hang on me till September.

You men will find out
That my apples are fine
When not taken by force,
When I drop them myself.

—trans. D. Woodruff

For Soloukhin the poet's task is to hear nature's groan, its prayer addressed to man. But he is also painfully conscious of the barbarity within nature itself. The world of nature has its own anthropomorphic martyrs, and the poet is quick to come to their aid when he can. For him a piece

°so lyōō´ kin, vlä dyē´ mir

of wood in a campfire is not simply burning itself out, it is dying in agony, and he "saves" it by keeping it aflame ("I Look upon a Dying Fire . . . "). A sea gull that has somehow strayed into a forest finds itself surrounded by hostile pines ("The Gull").

In the late forties and early fifties, Soloukhin wrote poetry in which he tried to combine his inherent lyricism with purely political motifs ("Fellow Countrymen," "It Happened in 1920," "The Party Membership Card"). These poems were most probably required student work, of a sort unavoidable for anyone at the Gorky Institute of Literature. In them one senses precisely the strong influence of Simonov and Lugovskoy. In the fifties and sixties Soloukhin's evolution as a poet proceeded in two directions. First, he freed himself from the uncharacteristic politicization of his verse, partly as a result of the revelations concerning Stalin's abuse of power and the changed atmosphere in the country that followed. Secondly, he concentrated more and more on his favorite theme, the conflict between man and nature. His first philosophical verse dates from 1960, and includes such poems as "The Threads Are Fastened in a Knot," "The Head," "How to Drink the Sun," and others from the collection *Imeyushchii v rukakh tsvety* (The Man with Flowers in his Arms, 1962). For these poems Soloukhin adopted a form of free verse not far from prose, a choice with numerous precedents in the history of Russian philosophical verse. In the world of this limited group of poems, nature is no longer the victim of man's barbarity, but a great mysterious laboratory, where man feels himself a timid learner.

Beyond the philosophical verse with its universal conclusions, however, man becomes a frightful force which threatens the world of nature. Soloukhin no longer hopes, as he did before, that man will listen to nature. A tragic break has taken place, and the process of mutual alienation is irreversible. Significant in this respect is a poem from the collection "Argument" (1972), "The Animals Flee from Me."

I go through the forests, parting the green branches,
I go through the meadows, parting the green grasses,
I go through the earth, parting the transparent air,
I am the same as tree, or cloud, or water,—
But the animals flee from me in horror,
The animals scatter from me in horror.
What a pity. What misfortune!

—trans. D. Woodruff

In "Argument" there are also two wreaths of sonnets, entitled "Georgia" and "A Wreath of Sonnets." Soloukhin wrote that he had long intended to test his technical mastery on this complicated form, which consists of fifteen thematically unified sonnets, each of whose first lines repeats the last line of the one preceding, while the fifteenth consists of the first lines of the other fourteen. This same collection includes translations from the Bulgarian of Liliana Stefanova and Blaga Dimitrova. Soloukhin translates Stefanova quite often, apparently attracted by the subtle intimacy of her lyrics.

It may be that the collection *Sedina* (Gray Hair, 1977) is Soloukhin's best, because in it he overcomes a certain strain of infantilism in his earlier verse and does not project childhood sorrows on universal problems, interpreted apocalyptically. Instead he chooses a classical, time-tested basis for poetic reflection: the relation between individual human life and the constant, eternal world of nature, which forms the background against which that life proceeds. In the following passage there are traces of a mother-child relationship, but there are no tormentors or victims. The false pathos of infantile philosophizing has given way to deep, steady feeling.

This whole worls grows hazy like a fable,
In the distance the battle of life grows faint.
We are left alone, the sky and I,
I on the earth and the sky above me.

And before the light of consciousness goes out
In my eyes,
I would if only I could
Be just one instant alone
With the countenance of the universe bending over me.

—trans. D. Woodruff

Soloukhin's achievements in prose—fiction, essays, literary criticism—are far more striking than in his poetry. He has characterized himself as a writer who describes what he has actually experienced, rather than one who relies primarily on fantasy and imagination, and it is sometimes impossible to distinguish sketch from story or essay from tale. His many stories and short novels are autobiographical, as a rule, introducing various incidents from his life and then revealing their symbolic significance. He says that life is the best storyteller.

Soloukhin first gained wide renown for the long story "Vladimirskie prosyolki" (Vladimir Country Roads, 1958; translated as: *A Walk in Rural Russia*), in which he recounts a journey he made to the region where he was born and raised, describing in detail the countryside around Vladimir and the life of its villages, while introducing a great many conversations with various people. Much of the story's success can be explained by Soloukhin's subordination of an abstractly ideological understanding of "motherland" to the traditional one. The story's great significance was that new Soviet man was returning to his roots, to the soil which had nourished him for a thousand years. Soloukhin offered the reader a new hero, one who would have been unthinkable during the Stalin era. By seeking his roots in the history of his native land rather than in the history of the Party, this hero narrows the gap between city and country that has been a constant feature of Soviet history.

Soloukhin extended the success of "Vladimir Country Roads" with another long story "Kaplya rosy" (The Dew-drop, 1960), in which he describes in detail the inhabitants of his native village, Alepino. He does not merely celebrate the beauty of the country landscape or the work of the collective farmers, however, but criticizes the village as well. He tells how the country dweller runs off to live in the city, how ancient folkways are nearly forgotten, and how fights and drunkenness are commonplaces of village life. The men are quick to kill any wild animal without considering its value to nature a a whole. To get at cones which they can sell, they are capable of cutting the branches off a fir and so destroying a fine large tree. The theme is that the country people are degenerating, losing their sense of beauty and feeling for the land, taking to drink and turning savage in spite of television sets and other attributes of modern civilization. He shares this theme with another Soviet writer, Vasily Shukshin, who felt the degradation of the Russian village just as keenly.

The relations between man and nature occupy as large a place in Soloukhin's prose as in his poetry. He cannot imagine living without frequent trips which afford him the kind of contact with nature that is well known to Russian readers from the works of such nineteenth-century classics as Sergei Aksakov and Turgenev. In three poetic nature sketches, "The Third Kind of Hunt," "The Grigorov Islands" and "Grass," Soloukhin discusses mushrooms and the art of gathering and preparing them, fishing, the varieties of herbs and their medicinal characteristics. The poetic quality of these studies is combined with interesting and useful information. Along with other Soviet writers like Prishvin and Paustovsky, he is consciously continuing the tradition of Sergei Aksakov, whom he considers the founder of this genre in Russian literature. "Beautiful Adygene" is the story of Soloukhin's climb up a Kazakhstan mountain, whose Greek name is "Adygene." He recounts his many impressions on what for him is a rather unusual journey. As always, contact with nature is valued both in itself and as a source of moral experience. The long story "The Sentence" is devoted to a sort of journey as well. It is not a journey to a forest, however, nor to a distant river, nor in search of mushrooms, but a journey into self. Soloukhin describes what he went through when doctors discovered that he had a cancerous tumor. The theme of life and death is developed with pointed drama.

Soloukhin's novel *Mat-i-machekha* (Coltsfoot) was published in 1966. Its title is the name of a wild flower, but it literally means "mother and stepmother" and refers to the hero's ambivalence about his country, which is both a loving mother and a hateful stepmother. Structurally the novel is a chronologically consecutive narrative of the life of Mitya Zoloshkin, starting with his village childhood and going on to his military service and study at the literary Institute. The theme of the novel is the ever-present threat of Russian society—arrest and imprisonment. The father of the girl Mitya loves is arrested, as is his best friend, and the drama of the story arises when Mitya himself is summoned by the secret police to implicate his friend.

Soloukhin's essays and sketches are marked by his concern for the cultural heritage of his country. He has performed a great service to Russian culture by focusing popular attention on the neglect of Old Russian painting. In 1969 the journal *Moskva* published his long non-fictional narrative "Chernye doski" (Black Boards; translated as *Searching for Icons in Russia*), with the subtitle "Notes of a Beginning Collector." Soloukhin maintains here that the art of the icon fully and profoundly reflected everyday Russian life, as well as its spiritual side. By providing an endless variety of profound subjects, the Bible expressed the icon's "literary" aspect, thus permitting the painter to concentrate on artistic problems. Moreover, it was always possible to incorporate local Russian color into the biblical subject, and so in fact the painter's freedom was unlimited. In the first chapter he relates how at the home of friends he unexpectedly learns that icons can be restored privately, not just in museums. The icon's beauty, emerging from what had seemed a "black board," makes a collector of him. He travels once more around his native Vladimir region, this time in search of the past. The trip leads him to the conclusion that the culture of the Russian people has been destroyed. With exaltation and bitterness he tells of astonishingly beautiful churches barbarously demolished and quantities of icons destroyed during the consolidation of Soviet power. Though he never speaks directly, it seems clear that Soloukhin thinks the new order has been unable to replace the culture it destroyed with anything as valuable. In one of the strongest episodes, an old woman, muisunderstanding the writer's intentions, is afraid that he wants to carry off an icon of the Mother of God; she shouts angrily that he and the others have mocked the icons long enough, that she remembers how they took axes to them. (He based one of his finest poems, "The Fairy Tale," on this incident.)

Here Soloukhin is developing ideas already

expressed in "Pisma iz russkogo muzeya" (Letters from the Russian Museum, 1966), an essay in which he attacks the prestige of genre painting in Soviet art, the preference accorded the "literary"—here meaning the social—side of art over the purely artistic, and implicitly condemns the nineteenth-century Russian school of painters called "The Wanderers," with their tendency to darken Russian reality and present it as culturally and intellectually disreputable and impoverished. He also proposes to enlarge the range of paintings on display in the Russian Museum, to expose the Soviet viewer to masterpieces now hidden away in storerooms, including modernist works as well as icons. He sharply condemns the destruction of churches in and around Moscow. In place of architectural masterpieces, he writes, one now sees only characterless modern constructions or empty squares. Once uniquely beautiful, Moscow has been turned into a faceless, architecturally mediocre city. He also criticizes the mania for renaming cities: knowledge of the past and historical memory are effaced along with the old names. Not surprisingly, "Letters from the Russian Museum" was strongly criticized in an article which appeared in *Oktyabr*, the literary journal that most closely follows the official line, describing Soloukhin as "a prisoner of preconceived ideas and arbitrary schemata."

The essays collected in *Vremya sobirat kamni* (A Time to Gather Stones Together, 1980) are devoted to the "literary places" of Russia, the places where such leading writers as Derzhavin ("A Visit to Zvanka"), Sergei Aksakov ("Where Aksakov Lived"), and Blok ("Bolshoe Shakhmatovo") lived. Soloukhin writes of the neglect these places have suffered and the red tape that may surround them even after they have been declared national preserves. While bureaucrats exchange letters, old parks fall into decay, houses are destroyed, and family graveyards disappear. In "Where Aksakov Lived" Soloukhin tells how as recently as 1960, Sergei Aksakov's well preserved old house was demolished. The title sketch, "A Time to Gather Stones Together," is devoted to the fate of the Optina Pustyn monastery, now in ruins, which before the revolution attracted pilgrims from all over Russia, including Gogol, the Kireevsky brothers, Dostoevsky, and Tolstoy. In discussing the dilapidated, ruined monastery, Soloukhin bitterly quotes from a reader's letter: " . . . we search for traces of extraterrestrial civilizations, and obliterate the traces of our own."

Much of Soloukhin's literary criticism, replies to letters from readers, and remarks on writers and artists, was collected in 1965 in *Sliricheskikh pozitsii* (From Lyrical Positions) and *Slovo*

zhivoe i mertvoe (Words Living and Dead). In an article published in the literary weekly *Literaturnaya Gazeta* (1958) Soloukhin had criticized the poet Evgeny Yevtushenko for his pro-western stance. Later ("Beautiful Adygene") he confessed that he felt ashamed of the article, presumably because he had attacked a fellow writer and because his own views had moderated in the meantime. In "An Angry Poetry Lover" he defended another poet, Andrei Voznesensky, from the attacks of a reader to whom Voznesensky's poetry seemed elitist. "Ilya Glazunov and his Painting" is Soloukhin's positive response to an artist whom many Soviet intellectuals consider a prime example of successful, time-serving conformism. In "What to Make of the National Culture Movement," Soloukhin maintains that the cultures of the various Soviet peoples must differ in national coloring but be one in their socialist world outlook. This seemingly contradicts the author's ideas about a Russian spiritual revival, which could hardly be compatible with atheistic socialism.

Soloukhin belongs to the generation of Soviet writers who came to the fore during the so-called "thaw," the relatively liberal period after Stalin's death. By the end of the 1960s the regime had decided once and for all against a more democratic Soviet society. This presented many writers of principle with the problem of reconciling their consciences with the ideological pressure of the regime. Soloukhin was no exception. Apparently his article "What to Make of the National Culture Movement" represents one of the compromises with which a writer must pay for the chance to express his more important ideas.

WORKS IN ENGLISH TRANSLATION: There are translations of two of Soloukhin's novels—*A Walk in Rural Russia*, by Stella Miskin, 1967, and *White Grass*, by Margaret Wettlin, 1977—and of a number of his short stories in collections, including D. Martin's *Sentenced and Other Stories*, 1983, V. Mikhailovich's *White Stones and Fir Trees*, 1977, and K. M. Cook's *Spring of Light*, 1974. His short stories have also appeared in the journal *Soviet Literature* in September 1960, February 1963, January 1964, February 1972, October 1976, and December 1982. His important non-fiction book *Searching for Icons in Russia* was translated by P.S. Falla, 1971; some of his shorter prose pieces are in *Soviet Literature* October 1959, October 1961, April 1972, October 1977, May 1979. Selections from his poetry are published in V. Markov and M. Sparks' *Modern Russian Poetry*, 1967, and in C. and E. Proffer's *Ardis Anthology of Recent Russian Literature*, 1975. There are also poems in *Soviet Literature* June 1980 and November 1981.

ABOUT: Brown, D. Soviet Russian Literature since Stalin, 1978; Columbia Dictionary of Modern European Literature, 1980; Encyclopedia of World Literature in the 20th Century III, 1971; International Who's Who 1983–84; Penguin Companion to European Literature 2, 1969; Prominent Personalities in the USSR, 1968; Slonim M. *Soviet Russian Literature*, 1977. *Periodicals*—World Literature Today Autumn 1978; Winter 1981.

GILBERT SORRENTINO

SORRENTINO, GILBERT (April 27, 1929–), American novelist and poet, writes: "I was born in Brooklyn, New York. I attended the public schools of the City of New York, and went to Brooklyn College. My education was interrupted by two years of service in the Army, after which I returned to Brooklyn College, but left without a degree. I began to write in about 1948. I have little to say about my work outside of what, one hopes, the work itself says. My life is, I should think, singularly uninteresting, and is centered on my family and my writing."

Gilbert Sorrentino's brief note does not detail the long struggle he had to become a professional writer. Brooklyn-born (to August E. and Ann Davis Sorrentino) and Brooklyn-educated, he supported himself with variety of jobs—packer, shipping-room supervisor, insurance company employee—while writing poetry and a vast novel which he eventually considered "hopeless" and abandoned. During this period, from 1956 to 1960, he was also editor and publisher of *Neon* magazine, whose contributors included William Carlos Williams, Hubert Selby, Jr., and Leroi Jones. In the early 1960s, Sorrentino served in various editorial capacities for *Kulchur,* a magazine that brought together a diverse group of writers from the Black Mountain School, the New York School, and the Beats, loosely united in their opposition to the poetry and fiction of the period. From 1965 to 1970, Sorrentino was an editor at Grove Press, an experience that further enlarged his acquaintance with avant-garde writing.

Sorrentino's first volume of poetry, *The Darkness Surrounds Us*, was published in 1960, and was followed later in the decade by *Black and White* and *The Perfect Fiction*. William M. Robins has described his early poetry as "black in tone, disciplined and tight in form, opaque in allusion, transcendant in intent." In *Black and White* and *The Perfect Fiction*, indebted to Robert Creeley and Wallace Stevens, Sorrentino writes as an "urban and interior" poet with a sense of reality as an "artificial" construct, able to give form to experience—but only momentarily. Richard Howard called *The Perfect Fiction*, which contains fifty-two poems of three-line

stanzas whose sentences lead from one poem to the next, "a yearbook of dissatisfactions," intentionally depressing in its effect. Duane R. Schneider, in assessing Sorrentino's esthetics, called attention to the large intellectual range of the poems and the bleakness of reality, as Sorrentino sees it, from which the poet cannot free himself.

Sorrentino's first novels, *The Sky Changes* and *Steelwork,* reflect his concerns as a poet, since their vision of life is both abstract and gloomy. In *The Sky Changes,* after seven years of marriage, a husband and wife, with their two children, pull up roots in New York and set out by car for Mexico. They are accompanied by another man, apparently the wife's lover. Very little happens, but in the course of the narrative the nature of their unfulfilled lives is painfully revealed. The pace and tone of the novel are deliberately down-beat, even numbing, suggesting, through various locales and on different levels of time, the entrapment of the characters. In an interview, Sorrentino said of the novel, whose chronology is scrambled, that "the past, the present, the future are mixed together in order to show very clearly that there is really no past that is worse than the present and there is no future that will be better than the present. I wanted to create a world that was black and without hope."

Steelwork takes place in a single setting, the Brooklyn neighborhood where Sorrentino grew up. The novel is often evocative, as Sorrentino creates vacant lots, poolroom legends, brawls, and neighborhood tragedies, but his disgust with the meanness and cruelty of life as it was lived there colors the narrative. Once again Sorrentino uses a scrambled chronology; ninety-six distinct but interlocking dramatic vignettes, spanning the years between 1935 and 1951, appear out of order. Shaun O'Connell remarked that "Sorrentino is at times too much under the sway of that other chronicler of Brooklyn lives, Hubert Selby. . . . Like Selby, Sorrentino sees a world circumscribed by unrelieved frustration and senseless violence. . . . But if the vision of *Steelwork* is, in the end, somewhat circumscribed and pat, there is more than enough included in Sorrentino's flexible style and inventive narrative to redeem his novel—artful, compressed and striking."

Imaginative Qualities of Actual Things, completed while Sorrentino was still an editor at Grove Press, draws from his experience of the avant-garde art and literary world in New York in the 1960s. Often sharply satiric, it punctures the illusions and pretensions of writers, painters, and hangers-on in the arts. Each of its chapters is devoted to a particular character, but the novel is filtered through the mind of the narrator, who digresses, tells anecdotes, provides comic "lists," and even informs the reader that his characters are "unreal" and not worth troubling about. *Imaginative Qualities of Actual Things* made a stronger impression than Sorrentino's earlier novels, and at its best has a delightful comic gusto. Reviewers generally enjoyed Sorrentino's humor—"savage, caustic, whimsical, and bitchy," as J. M. Warner called it—but felt that his parade of defeated characters who were not to be considered "real" did not quite make a wholly satisfactory novel.

After leaving Grove Press to devote himself to writing, Sorrentino held a number of interim academic posts, teaching at Columbia University in 1960, the Aspen Writers Workshop in 1967, Sarah Lawrence College in 1972, and the New School for Social Research from 1976 to 1979. Recognition of his work increased, and he was awarded a Guggenheim fellowship for 1973–74, and a National Endowment for the Arts grant for 1975–76 and again 1978–79. During the 1970s, he published new volumes of poetry, including *Corrosive Sublimate, Splendide-Hôtel, White Sail,* and *The Orangery,* which received generally favorable reviews. *Splendide-Hôtel,* a collection of fantasies or baroque prose poems wreathed about the letters of the alphabet from A to Z, draws its title from Rimbaud. Hayden Carruth called it a "discussion, in the form of an extended personal essay on motifs from Rimbaud and Williams, of the role of the poet in history and civilization." Its primary subject is the poet's isolation, his engagement in time at the moment of creation but "ultimate discontinuity with the world." This theme also runs through *White Sail,* in which Sorrentino's poems tend to

be "pure unto themselves," and to present figures "isolated out of time." *White Sail* also contains Sorrentino's first group of "orange" poems, later elaborated in *The Orangery,* a collection of short poems based on the sonnet form, each a variation on "orange." Wide-ranging, with surprising observations and moments of feeling, blending the serious with the humorous, *The Orangery* struck reviewers as a collection of poems with an unusually rich texture. The playfulness of the volume is symptomatic of the change taking place in Sorrentino's poetry of this time.

Playfulness is immediately noticeable in Sorrentino's novel *Mulligan Stew.* An "experimental" novel, and parody of "irrealist" or "sur-fiction," *Mulligan Stew* focuses on a writer, Anthony Lamont, as he attempts to write a novel whose characters attempt to "escape" from the artificial structures he has imposed on them. They even step forward at times to complain bitterly of Lamont as a "hack." To complicate matters, Lamont's notebooks, scrapbooks, and letters are introduced. Poor Lamont comes ever closer to psychic collapse as publishers send "comic" rejection letters, and a professor at first shows an interest in his work and then abandons him. Reviewers noted the influence of Joyce and Flann O'Brien, but in general praised the book, regarding it as one of the more notable comic novels of the 1970s.

Since *Mulligan Stew,* Sorrentino has published a new volume of verse, *Selected Poems, 1958–1980,* which marks, in the more recent poems, a new growth in his talent; and three novels, *Aberration of Starlight, Crystal Vision,* and *Blue Pastoral. Aberration of Starlight* concerns a Brooklyn family vacationing in New Jersey in 1939: Marie McGrath Recco, a youngish divorcée who is caring for her aging father; her ten-year-old son, Billy; a suitor, who might enlarge Marie's life; and Mr. McGrath, now enjoying the power he exerts over his daughter. Using a series of short narratives, letters, cathechism of questions and answers, and internal monologues, Sorrentino lays bare a world in which desire is thwarted by convention. Sad, whimsical, and humorous, it deals with "common people thinking common thoughts." It received generally favorable reviews, but some critics felt that Sorrentino's technical virtuosity attracted attention at the expense of his characters.

Crystal Vision deals with a crowd of Brookyn layabouts, from teen-agers to elderly alcoholics, overheard in a candy store, in bars, on street corners, and in letters and soliloquies as they tell stories about themselves, one another, and the neighborhood—ultimately to reveal the irredeemable barrenness of their lives. William Pritchard complained that "the voices all seem the same—this is Sorrentino's monochromatic voice talking—and so the men and their stories become murky and blur." J. D. O'Hara commented that Sorrentino patronized his characters, and was rehearsing an old theme once too often. *Blue Pastoral* received more enthusiastic reviews. Joel Conarroe called it "a wild and crazy book, lavishly inventive, full of surprises, sometimes exasperating, often exhilarating." The plot itself is a peripheral concern: a man named "Blue" Serge Gavotte and his wife drag their pushcart across America in search of the notes that will constitute the "Perfect Musical Phrase." More important are the virtuoso set pieces—a political oration, a fundamentalist sermon, parodies of everything from scholarly footnotes to country lyrics. Ray Sawhill, although admiring Sorrentino's effects, felt that *Blue Pastoral* "grows tedious . . . because the story interests [Sorrentino] as little but a display case for his [parodic] skills."

Sorrentino, who teaches at Stanford University, has received several awards and honors, including the John Dos Passos prize in 1981. He has been married twice, to Elsene Weissman, from whom he is divorced; and to Vivian Victoria Ortiz. The Sorrentinos have three children, a daughter, and two sons.

PRINCIPAL WORKS: *Fiction*—The Sky Changes, 1966; Steelwork, 1970; Imaginative Qualities of Actual Things, 1971; Splendide-Hôtel, 1973; Mulligan Stew, 1979; Aberration of Starlight, 1980; Crystal Vision, 1981; Blue Pastoral, 1983. *Poetry*—The Darkness Surrounds Us, 1960; Black and White, 1964; The Perfect Fiction, 1968; Corrosive Sublimate, 1971; White Sail, 1977; The Orangery, 1978; Selected Poems: 1958–1980, 1981.

ABOUT: American Poets Since World War II, 1980; Contemporary Authors 77–80, 1979; Contemporary Literary Criticism 3, 1975; vol. 7, 1977; Contemporary Novelists, 1982; Dictionary of Literary Biography 5, 1980; Vinson, J. (ed.) Contemporary Poets, 1980; Who's Who in America 1982–83. *Periodicals*—Grosseteste Review 1, 1973; Nation August 21, 1972; January 1982; New Republic August 30, 1980; Newsweek July 4, 1983; New York Times Book Review July 2, 1972; November 8, 1981; June 19, 1983; Review of Contemporary Fiction 1, 1981; TLS April 24, 1980; May 2, 1980; December 4, 1981; Vort Fall 1974.

SOTO, GARY (April 12, 1952–), American poet, was born in Fresno, California, and received his primary schooling there. He took a bachelor's degree from the California State University in Fresno (1974) and a master of fine arts

GARY SOTO

degree in creative writing from the University of California at Irvine (1976). Soto is a Chicano, and has apparently, from the personal evidence he offers in his poems, experienced many of the hardships that afflict his people in the western United States. He has been a field hand on the huge vegetable farms of California's San Joaquin Valley, and has worked in a tire factory in Fresno alongside illegal aliens from Mexico. In the early 1970s he began publishing poems in various reviews and magazines, including *Poetry,* the *Nation, Partisan Review,* and the *New Yorker.* In 1975 he won both a prize from the Academy of American Poets and the YMHA Discovery–the *Nation* award. For several years he has taught Chicano studies and English at the University of California at Berkeley. He is married, lives in Albany, California, and has a child.

The thirty-one lyrics in *The Elements of San Joaquin,* Soto's first collection, comprise in their entirety a gripping introduction to Chicano life. The San Joaquin Valley is the entire world of the poems—its endless fertility and the money that it begets, the families and friends who live and work in it and must come to terms with the hardness of their lives. Typical of the collection is the eight-part title poem, especially the first part of it, subtitled "Field":

The wind sprays pale dirt into my mouth
The small, almost invisible scars
On my hands.

The pores in my throat and elbows
Have taken in a seed of dirt of their own.

After a day in the grape fields near Rolinda
A fine silt, washed by sweat,
Has settled into the lines

On my wrists and palms.

Already I am becoming the valley,
A soil that sprouts nothing
For any of us.

The poem gives a good indication of the tenor of Soto's voice, which has not greatly varied throughout his several collections. It is angry, tough, ironic, and even suspicious, but it revels in life's richness, and the bitterness felt by the people he writes about is only recorded, rarely dwelt upon. His irony is a powerful weapon, never abandoned: it allows him a deep insight into the situations he describes and usually a compassionate conclusion. One critic commented on Soto's "fine sense of imagery and his ability to make the reader reflect on the inexorable processes of nature, on the interdependence of human beings, and on familial relationships." Another wrote that "his best poems are self-explanatory and as unadorned and unambiguous as the California desert he is so familiar with."

The Tale of Sunlight is composed of three groups of poems. The first group, about childhood, features a character called Molina, clearly the canny, resourceful persona already encountered in *The Elements of San Joaquin.* The second recounts travel adventures in Latin America and experiences with a *brujo,* a man of spiritual power. The third group consists of poems about Manuel Zaragoza, an unhappy man who owns a tawdry cantina but is able to imagine it and his life transformed by magical events.

The poems in *Where Sparrows Work Hard* seem less thematic and more spontaneous than those in the previous collections. They are mostly about life in and around Fresno, and at their best are more compressed and entire than any others Soto has written. He is often able to tell a complete story, including an ironic moral, in twenty lines or less, as in "Mexicans Begin Jogging," a stinging account of what is an everyday occurrence in many parts of the United States:

At the factory I worked
In the fleck of rubber, under the press
Of an oven yellow with flame,
Until the border patrol opened
Their vans and my boss waved for us to run.
"Over the fence, Soto," he shouted,
And I shouted that I was American.
"No time for lies," he said, and pressed
A dollar in my palm, hurrying me
Through the back door.

Since I was on his time, I ran
And became the wag to a short tail of Mexicans—
Ran past the amazed crowds that lined
The street and blurred like photographs, in rain.
I ran from that industrial road to the soft
Houses where people paled at the turn of an autumn sky.
What could I do but yell *vivas*

To baseball, milkshakes, and those sociologists
Who would clock me
As I jog into the next century
On the power of a great, silly grin.

Some critics have found Soto's plain style not at all appealing—one referred to a "monotonous prosody," a lack of extravagance, and "an understated style that fails to tap the power of understatement." There are also disturbingly frequent references throughout his work to routine cruelties committed on animals: "the cat dropped/By a .22, among/The slouched weeds/Of South Fresno"; "Flicking matches/Into a jar of flies, wingless/And frisking/Themselves empty"; "It was . . . Tuesday that I/Slapped a pillowcase/Of frogs against/A fence post, until/They grew silent." Yet his love for the people he writes about is absolutely evident: Alan Williamson has referred to his "vein of consolatory fantasy which passes beyond escapism into a pure imaginative generosity toward life." Soto is obviously still growing as a poet, and has been accorded by Williamson the limiting, even questionable title of "the most exciting poet of poverty in America to emerge since James Wright and Philip Levine."

In addition to a fourth collection of poems, *Black Hair,* Soto has also published a set of prose sketches, *Living Up the Street.*

WORKS: *Poetry*—Entrance: Four Chicano Poets, 1976; The Elements of San Joaquin, 1977; The Tale of Sunlight, 1978; Where Sparrows Work Hard, 1981; Black Hair, 1985. *Prose*—Living Up the Street, 1984.

ABOUT: Martinez, Julio A. Chicano Scholars and Writers: A Bio-Bibliographical Directory, 1977. *Periodicals*—Choice November 1977; January 1979; Library Journal March 1, 1977; Poetry March 1980.

STALLWORTHY, JON (HOWIE) (January 18, 1935–), English poet, translator of poetry, critic, and biographer, writes: "An eighteenth-century Stallworthy left his Buckinghamshire village to till the missionary field in the cannibal Marquesas Islands of the Pacific. His son went on to New Zealand as a sailor, worked there in a logging-yard, and climbed from the saw-pits into wood-pulp, newsprint, politics, and a seat in the cabinet. None of this was known to his great-grandson, born in London and brought up in Oxford during the Second World War. When I did discover it—and much more—in 1974, it helped explain me to myself and, incidentally, gave me my best poem, *A Familiar Tree.* I realized why, through the happiest of childhoods, I had an odd, exciting rather than disturbing, sense of not

JON H. STALLWORTHY

quite belonging in the middle-class world of my friends. My parents were New Zealanders, and their other world was always shimmering like a mirage at the edge of sight.

"Under my mother's Anglophile eye, I graduated from nursery rhymes—which she usually sang—to poetry, and by the age of seven was writing poems in the unshakeable belief that this was, and would remain, what I cared to do most. I was lucky to be at a school where any interest in anything was encouraged; where everyone was required to learn miles of poetry by heart; and where literature was taught by reading an author and then writing something in his or her manner. So by the time I left to go to Rugby, at thirteen, I had wrestled with Chaucerian couplets, Shakespearean sonnets, Housmanic quatrains, and knew that poetry was music and hard to write.

"At Rugby, I soon gave up every subject that had no intimate connection with literature, and munched my way through English—and some French—poetry like a calf through clover. I was writing poems all the time. They were very bad, but the *forms* of poetry were becoming second nature, and I was as comfortable in them as in my clothes. It would have been—and would now be—as unnatural for me to write in open forms as it would be for one of the heirs of Whitman to write in terza rima.

"My father was a surgeon, passionately concerned with the precision of his craft ('mistakes cost lives'), compassionately concerned with the lives of his patients, and in 1952 he was invited to lecture in Australia and New Zealand. My mother, my sisters, and I went with him—or, to be precise, went ahead by sea, while he flew after us—our migrant blood responding to a new rhythm, and the ports passed in sun-dazzled succession and the mirage drew nearer. On the voyage out and back I learnt more about 'the drunkenness of things being various' than I had in all the years before, and returned to Rugby, an impatient schoolboy, for one more term.

"In 1953 I exchanged the cloister for the barracks and, responding again to the magnetic tug of 'the round earth's imagined corners,' volunteered to spend my two years' mandatory National Service on the shrinking frontiers of the British Empire. Nigeria, its independence approaching, was an exciting country. My duties as a 2nd Lieutenant in the Royal West African Frontier Force were undemanding and, after the constraints of school, I found the new freedom intoxicating. I grew up. Only when the carousel had stopped and I found myself re-entering the cloister—as an undergraduate at Oxford—did I realize that for two years I had read nothing and written nothing. That omission was to some extent repaired over the years that followed. When it was time to leave and again earn my living, I joined the Oxford University Press, because I wanted to see more of the world and publish some of the world's best poets (which for more than a decade I did), while waiting for my own poems to emerge. Everything else that I have written since then—studies of Yeats' poetry, translations of Blok and Pasternak, a biography and an edition of Wilfred Owen—has been undertaken with one end in view: to prepare myself for the challenge of making great poems, should life ever offer that challenge.

"I came to Cornell in 1977 to further that preparation and also, if I'm honest, to preach—not my missionary ancestor's Book of Life, but literature as a book of lives all too easily forgotten in an advanced technological society."

———

A critic and student of Russian and Polish poetry, the writings of W. B. Yeats and many other twentieth-century poets, Jon Stallworthy was nevertheless best though somewhat startlingly described by a reviewer of his collection *A Familiar Tree* as "a Wordsworthian poet." Readers of his poignant, warmly humane and simply but fastidiously phrased poems will appreciate the comparison. Underlying all Stallworthy's work is a theme that he finds articulated in Tolstoy's *War and Peace*: "The movement of humanity, arising as it does from innumerable arbitrary human wills, is continuous." His vision of life is not one of flux, "a stream of random sense impressions most faithfully recorded by the stream-of-consciousness method," but of a natural cycle, with "patterns of recurrence." Thus home, family, roots, and tradition figure prominently in his poetry. In *A Familiar Tree* he traces his family's history from his ancestor in eighteenth-century England who went out to the Marquesas as a missionary, down to his own marriage and the births of his children:

Let me go down to them and learn
what they learned on their journeys
And in the looted cavern
of the skull, let me restore
their sight, their broken speech, before
from these worn steps or steps like these
speechless to the speechless I return.

The volume includes Stallworthy's most frequently anthologized and certainly most moving poem, "The Almond Tree," in which he welcomes the birth of his first son—"my best poem!"— only to learn from the doctors that "your son is a mongol":

How easily the word went in—
clean as a bullet
leaving no mark on the skin,
stopping the heart within it.

With time and nurturing love, the child grows and Stallworthy writes in "The Almond Tree Revisited" of "my light-headed son" at seven:

He looks up, wondering why
we've stopped to see a pink cloud cross
the untroubled blue of his eye
° ° °
I stand in your shadow again
troubled with loss: the loss of power,
not his, but mine, the poet's an-

cient power of giving praise and honour:
in gratitude, blessing a tree
above its kind with a continual flower.

Stallworthy received wide recognition for his biography of Wilfred Owen, one of the generation of young English poets who died in World War I. Working with Owen's letters, unpublished manuscripts, his library (now housed in All Souls College, Oxford), and the cooperation of Owen's younger brother Harold, to whom the book is dedicated, Stallworthy produced a sympathetic and detailed account of the poet's life, recreating, as John Bayley wrote in a review, "a rich domestic density of felt and feeling existence." The book was winner of the Duff Cooper Memorial Prize, the W. H. Smith Literary Award, and the E. M. Forster Award of the American Academy of Arts and Letters. Stallworthy has also written two critical studies of the poetry of Yeats, concentrating in the first of these, *Between the Lines: Yeats's Poetry in the Making*, on the composition of nine of the poet's most famous poems (including "The Second

Coming" and the Byzantium poems) and showing through a study of Yeats' revisions in his manuscripts, how conscious and expert a craftsman he was. Yeats'manuscripts, Stallworthy concludes, "show that of all the tools in the poet's workshop the most important is a razor-sharp self-critical faculty." In *Vision and Revision in Yeats's Later Poems* Stallworthy again produced illuminating interpretations of the poet's work based on a close study of the manuscripts. Stallworthy has also written on the poetry of Thomas Hardy, J. M. Synge, Seamus Heaney, and has edited a two-volume collection of Owen's poems and a collection of critical essays, *Yeats: Last Poems.*

The son of John Arthur and Margaret (Howie) Stallworthy, he received his B.A. from Magdalen College, Oxford, in 1958 and his B. Litt. in 1961. He married Gillian Waldock in 1960. They have two sons and a daughter.

PRINCIPAL WORKS: *Poetry*—The Astronomy of Love, 1961; Out of Bounds, 1963; Root and Branch, 1969; Hand in Hand, 1974; The Apple Barrel: Selected Poems 1956–63, 1974; A Familiar Tree, 1978. *Criticism*—Between the Lines: Yeats's Poetry in the Making, 1963; Vision and Revision in Yeats's Last Poems, 1969. *Biography*—Wilfred Owen, 1974; Poets of the First World War, 1974. *Translations*—(with P. France) Alexander Blok: The Twelve and Other Poems, 1970; (with P. France) Boris Pasternak: Selected Poems, 1983. *As editor*—Yeats: Last Poems, 1968; (with A. Brownjohn and S. Heaney) New Poems 1970–71, 1971; The Penguin Book of Love Poetry, 1973; The Oxford Book of War Poetry, 1974; The Complete Poems of Wilfred Owen, 1983.

ABOUT: Contemporary Authors, new revision series 8, 1983; Vinson, J. (ed.) Contemporary Poets, 1980; Who's Who, 1983–84. *Periodicals*—Christian Science Monitor January 3, 1979; Contemporary Literature 21, 1980; Cornell Alumni News May 1980; New Statesman and Nation February 28, 1969; Times Literary Supplement November 15, 1974.

STARK, RICHARD *See* WESTLAKE, DONALD E.

*STEPANCHEV, STEPHEN (January 30, 1915–   ), American poet, writes: "I was born in Mokrin, Yugoslavia, in the autonomous province of Vojvodina, where my ancestors farmed and served as soldiers in the Hapsburg armies in return for a measure of self-government and religious freedom: they belonged to the Serbian Orthodox Church. Some of them took part in the decisive battle of Senta on September 11, 1697,

°ste pan´ chev

STEPHEN STEPANCHEV

when the Ottoman Turks were driven out of the region. My father died when I was five years old, and two years later my mother decided to emigrate to America, to Chicago, where her father had already settled. I was educated in the public schools of Chicago and at the University of Chicago, earning a bachelor's degree in 1937 and a master's degree in 1938. I taught English composition and literature at Purdue University from 1938 to 1941. Then I was called up by the U.S. Army and served with it for four years. After World War II I studied American literature at New York University and earned a Ph.D. In 1949 I joined the English Department at Queens College and have been teaching there ever since.

"I think my interest in verse-writing began in grammar school, when my seventh-grade teacher, a Miss Armstrong, invited the class to join her in writing a poem. She put the first line on the blackboard and asked us to supply a second line that would be like it metrically and would rhyme. Our hands flew up. We found it a delightful word game, and soon the board was covered with lines of rather halting, hilarious verse. I have always had a warm feeling for words, and in those days I especially liked the way Edgar Allan Poe put them together. I remember memorizing 'Annabel Lee' and reciting it with great gusto to my astounded seventh-grade class. I enjoyed mouthing every syllable of that lambent, lugubrious poem.

"Since then, of course, I have read many other poets, American and European, and I have liked most of their poems, regardless of differences in style or philosophy. I have discovered that poets are god-like in their sense of the human predica-

ment, their understanding of the joys and agonies of an animal with a preternatural awareness of its own history and doom.

"I write about whatever I observe or hear about: experiences of love and death, gossip of friends, TV documentaries about far-off places, news reports, dreams, etc. These subjects seem to arrange themselves in such a way as to suggest the precariousness of life and the provisional character of human happiness. Like everyone else, I tend to see the world in terms of contraries: day and night, good and evil, fire and ice, life and death. My poems reflect these contraries. Without them, my poems would be static and lacking in verisimilitude. When I write about spring, I ask myself why it is still winter inside me. When I write about my mother, I describe two photographs of her in my album: the first taken at her wedding and the other in the year of her death.

"Since the world comes to me through my senses, I like to emphasize imagery, without which a poem is abstract, bare, opaque. I enjoy images of sight, sound, taste, and smell. I would rather write a poem deficient in philosophy than one devoid of imagery. After all, ideas merely provide structure for a poem; without images, a poem is lifeless. The rhythms of my poems are speech rhythms, but I must confess that, at the risk of artifice, I sometimes heighten these rhythms so as to avoid the flatness and monotony of ordinary conversation. I do this by dropping slack phrases and by increasing the number of accented syllables per line.

"My affinities with the various poetic movements and schools of the recent past are not very strong. I share with the projectivists a respect for objective reality and try to report it as exactly as I can, but I dislike their disparagement of emotion, of the lyric impulse. I share with the subjectivists and neo-surrealists an affection for the dreams and the inspired accidents of the subconscious realm, but I insist on scrutinizing every image that wells up and so make sure that it is useful and represents a true discovery. Too many neo-surreal poems are mechanical collections of incredible comparisons: 'The sea is like a screwdriver.' I have not been moved to emulate the raw, tasteless verse of the anti-establishment poets or the journalistic slogans of the political poets, but I think good poems can have political implications. In some of my poems a social or political message is implicit, I think. I enjoy the seemingly effortless, urbane poems of the New York School; they all sound like entries in a diary describing the wonders and terrors of the city scene; but I have not been impelled to write like the New York School poets because there is something cosy and 'fraternal' about their work. It would be virtually an invasion of copyright to assume their tone of voice. I admire ethnicity in poetry because it makes the reader aware of the experience of minorities in America: Spanish Americans, Japanese, Jews, American Indians, Slavs, etc. I have written some poems in this vein, but have tried to give them resonance so that they could, perhaps, become part of the 'mainstream.'"

One reviewer has suggested that the reason for the relative neglect of Stephen Stepanchev as a poet is the fact that he lives in Flushing—a middle-class family neighborhood in the characteristically "domestic" New York City borough of Queens that Stepanchev calls "the center of the universe." More likely, in this same writer's phrase, it is Stepanchev's "unanchored . . . bachelor persona" that has kept him aloof from and independent of poetic movements, circles, and makers. His poetry has been variously described as "imagistic," "modernist," "romantic" ("in the tradition of Dylan Thomas," Thom Gunn wrote of his first collection, *Three Priests in April*), "autumnal"; but in fact it defies labeling. As Edward Butscher observed in *Poets*: "What is remarkable about Stepanchev's quiet skill, besides its neo-classic restraint and contrary readiness to take surreal gambles, is the constant evolutionary development behind its individual voice."

In his early poems like "Three Priests in April," Stepanchev experimented with daring, sometimes eccentric imagery:

April burned in the grass, a green fire
In dusty snow, as three priests walked toward
    a bell
Telling above the season's pyre of hearts,
Above their flaming prayers, the difference
In blue, pulsing beyond their leaf-repeating
    eyes.

His images remain striking, but he has moved with later collections toward a more subtle and complex language. "Some poems undercut our easy recognition of things by dilating upon hitherto hidden latencies," John Robert Leo wrote in *Poetry* of *Mining the Darkness*. In these poems "images develop and expand off each other, almost like sequential analogies, aiming all the while at a revelation bringing the whole process to rest":

It is subtle and slow
Like a fire in the walls,
A pan rusting,
Invisible as radio signals.

Then it is, suddenly,
All there,

Like a screen lit,
A blast of emotion.

You see.

In recent years Stepanchev's interest in ethnicity has sent him back to his own roots in Yugoslavia where, indeed, he is more widely appreciated than in the United States. A bilingual edition of his poems, *Golubica na bagremu* or *The Dove in the Attic* (translated into Serbo-Croatian by Rasa Popov) was the first bilingual book by an American poet ever published in Yugoslavia. Reviewing the volume in *World Literature Today*, Branko Mikasinovich was impressed by its philosophical as well as its poetic interest: "As a whole, Stepanchev's poetry is inspiring and moving, and it proves once again that good poetry doesn't recognize any boundaries, including linguistic ones." Nevertheless, the tone of the poems reflects a stranger, lonely and alienated in a foreign land. In "A Visit to Mokrin," his birthplace, Stepanchev meets his "tractor-loving cousin" working in the fields and "looking like an East European cliché." He responds to his cousin's delight in progress with the melancholy sophistication of the modern Westerner: "Why should I infect him / With my own doubts, gropings, and malaise?" and he leaves him sadly:

I nod and sigh and move off in a cloud
Of questions that immobilize. He offers
Me a plum brandy and we drink to the sun
While an acacia rustles over our heads and a
    green
Dove moans softly for a change of state.

For more than thirty-five years Stepanchev taught English composition, literature, and poetry workshops in the English Department of Queens College, the City University of New York. He became professor emeritus in 1985. Author of a doctoral dissertation on the critical reception of the works of Theodore Dreiser, he has also written a book on contemporary American poetry that is widely used in high schools and colleges. He has been a Fulbright Professor of American literature at the University of Copenhagen (1957) and was awarded a National Education Association grant in 1968.

PRINCIPAL WORKS: *Poetry*—Three Priests in April, 1956; Spring in the Harbor, 1967; A Man Running in the Rain, 1969; The Mad Bomber, 1972; Mining the Darkness, 1975; Medusa and Others (A Chapbook), 1975; The Dove in the Acacia, 1977; What I Own (A Chapbook), 1978. *Prose*—American Poetry Since 1945, 1965.

ABOUT: Contemporary Authors, new revision series 7, 1982; Vinson, J. (ed.) Contemporary Poets, 1980; Who's Who in America, 1983–84. *Periodicals*—Falcon

Spring 1972; Poetry January 1957; November 1976; Poets May 1978; World Literature Today Summer 1978.

STEVENSON, ANNE (KATHARINE) (January 3, 1933–), American poet now living in England, writes: "I was born into an American academic family, but by accident my birthplace was Cambridge, England, not Cambridge, Massachusetts. My early childhood was spent in New England where my father taught at Harvard (after taking a Ph.D. there) and at Yale. I remember my father chiefly as a musician, although he was a well-known philosopher. He was a devoted pianist and cellist. My sister Diana and I were taught to play the violin and piano almost as soon as we could walk; and I can remember no time when there were not two grand pianos in our otherwise sparsely furnished living room. People came to play chamber music, two pianos, even Brandenburg concerti. I never expected to be anything but a musician when I grew up. We were a literary family, too. My father read the English poets aloud to us; his taste were Romantic, and I remember running upstairs in tears before the inevitable climax of 'Sohrab and Rustum.' I wrote ballads à la Scott and Byron when I should have been doing arithmetic at school. My mother, who was a novelist herself, read aloud to us during the summers: *Rob Roy, Tale of Two Cities, Pride and Prejudice, The Black Arrow.* I don't suppose children are brought up as we were any longer; television supplants the family readings, and the tradition of the amateur has fallen into abeyance. In any case, I realize now how much I owe to my parents' liberal, gentle assumption that beauty was more to be cherished than success or money, and that in fulfilling oneself one incurred an obligation to live for more than oneself. Both my parents were atheists, or at least, agnostics, but my maternal grandmother, who lived with us, was a devout Presbyterian and we children were sent to church with her, probably to appease my mother's conscience.

"I went to high school at the University High School in Ann Arbor, where I was fortunate in my English teachers. At the University of Michigan, which I entered in 1950, I acted, played the cello, wrote poetry, took up modern dance and generally tried to make myself into the universal artist. When I graduated in 1954, with a Phi Beta Kappa and a Major Hopwood Award in poetry, I felt in myself a confidence that it has taken thirty years to find again. I went to England, taught in a school, married, returned to America (to the South this time), divorced, went back to

ANNE STEVENSON

Michigan with my small daughter, studied poetry under Donald Hall and finally got a job in Cambridge, Massachusetts, teaching at the Cambridge School of Weston. Teaching was never a thing I did very well—I was both too sure of myself and not sure enough of my knowledge. But I wrote poetry in Cambridge in the early 1960s and married Mark Elvin, an English student of Chinese at Harvard, who took me back to Cambridge, England in 1964.

"Since 1964 I have lived almost entirely in Britain: in Cambridge where a son John was born in 1966; in Glasgow, where Charles was born in 1967; in Dundee where I was Fellow in Writing from 1973–1975; in Oxford, where I was a fellow of Lady Margaret Hall and a writing fellow in Reading; and in Hay-on-Wye on the Welsh Borders, where Michael Farley and I founded The Poetry Bookshop. The externals of my life in the sixties and seventies were only a gloss on profound disturbances within. I was fortunately, in the 1960s, under the spell of Elizabeth Bishop, on whom I wrote a book for Twayne's United States Authors Series (1965). Elizabeth and I corresponded when I was living in Watertown, Mass., and she in Brazil. (Her letters to me are now in the Library of Washington University in St. Louis, Mo.) It was through Elizabeth that I came to be suspicious of the hysteria which produced the 'suicide poetry' of the sixties. At the same time, both of us suffered profoundly from the anxieties of those days. Looking back, I feel the decade 1964–1974 (when I was writing *Correspondences*) was a period when, for me at least, a connection with the world of my family in New England snapped like a spine. *Correspondences* was written, with the help of Philip Hobsbaum, as a kind of document of survival. My mother died of cancer in 1962, and that death symbolized the death of a past I craved but to which I could not return.

"The poems I have written since the monologues of *Correspondences* have tried to answer the question, where to go now? *Enough of Green* was a black book with a core of forced stoicism. I was living alone on the East Coast of Scotland when I wrote it, having left all my family to what I thought of as 'the past age of the family.' Loneliness could be the only way of the artist (I thought) and I steeled myself to a despair I now marvel at surviving. Between that book and *Minute by Glass Minute* I met Michael Farley with whom I have lived since. Through Michael I have become a Christian. Although the poems of *Minute by Glass Minute* are not, I think, entirely religious poems, they are certainly poems of self-discovery through the world, or of discovery *of* the world. It's a matter of losing yourself to find yourself—losing a self-preoccupied ego to find what is valuable, even today, in living. I have come to think, too, that it is only when you become ignorant enough to *see* the world as given, that the imagination comes into its rightful inheritance as the instrument—finely tuned and delicate, yet as tough as humanity itself—on which poetry is played."

———

Anne Stevenson is the daughter of the philosopher Charles Leslie Stevenson and Louise Destler Stevenson. From her 1955 marriage to R. L. Hitchcock she has a daughter, and from her 1962 marriage to J.M.D. Elvin, two sons. Both marriages ended in divorce.

She has said she admires poetry that is "controlled, finely wrought and yet passionate," but describes her own as "quiet, somewhat cynical, more than usually domestic." Her work has been generally regarded by its critics as highly disciplined, effortlessly witty, and imbued with a keen sense of the particularities of the many places she knows well. These characteristics were already evident in the title poem of her earliest collection, *Living in America*:

"Living in America,"
the intelligent people at Harvard say,
"is the price you pay for living in New
    England."

Californians think
living in America is a reward
for managing not to live anywhere else.
The rest of the country?
Could it be sagging between two poles,
tastelessly decorated, dangerously overweight? . . .

"The poems of place," wrote Ralph Mills of her next collection, *Reversals*, "display a personal responsiveness to the features of a particular location that never let subjectivity overbalance them, so the resulting detail is always fresh, discriminating, and independent." She has come to be greatly appreciated in Britain, partly for the knowing irony of such poems as "England," included in *Reversals*, which displays a more robust sense than most English poets have been able to muster of that country's special attractions and peculiarities:

Without nostalgia who could love England?
Without a sentimental attachment to
    tolerance
who could delight in this cramped corner
    country
in no quarter savage, where everything
    done well
is touched with the melancholy of understanding? . . .

Correspondences: A Family History in Letters is based on 150 years of letters and other documents from the archives of the Chandler family of Clearfield, Vermont, which were turned into poetry by Stevenson. The *Choice* reviewer called the book "a remarkable fusion of the techniques of fiction, poetry, and cultural history." Richard Charnoff considered the poems "convenient touchstones of reliable feelings, intelligent, resolute, but externally determined. The alienation of self barely echoes through a genealogy of undifferentiated, inauthentic voices." Douglas Dunn disagreed, asserting that she chooses "different styles for her individual 'correspondents,' ranging from those of hell-fire commercialists to sensitive lady poets, freak-out contemporary sons, and ruined wives. Idiom changes as time moves on."

In *Enough of Green*, Stevenson was said by Andrew Motion to have "compressed and refined" the narrative style of *Correspondences* "to one of telegraphic, controlled impetuosity. Ellipsis and imperatives have replaced epistolary frankness, and the result is a marvellously tense diction which relishes physical detail and also admits abstract considerations." He compared her to her friend Elizabeth Bishop in "the manner of short-story telling in which natural descriptions are introduced as symbolic landscapes," as in "The Mudtower" from *Enough of Green*:

Watch the fierce, driven, hot-looking
scuttlings of redshanks, the beaks of the
    oystercatchers.
Struggle and panic. Struggle and panic.
Mud's rituals resume. The priest-gulls flap to
    the kill.
Now high flocks of sandpipers, wings made of
    sunlight,
flicker as snow flickers, blown from those in
    land hills.

The poems on Scotland in this collection were described by James Fenton as occasionally suffering from an outsider's impressionability. Lines such as "Reach Mallaig and discover / Heaven is real" sound to Fenton "as if she is writing for the Highlands and Islands Development Board."

The poems in *Minute by Glass Minute* mark, according to Carol Rumens, "a return to green, for the landscape is no longer primarily coastal but dominated by the mountains and pastures of South Wales." The collection includes as its centerpiece the sequence "Green Mountain, Black Mountain," which is, in Rumens' words, "subtly woven from connections, sometimes reluctant, sometimes celebratory, between the green mountain of Vermont and childhood and the black mountain of Wales and the present. Gradually the pastoral element is pushed back to become a setting for the sharp, frieze-like gestures of the human characters—the poet's mother 'dying / at us,' her father 'animate in argument, ash scattered / from your cigarette like punctuation.' Described as 'a species of cantata,' the sequence is often strikingly musical, particularly in the final section with its imaginative verbalizing of the thrush's and its two powerful, isolated final lines that give the effect of an affirmative *rallentando*:

Swifts twist on the syllables of the wind
   currents
Blackbirds are the cellos of the deep farms.

In 1981–82 Stevenson held a literary fellowship at Durham and Newcastle universities and lived in Sunderland, a town on the North Sea coast, with her husband, Michael Farley.

PRINCIPAL WORKS: *Poetry*—Living in America, 1965; Reversals, 1969; Correspondences, 1974; Travelling under Glass, 1974; Enough of Green, 1977; Minute by Glass Minute, 1982; Making Poetry, 1983. *Non-fiction*—Elizabeth Bishop, 1966.

ABOUT: Contemporary Authors, first revision series 17–20, 1976; Contemporary Literary Criticism 7, 1977; Vinson, J. (ed.) Contemporary Poets, 1975. *Periodicals*—Choice April 1968; January 1975; September 1978; Encounter December 1974; April 1978; Library Journal February 1, 1967; September 1, 1969; January 15, 1975; New Statesman September 12, 1969; December 6, 1974; February 10, 1978; Poetry February 1971; November 1975; Times Literary Supplement November 25, 1977; May 6, 1983.

STONE, ROBERT (ANTHONY) (August 21, 1937–), American novelist, was born in Brooklyn, New York, son of C. Homer and Gladys Catherine (Grant) Stone. His family back-

ROBERT STONE

ground was Scottish Presbyterian and Irish Catholic. Stone grew up on Manhattan's West Side in rooming houses and welfare hotels, and during a period of several years lived in an orphanage. He never knew his father, and his mother, once a schoolteacher and then a hotel maid, suffered from schizophrenia. An early, absorbed reader of books, Stone attended a Catholic high school, but was expelled before graduation. His rebellion took the form of rowdyism, drinking, and an avowed atheism. He later considered his loss of faith at seventeen one of the momentous events of his life. After dropping out of high school he enlisted in the Navy, becoming a journalist for the Armed Forces Press Service. In 1958 he enrolled at New York University, but remained for only one term. It was there, however, that he met his wife, Janice G. Burr, whom he married in 1959.

During 1958–1960 Stone worked as a reporter for the New York *Daily News* and for a sensation tabloid sold in supermarkets. On the basis of the opening chapters of his first novel, he received a Stegner fellowship at Stanford University in 1962. At this time he met Ken Kesey and became a member of his Merry Pranksters, crossing the country in a bus driven by Neal Cassady, the hero of Jack Kerouac's *On the Road.* He participated in the counter culture and for a time used drugs, which he says made him aware of his own "religious impulse." His first novel, *A Hall of Mirrors,* was awarded the Houghton Mifflin Literary Fellowship, and won the William Faulkner prize for 1967. Set in New Orleans, it concerns a set of maimed and displaced individuals who are drawn into a world of nightmare.

Rheinhardt, once a classical musician but now a disheveled alcoholic at the edge of nervous breakdown, takes a job as an announcer of biased news at a right-wing radio station. He lives in a rooming house with a young woman named Geraldine, whose face has been scarred by a psychotic boyfriend, and becomes involved with a homicidal con man posing as a preacher, and with Morgan Rainey, a tortured neurotic. Events impel these characters toward a climactic scene of a racist "Patriotic Revival," where anarchy erupts.

Reviews of *A Hall of Mirrors* were extraordinarily favorable. Howard Junker declared: "As a first novel this book can be ranked with Pynchon's *V.* and Donleavy's *The Ginger Man.* In some ways it is better than either." Emile Capouya remarked that Stone "has a breadth of mind and a seriousness that set him apart from any number of merely talented writers"; and Wallace Stegner commented that *A Hall of Mirrors* "would be notable in any season . . . whether it was the author's first novel or his tenth. . . . [The book] is exciting in a way that even promising first novels rarely are." Attempting to capture the book's special qualities, Fred Rotondaro wrote that "the nightmare quality of the work, the confusion of values, and specifically the riot which ends the novel, remind me of Nathanael West's *The Day of the Locust.*" Ivan Gold agreed, remarking that "*A Hall of Mirrors* is, one could say, *The Day of the Locust* as told to Malcolm Lowry. . . . Not the least of his achievements is to throw a bridge between the private person and the political act, illumine where and how the individual meets and fuses with the social body." *A Hall of Mirrors* is essentially a dramatization of the polarized values of the United States during the sixties.

In 1971 Stone was the recipient of a Guggenheim fellowship, and went to Vietnam to experience the war. He returned to the United States that year to begin his second novel, *Dog Soldiers,* which opens in Vietnam and, with hallucinatory effect, brings the war home. The work is set in 1970 against a background of the bleakest and most scarring disillusionment. A one-time playwright, Converse, a journalist in Vietnam, concocts a scheme to smuggle heroin back home to Berkeley, where his wife Marge is to give it to a waiting buyer. Hicks, a Navy friend and skilled dealer in the black market, delivers the contraband, only to find that the politically influential buyer (with links to the CIA) intends to steal it. Hicks and Marge flee to a mountain retreat, are pursued, and a horror scene takes place—a fantasia of drug-numbed greed and irrationality dramatizing the brutality, emptiness, and desolation of the United States in the shadow of Vietnam.

Dog Soldiers received the National Book Award for 1975 and was widely praised by reviewers. Paul Gray wrote that "this second novel confirms a talent betrayed in *A Hall of Mirrors* and reveals added discipline"; and Thomas Powers called *Dog Soldiers* "the best book so far about the spiritually corrupting effect on the United States of the war it fought in Vietnam." Certain other critics, however, pointed to weaknesses in the novel. Joan Joffe Hall found the principal characters unrealized, as did David Gleicher, who remarked that "the structural limit imposed by the author on his characters . . . is too narrow. They float in the vast moral limbo of the 60s. . . . One gets the feeling, indeed, that the people in the book are merely tacked on to the plot." But although flawed in various respects, and wallowing at times in "baroque bleakness," *Dog Soldiers* seemed to a majority of critics a work with the power to project a dark, horrendous vision of modern times.

In the later seventies Stone and his wife took several trips through Central America, acquiring a knowledge of Honduras, Guatemala, and El Salvador—an experience that inspired *A Flag for Sunrise.* This novel is set in the mythic Central American country of Tecan (based largely on Honduras), mired in poverty and official corruption, and teetering on the edge of revolution. Its four principal characters are North Americans: Father Egan, a whiskey priest whose failed mission is about to be closed down; Sister Justin Feeney, his assistant who, as her faith fails, commits herself to the revolutionary cause; Pablo Tabor, a benzedrine addict drifter who becomes involved in gun running; and Frank Holliwell, a disillusioned intellectual whose good intentions lead to catastrophe. The novel focuses, in turn, upon these characters who come together only late in the work, as events move toward political upheaval.

Upon its publication, *A Flag for Sunrise* was acclaimed as a major work, the richest and finest of Stone's books by far. Jack Beatty declared that the novel "seems destined to be one of the books that will justify our time before the bar of literary history." He went on to note the novel's resemblance to the fiction of Joseph Conrad, commenting that "the rhetoric is Conradian, and like Conrad's moralized geography, it both establishes a mood and propounds a philosophy. The philosophy is somber, an articulation of emptiness." The critic for the *New Yorker* made very much the same point, calling *A Flag for Sunrise* "a thriller that offers ideas . . . as well as adventure and suspense—a kind of latter day *Nostromo.* . . . Its characters take on mythic stature . . . a most notable novel." Frank McConnell described its theme, "the killing tension between politics and the religious sensibility," as worthy of comparison with both Conrad and Graham Greene. Other reviewers expressed reservations. Robert Towers, although decidedly impressed by *A Flag for Sunrise* as a work in a tradition of "existential adventure" (Conrad, Greene, Malraux), thought Stone's rendering of the political situation lacking in subtlety, his evil characters "stamped out of thin metal." He found Sister Justin "a sentimentally conceived heroine-victim, as inspirational and unconvincing as the women in Conrad and Hemingway"; and Father Egan "more the product of the author's attachment to drunks and losers than a character freshly perceived and freshly felt."

Stone adapted *A Hall of Mirrors* for the screen as *WUSA* (Paramount, 1970), and *Dog Soldiers* as *Who'll Stop the Rain?* (United Artists, 1978). He has held several academic appointments—as writer-in-residence at Princeton (1971–72), and at Harvard and Amherst. In recent years, he has lived in Amherst, Massachusetts with his wife, a social worker, and his two children, Deirdre, and Ian. Responding to an inquiry about a religious impulse in his novels, Stone has said: "I'm some sort of Catholic, though not a practicing one. If there's no transcendent place outside human life, then there's just primate behavior. I wish I could believe. That's the situation my characters are in. They get glimpses—or think they do—just on the edge of vision."

PRINCIPAL WORKS: A Hall of Mirrors, 1967; Dog Soldiers, 1974; A Flag for Sunrise, 1981.

ABOUT: Contemporary Authors 85–88, 1980; Contemporary Literary Criticism 5, 1976; Who's Who in America, 1983–84. *Periodicals*—Atlantic November 1981; Commentary March 1982; Commonweal March 12, 1982; Nation April 1, 1968; New Leader March 17, 1975; Newsweek October 26, 1981; New York Review of Books April 3, 1975; December 3, 1981; New York Times Book Review September 24, 1967; November 3, 1974; October 18, 1981.

*STRUGATSKY, ARKADY NATANO-VICH (August 28, 1925–) and BORIS NATANOVICH (April 15, 1933–), Russian science-fiction writers, write (in Russian): "After some consideration, my brother [Boris] and I have decided not to write an essay about impressions which, forced upon us by life, shaped our view of the world, but rather to limit ourselves to bare facts. Our mother, Alexandra Ivanovna Strugatsky, born to a large family of a minor trader in the northwestern Ukraine, was Russian by nationality. She married our father in 1927, to be ostracized by her family for marrying a

Jew, but was forgiven after my birth. Working in a cardboard factory, she simultaneously studied in a primary schoolteachers' college. Later, upon graduating from Gertzen Pedagogical Institute in Leningrad, she went on to teach Russian. At the end of the forties our mother was awarded a "Mark of Merit" medal. She died in 1979 at the age of seventy-nine. We were good sons to her; I hope she died in peace.

"Our father, Natan Zenovievich Strugatsky, was the oldest son in the family of a provincial lawyer. All three sons embraced the Revolution. The second oldest, Aron, died in 1919 in the liberation of Rostov from the White Army. The youngest, Alexander, died in the political purges of 1937. My father became a member of the Communist Party in 1916, fought throughout the Civil War—first as a commissar of a cavalry brigade, then in the political division of the Front under the legendary Mikhail Frunze (participating in the liberation of the Crimea from General Vrangel). As a party functionary, he took an active part in the restoration and development of the People's Economy in the time between the wars, but every now and then (two, and sometimes three years at a time) he worked in his own field (he had received a degree in Fine Arts from the University of St. Petersburg before the Revolution) first at the Hermitage Museum, then in the magnificent M. E. Saltykov-Shchedrin State public library in Leningrad. At the start of World War II he joined the People's Volunteer Corps. He died of hunger during the siege of Leningrad in January 1942.

"Arkady Natanovich Strugatsky, the older brother, was born in Batumi, Georgia, in 1925. Shortly afterward, our parents moved to Leningrad, where I lived and studied until 1942. I fell in love with science-fiction in early childhood. Perhaps it was my father's influence; busy as he was, he found time to tell me endless stories in which Jules Verne, H. G. Wells, and Conan Doyle were interwoven with one another. When World War II broke out, my schoolmates and I were sent off on the construction of military defenses that were to bar the Germans from Leningrad. The Germans broke through earlier than expected. At the end of July we were in our first battle, and I killed my first Nazi. In the dry July heat they marched on us, on kids, grinning, self-assured, almost naked—black underwear and helmets with horns—spraying us with bullets from sub-machine guns, and then we hit them with old, heavy Canadian (to this day I do not know why 'Canadian') rifles. The bastard that was marching straight toward me, I shot right in the naked belly from 20 paces, and I saw him double over, smashing his sweaty face into the ground he wanted to trample with his

°strū gat´ skē

boots. . . . Well, it is just lyricism, but how clearly it stayed in the memory! Then there was retreat, and then the siege, and we ate cats, and cooked wallpaper and made soup from carpenter's glue, and the city was hit by bombs from the air and heavy artillery from land and the people fell into snow, weak with hunger, and died on the streets, and mountains of corpses filled the sheds in the yards of Leningrad. And then I, half dead, was taken out into the Big Land in a truck by the Road of Life°, and the truck crashed through a bomb crater, under the ice of the Ladoga Lake, and the cargo of people dying of starvation was in the water—frost -40°F and a blizzard. . . . I was fished out. In a hospital I lost all my skin, fingers and toe nails, and the little toe from my left foot. I shall never forget it and someone will answer to me for all that . . . I do not want to go on, and I should not have told any of this, but the readers of your book, as I understood, are interested in the genesis of our ideology, our world outlook. Well, then here it is: father, a communist, the most noble man in the world, and the mocking, degenerative, sweat-covered face of the war and Nazism. All the love for mankind, all the concern for the fate of the world from my father, and also hatred of fascism, war, and narrow-mindedness.

"And Boris Natanovich Strugatsky, my younger brother and co-author, born in 1933, became so weak during the siege that taking him out of Leningrad was unthinkable. And my mother remained with him to die. She pushed me out to live, and stayed to die. By a miracle they survived; they outlived death, and the war ended. Boris, after finishing school, was accepted by Leningrad University, Department of Mathematics and Mechanics, graduated with honors and joined the staff of Pulkov Observatory. Stellar astronomer—that was the name of his profession: he was studying interactions of stars in binary and multiple systems and of stars and interstellar dust in our galaxy. I passed on to him the love for science-fiction, as my father had passed it on to me. Unlike me, my brother is a born traveler, member of archeological expeditions, choosing a site for our great telescope in the Trans-Caucasus. Even now he drives his car on the god-forsaken dirt roads of the Baltics and Karelia. We began writing together in 1956, becoming professional writers in 1964. He quit work, as I did, but aside from his literary activity he continues to busy himself with his astronomy, just as I continue with translations of medieval Japanese prose.

°The "Big Land" was Soviet territory unoccupied by the Nazis. The "Road of Life," the only way out of Leningrad, crossed the frozen Ladoga Lake, which was under bombardment.

"And, I suppose that is all that is worth knowing about us."

—trans. E. Braigen

———

Arkady and Boris Strugatsky are the authors of the most widely read science fiction in the Soviet Union. Their popularity is as immense as it is universal, extending across economic, social, and cultural groups. This popularity of science fiction writers cannot be explained only by the scarcity of good fiction in the USSR or by the public's hunger for good literature or an unusually intense interest in science fiction among the Soviet intelligensia. The popular appeal of the Strugatsky brothers has its roots in the allegorical nature of their works which eludes the watchful eye of Soviet censorship to bring readers new, fresh, and stimulating ideas and concepts, which would have been censored if submitted in a more direct and candid form. Arkady and Boris Strugatsky communicate to an attentive reader by placing subtle hints and inconsistencies in his path. If noticed and analyzed, those hints yield implied conclusions, not committed to paper. This literary technique, along with extensive use of symbolism, and other methods of "covert" creativity, common to literary circles world wide, are made into an art in the Soviet Union and the works of Strugatsky brothers take on a new meaning. However, they have not entirely escaped the rigors of official scrutiny. In 1969 *Gadkie lebedi* (*The Ugly Swans*), the manuscript of which had been published abroad without their authorization, was rejected by the Soviet censor, and while their works continue to be published in the USSR, the Strugatskys are, according to Patrick McGuire, "in a sort of limbo . . . [they] have neither been outlawed nor fully accepted as writers."

The first cycle of their works depicts a rather optimistic attitude toward the future, closely matching one entertained in official circles. *Strana bagrovykh tuch* (The Land of the Crimson Cloud, 1959) sets the stage for the first generation of Strugatsky heroes—Anton Bukov, Vladimir Yurovsky, and in later books, Ivan Zhilin. The first successful expedition to Venus for purposes of mining uranium ores is the backdrop for these idealistic characters, who lead the first entry of humanity into space. The remainder of the works in this cycle have similar subjects. *Destination: Amalthea,* 1960, is a portrayal of a rescue mission on one of the Jupiter moons. The same trio of characters find themselves marooned and drifting in Jupiter's gaseous atmosphere. They are rescued by the skill and bravery of Bukov, who is now well established as a central character of the imagined world. Subsequent books contain more exploits of the same characters, taking these heroes of the early days of space exploration well into middle age. As a prefiguring of more controversial subjects of future works, characters grow tired and plagued with doubts. Subsequent novels show them old and wise, but far from infallible. Yurovsky, true to his compulsive nature, dies taking a useless, suicidal risk. Other loosely connected stories were written in this period and later published under the title *Vozvrashchenie polden', XXII vek* (*Noon: 22nd Century*) in 1978.

Increasingly, from earlier to later writings, an element of pain invades the utopian world of Strugatsky fiction. The conflicts of personalities arise more often and marriages fail more frequently as the characters and authors mature. Still, the conflict is not yet the individual against society; it is individual against individual, and the question under examination is not man and evil, but the balance of stern caution and light-headed bravery of various space heroes. All these belong to an earlier set of works, in which the authors set man against the elements, steering clear of social and political questions. The cycle ends with *Dalekaia raduga* (*Far Rainbow*, 1964). Cataclysm, pain, and stress invade the utopian world, forcing characters to act in a way no enlightened communist should. The inhabitants of planet Rainbow, used by physicists for experimentation, are faced with immutable destruction from a deadly "wave" unleashed by an experiment on a planetary scale. The "wave" is unavoidable and everything on the planetary surface is doomed; the number of spaceships is inadequate for a total evacuation, as the new hero Gorbovsky has to decide who shall live and who shall die. This is the most dificult and stressful situation that the characters in the Strugatskys' books have to face; with ever-mounting frequency they fail the test. Something is amiss in utopia.

In the mid-1960s Arkady and Boris Strugatsky began writing in two genres. The bulk of their writing is still science fiction, set in the same future utopian world. The difference is the somber, at times pessimistic, approach of these works. An offshoot from the mainstream of science fiction are their satirical fantasy tales.

Ponedelnik nachinayetsya subbotu (*Monday Begins on Saturday*, 1965) opens a cycle of charming, humorous, and, most of all, satirical fantasy tales. It is a happy marriage of folk-tale, of magic and witchcraft, with sharp satire on a "scientific-administrative" institution. *Vtoroe nashestrie Marsian* (The Second Martian Invasion, 1968) is another funny and imaginative tale, a sequel to H. G. Wells' *War of the Worlds*. Martian aliens, failing to conquer Earth by military force, come back the second time to succeed by bribery and propaganda. Their satirical tales are lively, striking the target of ridicule with merciless precision. To many fans these works are the acme of the Strugatskys' creativity.

Their more conventional science fiction of the later period, written simultaneously with the fantasy tales, is very different from the earlier books. There the authors present a much less attractive side of a familiar setting with a new relationship between man and evil, particularly the unavoidable evil of history. A number of works examine the cruel march of history, every step of which is inevitable and necessary. *Obitayemy ostrov* (*Prisoners of Power*, 1969) gives an account of the disastrous effects of a well-meaning but thoughtless intervention by a marooned astronaut in the affairs of a planet governed by a tyranny. A young pilot in a noble attempt to lead the inhabitants to a better and brighter future, rallying them against the tyranny, causes death and havoc, while achieving nothing. An effective twist is added as the main character discovers that the tyrants are human agents engaged in a thankless task of directing and over-looking the development of the planet. The book raises interesting questions on the subject matter and authors' views alike. The message of the book is a somber one—history will progress along certain lines; it might move faster or slower but will take no short cuts; or, what seems more to the point in the Strugatskys' books—every step of progress must be earned with sweat, blood, and tears. Thus, the authors seem increasingly pessimistic on the subject, as they are in other books dealing with similar questions such as *Popytka ka begstuv* (*Escape Attempt*, 1962) and *Trudno byt bogom* (*Hard to Be a God*, 1964).

Of a particular interest is *Za milliard let do knotsa sveta* (*Definitely Maybe: A Manuscript Discovered Under Unusual Circumstances*, 1976). A science fiction tale set in the present, it brings up a current and controversial issue of integrity and freedom in scientific research. Parallel with this theme is another one, a study of shameful surrender and compromise executed with force, vividness, and pain unusual for a science fiction writer. The characters of *Definitely Maybe* are scientists, all of them on the verge of breakthrough in their work but all intimidated and frustrated by mysterious sentient aliens and the forces of the universe itself, threatening them, their sanity, their loved ones. Logically the choice is clear: "When a heavy tank is headed straight for you and the only weapon you have is the head on your shoulders, you should know enough to jump out of its way." If you can not win you must surrender, forget your own creative work and concentrate on dull and harmless official projects. However, "It's very unpleasant for a person to realize that he is not at all what he thought he was. He wants to remain the way he was all his life, and that's impossible if he capitulates." With this, the scientists withdraw one by one from the scene, trying not to look one another in the eye. Finally the two main characters are left to make their decision. Because the feeling of capitulation and compromise is familiar to most readers, the book with its masterful clarity touches a raw nerve in each of us.

WORKS IN ENGLISH TRANSLATION: Destination Amalthea (tr. Kolesnikov), 1962; Hard to Be a God (tr. W. Ackerman), 1973; The Final Circle of Paradise (tr. L. Renen), 1976; Monday Begins on Saturday (tr. L. Renen), 1977; Tale of the Troika: Roadside Picnic (tr. A.W. Bouis), 1977; Prisoners of Power (tr. H.S. Jacobson), 1977; Definitely Maybe (tr. A.W. Bouis), 1978; Noon: 22nd Century (tr. P.L. McGuire), 1978; The Ugly Swans (tr. A.S. and A. Nakhimovsky), 1979; The Second Invasion from Mars (tr. G. Kern), 1979; Far Rainbow (tr. A.W. Bouis), 1979; The Snail on the Slope, 1980; Beetle in the Anthill (tr. A.W. Bouis), 1980; Space Apprentice (tr. A.W. Bouis), 1981; Escape Attempt (tr. R. DeGaris), 1982.

ABOUT: Barron, N. Anatomy of Wonder: A Critical Guide to Science Fiction, 2nd ed., 1981; Columbia Dictionary of Modern European Literature, 1980; Contemporary Authors 106, 1982; Reginald, R. Science Fiction and Fantasy Literature II, 1979. Periodicals—Canadian-American Slavic Studies 5 Summer 1972; Critical Encounters II 1982; Galileo 7 1978; Russian Review 33 April 1974.

SULLIVAN, WALTER S(EAGER), JR.

(January 12, 1918–), American journalist and science writer, was born in New York City. His mother, Jeanet Ellinwood Loomis Sullivan, was a pianist and composer who instilled in him a lifelong love of music; his father, Walter Sr., an insurance executive, had managed advertising for the New York Times and helped save the ailing paper from bankruptcy when Adolph S. Ochs bought it in 1896. "My father wasn't a scientist," Sullivan told an interviewer in 1974, "but he was a very observant man. We'd often walk in the woods and he used to see something and would point things out about it. I think that's what science is pretty much—just observing and pointing things out."

The summer before his senior year at the Groton School, Connecticut, Sullivan convinced

WALTER S. SULLIVAN, JR.

the members of an American Museum of Natural History paleontological expedition to let him accompany them on a fossil hunt in Alaska. Digging in exposed permafrost outside Fairbanks, Sullivan made the major find of the trip—the frozen, preserved forefoot of a 20,000-year-old bison, complete with hair, skin, and tendon. The thrill of this discovery, Sullivan has said, was a major impetus toward his later fascination with science, as were the pre-med courses he took during his first year at Yale University. Sullivan moved restlessly from one discipline to another; he studied law in his second year, and composition and cello with Paul Hindemith in his third, then graduated with a bachelor's degree in English history in 1940. ("History," Sullivan says, "is the main thrust of my approach to science.") By then he already had a summer's experience with the New York Times as a $15-a-week copyboy—he had originally hoped to be hired as a music critic—and rejoined the paper after his graduation. As an ensign and later lieutenant-commander with the U.S. Navy during World War II, Sullivan won twelve combat stars in the western Pacific and ended his military service commanding a converted destroyer.

After his discharge in 1946 Sullivan became a reporter for the New York Times. His first story described the effects of nuclear fallout from bomb tests at Alamagordo, New Mexico, but usually he was handed typical cub reporter assignments—obituaries and club notes. His break as a correspondent came in late 1946 when he was sent by the paper to cover Admiral Richard E. Byrd's fourth Antarctic expedition. Following stints as a foreign correspondent in the Pacific, in China during the Communist takeover—he was one of the last Westerners to cross the Gobi Desert before the country's borders were closed—and in Germany as head of the *New York Times*' Berlin bureau from 1952 to 1956, Sullivan returned to the Antarctic as the sole reporter on a U.S. Navy survey of the continent's coast made in preparation for the International Geophysical Year, (1957–58). The reports he filed provided the basis for parts of *Quest for a Continent*, his first book.

Although partially superseded by the findings of subsequent polar researchers, especially in its descriptions of Antarctic fauna, *Quest for a Continent* remains one of the best introductions to the most alien of continents. Sullivan covered in detail the various Antarctic expeditions, giving particular emphasis to more recent international efforts to map and explore the coastline and icebound interior. As the last great unclaimed expanse of land left on earth, Antarctica, international treaties notwithstanding, is ripe for commercial and political exploitation; in his final chapter Sullivan contrasts the jockeying among nations for chunks of territory with "the ideals of the Antarctic heroes," explorers "whose epic feats are not likely to be repeated in an age of radio telephony, helicopters and jet aircraft." In the opinion of *New York Times* reviewer Charles Poore, Sullivan "achieved the impossible with fluent, splendid ease"—creating "one continuous narrative out of a thousand-and-one reports from frequently disparate sources." Drawing on his polar research, Sullivan also produced two books for juveniles: *White Land of Adventure* and *Polar Regions: The Geography, Climate, and Life of the Arctic and Antarctic and the Explorers who Discovered Them*.

The International Geophysical Year, which Sullivan covered in an extensive series of articles for the *New York Times* and which he called "a scientific adventure of awesome proportions," was the subject of his next book, *Assault on the Unknown: The International Geophysical Year*. In a unique example of international scientific cooperation, 30,000 IGY researchers from some seventy countries made the first comprehensive surveys of Antarctica and such global phenomena as ocean currents, the jet streams, hurricane movements, earthquake patterns, and the effects of fluctuations in solar radiation. "The immeasurable enlargement of man's horizons through the I.G.Y. exploration of space, the atmosphere, the seas, the poles, and the earth's interior has stirred the layman as well as the scientist," Sullivan wrote. "We have begun to learn that hurricanes, droughts, pestilence know no national frontiers and we have come a little closer to a cosmic view of our planet—a water-covered

sphere, crusted here and there with continents upon which there is the fragile green hue of life. . . . In studying itself, the world has grown closer together."

As the *New York Times*' chief science reporter from 1960 and science editor from 1964, Sullivan became interested in the possibility of extraterrestrial life. He had covered Project Ozma, the pioneering (but limited) search for interstellar radio transmissions by the Space Science Board of the National Academy of Science, and used this experience to write *We Are Not Alone: The Search for Intelligent Life on Other Worlds*. Published during a period of public fascination with UFOs (which Sullivan debunked in his book), *We Are Not Alone* entered the bestseller list on the strength of its subject matter alone. Basing his account of an extremely speculative area of science on the work of such astronomers as Carl Sagan, I. S. Shklovskii, Otto Struve, Freeman Dyson, Frank Drake, and Fred Hoyle, Sullivan began with a short history of astronomy, then discussed conflicting theories of the origin of life and intelligence, and ended with a survey of possible ways of detecting and contacting alien civilizations. Rocketeer Willy Ley called the book "not only very well-written" but also "perfectly researched," though *Science* reviewer L.W. Frederick was irritated by "the use of some very sloppy physics and astronomy" (for example, Sullivan had confused focal length and focal ratio), and worried that the book would be read "by just those people who should not be given erroneous science." Nonetheless, even Frederick concluded that " if one weeds out the mistakes, the book is worth reading for the vistas that it reveals and the thoughts that it provokes." *We Are Not Alone* won the 1965 International Nonfiction Book Prize.

"The best general introduction presently in print on the recent revolutionary developments in earth science" was how *Choice* described *Continents in Motion: The New Earth Debate*, Sullivan's fact-laden account of the theory of plate tectonics, popularly called "continental drift." The author pieced together information from hundreds of reports and interviews to provide a comprehensive, nontechnical overview of the new theory, which has as its foundation myriad bits of interlocking evidence from the fossil record. He carefully allocated credit for each discovery to the proper researchers. "Personalities and controversies in the development of the theory," continued *Choice*, "are woven throughout the book in a way that gives excitement to the narrative and provides a historical perspective that will be of interest to geoscience students and laymen alike." Sullivan, wrote S. S. Oddo in her *New York Times* review, "tells the story like a mystery story, clue by clue, investigator by investigator. . . . [his book] is also a history of discovery as revealing [of] the ways of science and scientists as J. D. Watson's account of unraveling the genetic code."

As science editor, Sullivan coordinated all science stories run in the *New York Times*. His greatest difficulty, he has said, was to balance the desire of his superiors for front-page "scoops" and the tendency of research institutions to publish "self-serving press releases" touting "minor developments in important fields" with his own desire for accurate and thorough coverage of major advances. For years he argued for the creation of a separate "science section," like the food or sports sections; in the late 1970s, the *Times* reorganized its weekly supplements and created "Science Times," which has proved extremely popular.

Sullivan professes to be fascinated by astronomical subjects and has reported on the discovery of pulsars, galactic gravitational lenses, and black holes. Certainly the most unlikely of all phenomena predicted by general relativity, black holes were the subject for Sullivan's 1980 book *Black Holes: The Edge of Space, the End of Time*. Created by the gravitational collapse of massive stars, black holes occupy infinitesimal space but possess infinite density, Sullivan explained; no energy or matter can escape once in the grip of their intense gravity. Though not a single black hole has yet been definitively identified (by their very nature they are difficult to detect), scientists speculate that black holes may be common throughout the universe, orbiting distorted stellar companions or gradually devouring the cores of galaxies (possibly including our own). Drawing on the recent work of cosmologists including Stephen Hawking and Stephen Weinberg, Sullivan described these and yet more bizarre speculations with what Timothy Ferris, calling him "the Walter Cronkite of the science beat," termed his "customary poise and lucidity." In his review of *Black Holes* John Leonard wrote: "Walter Sullivan, unabashed, proposes a romance of the stars . . . in *Black Holes* he is seized by wondrous possibilities, attacked by quarks and quasars and white dwarfs and 'little green men,' fights his way out of Massachusetts Institute of Technology 'bag models,' and achieves singularity."

The author, who currently lives in Riverside, Connecticut, with his wife, the former Mary Barrett, has won most of journalism's important awards, including the George Polk Memorial Award (1959) for his "distinguished coverage of the International Geophysical Year" and three prizes in natural science writing from the American Association for the Advancement of Science (1963, 1968, and 1972). He was awarded the National Science Foundation's outstanding public service award (1978), the first ever given to a writer, and the National Academy of Sciences' Public Welfare Medal (1980). He is a director of the American Polar Society, a governor of the Arctic Institute of North America, and a councilor of the American Geographical Society.

PRINCIPAL WORKS: Quest for a Continent, 1957; White Land of Adventure (juvenile), 1957; Assault on the Unknown: The International Geophysical Year, 1961; Polar Regions: The Geography, Climate, and Life of the Arctic and Antarctic and the Explorers Who Discovered Them (juvenile), 1962; (ed.) America's Race for the Moon, 1962; We Are Not Alone, 1964; Continents in Motion: The New Earth Debate, 1974; (co-ed.) Science in the Twentieth Century, 1976; Black Holes: The Edge of Space, the End of Time, 1979; (with William C. Harvard) A Band of Prophets, 1982; Landprints, 1984.

ABOUT: Contemporary Authors, new revision series 2, 1980; Current Biography, 1980; Who's Who in America, 1983–84. *Periodicals*—Choice February 1975; New York Times March 16, 1957; April 6, 1961; December 6, 1961; New York Times Book Review December 20, 1964; November 3, 1974; January 6, 1980; Saturday Review February 1, 1964; Science December 25, 1964; Science Digest August 1984; Stamford [Connecticut] Advocate December 21,1974; Time, March 30, 1959; January 13, 1975.

*SUNDMAN, PER OLOF (September 3, 1922–), Swedish novelist and short-story writer, writes in: "I dislike writing about myself. However, here are a few biographical notes, rambling and uninteresting.

"I have a name which can be spelled with letters. But above all I am a combination of numbers: 220904-0878. (Sweden can claim the world's oldest and most accurate continuous population registration!) This particular number is mine alone, and it is to be found on my driver's licence, my various insurance policies, tax instruments, passport—yes, on all my official documents. I *am* 220904-0878. The first six numerals indicate that I was born on September 4, 1922. However, this is not true. In fact, I was born on Sunday, September 3, 1922, just before midnight. The midwife happened to fill in the wrong date on the documents and my mother never was able to have it corrected. This error at the beginning of my life sincerely gratifies me. Must one live in 'perfectionist' Sweden to understand my feeling?

"I can say with certainty the moment I decided to become a writer. It was in September 1935,

°sŏōnd´ män, pâr ōō´ lôf

PER OLOF SUNDMAN

not long after my eleventh birthday. My Swedish teacher happened to be a brilliant pedagogue. He started a 'class newspaper' to which I frequently contributed. He taught me to write a story pretty much the way I would tell it orally; even as a child, it seems, I told a striking story. He also influenced, if in the opposite direction, my classmate Stig Dagerman.

"My classmates and I grew up during the 1940s. I wrote assiduously, but was unable to find a suitable literary style. The 1940s was a fertile period in Sweden's modern literary history. I did not fit there. For me it was too verbosely effervescent, there was too much of the 'inner monolog,' too much psychologizing. Stig Dagerman, on the other hand, became one of the major names of that decade, a brilliant writer and playwright. Aside from my unsuccessful literary endeavors, I read—probably I read far too much. I recall that after a short period of fascination, I rejected Freud and Adler, to name two. Ivan Pavlov and John B. Watson had all the more influence on me. I found a relation between them and the classic Icelandic sagas. And these I have read and reread all my life. Snorre Sturlason, now there's a writer! Reflexologist 850 years before Pavlov, behaviorist 900 years before Watson! These vivid, straightforward, epic sagas are actually not just Icelandic—they are also Danish, Norwegian, Finnish and Swedish. They are a joint 'Scandinavian' gift to world literature. We have here a narrative technique whose simplicity is only illusory. It transports the reader or listener out onto the most deep and dangerous waters. Read Snorre's account of the battle at Svolder in 'The Saga of Olav Trygveson'! Where

in literature is there to be found a more shifting, subtle and ambiguous tale, although ostensibly confining itself to the telling of what took place and what was said?

"I spent my whole childhood and adolescence in Stockholm. This was my one reality, yet it remained inaccessible to me among the city's throngs. Naturally one can dig in an anthill, but does one find there anything to write about? In autumn 1945 I traveled north. The northern parts of Sweden, with the exception of the coastal areas, consist of vast forests and bogs. Towards the northwest, the land rises to vast and forestless expanses of mountains, interspersed with deep vales of birch trees. There dwell solitary Swedish mountain-farmers, engaged in agriculture of the extensive type, and it is there one finds the Lapps with their herds of reindeer. During the summer the weather sometimes becomes hot. In the winter, it grows so cold at times that the birds fall down frozen from their perches in the bushes. It was to these parts I went.

"I remained there almost a year. It was there I discovered the individual people—or, rather, the individual. In these thinly populated areas, he made his choreographic spins against a backdrop so devoid of people that he became fully manifest. He became accessible to me. Yet the language I needed to capture this still eluded me. In summer 1949 I bought into a small tourist hotel in Frostviken, in the province of Jämtland. The name of the village was Jormlien, and it lay as far north as Archangel in the Soviet Union or Nome, Alaska. At my back I had the mountains, in front of me there opened a broad valley, with large and numerous lakes. The people there spoke an archaic Swedish-Norwegian dialect, closely related to modern Icelandic. It was a vernacular characterized by the spare use of words. When someone said something there was a clatter, as if he or she had dropped a handful of pebbles on the tabletop. The sparing use of words requires a language with a large vocabulary. What had happened might be told, but value judgments were almost never made. The wording was often very poetic.

"It was there that I finally found a language and a method of written story-telling. I made my literary debut in 1957, at the age of thirty-five, with the short-story collection *Jägarna* (The Hunters). The following year my first novel *Undersökningen* (The Investigation) was published, and two years later my second novel *Skytten* (Sagittarius) appeared. The subject matter of these books was firmly anchored in the landscape and social reality of northern Sweden. After this there followed the novel *Expeditionen* (The Expedition), based on Stanley's account of his journeys through Africa. With *The Expedition* I made my move out onto the international book market.

"At Frostviken I ran into a complication. I was hotel manager and writer, but without warning I also found myself a politician. Suddenly I was chairman of the county board of supervisors, and I actually turned out to be quite good at dealing with concrete political matters. However my workload grew too heavy and I moved back to the Stockholm region in 1963, my mind made up to concentrate solely on my writing. I wrote several books, in addition to material for film and television. *Ingenjör Andrées luftfärd* [translated as *The Flight of the Eagle*] was published in 1968. I know of seventeen languages into which it has been translated, but there are probably well over twenty. I was therefore an established writer, and by all means should remain one.

"My social concern and above mentioned political knack led to my becoming a member of the Swedish Riksdag in 1969. (No, I am not a Socialist like so many of my fellow writers in Sweden. I am a member of the Center Party, a political movement which strictly speaking is found only in Finland, Iceland, Norway and Sweden, and which has evolved from the peasant parties of the past.) I was a member of parliament for eleven years and for obvious reasons occupied myself mainly with cultural policy. False modesty will not prevent me from declaring that I accomplished a great deal of good. But I did not get much writing done during these years: a book about Lofoten in northern Norway, a few television scripts, and the novel *Berättelsen om Såm* (Sam's Saga), which has been translated into a dozen languages—but not English.

"I left parliament in 1979, and threw myself into writing a novel about the remarkable inventor Alfred Nobel. But in the summer of 1980 I was enticed into joining the great Swedish polar expedition on the icebreaker *Ymer*. The journey (a fantastic experience) and the book I wrote about it (*Ishav*) took me almost two years to complete. At present I am once again plugging away at the Nobel material. However, I am plagued by mounting problems. Due to the way in which society has evolved, there are now but three kinds of Swedes. The three categories are retired, employed, or 'owner of one's own business' (examples of the latter category are carpenter, lawyer, or doctor with a private practice). Writers and artists are also considered 'owners of a private business.' It is reckoned that Sweden suffers under the heaviest tax burden in the world. To put things simply, owners of private businesses are required to pay an extra tax, equaling thirty percent of their income. This is the equivalent of the employee benefits employers pay for their workers. In sum, the tax system is making it impossible for writers and artists to live in this country."

As a writer, Leif Sjöberg observes, Sundman makes a clear distinction "between what can and what can not be known." Concerned strictly with objectivity, he rejects the idea of the "isolated individual" and insists that characters must be portrayed in terms of their relationship to others, "and within an environment in which he or she has a position and a *Gestalt*." Sundman is careful to document much of his fiction with fact. In *The Expedition,* as he points out above, he drew on the account of the expedition to rescue Enim Pasha in Henry M. Stanley's *The Congo* and *In Darkest Africa*; and in his best-known novel *The Flight of the Eagle* he used the records of Salomon Andrée's attempt, with two other men, to fly over the North Pole in a dirigible balloon, "The Eagle," in 1897. Forced to land in the Arctic wilderness, all three perished.

The themes of Sundman's novels, however, are far larger than the mere recording of events and introduce deeply philosophical insights into the human passion for heroism and the human plights of loneliness and failure. To quote the subtitle of Sjöberg's essay on Sundman in *Books Abroad,* he is only "a reasonably unbiased observer." Fundamentally he remains an imaginative writer, creating an illusion of truth however closely he adheres to the manner of documentary reporting. In *Two Days, Two Nights,* for example (subject of successful film and television adaptations in Sweden). he tells the story of the contrasting attitudes of two men to the pursuit of a psychopathic killer. One, a policeman, is workmanlike, sympathetic to the criminal but intent on his duty to track him down. The other, the narrator, is a teacher who enjoys the pursuit as an opportunity to display his cleverness. The interplay between the two men reflects Sundman's fascination with behavioral psychology (in part the influence of the American psychologist John B. Watson), with the conscious rather than the subconscious: "I am just as lacking in interest for it [the subconscious]," he has written, "as I am for the 'inner' man in general." Not surprisingly, he cites Truman Capote's *In Cold Blood* as a book that has fascinated him.

The narrator in one of Sundman's stories reminds himself: "Avoid conclusions, avoid evaluations, avoid judgments!" Some critics have found this detachment, Sundman's "reluctance to go the whole way," frustrating. Nevertheless, as Paul West wrote of *The Flight of the Eagle* in *Book World,* "no matter how cipher-like the three protagonists emerge . . . the doom-hard Arctic comes through, and shocks the mind . . . and that, I think, is what Sundman had in mind." A reviewer in the *Times Literary Supplement* agreed that slow and circumstantial as the narrative may be, the reader gradually "becomes involved and before the end has almost the feeling of taking part himself in the trio's doomed wanderings." A similar sense of mounting tension and horror pervades *Two Days, Two Nights,* "an engrossing psychological chiaroscuro," as Wayne Wonderley described it in *Library Journal.* In 1968 *The Flight of the Eagle* received the literature prize of the Nordic Council and the Grand Prize from *Literaturfrämjandet* in Stockholm. In 1982 it was made into an internationally successful film by Jan Troell, with Max von Sydow playing Andrée. Long active in the promotion of Scandinavian culture, Sundman was president of the Nordic Council and is a member of the Swedish Academy which awards the Nobel Prize in literature.

THOMAS SZASZ

WORKS IN ENGLISH TRANSLATION: Alan Blair translated *Two Days, Two Nights* in 1969. *The Expedition* and *The Flight of the Eagle* were translated by Mary Sandbach in 1970.

ABOUT: Columbia Dictionary of Modern European Literature, 1980; Rossel, S. H. A History of Scandinavian Literature 1870–1980, 1982. *Periodicals*—Books Abroad Spring 1973; World Literature Today Spring 1981; Autumn 1983.

SUTHERLAND, ROBERT GARIOCH *See* GARIOCH, ROBERT

*SZASZ, THOMAS STEPHEN (April 15, 1920–), American psychiatrist, son of Julius and Lily (Wellisch) Szasz, was born and raised in Budapest, Hungary, in a family of affluent, intellectually inclined Jewish landowners who came to the United States in 1938, shortly after Szasz finished high school, to escape Nazism. He went to the University of Cincinnati, where his uncle Otto Szasz was on the mathematics faculty, for both his B.A. and M.D. After an internship in Boston and a residency in Cincinnati, Szasz moved to the University of Chicago in 1946 to take further training in psychoanalysis.

During his training analysis at the Chicago Institute for Psychoanalysis Szasz's rebellious views

about his chosen profession began to take form. As was customary for all trainees, he had to be analyzed himself by a faculty member. In what Szasz regarded as an unpardonable breach of confidence, the results of his analysis were reported back to the Institute to be considered in evaluating his fitness as a therapist. This "completely despicable practice," which he likened to a "form of spying," crystallized doubts Szasz had begun to have about the scientific and moral values of psychiatry. In 1954, after several years in private psychoanalytic practice, Szasz was drafted into the Navy, and used this enforced break in his career to begin formalizing his doubts in a book manuscript. Upon his discharge in 1956, he got a position at the State University of New York Upstate Medical Center in Syracuse (where he has remained ever since) and in 1961 published *The Myth of Mental Illness,* thus launching his public career as a psychiatric gadfly.

From *The Myth of Mental Illness* to his 1980 book, *Sex By Prescription,* Szasz's line of analysis has been remarkably consistent. The starting point for all his critiques of modern society has been a deep commitment to the philosophy of libertarianism. Libertarians, who trace their intellectual heritage back to the mid-nineteenth century English philosopher John Stuart Mill, hold that whatever robs the individual of the right of self-determination is an unqualified moral and social evil. The only proper function of law, as they see it, is the protection of the individual from those who might seek to abrogate his personal freedom. As a psychoanalyst, Szasz gives libertarianism a special twist: the individual, as he sees him, is "born in chains, the innocent and hapless victim of internal passions and external controls that shape and possess him." Personal development consists of a "process of individual liberation" through which he learns to master both himself and his society. Any interference with that process of self-discovery, whether by brute force or subtle psychological manipulation, represents a threat to the "human enterprise," Szasz believes.

Psychiatry's worst sin against humanity, according to Szasz, is its unwarranted and extensive meddling in this difficult process of human growth. To acquire greater power and material rewards for themselves, psychiatrists have commandeered the moral crises engendered by modern society, labeling them erroneously as mental "diseases" and treating them ineffectively with medical measures. By telling unhappy people that they suffer from a mental disease, rather than a moral or social dilemma, psychiatrists allow their patients to escape full responsibility for their condition; and without accepting that responsibility, they cannot reach any valid or lasting resolution of their emotional problems. In the place of true growth, psychiatry offers only the spurious comfort of drugs and the enforced terror of involuntary hospitalization. For these reasons, Szasz believes that psychiatry has become one of the chief dehumanizing forces in modern society.

Szasz's critique of psychiatry rests on a thorough rejection of its claims to be a science. Drawing on the philosophy of logical positivism, he defines science in very strict terms as an enterprise concerned with measurable, verifiable physical properties and laws. Medicine is a science, he believes, because it deals with physical disorders caused by identifiable pathological mechanisms. Conversely, psychiatry is not a science, Szasz argues, because other than a few organic brain disorders, the mental "diseases" it treats have no known physiological basis; they are states of psychological or emotional distress.

Psychiatrists adopted the medical model of disease in the nineteenth century, Szasz argues in his historical analyses, so that they would acquire the authority of real scientists. In *Schizophrenia: The Sacred Symbol of Psychiatry,* he posits that the discovery of syphilitic insanity in the early 1900s gave them the opportunity to expand the disease model to include schizophrenia and the milder neuroses. In the process, psychiatrists substituted a supposedly neutral, scientific language of health and disease—what Szasz terms the "ideology of mental health"—for the language of right and wrong, sin and salvation, that had traditionally been used to label social deviance. In the short run, severely disturbed individuals benefited from the transformation in terminology and treatment; but the continual process of masking moral judgments in pseudo-scientific jargon has ultimately made psychiatry a repressive force in Western society.

Szasz has been particularly concerned with the legal implications of psychiatry's encroachments on the moral order. His writings on medical jurisprudence have focused on two primary issues, involuntary commitment to mental hospitals and the "psychiatrization" of criminal law. From his earliest work, Szasz has been a harsh and persistent critic of involuntary commitment. With Erving Goffman and R. D. Laing, he has been one of the most frequently cited authorities for the policy of deinstitutionalizing mental patients. Believing as he does that the vast majority of mental patients do not suffer from a disease, he sees the mental hospital solely as an institution of social control. Individuals are confined there not because they pose a threat to themselves or others, Szasz claims, but because they have transgressed important social norms. Their forcible removal from society is rationalized on the grounds that they are sick and need treatment. But since they are neither sick nor likely to receive treatment when confined in a mental hospital, he considers involuntary commitment as a gross violation of mental patients' legal rights. In *Law, Liberty and Psychiatry,* Szasz concludes, "like slavery, the entire oppressive-coercive pattern inherent in present-day involuntary mental hospitalization is an evil which must be done away with."

Szasz is equally critical of the "psychiatrization" of the criminal law, that is, the increasing tendency to equate crime with sickness. For example, he objects violently to the 1954 "Durham Rule," which abandoned the traditional right/wrong tests of criminal responsibility for a more liberal standard: that the unlawful act simply be shown to be the product of mental disease or mental defect. As Szasz told an interviewer in 1971: "The very essence of my work . . . is that we have replaced a theological outlook on life with a therapeutic one." If convicted under the rule, offenders are automatically placed in mental hospitals until such time as they are pronounced "cured." The substitution of a therapeutic rationale for the traditional moral function of the law, Szasz argues, is a crime against both the offender and society. By defining him as sick, the law discredits the criminal "as a self-responsible human being" and then subjects him to "humiliating punishment defined and disguised as treatment." This legal approach, Szasz concludes, "is hardly more than a refurbishing, with new terms, of the main ideas and techniques of the inquisitorial process."

Although extremely critical of the psychiatric establishment, Szasz has remained a staunch advocate of psychoanalysis as a means of human growth. In *The Ethics of Psychoanalysis,* he outlines a model of contractual or "autonomous" psychotherapy that he feels to be ethical. His conception of autonomous psychotherapy relies primarily on game theory: analyst and client agree upon rules governing their exchanges, then enter into a structured series of encounters exploring the client's psyche, the outcome of which is always uncertain. Conflict between the two players is a given, especially in the early stages of the game, and analyst and analysand must continually negotiate their demands and expectations. Such a therapeutic relationship must remain entirely voluntary: either partner can terminate it at any point. In many respects, Szasz's game model of therapy anticipates the transactional analysis developed by Eric Berne and his associates in the 1970s.

Not surprisingly, Szasz's denunciations of psychiatry have outraged his fellow psychiatrists, who consider him a dangerous extremist. In the revised edition of *The Myth of Mental Illness,* Szasz states that within a year of its original publication, the Commissioner of the New York State Department of Mental Hygiene demanded that he be dismissed from the Syracuse position because he did not "believe" in mental illness. Yet for a variety of reasons, Szasz's critiques found a receptive audience outside the medical profession. Dissatisfaction with the state mental hospital system, which had been growing in the 1950s, culminated in the Community Mental Health Act of 1964, setting aside federal funds for the establishment of community-based treatment centers. At the same time, new drugs, primarily the phenothiazines, made it increasingly feasible for chronically disabled mental patients to live outside institutions. In an atmosphere of general concern with civil rights, lawyers took up the cause of mental patients' legal entitlements, attacking the commitment process and the custodialism of hospital care. Although often disassociating themselves from Szasz's extreme views, mental health advocates invoked his name to justify their positions.

Szasz's views on drug addiction and suicide, which rest on the same philosophical assumptions as his critiques of psychiatry, have found much less support. In *Ceremonial Chemistry,* Szasz characterized the campaign against drug addiction as a modern-day witch hunt. As he sees it, a society increasingly dependent on culturally approved substances to avoid its moral

dilemmas has hypocritically and harshly persecuted those who become addicted to the "wrong" drugs. Coercive government control of drug traffic and drug use, he concludes, is as morally reprehensible as state-supported psychiatric abuses; all laws regulating drug use should be abolished. In *The Theology of Medicine,* Szasz makes a very similar libertarian argument for non-intervention in suicide.

Controversy over Szasz's views on drug addiction and suicide highlights the importance of timing and context in explaining his influence. His early work on psychiatry was enormously successful because its publication coincided with a broad-based reform movement in the mental health field. In the early sixties, when a decade of fiscal, therapeutic, and social dissatisfactions with the state hospital system peaked, Szasz presented a timely set of arguments against institutional psychiatry. In contrast, his later work has had less impact because his libertarian philosophy of non-intervention in problems such as drug abuse and suicide has had far less public support.

Critics point to a number of flaws in Szasz's formulations. He has been taken to task for exaggerating the scientific exactitude of medicine at psychiatry's expense. His argument posits a rigid mind/body dualism in the disease process that the vast majority of scientists find much too simplistic. Moreover, medical research has identified abnormalities in the brain chemistry of schizophrenics, undercutting his contention that no disease process exists in that illness. Szasz's views have also been attacked on social policy grounds, especially as the drawbacks of the deinstitutionalization movement have become apparent. The potential dangers to society as a whole, critics argue, require some coercive measures in dealing with mentally disturbed individuals. Liberal reformers accuse Szasz of a callous disregard for the poor who cannot afford the expensive private therapy he prescribes. Because of his laissez-faire philosophy of social welfare, Peter Sedgwick has likened Szasz to the "social Darwinists" of the nineteenth century who disapproved of any measures that allowed the "unfit" to survive. Szasz may not preach outright genocide, Sedgwick concludes, but he seems "content to redefine out of existence the structured social problems of the exploited communities of America."

However flawed they may find his arguments, few critics would deny that Szasz's passionate advocacy helped to improve the lot of the modern mental patient. And although his libertarian philosophy may seem extreme, his warnings about the dangers of the therapeutic state are undeniably relevant. In the last analysis, Szasz's work remains powerful because it addresses a central issue in modern society: the balance between individual freedom and collective good.

PRINCIPAL WORKS: Pain and Pleasure, 1957; The Myth of Mental Illness, 1961 (rev. ed. 1974); Law, Liberty, and Psychiatry, 1963; Psychiatric Justice, 1965; The Ethics of Psychoanalysis, 1965; Ideology and Insanity, 1970; The Manufacture of Madness, 1970; The Second Sin, 1973; Ceremonial Chemistry, 1974; Heresies, 1976; Karl Kraus and the Soul-Doctors, 1976; Schizophrenia, 1976; Psychiatric Slavery, 1977; The Theology of Medicine, 1977; The Myth of Psychotherapy, 1978; Sex By Prescription, 1980.

ABOUT: Contemporary Authors, new revision series 9, 1983; Current Biography, 1975; Sedgwick, P. Psychopolitics, 1982; Vatz, R.E. and L.S. Weinberg (eds.) Thomas Szasz: Primary Values and Major Contentions, 1983. *Periodicals*—Human Behavior 1 1972; New York Times Magazine October 3, 1971.

GAY TALESE

*TALESE, GAY (February 7, 1932–), American journalist and non-fiction writer, writes: "I was born on the southern shore of New Jersey on an island resort called Ocean City that was founded in 1879 by devout Methodist ministers who wished to establish a presence of God on the beach, to shade the summer from the corrupting exposure of the flesh, and to eliminate the temptations of alcohol and other evil spirits that they saw buzzing around them as freely as the mosquitos in the surrounding marshlands.

"And while these sober-suited ministers in straw hats did not achieve all of their virtuous ambitions, they did establish a tone of Victorian restraint in Ocean City that exists to this day. The sale of liquor is still forbidden on the island. Cinemas and most other businesses are closed on the sabbath. The steeples of churches rise prominently in an open sky. In the center of town there are white gingerbread houses with large porches, turrets and finials that retain the look of America before the turn of the century. And a modern young woman of the 1980s who strolls on the beach wearing a slim bikini will often prompt mild frowns from the town's proper matrons, if not from the middle-aged men concealing their interest behind mirrored sun-glasses.

"In this setting where sensuality and sin are always in delicate balance, I was born on the seventh day of February in 1932, ten years after my father had first visited the island on vacation. Having emigrated to the United States from a priest-ridden village in southern Italy where church bells rang incessantly, and where any

sign of personal interest between a young man and woman prior to marriage was scandalous, Ocean City appealed to him immediately. I also think it significant that this coastal area of New Jersey, fifteen miles south of Atlantic City, lies at the same latitude as my father's birthplace in southern Italy. And another reason he settled in Ocean City was his noticing, during his first walk through the town's main street, a "For Sale" sign on a tailor shop that was owned by a white-haired asthmatic gentleman who, desperate to leave the shore for the drier climate of Arizona, enticed my father with irresistible terms into buying the store.

"Though trained as a master tailor in Italy and France, where his Paris-based cousins and nephews of the Rue de la Paix are still renowned for the special cut and craft of their clothes for men, my father soon learned in Ocean City that the ministers and other staid citizens were unlikely candidates for the sharply-pointed lapels, slashed pockets, and flamboyant waistcoats of continental tailoring. So he wisely focused on the more stylish world of women's wear, specializing at first in the remodeling and altering of fur coats, and later—after his marriage in 1929 to my mother, who had worked in Brooklyn as a buyer for a large department store—in the establishment of a boutique featuring well-tailored dresses and coats for middle-aged women of ample figures and means.

"These women formed the moral fiber of the community. They were the ministers' wives, the bankers' wives, the bridge players, the town gossips. They were the white-gloved ladies who in summer avoided the beach and the boardwalk, and after a late breakfast and perhaps a few furtive sips of wine in their bedrooms, they would spend considerable amounts of time and money shopping along the avenue in places like my parent's store—where, amid the low humming of the fans and under the coddling care of my mother in the dressing rooms, they would try on clothes while discussing their personal lives and the town's latest social events, to which my mother paid close attention as she kept them engaged with polite questions and her disarming manner, all the while selling them more dresses.

"As a small boy observing my mother in the store I learned much about the subtle ways of drawing people out in conversation, the sales manner that gains a subject's trust and cooperation—techniques that years later served me well as a journalist. I also enjoyed during my youth overhearing the customers' tales of the town, the daily common concerns and secret lives of ordinary people, the human interest stories that would in the future become my specialty as a feature-writer on the *New York Times,* as a profile writer at *Esquire* magazine, and finally as the author of books that often reveal the discrepancy that exists between people's appearance and their reality. Indeed, each of my books draws inspiration from a sense of boyhood wonder and curiosity that evolved out of watching people parade in and out of the store, and in growing up in the intimate environment of a tiny island. My first book, *New York—a Serendipiter's Journey,* presents the smalltown character of New York neighborhoods and reveals the interesting lives of certain obscure individuals dwelling within the city's shadows. The next book, *The Bridge,* focuses on the private lives and loves of steel-workers as they link a bridge to an island and the character of the land.

"My first best-seller, *The Kingdom and the Power,* describes the backgrounds and interpersonal relationships of my former colleagues on the *New York Times,* where I had worked for ten years as a staff writer (from 1955–65); the *Times* provided me with the only fulltime job I ever had. Its newsroom was my 'store.'

"In reaction ot my father's embarrassment and anger over the prevalence of Italo-Americans in organized crime, I contrived a way to obtain personal interviews as well as the companionship of Mafia members themselves in order to understand better their private lives and rationalizations. This book was entitled *Honor Thy Father.* And in response to the sexual repression and hypocrisy that characterized the island of my birth, I wrote—almost as a dedication to the ladies in my mother's dressing rooms—*Thy Neighbor's Wife.*

"Now I am involved with a book that goes more deeply into my own roots, a long work that includes the history of Ocean City back to the days when Indians went clam-digging each day along the beach. I have also spent much of the last three years in Italy researching the history of my father's village. This background will form the basis of a saga about emigrating to America, about leaving home forever and being forever tied emotionally to the time and place of one's birth. My father's village has a history going back 2,000 years, back to the eras of the ancient Romans and Greeks. In my research I have recently arrived at the sixteenth century."

———

Gay Talese was born Gaetano Talese in the resort town of Ocean City, New Jersey, the son of Joseph Talese, an Italian immigrant who owned a women's clothing store in the town, and the former Catherine DePaulo. After a strict Roman Catholic upbringing he entered the University of Alabama to study journalism, earning his bachelor's degree in 1953. He was fortunate enough the same year to land a job with the *New York Times.* Starting as a copy boy, he was appointed staff writer in 1955 and held that post for a decade, earning a reputation as an adroit reporter of local-color stories, those slices of big-city life then exemplified on the newspaper by the work of Meyer Berger. Upon Berger's death in 1959, Talese took over the column "About New York."

New York: A Serendipiter's Journey, Talese's first book, consists of his articles on the city originally published in the *Times.* Accompanied by dozens of grittily evocative, black-and-white photographs by Marvin Lichtner, the text is divided into five sections descriptive of the city and its people, at least as seen by the author: "Of Things Unnoticed," "Of the Anonymous," "Of Characters," "Of Odd Occupations," and "Of the Forgotten." The short essays consider a multitude of subjects, from a catalogue of the types of stray cat in the city to the sad permanence of Potter's Field, the paupers' burial ground. Most critics liked the book, but few copies were sold outside New York.

While still working for the *Times,* in 1960, Talese was engaged by Harold Hayes, the innovative editor of *Esquire,* to write several extended profiles for that magaizne. One of them, "The King as a Middle-Aged Man," about the private life of Joe Louis, which appeared in the June 1962 issue, was later considered by Tom Wolfe to be the earliest example and inspiration of the "new journalism," entirely unlike any piece of non-fiction reportage he had ever read. "Really stylish reporting," Wolfe wrote in 1972, recalling the revelation the article represented for himself and others, "was something no one knew how to deal with, since no one was used to thinking of reporting as having an *esthetic* dimension." *The Overreachers,* Talese's second collection of previously published pieces, reprints the article on Louis along with memorable profiles of such figures as Frank Sinatra, Floyd Patterson, Joshua Logan, Peter O'Toole, and Joe DiMaggio.

Talese's first two collections, together with *The Bridge,* a short study of the people involved in building New York's Verrazano Narrows Bridge, were reprinted as *Fame and Obscurity.* In an "Author's Note" discussing the book and the genesis of its disparate parts, he gives a succinct definition of the school of journalism of which he is generally considered the founder and foremost practitioner: "The new journalism, though often reading like fiction, is not fiction. It is, or should be, as reliable as the most reliable reportage although it seeks a larger truth than is possible through the mere compilation of verifiable facts, the use of direct quotations, and adherence to the rigid organizational style of the older form. The new journalism allows, demands in fact, a more imaginative approach to reporting, and it permits the writer to inject himself into the narrative if he wishes, as many writers do, or to assume the role of a detached observer, as other writers do, including myself."

A profile Talese wrote for *Esquire* on Clifton Daniel, managing editor of the *Times,* led to a full-length study of that newspaper, *The Kingdom and the Power,* his first best-selling book. He spent the better part of two years talking with former colleagues and examining many private files of *Times*-related material, notably those maintained by the Ochs and Sulzberger families. Such copious research—always a characteristic of this author's working method—resulted at last in what he described as "the kind of book that I knew I wanted to write—a human history of an institution in transition, a book that would tell more about the men who report the news than the news they report, a factual story about several generations of *Times* men and the interplay within those generations, the internal scenes and confrontations and adjustments that are part of the vitality and growth of any enduring institution." The book traces the history of the newspaper and its best-known proprietors and editors but is generally reckoned best at describing, in the author's words, "the tense incidents that transpired within the *Times* during the nineteen-sixties." The most vivid character studies are of those journalists who were Talese's superiors: Meyer Berger, Turner Catledge, Clif-

ton Daniel, James Reston, and others. Erwin D. Canham, the veteran editor of the *Christian Science Monitor,* wrote that he knew "of no book about a great institution which is so detailed, so intensely personalized, or so dramatized as this volume." Yet Canham also held, as did several other reviewers, that the result was "overdramatized," the characters "all touched with more than a little theatrical makeup."

On several occasions in the years before the publication of *Honor Thy Father,* Talese referred to his continuing project as "a study of tradition and change within three successive generations of an Italo-American family between 1900 and 1970." The family in question turned out to be the notorious Bonanno clan, at the very center of organized crime in America. The author gradually gained their confidence, particularly that of Bill Bonanno, the son, and, to a lesser extent, of his father, the Mafia chief Joe ("Bananas") Bonanno. The book was extremely successful, selling nearly a third of a million copies in hardcover within four months of publication, but several critics raised questions about the tone of Talese's largely sympathetic portrayal of the family. F. J. Cook complained that he "creates the impression that the racketeering of the Mafioso has been grossly exaggerated by government crime-busters"; Colin MacInnes made a similar point, that Talese "conveys the impression that being a mobster is much the same as being a sportsman, film star or any other kind of public 'personality.'" Other reviewers recognized that, having made such effort and run such risk in achieving the trust of a Mafia family, Talese would have been unwise, to say the least, to make public fun of them in print.

Thy Neighbor's Wife, a study of heterosexual experimentation in contemporary America, became the best-known non-fiction work in progress during the 1970s. Talese's extensive research, coupled with a long writer's block, cause him to miss his publishers' deadline by five years, and several magazine articles on the nature of that research, notably *New York* magazine's "An Evening in the Nude with Gay Talese," ensured strong advance interest in the book. Several months before publication, furthermore, United Artists bought film rights for the record-breaking sum of $2.5 million. The book became an instant best-seller and remained the number-one non-fiction seller in the United States for three months. The author intended it to be a substantial work "that would reflect the social and sexual trends of the entire nation: a book that would deal with the history of sex laws and censorship, as well as describe some of the people and events that in recent decades influenced or reflected the redefinition of morality in America." Although he treats the history of American sexuality at some length, "going back to the founding of the Puritan republic," as usual his best writing is devoted to describing the people he is most concerned about, such as the married couple who in 1967 started Sandstone, a Reichian center for sexual experimentation in Los Angeles. "I wanted to report the bedroom," he said in an interview about the time of the book's publication. "I wanted to *report*—not fictionalize and create, as a novelist might do. The bedroom has been traditionally out of bounds for the serious reporter. If there is anything pioneering about this book—and I think there is—it is that it uses real names." *Thy Neighbor's Wife* was not a success with many of its reviewers. "If obscenity," wrote Rhoda Koenig in a critique typical of many the book received, "is determined not by the number and choice of certain words a writer uses, but by his vision, then the conclusion is inescapable that Talese has written a dirty book. There is not a trace of humanity or warmth in it." The sociologist Robert Coles, on the other hand, praised the author's seriousness of purpose and honesty of presentation: "He has a gift, through a phrase here, a sentence there, of making important narrative and historical connections. We are given, really, a number of well-told stories, their social message cumulative."

Talese married Nan Ahearn in June 1959; they have two daughters. He has called his wife, who is at present vice-president and head of the New York office of Houghton Mifflin Company, "the finest editor I have ever known" who "has had a hand in every paragraph I have written in the past twenty years." Talese describes himself as "very vain and egotistical"; like Tom Wolfe, the other best-known new journalist, he is a renowned dandy with a vast wardrobe, and is often reported as paying up to fifteen hundred dollars apiece for his many suits. He lives on Manhattan's Upper East Side and spends his summers in Ocean City.

PRINCIPAL WORKS: *Non-fiction*—New York, A Serendipiter's Journey, 1961; The Bridge, 1964; The Overreachers, 1965; The Kingdom and the Power, 1969; Fame and Obscurity, 1970; Honor Thy Father, 1971; Thy Neighbor's Wife, 1980.

ABOUT: Contemporary Authors revised series 9–12, 1974 and new revision series, 1983; Current Biography, 1972. *Periodicals*—Atlantic May 1980; Book World June 15, 1969; November 7, 1971; Christian Science Monitor July 3, 1969; December 9, 1971; Commentary September 1969; Library Journal November 15, 1964; September 15, 1969; May 15, 1970; June 15, 1980; Nation September 15, 1969; New Republic May 3, 1980; New York Herald Tribune Books August 8, 1961; New York Review of Books July 20, 1972; May 29, 1980; New York Times Book Review July 23, 1961; January 17, 1965; June 8, 1969; August 2, 1970; October 31, 1971; May 4, 1980; New Yorker July 8, 1961; November 28, 1964; Newsweek July 21, 1969; October 4, 1971; April 28, 1980; Playboy May 1980; Saturday Review June 14, 1969; October 9, 1971; May 1980; Time July 4, 1969; October 4, 1971; April 28, 1980; Times Literary Supplement May 14, 1971; April 14, 1972; July 4, 1980.

TEVIS, WALTER (1928–August 9, 1984), American novelist and science fiction writer, sent the following sketch to *World Authors* in early 1984: "I was born in San Francisco and reared by a hypochondriac mother and a nearly-invisible father; I spent most of my childhood either being sick or pretending to be, to please my mother. This meant a lot of time in bed, reading. What I read were fantasies of one kind or another. They included all of the Oz books, from *Glinda the Good* to *The Emerald City of Oz*, intermixed with books of Norse and Greek mythology, and whatever stories of gods or fairies I could lay my hands on in the San Francisco Public Library. I discovered realistic fiction only much later, in my teens, after my family had moved to Lexington, Kentucky. A few years later I began reading serious poetry, in a very eclectic manner—often barely understanding what I was reading. I was a college freshman at the time, majoring in chemistry: I found myself more and more often seated at the plywood booths at what must surely have been the only beer hall in Lexington where the poems of Ezra Pound and Wallace Stevens were being discussed. I became hooked. I wanted to be a poet. Although I liked chemistry well enough, I changed my major to English. After graduating I was surprised by an offer to teach at Science Hill, Kentucky, whose high school had an enrollment of seventy-three students. I would be the whole English department. I had not been trained for teaching and the salary was miniscule; but no one was buying my poems either.

"I took the job and loved it. This led to five years of teaching basic grammar and literature—both to my students and myself—in several tiny high schools in rural Kentucky. It was a wonderful kind of work to do with those years of my life.

"In college I had spent a lot of time playing pool. Often I would find myself hurrying through whatever poem I was working on in order to get downtown to the poolroom. After doing this for several months it dawned on me that I could combine the two activities and write po-

WALTER TEVIS

ems about pool playing. I tried it but it didn't work. Or possibly it did, since it showed me how uncongenial poems were when I had something other than myself to write about. In any case I began to write short stories about pool players. During my last few years of high school teaching, these stories, to my surprise, began to sell to national magazines. *Esquire* bought the first of them, 'The Best in the Country.' I decided to quit high school teaching and go back to college.

"The next few years were divided between graduate study in English literature and the writing of two novels—one about a pool player and the other about an extraterrestrial. Although both books found sizeable audiences—in fact, both were eventually made into films—for some reason I was devoting more time to the academic side of my life than to writing. Eventually I became a Professor of English Literature and Creative Writing [Ohio University]. Over the next fifteen years I would start novels but somehow be unable to finish them. I began drinking too much. The classes and the students were a pleasure to deal with, but I knew I ought to be writing and I wasn't.

"By the time I was in my late forties this was driving me crazy; I was presumably teaching people how to write but doing less and less of it myself. I wasn't sure I could even write decent fiction anymore. I was drinking heavily every evening and when I tried to stop found I couldn't; I had become an alcoholic. It took me a long time to discover that the first step in overcoming alcoholism was to admit the problem existed and the second was to look for help. After several years of fighting these unpleasant truths, I put myself into a treatment center for alcoholics and managed to stop drinking altogether. That made a radical change in my life which emboldened me to make another: two years after getting sober, at the age of fifty, I took a leave of absence from my professorship at Ohio University and moved to New York City, where I began writing novels for a living. It has been six years now; that leave of absence has become a resignation, and I have published four novels and a collection of short stories since.

"During the first few years in New York I found myself drawn to the fantasies I had begun my literary life with; I wrote what is called science fiction. In the first of these, *Mockingbird,* I attempted a statement about college teaching, feeling I should make some use of all those teaching years. But my satirical intentions, though present in the book, became subordinate to the aspirations of the characters, and I am now glad it turned out that way. I have loved fable ever since I discovered the land of Oz, and I love re-inventing the world—or disguising it in such a way as to make certain things about it more real. My novels about the 'future' are of course not about the future at all; they are ways of configuring my own times and places in the manner most meaningful to me. What I love most about fables is their ability to tell the truth.

"But after several books of that kind I began to tire of inventing the world and turned to doing realistic fiction again. My first novel, twenty years earlier, had structured itself around a game: pool. I had strong feelings about one other game, chess, and decided to try a novel about a chessplayer. (The real subject turned out to be about obsession.) I had never been consciously autobiographical before; in this novel I drew on my early experience of a year in a children's hospital. But I found a good deal of disguise necessary. My character became a girl; the hospital became an orphanage (I suppose I felt like an orphan as a child, with my two very withdrawn parents) and the reading I was obsessed with in the hospital became, for my heroine, an obsession with chess. I found strength in that use of my life and have come to feel that where there is strength in my work it almost invariably comes from material dredged, consciously or not, from the first dozen years. I suspect I am not the only writer for whom this is true. In any case I hope to be able to draw on some of the same sources in my future work. Whether that work will be the self-announced fable of science fiction, or fable in some more naturalistic dress, I don't yet know."

Walter Tevis enlisted in the U.S. Navy on his seventeenth birthday, and for a year and a half was stationed at Okinawa. Returning to Lexington, he worked for the Kentucky Highway Department while writing his first novel, *The Hustler,* which quickly brought him to attention, and was subsequently made into a well-known film starring Paul Newman. *The Hustler* tells the story of Eddie Felson, a young pool shark from Lexington, Kentucky, who breezes into Chicago, confident that he can beat Minnesota Fats, the best straight-pool player in the country. They meet at Bennington's Pool Hall, and engage in a forty-hour pool marathon, which results in the worst beating of his life. After a series of later experiences, including one in which his thumbs are broken by small-time gangsters, Felson challenges Minnesota Fats again, this time destroying his opponent. Although the reviewer for *Time* found the moral of the story "sententious" and the love story attached to it a "cliché," he praised its "succession of scenes in which a smoky, seedy world becomes sharply alive." The *New Yorker's* reviewer was impressed by the novel's "swift, effective style," and other reviewers called the novel "tightly plotted" and even spellbinding. Rex Lardner, in the *New York Times,* remarked that Tevis' novel "is a tense, jolting trip to the tough, dusty, smoky, ball-clackety, money-filled world of the pool shark . . . night-peopled with gamblers, suckers, steerers, . . . hoods, compulsive losers, the placid rich, the desperate broke. . . . Tevis writes like a streak. . . . This is a fine, swift, wanton, offbeat novel."

In his second novel, *The Man Who Fell to Earth,* Tevis chose a different world to explore, that of science fiction. The novel quickly became a cult classic, and in 1976 was adapted by Nicholas Roeg as a film, starring David Bowie. The central character is Newton, a lone extraterrestrial from Anthea, disguised as a human, who lands on Earth secretly to save his own species from extinction by preparing the way for their migration to our planet. He effortlessly amasses a fortune, using superior extraterrestrial technology, and builds a spaceship with which to ferry Anthea's remaining three hundred inhabitants (sole survivors of five nuclear wars) to Earth. However, he is foiled by government agents, blinded, and rendered pathetic and helpless.

The novel was published in paperback and received no reviews in literary magazines, but it has since been reissued in hardcover, with an introduction by Norman Spinrad. As Spinrad points out, the novel is remarkable in its "psychological realism." What Tevis has done, he wrote, "is [to have] written an utterly realistic novel about an alien human on Earth. . . . Re-

alistic in its portrait of his strengths and failures and confusion. Realistic in its description of what it is like to be an alien human. Realistic enough to become a metaphor for something inside us all, some existential aloneness." As such, the novel seemed to Spinrad and many others to have something like classic status.

Tevis has taught English and creative writing at Southern Connecticut College in New Haven and at Ohio University in Athens. In a *New York Times* interview, Tevis explained that his teaching did not turn out to be entirely compatible with his writing. "I found myself leaving my enthusiasm in the classroom," he said. "I enjoyed the students, but as long as I had a live audience, I didn't have a second need for a reading audience. It's scary to write—teaching is easier." In 1978, taking a gambler's risk, Tevis left his job at Ohio University to go to New York and devote himself entirely to writing fiction. His gamble led to the publication of a series of new books, beginning with *Mockingbird,* a main selection of the Science Fiction Book Club.

Mockingbird is concerned in part with a "Mike Nine" robot, Robert Spofforth, "the most sophisticated piece of equipment ever to be fashioned by human ingenuity." In the artificially grown body of a powerfully built black man he possesses all of recorded knowledge, and is chief manager of a post nuclear-war society set five hundred years in the future. The human inhabitants of this America are illiterate, docile, addicted to soporific drugs, TV, and selfish individualism, while robot drones and super robots have charge of the everyday workings of society. As robot Spofforth longs only for death, two lovers, Paul Bentley and Mary Lou Borne, defy the dictates of the state ("Don't ask; relax," "Quick sex is best") to teach themselves to read, and to establish a small community of family love. The novel ends with Spofforth's death and a small glimmer of hope for humanity's survival. Reviewers inevitably compared *Mockingbird* to *Brave New World* and *1984,* but found it nevertheless, fresh and original. Michael Bishop, in *Book World,* speculated that "future generations will periodically rediscover [the book] with wonder and delight." Susan Jeffreys and Mary Anne Bonney, in their Science Fiction column in *Punch,* praised the novel for its "great style and wit," and judged it as a distinctly superior piece of work.

Far From Home is a collection of thirteen tales, some of which had appeared previously in *Galaxy* and *The Magazine of Fantasy and Science Fiction.* Some were written earlier in Tevis' career, but slightly more than half were new, and these were generally regarded as his best.

The reviewer for *Library Journal* noted that they reveal "the keen eye for realistic detail" that makes the most fantastic events seem somehow plausible; and other critics praised the stories for their craft, and for the exactness and precision of Tevis' prose. Michael Bishop summed up the attitude of many in referring to Tevis' special gift for "psychological verisimilitude." Tevis' next science fiction novel, *The Steps of the Sun*, is set in the year 2064 in an America that has become a second-class power and is energy poor. The hero is a Ben Belson, a millionaire tycoon and adventurer, who embarks upon interstellar flight to search for "safe uranium" on a distant planet. Ironically, while Belson finds a new Eden on a foreign planet, he returns to confront a failure of communication between people, and between himself and the state, at home. David Lehman, in *Newsweek*, praised the novel as an acutely observed work, lighted by wit and intelligence; and the reviewer for *Publishers Weekly* called *The Steps of the Sun* "engaging and effortlessly readable, Tevis's best science fiction since *The Man Who Fell to Earth*."

Tevis' widely praised *The Queen's Gambit* does for chess what Tevis had formerly done for pool in *The Hustler*—made it, unpredictably, the source of extraordinarily suspenseful drama. His protagonist this time is a girl, Beth Harmon, who is raised in a Kentucky orphanage where, at eight, she first plays chess with the institution's janitor and discovers that she has a genius for the game. A plain girl with few outside interests and little worldly grace, she becomes the American chess champion at fourteen, and starts on the international circuit, in the end, at the climax of ever-mounting suspense, claiming the world chess championship.

Harold Schonberg, in the *New York Times*, wondered if it were really credible that a young woman could perform with such power and originality of mind in a game wholly dominated by men. But he conceded that "one does get involved with this strange, unhappy gifted heroine. Beth Harmon may not be prepossessing, but she has the dedication of a Biblical saint, a freak memory and an ability to synthesize and create and blow her little world apart . . . that nobody else can match." A. Alvarez, in the *New York Review of Books*, commented that "Tevis's prose is pure and emphatic, Like Beth's lucid, one-track mind, but he knows how to generate tension. As the book progresses and the games become more and more complex, this sense of excitement, stillness, and silence builds until it reaches an extraordinary climax in Moscow. Without any exterior action to speak of, *The Queen's Gambit* in a thriller in the most genuine sense of the term."

Tevis, who was himself a Class C chess player, said that his protagonists are "loners," who are up against formidable odds, and that he was "obsessed with the struggle between winning and losing." Married and the father of a son and a daughter, he lived in Manhattan, where he died of lung cancer at the age of fifty-six. His most recent novel, *The Color of Money*, is a sequel to *The Hustler*.

PRINCIPAL WORKS: The Hustler, 1959; The Man Who Fell to Earth, 1963; Mockingbird, 1980; Far From Home, 1981; The Steps of the Sun, 1983; The Queen's Gambit, 1983; The Color of Money, 1984.

ABOUT: Book World March 23, 1980; March 22, 1981; Newsweek February 20, 1984; New Yorker April 4, 1983; New York Review of Books November 10, 1983; New York Times April 6, 1983; August 11, 1984; New York Times Book Review January 11, 1959; April 3, 1983; Punch June 25, 1980; Time January 12, 1959; Times Literary Supplement February 19, 1960.

*THESIGER, WILFRED (PATRICK) (June 3, 1910–),

British explorer and travel writer, was born in the compound of the British legation in Addis, Ababa, Ethiopia, several months after the arrival there of his parents, Capt. the Hon. Wilfred Gilbert Thesiger, British minister to Ethiopia, and the former Kathleen Mary Vigors. He was the first Englishman born in that East African country. Having received his first gun—a double barrelled .410—when he was seven, at the age of eight he took part in a tiger shoot in India, where he had gone on holiday with his parents and where his uncle, Viscount Chelmsford, was viceroy. Thesiger was educated at Eton and at Magdalen College, Oxford, where he was captain of the boxing team. In October 1930, at the beginning of his second year at Oxford, he was invited by Haile Selassie, who had been a friend of his late father, to the imperial coronation in Addis Ababa. He got his first taste of exploration following the official celebrations, when he obtained the emperor's permission to travel into the country of the Danakil, a murderously fierce tribe living hundreds of miles east of the capital, an experience he described in an article in the *Times Literary Supplement* of June 22, 1984. December 1930, he later wrote, was "the most decisive month of my life." The course of that life—travel, adventure, and freedom—was set from then on.

In 1935, Thesiger joined the Sudan Political Service, serving in Northern Darfur and the Upper Nile, and managing to travel during his frequent leaves through Syria and Palestine, Morocco, and French Equatorial Africa. He

°thā´ si jur

WILFRED THESIGER

fought with the Sudan Defense Force early in World War II and against the Italians in the liberation of Ethiopia in 1941, receiving the DSO for valor.

Thesiger's travels in Arabia began in 1945, when he was attached to a government locust-control project. After extensive trips through the Western Aden Protectorate, Dhaufar, and the Qarra Mountains, he first saw in November–December 1945 the Rub al-Khali, or Empty Quarter, of southern Arabia. In his first book, *Arabian Sands*, he recounts two journeys on foot and on camel across the Rub al-Khali, the many friends he made among the Bedouin, and the hardships he endured. "The Empty Quarter," he wrote, "offered me the chance to win distinction as a traveller; but I believed that it could give me more than this, that in those empty wastes I could find the peace that comes with solitude, and, among the Bedu, comradeship in a hostile world. Many who venture into dangerous places have found this comradeship among members of their own race; a few find it more easily among people from other lands, the very differences which separate them binding them ever more closely. I found it among the Bedu. Without it these journeys would have been a meaningless penance." These sentences from the book are, to Thesiger, "the heart of the matter."

Many knowledgable readers had been for years eagerly anticipating *Arabian Sands*, which Thesiger undertook to write with some reluctance, considering it an encroachment on his freedom to travel. Most critics thought the wait worthwhile. Peter Quennell called it "a work of considerable art," and V. S. Pritchett wrote,

"This is the excellent book we hoped for from a man of great fortitude who has lived hard and wild, sought unknown places where life is 'bad.' As a traveller he is formidable; and as a writer he has the power to disclose the extraordinary experience, physical and mental, that has been shut up in himself with stern determination for half an active life-time."

From 1951, Thesiger had also been spending substantial parts of each year in the Marshes of Iraq, the vast lowland area formed by the confluence of the Tigris and Euphrates rivers. *The Marsh Arabs* treats the Madan and other tribes of Shiite Muslims who inhabit this relatively unexplored region, their feuds and wars, their kinship system, marriages, and mass circumcisions, their hunting and boating, and their suffering. "For myself," wrote Robert Payne, "I do not hope to read a better travel book this year or in any other year, for he tells his story so memorably and quietly that it becomes a part of oneself."

Thesiger's unadorned, straightforward style has often received high praise. According to Bruce Chatwin, he "has so absorbed the temper of the heroic world that his descriptions of raids, blood-feuds and reconciliations give his prose the character of an ancient epic or saga. Even plodding passages, full of what E. M. Forster called 'those dreadful Oriental names,' will suddenly break into images of great beauty that suggest far more than they state: 'The sun was on the desert rim, a red ball without heat.' 'The wind blew cold off dark water and I heard waves lapping on an unseen shore.'" Hal Lehrman described the prose as "unadorned by artifice, so simple, so clean and yet so flowing that it never tires—even when recounting the smallest details of an endless succession of apparently similar days—and sometimes approaches poetry."

Most of the beautiful and striking photographs, all taken by the author himself, which illustrate the first two books, and dozens more, are included in *The Last Nomad: One Man's Forty Year Adventure in the World's Most Remote Deserts, Mountains and Marshes* (the English title, terse and more appropriate, is *Desert, Marsh and Mountain: The World of a Nomad*). This book is essentially a pictorial autobiographical essay recapitulating his other two books and embracing also his earlier and later travels through Ethiopia, Kurdistan, Afghanistan, and Yemen. In the last country, he was present during the late 1960s when Nasser's air force destroyed the medieval mountain fortresses of the royalist Arab chieftains. In an epilogue written in 1977 he returns to Arabia to find that the desert life he had known and loved has almost entirely vanished, victim of the oil boom. "He has seen," wrote Peter Levi, "what no longer exists. He knew the great cities of the oil coast when they were villages. He knew tribesmen who had about them 'the special polish of the inner desert' when that was still a way of life. . . . The story ends ten years ago. The epilogue he writes now is elegy sharpened by some of bitterness. . . . He writes with lucidity and grace, with the authority of experience, about some of the most interesting people and places in the world."

Mingled with the elegiac tone of Thesiger's most recent reminiscences is a great deal of anger and foreboding. He expresses profound disillusionment with much of humanity. "We are like dinosaurs," he wrote, "—the last of a dying race. . . . The new technological civilization which we have evolved destroys or corrupts every culture with which it comes into contact. . . . I'm left feeling that every technical and scientific achievement in the last 150 years has been another nail in the human coffin." He has spent nine months of each year since 1968 in East Africa, mainly on safari among the Samburu cattle herdsmen of northern Kenya. Thesiger has always enjoyed an exalted reputation among Arabists, particularly those in Britain. He has been an important contributor to the Royal Geographical Society's *Geographical Journal* and to the *Royal Central Asian Journal* of the Royal Central Asian Society. The former society awarded him its Founder's Medal; the latter, its Lawrence of Arabia Medal. He has also won the Livingstone Medal of the Royal Scottish Geographical Society and the Burton Memorial Medal of the Royal Asiatic Society. He is a fellow of the Royal Society of Literature, an honorary doctor of letters of Leicester University, and an honorary fellow of Magdalen, his old college. He was made CBE in 1968.

PRINCIPAL WORKS: Arabian Sands, 1959; The Marsh Arabs, 1964; Desert, Marsh, and Mountain, 1979 (U.S. The Last Nomad).

ABOUT: Contemporary Authors 2, 1978; Green, Timothy, The Adventurers: Four Profiles of Contemporary Travellers, 1970. *Periodicals*—Economist August 8, 1964; October 6, 1979; New Statesman October 24, 1959; January 12, 1964; October 26, 1979; New York Herald Tribune Book Review November 29, 1959; New York Review of Books November 19, 1964; New York Times Book Review November 1, 1959; October 4, 1964; April 20, 1980; New Yorker December 12, 1959; May 29, 1965; Saturday Review January 9, 1960; January 2, 1965; Spectator October 23, 1959; Time March 31, 1980; Times Literary Supplement November 13, 1959; January 11, 1964.

THOMAS, D(ONALD) M(ICHAEL) (January 27, 1935–), British novelist, poet, and translator, was born in Redruth, Cornwall, the son of Harold Redvers Thomas, a tin miner who went as a youth to California, and Amy Thomas. After completing his secondary schooling and national service, he attended New College, Oxford, taking in 1958 a first-class degree in English. He was English master at a grammar school in Teignmouth, Devon, from 1960 to 1964, then spent thirteen years as lecturer, then senior lecturer and head of the English department, at a teacher-training college in Hereford. The college was closed by the government in 1979 as part of a series of cuts in aid to education. Since then he has been able to devote all his energies to writing.

Although Thomas' literary celebrity is due to his fiction, notably to the success in the United States in 1981 of his third novel, *The White Hotel,* he has for fifteen years been a prominent British poet, with a half-dozen substantial volumes of his own verse and three major translations to his credit. In his *Selected Poems* he arranged his verse into three sections: poems of love or sexuality, poems of Cornwall, and poems with historical or mythological themes. The erotic, however, in the words of Neil Corcoran, a reviewer of this collection, "is always a shimmer on the skin of Thomas's poems." It is an impulse frequently so unrestrained, striving so hard for resonant meaning, that it can provoke in the reader, according to Corcoran, "the critical equivalent of not knowing quite where to look."

From the beginning, Thomas has shown himself adept at longer lyrics and at combining in one poem various meters, dictions, and tones. His subjects are similarly multifarious, ranging in his early volumes from American Indian mythology, Freudianism, and the *I Ching* to such often-encountered later obsessions as the Freud-Jung relationship, Pushkin, García Lorca, and the great lyricists of modern Russian literature: Mandelstam, Akhmatova, Pasternak, and Tsvetayeva. To some critics, however, his most satisfying poems are those in which he treats love of family, and how that feeling becomes intensified by dreams and death—these two forces, indeed, being leitmotifs in all his work. *Love and Other Deaths,* one of his richest collections, includes "Cecie," a strong, moving elegy on the death of a favorite aunt, whose cheerful simplicity he is able to convey with equally simple language:

. . . Dear aunt, if Christ had come, as well he might, to you,
You'd have scrubbed his feet with good soapy water
Left from Monday's wash, pocketed a few
Fresh loaves and fishes for your poor sister;
Burnt your hand on the boiler, muttered, "That's nothin'",
Run out, lisle stocking flapping, to dig the garden. . . .

© 1984 Thomas Victor

D. M. THOMAS

You had no life. No lovers that I know of.
Yet we all loved you. You were filled with love
No-one repaid. . . .

"I think Thomas is at his best," wrote John Matthias, " . . . when he writes poems deriving from his family experience and his search for roots in Cornwall." His home county has inspired much industry on his part: an anthology of Cornish poems, *The Granite Kingdom,* in which he includes several of his own; *The Shaft,* a long poem about the reopening of some ancient Cornish tin mines; and his edition of *Songs from the Earth,* selections of the prose and poetry of John Harris (1820–84), a miner and an almost forgotten poet.

Thomas' knowledge of Russian, which he acquired in the army, was put to good use in his two volumes of translations of the poetry of Anna Akhmatova: her long masterpieces, *Requiem* and *Poem without a Hero,* and her lyrics, *Way of All the Earth.* In his introduction to the latter volume, he writes of this tragic poet, who, with her three compeers, "must be accounted largely responsible for the continuity of Russian poetic tradition" in that "her incorruptibility as a person is closely linked to her most fundamental characteristic as a poet: fidelity to things as they are, to 'the clear, familiar, material world.' [She] was able to speak, not to a small élite, but to the Russian people with whom she so closely and proudly identified." John Bayley, whose familiarity with twentieth-century Russian poetry is considered without equal in the English-speaking world, called Thomas' version of *Requiem* "to my mind the best so far" and re-

marked of his translation of *Poem without a Hero* that although it "is not of course itself a great poem, . . it makes us feel the original is one, and that is a remarkable achievement." Thomas has also translated *The Bronze Horseman: Selected Poetry of Alexander Pushkin.*

The Flute Player, Thomas' first novel, is a highly erotic, imaginative meditation on the major themes of modern Russian poetry. Its heroine, the flute player of the title, embodies love and inspiration although she lives in the midst of an inhuman and totalitarian system. Through her room, and often her bed, pass all the men of power in the book's imaginary city (which very much resembles Leningrad), but she is of greatest interest as a living muse: genuine masterpieces are summoned forth by her productive influence. In *Birthstone,* published in 1980 only six months after its predecessor, the central character is a woman with a split personality who is seeking a firm sense of identity. Andrew Motion found her, even when "relatively stable," to be "an unreliable witness, with the result that she persistently baffles and alienates the reader." Thomas manages the dreamy opacity of the novel with what Motion calls "a good deal of skill, and the end product is impressively unlikable."

The American success of *The White Hotel,* after its friendly but not overenthusiastic reception in Britain, surprised even the author himself, although the novel's preoccupation with sex, psychoanalysis, and the Holocaust, almost guaranteed its success. The heroine, Lisa Erdman, is a Russian Jewish opera singer, who just after World War II becomes a patient of Freud. She wants to rid herself of hysterical sexual fantasies, which she always imagines take place in a white hotel. She is at least partially cured after years with the master, then returns to Russia to resume her career, but loses her life during the Nazi massacre at Babi Yar in the Ukraine. The tones of the novel are extremely various, from the ballad form of Lisa's morbid hallucinations, through Freud's exchange of authentic-sounding letters on the case with other analysts, the careful, straightforward prose of the analysis itself, and what one reviewer called the book's "monolithic, appallingly grey panel"—the killings at Babi Yar—to a kind of idyllic coda, in which all the novel's characters, including Freud, meet in a Promised Land that resembles Palestine but may be Heaven. Critics were about evenly divided on the merits of *The White Hotel:* Paul Ableman called it "a work of vast ambition and impressive achievement"; to Brian Martin it is "a failure" that "starts with the pornography of sex . . . and works its way round to the pornography of violence."

Ararat is a novel, like *The White Hotel,* concerned with sex, death, fantasies, and mass killing; it also displays Thomas' skill at poetry, prose, and translation. Much of its structure consists of stories, often of such technical subtlety that the author, in Diane Johnson's words, "becomes Russian." She called the novel "a work of artifice about artifice, a formal work about form, . . . [it] seems a work of perfect proportion." The book, unlike its predecessor, was not a great commercial success. Its sequel, *Swallow,* is even more intricate in structure, a literary *jeu d'esprit* celebrating literary improvisation as each of the contestants in an international writing Olympics offers a manuscript. The only thing the fragments have in common is a preoccupation with sex. The book is wildly imaginative but also very personal—including one character's withdrawal from the contest because he has been charged with plagiarism. Generally critics were not impressed—some offended by its explicit sexuality, others by its personal reference. "To know the author's recent history is to know that *Swallow* is partly a defensive work," Galen Strawson wrote in the *Times Literary Supplement* "for in so far as it argues for anything, it argues for the inevitability and (hence) innocence of promiscuous influence in art; it examines the general phenomenon of literary emulation, of which flagrant plagiarism is just the limiting case."

The reference is to a heated controversy in the pages of the *Times Literary Supplement* and the *New York Times Book Review* in 1981–82, when Thomas was accused of plagiarism in the Babi Yar section of *The White Hotel* and in his translations from Akhmatova and Pushkin. He denied all charges at length, pointing out that he had declared his indebtedness to Anatoli Kuznetsov's *Babi Yar* in the acknowledgments to *The White Hotel* and that the parallels between his and others' translations of Pushkin were accidental and insignificant. To the charge that he had used notes from another translation without acknowledgment in his translations of Anna Akhmatova, he simply offered Pushkin's words: "Receive with indifference both flattery and slander, / and do not argue with a fool."

Thomas came to the United States in the winter of 1981–82 to teach for a semester at American University in Washington, D.C. In an article "On Literary Celebrity," published in the *New York Times Magazine,* he described this, to him nerve-shattering, experience which lasted, in fact, for only one week. Treated with awe and deference as a famous author, but isolated, in a freezing winter, in a campus apartment with several locks on the door, he felt that he was becoming a "media monster," and he left abruptly

to return to his more sheltered and serene life in Hereford.

PRINCIPAL WORKS: *Fiction*—The Flute Player, 1979; Birthstone, 1980; The White Hotel, 1981; Ararat, 1983; Swallow, 1984. *Poetry*—Personal and Possessive, 1964; Two Voices, 1968; Logan Stone, 1971; The Shaft, 1973; Lilith-Prints, 1974; Symphony in Moscow, 1974; Love and Other Deaths, 1975; The Rock, 1975; Orpheus in Hell, 1977; The Honeymoon Voyage, 1978; Selected Poems, 1983. *Translations*—Akhmatova, Requiem and Poem without a Hero, 1976; Akhmatova, Way of All the Earth, 1979; Pushkin, The Bronze Horseman, 1982. *As editor*—Penguin Modern Poets II, 1968; The Granite Kingdom, 1970; Harris, J. Songs from the Earth, n.d.

ABOUT: Contemporary Authors 61–64, 1976; Dictionary of Literary Biography Yearbook 1982. *Periodicals*—Commentary August 1981; Encounter August 1981; Esquire November 1982; Nation May 2, 1981; New Republic March 28, 1981; New Statesman July 11, 1975; June 22, 1979; March 21, 1980; January 16, 1981; New York Review of Books May 28, 1981; November 19, 1981; February 3, 1983; New York Times March 13, 1981; September 21, 1982; November 12, 1982; New York Times Book Review March 15, 1981; June 28, 1981; September 26, 1982; October 24, 1982; March 27, 1983; New York Times Magazine June 13, 1982; Newsweek March 10, 1981; March 15, 1982; Poetry May 1971; March 1977; Publishers Weekly March 27, 1981; Spectator July 7, 1979; January 17, 1981; Times Literary Supplement August 1, 1975; April 16, 1976; June 30, 1978; November 30, 1979; March 14, 1980; January 16, 1981; January 22, 1982; March 26, 1982 through April 30, 1982; January 28, 1983; February 25, 1983; July 29, 1983; June 29, 1984.

THOMAS, LEWIS (November 25, 1913–   ), American physician, medical administrator, educator, and essayist, was born in Flushing, New York, to Joseph S. Thomas, chief surgeon at Flushing Hospital, and Grace Emma Peck Thomas. In *The Youngest Science: Notes of a Medicine Watcher,* Thomas described the practice of medicine as he observed it while accompanying his father on his rounds in what was then a semirural section of Queens. Medicine before the discovery of antibiotics, Thomas came to realize, was largely a matter of the personal reassurances of the doctor, who could provide diagnosis and comfort but little effective treatment. The pharmacopoeia of the day was made up, by and large, of placebos—"the principal mainstay of medicine," Thomas wrote, "the sole technology, for so long a time—millenia—that they had the incantatory power of religious ritual. My father had little faith in the effectiveness of any of them, but he used them daily in his practice."

© 1983 Thomas Victor

LEWIS THOMAS

When Thomas entered Princeton in 1929 his inclination was already toward basic biological research—he was determined to increase, in some way, the effectiveness of treatment—but he also had a revealing secondary interest in the poetry of Pound and Eliot. (Thomas has noted: "Doctors are trained to observe and express their ideas precisely. Medical training is good training for a writing career.") He took an M.D. from Harvard in 1937, served his internship at Boston City Hospital, and a residency at the Neurological Institute of New York—Boston and New York were to remain the principal geographic poles of his career—but, rather than take up a general practice like his father's, he specialized in clinical research, particularly the neurology of meningitis. In 1941, while Tilner Memorial Fellow at Boston Hospital's Thorndike Laboratory, he married Beryl Dawson; they have three daughters. During World War II Thomas did field research on typhus and encephalitis for the U.S. Navy; he landed with the Marines during the invasion of Okinawa carrying a special case full of laboratory white mice.

After spending the years 1946–56 building his academic credentials in pediatrics, rheumatology, and pathology at the medical schools of Johns Hopkins, Tulane, and Minnesota universities, Thomas joined the staff of the New York University School of Medicine. Though he always found time to pursue some line of basic research—for example, in 1957 he and Benjamin Zweifach reported important discoveries in the pathology of endotoxins and the effect on cell walls of the enzyme papain—he was inexorably pushed up the administrative ladder, finally be-

coming dean of the School of Medicine in 1966. He also served for many years on the New York City Board of Health. The city hospital system, already grown to unmanageable proportions, drew his repeated criticisms. "The great and central trouble with the present system," he said in one report, "is the system itself"—and it was with some relief that he agreed in 1969 to chair the pathology department of Yale University's School of Medicine. For his first years there he had more time for research, but in 1971 he was asked to become the school's dean, and time to pursue his own interests was again sacrificed. In 1973 Thomas took his last major administrative post: president of the Sloan-Kettering Institute in New York City, heading one of the world's largest facilities devoted to cancer research.

Though Thomas was now at the top of his profession, one of the most respected medical administrators in the country and still an active scientist, he attained popular recognition for work of an entirely different sort: his series of short, lapidary essays which had been appearing in the back pages of the *New England Journal of Medicine* since 1971. Called "Notes of a Biology Watcher," they were written in everyday, but eloquent, prose and, though crammed with biological and medical information, addressed matters of general interest rather than scientific or scholarly questions. In these essays, originally conceived as poems (as a young medical student Thomas had written poetry), Thomas revealed a gift for the biological metaphor that illuminates some profound area of human experience expressing an exultation in the mysteries of the physical world with equal parts of clinical accuracy, irreverent optimism, and pure delight in the complexities of life. In what John Updike called "flights of fancy," Thomas suggested that the earth can best be understood *in toto* as a single cell ("for sheer size and perfection of function, it is far and away the grandest product of collaboration in all of nature"); that human society bears a remarkable resemblance to that of the ant; that the *St. Matthew Passion* of Bach captures "the sound of the whole central nervous system of human beings, all at once," and that the composer's music should be beamed to the stars ("we would be bragging, of course"); that, despite their many shortcomings, human beings "may be engaged in the formation of something like a mind for the life of this planet." In Thomas' view, symbiosis, rather than bloody Darwinian competition, is the dominant theme of life on earth. Nor is man separate in any way from nature: "The whole dear notion of one's own self—marvelous old free-willed, free-enterprising, autonomous, independent, isolated island of a self—is a myth."

The novelist Joyce Carol Oates (one of Thomas' earliest and staunchest admirers), reviewing *The Lives of a Cell: Notes of a Biology Watcher,* a collection of twenty-nine essays, put him in the company of such scientist-philosophers as Gregory Bateson, R. Buckminster Fuller, and Robert Ornstein—writers "as valuable to our humanistic culture as our most prized poets or artists," who "take on the language of poetry in order to communicate human truths too mysterious for old-fashioned common sense." These short "masterpieces of 'art of the essay,'" Oates continued, outline Thomas' vision of "the mystery that lies at the core of all life." Noted Paul Grey in his *Newsweek* profile of the author: "What Thomas does is extraordinarily rare. It is hard enough to explain specialized scientific findings to scientists in other fields, and harder still to get it right and still hold the attention of untutored novices. Add touches of poetry, joyful optimism, and an awe-inspired mysticism, and the job becomes impossible. Except that the impossible, like so many of the natural phenomena that Thomas describes, happens."

A second collection, *The Medusa and the Snail: More Notes of a Biology Watcher,* was, if anything, more enthusiastically received than *The Lives of a Cell.* Both were unanticipated best-sellers, an indication of the prevailing rarity of good writing on science and the eagerness with which readers wished to embrace the sincere optimism of an eminent physician. *The Lives of a Cell* was awarded a National Book Award in 1974, not in the category of science writing but in arts and letters.

The Youngest Science, Thomas' autobiography, was described by naturalist Stephen Jay Gould in the *New York Review of Books* as a "profound, and even disturbing book" that effectively delineated the revolution in American medicine within the compass of Thomas' own lifetime. Each of the book's two sections—the description of his father's career, with its ineffective but personalized brand of medicine, and then Thomas' own progress as a modern physician, researcher, and administrator of vast health-care institutions—illuminated, according to Gould, the "trade-offs made necessary, and surely in large part desirable, by improving technology—specifically, the sacrifice of heart for efficiency." Gould saw Thomas as embodying the solution to the problem of medicine's increasing dehumanization: "If medicine attracted more rational humanists, then a force of strong personal commitment might just balance or even overcome the shaping role of institutions. Thomas himself is the prototype of such a man, a medical administrator (the stereotypical role for the heartless) who exudes in his writing and exemplifies by his life all the old-fashioned traits of care and compassion that we must try again to bring into prominence."

A firm believer in the serendipity of error and "the essential wildness of science" from which "suddenly emerges with the purity of a slow phrase of music a single new truth about nature," Thomas encourages an undirected, evolutionary approach to research. "The only solid piece of scientific truth about which I feel totally confident is that we are profoundly ignorant about nature," he has said, but "if the air is right, the science will come in its own season, like pure honey."

PRINCIPAL WORKS: The Lives of a Cell: Notes of a Biology Watcher, 1974; The Medusa and the Snail: More Notes of a Biology Watcher, 1979; The Youngest Science: Notes of a Medicine Watcher, 1983; Late Night Thoughts on Mahler's Ninth Symphony, 1984.

ABOUT: Contemporary Authors 85–88, 1980; Current Biography 1975; Who's Who in America, 1983–84. *Periodicals*—Natural History August 1971; New York Post February 23, 1973; June 29, 1974; New York Review of Books November 28, 1974; July 21, 1983; New York Times July 29, 1974; New York Times Book Review May 26, 1974; July 15, 1979; February 27, 1983; New Yorker July 15, 1974; Newsweek June 24, 1974; Time May 14, 1979.

*THORDARSON, THORBERGUR** (March 12, 1889–November 12, 1974), Icelandic poet, essayist, biographer, satirist, and folklorist, was born at the farm Hali in Sudursveit, southeast Iceland, where he spent his first sixteen years in the parental home. Then he went to sea as a cook on a small fishing boat for three seasons, after which he attended secondary school in Reykjavík for a while and then studied at the Teacher Training College of Iceland for one winter before giving up his studies. For a number of years he was allowed to attend lectures at the University of Iceland without having matriculated. Just before his death in 1974 he was awarded a doctorate *honoris causa* at the same university. During the years 1919-1935 he intermittently earned his living by teaching at various secondary schools and collecting rare words for a dictionary in preparation. From early on he was active in left-wing politics and wrote a large number of articles for newspapers and magazines. He was also an ardent supporter of the international language Esperanto and taught it for a number of years. After 1935 he made his living as a writer and enjoyed great popularity and respect the rest of his life.

Thórdarson shares with Halldór Laxness (No-

°thôr´ dä sen, thôr´ ber gə

bel Prize 1955) the distinction of being the most original and linguistically dexterous Icelandic author of this century, even though they are in most other respects very dissimilar. Thórdarson occupies a place all by himself, being so peculiarly Icelandic in subject matter, tone, and treatment that only one of his numerous books has been translated into foreign languages (Danish, German, English), and that one only in an abbreviated version. In a sense he concentrated all his creative efforts on what was most peculiar and exclusive in the Icelandic character and created a kind of personal mythology which is largely alien to foreign readers.

Thórdarson's literary endeavors started about the time he left the fishing boat and settled in Reykjavík. There he joined a group of young and boisterous bohemians and started writing verse in a fumbling sort of way. His first three books (two of them published under a pseudonym) appeared during and just after World War I, the last in 1922. They were clever satires and parodies of established poets, very much in the vein of Heinrich Heine, with eye-catching futuristic effects and lyric interludes.

For some years he buried himself in the study of oriental philosophy, theosophy, and spiritualism, practicing yoga with considerable success. That rebirth he described in *Ljós úr austri* (Ex oriente lux, 1919), the first in a series of brilliant personal essays, written in a caustic, logical manner. Sincerely attracted to the theosophic ideal of the brotherhood of mankind, he was soon disillusioned when he felt that its adherents and propagandists did very little in order to attain it.

In his disillusionment Thórdarson turned to the study of socialism, reading authors like Upton Sinclair, H. G. Wells and George Bernard Shaw, and this preoccupation bore an unexpectedly fine fruit in his next book, *Bréf til Láru* (Letter to Laura, 1924), the most revolutionary and influential book of the 1920s in Iceland. It was intended as a manifesto of socialism, and it contained sharp attacks on the existing order, not least the Protestant and Catholic churches as well as the theosophists and spiritualists, for their hypocrisy and easy-going life—for the author had no quarrel with the teachings of Christ, nor did he doubt the existence of life after death. All these controversial matters were embedded in a picturesque frame of personal essays and sketches, anecdotes and tales quite often autobiographical, always witty and humorous, frequently at his own expense. And the book was written in a hitherto unknown style, fresh and brilliant, paradoxical and shocking to the bourgeois sensibilities of the epoch. These qualities made *Bréf til Láru* a milestone in the development of Icelandic letters and prose style, paving the way for Laxness and many younger authors to leave behind them the puristic classical style modeled on the famous *Sagas*. This strangely heterogeneous book may in some respects be termed the first *modern* book of Icelandic prose.

Bréf til Láru involved Thórdarson in a fierce controversy with the representatives of church and capital. Laxness, who had recently been converted to Catholicism, even wrote a booklet against him. During the controversy Thórdarson wrote perhaps his most brilliant essay, "Eldvígslan" (Initiation by Fire, 1925), in answer to a young bourgeois critic. Almost equally fascinating was the autobiographical *Lifandi kristindómur og ég* (Living Christianity and I, 1929).

For a number of years Thórdarson worked on scholarly projects, collecting rare words and folk tales, which appealed to his scientific meticulousness as well as his almost gullible mysticism. He embraced Esperanto enthusiastically, taught it, wrote it, and espoused its cause in a luminous little book. He also visited the Soviet Union and wrote the satirical *Rauda haettan* (The Red Scare, 1935), praising and defending Soviet society. At about the same time he wrote a newspaper column for which he was condemned and fined by the Icelandic Supreme Court for offending Adolf Hitler.

The unusually pronounced personal note present in all of Thórdarson's work first prompted him to write a sheaf of letters (1933) and finally resulted in a resolve to write his autobiography with all names unchanged and with the fullest exercise of truthfulness he could muster. It was published as *Íslenskur adall* (Icelandic Nobility, 1938) and the two-volume *Ofvitinn* (The Genius, 1940–1941), covering the period 1909–1913, from the time he left the fishing boat until he entered the notorious bohemian group. Though realistically written and claiming to tell nothing but the unadulterated truth, it is nonetheless a highly imaginative three-part novel, filled with eccentric personalities, odd happenings, and hilarious scenes. Here is not only the story of a diffident lover, romantic dreamer, sarcastic cynic, and fumbling philosopher, but also a canvas of the age on which move many celebrities and a host of minor figures, all intensely alive.

After World War II Thórdarson assumed the role of Boswell to write the memoirs of an old country parson in six volumes (1945–1950). Wagging tongues maintained that here the fastest liar in Iceland had met the most gullible scribe, but however that may be, the work is as prominent in Icelandic literature as Boswell's

Life of Samuel Johnson is in English. It is a veritable treasure trove of tall tales, gossip, miracles, prejudices, superstitions, and malice, all told in a personal style which sparkles on every single page.

From the voluble and hyperbolic octogenarian Thórdarson turned his acute observation and keen ear to the life and babble of a baby, a niece in the family born in 1943, to whom he devoted the two-volume *Sálmurinn um blómid* (The Hymn to the Flower, 1954–1955), an engrossing book written from the point of view of the child, with baby-talk and infantile perceptions mingling with the wisdom and perspicacity of old age.

From the precocious niece Thórdarson turned again to himself and now to his very first years, describing in three volumes his childhood at the parental farm, interweaving straightforward accounts of daily pastoral life with surreal tales of encounters with unearthly beings and preternatural phenomena, all told in a simple, matter-of-fact style which tends to become monotonous and longwinded. Apparently the author himself was aware of this potential defect, for he took pains to defend and expound his "scientific" method, ridiculing the poetic flights and syntactical embroideries of less earnest and accurate authors. Whatever the reason, Thórdarson did not in his later work achieve the stylistic brilliance of his heyday, neither in his childhood reminiscences nor in a three-volume biography of a renowned local entrepreneur (1967–1971). But his occasional essays retained the old bite and rhetorical exuberance characterizing his best books.

Much of Thórdarson's writing has been published in multiple editions and he is still a strongly felt presence in Icelandic literature, two collections of his letters and a fourth volume of his childhood memoirs having appeared posthumously. He also translated several books from Danish and English, including two tales of Edgar Allan Poe.

Thórbergur Thórdarson is very hard to classify in a literary context, since ultimately his distinction as a writer rests upon a unique personality that was exploited in an ingenious and self-mocking way to create memorable works of art, combining tradition and innovation, poetry and parody, theory and activism, supernaturalism and rationalism, credulity and a highly scientific turn of mind. Wherever we place him, he is one of the uncontested masters of Icelandic prose and has had strong and lasting influence on all younger writers through his innovative approach, daring style, and contagious humor.

WORKS IN ENGLISH TRANSLATION: The only book by Thórdarson available in English is *In Search of My Beloved*, Kenneth G. Chapman's translation of *Íslenskur adall* (1938), an autobiography, published in 1967 with an introduction by Kristján Karlsson. A short sketch, "The Brindled Monster," is published in *Anthology of Scandinavian Literature*, edited by H. Hallmundsson, 1966.

ABOUT: Columbia Dictionary of Modern European Literature, 1980; Einarsson, S. History of Icelandic Prose Writers, 1950; Einarsson, S. A History of Icelandic Literature, 1957; Encyclopedia of World Literature in the 20th Century III, 1971; Magnússon, S. A. Northern Sphinx, 1977; Magnússon, S. A. (ed.) Icelandic Writing Today, 1982. *Periodicals*—World Literature Today Winter 1982.

*TOER (TUR), PRAMOEDYA ANANTA

(February 6, 1925–), Indonesian short-story writer and novelist, was born in the village of Blora, in East Java, where, he writes, "all live in poverty," and those who can afford to buy meat "are no longer commoners but 'lords.'" His father was the headmaster of a private school under the strict control of the then Dutch government, a figure of some social prominence but as poor as the rest of the community, and addicted to gambling, which reduced the family to even greater poverty. Educated first in his father's school, where he showed little promise as a student, the boy managed finally, at the age of fourteen, to raise enough money to go to Surabaya. Here he attended a radio vocational school for a year. With the Japanese invasion of his country, he returned to his native village to help support his ailing mother and eight younger brothers and sisters by selling tobacco and cigarettes in the local street market.

After his mother's death in 1942, Toer settled in Jakarta, working as a typist and clerk for the Japanese news agency Domei. At first the Japanese occupation promised relief from the long domination of his country by the Dutch: "The Japanese had destroyed the whole glory of the white man's realm both in mainland Asia and throughout the archipelago," he writes in one of his semiautobiographical short stories. But the cruelty of the Japanese occupiers dispelled any hope of freedom, and he returned to East Java to join a paramilitary organization of the emerging Indonesian nationalist movement.

Largely self-educated, Toer had by now become interested in literature and edited a journal for the Free Indonesia movement. When the Dutch were restored to power after World War II, he was imprisoned from 1947 to 1949 for his political activities. This was the beginning of a series of imprisonments during which Toer developed a powerful mystical philosophy which made it possible not only for him to survive but to write the many stories and novels that transcend even while they record his personal suffering and the suffering of his people. In the Dutch prison he had access to a library where he studied English by reading John Steinbeck's *Of Mice and Men,* William Saroyan's *The Human Comedy,* and the Dutch writer Lode Zielens. From these writers he developed his own simple, direct, and moving prose style. As he recalls in an essay in *Indonesia* (Volume 36, October 1983), in Benedict Anderson's translation: "Steinbeck arranged his plain, terse, highly charged words in neat, completed sentences. With Saroyan, however, it was rather different: he taught me how the most basic human feelings are the quickest bridge to communicate with one's fellow human beings and thus his sentences were steered towards scenes in which these basic feelings could be displayed."

The result was Toer's first novel, *Perburuan* (The Fugitive), published in 1950 but written during his imprisonment ("in moments when I was not doing forced labor") on paper smuggled in to him by his sweetheart. This was followed in the same year by *Keluarga Gerilya* (A Guerrilla Family). Both novels marked Toer's dedication to revolution in the cause of his country's liberation from foreign rule and record the suffering of Indonesian freedom fighters who, even in defeat, preserve their integrity and their ideals. Both also are drawn from deeply felt personal experience. Released from prison, he learned to his surprise that *Perburuan* had won the Balai Putaska literary prize and with that money he was able to marry. He joined the newly formed Lekra, a Marxist literary group committed to "service to the masses," and was soon recognized as a leading figure in the movement although he continued to write in a distinctly individual and subjective style characterized not by socialist realism but by a personal vision that "the fusion of writer and protagonist is only made possible by understanding, love, and spiritual affinity. Yet the writer does not only put forward a main character, he also creates supporting and minor characters, some showing up only for a moment and others reappearing over and over again. Here too the writer fuses himself with them, no matter whether they are antagonists of the main character or are on his side. The problem is understanding human beings with all their sorrows and moments of happiness, with their dreams and with their stumblings, their successes and their failures, their resistance and their surrender to the conditions of their lives. The truth is that the problematic of literature is the problem-

atic of man in his living existence. Understanding literature means understanding man, and it may be that the reverse is also true."

Indonesian independence in 1949 brought no permanent peace to the internally divided country. When, after the Communist coup of 1965, the government of President Sukarno fell, Toer—along with thousands of other political activists—was imprisoned. Without trial he was exiled to an internment camp on the island of Buru, in East Indonesia, where for most of the next fourteen years, deprived of paper and pen, he composed orally, telling stories to his fellow prisoners. In the last years of his confinement, however, he managed to write four historical novels which he published on his release—brought about largely by international appeals to the Indonesian government—in 1979. These include *Bumi Manusia* (*This Earth of Mankind*) in 1980, and its sequels *Anak Semua Bangsa* (Child of All Nations), *Jejak Langkah* (Steps Forward), and *Rumah Kaca* (Glasshouse). *Bumi Manusia* was an immediate success. Keith Foulcher reports in the *Times Literary Supplement* (August 7, 1981) that the 10,000 copies of the first printing sold out within two weeks. Set in colonial Surabaya in 1898, it is the story of a young Dutch-educated Indonesian student who becomes disillusioned with Western culture only to discover that he is powerless against "caste, social convention and heartless, unprincipled bureaucracy." Though it takes place in the past and is written in an episodic and occasionally awkward style, the novel had a striking timeliness in the Indonesia of 1980. Jim Crace writes in the *Times Literary Supplement* (September 10, 1982) that " . . . the oddities and the blemishes as well as the eloquence of this courageous work are best comprehended in the light of Pramoedya's Buru experience."

Government censors failed at first to detect "the subversive resonance of the book's tragiromantic plot," but by 1981 its popularity with large numbers of young Indonesians alarmed the Attorney General who banned both *Bumi Manusia* and *Anak Semua Bangsa* (which continues the story of the young hero's struggles against the Dutch and for the peasant masses) for Marxist and Leninist leanings. An immediate jump in sales of the books followed, and the Attorney General thereupon ordered all remaining copies burnt. Though not imprisoned again, Toer remains under strict government surveillance, obliged to report regularly to the authorities. As Foulcher wrote in 1981: "His situation, just eighteen months after his release, may again be precarious. For the rest of the world, the ban serves as an indication that Indonesia's one major novelist to date still awaits the basic freedom to practise his art, let alone official recognition of it."

WORKS IN ENGLISH TRANSLATION: A translator himself of Pascal, Tolstoy, Sholokhov, Gorki, and Steinbeck among others, Pramoedya Toer has been more widely translated into Dutch, Russian, and other foreign languages than into English. A few of his short stories are available in two anthologies—J. Echols' *Indonesian Writing in Translation*, 1956, and R. Hendon's *Six Indonesian Short Stories*, 1968—and in the periodicals *Atlantic Monthly* June 1956, *Meanjin Quarterly* 4, 1963, and *Indonesia* 26, 1973. Harry Aveling translated a small collection of his short stories as *A Heap of Ashes* in 1975, and *Bumi Manusia* was translated as *This Earth of Mankind* by Max Lane for Penguin Books in 1982.

ABOUT: Aveling, H. *Introduction to* A Heap of Ashes, 1975; Dictionary of Oriental Literature II, 1974; Lane, M. *Introduction to* This Earth of Mankind, 1982; Lang, D. M. A Guide to Eastern Literature, 1971; Teeuw, A. Modern Indonesian Literature, 1967. *Periodicals*—Indonesia 30 1980; 36 1983; London Review of Books December 2–29 1982; Meanjin Quarterly 4 1963; (London) Times September 2, 1981; November 17, 1981; Times Literary Supplement August 7, 1981; September 10, 1982.

TOOLE, JOHN KENNEDY (1937–March 26, 1969), American novelist, was born in New Orleans, Louisiana, the son of John and Thelma (Ducoing) Toole. A precocious boy, Toole skipped several school grades and entered Tulane University at the age of sixteen. In the same year, according to Thelma Toole, he wrote an unpublished but still extant novel, "Neon Bible," which dealt with "the violence and the poverty and the frustration of the Bible Belt." Toole graduated from Tulane in 1958, and received his M.A. from Columbia University in 1959. He taught for a year in New York City, and then at St. Mary's Dominican College in New Orleans. Toole served for two years in the U.S. Army (1962–1963), and while teaching English as a second language to recruits in Puerto Rico wrote his novel *A Confederacy of Dunces*.

In 1963 he returned to teach at Dominican College and attempted to find a publisher for his novel. At some point he entered into correspondence with Robert Gottlieb, then an editor at Simon & Schuster, who may have been encouraging, because Toole made a number of revisions to his novel at this time. By 1966, however, Gottlieb decided to reject the novel, and Toole made no further efforts to find a publisher. In December 1968, having become increasingly withdrawn, he stopped teaching. Three months later he was found in his car, asphyxiated by carbon monoxide fumes.

JOHN KENNEDY TOOLE

Following his death, Toole's mother began a crusade to have her son's novel published. For nearly a decade she sent the single copy she had of the manuscript, a smudged carbon, to publishers in New York City. Years passed while at least eight publishing houses declined it. In 1976, having seen an announcement that Walker Percy was giving a seminar at Loyola University in New Orleans, she telephoned the novelist: "I told him I had a great novel of my son's," she said, and, with some reluctance, Percy agreed to read it. He was so impressed that he approached the Louisiana State University Press, which had only recently begun to publish fiction, and the novel was published in May 1980 to unusually enthusiastic reviews. *A Confederacy of Dunces* sold 70,000 copies in hardcover alone, and over a half million copies in its Grove Press paperback edition. The novel was awarded the Pulitzer Prize for fiction in 1981.

In his foreword to the novel, Walker Percy captured the quality of Toole's unusual hero by describing him as "without progenitor in any literature I know of—slob extraordinary, a mad Oliver Hardy, a fat Don Quixote, a perverse Thomas Aquinas rolled into one—who is in violent revolt against the entire modern age, lying in his flannel nightshirt, in a back bedroom on Constantinople Street in New Orleans, who between gigantic seizures of flatulence and eructations is filling dozens of Big Chief tablets with invective." He went on to praise the novel's rendering of the peculiarities of New Orleans, "its back streets, its out-of-the-way neighborhoods, its odd speech, its ethnic whites—and one black in whom Toole has achieved the near impossible, a superb comic character of immense wit and re-sourcefulness without the least trace of Rastus minstrelsy." In summary, Percy called the novel "a great rumbling farce of Falstaffian dimensions."

A Confederacy of Dunces concerns an educat-ed, grossly overweight, thirty-year-old man, Ig-natius J. Reilly, who lives in a small house in a shabby section of New Orleans with his eccen-tric mother. As he searches for employment, Ig-natius meets with a series of calamities that disrupt his digestive functions and cause severe flatulence. In the poisoned air of bedroom, and in his bathtub, he indites a condemnation of modern civilization.

He also conducts a correspondence with Myrna Minkoff, a New York activist who urges him to embrace liberal political causes. Instead, Ignatius skirmishes with Patrolman Mancuso, who dons grotesque disguises in order to arrest suspicious characters; Mr. Robichaux, an elderly anti-Communist; a youth who peddles pornogra-phy; an octogenarian bag-lady named Miss Trix-ie; and the proprietress of the Night of Joy, a seedy bar. At the end, when Ignatius is at the point of breakdown, Myrna Minkoff arrives to rescue him. Leaving the city, they pass the chari-ty mental asylum ambulance that has been sent for his committal.

Brad Owens, in the *Christian Science Monitor,* called Ignatius "one of the most repel-ling, entertaining, and, in some strange way, sympathetic characters I have ever encoun-tered. . . . There was an unmistakable comic genius in the creator of this book." Jeffrey Burke, in *Harper's,* divided his praise between Toole's exuberant conception of Ignatius and his depiction of the subordinate characters. "Toole's minor characters," he wrote, "his depiction of New Orleans street life, and his use of dialect all testify to his energetically imaginative mind and immense gifts as a writer." In his review in the *Times Literary Supplement,* Harold Beaver cal-led *A Confederacy of Dunces* "a masterpiece."

But *A Confederacy of Dunces* did not please all of its critics, some of whom found the comedy coarse and contrived. Alan Friedman, writing in the *New York Times,* acknowledged that the novel was "flawed in places. . . . Characters are overdone; caricatures are done to death." Many critics noted the novel's undercurrent of melan-choly. Stephen Goodwin, in *Book World,* ob-served that Toole's characters can "meet only at the absurd level of plot. The sadness arises from the sense of all the connections missed, of possi-bilities closed." Jean Strouse, in *Newsweek,* con-cluded that "at the heart of [this] splendid mock-heroic . . . lies a profound sense of solitude.

Like everything else in Ignatius J. Reilly's world, the absence of love is larger than life."

In 1984 it was reported that a New Orleans publisher was planning to issue Toole's early "Neon Bible." Ironically, his mother, who had so vigorously promoted the cause of *Confederacy,* threatened action to prevent its publication, claiming that the work was "immature." Chris-topher Hitchens speculated, in the *Times Liter-ary Supplement,* that "since the action of the novel describes a silly and sad mother figure, desperate and over-made-up, there may be oth-er reasons for Mrs. Toole's apparently inconsis-tent conduct on this occasion. And Louisiana inheritance law, which made her an executor along with other surviving relatives, means that she has the power to delay publication indefinitely." Mrs. Toole died in 1984.

ABOUT: Contemporary Authors 104, 1982; Contempo-rary Literary Criticism 19, 1981; Dictionary of Liter-ary Biography Yearbook, 1981. *Periodicals*—America July 4, 1981; American Spectator October 1980; Atlan-tic July 1980; Book World July 22, 1980; Christian Sci-ence Monitor June 4, 1980; June 8, 1981; Harper's March 1981; Horizon September 1980; June 1981; New Republic July 19, 1980; New Statesman June 5, 1981; New York Times Book Review June 22, 1980; August 19, 1981; Newsweek May 26, 1980; Publishers Weekly June 12, 1981; Rolling Stone August 21, 1981; Spectator September 12, 1981; Time June 2, 1980; Times Literary Supplement July 18, 1980; June 12, 1981; August 28, 1981; June 8, 1984; Virginia Quarter-ly Review Autumn 1980.

*TOURNIER, MICHEL (EDOUARD) (De-cember 19, 1924–   ), French novelist and essay-ist, writes (in English): "I was born in Paris, a city I hate, and I was so sickly there as a small child that my parents had to leave it for some time. They themselves were not originally from Paris. My father was the son of a glass-blower from the north of France. My mother was born in a vil-lage in Burgundy. They met at the Sorbonne where both were studying German, she prepar-ing her Master's degree, and he the *agrégation,* a competitive state examination for admission to the most important teaching jobs. The declara-tion of war in 1914 kept my father from passing the exam. He was wounded at the front, and when he returned he was no longer in the mood to work on it once again. But my mother, despite having stopped her studies when she married, remained faithful to the tradition of Germanism of her own family. Every summer she returned to Germany along with her children, to stay in the religious boarding house where she had been every year during her adolescence with her un-

°tŏŏr nyä′, mē shel′

MICHEL TOURNIER

cle, a priest and professor of German. That is how my sister, my two brothers, and I learned to speak German when we were little and witnessed the rise of Nazism closely enough to be forever vaccinated against its seductions.

"Words began to fascinate me very early. I discovered them, precise, mysterious, in the pharmacy of my maternal grandfather, written on the labels of jugs, demijohns, and bottles. I also listened for hours to the recorded texts which my father brought home often, for after giving up the idea of a teaching career he had started a business to take in royalties for authors' record rights. Finally, when I was about nine years old, I had the revelation of books thanks to the tales of Andersen and Selma Lagerlöf, and the novels by James Oliver Curwood. Despite my love for books, I had a chaotic school life until I got my baccalaureate. Undisciplined, allergic to mathematics, I was expelled from everywhere. So I went to a large number of private schools, mostly religious, where, despite my scholastic problems, I was very much impressed by the subtleties of theology, coupled with the magnificence of the ceremonies.

"I was fifteen years old when the war broke out, and I lived the first months as if it were a holiday, the welcome opportunity to turn my boring scholastic universe upside-down. I later discovered, in the village in Burgundy where my mother had taken refuge, its other aspects: the Resistance, the police round-ups, the reprisals. During the war I had passed my baccalaureate, majoring in philosophy, and I thought of starting to study medicine when, by chance, I discovered two books by Gaston Bachelard which were de-

cisive for my future. I would be a philosopher. I therefore got my Master's, and then higher degrees in both philosophy and law. The following year I should have passed the *agrégation,* in order to be able to teach. But by then it was once again possible to go to Germany, purged of its Nazism. Since for me philosophy meant essentially German philosophy, I spent four years at the University of Tübingen, convinced that I thus had the best possible preparation for my exam. But when I returned to France to pass the *agrégation,* I completely failed. Sick at heart, I had to give up my double vocation, philosophical and pedagogical, and earn my living by doing all sorts of jobs. Only later on did I realize that they had been an excellent preparation for writing. Already then I was thinking about writing novels, but without forgetting my training as a philosopher. It took me fifteen years to reconcile fiction and philosophy using myths as a vehicle. My first novel was based on the story of Robinson Crusoe.

"I live in the former vicarage of a remote village about twenty miles from Paris. I leave it frequently for short trips, but I write all of my books there."

———

The writing of Michel Tournier has a rare ability to draw the attention of both academic critics and children, who enjoy at least two of his books (*Friday* and *The Four Wise Men*). One of the most inventive and original of contemporary French novelists, he is nevertheless a traditionalist in form, a self-described "Flaubertian," working with history, myth, and folklore, in narrative that for all its complexity and sophistication is relatively straightforward. "Tournier's imagination," John Sturrock wrote in the *Times Literary Supplement,* "runs equally to the sublime and the macabre; he has no rival among French novelists of his generation for writing books that are at once vivid and intellectually provocative." Regarded as possibly the most important novelist writing in France today, Tournier remains little read abroad although most of his books are available in excellent English translations. His neglect is perhaps attributable to the fact that his work is not in the mainstream of current French literature, the *nouveau roman* and the critical theories of Alain Robbe-Grillet and Roland Barthes. "In the face of this influential set of ideas," Roger Shattuck wrote in an omnibus review of Tournier's novels in *New York Review of Books,* "any novelist who makes modest claims to represent reality and to maintain a stake in the principles and beliefs according to which his characters act and make decisions is likely to be seen as retrograde." Tournier is also seen by some of his critics as perverse, capricious, even pretentious. It is certain, however, that he is readable (his books have sold over 3,000,000 copies in France and he has been translated into twenty-five languages) and once read unforgettable.

The "all sorts of jobs" Tournier refers to in his sketch included journalism (1955–58), editing (chief editor for the publishing firm of Plon, 1958–68), and writing and producing for French radio and television. During this period he was also working on a first draft of the novel that years later became The Ogre. A slow, careful writer who spends several years on a single book, Tournier published his first novel in 1967 at the age of forty-three. This was Vendredi, ou Les Limbes du Pacifique (Friday), a brilliant retelling of Daniel Defoe's classic Robinson Crusoe, faithful to the letter though not to the spirit of that book. Tournier's Crusoe also survives shipwreck to find himself alone on an island—"the hero of solitude." After a period of intense despair ("He knew now that man resembles a person injured in a street riot, who can only stand upright while the crowd packed densely around him continues to prop him up. Exiled from the mass of his fellows, who had sustained him as a part of humanity without his realizing it, he felt that he no longer had the strength to stand on his own feet"), he accepts his fate and proceeds to "civilize" the island as Defoe's hero did. But in the course of doing so he develops a mystical and erotic relationship with the island itself (which he names Esperanza). His journal records his meditations, but more importantly his gradual metamorphosis into a creature of pure nature. His rescue of Friday completes the metamorphosis because the savage initiates him into that existence. When a ship appears after twenty-eight years, Tournier's Crusoe is repelled by the coarseness and brutality of civilization as he sees it reflected in the ship's crew, and chooses to remain on his island. Friday, ironically, chooses to leave. But Crusoe will not be alone, for he is joined by a young cabin boy who jumps ship. He names the boy "Sunday"—"the day of the resurrection."

This ingenious and paradoxical novel, an adventure story given a depth and dimension far beyond its original source, won immediate recognition in France. The Académie Française awarded it the Grand Prix de Roman for 1967, and three years later, with publication of Le Roi des aulnes (The Ogre), Tournier fulfilled the expectations of those who had hailed his first book by winning the Prix Goncourt with the only unanimous vote of its judges since the origin of the prize in 1903. The Ogre is an even more sub-

tle and complex novel than Friday and infinitely more controversial. It brings together a network of cultural influences on Tournier's life—his fascination with myth and religion, his studies at the anthropological Musée de l'Homme in Paris, his ambivalence toward Germany (torn as he is between his hatred for Nazism and his affinity for German culture), his avocation of photography, his love for children. The French title Le Roi des aulnes (King of the Alder Trees) is also the title of the French version of Goethe's poem "The Erl King" and more faithfully represents the spirit of the novel than its English translation The Ogre. Tournier's ogre, Abel Tiffauges, is a large, ungainly garage worker and amateur photographer in Paris, where the novel begins in 1938. He regards himself as an ogre, "issued from the mists of time," and he is in many ways monstrous and capable of mindless cruelty. But he is also curiously innocent—at once both an archetypal Erl King who steals and kills children and Saint Christopher who rescues them. Accused of child molestation, he evades prison when he is drafted into the French army. He is captured by the Germans and taken to Germany where gradually he forgets all his unhappy French associations and comes to love his new country. Germany is his promised land—"the country of strong, simplified, stylized drawing, easily read and remembered . . . the land of pure essences." He is appointed a guard in a Prussian military training camp, recruiting young boys (hence the Erl King). But one day, near the end of the war, he rescues a little Jewish boy running away from Auschwitz. He flees the advancing Russian troops carrying the boy on his shoulders (as Saint Christopher did with the infant Jesus) and perishes by drowning in a bog.

In preparation for writing The Ogre Tournier read widely in the history of Nazism, including all the transcripts of the Nuremberg trials. To some extent at least the character of Tiffauges mirrors that of Hitler (an attempt is made to assassinate Tiffauges on the same day as the abortive attempt to assassinate Hitler), and as Michael Popkin suggests, prompted by Tournier's interest in photography, Tiffauges, who is "fascinated by the relationship between the negative and the finished print," is a kind of negative of Nazism. Inevitably The Ogre aroused controversy among its readers—some of whom were shocked by its elements of pedophilia and sexual perversion, some by its politics, some by the strange mixture of realism and fable. It is, the reviewers agreed, a disturbing book. A representative reaction was novelist Marian Engel's in the New York Times Book Review: "My own perceptions and pretensions have been stripped so bare by this strange, rich, terrifying book that

I cannot stand with Tiffauges the protagonist and proclaim my sanity. . . . To follow his dark path is a magnificent experience." Calling *The Ogre* "one of the few major European novels of the past decade," George Steiner wrote in the London *Sunday Times*: "It illustrates precisely what is almost totally absent from current English fiction; the willingness to take major emotional and philosophical risks."

If less politically controversial, Tournier's next book, *Les Météores (Gemini)* is even more intellectually daunting. His longest novel to date, it is also his most ambitious, intricate, and sexually explicit. A philosophical tale imposed upon a family novel, *Gemini* is the story of twins ("a pair so profoundly one," he writes in his memoir *Le vent Paraclet* [Wind of the Holy Spirit], "that each of its members finds his destiny in the person of the other") and their quest for self-identity and of their eccentric uncle's quest for the ultimate homosexual union. The twins, Jean and Paul, are so closely united that the family refers to them by one name, Jean-Paul ("undistinguishable . . . both entrenched in a mutual rejection of everything outside the other"). Dualities and paradox figure everywhere. The family business—garbage disposal—is banal and revolting, yet to uncle Alexandre who inherits it, it is "a lunar landscape," full of revelations. When one twin runs away, the other pursues him all over the world even as Alexandre pursues his homosexual ideal (who turns out to be one of the twins) to Casablanca where he is murdered. "Sameness and difference, attachment, separation and loss," Galen Strawson wrote in a review of *Gemini* in the *Times Literary Supplement*: "Tournier offers no general survey of this vast area, but develops highly idiosyncratic positions—those of his characters—deep within it, where complicated insights jostle with sententious prejudices. The genre is doubtless not to everyone's taste, but Tournier at his best is master of it."

Tournier's fourth novel, *Gaspard, Melchior et Balthazar* (The Four Wise Men) reverts to the more childlike world of *Friday* and, like that novel, rings changes on a familiar legend. Here the story is what he calls "a Christian novel," the tale of the three kings who came to Bethlehem to honor the Messiah's birth. The three names are familiar (except that Tournier makes Gaspard black instead of Balthazar), but his treatment is characteristically original. Each king seeks an answer to his own problems. The fourth king—Tournier's contribution to the legend—comes from India, too late, as it turns out, to witness the miraculous birth but in time to rescue a group of children from the Massacre of the Innocents. He becomes a kind of surrogate savior,

suffering terrible torment but in the end redeemed through the Eucharist. Serious as *The Four Wise Men* sounds, it is also warmly humorous and richly evocative of the New Testament ethos. Kay Boyle observed of it: " . . . Tournier is telling the story of man's search for deliverance, and telling it with imagination and humor, as well as a respect for history. He writes of splendor and poverty, gentleness and fury, with a wisdom as timeless as scripture itself."

A collection of Tournier's short writings (monologues, sketches, stories) was published in France in 1978 titled *Le Coq de bruyère* (a grouse or woodcock), one of the stories included. The English translation took its title from another selection, a monologue *Le Fétichiste—The Fetishist*, which perhaps more accurately characterizes the spirit of these pieces. As in his earlier works, Tournier continues to play with the theme of human irrationality, resorting sometimes to the demonic and grotesque (the "sordid supernatural," as one critic described it) yet retaining a kind of childlike innocence and appeal. Granting that Tournier's work is "at times forced, didactic, culturally overdetermined, burdened with literary and legendary referents," the French scholar Victor Brombert nevertheless finds that such seeming flaws "enhance the thematic richness of Mr. Tournier's stories" and that "as a fiction maker, he is a worthy successor of Louis-Ferdinand Céline, Sartre, and Louis Guilloux." Similarly, John Weightman, reviewing *The Fetishist*, finds Tournier's "dominant tone . . . one of wild hilarity at the inextricable blend of ordinariness and strangeness in the world . . . a blessed relief after the pseudo-objectivity, and the deliberately stunted and refrigerated phenomenology, of the so-called 'New Novel,' which dominated the scene for so long before Tournier appeared to liven things up and restore to French fiction the vital human and philosophical content it had lost since the days of Sartre and Camus."

WORKS IN ENGLISH TRANSLATION: Tournier's novels are available in English translation—*Friday*, 1969, by Norman Denny; *The Ogre* (U.K. *The Erl King*), 1972, by Barbara Bray; *Gemini*, 1981, by Anne Carter; and *The Four Wise Men*, 1982, by Ralph Manheim. Tournier rewrote *Friday* for children (*Vendredi ou la Vie sauvage*), 1971, and it was translated by Ralph Manheim as *Friday and Robinson: Life on Esperanza Island*, 1972. His collection of short stories, *Le Coq de bruyère*, 1978, was translated by Barbara Wright as *The Fetishist* in 1984. Still untranslated are his literary autobiography *Le vent Paraclet*, 1977; *Le vol de vampire* (The Flight of the Vampire), 1981, a collection of critical notes on German and French fiction; *Gilles et Jeanne*, 1983, a story of the mass murderer nobleman Gilles de Rais, who fought at the side of Joan of Arc at Orléans; and two collections of prose poems on photography—*Des clefs et des serrures* (Of Keys and Locks), 1979, and *Vues de dos* (Views of Backs), 1981.

ABOUT: Contemporary Authors, new revision series 3, 1981; Contemporary Literary Criticism 6, 1976; Encyclopedia of World Literature in the 20th Century IV, 1975; International Who's Who, 1981–82; Popkin, D. and M. (eds.) Modern French Literature (Library of Literary Criticism) 2, 1977; Something about the Author 23, 1981; Tournier, M. Le vent Paraclet, 1977. *Periodicals*—French Review April 1979; New York Review of Books April 28, 1983; November 8, 1984; New York Times Book Review October 11, 1981; Times Literary Supplement October 16, 1981; World Literature Today Spring 1979.

YURI TRIFONOV

*TRIFONOV, YURI (VALENTINOVICH)

(August 28, 1925–March 28, 1981), Russian writer, was born in Moscow, the son of Valentin Trifonov, a prominent Bolshevik revolutionary, Red Army commander in the Civil War, Soviet trade commissioner to Finland in the late 1920s, and party official in Moscow in the mid-1930s. Trifonov's first tragic encounter with the reality of the Soviet system came at the age of twelve, when his parents fell victims to Stalin's purges. He lost his father in 1937; his mother was arrested in 1938 and returned from exile in 1946.

Yuri and his younger sister stayed with their maternal grandmother. During World War II they were evacuated to Tashkent, where Trifonov finished high school. Upon his return to Moscow he worked in an aircraft plant. From 1944 to 1949 he studied at the Gorky Literary Institute and began publishing in youth periodicals in 1947. Trifonov's first novel, *Studenty* (Students, 1950), published in the journal *Novy Mir,* won him a Stalin prize. Using fresh but carefully chosen colors, the young writer portrayed life at a pedagogical institute in post-war Moscow.

It took Trifonov almost thirteen years and several trips to Turkmenia to complete his next novel *Utolenie zhazhdy* (The Quenching of Thirst, 1963, or *The Acquenched,* in its English translation). This novel appeared in the journal *Znamia,* where he had previously published a collection of short stories *Puti v pustyne* (The Desert Roads, 1959) based on his travel notes. Although *The Acquenched* is a story about the construction of an irrigation canal, Trifonov's readers had no difficulty understanding the double meaning of the word "thirst." The Kara Kum desert needed water as desperately as the people longed for justice and a new life after Nikita Khrushchev's historic denunciation of Stalin at the twentieth Party Congress (1956). In this novel Trifonov also for the first time mentions the fate of people like his father. Soon afterward, he published a documentary work *Otblesk kostra* (Reflection of the Fire, 1965) dedicated to his father's activities during the Civil War.

In the late 1960s the influential journal *Novy Mir* published five of Trifonov's stories. They were followed by a cycle known as the "Moscow Novellas." The first novella, *Obmen* (The Exchange, 1969), marked a new stage in the writer's development. Its story is based on the housing shortage in Moscow. The protagonist's family wants to improve its living conditions by exchanging two single rooms in separate communal apartments, their own and that of the husband's dying mother, for a two-room apartment. The story ends with a successful exchange and with the death of the mother, of whose terminal condition the son and his wife were aware, although the mother was not. Her death, as the daughter-in-law intended, leaves the family in a new and larger apartment. Trifonov's main concern is not a single unethical exchange, but the general lack of moral values in a society that claims to be building a new life on revolutionary ideals, and what these ideals have been exchanged for. Soviet critics welcomed *The Exchange,* but they did everything to present it as an example of the writer's dedicated fight against the remnants of the petty bourgeois morals that occasionally infect an otherwise healthy Soviet society. Trifonov himself never agreed with such an interpretation.

In the following novellas, *Predvaritel'nye itogi* (Taking Stock, 1970), and *Dolgoe*

°tre′ fō nof

proshchanie (The Long Goodbye, 1971), Trifonov created characters who, experiencing alienation from a world in which they cannot find values worth cherishing, still must make moral compromises in order to be accepted by the existing society. Both novellas met with uneasiness among Soviet critics. A typical objection was voiced by the critic M. Sinel'nikov: "Trifonov is very precise in fulfilling his artistic objectives, in depicting the inner world of his heroes. . . . However, he is not always exact, and he often even contradicts himself when dealing with aspects of human relations and with conflicts which require a deep insight and understanding of social phenomena."

After an unfavorable official reaction to his new work, Trifonov retreated to the safe subject of the Russian revolutionary past. The historical novel *Neterpenie* (The Impatient Ones, 1973) is devoted to the life of Andrei Zheliabov, one of the leaders of the People's Will group that assassinated Alexander II in 1881. Trifonov's choice of a hero who believed that individual acts of terror would radically change czarist Russia presents a sharp contrast to subdued Soviet public life.

The fourth "Moscow Novella," *Drugaia zhizń* (Another Life, 1975), employs a narrative mode similar to that of Tolstoy's *Family Happiness;* the wife of historian Sergei Troitskii reviews their difficult marriage, which ended on Sergei's death from a heart attack at the age of forty-two. Behind this elaborate facade of everyday life and family problems one gradually makes out the story of an honest historian who was not allowed to defend his dissertation on the pre-revolutionary secret police.

In 1976 Trifonov published his most complex work, *Dom na naberezhnoi* (*The House on the Embankment*). The novel covers the years 1936–1974, examining the life of Vadim Glebov, a successful literary bureaucrat, and describing how fear of reprisal for political disobedience has produced a conformist without convictions who is preoccupied only with his immediate well-being.

The plot follows Glebov's reminiscences of the past, especially of the late 1930s and of the Zhdanov period following World War II. He remembers compromises with his conscience that advanced him to the next step on the ladder of success. The narrative in the third-person is interlaced with the voice of the first-person narrator, who knew Glebov as a school-mate. This semiautobiographical character watches for inconsistencies or accidental lapses in Glebov's involuntary memory. The house on the Moscow river embankment (in Muscovite slang "the government house"), where Trifonov lived as a child, hangs over the entire story as the symbol of a power able to inflict destruction upon those who choose to serve it and even upon itself.

The House on the Embankment was criticized at the Sixth Congress of Soviet Writers in 1976. Critic V. Ozerov warned Trifonov that his characters "act in a kind of spiritual vacuum," that they "are hermetically locked up in their own environment, while the author remains purposely on the sidelines, covering up his own intentions." Soviet readers, however, expressed a different opinion—the novel was an instant success and sold out immediately.

The novel *Starik* (*The Old Man,* 1978), published in the journal *Druzhba narodov*, expresses Trifonov's profound interest in the place and role of the individual in history. It attempts to reconcile memory, the reexamination of the past, with the reality of present-day life. The old man, Civil War veteran Pavel Letunov, lives in two different worlds. One of them turns around his reminiscences about the past, particularly about the heroic life and the tragic fate of Migulin, his Red Army commander in the Don district. (Migulin, who had a real historical double, Filipp Mironov, previously portrayed in *Reflections from the Fire,* was shot by the Reds in 1921 without any valid reason or court order.) The other world is the life of an ailing, elderly widower surrounded by his adult children and their families. They are outspokenly indifferent to their old man's 'schizophrenic' obsession with unveiling the historic truth and with his possible personal guilt for Migulin's death, preferring that he would fight now to help them to acquire a small country home needed for their growing families. For Letunov, however, only the first world is important; the outlook of his children appears to him pragmatic and pitifully shallow.

Trifonov's last novel, *Vremia i Mesto* (A Time and Place, 1981), was published posthumously also in *Druzhba narodov*. Its main character is a reworking of the superfluous figure Sasha Izvarin in *The Old Man* under a new name, Sasha Antipov. This novel spans the same period of Soviet history as *The House on the Embankment* (1936–1979), from Sasha's childhood to the moment when Antipov, already an accomplished writer, is in the process of creating an intricate multiple-mirror novel reflecting his own life. Critic A. Bocharov writes about *Vremia i Mesto*: "It is a novel about human destiny. . . . Everything in the novel is absolutely concrete and authentic and everything is charged with historic meaning, which highlights the ordinary things of life to a point where they become symbols, signs, pictographs. . . . [It] is a novel of memory: a memory that tries not to omit anything painful or difficult, but also not to forget the dazzling flashes of happiness that came at times along the road. And above all a memory intent on seeking out the causes and consequences that have shaped our present life."

Trifonov's memory seeks out these causes, namely Stalinism, in the last story of a collection of short sketches, *Oprokinutyi dom* (A Home Turned Over, 1981) published posthumously in *Novy Mir*. Trifonov gave this story the humble title "Seroe nebo, machty i ryzhaia loshad'" (The Grey Sky, the Masts and a Chesnut Horse). This is a fictionalized account of his busines trip to Finland, during which he also visits Helsinki, where he had spent a few happy years as a small child. There he unexpectedly meets an old woman who knew his father when he worked at the Soviet embassy. The writer remarks painfully that he has come as far as Finland before meeting someone who could remember his father, since "there were no such people left in Moscow." The story turns out to be an implied condemnation of the Stalinist system that killed Valentin Trifonov and many others like him. Thus in his final work the writer once again tries to find a mysterious link between time, place, and human destiny.

A good chess player and a sports fan, Trifonov also wrote three collections of stories and journalistic sketches about various sporting events: *V kontse sezona* (At the End of the Season, 1961), *Fakely na Flaminio* (The Torches at Flaminio, 1965), *Igry v sumerkakh* (The Games at Dusk, 1970) and a movie script, *Khokkeisty* (The Hockey Players, produced in 1965). His two novels, *Obmen* (The Exchange) and *The House on the Embankment*, adapted for the stage and produced by the well-known director Yuri Liubimov, were shown with enormous success in Moscow's avant-garde Taganka Theater. During his last years Trifonov taught at the Gorky Literary Institute.

In spite of the criticism at home, and due, apparently, to interest in his works among Western readers, Trifonov was frequently allowed to travel abroad. In 1978 he spent two months lecturing on Soviet literature at several American universities. At that time his first three "Moscow Novellas" appeared in English, published by Ardis (1978, *The Long Goodbye*). Trifonov's impressions of the visit to the United States, "Interv'iu o kontaktakh" (Interview: A Visit to the United States, 1978), were published in the journal *Inostrannaia Literatura*. His remark that "real Russian literature is created by Soviet writers, who live and 'officially' publish in their own country" was considered by many as an attack on Russian emigré writers and the *samizdat*. Trifonov himself was critical of the Soviet system, but he chose to live in his country and write what he was able to publish there. He died in Moscow at the age of fifty-five of coronary complications following kidney surgery and was given an official funeral by the Soviet Writers Union. The novelist Anatoly Rybakov delivered a eulogy before an audience of some 200 mourners, in which he said: "A writer's real material comes from his sufferings. The truest memory is the kind that leaves scars on the heart. Suffering was granted to Trifonov in full measure, to excess. Fate did not stint in that respect."

For Western readers, Trifonov is an excellent source of information about the life of a Soviet city-dweller. However, for profound understanding of his intentions, one has to read his work in the context of Russian and Soviet history, remembering Trifonov's own words: "I write for a sophisticated reader, for a reader who understands how one should read, who knows how to discern analogies, how to guess, how to see what is written between the lines."

WORKS IN ENGLISH TRANSLATION: *Students,* translated by Ivy Litvinova and M. Wettlin, was published in Moscow in 1953. *The Acquenched,* in Ralph Parker's translation, is in the periodical *Soviet Literature* 1 (1964), and Robert Daglish's translation of a chapter from one of Trifonov's novels, "The Side-Street behind Byelorussia Station," is in *Soviet Literature* 10 (1982). Additional English translations of his novels include: *The Impatient Ones,* by Robert Daglish, 1978; his trilogy *The Long Goodbye,* by H. Burlingame and E. Proffer, 1978; *Another Life* and *The House on the Embankment,* by M. Glenny, 1983. Jacqueline Edwards and Mitchell Schneider translated *The Old Man* in 1984. Tatiana Patera has published a book (in Russian) studying Trifonov's works, with special attention to the "Moscow Novellas," 1983 (Ardis).

ABOUT: Columbia Dictionary of Modern European Literature, 1980; Dunham, V. In Stalin's Time, 1976; Hosking, G. Beyond Socialist Realism, 1980; Proffer, E. *Introduction to* The Long Goodbye, 1978; Schneidman, N.N. Soviet Literature in the 1970s, 1979. *Periodicals*—Canadian-Slavonic Papers 19 (1977), 22 (1980), 25 (1983); New York Times October 23, 1977; March 29, 1981; April 2, 1981; New York Times Book Review March 18, 1984; New Yorker September 11, 1978; Russian Language Journal 34 1980; Slavic Review 37 1978; Slavic and East European Journal 26 1982; Soviet Literature 10 1982.

TRILLIN, CALVIN (December 5, 1935–   ), American journalist, novelist, and humorist, was born in Kansas City, Missouri, the son of Abe and Edyth (Weitzman) Trillin. He attended public schools in Kansas City, and graduated with a

CALVIN TRILLIN

B.A. degree from Yale University in 1957. After a period of service in the U.S. Army, he was employed, beginning in 1961, as a reporter for *Time* magazine, assigned partly to the South. In 1963 he became a staff writer for the *New Yorker*, a position he has retained ever since. In 1965 he married Alice Stewart, an English teacher and later a consultant to educational television.

Trillin's first pieces for the *New Yorker* were concerned with the entrance of the first two black students to the University of Georgia in 1961. The pieces were revised and expanded in Trillin's first book, *An Education in Georgia*. In the book Trillin chronicles the arrival of Charlayne Hunter and Hamilton Holmes at the previously all-white university; the tactics used by the state government and university administration to bar their entrance; the difficulties they experienced on campus and their graduation in 1964. The critic for the *Times Literary Supplement* praised Trillin's impartial coverage of the story, noting that he "writes with the sophisticated clarity and the eye for telling details which characterize the *New Yorker* magazine."

Trillin then ventured into fiction with *Barnett Frummer Is an Unbloomed Flower; and Other Adventures of Barnett Frummer, Rosalie Mondle, Roland Magruder, and Their Friends,* a collection of ten stories or vignettes which satirize radical chic in New York City during the 1960s. Poor Barnett Frummer, forever in pursuit of Rosalie Mondle, finds that he is out of step, cannot get invited to the parties Rosalie attends "where whites gathered to be castigated by some prominent Negro." Joyce Carol Oates, who liked

the light, sly humor of the work, commented that "Frummer's adventures never result in his blooming; he tries and tries again and again to establish himself in the center of the maniacally fluid fashionable world of New York City 'intellectuals,' but always the new issue, the new mania escapes him."

Runestruck, Trillin's first novel, is a comic account of what happens to the placid seacoast village of Berryville, Maine, when one of its inhabitants, while digging for clams, discovers a "real weird rock," believed to be a runestone left by Vikings. Acting on the doubtful assumption that Berryville is the fabled Vinland mentioned by Leif Erickson, the Chamber of Commerce sets out to transform the community into a tourist attraction, with an annual Runestone Festival. In the meantime, other residents stormily protest the new developments, and in the resulting furor Berryville is plunged into chaos. Phoebe-Lou Adams, in the *Atlantic,* remarked that the novel's "dialogue is amusing, the pace is supersonic." Robert Strozier, in the *New York Times,* thought that the plot eventually wore thin, but enjoyed the novel's constant flashes of wit. Critical response to *Floater,* Trillin's second novel, was also largely favorable. *Floater* is concerned with a young man, Fred Becker, who works for a national news magazine (based on Trillin's own apprenticeship at *Time*), who as a "floater" is a replacement writer, filling in one week for the business section and for religion the next. The story line, by Trillin's own admission, is rather tenuous, but the novel contains many engaging and cleverly struck off magazine types, including Waldo Brookside, the fired book editor, who says, "I certainly won't miss having to read all those books. I don't know which I hate more—books or authors." Nora Johnson, in the most enthusiastic review, observed that Trillin "has never been so funny as in this book, which is a denuding of some our most sacred Manhattan-based institutions."

U. S. Journal collected articles Trillin had written for the *New Yorker* from 1967 to 1970 in his column of the same title. They describe aspects of contemporary American life as observed by Trillin in his forays outside New York. John Hutchens observed that the book was "in the *New Yorker* tradition: low-keyed and precise, with reported fact allowed to make its own comment . . . nothing could be more chilling than the chronicle of the murder by a hillbilly of a Canadian documentary film-maker in the mountains of eastern Kentucky. . . . Mr. Trillin's instinct for oddity lurking in the apparently ordinary took him into all manner of curious corners." John Seelye, however, felt that Trillin's vignettes of hinterland life were too knowingly "packaged" for a Manhattan audience. His local eccentrics "are brought back to New York in the glass cages of Trillin's lucid prose," he concluded, "to confirm the smart city folks in their intellectual and moral superiority to the rest of (ugh) America."

Trillin's sense of humor, which enlivened his work in the sixties, was applied to food and the adventure of eating in *American Fried,* a droll account of his quest for a "decent meal" in America. "My interest in food," Trillin said in an interview, "came out of self defense, out of traveling a lot and facing, otherwise, dinner in the hotel." In *American Fried,* he asserts that the world capital of good food is his home town of Kansas City, particularly the spare ribs at Arthur Bryant's Barbecue and the hamburgers at Winstead's Drive-in. Spurning the standard fastfood outlets as well as pseudo-European cuisine served in "revolving" restaurants, he searches tirelessly for choice local food—Polish sausage and crab cakes in Baltimore, chili in Cincinnati, crawfish in New Orleans. *American Fried* delighted critics and public alike. Dorothy Rabinowitz, in the *Saturday Review,* commented that "Trillin is one of that rare breed of humor writers to whom literacy is not a burden. . . . Indeed, so far as humor is concerned, Mr. Trillin has here performed one of the most admirable and elegantly ordered entertainments to have come by in years."

Alice, Let's Eat continues Trillin's account of his passion for food as he travels to Kentucky for chicken, Vermont for wild game, and San Francisco for crab. Generally, reviewers found the book less piquant than *American Fried.* Ben Yagoda wrote that Trillin "ventures away from the U.S. too often: there's a trip to Martinique, one to France, and two to England. Transplanted from American soil, Trillin seems somehow out of place." For food expert Craig Claiborne, Trillin is "the Walt Whitman of American eats." But his truly cosmopolitan attitude to eating is summed up by his practice of carrying into Chinese restaurants a note in Chinese that reads: "Please bring me some of what that man at the next table is having." With *Third Helpings* his gourmand's odyssey became a trilogy. This time he roams to Louisiana, Kansas, Rhode Island, the West Indies, and Japan. As a food writer he is classed by Claiborne with Elizabeth David, M. F.K. Fisher and Waverley Root, but is "probably the most easily read, most joyous, and least sobersided of all." Christopher Lehmann-Haupt also praises his style, observing that he "almost never uses adjectives. . . . By shunning words like 'tangy,' 'soupy' and 'tender,' he steers clear of both clichés and wasted verbiage."

In 1978 Trillin began contributing a humorous current affairs column to the *Nation,* and has collected some of the pieces in *Uncivil Liberties.* In this book Trillin exercises a gift for social satire and parody that is often a healthy corrective to the fashions and pretensions of contemporary American society. "He is at his best," the critic for the *New Yorker* wrote, "where he does not seem to be making much effort, when he is just entertaining idle thoughts. . . . It would be wrong, however, to give the impression that Mr. Trillin is simply a genial humorist: he can leave his bite marks, and very often does." That Trillin is indeed also a serious writer was confirmed in *Killings,* a collection of pieces on violent deaths in America, intended, however, as Trillin writes, "to be more about how Americans live than about how some of them die." The sixteen cases reported here were pieces he wrote for the *New Yorker* between 1969 and 1982. They illustrated, according to William E. Geist in the *New York Times Book Review,* "reportage as art," thorough, straight-forward, and yet "much is revealed about human nature along the way."

Trillin is a prolific writer on the American scene not only in his books but also in the many articles he publishes in the *New Yorker,* the *Nation, Esquire,* the *Atlantic, Harper's, Life,* and other magazines. He lives with his wife and two daughters in a brownstone in Greenwich Village.

PRINCIPAL WORKS: An Education in Georgia, 1964; U.S. Journal, 1971; American Fried: Adventures of a Happy Eater, 1974; Alice, Let's Eat: Further Adventures of a Happy Eater, 1978; Uncivil Liberties, 1982; Third Helpings, 1983; Killings 1984. *Short stories*—Barnett Frummer Is an Unbloomed Flower, 1969. *Novels*—Runestruck, 1977; Floater, 1980.

ABOUT: Contemporary Authors, 85–88, 1980; Who's Who in America, 1983–84; Who's Who in the East, 1977. *Periodicals*—Book World October 26, 1969; Christian Science Monitor November 10, 1978; Life April 11, 1983; Nation March 3, 1984; National Review September 30, 1983; New Republic October 7, 1978; New York Review of Books, January 23, 1964; New York Times April 14, 1983; New York Times Book Review January 19, 1964; January 25, 1970; May 16, 1971; April 17, 1983; February 19, 1984; New Yorker May 23, 1977; June 14, 1982; Newsweek October 27, 1980; Playboy October, 1981; Publishers Weekly November 21, 1980; Saturday Review December 13, 1969; May 8, 1971; Time March 22, 1971; December 22, 1980; Times Literary Supplement August 20, 1964; Wall Street Journal May 16, 1977.

TRILLING, DIANA (July 21, 1905–), American literary and social critic, writes: "I was born in New York City and educated at Radcliffe. I graduated in 1925. Although it was my original intention to be a singer rather than a writer, I became seriously ill in 1930 and had to give up all hope of a musical career. By accident I fell into literary criticism in the early forties; several months after having started to write unsigned book notes for the *Nation*, I had a column in that magazine, 'Fiction in Review.' Soon I was a professional free-lance writer on literary, social, and political subjects, contributing to a varied list of periodicals including the *New York Times Book Review*, *Partisan Review*, *Commentary*, the *Reporter*, the *New Republic*, *Harper's*, the *Atlantic Monthly*, *Vogue*, *Harper's Bazaar*, *McCalls*, *Redbook*, *Look*, the *American Scholar* in this country and *Encounter*, the *Scotsman*, the *Times Literary Supplement* in Britain. In 1947 I edited and contributed a long introductory essay to the *Viking Portable D.H. Lawrence*, and in 1958 I similarly edited and introduced *The Selected Letters of D.H. Lawrence*. In 1964 I published my first collection of critical writings, *Claremont Essays*. This was followed in 1977 by *We Must March My Darlings*, also a collection of my critical essays, and in 1978 by a volume, *Reviewing the Forties*, which reprints a selection of my fiction reviews for the *Nation* during and following the second world war. My most recent book is of perhaps wider interest: in 1981 I published *Mrs. Harris*, a study of the trial of Jean Harris for the murder of Dr. Herman Tarnower, author of the famous Scarsdale diet.

"In 1929 I married Lionel Trilling, the noted literary critic and professor of English at Columbia University. I have one son, James, an historian of Byzantine art. After my husband's death in 1975 I edited a twelve-volume Uniform Edition of his work, published by Harcourt Brace Jovanovich.

"Over the years I have been fortunate enough to receive several grants and fellowships: in, I believe, 1950–51, I was the recipient of a Guggenheim fellowship; in 1977 and 1978 I received a joint grant from the National Endowment for the Humanities and the Rockefeller Foundation to do an oral history of the advanced literary-intellectual culture of New York City, 1925–75. The interviews done under this latter grant will eventually be on deposit at the Oral History division of the Columbia University Libraries. I am a member of the American Academy of Arts and Sciences and in 1982 I was elected to honorary membership in the Iota (Radcliffe) Chapter of Phi Beta Kappa.

"I still have a busy schedule of commitments."

———

© 1980 Thomas Victor

DIANA TRILLING

Daughter of Sadie (Forbert) and Joseph Rubin, a manufacturer, Diana Trilling was educated in schools in Westchester and at Erasmus Hall High School in Brooklyn and at Radcliffe, where she majored in fine arts, with a minor in music. Unable, because of her health, to pursue a career in vocal music, she worked briefly for the producer of a children's radio show. But it was not until 1942 when, on her husband's recommendation, she began writing brief, unsigned book reviews for the *Nation* that she found her vocation as a writer. By 1943 her perceptive critical observations and sharp, incisive prose had won her a regular signed column, "Fiction in Review."

Diana Trilling has acknowledged her husband's influence on her career, particularly in her practice of connecting works of literature with their social contexts. Her persistent search for what Paul Fussell described in his introduction to her *Reviewing the Forties* as "the fullest psychological, social, and political meanings" of what she reads marks her work as a critic. Among her most important critical writings is a long introduction to *The Portable D.H. Lawrence* (1947). Here, as Frank Kermode observed, she is an "Arnoldian" critic, applying those standards of high seriousness and social as well as artistic judgment that Lionel Trilling had explored so extensively in his biography of Matthew Arnold (1939, 1949). Lawrence's work, according to Mrs. Trilling, was his response to the world in which he lived: "What he saw around him drove him to extremes of loathing and fear: writing was his means of exorcizing his own demons and of trying to exorcize the demons of the rest of mankind." Writing at a time when Lawrence's literary reputation had declined, Mrs. Trilling stirred new appreciation of him. She acknowledged his shortcomings—"his intemperate tone" and lack of emotional control—and the disturbing implications of his philosophy: "[O]ne would be hard put it to name another writer, unless among the extreme *avant-garde* of this century, who so thoroughly rejects the moral and emotional premises of modern life—not alone the traditional literary forms, but also the whole modern Christian ethos." But after a brief but comprehensive survey of his life and works, she concludes that Lawrence offers his readers "what is often indicated instead of palliatives but almost never made available to us in art—a possible procedure for a fierce surgery upon our ailing world and selves."

Since 1949 Diana Trilling has been a freelance writer, contributing stimulating, often controversial articles on literature, politics, and contemporary culture to many journals. Her first collection of these pieces, *Claremont Essays,* includes essays on Enrico Caruso, the Alger Hiss case, Virginia Woolf, Edith Wharton, and Margaret Mead, this last ("Men, Women, and Sex") a survey of the ambiguous role of women in the early 1960s. Although she considers herself "the last living feminist," Mrs. Trilling has rejected what she considers the radicalism of the women's liberation movement which, she says, "actually turned out to be a kind of open season on gunning for men." She welcomes, however, the challenges with which feminism has confronted our culture. In an essay written in 1970, for example, she asks why women accepted the role of dependency and subordination to the male for so many generations and speculates "that women are considerably more flexible to the matter of how they are able to achieve fulfillment than we seem to recognize, and that it is perhaps only because our American culture requires women to find their best satisfaction in the activities of home or family that women obediently discover it there." Overall she seems to be sanguine about the cultural changes that the women's movement has initiated: "As I perceive it, or at least as I hoped, anything which rids us of false sexual assumptions and puts its stress on biological reality is bound to reduce men's and women's suspicions of each other and thus permit them a fuller expression of their human potentiality." ("Female Biology in a Male Culture," in *We Must March My Darlings*).

Seeking always the kind of intellectual middle ground that is the ideal of liberalism, both Trillings found themselves increasingly estranged from the political mainstream of the 1960s. Like many intellectuals of their generation, they had been attracted to Marxism in the early 1930s but were bitterly disenchanted by the Stalinist purges. In post-World War II America they found themselves politically isolated. "The anti-Communist liberal," she writes in her essay on Alger Hiss, "maintains . . . a very delicate position. He firmly opposes [Senator Joseph] McCarthy. But he doesn't automatically defend anyone McCarthy attacks." In another essay, "Liberal Anti-Communism Revisited," she alluded to the playwright Lillian Hellman's questioning of her and her husband's political position. The essay was included in a collection slated for publication by Little Brown, who had also published Hellman's book on the McCarthy era, *Scoundrel Time* (1976). When her publishers asked her to delete or modify some of the passages on Hellman, Mrs. Trilling refused, and her contract was cancelled. The book was subsequently published, the essay intact, as *We Must March My Darlings*. This collection included a first-hand account of the student uprising on the Columbia University campus in 1968. Sympathetic to the students, Mrs. Trilling sees them as victims of an apathetic university administration, a divided faculty, and a society hopelessly confused by the pressures of the Vietnam war and social radicalism ("On the Steps of the Low Library"). Among her other subjects were the popular film *Easy Rider*, Dr. Timothy Leary and the drug culture, and Norman Mailer's problems with the radical feminist movement.

Diana Trilling found a new and far larger reading public when in 1981 she published her book on the sensational trial of Mrs. Jean Harris for the murder of her lover, the famous Scarsdale diet doctor Herman Tarnower. The success of the book was not entirely gratifying to her. "It isn't as though I sold out by writing a trashy soap opera," she told Michiko Kakutani of the *New York Times*. "I wrote a serious book, but what scares me is that in the future I might automatically choose my subjects by whether or not I would have a big audience and the possibility of making money." The book is indeed not "a soap opera" or sob-sister reporting, but a literate and highly subjective examination as much of her own reactions as of the case itself. She attended the trial faithfully, visited the scene of the crime and the school where Mrs. Harris had been headmistress, and reported all the facts exhaustively. But she also, as she candidly admitted, responded emotionally and personally: "I'm fascinated by the kind of world that Dr. Tarnower and Mrs. Harris inhabited together and what happened between them for their relationship to ensue in such tragedy." Characteristically, Mrs. Trilling converted scandal into social and literary analysis, intrigued by another example of those events "which bring into conjunction our private and our public dilemmas." *Mrs. Harris,* Christopher Lehmann-Haupt wrote in the *New York Times,* "is about money, class, status, respectability, sex, power, feminism, and that peculiar but persisting state known as 'being a lady.'" It is also about literature, for Mrs. Trilling "reads" the case as she would read a classic novel, observing that while literature traditionally helped us discover "our own capacity for exaltation and pain," it no longer provides this function: "It has become abstract, remote from the objects of our immediate personal and social curiosity." She therefore reverts to literary parallels in F. Scott Fitzgerald (with Tarnower as a kind of Jay Gatsby and Mrs. Harris as Daisy), Stendhal, Flaubert, Tolstoy, and George Eliot. Among generally favorable reviewers of *Mrs. Harris,* Josephine Hendin, writing in the *New Republic,* found the book "the work of a seasoned writer with large resources of knowledge and intelligence."

PRINCIPAL WORKS: Claremont Essays, 1964; We Must March My Darlings, 1977; Reviewing the Forties, 1978; Mrs. Harris, 1981.

ABOUT: Contemporary Authors, first revision series 5–8, 1969; Contemporary Authors, new revision series 10, 1983; Current Biography, 1979; Who's Who in America, 1983–84. *Periodicals*—Commentary March 1978; New York Times November 16, 1981; Vogue September 1981.

*****UNDER, MARIE** (March 27, 1883– September 25, 1980), Estonian poet, was born in Tallinn, Estonia (now USSR). Her parents Fredrich Under, a schoolteacher, and Leena (née Kerner) were from Hiiumaa Island (Dagö) off the coast of Estonia. Marie Under was the best known poet in Estonia during its period of independence and later, in Sweden, she became one of the foremost Estonian writers in exile.

Having learned to read by the age of four, Marie Under attended a German school, as was customary at that time for children of the educated. There she also studied French and Russian and became acquainted with many cultural and political figures of her day through her association with the liberal newspaper *Teataja.* Although she published little until she was over thirty, Marie Under began writing verse at the age of thirteen. Her first poetry was written in German, but she was encouraged by the artist A. Laipman to write in Estonian. He also gave her the nickname Mutti, with which she signed her earliest poems. Before the age of twenty, however, she married K. Hacker, a librarian, with whom she moved to Moscow. In 1906 they re-

MARIE UNDER

turned to Tallinn with their two daughters. Marie Under then renewed her Estonian cultural ties and activities, especially through her work in the Estonia Theater, where she met Artur Adson, a young poet. They married in 1915 soon after Marie Under's divorce.

With the publication of *Sonetid* (Sonnets) in 1917, she acquired fame and cosiderable notoriety for erotic frankness. This book of youthful, sensuous, but skillful poems has been described as a "paean to the joy of living" by W. K. Matthews, her critic and translator. A member of the colorful Siuru group of poets, who had taken the name of a phoenix-like mythical bird, she was named "Princess of Siur."

Her second book of verse, *Eelõitseng* (First Flowering, 1918) contains poems written before those in *Sonetid.* Some of them had already appeared in publications of a group of poets known as Young Estonia who preceded Siuru and were influenced as much by West European symbolism as the later Siuru group was influenced by German expressionism. *Eelõitseng, Sonetid,* and *Sinine Puri* (Blue Sail, 1920), constitute Marie Under's work as a lyric of poet whose primary subjects were nature and erotic love.

During the politically insecure years following World War I, Marie Under visited European cities, especially Berlin, where she came to know the work of Kurt Weill and Gottfried Benn. The poetry she wrote between 1921 and 1923 reflects the moral and physical desolation of this world. No doubt German expressionist poetry that she translated during this period for an anthology also contributed to the radical change in her own work. From the flowering, emotion-filled

õon´ də

Sonetid her verse changed to the eerie, apocalyptic vistas of a shattered world found in *Verivalla* (Bloodbath, 1921) and *Pärisosa* (Heritage, 1923). The powerful emotionalism of these poems is masterfully rendered by broken rhythms and metaphors of violence. By this time, Marie Under had received many literary prizes and had been translated into several other languages. In 1937, she became an honorary member of International PEN.

It is generally conceded that *Hääl varjust* (Voice from the Shadows, 1927) marks the beginning of Marie Under's great poetry. According to Ants Oras, another of her critics, these poems have no equal in earlier Estonian literature. W. K. Matthews considers that her poetry then attained "an art that is classical in its balance between subjective and objective elements and between clarity and subtlety." This was a period of emotional extremes for the poet. She suffered from insomnia, a condition which remained with her throughout her life. Her poems carefully reconstruct the experience of illness and delirium.

It is only in the final poems of this volume that some relief and hope is afforded and an emotional bridge is formed to Marie Under's next book *Rõõm uhest ilusast päevast* (Delight in a Beautiful Day, 1928). Written in the same period as *Hääl varjust,* it reflects quite the opposite range of emotions and borders on religious ecstasy with its profound joy and unself-conscious absorption in nature, birds, trees, flowers, and children. Although it is not allegorical, the volume is reminiscent of Blake's *Songs of Innocence.* On reading some poems translated from these two books, the German poet-painter Oskar Kokoschka said, "I love this poetess honestly and affectionately; she has a power of vision comparable to that of those great German women who in the eleventh and twelfth centuries succeeded in depicting a Saviour utterly different from the Saviour of theology because their mysticism was rooted in sensory experience. This is the way our revered Marie Under writes and in this regard she is unique to our age."

Marie Under's next book, *Ønne varjutus* (Eclipse of Happiness, 1929), was written during a seemingly idyllic period of her life. As a permanent beneficiary of the National Fund for Culture, she was relieved from major financial concerns and left free to pursue her interests. During these years she translated Claudel, Baudelaire, Ibsen, Rilke, Pasternak, and Schiller among others. She kept a distance from literary circles and intrigues, preferring rural or semirural environments. Despite her outwardly harmonious existence, there was no ebb in the intensity of her poetry. *Ønne varjutus, ballaadid ja legendid* (Eclipse of Happiness, Ballads and Legends, 1929), a volume of narrative verse, including ballads on Estonian and biblical legendary themes, displays the grand, dramatic scope of her imagination. In it she handles tragic, phantasmal themes. These range from biblical Leah's use of magical Diedius berries to consummate her relationship with Jacob to the despair of a mother who had drowned her child and joins her in suicide in the crashing waves of the sea. This volume established Marie Under as a successful writer in the romantic ballad tradition.

After the publication of *Ønne varjutus,* Marie Under went into seclusion and a myth began to form around her for she was already considered one of the foremost poets in the country. During this time she published little. The appearance of *Lageda taeva all* (Under the Open Sky) in 1930 did little to clarify her state of mind to the public. It was *Kivi südamelt* (A Stone off the Heart), published in 1935, that gave an insight into her transformation. The volume is considered one of her peak achievements. It is a synthesis of the forms and genres found in her earlier poetry, now combined with a more subtle, complex style.

Metaphor and symbol, both of which she avoided in the past, are now used to portray a transcendental vision. Ants Oras sees in them parallels to the poetry of Gerard Manley Hopkins, Donne, Vaughan, and the lonely struggles of T. S. Eliot's *Four Quartets.* These are resolved by Marie Under in a new-found vitality and transfiguration of the world that is akin to the spirit of St. Francis. Images of wind, sea, and fire are used to render her visions of darkness, blinding light, and serenity.

Except for the anthology of her work *Ja liha sai sõnaks* (And Flesh Became Word) published in 1936, *Kivi südamelt* was the last volume of Marie Under's verse to be published before World War II. Her next book *Mureliku suuga* (With Sorrowful Mouth) was published in 1942 during the German occupation of Estonia. These poems describe the mental and physical agony suffered in her country from 1939, when Estonia was taken over by the USSR, and then occupied by the Germans during the following year. This book recounts the sufferings of the many families broken up and deported to distant parts of the USSR. Sorrow at the events of war and destruction, the sufferings of volunteers in the Russo-Finnish war, and images of cold, snow, stones, silence, and death permeate these poems. The poems themselves constitute a synthesis of personal and national sorrow.

In the mass exodus which took place from Estonia during 1944 upon renewed conflict between the German and Soviet forces, Marie Under and her family left for Sweden. There, uprooted in exile, she became once more one of the clearest, most powerful voices in Estonian literature. Her first volume of entirely new verse was not, however, published for a decade. But in *Sädemed tunas* (Sparks in Ash, 1954), as in *Ääremail* (On the Brink, 1963), she maintains the high level of her art and her transcendental vision. These poems, in all their indignation, plead for resistance and steadfastness without giving way to hatred. The emotions are now expressed in language that has become simple and more direct than that of her previous verse. Her collected poems (*Kogutud luulethused*) were published in 1958 in Sweden and several anthologies were published during this time in Estonia.

Her seventieth and seventy-fifth birthdays were celebrated by Estonians abroad and her eightieth birthday was observed in Soviet Estonia as well. Because of heavy arthritis, Marie Under spent the last six years of her life in a nursing home. Upon her death at the age of ninety-seven, she was survived by her daughters Dagmar Stock and Hedda Hacker. Her husband, Artur Adson, had died three years earlier. Marie Under's funeral was attended by over 400 people including an official representative of the Swedish Academy to which she had been nominated as a candidate for the Nobel Prize by the Finnish PEN Club.

At the funeral service it was announced to the dismayed mourners that her body had been confused with that of another elderly woman and mistakenly cremated, which was expressly against Marie Under's wishes. The coffin contained only her ashes. Some have seen this as symbolic of her storm-filled life.

WORKS IN ENGLISH TRANSLATION: A collection of Marie Under's poems was published in W.K. Matthews' translation as *Child of Man* in 1955. Twenty of her poems and ballads are included in Matthews' *Modern Estonian Poetry*, 1953. Selections from her work also appear in *The PEN in Exile*, I and II, 1954, 1966.

ABOUT: Cassell's Encyclopedia of World Literature, 1973; Columbia Dictionary of Modern European Literature, 1980; Encyclopedia of World Literature in the 20th Century III, 1971; Matthews, W.K. s *Introduction to* Child of Man, 1955; Oras, A. Marie Under, 1963.

*VACULIK, LUDVIK (July 23, 1926–), Czechoslovakian novelist, was born in the village of Brumov in Moravia and had little formal edu-

cation, though as a boy he read everything that came to hand from stories about the American Wild West to Verne, Dumas, and Sienkiewicz. His father worked during the depression of the 1930s as a laborer in Iran. At fourteen Vaculík joined the Bata shoe factory in Zlin and Zruc to become a shoemaker. After World War II he studied business and journalism. In 1946 he became a member of the Communist Party because, he told an interviewer, "I thought it had the most courageous program, the most logical one. As time went by and things didn't work, I thought it was because certain figures were no good." For a while he earned his living as a teacher in a vocational school for young workers where his wife, Marie Komarkova, was also a teacher, but by 1949 his free thinking led to his dismissal. After a period of army service, Vaculík moved to Prague, working first as a journalist for a Communist daily paper and then as a broadcaster for the official Prague radio station. In 1965 Vaculík joined the editorial board of the weekly *Literarni noviny* (later called *Literarni Listy*) published by the Czechoslovak Writers Union. The journal was influential in the developing democratic spirit in Czechoslovakia which, however, was halted by the 1968 Soviet invasion.

Vaculík's first novel, *Rusny dum* (A Noisy House), published in 1963, received little attention, but in 1966 his second novel, *Sekera* (*The Axe*), catapulted him to a leading position among Czech writers. A masterly book, frankly autobiographical, it is remarkable for its highly sensitive, almost Joycean, recall of the past; its internal structure is based on temporal expansion and restriction with shifts in time and place often occurring within the same sentence. The language is a mixture of poetic metaphors and crude dialect of his native village; and the overall effect is a mixture of subjective realism and surreal immediacy. To Czech intellectuals reading the novel in 1966 it also had a very real immediacy. His fellow editor on *Literarni noviny*, Antonin J. Liehm, described the impact the book had on him: "I read it through in two evenings and since . . . I have been breathing more easily in this world. Here was an author who had found a name for the incredible collapse of all structures—that collapse we all felt happening around us but could not define except on the level of political slogans. At the same time, this author demonstrated that life-giving impulses persist, that within the chaos there are still feelings that give meaning to life." Like Milan Kundera's celebrated novel *The Joke*, Vaculík's *The Axe* is the story of a cynical, disillusioned journalist who reviews the failure of his own life, contrasting it to that of his father, a dedicated, hard-working carpenter. The axe, a laborers' tool, is both literal and symbolic, and the character of the father, an idealist who becomes corrupted and ultimately destroyed as a tool of the Communist Party, is richly drawn. Vaculík calls him a "positive" hero: "The positive hero is characterized by the fact that he comes in conflict with a powerful force. And my hero is struggling not against the village, but against the irreconcilable conflict between his duties and himself. This hero's fate also provides proof of how distorted forms and structures may become as a result of realizing an ideal."

In 1967 Vaculík was expelled from the Communist Party for a speech at the Congress of the Czech Writers Association in which he denounced the power structure, saying, among other things: "The social revolution has triumphed in our country, but the problem of power is still with us. We have taken the bull by the horns and we are holding on, and yet something keeps butting us in the seat of the pants." His writings were immediately banned, but many Czech intellectuals defied the government by supporting him and, to the embarrassment of party officials, he was nominated for a prize as best journalist of the year. A year later Vaculík wrote a proclamation, "Two Thousand Words," signed by many prominent Czechs, which called for open protest against the restrictions imposed on free thought and expression.

Though under constant threat of arrest and trial, especially after the Soviet invasion of Czechoslovakia in 1968, he continued to write. *Morcata* (*The Guinea Pigs,* 1970) could not be published in Czechoslovakia, but when published abroad it was immediately hailed as a brilliant portrait of totalitarian society. Here Vaculík blended two components of the Czech literary tradition—the world of Jaroslav Hašek's *Good Soldier Schweik* and the world of Franz Kafka to produce a novel at once funny and chilling, realistic and absurdist. It tells the story of a bank clerk, his wife, and their two sons, who adopt two guinea pigs and perform some playful experiments in social conditioning upon them. The analogy between the caged guinea pigs performing their controlled experiments and the family living in a totalitarian state is all the more impressive as the satire moves from homely domestic comedy to nightmare horror.

In 1973 Vaculík again faced arrest for an interview that he gave British television. The trial never took place, but his passport was revoked and he was placed under police surveillance. His apartment was searched, and in 1975 he reported, in an open letter to Kurt Waldheim, then secretary general of the United Nations, that the manuscript of a book on which he had been working for several years had been removed. By now the key figure in underground publishing activities in Czechoslovakia, he helped many writers whose books were banned by authorities to reach their readers at home and abroad. He was instrumental in reviving a genre which has played an important role in Czech literature— the *feuilleton,* short essays such as earlier writers like Jan Neruda and Karel Čapek had produced.

In 1980 Vaculík published in *samizdat* what many consider his most important book, *Cesky snář* (A Czech Dreambook). Its protagonist is the writer Vaculík, a non-person for the authorities, who is continuously harassed by the police and prevented from having a normal life. He is also the organizer of underground publishing activities, an angry man, a philosopher. But above all, he is a sensitive human being struggling with a situation that has been forced upon him. This portrait of a "dissident as a human being" is based on its protagonist's diaries and notations of dreams from January 1979 to April 1980—a poem, a novel, an x-ray picture of a totalitarian world, an ironic and faithful description of what is called "dissidence" by one of its most indomitable heroes. In January 1982 the *New York Times* reported that Vaculík was still living in Prague.

WORKS IN ENGLISH TRANSLATION: Both *The Axe,* in Marian Sling's translation, and *The Guinea Pigs,* translated by Kaca Polackova, were published in 1973. *The Guinea Pigs* was reprinted by Penguin in 1975 as part of the "Writers from the Other Europe" series. Vaculík's *feuilletons,* along with those of fellow dissidents, were edited and translated by A.J. Liehm and P. Kussi in 1983 as *Writing on the Wall.*

ABOUT: Columbia Dictionary of Modern European Literature, 1980; Contemporary Authors 53–56, 1975; French, A. Czech Writers and Politics, 1945–1969, 1982; Liehm, A.J. The Politics of Culture, 1972. *Periodicals*—New Republic August 30, 1975; New York Review of Books October 30, 1975; New York Times September 20, 1967; February 14, 1977; Washington Post January 3, 1974.

VALENTINE, JEAN (April 27, 1934–), American poet, was born in Chicago, the daughter of John W. Valentine and the former Jean Purcell. She attended Milton Academy and graduated from Radcliffe College in 1956, was married to James Chace in 1957 and divorced in 1968, and is the mother of two daughters. Since 1968 she has taught poetry and the writing of it at various Eastern colleges and universities, including Swarthmore, Barnard, Hunter, Yale, and Sarah Lawrence.

© 1985 Thomas Victor

JEAN VALENTINE

Valentine's first published collection, *Dream Barker and Other Poems,* won the Yale Series of Younger Poets award the year it appeared. In a warm introduction to the volume, Dudley Fitts wrote: "Her ideas, her images, her very modes of saying, spring from love in its various aspects: from love of persons and places revisited, from love in experience, in contemplation, in dream. . . . The poems constitute a dialectic, a true conversation. The themes are ancient and common, the proper themes of lyric—youth, passion, loss, the human outrage, death. They are as old as poetry itself. What renews them here is a quirkily singular intelligence, a fusion of wit and tenderness, subserved by an unusual accuracy of pitch and rightness of tone. Insight and art work a transmutation." The collection contains many memorable poems, including "The Little Flower," a grandmother's lengthy monologue, full of sad, fragmented memories; although written as prose, it has poetry's flow, cadence, and significant repetition. Also notable is the witty "To My Soul," a short epigraph whose classical models are the Emperor Hadrian's address to his soul (*Animula vagula blandula/hospes comesque corporis* . . .) and Ronsard's deathbed variation of 1585 (*Amelette Ronsardelette,/mignonnelette doucelette,/ treschere hostesse de mon corps,* . . .). Valentine's version loses none of her originals' startling freshness and delight in word-play:

Scattered milkweed, valentine,
Moonlighting darling, leonine
Host and guest of my château,
Tender, yawning concubine,
Vine of my summer in decline,
Uncut, unribboned mistletoe,

Monstrous footprint in the snow,
Hypnotizing, gemmy toad,
My generation's cameo,

Symplegadês of every road,
Closet bones, unflowered sod,
Laugh, my little nuncio!

The poems in *Pilgrims* show markedly greater syntactical compression than those in her first book; their subject matter includes, in Anne Stevenson's words, "more than her own experience of life and change in the twentieth century." Love in its many variations is still, however, her guiding poetic principle. She can capture in a poem of a few words—even a single sentence—a sharply etched story and a way of behavior:

From this night on God let me eat
like that blind child on the train
touching her yogurt as I'd touch a spiderweb
the first morning in the country—sky red—

holding the carton and spoon to her mouth
with all her eyeless body, and then
orientally resting, the whole time smiling
a little to one side of straight ahead.

("Night")

Adrienne Rich wrote of the collection: "Almost every poem is life lived at the edge, but lived by someone who is without cessation a poet, and who moves back and forth between a special kind of blackness and a special kind of radiance."

Valentine has made a few much-acclaimed translations of poems by the Dutch lyricist Huub Oosterhuis. The first of these, the long sequence "Twenty Days' Journey," appeared with twenty-two of her short lyrics in *Ordinary Things.* Many of her poems still tell of love, but an increasing number concern death, the failure of family life, even random violence. Her style has here become so spare, her use of punctuation so idiosyncratic, that the images—individually often striking—tend to pile on one another and her voice becomes nearly incoherent, as in "Force (2): Song":

Weeds breaking up through stone:
our hold on our own hollows, the quick,
curved line of a smile: bare, our own
ribs shelter us: a boy's cold, white
fingers around a match:
heart belling: hollow, quick,
through the live horn, the bone, to this
day, calm.

Several of the poems in this collection contain allusions to Rilke and Jung, which are explained on a page of brief, enigmatic notes at the end of the volume. These poems, in one critic's words, "intensify the impression of subliminal, universal, larger-than-life experience."

Translations of Oosterhuis' "Orpheus" and Osip Mandelstam's "394" form one of the three parts of *The Messenger,* Valentine's fourth book. In her own poems in this collection she occasionally eases her strict control over syntax, but her work seems, if anything, even more complex, demanding of the reader's concentrated attention. "Human correlations are induced," in Hugh Seidman's phrase, " . . . in an atmosphere of remoteness. . . . Incoherence in the transition from the specific catalogue to the emotional concerns is the most obvious problem Miss Valentine's method poses." Depths of personal reference still resonate in her work, and are often unidentifiable, as in the short monologue "Letter from a Stranger":

You said, you know what I mean: one winter, you looked
    and saw
a river branching in the black sycamore branches, silver
veins of roads rising and ending in icy twigs at your
    window;
an awful time. Then spring came
    and you said
you *learned to love Lincoln again*; the first leaves came
and you saw Lincoln's *kind, grave face, drawn there*
in the leaves, in the light.
How can I answer your letter? words from your life
bring me home to my life. So safe
now, that I can leave it again, now
the milky quiet. The warm straw.

PRINCIPAL WORKS: *Poetry*—Dream Barker, 1965; Pilgrims, 1969; Ordinary Things, 1974; The Messenger, 1979.

ABOUT: Contemporary Authors 65–68, 1977; Vinson, J. (ed.) Contemporary Poets, 1980. *Periodicals*—Choice May 1975; January 1980; Christian Science Monitor October 28, 1969; Commonweal July 4, 1975; Harper January 1980; Library Journal November 1, 1969; June 1, 1979; New York Times Book Review August 2, 1970; October 21, 1979; Poetry December 1970; October 1975; August 1980; Virginia Quarterly Review Summer 1970.

*VARNALIS (BARNALES), KOSTAS (KONSTANDINOS), (February 15, 1884–December 16, 1974), Greek poet, playwright, prose satirist, and translator, was born of Greek parents in Pyrgos, Bulgaria, where he received his early education. In 1903 he enrolled in the School of Philosophy of the University of Athens, taking his degree in literature and classics in 1908. He then returned to Bulgaria to teach in the Greek high schools, but two years later settled permanently in Greece where, from 1911 to 1917, he was director of several secondary schools. In 1918 Várnalis became a professor of secondary education in Piraeus.

Várnalis' early poems, collected in 1905 in *Kerithes* (Honeycombs), reflected a high roman-

tic idealism similar to the mystic visionary work of his contemporary Angelos Sikelianós. Kimon Friar attributes this early manner in part to his Bulgarian birth and childhood—"the nostalgia of an exile"—and in part to his education in the classics. At first he wrote in the purist or erudite Greek language observing strict traditional meter and stanzaic forms. But in 1919 he went to France on a scholarship to study literature, philosophy, and sociology at the Sorbonne, where his exposure to the political upheavals of post-World War I Europe—to the influences of pacifist writers like Romain Rolland and Henry Barbusse and to Marxism in the turbulent years of the Russian Revolution—produced a radical change in his outlook and his writing. When he returned to Greece a year later, he found himself divided between his enduring passion for the ancient classical past and the modern world, which he saw as one of chaos and political corruption. The result of this inner conflict was a dualism which, Friar observes, "he was to retain in some form or another throughout his life." He switched to the demotic language, for which he became a crusader, and like his fellow-writers Nikos Kazantzákis and Yánnis Rítsos, he was outspokenly left-wing in his politics. Although demotic had by now been adopted as the official language of Greece, Várnalis' radical political ideology made him vulnerable to official censure. In 1922 he published a collection of his poems and plays, *To fos poi kaiei* (The Burning Light) under a pseudonym, Dhimos Tánalis, in Alexandria, Egypt. The theme of the book—the struggles and martyrdom of fighters for human freedom from Prometheus and Christ to a modern symbolic labor leader—was inflammatory in the repressive political atmosphere of Greece under the dictatorship of General Theodorus Pangálos, and in 1925 Várnalis was dismissed from his teaching post.

From that time Várnalis supported himself as a free-lance journalist and translator. Refusing to compromise, he turned to the genre of satire where he could express his views with biting effect, often under the cloak of ancient history and myth. He also reverted, satirically, to the Romantic past of the great nineteenth-century patriot and poet Dionysios Solomós, author of "The Hymn to Liberty" which became the Greek national anthem, with a collection of poems entitled *Sklavoi poliorkimenoi* (The Slaves Besieged, 1927), a wordplay on the title of a famous poem by Solomós, *Eleftheroi poliorkimenoi* (The Free Besieged). Here he wrote an impassioned attack on the enslavement of his fellow Greeks to custom and superstition and urged rebellion of the poor and downtrodden.

In no work is Várnalis' satire better reflected

°vär´ nä lēs, kôs´ tas

than in his short prose piece *I alithini apologia tou Sokrati* (*The True Apology of Socrates,* 1931). By now recognized as the foremost Marxist poet of his age, Várnalis conceived a Socrates whose defense is presented under the same circumstances as the ancient trial of the philosopher recounted by Plato, but in a spirit and idiom unmistakably contemporary. Stephen Yaloussis describes his Socrates as "a man of flesh and blood; . . . a man fond of the paradox in thought and full of biting irony," whose chief talent was "the uncommon gift of proving everybody a fool," and whose downfall "was partly due to his irony and to his unfailing aptitude for putting everybody's back up." To some extent, Várnalis' Socrates is himself—cynical, proud, outspoken in his contempt for autocratic authority and the bourgeois complacency which supports it. As he remarks in an "author's note": "The reader must now rest assured that all books written previously on the subject—on the supposed apology of Socrates—bear no relation to the truth. They are merely figments of their authors' imaginations, petty efforts to prove that Socrates was innocent, that the Law was just."

Várnalis' disclaimer is characteristic of his irony, for his Socrates is indeed innocent of any evil. He is, however, guilty of the crime of absolute honesty, even to the extent of admitting to his accusers, "Had I been in your shoes, I would have done the same." His "apology" is divided into five short sections in which he first infuriates his accusers by ridiculing them: "Lately my mind has been acting the same way as the mule when suddenly confronted with a sharp precipice or a wooden bridge rotten with decay. Like the mule, it digs its heels in and refuses to move an inch. It makes me stop and look down; yes, look down my nose—and there to my horror, I can see the whole world, the vast world of ugliness, of truth." Then he narrates a fable of an honest society where the common people will be free "to get drunk, to dance, to procreate, and to die," and their leaders will guide them firmly but generously. In the third part he speaks personally of his own contempt for life—"our world is black and ugly . . . there is no purpose in this life save to die." Yet, perverse and indifferent to happiness, he nevertheless lived his own life in freedom, defying convention and celebrating the body and nature. He regards himself, he says, in the fourth part, not as a philosopher but as a cynic and satirist. But in the closing section he describes what he would do to reform society. *The Apology* ends with the corrupt jurors, who have of course found him guilty, rushing out to collect their pay while Socrates is "frustrated but smiling. His innate peace and moral courage radiated from his face." With no guards to watch him, he quietly summons Plato to show him the way to prison.

The Apology has the mixture of cynicism and compassion, inflamed rhetoric and delicate sensibility, imagination and realism, that is equally remarkable in Várnalis' poetry. His early poems, though written in demotic, are classical in idiom and theme, as Friar points out, "primarily an aesthetic reconstruction of the classical world, evoking his nostalgia for a vanished glory." They are, nevertheless, also sophisticated and cynical, as his "Aphrodite" of 1913 demonstrates:

The raucous laughter of the Immortal Gods
still rang and burned within her ears like flame!
And when her lame-legged husband's crafty net
was cut, golden-haired Aphrodite sprang

out of her bed, and speeding through blue skylanes,
reached Paphos' foam-flecked shores. There Eroses,
whose wings ordeals had never touched, played on
their lyres to cheer her mood. The Graces, too,

wiped off all trace of color or of shame
from her smooth snow-white skin and laved her flesh
with unguents incorruptible. Behold her now,

More chaste than ever, she leaps on the sea's calm;
and in the sun, that sets the sky afire,
not one drop clings to her not even one word.
                                               —trans. K. Friar

Várnalis' increasing cynicism reflects his exposure to Marxism and his awakening political consciousness. His "Magdalen" addresses herself boldly to Christ in a poem of 1920:

You never said anything new, nor clad old things afresh.
All had been said by many men in times long past.
But yours the power to hear the silence of the heavens;
and men and all inanimate things, and even the heart
of God became for you—for me—transparent glass.

No one (not wise men, students, parents or multitudes)
could sense the agony behind your miracles;
and if you ever hoped to be saved from a death unjust,
then only I, who once was whore and mud, have felt
how mortal you were, Christ! And I shall resurrect you!
                                               —trans. K. Friar

His later poems even more passionately evoke the spirit of rage and rebellion, as in "My Sun" (1965):

Read Shakespeare, Aeschylos, and Tolstoy too,
read Solomós' great "Hymn to Liberty,"
for in your vitals, wormwood conscience gnaws
and deep shame presses in your throat and chokes.

Sun, a great people wait for you with longing,
and all the people everywhere united!
But do not rise behind Hymettos as once
before, to drown at evening down the sea.

Like an unsetting source of light and joy,
honor and liberty, you shall be brought
and placed deep in the sky, on land and sea,
by the forerunner, the whole world's Pariah.
                                               —trans. K. Friar

Várnalis wrote short stories, literary criticism, including a socio-historical study of the poet Solomós, *Solomós horis metaphysiki* (Solomós without Metaphysics, 1925) and a drama about a slave rebellion in ancient Greece, *Attalos o tritos* (Attalos the Third, 1972). A three-volume edition of his complete works, *Ta apanta tou Várnali,* was published 1956–1971. He married the poet Dora Moátsu in 1929. Honored in his last years, he received the Lenin Peace Prize in 1958 and, presented to him in a clinic in Athens only two hours before his death, the Gold Medal of the Athens Union of Journalists.

WORKS IN ENGLISH TRANSLATION: Only one book by Várnalis, *The True Apology of Socrates,* is available in English in a translation by Stephen Yaloussis published in 1955. Selections from his poetry appear in several anthologies, including Kimon Friar's *Modern Greek Poetry,* 1973, and Rae Dalven's *Modern Greek Poetry,* 1971.

ABOUT: Columbia Dictionary of Modern European Literature, 1980; Contemporary Authors 53–56, 1975; Dalven, R. Modern Greek Poetry, 1971; Dimaras, C.T. A History of Modern Greek Literature, 1972; Friar, K. Modern Greek Poetry, 1973; Yaloussis, S. *Introduction to* Várnalis' The True Apology of Socrates, 1955.

VENDLER, HELEN (HENNESSY) (April 30, 1933–   ), American critic, writes: "Helen Vendler was born in Boston, Massachusetts, the daughter of two schoolteachers. Her father taught her Spanish, French, and Italian during her childhood; her mother introduced her to English and poetry. She learned Latin in high school and continued to pursue French in high school and college. In college, she majored in chemistry, receiving her A.B. summa cum laude in chemistry (Emmanuel College, 1954). In 1954-55, she was a Fulbright scholar in Belgium, where she studied Old French, Italian, French literature, and philosophy. She spent 1955-56 taking English literature courses at Boston University in preparation for entrance to the Ph.D. program in English and American Language and Literature at Harvard. She was at Harvard, as a graduate student and member of the Board of Tutors, from 1956-60, receiving the Ph.D. in 1960 with a thesis on W. B. Yeats, published as *Yeats's Vision and the Later Plays.* She married the philosopher Zeno Vendler and accompanied him to Cornell, where she taught from 1960-63, and where their child David James was born (1960). In 1963-64 she was a lecturer at Haverford and Swarthmore; she was divorced in 1964. From 1964-66, she taught at Smith; in 1966 she moved to Boston University, where she is profes-

HELEN VENDLER

sor of English. From 1981 on she has also been a continuing visiting professor at Harvard every fall.

"Vendler is a frequent reviewer of contemporary poetry in various journals, and is the poetry critic for the *New Yorker.* She has had Guggenheim, NEH, and ACLS fellowships, and received in 1975 an award from the American Academy and Institute of Arts and Letters. She is a member of the American Academy of Arts and Sciences and Senior Fellow of the Society of Fellows of Harvard University; she was, in 1980, president of the Modern Language Association. Her book on Wallace Stevens received in 1969 the Lowell Award of the MLA and the Explicator Prize; her book on modern poetry received the National Book Critics Circle Award in 1980.

"Vendler's work has always been centered on the lyric. She considers herself an eclectic critic, free to bring various approaches to bear on the work of elucidating poetry. In her view, poems resemble music, painting, sculpture, or choreography—other works, that is, directed centrally to an aesthetic end, whatever other ends (political, philosophical, etc.) they may also accomplish. She is interested chiefly in the aesthetic power of lyric—how it arises, how it functions, how it is structured. She sees poems in English as interlocking parts first, of a single genre, and then, as parts of their native literature with its classical origins. She wishes she could read Greek."

In 1966 Helen Vendler wrote a review of current American poetry for *Massachusetts Review,* discovering along the way, as she wrote in the foreword to *Part of Nature, Part of Us,* that although for her poetry was "the most immediate, natural, and accessible" of all literary forms, it was not so to many readers. Bridging this gap—that is, communicating her own sensitive and illuminating readings to her readers—has been the aim of her teaching and writing. Simplification or reductionism, however, has not been her method. Denis Donoghue calls her mainly "a descriptive critic," pointing out that even in a brief review she offers "a profile of the poetry," and in her longer essays, "a more elaborate iconography of the poet in the scene of his entire work." Her virtues, W. H. Pritchard writes, "are a rigorous attending to verbal structure and texture; the ability to quote appositely and economically; a sure though not a too-exclusive taste; above all, the ability to do the poem one better by putting into words the relevant responses we might have had if we'd been smarter and more feeling."

Vendler's best known book, *Part of Nature, Part of Us: Modern American Poets* (the title is taken from Stevens' observation in *Academic Discourse at Havana,* that "as part of nature, he is part of us") discusses the works of more than twenty-five contemporary poets, with major emphasis on Robert Lowell, Wallace Stevens, and James Merrill. The book is intended, she writes, for those counterparts of her "younger self" who discover modern poetry for themselves. To write about modern poets, she says, "is to try to explain, first to oneself and then to others, what common note they strike and how they make it new." Her response to poetry is personal and sympathetic, but her technique is rigorous. Harold Bloom considers her "one of the best 'close readers' of poetry we now have." She reads for pleasure but with the trained eye of a scholar, linguist, grammarian, semanticist and rhetorician.

From her earliest critical writing—her doctoral dissertation on Yeats' later plays—Vendler has approached a great poet's work "not in terms of esoteric doctrine, but in terms of experience, especially aesthetic experience." She saw Yeats' obscure, mystical *A Vision* as a work on poetic inspiration as it operates in the poet's mind; her book was a lucid and illuminating study that traced the poet's inspiration "in its unconscious sources as well as in its conscious labors." Similarly, in *On Extended Wings* she read Wallace Stevens' longer poems both "as things in themselves and as steps in a long progress toward his most complete incarnations of his sense of the world." Stevens emerges, in her book, not as "the doctrinal poet of ideas," but as a poet of sensibility, fluid and experimental, moving between polarities of poetic experience. J. Hillis Miller, though dis-

agreeing with some of her interpretations of specific poems, judged her book "the definitive study" of Stevens' later work, finding in "her concentrated, witty, and shrewd language of interpretation an extension of the poet's language" rather than a reduction of it to prose explication.

Vendler has not confined her attention to modern poetry but has written with equal perception on earlier English poets. In an essay on Shakespeare's sonnet 129 ("Th' expense of spirit"), published in a collection honoring the critic I. A. Richards (to whom she dedicated *On Extended Wings*), she argued against Roman Jakobson's strict formal interpretation of the poem. No method of analysis, she wrote, "can be applied at random to poems. Each poem will still dictate the method best suited to its own interpretation." She proceeded to a close study of the language of the sonnet, reading it not as a static statement but as a "progressive evolution of thought," moving dramatically from one attitude toward lust to another. And in her book on the poet George Herbert (whom she regards as "one of the purest and most ravishing of English poets"), she used the same method of close reading to show "that Herbert's apparent simplicity is deceptive" and that his poetry reflects "successive (and often conflicting) points of view." It is poetic or creative development that Vendler studies again in her long and richly detailed *The Odes of John Keats.* In the concentrated genius of those six poems, all written within a few months when Keats was twenty-three, she found a steady and complex growth, culminating in "To Autumn," to which she devotes some seventy pages of her book. The method here, Frank Kermode observed, "imposes some constraints" and "an occasional bout of academic huffing and puffing [that] may discourage the faint-hearted." Nevertheless, he finds her prose "unpedantic and sometimes movingly accurate . . . the instrument of a tenacious and resourceful mind."

Vendler's future writing plans include another book on Wallace Stevens and a study of Shakespeare's sonnets. She also says that she "hopes some day to write about Milton."

PRINCIPAL WORKS: Yeats' *Vision* and the Later Plays, 1963; On Extended Wings: Wallace Stevens' Longer Poems, 1969; The Poetry of George Herbert, 1975; Part of Nature, Part of Us: Modern American Poets, 1980; The Odes of John Keats, 1983. *As editor*—(with R. Brower and J. Hollander) I.A. Richards: Essays in His Honor, 1973.

ABOUT: Contemporary Authors, first revision series 41-

44, 1979; Who's Who in America, 1983-84; Who's Who of American Women, 1983-84. *Periodicals*—New York Review of Books April 12, 1984; New York Times Book Review October 5, 1969; November 27, 1983; Times Literary Supplement November 28, 1975; Yale Review Winter 1970.

*VIVANTE, ARTURO (October 17, 1923–), Italian-American novelist and short story writer, writes: "One day, in third grade, in Italy, where I was born, we were asked to write an essay on why we loved our mother. While everyone said they loved their mother because she did so much for them, worked so hard, looked after them so well, gave them presents, and so forth, I simply said I loved her because she was lovely and good and dear. Much to my and the other students' astonishment, my little essay was singled out as the best. That was my literary success. The next, in fifth grade, was a poem I wrote about the stars. My father liked it so well he read it aloud and had me read it aloud and showed it to friends and to my teacher, who had the class listen to it. That early encouragement set me on a course that, after forty years, I still keep. If, in life's vicissitudes, I have strayed from it sometimes, I have never lost sight of it, and I have always tried to return to it. Never am I in greater misery than when I find myself veering from that course, and never am I happier and more confident than when I am right on it. Then life seems true. Then I am not at odds with myself. Then I am at peace.

"Of my early influences what can I say? My father's appreciation and my mother's help were probably the most important. She was a painter and looked more at what she was painting than at the canvas. I tried to do the same while writing. Even before that, I remember her bedtime stories, how they held me, especially those that she said were 'from the truth.' Later, in middle school, she would sometimes help me with an essay. Through her I learned how one detail, accurately drawn, or one right word, can bring a picture to life.

"All through my school and college years I wrote poems. Neatly I recopied them in bound little notebooks I still have. My parents and a few of my teachers saw some merit in them. Not enough, I decided, for me to embark on a literary career. I would go on writing, but to make a living I had to do something else besides. Medicine seemed more humane than the humanities, and I studied medicine and became a doctor and practiced for a few years in Rome. But that first love for writing never waned, and when a patient came—I had a very meager practice—I

ARTURO VIVANTE

would reluctantly clear my desk of the leaves of paper I was writing on to make room for the heavier medical equipment.

"I was twenty-five and—except for a little volume of verse which I had printed at my own expense and which, as I was warned, only made 'a hole in water'—I hadn't published any of my poems, though, heaven knows, I had tried. My poems certainly weren't of a fashionable kind. My ear was attuned to the classics of another age and out of tune with my contemporaries. A voice said, try prose. In prose my verse found refuge. Hidden, in disguise, some of my poems found a secure place in my stories, just as later some of my stories were concealed within my novels. Prose seemed more accommodating, easier perhaps, and I reveled in it as in a wider bed. Prose, and particularly the short story, gave me new breath, new vigor. And my stories seemed closer to the times, too, than my poems. Some contemporary prose writers—Carson McCullers, Tennessee Williams, Dorothy Parker, Salinger, to mention but a few—said things to me that contemporary poets did not. Before long I had written several stories, plays, and a novel. In 1955 I sent a short story, 'The Snake,' to the *Manchester Guardian,* and it was published. At this point I should mention that, though I was born in Italy, I wrote both in Italian and in English, having spent the war years (from when I was fourteen till twenty-one) in England and Canada as a refugee. Also, my mother was half American, and we often spoke English at home.

"Next I published two stories in *Botteghe Oscure.* Then, in 1958, Dwight Macdonald, the literary critic, saw some of my short stories and sent one to the *New Yorker*. They took it, and took three more that year. The checks I got dwarfed what I made in my medical practice, and I gave it up. The study of medicine—let me add—was a great education for me, and its practice provided me with experience and ideas which I used in my writing. I have been contributing short stories to the *New Yorker* to this day, and have had some seventy stories in it. Other magazines that have published more than one story of mine are: the *London Magazine*, the *Cornhill*, *Vogue*, *Southern Review*, *TriQuarterly*, *Yankee*, *Canto*, *Antaeus*, the *Greensboro Review*. I have taught creative writing in several colleges (at present in Bennington) and my ideas about writing are expressed in 'Writing Fiction' (*The Writer*, 1980).

"When not teaching I live in Wellfleet, Cape Cod, with my wife, Nancy, and three children—Lucy, Lydia, and Benjamin.

"I write in order to know the mystery that even a small event holds. Much of my work has an autobiographical flavor, though sometimes I write of what might have been as though it had actually taken place. Whether it happened or not, I think that if the thing is well told, it is convincing and has a measure of truth."

Arturo Vivante was born in Rome, the son of Leone Vivante, a philosopher, and Elena De Bosis Vivante. He received his bachelor's degree in 1945 from McGill University, Montreal, and his M.D. degree from the University of Rome in 1949. He was, as he writes above, a general practitioner in Rome from 1950 to 1958. A full-time writer since then, he has been writer-in-residence at North Carolina (1968), Boston (1970), and Purdue (1972–74) universities, and has taught creative writing at Brandeis and Michigan universities. He is at present a member of the teaching staff of Bennington College.

Poesie (1951), published in Venice, comprises forty-seven conventionally romantic lyrics in Italian and another twenty in English. The latter convey not so much Vivante's command of the language in his late twenties as a peculiar mastery of old-fashioned verse forms; he makes extensive use of such "poetic" devices as word-inversion and such archaisms as "doth" and "nay." It has been in prose, as he says above, and especially in short fiction, that his particular talents have found their best expression. His stories, as a rule, are simple and straightforward, detailing small, but not unimportant, moments of recognition. His subjects are often drawn from a childhood in Italy, exile during wartime in Britain and Canada, or from married life. He has de-

veloped a keen ear for dialogue and an economical method of setting a scene. There is little feeling of experimentation or modernism in his tone or style, and his stories, over the many years of their appearance in the *New Yorker*, have come to seem easily the least oblique in meaning and most linear in narrative style—in short, the most comprehensible—of all the fiction regularly published by that magazine.

The first of his collections, *The French Girls of Killíni*, consists of twenty-one stories, all of which came from the *New Yorker*. The title story shows Vivante at his best: what might have been a disagreeable, solitary journey around Greece in an old car constantly in need of repair is rendered happy, even idyllic, in the retelling—the hero's rather ordinary adventures and the classical sites he manages to visit become elevated to the status of memorable occurrences and accomplishments by the sheer force of narrative. Another story, "The Secret," traces the inner musings of a painter, who moves with his family into an old house. He has decided to leave his wife, with whom he is constantly quarrelling, but the enormous demands of renovating the house force him to change his mind. This tale's strength lies in the persuasive penetration of the artist's mind and motivation: his decision to leave leads him naturally to work on the house, which labor in turn leads him to reconsider his original decision.

> Now it was all finished, his house. His? No—hers. He walked some forty feet away to get a better view of it. "She looks all right," he said.
> "It," his wife corrected him.
> But in truth he had come to think of the house as a sort of ship, with passengers inside, and could he abandon it? How could he? He couldn't, really. It was so frail, so fragile . . .

Susan de Lissovoy remarked that Vivante "convinces us that there is poetry, compassion, and the opportunity to achieve integrity in the commonplace experiences of life. This . . . book . . . provides a refreshing change from the hard-driving violence and the easy experience which informs so much of modern fiction."

Vivante's other story collections include *English Stories*, most of which detail the experiences of a teen-ager in England during World War II: finding, with his parents, a well-lit, pleasant restaurant in London during the blackout; discovering the narrow viciousness of the required rituals in an English public school. *Run to the Waterfall* consists of fifteen stories focusing on the narrator, Giacomo, and his life with his mother and father in the stately, sunny, placid city of Siena before and after the war. Anne Bernays called this collection of linked stories "an elegant, gentle book by a writer of marvelous skill." Marc Granetz, while observing that on occasion the author's "soft, simple message seems disingenuous, too easy," concluded that "most of the reflections and realizations are genuine and unadorned. There is no manufactured drama, no exaggeration, no attempt at psychological analysis. . . . Any convincing affirmation of life in fiction these days is rare and refreshing, and that alone is reason enough to read this book."

Vivante's novels, while far from discreditable, contain little of the freshness, economy, and energy so abundant in the stories. The sure and sustained delineation of character is not one of his strengths. *A Goodly Babe* is the rather morose account of Cosimo Lami, a Roman physician who seems less interested in practicing medicine than in proposing to attractive, English-speaking women. He marries Jessie Reynolds, an American tourist, and after they lose a malformed baby they move to America where their life picks up and they have a normal child. R. Z. Sheppard called the book an "unpretentious, neatly spun skein of cotton candy" and thought the hero "a good-natured, slightly distracted chap, of the sort Marcello Mastroianni has portrayed so engagingly and so often." To Helene Cantarella, the novel "captures the intensity of elementary human truth and transmutes it into rare, crystalline beauty." Vivante's other published novel is *Doctor Giovanni*, which he translated and published in Italy as *Il dottor Giovanni* in 1971.

The author has also published a translation of philosophical essays by his father, Leone Vivante: *Essays on Art and Ontology* (1980). These are intended as an introduction to, and compendium of, his father's ideas as set forth in his two major works, in Italian, on the concept of indetermination and the philosophy of potentiality. One critic described the pieces as "precise, perceptive, phenomenological observations of artistic creativity"; E. F. Kaelin wrote that the book's central intuition "that man's spiritual being is an active potentiality, i.e. an originary or underived activity expressing itself through its works."

PRINCIPAL WORKS: *Stories*—The French Girls of Killini, 1967; English Stories, 1975; Run to the Waterfall, 1979. *Novels*—A Goodly Babe, 1966; Doctor Giovanni, 1969. *Poems* (in Italian and English)—Poesie, 1951. *Non-fiction*—Writing Fiction, 1980.

ABOUT: Contemporary Authors 17–20R, 1976. *Periodicals*—Best Sellers April 1, 1966; August 15, 1967; Book Week April 3, 1966; Choice July 1966; November 1980; Christian Science Monitor June 29, 1967; November 14, 1979; Journal of Aesthetics Spring 1981; Library Journal March 1, 1966; May 15, 1967; November 15, 1979; New Republic September 15, 1979; New York Times Book Review March 20, 1966; May 28, 1967; November 11, 1979.

*VLADIMOV, GEORGY (NIKOLAEVICH) (February 19, 1931–), Russian novelist, was born in Kharkov to parents who were both teachers of Russian language and literature. His father was killed in action during World War II. In 1948, after graduating from the Suvorov Military Academy, Vladimov entered the Law School of Leningrad University. After the arrest of his mother as an enemy of the people in 1952, he completed his studies by correspondence while working as a stevedore and ditchdigger but was unable to find work in the legal profession, and took a job as a correspondent with a regional newspaper. He began publishing literary criticism in 1954 and attracted the attention of Alexander Tvardovsky, the editor of *Novy Mir*, who appointed him prose editor of that journal for the years 1956 to 1959. Vladimov's short novel *Bolshaya ruda* (*The Ore*, 1961) appeared in *Novy Mir*.

In many ways the novel is connected with the so-called "production novel," which depicts the life of a factory with close attention to the relations among workers on the job. Its hero is the truck driver Pronyakin, who arrives at the gigantic mine in the beginning of the novel and dies there tragically when his truck, loaded with the first ore from a new deposit uncovered at great depth, falls over a cliff. Vladimov is in fundamental conflict with the aesthetic of socialist realism, which makes the collective the bearer of all true principles; real harmony can therefore lie only in union with the collective. Vladimov maintains to the contrary that individuals develop toward *individuality*, not collectivism. This in fact is the leading idea of the novel as a whole. It is not the collective, in the form of the mine workers, but Pronyakin who is obsessed with the great goal of digging down to the main deposit of ore.

Vladimov places his hero in difficult circumstances. His truck is significantly smaller than those of the other drivers. He is constantly hurrying to overtake them on the road and comes up with clever dodges to fulfill the plan on time. His romantic enthusiasm, his love for his work, his dream of the ore which is so essential for the country coexist with a practical, peasant shrewdness. His fellow workers respect his driving skill but cannot appreciate his higher qualities, the profound uniqueness of his personality. From their point of view he is a money-hungry egotist. There is an element of tragic guilt in his death, which takes place when despite all rules to the

°vlä´ dē môf, gyē´ ôr gyē

contrary he sets out with the first ore along a rain-soaked road. He is punished by fate for his impatience and excessively passionate temperament. But the collective suffers as well when Pronyakin's death evokes a keen sense of guilt among his former co-workers. Thus Vladimov has reshaped the material of the novel of production to pose the question of the collective and the individual in a new way, one that emphasizes the personal aspect systematically excluded from the literature of socialist realism.

Vladimov's next novel, *Tri minuty molchaniya* (Three Minutes of Silence, 1969), also appeared in *Novy Mir*. The title refers to the three minutes of radio silence traditionally set aside to listen for emergency SOS calls, such as those sent by the ship on which Semyon Shalai, the main character, serves. During loading operations while still in port, the fishing trawler *Skakun* sustains damage to its hull. A hole needs to be repaired, but for the sake of fulfilling the plan, the officers decide to ignore the danger and go out again after more fish. During a storm the trawler springs a serious leak. Nevertheless they take on board the crew of a foreign vessel, also in distress. Everything ends happily, though Vladimov misses no opportunity to emphasize the danger threatening the ship. Vladimov's narrator, Semyon Shalai, is an intelligent, ironical, efficient sailor who recalls the truck driver Pronyakin, but who is perhaps more educated, and is completely free of Pronyakin's calculation. The back-breaking labor of the sailors, the oppressive atmosphere on board the trawler, and the officers' negligence and lack of courage form the background to the action.

Only the authority of Alexander Tvardovsky secured the novel's publication. In spite of numerous cuts made by the censor, it evoked an enormous positive response. In 1983 the author succeeded in publishing a complete edition, undistorted by censorship, but outside the Soviet Union. Just as the novel was being published for the first time, Vladimov wrote an open letter to the Presidium of the Fourth Congress of the Writers' Unoin. He called for frank discussion of Alexander Solzhenitsyn's letter to the Congress. Solzhenitsyn had written of the persecution of literature in general as well as of his own persecution at the hands of the KGB. Vladimov demanded that the Congress take up the question of censorship which, he said, was crushing Russian literature and had engendered the phenomenon of *samizdat* ("self-publishing," the clandestine reproduction and dissemination of writing which cannot be published officially). "Conduct a general search, confiscate all films, all copies, arrest the authors and the distributors; and yet at least one copy will survive, and surviv-

ing—multiply, and more abundantly than before, as forbidden fruit is sweet." A fierce campaign hounding Vladimov began in the press. *Three Minutes of Silence* was subjected to savage criticism, and there was an attempt to initiate legal proceedings against him. Vladimov was effectively isolated.

His next short novel, *Verny Ruslan (Faithful Ruslan*, 1975) was published by Posev in West Germany. "Ruslan" is a German shepherd which had been raised and trained for guard duty in a concentration camp. The first version of the story was written in 1963, when Vladimov saw that "not only the gates of the camps have opened a bit, but also the gate of the camp as a literary theme, Ivan Denisovich has managed to squeeze through." The reference is to Solzhenitsyn's 1962 story of a prison camp of the Stalin era, "One Day in the Life of Ivan Denisovich." Vladimov wanted to seize the opportunity to write about his own experience: as a youth he visited his mother in a camp near Leningrad and listened to her stories. In addition he himself had lived in fear of arrest in connection with a case started against him, which was dropped only after Stalin's death. The immediate stimulus for *Verny Ruslan* was provided, however, by an acquaintance's report of actual former guard dogs which had been abandoned when a camp closed and which, though starving, would walk along with any group that came by and drive stragglers back in line. At that time Vladimov wrote merely a light-hearted satire on the theme, identifying the guard dogs with the guards.

Alexander Tvardovsky was willing to publish the piece, but it seemed to him that the theme was too large and potentially too tragic for light satire. Vladimov took the manuscript back, but against his will the story became widely circulated in *samizdat*, where curiously enough it was attributed to Solzhenitsyn. By the time Vladimov had reworked it, enlarging it to a short novel, Khrushchev had been removed from his post and the camp theme had become impossible. Vladimov revised it once more in the early 1970s and published it in the West. In this novel, he had created an image of the true Stalinist, brought up in the Stalin era and saturated with ideas of faithful service and unquestioning, "dog-like" loyalty to the leader. It is Ruslan's tragedy to be free only in prison and to be utterly helpless when free. Thus the light satire was transformed into the tragic portrait of Soviet man, deceived by the lie of Sovietized history. The ending of the novel is significant. Free workers arrive at the site of the former camp. The dogs surround them and attack those who "break ranks." The frightened workers at first try to fend the dogs off, then strike at them with shovels and crowbars. Ruslan fights courageously but is killed.

The publication of the novel in the West and its great success had completely unexpected consequences for Vladimov. His novel *Tri minuty molchaniya* was published in book form after being blocked for seven years, and an interview with him appeared in the literary weekly *Literaturnaya gazeta*. This proved to be Vladimov's last publication in the Soviet Union. The authorities wanted to show that he had not broken with the system and was still a "Soviet writer." Vladimov, however, remained true to himself. In October 1977 he addressed a stinging letter to the Writers' Union, which ended with the following words: "Bear the burden of the gray; do what you are fit for and inclined to— oppress, persecute, never let go. But do it without me. I hereby return membership card no. 1471." Vladimov's open letters, like those of Solzhenitsyn, are brilliant examples of contemporary civic rhetoric.

After leaving the Writers' Union and especially after joining the Moscow branch of Amnesty International, Vladimov's situation took a final turn for the worse. He was followed; his telephone was disconnected; his mail was stopped; his apartment searched. He responded to all this with the story "Ne obrashchaite vnimanya, Maestro" (Pay No Attention, Maestro), in which he portrayed a famous writer and dissident under the observation of the KGB. The writer of course is Vladimov himself. He has said that during this period of unequal combat with the KGB, he often addressed the words "pay no attention" to himself. "Maestro" hints at some connection with the hero of Mikhail Bulgakov's famous novel *The Master and Margarita* (1966–67). Like Bulgakov's Master, Vladimov's writer is surrounded by evil forces and doomed to an agonizing, bitter existence. The story is narrated by a thirty-two-year-old graduate student who lives in a tiny apartment with his father and mother. All of a sudden KGB men take over the apartment in order to observe the dissident writer who lives across the way. Acting dumb, the father and son go to the regular police station and report that their apartment has been occupied by international bandits. The climax of the story is provided by the clash between the regular policemen and the KGB agents, a clash that reflects the real animosity of these two services. Vladimov also conveys the paradoxical idea that in gathering and preserving information about remarkable men of the times, the state as police spy is playing the role of historian of culture, and in the future this information may well be used to right the wrongs of history as it is now being written.

In May 1983 Vladimov and his wife Natalya (Kuznetsova) emigrated to West Germany. In 1984 he assumed the editorship of *Grani,* the oldest Russian emigré publication.

WORKS IN ENGLISH TRANSLATION: An English translation of *Bolshaya ruda* by J. Kuraga was published in Moscow in 1963 with the title *Striking It Rich.* The same short novel, titled "The Ore," is in A. McAndrew's *Four Soviet Masterpieces,* 1965. *Faithful Ruslan: The Story of a Guard Dog* was translated by Michael Glenny, 1979. A non-fiction "Dialogue on Prose" between Vladimov and Felix Kuznetsov, translated by Robert Daglish, was published in the periodical *Soviet Literature* 7, 1976.

ABOUT: Adams, R. *Introduction to* Faithful Ruslan, 1979; Brown, D. Soviet Russian Literature Since Stalin, 1978; Columbia Dictionary of Modern European Literature, 1980; Hosking, G. Beyond Socialist Realism, 1980; International Who's Who, 1983–84; Richardson, K. Twentieth Century Writing: A Reader's Guide to Contemporary Literature, 1969; Slonim, M. Soviet Russian Literature, 1977. *Periodicals*—National Review November 9, 1979; Time February 14, 1983; World Literature Today Summer 1979.

*VOINOVICH, VLADIMIR NIKOLAEVICH

(September 26, 1932–), Russian-born novelist and short storywriter, writes (in Russian): "I was born in the southern region of the Soviet Union, in the town of Dushanbe (Tadzikistan), as a result of a marriage which would have been impossible before the October revolution. My father was of Serbian origin, from a rather distinguished noble family, whose members played notable roles in the history of Yugoslavia and Russia. One of them was Ivo Voinovich, a dramatist and a classic of Serbo-Croatian literature. Another, Marko Voinovich, was an admiral during the reign of Catherine the Great. He was the founder and the first commander of the Black Sea Fleet. My mother was a Jew from a small town near Odessa. Her parents were poor, barely literate people, and there were no famous ancestors in her surveyable past. From my birth on, my parents evidently had an inclination toward 'changing of places' (Pushkin's expression). They got acquainted somewhere on a train, and at the time of my birth found themselves in the distant mid-Asian city where both of them worked for the local newspaper. My father (he was a member of the Communist Party) had an important position, and my mother (partyless) had an unimportant position. Subsequently, my mother completed her studies at the Pedagogical Institute and started teaching mathematics.

"I was three and a half years old when my father disappeared. In answer to my question, my

°vä ēn´äw vich, vla dē´meer ni kō lā´ə vich

VLADIMIR VOINOVICH

mother would say that he was on an assignment and would return soon. Weeks passed, months and years, and my father did not return, and I started forgetting him. I only remembered that he had a big birthmark on his upper lip. I attended kindergarten, where appropriately there were a hundred banners with the inscription: 'Thank you, Comrade Stalin, for our happy childhood.' There, as everywhere else, hung the portraits of Comrade Stalin. The first poem that I remember was also about Comrade Stalin. When I was eight years old, I entered the first grade. At that time, my mother was working and attending the Institute, and my grandmother had a difficult time with me. All the free time that I had I spent on the street. Once when I tried to straddle a neighbor's pig behind a shed, one of my friends came running to get me: 'Come, there is some guy asking for you!' The very guy appeared, very suspicious, with an overgrown beard, in an old padded jacket and torn army boots. 'What is your name?' he asked, smiling strangely. I answered. 'And what is your last name?' I mentioned my last name. 'Well, then, show me where you live.' And I led him home, guessing and not quite believing that this terrible tramp was my father. Even through the beard I could discern the birthmark on his upper lip. It was thus that our family got together for awhile. Certainly, I was never as happy as during the first days after my father returned. However, there was much that astonished me and darkened my joy. Why did he return from an assignment in such a state? Why during the night did he stand grinding his teeth, why did he jump and look around in fear?

"Six years later, I found out the truth from my grandmother, my father's mother. Once, in a conversation with two of his co-workers, my father had said that in his opinion, one cannot build socialism in a given separate country, that is, that one can do it only in all countries simultaneously after a world revolution takes place. In as much as this thought contradicted the general position of Comrade Stalin, my father was arrested. After a two-year investigation, during which he was prepared for execution, he received only a five-year camp term. In the camp, in contrast to some others, he bid a final goodbye to communist illusions. He was lucky since just before the war there was a wave of rehabilitation, and he got into it. He was even offered an opportunity to return to the Party, but he flatly refused. Without waiting for a second arrest, he grabbed me and took me to his sister (my aunt) in the Ukraine, without having spent even a month at home. My mother remained in Leninabad in order to complete her studies at the Pedagogical Institute. It is possible that they would have found my father in the Ukraine, but in a few months after our arrival there, the war with Germany started. During the first days of the war, he left for the front. The war was a terrible disaster for all. I fled twice from the Germans with the family of my aunt. And during the winter of '43 we lived through a very real period of hunger in the Kuijbyshevskii region. Shortly after that, my mother and my invalid father, who returned from the war, located me there.

"I will not dwell on it, but my life developed in such a way that I grew up not in a family but on the street, and my parents influenced me little in a positive sense. But their indirect influence was greater than they could imagine. And especially strong was my father's influence on me. My father returned from the front during the height of the war when the hatred of Germans, precisely of Germans, and not of Hitler or the Nazis, reached its limit. Soviet propaganda and literature (in general, they are one and the same thing) propagandized for hatred of all Germans. 'Kill the German,' invoked Ehrenburg. 'However many times you see him, that many times kill him,' wrote a famous Soviet poet, Konstantin Simonov. Under these circumstances, I posed a question to my father, the kind of question that most children asked their fathers who returned from the front. I asked him: 'Daddy, and how many Germans did you kill?' He looked at me attentively and said precisely: 'I did not kill even one, and I am very pleased with it.' These words astonished me but did not disappoint me. I have remembered them all my life.

"The arrest of my father and the war dealt

losses to our family from which we could not recover for many years. Our family lived in poverty. At the age of eleven, I started my laboring years as a shepherd of *kolkhoz* [collective farm] calves. After that, I worked as a joiner, carpenter, locksmith, railroad worker, and God knows what else. I served four years as a soldier. I studied from time to time. Out of ten classes in the middle school (high school), I completed exactly one half (first, fourth, sixth, seventh, and tenth classes), the last three in an evening school of working youth. For a year and a half, I studied at the historical faculty (I think that this would be a department of history in American terms) of the Pedagogical Institute in Moscow.

"I started writing (poetry at first) in 1955, while in the army. Soon thereafter, my work saw print, at first as a poet and then as a prose writer. My first story, 'My Zdes' Zhivem' ['We Live Here'] was published in *Novy Mir,* in 1961. I was admitted to the Union of Writers of the USSR in 1962. This period has been called the 'thaw' by some historians. The thaw did not last very long. In 1965, the writers Sinyavsky and Daniel were arrested. Preparations were made for a public trial. I understood that the Soviet party *tops* decided to return to the Stalinist form of government. After all that the people of the country and my own family had been through, I felt a revulsion and a hatred for it. Together with other Soviet intellectuals, I protested against the trial of Sinyavsky and Daniel and against the administration of justice over many other people. For these activities and for my books, I was subjected to repressions. In 1974, I was excluded from the Writers' Union. In 1980, I was forced to emigrate. On the 16th of June in 1981, I was deprived of my Soviet citizenship by Brezhnev's edict.

"My books have been translated into thirty languages. I am a member-correspondent of the Bavarian Academy of Fine Arts and the PEN Club. I am an honorary member of the American Society of Mark Twain. At this time [1983] I am teaching a course in Russian literature at Princeton University."

—trans. B. Kogan

Except for two short intervals, Voinovich's writings were prohibited from publication in the Soviet Union shortly after he signed the letter protesting the trial of authors Sinyavsky and Daniel and defended Solzhenitsyn and Sakharov. Not only was he expelled from the Writers' Union, in 1974, but he was not permitted to receive royalties from his works published abroad. He was thus placed in the anomalous situation of being labeled a "parasite" for not earning his living as a writer. To further exacerbate his position, in 1976 the government disconnected his home telephone, and for the rest of his stay in the USSR, kept him under surveillance. In addition, two years later, it subjected his sick father to a police interrogation, in the course of which it informed the elder Voinovich fallaciously that his son was not to be found and could be dead. This false report was transmitted to his mother, ill with a heart condition, and may have contributed to her death a fortnight later.

In *Putem Vzaimnoĭ Perepiski (In Plain Russian,* 1979) Voinovich collected some of his early and late fiction and non-fiction. His earliest stories rendered the contemporary Soviet experience with a subdued realism that derived from his firsthand acquaintance with various areas of Russian life and labor. His first work in fiction was therefore different in tone from the later fantastic satire of the celebrated Private Chonkin narratives. In a brief preface to this book, Voinovich observes that even his first published fiction was received unfavorably by some critics because, though not blatantly offensive to them like the later Chonkin books, his stories clearly reflected on the rigors and shortcomings of life in the Soviet Union. In his introduction to these tales Richard Lourie, the translator, identifies Voinovich as "something of an outsider" in the USSR, one who, because of his background and experiences, is free of Russian chauvinism, and has therefore been able to maintain his integrity. The early stories, Lourie contends, reflect the "modesty" and "plainness" of Voinovich's prose. What comes out of these fictions, according to Lourie, is "plain truth and plain speech." Voinovich was not at first overtly dissident or controversial, as he himself reminds us. He considers himself to have been nonpolitical to begin with and insists that he could have functioned as a writer within the limitations imposed by Premier Nikita Khrushchev's censorship. Indeed, during his poetry-writing period, the popular song, "Fourteen Minutes to Go," with his lyrics, stopped just short of becoming the official anthem of the Soviet cosmonauts; and Khrushchev himself was reported to have sung it to welcome flying heroes Nikolaev and Popovich on their return from outer space.

Also printed in *In Plain Russian* are four pieces of non-fiction, "open letters" (written from 1973 to 1977), that show clearly enough how Voinovich moved from his early "realism" to become a dissident protester in spite of himself. The letters, all relatively late, illustrate both the bitterness and the rollicking satire that inform the Chonkin novels. In the letter of February 19, 1974, to the secretariat of the Moscow branch of the Writers' Union of the Russian Republic Voinovich characteristically asserts that he will not attend a meeting of the Union to respond to a motion of expulsion: "I will not come to your meeting, because it is due to take place behind closed doors and in secret, that is to say illegally, and I have no desire to take part in illegal activities. We have nothing to discuss and nothing to argue about, because I express my own opinions while you say what you are told."

P. L. Adams, in the *Atlantic,* sees in the apparent realism of Voinovich's short stories a kind of covert satire, as contrasted with the wild and open mockery of the Chonkin novels. The ordinary people that Voinovich writes about, says Adams, are described "with an artless sympathy which is totally and mischievously fake, for what he presents as ordinary life is a morass of incompetence, stupidity, alcoholism, and lawlessness." John Bayley, in the *New York Times Book Review,* represents the stories as containing "the essence of Voinovich's unique talent in a purer, more naive and subtler form" than it assumes in the "often very funny burlesques" of the Chonkin fiction and the non-fiction *Ivankiad,* which employ picaresque and mock-heroic literary forms, respectively.

Zhizn' i Neobychainye Prikliucheniia Soldata Ivana Chonkina (*The Life and Extraordinary Adventures of Private Ivan Chonkin*), the first of two volumes chronicling Voinovich's anti-hero, is now world renowned. Drawing upon his four-year experience in the Soviet army for materials, Voinovich began writing about Chonkin in the early sixties and completed the first novel in 1970. Though in growing disfavor with Russian authorities, he had thought that *Novy Mir* would publish his *Chonkin,* and publication was in fact announced in that journal. *Novy Mir* decided to reject it, however; and after circulating copies of it through *samizdat* (the underground "self-duplicating" and "self-distributing" publishing network in the USSR), Voinovich sent it to the YMCA press in Paris, where it appeared, in Russian, in 1975.

Voinovich's picaresque fantasy concerns one Ivan Vasilyevich Chonkin, "a short, bowlegged private in the Red Army with one year left to serve, his field shirt hanging out over his belt, his forage cap down over his big red ears, his puttees slipping, . . . his eyes inflamed from the sun." Hardly a type of military hero, actual or potential, this unlikely protagonist, through force of circumstances in World War II, has a kind of notoriety thrust upon him, and before the end of the novel, appears to be contending victoriously against the Soviet military might. The predominant quality of this first Chonkin novel is clearly mock-heroism. Not only is Chonkin himself an anti-hero, but his more sophisticated and presumably knowledgeable contemporaries, in and out of the military, are either corrupt, incompetent, or simply stupid—in any case, less than heroic. As Geoffrey Hosking writes in the *Times Literary Supplement*: "Chonkin is the ideal central character for this satire because, though he is subject to the external coercion [of the oppressive Soviet system] as much as anyone else, he does not internalize it: indeed he does not even understand it, and in that way remains spiritually free from it. . . . He is the innocent fool [a throwback, Hosking suggests, to the *Ivan-durak,* the stupid fool, of Russian folklore] who gets everyone at cross-purposes and in the process reveals their hidden motives."

The second Chonkin novel, *Pretendent Na Prestol* (*Pretender to the Throne: The Further Adventures of Private Ivan Chonkin*), appeared in 1979. From his experience with the first book, Voinovich knew very well that the sequel would not be published in the USSR. Whatever softening of the satirical tone may appear in the first is consequently lacking in the second. There is a similar amalgam of realistic detail, fantasy, and earthy humor, but the predominant satire is now more severe, and some of the details of Soviet government brutality are not only unfunny but more like those of the interrogation scenes in *1984* and *Darkness at Noon.* The plot follows directly from the end of the first novel. The military is first inclined to make a hero of the lubberly private in recognition of his courage and tenacity. The official ruling countermands that inclination, however, and he is arrested and thrown into a jail charged with desertion and, ultimately, other high crimes and misdemeanors. For most of the rest of the novel, Chonkin is in his cell, and we see him only occasionally, principally when he is led to one officer or another for questioning and during his trial. As a character, Chonkin remains basically unchanged throughout the sequel. Uncomprehending, he is caught up in a series of grotesquely comic events (involving even Stalin and Hitler) which are more or less a mystery to him. After being brutally interrogated and beaten, he willingly owns up to all the villainies that he is accused of. All that he can be sure of is that he has fulfilled his military orders and experienced love with his mistress, Nyura. The reader, but not Chonkin, knows further that Nyura is carrying Chonkin's child, but Voinovich leaves this detail undeveloped.

Like the first novel, the sequel is episodic, diffuse, with Voinovich as intrusive author making occasional editorial comments. Critical response to Voinovich's two Chonkin books has been extensive and, for the most part favorable. In a comprehensive review of Voinovich's literary career and of his first Chonkin novel in the *New York Times Book Review,* Theodore Solotaroff refers to the author's skill in "rendering the transactions between reality and fantasy, the ordinary life haunted by the phantoms and phantasmagoria of the police state." The novel he calls "stunning" and "brave": "a tender, hilarious piece of rural naturalism leavened by a pure imagination, and a stinging, far-reaching burlesque of institutionalized fear, stupidity, treachery, delusion, and absurdity." D. M. Thomas, however, in the *Times Literary Supplement,* finds that the sequel becomes repetitious: "Where the novel seems to me less successful [than the Gogolian surrealistic portions of the narrative] is in its more believable satire on pretension, bureaucratic muddle, and vice: on the venality of everyday Soviet life. With this—the greater part of the book—Voinovich seems largely to be repeating what he wrote in the first book. The satire is effective enough, but becomes so unremitting that its effect is weakened." Thomas also calls attention to those portions of the second novel in which Voinovich forgoes laughing satire for the blackest kind of black humor. At such times, Thomas asserts, Voinovich gives us neither "Gogolian extravagance" nor "Swiftian *saeva indignatio.*" Instead, he concludes, "we are in the Inferno of Dante or Solzhenitsyn." John Leonard, in the *New York Times,* rating *Pretender to the Throne* as Voinovich's "best book so far," also emphasizes the second novel's darker tone.

Ivan'kiada, ili Rasskaz o Vselenii Pisatelia Voĭnovicha v Novuiu Kvartiru (*The Ivankiad, or the Tale of the Writer Voinovich's Installation in His New Apartment*), Voinovich's best-known work of non-fiction, reads like the fantasy-fiction of the Chonkin narratives and at the same time takes on the form of an expanded open letter of the sort contained in *In Plain Russian.* As the title suggests, this is a mock-epic, whose "hero" is one Sergei Sergievich Ivanko, a powerful latecomer to the Soviet Writers' Union, who engages in "battle" for a two-room apartment with Voinovich. Despite Voinovich's clear claim, Ivanko, a well-situated Party bigwig with all kinds of connections, including one to the KGB, continues his campaign to take over the apartment for himself. The short narrative, recounted episodically and with high good humor interlaced with bursts of indignation, tells of the protracted contest, which finally winds up with Voinovich declared the rightful owner of the apartment and occupying it. For obvious reasons *The Ivankiad* has never been published legally in the Soviet Union. Anatole Shub, in the *New York Times Book Review,* captures the essential

effect of this satire: "One cannot read the story of Ivanko's subtle and not-so-subtle pressures, and of Voinovich's determined and ultimately successful countermeasures, without laughing. But also, perhaps with occasional rage for the cowardice, inertia, and hypocrisy of so many of their fellow-citizens, caught between Voinovich's clear rights under the letter of Soviet law and Ivanko's invocation of powerful behind-the-scenes influences. . . . As in all great satire, the situation is both thoroughly real and utterly preposterous."

WORKS IN ENGLISH TRANSLATION: English translations of Voinovich's writings include Richard Lourie's *The Life and Extraordinary Adventures of Private Ivan Chonkin,* 1977, and its sequel, by Lourie, *Pretender to the Throne: The Further Adventures of Private Ivan Chonkin,* 1981. Lourie also translated *In Plain Russian* in 1979. *The Ivankiad, or the Tale of the Writer Voinovich's Installation in His New Apartment* was translated by David Lapeza in 1977.

ABOUT: Columbia Dictionary of Modern European Literature, 1980; Contemporary Authors 81–84, 1979. *Periodicals*—Atlantic March 1977; September 1979; July 1981; New York Review of Books February 19, 1976; New York Times March 25, 1977; New York Times Book Review January 23, 1977; October 7, 1979; September 20, 1981; Times (London) December 23, 1980; Times Literary Supplement January 23, 1976; March 25, 1977; February 1, 1980; October 9, 1981.

WALKER, ALICE (February 9, 1944–), American novelist and poet, writes: "At the time I was born my family already consisted of nine people: my five brothers and two sisters, and my mother and father. The house in which I was born was small, of unpainted wood, and stood beside a dirt road that wandered through the backwoods of Putnam County, Georgia. It is still a beautiful setting, though the house has long since disappeared; there are pecan and walnut trees lining the main road, and around where our house stood, oaks. My mother was at that house and at all the others we lived in a consummate gardener, and if flowers turn up in almost everything I write, it is because I have a hard time imagining worlds in which they don't exist in profusion.

"I have at least two first memories: in one, my grandmother Nettie (after whom I named a childless African missionary in my book, *The Color Purple*) who was the mother of my mother and her eleven sisters and brothers, is standing over a wood stove cooking an enormous dinner (I realize it must have been enormous in retrospect; her family was huge) with a harassed, if

ALICE WALKER

stoic, look on her face. She is very dark brown, heavy (her spirit as heavy as her large body) and I can't imagine her laughing, or even smiling. In the second memory, my father is approaching the front porch of our house, on which I am standing, waiting in delight and anticipation for him to begin dancing for me, which I know he often does, laughing with his face and his eyes. I know when he finishes dancing he willl pick me up for a kiss and a hug. My grandmother died when I was two; my father stopped picking me up, I'm sure, around the same time.

"I cherish these memories, and they stick with me. Perhaps it is from the harassed, trapped look on my grandmother's face that I received an interest in the oppression of women; perhaps it is from my father's playfulness and delight in me that I received faith in the possibility of companionableness with men. For certainly in everything I've written there is concern for women's freedom and the need to envision man as something other than master or marriage partner. My sister tells me I used to address Space when I was very small and continued to do so well into my teens. I would stand, with a very attentive expression—always out of doors—and listen to 'something' only I could hear. I would then reply in words only 'something' understood. I'm convinced that this is the beginning of myself as writer.

"I wrote my first book of poems while a student at Sarah Lawrence, which I attended on scholarship, as I had attended Spelman College before it, and also my first published short story (under the double lucky auspices of Muriel Rukeyser, my poetry teacher, and Langston

Hughes). Since then I have written many poems and stories and novels, and no longer write—as I used to say—to survive, but because when I am writing I am so deeply happy. I imagine I feel as many pregnant women say they feel (and as I never felt while pregnant myself) totally attentive to an inner reality, an inner compulsion, an inner conversation, to which I know I will respond in a way that will reveal me even more to myself, while at the same time connecting me to other people.

"As I look at what I have written, it seems plain to me that writing, for me, has simply been about filling the space I always felt around me, peopling it with—instead of spirits—real listeners who understand because I have told them, through my work, how it is. Realizing this makes me long to reassure the little girl who addressed Space. Look, I want to tell her, the people you listened to and spoke to long ago have come. And it was your faith that they were there, in space, that brought them! And I see that that is perhaps what writing is. Sending out a voice—sometimes feeble, sometimes confused, sometimes strong and confident—but always just a human voice that has listened to the world and seeks to answer it, to say to it, You see, because we both listen and respond to each other, neither of us is alone."

———

Alice Walker has become recognized in little more than a decade as one of the most gifted black American writers, equally at home, and effective in the novel, the short story, poetry, and the literary-political essay. The natural lyricism of her style is one reason for her books' great emotional appeal; another is her unfailingly sensitive treatment of human problems.

She was born in Eatonton, Georgia, the daughter of Willie Lee Walker and Minnie Tallulah Grant Walker. In her early childhood, she recalls, like Eudora Welty, she was "deeply influenced" by Southern speech and Southern story-telling, and also by the Bible, as she listened to Sunday church services. By early adolescence she was escaping into books—*Gulliver's Travels, Jane Eyre, Oedipus Rex,* and *Romeo and Juliet.* In college she read Tolstoy, Hardy, and Stendahl; but the "immediate influences on my life" were Bob Dylan, Doris Lessing, the Japanese haiku, and Flannery O'Connor. A little later she discovered black writers such as Jean Toomer, Zora Neale Hurston, James Baldwin, and the writers of the Third World. All this reading, she has said, "reaffirmed my faith in the power of the written word to reach, to teach, to empower and encourage—to change and save lives." She attended Spelman College from 1961 to 1963, and took her B.A. from Sarah Lawrence in 1965. Her first book, the poetry collection *Once,* was accepted by her longtime publisher Harcourt Brace Jovanovich just after her graduation. In the summer of 1966 she went to Mississippi in order "to be in the heart of the civil-rights movement," as she recalled in an interview in 1983, "helping people who had been thrown off the farms or taken off the welfare rolls for registering to vote." Since that time she has taught writing and black studies at several colleges and universities, including Jackson State (1968–69), Tougaloo (1970–71), Wellesley (1972–73), Yale (1977–78), Berkeley, and Brandeis (both 1982). For several years from 1974 she was a fiction editor of *Ms.* magazine.

Walker's first novel, *The Third Life of Grange Copeland,* is a harrowing story of three generations of a sharecropper's family who try to surmount a constant, deadening white oppression but succeed only in destroying themselves. "I was curious to know," she remarked in an interview in 1970, "why people in families, specifically black families, are often cruel to each other, and how much of this cruelty is caused by outside forces. . . . In the black family, love, cohesion, support, and concern are crucial since a racist society constantly acts to destroy the black individual, the black family unit, the black child. In America black people have only themselves and each other." The novel was highly praised by all its reviewers. "The violent scenes are numerous," wrote Paul Theroux, "but the arguments between husband and wife, father and son, are if anything more harrowing than the shotgun murders. It is hardly an idealized portrait of . . . a black family, but the passions are enacted against a landscape which is carefully drawn." The social psychologist Robert Coles felt that in this novel "the centuries of black life in America are virtually engraved on one's consciousness. Equally vivid is Grange Copeland. . . . In him Miss Walker has turned dry sociological facts into a whole and alive particular person rather than a bundle of problems and attitudes."

Meridian takes place during the civil-rights turmoil of the 1960s. It is the story of Meridian Hill, an intelligent and sensitive woman, who returns to work in the South after being expelled from a revolutionary group in New York for refusing to swear she would kill as well as die for the Revolution. Confronting the essential meaning of the civil-rights movement back home in Chicokema, she is at last able to connect the political intellectualization of the struggle with the daily, needy reality she sees about her. Greil Marcus called the novel's tone "flat, direct, measured, deliberate, with a distinct lack of dra-

ma. . . . And the tone is right; it's not the plot that carries the novel forward but Meridian's attempt to resolve, or preserve the reality of, the questions of knowledge, history, and murder that Miss Walker introduces early on." To Marge Piercy, the character of Meridian is "an attempt to make real in contemporary terms the notion of holiness and commitment. Is it possible to write a novel about the progress of a saint? Apparently, yes." The novel, Piercy adds, "accomplishes a remarkable amount. The issues she is concerned with are massive. . . . [It is] a lean book that . . . goes down like clean water."

The universal praise accorded *The Color Purple* on its publication increased and intensified when the book later won both the American Book Award and the Pulitzer Prize for fiction. At the beginning of the novel, Celie, a fourteen-year-old girl pregnant by her stepfather for the second time, begins a series of letters to God, the only one she can turn to. The letters, at first only intermittently eloquent yet highly expressive of Celie's numb sense of loss, mirror her gradual growth in self-possession, her struggle to take charge of her life. The last half of the book is an exchange of letters between Celie and her long-lost and dearest sister, Nettie, who has become a missionary in Africa. At the end of her story, Celie, saved and strengthened by her unflaggingly loving nature and gentleness of spirit, awaits her earthly reward, a joyous reunion with Nettie. Most reviewers were delighted with Walker's masterly use of the epistolary form, which has rarely in this century produced such forceful effects. Mel Watkins singled out as the book's focus "the role of male domination in the frustration of black women's struggle for independence," and several other reviewers, all male, complained rather mildly of the author's "feminist bias" in making all the novel's male characters insensitive to those around them and brutish in word and deed. Several reviewers, notably Robert Towers, chose to praise in particular Walker's expressive use of dialect; yet without the universal power of the novel's theme—that love redeems and meanness kills—such linguistic skill would have been nugatory. As the author said, remarking on her sense of the novel's importance, "Let's hope people can hear Celie's voice. There are so many people like Celie who make it, who come out of nothing. People who triumph."

Walker's poetry has always been admired for its ostensible simplicity of statement and construction and its easy accessibility. Although she often addresses the reader directly, speaking eloquently of the intensest sort of pain and struggle, there is nothing rhetorical or artificial in her work. *Revolutionary Petunias & Other Poems* contains poems, she writes in the preface, "about Revolutionaries and Lovers; and about the loss of compassion, trust, and the ability to expand in love that marks the end of hopeful strategy." In general, the love poems and those with overt political content lack the canny wit and the deep familiarity of the family poems, such as the wonderfully moving lament "For My Sister Molly Who in the Fifties" and the humorous "Three Dollars Cash":

Three dollars cash
For a pair of catalog shoes
Was what the midwife charged
My mama
For bringing me.
"We wasn't so country then," says Mom,
"You being the last one—
And we couldn't, like
We done
When she brought your
Brother,
Send her out to the
Pen
And let her pick
Out
A pig."

The poems in *Good Night, Willie Lee, I'll See You in the Morning* are, according to Walker, "a by-product of the struggle to be, finally, an adult—grown up, *responsible* in the world—to put large areas of the past to rest." One of her aims in them is "to demystify love." The book is divided into sections: "Confession" contains poems of love, and of the near-impossibility of finding a love that is mutually satisfying, enriching, and respectful; "On Stripping Bark from Myself" has poems of personal struggle and of black feminist history; in "Early Losses: A Requiem" there are poems of political involvement, and African stories; "Facing the Way" consists of reflections on a revolutionary decade and its aftermath; and "Forgiveness" has four short poems which intend just that. The best poems manifest a wry irony that is not sparing of feelings, but gives them life and wit. In most of the love poems, however, the persona is always right: the ex-lover is given no chance of rebuttal, and salvation is usually accomplished by women's kinship and fellow-feeling.

Never offer your heart
to someone who eats hearts
who finds heartmeat
delicious
but not rare
who sucks the juices
drop by drop
and bloody-chinned
grins
like a God. . . .
                    ("Never Offer Your Heart . . . ")

In March 1967, Walker married Melvyn Rosenman Leventhal, an attorney active in the civil-rights movement, whom she had met in Mississippi the year before. They had a daughter, and were divorced in 1976. Since 1978 she has lived in the Japantown neighborhood of San Francisco, and does much of her writing in a cabin she owns in Mendocino County.

PRINCIPAL WORKS: *Fiction*—The Third Life of Grange Copeland, 1970; Meridian, 1976; The Color Purple, 1982. *Short stories*—In Love and Trouble, 1973; You Can't Keep a Good Woman Down, 1981. *Poetry*—Once, 1968; Revolutionary Petunias, 1973; Good Night, Willie Lee, I'll See You in the Morning, 1979; Horses Make a Landscape Look More Beautiful, 1984. *Non-fiction*—In Search of Our Mothers' Gardens: Womanist Prose, 1983. *As editor*—I Love Myself When I'm Laughing, and Then Again When I Am Looking Mean and Impressive: A Zora Neale Hurston Reader, 1979.

ABOUT: Bell, R. P., B. F. Parker and B. Guy-Sheftall (eds.), Sturdy Black Bridges: Visions of Black Women in Literature, 1979; Contemporary Authors, first revision series 37–40, 1979; new revision series 9, 1983; Contemporary Literary Criticism 5, 1976; 6, 1976; 9, 1978; 19, 1983; Evans, M. Black Women Writers 1950–1980, 1984. *Periodicals*—American Scholar Winter 1970–71; Summer 1973; Best Sellers October 15, 1973; September 1976; Book World September 13, 1970; Christian Science Monitor September 19, 1973; Current Biography, 1984; Library Journal July 1970; January 1, 1973; August 1973; May 1, 1976; July 1979; November 15, 1979; June 1, 1982; Nation November 12, 1973; September 4, 1982; New York Review of Books August 12, 1982; New York Times April 16, 1983; New York Times Book Review March 17, 1974; May 23, 1976; December 30, 1979; July 25, 1982; May 13, 1984; New York Times Magazine January 8, 1984; New Yorker February 27, 1971; June 7, 1976; Newsweek May 31, 1976; June 21, 1982; Poetry March 1980; Saturday Review August 22, 1970; Times Literary Supplement August 19, 1977; June 18, 1982; Virginia Quarterly Review Autumn 1976; Yale Review Autumn 1976.

WARNER, FRANCIS (October 21, 1937–), British poet and dramatist, was born in the village of Bishopthorpe, Yorkshire, the son of the Rev. Hugh Compton Warner, vicar of the local Anglican church, and the former Nancy Le Plastrier Owen. He was educated at Christ's Hospital, a major public school, attended for a while the Royal College of Music, then read English at St. Catharine's College, Cambridge, taking his B.A. in 1958. Shortly after his graduation he married Mary Hall; they have two daughters and were divorced in 1972.

Warner taught English at St. Catharine's from 1958 to 1965, when he was elected to a fellowship in English at St. Peter's College, Oxford. St.

Peter's, with its tiny endowment and undistinguished buildings, is not considered a first-rate institution by Oxford standards, and has never been able to attract the best students or fellows. Yet Warner has been for nearly two decades quite prominent in academic politics in the university, both in the English faculty and, more notably, in the periodic elections to the professorship of poetry. He was, in particular, instrumental in securing the election of Edmund Blunden to the chair in 1967. He also gained attention in university circles by inviting Elizabeth Taylor and Richard Burton to Oxford for a memorable performance of Marlowe's *Doctor Faustus,* in which Miss Taylor made much of the mute role of Helen of Troy.

As a dramatist, Warner is often compared with Samuel Beckett. His plays are heavily symbolic, have no plots to speak of, do not undertake directly to represent reality, and are filled with oblique dialogue, significant tableaux, and a pervasive Christianity. The first of his two dramatic trilogies of 1972, *Maquettes,* consists of three one-act plays, *Emblems, Troat,* and *Lumen.* The London critic Harold Hobson, a great admirer of Warner's drama, wrote of the "journey" taken by the plays "through gloom and doubt and rejection to a faint but precious glimmering of tenderness and light at the end." The trilogy's text, continues Hobson, "in meanings, sub-meanings, and sub-sub-meanings, in allusions, references, and associations, is one of the richest encountered in the theatre for a long time." Other critics emphatically disagreed. "Few will trouble," wrote the reviewer for the *Times Literary Supplement,* "to work out the symbolism because . . . Warner shows himself to be without even the most basic dramatic gifts. He has almost invented a new genre—the Theatre of the Unspeakable."

Warner's second trilogy, *Requiem,* consists of full-length plays: *Lying Figures, Killing Time,* and *Meeting Ends.* The epigraph of the first is God's terrible promise in Genesis: "And I will wipe off the face of the earth every living thing that I have made." Much of the play takes place in a mortuary, with dead bodies talking to one another. There is a good deal of female nudity—always a Warner dramatic specialty—and one horrific scene of a woman, strung up by her feet, being attacked at her genitals by a man wielding a razor. Hobson called *Lying Figures* "a surrealist play in language of great subtlety, wit, and beauty. . . . However unhappy and full of domestic quarrels and betrayals life may be, it can yet be looked back upon at the end in serenity and joy. The land is covered in darkness but the light is not extinguished." *Killing Time,* a series of vignettes on the subject of war, is staged inside

a giant human brain. John Coleby called it "a theatrical and impressionist work about why we fight and what happens when we do. . . . [Warner] writes rather fancy dialogue which swings from the poetic via some awful jokes to the pompous." *Meeting Ends,* meditations on love, takes as its epigraph Job's lament, "yet in my flesh shall I see God." According to Hobson, the play "mingles Greek, Roman, Christian, and Australian mythology with an ultimately rejected Mithraism, and ranges from nudity in a telephone booth and the torture on the wheel of the God of Thunder to a theatrically very striking rendering of the Last Post by a figure representing Christian Love. It exults in the resurrection of the body; our little life, says Mr. Warner, is rounded by a lyrical cry." The critic for *Choice,* however, saw no such order or symmetry, calling the play "selfconsciously modern, poetically overweight, heavily and obscurely symbolic, and studded with remote literary allusions; but at the same time it is full of banalities, coarse—as well as recondite—puns, gossipy anecdotes, eroticism, and nudity. The characters . . . declaim to the audience in paradoxes and Wildean inverted aphorisms, now and then reaching a climax in long, ranting monologues." All the aforementioned plays were first performed under Warner's direction at the Edinburgh Festival Fringe by the Samuel Beckett Theatre Appeal Company, an Oxford group founded by him. His other plays include *A Conception of Love* and *Light Shadows.*

Warner's poems, generally speaking, are modern in theme yet traditional in tone and meter. They range from sonnets imitating Shakespeare to a ballad on the death of Brendan Behan in the meter of an Irish jig. One of his most notable, and earliest, *tours de force* is *Perennia,* a dream-vision describing the heroine's love for the boy-god Eros, written in sixty-seven Spenserian stanzas, all composed in a three-week period in 1961 at Cambridge. Some parts capture the Spenserian mood and flavor with exceptional fidelity:

And then more lovely than a well-played lute
The voice of Eros spoke beside her ear
Telling her to go in and eat the fruit
That lay upon the table, and to cheer
Herself with honey-mead, the country beer;
And tell him all that she had felt that day;
To lie down on the bed of maiden-hair
And spend the hours in happiness and play
Of childish innocence while he beside her lay.

Another of Warner's early poems, this one confronting the mystery of death, is *Plainsong,* a lengthy elegy written in memory of two of his pupils who committed suicide within months of each other in 1961. The emotional intensity and urgency of this poem is often lacking in Warner's later verse:

> Two warm and living friends
> Wasting in mud and loam; suddenly snuffed
> On reaching manhood. One, and now another.
> Why, why oh why is this bitterness of doubt,
> This thud of guilt and loneliness of despair,
> Impossible, titanic weight of a universe
> Balanced to try each one of us in turn?

The Poetry of Francis Warner, published only in the United States in 1970, collected most of his relatively slender poetic output. Since its appearance he has produced two short books, *Lucca Quartet,* poems of love and loss in classical Italian meter, and *Morning Vespers.*

Warner has often expressed his view of the exalted nature of the poet, and the important moral role he must play in society. In a newspaper essay, "The Poetic Imagination," he wrote, "The preference for taking the poet as the moral center of the nation's health springs from a belief that, whereas the others are intermittently concerned with moral choices, the poet continually is. To an extent even greater than the theologian, let alone the priest, he is concerned with choices in that his entire professional life is concerned with the central question of relevant juxtapositions."

In 1972, Warner won the Messing International Award for distinguished contributions to literature.

PRINCIPAL WORKS: *Poetry*—Perennia, 1962; Early Poems, 1964; Experimental Sonnets, 1965; Madrigals, 1967; The Poetry of Francis Warner, 1970; Lucca Quartet, 1975; Morning Vespers, 1980. *Drama*—Maquettes, 1972; Requiem: Part 1, Lying Figures, 1972; Part 2, Killing Time, 1976; Part 3, Meeting Ends, 1974; A Conception of Love, 1978; Light Shadows, 1980. *As editor*—Eleven Poems by Edmund Blunden, 1965; Garland, 1968; Studies in the Arts, 1968.

ABOUT: Contemporary Authors 53–56, 1975; Contemporary Literary Criticism 14, 1980; Prentki, T. (ed.) Francis Warner: Poet and Dramatist, 1977; Vinson, J. (ed.) Contemporary Poets, 1980; Who's Who, 1983–84. *Periodicals*—Choice April 1975; Drama Winter 1976; London Sunday Times August 2, 1970; August 29, 1971; August 26, 1973; April 28, 1974; September 7, 1975; Times Literary Supplement March 30, 1973.

WARNER, MARINA (November 9, 1946–), British historian and novelist, was born in London, the daughter of Esmund Warner, a bookseller, and the former Emilia Terzulli. She attended convent schools in Egypt, Belgium, and England, then read modern languages, specializing in French and Italian, at Lady Margaret Hall, Oxford, and received her

MARINA WARNER

bachelor's degree in 1967. In her last year at Oxford she was editor of the university magazine *Isis.* Warner worked as a journalist for such publications as the *Daily Telegraph, Spectator,* the *Sunday Times Magazine,* and British *Vogue* before turning her attention to the full-length historical studies that have won her an international readership. Her journalistic efforts resulted in the *Daily Telegraph* Young Writer of the Year award in 1970. In 1972 she married the journalist and editor William Shawcross.

Warner's work has been of special interest to feminists and those involved in women's studies: her subjects in every case are women of tremendous power and compelling interest who have left profound marks on history. She has been able to examine their lives both as their contemporaries saw them and as subsequent generations, including our own, have come to understand them. Her posture as a biographer is always sympathetic and cautious, her narrative style witty and allusive.

The Dragon Empress: Life and Times of Tz'u-hsi, 1835–1908, Empress Dowager of China describes how the daughter of a minor Manchu official became the absolute ruler of half a billion people during the waning years of the Ch'ing dynasty. Warner was considerably hampered in writing this, her first book, by her lack of thorough grounding in Chinese language and history, but the forceful personality of Tz'u-hsi nonetheless pervades the whole work: her love of power and intrigue, ritual and ceremony, her extravagance, vanity, cruelty, and corruption are all richly detailed. F. W. Drake called the book "a very readable and quite reliable account of the last decades of the Chinese empire"; the reviewer for the *Times Literary Supplement* thought the author reflected every foreigner's confusion "when confronted with the jumble of events which made up Chinese history" of the period, "although she does little by any emphasis or analysis of her own to guide the reader through them."

Warner is probably best known for her second book, *Alone of All Her Sex: The Myth and the Cult of the Virgin Mary.* She begins this comprehensive study by describing her own convent childhood as "a devout Mariolater," then hints at her break with the Catholic Church and with it the dawning of a "new intimation that in the very celebration of the perfect human woman, both humanity and women were subtly denigrated." With great sympathy and a thorough command of Marian iconography spanning the entire Christian era, Warner proceeds to examine in detail Mary's various aspects— Virgin, Queen, Bride, Mother, and Intercessor. "I have not undertaken a history of the cult of the Virgin as such, but in chronological order I have taken aspects of her composite personality at their zenith and then worked backwards and forwards in time showing the ideas that contributed to their genesis and growth and lingered on in the tiredness of old age." Academic historians and conservative Catholics generally disapproved of the book, occasionally even dismissing it as shallow and unoriginal: "She has only nibbled at the vast edifice of Mariological scholarship," Keith Thomas complained. Yet the book was revelatory to many, who saw in it a groundbreaking modern treatment of an ancient and attractive mystery. Margaret Mead, in a lengthy review, acclaimed it as "a lovely book, . . . a magnificent study of the whole development of the character of a single female deity. . . . Besides giving us access to a depth of feeling and controversy which are so distant as to be almost unbelievable, the author has accomplished what I believe to be a unique feat: she has treated the Roman Catholic church—in all its changes, transformations, heresies, counterreformations, papal decrees, and changes of practice—as one among the great historical religions, and she has done this as a scholar of comparative religions might, from the outside. At the same time, she communicates with warmth and certitude what that faith meant to those for whom it was and is the only true faith, the whole meaning of existence."

Warner's confidence that she could bring a fresh, contemporary, feminist perspective to the life of Joan of Arc—despite the many thousands of works published on the subject—was amply vindicated in *Joan of Arc: The Image of Female Heroism.* Her goal, simply expressed, is "to find out why Joan of Arc was believed, how that belief was expressed, what its expression affirmed, and what causes it has served." She holds Joan to be "a preeminent heroine because she belongs to the sphere of action, while so many feminine figures or models are assigned to the sphere of contemplation. She is anomalous in our culture, a woman renowned for doing something on her own, not by birthright. She has extended the taxonomy of female types; she makes evident the dimenison of women's dynamism. . . . We must develop a richer vocabulary for female activity than we use at present, with our restrictions of wife, mother, mistress, muse. Joan of Arc, in all her brightness, illuminates the operation of our present classification system, its rigidity on the one hand, its potential on the other." This book is somewhat more demanding than its predecessors, in that the author deliberately eschews any conventional, chronological account of Joan's life and military career. In Part One, "The Life and Death of Jeanne la Pucelle," Warner attempts "to restore her to her own context, to create a foreground of the religious beliefs and political struggles that made her activities acceptable and intelligible. So the starting points of this narrative are not her birthday and her birthplace, but instead the physical nature of her virginal body, because that is the starting point of her impact on her contemporaries." "The Afterlife of Joan of Arc," Part Two of the book, "follows the thread of posthumous tributes to the heroine, both visual and verbal, and the successive transformations her figure undergoes as different pressure groups make her their own. . . . Throughout this section I hope to have developed the underlying theme that when a story is told, it is told according to the perceptions of its hearers or its readers: the teller unconsciously provides points of reference to make the material intelligible." Francine Du Plessix Gray characterized the author's approach to this mythical figure as one of "high-minded abstraction and general lifelessness"; Julia Epstein, on the other hand, called the book "a fascinating portrait, . . . a persuasive iconological interpretation of Joan's meaning in history and of her spiritual and representational authority."

Warner's other works of non-fiction include *The Crack in the Teacup: Britain in the 20th Century,* a popular account, written primarily for older schoolchildren, of social upheaval in Britain from the Edwardian era to the present day; and *Queen Victoria's Sketchbook,* a biographical narrative accompanying the watercolors, sketches, and etchings produced by the queen throughout her lifetime.

She has also published two novels. *In a Dark*

Wood is an account of crises occuring in the lives of two brothers, one a Jesuit completing his life-long study of a seventeenth-century Portuguese missionary to China, the other a publisher who learns that his successful magazine has been funded from the start by the C.I.A. *The Skating Party* reworks the Oedipus myth in a modern setting. Both novels were criticized for unconvincing characterization and lack of sure control of tone.

WORKS: *Non-fiction*—The Dragon Empress, 1972; Alone of All Her Sex, 1976; Queen Victoria's Sketchbook, 1979; The Crack in the Teacup, 1980; Joan of Arc, 1981. *Fiction*—In a Dark Wood, 1977; The Skating Party, 1982.

ABOUT: Contemporary Authors 65–68, 1977. *Periodicals*—American Historical Review October 1977; April 1982; Best Sellers January 1977; Choice November 1981; Christian Century December 22, 1976; November 23, 1977; Commonweal January 7, 1977; June 4, 1982; Critic Summer 1977; Economist September 25, 1976; February 13, 1982; Harper October 1976; Horn Book April 1980; Library Journal December 15, 1972; January 1, 1977; November 1, 1977; January 15, 1980; June 1, 1981; Ms. July 1981; Nation September 11, 1976; May 30, 1981; New Republic October 22, 1977; New Statesman September 24, 1976; June 17, 1977; November 23, 1979; October 30, 1981; New York Review of Books November 11, 1976; February 7, 1980; June 25, 1981; New York Times Book Review October 24, 1976; February 2, 1979; August 2, 1981; New Yorker November 7, 1977; December 31, 1979; Newsweek June 29, 1981; Times (London) September 8, 1981; Times Literary Supplement January 5, 1973; November 5, 1976; June 17, 1977; December 14, 1979; January 4, 1980; August 28, 1981; April 30, 1982.

WARNER, WILLIAM W(HITESIDES)
(April 20, 1920–   ), American essayist, was born in New York City, the son of Charles Jolly Warner and the former Leonora Haberle. He was educated at St. Paul's School, Concord, New Hampshire, and Princeton University, where he majored in geology, graduating in 1943. After service in the Naval Reserve (1944–46), Warner taught high-school English and managed a ski lodge in Vermont before joining the United States Information Agency, a division of the State Department, in 1951. He served as public affairs officer in Chile, Guatemala, and Costa Rica. When the Peace Corps was founded, in 1962, he joined that organization as executive secretary and program coordinator for Latin America. He moved to the Smithsonian Institution in 1964, where he has been director of the Office of International Activities (1964–67), assistant secretary for public service (1967–73),

WILLIAM WARNER

and, since 1973, consultant and research associate. He has received the Smithsonian's Exceptional Service award. In June 1951 he married Kathleen Berryman McMahon; they have four daughters and two sons.

Warner's first book, *Beautiful Swimmers: Watermen, Crabs and the Chesapeake Bay,* was, in his own words, "a magazine article that grew." For several years he had been exploring the "benign and beautiful" waters of the Chesapeake, "from the choppy wavelets of the Susquehanna Flats to the rolling surges of the Virginia capes." Although well aware of the Bay's natural beauty, he realized that it "does not impress those who know it best as the grandest or most of anything. For all its size and gross statistics, it is an intimate place where land and water intertwine in infinite varieties of mood and pattern." So the desire to write about the place and the frank-talking people who make their living there came over him only gradually. He decided to focus his study on the natural history of the Bay's most important product, the pugnacious, succulent Atlantic blue crab, *Callinectes sapidus* (*callinectes* is Greek for "beautiful swimmer"). He learned that the literature on Chesapeake crabbing "is not voluminous. One learns mainly by rack of eye and yarning, which is to say looking around without preconceived plan and talking a great deal." It is the watermen, however, with their odd boats and their jargon, who most piqued his curiosity: "In my case the revelation began with the boats. In talking to the Chesapeake watermen I found it impossible to hear them casually drop such terms as 'bar cats,' 'one-sail bateaux,' 'dinky skifts,'

'Jenkins Creekers,' or 'Hooper Island draketails' and let it go at that. . . . 'Crabs are out there, but they ain't for everyone to catch. All those stumps, that's where the doublers are at, hiding in the stumps.' . . . One cannot sit around very long and listen passively to this kind of talk. I have not been able to, at least. Inevitably, there comes the effort to find out what it all means." *Beautiful Swimmers* follows the waterman's year on the Bay from the copious catches (in pots) of the autumnal crab migrations through wintertime oystering and the peculiar joys of dredging for crabs in subfreezing temperatures, the waterman's brief weeks of idleness from late March to the last of April when pots are repaired and shedding flats are built for the softshell crab market, and finally to the heat of the Chesapeake summer and scraping (shallow dredging) for crabs. The book was generally well received by reviewers; Peter Stoler considered it "a piece of popular oceanography worthy of shelf space alongside Rachel Carson's *Edge of the Sea* and Henry Beston's *Outermost House.*" In addition to the Phi Beta Kappa book award and the Christopher award, *Beautiful Swimmers* won the Pulitzer prize for general non-fiction in 1977.

In his second book, *Distant Water: The Fate of the North Atlantic Fisherman,* Warner turns from the study of "what were in many cases the smallest of all commercial fishing vessels"—the bar cats and their sister craft of the Chesapeake—to examine the oceangoing behemoths of the 1970s. He describes his voyages on ships of five nations: factory-equipped freezer stern trawlers, able to catch, clean, and freeze tons of fish without returning to port. In the introduction, to illustrate the size of these strange ships, he offers a striking "hypothetical analogy to dry land": "First, assume a vast continental forest, free for the cutting or only ineffectively guarded. Then try to imagine a mobile and completely self-contained timber-cutting machine that could smash through the roughest trails of the forest, cut down the trees, mill them, and deliver consumer-ready lumber in half the time of normal logging and milling operations. This was exactly what factory trawlers did—this was exactly their effect on fish—in the forests of the deep." In addition to analyzing how the ships work, the author is also well aware that he is witness to an experiment in the course of failure. Because these ships operated outside of any effective international regulation, generally stayed in the North Atlantic, and overfished many species to the point of exhaustion, many countries imposed 200-mile fishing limits and strictly enforced quotas on species caught.

Factory trawlers are almost gone now: "The leviathan ships once hailed as fishing technology's greatest leap forward are proving too costly to operate under the low quotas assigned them by coastal states around the world. . . . Rather than the most effective of all fishing machines, factory trawlers now seem like lumbering dinosaurs, unable to adapt to the changing environment of world fishing they themselves did so much to create." Yet the present world fishing situation is one that ought to give cheer to marine conservationists: "a larger number of smaller vessels are now competing for smaller amounts of a greater variety of fishes over a wider expanse of the world's oceans." Although it treats a seemingly more specialized subject than *Beautiful Swimmers, Distant Water* attracted even stronger critical praise, with several reviewers remarking on the author's "unblinking eye for detail and unerring ear for language" and "vivid, authoritative prose." William McCloskey wrote, "With exactness of word and fact and cheerful anecdotes, [Warner] beguiles the reader into wanting to know all that he learned."

Warner lives in Washington, D.C. "I don't know," he said in a 1983 interview, "what it is about the sea. I love fishing and the coasts, but it's more than that. I guess I have a strong isolation urge that is denied one with a busy bureaucratic career and six kids."

PRINCIPAL WORKS: Beautiful Swimmers, 1976; Distant Water, 1983.

ABOUT: Who's Who in America, 1983–84. *Periodicals*—Choice July–August 1976; Christian Science Monitor March 31, 1976; June 24, 1983; Library Journal March 15, 1983; New York Times April 19, 1977; May 13, 1983; New York Times Book Review June 13, 1976; April 17, 1983; Scientific American October 1983; Time March 29, 1976.

*WASTBERG, PER ERIK (November 20, 1933–), Swedish novelist, journalist, critic, poet, and activist, was born in Stockholm, the son of Erik Wästberg, a newspaper editor, and the former Greta Hirsch, a business executive. He received a B.A. from Harvard University in 1955 and graduate degrees from the University of Uppsala in 1956 and 1962.

Wästberg's career is multifaceted: he is known as an interesting popular novelist, a leading journalist, an Africa specialist, a connoisseur of Stockholm, and an extremely energetic international activist. His literary career began at age fifteen when he published *Pojke med såpbubblor* (Boy with Soap Bubbles, 1949), a collection of sensitive stories about childhood; this was followed by *Enskilt arbete* (Individual Assignment, 1952), another collection of his writ-

°väst´ berg, pâr

PER ERIK WASTBERG

ing; and *Ett gammalt skuggspel* (An Old Shadow Play, 1952), a novel of pastiche. His first full-scale work was *Halva kungariket* (Half the Kingdom, 1955), a picaresque novel of Stockholm and childhood, and his perspective broadened with *Arvtagaren* (The Heir, 1958), a *bildungsroman* in which the Swedish hero searches for his freedom in Europe. The early Wästberg has been described as a typical author of the fifties, with stylistic sophistication and an openness to new experience but lacking any essential message to communicate. Following his early writing there was a ten-year pause in his novel publishing; during this period and later he traveled widely, especially to South Africa and Rhodesia but also to the Middle East and the Soviet Union.

His major achievement in fiction is his trilogy of novels dedicated to the depiction of love in a new age, among intelligent modern people with political consciousness. *Vattenslottet* (The Water Palace, 1968), *Luftburen* (Airbound, 1969; translated as *The Air Cage*, 1972), and *Jordmånen* (The Soil, 1972; translated as *Love's Gravity*, 1976) became best-sellers in Sweden and also won much praise abroad. The first deals with the love of Jan Backman and his half-sister Gertrud in the family's summer place, called The Water Palace. Both have responsible jobs (he is an air controller, and she a natural scientist) and are concerned with major issues of the day—especially in Africa though also in their own country—but it is the subtle possibilities and limitations of love that interest them most as they explore each other's similarities and differences, their connections to one another and

friends. In *The Air Cage* the intricacies of a modern love triangle emerge as Jan enters into a passionate relationship with Jenny Jeger (an environmentalist) while he continues to love Gertrud. None of the parties is endowed with the traditional sense of human ownership, but their struggle to formulate a new moral code for loving is never problem-free and is often poignant. The third novel in the series, *Love's Gravity,* continues the author's investigation of the ties between sexualtiy and politics, between love, work, and liberation. Much has been made of the frequent and imaginative erotic episodes in this trilogy, but the author was equally concerned with the ethical problems of men and women living together in the seventies, a decade of experimental deviation from conventional sex-role patterns. The less glamorous but significant issues of work roles and political commitments (e.g., to environment preservation and Third World liberation) are always near at hand as love is placed in a larger social context.

The author's main political interest has been the liberation of Africans, as a list of his non-fiction titles will attest: *Förbjudet område* (Prohibited Area, 1960) and *På svarta listan* (On the Blacklist, 1960) were the products of his visit to Africa; *Angola-Moçambique* (Angola-Mozambique, 1962) is a political study written with Anders Ehnmark; *Afrika berättar* (Africa Narrates, 1961), *The Writer in Modern Africa* (1968), the survey *Afrikas moderna litteratur* (Africa's Modern Literature, 1969), and *Afrikansk lyrik* (African Poetry, 1970, edited with others) are anthologies; and *Afrika till uppdrag* (Assignment Africa, 1976) is a later study. The most popular of these, "On the Blacklist," a political analysis and travel book, was translated into nine languages and sold over 300,000 copies. Wästberg was the official delegate to the United Nations on racialism and colonialism from 1966 to 1973 and in the 1970s accompanied Prime Minister Olof Palme on an extensive African journey. Since 1959 Wästberg has been secretary of the Fund for Victims of Racial Oppression.

Also a distinguished chronicler of Stockholm life, he has written a number of tributes to the city and its environs, including *Klara* (with photographer Lennart af Petersen, 1957); *Östermalm* (1962); *Innan gaslågan slocknade* (Before the Gaslight Died Out, 1964); *Humlegårdsmästaren—Ett skolkvarter på Östermalm* (The Master of Humlegården—A School Block in Östermalm, 1971); and *Sommaröarna* (The Summer Islands, with photographer Nina Monastra, 1973).

He has also produced some biographical volumes including *Skördetid* (Harvest Time, 1955), his father's posthumous writing which he edited; *Ernst och Mimmi* (Ernst and Mimmi, 1964), correspondence between Ernst Wehtje and his fiancée, from the 1880s; and *Kära Hjalle Kära Bo* (Dear Hjalmar, Dear Bo, 1969), correspondence between Swedish authors Hjalmar Söderberg and Bo Bergman, 1891–1941. Other miscellaneous works include *Femtiotal (The Fifties)*, which he edited; *Varför skriver vi?* (Why Do We Write?, 1953); *Mötet med boken* (Encounter with the Book, 1958); *En dag på världsmarknaden* (One Day on the World Market, 1967), newspaper articles; *Berättarens ögonblick* (The Narrator's Moment, 1977); *An Anthology of Modern Swedish Literature*, 1979; *Ett hörntorn vid Riddargatan* (A Corner Tower at Riddargatan, 1980); *Obestämda artiklar* (Indefinite Articles, 1981); *Bestämda artiklar* (Definite Articles, 1982); *Tal i röda rummet* (Speech in the Red Room, 1982).

In 1960 Wästberg was awarded the Swedish Academy's Ida Bäckmann prize. A founding member and vice-president of the Swedish section of Amnesty International between 1964 and 1971 and member of the Amnesty International executive board from 1966 to 1970, he is one of Sweden's leading international activists. From 1967 to 1978 he was president of the Swedish PEN. He was editor-in-chief, arts editor, and member of the board of *Dagens Nyheter*, Sweden's leading daily paper, from 1976 to 1982; and in 1980 he was appointed to the European Academy of Arts and Sciences.

Per Wästberg lives in Stockholm and Heby.

WORKS IN ENGLISH TRANSLATION: The second and third novels of Wästberg's trilogy have had English translations: *The Air Cage* by Thomas Teal, 1972, and *Love's Gravity*, by Ann Henning, 1976.

ABOUT: Cassell's Encyclopedia of World Literature, 1973; Columbia Dictionary of Modern European Literature, 1980. *Periodicals*—Times Literary Supplement May 20, 1977.

---

*WAUGH, AUBERON (ALEXANDER) (November 17, 1939–   ), English novelist and essayist, writes: "I was born in rural Somerset, West England, in a large Georgian house owned by my mother's family. My father, the novelist Evelyn Waugh, was away in the army and I was brought up with a large number of cousins, later joined by about forty children evacuated from the East End of London at the time of the blitz. These were put on the top floor of the house in such a position as to be able to spit on people walking underneath them on the ground floor.

AUBERON WAUGH

This was my first taste of the class war. I later achieved revenge of a sort by reporting some of them, untruthfully, for having eaten rat poison. They were taken away to be stomach pumped.

"It is not easy to say whether these experiences influenced my later development as a writer. When just six years old at the end of the war, I was sent to a Catholic boarding school at the other end of Somerset and stayed there, apart from school holidays, for seven years. From this school I won a major scholarship in classics to Downside, a large Benedictine school, also in Somerset. From Downside I won an Exhibition in English to Christ Church, Oxford, where I briefly read politics, philosophy, and economics, leaving it after a year without taking a degree, on publication of my first novel, *The Foxglove Saga*. This was written before going up to Oxford in a period of six weeks after being released from the hospital where I had been confined for nine months after a machine gun accident while serving as a second lieutenant in the Royal Horse Guards (an armoured car regiment) during the Cyprus emergency. This military service followed a period of nine months spent doing nothing in Florence after leaving school. On my release from hospital I went to Bologna to write *The Foxglove Saga*, illustrating most of my life's experience to that date.

"After leaving Oxford I joined the editorial staff of the *Daily Telegraph*, and have been a full-time journalist ever since, while managing to publish four other novels and three nonfiction books, as well as various collections of journalism. Among the novels the most interesting is *Consider the Lilies*, about the life of a

Church of England clergyman. Among the non-fiction the most interesting is *The Last Word: An Eye Witness Account of the Trial of Jeremy Thorpe*. My collections of journalism include rural essays originally published in the *Evening Standard; Four Crowded Years: Diaries 1972-1976* from a column originally printed in *Private Eye*, London, and *In the Lion's Den*, from essays on social and political subjects originally printed in the *New Statesman*.

"Married with four children, I find I have to write at least four columns a week to earn my way. At the moment of writing these include a weekly column on general subjects in *Spectator* (London); a weekly book column in the *Daily Mail* (London); a fortnightly satirical column in *Private Eye*; a fortnightly political column in *Sunday Telegraph*; a monthly book review lead in *Sunday Telegraph*; a monthly book column in *Business Traveller*; a monthly wine column in *Tatler*; a monthly book column in *Books & Bookmen*; a monthly Wine Club report in *Spectator*; and innumerable irregular articles on travel, wine, and general subjects in many publications.

"With age I find I have attained a certain fluency and speed. I find journalism is more satisfactory as a medium, partly because of its greater reward, partly because of its more immediate impact, but chiefly simply because more people read it and it seems to me that the main function of the writer is to be read. If we can also stimulate our readers, whether to extremes of vexation or pleasure, we are doing all we can reasonably hope to do. Novel writing, by contrast, is lonely, self-regarding and, apart from a small circle of faithful admirers, largely overlooked. I would have liked to have written more novels, but feel that I wrote quite a good one in *Consider the Lilies* which nobody noticed, and have no great desire to try again."

Auberon Waugh was born in Dulverton, Somerset, the elder son of the celebrated novelist and the former Laura Herbert. In July 1961, a year after leaving Oxford and around the time of the U.S. publication of his first novel, he married Lady Teresa Onslow, daughter of the sixth Earl of Onslow and sister of the present earl. They have two daughters and two sons. Both as a novelist and as a widely read journalist, Waugh has retained nearly all his father's most remarkable characteristics as a writer: the satirical tone, love for the bizarre and for black humor, the sophistication and caustic wit, the highly polished, deceptively simple prose style, the conservative Catholicism imbued with deep-seated pessimism. Although he has described himself as a "Liberal-anarchist," Auberon Waugh's social views are not notably different from the High Tory opinions of his father.

The Foxglove Saga was received with great enthusiasm and a few reservations on both sides of the Atlantic. Evelyn Waugh's name and fiction figured prominently in nearly every review. It is the story of several schoolboys, one of whom is Martin Foxglove, and their subsequent misadventures in career and life. Anne Fremantle thought the author "no Montaigne—he is not laughing at life in order to avoid the sorrow of things. He is, rather, a latterday Swift, as savage, as sincere, as almost unbearably iconoclastic. Sometimes, I think, he goes too far." A reviewer for the *Times Literary Supplement* called it "a funny, successful and professional book." Yet to Honor Tracy, the good things in the book "do not so much derive from Mr. Evelyn Waugh as belong to him entirely. They are genuine chips off the old block. There is, in the better parts, the same rueful awareness of contradiction and confusion, the wry sense of human impotence, the appallingly sharp eye for human frightfulness, the savagery, the gorgeous fun." She felt, however, that the book lacked "a valid point of view. . . . Mr. Waugh is too young to have known the England whose passing drew such cries of pain from his father." Nigel Dennis found in the book "everything one expects from a Waugh novel. . . . It is lively, it is laughable, it is exhilarating and nauseating—and had it not all been done by the father, what honor would not be due the son?"

Path of Dalliance is an Oxford novel about the university career of Jamey Sligger, handsome but not especially bright, and Guy Frazer-Robinson, his wealthy school friend. The *Times Literary Supplement* reviewer called it "brilliantly and expertly written, with both wit and economy. . . . Echoing though it does both *Decline and Fall* and *Brideshead Revisited*, it also demonstrates a very assured and mature talent in its own right." Bernard Bergonzi, on the other hand, thought the novel "a casual picaresque affair" which "tries to maintain a satirical onslaught on modern errors, but merely results in interminable stretches of sub-Beachcomber facetiousness." Bergonzi identified what he called "the reason for Auberon Waugh's failure: quite simply, he doesn't know enough about what he's attacking. He looks at things like CND [the Campaign for Nuclear Disarmament], the Liberal Party, action painting and beatnik parties as though through the wrong end of a telescope. A stance of disgusted and uninformed aloofness isn't likely to produce good satire, which demands a certain intimate hatred."

Arthur Friendship, who has no friends, is the feckless young hero of *Who Are the Violets Now?* A writer under several pseudonyms for *Woman's Dream* magazine, he becomes dangerously involved in a sinister organization called the International Peace Movement. The book was not well received. According to W. F. Galvin, the author made "the worst mistake a satirist can make: . . . he loses his cool, and, instead of satire, we are given ill-humor." Frank Littler wrote, "If the parental *oeuvre,* in Evelyn Waugh's lifetime, revealed any excesses of vulgarity or ineptitude by which this effort could be explained, I cannot remember where they occurred. . . . The narrative manner and the dialogue are often a generation and a half out of date." The *Times Literary Supplement* reviewer called the novel "an intellectual sick joke which fails to come off."

Waugh considers *Consider the Lilies* his "most interesting" novel, and nearly all the critics agreed. Nicholas Trumpeter is a somewhat innocent, not very serious young Anglican priest who is perfectly willing, in his new country parish, to appear to be all things to all men. Guy Davenport thought the novel Waugh's "best to date": the comedy "finds most of its hilariousness in the desperate obsolescence of super-liberal ideas. Religion has become sociology, sex has become hygiene, life has become boredom. Mr. Waugh's testiness snaps in every line. He gives his brightly colored cardboard characters their every due, creating the delightful impression that Mr. Waugh is dispassionately recording all this idiocy out of an inexplicable sense of duty, and that there is nothing whatever that can be done about it short of divine intervention." Barry Baldwin called it "a delicious farce. . . . Mr. Waugh attacks many current social fads of the English scene in the grand comic manner."

"Auberon Waugh's Diary," appearing fortnightly in the iconoclastic magazine *Private Eye,* is a column relished by many in Britain for the fine hilarity of its venom, directed at every conceivable public issue, figure, and movement. He usually manages adroitly to antagonize several sectors of opinion in each issue. "Of all the disagreeable qualities of this disgusting woman," he wrote in 1983 about one of his many bêtes noires, a leader of the Social Democratic Party, " . . . the worst is that she is disunited. It is not widely known that she wears a wig, or that her teeth are false, her eyes are glass, her legs are wooden, her arms made of plastic, her bottom of rubber. When she goes to bed she takes them all off and there is nothing left. When she gets up in the morning, she never puts herself together properly and often leaves little bits behind." In an adjoining entry, he reported the jailing of a Chinese peasant for having killed and eaten a giant panda, attributing this to socialists being "fanatically opposed to gastronomy." "It is a sad thought that I who have eaten squirrels in Somerset, crocodile meat in Cuba, dogs in the Philippines, raw horse in Japan, toads in Egypt, and snakes in Northern Thailand may never eat a giant panda, unless this abominable curse of socialism can be driven from the earth."

Private Eye led the way in press reporting on the Jeremy Thorpe case, and Waugh calls his book on the trial, *The Last Word* (1980), his "most interesting" work of non-fiction. Thorpe, the leader of the Parliamentary Liberal Party, was acquitted of a charge of conspiracy to commit murder without once taking the stand in his own defense. The alleged intended victim, Norman Scott, was a male prostitute who had spoken widely about a past liaison with Thorpe. Waugh interspersed verbatim excerpts from the court proceedings with his own pointed commentary. Henry Steck granted that the book was a full account of the trial, "but not of the case in all its 'sociopsychological' ramifications." From the author's damning account of the judge's bias in Thorpe's favor there "emerges the hint of a corruption that may have tainted the London courtroom, if not the entire realm," according to David Bell. "In following the case, [Waugh] has tempered his biting wit and allowed the dramatis personae to speak up and condemn themselves. His own disinterested and perceptive comments completely avoid the predilection for moral posturing and melodrama that characterized much of the reportage of political corruption in our own country."

The most important subjects Waugh has not so far tried are, of course, his father's career and their life together. He shows no signs of doing so, unfortunately, or of returning to fiction. He has always felt himself "much disliked by English critics," though the acerbity of even the most waspish of them can hardly match his own.

PRINCIPAL WORKS: *Fiction*—the Foxglove Saga, 1960; Path of Dalliance, 1963; Who Are the Violets Now?, 1965; Consider the Lilies, 1968. *Non-fiction*—Biafra: Britain's Shame, 1969; A Bed of Flowers; or, As You Like It, 1972; Country Topics, 1974; Four Crowded Years, 1976; In the Lion's Den, 1978; The Last Word, 1980; Auberon Waugh's Yearbook, 1981.

ABOUT: Contemporary Authors 45-48, 1974; Who's Who, 1983–84. *Periodicals*—America July 18, 1964; May 14, 1966; Book World April 6, 1969; Catholic World December 1961; Commonweal November 17, 1961; Economist February 23, 1980; Guardian October 21, 1960; Library Journal July 1961; July 1964; May 1, 1966; February 1, 1969; December 1, 1980; National Review August 25, 1964; February 11, 1969;

New Republic August 7, 1961; New Statesman October 22, 1960; November 1, 1963; October 15, 1965; New York Times Book Review July 23, 1961; July 19, 1964; May 29, 1966; Newsweek July 13, 1964; Saturday Review August 5, 1961; July 25, 1964; May 28, 1966; January 4, 1969; November 1980; Spectator October 21, 1960; Time July 21, 1961; July 24, 1964; May 27, 1966; Times Literary Supplement October 21, 1960; November 1, 1963; October 21, 1965; May 2, 1968.

WEISS, PAUL (May 19, 1901–), American philosopher, was born on the lower East Side of New York City, the son of Samuel Weiss, a laborer, and the former Emma Rothschild. He had to go to work at an early age to earn a living, but eventually was able to attend the evening division of City College. Transferring to the regular college program, Weiss earned his bachelor's degree with honors in 1927, with election to Phi Beta Kappa. He then went on to study philosophy, concentrating on mathematical logic, at Harvard under Alfred North Whitehead, taking his M.A. in 1928 and his Ph.D. the following year. He began his career as an instructor at Radcliffe College (1930–31), then moved to Bryn Mawr, where he was a member of the philosophy department from 1931 to 1946—full professor from 1940 and departmental chairman from 1944. From 1946 to 1969 Weiss taught at Yale, the last six years as Sterling professor of philosophy. In 1969, well beyond the normal retirement age, he accepted appointment as Heffer professor of philosophy at the Catholic University of America in Washington, D.C.

Weiss' earliest published work involved mathematical logic, notably an article in *Mind* (July 1928) refining and partially refuting Whitehead's and Bertrand Russell's work on the theory of types in the second chapter of their *Principia Mathematica*. He also compiled an extensive bibliography of "modern logic and the foundations of mathematics" (1929), an article on relativity in logic (1928), and a monograph, "The Nature of Systems" (1929), whose grandly stated purpose is "analytically to characterize all possible systems, to justify their methodology, and to attempt a solution to some of the basic problems that arise in dealing with them."

Such largeness of purpose has ever since been a hallmark of Weiss' work; he is perhaps the foremost practitioner in the United States of speculative philosophy, a variety of thinking of very ancient lineage rarely encountered now. Most British and American philosophers today, as Irwin C. Lieb wrote in his preface to Weiss' *festschrift, Experience, Existence, and The Good: Essays in Honor of Paul Weiss* in 1961,

PAUL WEISS

"are interested in methods of analysis and techniques of logic; they are interested in using them to examine special, often narrow, problems in philosophy. They tend to think that speculative philosophy is not precise or exact enough, that it is vagrant and private, that its noble visions are often empty, and that sound logic and good precision do not support a system in philosophy." Yet Weiss, in all his books, has never followed fashion; nor has he shown much interest in the work of his philosophical contemporaries. He has rather sought to demonstrate, in Lieb's words, "without timidity or apology, that speculative thought is an exact but comprehensive discipline. He has urged that the great questions shall be asked and dealt with since they cannot be avoided, for they are always presupposed. . . . He has urged that the great questions shall be discussed, and that we shall not be so concerned to avoid mistakes that we give up trying to say what important things are true."

In his search to expound the ultimate realities, Weiss came to consider one among his books as a kind of key to the others, the cornerstone of all his work. *Modes of Being* contains more than 600 pages of distilled abstraction, the core of which is 441 brief propositions on the four modes of being: actuality, ideality, existence, and God; a negative consideration of these modes; and a final section on their interconnectedness in the topics of being, understanding, and the cosmos. The essential flavor of Weiss' writing style permeates the book: highly abstract, deadly serious, and unrelievedly assertive. "There is little invitation," in J. E. Smith's words, "to consider and discuss but only to listen." Many critics admired the book's daring and ambition, though almost none found it a success. "Despite his careful work and intense stress on unity," wrote Irving Sosensky, "neither the whole nor its parts emerge with force or clarity." "Whence is it," asked W.N. Clarke, "that these four modes are all present at once to each other and so admirably complementary and intrinsically correlated one to another? Until a firmer and more satisfactory answer to this fundamental question is provided than I can find in *Modes of Being,* that is, until Professor Weiss moves a little closer to the common insight of all the great metaphysicians of the past, namely, that there can be no many without a One, I fear that his four-fold universe neither is nor can ever really be."

In his preface to *History: Written and Lived,* an attempt at a philosophy of history, or of historiography, Weiss described his "conviction that philosophy ought to be carried out on two levels. It should have a speculative dimension, where the whole of being and knowledge is in principle dealt with systematically by a distinctive method and in a distinctive style." This first level he considered fulfilled by *Modes of Being.* A second level should comprise "an empirically oriented set of studies revealing the experienceable significance of the realities which the systematic study isolated." Most of his other principal works are devoted to this endeavor. *Reality* and *Nature and Man* describe "the way in which men privately and publicly interplay with Actuality." The latter book, in particular, intends to provide a systematic answer to a profound question: "Can an ethics be grounded deep in the bedrock of nature and still do justice to the fact of duty, the nature of the good, the problem of guilt and related topics?" *Man's Freedom* and *Our Public Life* are concerned with private and public human interplay with the Ideal. The former book means "to make evident how man through a series of free efforts can become more complete and thereby more human." *Our Public Life* treats political ethics as only one of many important ethical fields in "a systematic speculative account of the nature and need for such important groups as society, state, culture, and civilization." The way in which humankind "privately takes account of Existence" is considered in a pair of works on aesthetic theory: *The World of Art* attempts to state the defining properties of all art, "to discover what problems art confronts, what claims it makes, and how its activities and products contrast with those exhibited in other enterprises"; its sequel, *Nine Basic Arts,* distinguishes and characterizes the major arts.

Weiss' other monographs of note include *The Making of Men,* on educational theory; *Sport: A Philosophic Enquiry,* characterized by the author as "the beginning of a new enterprise, the examination of sport in terms of principles which are to be at once revelatory of the nature of sport and pertinent to other fields—indeed, to the whole of things and knowledge"; and *Cinematics,* a philosophically grounded examination of film that aims to fill a longstanding gap: "I have been unable to find a work which not only treats film as an art, but examines its main contributors and constituents systematically, points up its similarities and differences from other arts, and tries to benefit from previous extended reflections on man and what else there is."

One of Weiss' most curious projects is the seven volumes of *Philosophy in Process* (1964–78), his philosophical journals kept between 1955 and the mid-1970s. He characterizes them as "reflections on multiple topics, some . . . based on what I had previously published, but most prompted by questions which arose in class, in conversation, etc." These reflections are "presented exactly as they were jotted down on the typewriter, . . . and make it possible for others to observe the nature of one philosopher's thinking before it has been subjected to detailed critical examination, purification, and systematization." He recognizes that such work must include many contradictions and confusions, yet believes, nevertheless, that "there is value . . . in making evident the kind of hesitations and doubts . . . which occur to one given to daily reflection on both old and new matters." Considerable space is allotted to correcting old work: much of volume three, for example, is spent on the critical examination and revision of *Modes of Being.* That central work was also the springboard of *Beyond All Appearances,* which "offers one illustration of the way in which the final Ideal is realized. This Ideal, in the guise of the ultimate objective for knowledge, is filled out with a systematic account of what is real." *First Considerations: An Examination of Philosophical Evidence* is described by Weiss as "another fresh effort . . . perhaps my best and last attempt to understand what it is that we daily confront, the evidences this provides of final realities, and the process by which one can move from what everyone knows to what everyone should understand."

Weiss has been a frequent contributor to compilations of articles on various philosophical subjects. He was founder in 1947 and longtime editor of the *Review of Metaphysics,* a founder of the Metaphysical Society of America and of the Philosophy Education Society. He was coeditor, with Charles Hartshorne, of the eight-volume *Collected Papers of Charles Sanders*

Peirce (1931–66).

In 1928 he married Victoria Brodkin, who collaborated on several of his early books; she died in 1953. They had a daughter Judith, and a son, Jonathan, who collaborated with his father on the book *Right and Wrong*.

PRINCIPAL WORKS: Reality, 1938; Nature and Man, 1947; Man's Freedom, 1950; Modes of Being, 1958; Our Public Life, 1959; Nine Basic Arts, 1961; World of Art, 1961; History: Written and Lived, 1962; Religion and Art, 1963; Philosophy in Process, Volume I, 1964, Volume II, 1966, Volume III, 1968, Volume IV, 1969, Volume V, 1971, Volume VI, 1975, Volume VII, 1978; The God We Seek, 1964; The Making of Men, 1967; (with Jonathan Weiss) Right and Wrong: A Philosophical Dialogue between Father and Son, 1967; First Considerations: An Examination of Philosophical Evidence, 1967; Sport: A Philosophic Inquiry, 1969; Beyond All Appearances, 1974; Cinematics, 1975; You, I, and the Others, 1980.

ABOUT: Contemporary Authors, revised series 5–8, 1969 and new revised series, 1981; Lieb, I. C. (ed.) Experience, Existence, and The Good, 1961. *Periodicals*—America November 11, 1967; American Political Science Review June 1960; American Sociological Review February 1960; Annals of the American Academy November 1950; May 1960; Atlantic October 1950; Book World July 13, 1969; Choice February 1966; July 1967; June 1968; July 1969; September 1975; December 1977; September 1980; Criticism Winter 1967; Current History June 1947; Ethics October 1958; January 1960; October 1961; Journal of Philosophy November 6, 1947; September 28, 1950; December 3, 1959; Journal of Religion October 1966; Library Journal February 15, 1947; May 1, 1966; October 15, 1967; November 15, 1967; July 1969; June 1, 1975; August 1977; August 1980; National Review January 25, 1966; October 21, 1969; New York Herald Tribune Book Review October 1, 1950; New York Review of Books August 21, 1969; New York Times Book Review May 11, 1947; Saturday Review April 12, 1947; August 19, 1950; June 20, 1959; January 29, 1966; November 18, 1967; Yale Review September 1958; September 1959; June 1961; March 1966.

WELDON, FAY (September 22, 1933–   ), English novelist and dramatist, was born in Alvechurch, Worcester, England, the daughter of Frank Thornton, a doctor, and Margaret (Jepson) Birkinshaw. She was brought up in New Zealand where, after her parents' divorce, she lived with her mother, grandmother, and sister, and went to a girls' school. "For years," Weldon said, "I didn't even speak to a man. I assumed that the world was peopled by females." After her mother brought her back to England, a period of "hardship and deprivation," Weldon attended the South Hampstead High School, London, and with a scholarship studied at St.

FAY WELDON

Andrews University, Fife, graduating with an M.A. in economics and psychology in 1954. Following college, she became a successful advertising copywriter and married Ronald Weldon, a London antiques dealer.

Fay Weldon's literary career began in the mid-1960s, when she wrote plays for British television. Since 1966, she has written approximately thirty television scripts, including two episodes of *Upstairs, Downstairs*. Most of her work for television has consisted of original plays, but she has also adapted the work of other writers, including Elizabeth Bowen and Penelope Mortimer. Her five-part dramatization of Jane Austen's *Pride and Prejudice* (1980) was shown in the United States and in England. She has also written radio scripts and eight plays for the stage.

Her first novel—*And the Wife Ran Away* (U.K. *The Fat Woman's Joke*) concerns two women, Londoners who, as Benjamin De Mott writes, "chat away to each other, chapterlessly, in sentences often reminiscent of Ivy Compton-Burnett." One of the women has left her unfaithful husband and spends her time miserably in a basement flat eating herself into obesity. The other woman listens sympathetically to her confidences partly because she feels guilty for having seduced her friend's husband and partly because in her friend's unhappiness she foresees her own grim future as a middle-aged wife. Rapidly paced, relentlessly observed, and mordantly witty, the novel gained Weldon an immediate audience.

Down Among the Women, "a brief, brilliant second novel," as Melvin Maddocks wrote, "squeezes two generations of Englishwomen into a corner too tight for good manners." The mother, Wanda, forty-four when the novel begins in 1950, is a liberated "1930s-style feminist," who raises her daughter by her own credo of "free love." The virginal daughter, after stubbornly resisting her mother's advice, finally obeys and promptly becomes pregnant.

In *Female Friends,* Weldon extends her observations of the war between the sexes. The main characters are three women, now in their forties, who became friends as children during the evacuation of wartime London. "These women," Sara Blackburn wrote, "gossip unforgivably about one another, are exasperated by one another's dependencies, inflict devastating criticism upon one another, for they see mirrored in their friends' inadequacies their own unending struggles for self-esteem and autonomy." L. E. Sissman wrote that the "real triumph of *Female Friends* is the gritty replication of the gross texture of everyday life—the perfectly recorded dialogue; the shocking progression of events that, however rude, seem real; and the flat matter-of-factness in reporting disasters that makes them both funny and appalling."

Remember Me, which also concerns three women, was regarded as a slighter work than her earlier novels. Joyce Carol Oates remarked that "Miss Weldon's scorn for her characters is expressed in frequent authorial intrusions. The effect is that the reader soon loses sympathy with them. *Remember Me* has the breathlessness of an Iris Murdoch novel, and some of its inventiveness. But it lacks depth and resonance."

Words of Advice (U.K. *Little Sisters*) is "a black comedy of late twentieth-century girlish manners and medieval fairy tale combined." The novel concerns two couples—Victor, an antiques dealer, and his young mistress Elsa; and Hamish, a millionaire, and his wife Gemma, who is paralyzed from the waist down. Hamish offers a valuable group of antiques as the price for a night with Elsa; and Victor, facing a visit from his wife and daughter and anxious to have Elsa out of sight, is distinctly tempted by the offer. Gemma, who wants Elsa pregnant by Hamish so that she may adopt the child, relates a complicated fairy tale to the girl intended to enlighten her as to the ways of the world and to cure her of illusions about her lover. "Like all of Weldon's novels," Margot Jefferson wrote, "*Words of Advice* has considerable energy and cleverness." But, in common with other critics, she found the fairy tale aspect of the novel unsatisfactory.

Critical opinion has been divided on Weldon's best-known novel *Praxis,* which recounts the life and times of Praxis Duveen, a female victim, but ultimately a heroine of the women's movement. To some critics, *Praxis* seemed too unrelievedly a tale of women's victimization by men, but Katha Pollitt remarked that "the energy with which Weldon urges us to blunder our way into a fuller humanity could not be more exhilarating."

Weldon's recent work includes *Puffball, Watching Me, Watching You, The President's Wife,* and *The Life and Loves of a She-Devil. Puffball* is a whimsical novel about a couple, Liffey and Richard, who go to live in the country where, left alone by her husband, pregnant Liffey is subjected to the spells of a witch, but falls in love with the baby growing inside her and confounds the malignant forces besetting her. *Watching Me, Watching You* reprints Weldon's first novel with eleven of her short stories. Many critics relished the "caustic asperity" and "wicked sense of humor" of the stories; but some objected to Weldon's stereotyping of her male characters, always less interesting than her women and invariably their oppressors. *The President's Child* has as its theme the dispensability of women and children whenever their interests and those of potentially powerful men do not coincide.

The female "victim," most typically a discarded wife, takes spectacular vengeance in *The Life and Loves of a She-Devil,* transforming herself from an ugly and unloved housewife and mother into a near-mythic "she-devil," who ends up still unloved but firmly in control of her destiny and the lives of those who had thwarted and betrayed her. If this "heroine" was intended to be a symbol of the new feminism ("Out there in the world," she says, "everything is possible and exciting. We can be different women: we can tap our own energies and the energies of women like us. . . . "), Weldon may have gone too far. Michiko Kakutani found the author's "gift for irony and wit overshadowed by her didacticism," producing here "an unforgiving parody of the women's movement." But other reviewers, agreeing that the novel is a fable or a parable, nevertheless found it redeemed by Weldon's "devilishly delightful" wit. "This is a revenger's comedy," Patricia Craig wrote, "of its nature elaborate and theatrical."

Weldon has been described in an interview as a "warm, rather shy woman—at first sight not at all the type to dabble in black comedy." She lives with her husband in London, and is the mother of four sons ranging in age from four to twenty-seven years. Her writing is fitted in between her children's needs. She has told one interviewer that she was "an unmarried mother in the '50s," and had "messed up" her life hopelessly before meeting her husband, whom she describes as a male chauvinist.

PRINCIPAL WORKS:And the Wife Ran Away (U.K. The Fat Woman's Joke), 1968; Down Among the Women, 1972; Female Friends, 1975; Remember Me, 1976; Words of Advice (U.K. Little Sisters), 1977; Praxis, 1978; Puffball, 1980; Watching Me, Watching You, 1981; The President's Child, 1983; The Life and Loves of a She-Devil, 1984.

ABOUT: Contemporary Authors 23–24, 1970; Contemporary Dramatists, 1977; Contemporary Literary Criticism 6, 1976; 9, 1978; 11, 1979; Contemporary Novelists, 1982; Dictionary of Literary Biography 14 1983. *Periodicals*—Critique December 1978; London Observer February 21, 1980; Newsweek August 15, 1977; December 4, 1978; New Yorker March 10, 1975; September 5, 1977; New York Times August 21, 1984; New York Times Book Review March 3, 1968; February 11, 1973; November 10, 1974; November 21, 1976; October 2, 1977; February 8, 1979; August 24, 1980; December 27, 1981; September 30, 1984; Punch November 1, 1968; March 7, 1979; Spectator July 11, 1981; Time February 26, 1973; August 22, 1977; Times Literary Supplement September 10, 1971; February 28, 1975; September 24, 1976; February 22, 1980; May 22, 1981; September 24, 1982; January 20, 1984.

WESTLAKE, DONALD E(DWIN) (July 12, 1933–), American novelist, was born in New York City, the son of Albert Joseph Westlake, a salesman, and the former Lillian Bounds. He grew up in Albany, and for a while attended Champlain College and the State University of New York at Binghamton, then served in the U.S. Air Force (1954–56), and worked at various jobs, including that of associate editor at the Scott Meredith literary agency (1958–59). From 1959 he has been a full-time writer, and has produced, under his own name, more than two dozen crime novels, and under the pseudonyms Richard Stark and Tucker Coe, another two dozen. All his books are marked by great narrative speed and invention and by quick, quirky dialogue. "He's a genuine plotologist," wrote Sheldon Bart, "with a knack for inventing tricky situations."

Westlake's earliest novels, best represented by his first three, *The Mercenaries, Killing Time,* and *361,* are hard-boiled, extremely violent thrillers, by which he was thought to be staking a claim to the readership of Dashiell Hammett and Raymond Chandler. *361,* a story of gangsters and revenge, takes its title from the classification number in *Roget's Thesaurus* for "[Destruction of life; violent death] KILLING." One reviewer called it "unpleasant but

DONALD E. WESTLAKE

convincing"; Anthony Boucher, an admirer of Westlake's work from the beginning, remarked on the author's unusual skill "at arranging shocking, yet legitimate surprises": "Brutal, harsh, violent (and surprisingly sexless), it remains—in the best tough tradition descending from Hammett—an intelligent novel and even a sensitive one."

This strain in Westlake's work—tough stories of bloody revenge—has been continued in the Richard Stark books, most of which concern the adventures of Parker, a humorless professional robber, or of Alan Grofield, a robber and part-time actor. In the books published under his own name, Westlake has turned in an entirely different—many say unique—direction. "He seems," in Jerome Charyn's words, "to have established a new genre for himself: the screwball thriller." Some of the best of these books treat the elaborate capers organized by the amiably bumbling burglar John A. Dortmunder. In *The Hot Rock,* Dortmunder is retained by the secessionist African state of Talabwo to heist the Balambo Emerald, on display at the New York Coliseum; in *Bank Shot,* he and his crew of small-time criminals manage to steal the entire temporary headquarters (a trailer) of the Capitalists and Immigrants Trust Company; in *Why Me?,* Dortmunder more or less accidentally pockets a valuable ruby, then finds himself heatedly pursued by both the F.B.I. and organized crime.

Many of Westlake's other thrillers are part of no series, and he has published a few novels that do not touch on crime at all. *Up Your Banners,* published in 1969 at a time of great urban unrest in the United States, is the bitterly humorous story of a white teacher who goes to work in a city high school where ninety-three percent of the students are black and where his father is principal. "You would hardly think it possible," wrote the reviewer for the *Times Literary Supplement*, "at this stage of the game that an American could write a funny and intelligent and fundamentally loving novel with black-white strife as its background. This is what Donald Westlake has achieved." The author also has published a work of non-fiction, *Under an English Heaven*, an account of the Anguilla crisis of 1967, when the people of that Caribbean island revolted against the idea of independence from Britain, and for their loyalty found themselves invaded and occupied by British paratroopers and policemen.

Several rewiewers have remarked the Westlake's novels often seem like ready-made film scripts minus the directorial notes. In the late 1960s and early '70s, during the relatively small-scale revival in Hollywood of gangster-caper movies, several of his novels became films, including *The Hunter,* released in 1967 as *Point Blank, The Busy Body,* in 1967, and *The Hot Rock,* in 1972. He still produces, on average, a couple of novels a year, as funny and clever as ever and increasingly less violent, populated by the standard Westlake characters, the semilunatics whom Jerome Charyn called "cartoons, . . . instead of characters we might love, fear or despise, . . . energized masks that babble at us in all sorts of crazy tongues, come alive for a minute, and then return to their normal frozen position."

For so prolific a writer, Westlake has a very *laissez-aller* attitude toward work habits. "I never outline," he said in an interview in 1980. "I hate outlines. It's more fun to make it up as you go along. . . . I don't have a schedule or a quota or anything, I just get to the typewriter whenever possible, and gradually the stuff piles up."

Winner of an Edgar from the Mystery Writers of America in 1966, Westlake has established an important reputation in the genre of crime fiction. Commenting that he "adheres to no formula but readability," Francis M. Nevins, Jr., a mystery writer himself and also an Edgar winner, sums up his achievement: "When the history of contemporary suspense fiction is compiled, he is likely to be recognized as one of its new masters."

PRINCIPAL WORKS: *Novels*—The Mercenaries, 1960; Killing Time, 1961; 361, 1962; Killy, 1963; Pity Him Afterwards, 1964; The Fugitive Pigeon, 1965; The Busy Body, 1966; The Spy in the Ointment, 1966; God Save the Mark, 1967; Up Your Banners, 1969; Who Stole Sassi Manoon?, 1969; The Hot Rock, 1970; Somebody Owes Me Money, 1970; Adios, Scheherazade, 1970; I Gave at the Office, 1972; Bankshot, 1972; Cops and Robbers, 1972; Help I Am Being Held Prisoner, 1974; Jimmy the Kid, 1974; Two Much!, 1975; Brothers Keepers, 1975; Dancing Aztecs, 1976; Enough, 1977; Nobody's Perfect, 1977; A New York Dance, 1979; Castle in the Air, 1980; Why Me?, 1982; Kahawa, 1982; A Likely Story, 1984. *Short stories*—The Curious Facts Preceding My Execution and Other Fictions, 1968. *Non-fiction*—Under an English Heaven, 1972. *As Richard Stark*—The Hunter, 1962; Blackbird, 1969; Butcher's Moon, 1977. *As Tucker Coe*—Wax Apple, 1970; Don't Lie to Me, 1972; *As Curt Clark*—Anarchaos, 1967.

ABOUT: Contemporary Authors, first revision series 19–20, 1976; Contemporary Literary Criticism 7, 1977; Reilly, J. M. (ed.) Twentieth Century Crime and Mystery Writers, 1980; Who's Who in America, 1982–83. *Periodicals*—New Republic December 13, 1975; New Statesman January 9, 1981; New York Herald Tribune Book Review February 11, 1962; August 7, 1980; New York Times Book Review August 7, 1960; April 9, 1961; February 25, 1962; May 24, 1964; March 14, 1965; November 23, 1969; July 19, 1970; May 16, 1971; April 16, 1972; November 19, 1972; July 14, 1974; May 18, 1975; October 5, 1975; October 2, 1977; April 13, 1980; April 11, 1982; January 9, 1983; New Yorker May 30, 1964; April 29, 1972; Time July 22, 1974; Times Literary Supplement June 23, 1961; October 9, 1970; September 29, 1972; March 9, 1973; March 16, 1973; August 6, 1976; August 13, 1978; March 13, 1981.

WHARTON, WILLIAM is the pseudonym of an American novelist and artist now living in Paris. Because Wharton wants to avoid the kind of media attention that would "get in the way of the creative process," the author and his publisher, Afred A. Knopf, have concealed the details of his life and career. In telephone interviews, however, he has revealed that he is married and in his fifties, is a successful *plein air* painter working in a traditionally figurative style, and has drawn heavily on personal experiences in his novels, *Birdy, Dad, A Midnight Clear,* and *Scumbler.* Wharton confesses to being a born raconteur whose impulse to write sprang, in part, from his daily invention of stories for his children. His deliberately cultivated anonymity and accomplished novelistic imagination have given rise to speculation that he may be a well-known writer—even, it has been suggested, the elusive J. D. Salinger.

According to Wharton's own account, the manuscript of his first novel, *Birdy,* had been circulating privately for some time before an agent placed it, with some alterations, at Knopf. No one was more surprised than the publisher when this thoroughly unconventional and uncommercial novel became a best-seller in 1979, and, later, something of a cult book. It was released as a film in late 1984. Set in the Depression and war years, *Birdy* tells the story of the maturation of two youths: Birdy, a scrawny boy so obsessed with birds and the possibility of winged flight that he becomes submerged in a fantasy that he is a bird himself; and his only friend, Al, a typical jock who discovers in war that his macho self-image is also a fantasy. Disfigured in battle, and desperately trying to hide the fact of his cowardice under fire, Al is summoned to an Army psychiatric hospital to contact Birdy, who has been completely absorbed by his bird-persona and will not speak. In a series of interlocking flashbacks the two young men recall their boyhood. The longest and most striking section of the book—on which rests its reputation as an unusually rich and compelling fantasy—details Birdy's gradual rejection of the tawdry and cruel real world for a rhapsodic dream world in which he is a parakeet, and learns to fly, mates with an exceptionally desirable female, builds a nest, and raises generations of young. Wharton's use of precise (and profuse) ornithological detail (he has raised birds since youth), coupled with his eccentric poetic vision, made this passage particularly effective; a number of reviewers compared it (not very helpfully) with the chapter on cetology in *Moby Dick.* The book as a whole was also routinely likened (even by critics who did not believe Wharton was Salinger) to another classic of adolescent angst, *The Catcher in the Rye.*

"As adolescent dream," wrote Michael Moore in the *New York Arts Journal,* "Birdy's escape into birdhood—flying with its illusion of freedom, the vision of perfectly realized erotic love, connubial bliss and familial fulfillment—is satisfying, especially since Wharton does not overstress the misanthropic possibility of such an escape as Swift does with the Houyhnhms." Robert Towers, though impressed with the book's "many passages of almost incandescent beauty," thought the central fantasy "excessively detailed and repetitious, 'overdetermined' in the Freudian sense," and, like most reviewers, found the book's ending, in which Birdy suddenly snaps out of his dream, stands erect, and begins to lecture Al on the nature of reality, "too schematic and preachy." For his part, Wharton has complained, in a *Contemporary Authors* interview, that critics have, with few exceptions, failed to understand his meaning. "My idea is there are no endings, that there's only one vast, unending middle; no beginnings, no endings. . . . I feel one of the book's main themes is that neither fight nor flight is adequate, that fantasy is necessary as a coping system. No one has mentioned this."

Belying Tower's prediction that *Birdy* was a "once-in-a-lifetime" effort, Wharton published just two years later a semiautobiographical novel, *Dad.* The narrator of *Dad* is John Tremont, a thinly disguised version of Wharton himself. Tremont, a painter who leaves his home and family in Paris to visit his ailing mother, stays to care for his father, who is slowly dying but who summons a brief flash of intense life before sinking into senility and death. With the same mixture of heightened realism and lyrical subtext that he used in *Birdy,* Wharton vividly describes Dad's medical crises and emotional subjugation to his wife, a neurotic woman who uses guilt to manipulate her family; he also reveals Dad's happy dream life as a truck farmer surrounded by adoring family. Alternately elated, frightened, and determined, but finally defeated, John Tremont (and, one suspects, the author himself) is forced to confront his own inevitable aging and death.

"Wharton insists on the plain style," wrote Roger Sale in the *New York Review of Books*; "he allows himself only exclamation marks and an occasional loftiness, but no higher than that Mom 'is a steam engine inside a canoe.' He allows himself to invent some passages of Dad's alternative world, and to do some scenes between Johnny and his son told from the son's point of view; these are strained, overdone. The rest is written, and the result is the sense that nothing is as wonderful, as awful, as wearying, as mysterious, as growing old." Despite masterly passages, the novel does suffer from Wharton's not having fully assimilated his own experience; there are rough edges and awkwardnesses, and, as in *Birdy,* a deep if intermittent vein of misogyny. *Dad* struck Benjamin DeMott as "even more formula-ridden than its predecessor"; the reviewer cited its "density of stereotypes" and the "peculiar megalomanic thrust of [its] sentimentality" as particular faults.

A *Midnight Clear* was published in 1982. Written in the first-person present tense (as was much of *Birdy* and all of *Dad*), the novel details the unusual and tragic events that befall a company of bright and very young soldiers toward the end of World War II. As in *Birdy,* Wharton sees little glory or even necessity in war and tells much that is graphically horrible. But his real theme is, again, the sustaining power of fantasy and the tragic results when even a collective dream is exposed to the violence of the real world. Sergeant Will Knott and his men, holding a chateau in Ardennes in the winter of 1944, receive mysterious overtures from a squad of Germans anxious to surrender. In concocting a plot to stage a mock battle before the surrender, so that the Germans can save face and one of the

Americans can take credit for the coup, they fatally overcomplicate the scheme, and when a shot is mistakenly fired, the mock battle turns into a real one. For most reviewers, the vividness and originality of the tale outweighed its shortcomings of plot and voice. Though Wharton "doesn't strike the right distance between realism and fantasy," wrote Peter S. Prescott, and the plot is "just improbable," the reviewer had "a good time with this story; its suspense and pace, and its likable young men, unhappily disguised as warriors, easily overcome its awkwardnesses."

Though not directly autobiographical, *Scumbler,* Wharton's novel about an aging American painter living in Paris, is closer to the circumstances of his own life. The title refers to a technique of layering the surface of a painting with opaque color, but it is also an obvious wordplay with its echoes of *scum* (the artist calls himself "Old Scum") and *bumbler.* An anti-hero, an embittered expatriate, and a general incompetent, he literally "tells all" about his messy life. Several reviewers found the novel disappointing—one (Tom LeClair) suggesting that having produced three powerful novels in five years, Wharton should follow Kafka's advice to himself: "Wait."

Wharton sees himself as partaking in, even helping to lead, a major change in American fiction, away from what he calls "the New York School of writing" and toward a kind of "magic realism." "It's time for a breakout in American writing, a really big one. If I had to guess at directions, I think it would be a movement toward an oral, lyrical tradition as opposed to the verbal, literary tradition. Also a subject matter move away from Freudian prurience toward fantasy—supported, sustained fantasy."

PRINCIPAL WORKS: Birdy, 1979; Dad, 1981; A Midnight Clear, 1982; Scumbler, 1984.

ABOUT: Contemporary Authors 93–96, 1979. *Periodicals*—America April 7, 1979; Atlantic June 1981; Nation September 18, 1982; New York Arts Journal 18, 1980; New York Review of Books March 8, 1979; August 13, 1981; New York Times Book Review January 21, 1979; February 11, 1979; May 24, 1981; September 12, 1982; June 3, 1984; Newsweek June 1, 1981; September 13, 1982; Publishers Weekly April 24, 1981; April 10, 1982; Time June 1, 1981; Times Literary Supplement December 7, 1979, September 25, 1981.

WILLIAMS, C(HARLES) K(ENNETH) (November 4, 1936–), American poet, was born in Newark, New Jersey, the son of Paul B.

C(HARLES) K(ENNETH) WILLIAMS

Williams and the former Dossie Kasdin. After attending public schools and Bucknell University, he transferred to the University of Pennsylvania, where he earned his bachelor's degree in 1959. He married Sarah Jones in 1965, was divorced, then married Catherine Mauger in 1975. He has one child from each marriage, a son, Jed, and a daughter, Jessica. In recent years Williams has been teaching creative writing at George Mason University in Virginia and in the Writing Division of the school of Arts of Columbia University. Since 1972 he has been on the editorial board of *American Poetry Review,* of which he is now the editor.

In "One of the Muses," a long poem that concludes his 1983 collection *Tar,* C. K. Williams addresses a personal muse, a nameless "she" and traces the evolution of his poetic career which began, he writes, "Long ago, in another place, it seems sometimes in another realm of being altogether." That "long ago" was the late 1960s and early seventies, a period of now "ancient desperation" when she came to him "with intensity, directness, aggression even." His muse was not an easy mistress—"with her abrasive offerings and takings back, I'd been ground down like a lens." Over the years, in a process less of mellowing than of agonizing self-searching, she drifted away: "Here, in a relatively stable present, no cries across the gorge, no veils atremble, / it sometimes seems as though she may have been a fiction utterly, a symbol or a system of them."

Williams emerged first as a poet of the "angry decades." His early volumes—*Lies* and *I Am the Bitter Name*—are collections of short lyrics notable for their rage and energy of expression. They are heavy with "political message," their inspiration the Holocaust, Vietnam, Cambodia, the killing of students at Kent State and Jackson State. Their effectiveness now, some years later, is uncertain—"vitiated by a shrill vehemence and sentimentality," James Atlas writes, and scarred (the scar is a recurring image in his poems) by desperation and despair. In one of the poems in *Lies* he writes characteristically:

I hook my fingers into the old tennis court fence
and kneel down in an overgrowth of sharp weeds
to watch the troopers in their spare compound drill.

Do you remember when this was a park? When girls
swung their rackets here in the hot summer mornings
and came at night to open their bodies to us?

Now gun-butts stamp the pale clay like hooves.
Hard boots gleam.
And still, children play tag and hide-and-seek

beyond the barriers. Lovers sag in the brush.
It is not them, it is us: we know too much.
Soon only the past will know what we know.
                                        ("Of What Is Past")

And in *I Am the Bitter Name,* in a poem on a mutilated war veteran, he bitterly conveys the pathos of machismo:

crutches artifical arms have you seen that?
how they pick their cups up and use razors? amazing!
and the wives shine it for them at night
they're sleeping the wives take it out of the room
and polish it with its own special rag
it's late they hold it against their bellies
the leather laces dangle into their laps
the mechanisms slip noiselessly
lowering the hook softly onto their breasts
we men! aren't we something? I mean
we are worth thinking about aren't we?
we are the end we are the living end.
                                ("The Spirit the Triumph")

The violence and explicitness of Williams' language, the free form of his verse (a reviewer in *Choice* describes it as "at-first-glance-Cummings style") may have been "self-defeating," as T. E. Luddy judged the poems in *I Am the Bitter Name.* "His best poems," Luddy writes, are those "in which the social conscience does not control the poem, but merely provides a cause for the poet to meditate lyrically on a human dilemma."

By the mid-1970s, however, Michael True detected a note of hope, of saving grace, emerging in his poetry: "In its precision, intensity, fury, his work gives full imaginative expression to a kind of consciousness that many poets have only hinted at. It asks a great deal of the reader, as all truly exceptional poetry must. One can only guess, at this time—when Williams is still a young man—the possibilities in language and technique yet available to him." *With Ignorance* indeed marked a major stylistic departure for Williams. His characteristic short lyric with its considerable economy of expression gives way entirely: all fourteen of the poems in this collection are written in a very long line, closer to prose than to lyric, which lends the verse a colloquial, even chatty, tone, dense with detail. In the title poem of this volume, a long, erotic meditation on sex and human frustration, Morris Dickstein found "a vague ruminative bleakness, a feverish disgust, which looks morosely inward and puts the actualities of life in limbo." But in other poems here Dickstein was moved by "the solid realism, the clash of contending feelings and human interchange [that] give the book its most signal quality, its emotional range and intensity . . . [His] poems sacrifice eloquence for energy, epigram for affect, song for speech. I find them deeply inspiriting."

The poems in *Tar* are mainly personal and domestic. Still, Williams has not forgotten the bitterness of the past. In "From My Window" he contemplates a spring morning ("the first morning when that one true block of sweet, laminar, complex scent arrives / from somewhere west and I keep coming to lean on the sill, glorying in the end of the wretched winter") and the sight of a paraplegic Vietnam veteran who is being wheeled down the street by a friend. The horror of the sight blots out everything else. But in another poem, "Waking Jed," he recalls tenderly the flickering images on the face of his sleeping son:

Now I sense, although I can't say how, his awareness
    of me: I can feel him begin to *think,*
I even know what he's thinking—or thinking in a dream
    perhaps—of me here watching him.
Now I'm aware—again, with no notion how, nothing
    indicates it—that if there was a dream,
it's gone, and, yes, his eyes abruptly open although his gaze,
    straight before him,
seems not to register just yet, the mental operations still
    independent of his vision.
I say his name, the way we do it, softly, calling one another
    from a cove or cave,
as though something else were there with us, not to be
    disturbed, to be crept along beside.
The lids come down again, he yawns, widely, very
    consciously manifesting intentionality.

In still another poem he revisits his old grammar school and recalls a patriotic pageant when he played Uncle Sam in a cheap store-bought costume that he hated: "We were taught obsessively to be 'Good Citizens,' a concept I never quite understood." The neighborhood as changed; urban blight is everywhere; yet something precious remains:

The baskets on their court are still intact at least,
    although the metal nets are torn.
Some men who must be from the neighborhood have got
    a game going out there now.

The children circle shyly, hand in hand, as solemn as a
  frieze of Greeks, while a yard beyond,
the backboards boom, the players sweat and feint and
  drive, as though everything depended on it.

The title poem "Tar" juxtaposes the news of
the Three Mile Island accident with a roofing job
that he is watching—"I never realized what brutal work it is, how matter-of-factly and harrowingly dangerous":

a dense, malignant smoke shoots up, and someone has
  to fiddle with a cock, then hammer it,
before the gush and stench will deintensify, the dark,
  Dantean broth wearily subside

and he wonders why the memory of the roofers
remains so clear for him while the rest, "the terror of that time . . . dims so":

But, more vividly, the men, silvered with glitter from
  the shingles, clinging like starlings beneath the eaves.
Even the leftover carats of tar in the gutter, so black they
  seemed to suck the light out of the air.
By nightfall kids had come across them: every sidewalk on
  the block was scribbled with obscenities and hearts.

These later poems suggest that Williams today
is moving closer to a poetry of "moral or even
theological order," a quality Michael True had
detected even in his earlier work. Such a direction is indicated certainly by Williams' collaboration with Gregory W. Dickerson, a scholar of
classical Greek, on a verse translation of Sophocles' *Women of Trachis.* He is currently working
on a translation of Euripides' *Bacchae.*

PRINCIPAL WORKS: A Day for Anne Frank, 1968; Lies,
1969; I Am the Bitter Name, 1972; With Ignorance,
1977; The Lark, the Thrush. The Starling. (Poems
from Issa), 1983; Tar, 1983. *Translation*—(with G.
Dickerson) Women of Trachis, 1978.

ABOUT: Contemporary Authors, first revision series 37-
40, 1979; Dictionary of Literary Biography: American
Poets Since World War II, Part I, 1980; Vinson, J. (ed.)
Contemporary Poets, 1975. *Periodicals*—Choice April
1973; September 1977; Library Journal February 1,
1972; June 15, 1977; Nation June 18, 1977; New York
Times July 10, 1977; New York Times Book Review
July 10, 1977; Poetry February 1973.

WILLIAMS, HUGO (February 20, 1942–   ),
British poet and travel writer, was born in Windsor, Berkshire, the son of Hugh Williams, an actor and playwright, and the former Margaret
Vyner. He attended Eton from the ages of thirteen to eighteen, but went no further in formal
education. He was employed during the 1960s
and later on the staff of the *London Magazine,*
and also wrote occasional articles for the *Sunday
Telegraph Magazine.* In 1966 Williams edited

the poetry collection *"London Magazine" Poems, 1961–1966.* He was married in October
1965 to Hermine Demoriane; they have a
daughter.

Williams' favorite poetic form is the short lyric. His first three collections, *Symptoms of Loss,
Sugar Daddy,* and *Some Sweet Day,* are composed in large part of poems of a dozen lines at
most: intelligent, often witty, rarely brash or insistent, these lyrics always convey truths, small
or large, ironically perceived. They are sometimes mere impressions, devoid of conventional
"meaning," as in "Sussex":

Broken mauve lightning.
The rooks
Explode upwards
Out of the mauve bracken.

Yet he is best, perhaps, at suggesting the nuances
in human relationships, as in "Couple," a rueful
account of wedded ennui:

Sick of me, you search your hair
For the frayed ends
You love to split back to the root.

Your head is bowed.
That hair I would weigh in my hands
Is falling over your eyes.

I don't know what to do
As you pass your time
Perfecting the darkness between us.

And everywhere one finds his thoroughgoing,
even relentless wittiness, a somewhat stiff-
upper-lip Britishness, which are nevertheless fully human and understandable. The motivation
is often nicely ambiguous, as in a poem like
"Charge":

I want to charge down to that water,
Fall over with a bang and stumble
In among the boats and reeds, upsetting
The boatmen and fishermen, swim
Far out in my clothes and pretend to drown.

I am looking after my daughter on this hill.

Lately, Williams has been attempting longer
poems. A particularly successful example of this
extension of his talent occupied, in its initial publication, a full page of the *Times Literary
Supplement,* January 22, 1982. "An Actor's Life
for Me" is the poet's sad, affectionate consideration of his father, a forbidding, demanding,
mysterious, yet utterly fascinating figure. The
poem's final section confirms it as an elegy of
disquieting honesty:

Now that I'm the same age
as he was during the war,
now that I hold him up like a mirror
to look over my shoulder,
I'm given to wondering
what manner of man it was
who walked in on us that day

in his final uniform.
A soldier with two families?
An actor without a career?
"You didn't know who on earth I was," he told me.
"You just cried and cried."

Now that he has walked out again
leaving me no wiser,
now that I'm sitting here like an actor
waiting to go on,
I wish I could see again
that rude, forgiving man from World War II
and hear him goading me.
Dawdling in peacetime,
not having to fight in my lifetime, left alone
to write poetry on the dole and be happy,
I'm given to wondering
what manner of man I might be.

A year of travel in Asia, consisting of a mean-dering overland journey from Israel to Australia, resulted in Williams' first book of prose, *All the Time in the World*. The reviewer for the *Times Literary Supplement* called the book funny, re-freshing, and unpretentious, remarking further that the author comes across as "a young man who is fresh without being gauche, open but not soft-centered." A second book of travel writings which grew out of Williams' extended poetry-reading tour of North America was *No Particular Place to Go*, a wry, bemused account of seem-ingly endless drifting, via Greyhound buses, through a soulless, utterly promiscuous America. The author keeps his literary precursors on the American tour—Oscar Wilde, Aldous Huxley, W. H. Auden, Evelyn Waugh, and Thom Gunn—clearly in view, but constantly undercuts any of his own pretensions to literariness by a steadily deflating irony and a disarming willing-ness to immerse himself in all the ambient mind-lessness. He describes being offered quantities of drugs, most of which he accepts, and experienc-ing a truly prodigious number of joyless, dispirit-ing, yet comically rendered sexual encounters with complacent, neurotic women. Blake Morri-son's generally favorable review quotes Williams on the riches made by visiting writers: "A friend of mine tours America almost constantly, lectur-ing on, and committing, 'Adultery.' Another reads out his thesis on 'The Blurb.' I heard of a man who got $35,000 from the government for a single talk on Clearasil." But Williams himself remembers "petty quibbles over fees, demands for receipts before expenses can be paid, or promises of cheques to be forwarded to England in due course. . . . He mixes not with the rich and famous, nor even with Faculty Deans and their wives, but with a stream of bums and drift-ers. He stays at the seediest hotels, . . . or else he telephones the friends of friends of friends who've found their way into his address book and pleads with them to put him up."

PRINCIPAL WORKS: *Poetry*—Symptoms of Loss, 1965; Po-ems, 1969; Sugar Daddy, 1970; Cherry Blossom, 1972; Some Sweet Day, 1975. *Travel*—All the Time in the World, 1966; No Particular Place to Go, 1981. *As editor*—"London Magazine" Poems, 1961–1966, 1966.

ABOUT: Contemporary Authors, new revision series 19–20, 1976; Vinson, J. (ed.) Contemporary Poets, 1975. *Periodicals*—Choice October 1966; March 1976; En-counter November 1975; Library Journal December 1, 1970; New Statesman October 29, 1965; July 24, 1970; July 11, 1975; Poetry November 1966; Times Literary Supplement November 18, 1965; March 9, 1967; Sep-tember 11, 1970; August 29, 1975; October 30, 1981; January 22, 1982.

WILLS, GARRY (May 22, 1934–   ), Ameri-can historian, political essayist, and journalist, was born in Atlanta, the son of John H. Wills, an appliance salesman, and Mayno Collins Wills. He grew up in the northern Midwest in a strict Roman Catholic family environment, becoming, as he writes in the autobiographical *Confessions of a Conservative*, "a Catholic cold warrior, praying after Mass every day for the conversion of Russia, rallying to anti-Communism around the cold-war icon, the statue of 'Our Lady of Fatima.'" He entered the Society of Jesus, and was sent to study philosophy at St. Louis Univer-sity, a Jesuit institution, receiving his bachelor's degree in 1957. Although he stopped training for the priesthood about the time of his graduation, he nevertheless proceeded to Jesuit-run Xavier University in Cincinnati, where he took a mas-ter's degree in philosophy the following year. He has remained a practicing Catholic.

Wills began his journalistic career as a protégé of William F. Buckley, Jr., editor of the right-wing magazine the *National Review*. For more than a decade after 1957, he was an increasingly prominent contributor to that monthly but never joined its staff as a full-time employee. Although he eventually broke with Buckley (who consid-ers him a traitor to the American right), Wills has continued to style himself a conservative. Most of his admirers, however, would call him at best an idiosyncratic one. Wills has also worked for the *National Catholic Reporter*, *Esquire* magazine, and as a columnist, since 1970, for the United Press Syndicate. He has, at the same time, followed an academic career. Af-ter earning an M.A. (1959) and a Ph.D. (1961) in classics from Yale University, he taught clas-sics at Johns Hopkins University (1961–67, 1968–69), and was adjunct professor of the hu-manities at that institution (1973–81). Since 1980 he has held the Henry R. Luce chair of Ameri-can culture and public policy at Northwestern

GARRY WILLS

University. He married Natalie Carvallo in May 1959; they have two sons and a daughter and live in Chicago.

Wills' many books, whether on politics or religion, have usually provoked controversy for their contentious, debunking, and ardently revisionist spirit. In *Politics and Catholic Freedom* he registered his disagreement with Pope John XXIII's encyclical *Mater et Magistra* (1961), arguing that papal stands on social problems are not binding on Catholics, who remain free, if they wish, to formulate their own politically based solutions. *The Second Civil War: Arming for Armageddon,* written after a tour of the black ghettos in the big cities in the North and West after the 1967 riots, demanded that Americans completely change their attitudes toward race relations or face the almost certain prospect of race wars. The essays in *Bare Ruined Choirs: Doubt, Prophecy, and Radical Religion* examine the disarray within the Roman Catholic church as cases of a general institutional breakdown and an individual crisis of authority.

Wills is midway through a series of books, generally entitled America's Political Enlightenment, tracing the philosophical genesis of American political institutions. Future volumes are planned to cover the history of the ratifying of the Constitution and the origins of the Supreme Court. *Inventing America: Jefferson's Declaration of Independence,* which won a National Book Award, holds that Jefferson's vision of liberty derived primarily not from John Locke's Second Treatise of Government, as has been usually supposed, but instead from the political writings of the philosophers of the Scottish En-

lightenment—David Hume and Francis Hutcheson, among others. *Explaining America: The Federalist* suggests that Hume's political philosophy formed the common ground between Madison and Hamilton in their collaboration on the Federalist essays during the 1780s. "It is not surprising that we should misunderstand the Declaration," Wills writes in the Prologue to *Inventing America.* "It is written in the lost language of the Enlightenment. It is dark with unexamined lights." Our "misreading" is the result partly of our ignorance of the intellectual context of these documents, and partly of our idealized and romantic notions of our country's origins, such as those voiced in Lincoln's Gettysburg Address mythicizing America's "miraculous birth" and historic "mission." All this was alien to Jefferson and Madison, schooled in eighteenth-century empiricism.

In *Explaining America* Wills develops and expands the historian Douglass Adair's thesis that "the most direct influence on *The Federalist* is Hume's conception of government as a utilitarian division of labor within a generally benevolent set of social ties." Like Jefferson's, Madison's was "the world of the American Enlightenment—a world of the classical virtues reborn, of optimism about man's effort to order society rationally, of a new science of man. . . . It was the world of the Encyclopedists, of the Scottish social scientists . . . a kind of secular Eden." Academic critics, reviewing these two books, complained that Wills used historical facts selectively in what G. S. Woods, writing of *Explaining America,* describes as "a bundle of brilliance and perversity, intelligence and sophistry, ingenuity and wrong-headedness." They have conceded, however, that he has brilliantly illuminated the intellectual background of our national past: "But right or wrong," E. S. Morgan wrote, "Wills has an extraordinary gift for seeing and suggesting new meanings of familiar passages." The result, however questionable as history, has been stimulating and provocative. "If Wills is right—and his case is formidable—," Jack Beatty wrote in *Newsweek* of *Inventing America,* "the roots of our political culture are far less individualistic than they are communal."

Wills' two most popular books, both on prominent American politicians, are also his most controversial. *Nixon Agonistes: The Crisis of the Self-Made Man* is a broad attack on "classical liberalism," to Wills a nefarious doctrine that "lingers in our institutions, haunts out language, forms our assumptions"; Nixon, in his view the self-made man par excellence, is the "apt spokesman for and final product of classical liberalism." He was the perfect president for the times, "the man so stiff, constricted, so careful to keep things remote from him; and the country so uneasy, discontented, yearning back toward lost certitudes, daydreaming for itself a ruler from the past, only half-reanimated, to defend the emulative ethic, to make this once more a 'land of opportunity' for competitive individuals." D. W. Brogan characterized the book as "a long vendetta" and Wills as "a lively but extremely repetitive writer with very limited powers of literary organization." But the book seemed to some in retrospect a remarkably prescient account of a fatally flawed man; it was brought out in a revised edition in 1979.

The Kennedy Imprisonment: A Meditation on Power is a de-mythicizing of the Kennedy mystique, a phenomenon whose origins Wills traces to the machinations of Joseph P. Kennedy, the family patriarch, who "labored to create a separate world for his family, an aristocracy floating free of lesser ties, where image and power would be controllable, resources instantly mobilizable for the family's advantage." Not a single member of the family or their retinue of friends and apologists is spared, most particularly not President John F. Kennedy. "In his fury to demystify," Joe McGinniss wrote in the *New York Times Book Review*, [Wills] has reduced the forty-year saga of (like it or not) one of America's most extraordinary families to the level of adult soap opera—a mix of sex, violence, power struggle and intrigue." The book belies its subtitle, Burke Wilkinson observed in the *Christian Science Monitor*, in being an emotional, irreverent and free-wheeling "extravaganza . . . gossipy, trivial, flawed, and outrageous—illuminated by sudden flashes of insight, and never for an instant dull or boring." Wills' case against the Kennedys is strong but so tendentious that it reminded John Gregory Dunne, in *New York Review of Books*, of "a kangaroo court . . . the verdict was in the judge's pocket before the charges on the indictment were read."

PRINCIPAL WORKS: *Non-fiction*—Chesterton, 1961; Politics and Catholic Freedom, 1964; Roman Culture, 1966; Jack Ruby, 1967; The Second Civil War, 1968; Nixon Agonistes, 1970; Bare Ruined Choirs, 1972; Inventing America, 1978; Confessions of a Conservative, 1979; Explaining America, 1980; Cincinnatus, 1982; Lead Time, 1983. *Fiction*—At Button's, 1979.

ABOUT: Contemporary Authors, new revision series, 1, 1981; Current Biography 1982; Who's Who in America, 1983–84. *Periodicals*—America December 19, 1970; November 11, 1972; March 1973; June 2, 1979; June 30, 1979; April 18, 1981; June 19, 1982; Book World January 14, 1968; October 11, 1970; June 18, 1978; April 15, 1979; June 17, 1979; Commentary February 1971; February 1973; October 1978; July 1979;

Commonweal April 30, 1971; December 22, 1972; October 27, 1978; September 28, 1979; May 8, 1981; May 21, 1982; Harper November 1979; National Review April 9, 1968; June 4, 1968; July 18, 1970; November 24, 1972; October 20, 1975; July 7, 1978; May 25, 1979; September 4, 1981; March 5, 1982; New Republic May 19, 1979; January 24, 1981; March 24, 1982; New York Review of Books March 25, 1971; August 17, 1978; October 11, 1979; April 2, 1981; April 15, 1982; New York Times May 6, 1968; October 15, 1970; October 20, 1972; March 19, 1979; April 26, 1979; New York Times Book Review November 1, 1970; October 29, 1972; June 16, 1978; July 2, 1978; March 25, 1979; July 15, 1979; March 1, 1981; March 14, 1982; Saturday Review January 2, 1971; August 1978; March 1982; Time November 2, 1970; October 23, 1972; July 31, 1978; April 23, 1979; March 22, 1982; Times Literary Supplement October 13, 1978.

WILSON, LANFORD (EUGENE) (April 13, 1937–), American playwright, was born in Lebanon, Missouri, the son of Ralph Eugene Wilson and the former Violetta Careybelle Tate. His parents divorced when he was five, and he lived with his mother in Missouri until he completed high school and a year of study (1955–56) at Southwest Missouri State College, after which he left for San Diego, California, to live near his father. This was an unhappy experience for the young man, one he recorded more than a dozen years later in a highly autobiographical play, *Lemon Sky*, about a stern father and his lost, idealistic son whom he grievously harms. After a year of university study at San Diego State University (1956–57), Wilson moved to Chicago, where he worked in the art department of an advertising agency and for another year (1957–58) attended university, this time the University of Chicago's downtown extension. He was trying, without success, to sell the short stories he had been writing, and had become involved in the theater as a fledgling actor and playwright.

In the summer of 1962, Wilson moved to New York where his one-act plays began to appear Off-Off-Broadway about a year later, notably at Caffe Cino and Cafe La Mama. Largely representations of American small-town life and of difficulties within families, they are remarkable for showing the author's early command of the resources of dialogue as a developer of characterization. Layered and overlapping dialogue, now a Wilson trademark, can also be traced to these early dramatic efforts.

The playwright's reputation grew during this period of creative apprenticeship; his first full-length play, *Balm in Gilead,* was a sensational success when it opened at Cafe La Mama, with dozens of people being turned away every night and the fire marshal threatening frequently to

LANFORD WILSON

close down the place because of overcrowding. The play takes place in a seedy all-night café in New York and concerns the interaction of the whores, pimps, junkies, and pushers of all races and sexual orientations—young American losers, both tough and vulnerable—who frequent the place. The play received a highly acclaimed revival in New York in 1984, a production powerful enough, in Frank Rich's words, "to make yesterday's new theater new once more." Convincing ensemble work by the large cast "completely locked [the audience] into a seething nocturnal community with its own rituals, laws, loyalties, manners, and language." *The Rimers of Eldritch,* about the physical and moral decline of a small Midwestern town, was less of a popular success in 1966 but won Wilson his first major critical prize, the Vernon Rice–Drama Desk award for best Off-Broadway play of 1967.

In 1969, Wilson was cofounder, with Marshall W. Mason (who has directed nearly all his plays), Rob Thirkield, and Tanya Berezin, of Circle Repertory Company, which has since become one of America's leading theater ensembles. He became the company's resident playwright in 1970, but his work during this period was not successful. One play, *The Gingham Dog,* an account of the breakup of an interracial marriage, closed on Broadway after only five performances in 1969. The autobiographical *Lemon Sky* fared little better Off-Broadway a year later. Wilson entered a period, lasting eighteen months, during which he could not write plays. By 1978 he was able to describe this dark time from a humorous distance: "A writer . . .

doesn't like to think about those times when his muse packs up her bags, goes off to St. Martin with somebody's chauffeur, and can't be reached by phone."

The resounding success of *The Hot 1 Baltimore* in 1973 signaled the end of his writer's block. The scene is set on "a recent Memorial Day" around the front desk of the Hotel Baltimore, a nineteenth-century faded wreck, or in Wilson's words, "a five-story establishment intended to be an elegant and restful haven. . . . The marble stairs and floors, the carved wood paneling have aged as neglected ivory ages, into a dull gold. The Hotel Baltimore is scheduled for demolition." The hotel's workers and various residents—the latter mainly prostitutes—open their lives to us and each other in this setting of neglect and decay. The play's "old-fashioned humanity" and "purely American voice" appealed greatly to critics and audiences. It ran for nearly three years off Broadway, won the New York Drama Critics Circle and Obie awards for best play of its year, and even formed the basis of a short-lived situation comedy on television.

Wilson encountered similar success with what he considers "my best play," *The Mound Builders,* in which archaeologists vainly attempt to extract the truth from a series of Mississippian culture burial mounds in Illinois that are to be inundated by a man-made lake. He then embarked on his multipartite saga of the Talley family, where his most fruitful themes—the loss of idealism, the decline of families, the routine violation of natural order, the inert complexity of modern life—have reached their fullest expression. Set on "the old Talley place," a prosperous mid-nineteenth-century farmhouse in Lebanon, Missouri, the plays (which may eventually number half a dozen or more) consider episodes of importance in the latter-day history of a family shrunken in size and influence. *The 5th of July* takes place in 1976, and relates the desultory plan of Ken Talley, a legless Vietnam veteran, to sell the family house. *Talley's Folly* is a long one-act play for two characters showing the culmination of the courtship, on the 4th of July 1944, of Sally Talley, Ken's aunt, and Matt Friedman, an ebullient, warm-hearted refugee from Nazism. In *A Tale Told,* set on the same evening, Timmy Talley, Ken's uncle, returns as an unseen ghost to visit his family, having just been killed in World War II. Although some critics found the plays wordy and implausible, most agreed that Wilson's writing showed real compassion for the characters and that the playwright has certainly, in Robert Berkvist's words, "devoted himself to exposing layer after layer of life in the countryside of his theatrical imagination." The Talley cycle, according to

Wilson, "will run backward, starting the day after the Bicentennial . . . and ending back around 1860 or thereabouts, when the Talley house was built."

Wilson does most of his writing in his office at Circle Rep, constantly requiring the interplay of his colleagues in the process of creation. "I'm crazy about actors," he wrote in 1978. "I've always written for actors. 'Whom do you write for?' Actors. 'But what audience do you write for?' Anybody. One of the pleasures of being a playwright (count them on one hand) is watching an actor in the process of understanding, *believing,* the part."

PRINCIPAL WORKS: Balm in Gilead and Other Plays, 1965; The Rimers of Eldritch and Other Plays, 1967; The Gingham Dog, 1969; Lemon Sky, 1970; The Sand Castle and Three Other Plays, 1970; The Great Nebula in Orion and Three Other Plays, 1973; The Hot l Baltimore, 1973; The Mound Builders, 1976; The 5th of July, 1978; Talley's Folly, 1979; A Tale Told, 1981; Angels Fall, 1983.

ABOUT: Contemporary Authors 19–20R, 1976; Contemporary Literary Criticism 7, 1977 and 14, 1980; Current Biography, 1979. *Periodicals*—Nation March 15, 1975; May 26, 1979; New Republic March 1, 1975; June 9, 1979; New York May 24, 1976; May 15, 1978; May 21, 1979; New York Times October 12, 1970; April 23, 1978; April 28, 1978; May 7, 1978; May 13, 1979; February 17, 1980; June 21, 1981; June 27, 1983; January 1, 1984; New Yorker May 3, 1969; May 8, 1978; May 14, 1979; Newsweek February 26, 1973; Plays and Players May 1975; Village Voice September 30, 1965; May 15, 1978; May 14, 1979.

WINGFIELD, SHEILA (CLAUDE BEDDINGTON) (May 23, 1906–), British poet and memoirist, was born in Hampshire, the only daughter of Colonel Claude Beddington and the former Frances Ethel Homan-Mulock. She was sent to Roedean, an exclusive girls' school in Brighton, and passed the Cambridge entrance examination at fifteen. Firm opposition from her mother, however, prevented any university education. On December 16, 1932, she married Mervyn Patrick Wingfield, scion of one of Britain's most ancient families. When he became the ninth Viscount Powerscourt, she became mistress of Powerscourt, in County Wicklow, Northern Ireland, one of Europe's largest stately homes, which burned to the ground in 1974, a year after her husband's death. She is the mother of a daughter and two sons, the elder of whom succeeded his father in the title.

W.B. Yeats and Walter de la Mare admired several of her earliest published verses, and the thirty mostly short lyrics collected as *Poems* in 1938 established her control over a subject matter that has developed but not greatly varied since. She has described her most "deeply rooted" interests as "the Irish and English countryside and country ways in general, . . . history, archaeology, folklore, and the superb economy of the classical Greeks." A reviewer for the *Times Literary Supplement* called this first volume "distinguished," remarking further that the poems "have that indefinable quality of style which is more than craftsmanship, because it is the language of imagination, a lyrical magic distilled in the simplest words."

Her second book and according to some her finest achievement, *Beat Drum Beat Heart,* occupies an anomalous place in Wingfield's work. It is really a single long poem welcoming the coming of peace and trying to understand the deepest reasons for and effects of World War II, then just ended. She has described it as "a lengthy psychological-philosophical piece without one philosophical expression and I fancy hardly an abstract noun in it. It attempts to sweeep over whole cultures and peoples and histories—but invariably in terms of known or perhaps only suspected feelings, expressed in a way that makes such feelings recognizable by a great variety of human beings." The poem is in four sections—"Men and War," "Men at Peace," "Women in Love," and "Women at Peace"—and in various meters, from rhymed couplets of different lengths to ballad forms with recurrent refrains. She is good at capturing the men's bravado, but best when evoking the women's weariness:

By our crawling
Spaniel-race;
By deeds that seemed
To us brave
And are nothing but
A stupid smutch;
By all confusion,
Flaws, disaster
On earth; by affection
That plays in the sun,
Dies, droops and is done:
By the stretched tendons
Of the two robbers;
By him who loved
Each incarnate person
More humbly, more fiercely
Than soul since or before;
By the women who stood
Near those nailed planks—
We who spoke low
Under our hoods—
For pity's sake, no more.

Winfgield's later collections include *A Cloud Across the Sun,* which contains many poems about Ireland; *A Kite's Dinner,* a retrospective collection with several new poems included at the end; *The Leaves Darken*; and another retrospective collection, *Her Storms: Selected Poems 1938–1977.* In *Admissions: Poems 1974–1977,* she stands as always on familiar ground, although her irony is more resonant and uncompromising than ever, as in the mordant "One's Due," a nice particularization of eternal torment:

Wife-beaters of course and constant liars,
The delicately mean or wilfully feeble,
People bent on provoking a child's scream
Or its future downfall,
Those sick with envy
And the high boasters,
Merit that burning rubbish-dump
Of stinking corpses, sewage, and offal
In the long ditch running below Jerusalem,
Known as Ge-Hinnom.

I should be there
For a heap of quiet crimes:
Chances of good aborted
When my tongue was too quick
Or my heart too slow,
The lost moment,
Unmeant betrayals from sheer
Inadvertence or stupidity—
Huge or trifling,
These too call for the pit.

G.S. Fraser, in his preface to *Her Storms,* called Wingfield "an objectivist. She is more interested in all the wonderful, sad, and glorious detail of the world around her than in herself."

Wingfield's two volumes of prose memoirs retain the specific, precise, allusive, and careful qualities of her poetry. *Real People* was described by John Betjeman in his introduction as "a new kind of autobiography, a selfless one. It is a series of reminiscenses written with a poet's care for the sound and sense of words and all about other people." She writes about all manner of subjects, including the local postman and constable, the characteristics of tourists, her own and her husband's families, and her great pleasure in travel—there are good, sharp observations of her voyages to America, Africa, and the Near East. The *Times Literary Supplement* reviewer called the book "a quick succession of skillful etchings, and there are times when almost too much acid has bitten into the plate," but then revealed a distinct class bias by a characterization of Wingfield as "that by no means rare phenomenon, the competent sportswoman with a gift for exact observation of scenery. . . . The description of a day's hunting in the shires misses nothing that would satisfy an ardent reader of *Horse and Hound.* . . . There are portraits here of notable eccentrics and grandees, and of country house visits which now appear as stylized and remote as the woven landscapes of a French tapestry."

Sun Too Fast, published under the name Sheila Powerscourt, was written in the aftermath

of the fire that destroyed the great house she had come to love. The book, like its prose predecessor, consists of autobiographical fragments: essays on her friends Dr. Margaret Murray (the folklorist and historian), Lord Brabazon of Tara, and Sir Chester Beatty; a revealing account of several visits to Sissinghurst Castle to visit Vita Sackville-West and Harold Nicolson; evocative pieces on earlier visits to Greece and Crete. As a whole the collection has a somewhat distant, even valetudinarian air about it: the author chose to make it "a rough journal of thirteen months" from September 1953 to September 1954, a time when the "recurrent threads of preoccupation . . . were more forcibly interwoven than in any other comparable stretch of time" and also because that time "turned out to be my last year of health, and imprisonment by illness served to intensify the past."

In recent years Wingfield has made her home in Switzerland.

WORKS: *Poetry*—Poems, 1938; Beat Drum Beat Heart, 1946; A Cloud Across the Sun, 1949; A Kite's Dinner; 1954; The Leaves Darken, 1964; Her Storms, 1977; Admissions, 1977; Collected Poems 1938–1983, 1984. *Memoirs*—Real People, 1952; Sun Too Fast, 1974.

ABOUT: Contemporary Authors 108, 1983; Vinson, J. (ed.) Contemporary Poets, 1980. *Periodicals*—Choice September 1978; Times Literary Supplement December 24, 1938; June 13, 1952; June 2, 1978; July 27, 1984.

*WOIWODE, LARRY (ALFRED) (October 30, 1941–), American novelist and poet, was born in Carrington, North Dakota, near his family's home in Sykeston, a community populated by the descendants of German immigrants. His parents, Everett Carl and Audrey Leone (Johnston) Woiwode, moved the family to Manito, Illinois, when he was ten. He attended the University of Illinois at Champaign-Urbana from 1959 to 1964, took an A.A. degree in rhetoric, and left to become a freelance writer of fiction and poetry.

Woiwode's first novel, *What I'm Going to Do, I Think,* was published in 1969; parts of it appeared earlier in the *New Yorker.* A character study of a tormented graduate student unable to commit himself to his wife and unborn child, it earned Woiwode the immediate attention of critics and was awarded the 1970 William Faulkner Award for the best first novel of the year and the 1970 American Library Association notable book award. Anne Tyler identified him as "a master at portraying life as most of us know it—subtle, complicated, sometimes mystifying,

°wĭ´ wŏod ē

LARRY WOIWODE

seldom dramatic or conclusive. Not once, in chronicling the near-claustrophobic existence of a newly married couple in a wilderness cabin, did he reach for a startling event; yet he held his readers to the end by sheer craftsmanship." Webster Schott agreed that it is "the discipline of art that makes Woiwode's novel work" despite its lack of action, specifically the "rightness of language, unfaltering control of events, characters acting through need and fear, and environment unfolding as naturally as a leafing tree. . . . Yet the command of the novel comes less from literary urgency than from Woiwode's skill at touching primary human weaknesses. . . . He tells us of the self struggling against surrender within another, of dreams of perfection thwarting empathy, of suspicion and jealousy poisoning human relationships." The few critics who were put off by the protagonist's unrelenting egocentrism and Woiwode's heavy use of symbolism nonetheless thought the book an unusually accomplished first novel and praised Woiwode's ability to render the emotional states of his characters through evocative descriptions of the Michigan countryside.

Beyond the Bedroom Wall: A Family Album, Woiwode's second novel and a National Book Award nominee, was almost the antithesis of his first. Ten years in the making—fourteen of its forty-four chapters originally appeared as short stories in the *New Yorker*—it is a massive, infinitely detailed chronicle of ninety years and four generations in the life of a North Dakota family, from the arrival of the German immigrant Otto Neumiller in 1881 to the dispersal of his college-educated great-grandchildren in 1964. The central story concerns the courtship and marriage of Martin Neumiller, Otto's grandson, and the schoolteacher Alpha Jones; the births and childhoods of their five children; and the death of Alpha in her mid-thirties, shortly after the family uproots itself from North Dakota and moves to Illinois.

Although the story proceeds in general chronological order, it is not a conventional narrative, but a montage of reminiscences and documents—diaries, letters, job applications, poems, and descriptions of photographs—through which Woiwode re-creates the totality of the family's life, insofar as it can be grasped at all (and Woiwode is at pains to show his readers how rarely this understanding is attained by the characters themselves). As John Gardner pointed out in his review, the book is at the same time an old-fashioned family saga, faithfully reporting the events that befall a large cast of characters, and a contemporary novel in which "time leaps backward and forward in an original and spectacular yet fully controlled way" and in which the alternating voices of the different characters produce "narration by ventriloquy." "In essence," wrote Michael E. Connaughton in the *Dictionary of Literary Biography,* "it is a series of tightly interwoven situations and soliloquies rendered so vividly and with so palpable a sense of emotional involvement that it suggests autobiography."

Roger Sale was one of many reviewers who took the novel to be a personal journey by Woiwode into his own family's past. "Woiwode's love for the Neumillers and for North Dakota—which is unashamedly a love for his own family and childhood home—is a a matter of memory and reconstruction. He discovered at some point that he began to achieve his own life when his parents and grandparents achieved theirs, and an 'album,' a loosely connected series of pictures and episodes, is his way of honoring not only their achievement but his way of knowing it. . . . In order to imagine or reconstruct or remember this world, he has had to lay aside simple reminiscence, to find a real and vivid use for this nostalgia, and he has done so wonderfully. The moment he comes to himself, as it were, to his own more direct memories, his novelistic hold slackens. His last major effort is Alpha's death, which is, presumably for Woiwode himself but certainly for the novel, the pivot."

Despite the almost universal appreciation of the reviewers for Woiwode's lyricism, tenderness, and sincerity, there were many who felt that the novel's length and form hurt rather than helped his purpose. "What is missing from *Beyond the Bedroom Wall,*" said Robert V. Daniels, "is a unifying, discriminating intelligence that might lend this family album some reflective meaning. . . . Woiwode gives self-indulgent voice to all the torrents of memory. As a result, the significance of the unforgotten is too easily lost in the dishevelling flood of detail, and he is forced to take refuge in the fraudulent certainties of sentimentality." Stephen Koch found that the last third of the novel, after the death of Alpha, "falls victim to every literary device that the first two-thirds escapes—sentimentality, lack of proportion, arbitrariness, tedium." But Jonathan Yardley, replying to such critics, said: "Woiwode's errors are those of ambition and expansiveness rather than caution and timidity. He is not afraid of emotion . . . and he is not afraid to insist that the reader feel it with him; in fact he forces the reader to, in a number of scenes of absolutely withering power." Woiwode told an interviewer that "the book is as closely written as most poetry and any emotion in it is 'paid for,' as the Bible says about sin, by the absolute precision of how it's enacted and the precision of what comes before."

Michael E. Connaughton has described Woiwode's first two novels as "religious and intellectual in the broadest sense, with a recurrent emphasis on the meaning and impact of death and the intricate negotiations between one's psyche and personal moral code and the demands of family and society." These themes were sounded again in *Poppa John,* a short study of an elderly actor who finds that his identity may not be able to survive the on-screen death of the popular character he played for twelve years on a soap opera. Most reviewers found that the novel, though admirable, did not achieve the same power as its predecessors. *Poppa John,* wrote Joyce Carol Oates, "keeps us within the consciousness of one person and forbids, as a consequence of the chill, spare, pitilessly chiseled nature of Mr. Woiwode's prose, any deep emotional involvement with him." Further, she says, at the end of this "troubled, brooding, intransigent meditation upon mortality," Woiwode offers a contrived happy ending in which the actor's wife undertakes, on Christmas Day, to restore him to his lost faith. Other reviewers complained that Woiwode had indulged in didacticism and in a convoluted prose style that was more tedious than lyrical.

Forty-nine of Woiwode's free-verse confessional poems were collected in *Even Tide*; his poetry and prose have been widely anthologized. He was the recipient of a Guggenheim fellowship in 1971–72 and received fiction awards from the Friends of American Letters in 1976 and from the National Institute of Arts and Letters in 1980.

Woiwode married Carole Ann Petersen in 1965; they have two children, Newlyn Smith and Joseph William. They settled in the late 1970s on a farm in southwestern North Dakota.

PRINCIPAL WORKS: *Fiction*—What I'm Going to Do, I Think, 1969; Beyond the Bedroom Wall, 1975; Poppa John, 1982. *Poetry*—Even Tide, 1977.

ABOUT: Contemporary Authors 73–76, 1978; Contemporary Literary Criticism 6, 1976; 10, 1979; Dictionary of Literary Biography 6, 1980; McGill's Literary Annual 1976. *Periodicals*—Christian Century November 12, 1975; February 17, 1982; Nation May 11, 1979; New Leader October 13, 1975; New Republic May 3, 1969; November 29, 1975; December 9, 1981; New York Review of Books July 10, 1969; November 13, 1975; New York Times Book Review May 4, 1969; September 28, 1975; November 15, 1981; Saturday Review September 6, 1975; November 1981; Yale Review Spring 1976.

WOLFF, GEOFFREY (ANSELL) (November 5, 1937–   ), American biographer and novelist, was born in Hollywood, California, the elder son of Arthur Samuels "Duke" Wolff and Rosemary Loftus Wolff. According to Wolff's memoir *The Duke of Deception,* his father was a man of exceptional charm, talent, and taste who spent all his life perfecting an elaborate myth of himself as a Yale-bred Episcopalian gentleman when in fact he was the renegade son of an authoritarian Jewish doctor from Hartford. He made his living as a confidence man, lying his way into a series of engineering jobs with aviation companies and maintaining his household on credit.

Wolff's childhood was a fragmented one, the demoralized family crossing and recrossing the country to escape police and creditors and to find new sources of income. Growing up a "temperamental brat," Wolff eventually graduated from Choate School and enrolled in Princeton University, from which he graduated summa cum laude with a degree in literature in 1960. Disentangling himself from the financial and emotional wreckage of his father (who was by now an amphetamine addict, in and out of prison), he spent the years 1961–62 in Istanbul on a Woodrow Wilson fellowship, teaching at Roberts College and Istanbul University, and 1963–64 at Cambridge University on a Fulbright fellowship, studying with George Steiner. On his return to the United States in 1964 he joined the *Washington Post,* of which he became book review editor. After leaving the *Washington Post,* Wolff was a book reviewer for *Newsweek* (1969–71), *New Times* (1974), and

GEOFFREY WOLFF

Esquire (1979); during 1971–72 he held a Guggenheim fellowship in creative writing, and in 1974–75 he was a senior fellow of the National Endowment for the Humanities. During these years he also taught at Maryland Institute College of Art (1965–69), the Corcoran School of Art (1968–69), Princeton (1970–74), and Middlebury College (1976). Wolff was married in 1965 to Priscilla Porter; they have two sons, Nicholas and Justin.

Wolff's first novel, *Bad Debts,* was heavily autobiographical. His protagonist, Caxton, is a Washington bureaucrat whose life and career are sabotaged by his father, a habitual and professional liar. Sara Blackburn, like several other reviewers, thought the writer "better than his material": "His control is always perfect, but he is a writer of such imagination and skill that one feels he is being confined by his material instead of using it and taking risks." Richard P. Brickner, noting that Wolff "draws upon an extraordinarily rich bank of accurate and imaginative behavior," compared *Bad Debts* for comic bitterness to *Catch-22* and *Portnoy's Complaint,* "even though it ends up failing for lack of emotional thrust." According to the reviewer for the *New Yorker,* "The wonder is that a writer who has such obvious reserves of strength, energy, and special information, and who shows a ready talent for plain farce, should waste himself on the pitiful revelations these meagre lives afford."

In 1974 Wolff published his second novel, *The Sightseers,* about a documentary filmmaker unable to face life except through a camera lens. "Wolff is no dummy, and there are moments of good observation and others where Caleb's de-tachment is truly ghastly," wrote Roger Sale. "But for the most part the book drifts, a short story idea used to fill a whole novel." Michael Mewshaw also detected, "buried in the corpulence of Geoffrey Wolff's second novel, several fine short stories. . . . The best passages of prose, bristling with lean, vivid imagery, lie cheek by flabby jowl with maundering essays on Beauty, Art and Truth. . . . The *yalt,* or oriental palace, where Caleb Sharrow passes a summer, might stand as an example of the structure Wolff aimed for in his book—arabesque, lush, exotic, rambling, infuriating, and fascinating. But what Wolff wound up with was confusion, a house falling apart, because, despite touches of elegance, taste and talent, it was built on a foundation far wider than it was deep."

Black Sun: The Brief Transit and Violent Eclipse of Harry Crosby was a biography of the Boston publisher and would-be poet, the intimate of MacLeish, Hemingway, Hart Crane, and Malcolm Cowley, who worshipped death and the sun and who shot himself and his mistress in a suicide pact when he was thirty-two. John Skow thought the book "a pure, self-indulgent, historical amusement" from which "no lessons are to be drawn." Hugh Kenner derided Wolff's "skill at composing pure newsmagazinese" and his "need to hint at significance" by conjuring "portentousness . . . out of numb fact." But where Kenner saw exaggeration, Paul Fussell saw honesty—"an unstylish refusal to euphemize or sentimentalize Crosby's murderousness." Wolff, he added, "understands his man admirably, sympathizing with him while remaining deeply critical, not just of Harry but of his absurd conception of literature and art as mechanisms of personal rebellion and Making It."

Wolff the book reviewer appears as a character in Wolff the novelist's *Inklings,* which H. C. Veit called "a marvelously funny and acid view of the current New York literary scene, expertly written and knowledgeable." The hero, Jupe, an embittered book critic who yearns to write fiction, is seduced by a groupie named Mouse and kidnapped by a novelist named Mole, who forces Jupe at gunpoint to edit, and then write a critical appreciation of, his monstrous book. According to Thomas LeClair, *Inklings* is "a frame-up, with Wolff as victim and enforcer. His elaborate framing devices, the trap-doors of fictions within fiction, the Shandyian mixture of footnotes and reality, the word play on Mouse, Mole, and the small details of the novel's first pages that reveal characters as Jupe's inventions—they all remind me of the high-wire art of Borges, Nabokov, and Barth where play, risk, and conceptual assault are one. Wolff, though, is just playing. . . . Despite the self-irony, *Inklings* is a smug book in its witty condescension to high art and its satisfaction with its own entertaining facileness."

Fiction and biography came together in *The Duke of Deception,* a memoir of the father whose life had been a complete falsehood but who always demanded absolute honesty and loyalty from his son. Wolff began writing the book in 1970, three months after Duke Wolff's death, as a way of explaining his father to his sons and to himself. The book functions as an extended meditation on the nature of fatherhood—the mysterious and unconscious transmission of self from father to child; it resonates with irony, for the confidence man, who practiced the art of fiction without documentation, is at last smuggled into literature by his son, who is by vocation a fictioneer. "I cannot now shake this conviction," writes Wolff, "that I was trained as his instrument of perpetuation, put here to put him into the record."

The Duke of Deception is, in the opinion of Frank Conroy and other reviewers, Wolff's best book so far. According to Tim O'Brien, "*The Duke of Deception . . .* traces a son's attempt fo find his father, to strip away the camouflage that hides not only Duke Wolff but all fathers. . . . It is straight and tough and unrelenting in its pursuit of truth. It is also, finally, a book of love." John Irving thought it "a book abundant with the complexities and contradictions of family sympathy. Keenly perceptive of family ties and family shame, Geoffrey Wolff has succeeded in being true to his emotionally complicated subject while also being divinely easy to read. . . . *The Duke of Deception* is not only first-rate autobiography, conscientious and intimate; it is a wholly instructive and provocative biography of the father and swindler, Arthur S. Wolff III; and it is as lucid and complicated a story as a good novel."

Wolff, who lives with his family in Warren, Vermont, quit reviewing in 1979 to work on two projects, a biography of Herman Melville and an anthology of American autobiographical literature. "Fiction at its very best is encountered very rarely these days," he told *Publishers Weekly*, "but autobiography at an uncommonly very good level is simply around, in the air."

PRINCIPAL WORKS: *Novels*—Bad Debts, 1969; The Sightseer, 1974; Inklings, 1977. *Biography*—Black Sun: The Brief Transit and Violent Eclipse of Harry Crosby, 1976; The Duke of Deception: Memories of My Father, 1979. *As editor*—The Edward Hoagland Reader, 1979.

ABOUT: Contemporary Authors 29–32, 1978.

Periodicals—Book World November 23, 1969; Harper's September 1976; February 1978; Library Journal February 1, 1978; December 1, 1979; New Republic April 27, 1974; November 6, 1976; March 11, 1978; August 18, 1979; Newsweek September 6, 1976; August 27, 1979; New Yorker November 22, 1969; October 8, 1979; New York Review of Books February 26, 1970; June 27, 1974; New York Times Book Review February 1, 1970; March 3, 1974; August 22, 1976; January 8, 1978; August 12, 1979; People October 1, 1979; Publishers Weekly September 3, 1979; Saturday Review September 29, 1979; Time September 6, 1979; August 13, 1979; Times Literary Supplement July 4, 1980.

WOODS, SARA (SARA HUTTON BOWEN-JUDD) (March 7, 1922–), British-born detective-story writer, was born in the industrial city of Bradford in western Yorkshire, the daughter of Francis Burton Hutton and Sara Roberta Woods Hutton. Her only formal education was at the Roman Catholic Convent of the Sacred Heart in Filey, Yorkshire. After leaving school, just at the beginning of World War II, she found work in London as a clerk, first for a bank and then in a solicitor's office, the latter job being her only firsthand exposure to courtrooms and criminals. She also worked as a pig breeder (1948–54), and as assistant to a company secretary in Gloucester (1954–58). She then emigrated to Canada to take up a position as registrar of St. Mary's University, Halifax, Nova Scotia, where she remained until 1964. She has continued to live in Canada, at present in Niagara-on-the-Lake, Ontario. In April 1946 she married Anthony George Bowen-Judd, an electrical engineer; they have no children.

Woods has published nearly three dozen crime novels since *Bloody Instructions* appeared in 1962. Her books are so remarkably alike in so many respects that at first glance it is difficult to understand her very considerable international appeal. All have Shakespearean titles, carefully identified as to source. All are just over two hundred pages in length. All feature the urbane legal sleuthing and eventual quiet triumph of Antony Maitland, an even-tempered London barrister and Queen's Counsel. The regular supporting characters almost invariably include his pretty, witty, but never sharp-tongued wife, Jenny; his irascible uncle and boss, the eminent barrister Sir Nicholas Harding; his blunt, dim-witted antagonist, Chief Superintendent Briggs of Scotland Yard; and the brusque woman who often pushes him into cases against his better judgment, Vera Langhorne, who eventually becomes Lady Harding. The settings are, again almost invariably, London, the villages of Burton

Cecil and Arkenshaw in Yorkshire, and the "particularly attractive market town" of Chedcombe, whose exact location is unclear although it is a couple of hours from London by train. All the novels begin with the same rather arch disclaimer: "Any work of fiction whose characters were of uniform excellence would rightly be condemned—by that fact if by no other—as being incredibly dull. Therefore no excuse can be considered necessary for the villainy or folly of the people appearing in this book. It seems extremely unlikely that any one of them should resemble a real person, alive or dead. Any such resemblance is completely unintentional and without malice." Finally, there are never any sexually explicit descriptions in Woods' books, and rarely any overt violence.

Re-using characters and settings is by no means rare in the genre of detective fiction, though few novelists, perhaps, have dared to employ quite so many congruities quite so often. That Woods has flourished while doing so is a testimony to her skill at characterization and plot construction and to her unfailingly fluent style. "In the Sara Woods books," wrote Newgate Callendar, "there is nothing highly original about the plotting, which generally follows the orthodoxies of the genre. What is unusual . . . is the style. Sara Woods is something of a combination of Galsworthy and C. P. Snow. Indeed, the quiet, civilized talk and the stiff-upper-lip mannerisms would approach caricatures were it not for Woods' sharp insights into character. Those who must have heavy-breathing action in their crime novels had best avoid the Woods/Maitland series. But those who relish intricate plotting and urbane dialogue will find these books a delight." Although the English countryside and the details of farming are encountered frequently in her work, neither is romanticized. She is most interested in using dialogue as a developer of character, pays great attention to tone of voice, and is able to invest meaning and importance even in idle gossip. The standard Woods scene features a quiet, eventually illuminating conversation in an unremarkable or familiar interior. A reviewer for the *Times Literary Supplement* described her invariable denouement: "Gently, gradually, almost inefficiently, Maitland pulls out threads until the pattern is clear, and justice done. The legal atmosphere is quietly convincing, and, thankfully, domesticity is kept to a minimum."

The following may be included among Woods' most popular novels: *They Love Not Poison* features Antony and Jenny, just starting out in 1947, solving a murder in Yorkshire while contending with elements of witchcraft, black magic, and hidden treasure; *Yet She Must Die* and *Serpent's Tooth* contain lengthy courtroom scenes that resolve rather ordinary domestic murders—Sir Nicholas has his finest hour appearing for the defense in the former novel; in *Done to Death,* Jenny, with Antony's sporadic help, solves a Yorkshire murder, a suicide, and a case of counterfeiting; in *They Stay for Death* (1980), Antony investigates multiple murders in the Restawhile Hotel, Chedcombe—a sinister and expensive private nursing home.

Woods is a member of the Society of Authors and the Crime Writers Association in Britain and of the Authors League of America and Mystery Writers of America. Her books are regularly published in German, Dutch, Italian, and Spanish translations.

PRINCIPAL WORKS: Bloody Instructions, 1962; Malice Domestic, 1962; The Third Encounter, 1963 in (U.K. The Taste of Fears, 1963); Error of the Moon, 1963; Trusted Like the Fox, 1964; This Little Measure, 1964; The Windy Side of the Law, 1965; Though I Know She Lies, 1965; Enter Certain Murderers, 1966; Let's Choose Executors, 1966; And Shame the Devil, 1967; The Case Is Altered, 1967; Past Praying For, 1968; Knives Have Edges, 1968; Tarry and Be Hanged, 1969; An Improbable Fiction, 1970; Serpent's Tooth, 1971; The Knavish Crows, 1971; They Love Not Poison, 1972; Yet She Must Die, 1973; Enter the Corpse, 1973; Done to Death, 1974; A Show of Violence, 1975; My Life Is Done, 1976; The Law's Delay, 1977; A Thief or Two, 1977; Exit Murderer, 1978; This Fatal Writ, 1979; Proceed to Judgment, 1979. They Stay for Death, 1980; Weep for Her, 1980; Cry Guilty, 1981.

ABOUT: Contemporary Authors, revised series 9–12, 1974 and new revision 5, 1982. *Periodicals*—Book World December 29, 1968; Christian Science Monitor December 5, 1968; New York Times Book Review February 11, 1968; December 8, 1968; July 19, 1970; July 29, 1973; March 3, 1974; November 9, 1975; April 24, 1977; January 1, 1978; New Yorker March 4, 1974; Observer July 6, 1975; January 25, 1976; November 25, 1979; Times Literary Supplement December 21, 1967; June 11, 1970; March 16, 1973.

WRIGHT, CHARLES (PENZEL, JR.) (August 25, 1935–), American poet, writes: "I was born on my father's birthday, in Hardin County, Tennessee, in a place called Pickwick Dam. We moved around a good bit during my early years. After the war we moved to Kingsport, Tennessee, where we stayed. It's in the upper wedge of Tennessee, about eight miles from Gate City, Virginia, where the Carter family lived, the great American poet-singers. Their songs have had a big influence on my later poems. In the tenth grade I was sent to a school that had eight students, a place called Sky Valley, outside Hendersonville, North Carolina. I lasted a year

CHARLES WRIGHT

there and my last two years of high school were spent at an Episcopal boarding school, Christ School, in Arden, North Carolina. Both these schools, Sky Valley and Christ School, made profound impressions on me and gave me a lot to write about later, mostly in *Hard Freight* and *Bloodlines*.

"After high school I went to Davidson College, also in North Carolina. This turned out to be four years of amnesia, as much my fault as theirs. Probably more. Then, in 1957, I went into the Army for four years, three of them spent in Italy. After the Army I went to the University of Iowa for two years. . . . All of which boils down to the fact that I grew up in east Tennessee and western North Carolina, a fact which had a lot to do with my poems. Place, of course, has a lot to do with many people's poems. It has almost everything to do with mine. From 1966–83 I lived in a small town in southern California, Laguna Beach. It was a good place for a writer as there was little to do there but write. In the summer of 1983 I moved to Charlottesville, Virginia, where I presently live.

"My biography is pretty much the biography of most middle-class Americans in mid-century. I happened to be in this place or that place while someone else was in another place, but most of us in my generation went through the same experiences. During the 1950s, in our 'coming of age' we were known as the Silent Generation. I discovered poetry when I was sitting under an olive tree, like Ferdinand the bull. Or was that a fig tree? In any case, it was rather late in life, when I was in Italy in the Army, and almost Saul-like in its intensity. I had been a history ma-

jor in college, for reasons I suspect had something to do with my interest in the Civil War, and the doomed lot of my people in that and subsequent situations. As I said, amnesia period.

"I suppose my original impetus for writing came from my mother. I discovered, once, after I had begun to publish a few things, some old stories of hers from her college days and early married life. She always tried to encourage me to write but it didn't take hold until very late, probably because I tend not to have a 'narrative' cast of mind. I seem to work and think synaptically, and exclusively—like Emily Dickinson, say—and not discursively, narratively and inclusively—say like Walt Whitman, as most prose writers do. I continue to be the only Southerner I know who cannot tell a story. I always want to get right to the point and everyone knows that the point of a story is the story, not its end. It wasn't until I was given a book, *The Selected Poems of Ezra Pound,* when I was living in Verona, Italy (to return to my story line), that things started to take a certain shape for me. I was told, in 1958, by a friend, to take the Pound book out to Sirmione, on Lake Garda where the Latin poet, Catullus, supposedly had a villa, and to read it there. It was, and continues to be, one of the most beautiful places I have ever been, or expect to go to. Lake Garda in front of you, the Italian Alps on three sides of you, the ruined and romantic villa around you, and I read a poem, "Blandula, Tenulla, Vagula," that Pound had written about the place, about how Sirmione was more beautiful and desirable than Paradise itself, and my life was changed forever, at the age of twenty-three.

"After the Army I went to the University of Iowa, as I said earlier, at the age of twenty-six, and started to try to learn how to write poems. And I have been at it, trying to learn how, ever since. By design, most of my biography is included in my poems, an attempt at trying to get it right. The two poles in my poems seem to be Italy, especially northern Italy, Verona, and Venice, and my childhood in the American South. I spent a year in 1968-69 in Venice as a Fulbright lecturer, and since then I have written a good bit that seems to me to be influenced by that year. And, in a way, almost everything I've written since that time seems to me to be influenced by the city. There is a connection, a lushness connective, in my mind, between the southern foliage and Venetian leafage, gold leafage, that has stayed with me ever since, and it keeps coming back in my poems, a sumptuousness the city has, like foliage. I believe the city had a lot to do with how, as they say in music, I went up a step. The intensity and texture and line of my poems picked up a step. A lusher and more sculptured energy.

"As for literary influences on my work, there have been two major direct ones, and a third, ghostly presence. Ezra Pound and Eugenio Montale are the first two, Dante Alighieri is the third. Pound was a tremendous influence as he was the first poet I ever read seriously. He had a golden ear, he directed my reading to valuable texts, and his own poems and translations opened areas that have been major mines for me—the T'ang Dynasty poets in China, for instance. Montale taught me a little about Hermeticism, or at least his approach to it, his hard-edge images, an image that Italian poetry hadn't seen since Dante, really. I learned from translating him a little about how to manipulate lines, how to move an image from one stage to the next. How to create imaginary bridges between images and stanzas and then to cross them, making them real, image to image, block to block. And compression from Pound. Condense, compress. 'Rhythm is a form cut into time. . . . ' And Dante broods over us all with his great white wings."

Charles Wright is the son of Charles Penzel Wright and the former Mary Castleman Winter. He took his B.A. from Davidson in 1957, a master of fine arts degree from Iowa in 1963, and did post-graduate work on a Fulbright scholarsip at the University of Rome in 1963–64. In April 1969 he married Holly McIntire; they have a son. He was a member of the English department of the University of California, Irvine, from 1966 to 1983, a professor since 1976. He is now a professor at the University of Virginia. His first collection, *The Grave of the Right Hand,* was admired, especially for what John N. Morris called "the permanent and classic weight" of its title poem. It is the trilogy of *Hard Freight, Bloodlines,* and *China Trace,* however, that has won him a growing reputation as a poet of considerable sensitivity and exactness of expression.

Hard Freight opens with a poem that has become rather famous as an ironic statement of negative capability, "The New Poem":

It will not resemble the sea.
It will not have dirt on its thick hands.
It will not be part of the weather.

It will not reveal its name.
It will not have dreams you can count on.
It will not be photogenic.

It will not attend our sorrow.
It will not console our children
It will not be able to help us.

Also included are a sequence called "Firstborn," a celebration of his son's birth, as well as a number of poems of sharply remembered scenes from a county childhood. Dave Smith praised

the collection highly: "Grim verities, Tennessee rivers, and the past: the past tempers and flavors these forty poems that are tough, spare, and honest. . . . Wright reminds me of Wendell Berry's sly ritualism and Ammons' flint intelligence. These goods are genuine."

With the publication of *Bloodlines,* Wright was felt by the *Choice* reviewer to have emerged as "a major American poet; the promise of his previous work is richly fulfilled." His poems have a warm, assured quality, a sense of the worthiness of what he is saying; he was called by the same critic "a mature poet at ease with his craft." The book includes, along with two sequences of irregular sonnets, two deeply moving elegies, one to his mother and another to his father. Wright's work here was said by Helen Vendler to have "the single indispensable quality needed for poetry—a self-sustaining language, where meaning scarcely matters till the second time round. . . . A poem has an independent life where language and meaning are inseparable, and in his lucky moments, Wright . . . lives in that unstable synthesis."

The final volume of the trilogy, *China Trace,* consists mainly of shorter pieces. It was called by Joseph Garrison "Wright's best and most accessible book to date," with the poems "full of the strengths of compression." A key to the mood of the collection is found in the epigraph, from the Ming dynasty poet T'u Lung: "I would like to house my spirit within my body, to nourish my virtue by mildness, and to travel in ether by becoming a void. But I cannot do it yet. . . . And so, being unable to find peace within myself, I made use of the external surroundings to calm my spirit, and being unable to find delight within my heart, I borrowed a landscape to please it." This sense of emotional minimalism is present again and again in the poems of this volume, as in the opening to "April":

The plum tree breaks out in bees.
A gull is locked like a ghost in the blue
     attic of heaven.
The wind goes nattering on,
Gossipy, ill at ease, in the damp rooms
     it will air.
I count off the grace and stays
My life has come to, and know I want less— . . .

The assured, professional quality of Wright's work, especially in this collection, nettled a few critics such as David Bromwich, who called the local texture "*echt*-1970s" (an odd complaint, considering the book appeared in 1977), and thought the poet "would be more intriguing if he found it not so fine a thing to relax into each inexpensive but portentous phrase as it rose to his mind and fell from his pen." Yet the *Choice* reviewer wrote that *China Trace* was proof that

Wright "should be counted among those in the absolute top flight of current American poets." And David Kalstone, reviewing Wright's 1984 collection, *The Other Side of the River,* observed: "He is one of our best middle-generation poets, writing at the peak of his form."

Among Wright's other books are the melange of criticism, interviews, and obiter dicta contained in *Wright: A Profile* and a new collection of verse, *The Southern Cross.* He won the PEN translation prize for his complete version of the difficult collection by Eugenio Montale, *The Storm and Other Poems* (1979).

WORKS: *Poetry*—The Grave of the Right Hand, 1970; Hard Freight, 1973; Bloodlines, 1975; China Trace, 1977; The Southern Cross, 1981; The Other Side of the River, 1984. *Translation*—The Storm and Other Poems by Eugenio Montale, 1979.

ABOUT: Contemporary Authors 29-32, 1978; Contemporary Literary Criticism 6, 1976 and 13, 1980; Vendler, H. Part of Nature, Part of Us, 1980; Who's Who in America, 1982-83. *Periodicals*—Choice April 1974; September 1975; March 1978; Hudson Review Spring 1974; Autumn 1975; Library Journal February 1, 1974; February 15, 1975; August 1977; New Republic November 24, 1973; New York Times Book Review February 17, 1974; September 7, 1975; January 1, 1978; July 1, 1984; Poetry December 1974; December 1978; Times Literary Supplement March 29, 1974; Yale Review Autumn 1975.

WRIGHT, RICHARD B(RUCE) (March 4, 1937–), Canadian novelist, was born in Midland, Ontario, the son of Laverne Wright and the former Laura Willette Thomas. After graduating from the Ryerson Polytechnic Institute in 1959, he took a job as a copywriter for radio station CFOR in Orilla, Ontario, then worked from 1960 to 1968 as an editor and sales manager for the Macmillan Publishing Company of Canada, based in Toronto. During this period he wrote his first book, a juvenile, *Andrew Tolliver.* Wright left his job to enter Trent University, a small institution in Peterborough, Ontario, from which he took his bachelor's degree in 1972, by which time he had published one well-received novel and had nearly completed a second. Since 1975 he has taught English and served as head of the department at Ridley College, St. Catharines, Ontario, a town very near Niagara Falls. He married Phyllis Mary Cotton, a librarian, in September 1966; they have two sons.

Wes Wakeham, the protagonist of *The Weekend Man,* Wright's first novel, is a profoundly alienated textbook salesman who, the weekend before Christmas, being temporarily estranged from his wife, undergoes a series of quite modest adventures before returning home. The operation of irony in the first-person narrative is exceptionally interesting: it is Wes' shield and weapon, but it ultimately works to undo him, in his own eyes as well as in the reader's. J. R. Frakes called the book "a tight, sour distillation of *nada,* . . . accomplished enough to put . . . Wright on the brink of anguished prominence. The brew is harsh, but the kick is honest." To L. J. Davis, *The Weekend Man* was "a brilliant first effort, a breathtaking stylistic tightrope act, . . . a haunting book, and very nearly a perfect one."

In the Middle of a Life is the third-person account of the failing life of Fred Landon, aged forty-two, an absolutely colorless salesman with an observant intelligence and the same predisposition to flat, revealing irony possessed by the hero of Wright's first novel. The two books were often compared by critics. Richard P. Brickner wrote that he was not "prepared . . . for the literalness of Wright's repetition." The author's evident fascination with the meaninglessness of his heroes' lives suggests to Brickner that "salesmanship must be for him a clamorous metaphor—man as salesman: if successful, a suffering fraud; if a failure, left behind." Walter Clemons thought the novel had "an added depth of feeling" over its predecessor and praised Wright's "gift of making ordinariness enthralling . . . [and] the even rarer ability to arouse affection for his characters."

Wright ventured beyond the bounds of contemporary middle-class anxiety in his third novel, *Farthing's Fortunes,* even though the passive purposelessness of its protagonist's life is a strong echo of his previous work. Billy Farthing, a ninety-five-year-old man in an Ontario nursing home, tells the story of his wanderings across the North American continent, from his birth in Ontario in 1880 to his final adventure in Florida in 1946. A fictive "publisher" supplies an afterword summarizing the last three decades of Farthing's life. The reviewer for *Choice* thought that Wright, in dwelling on the picaresque randomness of that life, and in other ways, "suggests that Farthing's lack of initiative is typically Canadian." Douglas Hill commented that all the book's adventures, places, characters, and circumstances amount only to "stories and surfaces. . . . There is at best only a negative and undefined sense of a personality—a human spirit—at the book's core. . . . Wright will not allow [Farthing] to open up to the implications of his narrative."

Charlie Farris, the hero of *Final Things,* is a failed novelist, a failed husband (he often sees his second wife, now happily remarried), and an alcoholic. His quiet son, on a weekly visit to his house, is horribly murdered, and Farris is tipped off about the identity of his killers. "Throughout the book," wrote David Profumo, "the focus is upon the inadequacies and pressures which undermine Farris as this personal disaster crushes his weary attempts to reorganize his life." He becomes even more ineffectual than before as he gradually comes to understand the killers' world, populated by human beings more evil than any he has ever known. The novel's low-keyed irony, terse observations, and utterly convincing dialogue make the reader deeply aware of Farris' vulnerability, and its conclusion is inevitable but wrenching, as he first kills his son's killers, then dies himself. "The fact to be celebrated here," wrote I. M. Owen in a general encomium of the book, "without reservation, is that Richard Wright has now completely mastered the art of telling a story. In addition, his narrative pose is faultless."

Wright, who considers himself conservative in politics and Anglican in religion, has been thrice a Canada Council fellow and twice a fellow of the Ontario Arts Council. He also won the Faber & Faber book award in 1975.

PRINCIPAL WORKS: *Fiction*—The Weekend Man, 1971; In the Middle of a Life, 1973; Farthing's Fortunes, 1976; Final Things, 1980. *Juvenile*—Andrew Tolliver, 1965.

ABOUT: Contemporary Authors 85–88, 1980; Contemporary Literary Criticism 6, 1976; Oxford Companion to Canadian Literature, 1983; Who's Who in America, 1983–84. *Periodicals*—Atlantic December 1973; Best Sellers May 15, 1971; March 1977; Book World June 6, 1971; Books in Canada November 1980; Canadian Forum December 1976–January 1977; Canadian Literature September 1981; Choice December 1973; April 1977; Library Journal April 1, 1971; September 15, 1973; September 15, 1976; November 1, 1980; New Republic May 29, 1971; New York Times Book Review September 23, 1973; January 2, 1977; December 14, 1980; New Yorker June 12, 1971; Newsweek October 1, 1973; Quill & Quire December 1980; Saturday Review July 3, 1971; Times Literary Supplement April 2, 1971; February 15, 1974; November 13, 1981.

*XIAO HONG (also rendered as **Hsiao Hung**) (1911–January 22, 1942), Chinese novelist, short story writer, and poet, was born Chang Nai Ying to a landlord family in Hulan county near Harbin city. Xiao Hong spent an unhappy childhood under a domineering father who, she later recalled in a memoir, "buried his humanity in greed. In his treatment of the servants, of us children and even of our grandfather, he was equally cruel and distant."

In 1926 she enrolled in a famous girls' school of Harbin, which opened up a totally new world to her. Here Xiao Hong came into contact with new writers and new ideas. She read avidly the works of Lu Xun, Xie Bingxin, and translations of Upton Sinclair as well as Russian and Soviet writers. In 1928 she became involved in the student movement against the growing Japanese aggression. From an unhappy, moody little girl, Xiao Hong grew into a youthful seeker of freedom and democracy. Her father arranged a marriage for her in the hope of checking her ways, but this only precipitated the final break. Penniless, she left Harbin for Beijing (Peking), where her intended husband followed. She finally agreed to live with him in order to get support for further studies, but two years later, in 1932, when the couple had moved back to Harbin, he left her, penniless and pregnant, in a hotel, unable to pay the bills. Xiao Jun, a young writer then working for a local paper, sneaked her out of the hotel when the city was threatened by flood; thus began Xiao Hong's bohemian life with Xiao Jun. Both were radical youths, fired with patriotic zeal and dedicated to writing. They both started to publish in the local papers and brought out a joint collection of short stories, *Bashe* (The Long Journey) in 1933. In 1934 they left Harbin, then part of Manchukuo (Manchuria), the puppet kingdom set up by the Japanese, for Qingdao, the seaside city of Shandong, where they wrote some of their best works, and finally landed in Shanghai, where they were under the patronage of the distinguished and influential writer Lu Xun. It was with his personal help that Xiao Hong's major work *Shengsi Chang* (*The Field of Life and Death,* 1935) along with Xiao Jun's *Bayue Di Xiang Cun* (1934, translated in 1974 as *Village in August*), was published. It was an instant success, and Xiao Hong found herself a celebrity overnight. Following the success of her first book, Xiao Hong wrote intensively during the years 1935–36. The works of this period, mostly short stories and essays, were later collected in *Shangshi Jie* (Market Street), *Qiao* (Bridge), and *Niuche Shang* (On the Ox Cart).

When war broke out in Shanghai, Xiao Hong moved with other progressive literary figures to Wuhan, after a brief stay in Tokyo, then to Shanxi, and eventually settled in Chongqing. During all these peregrinations she took an active part in leftist literary circles, especially in collaborating with Hu Feng to publish a leftist journal *Qi-yne* (July). In Chongqing she published her remembrance of Lu Xun (*Huiyi Lu Xun Xiansheng,* 1940), and short stories of the war against Japanese aggression, later collected in *Kuangye Li Di Hukan* (The Call of the Wilderness). In 1940, having broken with Xiao Jun,

°shou hŏong

she left for Hong Kong in the company of another leftist writer, Duanmu Hongliang. Here, in spite of ill health, she continued writing. Her *Minzu Hun* (Soul of a Nation), a pantomime in commemoration of Lu Xun, was greatly acclaimed. Also in Hong Kong she wrote her major work, *Hulan He Chuan* (*Tales of Hulan River*). She entrusted Agnes Smedley, en route to the United States, with a copy of *The Field of Life and Death* for Upton Sinclair, who responded by sending her a warm letter and a copy of his novel *Co-op*. In 1942 Xiao Hong published her "Letters to My Countrymen from the Northeast," urging them to "carry on the struggle with a cool head and persist until the very last." She died that same year, only thirty-one years old, her brain teeming with plans for writing and her desk littered with manuscripts, with less than a decade of writing behind her.

During the 1930s, after the Japanese occupation of northeast China, a group of writers emerged, later called "the Northeast group"; of them, Xiao Hong was undisputably the most talented. Her first important work, *The Field of Life and Death,* conjures up a picture of primitive village life during the thirties in northeast China, where people are perpetually engaged in the business of living and dying, benumbed by the grinding life, until they are finally roused to revolt by the bloody invasion of the Japanese. Lu Xun, in his preface to the first edition, wrote that in this work, "the fierce struggle for life against death of the Northern people seems to start out from the pages. Here feminine sensitivity and extraordinary portraiture add to the beauty and novelty of theme." Appearing at the outset of the war against Japanese aggression, *The Field of Life and Death* played an important part in rousing national consciousness, and the book is an acknowledged masterpiece of modern Chinese fiction.

Howard Goldblatt writes that Xiao Hong's *Tales of Hulan River,* published posthumously in 1942, "is generally acclaimed her masterpiece. It is a moving and highly artistic reminiscence of the author's Manchurian home. Thus, only after the national wartime emotions had cooled did this novel begin to enjoy the acclaim and popularity it rightly deserves." The tales conjure up scenes from her little hometown in Hulan county seen through a mist of nostalgic memories. The curse of the feudal heritage is starkly brought out, mirrored against the revolt it engendered, while the author reveals throughout her deep pity and understanding for a people doomed to a life of ignorance and sprititual poverty. The work is not a novel in the ordinary sense, having no tight plot or single protagonist, but as Mao Dun writes in his preface to the 1947

edition: "The point is not that *Tales of Hulan River* is not a novel in the strict sense of the word; the point is that it has other qualities which are more important than the regular elements of the novel, more captivating. It is a narrative poem, a colorful scenery, a series of plaintive ballads."

In her short story "Shou" (Hands), she writes of a disadvantaged girl growing up in an old-style family, deprived of everything she yearns for—knowledge, love, freedom. She dies in silent misery. "Hands" echoes much of the author's own inner experience and is artistically the best executed of her stories. Besides her stories and essays, Xiao Hong also wrote a number of poems, which she collected but were not published until 1980. Of these poems, one commemorates a comrade killed by the Japanese, while others reveal her mental anguish during the break-up of her love affair with Xiao Jun. Of late, Xiao Hong has been much studied both in China and abroad. Especially interesting today are her sympathetic portraits of women victimized as much by the men in their lives as by a repressive society. As Goldblatt observes, her ardent feminism is not surprising, "since on a personal level she was a constant victim of male arrogance and mistreatment and of a social system in which men viewed women as playthings, alter egos, supporters, servants—everything but equals."

WORKS IN ENGLISH TRANSLATION: *The Field of Life and Death,* translated by Howard Goldblatt and Ellen Yeung, and *Tales of Hulan River,* translated by Goldblatt, were published in one volume in 1979. Two of Xiao Hong's short stories, "Hands" and "Family Outsider," are included in C. T. Hsia's *Anthology of Modern Chinese Short Stories and Novels,* 1980, and others are in periodicals—*Asia Magazine* September 1941, and *Chinese Literature* 8, August 1959 ("Hands"), and August 1961 ("Spring in a Small Town"), and in the new series 2, February 1963 ("Harelip Feng," a chapter from *Tales of Hulan River*). A bibliography of her works in Chinese is included in Goldblatt's *Hsiao Hung* listed below.

ABOUT: Chen, C. Biographical and Bibliographical Dictionary of Chinese Authors, 1971; Goldblatt, H. Hsiao Hung, 1976; Smedley, A. Battle Hymn of China, 1943; Snow, E. Living China, 1936; Yang, W. L. Y. and N.K. Mao, Modern Chinese Fiction, 1981. *Periodicals*—New York Review of Books April 17, 1980.

*YACINE, KATEB (August 26, 1929–   ), Algerian novelist, playwright, and poet, was born in Condé-Smendou, near Constantine, Algeria, into an ancient, highly literate family, the son of

Kateb Mohamed and Kateb Jasmina (the name "Kateb" means "writer" in Arabic). His studies at the Collège de Sétif were interrupted by his arrest, at the age of sixteen, following a demonstration on May 8, 1945, and by his subsequent imprisonment without trial. He was freed a few months later.

Yacine published his first book, a short collection of poems, *Soliloques* (1946), when he was only seventeen. The first of several trips to France occurred in 1947, when he stayed nine months. During the course of his second stay there, the following year, a long poem, "Nedjma; ou, le poème ou le couteau" (Nedjma; Or, The Poem or the Knife) appeared in *Le Mercure de France*. This was his first use of the character of Nedjma (a name meaning "star" in Arabic), a mysterious spirit-woman who reappears in much of his subsequent work and comes to symbolize revolutionary Algeria.

From 1949 to 1951, Yacine worked as a journalist, principally for *Alger Républicain*, and travelled through Saudi Arabia, Sudan, and Soviet Central Asia. He broke with journalism in 1951, became for a time a dockworker in Algiers, then worked at several jobs in Paris. In 1952 he was at last enabled to write full time.

Nedjma (1956), a novel at once realistic and symbolic, captured the spirit of the Algerian national struggle for identity. It is one of the finest works in French to come out of North Africa, and has since acquired the status of national revolutionary novel. Its simple story, set in Bône, Algeria, concerns the obsessive love shared by four friends for Nedjma, a married woman of great beauty and uncertain past, a character both central and evanescent, inaccessible. The more they discover about her, the less they really know. The novel follows each of the men, who are all ardent revolutionaries, through many and yet illuminating adventures, with the ideal vision of Nedjma pervading all their stories. Critical attention, particularly in France, concentrated on the novel's unusual structure. Maurice Nadeau likened it to a "stellar universe. In its center [Yacine] has put a sun, Nedjma, around whom gravitate a number of large and small stars, themselves endowed with satellites. . . . Because all these stars are prisoners of the same movement which, at fixed intervals, brings each of them into the novel, there ensues a kind of 'eternal return,' a complete conclusion of past, present, and future. The story begins at a certain moment, develops, stops, begins again at the same point, takes another direction that it follows for a time before returning to its starting point, and so on. . . . Except for Nedjma, who is happy simply to be and who never

changes, . . . the other characters pass through all the ages of life, sometimes young, sometimes old, sometimes adults, sometimes children." American reviewers, in the main, found the book difficult yet passionate and compelling. In Robert Phelps' words, "Yacine writes in a swift, elliptic manner which is often extraordinarily vivid. Moving in a sort of sporadic, backward spiral, he touches on an exceptionally dense maze of events, but leaves sequence to establish itself; and his narrative devices seem wholly arbitrary. Some novels have to risk a complex technique. I doubt if *Nedjma* did."

Yacine's other major prose work, *Le polygone étoilé* (The Starry Polygon, 1966), exhibits a similarly oblique structure. Ostensibly the long monologue of a wandering writer, the book introduces several of the characters from *Nedjma,* including the heroine herself. The author has claimed an essential unity for all his work, including *Polygone*: everything he had done constitutes "a long, single work, always in gestation."

Of Yacine's dramatic works, only the first possesses the symbolic resonance of his major prose works. *Le cercle des représailles* (Circle of Reprisals, 1959) consists of four short plays—*Le cadavre encerclé, La poudre d'intelligence, Les ancêtres redoublent en férocité*, and *Le vautour* (The Encircled Corpse, Intelligence Powder, The Ancestors Redouble in Ferocity, The Vulture). Nedjma and many of her satellites appear again in identical roles, representing the same ideas—the Algerian sense of identity, the importance of the desert and of kinship ties in forging a new national life. The plays were successfully performed in Paris.

Yacine's subsequent French-language dramatic works are thematically centered on the Vietnam war. *L'homme aux sandales de caoutchouc* (The Man in Rubber Sandals, 1970) is a series of vignettes of Vietnamese and Algerian history, in which small roles are allotted to such historical characters as Mao Zedong, Chiang Kai-shek, Pierre Loti, and Marie-Antoinette, and there is an obtuse American Everyman called Captain Supermac, whose war-crimes trial occupies the last third of the play. The revolutionary conflicts of other regions are also introduced: the guerrillas of South America, the racial struggle in America, and the Arab-Israeli conflict are likened to the experiences of the Algerians and the Vietnamese. To the author, revolutionary Vietnam represented "my country as I wish her to be—I saw her born on Vietnamese soil. Algeria projected into the future. Colonial peoples, if they wish to overcome their immense historical retardation, must take the road of socialism." In another interview at about the same time, he said, "The revolutionary writer's role is to realize the struggles that envelop the entire world. He must transmit a living message, placing the public at the heart of a theater that partakes of the neverending combat opposing the proletariat to the bourgeoisie. That is the great confrontation of our time."

In a later short play, *Mohamed, prends ta valise* (Mohamed, Take Your Suitcase, ca. 1973), Yacine intended a specific cultural message. He remarked at the time, "In this play I wanted to show, and I think that the immigrant workers understood it, the class complicity that exists between the French bourgeoisie and the Algerian bourgeoisie at present in power. The immigration accords between Algeria and France have been signed on these workers' backs."

Yacine has lived exclusively in Algeria since the early 1970s. His current writing, mainly for the theater, is more overtly political than ever, and, most important of all, is in Arabic. His aim has been to accomplish "what I have always wanted o do, a *political theater* in *popular language*. . . . I shall continue to write in French, but it will no longer be the essential part of my work." The strength of the people has continued to be his mainstay. "The people for me," he remarked in 1972, "are not an abstract entity, sacred or mythic. I do not profess the People as a religion—that would be only another mystification. . . . The people are above all men of flesh and blood plunged into a particular situation, with their problems, certainties, doubts, ignorance, and contradictions—men who hate, dream, fear, err, and struggle."

PRINCIPAL WORKS IN ENGLISH TRANSLATION: *Nedjma* was translated by Richard Howard in 1961.

ABOUT: Le Sage, L. The French New Novel, 1962; Sarter, P. Kolonialismus im Roman, 1977; Dictionary of Oriental Literature 3, 1974; Encyclopedia of World Literature in the 20th Century (rev. ed.) 2; Contemporary Authors, revised series 11–12, 1974. *Periodicals*—Library Journal March 15, 1961; New York Herald Tribune Lively Arts February 26, 1961; New York Times Book Review February 26, 1961; Saturday Review May 13, 1961; Yale French Studies Summer 1959.

*YEHOSHUA, A(VRAHAM) B(EN) (December 9, 1936–   ), Israeli essayist, dramatist, short-story writer, and novelist, writes in 1983 (in Hebrew): "Some writers are bound to their own biography. And in fact, all of their writing is intended to report on their own lives, which they see as a story in which every detail is signifi-

A. B. YEHOSHUA

cant. Perhaps through their writing they want to understand and relive their lives. This is an endless effort, living for the sake of writing. Any imaginary plot seems artificial to them compared with the authenticity of their own lives. In contrast to them, other writers seem constantly to be running away from their biography, their own life courses, family and friends not seeming worthy for the writer's anvil; instead, they write to express a different and imaginary biography.

"Until a year or so ago, I considered myself a writer belonging clearly to the second type. I had no interest in my own biography, did not see the events surrounding my family a subject worthy of being elevated by writing. True, once in a while I would snatch some actual occurrence, some element about a relative and weave it into the imaginary cloth of my stories. I never had to preface my book with the statement—'any resemblance between my characters and living people is entirely accidental,' because I felt myself completely protected by my imagination. However, only a year or two ago, I began feeling a mild pull toward my own biography, and only a few months ago I completed an autobiographical play containing large portions from real episodes drawn from my life of the previous year. Am I indeed changing directions? or am I aging? or perhaps my father's death a year ago incited me to a different course.

"I was born in Jerusalem. My father, Ja'acov Yehoshua, also born in the old city of Jerusalem, belonged on his mother's side to a Sephardic family already four generations in Jerusalem. His father, who arrived as a baby from the city of Saloniki, was a rabbi and chief judge on the

Sephardic court. I still remember encountering him on the streets of Jerusalem, dressed in a black caftan and turban, while I wore my youth movement khaki uniform. We both grew up in the same city, living only a few hundred meters apart, yet in those days, several light-years separated us. My mother Malka, of the Rosili family, was a 'new immigrant.' She was born in Mogador, a small town in Morocco on the Atlantic ocean. Her father Avraham was an important rich man who, after the death of his beloved wife, decided in 1932 to come to Palestine with his three youngest children, leaving behind him his eight older children, his business, and all his property. His was not a Zionist ideological immigration but a result of religious longings and a response to a certain personal emptiness born of bereavement. The younger son returned to Morocco, but the two other daughters married two Sephardic youths from the older settlement; one of them was my father.

"My grandfather did not live much longer. He died in 1936 and I was named after him. Though both my parents belonged to the oriental Jewish community and, formally, both were considered orientals, they really were of two separate worlds. The community from which my father came could, speaking romantically, be referred to as a 'decadent aristocracy.' It was no longer at the center of events in Israel, although it had existed there for over a hundred years, but remained marginal to the Eastern European thrusts of the new Zionism. My mother seemed like an odd bird, a first sparrow from an enormous flock of Moroccan Jews which would flood the State of Israel in several great waves in the early fifties. In the thirties my mother felt herself uprooted from her family and world due to the capricious act of her father. After her marriage, however, she came to terms with the idea of remaining in Israel and directed her children toward the Ashkenazic Zionist community.

"I was raised and educated in the British mandated Jerusalem of the 1940s, a period which, beginning with World War II, was one of economic security and peace, but at the same time filled with terrible anxiety for the fate of millions of Jews trapped in Nazi Europe. I spent the War of Independence, the greatest hour of the State of Israel, as a child of twelve, playing with my toy pistols in a shelter in besieged Jerusalem, deeply worried about my father who would run between shellings to the secret listening center of the Underground. (He was an expert in Middle Eastern studies and the Arab language.) This heroic and glorious period in my life is but hinted at in my writings. As a student at the Gymnasium I was enthusiatic about history and politics and considered becoming a lawyer. Literature

was not my first, but only my second or third choice, and my compositions were mediocre and gray. I began to have writer's itch only when I started to compose for the social parties of the class, the school, and the Scouts. For these occasions I wrote several kinds of feuilletons and humoristic sketches into which I mixed various strange and surrealistic elements such as a conversation between the classroom chairs, a fight between the door and the garbage-can, or the story of a bag, etc. These sketches I would read out loud to my friends for whatever feedback I could get—silence, attentive listening, laughter, shock, or murmur due to loss of interest. Thus, in the beginning, I experienced directly detailed interaction between author and audience.

"In my senior year I became more seriously involved with literature thanks to an excellent teacher of literature, despite his greater interest in ideology than in aesthetic forms. I began reading poetry, kept poetry books in my knapsack during the military training, and started to warm my literary rifle with poetic phrases, writing only for myself. Poetry seemed more suitable for the service in the parachutists unit than prose. My first story *Mot Ha-za-ken* (Death of the Old Man) appeared in one of the literary supplements in 1957. It is written in the first person, and it tells about a very old man with extraordinary vitality, living in a large apartment house where the narrator is staying. One strong-willed old lady, also living in that house, decides that it is time for the old man to die, and since he does not show any sign that he is ready to do so, she decides to perform a funeral and bury him alive. The story focuses on the process by which all the tenants help the old lady in her act. This story, written in the style of [S.Y.] Agnon, was received appreciatively, and I realized that my fantastic stories had an appeal beyond my classroom and military unit.

"In those same years, the late fifties, a new generation in Hebrew literature came into its own, distinguished by an abandonment of the collectivist ideological sentiment of the previous generation, the writers and poets of the War of Independence. A total change of topics and choice of characters took place. The new hero was a marginal, perverted and somewhat estranged character; time and place became completely blurred. An escape from ideology and search situations gave it a surrealist atmosphere sundering realism. In a certain sense I was the most extreme example of this literary genre. In 1962 I published my first volume of stories.

"In 1963 I went with my wife Rivka to Paris. She wanted to continue her studies for a doctorate in clinical psychology. (I already had a B.A.

in literature and philosophy and felt I did not need more theoretical studies but instead should concentrate all my energy on creating literature.) The four years we spent in Paris were the richest and most wonderful of our lives. We were young Israelis entering deeply into European culture, falling in love with it emotionally and intellectually and greedily swallowing the history and the beauty which is on every corner. We began to understand what a continuous culture and a live tradition was, existing not only in books but in all aspects of life, the wonderful meeting between the matter and the spirit. What added to our elation was our sense of freedom, freedom from family and from Israel. (Israel of the 1960s was quiet; it did not daily appear on the news, no territories, no war, a normal Israel.) We were tourist-residents, indulging in the wonder around us without having to be responsible for it. But it was precisely in Paris that I began writing about Israel, coming back to its reality (I served as general secretary of the World Federation of Jewish students). I began mentioning places by their names and identifying Israelis with their particular mentality. The distance seemed to help me accept Israeli reality and realism. The stories became longer, still containing fantastic, grotesque, absurd, and surrealistic elements, but these became much milder, mixed with psychological reality. These gave birth to my second collection of stories *Mul Ha-Ye-a-rot* (Facing the Forests, 1968). The story by this name tells of a thirty-year-old student who does not succeed in finishing his master's thesis, and in order to do so is sent by his friends to become a watchman in a remote forest. It is obvious that he will not succeed in completing his work, but instead he joins in with his Arab helper to burn the forest in order to uncover the ruins of an Arab village buried underneath it.

"In all these stories Israeli places appear, but time is not yet defined in terms of its historical setting. Time re-entered in a brutal way with the outburst of the Six-Day War. We were then still in Paris, packing our suitcases in preparation for our return home. The war passed by us in weeks of terrified waiting, followed by a fantastic and dramatic turn of events. We suddenly realized how dear Israel was to us, how it is the most important part of our identity. Beautiful Paris became intolerable to us during the war; the center of our lives was again in the East. We returned to our home and to history. We then discovered that the danger existed not only in the external threat, but that it was also inside Israel itself, in the way Jews grasped themselves, in the reawakened mythological concepts, and in a new religious mysticism. Out of the past a dangerous lava streamed forth, sweeping over our small

modern Israel. From there on a new period started. The ideological and political reality imposed itself within literary creation. After I had published my second volume of stories I turned to a new genre, the drama. It was a good way for me to get out of my detached stand of storyteller, who sees the world only through his own experiences. The breakthrough to other characters was easier for me in drama. The play *Leila be mai* (A Night in May) was written in 1968, describing a family amidst a neurotic turmoil during May 1967, when the Straits of Tiran closed up and the escalation toward the Six-Day War began. It represented the transformation of family drama into national drama. The play was soon produced and enjoyed great success. Suddenly I saw myself not only a popular writer, beyond literary circles, but also a politically involved author. After that I found myself wandering between novels and playwriting. My stories became longer, turning into long novellas; and my characters, who actually were the same as those in the stories prior to the Six-Day War, began now facing not only place but time as well—the stormy history of the world between the two wars. I did not dare as yet approach the novel. I did not feel that I understood sufficiently the reality around me to write a real novel.

"The Yom Kippur War, which shook us all, brought about that reversal in me. This feeling we all shared, regardless of political affiliation, wishing to be more involved in reality in order to try to change it, brought me, at age forty, to write my first novel. The technique I employed for it, of monologues exchanged among several characters, was Faulkner's. The classical style of the novel did not suit me. I did not think I could become an omniscient author leading his characters in a complex plot, judging them and speaking on their behalf. I tried to uncover the Israeli reality and understand it through the eyes of six characters without definitely placing myself behind any one of them. I felt that the Israeli reality can be interpreted so differently by each character that one is not able to speak of a unified reality. In Israel, the gap in the interpretation of reality is much greater than in other countries, and it is deeper than psychological, political, and age differences. *Ha-me-a-hev* (*The Lover*) was published in 1977, became a best-seller, and was translated into many languages. The sensitive critics justly felt that one cannot call it a novel but a mixed breed between the short story and the novel. It tells the story of an Israeli family, a husband who brings his wife a lover, an Israeli who had been living as an expatriate in Paris and returned to Israel to collect an inheritance. The lover disappears in the Yom Kippur War. The novel concerns itself with the search after this lover until it becomes known that he defected from the front, masquerading as a religious Chassid, and has escaped into the ultra-Orthodox community in Jerusalem. The husband succeeds in finding him there and pulling him back into the Israeli reality. For history never stops for a moment in spite of the fact that the Jews try to escape it from time to time. In Israel the famous political reversal took place; government passed into the hands of the extreme political right. For my friends and myself the labor movement seemed, in recent years, to be sufficiently right wing; suddenly we found ourselves flanked by the right itself, and the labor movement, which we attacked, became the opposition. The ideological struggle in Israel became more intense. As an active member in this struggle I felt the necessity to lay down my literary pen and write an ideological book (not a political one), in order to redefine Zionism, the problem of Golah and its essence, the moral questions concerning the Arab-Israeli conflict, and basic definitions of Judaism. That's how my book *Biz-chut Ha-ro-ma-li-yut* (*Between Right and Right*, 1981) appeared.

"In the 1980s I again immersed myself in a novel. *Gei-ru-shim Me-u-cha-rim* (*A Late Divorce*, 1982) is not a political book nor is it connected to a concrete time overtly, but in its covert meaning there are several ideological themes. It still is not a novel in its classical form, and I kept the technique of monologues, but instead of several short monologues among the characters I used nine consecutive monologues for the nine characters in the story. Each monologue is long, describing one day in the life of a family, whose head—the grandfather in his sixties—returns from the United States (where he had lived for several years) to terminate his separation from his wife, now in a psychiatric hospital, and obtain a final divorce. Even though this novel devotes itself to a detailed and epic description of Israel's reality, its structure is still midway between the story and the novel. It seems to me that my literary career can be defined as: 'on the road to the novel.'"

—trans. R. Beizer-Bohrer

* * *

Yehoshua's life, like that of many Israeli writers, combines intellectual creativity with political activism. After serving in the army and graduating from the Hebrew University, Yehoshua, a leading dove, became a professor of Hebrew literature at Haifa University. In his fiction he is acutely aware of political issues, depicting an Israel straining under the pressure of war and political conflict, or enjoying an uneasy peace. Yet his deepest imaginary concerns lie elsewhere, in the delicate shifting tensions of the political surface, and what Robert Alter calls "an elemental depth, which is the principal source of his fiction's piquancy, its hallucinatory intensity, and its elusive, haunting appeal." These qualities result from Yehoshua's probing into the individual's inner psychological world, which constitutes the center of all his stories. Irrational and paradoxical impulses motivate the characters' mad or hallucinatory behavior and determine the stories' structure and plot. The external events are projections of psychological drives, revealing the logic of dream psychology rather than of ordinary reality and rendering the stories comically absurd and grotesquely uncanny.

Yehoshua's early stories, devoid of specific time and place and marked by allegory and symbolism, are strongly influenced by S. Y. Agnon's symbolic stories from his *Book of Deeds,* where time and place are obliterated, presenting an absurd world without unity or coherence. But while Agnon's metaphysical yearnings led him to utilize symbols from the venerated world of tradition, Yehoshua's secular world led him to look for universal cultural symbols as settings for his bizarre characters. Consequently, Yehoshua's first allegorical stories, although well received, have also been criticized for their lack of anchor in specific social reality to support the symbolic interpretations. The author's later work has indeed been steadily moving toward a greater representation of reality, and a fusion of reality with a grotesque artistic vision. This progress can be noted in his second collection of short stories *Mul-Ha-Ye-a-rot,* where the scenes take place in the Jewish national forests, in Jerusalem, Haifa, and Africa. In these stories Yehoshua seeks to penetrate into the archetypal depth of society as a whole by means of representative individuals. In each a fundamental human paradox, with a logic of its own, underlies the social situation. The main character in the stories must see the paradox to its very end, being both attracted to it and too weak to resist it.

Yehoshua's artistic growth is evident in several differences between the earlier and the later stories which account for his successful movement from short story to novel. In the earlier stories a fantastic and destructive idea or act, contradicting all norms and common notions of what is proper and good, begins to take over with a crazy consistency until all familiar reality becomes distorted. The central character, presented as a type, displays characteristic qualities of that type, such as forest guard, prison warden, etc., in an extreme and fanatic manner that borders on comic absurdity. The external plot, revealing the trouble that oppresses the character, erupts in a final catastropic climax. The later stories become more subtle, subordinating the fantastic external and dramatic events to the trivial realities of life. The main character, who is experiencing unusual and peculiar events, attempts to trivialize these events and explain them in a rational way, despite their disquieting nature. This creates an ironic gap between the point of view of the main character and that of the reader, who is aware of the hidden grotesqueness and absurdity that lie beneath the surface.

Yehoshua's first and impressive novel *The Lover* plunges fully into the reality of Israeli society. Some local critics saw the book only as an extended novella rather than a fully developed novel, but American critics praised this haunting work for its sensitivity and psychological insight. The novel is told in a realistic style. The characters, unlike those in the author's previous stories, are psychologically individualized with typical speech patterns, behaving like ordinary Jews and Arabs in everyday life. Yet in a broader sense the characters behave in a paradoxical manner bordering on madness. Similarly, the plot itself, which contains realistic materials, is structured in a grotesque pattern, reversing the conventional relations in society. Thus Adam, a husband and father, is obsessively seeking to provide both his wife and daughter with lovers (the reverse of the jealous husband and protective father); the Arab youth, who is trying to assimilate into Hebrew culture, helps an aging garage owner to find a missing Israeli soldier; the soldier, a deserter and a "yored" (one who emigrated from Israel), from an old Sephardic family, joins the Ashkenazic marginal Orthodox group. These social paradoxes seem to point to some of the existential paradoxes underlying Israeli society, as the Israeli critic Gershon Shaked has pointed out. Alfred Kazin, reviewing *The Lover* in the *New York Times Book Review,* praised Yehoshua for "bringing to his stories of alienation and antagonism within the Israeli family such fine political shadings. The parallel comedy of Arab-Israeli distrust attests to Yehoshua's ability for rendering both presences relieved of all sentimentality." Robert Alter writes: "What Yehoshua learned how to do adeptly from his second book onward, was to make the familiar world, rendered in realistic detail, imperceptibly merge with, or suddenly collapse into the uncanny. His informing vision is grotesquely comic, because that matches the writer's sense of the fundamental bizarreness of living as a human being. He is a writer who exhibits the vigorous fidelity to his own perceptions that produce real originality."

The novel *A Late Divorce* takes the Israeli family into the 1970s, probing with greater depth into its social, familial, and psychological makeup. Yehoshua continues to utilize the technique of interior monologue, but in this novel he lets each of the nine main characters tell the story of one day in the visit of the grandfather. Yehuda Kaminka, the father and grandfather, in his sixties, has returned to Israel after several years in the United States to obtain a divorce. He had fled from his wife when she tried to kill him with a kitchen knife, and is soon to become a father again in America. It is Passover and in the few days of his visit to this children and their households he discovers how much of himself remains in Tel-Aviv, Haifa, and Jerusalem. It its a story of a painful divorce and death. The members of the family are plagued by marital calamity, madness, estrangement between generations, and sexual malaise, but at the same time they cling to what the family, which is their life support, means to them. The hidden subject of the novel is Yehoshua's obsessive theme of the great debate between Israel and the Gola (exile), a theme he openly and polemically addresses in his political book of 1981, *Between Right and Right.* Here he fiercely argues that the Diaspora has no future, except in Israel, and he probes into the essence of the Jewish people, trying to reformulate the terms of identity, Jew, Zionist, Israeli. *A Late Divorce* echoes this argument on several points. In a personal interview during one of his recent visits to the United States, Yehoshua responded to the question whether *A Late Divorce* is really about Israel: "I don't claim this family is really a symbol of Israel, but there is a layer of allegory—the imbalance between the father and mother, which does not create proper relations for the health of the family. [And], like the father, who gives up his responsibilities and goes to America, Jews who leave Israel for America are escaping their responsibility." In his fiction Yehoshua integrates his argument about Zionism and his art, as Harold Bloom observed in his review in the *New York Times Book Review,* dealing with the subject in a subtle and indirect way, which is at times visionary and even phantasmagoric.

Yehoshua is dean of students and professor of literature at Haifa University. He is married to Rivka Kirsminski, a psychologist, and has a daughter and two sons. A frequent visitor to the United States, he has spent eight months in the writers' program at the University of Iowa.

WORKS IN ENGLISH TRANSLATION: Collections of Yehoshua's short stories in English translation include *Three Days and a Child,* translated by Miriam Arad in 1970, and *Early in the Summer of 1970,* by Miriam Arad and Pauline Schrier in 1977. Individual stories appear in a number of anthologies of Hebrew literature, among them Robert Alter's *Modern Hebrew Literature,* 1975. His novel *The Lover* was translated by Philip Simpson in 1978, and Hillel Halkin translated *A Late Divorce* in 1983. *Betwen Right and Right,* Yehoshua's political essays, was published in 1981 in Arnold Schwartz' translation, and *A Night in May,* translated by Arad, and *Last Treatment* (*Tipulim Aharonim*) were published as *Two Plays* in 1975.

ABOUT:Alter, R. *Introduction to* Modern Hebrew Literature, 1975; Contemporary Authors, first revision series 33–36, 1978. *Periodicals*—Books Abroad 45 (1971); 52 (1978); Choice April 1979; Commentary August 1972; January 1978; Hebrew Annual Review 5 (1981); Jerusalem Quarterly Summer 1980; Jewish Quarterly Autumn 1970; Literature East and West March 1970; Modern Hebrew Literature Spring 1975; Nation February 6, 1982; New Yorker December 25, 1978; New York Review of Books December 21, 1978; June 14, 1984; New York Times Book Review October 29, 1976; November 19, 1978; February 7, 19, 1984.

© 1982 Layle Silbert

HELEN YGLESIAS

*YGLESIAS, HELEN (March 19, 1915–), American novelist and memoirist, was born in New York City to Solomon and Kate (Goldstein) Bassine, Jewish immigrants from Eastern Europe. The youngest of seven children, she grew up in the Bronx, where her father ran a small grocery store. At sixteen, after graduating from James Monroe High School, she began writing a novel, but "it was the time of the Great Depression . . . a climate of harshness that beat my hopes to a pulp." Pressed by her family to go to work, she stopped writing and took a series of low-paying jobs, including several for socialist and communist organizations. In her free time she educated herself at the New York Public Library. In 1937 she married Bernard Cole, a union official (later a professional photographer), with whom she had two children, Tamar and Lewis; the marriage ended in divorce. In 1950 she married Jose Yglesias, a former executive with a pharmaceuticals company, who has written a number of novels and works of nonfiction on life in Spain and Latin America. They have one son, Rafael, also a novelist. During her years of childrearing, Yglesias was too busy to write fiction, although she occasionally did editing work and wrote book reviews. When her husband left his job in the early 1960s to become a full-time writer, she returned to work, becoming a literary editor of the *Nation* in 1966. Three years later she left the job to begin a new career as a novelist.

How She Died was published in 1972, when Yglesias was fifty-seven. The "she" of the title is Mary Moody Schwartz, a twenty-eight-year-old woman dying of cancer amid the disorder of her marriage and the confusion of her friends, a

group of socialists who raised her after her mother was imprisoned for spying. As Mary degenerates into paranoia, the narration is taken over by her friend Jean, who involves herself in Mary's dying and becomes the lover of Mary's husband.

Some reviewers were unable to tolerate the book's claustrophobic atmosphere or the obsessive soul-searchings of its characters. Muriel Haynes called it "a soap opera" about "a sociopolitical card catalogue of stock figures." But many were impressed by Yglesias' craftsmanlike prose and her ability to create believable New Yorkers and to recreate the sounds and smells of New York. "*How She Died* assails away like mad," wrote the reviewer for the *Times Literary Supplement,* "understating nothing in its treatment of those two towering fears of twentieth-century man: death by cancer and death by politics. . . . The committee members . . . serve as convenient vehicles for those stunning insights into human nature which Helen Yglesias has been saving for us." Wrote Roger Baker: "Rarely, in my experience, does a writer expose the nerve-endings of people, probe their interpersonal relationships and isolate the tensions operating upon them with such simplicity and directness. . . . The book can be read on several levels: as a bleeding chunk of life; as an affecting study of how an individual faces death; as an illustration of the way in which the best wills in the world can make an unutterable mess of things." *How She Died* won the Houghton Mifflin Literary Fellowship Award.

Yglesias' second book, *Family Feeling,* was an exploration of the workings of a family much like her own: seven children born to immigrant

°ē´´ glä´ sē əs

Jewish parents. The story is told from the point of view of Anne, the youngest, and takes the form of an extended reminiscence in which she reconstructs the network of familial tensions and affections and tries to resolve the contradictions of her own life. A communist in her youth, now a well-do-do widow with Marxist ideals, she is unable to repudiate the dominating older brother whose success in business has brought the family into the mainstream of American life, and she adopts as her "legendary grandfather" Frederick Law Olmsted, the architect who designed New York's great public parks.

The unorthodox narrative technique posed difficulties for reviewers such as Irma P. Feldman, who thought *Family Feeling* "rich in detail" but "unmoving," written with a self-consciousness that suggested that "less is invention than [Yglesias] would like us to believe." The reviewer for *Saturday Review* said: "Anne's growth is crucially linked to the national traumas of her lifespan: the Depression, the hopeful communism of the late Thirties, World War II, Vietnam, and the rise of brutal, random street crime. The failure to merge successfully the epic and the subjective . . . leaves both aspects unrealized and tantalizing." Dean Flower noted that Yglesias "keeps our attention fixed on hypocrisies of gesture and voice, unspoken motives, and subtle positionings," adding: "Yglesias masters this story by her relentless, almost Jamesian concentration on the issue of her title: the continuing power of family feeling to unite and divide, aggravate and bless, its members. The novel lucidly shows how family feeling disintegrates and then magically—or terribly?—renews itself."

Sweetsir is the story of a working-class New England woman who marries a violent man and kills him accidentally while defending herself from a beating. The novel has a circular design, opening with the murder and then retracing the heroine's life from her pregnancy at sixteen through an unhappy first marriage, the stillbirth of her second child, her successful efforts at self-improvement after a divorce, her attraction and marriage to a hard-drinking, abusive construction worker, and finally the killing and her trial for murder. "The metaphoric subject of this book," according to Vivian Gornick, "is the psychic history of two human beings who come together, thrash wildly about in an attempt to reduce their mutual isolation, fail miserably and are punished brutally for their failure."

Although, as Elizabeth Duvall pointed out, *Sweetsir* is "clearly a feminist tale," it is not doctrinaire (indeed, Yglesias satirizes a group of feminists who exploit the case for political ends). Rosellen Brown wrote that Yglesias "brought her

characters to the kind of desperation that so often leads people these days to rhetorical questions and polemical answers, and instead has let us hear a real, anguished voice in the act of self-discovery." According to David Roberts, " . . . there is an unmistakable authenticity in Yglesias' handling of Eatonville's impoverished Italians and Irish. The spareness of language and the simplicity of syntax in Yglesias' prose serve, at their best, to mirror . . . the drab currents of feeling that make up American life." Roberts nonetheless complained of a lack of suspense, and Gornick felt that the novel stopped just short of attaining "the fearfulness of the inevitable . . . achieved not through the recital of the event but the creation of texture."

In 1979 Yglesias published a non-fiction work, *Starting: Early, Anew, Over, and Late,* a compilation of oral histories of a variety of people who chose or were forced by circumstances to remake their lives. A few of them—Mother Jones, Grandma Moses, Alberta Hunter, Helen and Scott Nearing—are well known; the rest are acquaintances of Yglesias', including a widow who opened a social club for singles, a teacher who became a business consultant, a housewife who became a real-estate entrepreneur, and Yglesias' son Rafael, who left school at the age of fifteen to become a writer (the publication of his first novel coincided with that of *How She Died*). The first section of the book is an "autobiographical fragment" by Yglesias in which she describes the delays and false starts that preceded the writing of *How She Died* and the stimuli that impelled her to begin it, particularly a rebuke of her procrastination by the novelist Christina Stead. Of her decision to begin writing at the age of fifty-four, she writes: "I gave up work that I really did love doing on the magazine, gave up the infinitesimal measure of prestige my post carried in the literary world, gave up a good salary (for a woman), gave up the strictures and the securities of the spot I had wormed my way into. . . . This vehicle, however comfortable, wasn't taking me where I really wanted to go. I wanted to be on my way as a story-teller." On the subject of starting in general, Yglesias writes: "To start is to bring the self into active existence in society. It is a commitment to trust the self in the world . . . a declaration of unique existence, affirmed again and again in continuing action."

Reviewers judged *Starting* interesting but unfocused. "The book's strength," wrote Marjorie Pryse, "lies in Yglesias' ability to tell stories. Its weakness derives from her insistence . . . that the stories are closely related. She makes general statements about the lives of women and men in our society that have become commonplaces. . . . Still, anyone dreaming of beginning a new life will take courage from the stories in this book."

Most of Yglesias' writing is done in North Brooklin, Maine, in a two-hundred-year-old farmhouse that is also the writing headquarters of her husband and her two sons (the elder son writes social commentary). Her daughter too is a freelance writer. Nan Robertson calls Yglesias "a pivotal part of a literary family phenomenon like the Brontës, the Benchleys, the Lardners, and the Irving Wallaces."

PRINCIPAL WORKS: *Novels*—How She Died, 1972; Family Feeling, 1976; Sweetsir, 1981. *Non-fiction*—Starting, 1979.

ABOUT: Contemporary Authors 37–40, first revised edition, 1979; Contemporary Literary Criticism 7, 1977; 22, 1982. *Periodicals*—Atlantic May 1981; Books and Bookmen May 1973; Horizon April 1981; Hudson Review Summer 1976; Nation June 19, 1972; May 1, 1976; March 17, 1979; June 20, 1981; New York Times February 8, 1972; October 10, 1976; New York Times Book Review February 13, 1972; February 1, 1976; March 4, 1979; April 6, 1981; June 14, 1981; Parents March 1979; Publishers Weekly April 19, 1976; Saturday Review March 18, 1972; March 6, 1976; Times Literary Supplement January 26, 1973; Village Voice March 15, 1976; Working Woman December 1979.

*ZHAO SHULI** (also rendered as **Chao Shu-Li**) (1906–September 23, 1970), Chinese novelist and short story writer, was one of the few modern Chinese writers to have come from peasant stock. He is regarded as the most outstanding member of the popular literary movement of the "base-area" (i.e. the border region of northwest China where the Communist Party led the war of national resistance against the Japanese). Born to a poor peasant family in Xin Shui county, Shanxi province, from childhood he herded cattle, raked manure, and did all kinds of farm work. What distinguished Zhao from other boys in his society was that he was keenly interested in popular art forms such as song recitals, local opera, and popular music. The family made sacrifices to give him a good education, and in 1925 he was enrolled at a teachers' institute in the provincial city of Changzhi.

There, under the influence of the revolutionary May Fourth Movement of 1919, Zhao acquired more sophisticated ideas, and became involved in the radical student movement. From the late 1920s to the early thirties he led an itinerant life, doing odd jobs for a living. But he did not give up his interest in literature, especially his passion for popular art forms. He was convinced that modern urban culture, engendered by the May Fourth Movement with its strong echoes of foreign influence, could not reach the vast majority of the rural population, locked as they were in the obscurantism of the feudal tradition. As a budding writer himself, he saw his own role cut out: "I do not aspire to make a figure on the literary scene. I do not want to be a literary writer. What I need is just a literary 'stall,' that is, to write and sell for a few coppers some short pieces by inserting them into the ballad-sheets sold at the stalls during the fairs when the peasants visit the temple shrines, thus gradually taking over the market for those feudal ballad-sheets."

The launching of all-out war against the Japanese marked a new phase of development for Zhao Shuli. By then a full-time language teacher in Changzhi, he threw himself wholeheartedly into the propaganda campaign to forward the national cause. By the end of the 1930s he had established himself as a noted editor and author of patriotic writings. He published voluminously, using popular art forms—the tale, songs and lyrics, ballads, stories for recital, improvised plays, plays in verse, etc. Regrettably, because of the vicissitudes of the war, all these works have been lost.

By the beginning of the 1940s, Zhao was recognized as a representative writer and spokesman for popular art in the vast regions of the interior under Communist rule. In 1943, during one of the enemy's "mopping-up" operations, Zhao was evacuated into the Tai-hang mountains. There he heard a true story of a pair of village lovers, and from this material wrote the first work to win him lasting fame, *Xiao Erhei Jihan* (Little Erhei's Marriage, 1943). This is about a pair of village lovers, Little Erhei and Little Qin, who are thwarted in their love by the forces of feudalism and superstition. But Zhao Shuli turned the original tragic story into a satiric comedy with a generous sprinkling of earthy humor and now and then a dash of farce. The two protagonists, embodiments of the young generation's struggle for individual freedom and happiness, are no more than props for the story. The two characters who instantly caught the public imagination are the two villains of the piece: the boy's father, nicknamed "Second Zhu Ge" for his self-styled wisdom (Zhu Ge being a famous statesman and strategist of ancient China), and the girl's mother, nicknamed "third fairy" for her magic and witchcraft. Of course the villains are foiled and true love prevails. Appearing during the period when China was emerging from feudalism, "Little Erhei's Marriage," written in a pithy, homespun peasant vernacular, was like a breath of fresh air with its vindication of the

°jou shōo lē

rights of the individual, and it had a wide appeal for the peasants. In the Tai-hang region alone it sold in tens of thousands of copies and was adapted for performances in many different forms.

Zhao Shuli's next major work, *Li Yucai Banhua* (*The Rhymes of Li Yu-ts'ai*), is also set in the author's familiar territory—the countryside of Shanxi during the struggle led by the Communist Party to establish democratic rule. Although dealing with the class struggle, the subject is enlivened by the main character, Li Yu-ts'ai, who improvises comic rhymes to expose the conspiracy of the landlords and at the same time to make sly digs at the obtuseness of petty bureaucrats in charge of public affairs. From then until the liberation in 1949, Zhao Shuli, while active in cultural affairs of the base-area, kept on writing. A host of novels, novelettes, and short stories appeared in quick succession. Notable among these is the full-length novel of 1950 *Lijiazhuang Bianqian* (*Changes in Li Village*). It is a huge panorama of historic changes in old China as reflected in a village in southern Shanxi, covering the period from the late 1920s, after the failure of the revolution of 1927, to the victory of the war of national resistance in 1945. This saga of peasant life, based on Zhao Shuli's personal experience, focuses on the struggle of the peasants against an array of war lords, landlords, collaborators, and other parasites and oppressors. In 1946, Marxist critic and leader of cultural affairs in the Communist base-area Zhou Yang pointed out that Zhao Shuli's three major works—"Little Erhei's Marriage," *The Rhymes of Li Yu-ts'ai*, and *Changes in Li Village*—are "grand and exquisitely executed portraits of the stupendous changes that have taken place in the countryside." Likewise, in the "white areas" (areas still under Guomindang control), such prestigious figures as Guo Moruo and Mao Dun praised Zhao Shuli highly. In 1946 Guo wrote of him: "How I envy this writer. He is in a free element, expanding freely. From 'Little Erhei's Marriage' to *The Rhymes of Li Yu-ts'ai* to *Changes in Li Village*, this writer is flourishing and growing like a tree. Zhao Shuli is without doubt a great tree." And Mao Dun pointed out that Zhao Shuli's work is a milestone in the search for national form in modern Chinese literature.

After the liberation, Zhao Shuli settled in Beijing (Peking) and headed the Beijing Writers' Union. Though a busy man, he continued writing and also remained in touch with his rural origins. Most of the changes that took place in rural areas after the liberation are portrayed in his works of this period. Conspicuous among these are stories that reflect social changes as perceived by different generations of women, and a novelette, *Sanliwan* (*Sanliwan Village*), full of gusto and humor, depicting problems and perplexities in the rural collectivization programs when different ideologies and temperaments collided. To the end, Zhao Shuli preserved his blood ties with the peasant, his straightforward, vigorous prose style, his rustic humor, and his down-to-earth attitude with no hint of cant. Well-read, proficient in calligraphy and Chinese painting and seal-cutting, he remained a peasant writer. Because he so honestly represents the land, using the techniques of traditional storytelling, Zhao Shuli has excited much interest abroad. Translations and studies of his works are especially widespread in the Soviet Union and other eastern European countries. But in the West too, in France, Great Britain, and the United States, Zhao Shuli is regarded as a major figure in contemporary Chinese literature.

WORKS IN ENGLISH TRANSLATION: The short story "Erhei's Marriage" was translated in *Chinese Literature* 5, May 1979; another short story, "The Unglovable Hands," translated by Nathan K. Mao and W. L. Y. Yang, is in Kai-yu Hsu's *Literature of the People's Republic of China*, 1980. *The Rhymes of Li Yu-ts'ai and Other Stories*, translated by Sidney Shapiro (the collection includes "Little Erhei's Marriage"), was published in 1950 and again in 1955. Other short stories in English translation include "A New Canteen and Old Memories," in W. J. and R. I. Meserve's *Modern Literature from China*, 1974, and "Patriarch" in *Chinese Literature* 9, September 1964. Gladys Yang translated the two novels *Changes in Li Village*, 1953, and *Sanliwan Village*, 1957.

ABOUT: Birch, C. Chinese Communist Literature, 1963; Dictionary of Oriental Literature 1, 1974; Encyclopedia of World Literature in the 20th Century (rev. ed.) I, 1981; Hsia, C. T. A History of Modern Chinese Fiction, 1971; Huang, J. C. Heroes and Villains in Communist China, 1973; Yang, W. and N. K. Mao, Modern Chinese Fiction, 1981. *Periodicals*—Chinese Literature 9, September 1964; New Mexico Quarterly 25, 1955.

---

*ZHOU LIBO (also rendered as **Chou Li-po**) (August 9, 1908–September 25, 1979), Chinese novelist and short story writer, originally named Zhou Shao Yi, was born in YiYang county, Hunan province, to a peasant family. He was a proficient student and by the time he graduated from the prestigious No.1 Middle School of Changsha city, he had read extensively in Chinese classical literature and the work of modern thinkers. He was also deeply interested in the new literature that had sprung up after the May Fourth Movement. But a more turbulent fate

°jou lē pō

was in store for him for the time being. It was a period of revolutionary upheaval in Hunan, especially in the countryside. A radical friend recruited Zhou into revolutionary circles and he joined street demonstrations and meetings, until Changsha became too hot to hold him.

Zhou next landed in Shanghai in 1927, where he enrolled in college but also took part in the underground movement. One of the important results of his stay in Shanghai was that he taught himself English and translated a number of works of Soviet fiction from the English. It was at this time that he first adopted the pen-name Zhou Libo, "libo" corresponding phonetically with the English word "liberty," to which he vowed to dedicate himself. In 1932, he was arrested for his revolutionary activities and spent two harrowing years in jail. Other works which he translated after his release include Mark Twain's "The Celebrated Jumping Frog of Calaveras County," short stories of James Joyce, and Pushkin's "Dubrovsky." One of Zhou's most important translations was of the Soviet writer Mikhail Sholokov's *Seeds of Tomorrow* (published in the U.K. as *Virgin Soil Upturned*), a novel that was to have an important influence on his later writing.

On the outbreak of the war of resistance against the Japanese, Zhou, with other leftist writers, retreated from Shanghai and settled in Xian, in Shaanxi province, then capital of the base-area under Communist control. He wanted at first to do some reporting at the front. It happened that the American writer and reporter Agnes Smedley had planned to visit the Shaanxi front, so Zhou accompanied her as translator. They toured the battle front and the base-area, traveling more than a thousand kilometers altogether. In 1938 Zhou collected his notes on this trip and published them as *Jin-Cha-Ji Bianqu Yinxiang Ji* (Impressions of the Border Region, and Diary of the Front). These carry vivid reports of the fighting, the spirit of self-sacrifice of the Communist-led army, the atrocities committed by the invaders, as well as observations of the lives and struggles of the people in the base-area, the mainstay of the resistance movement.

In 1941 Zhou Libo finally settled in Yanan as a language teacher at the Lu Xun Institute of the Arts, the only one of its kind in the area. He was active in the cultural affairs of the region, edited the literature page of the chief newspaper, and took part in the famous Yanan Forum on Art and Literature where Mao Zedong gave his famous speeches that, as C.T. Hsia writes, "became the new oracle for all literary and art workers in Communist areas." It was then also that he finally settled down to the writing of fiction, producing first a series of short stories drawing on memories of his prison life. But in the mid-1940s, after the end of the war of national resistance and with the outbreak of the civil war, Zhou Libo returned to the interior, running two newspapers, and even serving as interpreter during the peace talks between the Communist Party and the Guomindang when the United States acted as mediator.

In 1946 Zhou went to the northeast part of China, formerly Manchuria, a move that was decisive for his own career as writer. He was there to start a newspaper and take part in the land reform movement, as the northeast was under Communist control immediately after the Japanese surrender. Zhou lived with the peasants, sharing their lives and earning their confidence. Together they carried out the fight against the landlords and the remnants of the Japanese domination, and put the land back into the hands of the peasants. Zhou was deeply stirred by this experience and in 1949 wrote his first major work, *Baofeng Zhouyu* (*The Hurricane*). It was an immediate success and won the third place in the Stalin Prize for Literature in 1951. It was also successfully adapted for the screen.

After the liberation in 1949, Zhou Libo settled in Beijing (Peking) and worked at the Ministry of Culture. He tried, with little success, to write about steel workers and then decided to give up his job in Beijing to settle back in his own familiar elements. By 1955 he was back in his home village in the south. Once again, he immersed himself in the lives and struggles of the peasants, this time during the height of the movement for collectivization. From 1957–1959, he finished his best work—*Shanxiang Jubian* (*Great Changes in a Mountain Village*), a novel in two volumes. He continued to write, publishing short stories until the outbreak of the cultural revolution when it was impossible for him to work any more. After the "cultural revolution," he mapped out vast work plans, but died before completing any of them.

Zhou's fame rests on his two major novels—*Hurricane* and *Great Changes in a Mountain Village*—complementary works that reflect the drastic changes that have taken place in the Chinese countryside, that is, the land reforms that gave the land to the peasants and then to the socialist collectivization movement which began during the 1950s. Zhou describes the feelings of the peasants who were forced to relinquish their land to cooperatives, their uprightness, strength of character, and unswerving loyalty to the revolutionary cause when once their zeal was fired. Zhou makes it clear that it is the great mass of peasants, their struggles and sacrifices, that made possible the profound changes in China.

Great Changes in a Mountain Village, more finished than its predecessor, presents a set of vivid portraits of peasants; their relationships and confrontations during the collectivization movement are described with great psychological subtlety. It is at the same time a charming novel of local color with vivid descriptions of southern scenes and manners.

WORKS IN ENGLISH TRANSLATION: Derek Bryan translated *Great Changes in a Mountain Village* in 1961, and Kai-yu Hsü includes one chapter from Volume II of the novel, in Donald A. Gibbs' translation, in *Literature of the People's Republic of China,* 1980. *The Hurricane* was translated by Hsü Meng-Hsiung in 1955. One of Zhou Libo's six short stories, translated as "The Family on the Other Side of the Mountain," is in *Modern Literature from China,* edited by W. J. and R. I. Meserve, 1974.

ABOUT: Birch, C. (ed.) Chinese Communist Literature, 1963; Cassell's Encyclopedia of World Literature, 1973; Dictionary of Oriental Literature I, 1974; Encyclopedia of World Literature in the 20th Century (rev. ed.) I, 1981; Hsia, C. T. A History of Modern Chinese Fiction, 1971; Hsü, K. Literature of the People's Republic of China, 1980; Huang, J. C. Heroes and Villains in Communist China: The Contemporary Chinese Novel as a Reflection of Life, 1973; Yang, W. L. Y. and N. K. Mao, Modern Chinese Fiction, 1981.

*ZINOVIEV, ALEXANDER (October 29, 1922–), Russian philosopher and novelist, writes: "I was born in a small Russian village. My mother was a peasant. My father was a worker, a house-painter. There were eleven children in our family. In accordance with local tradition our family lived partly in the country (my mother and the younger children) and partly in Moscow (my father and the elder children). In 1946 the whole family moved to Moscow. We lived in a damp basement room measuring ten square metres and there were always at least eight or ten people in it.

"From 1933 onward I lived and studied in Moscow. In 1939 I finished school and entered the Faculty of Philosophy at the Institute of Philosophy, Literature and History. In the same year I was expelled from the Komsomol and the Institute for speaking out against the Stalin cult. First I was sent to a psychiatric clinic, but after the clinic had pronounced me mentally normal I was taken to the KGB (or whatever the organization was called at the time) building on the Lubyanka. I was interrogated several times over in an effort to discover who had taught me to think such thoughts. After a short time I was re-

ALEXANDER ZINOVIEV

leased. This was done in the hope of identifying my connections and 'confederates.' However, I did not go home; instead I went straight to my mother in the country. In my village I had been working on a collective farm. Although I had had my military service deferred, I now persuaded them to issue me with my call-up papers all the same. In this way I escaped both the security organs and starvation.

"In my military service I served in the cavalry, tank forces, and the air force. I began the war in the ground forces and ended it in the air. I was a pilot and as such took part in several dozen missions raiding targets in the enemy rear. For my record in battle I was decorated and awarded medals. I was demobilized in 1946. After the army I entered the Philosophy Faculty at Moscow University. In 1951 I graduated and embarked on postgraduate study which I completed in 1954. While studying I also worked as a loader, navvy, laboratory assistant, translator, and schoolteacher. In 1954 I was given a post at the Academy of Sciences' Institute of Philosophy, where I remained in regular and continuous employment right up to my dismissal in January 1977, i.e. for over twenty-two years. I held a combined post in the University Philosophy Faculty. At one time I was head of the department of logic. In 1966 I was awarded a professorship. In 1974 I was elected a member of the Finnish Academy of Sciences.

"I did not begin to publish until fairly late on—in 1958. Furthermore, my first articles were published in Poland, Czechoslovakia, and elsewhere in the West. In 1959 I started working in the field of mathematical logic and the logical methodology of science. I have had six books and over 100 articles published in Russian as well as several books and a great many articles in other languages. On many occasions I was invited to attend international professional gatherings, included in delegations to congresses; I received private invitations and so on, but I was not once allowed out of the Soviet Union.

"If I did achieve any success during that time it was thanks to the leniencies of the 'liberal' period and because my works were being published in the West, and foreign logicians and philosophers were showing an interest in me. The 1970s saw the start of a campaign among my colleagues to discredit me as a scholar which ended in the total dissolution of my group, the banning of my works from publication, and the prohibition of all references to my works. My activities at the University were reduced to an insignificant course of lectures. So, long before the appearance of *The Yawning Heights* I was already in a situation of total creative isolation.

"As the saying goes, every cloud has a silver lining. Prevented from doing any active work in the field of logic, I found myself for the first time for many years with free time at my disposal. I embarked on the writing of *The Yawning Heights*. However, the book was no casual venture for me. In my young days I had devoted quite a lot of time to literary activity—poems, caricatures and satirical sketches in wall newspapers, story-telling, 'playing around.' After the army I thought about becoming a writer but decided that such an enterprise would be foolish at that time. I went on as before writing for the wall newspaper, contributing to the composition of anecdotes and jokes and practicing oral story-telling. All the time I was dreaming of writing a full-scale book. I did write a thing or two, and I did publish one or two things. I gave dozens of public lectures, many of which I later incorporated almost word for word in *The Yawning Heights*. I continually indulged in literary digressions in my lectures on logic. Nor did my experience of writing books and articles on logic and philosophy go to waste. In short, I was perfectly well prepared for writing *The Yawning Heights*. The book was practically 'written' already in my head and all I had to do was get it down on paper. This I did in six months from start to finish.

"In September 1976 the book was published in the West. My colleagues, fellow-employees, and old acquaintances declared a total boycott of me and my family. I lost my job and was stripped of all my degrees, titles, and state awards. My family survived all this time by selling books and any articles of the slightest value,

and also thanks to the help of relatives and new friends. We became used to living in an atmosphere of constant surveillance, intimidation, and false rumors. In August 1978 I was ordered to leave the Soviet Union with my family.

"When, as a young man, I used to wander round Moscow, hungry and alone, and waiting for arrest to relieve me from my misery, I would dream of becoming a writer and telling the truth about the society which was taking shape inexorably before my very eyes. Since then almost forty years have gone by. I have written books in which I have set forth what seems to me to be the truth about our life. For doing that I got off relatively lightly: I found myself in the West, and not at hard labor in a prison camp, which is what I had been expecting. What more could one want?—Life's aim achieved. Simply enjoy the delight of Western civilization! But I don't want to look at beautiful cities, eat tasty dishes, or take advantage of democratic freedoms. I feel nostalgic, because my heart is still there, in my ugly but native Moscow. The point is not so much that I have lived my life and left my roots there; it is rather that, as that terrible new society grew, it was linked, however tenuously with my own heart; it was mine and it remains mine, whatever happens. That monster is my child too."

———

Aleksandr Nekrich wrote in a review of *The Yawning Heights* that Zinoviev's training as a logician is reflected in the satire of that novel. Every form of modern logic—mathematical, symbolic, Wittgensteinian, structuralist, and especially Marxist dialectical—becomes his instrument and his target: "Indeed," Nekrich observed, "the tone of the book is that of a mordant logical mind reassembling from shards of evidence the mad yet brutally effective logic of a closed society." Every political satirist from Swift, Voltaire, and Gogol to Kafka and Orwell has been cited in comments on Zinoviev's novel. But the fact remains that as a satirist he is an original, his own man, expressing a deeply personal vision of his native country from which he is now an exile. He insists that his work is not satire: "It is Soviet life that is the 'real' satire," he told an interviewer during a visit to New York in 1979; "My description of the Soviet 'satire' is not a satire. It is traditional realism."

Despite his disclaimer, Zinoviev writes satire, and with a heavy hand—"Gogol with elephantiasis" was John Leonard's description of *The Yawning Heights*. This large (more than 800 pages), sprawling, and—for many readers— tasteless allegory of a society paralyzed by its appalling banality and mediocrity is of larger scope than most familiar classic examples of political satire, attacking everything in the huge Soviet state from its politics to its education, cultural life, and the personal morality of its citizens. Nothing and nobody is spared—with the result, ironically, that Zinoviev undermines even the opposition, the dissidents who express their protests both from within and outside their country. Dissidence is futile because, as *The Yawning Heights* portrays it, Soviet society is normal and natural. As Geoffrey Hosking pointed out in a review of the book, "its arrangements are those which natural man would create for himself without the restraints imposed by centuries of civilized society."

The title *The Yawning Heights* is a pun. As Gordon Clough, its English translator, explains in his Preface, in the Russian title *Ziyayushchie Vysoty* the verb *zivat* "means to gape or to yawn, as an abyss. But in the jargon of Soviet speech-makers and leader-writers, the word which often prefaces *vysoty* (heights) is *siyayushchie* (with a s, not a z): 'gleaming' or 'radiant,' as in phrases like 'the gleaming heights of socialism'—the radiant future toward which the Communist Party of the Soviet Union claims to be leading the progressive forces of mankind. So the title *The Yawning Heights* both encapsulates the paradox and snipes accurately at the jargon of the Soviet gospel." The scene of the novel, an imaginary town called Ibansk, is also a pun, combining the familiar Russian name Ivan with the Russian verb *yebat*, meaning sexual intercourse. All of the characters, residents of Ibansk, have the same name, Ibanov, but they are distinguished by epithets that designate their symbolic functions and they are all easily recognized—Boss is Stalin, Hog is Khrushchev, the Great Veterinarian is the scientist Lysenko, Writer is the poet Yevtushenko, Truthteller is Solzhenitsyn. The manuscript on which the book is purportedly based, according to the Author's Note, was a collection of fragments found on a rubbish dump, and fragments it truly is, a series of episodes and essays held together tenuously but in strict logical form, with a statement of methodological principles which are, of course, a group of absurdist paradoxes: "The history of Ibansk is made up of events which almost failed to happen; which almost happened but at the last moment somehow didn't; were expected but never happened despite that; were not expected but did happen despite that; happened but in the wrong way at the wrong time, in the wrong place; happened, but are acknowledged not to have happened; did not happen but were generally accepted as having happened." Interspersed with the prose are numerous doggerel

poems—"A correct position in life / If you want to live in ease / Learn the art of catching fleas." And, from the closing section, mainly in prose though titled "Poem on Boredom"—"It's perfectly true that the world's a sty,/ Perfectly true that men are scum."

Writing with what John Bayley calls "a passionate self-indulgence, " Zinoviev exposes Soviet society from an inside point of view as few other Russian dissidents have done: " . . . it is the most thorough and profound examination of the Soviet regime, from the viewpoint of a disaffected intellectual, that has yet appeared. . . . " Deming Brown wrote of *The Yawning Heights*. Even the better-known Solzhenitsyn, whom Zinoviev respects and admires, fails because his cause is hopeless: "He is problem number one of our time," Zinoviev writes, "He is something much bigger than ideology, politics, and morality. He is the focal point where all problems are concentrated. If only men can contrive to preserve all this long enough!"

In contrast to *The Yawning Heights*, the novel which followed, *The Radiant Future*, is relatively short, easy to read, and less despairing. Described as a "non-novel," it begins on a note of cynicism characteristic of its predecessor with Zinoviev reporting a conversation of two Moscow intellectuals, summed up in "What a bloody awful life it is" and an obscenity. But immediately following, he writes: "There can be no more definitive comment on the life we lead. And yet in that life we sometimes see some vague hints at something different. And those hints merit at least a moment's consideration." The narrator here is a far more human and recognizable figure, a philosophy professor with a wife and children living a mediocre life. In a series of philosophic dialogues with a dissident friend and in the metaphor running through the book of a steadily deteriorating billboard that proclaims, "Long Live Communism—the Radiant Future of Mankind," we watch the gradual erosion of his faith in Communism. In this novel Clive James finds "an expiatory quality that gives a dimension missing from *The Yawning Heights*, in which squalor is without pathos." Here Zinoviev speaks more directly, as when the professor sums up the book his friend will publish outside the Soviet Union: "The aim of the book is to give an objective description of communism as it really is from the point of view of its deepest underlying laws, its tendencies and its future prospects. What attitude to take up vis-à-vis this society is the personal affair of each reader. The author is not trying to dictate any line of response to him. The only thing he can advise is: if you are not content, if you don't like it, fight against it. How? However you are able."

In August 1978, one month before Soviet President Brezhnev revoked Zinoviev's citizenship for "behavior damaging to Soviet prestige," he and his family were allowed to leave the USSR to attend a philosophy seminar at the University of Munich. He now lives in Munich and teaches at the University.

WORKS IN ENGLISH TRANSLATION: Two of Zinoviev's studies in logic were translated into English and published in the Netherlands—*Philosophical Problems of Many-Valued Logic,* by G. Küng and D. D. Comey in 1963, *Foundations of the Logical Theory of Scientific Knowledge,* by T. J. Blakeley in 1973. Graham Clough translated *The Yawning Heights* in 1978 and *The Radiant Future* in 1980. Zinoviev's essays on Communist society and ideology, *The Reality of Communism,* were translated by Charles Janson in 1984.

ABOUT: Contemporary Literary Criticism 19, 1981; International Who's Who, 1981-82. *Periodicals*—New York Review of Books April 14, 1977; March 19, 1981; New York Times June 7, 1979; June 21, 1979; New York Times Book Review June 24, 1979; March 15, 1981; Observer March 29, 1981; Times Literary Supplement May 23, 1980; March 27, 1981; April 6, 1984; Washington Post Book World July 1, 1979.

THEODORE ZIOLKOWSKI

*ZIOLKOWSKI, THEODORE (JOSEPH) (September 30, 1932–   ), American literary critic, was born in Montevallo, Alabama, the son of two pianists, Professor Miecislaw Ziolkowski and Cecilia (Jankowski) Ziolkowski. After receiving his bachelor's (1951) and master's (1952) degrees from Duke University, he did a year's graduate study on a Fulbright grant at the University of Innsbruck, Austria, and earned a Ph.D. from Yale in 1957. Hired as an instructor in the German department in 1956, he became an assistant professor in 1960, then moved for two years (1962–64) to Columbia University, and was named professor of German at Princeton University in 1964. At Princeton he held the Class of 1900 Professorship in Modern Languages from 1969, was chairman of the German department from 1973, and since 1979 has been dean of the Graduate School.

Ziolkowski is one of the English-speaking world's foremost authorities on the works of Hermann Hesse, the German Nobel laureate in literature whose novels, especially *Siddhartha* and *Steppenwolf,* were avidly read and discussed by American college students during the 1950s and '60s. *The Novels of Hermann Hesse: A Study in Theme and Structure* is a much-praised general consideration of the six major novels, showing how Hesse's principal themes grew out of his experiences in World War I, discussing his interest in German Romanticism and

Oriental philosophy, and tracing the chief intellectual influences on his development. Ziolkowski has also published two other works of Hesse criticism, *Hermann Hesse* and *Der Schriftsteller Hermann Hesse* (The Writer Hermann Hesse), and has edited five volumes of the American edition of Hesse's complete works. He is also the editor of a collection of critical essays on Hesse and of the Hermann Hesse–Thomas Mann letters.

Ziolkowski's other critical works have been appreciated by a somewhat more specialized audience which is not, however, confined to scholars of German literature. An essay, for example, first published in *PMLA* (*Publications of the Modern Language Association*) in January 1976, with the intriguing title "The Telltale Teeth: Psychodontia to Sociodontia," dazzled its readers with its wit and erudition. *PMLA*'s editor, William D. Schaeffer, wrote: "I suspect that anyone with a good set of uppers and lowers will find Ziolkowski's story to be a fascinating one." It is indeed a "story," ranging widely over Western literature from biblical and patristic writings (St. Augustine's analogy of the saints and "the healthy teeth of the Church") to images of aching teeth in Thomas Mann, Arthur Koestler, Graham Green, Saul Bellow, and Günter Grass. Such images, Ziolkowski writes, reflect "the shift in emphasis from psychodontia to sociodontia: decaying teeth now represent with increasing frequency society as a whole and not just the esthetic or moral agony of the individual." In contemporary literature, he wryly observes, dentists are "philosophers of decay, who assign psychological and political significance to tartar and

°zol˝ kou´ skē

caries and who gaze into their patients' mouths as raptly as any soothsayer into a crystal ball."

In *Dimensions of the Modern Novel: German Texts and European Contexts* Ziolkowski discusses certain common themes and images in Rilke's *The Notebooks of Malte Laurids Brigge,* Kafka's *The Trial,* Mann's *The Magic Mountain,* Alfred Döblin's *Berlin Alexanderplatz,* and Hermann Broch's *The Sleepwalkers. Fictional Transfigurations of Jesus* studies some twenty novels of the last hundred years in which the action is in various ways prefigured by the life of Jesus. His *Disenchanted Images: A Literary Iconology* "traces," in the author's words, "the motifs of walking statues, haunted portraits, and magic mirrors through European and American fiction of the nineteenth and twentieth centuries." He analyzes the cultural and historical dynamics of these motifs, arriving at their "disenchantment"—"The paradigm," according to M. G. Fuchs, " . . . is initial acceptance, to rationalization and psychological interpretation, to parody and fantasy." Fuchs concluded that the book is "a vividly narrated yet immaculately analytic touch of magic for our oft-disenchanted world of literary criticism."

One of Ziolkowski's best received books was *The Classical German Elegy, 1795–1950,* a work of generic discovery that begins with the analysis of Schiller's "Der Spaziergang" (1795) as an entirely new literary form, then investigates the tradition the poem created with regard to image, setting, form, and mode in major and minor works by some twenty poets, down to the genre's eventual exhaustion in our own era. What the author calls "a chapter in the history of genre" seemed "utterly convincing" to Idris Parry: "No simplification can do justice to the subtlety and erudition of this work. It is dense with detail, connected to form a stimulating contribution to the cultural history of the period. It is appropriate that a book about the impact of poetry, a particular organization of words, should itself be notable for precision, controlled arrangement and easy style." Ziolkowski collected a number of his critical essays in *Varieties of Literary Thematics,* in which, in his own words, he "uses such images as symbolic teeth, mystic carbuncles, and talking dogs as the basis for a methodology of thematic studies."

In March 1951, Ziolkowski married Yetta Goldstein; they have a daughter and two sons. Yetta Ziolkowski has collaborated with her husband on several projects, notably the translations of Herman Meyer's *The Poetics of Quotation in the European Novel* (1969) and *Hermann Hesse: A Pictorial Biography* (1975). He has been a visiting professor at Rutgers, Yale, and the City University of New York, a lecturer at U.S., Canadian, and European universities, and is a frequent contributor of articles and reviews to scholarly journals. In addition to English and German, he is fluent in French, Italian, and Dutch.

PRINCIPAL WORKS: Hermann Broch, 1964; The Novels of Hermann Hessee, 1965; Hermann Hesse, 1966; Dimensions of the Modern Novel, 1969; Fictional Transfigurations of Jesus, 1972; Disenchanted Images, 1977; Der Schriftsteller Hermann Hesse, 1979; The Classical German Elegy, 1795–1950, 1980; Varieties of Literary Thematics, 1983. *As translator*—Herman Meyer, The Poetics of Quotation in the European Novel, 1968; (with Y. Ziolkowski) Hermann Hesse: A Pictorial Biography, 1975. *As editor*—Hermann Hesse, Autobiographical Writings, 1972; Hermann Hesse, Stories of Five Decades, 1972; Hesse: A Collection of Critical Essays, 1973; Hermann Hesse, My Belief, 1973; Hermann Hesse, Tales of Student Life, 1976; Hermann Hesse, Pictor's Metamorphoses and Other Fantasies, 1982.

ABOUT: Contemporary Authors, first revision series 13–16, 1975; Who's Who in America, 1983–84. *Periodicals*—America July 2–9, 1977; Choice October 1969; March 1973; October 1977; November 1980; Christian Century October 18, 1972; Commonweal April 20, 1973; Library Journal June 1, 1969; November 15, 1972; March 15, 1977; Modern Language Journal March 1966; Modern Philology February 1967; Times Literary Supplement August 17, 1973; October 3, 1980; World Literature Today Spring 1981; Yale Review March 1973.

*ZWEIG, PAUL (July 14, 1935–August 29, 1984), American poet, essayist, and critic, was born in New York City, the son of Samuel H. and Celia Berkin Zweig. After taking his bachelor's (1956) and master's (1958) degrees from Columbia University, he left for France, where for a decade he lived the life of an alienated Parisian intellectual. After receiving a Ph.D from the Sorbonne Zweig returned to New York in the mid-1960s, held an assistant professorship at Columbia (1966–68), and from then until the time of his death was a member and chairman of the comparative literature department at Queens College of the City University of New York.

Zweig's first books were English translations, published in Paris: the first was selections from Aloysius Bertrand's prose poem *Gaspard de la Nuit;* the second, a work by Antonin Artaud, *Black Poet.* The book marking his critical debut, written in French and first published in Paris (1967), was a study of Lautréamont, the nineteenth-century precursor of symbolism, and of his major work, the bizarre, neo-Gothic *Les Chants de Maldoror.* Zweig subsequently

© 1975 Layle Silbert

PAUL ZWEIG

brought out the book in English as *Lautréamont: The Violent Narcissus,* a revised version of his French original accompanied by a new general introduction to the poet and his themes and several passages from *Maldoror* in translation.

Against Emptiness: Poems collected much of the poetry that Zweig had published over several years in such national magazines as the *New Yorker,* the *Nation,* and *Harper's.* These are somber, anxious poems, for the most part resolutely unmusical, treating over and over again the themes of death, failure, and loneliness. Among the best-known is the often-anthologized poem whose first line is its title:

Afraid that I am not a poet,
Yet willing to write
Even about that;
Holding up words I have loved,
Their exploded joys
Have scarred me into life,

And I am frightened suddenly.
For nothing I have been resembles them;
Nothing has stuck to these
Irretrievable bones.

How can I be sane with borrowed faces?
When the fears and pleasures
That tumble my words
Like seasons harvested in love,
Are only empty mirrors,
Images floating in a dry sea.

This dissatisfaction with the limitations of his art becomes, in John Demos' words, the poet's "artifice, becomes the metaphor of life-in-death which recurs again and again as if life itself was a false start. . . . Zweig despairs of making

sense of the world, and . . . though he gasps and struggles for meaning, he frequently does so with a set of private associations that leaves the reader in his wake." Even a simple childhood recollection can pose the most dreadfully final of questions, as in this section from the sequence "The Natural History of Death":

I liked standing naked in the basement
Shoveling coal into the open furnace.
The heat taught me I had a body
Long before women ever tried.
That is why, even now, love begins for me
In madness, as if this were an answer
To the old question:
What have you done to need life so badly?

The poems in *The Dark Side of the Earth* are generally similar in theme and tone to those of the preceding book. "I stand in a frozen year,/ And hear the whisper of darkened lives." is a couplet expressing the collection's dominant melancholia. Death seems to be everywhere, winking or beckoning; in "Amanita Phalloidus" the poet discovers a deadly mushroom in a sexually burgeoning forest:

. . . I know that one bite would be suicide,
Like a pause in the wind, when the faintest hum
Of insects can be heard. I am not tempted,
Yet I find it hard to look away,
As if I were leaning over a well
Whose moist echoes urged me to lean over more,
Still more, until my arms lurched forward,
And I fell into the perfect night of the earth.

The *Choice* reviewer remarked on "the limits of the author's interests and . . . the repetition of some images and phrases," adding that Zweig "is unusually intelligent, and at his best . . . he is an original." Joseph Garrison wrote, "*The Dark Side of the Earth* does not attempt to console distress: rather, it clarifies the depths of darkness."

Zweig was also the author of two well-regarded comparative literary studies. The first of these, *The Heresy of Self-Love: A Study of Subversive Individualism,* considers the prevalence in the Western cultural tradition, despite constant condemnation, of the experience of the self and the glorification of individual worth as primary literary and philosophical attitudes. Narcissism in its many forms is traced from the Gnostic writings, the Tristan legends, and Provençal love poetry through the works of Shakespeare and Milton, Descartes, Spinoza, Rousseau, and Kierkegaard, down to the nineteenth century and the works of Melville and Baudelaire. "One is steadily conscious," wrote Mary Ellmann in a review, "of a quiet, comprehensive, and generous intelligence. . . . Zweig's thesis is both persuasive and revelatory. . . . I am not sure that it is any more exhilarating than distressing to be shown the persistent sameness of this one Western posture, but Zweig shows it beyond disbelief." *The Adventurer* examines the cultural role of adventure and the adventurer from the early epics of Gilgamesh, Odysseus, and Beowulf, through the domesticated adventures of Robinson Crusoe and the frivolous adventures of Casanova. Zweig shows how adventure lost out to sensibility in the novels of Jane Austen and her spiritual descendants, yet simultaneously reemerged in the Gothic romances and later in the works of Nietzsche, Conrad, T. E. Lawrence, Malraux, Sartre, and Mailer. To John Gardner, Zweig's argument "throws startling light on where we are and where we've been and provides what every first-rate theory is supposed to provide, a new way of seeing not only the books and men he chooses to talk about but also those he passes over in silence. . . . When he turns to the adventurer in modern times, Zweig's book takes wings. In a series of brilliant analyses, . . . he traces what happened to us: how the adventurer's fight and flight turned inward." George Steiner thought the book "shows real verve and perception," but complained that the author had ignored the adventure content of modern science fiction. Had he explored this area, Steiner continued, he "would have discovered those great currents of action and adventure he finds lacking in the modern novel."

By most accounts, Zweig's most widely admired book is the autobiographical *Three Journeys: An Automythology*. In a kind of parallel to the spiritual quests described in *The Adventurer*, Zweig recounts three of the most significant episodes of his life. The first chapter, "Against Emptiness"—a title he here puts to new use—describes a month traveling in the Sahara in the spring of 1974. "My determination to go," he writes in the preface to the book, "even if no one else could, seemed strange and a little grim, even to myself. I was dimly aware that my age had something to do with it. I was thirty-eight, and had gotten much of what I'd spent a great deal of time wanting. I loved my wife; I had a reasonable job; several of my books had been published and praised. All this was good, but somehow it wasn't good enough. I suspected that I didn't know how to want properly, that I had a way of giving things back merely by having them." Although he relates the external circumstances of the journey with a good deal of ironic humor, he experiences the desert, according to Francine du Plessix Gray, "not as an objective material entity in which to fight for survival but as a 'personal space' in which to struggle for heightened self-awareness, in which to meditate

on that space's spiritual associations"—the desert as a place for contemplation and asceticism, as the cradle of the great monotheistic religions, as a place of intensified revelation, and finally, in Gray's words, "as a kind of magnifying lens that enlarges and clarifies the meaning of the two other inner journeys which Zweig describes in his book." The second chapter, "Automythology," is a frequently hilarious account of the rebellion of his twenties when he lived as a Communist in Paris during the Algerian War. "Against Communism," he writes, "the only reliable protection is a cheerful nature combined with a great deal of ballroom dancing." The final chapter, "The Bright Yellow Circus," remains perhaps the most startling thing Zweig has so far written: an account of his conversion, sometime after his return from the Sahara, to Indian mysticism as a disciple of Swami Muktananda. The conversion is immediate: within the first hour of being in the swami's presence, the urbane professor of poetry is weeping uncontrollably. It is also utterly fulfilling: the author feels once again—but not this time so fleetingly—the sense of belonging to a cosmic entity, the wholeness that he first experienced in the Sahara: "like being inside God, moving wholly within him." "The desert blooms," wrote Gray, "in this most inner of the three adventures, and so does Zweig's translucent prose." Around the time of the publication of *Three Journeys*, Zweig set off on a lecture tour to promote Muktananda's brand of cosmic consciousness. He also published *Muktananda: Selected Essays*.

Only a few months before his death Zweig published *Walt Whitman: The Making of the Poet*, a study that was almost immediately acclaimed as major and indispensable. Less a biography of the poet than a biography of his mind, the book focuses on Whitman's development from drifter-journalist to a veritable American culture hero. The crucial question of the book, as Harold Bloom pointed out, is "How did someone of Whitman's extraordinarily idiosyncratic nature become so absolutely central to nearly all subsequent American literary high culture?" Zweig offered no answer to the question; Whitman, like all creative artists, remains a mystery. But moving outward from the poetry itself and from Whitman's notebooks ("the voice of the poet himself"), he wrote a sensitive and illuminating account of the genesis of a poet and his place in the context of Western literature. In their reviews of the book, both Quentin Anderson and Bloom found only one weakness: both dissented from Zweig's conclusion that Whitman's poetry "laid the groundwork for the anticultural ambition of much modernist writing . . . of all who have made of their writing an attack on the act of writing and on culture itself," thus linking him with writers like Henry Miller and Allen Ginsberg, as well as Kafka, Beckett, and Borges. Bloom writes that here Zweig not only misinterprets Kafka, Beckett, and Borges (whose "assault upon certain interpretive conventions" was not "a war against literary culture") but also misinterprets "the subtle artistry, delicate and evasive, of Whitman's greatest poems." And Anderson objects that here Zweig "fails to give Whitman his due as a force in the history of our culture."

For some years before his death Zweig knew that he had lymphatic cancer, but he continued teaching and writing prolifically. In the summer of 1984, while abroad to do research for a book on cave painting in France, he died in the American Hospital in Paris, aged forty-nine. He was survived by his wife Vikki Stark and a daughter from an earlier marriage.

PRINCIPAL WORKS: *Poetry*—Against Emptiness, 1971; Images & Footsteps, 1971; The Dark Side of the Earth, 1974; The River, 1981; Eternity's Woods, 1985. *Criticism*—The Heresy of Self-Love, 1968; Lautréamont, 1972; The Adventurer, 1974; Muktananda: Selected Essays, 1977; Walt Whitman: The Making of the Poet, 1984. *Autobiography*—Three Journeys, 1976. *As editor and translator*—A. Bertrand, From Gaspard of the Night, 1964; A. Artaud, Black Poet, 1966; Yuan Goll: Selected Poems, 1968.

ABOUT: Contemporary Authors 85–88, 1980. *Periodicals*—Choice June 1969; June 1973; January 1975; July–August 1975; Library Journal October 15, 1968; March 15, 1971; October 15, 1972; March 15, 1974; January 15, 1975; April 15, 1976; Nation March 31, 1969; New York Review of Books September 30, 1976; April 26, 1984; New York Times August 31, 1984; New York Times Book Review December 26, 1971; December 22, 1974; May 2, 1976; May 6, 1984; New Yorker January 20, 1975; Poetry May 1972; December 1975; Times Literary Supplement July 18, 1975; Virginia Quarterly Review Spring 1973.

Photographic Credits

© *Bob Adelman*, Martin Cruz Smith; © *Bert Andrews*, Toni Morrison; *Aliza Auerbach*, Abraham Yehoshua; *Pilar Ayamerich, Barcelona*, Juan Marse John M. Baker, Bienvenido N. Santos; © *Seix Barral*, Manuel Puig; © *Jerry Bauer*, Carolyn Blackwood, Breyten Breytenbach, A.S. Byatt, Nigel Calder, Alice Childress, Richard M. Elman, J.G. Farrell, Julian Gloag, Russell Hoban, P.D. James, Jennifer Johnston, Jacques Lacan, Ana Maria Matute, James McClure, Colleen McCullough, Ian McEwan, A.G. Mojtabai, Sandro Penna, Fay Weldon; *M. Bedford*, Pierre Berton; © *Rosalind Bell*, Dirk Bogarde; *Leslie A. Beran*, Hilton Kramer; *The Bettman Archive/BBC Hulton*, R. F. Delderfield; © *Gervas Blakely*, Mary Gordon; *Stuart Bratesman*, Frances Fitzgerald; © *Aaron Broches*, Chaim Grade; *Linda L. Brown*, Dee Brown

Eduardo Chamorro, Juan Benet; *Columbia University, Office of Public Information*, David Shapiro; *Tessa Colvin*, Gabriel Okara © 1983; *Andre Le Coz*, Paul-Marie Lapointe; *Nancy Crampton*, Michael J. Arlen ©, John Brooks © 1980, Laurie Colwin © 1982, Gail Godwin, Alix Kates Shulman © 1981; *Creative Photographers*, L. E. Sissman; © *Anthony Crickmay*, Andrew Porter; *Wayne Crosslin*, Jonathan Raban

© *Royal Danish Ministry for Foreign Affairs*, Anders Bodelsen; *Alex Darrow Photography*, Charles Edward Eaton; *Renee DeKona/Cape Cod Times*, Annie Dillard; *Dotman Pretorius Fotograaf*, Etienne Leroux; © *Fred Dubetsky*, Stephen Stepanchev; *Quintana Roo Dunne*, John Gregory Dunne

Chris Ellis, Michael Moorcock; *Barbara Ellman*, Joseph McElroy; *T. Charles Erickson, Yale University Office of Public Information*, Geoffrey H. Hartman; *David A. Evans*, Jerre Gerlando Mangione

Jean Faust, Irvin Faust; *Ivor Fields*, Ronald Hingley; *Graham Finlayson*, Frederick Forsyth; © *Nikky Finney*, Toni Cade Bambara; *Deborah Flomenhaft*, Jerome Charyn; *John Foraste*, Michael S. Harper; *Gyldendal Norsk Forlag*, Johan Borges; *Berhi Frick, 1984*, Goran Palm; *Marti Friedlander*, Maurice Duggan

© *Tess Gallagher*, Raymond Carver; © *Kevin Galvin*, George V. Higgins; *Jan Gauthier*, Theodore Roszak; *Courtesy of the German Information Center*, Alfred Andersch, Franz Xaver Kroetz, Siegfried Lenz; *Donald A. Gibbs*, Ding Ling; *Graeme Gibson*, Norman Levine; © *Fay Godwin*, Desmond Morris, David Robert Plante; *Alex Gotfryd*, William Barrett, Alex Haley; © *Beryl Gray*, Simon Gray; *Albert Greenberg*, Joanne Greenberg; *J. -F. Grousset*, Jacques Ellul

John Patrick Hart, Donald E. Westlake; *Harvard University Press*, Robert Nozick; *Tara Heinimann*, Marina Warner; *Morris Helprin*, Mark Helprin; *Alan Hillyer*, Wilfred Thesiger; *Marv Hoffman*, Rosellen Brown; *Loretta Howard*, Maureen Howard; *Jean Humez*, Thomas McMahon

© *Marcel Imsand*, Jacques Chessex; *Shyla Irving*, Stratis Haviaras, John Irving; *Italian Cultural Institute*, Antonio Gramsci

Paul Jaronski, The University of Michigan News and Information Services, Lemuel Johnston

© *Jim Kalett*, C. K. Williams; © *Martha Kaplan*, Robert K. Massie, Richard Sennett; *Mamoru Kasahara*, Junji Kinoshita; *Paul Kasmin*, Bruce Chatwin; © *Bhupendra Kavia*, Ayi Kwei Armah; *Photo by V. Koshevoy, Fotokhronika TASS*, Chingiz Aitmatov

Herman Laesker, Trenton Times, Fletcher Knebel; *J.D. Levine/Yale University Office of Public Information*, Peter Gay; *Lawrence Lipke*, Lois Gould Helen Marcus, Cecilia Holland; *Mark Marraccini*, Walter Tevis; *Jessie Ann Matthew*, Robert Garioch; *Jane Melnick*, Lisa Alther; *Diana Michener*, Carolyn Heilbrun; *Jack Mitchell*, Agnes De Mille; *Moldvay*, Agnes Nemes Nagy; *Tom Monaster*, Gay Talese; *Paul Morby*, David Lodge; *Allan Myrman*, Per Olof Sundman

Timothy Neal, Sorley Maclean © 1983; *Martha Nelson*, Gerda Lerner; *Arnold Newman*, Robert A. Caro © 1982; © *Novosti Press Agency*, Yuri Trifonov

© *The Observer*, Clive James; *Ken T. O'Hara*, Craig Nova; © *Isolde Ohlbaum*, Thomas Bernhard, Salman Rushdie, Hans Werner Richter; *Quentin Ondaatje*, Michael Ondaatje; *Susan Oristaglio*, Judith Rossner; *Lutfi Ozkok, Sweden*, Osten Sjostrand; *Lufti Ozkok, Courtesy of New Publishing Corp.*, Lars Gustafsson

Pach Bros., N. Y., Ned Rorem; *Paramount Pictures Corporation*, Nicholas Meyer © 1981; *H. Perten, Stockholm*, Marie Under; *University of Pittsburgh Press*, Gary Soto; *Eric Poppenpohl*, Gary Wills; *Princeton University*, Joseph Frank

© *Nelson Redland*, John Brunner; *Jon Reis Photography*, Jon Stallworthy © 1983; *Jacques Robert*, Edmond Jabès, Emmanuel Le Roy Ladurie, Michel Tournier; *Jacques Robert/Editors Gallimard*, Vladimir Y. Maksimov, Patrick Modiano; *The Rockefeller University Archives*, Rene J. Dubois; *Tony Rollo, Newsweek*, Berton Roueché

Serge Sachno, Marilyn French; © *Charles Salaquarda*, Josef Skvorecky; *San Diego Tribune/Thane McIntosh*, Calvin Trillin; *Laurie Sapakoff*, Lucy Dawidowicz; *Peter Schaaf*, Charles Rosen; *Virginia Schendler, Courtesy of New Directions Publishing Corp.*, James Laughlin; *Bonnie Schiffman*, Andrew M. Greeley; *Joel Siegel, 1983*, Thomas Szasz; *Layle Silbert*, Pablo Antonio Cuadra, Elaine Feinstein © 1985, Marilyn Hacker © 1982, Enrique Lihn © 1982, Audre Lorde, José Emilio Pacheco © 1985, Helen Yglesias © 1982, Paul Zweig © 1975; *Roger B. Smith*, Christopher Lasch; *Jamie Spracher*, Thomas M. Disch; *Gene Stamm*, David Shapiro; *Nina Subin*, Clayton Eshleman; *Courtesy of the Swedish Institute*, Lars Ahlin, Per Olov Enquist; *Geraldine Sweeney*, Derek Mahon

Technical Photo Service, Vine Deloria; © *Thomas Studios*, Jane Jacobs

UPI/BETTMAN Newsphotos, Michael Harrington, Jaroslav Seifert, Lanford Wilson

Maristella Velickovic, Danilo Kiš; *Thomas Victor*, Roger Angell ©, Ann Beattie ©, David Bradley © 1980, Richard P. Brickner © 1985, Anita Brookner © 1985, Don De Lillo ©, Paul Fussell © 1982, William Kennedy © 1984, Maxine Hong Kingston © 1979, Jane Kramer ©, N. Scott Momaday © 1985, Ted Morgan © 1985, James Schuyler © 1985, Red

Smith ©, Gilbert Sorrentino ©, D.M. Thomas © 1984, Lewis Thomas © 1983, Diana Trilling © 1980, Jean Valentine © 1985, Helen Vendler © 1985

Diana H. Walker, Larry McMurtry; *Hildegard Weber*, Lev Kopelev; *Herb Weitman*, Geoffrey Wolff © 1979; © *Susan Mullally Well*, Maya Angelou; *Welsh Arts Council*, Leslie Norris; © *Wide World*

Photos, Andrei Aleseyevich Amalrik; © *Valerie Wilmer*, Buchi Emechetta; *James D. Wilson*, M. F. K. Fisher © 1982; © *Kelly Wise*, Robert Stone; © *Carole Woiwode*, Larry Woiwode; *Susan Wood*, Betty Friedan

Yale University Office of Public Information, Jaroslav Pelikan